Proverbs 13:20

Walk with the w … e;
associate with fo … ouble

Love Dad
29 May 2011

Student's Life Application Study Bible

STUDENT'S LIFE APPLICATION® STUDY BIBLE

New Living Translation®

SECOND EDITION

Tyndale House Publishers, Inc.
Carol Stream, Illinois

Visit Tyndale's exciting Web site at www.tyndale.com

The publisher gratefully acknowledges the role of Youth for Christ/USA in preparing the Life Application Notes and Bible Helps.

ISBN-10: 0-8423-8511-8 ISBN-13: 978-0-8423-8511-4 Bonded Leather Burgundy
ISBN-10: 0-8423-8512-6 ISBN-13: 978-0-8423-8512-1 Bonded Leather Navy
ISBN-10: 0-8423-8510-X ISBN-13: 978-0-8423-8510-7 Hardcover Blue
ISBN-10: 1-4143-0605-9 ISBN-13: 978-1-4143-0605-6 Hardcover Orange
ISBN-10: 1-4143-0217-7 ISBN-13: 978-1-4143-0217-1 Softcover

Printed in the United States of America

14 13 12 11 10 09
14 13 12 11 10 9 8 7 6

Tyndale House Publishers and Wycliffe Bible Translators share the vision for an understandable, accurate translation of the Bible for every person in the world. Each sale of the *Holy Bible,* New Living Translation, benefits Wycliffe Bible Translators. Wycliffe is working with partners around the world to accomplish Vision 2025—an initiative to start a Bible translation program in every langauge group that needs it by the year 2025.

DESIGN TEAM
Dr. Bruce B. Barton
Ron Beers
Dr. James Galvin
LaVonne Neff
David R. Veerman

SENIOR EDITOR
David R. Veerman

EDITORS
Karen Ball
Kathryn S. Olson
Linda Taylor

REVISION EDITORS
Linda Washington
Leanne Roberts

GRAPHIC DESIGN
Jackie Noe
Julie Chen

TYPESETTER
Judy Stafford

WRITERS:
DR. RICHARD R. DUNN
Chairman, Department of Christian Education
Trinity Evangelical Divinity School
Deerfield, Illinois

TERRY PRISK
Youth Communicator/Consultant
Executive Director of Contemporary Communication
Detroit, Michigan

KENT KELLER
Pastor, Redeemer Presbyterian Church
Miami, Florida

JARED REED
Pastor, Faith Presbyterian Church
Miami, Florida

LEN WOODS
Former Editor of *Youthwalk*
Minister to Students, Christ Community Church
Ruston, Louisiana

GREG JOHNSON
Former Editor of *Breakaway*

BYRON EMMERT
Speaker and seminar leader
Youth for Christ
Mt. Lake, Minnesota

DIANE EBLE
Freelance editor/writer
Wheaton, Illinois

NEIL WILSON
Pastor, Eureka United Methodist Church
Omro, Wisconsin

BILL SANDERS
Author and speaker
Kalamazoo, Michigan

DAVID R. VEERMAN
Veteran youth worker and author
The Livingstone Corporation
Carol Stream, Illinois

NOTES AND FEATURES:
BOOK INTRODUCTIONS
Jared Reed
Len Woods
David R. Veerman

PERSONALITY PROFILES
Neil Wilson

"CHOICES" NOTES
Len Woods

"I WONDER" NOTES
Greg Johnson

"KEEPING IT REAL" NOTES
Terry Prisk
Diane Eble

MEGATHEMES
Dr. Richard R. Dunn
Dr. Bruce B. Barton

ULTIMATE ISSUES
Kent Keller

LIFE-CHANGER INDEX
Bill Sanders
Linda Taylor

MAPS
Adapted from the *Life Application Study Bible*

CHARTS
Adapted from the *Life Application Study Bible*

A LOOK AT THE BOOK
Neil Wilson

HELP FOR NEW BELIEVERS/14 ENCOUNTERS
Byron Emmert

LIFE APPLICATION NOTES
Adapted from the *Life Application Study Bible*
David R. Veerman

Thank you to the young people from the following youth groups for their invaluable assistance with this project:
Southern Gables Church, Denver, Colorado
Spring Hill Camps, Evart, Michigan
Pekin Bible Church, Pekin, Illinois
Ward Presbyterian Church, Livonia, Michigan
First Baptist Church, Holdrege, Nebraska
Naperville Presbyterian Church, Naperville, Illinois

contents

a note to readers

The *Holy Bible*, New Living Translation, was first published in 1996. It quickly became one of the most popular Bible translations in the English-speaking world. While the NLT's influence was rapidly growing, the Bible Translation Committee determined that an additional investment in scholarly review and text refinement could make it even better. So shortly after its initial publication, the committee began an eight-year process with the purpose of increasing the level of the NLT's precision without sacrificing its easy-to-understand quality. This second-generation text was completed in 2004 and is reflected in this edition of the New Living Translation.

The goal of any Bible translation is to convey the meaning and content of the ancient Hebrew, Aramaic, and Greek texts as accurately as possible to contemporary readers. The challenge for our translators was to create a text that would communicate as clearly and powerfully to today's readers as the original texts did to readers and listeners in the ancient biblical world. The resulting translation is easy to read and understand, while also accurately communicating the meaning and content of the original biblical texts. The NLT is a general-purpose text especially good for study, devotional reading, and reading aloud in worship services.

We believe that the New Living Translation—which combines the latest biblical scholarship with a clear, dynamic writing style—will communicate God's word powerfully to all who read it. We publish it with the prayer that God will use it to speak his timeless truth to the church and the world in a fresh, new way.

The Publishers
July 2004

Introduction TO THE NEW LIVING TRANSLATION

TRANSLATION PHILOSOPHY AND METHODOLOGY

English Bible translations tend to be governed by one of two general translation theories. The first theory has been called "formal-equivalence," "literal," or "word-for-word" translation. According to this theory, the translator attempts to render each word of the original language into English and seeks to preserve the original syntax and sentence structure as much as possible in translation. The second theory has been called "dynamic-equivalence," "functional-equivalence," or "thought-for-thought" translation. The goal of this translation theory is to produce in English the closest natural equivalent of the message expressed by the original-language text, both in meaning and in style.

Both of these translation theories have their strengths. A formal-equivalence translation preserves aspects of the original text—including ancient idioms, term consistency, and original-language syntax—that are valuable for scholars and professional study. It allows a reader to trace formal elements of the original-language text through the English translation. A dynamic-equivalence translation, on the other hand, focuses on translating the message of the original-language text. It ensures that the meaning of the text is readily apparent to the contemporary reader. This allows the message to come through with immediacy, without requiring the reader to struggle with foreign idioms and awkward syntax. It also facilitates serious study of the text's message and clarity in both devotional and public reading.

The pure application of either of these translation philosophies would create translations at opposite ends of the translation spectrum. But in reality, all translations contain a mixture of these two philosophies. A purely formal-equivalence translation would be unintelligible in English, and a purely dynamic-equivalence translation would risk being unfaithful to the original. That is why translations shaped by dynamic-equivalence theory are usually quite literal when the original text is relatively clear, and the translations shaped by formal-equivalence theory are sometimes quite dynamic when the original text is obscure.

The translators of the New Living Translation set out to render the message of the original texts of Scripture into clear, contemporary English. As they did so, they kept the concerns of both formal-equivalence and dynamic-equivalence in mind. On the one hand, they translated as simply and literally as possible when that approach yielded an accurate, clear, and natural English text. Many words and phrases were rendered literally and consistently into English, preserving essential literary and rhetorical devices, ancient metaphors, and word choices that give structure to the text and provide echoes of meaning from one passage to the next.

On the other hand, the translators rendered the message more dynamically when the literal rendering was hard to understand, was misleading, or yielded archaic or foreign wording. They clarified difficult metaphors and terms to aid in the reader's understanding. The translators first struggled with the meaning of the words and phrases in the ancient context; then they rendered the message into clear, natural English. Their goal was to be both faithful to the ancient texts and eminently readable. The result is a translation that is both exegetically accurate and idiomatically powerful.

TRANSLATION PROCESS AND TEAM

To produce an accurate translation of the Bible into contemporary English, the translation team needed the skills necessary to enter into the thought patterns of the ancient authors and then to render their ideas, connotations, and effects into clear, contemporary English. To begin this process, qualified biblical scholars were needed to interpret the meaning of the original text and to check it against our base English translation. In order to guard against personal and theological biases, the scholars needed to represent a diverse group of Evangelicals who would employ the best exegetical tools. Then to work alongside the scholars, skilled English stylists were needed to shape the text into clear, contemporary English.

With these concerns in mind, the Bible Translation Committee recruited teams of scholars that represented a broad spectrum of denominations, theological perspectives, and backgrounds within the worldwide Evangelical community. (These scholars are listed at the end of this introduction.) Each book of the Bible was assigned to three different scholars with proven expertise in the book or group of books to be reviewed. Each of these scholars made a thorough review of a base translation and submitted suggested revisions to the appropriate Senior Translator. The Senior Translator then reviewed and summarized these suggestions and proposed a first-draft revision of the base text. This draft served as the basis for several additional phases of exegetical and stylistic committee review. Then the Bible Translation Committee jointly reviewed and approved every verse of the final translation.

Throughout the translation and editing process, the Senior Translators and their scholar teams were given a chance to review the editing done by the team of stylists. This ensured that exegetical errors would not be introduced late in the process and that the entire Bible Translation Committee was happy with the final result. By choosing a team of qualified scholars and skilled stylists and by setting up a process that allowed their interaction throughout the process, the New Living Translation has been refined to preserve the essential formal elements of the original biblical texts, while also creating a clear, understandable English text.

The New Living Translation was first published in 1996. Shortly after its initial publication, the Bible Translation Committee began a process of further committee review and translation refinement. The purpose of this continued revision was to increase the level of precision without sacrificing the text's easy-to-understand quality. This second-edition text was completed in 2004, and this printing of the New Living Translation reflects the updated text.

WRITTEN TO BE READ ALOUD

It is evident in Scripture that the biblical documents were written to be read aloud, often in public worship (see Nehemiah 8; Luke 4:16-20; 1 Timothy 4:13; Revelation 1:3). It is still the case today that more people will hear the Bible read aloud in church than are likely to read it for themselves. Therefore, a new translation must communicate with clarity and power when it is read publicly. Clarity was a primary goal for the NLT translators, not only to facilitate private reading and understanding, but also to ensure that it would be excellent for public reading and make an immediate and powerful impact on any listener.

THE TEXTS BEHIND THE NEW LIVING TRANSLATION

The Old Testament translators used the Masoretic Text of the Hebrew Bible as represented in *Biblia Hebraica Stuttgartensia* (1977), with its extensive system of textual notes; this is an update of Rudolf Kittel's *Biblia Hebraica* (Stuttgart, 1937). The translators also further compared the Dead Sea Scrolls, the Septuagint and other Greek manuscripts, the Samaritan Pentateuch, the Syriac Peshitta, the Latin Vulgate, and any other versions or manuscripts that shed light on the meaning of difficult passages.

The New Testament translators used the two standard editions of the Greek New Testament: the *Greek New Testament*, published by the United Bible Societies (UBS, fourth revised edition, 1993), and *Novum Testamentum Graece*, edited by Nestle and Aland (NA, twenty-seventh edition, 1993). These two editions, which have the same text but differ in punctuation and textual notes, represent, for the most part, the best in modern textual scholarship. However, in cases where strong textual or other scholarly evidence supported the decision, the translators sometimes chose to differ from the UBS and NA Greek texts and followed variant readings found in other ancient witnesses. Significant textual variants of this sort are always noted in the textual notes of the New Living Translation.

TRANSLATION ISSUES

The translators have made a conscious effort to provide a text that can be easily understood by the typical reader of modern English. To this end, we sought to use only vocabulary and language structures in common use today. We avoided using language likely to become quickly dated or that reflects only a narrow sub-dialect of English, with the goal of making the New Living Translation as broadly useful and timeless as possible.

But our concern for readability goes beyond the concerns of vocabulary and sentence structure. We are also concerned about historical and cultural barriers to understanding the Bible, and we have sought to translate terms shrouded in history and culture in ways that can be immediately understood. To this end:

- We have converted ancient weights and measures (for example, "ephah" [a unit of dry volume] or "cubit" [a unit of length]) to modern English (American) equivalents, since the ancient measures are not generally meaningful to today's readers. Then in the textual footnotes we offer the literal Hebrew, Aramaic, or Greek measures, along with modern metric equivalents.
- Instead of translating ancient currency values literally, we have expressed them in common terms that communicate the message. For example, in the Old Testament, "ten shekels of silver" becomes "ten pieces of silver" to convey the intended message. In the New Testament, we have often translated the "denarius" as "the normal daily wage" to facilitate

understanding. Then a footnote offers: "Greek *a denarius*, the payment for a full day's wage." In general, we give a clear English rendering and then state the literal Hebrew, Aramaic, or Greek in a textual footnote.

- Since the names of Hebrew months are unknown to most contemporary readers, and since the Hebrew lunar calendar fluctuates from year to year in relation to the solar calendar used today, we have looked for clear ways to communicate the time of year the Hebrew months (such as Abib) refer to. When an expanded or interpretive rendering is given in the text, a textual note gives the literal rendering. Where it is possible to define a specific ancient date in terms of our modern calendar, we use modern dates in the text. A textual footnote then gives the literal Hebrew date and states the rationale for our rendering. For example, Ezra 6:15 pinpoints the date when the post-exilic Temple was completed in Jerusalem: "the third day of the month Adar." This was during the sixth year of King Darius's reign (that is, 515 B.C.). We have translated that date as March 12, with a footnote giving the Hebrew and identifying the year as 515 B.C.
- Since ancient references to the time of day differ from our modern methods of denoting time, we have used renderings that are instantly understandable to the modern reader. Accordingly, we have rendered specific times of day by using approximate equivalents in terms of our common "o'clock" system. On occasion, translations such as "at dawn the next morning" or "as the sun began to set" have been used when the biblical reference is more general.
- When the meaning of a proper name (or a wordplay inherent in a proper name) is relevant to the message of the text, its meaning is often illuminated with a textual footnote. For example, in Exodus 2:10 the text reads: "The princess named him Moses, for she explained, 'I lifted him out of the water.' " The accompanying footnote reads: "*Moses* sounds like a Hebrew term that means 'to lift out.' "

  Sometimes, when the actual meaning of a name is clear, that meaning is included in parentheses within the text itself. For example, the text at Genesis 16:11 reads: "You are to name him Ishmael *(which means 'God hears')*, for the LORD has heard your cry of distress." Since the original hearers and readers would have instantly understood the meaning of the name "Ishmael," we have provided modern readers with the same information so they can experience the text in a similar way.
- Many words and phrases carry a great deal of cultural meaning that was obvious to the original readers but needs explanation in our own culture. For example, the phrase "they beat their breasts" (Luke 23:48) in ancient times meant that people were very upset, often in mourning. In our translation we chose to translate this phrase dynamically for clarity: "They went home *in deep sorrow*." Then we included a footnote with the literal Greek, which reads: "Greek *went home beating their breasts*." In other similar cases, however, we have sometimes chosen to illuminate the existing literal expression to make it immediately understandable. For example, here we might have expanded the literal Greek phrase to read: "They went home beating their breasts *in sorrow*." If we had done this, we would not have included a textual footnote, since the literal Greek clearly appears in translation.
- Metaphorical language is sometimes difficult for contemporary readers to understand, so at times we have chosen to translate or illuminate the meaning of a metaphor. For example, the ancient poet writes, "Your neck is *like* the tower of David" (Song of Songs 4:4). We have rendered it "Your neck is *as beautiful as* the tower of David" to clarify the intended positive meaning of the simile. Another example comes in Ecclesiastes 12:3, which can be literally rendered: "Remember him . . . when the grinding women cease because they are few, and the women who look through the windows see dimly." We have rendered it: "Remember him before your teeth—your few remaining servants—stop grinding; and before your eyes—the women looking through the windows—see dimly." We clarified such metaphors only when we believed a typical reader might be confused by the literal text.
- When the content of the original language text is poetic in character, we have rendered it in English poetic form. We sought to break lines in ways that clarify and highlight the relationships between phrases of the text. Hebrew poetry often uses parallelism, a literary form where a second phrase (or in some instances a third or fourth) echoes the initial phrase in some way. In Hebrew parallelism, the subsequent parallel phrases continue, while also furthering and sharpening, the thought expressed in the initial line or phrase. Whenever possible, we sought to represent these parallel phrases in natural poetic English.

- The Greek term *hoi Ioudaioi* is literally translated "the Jews" in many English translations. In the Gospel of John, however, this term doesn't always refer to the Jewish people generally. In some contexts, it refers more particularly to the Jewish religious leaders. We have attempted to capture the meaning in these different contexts by using terms such as "the people" (with a footnote: Greek *the Jewish people*) or "the religious leaders," where appropriate.
- One challenge we faced was how to translate accurately the ancient biblical text that was originally written in a context where male-oriented terms were used to refer to humanity generally. We needed to respect the nature of the ancient context while also trying to make the translation clear to a modern audience that tends to read male-oriented language as applying only to males. Often the original text, though using masculine nouns and pronouns, clearly intends that the message be applied to both men and women. A typical example is found in the New Testament letters, where the believers are called "brothers" (*adelphoi*). Yet it is clear from the content of these letters that they were addressed to all the believers—male and female. Thus, we have usually translated this Greek word as "brothers and sisters" in order to represent the historical situation more accurately.

  We have also been sensitive to passages where the text applies generally to human beings or to the human condition. In some instances we have used plural pronouns (they, them) in place of the masculine singular (he, him). For example, a traditional rendering of Proverbs 22:6 is: "Train up a child in the way he should go, and when he is old he will not turn from it." We have rendered it: "Teach your children to choose the right path, and when they are older, they will remain upon it." At times, we have also replaced third person pronouns with the second person to ensure clarity. A traditional rendering of Proverbs 26:27 is: "He who digs a pit will fall into it, and he who rolls a stone, it will come back on him." We have rendered it: "If you set a trap for others, you will get caught in it yourself. If you roll a boulder down on others, it will crush you instead."

  We should emphasize, however, that all masculine nouns and pronouns used to represent God (for example, "Father") have been maintained without exception. All decisions of this kind have been driven by the concern to reflect accurately the intended meaning of the original texts of Scripture.

LEXICAL CONSISTENCY IN TERMINOLOGY

For the sake of clarity, we have translated certain original-language terms consistently, especially within synoptic passages and for commonly repeated rhetorical phrases, and within certain word categories such as divine names and non-theological technical terminology (e.g., liturgical, legal, cultural, zoological, and botanical terms). For theological terms, we have allowed a greater semantic range of acceptable English words or phrases for a single Hebrew or Greek word. We have avoided some theological terms that are not readily understood by many modern readers. For example, we avoided using words such as "justification" and "sanctification," which are carryovers from Latin translations. In place of these words, we have provided renderings such as "we are made right with God" and "we are made holy."

THE SPELLING OF PROPER NAMES

Many individuals in the Bible, especially the Old Testament, are known by more than one name (e.g., Uzziah/Azariah). For the sake of clarity, we have tried to use a single spelling for any one individual, footnoting the literal spelling whenever we differ from it. This is especially helpful in delineating the kings of Israel and Judah. King Joash/Jehoash of Israel has been consistently called Jehoash, while King Joash/Jehoash of Judah is called Joash. A similar distinction has been used to distinguish between Joram/Jehoram of Israel and Joram/Jehoram of Judah. All such decisions were made with the goal of clarifying the text for the reader. When the ancient biblical writers clearly had a theological purpose in their choice of a variant name (e.g., Eshbaal/Ishbosheth), the different names have been maintained with an explanatory footnote.

For the names Jacob and Israel, which are used interchangeably for both the individual patriarch and the nation, we generally render it "Israel" when it refers to the nation and "Jacob" when it refers to the individual. When our rendering of the name differs from the underlying Hebrew text, we provide a textual footnote, which includes this explanation: "The names 'Jacob' and 'Israel' are often interchanged throughout the Old Testament, referring sometimes to the individual patriarch and sometimes to the nation."

THE RENDERING OF DIVINE NAMES

All appearances of *'el, 'elohim,* or *'eloah* have been translated "God," except where the context demands the translation "god(s)." We have generally rendered the tetragrammaton (*YHWH*) consistently as "the LORD," utilizing a form with small capitals that is common among English translations. This will distinguish it from the name *'adonai,* which we render "Lord." When *'adonai* and *YHWH* appear together, we have rendered it "Sovereign LORD." This also distinguishes *'adonai YHWH* from cases where *YHWH* appears with *'elohim,* which is rendered "LORD God." When *YH* (the short form of *YHWH*) and *YHWH* appear together, we have rendered it "LORD GOD." When *YHWH* appears with the term *tseba'oth,* we have rendered it "LORD of Heaven's Armies" to translate the meaning of the name. In a few cases, we have utilized the transliteration, *Yahweh,* when the personal character of the name is being invoked in contrast to another divine name or the name of some other god (for example, see Exodus 3:15; 6:2-3).

In the New Testament, the Greek word *christos* has been translated as "Messiah" when the context assumes a Jewish audience. When a Gentile audience can be assumed, *christos* has been translated as "Christ." The Greek word *kurios* is consistently translated "Lord," except that it is translated "LORD" wherever the New Testament text explicitly quotes from the Old Testament, and the text there has it in small capitals.

TEXTUAL FOOTNOTES

The New Living Translation provides several kinds of textual footnotes, all designated in the text with an asterisk:

- When for the sake of clarity the NLT renders a difficult or potentially confusing phrase dynamically, we generally give the literal rendering in a textual footnote. This allows the reader to see the literal source of our dynamic rendering and how our translation relates to other more literal translations. These notes are prefaced with "Hebrew," "Aramaic," or "Greek," identifying the language of the underlying source text. For example, in Acts 2:42 we translated the literal "breaking of bread" (from the Greek) as "the Lord's Supper" to clarify that this verse refers to the ceremonial practice of the church rather than just an ordinary meal. Then we attached a footnote to "the Lord's Supper," which reads: "Greek *the breaking of bread.*"
- Textual footnotes are also used to show alternative renderings, prefaced with the word "Or." These normally occur for passages where an aspect of the meaning is debated. On occasion, we also provide notes on words or phrases that represent a departure from long-standing tradition. These notes are prefaced with "Traditionally rendered." For example, the footnote to the translation "serious skin disease" at Leviticus 13:2 says: "Traditionally rendered *leprosy.* The Hebrew word used throughout this passage is used to describe various skin diseases."
- When our translators follow a textual variant that differs significantly from our standard Hebrew or Greek texts (listed earlier), we document that difference with a footnote. We also footnote cases when the NLT excludes a passage that is included in the Greek text known as the *Textus Receptus* (and familiar to readers through its translation in the King James Version). In such cases, we offer a translation of the excluded text in a footnote, even though it is generally recognized as a later addition to the Greek text and not part of the original Greek New Testament.
- All Old Testament passages that are quoted in the New Testament are identified by a textual footnote at the New Testament location. When the New Testament clearly quotes from the Greek translation of the Old Testament, and when it differs significantly in wording from the Hebrew text, we also place a textual footnote at the Old Testament location. This note includes a rendering of the Greek version, along with a cross-reference to the New Testament passage(s) where it is cited (for example, see notes on Proverbs 3:12; Psalms 8:2; 53:3).
- Some textual footnotes provide cultural and historical information on places, things, and people in the Bible that are probably obscure to modern readers. Such notes should aid the reader in understanding the message of the text. For example, in Acts 12:1, "King Herod" is named in this translation as "King Herod Agrippa" and is identified in a footnote as being "the nephew of Herod Antipas and a grandson of Herod the Great."
- When the meaning of a proper name (or a wordplay inherent in a proper name) is relevant to the meaning of the text, it is either illuminated with a textual footnote or included within parentheses in the text itself. For example, the footnote concerning the name "Eve" at Genesis 3:20 reads: "Eve sounds like a Hebrew term that means 'to give life.' " This wordplay in the Hebrew illuminates the meaning of the text, which goes on to say that Eve "would be the mother of all who live."

As we submit this translation for publication, we recognize that any translation of the Scriptures is subject to limitations and imperfections. Anyone who has attempted to communicate the richness of God's Word into another language will realize it is impossible to make a perfect translation. Recognizing these limitations, we sought God's guidance and wisdom throughout this project. Now we pray that he will accept our efforts and use this translation for the benefit of the church and of all people.

We pray that the New Living Translation will overcome some of the barriers of history, culture, and language that have kept people from reading and understanding God's Word. We hope that readers unfamiliar with the Bible will find the words clear and easy to understand and that readers well versed in the Scriptures will gain a fresh perspective. We pray that readers will gain insight and wisdom for living, but most of all that they will meet the God of the Bible and be forever changed by knowing him.

The Bible Translation Committee
July 2004

bible translation team HOLY BIBLE, NEW LIVING TRANSLATION

PENTATEUCH
Daniel I. Block, Senior Translator
Wheaton College

GENESIS
Allen Ross, *Beeson Divinity School, Samford University*
Gordon Wenham, *University of Gloucester*

EXODUS
Robert Bergen, *Hannibal-LaGrange College*
Daniel I. Block, *Wheaton College*
Eugene Carpenter, *Bethel College, Mishawaka, Indiana*

LEVITICUS
David Baker, *Ashland Theological Seminary*
Victor Hamilton, *Asbury College*
Kenneth Mathews, *Beeson Divinity School, Samford University*

NUMBERS
Dale A. Brueggemann, *Assemblies of God Division of Foreign Missions*
R. K. Harrison (deceased), *Wycliffe College*
Paul R. House, *Wheaton College*
Gerald L. Mattingly, *Johnson Bible College*

DEUTERONOMY
J. Gordon McConville, *University of Gloucester*
Eugene H. Merrill, *Dallas Theological Seminary*
John A. Thompson (deceased), *University of Melbourne*

HISTORICAL BOOKS
Barry J. Beitzel, Senior Translator
Trinity Evangelical Divinity School

JOSHUA, JUDGES
Carl E. Armerding, *Schloss Mittersill Study Centre*
Barry J. Beitzel, *Trinity Evangelical Divinity School*
Lawson Stone, *Asbury Theological Seminary*

1 & 2 SAMUEL
Robert Gordon, *Cambridge University*
V. Philips Long, *Regent College*
J. Robert Vannoy, *Biblical Theological Seminary*

1 & 2 KINGS
Bill T. Arnold, *Asbury Theological Seminary*
William H. Barnes, *North Central University*
Frederic W. Bush, *Fuller Theological Seminary*

1 & 2 CHRONICLES
Raymond B. Dillard (deceased), *Westminster Theological Seminary*
David A. Dorsey, *Evangelical School of Theology*
Terry Eves, *Erskine College*

RUTH, EZRA–ESTHER
William C. Williams, *Vanguard University*
H. G. M. Williamson, *Oxford University*

WISDOM BOOKS
Tremper Longman III, Senior Translator
Westmont College

JOB
August Konkel, *Providence Theological Seminary*
Tremper Longman III, *Westmont College*
Al Wolters, *Redeemer College*

PSALMS 1–75
Mark D. Futato, *Reformed Theological Seminary*
Douglas Green, *Westminster Theological Seminary*
Richard Pratt, *Reformed Theological Seminary*

PSALMS 76–150
David M. Howard Jr., *Bethel Theological Seminary*
Raymond C. Ortlund Jr., *Trinity Evangelical Divinity School*
Willem VanGemeren, *Trinity Evangelical Divinity School*

PROVERBS
Ted Hildebrandt, *Gordon College*
Richard Schultz, *Wheaton College*
Raymond C. Van Leeuwen, *Eastern College*

ECCLESIASTES, SONG OF SONGS
Daniel C. Fredericks, *Belhaven College*
David Hubbard (deceased), *Fuller Theological Seminary*
Tremper Longman III, *Westmont College*

PROPHETS
John N. Oswalt, Senior Translator
Wesley Biblical Seminary

ISAIAH
John N. Oswalt, *Wesley Biblical Seminary*
Gary Smith, *Midwestern Baptist Theological Seminary*
John Walton, *Wheaton College*

JEREMIAH, LAMENTATIONS
G. Herbert Livingston, *Asbury Theological Seminary*
Elmer A. Martens, *Mennonite Brethren Biblical Seminary*

EZEKIEL
Daniel I. Block, *Wheaton College*
David H. Engelhard, *Calvin Theological Seminary*
David Thompson, *Asbury Theological Seminary*

DANIEL, HAGGAI–MALACHI
Joyce Baldwin Caine (deceased), *Trinity College, Bristol*
Douglas Gropp, *Catholic University of America*
Roy Hayden, *Oral Roberts School of Theology*
Andrew Hill, *Wheaton College*
Tremper Longman III, *Westmont College*

HOSEA–ZEPHANIAH
Joseph Coleson, *Nazarene Theological Seminary*
Roy Hayden, *Oral Roberts School of Theology*
Andrew Hill, *Wheaton College*
Richard Patterson, *Liberty University*

GOSPELS AND ACTS
Grant R. Osborne, Senior Translator
Trinity Evangelical Divinity School

MATTHEW
Craig Blomberg, *Denver Seminary*
Donald A. Hagner, *Fuller Theological Seminary*
David Turner, *Grand Rapids Baptist Seminary*

MARK
Robert Guelich (deceased), *Fuller Theological Seminary*
George Guthrie, *Union University*
Grant R. Osborne, *Trinity Evangelical Divinity School*

LUKE
Darrell Bock, *Dallas Theological Seminary*
Scot McKnight, *North Park University*
Robert Stein, *The Southern Baptist Theological Seminary*

JOHN
Gary M. Burge, *Wheaton College*
Philip W. Comfort, *Coastal Carolina University*
Marianne Meye Thompson, *Fuller Theological Seminary*

ACTS
D. A. Carson, *Trinity Evangelical Divinity School*
William J. Larkin, *Columbia International University*
Roger Mohrlang, *Whitworth University*

LETTERS AND REVELATION
Norman R. Ericson, Senior Translator
Wheaton College

ROMANS, GALATIANS
Gerald Borchert, *Northern Baptist Theological Seminary*
Douglas J. Moo, *Wheaton College*
Thomas R. Schreiner, *The Southern Baptist Theological Seminary*

1 & 2 CORINTHIANS
Joseph Alexanian, *Trinity International University*
Linda Belleville, *Bethel College, Mishawaka, Indiana*
Douglas A. Oss, *Central Bible College*
Robert Sloan, *Baylor University*

EPHESIANS–PHILEMON
Harold W. Hoehner, *Dallas Theological Seminary*
Moises Silva, *Gordon-Conwell Theological Seminary*
Klyne Snodgrass, *North Park Theological Seminary*

HEBREWS, JAMES, 1 & 2 PETER, JUDE
Peter Davids, *Schloss Mittersill Study Centre*
Norman R. Ericson, *Wheaton College*
William Lane (deceased), *Seattle Pacific University*
J. Ramsey Michaels, *S. W. Missouri State University*

1–3 JOHN, REVELATION
Greg Beale, *Wheaton College*
Robert Mounce, *Whitworth University*
M. Robert Mulholland Jr., *Asbury Theological Seminary*

SPECIAL REVIEWERS
F. F. Bruce (deceased), *University of Manchester*
Kenneth N. Taylor (deceased), *Translator,* The Living Bible

COORDINATING TEAM
Mark D. Taylor, *Director and Chief Stylist*
Ronald A. Beers, *Executive Director and Stylist*
Mark R. Norton, *Managing Editor and O.T. Coordinating Editor*
Philip W. Comfort, *N.T. Coordinating Editor*
Daniel W. Taylor, *Bethel University, Senior Stylist*

Welcome to the *Student's Life Application Study Bible*. Most power tools come with a user's manual or instructions of some kind. This book is no exception! God gave us his Word to tell us about himself: how he operates, what he's done, and what his plans are for the people he created. This book is a "power tool" you can use. Wanna know more? Check this out: "All Scripture is inspired by God and is useful to teach us what is true and to make us realize what is wrong in our lives. It corrects us when we are wrong and teaches us to do what is right. God uses it to prepare and equip his people to do every good work" (2 Timothy 3:16-17).

So, what're we to make of that? For starters, it reminds us to make Bible reading a priority. That's why the *Student's Life Application Study Bible* was written—to help you understand and apply God's Word. It's easy to use and packed with helpful notes and other features. You'll find the notes within the text, at the beginnings and endings of books, and at the back of the Bible.

At the back of the Bible you'll find . . .

A LOOK AT THE BOOK

By following this simple Bible reading plan, you'll read through all the important biblical stories and passages in a year.

LIFE CHOICES REFERENCE INDEX

You'll face many choices and questions in life—questions that need answers; choices that need wisdom. More than 100 topics are listed in this index. Each topic has a selection of relevant Bible passages and notes that relate.

INDEXES FOR "CHOICES," "I WONDER," ULTIMATE ISSUES, CHARTS, PERSONALITY PROFILES, MAPS, AND "KEEPING IT REAL"

Again, Scripture references listed for these notes are to help you locate the notes easily. The notes may or may not actually relate to the Scripture listed.

"WHERE TO FIND IT" INDEX

More than 70 of the best-known Bible stories are listed in this index, along with Jesus' parables and miracles. Use either the Scripture references or the page numbers to quickly and easily find the story, parable, or miracle you want.

It's all here. Just about everything you'll need to understand and apply God's word. The next step—actually taking time to read and study the Bible—is yours. *So, what are you waiting for?*

The following spread is a quick look at each of the special features:

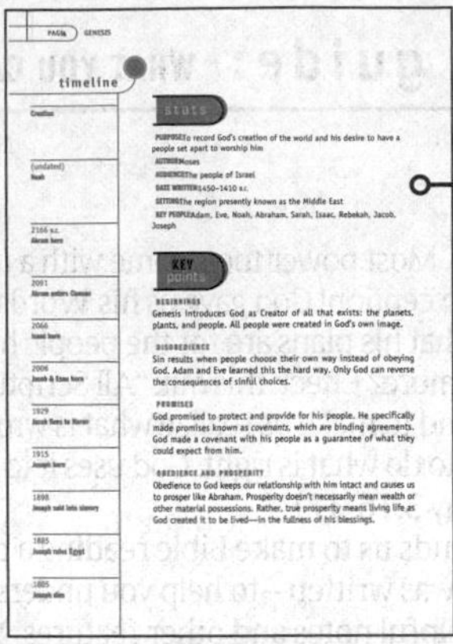

BOOK INTRODUCTIONS

Want to know the who, what, when, where, and how of a particular book of the Bible? Check out the introduction. (Every story has to start somewhere.) Need info about the time period (like maybe a timeline)? It's all right there. You will also find a list of "Key Points"—the main themes found in each book. What more could you ask for?

LIFE APPLICATION NOTES

Throughout the Bible, you'll find notes to help you understand and apply a specific passage of Scripture to your life. Cool, huh?

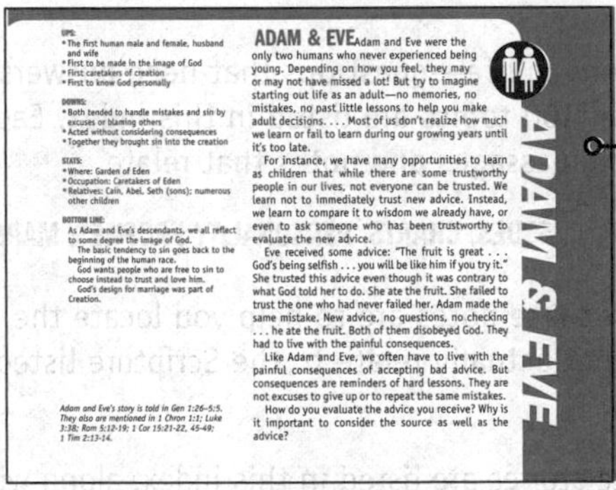

PERSONALITY PROFILE

Each personality profile is a mini-biography of a key person in the Bible. It's like watching *Biography*, but without the commercials.

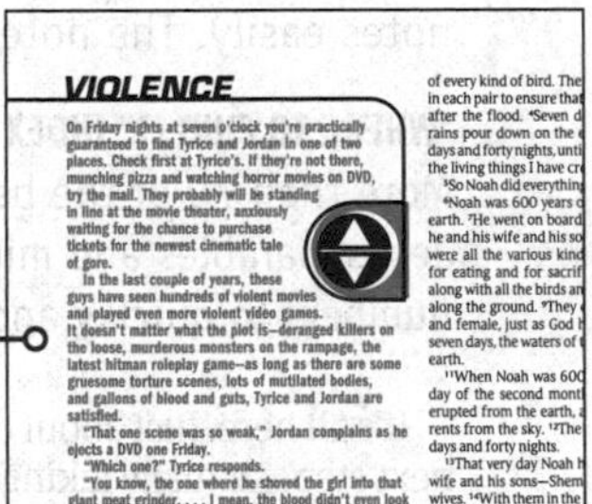

CHOICES

You face choices each day. This feature shows some of the choices many teens face, choices that lead to triumph or tragedy. You can choose to read these notes.

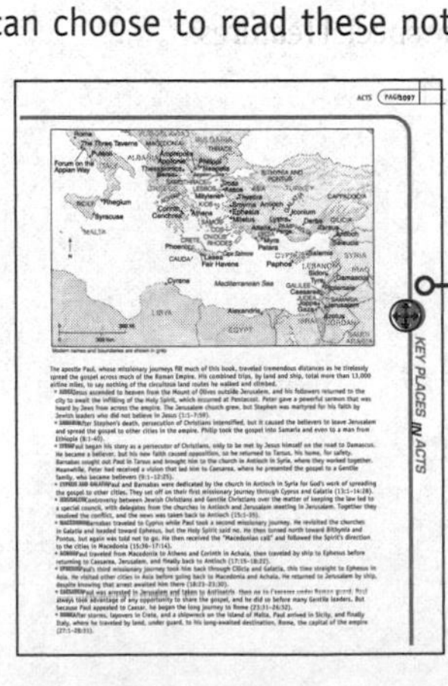

MAPS

Your atlas to Bible locations. Hunting for Ur of the Chaldeans? Check out a map. You won't have to stop and ask for directions.

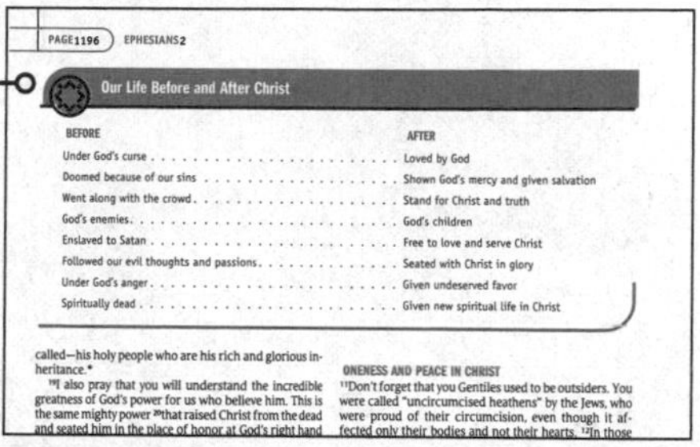
PAGE1196 EPHESIANS2

Our Life Before and After Christ

BEFORE	AFTER
Under God's curse	Loved by God
Doomed because of our sins	Shown God's mercy and given salvation
Went along with the crowd	Stand for Christ and truth
God's enemies	God's children
Enslaved to Satan	Free to love and serve Christ
Followed our evil thoughts and passions	Seated with Christ in glory
Under God's anger	Given undeserved favor
Spiritually dead	Given new spiritual life in Christ

called—his holy people who are his rich and glorious inheritance.* [19]I also pray that you will understand the incredible greatness of God's power for us who believe him. This is the same mighty power [20]that raised Christ from the dead and seated him in the place of honor at God's right hand

ONENESS AND PEACE IN CHRIST
[11]Don't forget that you Gentiles used to be outsiders. You were called "uncircumcised heathens" by the Jews, who were proud of their circumcision, even though it affected only their bodies and not their hearts. [12]In those

CHARTS

Love lists of related Bible facts (days of creation; the judges of Israel)? Look and learn throughout.

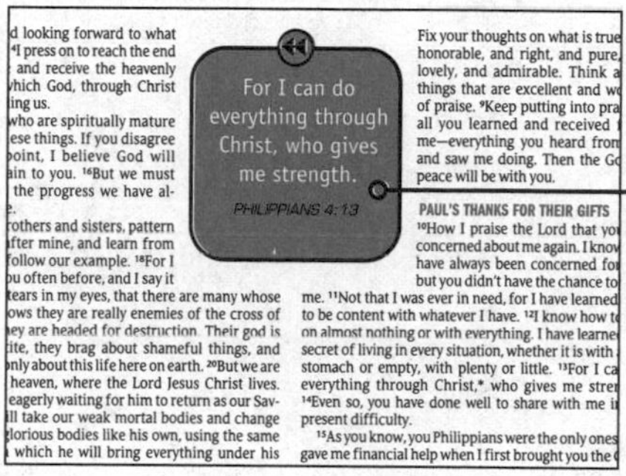

For I can do everything through Christ, who gives me strength.
PHILIPPIANS 4:13
PAUL'S THANKS FOR THEIR GIFTS

KEY VERSES

You'll find a verse highlighted in each book. (Like a Post-it note on a bathroom mirror, these stand out.) Each verse can remind you of the hope and strength God provides.

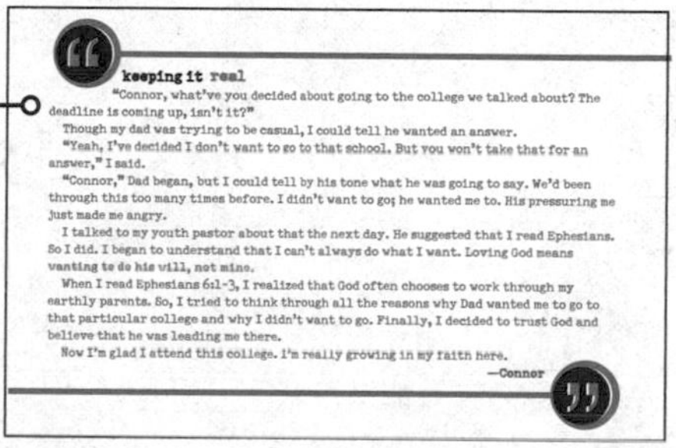
keeping it real

"Connor, what've you decided about going to the college we talked about? The deadline is coming up, isn't it?"

Though my dad was trying to be casual, I could tell he wanted an answer.

"Yeah, I've decided I don't want to go to that school. But you won't take that for an answer," I said.

"Connor," Dad began, but I could tell by his tone what he was going to say. We'd been through this too many times before. I didn't want to go; he wanted me to. His pressuring me just made me angry.

I talked to my youth pastor about that the next day. He suggested that I read Ephesians. So I did. I began to understand that I can't always do what I want. Loving God means wanting to do his will, not mine.

When I read Ephesians 6:1-3, I realized that God often chooses to work through my earthly parents. So, I tried to think through all the reasons why Dad wanted me to go to that particular college and why I didn't want to go. Finally, I decided to trust God and believe that he was leading me there.

Now I'm glad I attend this college. I'm really growing in my faith here.

—Connor

KEEPING IT REAL

Everyone has a story. Throughout the Bible, you'll find stories that will help you see how God's Word can be applied to specific, real-life situations today.

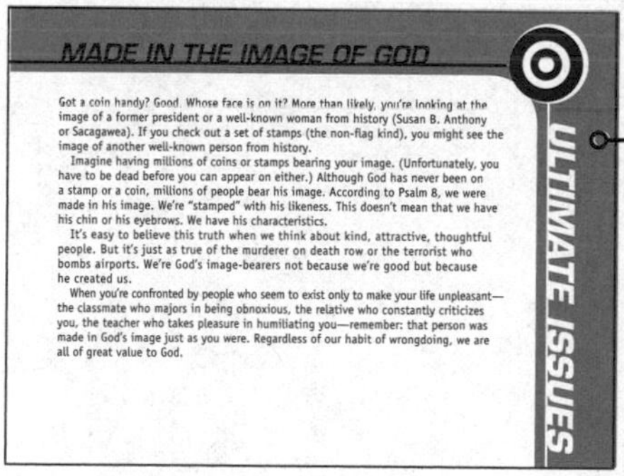
MADE IN THE IMAGE OF GOD

ULTIMATE ISSUES

Got a coin handy? Good. Whose face is on it? More than likely, you're looking at the image of a former president or a well-known woman from history (Susan B. Anthony or Sacagawea). If you check out a set of stamps (the non-flag kind), you might see the image of another well-known person from history.

Imagine having millions of coins or stamps bearing your image. (Unfortunately, you have to be dead before you can appear on either.) Although God has never been on a stamp or a coin, millions of people bear his image. According to Psalm 8, we were made in his image. We're "stamped" with his likeness. This doesn't mean that we have his chin or his eyebrows. We have his characteristics.

It's easy to believe this truth when we think about kind, attractive, thoughtful people. But it's just as true of the murderer on death row or the terrorist who bombs airports. We're God's image-bearers not because we're good but because he created us.

When you're confronted by people who seem to exist only to make your life unpleasant—the classmate who majors in being obnoxious, the relative who constantly criticizes you, the teacher who takes pleasure in humiliating you—remember: that person was made in God's image just as you were. Regardless of our habit of wrongdoing, we are all of great value to God.

ULTIMATE ISSUES

This feature explores hard issues about God, the Bible, and life in general. Curious? Check 'em out.

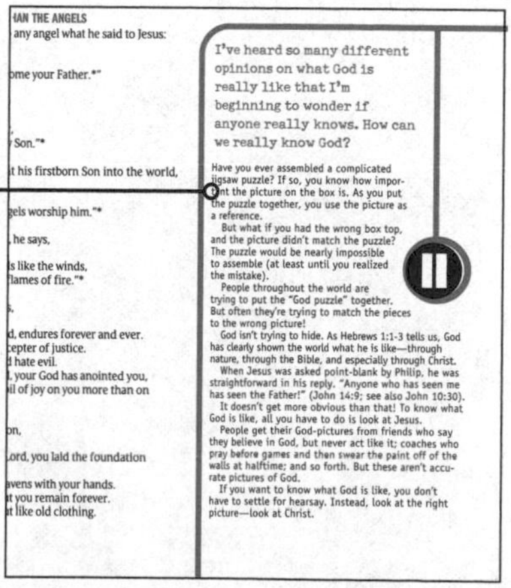
I've heard so many different opinions on what God is really like that I'm beginning to wonder if anyone really knows. How can we really know God?

Have you ever assembled a complicated jigsaw puzzle? If so, you know how important the picture on the box is. As you put the puzzle together, you use the picture as a reference.

But what if you had the wrong box top, and the picture didn't match the puzzle? The puzzle would be nearly impossible to assemble (at least until you realized the mistake).

People throughout the world are trying to put the "God puzzle" together. But often they're trying to match the pieces to the wrong picture!

God isn't trying to hide. As Hebrews 1:1-3 tells us, God has clearly shown the world what he is like—through nature, through the Bible, and especially through Christ.

When Jesus was asked point-blank by Philip, he was straightforward in his reply. "Anyone who has seen me has seen the Father!" (John 14:9; see also John 10:30).

It doesn't get more obvious than that! To know what God is like, all you have to do is look at Jesus.

People get their God-pictures from friends who say they believe in God, but never act like it; coaches who pray before games and then swear the paint off of the walls at halftime; and so forth. But these aren't accurate pictures of God.

If you want to know what God is like, you don't have to settle for hearsay. Instead, look at the right picture—look at Christ.

I WONDER . . .

Got questions about the Bible? You might find some of the ones you've asked, along with answers anchored to specific Scriptures.

old testament

GENESIS

EVER TURN ON a TV show a few minutes after it began? Chances are you turned it off before the show ended or flipped to a different channel because you couldn't figure out what was going on. To fully understand the plot, you needed to see the beginning of the show.

The same truth applies to the Bible. If you're having a hard time figuring out the "plot," Genesis is the right place to begin your search for answers. Why? Genesis is the book of beginnings. In it you see the creation of the universe, the introduction of sin into the world, the beginning of God's plan to rescue his people from the sin habit, and the birth of the nation of Israel.

In Genesis we also get our first glimpse into God's character. Unlike everything else, God didn't have a beginning. He always existed. Chapters 1 and 2 showcase his creativeness and power, while chapter 3 reveals his holiness and judgment of sin. Through the sad saga of Adam and Eve and their descendants, we view God's incredible love for his people even when they constantly disobey him.

As you read Genesis, what other beginnings do you see? How do they enlarge your view of God?

genesis

timeline

Creation

(undated)
Noah

2166 B.C.
Abram born

2091
Abram enters Canaan

2066
Isaac born

2006
Jacob & Esau born

1929
Jacob flees to Haran

1915
Joseph born

1898
Joseph sold into slavery

1885
Joseph rules Egypt

1805
Joseph dies

stats

PURPOSE: To record God's creation of the world and his desire to have a people set apart to worship him

AUTHOR: Moses

AUDIENCE: The people of Israel

DATE WRITTEN: 1450–1410 B.C.

SETTING: The region presently known as the Middle East

KEY PEOPLE: Adam, Eve, Noah, Abraham, Sarah, Isaac, Rebekah, Jacob, Joseph

KEY points

BEGINNINGS
Genesis introduces God as Creator of all that exists: the planets, plants, and people. All people were created in God's own image.

DISOBEDIENCE
Sin results when people choose their own way instead of obeying God. Adam and Eve learned this the hard way. Only God can reverse the consequences of sinful choices.

PROMISES
God promised to protect and provide for his people. He specifically made promises known as *covenants,* which are binding agreements. God made a covenant with his people as a guarantee of what they could expect from him.

OBEDIENCE AND PROSPERITY
Obedience to God keeps our relationship with him intact and causes us to prosper like Abraham. Prosperity doesn't necessarily mean wealth or other material possessions. Rather, true prosperity means living life as God created it to be lived—in the fullness of his blessings.

KEY PLACES IN GENESIS

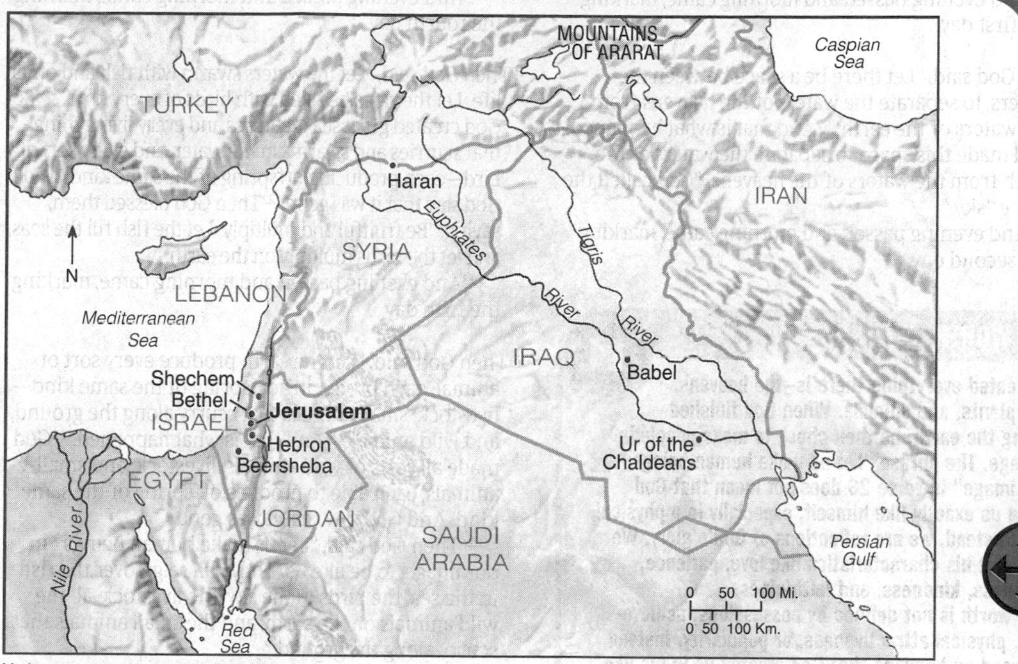

Modern names and boundaries are shown in gray.

God created the universe and the earth. Then he made man and woman, giving them a home in a beautiful garden. Unfortunately, Adam and Eve disobeyed God and were expelled from the garden (3:24).

- **MOUNTAINS OF ARARAT** Adam and Eve's sin brought sin into the human race. Years later, sin had run rampant and God decided to destroy the earth with a great flood. All except for Noah, his family, and two of each animal who were all safe in a huge boat. When the floods receded, the boat rested on the mountains of Ararat (8:4).
- **BABEL** People never learn. Again sin abounded and the pride of the people led them to build a huge tower as a monument to their own greatness—obviously they had no thought of God. As punishment, God scattered the people by giving them different languages (11:8-9).
- **UR OF THE CHALDEANS** Abram, a descendant of Shem, was born in this great city (11:27-28).
- **HARAN** Terah, Lot, Abram, and Sarai left Ur and, following the fertile crescent of the Euphrates River, headed toward the land of Canaan. Along the way, they settled in the city of Haran for a while (11:31).
- **SHECHEM** God urged Abram to leave Haran and go to a place where he would become the father of a great nation (12:1-2). So Abram, Lot, and Sarai traveled to the land of Canaan and settled near a city called Shechem (12:5-6).
- **HEBRON** Abraham moved on to Hebron, to "the oak grove belonging to Mamre," where he put down his deepest roots (13:18). Abraham, Isaac, and Jacob all lived and were buried there.
- **BEERSHEBA** After a dispute over ownership of the well here, Abraham made a covenant with Abimelech (21:31). Years later, as Isaac was moving from place to place, God appeared to him here and passed on to him the covenant he had made with his father, Abraham (26:23-25).
- **BETHEL** After deceiving his brother out of both his birthright and his blessing, Jacob left Beersheba and fled to Haran. Along the way God revealed himself to Jacob in a dream and again passed on the covenant he had made with Abraham and Isaac (28:10-22). Jacob lived in Haran, worked for Laban, and married Leah and Rachel (29:15-28). After a tense meeting with his brother, Esau, Jacob returned to Bethel (35:1).
- **EGYPT** Jacob had 12 sons, including Joseph, Jacob's favorite. The other brothers grew jealous, until one day, out in the fields, the brothers sold him to Ishmaelite traders who were going to Egypt. Eventually, Joseph rose from Egyptian slave to Pharaoh's "right hand man," saving Egypt and the surrounding country from famine. His entire family moved from Canaan to Egypt and settled there during the severe famine (46:3-4).

1

THE ACCOUNT OF CREATION

In the beginning God created the heavens and the earth.*
2The earth was formless and empty, and darkness covered the deep waters. And the Spirit of God was hovering
over the surface of the waters.
3Then God said, "Let there be light," and there
was light. 4And God saw that the light was good.
Then he separated the light from the darkness.
5God called the light "day" and the darkness
"night."

1:1 Or *In the beginning when God created the heavens and the earth, . . .* Or *When God began to create the heavens and the earth, . . .*

And evening passed and morning came, marking
the first day.

6 Then God said, "Let there be a space between the
waters, to separate the waters of the heavens from
the waters of the earth." 7 And that is what happened.
God made this space to separate the waters of the
earth from the waters of the heavens. 8 God called the
space "sky."
And evening passed and morning came, marking
the second day.

TRUE WORTH 1:1-26

God created everything there is—the heavens, earth, plants, and animals. When God finished creating the earth, he then chose to make people in his image. The phrase "Let *us* make human beings in *our* image" in verse 26 does not mean that God created us exactly like himself, especially in a physical sense. Instead, we are reflections of God's glory. We can reflect his characteristics like love, patience, forgiveness, kindness, and faithfulness.

Our worth is not defined by possessions, achievements, physical attractiveness, or popularity. Instead, it is based on knowing that God created us in his likeness. Knowing that you are a person of infinite worth gives you the freedom to love God, know him personally, and make a valuable contribution to the lives of those around you. ■

9 Then God said, "Let the waters beneath the sky flow
together into one place, so dry ground may appear."
And that is what happened. 10 God called the dry
ground "land" and the waters "seas." And God saw
that it was good. 11 Then God said, "Let the land
sprout with vegetation—every sort of seed-bearing
plant, and trees that grow seed-bearing fruit. These
seeds will then produce the kinds of plants and trees
from which they came." And that is what happened.
12 The land produced vegetation—all sorts of seed-
bearing plants, and trees with seed-bearing fruit.
Their seeds produced plants and trees of the same
kind. And God saw that it was good.
13 And evening passed and morning came, marking
the third day.

14 Then God said, "Let lights appear in the sky to
separate the day from the night. Let them mark
off the seasons, days, and years. 15 Let these lights in
the sky shine down on the earth." And that is what
happened. 16 God made two great lights—the larger
one to govern the day, and the smaller one to govern
the night. He also made the stars. 17 God set these
lights in the sky to light the earth, 18 to govern the
day and night, and to separate the light from the
darkness. And God saw that it was good.

19 And evening passed and morning came, marking
the fourth day.

20 Then God said, "Let the waters swarm with fish and other
life. Let the skies be filled with birds of every kind." 21 So
God created great sea creatures and every living thing
that scurries and swarms in the water, and every sort of
bird—each producing offspring of the same kind. And
God saw that it was good. 22 Then God blessed them,
saying, "Be fruitful and multiply. Let the fish fill the seas,
and let the birds multiply on the earth."
23 And evening passed and morning came, marking
the fifth day.

24 Then God said, "Let the earth produce every sort of
animal, each producing offspring of the same kind—
livestock, small animals that scurry along the ground,
and wild animals." And that is what happened. 25 God
made all sorts of wild animals, livestock, and small
animals, each able to produce offspring of the same
kind. And God saw that it was good.
26 Then God said, "Let us make human beings* in
our image, to be like us. They will reign over the fish
in the sea, the birds in the sky, the livestock, all the
wild animals on the earth, and the small animals that
scurry along the ground."

27 So God created human beings* in his own image.
In the image of God he created them;
male and female he created them.

28 Then God blessed them and said, "Be fruitful and
multiply. Fill the earth and govern it. Reign over the
fish in the sea, the birds in the sky, and all the animals
that scurry along the ground."

MARRIAGE 2:18-24

God's creative work was not complete until he made woman. He could have made her from the dust of the ground, as he made man. God chose, however, to make her from the man's flesh and bone. In so doing, he illustrated that in marriage man and woman symbolically become one flesh. This is a mystical union of the couple's hearts and lives. Throughout the Bible, God treats this special partnership seriously. If you are planning to be married, are you willing to keep the commitment that makes the two of you one? What are some helpful habits you can begin to develop that will help you honor that commitment? ■

29 Then God said, "Look! I have given you every seed-
bearing plant throughout the earth and all the fruit trees
for your food. 30 And I have given every green plant as
food for all the wild animals, the birds in the sky, and the
small animals that scurry along the ground—everything
that has life." And that is what happened.

1:26 Or *man;* Hebrew reads *adam.* **1:27** Or *the man;* Hebrew reads *ha-adam.*

THE ORIGIN OF HUMANITY

ULTIMATE ISSUES

Ever been part of the great ape debate? Wondering what that is? If you've read a biology textbook or those of other life sciences lately, you'll find the theory that humans descended from apes. Or so Darwin's theory of evolution goes. On the other side of the coin, however, is a quote like this from Genesis: "In the beginning God created the heavens and the earth."

But many educators, philosophers, and others tell us that we evolved from nothing into one-celled animals, then progressed up the zoological chain to evolve into *Homo sapiens*. Or perhaps a third option exists—God created people, using the process of evolution as his "laboratory."

An uneasy tension exists between these views. Are you feeling it? Maybe you're wondering which viewpoint is the "right" viewpoint.

According to the Bible, humans, animals, and everything else in the universe were created by God. The idea that we simply materialized out of nothing is a logical and scientific impossibility. Check this out. The first law of thermodynamics tells us that matter can neither be created nor destroyed by natural causes. That's a big problem for an evolutionist. If only natural causes are involved, how did nothing turn into something? Also, how did that "something" develop intelligence, a definite personality, morality, and spirituality? By chance? Impossible!

So, what does this all add up to? Three words: *God did it.* This truth does not rule out the possibility of some kind of God-directed evolution; neither does it give it any support. And frankly, honest evolutionists will admit that their beliefs involve as much faith and speculation—if not more—as the creationists'.

The Bible (Genesis in particular) gives us one core fact about the origin of humanity: God created us in his own image. Exactly how he did that remains a matter of faith. So, what do you believe?

31Then God looked over all he had made, and he
saw that it was very good!
And evening passed and morning came, marking
the sixth day.

2 So the creation of the heavens and the earth and
everything in them was completed. 2On the seventh
day God had finished his work of creation, so he
rested* from all his work. 3And God blessed the
seventh day and declared it holy, because it was
the day when he rested from all his work of
creation.

4This is the account of the creation of the heavens and
the earth.

THE MAN AND WOMAN IN EDEN

When the LORD God made the earth and the heavens,
5neither wild plants nor grains were growing on the earth.
For the LORD God had not yet sent rain to water the earth,
and there were no people to cultivate the soil. 6Instead,
springs* came up from the ground and watered all the
land. 7Then the LORD God formed the man from the dust
of the ground. He breathed the breath of life into the
man's nostrils, and the man became a living person.
8Then the LORD God planted a garden in Eden in the
east, and there he placed the man he had made. 9The LORD
God made all sorts of trees grow up from the ground—
trees that were beautiful and that produced delicious
fruit. In the middle of the garden he placed the tree of life
and the tree of the knowledge of good and evil.
10A river flowed from the land of Eden, watering the
garden and then dividing into four branches. 11The first
branch, called the Pishon, flowed around the entire land
of Havilah, where gold is found. 12The gold of that land is
exceptionally pure; aromatic resin and onyx stone are
also found there. 13The second branch, called the Gihon,
flowed around the entire land of Cush. 14The third
branch, called the Tigris, flowed east of the land of Asshur. The fourth branch is called the Euphrates.
15The LORD God placed the man in the Garden of Eden
to tend and watch over it. 16But the LORD God warned
him, "You may freely eat the fruit of every tree in the garden—17except the tree of the knowledge of good and evil.
If you eat its fruit, you are sure to die."
18Then the LORD God said, "It is not good for the man to
be alone. I will make a helper who is just right for him."

2:2 Or *ceased;* also in 2:3. 2:6 Or *mist.*

Days of Creation

DAY 1	LIGHT so there was light and darkness
DAY 2	SKY AND WATER waters separated
DAY 3	SEA AND LAND waters gathered
DAY 4	SUN, MOON, AND STARS to preside over day and night, to mark off seasons, days, and years
DAY 5	FISH AND BIRDS to fill the waters and the sky
DAY 6	ANIMALS to fill the earth MAN AND WOMAN to care for the earth and commune with God
DAY 7	GOD RESTED AND WAS PLEASED

19So the LORD God formed from the ground all the wild
animals and all the birds of the sky. He brought them to
the man* to see what he would call them, and the man
chose a name for each one. 20He gave names to all the
livestock, all the birds of the sky, and all the wild animals.
But still there was no helper just right for him.
21So the LORD God caused the man to fall into a deep
sleep. While the man slept, the LORD God took out one of
the man's ribs* and closed up the opening. 22Then the
LORD God made a woman from the rib, and he brought
her to the man.
23"At last!" the man exclaimed.

"This one is bone from my bone,
 and flesh from my flesh!
She will be called 'woman,'
 because she was taken from 'man.'"

24This explains why a man leaves his father and
mother and is joined to his wife, and the two are united
into one.
25Now the man and his wife were both naked, but they
felt no shame.

3 THE MAN AND WOMAN SIN

The serpent was the shrewdest of all the wild animals the
LORD God had made. One day he asked the woman, "Did
God really say you must not eat the fruit from any of the
trees in the garden?"
2"Of course we may eat fruit from the trees in the garden," the woman replied. 3"It's only the fruit from the
tree in the middle of the garden that we are not allowed
to eat. God said, 'You must not eat it or even touch it; if
you do, you will die.'"
4"You won't die!" the serpent replied to the woman.
5"God knows that your eyes will be opened as soon as you
eat it, and you will be like God, knowing both good and
evil."
6The woman was convinced. She saw that the tree was
beautiful and its fruit looked delicious, and she wanted
the wisdom it would give her. So she took some of the
fruit and ate it. Then she gave some to her husband, who
was with her, and he ate it, too. 7At that moment their
eyes were opened, and they suddenly felt shame at their
nakedness. So they sewed fig leaves together to cover
themselves.
8When the cool evening breezes were blowing, the
man* and his wife heard the LORD God walking about in
the garden. So they hid from the LORD God among the
trees. 9Then the LORD God called to the man, "Where are
you?"
10He replied, "I heard you walking in the garden, so I
hid. I was afraid because I was naked."

Satan's Plan

DOUBT	Makes you question God's Word and his goodness
DISCOURAGEMENT	Makes you look at your problems rather than at God
DIVERSION	Makes the wrong things seem attractive so you want them more than the right things
DEFEAT	Makes you feel like a failure, so you don't even try
DELAY	Makes you put off doing something, so it never gets done

11"Who told you that you were naked?" the LORD God
asked. "Have you eaten from the tree whose fruit I commanded you not to eat?"
12The man replied, "It was the woman you gave me who
gave me the fruit, and I ate it."
13Then the LORD God asked the woman, "What have
you done?"

2:19 Or *Adam*, and so throughout the chapter. 2:21 Or *took a part of the man's side*. 3:8 Or *Adam*, and so throughout the chapter.

"The serpent deceived me," she replied. "That's why I ate it."

14Then the LORD God said to the serpent,

"Because you have done this, you are cursed
more than all animals, domestic and wild.
You will crawl on your belly,
groveling in the dust as long as you live.
15 And I will cause hostility between you and the woman,
and between your offspring and her offspring.
He will strike* your head,
and you will strike his heel."

16Then he said to the woman,

"I will sharpen the pain of your pregnancy,
and in pain you will give birth.
And you will desire to control your husband,
but he will rule over you.*"

17And to the man he said,

"Since you listened to your wife and ate from the tree
whose fruit I commanded you not to eat,
the ground is cursed because of you.
All your life you will struggle to scratch a living
from it.
18 It will grow thorns and thistles for you,
though you will eat of its grains.
19 By the sweat of your brow
will you have food to eat
until you return to the ground
from which you were made.
For you were made from dust,
and to dust you will return."

PARADISE LOST: GOD'S JUDGMENT

20Then the man—Adam—named his wife Eve, because
she would be the mother of all who live.* 21And the LORD
God made clothing from animal skins for Adam and his
wife.

22Then the LORD God said, "Look, the human beings*
have become like us, knowing both good and evil. What if
they reach out, take fruit from the tree of life, and eat it?
Then they will live forever!" 23So the LORD God banished
them from the Garden of Eden, and he sent Adam out to
cultivate the ground from which he had been made.

3:15 Or *bruise;* also in 3:15b. 3:16 Or *And though you will have desire for your husband, / he will rule over you.* 3:20 *Eve* sounds like a Hebrew term that means "to give life." 3:22 Or *the man;* Hebrew reads *ha-adam.*

ADAM & EVE

Adam and Eve were the only two humans who never experienced being young. Depending on how you feel, they may or may not have missed a lot! But try to imagine starting out life as an adult—no memories, no mistakes, no past little lessons to help you make adult decisions. . . . Most of us don't realize how much we learn or fail to learn during our growing years until it's too late.

For instance, we have many opportunities to learn as children that while there are some trustworthy people in our lives, not everyone can be trusted. We learn not to immediately trust new advice. Instead, we learn to compare it to wisdom we already have, or even to ask someone who has been trustworthy to evaluate the new advice.

Eve received some advice: "The fruit is great . . . God's being selfish . . . you will be like him if you try it." She trusted this advice even though it was contrary to what God told her to do. She ate the fruit. She failed to trust the one who had never failed her. Adam made the same mistake. New advice, no questions, no checking . . . he ate the fruit. Both of them disobeyed God. They had to live with the painful consequences.

Like Adam and Eve, we often have to live with the painful consequences of accepting bad advice. But consequences are reminders of hard lessons. They are not excuses to give up or to repeat the same mistakes.

How do you evaluate the advice you receive? Why is it important to consider the source as well as the advice?

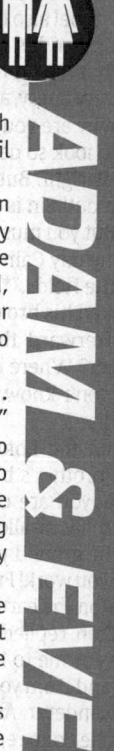

UPS:
- The first human male and female, husband and wife
- First to be made in the image of God
- First caretakers of creation
- First to know God personally

DOWNS:
- Both tended to handle mistakes and sin by excuses or blaming others
- Acted without considering consequences
- Together they brought sin into the creation

STATS:
- Where: Garden of Eden
- Occupation: Caretakers of Eden
- Relatives: Cain, Abel, Seth (sons); numerous other children

BOTTOM LINE:

As Adam and Eve's descendants, we all reflect to some degree the image of God.

The basic tendency to sin goes back to the beginning of the human race.

God wants people who are free to sin to choose instead to trust and love him.

God's design for marriage was part of Creation.

Adam and Eve's story is told in Gen 1:26–5:5. They also are mentioned in 1 Chron 1:1; Luke 3:38; Rom 5:12-19; 1 Cor 15:21-22, 45-49; 1 Tim 2:13-14.

BIG MISTAKE 4:3-10

Adam and Eve's disobedience (Gen 3) brought sin into the human race. They may have thought their sin (eating a "harmless" piece of fruit) wasn't very bad, but notice how quickly the sin habit developed in the lives of their children. Simple disobedience blossomed into outright murder. Adam and Eve acted only against God, but Cain acted against both God and man. A small sin has a way of growing out of control. Feeling controlled by the sin habit? The best way to break free is to put yourself under God's control. ■

24After sending them out, the LORD God stationed mighty
cherubim to the east of the Garden of Eden. And he
placed a flaming sword that flashed back and forth to
guard the way to the tree of life.

4 CAIN AND ABEL

Now Adam* had sexual relations with his wife, Eve, and
she became pregnant. When she gave birth to Cain, she
said, "With the LORD's help, I have produced* a man!"
2Later she gave birth to his brother and named him
Abel.

When they grew up, Abel became a shepherd, while
Cain cultivated the ground. 3When it was time for the
harvest, Cain presented some of his crops as a gift to the
LORD. 4Abel also brought a gift—the best of the firstborn
lambs from his flock. The LORD accepted Abel and his
gift, 5but he did not accept Cain and his gift. This made
Cain very angry, and he looked dejected.

6"Why are you so angry?" the LORD asked Cain. "Why
do you look so dejected? 7You will be accepted if you do
what is right. But if you refuse to do what is right, then
watch out! Sin is crouching at the door, eager to control
you. But you must subdue it and be its master."

8One day Cain suggested to his brother, "Let's go out
into the fields."* And while they were in the field, Cain
attacked his brother, Abel, and killed him.

9Afterward the LORD asked Cain, "Where is your
brother? Where is Abel?"

"I don't know," Cain responded. "Am I my brother's
guardian?"

10But the LORD said, "What have you done? Listen!
Your brother's blood cries out to me from the ground!
11Now you are cursed and banished from the ground,
which has swallowed your brother's blood. 12No longer
will the ground yield good crops for you, no matter how
hard you work! From now on you will be a homeless wanderer on the earth."

13Cain replied to the LORD, "My punishment* is too
great for me to bear! 14You have banished me from the
land and from your presence; you have made me a homeless wanderer. Anyone who finds me will kill me!"

15The LORD replied, "No, for I will give a sevenfold punishment to anyone who kills you." Then the LORD put a
mark on Cain to warn anyone who might try to kill him.
16So Cain left the LORD's presence and settled in the land
of Nod,* east of Eden.

THE DESCENDANTS OF CAIN

17Cain had sexual relations with his wife, and she became
pregnant and gave birth to Enoch. Then Cain founded a
city, which he named Enoch, after his son. 18Enoch had a
son named Irad. Irad became the father of* Mehujael.
Mehujael became the father of Methushael. Methushael
became the father of Lamech.

19Lamech married two women. The first was named
Adah, and the second was Zillah. 20Adah gave birth to Jabal, who was the first of those who raise livestock and live
in tents. 21His brother's name was Jubal, the first of all
who play the harp and flute. 22Lamech's other wife, Zillah, gave birth to a son named Tubal-cain. He became an

4:1a Or *the man;* also in 4:25. **4:1b** Or *I have acquired. Cain* sounds like a Hebrew term that can mean "produce" or "acquire." **4:8** As in Samaritan Pentateuch, Greek and Syriac versions, and Latin Vulgate; Masoretic Text lacks *"Let's go out into the fields."* **4:13** Or *My sin.* **4:16** *Nod* means "wandering." **4:18** Or *the ancestor of,* and so throughout the verse.

What does God really expect from me? Do I have to be perfect in order to please him?

When you look at Abel's life (Genesis 4), do you ever think that you have to be perfect in order to please God?

Some people view God as an impossible taskmaster with impossibly high expectations. Ever think that way?

Here's the deal: like any loving parent, God has expects his kids to act a certain way. (Think of your parents' expectations for you.) Some Christians may tell you about God's expectations based on where they are in their walk with him. An abundance of advice often contributes to the belief that God expects way too much. If you are feeling overwhelmed, you might be listening to others' expectations, rather than God's.

So, how can you please God? The story of Cain and Abel gives a significant piece to the puzzle. Both of these men brought something to God; yet only Abel's sacrifice pleased God. One reason was because Cain's heart was not really in his offering. He tried to please God out of obligation instead of love.

The first step in pleasing God is to examine our motivation for doing so. Do we really want to please him, or are we going through the motions because someone told us we should?

Obedience is the second step to pleasing God. It means loving him enough to listen to what he says, then following through on what we know he tells us to do.

Through the Holy Spirit, God speaks to us as we come to him with willing hearts. He gently shows us areas in our lives that we need to examine and change according to his timetable, not someone else's.

expert in forging tools of bronze and iron. Tubal-cain
had a sister named Naamah. 23One day Lamech said to
his wives,

> "Adah and Zillah, hear my voice;
> listen to me, you wives of Lamech.
> I have killed a man who attacked me,
> a young man who wounded me.
> 24 If someone who kills Cain is punished seven times,
> then the one who kills me will be punished seventy-seven times!"

THE BIRTH OF SETH

25Adam had sexual relations with his wife again, and she
gave birth to another son. She named him Seth,* for she
said, "God has granted me another son in place of Abel,
whom Cain killed." 26When Seth grew up, he had a son
and named him Enosh. At that time people first began to
worship the LORD by name.

5 THE DESCENDANTS OF ADAM

This is the written account of the descendants of Adam.
When God created human beings,* he made them to be
like himself. 2He created them male and female, and he
blessed them and called them "human."

3When Adam was 130 years old, he became the father
of a son who was just like him—in his very image.
He named his son Seth. 4After the birth of Seth,
Adam lived another 800 years, and he had other
sons and daughters. 5Adam lived 930 years, and
then he died.

6When Seth was 105 years old, he became the father
of* Enosh. 7After the birth of* Enosh, Seth lived
another 807 years, and he had other sons and
daughters. 8Seth lived 912 years, and then he
died.

9When Enosh was 90 years old, he became the father
of Kenan. 10After the birth of Kenan, Enosh lived
another 815 years, and he had other sons and
daughters. 11Enosh lived 905 years, and then
he died.

12When Kenan was 70 years old, he became the father
of Mahalalel. 13After the birth of Mahalalel, Kenan
lived another 840 years, and he had other sons
and daughters. 14Kenan lived 910 years, and then
he died.

15When Mahalalel was 65 years old, he became the
father of Jared. 16After the birth of Jared, Mahalalel
lived another 830 years, and he had other sons and
daughters. 17Mahalalel lived 895 years, and then
he died.

18When Jared was 162 years old, he became the
father of Enoch. 19After the birth of Enoch, Jared
lived another 800 years, and he had other sons
and daughters. 20Jared lived 962 years, and then
he died.

21When Enoch was 65 years old, he became the father

4:25 *Seth* probably means "granted"; the name may also mean "appointed." 5:1 Or *man;* Hebrew reads *adam;* similarly in 5:2. 5:6 Or *the ancestor of;* also in 5:9, 12, 15, 18, 21, 25. 5:7 Or *the birth of this ancestor of;* also in 5:10, 13, 16, 19, 22, 26.

UPS:
- First member of the Hall of Faith in Hebrews 11
- First shepherd
- First martyr for truth (Matt 23:35)

STATS:
- Where: Just outside of Eden
- Occupation: Shepherd
- Relatives: Adam and Eve (parents); Cain (brother)

BOTTOM LINE:

God hears those who come to him.

God recognizes the innocent person, and sooner or later he judges the guilty.

God prefers wholehearted, rather than halfhearted offerings.

Abel's story is told in Gen 4:1-10. He also is mentioned in Matt 23:35; Luke 11:51; Heb 11:4; 12:24.

ABEL Let's face it. The first time you read Abel's story, maybe you thought you knew all about him. Maybe you had him pegged as the teacher's pet—the one who got all A's in class and always raised his hand with the right answer on his lips. Or maybe he's too close in personality to someone in your family who seems "perfect." Does that sound like your view of him?

Abel was the second child born into the world, but the first one to obey God. He worshiped in a way that pleased God. That really bothered his brother Cain. Maybe Abel suspected that Cain was angry with him. Brothers and sisters know things like that about each other. Yet Abel trusted his brother even when Cain suggested they go out to the field together.

The Bible doesn't tell us why God accepted Abel's gift and rejected Cain's, but both brothers knew what God expected. Cain seemed to take a shortcut. Only Abel fully obeyed. He is remembered for his obedience and faith (Heb 11:4), and he is called "righteous" (Matt 23:35).

When it comes to obeying God, what's your style? Wholehearted like Abel? Halfhearted like Cain?

keeping it real

I admit I want my own way most of the time. I'm not going to lie to you. And I want God to accept my will, rather than the other way around. Sometimes, I find myself reacting like Cain—y'know, mad at God for not accepting my half-hearted efforts.

Submitting to God's will is the hardest part for me about being a Christian. I know it means giving up what I want and totally giving in to what God wants. It also means giving God my best instead of the least I can give. Sometimes, I want to say, "Cut me some slack, God!" But when I think about what God's done for me and how much he's always willing to give up for me, I find myself wanting to do things his way. —Tynisha

of Methuselah. 22After the birth of Methuselah,
Enoch lived in close fellowship with God for another
300 years, and he had other sons and daughters.
23Enoch lived 365 years, 24walking in close fellowship
with God. Then one day he disappeared, because God
took him.
25When Methuselah was 187 years old, he became
the father of Lamech. 26After the birth of Lamech,
Methuselah lived another 782 years, and he had
other sons and daughters. 27Methuselah lived
969 years, and then he died.
28When Lamech was 182 years old, he became the
father of a son. 29Lamech named his son Noah, for
he said, "May he bring us relief* from our work and
the painful labor of farming this ground that the
LORD has cursed." 30After the birth of Noah, Lamech
lived another 595 years, and he had other sons and
daughters. 31Lamech lived 777 years, and then
he died.
32By the time Noah was 500 years old, he was the father
of Shem, Ham, and Japheth.

6 A WORLD GONE WRONG

Then the people began to multiply on the earth, and
daughters were born to them. 2The sons of God saw the
beautiful women* and took any they wanted as their
wives. 3Then the LORD said, "My Spirit will not put up
with* humans for such a long time, for they are only mortal flesh. In the future, their normal lifespan will be no
more than 120 years."
4In those days, and for some time after, giant
Nephilites lived on the earth, for whenever the sons of
God had intercourse with women, they gave birth to children who became the heroes and famous warriors of ancient times.
5The LORD observed the extent of human wickedness
on the earth, and he saw that everything they thought or
imagined was consistently and totally evil. 6So the LORD
was sorry he had ever made them and put them on the
earth. It broke his heart. 7And the LORD said, "I will wipe
this human race I have created from the face of the
earth. Yes, and I will destroy every living thing—all the
people, the large animals, the small animals that scurry
along the ground, and even the birds of the sky. I am
sorry I ever made them." 8But Noah found favor with the
LORD.

THE STORY OF NOAH

9This is the account of Noah and his family. Noah was a
righteous man, the only blameless person living on earth
at the time, and he walked in close fellowship with God.
10Noah was the father of three sons: Shem, Ham, and Japheth.
11Now God saw that the earth had become corrupt
and was filled with violence. 12God observed all this
corruption in the world, for everyone on earth was corrupt. 13So God said to Noah, "I have decided to destroy
all living creatures, for they have filled the earth with
violence. Yes, I will wipe them all out along with the
earth!
14"Build a large boat* from cypress wood* and waterproof it with tar, inside and out. Then construct decks
and stalls throughout its interior. 15Make the boat
450 feet long, 75 feet wide, and 45 feet high.* 16Leave an
18-inch opening* below the roof all the way around the
boat. Put the door on the side, and build three decks inside the boat—lower, middle, and upper.
17"Look! I am about to cover the earth with a flood that
will destroy every living thing that breathes. Everything
on earth will die. 18But I will confirm my covenant with
you. So enter the boat—you and your wife and your sons
and their wives. 19Bring a pair of every kind of animal—a
male and a female—into the boat with you to keep them

5:29 *Noah* sounds like a Hebrew term that can mean "relief" or "comfort." 6:2 Hebrew *daughters of men;* also in 6:4. 6:3 Greek version reads *will not remain in.* 6:14a Traditionally rendered *an ark.* 6:14b Or *gopher wood.* 6:15 Hebrew *300 cubits* [138 meters] *long, 50 cubits* [23 meters] *wide, and 30 cubits* [13.8 meters] *high.* 6:16 Hebrew *an opening of 1 cubit* [46 centimeters].

VIOLENCE

On Friday nights at seven o'clock you're practically guaranteed to find Tyrice and Jordan in one of two places. Check first at Tyrice's. If they're not there, munching pizza and watching horror movies on DVD, try the mall. They probably will be standing in line at the movie theater, anxiously waiting for the chance to purchase tickets for the newest cinematic tale of gore.

In the last couple of years, these guys have seen hundreds of violent movies and played even more violent video games. It doesn't matter what the plot is—deranged killers on the loose, murderous monsters on the rampage, the latest hitman roleplay game—as long as there are some gruesome torture scenes, lots of mutilated bodies, and gallons of blood and guts, Tyrice and Jordan are satisfied.

"That one scene was so weak," Jordan complains as he ejects a DVD one Friday.

"Which one?" Tyrice responds.

"You know, the one where he shoved the girl into that giant meat grinder. . . . I mean, the blood didn't even look real."

"Tell me about it!" Tyrice agrees. "Every scene in the whole movie was just ripped off from another movie."

"Want to watch *Babies with Rabies* now?"

"Naw, let's play *Hitman Heist.* I wanna try out your new game system. But let me go get some more cherry soda first."

Ever think that the violent scenes on the news, in movies, or in video games seem almost "tame"? That's what's known as being desensitized. It means you're so used to violence, it doesn't bother you anymore. Know what? Even though God has seen it all, he'll never be desensitized.

Check out his response to violence in Genesis 6:11-13. What's your response?

alive during the flood. 20Pairs of every kind of bird, and
every kind of animal, and every kind of small animal that
scurries along the ground, will come to you to be kept
alive. 21And be sure to take on board enough food for
your family and for all the animals."
22So Noah did everything exactly as God had commanded him.

7

THE FLOOD COVERS THE EARTH

When everything was ready, the LORD said to Noah, "Go
into the boat with all your family, for among all the people of the earth, I can see that you alone are righteous.
2Take with you seven pairs—male and female—of each
animal I have approved for eating and for sacrifice,* and
take one pair of each of the others. 3Also take seven pairs
of every kind of bird. There must be a male and a female
in each pair to ensure that all life will survive on the earth
after the flood. 4Seven days from now I will make the
rains pour down on the earth. And it will rain for forty
days and forty nights, until I have wiped from the earth all
the living things I have created."
5So Noah did everything as the LORD commanded him.
6Noah was 600 years old when the flood covered the
earth. 7He went on board the boat to escape the flood—
he and his wife and his sons and their wives. 8With them
were all the various kinds of animals—those approved
for eating and for sacrifice and those that were not—
along with all the birds and the small animals that scurry
along the ground. 9They entered the boat in pairs, male
and female, just as God had commanded Noah. 10After
seven days, the waters of the flood came and covered the
earth.
11When Noah was 600 years old, on the seventeenth
day of the second month, all the underground waters
erupted from the earth, and the rain fell in mighty torrents from the sky. 12The rain continued to fall for forty
days and forty nights.
13That very day Noah had gone into the boat with his
wife and his sons—Shem, Ham, and Japheth—and their
wives. 14With them in the boat were pairs of every kind of
animal—domestic and wild, large and small—along with
birds of every kind. 15Two by two they came into the boat,
representing every living thing that breathes. 16A male
and female of each kind entered, just as God had commanded Noah. Then the LORD closed the door behind
them.
17For forty days the floodwaters grew deeper, covering
the ground and lifting the boat high above the earth. 18As
the waters rose higher and higher above the ground, the
boat floated safely on the surface. 19Finally, the water
covered even the highest mountains on the earth, 20rising
more than twenty-two feet* above the highest peaks.
21All the living things on earth died—birds, domestic animals, wild animals, small animals that scurry along the
ground, and all the people. 22Everything that breathed
and lived on dry land died. 23God wiped out every living
thing on the earth—people, livestock, small animals that

WHY WORRY? 7:15-16

Many have wondered how this animal kingdom roundup happened. Did Noah and his sons spend years collecting them? Actually, God took care of that job while Noah and his sons built the boat. They didn't have to worry about how the animals would arrive. Often we do just the opposite of Noah. We worry about details in our lives over which we have no control, while neglecting specific areas (such as attitudes, relationships, responsibilities) that *are* under our control. What task has God given you? What aspects of your life seem out of your control? Are you willing to put aside worry over the things you can't change and concentrate on what God has given you to do? ■

7:2 Hebrew *of each clean animal;* similarly in 7:8. 7:20 Hebrew *15 cubits* [6.9 meters].

scurry along the ground, and the birds of the sky. All were destroyed. The only people who survived were Noah and those with him in the boat. 24And the floodwaters covered the earth for 150 days.

8 THE FLOOD RECEDES

But God remembered Noah and all the wild animals and livestock with him in the boat. He sent a wind to blow across the earth, and the floodwaters began to recede.
2The underground waters stopped flowing, and the torrential rains from the sky were stopped. 3So the floodwaters gradually receded from the earth. After 150 days,
4exactly five months from the time the flood began,* the boat came to rest on the mountains of Ararat. 5Two and a half months later,* as the waters continued to go down, other mountain peaks became visible.

6After another forty days, Noah opened the window he had made in the boat 7and released a raven. The bird flew back and forth until the floodwaters on the earth had dried up. 8He also released a dove to see if the water had receded and it could find dry ground. 9But the dove could find no place to land because the water still covered the ground. So it returned to the boat, and Noah held out his hand and drew the dove back inside. 10After waiting another seven days, Noah released the dove again. 11This time the dove returned to him in the evening with a fresh olive leaf in its beak. Then Noah knew that the floodwaters were almost gone. 12He waited another seven days and then released the dove again. This time it did not come back.

13Noah was now 601 years old. On the first day of the new year, ten and a half months after the flood began,* the floodwaters had almost dried up from the earth. Noah lifted back the covering of the boat and saw that the surface of the ground was drying. 14Two more months went by,* and at last the earth was dry!

15Then God said to Noah, 16"Leave the boat, all of you—you and your wife, and your sons and their wives.
17Release all the animals—the birds, the livestock, and the small animals that scurry along the ground—so they can be fruitful and multiply throughout the earth."

18So Noah, his wife, and his sons and their wives left the boat. 19And all of the large and small animals and birds came out of the boat, pair by pair.

20Then Noah built an altar to the LORD, and there he sacrificed as burnt offerings the animals and birds that had been approved for that purpose.* 21And the LORD was pleased with the aroma of the sacrifice and said to himself, "I will never again curse the ground because of the human race, even though everything they think or imagine is bent toward evil from childhood. I will never again destroy all living things. 22As long as the

8:4 Hebrew *on the seventeenth day of the seventh month;* see 7:11. **8:5** Hebrew *On the first day of the tenth month;* see 7:11 and note on 8:4. **8:13** Hebrew *On the first day of the first month;* see 7:11. **8:14** Hebrew *The twenty-seventh day of the second month arrived;* see note on 8:13. **8:20** Hebrew *every clean animal and every clean bird.*

NOAH

UPS:
- Only follower of God left in his generation
- Second father of the human race
- Man of patience, consistency, and obedience
- First major shipbuilder in history

DOWN:
- Got drunk and later cursed Canaan because his son Ham saw him naked

STATS:
- Where: We're not told how far from the Garden of Eden people had settled.
- Occupations: Farmer, shipbuilder, preacher
- Relatives: Methuselah (grandfather); Lamech (father); Ham, Shem, and Japheth (sons)

BOTTOM LINE:
God is faithful.
God does not always protect us from trouble, but cares for us in spite of trouble.
Obedience is a long-term commitment.
A man may be faithful, but his sinful nature always travels with him.

Noah's story is told in Gen 5:29–10:32. He also is mentioned in 1 Chron 1:4; Isa 54:9; Ezek 14:14, 20; Matt 24:37-38; Luke 3:36; 17:26-27; Heb 11:7; 1 Pet 3:20; 2 Pet 2:5.

NOAH Ever been disgusted by the amount of evil you hear about in the world? Welcome to Noah's world. The story of Noah's life involved not one, but two great and tragic floods. The first was a flood of evil. The world had become so bad that there was only one person left who remembered the God of creation, perfection, and love.

God's response to this flood of evil was a 120-year-long last chance. During those years, he had Noah build a large advertisement of what God was going to do. There's nothing like a huge boat built on dry land to make a point! Of course, everyone thought Noah was crazy. Despite the jeers of his friends and neighbors, Noah continued to build. When the flood came, no one could say he or she hadn't been warned. For Noah, obedience to God meant a long-term courageous commitment to a project.

Many of us have trouble sticking to any project, whether or not it is directed by God. (Does that describe you?) Or we back off when opposition occurs. Noah obeyed God and worked on one project longer than we even expect to live. The only project we have that is like Noah's is our life. What is God building in your life? A stronger faith? Perseverance? How are you aiding or hindering his building plan?

earth remains, there will be planting and harvest, cold
and heat, summer and winter, day and night."

9

GOD CONFIRMS HIS COVENANT

Then God blessed Noah and his sons and told them, "Be
fruitful and multiply. Fill the earth. 2All the animals of the
earth, all the birds of the sky, all the small animals that
scurry along the ground, and all the fish in the sea will
look on you with fear and terror. I have placed them in
your power. 3I have given them to you for food, just as I
have given you grain and vegetables. 4But you must never
eat any meat that still has the lifeblood in it.

5"And I will require the blood of anyone who takes
another person's life. If a wild animal kills a person, it
must die. And anyone who murders a fellow human
must die. 6If anyone takes a human life, that person's
life will also be taken by human hands. For God made
human beings* in his own image. 7Now be fruitful and
multiply, and repopulate the earth."

WHAT'S WRONG WITH MURDER? 9:5-6

Here God explains why murder is so wrong: to kill a person is to kill someone made in God's image. All people possess the qualities that distinguish us from animals: morality, reason, creativity, and self-worth. When we interact with others, we interact with beings made by God, beings to whom God offers eternal life. How do your actions show the value you place on human life? ■

8Then God told Noah and his sons, 9"I hereby confirm
my covenant with you and your descendants, 10and with
all the animals that were on the boat with you—the birds,
the livestock, and all the wild animals—every living creature on earth. 11Yes, I am confirming my covenant with
you. Never again will floodwaters kill all living creatures;
never again will a flood destroy the earth."

12Then God said, "I am giving you a sign of my covenant
with you and with all living creatures, for all generations
to come. 13I have placed my rainbow in the clouds. It is
the sign of my covenant with you and with all the earth.
14When I send clouds over the earth, the rainbow will appear in the clouds, 15and I will remember my covenant
with you and with all living creatures. Never again will the
floodwaters destroy all life. 16When I see the rainbow in
the clouds, I will remember the eternal covenant between God and every living creature on earth." 17Then
God said to Noah, "Yes, this rainbow is the sign of the covenant I am confirming with all the creatures on earth."

NOAH'S SONS

18The sons of Noah who came out of the boat with their
father were Shem, Ham, and Japheth. (Ham is the father
of Canaan.) 19From these three sons of Noah came all the
people who now populate the earth.

20After the flood, Noah began to cultivate the ground,
and he planted a vineyard. 21One day he drank some wine
he had made, and he became drunk and lay naked inside
his tent. 22Ham, the father of Canaan, saw that his father
was naked and went outside and told his brothers.
23Then Shem and Japheth took a robe, held it over their
shoulders, and backed into the tent to cover their father.
As they did this, they looked the other way so they would
not see him naked.

24When Noah woke up from his stupor, he learned
what Ham, his youngest son, had done. 25Then he cursed
Canaan, the son of Ham:

"May Canaan be cursed!
May he be the lowest of servants to his relatives."

26Then Noah said,

"May the LORD, the God of Shem, be blessed,
and may Canaan be his servant!
27 May God expand the territory of Japheth!
May Japheth share the prosperity of Shem,*
and may Canaan be his servant."

28Noah lived another 350 years after the great flood.
29He lived 950 years, and then he died.

10

This is the account of the families of Shem,
Ham, and Japheth, the three sons of Noah. Many children
were born to them after the great flood.

DESCENDANTS OF JAPHETH

2The descendants of Japheth were Gomer, Magog,
Madai, Javan, Tubal, Meshech, and Tiras.
3The descendants of Gomer were Ashkenaz, Riphath,
and Togarmah.
4The descendants of Javan were Elishah, Tarshish,
Kittim, and Rodanim.* 5Their descendants became
the seafaring peoples that spread out to various
lands, each identified by its own language, clan,
and national identity.

DESCENDANTS OF HAM

6The descendants of Ham were Cush, Mizraim, Put, and
Canaan.
7The descendants of Cush were Seba, Havilah, Sabtah,
Raamah, and Sabteca. The descendants of Raamah
were Sheba and Dedan.
8Cush was also the ancestor of Nimrod, who was
the first heroic warrior on earth. 9Since he was the
greatest hunter in the world,* his name became
proverbial. People would say, "This man is like
Nimrod, the greatest hunter in the world." 10He built
his kingdom in the land of Babylonia,* with the cities
of Babylon, Erech, Akkad, and Calneh. 11From there

9:6 Or *man;* Hebrew reads *ha-adam.* **9:27** Hebrew *May he live in the tents of Shem.* **10:4** As in some Hebrew manuscripts and Greek version (see also 1 Chr 1:7); most Hebrew manuscripts read *Dodanim.* **10:9** Hebrew *a great hunter before the LORD;* also in 10:9b. **10:10** Hebrew *Shinar.*

he expanded his territory to Assyria,* building the
cities of Nineveh, Rehoboth-ir, Calah, 12and Resen
(the great city located between Nineveh and Calah).
13Mizraim was the ancestor of the Ludites, Anamites,
Lehabites, Naphtuhites, 14Pathrusites, Casluhites, and
the Caphtorites, from whom the Philistines came.*
15Canaan's oldest son was Sidon, the ancestor of the
Sidonians. Canaan was also the ancestor of the Hittites,
16Jebusites, Amorites, Girgashites, 17Hivites, Arkites,
Sinites, 18Arvadites, Zemarites, and Hamathites. The
Canaanite clans eventually spread out, 19and the
territory of Canaan extended from Sidon in the north
to Gerar and Gaza in the south, and east as far as
Sodom, Gomorrah, Admah, and Zeboiim, near Lasha.
20These were the descendants of Ham, identified by clan,
language, territory, and national identity.

DESCENDANTS OF SHEM

21Sons were also born to Shem, the older brother
of Japheth.* Shem was the ancestor of all the
descendants of Eber.
22The descendants of Shem were Elam, Asshur,
Arphaxad, Lud, and Aram.
23The descendants of Aram were Uz, Hul, Gether, and
Mash.
24Arphaxad was the father of Shelah,* and Shelah was
the father of Eber.
25Eber had two sons. The first was named Peleg (which
means "division"), for during his lifetime the people
of the world were divided into different language
groups. His brother's name was Joktan.
26Joktan was the ancestor of Almodad, Sheleph,
Hazarmaveth, Jerah, 27Hadoram, Uzal, Diklah, 28Obal,
Abimael, Sheba, 29Ophir, Havilah, and Jobab. All these
were descendants of Joktan. 30The territory they
occupied extended from Mesha all the way to Sephar
in the eastern mountains.
31These were the descendants of Shem, identified by
clan, language, territory, and national identity.

CONCLUSION

32These are the clans that descended from Noah's sons,
arranged by nation according to their lines of descent. All
the nations of the earth descended from these clans after
the great flood.

11 THE TOWER OF BABEL

At one time all the people of the world spoke the same
language and used the same words. 2As the people migrated to the east, they found a plain in the land of Babylonia* and settled there.
3They began saying to each other, "Let's make bricks and
harden them with fire." (In this region bricks were used instead of stone, and tar was used for mortar.) 4Then they
said, "Come, let's build a great city for ourselves with a
tower that reaches into the sky. This will make us famous
and keep us from being scattered all over the world."

TOWERING PRIDE 11:4

The tower of Babel was a great human achievement, a wonder of the ancient world. But it was a monument to the builders rather than to God. We often build monuments to ourselves (closets full of expensive clothes, the best CD collection in the state, shelves crammed with trophies) to call attention to our achievements. These may not be wrong in themselves, but when we depend on what we have to gain our identity and value, they take God's place in our lives. What are the "monuments" in your life? ■

5But the LORD came down to look at the city and the
tower the people were building. 6"Look!" he said. "The
people are united, and they all speak the same language.
After this, nothing they set out to do will be impossible
for them! 7Come, let's go down and confuse the people
with different languages. Then they won't be able to
understand each other."
8In that way, the LORD scattered them all over the
world, and they stopped building the city. 9That is why
the city was called Babel,* because that is where the LORD
confused the people with different languages. In this way
he scattered them all over the world.

THE LINE OF DESCENT FROM SHEM TO ABRAM

10This is the account of Shem's family.

Two years after the great flood, when Shem was
100 years old, he became the father of* Arphaxad.
11After the birth of* Arphaxad, Shem lived another
500 years and had other sons and daughters.
12When Arphaxad was 35 years old, he became the
father of Shelah. 13After the birth of Shelah,
Arphaxad lived another 403 years and had other
sons and daughters.*
14When Shelah was 30 years old, he became the father
of Eber. 15After the birth of Eber, Shelah lived another
403 years and had other sons and daughters.
16When Eber was 34 years old, he became the father of
Peleg. 17After the birth of Peleg, Eber lived another
430 years and had other sons and daughters.
18When Peleg was 30 years old, he became the father of
Reu. 19After the birth of Reu, Peleg lived another
209 years and had other sons and daughters.
20When Reu was 32 years old, he became the father of

10:11 Or *From that land Assyria went out.* **10:14** Hebrew *Casluhites, from whom the Philistines came, and Caphtorites.* Compare Jer 47:4; Amos 9:7. **10:21** Or *Shem, whose older brother was Japheth.* **10:24** Greek version reads *Arphaxad was the father of Cainan, Cainan was the father of Shelah.* Compare Luke 3:36. **11:2** Hebrew *Shinar.* **11:9** Or *Babylon. Babel* sounds like a Hebrew term that means "confusion." **11:10** Or *the ancestor of;* also in 11:12, 14, 16, 18, 20, 22, 24. **11:11** Or *the birth of this ancestor of;* also in 11:13, 15, 17, 19, 21, 23, 25. **11:12-13** Greek version reads *12When Arphaxad was 135 years old, he became the father of Cainan. 13After the birth of Cainan, Arphaxad lived another 430 years and had other sons and daughters, and then he died. When Cainan was 130 years old, he became the father of Shelah. After the birth of Shelah, Cainan lived another 330 years and had other sons and daughters, and then he died.* Compare Luke 3:35-36.

Serug. [21]After the birth of Serug, Reu lived another
207 years and had other sons and daughters.
[22]When Serug was 30 years old, he became the father of
Nahor. [23]After the birth of Nahor, Serug lived another
200 years and had other sons and daughters.
[24]When Nahor was 29 years old, he became the father
of Terah. [25]After the birth of Terah, Nahor lived
another 119 years and had other sons and daughters.
[26]When Terah was 70 years old, he had become the
father of Abram, Nahor, and Haran.

THE FAMILY OF TERAH

[27]This is the account of Terah's family. Terah was the
father of Abram, Nahor, and Haran; and Haran was the
father of Lot. [28]But Haran died in Ur of the Chaldeans,
the land of his birth, while his father, Terah, was still living. [29]Meanwhile, Abram and Nahor both married. The
name of Abram's wife was Sarai, and the name of Nahor's wife was Milcah. (Milcah and her sister Iscah were
daughters of Nahor's brother Haran.) [30]But Sarai was
unable to become pregnant and had no children.
[31]One day Terah took his son Abram, his daughter-in-
law Sarai (his son Abram's wife), and his grandson Lot (his
son Haran's child) and moved away from Ur of the Chaldeans. He was headed for the land of Canaan, but they
stopped at Haran and settled there. [32]Terah lived for
205 years* and died while still in Haran.

12 THE CALL OF ABRAM

The LORD had said to Abram, "Leave your native country,
your relatives, and your father's family, and go to the land
that I will show you. [2]I will make you into a great nation. I
will bless you and make you famous, and you will be a
blessing to others. [3]I will bless those who bless you and
curse those who treat you with contempt. All the families
on earth will be blessed through you."
[4]So Abram departed as the LORD had instructed, and
Lot went with him. Abram was seventy-five years old
when he left Haran. [5]He took his wife, Sarai, his nephew
Lot, and all his wealth—his livestock and all the people
he had taken into his household at Haran—and headed
for the land of Canaan. When they arrived in Canaan,
[6]Abram traveled through the land as far as Shechem.
There he set up camp beside the oak of Moreh. At that
time, the area was inhabited by Canaanites.
[7]Then the LORD appeared to Abram and said, "I will
give this land to your descendants.*" And Abram built an
altar there and dedicated it to the LORD, who had appeared to him. [8]After that, Abram traveled south and set
up camp in the hill country, with Bethel to the west and Ai
to the east. There he built another altar and dedicated it
to the LORD, and he worshiped the LORD. [9]Then Abram
continued traveling south by stages toward the Negev.

11:32 Some ancient versions read *145 years;* compare 11:26 and 12:4. 12:7 Hebrew *seed.*

LOT

Have you noticed how some people simply drift through life? They don't really make choices; they just take the easiest way. Usually, that choice turns out to be the wrong way.

Lot, Abram's nephew, often took the easy way out. Although his father died early on, Lot was cared for by his grandfather, Terah, and his uncle Abram. Though they were good role models, Lot's life was full of unwise decisions. Despite Abram's attention and God's help, Lot went his own way.

By the time Lot drifted away from Abram, his life had taken an ugly turn. He had become so blended into the culture of his day that he did not want to leave it. During the family's narrow escape from the destruction of Sodom and Gomorrah, his wife's disobedience caused her to be turned into a pillar of salt. Later, his daughters committed incest with him. His drifting finally led him to destruction.

But God brought good out of failure. The New Testament describes Lot as a righteous man (2 Pet 2:7-8). Even though he didn't do much about the evil surrounding him, it still bothered him deeply. And Ruth—a descendant of Moab, the child born from the incest between Lot and one of his daughters—was an ancestor of Jesus Christ.

Are you headed toward God or drifting away from him? What circumstances tempt you to drift?

UPS:
- Successful businessman
- Called a righteous man by Peter (2 Pet 2:7-8)

DOWNS:
- Wishy-washy about decision; usually chose the easy way out
- Usually thought of himself when decisions were made

STATS:
- Where: Lived first in Ur of the Chaldeans, then moved to Canaan with Abram
- Occupations: Wealthy sheep and cattle rancher, city official
- Relatives: Haran (father); Abraham (uncle who later adopted him at Haran's death); wife (unnamed); two unnamed daughters

BOTTOM LINE:

God wants us to do more than drift through life; he wants people to be an influence for him.

Lot's story is told in Gen 11:27; 12:5; 13–14; 19. He also is mentioned in Deut 2:9; Luke 17:28-32; 2 Pet 2:7-8.

WILLING TO GO 12:2

God promised to bless Abram by making him the father of a great nation. However, there was one condition. Abram had to do what God wanted him to do. This meant leaving his home and friends and traveling to a new land. Abram obeyed, leaving his home for God's promise of even greater blessings in the future. God may be trying to lead you to a place of greater service and usefulness for him. In what ways do you recognize his leading? Are you willing to go where he sends you? ■

ABRAM AND SARAI IN EGYPT

10At that time a severe famine struck the land of Canaan,
forcing Abram to go down to Egypt, where he lived as a
foreigner. 11As he was approaching the border of Egypt,
Abram said to his wife, Sarai, "Look, you are a very beautiful woman. 12When the Egyptians see you, they will
say, 'This is his wife. Let's kill him; then we can have her!'
13So please tell them you are my sister. Then they will
spare my life and treat me well because of their interest
in you."
14And sure enough, when Abram arrived in Egypt,
everyone spoke of Sarai's beauty. 15When the palace officials saw her, they sang her praises to Pharaoh, their king,
and Sarai was taken into his palace. 16Then Pharaoh gave
Abram many gifts because of her—sheep, goats, cattle,
male and female donkeys, male and female servants, and
camels.
17But the LORD sent terrible plagues upon Pharaoh and
his household because of Sarai, Abram's wife. 18So Pharaoh summoned Abram and accused him sharply. "What
have you done to me?" he demanded. "Why didn't you
tell me she was your wife? 19Why did you say, 'She is my
sister,' and allow me to take her as my wife? Now then,
here is your wife. Take her and get out of here!" 20Pha-
raoh ordered some of his men to escort them, and he sent
Abram out of the country, along with his wife and all his
possessions.

13 ABRAM AND LOT SEPARATE

So Abram left Egypt and traveled north into the Negev,
along with his wife and Lot and all that they owned.
2(Abram was very rich in livestock, silver, and gold.)
3From the Negev, they continued traveling by stages toward Bethel, and they pitched their tents between Bethel
and Ai, where they had camped before. 4This was the
same place where Abram had built the altar, and there he
worshiped the LORD again.
5Lot, who was traveling with Abram, had also become
very wealthy with flocks of sheep and goats, herds of cattle, and many tents. 6But the land could not support both
Abram and Lot with all their flocks and herds living so
close together. 7So disputes broke out between the
herdsmen of Abram and Lot. (At that time Canaanites
and Perizzites were also living in the land.)
8Finally Abram said to Lot, "Let's not allow this conflict
to come between us or our herdsmen. After all, we are
close relatives! 9The whole countryside is open to you.
Take your choice of any section of the land you want, and
we will separate. If you want the land to the left, then I'll
take the land on the right. If you prefer the land on the
right, then I'll go to the left."
10Lot took a long look at the fertile plains of the Jordan
Valley in the direction of Zoar. The whole area was well
watered everywhere, like the garden of the LORD or the
beautiful land of Egypt. (This was before the LORD destroyed Sodom and Gomorrah.) 11Lot chose for himself
the whole Jordan Valley to the east of them. He went
there with his flocks and servants and parted company
with his uncle Abram. 12So Abram settled in the land of
Canaan, and Lot moved his tents to a place near Sodom
and settled among the cities of the plain. 13But the people
of this area were extremely wicked and constantly
sinned against the LORD.

FAMILY FEUD 13:5-9

Facing a potential conflict with his nephew Lot, Abram took the initiative in settling the dispute. He gave Lot the first choice of land and showed a willingness to risk being cheated. Abram's example shows us how to respond to difficult family situations: (1) take the initiative in resolving conflicts; (2) let others have first choice, even if that means not getting what we want; (3) put family peace above personal desires. ■

14After Lot had gone, the LORD said to Abram, "Look as
far as you can see in every direction—north and south,
east and west. 15I am giving all this land, as far as you can
see, to you and your descendants* as a permanent possession. 16And I will give you so many descendants that,
like the dust of the earth, they cannot be counted! 17Go
and walk through the land in every direction, for I am giving it to you."
18So Abram moved his camp to Hebron and settled
near the oak grove belonging to Mamre. There he built
another altar to the LORD.

14 ABRAM RESCUES LOT

About this time war broke out in the region. King Amra-
phel of Babylonia,* King Arioch of Ellasar, King Kedorlaomer of Elam, and King Tidal of Goiim 2fought against
King Bera of Sodom, King Birsha of Gomorrah, King Shi-
nab of Admah, King Shemeber of Zeboiim, and the king
of Bela (also called Zoar).
3This second group of kings joined forces in Siddim
Valley (that is, the valley of the Dead Sea*). 4For twelve
years they had been subject to King Kedorlaomer, but in
the thirteenth year they rebelled against him.

13:15 Hebrew *seed*; also in 13:16. **14:1** Hebrew *Shinar*; also in 14:9. **14:3** Hebrew *Salt Sea*.

5One year later Kedorlaomer and his allies arrived and
defeated the Rephaites at Ashteroth-karnaim, the Zu-
zites at Ham, the Emites at Shaveh-kiriathaim, 6and the
Horites at Mount Seir, as far as El-paran at the edge of the
wilderness. 7Then they turned back and came to En-
mishpat (now called Kadesh) and conquered all the territory of the Amalekites, and also the Amorites living in
Hazazon-tamar.

8Then the rebel kings of Sodom, Gomorrah, Admah,
Zeboiim, and Bela (also called Zoar) prepared for battle in
the valley of the Dead Sea.* 9They fought against King
Kedorlaomer of Elam, King Tidal of Goiim, King Amra-
phel of Babylonia, and King Arioch of Ellasar—four kings
against five. 10As it happened, the valley of the Dead Sea
was filled with tar pits. And as the army of the kings of
Sodom and Gomorrah fled, some fell into the tar pits,
while the rest escaped into the mountains. 11The victorious invaders then plundered Sodom and Gomorrah and
headed for home, taking with them all the spoils of war
and the food supplies. 12They also captured Lot—
Abram's nephew who lived in Sodom—and carried off
everything he owned.

13But one of Lot's men escaped and reported everything to Abram the Hebrew, who was living near the oak
grove belonging to Mamre the Amorite. Mamre and his
relatives, Eshcol and Aner, were Abram's allies.

14When Abram heard that his nephew Lot had been
captured, he mobilized the 318 trained men who had
been born into his household. Then he pursued Kedorlaomer's army until he caught up with them at Dan. 15There
he divided his men and attacked during the night. Kedorlaomer's army fled, but Abram chased them as far as
Hobah, north of Damascus. 16Abram recovered all the
goods that had been taken, and he brought back his
nephew Lot with his possessions and all the women and
other captives.

MELCHIZEDEK BLESSES ABRAM

17After Abram returned from his victory over Kedorlaomer and all his allies, the king of Sodom went out to meet
him in the valley of Shaveh (that is, the King's Valley).

18And Melchizedek, the king of Salem and a priest of
God Most High,* brought Abram some bread and wine.
19Melchizedek blessed Abram with this blessing:

"Blessed be Abram by God Most High,
Creator of heaven and earth.
20 And blessed be God Most High,
who has defeated your enemies for you."

Then Abram gave Melchizedek a tenth of all the goods he
had recovered.

21The king of Sodom said to Abram, "Give back my
people who were captured. But you may keep for yourself all the goods you have recovered."

22Abram replied to the king of Sodom, "I solemnly

14:8 Hebrew *Siddim Valley* (see 14:3); also in 14:10. **14:18** Hebrew *El-Elyon;* also in 14:19, 20, 22.

UPS:
- Had a faith that pleased God
- Became the founder of the Jewish nation
- Was a successful and wealthy rancher
- Usually avoided conflicts, but when they happened, he let his opponent set the rules for settling the disputes

DOWN:
- Had a lifelong tendency to lie when under pressure

STATS:
- Where: Born in Ur of the Chaldeans; spent most of his life in the land of Canaan
- Occupation: Wealthy livestock owner
- Relatives: Terah (father); Nahor and Haran (brothers); Sarah (wife); Ishmael and Isaac (sons); Lot (nephew)
- Contemporaries: Abimelech, Melchizedek

BOTTOM LINE:
God desires dependence, trust, and faith in him—not faith in our ability to please him.
God's plan from the beginning has been to make himself known to all people.

Abraham's story is told in Gen 11:27–25:11. He also is mentioned in Exod 2:24; John 8:33-59; Acts 7:2-8, 32; Rom 4; Gal 3:6-29; Heb 6:13–7:10; 11.

ABRAHAM

As you read about Abraham's life, you might ask: "What on earth made God like this man so much?" Abraham made a lot of mistakes, and some of his mistakes had long-range consequences.

Yet what you will find if you read carefully is that in spite of his mistakes, Abraham trusted God with his life. This is the main fact the Bible tells us about him in both the Old and New Testaments (Gen 15:6; Rom 4:3).

Early in life, Abraham had to make an important decision. God asked him to choose between staying at home or following God's leading. It was a choice between doing what Abraham wanted to do or doing what God wanted Abraham to do.

Of course Abraham couldn't know how his decision would affect the future, but God used Abraham's obedience to affect millions of people. Through Abraham the Jewish nation developed and eventually Jesus Christ came into the world.

God gives us exactly the same choice he gave Abraham: go his way or the world's. Once Abraham gave his life to God, he never tried to take it back. He may have taken some wrong turns on the journey . . . but he never turned around. What about you? Is your basic desire to trust God and live his way, or is your goal to live life your way? Explain.

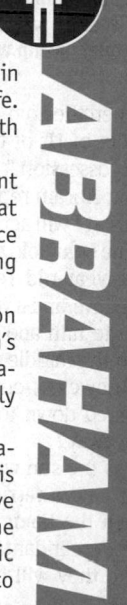

ABRAHAM

swear to the LORD, God Most High, Creator of heaven and earth, [23]that I will not take so much as a single thread or sandal thong from what belongs to you. Otherwise you might say, 'I am the one who made Abram rich.' [24]I will accept only what my young warriors have already eaten, and I request that you give a fair share of the goods to my allies—Aner, Eshcol, and Mamre."

15 THE LORD'S COVENANT PROMISE TO ABRAM

Some time later, the LORD spoke to Abram in a vision and said to him, "Do not be afraid, Abram, for I will protect you, and your reward will be great."

[2]But Abram replied, "O Sovereign LORD, what good are all your blessings when I don't even have a son? Since you've given me no children, Eliezer of Damascus, a servant in my household, will inherit all my wealth. [3]You have given me no descendants of my own, so one of my servants will be my heir."

[4]Then the LORD said to him, "No, your servant will not be your heir, for you will have a son of your own who will be your heir." [5]Then the LORD took Abram outside and said to him, "Look up into the sky and count the stars if you can. That's how many descendants you will have!"

[6]And Abram believed the LORD, and the LORD counted him as righteous because of his faith.

GETTING IT RIGHT 15:6

Although Abram demonstrated his faith through his actions, his belief in the Lord made him right with God (Rom 4:1-5). We can be right with God by trusting him with our lives. Church attendance, prayer, and good deeds will not make us right with God. A right relationship is based on faith—the heartfelt inner confidence that God is who he says he is and does what he says he will do. Obedience is a result of a good relationship with God. ■

[7]Then the LORD told him, "I am the LORD who brought you out of Ur of the Chaldeans to give you this land as your possession."

[8]But Abram replied, "O Sovereign LORD, how can I be sure that I will actually possess it?"

[9]The LORD told him, "Bring me a three-year-old heifer, a three-year-old female goat, a three-year-old ram, a turtledove, and a young pigeon." [10]So Abram presented all these to him and killed them. Then he cut each animal down the middle and laid the halves side by side; he did not, however, cut the birds in half. [11]Some vultures swooped down to eat the carcasses, but Abram chased them away.

[12]As the sun was going down, Abram fell into a deep sleep, and a terrifying darkness came down over him. [13]Then the LORD said to Abram, "You can be sure that your descendants will be strangers in a foreign land, where they will be oppressed as slaves for 400 years. [14]But I will punish the nation that enslaves them, and in the end they will come away with great wealth. [15](As for you, you will die in peace and be buried at a ripe old age.) [16]After four generations your descendants will return here to this land, for the sins of the Amorites do not yet warrant their destruction."

[17]After the sun went down and darkness fell, Abram saw a smoking firepot and a flaming torch pass between the halves of the carcasses. [18]So the LORD made a covenant with Abram that day and said, "I have given this land to your descendants, all the way from the border of Egypt* to the great Euphrates River—[19]the land now occupied by the Kenites, Kenizzites, Kadmonites, [20]Hittites, Perizzites, Rephaites, [21]Amorites, Canaanites, Girgashites, and Jebusites."

16 THE BIRTH OF ISHMAEL

Now Sarai, Abram's wife, had not been able to bear children for him. But she had an Egyptian servant named Hagar. [2]So Sarai said to Abram, "The LORD has prevented me from having children. Go and sleep with my servant. Perhaps I can have children through her." And Abram agreed with Sarai's proposal. [3]So Sarai, Abram's wife, took Hagar the Egyptian servant and gave her to Abram as a wife. (This happened ten years after Abram had settled in the land of Canaan.)

[4]So Abram had sexual relations with Hagar, and she became pregnant. But when Hagar knew she was pregnant, she began to treat her mistress, Sarai, with contempt. [5]Then Sarai said to Abram, "This is all your fault! I put my servant into your arms, but now that she's pregnant she treats me with contempt. The LORD will show who's wrong—you or me!"

[6]Abram replied, "Look, she is your servant, so deal with her as you see fit." Then Sarai treated Hagar so harshly that she finally ran away.

[7]The angel of the LORD found Hagar beside a spring of water in the wilderness, along the road to Shur. [8]The angel said to her, "Hagar, Sarai's servant, where have you come from, and where are you going?"

RUNAWAY 16:6-14

When Hagar ran away after a fight with her mistress Sarai, the Angel of the Lord instructed her to return to her mistress. Hagar needed to work on her attitude toward Sarai, no matter how unfairly Sarai might have treated her. Running away from our problems rarely solves them. Tempted to run away from a problem? The wise person accepts God's help to face problems squarely. ■

"I'm running away from my mistress, Sarai," she replied.

[9]The angel of the LORD said to her, "Return to your mistress, and submit to her authority." [10]Then he added, "I will give you more descendants than you can count."

15:18 Hebrew *the river of Egypt,* referring either to an eastern branch of the Nile River or to the Brook of Egypt in the Sinai (see Num 34:5).

[11]And the angel also said, "You are now pregnant and
will give birth to a son. You are to name him Ishmael
(which means 'God hears'), for the LORD has heard your
cry of distress. [12]This son of yours will be a wild man, as
untamed as a wild donkey! He will raise his fist against
everyone, and everyone will be against him. Yes, he will
live in open hostility against all his relatives."

[13]Thereafter, Hagar used another name to refer to the
LORD, who had spoken to her. She said, "You are the God
who sees me."* She also said, "Have I truly seen the One
who sees me?" [14]So that well was named Beer-lahai-roi
(which means "well of the Living One who sees me"). It
can still be found between Kadesh and Bered.

[15]So Hagar gave Abram a son, and Abram named him
Ishmael. [16]Abram was eighty-six years old when Ishmael
was born.

17 ABRAM IS NAMED ABRAHAM

When Abram was ninety-nine years old, the LORD appeared to him and said, "I am El-Shaddai—'God Almighty.' Serve me faithfully and live a blameless life. [2]I
will make a covenant with you, by which I will guarantee
to give you countless descendants."

[3]At this, Abram fell face down on the ground. Then
God said to him, [4]"This is my covenant with you: I will
make you the father of a multitude of nations! [5]What's
more, I am changing your name. It will no longer be
Abram. Instead, you will be called Abraham,* for you will
be the father of many nations. [6]I will make you extremely
fruitful. Your descendants will become many nations,
and kings will be among them!

[7]"I will confirm my covenant with you and your descendants* after you, from generation to generation.
This is the everlasting covenant: I will always be your God
and the God of your descendants after you. [8]And I will
give the entire land of Canaan, where you now live as a
foreigner, to you and your descendants. It will be their
possession forever, and I will be their God."

THE MARK OF THE COVENANT

[9]Then God said to Abraham, "Your responsibility is to
obey the terms of the covenant. You and all your descendants have this continual responsibility. [10]This is the covenant that you and your descendants must keep: Each
male among you must be circumcised. [11]You must cut off
the flesh of your foreskin as a sign of the covenant between me and you. [12]From generation to generation,
every male child must be circumcised on the eighth day
after his birth. This applies not only to members of your
family but also to the servants born in your household
and the foreign-born servants whom you have purchased. [13]All must be circumcised. Your bodies will bear
the mark of my everlasting covenant. [14]Any male who
fails to be circumcised will be cut off from the covenant
family for breaking the covenant."

16:13 Hebrew *El-roi.* 17:5 *Abram* means "exalted father"; *Abraham* sounds like a Hebrew term that means "father of many." 17:7 Hebrew *seed;* also in 17:7b, 8, 9, 10, 19.

SARAH

UPS:
- Was intensely loyal to her own child
- Became the mother of a nation and an ancestor of Jesus
- Was the first woman listed in the Hall of Faith in Hebrews 11

DOWNS:
- Had trouble believing God's promises to her
- Attempted to work problems out on her own, without consulting God
- Tried to cover her own faults by blaming others

STATS:
- Where: Married Abram in Ur of the Chaldeans, then moved with him to Canaan
- Occupation: Household manager
- Relatives: Terah (father); Abraham (husband); Nahor and Haran (half-brothers); Lot (nephew); Isaac (son)

BOTTOM LINE:

God responds to faith even in the midst of failure.

God is not bound by what usually happens. He can stretch the limits and cause unheard-of events to occur.

Sarah's story is told in Gen 11:29–24:67. She also is mentioned in Isa 51:2; Rom 4:19; 9:9; Heb 11:11; 1 Pet 3:6.

SARAH Have you ever laughed out loud because you thought something was funny, only to discover that what you heard wasn't supposed to be funny? If so, you know how Sarah felt. When told that she was going to have a baby, Sarah burst out laughing (Gen 18:10-12). After all, she was 90 years old and had not been able to conceive. Doing the impossible seemed . . . well . . . funny. But when God called her on that, she tried to fake her way out.

God promised to give Abraham a son through Sarah (Gen 17:16-21). Earlier, Sarah took matters into her own hands by giving her servant, Hagar, to Abraham to produce a son. (See Gen 16.) But that scheme inspired anger and tears, rather than laughter.

God got the last laugh when Sarah's son was born. The impossible had become possible! God had her name the baby *Isaac,* which means "laughter" (Gen 17:19).

Like Sarah, are you tempted to laugh when faced with an impossible situation? God likes to do the impossible! Are you willing to trust him?

SARAI IS NAMED SARAH

15 Then God said to Abraham, "Regarding Sarai, your wife—her name will no longer be Sarai. From now on her name will be Sarah.* 16 And I will bless her and give you a son from her! Yes, I will bless her richly, and she will become the mother of many nations. Kings of nations will be among her descendants."

17 Then Abraham bowed down to the ground, but he laughed to himself in disbelief. "How could I become a father at the age of 100?" he thought. "And how can Sarah have a baby when she is ninety years old?" 18 So Abraham said to God, "May Ishmael live under your special blessing!"

19 But God replied, "No—Sarah, your wife, will give birth to a son for you. You will name him Isaac,* and I will confirm my covenant with him and his descendants as an everlasting covenant. 20 As for Ishmael, I will bless him also, just as you have asked. I will make him extremely fruitful and multiply his descendants. He will become the father of twelve princes, and I will make him a great nation. 21 But my covenant will be confirmed with Isaac, who will be born to you and Sarah about this time next year." 22 When God had finished speaking, he left Abraham.

23 On that very day Abraham took his son, Ishmael, and every male in his household, including those born there and those he had bought. Then he circumcised them, cutting off their foreskins, just as God had told him. 24 Abraham was ninety-nine years old when he was circumcised, 25 and Ishmael, his son, was thirteen. 26 Both Abraham and his son, Ishmael, were circumcised on that same day, 27 along with all the other men and boys of the household, whether they were born there or bought as servants. All were circumcised with him.

18 A SON IS PROMISED TO SARAH

The LORD appeared again to Abraham near the oak grove belonging to Mamre. One day Abraham was sitting at the entrance to his tent during the hottest part of the day. 2 He looked up and noticed three men standing nearby. When he saw them, he ran to meet them and welcomed them, bowing low to the ground.

3 "My lord," he said, "if it pleases you, stop here for a while. 4 Rest in the shade of this tree while water is brought to wash your feet. 5 And since you've honored your servant with this visit, let me prepare some food to refresh you before you continue on your journey."

"All right," they said. "Do as you have said."

6 So Abraham ran back to the tent and said to Sarah, "Hurry! Get three large measures* of your best flour, knead it into dough, and bake some bread." 7 Then Abraham ran out to the herd and chose a tender calf and gave it to his servant, who quickly prepared it. 8 When the food was ready, Abraham took some yogurt and milk and the roasted meat, and he served it to the men. As they ate, Abraham waited on them in the shade of the trees.

9 "Where is Sarah, your wife?" the visitors asked.

"She's inside the tent," Abraham replied.

10 Then one of them said, "I will return to you about this time next year, and your wife, Sarah, will have a son!"

LYING 18:10-15

Sarah lied about her laughter at God's promise that she would have a son. Fear is the most common motive for lying. Sometimes we fear that we'll look foolish if we're caught in a lie. Other times, we fear that our wrongdoing will be discovered. But lying causes greater complications than telling the truth. If God can't be trusted with our thoughts and fears, we are in greater trouble than we first imagined. ■

Sarah was listening to this conversation from the tent. 11 Abraham and Sarah were both very old by this time, and Sarah was long past the age of having children. 12 So she laughed silently to herself and said, "How could a worn-out woman like me enjoy such pleasure, especially when my master—my husband—is also so old?"

13 Then the LORD said to Abraham, "Why did Sarah laugh? Why did she say, 'Can an old woman like me have a baby?' 14 Is anything too hard for the LORD? I will return about this time next year, and Sarah will have a son."

15 Sarah was afraid, so she denied it, saying, "I didn't laugh."

But the LORD said, "No, you did laugh."

> Is anything too hard for the LORD?
>
> *GENESIS 18:14*

ABRAHAM INTERCEDES FOR SODOM

16 Then the men got up from their meal and looked out toward Sodom. As they left, Abraham went with them to send them on their way.

17 "Should I hide my plan from Abraham?" the LORD asked. 18 "For Abraham will certainly become a great and mighty nation, and all the nations of the earth will be blessed through him. 19 I have singled him out so that he will direct his sons and their families to keep the way of the LORD by doing what is right and just. Then I will do for Abraham all that I have promised."

20 So the LORD told Abraham, "I have heard a great outcry from Sodom and Gomorrah, because their sin is so flagrant. 21 I am going down to see if their actions are as wicked as I have heard. If not, I want to know."

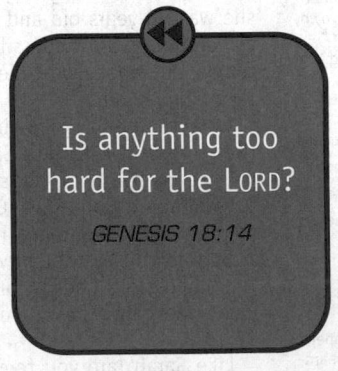

22 The other men turned and headed toward Sodom, but the LORD remained with Abraham. 23 Abraham approached him and said, "Will you sweep away both the righteous and

17:15 *Sarai* and *Sarah* both mean "princess." **17:19** *Isaac* means "he laughs." **18:6** Hebrew *3 seahs,* about 15 quarts or 18 liters.

the wicked? 24Suppose you find fifty righteous people living there in the city—will you still sweep it away and not spare it for their sakes? 25Surely you wouldn't do such a thing, destroying the righteous along with the wicked. Why, you would be treating the righteous and the wicked exactly the same! Surely you wouldn't do that! Should not the Judge of all the earth do what is right?"

26And the LORD replied, "If I find fifty righteous people in Sodom, I will spare the entire city for their sake."

27Then Abraham spoke again. "Since I have begun, let me speak further to my Lord, even though I am but dust and ashes. 28Suppose there are only forty-five righteous people rather than fifty? Will you destroy the whole city for lack of five?"

And the LORD said, "I will not destroy it if I find forty-five righteous people there."

29Then Abraham pressed his request further. "Suppose there are only forty?"

And the LORD replied, "I will not destroy it for the sake of the forty."

30"Please don't be angry, my Lord," Abraham pleaded. "Let me speak—suppose only thirty righteous people are found?"

And the LORD replied, "I will not destroy it if I find thirty."

31Then Abraham said, "Since I have dared to speak to the Lord, let me continue—suppose there are only twenty?"

And the LORD replied, "Then I will not destroy it for the sake of the twenty."

32Finally, Abraham said, "Lord, please don't be angry with me if I speak one more time. Suppose only ten are found there?"

And the LORD replied, "Then I will not destroy it for the sake of the ten."

33When the LORD had finished his conversation with Abraham, he went on his way, and Abraham returned to his tent.

19 SODOM AND GOMORRAH DESTROYED

That evening the two angels came to the entrance of the city of Sodom. Lot was sitting there, and when he saw them, he stood up to meet them. Then he welcomed them and bowed with his face to the ground. 2"My lords," he said, "come to my home to wash your feet, and be my guests for the night. You may then get up early in the morning and be on your way again."

"Oh no," they replied. "We'll just spend the night out here in the city square."

3But Lot insisted, so at last they went home with him. Lot prepared a feast for them, complete with fresh bread made without yeast, and they ate. 4But before they retired for the night, all the men of Sodom, young and old, came from all over the city and surrounded the house. 5They shouted to Lot, "Where are the men who came to spend the night with you? Bring them out to us so we can have sex with them!"

6So Lot stepped outside to talk to them, s[illegible] door behind him. 7"Please, my brothers," he beg[illegible] "don't do such a wicked thing. 8Look, I have two virgin daughters. Let me bring them out to you, and you can do with them as you wish. But please, leave these men alone, for they are my guests and are under my protection."

9"Stand back!" they shouted. "This fellow came to town as an outsider, and now he's acting like our judge! We'll treat you far worse than those other men!" And they lunged toward Lot to break down the door.

10But the two angels* reached out, pulled Lot into the house, and bolted the door. 11Then they blinded all the men, young and old, who were at the door of the house, so they gave up trying to get inside.

12Meanwhile, the angels questioned Lot. "Do you have any other relatives here in the city?" they asked. "Get them out of this place—your sons-in-law, sons, daughters, or anyone else. 13For we are about to destroy this city completely. The outcry against this place is so great it has reached the LORD, and he has sent us to destroy it."

14So Lot rushed out to tell his daughters' fiancés, "Quick, get out of the city! The LORD is about to destroy it." But the young men thought he was only joking.

CHAMELEON OR CHAMPION? 19:14

Lot had lived so long among ungodly people that he was no longer a believable witness for God. He had allowed his environment to shape him, rather than shaping his environment. Also, he had compromised to the point that he was almost useless to God. When he finally took a stand, nobody listened. Do those who know you see you as a witness for God? Or, are you a chameleon like Lot—blending into your environment? If you want to make a difference, you must first decide to be different and take a stand for what's right. ■

15At dawn the next morning the angels became insistent. "Hurry," they said to Lot. "Take your wife and your two daughters who are here. Get out right now, or you will be swept away in the destruction of the city!"

16When Lot still hesitated, the angels seized his hand and the hands of his wife and two daughters and rushed them to safety outside the city, for the LORD was merciful. 17When they were safely out of the city, one of the angels ordered, "Run for your lives! And don't look back or stop anywhere in the valley! Escape to the mountains, or you will be swept away!"

18"Oh no, my lord!" Lot begged. 19"You have been so gracious to me and saved my life, and you have shown such great kindness. But I cannot go to the mountains. Disaster would catch up to me there, and I would soon die. 20See, there is a small village nearby. Please let me go there instead; don't you see how small it is? Then my life will be saved."

19:10 Hebrew *men;* also in 19:12, 16.

21"All right," the angel said, "I will grant your request. I
will not destroy the little village. 22But hurry! Escape to it,
for I can do nothing until you arrive there." (This explains
why that village was known as Zoar, which means "little
place.")
23Lot reached the village just as the sun was rising over
the horizon. 24Then the LORD rained down fire and burning sulfur from the sky on Sodom and Gomorrah. 25He
utterly destroyed them, along with the other cities and
villages of the plain, wiping out all the people and every
bit of vegetation. 26But Lot's wife looked back as she was
following behind him, and she turned into a pillar of salt.
27Abraham got up early that morning and hurried out
to the place where he had stood in the LORD's presence.
28He looked out across the plain toward Sodom and Gomorrah and watched as columns of smoke rose from the
cities like smoke from a furnace.
29But God had listened to Abraham's request and kept
Lot safe, removing him from the disaster that engulfed
the cities on the plain.

LOT AND HIS DAUGHTERS

30Afterward Lot left Zoar because he was afraid of the
people there, and he went to live in a cave in the mountains with his two daughters. 31One day the older daughter said to her sister, "There are no men left anywhere in
this entire area, so we can't get married like everyone
else. And our father will soon be too old to have children.
32Come, let's get him drunk with wine, and then we will
have sex with him. That way we will preserve our family
line through our father."
33So that night they got him drunk with wine, and the
older daughter went in and had intercourse with her father. He was unaware of her lying down or getting up
again.
34The next morning the older daughter said to her
younger sister, "I had sex with our father last night. Let's
get him drunk with wine again tonight, and you go in and
have sex with him. That way we will preserve our family
line through our father." 35So that night they got him
drunk with wine again, and the younger daughter went in

ISAAC

UPS:

- Was the miracle child born to 90-year-old Sarah and 100-year-old Abraham
- The first descendant in fulfillment of God's promise to Abraham
- Seems to have been a caring and consistent husband, at least until his sons were born
- Demonstrated great patience

DOWNS:

- Tended to imitate his father and lie when under pressure
- Tried to avoid confrontation by bargaining
- Played favorites between his sons and alienated his wife

STATS:

- Where: The area called the Negev, in the southern part of Palestine, between Kadesh and Shur (Gen 20:1)
- Occupation: Wealthy livestock owner
- Relatives: Abraham and Sarah (parents); Ishmael (half-brother); Rebekah (wife); Esau and Jacob (twin sons)

BOTTOM LINE:

Patience often brings rewards.

Both God's plans and his promises are larger than people.

God keeps his promises! He remains faithful though we are often faithless.

Isaac's story is told in Gen 17:19; 21–22; 24:1–28:22; 35:39. He also is mentioned in Rom 9:7; Heb 11:17-20; James 2:21.

ISAAC Like it or not, your name is powerful. It sets you apart. It undoubtedly triggers some kind of reaction in people—based on the way you've treated them. When you hear your name said, you almost have to look. When people heard Isaac's name, they almost had to laugh!

Isaac's name means "laughter." As with many Bible characters, there were several reasons Isaac got his name. Isaac's name reminded his parents of their first reaction of shocked laughter when God told them they would have a son though they were quite old. At other times, his name must have reminded them of the great joy they had when Isaac was born. His name was also a reminder of God's presence, for God had told Isaac's parents to give their child that name.

In a family of active leaders, Isaac was the quiet, "mind-my-own-business" type unless he had to be involved. He was the protected only child until Abraham arranged his marriage to Rebekah. Then Isaac allowed his wife to run their family. He rarely stood his ground and found it easier to compromise or lie than to face a confrontation.

In spite of these problems, Isaac was still a vital part of God's plan. Isaac learned the importance of faith in the one true God from his father. God's promise to Abraham to create a great nation through which he would bless the world was passed on to Isaac and to his twin sons.

Ever feel like Isaac—like you just go along with what your friends say or do, even though you believe otherwise? God works through people in spite of their weaknesses. Are you willing to tell God you're available to him, weaknesses and all? You will discover that his willingness to use you is even greater than your desire to be used.

and had intercourse with him. As before, he was unaware
of her lying down or getting up again.
36As a result, both of Lot's daughters became pregnant
by their own father. 37When the older daughter gave
birth to a son, she named him Moab.* He became the ancestor of the nation now known as the Moabites. 38When
the younger daughter gave birth to a son, she named him
Ben-ammi.* He became the ancestor of the nation now
known as the Ammonites.

20 ABRAHAM DECEIVES ABIMELECH

Abraham moved south to the Negev and lived for a while
between Kadesh and Shur, and then he moved on to
Gerar. While living there as a foreigner, 2Abraham introduced his wife, Sarah, by saying, "She is my sister." So
King Abimelech of Gerar sent for Sarah and had her
brought to him at his palace.
3But that night God came to Abimelech in a dream and
told him, "You are a dead man, for that woman you have
taken is already married!"
4But Abimelech had not slept with her yet, so he said,
"Lord, will you destroy an innocent nation? 5Didn't Abraham tell me, 'She is my sister'? And she herself said, 'Yes,
he is my brother.' I acted in complete innocence! My
hands are clean."
6In the dream God responded, "Yes, I know you are innocent. That's why I kept you from sinning against me,
and why I did not let you touch her. 7Now return the
woman to her husband, and he will pray for you, for he is
a prophet. Then you will live. But if you don't return her
to him, you can be sure that you and all your people will
die."
8Abimelech got up early the next morning and quickly
called all his servants together. When he told them what
had happened, his men were terrified. 9Then Abimelech
called for Abraham. "What have you done to us?" he demanded. "What crime have I committed that deserves
treatment like this, making me and my kingdom guilty of
this great sin? No one should ever do what you have done!
10Whatever possessed you to do such a thing?"
11Abraham replied, "I thought, 'This is a godless place.
They will want my wife and will kill me to get her.' 12And
she really is my sister, for we both have the same father,
but different mothers. And I married her. 13When God
called me to leave my father's home and to travel from
place to place, I told her, 'Do me a favor. Wherever we go,
tell the people that I am your brother.'"
14Then Abimelech took some of his sheep and goats,
cattle, and male and female servants, and he presented
them to Abraham. He also returned his wife, Sarah, to
him. 15Then Abimelech said, "Look over my land and
choose any place where you would like to live." 16And he
said to Sarah, "Look, I am giving your 'brother' 1,000
pieces of silver* in the presence of all these witnesses.
This is to compensate you for any wrong I may have done
to you. This will settle any claim against me, and your reputation is cleared."
17Then Abraham prayed to God, and God healed Abimelech, his wife, and his female servants, so they could
have children. 18For the LORD had caused all the women
to be infertile because of what happened with Abraham's
wife, Sarah.

21 THE BIRTH OF ISAAC

The LORD kept his word and did for Sarah exactly what he
had promised. 2She became pregnant, and she gave birth
to a son for Abraham in his old age. This happened at just
the time God had said it would. 3And Abraham named
their son Isaac. 4Eight days after Isaac was born, Abraham circumcised him as God had commanded. 5Abra-
ham was 100 years old when Isaac was born.
6And Sarah declared, "God has brought me laughter.*
All who hear about this will laugh with me. 7Who would
have said to Abraham that Sarah would nurse a baby? Yet
I have given Abraham a son in his old age!"

HAGAR AND ISHMAEL ARE SENT AWAY

8When Isaac grew up and was about to be weaned, Abraham prepared a huge feast to celebrate the occasion. 9But
Sarah saw Ishmael—the son of Abraham and her Egyptian servant Hagar—making fun of her son, Isaac.* 10So
she turned to Abraham and demanded, "Get rid of that
slave woman and her son. He is not going to share the inheritance with my son, Isaac. I won't have it!"
11This upset Abraham very much because Ishmael was
his son. 12But God told Abraham, "Do not be upset over
the boy and your servant. Do whatever Sarah tells you, for
Isaac is the son through whom your descendants will be
counted. 13But I will also make a nation of the descendants of Hagar's son because he is your son, too."
14So Abraham got up early the next morning, prepared
food and a container of water, and strapped them on
Hagar's shoulders. Then he sent her away with their son,
and she wandered aimlessly in the wilderness of
Beersheba.
15When the water was gone, she put the boy in the
shade of a bush. 16Then she went and sat down by herself
about a hundred yards* away. "I don't want to watch the
boy die," she said, as she burst into tears.
17But God heard the boy crying, and the angel of God
called to Hagar from heaven, "Hagar, what's wrong? Do
not be afraid! God has heard the boy crying as he lies
there. 18Go to him and comfort him, for I will make a
great nation from his descendants."
19Then God opened Hagar's eyes, and she saw a well
full of water. She quickly filled her water container and
gave the boy a drink.
20And God was with the boy as he grew up in the wilderness. He became a skillful archer, 21and he settled in
the wilderness of Paran. His mother arranged for him to
marry a woman from the land of Egypt.

19:37 *Moab* sounds like a Hebrew term that means "from father." **19:38** *Ben-ammi* means "son of my kinsman." **20:16** Hebrew *1,000 shekels of silver,* about 25 pounds or 11.4 kilograms in weight. **21:6** The name *Isaac* means "he laughs." **21:9** As in Greek version and Latin Vulgate; Hebrew omits *of her son, Isaac.* **21:16** Hebrew *a bowshot.*

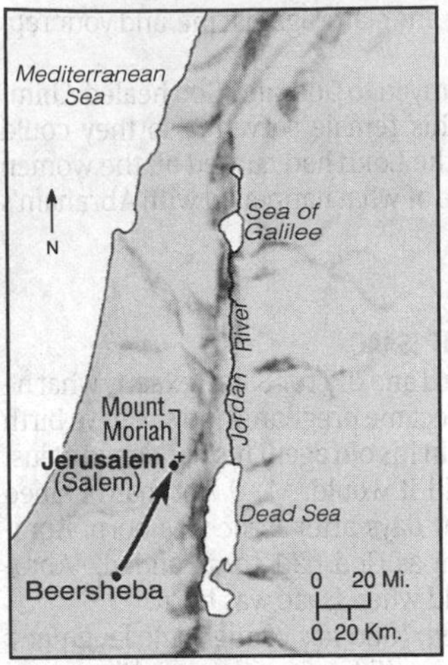

ABRAHAM'S TRIP TO MOUNT MORIAH
Abraham and Isaac traveled the 50 or 60 miles from Beersheba to Mount Moriah in about three days. This was a very difficult three days for Abraham, who was on his way to sacrifice his beloved son, Isaac.

ABRAHAM'S COVENANT WITH ABIMELECH

22About this time, Abimelech came with Phicol, his army commander, to visit Abraham. "God is obviously with you, helping you in everything you do," Abimelech said. 23"Swear to me in God's name that you will never deceive me, my children, or any of my descendants. I have been loyal to you, so now swear that you will be loyal to me and to this country where you are living as a foreigner."

24Abraham replied, "Yes, I swear to it!" 25Then Abraham complained to Abimelech about a well that Abimelech's servants had taken by force from Abraham's servants.

26"This is the first I've heard of it," Abimelech answered. "I have no idea who is responsible. You have never complained about this before."

27Abraham then gave some of his sheep, goats, and cattle to Abimelech, and they made a treaty. 28But Abraham also took seven additional female lambs and set them off by themselves. 29Abimelech asked, "Why have you set these seven apart from the others?"

30Abraham replied, "Please accept these seven lambs to show your agreement that I dug this well." 31Then he named the place Beersheba (which means "well of the oath"), because that was where they had sworn the oath.

32After making their covenant at Beersheba, Abimelech left with Phicol, the commander of his army, and they returned home to the land of the Philistines. 33Then Abraham planted a tamarisk tree at Beersheba, and there he worshiped the LORD, the Eternal God.* 34And Abraham lived as a foreigner in Philistine country for a long time.

22 ABRAHAM'S FAITH TESTED

Some time later, God tested Abraham's faith. "Abraham!" God called.

"Yes," he replied. "Here I am."

2"Take your son, your only son—yes, Isaac, whom you love so much—and go to the land of Moriah. Go and sacrifice him as a burnt offering on one of the mountains, which I will show you."

3The next morning Abraham got up early. He saddled his donkey and took two of his servants with him, along with his son, Isaac. Then he chopped wood for a fire for a burnt offering and set out for the place God had told him about. 4On the third day of their journey, Abraham looked up and saw the place in the distance. 5"Stay here with the donkey," Abraham told the servants. "The boy and I will travel a little farther. We will worship there, and then we will come right back."

6So Abraham placed the wood for the burnt offering on Isaac's shoulders, while he himself carried the fire and the knife. As the two of them walked on together, 7Isaac turned to Abraham and said, "Father?"

"Yes, my son?" Abraham replied.

"We have the fire and the wood," the boy said, "but where is the sheep for the burnt offering?"

8"God will provide a sheep for the burnt offering, my son," Abraham answered. And they both walked on together.

9When they arrived at the place where God had told him to go, Abraham built an altar and arranged the wood on it. Then he tied his son, Isaac, and laid him on the altar on top of the wood. 10And Abraham picked up the knife to kill his son as a sacrifice. 11At that moment the angel of the LORD called to him from heaven, "Abraham! Abraham!"

"Yes," Abraham replied. "Here I am!"

12"Don't lay a hand on the boy!" the angel said. "Do not hurt him in any way, for now I know that you truly fear God. You have not withheld from me even your son, your only son."

PASSING THE TEST 22:1-2

Why did God ask Abraham to sacrifice his son? Enemy nations practiced human sacrifice, but God condemned this as a terrible sin (Lev 20:1-5). God did not want Isaac to die; he wanted Abraham to prove that he loved God more than he loved his long-awaited son. Through this difficult experience, Abraham strengthened his commitment to God. He also learned about God's ability to provide. The purpose of testing is to strengthen our character and deepen our commitment to God. Are you feeling like you're being tested right now? How will you respond? ■

13Then Abraham looked up and saw a ram caught by its horns in a thicket. So he took the ram and sacrificed it as a burnt offering in place of his son. 14Abraham named the place Yahweh-Yireh (which means "the LORD will provide"). To this day, people still use that name as a proverb: "On the mountain of the LORD it will be provided."

15Then the angel of the LORD called again to Abraham from heaven. 16"This is what the LORD says: Because you have obeyed me and have not withheld even your son,

21:33 Hebrew *El-Olam.*

your only son, I swear by my own name that 17I will certainly bless you. I will multiply your descendants* beyond number, like the stars in the sky and the sand on the seashore. Your descendants will conquer the cities of their enemies. 18And through your descendants all the nations of the earth will be blessed—all because you have obeyed me."

19Then they returned to the servants and traveled back to Beersheba, where Abraham continued to live.

20Soon after this, Abraham heard that Milcah, his brother Nahor's wife, had borne Nahor eight sons. 21The oldest was named Uz, the next oldest was Buz, followed by Kemuel (the ancestor of the Arameans), 22Kesed, Hazo, Pildash, Jidlaph, and Bethuel. 23(Bethuel became the father of Rebekah.) In addition to these eight sons from Milcah, 24Nahor had four other children from his concubine Reumah. Their names were Tebah, Gaham, Tahash, and Maacah.

23 THE BURIAL OF SARAH

When Sarah was 127 years old, 2she died at Kiriath-arba (now called Hebron) in the land of Canaan. There Abraham mourned and wept for her.

3Then, leaving her body, he said to the Hittite elders, 4"Here I am, a stranger and a foreigner among you. Please sell me a piece of land so I can give my wife a proper burial."

5The Hittites replied to Abraham, 6"Listen, my lord, you are an honored prince among us. Choose the finest of our tombs and bury her there. No one here will refuse to help you in this way."

7Then Abraham bowed low before the Hittites and said, 8"Since you are willing to help me in this way, be so kind as to ask Ephron son of Zohar 9to let me buy his cave at Machpelah, down at the end of his field. I will pay the full price in the presence of witnesses, so I will have a permanent burial place for my family."

10Ephron was sitting there among the others, and he answered Abraham as the others listened, speaking publicly before all the Hittite elders of the town. 11"No, my lord," he said to Abraham, "please listen to me. I will give you the field and the cave. Here in the presence of my people, I give it to you. Go and bury your dead."

12Abraham again bowed low before the citizens of the land, 13and he replied to Ephron as everyone listened. "No, listen to me. I will buy it from you. Let me pay the full price for the field so I can bury my dead there."

14Ephron answered Abraham, 15"My lord, please listen to me. The land is worth 400 pieces* of silver, but what is that between friends? Go ahead and bury your dead."

16So Abraham agreed to Ephron's price and paid the amount he had suggested—400 pieces of silver, weighed according to the market standard. The Hittite elders witnessed the transaction.

17So Abraham bought the plot of land belonging to Ephron at Machpelah, near Mamre. This included the field itself, the cave that was in it, and all the surrounding trees. 18It was transferred to Abraham as his permanent possession in the presence of the Hittite elders at the city gate. 19Then Abraham buried his wife, Sarah, there in Canaan, in the cave of Machpelah, near Mamre (also called Hebron). 20So the field and the cave were transferred from the Hittites to Abraham for use as a permanent burial place.

24 A WIFE FOR ISAAC

Abraham was now a very old man, and the LORD had blessed him in every way. 2One day Abraham said to his oldest servant, the man in charge of his household, "Take an oath by putting your hand under my thigh. 3Swear by the LORD, the God of heaven and earth, that you will not allow my son to marry one of these local Canaanite women. 4Go instead to my homeland, to my relatives, and find a wife there for my son Isaac."

HERE COMES THE BRIDE! 24:4

Abraham wanted Isaac to marry a relative. This was a common and acceptable practice that had the added advantage of avoiding intermarriage with enemy nations. Also, parents usually chose their sons' wives. Many of the chosen brides were teens! Are you thinking about getting married someday? What characteristics are you looking for in a future spouse? How much of a part will your parents play in your choice of spouse? ■

5The servant asked, "But what if I can't find a young woman who is willing to travel so far from home? Should I then take Isaac there to live among your relatives in the land you came from?"

6"No!" Abraham responded. "Be careful never to take my son there. 7For the LORD, the God of heaven, who took me from my father's house and my native land, solemnly promised to give this land to my descendants.* He will send his angel ahead of you, and he will see to it that you find a wife there for my son. 8If she is unwilling to come back with you, then you are free from this oath of mine. But under no circumstances are you to take my son there."

9So the servant took an oath by putting his hand under the thigh of his master, Abraham. He swore to follow Abraham's instructions. 10Then he loaded ten of Abraham's camels with all kinds of expensive gifts from his master, and he traveled to distant Aram-naharaim. There he went to the town where Abraham's brother Nahor had settled. 11He made the camels kneel beside a well just outside the town. It was evening, and the women were coming out to draw water.

12"O LORD, God of my master, Abraham," he prayed. "Please give me success today, and show unfailing love to my master, Abraham. 13See, I am standing here beside this spring, and the young women of the town are coming

22:17 Hebrew *seed;* also in 22:17b, 18. **23:15** Hebrew *400 shekels,* about 10 pounds or 4.6 kilograms in weight; also in 23:16. **24:7** Hebrew *seed;* also in 24:60.

out to draw water. 14This is my request. I will ask one of them, 'Please give me a drink from your jug.' If she says, 'Yes, have a drink, and I will water your camels, too!'—let her be the one you have selected as Isaac's wife. This is how I will know that you have shown unfailing love to my master."

15Before he had finished praying, he saw a young woman named Rebekah coming out with her water jug on her shoulder. She was the daughter of Bethuel, who was the son of Abraham's brother Nahor and his wife, Milcah. 16Rebekah was very beautiful and old enough to be married, but she was still a virgin. She went down to the spring, filled her jug, and came up again. 17Running over to her, the servant said, "Please give me a little drink of water from your jug."

INNER BEAUTY 24:15-16

Rebekah had physical beauty, but Abraham's servant looked for a sign of inner beauty. Our appearance is important to us. Many of us spend time and money to improve the way we look. But inner beauty is important also. How do we develop inner beauty? Patience, kindness, and joy are the beauty treatments that help us become truly lovely on the inside. ■

18"Yes, my lord," she answered, "have a drink." And she quickly lowered her jug from her shoulder and gave him a drink. 19When she had given him a drink, she said, "I'll draw water for your camels, too, until they have had enough to drink." 20So she quickly emptied her jug into the watering trough and ran back to the well to draw water for all his camels.

21The servant watched her in silence, wondering whether or not the LORD had given him success in his mission. 22Then at last, when the camels had finished drinking, he took out a gold ring for her nose and two large gold bracelets* for her wrists.

23"Whose daughter are you?" he asked. "And please tell me, would your father have any room to put us up for the night?"

24"I am the daughter of Bethuel," she replied. "My grandparents are Nahor and Milcah. 25Yes, we have plenty of straw and feed for the camels, and we have room for guests."

26The man bowed low and worshiped the LORD. 27"Praise the LORD, the God of my master, Abraham," he said. "The LORD has shown unfailing love and faithfulness to my master, for he has led me straight to my master's relatives."

28The young woman ran home to tell her family everything that had happened. 29Now Rebekah had a brother named Laban, who ran out to meet the man at the spring. 30He had seen the nose-ring and the bracelets on his sister's wrists, and had heard Rebekah tell what the man had said. So he rushed out to the spring, where the man was still standing beside his camels. Laban said to him, 31"Come and stay with us, you who are blessed by the LORD! Why are you standing here outside the town when I have a room all ready for you and a place prepared for the camels?"

32So the man went home with Laban, and Laban unloaded the camels, gave him straw for their bedding, fed them, and provided water for the man and the camel drivers to wash their feet. 33Then food was served. But Abraham's servant said, "I don't want to eat until I have told you why I have come."

"All right," Laban said, "tell us."

34"I am Abraham's servant," he explained. 35"And the LORD has greatly blessed my master; he has become a wealthy man. The LORD has given him flocks of sheep and goats, herds of cattle, a fortune in silver and gold, and many male and female servants and camels and donkeys.

36"When Sarah, my master's wife, was very old, she gave birth to my master's son, and my master has given him everything he owns. 37And my master made me take an oath. He said, 'Do not allow my son to marry one of these local Canaanite women. 38Go instead to my father's house, to my relatives, and find a wife there for my son.'

39"But I said to my master, 'What if I can't find a young woman who is willing to go back with me?' 40He responded, 'The LORD, in whose presence I have lived, will send his angel with you and will make your mission successful. Yes, you must find a wife for my son from among my relatives, from my father's family. 41Then you will have fulfilled your obligation. But if you go to my relatives and they refuse to let her go with you, you will be free from my oath.'

42"So today when I came to the spring, I prayed this prayer: 'O LORD, God of my master, Abraham, please give me success on this mission. 43See, I am standing here beside this spring. This is my request. When a young woman comes to draw water, I will say to her, "Please give me a little drink of water from your jug." 44If she says, "Yes, have a drink, and I will draw water for your camels, too," let her be the one you have selected to be the wife of my master's son.'

45"Before I had finished praying in my heart, I saw Rebekah coming out with her water jug on her shoulder. She went down to the spring and drew water. So I said to her, 'Please give me a drink.' 46She quickly lowered her jug from her shoulder and said, 'Yes, have a drink, and I will water your camels, too!' So I drank, and then she watered the camels.

47"Then I asked, 'Whose daughter are you?' She replied, 'I am the daughter of Bethuel, and my grandparents are Nahor and Milcah.' So I put the ring on her nose, and the bracelets on her wrists.

48"Then I bowed low and worshiped the LORD. I praised the LORD, the God of my master, Abraham, because he had led me straight to my master's niece to be his son's wife. 49So tell me—will you or won't you show

24:22 Hebrew *a gold nose-ring weighing a half shekel* [0.2 ounces or 6 grams] *and two gold bracelets weighing 10 shekels* [4 ounces or 114 grams].

unfailing love and faithfulness to my master? Please tell
me yes or no, and then I'll know what to do next."
50 Then Laban and Bethuel replied, "The LORD has
obviously brought you here, so there is nothing we can
say. 51 Here is Rebekah; take her and go. Yes, let her be
the wife of your master's son, as the LORD has directed."
52 When Abraham's servant heard their answer, he
bowed down to the ground and worshiped the LORD.
53 Then he brought out silver and gold jewelry and clothing and presented them to Rebekah. He also gave expensive presents to her brother and mother. 54 Then they ate
their meal, and the servant and the men with him stayed
there overnight.
But early the next morning, Abraham's servant said,
"Send me back to my master."
55 "But we want Rebekah to stay with us at least ten
days," her brother and mother said. "Then she can go."
56 But he said, "Don't delay me. The LORD has made my
mission successful; now send me back so I can return to
my master."
57 "Well," they said, "we'll call Rebekah and ask her
what she thinks." 58 So they called Rebekah. "Are you willing to go with this man?" they asked her.
And she replied, "Yes, I will go."
59 So they said good-bye to Rebekah and sent her away
with Abraham's servant and his men. The woman who
had been Rebekah's childhood nurse went along with
her. 60 They gave her this blessing as she parted:

"Our sister, may you become
the mother of many millions!
May your descendants be strong
and conquer the cities of their enemies."

61 Then Rebekah and her servant girls mounted the camels and followed the man. So Abraham's servant took
Rebekah and went on his way.
62 Meanwhile, Isaac, whose home was in the Negev, had
returned from Beer-lahai-roi. 63 One evening as he was
walking and meditating in the fields, he looked up and
saw the camels coming. 64 When Rebekah looked up and
saw Isaac, she quickly dismounted from her camel.
65 "Who is that man walking through the fields to meet
us?" she asked the servant.
And he replied, "It is my master." So Rebekah covered
her face with her veil. 66 Then the servant told Isaac everything he had done.
67 And Isaac brought Rebekah into his mother Sarah's
tent, and she became his wife. He loved her deeply, and
she was a special comfort to him after the death of his
mother.

REBEKAH

Some people know how to get things started. They're initiators. They naturally make the first moves. Know anyone like this? Then you know what Rebekah was like.

When Rebekah saw something that needed to be done, she took action. Look at what she did at the well near her home. She gave a drink to Eliezer, Abraham's servant who searched for a wife for Isaac. That was kind. Then she offered to give a drink to his 10 thirsty camels. That really caught his attention—and led to a marriage between Isaac and Rebekah! Often, a person's helpfulness makes a deeper impression than his or her appearance.

Other times, though, Rebekah acted without such good results. She found ways to help her favorite son, Jacob, do better than his brother, Esau. But Esau, an outdoorsy kind of guy, was Isaac's favorite. Rebekah later tricked her husband into giving to Jacob the special blessing meant for Esau. She tried to accomplish God's plan *her* way and made a mess.

Most of us, if we're honest, will admit that we sometimes try to justify our actions in order to get our own way. (Sound like anyone you know?) Often we even want God's approval for our plans! Before we take action we need to be truthful about our real motives. Asking ourselves this question can help: "Am I sure God wants me to do this, or do I just want him to approve my plan?" The choice is up to you.

UPS:
- Took immediate action when confronted with a need
- Persistent in her plans

DOWNS:
- Showed more initiative than wisdom
- Played favorites with her sons
- Deceived her husband

STATS:
- Where: Haran, Canaan
- Occupation: Household manager
- Relatives: Bethuel and Milcah (parents); Isaac (husband); Laban (brother); Esau and Jacob (twin sons)

BOTTOM LINE:
True followers of God are guided by his Word.
God even makes use of our mistakes in his plan.
Parental favoritism hurts a family.

Rebekah's story is told in Gen 24–27.
She also is mentioned in Rom 9:10-12.

REBEKAH

What the Bible Says about Marriage

GENESIS 2:18-24	Marriage is God's idea
GENESIS 24:58-60	Commitment is essential to a successful marriage
GENESIS 29:10-11	Romance is important
JEREMIAH 33:10-11	Marriage holds times of great joy
MALACHI 2:14-15	Marriage creates the best environment for raising children
MATTHEW 5:32	Unfaithfulness breaks the bond of trust, the foundation of all relationships
MATTHEW 19:6	Marriage is permanent
ROMANS 7:2-3	Ideally, only death should dissolve marriage
EPHESIANS 5:21-33	Marriage is based on the principled practice of love, not on feelings
EPHESIANS 5:23, 32	Marriage is a living symbol of Christ and the church
HEBREWS 13:4	Marriage is good and honorable

25

THE DEATH OF ABRAHAM

Abraham married another wife, whose name was Keturah. 2She gave birth to Zimran, Jokshan, Medan, Midian,
Ishbak, and Shuah. 3Jokshan was the father of Sheba and
Dedan. Dedan's descendants were the Asshurites, Letu-
shites, and Leummites. 4Midian's sons were Ephah,
Epher, Hanoch, Abida, and Eldaah. These were all descendants of Abraham through Keturah.
5Abraham gave everything he owned to his son Isaac.
6But before he died, he gave gifts to the sons of his concubines and sent them off to a land in the east, away from
Isaac.
7Abraham lived for 175 years, 8and he died at a ripe
old age, having lived a long and satisfying life. He
breathed his last and joined his ancestors in death. 9His
sons Isaac and Ishmael buried him in the cave of Machpelah, near Mamre, in the field of Ephron son of Zohar
the Hittite. 10This was the field Abraham had purchased
from the Hittites and where he had buried his wife Sarah.
11After Abraham's death, God blessed his son Isaac, who
settled near Beer-lahai-roi in the Negev.

ISHMAEL'S DESCENDANTS

12This is the account of the family of Ishmael, the son of
Abraham through Hagar, Sarah's Egyptian servant.
13Here is a list, by their names and clans, of Ishmael's descendants: The oldest was Nebaioth, followed by Kedar,
Adbeel, Mibsam, 14Mishma, Dumah, Massa, 15Hadad,
Tema, Jetur, Naphish, and Kedemah. 16These twelve
sons of Ishmael became the founders of twelve tribes
named after them, listed according to the places they
settled and camped. 17Ishmael lived for 137 years. Then
he breathed his last and joined his ancestors in death.
18Ishmael's descendants occupied the region from Havilah to Shur, which is east of Egypt in the direction of Asshur. There they lived in open hostility toward all their
relatives.*

THE BIRTHS OF ESAU AND JACOB

19This is the account of the family of Isaac, the son of
Abraham. 20When Isaac was forty years old, he married
Rebekah, the daughter of Bethuel the Aramean from
Paddan-aram and the sister of Laban the Aramean.
21Isaac pleaded with the LORD on behalf of his wife, because she was unable to have children. The LORD answered Isaac's prayer, and Rebekah became pregnant
with twins. 22But the two children struggled with each
other in her womb. So she went to ask the LORD about it.
"Why is this happening to me?" she asked.
23And the LORD told her, "The sons in your womb will
become two nations. From the very beginning, the two nations will be rivals. One nation will be stronger than the
other; and your older son will serve your younger son."

IMPULSE BUYING 25:29-33

Esau traded the lasting benefits of his birthright for the immediate pleasure of food. The pressure of the moment distorted his perspective and made his decision seem urgent. Can you relate? When you see something you want, what's your first impulse? Do you have to have what you want right away? Or, are you usually willing to wait? We can avoid making Esau's mistake by comparing the short-term satisfaction with its long-range consequences before we act. ■

24And when the time came to give birth, Rebekah discovered that she did indeed have twins! 25The first one
was very red at birth and covered with thick hair like a fur
coat. So they named him Esau.* 26Then the other twin
was born with his hand grasping Esau's heel. So they

25:18 The meaning of the Hebrew is uncertain. **25:25** *Esau* sounds like a Hebrew term that means "hair."

named him Jacob.* Isaac was sixty ye
twins were born.

ESAU SELLS HIS BIRTHRIGHT

27As the boys grew up, Esau became a skillful hunt
was an outdoorsman, but Jacob had a quiet tempe
ment, preferring to stay at home. 28Isaac loved Esau be
cause he enjoyed eating the wild game Esau brought
home, but Rebekah loved Jacob.
29One day when Jacob was cooking some stew, Esau arrived home from the wilderness exhausted and hungry.
30Esau said to Jacob, "I'm starved! Give me some of that
red stew!" (This is how Esau got his other name, Edom,
which means "red.")
31"All right," Jacob replied, "but trade me your rights as
the firstborn son."
32"Look, I'm dying of starvation!" said Esau. "What
good is my birthright to me now?"
33But Jacob said, "First you must swear that your birthright is mine." So Esau swore an oath, thereby selling all
his rights as the firstborn to his brother, Jacob.
34Then Jacob gave Esau some bread and lentil stew.
Esau ate the meal, then got up and left. He showed contempt for his rights as the firstborn.

26 ISAAC DECEIVES ABIMELECH

vere famine now struck the land, as had happened
in Abraham's time. So Isaac moved to Gerar,
2 imelech, king of the Philistines, lived.
to Egyp appeared to Isaac and said, "Do not go down
this land, do as I tell you. 3Live here as a foreigner in
confirm that will be with you and bless you. I hereby
scendants,* just give all these lands to you and your de-
father. 4I will cause solemnly promised Abraham, your
merous as the stars o r descendants to become as nu-
these lands. And throug sky, and I will give them all
tions of the earth will be ble your descendants all the na-
Abraham listened to me and obeyed all my requirements, sed. 5I will do this because
commands, decrees, and instructions." 6So Isaac stayed
in Gerar.

25:26 *Jacob* sounds like the Hebrew words for "heel" and "deceiver." 26:3 Hebrew *seed;* also in 26:4, 24.

UPS:
- Ancestor of the Edomites
- Known for his archery skill
- Able to forgive after explosive anger

DOWNS:
- When faced with important decisions, tended to choose according to the immediate need rather than the long-range effect
- Angered his parents by poor marriage choices

STATS:
- Where: Canaan
- Occupation: Skillful hunter
- Relatives: Isaac and Rebekah (parents); Jacob (twin brother); Judith, Basemath, and Mahalath (wives)

BOTTOM LINE:
Although God allows certain events in our lives to accomplish his overall purposes, we are still responsible for our actions.
Consequences are important to consider.
It is possible to have great anger and yet not sin.

Esau's story is told in Gen 25:19–28:9; 32–33; 36. He also is mentioned in Mal 1:2-4; Rom 9:13; Heb 12:16-17.

ESAU At some point in your life, you probably have had people tell you to use common sense. But did anyone ever explain what that meant? "Using common sense" means refusing to do something that you know will bring results you won't like.

Esau had a real problem with common sense. He made many wrong decisions because he didn't stop to think about what could happen. He wanted things right away without figuring out what he would have to pay later. Trading his birthright for a bowl of stew was one example of this problem. He also chose wives in direct opposition to his parents' wishes. (See Gen 28:6-9.)

What are you willing to trade for the things you want? Do you find yourself willing at times to give anything—even your relationships with family and friends, reputation, body, or soul—to get what you feel you need *now?* Maybe, like Esau, you haven't been using common sense. If so, your first response, also like Esau, may be to get angry. That isn't necessarily wrong, as long as you direct the energy of that anger toward finding a solution and not toward punishing yourself or others.

Your greatest need probably is to find a new way to measure how important things are to you. Up until now, your only measurement may have been to ask, "Do I need this now?" But the best measurement of value comes from God and his Word. In other words, you could ask: "Is this what God wants?" A relationship with him will not only give an ultimate purpose to your life, but will also be a daily guideline for real commonsense living.

ESAU

7When the men who lived there asked Isaac about his wife, Rebekah, he said, "She is my sister." He was afraid to say, "She is my wife." He thought, "They will kill me to get her, because she is so beautiful." 8But some time lat Abimelech, king of the Philistines, looked out his win and saw Isaac caressing Rebekah.

9Immediately, Abimelech called for Isaac ay, claimed, "She is obviously your wife! Why di 'She is my sister'?"

"Because I was afraid someone would ki o get her from me," Isaac replied.

10"How could you do this to us imelech exclaimed. "One of my people might have taken your wife and slept with her, and yo uld have made us guilty of great sin."

11Then Abimelech issued a blic proclamation: "Anyone who touches this ma or his wife will be put to death!"

CONFLICT OVER WATER RIGHTS

12When Isaac planted his crops that year, he harvested a hundred times more grain than he planted, for the LORD blessed him. 13He became a very rich man, and his wealth continued to grow. 14He acquired so many flocks of sheep and goats, herds of cattle, and servants that the Philistines became jealous of him. 15So the Philistines filled up all of Isaac's wells with dirt. These were the wells that had been dug by the servants of his father, Abraham.

16Finally, Abimelech ordered Isaac to leave the country. "Go somewhere else," he said, "for you have become too powerful for us."

ENVY 26:12-16

God kept his promise to bless Isaac. The neighboring Philistines grew envious because everything Isaac did seemed to go right. So they filled up his wells and tried to get rid of him. Envy is a dividing force strong enough to tear apart the mightiest of nations or the closest of friends. Bugged by the green-eyed monster lately? A thankful attitude is just what the doctor ordered. You might thank God for what he's already given you. A thankful attitude is a helpful way to keep anger under control. ■

17So Isaac moved away to the Gerar Valley, where he set up their tents and settled down. 18He reopened the wells his father had dug, which the Philistines had filled in after Abraham's death. Isaac also restored the names Abraham had given them.

19Isaac's servants also dug in the Gerar Valley and discovered a well of fresh water. 20But then the shepherds from Gerar came and claimed the spring. "This is our water," they said, and they argued over it with Isaac's herdsmen. So Isaac named the well Esek (which means "argument"). 21Isaac's men then dug another well, but again there was a dispute over it. So Isaac named it ich means "hostility"). 22Abandoning that c moved on and dug another well. This time was no dispute over it, so Isaac named the place oboth (which means "open space"), for he said, "At st the LORD has created enough space for us to prosper in this land."

23From there Isaac moved to Beersheba, 24where the LORD appeared to him on the night of his arrival. "I am the God of your father, Abraham," he said. "Do not be afraid, for I am with you and will bless you. I will multiply your descendants, and they will become a great nation. I will do this because of my promise to Abraham, my servant." 25Then Isaac built an altar there and worshiped the LORD. He set up his camp at that place, and his servants dug another well.

PARENTS AND CHOICES 26:34-35

Esau's marriage to women from an enemy nation caused his parents grief. After all, he didn't allow them to have any say over his choice of brides. Since parents usually arranged marriages for their offspring, Esau's decision spoke volumes about his relationship with his folks. What do your decisions reveal about your relationship with your parent or parents? What, if anything, would you be willing to change about that relationship? ■

ISAAC'S COVENANT WITH ABIMELECH

26One day King Abimelech came from Gerar with his adviser, Ahuzzath, and also Phicol, his army commander. 27"Why have you come here?" Isaac asked. "You obviously hate me, since you kicked me off your land."

28They replied, "We can plainly see that the LORD is with you. So we want to enter into a sworn treaty with you. Let's make a covenant. 29Swear that you will not harm us, just as we have never troubled you. We have always treated you well, and we sent you away from us in peace. And now look how the LORD has blessed you!"

30So Isaac prepared a covenant feast to celebrate the treaty, and they ate and drank together. 31Early the next morning, they each took a solemn oath not to interfere with each other. Then Isaac sent them home again, and they left him in peace.

32That very day Isaac's servants came and told him about a new well they had dug. "We've found water!" they exclaimed. 33So Isaac named the well Shibah (which means "oath"). And to this day the town that grew up there is called Beersheba (which means "well of the oath").

34At the age of forty, Esau married two Hittite wives: Judith, the daughter of Beeri, and Basemath, the daughter of Elon. 35But Esau's wives made life miserable for Isaac and Rebekah.

27 JACOB STEALS ESAU'S BLESSING

One day when Isaac was old and turning blind, he called for Esau, his older son, and said, "My son."

"Yes, Father?" Esau replied.
2"I am an old man now," Isaac said, "and I don't know
when I may die. 3Take your bow and a quiver full of arrows, and go out into the open country to hunt some wild
game for me. 4Prepare my favorite dish, and bring it here
for me to eat. Then I will pronounce the blessing that belongs to you, my firstborn son, before I die."
5But Rebekah overheard what Isaac had said to his son
Esau. So when Esau left to hunt for the wild game, 6she
said to her son Jacob, "Listen. I overheard your father say
to Esau, 7'Bring me some wild game and prepare me a delicious meal. Then I will bless you in the LORD's presence
before I die.' 8Now, my son, listen to me. Do exactly as I
tell you. 9Go out to the flocks, and bring me two fine
young goats. I'll use them to prepare your father's favorite dish. 10Then take the food to your father so he can eat
it and bless you before he dies."
11"But look," Jacob replied to Rebekah, "my brother,
Esau, is a hairy man, and my skin is smooth. 12What if my
father touches me? He'll see that I'm trying to trick him,
and then he'll curse me instead of blessing me."
13But his mother replied, "Then let the curse fall on me,
my son! Just do what I tell you. Go out and get the goats
for me!"
14So Jacob went out and got the young goats for his
mother. Rebekah took them and prepared a delicious
meal, just the way Isaac liked it. 15Then she took Esau's favorite clothes, which were there in the house, and gave
them to her younger son, Jacob. 16She covered his arms
and the smooth part of his neck with the skin of the
young goats. 17Then she gave Jacob the delicious meal, including freshly baked bread.
18So Jacob took the food to his father. "My father?" he
said.
"Yes, my son," Isaac answered. "Who are you—Esau or
Jacob?"

UPS:
- Father of the 12 tribes of Israel
- Third in the Abrahamic line of God's plan
- Determined; willing to work long and hard for what he wanted
- Successful livestock owner

DOWNS:
- When faced with conflict, he relied on his own resources rather than going to God for help
- Wanted to fill his life with things

STATS:
- Where: Canaan
- Occupations: Shepherd, livestock owner
- Relatives: Isaac and Rebekah (parents); Esau (twin brother); Laban (father-in-law); Rachel and Leah (wives); twelve sons and one daughter

BOTTOM LINE:
True security comes from God, rather than the material things you have.

All human intentions and actions—for good or for evil—are woven by God into his ongoing plan.

Jacob's story is told in Gen 25:19–35; 37; 42:1–49:33. He also is mentioned in Hos 12:2-13; Matt 1:2; 22:31-32; Acts 3:13; 7:46; Rom 9:10-13; Heb 11:9, 20-21.

JACOB Know anyone who's a born opportunist? You know—someone who makes the most of every opportunity to get what he or she wants. That's what Jacob was known for.

Jacob's name means "Usurper," or "Grabber," and he certainly lived up to it. He got the name by grabbing his twin brother Esau's heel while they were being born. Later, after he grabbed his brother's birthright and blessing, he had to run for his life.

When Jacob ran away from home, God appeared to him. God revealed his plans to work through Jacob despite Jacob's weakness. Shortly after this, Jacob had to live with his uncle Laban who was the king of opportunists!

Jacob agreed to seven years of labor for Laban in order to marry Laban's daughter, Rachel. But Laban pulled a fast one and gave his oldest daughter, Leah, to Jacob instead. To gain the woman he really wanted, Jacob was forced to work another seven years.

Although Jacob gained 20 years' worth of patience lessons through his uncle's schemes (see Gen 31:38), he realized that he was where God wanted him to be. When Jacob finally left Laban, he had become a different kind of grabber. This time, by the Jordan River, he grabbed on to God and wouldn't let go. He realized the value of God's presence and blessing.

Since God had changed Jacob, he also changed Jacob's name. He would now be called Israel. By the time Jacob (Israel) was an old man, he wasn't so much a *grabber* as someone who had been *grabbed* by God. He no longer made plans without including God.

At what times and places has God made himself known to you? Are you more like the young Jacob, forcing God to track you down in the wilderness of your own plans and mistakes? Or are you more like the Jacob who placed his desires and plans before God for his approval before taking any action?

JACOB

19 Jacob replied, "It's Esau, your firstborn son. I've done
as you told me. Here is the wild game. Now sit up and eat
it so you can give me your blessing."
20 Isaac asked, "How did you find it so quickly, my
son?"

GOING FOR THE GOAL? 27:5-10

When Rebekah learned that Isaac was preparing to bless Esau, she quickly devised a plan to trick him into blessing Jacob instead. Although God had already told her that Jacob would become the family leader (25:23), Rebekah took matters into her own hands. Does that behavior sound familiar? Think about the goals you have. Like Rebekah, are you tempted to take matters into your own hands in order to make those goals a reality? Rebekah compromised her integrity to get what she wanted. No goal is worth that. ■

"The LORD your God put it in my path!" Jacob replied.
21 Then Isaac said to Jacob, "Come closer so I can
touch you and make sure that you really are Esau." 22 So
Jacob went closer to his father, and Isaac touched him.
"The voice is Jacob's, but the hands are Esau's," Isaac
said. 23 But he did not recognize Jacob, because Jacob's
hands felt hairy just like Esau's. So Isaac prepared to
bless Jacob. 24 "But are you really my son Esau?" he
asked.
"Yes, I am," Jacob replied.
25 Then Isaac said, "Now, my son, bring me the wild
game. Let me eat it, and then I will give you my blessing."
So Jacob took the food to his father, and Isaac ate it. He
also drank the wine that Jacob served him. Then Isaac
said to Jacob, 26 "Please come a little closer and kiss me,
my son."
27 So Jacob went over and kissed him. And when Isaac
caught the smell of his clothes, he was finally convinced,
and he blessed his son. He said, "Ah! The smell of my son
is like the smell of the outdoors, which the LORD has
blessed!

28 "From the dew of heaven
and the richness of the earth,
may God always give you abundant harvests of grain
and bountiful new wine.
29 May many nations become your servants,
and may they bow down to you.
May you be the master over your brothers,
and may your mother's sons bow down to you.
All who curse you will be cursed,
and all who bless you will be blessed."

30 As soon as Isaac had finished blessing Jacob, and almost before Jacob had left his father, Esau returned from
his hunt. 31 Esau prepared a delicious meal and brought it
to his father. Then he said, "Sit up, my father, and eat my
wild game so you can give me your blessing."

32 But Isaac asked him, "Who are you?"
Esau replied, "It's your son, your firstborn son, Esau."
33 Isaac began to tremble uncontrollably and said,
"Then who just served me wild game? I have already
eaten it, and I blessed him just before you came. And yes,
that blessing must stand!"
34 When Esau heard his father's words, he let out a loud
and bitter cry. "Oh my father, what about me? Bless me,
too!" he begged.
35 But Isaac said, "Your brother was here, and he tricked
me. He has taken away your blessing."
36 Esau exclaimed, "No wonder his name is Jacob, for
now he has cheated me twice.* First he took my rights as
the firstborn, and now he has stolen my blessing. Oh,
haven't you saved even one blessing for me?"
37 Isaac said to Esau, "I have made Jacob your master
and have declared that all his brothers will be his servants. I have guaranteed him an abundance of grain and
wine—what is left for me to give you, my son?"
38 Esau pleaded, "But do you have only one blessing?
Oh my father, bless me, too!" Then Esau broke down and
wept.
39 Finally, his father, Isaac, said to him,

"You will live away from the richness of the earth,
and away from the dew of the heaven above.
40 You will live by your sword,
and you will serve your brother.
But when you decide to break free,
you will shake his yoke from your neck."

WARNING! 27:11-12

How we react to a problem or temptation often exposes our attitudes or agendas. Sometimes we're more worried about getting caught than about doing what's right. Jacob did not seem concerned about the deceitfulness of his mother's plan; instead he feared getting in trouble while carrying it out. If you are worried about getting caught, you are probably in a position that is less than honest. The fear of getting caught is a warning to do right. Jacob paid a huge price for carrying out this dishonest plan. You can choose to do the right thing! ■

JACOB FLEES TO PADDAN-ARAM

41 From that time on, Esau hated Jacob because their father had given Jacob the blessing. And Esau began to
scheme: "I will soon be mourning my father's death.
Then I will kill my brother, Jacob."
42 But Rebekah heard about Esau's plans. So she sent
for Jacob and told him, "Listen, Esau is consoling himself
by plotting to kill you. 43 So listen carefully, my son. Get
ready and flee to my brother, Laban, in Haran. 44 Stay
there with him until your brother cools off. 45 When he
calms down and forgets what you have done to him, I will

27:36 *Jacob* sounds like the Hebrew words for "heel" and "deceiver."

send for you to come back. Why should I lose both of you in one day?"

[46]Then Rebekah said to Isaac, "I'm sick and tired of these local Hittite women! I would rather die than see Jacob marry one of them."

28 So Isaac called for Jacob, blessed him, and said, "You must not marry any of these Canaanite women. [2]Instead, go at once to Paddan-aram, to the house of your grandfather Bethuel, and marry one of your uncle Laban's daughters. [3]May God Almighty* bless you and give you many children. And may your descendants multiply and become many nations! [4]May God pass on to you and your descendants* the blessings he promised to Abraham. May you own this land where you are now living as a foreigner, for God gave this land to Abraham."

[5]So Isaac sent Jacob away, and he went to Paddan-aram to stay with his uncle Laban, his mother's brother, the son of Bethuel the Aramean.

[6]Esau knew that his father, Isaac, had blessed Jacob and sent him to Paddan-aram to find a wife, and that he had warned Jacob, "You must not marry a Canaanite woman." [7]He also knew that Jacob had obeyed his parents and gone to Paddan-aram. [8]It was now very clear to Esau that his father did not like the local Canaanite women. [9]So Esau visited his uncle Ishmael's family and married one of Ishmael's daughters, in addition to the wives he already had. His new wife's name was Mahalath. She was the sister of Nebaioth and the daughter of Ishmael, Abraham's son.

OWNING YOUR FAITH 28:10-15

God's covenant promise to Abraham and Isaac was offered to Jacob as well. But it was not enough to be Abraham's grandson; Jacob had to establish his own relationship with God. God has no grandchildren; each of us must have a relationship with him. Owned your faith lately? How were you encouraged by the faith stories of your family members? ■

JACOB'S DREAM AT BETHEL

[10]Meanwhile, Jacob left Beersheba and traveled toward Haran. [11]At sundown he arrived at a good place to set up camp and stopped there for the night. Jacob found a stone to rest his head against and lay down to sleep. [12]As he slept, he dreamed of a stairway that reached from the earth up to heaven. And he saw the angels of God going up and down the stairway.

[13]At the top of the stairway stood the LORD, and he said, "I am the LORD, the God of your grandfather Abraham, and the God of your father, Isaac. The ground you are lying on belongs to you. I am giving it to you and your descendants. [14]Your descendants will be as numerous as the dust of the earth! They will spread out in all directions—to the west and the east, to the north and the south. And all the families of the earth will be blessed through you and your descendants. [15]What's more, I am with you, and I will protect you wherever you go. One day I will bring you back to this land. I will not leave you until I have finished giving you everything I have promised you."

[16]Then Jacob awoke from his sleep and said, "Surely the LORD is in this place, and I wasn't even aware of it!" [17]But he was also afraid and said, "What an awesome place this is! It is none other than the house of God, the very gateway to heaven!"

[18]The next morning Jacob got up very early. He took the stone he had rested his head against, and he set it upright as a memorial pillar. Then he poured olive oil over it. [19]He named that place Bethel (which means "house of God"), although the name of the nearby village was Luz.

[20]Then Jacob made this vow: "If God will indeed be with me and protect me on this journey, and if he will provide me with food and clothing, [21]and if I return safely to my father's home, then the LORD will certainly be my God. [22]And this memorial pillar I have set up will become a place for worshiping God, and I will present to God a tenth of everything he gives me."

29 **JACOB ARRIVES AT PADDAN-ARAM**

Then Jacob hurried on, finally arriving in the land of the east. [2]He saw a well in the distance. Three flocks of sheep and goats lay in an open field beside it, waiting to be watered. But a heavy stone covered the mouth of the well.

[3]It was the custom there to wait for all the flocks to arrive before removing the stone and watering the animals. Afterward the stone would be placed back over the mouth of the well. [4]Jacob went over to the shepherds and asked, "Where are you from, my friends?"

"We are from Haran," they answered.

[5]"Do you know a man there named Laban, the grandson of Nahor?" he asked.

"Yes, we do," they replied.

[6]"Is he doing well?" Jacob asked.

"Yes, he's well," they answered. "Look, here comes his daughter Rachel with the flock now."

[7]Jacob said, "Look, it's still broad daylight—too early to round up the animals. Why don't you water the sheep and goats so they can get back out to pasture?"

[8]"We can't water the animals until all the flocks have arrived," they replied. "Then the shepherds move the stone from the mouth of the well, and we water all the sheep and goats."

[9]Jacob was still talking with them when Rachel arrived with her father's flock, for she was a shepherd. [10]And because Rachel was his cousin—the daughter of Laban, his mother's brother—and because the sheep and goats belonged to his uncle Laban, Jacob went over to the well and moved the stone from its mouth and watered his uncle's flock. [11]Then Jacob kissed Rachel, and he wept aloud. [12]He explained to Rachel that he was her cousin on her

28:3 Hebrew *El-Shaddai*. **28:4** Hebrew *seed;* also in 28:13, 14.

father's side—the son of her aunt Rebekah. So Rachel
quickly ran and told her father, Laban.
13As soon as Laban heard that his nephew Jacob had
arrived, he ran out to meet him. He embraced and kissed
him and brought him home. When Jacob had told him
his story, 14Laban exclaimed, "You really are my own flesh
and blood!"

JACOB MARRIES LEAH AND RACHEL

After Jacob had stayed with Laban for about a month,
15Laban said to him, "You shouldn't work for me without
pay just because we are relatives. Tell me how much your
wages should be."
16Now Laban had two daughters. The older daughter
was named Leah, and the younger one was Rachel.
17There was no sparkle in Leah's eyes,* but Rachel had a
beautiful figure and a lovely face. 18Since Jacob was in
love with Rachel, he told her father, "I'll work for you for
seven years if you'll give me Rachel, your younger daughter, as my wife."
19"Agreed!" Laban replied. "I'd rather give her to you
than to anyone else. Stay and work with me." 20So Jacob
worked seven years to pay for Rachel. But his love for her
was so strong that it seemed to him but a few days.

WORTH THE WAIT 29:20-28

Jacob waited seven years to marry Rachel. After being tricked into marrying her sister, he agreed to work seven more years after their father, Laban, allowed him to marry Rachel! People often wonder if a goal (earning enough money to buy a car; abstaining from sex until marriage) is worth the wait. In our instant society, waiting for anything is seldom encouraged. The most important goals and desires are worth waiting for. Patience is hardest when we need it the most, but it is the key to achieving our goals. ■

21Finally, the time came for him to marry her. "I have
fulfilled my agreement," Jacob said to Laban. "Now give
me my wife so I can marry her."
22So Laban invited everyone in the neighborhood and
prepared a wedding feast. 23But that night, when it was
dark, Laban took Leah to Jacob, and he slept with her.
24(Laban had given Leah a servant, Zilpah, to be her maid.)
25But when Jacob woke up in the morning—it was Leah!
"What have you done to me?" Jacob raged at Laban. "I
worked seven years for Rachel! Why have you tricked me?"

29:17 Or *Leah had dull eyes,* or *Leah had soft eyes.* The meaning of the Hebrew is uncertain.

RACHEL

UPS:
- Showed great loyalty to her family
- Had two sons (Joseph and Benjamin) after being barren for many years

DOWNS:
- Envy and competitiveness spoiled her relationship with her sister, Leah
- Was capable of dishonesty by taking her loyalty too far
- Failed to recognize that Jacob's devotion was not dependent on her ability to have children

STATS:
- Where: Haran
- Occupations: Shepherdess, homemaker
- Relatives: Laban (father); Rebekah (aunt); Leah (sister); Jacob (husband); Joseph and Benjamin (sons)

BOTTOM LINE:
Loyalty must be controlled by what is true and right.
Love is accepted, not earned.

Rachel's story is told in Gen 29:6–35:20. She also is mentioned in Ruth 4:11.

RACHEL Got any siblings? Ever feel a sense of competitiveness in regard to a brother or sister? Sometimes competitiveness is sparked by what you have in common. For example, maybe you felt you had to compete for the love of your mom or dad. Or, maybe you had to live up to the reputation of a stellar sib who was a legend at your school.

Rachel and her sister Leah had something in common. Not only did they share the same parents, they also shared the same husband—Jacob. But for Rachel, the urge to compete grew stronger when she found that Leah could easily provide their husband with something she could not: children.

Let's backtrack a bit. Rachel had been Jacob's choice for a wife in the first place. But through circumstances highly unforeseen, her sister beat her to the altar. Although she still retained Jacob's love and loyalty, she feared that her barrenness would soon eclipse her position as the number one wife. So, when Leah had son after son, Rachel grew desperate enough to gain children by any means necessary. Her envy and competitiveness caused a rift in her relationship with her sister and her husband.

Ever think you have to earn the love and loyalty of the people in your life? Perhaps you've even thought that you can somehow earn God's love by what you do. But none of us can earn what God has already given us. He loves us! His love has no beginning and is incredibly patient. All we need to do is respond to God's love, which he has offered freely to us.

26"It's not our custom here to marry off a younger
daughter ahead of the firstborn," Laban replied. 27"But
wait until the bridal week is over, then we'll give you Rachel, too—provided you promise to work another seven
years for me."
28So Jacob agreed to work seven more years. A week after Jacob had married Leah, Laban gave him Rachel, too.
29(Laban gave Rachel a servant, Bilhah, to be her maid.)
30So Jacob slept with Rachel, too, and he loved her much
more than Leah. He then stayed and worked for Laban
the additional seven years.

JACOB'S MANY CHILDREN

31When the LORD saw that Leah was unloved, he enabled
her to have children, but Rachel could not conceive. 32So
Leah became pregnant and gave birth to a son. She
named him Reuben,* for she said, "The LORD has noticed
my misery, and now my husband will love me."
33She soon became pregnant again and gave birth to
another son. She named him Simeon,* for she said, "The
LORD heard that I was unloved and has given me another
son."
34Then she became pregnant a third time and gave
birth to another son. She named him Levi,* for she said,
"Surely this time my husband will feel affection for me,
since I have given him three sons!"
35Once again Leah became pregnant and gave birth to
another son. She named him Judah,* for she said, "Now I
will praise the LORD!" And then she stopped having
children.

30

When Rachel saw that she wasn't having any
children for Jacob, she became jealous of her sister. She
pleaded with Jacob, "Give me children, or I'll die!"

WHAT'S RIGHT? 30:1-12

Rachel and Leah were locked in a cruel contest. In their race to have children, they both gave their servant girls to Jacob as concubines. Although taking a concubine was an accepted custom of the day, God never delighted in this practice. He knew the potential heartache it could cause. Have you been wondering about a choice or lifestyle that everyone else seems to think is okay? Some socially acceptable practices might not be wise or right. Want to be wise? Base your choices on the truth of God's Word. ■

2Then Jacob became furious with Rachel. "Am I God?"
he asked. "He's the one who has kept you from having
children!"
3Then Rachel told him, "Take my maid, Bilhah, and
sleep with her. She will bear children for me,* and
through her I can have a family, too." 4So Rachel gave her
servant, Bilhah, to Jacob as a wife, and he slept with her.
5Bilhah became pregnant and presented him with a son.
6Rachel named him Dan,* for she said, "God has vindicated me! He has heard my request and given me a son."
7Then Bilhah became pregnant again and gave Jacob a
second son. 8Rachel named him Naphtali,* for she said, "I
have struggled hard with my sister, and I'm winning!"

WAIT FOR GOD 30:22-24

Eventually God answered Rachel's prayers and gave her a child of her own. In the meantime, however, she had given her servant girl to Jacob to gain children that way. The consequences of that decision were long lasting. Trusting God when nothing seems to happen is difficult. But it is harder still to live with the consequences of taking matters into our own hands. Feeling forgotten? Tired of waiting for God? Are you willing to wait just a little while longer for him to act? He may not act when you want him to, but he's always on time. ■

9Meanwhile, Leah realized that she wasn't getting
pregnant anymore, so she took her servant, Zilpah, and
gave her to Jacob as a wife. 10Soon Zilpah presented him
with a son. 11Leah named him Gad,* for she said, "How
fortunate I am!" 12Then Zilpah gave Jacob a second son.
13And Leah named him Asher,* for she said, "What joy is
mine! Now the other women will celebrate with me."
14One day during the wheat harvest, Reuben found
some mandrakes growing in a field and brought them to
his mother, Leah. Rachel begged Leah, "Please give me
some of your son's mandrakes."
15But Leah angrily replied, "Wasn't it enough that you
stole my husband? Now will you steal my son's mandrakes, too?"
Rachel answered, "I will let Jacob sleep with you tonight if you give me some of the mandrakes."
16So that evening, as Jacob was coming home from the
fields, Leah went out to meet him. "You must come and
sleep with me tonight!" she said. "I have paid for you with
some mandrakes that my son found." So that night he
slept with Leah. 17And God answered Leah's prayers. She
became pregnant again and gave birth to a fifth son for
Jacob. 18She named him Issachar,* for she said, "God has
rewarded me for giving my servant to my husband as a
wife." 19Then Leah became pregnant again and gave birth
to a sixth son for Jacob. 20She named him Zebulun,* for
she said, "God has given me a good reward. Now my husband will treat me with respect, for I have given him six
sons." 21Later she gave birth to a daughter and named her
Dinah.
22Then God remembered Rachel's plight and answered

29:32 *Reuben* means "Look, a son!" It also sounds like the Hebrew for "He has seen my misery." **29:33** *Simeon* probably means "one who hears." **29:34** *Levi* sounds like a Hebrew term that means "being attached" or "feeling affection for." **29:35** *Judah* sounds like the Hebrew term for "praise." **30:3** Hebrew *bear children on my knees.* **30:6** *Dan* means "he judged" or "he vindicated." **30:8** *Naphtali* means "my struggle." **30:11** *Gad* means "good fortune." **30:13** *Asher* means "happy." **30:18** *Issachar* sounds like a Hebrew term that means "reward." **30:20** *Zebulun* probably means "honor."

her prayers by enabling her to have children. [23]She became pregnant and gave birth to a son. "God has removed
my disgrace," she said. [24]And she named him Joseph,*
for she said, "May the LORD add yet another son to my
family."

JACOB'S WEALTH INCREASES

[25]Soon after Rachel had given birth to Joseph, Jacob said
to Laban, "Please release me so I can go home to my own
country. [26]Let me take my wives and children, for I have
earned them by serving you, and let me be on my way.
You certainly know how hard I have worked for you."

[27]"Please listen to me," Laban replied. "I have become wealthy, for* the LORD has blessed me because of
you. [28]Tell me how much I owe you. Whatever it is, I'll
pay it."

[29]Jacob replied, "You know how hard I've worked for
you, and how your flocks and herds have grown under
my care. [30]You had little indeed before I came, but your
wealth has increased enormously. The LORD has
blessed you through everything I've done. But now,
what about me? When can I start providing for my own
family?"

[31]"What wages do you want?" Laban asked again.

Jacob replied, "Don't give me anything. Just do this one
thing, and I'll continue to tend and watch over your
flocks. [32]Let me inspect your flocks today and remove all
the sheep and goats that are speckled or spotted, along
with all the black sheep. Give these to me as my wages.
[33]In the future, when you check on the animals you have
given me as my wages, you'll see that I have been honest.
If you find in my flock any goats without speckles or
spots, or any sheep that are not black, you will know that I
have stolen them from you."

[34]"All right," Laban replied. "It will be as you say." [35]But
that very day Laban went out and removed the male goats
that were streaked and spotted, all the female goats that
were speckled and spotted or had white patches, and all
the black sheep. He placed them in the care of his own
sons, [36]who took them a three-days' journey from where
Jacob was. Meanwhile, Jacob stayed and cared for the rest
of Laban's flock.

[37]Then Jacob took some fresh branches from poplar,
almond, and plane trees and peeled off strips of bark,
making white streaks on them. [38]Then he placed these
peeled branches in the watering troughs where the
flocks came to drink, for that was where they mated.
[39]And when they mated in front of the white-streaked
branches, they gave birth to young that were streaked,
speckled, and spotted. [40]Jacob separated those lambs
from Laban's flock. And at mating time he turned the
flock to face Laban's animals that were streaked or black.
This is how he built his own flock instead of increasing
Laban's.

[41]Whenever the stronger females were ready to mate,
Jacob would place the peeled branches in the watering
troughs in front of them. Then they would mate in front
of the branches. [42]But he didn't do this with the weaker
ones, so the weaker lambs belonged to Laban, and the
stronger ones were Jacob's. [43]As a result, Jacob became
very wealthy, with large flocks of sheep and goats, male
and female servants, and many camels and donkeys.

30:24 *Joseph* means "may he add." **30:27** Or *I have learned by divination that.*

REUBEN

UPS:

- Saved Joseph's life by talking the other brothers out of murder
- Showed intense love for his father by offering his own sons as a guarantee that Benjamin's life would be safe

DOWNS:

- Gave in quickly to group pressure
- Did not directly protect Joseph from his brothers, although as eldest son he had the authority to do so
- Slept with his father's concubine

STATS:

- Where: Canaan, Egypt
- Occupation: Shepherd
- Relatives: Jacob and Leah (parents); eleven brothers, one sister

BOTTOM LINE:

Public and private lives must show the same integrity, or one will destroy the other.

Punishment for sin may not be immediate, but it is certain.

Reuben's story is told in Gen 29:31; 35:23; 37; 42–50.

REUBEN How would your mom or dad describe your personality? Jacob summarized the personality of his son Reuben by comparing him to the waves of the sea. He knew that Reuben lacked stability. Reuben usually wanted to do the right thing, but seemed unable to stand against a crowd. His instability made him hard to trust. His private and public values contradicted each other. He went along with his brothers in their actions against Joseph while hoping he could do something helpful when they weren't looking. His plan failed.

Compromise has a way of destroying convictions. Without convictions, there is no direction. And lack of direction will destroy life. In Reuben's case, his early mistakes led to a real mess later on in life. Because of the decision he made in regard to his father's concubine, he lost the blessing and status usually given to the firstborn.

For many of us Jacob's description of his son, "unruly as the waves of the sea," is an accurate description of our lives. How about you? Are you the same person on the inside that you are on the outside? How do your actions show your integrity?

31 JACOB FLEES FROM LABAN

But Jacob soon learned that Laban's sons were grumbling
about him. "Jacob has robbed our father of everything!"
they said. "He has gained all his wealth at our father's expense." [2]And Jacob began to notice a change in Laban's
attitude toward him.
[3]Then the LORD said to Jacob, "Return to the land of
your father and grandfather and to your relatives there,
and I will be with you."
[4]So Jacob called Rachel and Leah out to the field where
he was watching his flock. [5]He said to them, "I have noticed that your father's attitude toward me has changed.
But the God of my father has been with me. [6]You know
how hard I have worked for your father, [7]but he has
cheated me, changing my wages ten times. But God has
not allowed him to do me any harm. [8]For if he said, 'The
speckled animals will be your wages,' the whole flock began to produce speckled young. And when he changed
his mind and said, 'The striped animals will be your
wages,' then the whole flock produced striped young. [9]In
this way, God has taken your father's animals and given
them to me.
[10]"One time during the mating season, I had a dream
and saw that the male goats mating with the females
were streaked, speckled, and spotted. [11]Then in my
dream, the angel of God said to me, 'Jacob!' And I replied,
'Yes, here I am.'
[12]"The angel said, 'Look up, and you will see that only
the streaked, speckled, and spotted males are mating
with the females of your flock. For I have seen how Laban
has treated you. [13]I am the God who appeared to you at
Bethel,* the place where you anointed the pillar of stone
and made your vow to me. Now get ready and leave this
country and return to the land of your birth.'"
[14]Rachel and Leah responded, "That's fine with us! We
won't inherit any of our father's wealth anyway. [15]He has
reduced our rights to those of foreign women. And after
he sold us, he wasted the money you paid him for us. [16]All
the wealth God has given you from our father legally belongs to us and our children. So go ahead and do whatever God has told you."
[17]So Jacob put his wives and children on camels, [18]and
he drove all his livestock in front of him. He packed all
the belongings he had acquired in Paddan-aram and set
out for the land of Canaan, where his father, Isaac, lived.
[19]At the time they left, Laban was some distance away,
shearing his sheep. Rachel stole her father's household
idols and took them with her. [20]Jacob outwitted Laban
the Aramean, for they set out secretly and never told Laban they were leaving. [21]So Jacob took all his possessions
with him and crossed the Euphrates River,* heading for
the hill country of Gilead.

31:13 As in Greek version and an Aramaic Targum; Hebrew reads *the God of Bethel*. **31:21** Hebrew *the river*.

JUDAH

JUDAH People who are leaders stand out at the right time. They don't necessarily act or look a certain way until the need for action comes along. Among their skills are the abilities to speak up, make decisions, take action, or take control. (Does that describe you?) Leaders can use their skills for great good or great evil.

Jacob's fourth son, Judah, was a natural leader. His life included many opportunities to exercise his skills. Unfortunately, Judah's decisions were often shaped more by the pressures of the moment than by a desire to cooperate with God's plan. But when he recognized his mistakes, he was willing to admit them. His experience with Tamar and the final confrontation with Joseph are both examples of his willingness to take responsibility for his sins when confronted. That quality was a strength Judah passed on to his descendant David.

Taking responsibility for one's sins isn't always easy, but it's necessary. Through Judah's life we can learn that it is not wise to avoid owning up to wrongdoing. It is better to openly admit our mistakes, shoulder the blame, and seek forgiveness. Wouldn't you agree?

UPS:
- Was a natural leader—outspoken and decisive
- Thought clearly and took action in pressure situations
- Was willing to stand by his word and put himself on the line when necessary
- Was the fourth son of 12, and the one through whom God would eventually bring King David and Jesus, the Messiah

DOWNS:
- Suggested to his brothers they sell Joseph into slavery
- Failed to keep his promise to his daughter-in-law, Tamar

STATS:
- Where: Canaan, Egypt
- Occupation: Shepherd
- Relatives: Jacob and Leah (parents); Bathshua (wife—see 1 Chron 2:3); Tamar (daughter-in-law); eleven brothers, one sister, and at least five sons (Gen 38:3-5, 27-30)

BOTTOM LINE:

God is in control far beyond the immediate situation.

Procrastination often brings about a worse result.

Judah's offer to substitute his life for Benjamin's is a picture of what his descendant Jesus would do for all people.

Judah's story is told in Gen 29:35; 35:23; 37–50. He also is mentioned in 1 Chron 2:1-4.

LABAN PURSUES JACOB

22 Three days later, Laban was told that Jacob had fled.
23 So he gathered a group of his relatives and set out in hot
pursuit. He caught up with Jacob seven days later in the
hill country of Gilead. 24 But the previous night God had
appeared to Laban the Aramean in a dream and told him,
"I'm warning you—leave Jacob alone!"
25 Laban caught up with Jacob as he was camped in the
hill country of Gilead, and he set up his camp not far from
Jacob's. 26 "What do you mean by stealing away like this?"
Laban demanded. "How dare you drag my daughters
away like prisoners of war? 27 Why did you slip away secretly? Why did you steal away? And why didn't you say
you wanted to leave? I would have given you a farewell
feast, with singing and music, accompanied by tambourines and harps. 28 Why didn't you let me kiss my daughters and grandchildren and tell them good-bye? You have
acted very foolishly! 29 I could destroy you, but the God of
your father appeared to me last night and warned me,
'Leave Jacob alone!' 30 I can understand your feeling that
you must go, and your intense longing for your father's
home. But why have you stolen my gods?"
31 "I rushed away because I was afraid," Jacob answered. "I thought you would take your daughters from
me by force. 32 But as for your gods, see if you can find
them, and let the person who has taken them die! And if
you find anything else that belongs to you, identify it before all these relatives of ours, and I will give it back!" But
Jacob did not know that Rachel had stolen the household
idols.
33 Laban went first into Jacob's tent to search there,
then into Leah's, and then the tents of the two servant
wives—but he found nothing. Finally, he went into Rachel's tent. 34 But Rachel had taken the household idols
and hidden them in her camel saddle, and now she was
sitting on them. When Laban had thoroughly searched
her tent without finding them, 35 she said to her father,
"Please, sir, forgive me if I don't get up for you. I'm having
my monthly period." So Laban continued his search, but
he could not find the household idols.
36 Then Jacob became very angry, and he challenged
Laban. "What's my crime?" he demanded. "What have I
done wrong to make you chase after me as though I were
a criminal? 37 You have rummaged through everything I
own. Now show me what you found that belongs to you!
Set it out here in front of us, before our relatives, for all to
see. Let them judge between us!
38 "For twenty years I have been with you, caring for
your flocks. In all that time your sheep and goats never
miscarried. In all those years I never used a single ram of
yours for food. 39 If any were attacked and killed by wild
animals, I never showed you the carcass and asked you to
reduce the count of your flock. No, I took the loss myself!
You made me pay for every stolen animal, whether it was
taken in broad daylight or in the dark of night.
40 "I worked for you through the scorching heat of the
day and through cold and sleepless nights. 41 Yes, for
twenty years I slaved in your house! I worked for fourteen
years earning your two daughters, and then six more
years for your flock. And you changed my wages ten
times! 42 In fact, if the God of my father had not been on
my side—the God of Abraham and the fearsome God of
Isaac*—you would have sent me away empty-handed.
But God has seen your abuse and my hard work. That is
why he appeared to you last night and rebuked you!"

THE DILIGENCE PAYOFF 31:38-42

Jacob had the habit of doing more than was expected of him. When his flocks were attacked, he took the losses rather than splitting them with Laban. He worked hard even after several pay cuts. His diligence eventually paid off; his flocks began to multiply. Diligence (1) pleases God, (2) earns recognition and advancement, (3) enhances your reputation, (4) builds others' confidence in you, (5) gives you more experience and knowledge, and (6) develops your spiritual maturity. Do you have the diligence habit? ■

JACOB'S TREATY WITH LABAN

43 Then Laban replied to Jacob, "These women are my
daughters, these children are my grandchildren, and
these flocks are my flocks—in fact, everything you see is
mine. But what can I do now about my daughters and
their children? 44 So come, let's make a covenant, you and
I, and it will be a witness to our commitment."
45 So Jacob took a stone and set it up as a monument.
46 Then he told his family members, "Gather some
stones." So they gathered stones and piled them in a
heap. Then Jacob and Laban sat down beside the pile of
stones to eat a covenant meal. 47 To commemorate the
event, Laban called the place Jegar-sahadutha (which
means "witness pile" in Aramaic), and Jacob called it Galeed (which means "witness pile" in Hebrew).
48 Then Laban declared, "This pile of stones will stand
as a witness to remind us of the covenant we have made
today." This explains why it was called Galeed—"Witness
Pile." 49 But it was also called Mizpah (which means
"watchtower"), for Laban said, "May the LORD keep watch
between us to make sure that we keep this covenant
when we are out of each other's sight. 50 If you mistreat
my daughters or if you marry other wives, God will see it
even if no one else does. He is a witness to this covenant
between us.
51 "See this pile of stones," Laban continued, "and see
this monument I have set between us. 52 They stand between us as witnesses of our vows. I will never pass this
pile of stones to harm you, and you must never pass these
stones or this monument to harm me. 53 I call on the God
of our ancestors—the God of your grandfather Abraham
and the God of my grandfather Nahor—to serve as a
judge between us."
So Jacob took an oath before the fearsome God of his
father, Isaac,* to respect the boundary line. 54 Then Jacob
offered a sacrifice to God there on the mountain and

31:42 Or *and the Fear of Isaac.* 31:53 Or *the Fear of his father, Isaac.*

invited everyone to a covenant feast. After they had
eaten, they spent the night on the mountain.
55*Laban got up early the next morning, and he kissed
his grandchildren and his daughters and blessed them.
Then he left and returned home.

32

1*As Jacob started on his way again, angels of
God came to meet him. 2When Jacob saw them, he ex-
claimed, "This is God's camp!" So he named the place
Mahanaim.*

JACOB SENDS GIFTS TO ESAU

3Then Jacob sent messengers ahead to his brother, Esau,
who was living in the region of Seir in the land of Edom.
4He told them, "Give this message to my master Esau:
'Humble greetings from your servant Jacob. Until now I
have been living with Uncle Laban, 5and now I own cattle,
donkeys, flocks of sheep and goats, and many servants,
both men and women. I have sent these messengers to
inform my lord of my coming, hoping that you will be
friendly to me.'"
6After delivering the message, the messengers returned to Jacob and reported, "We met your brother,
Esau, and he is already on his way to meet you—with an
army of 400 men!" 7Jacob was terrified at the news. He
divided his household, along with the flocks and herds
and camels, into two groups. 8He thought, "If Esau meets
one group and attacks it, perhaps the other group can
escape."

FRANTIC WITH FEAR 32:6-12

How would you feel knowing you were about to meet the person you had cheated out of his most precious possession? Jacob had taken Esau's birthright (25:33) and his blessing (27:27-40). Now that he was about to meet this brother for the first time in 20 years, he was frantic with fear. He collected his thoughts, however, and decided to pray. When we face a difficult conflict, we can run about frantically or we can pause to pray. Which approach will be more effective? ■

9Then Jacob prayed, "O God of my grandfather Abraham, and God of my father, Isaac—O LORD, you told me,
'Return to your own land and to your relatives.' And you
promised me, 'I will treat you kindly.' 10I am not worthy of
all the unfailing love and faithfulness you have shown to
me, your servant. When I left home and crossed the Jordan River, I owned nothing except a walking stick. Now
my household fills two large camps! 11O LORD, please rescue me from the hand of my brother, Esau. I am afraid
that he is coming to attack me, along with my wives and
children. 12But you promised me, 'I will surely treat you
kindly, and I will multiply your descendants until they become as numerous as the sands along the seashore—too
many to count.'"
13Jacob stayed where he was for the night. Then he selected these gifts from his possessions to present to his
brother, Esau: 14200 female goats, 20 male goats,
200 ewes, 20 rams, 1530 female camels with their young,
40 cows, 10 bulls, 20 female donkeys, and 10 male donkeys. 16He divided these animals into herds and assigned
each to different servants. Then he told his servants, "Go
ahead of me with the animals, but keep some distance
between the herds."
17He gave these instructions to the men leading the
first group: "When my brother, Esau, meets you, he will
ask, 'Whose servants are you? Where are you going? Who
owns these animals?' 18You must reply, 'They belong to
your servant Jacob, but they are a gift for his master Esau.
Look, he is coming right behind us.'"
19Jacob gave the same instructions to the second and
third herdsmen and to all who followed behind the
herds: "You must say the same thing to Esau when you
meet him. 20And be sure to say, 'Look, your servant Jacob
is right behind us.'"
Jacob thought, "I will try to appease him by sending
gifts ahead of me. When I see him in person, perhaps he
will be friendly to me." 21So the gifts were sent on ahead,
while Jacob himself spent that night in the camp.

JACOB WRESTLES WITH GOD

22During the night Jacob got up and took his two wives,
his two servant wives, and his eleven sons and crossed the
Jabbok River with them. 23After taking them to the other
side, he sent over all his possessions.
24This left Jacob all alone in the camp, and a man
came and wrestled with him until the dawn began to
break. 25When the man saw that he would not win the
match, he touched Jacob's hip and wrenched it out of its
socket. 26Then the man said, "Let me go, for the dawn is
breaking!"
But Jacob said, "I will not let you go unless you bless
me."
27"What is your name?" the man asked.
He replied, "Jacob."
28"Your name will no longer be Jacob," the man told
him. "From now on you will be called Israel,* because you
have fought with God and with men and have won."
29"Please tell me your name," Jacob said.
"Why do you want to know my name?" the man replied. Then he blessed Jacob there.
30Jacob named the place Peniel (which means "face
of God"), for he said, "I have seen God face to face, yet
my life has been spared." 31The sun was rising as Jacob
left Peniel,* and he was limping because of the injury
to his hip. 32(Even today the people of Israel don't eat
the tendon near the hip socket because of what happened that night when the man strained the tendon of
Jacob's hip.)

31:55 Verse 31:55 is numbered 32:1 in Hebrew text. **32:1** Verses 32:1-32 are numbered 32:2-33 in Hebrew text. **32:2** *Mahanaim* means "two camps." **32:28** *Jacob* sounds like the Hebrew words for "heel" and "deceiver." *Israel* means "God fights." **32:31** Hebrew *Penuel,* a variant spelling of Peniel.

33 JACOB AND ESAU MAKE PEACE

Then Jacob looked up and saw Esau coming with his 400 men. So he divided the children among Leah, Rachel, and his two servant wives. 2He put the servant wives and their children at the front, Leah and her children next, and Rachel and Joseph last. 3Then Jacob went on ahead. As he approached his brother, he bowed to the ground seven times before him. 4Then Esau ran to meet him and embraced him, threw his arms around his neck, and kissed him. And they both wept.

BITTERNESS 33:1-11

It is refreshing to see Esau's change of heart when the two brothers meet again. The bitterness over losing his birthright and blessing (25:29-34) seems gone. Instead Esau is content with what he has. Jacob even exclaims how great it is to see his brother's friendly smile (33:10). Ever feel the bite of bitterness after being cheated by someone? Many of us have. We can remove bitterness from our lives by honestly expressing our feelings to God, forgiving those who have wronged us, and being content with what we have. ■

5Then Esau looked at the women and children and asked, "Who are these people with you?"

"These are the children God has graciously given to me, your servant," Jacob replied. 6Then the servant wives came forward with their children and bowed before him. 7Next came Leah with her children, and they bowed before him. Finally, Joseph and Rachel came forward and bowed before him.

8"And what were all the flocks and herds I met as I came?" Esau asked.

Jacob replied, "They are a gift, my lord, to ensure your friendship."

9"My brother, I have plenty," Esau answered. "Keep what you have for yourself."

10But Jacob insisted, "No, if I have found favor with you, please accept this gift from me. And what a relief to see your friendly smile. It is like seeing the face of God! 11Please take this gift I have brought you, for God has been very gracious to me. I have more than enough." And because Jacob insisted, Esau finally accepted the gift.

12"Well," Esau said, "let's be going. I will lead the way."

13But Jacob replied, "You can see, my lord, that some of the children are very young, and the flocks and herds have their young, too. If they are driven too hard, even for one day, all the animals could die. 14Please, my lord, go ahead of your servant. We will follow slowly, at a pace that is comfortable for the livestock and the children. I will meet you at Seir."

15"All right," Esau said, "but at least let me assign some of my men to guide and protect you."

Jacob responded, "That's not necessary. It's enough that you've received me warmly, my lord!"

16So Esau turned around and started back to Seir that same day. 17Jacob, on the other hand, traveled on to Succoth. There he built himself a house and made shelters for his livestock. That is why the place was named Succoth (which means "shelters").

18Later, having traveled all the way from Paddan-aram, Jacob arrived safely at the town of Shechem, in the land of Canaan. There he set up camp outside the town. 19Jacob bought the plot of land where he camped from the family of Hamor, the father of Shechem, for 100 pieces of silver.* 20And there he built an altar and named it El-Elohe-Israel.*

34 REVENGE AGAINST SHECHEM

One day Dinah, the daughter of Jacob and Leah, went to visit some of the young women who lived in the area. 2But when the local prince, Shechem son of Hamor the Hivite, saw Dinah, he seized her and raped her. 3But then he fell in love with her, and he tried to win her affection with tender words. 4He said to his father, Hamor, "Get me this young girl. I want to marry her."

5Soon Jacob heard that Shechem had defiled his daughter, Dinah. But since his sons were out in the fields herding his livestock, he said nothing until they returned. 6Hamor, Shechem's father, came to discuss the matter with Jacob. 7Meanwhile, Jacob's sons had come in from the field as soon as they heard what had happened. They were shocked and furious that their sister had been raped. Shechem had done a disgraceful thing against Jacob's family,* something that should never be done.

CAN'T EXCUSE EVIL 34:1-4

Shechem may have been a victim of "love at first sight," but his actions were impulsive and evil. His declared love for Dinah could not excuse the wrong that he did. Many of us would admit that an excuse for a wrongdoing comes more readily to mind than an apology. But God prefers our repentance to our excuses. How about you? ■

8Hamor tried to speak with Jacob and his sons. "My son Shechem is truly in love with your daughter," he said. "Please let him marry her. 9In fact, let's arrange other marriages, too. You give us your daughters for our sons, and we will give you our daughters for your sons. 10And you may live among us; the land is open to you! Settle here and trade with us. And feel free to buy property in the area."

11Then Shechem himself spoke to Dinah's father and brothers. "Please be kind to me, and let me marry her," he begged. "I will give you whatever you ask. 12No matter what dowry or gift you demand, I will gladly pay it—just give me the girl as my wife."

13But since Shechem had defiled their sister, Dinah,

33:19 Hebrew *100 kesitahs;* the value or weight of the kesitah is no longer known. 33:20 *El-Elohe-Israel* means "God, the God of Israel."
34:7 Hebrew *a disgraceful thing in Israel.*

Jacob's sons responded deceitfully to Shechem and his father, Hamor. 14They said to them, "We couldn't possibly allow this, because you're not circumcised. It would be a disgrace for our sister to marry a man like you! 15But here is a solution. If every man among you will be circumcised like we are, 16then we will give you our daughters, and we'll take your daughters for ourselves. We will live among you and become one people. 17But if you don't agree to be circumcised, we will take her and be on our way."

18Hamor and his son Shechem agreed to their proposal. 19Shechem wasted no time in acting on this request, for he wanted Jacob's daughter desperately. Shechem was a highly respected member of his family, 20and he went with his father, Hamor, to present this proposal to the leaders at the town gate.

21"These men are our friends," they said. "Let's invite them to live here among us and trade freely. Look, the land is large enough to hold them. We can take their daughters as wives and let them marry ours. 22But they will consider staying here and becoming one people with us only if all of our men are circumcised, just as they are. 23But if we do this, all their livestock and possessions will eventually be ours. Come, let's agree to their terms and let them settle here among us."

24So all the men in the town council agreed with Hamor and Shechem, and every male in the town was circumcised. 25But three days later, when their wounds were still sore, two of Jacob's sons, Simeon and Levi, who were Dinah's full brothers, took their swords and entered the town without opposition. Then they slaughtered every male there, 26including Hamor and his son Shechem. They killed them with their swords, then took Dinah from Shechem's house and returned to their camp.

27Meanwhile, the rest of Jacob's sons arrived. Finding the men slaughtered, they plundered the town because their sister had been defiled there. 28They seized all the flocks and herds and donkeys—everything they could lay their hands on, both inside the town and outside in the fields. 29They looted all their wealth and plundered their houses. They also took all their little children and wives and led them away as captives.

30Afterward Jacob said to Simeon and Levi, "You have ruined me! You've made me stink among all the people of this land—among all the Canaanites and Perizzites. We are so few that they will join forces and crush us. I will be ruined, and my entire household will be wiped out!"

31"But why should we let him treat our sister like a prostitute?" they retorted angrily.

35

JACOB'S RETURN TO BETHEL

Then God said to Jacob, "Get ready and move to Bethel and settle there. Build an altar there to the God who appeared to you when you fled from your brother, Esau."

2So Jacob told everyone in his household, "Get rid of all your pagan idols, purify yourselves, and put on clean clothing. 3We are now going to Bethel, where I will build an altar to the God who answered my prayers when I was in distress. He has been with me wherever I have gone."

4So they gave Jacob all their pagan idols and earrings, and he buried them under the great tree near Shechem. 5As they set out, a terror from God spread over the people in all the towns of that area, so no one attacked Jacob's family.

6Eventually, Jacob and his household arrived at Luz (also called Bethel) in Canaan. 7Jacob built an altar there and named the place El-bethel (which means "God of Bethel"), because God had appeared to him there when he was fleeing from his brother, Esau.

8Soon after this, Rebekah's old nurse, Deborah, died. She was buried beneath the oak tree in the valley below Bethel. Ever since, the tree has been called Allon-bacuth (which means "oak of weeping").

9Now that Jacob had returned from Paddan-aram, God appeared to him again at Bethel. God blessed him, 10saying, "Your name is Jacob, but you will not be called Jacob any longer. From now on your name will be Israel."* So God renamed him Israel.

11Then God said, "I am El-Shaddai—'God Almighty.' Be fruitful and multiply. You will become a great nation, even many nations. Kings will be among your descendants! 12And I will give you the land I once gave to Abraham and Isaac. Yes, I will give it to you and your descendants after you." 13Then God went up from the place where he had spoken to Jacob.

14Jacob set up a stone pillar to mark the place where God had spoken to him. Then he poured wine over it as an offering to God and anointed the pillar with olive oil. 15And Jacob named the place Bethel (which means "house of God"), because God had spoken to him there.

THE DEATHS OF RACHEL AND ISAAC

16Leaving Bethel, Jacob and his clan moved on toward Ephrath. But Rachel went into labor while they were still some distance away. Her labor pains were intense. 17After a very hard delivery, the midwife finally exclaimed, "Don't be afraid—you have another son!" 18Rachel was about to die, but with her last breath she named the baby Ben-oni (which means "son of my sorrow"). The baby's father, however, called him Benjamin (which means "son of my right hand"). 19So Rachel died and was buried on the way to Ephrath (that is, Bethlehem). 20Jacob set up a stone monument over Rachel's grave, and it can be seen there to this day.

21Then Jacob* traveled on and camped beyond Migdal-eder. 22While he was living there, Reuben had intercourse with Bilhah, his father's concubine, and Jacob soon heard about it.

These are the names of the twelve sons of Jacob:

23The sons of Leah were Reuben (Jacob's oldest son),
Simeon, Levi, Judah, Issachar, and Zebulun.

35:10 *Jacob* sounds like the Hebrew words for "heel" and "deceiver." *Israel* means "God fights." **35:21** Hebrew *Israel;* also in 35:22a. The names "Jacob" and "Israel" are often interchanged throughout the Old Testament, referring sometimes to the individual patriarch and sometimes to the nation.

24The sons of Rachel were Joseph and Benjamin.
25The sons of Bilhah, Rachel's servant, were Dan and
Naphtali.
26The sons of Zilpah, Leah's servant, were Gad and
Asher.
These are the names of the sons who were born to Jacob
at Paddan-aram.

SIN'S CONSEQUENCES 35:22

When Reuben slept with his father's concubine, maybe he thought he would get away with it. But on his deathbed, Jacob brought up Reuben's action. Instead of the double portion of the family inheritance that Reuben would have received as the oldest son, Jacob took away his status and gave it to someone else (49:4). Sin's consequences can plague us long after the sin is committed. We can run, but we can't hide from the consequences of wrong actions. ■

27So Jacob returned to his father, Isaac, in Mamre,
which is near Kiriath-arba (now called Hebron), where
Abraham and Isaac had both lived as foreigners. 28Isaac
lived for 180 years. 29Then he breathed his last and died
at a ripe old age, joining his ancestors in death. And his
sons, Esau and Jacob, buried him.

36 DESCENDANTS OF ESAU

This is the account of the descendants of Esau (also
known as Edom). 2Esau married two young women from
Canaan: Adah, the daughter of Elon the Hittite; and
Oholibamah, the daughter of Anah and granddaughter
of Zibeon the Hivite. 3He also married his cousin Basemath, who was the daughter of Ishmael and the sister of
Nebaioth. 4Adah gave birth to a son named Eliphaz for
Esau. Basemath gave birth to a son named Reuel. 5Oho-
libamah gave birth to sons named Jeush, Jalam, and Korah. All these sons were born to Esau in the land of
Canaan.

6Esau took his wives, his children, and his entire
household, along with his livestock and cattle—all the
wealth he had acquired in the land of Canaan—and
moved away from his brother, Jacob. 7There was not
enough land to support them both because of all the livestock and possessions they had acquired. 8So Esau (also
known as Edom) settled in the hill country of Seir.

9This is the account of Esau's descendants, the Edomites, who lived in the hill country of Seir.

10These are the names of Esau's sons: Eliphaz, the son of
Esau's wife Adah; and Reuel, the son of Esau's wife
Basemath.
11The descendants of Eliphaz were Teman, Omar,
Zepho, Gatam, and Kenaz. 12Timna, the concubine of
Esau's son Eliphaz, gave birth to a son named Amalek.
These are the descendants of Esau's wife Adah.
13The descendants of Reuel were Nahath, Zerah,
Shammah, and Mizzah. These are the descendants of
Esau's wife Basemath.
14Esau also had sons through Oholibamah, the daughter
of Anah and granddaughter of Zibeon. Their names
were Jeush, Jalam, and Korah.

15These are the descendants of Esau who became the
leaders of various clans:

The descendants of Esau's oldest son, Eliphaz, became
the leaders of the clans of Teman, Omar, Zepho,
Kenaz, 16Korah, Gatam, and Amalek. These are the
clan leaders in the land of Edom who descended
from Eliphaz. All these were descendants of Esau's
wife Adah.
17The descendants of Esau's son Reuel became the
leaders of the clans of Nahath, Zerah, Shammah, and
Mizzah. These are the clan leaders in the land of
Edom who descended from Reuel. All these were
descendants of Esau's wife Basemath.
18The descendants of Esau and his wife Oholibamah
became the leaders of the clans of Jeush, Jalam, and
Korah. These are the clan leaders who descended
from Esau's wife Oholibamah, the daughter of Anah.
19These are the clans descended from Esau (also known
as Edom), identified by their clan leaders.

ORIGINAL PEOPLES OF EDOM

20These are the names of the tribes that descended from
Seir the Horite. They lived in the land of Edom: Lotan,
Shobal, Zibeon, Anah, 21Dishon, Ezer, and Dishan. These
were the Horite clan leaders, the descendants of Seir,
who lived in the land of Edom.

22The descendants of Lotan were Hori and Heman.
Lotan also had a sister named Timna.
23The descendants of Shobal were Alvan, Manahath,
Ebal, Shepho, and Onam.
24The descendants of Zibeon were Aiah and Anah. (This
is the Anah who discovered the hot springs in the
wilderness while he was grazing his father's
donkeys.)
25The descendants of Anah were his son, Dishon, and
his daughter, Oholibamah.
26The descendants of Dishon* were Hemdan, Eshban,
Ithran, and Keran.
27The descendants of Ezer were Bilhan, Zaavan, and
Akan.
28The descendants of Dishan were Uz and Aran.
29So these were the leaders of the Horite clans: Lotan,
Shobal, Zibeon, Anah, 30Dishon, Ezer, and Dishan. The
Horite clans are named after their clan leaders, who lived
in the land of Seir.

RULERS OF EDOM

31These are the kings who ruled in the land of Edom before any king ruled over the Israelites*:

36:26 Hebrew *Dishan,* a variant spelling of Dishon; compare 36:21, 28. 36:31 Or *before an Israelite king ruled over them.*

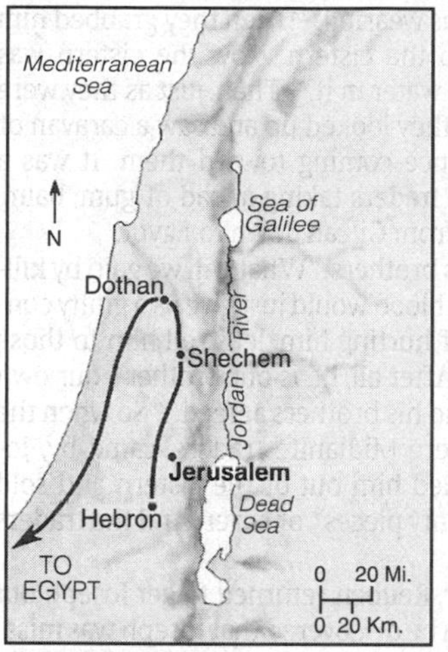

JOSEPH GOES TO MEET HIS BROTHERS
Jacob asked Joseph to go find his brothers, who were grazing their flocks near Shechem. When Joseph arrived, he learned that his brothers had gone on to Dothan, which lay along a major trade route to Egypt. There the jealous brothers sold Joseph as a slave to a group of Ishmaelite traders who were on their way to Egypt.

32Bela son of Beor, who ruled in Edom from the city of Dinhabah.
33After Bela died, Jobab son of Zerah from Bozrah became king in his place.
34After Jobab died, Husham from the land of the Temanites became king in his place.
35After Husham died, Hadad son of Bedad became king in his place and ruled from the city of Avith. He was the one who defeated the Midianites in the land of Moab.
36After Hadad died, Samlah from the city of Masrekah became king in his place.
37After Samlah died, Shaul from the city of Rehoboth-on-the-River became king in his place.
38After Shaul died, Baal-hanan son of Acbor became king in his place.
39After Baal-hanan son of Acbor died, Hadad* became king in his place and ruled from the city of Pau. Hadad's wife was Mehetabel, the daughter of Matred and granddaughter of Me-zahab.

40These are the names of the leaders of the clans descended from Esau, who lived in the places named for
them: Timna, Alvah, Jetheth, 41Oholibamah, Elah, Pinon,
42Kenaz, Teman, Mibzar, 43Magdiel, and Iram. These are
the leaders of the clans of Edom, listed according to their
settlements in the land they occupied. They all descended from Esau, the ancestor of the Edomites.

37 JOSEPH'S DREAMS

So Jacob settled again in the land of Canaan, where his father had lived as a foreigner.
2This is the account of Jacob and his family. When Joseph was seventeen years old, he often tended his father's flocks. He worked for his half brothers, the sons of
his father's wives Bilhah and Zilpah. But Joseph reported
to his father some of the bad things his brothers were
doing.
3Jacob* loved Joseph more than any of his other children because Joseph had been born to him in his old age.
So one day Jacob had a special gift made for Joseph—a
beautiful robe.* 4But his brothers hated Joseph because
their father loved him more than the rest of them. They
couldn't say a kind word to him.
5One night Joseph had a dream, and when he told his
brothers about it, they hated him more than ever. 6"Listen
to this dream," he said. 7"We were out in the field, tying up
bundles of grain. Suddenly my bundle stood up, and your
bundles all gathered around and bowed low before mine!"
8His brothers responded, "So you think you will be our
king, do you? Do you actually think you will reign over
us?" And they hated him all the more because of his
dreams and the way he talked about them.
9Soon Joseph had another dream, and again he told his
brothers about it. "Listen, I have had another dream," he
said. "The sun, moon, and eleven stars bowed low before
me!"
10This time he told the dream to his father as well as to
his brothers, but his father scolded him. "What kind of
dream is that?" he asked. "Will your mother and I and
your brothers actually come and bow to the ground before you?" 11But while his brothers were jealous of Joseph, his father wondered what the dreams meant.
12Soon after this, Joseph's brothers went to pasture
their father's flocks at Shechem. 13When they had been
gone for some time, Jacob said to Joseph, "Your brothers
are pasturing the sheep at Shechem. Get ready, and I will
send you to them."
"I'm ready to go," Joseph replied.

UGLY RAGE 37:19-20

Could jealousy ever make you feel like killing someone? Before saying, "No way!" look at what happened in this story. Ten men were willing to kill their youngest brother because of his status as the favorite son. Their deep jealousy had grown into ugly rage, blinding them completely to what was right. Jealousy can be hard to recognize, because our reasons for it seem to make sense. But left unchecked, jealousy grows quickly and leads to serious sins. The longer you cultivate jealous feelings, the harder it is to uproot them. The time to deal with jealousy is when you notice yourself keeping score of what others have. ■

14"Go and see how your brothers and the flocks are
getting along," Jacob said. "Then come back and bring me
a report." So Jacob sent him on his way, and Joseph traveled to Shechem from their home in the valley of Hebron.
15When he arrived there, a man from the area noticed
him wandering around the countryside. "What are you
looking for?" he asked.

36:39 As in some Hebrew manuscripts, Samaritan Pentateuch, and Syriac version (see also 1 Chr 1:50); most Hebrew manuscripts read *Hadar*. **37:3a** Hebrew *Israel;* also in 37:13. See note on 35:21. **37:3b** Traditionally rendered *a coat of many colors.* The exact meaning of the Hebrew is uncertain.

16"I'm looking for my brothers," Joseph replied. "Do
you know where they are pasturing their sheep?"
17"Yes," the man told him. "They have moved on from
here, but I heard them say, 'Let's go on to Dothan.'" So Joseph followed his brothers to Dothan and found them
there.

JOSEPH SOLD INTO SLAVERY

18When Joseph's brothers saw him coming, they recognized him in the distance. As he approached, they made
plans to kill him. 19"Here comes the dreamer!" they said.
20"Come on, let's kill him and throw him into one of these
cisterns. We can tell our father, 'A wild animal has eaten
him.' Then we'll see what becomes of his dreams!"
21But when Reuben heard of their scheme, he came to
Joseph's rescue. "Let's not kill him," he said. 22"Why
should we shed any blood? Let's just throw him into this
empty cistern here in the wilderness. Then he'll die without our laying a hand on him." Reuben was secretly planning to rescue Joseph and return him to his father.
23So when Joseph arrived, his brothers ripped off the
beautiful robe he was wearing. 24Then they grabbed him
and threw him into the cistern. Now the cistern was
empty; there was no water in it. 25Then, just as they were
sitting down to eat, they looked up and saw a caravan of
camels in the distance coming toward them. It was a
group of Ishmaelite traders taking a load of gum, balm,
and aromatic resin from Gilead down to Egypt.
26Judah said to his brothers, "What will we gain by killing our brother? His blood would just give us a guilty conscience. 27Instead of hurting him, let's sell him to those
Ishmaelite traders. After all, he is our brother—our own
flesh and blood!" And his brothers agreed. 28So when the
Ishmaelites, who were Midianite traders, came by, Joseph's brothers pulled him out of the cistern and sold
him to them for twenty pieces* of silver. And the traders
took him to Egypt.
29Some time later, Reuben returned to get Joseph out
of the cistern. When he discovered that Joseph was missing, he tore his clothes in grief. 30Then he went back to
his brothers and lamented, "The boy is gone! What will I
do now?"

37:28 Hebrew *20 shekels,* about 8 ounces or 228 grams in weight.

JOSEPH

UPS:
- Rose in power from slave to ruler of Egypt
- Was known for his personal integrity
- Was a man of spiritual sensitivity
- Prepared a nation to survive a famine

DOWN:
- Youthful pride caused friction with his brothers

STATS:
- Where: Canaan, Egypt
- Occupations: Shepherd, slave, ruler
- Relatives: Jacob and Rachel (parents); eleven brothers, one sister; Asenath (wife); Manasseh and Ephraim (sons)

BOTTOM LINE:
How we respond to different circumstances in life shows our belief or unbelief.

With God's help, any situation can be used for good—even when others intend it for evil.

Joseph's story is told in Gen 30:22-24; 35:24; 37; 39–50. He also is mentioned in Heb 11:21-22.

JOSEPH Ever been told that you can be or do anything? Joseph believed that. He was naturally self-confident. He was also Jacob's favorite son. God had given Joseph hints of great plans for his life.

Sometimes, though, he wasn't very sensitive of others' feelings. When he had dreams of greatness, he didn't hesitate to share them with his brothers and father. His dreams and status as the favorite of the family triggered his brothers' jealousy and anger. Eventually they tried to get rid of him.

As he grew, Joseph learned. The painful experiences in his life changed his self-confidence into a quiet but powerful confidence in God. He was able to survive and do well where most people would have failed. He added practical wisdom to his confidence and won the hearts of almost everyone who got to know him, including Potiphar, the jailer, other prisoners, the king, and after many years even his 10 older brothers.

Perhaps you can identify with one or more of these hardships Joseph experienced: betrayal and desertion by family members, sexual temptation, punishment for doing the right thing, long imprisonment, and being forgotten by those he helped. As you read his story, note what Joseph did in each case. His positive response transformed each setback into a step forward. He didn't spend much time asking why. Instead, he kept doing what was right. Those who watched his life were aware that wherever Joseph went and whatever he did, God was with him.

What's your attitude when things go wrong? Are you tempted to complain? Or will you, like Joseph, let the hard times shape you?

ME FIRST? 37:29-30

Reuben returned to the pit to find Joseph, but his little brother was gone. His first response, in effect, was *What is going to happen to me?* rather than *What is going to happen to Joseph?* In a tough situation, what's your first concern? Consider the person most affected by the problem, and you are more likely to find a solution for it. ■

31Then the brothers killed a young goat and dipped Joseph's robe in its blood. 32They sent the beautiful robe to
their father with this message: "Look at what we found.
Doesn't this robe belong to your son?"
33Their father recognized it immediately. "Yes," he
said, "it is my son's robe. A wild animal must have eaten
him. Joseph has clearly been torn to pieces!" 34Then Jacob
tore his clothes and dressed himself in burlap. He
mourned deeply for his son for a long time. 35His family
all tried to comfort him, but he refused to be comforted.
"I will go to my grave* mourning for my son," he would
say, and then he would weep.
36Meanwhile, the Midianite traders* arrived in Egypt,
where they sold Joseph to Potiphar, an officer of Pharaoh,
the king of Egypt. Potiphar was captain of the palace
guard.

38

JUDAH AND TAMAR

About this time, Judah left home and moved to Adullam,
where he stayed with a man named Hirah. 2There he saw
a Canaanite woman, the daughter of Shua, and he married her. When he slept with her, 3she became pregnant
and gave birth to a son, and he named the boy Er. 4Then
she became pregnant again and gave birth to another
son, and she named him Onan. 5And when she gave birth
to a third son, she named him Shelah. At the time of Shelah's birth, they were living at Kezib.
6In the course of time, Judah arranged for his firstborn
son, Er, to marry a young woman named Tamar. 7But Er
was a wicked man in the LORD's sight, so the LORD took his
life. 8Then Judah said to Er's brother Onan, "Go and marry
Tamar, as our law requires of the brother of a man who
has died. You must produce an heir for your brother."
9But Onan was not willing to have a child who would
not be his own heir. So whenever he had intercourse with
his brother's wife, he spilled the semen on the ground.
This prevented her from having a child who would belong to his brother. 10But the LORD considered it evil for
Onan to deny a child to his dead brother. So the LORD
took Onan's life, too.
11Then Judah said to Tamar, his daughter-in-law, "Go
back to your parents' home and remain a widow until my
son Shelah is old enough to marry you." (But Judah didn't
really intend to do this because he was afraid Shelah
would also die, like his two brothers.) So Tamar went
back to live in her father's home.
12Some years later Judah's wife died. After the time of
mourning was over, Judah and his friend Hirah the Adullamite went up to Timnah to supervise the shearing of his
sheep. 13Someone told Tamar, "Look, your father-in-law
is going up to Timnah to shear his sheep."
14Tamar was aware that Shelah had grown up, but no
arrangements had been made for her to come and marry
him. So she changed out of her widow's clothing and covered herself with a veil to disguise herself. Then she sat
beside the road at the entrance to the village of Enaim,
which is on the road to Timnah. 15Judah noticed her and
thought she was a prostitute, since she had covered her
face. 16So he stopped and propositioned her. "Let me
have sex with you," he said, not realizing that she was his
own daughter-in-law.
"How much will you pay to have sex with me?" Tamar
asked.
17"I'll send you a young goat from my flock," Judah
promised.
"But what will you give me to guarantee that you will
send the goat?" she asked.
18"What kind of guarantee do you want?" he replied.
She answered, "Leave me your identification seal and
its cord and the walking stick you are carrying." So Judah
gave them to her. Then he had intercourse with her, and
she became pregnant. 19Afterward she went back home,
took off her veil, and put on her widow's clothing as usual.

Women in Jesus' Family Tree

TAMAR	Canaanite Genesis 38:1-30
RAHAB	Canaanite Joshua 6:22-25
RUTH	Moabite Ruth 4:13-22
BATHSHEBA	Israelite 2 Samuel 12:24-25

20Later Judah asked his friend Hirah the Adullamite to
take the young goat to the woman and to pick up the
things he had given her as his guarantee. But Hirah
couldn't find her. 21So he asked the men who lived there,
"Where can I find the shrine prostitute who was sitting
beside the road at the entrance to Enaim?"
"We've never had a shrine prostitute here," they
replied.
22So Hirah returned to Judah and told him, "I couldn't
find her anywhere, and the men of the village claim
they've never had a shrine prostitute there."

37:35 Hebrew *go down to Sheol.* 37:36 Hebrew *the Medanites.* The relationship between the Midianites and Medanites is unclear; compare 37:28. See also 25:2.

[23]"Then let her keep the things I gave her," Judah said. "I sent the young goat as we agreed, but you couldn't find her. We'd be the laughingstock of the village if we went back again to look for her."

[24]About three months later, Judah was told, "Tamar, your daughter-in-law, has acted like a prostitute. And now, because of this, she's pregnant."

"Bring her out, and let her be burned!" Judah demanded.

[25]But as they were taking her out to kill her, she sent this message to her father-in-law: "The man who owns these things made me pregnant. Look closely. Whose seal and cord and walking stick are these?"

[26]Judah recognized them immediately and said, "She is more righteous than I am, because I didn't arrange for her to marry my son Shelah." And Judah never slept with Tamar again.

[27]When the time came for Tamar to give birth, it was discovered that she was carrying twins. [28]While she was in labor, one of the babies reached out his hand. The midwife grabbed it and tied a scarlet string around the child's wrist, announcing, "This one came out first." [29]But then he pulled back his hand, and out came his brother! "What!" the midwife exclaimed. "How did you break out first?" So he was named Perez.* [30]Then the baby with the scarlet string on his wrist was born, and he was named Zerah.*

39

JOSEPH IN POTIPHAR'S HOUSE

When Joseph was taken to Egypt by the Ishmaelite traders, he was purchased by Potiphar, an Egyptian officer. Potiphar was captain of the guard for Pharaoh, the king of Egypt.

TURN AND RUN 39:7-15

Joseph avoided Potiphar's wife as much as possible. He refused her sexual advances and finally *ran* from her. Sometimes merely trying to avoid temptation is not enough. We must turn and run, especially when the temptations seem very strong. Running from sin isn't cowardly. It could save your life. ■

[2]The LORD was with Joseph, so he succeeded in everything he did as he served in the home of his Egyptian master. [3]Potiphar noticed this and realized that the LORD was with Joseph, giving him success in everything he did. [4]This pleased Potiphar, so he soon made Joseph his personal attendant. He put him in charge of his entire household and everything he owned. [5]From the day Joseph was put in charge of his master's household and property, the LORD began to bless Potiphar's household for Joseph's sake. All his household affairs ran smoothly, and his crops and livestock flourished. [6]So Potiphar gave Joseph complete administrative responsibility over everything he owned. With Joseph there, he didn't worry about a thing—except what kind of food to eat!

Joseph was a very handsome and well-built young man, [7]and Potiphar's wife soon began to look at him lustfully. "Come and sleep with me," she demanded.

[8]But Joseph refused. "Look," he told her, "my master trusts me with everything in his entire household. [9]No one here has more authority than I do. He has held back nothing from me except you, because you are his wife. How could I do such a wicked thing? It would be a great sin against God."

HIS PRESENCE POWER 39:21-23

As a prisoner and slave, Joseph could have believed that his situation was hopeless. Instead, he did his best with each assigned task. The chief jailer, who promoted him to prison administrator, soon noticed his diligence and positive attitude. Are you in the midst of a seemingly hopeless predicament? Perhaps you've wondered whether you're suppose to fake a positive attitude. You don't have to fake it. Instead, you might ask God to help you recognize his presence, even in the midst of an impossibly difficult situation. ■

[10]She kept putting pressure on Joseph day after day, but he refused to sleep with her, and he kept out of her way as much as possible. [11]One day, however, no one else was around when he went in to do his work. [12]She came and grabbed him by his cloak, demanding, "Come on, sleep with me!" Joseph tore himself away, but he left his cloak in her hand as he ran from the house.

[13]When she saw that she was holding his cloak and he had fled, [14]she called out to her servants. Soon all the men came running. "Look!" she said. "My husband has brought this Hebrew slave here to make fools of us! He came into my room to rape me, but I screamed. [15]When he heard me scream, he ran outside and got away, but he left his cloak behind with me."

[16]She kept the cloak with her until her husband came home. [17]Then she told him her story. "That Hebrew slave you've brought into our house tried to come in and fool around with me," she said. [18]"But when I screamed, he ran outside, leaving his cloak with me!"

JOSEPH PUT IN PRISON

[19]Potiphar was furious when he heard his wife's story about how Joseph had treated her. [20]So he took Joseph and threw him into the prison where the king's prisoners were held, and there he remained. [21]But the LORD was with Joseph in the prison and showed him his faithful love. And the LORD made Joseph a favorite with the prison warden. [22]Before long, the warden put Joseph in charge of all the other prisoners and over everything that happened in the prison. [23]The warden had no more worries, because Joseph took care of everything. The LORD was with him and caused everything he did to succeed.

38:29 *Perez* means "breaking out." **38:30** *Zerah* means "scarlet" or "brightness."

40 JOSEPH INTERPRETS TWO DREAMS

Some time later, Pharaoh's chief cup-bearer and chief
baker offended their royal master. 2Pharaoh became
angry with these two officials, 3and he put them in the
prison where Joseph was, in the palace of the captain of
the guard. 4They remained in prison for quite some time,
and the captain of the guard assigned them to Joseph,
who looked after them.

5While they were in prison, Pharaoh's cup-bearer and
baker each had a dream one night, and each dream had
its own meaning. 6When Joseph saw them the next
morning, he noticed that they both looked upset. 7"Why
do you look so worried today?" he asked them.

8And they replied, "We both had dreams last night, but
no one can tell us what they mean."

"Interpreting dreams is God's business," Joseph replied. "Go ahead and tell me your dreams."

OPPORTUNITY 40:8

When the subject of interpreting dreams came up, Joseph focused everyone's attention on God. Rather than using the situation to make himself look good, he turned it into a powerful witness for the Lord. One secret of effective witnessing is to recognize opportunities to relate God to the other person's experience. On the hunt for opportunities to give glory to God? Go for it! ■

9So the chief cup-bearer told Joseph his dream first.
"In my dream," he said, "I saw a grapevine in front of me.
10The vine had three branches that began to bud and
blossom, and soon it produced clusters of ripe grapes. 11I
was holding Pharaoh's wine cup in my hand, so I took a
cluster of grapes and squeezed the juice into the cup.
Then I placed the cup in Pharaoh's hand."

12"This is what the dream means," Joseph said. "The
three branches represent three days. 13Within three days
Pharaoh will lift you up and restore you to your position as
his chief cup-bearer. 14And please remember me and do
me a favor when things go well for you. Mention me to Pharaoh, so he might let me out of this place. 15For I was kid-
napped from my homeland, the land of the Hebrews, and
now I'm here in prison, but I did nothing to deserve it."

16When the chief baker saw that Joseph had given the
first dream such a positive interpretation, he said to Joseph, "I had a dream, too. In my dream there were three
baskets of white pastries stacked on my head. 17The top
basket contained all kinds of pastries for Pharaoh, but the
birds came and ate them from the basket on my head."

18"This is what the dream means," Joseph told him.
"The three baskets also represent three days. 19Three
days from now Pharaoh will lift you up and impale your
body on a pole. Then birds will come and peck away at
your flesh."

20Pharaoh's birthday came three days later, and he
prepared a banquet for all his officials and staff. He summoned* his chief cup-bearer and chief baker to join the
other officials. 21He then restored the chief cup-bearer
to his former position, so he could again hand Pharaoh
his cup. 22But Pharaoh impaled the chief baker, just as
Joseph had predicted when he interpreted his dream.
23Pharaoh's chief cup-bearer, however, forgot all about
Joseph, never giving him another thought.

41 PHARAOH'S DREAMS

Two full years later, Pharaoh dreamed that he was standing
on the bank of the Nile River. 2In his dream he saw seven fat,
healthy cows come up out of the river and begin grazing in
the marsh grass. 3Then he saw seven more cows come up
behind them from the Nile, but these were scrawny and
thin. These cows stood beside the fat cows on the riverbank.
4Then the scrawny, thin cows ate the seven healthy, fat
cows! At this point in the dream, Pharaoh woke up.

5But he fell asleep again and had a second dream. This
time he saw seven heads of grain, plump and beautiful,
growing on a single stalk. 6Then seven more heads of
grain appeared, but these were shriveled and withered by
the east wind. 7And these thin heads swallowed up the
seven plump, well-formed heads! Then Pharaoh woke up
again and realized it was a dream.

8The next morning Pharaoh was very disturbed by the
dreams. So he called for all the magicians and wise men
of Egypt. When Pharaoh told them his dreams, not one of
them could tell him what they meant.

9Finally, the king's chief cup-bearer spoke up. "Today I
have been reminded of my failure," he told Pharaoh.
10"Some time ago, you were angry with the chief baker
and me, and you imprisoned us in the palace of the captain of the guard. 11One night the chief baker and I each
had a dream, and each dream had its own meaning.
12There was a young Hebrew man with us in the prison
who was a slave of the captain of the guard. We told him
our dreams, and he told us what each of our dreams
meant. 13And everything happened just as he had predicted. I was restored to my position as cup-bearer, and
the chief baker was executed and impaled on a pole."

14Pharaoh sent for Joseph at once, and he was quickly
brought from the prison. After he shaved and changed
his clothes, he went in and stood before Pharaoh. 15Then
Pharaoh said to Joseph, "I had a dream last night, and no
one here can tell me what it means. But I have heard that
when you hear about a dream you can interpret it."

16"It is beyond my power to do this," Joseph replied.
"But God can tell you what it means and set you at ease."

17So Pharaoh told Joseph his dream. "In my dream," he
said, "I was standing on the bank of the Nile River, 18and I
saw seven fat, healthy cows come up out of the river and
begin grazing in the marsh grass. 19But then I saw seven
sick-looking cows, scrawny and thin, come up after
them. I've never seen such sorry-looking animals in all
the land of Egypt. 20These thin, scrawny cows ate the
seven fat cows. 21But afterward you wouldn't have known

40:20 Hebrew *He lifted up the head of.*

it, for they were still as thin and scrawny as before! Then I woke up.

22"Then I fell asleep again, and I had another dream. This time I saw seven heads of grain, full and beautiful, growing on a single stalk. 23Then seven more heads of grain appeared, but these were blighted, shriveled, and withered by the east wind. 24And the shriveled heads swallowed the seven healthy heads. I told these dreams to the magicians, but no one could tell me what they mean."

PREPARATION 41:14

Our most important opportunities may come when we are least prepared for them. Joseph was brought hastily from the dungeon and pushed before Pharaoh. Did he have time to prepare? Yes and no. He had no warning that he suddenly would be pulled from prison and questioned by the king. Yet Joseph was ready for almost anything because he kept cool with God. Are you and God tight? If not, do you need to make things right? Keeping close to God can help you be prepared for anything that comes your way. ■

25Joseph responded, "Both of Pharaoh's dreams mean the same thing. God is telling Pharaoh in advance what he is about to do. 26The seven healthy cows and the seven healthy heads of grain both represent seven years of prosperity. 27The seven thin, scrawny cows that came up later and the seven thin heads of grain, withered by the east wind, represent seven years of famine.

28"This will happen just as I have described it, for God has revealed to Pharaoh in advance what he is about to do. 29The next seven years will be a period of great prosperity throughout the land of Egypt. 30But afterward there will be seven years of famine so great that all the prosperity will be forgotten in Egypt. Famine will destroy the land. 31This famine will be so severe that even the memory of the good years will be erased. 32As for having two similar dreams, it means that these events have been decreed by God, and he will soon make them happen.

33"Therefore, Pharaoh should find an intelligent and wise man and put him in charge of the entire land of Egypt. 34Then Pharaoh should appoint supervisors over the land and let them collect one-fifth of all the crops during the seven good years. 35Have them gather all the food produced in the good years that are just ahead and bring it to Pharaoh's storehouses. Store it away, and guard it so there will be food in the cities. 36That way there will be enough to eat when the seven years of famine come to the land of Egypt. Otherwise this famine will destroy the land."

JOSEPH MADE RULER OF EGYPT

37Joseph's suggestions were well received by Pharaoh and his officials. 38So Pharaoh asked his officials, "Can we find anyone else like this man so obviously filled with the spirit of God?" 39Then Pharaoh said to Joseph, "Since God has revealed the meaning of the dreams to you, clearly no one else is as intelligent or wise as you are. 40You will be in charge of my court, and all my people will take orders from you. Only I, sitting on my throne, will have a rank higher than yours."

41Pharaoh said to Joseph, "I hereby put you in charge of the entire land of Egypt." 42Then Pharaoh removed his signet ring from his hand and placed it on Joseph's finger. He dressed him in fine linen clothing and hung a gold chain around his neck. 43Then he had Joseph ride in the chariot reserved for his second-in-command. And wherever Joseph went, the command was shouted, "Kneel down!" So Pharaoh put Joseph in charge of all Egypt. 44And Pharaoh said to him, "I am Pharaoh, but no one will lift a hand or foot in the entire land of Egypt without your approval."

45Then Pharaoh gave Joseph a new Egyptian name, Zaphenath-paneah.* He also gave him a wife, whose name was Asenath. She was the daughter of Potiphera, the priest of On.* So Joseph took charge of the entire land of Egypt. 46He was thirty years old when he began serving in the court of Pharaoh, the king of Egypt. And when Joseph left Pharaoh's presence, he inspected the entire land of Egypt.

47As predicted, for seven years the land produced bumper crops. 48During those years, Joseph gathered all the crops grown in Egypt and stored the grain from the surrounding fields in the cities. 49He piled up huge amounts of grain like sand on the seashore. Finally, he stopped keeping records because there was too much to measure.

50During this time, before the first of the famine years, two sons were born to Joseph and his wife, Asenath, the daughter of Potiphera, the priest of On. 51Joseph named his older son Manasseh,* for he said, "God has made me forget all my troubles and everyone in my father's family." 52Joseph named his second son Ephraim,* for he said, "God has made me fruitful in this land of my grief."

53At last the seven years of bumper crops throughout the land of Egypt came to an end. 54Then the seven years of famine began, just as Joseph had predicted. The famine also struck all the surrounding countries, but throughout Egypt there was plenty of food. 55Eventually, however, the famine spread throughout the land of Egypt as well. And when the people cried out to Pharaoh for food, he told them, "Go to Joseph, and do whatever he tells you." 56So with severe famine everywhere, Joseph opened up the storehouses and distributed grain to the Egyptians, for the famine was severe throughout the land of Egypt. 57And people from all around came to Egypt to buy grain from Joseph because the famine was severe throughout the world.

42 JOSEPH'S BROTHERS GO TO EGYPT

When Jacob heard that grain was available in Egypt, he said to his sons, "Why are you standing around looking at one another? 2I have heard there is grain in Egypt. Go

41:45a *Zaphenath-paneah* probably means "God speaks and lives." **41:45b** Greek version reads *of Heliopolis;* also in 41:50. **41:51** *Manasseh* sounds like a Hebrew term that means "causing to forget." **41:52** *Ephraim* sounds like a Hebrew term that means "fruitful."

down there, and buy enough grain to keep us alive. Otherwise we'll die."

3So Joseph's ten older brothers went down to Egypt to buy grain. 4But Jacob wouldn't let Joseph's younger brother, Benjamin, go with them, for fear some harm might come to him. 5So Jacob's* sons arrived in Egypt along with others to buy food, for the famine was in Canaan as well.

6Since Joseph was governor of all Egypt and in charge of selling grain to all the people, it was to him that his brothers came. When they arrived, they bowed before him with their faces to the ground. 7Joseph recognized his brothers instantly, but he pretended to be a stranger and spoke harshly to them. "Where are you from?" he demanded.

"From the land of Canaan," they replied. "We have come to buy food."

8Although Joseph recognized his brothers, they didn't recognize him. 9And he remembered the dreams he'd had about them many years before. He said to them, "You are spies! You have come to see how vulnerable our land has become."

10"No, my lord!" they exclaimed. "Your servants have simply come to buy food. 11We are all brothers—members of the same family. We are honest men, sir! We are not spies!"

12"Yes, you are!" Joseph insisted. "You have come to see how vulnerable our land has become."

13"Sir," they said, "there are actually twelve of us. We, your servants, are all brothers, sons of a man living in the land of Canaan. Our youngest brother is back there with our father right now, and one of our brothers is no longer with us."

14But Joseph insisted, "As I said, you are spies! 15This is how I will test your story. I swear by the life of Pharaoh that you will never leave Egypt unless your youngest brother comes here! 16One of you must go and get your brother. I'll keep the rest of you here in prison. Then we'll find out whether or not your story is true. By the life of Pharaoh, if it turns out that you don't have a younger brother, then I'll know you are spies."

17So Joseph put them all in prison for three days. 18On the third day Joseph said to them, "I am a God-fearing man. If you do as I say, you will live. 19If you really are honest men, choose one of your brothers to remain in prison. The rest of you may go home with grain for your starving families. 20But you must bring your youngest brother back to me. This will prove that you are telling the truth, and you will not die." To this they agreed.

21Speaking among themselves, they said, "Clearly we are being punished because of what we did to Joseph long ago. We saw his anguish when he pleaded for his life, but we wouldn't listen. That's why we're in this trouble."

22"Didn't I tell you not to sin against the boy?" Reuben asked. "But you wouldn't listen. And now we have to answer for his blood!"

23Of course, they didn't know that Joseph understood them, for he had been speaking to them through an interpreter. 24Now he turned away from them and began to weep. When he regained his composure, he spoke to them again. Then he chose Simeon from among them and had him tied up right before their eyes.

25Joseph then ordered his servants to fill the men's sacks with grain, but he also gave secret instructions to return each brother's payment at the top of his sack. He also gave them supplies for their journey home. 26So the brothers loaded their donkeys with the grain and headed for home.

27But when they stopped for the night and one of them opened his sack to get grain for his donkey, he found his money in the top of his sack. 28"Look!" he exclaimed to his brothers. "My money has been returned; it's here in my sack!" Then their hearts sank. Trembling, they said to each other, "What has God done to us?"

29When the brothers came to their father, Jacob, in the land of Canaan, they told him everything that had happened to them. 30"The man who is governor of the land spoke very harshly to us," they told him. "He accused us of being spies scouting the land. 31But we said, 'We are honest men, not spies. 32We are twelve brothers, sons of one father. One brother is no longer with us, and the youngest is at home with our father in the land of Canaan.'

33"Then the man who is governor of the land told us, 'This is how I will find out if you are honest men. Leave one of your brothers here with me, and take grain for your starving families and go on home. 34But you must bring your youngest brother back to me. Then I will know you are honest men and not spies. Then I will give you back your brother, and you may trade freely in the land.'"

35As they emptied out their sacks, there in each man's sack was the bag of money he had paid for the grain! The brothers and their father were terrified when they saw the bags of money. 36Jacob exclaimed, "You are robbing me of my children! Joseph is gone! Simeon is gone! And now you want to take Benjamin, too. Everything is going against me!"

37Then Reuben said to his father, "You may kill my two sons if I don't bring Benjamin back to you. I'll be responsible for him, and I promise to bring him back."

38But Jacob replied, "My son will not go down with you. His brother Joseph is dead, and he is all I have left. If anything should happen to him on your journey, you would send this grieving, white-haired man to his grave.*"

43 THE BROTHERS RETURN TO EGYPT

But the famine continued to ravage the land of Canaan. 2When the grain they had brought from Egypt was almost gone, Jacob said to his sons, "Go back and buy us a little more food."

3But Judah said, "The man was serious when he warned us, 'You won't see my face again unless your brother is with you.' 4If you send Benjamin with us, we will go down and buy more food. 5But if you don't let Benjamin go, we

42:5 Hebrew *Israel's*. See note on 35:21. **42:38** Hebrew *to Sheol*.

won't go either. Remember, the man said, 'You won't see my face again unless your brother is with you.'"

6"Why were you so cruel to me?" Jacob* moaned. "Why did you tell him you had another brother?"

7"The man kept asking us questions about our family," they replied. "He asked, 'Is your father still alive? Do you have another brother?' So we answered his questions. How could we know he would say, 'Bring your brother down here'?"

8Judah said to his father, "Send the boy with me, and we will be on our way. Otherwise we will all die of starvation—and not only we, but you and our little ones. 9I personally guarantee his safety. You may hold me responsible if I don't bring him back to you. Then let me bear the blame forever. 10If we hadn't wasted all this time, we could have gone and returned twice by now."

FULL RESPONSIBILITY 43:8-9

Judah accepted full responsibility for Benjamin's safety. He did not know what that might mean for him, but he was determined to carry it out. In the end, Judah's stirring words caused Joseph to break down and reveal himself to his brothers (44:18-34). Accepting the responsibility can be difficult at times. But on the flip side, it builds character and confidence, earns others' respect, and motivates us to complete our work. Got any new responsibilities? Are you willing to see them through to the end? ■

11So their father, Jacob, finally said to them, "If it can't be avoided, then at least do this. Pack your bags with the best products of this land. Take them down to the man as gifts—balm, honey, gum, aromatic resin, pistachio nuts, and almonds. 12Also take double the money that was put back in your sacks, as it was probably someone's mistake. 13Then take your brother, and go back to the man. 14May God Almighty* give you mercy as you go before the man, so that he will release Simeon and let Benjamin return. But if I must lose my children, so be it."

15So the men packed Jacob's gifts and double the money and headed off with Benjamin. They finally arrived in Egypt and presented themselves to Joseph. 16When Joseph saw Benjamin with them, he said to the manager of his household, "These men will eat with me this noon. Take them inside the palace. Then go slaughter an animal, and prepare a big feast." 17So the man did as Joseph told him and took them into Joseph's palace.

18The brothers were terrified when they saw that they were being taken into Joseph's house. "It's because of the money someone put in our sacks last time we were here," they said. "He plans to pretend that we stole it. Then he will seize us, make us slaves, and take our donkeys."

A FEAST AT JOSEPH'S PALACE

19The brothers approached the manager of Joseph's household and spoke to him at the entrance to the palace. 20"Sir," they said, "we came to Egypt once before to buy food. 21But as we were returning home, we stopped for the night and opened our sacks. Then we discovered that each man's money—the exact amount paid—was in the top of his sack! Here it is; we have brought it back with us. 22We also have additional money to buy more food. We have no idea who put our money in our sacks."

23"Relax. Don't be afraid," the household manager told them. "Your God, the God of your father, must have put this treasure into your sacks. I know I received your payment." Then he released Simeon and brought him out to them.

24The manager then led the men into Joseph's palace. He gave them water to wash their feet and provided food for their donkeys. 25They were told they would be eating there, so they prepared their gifts for Joseph's arrival at noon.

26When Joseph came home, they gave him the gifts they had brought him, then bowed low to the ground before him. 27After greeting them, he asked, "How is your father, the old man you spoke about? Is he still alive?"

28"Yes," they replied. "Our father, your servant, is alive and well." And they bowed low again.

29Then Joseph looked at his brother Benjamin, the son of his own mother. "Is this your youngest brother, the one you told me about?" Joseph asked. "May God be gracious to you, my son." 30Then Joseph hurried from the room because he was overcome with emotion for his brother. He went into his private room, where he broke down and wept. 31After washing his face, he came back out, keeping himself under control. Then he ordered, "Bring out the food!"

32The waiters served Joseph at his own table, and his brothers were served at a separate table. The Egyptians who ate with Joseph sat at their own table, because Egyptians despise Hebrews and refuse to eat with them. 33Joseph told each of his brothers where to sit, and to their amazement, he seated them according to age, from oldest to youngest. 34And Joseph filled their plates with food from his own table, giving Benjamin five times as much as he gave the others. So they feasted and drank freely with him.

44

JOSEPH'S SILVER CUP

When his brothers were ready to leave, Joseph gave these instructions to his palace manager: "Fill each of their sacks with as much grain as they can carry, and put each man's money back into his sack. 2Then put my personal silver cup at the top of the youngest brother's sack, along with the money for his grain." So the manager did as Joseph instructed him.

3The brothers were up at dawn and were sent on their journey with their loaded donkeys. 4But when they had gone only a short distance and were barely out of the city, Joseph said to his palace manager, "Chase after them and stop them. When you catch up with them, ask them, 'Why have you repaid my kindness with such evil? 5Why have you stolen my master's silver cup,* which he

43:6 Hebrew *Israel;* also in 43:11. See note on 35:21. 43:14 Hebrew *El-Shaddai.* 44:5 As in Greek version; Hebrew lacks this phrase.

uses to predict the future? What a wicked thing you have
done!'"
6When the palace manager caught up with the men, he
spoke to them as he had been instructed.
7"What are you talking about?" the brothers responded. "We are your servants and would never do such
a thing! 8Didn't we return the money we found in our
sacks? We brought it back all the way from the land of
Canaan. Why would we steal silver or gold from your
master's house? 9If you find his cup with any one of us, let
that man die. And all the rest of us, my lord, will be your
slaves."
10"That's fair," the man replied. "But only the one who
stole the cup will be my slave. The rest of you may go
free."
11They all quickly took their sacks from the backs of
their donkeys and opened them. 12The palace manager
searched the brothers' sacks, from the oldest to the youngest. And the cup was found in Benjamin's sack! 13When
the brothers saw this, they tore their clothing in despair.
Then they loaded their donkeys again and returned to the
city.
14Joseph was still in his palace when Judah and his
brothers arrived, and they fell to the ground before him.
15"What have you done?" Joseph demanded. "Don't you
know that a man like me can predict the future?"
16Judah answered, "Oh, my lord, what can we say to
you? How can we explain this? How can we prove our innocence? God is punishing us for our sins. My lord, we
have all returned to be your slaves—all of us, not just our
brother who had your cup in his sack."
17"No," Joseph said. "I would never do such a thing!
Only the man who stole the cup will be my slave. The rest
of you may go back to your father in peace."

JUDAH SPEAKS FOR HIS BROTHERS

18Then Judah stepped forward and said, "Please, my lord,
let your servant say just one word to you. Please, do not be
angry with me, even though you are as powerful as Pharaoh himself.
19"My lord, previously you asked us, your servants, 'Do
you have a father or a brother?' 20And we responded, 'Yes,
my lord, we have a father who is an old man, and his youngest son is a child of his old age. His full brother is dead,
and he alone is left of his mother's children, and his father loves him very much.'
21"And you said to us, 'Bring him here so I can see him
with my own eyes.' 22But we said to you, 'My lord, the boy
cannot leave his father, for his father would die.' 23But
you told us, 'Unless your youngest brother comes with
you, you will never see my face again.'
24"So we returned to your servant, our father, and told
him what you had said. 25Later, when he said, 'Go back
again and buy us more food,' 26we replied, 'We can't go
unless you let our youngest brother go with us. We'll
never get to see the man's face unless our youngest
brother is with us.'
27"Then my father said to us, 'As you know, my wife
had two sons, 28and one of them went away and never
returned. Doubtless he was torn to pieces by some wild
animal. I have never seen him since. 29Now if you take his
brother away from me, and any harm comes to him, you
will send this grieving, white-haired man to his grave.*'
30"And now, my lord, I cannot go back to my father
without the boy. Our father's life is bound up in the boy's
life. 31If he sees that the boy is not with us, our father will
die. We, your servants, will indeed be responsible for
sending that grieving, white-haired man to his grave.
32My lord, I guaranteed to my father that I would take
care of the boy. I told him, 'If I don't bring him back to
you, I will bear the blame forever.'

CHANGED LIFE 44:16-34

When Judah was younger, he showed no regard for his brother Joseph or his father, Jacob. First, he convinced his brothers to sell Joseph as a slave (37:27). Second, he joined his brothers in lying to his father about Joseph's outcome (37:32). But what a change had taken place in Judah! The man who sold one favored little brother into slavery now offered to become a slave himself to save another favored little brother. What are the evidences of your changed life? Would your family members agree? ■

33"So please, my lord, let me stay here as a slave instead
of the boy, and let the boy return with his brothers. 34For
how can I return to my father if the boy is not with me? I
couldn't bear to see the anguish this would cause my
father!"

45 JOSEPH REVEALS HIS IDENTITY

Joseph could stand it no longer. There were many people
in the room, and he said to his attendants, "Out, all of
you!" So he was alone with his brothers when he told
them who he was. 2Then he broke down and wept. He
wept so loudly the Egyptians could hear him, and word of
it quickly carried to Pharaoh's palace.
3"I am Joseph!" he said to his brothers. "Is my father
still alive?" But his brothers were speechless! They were
stunned to realize that Joseph was standing there in front
of them. 4"Please, come closer," he said to them. So they
came closer. And he said again, "I am Joseph, your
brother, whom you sold into slavery in Egypt. 5But don't
be upset, and don't be angry with yourselves for selling
me to this place. It was God who sent me here ahead of
you to preserve your lives. 6This famine that has ravaged
the land for two years will last five more years, and there
will be neither plowing nor harvesting. 7God has sent me
ahead of you to keep you and your families alive and to
preserve many survivors.* 8So it was God who sent me
here, not you! And he is the one who made me an adviser*
to Pharaoh—the manager of his entire palace and the
governor of all Egypt.

44:29 Hebrew *to Sheol;* also in 44:31. **45:7** Or *and to save you with an extraordinary rescue.* The meaning of the Hebrew is uncertain.
45:8 Hebrew *a father.*

INTENTIONS 45:4-8

Although Joseph's brothers had wanted to get rid of him, God used even their evil actions to fulfill his ultimate plan. He sent Joseph ahead to preserve their lives and the lives of many others. When people intend evil toward you, do you have trouble believing that God is still in control? Although evil is never God's intent, he doesn't always save us from bad situations. He can, however, bring good out of evil. ■

9"Now hurry back to my father and tell him, 'This is what your son Joseph says: God has made me master over all the land of Egypt. So come down to me immediately! 10You can live in the region of Goshen, where you can be near me with all your children and grandchildren, your flocks and herds, and everything you own. 11I will take care of you there, for there are still five years of famine ahead of us. Otherwise you, your household, and all your animals will starve.'"

12Then Joseph added, "Look! You can see for yourselves, and so can my brother Benjamin, that I really am Joseph! 13Go tell my father of my honored position here in Egypt. Describe for him everything you have seen, and then bring my father here quickly." 14Weeping with joy, he embraced Benjamin, and Benjamin did the same. 15Then Joseph kissed each of his brothers and wept over them, and after that they began talking freely with him.

PHARAOH INVITES JACOB TO EGYPT

16The news soon reached Pharaoh's palace: "Joseph's brothers have arrived!" Pharaoh and his officials were all delighted to hear this.

17Pharaoh said to Joseph, "Tell your brothers, 'This is what you must do: Load your pack animals, and hurry back to the land of Canaan. 18Then get your father and all of your families, and return here to me. I will give you the very best land in Egypt, and you will eat from the best that the land produces.'"

19Then Pharaoh said to Joseph, "Tell your brothers, 'Take wagons from the land of Egypt to carry your little children and your wives, and bring your father here. 20Don't worry about your personal belongings, for the best of all the land of Egypt is yours.'"

21So the sons of Jacob* did as they were told. Joseph provided them with wagons, as Pharaoh had commanded, and he gave them supplies for the journey. 22And he gave each of them new clothes—but to Benjamin he gave five changes of clothes and 300 pieces* of silver. 23He also sent his father ten male donkeys loaded with the finest products of Egypt, and ten female donkeys loaded with grain and bread and other supplies he would need on his journey.

24So Joseph sent his brothers off, and as they left, he called after them, "Don't quarrel about all this along the way!" 25And they left Egypt and returned to their father, Jacob, in the land of Canaan.

26"Joseph is still alive!" they told him. "And he is governor of all the land of Egypt!" Jacob was stunned at the news—he couldn't believe it. 27But when they repeated to Jacob everything Joseph had told them, and when he saw the wagons Joseph had sent to carry him, their father's spirits revived.

28Then Jacob exclaimed, "It must be true! My son Joseph is alive! I must go and see him before I die."

46 JACOB'S JOURNEY TO EGYPT

So Jacob* set out for Egypt with all his possessions. And when he came to Beersheba, he offered sacrifices to the God of his father, Isaac. 2During the night God spoke to him in a vision. "Jacob! Jacob!" he called.

"Here I am," Jacob replied.

3"I am God,* the God of your father," the voice said. "Do not be afraid to go down to Egypt, for there I will make your family into a great nation. 4I will go with you down to Egypt, and I will bring you back again. But you will die in Egypt with Joseph attending to you."

STRANGE PLACES 46:1-4

Before Jacob moved his household to Egypt, God promised to go with him and take care of his family. That reassurance probably helped Jacob to put aside his fear of change. Feeling fearful about the future? The same reassurance that God offered to Jacob is yours for the taking. ■

5So Jacob left Beersheba, and his sons took him to Egypt. They carried him and their little ones and their wives in the wagons Pharaoh had provided for them. 6They also took all their livestock and all the personal belongings they had acquired in the land of Canaan. So Jacob and his entire family went to Egypt—7sons and grandsons, daughters and granddaughters—all his descendants.

8These are the names of the descendants of Israel—the sons of Jacob—who went to Egypt:

Reuben was Jacob's oldest son. 9The sons of Reuben were Hanoch, Pallu, Hezron, and Carmi.
10The sons of Simeon were Jemuel, Jamin, Ohad, Jakin, Zohar, and Shaul. (Shaul's mother was a Canaanite woman.)
11The sons of Levi were Gershon, Kohath, and Merari.
12The sons of Judah were Er, Onan, Shelah, Perez, and Zerah (though Er and Onan had died in the land of Canaan). The sons of Perez were Hezron and Hamul.
13The sons of Issachar were Tola, Puah,* Jashub,* and Shimron.

45:21 Hebrew *Israel;* also in 45:28. See note on 35:21. **45:22** Hebrew *300 shekels,* about 7.5 pounds or 3.4 kilograms in weight. **46:1** Hebrew *Israel;* also in 46:29, 30. See note on 35:21. **46:3** Hebrew *I am El.* **46:13a** As in Syriac version and Samaritan Pentateuch (see also 1 Chr 7:1); Hebrew reads *Puvah.* **46:13b** As in some Greek manuscripts and Samaritan Pentateuch (see also Num 26:24; 1 Chr 7:1); Hebrew reads *Iob.*

14 The sons of Zebulun were Sered, Elon, and Jahleel.
15 These were the sons of Leah and Jacob who were born
in Paddan-aram, in addition to their daughter, Dinah.
The number of Jacob's descendants (male and female)
through Leah was thirty-three.

16 The sons of Gad were Zephon,* Haggi, Shuni, Ezbon,
Eri, Arodi, and Areli.
17 The sons of Asher were Imnah, Ishvah, Ishvi, and
Beriah. Their sister was Serah. Beriah's sons were
Heber and Malkiel.
18 These were the sons of Zilpah, the servant given to Leah
by her father, Laban. The number of Jacob's descendants
through Zilpah was sixteen.

19 The sons of Jacob's wife Rachel were Joseph and
Benjamin.
20 Joseph's sons, born in the land of Egypt, were
Manasseh and Ephraim. Their mother was Asenath,
daughter of Potiphera, the priest of On.*
21 Benjamin's sons were Bela, Beker, Ashbel, Gera,
Naaman, Ehi, Rosh, Muppim, Huppim, and Ard.
22 These were the sons of Rachel and Jacob. The number
of Jacob's descendants through Rachel was fourteen.

23 The son of Dan was Hushim.
24 The sons of Naphtali were Jahzeel, Guni, Jezer, and
Shillem.
25 These were the sons of Bilhah, the servant given to Rachel by her father, Laban. The number of Jacob's descendants through Bilhah was seven.

26 The total number of Jacob's direct descendants who
went with him to Egypt, not counting his sons' wives, was
sixty-six. 27 In addition, Joseph had two sons* who were
born in Egypt. So altogether, there were seventy* members of Jacob's family in the land of Egypt.

JACOB'S FAMILY ARRIVES IN GOSHEN

28 As they neared their destination, Jacob sent Judah
ahead to meet Joseph and get directions to the region of
Goshen. And when they finally arrived there, 29 Joseph
prepared his chariot and traveled to Goshen to meet his
father, Jacob. When Joseph arrived, he embraced his father and wept, holding him for a long time. 30 Finally, Jacob said to Joseph, "Now I am ready to die, since I have
seen your face again and know you are still alive."
31 And Joseph said to his brothers and to his father's entire family, "I will go to Pharaoh and tell him, 'My brothers
and my father's entire family have come to me from the
land of Canaan. 32 These men are shepherds, and they
raise livestock. They have brought with them their flocks
and herds and everything they own.'"
33 Then he said, "When Pharaoh calls for you and asks
you about your occupation, 34 you must tell him, 'We, your
servants, have raised livestock all our lives, as our ancestors have always done.' When you tell him this, he will let
you live here in the region of Goshen, for the Egyptians
despise shepherds."

47 JACOB BLESSES PHARAOH

Then Joseph went to see Pharaoh and told him, "My father and my brothers have arrived from the land of Canaan. They have come with all their flocks and herds and
possessions, and they are now in the region of Goshen."
2 Joseph took five of his brothers with him and presented them to Pharaoh. 3 And Pharaoh asked the brothers, "What is your occupation?"
They replied, "We, your servants, are shepherds, just
like our ancestors. 4 We have come to live here in Egypt
for a while, for there is no pasture for our flocks in Canaan. The famine is very severe there. So please, we request permission to live in the region of Goshen."
5 Then Pharaoh said to Joseph, "Now that your father
and brothers have joined you here, 6 choose any place in
the entire land of Egypt for them to live. Give them the
best land of Egypt. Let them live in the region of Goshen.
And if any of them have special skills, put them in charge
of my livestock, too."

KEEP THE FAITH 47:1-6

The faithfulness of Joseph affected his entire family. When he was in prison, Joseph must have wondered about his future. Instead of despairing, he faithfully obeyed God and did what was right. Does that describe you? We may not always see the effects of our faith, but we can be sure that God will honor faithfulness. ■

7 Then Joseph brought in his father, Jacob, and presented him to Pharaoh. And Jacob blessed Pharaoh.
8 "How old are you?" Pharaoh asked him.
9 Jacob replied, "I have traveled this earth for 130 hard
years. But my life has been short compared to the lives of
my ancestors." 10 Then Jacob blessed Pharaoh again before leaving his court.
11 So Joseph assigned the best land of Egypt—the region of Rameses—to his father and his brothers, and he
settled them there, just as Pharaoh had commanded.
12 And Joseph provided food for his father and his brothers in amounts appropriate to the number of their de-
pendents, including the smallest children.

JOSEPH'S LEADERSHIP IN THE FAMINE

13 Meanwhile, the famine became so severe that all the
food was used up, and people were starving throughout
the lands of Egypt and Canaan. 14 By selling grain to the
people, Joseph eventually collected all the money in
Egypt and Canaan, and he put the money in Pharaoh's
treasury. 15 When the people of Egypt and Canaan ran out
of money, all the Egyptians came to Joseph. "Our money

46:16 As in Greek version and Samaritan Pentateuch (see also Num 26:15); Hebrew reads *Ziphion.* **46:20** Greek version reads *of Heliopolis.*
46:27a Greek version reads *nine sons,* probably including Joseph's grandsons through Ephraim and Manasseh (see 1 Chr 7:14-20).
46:27b Greek version reads *seventy-five;* see note on Exod 1:5.

is gone!" they cried. "But please give us food, or we will die before your very eyes!"

16Joseph replied, "Since your money is gone, bring me your livestock. I will give you food in exchange for your livestock." 17So they brought their livestock to Joseph in exchange for food. In exchange for their horses, flocks of sheep and goats, herds of cattle, and donkeys, Joseph provided them with food for another year.

KEEPING YOUR WORD 47:29-31

As Jacob lay dying, Joseph promised to bury his father in his homeland of Canaan. In this culture, a person's word carried as much force as a written contract today. Yet many people today seem to find it easy to say, "I didn't mean what I said." God wants his people to say what they mean and mean what they say. Do you consider your words to be as binding as a written contract? ■

18But that year ended, and the next year they came again and said, "We cannot hide the truth from you, my lord. Our money is gone, and all our livestock and cattle are yours. We have nothing left to give but our bodies and our land. 19Why should we die before your very eyes? Buy us and our land in exchange for food; we offer our land and ourselves as slaves for Pharaoh. Just give us grain so we may live and not die, and so the land does not become empty and desolate."

20So Joseph bought all the land of Egypt for Pharaoh. All the Egyptians sold him their fields because the famine was so severe, and soon all the land belonged to Pharaoh. 21As for the people, he made them all slaves,* from one end of Egypt to the other. 22The only land he did not buy was the land belonging to the priests. They received an allotment of food directly from Pharaoh, so they didn't need to sell their land.

23Then Joseph said to the people, "Look, today I have bought you and your land for Pharaoh. I will provide you with seed so you can plant the fields. 24Then when you harvest it, one-fifth of your crop will belong to Pharaoh. You may keep the remaining four-fifths as seed for your fields and as food for you, your households, and your little ones."

25"You have saved our lives!" they exclaimed. "May it please you, my lord, to let us be Pharaoh's servants." 26Joseph then issued a decree still in effect in the land of Egypt, that Pharaoh should receive one-fifth of all the crops grown on his land. Only the land belonging to the priests was not given to Pharaoh.

27Meanwhile, the people of Israel settled in the region of Goshen in Egypt. There they acquired property, and they were fruitful, and their population grew rapidly. 28Jacob lived for seventeen years after his arrival in Egypt, so he lived 147 years in all.

29As the time of his death drew near, Jacob* called for his son Joseph and said to him, "Please do me this favor. Put your hand under my thigh and swear that you will treat me with unfailing love by honoring this last request: Do not bury me in Egypt. 30When I die, please take my body out of Egypt and bury me with my ancestors."

So Joseph promised, "I will do as you ask."

31"Swear that you will do it," Jacob insisted. So Joseph gave his oath, and Jacob bowed humbly at the head of his bed.*

48 JACOB BLESSES MANASSEH AND EPHRAIM

One day not long after this, word came to Joseph, "Your father is failing rapidly." So Joseph went to visit his father, and he took with him his two sons, Manasseh and Ephraim.

2When Joseph arrived, Jacob was told, "Your son Joseph has come to see you." So Jacob* gathered his strength and sat up in his bed.

3Jacob said to Joseph, "God Almighty* appeared to me at Luz in the land of Canaan and blessed me. 4He said to me, 'I will make you fruitful, and I will multiply your descendants. I will make you a multitude of nations. And I will give this land of Canaan to your descendants* after you as an everlasting possession.'

5"Now I am claiming as my own sons these two boys of yours, Ephraim and Manasseh, who were born here in the land of Egypt before I arrived. They will be my sons, just as Reuben and Simeon are. 6But any children born to you in the future will be your own, and they will inherit land within the territories of their brothers Ephraim and Manasseh.

7"Long ago, as I was returning from Paddan-aram, Rachel died in the land of Canaan. We were still on the way, some distance from Ephrath (that is, Bethlehem). So with great sorrow I buried her there beside the road to Ephrath."

8Then Jacob looked over at the two boys. "Are these your sons?" he asked.

9"Yes," Joseph told him, "these are the sons God has given me here in Egypt."

And Jacob said, "Bring them closer to me, so I can bless them."

NEVER SO BAD 48:11

When Joseph became a slave, Jacob thought he was dead and wept in despair (37:34). But eventually God's plan allowed Jacob to regain not only his son, but his grandchildren as well. Circumstances are never so bad that they are beyond God's help. Jacob regained his son. Because we belong to a loving God, we need never despair. We never know what good he will bring out of a seemingly hopeless situation. ■

10Jacob was half blind because of his age and could hardly see. So Joseph brought the boys close to him, and Jacob kissed and embraced them. 11Then Jacob said to Joseph, "I never thought I would see your face again, but now God has let me see your children, too!"

47:21 As in Greek version and Samaritan Pentateuch; Hebrew reads *he moved them all into the towns.* **47:29** Hebrew *Israel;* also in 47:31b. See note on 35:21. **47:31** Greek version reads *and Israel bowed in worship as he leaned on his staff.* Compare Heb 11:21. **48:2** Hebrew *Israel;* also in 48:8, 10, 11, 13, 14, 21. See note on 35:21. **48:3** Hebrew *El-Shaddai.* **48:4** Hebrew *seed;* also in 48:19.

12 Joseph moved the boys, who were at their grandfather's knees, and he bowed with his face to the ground.
13 Then he positioned the boys in front of Jacob. With his
right hand he directed Ephraim toward Jacob's left hand,
and with his left hand he put Manasseh at Jacob's right
hand. 14 But Jacob crossed his arms as he reached out to
lay his hands on the boys' heads. He put his right hand on
the head of Ephraim, though he was the younger boy, and
his left hand on the head of Manasseh, though he was the
firstborn. 15 Then he blessed Joseph and said,

"May the God before whom my grandfather Abraham
and my father, Isaac, walked—
the God who has been my shepherd
all my life, to this very day,
16 the Angel who has redeemed me from all harm—
may he bless these boys.
May they preserve my name
and the names of Abraham and Isaac.
And may their descendants multiply greatly
throughout the earth."

17 But Joseph was upset when he saw that his father
placed his right hand on Ephraim's head. So Joseph lifted
it to move it from Ephraim's head to Manasseh's head.
18 "No, my father," he said. "This one is the firstborn. Put
your right hand on his head."
19 But his father refused. "I know, my son; I know," he
replied. "Manasseh will also become a great people, but
his younger brother will become even greater. And his
descendants will become a multitude of nations."
20 So Jacob blessed the boys that day with this blessing:
"The people of Israel will use your names when they give
a blessing. They will say, 'May God make you as prosperous as Ephraim and Manasseh.'" In this way, Jacob put
Ephraim ahead of Manasseh.
21 Then Jacob said to Joseph, "Look, I am about to die,
but God will be with you and will take you back to Canaan,
the land of your ancestors. 22 And beyond what I have
given your brothers, I am giving you an extra portion of
the land* that I took from the Amorites with my sword
and bow."

49 JACOB'S LAST WORDS TO HIS SONS

Then Jacob called together all his sons and said, "Gather
around me, and I will tell you what will happen to each of
you in the days to come.

2 "Come and listen, you sons of Jacob;
listen to Israel, your father.

3 "Reuben, you are my firstborn, my strength,
the child of my vigorous youth.
You are first in rank and first in power.
4 But you are as unruly as a flood,
and you will be first no longer.
For you went to bed with my wife;
you defiled my marriage couch.

5 "Simeon and Levi are two of a kind;
their weapons are instruments of violence.
6 May I never join in their meetings;
may I never be a party to their plans.
For in their anger they murdered men,
and they crippled oxen just for sport.
7 A curse on their anger, for it is fierce;
a curse on their wrath, for it is cruel.
I will scatter them among the descendants of Jacob;
I will disperse them throughout Israel.

FUTURE CHOICE 49:3-28

Jacob blessed each of his sons and then made a prediction about each one's future. The way the men had lived played an important part in Jacob's blessing and prophecy. Our past affects our present and future. By sunrise tomorrow, our actions of today will have become part of the past. Yet they will already have begun to shape the future. What actions can you choose or avoid in order to positively shape your future? ■

8 "Judah, your brothers will praise you.
You will grasp your enemies by the neck.
All your relatives will bow before you.
9 Judah, my son, is a young lion
that has finished eating its prey.
Like a lion he crouches and lies down;
like a lioness—who dares to rouse him?
10 The scepter will not depart from Judah,
nor the ruler's staff from his descendants,*
until the coming of the one to whom it belongs,*
the one whom all nations will honor.
11 He ties his foal to a grapevine,
the colt of his donkey to a choice vine.
He washes his clothes in wine,
his robes in the blood of grapes.
12 His eyes are darker than wine,
and his teeth are whiter than milk.

13 "Zebulun will settle by the seashore
and will be a harbor for ships;
his borders will extend to Sidon.

14 "Issachar is a sturdy donkey,
resting between two saddlepacks.*
15 When he sees how good the countryside is
and how pleasant the land,
he will bend his shoulder to the load
and submit himself to hard labor.

16 "Dan will govern his people,
like any other tribe in Israel.

48:22 Or *an extra ridge of land.* The meaning of the Hebrew is uncertain. **49:10a** Hebrew *from between his feet.* **49:10b** Or *until tribute is brought to him and the peoples obey;* traditionally rendered *until Shiloh comes.* **49:14** Or *sheepfolds,* or *hearths.*

17 Dan will be a snake beside the road,
a poisonous viper along the path
that bites the horse's hooves
so its rider is thrown off.
18 I trust in you for salvation, O LORD!

19 "Gad will be attacked by marauding bands,
but he will attack them when they retreat.

20 "Asher will dine on rich foods
and produce food fit for kings.

21 "Naphtali is a doe set free
that bears beautiful fawns.

GOOD GRIEF 50:1-11

When Jacob died at the age of 147 (see also Gen 47:28), Joseph wept and mourned for months. Often in society we ostracize those who are grieving, especially if we think they have grieved "too long." But grief has its own time frame. It's over when it's over. Grieving the loss of a loved one or know someone who is? Give yourself time. ■

22 "Joseph is the foal of a wild donkey,
the foal of a wild donkey at a spring—
one of the wild donkeys on the ridge.*
23 Archers attacked him savagely;
they shot at him and harassed him.
24 But his bow remained taut,
and his arms were strengthened
by the hands of the Mighty One of Jacob,
by the Shepherd, the Rock of Israel.
25 May the God of your father help you;
May the Almighty bless you
with the blessings of the heavens above,
and blessings of the watery depths below,
and blessings of the breasts and womb.
26 May the blessings of your father
surpass the blessings of the ancient mountains,*
reaching to the heights of the eternal hills.
May these blessings rest on the head of Joseph,
who is a prince among his brothers.

27 "Benjamin is a ravenous wolf,
devouring his enemies in the morning
and dividing his plunder in the evening."

28These are the twelve tribes of Israel, and this is what
their father said as he told his sons good-bye. He blessed
each one with an appropriate message.

JACOB'S DEATH AND BURIAL

29Then Jacob instructed them, "Soon I will die and join
my ancestors. Bury me with my father and grandfather in
the cave in the field of Ephron the Hittite. 30This is the
cave in the field of Machpelah, near Mamre in Canaan,
that Abraham bought from Ephron the Hittite as a permanent burial site. 31There Abraham and his wife Sarah
are buried. There Isaac and his wife, Rebekah, are buried.
And there I buried Leah. 32It is the plot of land and the
cave that my grandfather Abraham bought from the Hittites."
33When Jacob had finished this charge to his sons, he
drew his feet into the bed, breathed his last, and joined
his ancestors in death.

50

Joseph threw himself on his father and wept
over him and kissed him. 2Then Joseph told the physicians who served him to embalm his father's body; so Jacob* was embalmed. 3The embalming process took the
usual forty days. And the Egyptians mourned his death
for seventy days.
4When the period of mourning was over, Joseph approached Pharaoh's advisers and said, "Please do me this
favor and speak to Pharaoh on my behalf. 5Tell him that
my father made me swear an oath. He said to me, 'Listen, I
am about to die. Take my body back to the land of Canaan, and bury me in the tomb I prepared for myself.' So
please allow me to go and bury my father. After his burial,
I will return without delay."
6Pharaoh agreed to Joseph's request. "Go and bury
your father, as he made you promise," he said. 7So Joseph
went up to bury his father. He was accompanied by all of
Pharaoh's officials, all the senior members of Pharaoh's
household, and all the senior officers of Egypt. 8Joseph
also took his entire household and his brothers and their
households. But they left their little children and flocks
and herds in the land of Goshen. 9A great number of
chariots and charioteers accompanied Joseph.

RELIABLE 50:5-6

Joseph had proven himself trustworthy as Pharaoh's adviser. Because of his good record, Pharaoh was sure that he would return to Egypt as promised after burying his father in Canaan. Privileges and freedom often result when we have demonstrated our trustworthiness. In what ways have you demonstrated your trustworthiness? ■

10When they arrived at the threshing floor of Atad,
near the Jordan River, they held a very great and solemn
memorial service, with a seven-day period of mourning
for Joseph's father. 11The local residents, the Canaanites,
watched them mourning at the threshing floor of Atad.
Then they renamed that place (which is near the Jordan)
Abel-mizraim,* for they said, "This is a place of deep
mourning for these Egyptians."
12So Jacob's sons did as he had commanded them.
13They carried his body to the land of Canaan and buried

49:22 Or *Joseph is a fruitful tree, / a fruitful tree beside a spring. / His branches reach over the wall.* The meaning of the Hebrew is uncertain.
49:26 Or *of my ancestors.* 50:2 Hebrew *Israel.* See note on 35:21. 50:11 *Abel-mizraim* means "mourning of the Egyptians."

him in the cave in the field of Machpelah, near Mamre. This is the cave that Abraham had bought as a permanent burial site from Ephron the Hittite.

JOSEPH REASSURES HIS BROTHERS

[14]After burying Jacob, Joseph returned to Egypt with his brothers and all who had accompanied him to his father's burial. [15]But now that their father was dead, Joseph's brothers became fearful. "Now Joseph will show his anger and pay us back for all the wrong we did to him," they said.

MUSCLE BUILDING 50:22-24

Joseph was ready to die. He believed that God would keep his promise and one day bring the Israelites back to their homeland. What a tremendous example! The secret of that kind of faith is a lifetime of trusting God. Your faith is like a muscle—it grows with exercise, gaining strength over time. How are you exercising your faith? ■

[16]So they sent this message to Joseph: "Before your father died, he instructed us [17]to say to you: 'Please forgive your brothers for the great wrong they did to you—for their sin in treating you so cruelly.' So we, the servants of the God of your father, beg you to forgive our sin." When Joseph received the message, he broke down and wept. [18]Then his brothers came and threw themselves down before Joseph. "Look, we are your slaves!" they said.

[19]But Joseph replied, "Don't be afraid of me. Am I God, that I can punish you? [20]You intended to harm me, but God intended it all for good. He brought me to this position so I could save the lives of many people. [21]No, don't be afraid. I will continue to take care of you and your children." So he reassured them by speaking kindly to them.

THE DEATH OF JOSEPH

[22]So Joseph and his brothers and their families continued to live in Egypt. Joseph lived to the age of 110. [23]He lived to see three generations of descendants of his son Ephraim, and he lived to see the birth of the children of Manasseh's son Makir, whom he claimed as his own.*

[24]"Soon I will die," Joseph told his brothers, "but God will surely come to help you and lead you out of this land of Egypt. He will bring you back to the land he solemnly promised to give to Abraham, to Isaac, and to Jacob."

[25]Then Joseph made the sons of Israel swear an oath, and he said, "When God comes to help you and lead you back, you must take my bones with you." [26]So Joseph died at the age of 110. The Egyptians embalmed him, and his body was placed in a coffin in Egypt.

50:23 Hebrew *who were born on Joseph's knees.*

EXODUS

PROMISES—FROM innocent childhood pledges to earnest, romantic commitments—are an important part of life. Think about all of the promises made to you or through you recently. We promise to perform an action, be a certain place at a certain time, or give to a cause. Whether we keep those promises is another story! Yet when others make promises to us, we expect them to keep their word. If not, we become angry, disappointed, and even heartbroken.

The book of Exodus is all about promises: God's promises to his people. We're invited to walk along with Moses and the people of Israel as they make their exodus from Egypt. We're also on the front row of the giving and receiving of the Ten Commandments—God's rules for living.

Knowing that God kept his promise to deliver the Israelites from slavery and lead them to a home of their own can increase our trust in him. Just as God was faithful to keep the promises he made to Israel, he will keep every promise he has made to us. He promises to love us no matter what, to care for and protect us, to help us overcome any temptation, to comfort and teach us, and to bring us to heaven someday. That's what you believe, right?

exodus

timeline

1526 B.C.
Moses born

1446
Exodus from Egypt

1445
Ten Commandments given

1406
Israel enters Canaan

1375
Judges begin to rule

stats

PURPOSE: To record the events of Israel's deliverance from Egypt and development as a nation

AUTHOR: Moses

DATE WRITTEN: 1450–1410 B.C., approximately the same as Genesis

WHERE WRITTEN: In the wilderness during Israel's wanderings, somewhere in the Sinai Peninsula

SETTING: Egypt. God's people, once highly favored in the land during the time of Joseph, are now slaves. God is about to set them free.

KEY PEOPLE: Moses, Moses' mother (Jochebed), Miriam, Pharaoh, Pharaoh's daughter, Jethro, Aaron, Joshua, Bezalel

KEY PLACES: Egypt, Goshen, Nile River, Land of Midian, Red Sea, Sinai Peninsula, Mount Sinai

SPECIAL FEATURES: Exodus relates more miracles than any other Old Testament book and is noted for containing the Ten Commandments

KEY points

SLAVERY
The Israelites were slaves for 400 years. Physical slavery is like slavery to sin. The longer you are a slave, the more difficult breaking free becomes. Gaining freedom from sin requires God's power.

GUIDANCE
God guided Israel out of slavery by using the plagues, Moses' leadership, the miracle of the Red Sea, and the Ten Commandments. God demonstrates his power in our life through the guidance of wise leaders and the effort of Christian friends working together. He can be trusted to give us the guidance we need to follow his will.

TEN COMMANDMENTS
Through the Ten Commandments, God taught Israel the importance of making the right choices and accepting responsibility for one's actions. Both are key to our growth as Christians.

THE NATION
God established the nation of Israel to be the source of truth and salvation to all the world. Israel's newly formed nation models for us the need to depend upon God. Whether we are rebellious or obedient, God remains our only source of absolute, eternal truth and life.

KEY PLACES IN EXODUS

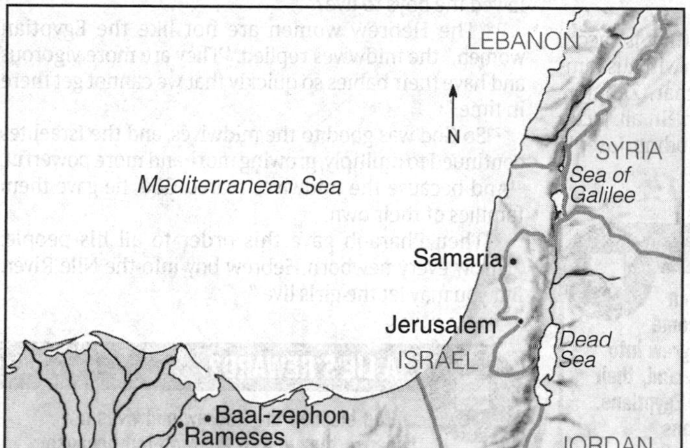

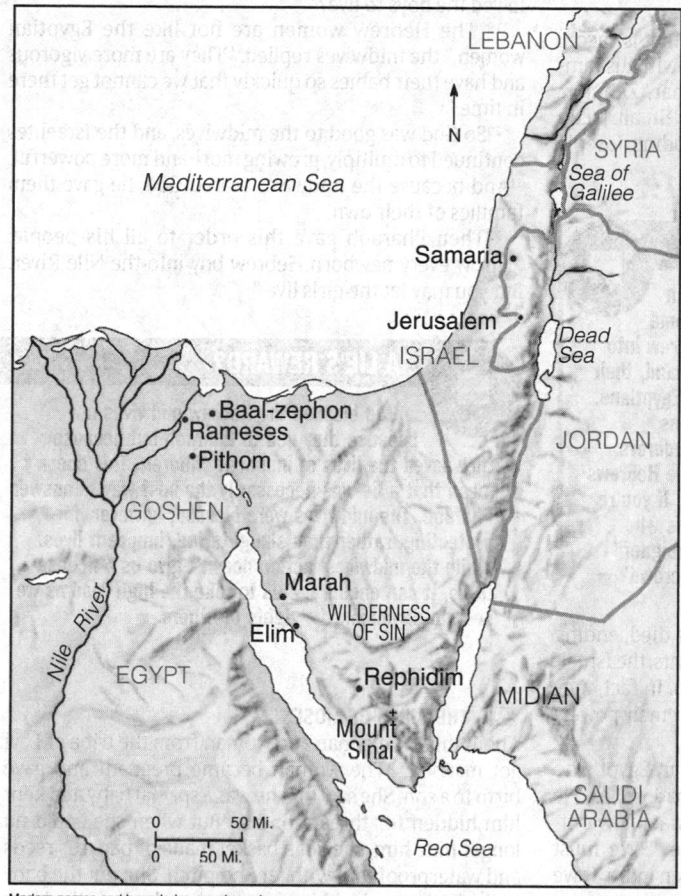

Modern names and boundaries are shown in gray.

- **LAND OF GOSHEN** This area was given to Jacob and his family when they moved to Egypt (Genesis 47:5-6). It became the Hebrews' homeland for 400 years, and remained separate from the main Egyptian centers, for Egyptian culture looked down on shepherds and nomads. As the years passed, Jacob's family grew into a large nation (1:7).
- **PITHOM AND RAMESES** After 400 years, a pharaoh came to the throne who had no respect for these descendants of Joseph and feared their large numbers. He forced them into slavery in order to oppress and subdue them. Out of their slave labor, the supply cities of Pithom and Rameses were built (1:11).
- **LAND OF MIDIAN** Moses, an Egyptian prince who was born a Hebrew, killed an Egyptian taskmaster and fled for his life to the land of Midian. There he became a shepherd and married a woman named Zipporah. It was while he was here that God commissioned him for the job of leading the Hebrew people out of Egypt (2:15–4:31).
- **BAAL-ZEPHON** Slavery was not to last, because God planned to deliver his people. After choosing Moses and Aaron to be his spokesmen to Pharaoh, God worked a series of dramatic miracles in the land of Egypt to convince Pharaoh to let the Hebrews go (5:1–12:33). When finally freed, the entire nation set out with the riches of Egypt (12:34-36). One of their first stops was at Baal-zephon (14:2), where Pharaoh, who had changed his mind, chased the Hebrews and trapped them against the Red Sea. But God parted the waters and led the people through the sea on dry land. When Pharaoh's army tried to pursue, the waters collapsed around them, and they were drowned (14:5-31).
- **MARAH** Moses now led the people southward. The long trek across the desert brought hot tempers and parched throats to this mass of people. At Marah, the water they found was bitter, but God sweetened it (15:22-25).
- **ELIM** As they continued their journey, the Hebrews (now called Israelites) came to Elim, an oasis with twelve springs (15:27).
- **WILDERNESS OF SIN** Leaving Elim, the people headed into the Wilderness of Sin. Here the people became hungry, so God provided them with manna that came from heaven and covered the ground each morning (16:1, 13-15). The people ate this manna until they entered the Promised Land.
- **REPHIDIM** Moses led the people to Rephidim, where they found no water. But God miraculously provided water from a rock (17:1, 5-6). Here the Israelites encountered their first test in battle: The Amalekites attacked and were defeated (17:9-13). Moses' father-in-law, Jethro, then arrived on the scene with some sound advice on delegating responsibilities (18).
- **MOUNT SINAI** God had previously appeared to Moses on this mountain and commissioned him to lead Israel (3:1-2). Now Moses returned with the people God had asked him to lead. For almost a year the people camped at the foot of Mount Sinai. During this time God gave them his Ten Commandments as well as other laws for right living. He also provided the blueprint for building the Tabernacle (19–40). God was forging a holy nation that was prepared to live for and serve him alone.

1 THE ISRAELITES IN EGYPT

These are the names of the sons of Israel (that is, Jacob) who moved to Egypt with their father, each with his family: 2Reuben, Simeon, Levi, Judah, 3Issachar, Zebulun, Benjamin, 4Dan, Naphtali, Gad, and Asher. 5In all, Jacob had seventy* descendants in Egypt, including Joseph, who was already there.

FOREIGNERS 1:1

Jacob's family moved to Egypt at the invitation of Joseph, one of Jacob's sons, who had become a great ruler under Pharaoh. Jacob's family grew into a large nation. But, as foreigners within the land, their lifestyle was quite different from that of the Egyptians. The Hebrews worshiped one God; the Egyptians worshiped many gods. The Hebrews were wanderers; the Egyptians had a deeply rooted culture. The Hebrews were shepherds; the Egyptians were builders. If you're a Christian, your lifestyle is "foreign" to those who lack your knowledge of Christ. Are you "a foreigner" or a chameleon—one who blends in with the crowd? ■

6In time, Joseph and all of his brothers died, ending that entire generation. 7But their descendants, the Israelites, had many children and grandchildren. In fact, they multiplied so greatly that they became extremely powerful and filled the land.

8Eventually, a new king came to power in Egypt who knew nothing about Joseph or what he had done. 9He said to his people, "Look, the people of Israel now outnumber us and are stronger than we are. 10We must make a plan to keep them from growing even more. If we don't, and if war breaks out, they will join our enemies and fight against us. Then they will escape from the country.*"

11So the Egyptians made the Israelites their slaves. They appointed brutal slave drivers over them, hoping to wear them down with crushing labor. They forced them to build the cities of Pithom and Rameses as supply centers for the king. 12But the more the Egyptians oppressed them, the more the Israelites multiplied and spread, and the more alarmed the Egyptians became. 13So the Egyptians worked the people of Israel without mercy. 14They made their lives bitter, forcing them to mix mortar and make bricks and do all the work in the fields. They were ruthless in all their demands.

15Then Pharaoh, the king of Egypt, gave this order to the Hebrew midwives, Shiphrah and Puah: 16"When you help the Hebrew women as they give birth, watch as they deliver.* If the baby is a boy, kill him; if it is a girl, let her live." 17But because the midwives feared God, they refused to obey the king's orders. They allowed the boys to live, too.

18So the king of Egypt called for the midwives. "Why have you done this?" he demanded. "Why have you allowed the boys to live?"

19"The Hebrew women are not like the Egyptian women," the midwives replied. "They are more vigorous and have their babies so quickly that we cannot get there in time."

20So God was good to the midwives, and the Israelites continued to multiply, growing more and more powerful. 21And because the midwives feared God, he gave them families of their own.

22Then Pharaoh gave this order to all his people: "Throw every newborn Hebrew boy into the Nile River. But you may let the girls live."

A LIE'S REWARD? 1:15-21

God blessed the Hebrew midwives not because they lied to Pharaoh but because they saved the lives of innocent children. This doesn't mean that a lie was necessarily the best way to answer Pharaoh. The midwives were blessed, however, for protecting, rather than slaughtering, innocent lives. While the midwives' action doesn't give us a license to lie, it can encourage us to take the high road as we seek to champion the rights of others. ■

2 THE BIRTH OF MOSES

About this time, a man and woman from the tribe of Levi got married. 2The woman became pregnant and gave birth to a son. She saw that he was a special baby and kept him hidden for three months. 3But when she could no longer hide him, she got a basket made of papyrus reeds and waterproofed it with tar and pitch. She put the baby in the basket and laid it among the reeds along the bank of the Nile River. 4The baby's sister then stood at a distance, watching to see what would happen to him.

5Soon Pharaoh's daughter came down to bathe in the river, and her attendants walked along the riverbank. When the princess saw the basket among the reeds, she sent her maid to get it for her. 6When the princess opened it, she saw the baby. The little boy was crying, and she felt sorry for him. "This must be one of the Hebrew children," she said.

7Then the baby's sister approached the princess. "Should I go and find one of the Hebrew women to nurse the baby for you?" she asked.

8"Yes, do!" the princess replied. So the girl went and called the baby's mother.

9"Take this baby and nurse him for me," the princess told the baby's mother. "I will pay you for your help." So the woman took her baby home and nursed him.

10Later, when the boy was older, his mother brought him back to Pharaoh's daughter, who adopted him as her own son. The princess named him Moses,* for she explained, "I lifted him out of the water."

1:5 Dead Sea Scrolls and Greek version read *seventy-five;* see notes on Gen 46:27. **1:10** Or *will take the country.* **1:16** Hebrew *look upon the two stones;* perhaps the reference is to a birthstool. **2:10** *Moses* sounds like a Hebrew term that means "to lift out."

MOSES ESCAPES TO MIDIAN

11 Many years later, when Moses had grown up, he went out to visit his own people, the Hebrews, and he saw how hard they were forced to work. During his visit, he saw an Egyptian beating one of his fellow Hebrews. 12 After looking in all directions to make sure no one was watching, Moses killed the Egyptian and hid the body in the sand.

> **A SMALL FIGHT AGAINST EVIL** 2:1-3
>
> **Moses' mother wanted her child to live. But there was little she could do to change Pharaoh's new law. Her only alternative was to hide her son and later place him in a tiny basket on the river. God used her courageous act to place her son in the house of Pharaoh. Do you sometimes feel surrounded by evil and frustrated by how little you can do about it? With God, no effort, however small it may seem, will go to waste. He can turn a small act for good into a great triumph over evil.** ■

13 The next day, when Moses went out to visit his people again, he saw two Hebrew men fighting. "Why are you beating up your friend?" Moses said to the one who had started the fight.

14 The man replied, "Who appointed you to be our prince and judge? Are you going to kill me as you killed that Egyptian yesterday?"

Then Moses was afraid, thinking, "Everyone knows what I did." 15 And sure enough, Pharaoh heard what had happened, and he tried to kill Moses. But Moses fled from Pharaoh and went to live in the land of Midian.

When Moses arrived in Midian, he sat down beside a well. 16 Now the priest of Midian had seven daughters who came as usual to draw water and fill the water troughs for their father's flocks. 17 But some other shepherds came and chased them away. So Moses jumped up and rescued the girls from the shepherds. Then he drew water for their flocks.

18 When the girls returned to Reuel, their father, he asked, "Why are you back so soon today?"

19 "An Egyptian rescued us from the shepherds," they answered. "And then he drew water for us and watered our flocks."

20 "Then where is he?" their father asked. "Why did you leave him there? Invite him to come and eat with us."

21 Moses accepted the invitation, and he settled there with him. In time, Reuel gave Moses his daughter Zipporah to be his wife. 22 Later she gave birth to a son, and Moses named him Gershom,* for he explained, "I have been a foreigner in a foreign land."

23 Years passed, and the king of Egypt died. But the Israelites continued to groan under their burden of slavery. They cried out for help, and their cry rose up to God. 24 God heard their groaning, and he remembered his covenant promise to Abraham, Isaac, and Jacob. 25 He looked down on the people of Israel and knew it was time to act.*

3 MOSES AND THE BURNING BUSH

One day Moses was tending the flock of his father-in-law, Jethro,* the priest of Midian. He led the flock far into the wilderness and came to Sinai,* the mountain of God. 2 There the angel of the LORD appeared to him in a blazing fire from the middle of a bush. Moses stared in amazement. Though the bush was engulfed in flames, it didn't burn up. 3 "This is amazing," Moses said to himself. "Why isn't that bush burning up? I must go see it."

4 When the LORD saw Moses coming to take a closer look, God called to him from the middle of the bush, "Moses! Moses!"

"Here I am!" Moses replied.

5 "Do not come any closer," the LORD warned. "Take off your sandals, for you are standing on holy ground. 6 I am the God of your father*—the God of Abraham, the God of Isaac, and the God of Jacob." When Moses heard this, he covered his face because he was afraid to look at God.

7 Then the LORD told him, "I have certainly seen the oppression of my people in Egypt. I have heard their cries of distress because of their harsh slave drivers. Yes, I am aware of their suffering. 8 So I have come down to rescue them from the power of the Egyptians and lead them out of Egypt into their own fertile and spacious land. It is a land flowing with milk and honey—the land where the Canaanites, Hittites, Amorites, Perizzites, Hivites, and Jebusites now live. 9 Look! The cry of the people of Israel has reached me, and I have seen how harshly the Egyptians abuse them. 10 Now go, for I am sending you to Pharaoh. You must lead my people Israel out of Egypt."

11 But Moses protested to God, "Who am I to appear before Pharaoh? Who am I to lead the people of Israel out of Egypt?"

12 God answered, "I will be with you. And this is your sign that I am the one who has sent you: When you have brought the people out of Egypt, you will worship God at this very mountain."

13 But Moses protested, "If I go to the people of Israel and tell them, 'The God of your ancestors has sent me to you,' they will ask me, 'What is his name?' Then what should I tell them?"

14 God replied to Moses, "I AM WHO I AM.* Say this to the people of Israel: I AM has sent me to you." 15 God also said to Moses, "Say this to the people of Israel: Yahweh,* the God of your ancestors—the God of Abraham, the God of Isaac, and the God of Jacob—has sent me to you.

This is my eternal name,
my name to remember for all generations.

16 "Now go and call together all the elders of Israel. Tell them, 'The LORD, the God of your ancestors—the God of

2:22 *Gershom* sounds like a Hebrew term that means "a foreigner there." 2:25 Or *and acknowledged his obligation to help them.* 3:1a Moses' father-in-law went by two names, Jethro and Reuel. 3:1b Hebrew *Horeb,* another name for Sinai. 3:6 Greek version reads *your fathers.* 3:14 Or *I WILL BE WHAT I WILL BE.* 3:15 *Yahweh* is a transliteration of the proper name *YHWH* that is sometimes rendered "Jehovah"; in this translation it is usually rendered "the LORD" (note the use of small capitals).

Abraham, Isaac, and Jacob—has appeared to me. He told me, "I have been watching closely, and I see how the Egyptians are treating you. 17I have promised to rescue you from your oppression in Egypt. I will lead you to a land flowing with milk and honey—the land where the Canaanites, Hittites, Amorites, Perizzites, Hivites, and Jebusites now live."'

18"The elders of Israel will accept your message. Then you and the elders must go to the king of Egypt and tell him, 'The LORD, the God of the Hebrews, has met with us. So please let us take a three-day journey into the wilderness to offer sacrifices to the LORD, our God.'

19"But I know that the king of Egypt will not let you go unless a mighty hand forces him.* 20So I will raise my hand and strike the Egyptians, performing all kinds of miracles among them. Then at last he will let you go. 21And I will cause the Egyptians to look favorably on you. They will give you gifts when you go so you will not leave empty-handed. 22Every Israelite woman will ask for articles of silver and gold and fine clothing from her Egyptian neighbors and from the foreign women in their houses. You will dress your sons and daughters with these, stripping the Egyptians of their wealth."

> Now go! I will be with you as you speak, and I will instruct you in what to say.
>
> *EXODUS 4:12*

4 SIGNS OF THE LORD'S POWER

But Moses protested again, "What if they won't believe me or listen to me? What if they say, 'The LORD never appeared to you'?"

ORDINARY TO EXTRAORDINARY 4:2-4

A shepherd's staff was commonly a three- to six-foot wooden rod with a curved hook at the top. The shepherd used it for walking, guiding his sheep, killing snakes, and many other tasks. Still, it was just a stick. But with God's power, the ordinary shepherd's staff Moses carried became extraordinary. Think about the ordinary things in your life—your voice, a pen, a hammer, a broom, a musical instrument. It's easy to assume that God only uses special items and skills for his work. We assume that he only works with an artistic genius like Michelangelo or an amazingly gifted bass guitarist. But he takes delight in using ordinary items and skills for extraordinary purposes. ■

2Then the LORD asked him, "What is that in your hand?"

"A shepherd's staff," Moses replied.

3"Throw it down on the ground," the LORD told him. So Moses threw down the staff, and it turned into a snake! Moses jumped back.

4Then the LORD told him, "Reach out and grab its tail." So Moses reached out and grabbed it, and it turned back into a shepherd's staff in his hand.

5"Perform this sign," the LORD told him. "Then they will believe that the LORD, the God of their ancestors—the God of Abraham, the God of Isaac, and the God of Jacob—really has appeared to you."

6Then the LORD said to Moses, "Now put your hand inside your cloak." So Moses put his hand inside his cloak, and when he took it out again, his hand was white as snow with a severe skin disease.* 7"Now put your hand back into your cloak," the LORD said. So Moses put his hand back in, and when he took it out again, it was as healthy as the rest of his body.

8The LORD said to Moses, "If they do not believe you and are not convinced by the first miraculous sign, they will be convinced by the second sign. 9And if they don't believe you or listen to you even after these two signs, then take some water from the Nile River and pour it out on the dry ground. When you do, the water from the Nile will turn to blood on the ground."

10But Moses pleaded with the LORD, "O Lord, I'm not very good with words. I never have been, and I'm not now, even though you have spoken to me. I get tongue-tied, and my words get tangled."

11Then the LORD asked Moses, "Who makes a person's mouth? Who decides whether people speak or do not speak, hear or do not hear, see or do not see? Is it not I, the LORD? 12Now go! I will be with you as you speak, and I will instruct you in what to say."

13But Moses again pleaded, "Lord, please! Send anyone else."

14Then the LORD became angry with Moses. "All right," he said. "What about your brother, Aaron the Levite? I know he speaks well. And look! He is on his way to meet you now. He will be delighted to see you. 15Talk to him, and put the words in his mouth. I will be with both of you as you speak, and I will instruct you both in what to do. 16Aaron will be your spokesman to the people. He will be your mouthpiece, and you will stand in the place of God for him, telling him what to say. 17And take your shepherd's staff with you, and use it to perform the miraculous signs I have shown you."

MOSES RETURNS TO EGYPT

18So Moses went back home to Jethro, his father-in-law. "Please let me return to my relatives in Egypt," Moses said. "I don't even know if they are still alive."

"Go in peace," Jethro replied.

19Before Moses left Midian, the LORD said to him, "Return to Egypt, for all those who wanted to kill you have died."

20So Moses took his wife and sons, put them on a

3:19 As in Greek and Latin versions; Hebrew reads *will not let you go, not by a mighty hand.* **4:6** Or *with leprosy.* The Hebrew word used here can describe various skin diseases.

donkey, and headed back to the land of Egypt. In his hand he carried the staff of God.

21 And the LORD told Moses, "When you arrive back in Egypt, go to Pharaoh and perform all the miracles I have empowered you to do. But I will harden his heart so he will refuse to let the people go. 22 Then you will tell him, 'This is what the LORD says: Israel is my firstborn son. 23 I commanded you, "Let my son go, so he can worship me." But since you have refused, I will now kill your firstborn son!'"

24 On the way to Egypt, at a place where Moses and his family had stopped for the night, the LORD confronted him and was about to kill him. 25 But Moses' wife, Zipporah, took a flint knife and circumcised her son. She touched his feet* with the foreskin and said, "Now you are a bridegroom of blood to me." 26 (When she said "a bridegroom of blood," she was referring to the circumcision.) After that, the LORD left him alone.

27 Now the LORD had said to Aaron, "Go out into the wilderness to meet Moses." So Aaron went and met Moses at the mountain of God, and he embraced him. 28 Moses then told Aaron everything the LORD had commanded him to say. And he told him about the miraculous signs the LORD had commanded him to perform.

29 Then Moses and Aaron returned to Egypt and called all the elders of Israel together. 30 Aaron told them everything the LORD had told Moses, and Moses performed the miraculous signs as they watched. 31 Then the people of Israel were convinced that the LORD had sent Moses and Aaron. When they heard that the LORD was concerned about them and had seen their misery, they bowed down and worshiped.

5

MOSES AND AARON SPEAK TO PHARAOH

After this presentation to Israel's leaders, Moses and Aaron went and spoke to Pharaoh. They told him, "This is what the LORD, the God of Israel, says: Let my people go so they may hold a festival in my honor in the wilderness."

KEEP TALKING 5:1-3

Pharaoh would not listen to Moses and Aaron because he did not know about the God of Israel. People who do not know God may choose to ignore his Word or his messengers. But that is no excuse to give up trying. Like Moses and Aaron, persistence counts. When others reject you or your faith, don't be surprised or discouraged. Instead, continue to tell them about God, trusting him to open closed minds and soften stubborn hearts. ■

2 "Is that so?" retorted Pharaoh. "And who is the LORD? Why should I listen to him and let Israel go? I don't know the LORD, and I will not let Israel go."

3 But Aaron and Moses persisted. "The God of the Hebrews has met with us," they declared. "So let us take a three-day journey into the wilderness so we can offer sacrifices to the LORD our God. If we don't, he will kill us with a plague or with the sword."

4 Pharaoh replied, "Moses and Aaron, why are you distracting the people from their tasks? Get back to work! 5 Look, there are many of your people in the land, and you are stopping them from their work."

MAKING BRICKS WITHOUT STRAW

6 That same day Pharaoh sent this order to the Egyptian slave drivers and the Israelite foremen: 7 "Do not supply any more straw for making bricks. Make the people get it themselves! 8 But still require them to make the same number of bricks as before. Don't reduce the quota. They are lazy. That's why they are crying out, 'Let us go and offer sacrifices to our God.' 9 Load them down with more work. Make them sweat! That will teach them to listen to lies!"

10 So the slave drivers and foremen went out and told the people: "This is what Pharaoh says: I will not provide any more straw for you. 11 Go and get it yourselves. Find it wherever you can. But you must produce just as many bricks as before!" 12 So the people scattered throughout the land of Egypt in search of stubble to use as straw.

13 Meanwhile, the Egyptian slave drivers continued to push hard. "Meet your daily quota of bricks, just as you did when we provided you with straw!" they demanded. 14 Then they whipped the Israelite foremen they had put in charge of the work crews. "Why haven't you met your quotas either yesterday or today?" they demanded.

15 So the Israelite foremen went to Pharaoh and pleaded with him. "Please don't treat your servants like this," they begged. 16 "We are given no straw, but the slave drivers still demand, 'Make bricks!' We are being beaten, but it isn't our fault! Your own people are to blame!"

17 But Pharaoh shouted, "You're just lazy! Lazy! That's why you're saying, 'Let us go and offer sacrifices to the LORD.' 18 Now get back to work! No straw will be given to you, but you must still produce the full quota of bricks."

19 The Israelite foremen could see that they were in serious trouble when they were told, "You must not reduce the number of bricks you make each day." 20 As they left Pharaoh's court, they confronted Moses and Aaron, who were waiting outside for them. 21 The foremen said to them, "May the LORD judge and punish you for making us stink before Pharaoh and his officials. You have put a sword into their hands, an excuse to kill us!"

22 Then Moses went back to the LORD and protested, "Why have you brought all this trouble on your own people, Lord? Why did you send me? 23 Ever since I came to Pharaoh as your spokesman, he has been even more brutal to your people. And you have done nothing to rescue them!"

6

PROMISES OF DELIVERANCE

Then the LORD told Moses, "Now you will see what I will do to Pharaoh. When he feels the force of my strong hand, he will let the people go. In fact, he will force them to leave his land!"

4:25 The Hebrew word for "feet" may refer here to the male sex organ.

2 And God said to Moses, "I am Yahweh—'the LORD.'* 3 I
appeared to Abraham, to Isaac, and to Jacob as El-
Shaddai—'God Almighty'*—but I did not reveal my name,
Yahweh, to them. 4 And I reaffirmed my covenant with
them. Under its terms, I promised to give them the land
of Canaan, where they were living as foreigners. 5 You can
be sure that I have heard the groans of the people of Israel, who are now slaves to the Egyptians. And I am well
aware of my covenant with them.

6 "Therefore, say to the people of Israel: 'I am the LORD.
I will free you from your oppression and will rescue you
from your slavery in Egypt. I will redeem you with a powerful arm and great acts of judgment. 7 I will claim you as
my own people, and I will be your God. Then you will
know that I am the LORD your God who has freed you
from your oppression in Egypt. 8 I will bring you into the
land I swore to give to Abraham, Isaac, and Jacob. I will
give it to you as your very own possession. I am the
LORD!'"

9 So Moses told the people of Israel what the LORD had
said, but they refused to listen anymore. They had become too discouraged by the brutality of their slavery.

10 Then the LORD said to Moses, 11 "Go back to Pharaoh,
the king of Egypt, and tell him to let the people of Israel
leave his country."

12 "But LORD!" Moses objected. "My own people won't
listen to me anymore. How can I expect Pharaoh to listen? I'm such a clumsy speaker!*"

13 But the LORD spoke to Moses and Aaron and gave
them orders for the Israelites and for Pharaoh, the king
of Egypt. The LORD commanded Moses and Aaron to lead
the people of Israel out of Egypt.

THE ANCESTORS OF MOSES AND AARON

14 These are the ancestors of some of the clans of Israel:

The sons of Reuben, Israel's oldest son, were Hanoch,
Pallu, Hezron, and Carmi. Their descendants became
the clans of Reuben.

15 The sons of Simeon were Jemuel, Jamin, Ohad, Jakin,
Zohar, and Shaul. (Shaul's mother was a Canaanite
woman.) Their descendants became the clans of
Simeon.

16 These are the descendants of Levi, as listed in their
family records: The sons of Levi were Gershon,
Kohath, and Merari. (Levi lived to be 137 years old.)

17 The descendants of Gershon included Libni and
Shimei, each of whom became the ancestor of a clan.

18 The descendants of Kohath included Amram,
Izhar, Hebron, and Uzziel. (Kohath lived to be
133 years old.)

19 The descendants of Merari included Mahli and
Mushi.

These are the clans of the Levites, as listed in their family
records.

20 Amram married his father's sister Jochebed, and she
gave birth to his sons, Aaron and Moses. (Amram
lived to be 137 years old.)

21 The sons of Izhar were Korah, Nepheg, and Zicri.

22 The sons of Uzziel were Mishael, Elzaphan, and Sithri.

23 Aaron married Elisheba, the daughter of Amminadab
and sister of Nahshon, and she gave birth to his sons,
Nadab, Abihu, Eleazar, and Ithamar.

6:2 *Yahweh* is a transliteration of the proper name *YHWH* that is sometimes rendered "Jehovah"; in this translation it is usually rendered "the LORD" (note the use of small capitals). **6:3** *El-Shaddai,* which means "God Almighty," is the name for God used in Gen 17:1; 28:3; 35:11; 43:14; 48:3. **6:12** Hebrew *I have uncircumcised lips;* also in 6:30.

MOSES

UPS:
- Egyptian education; wilderness training
- Greatest Jewish leader; set the Exodus in motion
- Prophet and lawgiver; recorder of the Ten Commandments

DOWNS:
- Failed to enter the Promised Land because of disobedience to God
- Did not always recognize and use the talents of others

STATS:
- Where: Egypt, Midian, Wilderness of Sinai
- Occupation: Prince, shepherd, leader of the Israelites
- Relatives: Miriam (sister); Aaron (brother); Zipporah (wife); Gershom and Eliezer (sons)

LESSONS

God first prepares his people, then uses them to do his work.

God does his greatest work through frail people.

Moses' story is told in the books of Exodus through Deuteronomy. He also is mentioned in Matt 17:3-4; Acts 7:20-44; Heb 11:23-28.

MOSES Some people can't stay out of trouble. (Know anyone like that?) Moses was that kind of person. He wasn't a troublemaker; he was usually trying to do the right thing. When he saw something wrong, he tried to make it right—and often ended up in trouble.

Moses was a reactor. When there was action, he reacted. Whether checking out a burning bush that didn't burn, defending a Hebrew slave, or trying to stop a fight, Moses reacted to the world around him.

Moses became a great leader because he learned to act, rather than react. He wasn't perfect—he even made a mistake that kept him out of the Promised Land. But God shaped and used his life anyway. God didn't change *who* or *what* Moses was; he worked on *how* Moses used what he'd been given.

God wants to change us in the same way. He will make the best version of us there could ever be, if we let him. When God changes us, he enhances the good qualities he gave us at the start. He also forgives us and straightens us out.

24 The sons of Korah were Assir, Elkanah, and Abiasaph.
Their descendants became the clans of Korah.
25 Eleazar son of Aaron married one of the daughters of
Putiel, and she gave birth to his son, Phinehas.
These are the ancestors of the Levite families, listed according to their clans.

26 The Aaron and Moses named in this list are the same ones to whom the LORD said, "Lead the people of Israel out of the land of Egypt like an army." 27 It was Moses and Aaron who spoke to Pharaoh, the king of Egypt, about leading the people of Israel out of Egypt.

28 When the LORD spoke to Moses in the land of Egypt, 29 he said to him, "I am the LORD! Tell Pharaoh, the king of Egypt, everything I am telling you." 30 But Moses argued with the LORD, saying, "I can't do it! I'm such a clumsy speaker! Why should Pharaoh listen to me?"

7

AARON'S STAFF BECOMES A SERPENT

Then the LORD said to Moses, "Pay close attention to this. I will make you seem like God to Pharaoh, and your brother, Aaron, will be your prophet. 2 Tell Aaron everything I command you, and Aaron must command Pharaoh to let the people of Israel leave his country. 3 But I will make Pharaoh's heart stubborn so I can multiply my miraculous signs and wonders in the land of Egypt. 4 Even then Pharaoh will refuse to listen to you. So I will bring down my fist on Egypt. Then I will rescue my forces—my people, the Israelites—from the land of Egypt with great acts of judgment. 5 When I raise my powerful hand and bring out the Israelites, the Egyptians will know that I am the LORD."

GOD'S AMBASSADOR 7:1

God made Moses his representative; he was "like God to Pharaoh." Christians are God's representatives, showing the world a lifestyle that differs from the world's. Much of the world knows little about God except what can be seen through the lives of God's people. What kind of God do they think you represent? ■

6 So Moses and Aaron did just as the LORD had commanded them. 7 Moses was eighty years old, and Aaron was eighty-three when they made their demands to Pharaoh.

8 Then the LORD said to Moses and Aaron, 9 "Pharaoh will demand, 'Show me a miracle.' When he does this, say to Aaron, 'Take your staff and throw it down in front of Pharaoh, and it will become a serpent.*'"

10 So Moses and Aaron went to Pharaoh and did what the LORD had commanded them. Aaron threw down his staff before Pharaoh and his officials, and it became a serpent! 11 Then Pharaoh called in his own wise men and sorcerers, and these Egyptian magicians did the same thing with their magic. 12 They threw down their staffs, which also became serpents! But then Aaron's staff swallowed up their staffs. 13 Pharaoh's heart, however, remained hard. He still refused to listen, just as the LORD had predicted.

DOUBLE TROUBLE 7:11

How were Pharaoh's wise men and magicians able to duplicate Moses' miracles? Some of their feats involved deception or illusions. But some may have used satanic power. Ironically, whenever the magicians duplicated one of Moses' plagues, it only made matters worse. If the magicians had been as powerful as God, they would have reversed the plagues, not added to them! Have you ever known someone who made matters worse for himself or herself? Using deception and other tricks of Satan usually turns matters from bad to worse. ■

A PLAGUE OF BLOOD

14 Then the LORD said to Moses, "Pharaoh's heart is stubborn,* and he still refuses to let the people go. 15 So go to Pharaoh in the morning as he goes down to the river. Stand on the bank of the Nile and meet him there. Be sure to take along the staff that turned into a snake. 16 Then announce to him, 'The LORD, the God of the Hebrews, has sent me to tell you, "Let my people go, so they can worship me in the wilderness." Until now, you have refused to listen to him. 17 So this is what the LORD says: "I will show you that I am the LORD." Look! I will strike the water of the Nile with this staff in my hand, and the river will turn to blood. 18 The fish in it will die, and the river will stink. The Egyptians will not be able to drink any water from the Nile.'"

19 Then the LORD said to Moses: "Tell Aaron, 'Take your staff and raise your hand over the waters of Egypt—all its rivers, canals, ponds, and all the reservoirs. Turn all the water to blood. Everywhere in Egypt the water will turn to blood, even the water stored in wooden bowls and stone pots.'"

20 So Moses and Aaron did just as the LORD commanded them. As Pharaoh and all of his officials watched, Aaron raised his staff and struck the water of the Nile. Suddenly, the whole river turned to blood! 21 The fish in the river died, and the water became so foul that the Egyptians couldn't drink it. There was blood everywhere throughout the land of Egypt. 22 But again the magicians of Egypt used their magic, and they, too, turned water into blood. So Pharaoh's heart remained hard. He refused to listen to Moses and Aaron, just as the LORD had predicted. 23 Pharaoh returned to his palace and put the whole thing out of his mind. 24 Then all the Egyptians dug along the riverbank to find drinking water, for they couldn't drink the water from the Nile.

25 Seven days passed from the time the LORD struck the Nile.

7:9 Hebrew *tannin,* which elsewhere refers to a sea monster. Greek version translates it "dragon." 7:14 Hebrew *heavy.*

The Plagues	What Happened/Result
BLOOD	Fish die, the river stinks, the people are without water/Pharaoh's magicians duplicate the miracle by their magic, so Pharaoh is unmoved 7:14-24
FROGS	Frogs come up from the water and completely cover the land/Again Pharaoh's magicians duplicate the miracle by sorcery, and Pharaoh is unmoved 8:1-15
GNATS	All the dust of Egypt becomes a massive swarm of gnats/Magicians are unable to duplicate this and say it is the "finger of God," but Pharaoh's heart remains hard 8:16-19
FLIES	Swarms of flies cover the land/Pharaoh promises to let the Hebrews go but then hardens his heart and refuses 8:20-32
BOILS	Horrible boils break out on everyone in Egypt/Magicians cannot respond as they are struck down with boils as well—Pharaoh refuses to listen 9:8-12
HAIL	Hailstorms kill all the servants and animals left out or unprotected and strip or destroy almost every plant/Pharaoh admits his fault but then changes his mind and refuses to let the people go 9:13-35
LOCUSTS	Locusts cover Egypt and eat everything left by the hail/Pharaoh confesses his sin, but the Lord makes him stubborn once again 10:1-20
LIVESTOCK	All the Egyptians' livestock die—but none of Israel's is even sick/Pharaoh still refuses to let the people go 9:1-7
DEATH OF FIRSTBORN	The firstborn of all the people and animals of Egypt die—but Israel is spared/Pharaoh urges Israel to leave but changes his mind and chases after them 11:1–12:33
DARKNESS	Total darkness covers Egypt for three days so no one can even move—except the Hebrews, who have light as usual/Pharaoh again promises to let Israel go but again changes his mind 10:21-29

8

A PLAGUE OF FROGS

1*Then the LORD said to Moses, "Go back to Pharaoh and
announce to him, 'This is what the LORD says: Let my people go, so they can worship me. 2If you refuse to let them
go, I will send a plague of frogs across your entire land.
3The Nile River will swarm with frogs. They will come up
out of the river and into your palace, even into your bedroom and onto your bed! They will enter the houses of your
officials and your people. They will even jump into your
ovens and your kneading bowls. 4Frogs will jump on you,
your people, and all your officials.'"

5*Then the LORD said to Moses, "Tell Aaron, 'Raise the
staff in your hand over all the rivers, canals, and ponds of
Egypt, and bring up frogs over all the land.'" 6So Aaron
raised his hand over the waters of Egypt, and frogs came
up and covered the whole land! 7But the magicians were
able to do the same thing with their magic. They, too,
caused frogs to come up on the land of Egypt.

8Then Pharaoh summoned Moses and Aaron and
begged, "Plead with the LORD to take the frogs away from
me and my people. I will let your people go, so they can
offer sacrifices to the LORD."

9"You set the time!" Moses replied. "Tell me when you
want me to pray for you, your officials, and your people.
Then you and your houses will be rid of the frogs. They
will remain only in the Nile River."

10"Do it tomorrow," Pharaoh said.

"All right," Moses replied, "it will be as you have said.
Then you will know that there is no one like the LORD our
God. 11The frogs will leave you and your houses, your of-
ficials, and your people. They will remain only in the Nile
River."

12So Moses and Aaron left Pharaoh's palace, and Moses
cried out to the LORD about the frogs he had inflicted on

8:1 Verses 8:1-4 are numbered 7:26-29 in Hebrew text. 8:5 Verses 8:5-32 are numbered 8:1-28 in Hebrew text.

Pharaoh. 13And the LORD did just what Moses had predicted. The frogs in the houses, the courtyards, and the fields all died. 14The Egyptians piled them into great heaps, and a terrible stench filled the land. 15But when Pharaoh saw that relief had come, he became stubborn.* He refused to listen to Moses and Aaron, just as the LORD had predicted.

A PLAGUE OF GNATS

16So the LORD said to Moses, "Tell Aaron, 'Raise your staff and strike the ground. The dust will turn into swarms of gnats throughout the land of Egypt.'" 17So Moses and Aaron did just as the LORD had commanded them. When Aaron raised his hand and struck the ground with his staff, gnats infested the entire land, covering the Egyptians and their animals. All the dust in the land of Egypt turned into gnats. 18Pharaoh's magicians tried to do the same thing with their secret arts, but this time they failed. And the gnats covered everyone, people and animals alike.

19"This is the finger of God!" the magicians exclaimed to Pharaoh. But Pharaoh's heart remained hard. He wouldn't listen to them, just as the LORD had predicted.

A PLAGUE OF FLIES

20Then the LORD told Moses, "Get up early in the morning and stand in Pharaoh's way as he goes down to the river. Say to him, 'This is what the LORD says: Let my people go, so they can worship me. 21If you refuse, then I will send swarms of flies on you, your officials, your people, and all the houses. The Egyptian homes will be filled with flies, and the ground will be covered with them. 22But this time I will spare the region of Goshen, where my people live. No flies will be found there. Then you will know that I am the LORD and that I am present even in the heart of your land. 23I will make a clear distinction between* my people and your people. This miraculous sign will happen tomorrow.'"

24And the LORD did just as he had said. A thick swarm of flies filled Pharaoh's palace and the houses of his officials. The whole land of Egypt was thrown into chaos by the flies.

25Pharaoh called for Moses and Aaron. "All right! Go ahead and offer sacrifices to your God," he said. "But do it here in this land."

26But Moses replied, "That wouldn't be right. The Egyptians detest the sacrifices that we offer to the LORD our God. Look, if we offer our sacrifices here where the Egyptians can see us, they will stone us. 27We must take a three-day trip into the wilderness to offer sacrifices to the LORD our God, just as he has commanded us."

28 "All right, go ahead," Pharaoh replied. "I will let you go into the wilderness to offer sacrifices to the LORD your God. But don't go too far away. Now hurry and pray for me."

29Moses answered, "As soon as I leave you, I will pray to the LORD, and tomorrow the swarms of flies will disappear from you and your officials and all your people. But I am warning you, Pharaoh, don't lie to us again and refuse to let the people go to sacrifice to the LORD."

30So Moses left Pharaoh's palace and pleaded with the LORD to remove all the flies. 31And the LORD did as Moses asked and caused the swarms of flies to disappear from Pharaoh, his officials, and his people. Not a single fly remained. 32But Pharaoh again became stubborn and refused to let the people go.

9

A PLAGUE AGAINST LIVESTOCK

"Go back to Pharaoh," the LORD commanded Moses. "Tell him, 'This is what the LORD, the God of the Hebrews, says: Let my people go, so they can worship me. 2If you continue to hold them and refuse to let them go, 3the hand of the LORD will strike all your livestock—your horses, donkeys, camels, cattle, sheep, and goats—with a deadly plague. 4But the LORD will again make a distinction between the livestock of the Israelites and that of the Egyptians. Not a single one of Israel's animals will die! 5The LORD has already set the time for the plague to begin. He has declared that he will strike the land tomorrow.'"

DON'T GIVE UP! 9:1

God sent Moses a fifth time to Pharaoh with the demand to let his people go! Moses may have been tired and discouraged by this time, but he continued to obey. Is there a difficult conflict you must face again and again? As Moses discovered, persistence is rewarded. Don't give up! ■

6And the LORD did just as he had said. The next morning all the livestock of the Egyptians died, but the Israelites didn't lose a single animal. 7Pharaoh sent his officials to investigate, and they discovered that the Israelites had not lost a single animal! But even so, Pharaoh's heart remained stubborn,* and he still refused to let the people go.

A PLAGUE OF FESTERING BOILS

8Then the LORD said to Moses and Aaron, "Take handfuls of soot from a brick kiln, and have Moses toss it into the air while Pharaoh watches. 9The ashes will spread like fine dust over the whole land of Egypt, causing festering boils to break out on people and animals throughout the land."

10So they took soot from a brick kiln and went and stood before Pharaoh. As Pharaoh watched, Moses threw the soot into the air, and boils broke out on people and animals alike. 11Even the magicians were unable to stand before Moses, because the boils had broken out on them and all the Egyptians. 12But the LORD hardened Pharaoh's heart, and just as the LORD had predicted to Moses, Pharaoh refused to listen.

A PLAGUE OF HAIL

13Then the LORD said to Moses, "Get up early in the morning and stand before Pharaoh. Tell him, 'This is what the

8:15 Hebrew *made his heart heavy;* also in 8:32. **8:23** As in Greek and Latin versions; Hebrew reads *I will set redemption between.*
9:7 Hebrew *heavy.*

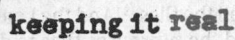

keeping it real

Whenever I get discouraged because I can't persuade a friend to believe the gospel, I remind myself that I can't convince someone who doesn't want to be convinced. See, there are some people that I wish were Christians. The fact that they don't believe has been tough for me to accept. But the story of Moses and Pharaoh helps me feel better. Nothing would convince Pharaoh that Moses represented the one true God—not plagues, not miracles, not even the death of Egypt's firstborn. If this kind of stuff couldn't move Pharaoh to believe in God, then I'm not surprised that Christians today have trouble convincing people about God.

Maybe the best tactic is the slow, steady work of Christ in our lives, coupled with prayer and our attempts to live the Christian life. I'm learning to place the rest in God's hands.

—Richard

LORD, the God of the Hebrews, says: Let my people go, so
they can worship me. 14If you don't, I will send more
plagues on you* and your officials and your people. Then
you will know that there is no one like me in all the earth.
15By now I could have lifted my hand and struck you and
your people with a plague to wipe you off the face of the
earth. 16But I have spared you for a purpose—to show you
my power* and to spread my fame throughout the earth.
17But you still lord it over my people and refuse to let
them go. 18So tomorrow at this time I will send a hailstorm more devastating than any in all the history of
Egypt. 19Quick! Order your livestock and servants to
come in from the fields to find shelter. Any person or animal left outside will die when the hail falls.'"
20Some of Pharaoh's officials were afraid because of
what the LORD had said. They quickly brought their servants and livestock in from the fields. 21But those who
paid no attention to the word of the LORD left theirs out in
the open.
22Then the LORD said to Moses, "Lift your hand toward
the sky so hail may fall on the people, the livestock, and all
the plants throughout the land of Egypt."
23So Moses lifted his staff toward the sky, and the LORD
sent thunder and hail, and lightning flashed toward the
earth. The LORD sent a tremendous hailstorm against all
the land of Egypt. 24Never in all the history of Egypt had
there been a storm like that, with such devastating hail
and continuous lightning. 25It left all of Egypt in ruins.
The hail struck down everything in the open field—people, animals, and plants alike. Even the trees were destroyed. 26The only place without hail was the region of
Goshen, where the people of Israel lived.
27Then Pharaoh quickly summoned Moses and Aaron.
"This time I have sinned," he confessed. "The LORD is the
righteous one, and my people and I are wrong. 28Please
beg the LORD to end this terrifying thunder and hail.
We've had enough. I will let you go; you don't need to stay
any longer."
29"All right," Moses replied. "As soon as I leave the city,
I will lift my hands and pray to the LORD. Then the thunder and hail will stop, and you will know that the earth belongs to the LORD. 30But I know that you and your officials
still do not fear the LORD God."
31(All the flax and barley were ruined by the hail, because the barley had formed heads and the flax was bud-
ding. 32But the wheat and the emmer wheat were spared,
because they had not yet sprouted from the ground.)
33So Moses left Pharaoh's court and went out of the
city. When he lifted his hands to the LORD, the thunder
and hail stopped, and the downpour ceased. 34But when
Pharaoh saw that the rain, hail, and thunder had stopped,
he and his officials sinned again, and Pharaoh again became stubborn.* 35Because his heart was hard, Pharaoh
refused to let the people leave, just as the LORD had predicted through Moses.

10 A PLAGUE OF LOCUSTS

Then the LORD said to Moses, "Return to Pharaoh and
make your demands again. I have made him and his officials stubborn* so I can display my miraculous signs
among them. 2I've also done it so you can tell your children and grandchildren about how I made a mockery of
the Egyptians and about the signs I displayed among
them—and so you will know that I am the LORD."
3So Moses and Aaron went to Pharaoh and said, "This
is what the LORD, the God of the Hebrews, says: How long
will you refuse to submit to me? Let my people go, so they
can worship me. 4If you refuse, watch out! For tomorrow I
will bring a swarm of locusts on your country. 5They will
cover the land so that you won't be able to see the ground.

9:14 Hebrew *on your heart*. 9:16 Greek version reads *to display my power in you;* compare Rom 9:17. 9:34 Hebrew *made his heart heavy*.
10:1 Hebrew *have made his heart and his officials' hearts heavy*.

They will devour what little is left of your crops after the hailstorm, including all the trees growing in the fields. 6They will overrun your palaces and the homes of your officials and all the houses in Egypt. Never in the history of Egypt have your ancestors seen a plague like this one!" And with that, Moses turned and left Pharaoh.

7Pharaoh's officials now came to Pharaoh and appealed to him. "How long will you let this man hold us hostage? Let the men go to worship the LORD their God! Don't you realize that Egypt lies in ruins?"

8So Moses and Aaron were brought back to Pharaoh. "All right," he told them, "go and worship the LORD your God. But who exactly will be going with you?"

9Moses replied, "We will all go—young and old, our sons and daughters, and our flocks and herds. We must all join together in celebrating a festival to the LORD."

10Pharaoh retorted, "The LORD will certainly need to be with you if I let you take your little ones! I can see through your evil plan. 11Never! Only the men may go and worship the LORD, since that is what you requested." And Pharaoh threw them out of the palace.

12Then the LORD said to Moses, "Raise your hand over the land of Egypt to bring on the locusts. Let them cover the land and devour every plant that survived the hailstorm."

13So Moses raised his staff over Egypt, and the LORD caused an east wind to blow over the land all that day and through the night. When morning arrived, the east wind had brought the locusts. 14And the locusts swarmed over the whole land of Egypt, settling in dense swarms from one end of the country to the other. It was the worst locust plague in Egyptian history, and there has never been another one like it. 15For the locusts covered the whole country and darkened the land. They devoured every plant in the fields and all the fruit on the trees that had survived the hailstorm. Not a single leaf was left on the trees and plants throughout the land of Egypt.

16Pharaoh quickly summoned Moses and Aaron. "I have sinned against the LORD your God and against you," he confessed. 17"Forgive my sin, just this once, and plead with the LORD your God to take away this death from me."

18So Moses left Pharaoh's court and pleaded with the LORD. 19The LORD responded by shifting the wind, and the strong west wind blew the locusts into the Red Sea.* Not a single locust remained in all the land of Egypt. 20But the LORD hardened Pharaoh's heart again, so he refused to let the people go.

A PLAGUE OF DARKNESS

21Then the LORD said to Moses, "Lift your hand toward heaven, and the land of Egypt will be covered with a darkness so thick you can feel it." 22So Moses lifted his hand to the sky, and a deep darkness covered the entire land of Egypt for three days. 23During all that time the people could not see each other, and no one moved. But there was light as usual where the people of Israel lived.

24Finally, Pharaoh called for Moses. "Go and worship the LORD," he said. "But leave your flocks and herds here. You may even take your little ones with you."

25"No," Moses said, "you must provide us with animals for sacrifices and burnt offerings to the LORD our God. 26All our livestock must go with us, too; not a hoof can be left behind. We must choose our sacrifices for the LORD our God from among these animals. And we won't know how we are to worship the LORD until we get there."

27But the LORD hardened Pharaoh's heart once more, and he would not let them go. 28"Get out of here!" Pharaoh shouted at Moses. "I'm warning you. Never come back to see me again! The day you see my face, you will die!"

29"Very well," Moses replied. "I will never see your face again."

11 DEATH FOR EGYPT'S FIRSTBORN

Then the LORD said to Moses, "I will strike Pharaoh and the land of Egypt with one more blow. After that, Pharaoh will let you leave this country. In fact, he will be so eager to get rid of you that he will force you all to leave. 2Tell all the Israelite men and women to ask their Egyptian neighbors for articles of silver and gold." 3(Now the LORD had caused the Egyptians to look favorably on the people of Israel. And Moses was considered a very great man in the land of Egypt, respected by Pharaoh's officials and the Egyptian people alike.)

HARD-HEARTED 11:10

Did God really harden Pharaoh's heart and force him to do wrong? Before the ten plagues began, Moses and Aaron announced what God would do if Pharaoh didn't let the people go. When it became evident that Pharaoh wouldn't change, God confirmed Pharaoh's prideful decision and set the painful consequences of his actions in motion. These days, are you tempted to say, "My will be done?" When God says, "Okay, *your* will be done," look out! ■

4Moses had announced to Pharaoh, "This is what the LORD says: At midnight tonight I will pass through the heart of Egypt. 5All the firstborn sons will die in every family in Egypt, from the oldest son of Pharaoh, who sits on his throne, to the oldest son of his lowliest servant girl who grinds the flour. Even the firstborn of all the livestock will die. 6Then a loud wail will rise throughout the land of Egypt, a wail like no one has heard before or will ever hear again. 7But among the Israelites it will be so peaceful that not even a dog will bark. Then you will know that the LORD makes a distinction between the Egyptians and the Israelites. 8All the officials of Egypt will run to me and fall to the ground before me. 'Please leave!' they will beg. 'Hurry! And take all your followers with you.' Only then will I go!" Then, burning with anger, Moses left Pharaoh.

9Now the LORD had told Moses earlier, "Pharaoh will

10:19 Hebrew *sea of reeds.*

not listen to you, but then I will do even more mighty miracles in the land of Egypt." 10 Moses and Aaron performed these miracles in Pharaoh's presence, but the LORD hardened Pharaoh's heart, and he wouldn't let the Israelites leave the country.

12 THE FIRST PASSOVER

While the Israelites were still in the land of Egypt, the LORD gave the following instructions to Moses and Aaron: 2 "From now on, this month will be the first month of the year for you. 3 Announce to the whole community of Israel that on the tenth day of this month each family must choose a lamb or a young goat for a sacrifice, one animal for each household. 4 If a family is too small to eat a whole animal, let them share with another family in the neighborhood. Divide the animal according to the size of each family and how much they can eat. 5 The animal you select must be a one-year-old male, either a sheep or a goat, with no defects.

6 "Take special care of this chosen animal until the evening of the fourteenth day of this first month. Then the whole assembly of the community of Israel must slaughter their lamb or young goat at twilight. 7 They are to take some of the blood and smear it on the sides and top of the doorframes of the houses where they eat the animal. 8 That same night they must roast the meat over a fire and eat it along with bitter salad greens and bread made without yeast. 9 Do not eat any of the meat raw or boiled in water. The whole animal—including the head, legs, and internal organs—must be roasted over a fire. 10 Do not leave any of it until the next morning. Burn whatever is not eaten before morning.

11 "These are your instructions for eating this meal: Be fully dressed,* wear your sandals, and carry your walking stick in your hand. Eat the meal with urgency, for this is the LORD's Passover. 12 On that night I will pass through the land of Egypt and strike down every firstborn son and firstborn male animal in the land of Egypt. I will execute judgment against all the gods of Egypt, for I am the LORD! 13 But the blood on your doorposts will serve as a sign, marking the houses where you are staying. When I see the blood, I will pass over you. This plague of death will not touch you when I strike the land of Egypt.

14 "This is a day to remember. Each year, from generation to generation, you must celebrate it as a special festival to the LORD. This is a law for all time. 15 For seven days the bread you eat must be made without yeast. On the first day of the festival, remove every trace of yeast from your homes. Anyone who eats bread made with yeast during the seven days of the festival will be cut off from the community of Israel. 16 On the first day of the festival and again on the seventh day, all the people must observe an official day for holy assembly. No work of any kind may be done on these days except in the preparation of food.

17 "Celebrate this Festival of Unleavened Bread, for it will remind you that I brought your forces out of the land of Egypt on this very day. This festival will be a permanent law for you; celebrate this day from generation to generation. 18 The bread you eat must be made without yeast from the evening of the fourteenth day of the first month until the evening of the twenty-first day of that month. 19 During those seven days, there must be no trace of yeast in your homes. Anyone who eats anything made with yeast during this week will be cut off from the community of Israel. These regulations apply both to the foreigners living among you and to the native-born Israelites. 20 During those days you must not eat anything made with yeast. Wherever you live, eat only bread made without yeast."

21 Then Moses called all the elders of Israel together and said to them, "Go, pick out a lamb or young goat for each of your families, and slaughter the Passover animal. 22 Drain the blood into a basin. Then take a bundle of hyssop branches and dip it into the blood. Brush the hyssop across the top and sides of the doorframes of your houses. And no one may go out through the door until morning. 23 For the LORD will pass through the land to strike down the Egyptians. But when he sees the blood on the top and sides of the doorframe, the LORD will pass over your home. He will not permit his death angel to enter your house and strike you down.

SUBSTITUTE 12:1-30

While every firstborn child of the Egyptians died, the Israelite children were spared. Why? Because of the lambs' blood on the doorposts of their homes, the angel of death passed them by. This is a story of redemption, the central theme of the Bible. *Redemption* means "to buy back." But the Passover story is not the only redemption story. Jesus Christ redeemed us by his death on the cross. Our part is to trust him and accept his gift of eternal life (Titus 2:14; Heb 9:13-15, 23-28). Have you? ■

24 "Remember, these instructions are a permanent law that you and your descendants must observe forever. 25 When you enter the land the LORD has promised to give you, you will continue to observe this ceremony. 26 Then your children will ask, 'What does this ceremony mean?' 27 And you will reply, 'It is the Passover sacrifice to the LORD, for he passed over the houses of the Israelites in Egypt. And though he struck the Egyptians, he spared our families.' " When Moses had finished speaking, all the people bowed down to the ground and worshiped.

28 So the people of Israel did just as the LORD had commanded through Moses and Aaron. 29 And that night at midnight, the LORD struck down all the firstborn sons in the land of Egypt, from the firstborn son of Pharaoh, who sat on his throne, to the firstborn son of the prisoner in the dungeon. Even the firstborn of their livestock were killed. 30 Pharaoh and all his officials and all the people of Egypt woke up during the night, and loud wailing was heard throughout the land of Egypt. There was not a single house where someone had not died.

12:11 Hebrew *Bind up your loins.*

ISRAEL'S EXODUS FROM EGYPT

31 Pharaoh sent for Moses and Aaron during the night. "Get out!" he ordered. "Leave my people—and take the rest of the Israelites with you! Go and worship the LORD as you have requested. 32 Take your flocks and herds, as you said, and be gone. Go, but bless me as you leave." 33 All the Egyptians urged the people of Israel to get out of the land as quickly as possible, for they thought, "We will all die!"

34 The Israelites took their bread dough before yeast was added. They wrapped their kneading boards in their cloaks and carried them on their shoulders. 35 And the people of Israel did as Moses had instructed; they asked the Egyptians for clothing and articles of silver and gold. 36 The LORD caused the Egyptians to look favorably on the Israelites, and they gave the Israelites whatever they asked for. So they stripped the Egyptians of their wealth!

37 That night the people of Israel left Rameses and started for Succoth. There were about 600,000 men,* plus all the women and children. 38 A rabble of non-Israelites went with them, along with great flocks and herds of livestock. 39 For bread they baked flat cakes from the dough without yeast they had brought from Egypt. It was made without yeast because the people were driven out of Egypt in such a hurry that they had no time to prepare the bread or other food.

40 The people of Israel had lived in Egypt* for 430 years. 41 In fact, it was on the last day of the 430th year that all the LORD's forces left the land. 42 On this night the LORD kept his promise to bring his people out of the land of Egypt. So this night belongs to him, and it must be commemorated every year by all the Israelites, from generation to generation.

INSTRUCTIONS FOR THE PASSOVER

43 Then the LORD said to Moses and Aaron, "These are the instructions for the festival of Passover. No outsiders are allowed to eat the Passover meal. 44 But any slave who has been purchased may eat it if he has been circumcised. 45 Temporary residents and hired servants may not eat it. 46 Each Passover lamb must be eaten in one house. Do not carry any of its meat outside, and do not break any of its bones. 47 The whole community of Israel must celebrate this Passover festival.

48 "If there are foreigners living among you who want to celebrate the LORD's Passover, let all their males be circumcised. Only then may they celebrate the Passover with you like any native-born Israelite. But no uncircumcised male may ever eat the Passover meal. 49 This instruction applies to everyone, whether a native-born Israelite or a foreigner living among you."

50 So all the people of Israel followed all the LORD's commands to Moses and Aaron. 51 On that very day the LORD brought the people of Israel out of the land of Egypt like an army.

13

DEDICATION OF THE FIRSTBORN

Then the LORD said to Moses, 2 "Dedicate to me every firstborn among the Israelites. The first offspring to be born, of both humans and animals, belongs to me."

BRANDED 13:9

The Festival of Unleavened Bread marked the Hebrews as a unique people—as though they were branded on their hands and foreheads. What actions or attitudes mark you as a follower of God? Think about the way you act at school, in the neighborhood, and at home. What you do in these areas will leave visible marks for all to see. Do you bear the marks of God's love? ■

3 So Moses said to the people, "This is a day to remember forever—the day you left Egypt, the place of your slavery. Today the LORD has brought you out by the power of his mighty hand. (Remember, eat no food containing yeast.) 4 On this day in early spring, in the month of Abib,* you have been set free. 5 You must celebrate this event in this month each year after the LORD brings you into the land of the Canaanites, Hittites, Amorites, Hivites, and Jebusites. (He swore to your ancestors that he would give you this land—a land flowing with milk and honey.) 6 For seven days the bread you eat must be made without yeast. Then on the seventh day, celebrate a feast to the LORD. 7 Eat bread without yeast during those seven days. In fact, there must be no yeast bread or any yeast at all found within the borders of your land during this time.

OBSTACLES 13:17-18

God doesn't always work in the way that seems best to us. Instead of guiding the Israelites along the direct route from Egypt to the Promised Land, he decided to take them by a longer route. By going that way, they would avoid a conflict with the Philistines. When God doesn't lead you along the shortest path to your goal, are you tempted to complain or resist? If not, are you willing to trust him to lead you safely around unseen obstacles? Since he can see your whole journey from the beginning to the end, he knows the safest and best route to take you. ■

8 "On the seventh day you must explain to your children, 'I am celebrating what the LORD did for me when I left Egypt.' 9 This annual festival will be a visible sign to you, like a mark branded on your hand or your forehead. Let it remind you always to recite this teaching of the LORD: 'With a strong hand, the LORD rescued you from Egypt.'* 10 So observe the decree of this festival at the appointed time each year.

12:37 Or *fighting men;* Hebrew reads *men on foot.* 12:40 Samaritan Pentateuch reads *in Canaan and Egypt;* Greek version reads *in Egypt and Canaan.* 13:4 Hebrew *On this day in the month of Abib.* This first month of the ancient Hebrew lunar calendar usually occurs within the months of March and April. 13:9 Or *Let it remind you always to keep the instructions of the LORD on the tip of your tongue, because with a strong hand, the LORD rescued you from Egypt.*

The Hebrew Calendar

The Hebrew lunar months, based on the earth's relationship with the moon, fluctuate in relationship to our modern calendar, which is based on the the earth's relationship to the sun. Thus, the Hebrew months often begin in the middle of the months of our modern calendar. Food crops in the Ancient Near East were normally planted in the fall months of October and November and then harvested the next spring between March and June.

MONTH	TODAY'S CALENDAR	BIBLE REFERENCE	ISRAEL'S HOLIDAYS
1 Nisan (Abib)	March–April	Exodus 13:4; 23:15; 34:18; Deuteronomy 16:1; Esther 3:7	Passover (Lev 23:5); Unleavened Bread (Lev 23:6) Firstfruits (Lev 23:10)
2 Iyyar (Ziv)	April–May	1 Kings 6:1-37	
3 Sivan	May–June	Esther 8:9	Harvest (Pentecost) (Lev 23:15)
4 Tammuz	June–July		
5 Ab	July–August		
6 Elul	August–September	Nehemiah 6:15	
7 Tishri (Ethanim)	September–October	1 Kings 8:2	Trumpets (Lev 23:24; Num 29:1); Day of Atonement (Lev 23:27); Shelters (Tabernacles) (Lev 23:34)
8 Marchesvan (Bul)	October–November	1 Kings 6:38	
9 Chislev (Kislev)	November–December	Nehemiah 1:1	Hanukkah (John 10:22)
10 Tebeth	December–January	Zechariah 1:7	
12 Adar	February–March	Esther 3:7	Purim (Esther 9:24-32)

11"This is what you must do when the LORD fulfills the
promise he swore to you and to your ancestors. When he
gives you the land where the Canaanites now live, 12you
must present all firstborn sons and firstborn male animals to the LORD, for they belong to him. 13A firstborn
donkey may be bought back from the LORD by presenting
a lamb or young goat in its place. But if you do not buy it
back, you must break its neck. However, you must buy
back every firstborn son.
14"And in the future, your children will ask you, 'What
does all this mean?' Then you will tell them, 'With the
power of his mighty hand, the LORD brought us out of
Egypt, the place of our slavery. 15Pharaoh stubbornly refused to let us go, so the LORD killed all the firstborn
males throughout the land of Egypt, both people and
animals. That is why I now sacrifice all the firstborn
males to the LORD—except that the firstborn sons are always bought back.' 16This ceremony will be like a mark
branded on your hand or your forehead. It is a reminder
that the power of the LORD's mighty hand brought us out
of Egypt."

ISRAEL'S WILDERNESS DETOUR

17When Pharaoh finally let the people go, God did not
lead them along the main road that runs through Philistine territory, even though that was the shortest
route to the Promised Land. God said, "If the people
are faced with a battle, they might change their minds
and return to Egypt." 18So God led them in a roundabout way through the wilderness toward the Red

Sea.* Thus the Israelites left Egypt like an army ready for
battle.*
[19]Moses took the bones of Joseph with him, for Joseph
had made the sons of Israel swear to do this. He said,
"God will certainly come to help you. When he does, you
must take my bones with you from this
place."
[20]The Israelites left Succoth and
camped at Etham on the edge of the
wilderness. [21]The LORD went ahead of
them. He guided them during the day
with a pillar of cloud, and he provided
light at night with a pillar of fire. This
allowed them to travel by day or by
night. [22]And the LORD did not remove
the pillar of cloud or pillar of fire from
its place in front of the people.

> Don't be afraid. Just stand still and watch the LORD rescue you today.
>
> EXODUS 14:13

14 Then the LORD gave these
instructions to Moses: [2]"Order the Israelites to turn back and camp by Pi-hahiroth between
Migdol and the sea. Camp there along the shore, across
from Baal-zephon. [3]Then Pharaoh will think, 'The Israelites are confused. They are trapped in the wilderness!'
[4]And once again I will harden Pharaoh's heart, and he will
chase after you.* I have planned this in order to display
my glory through Pharaoh and his whole army. After this
the Egyptians will know that I am the LORD!" So the Israelites camped there as they were told.

THE EGYPTIANS PURSUE ISRAEL

[5]When word reached the king of Egypt that the Israelites
had fled, Pharaoh and his officials changed their minds.
"What have we done, letting all those Israelite slaves get
away?" they asked. [6]So Pharaoh har-
nessed his chariot and called up his
troops. [7]He took with him 600 of
Egypt's best chariots, along with the
rest of the chariots of Egypt, each with
its commander. [8]The LORD hardened
the heart of Pharaoh, the king of Egypt,
so he chased after the people of Israel,
who had left with fists raised in defiance. [9]The Egyptians chased after
them with all the forces in Pharaoh's
army—all his horses and chariots, his
charioteers, and his troops. The Egyptians caught up with the people of Israel as they were camped beside the
shore near Pi-hahiroth, across from
Baal-zephon.
[10]As Pharaoh approached, the people of Israel looked
up and panicked when they saw the Egyptians overtaking
them. They cried out to the LORD, [11]and they said to
Moses, "Why did you bring us out here to die in the wilderness? Weren't there enough graves for us in Egypt?
What have you done to us? Why did you make us leave
Egypt? [12]Didn't we tell you this would happen while we
were still in Egypt? We said, 'Leave us alone! Let us be
slaves to the Egyptians. It's better to be a slave in Egypt
than a corpse in the wilderness!'"
[13]But Moses told the people, "Don't be afraid. Just
stand still and watch the LORD rescue
you today. The Egyptians you see today
will never be seen again. [14]The LORD
himself will fight for you. Just stay
calm."

ESCAPE THROUGH THE RED SEA

[15]Then the LORD said to Moses, "Why
are you crying out to me? Tell the people to get moving! [16]Pick up your staff
and raise your hand over the sea. Divide the water so the Israelites can
walk through the middle of the sea on
dry ground. [17]And I will harden the
hearts of the Egyptians, and they will
charge in after the Israelites. My great
glory will be displayed through Pharaoh and his troops,
his chariots, and his charioteers. [18]When my glory is displayed through them, all Egypt will see my glory and
know that I am the LORD!"
[19]Then the angel of God, who had been leading the
people of Israel, moved to the rear of the camp. The pillar
of cloud also moved from the front and stood behind
them. [20]The cloud settled between the Egyptian and Israelite camps. As darkness fell, the cloud turned to fire,
lighting up the night. But the Egyptians and Israelites did
not approach each other all night.
[21]Then Moses raised his hand over the sea, and the
LORD opened up a path through the water with a strong
east wind. The wind blew all that night, turning the sea-
bed into dry land. [22]So the people of Israel walked through the middle of the
sea on dry ground, with walls of water
on each side!
[23]Then the Egyptians—all of Pharaoh's horses, chariots, and charioteers—chased them into the middle
of the sea. [24]But just before dawn the
LORD looked down on the Egyptian
army from the pillar of fire and cloud,
and he threw their forces into total
confusion. [25]He twisted* their chariot
wheels, making their chariots difficult
to drive. "Let's get out of here—away
from these Israelites!" the Egyptians
shouted. "The LORD is fighting for
them against Egypt!"

> The LORD himself will fight for you.
>
> EXODUS 14:14

[26]When all the Israelites had reached the other side,
the LORD said to Moses, "Raise your hand over the sea
again. Then the waters will rush back and cover the Egyptians and their chariots and charioteers." [27]So as the sun
began to rise, Moses raised his hand over the sea, and the
water rushed back into its usual place. The Egyptians

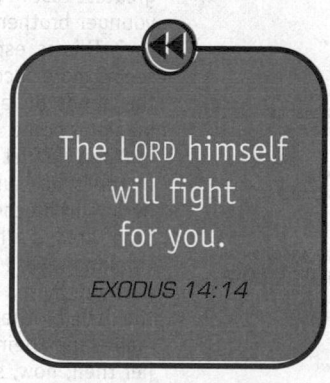

13:18a Hebrew *sea of reeds.* 13:18b Greek version reads *left Egypt in the fifth generation.* 14:4 Hebrew *after them.* 14:25 As in Greek version, Samaritan Pentateuch, and Syriac version; Hebrew reads *He removed.*

tried to escape, but the LORD swept them into the sea. 28Then the waters returned and covered all the chariots and charioteers—the entire army of Pharaoh. Of all the Egyptians who had chased the Israelites into the sea, not a single one survived.

GET MOVING! 14:15

While the people of Israel grumbled at the Red Sea, God told Moses to stop praying and get moving! He promised to help the Israelites once they moved forward in faith. Although prayer deserves a vital place in our life, there also is a place for action. Sometimes we know what to do, but we pray for more guidance as an excuse to postpone a faith action. Got a Red Sea in your life? If you know what you need to do, what are you waiting for? ■

29But the people of Israel had walked through the middle of the sea on dry ground, as the water stood up like a wall on both sides. 30That is how the LORD rescued Israel from the hand of the Egyptians that day. And the Israelites saw the bodies of the Egyptians washed up on the seashore. 31When the people of Israel saw the mighty power that the LORD had unleashed against the Egyptians, they were filled with awe before him. They put their faith in the LORD and in his servant Moses.

15 A SONG OF DELIVERANCE

Then Moses and the people of Israel sang this song to the LORD:

"I will sing to the LORD,
for he has triumphed gloriously;
he has hurled both horse and rider
into the sea.
2 The LORD is my strength and my song;
he has given me victory.
This is my God, and I will praise him—
my father's God, and I will exalt him!
3 The LORD is a warrior;
Yahweh* is his name!
4 Pharaoh's chariots and army
he has hurled into the sea.
The finest of Pharaoh's officers
are drowned in the Red Sea.*
5 The deep waters gushed over them;
they sank to the bottom like a stone.

6 "Your right hand, O LORD,
is glorious in power.
Your right hand, O LORD,
smashes the enemy.
7 In the greatness of your majesty,
you overthrow those who rise against you.

15:3 *Yahweh* is a transliteration of the proper name *YHWH* that is sometimes rendered "Jehovah"; in this translation it is usually rendered "the LORD" (note the use of small capitals). 15:4 Hebrew *sea of reeds;* also in 15:22.

MIRIAM

UPS:
- Quick thinker under pressure
- Able leader
- Songwriter
- Prophetess

DOWNS:
- Was envious of Moses' authority
- Openly criticized Moses' leadership

STATS:
- Where: Egypt, Sinai Peninsula
- Relatives: Aaron and Moses (brothers)

LESSON:
The motives behind criticism are often more important to deal with than the criticism itself.

Miriam's story is told in Exod 2 and 15; Num 12 and 20:1. She also is mentioned in Deut 24:9; 1 Chron 6:3; Mic 6:4.

MIRIAM Ask older brothers or sisters what their greatest test in life is and they will often answer, "My younger brother (or sister)!" Is that what you would say? This is especially true when the younger one seems more successful than the older. At such times, the bonds of family loyalty can be stretched to the breaking point.

When we first meet Miriam, she is involved in one of history's most unusual baby-sitting jobs: She watches her infant brother float down the Nile River in a waterproof cradle. When the baby is found, Miriam's quick thinking saves Moses and even allows him to be raised partially by his own mother. But it isn't long before the little brother she had protected grows into a great man—and their relationship changes. Moses needed her then; now, she needed him. The change probably wasn't easy for Miriam.

Instead of appreciating what God was doing in her brother's life, Miriam chose to criticize. Sound familiar? God had to teach Miriam and her other brother Aaron that each had a unique part in his plans. Being envious of one another was wrong.

The same lesson applies to our families. What difference would it make in your family if every criticism were changed into an encouraging or loving statement? Are you willing to model this new trend?

Famous Songs in the Bible

WHERE	PURPOSE OF SONG
Exodus 15:1-21	Moses' song of victory and praise after God led Israel out of Egypt and saved them by parting the Red Sea; Miriam joined in the singing, too
Numbers 21:17-18	Israel's song of praise to God for giving them water in the wilderness
Deuteronomy 32:1-43	Moses' song of Israel's history with thanksgiving and praise as the Hebrews were about to enter the Promised Land
Judges 5:2-31	Deborah and Barak's song of praise thanking God for Israel's victory over King Jabin's army at Mount Tabor
2 Samuel 22:1-51	David's song of thanks and praise to God for rescuing him from Saul and his other enemies
Song of Songs	Solomon's song of love celebrating the union of husband and wife
Isaiah 26:1	Isaiah's prophetic song about how the redeemed will sing in the new Jerusalem
Ezra 3:11	Israel's song of praise at the completion of the Temple's foundation
Luke 1:46-55	Mary's song of praise to God for the conception of Jesus
Luke 1:68-79	Zechariah's song of praise for the promise of a son
Acts 16:25	Paul and Silas sang hymns in prison
Revelation 5:9-10	The "new song" of the 24 elders acclaiming Christ as worthy to break the seven seals of God's scroll
Revelation 14:3	The song of the 144,000 redeemed from the earth
Revelation 15:3-4	The song of all the redeemed in praise of the Lamb who redeemed them

You unleash your blazing fury;
it consumes them like straw.
8 At the blast of your breath,
the waters piled up!
The surging waters stood straight like a wall;
in the heart of the sea the deep waters became hard.

9 "The enemy boasted, 'I will chase them
and catch up with them.
I will plunder them
and consume them.
I will flash my sword;
my powerful hand will destroy them.'
10 But you blew with your breath,
and the sea covered them.
They sank like lead
in the mighty waters.

11 "Who is like you among the gods, O LORD—
glorious in holiness,
awesome in splendor,
performing great wonders?
12 You raised your right hand,
and the earth swallowed our enemies.

13 "With your unfailing love you lead
the people you have redeemed.
In your might, you guide them
to your sacred home.
14 The peoples hear and tremble;
anguish grips those who live in Philistia.
15 The leaders of Edom are terrified;
the nobles of Moab tremble.
All who live in Canaan melt away;
16 terror and dread fall upon them.

The power of your arm
makes them lifeless as stone
until your people pass by, O LORD,
until the people you purchased pass by.
17 You will bring them in and plant them on your own
mountain—
the place, O LORD, reserved for your own dwelling,
the sanctuary, O Lord, that your hands have
established.
18 The LORD will reign forever and ever!"

19When Pharaoh's horses, chariots, and charioteers
rushed into the sea, the LORD brought the water crashing
down on them. But the people of Israel had walked
through the middle of the sea on dry ground!
20Then Miriam the prophet, Aaron's sister, took a tambourine and led all the women as they played their tambourines and danced. 21And Miriam sang this song:

"Sing to the LORD,
for he has triumphed gloriously;
he has hurled both horse and rider
into the sea."

BITTER WATER AT MARAH

22Then Moses led the people of Israel away from the Red
Sea, and they moved out into the desert of Shur. They
traveled in this desert for three days without finding any
water. 23When they came to the oasis of Marah, the water
was too bitter to drink. So they called the place Marah
(which means "bitter").
24Then the people complained and turned against
Moses. "What are we going to drink?" they demanded.
25So Moses cried out to the LORD for help, and the LORD
showed him a piece of wood. Moses threw it into the water, and this made the water good to drink.

PROTECTION FROM DISEASES 15:26

God promised that if the people obeyed him they would be free from the diseases that plagued the Egyptians. Little did they know that following his rules would help keep them free from diseases. For example, following God's law against prostitution would guard them against sexually transmitted diseases. Today, God's laws still keep us from harm. But he can't protect us if we don't submit to his directions for living. ■

It was there at Marah that the LORD set before them the
following decree as a standard to test their faithfulness
to him. 26He said, "If you will listen carefully to the voice
of the LORD your God and do what is right in his sight,
obeying his commands and keeping all his decrees, then I
will not make you suffer any of the diseases I sent on the
Egyptians; for I am the LORD who heals you."
27After leaving Marah, the Israelites traveled on to the
oasis of Elim, where they found twelve springs and seventy palm trees. They camped there beside the water.

16 MANNA AND QUAIL FROM HEAVEN

Then the whole community of Israel set out from Elim
and journeyed into the wilderness of Sin,* between Elim
and Mount Sinai. They arrived there on the fifteenth day
of the second month, one month after leaving the land of
Egypt.* 2There, too, the whole community of Israel complained about Moses and Aaron.

STRESSED OUT 16:1-3

It happened again. As the Israelites encountered danger, shortages, and inconvenience, they complained bitterly and longed to be back in Egypt. They didn't really want to be back in Egypt; they just wanted life to get a little easier. In the pressure of the moment, they couldn't focus on the cause of their stress (in this case, lack of trust in God). Instead, they could only think about the quickest way of escape. When you're in a tight spot, do you complain or carry on? Focusing on God's power and wisdom can help you deal with the cause of your stress and possibly overcome it. ■

3"If only the LORD had killed us back in Egypt," they
moaned. "There we sat around pots filled with meat and
ate all the bread we wanted. But now you have brought us
into this wilderness to starve us all to death."
4Then the LORD said to Moses, "Look, I'm going to rain
down food from heaven for you. Each day the people can
go out and pick up as much food as they need for that
day. I will test them in this to see whether or not they will
follow my instructions. 5On the sixth day they will gather
food, and when they prepare it, there will be twice as
much as usual."
6So Moses and Aaron said to all the people of Israel, "By
evening you will realize it was the LORD who brought you
out of the land of Egypt. 7In the morning you will see the
glory of the LORD, because he has heard your complaints,
which are against him, not against us. What have we done
that you should complain about us?" 8Then Moses added,
"The LORD will give you meat to eat in the evening and
bread to satisfy you in the morning, for he has heard all
your complaints against him. What have we done? Yes,
your complaints are against the LORD, not against us."
9Then Moses said to Aaron, "Announce this to the entire community of Israel: 'Present yourselves before the
LORD, for he has heard your complaining.'" 10And as
Aaron spoke to the whole community of Israel, they
looked out toward the wilderness. There they could see
the awesome glory of the LORD in the cloud.
11Then the LORD said to Moses, 12"I have heard the Israelites' complaints. Now tell them, 'In the evening you will
have meat to eat, and in the morning you will have all the

16:1a The geographical name *Sin* is related to *Sinai* and should not be confused with the English word *sin*. 16:1b The Exodus had occurred on the fifteenth day of the first month (see Num 33:3).

bread you want. Then you will know that I am the LORD your God.'"

13That evening vast numbers of quail flew in and covered the camp. And the next morning the area around the camp was wet with dew. 14When the dew evaporated, a flaky substance as fine as frost blanketed the ground. 15The Israelites were puzzled when they saw it. "What is it?" they asked each other. They had no idea what it was.

And Moses told them, "It is the food the LORD has given you to eat. 16These are the LORD's instructions: Each household should gather as much as it needs. Pick up two quarts* for each person in your tent."

17So the people of Israel did as they were told. Some gathered a lot, some only a little. 18But when they measured it out,* everyone had just enough. Those who gathered a lot had nothing left over, and those who gathered only a little had enough. Each family had just what it needed.

19Then Moses told them, "Do not keep any of it until morning." 20But some of them didn't listen and kept some of it until morning. But by then it was full of maggots and had a terrible smell. Moses was very angry with them.

21After this the people gathered the food morning by morning, each family according to its need. And as the sun became hot, the flakes they had not picked up melted and disappeared. 22On the sixth day, they gathered twice as much as usual—four quarts* for each person instead of two. Then all the leaders of the community came and asked Moses for an explanation. 23He told them, "This is what the LORD commanded: Tomorrow will be a day of complete rest, a holy Sabbath day set apart for the LORD. So bake or boil as much as you want today, and set aside what is left for tomorrow."

A TIME OUT WITH GOD 16:23

The Israelites were not supposed to work on the Sabbath. Even cooking food was viewed as work. God knew that the busy routine of daily living could distract people from worshiping him. He wanted his people to rest from their labors and focus on him. It is so easy to let school, friends, and other activities crowd our schedules so tightly that we don't spend regular time with God. How do you guard your time with God? ■

24So they put some aside until morning, just as Moses had commanded. And in the morning the leftover food was wholesome and good, without maggots or odor. 25Moses said, "Eat this food today, for today is a Sabbath day dedicated to the LORD. There will be no food on the ground today. 26You may gather the food for six days, but the seventh day is the Sabbath. There will be no food on the ground that day."

27Some of the people went out anyway on the seventh day, but they found no food. 28The LORD asked Moses, "How long will these people refuse to obey my commands and instructions? 29They must realize that the Sabbath is the LORD's gift to you. That is why he gives you a two-day supply on the sixth day, so there will be enough for two days. On the Sabbath day you must each stay in your place. Do not go out to pick up food on the seventh day." 30So the people did not gather any food on the seventh day.

31The Israelites called the food manna.* It was white like coriander seed, and it tasted like honey wafers.

32Then Moses said, "This is what the LORD has commanded: Fill a two-quart container with manna to preserve it for your descendants. Then later generations will be able to see the food I gave you in the wilderness when I set you free from Egypt."

33Moses said to Aaron, "Get a jar and fill it with two quarts of manna. Then put it in a sacred place before the LORD to preserve it for all future generations." 34Aaron did just as the LORD had commanded Moses. He eventually placed it in the Ark of the Covenant—in front of the stone tablets inscribed with the terms of the covenant.* 35So the people of Israel ate manna for forty years until they arrived at the land where they would settle. They ate manna until they came to the border of the land of Canaan.

36The container used to measure the manna was an omer, which was one tenth of an ephah; it held about two quarts.*

17 WATER FROM THE ROCK

At the LORD's command, the whole community of Israel left the wilderness of Sin* and moved from place to place. Eventually they camped at Rephidim, but there was no water there for the people to drink. 2So once more the people complained against Moses. "Give us water to drink!" they demanded.

"Quiet!" Moses replied. "Why are you complaining against me? And why are you testing the LORD?"

3But tormented by thirst, they continued to argue with Moses. "Why did you bring us out of Egypt? Are you trying to kill us, our children, and our livestock with thirst?"

4Then Moses cried out to the LORD, "What should I do with these people? They are ready to stone me!"

5The LORD said to Moses, "Walk out in front of the people. Take your staff, the one you used when you struck the water of the Nile, and call some of the elders of Israel to join you. 6I will stand before you on the rock at Mount Sinai.* Strike the rock, and water will come gushing out. Then the people will be able to drink." So Moses struck the rock as he was told, and water gushed out as the elders looked on.

7Moses named the place Massah (which means "test") and Meribah (which means "arguing") because the

16:16 Hebrew *1 omer* [2 liters]; also in 16:32, 33. 16:18 Hebrew *measured it with an omer*. 16:22 Hebrew *2 omers* [4 liters]. 16:31 *Manna* means "What is it?" See 16:15. 16:34 Hebrew *He placed it in front of the Testimony;* see note on 25:16. 16:36 Hebrew *An omer is one tenth of an ephah*. 17:1 The geographical name *Sin* is related to *Sinai* and should not be confused with the English word *sin*. 17:6 Hebrew *Horeb*, another name for Sinai.

people of Israel argued with Moses and tested the LORD by saying, "Is the LORD here with us or not?"

ISRAEL DEFEATS THE AMALEKITES

8While the people of Israel were still at Rephidim, the warriors of Amalek attacked them. 9Moses commanded Joshua, "Choose some men to go out and fight the army of Amalek for us. Tomorrow, I will stand at the top of the hill, holding the staff of God in my hand."

10So Joshua did what Moses had commanded and fought the army of Amalek. Meanwhile, Moses, Aaron, and Hur climbed to the top of a nearby hill. 11As long as Moses held up the staff in his hand, the Israelites had the advantage. But whenever he dropped his hand, the Amalekites gained the advantage. 12Moses' arms soon became so tired he could no longer hold them up. So Aaron and Hur found a stone for him to sit on. Then they stood on each side of Moses, holding up his hands. So his hands held steady until sunset. 13As a result, Joshua overwhelmed the army of Amalek in battle.

14After the victory, the LORD instructed Moses, "Write this down on a scroll as a permanent reminder, and read it aloud to Joshua: I will erase the memory of Amalek from under heaven." 15Moses built an altar there and named it Yahweh-nissi (which means "the LORD is my banner"). 16He said, "They have raised their fist against the LORD's throne, so now* the LORD will be at war with Amalek generation after generation."

18 JETHRO'S VISIT TO MOSES

Moses' father-in-law, Jethro, the priest of Midian, heard about everything God had done for Moses and his people, the Israelites. He heard especially about how the LORD had rescued them from Egypt.

2Earlier, Moses had sent his wife, Zipporah, and his two sons back to Jethro, who had taken them in. 3(Moses' first son was named Gershom,* for Moses had said when the boy was born, "I have been a foreigner in a foreign land." 4His second son was named Eliezer,* for Moses had said, "The God of my ancestors was my helper; he rescued me from the sword of Pharaoh.") 5Jethro, Moses' father-in-law, now came to visit Moses in the wilderness. He brought Moses' wife and two sons with him, and they arrived while Moses and the people were camped near the mountain of God. 6Jethro had sent a message to Moses, saying, "I, Jethro, your father-in-law, am coming to see you with your wife and your two sons."

7So Moses went out to meet his father-in-law. He bowed low and kissed him. They asked about each other's welfare and then went into Moses' tent. 8Moses told his father-in-law everything the LORD had done to Pharaoh and Egypt on behalf of Israel. He also told about all the hardships they had experienced along the way and how the LORD had rescued his people from all their troubles. 9Jethro was delighted when he heard about all the good things the LORD had done for Israel as he rescued them from the hand of the Egyptians.

10"Praise the LORD," Jethro said, "for he has rescued you from the Egyptians and from Pharaoh. Yes, he has rescued Israel from the powerful hand of Egypt! 11I know now that the LORD is greater than all other gods, because he rescued his people from the oppression of the proud Egyptians."

FAMILY TALK 18:1-11

Moses told his father-in-law about the great deeds God performed to free the people of Israel from slavery in Egypt. Our relatives and friends often are the hardest people to talk with about God. Yet we can have an important influence over them. What are some opportunities you have to tell your friends and relatives about God? Do you take advantage of those opportunities? ■

12Then Jethro, Moses' father-in-law, brought a burnt offering and sacrifices to God. Aaron and all the elders of Israel came out and joined him in a sacrificial meal in God's presence.

JETHRO'S WISE ADVICE

13The next day, Moses took his seat to hear the people's disputes against each other. They waited before him from morning till evening.

14When Moses' father-in-law saw all that Moses was doing for the people, he asked, "What are you really accomplishing here? Why are you trying to do all this alone while everyone stands around you from morning till evening?"

15Moses replied, "Because the people come to me to get a ruling from God. 16When a dispute arises, they come to me, and I am the one who settles the case between the quarreling parties. I inform the people of God's decrees and give them his instructions."

17"This is not good!" Moses' father-in-law exclaimed. 18"You're going to wear yourself out—and the people, too. This job is too heavy a burden for you to handle all by yourself. 19Now listen to me, and let me give you a word of advice, and may God be with you. You should continue to be the people's representative before God, bringing their disputes to him. 20Teach them God's decrees, and give them his instructions. Show them how to conduct their lives. 21But select from all the people some capable, honest men who fear God and hate bribes. Appoint them as leaders over groups of one thousand, one hundred, fifty, and ten. 22They should always be available to solve the people's common disputes, but have them bring the major cases to you. Let the leaders decide the smaller matters themselves. They will help you carry the load, making the task easier for you. 23If you follow this advice, and if God commands you to do so, then you will be able to

17:16 Or *Hands have been lifted up to the LORD's throne, and now.* **18:3** *Gershom* sounds like a Hebrew term that means "a foreigner there." **18:4** *Eliezer* means "God is my helper."

endure the pressures, and all these people will go home
in peace."
24Moses listened to his father-in-law's advice and followed his suggestions. 25He chose capable men from all
over Israel and appointed them as leaders over the people. He put them in charge of groups of one thousand,
one hundred, fifty, and ten. 26These men were always
available to solve the people's common disputes. They
brought the major cases to Moses, but they took care of
the smaller matters themselves.
27Soon after this, Moses said good-bye to his father-in-
law, who returned to his own land.

19 THE LORD REVEALS HIMSELF AT SINAI

Exactly two months after the Israelites left Egypt,* they
arrived in the wilderness of Sinai. 2After breaking camp
at Rephidim, they came to the wilderness of Sinai and set
up camp there at the base of Mount Sinai.
3Then Moses climbed the mountain to appear before
God. The LORD called to him from the mountain and said,
"Give these instructions to the family of Jacob; announce
it to the descendants of Israel: 4'You have seen what I did
to the Egyptians. You know how I carried you on eagles'
wings and brought you to myself. 5Now if you will obey
me and keep my covenant, you will be my own special
treasure from among all the peoples on earth; for all the
earth belongs to me. 6And you will be my kingdom of
priests, my holy nation.' This is the message you must
give to the people of Israel."
7So Moses returned from the mountain and called together the elders of the people and told them everything
the LORD had commanded him. 8And all the people responded together, "We will do everything the LORD has
commanded." So Moses brought the people's answer
back to the LORD.
9Then the LORD said to Moses, "I will come to you in a
thick cloud, Moses, so the people themselves can hear me
when I speak with you. Then they will always trust you."
Moses told the LORD what the people had said. 10Then
the LORD told Moses, "Go down and prepare the people
for my arrival. Consecrate them today and tomorrow, and
have them wash their clothing. 11Be sure they are ready
on the third day, for on that day the LORD will come down
on Mount Sinai as all the people watch. 12Mark off a
boundary all around the mountain. Warn the people, 'Be
careful! Do not go up on the mountain or even touch its
boundaries. Anyone who touches the mountain will certainly be put to death. 13No hand may touch the person or
animal that crosses the boundary; instead, stone them or
shoot them with arrows. They must be put to death.'
However, when the ram's horn sounds a long blast, then
the people may go up on the mountain.*"
14So Moses went down to the people. He consecrated
them for worship, and they washed their clothes. 15He
told them, "Get ready for the third day, and until then
abstain from having sexual intercourse."
16On the morning of the third day, thunder roared and
lightning flashed, and a dense cloud came down on the
mountain. There was a long, loud blast from a ram's horn,
and all the people trembled. 17Moses led them out from
the camp to meet with God, and they stood at the foot of
the mountain. 18All of Mount Sinai was covered with
smoke because the LORD had descended on it in the form
of fire. The smoke billowed into the sky like smoke from a
brick kiln, and the whole mountain shook violently. 19As
the blast of the ram's horn grew louder and louder, Moses
spoke, and God thundered his reply. 20The LORD came
down on the top of Mount Sinai and called Moses to the
top of the mountain. So Moses climbed the mountain.
21Then the LORD told Moses, "Go back down and warn
the people not to break through the boundaries to see the
LORD, or they will die. 22Even the priests who regularly
come near to the LORD must purify themselves so that the
LORD does not break out and destroy them."
23"But LORD," Moses protested, "the people cannot
come up to Mount Sinai. You already warned us. You told
me, 'Mark off a boundary all around the mountain to set
it apart as holy.'"
24But the LORD said, "Go down and bring Aaron back
up with you. In the meantime, do not let the priests or the
people break through to approach the LORD, or he will
break out and destroy them."
25So Moses went down to the people and told them
what the LORD had said.

GOD'S NAME 20:7

What's in a name? Everything, in God's case. His name reveals his character. Through the Ten Commandments, God reminded his people of the sacredness of his name. No one was to misuse it. Yet we often hear it used frivolously or in a curse today. The way we use God's name shows how we really feel about him. His name deserves respect. How do your conversations with others support this view? ■

20 TEN COMMANDMENTS FOR THE COVENANT COMMUNITY

Then God gave the people all these instructions*:

2"I am the LORD your God, who rescued you from the
land of Egypt, the place of your slavery.
3"You must not have any other god but me.
4"You must not make for yourself an idol of any kind or
an image of anything in the heavens or on the earth
or in the sea. 5You must not bow down to them or
worship them, for I, the LORD your God, am a jealous
God who will not tolerate your affection for any other
gods. I lay the sins of the parents upon their children;
the entire family is affected—even children in the

19:1 Hebrew *In the third month after the Israelites left Egypt, on the very day*, i.e., two lunar months to the day after leaving Egypt. Compare Num 33:3. **19:13** Or *up to the mountain*. **20:1** Hebrew *all these words*.

third and fourth generations of those who reject me.
[6]But I lavish unfailing love for a thousand generations on those* who love me and obey my commands.
[7]"You must not misuse the name of the LORD your God. The LORD will not let you go unpunished if you misuse his name.
[8]"Remember to observe the Sabbath day by keeping it holy. [9]You have six days each week for your ordinary work, [10]but the seventh day is a Sabbath day of rest dedicated to the LORD your God. On that day no one in your household may do any work. This includes you, your sons and daughters, your male and female servants, your livestock, and any foreigners living among you. [11]For in six days the LORD made the heavens, the earth, the sea, and everything in them; but on the seventh day he rested. That is why the LORD blessed the Sabbath day and set it apart as holy.
[12]"Honor your father and mother. Then you will live a long, full life in the land the LORD your God is giving you.
[13]"You must not murder.
[14]"You must not commit adultery.
[15]"You must not steal.
[16]"You must not testify falsely against your neighbor.
[17]"You must not covet your neighbor's house. You must not covet your neighbor's wife, male or female servant, ox or donkey, or anything else that belongs to your neighbor."

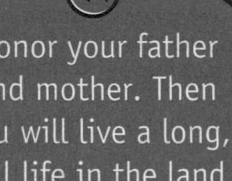

> Honor your father and mother. Then you will live a long, full life in the land the LORD your God is giving you.
>
> EXODUS 20:12

HONORING PARENTS 20:12

This is the first commandment with a promise attached. To live in peace for generations in the Promised Land, the Israelites would need to respect authority and build strong families. But how is the command to "honor" parents lived out? Speaking well of them is one way. Showing them courtesy and respect—but not at the cost of disobeying God—also is a way to honor them. Parents have a special place in God's sight. The command to honor them is for everyone—even for those who find it difficult to get along with their parents. How do you honor yours? ■

[18]When the people heard the thunder and the loud blast of the ram's horn, and when they saw the flashes of lightning and the smoke billowing from the mountain, they stood at a distance, trembling with fear.

[19]And they said to Moses, "You speak to us, and we will listen. But don't let God speak directly to us, or we will die!"

[20]"Don't be afraid," Moses answered them, "for God has come in this way to test you, and so that your fear of him will keep you from sinning!"

[21]As the people stood in the distance, Moses approached the dark cloud where God was.

PROPER USE OF ALTARS

[22]And the LORD said to Moses, "Say this to the people of Israel: You saw for yourselves that I spoke to you from heaven. [23]Remember, you must not make any idols of silver or gold to rival me.

[24]"Build for me an altar made of earth, and offer your sacrifices to me—your burnt offerings and peace offerings, your sheep and goats, and your cattle. Build my altar wherever I cause my name to be remembered, and I will come to you and bless you. [25]If you use stones to build my altar, use only natural, uncut stones. Do not shape the stones with a tool, for that would make the altar unfit for holy use. [26]And do not approach my altar by going up steps. If you do, someone might look up under your clothing and see your nakedness.

21

FAIR TREATMENT OF SLAVES

"These are the regulations you must present to Israel.

[2]"If you buy a Hebrew slave, he may serve for no more than six years. Set him free in the seventh year, and he will owe you nothing for his freedom. [3]If he was single when he became your slave, he shall leave single. But if he was married before he became a slave, then his wife must be freed with him.

[4]"If his master gave him a wife while he was a slave and they had sons or daughters, then only the man will be free in the seventh year, but his wife and children will still belong to his master. [5]But the slave may declare, 'I love my master, my wife, and my children. I don't want to go free.' [6]If he does this, his master must present him before God.* Then his master must take him to the door or doorpost and publicly pierce his ear with an awl. After that, the slave will serve his master for life.

[7]"When a man sells his daughter as a slave, she will not be freed at the end of six years as the men are. [8]If she does not satisfy her owner, he must allow her to be bought back again. But he is not allowed to sell her to foreigners, since he is the one who broke the contract with her. [9]But if the slave's owner arranges for her to marry his son, he may no longer treat her as a slave but as a daughter.

[10]"If a man who has married a slave wife takes another wife for himself, he must not neglect the rights of the first wife to food, clothing, and sexual intimacy. [11]If he fails in any of these three obligations, she may leave as a free woman without making any payment.

CASES OF PERSONAL INJURY

[12]"Anyone who assaults and kills another person must be put to death. [13]But if it was simply an accident permitted by God, I will appoint a place of refuge where the slayer

20:6 Hebrew *for thousands of those.* 21:6 Or *before the judges.*

can run for safety. 14However, if someone deliberately
kills another person, then the slayer must be dragged
even from my altar and be put to death.
15"Anyone who strikes father or mother must be put to
death.

RIGHTING WRONGS 22:1-15

Throughout chapter 22, we find examples of the principle of restitution—making wrongs right. For example, if a man stole an animal, he had to repay up to four or five times its market value, depending on the circumstances. If you have done someone wrong, you could go beyond what is expected to make things right. This will help ease any pain you might have caused. It can also help the other person to be more forgiving and make you more likely to think before you do the same thing again. ■

16"Kidnappers must be put to death, whether they are
caught in possession of their victims or have already sold
them as slaves.
17"Anyone who dishonors* father or mother must be
put to death.
18"Now suppose two men quarrel, and one hits the
other with a stone or fist, and the injured person does not
die but is confined to bed. 19If he is later able to walk outside again, even with a crutch, the assailant will not be
punished but must compensate his victim for lost wages
and provide for his full recovery.
20"If a man beats his male or female slave with a club
and the slave dies as a result, the owner must be punished. 21But if the slave recovers within a day or two, then
the owner shall not be punished, since the slave is his
property.
22"Now suppose two men are fighting, and in the process they accidentally strike a pregnant woman so she
gives birth prematurely.* If no further injury results, the
man who struck the woman must pay the amount of
compensation the woman's husband demands and the
judges approve. 23But if there is further injury, the punishment must match the injury: a life for a life, 24an eye
for an eye, a tooth for a tooth, a hand for a hand, a foot for
a foot, 25a burn for a burn, a wound for a wound, a bruise
for a bruise.
26"If a man hits his male or female slave in the eye and
the eye is blinded, he must let the slave go free to compensate for the eye. 27And if a man knocks out the tooth
of his male or female slave, he must let the slave go free to
compensate for the tooth.
28"If an ox* gores a man or woman to death, the ox
must be stoned, and its flesh may not be eaten. In such a
case, however, the owner will not be held liable. 29But
suppose the ox had a reputation for goring, and the
owner had been informed but failed to keep it under
control. If the ox then kills someone, it must be stoned,
and the owner must also be put to death. 30However, the
dead person's relatives may accept payment to compensate for the loss of life. The owner of the ox may redeem
his life by paying whatever is demanded.
31"The same regulation applies if the ox gores a boy or
a girl. 32But if the ox gores a slave, either male or female,
the animal's owner must pay the slave's owner thirty silver coins,* and the ox must be stoned.
33"Suppose someone digs or uncovers a pit and fails to
cover it, and then an ox or a donkey falls into it. 34The
owner of the pit must pay full compensation to the owner
of the animal, but then he gets to keep the dead animal.
35"If someone's ox injures a neighbor's ox and the injured ox dies, then the two owners must sell the live ox
and divide the price equally between them. They must
also divide the dead animal. 36But if the ox had a reputation for goring, yet its owner failed to keep it under control, he must pay full compensation—a live ox for the
dead one—but he may keep the dead ox.

22 PROTECTION OF PROPERTY

1*"If someone steals an ox* or sheep and then kills or
sells it, the thief must pay back five oxen for each ox stolen, and four sheep for each sheep stolen.
2*"If a thief is caught in the act of breaking into a
house and is struck and killed in the process, the person
who killed the thief is not guilty of murder. 3But if it happens in daylight, the one who killed the thief is guilty of
murder.
"A thief who is caught must pay in full for everything
he stole. If he cannot pay, he must be sold as a slave to pay
for his theft. 4If someone steals an ox or a donkey or a
sheep and it is found in the thief's possession, then the
thief must pay double the value of the stolen animal.
5"If an animal is grazing in a field or vineyard and the
owner lets it stray into someone else's field to graze, then
the animal's owner must pay compensation from the
best of his own grain or grapes.
6"If you are burning thornbushes and the fire gets out
of control and spreads into another person's field, destroying the sheaves or the uncut grain or the whole crop,
the one who started the fire must pay for the lost crop.
7"Suppose someone leaves money or goods with a
neighbor for safekeeping, and they are stolen from the
neighbor's house. If the thief is caught, the compensation is double the value of what was stolen. 8But if the
thief is not caught, the neighbor must appear before
God,* who will determine if he stole the property.
9"Suppose there is a dispute between two people who
both claim to own a particular ox, donkey, sheep, article
of clothing, or any lost property. Both parties must come
before God, and the person whom God declares* guilty
must pay double compensation to the other.
10"Now suppose someone leaves a donkey, ox, sheep,

21:17 Greek version reads *Anyone who speaks disrespectfully of.* Compare Matt 15:4; Mark 7:10. **21:22** Or *so she has a miscarriage;* Hebrew reads *so her children come out.* **21:28** Or *bull,* or *cow;* also in 21:29-36. **21:32** Hebrew *30 shekels of silver,* about 12 ounces or 342 grams in weight. **22:1a** Verse 22:1 is numbered 21:37 in Hebrew text. **22:1b** Or *bull,* or *cow;* also in 22:4, 9, 10. **22:2** Verses 22:2-31 are numbered 22:1-30 in Hebrew text. **22:8** Or *before the judges.* **22:9** Or *before the judges, and the person whom the judges declare.*

or any other animal with a neighbor for safekeeping, but it dies or is injured or gets away, and no one sees what happened. [11]The neighbor must then take an oath in the presence of the LORD. If the LORD confirms that the neighbor did not steal the property, the owner must accept the verdict, and no payment will be required. [12]But if the animal was indeed stolen, the guilty person must pay compensation to the owner. [13]If it was torn to pieces by a wild animal, the remains of the carcass must be shown as evidence, and no compensation will be required.

[14]"If someone borrows an animal from a neighbor and it is injured or dies when the owner is absent, the person who borrowed it must pay full compensation. [15]But if the owner was present, no compensation is required. And no compensation is required if the animal was rented, for this loss is covered by the rental fee.

SOCIAL RESPONSIBILITY

[16]"If a man seduces a virgin who is not engaged to anyone and has sex with her, he must pay the customary bride price and marry her. [17]But if her father refuses to let him marry her, the man must still pay him an amount equal to the bride price of a virgin.

[18]"You must not allow a sorceress to live.

[19]"Anyone who has sexual relations with an animal must certainly be put to death.

[20]"Anyone who sacrifices to any god other than the LORD must be destroyed.*

[21]"You must not mistreat or oppress foreigners in any way. Remember, you yourselves were once foreigners in the land of Egypt.

STRANGERS 22:21

God warned the Israelites not to treat foreigners unfairly, because they were once foreigners in Egypt. It is not easy coming to a new environment where you feel alone and out of place. Are there newcomers in your corner of the world? Perhaps they're new to your school or newly arrived in this country. How can you show sensitivity to their struggles and express God's love by your kindness and generosity? ■

[22]"You must not exploit a widow or an orphan. [23]If you exploit them in any way and they cry out to me, then I will certainly hear their cry. [24]My anger will blaze against you, and I will kill you with the sword. Then your wives will be widows and your children fatherless.

[25]"If you lend money to any of my people who are in need, do not charge interest as a money lender would. [26]If you take your neighbor's cloak as security for a loan, you must return it before sunset. [27]This coat may be the only blanket your neighbor has. How can a person sleep without it? If you do not return it and your neighbor cries out to me for help, then I will hear, for I am merciful.

[28]"You must not dishonor God or curse any of your rulers.

[29]"You must not hold anything back when you give me offerings from your crops and your wine.

"You must give me your firstborn sons.

[30]"You must also give me the firstborn of your cattle, sheep, and goats. But leave the newborn animal with its mother for seven days; then give it to me on the eighth day.

[31]"You must be my holy people. Therefore, do not eat any animal that has been torn up and killed by wild animals. Throw it to the dogs.

GOSSIP 23:1-3

Making up or passing along false reports was strictly forbidden by God. Gossip/rumors, slander, and false witnessing undermine families, strain relationships, and add chaos to the justice system. Yet we often pass on unverified information in the form of prayer requests or "news." Even if you do not initiate a lie, you become responsible if you pass it along. What will you do the next time you hear a rumor? ■

23 A CALL FOR JUSTICE

"You must not pass along false rumors. You must not cooperate with evil people by lying on the witness stand.

[2]"You must not follow the crowd in doing wrong. When you are called to testify in a dispute, do not be swayed by the crowd to twist justice. [3]And do not slant your testimony in favor of a person just because that person is poor.

[4]"If you come upon your enemy's ox or donkey that has strayed away, take it back to its owner. [5]If you see that the donkey of someone who hates you has collapsed under its load, do not walk by. Instead, stop and help.

[6]"In a lawsuit, you must not deny justice to the poor.

[7]"Be sure never to charge anyone falsely with evil. Never sentence an innocent or blameless person to death, for I never declare a guilty person to be innocent.

[8]"Take no bribes, for a bribe makes you ignore something that you clearly see. A bribe makes even a righteous person twist the truth.

[9]"You must not oppress foreigners. You know what it's like to be a foreigner, for you yourselves were once foreigners in the land of Egypt.

[10]"Plant and harvest your crops for six years, [11]but let the land be renewed and lie uncultivated during the seventh year. Then let the poor among you harvest whatever grows on its own. Leave the rest for wild animals to eat. The same applies to your vineyards and olive groves.

[12]"You have six days each week for your ordinary work, but on the seventh day you must stop working. This gives your ox and your donkey a chance to rest. It also allows

22:20 The Hebrew term used here refers to the complete consecration of things or people to the LORD, either by destroying them or by giving them as an offering.

your slaves and the foreigners living among you to be refreshed.

13"Pay close attention to all my instructions. You must not call on the name of any other gods. Do not even speak their names.

PEER PRESSURE

Mike and Cody stare in horror at the wrecked family room in Mike's house. Stacks of greasy pizza boxes, mud and beer stains on the carpet, and a broken lamp meet their gaze. In the downstairs bathroom, Mike is sickened by the sight and smell of vomit. The toilet is clogged and overflowing.

The scene upstairs is even worse. There they find a leaking waterbed, beer spills and cans everywhere, a framed print lying broken beside a bed, and a trashed bathroom.

"I'm history!" Mike groans. "My parents will be back tomorrow!"

"Don't panic," Cody reassures him. "We can clean all night. Your folks will never know we had a party."

Mike gives his friend a you-must-be-brain-dead look. "Come on, Cody! It'll take a week to fix this mess!"

How did this disaster happen? Cody and some friends talked Mike into throwing a "Party for Profit" while his parents were away. They could get a couple of kegs, invite about 50 friends, and charge them each $15. It was a guaranteed success!

Mike refused at first but soon changed his mind. "Okay," he finally said. "But only a few people!" Well, the "few" turned into more than 100, and the low-key party quickly turned into a wild nightmare.

Suppose Mike had listened to the advice of Exodus 23:2 instead of the counsel of his friends. How would this situation have changed?

When are you most tempted to give in to the crowd's wishes? After reading Exodus 23:2, what will you do the next time you're tempted?

THREE ANNUAL FESTIVALS

14"Each year you must celebrate three festivals in my honor. 15First, celebrate the Festival of Unleavened Bread. For seven days the bread you eat must be made without yeast, just as I commanded you. Celebrate this festival annually at the appointed time in early spring, in the month of Abib,* for that is the anniversary of your departure from Egypt. No one may appear before me without an offering.

16"Second, celebrate the Festival of Harvest,* when you bring me the first crops of your harvest.

"Finally, celebrate the Festival of the Final Harvest* at the end of the harvest season, when you have harvested all the crops from your fields. 17At these three times each year, every man in Israel must appear before the Sovereign, the LORD.

18"You must not offer the blood of my sacrificial offerings together with any baked goods containing yeast. And do not leave the fat from the festival offerings until the next morning.

19"As you harvest your crops, bring the very best of the first harvest to the house of the LORD your God.

"You must not cook a young goat in its mother's milk.

A PROMISE OF THE LORD'S PRESENCE

20"See, I am sending an angel before you to protect you on your journey and lead you safely to the place I have prepared for you. 21Pay close attention to him, and obey his instructions. Do not rebel against him, for he is my representative, and he will not forgive your rebellion. 22But if you are careful to obey him, following all my instructions, then I will be an enemy to your enemies, and I will oppose those who oppose you. 23For my angel will go before you and bring you into the land of the Amorites, Hittites, Perizzites, Canaanites, Hivites, and Jebusites, so you may live there. And I will destroy them completely. 24You must not worship the gods of these nations or serve them in any way or imitate their evil practices. Instead, you must utterly destroy them and smash their sacred pillars.

25"You must serve only the LORD your God. If you do, I* will bless you with food and water, and I will protect you from illness. 26There will be no miscarriages or infertility in your land, and I will give you long, full lives.

27"I will send my terror ahead of you and create panic among all the people whose lands you invade. I will make all your enemies turn and run. 28I will send terror* ahead of you to drive out the Hivites, Canaanites, and Hittites. 29But I will not drive them out in a single year, because the land would become desolate and the wild animals would multiply and threaten you. 30I will drive them out a little at a time until your population has increased enough to take possession of the land. 31And I will fix your boundaries from the Red Sea to the Mediterranean Sea,* and from the eastern wilderness to the Euphrates River.* I will hand over to you the people now living in the land, and you will drive them out ahead of you.

32"Make no treaties with them or their gods. 33They must not live in your land, or they will cause you to sin against me. If you serve their gods, you will be caught in the trap of idolatry."

24 ISRAEL ACCEPTS THE LORD'S COVENANT

Then the LORD instructed Moses: "Come up here to me, and bring along Aaron, Nadab, Abihu, and seventy of Israel's elders. All of you must worship from a distance. 2Only Moses is allowed to come near to the LORD. The

23:15 Hebrew *appointed time in the month of Abib.* This first month of the ancient Hebrew lunar calendar usually occurs within the months of March and April. **23:16a** Or *Festival of Weeks.* This was later called the Festival of Pentecost (see Acts 2:1). It is celebrated today as Shavuat (or Shabuoth). **23:16b** Or *Festival of Ingathering.* This was later called the Festival of Shelters or Festival of Tabernacles (see Lev 23:33-36). It is celebrated today as Sukkot (or Succoth). **23:25** As in Greek and Latin versions; Hebrew reads *he.* **23:28** Often rendered *the hornet.* The meaning of the Hebrew is uncertain. **23:31a** Hebrew *from the sea of reeds to the sea of the Philistines.* **23:31b** Hebrew *from the wilderness to the river.*

others must not come near, and none of the other people
are allowed to climb up the mountain with him."
3Then Moses went down to the people and repeated all
the instructions and regulations the LORD had given him.
All the people answered with one voice, "We will do
everything the LORD has commanded."
4Then Moses carefully wrote down all the LORD's instructions. Early the next morning Moses got up and
built an altar at the foot of the mountain. He also set up
twelve pillars, one for each of the twelve tribes of Israel.
5Then he sent some of the young Israelite men to present burnt offerings and to sacrifice bulls as peace offerings to the LORD. 6Moses drained half the blood from
these animals into basins. The other half he splattered
against the altar.
7Then he took the Book of the Covenant and read it
aloud to the people. Again they all responded, "We will
do everything the LORD has commanded. We will obey."
8Then Moses took the blood from the basins and splattered it over the people, declaring, "Look, this blood confirms the covenant the LORD has made with you in giving
you these instructions."
9Then Moses, Aaron, Nadab, Abihu, and the seventy elders of Israel climbed up the mountain. 10There they saw
the God of Israel. Under his feet there seemed to be a surface of brilliant blue lapis lazuli, as clear as the sky itself.
11And though these nobles of Israel gazed upon God, he
did not destroy them. In fact, they ate a covenant meal,
eating and drinking in his presence!
12Then the LORD said to Moses, "Come up to me on the
mountain. Stay there, and I will give you the tablets of
stone on which I have inscribed the instructions and
commands so you can teach the people." 13So Moses and
his assistant Joshua set out, and Moses climbed up the
mountain of God.
14Moses told the elders, "Stay here and wait for us until
we come back. Aaron and Hur are here with you. If anyone has a dispute while I am gone, consult with them."
15Then Moses climbed up the mountain, and the cloud
covered it. 16And the glory of the LORD settled down on
Mount Sinai, and the cloud covered it for six days. On
the seventh day the LORD called to Moses from inside the
cloud. 17To the Israelites at the foot of the mountain, the
glory of the LORD appeared at the summit like a consuming fire. 18Then Moses disappeared into the cloud as he
climbed higher up the mountain. He remained on the
mountain forty days and forty nights.

25

OFFERINGS FOR THE TABERNACLE

The LORD said to Moses, 2"Tell the people of Israel to
bring me their sacred offerings. Accept the contributions from all whose hearts are moved to offer them.
3Here is a list of sacred offerings you may accept from
them:

gold, silver, and bronze;
4 blue, purple, and scarlet thread;
fine linen and goat hair for cloth;
5 tanned ram skins and fine goatskin leather;
acacia wood;
6 olive oil for the lamps;
spices for the anointing oil and the fragrant incense;
7 onyx stones, and other gemstones to be set in the
ephod and the priest's chestpiece.

8"Have the people of Israel build me a holy sanctuary
so I can live among them. 9You must build this Tabernacle and its furnishings exactly according to the pattern I
will show you.

PLANS FOR THE ARK OF THE COVENANT

10"Have the people make an Ark of acacia wood—a sacred
chest 45 inches long, 27 inches wide, and 27 inches
high.* 11Overlay it inside and outside with pure gold, and
run a molding of gold all around it. 12Cast four gold rings
and attach them to its four feet, two rings on each side.
13Make poles from acacia wood, and overlay them with
gold. 14Insert the poles into the rings at the sides of the
Ark to carry it. 15These carrying poles must stay inside the
rings; never remove them. 16When the Ark is finished,
place inside it the stone tablets inscribed with the terms
of the covenant,* which I will give to you.
17"Then make the Ark's cover—the place of atonement—from pure gold. It must be 45 inches long and
27 inches wide.* 18Then make two cherubim from
hammered gold, and place them on the two ends of the
atonement cover. 19Mold the cherubim on each end of
the atonement cover, making it all of one piece of gold.
20The cherubim will face each other and look down on
the atonement cover. With their wings spread above it,
they will protect it. 21Place inside the Ark the stone tablets inscribed with the terms of the covenant, which I
will give to you. Then put the atonement cover on top
of the Ark. 22I will meet with you there and talk to you
from above the atonement cover between the gold
cherubim that hover over the Ark of the Covenant.*
From there I will give you my commands for the people
of Israel.

PLANS FOR THE TABLE

23"Then make a table of acacia wood, 36 inches long,
18 inches wide, and 27 inches high.* 24Overlay it with
pure gold and run a gold molding around the edge.
25Decorate it with a 3-inch border* all around, and run a
gold molding along the border. 26Make four gold rings
for the table and attach them at the four corners next to
the four legs. 27Attach the rings near the border to hold
the poles that are used to carry the table. 28Make these
poles from acacia wood, and overlay them with gold.
29Make special containers of pure gold for the table—

25:10 Hebrew *2.5 cubits* [115 centimeters] *long, 1.5 cubits* [69 centimeters] *wide, and 1.5 cubits high.* **25:16** Hebrew *Place inside the Ark the Testimony;* similarly in 25:21. The Hebrew word for "testimony" refers to the terms of the LORD's covenant with Israel as written on stone tablets, and also to the covenant itself. **25:17** Hebrew *2.5 cubits* [115 centimeters] *long and 1.5 cubits* [69 centimeters] *wide.* **25:22** Or *Ark of the Testimony.* **25:23** Hebrew *2 cubits* [92 centimeters] *long, 1 cubit* [46 centimeters] *wide, and 1.5 cubits* [69 centimeters] *high.* **25:25** Hebrew *a border of a handbreadth* [8 centimeters].

ABSOLUTE ANSWERS

Have you ever heard anyone say that truth is relative? Maybe you've even heard someone say, "Your truth isn't necessarily my truth. What's true for you may not be true for me." Ever say that yourself?

Some people think that truth and standards of right and wrong change from decade to decade or from person to person. They make choices based on society's or their peers' definitions of right and wrong. Like Judges 21:25 says, "The people [do] whatever seem[s] right in their own eyes" (Judg 21:25). Does that describe anyone you know?

Magazines, newspapers, and Internet carry story after story about lifestyle choices: a unmarried couple who lives together before marriage ("After all, we're in love"); a person who finally decides to break "free" of the shackles of heterosexual life to explore his or her "true" nature as a homosexual; a teen who just wants to be free to express his or her sexuality; a pastor who decides to bless the union of a same-sex couple—the list goes on. If you didn't catch those, just wait for the follow-up talk shows and movies. Many of these choices are made in the name of tolerance and other forms of political correctness. Those opposed to these lifestyle choices are viewed as intolerant, especially if society gives them the green light.

Wondering what's truly right or wrong? The Bible provides definite answers. The Ten Commandments and other laws reveal God's standards of right and wrong. Take murder for example. God says no to that. What about adultery? Don't even think about it. Stealing? Ditto. But honoring God and your parents are good moves.

Although times change, God's standards never do. "Your eternal word, O LORD, stands firm in heaven" (Ps 119:89). "The very essence of your words is truth; all your just regulations will stand forever" (Ps 119:160). Because God's standards always are the same, some are quick to describe the Bible as old-fashioned or lacking in relevance. Others might ignore it because they resent being measured by its standards. What's your view?

ULTIMATE ISSUES

bowls, pans, pitchers, and jars—to be used in pouring out
liquid offerings. 30Place the Bread of the Presence on the
table to remain before me at all times.

PLANS FOR THE LAMPSTAND

31"Make a lampstand of pure, hammered gold. Make the
entire lampstand and its decorations of one piece—the
base, center stem, lamp cups, buds, and petals. 32Make it
with six branches going out from the center stem, three
on each side. 33Each of the six branches will have three
lamp cups shaped like almond blossoms, complete with
buds and petals. 34Craft the center stem of the lampstand
with four lamp cups shaped like almond blossoms, complete with buds and petals. 35There will also be an almond
bud beneath each pair of branches where the six
branches extend from the center stem. 36The almond
buds and branches must all be of one piece with the center stem, and they must be hammered from pure gold.
37Then make the seven lamps for the lampstand, and set
them so they reflect their light forward. 38The lamp
snuffers and trays must also be made of pure gold. 39You
will need seventy-five pounds* of pure gold for the lampstand and its accessories.

40"Be sure that you make everything according to the
pattern I have shown you here on the mountain.

26 PLANS FOR THE TABERNACLE

"Make the Tabernacle from ten curtains of finely woven
linen. Decorate the curtains with blue, purple, and scarlet
thread and with skillfully embroidered cherubim. 2These
ten curtains must all be exactly the same size—42 feet
long and 6 feet wide.* 3Join five of these curtains together to make one long curtain, then join the other five
into a second long curtain. 4Put loops of blue yarn along
the edge of the last curtain in each set. 5The fifty loops
along the edge of one curtain are to match the fifty loops
along the edge of the other curtain. 6Then make fifty gold
clasps and fasten the long curtains together with the
clasps. In this way, the Tabernacle will be made of one
continuous piece.

7"Make eleven curtains of goat-hair cloth to serve as a
tent covering for the Tabernacle. 8These eleven curtains
must all be exactly the same size—45 feet long and 6 feet
wide.* 9Join five of these curtains together to make one
long curtain, and join the other six into a second long

25:39 Hebrew *1 talent* [34 kilograms]. 26:2 Hebrew *28 cubits* [12.9 meters] *long and 4 cubits* [1.8 meters] *wide.* 26:8 Hebrew *30 cubits* [13.8 meters] *long and 4 cubits* [1.8 meters] *wide.*

curtain. Allow 3 feet of material from the second set of
curtains to hang over the front* of the sacred tent.
10Make fifty loops for one edge of each large curtain.
11Then make fifty bronze clasps, and fasten the loops of
the long curtains with the clasps. In this way, the tent covering will be made of one continuous piece. 12The remaining 3 feet* of this tent covering will be left to hang
over the back of the Tabernacle. 13Allow 18 inches* of
remaining material to hang down over each side, so the
Tabernacle is completely covered. 14Complete the tent
covering with a protective layer of tanned ram skins and
a layer of fine goatskin leather.

EASY ACCESS 26:31

A linen curtain separated the two sacred rooms—the Holy Place and the Most Holy Place—in the Tabernacle. The priest entered the Holy Place each day to commune with God and tend to the altar of incense, the lampstand, and the table of the Bread of the Presence. The Most Holy Place housed the Ark of the Covenant. Only the high priest could enter the Most Holy Place. Even he could do so only once a year—on the Day of Atonement—to offer a sacrifice for the sins of the nation. (See Lev 16.)

When Jesus Christ later died on the cross, the curtain in the Temple (which had replaced the Tabernacle) tore from top to bottom (Mark 15:38), symbolizing our free access to God because of Jesus' death. We no longer need priests and sacrifices to approach God. ■

15"For the framework of the Tabernacle, construct
frames of acacia wood. 16Each frame must be 15 feet
high and 27 inches wide,* 17with two pegs under each
frame. Make all the frames identical. 18Make twenty of
these frames to support the curtains on the south side of
the Tabernacle. 19Also make forty silver bases—two bases
under each frame, with the pegs fitting securely into the
bases. 20For the north side of the Tabernacle, make another twenty frames, 21with their forty silver bases, two
bases under each frame. 22Make six frames for the rear—
the west side of the Tabernacle—23along with two additional frames to reinforce the rear corners of the Tabernacle. 24These corner frames will be matched at the
bottom and firmly attached at the top with a single ring,
forming a single corner unit. Make both of these corner
units the same way. 25So there will be eight frames at the
rear of the Tabernacle, set in sixteen silver bases—two
bases under each frame.

26"Make crossbars of acacia wood to link the frames,
five crossbars for the north side of the Tabernacle 27and
five for the south side. Also make five crossbars for the
rear of the Tabernacle, which will face west. 28The middle crossbar, attached halfway up the frames, will run all
the way from one end of the Tabernacle to the other.
29Overlay the frames with gold, and make gold rings to
hold the crossbars. Overlay the crossbars with gold as
well.

30"Set up this Tabernacle according to the pattern you
were shown on the mountain.

31"For the inside of the Tabernacle, make a special curtain of finely woven linen. Decorate it with blue, purple,
and scarlet thread and with skillfully embroidered cherubim. 32Hang this curtain on gold hooks attached to four
posts of acacia wood. Overlay the posts with gold, and set
them in four silver bases. 33Hang the inner curtain from
clasps, and put the Ark of the Covenant* in the room behind it. This curtain will separate the Holy Place from the
Most Holy Place.

34"Then put the Ark's cover—the place of atonement—
on top of the Ark of the Covenant inside the Most Holy
Place. 35Place the table outside the inner curtain on the
north side of the Tabernacle, and place the lampstand
across the room on the south side.

36"Make another curtain for the entrance to the sacred
tent. Make it of finely woven linen and embroider it with
exquisite designs, using blue, purple, and scarlet thread.
37Craft five posts from acacia wood. Overlay them with
gold, and hang the curtain from them with gold hooks.
Cast five bronze bases for the posts.

27 PLANS FOR THE ALTAR OF BURNT OFFERING

"Using acacia wood, construct a square altar 7½ feet
wide, 7½ feet long, and 4½ feet high.* 2Make horns for
each of its four corners so that the horns and altar are all
one piece. Overlay the altar with bronze. 3Make ash buckets, shovels, basins, meat forks, and firepans, all of
bronze. 4Make a bronze grating for it, and attach four
bronze rings at its four corners. 5Install the grating halfway down the side of the altar, under the ledge. 6For carrying the altar, make poles from acacia wood, and overlay
them with bronze. 7Insert the poles through the rings on
the two sides of the altar. 8The altar must be hollow, made
from planks. Build it just as you were shown on the
mountain.

PLANS FOR THE COURTYARD

9"Then make the courtyard for the Tabernacle, enclosed
with curtains made of finely woven linen. On the south
side, make the curtains 150 feet long.* 10They will be
held up by twenty posts set securely in twenty bronze
bases. Hang the curtains with silver hooks and rings.
11Make the curtains the same on the north side—150 feet
of curtains held up by twenty posts set securely in bronze
bases. Hang the curtains with silver hooks and rings.
12The curtains on the west end of the courtyard will be
75 feet long,* supported by ten posts set into ten bases.
13The east end of the courtyard, the front, will also be
75 feet long. 14The courtyard entrance will be on the east
end, flanked by two curtains. The curtain on the right

26:9 Hebrew *Double over the sixth sheet at the front.* 26:12 Hebrew *The half sheet that is left over.* 26:13 Hebrew *1 cubit* [46 centimeters]. 26:16 Hebrew *10 cubits* [4.6 meters] *high and 1.5 cubits* [69 centimeters] *wide.* 26:33 Or *Ark of the Testimony;* also in 26:34. 27:1 Hebrew *5 cubits* [2.3 meters] *wide, 5 cubits long, a square, and 3 cubits* [1.4 meters] *high.* 27:9 Hebrew *100 cubits* [46 meters]; also in 27:11. 27:12 Hebrew *50 cubits* [23 meters]; also in 27:13.

side will be 22½ feet long,* supported by three posts set into three bases. 15The curtain on the left side will also be 22½ feet long, supported by three posts set into three bases.

16"For the entrance to the courtyard, make a curtain that is 30 feet long.* Make it from finely woven linen, and decorate it with beautiful embroidery in blue, purple, and scarlet thread. Support it with four posts, each securely set in its own base. 17All the posts around the courtyard must have silver rings and hooks and bronze bases. 18So the entire courtyard will be 150 feet long and 75 feet wide, with curtain walls 7½ feet high,* made from finely woven linen. The bases for the posts will be made of bronze.

19"All the articles used in the rituals of the Tabernacle, including all the tent pegs used to support the Tabernacle and the courtyard curtains, must be made of bronze.

LIGHT FOR THE TABERNACLE

20"Command the people of Israel to bring you pure oil of pressed olives for the light, to keep the lamps burning continually. 21The lampstand will stand in the Tabernacle, in front of the inner curtain that shields the Ark of the Covenant.* Aaron and his sons must keep the lamps burning in the LORD's presence all night. This is a permanent law for the people of Israel, and it must be observed from generation to generation.

28

CLOTHING FOR THE PRIESTS

"Call for your brother, Aaron, and his sons, Nadab, Abihu, Eleazar, and Ithamar. Set them apart from the rest of the people of Israel so they may minister to me and be my priests. 2Make sacred garments for Aaron that are glorious and beautiful. 3Instruct all the skilled craftsmen whom I have filled with the spirit of wisdom. Have them make garments for Aaron that will distinguish him as a priest set apart for my service. 4These are the garments they are to make: a chestpiece, an ephod, a robe, a patterned tunic, a turban, and a sash. They are to make these sacred garments for your brother, Aaron, and his sons to wear when they serve me as priests. 5So give them fine linen cloth, gold thread, and blue, purple, and scarlet thread.

DESIGN OF THE EPHOD

6"The craftsmen must make the ephod of finely woven linen and skillfully embroider it with gold and with blue, purple, and scarlet thread. 7It will consist of two pieces, front and back, joined at the shoulders with two shoulder-pieces. 8The decorative sash will be made of the same materials: finely woven linen embroidered with gold and with blue, purple, and scarlet thread.

9"Take two onyx stones, and engrave on them the names of the tribes of Israel. 10Six names will be on each stone, arranged in the order of the births of the original sons of Israel. 11Engrave these names on the two stones in the same way a jeweler engraves a seal. Then mount the stones in settings of gold filigree. 12Fasten the two stones on the shoulder-pieces of the ephod as a reminder that Aaron represents the people of Israel. Aaron will carry these names on his shoulders as a constant reminder whenever he goes before the LORD. 13Make the settings of gold filigree, 14then braid two cords of pure gold and attach them to the filigree settings on the shoulders of the ephod.

DESIGN OF THE CHESTPIECE

15"Then, with great skill and care, make a chestpiece to be worn for seeking a decision from God.* Make it to match the ephod, using finely woven linen embroidered with gold and with blue, purple, and scarlet thread. 16Make the chestpiece of a single piece of cloth folded to form a pouch nine inches* square. 17Mount four rows of gemstones* on it. The first row will contain a red carnelian, a pale-green peridot, and an emerald. 18The second row will contain a turquoise, a blue lapis lazuli, and a white moonstone. 19The third row will contain an orange jacinth, an agate, and a purple amethyst. 20The fourth row will contain a blue-green beryl, an onyx, and a green jasper. All these stones will be set in gold filigree. 21Each stone will represent one of the twelve sons of Israel, and the name of that tribe will be engraved on it like a seal.

22"To attach the chestpiece to the ephod, make braided cords of pure gold thread. 23Then make two gold rings and attach them to the top corners of the chestpiece. 24Tie the two gold cords to the two rings on the chestpiece. 25Tie the other ends of the cords to the gold settings on the shoulder-pieces of the ephod. 26Then make two more gold rings and attach them to the inside edges of the chestpiece next to the ephod. 27And make two more gold rings and attach them to the front of the ephod, below the shoulder-pieces, just above the knot where the decorative sash is fastened to the ephod. 28Then attach the bottom rings of the chestpiece to the rings on the ephod with blue cords. This will hold the chestpiece securely to the ephod above the decorative sash.

29"In this way, Aaron will carry the names of the tribes of Israel on the sacred chestpiece* over his heart when he goes into the Holy Place. This will be a continual reminder that he represents the people when he comes before the LORD. 30Insert the Urim and Thummim into the sacred chestpiece so they will be carried over Aaron's heart when he goes into the LORD's presence. In this way, Aaron will always carry over his heart the objects used to determine the LORD's will for his people whenever he goes in before the LORD.

ADDITIONAL CLOTHING FOR THE PRIESTS

31"Make the robe that is worn with the ephod from a single piece of blue cloth, 32with an opening for Aaron's

27:14 Hebrew *15 cubits* [6.9 meters]; also in 27:15. 27:16 Hebrew *20 cubits* [9.2 meters]. 27:18 Hebrew *100 cubits* [46 meters] *long and 50 cubits* [23 meters] *wide and 5 cubits* [2.3 meters] *high.* 27:21 Hebrew *in the Tent of Meeting, outside the inner curtain that is in front of the Testimony.* See note on 25:16. 28:15 Hebrew *a chestpiece for decision.* 28:16 Hebrew *1 span* [23 centimeters]. 28:17 The identification of some of these gemstones is uncertain. 28:29 Hebrew *the chestpiece for decision;* also in 28:30. See 28:15.

head in the middle of it. Reinforce the opening with a woven collar* so it will not tear. [33]Make pomegranates out of blue, purple, and scarlet yarn, and attach them to the hem of the robe, with gold bells between them. [34]The gold bells and pomegranates are to alternate all around the hem. [35]Aaron will wear this robe whenever he ministers before the LORD, and the bells will tinkle as he goes in and out of the LORD's presence in the Holy Place. If he wears it, he will not die.

[36]"Next make a medallion of pure gold, and engrave it like a seal with these words: HOLY TO THE LORD. [37]Attach the medallion with a blue cord to the front of Aaron's turban, where it must remain. [38]Aaron must wear it on his forehead so he may take on himself any guilt of the people of Israel when they consecrate their sacred offerings. He must always wear it on his forehead so the LORD will accept the people.

[39]"Weave Aaron's patterned tunic from fine linen cloth. Fashion the turban from this linen as well. Also make a sash, and decorate it with colorful embroidery.

[40]"For Aaron's sons, make tunics, sashes, and special head coverings that are glorious and beautiful. [41]Clothe your brother, Aaron, and his sons with these garments, and then anoint and ordain them. Consecrate them so they can serve as my priests. [42]Also make linen undergarments for them, to be worn next to their bodies, reaching from their hips to their thighs. [43]These must be worn whenever Aaron and his sons enter the Tabernacle* or approach the altar in the Holy Place to perform their priestly duties. Then they will not incur guilt and die. This is a permanent law for Aaron and all his descendants after him.

29

DEDICATION OF THE PRIESTS

"This is the ceremony you must follow when you consecrate Aaron and his sons to serve me as priests: Take a young bull and two rams with no defects. [2]Then, using choice wheat flour and no yeast, make loaves of bread, thin cakes mixed with olive oil, and wafers spread with oil. [3]Place them all in a single basket, and present them at the entrance of the Tabernacle, along with the young bull and the two rams.

[4]"Present Aaron and his sons at the entrance of the Tabernacle,* and wash them with water. [5]Dress Aaron in his priestly garments—the tunic, the robe worn with the ephod, the ephod itself, and the chestpiece. Then wrap the decorative sash of the ephod around him. [6]Place the turban on his head, and fasten the sacred medallion to the turban. [7]Then anoint him by pouring the anointing oil over his head. [8]Next present his sons, and dress them in their tunics. [9]Wrap the sashes around the waists of Aaron and his sons, and put their special head coverings on them. Then the right to the priesthood will be theirs by law forever. In this way, you will ordain Aaron and his sons.

[10]"Bring the young bull to the entrance of the Tabernacle, where Aaron and his sons will lay their hands on its head. [11]Then slaughter the bull in the LORD's presence at the entrance of the Tabernacle. [12]Put some of its blood on the horns of the altar with your finger, and pour out the rest at the base of the altar. [13]Take all the fat around the internal organs, the long lobe of the liver, and the two kidneys and the fat around them, and burn it all on the altar. [14]Then take the rest of the bull, including its hide, meat, and dung, and burn it outside the camp as a sin offering.

RULES FOR WORSHIP 29:10-46

Ever wonder why there were so many rules for sacrifices? The rules were partially for quality control. A set standard of worship prevented problems from arising when individuals worshiped by their own rules. Also, following established patterns for worship separated the Hebrews from the pagan nations they would meet in the Promised Land.

People from other nations performed sacrifices to their gods wherever, however, and whenever they wanted to. Finally, the Hebrew form of worship showed Israel that they should be as serious about their relationship with God as he was about his relationship with them. Is serious a good description of your relationship with God? ■

[15]"Next Aaron and his sons must lay their hands on the head of one of the rams. [16]Then slaughter the ram, and splatter its blood against all sides of the altar. [17]Cut the ram into pieces, and wash off the internal organs and the legs. Set them alongside the head and the other pieces of the body, [18]then burn the entire animal on the altar. This is a burnt offering to the LORD; it is a pleasing aroma, a special gift presented to the LORD.

[19]"Now take the other ram, and have Aaron and his sons lay their hands on its head. [20]Then slaughter it, and apply some of its blood to the right earlobes of Aaron and his sons. Also put it on the thumbs of their right hands and the big toes of their right feet. Splatter the rest of the blood against all sides of the altar. [21]Then take some of the blood from the altar and some of the anointing oil, and sprinkle it on Aaron and his sons and on their garments. In this way, they and their garments will be set apart as holy.

[22]"Since this is the ram for the ordination of Aaron and his sons, take the fat of the ram, including the fat of the broad tail, the fat around the internal organs, the long lobe of the liver, and the two kidneys and the fat around them, along with the right thigh. [23]Then take one round loaf of bread, one thin cake mixed with olive oil, and one wafer from the basket of bread without yeast that was placed in the LORD's presence. [24]Put all these in the hands of Aaron and his sons to be lifted up as a special offering to the LORD. [25]Afterward take the various breads from their hands, and burn them on the altar along with the burnt offering. It is a pleasing aroma to the LORD, a special gift for him. [26]Then take the breast of Aaron's

28:32 The meaning of the Hebrew is uncertain. **28:43** Hebrew *Tent of Meeting*. **29:4** Hebrew *Tent of Meeting;* also in 29:10, 11, 30, 32, 42, 44.

ordination ram, and lift it up in the LORD's presence as a special offering to him. Then keep it as your own portion. 27"Set aside the portions of the ordination ram that belong to Aaron and his sons. This includes the breast and the thigh that were lifted up before the LORD as a special offering. 28In the future, whenever the people of Israel lift up a peace offering, a portion of it must be set aside for Aaron and his descendants. This is their permanent right, and it is a sacred offering from the Israelites to the LORD.

29"Aaron's sacred garments must be preserved for his descendants who succeed him, and they will wear them when they are anointed and ordained. 30The descendant who succeeds him as high priest will wear these clothes for seven days as he ministers in the Tabernacle and the Holy Place.

31"Take the ram used in the ordination ceremony, and boil its meat in a sacred place. 32Then Aaron and his sons will eat this meat, along with the bread in the basket, at the Tabernacle entrance. 33They alone may eat the meat and bread used for their purification* in the ordination ceremony. No one else may eat them, for these things are set apart and holy. 34If any of the ordination meat or bread remains until the morning, it must be burned. It may not be eaten, for it is holy.

35"This is how you will ordain Aaron and his sons to their offices, just as I have commanded you. The ordination ceremony will go on for seven days. 36Each day you must sacrifice a young bull as a sin offering to purify them, making them right with the LORD.* Afterward, cleanse the altar by purifying it*; make it holy by anointing it with oil. 37Purify the altar, and consecrate it every day for seven days. After that, the altar will be absolutely holy, and whatever touches it will become holy.

38"These are the sacrifices you are to offer regularly on the altar. Each day, offer two lambs that are a year old, 39one in the morning and the other in the evening. 40With one of them, offer two quarts of choice flour mixed with one quart of pure oil of pressed olives; also, offer one quart of wine* as a liquid offering. 41Offer the other lamb in the evening, along with the same offerings of flour and wine as in the morning. It will be a pleasing aroma, a special gift presented to the LORD.

42"These burnt offerings are to be made each day from generation to generation. Offer them in the LORD's presence at the Tabernacle entrance; there I will meet with you and speak with you. 43I will meet the people of Israel there, in the place made holy by my glorious presence. 44Yes, I will consecrate the Tabernacle and the altar, and I will consecrate Aaron and his sons to serve me as priests. 45Then I will live among the people of Israel and be their God, 46and they will know that I am the LORD their God. I am the one who brought them out of the land of Egypt so that I could live among them. I am the LORD their God.

30

PLANS FOR THE INCENSE ALTAR

"Then make another altar of acacia wood for burning incense. 2Make it 18 inches square and 36 inches high,* with horns at the corners carved from the same piece of wood as the altar itself. 3Overlay the top, sides, and horns of the altar with pure gold, and run a gold molding around the entire altar. 4Make two gold rings, and attach them on opposite sides of the altar below the gold molding to hold the carrying poles. 5Make the poles of acacia wood and overlay them with gold. 6Place the incense altar just outside the inner curtain that shields the Ark of the Covenant,* in front of the Ark's cover—the place of atonement—that covers the tablets inscribed with the terms of the covenant.* I will meet with you there.

7"Every morning when Aaron maintains the lamps, he must burn fragrant incense on the altar. 8And each evening when he lights the lamps, he must again burn incense in the LORD's presence. This must be done from generation to generation. 9Do not offer any unholy incense on this altar, or any burnt offerings, grain offerings, or liquid offerings.

10"Once a year Aaron must purify* the altar by smearing its horns with blood from the offering made to purify the people from their sin. This will be a regular, annual event from generation to generation, for this is the LORD's most holy altar."

A PAYMENT FOR SIN 30:11-16

The ransom money was like a census tax. It continued the principle that all of the people of Israel belonged to God and therefore needed to be redeemed (bought) by the payment of a sacrifice. Whenever a census took place, everyone—rich and poor alike—was required to pay a ransom.

All of us need mercy and forgiveness because of our sinful thoughts and actions. God does not discriminate between people (see Acts 10:34-35; Gal 3:28). His offer of mercy through Jesus is for all. ■

MONEY FOR THE TABERNACLE

11Then the LORD said to Moses, 12"Whenever you take a census of the people of Israel, each man who is counted must pay a ransom for himself to the LORD. Then no plague will strike the people as you count them. 13Each person who is counted must give a small piece of silver as a sacred offering to the LORD. (This payment is half a shekel,* based on the sanctuary shekel, which equals twenty gerahs.) 14All who have reached their twentieth birthday must give this sacred offering to the LORD. 15When this offering is given to the LORD to purify your lives, making you right with him,* the rich must not give more than the specified amount, and the poor must not

29:33 Or *their atonement.* **29:36a** Or *to make atonement.* **29:36b** Or *by making atonement for it;* similarly in 29:37. **29:40** Hebrew *1/10 of an ephah* [2.2 liters] *of choice flour . . . 1/4 of a hin* [1 liter] *of pure oil . . . 1/4 of a hin of wine.* **30:2** Hebrew *1 cubit* [46 centimeters] *long and 1 cubit wide, a square, and 2 cubits* [92 centimeters] *high.* **30:6a** Or *Ark of the Testimony;* also in 30:26. **30:6b** Hebrew *that covers the Testimony;* see note on 25:16. **30:10** Or *make atonement for;* also in 30:10b. **30:13** Or *0.2 ounces,* or *6 grams.* **30:15** Or *to make atonement for your lives;* similarly in 30:16.

give less. [16]Receive this ransom money from the Israelites, and use it for the care of the Tabernacle.* It will bring the Israelites to the LORD's attention, and it will purify your lives."

PLANS FOR THE WASHBASIN

[17]Then the LORD said to Moses, [18]"Make a bronze washbasin with a bronze stand. Place it between the Tabernacle and the altar, and fill it with water. [19]Aaron and his sons will wash their hands and feet there. [20]They must wash with water whenever they go into the Tabernacle to appear before the LORD and when they approach the altar to burn up their special gifts to the LORD—or they will die! [21]They must always wash their hands and feet, or they will die. This is a permanent law for Aaron and his descendants, to be observed from generation to generation."

THE ANOINTING OIL

[22]Then the LORD said to Moses, [23]"Collect choice spices—12½ pounds of pure myrrh, 6¼ pounds of fragrant cinnamon, 6¼ pounds of fragrant calamus,* [24]and 12½ pounds of cassia*—as measured by the weight of the sanctuary shekel. Also get one gallon of olive oil.* [25]Like a skilled incense maker, blend these ingredients to make a holy anointing oil. [26]Use this sacred oil to anoint the Tabernacle, the Ark of the Covenant, [27]the table and all its utensils, the lampstand and all its accessories, the incense altar, [28]the altar of burnt offering and all its utensils, and the washbasin with its stand. [29]Consecrate them to make them absolutely holy. After this, whatever touches them will also become holy.

[30]"Anoint Aaron and his sons also, consecrating them to serve me as priests. [31]And say to the people of Israel, 'This holy anointing oil is reserved for me from generation to generation. [32]It must never be used to anoint anyone else, and you must never make any blend like it for yourselves. It is holy, and you must treat it as holy. [33]Anyone who makes a blend like it or anoints someone other than a priest will be cut off from the community.' "

THE INCENSE

[34]Then the LORD said to Moses, "Gather fragrant spices—resin droplets, mollusk shell, and galbanum—and mix these fragrant spices with pure frankincense, weighed out in equal amounts. [35]Using the usual techniques of the incense maker, blend the spices together and sprinkle them with salt to produce a pure and holy incense. [36]Grind some of the mixture into a very fine powder and put it in front of the Ark of the Covenant,* where I will meet with you in the Tabernacle. You must treat this incense as most holy. [37]Never use this formula to make this incense for yourselves. It is reserved for the LORD, and you must treat it as holy. [38]Anyone who makes incense like this for personal use will be cut off from the community."

31

CRAFTSMEN: BEZALEL AND OHOLIAB

Then the LORD said to Moses, [2]"Look, I have specifically chosen Bezalel son of Uri, grandson of Hur, of the tribe of Judah. [3]I have filled him with the Spirit of God, giving him great wisdom, ability, and expertise in all kinds of crafts. [4]He is a master craftsman, expert in working with gold, silver, and bronze. [5]He is skilled in engraving and mounting gemstones and in carving wood. He is a master at every craft!

[6]"And I have personally appointed Oholiab son of Ahisamach, of the tribe of Dan, to be his assistant. Moreover, I have given special skill to all the gifted craftsmen so they can make all the things I have commanded you to make:

7 the Tabernacle;*
the Ark of the Covenant;*
the Ark's cover—the place of atonement;
all the furnishings of the Tabernacle;
8 the table and its utensils;
the pure gold lampstand with all its accessories;
the incense altar;
9 the altar of burnt offering with all its utensils;
the washbasin with its stand;
10 the beautifully stitched garments—the sacred garments for Aaron the priest, and the garments for his sons to wear as they minister as priests;
11 the anointing oil;
the fragrant incense for the Holy Place.

The craftsmen must make everything as I have commanded you."

INSTRUCTIONS FOR THE SABBATH

[12]The LORD then gave these instructions to Moses: [13]"Tell the people of Israel: 'Be careful to keep my Sabbath day, for the Sabbath is a sign of the covenant between me and you from generation to generation. It is given so you may know that I am the LORD, who makes you holy. [14]You must keep the Sabbath day, for it is a holy day for you. Anyone who desecrates it must be put to death; anyone who works on that day will be cut off from the community. [15]You have six days each week for your ordinary work, but the seventh day must be a Sabbath day of complete rest, a holy day dedicated to the LORD. Anyone who works on the Sabbath must be put to death. [16]The people of Israel must keep the Sabbath day by observing it from generation to generation. This is a covenant obligation for all time. [17]It is a permanent sign of my covenant with the people of Israel. For in six days the LORD made heaven and earth, but on the seventh day he stopped working and was refreshed.' "

[18]When the LORD finished speaking with Moses on Mount Sinai, he gave him the two stone tablets inscribed with the terms of the covenant,* written by the finger of God.

30:16 Hebrew *Tent of Meeting;* also in 30:18, 20, 26, 36. **30:23** Hebrew *500 shekels* [5.7 kilograms] *of pure myrrh, 250 shekels* [2.9 kilograms] *of fragrant cinnamon, 250 shekels of fragrant calamus.* **30:24a** Hebrew *500 shekels* [5.7 kilograms] *of cassia.* **30:24b** Hebrew *1 hin* [3.8 liters] *of olive oil.* **30:36** Hebrew *in front of the Testimony;* see note on 25:16. **31:7a** Hebrew *the Tent of Meeting.* **31:7b** Hebrew *the Ark of the Testimony.* **31:18** Hebrew *the two tablets of the Testimony;* see note on 25:16.

keeping it real

I loved ballet. I learned how to dance when I was five years old and have been doing it ever since. In the past I practiced every day and took lessons at least once a week. I dreamed of someday joining the American Ballet Theatre.

By the time I got to high school, ballet had become my life. Everything revolved around my dancing—even my social life. If I had a recital, I dropped out of every other activity in order to practice. And I was obsessed with my weight, unwilling to gain even a few extra ounces.

When I became a Christian, I never dreamed that it would affect my ballet. But one day in church the sermon was on the first commandment. The pastor talked about how certain things can become gods to us if we let them become more important than God. I compared the amount of time I spent practicing my ballet to the amount of time I spent reading the Bible and praying. Had ballet become my idol?

I began to pray about it. God showed me that I had allowed ballet to become more important than him. I decided to spend no more time practicing than I did reading the Bible and praying. I cut down on my dancing lessons and got involved in our church's youth group. It's been difficult to let up on dancing, but now it's okay that dancing is my second love. My first love is Jesus. —Kristy

32 THE GOLD CALF

When the people saw how long it was taking Moses to
come back down the mountain, they gathered around
Aaron. "Come on," they said, "make us some gods who
can lead us. We don't know what happened to this fellow
Moses, who brought us here from the land of Egypt."
2So Aaron said, "Take the gold rings from the ears of
your wives and sons and daughters, and bring them to
me."
3All the people took the gold rings from their ears and
brought them to Aaron. 4Then Aaron took the gold,
melted it down, and molded it into the shape of a calf.
When the people saw it, they exclaimed, "O Israel, these
are the gods who brought you out of the land of Egypt!"
5Aaron saw how excited the people were, so he built an
altar in front of the calf. Then he announced, "Tomorrow
will be a festival to the LORD!"
6The people got up early the next morning to sacrifice
burnt offerings and peace offerings. After this, they celebrated with feasting and drinking, and they indulged in
pagan revelry.
7The LORD told Moses, "Quick! Go down the mountain!
Your people whom you brought from the land of Egypt
have corrupted themselves. 8How quickly they have
turned away from the way I commanded them to live!
They have melted down gold and made a calf, and they
have bowed down and sacrificed to it. They are saying,
'These are your gods, O Israel, who brought you out of the
land of Egypt.'"
9Then the LORD said, "I have seen how stubborn and
rebellious these people are. 10Now leave me alone so my
fierce anger can blaze against them, and I will destroy
them. Then I will make you, Moses, into a great nation."
11But Moses tried to pacify the LORD his God. "O LORD!"
he said. "Why are you so angry with your own people
whom you brought from the land of Egypt with such
great power and such a strong hand? 12Why let the Egyptians say, 'Their God rescued them with the evil intention
of slaughtering them in the mountains and wiping them
from the face of the earth'? Turn away from your fierce
anger. Change your mind about this terrible disaster you
have threatened against your people! 13Remember your
servants Abraham, Isaac, and Jacob.* You bound yourself
with an oath to them, saying, 'I will make your descendants as numerous as the stars of heaven. And I will give
them all of this land that I have promised to your descendants, and they will possess it forever.'"
14So the LORD changed his mind about the terrible disaster he had threatened to bring on his people.
15Then Moses turned and went down the mountain.
He held in his hands the two stone tablets inscribed with
the terms of the covenant.* They were inscribed on both

32:13 Hebrew *Israel*. The names "Jacob" and "Israel" are often interchanged throughout the Old Testament, referring sometimes to the individual patriarch and sometimes to the nation. 32:15 Hebrew *the two tablets of the Testimony;* see note on 25:16.

sides, front and back. [16]These tablets were God's work;
the words on them were written by God himself.
[17]When Joshua heard the boisterous noise of the people shouting below them, he exclaimed to Moses, "It
sounds like war in the camp!"

IDOLS 32:1-10

Idols again! Even though Israel had seen the invisible God in action, they still wanted the familiar gods they could see and shape into whatever image they desired. How like them we sometimes are! Our great temptation is still to shape God to our liking, to make him convenient to obey or ignore. God responds in great anger when his mercy is trampled on. The gods we create blind us to the love God wants to shower on us. God cannot work in us when we elevate anyone or anything above him. Are there any idols in your life? If so, what will you do about them? ■

[18]But Moses replied, "No, it's not a shout of victory nor
the wailing of defeat. I hear the sound of a celebration."
[19]When they came near the camp, Moses saw the calf
and the dancing, and he burned with anger. He threw the
stone tablets to the ground, smashing them at the foot of
the mountain. [20]He took the calf they had made and
burned it. Then he ground it into powder, threw it into
the water, and forced the people to drink it.
[21]Finally, he turned to Aaron and demanded, "What
did these people do to you to make you bring such terrible sin upon them?"
[22]"Don't get so upset, my lord," Aaron replied. "You
yourself know how evil these people are. [23]They said to
me, 'Make us gods who will lead us. We don't know what
happened to this fellow Moses, who brought us here
from the land of Egypt.' [24]So I told them, 'Whoever has
gold jewelry, take it off.' When they brought it to me, I
simply threw it into the fire—and out came this calf!"
[25]Moses saw that Aaron had let the people get completely out of control, much to the amusement of their enemies.* [26]So he stood at the entrance to the camp and
shouted, "All of you who are on the LORD's side, come here
and join me." And all the Levites gathered around him.
[27]Moses told them, "This is what the LORD, the God of
Israel, says: Each of you, take your swords and go back
and forth from one end of the camp to the other. Kill
everyone—even your brothers, friends, and neighbors."
[28]The Levites obeyed Moses' command, and about 3,000
people died that day.
[29]Then Moses told the Levites, "Today you have ordained yourselves* for the service of the LORD, for you
obeyed him even though it meant killing your own sons
and brothers. Today you have earned a blessing."

MOSES INTERCEDES FOR ISRAEL

[30]The next day Moses said to the people, "You have committed a terrible sin, but I will go back up to the LORD on
the mountain. Perhaps I will be able to obtain forgiveness* for your sin."
[31]So Moses returned to the LORD and said, "Oh, what a
terrible sin these people have committed. They have
made gods of gold for themselves. [32]But now, if you will
only forgive their sin—but if not, erase my name from the
record you have written!"
[33]But the LORD replied to Moses, "No, I will erase the
name of everyone who has sinned against me. [34]Now go,
lead the people to the place I told you about. Look! My angel will lead the way before you. And when I come to call
the people to account, I will certainly hold them responsible for their sins."
[35]Then the LORD sent a great plague upon the people
because they had worshiped the calf Aaron had made.

PRAYER POWER 32:9-14

God was ready to destroy the whole nation of Israel because they sinned. But when Moses pleaded for mercy, God spared them. This is one of the countless examples in Scripture of how prayer can make a difference. Many times, however, we neglect prayer because a situation seems irreversible. Can you relate? Knowing that God has the power to change the impossible into the possible can help you persist in the prayer habit. ■

33

The LORD said to Moses, "Get going, you and
the people you brought up from the land of Egypt. Go up
to the land I swore to give to Abraham, Isaac, and Jacob. I
told them, 'I will give this land to your descendants.' [2]And
I will send an angel before you to drive out the Canaanites, Amorites, Hittites, Perizzites, Hivites, and Jebusites.
[3]Go up to this land that flows with milk and honey. But I
will not travel among you, for you are a stubborn and rebellious people. If I did, I would surely destroy you along
the way."
[4]When the people heard these stern words, they went
into mourning and stopped wearing their jewelry and
fine clothes. [5]For the LORD had told Moses to tell them,
"You are a stubborn and rebellious people. If I were to
travel with you for even a moment, I would destroy you.
Remove your jewelry and fine clothes while I decide what
to do with you." [6]So from the time they left Mount Sinai,*
the Israelites wore no more jewelry or fine clothes.
[7]It was Moses' practice to take the Tent of Meeting*
and set it up some distance from the camp. Everyone who
wanted to make a request of the LORD would go to the
Tent of Meeting outside the camp.
[8]Whenever Moses went out to the Tent of Meeting, all
the people would get up and stand in the entrances of
their own tents. They would all watch Moses until he disappeared inside. [9]As he went into the tent, the pillar of
cloud would come down and hover at its entrance while

32:25 Or *out of control, and they mocked anyone who opposed them.* The meaning of the Hebrew is unclear. 32:29 As in Greek and Latin versions; Hebrew reads *Today ordain yourselves.* 32:30 Or *to make atonement.* 33:6 Hebrew *Horeb,* another name for Sinai. 33:7 This "Tent of Meeting" is different from the Tabernacle described in chapters 26 and 36.

the LORD spoke with Moses. 10When the people saw the cloud standing at the entrance of the tent, they would stand and bow down in front of their own tents. 11Inside the Tent of Meeting, the LORD would speak to Moses face to face, as one speaks to a friend. Afterward Moses would return to the camp, but the young man who assisted him, Joshua son of Nun, would remain behind in the Tent of Meeting.

A FRIEND OF GOD 33:11

God and Moses talked face to face, just as friends do. Moses relied on God's wisdom and direction. His personality and skills did not earn him God's friendship. God simply chose him as a friend. Thanks to Jesus, God chooses us to be his friends. (See John 15:15.) Have you accepted his friendship? ■

MOSES SEES THE LORD'S GLORY

12One day Moses said to the LORD, "You have been telling me, 'Take these people up to the Promised Land.' But you haven't told me whom you will send with me. You have told me, 'I know you by name, and I look favorably on you.' 13If it is true that you look favorably on me, let me know your ways so I may understand you more fully and continue to enjoy your favor. And remember that this nation is your very own people."

14The LORD replied, "I will personally go with you, Moses, and I will give you rest—everything will be fine for you."

15Then Moses said, "If you don't personally go with us, don't make us leave this place. 16How will anyone know that you look favorably on me—on me and on your people—if you don't go with us? For your presence among us sets your people and me apart from all other people on the earth."

17The LORD replied to Moses, "I will indeed do what you have asked, for I look favorably on you, and I know you by name."

18Moses responded, "Then show me your glorious presence."

19The LORD replied, "I will make all my goodness pass before you, and I will call out my name, Yahweh,* before you. For I will show mercy to anyone I choose, and I will show compassion to anyone I choose. 20But you may not look directly at my face, for no one may see me and live." 21The LORD continued, "Look, stand near me on this rock. 22As my glorious presence passes by, I will hide you in the crevice of the rock and cover you with my hand until I have passed by. 23Then I will remove my hand and let you see me from behind. But my face will not be seen."

34 A NEW COPY OF THE COVENANT

Then the LORD told Moses, "Chisel out two stone tablets like the first ones. I will write on them the same words that were on the tablets you smashed. 2Be ready in the morning to climb up Mount Sinai and present yourself to me on the top of the mountain. 3No one else may come with you. In fact, no one is to appear anywhere on the mountain. Do not even let the flocks or herds graze near the mountain."

4So Moses chiseled out two tablets of stone like the first ones. Early in the morning he climbed Mount Sinai as the LORD had commanded him, and he carried the two stone tablets in his hands.

5Then the LORD came down in a cloud and stood there with him; and he called out his own name, Yahweh.* 6The LORD passed in front of Moses, calling out,

"Yahweh!* The LORD!
  The God of compassion and mercy!
I am slow to anger
  and filled with unfailing love and faithfulness.
7 I lavish unfailing love to a thousand generations.*
  I forgive iniquity, rebellion, and sin.
But I do not excuse the guilty.
  I lay the sins of the parents upon their children and grandchildren;
the entire family is affected—
  even children in the third and fourth generations."

GOD'S CHARACTER 34:6-7

Moses had asked to see God's glorious presence (33:18), and this was God's response. He wanted to give Moses a brief overview of his character. Notice that God did not give Moses a vision of his power and majesty, but rather of his love. God's glory is revealed in his mercy, grace, compassion, faithfulness, forgiveness, and justice. We give glory to God when we show his characteristics. Do your actions resemble his? ■

8Moses immediately threw himself to the ground and worshiped. 9And he said, "O Lord, if it is true that I have found favor with you, then please travel with us. Yes, this is a stubborn and rebellious people, but please forgive our iniquity and our sins. Claim us as your own special possession."

10The LORD replied, "Listen, I am making a covenant with you in the presence of all your people. I will perform miracles that have never been performed anywhere in all the earth or in any nation. And all the people around you will see the power of the LORD—the awesome power I will display for you. 11But listen carefully to everything I command you today. Then I will go ahead of you and drive out the Amorites, Canaanites, Hittites, Perizzites, Hivites, and Jebusites.

12"Be very careful never to make a treaty with the people who live in the land where you are going. If you do, you will follow their evil ways and be trapped. 13Instead,

33:19 *Yahweh* is a transliteration of the proper name *YHWH* that is sometimes rendered "Jehovah"; in this translation it is usually rendered "the LORD" (note the use of small capitals). **34:5** *Yahweh* is a transliteration of the proper name *YHWH* that is sometimes rendered "Jehovah"; in this translation it is usually rendered "the LORD" (note the use of small capitals). **34:6** See note on 34:5. **34:7** Hebrew *for thousands.*

you must break down their pagan altars, smash their sacred pillars, and cut down their Asherah poles. [14]You
must worship no other gods, for the LORD, whose very
name is Jealous, is a God who is jealous about his relationship with you.

[15]"You must not make a treaty of any kind with the
people living in the land. They lust after their gods, offering sacrifices to them. They will invite you to join them in
their sacrificial meals, and you will go with them. [16]Then
you will accept their daughters, who sacrifice to other
gods, as wives for your sons. And they will seduce your
sons to commit adultery against me by worshiping other
gods. [17]You must not make any gods of molten metal for
yourselves.

[18]"You must celebrate the Festival of Unleavened
Bread. For seven days the bread you eat must be made
without yeast, just as I commanded you. Celebrate this
festival annually at the appointed time in early spring, in
the month of Abib,* for that is the anniversary of your departure from Egypt.

[19]"The firstborn of every animal belongs to me, including the firstborn males from your herds of cattle and
your flocks of sheep and goats. [20]A firstborn donkey may
be bought back from the LORD by presenting a lamb or
young goat in its place. But if you do not buy it back, you
must break its neck. However, you must buy back every
firstborn son.

"No one may appear before me without an offering.

[21]"You have six days each week for your ordinary work,
but on the seventh day you must stop working, even during the seasons of plowing and harvest.

[22]"You must celebrate the Festival of Harvest* with the
first crop of the wheat harvest, and celebrate the Festival
of the Final Harvest* at the end of the harvest season.
[23]Three times each year every man in Israel must appear
before the Sovereign, the LORD, the God of Israel. [24]I will
drive out the other nations ahead of you and expand your
territory, so no one will covet and conquer your land
while you appear before the LORD your God three times
each year.

[25]"You must not offer the blood of my sacrificial offerings together with any baked goods containing yeast.
And none of the meat of the Passover sacrifice may be
kept over until the next morning.

[26]"As you harvest your crops, bring the very best of the
first harvest to the house of the LORD your God.

"You must not cook a young goat in its mother's milk."

[27]Then the LORD said to Moses, "Write down all these
instructions, for they represent the terms of the covenant
I am making with you and with Israel."

[28]Moses remained there on the mountain with the
LORD forty days and forty nights. In all that time he ate no
bread and drank no water. And the LORD* wrote the
terms of the covenant—the Ten Commandments*—on
the stone tablets.

[29]When Moses came down Mount Sinai carrying the
two stone tablets inscribed with the terms of the covenant,* he wasn't aware that his face had become radiant
because he had spoken to the LORD. [30]So when Aaron and
the people of Israel saw the radiance of Moses' face, they
were afraid to come near him.

[31]But Moses called out to them and asked Aaron and all
the leaders of the community to come over, and he talked
with them. [32]Then all the people of Israel approached
him, and Moses gave them all the instructions the LORD
had given him on Mount Sinai. [33]When Moses finished
speaking with them, he covered his face with a veil. [34]But
whenever he went into the Tent of Meeting to speak with
the LORD, he would remove the veil until he came out
again. Then he would give the people whatever instructions the LORD had given him, [35]and the people of Israel
would see the radiant glow of his face. So he would put
the veil over his face until he returned to speak with the
LORD.

35

INSTRUCTIONS FOR THE SABBATH

Then Moses called together the whole community of Israel and told them, "These are the instructions the LORD
has commanded you to follow. [2]You have six days each
week for your ordinary work, but the seventh day must be
a Sabbath day of complete rest, a holy day dedicated to
the LORD. Anyone who works on that day must be put to
death. [3]You must not even light a fire in any of your
homes on the Sabbath."

OFFERINGS FOR THE TABERNACLE

[4]Then Moses said to the whole community of Israel, "This
is what the LORD has commanded: [5]Take a sacred offering for the LORD. Let those with generous hearts present
the following gifts to the LORD:

gold, silver, and bronze;
6 blue, purple, and scarlet thread;
fine linen and goat hair for cloth;
7 tanned ram skins and fine goatskin leather;
acacia wood;
8 olive oil for the lamps;
spices for the anointing oil and the fragrant incense;
9 onyx stones, and other gemstones to be set in the
ephod and the priest's chestpiece.

[10]"Come, all of you who are gifted craftsmen. Construct everything that the LORD has commanded:

11 the Tabernacle and its sacred tent, its covering,
clasps, frames, crossbars, posts, and bases;
12 the Ark and its carrying poles;
the Ark's cover—the place of atonement;
the inner curtain to shield the Ark;

34:18 Hebrew *appointed time in the month of Abib.* This first month of the ancient Hebrew lunar calendar usually occurs within the months of March and April. **34:22a** Hebrew *Festival of Weeks;* compare 23:16. This was later called the Festival of Pentecost. It is celebrated today as Shavuat (or Shabuoth). **34:22b** Or *Festival of Ingathering.* This was later called the Festival of Shelters or Festival of Tabernacles (see Lev 23:33-36). It is celebrated today as Sukkot (or Succoth). **34:28a** Hebrew *he.* **34:28b** Hebrew *the ten words.* **34:29** Hebrew *the two tablets of the Testimony;* see note on 25:16.

13 the table, its carrying poles, and all its utensils;
the Bread of the Presence;
14 for light, the lampstand, its accessories, the lamp
cups, and the olive oil for lighting;
15 the incense altar and its carrying poles;
the anointing oil and fragrant incense;
the curtain for the entrance of the Tabernacle;
16 the altar of burnt offering;
the bronze grating of the altar and its carrying poles
and utensils;
the washbasin with its stand;
17 the curtains for the walls of the courtyard;
the posts and their bases;
the curtain for the entrance to the courtyard;
18 the tent pegs of the Tabernacle and courtyard and
their ropes;
19 the beautifully stitched garments for the priests to
wear while ministering in the Holy Place—the
sacred garments for Aaron the priest, and the
garments for his sons to wear as they minister
as priests."

CHEERFUL GIVING 35:21

Those whose hearts were stirred by God gave cheerfully to the Tabernacle. They gave with great enthusiasm, because they knew how important their giving was to the completion of God's house. Their cheerful giving showed their level of commitment to God. Generous people aren't necessarily faithful to God. But faithful people are usually generous. Feeling generous? ■

20 So the whole community of Israel left Moses and returned to their tents. 21 All whose hearts were stirred and
whose spirits were moved came and brought their sacred
offerings to the LORD. They brought all the materials
needed for the Tabernacle,* for the performance of its
rituals, and for the sacred garments. 22 Both men and
women came, all whose hearts were willing. They
brought to the LORD their offerings of gold—brooches,
earrings, rings from their fingers, and necklaces. They
presented gold objects of every kind as a special offering
to the LORD. 23 All those who owned the following items
willingly brought them: blue, purple, and scarlet thread;
fine linen and goat hair for cloth; and tanned ram skins
and fine goatskin leather. 24 And all who had silver and
bronze objects gave them as a sacred offering to the
LORD. And those who had acacia wood brought it for use
in the project.

25 All the women who were skilled in sewing and spinning prepared blue, purple, and scarlet thread, and fine
linen cloth. 26 All the women who were willing used their
skills to spin the goat hair into yarn. 27 The leaders
brought onyx stones and the special gemstones to be set
in the ephod and the priest's chestpiece. 28 They also
brought spices and olive oil for the light, the anointing
oil, and the fragrant incense. 29 So the people of Israel—
every man and woman who was eager to help in the work
the LORD had given them through Moses—brought their
gifts and gave them freely to the LORD.

30 Then Moses told the people of Israel, "The LORD has
specifically chosen Bezalel son of Uri, grandson of Hur,
of the tribe of Judah. 31 The LORD has filled Bezalel with
the Spirit of God, giving him great wisdom, ability, and
expertise in all kinds of crafts. 32 He is a master craftsman, expert in working with gold, silver, and bronze. 33 He
is skilled in engraving and mounting gemstones and in
carving wood. He is a master at every craft. 34 And the
LORD has given both him and Oholiab son of Ahisamach,
of the tribe of Dan, the ability to teach their skills to others. 35 The LORD has given them special skills as engravers,
designers, embroiderers in blue, purple, and scarlet
thread on fine linen cloth, and weavers. They excel as
craftsmen and as designers.

36

"The LORD has gifted Bezalel, Oholiab, and the
other skilled craftsmen with wisdom and ability to perform any task involved in building the sanctuary. Let
them construct and furnish the Tabernacle, just as the
LORD has commanded."

2 So Moses summoned Bezalel and Oholiab and all the
others who were specially gifted by the LORD and were
eager to get to work. 3 Moses gave them the materials donated by the people of Israel as sacred offerings for the
completion of the sanctuary. But the people continued to
bring additional gifts each morning. 4 Finally the craftsmen who were working on the sanctuary left their work.
5 They went to Moses and reported, "The people have
given more than enough materials to complete the job
the LORD has commanded us to do!"

6 So Moses gave the command, and this message was
sent throughout the camp: "Men and women, don't prepare any more gifts for the sanctuary. We have enough!"
So the people stopped bringing their sacred offerings.
7 Their contributions were more than enough to complete the whole project.

BUILDING THE TABERNACLE

8 The skilled craftsmen made ten curtains of finely woven
linen for the Tabernacle. Then Bezalel* decorated the
curtains with blue, purple, and scarlet thread and with
skillfully embroidered cherubim. 9 All ten curtains were
exactly the same size—42 feet long and 6 feet wide.*
10 Five of these curtains were joined together to make one
long curtain, and the other five were joined to make a second long curtain. 11 He made fifty loops of blue yarn and
put them along the edge of the last curtain in each set.
12 The fifty loops along the edge of one curtain matched
the fifty loops along the edge of the other curtain. 13 Then
he made fifty gold clasps and fastened the long curtains
together with the clasps. In this way, the Tabernacle was
made of one continuous piece.

14 He made eleven curtains of goat-hair cloth to serve

35:21 Hebrew *Tent of Meeting*. 36:8 Hebrew *he;* also in 36:16, 20, 35. See 37:1. 36:9 Hebrew *28 cubits* [12.9 meters] *long and 4 cubits* [1.8 meters] *wide*.

as a tent covering for the Tabernacle. [15]These eleven curtains were all exactly the same size—45 feet long and 6 feet wide.* [16]Bezalel joined five of these curtains together to make one long curtain, and the other six were joined to make a second long curtain. [17]He made fifty loops for the edge of each large curtain. [18]He also made fifty bronze clasps to fasten the long curtains together. In this way, the tent covering was made of one continuous piece. [19]He completed the tent covering with a layer of tanned ram skins and a layer of fine goatskin leather.

TEAMWORK 36:8-9

Making cloth (spinning and weaving) took a great deal of time in Moses' day. To own more than two or three changes of clothing was a sign of wealth! So you can imagine the huge effort involved in making enough cloth for the Tabernacle. It demonstrated a tremendous community effort. This same kind of teamwork is needed in churches and neighborhoods today. Without it, many essential services just wouldn't get done. Are you a team player? What part can you play in your church or community "team"? ■

[20]For the framework of the Tabernacle, Bezalel constructed frames of acacia wood. [21]Each frame was 15 feet high and 27 inches wide,* [22]with two pegs under each frame. All the frames were identical. [23]He made twenty of these frames to support the curtains on the south side of the Tabernacle. [24]He also made forty silver bases—two bases under each frame, with the pegs fitting securely into the bases. [25]For the north side of the Tabernacle, he made another twenty frames, [26]with their forty silver bases, two bases under each frame. [27]He made six frames for the rear—the west side of the Tabernacle—[28]along with two additional frames to reinforce the rear corners of the Tabernacle. [29]These corner frames were matched at the bottom and firmly attached at the top with a single ring, forming a single corner unit. Both of these corner units were made the same way. [30]So there were eight frames at the rear of the Tabernacle, set in sixteen silver bases—two bases under each frame.

[31]Then he made crossbars of acacia wood to link the frames, five crossbars for the north side of the Tabernacle [32]and five for the south side. He also made five crossbars for the rear of the Tabernacle, which faced west. [33]He made the middle crossbar to attach halfway up the frames; it ran all the way from one end of the Tabernacle to the other. [34]He overlaid the frames with gold and made gold rings to hold the crossbars. Then he overlaid the crossbars with gold as well.

[35]For the inside of the Tabernacle, Bezalel made a special curtain of finely woven linen. He decorated it with blue, purple, and scarlet thread and with skillfully embroidered cherubim. [36]For the curtain, he made four posts of acacia wood and four gold hooks. He overlaid the posts with gold and set them in four silver bases.

[37]Then he made another curtain for the entrance to the sacred tent. He made it of finely woven linen and embroidered it with exquisite designs using blue, purple, and scarlet thread. [38]This curtain was hung on gold hooks attached to five posts. The posts with their decorated tops and hooks were overlaid with gold, and the five bases were cast from bronze.

37

BUILDING THE ARK OF THE COVENANT

Next Bezalel made the Ark of acacia wood—a sacred chest 45 inches long, 27 inches wide, and 27 inches high.* [2]He overlaid it inside and outside with pure gold, and he ran a molding of gold all around it. [3]He cast four gold rings and attached them to its four feet, two rings on each side. [4]Then he made poles from acacia wood and overlaid them with gold. [5]He inserted the poles into the rings at the sides of the Ark to carry it.

[6]Then he made the Ark's cover—the place of atonement—from pure gold. It was 45 inches long and 27 inches wide.* [7]He made two cherubim from hammered gold and placed them on the two ends of the atonement cover. [8]He molded the cherubim on each end of the atonement cover, making it all of one piece of gold. [9]The cherubim faced each other and looked down on the atonement cover. With their wings spread above it, they protected it.

BUILDING THE TABLE

[10]Then Bezalel* made the table of acacia wood, 36 inches long, 18 inches wide, and 27 inches high.* [11]He overlaid it with pure gold and ran a gold molding around the edge. [12]He decorated it with a 3-inch border* all around, and he ran a gold molding along the border. [13]Then he cast four gold rings for the table and attached them at the four corners next to the four legs. [14]The rings were attached near the border to hold the poles that were used to carry the table. [15]He made these poles from acacia wood and overlaid them with gold. [16]Then he made special containers of pure gold for the table—bowls, pans, jars, and pitchers—to be used in pouring out liquid offerings.

BUILDING THE LAMPSTAND

[17]Then Bezalel made the lampstand of pure, hammered gold. He made the entire lampstand and its decorations of one piece—the base, center stem, lamp cups, buds, and petals. [18]The lampstand had six branches going out from the center stem, three on each side. [19]Each of the six branches had three lamp cups shaped like almond blossoms, complete with buds and petals. [20]The center stem of the lampstand was crafted with four lamp cups shaped like almond blossoms, complete with buds and petals.

36:15 Hebrew *30 cubits* [13.8 meters] *long and 4 cubits* [1.8 meters] *wide.* **36:21** Hebrew *10 cubits* [4.6 meters] *high and 1.5 cubits* [69 centimeters] *wide.* **37:1** Hebrew *2.5 cubits* [115 centimeters] *long, 1.5 cubits* [69 centimeters] *wide, and 1.5 cubits high.* **37:6** Hebrew *2.5 cubits* [115 centimeters] *long and 1.5 cubits* [69 centimeters] *wide.* **37:10a** Hebrew *he;* also in 37:17, 25. **37:10b** Hebrew *2 cubits* [92 centimeters] *long, 1 cubit* [46 centimeters] *wide, and 1.5 cubits* [69 centimeters] *high.* **37:12** Hebrew *a border of a handbreadth* [8 centimeters].

[21]There was an almond bud beneath each pair of
branches where the six branches extended from the center stem, all made of one piece. [22]The almond buds and
branches were all of one piece with the center stem, and
they were hammered from pure gold.
[23]He also made seven lamps for the lampstand, lamp
snuffers, and trays, all of pure gold. [24]The entire lampstand, along with its accessories, was made from seventy-
five pounds* of pure gold.

BUILDING THE INCENSE ALTAR

[25]Then Bezalel made the incense altar of acacia wood. It
was 18 inches square and 36 inches high,* with horns at
the corners carved from the same piece of wood as the altar itself. [26]He overlaid the top, sides, and horns of the altar with pure gold, and he ran a gold molding around the
entire altar. [27]He made two gold rings and attached them
on opposite sides of the altar below the gold molding to
hold the carrying poles. [28]He made the poles of acacia
wood and overlaid them with gold.
[29]Then he made the sacred anointing oil and the fragrant incense, using the techniques of a skilled incense
maker.

38

BUILDING THE ALTAR OF BURNT OFFERING

Next Bezalel* used acacia wood to construct the square
altar of burnt offering. It was 7½ feet wide, 7½ feet long,
and 4½ feet high.* [2]He made horns for each of its four
corners so that the horns and altar were all one piece. He
overlaid the altar with bronze. [3]Then he made all the altar
utensils of bronze—the ash buckets, shovels, basins,
meat forks, and firepans. [4]Next he made a bronze grating
and installed it halfway down the side of the altar, under
the ledge. [5]He cast four rings and attached them to the
corners of the bronze grating to hold the carrying poles.
[6]He made the poles from acacia wood and overlaid them
with bronze. [7]He inserted the poles through the rings on
the sides of the altar. The altar was hollow and was made
from planks.

BUILDING THE WASHBASIN

[8]Bezalel made the bronze washbasin and its bronze stand
from bronze mirrors donated by the women who served
at the entrance of the Tabernacle.*

BUILDING THE COURTYARD

[9]Then Bezalel made the courtyard, which was enclosed
with curtains made of finely woven linen. On the south
side the curtains were 150 feet long.* [10]They were held
up by twenty posts set securely in twenty bronze bases.
He hung the curtains with silver hooks and rings. [11]He
made a similar set of curtains for the north side—
150 feet of curtains held up by twenty posts set securely
in bronze bases. He hung the curtains with silver hooks
and rings. [12]The curtains on the west end of the courtyard were 75 feet long,* hung with silver hooks and rings
and supported by ten posts set into ten bases. [13]The east
end, the front, was also 75 feet long.
[14]The courtyard entrance was on the east end,
flanked by two curtains. The curtain on the right side
was 22½ feet long* and was supported by three posts
set into three bases. [15]The curtain on the left side was
also 22½ feet long and was supported by three posts set
into three bases. [16]All the curtains used in the courtyard
were made of finely woven linen. [17]Each post had a
bronze base, and all the hooks and rings were silver. The
tops of the posts of the courtyard were overlaid with
silver, and the rings to hold up the curtains were made
of silver.
[18]He made the curtain for the entrance to the courtyard of finely woven linen, and he decorated it with beautiful embroidery in blue, purple, and scarlet thread. It
was 30 feet long, and its height was 7½ feet,* just like the
curtains of the courtyard walls. [19]It was supported by
four posts, each set securely in its own bronze base. The
tops of the posts were overlaid with silver, and the hooks
and rings were also made of silver.
[20]All the tent pegs used in the Tabernacle and courtyard were made of bronze.

INVENTORY OF MATERIALS

[21]This is an inventory of the materials used in building
the Tabernacle of the Covenant.* The Levites compiled
the figures, as Moses directed, and Ithamar son of Aaron
the priest served as recorder. [22]Bezalel son of Uri, grandson of Hur, of the tribe of Judah, made everything just as
the LORD had commanded Moses. [23]He was assisted by
Oholiab son of Ahisamach, of the tribe of Dan, a craftsman expert at engraving, designing, and embroidering
with blue, purple, and scarlet thread on fine linen cloth.
[24]The people brought special offerings of gold total-
ing 2,193 pounds,* as measured by the weight of the
sanctuary shekel. This gold was used throughout the
Tabernacle.
[25]The whole community of Israel gave 7,545 pounds*
of silver, as measured by the weight of the sanctuary
shekel. [26]This silver came from the tax collected from
each man registered in the census. (The tax is one beka,
which is half a shekel,* based on the sanctuary shekel.)
The tax was collected from 603,550 men who had
reached their twentieth birthday. [27]The hundred bases
for the frames of the sanctuary walls and for the posts
supporting the inner curtain required 7,500 pounds of
silver, about 75 pounds for each base.* [28]The remaining
45 pounds* of silver was used to make the hooks and
rings and to overlay the tops of the posts.

37:24 Hebrew *1 talent* [34 kilograms]. **37:25** Hebrew *1 cubit* [46 centimeters] *long and 1 cubit wide, a square, and 2 cubits* [92 centimeters] *high.* **38:1a** Hebrew *he;* also in 38:8, 9. **38:1b** Hebrew *5 cubits* [2.3 meters] *wide, 5 cubits long, a square, and 3 cubits* [1.4 meters] *high.* **38:8** Hebrew *Tent of Meeting;* also in 38:30. **38:9** Hebrew *100 cubits* [46 meters]; also in 38:11. **38:12** Hebrew *50 cubits* [23 meters]; also in 38:13. **38:14** Hebrew *15 cubits* [6.9 meters]; also in 38:15. **38:18** Hebrew *20 cubits* [9.2 meters] *long and 5 cubits* [2.3 meters] *high.* **38:21** Hebrew *the Tabernacle, the Tabernacle of the Testimony.* **38:24** Hebrew *29 talents and 730 shekels* [994 kilograms]. Each shekel weighed about 0.4 ounces. **38:25** Hebrew *100 talents and 1,775 shekels* [3,420 kilograms]. **38:26** Or *0.2 ounces,* or *6 grams.* **38:27** Hebrew *100 talents* [3,400 kilograms] *of silver, 1 talent* [34 kilograms] *for each base.* **38:28** Hebrew *1,775 shekels* [20.2 kilograms].

29The people also brought as special offerings 5,310 pounds* of bronze, 30which was used for casting the bases for the posts at the entrance to the Tabernacle, and for the bronze altar with its bronze grating and all the altar utensils. 31Bronze was also used to make the bases for the posts that supported the curtains around the courtyard, the bases for the curtain at the entrance of the courtyard, and all the tent pegs for the Tabernacle and the courtyard.

39

CLOTHING FOR THE PRIESTS

The craftsmen made beautiful sacred garments of blue, purple, and scarlet cloth—clothing for Aaron to wear while ministering in the Holy Place, just as the LORD had commanded Moses.

MAKING THE EPHOD

2Bezalel* made the ephod of finely woven linen and embroidered it with gold and with blue, purple, and scarlet thread. 3He made gold thread by hammering out thin sheets of gold and cutting it into fine strands. With great skill and care, he worked it into the fine linen with the blue, purple, and scarlet thread.

4The ephod consisted of two pieces, front and back, joined at the shoulders with two shoulder-pieces. 5The decorative sash was made of the same materials: finely woven linen embroidered with gold and with blue, purple, and scarlet thread, just as the LORD had commanded Moses. 6They mounted the two onyx stones in settings of gold filigree. The stones were engraved with the names of the tribes of Israel, just as a seal is engraved. 7He fastened these stones on the shoulder-pieces of the ephod as a reminder that the priest represents the people of Israel. All this was done just as the LORD had commanded Moses.

MAKING THE CHESTPIECE

8Bezalel made the chestpiece with great skill and care. He made it to match the ephod, using finely woven linen embroidered with gold and with blue, purple, and scarlet thread. 9He made the chestpiece of a single piece of cloth folded to form a pouch nine inches* square. 10They mounted four rows of gemstones* on it. The first row contained a red carnelian, a pale-green peridot, and an emerald. 11The second row contained a turquoise, a blue lapis lazuli, and a white moonstone. 12The third row contained an orange jacinth, an agate, and a purple amethyst. 13The fourth row contained a blue-green beryl, an onyx, and a green jasper. All these stones were set in gold filigree. 14Each stone represented one of the twelve sons of Israel, and the name of that tribe was engraved on it like a seal.

15To attach the chestpiece to the ephod, they made braided cords of pure gold thread. 16They also made two settings of gold filigree and two gold rings and attached them to the top corners of the chestpiece. 17They tied the two gold cords to the rings on the chestpiece. 18They tied the other ends of the cords to the gold settings on the shoulder-pieces of the ephod. 19Then they made two more gold rings and attached them to the inside edges of the chestpiece next to the ephod. 20Then they made two more gold rings and attached them to the front of the ephod, below the shoulder-pieces, just above the knot where the decorative sash was fastened to the ephod. 21They attached the bottom rings of the chestpiece to the rings on the ephod with blue cords. In this way, the chestpiece was held securely to the ephod above the decorative sash. All this was done just as the LORD had commanded Moses.

ADDITIONAL CLOTHING FOR THE PRIESTS

22Bezalel made the robe that is worn with the ephod from a single piece of blue woven cloth, 23with an opening for Aaron's head in the middle of it. The opening was reinforced with a woven collar* so it would not tear. 24They made pomegranates of blue, purple, and scarlet yarn, and attached them to the hem of the robe. 25They also made bells of pure gold and placed them between the pomegranates along the hem of the robe, 26with bells and pomegranates alternating all around the hem. This robe was to be worn whenever the priest ministered before the LORD, just as the LORD had commanded Moses.

27They made tunics for Aaron and his sons from fine linen cloth. 28The turban and the special head coverings were made of fine linen, and the undergarments were also made of finely woven linen. 29The sashes were made of finely woven linen and embroidered with blue, purple, and scarlet thread, just as the LORD had commanded Moses.

30Finally, they made the sacred medallion—the badge of holiness—of pure gold. They engraved it like a seal with these words: HOLY TO THE LORD. 31They attached the medallion with a blue cord to Aaron's turban, just as the LORD had commanded Moses.

SMALL DETAILS 39:32

The Tabernacle was finally complete, down to the last detail. God was keenly interested in every detail—even the minor ones. Know what's cool? He cares infinitely more about you. You can talk with him about any of your concerns—no matter how small or unimportant they might seem. ■

MOSES INSPECTS THE WORK

32And so at last the Tabernacle* was finished. The Israelites had done everything just as the LORD had commanded Moses. 33And they brought the entire Tabernacle to Moses:

> the sacred tent with all its furnishings, clasps,
> frames, crossbars, posts, and bases;

38:29 Hebrew *70 talents and 2,400 shekels* [2,407 kilograms]. 39:2 Hebrew *He;* also in 39:8, 22. 39:9 Hebrew *1 span* [23 centimeters]. 39:10 The identification of some of these gemstones is uncertain. 39:23 The meaning of the Hebrew is uncertain. 39:32 Hebrew *the Tabernacle, the Tent of Meeting;* also in 39:40.

34 the tent coverings of tanned ram skins and fine
goatskin leather;
the inner curtain to shield the Ark;
35 the Ark of the Covenant* and its carrying poles;
the Ark's cover—the place of atonement;
36 the table and all its utensils;
the Bread of the Presence;
37 the pure gold lampstand with its symmetrical lamp
cups, all its accessories, and the olive oil for
lighting;
38 the gold altar;
the anointing oil and fragrant incense;
the curtain for the entrance of the sacred tent;
39 the bronze altar;
the bronze grating and its carrying poles and
utensils;
the washbasin with its stand;
40 the curtains for the walls of the courtyard;
the posts and their bases;
the curtain for the entrance to the courtyard;
the ropes and tent pegs;
all the furnishings to be used in worship at the
Tabernacle;
41 the beautifully stitched garments for the priests to
wear while ministering in the Holy Place—the
sacred garments for Aaron the priest, and the
garments for his sons to wear as they minister as
priests.

42So the people of Israel followed all of the LORD's instructions to Moses. 43Then Moses inspected all their work. When he found it had been done just as the LORD had commanded him, he blessed them.

40 THE TABERNACLE COMPLETED

Then the LORD said to Moses, 2"Set up the Tabernacle* on the first day of the new year.* 3Place the Ark of the Covenant* inside, and install the inner curtain to enclose the Ark within the Most Holy Place. 4Then bring in the table, and arrange the utensils on it. And bring in the lampstand, and set up the lamps.

5"Place the gold incense altar in front of the Ark of the Covenant. Then hang the curtain at the entrance of the Tabernacle. 6Place the altar of burnt offering in front of the Tabernacle entrance. 7Set the washbasin between the Tabernacle* and the altar, and fill it with water. 8Then set up the courtyard around the outside of the tent, and hang the curtain for the courtyard entrance.

9"Take the anointing oil and anoint the Tabernacle and all its furnishings to consecrate them and make them holy. 10 Anoint the altar of burnt offering and its utensils to consecrate them. Then the altar will become absolutely holy. 11Next anoint the washbasin and its stand to consecrate them.

12"Present Aaron and his sons at the entrance of the Tabernacle, and wash them with water. 13Dress Aaron with the sacred garments and anoint him, consecrating him to serve me as a priest. 14Then present his sons and dress them in their tunics. 15Anoint them as you did their father, so they may also serve me as priests. With their anointing, Aaron's descendants are set apart for the priesthood forever, from generation to generation."

16Moses proceeded to do everything just as the LORD had commanded him. 17So the Tabernacle was set up on the first day of the first month of the second year. 18Moses erected the Tabernacle by setting down its bases, inserting the frames, attaching the crossbars, and setting up the posts. 19Then he spread the coverings over the Tabernacle framework and put on the protective layers, just as the LORD had commanded him.

20He took the stone tablets inscribed with the terms of the covenant and placed them* inside the Ark. Then he attached the carrying poles to the Ark, and he set the Ark's cover—the place of atonement—on top of it. 21Then he brought the Ark of the Covenant into the Tabernacle and hung the inner curtain to shield it from view, just as the LORD had commanded him.

22Next Moses placed the table in the Tabernacle, along the north side of the Holy Place, just outside the inner curtain. 23And he arranged the Bread of the Presence on the table before the LORD, just as the LORD had commanded him.

24He set the lampstand in the Tabernacle across from the table on the south side of the Holy Place. 25Then he lit the lamps in the LORD's presence, just as the LORD had commanded him. 26He also placed the gold incense altar in the Tabernacle, in the Holy Place in front of the inner curtain. 27On it he burned the fragrant incense, just as the LORD had commanded him.

BIG CHANGES 40:38

Exodus began in gloom and ends in glory. The Israelites were once Egyptian slaves making bricks without straw. Now they're free and on their way to the land God promised them. This parallels our progress as Christians. We begin as slaves to sin, are bought at a price by God, and end our lives on Earth with the promise of living with God forever. Is that a promise you're counting on? ■

28He hung the curtain at the entrance of the Tabernacle, 29and he placed the altar of burnt offering near the Tabernacle entrance. On it he offered a burnt offering and a grain offering, just as the LORD had commanded him.

30Next Moses placed the washbasin between the Tabernacle and the altar. He filled it with water so the priests could wash themselves. 31Moses and Aaron and Aaron's sons used water from it to wash their hands and feet. 32Whenever they approached the altar and entered the Tabernacle, they washed themselves, just as the LORD had commanded Moses.

39:35 Or *Ark of the Testimony.* **40:2a** Hebrew *the Tabernacle, the Tent of Meeting;* also in 40:6, 29. **40:2b** Hebrew *the first day of the first month.* This day of the ancient Hebrew lunar calendar occurred in March or April. **40:3** Or *Ark of the Testimony;* also in 40:5, 21. **40:7** Hebrew *Tent of Meeting;* also in 40:12, 22, 24, 26, 30, 32, 34, 35. **40:20** Hebrew *He placed the Testimony;* see note on 25:16.

33Then he hung the curtains forming the courtyard
around the Tabernacle and the altar. And he set up the
curtain at the entrance of the courtyard. So at last Moses
finished the work.

THE LORD'S GLORY FILLS THE TABERNACLE

34Then the cloud covered the Tabernacle, and the glory
of the LORD filled the Tabernacle. 35Moses could no longer enter the Tabernacle because the cloud had settled
down over it, and the glory of the LORD filled the Tabernacle.

36Now whenever the cloud lifted from the Tabernacle,
the people of Israel would set out on their journey, following it. 37But if the cloud did not rise, they remained where
they were until it lifted. 38The cloud of the LORD hovered
over the Tabernacle during the day, and at night fire
glowed inside the cloud so the whole family of Israel could
see it. This continued throughout all their journeys.

LEVITICUS

TREY, ONE OF the star players on the high school football team, was the coach's son. During the practices he tried hard to pay attention, but he knew he was doomed when Yolonda, the cutest cheerleader, stopped by one day. As soon as he saw her, Trey could barely keep his mind on what the coach was saying.

But soon, Trey heard his father calling for his attention. "You need to stay focused, Trey," his dad advised. After that, Trey remained attentive for the rest of the practice.

The coach expected Trey to listen—not because he was better than the other players, but because Trey was his son. Trey's actions reflected on his father.

The Israelites were in a similar situation. God demanded they "pay attention" because they were his chosen people, his children. God told them, "You must be holy because I, the LORD your God, am holy" (19:2). *Holy* means set apart for God's service. That's why God gave them the laws recorded in the book of Leviticus. These laws would help them live holy lives. God also established the Day of Atonement (chapter 16) to allow them to come to him for forgiveness.

As you read Leviticus, consider your relationship with God. Is living a life that pleases him your first priority?

timeline

1446 B.C.
Exodus from Egypt

1445
Ten Commandments given

1444
Israel camps at Mt. Sinai

1406
Moses dies, Canaan entered

1375
Judges begin to rule

1050
United kingdom under Saul

stats

PURPOSE: A handbook for the Levites outlining their priestly duties in worship; a guidebook of holy living for the Hebrews

AUTHOR: Moses

DATE OF EVENTS: 1445–1444 B.C.

SETTING: At the foot of Mount Sinai, God teaches the Israelites how to live as holy people.

KEY PEOPLE: Moses, Aaron, Nadab, Abihu, Eleazar, Ithamar

SPECIAL FEATURE: Holiness is mentioned more often (152 times) than in any other book of the Bible.

KEY points

SACRIFICES
The system of sacrifices that God established for Israel helps us understand the high cost of sin. An animal had to be sacrificed to pay the price for someone's sin. Jesus' death, however, did away with this temporary system by permanently paying the penalty for all sin.

HEALTH
God established rules for all aspects of life. He wanted his people to be different from the surrounding nations. Through these rules, God preserved them from diseases and genetic problems while teaching them spiritual principles. Following his rules will make our lives different from those of unbelievers around us.

HOLINESS
Holy means "separated" or "devoted to God." God called his people to be committed to his ways and forsake the lifestyle they had in Egypt. God calls us to this level of commitment.

LEVITES
The Levites and priests taught the people how to worship God. They regulated the moral, civil, and ceremonial laws of the people. Understanding their role enables us to comprehend more of Jesus' role as our High Priest and our role as priestly believers.

1

PROCEDURES FOR THE BURNT OFFERING

The LORD called to Moses from the Tabernacle* and said to him, 2"Give the following instructions to the people of Israel. When you present an animal as an offering to the LORD, you may take it from your herd of cattle or your flock of sheep and goats.

3"If the animal you present as a burnt offering is from the herd, it must be a male with no defects. Bring it to the entrance of the Tabernacle so you* may be accepted by the LORD. 4Lay your hand on the animal's head, and the LORD will accept its death in your place to purify you, making you right with him.* 5Then slaughter the young bull in the LORD's presence, and Aaron's sons, the priests, will present the animal's blood by splattering it against all sides of the altar that stands at the entrance to the Tabernacle. 6Then skin the animal and cut it into pieces. 7The sons of Aaron the priest will build a wood fire on the altar. 8They will arrange the pieces of the offering, including the head and fat, on the wood burning on the altar. 9But the internal organs and the legs must first be washed with water. Then the priest will burn the entire sacrifice on the altar as a burnt offering. It is a special gift, a pleasing aroma to the LORD.

10"If the animal you present as a burnt offering is from the flock, it may be either a sheep or a goat, but it must be a male with no defects. 11Slaughter the animal on the north side of the altar in the LORD's presence, and Aaron's sons, the priests, will splatter its blood against all sides of the altar. 12Then cut the animal in pieces, and the priests will arrange the pieces of the offering, including the head and fat, on the wood burning on the altar. 13But the internal organs and the legs must first be washed with water. Then the priest will burn the entire sacrifice on the altar as a burnt offering. It is a special gift, a pleasing aroma to the LORD.

THE HIGH COST OF SIN 1:1

God used a system of sacrifices to teach his people about faith. The deaths of so many animals helped them see the high cost of their sin.

God's laws were intended to bring out true devotion of the heart. Our culture's casual attitude toward wrongdoing shows a forgetfulness of the cost of sin. Have you counted the cost? Jesus already paid it for you. ■

14"If you present a bird as a burnt offering to the LORD, choose either a turtledove or a young pigeon. 15The priest will take the bird to the altar, wring off its head, and burn it on the altar. But first he must drain its blood against the side of the altar. 16The priest must also remove the crop and the feathers* and throw them in the ashes on the east side of the altar. 17Then, grasping the bird by its wings, the priest will tear the bird open, but without tearing it apart. Then he will burn it as a burnt offering on the wood burning on the altar. It is a special gift, a pleasing aroma to the LORD.

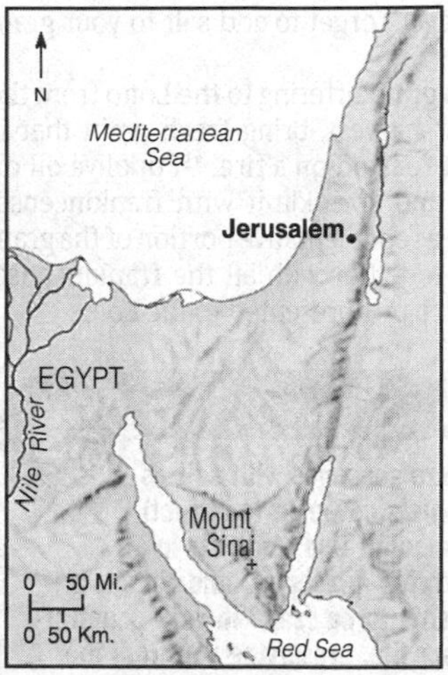

THE ISRAELITES AT MOUNT SINAI
Throughout the book of Leviticus, the Israelites were camped at the foot of Mount Sinai. It was time to regroup as a nation and learn the importance of following God as they prepared to march toward the Promised Land.

2

PROCEDURES FOR THE GRAIN OFFERING

"When you present grain as an offering to the LORD, the offering must consist of choice flour. You are to pour olive oil on it, sprinkle it with frankincense, 2and bring it to Aaron's sons, the priests. The priest will scoop out a handful of the flour moistened with oil, together with all the frankincense, and burn this representative portion on the altar. It is a special gift, a pleasing aroma to the LORD. 3The rest of the grain offering will then be given to Aaron and his sons. This offering will be considered a most holy part of the special gifts presented to the LORD.

4"If your offering is a grain offering baked in an oven, it must be made of choice flour, but without any yeast. It may be presented in the form of thin cakes mixed with olive oil or wafers spread with olive oil. 5If your grain offering is cooked on a griddle, it must be made of choice flour mixed with olive oil but without any yeast. 6Break it in pieces and pour olive oil on it; it is a grain offering. 7If your grain offering is prepared in a pan, it must be made of choice flour and olive oil.

8"No matter how a grain offering for the LORD has been prepared, bring it to the priest, who will present it at the altar. 9The priest will take a representative portion of the grain offering and burn it on the altar. It is a special gift, a pleasing aroma to the LORD. 10The rest of the grain offering will then be given to Aaron and his sons as their food. This offering will be considered a most holy part of the special gifts presented to the LORD.

11"Do not use yeast in preparing any of the grain offerings you present to the LORD, because no yeast or honey may be burned as a special gift presented to the LORD. 12You may add yeast and honey to an offering of the first crops of your harvest, but these must never be offered on the altar as a pleasing aroma to the LORD. 13Season all your grain offerings with salt to remind you of God's

1:1 Hebrew *Tent of Meeting;* also in 1:3, 5. **1:3** Or *it.* **1:4** Or *to make atonement for you.* **1:16** Or *the crop and its contents.* The meaning of the Hebrew is uncertain.

eternal covenant. Never forget to add salt to your grain offerings.

14"If you present a grain offering to the LORD from the first portion of your harvest, bring fresh grain that is coarsely ground and roasted on a fire. 15Put olive oil on this grain offering, and sprinkle it with frankincense. 16The priest will take a representative portion of the grain moistened with oil, together with all the frankincense, and burn it as a special gift presented to the LORD.

SALT 2:13

The grain offerings were seasoned with salt as a reminder of the people's covenant (contract) with God. Salt is a symbol of God's activity in a person's life—it penetrates, preserves, and acts as a healing agent. God wants to be "salt" in you—penetrating every aspect of your life, preserving you from the evil all around, and cleansing you when you sin.

3

PROCEDURES FOR THE PEACE OFFERING

"If you present an animal from the herd as a peace offering to the LORD, it may be a male or a female, but it must have no defects. 2Lay your hand on the animal's head, and slaughter it at the entrance of the Tabernacle.* Then Aaron's sons, the priests, will splatter its blood against all sides of the altar. 3The priest must present part of this peace offering as a special gift to the LORD. This includes all the fat around the internal organs, 4the two kidneys and the fat around them near the loins, and the long lobe of the liver. These must be removed with the kidneys, 5and Aaron's sons will burn them on top of the burnt offering on the wood burning on the altar. It is a special gift, a pleasing aroma to the LORD.

6"If you present an animal from the flock as a peace offering to the LORD, it may be a male or a female, but it must have no defects. 7If you present a sheep as your offering, bring it to the LORD, 8lay your hand on its head, and slaughter it in front of the Tabernacle. Aaron's sons will then splatter the sheep's blood against all sides of the altar. 9The priest must present the fat of this peace offering as a special gift to the LORD. This includes the fat of the broad tail cut off near the backbone, all the fat around the internal organs, 10the two kidneys and the fat around them near the loins, and the long lobe of the liver. These must be removed with the kidneys, 11and the priest will burn them on the altar. It is a special gift of food presented to the LORD.

12"If you present a goat as your offering, bring it to the LORD, 13lay your hand on its head, and slaughter it in front of the Tabernacle. Aaron's sons will then splatter the goat's blood against all sides of the altar. 14The priest must present part of this offering as a special gift to the LORD. This includes all the fat around the internal organs, 15the two kidneys and the fat around them near the loins, and the long lobe of the liver. These must be removed with the kidneys, 16and the priest will burn them on the altar. It is a special gift of food, a pleasing aroma to the LORD. All the fat belongs to the LORD.

17"You must never eat any fat or blood. This is a permanent law for you, and it must be observed from generation to generation, wherever you live."

4

PROCEDURES FOR THE SIN OFFERING

Then the LORD said to Moses, 2"Give the following instructions to the people of Israel. This is how you are to deal with those who sin unintentionally by doing anything that violates one of the LORD's commands.

3"If the high priest* sins, bringing guilt upon the entire community, he must give a sin offering for the sin he has committed. He must present to the LORD a young bull with no defects. 4He must bring the bull to the LORD at the entrance of the Tabernacle,* lay his hand on the bull's head, and slaughter it before the LORD. 5The high priest will then take some of the bull's blood into the Tabernacle, 6dip his finger in the blood, and sprinkle it seven times before the LORD in front of the inner curtain of the sanctuary. 7The priest will then put some of the blood on the horns of the altar for fragrant incense that stands in the LORD's presence inside the Tabernacle. He will pour out the rest of the bull's blood at the base of the altar for burnt offerings at the entrance of the Tabernacle. 8Then the priest must remove all the fat of the bull to be offered as a sin offering. This includes all the fat around the internal organs, 9the two kidneys and the fat around them near the loins, and the long lobe of the liver. He must remove these along with the kidneys, 10just as he does with cattle offered as a peace offering, and burn them on the altar of burnt offerings. 11But he must take whatever is left of the bull—its hide, meat, head, legs, internal organs, and dung—12and carry it away to a place outside the camp that is ceremonially clean, the place where the ashes are dumped. There, on the ash heap, he will burn it on a wood fire.

I DIDN'T MEAN IT! 4–5

Have you ever done something wrong without realizing it until later? Although your sin was unintentional, it was still sin. One of the purposes of God's law was to make the Israelites aware of their unintentional sins so they would not repeat them. Leviticus 4 and 5 mention some of these unintentional sins and God's remedies for them. The Holy Spirit reminds us of our intentional and unintentional sins. Are you listening?

13"If the entire Israelite community sins by violating one of the LORD's commands, but the people don't realize it, they are still guilty. 14When they become aware of their sin, the people must bring a young bull as an offering for

3:2 Hebrew *Tent of Meeting;* also in 3:8, 13. 4:3 Hebrew *the anointed priest;* also in 4:5, 16. 4:4 Hebrew *Tent of Meeting;* also in 4:5, 7, 14, 16, 18.

The Offerings

Listed here are the five key offerings the Israelites made to God. The Jews made these offerings in order to have their sins forgiven and to restore their fellowship with God. The death of Jesus Christ made these sacrifices unnecessary. Because of Jesus' death our sins are completely forgiven and fellowship with God has been restored.

OFFERING	Burnt Offering (Lev 1—voluntary)	Grain Offering (Lev 2—voluntary)	Peace Offering (Lev 3—voluntary)	Sin Offering (Lev 4—required)	Guilt Offering (Lev 5—required)
PURPOSE	To make payment for sins in general	To show honor and respect to God in worship	To express gratitude to God	To make payment for unintentional sins of uncleanness, neglect, or thoughtlessness	To make payment for sins against God and others. A sacrifice was made to God and the injured person repaid or compensated.
SIGNIFICANCE	Showed a person's devotion to God	Acknowledged that everything we have belongs to God	Symbolized peace and fellowship with God	Restored the sinner to fellowship with God; showed seriousness of sin	Provided compensation for injured parties
CHRIST, THE PERFECT OFFERING	Christ's death was the perfect offering	Christ was the perfect man, who gave all of himself to God and others	Christ is the only way to fellowship with God	Christ's death restores our fellowship with God	Christ's death takes away the deadly consequences of sin

their sin and present it before the Tabernacle. [15]The elders of the community must then lay their hands on the bull's head and slaughter it before the LORD. [16]The high priest will then take some of the bull's blood into the Tabernacle, [17]dip his finger in the blood, and sprinkle it seven times before the LORD in front of the inner curtain. [18]He will then put some of the blood on the horns of the altar for fragrant incense that stands in the LORD's presence inside the Tabernacle. He will pour out the rest of the blood at the base of the altar for burnt offerings at the entrance of the Tabernacle. [19]Then the priest must remove all the animal's fat and burn it on the altar, [20]just as he does with the bull offered as a sin offering for the high priest. Through this process, the priest will purify the people, making them right with the LORD,* and they will be forgiven. [21]Then the priest must take what is left of the bull and carry it outside the camp and burn it there, just as is done with the sin offering for the high priest. This offering is for the sin of the entire congregation of Israel.

[22]"If one of Israel's leaders sins by violating one of the commands of the LORD his God but doesn't realize it, he is still guilty. [23]When he becomes aware of his sin, he must bring as his offering a male goat with no defects. [24]He must lay his hand on the goat's head and slaughter it at the place where burnt offerings are slaughtered before the LORD. This is an offering for his sin. [25]Then the priest will dip his finger in the blood of the sin offering and put it on the horns of the altar for burnt offerings. He will pour out the rest of the blood at the base of the altar. [26]Then he must burn all the goat's fat on the altar, just as he does with the peace offering. Through this process, the priest will purify the leader from his sin, making him right with the LORD, and he will be forgiven.

[27]"If any of the common people sin by violating one of the LORD's commands, but they don't realize it, they are still guilty. [28]When they become aware of their sin, they must bring as an offering for their sin a female goat with no defects. [29]They must lay a hand on the head of the sin

4:20 Or *will make atonement for the people;* similarly in 4:26, 31, 35.

offering and slaughter it at the place where burnt offerings are slaughtered. [30]Then the priest will dip his finger
in the blood and put it on the horns of the altar for burnt
offerings. He will pour out the rest of the blood at the base
of the altar. [31]Then he must remove all the goat's fat, just
as he does with the fat of the peace offering. He will burn
the fat on the altar, and it will be a pleasing aroma to the
LORD. Through this process, the priest will purify the people, making them right with the LORD, and they will be
forgiven.

[32]"If the people bring a sheep as their sin offering, it
must be a female with no defects. [33]They must lay a hand
on the head of the sin offering and slaughter it at the
place where burnt offerings are slaughtered. [34]Then the
priest will dip his finger in the blood of the sin offering
and put it on the horns of the altar for burnt offerings. He
will pour out the rest of the blood at the base of the altar.
[35]Then he must remove all the sheep's fat, just as he does
with the fat of a sheep presented as a peace offering. He
will burn the fat on the altar on top of the special gifts
presented to the LORD. Through this process, the priest
will purify the people from their sin, making them right
with the LORD, and they will be forgiven.

5

SINS REQUIRING A SIN OFFERING

"If you are called to testify about something you have
seen or that you know about, it is sinful to refuse to testify, and you will be punished for your sin.

[2]"Or suppose you unknowingly touch something that
is ceremonially unclean, such as the carcass of an unclean animal. When you realize what you have done, you
must admit your defilement and your guilt. This is true
whether it is a wild animal, a domestic animal, or an animal that scurries along the ground.

[3]"Or suppose you unknowingly touch something that
makes a person unclean. When you realize what you have
done, you must admit your guilt.

[4]"Or suppose you make a foolish vow of any kind,
whether its purpose is for good or for bad. When you realize its foolishness, you must admit your guilt.

AVOID RASH VOWS 5:4

Have you ever sworn to do or not do something and then wished you could take back that vow? God's people are called to keep their word, even when they make promises that are tough to keep. Our word should be enough. Strengthening a promise with a vow is not necessary. The wise person avoids making rash vows. ■

[5]"When you become aware of your guilt in any of these
ways, you must confess your sin. [6]Then you must bring to
the LORD as the penalty for your sin a female from the
flock, either a sheep or a goat. This is a sin offering with
which the priest will purify you from your sin, making
you right with the LORD.*

[7]"But if you cannot afford to bring a sheep, you may
bring to the LORD two turtledoves or two young pigeons
as the penalty for your sin. One of the birds will be for a
sin offering, and the other for a burnt offering. [8]You
must bring them to the priest, who will present the first
bird as the sin offering. He will wring its neck but without
severing its head from the body. [9]Then he will sprinkle
some of the blood of the sin offering against the sides of
the altar, and the rest of the blood will be drained out
at the base of the altar. This is an offering for sin. [10]The
priest will then prepare the second bird as a burnt offering, following all the procedures that have been prescribed. Through this process the priest will purify you
from your sin, making you right with the LORD, and you
will be forgiven.

[11]"If you cannot afford to bring two turtledoves or two
young pigeons, you may bring two quarts* of choice flour
for your sin offering. Since it is an offering for sin, you
must not moisten it with olive oil or put any frankincense
on it. [12]Take the flour to the priest, who will scoop out a
handful as a representative portion. He will burn it on the
altar on top of the special gifts presented to the LORD. It is
an offering for sin. [13]Through this process, the priest will
purify those who are guilty of any of these sins, making
them right with the LORD, and they will be forgiven. The
rest of the flour will belong to the priest, just as with the
grain offering."

PROCEDURES FOR THE GUILT OFFERING

[14]Then the LORD said to Moses, [15]"If one of you commits a
sin by unintentionally defiling the LORD's sacred property, you must bring a guilt offering to the LORD. The offering must be your own ram with no defects, or you may
buy one of equal value with silver, as measured by the
weight of the sanctuary shekel.* [16]You must make restitution for the sacred property you have harmed by paying for the loss, plus an additional 20 percent. When you
give the payment to the priest, he will purify you with the
ram sacrificed as a guilt offering, making you right with
the LORD, and you will be forgiven.

[17]"Suppose you sin by violating one of the LORD's commands. Even if you are unaware of what you have done,
you are guilty and will be punished for your sin. [18]For a
guilt offering, you must bring to the priest your own ram
with no defects, or you may buy one of equal value.
Through this process the priest will purify you from your
unintentional sin, making you right with the LORD, and
you will be forgiven. [19]This is a guilt offering, for you have
been guilty of an offense against the LORD."

6

SINS REQUIRING A GUILT OFFERING

[1]*Then the LORD said to Moses, [2]"Suppose one of you sins
against your associate and is unfaithful to the LORD. Suppose you cheat in a deal involving a security deposit, or

5:6 Or *will make atonement for you;* similarly in 5:10, 13, 16, 18. 5:11 Hebrew *1/10 of an ephah* [2.2 liters]. 5:15 Each shekel was about 0.4 ounces or 11 grams in weight. 6:1 Verses 6:1-7 are numbered 5:20-26 in Hebrew text.

you steal or commit fraud, 3or you find lost property and lie about it, or you lie while swearing to tell the truth, or you commit any other such sin. 4If you have sinned in any of these ways, you are guilty. You must give back whatever you stole, or the money you took by extortion, or the security deposit, or the lost property you found, 5or anything obtained by swearing falsely. You must make restitution by paying the full price plus an additional 20 percent to the person you have harmed. On the same day you must present a guilt offering. 6As a guilt offering to the LORD, you must bring to the priest your own ram with no defects, or you may buy one of equal value. 7Through this process, the priest will purify you before the LORD, making you right with him,* and you will be forgiven for any of these sins you have committed."

STEALING 6:1-7

Here we discover that stealing involves more than just taking from someone. Finding something and not returning it or refusing to return something borrowed are other forms of stealing. Both are sins against God—not just a neighbor, a stranger, or a business. Instead of justifying our reason for keeping that overdue DVD from the video store or that library book we've had for five years, maybe we need to call it what it is: wrong. ■

FURTHER INSTRUCTIONS FOR THE BURNT OFFERING

8*Then the LORD said to Moses, 9"Give Aaron and his sons the following instructions regarding the burnt offering. The burnt offering must be left on top of the altar until the next morning, and the fire on the altar must be kept burning all night. 10In the morning, after the priest on duty has put on his official linen clothing and linen undergarments, he must clean out the ashes of the burnt offering and put them beside the altar. 11Then he must take off these garments, change back into his regular clothes, and carry the ashes outside the camp to a place that is ceremonially clean. 12Meanwhile, the fire on the altar must be kept burning; it must never go out. Each morning the priest will add fresh wood to the fire and arrange the burnt offering on it. He will then burn the fat of the peace offerings on it. 13Remember, the fire must be kept burning on the altar at all times. It must never go out.

FURTHER INSTRUCTIONS FOR THE GRAIN OFFERING

14"These are the instructions regarding the grain offering. Aaron's sons must present this offering to the LORD in front of the altar. 15The priest on duty will take from the grain offering a handful of the choice flour moistened with olive oil, together with all the frankincense. He will burn this representative portion on the altar as a pleasing aroma to the LORD. 16Aaron and his sons may eat the rest of the flour, but it must be baked without yeast and eaten in a sacred place within the courtyard of the Tabernacle.* 17Remember, it must never be prepared with yeast. I have given it to the priests as their share of the special gifts presented to me. Like the sin offering and the guilt offering, it is most holy. 18Any of Aaron's male descendants may eat from the special gifts presented to the LORD. This is their permanent right from generation to generation. Anyone or anything that touches these offerings will become holy."

PROCEDURES FOR THE ORDINATION OFFERING

19Then the LORD said to Moses, 20"On the day Aaron and his sons are anointed, they must present to the LORD a grain offering of two quarts* of choice flour, half to be offered in the morning and half to be offered in the evening. 21It must be carefully mixed with olive oil and cooked on a griddle. Then slice* this grain offering and present it as a pleasing aroma to the LORD. 22In each generation, the high priest* who succeeds Aaron must prepare this same offering. It belongs to the LORD and must be burned up completely. This is a permanent law. 23All such grain offerings of a priest must be burned up entirely. None of it may be eaten."

FURTHER INSTRUCTIONS FOR THE SIN OFFERING

24Then the LORD said to Moses, 25"Give Aaron and his sons the following instructions regarding the sin offering. The animal given as an offering for sin is a most holy offering, and it must be slaughtered in the LORD's presence at the place where the burnt offerings are slaughtered. 26The priest who offers the sacrifice as a sin offering must eat his portion in a sacred place within the courtyard of the Tabernacle. 27Anyone or anything that touches the sacrificial meat will become holy. If any of the sacrificial blood spatters on a person's clothing, the soiled garment must be washed in a sacred place. 28If a clay pot is used to boil the sacrificial meat, it must then be broken. If a bronze pot is used, it must be scoured and thoroughly rinsed with water. 29Any male from a priest's family may eat from this offering; it is most holy. 30But the offering for sin may not be eaten if its blood was brought into the Tabernacle as an offering for purification* in the Holy Place. It must be completely burned with fire.

7

FURTHER INSTRUCTIONS FOR THE GUILT OFFERING

"These are the instructions for the guilt offering. It is most holy. 2The animal sacrificed as a guilt offering must be slaughtered at the place where the burnt offerings are slaughtered, and its blood must be splattered against all sides of the altar. 3The priest will then offer all its fat on the altar, including the fat of the broad tail, the fat around the internal organs, 4the two kidneys and the fat around them near the loins, and the long lobe of the liver. These are to be removed with the kidneys, 5and the priests will burn them on the altar as a special gift presented to the LORD. This is the guilt offering. 6Any male from a priest's

6:7 Or *will make atonement for you before the LORD.* 6:8 Verses 6:8-30 are numbered 6:1-23 in Hebrew text. 6:16 Hebrew *Tent of Meeting;* also in 6:26, 30. 6:20 Hebrew *1/10 of an ephah* [2.2 liters]. 6:21 The meaning of this Hebrew term is uncertain. 6:22 Hebrew *the anointed priest.* 6:30 Or *an offering to make atonement.*

family may eat the meat. It must be eaten in a sacred place, for it is most holy.

7"The same instructions apply to both the guilt offering and the sin offering. Both belong to the priest who uses them to purify someone, making that person right with the LORD.* 8In the case of the burnt offering, the priest may keep the hide of the sacrificed animal. 9Any grain offering that has been baked in an oven, prepared in a pan, or cooked on a griddle belongs to the priest who presents it. 10All other grain offerings, whether made of dry flour or flour moistened with olive oil, are to be shared equally among all the priests, the descendants of Aaron.

FURTHER INSTRUCTIONS FOR THE PEACE OFFERING

11"These are the instructions regarding the different kinds of peace offerings that may be presented to the LORD. 12If you present your peace offering as an expression of thanksgiving, the usual animal sacrifice must be accompanied by various kinds of bread made without yeast—thin cakes mixed with olive oil, wafers spread with oil, and cakes made of choice flour mixed with olive oil. 13This peace offering of thanksgiving must also be accompanied by loaves of bread made with yeast. 14One of each kind of bread must be presented as a gift to the LORD. It will then belong to the priest who splatters the blood of the peace offering against the altar. 15The meat of the peace offering of thanksgiving must be eaten on the same day it is offered. None of it may be saved for the next morning.

16"If you bring an offering to fulfill a vow or as a voluntary offering, the meat must be eaten on the same day the sacrifice is offered, but whatever is left over may be eaten on the second day. 17Any meat left over until the third day must be completely burned up. 18If any of the meat from the peace offering is eaten on the third day, the person who presented it will not be accepted by the LORD. You will receive no credit for offering it. By then the meat will be contaminated; if you eat it, you will be punished for your sin.

19"Meat that touches anything ceremonially unclean may not be eaten; it must be completely burned up. The rest of the meat may be eaten, but only by people who are ceremonially clean. 20If you are ceremonially unclean and you eat meat from a peace offering that was presented to the LORD, you will be cut off from the community. 21If you touch anything that is unclean (whether it is human defilement or an unclean animal or any other unclean, detestable thing) and then eat meat from a peace offering presented to the LORD, you will be cut off from the community."

THE FORBIDDEN BLOOD AND FAT

22Then the LORD said to Moses, 23"Give the following instructions to the people of Israel. You must never eat fat, whether from cattle, sheep, or goats. 24The fat of an animal found dead or torn to pieces by wild animals must never be eaten, though it may be used for any other purpose. 25Anyone who eats fat from an animal presented as a special gift to the LORD will be cut off from the community. 26No matter where you live, you must never consume the blood of any bird or animal. 27Anyone who consumes blood will be cut off from the community."

A PORTION FOR THE PRIESTS

28Then the LORD said to Moses, 29"Give the following instructions to the people of Israel. When you present a peace offering to the LORD, bring part of it as a gift to the LORD. 30Present it to the LORD with your own hands as a special gift to the LORD. Bring the fat of the animal, together with the breast, and lift up the breast as a special offering to the LORD. 31Then the priest will burn the fat on the altar, but the breast will belong to Aaron and his descendants. 32Give the right thigh of your peace offering to the priest as a gift. 33The right thigh must always be given to the priest who offers the blood and the fat of the peace offering. 34For I have reserved the breast of the special offering and the right thigh of the sacred offering for the priests. It is the permanent right of Aaron and his descendants to share in the peace offerings brought by the people of Israel. 35This is their rightful share. The special gifts presented to the LORD have been reserved for Aaron and his descendants from the time they were set apart to serve the LORD as priests. 36On the day they were anointed, the LORD commanded the Israelites to give these portions to the priests as their permanent share from generation to generation."

37These are the instructions for the burnt offering, the grain offering, the sin offering, and the guilt offering, as well as the ordination offering and the peace offering. 38The LORD gave these instructions to Moses on Mount Sinai when he commanded the Israelites to present their offerings to the LORD in the wilderness of Sinai.

MEANINGLESS WORSHIP 7:38

God gave his people many worship rules to follow. The rules and ceremonies in Leviticus were meant to teach the people valuable spiritual lessons. But over time, the people became indifferent to the meanings of these ceremonies. As a result, they began to lose touch with God. When you consider your response to worship these days, can you relate? Want worship to come alive once more? Start by admitting where you are. Don't worry. God can take it. ■

8 ORDINATION OF THE PRIESTS

Then the LORD said to Moses, 2"Bring Aaron and his sons, along with their sacred garments, the anointing oil, the bull for the sin offering, the two rams, and the basket of bread made without yeast, 3and call the entire community of Israel together at the entrance of the Tabernacle.*"

4So Moses followed the LORD's instructions, and the whole community assembled at the Tabernacle entrance. 5Moses announced to them, "This is what the

7:7 Or *to make atonement.* 8:3 Hebrew *Tent of Meeting;* also in 8:4, 31, 33, 35.

LORD has commanded us to do!" 6Then he presented
Aaron and his sons and washed them with water. 7He put
the official tunic on Aaron and tied the sash around his
waist. He dressed him in the robe, placed the ephod on
him, and attached the ephod securely with its decorative
sash. 8Then Moses placed the chestpiece on Aaron and
put the Urim and the Thummim inside it. 9He placed the
turban on Aaron's head and attached the gold medallion—the badge of holiness—to the front of the turban,
just as the LORD had commanded him.

10Then Moses took the anointing oil and anointed the
Tabernacle and everything in it, making them holy. 11He
sprinkled the oil on the altar seven times, anointing it and
all its utensils, as well as the washbasin and its stand,
making them holy. 12Then he poured some of the anointing oil on Aaron's head, anointing him and making him
holy for his work. 13Next Moses presented Aaron's sons.
He clothed them in their tunics, tied their sashes around
them, and put their special head coverings on them, just
as the LORD had commanded him.

14Then Moses presented the bull for the sin offering.
Aaron and his sons laid their hands on the bull's head,
15and Moses slaughtered it. Moses took some of the
blood, and with his finger he put it on the four horns of
the altar to purify it. He poured out the rest of the blood
at the base of the altar. Through this process, he made
the altar holy by purifying it.* 16Then Moses took all the
fat around the internal organs, the long lobe of the liver,
and the two kidneys and the fat around them, and he
burned it all on the altar. 17He took the rest of the bull,
including its hide, meat, and dung, and burned it on a
fire outside the camp, just as the LORD had commanded
him.

18Then Moses presented the ram for the burnt offering. Aaron and his sons laid their hands on the ram's
head, 19and Moses slaughtered it. Then Moses took the
ram's blood and splattered it against all sides of the altar. 20Then he cut the ram into pieces, and he burned
the head, some of its pieces, and the fat on the altar.
21After washing the internal organs and the legs with
water, Moses burned the entire ram on the altar as a
burnt offering. It was a pleasing aroma, a special gift
presented to the LORD, just as the LORD had commanded him.

22Then Moses presented the other ram, which was the
ram of ordination. Aaron and his sons laid their hands on
the ram's head, 23and Moses slaughtered it. Then Moses
took some of its blood and applied it to the lobe of
Aaron's right ear, the thumb of his right hand, and the big
toe of his right foot. 24Next Moses presented Aaron's
sons and applied some of the blood to the lobes of their
right ears, the thumbs of their right hands, and the big
toes of their right feet. He then splattered the rest of the
blood against all sides of the altar.

25Next Moses took the fat, including the fat of the
broad tail, the fat around the internal organs, the long
lobe of the liver, and the two kidneys and the fat around
them, along with the right thigh. 26On top of these he
placed a thin cake of bread made without yeast, a cake
of bread mixed with olive oil, and a wafer spread with
olive oil. All these were taken from the basket of bread
made without yeast that was placed in the LORD's presence. 27He put all these in the hands of Aaron and his
sons, and he lifted them up as a special offering to the
LORD. 28Moses then took all the offerings back from
them and burned them on the altar on top of the burnt
offering. This was the ordination offering. It was a
pleasing aroma, a special gift presented to the LORD.
29Then Moses took the breast and lifted it up as a special
offering to the LORD. This was Moses' portion of the ram
of ordination, just as the LORD had commanded him.

30Next Moses took some of the anointing oil and some
of the blood that was on the altar, and he sprinkled them
on Aaron and his garments and on his sons and their garments. In this way, he made Aaron and his sons and their
garments holy.

TOTALLY HOLY 8:36

Aaron and his sons did all that the Lord told them to do. Considering the many lists of rules in Leviticus, that was a remarkable feat. They knew what God wanted, how he wanted it done, and with what attitude his instructions were to be carried out. God wants us to be thoroughly holy people with the same zealous attitude as Aaron and his sons. That's your attitude, right? ■

31Then Moses said to Aaron and his sons, "Boil the remaining meat of the offerings at the Tabernacle entrance, and eat it there, along with the bread that is in
the basket of offerings for the ordination, just as I commanded when I said, 'Aaron and his sons will eat it.'
32Any meat or bread that is left over must then be
burned up. 33You must not leave the Tabernacle entrance for seven days, for that is when the ordination
ceremony will be completed. 34Everything we have done
today was commanded by the LORD in order to purify
you, making you right with him.* 35Now stay at the entrance of the Tabernacle day and night for seven days,
and do everything the LORD requires. If you fail to do
this, you will die, for this is what the LORD has commanded." 36So Aaron and his sons did everything the
LORD had commanded through Moses.

9 THE PRIESTS BEGIN THEIR WORK

After the ordination ceremony, on the eighth day, Moses
called together Aaron and his sons and the elders of Israel. 2He said to Aaron, "Take a young bull for a sin offering
and a ram for a burnt offering, both without defects, and
present them to the LORD. 3Then tell the Israelites, 'Take a
male goat for a sin offering, and take a calf and a lamb,
both a year old and without defects, for a burnt offering.
4Also take a bull* and a ram for a peace offering and flour

8:15 Or *by making atonement for it;* or *that offerings for purification might be made on it.* 8:34 Or *to make atonement for you.* 9:4 Or *cow;* also in 9:18, 19.

moistened with olive oil for a grain offering. Present all these offerings to the LORD because the LORD will appear to you today.'"

[5]So the people presented all these things at the entrance of the Tabernacle,* just as Moses had commanded. Then the whole community came forward and stood before the LORD. [6]And Moses said, "This is what the LORD has commanded you to do so that the glory of the LORD may appear to you."

[7]Then Moses said to Aaron, "Come to the altar and sacrifice your sin offering and your burnt offering to purify yourself and the people. Then present the offerings of the people to purify them, making them right with the LORD,* just as he has commanded."

[8]So Aaron went to the altar and slaughtered the calf as a sin offering for himself. [9]His sons brought him the blood, and he dipped his finger in it and put it on the horns of the altar. He poured out the rest of the blood at the base of the altar. [10]Then he burned on the altar the fat, the kidneys, and the long lobe of the liver from the sin offering, just as the LORD had commanded Moses. [11]The meat and the hide, however, he burned outside the camp.

[12]Next Aaron slaughtered the animal for the burnt offering. His sons brought him the blood, and he splattered it against all sides of the altar. [13]Then they handed him each piece of the burnt offering, including the head, and he burned them on the altar. [14]Then he washed the internal organs and the legs and burned them on the altar along with the rest of the burnt offering.

[15]Next Aaron presented the offerings of the people. He slaughtered the people's goat and presented it as an offering for their sin, just as he had first done with the offering for his own sin. [16]Then he presented the burnt offering and sacrificed it in the prescribed way. [17]He also presented the grain offering, burning a handful of the flour mixture on the altar, in addition to the regular burnt offering for the morning.

[18]Then Aaron slaughtered the bull and the ram for the people's peace offering. His sons brought him the blood, and he splattered it against all sides of the altar. [19]Then he took the fat of the bull and the ram—the fat of the broad tail and from around the internal organs—along with the kidneys and the long lobes of the livers. [20]He placed these fat portions on top of the breasts of these animals and burned them on the altar. [21]Aaron then lifted up the breasts and right thighs as a special offering to the LORD, just as Moses had commanded.

[22]After that, Aaron raised his hands toward the people and blessed them. Then, after presenting the sin offering, the burnt offering, and the peace offering, he stepped down from the altar. [23]Then Moses and Aaron went into the Tabernacle, and when they came back out, they blessed the people again, and the glory of the LORD appeared to the whole community. [24]Fire blazed forth from the LORD's presence and consumed the burnt offering and the fat on the altar. When the people saw this, they shouted with joy and fell face down on the ground.

10

THE SIN OF NADAB AND ABIHU

Aaron's sons Nadab and Abihu put coals of fire in their incense burners and sprinkled incense over them. In this way, they disobeyed the LORD by burning before him the wrong kind of fire, different than he had commanded. [2]So fire blazed forth from the LORD's presence and burned them up, and they died there before the LORD.

A HOLY REMINDER 10:2

Sadly, after the good report of Leviticus 8:36, we see how careless Aaron's sons had become about following the laws for sacrifices. In response, God destroyed them with a blast of fire. Performing the sacrifices was an act of obedience. Doing them correctly showed respect for God and reminded the Israelites of God's holiness.

It's easy to grow careless about obeying God. At times, we want to do what we want instead of what he wants. Yet the punishment of Aaron's sons is a chilling reminder of how seriously God takes obedience. How serious are you about obeying God? ■

[3]Then Moses said to Aaron, "This is what the LORD meant when he said,

'I will display my holiness
through those who come near me.
I will display my glory
before all the people.'"

And Aaron was silent.

[4]Then Moses called for Mishael and Elzaphan, Aaron's cousins, the sons of Aaron's uncle Uzziel. He said to them, "Come forward and carry away the bodies of your relatives from in front of the sanctuary to a place outside the camp." [5]So they came forward and picked them up by their garments and carried them out of the camp, just as Moses had commanded.

[6]Then Moses said to Aaron and his sons Eleazar and Ithamar, "Do not show grief by leaving your hair uncombed* or by tearing your clothes. If you do, you will die, and the LORD's anger will strike the whole community of Israel. However, the rest of the Israelites, your relatives, may mourn because of the LORD's fiery destruction of Nadab and Abihu. [7]But you must not leave the entrance of the Tabernacle* or you will die, for you have been anointed with the LORD's anointing oil." So they did as Moses commanded.

INSTRUCTIONS FOR PRIESTLY CONDUCT

[8]Then the LORD said to Aaron, [9]"You and your descendants must never drink wine or any other alcoholic drink before going into the Tabernacle. If you do, you will die. This is a permanent law for you, and it must be observed from generation to generation. [10]You must distinguish

9:5 Hebrew *Tent of Meeting;* also in 9:23. **9:7** Or *to make atonement for them.* **10:6** Or *by uncovering your heads.* **10:7** Hebrew *Tent of Meeting;* also in 10:9.

between what is sacred and what is common, between what is ceremonially unclean and what is clean. 11 And you must teach the Israelites all the decrees that the LORD has given them through Moses."

12 Then Moses said to Aaron and his remaining sons, Eleazar and Ithamar, "Take what is left of the grain offering after a portion has been presented as a special gift to the LORD, and eat it beside the altar. Make sure it contains no yeast, for it is most holy. 13 You must eat it in a sacred place, for it has been given to you and your descendants as your portion of the special gifts presented to the LORD. These are the commands I have been given. 14 But the breast and thigh that were lifted up as a special offering may be eaten in any place that is ceremonially clean. These parts have been given to you and your descendants as your portion of the peace offerings presented by the people of Israel. 15 You must lift up the thigh and breast as a special offering to the LORD, along with the fat of the special gifts. These parts will belong to you and your descendants as your permanent right, just as the LORD has commanded."

16 Moses then asked them what had happened to the goat of the sin offering. When he discovered it had been burned up, he became very angry with Eleazar and Ithamar, Aaron's remaining sons. 17 "Why didn't you eat the sin offering in the sacred area?" he demanded. "It is a holy offering! The LORD has given it to you to remove the guilt of the community and to purify the people, making them right with the LORD.* 18 Since the animal's blood was not brought into the Holy Place, you should have eaten the meat in the sacred area as I ordered you."

19 Then Aaron answered Moses, "Today my sons presented both their sin offering and their burnt offering to the LORD. And yet this tragedy has happened to me. If I had eaten the people's sin offering on such a tragic day as this, would the LORD have been pleased?" 20 And when Moses heard this, he was satisfied.

KEEP AWAY 11:8

God had strictly forbidden eating the meat of certain animals. The people of Israel were not even allowed to touch these animals after they were dead. God wanted his people to keep away from forbidden items. Often we flirt with temptation with the rationalization that we haven't committed the sin . . . yet. But God wants us to separate ourselves from what's forbidden. If necessary that might mean running from temptation like Joseph. (See Gen 39:12.) ■

11 CEREMONIALLY CLEAN AND UNCLEAN ANIMALS

Then the LORD said to Moses and Aaron, 2 "Give the following instructions to the people of Israel.

"Of all the land animals, these are the ones you may use for food. 3 You may eat any animal that has completely split hooves and chews the cud. 4 You may not, however, eat the following animals* that have split hooves or that chew the cud, but not both. The camel chews the cud but does not have split hooves, so it is ceremonially unclean for you. 5 The hyrax* chews the cud but does not have split hooves, so it is unclean. 6 The hare chews the cud but does not have split hooves, so it is unclean. 7 The pig has evenly split hooves but does not chew the cud, so it is unclean. 8 You may not eat the meat of these animals or even touch their carcasses. They are ceremonially unclean for you.

BE PREPARED 11:24-47

Leviticus contains rules that the people of Israel used to prepare themselves for worship. Certain things could make a person ceremonially unclean, thus disqualifying him from worship. Similarly, we cannot live any way we want during the week and then rush into God's presence on Sunday. Our relationship with him must be one of constant repentance and cleansing so that we are prepared to worship him anytime. ■

9 "Of all the marine animals, these are ones you may use for food. You may eat anything from the water if it has both fins and scales, whether taken from salt water or from streams. 10 But you must never eat animals from the sea or from rivers that do not have both fins and scales. They are detestable to you. This applies both to little creatures that live in shallow water and to all creatures that live in deep water. 11 They will always be detestable to you. You must never eat their meat or even touch their dead bodies. 12 Any marine animal that does not have both fins and scales is detestable to you.

13 "These are the birds that are detestable to you. You must never eat them: the griffon vulture, the bearded vulture, the black vulture, 14 the kite, falcons of all kinds, 15 ravens of all kinds, 16 the eagle owl, the short-eared owl, the seagull, hawks of all kinds, 17 the little owl, the cormorant, the great owl, 18 the barn owl, the desert owl, the Egyptian vulture, 19 the stork, herons of all kinds, the hoopoe, and the bat.

20 "You must not eat winged insects that walk along the ground; they are detestable to you. 21 You may, however, eat winged insects that walk along the ground and have jointed legs so they can jump. 22 The insects you are permitted to eat include all kinds of locusts, bald locusts, crickets, and grasshoppers. 23 All other winged insects that walk along the ground are detestable to you.

24 "The following creatures will make you ceremonially unclean. If any of you touch their carcasses, you will be defiled until evening. 25 If you pick up their carcasses, you must wash your clothes, and you will remain defiled until evening.

26 "Any animal that has split hooves that are not evenly divided or that does not chew the cud is unclean for you. If you touch the carcass of such an animal, you will be defiled. 27 Of the animals that walk on all fours, those that

10:17 Or *to make atonement for the people before the LORD.* **11:4** The identification of some of the animals, birds, and insects in this chapter is uncertain. **11:5** Or *coney*, or *rock badger*.

have paws are unclean. If you touch the carcass of such an animal, you will be defiled until evening. 28If you pick up its carcass, you must wash your clothes, and you will remain defiled until evening. These animals are unclean for you.

29"Of the small animals that scurry along the ground, these are unclean for you: the mole rat, the rat, large lizards of all kinds, 30the gecko, the monitor lizard, the common lizard, the sand lizard, and the chameleon. 31All these small animals are unclean for you. If any of you touch the dead body of such an animal, you will be defiled until evening. 32If such an animal dies and falls on something, that object will be unclean. This is true whether the object is made of wood, cloth, leather, or burlap. Whatever its use, you must dip it in water, and it will remain defiled until evening. After that, it will be ceremonially clean and may be used again.

HOLY DESIGN 11:44-45

There is more to this chapter than eating right. These verses provide a key to understanding all of the laws in Leviticus. God wanted his people to be *holy* (set apart for a special purpose) to reflect his holiness. He established laws to help them remain separate—socially and spiritually—from the pagan nations they would encounter in Canaan.

Christians also are called to be holy (1 Pet 1:15-16). Like the Israelites, we have the task of maintaining God's standards, rather than the world's. Being holy in an unholy world isn't easy. But God doesn't expect you to accomplish this on your own. You can rely on the Holy Spirit's help. ■

33"If such an animal falls into a clay pot, everything in the pot will be defiled, and the pot must be smashed. 34If the water from such a container spills on any food, the food will be defiled. And any beverage in such a container will be defiled. 35Any object on which the carcass of such an animal falls will be defiled. If it is an oven or hearth, it must be destroyed, for it is defiled, and you must treat it accordingly.

36"However, if the carcass of such an animal falls into a spring or a cistern, the water will still be clean. But anyone who touches the carcass will be defiled. 37If the carcass falls on seed grain to be planted in the field, the seed will still be considered clean. 38But if the seed is wet when the carcass falls on it, the seed will be defiled.

39"If an animal you are permitted to eat dies and you touch its carcass, you will be defiled until evening. 40If you eat any of its meat or carry away its carcass, you must wash your clothes, and you will remain defiled until evening.

41"All small animals that scurry along the ground are detestable, and you must never eat them. 42This includes all animals that slither along on their bellies, as well as those with four legs and those with many feet. All such animals that scurry along the ground are detestable, and you must never eat them. 43Do not defile yourselves by touching them. You must not make yourselves ceremonially unclean because of them. 44For I am the LORD your God. You must consecrate yourselves and be holy, because I am holy. So do not defile yourselves with any of these small animals that scurry along the ground. 45For I, the LORD, am the one who brought you up from the land of Egypt, that I might be your God. Therefore, you must be holy because I am holy.

46"These are the instructions regarding land animals, birds, marine creatures, and animals that scurry along the ground. 47By these instructions you will know what is unclean and clean, and which animals may be eaten and which may not be eaten."

12

PURIFICATION AFTER CHILDBIRTH

The LORD said to Moses, "Give the following instructions to the people of Israel. 2If a woman becomes pregnant and gives birth to a son, she will be ceremonially unclean for seven days, just as she is unclean during her menstrual period. 3On the eighth day the boy's foreskin must be circumcised. 4After waiting thirty-three days, she will be purified from the bleeding of childbirth. During this time of purification, she must not touch anything that is set apart as holy. And she must not enter the sanctuary until her time of purification is over. 5If a woman gives birth to a daughter, she will be ceremonially unclean for two weeks, just as she is unclean during her menstrual period. After waiting sixty-six days, she will be purified from the bleeding of childbirth.

6"When the time of purification is completed for either a son or a daughter, the woman must bring a one-year-old lamb for a burnt offering and a young pigeon or turtledove for a purification offering. She must bring her offerings to the priest at the entrance of the Tabernacle.* 7The priest will then present them to the LORD to purify her.* Then she will be ceremonially clean again after her bleeding at childbirth. These are the instructions for a woman after the birth of a son or a daughter.

A WORSHIP STOPPER 12:1-8

***Unclean* did not mean "sinful," implying that sex or childbirth is dirty. Instead, it meant "not appropriate to make a sacrifice." In other words, the person could not worship at the Tabernacle until a specified time had passed. Again, this doesn't mean that sex is unclean. It just means that there are appropriate (and inappropriate) times and places for everything. ■**

8"If a woman cannot afford to bring a lamb, she must bring two turtledoves or two young pigeons. One will be for the burnt offering and the other for the purification offering. The priest will sacrifice them to purify her, and she will be ceremonially clean."

12:6 Hebrew *Tent of Meeting.* **12:7** Or *to make atonement for her;* also in 12:8.

13 SERIOUS SKIN DISEASES

The LORD said to Moses and Aaron, 2"If anyone has a swelling or a rash or discolored skin that might develop into a serious skin disease,* that person must be brought to Aaron the priest or to one of his sons.* 3The priest will examine the affected area of the skin. If the hair in the affected area has turned white and the problem appears to be more than skin-deep, it is a serious skin disease, and the priest who examines it must pronounce the person ceremonially unclean.

4"But if the affected area of the skin is only a white discoloration and does not appear to be more than skin-deep, and if the hair on the spot has not turned white, the priest will quarantine the person for seven days. 5On the seventh day the priest will make another examination. If he finds the affected area has not changed and the problem has not spread on the skin, the priest will quarantine the person for seven more days. 6On the seventh day the priest will make another examination. If he finds the affected area has faded and has not spread, the priest will pronounce the person ceremonially clean. It was only a rash. The person's clothing must be washed, and the person will be ceremonially clean. 7But if the rash continues to spread after the person has been examined by the priest and has been pronounced clean, the infected person must return to be examined again. 8If the priest finds that the rash has spread, he must pronounce the person ceremonially unclean, for it is indeed a skin disease.

9"Anyone who develops a serious skin disease must go to the priest for an examination. 10If the priest finds a white swelling on the skin, and some hair on the spot has turned white, and there is an open sore in the affected area, 11it is a chronic skin disease, and the priest must pronounce the person ceremonially unclean. In such cases the person need not be quarantined, for it is obvious that the skin is defiled by the disease.

12"Now suppose the disease has spread all over the person's skin, covering the body from head to foot. 13When the priest examines the infected person and finds that the disease covers the entire body, he will pronounce the person ceremonially clean. Since the skin has turned completely white, the person is clean. 14But if any open sores appear, the infected person will be pronounced ceremonially unclean. 15The priest must make this pronouncement as soon as he sees an open sore, since open sores indicate the presence of a skin disease. 16However, if the open sores heal and turn white like the rest of the skin, the person must return to the priest 17for another examination. If the affected areas have indeed turned white, the priest will then pronounce the person ceremonially clean by declaring, 'You are clean!'

18"If anyone has a boil on the skin that has started to heal, 19but a white swelling or a reddish white spot develops in its place, that person must go to the priest to be examined. 20If the priest examines it and finds it to be more than skin-deep, and if the hair in the affected area has turned white, the priest must pronounce the person ceremonially unclean. The boil has become a serious skin disease. 21But if the priest finds no white hair on the affected area and the problem appears to be no more than skin-deep and has faded, the priest must quarantine the person for seven days. 22If during that time the affected area spreads on the skin, the priest must pronounce the person ceremonially unclean, because it is a serious disease. 23But if the area grows no larger and does not spread, it is merely the scar from the boil, and the priest will pronounce the person ceremonially clean.

24"If anyone has suffered a burn on the skin and the burned area changes color, becoming either reddish white or shiny white, 25the priest must examine it. If he finds that the hair in the affected area has turned white and the problem appears to be more than skin-deep, a skin disease has broken out in the burn. The priest must then pronounce the person ceremonially unclean, for it is clearly a serious skin disease. 26But if the priest finds no white hair on the affected area and the problem appears to be no more than skin-deep and has faded, the priest must quarantine the infected person for seven days. 27On the seventh day the priest must examine the person again. If the affected area has spread on the skin, the priest must pronounce that person ceremonially unclean, for it is clearly a serious skin disease. 28But if the affected area has not changed or spread on the skin and has faded, it is simply a swelling from the burn. The priest will then pronounce the person ceremonially clean, for it is only the scar from the burn.

29"If anyone, either a man or woman, has a sore on the head or chin, 30the priest must examine it. If he finds it is more than skin-deep and has fine yellow hair on it, the priest must pronounce the person ceremonially unclean. It is a scabby sore of the head or chin. 31If the priest examines the scabby sore and finds that it is only skin-deep but there is no black hair on it, he must quarantine the person for seven days. 32On the seventh day the priest must examine the sore again. If he finds that the scabby sore has not spread, and there is no yellow hair on it, and it appears to be only skin-deep, 33the person must shave off all hair except the hair on the affected area. Then the priest must quarantine the person for another seven days. 34On the seventh day he will examine the sore again. If it has not spread and appears to be no more than skin-deep, the priest will pronounce the person ceremonially clean. The person's clothing must be washed, and the person will be ceremonially clean. 35But if the scabby sore begins to spread after the person is pronounced clean, 36the priest must do another examination. If he finds that the sore has spread, the priest does not need to look for yellow hair. The infected person is ceremonially unclean. 37But if the color of the scabby sore does not change and black hair has grown on it, it has healed. The priest will then pronounce the person ceremonially clean.

38"If anyone, either a man or woman, has shiny white patches on the skin, 39the priest must examine the affected

13:2a Traditionally rendered *leprosy*. The Hebrew word used throughout this passage is used to describe various skin diseases. **13:2b** Or *one of his descendants*.

area. If he finds that the shiny patches are only pale
white, this is a harmless skin rash, and the person is ceremonially clean.
40"If a man loses his hair and his head becomes bald,
he is still ceremonially clean. 41And if he loses hair on his
forehead, he simply has a bald forehead; he is still clean.
42However, if a reddish white sore appears on the bald
area at the top or back of his head, this is a skin disease.
43The priest must examine him, and if he finds swelling
around the reddish white sore anywhere on the man's
head and it looks like a skin disease, 44the man is indeed
infected with a skin disease and is unclean. The priest
must pronounce him ceremonially unclean because of
the sore on his head.
45"Those who suffer from a serious skin disease must
tear their clothing and leave their hair uncombed.* They
must cover their mouth and call out, 'Unclean! Unclean!'
46As long as the serious disease lasts, they will be ceremonially unclean. They must live in isolation in their place
outside the camp.

TREATMENT OF CONTAMINATED CLOTHING

47"Now suppose mildew* contaminates some woolen or
linen clothing, 48woolen or linen fabric, the hide of an animal, or anything made of leather. 49If the contaminated
area in the clothing, the animal hide, the fabric, or the
leather article has turned greenish or reddish, it is contaminated with mildew and must be shown to the priest.
50After examining the affected spot, the priest will put
the article in quarantine for seven days. 51On the seventh
day the priest must inspect it again. If the contaminated
area has spread, the clothing or fabric or leather is clearly
contaminated by a serious mildew and is ceremonially
unclean. 52The priest must burn the item—the clothing,
the woolen or linen fabric, or piece of leather—for it has
been contaminated by a serious mildew. It must be completely destroyed by fire.
53"But if the priest examines it and finds that the contaminated area has not spread in the clothing, the fabric,
or the leather, 54the priest will order the object to be
washed and then quarantined for seven more days.
55Then the priest must examine the object again. If he
finds that the contaminated area has not changed color
after being washed, even if it did not spread, the object is
defiled. It must be completely burned up, whether the
contaminated spot* is on the inside or outside. 56But if
the priest examines it and finds that the contaminated
area has faded after being washed, he must cut the spot
from the clothing, the fabric, or the leather. 57If the spot
later reappears on the clothing, the fabric, or the leather
article, the mildew is clearly spreading, and the contaminated object must be burned up. 58But if the spot disappears from the clothing, the fabric, or the leather
article after it has been washed, it must be washed again;
then it will be ceremonially clean.
59"These are the instructions for dealing with mildew
that contaminates woolen or linen clothing or fabric or
anything made of leather. This is how the priest will determine whether these items are ceremonially clean or
unclean."

14 CLEANSING FROM SKIN DISEASES

And the LORD said to Moses, 2"The following instructions
are for those seeking ceremonial purification from a skin
disease.* Those who have been healed must be brought
to the priest, 3who will examine them at a place outside
the camp. If the priest finds that someone has been
healed of a serious skin disease, 4he will perform a purification ceremony, using two live birds that are ceremonially clean, a stick of cedar,* some scarlet yarn, and a
hyssop branch. 5The priest will order that one bird be
slaughtered over a clay pot filled with fresh water. 6He
will take the live bird, the cedar stick, the scarlet yarn, and
the hyssop branch, and dip them into the blood of the
bird that was slaughtered over the fresh water. 7The
priest will then sprinkle the blood of the dead bird seven
times on the person being purified of the skin disease.
When the priest has purified the person, he will release
the live bird in the open field to fly away.
8"The persons being purified must then wash their
clothes, shave off all their hair, and bathe themselves in
water. Then they will be ceremonially clean and may return to the camp. However, they must remain outside
their tents for seven days. 9On the seventh day they must
again shave all the hair from their heads, including the
hair of the beard and eyebrows. They must also wash
their clothes and bathe themselves in water. Then they
will be ceremonially clean.
10"On the eighth day each person being purified must
bring two male lambs and a one-year-old female lamb, all
with no defects, along with a grain offering of six quarts*
of choice flour moistened with olive oil, and a cup* of olive oil. 11Then the officiating priest will present that person for purification, along with the offerings, before the
LORD at the entrance of the Tabernacle.* 12The priest will
take one of the male lambs and the olive oil and present
them as a guilt offering, lifting them up as a special offering before the LORD. 13He will then slaughter the male
lamb in the sacred area where sin offerings and burnt offerings are slaughtered. As with the sin offering, the guilt
offering belongs to the priest. It is a most holy offering.
14The priest will then take some of the blood of the guilt
offering and apply it to the lobe of the right ear, the
thumb of the right hand, and the big toe of the right foot
of the person being purified.
15"Then the priest will pour some of the olive oil into
the palm of his own left hand. 16He will dip his right finger into the oil in his palm and sprinkle some of it with
his finger seven times before the LORD. 17The priest will
then apply some of the oil in his palm over the blood
from the guilt offering that is on the lobe of the right ear,

13:45 Or *and uncover their heads.* **13:47** Traditionally rendered *leprosy.* The Hebrew term used throughout this passage is the same term used for the various skin diseases described in 13:1-46. **13:55** The meaning of the Hebrew is uncertain. **14:2** Traditionally rendered *leprosy;* see note on 13:2a. **14:4** Or *juniper;* also in 14:6, 49, 51. **14:10a** Hebrew *3/10 of an ephah* [6.6 liters]. **14:10b** Hebrew *1 log* [0.3 liters]; also in 14:21. **14:11** Hebrew *Tent of Meeting;* also in 14:23.

the thumb of the right hand, and the big toe of the right
foot of the person being purified. 18The priest will apply
the oil remaining in his hand to the head of the person
being purified. Through this process, the priest will purify* the person before the Lord.

19"Then the priest must present the sin offering to purify the person who was cured of the skin disease. After
that, the priest will slaughter the burnt offering 20and offer it on the altar along with the grain offering. Through
this process, the priest will purify the person who was
healed, and the person will be ceremonially clean.

21"But anyone who is too poor and cannot afford these
offerings may bring one male lamb for a guilt offering, to
be lifted up as a special offering for purification. The
person must also bring two quarts* of choice flour
moistened with olive oil for the grain offering and a cup
of olive oil. 22The offering must also include two
turtledoves or two young pigeons, whichever the person
can afford. One of the pair must be used for the sin offering and the other for a burnt offering. 23On the eighth
day of the purification ceremony, the person being purified must bring the offerings to the priest in the Lord's
presence at the entrance of the Tabernacle. 24The priest
will take the lamb for the guilt offering, along with the olive oil, and lift them up as a special offering to the Lord.
25Then the priest will slaughter the lamb for the guilt offering. He will take some of its blood and apply it to the
lobe of the right ear, the thumb of the right hand, and the
big toe of the right foot of the person being purified.

26"The priest will also pour some of the olive oil into
the palm of his own left hand. 27He will dip his right finger into the oil in his palm and sprinkle some of it seven
times before the Lord. 28The priest will then apply some
of the oil in his palm over the blood from the guilt offering that is on the lobe of the right ear, the thumb of the
right hand, and the big toe of the right foot of the person
being purified. 29The priest will apply the oil remaining
in his hand to the head of the person being purified.
Through this process, the priest will purify the person
before the Lord.

30"Then the priest will offer the two turtledoves or the
two young pigeons, whichever the person can afford.
31One of them is for a sin offering and the other for a
burnt offering, to be presented along with the grain offering. Through this process, the priest will purify the
person before the Lord. 32These are the instructions for
purification for those who have recovered from a serious
skin disease but who cannot afford to bring the offerings
normally required for the ceremony of purification."

TREATMENT OF CONTAMINATED HOUSES

33Then the Lord said to Moses and Aaron, 34"When you
arrive in Canaan, the land I am giving you as your own
possession, I may contaminate some of the houses in
your land with mildew.* 35The owner of such a house
must then go to the priest and say, 'It appears that my
house has some kind of mildew.' 36Before the priest goes
in to inspect the house, he must have the house emptied
so nothing inside will be pronounced ceremonially unclean. 37Then the priest will go in and examine the mildew on the walls. If he finds greenish or reddish streaks
and the contamination appears to go deeper than the
wall's surface, 38the priest will step outside the door and
put the house in quarantine for seven days. 39On the seventh day the priest must return for another inspection. If
he finds that the mildew on the walls of the house has
spread, 40the priest must order that the stones from those
areas be removed. The contaminated material will then
be taken outside the town to an area designated as ceremonially unclean. 41Next the inside walls of the entire
house must be scraped thoroughly and the scrapings
dumped in the unclean place outside the town. 42Other
stones will be brought in to replace the ones that were removed, and the walls will be replastered.

43"But if the mildew reappears after all the stones have
been replaced and the house has been scraped and replastered, 44the priest must return and inspect the house
again. If he finds that the mildew has spread, the walls are
clearly contaminated with a serious mildew, and the
house is defiled. 45It must be torn down, and all its stones,
timbers, and plaster must be carried out of town to the
place designated as ceremonially unclean. 46Those who
enter the house during the period of quarantine will be
ceremonially unclean until evening, 47and all who sleep
or eat in the house must wash their clothing.

FUNGUS FACTS 14:33-53

Here are instructions concerning "serious mildew" on clothing or house walls. This was probably a mold, fungus, or bacteria. Like mildew, this fungus could spread rapidly and promote disease. It was therefore important to check its spread as soon as possible. Is there anything in your life—an activity or relationship—that has a similar, destructive effect on you or your faith? ■

48"But if the priest returns for his inspection and finds
that the mildew has not reappeared in the house after the
fresh plastering, he will pronounce it clean because the
mildew is clearly gone. 49To purify the house the priest
must take two birds, a stick of cedar, some scarlet yarn,
and a hyssop branch. 50He will slaughter one of the birds
over a clay pot filled with fresh water. 51He will take the
cedar stick, the hyssop branch, the scarlet yarn, and the
live bird, and dip them into the blood of the slaughtered
bird and into the fresh water. Then he will sprinkle the
house seven times. 52When the priest has purified the
house in exactly this way, 53he will release the live bird in
the open fields outside the town. Through this process,
the priest will purify the house, and it will be ceremonially clean.

54"These are the instructions for dealing with serious

14:18 Or *will make atonement for;* similarly in 14:19, 20, 21, 29, 31, 53. **14:21** Hebrew *1/10 of an ephah* [2.2 liters]. **14:34** Traditionally rendered *leprosy;* see note on 13:47.

skin diseases,* including scabby sores; 55and mildew,* whether on clothing or in a house; 56and a swelling on the skin, a rash, or discolored skin. 57This procedure will determine whether a person or object is ceremonially clean or unclean.

"These are the instructions regarding skin diseases and mildew."

15 BODILY DISCHARGES

The LORD said to Moses and Aaron, 2"Give the following instructions to the people of Israel.

"Any man who has a bodily discharge is ceremonially unclean. 3This defilement is caused by his discharge, whether the discharge continues or stops. In either case the man is unclean. 4Any bed on which the man with the discharge lies and anything on which he sits will be ceremonially unclean. 5So if you touch the man's bed, you must wash your clothes and bathe yourself in water, and you will remain unclean until evening. 6If you sit where the man with the discharge has sat, you must wash your clothes and bathe yourself in water, and you will remain unclean until evening. 7If you touch the man with the discharge, you must wash your clothes and bathe yourself in water, and you will remain unclean until evening. 8If the man spits on you, you must wash your clothes and bathe yourself in water, and you will remain unclean until evening. 9Any saddle blanket on which the man rides will be ceremonially unclean. 10If you touch anything that was under the man, you will be unclean until evening. You must wash your clothes and bathe yourself in water, and you will remain unclean until evening. 11If the man touches you without first rinsing his hands, you must wash your clothes and bathe yourself in water, and you will remain unclean until evening. 12Any clay pot the man touches must be broken, and any wooden utensil he touches must be rinsed with water.

13"When the man with the discharge is healed, he must count off seven days for the period of purification. Then he must wash his clothes and bathe himself in fresh water, and he will be ceremonially clean. 14On the eighth day he must get two turtledoves or two young pigeons and come before the LORD at the entrance of the Tabernacle* and give his offerings to the priest. 15The priest will offer one bird for a sin offering and the other for a burnt offering. Through this process, the priest will purify* the man before the LORD for his discharge.

16"Whenever a man has an emission of semen, he must bathe his entire body in water, and he will remain ceremonially unclean until the next evening.* 17Any clothing or leather with semen on it must be washed in water, and it will remain unclean until evening. 18After a man and a woman have sexual intercourse, they must each bathe in water, and they will remain unclean until the next evening.

19"Whenever a woman has her menstrual period, she will be ceremonially unclean for seven days. Anyone who touches her during that time will be unclean until evening. 20Anything on which the woman lies or sits during the time of her period will be unclean. 21If any of you touch her bed, you must wash your clothes and bathe yourself in water, and you will remain unclean until evening. 22If you touch any object she has sat on, you must wash your clothes and bathe yourself in water, and you will remain unclean until evening. 23This includes her bed or any other object she has sat on; you will be unclean until evening if you touch it. 24If a man has sexual intercourse with her and her blood touches him, her menstrual impurity will be transmitted to him. He will remain unclean for seven days, and any bed on which he lies will be unclean.

25"If a woman has a flow of blood for many days that is unrelated to her menstrual period, or if the blood continues beyond the normal period, she is ceremonially unclean. As during her menstrual period, the woman will be unclean as long as the discharge continues. 26Any bed she lies on and any object she sits on during that time will be unclean, just as during her normal menstrual period. 27If any of you touch these things, you will be ceremonially unclean. You must wash your clothes and bathe yourself in water, and you will remain unclean until evening.

28"When the woman's bleeding stops, she must count off seven days. Then she will be ceremonially clean. 29On the eighth day she must bring two turtledoves or two young pigeons and present them to the priest at the entrance of the Tabernacle. 30The priest will offer one for a sin offering and the other for a burnt offering. Through this process, the priest will purify her before the LORD for the ceremonial impurity caused by her bleeding.

31"This is how you will guard the people of Israel from ceremonial uncleanness. Otherwise they would die, for their impurity would defile my Tabernacle that stands among them. 32These are the instructions for dealing with anyone who has a bodily discharge—a man who is unclean because of an emission of semen 33or a woman during her menstrual period. It applies to any man or woman who has a bodily discharge, and to a man who has sexual intercourse with a woman who is ceremonially unclean."

16 THE DAY OF ATONEMENT

The LORD spoke to Moses after the death of Aaron's two sons, who died after they entered the LORD's presence and burned the wrong kind of fire before him. 2The LORD said to Moses, "Warn your brother, Aaron, not to enter the Most Holy Place behind the inner curtain whenever he chooses; if he does, he will die. For the Ark's cover—the place of atonement—is there, and I myself am present in the cloud above the atonement cover.

3"When Aaron enters the sanctuary area, he must follow these instructions fully. He must bring a young bull for a sin offering and a ram for a burnt offering. 4He must put on his linen tunic and the linen undergarments worn next to his body. He must tie the linen sash around his

14:54 Traditionally rendered *leprosy;* see note on 13:2a. **14:55** Traditionally rendered *leprosy;* see note on 13:47. **15:14** Hebrew *Tent of Meeting;* also in 15:29. **15:15** Or *will make atonement for;* also in 15:30. **15:16** Hebrew *until evening;* also in 15:18.

GET READY 16:1-25

Aaron had to spend hours preparing himself to meet God on the Day of Atonement. But we can approach God anytime. Because of Jesus, the way to God has been opened. (See Heb 4:16.) What a privilege! We are offered easier access to God than the high priests of Old Testament times! But easy access to God does not eliminate our need to prepare our hearts as we draw near in prayer. ■

waist and put the linen turban on his head. These are sacred garments, so he must bathe himself in water before
he puts them on. 5Aaron must take from the community
of Israel two male goats for a sin offering and a ram for a
burnt offering.
6"Aaron will present his own bull as a sin offering to
purify himself and his family, making them right with the
LORD.* 7Then he must take the two male goats and present them to the LORD at the entrance of the Tabernacle.*
8He is to cast sacred lots to determine which goat will be
reserved as an offering to the LORD and which will carry
the sins of the people to the wilderness of Azazel. 9Aaron
will then present as a sin offering the goat chosen by lot
for the LORD. 10The other goat, the scapegoat chosen by
lot to be sent away, will be kept alive, standing before the
LORD. When it is sent away to Azazel in the wilderness,
the people will be purified and made
right with the LORD.*
11"Aaron will present his own bull as
a sin offering to purify himself and his
family, making them right with the
LORD. After he has slaughtered the bull
as a sin offering, 12he will fill an incense burner with burning coals from
the altar that stands before the LORD.
Then he will take two handfuls of fragrant powdered incense and will carry
the burner and the incense behind the
inner curtain. 13There in the LORD's
presence he will put the incense on the
burning coals so that a cloud of incense will rise over the Ark's cover—
the place of atonement—that rests on
the Ark of the Covenant.* If he follows
these instructions, he will not die.
14Then he must take some of the blood of the bull, dip his
finger in it, and sprinkle it on the east side of the atonement cover. He must sprinkle blood seven times with his
finger in front of the atonement cover.
15"Then Aaron must slaughter the first goat as a sin offering for the people and carry its blood behind the inner
curtain. There he will sprinkle the goat's blood over the
atonement cover and in front of it, just as he did with
the bull's blood. 16Through this process, he will purify*
the Most Holy Place, and he will do the same for the entire
Tabernacle, because of the defiling sin and rebellion of
the Israelites. 17No one else is allowed inside the Tabernacle when Aaron enters it for the purification ceremony in
the Most Holy Place. No one may enter until he comes out
again after purifying himself, his family, and all the congregation of Israel, making them right with the LORD.
18"Then Aaron will come out to purify the altar that
stands before the LORD. He will do this by taking some of
the blood from the bull and the goat and putting it on
each of the horns of the altar. 19Then he must sprinkle
the blood with his finger seven times over the altar. In
this way, he will cleanse it from Israel's defilement and
make it holy.
20"When Aaron has finished purifying the Most Holy
Place and the Tabernacle and the altar, he must present
the live goat. 21He will lay both of his hands on the goat's
head and confess over it all the wickedness, rebellion, and
sins of the people of Israel. In this way, he will transfer the
people's sins to the head of the goat. Then a man specially
chosen for the task will drive the goat into the wilderness.
22As the goat goes into the wilderness, it will carry all the
people's sins upon itself into a desolate land.
23"When Aaron goes back into the Tabernacle, he
must take off the linen garments he was wearing when he
entered the Most Holy Place, and he must leave the garments there. 24Then he must bathe himself with water in
a sacred place, put on his regular gar-
ments, and go out to sacrifice a burnt
offering for himself and a burnt offering for the people. Through this process, he will purify himself and the
people, making them right with the
LORD. 25He must then burn all the fat
of the sin offering on the altar.
26"The man chosen to drive the
scapegoat into the wilderness of Azazel must wash his clothes and bathe
himself in water. Then he may return
to the camp.
27"The bull and the goat presented as
sin offerings, whose blood Aaron takes
into the Most Holy Place for the purification ceremony, will be carried outside
the camp. The animals' hides, internal
organs, and dung are all to be burned.
28The man who burns them must wash his clothes and
bathe himself in water before returning to the camp.
29"On the tenth day of the appointed month in early autumn,* you must deny yourselves.* Neither native-born
Israelites nor foreigners living among you may do any
kind of work. This is a permanent law for you. 30On that
day offerings of purification will be made for you,* and
you will be purified in the LORD's presence from all your
sins. 31It will be a Sabbath day of complete rest for you,

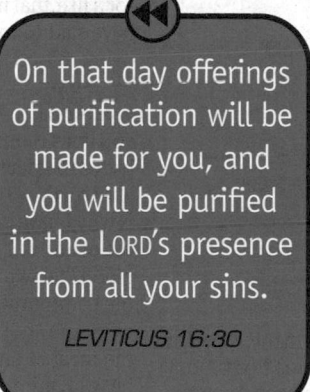

On that day offerings of purification will be made for you, and you will be purified in the LORD's presence from all your sins.

LEVITICUS 16:30

16:6 Or *to make atonement for himself and his family;* similarly in 16:11, 17b, 24, 34. **16:7** Hebrew *Tent of Meeting;* also in 16:16, 17, 20, 23, 33. **16:10** Or *wilderness, it will make atonement for the people.* **16:13** Hebrew *that is above the Testimony.* The Hebrew word for "testimony" refers to the terms of the LORD's covenant with Israel as written on stone tablets, which were kept in the Ark, and also to the covenant itself. **16:16** Or *make atonement for;* similarly in 16:17a, 18, 20, 27, 33. **16:29a** Hebrew *On the tenth day of the seventh month.* This day in the ancient Hebrew lunar calendar occurred in September or October. **16:29b** Or *must fast;* also in 16:31. **16:30** Or *atonement will be made for you, to purify you.*

Old/New System of Sacrifice

OLD SYSTEM OF SACRIFICE	NEW SYSTEM OF SACRIFICE
Was temporary (Heb 7:21)	Is permanent (Heb 7:21)
Aaron first high priest (Lev 16:32)	Jesus only High Priest (Heb 4:14)
From tribe of Levi (Heb 7:16)	From tribe of Judah (Heb 7:14)
Ministered on earth (Heb 8:4)	Ministers in heaven (Heb 8:12)
Used blood of animals (Lev 16:15)	Uses blood of Christ (Heb 10:4-12)
Required many sacrifices (Heb 10:1-3)	Requires one sacrifice (Heb 9:28)
Needed perfect animals (Lev 22:19)	Needs perfect life (Heb 5:9)
Required careful approach to tabernacle (Lev 16:2)	Encourages bold approach to throne (Heb 4:16)
Looked forward to new system (Heb 10:1)	Cancels old system (Heb 10:9)

and you must deny yourselves. This is a permanent law for you. 32In future generations, the purification* ceremony will be performed by the priest who has been anointed and ordained to serve as high priest in place of his ancestor Aaron. He will put on the holy linen garments 33and purify the Most Holy Place, the Tabernacle, the altar, the priests, and the entire congregation. 34This is a permanent law for you, to purify the people of Israel from their sins, making them right with the LORD once each year."

Moses followed all these instructions exactly as the LORD had commanded him.

17

PROHIBITIONS AGAINST EATING BLOOD

Then the LORD said to Moses, 2"Give the following instructions to Aaron and his sons and all the people of Israel. This is what the LORD has commanded.

3"If any native Israelite sacrifices a bull* or a lamb or a goat anywhere inside or outside the camp 4instead of bringing it to the entrance of the Tabernacle* to present it as an offering to the LORD, that person will be as guilty as a murderer.* Such a person has shed blood and will be cut off from the community. 5The purpose of this rule is to stop the Israelites from sacrificing animals in the open fields. It will ensure that they bring their sacrifices to the priest at the entrance of the Tabernacle, so he can present them to the LORD as peace offerings. 6Then the priest will be able to splatter the blood against the LORD's altar at the entrance of the Tabernacle, and he will burn the fat as a pleasing aroma to the LORD. 7The people must no longer be unfaithful to the LORD by offering sacrifices to the goat idols.* This is a permanent law for them, to be observed from generation to generation.

8"Give them this command as well. If any native Israelite or foreigner living among you offers a burnt offering or a sacrifice 9but does not bring it to the entrance of the Tabernacle to offer it to the LORD, that person will be cut off from the community.

10"And if any native Israelite or foreigner living among you eats or drinks blood in any form, I will turn against that person and cut him off from the community of your people, 11for the life of the body is in its blood. I have given you the blood on the altar to purify you, making you right with the LORD.* It is the blood, given in exchange for a life, that makes purification possible. 12That is why I have said to the people of Israel, 'You must never eat or drink blood—neither you nor the foreigners living among you.'

13"And if any native Israelite or foreigner living among you goes hunting and kills an animal or bird that is approved for eating, he must drain its blood and cover it with earth. 14The life of every creature is in its blood. That is why I have said to the people of Israel, 'You must never eat or drink blood, for the life of any creature is in its blood.' So whoever consumes blood will be cut off from the community.

15"And if any native-born Israelites or foreigners eat the meat of an animal that died naturally or was torn up by wild animals, they must wash their clothes and bathe themselves in water. They will remain ceremonially unclean until evening, but then they will be clean. 16But if they do not wash their clothes and bathe themselves, they will be punished for their sin."

18

FORBIDDEN SEXUAL PRACTICES

Then the LORD said to Moses, 2"Give the following instructions to the people of Israel. I am the LORD your God. 3So do not act like the people in Egypt, where you used to live, or like the people of Canaan, where I am taking you. You must not imitate their way of life. 4You must obey all my regulations and be careful to obey my decrees, for I am the LORD your God. 5If you obey my decrees and my

16:32 Or *atonement.* 17:3 Or *cow.* 17:4a Hebrew *Tent of Meeting;* also in 17:5, 6, 9. 17:4b Hebrew *will be guilty of blood.* 17:7 Or *goat demons.* 17:11 Or *to make atonement for you.*

ULTIMATE ISSUES

THE LAW

It's universal: We see a sign that says *Wet Paint* and we want to touch it. We walk by a sign in a zoo that says *Do Not Feed the Animals* and what do we do? Slip the monkeys the rest of our jelly doughnut.

A law of human nature seems to be that rules are made to be broken. We wonder, "What happens if I cross the line?"

The people of Israel could relate to this temptation. During the Old Testament, God gave them his laws to follow.

So what does the law do?

- *It measures our behavior.* If you had a three-year-old draw a line on a chalkboard, you'd probably get a crooked line. If you drew a line next to it and compared them, you might think, *My line really is straight, especially compared to little Kayla's.* But if someone else drew a line next to yours using a ruler, you'd see the imperfections of your line. In the same way, the law measures our behavior. When compared to God's perfect standard, we don't measure up. That's why we need a Savior.
- *The law also acts as an instructor.* These rules showed the Israelites how to live before a holy God. (See Lev 19:2.) God's law also set Israel apart from pagan nations. With God's law as instructor, there was no "grading on the curve."

Think of the law as training wheels. Training wheels help a beginning bike rider to stay upright until he or she "gets the hang of riding." The law shows you how to walk uprightly before a holy God.

The law pointed the people of the Old Testament toward a coming Savior, who would fulfill the law and set his people free. We don't need to wait until the Savior comes. He has come already and has written his law on our hearts. (See Rom 2:15.)

regulations, you will find life through them. I am the LORD.

6"You must never have sexual relations with a close relative, for I am the LORD.

7"Do not violate your father by having sexual relations with your mother. She is your mother; you must not have sexual relations with her.

8"Do not have sexual relations with any of your father's wives, for this would violate your father.

9"Do not have sexual relations with your sister or half sister, whether she is your father's daughter or your mother's daughter, whether she was born into your household or someone else's.

10"Do not have sexual relations with your granddaughter, whether she is your son's daughter or your daughter's daughter, for this would violate yourself.

11"Do not have sexual relations with your stepsister, the daughter of any of your father's wives, for she is your sister.

12"Do not have sexual relations with your father's sister, for she is your father's close relative.

13"Do not have sexual relations with your mother's sister, for she is your mother's close relative.

14"Do not violate your uncle, your father's brother, by having sexual relations with his wife, for she is your aunt.

15"Do not have sexual relations with your daughter-in-law; she is your son's wife, so you must not have sexual relations with her.

16"Do not have sexual relations with your brother's wife, for this would violate your brother.

17"Do not have sexual relations with both a woman and her daughter. And do not take* her granddaughter, whether her son's daughter or her daughter's daughter, and have sexual relations with her. They are close relatives, and this would be a wicked act.

18"While your wife is living, do not marry her sister and have sexual relations with her, for they would be rivals.

19"Do not have sexual relations with a woman during her period of menstrual impurity.

20"Do not defile yourself by having sexual intercourse with your neighbor's wife.

21"Do not permit any of your children to be offered as a sacrifice to Molech, for you must not bring shame on the name of your God. I am the LORD.

22"Do not practice homosexuality, having sex with another man as with a woman. It is a detestable sin.

18:17 Or *do not marry.*

MOLDER OR MOLDED? 18:3

The Israelites moved from one idol-infested region to another. As God helped them form a new culture, he warned them to stop imitating the people of Egypt. He also did not want his people to absorb the culture of Canaan. The same warning goes for us. Society may pressure us to conform to its way of life, but yielding to that pressure can eliminate our effectiveness in serving God. You don't have to be like gelatin—easily molded. Instead, you can help mold others by your strong faith. ■

23"A man must not defile himself by having sex with an
animal. And a woman must not offer herself to a male animal to have intercourse with it. This is a perverse act.
24"Do not defile yourselves in any of these ways, for
the people I am driving out before you have defiled
themselves in all these ways. 25Because the entire land
has become defiled, I am punishing the people who live
there. I will cause the land to vomit them out. 26You
must obey all my decrees and regulations. You must not
commit any of these detestable sins. This applies both
to native-born Israelites and to the foreigners living
among you.
27"All these detestable activities are practiced by the
people of the land where I am taking you, and this is how
the land has become defiled. 28So do not defile the land
and give it a reason to vomit you out, as it will vomit out
the people who live there now. 29Whoever commits any
of these detestable sins will be cut off from the community of Israel. 30So obey my instructions, and do not defile
yourselves by committing any of these detestable practices that were committed by the people who lived in the
land before you. I am the LORD your God."

19 HOLINESS IN PERSONAL CONDUCT

The LORD also said to Moses, 2"Give the following instructions to the entire community of Israel. You must be holy
because I, the LORD your God, am holy.
3"Each of you must show great respect for your mother
and father, and you must always observe my Sabbath
days of rest. I am the LORD your God.
4"Do not put your trust in idols or make metal images
of gods for yourselves. I am the LORD your God.
5"When you sacrifice a peace offering to the LORD, offer it properly so you* will be accepted by God. 6The sacrifice must be eaten on the same day you offer it or on the
next day. Whatever is left over until the third day must be
completely burned up. 7If any of the sacrifice is eaten on
the third day, it will be contaminated, and I will not accept it. 8Anyone who eats it on the third day will be punished for defiling what is holy to the LORD and will be cut
off from the community.
9"When you harvest the crops of your land, do not harvest the grain along the edges of your fields, and do not
pick up what the harvesters drop. 10It is the same with
your grape crop—do not strip every last bunch of grapes
from the vines, and do not pick up the grapes that fall to
the ground. Leave them for the poor and the foreigners
living among you. I am the LORD your God.
11"Do not steal.
"Do not deceive or cheat one another.
12"Do not bring shame on the name of your God by using it to swear falsely. I am the LORD.
13"Do not defraud or rob your neighbor.
"Do not make your hired workers wait until the next
day to receive their pay.
14"Do not insult the deaf or cause the blind to stumble.
You must fear your God; I am the LORD.
15"Do not twist justice in legal matters by favoring the
poor or being partial to the rich and powerful. Always
judge people fairly.

19:5 Or *it*.

When I read a verse like Leviticus 19:28, I have to wonder: Is body piercing okay? What about tattoos?

Keep up with the latest trends? Although body piercing and tattoos have been around for centuries, they're really trendy these days. You can't go very far without seeing some form of piercing, from the more conventional one-hole in the earlobe to tongue piercing. And as for tattoos and other body decorations, well, let's just say that they're not confined to sailors, bikers, and others celebrating rites of passage. Suddenly, even your mom might consider getting a rose on her ankle!

But are tattoos and body piercing allowable, according to the Bible? Leviticus 19:28 says, "Do not cut your bodies for the dead, and do not mark your skin with tattoos. I am the Lord." Taking that verse at face value, one would assume that God says no to all piercing and tattoos. So, does that mean everyone with a tattoo needs to head to the nearest doctor to have it removed immediately? Does that mean no more earrings?

Actually, the best thing to do with a verse like this is to check out the context—the situation described in this passage. God knew that the nations in the land of Canaan used tattoos and body piercing as part of their religion. God vetoed both practices for Israel, because he did not want his people to imitate the worship practices of these nations. In other words, he looked at the attitude behind the practice.

To sum up, the Bible does not say that body piercing and tattoos are wrong. Does that make either okay to do? A better question to ask yourself is *What's my reason for doing this?* Before you act, consider these questions: How carefully have you considered this issue? Have you weighed the pros and cons (the possible infection factor; the cost of removal if you grow bored with a tattoo)? Do you just want to do what everyone else is doing? If you've already made your choice, how does your decision show your desire to bring glory to God?

STEALING

Kelli and Cheyenne work together at Quackers, the newest fast-food restaurant in town. It's not such a bad job. The hours are good, the uniforms—surprise!—don't look like circus costumes, and the pay is more than minimum wage. Besides, the girls have great fun (and a lot of laughs) checking out the cute guys from a rival high school who frequent the place on weekends.

Today, however, when the girls come to work, they discover a terse note from the boss: *I want to talk to both of you. It's very important!*

Kelli's heart drops to her shoes, and Cheyenne's stomach does a cartwheel. What could it mean? A raise? A promotion? Not likely. In fact, the girls are expecting the worst. See, they've been giving away free food and Quackers T-shirts to certain male customers. And Cheyenne took a whole box of burgers from the freezer late last Friday night to use at her Saturday pool party.

"We're dead!" Kelli moans. "We've done everything but actually take money out of the cash register!"

Cheyenne looks sheepish. "No—I even did that one night."

"Cheyenne! You didn't! How much did you take?"

"Fifty bucks."

"Oh no! What are we gonna say?"

Leviticus 19:11 could have helped Kelli and Cheyenne avoid this whole horrible headache. But God's command against stealing needs something else. It needs cooperation from people . . . like you.

16"Do not spread slanderous gossip among your people.*

"Do not stand idly by when your neighbor's life is threatened. I am the LORD.

17"Do not nurse hatred in your heart for any of your relatives.* Confront people directly so you will not be held guilty for their sin.

18"Do not seek revenge or bear a grudge against a fellow Israelite, but love your neighbor as yourself. I am the LORD.

19"You must obey all my decrees.

"Do not mate two different kinds of animals. Do not plant your field with two different kinds of seed. Do not wear clothing woven from two different kinds of thread.

20"If a man has sex with a slave girl whose freedom has never been purchased but who is committed to become another man's wife, he must pay full compensation to her master. But since she is not a free woman, neither the man nor the woman will be put to death. 21The man, however, must bring a ram as a guilt offering and present it to the LORD at the entrance of the Tabernacle.* 22The priest will then purify him* before the LORD with the ram of the guilt offering, and the man's sin will be forgiven.

23"When you enter the land and plant fruit trees, leave the fruit unharvested for the first three years and consider it forbidden.* Do not eat it. 24In the fourth year the entire crop must be consecrated to the LORD as a celebration of praise. 25Finally, in the fifth year you may eat the fruit. If you follow this pattern, your harvest will increase. I am the LORD your God.

26"Do not eat meat that has not been drained of its blood.

"Do not practice fortune-telling or witchcraft.

27"Do not trim off the hair on your temples or trim your beards.

28"Do not cut your bodies for the dead, and do not mark your skin with tattoos. I am the LORD.

29"Do not defile your daughter by making her a prostitute, or the land will be filled with prostitution and wickedness.

30"Keep my Sabbath days of rest, and show reverence toward my sanctuary. I am the LORD.

31"Do not defile yourselves by turning to mediums or to those who consult the spirits of the dead. I am the LORD your God.

32"Stand up in the presence of the elderly, and show respect for the aged. Fear your God. I am the LORD.

33"Do not take advantage of foreigners who live among you in your land. 34Treat them like native-born Israelites, and love them as you love yourself. Remember that you were once foreigners living in the land of Egypt. I am the LORD your God.

35"Do not use dishonest standards when measuring length, weight, or volume. 36Your scales and weights must be accurate. Your containers for measuring dry materials or liquids must be accurate.* I am the LORD your God who brought you out of the land of Egypt.

37"You must be careful to keep all of my decrees and regulations by putting them into practice. I am the LORD."

TWO SIMPLE COMMANDS 19:18

Don't, don't, don't. Some people think the Bible is nothing but a book of don'ts. But here we find two "do's" that sum up all of the other commandments. In Matthew 22:37-40, Jesus called these commandments—to love God and one's neighbors—the greatest commandments of all. Are these commandments high on your priorities list? ■

20 PUNISHMENTS FOR DISOBEDIENCE

The LORD said to Moses, 2"Give the people of Israel these instructions, which apply both to native Israelites and to the foreigners living in Israel.

"If any of them offer their children as a sacrifice to Molech, they must be put to death. The people of the community must stone them to death. 3I myself will turn against them and cut them off from the community,

19:16 Hebrew *Do not act as a merchant toward your own people.* 19:17 Hebrew *for your brother.* 19:21 Hebrew *Tent of Meeting.* 19:22 Or *make atonement for him.* 19:23 Hebrew *consider it uncircumcised.* 19:36 Hebrew *Use an honest ephah* [a dry measure] *and an honest hin* [a liquid measure].

because they have defiled my sanctuary and brought shame on my holy name by offering their children to Molech. 4And if the people of the community ignore those who offer their children to Molech and refuse to execute them, 5I myself will turn against them and their families and will cut them off from the community. This will happen to all who commit spiritual prostitution by worshiping Molech.

JUST SAY NO TO THE OCCULT 20:6

Everyone is interested in what the future holds. We often look to others for guidance. But God warned the Israelites against looking to the occult for advice. Mediums and psychics were outlawed because God was not the source of their information. At best, occult practitioners are fakes whose predictions cannot be trusted. At worst, they are in contact with evil spirits and are thus extremely dangerous. We don't need to look to the occult for information about the future. God has given us the Bible—a trustworthy source—for guidance. Is it your one-stop wisdom check? ■

6"I will also turn against those who commit spiritual prostitution by putting their trust in mediums or in those who consult the spirits of the dead. I will cut them off from the community. 7So set yourselves apart to be holy, for I am the LORD your God. 8Keep all my decrees by putting them into practice, for I am the LORD who makes you holy.

9"Anyone who dishonors* father or mother must be put to death. Such a person is guilty of a capital offense.

10"If a man commits adultery with his neighbor's wife, both the man and the woman who have committed adultery must be put to death.

11"If a man violates his father by having sex with one of his father's wives, both the man and the woman must be put to death, for they are guilty of a capital offense.

12"If a man has sex with his daughter-in-law, both must be put to death. They have committed a perverse act and are guilty of a capital offense.

13"If a man practices homosexuality, having sex with another man as with a woman, both men have committed a detestable act. They must both be put to death, for they are guilty of a capital offense.

14"If a man marries both a woman and her mother, he has committed a wicked act. The man and both women must be burned to death to wipe out such wickedness from among you.

15"If a man has sex with an animal, he must be put to death, and the animal must be killed.

16"If a woman presents herself to a male animal to have intercourse with it, she and the animal must both be put to death. You must kill both, for they are guilty of a capital offense.

17"If a man marries his sister, the daughter of either his father or his mother, and they have sexual relations, it is a shameful disgrace. They must be publicly cut off from the community. Since the man has violated his sister, he will be punished for his sin.

18"If a man has sexual relations with a woman during her menstrual period, both of them must be cut off from the community, for together they have exposed the source of her blood flow.

19"Do not have sexual relations with your aunt, whether your mother's sister or your father's sister. This would dishonor a close relative. Both parties are guilty and will be punished for their sin.

20"If a man has sex with his uncle's wife, he has violated his uncle. Both the man and woman will be punished for their sin, and they will die childless.

21"If a man marries his brother's wife, it is an act of impurity. He has violated his brother, and the guilty couple will remain childless.

22"You must keep all my decrees and regulations by putting them into practice; otherwise the land to which I am bringing you as your new home will vomit you out. 23Do not live according to the customs of the people I am driving out before you. It is because they do these shameful things that I detest them. 24But I have promised you, 'You will possess their land because I will give it to you as your possession—a land flowing with milk and honey.' I am the LORD your God, who has set you apart from all other people.

SELF-DESTRUCTION 20:22-23

God gave many rules to his people—but not without reason. He did not withhold good from them; he only prohibited those acts that would bring them to ruin. All of us understand God's physical laws of nature. For example, jumping off a ten-story building means death because of the law of gravity. But some of us don't understand how God's spiritual laws work. God forbids us to do certain things because he wants to keep us from self-destruction. Understand? ■

25"You must therefore make a distinction between ceremonially clean and unclean animals, and between clean and unclean birds. You must not defile yourselves by eating any unclean animal or bird or creature that scurries along the ground. I have identified them as being unclean for you. 26You must be holy because I, the LORD, am holy. I have set you apart from all other people to be my very own.

27"Men and women among you who act as mediums or who consult the spirits of the dead must be put to death by stoning. They are guilty of a capital offense."

21 INSTRUCTIONS FOR THE PRIESTS

The LORD said to Moses, "Give the following instructions to the priests, the descendants of Aaron.

"A priest must not make himself ceremonially unclean by touching the dead body of a relative. 2The only exceptions are his closest relatives—his mother or father, son

20:9 Greek version reads *Anyone who speaks disrespectfully of.* Compare Matt 15:4; Mark 7:10.

or daughter, brother, [3]or his virgin sister who depends on him because she has no husband. [4]But a priest must not defile himself and make himself unclean for someone who is related to him only by marriage.

[5]"The priests must not shave their heads or trim their beards or cut their bodies. [6]They must be set apart as holy to their God and must never bring shame on the name of God. They must be holy, for they are the ones who present the special gifts to the LORD, gifts of food for their God.

[7]"Priests may not marry a woman defiled by prostitution, and they may not marry a woman who is divorced from her husband, for the priests are set apart as holy to their God. [8]You must treat them as holy because they offer up food to your God. You must consider them holy because I, the LORD, am holy, and I make you holy.

> I, the LORD, am holy, and I make you holy.
>
> *LEVITICUS 21:8*

[9]"If a priest's daughter defiles herself by becoming a prostitute, she also defiles her father's holiness, and she must be burned to death.

[10]"The high priest has the highest rank of all the priests. The anointing oil has been poured on his head, and he has been ordained to wear the priestly garments. He must never leave his hair uncombed* or tear his clothing. [11]He must not defile himself by going near a dead body. He may not make himself ceremonially unclean even for his father or mother. [12]He must not defile the sanctuary of his God by leaving it to attend to a dead person, for he has been made holy by the anointing oil of his God. I am the LORD.

[13]"The high priest may marry only a virgin. [14]He may not marry a widow, a woman who is divorced, or a woman who has defiled herself by prostitution. She must be a virgin from his own clan, [15]so that he will not dishonor his descendants among his clan, for I am the LORD who makes him holy."

[16]Then the LORD said to Moses, [17]"Give the following instructions to Aaron: In all future generations, none of your descendants who has any defect will qualify to offer food to his God. [18]No one who has a defect qualifies, whether he is blind, lame, disfigured, deformed, [19]or has a broken foot or arm, [20]or is hunchbacked or dwarfed, or has a defective eye, or skin sores or scabs, or damaged testicles. [21]No descendant of Aaron who has a defect may approach the altar to present special gifts to the LORD. Since he has a defect, he may not approach the altar to offer food to his God. [22]However, he may eat from the food offered to God, including the holy offerings and the most holy offerings. [23]Yet because of his physical defect, he may not enter the room behind the inner curtain or approach the altar, for this would defile my holy places. I am the LORD who makes them holy."

[24]So Moses gave these instructions to Aaron and his sons and to all the Israelites.

22 The LORD said to Moses, [2]"Tell Aaron and his sons to be very careful with the sacred gifts that the Israelites set apart for me, so they do not bring shame on my holy name. I am the LORD. [3]Give them the following instructions.

"In all future generations, if any of your descendants is ceremonially unclean when he approaches the sacred offerings that the people of Israel consecrate to the LORD, he must be cut off from my presence. I am the LORD.

[4]"If any of Aaron's descendants has a skin disease* or any kind of discharge that makes him ceremonially unclean, he may not eat from the sacred offerings until he has been pronounced clean. He also becomes unclean by touching a corpse, or by having an emission of semen, [5]or by touching a small animal that is unclean, or by touching someone who is ceremonially unclean for any reason. [6]The man who is defiled in any of these ways will remain unclean until evening. He may not eat from the sacred offerings until he has bathed himself in water. [7]When the sun goes down, he will be ceremonially clean again and may eat from the sacred offerings, for this is his food. [8]He may not eat an animal that has died a natural death or has been torn apart by wild animals, for this would defile him. I am the LORD.

[9]"The priests must follow my instructions carefully. Otherwise they will be punished for their sin and will die for violating my instructions. I am the LORD who makes them holy.

[10]"No one outside a priest's family may eat the sacred offerings. Even guests and hired workers in a priest's home are not allowed to eat them. [11]However, if the priest buys a slave for himself, the slave may eat from the sacred offerings. And if his slaves have children, they also may share his food. [12]If a priest's daughter marries someone outside the priestly family, she may no longer eat the sacred offerings. [13]But if she becomes a widow or is divorced and has no children to support her, and she returns to live in her father's home as in her youth, she may eat her father's food again. Otherwise, no one outside a priest's family may eat the sacred offerings.

[14]"Any such person who eats the sacred offerings without realizing it must pay the priest for the amount eaten, plus an additional 20 percent. [15]The priests must not let the Israelites defile the sacred offerings brought to the LORD [16]by allowing unauthorized people to eat them. This would bring guilt upon them and require them to pay compensation. I am the LORD who makes them holy."

WORTHY AND UNWORTHY OFFERINGS

[17]And the LORD said to Moses, [18]"Give Aaron and his sons and all the Israelites these instructions, which apply both to native Israelites and to the foreigners living among you.

21:10 Or *never uncover his head.* **22:4** Traditionally rendered *leprosy;* see note on 13:2a.

"If you present a gift as a burnt offering to the LORD, whether it is to fulfill a vow or is a voluntary offering, 19you* will be accepted only if your offering is a male animal with no defects. It may be a bull, a ram, or a male goat. 20Do not present an animal with defects, because the LORD will not accept it on your behalf.

ONLY THE BEST 22:19-25

Animals with defects were not acceptable as sacrifices because they did not represent God's holy nature. Only "perfect" animals were used. God also prefers that we give our best, whether we offer him time, talents, or treasures. When we offer our best, instead of the leftovers, we show the true meaning of worship and testify to God's supreme worth. ■

21"If you present a peace offering to the LORD from the herd or the flock, whether it is to fulfill a vow or is a voluntary offering, you must offer a perfect animal. It may have no defect of any kind. 22You must not offer an animal that is blind, crippled, or injured, or that has a wart, a skin sore, or scabs. Such animals must never be offered on the altar as special gifts to the LORD. 23If a bull* or lamb has a leg that is too long or too short, it may be offered as a voluntary offering, but it may not be offered to fulfill a vow. 24If an animal has damaged testicles or is castrated, you may not offer it to the LORD. You must never do this in your own land, 25and you must not accept such an animal from foreigners and then offer it as a sacrifice to your God. Such animals will not be accepted on your behalf, for they are mutilated or defective."

26And the LORD said to Moses, 27"When a calf or lamb or goat is born, it must be left with its mother for seven days. From the eighth day on, it will be acceptable as a special gift to the LORD. 28But you must not slaughter a mother animal and her offspring on the same day, whether from the herd or the flock. 29When you bring a thanksgiving offering to the LORD, sacrifice it properly so you will be accepted. 30Eat the entire sacrificial animal on the day it is presented. Do not leave any of it until the next morning. I am the LORD.

31"You must faithfully keep all my commands by putting them into practice, for I am the LORD. 32Do not bring shame on my holy name, for I will display my holiness among the people of Israel. I am the LORD who makes you holy. 33It was I who rescued you from the land of Egypt, that I might be your God. I am the LORD."

23 THE APPOINTED FESTIVALS

The LORD said to Moses, 2"Give the following instructions to the people of Israel. These are the LORD's appointed festivals, which you are to proclaim as official days for holy assembly.

3"You have six days each week for your ordinary work, but the seventh day is a Sabbath day of complete rest, an official day for holy assembly. It is the LORD's Sabbath day, and it must be observed wherever you live.

4"In addition to the Sabbath, these are the LORD's appointed festivals, the official days for holy assembly that are to be celebrated at their proper times each year.

PASSOVER AND THE FESTIVAL OF UNLEAVENED BREAD

5"The LORD's Passover begins at sundown on the fourteenth day of the first month.* 6On the next day, the fifteenth day of the month, you must begin celebrating the Festival of Unleavened Bread. This festival to the LORD continues for seven days, and during that time the bread you eat must be made without yeast. 7On the first day of the festival, all the people must stop their ordinary work and observe an official day for holy assembly. 8For seven days you must present special gifts to the LORD. On the seventh day the people must again stop all their ordinary work to observe an official day for holy assembly."

TRADITIONS 23:1-4

God established several national holidays each year for celebration, fellowship, and worship. Much can be learned about people by observing the holidays they celebrate and the way they celebrate them. What do your holiday traditions say about your values? ■

CELEBRATION OF FIRST HARVEST

9Then the LORD said to Moses, 10"Give the following instructions to the people of Israel. When you enter the land I am giving you and you harvest its first crops, bring the priest a bundle of grain from the first cutting of your grain harvest. 11On the day after the Sabbath, the priest will lift it up before the LORD so it may be accepted on your behalf. 12On that same day you must sacrifice a one-year-old male lamb with no defects as a burnt offering to the LORD. 13With it you must present a grain offering consisting of four quarts* of choice flour moistened with olive oil. It will be a special gift, a pleasing aroma to the LORD. You must also offer one quart* of wine as a liquid offering. 14Do not eat any bread or roasted grain or fresh kernels on that day until you bring this offering to your God. This is a permanent law for you, and it must be observed from generation to generation wherever you live.

THE FESTIVAL OF HARVEST

15"From the day after the Sabbath—the day you bring the bundle of grain to be lifted up as a special offering—count off seven full weeks. 16Keep counting until the day after the seventh Sabbath, fifty days later. Then present an offering of new grain to the LORD. 17From wherever you live, bring two loaves of bread to be lifted up before the LORD as a special offering.

22:19 Or *it.* **22:23** Or *cow.* **23:5** This day in the ancient Hebrew lunar calendar occurred in late March, April, or early May. **23:13a** Hebrew *2/10 of an ephah* [4.4 liters]; also in 23:17. **23:13b** Hebrew *1/4 of a hin* [1 liter].

The Festivals

Besides enjoying one Sabbath day of rest each week, the Israelites also enjoyed 19 days when national holidays were celebrated.

FESTIVAL	WHEN IT CELEBRATED	ITS IMPORTANCE
Passover One day (Lev 23:5)	When God spared the lives of Israel's firstborn children in Egypt and freed the Hebrews from slavery	Reminded the people of God's deliverance
Unleavened Bread Seven days (Lev 23:6-8)	The Exodus from Egypt	Reminded the people they were leaving the old life behind and entering a new way of living
Firstfruits One day (Lev 23:9-14)	The first crops of the barley harvest	Reminded the people how God provided for them
Harvest (Pentecost) One day (Lev 23:15-22)	The end of the barley harvest and beginning of the wheat harvest	Showed joy and thanksgiving over the bountiful harvest
Trumpets One day (Lev 23:23-25)	The beginning of the seventh month (civil new year)	Restored fellowship with God
Day of Atonement One day (Lev 23:26-32)	The removal of sin from the people and the nation	Restored fellowship with God
Shelters (Tabernacles) Seven days (Lev 23:33-43)	God's protection and guidance in the wilderness	Renewed Israel's commitment to God and trust in his guidance and protection

Make these loaves from four quarts of choice flour, and bake them with yeast. They will be an offering to the LORD from the first of your crops. 18Along with the
bread, present seven one-year-old male lambs with no defects, one young bull, and two rams as burnt offerings to the LORD. These burnt offerings, together with the grain offerings and liquid offerings, will be a special gift, a pleasing aroma to the LORD. 19Then you must offer one
male goat as a sin offering and two one-year-old male lambs as a peace offering.
20"The priest will lift up the two lambs as a special offering to the LORD, together with the loaves representing the first of your crops. These offerings, which are holy to the LORD, belong to the priests. 21That same day will be
proclaimed an official day for holy assembly, a day on which you do no ordinary work. This is a permanent law for you, and it must be observed from generation to generation wherever you live.*
22"When you harvest the crops of your land, do not harvest the grain along the edges of your fields, and do not pick up what the harvesters drop. Leave it for the poor and the foreigners living among you. I am the LORD your God."

THE FESTIVAL OF TRUMPETS

23The LORD said to Moses, 24"Give the following instructions to the people of Israel. On the first day of the appointed month in early autumn,* you are to observe a day of complete rest. It will be an official day for holy assembly, a day commemorated with loud blasts of a trumpet.
25You must do no ordinary work on that day. Instead, you are to present special gifts to the LORD."

THE DAY OF ATONEMENT

26Then the LORD said to Moses, 27"Be careful to celebrate the Day of Atonement on the tenth day of that same

23:21 This celebration, called the Festival of Harvest or the Festival of Weeks, was later called the Festival of Pentecost (see Acts 2:1). It is celebrated today as Shavuat (or Shabuoth). 23:24 Hebrew *On the first day of the seventh month.* This day in the ancient Hebrew lunar calendar occurred in September or October. This festival is celebrated today as Rosh Hashanah, the Jewish new year.

month—nine days after the Festival of Trumpets.* You
must observe it as an official day for holy assembly, a day
to deny yourselves* and present special gifts to the LORD.
28Do no work during that entire day because it is the Day
of Atonement, when offerings of purification are made
for you, making you right with* the LORD your God. 29All
who do not deny themselves that day will be cut off from
God's people. 30And I will destroy anyone among you who
does any work on that day. 31You must not do any work at
all! This is a permanent law for you, and it must be observed from generation to generation wherever you live.
32This will be a Sabbath day of complete rest for you, and
on that day you must deny yourselves. This day of rest will
begin at sundown on the ninth day of the month and extend until sundown on the tenth day."

THE FESTIVAL OF SHELTERS

33And the LORD said to Moses, 34"Give the following instructions to the people of Israel. Begin celebrating the
Festival of Shelters* on the fifteenth day of the appointed month—five days after the Day of Atonement.*
This festival to the LORD will last for seven days. 35On the
first day of the festival you must proclaim an official day
for holy assembly, when you do no ordinary work. 36For
seven days you must present special gifts to the LORD.
The eighth day is another holy day on which you present
your special gifts to the LORD. This will be a solemn occasion, and no ordinary work may be done that day.

37("These are the LORD's appointed festivals. Celebrate
them each year as official days for holy assembly by presenting special gifts to the LORD—burnt offerings, grain
offerings, sacrifices, and liquid offerings—each on its
proper day. 38These festivals must be observed in addition to the LORD's regular Sabbath days, and the offerings
are in addition to your personal gifts, the offerings you
give to fulfill your vows, and the voluntary offerings you
present to the LORD.)

39"Remember that this seven-day festival to the LORD—
the Festival of Shelters—begins on the fifteenth day of the
appointed month,* after you have harvested all the produce
of the land. The first day and the eighth day of the festival
will be days of complete rest. 40On the first day gather
branches from magnificent trees*—palm fronds, boughs
from leafy trees, and willows that grow by the streams. Then
celebrate with joy before the LORD your God for seven days.
41You must observe this festival to the LORD for seven days
every year. This is a permanent law for you, and it must be
observed in the appointed month* from generation to generation. 42For seven days you must live outside in little shelters. All native-born Israelites must live in shelters. 43This
will remind each new generation of Israelites that I made
their ancestors live in shelters when I rescued them from
the land of Egypt. I am the LORD your God."

44So Moses gave the Israelites these instructions regarding the annual festivals of the LORD.

24

PURE OIL AND HOLY BREAD

The LORD said to Moses, 2"Command the people of Israel
to bring you pure oil of pressed olives for the light, to
keep the lamps burning continually. 3This is the lampstand that stands in the Tabernacle, in front of the inner
curtain that shields the Ark of the Covenant.* Aaron
must keep the lamps burning in the LORD's presence all
night. This is a permanent law for you, and it must be observed from generation to generation. 4Aaron and the
priests must tend the lamps on the pure gold lampstand
continually in the LORD's presence.

5"You must bake twelve loaves of bread from choice
flour, using four quarts* of flour for each loaf. 6Place the
bread before the LORD on the pure gold table, and arrange the loaves in two rows, with six loaves in each row.
7Put some pure frankincense near each row to serve as a
representative offering, a special gift presented to the
LORD. 8Every Sabbath day this bread must be laid out before the LORD. The bread is to be received from the people of Israel as a requirement of the eternal covenant.
9The loaves of bread will belong to Aaron and his descendants, who must eat them in a sacred place, for they are
most holy. It is the permanent right of the priests to claim
this portion of the special gifts presented to the LORD."

AN EXAMPLE OF JUST PUNISHMENT

10One day a man who had an Israelite mother and an
Egyptian father came out of his tent and got into a fight
with one of the Israelite men. 11During the fight, this son
of an Israelite woman blasphemed the Name of the
LORD* with a curse. So the man was brought to Moses for
judgment. His mother was Shelomith, the daughter of
Dibri of the tribe of Dan. 12They kept the man in custody
until the LORD's will in the matter should become clear to
them.

13Then the LORD said to Moses, 14"Take the blasphemer outside the camp, and tell all those who heard
the curse to lay their hands on his head. Then let the entire community stone him to death. 15Say to the people of
Israel: Those who curse their God will be punished for
their sin. 16Anyone who blasphemes the Name of the
LORD must be stoned to death by the whole community
of Israel. Any native-born Israelite or foreigner among
you who blasphemes the Name of the LORD must be put
to death.

17"Anyone who takes another person's life must be put
to death.

18"Anyone who kills another person's animal must pay
for it in full—a live animal for the animal that was killed.

23:27a Hebrew *on the tenth day of the seventh month;* see 23:24 and the note there. This day in the ancient Hebrew lunar calendar occurred in September or October. It is celebrated today as Yom Kippur. **23:27b** Or *to fast;* similarly in 23:29, 32. **23:28** Or *when atonement is made for you before.* **23:34a** Or *Festival of Booths,* or *Festival of Tabernacles.* This was earlier called the Festival of the Final Harvest or Festival of Ingathering (see Exod 23:16b). It is celebrated today as Sukkot (or Succoth). **23:34b** Hebrew *on the fifteenth day of the seventh month;* see 23:27a and the note there. **23:39** Hebrew *on the fifteenth day of the seventh month.* **23:40** Or *gather fruit from majestic trees.* **23:41** Hebrew *the seventh month.* **24:3** Hebrew *in the Tent of Meeting, outside the inner curtain of the Testimony;* see note on 16:13. **24:5** Hebrew *2/10 of an ephah* [4.4 liters]. **24:11** Hebrew *the Name;* also in 24:16b.

19"Anyone who injures another person must be dealt with according to the injury inflicted—20a fracture for a fracture, an eye for an eye, a tooth for a tooth. Whatever anyone does to injure another person must be paid back in kind.

21"Whoever kills an animal must pay for it in full, but whoever kills another person must be put to death.

22"This same standard applies both to native-born Israelites and to the foreigners living among you. I am the LORD your God."

23After Moses gave all these instructions to the Israelites, they took the blasphemer outside the camp and stoned him to death. The Israelites did just as the LORD had commanded Moses.

25

THE SABBATH YEAR

While Moses was on Mount Sinai, the LORD said to him, 2"Give the following instructions to the people of Israel. When you have entered the land I am giving you, the land itself must observe a Sabbath rest before the LORD every seventh year. 3For six years you may plant your fields and prune your vineyards and harvest your crops, 4but during the seventh year the land must have a Sabbath year of complete rest. It is the LORD's Sabbath. Do not plant your fields or prune your vineyards during that year. 5And don't store away the crops that grow on their own or gather the grapes from your unpruned vines. The land must have a year of complete rest. 6But you may eat whatever the land produces on its own during its Sabbath. This applies to you, your male and female servants, your hired workers, and the temporary residents who live with you. 7Your livestock and the wild animals in your land will also be allowed to eat what the land produces.

THE YEAR OF JUBILEE

8"In addition, you must count off seven Sabbath years, seven sets of seven years, adding up to forty-nine years in all. 9Then on the Day of Atonement in the fiftieth year,* blow the ram's horn loud and long throughout the land. 10Set this year apart as holy, a time to proclaim freedom throughout the land for all who live there. It will be a jubilee year for you, when each of you may return to the land that belonged to your ancestors and return to your own clan. 11This fiftieth year will be a jubilee for you. During that year you must not plant your fields or store away any of the crops that grow on their own, and don't gather the grapes from your unpruned vines. 12It will be a jubilee year for you, and you must keep it holy. But you may eat whatever the land produces on its own. 13In the Year of Jubilee each of you may return to the land that belonged to your ancestors.

14"When you make an agreement with your neighbor to buy or sell property, you must not take advantage of each other. 15When you buy land from your neighbor, the price you pay must be based on the number of years since the last jubilee. The seller must set the price by taking into account the number of years remaining until the next Year of Jubilee. 16The more years until the next jubilee, the higher the price; the fewer years, the lower the price. After all, the person selling the land is actually selling you a certain number of harvests. 17Show your fear of God by not taking advantage of each other. I am the LORD your God.

18"If you want to live securely in the land, follow my decrees and obey my regulations. 19Then the land will yield large crops, and you will eat your fill and live securely in it. 20But you might ask, 'What will we eat during the seventh year, since we are not allowed to plant or harvest crops that year?' 21Be assured that I will send my blessing for you in the sixth year, so the land will produce a crop large enough for three years. 22When you plant your fields in the eighth year, you will still be eating from the large crop of the sixth year. In fact, you will still be eating from that large crop when the new crop is harvested in the ninth year.

REDEMPTION OF PROPERTY

23"The land must never be sold on a permanent basis, for the land belongs to me. You are only foreigners and tenant farmers working for me.

24"With every purchase of land you must grant the seller the right to buy it back. 25If one of your fellow Israelites falls into poverty and is forced to sell some family land, then a close relative should buy it back for him. 26If there is no close relative to buy the land, but the person who sold it gets enough money to buy it back, 27he then has the right to redeem it from the one who bought it. The price of the land will be discounted according to the number of years until the next Year of Jubilee. In this way the original owner can then return to the land. 28But if the original owner cannot afford to buy back the land, it will remain with the new owner until the next Year of Jubilee. In the jubilee year, the land must be returned to the original owners so they can return to their family land.

29"Anyone who sells a house inside a walled town has the right to buy it back for a full year after its sale. During that year, the seller retains the right to buy it back. 30But if it is not bought back within a year, the sale of the house within the walled town cannot be reversed. It will become the permanent property of the buyer. It will not be returned to the original owner in the Year of Jubilee. 31But a house in a village—a settlement without fortified walls—will be treated like property in the countryside. Such a house may be bought back at any time, and it must be returned to the original owner in the Year of Jubilee.

32"The Levites always have the right to buy back a house they have sold within the towns allotted to them. 33And any property that is sold by the Levites—all houses within the Levitical towns—must be returned in the Year of Jubilee. After all, the houses in the towns reserved for the Levites are the only property they own in all Israel. 34The open pastureland around the Levitical towns may never be sold. It is their permanent possession.

25:9 Hebrew *on the tenth day of the seventh month, on the Day of Atonement;* see 23:27a and the note there.

REDEMPTION OF THE POOR AND ENSLAVED

35"If one of your fellow Israelites falls into poverty and cannot support himself, support him as you would a foreigner or a temporary resident and allow him to live with you. 36Do not charge interest or make a profit at his expense. Instead, show your fear of God by letting him live with you as your relative. 37Remember, do not charge interest on money you lend him or make a profit on food you sell him. 38I am the LORD your God, who brought you out of the land of Egypt to give you the land of Canaan and to be your God.

39"If one of your fellow Israelites falls into poverty and is forced to sell himself to you, do not treat him as a slave. 40Treat him instead as a hired worker or as a temporary resident who lives with you, and he will serve you only until the Year of Jubilee. 41At that time he and his children will no longer be obligated to you, and they will return to their clans and go back to the land originally allotted to their ancestors. 42The people of Israel are my servants, whom I brought out of the land of Egypt, so they must never be sold as slaves. 43Show your fear of God by not treating them harshly.

44"However, you may purchase male and female slaves from among the nations around you. 45You may also purchase the children of temporary residents who live among you, including those who have been born in your land. You may treat them as your property, 46passing them on to your children as a permanent inheritance. You may treat them as slaves, but you must never treat your fellow Israelites this way.

47"Suppose a foreigner or temporary resident becomes rich while living among you. If any of your fellow Israelites fall into poverty and are forced to sell themselves to such a foreigner or to a member of his family, 48they still retain the right to be bought back, even after they have been purchased. They may be bought back by a brother, 49an uncle, or a cousin. In fact, anyone from the extended family may buy them back. They may also redeem themselves if they have prospered. 50They will negotiate the price of their freedom with the person who bought them. The price will be based on the number of years from the time they were sold until the next Year of Jubilee—whatever it would cost to hire a worker for that period of time. 51If many years still remain until the jubilee, they will repay the proper proportion of what they received when they sold themselves. 52If only a few years remain until the Year of Jubilee, they will repay a small amount for their redemption. 53The foreigner must treat them as workers hired on a yearly basis. You must not allow a foreigner to treat any of your fellow Israelites harshly. 54If any Israelites have not been bought back by the time the Year of Jubilee arrives, they and their children must be set free at that time. 55For the people of Israel belong to me. They are my servants, whom I brought out of the land of Egypt. I am the LORD your God.

26

BLESSINGS FOR OBEDIENCE

"Do not make idols or set up carved images, or sacred pillars, or sculptured stones in your land so you may worship them. I am the LORD your God. 2You must keep my Sabbath days of rest and show reverence for my sanctuary. I am the LORD.

WARNINGS 26:1

The people of Israel were warned over and over against worshiping idols. We wonder how they could deceive themselves with these objects of wood and stone. Yet God could give us the same warning about the idols in our lives. An idol is anything more important to us than God. Money, looks, success, security, and popularity are just a few of today's idols. As you look at these false gods that promise everything you want but nothing you need, does idolatry seem so far removed from your experience? ■

3"If you follow my decrees and are careful to obey my commands, 4I will send you the seasonal rains. The land will then yield its crops, and the trees of the field will produce their fruit. 5Your threshing season will overlap with the grape harvest, and your grape harvest will overlap with the season of planting grain. You will eat your fill and live securely in your own land.

6"I will give you peace in the land, and you will be able to sleep with no cause for fear. I will rid the land of wild animals and keep your enemies out of your land. 7In fact, you will chase down your enemies and slaughter them with your swords. 8Five of you will chase a hundred, and a hundred of you will chase ten thousand! All your enemies will fall beneath your sword.

9"I will look favorably upon you, making you fertile and multiplying your people. And I will fulfill my covenant with you. 10You will have such a surplus of crops that you will need to clear out the old grain to make room for the new harvest! 11I will live among you, and I will not despise you. 12I will walk among you; I will be your God, and you will be my people. 13I am the LORD your God, who brought you out of the land of Egypt so you would no longer be their slaves. I broke the yoke of slavery from your neck so you can walk with your heads held high.

PUNISHMENTS FOR DISOBEDIENCE

14"However, if you do not listen to me or obey all these commands, 15and if you break my covenant by rejecting my decrees, treating my regulations with contempt, and refusing to obey my commands, 16I will punish you. I will bring sudden terrors upon you—wasting diseases and burning fevers that will cause your eyes to fail and your life to ebb away. You will plant your crops in vain because your enemies will eat them. 17I will turn against you, and you will be defeated by your enemies. Those who hate you will rule over you, and you will run even when no one is chasing you!

18"And if, in spite of all this, you still disobey me, I will punish you seven times over for your sins. 19I will break your proud spirit by making the skies as unyielding as iron and the earth as hard as bronze. 20All your work will

keeping it real

Okay, I know that most people don't usually read Leviticus unless they have to. I'm one of them. But since I was involved in a read-through-the-Bible-in-a-year program, I had to read every word of this book.

What hit me most as I read all this stuff about laws and sacrifices was how seriously God takes the way his people obey or disobey him. And he stated it so clearly for the Israelites. For example, in chapter 26 God says that obedience will bring prosperity in the Promised Land, but disobedience will bring nothing but trouble. **How could the people be so stupid,** I thought as I read. **Why would they ever disobey?** Easy for me to say, right? But even though I have more evidence of God's love than those people had, I still take God for granted and even disobey him on purpose at times.

Sometimes, what God wants me to do seems pretty clear. Like the time I needed to apologize to my mom for something I had said. I asked God to forgive me and went to talk with Mom.

God takes obedience seriously. That's what I need to do. **—Kara**

be for nothing, for your land will yield no crops, and your
trees will bear no fruit.
21 "If even then you remain hostile toward me and refuse to obey me, I will inflict disaster on you seven times
over for your sins. 22 I will send wild animals that will rob
you of your children and destroy your livestock. Your
numbers will dwindle, and your roads will be deserted.
23 "And if you fail to learn the lesson and continue your
hostility toward me, 24 then I myself will be hostile toward
you. I will personally strike you with calamity seven times
over for your sins. 25 I will send armies against you to carry
out the curse of the covenant you have broken. When you
run to your towns for safety, I will send a plague to destroy you there, and you will be handed over to your enemies. 26 I will destroy your food supply, so that ten women
will need only one oven to bake bread for their families.
They will ration your food by weight, and though you
have food to eat, you will not be satisfied.
27 "If in spite of all this you still refuse to listen and still
remain hostile toward me, 28 then I will give full vent to my
hostility. I myself will punish you seven times over for
your sins. 29 Then you will eat the flesh of your own sons
and daughters. 30 I will destroy your pagan shrines and
knock down your places of worship. I will leave your lifeless corpses piled on top of your lifeless idols,* and I will
despise you. 31 I will make your cities desolate and destroy
your places of pagan worship. I will take no pleasure in
your offerings that should be a pleasing aroma to me.
32 Yes, I myself will devastate your land, and your enemies
who come to occupy it will be appalled at what they see.
33 I will scatter you among the nations and bring out my
sword against you. Your land will become desolate, and
your cities will lie in ruins. 34 Then at last the land will enjoy its neglected Sabbath years as it lies desolate while
you are in exile in the land of your enemies. Then the
land will finally rest and enjoy the Sabbaths it missed.
35 As long as the land lies in ruins, it will enjoy the rest you
never allowed it to take every seventh year while you lived
in it.
36 "And for those of you who survive, I will demoralize
you in the land of your enemies. You will live in such fear
that the sound of a leaf driven by the wind will send you
fleeing. You will run as though fleeing from a sword, and
you will fall even when no one pursues you. 37 Though no
one is chasing you, you will stumble over each other as
though fleeing from a sword. You will have no power to
stand up against your enemies. 38 You will die among the
foreign nations and be devoured in the land of your enemies. 39 Those of you who survive will waste away in your
enemies' lands because of their sins and the sins of their
ancestors.
40 "But at last my people will confess their sins and the
sins of their ancestors for betraying me and being hostile
toward me. 41 When I have turned their hostility back on
them and brought them to the land of their enemies, then
at last their stubborn hearts will be humbled, and they
will pay for their sins. 42 Then I will remember my covenant with Jacob and my covenant with Isaac and my covenant with Abraham, and I will remember the land. 43 For
the land must be abandoned to enjoy its years of Sabbath

26:30 The Hebrew term (literally *round things*) probably alludes to dung.

rest as it lies deserted. At last the people will pay for their sins, for they have continually rejected my regulations and despised my decrees.

44"But despite all this, I will not utterly reject or despise them while they are in exile in the land of their enemies. I will not cancel my covenant with them by wiping them out, for I am the LORD their God. 45For their sakes I will remember my ancient covenant with their ancestors, whom I brought out of the land of Egypt in the sight of all the nations, that I might be their God. I am the LORD."

GROWTH 26:40-45

In Exodus 34:6, God declared his mercy, grace, love, and faithfulness to Moses. This passage in Leviticus shows these characteristics in action. Even if the Israelites chose to disobey him, God refused to give up on them. He would still give them the opportunity to seek his forgiveness. His purpose was not to destroy them, but to help them grow. His faithfulness to Israel can provide encouragement for us today. ■

46These are the decrees, regulations, and instructions that the LORD gave through Moses on Mount Sinai as evidence of the relationship between himself and the Israelites.

27

REDEMPTION OF GIFTS OFFERED TO THE LORD

The LORD said to Moses, 2"Give the following instructions to the people of Israel. If anyone makes a special vow to dedicate someone to the LORD by paying the value of that person, 3here is the scale of values to be used. A man between the ages of twenty and sixty is valued at fifty shekels* of silver, as measured by the sanctuary shekel. 4A woman of that age is valued at thirty shekels* of silver. 5A boy between the ages of five and twenty is valued at twenty shekels of silver; a girl of that age is valued at ten shekels* of silver. 6A boy between the ages of one month and five years is valued at five shekels of silver; a girl of that age is valued at three shekels* of silver. 7A man older than sixty is valued at fifteen shekels of silver; a woman of that age is valued at ten shekels* of silver. 8If you desire to make such a vow but cannot afford to pay the required amount, take the person to the priest. He will determine the amount for you to pay based on what you can afford.

9"If your vow involves giving an animal that is acceptable as an offering to the LORD, any gift to the LORD will be considered holy. 10You may not exchange or substitute it for another animal—neither a good animal for a bad one nor a bad animal for a good one. But if you do exchange one animal for another, then both the original animal and its substitute will be considered holy. 11If your vow involves an unclean animal—one that is not acceptable as an offering to the LORD—then you must bring the animal to the priest. 12He will assess its value, and his assessment will be final, whether high or low. 13If you want to buy back the animal, you must pay the value set by the priest, plus 20 percent.

14"If someone dedicates a house to the LORD, the priest will come to assess its value. The priest's assessment will be final, whether high or low. 15If the person who dedicated the house wants to buy it back, he must pay the value set by the priest, plus 20 percent. Then the house will again be his.

16"If someone dedicates to the LORD a piece of his family property, its value will be assessed according to the amount of seed required to plant it—fifty shekels of silver for a field planted with five bushels of barley seed.* 17If the field is dedicated to the LORD in the Year of Jubilee, then the entire assessment will apply. 18But if the field is dedicated after the Year of Jubilee, the priest will assess the land's value in proportion to the number of years left until the next Year of Jubilee. Its assessed value is reduced each year. 19If the person who dedicated the field wants to buy it back, he must pay the value set by the priest, plus 20 percent. Then the field will again be legally his. 20But if he does not want to buy it back, and it is sold to someone else, the field can no longer be bought back. 21When the field is released in the Year of Jubilee, it will be holy, a field specially set apart* for the LORD. It will become the property of the priests.

ALWAYS THE SAME 27:34

The book of Leviticus is filled with the commands God gave his people at the foot of Mount Sinai. From these commands we can learn much about God's nature. At first glance, Leviticus seems irrelevant to our high-tech world. But digging a little deeper, we realize that the book still speaks to us today. After all, God has not changed! (See Heb 13:8.) His principles are for all times. As people and society change, we need to continue searching for ways to apply the principles of God's law to our present circumstances. ■

22"If someone dedicates to the LORD a field he has purchased but which is not part of his family property, 23the priest will assess its value based on the number of years left until the next Year of Jubilee. On that day he must give the assessed value of the land as a sacred donation to the LORD. 24In the Year of Jubilee the field must be returned to the person from whom he purchased it, the one who inherited it as family property. 25(All the payments must be measured by the weight of the sanctuary shekel,* which equals twenty gerahs.)

27:3 Or *20 ounces* [570 grams]. 27:4 Or *12 ounces* [342 grams]. 27:5 Or *A boy . . . 8 ounces* [228 grams] *of silver; a girl . . . 4 ounces* [114 grams]. 27:6 Or *A boy . . . 2 ounces* [57 grams] *of silver; a girl . . . 1.2 ounces* [34 grams]. 27:7 Or *A man . . . 6 ounces* [171 grams] *of silver; a woman . . . 4 ounces* [114 grams]. 27:16 Hebrew *50 shekels* [20 ounces, or 570 grams] *of silver for a homer* [182 liters] *of barley seed.* 27:21 The Hebrew term used here refers to the complete consecration of things or people to the LORD, either by destroying them or by giving them as an offering; also in 27:28, 29. 27:25 Each shekel was about 0.4 ounces [11 grams] in weight.

[26]"You may not dedicate a firstborn animal to the
LORD, for the firstborn of your cattle, sheep, and goats already belong to him. [27]However, you may buy back the
firstborn of a ceremonially unclean animal by paying the
priest's assessment of its worth, plus 20 percent. If you
do not buy it back, the priest will sell it at its assessed
value.

[28]"However, anything specially set apart for the LORD—
whether a person, an animal, or family property—must
never be sold or bought back. Anything devoted in this
way has been set apart as holy, and it belongs to the LORD.
[29]No person specially set apart for destruction may be
bought back. Such a person must be put to death.

[30]"One tenth of the produce of the land, whether grain
from the fields or fruit from the trees, belongs to the
LORD and must be set apart to him as holy. [31]If you want to
buy back the LORD's tenth of the grain or fruit, you must
pay its value, plus 20 percent. [32]Count off every tenth animal from your herds and flocks and set them apart for
the LORD as holy. [33]You may not pick and choose between
good and bad animals, and you may not substitute one
for another. But if you do exchange one animal for another, then both the original animal and its substitute will
be considered holy and cannot be bought back."

[34]These are the commands that the LORD gave through
Moses on Mount Sinai for the Israelites.

AT NOON, two weary travelers who had been walking all day wanted to rest. They noticed a huge tree with a lot of shade. They stumbled over to the tree, threw down their packs, and were soon asleep. When they awoke, one of the travelers, feeling refreshed, gazed into the tree and complained: "What a useless tree. There's no fruit!"

That traveler was a lot like the people of Israel. At the start of the book of Numbers, the Israelites seemed to be sitting in God's "shade." They were about to enter the Promised Land—the future looked great. But life took a bleak turn when the twelve spies returned. Instead of believing the two spies' good report, the people chose to focus on the ten spies' negative report. They had forgotten God's promise to give them the land.

After hearing little but complaints from the people of Israel, God gave them a taste of his judgment. This generation would never enter the Promised Land.

Are we much different from the complaining Israelites? God has done, is doing, and will do so much for us. Yet we complain. "God, what are you doing?" "God, you don't care!" "God, how could you do this to me?" We don't trust him even though he proves himself trustworthy. Are you trusting or complaining?

numbers

timeline

1805 B.C.
Joseph dies

SLAVERY IN EGYPT

1446
Exodus from Egypt

1445
Ten Commandments given

1444
First census

1443
First spy mission

WILDERNESS WANDERINGS

1407
Second census; Balaam prophesies

1406
Joshua appointed; Canaan entered

1375
Judges begin to rule

1050
United kingdom under Saul

stats

PURPOSE: To tell the story of how Israel prepared to enter the Promised Land, how they sinned and were punished, and how they prepared to try again

AUTHOR: Moses

TO WHOM WRITTEN: The people of Israel

DATE WRITTEN: 1450–1410 B.C.

SETTING: The vast wilderness of the Sinai region, as well as lands just south and east of Canaan

KEY PEOPLE: Moses, Aaron, Miriam, Joshua, Caleb, Eleazar, Korah, Balaam

KEY PLACES: Mount Sinai, Promised Land (Canaan), Kadesh, Mount Hor, the plains of Moab

KEY points

CENSUS
Moses counted the Israelites twice for the defense of Israel as they entered the Promise Land. People have to be organized, trained, and led to be effective in making a difference in their world. Before beginning great tasks, it is always wise to count the cost of what lies ahead.

REBELLION
At Kadesh, the people of Israel rebelled, having accepted the negative report of ten out of twelve spies. Rebellion against God is always serious. Usually, rebellion is not an abrupt, radical departure from God; instead, it is the result of long-term drifting, often characterized by complaining and criticizing.

WANDERING
Because they rebelled, the Israelites had a forty-year stay in the wilderness. During this time, God trained a new generation to follow him while those who still had wrong attitudes died. He judges sin not just because he dislikes it but because he is holy and cannot tolerate it.

CANAAN
Canaan was the Promised Land—the land God promised to Abraham, Isaac, and Jacob. Canaan was to be the dwelling place of God's people, those set apart for true worship. Today, the place for true worship can be found in the human heart—the home of the Holy Spirit.

KEY PLACES IN NUMBERS

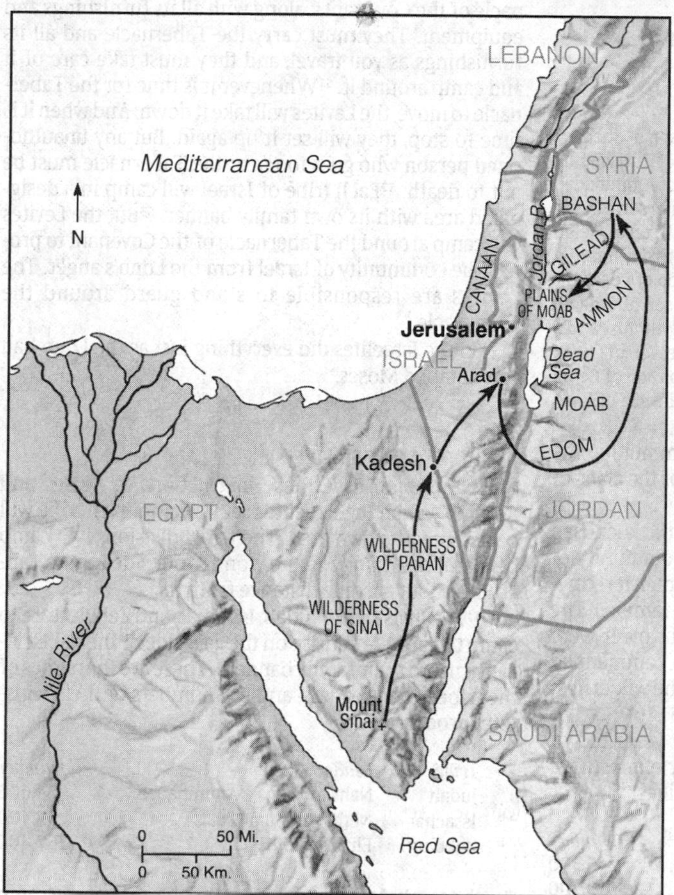

Modern names and boundaries are shown in gray.

- **MOUNT SINAI** Numbers begins at Mount Sinai with Moses taking a census of the men eligible for battle. As the battle preparations began, the people also prepared for the spiritual warfare they would face. The Promised Land was full of wicked people who would try to entice the Israelites to sin. God, therefore, taught Moses and the Israelites how to live rightly (1:1–12:15).
- **WILDERNESS OF PARAN** After a full year at Mount Sinai, the Israelites broke camp and began their march toward the Promised Land by moving into the wilderness of Paran. From there, one leader from each tribe was sent to explore the new land. After 40 days they returned, and all but Joshua and Caleb were too afraid to enter. Because of their lack of faith, the Israelites were made to wander in the wilderness for 40 years (12:16–19:22).
- **KADESH** With the years of wandering nearing an end, the Israelites set their sights once again on the Promised Land. Kadesh was the oasis where they spent most of their wilderness years. Miriam died here. And it was here that Moses angrily struck the rock, which kept him from entering the Promised Land (20).
- **ARAD** When the king of Arad heard that Israel was on the move, he attacked, but he was soundly defeated. Moses then led the people southward and eastward around the Dead Sea (21:1-3).
- **EDOM** The Israelites wanted to travel through Edom, but the king of Edom refused them passage (20:14-22). So they traveled around Edom and became very discouraged. The people complained, and God sent poisonous snakes to punish them. Only by looking at a bronze snake on a pole could those bitten be healed (21:4-9).
- **AMMON** Next, King Sihon of the Amorites refused Israel passage. When he attacked, Israel defeated them (21:21-32).
- **BASHAN** After capturing the Amorite country, the Israelites moved up to Bashan. King Og attacked, but he was also defeated (21:33-35).
- **PLAINS OF MOAB** The people camped on the plains of Moab, east of the Jordan River opposite Jericho. They were on the verge of entering the Promised Land (22:1).
- **MOAB** King Balak of Moab, terrified of the Israelites, called upon Balaam, a famous sorcerer, to curse Israel from the mountains above where the Israelites camped. But the Lord caused Balaam to bless them instead (22:2–24:25).
- **GILEAD** The tribes of Reuben and Gad decided to settle in the fertile country of Gilead east of the Jordan River because it was a good land for their sheep. But first they promised to help the other tribes conquer the land west of the Jordan River (32).

1

REGISTRATION OF ISRAEL'S TROOPS

A year after Israel's departure from Egypt, the LORD
spoke to Moses in the Tabernacle* in the wilderness of
Sinai. On the first day of the second month* of that
year he said, 2"From the whole community of Israel, record the names of all the warriors by their clans and
families. List all the men 3twenty years old or older who
are able to go to war. You and Aaron must register the

1:1a Hebrew *the Tent of Meeting.* 1:1b This day in the ancient Hebrew lunar calendar occurred in April or May.

troops, 4and you will be assisted by one family leader
from each tribe.
5"These are the tribes and the names of the leaders
who will assist you:

	Tribe	Leader
	Reuben	Elizur son of Shedeur
6	Simeon	Shelumiel son of Zurishaddai
7	Judah	Nahshon son of Amminadab
8	Issachar	Nethanel son of Zuar
9	Zebulun	Eliab son of Helon
10	Ephraim son of Joseph	Elishama son of Ammihud
	Manasseh son of Joseph	Gamaliel son of Pedahzur
11	Benjamin	Abidan son of Gideoni
12	Dan	Ahiezer son of Ammishaddai
13	Asher	Pagiel son of Ocran
14	Gad	Eliasaph son of Deuel
15	Naphtali	Ahira son of Enan

16These are the chosen leaders of the community, the
leaders of their ancestral tribes, the heads of the clans of
Israel."
17So Moses and Aaron called together these chosen
leaders, 18and they assembled the whole community of
Israel on that very day.* All the people were registered according to their ancestry by their clans and families. The
men of Israel who were twenty years old or older were
listed one by one, 19just as the LORD had commanded
Moses. So Moses recorded their names in the wilderness
of Sinai.
20-21This is the number of men twenty years old or
older who were able to go to war, as their names were
listed in the records of their clans and families*:

	Tribe	Number
	Reuben (Jacob's* oldest son)	46,500
22-23	Simeon	59,300
24-25	Gad	45,650
26-27	Judah	74,600
28-29	Issachar	54,400
30-31	Zebulun	57,400
32-33	Ephraim son of Joseph	40,500
34-35	Manasseh son of Joseph	32,200
36-37	Benjamin	35,400
38-39	Dan	62,700
40-41	Asher	41,500
42-43	Naphtali	53,400

44These were the men registered by Moses and Aaron
and the twelve leaders of Israel, all listed according to
their ancestral descent. 45They were registered by families—all the men of Israel who were twenty years old or
older and able to go to war. 46The total number was
603,550.
47But this total did not include the Levites. 48For the
LORD had said to Moses, 49"Do not include the tribe of
Levi in the registration; do not count them with the rest
of the Israelites. 50Put the Levites in charge of the Tabernacle of the Covenant,* along with all its furnishings and
equipment. They must carry the Tabernacle and all its
furnishings as you travel, and they must take care of it
and camp around it. 51Whenever it is time for the Tabernacle to move, the Levites will take it down. And when it is
time to stop, they will set it up again. But any unauthorized person who goes too near the Tabernacle must be
put to death. 52Each tribe of Israel will camp in a designated area with its own family banner. 53But the Levites
will camp around the Tabernacle of the Covenant to protect the community of Israel from the LORD's anger. The
Levites are responsible to stand guard around the
Tabernacle."
54So the Israelites did everything just as the LORD had
commanded Moses.

2 ORGANIZATION FOR ISRAEL'S CAMP

Then the LORD gave these instructions to Moses and
Aaron: 2"When the Israelites set up camp, each tribe will
be assigned its own area. The tribal divisions will camp
beneath their family banners on all four sides of the Tabernacle,* but at some distance from it.
3-4"The divisions of Judah, Issachar, and Zebulun are to
camp toward the sunrise on the east side of the Tabernacle, beneath their family banners. These are the names of
the tribes, their leaders, and the numbers of their registered troops:

	Tribe	Leader	Number
	Judah	Nahshon son of Amminadab	74,600
5-6	Issachar	Nethanel son of Zuar	54,400
7-8	Zebulun	Eliab son of Helon	57,400

9So the total of all the troops on Judah's side of the camp
is 186,400. These three tribes are to lead the way whenever the Israelites travel to a new campsite.
10-11"The divisions of Reuben, Simeon, and Gad are to
camp on the south side of the Tabernacle, beneath their
family banners. These are the names of the tribes, their
leaders, and the numbers of their registered troops:

	Tribe	Leader	Number
	Reuben	Elizur son of Shedeur	46,500
12-13	Simeon	Shelumiel son of Zurishaddai	59,300
14-15	Gad	Eliasaph son of Deuel*	45,650

16So the total of all the troops on Reuben's side of the
camp is 151,450. These three tribes will be second in
line whenever the Israelites travel.
17"Then the Tabernacle, carried by the Levites, will set
out from the middle of the camp. All the tribes are to
travel in the same order that they camp, each in position
under the appropriate family banner.

1:18 Hebrew *on the first day of the second month;* see 1:1. **1:20-21a** In the Hebrew text, this phrase (*This is the number of men twenty years old or older who were able to go to war, as their names were listed in the records of their clans and families*) is repeated in 1:22, 24, 26, 28, 30, 32, 34, 36, 38, 40, 42. **1:20-21b** Hebrew *Israel's.* The names "Jacob" and "Israel" are often interchanged throughout the Old Testament, referring sometimes to the individual patriarch and sometimes to the nation. **1:50** Or *Tabernacle of the Testimony;* also in 1:53. **2:2** Hebrew *the Tent of Meeting;* also in 2:17. **2:14-15** As in many Hebrew manuscripts, Samaritan Pentateuch, and Latin Vulgate (see also 1:14); most Hebrew manuscripts read *son of Reuel.*

18-19 "The divisions of Ephraim, Manasseh, and Benjamin are to camp on the west side of the Tabernacle, beneath their family banners. These are the names of the
tribes, their leaders, and the numbers of their registered
troops:

	Tribe	*Leader*	*Number*
	Ephraim	Elishama son of Ammihud	40,500
20-21	Manasseh	Gamaliel son of Pedahzur	32,200
22-23	Benjamin	Abidan son of Gideoni	35,400

24 So the total of all the troops on Ephraim's side of the
camp is 108,100. These three tribes will be third in line
whenever the Israelites travel.
25-26 "The divisions of Dan, Asher, and Naphtali are to
camp on the north side of the Tabernacle, beneath their
family banners. These are the names of the tribes, their
leaders, and the numbers of their registered troops:

	Tribe	*Leader*	*Number*
	Dan	Ahiezer son of Ammishaddai	62,700
27-28	Asher	Pagiel son of Ocran	41,500
29-30	Naphtali	Ahira son of Enan	53,400

31 So the total of all the troops on Dan's side of the camp is
157,600. These three tribes will be last, marching under
their banners whenever the Israelites travel."

CONTRAST 2:34

This must have been one of the biggest campsites the world has ever seen! It would have taken about 12 square miles to set up tents for just the 600,000 fighting men—not to mention the women and children. Moses must have had a difficult time managing such a group. In the early stages of the journey and at Mount Sinai, the people were generally obedient to both God and Moses. But when the people left Mount Sinai and traveled across the rugged wilderness, they began to grumble and disobey. Soon problems erupted. The books of Exodus, Leviticus, and Numbers present a striking contrast between how much we can accomplish when we obey God, and how little we can accomplish when we don't. ■

32 In summary, the troops of Israel listed by their families totaled 603,550. 33 But as the LORD had commanded,
the Levites were not included in this registration. 34 So the
people of Israel did everything as the LORD had commanded Moses. Each clan and family set up camp and
marched under their banners exactly as the LORD had instructed them.

3 LEVITES APPOINTED FOR SERVICE

This is the family line of Aaron and Moses as it was recorded when the LORD spoke to Moses on Mount Sinai:
2 The names of Aaron's sons were Nadab (the oldest), Abihu, Eleazar, and Ithamar. 3 These sons of Aaron were
anointed and ordained to minister as priests. 4 But Nadab
and Abihu died in the LORD's presence in the wilderness
of Sinai when they burned before the LORD the wrong
kind of fire, different than he had commanded. Since
they had no sons, this left only Eleazar and Ithamar to
serve as priests with their father, Aaron.
5 Then the LORD said to Moses, 6 "Call forward the tribe
of Levi, and present them to Aaron the priest to serve as
his assistants. 7 They will serve Aaron and the whole community, performing their sacred duties in and around the
Tabernacle.* 8 They will also maintain all the furnishings
of the sacred tent,* serving in the Tabernacle on behalf of
all the Israelites. 9 Assign the Levites to Aaron and his
sons. They have been given from among all the people of
Israel to serve as their assistants. 10 Appoint Aaron and his
sons to carry out the duties of the priesthood. But any unauthorized person who goes too near the sanctuary must
be put to death."
11 And the LORD said to Moses, 12 "Look, I have chosen
the Levites from among the Israelites to serve as substitutes for all the firstborn sons of the people of Israel. The
Levites belong to me, 13 for all the firstborn males are
mine. On the day I struck down all the firstborn sons of
the Egyptians, I set apart for myself all the firstborn in Israel, both of people and of animals. They are mine; I am
the LORD."

REGISTRATION OF THE LEVITES

14 The LORD spoke again to Moses in the wilderness of Sinai. He said, 15 "Record the names of the members of the
tribe of Levi by their families and clans. List every male
who is one month old or older." 16 So Moses listed them,
just as the LORD had commanded.

17 Levi had three sons, whose names were Gershon,
Kohath, and Merari.
18 The clans descended from Gershon were named after
two of his descendants, Libni and Shimei.
19 The clans descended from Kohath were named after
four of his descendants, Amram, Izhar, Hebron, and
Uzziel.
20 The clans descended from Merari were named after
two of his descendants, Mahli and Mushi.
These were the Levite clans, listed according to their
family groups.

21 The descendants of Gershon were composed of the
clans descended from Libni and Shimei. 22 There were
7,500 males one month old or older among these Gershonite clans. 23 They were assigned the area to the west
of the Tabernacle for their camp. 24 The leader of the Gershonite clans was Eliasaph son of Lael. 25 These two clans
were responsible to care for the Tabernacle, including
the sacred tent with its layers of coverings, the curtain at
its entrance, 26 the curtains of the courtyard that surrounded the Tabernacle and altar, the curtain at the
courtyard entrance, the ropes, and all the equipment
related to their use.
27 The descendants of Kohath were composed of the

3:7 Hebrew *around the Tent of Meeting, doing service at the Tabernacle.* 3:8 Hebrew *the Tent of Meeting;* also in 3:25.

clans descended from Amram, Izhar, Hebron, and Uzziel. 28There were 8,600* males one month old or older among these Kohathite clans. They were responsible for the care of the sanctuary, 29and they were assigned the area south of the Tabernacle for their camp. 30The leader of the Kohathite clans was Elizaphan son of Uzziel. 31These four clans were responsible for the care of the Ark, the table, the lampstand, the altars, the various articles used in the sanctuary, the inner curtain, and all the equipment related to their use. 32Eleazar, son of Aaron the priest, was the chief administrator over all the Levites, with special responsibility for the oversight of the sanctuary.

33The descendants of Merari were composed of the clans descended from Mahli and Mushi. 34There were 6,200 males one month old or older among these Merarite clans. 35They were assigned the area north of the Tabernacle for their camp. The leader of the Merarite clans was Zuriel son of Abihail. 36These two clans were responsible for the care of the frames supporting the Tabernacle, the crossbars, the pillars, the bases, and all the equipment related to their use. 37They were also responsible for the posts of the courtyard and all their bases, pegs, and ropes.

38The area in front of the Tabernacle, in the east toward the sunrise,* was reserved for the tents of Moses and of Aaron and his sons, who had the final responsibility for the sanctuary on behalf of the people of Israel. Anyone other than a priest or Levite who went too near the sanctuary was to be put to death.

39When Moses and Aaron counted the Levite clans at the LORD's command, the total number was 22,000 males one month old or older.

REDEEMING THE FIRSTBORN SONS

40Then the LORD said to Moses, "Now count all the firstborn sons in Israel who are one month old or older, and make a list of their names. 41The Levites must be reserved for me as substitutes for the firstborn sons of Israel; I am the LORD. And the Levites' livestock must be reserved for me as substitutes for the firstborn livestock of the whole nation of Israel."

42So Moses counted the firstborn sons of the people of Israel, just as the LORD had commanded. 43The number of firstborn sons who were one month old or older was 22,273.

44Then the LORD said to Moses, 45"Take the Levites as substitutes for the firstborn sons of the people of Israel. And take the livestock of the Levites as substitutes for the firstborn livestock of the people of Israel. The Levites belong to me; I am the LORD. 46There are 273 more firstborn sons of Israel than there are Levites. To redeem these extra firstborn sons, 47collect five pieces of silver* for each of them (each piece weighing the same as the sanctuary shekel, which equals twenty gerahs). 48Give the silver to Aaron and his sons as the redemption price for the extra firstborn sons."

49So Moses collected the silver for redeeming the firstborn sons of Israel who exceeded the number of Levites. 50He collected 1,365 pieces of silver* on behalf of these firstborn sons of Israel (each piece weighing the same as the sanctuary shekel). 51And Moses gave the silver for the redemption to Aaron and his sons, just as the LORD had commanded.

4 DUTIES OF THE KOHATHITE CLAN

Then the LORD said to Moses and Aaron, 2"Record the names of the members of the clans and families of the Kohathite division of the tribe of Levi. 3List all the men between the ages of thirty and fifty who are eligible to serve in the Tabernacle.*

4"The duties of the Kohathites at the Tabernacle will relate to the most sacred objects. 5When the camp moves, Aaron and his sons must enter the Tabernacle first to take down the inner curtain and cover the Ark of the Covenant* with it. 6Then they must cover the inner curtain with fine goatskin leather and spread over that a single piece of blue cloth. Finally, they must put the carrying poles of the Ark in place.

7"Next they must spread a blue cloth over the table where the Bread of the Presence is displayed, and on the cloth they will place the bowls, pans, jars, pitchers, and the special bread. 8They must spread a scarlet cloth over all of this, and finally a covering of fine goatskin leather on top of the scarlet cloth. Then they must insert the carrying poles into the table.

9"Next they must cover the lampstand with a blue cloth, along with its lamps, lamp snuffers, trays, and special jars of olive oil. 10Then they must cover the lampstand and its accessories with fine goatskin leather and place the bundle on a carrying frame.

11"Next they must spread a blue cloth over the gold incense altar and cover this cloth with fine goatskin leather. Then they must attach the carrying poles to the altar. 12They must take all the remaining furnishings of the sanctuary and wrap them in a blue cloth, cover them with fine goatskin leather, and place them on the carrying frame.

13"They must remove the ashes from the altar for sacrifices and cover the altar with a purple cloth. 14All the altar utensils—the firepans, meat forks, shovels, basins, and all the containers—must be placed on the cloth, and a covering of fine goatskin leather must be spread over them. Finally, they must put the carrying poles in place. 15The camp will be ready to move when Aaron and his sons have finished covering the sanctuary and all the sacred articles. The Kohathites will come and carry these things to the next destination. But they must not touch the sacred objects, or they will die. So these are the things from the Tabernacle that the Kohathites must carry.

16"Eleazar son of Aaron the priest will be responsible for the oil of the lampstand, the fragrant incense, the daily grain offering, and the anointing oil. In fact, Eleazar

3:28 Some Greek manuscripts read *8,300;* see total in 3:39. **3:38** Hebrew *toward the sunrise, in front of the Tent of Meeting.* **3:47** Hebrew *5 shekels* [2 ounces or 57 grams]. **3:50** Hebrew *1,365 shekels* [34 pounds or 15.5 kilograms]. **4:3** Hebrew *the Tent of Meeting;* also in 4:4, 15, 23, 25, 28, 30, 31, 33, 35, 37, 39, 41, 43, 47. **4:5** Or *Ark of the Testimony.*

will be responsible for the entire Tabernacle and everything in it, including the sanctuary and its furnishings."

17Then the LORD said to Moses and Aaron, 18"Do not let the Kohathite clans be destroyed from among the Levites! 19This is what you must do so they will live and not die when they approach the most sacred objects. Aaron and his sons must always go in with them and assign a specific duty or load to each person. 20The Kohathites must never enter the sanctuary to look at the sacred objects for even a moment, or they will die."

DUTIES OF THE GERSHONITE CLAN

21And the LORD said to Moses, 22"Record the names of the members of the clans and families of the Gershonite division of the tribe of Levi. 23List all the men between the ages of thirty and fifty who are eligible to serve in the Tabernacle.

24"These Gershonite clans will be responsible for general service and carrying loads. 25They must carry the curtains of the Tabernacle, the Tabernacle itself with its coverings, the outer covering of fine goatskin leather, and the curtain for the Tabernacle entrance. 26They are also to carry the curtains for the courtyard walls that surround the Tabernacle and altar, the curtain across the courtyard entrance, the ropes, and all the equipment related to their use. The Gershonites are responsible for all these items. 27Aaron and his sons will direct the Gershonites regarding all their duties, whether it involves moving the equipment or doing other work. They must assign the Gershonites responsibility for the loads they are to carry. 28So these are the duties assigned to the Gershonite clans at the Tabernacle. They will be directly responsible to Ithamar son of Aaron the priest.

DUTIES OF THE MERARITE CLAN

29"Now record the names of the members of the clans and families of the Merarite division of the tribe of Levi. 30List all the men between the ages of thirty and fifty who are eligible to serve in the Tabernacle.

31"Their only duty at the Tabernacle will be to carry loads. They will carry the frames of the Tabernacle, the crossbars, the posts, and the bases; 32also the posts for the courtyard walls with their bases, pegs, and ropes; and all the accessories and everything else related to their use. Assign the various loads to each man by name. 33So these are the duties of the Merarite clans at the Tabernacle. They are directly responsible to Ithamar son of Aaron the priest."

SUMMARY OF THE REGISTRATION

34So Moses, Aaron, and the other leaders of the community listed the members of the Kohathite division by their clans and families. 35The list included all the men between thirty and fifty years of age who were eligible for service in the Tabernacle, 36and the total number came to 2,750. 37So this was the total of all those from the Kohathite clans who were eligible to serve at the Tabernacle. Moses and Aaron listed them, just as the LORD had commanded through Moses.

38The Gershonite division was also listed by its clans and families. 39The list included all the men between thirty and fifty years of age who were eligible for service in the Tabernacle, 40and the total number came to 2,630. 41So this was the total of all those from the Gershonite clans who were eligible to serve at the Tabernacle. Moses and Aaron listed them, just as the LORD had commanded.

42The Merarite division was also listed by its clans and families. 43The list included all the men between thirty and fifty years of age who were eligible for service in the Tabernacle, 44and the total number came to 3,200. 45So this was the total of all those from the Merarite clans who were eligible for service. Moses and Aaron listed them, just as the LORD had commanded through Moses.

46So Moses, Aaron, and the leaders of Israel listed all the Levites by their clans and families. 47All the men between thirty and fifty years of age who were eligible for service in the Tabernacle and for its transportation 48numbered 8,580. 49When their names were recorded, as the LORD had commanded through Moses, each man was assigned his task and told what to carry.

And so the registration was completed, just as the LORD had commanded Moses.

5 PURITY IN ISRAEL'S CAMP

The LORD gave these instructions to Moses: 2"Command the people of Israel to remove from the camp anyone who has a skin disease* or a discharge, or who has become ceremonially unclean by touching a dead person. 3This command applies to men and women alike. Remove them so they will not defile the camp in which I live among them." 4So the Israelites did as the LORD had commanded Moses and removed such people from the camp.

SET THINGS RIGHT 5:5-8

God included restitution, a unique concept for that day, as part of his law for Israel. When someone was robbed, the guilty person was required to restore to the victim what had been taken and pay an additional interest penalty. This can inspire us to look for ways to set things right when we have wronged someone. ■

5Then the LORD said to Moses, 6"Give the following instructions to the people of Israel: If any of the people—men or women—betray the LORD by doing wrong to another person, they are guilty. 7They must confess their sin and make full restitution for what they have done, adding an additional 20 percent and returning it to the person who was wronged. 8But if the person who was wronged is dead, and there are no near relatives to whom restitution can be made, the payment belongs to the LORD and must be given to the priest. Those who are guilty must also bring a ram as a sacrifice, and they will be purified and made right with the LORD.* 9All the sacred offerings that

5:2 Traditionally rendered *leprosy*. The Hebrew word used here describes various skin diseases. **5:8** Or *bring a ram for atonement, which will make atonement for them.*

the Israelites bring to a priest will belong to him. 10Each priest may keep all the sacred donations that he receives."

PROTECTING MARITAL FAITHFULNESS

11And the LORD said to Moses, 12"Give the following instructions to the people of Israel.

"Suppose a man's wife goes astray, and she is unfaithful to her husband 13and has sex with another man, but neither her husband nor anyone else knows about it. She has defiled herself, even though there was no witness and she was not caught in the act. 14If her husband becomes jealous and is suspicious of his wife and needs to know whether or not she has defiled herself, 15the husband must bring his wife to the priest. He must also bring an offering of two quarts* of barley flour to be presented on her behalf. Do not mix it with olive oil or frankincense, for it is a jealousy offering—an offering to prove whether or not she is guilty.

16"The priest will then present her to stand trial before the LORD. 17He must take some holy water in a clay jar and pour into it dust he has taken from the Tabernacle floor. 18When the priest has presented the woman before the LORD, he must unbind her hair and place in her hands the offering of proof—the jealousy offering to determine whether her husband's suspicions are justified. The priest will stand before her, holding the jar of bitter water that brings a curse to those who are guilty. 19The priest will then put the woman under oath and say to her, 'If no other man has had sex with you, and you have not gone astray and defiled yourself while under your husband's authority, may you be immune from the effects of this bitter water that brings on the curse. 20But if you have gone astray by being unfaithful to your husband, and have defiled yourself by having sex with another man—'

21"At this point the priest must put the woman under oath by saying, 'May the people know that the LORD's curse is upon you when he makes you infertile, causing your womb to shrivel* and your abdomen to swell. 22Now may this water that brings the curse enter your body and cause your abdomen to swell and your womb to shrivel.*' And the woman will be required to say, 'Yes, let it be so.' 23And the priest will write these curses on a piece of leather and wash them off into the bitter water. 24He will make the woman drink the bitter water that brings on the curse. When the water enters her body, it will cause bitter suffering if she is guilty.

25"The priest will take the jealousy offering from the woman's hand, lift it up before the LORD, and carry it to the altar. 26He will take a handful of the flour as a token portion and burn it on the altar, and he will require the woman to drink the water. 27If she has defiled herself by being unfaithful to her husband, the water that brings on the curse will cause bitter suffering. Her abdomen will swell and her womb will shrink,* and her name will become a curse among her people. 28But if she has not defiled herself and is pure, then she will be unharmed and will still be able to have children.

29"This is the ritual law for dealing with suspicion. If a woman goes astray and defiles herself while under her husband's authority, 30or if a man becomes jealous and is suspicious that his wife has been unfaithful, the husband must present his wife before the LORD, and the priest will apply this entire ritual law to her. 31The husband will be innocent of any guilt in this matter, but his wife will be held accountable for her sin."

6

NAZIRITE LAWS

Then the LORD said to Moses, "Give the following instructions to the people of Israel.

2"If any of the people, either men or women, take the special vow of a Nazirite, setting themselves apart to the LORD in a special way, 3they must give up wine and other alcoholic drinks. They must not use vinegar made from wine or from other alcoholic drinks, they must not drink fresh grape juice, and they must not eat grapes or raisins. 4As long as they are bound by their Nazirite vow, they are not allowed to eat or drink anything that comes from a grapevine—not even the grape seeds or skins.

5"They must never cut their hair throughout the time of their vow, for they are holy and set apart to the LORD. Until the time of their vow has been fulfilled, they must let their hair grow long. 6And they must not go near a dead body during the entire period of their vow to the LORD. 7Even if the dead person is their own father, mother, brother, or sister, they must not defile themselves, for the hair on their head is the symbol of their separation to God. 8This requirement applies as long as they are set apart to the LORD.

9"If someone falls dead beside them, the hair they have dedicated will be defiled. They must wait for seven days and then shave their heads. Then they will be cleansed from their defilement. 10On the eighth day they must bring two turtledoves or two young pigeons to the priest at the entrance of the Tabernacle.* 11The priest will offer one of the birds for a sin offering and the other for a burnt offering. In this way, he will purify them* from the guilt they incurred through contact with the dead body. Then they must reaffirm their commitment and let their hair begin to grow again. 12The days of their vow that were completed before their defilement no longer count. They must rededicate themselves to the LORD as a Nazirite for the full term of their vow, and each must bring a one-year-old male lamb for a guilt offering.

13"This is the ritual law for Nazirites. At the conclusion of their time of separation as Nazirites, they must each go to the entrance of the Tabernacle 14and offer their sacrifices to the LORD: a one-year-old male lamb without defect for a burnt offering, a one-year-old female lamb without defect for a sin offering, a ram without defect for a peace offering, 15a basket of bread made without yeast—cakes of choice flour mixed with olive oil and wafers spread with olive oil—along with their prescribed grain offerings and liquid offerings. 16The priest will

5:15 Hebrew *1/10 of an ephah* [2.2 liters]. 5:21 Hebrew *when he causes your thigh to waste away.* 5:22 Hebrew *and your thigh to waste away.* 5:27 Hebrew *and her thigh will waste away.* 6:10 Hebrew *the Tent of Meeting;* also in 6:13, 18. 6:11 Or *make atonement for them.*

present these offerings before the LORD: first the sin offering and the burnt offering; 17then the ram for a peace
offering, along with the basket of bread made without
yeast. The priest must also present the prescribed grain
offering and liquid offering to the LORD.
18"Then the Nazirites will shave their heads at the entrance of the Tabernacle. They will take the hair that had
been dedicated and place it on the fire beneath the
peace-offering sacrifice. 19After the Nazirite's head has
been shaved, the priest will take for each of them the
boiled shoulder of the ram, and he will take from the basket a cake and a wafer made without yeast. He will put
them all into the Nazirite's hands. 20Then the priest will
lift them up as a special offering before the LORD. These
are holy portions for the priest, along with the breast of
the special offering and the thigh of the sacred offering
that are lifted up before the LORD. After this ceremony
the Nazirites may again drink wine.
21"This is the ritual law of the Nazirites, who vow to
bring these offerings to the LORD. They may also bring
additional offerings if they can afford it. And they must
be careful to do whatever they vowed when they set
themselves apart as Nazirites."

THE PRIESTLY BLESSING

22Then the LORD said to Moses, 23"Tell Aaron and his sons
to bless the people of Israel with this special blessing:

24 'May the LORD bless you
and protect you.
25 May the LORD smile on you
and be gracious to you.
26 May the LORD show you his favor
and give you his peace.'

27Whenever Aaron and his sons bless the people of Israel
in my name, I myself will bless them."

7

OFFERINGS OF DEDICATION

On the day Moses set up the Tabernacle, he anointed it
and set it apart as holy. He also anointed and set apart all
its furnishings and the altar with its utensils. 2Then the
leaders of Israel—the tribal leaders who had registered
the troops—came and brought their offerings. 3Together
they brought six large wagons and twelve oxen. There
was a wagon for every two leaders and an ox for each
leader. They presented these to the LORD in front of the
Tabernacle.
4Then the LORD said to Moses, 5"Receive their gifts,
and use these oxen and wagons for transporting the Tabernacle.* Distribute them among the Levites according
to the work they have to do." 6So Moses took the wagons
and oxen and presented them to the Levites. 7He gave two
wagons and four oxen to the Gershonite division for their
work, 8and he gave four wagons and eight oxen to the Merarite division for their work. All their work was done
under the leadership of Ithamar son of Aaron the priest.
9But he gave none of the wagons or oxen to the Kohathite
division, since they were required to carry the sacred objects of the Tabernacle on their shoulders.
10The leaders also presented dedication gifts for the
altar at the time it was anointed. They each placed their
gifts before the altar. 11The LORD said to Moses, "Let one
leader bring his gift each day for the dedication of the
altar."

12On the first day Nahshon son of Amminadab, leader of
the tribe of Judah, presented his offering.
13His offering consisted of a silver platter weighing
3¼ pounds and a silver basin weighing 1¾ pounds*
(as measured by the weight of the sanctuary shekel).
These were both filled with grain offerings of choice
flour moistened with olive oil. 14He also brought a
gold container weighing four ounces,* which was
filled with incense. 15He brought a young bull, a ram,
and a one-year-old male lamb for a burnt offering,
16and a male goat for a sin offering. 17For a peace
offering he brought two bulls, five rams, five male
goats, and five one-year-old male lambs. This was the
offering brought by Nahshon son of Amminadab.

18On the second day Nethanel son of Zuar, leader of the
tribe of Issachar, presented his offering.
19His offering consisted of a silver platter weighing
3¼ pounds and a silver basin weighing 1¾ pounds
(as measured by the weight of the sanctuary shekel).
These were both filled with grain offerings of choice
flour moistened with olive oil. 20He also brought a
gold container weighing four ounces, which was
filled with incense. 21He brought a young bull, a ram,
and a one-year-old male lamb for a burnt offering,
22and a male goat for a sin offering. 23For a peace
offering he brought two bulls, five rams, five male
goats, and five one-year-old male lambs. This was the
offering brought by Nethanel son of Zuar.

24On the third day Eliab son of Helon, leader of the tribe
of Zebulun, presented his offering.
25His offering consisted of a silver platter weighing
3¼ pounds and a silver basin weighing 1¾ pounds
(as measured by the weight of the sanctuary shekel).
These were both filled with grain offerings of choice
flour moistened with olive oil. 26He also brought a
gold container weighing four ounces, which was
filled with incense. 27He brought a young bull, a ram,
and a one-year-old male lamb for a burnt offering,
28and a male goat for a sin offering. 29For a peace
offering he brought two bulls, five rams, five male
goats, and five one-year-old male lambs. This was
the offering brought by Eliab son of Helon.

30On the fourth day Elizur son of Shedeur, leader of the
tribe of Reuben, presented his offering.

7:5 Hebrew *the Tent of Meeting;* also in 7:89. 7:13 Hebrew *silver platter weighing 130 shekels* [1.5 kilograms] *and a silver basin weighing 70 shekels* [800 grams]; also in 7:19, 25, 31, 37, 43, 49, 55, 61, 67, 73, 79, 85. 7:14 Hebrew *10 shekels* [114 grams]; also in 7:20, 26, 32, 38, 44, 50, 56, 62, 68, 74, 80, 86.

[31]His offering consisted of a silver platter weighing 3¼ pounds and a silver basin weighing 1¾ pounds (as measured by the weight of the sanctuary shekel). These were both filled with grain offerings of choice flour moistened with olive oil. [32]He also brought a gold container weighing four ounces, which was filled with incense. [33]He brought a young bull, a ram, and a one-year-old male lamb for a burnt offering, [34]and a male goat for a sin offering. [35]For a peace offering he brought two bulls, five rams, five male goats, and five one-year-old male lambs. This was the offering brought by Elizur son of Shedeur.

[36]On the fifth day Shelumiel son of Zurishaddai, leader of the tribe of Simeon, presented his offering.

[37]His offering consisted of a silver platter weighing 3¼ pounds and a silver basin weighing 1¾ pounds (as measured by the weight of the sanctuary shekel). These were both filled with grain offerings of choice flour moistened with olive oil. [38]He also brought a gold container weighing four ounces, which was filled with incense. [39]He brought a young bull, a ram, and a one-year-old male lamb for a burnt offering, [40]and a male goat for a sin offering. [41]For a peace offering he brought two bulls, five rams, five male goats, and five one-year-old male lambs. This was the offering brought by Shelumiel son of Zurishaddai.

[42]On the sixth day Eliasaph son of Deuel, leader of the tribe of Gad, presented his offering.

[43]His offering consisted of a silver platter weighing 3¼ pounds and a silver basin weighing 1¾ pounds (as measured by the weight of the sanctuary shekel). These were both filled with grain offerings of choice flour moistened with olive oil. [44]He also brought a gold container weighing four ounces, which was filled with incense. [45]He brought a young bull, a ram, and a one-year-old male lamb for a burnt offering, [46]and a male goat for a sin offering. [47]For a peace offering he brought two bulls, five rams, five male goats, and five one-year-old male lambs. This was the offering brought by Eliasaph son of Deuel.

[48]On the seventh day Elishama son of Ammihud, leader of the tribe of Ephraim, presented his offering.

[49]His offering consisted of a silver platter weighing 3¼ pounds and a silver basin weighing 1¾ pounds (as measured by the weight of the sanctuary shekel). These were both filled with grain offerings of choice flour moistened with olive oil. [50]He also brought a gold container weighing four ounces, which was filled with incense. [51]He brought a young bull, a ram, and a one-year-old male lamb for a burnt offering, [52]and a male goat for a sin offering. [53]For a peace offering he brought two bulls, five rams, five male goats, and five one-year-old male lambs. This was the offering brought by Elishama son of Ammihud.

[54]On the eighth day Gamaliel son of Pedahzur, leader of the tribe of Manasseh, presented his offering.

[55]His offering consisted of a silver platter weighing 3¼ pounds and a silver basin weighing 1¾ pounds (as measured by the weight of the sanctuary shekel). These were both filled with grain offerings of choice flour moistened with olive oil. [56]He also brought a gold container weighing four ounces, which was filled with incense. [57]He brought a young bull, a ram, and a one-year-old male lamb for a burnt offering, [58]and a male goat for a sin offering. [59]For a peace offering he brought two bulls, five rams, five male goats, and five one-year-old male lambs. This was the offering brought by Gamaliel son of Pedahzur.

[60]On the ninth day Abidan son of Gideoni, leader of the tribe of Benjamin, presented his offering.

[61]His offering consisted of a silver platter weighing 3¼ pounds and a silver basin weighing 1¾ pounds (as measured by the weight of the sanctuary shekel). These were both filled with grain offerings of choice flour moistened with olive oil. [62]He also brought a gold container weighing four ounces, which was filled with incense. [63]He brought a young bull, a ram, and a one-year-old male lamb for a burnt offering, [64]and a male goat for a sin offering. [65]For a peace offering he brought two bulls, five rams, five male goats, and five one-year-old male lambs. This was the offering brought by Abidan son of Gideoni.

[66]On the tenth day Ahiezer son of Ammishaddai, leader of the tribe of Dan, presented his offering.

[67]His offering consisted of a silver platter weighing 3¼ pounds and a silver basin weighing 1¾ pounds (as measured by the weight of the sanctuary shekel). These were both filled with grain offerings of choice flour moistened with olive oil. [68]He also brought a gold container weighing four ounces, which was filled with incense. [69]He brought a young bull, a ram, and a one-year-old male lamb for a burnt offering, [70]and a male goat for a sin offering. [71]For a peace offering he brought two bulls, five rams, five male goats, and five one-year-old male lambs. This was the offering brought by Ahiezer son of Ammishaddai.

[72]On the eleventh day Pagiel son of Ocran, leader of the tribe of Asher, presented his offering.

[73]His offering consisted of a silver platter weighing 3¼ pounds and a silver basin weighing 1¾ pounds (as measured by the weight of the sanctuary shekel). These were both filled with grain offerings of choice flour moistened with olive oil. [74]He also brought a gold container weighing four ounces, which was filled with incense. [75]He brought a young bull, a ram, and a one-year-old male lamb for a burnt offering, [76]and a male goat for a sin offering. [77]For a peace offering he brought two bulls, five rams, five male goats, and five one-year-old male lambs. This was the offering brought by Pagiel son of Ocran.

[78]On the twelfth day Ahira son of Enan, leader of the tribe of Naphtali, presented his offering.

79His offering consisted of a silver platter weighing
3¼ pounds and a silver basin weighing 1¾ pounds
(as measured by the weight of the sanctuary shekel).
These were both filled with grain offerings of choice
flour moistened with olive oil. 80He also brought a
gold container weighing four ounces, which was
filled with incense. 81He brought a young bull, a ram,
and a one-year-old male lamb for a burnt offering,
82and a male goat for a sin offering. 83For a peace
offering he brought two bulls, five rams, five male
goats, and five one-year-old male lambs. This was
the offering brought by Ahira son of Enan.

84So this was the dedication offering brought by the
leaders of Israel at the time the altar was anointed: twelve
silver platters, twelve silver basins, and twelve gold incense containers. 85Each silver platter weighed 3¼ pounds,
and each silver basin weighed 1¾ pounds. The total
weight of the silver was 60 pounds* (as measured by the
weight of the sanctuary shekel). 86Each of the twelve gold
containers that was filled with incense weighed four
ounces (as measured by the weight of the sanctuary
shekel). The total weight of the gold was three pounds.*
87Twelve young bulls, twelve rams, and twelve one-year-
old male lambs were donated for the burnt offerings,
along with their prescribed grain offerings. Twelve male
goats were brought for the sin offerings. 88Twenty-four
bulls, sixty rams, sixty male goats, and sixty one-year-old
male lambs were donated for the peace offerings. This
was the dedication offering for the altar after it was
anointed.

HEARING GOD 7:89

Imagine hearing the audible voice of God! Moses must have trembled at the sound. God sometimes spoke directly to his people to tell them the proper way to live. The Bible records these conversations to give us insights into God's character. Wondering what God sounds like? Check out his Word. Also, if you're a believer, the Holy Spirit lives within you. Have you paid attention to his "gentle whisper" (see 1 Kings 19:12) recently? ■

89Whenever Moses went into the Tabernacle to speak
with the LORD, he heard the voice speaking to him from
between the two cherubim above the Ark's cover—the
place of atonement—that rests on the Ark of the Covenant.* The LORD spoke to him from there.

8

PREPARING THE LAMPS

The LORD said to Moses, 2"Give Aaron the following instructions: When you set up the seven lamps in the lampstand, place them so their light shines forward in front of
the lampstand." 3So Aaron did this. He set up the seven
lamps so they reflected their light forward, just as the
LORD had commanded Moses. 4The entire lampstand,
from its base to its decorative blossoms, was made of
beaten gold. It was built according to the exact design the
LORD had shown Moses.

THE LEVITES DEDICATED

5Then the LORD said to Moses, 6"Now set the Levites apart
from the rest of the people of Israel and make them ceremonially clean. 7Do this by sprinkling them with the water of purification, and have them shave their entire body
and wash their clothing. Then they will be ceremonially
clean. 8Have them bring a young bull and a grain offering
of choice flour moistened with olive oil, along with a second young bull for a sin offering. 9Then assemble the
whole community of Israel, and present the Levites at the
entrance of the Tabernacle.* 10When you present the Levites before the LORD, the people of Israel must lay their
hands on them. 11Raising his hands, Aaron must then
present the Levites to the LORD as a special offering from
the people of Israel, thus dedicating them to the LORD's
service.

12"Next the Levites will lay their hands on the heads of
the young bulls. Present one as a sin offering and the
other as a burnt offering to the LORD, to purify the Levites
and make them right with the LORD.* 13Then have the Levites stand in front of Aaron and his sons, and raise your
hands and present them as a special offering to the LORD.
14In this way, you will set the Levites apart from the rest of
the people of Israel, and the Levites will belong to me.
15After this, they may go into the Tabernacle to do their
work, because you have purified them and presented
them as a special offering.

16"Of all the people of Israel, the Levites are reserved
for me. I have claimed them for myself in place of all the
firstborn sons of the Israelites; I have taken the Levites as
their substitutes. 17For all the firstborn males among the
people of Israel are mine, both of people and of animals. I
set them apart for myself on the day I struck down all the
firstborn sons of the Egyptians. 18Yes, I have claimed the
Levites in place of all the firstborn sons of Israel. 19And of
all the Israelites, I have assigned the Levites to Aaron and
his sons. They will serve in the Tabernacle on behalf of
the Israelites and make sacrifices to purify* the people so
no plague will strike them when they approach the
sanctuary."

20So Moses, Aaron, and the whole community of Israel
dedicated the Levites, carefully following all the LORD's
instructions to Moses. 21The Levites purified themselves
from sin and washed their clothes, and Aaron lifted them
up and presented them to the LORD as a special offering.
He then offered a sacrifice to purify them and make
them right with the LORD.* 22After that the Levites went
into the Tabernacle to perform their duties, assisting
Aaron and his sons. So they carried out all the commands
that the LORD gave Moses concerning the Levites.

23The LORD also instructed Moses, 24"This is the rule

7:85 Hebrew *2,400 shekels* [27.6 kilograms]. 7:86 Hebrew *120 shekels* [1.4 kilograms]. 7:89 Or *Ark of the Testimony*. 8:9 Hebrew *the Tent of Meeting;* also in 8:15, 19, 22, 24, 26. 8:12 Or *to make atonement for the Levites.* 8:19 Or *make atonement for.* 8:21 Or *then made atonement for them to purify them.*

the Levites must follow: They must begin serving in the Tabernacle at the age of twenty-five, 25and they must retire at the age of fifty. 26After retirement they may assist their fellow Levites by serving as guards at the Tabernacle, but they may not officiate in the service. This is how you must assign duties to the Levites."

9

THE SECOND PASSOVER

A year after Israel's departure from Egypt, the LORD spoke to Moses in the wilderness of Sinai. In the first month* of that year he said, 2"Tell the Israelites to celebrate the Passover at the prescribed time, 3at twilight on the fourteenth day of the first month.* Be sure to follow all my decrees and regulations concerning this celebration."

SAME LAWS FOR ALL 9:14

Sometimes we are tempted to excuse non-Christians from following God's guidelines for worship. Yet foreigners at this time were expected to follow the same laws as the Israelites. God did not have a separate set of standards for unbelievers, and he still does not today. God's statement that "the same laws apply both to you and to the foreigners living among you" emphasizes this truth. Although God singled out Israel to be his people, his ultimate aim was to have all people obey and worship him. ■

4So Moses told the people to celebrate the Passover 5in the wilderness of Sinai as twilight fell on the fourteenth day of the month. And they celebrated the festival there, just as the LORD had commanded Moses. 6But some of the men had been ceremonially defiled by touching a dead body, so they could not celebrate the Passover that day. They came to Moses and Aaron that day 7and said, "We have become ceremonially unclean by touching a dead body. But why should we be prevented from presenting the LORD's offering at the proper time with the rest of the Israelites?"

8Moses answered, "Wait here until I have received instructions for you from the LORD."

9This was the LORD's reply to Moses. 10"Give the following instructions to the people of Israel: If any of the people now or in future generations are ceremonially unclean at Passover time because of touching a dead body, or if they are on a journey and cannot be present at the ceremony, they may still celebrate the LORD's Passover. 11They must offer the Passover sacrifice one month later, at twilight on the fourteenth day of the second month.* They must eat the Passover lamb at that time with bitter salad greens and bread made without yeast. 12They must not leave any of the lamb until the next morning, and they must not break any of its bones. They must follow all the normal regulations concerning the Passover.

13"But those who neglect to celebrate the Passover at the regular time, even though they are ceremonially clean and not away on a trip, will be cut off from the community of Israel. If they fail to present the LORD's offering at the proper time, they will suffer the consequences of their guilt. 14And if foreigners living among you want to celebrate the Passover to the LORD, they must follow these same decrees and regulations. The same laws apply both to native-born Israelites and to the foreigners living among you."

THE FIERY CLOUD

15On the day the Tabernacle was set up, the cloud covered it.* But from evening until morning the cloud over the Tabernacle looked like a pillar of fire. 16This was the regular pattern—at night the cloud that covered the Tabernacle had the appearance of fire. 17Whenever the cloud lifted from over the sacred tent, the people of Israel would break camp and follow it. And wherever the cloud settled, the people of Israel would set up camp. 18In this way, they traveled and camped at the LORD's command wherever he told them to go. Then they remained in their camp as long as the cloud stayed over the Tabernacle. 19If the cloud remained over the Tabernacle for a long time, the Israelites stayed and performed their duty to the LORD. 20Sometimes the cloud would stay over the Tabernacle for only a few days, so the people would stay for only a few days, as the LORD commanded. Then at the LORD's command they would break camp and move on. 21Sometimes the cloud stayed only overnight and lifted the next morning. But day or night, when the cloud lifted, the people broke camp and moved on. 22Whether the cloud stayed above the Tabernacle for two days, a month, or a year, the people of Israel stayed in camp and did not move on. But as soon as it lifted, they broke camp and moved on. 23So they camped or traveled at the LORD's command, and they did whatever the LORD told them through Moses.

IN THE RIGHT SPOT 9:23

The Hebrews traveled and camped as God guided. When you follow God's guidance, you can be confident that you're where God wants you, whether you're moving or staying in one place. Instead of praying, "God, what do you want me to do next?" you might ask, "God, what do you want me to do while I'm right here?" Direction from God is not just for your next big move. He has a purpose in placing you where you are right now. ■

10

THE SILVER TRUMPETS

Now the LORD said to Moses, 2"Make two trumpets of hammered silver for calling the community to assemble and for signaling the breaking of camp. 3When both

9:1 The first month of the ancient Hebrew lunar calendar usually occurs within the months of March and April. 9:3 This day in the ancient Hebrew lunar calendar occurred in late March, April, or early May. 9:11 This day in the ancient Hebrew lunar calendar occurred in late April, May, or early June. 9:15 Hebrew *covered the Tabernacle, the Tent of the Testimony.*

trumpets are blown, everyone must gather before you at the entrance of the Tabernacle.* 4But if only one trumpet is blown, then only the leaders—the heads of the clans of Israel—must present themselves to you.

5"When you sound the signal to move on, the tribes camped on the east side of the Tabernacle must break camp and move forward. 6When you sound the signal a second time, the tribes camped on the south will follow. You must sound short blasts as the signal for moving on. 7But when you call the people to an assembly, blow the trumpets with a different signal. 8Only the priests, Aaron's descendants, are allowed to blow the trumpets. This is a permanent law for you, to be observed from generation to generation.

9"When you arrive in your own land and go to war against your enemies who attack you, sound the alarm with the trumpets. Then the LORD your God will remember you and rescue you from your enemies. 10Blow the trumpets in times of gladness, too, sounding them at your annual festivals and at the beginning of each month. And blow the trumpets over your burnt offerings and peace offerings. The trumpets will remind the LORD your God of his covenant with you. I am the LORD your God."

THE ISRAELITES LEAVE SINAI

11In the second year after Israel's departure from Egypt—on the twentieth day of the second month*—the cloud lifted from the Tabernacle of the Covenant.* 12So the Israelites set out from the wilderness of Sinai and traveled on from place to place until the cloud stopped in the wilderness of Paran.

13When the people set out for the first time, following the instructions the LORD had given through Moses, 14Judah's troops led the way. They marched behind their banner, and their leader was Nahshon son of Amminadab. 15They were joined by the troops of the tribe of Issachar, led by Nethanel son of Zuar, 16and the troops of the tribe of Zebulun, led by Eliab son of Helon.

17Then the Tabernacle was taken down, and the Gershonite and Merarite divisions of the Levites were next in the line of march, carrying the Tabernacle with them. 18Reuben's troops went next, marching behind their banner. Their leader was Elizur son of Shedeur. 19They were joined by the troops of the tribe of Simeon, led by Shelumiel son of Zurishaddai, 20and the troops of the tribe of Gad, led by Eliasaph son of Deuel.

21Next came the Kohathite division of the Levites, carrying the sacred objects from the Tabernacle. Before they arrived at the next camp, the Tabernacle would already be set up at its new location. 22Ephraim's troops went next, marching behind their banner. Their leader was Elishama son of Ammihud. 23They were joined by the troops of the tribe of Manasseh, led by Gamaliel son of Pedahzur, 24and the troops of the tribe of Benjamin, led by Abidan son of Gideoni.

25Dan's troops went last, marching behind their banner and serving as the rear guard for all the tribal camps. Their leader was Ahiezer son of Ammishaddai. 26They were joined by the troops of the tribe of Asher, led by Pagiel son of Ocran, 27and the troops of the tribe of Naphtali, led by Ahira son of Enan.

28This was the order in which the Israelites marched, division by division.

29One day Moses said to his brother-in-law, Hobab son of Reuel the Midianite, "We are on our way to the place the LORD promised us, for he said, 'I will give it to you.' Come with us and we will treat you well, for the LORD has promised wonderful blessings for Israel!"

30But Hobab replied, "No, I will not go. I must return to my own land and family."

31"Please don't leave us," Moses pleaded. "You know the places in the wilderness where we should camp. Come, be our guide. 32If you do, we'll share with you all the blessings the LORD gives us."

COMPLIMENTS 10:29-32

By complimenting Hobab's wilderness skills, Moses let Hobab know that he was needed. The people in your life won't know that you appreciate them if you don't tell them. Complimenting the people in your life builds lasting relationships and helps them know their strengths and value. Think about those who have helped you this month. What can you do to let them know how much you need and appreciate them? ■

33They marched for three days after leaving the mountain of the LORD, with the Ark of the LORD's Covenant moving ahead of them to show them where to stop and rest. 34As they moved on each day, the cloud of the LORD hovered over them. 35And whenever the Ark set out, Moses would shout, "Arise, O LORD, and let your enemies be scattered! Let them flee before you!" 36And when the Ark was set down, he would say, "Return, O LORD, to the countless thousands of Israel!"

11 THE PEOPLE COMPLAIN TO MOSES

Soon the people began to complain about their hardship, and the LORD heard everything they said. Then the LORD's anger blazed against them, and he sent a fire to rage among them, and he destroyed some of the people in the outskirts of the camp. 2Then the people screamed to Moses for help, and when he prayed to the LORD, the fire stopped. 3After that, the area was known as Taberah (which means "the place of burning"), because fire from the LORD had burned among them there.

4Then the foreign rabble who were traveling with the Israelites began to crave the good things of Egypt. And the people of Israel also began to complain. "Oh, for some meat!" they exclaimed. 5"We remember the fish we used to eat for free in Egypt. And we had all the cucumbers, melons, leeks, onions, and garlic we wanted. 6But now our appetites are gone. All we ever see is this manna!"

10:3 Hebrew *Tent of Meeting.* **10:11a** This day in the ancient Hebrew lunar calendar occurred in late April, May, or early June. **10:11b** Or *Tabernacle of the Testimony.*

GRATITUDE ATTITUDE 11:1-6

Dissatisfaction comes when our attention shifts from what we have to what we don't have. The people of Israel didn't seem to notice what God was doing for them—setting them free, making them a nation, giving them a new land—because they were so wrapped up in what God wasn't doing for them. They could think of nothing but the delicious Egyptian food they had left behind. Somehow they forgot that the brutal whip of Egyptian slavery was the cost of eating that food. Before we judge the Israelites too harshly, it's helpful to think about what occupies our attention most of the time. Are we grateful for what God has given us, or are we always thinking about what we would like to have? ■

7The manna looked like small coriander seeds, and it was pale yellow like gum resin. 8The people would go out and gather it from the ground. They made flour by grinding it with hand mills or pounding it in mortars. Then they boiled it in a pot and made it into flat cakes. These cakes tasted like pastries baked with olive oil. 9The manna came down on the camp with the dew during the night.

10Moses heard all the families standing in the doorways of their tents whining, and the LORD became extremely angry. Moses was also very aggravated. 11And Moses said to the LORD, "Why are you treating me, your servant, so harshly? Have mercy on me! What did I do to deserve the burden of all these people? 12Did I give birth to them? Did I bring them into the world? Why did you tell me to carry them in my arms like a mother carries a nursing baby? How can I carry them to the land you swore to give their ancestors? 13Where am I supposed to get meat for all these people? They keep whining to me, saying, 'Give us meat to eat!' 14I can't carry all these people by myself! The load is far too heavy! 15If this is how you intend to treat me, just go ahead and kill me. Do me a favor and spare me this misery!"

MOSES CHOOSES SEVENTY LEADERS

16Then the LORD said to Moses, "Gather before me seventy men who are recognized as elders and leaders of Israel. Bring them to the Tabernacle* to stand there with you. 17I will come down and talk to you there. I will take some of the Spirit that is upon you, and I will put the Spirit upon them also. They will bear the burden of the people along with you, so you will not have to carry it alone.

18"And say to the people, 'Purify yourselves, for tomorrow you will have meat to eat. You were whining, and the LORD heard you when you cried, "Oh, for some meat! We were better off in Egypt!" Now the LORD will give you meat, and you will have to eat it. 19And it won't be for just a day or two, or for five or ten or even twenty. 20You will eat it for a whole month until you gag and are sick of it. For you have rejected the LORD, who is here among you, and you have whined to him, saying, "Why did we ever leave Egypt?"'"

21But Moses responded to the LORD, "There are 600,000 foot soldiers here with me, and yet you say, 'I will give them meat for a whole month!' 22Even if we butchered all our flocks and herds, would that satisfy them? Even if we caught all the fish in the sea, would that be enough?"

23Then the LORD said to Moses, "Has my arm lost its power? Now you will see whether or not my word comes true!"

24So Moses went out and reported the LORD's words to the people. He gathered the seventy elders and stationed them around the Tabernacle.* 25And the LORD came down in the cloud and spoke to Moses. Then he gave the seventy elders the same Spirit that was upon Moses. And when the Spirit rested upon them, they prophesied. But this never happened again.

26Two men, Eldad and Medad, had stayed behind in the camp. They were listed among the elders, but they had not gone out to the Tabernacle. Yet the Spirit rested upon them as well, so they prophesied there in the camp. 27A young man ran and reported to Moses, "Eldad and Medad are prophesying in the camp!"

28Joshua son of Nun, who had been Moses' assistant since his youth, protested, "Moses, my master, make them stop!"

29But Moses replied, "Are you jealous for my sake? I wish that all the LORD's people were prophets and that the LORD would put his Spirit upon them all!" 30Then Moses returned to the camp with the elders of Israel.

THE LORD SENDS QUAIL

31Now the LORD sent a wind that brought quail from the sea and let them fall all around the camp. For miles in every direction there were quail flying about three feet above the ground.* 32So the people went out and caught quail all that day and throughout the night and all the next day, too. No one gathered less than fifty bushels*! They spread the quail all around the camp to dry. 33But while they were gorging themselves on the meat—while it was still in their mouths—the anger of the LORD blazed against the people, and he struck them with a severe plague. 34So that place was called Kibroth-hattaavah (which means "graves of gluttony") because there they buried the people who had craved meat from Egypt. 35From Kibroth-hattaavah the Israelites traveled to Hazeroth, where they stayed for some time.

12 THE COMPLAINTS OF MIRIAM AND AARON

While they were at Hazeroth, Miriam and Aaron criticized Moses because he had married a Cushite woman. 2They said, "Has the LORD spoken only through Moses? Hasn't he spoken through us, too?" But the LORD heard them. 3(Now Moses was very humble—more humble than any other person on earth.)

4So immediately the LORD called to Moses, Aaron, and

11:16 Hebrew *the Tent of Meeting.* **11:24** Hebrew *the tent;* also in 11:26. **11:31** Or *there were quail 3 feet* [2 cubits or 92 centimeters] *deep on the ground.* **11:32** Hebrew *10 homers* [1.8 kiloliters].

Miriam and said, "Go out to the Tabernacle,* all three of
you!" So the three of them went to the Tabernacle. [5]Then
the LORD descended in the pillar of cloud and stood at the
entrance of the Tabernacle.* "Aaron and Miriam!" he
called, and they stepped forward. [6]And the LORD said to
them, "Now listen to what I say:

"If there were prophets among you,
I, the LORD, would reveal myself in visions.
I would speak to them in dreams.
[7] But not with my servant Moses.
Of all my house, he is the one I trust.
[8] I speak to him face to face,
clearly, and not in riddles!
He sees the LORD as he is.
So why were you not afraid
to criticize my servant Moses?"

[9]The LORD was very angry with them, and he departed.
[10]As the cloud moved from above the Tabernacle, there
stood Miriam, her skin as white as snow from leprosy.*
When Aaron saw what had happened to her, [11]he cried
out to Moses, "Oh, my master! Please don't punish us for
this sin we have so foolishly committed. [12]Don't let her be
like a stillborn baby, already decayed at birth."
[13]So Moses cried out to the LORD, "O God, I beg you,
please heal her!"
[14]But the LORD said to Moses, "If her father had done
nothing more than spit in her face, wouldn't she be defiled for seven days? So keep her outside the camp for
seven days, and after that she may be accepted back."
[15]So Miriam was kept outside the camp for seven days,
and the people waited until she was brought back before
they traveled again. [16]Then they left Hazeroth and
camped in the wilderness of Paran.

13 TWELVE SCOUTS EXPLORE CANAAN

The LORD now said to Moses, [2]"Send out men to explore
the land of Canaan, the land I am giving to the Israelites.
Send one leader from each of the twelve ancestral
tribes." [3]So Moses did as the LORD commanded him. He
sent out twelve men, all tribal leaders of Israel, from their
camp in the wilderness of Paran. [4]These were the tribes
and the names of their leaders:

Tribe	*Leader*
Reuben	Shammua son of Zaccur
[5] Simeon	Shaphat son of Hori
[6] Judah	Caleb son of Jephunneh
[7] Issachar	Igal son of Joseph
[8] Ephraim	Hoshea son of Nun
[9] Benjamin	Palti son of Raphu
[10] Zebulun	Gaddiel son of Sodi
[11] Manasseh son of Joseph	Gaddi son of Susi
[12] Dan	Ammiel son of Gemalli
[13] Asher	Sethur son of Michael
[14] Naphtali	Nahbi son of Vophsi
[15] Gad	Geuel son of Maki

[16]These are the names of the men Moses sent out to explore the land. (Moses called Hoshea son of Nun by the
name Joshua.)
[17]Moses gave the men these instructions as he sent
them out to explore the land: "Go north through the Negev into the hill country. [18]See what the land is like, and
find out whether the people living there are strong or
weak, few or many. [19]See what kind of land they live in. Is
it good or bad? Do their towns have walls, or are they unprotected like open camps? [20]Is the soil fertile or poor?
Are there many trees? Do your best to bring back samples
of the crops you see." (It happened to be the season for
harvesting the first ripe grapes.)
[21]So they went up and explored the land from the
wilderness of Zin as far as Rehob, near Lebo-hamath.
[22]Going north, they passed through the Negev and arrived at Hebron, where Ahiman, Sheshai, and Talmai—all
descendants of Anak—lived. (The ancient town of Hebron was founded seven years before the Egyptian city of
Zoan.) [23]When they came to the valley of Eshcol, they cut
down a branch with a single cluster of grapes so large that
it took two of them to carry it on a pole between them!
They also brought back samples of the pomegranates
and figs. [24]That place was called the valley of Eshcol
(which means "cluster"), because of the cluster of grapes
the Israelite men cut there.

FEAR OR FOCUS ON GOD? 13:25-29

God told the Israelites that the rich and plentiful Promised Land would be theirs. But when the scouting party reported back to Moses, they couldn't stop focusing on their fears. God's promise to help had been forgotten. When facing tough decisions, do you tend to focus on the fear of potential difficulties or God's power to help? The Israelites wandered in the desert for 40 years because they chose to give in to fear. The consequences of disobedience can be far greater than any imagined fear. ■

THE SCOUTING REPORT

[25]After exploring the land for forty days, the men returned
[26]to Moses, Aaron, and the whole community of Israel at
Kadesh in the wilderness of Paran. They reported to the
whole community what they had seen and showed them
the fruit they had taken from the land. [27]This was their report to Moses: "We entered the land you sent us to explore,
and it is indeed a bountiful country—a land flowing with
milk and honey. Here is the kind of fruit it produces. [28]But
the people living there are powerful, and their towns are
large and fortified. We even saw giants there, the descendants of Anak! [29]The Amalekites live in the Negev, and the
Hittites, Jebusites, and Amorites live in the hill country.
The Canaanites live along the coast of the Mediterranean
Sea* and along the Jordan Valley."
[30]But Caleb tried to quiet the people as they stood before Moses. "Let's go at once to take the land," he said.
"We can certainly conquer it!"

12:4 Hebrew *the Tent of Meeting.* **12:5** Hebrew *the tent;* also in 12:10. **12:10** Or *with a skin disease.* The Hebrew word used here can describe various skin diseases. **13:29** Hebrew *the sea.*

31But the other men who had explored the land with
him disagreed. "We can't go up against them! They are
stronger than we are!" 32So they spread this bad report
about the land among the Israelites:
"The land we traveled through and explored will devour anyone who goes to
live there. All the people we saw were
huge. 33We even saw giants* there, the
descendants of Anak. Next to them we
felt like grasshoppers, and that's what
they thought, too!"

14 THE PEOPLE REBEL

Then the whole community began
weeping aloud, and they cried all night.
2Their voices rose in a great chorus of
protest against Moses and Aaron. "If
only we had died in Egypt, or even here
in the wilderness!" they complained.
3"Why is the LORD taking us to this country only to have
us die in battle? Our wives and our little ones will be carried off as plunder! Wouldn't it be better for us to return
to Egypt?" 4Then they plotted among themselves, "Let's
choose a new leader and go back to Egypt!"

5Then Moses and Aaron fell face down on the ground
before the whole community of Israel. 6Two of the men
who had explored the land, Joshua son of Nun and Caleb
son of Jephunneh, tore their clothing. 7They said to all the
people of Israel, "The land we traveled through and explored is a wonderful land! 8And if the LORD is pleased
with us, he will bring us safely into that land and give it to
us. It is a rich land flowing with milk and honey. 9Do not
rebel against the LORD, and don't be afraid of the people
of the land. They are only helpless prey to us! They have
no protection, but the LORD is with us! Don't be afraid of
them!"

> The LORD is slow to anger and filled with unfailing love, forgiving every kind of sin and rebellion.
>
> *NUMBERS 14:18*

ADVICE 14:6-10

Two wise men, Joshua and Caleb, encouraged the people to act on God's promise to give them the land of Canaan. But the people rejected their advice and even talked of killing them. Have you ever rejected advice that you didn't like? Next time you receive advice, why not evaluate it carefully and weigh it against God's Word. That advice could be God's message to you. ■

10But the whole community began to talk about stoning Joshua and Caleb. Then the glorious presence of the
LORD appeared to all the Israelites at the Tabernacle.*
11And the LORD said to Moses, "How long will these people treat me with contempt? Will they never believe me,
even after all the miraculous signs I have done among
them? 12I will disown them and destroy them with a
plague. Then I will make you into a nation greater and
mightier than they are!"

MOSES INTERCEDES FOR THE PEOPLE

13But Moses objected. "What will the Egyptians think
when they hear about it?" he asked the LORD. "They know
full well the power you displayed in
rescuing your people from Egypt.
14Now if you destroy them, the Egyptians will send a report to the inhabitants of this land, who have already
heard that you live among your people.
They know, LORD, that you have appeared to your people face to face and
that your pillar of cloud hovers over
them. They know that you go before
them in the pillar of cloud by day and
the pillar of fire by night. 15Now if you
slaughter all these people with a single
blow, the nations that have heard of
your fame will say, 16'The LORD was not
able to bring them into the land he
swore to give them, so he killed them
in the wilderness.'

17"Please, Lord, prove that your power is as great as you
have claimed. For you said, 18'The LORD is slow to anger
and filled with unfailing love, forgiving every kind of sin
and rebellion. But he does not excuse the guilty. He lays
the sins of the parents upon their children; the entire
family is affected—even children in the third and fourth
generations.' 19In keeping with your magnificent, unfailing love, please pardon the sins of this people, just as you
have forgiven them ever since they left Egypt."

20Then the LORD said, "I will pardon them as you have requested. 21But as surely as I live, and as surely as the earth is
filled with the LORD's glory, 22not one of these people will
ever enter that land. They have all seen my glorious presence and the miraculous signs I performed both in Egypt
and in the wilderness, but again and again they have tested
me by refusing to listen to my voice. 23They will never even
see the land I swore to give their ancestors. None of those
who have treated me with contempt will ever see it. 24But
my servant Caleb has a different attitude than the others
have. He has remained loyal to me, so I will bring him into
the land he explored. His descendants will possess their
full share of that land. 25Now turn around, and don't go on
toward the land where the Amalekites and Canaanites live.
Tomorrow you must set out for the wilderness in the direction of the Red Sea.*"

THE LORD PUNISHES THE ISRAELITES

26Then the LORD said to Moses and Aaron, 27"How long
must I put up with this wicked community and its complaints about me? Yes, I have heard the complaints the Israelites are making against me. 28Now tell them this: 'As
surely as I live, declares the LORD, I will do to you the very
things I heard you say. 29You will all drop dead in this wilderness! Because you complained against me, every one
of you who is twenty years old or older and was included
in the registration will die. 30You will not enter and occupy the land I swore to give you. The only exceptions
will be Caleb son of Jephunneh and Joshua son of Nun.

13:33 Hebrew *nephilim.* 14:10 Hebrew *the Tent of Meeting.* 14:25 Hebrew *sea of reeds.*

Israel's Complaining

COMPLAINT	SIN	RESULT
11:1 About their hardships	Complained about their problems instead of praying to God	Thousands of people were destroyed when God sent fire to punish them
11:4 About the lack of meat	Lusted after things they didn't have	God sent quail, but as the people began to eat, God struck them with a plague that killed many
11:1-4 About being stuck in the wilderness, facing the giants of the Promised Land, and wishing to return to Egypt	Openly rebelled against God's leaders and failed to trust in his promises	All who complained were not allowed to enter the Promised Land; they were doomed to wander in the wilderness until they died
16:3 About Moses' and Aaron's authority and leadership	Were greedy for more power and authority	The families, friends, and possessions of Korah, Dathan, and Abiram were swallowed up by the earth. Fire then burned up the 250 other men who rebelled
16:41 That Moses and Aaron caused the deaths of Korah and his conspirators	Blamed others for their own troubles	God began to destroy Israel with a plague. Moses and Aaron made atonement for the people, but 14,700 of them were killed
20:2-3 About the lack of water	Refused to believe that God would provide as he had promised	Moses sinned along with the people. For this he was barred from entering the Promised Land
21:5 That God and Moses brought them into the wilderness	Failed to recognize that their problems were brought on by their own disobedience	God sent poisonous snakes that killed many people and seriously injured many others

31" 'You said your children would be carried off as
plunder. Well, I will bring them safely into the land, and
they will enjoy what you have despised. 32But as for you,
you will drop dead in this wilderness. 33And your children will be like shepherds, wandering in the wilderness
for forty years. In this way, they will pay for your faithlessness, until the last of you lies dead in the wilderness.
34" 'Because your men explored the land for forty days,
you must wander in the wilderness for forty years—a year
for each day, suffering the consequences of your sins.
Then you will discover what it is like to have me for an enemy.' 35I, the LORD, have spoken! I will certainly do these
things to every member of the community who has conspired against me. They will be destroyed here in this wilderness, and here they will die!"

36The ten men Moses had sent to explore the land—the
ones who incited rebellion against the LORD with their
bad report—37were struck dead with a plague before the
LORD. 38Of the twelve who had explored the land, only
Joshua and Caleb remained alive.
39When Moses reported the LORD's words to all the Israelites, the people were filled with grief. 40Then they got
up early the next morning and went to the top of the
range of hills. "Let's go," they said. "We realize that we
have sinned, but now we are ready to enter the land the
LORD has promised us."
41But Moses said, "Why are you now disobeying the
LORD's orders to return to the wilderness? It won't work.
42Do not go up into the land now. You will only be
crushed by your enemies because the LORD is not with

you. [43]When you face the Amalekites and Canaanites in battle, you will be slaughtered. The LORD will abandon you because you have abandoned the LORD."

[44]But the people defiantly pushed ahead toward the hill country, even though neither Moses nor the Ark of the LORD's Covenant left the camp. [45]Then the Amalekites and the Canaanites who lived in those hills came down and attacked them and chased them back as far as Hormah.

15

LAWS CONCERNING OFFERINGS

Then the LORD told Moses, [2]"Give the following instructions to the people of Israel.

"When you finally settle in the land I am giving you, [3]you will offer special gifts as a pleasing aroma to the LORD. These gifts may take the form of a burnt offering, a sacrifice to fulfill a vow, a voluntary offering, or an offering at any of your annual festivals, and they may be taken from your herds of cattle or your flocks of sheep and goats. [4]When you present these offerings, you must also give the LORD a grain offering of two quarts* of choice flour mixed with one quart* of olive oil. [5]For each lamb offered as a burnt offering or a special sacrifice, you must also present one quart of wine as a liquid offering.

[6]"If the sacrifice is a ram, give a grain offering of four quarts* of choice flour mixed with a third of a gallon* of olive oil, [7]and give a third of a gallon of wine as a liquid offering. This will be a pleasing aroma to the LORD.

[8]"When you present a young bull as a burnt offering or as a sacrifice to fulfill a vow or as a peace offering to the LORD, [9]you must also give a grain offering of six quarts* of choice flour mixed with two quarts* of olive oil, [10]and give two quarts of wine as a liquid offering. This will be a special gift, a pleasing aroma to the LORD.

[11]"Each sacrifice of a bull, ram, lamb, or young goat should be prepared in this way. [12]Follow these instructions with each offering you present. [13]All of you native-born Israelites must follow these instructions when you offer a special gift as a pleasing aroma to the LORD. [14]And if any foreigners visit you or live among you and want to present a special gift as a pleasing aroma to the LORD, they must follow these same procedures. [15]Native-born Israelites and foreigners are equal before the LORD and are subject to the same decrees. This is a permanent law for you, to be observed from generation to generation. [16]The same instructions and regulations will apply both to you and to the foreigners living among you."

[17]Then the LORD said to Moses, [18]"Give the following instructions to the people of Israel.

"When you arrive in the land where I am taking you, [19]and you eat the crops that grow there, you must set some aside as a sacred offering to the LORD. [20]Present a cake from the first of the flour you grind, and set it aside as a sacred offering, as you do with the first grain from the threshing floor. [21]Throughout the generations to come, you are to present a sacred offering to the LORD each year from the first of your ground flour.

[22]"But suppose you unintentionally fail to carry out all these commands that the LORD has given you through Moses. [23]And suppose your descendants in the future fail to do everything the LORD has commanded through Moses. [24]If the mistake was made unintentionally, and the community was unaware of it, the whole community must present a young bull for a burnt offering as a pleasing aroma to the LORD. It must be offered along with its prescribed grain offering and liquid offering and with one male goat for a sin offering. [25]With it the priest will purify the whole community of Israel, making them right with the LORD,* and they will be forgiven. For it was an unintentional sin, and they have corrected it with their offerings to the LORD—the special gift and the sin offering. [26]The whole community of Israel will be forgiven, including the foreigners living among you, for all the people were involved in the sin.

[27]"If one individual commits an unintentional sin, the guilty person must bring a one-year-old female goat for a sin offering. [28]The priest will sacrifice it to purify* the guilty person before the LORD, and that person will be forgiven. [29]These same instructions apply both to native-born Israelites and to the foreigners living among you.

[30]"But those who brazenly violate the LORD's will, whether native-born Israelites or foreigners, have blasphemed the LORD, and they must be cut off from the community. [31]Since they have treated the LORD's word with contempt and deliberately disobeyed his command, they must be completely cut off and suffer the punishment for their guilt."

PENALTY FOR BREAKING THE SABBATH

[32]One day while the people of Israel were in the wilderness, they discovered a man gathering wood on the Sabbath day. [33]The people who found him doing this took him before Moses, Aaron, and the rest of the community. [34]They held him in custody because they did not know what to do with him. [35]Then the LORD said to Moses, "The man must be put to death! The whole community must stone him outside the camp." [36]So the whole community took the man outside the camp and stoned him to death, just as the LORD had commanded Moses.

TASSELS ON CLOTHING

[37]Then the LORD said to Moses, [38]"Give the following instructions to the people of Israel: Throughout the generations to come you must make tassels for the hems of your clothing and attach them with a blue cord. [39]When you see the tassels, you will remember and obey all the commands of the LORD instead of following your own desires and defiling yourselves, as you are prone to do. [40]The tassels will help you remember that you must obey all my commands and be holy to your God. [41]I am the LORD your God who brought you out of the land of Egypt that I might be your God. I am the LORD your God!"

15:4a Hebrew 1/10 *of an ephah* [2.2 liters]. **15:4b** Hebrew 1/4 *of a hin* [1 liter]; also in 15:5. **15:6a** Hebrew 2/10 *of an ephah* [4.4 liters]. **15:6b** Hebrew 1/3 *of a hin* [1.3 liters]; also in 15:7. **15:9a** Hebrew 3/10 *of an ephah* [6.6 liters]. **15:9b** Hebrew 1/2 *of a hin* [2 liters]; also in 15:10. **15:25** Or *will make atonement for the whole community of Israel.* **15:28** Or *to make atonement for.*

16

KORAH'S REBELLION

One day Korah son of Izhar, a descendant of Kohath son of Levi, conspired with Dathan and Abiram, the sons of Eliab, and On son of Peleth, from the tribe of Reuben. 2They incited a rebellion against Moses, along with 250 other leaders of the community, all prominent members of the assembly. 3They united against Moses and Aaron and said, "You have gone too far! The whole community of Israel has been set apart by the LORD, and he is with all of us. What right do you have to act as though you are greater than the rest of the LORD's people?"

A SELFISH AMBITION 16:1-10

Korah wanted the special qualities God had given to Moses and other leaders, even though he had his own worthwhile abilities and responsibilities. In the end, his ambition caused him to lose everything. Sometimes we want the fame, power, or material possessions that someone else has. Trouble results when we try to gain what others have. If you've fallen into that trap, consider the chilling example of Korah, who gambled and lost. ■

4When Moses heard what they were saying, he fell face down on the ground. 5Then he said to Korah and his followers, "Tomorrow morning the LORD will show us who belongs to him* and who is holy. The LORD will allow only those whom he selects to enter his own presence. 6Korah, you and all your followers must prepare your incense burners. 7Light fires in them tomorrow, and burn incense before the LORD. Then we will see whom the LORD chooses as his holy one. You Levites are the ones who have gone too far!"

8Then Moses spoke again to Korah: "Now listen, you Levites! 9Does it seem insignificant to you that the God of Israel has chosen you from among all the community of Israel to be near him so you can serve in the LORD's Tabernacle and stand before the people to minister to them? 10Korah, he has already given this special ministry to you and your fellow Levites. Are you now demanding the priesthood as well? 11The LORD is the one you and your followers are really revolting against! For who is Aaron that you are complaining about him?"

12Then Moses summoned Dathan and Abiram, the sons of Eliab, but they replied, "We refuse to come before you! 13Isn't it enough that you brought us out of Egypt, a land flowing with milk and honey, to kill us here in this wilderness, and that you now treat us like your subjects? 14What's more, you haven't brought us into another land flowing with milk and honey. You haven't given us a new homeland with fields and vineyards. Are you trying to fool these men?* We will not come."

15Then Moses became very angry and said to the LORD, "Do not accept their grain offerings! I have not taken so much as a donkey from them, and I have never hurt a single one of them." 16And Moses said to Korah, "You and all your followers must come here tomorrow and present yourselves before the LORD. Aaron will also be here. 17You and each of your 250 followers must prepare an incense burner and put incense on it, so you can all present them before the LORD. Aaron will also bring his incense burner."

18So each of these men prepared an incense burner, lit the fire, and placed incense on it. Then they all stood at the entrance of the Tabernacle* with Moses and Aaron. 19Meanwhile, Korah had stirred up the entire community against Moses and Aaron, and they all gathered at the Tabernacle entrance. Then the glorious presence of the LORD appeared to the whole community, 20and the LORD said to Moses and Aaron, 21"Get away from all these people so that I may instantly destroy them!"

22But Moses and Aaron fell face down on the ground. "O God," they pleaded, "you are the God who gives breath to all creatures. Must you be angry with all the people when only one man sins?"

23And the LORD said to Moses, 24"Then tell all the people to get away from the tents of Korah, Dathan, and Abiram."

25So Moses got up and rushed over to the tents of Dathan and Abiram, followed by the elders of Israel. 26"Quick!" he told the people. "Get away from the tents of these wicked men, and don't touch anything that belongs to them. If you do, you will be destroyed for their sins." 27So all the people stood back from the tents of Korah, Dathan, and Abiram. Then Dathan and Abiram came out and stood at the entrances of their tents, together with their wives and children and little ones.

REVENGE 16:22-27

Moses and Aaron prayed for those with whom they were most angry and frustrated. Do you pray for those who hurt you or do you seek revenge? God promises to settle the score with wrongdoers. It is not our job to take revenge. God will make certain that, in the end, justice is done. ■

28And Moses said, "This is how you will know that the LORD has sent me to do all these things that I have done—for I have not done them on my own. 29If these men die a natural death, or if nothing unusual happens, then the LORD has not sent me. 30But if the LORD does something entirely new and the ground opens its mouth and swallows them and all their belongings, and they go down alive into the grave,* then you will know that these men have shown contempt for the LORD."

31He had hardly finished speaking the words when the ground suddenly split open beneath them. 32The earth opened its mouth and swallowed the men, along with their households and all their followers who were standing with them, and everything they owned. 33So they went down alive into the grave, along with all their belongings.

16:5 Greek version reads *God has visited and knows those who are his.* Compare 2 Tim 2:19. **16:14** Hebrew *Are you trying to put out the eyes of these men?* **16:18** Hebrew *the Tent of Meeting;* also in 16:19, 42, 43, 50. **16:30** Hebrew *into Sheol;* also in 16:33.

The earth closed over them, and they all vanished from
among the people of Israel. 34All the people around them
fled when they heard their screams. "The earth will swallow us, too!" they cried. 35Then fire blazed forth from the
LORD and burned up the 250 men who were offering
incense.

36*And the LORD said to Moses, 37"Tell Eleazar son of
Aaron the priest to pull all the incense burners from the
fire, for they are holy. Also tell him to scatter the burning
coals. 38Take the incense burners of these men who have
sinned at the cost of their lives, and hammer the metal
into a thin sheet to overlay the altar. Since these burners
were used in the LORD's presence, they have become holy.
Let them serve as a warning to the people of Israel."

39So Eleazar the priest collected the 250 bronze incense burners that had been used by the men who died in
the fire, and he hammered them into a thin sheet to overlay the altar. 40This would warn the Israelites that no unauthorized person—no one who was not a descendant of
Aaron—should ever enter the LORD's presence to burn incense. If anyone did, the same thing would happen to
him as happened to Korah and his followers. So the
LORD's instructions to Moses were carried out.

41But the very next morning the whole community of
Israel began muttering again against Moses and Aaron,
saying, "You have killed the LORD's people!" 42As the community gathered to protest against Moses and Aaron,
they turned toward the Tabernacle and saw that the
cloud had covered it, and the glorious presence of the
LORD appeared.

43Moses and Aaron came and stood in front of the Tabernacle, 44and the LORD said to Moses, 45"Get away from
all these people so that I can instantly destroy them!" But
Moses and Aaron fell face down on the ground.

46And Moses said to Aaron, "Quick, take an incense
burner and place burning coals on it from the altar. Lay
incense on it, and carry it out among the people to purify
them and make them right with the LORD.* The LORD's
anger is blazing against them—the plague has already
begun."

47Aaron did as Moses told him and ran out among the
people. The plague had already begun to strike down
the people, but Aaron burned the incense and purified*
the people. 48He stood between the dead and the living,
and the plague stopped. 49But 14,700 people died in
that plague, in addition to those who had died in the affair involving Korah. 50Then because the plague had
stopped, Aaron returned to Moses at the entrance of the
Tabernacle.

17 THE BUDDING OF AARON'S STAFF

1*Then the LORD said to Moses, 2"Tell the people of Israel
to bring you twelve wooden staffs, one from each leader
of Israel's ancestral tribes, and inscribe each leader's
name on his staff. 3Inscribe Aaron's name on the staff of
the tribe of Levi, for there must be one staff for the leader
of each ancestral tribe. 4Place these staffs in the Tabernacle in front of the Ark containing the tablets of the Covenant,* where I meet with you. 5Buds will sprout on the
staff belonging to the man I choose. Then I will finally
put an end to the people's murmuring and complaining
against you."

REBELLION 17:5, 10

After witnessing spectacular miracles, seeing the Egyptians punished by the plagues, and experiencing the presence of God, the Israelites still rebelled. We wonder how they could be so blind and ignorant. But let's be honest—we often behave in the same way. We can escape this pattern only by paying attention to the signs of God's presence that we have been given. How has God guided and protected you in the past? How has he answered your prayers? If you focus your thoughts on these things, rebellion will become unthinkable. ■

6So Moses gave the instructions to the people of Israel,
and each of the twelve tribal leaders, including Aaron,
brought Moses a staff. 7Moses placed the staffs in the
LORD's presence in the Tabernacle of the Covenant.*
8When he went into the Tabernacle of the Covenant the
next day, he found that Aaron's staff, representing the
tribe of Levi, had sprouted, budded, blossomed, and produced ripe almonds!

9When Moses brought all the staffs out from the
LORD's presence, he showed them to the people. Each
man claimed his own staff. 10And the LORD said to Moses:
"Place Aaron's staff permanently before the Ark of the
Covenant* to serve as a warning to rebels. This should
put an end to their complaints against me and prevent
any further deaths." 11So Moses did as the LORD commanded him.

12Then the people of Israel said to Moses, "Look, we are
doomed! We are dead! We are ruined! 13Everyone who
even comes close to the Tabernacle of the LORD dies. Are
we all doomed to die?"

18 DUTIES OF PRIESTS AND LEVITES

Then the LORD said to Aaron: "You, your sons, and your
relatives from the tribe of Levi will be held responsible
for any offenses related to the sanctuary. But you and
your sons alone will be held responsible for violations
connected with the priesthood.

2"Bring your relatives of the tribe of Levi—your ancestral tribe—to assist you and your sons as you perform the
sacred duties in front of the Tabernacle of the Covenant.* 3But as the Levites go about all their assigned

16:36 Verses 16:36-50 are numbered 17:1-15 in Hebrew text. **16:46** Or *to make atonement for them.* **16:47** Or *and made atonement for.* **17:1** Verses 17:1-13 are numbered 17:16-28 in Hebrew text. **17:4** Hebrew *in the Tent of Meeting before the Testimony.* The Hebrew word for "testimony" refers to the terms of the LORD's covenant with Israel as written on stone tablets, which were kept in the Ark, and also to the covenant itself. **17:7** Or *Tabernacle of the Testimony;* also in 17:8. **17:10** Hebrew *before the Testimony;* see note on 17:4. **18:2** Or *Tabernacle of the Testimony.*

duties at the Tabernacle, they must be careful not to go near any of the sacred objects or the altar. If they do, both you and they will die. 4The Levites must join you in fulfilling their responsibilities for the care and maintenance of the Tabernacle,* but no unauthorized person may assist you.

5"You yourselves must perform the sacred duties inside the sanctuary and at the altar. If you follow these instructions, the LORD's anger will never again blaze against the people of Israel. 6I myself have chosen your fellow Levites from among the Israelites to be your special assistants. They are a gift to you, dedicated to the LORD for service in the Tabernacle. 7But you and your sons, the priests, must personally handle all the priestly rituals associated with the altar and with everything behind the inner curtain. I am giving you the priesthood as your special privilege of service. Any unauthorized person who comes too near the sanctuary will be put to death."

SUPPORT FOR THE PRIESTS AND LEVITES

8The LORD gave these further instructions to Aaron: "I myself have put you in charge of all the holy offerings that are brought to me by the people of Israel. I have given all these consecrated offerings to you and your sons as your permanent share. 9You are allotted the portion of the most holy offerings that is not burned on the fire. This portion of all the most holy offerings—including the grain offerings, sin offerings, and guilt offerings—will be most holy, and it belongs to you and your sons. 10You must eat it as a most holy offering. All the males may eat of it, and you must treat it as most holy.

11"All the sacred offerings and special offerings presented to me when the Israelites lift them up before the altar also belong to you. I have given them to you and to your sons and daughters as your permanent share. Any member of your family who is ceremonially clean may eat of these offerings.

12"I also give you the harvest gifts brought by the people as offerings to the LORD—the best of the olive oil, new wine, and grain. 13All the first crops of their land that the people present to the LORD belong to you. Any member of your family who is ceremonially clean may eat this food.

14"Everything in Israel that is specially set apart for the LORD* also belongs to you.

15"The firstborn of every mother, whether human or animal, that is offered to the LORD will be yours. But you must always redeem your firstborn sons and the firstborn of ceremonially unclean animals. 16Redeem them when they are one month old. The redemption price is five pieces of silver* (as measured by the weight of the sanctuary shekel, which equals twenty gerahs).

17"However, you may not redeem the firstborn of cattle, sheep, or goats. They are holy and have been set apart for the LORD. Sprinkle their blood on the altar, and burn their fat as a special gift, a pleasing aroma to the LORD. 18The meat of these animals will be yours, just like the breast and right thigh that are presented by lifting them up as a special offering before the altar. 19Yes, I am giving you all these holy offerings that the people of Israel bring to the LORD. They are for you and your sons and daughters, to be eaten as your permanent share. This is an eternal and unbreakable covenant* between the LORD and you, and it also applies to your descendants."

20And the LORD said to Aaron, "You priests will receive no allotment of land or share of property among the people of Israel. I am your share and your allotment. 21As for the tribe of Levi, your relatives, I will compensate them for their service in the Tabernacle. Instead of an allotment of land, I will give them the tithes from the entire land of Israel.

22"From now on, no Israelites except priests or Levites may approach the Tabernacle. If they come too near, they will be judged guilty and will die. 23Only the Levites may serve at the Tabernacle, and they will be held responsible for any offenses against it. This is a permanent law for you, to be observed from generation to generation. The Levites will receive no allotment of land among the Israelites, 24because I have given them the Israelites' tithes, which have been presented as sacred offerings to the LORD. This will be the Levites' share. That is why I said they would receive no allotment of land among the Israelites."

GIVING TO GOD 18:25-29

The Levites, who helped the priests, were required to tithe to support the work of the Tabernacle just like all of the other Israelites. No one was exempt from returning to God a portion of what was received from him. Though the Levites owned no land and operated no great enterprises, they were to treat their income the same as everyone else's by giving a portion to care for the needs of the other Levites and of the Tabernacle. The tithing principle is still relevant today. What can you give to help meet the needs of God's workers and to help build his kingdom? ■

25The LORD also told Moses, 26"Give these instructions to the Levites: When you receive from the people of Israel the tithes I have assigned as your allotment, give a tenth of the tithes you receive—a tithe of the tithe—to the LORD as a sacred offering. 27The LORD will consider this offering to be your harvest offering, as though it were the first grain from your own threshing floor or wine from your own winepress. 28You must present one-tenth of the tithe received from the Israelites as a sacred offering to the LORD. This is the LORD's sacred portion, and you must present it to Aaron the priest. 29Be sure to give to the LORD the best portions of the gifts given to you.

30"Also, give these instructions to the Levites: When you present the best part as your offering, it will be considered as though it came from your own threshing floor or winepress. 31You Levites and your families may eat this

18:4 Hebrew *the Tent of Meeting;* also in 18:6, 21, 22, 23, 31. **18:14** The Hebrew term used here refers to the complete consecration of things or people to the LORD, either by destroying them or by giving them as an offering. **18:16** Hebrew *5 shekels* [2 ounces or 57 grams] *of silver.* **18:19** Hebrew *a covenant of salt.*

food anywhere you wish, for it is your compensation for serving in the Tabernacle. 32You will not be considered guilty for accepting the LORD's tithes if you give the best portion to the priests. But be careful not to treat the holy gifts of the people of Israel as though they were common. If you do, you will die."

19 THE WATER OF PURIFICATION

The LORD said to Moses and Aaron, 2"Here is another legal requirement commanded by the LORD: Tell the people of Israel to bring you a red heifer, a perfect animal that has no defects and has never been yoked to a plow. 3Give it to Eleazar the priest, and it will be taken outside the camp and slaughtered in his presence. 4Eleazar will take some of its blood on his finger and sprinkle it seven times toward the front of the Tabernacle.* 5As Eleazar watches, the heifer must be burned—its hide, meat, blood, and dung. 6Eleazar the priest must then take a stick of cedar,* a hyssop branch, and some scarlet yarn and throw them into the fire where the heifer is burning.

7"Then the priest must wash his clothes and bathe himself in water. Afterward he may return to the camp, though he will remain ceremonially unclean until evening. 8The man who burns the animal must also wash his clothes and bathe himself in water, and he, too, will remain unclean until evening. 9Then someone who is ceremonially clean will gather up the ashes of the heifer and deposit them in a purified place outside the camp. They will be kept there for the community of Israel to use in the water for the purification ceremony. This ceremony is performed for the removal of sin. 10The man who gathers up the ashes of the heifer must also wash his clothes, and he will remain ceremonially unclean until evening. This is a permanent law for the people of Israel and any foreigners who live among them.

11"All those who touch a dead human body will be ceremonially unclean for seven days. 12They must purify themselves on the third and seventh days with the water of purification; then they will be purified. But if they do not do this on the third and seventh days, they will continue to be unclean even after the seventh day. 13All those who touch a dead body and do not purify themselves in the proper way defile the LORD's Tabernacle, and they will be cut off from the community of Israel. Since the water of purification was not sprinkled on them, their defilement continues.

14"This is the ritual law that applies when someone dies inside a tent: All those who enter that tent and those who were inside when the death occurred will be ceremonially unclean for seven days. 15Any open container in the tent that was not covered with a lid is also defiled. 16And if someone in an open field touches the corpse of someone who was killed with a sword or who died a natural death, or if someone touches a human bone or a grave, that person will be defiled for seven days.

17"To remove the defilement, put some of the ashes from the burnt purification offering in a jar, and pour fresh water over them. 18Then someone who is ceremonially clean must take a hyssop branch and dip it into the water. That person must sprinkle the water on the tent, on all the furnishings in the tent, and on the people who were in the tent; also on the person who touched a human bone, or touched someone who was killed or who died naturally, or touched a grave. 19On the third and seventh days the person who is ceremonially clean must sprinkle the water on those who are defiled. Then on the seventh day the people being cleansed must wash their clothes and bathe themselves, and that evening they will be cleansed of their defilement.

20"But those who become defiled and do not purify themselves will be cut off from the community, for they have defiled the sanctuary of the LORD. Since the water of purification has not been sprinkled on them, they remain defiled. 21This is a permanent law for the people. Those who sprinkle the water of purification must afterward wash their clothes, and anyone who then touches the water used for purification will remain defiled until evening. 22Anything and anyone that a defiled person touches will be ceremonially unclean until evening."

20 MOSES STRIKES THE ROCK

In the first month of the year,* the whole community of Israel arrived in the wilderness of Zin and camped at Kadesh. While they were there, Miriam died and was buried.

CONFLICT 20:14-21

Moses negotiated and reasoned with the Edomite king. When nothing worked, he was left with two choices—force a conflict or avoid it. Moses knew there would be enough barriers in the days and months ahead. There was no point in adding another one unnecessarily. Sometimes conflict is unavoidable. At other times, however, it isn't worth the consequences. Open warfare may seem heroic, courageous, and even righteous, but it is not always the best choice. When we can find another way to solve our problems, even if it is harder for us to do, we should consider Moses' example. ■

2There was no water for the people to drink at that place, so they rebelled against Moses and Aaron. 3The people blamed Moses and said, "If only we had died in the LORD's presence with our brothers! 4Why have you brought the congregation of the LORD's people into this wilderness to die, along with all our livestock? 5Why did you make us leave Egypt and bring us here to this terrible place? This land has no grain, no figs, no grapes, no pomegranates, and no water to drink!"

6Moses and Aaron turned away from the people and went to the entrance of the Tabernacle,* where they fell

19:4 Hebrew *the Tent of Meeting*. 19:6 Or *juniper*. 20:1 The first month of the ancient Hebrew lunar calendar usually occurs within the months of March and April. The number of years since leaving Egypt is not specified. 20:6 Hebrew *the Tent of Meeting*.

face down on the ground. Then the glorious presence of the LORD appeared to them, 7and the LORD said to Moses, 8"You and Aaron must take the staff and assemble the entire community. As the people watch, speak to the rock over there, and it will pour out its water. You will provide enough water from the rock to satisfy the whole community and their livestock."

9So Moses did as he was told. He took the staff from the place where it was kept before the LORD. 10Then he and Aaron summoned the people to come and gather at the rock. "Listen, you rebels!" he shouted. "Must we bring you water from this rock?" 11Then Moses raised his hand and struck the rock twice with the staff, and water gushed out. So the entire community and their livestock drank their fill.

ANGER

Jacob's father always cautions him about his temper: "Son, someday your temper will get you into big trouble. Learn to express yourself without getting so mad. Go read Galatians 5:22-23 and pray about your attitude, okay?"

Each time Jacob nods and apologizes. But the talks don't seem to accomplish much. Jacob still blows up. And he ends up in at least one fistfight per month.

Finally, Jacob's dad's prediction comes true.

At a postgame party, some guys from a rival school show up and start mouthing off. Words are exchanged. Tempers flare. Someone gets shoved. A punch is thrown. Suddenly, the friendly get-together erupts into a small-scale riot!

Jacob is in the thick of things, throwing punches left and right. He even chases both guys to their pickup truck. Before they can pull away, Jacob smashes the truck's rear window and headlight, and puts some major dents in the driver's door!

And that's when the police get involved. After receiving a call, they show up at Jacob's house. In his state of semi-shock, Jacob hears words like *assault, lawyer,* and *arrest.*

A few minutes of unchecked anger can produce serious heartache!

Read Numbers 20:1-12. Moses learned the terrible consequences of unchecked anger the hard way. You don't have to.

12But the LORD said to Moses and Aaron, "Because you did not trust me enough to demonstrate my holiness to the people of Israel, you will not lead them into the land I am giving them!" 13This place was known as the waters of Meribah (which means "arguing") because there the people of Israel argued with the LORD, and there he demonstrated his holiness among them.

EDOM REFUSES ISRAEL PASSAGE

14While Moses was at Kadesh, he sent ambassadors to the king of Edom with this message:

"This is what your relatives, the people of Israel, say: You know all the hardships we have been through. 15Our ancestors went down to Egypt, and we lived there a long time, and we and our ancestors were brutally mistreated by the Egyptians. 16But when we cried out to the LORD, he heard us and sent an angel who brought us out of Egypt. Now we are camped at Kadesh, a town on the border of your land. 17Please let us travel through your land. We will be careful not to go through your fields and vineyards. We won't even drink water from your wells. We will stay on the king's road and never leave it until we have passed through your territory."

18But the king of Edom said, "Stay out of my land, or I will meet you with an army!"

19The Israelites answered, "We will stay on the main road. If our livestock drink your water, we will pay for it. Just let us pass through your country. That's all we ask."

20But the king of Edom replied, "Stay out! You may not pass through our land." With that he mobilized his army and marched out against them with an imposing force. 21Because Edom refused to allow Israel to pass through their country, Israel was forced to turn around.

THE DEATH OF AARON

22The whole community of Israel left Kadesh and arrived at Mount Hor. 23There, on the border of the land of Edom, the LORD said to Moses and Aaron, 24"The time has come for Aaron to join his ancestors in death. He will not enter the land I am giving the people of Israel, because the two of you rebelled against my instructions concerning the water at Meribah. 25Now take Aaron and his son Eleazar up Mount Hor. 26There you will remove Aaron's priestly garments and put them on Eleazar, his son. Aaron will die there and join his ancestors."

27So Moses did as the LORD commanded. The three of them went up Mount Hor together as the whole community watched. 28At the summit, Moses removed the priestly garments from Aaron and put them on Eleazar, Aaron's son. Then Aaron died there on top of the mountain, and Moses and Eleazar went back down. 29When the people realized that Aaron had died, all Israel mourned for him thirty days.

21 VICTORY OVER THE CANAANITES

The Canaanite king of Arad, who lived in the Negev, heard that the Israelites were approaching on the road through Atharim. So he attacked the Israelites and took some of them as prisoners. 2Then the people of Israel made this vow to the LORD: "If you will hand these people over to us, we will completely destroy* all their towns."

21:2 The Hebrew term used here refers to the complete consecration of things or people to the LORD, either by destroying them or by giving them as an offering; also in 21:3.

3The LORD heard the Israelites' request and gave them
victory over the Canaanites. The Israelites completely destroyed them and their towns, and the place has been
called Hormah* ever since.

THE BRONZE SNAKE

4Then the people of Israel set out from Mount Hor, taking the road to the Red Sea* to go around the land of
Edom. But the people grew impatient with the long journey, 5and they began to speak against God and Moses.
"Why have you brought us out of Egypt to die here in the
wilderness?" they complained. "There is nothing to eat
here and nothing to drink. And we hate this horrible
manna!"

> **COMPLAINTS 21:5**
>
> **In Psalm 78, we learn the sources of Israel's complaining: (1) they forgot the miracles God did for them, (2) they demanded more than what God had given them, (3) their repentance was insincere, and (4) they were ungrateful for what God had done for them. Our complaining often has its roots in one of these actions and attitudes. It's like a weed. If we can cut off the source of complaining, it will not take hold and grow into bitterness or rebellion.** ■

6So the LORD sent poisonous snakes among the people,
and many were bitten and died. 7Then the people came to
Moses and cried out, "We have sinned by speaking
against the LORD and against you. Pray that the LORD will
take away the snakes." So Moses prayed for the people.
8Then the LORD told him, "Make a replica of a poisonous
snake and attach it to a pole. All who are bitten will live if
they simply look at it!" 9So Moses made a snake out of
bronze and attached it to a pole. Then anyone who was bitten by a snake could look at the bronze snake and be
healed!

ISRAEL'S JOURNEY TO MOAB

10The Israelites traveled next to Oboth and camped
there. 11Then they went on to Iye-abarim, in the wilderness on the eastern border of Moab. 12From there they
traveled to the valley of Zered Brook and set up camp.
13Then they moved out and camped on the far side of the
Arnon River, in the wilderness adjacent to the territory of
the Amorites. The Arnon is the boundary line between
the Moabites and the Amorites. 14For this reason *The
Book of the Wars of the LORD* speaks of "the town of Wa-
heb in the area of Suphah, and the ravines of the Arnon
River, 15and the ravines that extend as far as the settlement of Ar on the border of Moab."
16From there the Israelites traveled to Beer,* which is
the well where the LORD said to Moses, "Assemble the
people, and I will give them water." 17There the Israelites
sang this song:

"Spring up, O well!
Yes, sing its praises!
18 Sing of this well,
which princes dug,
which great leaders hollowed out
with their scepters and staffs."

Then the Israelites left the wilderness and proceeded
on through Mattanah, 19Nahaliel, and Bamoth. 20After
that they went to the valley in Moab where Pisgah Peak
overlooks the wasteland.*

VICTORY OVER SIHON AND OG

21The Israelites sent ambassadors to King Sihon of the
Amorites with this message:

22"Let us travel through your land. We will be careful
not to go through your fields and vineyards. We
won't even drink water from your wells. We will stay
on the king's road until we have passed through your
territory."

23But King Sihon refused to let them cross his territory. Instead, he mobilized his entire army and attacked
Israel in the wilderness, engaging them in battle at Jahaz.
24But the Israelites slaughtered them with their swords
and occupied their land from the Arnon River to the
Jabbok River. They went only as far as the Ammonite border because the boundary of the Ammonites was
fortified.*
25So Israel captured all the towns of the Amorites and
settled in them, including the city of Heshbon and its surrounding villages. 26Heshbon had been the capital of
King Sihon of the Amorites. He had defeated a former
Moabite king and seized all his land as far as the Arnon
River. 27Therefore, the ancient poets wrote this about
him:

"Come to Heshbon and let it be rebuilt!
Let the city of Sihon be restored.
28 A fire flamed forth from Heshbon,
a blaze from the city of Sihon.
It burned the city of Ar in Moab;
it destroyed the rulers of the Arnon heights.
29 What sorrow awaits you, O people of Moab!
You are finished, O worshipers of Chemosh!
Chemosh has left his sons as refugees,
his daughters as captives of Sihon, the Amorite
king.
30 We have utterly destroyed them,
from Heshbon to Dibon.
We have completely wiped them out
as far away as Nophah and Medeba.*"

31So the people of Israel occupied the territory of the
Amorites. 32After Moses sent men to explore the Jazer
area, they captured all the towns in the region and drove

21:3 *Hormah* means "destruction." 21:4 Hebrew *sea of reeds.* 21:16 *Beer* means "well." 21:20 Or *overlooks Jeshimon.* 21:24 Or *because the terrain of the Ammonite frontier was rugged;* Hebrew reads *because the boundary of the Ammonites was strong.* 21:30 Or *until fire spread to Medeba.* The meaning of the Hebrew is uncertain.

out the Amorites who lived there. 33Then they turned and marched up the road to Bashan, but King Og of Bashan and all his people attacked them at Edrei. 34The LORD said to Moses, "Do not be afraid of him, for I have handed him over to you, along with all his people and his land. Do the same to him as you did to King Sihon of the Amorites, who ruled in Heshbon." 35And Israel killed King Og, his sons, and all his subjects; not a single survivor remained. Then Israel occupied their land.

STEPS TO VICTORY 21:34-35

God assured Moses that Israel's enemy was conquered even before the battle began! God wants to give us victory over our enemies, which usually are problems related to sin, rather than armed soldiers. First, we must believe that he can help us. Second, we must trust him to help us. Third, we must take the steps he shows us. ■

22

BALAK SENDS FOR BALAAM

Then the people of Israel traveled to the plains of Moab and camped east of the Jordan River, across from Jericho. 2Balak son of Zippor, the Moabite king, had seen everything the Israelites did to the Amorites. 3And when the people of Moab saw how many Israelites there were, they were terrified. 4The king of Moab said to the elders of Midian, "This mob will devour everything in sight, like an ox devours grass in the field!"

So Balak, king of Moab, 5sent messengers to call Balaam son of Beor, who was living in his native land of Pethor* near the Euphrates River.* His message said:

> "Look, a vast horde of people has arrived from Egypt. They cover the face of the earth and are threatening me. 6Please come and curse these people for me because they are too powerful for me. Then perhaps I will be able to conquer them and drive them from the land. I know that blessings fall on any people you bless, and curses fall on people you curse."

7Balak's messengers, who were elders of Moab and Midian, set out with money to pay Balaam to place a curse upon Israel.* They went to Balaam and delivered Balak's message to him. 8"Stay here overnight," Balaam said. "In the morning I will tell you whatever the LORD directs me to say." So the officials from Moab stayed there with Balaam.

9That night God came to Balaam and asked him, "Who are these men visiting you?"

10Balaam said to God, "Balak son of Zippor, king of Moab, has sent me this message: 11'Look, a vast horde of people has arrived from Egypt, and they cover the face of the earth. Come and curse these people for me. Then perhaps I will be able to stand up to them and drive them from the land.'"

12But God told Balaam, "Do not go with them. You are not to curse these people, for they have been blessed!"

13The next morning Balaam got up and told Balak's officials, "Go on home! The LORD will not let me go with you."

14So the Moabite officials returned to King Balak and reported, "Balaam refused to come with us." 15Then Balak tried again. This time he sent a larger number of even more distinguished officials than those he had sent the first time. 16They went to Balaam and delivered this message to him:

> "This is what Balak son of Zippor says: Please don't let anything stop you from coming to help me. 17I will pay you very well and do whatever you tell me. Just come and curse these people for me!"

18But Balaam responded to Balak's messengers, "Even if Balak were to give me his palace filled with silver and gold, I would be powerless to do anything against the will of the LORD my God. 19But stay here one more night, and I will see if the LORD has anything else to say to me."

20That night God came to Balaam and told him, "Since these men have come for you, get up and go with them. But do only what I tell you to do."

BLIND GREED 22:20-23

Although God allowed Balaam to go with Balak's messengers, he was angry about Balaam's greedy attitude. The wealth offered by the king blinded Balaam to God's efforts to stop him. Though we may know what God wants us to do, we can become blinded by our desire for money, possessions, or prestige. We can avoid Balaam's mistake by looking past the allure of fame or fortune to the long-range benefits of following God. ■

BALAAM AND HIS DONKEY

21So the next morning Balaam got up, saddled his donkey, and started off with the Moabite officials. 22But God was angry that Balaam was going, so he sent the angel of the LORD to stand in the road to block his way. As Balaam and two servants were riding along, 23Balaam's donkey saw the angel of the LORD standing in the road with a drawn sword in his hand. The donkey bolted off the road into a field, but Balaam beat it and turned it back onto the road. 24Then the angel of the LORD stood at a place where the road narrowed between two vineyard walls. 25When the donkey saw the angel of the LORD, it tried to squeeze by and crushed Balaam's foot against the wall. So Balaam beat the donkey again. 26Then the angel of the LORD moved farther down the road and stood in a place too narrow for the donkey to get by at all. 27This time when the donkey saw the angel, it lay down under Balaam. In a fit of rage Balaam beat the animal again with his staff.

22:5a Or *who was at Pethor in the land of the Amavites.* **22:5b** Hebrew *the river.* **22:7** Hebrew *set out with the money of divination in their hand.*

28 Then the LORD gave the donkey the ability to speak. "What have I done to you that deserves your beating me three times?" it asked Balaam.

29 "You have made me look like a fool!" Balaam shouted. "If I had a sword with me, I would kill you!"

30 "But I am the same donkey you have ridden all your life," the donkey answered. "Have I ever done anything like this before?"

"No," Balaam admitted.

31 Then the LORD opened Balaam's eyes, and he saw the angel of the LORD standing in the roadway with a drawn sword in his hand. Balaam bowed his head and fell face down on the ground before him.

32 "Why did you beat your donkey those three times?" the angel of the LORD demanded. "Look, I have come to block your way because you are stubbornly resisting me. 33 Three times the donkey saw me and shied away; otherwise, I would certainly have killed you by now and spared the donkey."

34 Then Balaam confessed to the angel of the LORD, "I have sinned. I didn't realize you were standing in the road to block my way. I will return home if you are against my going."

35 But the angel of the LORD told Balaam, "Go with these men, but say only what I tell you to say." So Balaam went on with Balak's officials. 36 When King Balak heard that Balaam was on the way, he went out to meet him at a Moabite town on the Arnon River at the farthest border of his land.

37 "Didn't I send you an urgent invitation? Why didn't you come right away?" Balak asked Balaam. "Didn't you believe me when I said I would reward you richly?"

38 Balaam replied, "Look, now I have come, but I have no power to say whatever I want. I will speak only the message that God puts in my mouth." 39 Then Balaam accompanied Balak to Kiriath-huzoth, 40 where the king sacrificed cattle and sheep. He sent portions of the meat to Balaam and the officials who were with him. 41 The next morning Balak took Balaam up to Bamoth-baal. From there he could see some of the people of Israel spread out below him.

23

BALAAM BLESSES ISRAEL

Then Balaam said to King Balak, "Build me seven altars here, and prepare seven young bulls and seven rams for me to sacrifice." 2 Balak followed his instructions, and the two of them sacrificed a young bull and a ram on each altar.

3 Then Balaam said to Balak, "Stand here by your burnt offerings, and I will go to see if the LORD will respond to me. Then I will tell you whatever he reveals to me." So Balaam went alone to the top of a bare hill, 4 and God met him there. Balaam said to him, "I have prepared seven altars and have sacrificed a young bull and a ram on each altar."

5 The LORD gave Balaam a message for King Balak. Then he said, "Go back to Balak and give him my message."

6 So Balaam returned and found the king standing beside his burnt offerings with all the officials of Moab. 7 This was the message Balaam delivered:

"Balak summoned me to come from Aram;
the king of Moab brought me from the eastern hills.
'Come,' he said, 'curse Jacob for me!
Come and announce Israel's doom.'
8 But how can I curse those
whom God has not cursed?
How can I condemn those
whom the LORD has not condemned?
9 I see them from the cliff tops;
I watch them from the hills.
I see a people who live by themselves,
set apart from other nations.
10 Who can count Jacob's descendants, as numerous as dust?
Who can count even a fourth of Israel's people?
Let me die like the righteous;
let my life end like theirs."

11 Then King Balak demanded of Balaam, "What have you done to me? I brought you to curse my enemies. Instead, you have blessed them!"

12 But Balaam replied, "I will speak only the message that the LORD puts in my mouth."

BALAAM'S SECOND MESSAGE

13 Then King Balak told him, "Come with me to another place. There you will see another part of the nation of Israel, but not all of them. Curse at least that many!" 14 So Balak took Balaam to the plateau of Zophim on Pisgah Peak. He built seven altars there and offered a young bull and a ram on each altar.

15 Then Balaam said to the king, "Stand here by your burnt offerings while I go over there to meet the LORD."

16 And the LORD met Balaam and gave him a message. Then he said, "Go back to Balak and give him my message."

17 So Balaam returned and found the king standing beside his burnt offerings with all the officials of Moab. "What did the LORD say?" Balak asked eagerly.

18 This was the message Balaam delivered:

"Rise up, Balak, and listen!
Hear me, son of Zippor.
19 God is not a man, so he does not lie.
He is not human, so he does not change his mind.
Has he ever spoken and failed to act?
Has he ever promised and not carried it through?
20 Listen, I received a command to bless;
God has blessed, and I cannot reverse it!
21 No misfortune is in his plan for Jacob;
no trouble is in store for Israel.
For the LORD their God is with them;
he has been proclaimed their king.
22 God brought them out of Egypt;
for them he is as strong as a wild ox.

23 No curse can touch Jacob;
no magic has any power against Israel.
For now it will be said of Jacob,
'What wonders God has done for Israel!'
24 These people rise up like a lioness,
like a majestic lion rousing itself.
They refuse to rest
until they have feasted on prey,
drinking the blood of the slaughtered!"

25Then Balak said to Balaam, "Fine, but if you won't curse them, at least don't bless them!"

26But Balaam replied to Balak, "Didn't I tell you that I can do only what the LORD tells me?"

BALAAM'S THIRD MESSAGE

27Then King Balak said to Balaam, "Come, I will take you to one more place. Perhaps it will please God to let you curse them from there."

A NEW VIEW 23:27

King Balak took Balaam to several places to entice him to curse the Israelites. He thought a change of scenery might help change Balaam's mind. But changing locations won't change God's will. Facing the source of our problems, especially if that source is an attitude we have, is a better choice. To make a change in geography or a change in jobs may only cloud the need for a change in heart. ■

28So Balak took Balaam to the top of Mount Peor, overlooking the wasteland.* 29Balaam again told Balak, "Build me seven altars, and prepare seven young bulls and seven rams for me to sacrifice." 30So Balak did as Balaam ordered and offered a young bull and a ram on each altar.

24 By now Balaam realized that the LORD was
determined to bless Israel, so he did not resort to divination as before. Instead, he turned and looked out toward
the wilderness, 2where he saw the people of Israel
camped, tribe by tribe. Then the Spirit of God came upon
him, 3and this is the message he delivered:

"This is the message of Balaam son of Beor,
the message of the man whose eyes see clearly,
4 the message of one who hears the words of God,
who sees a vision from the Almighty,
who bows down with eyes wide open:
5 How beautiful are your tents, O Jacob;
how lovely are your homes, O Israel!
6 They spread before me like palm groves,*
like gardens by the riverside.
They are like tall trees planted by the LORD,
like cedars beside the waters.
7 Water will flow from their buckets;
their offspring have all they need.
Their king will be greater than Agag;
their kingdom will be exalted.
8 God brought them out of Egypt;
for them he is as strong as a wild ox.
He devours all the nations that oppose him,
breaking their bones in pieces,
shooting them with arrows.
9 Like a lion, Israel crouches and lies down;
like a lioness, who dares to arouse her?
Blessed is everyone who blesses you, O Israel,
and cursed is everyone who curses you."

10King Balak flew into a rage against Balaam. He angrily clapped his hands and shouted, "I called you to
curse my enemies! Instead, you have blessed them three
times. 11Now get out of here! Go back home! I promised
to reward you richly, but the LORD has kept you from your
reward."
12Balaam told Balak, "Don't you remember what I told
your messengers? I said, 13'Even if Balak were to give me
his palace filled with silver and gold, I would be powerless to do anything against the will of the LORD.' I told you
that I could say only what the LORD says! 14Now I am returning to my own people. But first let me tell you what
the Israelites will do to your people in the future."

BALAAM'S FINAL MESSAGES

15This is the message Balaam delivered:

"This is the message of Balaam son of Beor,
the message of the man whose eyes see clearly,
16 the message of one who hears the words of God,
who has knowledge from the Most High,
who sees a vision from the Almighty,
who bows down with eyes wide open:
17 I see him, but not here and now.
I perceive him, but far in the distant future.
A star will rise from Jacob;
a scepter will emerge from Israel.
It will crush the foreheads of Moab's people,
cracking the skulls of the people of Sheth.
18 Edom will be taken over,
and Seir, its enemy, will be conquered,
while Israel marches on in triumph.
19 A ruler will rise in Jacob
who will destroy the survivors of Ir."

20Then Balaam looked over toward the people of Amalek and delivered this message:

"Amalek was the greatest of nations,
but its destiny is destruction!"

21Then he looked over toward the Kenites and delivered this message:

"Your home is secure;
your nest is set in the rocks.

23:28 Or *overlooking Jeshimon.* 24:6 Or *like a majestic valley.*

[22] But the Kenites will be destroyed
when Assyria* takes you captive."

[23]Balaam concluded his messages by saying:

"Alas, who can survive
unless God has willed it?
[24] Ships will come from the coasts of Cyprus*;
they will oppress Assyria and afflict Eber,
but they, too, will be utterly destroyed."

[25]Then Balaam and Balak returned to their homes.

25 MOAB SEDUCES ISRAEL

While the Israelites were camped at Acacia Grove,* some of the men defiled themselves by having* sexual relations with local Moabite women. [2]These women invited them to attend sacrifices to their gods, so the Israelites feasted with them and worshiped the gods of Moab. [3]In this way, Israel joined in the worship of Baal of Peor, causing the LORD's anger to blaze against his people.

[4]The LORD issued the following command to Moses: "Seize all the ringleaders and execute them before the LORD in broad daylight, so his fierce anger will turn away from the people of Israel."

[5]So Moses ordered Israel's judges, "Each of you must put to death the men under your authority who have joined in worshiping Baal of Peor."

RIGHTEOUS ANGER 25:6-11

It is clear from Phinehas's story that some anger is proper and justified. (Phinehas's case was unique, however.) But how can we know when our anger is appropriate and when it should be restrained? You might ask yourself these questions when you become angry: (1) Why am I angry? (2) Whose rights are being violated (mine or another's)? (3) Is the truth (a principle of God) being violated? If only your rights are at stake, it may be wiser to keep angry feelings under control. But if the truth is at stake, anger often is justified, although violence and revenge are usually the wrong way to express it. ■

[6]Just then one of the Israelite men brought a Midianite woman into his tent, right before the eyes of Moses and all the people, as everyone was weeping at the entrance of the Tabernacle.* [7]When Phinehas son of Eleazar and grandson of Aaron the priest saw this, he jumped up and left the assembly. He took a spear [8]and rushed after the man into his tent. Phinehas thrust the spear all the way through the man's body and into the woman's stomach. So the plague against the Israelites was stopped, [9]but not before 24,000 people had died.

[10]Then the LORD said to Moses, [11]"Phinehas son of Eleazar and grandson of Aaron the priest has turned my anger away from the Israelites by being as zealous among them as I was. So I stopped destroying all Israel as I had intended to do in my zealous anger. [12]Now tell him that I am making my special covenant of peace with him. [13]In this covenant, I give him and his descendants a permanent right to the priesthood, for in his zeal for me, his God, he purified the people of Israel, making them right with me.*"

[14]The Israelite man killed with the Midianite woman was named Zimri son of Salu, the leader of a family from the tribe of Simeon. [15]The woman's name was Cozbi; she was the daughter of Zur, the leader of a Midianite clan.

[16]Then the LORD said to Moses, [17]"Attack the Midianites and destroy them, [18]because they assaulted you with deceit and tricked you into worshiping Baal of Peor, and because of Cozbi, the daughter of a Midianite leader, who was killed at the time of the plague because of what happened at Peor."

26 THE SECOND REGISTRATION OF ISRAEL'S TROOPS

After the plague had ended, the LORD said to Moses and to Eleazar son of Aaron the priest, [2]"From the whole community of Israel, record the names of all the warriors by their families. List all the men twenty years old or older who are able to go to war."

[3]So there on the plains of Moab beside the Jordan River, across from Jericho, Moses and Eleazar the priest issued these instructions to the leaders of Israel: [4]"List all the men of Israel twenty years old and older, just as the LORD commanded Moses."

This is the record of all the descendants of Israel who came out of Egypt.

THE TRIBE OF REUBEN

[5]These were the clans descended from the sons of Reuben, Jacob's* oldest son:

The Hanochite clan, named after their ancestor Hanoch.
The Palluite clan, named after their ancestor Pallu.
[6] The Hezronite clan, named after their ancestor Hezron.
The Carmite clan, named after their ancestor Carmi.

[7]These were the clans of Reuben. Their registered troops numbered 43,730.

[8]Pallu was the ancestor of Eliab, [9]and Eliab was the father of Nemuel, Dathan, and Abiram. This Dathan and Abiram are the same community leaders who conspired with Korah against Moses and Aaron, rebelling against the LORD. [10]But the earth opened up its mouth and swallowed them with Korah, and fire devoured 250 of their followers. This served as a warning to the entire nation of Israel. [11]However, the sons of Korah did not die that day.

24:22 Hebrew *Asshur;* also in 24:24. **24:24** Hebrew *Kittim.* **25:1a** Hebrew *Shittim.* **25:1b** As in Greek version; Hebrew reads *some of the men began having.* **25:6** Hebrew *the Tent of Meeting.* **25:13** Or *he made atonement for the people of Israel.* **26:5** Hebrew *Israel's;* see note on 1:20-21b.

THE TRIBE OF SIMEON

[12]These were the clans descended from the sons of Simeon:
The Jemuelite clan, named after their ancestor Jemuel.*
The Jaminite clan, named after their ancestor Jamin.
The Jakinite clan, named after their ancestor Jakin.
13 The Zoharite clan, named after their ancestor Zohar.*
The Shaulite clan, named after their ancestor Shaul.

[14]These were the clans of Simeon. Their registered troops numbered 22,200.

THE TRIBE OF GAD

[15]These were the clans descended from the sons of Gad:
The Zephonite clan, named after their ancestor Zephon.
The Haggite clan, named after their ancestor Haggi.
The Shunite clan, named after their ancestor Shuni.
16 The Oznite clan, named after their ancestor Ozni.
The Erite clan, named after their ancestor Eri.
17 The Arodite clan, named after their ancestor Arodi.*
The Arelite clan, named after their ancestor Areli.

[18]These were the clans of Gad. Their registered troops numbered 40,500.

THE TRIBE OF JUDAH

[19]Judah had two sons, Er and Onan, who had died in the land of Canaan. [20]These were the clans descended from Judah's surviving sons:
The Shelanite clan, named after their ancestor Shelah.
The Perezite clan, named after their ancestor Perez.
The Zerahite clan, named after their ancestor Zerah.

[21]These were the subclans descended from the Perezites:
The Hezronites, named after their ancestor Hezron.
The Hamulites, named after their ancestor Hamul.

[22]These were the clans of Judah. Their registered troops numbered 76,500.

THE TRIBE OF ISSACHAR

[23]These were the clans descended from the sons of Issachar:
The Tolaite clan, named after their ancestor Tola.
The Puite clan, named after their ancestor Puah.*
24 The Jashubite clan, named after their ancestor Jashub.
The Shimronite clan, named after their ancestor Shimron.

[25]These were the clans of Issachar. Their registered troops numbered 64,300.

THE TRIBE OF ZEBULUN

[26]These were the clans descended from the sons of Zebulun:
The Seredite clan, named after their ancestor Sered.
The Elonite clan, named after their ancestor Elon.
The Jahleelite clan, named after their ancestor Jahleel.

[27]These were the clans of Zebulun. Their registered troops numbered 60,500.

THE TRIBE OF MANASSEH

[28]Two clans were descended from Joseph through Manasseh and Ephraim.

[29]These were the clans descended from Manasseh:
The Makirite clan, named after their ancestor Makir.
The Gileadite clan, named after their ancestor Gilead, Makir's son.

[30]These were the subclans descended from the Gileadites:
The Iezerites, named after their ancestor Iezer.
The Helekites, named after their ancestor Helek.
31 The Asrielites, named after their ancestor Asriel.
The Shechemites, named after their ancestor Shechem.
32 The Shemidaites, named after their ancestor Shemida.
The Hepherites, named after their ancestor Hepher.
33 (One of Hepher's descendants, Zelophehad, had no sons, but his daughters' names were Mahlah, Noah, Hoglah, Milcah, and Tirzah.)

[34]These were the clans of Manasseh. Their registered troops numbered 52,700.

THE TRIBE OF EPHRAIM

[35]These were the clans descended from the sons of Ephraim:
The Shuthelahite clan, named after their ancestor Shuthelah.
The Bekerite clan, named after their ancestor Beker.
The Tahanite clan, named after their ancestor Tahan.

[36]This was the subclan descended from the Shuthelahites:
The Eranites, named after their ancestor Eran.

[37]These were the clans of Ephraim. Their registered troops numbered 32,500.

These clans of Manasseh and Ephraim were all descendants of Joseph.

THE TRIBE OF BENJAMIN

[38]These were the clans descended from the sons of Benjamin:
The Belaite clan, named after their ancestor Bela.
The Ashbelite clan, named after their ancestor Ashbel.

26:12 As in Syriac version (see also Gen 46:10; Exod 6:15); Hebrew reads *Nemuelite . . . Nemuel.* **26:13** As in parallel texts at Gen 46:10 and Exod 6:15; Hebrew reads *Zerahite . . . Zerah.* **26:17** As in Samaritan Pentateuch and Greek and Syriac versions (see also Gen 46:16); Hebrew reads *Arod.* **26:23** As in Samaritan Pentateuch, Greek and Syriac versions, and Latin Vulgate (see also 1 Chr 7:1); Hebrew reads *The Punite clan, named after its ancestor Puvah.*

The Ahiramite clan, named after their ancestor Ahiram.
39 The Shuphamite clan, named after their ancestor Shupham.*
The Huphamite clan, named after their ancestor Hupham.

40These were the subclans descended from the Belaites:
The Ardites, named after their ancestor Ard.*
The Naamites, named after their ancestor Naaman.

41These were the clans of Benjamin. Their registered troops numbered 45,600.

THE TRIBE OF DAN

42These were the clans descended from the sons of Dan:
The Shuhamite clan, named after their ancestor Shuham.

43These were the Shuhamite clans of Dan. Their registered troops numbered 64,400.

THE TRIBE OF ASHER

44These were the clans descended from the sons of Asher:
The Imnite clan, named after their ancestor Imnah.
The Ishvite clan, named after their ancestor Ishvi.
The Beriite clan, named after their ancestor Beriah.

45These were the subclans descended from the Beriites:
The Heberites, named after their ancestor Heber.
The Malkielites, named after their ancestor Malkiel.

46Asher also had a daughter named Serah.

47These were the clans of Asher. Their registered troops numbered 53,400.

THE TRIBE OF NAPHTALI

48These were the clans descended from the sons of Naphtali:
The Jahzeelite clan, named after their ancestor Jahzeel.
The Gunite clan, named after their ancestor Guni.
49 The Jezerite clan, named after their ancestor Jezer.
The Shillemite clan, named after their ancestor Shillem.

50These were the clans of Naphtali. Their registered troops numbered 45,400.

RESULTS OF THE REGISTRATION

51In summary, the registered troops of all Israel numbered 601,730.

52Then the Lord said to Moses, 53"Divide the land among the tribes, and distribute the grants of land in proportion to the tribes' populations, as indicated by the number of names on the list. 54Give the larger tribes more land and the smaller tribes less land, each group receiving a grant in proportion to the size of its population. 55But you must assign the land by lot, and give land to each ancestral tribe according to the number of names on the list. 56Each grant of land must be assigned by lot among the larger and smaller tribal groups."

THE TRIBE OF LEVI

57This is the record of the Levites who were counted according to their clans:
The Gershonite clan, named after their ancestor Gershon.
The Kohathite clan, named after their ancestor Kohath.
The Merarite clan, named after their ancestor Merari.

58The Libnites, the Hebronites, the Mahlites, the Mushites, and the Korahites were all subclans of the Levites.
Now Kohath was the ancestor of Amram, 59and Amram's wife was named Jochebed. She also was a descendant of Levi, born among the Levites in the land of Egypt. Amram and Jochebed became the parents of Aaron, Moses, and their sister, Miriam. 60To Aaron were born Nadab, Abihu, Eleazar, and Ithamar. 61But Nadab and Abihu died when they burned before the Lord the wrong kind of fire, different than he had commanded.

62The men from the Levite clans who were one month old or older numbered 23,000. But the Levites were not included in the registration of the rest of the people of Israel because they were not given an allotment of land when it was divided among the Israelites.

QUIET WORK 26:1-65

Thirty-eight years had elapsed since the first great census in chapter one of Numbers. During that time, every Israelite man and woman over 20 years of age—except Caleb, Joshua, and Moses—had died; yet God's laws and the spiritual character of the nation were still intact. This quiet but powerful miracle is often overlooked. God often works in quiet ways in our day to bring about his long-range purposes. ■

63So these are the results of the registration of the people of Israel as conducted by Moses and Eleazar the priest on the plains of Moab beside the Jordan River, across from Jericho. 64Not one person on this list had been among those listed in the previous registration taken by Moses and Aaron in the wilderness of Sinai. 65For the Lord had said of them, "They will all die in the wilderness." Not one of them survived except Caleb son of Jephunneh and Joshua son of Nun.

26:39 As in some Hebrew manuscripts, Samaritan Pentateuch, Greek and Syriac versions, and Latin Vulgate; most Hebrew manuscripts read *Shephupham*. 26:40 As in Samaritan Pentateuch, some Greek manuscripts, and Latin Vulgate; Hebrew lacks *named after their ancestor Ard.*

27 THE DAUGHTERS OF ZELOPHEHAD

One day a petition was presented by the daughters of Zelophehad—Mahlah, Noah, Hoglah, Milcah, and Tirzah. Their father, Zelophehad, was a descendant of Hepher son of Gilead, son of Makir, son of Manasseh, son of Joseph. 2These women stood before Moses, Eleazar the priest, the tribal leaders, and the entire community at the entrance of the Tabernacle.* 3"Our father died in the wilderness," they said. "He was not among Korah's followers, who rebelled against the LORD; he died because of his own sin. But he had no sons. 4Why should the name of our father disappear from his clan just because he had no sons? Give us property along with the rest of our relatives."

5So Moses brought their case before the LORD. 6And the LORD replied to Moses, 7"The claim of the daughters of Zelophehad is legitimate. You must give them a grant of land along with their father's relatives. Assign them the property that would have been given to their father.

8"And give the following instructions to the people of Israel: If a man dies and has no son, then give his inheritance to his daughters. 9And if he has no daughter either, transfer his inheritance to his brothers. 10If he has no brothers, give his inheritance to his father's brothers. 11But if his father has no brothers, give his inheritance to the nearest relative in his clan. This is a legal requirement for the people of Israel, just as the LORD commanded Moses."

JOSHUA CHOSEN TO LEAD ISRAEL

12One day the LORD said to Moses, "Climb one of the mountains east of the river,* and look out over the land I have given the people of Israel. 13After you have seen it, you will die like your brother, Aaron, 14for you both rebelled against my instructions in the wilderness of Zin. When the people of Israel rebelled, you failed to demonstrate my holiness to them at the waters." (These are the waters of Meribah at Kadesh* in the wilderness of Zin.)

15Then Moses said to the LORD, 16"O LORD, you are the God who gives breath to all creatures. Please appoint a new man as leader for the community. 17Give them someone who will guide them wherever they go and will lead them into battle, so the community of the LORD will not be like sheep without a shepherd."

18The LORD replied, "Take Joshua son of Nun, who has the Spirit in him, and lay your hands on him. 19Present him to Eleazar the priest before the whole community, and publicly commission him to lead the people. 20Transfer some of your authority to him so the whole community of Israel will obey him. 21When direction from the LORD is needed, Joshua will stand before Eleazar the priest, who will use the Urim—one of the sacred lots cast before the LORD—to determine his will. This is how Joshua and the rest of the community of Israel will determine everything they should do."

22So Moses did as the LORD commanded. He presented Joshua to Eleazar the priest and the whole community. 23Moses laid his hands on him and commissioned him to lead the people, just as the LORD had commanded through Moses.

28 THE DAILY OFFERINGS

The LORD said to Moses, 2"Give these instructions to the people of Israel: The offerings you present as special gifts are a pleasing aroma to me; they are my food. See to it that they are brought at the appointed times and offered according to my instructions.

> **GETTING READY FOR WORSHIP 28:1-2**
>
> **Offerings had to be brought to the Tabernacle regularly and carried out a certain way under the supervision of the priests. The people had to undergo a period of preparation to be sure they were ready for worship. During this time of preparation, they didn't have time to focus on idols or other distractions. God is pleased today when we allow nothing to come between him and us. How do you prepare to worship God?** ■

3"Say to the people: This is the special gift you must present to the LORD as your daily burnt offering. You must offer two one-year-old male lambs with no defects. 4Sacrifice one lamb in the morning and the other in the evening. 5With each lamb you must offer a grain offering of two quarts* of choice flour mixed with one quart* of pure oil of pressed olives. 6This is the regular burnt offering instituted at Mount Sinai as a special gift, a pleasing aroma to the LORD. 7Along with it you must present the proper liquid offering of one quart of alcoholic drink with each lamb, poured out in the Holy Place as an offering to the LORD. 8Offer the second lamb in the evening with the same grain offering and liquid offering. It, too, is a special gift, a pleasing aroma to the LORD.

THE SABBATH OFFERINGS

9"On the Sabbath day, sacrifice two one-year-old male lambs with no defects. They must be accompanied by a grain offering of four quarts* of choice flour moistened with olive oil, and a liquid offering. 10This is the burnt offering to be presented each Sabbath day, in addition to the regular burnt offering and its accompanying liquid offering.

THE MONTHLY OFFERINGS

11"On the first day of each month, present an extra burnt offering to the LORD of two young bulls, one ram, and seven one-year-old male lambs, all with no defects. 12These must be accompanied by grain offerings of choice flour moistened with olive oil—six quarts* with

27:2 Hebrew *the Tent of Meeting.* **27:12** Or *the mountains of Abarim.* **27:14** Hebrew *waters of Meribah-kadesh.* **28:5a** Hebrew *1/10 of an ephah* [2.2 liters]; also in 28:13, 21, 29. **28:5b** Hebrew *1/4 of a hin* [1 liter]; also in 28:7. **28:9** Hebrew *2/10 of an ephah* [4.4 liters]; also in 28:12, 20, 28. **28:12** Hebrew *3/10 of an ephah* [6.6 liters]; also in 28:20, 28.

each bull, four quarts with the ram, 13and two quarts with each lamb. This burnt offering will be a special gift, a pleasing aroma to the LORD. 14You must also present a liquid offering with each sacrifice: two quarts* of wine for each bull, a third of a gallon* for the ram, and one quart* for each lamb. Present this monthly burnt offering on the first day of each month throughout the year.

15"On the first day of each month, you must also offer one male goat for a sin offering to the LORD. This is in addition to the regular burnt offering and its accompanying liquid offering.

OFFERINGS FOR THE PASSOVER

16"On the fourteenth day of the first month,* you must celebrate the LORD's Passover. 17On the following day—the fifteenth day of the month—a joyous, seven-day festival will begin, but no bread made with yeast may be eaten. 18The first day of the festival will be an official day for holy assembly, and no ordinary work may be done on that day. 19As a special gift you must present a burnt offering to the LORD—two young bulls, one ram, and seven one-year-old male lambs, all with no defects. 20These will be accompanied by grain offerings of choice flour moistened with olive oil—six quarts with each bull, four quarts with the ram, 21and two quarts with each of the seven lambs. 22You must also offer a male goat as a sin offering to purify yourselves and make yourselves right with the LORD.* 23Present these offerings in addition to your regular morning burnt offering. 24On each of the seven days of the festival, this is how you must prepare the food offering that is presented as a special gift, a pleasing aroma to the LORD. These will be offered in addition to the regular burnt offerings and liquid offerings. 25The seventh day of the festival will be another official day for holy assembly, and no ordinary work may be done on that day.

OFFERINGS FOR THE FESTIVAL OF HARVEST

26"At the Festival of Harvest,* when you present the first of your new grain to the LORD, you must call an official day for holy assembly, and you may do no ordinary work on that day. 27Present a special burnt offering on that day as a pleasing aroma to the LORD. It will consist of two young bulls, one ram, and seven one-year-old male lambs. 28These will be accompanied by grain offerings of choice flour moistened with olive oil—six quarts with each bull, four quarts with the ram, 29and two quarts with each of the seven lambs. 30Also, offer one male goat to purify yourselves and make yourselves right with the LORD. 31Prepare these special burnt offerings, along with their liquid offerings, in addition to the regular burnt offering and its accompanying grain offering. Be sure that all the animals you sacrifice have no defects.

29

OFFERINGS FOR THE FESTIVAL OF TRUMPETS

"Celebrate the Festival of Trumpets each year on the first day of the appointed month in early autumn.* You must call an official day for holy assembly, and you may do no ordinary work. 2On that day you must present a burnt offering as a pleasing aroma to the LORD. It will consist of one young bull, one ram, and seven one-year-old male lambs, all with no defects. 3These must be accompanied by grain offerings of choice flour moistened with olive oil—six quarts* with the bull, four quarts* with the ram, 4and two quarts* with each of the seven lambs. 5In addition, you must sacrifice a male goat as a sin offering to purify yourselves and make yourselves right with the LORD.* 6These special sacrifices are in addition to your regular monthly and daily burnt offerings, and they must be given with their prescribed grain offerings and liquid offerings. These offerings are given as a special gift to the LORD, a pleasing aroma to him.

WORSHIP TODAY 29:1-2

The Festival of Trumpets demonstrated three important principles that we can follow as we worship God: (1) The people gathered together to celebrate and worship. There is something special about worshiping with other believers. (2) The normal daily routine was suspended and no hard work was done. Setting aside the time to worship without distractions allows us to prepare our hearts before and reflect afterward. (3) The people sacrificed animals as burnt offerings to God. We show our commitment to God when we give something of value to him. The best gift, of course, is our complete loyalty to God. ■

OFFERINGS FOR THE DAY OF ATONEMENT

7"Ten days later, on the tenth day of the same month,* you must call another holy assembly. On that day, the Day of Atonement, the people must go without food and must do no ordinary work. 8You must present a burnt offering as a pleasing aroma to the LORD. It will consist of one young bull, one ram, and seven one-year-old male lambs, all with no defects. 9These offerings must be accompanied by the prescribed grain offerings of choice flour moistened with olive oil—six quarts of choice flour with the bull, four quarts of choice flour with the ram, 10and two quarts of choice flour with each of the seven lambs. 11You must also sacrifice one male goat for a sin offering. This is in addition to the sin offering of atonement and the regular daily burnt offering with its grain offering, and their accompanying liquid offerings.

28:14a Hebrew *½ of a hin* [2 liters]. **28:14b** Hebrew *⅓ of a hin* [1.3 liters]. **28:14c** Hebrew *¼ of a hin* [1 liter]. **28:16** This day in the ancient Hebrew lunar calendar occurred in late March, April, or early May. **28:22** Or *to make atonement for yourselves;* also in 28:30. **28:26** Hebrew *Festival of Weeks.* This was later called the Festival of Pentecost (see Acts 2:1). It is celebrated today as Shavuat (or Shabuoth). **29:1** Hebrew *the first day of the seventh month.* This day in the ancient Hebrew lunar calendar occurred in September or October. This festival is celebrated today as Rosh Hashanah, the Jewish new year. **29:3a** Hebrew *3/10 of an ephah* [6.6 liters]; also in 29:9, 14. **29:3b** Hebrew *2/10 of an ephah* [4.4 liters]; also in 29:9, 14. **29:4** Hebrew *1/10 of an ephah* [2.2 liters]; also in 29:10, 15. **29:5** Or *to make atonement for yourselves.* **29:7** Hebrew *On the tenth day of the seventh month;* see 29:1 and the note there. This day in the ancient Hebrew lunar calendar occurred in September or October. It is celebrated today as Yom Kippur.

OFFERINGS FOR THE FESTIVAL OF SHELTERS

12"Five days later, on the fifteenth day of the same
month,* you must call another holy assembly of all the
people, and you may do no ordinary work on that day. It is
the beginning of the Festival of Shelters,* a seven-day
festival to the LORD. 13On the first day of the festival, you
must present a burnt offering as a special gift, a pleasing
aroma to the LORD. It will consist of thirteen young bulls,
two rams, and fourteen one-year-old male lambs, all with
no defects. 14Each of these offerings must be accompanied by a grain offering of choice flour moistened with
olive oil—six quarts for each of the thirteen bulls, four
quarts for each of the two rams, 15and two quarts for each
of the fourteen lambs. 16You must also sacrifice a male
goat as a sin offering, in addition to the regular burnt offering with its accompanying grain offering and liquid
offering.

17"On the second day of this seven-day festival, sacrifice twelve young bulls, two rams, and fourteen one-year-
old male lambs, all with no defects. 18Each of these offerings of bulls, rams, and lambs must be accompanied by
its prescribed grain offering and liquid offering. 19You
must also sacrifice a male goat as a sin offering, in addition to the regular burnt offering with its accompanying
grain offering and liquid offering.

20"On the third day of the festival, sacrifice eleven
young bulls, two rams, and fourteen one-year-old male
lambs, all with no defects. 21Each of these offerings of
bulls, rams, and lambs must be accompanied by its prescribed grain offering and liquid offering. 22You must
also sacrifice a male goat as a sin offering, in addition to
the regular burnt offering with its accompanying grain
offering and liquid offering.

23"On the fourth day of the festival, sacrifice ten young
bulls, two rams, and fourteen one-year-old male lambs,
all with no defects. 24Each of these offerings of bulls,
rams, and lambs must be accompanied by its prescribed
grain offering and liquid offering. 25You must also sacrifice a male goat as a sin offering, in addition to the regular burnt offering with its accompanying grain offering
and liquid offering.

26"On the fifth day of the festival, sacrifice nine young
bulls, two rams, and fourteen one-year-old male lambs,
all with no defects. 27Each of these offerings of bulls,
rams, and lambs must be accompanied by its prescribed
grain offering and liquid offering. 28You must also sacrifice a male goat as a sin offering, in addition to the regular burnt offering with its accompanying grain offering
and liquid offering.

29"On the sixth day of the festival, sacrifice eight young
bulls, two rams, and fourteen one-year-old male lambs,
all with no defects. 30Each of these offerings of bulls,
rams, and lambs must be accompanied by its prescribed
grain offering and liquid offering. 31You must also sacrifice a male goat as a sin offering, in addition to the
regular burnt offering with its accompanying grain offering and liquid offering.

32"On the seventh day of the festival, sacrifice seven
young bulls, two rams, and fourteen one-year-old male
lambs, all with no defects. 33Each of these offerings of
bulls, rams, and lambs must be accompanied by its prescribed grain offering and liquid offering. 34You must
also sacrifice one male goat as a sin offering, in addition
to the regular burnt offering with its accompanying grain
offering and liquid offering.

35"On the eighth day of the festival, proclaim another
holy day. You must do no ordinary work on that day.
36You must present a burnt offering as a special gift, a
pleasing aroma to the LORD. It will consist of one young
bull, one ram, and seven one-year-old male lambs, all
with no defects. 37Each of these offerings must be accompanied by its prescribed grain offering and liquid offering. 38You must also sacrifice one male goat as a sin
offering, in addition to the regular burnt offering with its
accompanying grain offering and liquid offering.

39"You must present these offerings to the LORD at
your annual festivals. These are in addition to the sacrifices and offerings you present in connection with vows,
or as voluntary offerings, burnt offerings, grain offerings, liquid offerings, or peace offerings."

40*So Moses gave all of these instructions to the people
of Israel as the LORD had commanded him.

PROMISES 30:1-2

Moses reminded the people that their promises to God and others must be kept. In ancient times, people did not sign written contracts. A person's word was as binding as a signature. To make a vow even more binding, an offering was given along with it. No one was forced by law to make a vow; but once made, vows had to be fulfilled. Breaking a vow meant a broken trust and a broken relationship. Trust is still the basis of our relationships with God and others. Thus a broken promise today is just as harmful as it was in Moses' day. ■

30 LAWS CONCERNING VOWS

1*Then Moses summoned the leaders of the tribes of Israel and told them, "This is what the LORD has commanded: 2A man who makes a vow to the LORD or makes
a pledge under oath must never break it. He must do
exactly what he said he would do.

3"If a young woman makes a vow to the LORD or a
pledge under oath while she is still living at her father's
home, 4and her father hears of the vow or pledge and
does not object to it, then all her vows and pledges will
stand. 5But if her father refuses to let her fulfill the vow
or pledge on the day he hears of it, then all her vows and

29:12a Hebrew *On the fifteenth day of the seventh month;* see 29:1, 7 and the notes there. This day in the ancient Hebrew lunar calendar occurred in late September, October, or early November. **29:12b** Or *Festival of Booths,* or *Festival of Tabernacles.* This was earlier called the Festival of the Final Harvest or Festival of Ingathering (see Exod 23:16b). It is celebrated today as Sukkot (or Succoth). **29:40** Verse 29:40 is numbered 30:1 in Hebrew text. **30:1** Verses 30:1-16 are numbered 30:2-17 in Hebrew text.

pledges will become invalid. The LORD will forgive her
because her father would not let her fulfill them.
6"Now suppose a young woman makes a vow or binds
herself with an impulsive pledge and later marries. 7If
her husband learns of her vow or pledge and does not object on the day he hears of it, her vows and pledges will
stand. 8But if her husband refuses to accept her vow or
impulsive pledge on the day he hears of it, he nullifies her
commitments, and the LORD will forgive her. 9If, however, a woman is a widow or is divorced, she must fulfill
all her vows and pledges.

A PARENT'S ADVICE 30:3-5

Under Israelite law, parents could overrule their children's vows. This helped young people avoid making foolish promises or costly commitments. From this law comes an important principle for both parents and children. A parent's advice is worth seeking. His or her experience could save you from making a serious mistake. Parents, however, are encouraged to exercise their authority with caution and grace. How have your parents helped you in your decision making recently? ■

10"But suppose a woman is married and living in her
husband's home when she makes a vow or binds herself
with a pledge. 11If her husband hears of it and does not
object to it, her vow or pledge will stand. 12But if her husband refuses to accept it on the day he hears of it, her vow
or pledge will be nullified, and the LORD will forgive her.
13So her husband may either confirm or nullify any vows
or pledges she makes to deny herself. 14But if he does not
object on the day he hears of it, then he is agreeing to all
her vows and pledges. 15If he waits more than a day and
then tries to nullify a vow or pledge, he will be punished
for her guilt."
16These are the regulations the LORD gave Moses concerning relationships between a man and his wife, and
between a father and a young daughter who still lives at
home.

31 CONQUEST OF THE MIDIANITES

Then the LORD said to Moses, 2"On behalf of the people of
Israel, take revenge on the Midianites for leading them
into idolatry. After that, you will die and join your ancestors."
3So Moses said to the people, "Choose some men, and
arm them to fight the LORD's war of revenge against Midian. 4From each tribe of Israel, send 1,000 men into battle." 5So they chose 1,000 men from each tribe of Israel, a
total of 12,000 men armed for battle. 6Then Moses sent
them out, 1,000 men from each tribe, and Phinehas son
of Eleazar the priest led them into battle. They carried
along the holy objects of the sanctuary and the trumpets
for sounding the charge. 7They attacked Midian as the
LORD had commanded Moses, and they killed all the men.
8All five of the Midianite kings—Evi, Rekem, Zur, Hur,
and Reba—died in the battle. They also killed Balaam son
of Beor with the sword.
9Then the Israelite army captured the Midianite
women and children and seized their cattle and flocks
and all their wealth as plunder. 10They burned all the
towns and villages where the Midianites had lived.
11After they had gathered the plunder and captives, both
people and animals, 12they brought them all to Moses and
Eleazar the priest, and to the whole community of Israel,
which was camped on the plains of Moab beside the Jordan River, across from Jericho. 13Moses, Eleazar the
priest, and all the leaders of the community went to meet
them outside the camp. 14But Moses was furious with all
the generals and captains* who had returned from the
battle.
15"Why have you let all the women live?" he demanded. 16"These are the very ones who followed Balaam's advice and caused the people of Israel to rebel
against the LORD at Mount Peor. They are the ones who
caused the plague to strike the LORD's people. 17So kill all
the boys and all the women who have had intercourse
with a man. 18Only the young girls who are virgins may
live; you may keep them for yourselves. 19And all of you
who have killed anyone or touched a dead body must stay
outside the camp for seven days. You must purify yourselves and your captives on the third and seventh days.
20Purify all your clothing, too, and everything made of
leather, goat hair, or wood."
21Then Eleazar the priest said to the men who were in
the battle, "The LORD has given Moses this legal requirement: 22Anything made of gold, silver, bronze, iron, tin, or
lead—23that is, all metals that do not burn—must be
passed through fire in order to be made ceremonially
pure. These metal objects must then be further purified
with the water of purification. But everything that burns
must be purified by the water alone. 24On the seventh day
you must wash your clothes and be purified. Then you
may return to the camp."

DIVIDING THE SPOILS 31:25-30

Moses told the Israelites to give God a portion of the spoils from the war with Midian. Another portion was to go to the soldiers and to the people who remained behind. Similarly, the money we earn is not ours alone. Everything we possess comes directly or indirectly from God and ultimately belongs to him. God is pleased when we return a portion to him and also share a portion with those in need. ■

DIVISION OF THE PLUNDER

25And the LORD said to Moses, 26"You and Eleazar the priest
and the family leaders of each tribe are to make a list of all
the plunder taken in the battle, including the people and
animals. 27Then divide the plunder into two parts, and give
half to the men who fought the battle and half to the rest of
the people. 28From the army's portion, first give the LORD

31:14 Hebrew *the commanders of thousands, and the commanders of hundreds;* also in 31:48, 52, 54.

HOLY WAR?

ULTIMATE ISSUES

The involvement of our country in the war in Iraq inspired many polls for or against the war on the Internet. While many people are quick to point out the need for the war (to gain justice for the human rights violations and acts of terrorism suffered by many; to punish the terrorists), others seem doubtful. Some Christians have asked themselves, *Should a Christian ever go to war? Or should Christians be pacifists, refusing to take up arms no matter what the cause?* Have you asked yourself those questions as well?

Let's examine God's orders for his chosen nation of Israel in the Old Testament. In Numbers 31, God tells his people to go to war with the Midianites and to utterly destroy them. Why did God require such terrible punishment for Israel's enemies? Aren't Christians supposed to be loving and kind peacemakers?

To answer this, we have to understand some basic differences between the Old Testament nation of Israel and God's people today. In the Old Testament, God led his nation to their new home—Canaan. Along the way, they were opposed by numerous other nations, like the Midianites. (After all, who would voluntarily give up his or her home?)

The problem wasn't simply that these other people were in the way. They also worshiped idols and routinely sacrificed children to these idols.

For Christians today, however, our war is a spiritual one. "For we are not fighting against flesh-and-blood enemies, but against evil rulers and authorities of the unseen world, against mighty powers in this dark world, and against evil spirits in the heavenly places" (Eph 6:12). God's people today are not determined by *nationality,* but by *spirituality.* Whereas God's blessings and promises before belonged to Abraham's physical descendants, they now belong to those who are spiritually "grafted" into Abraham's line (Rom 11:17). Therefore, when any nation goes to war today, its cause may be just, but it cannot be considered holy in the way Israel's wars were. Israel had God himself fighting battles for them, and he often gave Israel miraculous assistance and assurance of victory. No modern nation can make that claim.

So, should a Christian go to war? Unfortunately, you won't find the final answer here. We see in God's Word that God has, at times, told his people to go to war with other people; therefore, those who believe war is never right should reconsider.

his share of the plunder—one of every 500 of the prisoners and of the cattle, donkeys, sheep, and goats. [29]Give this share of the army's half to Eleazar the priest as an offering to the LORD. [30]From the half that belongs to the people of Israel, take one of every fifty of the prisoners and of the cattle, donkeys, sheep, goats, and other animals. Give this share to the Levites, who are in charge of maintaining the LORD's Tabernacle." [31]So Moses and Eleazar the priest did as the LORD commanded Moses.

[32]The plunder remaining from everything the fighting men had taken totaled 675,000 sheep and goats, [33]72,000 cattle, [34]61,000 donkeys, [35]and 32,000 virgin girls.

[36]Half of the plunder was given to the fighting men. It totaled 337,500 sheep and goats, [37]of which 675 were the LORD's share; [38]36,000 cattle, of which 72 were the LORD's share; [39]30,500 donkeys, of which 61 were the LORD's share; [40]and 16,000 virgin girls, of whom 32 were the LORD's share. [41]Moses gave all the LORD's share to Eleazar the priest, just as the LORD had directed him.

[42]Half of the plunder belonged to the people of Israel, and Moses separated it from the half belonging to the fighting men. [43]It totaled 337,500 sheep and goats, [44]36,000 cattle, [45]30,500 donkeys, [46]and 16,000 virgin girls. [47]From the half-share given to the people, Moses took one of every fifty prisoners and animals and gave them to the Levites, who maintained the LORD's Tabernacle. All this was done as the LORD had commanded Moses.

[48]Then all the generals and captains came to Moses [49]and said, "We, your servants, have accounted for all the men who went out to battle under our command; not one of us is missing! [50]So we are presenting the items of gold we captured as an offering to the LORD from our share of the plunder—armbands, bracelets, rings, earrings, and necklaces. This will purify our lives before the LORD and make us right with him.*"

[51]So Moses and Eleazar the priest received the gold from all the military commanders—all kinds of jewelry and crafted objects. [52]In all, the gold that the generals and

31:50 Or *will make atonement for our lives before the LORD.*

captains presented as a gift to the LORD weighed about 420 pounds.* 53All the fighting men had taken some of the plunder for themselves. 54So Moses and Eleazar the priest accepted the gifts from the generals and captains and brought the gold to the Tabernacle* as a reminder to the LORD that the people of Israel belong to him.

32 THE TRIBES EAST OF THE JORDAN

The tribes of Reuben and Gad owned vast numbers of livestock. So when they saw that the lands of Jazer and Gilead were ideally suited for their flocks and herds, 2they came to Moses, Eleazar the priest, and the other leaders of the community. They said, 3"Notice the towns of Ataroth, Dibon, Jazer, Nimrah, Heshbon, Elealeh, Sibmah,* Nebo, and Beon. 4The LORD has conquered this whole area for the community of Israel, and it is ideally suited for all our livestock. 5If we have found favor with you, please let us have this land as our property instead of giving us land across the Jordan River."

6"Do you intend to stay here while your brothers go across and do all the fighting?" Moses asked the men of Gad and Reuben. 7"Why do you want to discourage the rest of the people of Israel from going across to the land the LORD has given them? 8Your ancestors did the same thing when I sent them from Kadesh-barnea to explore the land. 9After they went up to the valley of Eshcol and explored the land, they discouraged the people of Israel from entering the land the LORD was giving them. 10Then the LORD was very angry with them, and he vowed, 11'Of all those I rescued from Egypt, no one who is twenty years old or older will ever see the land I swore to give to Abraham, Isaac, and Jacob, for they have not obeyed me wholeheartedly. 12The only exceptions are Caleb son of Jephunneh the Kenizzite and Joshua son of Nun, for they have wholeheartedly followed the LORD.'

13"The LORD was angry with Israel and made them wander in the wilderness for forty years until the entire generation that sinned in the LORD's sight had died. 14But here you are, a brood of sinners, doing exactly the same thing! You are making the LORD even angrier with Israel. 15If you turn away from him like this and he abandons them again in the wilderness, you will be responsible for destroying this entire nation!"

16But they approached Moses and said, "We simply want to build pens for our livestock and fortified towns for our wives and children. 17Then we will arm ourselves and lead our fellow Israelites into battle until we have brought them safely to their land. Meanwhile, our families will stay in the fortified towns we build here, so they will be safe from any attacks by the local people. 18We will not return to our homes until all the people of Israel have received their portions of land. 19But we do not claim any of the land on the other side of the Jordan. We would rather live here on the east side and accept this as our grant of land."

20Then Moses said, "If you keep your word and arm yourselves for the LORD's battles, 21and if your troops cross the Jordan and keep fighting until the LORD has driven out his enemies, 22then you may return when the LORD has conquered the land. You will have fulfilled your duty to the LORD and to the rest of the people of Israel. And the land on the east side of the Jordan will be your property from the LORD. 23But if you fail to keep your word, then you will have sinned against the LORD, and you may be sure that your sin will find you out. 24Go ahead and build towns for your families and pens for your flocks, but do everything you have promised."

25Then the men of Gad and Reuben replied, "We, your servants, will follow your instructions exactly. 26Our children, wives, flocks, and cattle will stay here in the towns of Gilead. 27But all who are able to bear arms will cross over to fight for the LORD, just as you have said."

28So Moses gave orders to Eleazar the priest, Joshua son of Nun, and the leaders of the clans of Israel. 29He said, "The men of Gad and Reuben who are armed for battle must cross the Jordan with you to fight for the LORD. If they do, give them the land of Gilead as their property when the land is conquered. 30But if they refuse to arm themselves and cross over with you, then they must accept land with the rest of you in the land of Canaan."

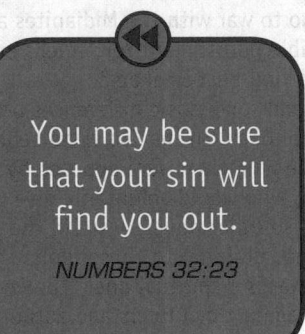

> You may be sure that your sin will find you out.
>
> *NUMBERS 32:23*

WRONG ASSUMPTIONS 32:1-33

Three tribes (Reuben, Gad, and the half-tribe of Manasseh) wanted to live east of the Jordan River on land they had already conquered. Moses immediately assumed they had selfish motives and were trying to avoid helping the others fight for the land across the river. But Moses jumped to the wrong conclusion. Have you done something similar recently? In dealing with people, we must find out all the facts before making up our mind. We shouldn't automatically assume that their motives are wrong, even if their plans sound suspicious. ■

31The tribes of Gad and Reuben said again, "We are your servants, and we will do as the LORD has commanded! 32We will cross the Jordan into Canaan fully armed to fight for the LORD, but our property will be here on this side of the Jordan."

33So Moses assigned land to the tribes of Gad, Reuben, and half the tribe of Manasseh son of Joseph. He gave them the territory of King Sihon of the Amorites and the

31:52 Hebrew *16,750 shekels* [191 kilograms]. 31:54 Hebrew *the Tent of Meeting*. 32:3 As in Samaritan Pentateuch and Greek version (see also 32:38); Hebrew reads *Sebam*.

land of King Og of Bashan—the whole land with its cities
and surrounding lands.
34 The descendants of Gad built the towns of Dibon, Ataroth, Aroer, 35 Atroth-shophan, Jazer, Jogbehah, 36 Beth-
nimrah, and Beth-haran. These were all fortified towns
with pens for their flocks.
37 The descendants of Reuben built the towns of Heshbon, Elealeh, Kiriathaim, 38 Nebo, Baal-meon, and Sibmah. They changed the names of some of the towns they
conquered and rebuilt.
39 Then the descendants of Makir of the tribe of Manasseh went to Gilead and conquered it, and they drove
out the Amorites living there. 40 So Moses gave Gilead to
the Makirites, descendants of Manasseh, and they settled
there. 41 The people of Jair, another clan of the tribe of
Manasseh, captured many of the towns in Gilead and
changed the name of that region to the Towns of Jair.*
42 Meanwhile, a man named Nobah captured the town of
Kenath and its surrounding villages, and he renamed that
area Nobah after himself.

33

REMEMBERING ISRAEL'S JOURNEY

This is the route the Israelites followed as they marched
out of Egypt under the leadership of Moses and Aaron. 2 At
the LORD's direction, Moses kept a written record of their
progress. These are the stages of their march, identified by
the different places where they stopped along the way.

A TRAVEL JOURNAL 33:2

Moses recorded the Israelites' journeys as God instructed him, providing a written record of their spiritual as well as geographic progress. Have you made spiritual progress lately? Recording your thoughts about God and lessons you have learned over a period of time can be a valuable aid to spiritual growth. A record of your spiritual pilgrimage will let you check up on your progress and avoid repeating past mistakes. ■

3 They set out from the city of Rameses in early
spring—on the fifteenth day of the first month*—on the
morning after the first Passover celebration. The people
of Israel left defiantly, in full view of all the Egyptians.
4 Meanwhile, the Egyptians were burying all their firstborn sons, whom the LORD had killed the night before.
The LORD had defeated the gods of Egypt that night with
great acts of judgment!

5 After leaving Rameses, the Israelites set up camp at Succoth.
6 Then they left Succoth and camped at Etham on the edge of the wilderness.
7 They left Etham and turned back toward Pi-hahiroth, opposite Baal-zephon, and camped near Migdol.
8 They left Pi-hahiroth and crossed the Red Sea* into the wilderness beyond. Then they traveled for three days into the Etham wilderness and camped at Marah.
9 They left Marah and camped at Elim, where there were twelve springs of water and seventy palm trees.
10 They left Elim and camped beside the Red Sea.*
11 They left the Red Sea and camped in the wilderness of Sin.*
12 They left the wilderness of Sin and camped at Dophkah.
13 They left Dophkah and camped at Alush.
14 They left Alush and camped at Rephidim, where there was no water for the people to drink.
15 They left Rephidim and camped in the wilderness of Sinai.
16 They left the wilderness of Sinai and camped at Kibroth-hattaavah.
17 They left Kibroth-hattaavah and camped at Hazeroth.
18 They left Hazeroth and camped at Rithmah.
19 They left Rithmah and camped at Rimmon-perez.
20 They left Rimmon-perez and camped at Libnah.
21 They left Libnah and camped at Rissah.
22 They left Rissah and camped at Kehelathah.
23 They left Kehelathah and camped at Mount Shepher.
24 They left Mount Shepher and camped at Haradah.
25 They left Haradah and camped at Makheloth.
26 They left Makheloth and camped at Tahath.
27 They left Tahath and camped at Terah.
28 They left Terah and camped at Mithcah.
29 They left Mithcah and camped at Hashmonah.
30 They left Hashmonah and camped at Moseroth.
31 They left Moseroth and camped at Bene-jaakan.
32 They left Bene-jaakan and camped at Hor-haggidgad.
33 They left Hor-haggidgad and camped at Jotbathah.
34 They left Jotbathah and camped at Abronah.
35 They left Abronah and camped at Ezion-geber.
36 They left Ezion-geber and camped at Kadesh in the wilderness of Zin.
37 They left Kadesh and camped at Mount Hor, at the
border of Edom. 38 While they were at the foot of
Mount Hor, Aaron the priest was directed by the
LORD to go up the mountain, and there he died. This
happened in midsummer, on the first day of the fifth
month* of the fortieth year after Israel's departure
from Egypt. 39 Aaron was 123 years old when he died
there on Mount Hor.
40 At that time the Canaanite king of Arad, who lived in the Negev in the land of Canaan, heard that the people of Israel were approaching his land.
41 Meanwhile, the Israelites left Mount Hor and camped at Zalmonah.
42 Then they left Zalmonah and camped at Punon.
43 They left Punon and camped at Oboth.
44 They left Oboth and camped at Iye-abarim on the border of Moab.
45 They left Iye-abarim* and camped at Dibon-gad.

32:41 Hebrew *Havvoth-jair.* **33:3** This day in the ancient Hebrew lunar calendar occurred in late March, April, or early May. **33:8** Hebrew *the sea.* **33:10** Hebrew *sea of reeds;* also in 33:11. **33:11** The geographical name *Sin* is related to *Sinai* and should not be confused with the English word *sin.* **33:38** This day in the ancient Hebrew lunar calendar occurred in July or August. **33:45** As in 33:44; Hebrew reads *Iyim,* another name for Iye-abarim.

46They left Dibon-gad and camped at Almon-
diblathaim.
47They left Almon-diblathaim and camped in the
mountains east of the river,* near Mount Nebo.
48They left the mountains east of the river and camped
on the plains of Moab beside the Jordan River, across
from Jericho. 49Along the Jordan River they camped
from Beth-jeshimoth as far as the meadows of
Acacia* on the plains of Moab.

50While they were camped near the Jordan River on
the plains of Moab opposite Jericho, the LORD said to
Moses, 51"Give the following instructions to the people of
Israel: When you cross the Jordan River into the land of
Canaan, 52you must drive out all the people living there.
You must destroy all their carved and molten images and
demolish all their pagan shrines. 53Take possession of
the land and settle in it, because I have given it to you to
occupy. 54You must distribute the land among the clans
by sacred lot and in proportion to their size. A larger portion of land will be allotted to each of the larger clans, and
a smaller portion will be allotted to each of the smaller
clans. The decision of the sacred lot is final. In this way,
the portions of land will be divided among your ancestral
tribes. 55But if you fail to drive out the people who live in
the land, those who remain will be like splinters in your
eyes and thorns in your sides. They will harass you in the
land where you live. 56And I will do to you what I had
planned to do to them."

ORGANIZING GOD'S WAY 34:16-29

In God's plan for settling the land, he explained what to do in a clear fashion to Moses and assigned specific people to oversee the division of the land. No plan is complete until each job is assigned and everyone understands his or her responsibilities. Need to organize some people for a task? God's plan is a good one to follow. ■

34 BOUNDARIES OF THE LAND

Then the LORD said to Moses, 2"Give these instructions to
the Israelites: When you come into the land of Canaan,
which I am giving you as your special possession, these
will be the boundaries. 3The southern portion of your
country will extend from the wilderness of Zin, along the
edge of Edom. The southern boundary will begin on the
east at the Dead Sea.* 4It will then run south past Scorpion Pass* in the direction of Zin. Its southernmost point
will be Kadesh-barnea, from which it will go to Hazar-
addar, and on to Azmon. 5From Azmon the boundary will
turn toward the Brook of Egypt and end at the Mediterranean Sea.*
6"Your western boundary will be the coastline of the
Mediterranean Sea.

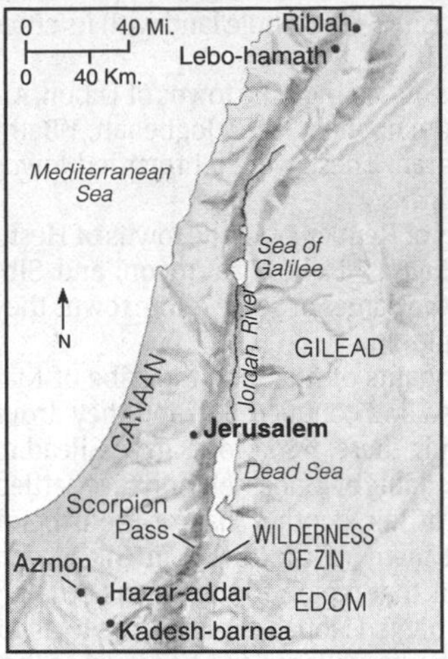

THE BORDERS OF THE PROMISED LAND
The borders of the Promised Land stretched from the wilderness of Zin and Kadesh-barnea in the south to Lebo-hamath and Riblah in the north, and from the Mediterranean seacoast on the west to the Jordan River on the east. The land of Gilead was also included.

7"Your northern boundary will begin at the Mediterranean Sea and run east to Mount Hor, 8then to Lebo-
hamath, and on through Zedad 9and Ziphron to Hazar-
enan. This will be your northern boundary.
10"The eastern boundary will start at Hazar-enan and
run south to Shepham, 11then down to Riblah on the east
side of Ain. From there the boundary will run down along
the eastern edge of the Sea of Galilee,* 12and then along
the Jordan River to the Dead Sea. These are the boundaries of your land."
13Then Moses told the Israelites, "This territory is the
homeland you are to divide among yourselves by sacred
lot. The LORD has commanded that the land be divided
among the nine and a half remaining tribes. 14The families of the tribes of Reuben, Gad, and half the tribe of Manasseh have already received their grants of land 15on the
east side of the Jordan River, across from Jericho toward
the sunrise."

LEADERS TO DIVIDE THE LAND

16And the LORD said to Moses, 17"Eleazar the priest and
Joshua son of Nun are the men designated to divide the
grants of land among the people. 18Enlist one leader from
each tribe to help them with the task. 19These are the
tribes and the names of the leaders:

	Tribe	*Leader*
	Judah	Caleb son of Jephunneh
20	Simeon	Shemuel son of Ammihud
21	Benjamin	Elidad son of Kislon
22	Dan	Bukki son of Jogli
23	Manasseh son of Joseph	Hanniel son of Ephod
24	Ephraim son of Joseph	Kemuel son of Shiphtan
25	Zebulun	Elizaphan son of Parnach
26	Issachar	Paltiel son of Azzan
27	Asher	Ahihud son of Shelomi
28	Naphtali	Pedahel son of Ammihud

29These are the men the LORD has appointed to divide the
grants of land in Canaan among the Israelites."

33:47 Or *the mountains of Abarim;* also in 33:48. 33:49 Hebrew *as far as Abel-shittim.* 34:3 Hebrew *Salt Sea;* also in 34:12. 34:4 Or *the ascent of Akrabbim.* 34:5 Hebrew *the sea;* also in 34:6, 7. 34:11 Hebrew *Sea of Kinnereth.*

35 TOWNS FOR THE LEVITES

While Israel was camped beside the Jordan on the plains of Moab across from Jericho, the LORD said to Moses, 2"Command the people of Israel to give to the Levites from their property certain towns to live in, along with the surrounding pasturelands. 3These towns will be for the Levites to live in, and the surrounding lands will provide pasture for their cattle, flocks, and other livestock. 4The pastureland assigned to the Levites around these towns will extend 1,500 feet* from the town walls in every direction. 5Measure off 3,000 feet* outside the town walls in every direction—east, south, west, north—with the town at the center. This area will serve as the larger pastureland for the towns.

6"Six of the towns you give the Levites will be cities of refuge, where a person who has accidentally killed someone can flee for safety. In addition, give them forty-two other towns. 7In all, forty-eight towns with the surrounding pastureland will be given to the Levites. 8These towns will come from the property of the people of Israel. The larger tribes will give more towns to the Levites, while the smaller tribes will give fewer. Each tribe will give property in proportion to the size of its land."

TRUE JUSTICE 35:9-28

At this time in Israel's history, if someone died because of violence, the murder suspect was not automatically considered guilty, even if murder was assumed. The people were to be intolerant of the sin, yet impartial to the accused so that he or she could have a fair trial. The cities of refuge represented God's concern for justice in a culture that did not always protect the innocent. It is unjust both to overlook wrongdoing and to jump to conclusions about guilt. When someone is accused of wrongdoing, are you willing to stand up for justice, protect those not yet proven guilty, and listen carefully to all sides of the story? ■

CITIES OF REFUGE

9The LORD said to Moses, 10"Give the following instructions to the people of Israel.

"When you cross the Jordan into the land of Canaan, 11designate cities of refuge to which people can flee if they have killed someone accidentally. 12These cities will be places of protection from a dead person's relatives who want to avenge the death. The slayer must not be put to death before being tried by the community. 13Designate six cities of refuge for yourselves, 14three on the east side of the Jordan River and three on the west in the land of Canaan. 15These cities are for the protection of Israelites, foreigners living among you, and traveling merchants. Anyone who accidentally kills someone may flee there for safety.

16"But if someone strikes and kills another person with a piece of iron, it is murder, and the murderer must be executed. 17Or if someone with a stone in his hand strikes and kills another person, it is murder, and the murderer must be put to death. 18Or if someone strikes and kills another person with a wooden object, it is murder, and the murderer must be put to death. 19The victim's nearest relative is responsible for putting the murderer to death. When they meet, the avenger must put the murderer to death. 20So if someone hates another person and pushes him or throws a dangerous object at him and he dies, it is murder. 21Or if someone hates another person and hits him with a fist and he dies, it is murder. In such cases, the avenger must put the murderer to death when they meet.

A CORRUPTING INFLUENCE 35:33

According to God's law, murderers were to be executed because they corrupted the land. Murder and anger stem from the same root. While anger seems a lesser sin, it can often lead to more sin. Unchecked bitterness and anger will ultimately destroy us. We need to deal with these strong emotions in an appropriate way, before they get out of control. ■

22"But suppose someone pushes another person without having shown previous hostility, or throws something that unintentionally hits another person, 23or accidentally drops a huge stone on someone, though they were not enemies, and the person dies. 24If this should happen, the community must follow these regulations in making a judgment between the slayer and the avenger, the victim's nearest relative: 25The community must protect the slayer from the avenger and must escort the slayer back to live in the city of refuge to which he fled. There he must remain until the death of the high priest, who was anointed with the sacred oil.

26"But if the slayer ever leaves the limits of the city of refuge, 27and the avenger finds him outside the city and kills him, it will not be considered murder. 28The slayer should have stayed inside the city of refuge until the death of the high priest. But after the death of the high priest, the slayer may return to his own property. 29These are legal requirements for you to observe from generation to generation, wherever you may live.

30"All murderers must be put to death, but only if evidence is presented by more than one witness. No one may be put to death on the testimony of only one witness. 31Also, you must never accept a ransom payment for the life of someone judged guilty of murder and subject to execution; murderers must always be put to death. 32And never accept a ransom payment from someone who has fled to a city of refuge, allowing a slayer to return to his property before the death of the high priest. 33This will ensure that the land where you live will not be polluted, for murder pollutes the land. And no sacrifice except the execution of the murderer can purify the land from murder.* 34You must not defile the land where you live, for I live there myself. I am the LORD, who lives among the people of Israel."

35:4 Hebrew *1,000 cubits* [460 meters]. 35:5 Hebrew *2,000 cubits* [920 meters]. 35:33 Or *can make atonement for murder.*

36 WOMEN WHO INHERIT PROPERTY

Then the heads of the clans of Gilead—descendants of Makir, son of Manasseh, son of Joseph—came to Moses and the family leaders of Israel with a petition. [2]They said, "Sir, the LORD instructed you to divide the land by sacred lot among the people of Israel. You were told by the LORD to give the grant of land owned by our brother Zelophehad to his daughters. [3]But if they marry men from another tribe, their grants of land will go with them to the tribe into which they marry. In this way, the total area of our tribal land will be reduced. [4]Then when the Year of Jubilee comes, their portion of land will be added to that of the new tribe, causing it to be lost forever to our ancestral tribe."

[5]So Moses gave the Israelites this command from the LORD: "The claim of the men of the tribe of Joseph is legitimate. [6]This is what the LORD commands concerning the daughters of Zelophehad: Let them marry anyone they like, as long as it is within their own ancestral tribe. [7]None of the territorial land may pass from tribe to tribe, for all the land given to each tribe must remain within the tribe to which it was first allotted. [8]The daughters throughout the tribes of Israel who are in line to inherit property must marry within their tribe, so that all the Israelites will keep their ancestral property. [9]No grant of land may pass from one tribe to another; each tribe of Israel must keep its allotted portion of land."

[10]The daughters of Zelophehad did as the LORD commanded Moses. [11]Mahlah, Tirzah, Hoglah, Milcah, and Noah all married cousins on their father's side. [12]They married into the clans of Manasseh son of Joseph. Thus, their inheritance of land remained within their ancestral tribe.

[13]These are the commands and regulations that the LORD gave to the people of Israel through Moses while they were camped on the plains of Moab beside the Jordan River across from Jericho.

DEUTERONOMY

GOT A "MEMORIES" drawer or some other place where you keep various reminders from your past? Maybe you have a scrapbook. Some keep ticket stubs; Others store especially meaningful letters or old pictures.

If you're like most people, these treasures become even more meaningful when you are going through tough times: when you're sad or lonely or scared about the future. There is something comforting in remembering the good times you've had.

Deuteronomy is a book of memories. God had made a Promised Land covenant with the Israelites who came out of Egypt, but they refused to obey or trust God. So he let them wander in the wilderness until they died.

But since a new generation had grown up, God used Moses to remind them of the covenant. Moses first reviewed the mighty acts God had done for Israel. Then he let them know that, based on the past, they must trust, obey, and love God as they prepared to enter their new homeland. Only such an attitude would enable them to conquer the Promised Land.

As you read Deuteronomy, think about your "spiritual memories" collection. How did God help you in the past? Are you willing to trust him with your deepest fears?

deuteronomy

timeline

1805 B.C.
Joseph dies

SLAVERY IN EGYPT

1446
Exodus from Egypt

1445
Ten Commandments given

WILDERNESS WANDERINGS

1406
Moses' death; Israelites enter Canaan

1375
Judges begin to rule

1050
United kingdom under Saul

stats

PURPOSE: To remind the people of what God has done and encourage them to rededicate their lives to him

AUTHOR: Moses (except for the final summary which was probably written by Joshua after Moses' death)

TO WHOM WRITTEN: Israel (the new generation entering the Promised Land)

DATE WRITTEN: About 1407/6 B.C.

SETTING: The east side of the Jordan River, in view of the Promised Land

KEY PEOPLE: Moses, Joshua

KEY PLACE: The valley of Arabah in Moab, east of the Jordan River

KEY points

HISTORY
Moses reviews God's efforts to set Israel free from slavery in Egypt. By reviewing God's promises and mighty acts, we can learn about his character and grow in faith.

LAWS
The legal contract between God and his people had to be renewed for the new generation entering the Promised Land. Commitment to God and his truth cannot be taken for granted. Every person in each generation must respond anew to God's call.

LOVE
God's faithful and patient love is portrayed more often than his punishment. His love forms the foundation for our trust in him. We can be confident that the one who loves us perfectly can be trusted with our lives.

CHOICES
God reminded his people that in order to enjoy the blessings of his will for them, they would have to continue in obedience. Our choices make a difference. Choosing to follow God produces good results in our lives and in our relationships with others. Choosing to abandon God's ways brings harmful results to us and to others.

TEACHING
God commanded the Israelites to teach their children his ways. God's truth must be passed on to future generations. It is not, however, just the traditions or commands that are to be passed on. Rather, we are to teach each new generation to know and love God personally.

1

INTRODUCTION TO MOSES' FIRST ADDRESS

These are the words that Moses spoke to all the people of Israel while they were in the wilderness east of the Jordan River. They were camped in the Jordan Valley* near Suph, between Paran on one side and Tophel, Laban, Hazeroth, and Di-zahab on the other.

2Normally it takes only eleven days to travel from Mount Sinai* to Kadesh-barnea, going by way of Mount Seir. 3But forty years after the Israelites left Egypt, on the first day of the eleventh month,* Moses addressed the people of Israel, telling them everything the LORD had commanded him to say. 4This took place after he had defeated King Sihon of the Amorites, who had ruled in Heshbon, and King Og of Bashan, who had ruled in Ashtaroth and Edrei.

5While the Israelites were in the land of Moab east of the Jordan River, Moses carefully explained the LORD's instructions as follows.

THE COMMAND TO LEAVE SINAI

6"When we were at Mount Sinai, the LORD our God said to us, 'You have stayed at this mountain long enough. 7It is time to break camp and move on. Go to the hill country of the Amorites and to all the neighboring regions—the Jordan Valley, the hill country, the western foothills,* the Negev, and the coastal plain. Go to the land of the Canaanites and to Lebanon, and all the way to the great Euphrates River. 8Look, I am giving all this land to you! Go in and occupy it, for it is the land the LORD swore to give to your ancestors Abraham, Isaac, and Jacob, and to all their descendants.'"

LEADERSHIP QUALITIES 1:13-18

Moses identified some of the qualities of a good leader: wisdom, understanding, a good reputation, and fairness. These characteristics differ greatly from the ones that often help elect leaders today: good looks, wealth, popularity, and a willingness to do anything to get to the top. Think you've got what it takes to be a leader? Which set of qualities do you value most: the ones on Moses' list or the second list? ■

MOSES APPOINTS LEADERS FROM EACH TRIBE

9Moses continued, "At that time I told you, 'You are too great a burden for me to carry all by myself. 10The LORD your God has increased your population, making you as numerous as the stars! 11And may the LORD, the God of your ancestors, multiply you a thousand times more and bless you as he promised! 12But you are such a heavy load to carry! How can I deal with all your problems and bickering? 13Choose some well-respected men from each tribe who are known for their wisdom and understanding, and I will appoint them as your leaders.'

14"Then you responded, 'Your plan is a good one.' 15So I took the wise and respected men you had selected from your tribes and appointed them to serve as judges and officials over you. Some were responsible for a thousand people, some for a hundred, some for fifty, and some for ten.

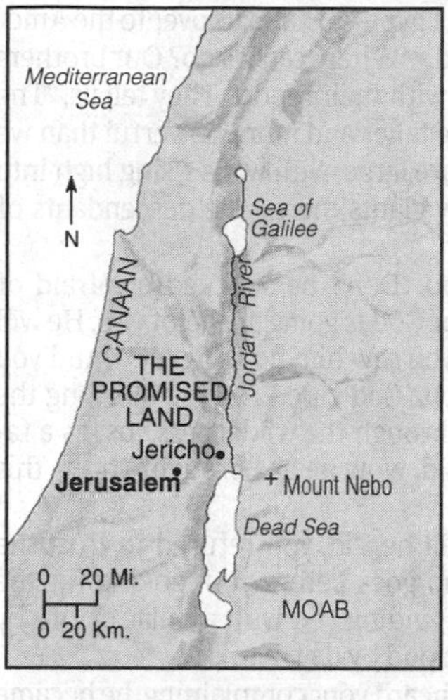

EVENTS IN DEUTERONOMY
The book of Deuteronomy opens with Israel camped east of the Jordan River in the Jordan Valley in the land of Moab. Just before the people crossed the river into the Promised Land, Moses delivered an inspirational speech indicating how they were to live.

16"At that time I instructed the judges, 'You must hear the cases of your fellow Israelites and the foreigners living among you. Be perfectly fair in your decisions 17and impartial in your judgments. Hear the cases of those who are poor as well as those who are rich. Don't be afraid of anyone's anger, for the decision you make is God's decision. Bring me any cases that are too difficult for you, and I will handle them.'

18"At that time I gave you instructions about everything you were to do.

SCOUTS EXPLORE THE LAND

19"Then, just as the LORD our God commanded us, we left Mount Sinai and traveled through the great and terrifying wilderness, as you yourselves remember, and headed toward the hill country of the Amorites. When we arrived at Kadesh-barnea, 20I said to you, 'You have now reached the hill country of the Amorites that the LORD our God is giving us. 21Look! He has placed the land in front of you. Go and occupy it as the LORD, the God of your ancestors, has promised you. Don't be afraid! Don't be discouraged!'

22"But you all came to me and said, 'First, let's send out scouts to explore the land for us. They will advise us on the best route to take and which towns we should enter.'

23"This seemed like a good idea to me, so I chose twelve scouts, one from each of your tribes. 24They headed for the hill country and came to the valley of Eshcol and explored it. 25They picked some of its fruit and brought it back to us. And they reported, 'The land the LORD our God has given us is indeed a good land.'

ISRAEL'S REBELLION AGAINST THE LORD

26"But you rebelled against the command of the LORD your God and refused to go in. 27You complained in your tents and said, 'The LORD must hate us. That's why he has

1:1 Hebrew *the Arabah;* also in 1:7. **1:2** Hebrew *Horeb,* another name for Sinai; also in 1:6, 19. **1:3** Hebrew *In the fortieth year, on the first day of the eleventh month.* This day in the ancient Hebrew lunar calendar occurred in January or February. **1:7** Hebrew *the Shephelah.*

brought us here from Egypt—to hand us over to the Amorites to be slaughtered. 28Where can we go? Our brothers have demoralized us with their report. They tell us, "The people of the land are taller and more powerful than we are, and their towns are large, with walls rising high into the sky! We even saw giants there—the descendants of Anak!"'

29"But I said to you, 'Don't be shocked or afraid of them! 30The LORD your God is going ahead of you. He will fight for you, just as you saw him do in Egypt. 31And you saw how the LORD your God cared for you all along the way as you traveled through the wilderness, just as a father cares for his child. Now he has brought you to this place.'

32"But even after all he did, you refused to trust the LORD your God, 33who goes before you looking for the best places to camp, guiding you with a pillar of fire by night and a pillar of cloud by day.

34"When the LORD heard your complaining, he became very angry. So he solemnly swore, 35'Not one of you from this wicked generation will live to see the good land I swore to give your ancestors, 36except Caleb son of Jephunneh. He will see this land because he has followed the LORD completely. I will give to him and his descendants some of the very land he explored during his scouting mission.'

37"And the LORD was also angry with me because of you. He said to me, 'Moses, not even you will enter the Promised Land! 38Instead, your assistant, Joshua son of Nun, will lead the people into the land. Encourage him, for he will lead Israel as they take possession of it. 39I will give the land to your little ones—your innocent children. You were afraid they would be captured, but they will be the ones who occupy it. 40As for you, turn around now and go on back through the wilderness toward the Red Sea.*'

41"Then you confessed, 'We have sinned against the LORD! We will go into the land and fight for it, as the LORD our God has commanded us.' So your men strapped on their weapons, thinking it would be easy to attack the hill country.

42"But the LORD told me to tell you, 'Do not attack, for I am not with you. If you go ahead on your own, you will be crushed by your enemies.'

43"This is what I told you, but you would not listen. Instead, you again rebelled against the LORD's command and arrogantly went into the hill country to fight. 44But the Amorites who lived there came out against you like a swarm of bees. They chased and battered you all the way from Seir to Hormah. 45Then you returned and wept before the LORD, but he refused to listen. 46So you stayed there at Kadesh for a long time.

2 REMEMBERING ISRAEL'S WANDERINGS

"Then we turned around and headed back across the wilderness toward the Red Sea,* just as the LORD had instructed me, and we wandered around in the region of Mount Seir for a long time.

2"Then at last the LORD said to me, 3'You have been wandering around in this hill country long enough; turn to the north. 4Give these orders to the people: "You will pass through the country belonging to your relatives the Edomites, the descendants of Esau, who live in Seir. The Edomites will feel threatened, so be careful. 5Do not bother them, for I have given them all the hill country around Mount Seir as their property, and I will not give you even one square foot of their land. 6If you need food to eat or water to drink, pay them for it. 7For the LORD your God has blessed you in everything you have done. He has watched your every step through this great wilderness. During these forty years, the LORD your God has been with you, and you have lacked nothing."'

8"So we bypassed the territory of our relatives, the descendants of Esau, who live in Seir. We avoided the road through the Arabah Valley that comes up from Elath and Ezion-geber.

"Then as we turned north along the desert route through Moab, 9the LORD warned us, 'Do not bother the Moabites, the descendants of Lot, or start a war with them. I have given them Ar as their property, and I will not give you any of their land.'"

10(A race of giants called the Emites had once lived in the area of Ar. They were as strong and numerous and tall as the Anakites, another race of giants. 11Both the Emites and the Anakites are also known as the Rephaites, though the Moabites call them Emites. 12In earlier times the Horites had lived in Seir, but they were driven out and displaced by the descendants of Esau, just as Israel drove out the people of Canaan when the LORD gave Israel their land.)

13Moses continued, "Then the LORD said to us, 'Get moving. Cross the Zered Brook.' So we crossed the brook.

14"Thirty-eight years passed from the time we first left Kadesh-barnea until we finally crossed the Zered Brook! By then, all the men old enough to fight in battle had died in the wilderness, as the LORD had vowed would happen. 15The LORD struck them down until they had all been eliminated from the community.

16"When all the men of fighting age had died, 17the LORD said to me, 18'Today you will cross the border of Moab at Ar 19and enter the land of the Ammonites, the descendants of Lot. But do not bother them or start a war with them. I have given the land of Ammon to them as their property, and I will not give you any of their land.'"

20(That area was once considered the land of the Rephaites, who had lived there, though the Ammonites call them Zamzummites. 21They were also as strong and numerous and tall as the Anakites. But the LORD destroyed them so the Ammonites could occupy their land. 22He had done the same for the descendants of Esau who lived in Seir, for he destroyed the Horites so they could settle there in their place. The descendants of Esau live there to this day. 23A similar thing happened when the Caphtorites from Crete* invaded and destroyed the Avvites, who had lived in villages in the area of Gaza.)

24Moses continued, "Then the LORD said, 'Now get

1:40 Hebrew *sea of reeds*. **2:1** Hebrew *sea of reeds*. **2:23** Hebrew *from Caphtor*.

moving! Cross the Arnon Gorge. Look, I will hand over to
you Sihon the Amorite, king of Heshbon, and I will give
you his land. Attack him and begin to occupy the land.
25Beginning today I will make people throughout the
earth terrified because of you. When they hear reports
about you, they will tremble with dread and fear.'"

VICTORY OVER SIHON OF HESHBON

26Moses continued, "From the wilderness of Kedemoth I
sent ambassadors to King Sihon of Heshbon with this
proposal of peace:

27'Let us travel through your land. We will stay on the
main road and won't turn off into the fields on either
side. 28Sell us food to eat and water to drink, and we
will pay for it. All we want is permission to pass
through your land. 29The descendants of Esau who
live in Seir allowed us to go through their country,
and so did the Moabites, who live in Ar. Let us pass
through until we cross the Jordan into the land the
LORD our God is giving us.'

30"But King Sihon of Heshbon refused to allow us to
pass through, because the LORD your God made Sihon
stubborn and defiant so he could help you defeat him, as
he has now done.
31"Then the LORD said to me, 'Look, I have begun to
hand King Sihon and his land over to you. Begin now to
conquer and occupy his land.'
32"Then King Sihon declared war on us and mobilized
his forces at Jahaz. 33But the LORD our God handed him
over to us, and we crushed him, his sons, and all his people. 34We conquered all his towns and completely destroyed* everyone—men, women, and children. Not a
single person was spared. 35We took all the livestock as
plunder for ourselves, along with anything of value from
the towns we ransacked.
36"The LORD our God also helped us conquer Aroer on
the edge of the Arnon Gorge, and the town in the gorge,
and the whole area as far as Gilead. No town had walls too
strong for us. 37However, we avoided the land of the Ammonites all along the Jabbok River and the towns in the
hill country—all the places the LORD our God had commanded us to leave alone.

3

VICTORY OVER OG OF BASHAN

"Next we turned and headed for the land of Bashan,
where King Og and his entire army attacked us at Edrei.
2But the LORD told me, 'Do not be afraid of him, for I have
given you victory over Og and his entire army, and I will
give you all his land. Treat him just as you treated King
Sihon of the Amorites, who ruled in Heshbon.'
3"So the LORD our God handed King Og and all his people over to us, and we killed them all. Not a single person
survived. 4We conquered all sixty of his towns—the entire
Argob region in his kingdom of Bashan. Not a single town
escaped our conquest. 5These towns were all fortified
with high walls and barred gates. We also took many
unwalled villages at the same time. 6We completely destroyed* the kingdom of Bashan, just as we had destroyed
King Sihon of Heshbon. We destroyed all the people in
every town we conquered—men, women, and children
alike. 7But we kept all the livestock for ourselves and took
plunder from all the towns.
8"So we took the land of the two Amorite kings east of
the Jordan River—all the way from the Arnon Gorge to
Mount Hermon. 9(Mount Hermon is called Sirion by the
Sidonians, and the Amorites call it Senir.) 10We had now
conquered all the cities on the plateau and all Gilead and
Bashan, as far as the towns of Salecah and Edrei, which
were part of Og's kingdom in Bashan. 11(King Og of Bashan was the last survivor of the giant Rephaites. His bed
was made of iron and was more than thirteen feet long
and six feet wide.* It can still be seen in the Ammonite
city of Rabbah.)

IMPOSSIBLE ODDS? 3:1-3

The Israelites faced a big problem: the well-trained army of Og, the king of Bashan, was much stronger. But Israel defeated them because God fought for them. Facing a huge problem like the Israelites? Maybe the odds you face seem impossible to beat. The same God who saw Og's army as no challenge at all is right there with you. ■

LAND DIVISION EAST OF THE JORDAN

12"When we took possession of this land, I gave to the
tribes of Reuben and Gad the territory beyond Aroer
along the Arnon Gorge, plus half of the hill country of Gilead with its towns. 13Then I gave the rest of Gilead and all
of Bashan—Og's former kingdom—to the half-tribe of
Manasseh. (This entire Argob region of Bashan used to be
known as the land of the Rephaites. 14Jair, a leader from
the tribe of Manasseh, conquered the whole Argob region in Bashan, all the way to the border of the Geshurites
and Maacathites. Jair renamed this region after himself,
calling it the Towns of Jair,* as it is still known today.) 15I
gave Gilead to the clan of Makir. 16But I also gave part of
Gilead to the tribes of Reuben and Gad. The area I gave
them extended from the middle of the Arnon Gorge in
the south to the Jabbok River on the Ammonite frontier.
17They also received the Jordan Valley, all the way from
the Sea of Galilee down to the Dead Sea,* with the Jordan
River serving as the western boundary. To the east were
the slopes of Pisgah.
18"At that time I gave this command to the tribes that
would live east of the Jordan: 'Although the LORD your God
has given you this land as your property, all your fighting
men must cross the Jordan ahead of your Israelite relatives,

2:34 The Hebrew term used here refers to the complete consecration of things or people to the LORD, either by destroying them or by giving them as an offering. **3:6** The Hebrew term used here refers to the complete consecration of things or people to the LORD, either by destroying them or by giving them as an offering; also in 3:6b. **3:11** Hebrew *9 cubits* [4.1 meters] *long and 4 cubits* [1.8 meters] *wide.* **3:14** Hebrew *Havvoth-jair.* **3:17** Hebrew *from Kinnereth to the Sea of the Arabah, the Salt Sea.*

armed and ready to assist them. 19Your wives, children,
and numerous livestock, however, may stay behind in the
towns I have given you. 20When the LORD has given security to the rest of the Israelites, as he has to you, and when
they occupy the land the LORD your God is giving them
across the Jordan River, then you may all return here to
the land I have given you.'

A SECRET WEAPON 3:21-22

"The LORD your God will fight for you." What encouraging news for Joshua, who was to lead his men against army after army in the Promised Land! Since God promised to help him win every battle, he had nothing to fear. Our battles may not be against godless armies, but they are just as real as Joshua's. Whether we have a need to resist temptation or are battling fear, God has promised to fight with and for us as we obey him. ■

MOSES FORBIDDEN TO ENTER THE LAND

21"At that time I gave Joshua this charge: 'You have seen
for yourself everything the LORD your God has done to
these two kings. He will do the same to all the kingdoms
on the west side of the Jordan. 22Do not be afraid of the
nations there, for the LORD your God will fight for you.'

23"At that time I pleaded with the LORD and said,
24'O Sovereign LORD, you have only begun to show your
greatness and the strength of your hand to me, your servant. Is there any god in heaven or on earth who can perform such great and mighty deeds as you do? 25Please let
me cross the Jordan to see the wonderful land on the
other side, the beautiful hill country and the Lebanon
mountains.'

26"But the LORD was angry with me because of you, and
he would not listen to me. 'That's enough!' he declared.
'Speak of it no more. 27But go up to Pisgah Peak, and look
over the land in every direction. Take a good look, but you
may not cross the Jordan River. 28Instead, commission
Joshua and encourage and strengthen him, for he will
lead the people across the Jordan. He will give them all
the land you now see before you as their possession.' 29So
we stayed in the valley near Beth-peor.

4

MOSES URGES ISRAEL TO OBEY

"And now, Israel, listen carefully to these decrees and
regulations that I am about to teach you. Obey them so
that you may live, so you may enter and occupy the land
that the LORD, the God of your ancestors, is giving you.
2Do not add to or subtract from these commands I am
giving you. Just obey the commands of the LORD your God
that I am giving you.

3"You saw for yourself what the LORD did to you at Baal-
peor. There the LORD your God destroyed everyone who
had worshiped Baal, the god of Peor. 4But all of you who
were faithful to the LORD your God are still alive today—
every one of you.

5"Look, I now teach you these decrees and regulations
just as the LORD my God commanded me, so that you may
obey them in the land you are about to enter and occupy.
6Obey them completely, and you will display your wisdom and intelligence among the surrounding nations.
When they hear all these decrees, they will exclaim, 'How
wise and prudent are the people of this great nation!' 7For
what great nation has a god as near to them as the LORD
our God is near to us whenever we call on him? 8And what
great nation has decrees and regulations as righteous and
fair as this body of instructions that I am giving you
today?

9"But watch out! Be careful never to forget what you
yourself have seen. Do not let these memories escape
from your mind as long as you live! And be sure to pass
them on to your children and grandchildren. 10Never forget the day when you stood before the LORD your God at
Mount Sinai,* where he told me, 'Summon the people before me, and I will personally instruct them. Then they
will learn to fear me as long as they live, and they will
teach their children to fear me also.'

DON'T FORGET 4:9-10

Moses wanted to make sure that the people of Israel did not forget what God had accomplished for them. That's why he urged parents to tell their children about God's great miracles. You can keep God's great acts of faithfulness fresh in your mind by telling your friends what you have seen him do. ■

11"You came near and stood at the foot of the mountain, while flames from the mountain shot into the sky.
The mountain was shrouded in black clouds and deep
darkness. 12And the LORD spoke to you from the heart of
the fire. You heard the sound of his words but didn't see
his form; there was only a voice. 13He proclaimed his covenant—the Ten Commandments*—which he com-
manded you to keep, and which he wrote on two stone
tablets. 14It was at that time that the LORD commanded
me to teach you his decrees and regulations so you would
obey them in the land you are about to enter and occupy.

A WARNING AGAINST IDOLATRY

15"But be very careful! You did not see the LORD's form on
the day he spoke to you from the heart of the fire at
Mount Sinai. 16So do not corrupt yourselves by making an
idol in any form—whether of a man or a woman, 17an animal on the ground, a bird in the sky, 18a small animal that
scurries along the ground, or a fish in the deepest sea.
19And when you look up into the sky and see the sun,
moon, and stars—all the forces of heaven—don't be seduced into worshiping them. The LORD your God gave
them to all the peoples of the earth. 20Remember that the
LORD rescued you from the iron-smelting furnace of
Egypt in order to make you his very own people and his
special possession, which is what you are today.

21"But the LORD was angry with me because of you. He

4:10 Hebrew *Horeb*, another name for Sinai; also in 4:15. 4:13 Hebrew *the ten words*.

vowed that I would not cross the Jordan River into the
good land the LORD your God is giving you as your special
possession. 22You will cross the Jordan to occupy the
land, but I will not. Instead, I will die here on the east side
of the river. 23So be careful not to break the covenant the
LORD your God has made with you. Do not make idols of
any shape or form, for the LORD your God has forbidden
this. 24The LORD your God is a devouring fire; he is a jealous God.

ASTROLOGY

"What's that?" Kevin asks, pointing to a book in Kim's locker.

"Oh, that," Kim responds, picking up the skinny paperback. "That's a new book on astrology I got at a bookstore yesterday."

"Astrology?!" Kevin half screams. "Don't tell me you believe all that junk!"

"Laugh if you want," Kim responds matter-of-factly. "But I've seen it come true in my life so many times it's scary! Besides, lots of people in this country believe in astrology. So really, Kevin, if you don't read your horoscope, you're the one who's out of it."

Lauren (the noisiest girl at school) walks up. "What are you guys looking at? Oh, I have that book. It's so good! What sign are you, Kevin? . . . Or aren't you into astrology?"

Kevin hesitates before replying, "Well, it's not like I don't ever read my horoscope. I'm a Leo. Sometimes it's pretty accurate, I guess."

Kim smiles. "Well, you're welcome to borrow my copy. My mom has another one at home."

Kevin coughs nervously, "I don't know—I, uh . . ."

"Kevin, it's completely harmless!" Lauren urges. "Astrology is interesting . . . and a lot of fun. Take the book!"

Kim stands there offering the book. Kevin reluctantly takes it as the bell rings.

Is looking to the stars for guidance just an innocent diversion?

Check out Deuteronomy 4:19 and 17:2-5. The next time someone brings up your horoscope, what will you say?

25"In the future, when you have children and grandchildren and have lived in the land a long time, do not
corrupt yourselves by making idols of any kind. This is
evil in the sight of the LORD your God and will arouse his
anger.
26"Today I call on heaven and earth as witnesses
against you. If you break my covenant, you will quickly
disappear from the land you are crossing the Jordan to
occupy. You will live there only a short time; then you will
be utterly destroyed. 27For the LORD will scatter you
among the nations, where only a few of you will survive.
28There, in a foreign land, you will worship idols made
from wood and stone—gods that neither see nor hear nor
eat nor smell. 29But from there you will search again for
the LORD your God. And if you search for him with all
your heart and soul, you will find him.
30"In the distant future, when you are suffering all
these things, you will finally return to the LORD your God
and listen to what he tells you. 31For the LORD your God is
a merciful God; he will not abandon you or destroy you or
forget the solemn covenant he made with your ancestors.

THERE IS ONLY ONE GOD

32"Now search all of history, from the time God created
people on the earth until now, and search from one end
of the heavens to the other. Has anything as great as this
ever been seen or heard before? 33Has any nation ever
heard the voice of God* speaking from fire—as you did—
and survived? 34Has any other god dared to take a nation
for himself out of another nation by means of trials, miraculous signs, wonders, war, a strong hand, a powerful
arm, and terrifying acts? Yet that is what the LORD your
God did for you in Egypt, right before your eyes.
35"He showed you these things so you would know that
the LORD is God and there is no other. 36He let you hear
his voice from heaven so he could instruct you. He let you
see his great fire here on earth so he could speak to you
from it. 37Because he loved your ancestors, he chose to
bless their descendants, and he personally brought you
out of Egypt with a great display of power. 38He drove out
nations far greater than you, so he could bring you in and
give you their land as your special possession, as it is
today.
39"So remember this and keep it firmly in mind: The
LORD is God both in heaven and on earth, and there is no
other. 40If you obey all the decrees and commands I am
giving you today, all will be well with you and your children. I am giving you these instructions so you will enjoy
a long life in the land the LORD your God is giving you for
all time."

EASTERN CITIES OF REFUGE

41Then Moses set apart three cities of refuge east of the
Jordan River. 42Anyone who killed another person unintentionally, without previous hostility, could flee there to
live in safety. 43These were the cities: Bezer on the wilderness plateau for the tribe of Reuben; Ramoth in Gilead
for the tribe of Gad; Golan in Bashan for the tribe of
Manasseh.

INTRODUCTION TO MOSES' SECOND ADDRESS

44This is the body of instruction that Moses presented to
the Israelites. 45These are the laws, decrees, and regulations that Moses gave to the people of Israel when they
left Egypt, 46and as they camped in the valley near Beth-
peor east of the Jordan River. (This land was formerly
occupied by the Amorites under King Sihon, who ruled
from Heshbon. But Moses and the Israelites destroyed
him and his people when they came up from Egypt. 47Israel

4:33 Or *voice of a god.*

keeping it real

My parents are Christians, and even though they are stricter than I'd like, I have to admit they're good parents. One day while reading the Bible, I came across the fifth commandment, the one about honoring your parents. The note in the margin pointed out that there is a promise attached to this commandment: If you follow it, you will lead a long and happy life.

What struck me is that my parents are always saying things like, "We're only saying this for your own good. We want you to be happy." It seemed like God was saying, "Your parents love you, they are trying to help you lead a happy life, so if you listen to them, your life will go better." It all made sense. For a while I felt guilty that I didn't listen to them as much as I should, but I determined to consult them more.

A few nights later I decided to talk to them about a relationship I was having trouble with. I was surprised to find that they really understood, and my mom even had some helpful advice about what she had done in a similar situation. I hadn't realized before how much wisdom my parents really have to give me. **—Amy**

took possession of his land and that of King Og of Bashan—the two Amorite kings east of the Jordan. 48So Israel conquered the entire area from Aroer at the edge of
the Arnon Gorge all the way to Mount Sirion,* also called
Mount Hermon. 49And they conquered the eastern bank
of the Jordan River as far south as the Dead Sea,* below
the slopes of Pisgah.)

REMEMBERING THE COVENANT 5:1

As the people of Israel reviewed their covenant with God, Moses commanded them to listen, learn, and obey God's laws and regulations. Moses' threefold command to the Israelites is excellent advice for all of God's followers. *Listening* means absorbing and accepting information about God. *Learning* means understanding the meaning and consequences of this information. *Obeying* means putting into action all we have learned and understood. All three parts are essential to a growing relationship with God. Which of the three is easiest for you? Which is hardest? ■

5

TEN COMMANDMENTS FOR THE COVENANT COMMUNITY

Moses called all the people of Israel together and said,
"Listen carefully, Israel. Hear the decrees and regulations
I am giving you today, so you may learn them and obey
them!
2"The LORD our God made a covenant with us at Mount
Sinai.* 3The LORD did not make this covenant with our
ancestors, but with all of us who are alive today. 4At the
mountain the LORD spoke to you face to face from the
heart of the fire. 5I stood as an intermediary between you
and the LORD, for you were afraid of the fire and did not
want to approach the mountain. He spoke to me, and I
passed his words on to you. This is what he said:

6"I am the LORD your God, who rescued you from the
land of Egypt, the place of your slavery.
7"You must not have any other god but me.
8"You must not make for yourself an idol of any kind,
or an image of anything in the heavens or on the earth
or in the sea. 9You must not bow down to them or
worship them, for I, the LORD your God, am a jealous
God who will not tolerate your affection for any other
gods. I lay the sins of the parents upon their children;
the entire family is affected—even children in the
third and fourth generations of those who reject me.
10But I lavish unfailing love for a thousand generations
on those* who love me and obey my commands.
11"You must not misuse the name of the LORD your God.
The LORD will not let you go unpunished if you
misuse his name.
12"Observe the Sabbath day by keeping it holy, as the LORD
your God has commanded you. 13You have six days each
week for your ordinary work, 14but the seventh day is a
Sabbath day of rest dedicated to the LORD your God. On
that day no one in your household may do any work.
This includes you, your sons and daughters, your male

4:48 As in Syriac version (see also 3:9); Hebrew reads *Mount Sion.* 4:49 Hebrew *took the Arabah on the east side of the Jordan as far as the sea of the Arabah.* 5:2 Hebrew *Horeb,* another name for Sinai. 5:10 Hebrew *for thousands of those.*

and female servants, your oxen and donkeys and
other livestock, and any foreigners living among you.
All your male and female servants must rest as you do.
15 Remember that you were once slaves in Egypt, but the
LORD your God brought you out with his strong hand
and powerful arm. That is why the LORD your God has
commanded you to rest on the Sabbath day.
16 "Honor your father and mother, as the LORD your God
commanded you. Then you will live a long, full life in
the land the LORD your God is giving you.
17 "You must not murder.
18 "You must not commit adultery.
19 "You must not steal.
20 "You must not testify falsely against your neighbor.
21 "You must not covet your neighbor's wife. You must
not covet your neighbor's house or land, male or
female servant, ox or donkey, or anything else that
belongs to your neighbor.

22 "The LORD spoke these words to all of you assembled
there at the foot of the mountain. He spoke with a loud
voice from the heart of the fire, surrounded by clouds and
deep darkness. This was all he said at that time, and he
wrote his words on two stone tablets and gave them to me.
23 "But when you heard the voice from the heart of the
darkness, while the mountain was blazing with fire, all
your tribal leaders and elders came to me. 24 They said,
'Look, the LORD our God has shown us his glory and greatness, and we have heard his voice from the heart of the
fire. Today we have seen that God can speak to us humans,
and yet we live! 25 But now, why should we risk death
again? If the LORD our God speaks to us again, we will certainly die and be consumed by this awesome fire. 26 Can
any living thing hear the voice of the living God from the
heart of the fire as we did and yet survive? 27 Go yourself
and listen to what the LORD our God says. Then come and
tell us everything he tells you, and we will listen and obey.'
28 "The LORD heard the request you made to me. And he
said, 'I have heard what the people said to you, and they
are right. 29 Oh, that they would always have hearts like
this, that they might fear me and obey all my commands!
If they did, they and their descendants would prosper
forever. 30 Go and tell them, "Return to your tents." 31 But
you stand here with me so I can give you all my commands, decrees, and regulations. You must teach them to
the people so they can obey them in the land I am giving
them as their possession.'"
32 So Moses told the people, "You must be careful to
obey all the commands of the LORD your God, following
his instructions in every detail. 33 Stay on the path that the
LORD your God has commanded you to follow. Then you
will live long and prosperous lives in the land you are
about to enter and occupy.

6

A CALL FOR WHOLEHEARTED COMMITMENT

"These are the commands, decrees, and regulations that
the LORD your God commanded me to teach you. You
must obey them in the land you are about to enter and
occupy, 2 and you and your children and grandchildren
must fear the LORD your God as long as you live. If you
obey all his decrees and commands, you will enjoy a long
life. 3 Listen closely, Israel, and be careful to obey. Then all
will go well with you, and you will have many children in
the land flowing with milk and honey, just as the LORD,
the God of your ancestors, promised you.
4 "Listen, O Israel! The LORD is our God, the LORD
alone.* 5 And you must love the LORD your God with all
your heart, all your soul, and all your strength. 6 And you
must commit yourselves wholeheartedly to these commands that I am giving you today. 7 Repeat them again
and again to your children. Talk about them when you
are at home and when you are on the road, when you are
going to bed and when you are getting up. 8 Tie them to
your hands and wear them on your forehead as reminders. 9 Write them on the doorposts of your house and on
your gates.

TEACHING CHILDREN 6:4-9

This passage often is said to be the central theme of Deuteronomy. It sets a pattern that helps us relate the Word of God to daily life. We are to love God, obey his commandments, and teach them to our children. God emphasized the importance of teaching children about his commandments. Even if you don't have any children, you can still take part in a younger person's faith education. Maybe you have a niece, a younger cousin, or work with younger kids in a community center. How do you model your commitment to God's Word? ■

10 "The LORD your God will soon bring you into the land
he swore to give you when he made a vow to your ancestors Abraham, Isaac, and Jacob. It is a land with large,
prosperous cities that you did not build. 11 The houses
will be richly stocked with goods you did not produce.
You will draw water from cisterns you did not dig, and
you will eat from vineyards and olive trees you did not
plant. When you have eaten your fill in this land, 12 be
careful not to forget the LORD, who rescued you from
slavery in the land of Egypt. 13 You must fear the LORD
your God and serve him. When you take an oath, you
must use only his name.
14 "You must not worship any of the gods of neighboring nations, 15 for the LORD your God, who lives among
you, is a jealous God. His anger will flare up against you,
and he will wipe you from the face of the earth. 16 You
must not test the LORD your God as you did when you
complained at Massah. 17 You must diligently obey the
commands of the LORD your God—all the laws and decrees he has given you. 18 Do what is right and good in the
LORD's sight, so all will go well with you. Then you will enter and occupy the good land that the LORD swore to give
your ancestors. 19 You will drive out all the enemies living
in the land, just as the LORD said you would.

6:4 Or *The LORD our God is one LORD;* or *The LORD our God, the LORD is one;* or *The LORD is our God, the LORD is one.*

20"In the future your children will ask you, 'What is the
meaning of these laws, decrees, and regulations that the
LORD our God has commanded us to
obey?'
21"Then you must tell them, 'We
were Pharaoh's slaves in Egypt, but the
LORD brought us out of Egypt with his
strong hand. 22The LORD did miraculous signs and wonders before our
eyes, dealing terrifying blows against
Egypt and Pharaoh and all his people.
23He brought us out of Egypt so he
could give us this land he had sworn to
give our ancestors. 24And the LORD our
God commanded us to obey all these
decrees and to fear him so he can continue to bless us and preserve our lives,
as he has done to this day. 25For we will
be counted as righteous when we obey
all the commands the LORD our God
has given us.'

The LORD your God is indeed God. He is the faithful God who keeps his covenant for a thousand generations.

DEUTERONOMY 7:9

7

THE PRIVILEGE OF HOLINESS

"When the LORD your God brings you into the land you are
about to enter and occupy, he will clear away many nations
ahead of you: the Hittites, Girgashites, Amorites, Canaanites, Perizzites, Hivites, and Jebusites. These seven nations
are greater and more numerous than you. 2When the LORD
your God hands these nations over to you and you conquer
them, you must completely destroy* them. Make no treaties with them and show them no mercy. 3You must not
intermarry with them. Do not let your daughters and sons
marry their sons and daughters, 4for they will lead your
children away from me to worship other gods. Then the
anger of the LORD will burn against you, and he will quickly
destroy you. 5This is what you must do. You must break
down their pagan altars and shatter their sacred pillars. Cut
down their Asherah poles and burn their idols. 6For you are
a holy people, who belong to the LORD your God. Of all the
people on earth, the LORD your God has chosen you to be
his own special treasure.
7"The LORD did not set his heart on you and choose you
because you were more numerous than other nations, for
you were the smallest of all nations! 8Rather, it was simply
that the LORD loves you, and he was keeping the oath he
had sworn to your ancestors. That is why the LORD rescued you with such a strong hand from your slavery and
from the oppressive hand of Pharaoh, king of Egypt.
9Understand, therefore, that the LORD your God is indeed
God. He is the faithful God who keeps his covenant for a
thousand generations and lavishes his unfailing love on
those who love him and obey his commands. 10But he
does not hesitate to punish and destroy those who reject
him. 11Therefore, you must obey all these commands, decrees, and regulations I am giving you today.
12"If you listen to these regulations and faithfully obey
them, the LORD your God will keep his covenant of
unfailing love with you, as he promised with an oath to
your ancestors. 13He will love you and
bless you, and he will give you many
children. He will give fertility to your
land and your animals. When you arrive in the land he swore to give your
ancestors, you will have large harvests
of grain, new wine, and olive oil, and
great herds of cattle, sheep, and goats.
14You will be blessed above all the nations of the earth. None of your men
or women will be childless, and all
your livestock will bear young. 15And
the LORD will protect you from all
sickness. He will not let you suffer
from the terrible diseases you knew in
Egypt, but he will inflict them on all
your enemies!
16"You must destroy all the nations the LORD your God hands over
to you. Show them no mercy, and do not worship their
gods, or they will trap you. 17Perhaps you will think to
yourselves, 'How can we ever conquer these nations
that are so much more powerful than we are?' 18But
don't be afraid of them! Just remember what the LORD
your God did to Pharaoh and to all the land of Egypt.
19Remember the great terrors the LORD your God sent
against them. You saw it all with your own eyes! And remember the miraculous signs and wonders, and the
strong hand and powerful arm with which he brought
you out of Egypt. The LORD your God will use this same
power against all the people you fear. 20And then the
LORD your God will send terror* to drive out the few
survivors still hiding from you!

ONE STEP AT A TIME 7:21-24

Moses told the Israelites that God would destroy their enemies, but not all at once. God had the power to destroy those nations instantly, but he chose to do it in stages. In the same way and with the same power, God could miraculously and instantaneously change your life. Ever wish that? Many times God chooses to help people gradually, teaching them one lesson at a time. Are you willing to trust God's step-by-step process? ■

21"No, do not be afraid of those nations, for the LORD
your God is among you, and he is a great and awesome
God. 22The LORD your God will drive those nations out
ahead of you little by little. You will not clear them away
all at once, otherwise the wild animals would multiply too
quickly for you. 23But the LORD your God will hand them
over to you. He will throw them into complete confusion
until they are destroyed. 24He will put their kings in your
power, and you will erase their names from the face of

7:2 The Hebrew term used here refers to the complete consecration of things or people to the LORD, either by destroying them or by giving them as an offering; also in 7:26. 7:20 Often rendered *the hornet*. The meaning of the Hebrew is uncertain.

COVENANTS

ULTIMATE ISSUES

You've seen it in the movies or maybe on the news—leaders of two warring countries decide to end the fighting and sign a peace treaty. The representative of the losing side agrees to terms of surrender, perhaps giving up contested land or paying back some money as a war debt. The winning country's spokesman agrees that his military forces will pull out, so long as the losing side keeps up its end of the agreement. Should they ever break their word and resume the hostilities, the conquering armies will come back in full force.

What we call a peace treaty was called a *covenant* in Old Testament times. It was used in situations where one kingdom defeated another in battle, or when a weaker empire wanted to avoid going to war with a more powerful one. In short, a covenant is an agreement between two parties that binds them to do certain things for each other. For example, the stronger party agrees not to destroy the weaker one; in return, the weaker one agrees to pay taxes or tribute. Also, the covenant agreement included sections explaining what would happen if the rules were kept and if they were broken. These sections were called "blessings" and "curses." (See Deut 11:26-32.)

God's covenant with Israel started with Abram. God promised to give Abram many descendants and a wonderful land for their home. After establishing this covenant, God promised to take the curse on himself if he should ever break his part of the agreement.

You might be thinking, *That's a fascinating bit of historical trivia—but what does it have to do with me?* Just this: in Romans, Paul tells us that Christians will inherit the blessings promised to Abram (Abraham). Romans 11:17 says, "But some of these branches from Abraham's tree—some of the people of Israel—have been broken off. And you Gentiles, who were branches from a wild olive tree, were grafted in. So now you also receive the blessing God has promised Abraham and his children, sharing in the rich nourishment of God's special olive tree." So, if you're a Christian, this promise is for you!

No, that doesn't mean you can pick up and head to the Holy Land to stake out some prime real estate. Our Promised Land is in another place—a new heaven and a new earth. But as you read about God's covenant with Abram and with the nation of Israel, know with absolute certainty that God will keep his promises to you—all of them—just as he did with Israel. Your part is to enter into an agreement with him about your sin and his forgiveness through Jesus, the author of the new covenant.

the earth. No one will be able to stand against you, and
you will destroy them all.
25"You must burn their idols in fire, and you must not
covet the silver or gold that covers them. You must not
take it or it will become a trap to you, for it is detestable to
the LORD your God. 26Do not bring any detestable objects
into your home, for then you will be destroyed, just like
them. You must utterly detest such things, for they are set
apart for destruction.

8 A CALL TO REMEMBER AND OBEY

"Be careful to obey all the commands I am giving you today. Then you will live and multiply, and you will enter
and occupy the land the LORD swore to give your ancestors. 2Remember how the LORD your God led you through
the wilderness for these forty years, humbling you and
testing you to prove your character, and to find out
whether or not you would obey his commands. 3Yes, he
humbled you by letting you go hungry and then feeding
you with manna, a food previously unknown to you and
your ancestors. He did it to teach you that people do not
live by bread alone; rather, we live by every word that
comes from the mouth of the LORD. 4For all these forty
years your clothes didn't wear out, and your feet didn't
blister or swell. 5Think about it: Just as a parent disciplines a child, the LORD your God disciplines you for your
own good.
6"So obey the commands of the LORD your God by
walking in his ways and fearing him. 7For the LORD your
God is bringing you into a good land of flowing streams
and pools of water, with fountains and springs that gush
out in the valleys and hills. 8It is a land of wheat and barley; of grapevines, fig trees, and pomegranates; of olive oil

Obedience

Deuteronomy 8:1 tells us to obey God's commands. We do this by obeying God with . . .

OUR HEART	By loving him more than any relationship, activity, achievement, or possession
OUR WILL	By committing ourselves completely to him
OUR MIND	By seeking to know him and his Word, so his principles and values form the foundation of all we think and do
OUR BODY	By recognizing that our strengths, talents, and sexuality are given to us by God to be used for pleasure and fulfillment according to his rules, not ours
OUR FINANCES	By deciding that all of the resources we have ultimately come from God, and that we are to be managers of them and not owners
OUR FUTURE	By deciding to make service to God and people the main purpose of our life's work

and honey. 9It is a land where food is plentiful and nothing is lacking. It is a land where iron is as common as
stone, and copper is abundant in the hills. 10When you
have eaten your fill, be sure to praise the LORD your God
for the good land he has given you.
11"But that is the time to be careful! Beware that in your
plenty you do not forget the LORD your God and disobey
his commands, regulations, and decrees that I am giving
you today. 12For when you have become full and prosperous and have built fine homes to live in, 13and when your
flocks and herds have become very large and your silver
and gold have multiplied along with everything else, be
careful! 14Do not become proud at that time and forget
the LORD your God, who rescued you from slavery in the
land of Egypt. 15Do not forget that he led you through the
great and terrifying wilderness with its poisonous snakes
and scorpions, where it was so hot and dry. He gave you
water from the rock! 16He fed you with manna in the wilderness, a food unknown to your ancestors. He did this to
humble you and test you for your own good. 17He did all
this so you would never say to yourself, 'I have achieved
this wealth with my own strength and energy.' 18Remember
the LORD your God. He is the one who gives you power to
be successful, in order to fulfill the covenant he confirmed to your ancestors with an oath.
19"But I assure you of this: If you ever forget the LORD
your God and follow other gods, worshiping and bowing
down to them, you will certainly be destroyed. 20Just as
the LORD has destroyed other nations in your path, you
also will be destroyed if you refuse to obey the LORD your
God.

9 VICTORY BY GOD'S GRACE

"Listen, O Israel! Today you are about to cross the Jordan
River to take over the land belonging to nations much
greater and more powerful than you. They live in cities
with walls that reach to the sky! 2The people are strong
and tall—descendants of the famous Anakite giants.
You've heard the saying, 'Who can stand up to the Anakites?' 3But recognize today that the LORD your God is the
one who will cross over ahead of you like a devouring fire
to destroy them. He will subdue them so that you will
quickly conquer them and drive them out, just as the
LORD has promised.
4"After the LORD your God has done this for you, don't
say in your hearts, 'The LORD has given us this land because we are such good people!' No, it is because of the
wickedness of the other nations that he is pushing them
out of your way. 5It is not because you are so good or have
such integrity that you are about to occupy their land.
The LORD your God will drive these nations out ahead of
you only because of their wickedness, and to fulfill the
oath he swore to your ancestors Abraham, Isaac, and Jacob. 6You must recognize that the LORD your God is not
giving you this good land because you are good, for you
are not—you are a stubborn people.

REMEMBERING THE GOLD CALF

7"Remember and never forget how angry you made the
LORD your God out in the wilderness. From the day you
left Egypt until now, you have been constantly rebelling
against him. 8Even at Mount Sinai* you made the LORD so
angry he was ready to destroy you. 9This happened when
I was on the mountain receiving the tablets of stone inscribed with the words of the covenant that the LORD had
made with you. I was there for forty days and forty nights,
and all that time I ate no food and drank no water. 10The
LORD gave me the two tablets on which God had written
with his own finger all the words he had spoken to you
from the heart of the fire when you were assembled at
the mountain.
11"At the end of the forty days and nights, the LORD
handed me the two stone tablets inscribed with the
words of the covenant. 12Then the LORD said to me, 'Get

9:8 Hebrew *Horeb*, another name for Sinai.

up! Go down immediately, for the people you brought out of Egypt have corrupted themselves. How quickly they have turned away from the way I commanded them to live! They have melted gold and made an idol for themselves!'

GOD'S MERCY 9:1-6

If the Israelites were unrighteous and stubborn, why did God make such wonderful promises to them? There are two good reasons. (1) God and Israel had made a covenant (Gen 15; 17; Exod 19–20). God promised to be faithful to them and they promised to obey him. Even though the Israelites rarely held up their end of the bargain, God remained faithful. (2) God's unconditional mercy made him willing to restore his people no matter how many times they turned from him.

It is comforting to know that despite our inconsistencies and sins, God loves us unconditionally. Eternal life is not achieved on the merit system, but on the mercy system. God loves us no matter who we are or what we have done. Believe that? ■

13"The LORD also said to me, 'I have seen how stubborn and rebellious these people are. 14Leave me alone so I may destroy them and erase their name from under heaven. Then I will make a mighty nation of your descendants, a nation larger and more powerful than they are.'

15"So while the mountain was blazing with fire I turned and came down, holding in my hands the two stone tablets inscribed with the terms of the covenant. 16There below me I could see that you had sinned against the LORD your God. You had melted gold and made a calf idol for yourselves. How quickly you had turned away from the path the LORD had commanded you to follow! 17So I took the stone tablets and threw them to the ground, smashing them before your eyes.

18"Then, as before, I threw myself down before the LORD for forty days and nights. I ate no bread and drank no water because of the great sin you had committed by doing what the LORD hated, provoking him to anger. 19I feared that the furious anger of the LORD, which turned him against you, would drive him to destroy you. But again he listened to me. 20The LORD was so angry with Aaron that he wanted to destroy him, too. But I prayed for Aaron, and the LORD spared him. 21I took your sin—the calf you had made—and I melted it down in the fire and ground it into fine dust. Then I threw the dust into the stream that flows down the mountain.

22"You also made the LORD angry at Taberah,* Massah,* and Kibroth-hattaavah.* 23And at Kadesh-barnea the LORD sent you out with this command: 'Go up and take over the land I have given you.' But you rebelled against the command of the LORD your God and refused to put your trust in him or obey him. 24Yes, you have been rebelling against the LORD as long as I have known you.

25"That is why I threw myself down before the LORD for forty days and nights—for the LORD said he would destroy you. 26I prayed to the LORD and said, 'O Sovereign LORD, do not destroy them. They are your own people. They are your special possession, whom you redeemed from Egypt by your mighty power and your strong hand. 27Please overlook the stubbornness and the awful sin of these people, and remember instead your servants Abraham, Isaac, and Jacob. 28If you destroy these people, the Egyptians will say, "The Israelites died because the LORD wasn't able to bring them to the land he had promised to give them." Or they might say, "He destroyed them because he hated them; he deliberately took them into the wilderness to slaughter them." 29But they are your people and your special possession, whom you brought out of Egypt by your great strength and powerful arm.'

10 A NEW COPY OF THE COVENANT

"At that time the LORD said to me, 'Chisel out two stone tablets like the first ones. Also make a wooden Ark—a sacred chest to store them in. Come up to me on the mountain, 2and I will write on the tablets the same words that were on the ones you smashed. Then place the tablets in the Ark.'

3"So I made an Ark of acacia wood and cut two stone tablets like the first two. Then I went up the mountain with the tablets in my hand. 4Once again the LORD wrote the Ten Commandments* on the tablets and gave them to me. They were the same words the LORD had spoken to you from the heart of the fire on the day you were assembled at the foot of the mountain. 5Then I turned and came down the mountain and placed the tablets in the Ark of the Covenant, which I had made, just as the LORD commanded me. And the tablets are still there in the Ark."

6(The people of Israel set out from the wells of the people of Jaakan* and traveled to Moserah, where Aaron died and was buried. His son Eleazar ministered as high priest in his place. 7Then they journeyed to Gudgodah, and from there to Jotbathah, a land with many brooks and streams. 8At that time the LORD set apart the tribe of Levi to carry the Ark of the LORD's Covenant, and to stand before the LORD as his ministers, and to pronounce blessings in his name. These are their duties to this day. 9That is why the Levites have no share of property or possession of land among the other Israelite tribes. The LORD himself is their special possession, as the LORD your God told them.)

10"As for me, I stayed on the mountain in the LORD's presence for forty days and nights, as I had done the first time. And once again the LORD listened to my pleas and agreed not to destroy you. 11Then the LORD said to me, 'Get up and resume the journey, and lead the people to the land I swore to give to their ancestors, so they may take possession of it.'

9:22a *Taberah* means "place of burning." See Num 11:1-3. **9:22b** *Massah* means "place of testing." See Exod 17:1-7. **9:22c** *Kibroth-hattaavah* means "graves of craving." See Num 11:31-34. **10:4** Hebrew *the ten words.* **10:6** Or *set out from Beeroth of Bene-jaakan.*

A CALL TO LOVE AND OBEDIENCE

[12]"And now, Israel, what does the LORD your God require of you? He requires only that you fear the LORD your God, and live in a way that pleases him, and love him and serve him with all your heart and soul. [13]And you must always obey the LORD's commands and decrees that I am giving you today for your own good.

GREAT EXPECTATIONS 10:12-13

Often we ask, "What does God expect of me?" Here Moses gives a summary that's easy to remember. Here are the essentials: (1) Fear God (have a deep respect for his authority). (2) Live according to his will. (3) Love him. (4) Worship him wholeheartedly. (5) Obey his commands. How often we complicate faith with man-made rules, regulations, and requirements. Are you frustrated or feeling burned out from trying hard to please God? You don't have to jump over hoops to please God. Just love and obey him. ■

[14]"Look, the highest heavens and the earth and everything in it all belong to the LORD your God. [15]Yet the LORD chose your ancestors as the objects of his love. And he chose you, their descendants, above all other nations, as is evident today. [16]Therefore, change your hearts* and stop being stubborn.

[17]"For the LORD your God is the God of gods and Lord of lords. He is the great God, the mighty and awesome God, who shows no partiality and cannot be bribed. [18]He ensures that orphans and widows receive justice. He shows love to the foreigners living among you and gives them food and clothing. [19]So you, too, must show love to foreigners, for you yourselves were once foreigners in the land of Egypt. [20]You must fear the LORD your God and worship him and cling to him. Your oaths must be in his name alone. [21]He alone is your God, the only one who is worthy of your praise, the one who has done these mighty miracles that you have seen with your own eyes. [22]When your ancestors went down into Egypt, there were only seventy of them. But now the LORD your God has made you as numerous as the stars in the sky!

11 "You must love the LORD your God and obey all his requirements, decrees, regulations, and commands. [2]Keep in mind that I am not talking now to your children, who have never experienced the discipline of the LORD your God or seen his greatness and his strong hand and powerful arm. [3]They didn't see the miraculous signs and wonders he performed in Egypt against Pharaoh and all his land. [4]They didn't see what the LORD did to the armies of Egypt and to their horses and chariots—how he drowned them in the Red Sea* as they were chasing you. He destroyed them, and they have not recovered to this very day!

[5]"Your children didn't see how the LORD cared for you in the wilderness until you arrived here. [6]They didn't see what he did to Dathan and Abiram (the sons of Eliab, a descendant of Reuben) when the earth opened its mouth in the Israelite camp and swallowed them, along with their households and tents and every living thing that belonged to them. [7]But you have seen the LORD perform all these mighty deeds with your own eyes!

THE BLESSINGS OF OBEDIENCE

[8]"Therefore, be careful to obey every command I am giving you today, so you may have strength to go in and take over the land you are about to enter. [9]If you obey, you will enjoy a long life in the land the LORD swore to give to your ancestors and to you, their descendants—a land flowing with milk and honey! [10]For the land you are about to enter and take over is not like the land of Egypt from which you came, where you planted your seed and made irrigation ditches with your foot as in a vegetable garden. [11]Rather, the land you will soon take over is a land of hills and valleys with plenty of rain—[12]a land that the LORD your God cares for. He watches over it through each season of the year!

[13]"If you carefully obey all the commands I am giving you today, and if you love the LORD your God and serve him with all your heart and soul, [14]then he will send the rains in their proper seasons—the early and late rains—so you can bring in your harvests of grain, new wine, and olive oil. [15]He will give you lush pastureland for your livestock, and you yourselves will have all you want to eat.

[16]"But be careful. Don't let your heart be deceived so that you turn away from the LORD and serve and worship other gods. [17]If you do, the LORD's anger will burn against you. He will shut up the sky and hold back the rain, and the ground will fail to produce its harvests. Then you will quickly die in that good land the LORD is giving you.

[18]"So commit yourselves wholeheartedly to these words of mine. Tie them to your hands and wear them on your forehead as reminders. [19]Teach them to your children. Talk about them when you are at home and when you are on the road, when you are going to bed and when you are getting up. [20]Write them on the doorposts of your house and on your gates, [21]so that as long as the sky remains above the earth, you and your children may flourish in the land the LORD swore to give your ancestors.

[22]"Be careful to obey all these commands I am giving you. Show love to the LORD your God by walking in his ways and holding tightly to him. [23]Then the LORD will drive out all the nations ahead of you, though they are much greater and stronger than you, and you will take over their land. [24]Wherever you set foot, that land will be yours. Your frontiers will stretch from the wilderness in the south to Lebanon in the north, and from the Euphrates River in the east to the Mediterranean Sea in the west.* [25]No one will be able to stand against you, for the LORD your God will cause the people to fear and dread you, as he promised, wherever you go in the whole land.

[26]"Look, today I am giving you the choice between a blessing and a curse! [27]You will be blessed if you obey the

10:16 Hebrew *circumcise the foreskin of your hearts.* **11:4** Hebrew *sea of reeds.* **11:24** Hebrew *to the western sea.*

commands of the LORD your God that I am giving you today. 28But you will be cursed if you reject the commands of the LORD your God and turn away from him and worship gods you have not known before.

29"When the LORD your God brings you into the land and helps you take possession of it, you must pronounce the blessing at Mount Gerizim and the curse at Mount Ebal. 30(These two mountains are west of the Jordan River in the land of the Canaanites who live in the Jordan Valley,* near the town of Gilgal, not far from the oaks of Moreh.) 31For you are about to cross the Jordan River to take over the land the LORD your God is giving you. When you take that land and are living in it, 32you must be careful to obey all the decrees and regulations I am giving you today.

12

THE LORD'S CHOSEN PLACE FOR WORSHIP

"These are the decrees and regulations you must be careful to obey when you live in the land that the LORD, the God of your ancestors, is giving you. You must obey them as long as you live.

2"When you drive out the nations that live there, you must destroy all the places where they worship their gods—high on the mountains, up on the hills, and under every green tree. 3Break down their altars and smash their sacred pillars. Burn their Asherah poles and cut down their carved idols. Completely erase the names of their gods!

4"Do not worship the LORD your God in the way these pagan peoples worship their gods. 5Rather, you must seek the LORD your God at the place of worship he himself will choose from among all the tribes—the place where his name will be honored. 6There you will bring your burnt offerings, your sacrifices, your tithes, your sacred offerings, your offerings to fulfill a vow, your voluntary offerings, and your offerings of the firstborn animals of your herds and flocks. 7There you and your families will feast in the presence of the LORD your God, and you will rejoice in all you have accomplished because the LORD your God has blessed you.

8"Your pattern of worship will change. Today all of you are doing as you please, 9because you have not yet arrived at the place of rest, the land the LORD your God is giving you as your special possession. 10But you will soon cross the Jordan River and live in the land the LORD your God is giving you. When he gives you rest from all your enemies and you're living safely in the land, 11you must bring everything I command you—your burnt offerings, your sacrifices, your tithes, your sacred offerings, and your offerings to fulfill a vow—to the designated place of worship, the place the LORD your God chooses for his name to be honored.

12"You must celebrate there in the presence of the LORD your God with your sons and daughters and all your servants. And remember to include the Levites who live in your towns, for they will receive no allotment of land among you. 13Be careful not to sacrifice your burnt offerings just anywhere you like. 14You may do so only at the place the LORD will choose within one of your tribal territories. There you must offer your burnt offerings and do everything I command you.

15"But you may butcher your animals and eat their meat in any town whenever you want. You may freely eat the animals with which the LORD your God blesses you. All of you, whether ceremonially clean or unclean, may eat that meat, just as you now eat gazelle and deer. 16But you must not eat the blood. You must pour it out on the ground like water.

17"But you may not eat your offerings in your hometown—neither the tithe of your grain and new wine and olive oil, nor the firstborn of your flocks and herds, nor any offering to fulfill a vow, nor your voluntary offerings, nor your sacred offerings. 18You must eat these in the presence of the LORD your God at the place he will choose. Eat them there with your children, your servants, and the Levites who live in your towns, celebrating in the presence of the LORD your God in all you do. 19And be very careful never to neglect the Levites as long as you live in your land.

FAMILY WORSHIP 12:12, 18

The Hebrews placed great emphasis on family worship, which often involved sacrificial offerings or attending the required festivals. Worshiping as a family gave the children a healthy attitude toward worship and made it more meaningful for the adults. How has your family's worship traditions affected your view of worship? ■

20"When the LORD your God expands your territory as he has promised, and you have the urge to eat meat, you may freely eat meat whenever you want. 21It might happen that the designated place of worship—the place the LORD your God chooses for his name to be honored—is a long way from your home. If so, you may butcher any of the cattle, sheep, or goats the LORD has given you, and you may freely eat the meat in your hometown, as I have commanded you. 22Anyone, whether ceremonially clean or unclean, may eat that meat, just as you do now with gazelle and deer. 23But never eat the blood, for the blood is the life, and you must not eat the lifeblood with the meat. 24Instead, pour out the blood on the ground like water. 25Do not eat the blood, so that all may go well with you and your children after you, because you will be doing what pleases the LORD.

26"Take your sacred gifts and your offerings given to fulfill a vow to the place the LORD chooses. 27You must offer the meat and blood of your burnt offerings on the altar of the LORD your God. The blood of your other sacrifices must be poured out on the altar of the LORD your God, but you may eat the meat. 28Be careful to obey all my commands, so that all will go well with you and your children after you, because you will be doing what is good and pleasing to the LORD your God.

11:30 Hebrew *the Arabah.*

29"When the LORD your God goes ahead of you and destroys the nations and you drive them out and live in their land, 30do not fall into the trap of following their customs and worshiping their gods. Do not inquire about their gods, saying, 'How do these nations worship their gods? I want to follow their example.' 31You must not worship the LORD your God the way the other nations worship their gods, for they perform for their gods every detestable act that the LORD hates. They even burn their sons and daughters as sacrifices to their gods.

32*"So be careful to obey all the commands I give you. You must not add anything to them or subtract anything from them.

13 A WARNING AGAINST IDOLATRY

1*"Suppose there are prophets among you or those who dream dreams about the future, and they promise you signs or miracles, 2and the predicted signs or miracles occur. If they then say, 'Come, let us worship other gods'—gods you have not known before—3do not listen to them. The LORD your God is testing you to see if you truly love him with all your heart and soul. 4Serve only the LORD your God and fear him alone. Obey his commands, listen to his voice, and cling to him. 5The false prophets or visionaries who try to lead you astray must be put to death, for they encourage rebellion against the LORD your God, who redeemed you from slavery and brought you out of the land of Egypt. Since they try to lead you astray from the way the LORD your God commanded you to live, you must put them to death. In this way you will purge the evil from among you.

WHISPERED TEMPTATIONS 13:1-11

The Israelites were warned not to listen to false prophets or anyone else who tried to get them to worship other gods. The temptation to abandon God's commands often sneaks up on us. It may come not with a loud shout, but in a whispering doubt. Whispers can be very persuasive, especially if they come from loved ones. But love for relatives should not take precedence over devotion to God. We can overcome whispered temptations by pouring out our feelings to God in prayer and by studying his Word. ■

6"Suppose someone secretly entices you—even your brother, your son or daughter, your beloved wife, or your closest friend—and says, 'Let us go worship other gods'—gods that neither you nor your ancestors have known. 7They might suggest that you worship the gods of peoples who live nearby or who come from the ends of the earth. 8But do not give in or listen. Have no pity, and do not spare or protect them. 9You must put them to death! Strike the first blow yourself, and then all the people must join in. 10Stone the guilty ones to death because they have tried to draw you away from the LORD your God, who rescued you from the land of Egypt, the place of slavery. 11Then all Israel will hear about it and be afraid, and no one will act so wickedly again.

12"When you begin living in the towns the LORD your God is giving you, you may hear 13that scoundrels among you are leading their fellow citizens astray by saying, 'Let us go worship other gods'—gods you have not known before. 14In such cases, you must examine the facts carefully. If you find that the report is true and such a detestable act has been committed among you, 15you must attack that town and completely destroy* all its inhabitants, as well as all the livestock. 16Then you must pile all the plunder in the middle of the open square and burn it. Burn the entire town as a burnt offering to the LORD your God. That town must remain a ruin forever; it may never be rebuilt. 17Keep none of the plunder that has been set apart for destruction. Then the LORD will turn from his fierce anger and be merciful to you. He will have compassion on you and make you a large nation, just as he swore to your ancestors.

18"The LORD your God will be merciful only if you listen to his voice and keep all his commands that I am giving you today, doing what pleases him.

14 CEREMONIALLY CLEAN AND UNCLEAN ANIMALS

"Since you are the people of the LORD your God, never cut yourselves or shave the hair above your foreheads in mourning for the dead. 2You have been set apart as holy to the LORD your God, and he has chosen you from all the nations of the earth to be his own special treasure.

3"You must not eat any detestable animals that are ceremonially unclean. 4These are the animals* you may eat: the ox, the sheep, the goat, 5the deer, the gazelle, the roe deer, the wild goat, the addax, the antelope, and the mountain sheep.

6"You may eat any animal that has completely split hooves and chews the cud, 7but if the animal doesn't have both, it may not be eaten. So you may not eat the camel, the hare, or the hyrax.* They chew the cud but do not have split hooves, so they are ceremonially unclean for you. 8And you may not eat the pig. It has split hooves but does not chew the cud, so it is ceremonially unclean for you. You may not eat the meat of these animals or even touch their carcasses.

9"Of all the marine animals, you may eat whatever has both fins and scales. 10You may not, however, eat marine animals that do not have both fins and scales. They are ceremonially unclean for you.

11"You may eat any bird that is ceremonially clean. 12These are the birds you may not eat: the griffon vulture, the bearded vulture, the black vulture, 13the kite, the falcon, buzzards of all kinds, 14ravens of all kinds, 15the eagle owl, the short-eared owl, the seagull, hawks of all kinds, 16the little owl, the great owl, the barn owl, 17the

12:32 Verse 12:32 is numbered 13:1 in Hebrew text. **13:1** Verses 13:1-18 are numbered 13:2-19 in Hebrew text. **13:15** The Hebrew term used here refers to the complete consecration of things or people to the LORD, either by destroying them or by giving them as an offering; similarly in 13:17. **14:4** The identification of some of the animals and birds listed in this chapter is uncertain. **14:7** Or *coney*, or *rock badger*.

desert owl, the Egyptian vulture, the cormorant, [18]the
stork, herons of all kinds, the hoopoe, and the bat.
[19]"All winged insects that walk along the ground are
ceremonially unclean for you and may not be eaten. [20]But
you may eat any winged bird or insect that is ceremonially clean.
[21]"You must not eat anything that has died a natural
death. You may give it to a foreigner living in your town,
or you may sell it to a stranger. But do not eat it yourselves, for you are set apart as holy to the LORD your God.

"You must not cook a young goat in its mother's milk.

THE GIVING OF TITHES

[22]"You must set aside a tithe of your crops—one-tenth of
all the crops you harvest each year. [23]Bring this tithe to
the designated place of worship—the place the LORD
your God chooses for his name to be honored—and eat it
there in his presence. This applies to your tithes of grain,
new wine, olive oil, and the firstborn males of your flocks
and herds. Doing this will teach you always to fear the
LORD your God.
[24]"Now when the LORD your God blesses you with a
good harvest, the place of worship he chooses for his
name to be honored might be too far for you to bring the
tithe. [25]If so, you may sell the tithe portion of your crops
and herds, put the money in a pouch, and go to the place
the LORD your God has chosen. [26]When you arrive, you
may use the money to buy any kind of food you want—
cattle, sheep, goats, wine, or other alcoholic drink. Then
feast there in the presence of the LORD your God and celebrate with your household. [27]And do not neglect the Levites in your town, for they will receive no allotment of
land among you.
[28]"At the end of every third year, bring the entire tithe
of that year's harvest and store it in the nearest town.
[29]Give it to the Levites, who will receive no allotment of
land among you, as well as to the foreigners living among
you, the orphans, and the widows in your towns, so they
can eat and be satisfied. Then the LORD your God will
bless you in all your work.

15 RELEASE FOR DEBTORS

"At the end of every seventh year you must cancel the
debts of everyone who owes you money. [2]This is how it
must be done. Everyone must cancel the loans they have
made to their fellow Israelites. They must not demand
payment from their neighbors or relatives, for the LORD's
time of release has arrived. [3]This release from debt, however, applies only to your fellow Israelites—not to the foreigners living among you.
[4]"There should be no poor among you, for the LORD
your God will greatly bless you in the land he is giving you
as a special possession. [5]You will receive this blessing if
you are careful to obey all the commands of the LORD
your God that I am giving you today. [6]The LORD your God
will bless you as he has promised. You will lend money to
many nations but will never need to borrow. You will rule
many nations, but they will not rule over you.
[7]"But if there are any poor Israelites in your towns
when you arrive in the land the LORD your God is giving
you, do not be hard-hearted or tightfisted toward them.
[8]Instead, be generous and lend them whatever they need.
[9]Do not be mean-spirited and refuse someone a loan because the year for canceling debts is close at hand. If you
refuse to make the loan and the needy person cries out to
the LORD, you will be considered guilty of sin. [10]Give generously to the poor, not grudgingly, for the LORD your God
will bless you in everything you do. [11]There will always be
some in the land who are poor. That is why I am commanding you to share freely with the poor and with other
Israelites in need.

> **POVERTY 15:7-11**
>
> **God told the Israelites to help the poor among them when they arrived in the Promised Land. This was an important part of possessing the land. (See also Deut 24:17-22.) Some people make the assumption that people are poor through some fault of their own. Ever hear someone voice an opinion like that? This kind of reasoning makes it easy to close our hearts and hands against them. But we are not to invent reasons for ignoring the care of the poor. We are to respond to their needs no matter who or what was responsible for their condition. Who are the poor in your community? How will you help them? ■**

RELEASE FOR HEBREW SLAVES

[12]"If a fellow Hebrew sells himself or herself to be your
servant* and serves you for six years, in the seventh year
you must set that servant free.
[13]"When you release a male servant, do not send him
away empty-handed. [14]Give him a generous farewell gift
from your flock, your threshing floor, and your winepress. Share with him some of the bounty with which the
LORD your God has blessed you. [15]Remember that you
were once slaves in the land of Egypt and the LORD your
God redeemed you! That is why I am giving you this
command.
[16]"But suppose your servant says, 'I will not leave you,'
because he loves you and your family, and he has done
well with you. [17]In that case, take an awl and push it
through his earlobe into the door. After that, he will be
your servant for life. And do the same for your female
servants.
[18]"You must not consider it a hardship when you release
your servants. Remember that for six years they have given
you services worth double the wages of hired workers, and
the LORD your God will bless you in all you do.

SACRIFICING FIRSTBORN MALE ANIMALS

[19]"You must set aside for the LORD your God all the firstborn males from your flocks and herds. Do not use the

15:12 Or *If a Hebrew man or woman is sold to you.*

firstborn of your herds to work your fields, and do not shear the firstborn of your flocks. 20Instead, you and your family must eat these animals in the presence of the LORD your God each year at the place he chooses. 21But if this firstborn animal has any defect, such as lameness or blindness, or if anything else is wrong with it, you must not sacrifice it to the LORD your God. 22Instead, use it for food for your family in your hometown. Anyone, whether ceremonially clean or unclean, may eat it, just as anyone may eat a gazelle or deer. 23But you must not eat the blood. You must pour it out on the ground like water.

16 PASSOVER AND THE FESTIVAL OF UNLEAVENED BREAD

"In honor of the LORD your God, celebrate the Passover each year in the early spring, in the month of Abib,* for that was the month in which the LORD your God brought you out of Egypt by night. 2Your Passover sacrifice may be from either the flock or the herd, and it must be sacrificed to the LORD your God at the designated place of worship—the place he chooses for his name to be honored. 3Eat it with bread made without yeast. For seven days the bread you eat must be made without yeast, as when you escaped from Egypt in such a hurry. Eat this bread—the bread of suffering—so that as long as you live you will remember the day you departed from Egypt. 4Let no yeast be found in any house throughout your land for those seven days. And when you sacrifice the Passover lamb on the evening of the first day, do not let any of the meat remain until the next morning.

5"You may not sacrifice the Passover in just any of the towns that the LORD your God is giving you. 6You must offer it only at the designated place of worship—the place the LORD your God chooses for his name to be honored. Sacrifice it there in the evening as the sun goes down on the anniversary of your exodus from Egypt. 7Roast the lamb and eat it in the place the LORD your God chooses. Then you may go back to your tents the next morning. 8For the next six days you may not eat any bread made with yeast. On the seventh day proclaim another holy day in honor of the LORD your God, and no work may be done on that day.

THE FESTIVAL OF HARVEST

9"Count off seven weeks from when you first begin to cut the grain at the time of harvest. 10Then celebrate the Festival of Harvest* to honor the LORD your God. Bring him a voluntary offering in proportion to the blessings you have received from him. 11This is a time to celebrate before the LORD your God at the designated place of worship he will choose for his name to be honored. Celebrate with your sons and daughters, your male and female servants, the Levites from your towns, and the foreigners, orphans, and widows who live among you. 12Remember that you were once slaves in Egypt, so be careful to obey all these decrees.

THE FESTIVAL OF SHELTERS

13"You must observe the Festival of Shelters* for seven days at the end of the harvest season, after the grain has been threshed and the grapes have been pressed. 14This festival will be a happy time of celebrating with your sons and daughters, your male and female servants, and the Levites, foreigners, orphans, and widows from your towns. 15For seven days you must celebrate this festival to honor the LORD your God at the place he chooses, for it is he who blesses you with bountiful harvests and gives you success in all your work. This festival will be a time of great joy for all.

16"Each year every man in Israel must celebrate these three festivals: the Festival of Unleavened Bread, the Festival of Harvest, and the Festival of Shelters. On each of these occasions, all men must appear before the LORD your God at the place he chooses, but they must not appear before the LORD without a gift for him. 17All must give as they are able, according to the blessings given to them by the LORD your God.

GIVING BACK TO GOD 16:16-17

Three times a year every Hebrew male was required to attend three feasts wherever the Tabernacle happened to be. (See also Exod 23:17; 34:23.) At these feasts, each participant was encouraged to give what he could in proportion to what God had given him. Although God does not expect us to give more than we can, we are blessed when we are able to give cheerfully. For some of us, 10 percent may be a burden. For most of us, it is far too little. If you were to give in proportion to what you have been given, what would you give? ■

JUSTICE FOR THE PEOPLE

18"Appoint judges and officials for yourselves from each of your tribes in all the towns the LORD your God is giving you. They must judge the people fairly. 19You must never twist justice or show partiality. Never accept a bribe, for bribes blind the eyes of the wise and corrupt the decisions of the godly. 20Let true justice prevail, so you may live and occupy the land that the LORD your God is giving you.

21"You must never set up a wooden Asherah pole beside the altar you build for the LORD your God. 22And never set up sacred pillars for worship, for the LORD your God hates them.

17 "Never sacrifice sick or defective cattle, sheep, or goats to the LORD your God, for he detests such gifts.

16:1 Hebrew *Observe the month of Abib, and keep the Passover unto the LORD your God.* Abib, the first month of the ancient Hebrew lunar calendar, usually occurs within the months of March and April. 16:10 Hebrew *Festival of Weeks;* also in 16:16. This was later called the Festival of Pentecost (see Acts 2:1). It is celebrated today as Shavuat (or Shabuoth). 16:13 Or *Festival of Booths,* or *Festival of Tabernacles;* also in 16:16. This was earlier called the Festival of the Final Harvest or Festival of Ingathering (see Exod 23:16b). It is celebrated today as Sukkot (or Succoth).

2"When you begin living in the towns the LORD your
God is giving you, a man or woman among you might do
evil in the sight of the LORD your God and violate the covenant. 3For instance, they might serve other gods or worship the sun, the moon, or any of the stars—the forces of
heaven—which I have strictly forbidden. 4When you hear
about it, investigate the matter thoroughly. If it is true
that this detestable thing has been done in Israel, 5then
the man or woman who has committed such an evil act
must be taken to the gates of the town and stoned to
death. 6But never put a person to death on the testimony
of only one witness. There must always be two or three
witnesses. 7The witnesses must throw the first stones,
and then all the people may join in. In this way, you will
purge the evil from among you.

A RULE FOR WITNESSES 17:2-7

During this time in Israel's history, a law concerning capital punishment was established. A person accused of worshiping idols could not be stoned to death based on the testimony of only one witness. A death sentence required two or three witnesses. This system prevented angry individuals from giving false testimony. (See Exod 20:16.) Also, since the accusers threw the first stones, they thought twice about accusing unjustly. Maybe we need to do the same before we accuse someone of a wrongdoing. ■

8"Suppose a case arises in a local court that is too hard
for you to decide—for instance, whether someone is
guilty of murder or only of manslaughter, or a difficult
lawsuit, or a case involving different kinds of assault.
Take such legal cases to the place the LORD your God will
choose, 9and present them to the Levitical priests or the
judge on duty at that time. They will hear the case and declare the verdict. 10You must carry out the verdict they
announce and the sentence they prescribe at the place
the LORD chooses. You must do exactly what they say.
11After they have interpreted the law and declared their
verdict, the sentence they impose must be fully executed;
do not modify it in any way. 12Anyone arrogant enough to
reject the verdict of the judge or of the priest who represents the LORD your God must die. In this way you will
purge the evil from Israel. 13Then everyone else will hear
about it and be afraid to act so arrogantly.

GUIDELINES FOR A KING

14"You are about to enter the land the LORD your God is
giving you. When you take it over and settle there, you
may think, 'We should select a king to rule over us like the
other nations around us.' 15If this happens, be sure to select as king the man the LORD your God chooses. You
must appoint a fellow Israelite; he may not be a foreigner.
16"The king must not build up a large stable of horses
for himself or send his people to Egypt to buy horses, for
the LORD has told you, 'You must never return to Egypt.'
17The king must not take many wives for himself, because they will turn his heart away from the LORD. And he
must not accumulate large amounts of wealth in silver
and gold for himself.
18"When he sits on the throne as king, he must copy
for himself this body of instruction on a scroll in the
presence of the Levitical priests. 19He must always keep
that copy with him and read it daily as long as he lives.
That way he will learn to fear the LORD his God by obeying all the terms of these instructions and decrees.
20This regular reading will prevent him from becoming
proud and acting as if he is above his fellow citizens. It
will also prevent him from turning away from these
commands in the smallest way. And it will ensure that
he and his descendants will reign for many generations
in Israel.

18

GIFTS FOR THE PRIESTS AND LEVITES

"Remember that the Levitical priests—that is, the whole
of the tribe of Levi—will receive no allotment of land
among the other tribes in Israel. Instead, the priests and
Levites will eat from the special gifts given to the LORD,
for that is their share. 2They will have no land of their
own among the Israelites. The LORD himself is their special possession, just as he promised them.
3"These are the parts the priests may claim as their
share from the cattle, sheep, and goats that the people
bring as offerings: the shoulder, the cheeks, and the
stomach. 4You must also give to the priests the first share
of the grain, the new wine, the olive oil, and the wool at
shearing time. 5For the LORD your God chose the tribe of
Levi out of all your tribes to minister in the LORD's name
forever.

A DANGEROUS FASCINATION 18:9-14

Just as most of us are naturally curious about a magician's trick, the Israelites were curious about the occult practices of the Canaanites. Because Satan was involved in these practices, God warned Israel to avoid them. People today are still fascinated by horoscopes, fortune-telling, witchcraft, and cults. Often their interest comes from a desire to know and control the future. But the information Satan offers is likely to be distorted or completely false. With the trustworthy guidance of the Holy Spirit through the Scriptures and the church, we don't need to turn to occult sources for information. ■

6"Suppose a Levite chooses to move from his town in
Israel, wherever he is living, to the place the LORD chooses
for worship. 7He may minister there in the name of the
LORD his God, just like all his fellow Levites who are serving the LORD there. 8He may eat his share of the sacrifices
and offerings, even if he also receives support from his
family.

A CALL TO HOLY LIVING

9"When you enter the land the LORD your God is giving
you, be very careful not to imitate the detestable customs

keeping it real

It was strange how this one passage of Scripture—Ephesians 6:10-18, about putting on the whole armor of God—kept coming up again and again in one week. First it came up in my quiet time. Then we studied the same passage in the youth Bible study. Finally, my pastor preached a sermon on spiritual warfare.

Later that week my friend brought out a Ouija board and asked me to try it with her. I felt uneasy about it, but it seemed like just a game, so I said yes. Some weird things happened; the piece that you put your fingers on really seemed to move of its own accord, and it spelled out some weird answers. I had a very creepy feeling that this was not of God. I told my friend I wanted to quit right now, that I didn't think God wanted us to do this. That night I called my youth pastor and told him about it. He pointed out that Deuteronomy 18:9-14 warns us against trying to seek the future from means other than God. He reminded me that Satan is always trying to find a way to sneak into our lives. And he reminded me of Ephesians 6 and the armor God gives us to fight the devil. I realized that God had been trying to prepare me for the temptation to use the Ouija board, but I wasn't paying close enough attention at the time.

I learned from my mistake. I will never touch or mess with a Ouija board or horoscopes or anything like that again.

—**Meagan**

of the nations living there. 10For example, never sacrifice
your son or daughter as a burnt offering.* And do not let
your people practice fortune-telling, or use sorcery, or interpret omens, or engage in witchcraft, 11or cast spells, or
function as mediums or psychics, or call forth the spirits
of the dead. 12Anyone who does these things is detestable
to the LORD. It is because the other nations have done
these detestable things that the LORD your God will drive
them out ahead of you. 13But you must be blameless before the LORD your God. 14The nations you are about to
displace consult sorcerers and fortune-tellers, but the
LORD your God forbids you to do such things."

TRUE AND FALSE PROPHETS

15Moses continued, "The LORD your God will raise up for
you a prophet like me from among your fellow Israelites.
You must listen to him. 16For this is what you yourselves
requested of the LORD your God when you were assembled at Mount Sinai.* You said, 'Don't let us hear the voice
of the LORD our God anymore or see this blazing fire, for
we will die.'

17"Then the LORD said to me, 'What they have said is
right. 18I will raise up a prophet like you from among
their fellow Israelites. I will put my words in his mouth,
and he will tell the people everything I command him. 19I
will personally deal with anyone who will not listen to the
messages the prophet proclaims on my behalf. 20But any
prophet who falsely claims to speak in my name or who
speaks in the name of another god must die.'

21"But you may wonder, 'How will we know whether or
not a prophecy is from the LORD?' 22If the prophet speaks
in the LORD's name but his prediction does not happen or
come true, you will know that the LORD did not give that
message. That prophet has spoken without my authority
and need not be feared.

19 CITIES OF REFUGE

"When the LORD your God destroys the nations whose
land he is giving you, you will take over their land and settle in their towns and homes. 2Then you must set apart
three cities of refuge in the land the LORD your God is giving you. 3Survey the territory,* and divide the land the
LORD your God is giving you into three districts, with one
of these cities in each district. Then anyone who has
killed someone can flee to one of the cities of refuge for
safety.

4"If someone kills another person unintentionally,
without previous hostility, the slayer may flee to any of
these cities to live in safety. 5For example, suppose someone goes into the forest with a neighbor to cut wood. And
suppose one of them swings an ax to chop down a tree,

18:10 Or *never make your son or daughter pass through the fire.* **18:16** Hebrew *Horeb,* another name for Sinai. **19:3** Or *Keep the roads in good repair.*

and the ax head flies off the handle, killing the other person. In such cases, the slayer may flee to one of the cities
of refuge to live in safety.
6"If the distance to the nearest city of refuge is too far,
an enraged avenger might be able to chase down and kill
the person who caused the death. Then the slayer would
die unfairly, since he had never shown hostility toward
the person who died. 7That is why I am commanding you
to set aside three cities of refuge.

8"And if the LORD your God enlarges your territory, as he
swore to your ancestors, and gives you all the land he promised them, 9you must designate three additional cities of
refuge. (He will give you this land if you are careful to obey
all the commands I have given you—if you always love the
LORD your God and walk in his ways.) 10That way you will
prevent the death of innocent people in the land the LORD
your God is giving you as your special possession. You will
not be held responsible for the death of innocent people.

11"But suppose someone is hostile toward a neighbor
and deliberately ambushes and murders him and then
flees to one of the cities of refuge. 12In that case, the elders
of the murderer's hometown must send agents to the city
of refuge to bring him back and hand him over to the
dead person's avenger to be put to death. 13Do not feel
sorry for that murderer! Purge from Israel the guilt of
murdering innocent people; then all will go well with you.

CONCERN FOR JUSTICE

14"When you arrive in the land the LORD your God is giving you as your special possession, you must never steal
anyone's land by moving the boundary markers your
ancestors set up to mark their property.

15"You must not convict anyone of a crime on the testimony of only one witness. The facts of the case must be
established by the testimony of two or three witnesses.

16"If a malicious witness comes forward and accuses
someone of a crime, 17then both the accuser and accused
must appear before the LORD by coming to the priests
and judges in office at that time. 18The judges must investigate the case thoroughly. If the accuser has brought
false charges against his fellow Israelite, 19you must impose on the accuser the sentence he intended for the
other person. In this way, you will purge such evil from
among you. 20Then the rest of the people will hear about
it and be afraid to do such an evil thing. 21You must show
no pity for the guilty! Your rule should be life for life, eye
for eye, tooth for tooth, hand for hand, foot for foot.

20 REGULATIONS CONCERNING WAR

"When you go out to fight your enemies and you face
horses and chariots and an army greater than your own, do
not be afraid. The LORD your God, who brought you out of
the land of Egypt, is with you! 2When you prepare for battle, the priest must come forward to speak to the troops.
3He will say to them, 'Listen to me, all you men of Israel! Do
not be afraid as you go out to fight your enemies today! Do
not lose heart or panic or tremble before them. 4For the
LORD your God is going with you! He will fight for you
against your enemies, and he will give you victory!'

GOD'S VICTORY EQUATION 20:1

When the Israelites worried that powerful enemies outnumbered them, God reminded them that he was always with them. When big problems arise, many of us can relate to feelings of helplessness and hopelessness. Is that where you are now? If so, God wants you to consider a new equation: God + you = victory. ■

5"Then the officers of the army must address the
troops and say, 'Has anyone here just built a new house
but not yet dedicated it? If so, you may go home! You
might be killed in the battle, and someone else would
dedicate your house. 6Has anyone here just planted a
vineyard but not yet eaten any of its fruit? If so, you may
go home! You might die in battle, and someone else
would eat the first fruit. 7Has anyone here just become
engaged to a woman but not yet married her? Well, you
may go home and get married! You might die in the battle, and someone else would marry her.'

8"Then the officers will also say, 'Is anyone here afraid
or worried? If you are, you may go home before you
frighten anyone else.' 9When the officers have finished
speaking to their troops, they will appoint the unit
commanders.

10"As you approach a town to attack it, you must first
offer its people terms for peace. 11If they accept your
terms and open the gates to you, then all the people inside will serve you in forced labor. 12But if they refuse to
make peace and prepare to fight, you must attack the
town. 13When the LORD your God hands the town over to
you, use your swords to kill every man in the town. 14But
you may keep for yourselves all the women, children,
livestock, and other plunder. You may enjoy the plunder
from your enemies that the LORD your God has given you.

15"But these instructions apply only to distant towns,
not to the towns of the nations in the land you will enter.
16In those towns that the LORD your God is giving you as a
special possession, destroy every living thing. 17You must
completely destroy* the Hittites, Amorites, Canaanites,
Perizzites, Hivites, and Jebusites, just as the LORD your
God has commanded you. 18This will prevent the people
of the land from teaching you to imitate their detestable
customs in the worship of their gods, which would cause
you to sin deeply against the LORD your God.

19"When you are attacking a town and the war drags
on, you must not cut down the trees with your axes. You
may eat the fruit, but do not cut down the trees. Are the
trees your enemies, that you should attack them? 20You
may only cut down trees that you know are not valuable
for food. Use them to make the equipment you need to
attack the enemy town until it falls.

20:17 The Hebrew term used here refers to the complete consecration of things or people to the LORD, either by destroying them or by giving them as an offering.

21

CLEANSING FOR UNSOLVED MURDER

"When you are in the land the LORD your God is giving you,
someone may be found murdered in a field, and you don't
know who committed the murder. 2In such a case, your elders and judges must measure the distance from the site of
the crime to the nearby towns. 3When the nearest town has
been determined, that town's elders must select from the
herd a young cow that has never been trained or yoked to a
plow. 4They must lead it down to a valley that has not been
plowed or planted and that has a stream running through
it. There in the valley they must break the young cow's
neck. 5Then the Levitical priests must step forward, for the
LORD your God has chosen them to minister before him
and to pronounce blessings in the LORD's name. They are to
decide all legal and criminal cases.

6"The elders of the town must wash their hands over
the young cow whose neck was broken. 7Then they must
say, 'Our hands did not shed this person's blood, nor did
we see it happen. 8O LORD, forgive your people Israel
whom you have redeemed. Do not charge your people
with the guilt of murdering an innocent person.' Then
they will be absolved of the guilt of this person's blood.
9By following these instructions, you will do what is right
in the LORD's sight and will cleanse the guilt of murder
from your community.

MARRIAGE TO A CAPTIVE WOMAN

10"Suppose you go out to war against your enemies and
the LORD your God hands them over to you, and you take
some of them as captives. 11And suppose you see among
the captives a beautiful woman, and you are attracted to
her and want to marry her. 12If this happens, you may take
her to your home, where she must shave her head, cut her
nails, 13and change the clothes she was wearing when
she was captured. She will stay in your home, but let her
mourn for her father and mother for a full month. Then
you may marry her, and you will be her husband and she
will be your wife. 14But if you marry her and she does not
please you, you must let her go free. You may not sell her
or treat her as a slave, for you have humiliated her.

RIGHTS OF THE FIRSTBORN

15"Suppose a man has two wives, but he loves one and not
the other, and both have given him sons. And suppose the
firstborn son is the son of the wife he does not love.
16When the man divides his inheritance, he may not give
the larger inheritance to his younger son, the son of the
wife he loves, as if he were the firstborn son. 17He must
recognize the rights of his oldest son, the son of the wife
he does not love, by giving him a double portion. He is the
first son of his father's virility, and the rights of the firstborn belong to him.

DEALING WITH A REBELLIOUS SON

18"Suppose a man has a stubborn and rebellious son who
will not obey his father or mother, even though they discipline him. 19In such a case, the father and mother must
take the son to the elders as they hold court at the town
gate. 20The parents must say to the elders, 'This son of
ours is stubborn and rebellious and refuses to obey. He is
a glutton and a drunkard.' 21Then all the men of his town
must stone him to death. In this way, you will purge this
evil from among you, and all Israel will hear about it and
be afraid.

VARIOUS REGULATIONS

22"If someone has committed a crime worthy of death
and is executed and hung on a tree,* 23the body must not
remain hanging from the tree overnight. You must bury
the body that same day, for anyone who is hung* is
cursed in the sight of God. In this way, you will prevent
the defilement of the land the LORD your God is giving
you as your special possession.

22

"If you see your neighbor's ox or sheep or
goat wandering away, don't ignore your responsibility.*
Take it back to its owner. 2If its owner does not live
nearby or you don't know who the owner is, take it to your
place and keep it until the owner comes looking for it.
Then you must return it. 3Do the same if you find your
neighbor's donkey, clothing, or anything else your neighbor loses. Don't ignore your responsibility.

4"If you see that your neighbor's donkey or ox has collapsed on the road, do not look the other way. Go and
help your neighbor get it back on its feet!

SEX ROLES 22:5

This verse is not merely a discussion of Old Testament fashions. It describes a command to men and women to avoid reversing their sexual roles. Yet rejecting these roles is not uncommon today. Many talk shows feature the stories of individuals who feel "trapped" in their bodies and seek ways to make themselves "whole." Some of their paths to wholeness include homosexuality or sex-change operations. But neither path leads to the desired goal.

Ever struggle with questions about this issue? God had a purpose for making us uniquely male and female. He understands our struggles and wants us to trust that his plans for us are good. ■

5"A woman must not put on men's clothing, and a man
must not wear women's clothing. Anyone who does this
is detestable in the sight of the LORD your God.

6"If you happen to find a bird's nest in a tree or on the
ground, and there are young ones or eggs in it with the
mother sitting in the nest, do not take the mother with
the young. 7You may take the young, but let the mother
go, so that you may prosper and enjoy a long life.

8"When you build a new house, you must build a rail-
ing around the edge of its flat roof. That way you will not

21:22 Or *impaled on a pole;* similarly in 21:23. 21:23 Greek version reads *for everyone who is hung on a tree.* Compare Gal 3:13.
22:1 Hebrew *don't hide yourself;* similarly in 22:3.

be considered guilty of murder if someone falls from the
roof.
9"You must not plant any other crop between the rows
of your vineyard. If you do, you are forbidden to use either the grapes from the vineyard or the other crop.
10"You must not plow with an ox and a donkey har-
nessed together.
11"You must not wear clothing made of wool and linen
woven together.
12"You must put four tassels on the hem of the cloak
with which you cover yourself—on the front, back, and
sides.

REGULATIONS FOR SEXUAL PURITY

13"Suppose a man marries a woman, but after sleeping
with her, he turns against her 14and publicly accuses her
of shameful conduct, saying, 'When I married this
woman, I discovered she was not a virgin.' 15Then the
woman's father and mother must bring the proof of her
virginity to the elders as they hold court at the town gate.
16Her father must say to them, 'I gave my daughter to this
man to be his wife, and now he has turned against her.
17He has accused her of shameful conduct, saying, "I discovered that your daughter was not a virgin." But here is
the proof of my daughter's virginity.' Then they must
spread her bed sheet before the elders. 18The elders must
then take the man and punish him. 19They must also fine
him 100 pieces of silver,* which he must pay to the
woman's father because he publicly accused a virgin of
Israel of shameful conduct. The woman will then remain
the man's wife, and he may never divorce her.
20"But suppose the man's accusations are true, and he
can show that she was not a virgin. 21The woman must be
taken to the door of her father's home, and there the men
of the town must stone her to death, for she has committed a disgraceful crime in Israel by being promiscuous
while living in her parents' home. In this way, you will
purge this evil from among you.
22"If a man is discovered committing adultery, both he
and the woman must die. In this way, you will purge Israel
of such evil.
23"Suppose a man meets a young woman, a virgin who is
engaged to be married, and he has sexual intercourse with
her. If this happens within a town, 24you must take both of
them to the gates of that town and stone them to death.
The woman is guilty because she did not scream for help.
The man must die because he violated another man's wife.
In this way, you will purge this evil from among you.
25"But if the man meets the engaged woman out in the
country, and he rapes her, then only the man must die.
26Do nothing to the young woman; she has committed no
crime worthy of death. She is as innocent as a murder victim. 27Since the man raped her out in the country, it must
be assumed that she screamed, but there was no one to
rescue her.
28"Suppose a man has intercourse with a young
woman who is a virgin but is not engaged to be married.
If they are discovered, 29he must pay her father fifty
pieces of silver.* Then he must marry the young woman
because he violated her, and he may never divorce her as
long as he lives.
30*"A man must not marry his father's former wife, for
this would violate his father.

23 REGULATIONS CONCERNING WORSHIP

1*"If a man's testicles are crushed or his penis is cut off,
he may not be admitted to the assembly of the LORD.
2"If a person is illegitimate by birth, neither he nor his
descendants for ten generations may be admitted to the
assembly of the LORD.
3"No Ammonite or Moabite or any of their descendants for ten generations may be admitted to the assembly of the LORD. 4These nations did not welcome you with
food and water when you came out of Egypt. Instead, they
hired Balaam son of Beor from Pethor in distant Aram-
naharaim to curse you. 5But the LORD your God refused
to listen to Balaam. He turned the intended curse into a
blessing because the LORD your God loves you. 6As long as
you live, you must never promote the welfare and prosperity of the Ammonites or Moabites.
7"Do not detest the Edomites or the Egyptians, because
the Edomites are your relatives and you lived as foreigners among the Egyptians. 8The third generation of Edomites and Egyptians may enter the assembly of the LORD.

THE PURPOSE FOR SEX 23:17-18

Although other nations in Canaan included prostitution in their worship rituals, this practice was off-limits for the Israelites. Prostitution is a mockery of God's original idea for sex. It treats sex as an isolated physical act rather than an act of commitment within a marriage. Outside of marriage, sex destroys relationships. Within a marriage it can be a relationship builder, if approached with the right attitude. God frequently warned his people against indulging in sex outside of marriage. This warning is still in force today. ■

MISCELLANEOUS REGULATIONS

9"When you go to war against your enemies, be sure to
stay away from anything that is impure.
10"Any man who becomes ceremonially defiled because of a nocturnal emission must leave the camp and
stay away all day. 11Toward evening he must bathe himself, and at sunset he may return to the camp.
12"You must have a designated area outside the camp
where you can go to relieve yourself. 13Each of you must
have a spade as part of your equipment. Whenever you
relieve yourself, dig a hole with the spade and cover the
excrement. 14The camp must be holy, for the LORD your
God moves around in your camp to protect you and to defeat your enemies. He must not see any shameful thing
among you, or he will turn away from you.

22:19 Hebrew *100 shekels of silver,* about 2.5 pounds or 1.1 kilograms in weight. 22:29 Hebrew *50 shekels of silver,* about 1.25 pounds or 570 grams in weight. 22:30 Verse 22:30 is numbered 23:1 in Hebrew text. 23:1 Verses 23:1-25 are numbered 23:2-26 in Hebrew text.

15"If slaves should escape from their masters and take
refuge with you, you must not hand them over to their
masters. 16Let them live among you in any town they
choose, and do not oppress them.

17"No Israelite, whether man or woman, may become a
temple prostitute. 18When you are bringing an offering
to fulfill a vow, you must not bring to the house of the
LORD your God any offering from the earnings of a prostitute, whether a man* or a woman, for both are detestable to the LORD your God.

19"Do not charge interest on the loans you make to a
fellow Israelite, whether you loan money, or food, or anything else. 20You may charge interest to foreigners, but
you may not charge interest to Israelites, so that the LORD
your God may bless you in everything you do in the land
you are about to enter and occupy.

21"When you make a vow to the LORD your God, be
prompt in fulfilling whatever you promised him. For the
LORD your God demands that you promptly fulfill all your
vows, or you will be guilty of sin. 22However, it is not a sin
to refrain from making a vow. 23But once you have voluntarily made a vow, be careful to fulfill your promise to the
LORD your God.

24"When you enter your neighbor's vineyard, you may
eat your fill of grapes, but you must not carry any away in
a basket. 25And when you enter your neighbor's field of
grain, you may pluck the heads of grain with your hand,
but you must not harvest it with a sickle.

24

"Suppose a man marries a woman but she
does not please him. Having discovered something
wrong with her, he writes her a letter of divorce, hands it
to her, and sends her away from his house. 2When she
leaves his house, she is free to marry another man. 3But if
the second husband also turns against her and divorces
her, or if he dies, 4the first husband may not marry her
again, for she has been defiled. That would be detestable
to the LORD. You must not bring guilt upon the land the
LORD your God is giving you as a special possession.

5"A newly married man must not be drafted into the
army or be given any other official responsibilities. He
must be free to spend one year at home, bringing happiness to the wife he has married.

6"It is wrong to take a set of millstones, or even just the
upper millstone, as security for a loan, for the owner uses
it to make a living.

7"If anyone kidnaps a fellow Israelite and treats him as
a slave or sells him, the kidnapper must die. In this way,
you will purge the evil from among you.

8"In all cases involving serious skin diseases,* be careful to follow the instructions of the Levitical priests; obey
all the commands I have given them. 9Remember what
the LORD your God did to Miriam as you were coming
from Egypt.

10"If you lend anything to your neighbor, do not enter
his house to pick up the item he is giving as security.
11You must wait outside while he goes in and brings it out
to you. 12If your neighbor is poor and gives you his cloak
as security for a loan, do not keep the cloak overnight.
13Return the cloak to its owner by sunset so he can stay
warm through the night and bless you, and the LORD your
God will count you as righteous.

14"Never take advantage of poor and destitute laborers, whether they are fellow Israelites or foreigners living
in your towns. 15You must pay them their wages each day
before sunset because they are poor and are counting on
it. If you don't, they might cry out to the LORD against you,
and it would be counted against you as sin.

16"Parents must not be put to death for the sins of their
children, nor children for the sins of their parents. Those
deserving to die must be put to death for their own
crimes.

17"True justice must be given to foreigners living
among you and to orphans, and you must never accept a
widow's garment as security for her debt. 18Always remember that you were slaves in Egypt and that the LORD
your God redeemed you from your slavery. That is why I
have given you this command.

19"When you are harvesting your crops and forget to
bring in a bundle of grain from your field, don't go back
to get it. Leave it for the foreigners, orphans, and widows.
Then the LORD your God will bless you in all you do.
20When you beat the olives from your olive trees, don't go
over the boughs twice. Leave the remaining olives for the
foreigners, orphans, and widows. 21When you gather the
grapes in your vineyard, don't glean the vines after they
are picked. Leave the remaining grapes for the foreigners, orphans, and widows. 22Remember that you were
slaves in the land of Egypt. That is why I am giving you
this command.

25

"Suppose two people take a dispute to court,
and the judges declare that one is right and the other is
wrong. 2If the person in the wrong is sentenced to be
flogged, the judge must command him to lie down and be
beaten in his presence with the number of lashes appropriate to the crime. 3But never give more than forty
lashes; more than forty lashes would publicly humiliate
your neighbor.

4"You must not muzzle an ox to keep it from eating as
it treads out the grain.

5"If two brothers are living together on the same property and one of them dies without a son, his widow may
not be married to anyone from outside the family. Instead, her husband's brother should marry her and have
intercourse with her to fulfill the duties of a brother-in-
law. 6The first son she bears to him will be considered the
son of the dead brother, so that his name will not be forgotten in Israel.

7"But if the man refuses to marry his brother's widow,
she must go to the town gate and say to the elders assembled there, 'My husband's brother refuses to preserve his
brother's name in Israel—he refuses to fulfill the duties
of a brother-in-law by marrying me.' 8The elders of the

23:18 Hebrew *a dog*. 24:8 Traditionally rendered *leprosy*. The Hebrew word used here can describe various skin diseases.

town will then summon him and talk with him. If he still refuses and says, 'I don't want to marry her,' 9the widow must walk over to him in the presence of the elders, pull his sandal from his foot, and spit in his face. Then she must declare, 'This is what happens to a man who refuses to provide his brother with children.' 10Ever afterward in Israel his family will be referred to as 'the family of the man whose sandal was pulled off'!

11"If two Israelite men get into a fight and the wife of one tries to rescue her husband by grabbing the testicles of the other man, 12you must cut off her hand. Show her no pity.

13"You must use accurate scales when you weigh out merchandise, 14and you must use full and honest measures. 15Yes, always use honest weights and measures, so that you may enjoy a long life in the land the LORD your God is giving you. 16All who cheat with dishonest weights and measures are detestable to the LORD your God.

17"Never forget what the Amalekites did to you as you came from Egypt. 18They attacked you when you were exhausted and weary, and they struck down those who were straggling behind. They had no fear of God. 19Therefore, when the LORD your God has given you rest from all your enemies in the land he is giving you as a special possession, you must destroy the Amalekites and erase their memory from under heaven. Never forget this!

A SPIRITUAL JOURNEY 26:1-11

The people of Israel were required to give an offering of thanks to God as soon as they settled in the Promised Land. They also were required to recite the history of God's dealings with his people. Who have you told about your spiritual journey? Talking about what God has done is a great way to tell him thanks. ■

26

HARVEST OFFERINGS AND TITHES

"When you enter the land the LORD your God is giving you as a special possession and you have conquered it and settled there, 2put some of the first produce from each crop you harvest into a basket and bring it to the designated place of worship—the place the LORD your God chooses for his name to be honored. 3Go to the priest in charge at that time and say to him, 'With this gift I acknowledge to the LORD your God that I have entered the land he swore to our ancestors he would give us.' 4The priest will then take the basket from your hand and set it before the altar of the LORD your God.

5"You must then say in the presence of the LORD your God, 'My ancestor Jacob was a wandering Aramean who went to live as a foreigner in Egypt. His family arrived few in number, but in Egypt they became a large and mighty nation. 6When the Egyptians oppressed and humiliated us by making us their slaves, 7we cried out to the LORD, the God of our ancestors. He heard our cries and saw our hardship, toil, and oppression. 8So the LORD brought us out of Egypt with a strong hand and powerful arm, with overwhelming terror, and with miraculous signs and wonders. 9He brought us to this place and gave us this land flowing with milk and honey! 10And now, O LORD, I have brought you the first portion of the harvest you have given me from the ground.' Then place the produce before the LORD your God, and bow to the ground in worship before him. 11Afterward you may go and celebrate because of all the good things the LORD your God has given to you and your household. Remember to include the Levites and the foreigners living among you in the celebration.

12"Every third year you must offer a special tithe of your crops. In this year of the special tithe you must give your tithes to the Levites, foreigners, orphans, and widows, so that they will have enough to eat in your towns. 13Then you must declare in the presence of the LORD your God, 'I have taken the sacred gift from my house and have given it to the Levites, foreigners, orphans, and widows, just as you commanded me. I have not violated or forgotten any of your commands. 14I have not eaten any of it while in mourning; I have not handled it while I was ceremonially unclean; and I have not offered any of it to the dead. I have obeyed the LORD my God and have done everything you commanded me. 15Now look down from your holy dwelling place in heaven and bless your people Israel and the land you swore to our ancestors to give us—a land flowing with milk and honey.'

A CALL TO OBEY THE LORD'S COMMANDS

16"Today the LORD your God has commanded you to obey all these decrees and regulations. So be careful to obey them wholeheartedly. 17You have declared today that the LORD is your God. And you have promised to walk in his ways, and to obey his decrees, commands, and regulations, and to do everything he tells you. 18The LORD has declared today that you are his people, his own special treasure, just as he promised, and that you must obey all his commands. 19And if you do, he will set you high above all the other nations he has made. Then you will receive praise, honor, and renown. You will be a nation that is holy to the LORD your God, just as he promised."

27

THE ALTAR ON MOUNT EBAL

Then Moses and the leaders of Israel gave this charge to the people: "Obey all these commands that I am giving you today. 2When you cross the Jordan River and enter the land the LORD your God is giving you, set up some large stones and coat them with plaster. 3Write this whole body of instruction on them when you cross the river to enter the land the LORD your God is giving you—a land flowing with milk and honey, just as the LORD, the God of your ancestors, promised you. 4When you cross the Jordan, set up these stones at Mount Ebal and coat them with plaster, as I am commanding you today.

5"Then build an altar there to the LORD your God, using natural, uncut stones. You must not shape the stones with an iron tool. 6Build the altar of uncut stones, and use it to offer burnt offerings to the LORD your God. 7Also sacrifice peace offerings on it, and celebrate by feasting there before the LORD your God. 8You must clearly write all these instructions on the stones coated with plaster."

[9]Then Moses and the Levitical priests addressed all Israel as follows: "O Israel, be quiet and listen! Today you have become the people of the LORD your God. [10]So you must obey the LORD your God by keeping all these commands and decrees that I am giving you today."

CURSES FROM MOUNT EBAL

[11]That same day Moses also gave this charge to the people:
[12]"When you cross the Jordan River, the tribes of Simeon, Levi, Judah, Issachar, Joseph, and Benjamin must stand on Mount Gerizim to proclaim a blessing over the people.
[13]And the tribes of Reuben, Gad, Asher, Zebulun, Dan, and Naphtali must stand on Mount Ebal to proclaim a curse.

[14]"Then the Levites will shout to all the people of Israel:

[15]'Cursed is anyone who carves or casts an idol and secretly sets it up. These idols, the work of craftsmen, are detestable to the LORD.'
And all the people will reply, 'Amen.'

CURSES AND BLESSINGS 27:15-26

These curses were a series of oaths, spoken by the priests and affirmed by the people, by which the people promised to stay away from wrong actions. By saying *Amen*, "So be it," the people took responsibility for their actions.

Looking at a list of curses like this might give us the idea that God is out to crush anyone who steps out of line. But that's not the case. Just as we warn children to stay away from hot stoves and busy streets, God warns us to stay away from dangerous actions. He does not leave us with only curses or consequences, however. Immediately following these curses, we discover the blessings that come from living for God (28:1-14). These give us extra incentive to obey his laws. ■

[16]'Cursed is anyone who dishonors father or mother.'
And all the people will reply, 'Amen.'

[17]'Cursed is anyone who steals property from a neighbor by moving a boundary marker.'
And all the people will reply, 'Amen.'

[18]'Cursed is anyone who leads a blind person astray on the road.'
And all the people will reply, 'Amen.'

[19]'Cursed is anyone who denies justice to foreigners, orphans, or widows.'
And all the people will reply, 'Amen.'

[20]'Cursed is anyone who has sexual intercourse with one of his father's wives, for he has violated his father.'
And all the people will reply, 'Amen.'

[21]'Cursed is anyone who has sexual intercourse with an animal.'
And all the people will reply, 'Amen.'

[22]'Cursed is anyone who has sexual intercourse with his sister, whether she is the daughter of his father or his mother.'
And all the people will reply, 'Amen.'

[23]'Cursed is anyone who has sexual intercourse with his mother-in-law.'
And all the people will reply, 'Amen.'

[24]'Cursed is anyone who attacks a neighbor in secret.'
And all the people will reply, 'Amen.'

[25]'Cursed is anyone who accepts payment to kill an innocent person.'
And all the people will reply, 'Amen.'

[26]'Cursed is anyone who does not affirm and obey the terms of these instructions.'
And all the people will reply, 'Amen.'

28 BLESSINGS FOR OBEDIENCE

"If you fully obey the LORD your God and carefully keep all his commands that I am giving you today, the LORD your God will set you high above all the nations of the world. [2]You will experience all these blessings if you obey the LORD your God:

[3] Your towns and your fields
will be blessed.
[4] Your children and your crops
will be blessed.
The offspring of your herds and flocks
will be blessed.
[5] Your fruit baskets and breadboards
will be blessed.
[6] Wherever you go and whatever you do,
you will be blessed.

[7]"The LORD will conquer your enemies when they attack you. They will attack you from one direction, but they will scatter from you in seven!
[8]"The LORD will guarantee a blessing on everything you do and will fill your storehouses with grain. The LORD your God will bless you in the land he is giving you.
[9]"If you obey the commands of the LORD your God and walk in his ways, the LORD will establish you as his holy people as he swore he would do. [10]Then all the nations of the world will see that you are a people claimed by the LORD, and they will stand in awe of you.
[11]"The LORD will give you prosperity in the land he swore to your ancestors to give you, blessing you with many children, numerous livestock, and abundant crops.
[12]The LORD will send rain at the proper time from his rich treasury in the heavens and will bless all the work you do. You will lend to many nations, but you will never need to borrow from them. [13]If you listen to these commands of the LORD your God that I am giving you today, and if you carefully obey them, the LORD will make you the head and not the tail, and you will always be on top and never at the

bottom. 14You must not turn away from any of the commands I am giving you today, nor follow after other gods
and worship them.

CURSES FOR DISOBEDIENCE

15"But if you refuse to listen to the LORD your God and do
not obey all the commands and decrees I am giving you
today, all these curses will come and overwhelm you:

16 Your towns and your fields
will be cursed.
17 Your fruit baskets and breadboards
will be cursed.
18 Your children and your crops
will be cursed.
The offspring of your herds and flocks
will be cursed.
19 Wherever you go and whatever you do,
you will be cursed.

20"The LORD himself will send on you curses, confusion, and frustration in everything you do, until at last you
are completely destroyed for doing evil and abandoning
me. 21The LORD will afflict you with diseases until none of
you are left in the land you are about to enter and occupy.
22The LORD will strike you with wasting diseases, fever,
and inflammation, with scorching heat and drought, and
with blight and mildew. These disasters will pursue you
until you die. 23The skies above will be as unyielding as
bronze, and the earth beneath will be as hard as iron.
24The LORD will change the rain that falls on your land
into powder, and dust will pour down from the sky until
you are destroyed.

25"The LORD will cause you to be defeated by your enemies. You will attack your enemies from one direction,
but you will scatter from them in seven! You will be an object of horror to all the kingdoms of the earth. 26Your
corpses will be food for all the scavenging birds and wild
animals, and no one will be there to chase them away.

THE CURSE OF INSANITY 28:34

Moses warned the people of Israel about the curses that resulted from rejecting God. One of these curses involved becoming mentally unhinged due to terrible hardships and tragedies. It's easy to become completely disheartened by the evil acts of others. Much of the world's evil is a result of the failure to acknowledge and serve God. When you hear bad news, do you find yourself groaning helplessly? There is hope. God has ultimate control and one day will come back to make everything right. ■

27"The LORD will afflict you with the boils of Egypt and
with tumors, scurvy, and the itch, from which you cannot
be cured. 28The LORD will strike you with madness, blindness, and panic. 29You will grope around in broad daylight like a blind person groping in the darkness, but you
will not find your way. You will be oppressed and robbed
continually, and no one will come to save you.

30"You will be engaged to a woman, but another man
will sleep with her. You will build a house, but someone
else will live in it. You will plant a vineyard, but you will
never enjoy its fruit. 31Your ox will be butchered before
your eyes, but you will not eat a single bite of the meat.
Your donkey will be taken from you, never to be returned.
Your sheep and goats will be given to your enemies, and
no one will be there to help you. 32You will watch as your
sons and daughters are taken away as slaves. Your heart
will break for them, but you won't be able to help them.
33A foreign nation you have never heard about will eat the
crops you worked so hard to grow. You will suffer under
constant oppression and harsh treatment. 34You will go
mad because of all the tragedy you see around you. 35The
LORD will cover your knees and legs with incurable boils.
In fact, you will be covered from head to foot.

36"The LORD will exile you and your king to a nation unknown to you and your ancestors. There in exile you will
worship gods of wood and stone! 37You will become an
object of horror, ridicule, and mockery among all the nations to which the LORD sends you.

38"You will plant much but harvest little, for locusts
will eat your crops. 39You will plant vineyards and care for
them, but you will not drink the wine or eat the grapes,
for worms will destroy the vines. 40You will grow olive
trees throughout your land, but you will never use the olive oil, for the fruit will drop before it ripens. 41You will
have sons and daughters, but you will lose them, for they
will be led away into captivity. 42Swarms of insects will
destroy your trees and crops.

43"The foreigners living among you will become stronger and stronger, while you become weaker and weaker.
44They will lend money to you, but you will not lend to
them. They will be the head, and you will be the tail!

45"If you refuse to listen to the LORD your God and to
obey the commands and decrees he has given you, all
these curses will pursue and overtake you until you are
destroyed. 46These horrors will serve as a sign and warning among you and your descendants forever. 47If you do
not serve the LORD your God with joy and enthusiasm for
the abundant benefits you have received, 48you will serve
your enemies whom the LORD will send against you. You
will be left hungry, thirsty, naked, and lacking in everything. The LORD will put an iron yoke on your neck, oppressing you harshly until he has destroyed you.

49"The LORD will bring a distant nation against you from
the end of the earth, and it will swoop down on you like a
vulture. It is a nation whose language you do not understand, 50a fierce and heartless nation that shows no respect
for the old and no pity for the young. 51Its armies will devour your livestock and crops, and you will be destroyed.
They will leave you no grain, new wine, olive oil, calves, or
lambs, and you will starve to death. 52They will attack your
cities until all the fortified walls in your land—the walls you
trusted to protect you—are knocked down. They will attack
all the towns in the land the LORD your God has given you.

53"The siege and terrible distress of the enemy's attack
will be so severe that you will eat the flesh of your own
sons and daughters, whom the LORD your God has given
you. 54The most tenderhearted man among you will have

no compassion for his own brother, his beloved wife, and his surviving children. 55He will refuse to share with them the flesh he is devouring—the flesh of one of his own children—because he has nothing else to eat during the siege and terrible distress that your enemy will inflict on all your towns. 56The most tender and delicate woman among you—so delicate she would not so much as touch the ground with her foot—will be selfish toward the husband she loves and toward her own son or daughter. 57She will hide from them the afterbirth and the new baby she has borne, so that she herself can secretly eat them. She will have nothing else to eat during the siege and terrible distress that your enemy will inflict on all your towns.

58"If you refuse to obey all the words of instruction that are written in this book, and if you do not fear the glorious and awesome name of the LORD your God, 59then the LORD will overwhelm you and your children with indescribable plagues. These plagues will be intense and without relief, making you miserable and unbearably sick. 60He will afflict you with all the diseases of Egypt that you feared so much, and you will have no relief. 61The LORD will afflict you with every sickness and plague there is, even those not mentioned in this Book of Instruction, until you are destroyed. 62Though you become as numerous as the stars in the sky, few of you will be left because you would not listen to the LORD your God.

63"Just as the LORD has found great pleasure in causing you to prosper and multiply, the LORD will find pleasure in destroying you. You will be torn from the land you are about to enter and occupy. 64For the LORD will scatter you among all the nations from one end of the earth to the other. There you will worship foreign gods that neither you nor your ancestors have known, gods made of wood and stone! 65There among those nations you will find no peace or place to rest. And the LORD will cause your heart to tremble, your eyesight to fail, and your soul to despair. 66Your life will constantly hang in the balance. You will live night and day in fear, unsure if you will survive. 67In the morning you will say, 'If only it were night!' And in the evening you will say, 'If only it were morning!' For you will be terrified by the awful horrors you see around you. 68Then the LORD will send you back to Egypt in ships, to a destination I promised you would never see again. There you will offer to sell yourselves to your enemies as slaves, but no one will buy you."

29

1*These are the terms of the covenant the LORD commanded Moses to make with the Israelites while they were in the land of Moab, in addition to the covenant he had made with them at Mount Sinai.*

MOSES REVIEWS THE COVENANT

2*Moses summoned all the Israelites and said to them, "You have seen with your own eyes everything the LORD did in the land of Egypt to Pharaoh and to all his servants and to his whole country—3all the great tests of strength, the miraculous signs, and the amazing wonders. 4But to this day the LORD has not given you minds that understand, nor eyes that see, nor ears that hear! 5For forty years I led you through the wilderness, yet your clothes and sandals did not wear out. 6You ate no bread and drank no wine or other alcoholic drink, but he gave you food so you would know that he is the LORD your God.

7"When we came here, King Sihon of Heshbon and King Og of Bashan came out to fight against us, but we defeated them. 8We took their land and gave it to the tribes of Reuben and Gad and to the half-tribe of Manasseh as their grant of land.

9"Therefore, obey the terms of this covenant so that you will prosper in everything you do. 10All of you—tribal leaders, elders, officers, all the men of Israel—are standing today in the presence of the LORD your God. 11Your little ones and your wives are with you, as well as the foreigners living among you who chop your wood and carry your water. 12You are standing here today to enter into the covenant of the LORD your God. The LORD is making this covenant, including the curses. 13By entering into the covenant today, he will establish you as his people and confirm that he is your God, just as he promised you and as he swore to your ancestors Abraham, Isaac, and Jacob.

14"But you are not the only ones with whom I am making this covenant with its curses. 15I am making this covenant both with you who stand here today in the presence of the LORD our God, and also with the future generations who are not standing here today.

AN EVIL SEED 29:18

Moses provided yet another warning for the people of Israel. If they rebelled against God, a root of bitterness would spring up within them. When we decide to do what we know is wrong, we plant an evil seed that eventually yields a crop of sorrow. But we can prevent that seed from taking root. We can do this by confessing wrongdoings to God and others immediately. If the seed never finds fertile soil, its bitter fruit will never ripen. ■

16"You remember how we lived in the land of Egypt and how we traveled through the lands of enemy nations as we left. 17You have seen their detestable practices and their idols* made of wood, stone, silver, and gold. 18I am making this covenant with you so that no one among you—no man, woman, clan, or tribe—will turn away from the LORD our God to worship these gods of other nations, and so that no root among you bears bitter and poisonous fruit.

19"Those who hear the warnings of this curse should not congratulate themselves, thinking, 'I am safe, even though I am following the desires of my own stubborn heart.' This would lead to utter ruin! 20The LORD will never pardon such people. Instead his anger and jealousy will burn against them. All the curses written in this book will

29:1a Verse 29:1 is numbered 28:69 in Hebrew text. 29:1b Hebrew *Horeb*, another name for Sinai. 29:2 Verses 29:2-29 are numbered 29:1-28 in Hebrew text. 29:17 The Hebrew term (literally *round things*) probably alludes to dung.

come down on them, and the LORD will erase their names
from under heaven. [21]The LORD will separate them from
all the tribes of Israel, to pour out on them all the curses of
the covenant recorded in this Book of Instruction.
[22]"Then the generations to come, both your own descendants and the foreigners who come from distant
lands, will see the devastation of the land and the diseases the LORD inflicts on it. [23]They will exclaim, 'The
whole land is devastated by sulfur and salt. It is a wasteland with nothing planted and nothing growing, not even
a blade of grass. It is like the cities of Sodom and Gomorrah, Admah and Zeboiim, which the LORD destroyed in
his intense anger.'
[24]"And all the surrounding nations will ask, 'Why has
the LORD done this to this land? Why was he so angry?'
[25]"And the answer will be, 'This happened because the
people of the land abandoned the covenant that the
LORD, the God of their ancestors, made with them when
he brought them out of the land of Egypt. [26]Instead, they
turned away to serve and worship gods they had not
known before, gods that were not from the LORD. [27]That
is why the LORD's anger has burned against this land,
bringing down on it every curse recorded in this book.
[28]In great anger and fury the LORD uprooted his people
from their land and banished them to another land,
where they still live today!'
[29]"The LORD our God has secrets known to no one. We
are not accountable for them, but we and our children
are accountable forever for all that he has revealed to us,
so that we may obey all the terms of these instructions.

30 A CALL TO RETURN TO THE LORD

"In the future, when you experience all these blessings
and curses I have listed for you, and when you are living
among the nations to which the LORD your God has exiled
you, take to heart all these instructions. [2]If at that time
you and your children return to the
LORD your God, and if you obey with all
your heart and all your soul all the
commands I have given you today,
[3]then the LORD your God will restore
your fortunes. He will have mercy on
you and gather you back from all the
nations where he has scattered you.
[4]Even though you are banished to the
ends of the earth, the LORD your God
will gather you from there and bring
you back again. [5]The LORD your God
will return you to the land that belonged to your ancestors, and you will
possess that land again. Then he will
make you even more prosperous and
numerous than your ancestors!
[6]"The LORD your God will change your heart* and the
hearts of all your descendants, so that you will love him
with all your heart and soul and so you may live! [7]The
LORD your God will inflict all these curses on your enemies and on those who hate and persecute you. [8]Then
you will again obey the LORD and keep all his commands
that I am giving you today.

> Oh, that you would choose life, so that you and your descendants might live!
>
> DEUTERONOMY 30:19

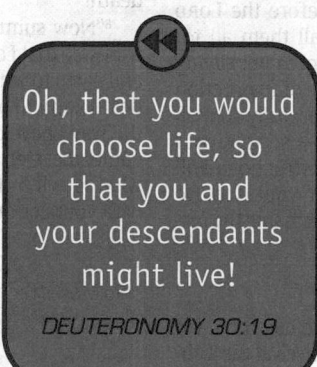

A FRESH START 30:1-6

Moses assured the people of Israel that when they were ready to return to God, he would be ready to receive them. Even if they deliberately walked away from him and ruined their lives, God would still take them back. He promises a fresh start to anyone separated from him by sin. Need a fresh start? His mercy goes far beyond what any of us can imagine. ■

[9]"The LORD your God will then make you successful in
everything you do. He will give you many children and
numerous livestock, and he will cause your fields to produce abundant harvests, for the LORD will again delight in
being good to you as he was to your ancestors. [10]The LORD
your God will delight in you if you obey his voice and keep
the commands and decrees written in this Book of Instruction, and if you turn to the LORD your God with all
your heart and soul.

THE CHOICE OF LIFE OR DEATH

[11]"This command I am giving you today is not too difficult for you to understand, and it is not beyond your
reach. [12]It is not kept in heaven, so distant that you must
ask, 'Who will go up to heaven and bring it down so we
can hear it and obey?' [13]It is not kept beyond the sea, so
far away that you must ask, 'Who will cross the sea to
bring it to us so we can hear it and obey?' [14]No, the message is very close at hand; it is on your lips and in your
heart so that you can obey it.
[15]"Now listen! Today I am giving you a choice between
life and death, between prosperity and disaster. [16]For I
command you this day to love the
LORD your God and to keep his commands, decrees, and regulations by
walking in his ways. If you do this, you
will live and multiply, and the LORD
your God will bless you and the land
you are about to enter and occupy.
[17]"But if your heart turns away and
you refuse to listen, and if you are
drawn away to serve and worship
other gods, [18]then I warn you now that
you will certainly be destroyed. You
will not live a long, good life in the land
you are crossing the Jordan to occupy.
[19]"Today I have given you the choice
between life and death, between blessings and curses. Now I call on heaven
and earth to witness the choice you make. Oh, that you
would choose life, so that you and your descendants
might live! [20]You can make this choice by loving the LORD
your God, obeying him, and committing yourself firmly
to him. This* is the key to your life. And if you love and

30:6 Hebrew *circumcise your heart*. 30:20 Or *He*.

obey the LORD, you will live long in the land the LORD
swore to give your ancestors Abraham, Isaac, and Jacob."

31 JOSHUA BECOMES ISRAEL'S LEADER

When Moses had finished giving these instructions* to
all the people of Israel, 2he said, "I am now 120 years old,
and I am no longer able to lead you. The LORD has told me,
'You will not cross the Jordan River.' 3But the LORD your
God himself will cross over ahead of you. He will destroy
the nations living there, and you will take possession of
their land. Joshua will lead you across the river, just as the
LORD promised.

4"The LORD will destroy the nations living in the land,
just as he destroyed Sihon and Og, the kings of the Amorites. 5The LORD will hand over to you the people who live
there, and you must deal with them as I have commanded
you. 6So be strong and courageous! Do not be afraid and
do not panic before them. For the LORD your God will
personally go ahead of you. He will neither fail you nor
abandon you."

7Then Moses called for Joshua, and as all Israel
watched, he said to him, "Be strong and courageous! For
you will lead these people into the land that the LORD
swore to their ancestors he would give them. You are the
one who will divide it among them as their grants of land.
8Do not be afraid or discouraged, for the LORD will personally go ahead of you. He will be with you; he will neither fail you nor abandon you."

PUBLIC READING OF THE BOOK OF INSTRUCTION

9So Moses wrote this entire body of instruction in a book
and gave it to the priests, who carried the Ark of the
LORD's Covenant, and to the elders of Israel. 10Then
Moses gave them this command: "At the end of every seventh year, the Year of Release, during the Festival of Shelters, 11you must read this Book of Instruction to all the
people of Israel when they assemble before the LORD
your God at the place he chooses. 12Call them all together—men, women, children, and the foreigners living
in your towns—so they may hear this Book of Instruction
and learn to fear the LORD your God and carefully obey all
the terms of these instructions. 13Do this so that your
children who have not known these instructions will
hear them and will learn to fear the LORD your God. Do
this as long as you live in the land you are crossing the Jordan to occupy."

ISRAEL'S DISOBEDIENCE PREDICTED

14Then the LORD said to Moses, "The time has come for
you to die. Call Joshua and present yourselves at the Tabernacle,* so that I may commission him there." So Moses
and Joshua went and presented themselves at the Tabernacle. 15And the LORD appeared to them in a pillar of
cloud that stood at the entrance to the sacred tent.

16The LORD said to Moses, "You are about to die and
join your ancestors. After you are gone, these people will
begin to worship foreign gods, the gods of the land where
they are going. They will abandon me and break my covenant that I have made with them. 17Then my anger will
blaze forth against them. I will abandon them, hiding my
face from them, and they will be devoured. Terrible trouble will come down on them, and on that day they will say,
'These disasters have come down on us because God is no
longer among us!' 18At that time I will hide my face from
them on account of all the evil they commit by worshiping other gods.

19"So write down the words of this song, and teach it
to the people of Israel. Help them learn it, so it may serve
as a witness for me against them. 20For I will bring them
into the land I swore to give their ancestors—a land
flowing with milk and honey. There they will become
prosperous, eat all the food they want, and become fat.
But they will begin to worship other gods; they will despise me and break my covenant. 21And when great disasters come down on them, this song will stand as
evidence against them, for it will never be forgotten by
their descendants. I know the intentions of these people, even now before they have entered the land I swore
to give them."

22So that very day Moses wrote down the words of the
song and taught it to the Israelites.

23Then the LORD commissioned Joshua son of Nun
with these words: "Be strong and courageous, for you
must bring the people of Israel into the land I swore to
give them. I will be with you."

24When Moses had finished writing this entire body of
instruction in a book, 25he gave this command to the Levites who carried the Ark of the LORD's Covenant: 26"Take
this Book of Instruction and place it beside the Ark of the
Covenant of the LORD your God, so it may remain there as
a witness against the people of Israel. 27For I know how
rebellious and stubborn you are. Even now, while I am
still alive and am here with you, you have rebelled against
the LORD. How much more rebellious will you be after my
death!

28"Now summon all the elders and officials of your
tribes, so that I can speak to them directly and call heaven
and earth to witness against them. 29I know that after my
death you will become utterly corrupt and will turn from
the way I have commanded you to follow. In the days to
come, disaster will come down on you, for you will do
what is evil in the LORD's sight, making him very angry
with your actions."

THE SONG OF MOSES

30So Moses recited this entire song publicly to the assembly of Israel:

32

1 "Listen, O heavens, and I will speak!
Hear, O earth, the words that I say!
2 Let my teaching fall on you like rain;
let my speech settle like dew.
Let my words fall like rain on tender grass,
like gentle showers on young plants.

31:1 As in Dead Sea Scrolls and Greek version; Masoretic Text reads *Moses went and spoke.* 31:14 Hebrew *Tent of Meeting;* also in 31:14b.

Variety in Worship

Israel's worship involved all of the senses. This reinforced the meaning of the ceremony and painted a dramatic picture that worship touches all areas of life.

SIGHT	The beauty and symbolism of the Tabernacle; every color and hue had a meaning
HEARING	The use of music; there were instructions for the use of a variety of instruments, and the Bible records many songs
SMELL	The sacrifices were burned, emitting a familiar aroma
TASTE	Israel's festivals were celebrations and memorials—much of the food had symbolic importance
TOUCH	At the sacrifice, they were to touch the head of the animal to symbolize the fact that it was taking their place.

3 I will proclaim the name of the LORD;
how glorious is our God!
4 He is the Rock; his deeds are perfect.
Everything he does is just and fair.
He is a faithful God who does no wrong;
how just and upright he is!

5 "But they have acted corruptly toward him;
when they act so perversely,
are they really his children?*
They are a deceitful and twisted generation.
6 Is this the way you repay the LORD,
you foolish and senseless people?
Isn't he your Father who created you?
Has he not made you and established you?
7 Remember the days of long ago;
think about the generations past.
Ask your father, and he will inform you.
Inquire of your elders, and they will tell you.
8 When the Most High assigned lands to the nations,
when he divided up the human race,
he established the boundaries of the peoples
according to the number in his heavenly court.*

9 "For the people of Israel belong to the LORD;
Jacob is his special possession.
10 He found them in a desert land,
in an empty, howling wasteland.
He surrounded them and watched over them;
he guarded them as he would guard his own eyes.*
11 Like an eagle that rouses her chicks
and hovers over her young,
so he spread his wings to take them up
and carried them safely on his pinions.
12 The LORD alone guided them;
they followed no foreign gods.
13 He let them ride over the highlands
and feast on the crops of the fields.
He nourished them with honey from the rock
and olive oil from the stony ground.
14 He fed them yogurt from the herd
and milk from the flock,
together with the fat of lambs.
He gave them choice rams from Bashan, and goats,
together with the choicest wheat.
You drank the finest wine,
made from the juice of grapes.

15 "But Israel* soon became fat and unruly;
the people grew heavy, plump, and stuffed!
Then they abandoned the God who had made them;
they made light of the Rock of their salvation.
16 They stirred up his jealousy by worshiping foreign
gods;
they provoked his fury with detestable deeds.
17 They offered sacrifices to demons, which are not
God,
to gods they had not known before,
to new gods only recently arrived,
to gods their ancestors had never feared.
18 You neglected the Rock who had fathered you;
you forgot the God who had given you birth.

19 "The LORD saw this and drew back,
provoked to anger by his own sons and daughters.
20 He said, 'I will abandon them;
then see what becomes of them.
For they are a twisted generation,
children without integrity.
21 They have roused my jealousy by worshiping things
that are not God;
they have provoked my anger with their useless
idols.
Now I will rouse their jealousy through people who
are not even a people;
I will provoke their anger through the foolish
Gentiles.
22 For my anger blazes forth like fire
and burns to the depths of the grave.*
It devours the earth and all its crops
and ignites the foundations of the mountains.

32:5 The meaning of the Hebrew is uncertain. 32:8 As in Dead Sea Scrolls, which read *the number of the sons of God,* and Greek version, which reads *the number of the angels of God;* Masoretic Text reads *the number of the sons of Israel.* 32:10 Hebrew *as the pupil of his eye.* 32:15 Hebrew *Jeshurun,* a term of endearment for Israel. 32:22 Hebrew *of Sheol.*

23 I will heap disasters upon them
and shoot them down with my arrows.
24 I will weaken them with famine,
burning fever, and deadly disease.
I will send the fangs of wild beasts
and poisonous snakes that glide in the dust.
25 Outside, the sword will bring death,
and inside, terror will strike
both young men and young women,
both infants and the aged.
26 I would have annihilated them,
wiping out even the memory of them.
27 But I feared the taunt of Israel's enemy,
who might misunderstand and say,
"Our own power has triumphed!
The LORD had nothing to do with this!"'

28 "But Israel is a senseless nation;
the people are foolish, without understanding.
29 Oh, that they were wise and could understand this!
Oh, that they might know their fate!
30 How could one person chase a thousand of them,
and two people put ten thousand to flight,
unless their Rock had sold them,
unless the LORD had given them up?
31 But the rock of our enemies is not like our Rock,
as even they recognize.*
32 Their vine grows from the vine of Sodom,
from the vineyards of Gomorrah.
Their grapes are poison,
and their clusters are bitter.
33 Their wine is the venom of serpents,
the deadly poison of cobras.

34 "The LORD says, 'Am I not storing up these things,
sealing them away in my treasury?
35 I will take revenge; I will pay them back.
In due time their feet will slip.
Their day of disaster will arrive,
and their destiny will overtake them.'

36 "Indeed, the LORD will give justice to his people,
and he will change his mind about* his servants,
when he sees their strength is gone
and no one is left, slave or free.
37 Then he will ask, 'Where are their gods,
the rocks they fled to for refuge?
38 Where now are those gods,
who ate the fat of their sacrifices
and drank the wine of their offerings?
Let those gods arise and help you!
Let them provide you with shelter!
39 Look now; I myself am he!
There is no other god but me!
I am the one who kills and gives life;
I am the one who wounds and heals;
no one can be rescued from my powerful hand!
40 Now I raise my hand to heaven
and declare, "As surely as I live,
41 when I sharpen my flashing sword
and begin to carry out justice,
I will take revenge on my enemies
and repay those who reject me.
42 I will make my arrows drunk with blood,
and my sword will devour flesh—
the blood of the slaughtered and the captives,
and the heads of the enemy leaders."'

43 "Rejoice with him, you heavens,
and let all of God's angels worship him.*
Rejoice with his people, you nations,
and let all the angels be strengthened in him.*
For he will avenge the blood of his servants;
he will take revenge against his enemies.
He will repay those who hate him*
and cleanse the land for his people."

44So Moses came with Joshua* son of Nun and recited
all the words of this song to the people.
45When Moses had finished reciting all these words to
the people of Israel, 46he added: "Take to heart all the
words of warning I have given you today. Pass them on as
a command to your children so they will obey every word
of these instructions. 47These instructions are not empty
words—they are your life! By obeying them you will enjoy
a long life in the land you will occupy when you cross the
Jordan River."

MOSES' DEATH FORETOLD

48That same day the LORD said to Moses, 49"Go to Moab, to
the mountains east of the river,* and climb Mount Nebo,
which is across from Jericho. Look out across the land of
Canaan, the land I am giving to the people of Israel as
their own special possession. 50Then you will die there on
the mountain. You will join your ancestors, just as Aaron,
your brother, died on Mount Hor and joined his ancestors. 51For both of you betrayed me with the Israelites at
the waters of Meribah at Kadesh* in the wilderness of
Zin. You failed to demonstrate my holiness to the people
of Israel there. 52So you will see the land from a distance,
but you may not enter the land I am giving to the people
of Israel."

33 MOSES BLESSES THE PEOPLE

This is the blessing that Moses, the man of God, gave to the people of Israel before his death:

2 "The LORD came from Mount Sinai
and dawned upon us* from Mount Seir;

32:31 The meaning of the Hebrew is uncertain. Greek version reads *our enemies are fools*. 32:36 Or *will take revenge for*. 32:43a As in Dead Sea Scrolls and Greek version; Masoretic Text lacks the first two lines. Compare Heb 1:6. 32:43b As in Greek version; Hebrew text lacks this line. 32:43c As in Dead Sea Scrolls and Greek version; Masoretic Text lacks this line. 32:44 Hebrew *Hoshea*, a variant name for Joshua. 32:49 Hebrew *the mountains of Abarim*. 32:51 Hebrew *waters of Meribath-kadesh*. 33:2a As in Greek and Syriac versions; Hebrew reads *upon them*.

he shone forth from Mount Paran
and came from Meribah-kadesh
with flaming fire at his right hand.*
3 Indeed, he loves his people;*
all his holy ones are in his hands.
They follow in his steps
and accept his teaching.
4 Moses gave us the LORD's instruction,
the special possession of the people of Israel.*
5 The LORD became king in Israel*—
when the leaders of the people assembled,
when the tribes of Israel gathered as one."

DIFFERENT BLESSINGS 33:6-25

God blessed each tribe of Israel in different ways. To one he gave the best land, to another strength, to another safety. Too often we see someone with a particular blessing or talent and think that God must love that person more than he loves us. But God chooses to equip each person in ways that he sees fit. We are not to compare ourselves with others. (See 2 Cor 10:12.) Instead, we are to work to build his kingdom. What gifts has God given you? How are you using them to help build his kingdom? ■

6 Moses said this about the tribe of Reuben:*

"Let the tribe of Reuben live and not die out,
though they are few in number."

7 Moses said this about the tribe of Judah:

"O LORD, hear the cry of Judah
and bring them together as a people.
Give them strength to defend their cause;
help them against their enemies!"

8 Moses said this about the tribe of Levi:

"O LORD, you have given your Thummim and Urim—
the sacred lots—
to your faithful servants the Levites.*
You put them to the test at Massah
and struggled with them at the waters of Meribah.
9 The Levites obeyed your word
and guarded your covenant.
They were more loyal to you
than to their own parents.
They ignored their relatives
and did not acknowledge their own children.
10 They teach your regulations to Jacob;
they give your instructions to Israel.
They present incense before you
and offer whole burnt offerings on the altar.
11 Bless the ministry of the Levites, O LORD,
and accept all the work of their hands.
Hit their enemies where it hurts the most;
strike down their foes so they never rise again."

12 Moses said this about the tribe of Benjamin:

"The people of Benjamin are loved by the LORD
and live in safety beside him.
He surrounds them continuously
and preserves them from every harm."

13 Moses said this about the tribes of Joseph:

"May their land be blessed by the LORD
with the precious gift of dew from the heavens
and water from beneath the earth;
14 with the rich fruit that grows in the sun,
and the rich harvest produced each month;
15 with the finest crops of the ancient mountains,
and the abundance from the everlasting hills;
16 with the best gifts of the earth and its bounty,
and the favor of the one who appeared in the
burning bush.
May these blessings rest on Joseph's head,
crowning the brow of the prince among his
brothers.
17 Joseph has the majesty of a young bull;
he has the horns of a wild ox.
He will gore distant nations,
driving them to the ends of the earth.
This is my blessing for the multitudes of Ephraim
and the thousands of Manasseh."

18 Moses said this about the tribes of Zebulun and Issachar*:

"May the people of Zebulun prosper in their travels.
May the people of Issachar prosper at home in
their tents.
19 They summon the people to the mountain
to offer proper sacrifices there.
They benefit from the riches of the sea
and the hidden treasures in the sand."

20 Moses said this about the tribe of Gad:

"Blessed is the one who enlarges Gad's territory!
Gad is poised there like a lion
to tear off an arm or a head.
21 The people of Gad took the best land for themselves;
a leader's share was assigned to them.
When the leaders of the people were assembled,
they carried out the LORD's justice
and obeyed his regulations for Israel."

33:2b Or *came from myriads of holy ones, from the south, from his mountain slopes.* The meaning of the Hebrew is uncertain. **33:3** As in Greek version; Hebrew reads *Indeed, lover of the peoples.* **33:4** Hebrew *of Jacob.* The names "Jacob" and "Israel" are often interchanged throughout the Old Testament, referring sometimes to the individual patriarch and sometimes to the nation. **33:5** Hebrew *in Jeshurun,* a term of endearment for Israel. **33:6** Hebrew lacks *Moses said this about the tribe of Reuben.* **33:8** As in Greek version; Hebrew lacks *the Levites.* **33:18** Hebrew lacks *and Issachar.*

[22]Moses said this about the tribe of Dan:

"Dan is a lion's cub,
leaping out from Bashan."

[23]Moses said this about the tribe of Naphtali:

"O Naphtali, you are rich in favor
and full of the LORD's blessings;
may you possess the west and the south."

[24]Moses said this about the tribe of Asher:

"May Asher be blessed above other sons;
may he be esteemed by his brothers;
may he bathe his feet in olive oil.
25 May the bolts of your gates be of iron and bronze;
may you be secure all your days."

26 "There is no one like the God of Israel.*
He rides across the heavens to help you,
across the skies in majestic splendor.
27 The eternal God is your refuge,
and his everlasting arms are under you.
He drives out the enemy before you;
he cries out, 'Destroy them!'
28 So Israel will live in safety,
prosperous Jacob in security,
in a land of grain and new wine,
while the heavens drop down dew.
29 How blessed you are, O Israel!
Who else is like you, a people saved by the LORD?
He is your protecting shield
and your triumphant sword!
Your enemies will cringe before you,
and you will stomp on their backs!"

34 THE DEATH OF MOSES

Then Moses went up to Mount Nebo from the plains of Moab and climbed Pisgah Peak, which is across from Jericho. And the LORD showed him the whole land, from Gilead as far as Dan; [2]all the land of Naphtali; the land of Ephraim and Manasseh; all the land of Judah, extending to the Mediterranean Sea*; [3]the Negev; the Jordan Valley with Jericho—the city of palms—as far as Zoar. [4]Then the LORD said to Moses, "This is the land I promised on oath to Abraham, Isaac, and Jacob when I said, 'I will give it to your descendants.' I have now allowed you to see it with your own eyes, but you will not enter the land."

FROM FAILURE TO SUCCESS 34:10-12

Moses, the man who did not want to be sent to Egypt because he had trouble speaking in public (Exod 4:10), delivered the three addresses to Israel that make up the book of Deuteronomy. God changed this stuttering shepherd into a powerful speaker and national leader. Moses' success story is a great example for us. Ever wonder whether or not you'll be successful? Or maybe you've wondered whether past failures have doomed your chances for success. If so, take a lesson from Moses' life. God can turn a failure into a success. ■

[5]So Moses, the servant of the LORD, died there in the land of Moab, just as the LORD had said. [6]The LORD buried him* in a valley near Beth-peor in Moab, but to this day no one knows the exact place. [7]Moses was 120 years old when he died, yet his eyesight was clear, and he was as strong as ever. [8]The people of Israel mourned for Moses on the plains of Moab for thirty days, until the customary period of mourning was over.

[9]Now Joshua son of Nun was full of the spirit of wisdom, for Moses had laid his hands on him. So the people of Israel obeyed him, doing just as the LORD had commanded Moses.

[10]There has never been another prophet in Israel like Moses, whom the LORD knew face to face. [11]The LORD sent him to perform all the miraculous signs and wonders in the land of Egypt against Pharaoh, and all his servants, and his entire land. [12]With mighty power, Moses performed terrifying acts in the sight of all Israel.

33:26 Hebrew *of Jeshurun,* a term of endearment for Israel. **34:2** Hebrew *the western sea.* **34:6** Hebrew *He buried him;* Samaritan Pentateuch and some Greek manuscripts read *They buried him.*

JOSHUA

WHAT CHARACTERISTICS do you think are important in a leader? If you were chosen as captain of the football or speech team or class president, what would you need to be like? Strong? Smart? Clever? Good with people? Good-looking? Enthusiastic? Devoted?

God called Joshua to be the leader of Israel as they were about to enter the Promised Land. Joshua was unsure about his leadership capabilities. But God told him: "No one will be able to stand against you as long as you live. For I will be with you as I was with Moses. I will not fail you or abandon you" (1:5). Then God explained the qualities Joshua needed in order to be a good leader for his people.

The first quality was obedience to God: "Be strong and very courageous. Be careful to obey all the instructions Moses gave you. Do not deviate from them, turning either to the right or to the left. Then you will be successful in everything you do" (1:7).

The second was total dependence on God for the victory. God had taken care of Israel in the past. He wanted Joshua to know that he would not win a single battle without God.

Have you been tapped to be a leader in your school or community? If so, take a second look at Joshua. Are obedience and dependence on God apparent in your life?

timeline

1446 B.C.
Exodus from Egypt

1406
Israelites enter Canaan

1375
Judges begin to rule

1050
United kingdom under Saul

1010
David becomes king

stats

PURPOSE: To give the history of Israel's conquest of the Promised Land

AUTHOR: Joshua, except for the ending, which may have been written by the high priest Phinehas, an eyewitness to the events recounted there

SETTING: Canaan, also called the Promised Land, which occupied the same general geographical territory of modern-day Israel

KEY PEOPLE: Joshua, Rahab, Achan, Phinehas, Eleazar

KEY PLACES: Jericho, Ai, Mount Ebal, Mount Gerizim, Gibeon, Gilgal, Shiloh, Shechem

SPECIAL FEATURE: Joshua and Caleb were the only two survivors out of the original group of adults who left Egypt to enter the Promised Land.

KEY points

SUCCESS

God gave success to the Israelites when they obeyed his master plan, not when they followed their own desires. Likewise, we must adjust our mind to God's way of thinking in order to see his standard for success.

GOD'S FAITHFULNESS

Remembering how God fulfilled his promises in the past assured the Israelites that he would be faithful in the future. In the same way, God's promises reassure us of his love, faithfulness, and guidance.

LEADERSHIP

Joshua's dependence on God made him a strong and effective leader. To be a strong leader like Joshua, we must be ready to listen and act on God's commands.

CONQUEST

God commanded his people to conquer the Canaanites and take their land. But Israel's commitment to the task didn't last. Commitment to God means more than being enthusiastic about him. We must complete all of the work he gives us and apply his instructions to every part of our lives.

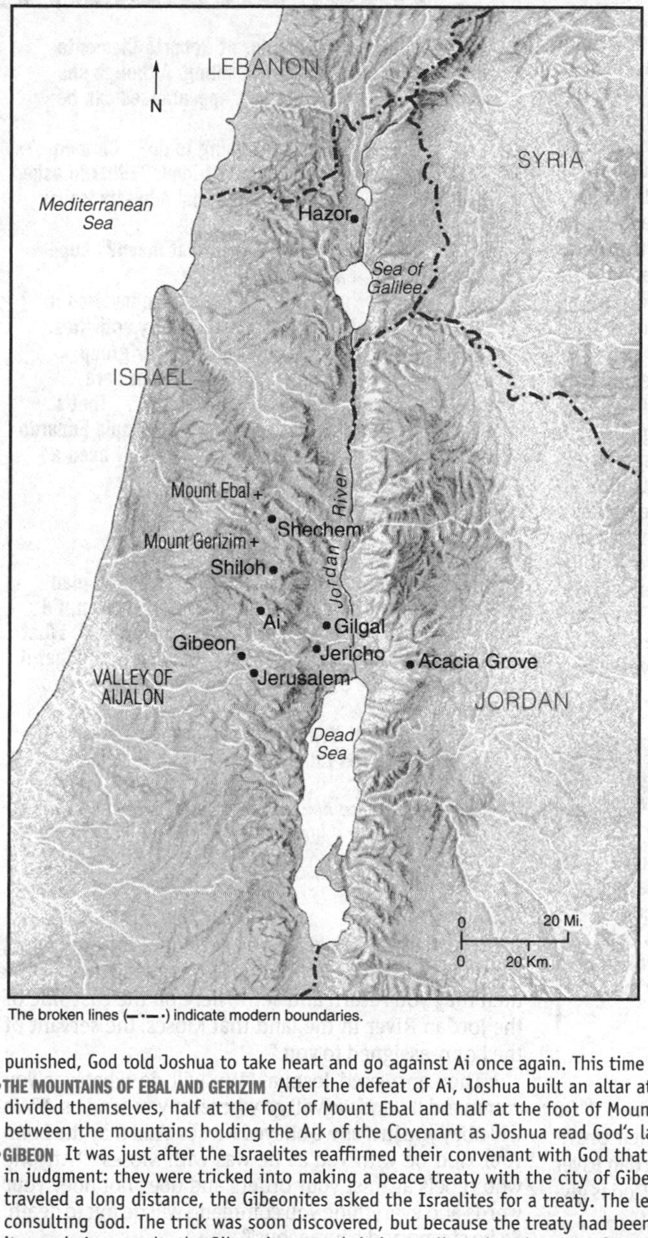

The broken lines (—·—·) indicate modern boundaries.

KEY PLACES IN JOSHUA

- **ACACIA GROVE** The story of Joshua begins with the Israelites camping at Acacia Grove. The Israelites under Joshua were ready to enter and conquer Canaan. But before the nation moved out, Joshua received instructions from God (1:1-18).
- **JORDAN RIVER** The entire nation prepared to cross this river, which was swollen from spring rains. After the scouts returned from Jericho with a positive report, Joshua prepared the priests and people for a miracle. As the priests carried the Ark into the Jordan River, the water stopped flowing and the entire nation crossed on dry ground into the Promised Land (2:1–4:24).
- **GILGAL** After crossing the Jordan River, the Israelites camped at Gilgal, where they renewed their commitment to God and celebrated the Passover, the feast commemorating their deliverance from Egypt (see Exodus). As Joshua made plans for the attack on Jericho, an angel appeared to him (5:1-15).
- **JERICHO** The walled city of Jericho seemed a formidable enemy. But when Joshua followed God's plans, the great walls were no obstacle. The city was conquered with only the obedient marching of the people (6:1-27).
- **AI** Victory could not continue without obedience to God. That is why the disobedience of one man, Achan, brought defeat to the entire nation in the first battle against Ai. But once the sin was recognized and punished, God told Joshua to take heart and go against Ai once again. This time the city was taken (7:1–8:29).
- **THE MOUNTAINS OF EBAL AND GERIZIM** After the defeat of Ai, Joshua built an altar at Mount Ebal. Then the people divided themselves, half at the foot of Mount Ebal and half at the foot of Mount Gerizim. The priests stood between the mountains holding the Ark of the Covenant as Joshua read God's laws to all the people (8:30-35).
- **GIBEON** It was just after the Israelites reaffirmed their convenant with God that their leaders made a major mistake in judgment: they were tricked into making a peace treaty with the city of Gibeon. Pretending that they had traveled a long distance, the Gibeonites asked the Israelites for a treaty. The leaders made the agreement without consulting God. The trick was soon discovered, but because the treaty had been made, Israel could not go back on its word. As a result, the Gibeonites saved their own lives, but they were forced to become Israel's slaves (9:1-27).
- **VALLEY OF AIJALON** The king of Jerusalem was very angry at the Gibeonites for making a peace treaty with Israel. He gathered armies from four other cities to attack Gibeon. Gibeon summoned Joshua for help, and Joshua took immediate action. Leaving Gilgal, he attacked the coalition by surprise. As the battle raged on and moved into the valley of Aijalon, Joshua prayed for the sun to stand still until the enemy could be destroyed (10:1-43).
- **HAZOR** Up north in Hazor, King Jabin mobilized the kings of the surrounding cities to unite and crush Israel. But God gave Joshua and Israel victory. Joshua conquered the entire federation (11:1-23).
- **SHILOH** After the armies of Canaan were conquered, Israel gathered at Shiloh to set up the Tabernacle. This movable building had been the nation's center of worship during their years of wandering. The seven tribes who had not received their land were given their allotments (18:1–19:51).
- **SHECHEM** Before Joshua died, he called the entire nation together at Shechem to remind them that it was God who had given them their land and that only with God's help could they keep it. The people vowed to follow God. As long as Joshua was alive, the land was at rest from war and trouble (24:1-33).

1 THE LORD'S CHARGE TO JOSHUA

After the death of Moses the LORD's servant, the LORD
spoke to Joshua son of Nun, Moses' assistant. He said,
2"Moses my servant is dead. Therefore, the time has
come for you to lead these people, the Israelites, across
the Jordan River into the land I am giving them. 3I promise you what I promised Moses: 'Wherever you set foot,
you will be on land I have given you—4from the Negev
wilderness in the south to the Lebanon mountains in the
north, from the Euphrates River in the east to the Mediterranean Sea* in the west, including all the land of the
Hittites.' 5No one will be able to stand against you as long
as you live. For I will be with you as I was with Moses. I will
not fail you or abandon you.

6"Be strong and courageous, for you are the one who
will lead these people to possess all the land I swore to
their ancestors I would give them. 7Be strong and very
courageous. Be careful to obey all the instructions
Moses gave you. Do not deviate from them, turning either to the right or to the left. Then you will be successful in everything you do. 8Study this Book of Instruction
continually. Meditate on it day and night so you will be
sure to obey everything written in it. Only then will you
prosper and succeed in all you do. 9This is my command—be strong and courageous! Do not be afraid or
discouraged. For the LORD your God is with you wherever you go."

RESPONSIBILITY

Carmen, a 16-year-old junior at Roberto Clemente High, is popular and always smiling. Although she seems to have it all together, appearances can be deceiving. Judge for yourself.

"Lupe, what am I going to do?" Carmen queries her best friend. "Eduardo asked me to be the girls' ministry leader this year."

"What does that mean?" Lupe asks.

"Well, I'd have to be involved in all of the campus ministry activities. You know—Bible studies, morning prayer group, outreaches—all that stuff. Ministry leaders are expected to talk a lot about their faith. . . . That's what's so weird. I mean, out of all the people Eduardo could have asked, he came to me! I've only been a Christian for three years."

"Sounds cool—"

"*Séi* . . ."

"—and a lot of responsibility."

"That's what worries me! I've never had to plan everything and give everybody direction. I mean, I'd kinda like to do it, but what if I can't handle it? What if I do something stupid or let Eduardo down? What if I turn out to be a horrible leader and they fire me or something?"

"Oh, Carmen! You'll do great and you know it."

"*No sée* (I don't know). . . ."

Can you relate to how Carmen feels? Read Joshua 1:5-9. If you were Lupe, how would you share this comfort and encouragement with Carmen, or anyone facing big responsibilities?

CHALLENGE 1:1-9

Joshua's new job consisted of leading more than two million people into a strange new land and conquering it. What a challenge—even for a man of Joshua's capability! We may never have to face such a challenge; still, we face tough situations, difficult people, and temptations every day. God promises that he will never abandon us or fail to help us, regardless of how we feel. With God's help, we can conquer many of life's challenges. ■

JOSHUA'S CHARGE TO THE ISRAELITES

10Joshua then commanded the officers of Israel, 11"Go
through the camp and tell the people to get their provisions ready. In three days you will cross the Jordan River
and take possession of the land the LORD your God is giving you."

12Then Joshua called together the tribes of Reuben,
Gad, and the half-tribe of Manasseh. He told them,
13"Remember what Moses, the servant of the LORD,
commanded you: 'The LORD your God is giving you a
place of rest. He has given you this land.' 14Your wives,
children, and livestock may remain here in the land
Moses assigned to you on the east side of the Jordan
River. But your strong warriors, fully armed, must lead
the other tribes across the Jordan to help them conquer
their territory. Stay with them 15until the LORD gives
them rest, as he has given you rest, and until they, too,
possess the land the LORD your God is giving them. Only
then may you return and settle here on the east side of
the Jordan River in the land that Moses, the servant of
the LORD, assigned to you."

16They answered Joshua, "We will do whatever you
command us, and we will go wherever you send us. 17We
will obey you just as we obeyed Moses. And may the LORD
your God be with you as he was with Moses. 18Anyone
who rebels against your orders and does not obey your
words and everything you command will be put to death.
So be strong and courageous!"

2 RAHAB PROTECTS THE SPIES

Then Joshua secretly sent out two spies from the Israelite
camp at Acacia Grove.* He instructed them, "Scout out
the land on the other side of the Jordan River, especially
around Jericho." So the two men set out and came to the
house of a prostitute named Rahab and stayed there that
night.

1:4 Hebrew *the Great Sea*. 2:1 Hebrew *Shittim*.

keeping it real

When I was in first grade, I memorized Joshua 1:9: "This is my command—be strong and courageous! Do not be afraid or discouraged. For the LORD your God is with you wherever you go." Man, I never thought that verse would come in handy when I went to high school!

Recently I took part in a school play. I developed a bad case of stage fright before the performance. I didn't think I was going to make it through. So, I asked God to help me feel more comfortable with my part. Know what? Joshua 1:9 came to mind again! It helped take away my fear. I remembered my lines and even did pretty well in the play, according to several people.

There have been many other times when I've recalled this verse and gained courage from it. Whenever I feel scared and alone, I remember this verse. It always comforts me.

—Steve

2But someone told the king of Jericho, "Some Israelites
have come here tonight to spy out the land." 3So the king
of Jericho sent orders to Rahab: "Bring out the men who
have come into your house, for they have come here to
spy out the whole land."
4Rahab had hidden the two men, but she replied, "Yes,
the men were here earlier, but I didn't know where they
were from. 5They left the town at dusk, as the gates were
about to close. I don't know where they went. If you
hurry, you can probably catch up with them." 6(Actually,
she had taken them up to the roof and hidden them beneath bundles of flax she had laid out.) 7So the king's men
went looking for the spies along the road leading to the
shallow crossings of the Jordan River. And as soon as the
king's men had left, the gate of Jericho was shut.
8Before the spies went to sleep that night, Rahab went
up on the roof to talk with them. 9"I know the LORD has
given you this land," she told them. "We are all afraid of
you. Everyone in the land is living in terror. 10For we have
heard how the LORD made a dry path for you through the
Red Sea* when you left Egypt. And we know what you did
to Sihon and Og, the two Amorite kings east of the Jordan
River, whose people you completely destroyed.* 11No
wonder our hearts have melted in fear! No one has the
courage to fight after hearing such things. For the LORD
your God is the supreme God of the heavens above and
the earth below.
12"Now swear to me by the LORD that you will be kind to
me and my family since I have helped you. Give me some
guarantee that 13when Jericho is conquered, you will let
me live, along with my father and mother, my brothers
and sisters, and all their families."
14"We offer our own lives as a guarantee for your
safety," the men agreed. "If you don't betray us, we will
keep our promise and be kind to you when the LORD gives
us the land."
15Then, since Rahab's house was built into the town
wall, she let them down by a rope through the window.
16"Escape to the hill country," she told them. "Hide there
for three days from the men searching for you. Then,
when they have returned, you can go on your way."
17Before they left, the men told her, "We will be bound
by the oath we have taken only if you follow these instructions. 18When we come into the land, you must leave
this scarlet rope hanging from the window through
which you let us down. And all your family members—
your father, mother, brothers, and all your relatives—
must be here inside the house. 19If they go out into the
street and are killed, it will not be our fault. But if anyone
lays a hand on people inside this house, we will accept the
responsibility for their death. 20If you betray us, however,
we are not bound by this oath in any way."
21"I accept your terms," she replied. And she sent them
on their way, leaving the scarlet rope hanging from the
window.
22The spies went up into the hill country and stayed
there three days. The men who were chasing them
searched everywhere along the road, but they finally returned without success.
23Then the two spies came down from the hill country,
crossed the Jordan River, and reported to Joshua all that
had happened to them. 24"The LORD has given us the
whole land," they said, "for all the people in the land are
terrified of us."

2:10a Hebrew *sea of reeds.* **2:10b** The Hebrew term used here refers to the complete consecration of things or people to the LORD, either by destroying them or by giving them as an offering.

A NEW ROLE 2:1

Rahab risked her life to help the two Israelite spies. She didn't allow her imperfect past to keep her from reaching out to God and helping his people. God often uses people with simple faith to accomplish his great purposes, no matter what kind of past they have had or how insignificant they seem to be. Feeling like the mistakes you've made will keep you from being used by God? Remember Rahab! ■

3 THE ISRAELITES CROSS THE JORDAN

Early the next morning Joshua and all the Israelites left Acacia Grove* and arrived at the banks of the Jordan River, where they camped before crossing. 2Three days later the Israelite officers went through the camp, 3giving these instructions to the people: "When you see the Levitical priests carrying the Ark of the Covenant of the LORD your God, move out from your positions and follow them. 4Since you have never traveled this way before, they will guide you. Stay about a half mile* behind them, keeping a clear distance between you and the Ark. Make sure you don't come any closer."

5Then Joshua told the people, "Purify yourselves, for tomorrow the LORD will do great wonders among you."

6In the morning Joshua said to the priests, "Lift up the Ark of the Covenant and lead the people across the river." And so they started out and went ahead of the people.

7The LORD told Joshua, "Today I will begin to make you a great leader in the eyes of all the Israelites. They will know that I am with you, just as I was with Moses. 8Give this command to the priests who carry the Ark of the Covenant: 'When you reach the banks of the Jordan River, take a few steps into the river and stop there.'"

9So Joshua told the Israelites, "Come and listen to what the LORD your God says. 10Today you will know that the living God is among you. He will surely drive out the Canaanites, Hittites, Hivites, Perizzites, Girgashites, Amorites, and Jebusites ahead of you. 11Look, the Ark of the Covenant, which belongs to the Lord of the whole earth, will lead you across the Jordan River! 12Now choose twelve men from the tribes of Israel, one from each tribe. 13The priests will carry the Ark of the LORD, the Lord of all the earth. As soon as their feet touch the water, the flow of water will be cut off upstream, and the river will stand up like a wall."

14So the people left their camp to cross the Jordan, and the priests who were carrying the Ark of the Covenant went ahead of them. 15It was the harvest season, and the Jordan was overflowing its banks. But as soon as the feet of the priests who were carrying the Ark touched the water at the river's edge, 16the water above that point began backing up a great distance away at a town called Adam, which is near Zarethan. And the water below that point flowed on to the Dead Sea* until the riverbed was dry. Then all the people crossed over near the town of Jericho.

17Meanwhile, the priests who were carrying the Ark of the LORD's Covenant stood on dry ground in the middle of the riverbed as the people passed by. They waited there until the whole nation of Israel had crossed the Jordan on dry ground.

4 MEMORIALS TO THE JORDAN CROSSING

When all the people had crossed the Jordan, the LORD said to Joshua, 2"Now choose twelve men, one from each tribe. 3Tell them, 'Take twelve stones from the very place where the priests are standing in the middle of the Jordan. Carry them out and pile them up at the place where you will camp tonight.'"

4So Joshua called together the twelve men he had chosen—one from each of the tribes of Israel. 5He told them, "Go into the middle of the Jordan, in front of the Ark of the LORD your God. Each of you must pick up one stone and carry it out on your shoulder—twelve stones in all, one for each of the twelve tribes of Israel. 6We will use these stones to build a memorial. In the future your children will ask you, 'What do these stones mean?' 7Then you can tell them, 'They remind us that the Jordan River stopped flowing when the Ark of the LORD's Covenant went across.' These stones will stand as a memorial among the people of Israel forever."

8So the men did as Joshua had commanded them. They took twelve stones from the middle of the Jordan River, one for each tribe, just as the LORD had told Joshua. They carried them to the place where they camped for the night and constructed the memorial there.

9Joshua also set up another pile of twelve stones in the middle of the Jordan, at the place where the priests who carried the Ark of the Covenant were standing. And they are there to this day.

10The priests who were carrying the Ark stood in the middle of the river until all of the LORD's commands that Moses had given to Joshua were carried out. Meanwhile, the people hurried across the riverbed. 11And when everyone was safely on the other side, the priests crossed over with the Ark of the LORD as the people watched.

12The armed warriors from the tribes of Reuben, Gad, and the half-tribe of Manasseh led the Israelites across the Jordan, just as Moses had directed. 13These armed men—about 40,000 strong—were ready for battle, and the LORD was with them as they crossed over to the plains of Jericho.

14That day the LORD made Joshua a great leader in the eyes of all the Israelites, and for the rest of his life they revered him as much as they had revered Moses.

15The LORD had said to Joshua, 16"Command the priests carrying the Ark of the Covenant* to come up out of the riverbed." 17So Joshua gave the command. 18As soon as the priests carrying the Ark of the LORD's Covenant came up out of the riverbed and their feet were on

3:1 Hebrew *Shittim.* **3:4** Hebrew *about 2,000 cubits* [920 meters]. **3:16** Hebrew *the sea of the Arabah, the Salt Sea.* **4:16** Hebrew *Ark of the Testimony.*

high ground, the water of the Jordan returned and overflowed its banks as before.
19The people crossed the Jordan on the tenth day of
the first month.* Then they camped at Gilgal, just east of
Jericho. 20It was there at Gilgal that Joshua piled up the
twelve stones taken from the Jordan River.
21Then Joshua said to the Israelites, "In the future your
children will ask, 'What do these stones mean?' 22Then
you can tell them, 'This is where the Israelites crossed the
Jordan on dry ground.' 23For the LORD your God dried up
the river right before your eyes, and he kept it dry until
you were all across, just as he did at the Red Sea* when he
dried it up until we had all crossed over. 24He did this so
all the nations of the earth might know that the LORD's
hand is powerful, and so you might fear the LORD your
God forever."

5

When all the Amorite kings west of the Jordan and
all the Canaanite kings who lived along the Mediterranean coast* heard how the LORD had dried up the Jordan
River so the people of Israel could cross, they lost heart
and were paralyzed with fear because of them.

ISRAEL REESTABLISHES COVENANT CEREMONIES

2At that time the LORD told Joshua, "Make flint knives and
circumcise this second generation of Israelites.*" 3So
Joshua made flint knives and circumcised the entire
male population of Israel at Gibeath-haaraloth.*
4Joshua had to circumcise them because all the men
who were old enough to fight in battle when they left
Egypt had died in the wilderness. 5Those who left Egypt
had all been circumcised, but none of those born after
the Exodus, during the years in the wilderness, had been
circumcised. 6The Israelites had traveled in the wilderness for forty years until all the men who were old
enough to fight in battle when they left Egypt had died.
For they had disobeyed the LORD, and the LORD vowed he
would not let them enter the land he had sworn to give
us—a land flowing with milk and honey. 7So Joshua circumcised their sons—those who had grown up to take
their fathers' places—for they had not been circumcised
on the way to the Promised Land. 8After all the males had
been circumcised, they rested in the camp until they
were healed.
9Then the LORD said to Joshua, "Today I have rolled
away the shame of your slavery in Egypt." So that place
has been called Gilgal* to this day.
10While the Israelites were camped at Gilgal on the
plains of Jericho, they celebrated Passover on the evening
of the fourteenth day of the first month.* 11The very next
day they began to eat unleavened bread and roasted grain
harvested from the land. 12No manna appeared on the
day they first ate from the crops of the land, and it was
never seen again. So from that time on the Israelites ate
from the crops of Canaan.

THE LORD'S COMMANDER CONFRONTS JOSHUA

13When Joshua was near the town of Jericho, he looked
up and saw a man standing in front of him with sword in
hand. Joshua went up to him and demanded, "Are you
friend or foe?"
14"Neither one," he replied. "I am the commander of
the LORD's army."
At this, Joshua fell with his face to the ground in reverence. "I am at your command," Joshua said. "What do you
want your servant to do?"
15The commander of the LORD's army replied, "Take
off your sandals, for the place where you are standing is
holy." And Joshua did as he was told.

6

THE FALL OF JERICHO

Now the gates of Jericho were tightly shut because the
people were afraid of the Israelites. No one was allowed
to go out or in. 2But the LORD said to Joshua, "I have
given you Jericho, its king, and all its strong warriors.
3You and your fighting men should march around the
town once a day for six days. 4Seven priests will walk
ahead of the Ark, each carrying a ram's horn. On the
seventh day you are to march around the town seven
times, with the priests blowing the horns. 5When you
hear the priests give one long blast on the rams' horns,
have all the people shout as loud as they can. Then the
walls of the town will collapse, and the people can
charge straight into the town."

A WAR ALREADY WON 6:2-5

God told Joshua that the enemy was defeated before the battle began! What confidence Joshua must have had as he went into battle! Christians also fight against a defeated enemy. Jesus defeated our enemy, Satan, when he died on the cross (Rom 8:37-39; Heb 2:14-15; 1 John 3:8). Although we still fight battles every day and evil continues in the world, we have the assurance that the war has already been won. ■

6So Joshua called together the priests and said, "Take
up the Ark of the LORD's Covenant, and assign seven
priests to walk in front of it, each carrying a ram's horn."
7Then he gave orders to the people: "March around the
town, and the armed men will lead the way in front of the
Ark of the LORD."
8After Joshua spoke to the people, the seven priests
with the rams' horns started marching in the presence of
the LORD, blowing the horns as they marched. And the
Ark of the LORD's Covenant followed behind them.
9Some of the armed men marched in front of the priests
with the horns and some behind the Ark, with the priests
continually blowing the horns. 10"Do not shout; do not
even talk," Joshua commanded. "Not a single word from

4:19 This day in the ancient Hebrew lunar calendar occurred in late March, April, or early May. **4:23** Hebrew *sea of reeds.* **5:1** Hebrew *along the sea.* **5:2** Or *circumcise the Israelites a second time.* **5:3** *Gibeath-haaraloth* means "hill of foreskins." **5:9** *Gilgal* sounds like the Hebrew word *galal,* meaning "to roll." **5:10** This day in the ancient Hebrew lunar calendar occurred in late March, April, or early May.

any of you until I tell you to shout. Then shout!" 11So the Ark of the LORD was carried around the town once that day, and then everyone returned to spend the night in the camp.

12Joshua got up early the next morning, and the priests again carried the Ark of the LORD. 13The seven priests with the rams' horns marched in front of the Ark of the LORD, blowing their horns. Again the armed men marched both in front of the priests with the horns and behind the Ark of the LORD. All this time the priests were blowing their horns. 14On the second day they again marched around the town once and returned to the camp. They followed this pattern for six days.

15On the seventh day the Israelites got up at dawn and marched around the town as they had done before. But this time they went around the town seven times. 16The seventh time around, as the priests sounded the long blast on their horns, Joshua commanded the people, "Shout! For the LORD has given you the town! 17Jericho and everything in it must be completely destroyed* as an offering to the LORD. Only Rahab the prostitute and the others in her house will be spared, for she protected our spies.

18"Do not take any of the things set apart for destruction, or you yourselves will be completely destroyed, and you will bring trouble on the camp of Israel. 19Everything made from silver, gold, bronze, or iron is sacred to the LORD and must be brought into his treasury."

20When the people heard the sound of the rams' horns, they shouted as loud as they could. Suddenly, the walls of Jericho collapsed, and the Israelites charged straight into the town and captured it. 21They completely destroyed everything in it with their swords—men and women, young and old, cattle, sheep, goats, and donkeys.

22Meanwhile, Joshua said to the two spies, "Keep your promise. Go to the prostitute's house and bring her out, along with all her family."

23The men who had been spies went in and brought out Rahab, her father, mother, brothers, and all the other relatives who were with her. They moved her whole family to a safe place near the camp of Israel.

24Then the Israelites burned the town and everything in it. Only the things made from silver, gold, bronze, or iron were kept for the treasury of the LORD's house. 25So Joshua spared Rahab the prostitute and her relatives who were with her in the house, because she had hidden the spies Joshua sent to Jericho. And she lives among the Israelites to this day.

26At that time Joshua invoked this curse:

"May the curse of the LORD fall on anyone
  who tries to rebuild the town of Jericho.
At the cost of his firstborn son,
  he will lay its foundation.
At the cost of his youngest son,
  he will set up its gates."

27So the LORD was with Joshua, and his reputation spread throughout the land.

6:17 The Hebrew term used here refers to the complete consecration of things or people to the LORD, either by destroying them or by giving them as an offering; similarly in 6:18, 21.

RAHAB

UPS:
- Relative of Boaz, and thus an ancestor of David and Jesus
- One of only two women listed in the Hall of Faith in Hebrews 11
- Resourceful, willing to help others at great cost to herself

DOWNS:
- Worked as a prostitute

STATS:
- Where: Jericho
- Occupation: Prostitute, innkeeper; later became a wife and mother
- Relatives: Ancestor of David and Jesus (Matt 1:5)
- Contemporary: Joshua

BOTTOM LINE:
She did not let fear affect her faith in God's ability to save her family from death.

Rahab's story is told in Josh 2 and 6. She also is mentioned in Matt 1:5; Heb 11:31; and James 2:25.

RAHAB Out of all the people you know, who is the most unlikely person you can think of to accomplish something great? Rahab was a surprise. She was one of those people we wouldn't expect God to use. But God looks at people differently than we do.

As a prostitute in the city of Jericho, Rahab lived on the edge of society. She was used in private and rejected in public. Her house, built right into the city wall, was a natural place for the Israelite spies to hide, since they would be mistaken for Rahab's customers.

Rumors about the coming Israelite invasion were all over the city, but having spies in her home convinced Rahab that war was on the horizon. Living on the city wall, Rahab probably felt especially vulnerable. Although she shared everyone's fears, she decided to do something about them—she decided to trust the God of the Israelites. Although she didn't know much about God, she knew enough to know that he could be trusted. God saved Rahab's family because of her faith, not her profession!

Through Rahab's family line came the ultimate sign of God's mercy—his Son. If at times you feel like a failure, remember that Rahab overcame failure through her trust in God. You can do the same!

As you read the Old Testament, you may wonder, *Why did God select the people of Israel as his chosen people?* That's a good question, and one that's not easy to answer.

First, God singled out a man named Abram (later Abraham) from the ancient city of Ur and promised to bless him and his descendants (Gen 12:1-3). But there was a condition attached: Abram had to remain faithful to God. Even though he had numerous lapses, Abram kept his end of the bargain. And God was true to his word, making Abram's descendants into the nation of Israel.

Second, God set the stage for his Son, the Messiah, who would be ushered into the world many centuries later. Because God chose to have his Son born of a woman, he needed to provide an appropriate backdrop for the woman and her ancestry. He chose the people of Israel, the descendants of Abraham.

Third, it has been suggested that the people of Israel were the perfect "display case" for God's mercy and patient love. They were stubborn, rebellious, unfaithful—just like many believers today. No one would have blamed God for giving up on them and starting over with a new nation. But God kept his word to Abraham and never abandoned Abraham's descendants. Although he punished them, scolded them, and sent them into exile, he never forgot them or his promise.

Many people today see the existence of the Jews as a powerful argument for the existence of God. In spite of overwhelming opposition throughout history, they are still here, while most of their enemies (at least from Old Testament times) are long gone. How else could they have survived, except for the protection of a powerful, loving God who refused to give up on them?

The people of Israel are not the only members of God's special covenant group. Now, all who follow Christ are God's chosen people as well. That includes you, right?

7 **AI DEFEATS THE ISRAELITES**
But Israel violated the instructions about the things set
apart for the LORD.* A man named Achan had stolen
some of these dedicated things, so the LORD was very angry with the Israelites. Achan was the son of Carmi, a descendant of Zimri* son of Zerah, of the tribe of Judah.
2Joshua sent some of his men from Jericho to spy out
the town of Ai, east of Bethel, near Beth-aven. 3When they
returned, they told Joshua, "There's no need for all of us
to go up there; it won't take more than two or three thousand men to attack Ai. Since there are so few of them,
don't make all our people struggle to go up there."
4So approximately 3,000 warriors were sent, but they
were soundly defeated. The men of Ai 5chased the Israelites from the town gate as far as the quarries,* and they
killed about thirty-six who were retreating down the
slope. The Israelites were paralyzed with fear at this turn
of events, and their courage melted away.
6Joshua and the elders of Israel tore their clothing in
dismay, threw dust on their heads, and bowed face down
to the ground before the Ark of the LORD until evening.
7Then Joshua cried out, "Oh, Sovereign LORD, why did you
bring us across the Jordan River if you are going to let the
Amorites kill us? If only we had been content to stay on
the other side! 8Lord, what can I say now that Israel has
fled from its enemies? 9For when the Canaanites and all
the other people living in the land hear about it, they will
surround us and wipe our name off the face of the earth.
And then what will happen to the honor of your great
name?"
10But the LORD said to Joshua, "Get up! Why are you lying on your face like this? 11Israel has sinned and broken
my covenant! They have stolen some of the things that I
commanded must be set apart for me. And they have not
only stolen them but have lied about it and hidden the
things among their own belongings. 12That is why the Israelites are running from their enemies in defeat. For
now Israel itself has been set apart for destruction. I will
not remain with you any longer unless you destroy the
things among you that were set apart for destruction.
13"Get up! Command the people to purify themselves
in preparation for tomorrow. For this is what the LORD,
the God of Israel, says: Hidden among you, O Israel, are
things set apart for the LORD. You will never defeat your
enemies until you remove these things from among you.

7:1a The Hebrew term used here refers to the complete consecration of things or people to the LORD, either by destroying them or by giving them as an offering; similarly in 7:11, 12, 13, 15. 7:1b As in Greek version (see also 1 Chr 2:6); Hebrew reads *Zabdi*. Also in 7:17, 18. 7:5 Or *as far as Shebarim*.

14"In the morning you must present yourselves by tribes, and the LORD will point out the tribe to which the guilty man belongs. That tribe must come forward with its clans, and the LORD will point out the guilty clan. That clan will then come forward, and the LORD will point out the guilty family. Finally, each member of the guilty family must come forward one by one. 15The one who has stolen what was set apart for destruction will himself be burned with fire, along with everything he has, for he has broken the covenant of the LORD and has done a horrible thing in Israel."

ACHAN'S SIN

16Early the next morning Joshua brought the tribes of Israel before the LORD, and the tribe of Judah was singled out. 17Then the clans of Judah came forward, and the clan of Zerah was singled out. Then the families of Zerah came forward, and the family of Zimri was singled out. 18Every member of Zimri's family was brought forward person by person, and Achan was singled out.

19Then Joshua said to Achan, "My son, give glory to the LORD, the God of Israel, by telling the truth. Make your confession and tell me what you have done. Don't hide it from me."

NO SMALL THING 7:20-25

Achan underestimated God and didn't take his commands seriously (6:18-19). Taking a robe, some coins, and a bar of gold may have seemed a small matter to Achan, but the effects of his action were felt by the entire nation, especially his family. Israel lost a battle and the lives of thirty-six men because of Achan. A small sin can have a big impact. When temptation comes, count the cost! ■

20Achan replied, "It is true! I have sinned against the LORD, the God of Israel. 21Among the plunder I saw a beautiful robe from Babylon,* 200 silver coins,* and a bar of gold weighing more than a pound.* I wanted them so much that I took them. They are hidden in the ground beneath my tent, with the silver buried deeper than the rest."

22So Joshua sent some men to make a search. They ran to the tent and found the stolen goods hidden there, just as Achan had said, with the silver buried beneath the rest. 23They took the things from the tent and brought them to Joshua and all the Israelites. Then they laid them on the ground in the presence of the LORD.

24Then Joshua and all the Israelites took Achan, the silver, the robe, the bar of gold, his sons, daughters, cattle, donkeys, sheep, goats, tent, and everything he had, and they brought them to the valley of Achor. 25Then Joshua said to Achan, "Why have you brought trouble on us? The LORD will now bring trouble on you." And all the Israelites stoned Achan and his family and burned their bodies. 26They piled a great heap of stones over Achan, which remains to this day. That is why the place has been called the Valley of Trouble* ever since. So the LORD was no longer angry.

8 THE ISRAELITES DEFEAT AI

Then the LORD said to Joshua, "Do not be afraid or discouraged. Take all your fighting men and attack Ai, for I have given you the king of Ai, his people, his town, and his land. 2You will destroy them as you destroyed Jericho and its king. But this time you may keep the plunder and the livestock for yourselves. Set an ambush behind the town."

3So Joshua and all the fighting men set out to attack Ai. Joshua chose 30,000 of his best warriors and sent them out at night 4with these orders: "Hide in ambush close behind the town and be ready for action. 5When our main army attacks, the men of Ai will come out to fight as they did before, and we will run away from them. 6We will let them chase us until we have drawn them away from the town. For they will say, 'The Israelites are running away from us as they did before.' Then, while we are running from them, 7you will jump up from your ambush and take possession of the town, for the LORD your God will give it to you. 8Set the town on fire, as the LORD has commanded. You have your orders."

9So they left and went to the place of ambush between Bethel and the west side of Ai. But Joshua remained among the people in the camp that night. 10Early the next morning Joshua roused his men and started toward Ai, accompanied by the elders of Israel. 11All the fighting men who were with Joshua marched in front of the town and camped on the north side of Ai, with a valley between them and the town. 12That night Joshua sent 5,000 men to lie in ambush between Bethel and Ai, on the west side of the town. 13So they stationed the main army north of the town and the ambush west of the town. Joshua himself spent that night in the valley.

14When the king of Ai saw the Israelites across the valley, he and all his army hurried out early in the morning and attacked the Israelites at a place overlooking the Jordan Valley.* But he didn't realize there was an ambush behind the town. 15Joshua and the Israelite army fled toward the wilderness as though they were badly beaten. 16Then all the men in the town were called out to chase after them. In this way, they were lured away from the town. 17There was not a man left in Ai or Bethel* who did not chase after the Israelites, and the town was left wide open.

18Then the LORD said to Joshua, "Point the spear in your hand toward Ai, for I will hand the town over to you." Joshua did as he was commanded. 19As soon as Joshua gave this signal, all the men in ambush jumped up from their position and poured into the town. They quickly captured it and set it on fire.

20When the men of Ai looked behind them, smoke from the town was filling the sky, and they had nowhere

7:21a Hebrew *Shinar*. 7:21b Hebrew *200 shekels of silver*, about 5 pounds or 2.3 kilograms in weight. 7:21c Hebrew *50 shekels*, about 20 ounces or 570 grams in weight. 7:26 Hebrew *valley of Achor*. 8:14 Hebrew *the Arabah*. 8:17 Some manuscripts lack *or Bethel*.

to go. For the Israelites who had fled in the direction of the wilderness now turned on their pursuers. [21]When Joshua and all the other Israelites saw that the ambush had succeeded and that smoke was rising from the town, they turned and attacked the men of Ai. [22]Meanwhile, the Israelites who were inside the town came out and attacked the enemy from the rear. So the men of Ai were caught in the middle, with Israelite fighters on both sides. Israel attacked them, and not a single person survived or escaped. [23]Only the king of Ai was taken alive and brought to Joshua.

[24]When the Israelite army finished chasing and killing all the men of Ai in the open fields, they went back and finished off everyone inside. [25]So the entire population of Ai, including men and women, was wiped out that day—12,000 in all. [26]For Joshua kept holding out his spear until everyone who had lived in Ai was completely destroyed.* [27]Only the livestock and the treasures of the town were not destroyed, for the Israelites kept these as plunder for themselves, as the LORD had commanded Joshua. [28]So Joshua burned the town of Ai,* and it became a permanent mound of ruins, desolate to this very day.

[29]Joshua impaled the king of Ai on a sharpened pole and left him there until evening. At sunset the Israelites took down the body, as Joshua commanded, and threw it in front of the town gate. They piled a great heap of stones over him that can still be seen today.

A FORK IN THE ROAD 8:33-35

After Israel's military victory at Ai, Joshua celebrated by thanking God and reading God's laws to the people of Israel. A victory is a fork in the road for each person. It can either be a reminder to stick closer to God more than ever or a time to congratulate oneself. Joshua chose to stick close to God. When the next victory comes in your life, what will you do? ■

THE LORD'S COVENANT RENEWED

[30]Then Joshua built an altar to the LORD, the God of Israel, on Mount Ebal. [31]He followed the commands that Moses the LORD's servant had written in the Book of Instruction: "Make me an altar from stones that are uncut and have not been shaped with iron tools."* Then on the altar they presented burnt offerings and peace offerings to the LORD. [32]And as the Israelites watched, Joshua copied onto the stones of the altar* the instructions Moses had given them.

[33]Then all the Israelites—foreigners and native-born alike—along with the elders, officers, and judges, were divided into two groups. One group stood in front of Mount Gerizim, the other in front of Mount Ebal. Each group faced the other, and between them stood the Levitical priests carrying the Ark of the LORD's Covenant. This was all done according to the commands that Moses, the servant of the LORD, had previously given for blessing the people of Israel.

[34]Joshua then read to them all the blessings and curses Moses had written in the Book of Instruction. [35]Every word of every command that Moses had ever given was read to the entire assembly of Israel, including the women and children and the foreigners who lived among them.

9

THE GIBEONITES DECEIVE ISRAEL

Now all the kings west of the Jordan River heard about what had happened. These were the kings of the Hittites, Amorites, Canaanites, Perizzites, Hivites, and Jebusites, who lived in the hill country, in the western foothills,* and along the coast of the Mediterranean Sea* as far north as the Lebanon mountains. [2]These kings combined their armies to fight as one against Joshua and the Israelites.

[3]But when the people of Gibeon heard what Joshua had done to Jericho and Ai, [4]they resorted to deception to save themselves. They sent ambassadors to Joshua, loading their donkeys with weathered saddlebags and old, patched wineskins. [5]They put on worn-out, patched sandals and ragged clothes. And the bread they took with them was dry and moldy. [6]When they arrived at the camp of Israel at Gilgal, they told Joshua and the men of Israel, "We have come from a distant land to ask you to make a peace treaty with us."

[7]The Israelites replied to these Hivites, "How do we know you don't live nearby? For if you do, we cannot make a treaty with you."

[8]They replied, "We are your servants."

"But who are you?" Joshua demanded. "Where do you come from?"

[9]They answered, "Your servants have come from a very distant country. We have heard of the might of the LORD your God and of all he did in Egypt. [10]We have also heard what he did to the two Amorite kings east of the Jordan River—King Sihon of Heshbon and King Og of Bashan (who lived in Ashtaroth). [11]So our elders and all our people instructed us, 'Take supplies for a long journey. Go meet with the people of Israel and tell them, "We are your servants; please make a treaty with us."'

[12]"This bread was hot from the ovens when we left our homes. But now, as you can see, it is dry and moldy. [13]These wineskins were new when we filled them, but now they are old and split open. And our clothing and sandals are worn out from our very long journey."

[14]So the Israelites examined their food, but they did not consult the LORD. [15]Then Joshua made a peace treaty with them and guaranteed their safety, and the leaders of the community ratified their agreement with a binding oath.

[16]Three days after making the treaty, they learned that these people actually lived nearby! [17]The Israelites set out

8:26 The Hebrew term used here refers to the complete consecration of things or people to the LORD, either by destroying them or by giving them as an offering. **8:28** *Ai* means "ruin." **8:31** Exod 20:25; Deut 27:5-6. **8:32** Or *onto stones.* **9:1a** Hebrew *the Shephelah.* **9:1b** Hebrew *the Great Sea.*

at once to investigate and reached their towns in three days. The names of these towns were Gibeon, Kephirah, Beeroth, and Kiriath-jearim. [18]But the Israelites did not attack the towns, for the Israelite leaders had made a vow to them in the name of the LORD, the God of Israel.

The people of Israel grumbled against their leaders because of the treaty. [19]But the leaders replied, "Since we have sworn an oath in the presence of the LORD, the God of Israel, we cannot touch them. [20]This is what we must do. We must let them live, for divine anger would come upon us if we broke our oath. [21]Let them live." So they made them woodcutters and water carriers for the entire community, as the Israelite leaders directed.

[22]Joshua called together the Gibeonites and said, "Why did you lie to us? Why did you say that you live in a distant land when you live right here among us? [23]May you be cursed! From now on you will always be servants who cut wood and carry water for the house of my God."

[24]They replied, "We did it because we—your servants—were clearly told that the LORD your God commanded his servant Moses to give you this entire land and to destroy all the people living in it. So we feared greatly for our lives because of you. That is why we have done this. [25]Now we are at your mercy—do to us whatever you think is right."

[26]So Joshua did not allow the people of Israel to kill them. [27]But that day he made the Gibeonites the woodcutters and water carriers for the community of Israel and for the altar of the LORD—wherever the LORD would choose to build it. And that is what they do to this day.

10 ISRAEL DEFEATS THE SOUTHERN ARMIES

Adoni-zedek, king of Jerusalem, heard that Joshua had captured and completely destroyed* Ai and killed its king, just as he had destroyed the town of Jericho and killed its king. He also learned that the Gibeonites had made peace with Israel and were now their allies. [2]He and his people became very afraid when they heard all this because Gibeon was a large town—as large as the royal cities and larger than Ai. And the Gibeonite men were strong warriors.

[3]So King Adoni-zedek of Jerusalem sent messengers to several other kings: Hoham of Hebron, Piram of Jarmuth, Japhia of Lachish, and Debir of Eglon. [4]"Come and help me destroy Gibeon," he urged them, "for they have made peace with Joshua and the people of Israel." [5]So these five Amorite kings combined their armies for a

10:1 The Hebrew term used here refers to the complete consecration of things or people to the LORD, either by destroying them or by giving them as an offering; also in 10:28, 35, 37, 39, 40.

JOSHUA

UPS:
- Moses' assistant and successor
- One of only two adults who experienced Egyptian slavery and lived to enter the Promised Land
- Led the Israelites into their God-given homeland
- Brilliant military strategist
- Faithful to ask God's direction in the challenges he faced

DOWNS:
- Was fooled by the Gibeonites

STATS:
- Where: Egypt, the wilderness of Sinai, and Canaan (the Promised Land)
- Occupation: Special assistant to Moses; warrior, leader
- Relatives: Nun (father)
- Contemporaries: Moses, Caleb, Miriam, Aaron

BOTTOM LINE:

Effective leadership is often the product of good preparation and encouragement.

The person we admire the most will have a definite effect on us and those who learn from us.

A person committed to God provides the best model for us.

Joshua is also mentioned in Exod 17:9-14; 24:13; 32:17; 33:11; Num 11:28; 13–14; 26:65; 27:18-23; 32:12, 28; 34:17; Deut 1:38; 3:21-22, 28; 31:3, 14-15, 23; 34:9; Josh; Judg 2:6-9; 1 Kings 16:34; and Heb 4:8.

JOSHUA Who is the leader you most admire? Being a good leader means more than being in charge. The best leaders are those who help others learn to lead. This is true for two reasons: (1) Sometimes the job is too big for one person to do alone, so leadership has to be shared; and (2) some jobs take so long that they don't get done unless the first leader trains others to take over after he's gone. Joshua helped Moses with the huge job of leading the people of Israel. At the same time he was being trained as the new leader.

Moses made an excellent decision when he chose Joshua as his assistant. Later, God told Moses that Joshua would take over as Israel's leader after his (Moses') death.

Joshua was an important part of the Exodus story. He led the army, and was the only person allowed to go with Moses partway up the mountain where Moses received the Ten Commandments. The first time twelve scouts were sent into the Promised Land, only Joshua and Caleb were willing to tell the people that God could help them conquer the land. Joshua was always with Moses, like a shadow. His "basic training" involved watching and imitating everything his leader did and said.

Who is your Moses? Who is your Joshua? You are part of the unbroken chain of God's work in the world. What are you learning from these leaders? Can those who are watching you see how important God is to you? Why or why not? Ask God to lead you to a Moses worth following. Ask him also to make you a good Joshua.

united attack. They moved all their troops into place and
attacked Gibeon.
6The men of Gibeon quickly sent messengers to Joshua
at his camp in Gilgal. "Don't abandon your servants now!"
they pleaded. "Come at once! Save us! Help us! For all the
Amorite kings who live in the hill country have joined
forces to attack us."
7So Joshua and his entire army, including his best warriors, left Gilgal and set out for Gibeon. 8"Do not be afraid
of them," the LORD said to Joshua, "for I have given you
victory over them. Not a single one of them will be able to
stand up to you."
9Joshua traveled all night from Gilgal and took the Amorite armies by surprise. 10The LORD threw them into a
panic, and the Israelites slaughtered great numbers of
them at Gibeon. Then the Israelites chased the enemy
along the road to Beth-horon, killing them all along the
way to Azekah and Makkedah. 11As the Amorites retreated down the road from Beth-horon, the LORD destroyed them with a terrible hailstorm from heaven that
continued until they reached Azekah. The hail killed
more of the enemy than the Israelites killed with the
sword.
12On the day the LORD gave the Israelites victory over
the Amorites, Joshua prayed to the LORD in front of all the
people of Israel. He said,

"Let the sun stand still over Gibeon,
and the moon over the valley of Aijalon."

13So the sun stood still and the moon stayed in place until
the nation of Israel had defeated its enemies.
Is this event not recorded in *The Book of Jashar**? The
sun stayed in the middle of the sky, and it did not set as on
a normal day.* 14There has never been a day like this one
before or since, when the LORD answered such a prayer.
Surely the LORD fought for Israel that day!
15Then Joshua and the Israelite army returned to their
camp at Gilgal.

JOSHUA KILLS THE FIVE SOUTHERN KINGS

16During the battle the five kings escaped and hid in a
cave at Makkedah. 17When Joshua heard that they had
been found, 18he issued this command: "Cover the opening of the cave with large rocks, and place guards at the
entrance to keep the kings inside. 19The rest of you continue chasing the enemy and cut them down from the
rear. Don't give them a chance to get back to their towns,
for the LORD your God has given you victory over them."
20So Joshua and the Israelite army continued the
slaughter and completely crushed the enemy. They totally wiped out the five armies except for a tiny remnant
that managed to reach their fortified towns. 21Then the
Israelites returned safely to Joshua in the camp at Makkedah. After that, no one dared to speak even a word
against Israel.
22Then Joshua said, "Remove the rocks covering the
opening of the cave, and bring the five kings to me." 23So
they brought the five kings out of the cave—the kings of
Jerusalem, Hebron, Jarmuth, Lachish, and Eglon. 24When
they brought them out, Joshua told the commanders of
his army, "Come and put your feet on the kings' necks."
And they did as they were told.
25"Don't ever be afraid or discouraged," Joshua told his
men. "Be strong and courageous, for the LORD is going to
do this to all of your enemies." 26Then Joshua killed each
of the five kings and impaled them on five sharpened
poles, where they hung until evening.

HOPE FOR THE FUTURE 10:25

With God's help, Israel won a battle against five Amorite armies (10:1-14). Joshua told his men never to be afraid, because God would give them similar victories over their enemies. The same God who empowered Joshua and his troops and led us in the past will help us with our present and future needs. Reminding ourselves of God's faithfulness will give us hope for the struggles that lie ahead. ■

27As the sun was going down, Joshua gave instructions
for the bodies of the kings to be taken down from the
poles and thrown into the cave where they had been hiding. Then they covered the opening of the cave with a pile
of large rocks, which remains to this very day.

ISRAEL DESTROYS THE SOUTHERN TOWNS

28That same day Joshua captured and destroyed the town
of Makkedah. He killed everyone in it, including the king,
leaving no survivors. He destroyed them all, and he killed
the king of Makkedah as he had killed the king of Jericho.
29Then Joshua and the Israelites went to Libnah and attacked it. 30There, too, the LORD gave them the town and
its king. He killed everyone in it, leaving no survivors.
Then Joshua killed the king of Libnah as he had killed the
king of Jericho.
31From Libnah, Joshua and the Israelites went to Lachish and attacked it. 32Here again, the LORD gave them
Lachish. Joshua took it on the second day and killed
everyone in it, just as he had done at Libnah. 33During the
attack on Lachish, King Horam of Gezer arrived with his
army to help defend the town. But Joshua's men killed
him and his army, leaving no survivors.
34Then Joshua and the Israelite army went on to Eglon
and attacked it. 35They captured it that day and killed
everyone in it. He completely destroyed everyone, just as
he had done at Lachish. 36From Eglon, Joshua and the Israelite army went up to Hebron and attacked it. 37They
captured the town and killed everyone in it, including its
king, leaving no survivors. They did the same thing to all
of its surrounding villages. And just as he had done at Eglon, he completely destroyed the entire population.
38Then Joshua and the Israelites turned back and attacked Debir. 39He captured the town, its king, and all of
its surrounding villages. He completely destroyed everyone in it, leaving no survivors. He did to Debir and its king

10:13a Or *The Book of the Upright*. **10:13b** Or *did not set for about a whole day*.

just what he had done to Hebron and to Libnah and its king.

40 So Joshua conquered the whole region—the kings and people of the hill country, the Negev, the western foothills,* and the mountain slopes. He completely destroyed everyone in the land, leaving no survivors, just as the LORD, the God of Israel, had commanded. 41 Joshua slaughtered them from Kadesh-barnea to Gaza and from the region around the town of Goshen up to Gibeon. 42 Joshua conquered all these kings and their land in a single campaign, for the LORD, the God of Israel, was fighting for his people.

43 Then Joshua and the Israelite army returned to their camp at Gilgal.

A THOROUGH RESPONSE 10:40-43

God had commanded Joshua to conquer the people of Canaan to allow God's people to settle in this territory. Joshua did his part thoroughly. When God orders us to eliminate elements in our lives that cause us to do wrong (for example, Internet porn; TV shows that make us unsatisfied with our lives), we must not pause to rationalize. Instead, like Joshua, our response must be swift and complete. ■

11

ISRAEL DEFEATS THE NORTHERN ARMIES

When King Jabin of Hazor heard what had happened, he sent messages to the following kings: King Jobab of Madon; the king of Shimron; the king of Acshaph; 2 all the kings of the northern hill country; the kings in the Jordan Valley south of Galilee*; the kings in the Galilean foothills*; the kings of Naphoth-dor on the west; 3 the kings of Canaan, both east and west; the kings of the Amorites, the Hittites, the Perizzites, the Jebusites in the hill country, and the Hivites in the towns on the slopes of Mount Hermon in the land of Mizpah.

4 All these kings came out to fight. Their combined armies formed a vast horde. And with all their horses and chariots, they covered the landscape like the sand on the seashore. 5 The kings joined forces and established their camp around the water near Merom to fight against Israel.

6 Then the LORD said to Joshua, "Do not be afraid of them. By this time tomorrow I will hand all of them over to Israel as dead men. Then you must cripple their horses and burn their chariots."

7 So Joshua and all his fighting men traveled to the water near Merom and attacked suddenly. 8 And the LORD gave them victory over their enemies. The Israelites chased them as far as Greater Sidon and Misrephoth-maim, and eastward into the valley of Mizpah, until not one enemy warrior was left alive. 9 Then Joshua crippled the horses and burned all the chariots, as the LORD had instructed.

10 Joshua then turned back and captured Hazor and killed its king. (Hazor had at one time been the capital of all these kingdoms.) 11 The Israelites completely destroyed* every living thing in the city, leaving no survivors. Not a single person was spared. And then Joshua burned the city.

12 Joshua slaughtered all the other kings and their people, completely destroying them, just as Moses, the servant of the LORD, had commanded. 13 But the Israelites did not burn any of the towns built on mounds except Hazor, which Joshua burned. 14 And the Israelites took all the plunder and livestock of the ravaged towns for themselves. But they killed all the people, leaving no survivors. 15 As the LORD had commanded his servant Moses, so Moses commanded Joshua. And Joshua did as he was told, carefully obeying all the commands that the LORD had given to Moses.

16 So Joshua conquered the entire region—the hill country, the entire Negev, the whole area around the town of Goshen, the western foothills, the Jordan Valley,* the mountains of Israel, and the Galilean foothills. 17 The Israelite territory now extended all the way from Mount Halak, which leads up to Seir in the south, as far north as Baal-gad at the foot of Mount Hermon in the valley of Lebanon. Joshua killed all the kings of those territories, 18 waging war for a long time to accomplish this. 19 No one in this region made peace with the Israelites except the Hivites of Gibeon. All the others were defeated. 20 For the LORD hardened their hearts and caused them to fight the Israelites. So they were completely destroyed without mercy, as the LORD had commanded Moses.

PROGRESS 11:16-23

Although the conquest of much of the land of Canaan seems to have happened quickly (we can read about it in one sitting), it actually took seven years. We often expect quick changes in our lives or quick victories over sin. But our journey with God is a lifelong process. Because changes and victories take time, many people grow impatient with God and feel like giving up hope. Are you wondering whether or not you see any progress in your life? Hold on to hope! One day you'll look back at this point in your life and be amazed at how much progress actually took place! ■

21 During this period Joshua destroyed all the descendants of Anak, who lived in the hill country of Hebron, Debir, Anab, and the entire hill country of Judah and Israel. He killed them all and completely destroyed their towns. 22 None of the descendants of Anak were left in all the land of Israel, though some still remained in Gaza, Gath, and Ashdod.

23 So Joshua took control of the entire land, just as the LORD had instructed Moses. He gave it to the people of Israel as their special possession, dividing the land among the tribes. So the land finally had rest from war.

10:40 Hebrew *the Shephelah.* 11:2a Hebrew *in the Arabah south of Kinnereth.* 11:2b Hebrew *the Shephelah;* also in 11:16. 11:11 The Hebrew term used here refers to the complete consecration of things or people to the LORD, either by destroying them or by giving them as an offering; also in 11:12, 20, 21. 11:16 Hebrew *the Shephelah, the Arabah.*

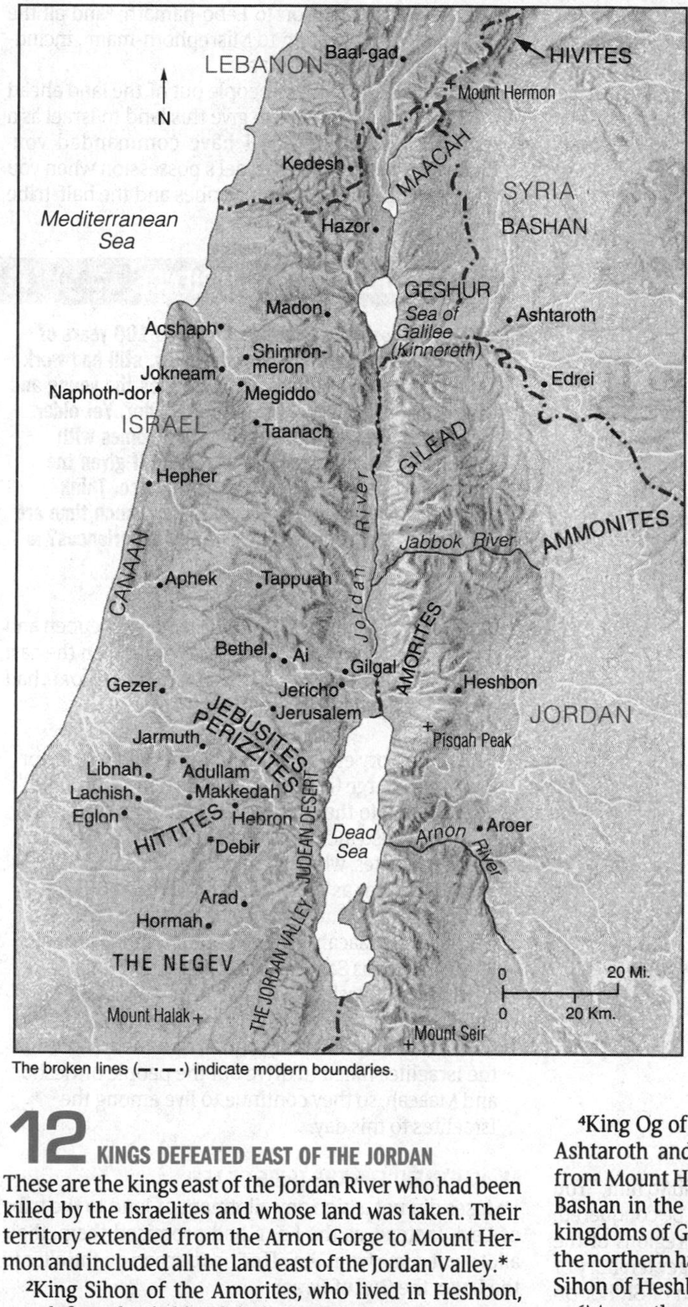

The broken lines (—·—·) indicate modern boundaries.

THE CONQUERED LAND
Joshua displayed brilliant military strategy in the way he went about conquering the land of Canaan. He first captured the well-fortified Jericho to gain a foothold in Canaan and to demonstrate the awesome might of the God of Israel. Then he gained the hill country around Bethel. From there he subdued towns in the lowlands. Then his army conquered important cities in the north, such as Hazor. In all, Israel conquered land both east (12:1-6) and west (12:7-24) of the Jordan River, from Mount Hermon in the north to beyond the Negev to Mount Halak in the south. Thirty-one kings and their cities had been defeated. The Israelites had overpowered the Hittites, the Amorites, the Canaanites, the Perizzites, the Hivites, and the Jebusites. Other people living in Canaan were yet to be conquered.

12 KINGS DEFEATED EAST OF THE JORDAN

These are the kings east of the Jordan River who had been
killed by the Israelites and whose land was taken. Their
territory extended from the Arnon Gorge to Mount Hermon and included all the land east of the Jordan Valley.*
2King Sihon of the Amorites, who lived in Heshbon,
was defeated. His kingdom included Aroer, on the edge
of the Arnon Gorge, and extended from the middle of the
Arnon Gorge to the Jabbok River, which serves as a border for the Ammonites. This territory included the
southern half of the territory of Gilead. 3Sihon also controlled the Jordan Valley and regions to the east—from as
far north as the Sea of Galilee to as far south as the Dead
Sea,* including the road to Beth-jeshimoth and southward to the slopes of Pisgah.
4King Og of Bashan, the last of the Rephaites, lived at
Ashtaroth and Edrei. 5He ruled a territory stretching
from Mount Hermon to Salecah in the north and to all of
Bashan in the east, and westward to the borders of the
kingdoms of Geshur and Maacah. This territory included
the northern half of Gilead, as far as the boundary of King
Sihon of Heshbon.
6Moses, the servant of the LORD, and the Israelites had
destroyed the people of King Sihon and King Og. And
Moses gave their land as a possession to the tribes of Reuben, Gad, and the half-tribe of Manasseh.

KINGS DEFEATED WEST OF THE JORDAN

7The following is a list of the kings that Joshua and the Israelite armies defeated on the west side of the Jordan,
from Baal-gad in the valley of Lebanon to Mount Halak,

12:1 Hebrew *the Arabah;* also in 12:3, 8. **12:3** Hebrew *from the Sea of Kinnereth to the Sea of the Arabah, which is the Salt Sea.*

which leads up to Seir. (Joshua gave this land to the tribes of Israel as their possession, [8]including the hill country, the western foothills,* the Jordan Valley, the mountain slopes, the Judean wilderness, and the Negev. The people who lived in this region were the Hittites, the Amorites, the Canaanites, the Perizzites, the Hivites, and the Jebusites.) These are the kings Israel defeated:

9 The king of Jericho
The king of Ai, near Bethel
10 The king of Jerusalem
The king of Hebron
11 The king of Jarmuth
The king of Lachish
12 The king of Eglon
The king of Gezer
13 The king of Debir
The king of Geder
14 The king of Hormah
The king of Arad
15 The king of Libnah
The king of Adullam
16 The king of Makkedah
The king of Bethel
17 The king of Tappuah
The king of Hepher
18 The king of Aphek
The king of Lasharon
19 The king of Madon
The king of Hazor
20 The king of Shimron-meron
The king of Acshaph
21 The king of Taanach
The king of Megiddo
22 The king of Kedesh
The king of Jokneam in Carmel
23 The king of Dor in the town of Naphoth-dor*
The king of Goyim in Gilgal*
24 The king of Tirzah.

In all, thirty-one kings were defeated.

13

THE LAND YET TO BE CONQUERED

When Joshua was an old man, the LORD said to him, "You are growing old, and much land remains to be conquered.
[2]This is the territory that remains: all the regions of the
Philistines and the Geshurites, [3]and the larger territory of
the Canaanites, extending from the stream of Shihor on
the border of Egypt, northward to the boundary of Ekron.
It includes the territory of the five Philistine rulers of
Gaza, Ashdod, Ashkelon, Gath, and Ekron. The land of the
Avvites [4]in the south also remains to be conquered. In the
north, the following area has not yet been conquered: all
the land of the Canaanites, including Mearah (which belongs to the Sidonians), stretching northward to Aphek on
the border of the Amorites; [5]the land of the Gebalites and
all of the Lebanon mountain area to the east, from Baal-
gad below Mount Hermon to Lebo-hamath; [6]and all the
hill country from Lebanon to Misrephoth-maim, including all the land of the Sidonians.

"I myself will drive these people out of the land ahead of the Israelites. So be sure to give this land to Israel as a special possession, just as I have commanded you.
[7]Include all this territory as Israel's possession when you
divide this land among the nine tribes and the half-tribe of Manasseh."

THE AGE OF EXPERIENCE 13:1

Joshua was between 85 and 100 years of age at this time. God, however, still had work for him to do. Our culture often glorifies the young and strong and sets aside those who are older. Yet older people are filled with the wisdom that comes with experience. They are capable of serving if given the chance and should be encouraged to do so. Think about the older people in your life. How much time are you willing to give to learn from their experiences? ■

THE LAND DIVIDED EAST OF THE JORDAN

[8]Half the tribe of Manasseh and the tribes of Reuben and Gad had already received their grants of land on the east side of the Jordan, for Moses, the servant of the LORD, had previously assigned this land to them.

[9]Their territory extended from Aroer on the edge of the Arnon Gorge (including the town in the middle of the gorge) to the plain beyond Medeba, as far as
Dibon. [10]It also included all the towns of King Sihon of the Amorites, who had reigned in Heshbon, and extended as far as the borders of Ammon. [11]It
included Gilead, the territory of the kingdoms of Geshur and Maacah, all of Mount Hermon, all of Bashan as far as Salecah, [12]and all the territory
of King Og of Bashan, who had reigned in Ashtaroth and Edrei. King Og was the last of the Rephaites, for Moses had attacked them and driven them out. [13]But
the Israelites failed to drive out the people of Geshur and Maacah, so they continue to live among the Israelites to this day.

AN ALLOTMENT FOR THE TRIBE OF LEVI

[14]Moses did not assign any allotment of land to the tribe of Levi. Instead, as the LORD had promised them, their allotment came from the offerings burned on the altar to the LORD, the God of Israel.

THE LAND GIVEN TO THE TRIBE OF REUBEN

[15]Moses had assigned the following area to the clans of the tribe of Reuben.

[16]Their territory extended from Aroer on the edge of the Arnon Gorge (including the town in the middle of the gorge) to the plain beyond Medeba. [17]It included
Heshbon and the other towns on the plain—Dibon,

12:8 Hebrew *the Shephelah.* 12:23a Hebrew *Naphath-dor,* a variant spelling of Naphoth-dor. 12:23b Greek version reads *Goyim in Galilee.*

Bamoth-baal, Beth-baal-meon, 18Jahaz, Kedemoth, Mephaath, 19Kiriathaim, Sibmah, Zereth-shahar on the hill above the valley, 20Beth-peor, the slopes of Pisgah, and Beth-jeshimoth.

21The land of Reuben also included all the towns of the plain and the entire kingdom of Sihon. Sihon was the Amorite king who had reigned in Heshbon and was killed by Moses along with the leaders of Midian—Evi, Rekem, Zur, Hur, and Reba—princes living in the region who were allied with Sihon. 22The Israelites had also killed Balaam son of Beor, who used magic to tell the future. 23The Jordan River marked the western boundary for the tribe of Reuben. The towns and their surrounding villages in this area were given as a homeland to the clans of the tribe of Reuben.

THE LAND GIVEN TO THE TRIBE OF GAD

24Moses had assigned the following area to the clans of the tribe of Gad.

25Their territory included Jazer, all the towns of Gilead, and half of the land of Ammon, as far as the town of Aroer just west of* Rabbah. 26It extended from Heshbon to Ramath-mizpeh and Betonim, and from Mahanaim to Lo-debar.* 27In the valley were Beth-haram, Beth-nimrah, Succoth, Zaphon, and the rest of the kingdom of King Sihon of Heshbon. The western boundary ran along the Jordan River, extended as far north as the tip of the Sea of Galilee,* and then turned eastward. 28The towns and their surrounding villages in this area were given as a homeland to the clans of the tribe of Gad.

THE LAND GIVEN TO THE HALF-TRIBE OF MANASSEH

29Moses had assigned the following area to the clans of the half-tribe of Manasseh.

30Their territory extended from Mahanaim, including all of Bashan, all the former kingdom of King Og, and the sixty towns of Jair in Bashan. 31It also included half of Gilead and King Og's royal cities of Ashtaroth and Edrei. All this was given to the clans of the descendants of Makir, who was Manasseh's son.

32These are the allotments Moses had made while he was on the plains of Moab, across the Jordan River, east of Jericho. 33But Moses gave no allotment of land to the tribe of Levi, for the LORD, the God of Israel, had promised that he himself would be their allotment.

14

THE LAND DIVIDED WEST OF THE JORDAN

The remaining tribes of Israel received land in Canaan as allotted by Eleazar the priest, Joshua son of Nun, and the tribal leaders. 2These nine and a half tribes received their grants of land by means of sacred lots, in accordance with the LORD's command through Moses. 3Moses had already given a grant of land to the two and a half tribes on the east side of the Jordan River, but he had given the Levites no such allotment. 4The descendants of Joseph had become two separate tribes—Manasseh and Ephraim. And the Levites were given no land at all, only towns to live in with surrounding pasturelands for their livestock and all their possessions. 5So the land was distributed in strict accordance with the LORD's commands to Moses.

AN EXACT OBEDIENCE 14:1-5

The land was divided exactly as God had instructed Moses years before. Joshua followed God's commands precisely. Often we believe that "almost" is close enough. This idea can carry over into our spiritual lives. For example, we may follow God's Word as long as we agree with it, but ignore it when the demands seem difficult. But God is looking for leaders who follow his instructions thoroughly. Does that describe you? ■

CALEB REQUESTS HIS LAND

6A delegation from the tribe of Judah, led by Caleb son of Jephunneh the Kenizzite, came to Joshua at Gilgal. Caleb said to Joshua, "Remember what the LORD said to Moses, the man of God, about you and me when we were at Kadesh-barnea. 7I was forty years old when Moses, the servant of the LORD, sent me from Kadesh-barnea to explore the land of Canaan. I returned and gave an honest report, 8but my brothers who went with me frightened the people from entering the Promised Land. For my part, I wholeheartedly followed the LORD my God. 9So that day Moses solemnly promised me, 'The land of Canaan on which you were just walking will be your grant of land and that of your descendants forever, because you wholeheartedly followed the LORD my God.'

PROMISE KEEPER 14:6-12

When Joshua gave Caleb his land, he fulfilled a promise God had made to Caleb 45 years earlier. How about you? Are you this reliable? God is. Even today he honors promises he made *thousands* of years ago. In fact, some of his greatest promises are yet to be fulfilled. How does the knowledge of God's faithfulness make you feel? ■

10"Now, as you can see, the LORD has kept me alive and well as he promised for all these forty-five years since Moses made this promise—even while Israel wandered in the wilderness. Today I am eighty-five years old. 11I am as strong now as I was when Moses sent me on that journey, and I can still travel and fight as well as I could then. 12So give me the hill country that the LORD promised me. You will remember that as scouts we found the descendants of Anak living there in great, walled towns. But if the LORD is with me, I will drive them out of the land, just as the LORD said."

13:25 Hebrew *in front of*. 13:26 Or *to the territory of Debir*. 13:27 Hebrew *Sea of Kinnereth*.

[13]So Joshua blessed Caleb son of Jephunneh and gave Hebron to him as his portion of land. [14]Hebron still belongs to the descendants of Caleb son of Jephunneh the Kenizzite because he wholeheartedly followed the LORD, the God of Israel. [15](Previously Hebron had been called Kiriath-arba. It had been named after Arba, a great hero of the descendants of Anak.)

And the land had rest from war.

15

THE LAND GIVEN TO THE TRIBE OF JUDAH

The allotment for the clans of the tribe of Judah reached southward to the border of Edom, as far south as the wilderness of Zin.

[2]The southern boundary began at the south bay of the Dead Sea,* [3]ran south of Scorpion Pass* into the wilderness of Zin, and then went south of Kadesh-barnea to Hezron. Then it went up to Addar, where it turned toward Karka. [4]From there it passed to Azmon until it finally reached the Brook of Egypt, which it followed to the Mediterranean Sea.* This was their* southern boundary.

[5]The eastern boundary extended along the Dead Sea to the mouth of the Jordan River.

The northern boundary began at the bay where the Jordan River empties into the Dead Sea, [6]went up from there to Beth-hoglah, then proceeded north of Beth-arabah to the Stone of Bohan. (Bohan was Reuben's son.) [7]From that point it went through the valley of Achor to Debir, turning north toward Gilgal, which is across from the slopes of Adummim on the south side of the valley. From there the boundary extended to the springs at En-shemesh and on to En-rogel. [8]The boundary then passed through the valley of Ben-Hinnom, along the southern slopes of the Jebusites, where the city of Jerusalem is located. Then it went west to the top of the mountain above the valley of Hinnom, and on up to the northern end of the valley of Rephaim. [9]From there the boundary extended from the top of the mountain to the spring at the waters of Nephtoah,* and from there to the towns on Mount Ephron. Then it turned toward Baalah (that is, Kiriath-jearim). [10]The boundary circled west of Baalah to Mount Seir, passed along to the town of Kesalon on the northern slope of Mount Jearim, and went down to Beth-shemesh and on to Timnah. [11]The boundary then proceeded to the slope of the hill north of Ekron, where it turned toward Shikkeron and Mount Baalah. It passed Jabneel and ended at the Mediterranean Sea.

[12]The western boundary was the shoreline of the Mediterranean Sea.*

These are the boundaries for the clans of the tribe of Judah.

THE LAND GIVEN TO CALEB

[13]The LORD commanded Joshua to assign some of Judah's territory to Caleb son of Jephunneh. So Caleb was given the town of Kiriath-arba (that is, Hebron), which had been named after Anak's ancestor. [14]Caleb drove out the three groups of Anakites—the descendants of Sheshai, Ahiman, and Talmai, the sons of Anak.

[15]From there he went to fight against the people living in the town of Debir (formerly called Kiriath-sepher). [16]Caleb said, "I will give my daughter Acsah in marriage to the one who attacks and captures Kiriath-sepher." [17]Othniel, the son of Caleb's brother Kenaz, was the one who conquered it, so Acsah became Othniel's wife.

[18]When Acsah married Othniel, she urged him* to ask her father for a field. As she got down off her donkey, Caleb asked her, "What's the matter?"

[19]She said, "Give me another gift. You have already given me land in the Negev; now please give me springs of water, too." So Caleb gave her the upper and lower springs.

THE TOWNS ALLOTTED TO JUDAH

[20]This was the homeland allocated to the clans of the tribe of Judah.

[21]The towns of Judah situated along the borders of Edom in the extreme south were Kabzeel, Eder, Jagur, [22]Kinah, Dimonah, Adadah, [23]Kedesh, Hazor, Ithnan, [24]Ziph, Telem, Bealoth, [25]Hazor-hadattah, Kerioth-hezron (that is, Hazor), [26]Amam, Shema, Moladah, [27]Hazar-gaddah, Heshmon, Beth-pelet, [28]Hazar-shual, Beersheba, Biziothiah, [29]Baalah, Iim, Ezem, [30]Eltolad, Kesil, Hormah, [31]Ziklag, Madmannah, Sansannah, [32]Lebaoth, Shilhim, Ain, and Rimmon—twenty-nine towns with their surrounding villages.

[33]The following towns situated in the western foothills* were also given to Judah: Eshtaol, Zorah, Ashnah, [34]Zanoah, En-gannim, Tappuah, Enam, [35]Jarmuth, Adullam, Socoh, Azekah, [36]Shaaraim, Adithaim, Gederah, and Gederothaim—fourteen towns with their surrounding villages.

[37]Also included were Zenan, Hadashah, Migdal-gad, [38]Dilean, Mizpeh, Joktheel, [39]Lachish, Bozkath, Eglon, [40]Cabbon, Lahmam, Kitlish, [41]Gederoth, Beth-dagon, Naamah, and Makkedah—sixteen towns with their surrounding villages.

[42]Besides these, there were Libnah, Ether, Ashan, [43]Iphtah, Ashnah, Nezib, [44]Keilah, Aczib, and Mareshah—nine towns with their surrounding villages.

[45]The territory of the tribe of Judah also included Ekron and its surrounding settlements and villages. [46]From Ekron the boundary extended west and included the towns near Ashdod with their surrounding villages. [47]It also included Ashdod with its surrounding settlements and villages and Gaza with its settlements and villages, as far as the Brook of Egypt and along the coast of the Mediterranean Sea.

15:2 Hebrew *the Salt Sea;* also in 15:5. **15:3** Hebrew *Akrabbim.* **15:4a** Hebrew *the sea;* also in 15:11. **15:4b** Hebrew *your.* **15:9** Or *the spring at Me-nephtoah.* **15:12** Hebrew *the Great Sea;* also in 15:47. **15:18** Some Greek manuscripts read *he urged her.* **15:33** Hebrew *the Shephelah.*

[48]Judah also received the following towns in the hill country: Shamir, Jattir, Socoh, [49]Dannah, Kiriath-sannah (that is, Debir), [50]Anab, Eshtemoh, Anim, [51]Goshen, Holon, and Giloh—eleven towns with their surrounding villages.

[52]Also included were the towns of Arab, Dumah, Eshan, [53]Janim, Beth-tappuah, Aphekah, [54]Humtah, Kiriath-arba (that is, Hebron), and Zior—nine towns with their surrounding villages.

[55]Besides these, there were Maon, Carmel, Ziph, Juttah, [56]Jezreel, Jokdeam, Zanoah, [57]Kain, Gibeah, and Timnah—ten towns with their surrounding villages.

[58]In addition, there were Halhul, Beth-zur, Gedor, [59]Maarath, Beth-anoth, and Eltekon—six towns with their surrounding villages.

[60]There were also Kiriath-baal (that is, Kiriath-jearim) and Rabbah—two towns with their surrounding villages.

[61]In the wilderness there were the towns of Beth-arabah, Middin, Secacah, [62]Nibshan, the City of Salt, and En-gedi—six towns with their surrounding villages.

[63]But the tribe of Judah could not drive out the Jebusites, who lived in the city of Jerusalem, so the Jebusites live there among the people of Judah to this day.

A DOUBLE PORTION 16:1-10

Though Joseph was one of Jacob's 12 sons, he did not have a tribe named after him. Yet his family group was due to receive a double portion of the land because Reuben messed up long ago (see Gen 49:3-4). This double portion was given to Joseph's two sons, Ephraim and Manasseh, whom Jacob considered as his own (Gen 48:5). If you believe in Jesus, you are one of God's own. What "portions" of God's mercy have you received recently? ■

16 THE LAND GIVEN TO EPHRAIM AND WEST MANASSEH

The allotment for the descendants of Joseph extended from the Jordan River near Jericho, east of the springs of Jericho, through the wilderness and into the hill country of Bethel. [2]From Bethel (that is, Luz)* it ran over to Ataroth in the territory of the Arkites. [3]Then it descended westward to the territory of the Japhletites as far as Lower Beth-horon, then to Gezer and over to the Mediterranean Sea.*

[4]This was the homeland allocated to the families of Joseph's sons, Manasseh and Ephraim.

THE LAND GIVEN TO EPHRAIM

[5]The following territory was given to the clans of the tribe of Ephraim.

The boundary of their homeland began at Ataroth-addar in the east. From there it ran to Upper Beth-horon, [6]then on to the Mediterranean Sea. From Micmethath on the north, the boundary curved eastward past Taanath-shiloh to the east of Janoah. [7]From Janoah it turned southward to Ataroth and Naarah, touched Jericho, and ended at the Jordan River. [8]From Tappuah the boundary extended westward, following the Kanah Ravine to the Mediterranean Sea. This is the homeland allocated to the clans of the tribe of Ephraim.

[9]In addition, some towns with their surrounding villages in the territory allocated to the half-tribe of Manasseh were set aside for the tribe of Ephraim. [10]They did not drive the Canaanites out of Gezer, however, so the people of Gezer live as slaves among the people of Ephraim to this day.

17 THE LAND GIVEN TO WEST MANASSEH

The next allotment of land was given to the half-tribe of Manasseh, the descendants of Joseph's older son. Makir, the firstborn son of Manasseh, was the father of Gilead. Because his descendants were experienced soldiers, the regions of Gilead and Bashan on the east side of the Jordan had already been given to them. [2]So the allotment on the west side of the Jordan was for the remaining families within the clans of the tribe of Manasseh: Abiezer, Helek, Asriel, Shechem, Hepher, and Shemida. These clans represent the male descendants of Manasseh son of Joseph.

[3]However, Zelophehad, a descendant of Hepher son of Gilead, son of Makir, son of Manasseh, had no sons. He had only daughters, whose names were Mahlah, Noah, Hoglah, Milcah, and Tirzah. [4]These women came to Eleazar the priest, Joshua son of Nun, and the Israelite leaders and said, "The LORD commanded Moses to give us a grant of land along with the men of our tribe."

TRADITION 17:3-4

By giving land to the daughters of Zelophehad, Joshua honored a promise that Moses had made earlier (see Num 27:1-11). Although Israelite women did not traditionally inherit property, Moses put justice ahead of tradition and gave these five women the land they deserved.

Ever allow a tradition to decide your actions? It's easy to refuse to honor a reasonable request because of tradition. God sometimes calls us to break one tradition and start a new one. ■

So Joshua gave them a grant of land along with their uncles, as the LORD had commanded. [5]As a result, Manasseh's total allocation came to ten parcels of land, in addition to the land of Gilead and Bashan across the Jordan River, [6]because the female descendants of Manasseh received a grant of land along with the male descendants. (The land of Gilead was given to the rest of the male descendants of Manasseh.)

16:2 As in Greek version (also see 18:13); Hebrew reads *From Bethel to Luz.* 16:3 Hebrew *the sea;* also in 16:6, 8.

7The boundary of the tribe of Manasseh extended from
the border of Asher to Micmethath, near Shechem.
Then the boundary went south from Micmethath to
the settlement near the spring of Tappuah. 8The land
surrounding Tappuah belonged to Manasseh, but the
town of Tappuah itself, on the border of Manasseh's
territory, belonged to the tribe of Ephraim. 9From the
spring of Tappuah, the boundary of Manasseh followed
the Kanah Ravine to the Mediterranean Sea.* Several
towns south of the ravine were inside Manasseh's
territory, but they actually belonged to the tribe of
Ephraim. 10In general, however, the land south of the
ravine belonged to Ephraim, and the land north of the
ravine belonged to Manasseh. Manasseh's boundary ran
along the northern side of the ravine and ended at the
Mediterranean Sea. North of Manasseh was the territory
of Asher, and to the east was the territory of Issachar.

11The following towns within the territory of
Issachar and Asher, however, were given to Manasseh:
Beth-shan,* Ibleam, Dor (that is, Naphoth-dor),*
Endor, Taanach, and Megiddo, each with their
surrounding settlements.

12But the descendants of Manasseh were unable to occupy these towns. They could not drive out the Canaanites who continued to live there. 13Later, however, when
the Israelites became strong enough, they forced the Canaanites to work as slaves. But they did not drive them
out of the land.

14The descendants of Joseph came to Joshua and
asked, "Why have you given us only one portion of land as
our homeland when the LORD has blessed us with so
many people?"

15Joshua replied, "If there are so many of you, and if the
hill country of Ephraim is not large enough for you, clear
out land for yourselves in the forest where the Perizzites
and Rephaites live."

16The descendants of Joseph responded, "It's true that
the hill country is not large enough for us. But all the Canaanites in the lowlands have iron chariots, both those in
Beth-shan and its surrounding settlements and those in
the valley of Jezreel. They are too strong for us."

17Then Joshua said to the tribes of Ephraim and Manasseh, the descendants of Joseph, "Since you are so large
and strong, you will be given more than one portion.
18The forests of the hill country will be yours as well.
Clear as much of the land as you wish, and take possession of its farthest corners. And you will drive out the
Canaanites from the valleys, too, even though they are
strong and have iron chariots."

18 THE ALLOTMENTS OF THE REMAINING LAND

Now that the land was under Israelite control, the entire
community of Israel gathered at Shiloh and set up the
Tabernacle.* 2But there remained seven tribes who had
not yet been allotted their grants of land.

3Then Joshua asked them, "How long are you going to
wait before taking possession of the remaining land the
LORD, the God of your ancestors, has given to you? 4Select
three men from each tribe, and I will send them out to explore the land and map it out. They will then return to me
with a written report of their proposed divisions of their
new homeland. 5Let them divide the land into seven sections, excluding Judah's territory in the south and Joseph's territory in the north. 6And when you record the
seven divisions of the land and bring them to me, I will
cast sacred lots in the presence of the LORD our God to
assign land to each tribe.

PUTTING IT OFF 18:3-6

Joshua wondered why some of the tribes were slow to claim their land. Like the Israelites, we sometimes delay doing jobs that seem large, difficult, boring, or disagreeable. Jobs we don't enjoy require concentration, teamwork, lots of encouragement, and accountability. Tempted to procrastinate? You might investigate the cause of the delay (fear; lack of confidence in your ability to finish the task). Then ask God to help you do what you need to do. Don't put it off! ■

7"The Levites, however, will not receive any allotment
of land. Their role as priests of the LORD is their allotment. And the tribes of Gad, Reuben, and the half-tribe
of Manasseh won't receive any more land, for they have
already received their grant of land, which Moses, the
servant of the LORD, gave them on the east side of the Jordan River."

8As the men started on their way to map out the land,
Joshua commanded them, "Go and explore the land and
write a description of it. Then return to me, and I will assign the land to the tribes by casting sacred lots here in
the presence of the LORD at Shiloh." 9The men did as they
were told and mapped the entire territory into seven sections, listing the towns in each section. They made a written record and then returned to Joshua in the camp at
Shiloh. 10And there at Shiloh, Joshua cast sacred lots in
the presence of the LORD to determine which tribe
should have each section.

THE LAND GIVEN TO BENJAMIN

11The first allotment of land went to the clans of the tribe
of Benjamin. It lay between the territory assigned to the
tribes of Judah and Joseph.

12The northern boundary of Benjamin's land began
at the Jordan River, went north of the slope of
Jericho, then west through the hill country and the
wilderness of Beth-aven. 13From there the boundary
went south to Luz (that is, Bethel) and proceeded
down to Ataroth-addar on the hill that lies south of
Lower Beth-horon.

17:9 Hebrew *the sea;* also in 17:10. **17:11a** Hebrew *Beth-shean,* a variant spelling of Beth-shan; also in 17:16. **17:11b** The meaning of the Hebrew here is uncertain. **18:1** Hebrew *Tent of Meeting.*

[14]The boundary then made a turn and swung south along the western edge of the hill facing Beth-horon, ending at the village of Kiriath-baal (that is, Kiriath-jearim), a town belonging to the tribe of Judah. This was the western boundary.

[15]The southern boundary began at the outskirts of Kiriath-jearim. From that western point it ran* to the spring at the waters of Nephtoah,* [16]and down to the base of the mountain beside the valley of Ben-Hinnom, at the northern end of the valley of Rephaim. From there it went down the valley of Hinnom, crossing south of the slope where the Jebusites lived, and continued down to En-rogel. [17]From En-rogel the boundary proceeded in a northerly direction and came to En-shemesh and on to Geliloth (which is across from the slopes of Adummim). Then it went down to the Stone of Bohan. (Bohan was Reuben's son.) [18]From there it passed along the north side of the slope overlooking the Jordan Valley.* The border then went down into the valley, [19]ran past the north slope of Beth-hoglah, and ended at the north bay of the Dead Sea,* which is the southern end of the Jordan River. This was the southern boundary.

[20]The eastern boundary was the Jordan River.

These were the boundaries of the homeland allocated to the clans of the tribe of Benjamin.

THE TOWNS GIVEN TO BENJAMIN

[21]These were the towns given to the clans of the tribe of Benjamin.

Jericho, Beth-hoglah, Emek-keziz, [22]Beth-arabah, Zemaraim, Bethel, [23]Avvim, Parah, Ophrah, [24]Kephar-ammoni, Ophni, and Geba—twelve towns with their surrounding villages. [25]Also Gibeon, Ramah, Beeroth, [26]Mizpah, Kephirah, Mozah, [27]Rekem, Irpeel, Taralah, [28]Zela, Haeleph, Jebus (that is, Jerusalem), Gibeah, and Kiriath-jearim*—fourteen towns with their surrounding villages.

This was the homeland allocated to the clans of the tribe of Benjamin.

19

THE LAND GIVEN TO SIMEON

The second allotment of land went to the clans of the tribe of Simeon. Their homeland was surrounded by Judah's territory.

[2]Simeon's homeland included Beersheba, Sheba, Moladah, [3]Hazar-shual, Balah, Ezem, [4]Eltolad, Bethul, Hormah, [5]Ziklag, Beth-marcaboth, Hazar-susah, [6]Beth-lebaoth, and Sharuhen—thirteen towns with their surrounding villages. [7]It also included Ain, Rimmon, Ether, and Ashan—four towns with their villages, [8]including all the surrounding villages as far south as Baalath-beer (also known as Ramah of the Negev).

This was the homeland allocated to the clans of the tribe of Simeon. [9]Their allocation of land came from part of what had been given to Judah because Judah's territory was too large for them. So the tribe of Simeon received an allocation within the territory of Judah.

THE LAND GIVEN TO ZEBULUN

[10]The third allotment of land went to the clans of the tribe of Zebulun.

The boundary of Zebulun's homeland started at Sarid. [11]From there it went west, going past Maralah, touching Dabbesheth, and proceeding to the brook east of Jokneam. [12]In the other direction, the boundary went east from Sarid to the border of Kisloth-tabor, and from there to Daberath and up to Japhia. [13]Then it continued east to Gath-hepher, Eth-kazin, and Rimmon and turned toward Neah. [14]The northern boundary of Zebulun passed Hannathon and ended at the valley of Iphtah-el. [15]The towns in these areas included Kattath, Nahalal, Shimron, Idalah, and Bethlehem—twelve towns with their surrounding villages.

[16]The homeland allocated to the clans of the tribe of Zebulun included these towns and their surrounding villages.

THE LAND GIVEN TO ISSACHAR

[17]The fourth allotment of land went to the clans of the tribe of Issachar.

[18]Its boundaries included the following towns: Jezreel, Kesulloth, Shunem, [19]Hapharaim, Shion, Anaharath, [20]Rabbith, Kishion, Ebez, [21]Remeth, En-gannim, En-haddah, and Beth-pazzez. [22]The boundary also touched Tabor, Shahazumah, and Beth-shemesh, ending at the Jordan River—sixteen towns with their surrounding villages.

[23]The homeland allocated to the clans of the tribe of Issachar included these towns and their surrounding villages.

THE LAND GIVEN TO ASHER

[24]The fifth allotment of land went to the clans of the tribe of Asher.

[25]Its boundaries included these towns: Helkath, Hali, Beten, Acshaph, [26]Allammelech, Amad, and Mishal. The boundary on the west touched Carmel and Shihor-libnath, [27]then it turned east toward Beth-dagon, and ran as far as Zebulun in the valley of Iphtah-el, going north to Beth-emek and Neiel. It

18:15a Or *From there it went to Mozah.* The meaning of the Hebrew is uncertain. **18:15b** Or *the spring at Me-nephtoah.* **18:18** Hebrew *overlooking the Arabah,* or *overlooking Beth-arabah.* **18:19** Hebrew *Salt Sea.* **18:28** As in Greek version; Hebrew reads *Kiriath.*

then continued north to Cabul, 28Abdon,* Rehob, Hammon, Kanah, and as far as Greater Sidon. 29Then the boundary turned toward Ramah and the fortress of Tyre, where it turned toward Hosah and came to the Mediterranean Sea.* The territory also included Mehebel, Aczib, 30Ummah, Aphek, and Rehob—twenty-two towns with their surrounding villages.

31The homeland allocated to the clans of the tribe of Asher included these towns and their surrounding villages.

THE LAND GIVEN TO NAPHTALI

32The sixth allotment of land went to the clans of the tribe of Naphtali.

33Its boundary ran from Heleph, from the oak at Zaanannim, and extended across to Adami-nekeb, Jabneel, and as far as Lakkum, ending at the Jordan River. 34The western boundary ran past Aznoth-tabor, then to Hukkok, and touched the border of Zebulun in the south, the border of Asher on the west, and the Jordan River* on the east. 35The fortified towns included in this territory were Ziddim, Zer, Hammath, Rakkath, Kinnereth, 36Adamah, Ramah, Hazor, 37Kedesh, Edrei, En-hazor, 38Yiron, Migdal-el, Horem, Beth-anath, and Beth-shemesh—nineteen towns with their surrounding villages.

39The homeland allocated to the clans of the tribe of Naphtali included these towns and their surrounding villages.

THE LAND GIVEN TO DAN

40The seventh allotment of land went to the clans of the tribe of Dan.

41The land allocated as their homeland included the following towns: Zorah, Eshtaol, Ir-shemesh, 42Shaalabbin, Aijalon, Ithlah, 43Elon, Timnah, Ekron, 44Eltekeh, Gibbethon, Baalath, 45Jehud, Bene-berak, Gath-rimmon, 46Me-jarkon, Rakkon, and the territory across from Joppa.

47But the tribe of Dan had trouble taking possession of their land,* so they attacked the town of Laish.* They captured it, slaughtered its people, and settled there. They renamed the town Dan after their ancestor.

48The homeland allocated to the clans of the tribe of Dan included these towns and their surrounding villages.

THE LAND GIVEN TO JOSHUA

49After all the land was divided among the tribes, the Israelites gave a piece of land to Joshua as his allocation. 50For the LORD had said he could have any town he wanted. He chose Timnath-serah in the hill country of Ephraim. He rebuilt the town and lived there.

51These are the territories that Eleazar the priest, Joshua son of Nun, and the tribal leaders allocated as grants of land to the tribes of Israel by casting sacred lots in the presence of the LORD at the entrance of the Tabernacle* at Shiloh. So the division of the land was completed.

WHEN THE GOING GETS TOUGH 19:47-48

When the tribe of Dan decided that some of their land looked too difficult to conquer, they headed to Laish where a victory would be easier. Can you relate to that decision? Anyone can trust God when the going is easy. Our faith and courage are put to the test when everything looks impossible. Do you believe that God is great enough to tackle your most difficult problem? ■

20 THE CITIES OF REFUGE

The LORD said to Joshua, 2"Now tell the Israelites to designate the cities of refuge, as I instructed Moses. 3Anyone who kills another person accidentally and unintentionally can run to one of these cities; they will be places of refuge from relatives seeking revenge for the person who was killed.

4"Upon reaching one of these cities, the one who caused the death will appear before the elders at the city gate and present his case. They must allow him to enter the city and give him a place to live among them. 5If the relatives of the victim come to avenge the killing, the leaders must not release the slayer to them, for he killed the other person unintentionally and without previous hostility. 6But the slayer must stay in that city and be tried by the local assembly, which will render a judgment. And he must continue to live in that city until the death of the high priest who was in office at the time of the accident. After that, he is free to return to his own home in the town from which he fled."

7The following cities were designated as cities of refuge: Kedesh of Galilee, in the hill country of Naphtali; Shechem, in the hill country of Ephraim; and Kiriath-arba (that is, Hebron), in the hill country of Judah. 8On the east side of the Jordan River, across from Jericho, the following cities were designated: Bezer, in the wilderness plain of the tribe of Reuben; Ramoth in Gilead, in the territory of the tribe of Gad; and Golan in Bashan, in the land of the tribe of Manasseh. 9These cities were set apart for all the Israelites as well as the foreigners living among them. Anyone who accidentally killed another person could take refuge in one of these cities. In this way, they could escape being killed in revenge prior to standing trial before the local assembly.

19:28 As in some Hebrew manuscripts (see also 21:30); most Hebrew manuscripts read *Ebron*. **19:29** Hebrew *the sea*. **19:34** Hebrew *and Judah at the Jordan River*. **19:47a** Or *had trouble holding onto their land*. **19:47b** Hebrew *Leshem*, a variant spelling of Laish. **19:51** Hebrew *Tent of Meeting*.

21 THE TOWNS GIVEN TO THE LEVITES

Then the leaders of the tribe of Levi came to consult with
Eleazar the priest, Joshua son of Nun, and the leaders of
the other tribes of Israel. 2They came to them at Shiloh in
the land of Canaan and said, "The LORD commanded
Moses to give us towns to live in and pasturelands for our
livestock." 3So by the command of the LORD the people of
Israel gave the Levites the following towns and pasturelands out of their own grants of land.

4The descendants of Aaron, who were members of the
Kohathite clan within the tribe of Levi, were allotted thir-
teen towns that were originally assigned to the tribes of
Judah, Simeon, and Benjamin. 5The other families of the
Kohathite clan were allotted ten towns from the tribes of
Ephraim, Dan, and the half-tribe of Manasseh.

6The clan of Gershon was allotted thirteen towns from
the tribes of Issachar, Asher, Naphtali, and the half-tribe
of Manasseh in Bashan.

7The clan of Merari was allotted twelve towns from the
tribes of Reuben, Gad, and Zebulun.

8So the Israelites obeyed the LORD's command to
Moses and assigned these towns and pasturelands to the
Levites by casting sacred lots.

9The Israelites gave the following towns from the
tribes of Judah and Simeon 10to the descendants of
Aaron, who were members of the Kohathite clan within
the tribe of Levi, since the sacred lot fell to them first:
11Kiriath-arba (that is, Hebron), in the hill country of Judah, along with its surrounding pasturelands. (Arba was
an ancestor of Anak.) 12But the open fields beyond the
town and the surrounding villages were given to Caleb
son of Jephunneh as his possession.

13The following towns with their pasturelands were
given to the descendants of Aaron the priest: Hebron (a
city of refuge for those who accidentally killed someone),
Libnah, 14Jattir, Eshtemoa, 15Holon, Debir, 16Ain, Juttah,
and Beth-shemesh—nine towns from these two tribes.

17From the tribe of Benjamin the priests were given the
following towns with their pasturelands: Gibeon, Geba,
18Anathoth, and Almon—four towns. 19So in all, thirteen
towns with their pasturelands were given to the priests,
the descendants of Aaron.

20The rest of the Kohathite clan from the tribe of Levi
was allotted the following towns and pasturelands from
the tribe of Ephraim: 21Shechem in the hill country of
Ephraim (a city of refuge for those who accidentally killed
someone), Gezer, 22Kibzaim, and Beth-horon—four towns.

23The following towns and pasturelands were allotted
to the priests from the tribe of Dan: Eltekeh, Gibbethon,
24Aijalon, and Gath-rimmon—four towns.

25The half-tribe of Manasseh allotted the following
towns with their pasturelands to the priests: Taanach and
Gath-rimmon—two towns. 26So in all, ten towns with their
pasturelands were given to the rest of the Kohathite clan.

27The descendants of Gershon, another clan within the
tribe of Levi, received the following towns with their
pasturelands from the half-tribe of Manasseh: Golan in
Bashan (a city of refuge for those who accidentally killed
someone) and Be-eshterah—two towns.

28From the tribe of Issachar they received the following towns with their pasturelands: Kishion, Daberath,
29Jarmuth, and En-gannim—four towns.

30From the tribe of Asher they received the following
towns with their pasturelands: Mishal, Abdon, 31Helkath,
and Rehob—four towns.

32From the tribe of Naphtali they received the following towns with their pasturelands: Kedesh in Galilee (a
city of refuge for those who accidentally killed someone),
Hammoth-dor, and Kartan—three towns. 33So in all, thirteen towns with their pasturelands were allotted to the
clan of Gershon.

34The rest of the Levites—the Merari clan—were given
the following towns with their pasturelands from the
tribe of Zebulun: Jokneam, Kartah, 35Dimnah, and Nahalal—four towns.

36From the tribe of Reuben they received the following
towns with their pasturelands: Bezer, Jahaz,* 37Kede-
moth, and Mephaath—four towns.

38From the tribe of Gad they received the following
towns with their pasturelands: Ramoth in Gilead (a city of
refuge for those who accidentally killed someone), Mahanaim, 39Heshbon, and Jazer—four towns. 40So in all,
twelve towns were allotted to the clan of Merari.

41The total number of towns and pasturelands within
Israelite territory given to the Levites came to forty-eight.
42Every one of these towns had pasturelands surrounding it.

43So the LORD gave to Israel all the land he had sworn to
give their ancestors, and they took possession of it and settled there. 44And the LORD gave them rest on every side, just
as he had solemnly promised their ancestors. None of their
enemies could stand against them, for the LORD helped
them conquer all their enemies. 45Not a single one of all the
good promises the LORD had given to the family of Israel
was left unfulfilled; everything he had spoken came true.

FINISH THE JOB 22:1-5

Before the conquest of Canaan had begun, the tribes of Reuben, Gad and the half-tribe of Manasseh were given land on the east side of the Jordan River. But before they could settle down, they had to help the other tribes to conquer the land on the west side (Num 32:20-24). After they had carried out their duties, they were permitted to return to their families and build their cities. Follow through is vital in God's work. How diligent are you to follow through on your promises? ■

22 THE EASTERN TRIBES RETURN HOME

Then Joshua called together the tribes of Reuben, Gad,
and the half-tribe of Manasseh. 2He told them, "You have
done as Moses, the servant of the LORD, commanded you,
and you have obeyed every order I have given you.

21:36 Hebrew *Jahzah*, a variant spelling of Jahaz.

3During all this time you have not deserted the other tribes. You have been careful to obey the commands of the LORD your God right up to the present day. 4And now the LORD your God has given the other tribes rest, as he promised them. So go back home to the land that Moses, the servant of the LORD, gave you as your possession on the east side of the Jordan River. 5But be very careful to obey all the commands and the instructions that Moses gave to you. Love the LORD your God, walk in all his ways, obey his commands, hold firmly to him, and serve him with all your heart and all your soul." 6So Joshua blessed them and sent them away, and they went home.

7Moses had given the land of Bashan, east of the Jordan River, to the half-tribe of Manasseh. (The other half of the tribe was given land west of the Jordan.) As Joshua sent them away and blessed them, 8he said to them, "Go back to your homes with the great wealth you have taken from your enemies—the vast herds of livestock, the silver, gold, bronze, and iron, and the large supply of clothing. Share the plunder with your relatives."

9So the men of Reuben, Gad, and the half-tribe of Manasseh left the rest of Israel at Shiloh in the land of Canaan. They started the journey back to their own land of Gilead, the territory that belonged to them according to the LORD's command through Moses.

THE EASTERN TRIBES BUILD AN ALTAR

10But while they were still in Canaan, and when they came to a place called Geliloth* near the Jordan River, the men of Reuben, Gad, and the half-tribe of Manasseh stopped to build a large and imposing altar.

REACTIONS 22:11-34

When the tribes of Reuben and Gad and the half-tribe of Manasseh built an altar at the Jordan River, the rest of Israel feared that these tribes were rebelling against God by worshiping idols. But before beginning an all-out war, a priest (Phinehas) led a delegation to learn the truth. We would benefit from a similar approach to resolving conflicts. Assuming the worst about the intentions of others only brings trouble. ■

11The rest of Israel heard that the people of Reuben, Gad, and the half-tribe of Manasseh had built an altar at Geliloth at the edge of the land of Canaan, on the west side of the Jordan River. 12So the whole community of Israel gathered at Shiloh and prepared to go to war against them. 13First, however, they sent a delegation led by Phinehas son of Eleazar, the priest, to talk with the tribes of Reuben, Gad, and the half-tribe of Manasseh. 14In this delegation were ten leaders of Israel, one from each of the ten tribes, and each the head of his family within the clans of Israel.

15When they arrived in the land of Gilead, they said to the tribes of Reuben, Gad, and the half-tribe of Manasseh, 16"The whole community of the LORD demands to know why you are betraying the God of Israel. How could you turn away from the LORD and build an altar for yourselves in rebellion against him? 17Was our sin at Peor not enough? To this day we are not fully cleansed of it, even after the plague that struck the entire community of the LORD. 18And yet today you are turning away from following the LORD. If you rebel against the LORD today, he will be angry with all of us tomorrow.

19"If you need the altar because the land you possess is defiled, then join us in the LORD's land, where the Tabernacle of the LORD is situated, and share our land with us. But do not rebel against the LORD or against us by building an altar other than the one true altar of the LORD our God. 20Didn't divine anger fall on the entire community of Israel when Achan, a member of the clan of Zerah, sinned by stealing the things set apart for the LORD*? He was not the only one who died because of his sin."

21Then the people of Reuben, Gad, and the half-tribe of Manasseh answered the heads of the clans of Israel: 22"The LORD, the Mighty One, is God! The LORD, the Mighty One, is God! He knows the truth, and may Israel know it, too! We have not built the altar in treacherous rebellion against the LORD. If we have done so, do not spare our lives this day. 23If we have built an altar for ourselves to turn away from the LORD or to offer burnt offerings or grain offerings or peace offerings, may the LORD himself punish us.

24"The truth is, we have built this altar because we fear that in the future your descendants will say to ours, 'What right do you have to worship the LORD, the God of Israel? 25The LORD has placed the Jordan River as a barrier between our people and you people of Reuben and Gad. You have no claim to the LORD.' So your descendants may prevent our descendants from worshiping the LORD.

26"So we decided to build the altar, not for burnt offerings or sacrifices, 27but as a memorial. It will remind our descendants and your descendants that we, too, have the right to worship the LORD at his sanctuary with our burnt offerings, sacrifices, and peace offerings. Then your descendants will not be able to say to ours, 'You have no claim to the LORD.'

28"If they say this, our descendants can reply, 'Look at this copy of the LORD's altar that our ancestors made. It is not for burnt offerings or sacrifices; it is a reminder of the relationship both of us have with the LORD.' 29Far be it from us to rebel against the LORD or turn away from him by building our own altar for burnt offerings, grain offerings, or sacrifices. Only the altar of the LORD our God that stands in front of the Tabernacle may be used for that purpose."

30When Phinehas the priest and the leaders of the community—the heads of the clans of Israel—heard this from the tribes of Reuben, Gad, and the half-tribe of Manasseh, they were satisfied. 31Phinehas son of Eleazar, the priest, replied to them, "Today we know the LORD is among us because you have not committed this treachery against the LORD as we thought. Instead, you have

22:10 Or *to the circle of stones;* similarly in 22:11. 22:20 The Hebrew term used here refers to the complete consecration of things or people to the LORD, either by destroying them or by giving them as an offering.

rescued Israel from being destroyed by the hand of the LORD."

[32]Then Phinehas son of Eleazar, the priest, and the other leaders left the tribes of Reuben and Gad in Gilead and returned to the land of Canaan to tell the Israelites what had happened. [33]And all the Israelites were satisfied and praised God and spoke no more of war against Reuben and Gad.

[34]The people of Reuben and Gad named the altar "Witness,"* for they said, "It is a witness between us and them that the LORD is our God, too."

CONSEQUENCES 23:12-16

This chilling prediction about the consequences of intermarriage with the Canaanite nations eventually became a reality. Numerous stories in the book of Judges show what Israel had to suffer because of their failure to follow God wholeheartedly. God was patient as usual with Israel, just as he is today with us. But his patience doesn't always mean that he approves of our plans. Tempted to demand your own way? Watch out! You may get your way—along with some painful consequences. ■

23

JOSHUA'S FINAL WORDS TO ISRAEL

The years passed, and the LORD had given the people of Israel rest from all their enemies. Joshua, who was now very old, [2]called together all the elders, leaders, judges, and officers of Israel. He said to them, "I am now a very old man. [3]You have seen everything the LORD your God has done for you during my lifetime. The LORD your God has fought for you against your enemies. [4]I have allotted to you as your homeland all the land of the nations yet unconquered, as well as the land of those we have already conquered—from the Jordan River to the Mediterranean Sea* in the west. [5]This land will be yours, for the LORD your God will himself drive out all the people living there now. You will take possession of their land, just as the LORD your God promised you.

[6]"So be very careful to follow everything Moses wrote in the Book of Instruction. Do not deviate from it, turning either to the right or to the left. [7]Make sure you do not associate with the other people still remaining in the land. Do not even mention the names of their gods, much less swear by them or serve them or worship them. [8]Rather, cling tightly to the LORD your God as you have done until now.

[9]"For the LORD has driven out great and powerful nations for you, and no one has yet been able to defeat you. [10]Each one of you will put to flight a thousand of the enemy, for the LORD your God fights for you, just as he has promised. [11]So be very careful to love the LORD your God.

[12]"But if you turn away from him and cling to the customs of the survivors of these nations remaining among you, and if you intermarry with them, [13]then know for certain that the LORD your God will no longer drive them out of your land. Instead, they will be a snare and a trap to you, a whip for your backs and thorny brambles in your eyes, and you will vanish from this good land the LORD your God has given you.

[14]"Soon I will die, going the way of everything on earth. Deep in your hearts you know that every promise of the LORD your God has come true. Not a single one has failed! [15]But as surely as the LORD your God has given you the good things he promised, he will also bring disaster on you if you disobey him. He will completely destroy you from this good land he has given you. [16]If you break the covenant of the LORD your God by worshiping and serving other gods, his anger will burn against you, and you will quickly vanish from the good land he has given you."

24

THE LORD'S COVENANT RENEWED

Then Joshua summoned all the tribes of Israel to Shechem, including their elders, leaders, judges, and officers. So they came and presented themselves to God.

[2]Joshua said to the people, "This is what the LORD, the God of Israel, says: Long ago your ancestors, including Terah, the father of Abraham and Nahor, lived beyond the Euphrates River,* and they worshiped other gods. [3]But I took your ancestor Abraham from the land beyond the Euphrates and led him into the land of Canaan. I gave him many descendants through his son Isaac. [4]To Isaac I gave Jacob and Esau. To Esau I gave the mountains of Seir, while Jacob and his children went down into Egypt.

IT'S YOUR CHOICE 24:15

The people had to decide whether they would obey the Lord, who had proven his trustworthiness, or obey the man-made idols of the people of Canaan. This is a decision each of us faces today. That includes you. Will you follow God's way or your own? The choice is yours. ■

[5]"Then I sent Moses and Aaron, and I brought terrible plagues on Egypt; and afterward I brought you out as a free people. [6]But when your ancestors arrived at the Red Sea,* the Egyptians chased after you with chariots and charioteers. [7]When your ancestors cried out to the LORD, I put darkness between you and the Egyptians. I brought the sea crashing down on the Egyptians, drowning them. With your very own eyes you saw what I did. Then you lived in the wilderness for many years.

[8]"Finally, I brought you into the land of the Amorites on the east side of the Jordan. They fought against you, but I destroyed them before you. I gave you victory over them, and you took possession of their land. [9]Then Balak son of Zippor, king of Moab, started a war against Israel.

22:34 Some manuscripts lack this word. **23:4** Hebrew *the Great Sea.* **24:2** Hebrew *the river;* also in 24:3, 14, 15. **24:6** Hebrew *sea of reeds.*

He summoned Balaam son of Beor to curse you, 10 but I would not listen to him. Instead, I made Balaam bless you, and so I rescued you from Balak.

11 "When you crossed the Jordan River and came to Jericho, the men of Jericho fought against you, as did the Amorites, the Perizzites, the Canaanites, the Hittites, the Girgashites, the Hivites, and the Jebusites. But I gave you victory over them. 12 And I sent terror* ahead of you to drive out the two kings of the Amorites. It was not your swords or bows that brought you victory. 13 I gave you land you had not worked on, and I gave you towns you did not build—the towns where you are now living. I gave you vineyards and olive groves for food, though you did not plant them.

14 "So fear the LORD and serve him wholeheartedly. Put away forever the idols your ancestors worshiped when they lived beyond the Euphrates River and in Egypt. Serve the LORD alone. 15 But if you refuse to serve the LORD, then choose today whom you will serve. Would you prefer the gods your ancestors served beyond the Euphrates? Or will it be the gods of the Amorites in whose land you now live? But as for me and my family, we will serve the LORD."

16 The people replied, "We would never abandon the LORD and serve other gods. 17 For the LORD our God is the one who rescued us and our ancestors from slavery in the land of Egypt. He performed mighty miracles before our very eyes. As we traveled through the wilderness among our enemies, he preserved us. 18 It was the LORD who drove out the Amorites and the other nations living here in the land. So we, too, will serve the LORD, for he alone is our God."

19 Then Joshua warned the people, "You are not able to serve the LORD, for he is a holy and jealous God. He will not forgive your rebellion and your sins. 20 If you abandon the LORD and serve other gods, he will turn against you and destroy you, even though he has been so good to you."

21 But the people answered Joshua, "No, we will serve the LORD!"

22 "You are a witness to your own decision," Joshua said. "You have chosen to serve the LORD."

"Yes," they replied, "we are witnesses to what we have said."

23 "All right then," Joshua said, "destroy the idols among you, and turn your hearts to the LORD, the God of Israel."

24 The people said to Joshua, "We will serve the LORD our God. We will obey him alone."

25 So Joshua made a covenant with the people that day at Shechem, committing them to follow the decrees and regulations of the LORD. 26 Joshua recorded these things in the Book of God's Instructions. As a reminder of their agreement, he took a huge stone and rolled it beneath the terebinth tree beside the Tabernacle of the LORD.

27 Joshua said to all the people, "This stone has heard everything the LORD said to us. It will be a witness to testify against you if you go back on your word to God."

28 Then Joshua sent all the people away to their own homelands.

LEADERS BURIED IN THE PROMISED LAND

29 After this, Joshua son of Nun, the servant of the LORD, died at the age of 110. 30 They buried him in the land he had been allocated, at Timnath-serah in the hill country of Ephraim, north of Mount Gaash.

31 The people of Israel served the LORD throughout the lifetime of Joshua and of the elders who outlived him—those who had personally experienced all that the LORD had done for Israel.

32 The bones of Joseph, which the Israelites had brought along with them when they left Egypt, were buried at Shechem, in the parcel of ground Jacob had bought from the sons of Hamor for 100 pieces of silver.* This land was located in the territory allotted to the descendants of Joseph.

33 Eleazar son of Aaron also died. He was buried in the hill country of Ephraim, in the town of Gibeah, which had been given to his son Phinehas.

24:12 Often rendered *the hornet*. The meaning of the Hebrew is uncertain. 24:32 Hebrew *100 kesitahs;* the value or weight of the kesitah is no longer known.

Why did Achan's whole family have to be killed just because Achan sinned? Does that seem fair?

Before we answer the above question, let's look at another. What happens if you wash a red shirt with a load of white clothes? The white clothes turn pink! Unless you happen to like the color pink, your clothes are ruined.

During the Old Testament, God operated under the principle that one person's wrongdoing affected everyone else. That wrongdoing was just a red shirt added to a load of white clothing—it colored everything else.

Since Achan was the head of his family, his guilt rubbed off on his family first, and the nation second (see Josh 7:11). This sin cost Israel a victory in battle and the lives of 36 soldiers. Because of the violation of God's command, Achan's whole family had to be put to death (see also Exod 19:13; Lev 24:16, 23). In that way, the guilt would be lifted off of the whole nation.

Centuries later, one man's death would pay the price of the wrongdoings of the whole world. In Jesus' case, it was like adding a white sock to a load of red laundry and turning that entire load white! As Isaiah 1:18 states, "Though your sins are like scarlet, I will make them white as snow. Though they are red like crimson, I will make them as white as wool." Because he never did anything wrong, Jesus' death wasn't exactly fair. But aren't you glad he was willing to die for you?

JUDGES

THINK ABOUT THE superheroes you've read about or seen recently. They always seem to arrive in the nick of time to defeat the bad guys and save the day. The world longs for superheroes. But superheroes like that don't exist. But that doesn't mean that the world lacks heroes. Think about that every time you pass a fire station.

The book of Judges is about heroes—twelve people known as the judges. Some didn't want the job. None were perfect. One was even a murderer! But God used them to rescue Israel from some pretty tough enemies.

The book of Judges is about the results of sin and about God's mercy. The people of Israel had become corrupt. Judges describes them this way: "In those days Israel had no king; all the people did whatever seemed right in their own eyes" (17:6). They intermarried with other nations and worshiped idols. Because of their actions God would allow a neighboring nation to conquer them. Then the people would call out to God and he would send a "judge" to rescue them. But the cycle continued.

Many of us can relate to such a cycle. We do our own thing, but when trouble comes, we turn to God. When life is good, we forget about God. The book of Judges is a reminder of how much we depend on God for mercy.

judges

timeline

1446 B.C.
Exodus from Egypt

1406
Israelites enter Canaan

1375
Period of the Judges begins

1367–1327
Othniel

1209–1169
Deborah

1162–1122
Gideon

1105
Samuel born

1075–1055
Samson

1050
Saul anointed

1010
David becomes king

stats

PURPOSE: To show that God's judgment against sin is certain, and his forgiveness of sin and restoration of fellowship is just as certain for those who call on him

AUTHOR: Probably Samuel

SETTING: The land of Canaan, later called Israel. God had helped the Israelites to conquer Canaan, which had been inhabited by a host of enemy nations. But the people of Israel were in danger of losing this Promised Land because they compromised their convictions and disobeyed God.

KEY PEOPLE: Othniel, Ehud, Deborah, Gideon, Abimelech, Jephthah, Samson, Delilah

SPECIAL FEATURE: Records Israel's first civil war

KEY points

DECLINE/COMPROMISE
The people of Israel faced decline and failure because they compromised their principles and began living like the people of other nations. Society offers many rewards to those who compromise their faith: wealth, acceptance, recognition, power, and influence. But God calls his people to a higher standard.

DECAY/REBELLION
Israel's compromising led them to rebel against God. We can expect things to fall apart when we choose to go our own way, rather than God's.

DEFEAT/OPPRESSION
God allowed the tough armies of other nations to torment the Israelites when they rebelled. God sometimes specializes in "tough love" when his people rebel.

REPENTANCE
Decline, decay, and defeat caused the people to cry out for help. They vowed to stop worshiping idols and obey God once more. In the same way, we must identify and renounce modern idols.

DELIVERANCE/HEROES
Because Israel repented, God helped ordinary people to do the extraordinary: deliver his people from their enemies. Anyone who is dedicated to God can be used for his service.

KEY PLACES IN JUDGES

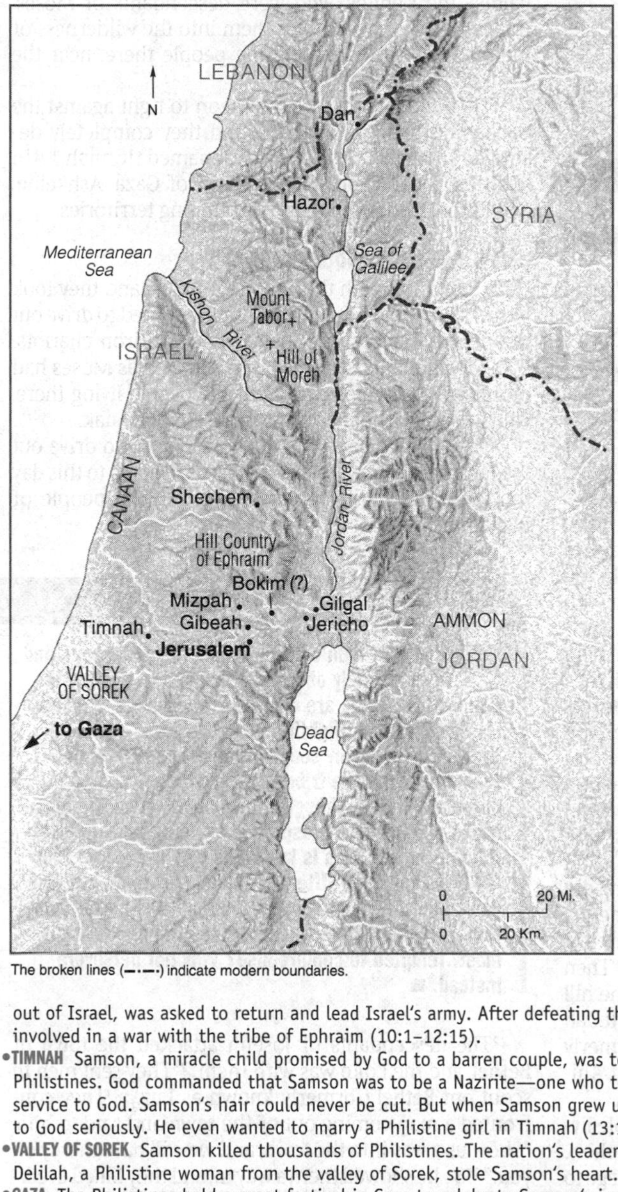

The broken lines (–·–) indicate modern boundaries.

- **BOKIM** The Angel of the Lord appeared at Bokim, informing the Israelites that their sin and disobedience had broken their agreement with God. Their punishment would be oppression (1:1–3:11).
- **JERICHO** King Eglon of Moab, one of Israel's first oppressors, conquered much of Israel—including Jericho. Ehud, who was supposed to deliver tax money to King Eglon, killed the Moabite king, escaped, then returned with an army that defeated the Moabites and freed Israel (3:12-31).
- **HAZOR** After Ehud's death, King Jabin of Hazor conquered Israel, oppressing them for 20 years. Then Deborah became Israel's leader (4:1–5:31).
- **HILL OF MOREH** After 40 years of peace, the Midianites began harassing the Israelites. God chose Gideon, a humble farmer, to be Israel's deliverer. Gideon attacked the Midianite army camped near the hill of Moreh and sent the enemy running away in confusion (6:1–7:25).
- **SHECHEM** From Gideon's relations with a concubine in Shechem came a son named Abimelech, who was treacherous and power hungry. Because he wanted to be king, he killed 69 of his 70 half brothers. Though men of Shechem rebelled against Abimelech, he gathered an army and defeated them. His lust for power led him to ransack two other cities. A woman finally killed him by dropping a millstone on his head (8:28–9:57).
- **LAND OF AMMON** Again Israel turned from God; so God turned from them. But when the Ammonite army got ready to attack, Israel threw away her idols and called upon God. Jephthah, a prostitute's son who had been run out of Israel, was asked to return and lead Israel's army. After defeating the Ammonites, Jephthah became involved in a war with the tribe of Ephraim (10:1–12:15).
- **TIMNAH** Samson, a miracle child promised by God to a barren couple, was to begin to free Israel from the Philistines. God commanded that Samson was to be a Nazirite—one who took a vow to be set apart for special service to God. Samson's hair could never be cut. But when Samson grew up, he did not take his responsibility to God seriously. He even wanted to marry a Philistine girl in Timnah (13:1–14:20).
- **VALLEY OF SOREK** Samson killed thousands of Philistines. The nation's leaders got their chance to stop him when Delilah, a Philistine woman from the valley of Sorek, stole Samson's heart. (15:1–16:20).
- **GAZA** The Philistines held a great festival in Gaza to celebrate Samson's imprisonment and to humiliate him before the crowds. When he was brought out as the entertainment, he pushed on the main pillars of the building, collapsing it and killing thousands of Philistines. The prophecy that he would begin to free Israel from the Philistines had come true (16:21-31).
- **HILL COUNTRY OF EPHRAIM** Here lived a man named Micah, who hired his own priest to perform priestly duties in the shrine that housed his collection of idols. Micah assumed that God's opinions of what was right would agree with his (17:1-13).
- **DAN** The tribe of Dan migrated north to find new territory. They sent warriors to scout out the land. They came upon the city of Laish and slaughtered the unarmed and innocent citizens, renaming the conquered city Dan (18:1-31).
- **GIBEAH** A man and his concubine stopped in Gibeah, thinking they would be safe. But some perverts gathered and demanded that the man have sex with them. Instead, the man and his host pushed the concubine out the door. She was raped and abused all night. When the man found her body the next morning, he cut it into 12 pieces and sent the parts to each tribe of Israel, demonstrating that the nation had sunk to its lowest spiritual level (19:1-30).
- **MIZPAH** The leaders of Israel came to Mizpah to decide how to punish Gibeah. But the city leaders refused to turn the criminals over, so Israel took vengeance upon the whole tribe of Benjamin. When the battle ended, the entire tribe had been destroyed except for a few men. Israel was now ready for spiritual renewal (20:1–21:25).

1

JUDGES AND SIMEON CONQUER THE LAND

After the death of Joshua, the Israelites asked the LORD,
"Which tribe should go first to attack the Canaanites?"
2The LORD answered, "Judah, for I have given them victory over the land."

A GREATER THREAT 1:1-33

Canaan—the Promised Land—was filled with many different people groups. They lived in city-states where each city had its own government, army, and laws. But Canaan's greatest threat to Israel was not its military, but its religion. Canaanite religion idealized evil traits: cruelty in war, sexual immorality, selfish greed, and materialism. It was a "me first, anything goes" society. Does that sound familiar? We face the same challenges these days. How will you stand up to these challenges? ■

3The men of Judah said to their relatives from the tribe
of Simeon, "Join with us to fight against the Canaanites
living in the territory allotted to us. Then we will help you
conquer your territory." So the men of Simeon went with
Judah.
4When the men of Judah attacked, the LORD gave them
victory over the Canaanites and Perizzites, and they
killed 10,000 enemy warriors at the town of Bezek.
5While at Bezek they encountered King Adoni-bezek and
fought against him, and the Canaanites and Perizzites
were defeated. 6Adoni-bezek escaped, but the Israelites
soon captured him and cut off his thumbs and big toes.
7Adoni-bezek said, "I once had seventy kings with
their thumbs and big toes cut off, eating scraps from
under my table. Now God has paid me back for what I did
to them." They took him to Jerusalem, and he died there.
8The men of Judah attacked Jerusalem and captured it,
killing all its people and setting the city on fire. 9Then
they went down to fight the Canaanites living in the hill
country, the Negev, and the western foothills.* 10Judah
marched against the Canaanites in Hebron (formerly
called Kiriath-arba), defeating the forces of Sheshai, Ahiman, and Talmai.
11From there they went to fight against the people living in the town of Debir (formerly called Kiriath-sepher).
12Caleb said, "I will give my daughter Acsah in marriage to
the one who attacks and captures Kiriath-sepher." 13Oth-
niel, the son of Caleb's younger brother, Kenaz, was the
one who conquered it, so Acsah became Othniel's wife.
14When Acsah married Othniel, she urged him* to ask
her father for a field. As she got down off her donkey, Caleb asked her, "What's the matter?"
15She said, "Let me have another gift. You have already
given me land in the Negev; now please give me springs
of water, too." So Caleb gave her the upper and lower
springs.
16When the tribe of Judah left Jericho—the city of
palms—the Kenites, who were descendants of Moses'
father-in-law, traveled with them into the wilderness of
Judah. They settled among the people there, near the
town of Arad in the Negev.
17Then Judah joined with Simeon to fight against the
Canaanites living in Zephath, and they completely destroyed* the town. So the town was named Hormah.* 18In
addition, Judah captured the towns of Gaza, Ashkelon,
and Ekron, along with their surrounding territories.

ISRAEL FAILS TO CONQUER THE LAND

19The LORD was with the people of Judah, and they took
possession of the hill country. But they failed to drive out
the people living in the plains, who had iron chariots.
20The town of Hebron was given to Caleb as Moses had
promised. And Caleb drove out the people living there,
who were descendants of the three sons of Anak.
21The tribe of Benjamin, however, failed to drive out
the Jebusites, who were living in Jerusalem. So to this day
the Jebusites live in Jerusalem among the people of
Benjamin.

PERSEVERE 1:19-36

Why didn't God's people follow through and completely obey his command to destroy the Canaanites? There are a number of possible reasons: (1) They had been fighting for a long time and were tired. (2) The enemy seemed too strong. (3) Since Joshua's death, the tribes were no longer unified in purpose. (4) They thought they could handle the temptation and be more prosperous by doing business with the Canaanites. This is known as compromising. Ever fall into that trap? Often we know what to do but just don't follow through. So, we gradually drift away from God. This is the time when we need to persevere the most. Tempted to compromise? Why not persevere instead. ■

22The descendants of Joseph attacked the town of
Bethel, and the LORD was with them. 23They sent men to
scout out Bethel (formerly known as Luz). 24They confronted a man coming out of the town and said to him,
"Show us a way into the town, and we will have mercy on
you." 25So he showed them a way in, and they killed everyone in the town except that man and his family. 26Later
the man moved to the land of the Hittites, where he built
a town. He named it Luz, which is its name to this day.
27The tribe of Manasseh failed to drive out the people
living in Beth-shan,* Taanach, Dor, Ibleam, Megiddo, and
all their surrounding settlements, because the Canaanites were determined to stay in that region. 28When the
Israelites grew stronger, they forced the Canaanites to
work as slaves, but they never did drive them completely
out of the land.

1:9 Hebrew *the Shephelah.* **1:14** Greek version and Latin Vulgate read *he urged her.* **1:17a** The Hebrew term used here refers to the complete consecration of things or people to the LORD, either by destroying them or by giving them as an offering. **1:17b** *Hormah* means "destruction." **1:27** Hebrew *Beth-shean,* a variant spelling of Beth-shan.

OTHER RELIGIONS

ULTIMATE ISSUES

If you've been paying attention as you've read so far, you have noticed that God takes a dim view (to put it mildly) of other religions that don't acknowledge him as the one true God. One of the Ten Commandments spoke against "other gods." And whenever the people of Israel encountered foreigners who worshiped idols, God instructed them to use harsh measures when dealing with them.

As you read passages like Joshua 10–12, where Joshua and the people of Israel conquered city after city, killing all of the inhabitants, you may wonder, "Why is God so intolerant? Why is he so rough on lifeless idols and the people who believe in them?"

Admittedly, such harsh measures seem strange to us, unaccustomed as we are to these cultures and their worship rituals. But God had good reason for wanting Israel to avoid these religions. First, some of these religions included child sacrificing in their worship ceremonies (see Deut 12:31)—a practice that disgusted God.

Second, God knew what prolonged contact with people who practiced these religions would do to his chosen people. It was like being exposed to a fatal virus. Because of God's concern for his people, he told them to eliminate the source of the disease as radically as a surgeon removing a malignant tumor. Though painful and costly, it was necessary for survival. If they failed to remove the cancer—as they often did—it would grow back and threaten to destroy them. Then it would be up to God to do the "surgery" himself, which he did in the form of persecution and exile. It was far better for Israel to do it right in the first place.

While some Christians struggle with the temptation to try other religions (Buddhism; Hinduism), many more struggle with worshiping "idols." Our "idols" today—money, sex, status, alcohol—don't look much like the idols the Israelites encountered. But they are just as real and just as dangerous as those others. Wouldn't you agree?

29The tribe of Ephraim failed to drive out the Canaanites living in Gezer, so the Canaanites continued to live
there among them.
30The tribe of Zebulun failed to drive out the residents
of Kitron and Nahalol, so the Canaanites continued to
live among them. But the Canaanites were forced to work
as slaves for the people of Zebulun.
31The tribe of Asher failed to drive out the residents of
Acco, Sidon, Ahlab, Aczib, Helbah, Aphik, and Rehob.
32Instead, the people of Asher moved in among the Canaanites, who controlled the land, for they failed to drive
them out.
33Likewise, the tribe of Naphtali failed to drive out the
residents of Beth-shemesh and Beth-anath. Instead, they
moved in among the Canaanites, who controlled the
land. Nevertheless, the people of Beth-shemesh and
Beth-anath were forced to work as slaves for the people
of Naphtali.
34As for the tribe of Dan, the Amorites forced them
back into the hill country and would not let them come
down into the plains. 35The Amorites were determined
to stay in Mount Heres, Aijalon, and Shaalbim, but when
the descendants of Joseph became stronger, they forced
the Amorites to work as slaves. 36The boundary of the
Amorites ran from Scorpion Pass* to Sela and continued
upward from there.

2 THE LORD'S MESSENGER COMES TO BOKIM

The angel of the Lord went up from Gilgal to Bokim and
said to the Israelites, "I brought you out of Egypt into this
land that I swore to give your ancestors, and I said I would
never break my covenant with you. 2For your part, you
were not to make any covenants with the people living in
this land; instead, you were to destroy their altars. But you
disobeyed my command. Why did you do this? 3So now I
declare that I will no longer drive out the people living in
your land. They will be thorns in your sides,* and their
gods will be a constant temptation to you."
4When the angel of the Lord finished speaking to all
the Israelites, the people wept loudly. 5So they called the
place Bokim (which means "weeping"), and they offered
sacrifices there to the Lord.

THE DEATH OF JOSHUA

6After Joshua sent the people away, each of the tribes left
to take possession of the land allotted to them. 7And the
Israelites served the Lord throughout the lifetime of

1:36 Hebrew *Akrabbim*. 2:3 Hebrew *They will be in your sides;* compare Num 33:55.

Joshua and the leaders who outlived him—those who had seen all the great things the LORD had done for Israel.

8Joshua son of Nun, the servant of the LORD, died at the age of 110. 9They buried him in the land he had been allocated, at Timnath-serah* in the hill country of Ephraim, north of Mount Gaash.

ISRAEL DISOBEYS THE LORD

10After that generation died, another generation grew up who did not acknowledge the LORD or remember the mighty things he had done for Israel.

> **PEER PRESSURE 2:11-15**
>
> **This generation of Israelites abandoned the faith of their parents and began worshiping the false gods of their neighbors. Many things can tempt us to abandon what we know is right. The desire to be accepted by others can lead us into behavior that is unacceptable to God. But God wants us to stand firm. When someone tries to pressure you into disobedience, what will you do? ■**

11The Israelites did evil in the LORD's sight and served the images of Baal. 12They abandoned the LORD, the God of their ancestors, who had brought them out of Egypt. They went after other gods, worshiping the gods of the people around them. And they angered the LORD. 13They abandoned the LORD to serve Baal and the images of Ashtoreth. 14This made the LORD burn with anger against Israel, so he handed them over to raiders who stole their possessions. He turned them over to their enemies all around, and they were no longer able to resist them. 15Every time Israel went out to battle, the LORD fought against them, causing them to be defeated, just as he had warned. And the people were in great distress.

> The LORD took pity on his people, who were burdened by oppression and suffering.
>
> *JUDGES 2:18*

THE LORD RESCUES HIS PEOPLE

16Then the LORD raised up judges to rescue the Israelites from their attackers. 17Yet Israel did not listen to the judges but prostituted themselves by worshiping other gods. How quickly they turned away from the path of their ancestors, who had walked in obedience to the LORD's commands.

18Whenever the LORD raised up a judge over Israel, he was with that judge and rescued the people from their enemies throughout the judge's lifetime. For the LORD took pity on his people, who were burdened by oppression and suffering. 19But when the judge died, the people returned to their corrupt ways, behaving worse than those who had lived before them. They went after other gods, serving and worshiping them. And they refused to give up their evil practices and stubborn ways.

20So the LORD burned with anger against Israel. He said, "Because these people have violated my covenant, which I made with their ancestors, and have ignored my commands, 21I will no longer drive out the nations that Joshua left unconquered when he died. 22I did this to test Israel—to see whether or not they would follow the ways of the LORD as their ancestors did." 23That is why the LORD left those nations in place. He did not quickly drive them out or allow Joshua to conquer them all.

3

THE NATIONS LEFT IN CANAAN

These are the nations that the LORD left in the land to test those Israelites who had not experienced the wars of Canaan. 2He did this to teach warfare to generations of Israelites who had no experience in battle. 3These are the nations: the Philistines (those living under the five Philistine rulers), all the Canaanites, the Sidonians, and the Hivites living in the mountains of Lebanon from Mount Baal-hermon to Lebo-hamath. 4These people were left to test the Israelites—to see whether they would obey the commands the LORD had given to their ancestors through Moses.

5So the people of Israel lived among the Canaanites, Hittites, Amorites, Perizzites, Hivites, and Jebusites, 6and they intermarried with them. Israelite sons married their daughters, and Israelite daughters were given in marriage to their sons. And the Israelites served their gods.

OTHNIEL BECOMES ISRAEL'S JUDGE

7The Israelites did evil in the LORD's sight. They forgot about the LORD their God, and they served the images of Baal and the Asherah poles. 8Then the LORD burned with anger against Israel, and he turned them over to King Cushan-rishathaim of Aram-naharaim.* And the Israelites served Cushan-rishathaim for eight years.

9But when the people of Israel cried out to the LORD for help, the LORD raised up a rescuer to save them. His name was Othniel, the son of Caleb's younger brother, Kenaz. 10The Spirit of the LORD came upon him, and he became Israel's judge. He went to war against King Cushan-rishathaim of Aram, and the LORD gave Othniel victory over him. 11So there was peace in the land for forty years. Then Othniel son of Kenaz died.

EHUD BECOMES ISRAEL'S JUDGE

12Once again the Israelites did evil in the LORD's sight, and the LORD gave King Eglon of Moab control over Israel because of their evil. 13Eglon enlisted the Ammonites and Amalekites as allies, and then he went out and defeated Israel, taking possession of Jericho, the city of palms. 14And the Israelites served Eglon of Moab for eighteen years.

15But when the people of Israel cried out to the LORD

2:9 As in parallel text at Josh 24:30; Hebrew reads *Timnath-heres,* a variant spelling of Timnath-serah. **3:8** *Aram-naharaim* means "Aram of the two rivers," thought to have been located between the Euphrates and Balih Rivers in northwestern Mesopotamia.

The Judges of Israel

OTHNIEL (40 YEARS)
He captured a powerful Canaanite city
Judges 3:7-11

EHUD (80 YEARS)
He killed Eglon and defeated the Moabites
Judges 3:12-30

SHAMGAR
He killed 600 Philistines with an ox goad
Judges 3:31

DEBORAH (40 YEARS)
She defeated General Sisera and the Canaanites and later sang a victory song with Barak
Judges 4–5

GIDEON (40 YEARS)
He used a fleece to determine God's will and defeated 135,000 Midianites with 300 men
Judges 6–8

TOLA (23 YEARS)
Judges 10:1-2

IBZAN (7 YEARS)
He had 30 sons and 30 daughters
Judges 12:8-10

JAIR (22 YEARS)
He had 30 sons
Judges 10:3-5

JEPHTHAH (6 YEARS)
He made a rash vow, defeated the Ammonites, and later battled Ephraim
Judges 10:6–12:7

SAMSON (20 YEARS)
He was betrayed by Delilah but destroyed thousands of Philistines
Judges 13–16

ELON (10 YEARS)
Judges 12:11-12

ABDON (8 YEARS)
He had 40 sons and 30 grandsons, each of whom had his own donkey
Judges 12:13-15

for help, the LORD again raised up a rescuer to save them. His name was Ehud son of Gera, a left-handed man of the tribe of Benjamin. The Israelites sent Ehud to deliver their tribute money to King Eglon of Moab.
16So Ehud made a double-edged dagger that was about a foot* long, and he strapped it to his right thigh, keeping it hidden under his clothing.
17He brought the tribute money to Eglon, who was very fat.
18After delivering the payment, Ehud started home with those who had helped carry the tribute.
19But when Ehud reached the stone idols near Gilgal, he turned back. He came to Eglon and said, "I have a secret message for you."

So the king commanded his servants, "Be quiet!" and he sent them all out of the room.
20Ehud walked over to Eglon, who was sitting alone in a cool upstairs room. And Ehud said, "I have a message from God for you!" As King Eglon rose from his seat,
21Ehud reached with his left hand, pulled out the dagger strapped to his right thigh, and plunged it into the king's belly.
22The dagger went so deep that the handle disappeared beneath the king's fat. So Ehud did not pull out the dagger, and the king's bowels emptied.*
23Then Ehud closed and locked the doors of the room and escaped down the latrine.*
24After Ehud was gone, the king's servants returned and found the doors to the upstairs room locked. They thought he might be using the latrine in the room,
25so they waited. But when the king didn't come out after a long delay, they became concerned and got a key. And when they opened the doors, they found their master dead on the floor.
26While the servants were waiting, Ehud escaped, passing the stone idols on his way to Seirah.
27When he arrived in the hill country of Ephraim, Ehud sounded a call to arms. Then he led a band of Israelites down from the hills.
28"Follow me," he said, "for the LORD has given you victory over Moab your enemy." So they followed him. And the Israelites took control of the shallow crossings of the Jordan River across from Moab, preventing anyone from crossing.
29They attacked the Moabites and killed about 10,000 of their strongest and most able-bodied warriors. Not one of them escaped.
30So Moab was conquered by Israel that day, and there was peace in the land for eighty years.

SHAMGAR BECOMES ISRAEL'S JUDGE

31After Ehud, Shamgar son of Anath rescued Israel. He once killed 600 Philistines with an ox goad.

4 DEBORAH BECOMES ISRAEL'S JUDGE

After Ehud's death, the Israelites again did evil in the LORD's sight.
2So the LORD turned them over to King Jabin

3:16 Hebrew *gomed,* the length of which is uncertain. 3:22 Or *and it came out behind.* 3:23 Or *and went out through the porch;* the meaning of the Hebrew is uncertain.

of Hazor, a Canaanite king. The commander of his army was Sisera, who lived in Harosheth-haggoyim. 3Sisera, who had 900 iron chariots, ruthlessly oppressed the Israelites for twenty years. Then the people of Israel cried out to the LORD for help.

HURTING GOD 4:1

Israel hurt themselves and God when they did wrong. Everything we do wrong ultimately is against God because it shows a disregard for his commands and his authority over our lives. As David prayed, "Against you, and you alone, have I sinned; I have done what is evil in your sight" (Ps 51:4). Need to make things right with God? There's no time like the present. ■

4Deborah, the wife of Lappidoth, was a prophet who was judging Israel at that time. 5She would sit under the Palm of Deborah, between Ramah and Bethel in the hill country of Ephraim, and the Israelites would go to her for judgment. 6One day she sent for Barak son of Abinoam, who lived in Kedesh in the land of Naphtali. She said to him, "This is what the LORD, the God of Israel, commands you: Call out 10,000 warriors from the tribes of Naphtali and Zebulun at Mount Tabor. 7And I will call out Sisera, commander of Jabin's army, along with his chariots and warriors, to the Kishon River. There I will give you victory over him."

8Barak told her, "I will go, but only if you go with me."

A TRUE LEADER 4:9

As a prophet and judge of Israel, Deborah guided the people on legal matters and told the soldiers when to go to battle. But more than that, she encouraged the people of Israel to live for God after the battle was over. Those who lead must not forget about the spiritual condition of those being led. A true leader is concerned for people, not just success. Does that describe you? ■

9"Very well," she replied, "I will go with you. But you will receive no honor in this venture, for the LORD's victory over Sisera will be at the hands of a woman." So Deborah went with Barak to Kedesh. 10At Kedesh, Barak called together the tribes of Zebulun and Naphtali, and 10,000 warriors went up with him. Deborah also went with him.

11Now Heber the Kenite, a descendant of Moses' brother-in-law* Hobab, had moved away from the other members of his tribe and pitched his tent by the oak of Zaanannim near Kedesh.

12When Sisera was told that Barak son of Abinoam had gone up to Mount Tabor, 13he called for all 900 of his iron chariots and all of his warriors, and they marched from Harosheth-haggoyim to the Kishon River.

14Then Deborah said to Barak, "Get ready! This is the day the LORD will give you victory over Sisera, for the LORD is marching ahead of you." So Barak led his 10,000 warriors down the slopes of Mount Tabor into battle. 15When Barak attacked, the LORD threw Sisera and all his chariots and warriors into a panic. Sisera leaped down from his chariot and escaped on foot. 16Then Barak chased the chariots and the enemy army all the way to Harosheth-haggoyim, killing all of Sisera's warriors. Not a single one was left alive.

17Meanwhile, Sisera ran to the tent of Jael, the wife of Heber the Kenite, because Heber's family was on friendly terms with King Jabin of Hazor. 18Jael went out to meet Sisera and said to him, "Come into my tent, sir. Come in. Don't be afraid." So he went into her tent, and she covered him with a blanket.

19"Please give me some water," he said. "I'm thirsty." So she gave him some milk from a leather bag and covered him again.

20"Stand at the door of the tent," he told her. "If anybody comes and asks you if there is anyone here, say no."

21But when Sisera fell asleep from exhaustion, Jael quietly crept up to him with a hammer and tent peg in her hand. Then she drove the tent peg through his temple and into the ground, and so he died.

22When Barak came looking for Sisera, Jael went out to meet him. She said, "Come, and I will show you the man you are looking for." So he followed her into the tent and found Sisera lying there dead, with the tent peg through his temple.

23So on that day Israel saw God defeat Jabin, the Canaanite king. 24And from that time on Israel became stronger and stronger against King Jabin until they finally destroyed him.

5 THE SONG OF DEBORAH

On that day Deborah and Barak son of Abinoam sang this song:

2 "Israel's leaders took charge,
and the people gladly followed.
Praise the LORD!

3 "Listen, you kings!
Pay attention, you mighty rulers!
For I will sing to the LORD.
I will make music to the LORD, the God of Israel.

4 "LORD, when you set out from Seir
and marched across the fields of Edom,
the earth trembled,
and the cloudy skies poured down rain.
5 The mountains quaked in the presence of the LORD,
the God of Mount Sinai—
in the presence of the LORD,
the God of Israel.

6 "In the days of Shamgar son of Anath,
and in the days of Jael,

4:11 Or *father-in-law*.

people avoided the main roads,
and travelers stayed on winding pathways.
7 There were few people left in the villages of Israel*—
until Deborah arose as a mother for Israel.
8 When Israel chose new gods,
war erupted at the city gates.
Yet not a shield or spear could be seen
among forty thousand warriors in Israel!
9 My heart is with the commanders of Israel,
with those who volunteered for war.
Praise the LORD!

10 "Consider this, you who ride on fine donkeys,
you who sit on fancy saddle blankets,
and you who walk along the road.
11 Listen to the village musicians*
gathered at the watering holes.
They recount the righteous victories of the LORD
and the victories of his villagers in Israel.
Then the people of the LORD
marched down to the city gates.

12 "Wake up, Deborah, wake up!
Wake up, wake up, and sing a song!
Arise, Barak!
Lead your captives away, son of Abinoam!

13 "Down from Tabor marched the few against the nobles.
The people of the LORD marched down against mighty warriors.
14 They came down from Ephraim—
a land that once belonged to the Amalekites;
they followed you, Benjamin, with your troops.
From Makir the commanders marched down;
from Zebulun came those who carry a commander's staff.
15 The princes of Issachar were with Deborah and Barak.
They followed Barak, rushing into the valley.
But in the tribe of Reuben
there was great indecision.
16 Why did you sit at home among the sheepfolds—
to hear the shepherds whistle for their flocks?
Yes, in the tribe of Reuben
there was great indecision.
17 Gilead remained east of the Jordan.
And why did Dan stay home?
Asher sat unmoved at the seashore,
remaining in his harbors.
18 But Zebulun risked his life,
as did Naphtali, on the heights of the battlefield.

19 "The kings of Canaan came and fought,
at Taanach near Megiddo's springs,
but they carried off no silver treasures.
20 The stars fought from heaven.
The stars in their orbits fought against Sisera.
21 The Kishon River swept them away—
that ancient torrent, the Kishon.
March on with courage, my soul!
22 Then the horses' hooves hammered the ground,
the galloping, galloping of Sisera's mighty steeds.
23 'Let the people of Meroz be cursed,' said the angel of the LORD.
'Let them be utterly cursed,
because they did not come to help the LORD—
to help the LORD against the mighty warriors.'

SONGS 5:1-31

After the defeat of Sisera and the army of Jabin, Barak and Deborah sang a praise song to God. Songs of praise focus our attention on God by reminding us of his character and actions. Whether you are in the middle of a great victory or a difficult problem, singing praises to God can have a positive effect on your attitude. ■

24 "Most blessed among women is Jael,
the wife of Heber the Kenite.
May she be blessed above all women who live in tents.
25 Sisera asked for water,
and she gave him milk.
In a bowl fit for nobles,
she brought him yogurt.
26 Then with her left hand she reached for a tent peg,
and with her right hand for the workman's hammer.
She struck Sisera with the hammer, crushing his head.
With a shattering blow, she pierced his temples.
27 He sank, he fell,
he lay still at her feet.
And where he sank,
there he died.

28 "From the window Sisera's mother looked out.
Through the window she watched for his return, saying,
'Why is his chariot so long in coming?
Why don't we hear the sound of chariot wheels?'

29 "Her wise women answer,
and she repeats these words to herself:
30 'They must be dividing the captured plunder—
with a woman or two for every man.
There will be colorful robes for Sisera,
and colorful, embroidered robes for me.
Yes, the plunder will include
colorful robes embroidered on both sides.'

31 "LORD, may all your enemies die like Sisera!
But may those who love you rise like the sun in all its power!"

Then there was peace in the land for forty years.

5:7 The meaning of the Hebrew is uncertain. 5:11 The meaning of the Hebrew is uncertain.

6 GIDEON BECOMES ISRAEL'S JUDGE

The Israelites did evil in the LORD's sight. So the LORD
handed them over to the Midianites for seven years. 2The
Midianites were so cruel that the Israelites made hiding
places for themselves in the mountains, caves, and
strongholds. 3Whenever the Israelites planted their
crops, marauders from Midian, Amalek, and the people
of the east would attack Israel, 4camping in the land and
destroying crops as far away as Gaza. They left the Israelites with nothing to eat, taking all the sheep, goats, cattle,
and donkeys. 5These enemy hordes, coming with their
livestock and tents, were as thick as locusts; they arrived
on droves of camels too numerous to count. And they
stayed until the land was stripped bare. 6So Israel was reduced to starvation by the Midianites. Then the Israelites
cried out to the LORD for help.

7When they cried out to the LORD because of Midian,
8the LORD sent a prophet to the Israelites. He said, "This is
what the LORD, the God of Israel, says: I brought you up out
of slavery in Egypt. 9I rescued you from the Egyptians and
from all who oppressed you. I drove out your enemies and
gave you their land. 10I told you, 'I am the LORD your God.
You must not worship the gods of the Amorites, in whose
land you now live.' But you have not listened to me."

11Then the angel of the LORD came and sat beneath the
great tree at Ophrah, which belonged to Joash of the clan
of Abiezer. Gideon son of Joash was threshing wheat at
the bottom of a winepress to hide the grain from the
Midianites. 12The angel of the LORD appeared to him and
said, "Mighty hero, the LORD is with you!"

13"Sir," Gideon replied, "if the LORD is with us, why has
all this happened to us? And where are all the miracles
our ancestors told us about? Didn't they say, 'The LORD
brought us up out of Egypt'? But now the LORD has abandoned us and handed us over to the Midianites."

14Then the LORD turned to him and said, "Go with the
strength you have, and rescue Israel from the Midianites.
I am sending you!"

15"But Lord," Gideon replied, "how can I rescue Israel?
My clan is the weakest in the whole tribe of Manasseh,
and I am the least in my entire family!"

16The LORD said to him, "I will be with you. And you
will destroy the Midianites as if you were fighting
against one man."

GIDEON

UPS:
- Israel's fifth judge
- A military strategist who was an expert at surprise
- A member of the Hall of Faith in Hebrews 11
- Led a victorious Israelite army against the Midianite army
- Was offered the title of king by the people of Israel
- Though slow to be convinced, acted on his convictions

DOWNS:
- Feared that his own limitations would prevent God from working
- Collected Midianite gold and made a symbol which became an object of worship
- Through a sexual relationship outside marriage, fathered a son who would bring great grief to both Gideon's family and the nation of Israel
- Failed to influence the nation in God's ways

STATS:
- Where: Ophrah, valley of Jezreel, well of Harod
- Occupation: Farmer, warrior, and judge
- Relatives: Joash (father); Abimelech (son)
- Contemporaries: King Zebah, King Zalmunna

BOTTOM LINE:

God expands and uses the abilities he has already built into us.

God uses us in spite of our limitations and failures.

Even those who make great spiritual progress can easily fall into sin if they don't consistently follow God.

Gideon's story is told in Judg 6–8. He also is mentioned in Heb 11:32-33.

GIDEON Most of us who call ourselves believers want to know God's plan for our lives; however, we're not always sure how to find it. It's easy to think that God's will for our lives is hidden and that we might miss it if we are not always on the lookout. But if we're always looking around for God's next assignment, we will probably not do a very good job on what he has us doing now.

Fortunately, the Bible gives us a better way to understand God's guidance. In the Bible's descriptions of how God guided people, we can see that God usually showed them what he wanted next while they were completely involved in obeying him right where they were. A good example of this kind of guidance is seen in Gideon's life.

Times were hard, thanks to the continual invasions of the Midianites. While Gideon tried his best to hide the little bit of wheat his family had left from the enemy, God's messenger showed up with an assignment. Gideon had been chosen to lead the Israelites against the Midianites. But Gideon had some questions that revealed his doubts. Was this really a task that God wanted him to do? Was he the right person for the job?

Sometimes we question God because we want to be sure what he requires of us. But sometimes we ask questions because we really don't want to obey. God was patient with Gideon's questions and doubts—he knew Gideon wanted to obey. Gideon made mistakes, but he was still God's servant. You can be sure that God will guide you as long as your desire is to serve and obey him wherever you are.

LAME EXCUSES 6:14-16

God chose Gideon to lead the Israelites in battle against their enemies. He also promised to give Gideon the strength he needed to overcome the opposition. Yet Gideon made excuses, seeing only his limitations and weaknesses. Like Gideon, we sometimes make excuses instead of serving God. Reminding God of our limitations only implies that he does not know all about us or that he has made a mistake in evaluating our character. Are you a Gideon—called to act on God's behalf? Instead of making excuses, what will you do instead? ■

17 Gideon replied, "If you are truly going to help me,
show me a sign to prove that it is really the LORD speaking
to me. 18 Don't go away until I come back and bring my
offering to you."
He answered, "I will stay here until you return."
19 Gideon hurried home. He cooked a young goat, and
with a basket* of flour he baked some bread without
yeast. Then, carrying the meat in a basket and the broth
in a pot, he brought them out and presented them to the
angel, who was under the great tree.
20 The angel of God said to him, "Place the meat and the
unleavened bread on this rock, and pour the broth over
it." And Gideon did as he was told. 21 Then the angel of the
LORD touched the meat and bread with the tip of the staff
in his hand, and fire flamed up from the rock and consumed all he had brought. And the angel of the LORD
disappeared.
22 When Gideon realized that it was the angel of the
LORD, he cried out, "Oh, Sovereign LORD, I'm doomed! I
have seen the angel of the LORD face to face!"
23 "It is all right," the LORD replied. "Do not be afraid.
You will not die." 24 And Gideon built an altar to the LORD
there and named it Yahweh-Shalom (which means "the
LORD is peace"). The altar remains in Ophrah in the land
of the clan of Abiezer to this day.
25 That night the LORD said to Gideon, "Take the second
bull from your father's herd, the one that is seven years
old. Pull down your father's altar to Baal, and cut down
the Asherah pole standing beside it. 26 Then build an altar
to the LORD your God here on this hilltop sanctuary, laying the stones carefully. Sacrifice the bull as a burnt offering on the altar, using as fuel the wood of the Asherah
pole you cut down."
27 So Gideon took ten of his servants and did as the
LORD had commanded. But he did it at night because he
was afraid of the other members of his father's household and the people of the town.
28 Early the next morning, as the people of the town began to stir, someone discovered that the altar of Baal had
been broken down and that the Asherah pole beside it
had been cut down. In their place a new altar had been
built, and on it were the remains of the bull that had been
sacrificed. 29 The people said to each other, "Who did
this?" And after asking around and making a careful
search, they learned that it was Gideon, the son of Joash.
30 "Bring out your son," the men of the town demanded
of Joash. "He must die for destroying the altar of Baal and
for cutting down the Asherah pole."
31 But Joash shouted to the mob that confronted him,
"Why are you defending Baal? Will you argue his case?
Whoever pleads his case will be put to death by morning!
If Baal truly is a god, let him defend himself and destroy
the one who broke down his altar!" 32 From then on Gideon was called Jerub-baal, which means "Let Baal defend
himself," because he broke down Baal's altar.

GIDEON ASKS FOR A SIGN

33 Soon afterward the armies of Midian, Amalek, and the
people of the east formed an alliance against Israel and
crossed the Jordan, camping in the valley of Jezreel.
34 Then the Spirit of the LORD took possession of Gideon.
He blew a ram's horn as a call to arms, and the men of the
clan of Abiezer came to him. 35 He also sent messengers
throughout Manasseh, Asher, Zebulun, and Naphtali,
summoning their warriors, and all of them responded.

WAITING FOR PROOF 6:36-40

Was Gideon really testing God or was he simply asking God for more encouragement? In either case, though his motive was right (to obey God and defeat the enemy), his method was less than ideal. Instead of acting, he delayed his obedience because he wanted more proof. Can you relate? Like Gideon, fear sometimes makes us wait for more confirmation instead of taking action. Visible signs are unnecessary if they only confirm what we already know to be true. Do you know what God wants you to do? If so, are you acting or waiting? ■

36 Then Gideon said to God, "If you are truly going to
use me to rescue Israel as you promised, 37 prove it to me
in this way. I will put a wool fleece on the threshing floor
tonight. If the fleece is wet with dew in the morning but
the ground is dry, then I will know that you are going to
help me rescue Israel as you promised." 38 And that is just
what happened. When Gideon got up early the next
morning, he squeezed the fleece and wrung out a whole
bowlful of water.
39 Then Gideon said to God, "Please don't be angry with
me, but let me make one more request. Let me use the
fleece for one more test. This time let the fleece remain
dry while the ground around it is wet with dew." 40 So that
night God did as Gideon asked. The fleece was dry in the
morning, but the ground was covered with dew.

7

GIDEON DEFEATS THE MIDIANITES

So Jerub-baal (that is, Gideon) and his army got up early
and went as far as the spring of Harod. The armies of

6:19 Hebrew *an ephah* [20 quarts or 22 liters].

Midian were camped north of them in the valley near the hill of Moreh. 2The LORD said to Gideon, "You have too many warriors with you. If I let all of you fight the Midianites, the Israelites will boast to me that they saved themselves by their own strength. 3Therefore, tell the people, 'Whoever is timid or afraid may leave this mountain* and go home.'" So 22,000 of them went home, leaving only 10,000 who were willing to fight.

4But the LORD told Gideon, "There are still too many! Bring them down to the spring, and I will test them to determine who will go with you and who will not." 5When Gideon took his warriors down to the water, the LORD told him, "Divide the men into two groups. In one group put all those who cup water in their hands and lap it up with their tongues like dogs. In the other group put all those who kneel down and drink with their mouths in the stream." 6Only 300 of the men drank from their hands. All the others got down on their knees and drank with their mouths in the stream.

7The LORD told Gideon, "With these 300 men I will rescue you and give you victory over the Midianites. Send all the others home." 8So Gideon collected the provisions and rams' horns of the other warriors and sent them home. But he kept the 300 men with him.

The Midianite camp was in the valley just below Gideon. 9That night the LORD said, "Get up! Go down into the Midianite camp, for I have given you victory over them! 10But if you are afraid to attack, go down to the camp with your servant Purah. 11Listen to what the Midianites are saying, and you will be greatly encouraged. Then you will be eager to attack."

THANK GOD 7:15

Gideon stood just outside the enemy camp and thanked God. Rituals, motions, or loud praise would have announced his presence to the enemy, so Gideon's praise must have been a silent attitude of joy, worship, and praise to God. Similarly, we can thank God silently and constantly even in the middle of difficult situations. ■

So Gideon took Purah and went down to the edge of the enemy camp. 12The armies of Midian, Amalek, and the people of the east had settled in the valley like a swarm of locusts. Their camels were like grains of sand on the seashore—too many to count! 13Gideon crept up just as a man was telling his companion about a dream. The man said, "I had this dream, and in my dream a loaf of barley bread came tumbling down into the Midianite camp. It hit a tent, turned it over, and knocked it flat!"

14His companion answered, "Your dream can mean only one thing—God has given Gideon son of Joash, the Israelite, victory over Midian and all its allies!"

15When Gideon heard the dream and its interpretation, he bowed in worship before the LORD.* Then he returned to the Israelite camp and shouted, "Get up! For the LORD has given you victory over the Midianite hordes!" 16He divided the 300 men into three groups and gave each man a ram's horn and a clay jar with a torch in it.

17Then he said to them, "Keep your eyes on me. When I come to the edge of the camp, do just as I do. 18As soon as I and those with me blow the rams' horns, blow your horns, too, all around the entire camp, and shout, 'For the LORD and for Gideon!'"

19It was just after midnight,* after the changing of the guard, when Gideon and the 100 men with him reached the edge of the Midianite camp. Suddenly, they blew the rams' horns and broke their clay jars. 20Then all three groups blew their horns and broke their jars. They held the blazing torches in their left hands and the horns in their right hands, and they all shouted, "A sword for the LORD and for Gideon!"

21Each man stood at his position around the camp and watched as all the Midianites rushed around in a panic, shouting as they ran to escape. 22When the 300 Israelites blew their rams' horns, the LORD caused the warriors in the camp to fight against each other with their swords. Those who were not killed fled to places as far away as Beth-shittah near Zererah and to the border of Abel-meholah near Tabbath.

23Then Gideon sent for the warriors of Naphtali, Asher, and Manasseh, who joined in chasing the army of Midian. 24Gideon also sent messengers throughout the hill country of Ephraim, saying, "Come down to attack the Midianites. Cut them off at the shallow crossings of the Jordan River at Beth-barah."

So all the men of Ephraim did as they were told. 25They captured Oreb and Zeeb, the two Midianite commanders, killing Oreb at the rock of Oreb, and Zeeb at the winepress of Zeeb. And they continued to chase the Midianites. Afterward the Israelites brought the heads of Oreb and Zeeb to Gideon, who was by the Jordan River.

8

GIDEON KILLS ZEBAH AND ZALMUNNA

Then the people of Ephraim asked Gideon, "Why have you treated us this way? Why didn't you send for us when you first went out to fight the Midianites?" And they argued heatedly with Gideon.

2But Gideon replied, "What have I accomplished compared to you? Aren't even the leftover grapes of Ephraim's harvest better than the entire crop of my little clan of Abiezer? 3God gave you victory over Oreb and Zeeb, the commanders of the Midianite army. What have I accomplished compared to that?" When the men of Ephraim heard Gideon's answer, their anger subsided.

4Gideon then crossed the Jordan River with his 300 men, and though exhausted, they continued to chase the enemy. 5When they reached Succoth, Gideon asked the leaders of the town, "Please give my warriors some food. They are very tired. I am chasing Zebah and Zalmunna, the kings of Midian."

6But the officials of Succoth replied, "Catch Zebah and Zalmunna first, and then we will feed your army."

7:3 Hebrew *may leave Mount Gilead.* The identity of Mount Gilead is uncertain in this context. It is perhaps used here as another name for Mount Gilboa. 7:15 As in Greek version; Hebrew reads *he bowed.* 7:19 Hebrew *at the beginning of the second watch.*

[7]So Gideon said, "After the LORD gives me victory over Zebah and Zalmunna, I will return and tear your flesh with the thorns and briers from the wilderness."

[8]From there Gideon went up to Peniel* and again asked for food, but he got the same answer. [9]So he said to the people of Peniel, "After I return in victory, I will tear down this tower."

[10]By this time Zebah and Zalmunna were in Karkor with 15,000 warriors—all that remained of the allied armies of the east, for 120,000 had already been killed. [11]Gideon circled around by the caravan route east of Nobah and Jogbehah, taking the Midianite army by surprise. [12]Zebah and Zalmunna, the two Midianite kings, fled, but Gideon chased them down and captured all their warriors.

[13]After this, Gideon returned from the battle by way of Heres Pass. [14]There he captured a young man from Succoth and demanded that he write down the names of all the seventy-seven officials and elders in the town. [15]Gideon then returned to Succoth and said to the leaders, "Here are Zebah and Zalmunna. When we were here before, you taunted me, saying, 'Catch Zebah and Zalmunna first, and then we will feed your exhausted army.'" [16]Then Gideon took the elders of the town and taught them a lesson, punishing them with thorns and briers from the wilderness. [17]He also tore down the tower of Peniel and killed all the men in the town.

[18]Then Gideon asked Zebah and Zalmunna, "The men you killed at Tabor—what were they like?"

"Like you," they replied. "They all had the look of a king's son."

[19]"They were my brothers, the sons of my own mother!" Gideon exclaimed. "As surely as the LORD lives, I wouldn't kill you if you hadn't killed them."

[20]Turning to Jether, his oldest son, he said, "Kill them!" But Jether did not draw his sword, for he was only a boy and was afraid.

[21]Then Zebah and Zalmunna said to Gideon, "Be a man! Kill us yourself!" So Gideon killed them both and took the royal ornaments from the necks of their camels.

GIDEON'S SACRED EPHOD

[22]Then the Israelites said to Gideon, "Be our ruler! You and your son and your grandson will be our rulers, for you have rescued us from Midian."

[23]But Gideon replied, "I will not rule over you, nor will my son. The LORD will rule over you! [24]However, I do have one request—that each of you give me an earring from the plunder you collected from your fallen enemies." (The enemies, being Ishmaelites, all wore gold earrings.)

[25]"Gladly!" they replied. They spread out a cloak, and each one threw in a gold earring he had gathered from the plunder. [26]The weight of the gold earrings was forty-three pounds,* not including the royal ornaments and pendants, the purple clothing worn by the kings of Midian, or the chains around the necks of their camels.

[27]Gideon made a sacred ephod from the gold and put it in Ophrah, his hometown. But soon all the Israelites prostituted themselves by worshiping it, and it became a trap for Gideon and his family.

[28]That is the story of how the people of Israel defeated Midian, which never recovered. Throughout the rest of Gideon's lifetime—about forty years—there was peace in the land.

[29]Then Gideon* son of Joash returned home. [30]He had seventy sons born to him, for he had many wives. [31]He also had a concubine in Shechem, who gave birth to a son, whom he named Abimelech. [32]Gideon died when he was very old, and he was buried in the grave of his father, Joash, at Ophrah in the land of the clan of Abiezer.

STAY ALERT 8:31

The relationship between Gideon and his concubine produced a son who tore apart Gideon's family and caused tragedy for the nation. Gideon may have won a battle for the nation, but lost the war with his family. His story is a sad reminder of how temptation can creep in right after we have experienced a spiritual victory. That's why we need to stay alert and keep on praying when temptations come. ■

[33]As soon as Gideon died, the Israelites prostituted themselves by worshiping the images of Baal, making Baal-berith their god. [34]They forgot the LORD their God, who had rescued them from all their enemies surrounding them. [35]Nor did they show any loyalty to the family of Jerub-baal (that is, Gideon), despite all the good he had done for Israel.

9

ABIMELECH RULES OVER SHECHEM

One day Gideon's* son Abimelech went to Shechem to visit his uncles—his mother's brothers. He said to them and to the rest of his mother's family, [2]"Ask the leading citizens of Shechem whether they want to be ruled by all seventy of Gideon's sons or by one man. And remember that I am your own flesh and blood!"

[3]So Abimelech's uncles gave his message to all the citizens of Shechem on his behalf. And after listening to this proposal, the people of Shechem decided in favor of Abimelech because he was their relative. [4]They gave him seventy silver coins from the temple of Baal-berith, which he used to hire some reckless troublemakers who agreed to follow him. [5]He went to his father's home at Ophrah, and there, on one stone, they killed all seventy of his half brothers, the sons of Gideon.* But the youngest brother, Jotham, escaped and hid.

[6]Then all the leading citizens of Shechem and Beth-millo called a meeting under the oak beside the pillar* at Shechem and made Abimelech their king.

JOTHAM'S PARABLE

[7]When Jotham heard about this, he climbed to the top of Mount Gerizim and shouted,

8:8 Hebrew *Penuel*, a variant spelling of Peniel; also in 8:9, 17. **8:26** Hebrew *1,700 shekels* [19.4 kilograms]. **8:29** Hebrew *Jerub-baal;* see 6:32. **9:1** Hebrew *Jerub-baal's* (see 6:32); also in 9:2, 24. **9:5** Hebrew *Jerub-baal* (see 6:32); also in 9:16, 19, 28, 57. **9:6** The meaning of the Hebrew is uncertain.

"Listen to me, citizens of Shechem!
Listen to me if you want God to listen to you!
8 Once upon a time the trees decided to elect a king.
First they said to the olive tree,
'Be our king!'

PRIORITIES 9:7-21

Jotham told the story about the trees in order to help the people of Israel to set good priorities. He did not want them to appoint a leader of low character. As we serve in leadership positions, we also need to examine our motives. Do we just want praise, prestige, or power? In the parable, the thornbush chose to be a servant to the trees under its care. Is being a servant to others your first priority as a leader? ■

9 But the olive tree refused, saying,
'Should I quit producing the olive oil
that blesses both God and people,
just to wave back and forth over the trees?'
10 "Then they said to the fig tree,
'You be our king!'
11 But the fig tree also refused, saying,
'Should I quit producing my sweet fruit
just to wave back and forth over the trees?'
12 "Then they said to the grapevine,
'You be our king!'
13 But the grapevine also refused, saying,
'Should I quit producing the wine
that cheers both God and people,
just to wave back and forth over the trees?'

14 "Then all the trees finally turned to the thornbush
and said,
'Come, you be our king!'
15 And the thornbush replied to the trees,
'If you truly want to make me your king,
come and take shelter in my shade.
If not, let fire come out from me
and devour the cedars of Lebanon.'"

16Jotham continued, "Now make sure you have acted
honorably and in good faith by making Abimelech your
king, and that you have done right by Gideon and all of his
descendants. Have you treated him with the honor he deserves for all he accomplished? 17For he fought for you
and risked his life when he rescued you from the Midianites. 18But today you have revolted against my father and
his descendants, killing his seventy sons on one stone.
And you have chosen his slave woman's son, Abimelech,
to be your king just because he is your relative.
19"If you have acted honorably and in good faith toward Gideon and his descendants today, then may you
find joy in Abimelech, and may he find joy in you. 20But
if you have not acted in good faith, then may fire come
out from Abimelech and devour the leading citizens of
Shechem and Beth-millo; and may fire come out from
the citizens of Shechem and Beth-millo and devour
Abimelech!"
21Then Jotham escaped and lived in Beer because he
was afraid of his brother Abimelech.

SHECHEM REBELS AGAINST ABIMELECH

22After Abimelech had ruled over Israel for three years,
23God sent a spirit that stirred up trouble between Abimelech and the leading citizens of Shechem, and they revolted. 24God was punishing Abimelech for murdering
Gideon's seventy sons, and the citizens of Shechem for
supporting him in this treachery of murdering his brothers. 25The citizens of Shechem set an ambush for Abimelech on the hilltops and robbed everyone who passed that
way. But someone warned Abimelech about their plot.
26One day Gaal son of Ebed moved to Shechem with
his brothers and gained the confidence of the leading
citizens of Shechem. 27During the annual harvest festival
at Shechem, held in the temple of the local god, the wine
flowed freely, and everyone began cursing Abimelech.
28"Who is Abimelech?" Gaal shouted. "He's not a true son
of Shechem,* so why should we be his servants? He's
merely the son of Gideon, and this Zebul is merely his
deputy. Serve the true sons of Hamor, the founder of
Shechem. Why should we serve Abimelech? 29If I were in
charge here, I would get rid of Abimelech. I would say* to
him, 'Get some soldiers, and come out and fight!'"
30But when Zebul, the leader of the city, heard what
Gaal was saying, he was furious. 31He sent messengers to
Abimelech in Arumah,* telling him, "Gaal son of Ebed
and his brothers have come to live in Shechem, and now
they are inciting the city to rebel against you. 32Come by
night with an army and hide out in the fields. 33In the
morning, as soon as it is daylight, attack the city. When
Gaal and those who are with him come out against you,
you can do with them as you wish."
34So Abimelech and all his men went by night and split
into four groups, stationing themselves around Shechem. 35Gaal was standing at the city gates when Abimelech and his army came out of hiding. 36When Gaal saw
them, he said to Zebul, "Look, there are people coming
down from the hilltops!"
Zebul replied, "It's just the shadows on the hills that
look like men."
37But again Gaal said, "No, people are coming down
from the hills.* And another group is coming down the
road past the Diviners' Oak.*"
38Then Zebul turned on him and asked, "Now where is
that big mouth of yours? Wasn't it you that said, 'Who is
Abimelech, and why should we be his servants?' The men
you mocked are right outside the city! Go out and fight
them!"
39So Gaal led the leading citizens of Shechem into battle against Abimelech. 40But Abimelech chased him, and

9:28 Hebrew *Who is Shechem?* **9:29** As in Greek version; Hebrew reads *And he said.* **9:31** Or *in secret;* Hebrew reads *in Tormah;* compare 9:41. **9:37a** Or *the center of the land.* **9:37b** Hebrew *Elon-meonenim.*

many of Shechem's men were wounded and fell along the road as they retreated to the city gate. [41]Abimelech returned to Arumah, and Zebul drove Gaal and his brothers out of Shechem.

[42]The next day the people of Shechem went out into the fields to battle. When Abimelech heard about it, [43]he divided his men into three groups and set an ambush in the fields. When Abimelech saw the people coming out of the city, he and his men jumped up from their hiding places and attacked them. [44]Abimelech and his group stormed the city gate to keep the men of Shechem from getting back in, while Abimelech's other two groups cut them down in the fields. [45]The battle went on all day before Abimelech finally captured the city. He killed the people, leveled the city, and scattered salt all over the ground.

[46]When the leading citizens who lived in the tower of Shechem heard what had happened, they ran and hid in the temple of Baal-berith.* [47]Someone reported to Abimelech that the citizens had gathered in the temple, [48]so he led his forces to Mount Zalmon. He took an ax and chopped some branches from a tree, then put them on his shoulder. "Quick, do as I have done!" he told his men. [49]So each of them cut down some branches, following Abimelech's example. They piled the branches against the walls of the temple and set them on fire. So all the people who had lived in the tower of Shechem died—about 1,000 men and women.

[50]Then Abimelech attacked the town of Thebez and captured it. [51]But there was a strong tower inside the town, and all the men and women—the entire population—fled to it. They barricaded themselves in and climbed up to the roof of the tower. [52]Abimelech followed them to attack the tower. But as he prepared to set fire to the entrance, [53]a woman on the roof dropped a millstone that landed on Abimelech's head and crushed his skull.

[54]He quickly said to his young armor bearer, "Draw your sword and kill me! Don't let it be said that a woman killed Abimelech!" So the young man ran him through with his sword, and he died. [55]When Abimelech's men saw that he was dead, they disbanded and returned to their homes.

[56]In this way, God punished Abimelech for the evil he had done against his father by murdering his seventy brothers. [57]God also punished the men of Shechem for all their evil. So the curse of Jotham son of Gideon was fulfilled.

10

TOLA BECOMES ISRAEL'S JUDGE

After Abimelech died, Tola son of Puah, son of Dodo, was the next person to rescue Israel. He was from the tribe of Issachar but lived in the town of Shamir in the hill country of Ephraim. [2]He judged Israel for twenty-three years. When he died, he was buried in Shamir.

JAIR BECOMES ISRAEL'S JUDGE

[3]After Tola died, Jair from Gilead judged Israel for twenty-two years. [4]His thirty sons rode around on thirty donkeys, and they owned thirty towns in the land of Gilead, which are still called the Towns of Jair.* [5]When Jair died, he was buried in Kamon.

NOTEWORTHY 10:1-5

In five verses we read about two men who judged Israel for a total of 45 years. Yet all we know about them besides the length of their rules is that one had 30 sons who rode around on 30 donkeys. What are you doing for God that is worth noting? When your life is over, will people remember more than just what was in your bank account or the number of years you lived? Why or why not? ■

THE AMMONITES OPPRESS ISRAEL

[6]Again the Israelites did evil in the LORD's sight. They served the images of Baal and Ashtoreth, and the gods of Aram, Sidon, Moab, Ammon, and Philistia. They abandoned the LORD and no longer served him at all. [7]So the LORD burned with anger against Israel, and he turned them over to the Philistines and the Ammonites, [8]who began to oppress them that year. For eighteen years they oppressed all the Israelites east of the Jordan River in the land of the Amorites (that is, in Gilead). [9]The Ammonites also crossed to the west side of the Jordan and attacked Judah, Benjamin, and Ephraim.

The Israelites were in great distress. [10]Finally, they cried out to the LORD for help, saying, "We have sinned against you because we have abandoned you as our God and have served the images of Baal."

PUNISHMENT 10:7-10

God permitted enemy nations to oppress the Israelites because of their sin (2:1-3). Sometimes God allows problems and pressures to plague us when we decide to turn away from him. When problems arise, before you ask, "Why me?" ask, "Is God trying to say something to me through this?" ■

[11]The LORD replied, "Did I not rescue you from the Egyptians, the Amorites, the Ammonites, the Philistines, [12]the Sidonians, the Amalekites, and the Maonites? When they oppressed you, you cried out to me for help, and I rescued you. [13]Yet you have abandoned me and served other gods. So I will not rescue you anymore. [14]Go and cry out to the gods you have chosen! Let them rescue you in your hour of distress!"

[15]But the Israelites pleaded with the LORD and said, "We have sinned. Punish us as you see fit, only rescue us today from our enemies." [16]Then the Israelites put aside their foreign gods and served the LORD. And he was grieved by their misery.

[17]At that time the armies of Ammon had gathered for war and were camped in Gilead, and the people of Israel assembled and camped at Mizpah. [18]The leaders of Gilead said to each other, "Whoever attacks the Ammonites first will become ruler over all the people of Gilead."

9:46 Hebrew *El-berith*, another name for Baal-berith; compare 9:4. 10:4 Hebrew *Havvoth-jair*.

God Uses Common People

GOD USES ALL SORTS OF PEOPLE TO DO HIS WORK—PEOPLE LIKE YOU AND ME!

Person	*Known as*	*Task*	*Reference*
JACOB	A liar	To "father" the Israelite nation	Genesis 27
JOSEPH	A slave	To save his family	Genesis 39–47
MOSES	A shepherd in exile (and a murderer)	To lead Israel out of bondage into the Promised Land	Exodus 3
GIDEON	A farmer	To deliver Israel from Midian	Judges 6:11
JEPHTHAH	The son of a prostitute	To deliver Israel from the Ammonites	Judges 11:1
HANNAH	A housewife	To be the mother of Samuel	1 Samuel 1
DAVID	A shepherd boy and youngest of the family	To be Israel's greatest king	1 Samuel 16
EZRA	A scribe	To lead the return to Judah and to write some of the Bible	Ezra, Nehemiah
ESTHER	An orphan	To save her people from massacre	Esther
MARY	A peasant girl	To be the mother of Christ	Luke 1:27-38
MATTHEW	A tax collector	To be an apostle and Gospel writer	Matthew 9:9
LUKE	A Greek physician	To be a companion of Paul and a Gospel writer	Colossians 4:14
PETER	A fisherman	To be an apostle, a leader of the early church, and a writer of two New Testament letters	Matthew 4:18-20

11

JEPHTHAH BECOMES ISRAEL'S JUDGE

Now Jephthah of Gilead was a great warrior. He was the
son of Gilead, but his mother was a prostitute. 2Gilead's
wife also had several sons, and when these half brothers
grew up, they chased Jephthah off the land. "You will not
get any of our father's inheritance," they said, "for you are
the son of a prostitute." 3So Jephthah fled from his brothers and lived in the land of Tob. Soon he had a band of
worthless rebels following him.

4At about this time, the Ammonites began their war
against Israel. 5When the Ammonites attacked, the elders of Gilead sent for Jephthah in the land of Tob. The
elders said, 6"Come and be our commander! Help us fight
the Ammonites!"

7But Jephthah said to them, "Aren't you the ones who
hated me and drove me from my father's house? Why do
you come to me now when you're in trouble?"

8"Because we need you," the elders replied. "If you lead
us in battle against the Ammonites, we will make you
ruler over all the people of Gilead."

9Jephthah said to the elders, "Let me get this straight. If
I come with you and if the LORD gives me victory over the
Ammonites, will you really make me ruler over all the
people?"

10"The LORD is our witness," the elders replied. "We
promise to do whatever you say."

11So Jephthah went with the elders of Gilead, and the
people made him their ruler and commander of the
army. At Mizpah, in the presence of the LORD, Jephthah
repeated what he had said to the elders.

12Then Jephthah sent messengers to the king of Ammon, asking, "Why have you come out to fight against my
land?"

13The king of Ammon answered Jephthah's messengers, "When the Israelites came out of Egypt, they stole

my land from the Arnon River to the Jabbok River and all the way to the Jordan. Now then, give back the land peaceably."

REJECTION 11:1-29

Jephthah, an illegitimate son of Gilead, was chased out of the country by his half brothers. He suffered as a result of a decision made by others and not for any wrong he had done. Yet in spite of his brothers' rejection, God used him. When you're feeling rejected, blaming others and becoming discouraged might come naturally. Yet neither solves the problem. God, however, is able to make something good out of a bad situation. Are you willing to trust him? ■

[14]Jephthah sent this message back to the Ammonite king:

[15]"This is what Jephthah says: Israel did not steal any land from Moab or Ammon. [16]When the people of Israel arrived at Kadesh on their journey from Egypt after crossing the Red Sea,* [17]they sent messengers to the king of Edom asking for permission to pass through his land. But their request was denied. Then they asked the king of Moab for similar permission, but he wouldn't let them pass through either. So the people of Israel stayed in Kadesh.

[18]"Finally, they went around Edom and Moab through the wilderness. They traveled along Moab's eastern border and camped on the other side of the Arnon River. But they never once crossed the Arnon River into Moab, for the Arnon was the border of Moab.

[19]"Then Israel sent messengers to King Sihon of the Amorites, who ruled from Heshbon, asking for permission to cross through his land to get to their destination. [20]But King Sihon didn't trust Israel to pass through his land. Instead, he mobilized his army at Jahaz and attacked them. [21]But the LORD, the God of Israel, gave his people victory over King Sihon. So Israel took control of all the land of the Amorites, who lived in that region, [22]from the Arnon River to the Jabbok River, and from the eastern wilderness to the Jordan.

[23]"So you see, it was the LORD, the God of Israel, who took away the land from the Amorites and gave it to Israel. Why, then, should we give it back to you? [24]You keep whatever your god Chemosh gives you, and we will keep whatever the LORD our God gives us. [25]Are you any better than Balak son of Zippor, king of Moab? Did he try to make a case against Israel for disputed land? Did he go to war against them?

[26]"Israel has been living here for 300 years, inhabiting Heshbon and its surrounding settlements, all the way to Aroer and its settlements, and in all the towns along the Arnon River. Why have you made no effort to recover it before now? [27]Therefore, I have not sinned against you. Rather, you have wronged me by attacking me. Let the LORD, who is judge, decide today which of us is right—Israel or Ammon."

[28]But the king of Ammon paid no attention to Jephthah's message.

JEPHTHAH'S VOW

[29]At that time the Spirit of the LORD came upon Jephthah, and he went throughout the land of Gilead and Manasseh, including Mizpah in Gilead, and from there he led an army against the Ammonites. [30]And Jephthah made a vow to the LORD. He said, "If you give me victory over the Ammonites, [31]I will give to the LORD whatever comes out of my house to meet me when I return in triumph. I will sacrifice it as a burnt offering."

[32]So Jephthah led his army against the Ammonites, and the LORD gave him victory. [33]He crushed the Ammonites, devastating about twenty towns from Aroer to an area near Minnith and as far away as Abel-keramim. In this way Israel defeated the Ammonites.

A RASH PROMISE 11:30-40

Jephthah's rash vow brought him unspeakable grief. In the heat of emotion or personal turmoil it is easy to make foolish promises to God. These promises might sound very spiritual when we make them, but they often produce only guilt and frustration when we are forced to fulfill them. Making spiritual "deals" only brings disappointment. God does not want promises for the future, but obedience for today. ■

[34]When Jephthah returned home to Mizpah, his daughter came out to meet him, playing on a tambourine and dancing for joy. She was his one and only child; he had no other sons or daughters. [35]When he saw her, he tore his clothes in anguish. "Oh, my daughter!" he cried out. "You have completely destroyed me! You've brought disaster on me! For I have made a vow to the LORD, and I cannot take it back."

[36]And she said, "Father, if you have made a vow to the LORD, you must do to me what you have vowed, for the LORD has given you a great victory over your enemies, the Ammonites. [37]But first let me do this one thing: Let me go up and roam in the hills and weep with my friends for two months, because I will die a virgin."

[38]"You may go," Jephthah said. And he sent her away for two months. She and her friends went into the hills and wept because she would never have children. [39]When she returned home, her father kept the vow he had made, and she died a virgin.

So it has become a custom in Israel [40]for young Israelite women to go away for four days each year to lament the fate of Jephthah's daughter.

11:16 Hebrew *sea of reeds.*

12 EPHRAIM FIGHTS WITH JEPHTHAH

Then the people of Ephraim mobilized an army and crossed over the Jordan River to Zaphon. They sent this message to Jephthah: "Why didn't you call for us to help you fight against the Ammonites? We are going to burn down your house with you in it!"

2Jephthah replied, "I summoned you at the beginning of the dispute, but you refused to come! You failed to help us in our struggle against Ammon. 3So when I realized you weren't coming, I risked my life and went to battle without you, and the LORD gave me victory over the Ammonites. So why have you now come to fight me?"

4The people of Ephraim responded, "You men of Gilead are nothing more than fugitives from Ephraim and Manasseh." So Jephthah gathered all the men of Gilead and attacked the men of Ephraim and defeated them.

5Jephthah captured the shallow crossings of the Jordan River, and whenever a fugitive from Ephraim tried to go back across, the men of Gilead would challenge him. "Are you a member of the tribe of Ephraim?" they would ask. If the man said, "No, I'm not," 6they would tell him to say "Shibboleth." If he was from Ephraim, he would say "Sibboleth," because people from Ephraim cannot pronounce the word correctly. Then they would take him and kill him at the shallow crossings of the Jordan. In all, 42,000 Ephraimites were killed at that time.

7Jephthah judged Israel for six years. When he died, he was buried in one of the towns of Gilead.

IBZAN BECOMES ISRAEL'S JUDGE

8After Jephthah died, Ibzan from Bethlehem judged Israel. 9He had thirty sons and thirty daughters. He sent his daughters to marry men outside his clan, and he brought in thirty young women from outside his clan to marry his sons. Ibzan judged Israel for seven years. 10When he died, he was buried at Bethlehem.

ELON BECOMES ISRAEL'S JUDGE

11After Ibzan died, Elon from the tribe of Zebulun judged Israel for ten years. 12When he died, he was buried at Aijalon in Zebulun.

ABDON BECOMES ISRAEL'S JUDGE

13After Elon died, Abdon son of Hillel, from Pirathon, judged Israel. 14He had forty sons and thirty grandsons, who rode on seventy donkeys. He judged Israel for eight years. 15When he died, he was buried at Pirathon in Ephraim, in the hill country of the Amalekites.

13 THE BIRTH OF SAMSON

Again the Israelites did evil in the LORD's sight, so the LORD handed them over to the Philistines, who oppressed them for forty years.

2In those days a man named Manoah from the tribe of Dan lived in the town of Zorah. His wife was unable to become pregnant, and they had no children. 3The angel of the LORD appeared to Manoah's wife and said, "Even though you have been unable to have children, you will soon become pregnant and give birth to a son. 4So be careful; you must not drink wine or any other alcoholic drink nor eat any forbidden food.* 5You will become pregnant and give birth to a son, and his hair must never be cut. For he will be dedicated to God as a Nazirite from birth. He will begin to rescue Israel from the Philistines."

A JOB TO DO 13:5

Although Manoah's wife was told that her son would rescue the Israelites from Philistine oppression, that goal wasn't reached until David's day (2 Sam 8:1). Samson's part in subduing the Philistines was just the beginning, but it was important nonetheless. What task has God called you to do? Are you willing to be faithful in following God even if you don't see instant results? ■

6The woman ran and told her husband, "A man of God appeared to me! He looked like one of God's angels, terrifying to see. I didn't ask where he was from, and he didn't tell me his name. 7But he told me, 'You will become pregnant and give birth to a son. You must not drink wine or any other alcoholic drink nor eat any forbidden food. For your son will be dedicated to God as a Nazirite from the moment of his birth until the day of his death.'"

8Then Manoah prayed to the LORD, saying, "Lord, please let the man of God come back to us again and give us more instructions about this son who is to be born."

9God answered Manoah's prayer, and the angel of God appeared once again to his wife as she was sitting in the field. But her husband, Manoah, was not with her. 10So she quickly ran and told her husband, "The man who appeared to me the other day is here again!"

11Manoah ran back with his wife and asked, "Are you the man who spoke to my wife the other day?"

"Yes," he replied, "I am."

12So Manoah asked him, "When your words come true, what kind of rules should govern the boy's life and work?"

13The angel of the LORD replied, "Be sure your wife follows the instructions I gave her. 14She must not eat grapes or raisins, drink wine or any other alcoholic drink, or eat any forbidden food."

15Then Manoah said to the angel of the LORD, "Please stay here until we can prepare a young goat for you to eat."

16"I will stay," the angel of the LORD replied, "but I will not eat anything. However, you may prepare a burnt offering as a sacrifice to the LORD." (Manoah didn't realize it was the angel of the LORD.)

17Then Manoah asked the angel of the LORD, "What is your name? For when all this comes true, we want to honor you."

18"Why do you ask my name?" the angel of the LORD replied. "It is too wonderful for you to understand."

13:4 Hebrew *any unclean thing;* also in 13:7, 14.

19Then Manoah took a young goat and a grain offering
and offered it on a rock as a sacrifice to the LORD. And as
Manoah and his wife watched, the LORD did an amazing
thing. 20As the flames from the altar shot up toward the
sky, the angel of the LORD ascended in the fire. When
Manoah and his wife saw this, they fell with their faces to
the ground.

21The angel did not appear again to Manoah and his
wife. Manoah finally realized it was the angel of the LORD,
22and he said to his wife, "We will certainly die, for we
have seen God!"

23But his wife said, "If the LORD were going to kill us, he
wouldn't have accepted our burnt offering and grain offering. He wouldn't have appeared to us and told us this
wonderful thing and done these miracles."

24When her son was born, she named him Samson.
And the LORD blessed him as he grew up. 25And the Spirit
of the LORD began to stir him while he lived in Mahaneh-
dan, which is located between the towns of Zorah and
Eshtaol.

14 SAMSON'S RIDDLE

One day when Samson was in Timnah, one of the Philistine women caught his eye. 2When he returned home, he
told his father and mother, "A young Philistine woman in
Timnah caught my eye. I want to marry her. Get her for
me."

3His father and mother objected. "Isn't there even one
woman in our tribe or among all the Israelites you could
marry?" they asked. "Why must you go to the pagan Philistines to find a wife?"

But Samson told his father, "Get her for me! She looks
good to me." 4His father and mother didn't realize the
LORD was at work in this, creating an opportunity to work
against the Philistines, who ruled over Israel at that time.

5As Samson and his parents were going down to
Timnah, a young lion suddenly attacked Samson near the
vineyards of Timnah. 6At that moment the Spirit of the
LORD came powerfully upon him, and he ripped the lion's
jaws apart with his bare hands. He did it as easily as if it
were a young goat. But he didn't tell his father or mother
about it. 7When Samson arrived in Timnah, he talked
with the woman and was very pleased with her.

8Later, when he returned to Timnah for the wedding,
he turned off the path to look at the carcass of the lion.
And he found that a swarm of bees had made some
honey in the carcass. 9He scooped some of the honey into
his hands and ate it along the way. He also gave some to
his father and mother, and they ate it. But he didn't tell
them he had taken the honey from the carcass of the lion.

10As his father was making final arrangements for the

UPS:
- Dedicated to God from birth as a Nazirite
- Known for his feats of strength
- Listed in the Hall of Faith in Hebrews 11
- Began to free Israel from Philistine oppression

DOWNS:
- Violated his vow and God's laws on many occasions
- Was controlled by his hormones
- Confided in the wrong people
- Used his gifts and abilities unwisely

STATS:
- Where: Zorah, Timnah, Ashkelon, Gaza, valley of Sorek
- Occupation: Judge
- Relatives: Manoah (father)
- Contemporaries: Delilah, Samuel (who might have been born while Samson was a judge)

BOTTOM LINE:

Great strength in one area of life does not make up for weaknesses in other areas.

God's presence does not overwhelm a person's will.

God can use people of faith in spite of their mistakes.

Samson's story is told in Judg 13–16. He also is mentioned in Heb 11:32-33.

SAMSON If it hasn't already happened, sooner or later someone is going to talk to you about your potential. "Potential" is what you could realize if you keep developing an ability or some other goal set for your improvement. It is the plan God set in motion to make you the coolest *you* possible.

Samson had the potential to be a great servant of God. God planned to use him to lead the Israelites against their enemies the Philistines. To help him, God gave Samson incredible physical strength. Unfortunately, Samson became an example of what happens when a person doesn't live up to his or her potential.

Samson's life included many opportunities to help his people. But he wasted most of his chances and even wound up being made a fool of by a woman. Yet, in spite of his mistakes, God still worked with him. The last thing Samson did before he died was an act that started the work God had planned for him all along.

The New Testament does not mention Samson's failures or his great feats of strength. In Hebrews 11:32-33, he is simply called one who "by faith . . . received what God had promised." In the end, Samson recognized his dependence on God. God turned his failure into victory.

Want to reach your full potential? Why not start by putting your life in God's hands? If you've already done that, but feel that you've wasted too much of your potential, take heart. Samson's story teaches us that it is never too late to start over.

marriage, Samson threw a party at Timnah, as was the
custom for elite young men. 11When the bride's parents*
saw him, they selected thirty young men from the town to
be his companions.
12Samson said to them, "Let me tell you a riddle. If you
solve my riddle during these seven days of the celebration, I will give you thirty fine linen robes and thirty sets
of festive clothing. 13But if you can't solve it, then you
must give me thirty fine linen robes and thirty sets of festive clothing."

"All right," they agreed, "let's hear your riddle."
14So he said:

"Out of the one who eats came something to eat;
out of the strong came something sweet."

Three days later they were still trying to figure it out.
15On the fourth* day they said to Samson's wife, "Entice
your husband to explain the riddle for us, or we will burn
down your father's house with you in it. Did you invite us
to this party just to make us poor?"
16So Samson's wife came to him in tears and said, "You
don't love me; you hate me! You have given my people a
riddle, but you haven't told me the answer."

"I haven't even given the answer to my father or
mother," he replied. "Why should I tell you?" 17So she
cried whenever she was with him and kept it up for the
rest of the celebration. At last, on the seventh day he told
her the answer because she was tormenting him with her
nagging. Then she explained the riddle to the young men.
18So before sunset of the seventh day, the men of the
town came to Samson with their answer:

"What is sweeter than honey?
What is stronger than a lion?"

Samson replied, "If you hadn't plowed with my heifer,
you wouldn't have solved my riddle!"
19Then the Spirit of the LORD came powerfully upon
him. He went down to the town of Ashkelon, killed thirty
men, took their belongings, and gave their clothing to the
men who had solved his riddle. But Samson was furious
about what had happened, and he went back home to live
with his father and mother. 20So his wife was given in
marriage to the man who had been Samson's best man at
the wedding.

15 SAMSON'S VENGEANCE ON THE PHILISTINES

Later on, during the wheat harvest, Samson took a young
goat as a present to his wife. He said, "I'm going into my
wife's room to sleep with her," but her father wouldn't let
him in.
2"I truly thought you must hate her," her father explained, "so I gave her in marriage to your best man. But
look, her younger sister is even more beautiful than she
is. Marry her instead."
3Samson said, "This time I cannot be blamed for
everything I am going to do to you Philistines." 4Then he
went out and caught 300 foxes. He tied their tails together in pairs, and he fastened a torch to each pair of
tails. 5Then he lit the torches and let the foxes run
through the grain fields of the Philistines. He burned all
their grain to the ground, including the sheaves and the
uncut grain. He also destroyed their vineyards and olive
groves.

BOOMERANG 15:1-20

Samson's reply in 15:11 is one to which many of us can relate: "I only did to them what they did to me." Revenge is an uncontrollable monster. Each act of retaliation brings another. It is a boomerang that cannot be thrown without cost to the thrower. Feeling the urge to "throw" revenge at someone? The revenge cycle can be halted only by forgiveness. ■

6"Who did this?" the Philistines demanded.

"Samson," was the reply, "because his father-in-law
from Timnah gave Samson's wife to be married to his
best man." So the Philistines went and got the woman
and her father and burned them to death.
7"Because you did this," Samson vowed, "I won't rest
until I take my revenge on you!" 8So he attacked the Philistines with great fury and killed many of them. Then he
went to live in a cave in the rock of Etam.
9The Philistines retaliated by setting up camp in Judah
and spreading out near the town of Lehi. 10The men of Judah asked the Philistines, "Why are you attacking us?"

The Philistines replied, "We've come to capture Samson. We've come to pay him back for what he did to us."
11So 3,000 men of Judah went down to get Samson at
the cave in the rock of Etam. They said to Samson, "Don't
you realize the Philistines rule over us? What are you doing to us?"

But Samson replied, "I only did to them what they did
to me."
12But the men of Judah told him, "We have come to tie
you up and hand you over to the Philistines."

"All right," Samson said. "But promise that you won't
kill me yourselves."
13"We will only tie you up and hand you over to the Philistines," they replied. "We won't kill you." So they tied
him up with two new ropes and brought him up from the
rock.
14As Samson arrived at Lehi, the Philistines came
shouting in triumph. But the Spirit of the LORD came
powerfully upon Samson, and he snapped the ropes on
his arms as if they were burnt strands of flax, and they fell
from his wrists. 15Then he found the jawbone of a recently killed donkey. He picked it up and killed 1,000
Philistines with it. 16Then Samson said,

"With the jawbone of a donkey,
I've piled them in heaps!

14:11 Hebrew *they*. **14:15** As in Greek version; Hebrew reads *seventh*.

With the jawbone of a donkey,
I've killed a thousand men!"

17When he finished his boasting, he threw away the jawbone; and the place was named Jawbone Hill.*

EXHAUSTION 15:18

Samson was physically and emotionally exhausted. After a great personal victory, his attitude declined quickly into self-pity—"Must I now die of thirst?" Emotionally, we are most vulnerable after a great effort or when faced with real physical needs. That's why depression often follows great achievements. When you're feeling exhausted, let the message of Isaiah 40:31 renew your hope: "Those who trust in the LORD will find new strength." ■

18Samson was now very thirsty, and he cried out to the LORD, "You have accomplished this great victory by the strength of your servant. Must I now die of thirst and fall into the hands of these pagans?" 19So God caused water to gush out of a hollow in the ground at Lehi, and Samson was revived as he drank. Then he named that place "The Spring of the One Who Cried Out,"* and it is still in Lehi to this day.

20Samson judged Israel for twenty years during the period when the Philistines dominated the land.

16 SAMSON CARRIES AWAY GAZA'S GATES

One day Samson went to the Philistine town of Gaza and spent the night with a prostitute. 2Word soon spread* that Samson was there, so the men of Gaza gathered together and waited all night at the town gates. They kept quiet during the night, saying to themselves, "When the light of morning comes, we will kill him."

3But Samson stayed in bed only until midnight. Then he got up, took hold of the doors of the town gate, including the two posts, and lifted them up, bar and all. He put them on his shoulders and carried them all the way to the top of the hill across from Hebron.

SAMSON AND DELILAH

4Some time later Samson fell in love with a woman named Delilah, who lived in the valley of Sorek. 5The rulers of the Philistines went to her and said, "Entice Samson to tell you what makes him so strong and how he can be overpowered and tied up securely. Then each of us will give you 1,100 pieces* of silver."

6So Delilah said to Samson, "Please tell me what makes you so strong and what it would take to tie you up securely."

7Samson replied, "If I were tied up with seven new bowstrings that have not yet been dried, I would become as weak as anyone else."

8So the Philistine rulers brought Delilah seven new bowstrings, and she tied Samson up with them. 9She had hidden some men in one of the inner rooms of her house, and she cried out, "Samson! The Philistines have come to capture you!" But Samson snapped the bowstrings as a piece of string snaps when it is burned by a fire. So the secret of his strength was not discovered.

10Afterward Delilah said to him, "You've been making fun of me and telling me lies! Now please tell me how you can be tied up securely."

11Samson replied, "If I were tied up with brand-new ropes that had never been used, I would become as weak as anyone else."

12So Delilah took new ropes and tied him up with them. The men were hiding in the inner room as before, and again Delilah cried out, "Samson! The Philistines have come to capture you!" But again Samson snapped the ropes from his arms as if they were thread.

13Then Delilah said, "You've been making fun of me and telling me lies! Now tell me how you can be tied up securely."

Samson replied, "If you were to weave the seven braids of my hair into the fabric on your loom and tighten it with the loom shuttle, I would become as weak as anyone else."

So while he slept, Delilah wove the seven braids of his hair into the fabric. 14Then she tightened it with the loom shuttle.* Again she cried out, "Samson! The Philistines have come to capture you!" But Samson woke up, pulled back the loom shuttle, and yanked his hair away from the loom and the fabric.

A FOOL FOR LOVE 16:15

Samson allowed himself to be deceived by Delilah, because he didn't want to lose her. How can you avoid being deceived like this? (1) Use wisdom as you consider who to date. (The best way to gain wisdom is to ask God for it.) (2) Avoid compromising your principles. (3) Be patient. You'll soon discover your potential date's true colors. ■

15Then Delilah pouted, "How can you tell me, 'I love you,' when you don't share your secrets with me? You've made fun of me three times now, and you still haven't told me what makes you so strong!" 16She tormented him with her nagging day after day until he was sick to death of it.

17Finally, Samson shared his secret with her. "My hair has never been cut," he confessed, "for I was dedicated to God as a Nazirite from birth. If my head were shaved, my strength would leave me, and I would become as weak as anyone else."

18Delilah realized he had finally told her the truth, so she sent for the Philistine rulers. "Come back one more time," she said, "for he has finally told me his secret." So

15:17 Hebrew *Ramath-lehi.* **15:19** Hebrew *En-hakkore.* **16:2** As in Greek and Syriac versions and Latin Vulgate; Hebrew lacks *Word soon spread.* **16:5** Hebrew *1,100 shekels,* about 28 pounds or 12.5 kilograms in weight. **16:13-14** As in Greek version and Latin Vulgate; Hebrew lacks *I would become as weak as anyone else. / So while he slept, Delilah wove the seven braids of his hair into the fabric.* [14]*Then she tightened it with the loom shuttle.*

COMPROMISE

Becca and her boyfriend James seem to have everything going for them:

- **They trust Jesus as their Savior.**
- **They come from solid Christian homes.**
- **Friends constantly tease them by saying, "You guys are so good together. . . . You're just like an old married couple!"**
- **They are seniors at one of the best Christian schools in the country.**
- **They both have been accepted to one of the top Christian colleges in the country.**
- **They plan to marry after they finish college.**
- **They want to go to Guatemala as missionaries.**

Amazing, isn't it? The relationship seems perfect. Proud parents, teachers, and church leaders agree that Becca and James are all that and a bag of chips. Great things will happen for them.

Well, if the scenario seems almost too good to be true, it is. In just about two weeks, this perfect couple will see their dream world collapse right before their eyes.

See, Becca and James have let their physical relationship get out of hand. And now Becca is pregnant.

Check out Judges 16. How is Samson's story like Becca and James's story? What would you do to avoid following the same path?

the Philistine rulers returned with the money in their
hands. 19Delilah lulled Samson to sleep with his head in
her lap, and then she called in a man to shave off the
seven locks of his hair. In this way she began to bring him
down,* and his strength left him.
20Then she cried out, "Samson! The Philistines have
come to capture you!"
When he woke up, he thought, "I will do as before and
shake myself free." But he didn't realize the LORD had left
him.
21So the Philistines captured him and gouged out his
eyes. They took him to Gaza, where he was bound with
bronze chains and forced to grind grain in the prison.
22But before long, his hair began to grow back.

SAMSON'S FINAL VICTORY

23The Philistine rulers held a great festival, offering sacrifices and praising their god, Dagon. They said, "Our god
has given us victory over our enemy Samson!"
24When the people saw him, they praised their god,
saying, "Our god has delivered our enemy to us! The one
who killed so many of us is now in our power!"
25Half drunk by now, the people demanded, "Bring out
Samson so he can amuse us!" So he was brought from the
prison to amuse them, and they had him stand between
the pillars supporting the roof.
26Samson said to the young servant who was leading
him by the hand, "Place my hands against the pillars that
hold up the temple. I want to rest against them." 27Now
the temple was completely filled with people. All the Philistine rulers were there, and there were about 3,000
men and women on the roof who were watching as Samson amused them.
28Then Samson prayed to the LORD, "Sovereign LORD,
remember me again. O God, please strengthen me just
one more time. With one blow let me pay back the Philistines for the loss of my two eyes." 29Then Samson put his
hands on the two center pillars that held up the temple.
Pushing against them with both hands, 30he prayed, "Let
me die with the Philistines." And the temple crashed
down on the Philistine rulers and all the people. So he
killed more people when he died than he had during his
entire lifetime.
31Later his brothers and other relatives went down to
get his body. They took him back home and buried him
between Zorah and Eshtaol, where his father, Manoah,
was buried. Samson had judged Israel for twenty years.

SALVAGED 16:28-30

In spite of Samson's mistakes, God still answered his prayer and destroyed the Philistine temple and worshipers.

One of the effects of sin is that it keeps us from feeling like praying. But being good is not a prerequisite for prayer. Feeling distant from God lately? No matter how long you have been away from him, he's ready to hear from you and restore you to a right relationship. ■

17

MICAH'S IDOLS

There was a man named Micah, who lived in the hill
country of Ephraim. 2One day he said to his mother, "I
heard you place a curse on the person who stole 1,100
pieces* of silver from you. Well, I have the money. I was
the one who took it."
"The LORD bless you for admitting it," his mother replied. 3He returned the money to her, and she said, "I now
dedicate these silver coins to the LORD. In honor of my
son, I will have an image carved and an idol cast."
4So when he returned the money to his mother, she
took 200 silver coins and gave them to a silversmith, who
made them into an image and an idol. And these were
placed in Micah's house. 5Micah set up a shrine for the
idol, and he made a sacred ephod and some household
idols. Then he installed one of his sons as his personal
priest.
6In those days Israel had no king; all the people did
whatever seemed right in their own eyes.
7One day a young Levite, who had been living in Bethlehem in Judah, arrived in that area. 8He had left Bethlehem
in search of another place to live, and as he traveled, he

16:19 Or *she began to torment him.* Greek version reads *He began to grow weak.* **17:2** Hebrew *1,100 shekels,* about 28 pounds or 12.5 kilograms in weight.

came to the hill country of Ephraim. He happened to stop
at Micah's house as he was traveling through. 9"Where
are you from?" Micah asked him.

He replied, "I am a Levite from Bethlehem in Judah, and I am looking for a
place to live."

10"Stay here with me," Micah said,
"and you can be a father and priest to
me. I will give you ten pieces* of silver
a year, plus a change of clothes and
your food." 11The Levite agreed to this,
and the young man became like one of
Micah's sons.

12So Micah installed the Levite as his
personal priest, and he lived in Micah's
house. 13"I know the LORD will bless
me now," Micah said, "because I have a
Levite serving as my priest."

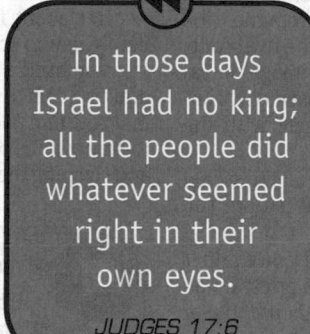

> In those days Israel had no king; all the people did whatever seemed right in their own eyes.
>
> JUDGES 17:6

18 IDOLATRY IN THE TRIBE OF DAN

Now in those days Israel had no king. And the tribe of
Dan was trying to find a place where they could settle, for
they had not yet moved into the land assigned to them
when the land was divided among the tribes of Israel. 2So
the men of Dan chose from their clans five capable warriors from the towns of Zorah and Eshtaol to scout out a
land for them to settle in.

When these warriors arrived in the hill country of
Ephraim, they came to Micah's house and spent the night
there. 3While at Micah's house, they recognized the
young Levite's accent, so they went over and asked him,
"Who brought you here, and what are you doing in this
place? Why are you here?" 4He told them about his agreement with Micah and that he had been hired as Micah's
personal priest.

5Then they said, "Ask God whether
or not our journey will be successful."

6"Go in peace," the priest replied.
"For the LORD is watching over your
journey."

7So the five men went on to the town
of Laish, where they noticed the people living carefree lives, like the Sidonians; they were peaceful and secure.*
The people were also wealthy because
their land was very fertile. And they
lived a great distance from Sidon and
had no allies nearby.

8When the men returned to Zorah
and Eshtaol, their relatives asked them,
"What did you find?"

9The men replied, "Come on, let's attack them! We
have seen the land, and it is very good. What are you waiting for? Don't hesitate to go and take possession of it.
10When you get there, you will find the people living carefree lives. God has given us a spacious and fertile land,
lacking in nothing!"

11So 600 men from the tribe of Dan, armed with weapons of war, set out from Zorah and Eshtaol. 12They
camped at a place west of Kiriath-jearim in Judah, which
is called Mahaneh-dan* to this day. 13Then they went on
from there into the hill country of Ephraim and came to
the house of Micah.

14The five men who had scouted out the land around
Laish explained to the others, "These buildings contain a

17:10 Hebrew *10 shekels*, about 4 ounces or 114 grams in weight. **18:7** The meaning of the Hebrew is uncertain. **18:12** *Mahaneh-dan* means "the camp of Dan."

UP:
- Persistent when faced with obstacles

DOWNS:
- Valued money more than relationships
- Betrayed the man who trusted her

STATS:
- Where: Valley of Sorek
- Contemporary: Samson

BOTTOM LINE:
We can either help or hinder people to reach their potential.

Delilah's story is told in Judg 16.

DELILAH What kind of reputation do you have? There are two very different ways to gain a reputation. One way is to help others do great things. Another is to keep others from doing great things. Delilah was only one person in Samson's life, but she almost completely ruined him. She persuaded him to go against what God wanted him to do. Because of what she thought she could get, Delilah used her persistence to wear Samson down. When others couldn't defeat his strength or even discover its source, Delilah used deception to gain that information.

Delilah is never mentioned again in the Bible. But she is frequently remembered as an example of someone who betrayed a friend. That earned her a permanent reputation of the worst kind.

Are people helped by knowing you? Does your friendship encourage them to be the best they can be? Even more important, does knowing you help their relationship with God?

DELILAH

sacred ephod, as well as some household idols, a carved image, and a cast idol. What do you think you should do?" 15Then the five men turned off the road and went over to Micah's house, where the young Levite lived, and greeted him kindly. 16As the 600 armed warriors from the tribe of Dan stood at the entrance of the gate, 17the five scouts entered the shrine and removed the carved image, the sacred ephod, the household idols, and the cast idol. Meanwhile, the priest was standing at the gate with the 600 armed warriors.

18When the priest saw the men carrying all the sacred objects out of Micah's shrine, he said, "What are you doing?"

19"Be quiet and come with us," they said. "Be a father and priest to all of us. Isn't it better to be a priest for an entire tribe and clan of Israel than for the household of just one man?"

20The young priest was quite happy to go with them, so he took along the sacred ephod, the household idols, and the carved image. 21They turned and started on their way again, placing their children, livestock, and possessions in front of them.

22When the people from the tribe of Dan were quite a distance from Micah's house, the people who lived near Micah came chasing after them. 23They were shouting as they caught up with them. The men of Dan turned around and said to Micah, "What's the matter? Why have you called these men together and chased after us like this?"

24"What do you mean, 'What's the matter?'" Micah replied. "You've taken away all the gods I have made, and my priest, and I have nothing left!"

25The men of Dan said, "Watch what you say! There are some short-tempered men around here who might get angry and kill you and your family." 26So the men of Dan continued on their way. When Micah saw that there were too many of them for him to attack, he turned around and went home.

27Then, with Micah's idols and his priest, the men of Dan came to the town of Laish, whose people were peaceful and secure. They attacked with swords and burned the town to the ground. 28There was no one to rescue the people, for they lived a great distance from Sidon and had no allies nearby. This happened in the valley near Beth-rehob.

Then the people of the tribe of Dan rebuilt the town and lived there. 29They renamed the town Dan after their ancestor, Israel's son, but it had originally been called Laish.

30Then they set up the carved image, and they appointed Jonathan son of Gershom, son of Moses,* as their priest. This family continued as priests for the tribe of Dan until the Exile. 31So Micah's carved image was worshiped by the tribe of Dan as long as the Tabernacle of God remained at Shiloh.

19 THE LEVITE AND HIS CONCUBINE

Now in those days Israel had no king. There was a man from the tribe of Levi living in a remote area of the hill country of Ephraim. One day he brought home a woman from Bethlehem in Judah to be his concubine. 2But she became angry with him* and returned to her father's home in Bethlehem.

After about four months, 3her husband set out for Bethlehem to speak personally to her and persuade her to come back. He took with him a servant and a pair of donkeys. When he arrived at* her father's house, her father saw him and welcomed him. 4Her father urged him to stay awhile, so he stayed three days, eating, drinking, and sleeping there.

CONCUBINES 19:1-26

While polygamy was an accepted practice in Israel, it was not what God intended (see Gen 2:24). A concubine or secondary wife had the duties, but not the privileges, of being a wife. Her primary purposes were to bear additional children and to contribute more help to the household or estate.

The man from Levi clearly thought more about himself than about his concubine. This awful story illustrates the fact that unthinkable sin can result when we choose to fulfill our own desires rather than following God's design. God's plan is for one husband and one wife to be committed to each other with a sacrificial, life-long love. Is that the kind of love you desire? ■

5On the fourth day the man was up early, ready to leave, but the woman's father said to his son-in-law, "Have something to eat before you go." 6So the two men sat down together and had something to eat and drink. Then the woman's father said, "Please stay another night and enjoy yourself." 7The man got up to leave, but his father-in-law kept urging him to stay, so he finally gave in and stayed the night.

8On the morning of the fifth day he was up early again, ready to leave, and again the woman's father said, "Have something to eat; then you can leave later this afternoon." So they had another day of feasting. 9Later, as the man and his concubine and servant were preparing to leave, his father-in-law said, "Look, it's almost evening. Stay the night and enjoy yourself. Tomorrow you can get up early and be on your way."

10But this time the man was determined to leave. So he took his two saddled donkeys and his concubine and headed in the direction of Jebus (that is, Jerusalem). 11It was late in the day when they neared Jebus, and the man's servant said to him, "Let's stop at this Jebusite town and spend the night there."

12"No," his master said, "we can't stay in this foreign town where there are no Israelites. Instead, we will go on to Gibeah. 13Come on, let's try to get as far as Gibeah or Ramah, and we'll spend the night in one of those towns." 14So they went on. The sun was setting as they came to Gibeah, a town in the land of Benjamin, 15so they stopped

18:30 As in an ancient Hebrew tradition, some Greek manuscripts, and Latin Vulgate; Masoretic Text reads *son of Manasseh.* **19:2** Or *she was unfaithful to him.* **19:3** As in Greek version; Hebrew reads *When she brought him to.*

there to spend the night. They rested in the town square, but no one took them in for the night.

16That evening an old man came home from his work in the fields. He was from the hill country of Ephraim, but he was living in Gibeah, where the people were from the tribe of Benjamin. 17When he saw the travelers sitting in the town square, he asked them where they were from and where they were going.

GOVERNMENT 19:30

The horrible crime described in this chapter wasn't Israel's worst offense. Even worse was the nation's failure to establish a government based upon God's laws. As a result, laws were usually not enforced. Sexual perversion and lawlessness were by-products of Israel's disobedience to God.

Whenever we drift away from God and his Word, all sorts of evil can follow. Our drifting away may be slow and almost imperceptible, but the effects can be long lasting. Want to know a sure cure for drifting? Return to God. ■

18"We have been in Bethlehem in Judah," the man replied. "We are on our way to a remote area in the hill country of Ephraim, which is my home. I traveled to Bethlehem, and now I'm returning home.* But no one has taken us in for the night, 19even though we have everything we need. We have straw and feed for our donkeys and plenty of bread and wine for ourselves."

20"You are welcome to stay with me," the old man said. "I will give you anything you might need. But whatever you do, don't spend the night in the square." 21So he took them home with him and fed the donkeys. After they washed their feet, they ate and drank together.

22While they were enjoying themselves, a crowd of troublemakers from the town surrounded the house. They began beating at the door and shouting to the old man, "Bring out the man who is staying with you so we can have sex with him."

23The old man stepped outside to talk to them. "No, my brothers, don't do such an evil thing. For this man is a guest in my house, and such a thing would be shameful. 24Here, take my virgin daughter and this man's concubine. I will bring them out to you, and you can abuse them and do whatever you like. But don't do such a shameful thing to this man."

25But they wouldn't listen to him. So the Levite took hold of his concubine and pushed her out the door. The men of the town abused her all night, taking turns raping her until morning. Finally, at dawn they let her go. 26At daybreak the woman returned to the house where her husband was staying. She collapsed at the door of the house and lay there until it was light.

27When her husband opened the door to leave, there lay his concubine with her hands on the threshold. 28He said, "Get up! Let's go!" But there was no answer.* So he put her body on his donkey and took her home.

29When he got home, he took a knife and cut his concubine's body into twelve pieces. Then he sent one piece to each tribe throughout all the territory of Israel.

30Everyone who saw it said, "Such a horrible crime has not been committed in all the time since Israel left Egypt. Think about it! What are we going to do? Who's going to speak up?"

20 ISRAEL'S WAR WITH BENJAMIN

Then all the Israelites were united as one man, from Dan in the north to Beersheba in the south, including those from across the Jordan in the land of Gilead. The entire community assembled in the presence of the LORD at Mizpah. 2The leaders of all the people and all the tribes of Israel—400,000 warriors armed with swords—took their positions in the assembly of the people of God. 3(Word soon reached the land of Benjamin that the other tribes had gone up to Mizpah.) The Israelites then asked how this terrible crime had happened.

4The Levite, the husband of the woman who had been murdered, said, "My concubine and I came to spend the night in Gibeah, a town that belongs to the people of Benjamin. 5That night some of the leading citizens of Gibeah surrounded the house, planning to kill me, and they raped my concubine until she was dead. 6So I cut her body into twelve pieces and sent the pieces throughout the territory assigned to Israel, for these men have committed a terrible and shameful crime. 7Now then, all of you—the entire community of Israel—must decide here and now what should be done about this!"

8And all the people rose to their feet in unison and declared, "None of us will return home! No, not even one of us! 9Instead, this is what we will do to Gibeah; we will draw lots to decide who will attack it. 10One tenth of the men* from each tribe will be chosen to supply the warriors with food, and the rest of us will take revenge on Gibeah* of Benjamin for this shameful thing they have done in Israel." 11So all the Israelites were completely united, and they gathered together to attack the town.

12The Israelites sent messengers to the tribe of Benjamin, saying, "What a terrible thing has been done among you! 13Give up those evil men, those troublemakers from Gibeah, so we can execute them and purge Israel of this evil."

But the people of Benjamin would not listen. 14Instead, they came from their towns and gathered at Gibeah to fight the Israelites. 15In all, 26,000 of their warriors armed with swords arrived in Gibeah to join the 700 elite troops who lived there. 16Among Benjamin's elite troops, 700 were left-handed, and each of them could sling a rock and hit a target within a hairsbreadth without missing. 17Israel had 400,000 experienced soldiers armed with swords, not counting Benjamin's warriors.

18Before the battle the Israelites went to Bethel and

19:18 As in Greek version (see also 19:29); Hebrew reads *now I'm going to the Tabernacle of the LORD.* **19:28** Greek version adds *for she was dead.* **20:10a** Hebrew *10 men from every hundred, 100 men from every thousand, and 1,000 men from every 10,000.* **20:10b** Hebrew *Geba,* in this case a variant spelling of Gibeah; also in 20:33.

asked God, "Which tribe should go first to attack the people of Benjamin?"
The LORD answered, "Judah is to go first."
19So the Israelites left early the next morning and
camped near Gibeah. 20Then they advanced toward Gibeah to attack the men of Benjamin. 21But Benjamin's warriors, who were defending the town, came out and killed
22,000 Israelites on the battlefield that day.
22But the Israelites encouraged each other and took
their positions again at the same place they had fought
the previous day. 23For they had gone up to Bethel and
wept in the presence of the LORD until evening. They had
asked the LORD, "Should we fight against our relatives
from Benjamin again?"
And the LORD had said, "Go out and fight against
them."
24So the next day they went out again to fight against
the men of Benjamin, 25but the men of Benjamin killed
another 18,000 Israelites, all of whom were experienced
with the sword.
26Then all the Israelites went up to Bethel and wept in
the presence of the LORD and fasted until evening. They
also brought burnt offerings and peace offerings to the
LORD. 27The Israelites went up seeking direction from the
LORD. (In those days the Ark of the Covenant of God was
in Bethel, 28and Phinehas son of Eleazar and grandson of
Aaron was the priest.) The Israelites asked the LORD,
"Should we fight against our relatives from Benjamin
again, or should we stop?"
The LORD said, "Go! Tomorrow I will hand them over to
you."
29So the Israelites set an ambush all around Gibeah.
30They went out on the third day and took their positions
at the same place as before. 31When the men of Benjamin
came out to attack, they were drawn away from the town.
And as they had done before, they began to kill the Israelites. About thirty Israelites died in the open fields and
along the roads, one leading to Bethel and the other leading back to Gibeah.
32Then the warriors of Benjamin shouted, "We're defeating them as we did before!" But the Israelites had
planned in advance to run away so that the men of Benjamin would chase them along the roads and be drawn
away from the town.
33When the main group of Israelite warriors reached
Baal-tamar, they turned and took up their positions.
Meanwhile, the Israelites hiding in ambush to the west*
of Gibeah jumped up to fight. 34There were 10,000 elite
Israelite troops who advanced against Gibeah. The fighting was so heavy that Benjamin didn't realize the impending disaster. 35So the LORD helped Israel defeat
Benjamin, and that day the Israelites killed 25,100 of
Benjamin's warriors, all of whom were experienced
swordsmen. 36Then the men of Benjamin saw that they
were beaten.
The Israelites had retreated from Benjamin's warriors
in order to give those hiding in ambush more room to
maneuver against Gibeah. 37Then those who were hiding
rushed in from all sides and killed everyone in the town.
38They had arranged to send up a large cloud of smoke
from the town as a signal. 39When the Israelites saw the
smoke, they turned and attacked Benjamin's warriors.
By that time Benjamin's warriors had killed about
thirty Israelites, and they shouted, "We're defeating them
as we did in the first battle!" 40But when the warriors of
Benjamin looked behind them and saw the smoke rising
into the sky from every part of the town, 41the men of Israel turned and attacked. At this point the men of Benjamin became terrified, because they realized disaster was
close at hand. 42So they turned around and fled before
the Israelites toward the wilderness. But they couldn't
escape the battle, and the people who came out of the
nearby towns were also killed.* 43The Israelites surrounded the men of Benjamin and chased them relentlessly, finally overtaking them east of Gibeah.* 44That day
18,000 of Benjamin's strongest warriors died in battle.
45The survivors fled into the wilderness toward the rock
of Rimmon, but Israel killed 5,000 of them along the
road. They continued the chase until they had killed another 2,000 near Gidom.
46So that day the tribe of Benjamin lost 25,000 strong
warriors armed with swords, 47leaving only 600 men who
escaped to the rock of Rimmon, where they lived for four
months. 48And the Israelites returned and slaughtered
every living thing in all the towns—the people, the livestock, and everything they found. They also burned down
all the towns they came to.

QUICK ACTION 20:46-48

The effects of the horrible rape and murder should never have been felt outside of the community where the crime happened. The local people should have brought the criminals to justice and corrected the negligence that originally permitted this crime. Instead, the nation of Israel had a civil war over it. This war almost wiped out the fighting men of Benjamin. To prevent problems from turning into major conflicts, firm action must be taken quickly, wisely, and forcefully *before* the situation gets out of hand. ■

21

ISRAEL PROVIDES WIVES FOR BENJAMIN

The Israelites had vowed at Mizpah, "We will never give
our daughters in marriage to a man from the tribe of Benjamin." 2Now the people went to Bethel and sat in the
presence of God until evening, weeping loudly and bitterly. 3"O LORD, God of Israel," they cried out, "why has
this happened in Israel? Now one of our tribes is missing
from Israel!"
4Early the next morning the people built an altar and
presented their burnt offerings and peace offerings on
it. 5Then they said, "Who among the tribes of Israel did
not join us at Mizpah when we held our assembly in the

20:33 As in Greek and Syriac versions and Latin Vulgate; Hebrew reads *hiding in the open space.* **20:42** Or *battle, for the people from the nearby towns also came out and killed them.* **20:43** The meaning of the Hebrew is uncertain.

presence of the LORD?" At that time they had taken a solemn oath in the LORD's presence, vowing that anyone who refused to come would be put to death.

6The Israelites felt sorry for their brother Benjamin and said, "Today one of the tribes of Israel has been cut off. 7How can we find wives for the few who remain, since we have sworn by the LORD not to give them our daughters in marriage?"

8So they asked, "Who among the tribes of Israel did not join us at Mizpah when we assembled in the presence of the LORD?" And they discovered that no one from Jabesh-gilead had attended the assembly. 9For after they counted all the people, no one from Jabesh-gilead was present.

HEROES 21:25

During the time of the judges, the people of Israel experienced trouble because they acted on their own opinions of right and wrong. This produced horrendous results. Our world is similar. Many individuals and groups have made themselves the final authorities of what's right or wrong. But God calls his people to live by his rules. That is the act of a true hero.

To be truly heroic, we must go into battle each day in our home, school, church, and society to make God's kingdom a reality. Our weapons are the standards and truths we receive from God's Word. We will lose the battle if we gather the spoils of earthly treasures rather than seeking the treasures of heaven. ■

10So the assembly sent 12,000 of their best warriors to Jabesh-gilead with orders to kill everyone there, including women and children. 11"This is what you are to do," they said. "Completely destroy* all the males and every woman who is not a virgin." 12Among the residents of Jabesh-gilead they found 400 young virgins who had never slept with a man, and they brought them to the camp at Shiloh in the land of Canaan.

13The Israelite assembly sent a peace delegation to the remaining people of Benjamin who were living at the rock of Rimmon. 14Then the men of Benjamin returned to their homes, and the 400 women of Jabesh-gilead who had been spared were given to them as wives. But there were not enough women for all of them.

15The people felt sorry for Benjamin because the LORD had made this gap among the tribes of Israel. 16So the elders of the assembly asked, "How can we find wives for the few who remain, since the women of the tribe of Benjamin are dead? 17There must be heirs for the survivors so that an entire tribe of Israel is not wiped out. 18But we cannot give them our own daughters in marriage because we have sworn with a solemn oath that anyone who does this will fall under God's curse."

19Then they thought of the annual festival of the LORD held in Shiloh, south of Lebonah and north of Bethel, along the east side of the road that goes from Bethel to Shechem. 20They told the men of Benjamin who still needed wives, "Go and hide in the vineyards. 21When you see the young women of Shiloh come out for their dances, rush out from the vineyards, and each of you can take one of them home to the land of Benjamin to be your wife! 22And when their fathers and brothers come to us in protest, we will tell them, 'Please be sympathetic. Let them have your daughters, for we didn't find wives for all of them when we destroyed Jabesh-gilead. And you are not guilty of breaking the vow since you did not actually give your daughters to them in marriage.'"

23So the men of Benjamin did as they were told. Each man caught one of the women as she danced in the celebration and carried her off to be his wife. They returned to their own land, and they rebuilt their towns and lived in them.

24Then the people of Israel departed by tribes and families, and they returned to their own homes.

25In those days Israel had no king; all the people did whatever seemed right in their own eyes.

21:11 The Hebrew term used here refers to the complete consecration of things or people to the LORD, either by destroying them or by giving them as an offering.

RUTH

"MOM, THAT FOOD looks awful!" "Dad, you always make me take out the garbage." "She's the worst teacher ever!" "My allowance isn't enough." "I hate the way I look." Sound familiar? Everyone likes to complain. When things don't go exactly as we think they should, we are quick to let others know we feel cheated and angry.

In the book of Ruth, we find Naomi's complaints. She blamed God for the deaths of her husband and two sons. She even wanted to be known as Mara, a name that means "bitterness" (1:20).

But Naomi later learned that God wasn't to be blamed for her family members' deaths; instead, he was to be thanked for his kindness. His kindness was revealed through the love and loyalty of Ruth—one of Naomi's daughters-in-law.

We're like Naomi sometimes. If something in life is wrong, we conclude that it must be his fault. The book of Ruth reminds us strongly and clearly that this is not the case. God is not to be blamed for our problems, but praised for his goodness.

Read the book of Ruth—a story of relationships, rescue, and romance—and thank God for his goodness in your life.

ruth

stats

PURPOSE: To show how three people remained strong in character and true to God even when the people around them chose to be disobedient.

AUTHOR: Unknown. Some think it was Samuel, but internal evidence suggests that it was written after his death.

DATE WRITTEN: Sometime after the period of the judges (1375–1050 B.C.)

SETTING: A dark time in Israel's history when people lived to please themselves, not God (Judg. 17:6)

KEY PEOPLE: Ruth, Naomi, Boaz

KEY PLACES: Moab, Bethlehem

KEY points

FAITHFULNESS

Ruth's faithfulness to Naomi as a daughter-in-law and friend is a great example of love and loyalty. We can imitate God's faithfulness by being loyal and loving in our relationships.

KINDNESS

Ruth showed great kindness to Naomi and received kindness from Boaz, the redeemer of her family's inheritance. In a similar way, Christ showed his kindness by purchasing us to guarantee our eternal life.

INTEGRITY

Ruth showed integrity by being loyal to Naomi, by her clean break from her former land and customs, and by her hard work in the field. God's faithfulness and kindness can encourage us to live lives characterized by integrity.

PROTECTION

God protected Naomi and Ruth as they traveled to Bethlehem and while Ruth worked in the barley field. We can count on God's protection and mercy.

PROSPERITY/BLESSING

Ruth and Naomi came to Bethlehem as poor widows, but soon became prosperous through Ruth's marriage to Boaz. Yet the greatest blessing was not material; it was the quality of love and respect between Ruth, Boaz, and Naomi. Relationships that God makes possible for us are one of his most special blessings.

1

ELIMELECH MOVES HIS FAMILY TO MOAB

In the days when the judges ruled in Israel, a severe famine came upon the land. So a man from Bethlehem in Judah left his home and went to live in the country of Moab,
taking his wife and two sons with him. 2The man's name
was Elimelech, and his wife was Naomi. Their two sons
were Mahlon and Kilion. They were Ephrathites from
Bethlehem in the land of Judah. And when they reached
Moab, they settled there.
3Then Elimelech died, and Naomi was left with her two
sons. 4The two sons married Moabite women. One married a woman named Orpah, and the other a woman
named Ruth. But about ten years later, 5both Mahlon and
Kilion died. This left Naomi alone, without her two sons
or her husband.

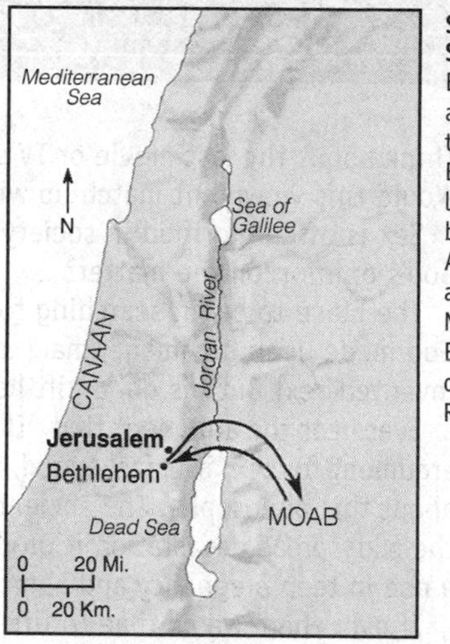

SETTING FOR THE STORY
Elimelech, Naomi, and their sons traveled from Bethlehem to the land of Moab because of a famine. After her husband and sons died, Naomi returned to Bethlehem with her daughter-in-law Ruth.

COMMITMENT

Aya and Kelsey have been friends ever since the third grade. Girl Scouts, softball, Sunday school—they've done it all together.

As they've grown older, however, the girls have developed vastly different interests. In fact, now, as teenagers, they couldn't be more opposite.

Aya is extremely outgoing, makes good grades and keeps everyone in the band in stitches. She's also very involved in the drama club. Kelsey is extremely shy. She's also an average student, dates quite a bit, and works at an expensive dress shop in the mall.

Since the two girls have such contrasting personalities, nobody can quite understand why they're still friends. But they are. They're best friends.

Just how close are they? Well, get this: Last week, Aya and Kelsey made Saturday plans to go shopping. The very next day, Kelsey got a call from the hottest guy at school (a guy she's secretly liked all year). The call went like this:

"Kelsey? Hi, this is Eric. Listen, I was just wondering if you'd like to go horseback riding this Saturday?"

"This weekend?" Kelsey paused. "Um, Eric, I'd really like to, but I've kinda made plans already. Can we do it some other time?"

Would you have been that loyal to a friend? Read about another woman who understood the meaning of commitment—Ruth 1:1-18. Like Ruth, how do you demonstrate loyalty to your friends?

NAOMI AND RUTH RETURN

6Then Naomi heard in Moab that the LORD had blessed
his people in Judah by giving them good crops again. So
Naomi and her daughters-in-law got ready to leave Moab
to return to her homeland. 7With her two daughters-in-
law she set out from the place where she had been living,
and they took the road that would lead them back to Judah.
8But on the way, Naomi said to her two daughters-in-
law, "Go back to your mothers' homes. And may the LORD
reward you for your kindness to your husbands and to
me. 9May the LORD bless you with the security of another
marriage." Then she kissed them good-bye, and they all
broke down and wept.
10"No," they said. "We want to go with you to your
people."
11But Naomi replied, "Why should you go on with me?
Can I still give birth to other sons who could grow up to
be your husbands? 12No, my daughters, return to your
parents' homes, for I am too old to marry again. And
even if it were possible, and I were to get married tonight and bear sons, then what? 13Would you wait for
them to grow up and refuse to marry someone else? No,
of course not, my daughters! Things are far more bitter
for me than for you, because the LORD himself has
raised his fist against me."
14And again they wept together, and Orpah kissed her
mother-in-law good-bye. But Ruth clung tightly to Naomi. 15"Look," Naomi said to her, "your sister-in-law has
gone back to her people and to her gods. You should do
the same."
16But Ruth replied, "Don't ask me to leave you and turn
back. Wherever you go, I will go; wherever you live, I will
live. Your people will be my people, and your God will be
my God. 17Wherever you die, I will die, and there I will be
buried. May the LORD punish me severely if I allow anything but death to separate us!" 18When Naomi saw that
Ruth was determined to go with her, she said nothing
more.
19So the two of them continued on their journey.
When they came to Bethlehem, the entire town was excited by their arrival. "Is it really Naomi?" the women
asked.
20"Don't call me Naomi," she responded. "Instead, call
me Mara,* for the Almighty has made life very bitter for
me. 21I went away full, but the LORD has brought me

1:20 *Naomi* means "pleasant"; *Mara* means "bitter."

ULTIMATE ISSUES

SEXUAL MORALITY

Think about the last movie or TV show you saw. What view of sexuality did it portray? Would this viewpoint match up with what's in the Bible? Probably not, right?

Sex is often glorified in society. For some, it is the end all and be all. But what is God's opinion on the matter?

The place to begin searching for answers is God's Word. Genesis 1:26-27 tells us that God made us in his image, male and female. God created us to be sexual beings. He invented sex! But his good gift has been cheapened and exploited in society.

Ever hear the argument that "If it feels good, do it"? Some single people use that argument for sex: if it feels good, they do it whenever they want. There's nothing new about this philosophy. The ancient Greeks called it *hedonism.* What *is* new, though, is the widespread devastation it produces in countless lives: sexually transmitted diseases; a rise in teen pregnancy and abortions; suicides as a result of broken relationships.

If ever there was a time to lift up the biblical standard of sexual morality, it's now. The Bible has some straightforward words about sexual behavior.

Hebrews 13:4 says, "Give honor to marriage, and remain faithful to one another in marriage. God will surely judge people who are immoral and those who commit adultery." (See also 1 Cor 6:13.) Since God made sex to be part of the bond between a husband and wife, sex outside of marriage is wrong.

Of course, this leaves a sizable gray area of what is and isn't acceptable in God's eyes. The issue isn't "How much can I do before I'm considered sinning?" If you want to please God, a better question to ask is "What would God have me do in my opposite-sex relationships? How can I best honor him and the other person?"

Navigating the waters of sexual morality can be challenging, but with the Bible, prayer, and other Christians' input as your compass, you can do it without crashing on the rocks of sexual sin.

home empty. Why call me Naomi when the LORD has
caused me to suffer* and the Almighty has sent such
tragedy upon me?"
22So Naomi returned from Moab,
accompanied by her daughter-in-law
Ruth, the young Moabite woman.
They arrived in Bethlehem in late
spring, at the beginning of the barley
harvest.

2 RUTH WORKS IN BOAZ'S FIELD

Now there was a wealthy and influential man in Bethlehem named Boaz,
who was a relative of Naomi's husband,
Elimelech.
2One day Ruth the Moabite said to
Naomi, "Let me go out into the harvest
fields to pick up the stalks of grain left
behind by anyone who is kind enough
to let me do it."
Naomi replied, "All right, my daughter, go ahead." 3So
Ruth went out to gather grain behind the harvesters. And
as it happened, she found herself working in a field that
belonged to Boaz, the relative of her father-in-law,
Elimelech.
4While she was there, Boaz arrived
from Bethlehem and greeted the harvesters. "The LORD be with you!" he
said.
"The LORD bless you!" the harvesters replied.
5Then Boaz asked his foreman,
"Who is that young woman over
there? Who does she belong to?"
6And the foreman replied, "She is
the young woman from Moab who
came back with Naomi. 7She asked
me this morning if she could gather
grain behind the harvesters. She has
been hard at work ever since, except
for a few minutes' rest in the shelter."
8Boaz went over and said to Ruth,
"Listen, my daughter. Stay right here
with us when you gather grain; don't
go to any other fields. Stay right behind the young
women working in my field. 9See which part of the field
they are harvesting, and then follow them. I have warned

> Wherever you go, I will go; wherever you live, I will live. Your people will be my people, and your God will be my God.
>
> RUTH 1:16

1:21 Or *has testified against me.*

the young men not to treat you roughly. And when you
are thirsty, help yourself to the water they have drawn
from the well."
10 Ruth fell at his feet and thanked him warmly. "What
have I done to deserve such kindness?" she asked. "I am
only a foreigner."
11 "Yes, I know," Boaz replied. "But I also know about
everything you have done for your mother-in-law since
the death of your husband. I have heard how you left your
father and mother and your own land to live here among
complete strangers. 12 May the LORD, the God of Israel,
under whose wings you have come to take refuge, reward
you fully for what you have done."
13 "I hope I continue to please you, sir," she replied.
"You have comforted me by speaking so kindly to me,
even though I am not one of your workers."
14 At mealtime Boaz called to her, "Come over here, and
help yourself to some food. You can dip your bread in the
sour wine." So she sat with his harvesters, and Boaz gave
her some roasted grain to eat. She ate all she wanted and
still had some left over.
15 When Ruth went back to work again, Boaz ordered
his young men, "Let her gather grain right among the
sheaves without stopping her. 16 And pull out some
heads of barley from the bundles and drop them on purpose for her. Let her pick them up, and don't give her a
hard time!"
17 So Ruth gathered barley there all day, and when she
beat out the grain that evening, it filled an entire basket.*
18 She carried it back into town and showed it to her
mother-in-law. Ruth also gave her the roasted grain that
was left over from her meal.
19 "Where did you gather all this grain today?" Naomi
asked. "Where did you work? May the LORD bless the one
who helped you!"
So Ruth told her mother-in-law about the man in
whose field she had worked. She said, "The man I worked
with today is named Boaz."
20 "May the LORD bless him!" Naomi told her daughter-
in-law. "He is showing his kindness to us as well as to your
dead husband.* That man is one of our closest relatives,
one of our family redeemers."
21 Then Ruth* said, "What's more, Boaz even told me to
come back and stay with his harvesters until the entire
harvest is completed."
22 "Good!" Naomi exclaimed. "Do as he said, my daughter. Stay with his young women right through the whole
harvest. You might be harassed in other fields, but you'll
be safe with him."
23 So Ruth worked alongside the women in Boaz's
fields and gathered grain with them until the end of the
barley harvest. Then she continued working with them
through the wheat harvest in early summer. And all the
while she lived with her mother-in-law.

2:17 Hebrew *it was about an ephah* [20 quarts or 22 liters]. 2:20 Hebrew *to the living and to the dead.* 2:21 Hebrew *Ruth the Moabite.*

RUTH & NAOMI

Who are your true friends? One of the greatest friendships described in the Bible was that of Ruth and Naomi. In fact, we know more about their friendship than we know about them as individuals.

Naomi and Ruth came from different cultures, families, and places. Naomi was older than Ruth. Ruth had been married to one of Naomi's sons. They had little but widowhood in common. Yet they forged a deep friendship.

Freedom was a key aspect of their friendship. Often in relationships people try to hold each other too tightly. Friendship can fade when there is no room to breathe. Naomi was willing to let Ruth return to her family. Ruth was willing to leave her homeland to go to Israel with Naomi. Naomi even helped arrange Ruth's marriage even though she knew their relationship would change because of it.

God was always part of Naomi and Ruth's friendship. Ruth met God through Naomi as the older woman allowed Ruth to see, hear, and feel all the joy and sorrow of her relationship with God. How much of your thoughts, feelings, and questions about God do you feel free to share with your best friends? God wants to be part of all of your friendships.

UPS:
- A relationship where the greatest bond was their faith in God
- A relationship of strong mutual commitment
- A relationship in which each person tried to do what was best for the other

STATS:
- Where: Moab, Bethlehem
- Occupation: Wives, widows, gleaners
- Relatives: Elimelech (Naomi's husband), Mahlon and Kilion (Naomi's sons), Orpah (Naomi's daughter-in-law and Ruth's sister-in-law), Boaz (Ruth's second husband)

BOTTOM LINE:
God's living presence in a relationship overcomes differences that might otherwise create division and disharmony.

Ruth and Naomi's story is told in the book of Ruth. Ruth also is mentioned in Matt 1:5.

3 RUTH AT THE THRESHING FLOOR

One day Naomi said to Ruth, "My daughter, it's time that I found a permanent home for you, so that you will be provided for. 2Boaz is a close relative of ours, and he's been very kind by letting you gather grain with his young women. Tonight he will be winnowing barley at the threshing floor. 3Now do as I tell you—take a bath and put on perfume and dress in your nicest clothes. Then go to the threshing floor, but don't let Boaz see you until he has finished eating and drinking. 4Be sure to notice where he lies down; then go and uncover his feet and lie down there. He will tell you what to do."

5"I will do everything you say," Ruth replied. 6So she went down to the threshing floor that night and followed the instructions of her mother-in-law.

GOOD ADVICE 3:5

As a foreigner, Ruth may have thought that Naomi's advice was odd. But Ruth followed the advice because she knew Naomi was kind and trustworthy. Each of us knows a parent, older friend, or relative who is always looking out for our best interests. The experience and knowledge of such a person can be invaluable. Who do you go to when you need good advice? ■

7After Boaz had finished eating and drinking and was in good spirits, he lay down at the far end of the pile of grain and went to sleep. Then Ruth came quietly, uncovered his feet, and lay down. 8Around midnight Boaz suddenly woke up and turned over. He was surprised to find a woman lying at his feet! 9"Who are you?" he asked.

"I am your servant Ruth," she replied. "Spread the corner of your covering over me, for you are my family redeemer."

10"The LORD bless you, my daughter!" Boaz exclaimed. "You are showing even more family loyalty now than you did before, for you have not gone after a younger man, whether rich or poor. 11Now don't worry about a thing, my daughter. I will do what is necessary, for everyone in town knows you are a virtuous woman. 12But while it's true that I am one of your family redeemers, there is another man who is more closely related to you than I am. 13Stay here tonight, and in the morning I will talk to him. If he is willing to redeem you, very well. Let him marry you. But if he is not willing, then as surely as the LORD lives, I will redeem you myself! Now lie down here until morning."

14So Ruth lay at Boaz's feet until the morning, but she got up before it was light enough for people to recognize each other. For Boaz had said, "No one must know that a woman was here at the threshing floor." 15Then Boaz said to her, "Bring your cloak and spread it out." He measured six scoops* of barley into the cloak and placed it on her back. Then he* returned to the town.

16When Ruth went back to her mother-in-law, Naomi asked, "What happened, my daughter?"

Ruth told Naomi everything Boaz had done for her, 17and she added, "He gave me these six scoops of barley and said, 'Don't go back to your mother-in-law empty-handed.'"

18Then Naomi said to her, "Just be patient, my daughter, until we hear what happens. The man won't rest until he has settled things today."

4 BOAZ MARRIES RUTH

Boaz went to the town gate and took a seat there. Just then the family redeemer he had mentioned came by, so Boaz called out to him, "Come over here and sit down, friend. I want to talk to you." So they sat down together. 2Then Boaz called ten leaders from the town and asked them to sit as witnesses. 3And Boaz said to the family redeemer, "You know Naomi, who came back from Moab. She is selling the land that belonged to our relative Elimelech. 4I thought I should speak to you about it so that you can redeem it if you wish. If you want the land, then buy it here in the presence of these witnesses. But if you don't want it, let me know right away, because I am next in line to redeem it after you."

The man replied, "All right, I'll redeem it."

5Then Boaz told him, "Of course, your purchase of the land from Naomi also requires that you marry Ruth, the Moabite widow. That way she can have children who will carry on her husband's name and keep the land in the family."

6"Then I can't redeem it," the family redeemer replied, "because this might endanger my own estate. You redeem the land; I cannot do it."

TOUGH TIMES 4:15

God brought great blessings out of Naomi's tragedy—even greater blessings than "seven sons" (indicating the great blessing of an abundance of heirs). Throughout her tough times, Naomi continued to trust God. And God, in his time, blessed her greatly. God can make something good happen even out of a hard situation. When hard times hit, will you trust God, instead of asking "How can God allow this to happen to me?" God will be with you even in the hard times. ■

7Now in those days it was the custom in Israel for anyone transferring a right of purchase to remove his sandal and hand it to the other party. This publicly validated the transaction. 8So the other family redeemer drew off his sandal as he said to Boaz, "You buy the land."

9Then Boaz said to the elders and to the crowd standing around, "You are witnesses that today I have bought from Naomi all the property of Elimelech, Kilion, and Mahlon. 10And with the land I have acquired Ruth, the

3:15a Hebrew *six measures,* an unknown quantity. **3:15b** Most Hebrew manuscripts read *he;* many Hebrew manuscripts, Syriac version, and Latin Vulgate read *she.*

Moabite widow of Mahlon, to be my wife. This way she can have a son to carry on the family name of her dead husband and to inherit the family property here in his hometown. You are all witnesses today."
11 Then the elders and all the people standing in the gate replied, "We are witnesses! May the LORD make this woman who is coming into your home like Rachel and Leah, from whom all the nation of Israel descended! May you prosper in Ephrathah and be famous in Bethlehem.
12 And may the LORD give you descendants by this young woman who will be like those of our ancestor Perez, the son of Tamar and Judah."

THE DESCENDANTS OF BOAZ

13 So Boaz took Ruth into his home, and she became his wife. When he slept with her, the LORD enabled her to become pregnant, and she gave birth to a son.
14 Then the women of the town said to Naomi, "Praise the LORD, who has now provided a redeemer for your family! May this child be famous in Israel.
15 May he restore your youth and care for you in your old age. For he is the son of your daughter-in-law who loves you and has been better to you than seven sons!"
16 Naomi took the baby and cuddled him to her breast. And she cared for him as if he were her own.
17 The neighbor women said, "Now at last Naomi has a son again!" And they named him Obed. He became the father of Jesse and the grandfather of David.
18 This is the genealogical record of their ancestor Perez:

Perez was the father of Hezron.
19 Hezron was the father of Ram.
Ram was the father of Amminadab.
20 Amminadab was the father of Nahshon.
Nahshon was the father of Salmon.*
21 Salmon was the father of Boaz.
Boaz was the father of Obed.
22 Obed was the father of Jesse.
Jesse was the father of David.

4:20 As in some Greek manuscripts (see also 4:21; Hebrew reads *Salma*.

"GIA, IS THAT YOU?" Gia had just answered her phone, expecting it to be her best friend, Vicki. Instead, the voice was unfamiliar. "It's Adam from school."

Gia knew Adam, but never paid much attention to him. She was one of the most popular seniors at their high school. So far, she'd only dated the hot, popular guys. "Hot" was not a word most people would use to describe Adam.

"Why'd you call me?" she asked. She had never hung out with him.

"I just wanted to talk," Adam said. So they did.

Gia was surprised to find herself looking forward to Adam's calls. Soon Adam's popularity or looks didn't matter. She started to understand that though we often judge people by their appearance, it's what's inside that counts.

First Samuel shows how looks can be deceiving. It features the stories of Israel's first kings: Saul and David. Saul looked like a king. David didn't look like a leader, much less a king. He was young and seemingly insignificant. But Saul proved he wasn't worthy, and David became a great king.

As you read 1 Samuel, remember that while people judge by appearances, God looks at thoughts and intentions (1 Sam 16:7).

timeline

1105 B.C.
Samuel born

1080
Saul born

1050
Saul becomes king

1040
David born

1025
David anointed; Goliath slain

1010
David becomes king of Judah

1003
David becomes king of Israel

970
Solomon becomes king

930
The kingdom is divided

stats

PURPOSE: To record the life of Samuel, Israel's last judge; the reign and decline of Saul, Israel's first king; and the choice and preparation of David, Israel's greatest king

AUTHOR: Probably Samuel, but also includes writings from the prophets Nathan and Gad (1 Chron 29:29)

SETTING: The book begins in the days of the judges and describes Israel's transition from a theocracy (a nation led by God) to a monarchy (a nation led by a king).

KEY PEOPLE: Eli, Hannah, Samuel, Saul, Jonathan, David

KEY points

KING
Because Israel had corrupt priests and judges, the people asked to have a king like other nations in the area. God warned them that they would soon regret this request. He wants each person to be devoted to him, rather than to a king or government leader.

GOD'S CONTROL
Israel prospered as long as the people regarded God as their true King. When the leaders strayed from God and his law, he overruled their actions. God is always at work in this world, even when we can't see what he is doing.

LEADERSHIP
God guided his people using different forms of leadership: judges, priests, prophets, and kings. But when these leaders disobeyed God, they faced tragic consequences. Being a true leader means letting God guide you as you make decisions.

OBEDIENCE
God wanted his people to follow him wholeheartedly, rather than maintaining a superficial commitment based on traditions or ceremonies. God wants our actions to be motivated by genuine, heartfelt devotion to him.

MERCY AND JUSTICE
God responded to his people with tender mercy and swift justice. In showing mercy, he acted with his people's best interests in mind. In showing justice, he was faithful to his word and perfect moral nature. Because God is faithful, he can be counted on to show us mercy.

KEY PLACES IN 1 SAMUEL

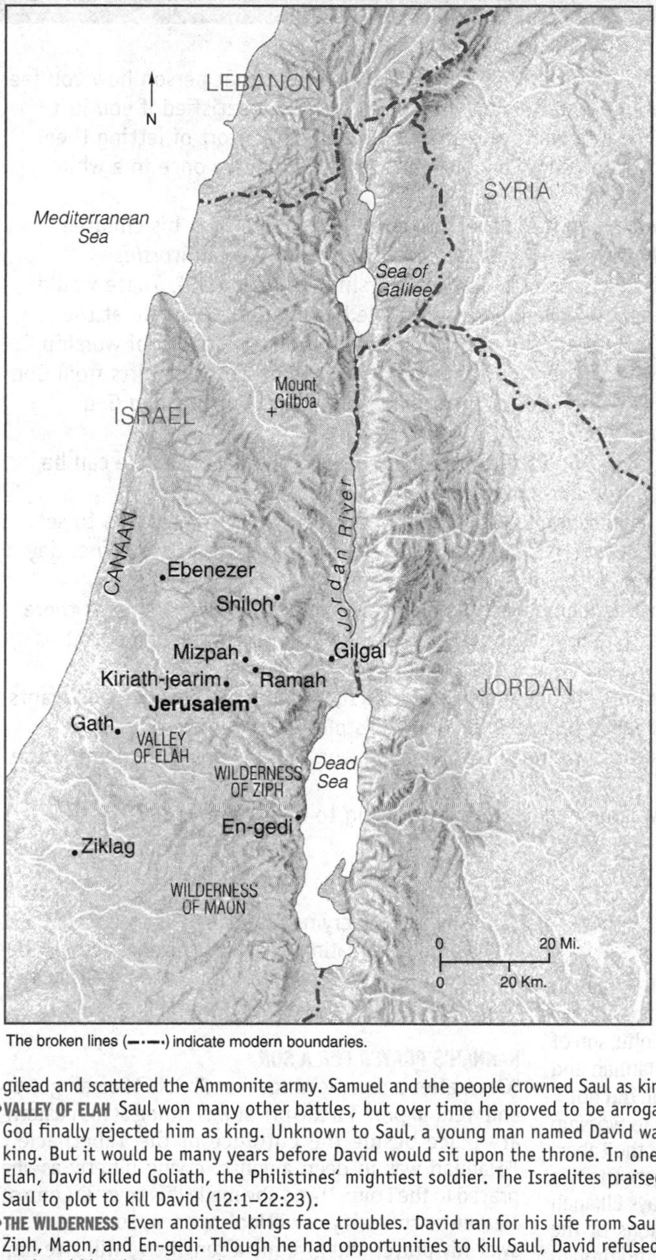

The broken lines (—·—·) indicate modern boundaries.

•**RAMAH** Samuel was born in Ramah. Before his birth, Samuel's mother, Hannah, made a promise to God that she would dedicate her son to serve God (1:1–2:11).

•**SHILOH** The focal point of Israel's worship was at Shiloh, where the Tabernacle and the Ark of the Covenant resided. (2:12–3:21).

•**KIRIATH-JEARIM** Hophni and Phinehas brought the Ark from Shiloh to the battlefield, believing that its mere presence would bring the Israelites victory. The Israelites were defeated by the Philistines at Ebenezer, and the Ark was captured. However, the Philistines found that the Ark was not the trophy they expected, because God sent plagues upon every Philistine city the Ark was brought to. Finally, the Philistines sent the Ark back to Kiriath-jearim in Israel (4:1–7:1).

•**MIZPAH** The Israelites' defeat made them realize that God was no longer blessing them. Samuel called the people together at Mizpah and asked them to fast and pray in sorrow for their sins. As Samuel grew old, the people came to him demanding a king so they could be like the other nations. At Mizpah, Saul was chosen by sacred lot to be Israel's first king with the blessing, but not the approval, of God and Samuel (7:2–10:27).

•**GILGAL** A battle with the Ammonites proved Saul's leadership abilities. He protected the people of Jabesh-gilead and scattered the Ammonite army. Samuel and the people crowned Saul as king of Israel at Gilgal (11:1-15).

•**VALLEY OF ELAH** Saul won many other battles, but over time he proved to be arrogant, sinful, and rebellious until God finally rejected him as king. Unknown to Saul, a young man named David was anointed to be Israel's next king. But it would be many years before David would sit upon the throne. In one particular battle in the valley of Elah, David killed Goliath, the Philistines' mightiest soldier. The Israelites praised David more than Saul, causing Saul to plot to kill David (12:1–22:23).

•**THE WILDERNESS** Even anointed kings face troubles. David ran for his life from Saul, hiding in the wildernesses of Ziph, Maon, and En-gedi. Though he had opportunities to kill Saul, David refused to do so because Saul was God's anointed king (23:1–26:25).

•**GATH** David moved his men and family to Gath, the Philistine city where King Achish lived. Saul then stopped chasing him. The Philistines seemed to welcome this famous fugitive from Israel (27:1-4).

•**ZIKLAG** In return for his pretended loyalty to King Achish, David asked for a city for his men and family. Achish gave him Ziklag. From there David conducted raids against the Geshurites, Girzites, and the Amalekites, making sure no one escaped to tell the tale (27:5-12). Later David conquered the Amalekites after they raided Ziklag (30:1-31).

•**MOUNT GILBOA** War with the Philistines broke out again in the north, near Mount Gilboa. Saul, who no longer relied on God, consulted a witch (a "medium") in a desperate attempt to contact Samuel for help. In the meantime, David was sent back to Ziklag because the Philistine commanders did not trust his loyalty in battle against Israel. The Philistines slaughtered the Israelites on Mount Gilboa, killing King Saul and his three sons, including David's loyal friend Jonathan. Without God, Saul had led a bitter and misguided life. His sinful actions affected him and hurt his family and nation (28:1–31:13).

ULTIMATE ISSUES

WORSHIP

Think you could date someone for a while without ever telling that person how you feel about him or her? How about your family? Think they would be satisfied if you just grunted at them every once in a while and spared yourself the effort of letting them know that you love them? Nope. Most people want to be told every once in a while that they are loved.

God is like that, too. Although he's never insecure, he likes to hear his children express their love directly to him. This is the essence of what we call *worship.*

Israel had a lengthy list of instructions about worship (see Exod 35). These would have been familiar to people like Hannah who traveled regularly to worship at the Tabernacle (see 1 Sam 1). Here are the *who, what, when, where,* and *why* of worship.

Who: Easy, right? We worship *God.* But at times the focus of worship shifts from God to *what God does for us.* Praising God for his goodness is okay. But praising God because he is God is good, too.

What: Worship means giving God the glory and obedience he deserves. We can be intentional about praising God and talking with him.

When: While any time is acceptable to worship God, the Scriptures teach us to set aside regular times for worship (Heb 10:24-25). The early church met on the first day of the week. Churches today often meet on Sunday and other days of the week.

Where: There are almost as many different places where Christians worship as there are Christians. Jesus clearly taught that where you worship God isn't as important as the worship itself (John 4:19-24). You can worship God anywhere.

Why: The *why* of worship is simple and twofold: First, we worship because God wants us to. But worship is not just for us; it's for God. He's pleased when we offer it.

Second, we worship because we need to. When we worship, we are reminded that he is God, and we are not.

So, are you ready to worship? Your Father is waiting to hear from you.

1

ELKANAH AND HIS FAMILY

There was a man named Elkanah who lived in Ramah in
the region of Zuph* in the hill country of Ephraim. He
was the son of Jeroham, son of Elihu, son of Tohu, son of
Zuph, of Ephraim. [2]Elkanah had two wives, Hannah and
Peninnah. Peninnah had children, but Hannah did not.
[3]Each year Elkanah would travel to Shiloh to worship
and sacrifice to the LORD of Heaven's Armies at the Tabernacle. The priests of the LORD at that time were the two
sons of Eli—Hophni and Phinehas. [4]On the days Elkanah
presented his sacrifice, he would give portions of the
meat to Peninnah and each of her chidren. [5]And though
he loved Hannah, he would give her only one choice portion* because the LORD had given her no children. [6]So Peninnah would taunt Hannah and make fun of her because
the LORD had kept her from having children. [7]Year after
year it was the same—Peninnah would taunt Hannah as
they went to the Tabernacle.* Each time, Hannah would
be reduced to tears and would not even eat.
[8]"Why are you crying, Hannah?" Elkanah would ask.
"Why aren't you eating? Why be downhearted just because you have no children? You have me—isn't that
better than having ten sons?"

HANNAH'S PRAYER FOR A SON

[9]Once after a sacrificial meal at Shiloh, Hannah got up
and went to pray. Eli the priest was sitting at his customary place beside the entrance of the Tabernacle.*
[10]Hannah was in deep anguish, crying bitterly as she
prayed to the LORD. [11]And she made this vow: "O LORD of
Heaven's Armies, if you will look upon my sorrow and answer my prayer and give me a son, then I will give him
back to you. He will be yours for his entire lifetime, and as
a sign that he has been dedicated to the LORD, his hair will
never be cut.*"
[12]As she was praying to the LORD, Eli watched her.
[13]Seeing her lips moving but hearing no sound, he
thought she had been drinking. [14]"Must you come here
drunk?" he demanded. "Throw away your wine!"

1:1 As in Greek version; Hebrew reads *in Ramathaim-zophim;* compare 1:19. 1:5 Or *And because he loved Hannah, he would give her a choice portion.* The meaning of the Hebrew is uncertain. 1:7 Hebrew *the house of the LORD;* also in 1:24. 1:9 Hebrew *the Temple of the LORD.* 1:11 Some manuscripts add *He will drink neither wine nor intoxicants.*

15"Oh no, sir!" she replied. "I haven't been drinking wine or anything stronger. But I am very discouraged, and I was pouring out my heart to the LORD. 16Don't think I am a wicked woman! For I have been praying out of great anguish and sorrow."

STILL INVOLVED 1:6-28

Part of God's plan for Hannah involved postponing her years of childbearing. While Peninnah and Elkanah looked at Hannah's seemingly dreary circumstances, God still had a plan. Know anyone who struggles with doubt about God's involvement in their lives? How can you encourage them to believe that God is still involved in their lives? ■

17"In that case," Eli said, "go in peace! May the God of Israel grant the request you have asked of him."

18"Oh, thank you, sir!" she exclaimed. Then she went back and began to eat again, and she was no longer sad.

SAMUEL'S BIRTH AND DEDICATION

19The entire family got up early the next morning and went to worship the LORD once more. Then they returned home to Ramah. When Elkanah slept with Hannah, the LORD remembered her plea, 20and in due time she gave birth to a son. She named him Samuel,* for she said, "I asked the LORD for him."

21The next year Elkanah and his family went on their annual trip to offer a sacrifice to the LORD. 22But Hannah did not go. She told her husband, "Wait until the boy is weaned. Then I will take him to the Tabernacle and leave him there with the LORD permanently.*"

DISCOURAGED 1:17-18

The change in Hannah's attitude may be attributed to three factors: (1) her honest prayer to God (1:10-11), (2) her resolve to leave the problem with God (1:18), and (3) the encouragement she received from Eli (1:17). These factors together make up the antidote for discouragement. When you feel discouraged, how could this antidote help? ■

23"Whatever you think is best," Elkanah agreed. "Stay here for now, and may the LORD help you keep your promise." So she stayed home and nursed the boy until he was weaned.

24When the child was weaned, Hannah took him to the Tabernacle in Shiloh. They brought along a three-year-old bull* for the sacrifice and a basket* of flour and some wine. 25After sacrificing the bull, they brought the boy to Eli. 26"Sir, do you remember me?" Hannah asked. "I am the woman who stood here several years ago praying to the LORD. 27I asked the LORD to give me this boy, and he has granted my request. 28Now I am giving him to the LORD, and he will belong to the LORD his whole life." And they* worshiped the LORD there.

2

HANNAH'S PRAYER OF PRAISE

Then Hannah prayed:

"My heart rejoices in the LORD!
The LORD has made me strong.*
Now I have an answer for my enemies;
I rejoice because you rescued me.
2 No one is holy like the LORD!
There is no one besides you;
there is no Rock like our God.

3 "Stop acting so proud and haughty!
Don't speak with such arrogance!
For the LORD is a God who knows what you have done;
he will judge your actions.
4 The bow of the mighty is now broken,
and those who stumbled are now strong.
5 Those who were well fed are now starving,
and those who were starving are now full.
The childless woman now has seven children,
and the woman with many children wastes away.
6 The LORD gives both death and life;
he brings some down to the grave* but raises others up.
7 The LORD makes some poor and others rich;
he brings some down and lifts others up.
8 He lifts the poor from the dust
and the needy from the garbage dump.
He sets them among princes,
placing them in seats of honor.
For all the earth is the LORD's,
and he has set the world in order.

9 "He will protect his faithful ones,
but the wicked will disappear in darkness.
No one will succeed by strength alone.
10 Those who fight against the LORD will be shattered.
He thunders against them from heaven;
the LORD judges throughout the earth.
He gives power to his king;
he increases the strength* of his anointed one."

11Then Elkanah returned home to Ramah without Samuel. And the boy served the LORD by assisting Eli the priest.

ELI'S WICKED SONS

12Now the sons of Eli were scoundrels who had no respect for the LORD 13or for their duties as priests. Whenever anyone offered a sacrifice, Eli's sons would send over a servant with a three-pronged fork. While the meat

1:20 *Samuel* sounds like the Hebrew term for "asked of God" or "heard by God." **1:22** Some manuscripts add *I will offer him as a Nazirite for all time.* **1:24a** As in Dead Sea Scrolls, Greek and Syriac versions; Masoretic Text reads *three bulls.* **1:24b** Hebrew *and an ephah* [20 quarts or 22 liters]. **1:28** Hebrew *he.* **2:1** Hebrew *has exalted my horn.* **2:6** Hebrew *to Sheol.* **2:10** Hebrew *he exalts the horn.*

HELP! 2:2

Hannah praised God for being a "rock"—firm, strong, and unchanging. In our fast-paced world, friends come and go and circumstances change. Those who devote their lives to causes, possessions, or other wealth are trusting things that will all pass away. None is a solid foundation for hope. But God is always present and ready to help, even when life seems to fall apart. Is he the foundation of your hope? ■

of the sacrificed animal was still boiling, 14the servant
would stick the fork into the pot and demand that whatever it brought up be given to Eli's sons. All the Israelites
who came to worship at Shiloh were treated this way.
15Sometimes the servant would come even before the animal's fat had been burned on the altar. He would demand raw meat before it had been boiled so that it could
be used for roasting.

16The man offering the sacrifice might reply, "Take as
much as you want, but the fat must be burned first." Then
the servant would demand, "No, give it to me now, or I'll
take it by force." 17So the sin of these young men was very
serious in the LORD's sight, for they treated the LORD's offerings with contempt.

18But Samuel, though he was only a boy, served the
LORD. He wore a linen garment like that of a priest.*
19Each year his mother made a small coat for him and
brought it to him when she came with her husband for
the sacrifice. 20Before they returned home, Eli would
bless Elkanah and his wife and say, "May the LORD give
you other children to take the place of this one she gave
to the LORD.*" 21And the LORD gave Hannah three sons
and two daughters. Meanwhile, Samuel grew up in the
presence of the LORD.

22Now Eli was very old, but he was aware of what his
sons were doing to the people of Israel. He knew, for instance, that his sons were seducing the young women
who assisted at the entrance of the Tabernacle.* 23Eli said
to them, "I have been hearing reports from all the people
about the wicked things you are doing. Why do you keep
sinning? 24You must stop, my sons! The reports I hear
among the LORD's people are not good. 25If someone sins
against another person, God* can mediate for the guilty
party. But if someone sins against the LORD, who can intercede?" But Eli's sons wouldn't listen to their father, for
the LORD was already planning to put them to death.

26Meanwhile, the boy Samuel grew taller and grew in
favor with the LORD and with the people.

A WARNING FOR ELI'S FAMILY

27One day a man of God came to Eli and gave him this
message from the LORD: "I revealed myself* to your ancestors when the people of Israel were slaves in Egypt. 28I
chose your ancestor Aaron* from among all the tribes of
Israel to be my priest, to offer sacrifices on my altar, to
burn incense, and to wear the priestly vest* as he served
me. And I assigned the sacrificial offerings to you priests.
29So why do you scorn my sacrifices and offerings? Why
do you give your sons more honor than you give me—for
you and they have become fat from the best offerings of
my people Israel!

30"Therefore, the LORD, the God of Israel, says: I promised that your branch of the tribe of Levi* would always
be my priests. But I will honor those who honor me, and I
will despise those who think lightly of me. 31The time is
coming when I will put an end to your family, so it will no
longer serve as my priests. All the members of your family will die before their time. None will reach old age.
32You will watch with envy as I pour out prosperity on the
people of Israel. But no members of your family will ever
live out their days. 33Those who survive will live in sadness and grief, and their children will die a violent
death.* 34And to prove that what I have said will come
true, I will cause your two sons, Hophni and Phinehas, to
die on the same day!

35"Then I will raise up a faithful priest who will serve
me and do what I desire. I will establish his family, and
they will be priests to my anointed kings forever. 36Then
all of your surviving family will bow before him, begging
for money and food. 'Please,' they will say, 'give us jobs
among the priests so we will have enough to eat.'"

LISTENING 3:1-15

During the days of Eli, messages from God were rare. Why? Look at the attitude of Eli's sons (2:12-25). They refused to listen to God and allowed greed to get in the way of any communication with him.

Listening and responding are vital in a relationship with God. Although God may not speak audibly, he speaks just as clearly today through his Word. To receive his messages, we must be ready to listen and act upon what he tells us. Like Samuel, are you ready to say "Speak, your servant is listening" (3:10) when God calls you to action? ■

3 THE LORD SPEAKS TO SAMUEL

Meanwhile, the boy Samuel served the LORD by assisting
Eli. Now in those days messages from the LORD were very
rare, and visions were quite uncommon.

2One night Eli, who was almost blind by now, had gone
to bed. 3The lamp of God had not yet gone out, and Samuel was sleeping in the Tabernacle* near the Ark of God.
4Suddenly the LORD called out, "Samuel!"

"Yes?" Samuel replied. "What is it?" 5He got up and ran
to Eli. "Here I am. Did you call me?"

"I didn't call you," Eli replied. "Go back to bed." So he did.

2:18 Hebrew *He wore a linen ephod.* 2:20 As in Dead Sea Scrolls and Greek version; Masoretic Text reads *this one she requested of the LORD in prayer.* 2:22 Hebrew *Tent of Meeting.* Some manuscripts lack this entire sentence. 2:25 Or *the judges.* 2:27 As in Greek and Syriac versions; Hebrew reads *Did I reveal myself.* 2:28a Hebrew *your father.* 2:28b Hebrew *an ephod.* 2:30 Hebrew *that your house and your father's house.* 2:33 As in Dead Sea Scrolls, which read *die by the sword;* Masoretic Text reads *die like mortals.* 3:3 Hebrew *the Temple of the LORD.*

6 Then the LORD called out again, "Samuel!"
Again Samuel got up and went to Eli. "Here I am. Did
you call me?"
"I didn't call you, my son," Eli said. "Go back to bed."
7 Samuel did not yet know the LORD because he had
never had a message from the LORD before. 8 So the LORD
called a third time, and once more Samuel got up and
went to Eli. "Here I am. Did you call me?"
Then Eli realized it was the LORD who was calling the
boy. 9 So he said to Samuel, "Go and lie down again, and if
someone calls again, say, 'Speak, LORD, your servant is listening.'" So Samuel went back to bed.
10 And the LORD came and called as before, "Samuel!
Samuel!"
And Samuel replied, "Speak, your servant is listening."
11 Then the LORD said to Samuel, "I am about to do a
shocking thing in Israel. 12 I am going to carry out all my
threats against Eli and his family, from beginning to end.
13 I have warned him that judgment is coming upon his
family forever, because his sons are blaspheming God*
and he hasn't disciplined them. 14 So I have vowed that the
sins of Eli and his sons will never be forgiven by sacrifices
or offerings."

SAMUEL SPEAKS FOR THE LORD

15 Samuel stayed in bed until morning, then got up and
opened the doors of the Tabernacle* as usual. He was
afraid to tell Eli what the LORD had said to him. 16 But Eli
called out to him, "Samuel, my son."
"Here I am," Samuel replied.
17 "What did the LORD say to you? Tell me everything.
And may God strike you and even kill you if you hide anything from me!" 18 So Samuel told Eli everything; he didn't
hold anything back. "It is the LORD's will," Eli replied. "Let
him do what he thinks best."
19 As Samuel grew up, the LORD was with him, and
everything Samuel said proved to be reliable. 20 And all Israel, from Dan in the north to Beersheba in the south,
knew that Samuel was confirmed as a prophet of the
LORD. 21 The LORD continued to appear at Shiloh and gave
messages to Samuel there at the Tabernacle. 4:1 And Samuel's words went out to all the people of Israel.

4 THE PHILISTINES CAPTURE THE ARK

At that time Israel was at war with the Philistines. The Israelite army was camped near Ebenezer, and the Philistines were at Aphek. 2 The Philistines attacked and
defeated the army of Israel, killing 4,000 men. 3 After the
battle was over, the troops retreated to their camp, and
the elders of Israel asked, "Why did the LORD allow us to
be defeated by the Philistines?" Then they said, "Let's
bring the Ark of the Covenant of the LORD from Shiloh. If

3:13 As in Greek version; Hebrew reads *his sons have made themselves contemptible.* 3:15 Hebrew *the house of the LORD.*

UPS:
- Used by God to assist Israel's transition from a loosely governed tribal people to a monarchy
- Anointed the first two kings of Israel
- The last and most effective of Israel's judges
- Listed in the Hall of Faith in Hebrews 11

DOWNS:
- Unable to instill in his sons the same relationship he had with God

STATS:
- Where: Ephraim
- Occupation: Judge, prophet, priest
- Relatives: Hannah (mother); Elkanah (father); Joel and Abijah (sons)
- Contemporaries: Eli, Saul, David

BOTTOM LINE:
The significance of what people accomplish in life is directly related to their relationship with God.
Being a person of integrity is more important than anything we might do.

Samuel's story is told in 1 Sam 1–16.13, 25.1, 28:3-20. He also is mentioned in Ps 99:6; Jer 15:1; Acts 3:24; 13:20; Heb 11:32.

SAMUEL Ever wonder what your favorite celebrity was like when he or she was your age? We have little information about the early years of most of the people mentioned in the Bible. One delightful exception is Samuel, who was born as a result of God's answer to Hannah's prayer for a child. (In fact, the name "Samuel" comes from the Hebrew expression, "asked of God.") God had plans for Samuel from the start. He used Samuel in many different and important ways. The reason God was able to use Samuel so much is because Samuel was willing to be one thing—God's servant.

Samuel's life teaches us that those who are faithful to God in small things will be trusted with greater things. Little jobs like helping the high priest may not have seemed very important, but God used those tasks to train Samuel for bigger responsibilities.

Samuel moved ahead because he listened to God's directions. Too often we ask God to control our life without being willing to give up the goals we've chosen. We ask God to help us get where *we* want to go. The first step in correcting this tendency is to turn over both the control and destination of our life to him. The second step is to be obedient to what we already know God wants us to do. The third step is to watch for further direction from his Word—God's roadmap for life.

we carry it into battle with us, it* will save us from our enemies."

[4]So they sent men to Shiloh to bring the Ark of the Covenant of the LORD of Heaven's Armies, who is enthroned between the cherubim. Hophni and Phinehas, the sons of Eli, were also there with the Ark of the Covenant of God. [5]When all the Israelites saw the Ark of the Covenant of the LORD coming into the camp, their shout of joy was so loud it made the ground shake!

DON'T TAKE HIM FOR GRANTED 4:5-8

The Philistines were frightened by stories of how God helped the people of Israel when they left Egypt. But Israel had turned away from God and now clung only to a form of godliness. They wrongly assumed that because God had given them victory in the past he would do it again, even though they had strayed far from him. Today, spiritual victories come when we stick with God, instead of taking him for granted. How do your actions show your willingness to stick with God? ■

[6]"What's going on?" the Philistines asked. "What's all the shouting about in the Hebrew camp?" When they were told it was because the Ark of the LORD had arrived, [7]they panicked. "The gods have* come into their camp!" they cried. "This is a disaster! We have never had to face anything like this before! [8]Help! Who can save us from these mighty gods of Israel? They are the same gods who destroyed the Egyptians with plagues when Israel was in the wilderness. [9]Fight as never before, Philistines! If you don't, we will become the Hebrews' slaves just as they have been ours! Stand up like men and fight!"

[10]So the Philistines fought desperately, and Israel was defeated again. The slaughter was great; 30,000 Israelite soldiers died that day. The survivors turned and fled to their tents. [11]The Ark of God was captured, and Hophni and Phinehas, the two sons of Eli, were killed.

THE DEATH OF ELI

[12]A man from the tribe of Benjamin ran from the battlefield and arrived at Shiloh later that same day. He had torn his clothes and put dust on his head to show his grief. [13]Eli was waiting beside the road to hear the news of the battle, for his heart trembled for the safety of the Ark of God. When the messenger arrived and told what had happened, an outcry resounded throughout the town.

[14]"What is all the noise about?" Eli asked.

The messenger rushed over to Eli, [15]who was ninety-eight years old and blind. [16]He said to Eli, "I have just come from the battlefield—I was there this very day."

"What happened, my son?" Eli demanded.

[17]"Israel has been defeated by the Philistines," the messenger replied. "The people have been slaughtered, and your two sons, Hophni and Phinehas, were also killed. And the Ark of God has been captured."

[18]When the messenger mentioned what had happened to the Ark of God, Eli fell backward from his seat beside the gate. He broke his neck and died, for he was old and overweight. He had been Israel's judge for forty years.

[19]Eli's daughter-in-law, the wife of Phinehas, was pregnant and near her time of delivery. When she heard that the Ark of God had been captured and that her father-in-law and husband were dead, she went into labor and gave birth. [20]She died in childbirth, but before she passed away the midwives tried to encourage her. "Don't be afraid," they said. "You have a baby boy!" But she did not answer or pay attention to them.

[21]She named the child Ichabod (which means "Where is the glory?"), for she said, "Israel's glory is gone." She named him this because the Ark of God had been captured and because her father-in-law and husband were dead. [22]Then she said, "The glory has departed from Israel, for the Ark of God has been captured."

THE TRUTH HURTS 5:1-7

After the Philistines stole the Ark of the Covenant, God showed the Philistines that he was the real God by breaking their idol, Dagon. But they didn't act upon that insight until they began suffering from tumors (probably boils). Similarly, many people don't respond to biblical truth until they experience pain and suddenly feel they have no place else to turn. Are you willing to listen to God for truth's sake, or do you turn to him only when you're suffering? ■

5

THE ARK IN PHILISTIA

After the Philistines captured the Ark of God, they took it from the battleground at Ebenezer to the town of Ashdod. [2]They carried the Ark of God into the temple of Dagon and placed it beside an idol of Dagon. [3]But when the citizens of Ashdod went to see it the next morning, Dagon had fallen with his face to the ground in front of the Ark of the LORD! So they took Dagon and put him in his place again. [4]But the next morning the same thing happened—Dagon had fallen face down before the Ark of the LORD again. This time his head and hands had broken off and were lying in the doorway. Only the trunk of his body was left intact. [5]That is why to this day neither the priests of Dagon nor anyone who enters the temple of Dagon in Ashdod will step on its threshold.

[6]Then the LORD's heavy hand struck the people of Ashdod and the nearby villages with a plague of tumors.* [7]When the people realized what was happening, they cried out, "We can't keep the Ark of the God of Israel here any longer! He is against us! We will all be destroyed along with Dagon, our god." [8]So they called together the rulers of the Philistine towns and asked, "What should we do with the Ark of the God of Israel?"

4:3 Or *he.* **4:7** Or *A god has.* **5:6** Greek version and Latin Vulgate read *tumors; and rats appeared in their land, and death and destruction were throughout the city.*

The rulers discussed it and replied, "Move it to the town of Gath." So they moved the Ark of the God of Israel to Gath. 9But when the Ark arrived at Gath, the LORD's heavy hand fell on its men, young and old; he struck them with a plague of tumors, and there was a great panic.

INGREDIENT OR THE SOURCE? 6:9

The Philistines acknowledged the existence of the God of Israel, but only as one of many "gods" whose favor they sought. Thinking of God in this way made it easy for them to ignore God's demand that people worship him alone. Many people "worship" God this way. They see him as just one ingredient in a successful life. But God is not an ingredient—he is the source of life itself. Is that how you see God? ■

10So they sent the Ark of God to the town of Ekron, but when the people of Ekron saw it coming they cried out, "They are bringing the Ark of the God of Israel here to kill us, too!" 11The people summoned the Philistine rulers again and begged them, "Please send the Ark of the God of Israel back to its own country, or it* will kill us all." For the deadly plague from God had already begun, and great fear was sweeping across the town. 12Those who didn't die were afflicted with tumors; and the cry from the town rose to heaven.

6 THE PHILISTINES RETURN THE ARK

The Ark of the LORD remained in Philistine territory seven months in all. 2Then the Philistines called in their priests and diviners and asked them, "What should we do about the Ark of the LORD? Tell us how to return it to its own country."

3"Send the Ark of the God of Israel back with a gift," they were told. "Send a guilt offering so the plague will stop. Then, if you are healed, you will know it was his hand that caused the plague."

4"What sort of guilt offering should we send?" they asked.

And they were told, "Since the plague has struck both you and your five rulers, make five gold tumors and five gold rats, just like those that have ravaged your land. 5Make these things to show honor to the God of Israel. Perhaps then he will stop afflicting you, your gods, and your land. 6Don't be stubborn and rebellious as Pharaoh and the Egyptians were. By the time God was finished with them, they were eager to let Israel go.

7"Now build a new cart, and find two cows that have just given birth to calves. Make sure the cows have never been yoked to a cart. Hitch the cows to the cart, but shut their calves away from them in a pen. 8Put the Ark of the LORD on the cart, and beside it place a chest containing the gold rats and gold tumors you are sending as a guilt offering. Then let the cows go wherever they want. 9If they cross the border of our land and go to Beth-shemesh, we will know it was the LORD who brought this great disaster upon us. If they don't, we will know it was not his hand that caused the plague. It came simply by chance."

10So these instructions were carried out. Two cows were hitched to the cart, and their newborn calves were shut up in a pen. 11Then the Ark of the LORD and the chest containing the gold rats and gold tumors were placed on the cart. 12And sure enough, without veering off in other directions, the cows went straight along the road toward Beth-shemesh, lowing as they went. The Philistine rulers followed them as far as the border of Beth-shemesh.

13The people of Beth-shemesh were harvesting wheat in the valley, and when they saw the Ark, they were overjoyed! 14The cart came into the field of a man named Joshua and stopped beside a large rock. So the people broke up the wood of the cart for a fire and killed the cows and sacrificed them to the LORD as a burnt offering. 15Several men of the tribe of Levi lifted the Ark of the LORD and the chest containing the gold rats and gold tumors from the cart and placed them on the large rock. Many sacrifices and burnt offerings were offered to the LORD that day by the people of Beth-shemesh. 16The five Philistine rulers watched all this and then returned to Ekron that same day.

17The five gold tumors sent by the Philistines as a guilt offering to the LORD were gifts from the rulers of Ashdod, Gaza, Ashkelon, Gath, and Ekron. 18The five gold rats represented the five Philistine towns and their surrounding villages, which were controlled by the five rulers. The large rock at Beth-shemesh, where they set the Ark of the LORD, still stands in the field of Joshua as a witness to what happened there.

THE ARK MOVED TO KIRIATH-JEARIM

19But the LORD killed seventy men* from Beth-shemesh because they looked into the Ark of the LORD. And the people mourned greatly because of what the LORD had done. 20"Who is able to stand in the presence of the LORD, this holy God?" they cried out. "Where can we send the Ark from here?"

21So they sent messengers to the people at Kiriath-jearim and told them, "The Philistines have returned the Ark of the LORD. Come here and get it!"

7

So the men of Kiriath-jearim came to get the Ark of the LORD. They took it to the hillside home of Abinadab and ordained Eleazar, his son, to be in charge of it. 2The Ark remained in Kiriath-jearim for a long time—twenty years in all. During that time all Israel mourned because it seemed the LORD had abandoned them.

SAMUEL LEADS ISRAEL TO VICTORY

3Then Samuel said to all the people of Israel, "If you are really serious about wanting to return to the LORD, get rid

5:11 Or *he*. **6:19** As in a few Hebrew manuscripts; most Hebrew manuscripts read *70 men, 50,000 men*. Perhaps the text should be understood to read *the LORD killed 70 men and 50 oxen*.

of your foreign gods and your images of Ashtoreth. Determine to obey only the LORD; then he will rescue you from the Philistines." 4So the Israelites got rid of their images of Baal and Ashtoreth and worshiped only the LORD.

ABANDONED OR JUST INACTIVE? 7:2-3

Sorrow gripped Israel for 20 years. The Ark was put away like an unwanted box in an attic. Many believed that the Lord had abandoned his people. But Samuel, now a grown man, roused them to action by calling them to do something, rather than complain.

How easy it is for us to complain to God about our problems, instead of doing what he requires. We don't even take the advice he has already given us. Do you ever feel as if God has abandoned you? Check to see if there is anything he has already told you to do. You might not receive new guidance until you have acted on his previous directions. ■

5Then Samuel told them, "Gather all of Israel to Mizpah, and I will pray to the LORD for you." 6So they gathered at Mizpah and, in a great ceremony, drew water from a well and poured it out before the LORD. They also went without food all day and confessed that they had sinned against the LORD. (It was at Mizpah that Samuel became Israel's judge.)

7When the Philistine rulers heard that Israel had gathered at Mizpah, they mobilized their army and advanced. The Israelites were badly frightened when they learned that the Philistines were approaching. 8"Don't stop pleading with the LORD our God to save us from the Philistines!" they begged Samuel. 9So Samuel took a young lamb and offered it to the LORD as a whole burnt offering. He pleaded with the LORD to help Israel, and the LORD answered him.

10Just as Samuel was sacrificing the burnt offering, the Philistines arrived to attack Israel. But the LORD spoke with a mighty voice of thunder from heaven that day, and the Philistines were thrown into such confusion that the Israelites defeated them. 11The men of Israel chased them from Mizpah to a place below Beth-car, slaughtering them all along the way.

12Samuel then took a large stone and placed it between the towns of Mizpah and Jeshanah.* He named it Ebenezer (which means "the stone of help"), for he said, "Up to this point the LORD has helped us!"

13So the Philistines were subdued and didn't invade Israel again for some time. And throughout Samuel's lifetime, the LORD's powerful hand was raised against the Philistines. 14The Israelite villages near Ekron and Gath that the Philistines had captured were restored to Israel, along with the rest of the territory that the Philistines had taken. And there was peace between Israel and the Amorites in those days.

15Samuel continued as Israel's judge for the rest of his life. 16Each year he traveled around, setting up his court first at Bethel, then at Gilgal, and then at Mizpah. He judged the people of Israel at each of these places. 17Then he would return to his home at Ramah, and he would hear cases there, too. And Samuel built an altar to the LORD at Ramah.

8

ISRAEL REQUESTS A KING

As Samuel grew old, he appointed his sons to be judges over Israel. 2Joel and Abijah, his oldest sons, held court in Beersheba. 3But they were not like their father, for they were greedy for money. They accepted bribes and perverted justice.

4Finally, all the elders of Israel met at Ramah to discuss the matter with Samuel. 5"Look," they told him, "you are now old, and your sons are not like you. Give us a king to judge us like all the other nations have."

6Samuel was displeased with their request and went to the LORD for guidance. 7"Do everything they say to you," the LORD replied, "for it is me they are rejecting, not you. They don't want me to be their king any longer. 8Ever since I brought them from Egypt they have continually abandoned me and followed other gods. And now they are giving you the same treatment. 9Do as they ask, but solemnly warn them about the way a king will reign over them."

7:12 As in Greek and Syriac versions; Hebrew reads *Shen*.

So many things crowd God out of my life. How much of my time does God want?

God does not want to be just another addition to your life—he wants everything you do to revolve around him!

Check this out: Bike tires are only as strong as the hub of the wheel. If a tire was made up only of rim and spokes, the wheel would soon collapse under the constant pounding and pressure.

The spokes in our lives are those things that are important to us: family, friends, school, sports, entertainment, etc. If life revolves around any one of these "spokes," eventually the constant pounding and pressures of our world will wear us down and possibly cause us to collapse! But God is a hub that can keep life together.

The people of Israel chose to reject God "the hub" of their lives by demanding a king to rule over them. What they were actually saying was, "God, since we can't see you, we can't trust you to take care of us. Give us someone we can see who will rule over us." Eventually God gave in to their request. (See 1 Sam 8:7.) The results, however, were devastating. The Old Testament graphically describes what happened when God's people rejected him as their leader.

When things begin to crowd out your relationship with God, try writing down a list of your priorities. Ask a trusted Christian friend if he or she thinks any one of these "spokes" is taking the place of God in your life.

SAMUEL WARNS AGAINST A KINGDOM

10So Samuel passed on the LORD's warning to the people
who were asking him for a king. 11"This is how a king
will reign over you," Samuel said. "The king will draft
your sons and assign them to his chariots and his charioteers, making them run before his chariots. 12Some
will be generals and captains in his army,* some will be
forced to plow in his fields and harvest his crops, and
some will make his weapons and chariot equipment.
13The king will take your daughters from you and force
them to cook and bake and make perfumes for him.
14He will take away the best of your fields and vineyards
and olive groves and give them to his own officials. 15He
will take a tenth of your grain and your grape harvest
and distribute it among his officers and attendants.
16He will take your male and female slaves and demand
the finest of your cattle* and donkeys for his own use.
17He will demand a tenth of your flocks, and you will be
his slaves. 18When that day comes, you will beg for relief from this king you are demanding, but then the
LORD will not help you."

19But the people refused to listen to Samuel's warning.
"Even so, we still want a king," they said. 20"We want to be
like the nations around us. Our king will judge us and
lead us into battle."

21So Samuel repeated to the LORD what the people had
said, 22and the LORD replied, "Do as they say, and give
them a king." Then Samuel agreed and sent the people
home.

9

SAUL MEETS SAMUEL

There was a wealthy, influential man named Kish from
the tribe of Benjamin. He was the son of Abiel, son of Ze-
ror, son of Becorath, son of Aphiah, of the tribe of Benjamin. 2His son Saul was the most handsome man in
Israel—head and shoulders taller than anyone else in the
land.

3One day Kish's donkeys strayed away, and he told
Saul, "Take a servant with you, and go look for the
donkeys." 4So Saul took one of the servants and traveled through the hill country of Ephraim, the land
of Shalishah, the Shaalim area, and the entire land
of Benjamin, but they couldn't find the donkeys
anywhere.

5Finally, they entered the region of Zuph, and Saul
said to his servant, "Let's go home. By now my father
will be more worried about us than about the donkeys!"

6But the servant said, "I've just thought of something!
There is a man of God who lives here in this town. He is
held in high honor by all the people because everything
he says comes true. Let's go find him. Perhaps he can tell
us which way to go."

7"But we don't have anything to offer him," Saul replied. "Even our food is gone, and we don't have a thing to
give him."

8"Well," the servant said, "I have one small silver
piece.* We can at least offer it to the man of God and see

8:12 Hebrew *commanders of thousands and commanders of fifties.* **8:16** As in Greek version; Hebrew reads *young men.* **9:8** Hebrew *¼ shekel of silver,* about 0.1 ounces or 3 grams in weight.

SAUL First impressions aren't always accurate. Sometimes a person with a great image looks very different when we discover his or her character or lack thereof.

Saul made a good first impression. He looked like a king, but lacked the traits that would have helped him be a good one. He often forgot or disobeyed God's directions. He was God's chosen leader, but God's choice did not mean that Saul was capable of being king on his own.

During his reign, Saul had his greatest successes when he obeyed God. His greatest failures resulted from acting on his own. His choices alienated him from God and eventually his own people.

While our strengths and abilities make us useful, our weaknesses often make us usable. Whatever we accomplish on our own is only a hint of what God could do through us. Does he control your life?

UPS:
- First God-appointed king of Israel
- Known for his courage and generosity
- Stood tall, with a striking appearance

DOWNS:
- Lacked integrity
- Jealousy of David led to attempted murder
- Deliberately disobeyed God on several occasions

STATS:
- Where: The land of Benjamin
- Occupation: King of Israel
- Relatives: Kish (father); Ahinoam (wife); Jonathan, Ishbosheth, Abinadab, and Malchishua (sons); Merab and Michal (daughters)

BOTTOM LINE:

God wants obedience from the heart, not empty rituals.

Obedience always involves sacrifice, but sacrifice does not always mean obedience.

God wants to make use of our strengths and weaknesses.

Our weaknesses can help us remember our need for God's guidance and help.

Saul's story is told in 1 Sam 9–31. He also is mentioned in Acts 13:21-22.

what happens!" 9(In those days if people wanted a message from God, they would say, "Let's go and ask the seer,"
for prophets used to be called seers.)
10"All right," Saul agreed, "let's try it!" So they started
into the town where the man of God lived.
11As they were climbing the hill to the town, they met
some young women coming out to draw water. So Saul
and his servant asked, "Is the seer here today?"
12"Yes," they replied. "Stay right on this road. He is at
the town gates. He has just arrived to take part in a public
sacrifice up at the place of worship. 13Hurry and catch
him before he goes up there to eat. The guests won't begin eating until he arrives to bless the food."
14So they entered the town, and as they passed through
the gates, Samuel was coming out toward them to go up
to the place of worship.
15Now the LORD had told Samuel the previous day,
16"About this time tomorrow I will send you a man from
the land of Benjamin. Anoint him to be the leader of my
people, Israel. He will rescue them from the Philistines,
for I have looked down on my people in mercy and have
heard their cry."
17When Samuel saw Saul, the LORD said, "That's the
man I told you about! He will rule my people."
18Just then Saul approached Samuel at the gateway and
asked, "Can you please tell me where the seer's house is?"
19"I am the seer!" Samuel replied. "Go up to the place of
worship ahead of me. We will eat there together, and in
the morning I'll tell you what you want to know and send
you on your way. 20And don't worry about those donkeys
that were lost three days ago, for they have been found.
And I am here to tell you that you and your family are the
focus of all Israel's hopes."
21Saul replied, "But I'm only from the tribe of Benjamin, the smallest tribe in Israel, and my family is the least
important of all the families of that tribe! Why are you
talking like this to me?"
22Then Samuel brought Saul and his servant into the
hall and placed them at the head of the table, honoring
them above the thirty special guests. 23Samuel then instructed the cook to bring Saul the finest cut of meat, the
piece that had been set aside for the guest of honor. 24So
the cook brought in the meat and placed it before Saul.
"Go ahead and eat it," Samuel said. "I was saving it for you
even before I invited these others!" So Saul ate with Samuel that day.
25When they came down from the place of worship
and returned to town, Samuel took Saul up to the roof of
the house and prepared a bed for him there.* 26At daybreak the next morning, Samuel called to Saul, "Get up!
It's time you were on your way." So Saul got ready, and
he and Samuel left the house together. 27When they
reached the edge of town, Samuel told Saul to send his
servant on ahead. After the servant was gone, Samuel
said, "Stay here, for I have received a special message for
you from God."

10

SAMUEL ANOINTS SAUL AS KING

Then Samuel took a flask of olive oil and poured it over
Saul's head. He kissed Saul and said, "I am doing this because the LORD has appointed you to be the ruler over Israel, his special possession.* 2When you leave me today,
you will see two men beside Rachel's tomb at Zelzah, on
the border of Benjamin. They will tell you that the donkeys have been found and that your father has stopped
worrying about them and is now worried about you. He is
asking, 'Have you seen my son?'
3"When you get to the oak of Tabor, you will see three
men coming toward you who are on their way to worship
God at Bethel. One will be bringing three young goats, another will have three loaves of bread, and the third will be
carrying a wineskin full of wine. 4They will greet you and
offer you two of the loaves, which you are to accept.
5"When you arrive at Gibeah of God,* where the garrison of the Philistines is located, you will meet a band of
prophets coming down from the place of worship. They
will be playing a harp, a tambourine, a flute, and a lyre,
and they will be prophesying. 6At that time the Spirit of
the LORD will come powerfully upon you, and you will
prophesy with them. You will be changed into a different
person. 7After these signs take place, do what must be
done, for God is with you. 8Then go down to Gilgal ahead
of me. I will join you there to sacrifice burnt offerings
and peace offerings. You must wait for seven days until I
arrive and give you further instructions."

YOUR LIFE, HIS DESIGN 9:1–10:16

Often we think that events just happen to us. But Saul's story shows us that God often uses common occurrences to guide us. Think of the good and bad circumstances that have affected you lately. Can you see God's purpose in them? Perhaps he is building a certain quality in your life or leading you to serve him in a new area. ■

SAMUEL'S SIGNS ARE FULFILLED

9As Saul turned and started to leave, God gave him a new
heart, and all Samuel's signs were fulfilled that day.
10When Saul and his servant arrived at Gibeah, they saw a
group of prophets coming toward them. Then the Spirit
of God came powerfully upon Saul, and he, too, began to
prophesy. 11When those who knew Saul heard about it,
they exclaimed, "What? Is even Saul a prophet? How did
the son of Kish become a prophet?"
12And one of those standing there said, "Can anyone
become a prophet, no matter who his father is?"* So that
is the origin of the saying "Is even Saul a prophet?"
13When Saul had finished prophesying, he went up to
the place of worship. 14"Where have you been?" Saul's
uncle asked him and his servant.
"We were looking for the donkeys," Saul replied, "but

9:25 As in Greek version; Hebrew reads *and talked with him there.* **10:1** Greek version reads *over Israel. And you will rule over the LORD's people and save them from their enemies around them. This will be the sign to you that the LORD has appointed you to be leader over his special possession.* **10:5** Hebrew *Gibeath-elohim.* **10:12** Hebrew *said, "Who is their father?"*

we couldn't find them. So we went to Samuel to ask him where they were."

[15]"Oh? And what did he say?" his uncle asked.

[16]"He told us that the donkeys had already been found," Saul replied. But Saul didn't tell his uncle what Samuel said about the kingdom.

SAUL IS ACCLAIMED KING

[17]Later Samuel called all the people of Israel to meet before the LORD at Mizpah. [18]And he said, "This is what the LORD, the God of Israel, has declared: I brought you from Egypt and rescued you from the Egyptians and from all of the nations that were oppressing you. [19]But though I have rescued you from your misery and distress, you have rejected your God today and have said, 'No, we want a king instead!' Now, therefore, present yourselves before the LORD by tribes and clans."

HIDE AND SEEK 10:22-24

When a king was to be chosen for Israel, Saul already knew that he was the one (10:1). Instead of coming forward, however, he hid. Often we hide from important responsibilities because we are afraid of failure, afraid of what others will think, or perhaps unsure about how to proceed. Tempted to run from your responsibilities? You can run, but you can't hide from God. Why not seek him instead. ■

[20]So Samuel brought all the tribes of Israel before the LORD, and the tribe of Benjamin was chosen by lot. [21]Then he brought each family of the tribe of Benjamin before the LORD, and the family of the Matrites was chosen. And finally Saul son of Kish was chosen from among them. But when they looked for him, he had disappeared! [22]So they asked the LORD, "Where is he?"

And the LORD replied, "He is hiding among the baggage." [23]So they found him and brought him out, and he stood head and shoulders above anyone else.

[24]Then Samuel said to all the people, "This is the man the LORD has chosen as your king. No one in all Israel is like him!"

And all the people shouted, "Long live the king!"

[25]Then Samuel told the people what the rights and duties of a king were. He wrote them down on a scroll and placed it before the LORD. Then Samuel sent the people home again.

[26]When Saul returned to his home at Gibeah, a group of men whose hearts God had touched went with him. [27]But there were some scoundrels who complained, "How can this man save us?" And they scorned him and refused to bring him gifts. But Saul ignored them.

[Nahash, king of the Ammonites, had been grievously oppressing the people of Gad and Reuben who lived east of the Jordan River. He gouged out the right eye of each of the Israelites living there, and he didn't allow anyone to come and rescue them. In fact, of all the Israelites east of the Jordan, there wasn't a single one whose right eye Nahash had not gouged out. But there were 7,000 men who had escaped from the Ammonites, and they had settled in Jabesh-gilead.]*

11

SAUL DEFEATS THE AMMONITES

About a month later,* King Nahash of Ammon led his army against the Israelite town of Jabesh-gilead. But all the citizens of Jabesh asked for peace. "Make a treaty with us, and we will be your servants," they pleaded.

[2]"All right," Nahash said, "but only on one condition. I will gouge out the right eye of every one of you as a disgrace to all Israel!"

[3]"Give us seven days to send messengers throughout Israel!" replied the elders of Jabesh. "If no one comes to save us, we will agree to your terms."

[4]When the messengers came to Gibeah of Saul and told the people about their plight, everyone broke into tears. [5]Saul had been plowing a field with his oxen, and when he returned to town, he asked, "What's the matter? Why is everyone crying?" So they told him about the message from Jabesh.

[6]Then the Spirit of God came powerfully upon Saul, and he became very angry. [7]He took two oxen and cut them into pieces and sent the messengers to carry them throughout Israel with this message: "This is what will happen to the oxen of anyone who refuses to follow Saul and Samuel into battle!" And the LORD made the people afraid of Saul's anger, and all of them came out together as one. [8]When Saul mobilized them at Bezek, he found that there were 300,000 men from Israel and 30,000* men from Judah.

APPROPRIATE ANGER 11:6

Anger is a powerful emotion. Often it is used wrongly to hurt others. But anger directed at the mistreatment of others is not wrong. Saul was angered by the Ammonites' threat to humiliate and mistreat his fellow Israelites. God used Saul's anger to bring justice and freedom. When evil or injustice makes you angry, ask God to help you use that anger in constructive ways to bring about a positive change. ■

[9]So Saul sent the messengers back to Jabesh-gilead to say, "We will rescue you by noontime tomorrow!" There was great joy throughout the town when that message arrived!

[10]The men of Jabesh then told their enemies, "Tomorrow we will come out to you, and you can do to us whatever you wish." [11]But before dawn the next morning, Saul arrived, having divided his army into three detachments. He launched a surprise attack against the Ammonites and slaughtered them the whole morning. The remnant of their army was so badly scattered that no two of them were left together.

10:27 This paragraph, which is not included in the Masoretic Text, is found in Dead Sea Scroll 4QSam[a]. **11:1** As in Greek version; Hebrew lacks *About a month later*. **11:8** Dead Sea Scrolls and Greek version read *70,000*.

12Then the people exclaimed to Samuel, "Now where are those men who said, 'Why should Saul rule over us?' Bring them here, and we will kill them!"

13But Saul replied, "No one will be executed today, for today the LORD has rescued Israel!"

14Then Samuel said to the people, "Come, let us all go to Gilgal to renew the kingdom." 15So they all went to Gilgal, and in a solemn ceremony before the LORD they made Saul king. Then they offered peace offerings to the LORD, and Saul and all the Israelites were filled with joy.

12 SAMUEL'S FAREWELL ADDRESS

Then Samuel addressed all Israel: "I have done as you asked and given you a king. 2Your king is now your leader. I stand here before you—an old, gray-haired man—and my sons serve you. I have served as your leader from the time I was a boy to this very day. 3Now testify against me in the presence of the LORD and before his anointed one. Whose ox or donkey have I stolen? Have I ever cheated any of you? Have I ever oppressed you? Have I ever taken a bribe and perverted justice? Tell me and I will make right whatever I have done wrong."

4"No," they replied, "you have never cheated or oppressed us, and you have never taken even a single bribe."

5"The LORD and his anointed one are my witnesses today," Samuel declared, "that my hands are clean."

"Yes, he is a witness," they replied.

6"It was the LORD who appointed Moses and Aaron," Samuel continued. "He brought your ancestors out of the land of Egypt. 7Now stand here quietly before the LORD as I remind you of all the great things the LORD has done for you and your ancestors.

8"When the Israelites were* in Egypt and cried out to the LORD, he sent Moses and Aaron to rescue them from Egypt and to bring them into this land. 9But the people soon forgot about the LORD their God, so he handed them over to Sisera, the commander of Hazor's army, and also to the Philistines and to the king of Moab, who fought against them.

10"Then they cried to the LORD again and confessed, 'We have sinned by turning away from the LORD and worshiping the images of Baal and Ashtoreth. But we will worship you and you alone if you will rescue us from our enemies.' 11Then the LORD sent Gideon,* Bedan,* Jephthah, and Samuel* to save you, and you lived in safety.

12"But when you were afraid of Nahash, the king of Ammon, you came to me and said that you wanted a king to reign over you, even though the LORD your God was already your king. 13All right, here is the king you have chosen. You asked for him, and the LORD has granted your request.

14"Now if you fear and worship the LORD and listen to his voice, and if you do not rebel against the LORD's commands, then both you and your king will show that you recognize the LORD as your God. 15But if you rebel against the LORD's commands and refuse to listen to him, then his hand will be as heavy upon you as it was upon your ancestors.

16"Now stand here and see the great thing the LORD is about to do. 17You know that it does not rain at this time of the year during the wheat harvest. I will ask the LORD to send thunder and rain today. Then you will realize how wicked you have been in asking the LORD for a king!"

18So Samuel called to the LORD, and the LORD sent thunder and rain that day. And all the people were terrified of the LORD and of Samuel. 19"Pray to the LORD your God for us, or we will die!" they all said to Samuel. "For now we have added to our sins by asking for a king."

> Be sure to fear the LORD and faithfully serve him. Think of all the wonderful things he has done for you.
>
> 1 SAMUEL 12:24

20"Don't be afraid," Samuel reassured them. "You have certainly done wrong, but make sure now that you worship the LORD with all your heart, and don't turn your back on him. 21Don't go back to worshiping worthless idols that cannot help or rescue you—they are totally useless! 22The LORD will not abandon his people, because that would dishonor his great name. For it has pleased the LORD to make you his very own people.

23"As for me, I will certainly not sin against the LORD by ending my prayers for you. And I will continue to teach you what is good and right. 24But be sure to fear the LORD and faithfully serve him. Think of all the wonderful things he has done for you. 25But if you continue to sin, you and your king will be swept away."

13 CONTINUED WAR WITH PHILISTIA

Saul was thirty* years old when he became king, and he reigned for forty-two years.*

2Saul selected 3,000 special troops from the army of Israel and sent the rest of the men home. He took 2,000 of the chosen men with him to Micmash and the hill country of Bethel. The other 1,000 went with Saul's son Jonathan to Gibeah in the land of Benjamin.

3Soon after this, Jonathan attacked and defeated the garrison of Philistines at Geba. The news spread quickly among the Philistines. So Saul blew the ram's horn throughout the land, saying, "Hebrews, hear this! Rise up in revolt!" 4All Israel heard the news that Saul had destroyed the Philistine garrison at Geba and that the

12:8 Hebrew *When Jacob was.* The names "Jacob" and "Israel" are often interchanged throughout the Old Testament, referring sometimes to the individual patriarch and sometimes to the nation. **12:11a** Hebrew *Jerub-baal,* another name for Gideon; see Judg 6:32. **12:11b** Greek and Syriac versions read *Barak.* **12:11c** Greek and Syriac versions read *Samson.* **13:1a** As in a few Greek manuscripts; the number is missing in the Hebrew. **13:1b** Hebrew *reigned . . . and two;* the number is incomplete in the Hebrew. Compare Acts 13:21.

Philistines now hated the Israelites more than ever. So
the entire Israelite army was summoned to join Saul at
Gilgal.
5The Philistines mustered a mighty army of 3,000*
chariots, 6,000 charioteers, and as many warriors as the
grains of sand on the seashore! They camped at Micmash
east of Beth-aven. 6The men of Israel saw what a tight
spot they were in; and because they were hard pressed by
the enemy, they tried to hide in caves, thickets, rocks,
holes, and cisterns. 7Some of them crossed the Jordan
River and escaped into the land of Gad and Gilead.

SAUL'S DISOBEDIENCE AND SAMUEL'S REBUKE

Meanwhile, Saul stayed at Gilgal, and his men were trembling with fear. 8Saul waited there seven days for Samuel,
as Samuel had instructed him earlier, but Samuel still
didn't come. Saul realized that his troops were rapidly
slipping away. 9So he demanded, "Bring me the burnt offering and the peace offerings!" And Saul sacrificed the
burnt offering himself.
10Just as Saul was finishing with the burnt offering,
Samuel arrived. Saul went out to meet and welcome him,
11but Samuel said, "What is this you have done?"
Saul replied, "I saw my men scattering from me, and
you didn't arrive when you said you would, and the Philistines are at Micmash ready for battle. 12So I said, 'The
Philistines are ready to march against us at Gilgal, and I
haven't even asked for the LORD's help!' So I felt compelled to offer the burnt offering myself before you
came."

EXCUSES, EXCUSES 13:8-13

Saul had plenty of excuses for his disobedience. But Samuel zeroed in on the real issue: "You have not kept the command the LORD your God gave you." By trying to hide his sins behind excuses, Saul lost his kingship (13:14). Like Saul, we sometimes gloss over our actions, trying to justify and spiritualize our actions because of our "special" circumstances. But an excuse is just that—an excuse. God knows our true motives. He forgives, restores, and blesses only when we are honest about our actions. ■

13"How foolish!" Samuel exclaimed. "You have not
kept the command the LORD your God gave you. Had you
kept it, the LORD would have established your kingdom
over Israel forever. 14But now your kingdom must end,
for the LORD has sought out a man after his own heart.
The LORD has already appointed him to be the leader of
his people, because you have not kept the LORD's
command."

13:5 As in Greek and Syriac versions; Hebrew reads *30,000*.

UPS:
- Greatest king of Israel
- Ancestor of Jesus Christ
- Listed in the Hall of Faith in Hebrews 11
- Described by God as "a man after his own heart" (1 Sam 13:14; Acts 13:22)

DOWNS:
- Committed adultery with Bathsheba
- Arranged the murder of Uriah, Bathsheba's husband
- Disobeyed God by taking a census of the people

STATS:
- Where: Bethlehem, Jerusalem
- Occupation: Shepherd, musician, poet, soldier, king
- Relatives: Jesse (father); seven brothers; Michal, Ahinoam, Bathsheba, Abigail (wives); Absalom, Amnon, Solomon, Adonijah (sons); Tamar (daughter)
- Contemporaries: Saul, Jonathan, Samuel, Nathan

BOTTOM LINE:

Being willing to admit our mistakes is the first step in dealing with them.

Forgiveness does not remove the consequences of sin.

God greatly desires our complete trust and worship.

David's story is told in 1 Sam 16—1 Kings 2. He also is mentioned in Amos 6:5; Matt 1:1, 6; 22:43-45; Luke 1:32; Rom 1:3; Heb 11:32.

DAVID Who is the coolest person you know? Does he or she have qualities like David? When we think of David, we think of a shepherd, poet, giant-killer, king, ancestor of Jesus—in short, we think of one of the greatest heroes in the Old Testament. But other words could also be used to describe David: betrayer, liar, adulterer, murderer.

The Bible makes no effort to hide David's failures. Yet he is remembered and respected as a godly man. Although he messed up many times, he was quick to confess his wrongdoings. His confessions were from the heart and his repentance was real. David never took God's forgiveness lightly. In return, God never held back from David either his forgiveness or the consequences of his actions. David experienced the joy of forgiveness even when he had to suffer the consequences of wrong behavior.

David didn't make the same mistakes over and over. Rather, he learned from his mistakes. Is that how you are? Looking back at the list of David's good qualities, how many are true of your life?

ISRAEL'S MILITARY DISADVANTAGE

15Samuel then left Gilgal and went on his way, but the rest of the troops went with Saul to meet the army. They went up from Gilgal to Gibeah in the land of Benjamin.* When Saul counted the men who were still with him, he found only 600 were left! 16Saul and Jonathan and the troops with them were staying at Geba in the land of Benjamin. The Philistines set up their camp at Micmash. 17Three raiding parties soon left the camp of the Philistines. One went north toward Ophrah in the land of Shual, 18another went west to Beth-horon, and the third moved toward the border above the valley of Zeboim near the wilderness.

19There were no blacksmiths in the land of Israel in those days. The Philistines wouldn't allow them for fear they would make swords and spears for the Hebrews. 20So whenever the Israelites needed to sharpen their plowshares, picks, axes, or sickles,* they had to take them to a Philistine blacksmith. 21(The charges were as follows: a quarter of an ounce of silver* for sharpening a plowshare or a pick, and an eighth of an ounce* for sharpening an ax, a sickle, or an ox goad.) 22So on the day of the battle none of the people of Israel had a sword or spear, except for Saul and Jonathan.

23The pass at Micmash had meanwhile been secured by a contingent of the Philistine army.

SURROUNDED 14:1-6

Jonathan and his armor bearer weren't much of a force to attack the huge Philistine army. But while everyone else was afraid, these men trusted God, knowing that the size of the enemy army had no relationship to God's ability to help them. God rewarded the faith and brave actions of these two men with a tremendous victory.

Have you ever faced an overwhelming problem? God is never intimidated by the size of an enemy or the complexity of a problem. With him, there are always enough resources to resist the pressures and win your battles. If God has called you to action, why not commit what few resources you have to God and rely on him to win the battle for you. ■

14 JONATHAN'S DARING PLAN

One day Jonathan said to his armor bearer, "Come on, let's go over to where the Philistines have their outpost." But Jonathan did not tell his father what he was doing.

2Meanwhile, Saul and his 600 men were camped on the outskirts of Gibeah, around the pomegranate tree* at Migron. 3Among Saul's men was Ahijah the priest, who was wearing the ephod, the priestly vest. Ahijah was the son of Ichabod's brother Ahitub, son of Phinehas, son of Eli, the priest of the LORD who had served at Shiloh.

No one realized that Jonathan had left the Israelite camp. 4To reach the Philistine outpost, Jonathan had to go down between two rocky cliffs that were called Bozez and Seneh. 5The cliff on the north was in front of Micmash, and the one on the south was in front of Geba. 6"Let's go across to the outpost of those pagans," Jonathan said to his armor bearer. "Perhaps the LORD will help us, for nothing can hinder the LORD. He can win a battle whether he has many warriors or only a few!"

7"Do what you think is best," the armor bearer replied. "I'm with you completely, whatever you decide."

8"All right then," Jonathan told him. "We will cross over and let them see us. 9If they say to us, 'Stay where you are or we'll kill you,' then we will stop and not go up to them. 10But if they say, 'Come on up and fight,' then we will go up. That will be the LORD's sign that he will help us defeat them."

11When the Philistines saw them coming, they shouted, "Look! The Hebrews are crawling out of their holes!" 12Then the men from the outpost shouted to Jonathan, "Come on up here, and we'll teach you a lesson!"

"Come on, climb right behind me," Jonathan said to his armor bearer, "for the LORD will help us defeat them!"

13So they climbed up using both hands and feet, and the Philistines fell before Jonathan, and his armor bearer killed those who came behind them. 14They killed some twenty men in all, and their bodies were scattered over about half an acre.*

15Suddenly, panic broke out in the Philistine army, both in the camp and in the field, including even the outposts and raiding parties. And just then an earthquake struck, and everyone was terrified.

ISRAEL DEFEATS THE PHILISTINES

16Saul's lookouts in Gibeah of Benjamin saw a strange sight—the vast army of Philistines began to melt away in every direction. 17"Call the roll and find out who's missing," Saul ordered. And when they checked, they found that Jonathan and his armor bearer were gone.

18Then Saul shouted to Ahijah, "Bring the ephod here!" For at that time Ahijah was wearing the ephod in front of the Israelites.* 19But while Saul was talking to the priest, the confusion in the Philistine camp grew louder and louder. So Saul said to the priest, "Never mind; let's get going!"*

20Then Saul and all his men rushed out to the battle and found the Philistines killing each other. There was terrible confusion everywhere. 21Even the Hebrews who had previously gone over to the Philistine army revolted and joined in with Saul, Jonathan, and the rest of the Israelites. 22Likewise, the men of Israel who were hiding in the hill country of Ephraim joined the chase when they saw the Philistines running away. 23So the LORD saved Israel that day, and the battle continued to rage even beyond Beth-aven.

13:15 As in Greek version; Hebrew reads *Samuel then left Gilgal and went to Gibeah in the land of Benjamin.* **13:20** As in Greek version; Hebrew reads *or plowshares.* **13:21a** Hebrew *1 pim* [8 grams]. **13:21b** Hebrew *⅓ of a shekel* [4 grams]. **14:2** Or *around the rock of Rimmon;* compare Judg 20:45, 47; 21:13. **14:14** Hebrew *half a yoke;* a "yoke" was the amount of land plowed by a pair of yoked oxen in one day. **14:18** As in some Greek manuscripts; Hebrew reads *"Bring the Ark of God." For at that time the Ark of God was with the Israelites.* **14:19** Hebrew *Withdraw your hand.*

SAUL'S FOOLISH OATH

24Now the men of Israel were pressed to exhaustion that day, because Saul had placed them under an oath, saying, "Let a curse fall on anyone who eats before evening—before I have full revenge on my enemies." So no one ate anything all day, 25even though they had all found honeycomb on the ground in the forest. 26They didn't dare touch the honey because they all feared the oath they had taken.

VOWS 14:24-46

Saul made an oath without thinking through the implications. The results? Saul's men were too tired to fight. Also, they were so hungry they ate meat without draining the blood, which was against God's law (Lev 7:26). Not only that, Saul almost killed his own son because Jonathan broke the vow (14:42-44).

Saul's impulsive vow sounded heroic, but its disastrous side effects made it little more than "shooting off at the mouth." If you are in the middle of a conflict, guard against impulsive statements that you may be forced to honor. ■

27But Jonathan had not heard his father's command, and he dipped the end of his stick into a piece of honeycomb and ate the honey. After he had eaten it, he felt refreshed.* 28But one of the men saw him and said, "Your father made the army take a strict oath that anyone who eats food today will be cursed. That is why everyone is weary and faint."

29"My father has made trouble for us all!" Jonathan exclaimed. "A command like that only hurts us. See how refreshed I am now that I have eaten this little bit of honey. 30If the men had been allowed to eat freely from the food they found among our enemies, think how many more Philistines we could have killed!"

31They chased and killed the Philistines all day from Micmash to Aijalon, growing more and more faint. 32That evening they rushed for the battle plunder and butchered the sheep, goats, cattle, and calves, but they ate them without draining the blood. 33Someone reported to Saul, "Look, the men are sinning against the LORD by eating meat that still has blood in it."

"That is very wrong," Saul said. "Find a large stone and roll it over here. 34Then go out among the troops and tell them, 'Bring the cattle, sheep, and goats here to me. Kill them here, and drain the blood before you eat them. Do not sin against the LORD by eating meat with the blood still in it.'"

So that night all the troops brought their animals and slaughtered them there. 35Then Saul built an altar to the LORD; it was the first of the altars he built to the LORD.

36Then Saul said, "Let's chase the Philistines all night and plunder them until sunrise. Let's destroy every last one of them."

His men replied, "We'll do whatever you think is best."

But the priest said, "Let's ask God first."

37So Saul asked God, "Should we go after the Philistines? Will you help us defeat them?" But God made no reply that day.

38Then Saul said to the leaders, "Something's wrong! I want all my army commanders to come here. We must find out what sin was committed today. 39I vow by the name of the LORD who rescued Israel that the sinner will surely die, even if it is my own son Jonathan!" But no one would tell him what the trouble was.

40Then Saul said, "Jonathan and I will stand over here, and all of you stand over there."

And the people responded to Saul, "Whatever you think is best."

41Then Saul prayed, "O LORD, God of Israel, please show us who is guilty and who is innocent.*" Then they cast sacred lots, and Jonathan and Saul were chosen as the guilty ones, and the people were declared innocent.

42Then Saul said, "Now cast lots again and choose between me and Jonathan." And Jonathan was shown to be the guilty one.

43"Tell me what you have done," Saul demanded of Jonathan.

"I tasted a little honey," Jonathan admitted. "It was only a little bit on the end of my stick. Does that deserve death?"

44"Yes, Jonathan," Saul said, "you must die! May God strike me and even kill me if you do not die for this."

45But the people broke in and said to Saul, "Jonathan has won this great victory for Israel. Should he die? Far from it! As surely as the LORD lives, not one hair on his head will be touched, for God helped him do a great deed today." So the people rescued Jonathan, and he was not put to death.

46Then Saul called back the army from chasing the Philistines, and the Philistines returned home.

SAUL'S MILITARY SUCCESSES

47Now when Saul had secured his grasp on Israel's throne, he fought against his enemies in every direction—against Moab, Ammon, Edom, the kings of Zobah, and the Philistines. And wherever he turned, he was victorious. 48He performed great deeds and conquered the Amalekites, saving Israel from all those who had plundered them.

49Saul's sons included Jonathan, Ishbosheth,* and Malkishua. He also had two daughters: Merab, who was older, and Michal. 50Saul's wife was Ahinoam, the daughter of Ahimaaz. The commander of Saul's army was Abner, the son of Saul's uncle Ner. 51Saul's father, Kish, and Abner's father, Ner, were both sons of Abiel.

52The Israelites fought constantly with the Philistines throughout Saul's lifetime. So whenever Saul observed a young man who was brave and strong, he drafted him into his army.

15

SAUL DESTROYS THE AMALEKITES

One day Samuel said to Saul, "It was the LORD who told me to anoint you as king of his people, Israel. Now listen

14:27 Or *his eyes brightened;* similarly in 14:29. 14:41 Greek version adds *If the fault is with me or my son Jonathan, respond with Urim; but if the men of Israel are at fault, respond with Thummim.* 14:49 Hebrew *Ishvi,* a variant name for Ishbosheth; also known as Esh-baal.

to this message from the LORD! 2This is what the LORD of
Heaven's Armies has declared: I have decided to settle accounts with the nation of Amalek for opposing Israel
when they came from Egypt. 3Now go and completely destroy* the entire Amalekite nation—men, women, children, babies, cattle, sheep, goats, camels, and donkeys."
4So Saul mobilized his army at Telaim. There were
200,000 soldiers from Israel and 10,000 men from Judah. 5Then Saul and his army went to a town of the Amalekites and lay in wait in the valley. 6Saul sent this
warning to the Kenites: "Move away from where the Amalekites live, or you will die with them. For you showed
kindness to all the people of Israel when they came up
from Egypt." So the Kenites packed up and left.

LYING

On her way out the door for a company party, Mrs. Richards addresses her sophomore daughter, whom she has just grounded. "Janelle, remember—no visitors, and under no circumstances may you leave the house."

"Okay," mumbles the hacked-off teen.

After her mom leaves, Janelle grabs the phone and dials her best friend. "Kat, everything's cool." Ten minutes later Katherine drops by.

"How 'bout checking the mall to see if Greg's there?" Janelle suggests.

"What if your mom calls?" Katherine asks.

"Oh, I'll just tell her I was taking a bath."

The girls go to the mall. They eat ice cream and return home. Janelle slides into bed, thinking, "My mom is so out of it . . . I could have stayed out till midnight."

The next morning, Mrs. Richards, obviously ticked, summons Janelle into the living room.

"Care to tell me about last night?" Mrs. Richards asks.

"Huh?" Janelle asks.

"Where did you go?"

"What are you talking about?" (It's an Oscar-caliber performance.)

"Look, Janelle," Mrs. Richards states, "I know what you did. On my way to the party, I got a run in my hose. I stopped at the mall to get another pair. Guess who I saw there?"

Janelle sees her life flash before her eyes!

For a reminder of the high cost of dishonesty and disobedience, read 1 Samuel 15:1-23. What problems has dishonesty created in your life?

7Then Saul slaughtered the Amalekites from Havilah
all the way to Shur, east of Egypt. 8He captured Agag, the
Amalekite king, but completely destroyed everyone else.
9Saul and his men spared Agag's life and kept the best of
the sheep and goats, the cattle, the fat calves, and the
lambs—everything, in fact, that appealed to them. They
destroyed only what was worthless or of poor quality.

FAILURE 15:13-14

Saul thought he had won a great victory over the Amalekites. God, however, saw it as a great failure because Saul had disobeyed him. Saul also lied to Samuel about the results of the battle. He may have thought that his lie wouldn't be detected, or that what he did wasn't wrong. He was mistaken.

Dishonest people soon begin to believe their own lies. This puts up a barrier between them and God. That's why honesty is so important in our relationships, both with God and with others. ■

THE LORD REJECTS SAUL

10Then the LORD said to Samuel, 11"I am sorry that I ever
made Saul king, for he has not been loyal to me and has
refused to obey my command." Samuel was so deeply
moved when he heard this that he cried out to the LORD
all night.
12Early the next morning Samuel went to find Saul.
Someone told him, "Saul went to the town of Carmel to
set up a monument to himself; then he went on to Gilgal."
13When Samuel finally found him, Saul greeted him
cheerfully. "May the LORD bless you," he said. "I have carried out the LORD's command!"
14"Then what is all the bleating of sheep and goats and
the lowing of cattle I hear?" Samuel demanded.
15"It's true that the army spared the best of the sheep,
goats, and cattle," Saul admitted. "But they are going to
sacrifice them to the LORD your God. We have destroyed
everything else."
16Then Samuel said to Saul, "Stop! Listen to what the
LORD told me last night!"
"What did he tell you?" Saul asked.
17And Samuel told him, "Although you may think little
of yourself, are you not the leader of the tribes of Israel?
The LORD has anointed you king of Israel. 18And the LORD
sent you on a mission and told you, 'Go and completely destroy the sinners, the Amalekites, until they are all dead.'
19Why haven't you obeyed the LORD? Why did you rush
for the plunder and do what was evil in the LORD's sight?"
20"But I did obey the LORD," Saul insisted. "I carried out
the mission he gave me. I brought back King Agag, but I
destroyed everyone else. 21Then my troops brought in the
best of the sheep, goats, cattle, and plunder to sacrifice to
the LORD your God in Gilgal."
22But Samuel replied,

"What is more pleasing to the LORD:
your burnt offerings and sacrifices
or your obedience to his voice?
Listen! Obedience is better than sacrifice,
and submission is better than offering the fat of
rams.
23 Rebellion is as sinful as witchcraft,
and stubbornness as bad as worshiping idols.

15:3 The Hebrew term used here refers to the complete consecration of things or people to the LORD, either by destroying them or by giving them as an offering; also in 15:8, 9, 15, 18, 20, 21.

So because you have rejected the command of the
LORD,
he has rejected you as king."

SAUL PLEADS FOR FORGIVENESS

[24]Then Saul admitted to Samuel, "Yes, I have sinned. I have disobeyed your instructions and the LORD's command, for I was afraid of the people and did what they demanded. [25]But now, please forgive my sin and come back with me so that I may worship the LORD."

[26]But Samuel replied, "I will not go back with you! Since you have rejected the LORD's command, he has rejected you as king of Israel."

[27]As Samuel turned to go, Saul tried to hold him back and tore the hem of his robe. [28]And Samuel said to him, "The LORD has torn the kingdom of Israel from you today and has given it to someone else—one who is better than you. [29]And he who is the Glory of Israel will not lie, nor will he change his mind, for he is not human that he should change his mind!"

[30]Then Saul pleaded again, "I know I have sinned. But please, at least honor me before the elders of my people and before Israel by coming back with me so that I may worship the LORD your God." [31]So Samuel finally agreed and went back with him, and Saul worshiped the LORD.

SAMUEL EXECUTES KING AGAG

[32]Then Samuel said, "Bring King Agag to me." Agag arrived full of hope, for he thought, "Surely the worst is over, and I have been spared!"* [33]But Samuel said, "As your sword has killed the sons of many mothers, now your mother will be childless." And Samuel cut Agag to pieces before the LORD at Gilgal.

[34]Then Samuel went home to Ramah, and Saul returned to his house at Gibeah of Saul. [35]Samuel never went to meet with Saul again, but he mourned constantly for him. And the LORD was sorry he had ever made Saul king of Israel.

16

SAMUEL ANOINTS DAVID AS KING

Now the LORD said to Samuel, "You have mourned long enough for Saul. I have rejected him as king of Israel, so fill your flask with olive oil and go to Bethlehem. Find a man named Jesse who lives there, for I have selected one of his sons to be my king."

[2]But Samuel asked, "How can I do that? If Saul hears about it, he will kill me."

"Take a heifer with you," the LORD replied, "and say that you have come to make a sacrifice to the LORD. [3]Invite Jesse to the sacrifice, and I will show you which of his sons to anoint for me."

[4]So Samuel did as the LORD instructed. When he arrived at Bethlehem, the elders of the town came trembling to meet him. "What's wrong?" they asked. "Do you come in peace?"

[5]"Yes," Samuel replied. "I have come to sacrifice to the LORD. Purify yourselves and come with me to the sacrifice." Then Samuel performed the purification rite for Jesse and his sons and invited them to the sacrifice, too.

[6]When they arrived, Samuel took one look at Eliab and thought, "Surely this is the LORD's anointed!"

[7]But the LORD said to Samuel, "Don't judge by his appearance or height, for I have rejected him. The LORD doesn't see things the way you see them. People judge by outward appearance, but the LORD looks at the heart."

> People judge by outward appearance, but the LORD looks at the heart.
>
> *1 SAMUEL 16:7*

[8]Then Jesse told his son Abinadab to step forward and walk in front of Samuel. But Samuel said, "This is not the one the LORD has chosen." [9]Next Jesse summoned Shimea,* but Samuel said, "Neither is this the one the LORD has chosen." [10]In the same way all seven of Jesse's sons were presented to Samuel. But Samuel said to Jesse, "The LORD has not chosen any of these." [11]Then Samuel asked, "Are these all the sons you have?"

"There is still the youngest," Jesse replied. "But he's out in the fields watching the sheep and goats."

"Send for him at once," Samuel said. "We will not sit down to eat until he arrives."

[12]So Jesse sent for him. He was dark and handsome, with beautiful eyes.

And the LORD said, "This is the one; anoint him."

[13]So as David stood there among his brothers, Samuel took the flask of olive oil he had brought and anointed David with the oil. And the Spirit of the LORD came powerfully upon David from that day on. Then Samuel returned to Ramah.

INNER BEAUTY 16:7

Since Saul was tall and handsome, Samuel may have been trying to find someone who looked like Saul to be Israel's next king. But God warned Samuel against judging by appearance alone.

When people judge by appearance, they may overlook quality individuals who simply lack the particular physical qualities that society currently admires. But appearance doesn't reveal what people are really like or what their true value is. Fortunately, God judges by character, not appearances. Inner beauty is what counts with God. Is that what counts with you? ■

DAVID SERVES IN SAUL'S COURT

[14]Now the Spirit of the LORD had left Saul, and the LORD sent a tormenting spirit* that filled him with depression and fear.

15:32 Dead Sea Scrolls and Greek version read *Agag arrived hesitantly, for he thought, "Surely this is the bitterness of death."* **16:9** Hebrew *Shammah*, a variant spelling of Shimea; compare 1 Chr 2:13; 20:7. **16:14** Or *an evil spirit;* also in 16:15, 16, 23.

15Some of Saul's servants said to him, "A tormenting spirit from God is troubling you. 16Let us find a good musician to play the harp whenever the tormenting spirit troubles you. He will play soothing music, and you will soon be well again."

17"All right," Saul said. "Find me someone who plays well, and bring him here."

18One of the servants said to Saul, "One of Jesse's sons from Bethlehem is a talented harp player. Not only that—he is a brave warrior, a man of war, and has good judgment. He is also a fine-looking young man, and the LORD is with him."

19So Saul sent messengers to Jesse to say, "Send me your son David, the shepherd." 20Jesse responded by sending David to Saul, along with a young goat, a donkey loaded with bread, and a wineskin full of wine.

21So David went to Saul and began serving him. Saul loved David very much, and David became his armor bearer.

22Then Saul sent word to Jesse asking, "Please let David remain in my service, for I am very pleased with him."

23And whenever the tormenting spirit from God troubled Saul, David would play the harp. Then Saul would feel better, and the tormenting spirit would go away.

GROWTH 16:19-21

When Saul asked David to join his palace staff, he obviously did not know that David had been secretly anointed king (16:12-13). Saul's invitation presented an excellent opportunity for the young, future king to gain firsthand information about leading a nation.

Sometimes our plans—even the ones we think God has approved—have to be put on hold indefinitely. Like David, we can use this waiting time profitably. How? By allowing our experiences to help us grow in wisdom. ■

17

GOLIATH CHALLENGES THE ISRAELITES

The Philistines now mustered their army for battle and camped between Socoh in Judah and Azekah at Ephesdammim. 2Saul countered by gathering his Israelite troops near the valley of Elah. 3So the Philistines and Israelites faced each other on opposite hills, with the valley between them.

4Then Goliath, a Philistine champion from Gath, came out of the Philistine ranks to face the forces of Israel. He was over nine feet* tall! 5He wore a bronze helmet, and his bronze coat of mail weighed 125 pounds.* 6He also wore bronze leg armor, and he carried a bronze javelin on his shoulder. 7The shaft of his spear was as heavy and thick as a weaver's beam, tipped with an iron spearhead that weighed 15 pounds.* His armor bearer walked ahead of him carrying a shield.

A CHANGE OF PERSPECTIVE 17:26-37

Two people can have two different perspectives on the same thing. As far as the fight with Goliath was concerned, Saul saw a big giant and a young, insignificant looking man. David, however, saw a mortal man defying an invincible God. He looked at his situation from God's point of view. Viewing impossible situations from God's point of view helps us put giant problems in perspective. ■

8Goliath stood and shouted a taunt across to the Israelites. "Why are you all coming out to fight?" he called. "I am the Philistine champion, but you are only the servants of Saul. Choose one man to come down here and fight me! 9If he kills me, then we will be your slaves. But if I kill him, you will be our slaves! 10I defy the armies of Israel today! Send me a man who will fight me!" 11When Saul and the Israelites heard this, they were terrified and deeply shaken.

JESSE SENDS DAVID TO SAUL'S CAMP

12Now David was the son of a man named Jesse, an Ephrathite from Bethlehem in the land of Judah. Jesse was an old man at that time, and he had eight sons. 13Jesse's three oldest sons—Eliab, Abinadab, and Shimea*—had already joined Saul's army to fight the Philistines. 14David was the youngest son. David's three oldest brothers stayed with Saul's army, 15but David went back and forth so he could help his father with the sheep in Bethlehem.

16For forty days, every morning and evening, the Philistine champion strutted in front of the Israelite army.

17One day Jesse said to David, "Take this basket* of roasted grain and these ten loaves of bread, and carry them quickly to your brothers. 18And give these ten cuts of cheese to their captain. See how your brothers are getting along, and bring back a report on how they are doing.*" 19David's brothers were with Saul and the Israelite army at the valley of Elah, fighting against the Philistines.

20So David left the sheep with another shepherd and set out early the next morning with the gifts, as Jesse had directed him. He arrived at the camp just as the Israelite army was leaving for the battlefield with shouts and battle cries. 21Soon the Israelite and Philistine forces stood facing each other, army against army. 22David left his things with the keeper of supplies and hurried out to the ranks to greet his brothers. 23As he was talking with them, Goliath, the Philistine champion from Gath, came out from the Philistine ranks. Then David heard him shout his usual taunt to the army of Israel.

24As soon as the Israelite army saw him, they began to run away in fright. 25"Have you seen the giant?" the men asked. "He comes out each day to defy Israel. The king has offered a huge reward to anyone who kills him. He

17:4 Hebrew *6 cubits and 1 span* [which totals about 9.75 feet or 3 meters]; Dead Sea Scrolls and Greek version read *4 cubits and 1 span* [which totals about 6.75 feet or 2 meters]. 17:5 Hebrew *5,000 shekels* [57 kilograms]. 17:7 Hebrew *600 shekels* [6.8 kilograms]. 17:13 Hebrew *Shammah,* a variant spelling of Shimea; compare 1 Chr 2:13; 20:7. 17:17 Hebrew *ephah* [20 quarts or 22 liters]. 17:18 Hebrew *and take their pledge.*

Simple Objects

God often uses simple, ordinary objects to accomplish his tasks in the world. They only need to be dedicated to him for his use. What do you have that God can use? Anything and everything is a possible "instrument" for him.

Object	*Reference*	*Who used it?*	*How was it used?*
A SHEPHERD'S STAFF	Exodus 4:2-4	Moses	To work miracles before Pharaoh
A RAM'S HORN	Joshua 6:3-5	Joshua	To flatten the walls of Jericho
A FLEECE	Judges 6:36-40	Gideon	To confirm God's will
HORNS, JARS, AND TORCHES	Judges 7:19-22	Gideon	To defeat the Midianites
JAWBONE	Judges 15:15	Samson	To kill 1,000 Philistines
SMALL STONE	1 Samuel 17:40	David	To kill Goliath
OIL	2 Kings 4:1-7	Elisha	To demonstrate God's power to provide
A RIVER	2 Kings 5:9-14	Elisha	To heal a man of leprosy
LINEN BELT	Jeremiah 13:1-11	Jeremiah	As an object lesson of God's wrath
POTTERY	Jeremiah 19:1-13	Jeremiah	As an object lesson of God's wrath
FOOD AND WATER	Ezekiel 4:9-17	Ezekiel	As an object lesson of judgment
FIVE LOAVES OF BREAD AND TWO FISH	Mark 6:30-44	Jesus	To feed a crowd of over 5,000 people

will give that man one of his daughters for a wife, and
the man's entire family will be exempted from paying
taxes!"
26David asked the soldiers standing nearby, "What
will a man get for killing this Philistine and ending his
defiance of Israel? Who is this pagan Philistine anyway, that he is allowed to defy the armies of the living
God?"
27And these men gave David the same reply. They said,
"Yes, that is the reward for killing him."
28But when David's oldest brother, Eliab, heard David
talking to the men, he was angry. "What are you doing
around here anyway?" he demanded. "What about those
few sheep you're supposed to be taking care of? I know
about your pride and deceit. You just want to see the
battle!"
29"What have I done now?" David replied. "I was only
asking a question!" 30He walked over to some others and
asked them the same thing and received the same answer. 31Then David's question was reported to King Saul,
and the king sent for him.

DAVID KILLS GOLIATH

32"Don't worry about this Philistine," David told Saul. "I'll
go fight him!"
33"Don't be ridiculous!" Saul replied. "There's no way
you can fight this Philistine and possibly win! You're only
a boy, and he's been a man of war since his youth."
34But David persisted. "I have been taking care of my
father's sheep and goats," he said. "When a lion or a bear
comes to steal a lamb from the flock, 35I go after it with a
club and rescue the lamb from its mouth. If the animal
turns on me, I catch it by the jaw and club it to death. 36I
have done this to both lions and bears, and I'll do it to this
pagan Philistine, too, for he has defied the armies of the
living God! 37The LORD who rescued me from the claws of
the lion and the bear will rescue me from this Philistine!"
Saul finally consented. "All right, go ahead," he said.
"And may the LORD be with you!"
38Then Saul gave David his own armor—a bronze helmet and a coat of mail. 39David put it on, strapped the
sword over it, and took a step or two to see what it was
like, for he had never worn such things before.

"I can't go in these," he protested to Saul. "I'm not used
to them." So David took them off again. 40He picked up
five smooth stones from a stream and put them into his
shepherd's bag. Then, armed only with his shepherd's staff
and sling, he started across the valley to fight the Philistine.

41Goliath walked out toward David with his shield
bearer ahead of him, 42sneering in contempt at this
ruddy-faced boy. 43"Am I a dog," he roared at David, "that
you come at me with a stick?" And he cursed David by the
names of his gods. 44"Come over here, and I'll give your
flesh to the birds and wild animals!" Goliath yelled.

45David replied to the Philistine, "You come to me with
sword, spear, and javelin, but I come to you in the name of
the LORD of Heaven's Armies—the God of the armies of Israel, whom you have defied. 46Today the LORD will conquer
you, and I will kill you and cut off your head. And then I will
give the dead bodies of your men to the birds and wild animals, and the whole world will know that there is a God in
Israel! 47And everyone assembled here will know that the
LORD rescues his people, but not with sword and spear.
This is the LORD's battle, and he will give you to us!"

48As Goliath moved closer to attack, David quickly ran
out to meet him. 49Reaching into his shepherd's bag and
taking out a stone, he hurled it with his sling and hit the
Philistine in the forehead. The stone sank in, and Goliath
stumbled and fell face down on the ground.

50So David triumphed over the Philistine with only a
sling and a stone, for he had no sword. 51Then David ran
over and pulled Goliath's sword from its sheath. David
used it to kill him and cut off his head.

ISRAEL ROUTS THE PHILISTINES

When the Philistines saw that their champion was dead,
they turned and ran. 52Then the men of Israel and Judah
gave a great shout of triumph and rushed after the Philistines, chasing them as far as Gath* and the gates of Ekron. The bodies of the dead and wounded Philistines
were strewn all along the road from Shaaraim, as far as
Gath and Ekron. 53Then the Israelite army returned and
plundered the deserted Philistine camp. 54(David took
the Philistine's head to Jerusalem, but he stored the
man's armor in his own tent.)

55As Saul watched David go out to fight the Philistine,
he asked Abner, the commander of his army, "Abner,
whose son is this young man?"

"I really don't know," Abner declared.

56"Well, find out who he is!" the king told him.

57As soon as David returned from killing Goliath, Abner
brought him to Saul with the Philistine's head still in his
hand. 58"Tell me about your father, young man," Saul said.

And David replied, "His name is Jesse, and we live in
Bethlehem."

18 SAUL BECOMES JEALOUS OF DAVID

After David had finished talking with Saul, he met Jonathan, the king's son. There was an immediate bond between them, for Jonathan loved David. 2From that day on
Saul kept David with him and wouldn't let him return
home. 3And Jonathan made a solemn pact with David,
because he loved him as he loved himself. 4Jonathan
sealed the pact by taking off his robe and giving it to David,
together with his tunic, sword, bow, and belt.

A TRUE FRIENDSHIP 18:1-4

Soon after David and Jonathan met, they became close friends. Although Jonathan was probably somewhat older than David, their friendship is one of the deepest and closest recorded in the Bible because they (1) based their friendship on commitment to God, not just each other; (2) let nothing come between them—not even career or family problems; (3) drew closer together when their friendship was tested; and (4) were able to remain friends to the end. Is that the kind of loyalty you have for your friends? ■

5Whatever Saul asked David to do, David did it successfully. So Saul made him a commander over the men
of war, an appointment that was welcomed by the people
and Saul's officers alike.

6When the victorious Israelite army was returning
home after David had killed the Philistine, women from
all the towns of Israel came out to meet King Saul. They
sang and danced for joy with tambourines and cymbals.*
7This was their song:

"Saul has killed his thousands,
and David his ten thousands!"

8This made Saul very angry. "What's this?" he said.
"They credit David with ten thousands and me with only
thousands. Next they'll be making him their king!" 9So
from that time on Saul kept a jealous eye on David.

10The very next day a tormenting spirit* from God
overwhelmed Saul, and he began to rave in his house like
a madman. David was playing the harp, as he did each
day. But Saul had a spear in his hand, 11and he suddenly
hurled it at David, intending to pin him to the wall. But
David escaped him twice.

12Saul was then afraid of David, for the LORD was with
David and had turned away from Saul. 13Finally, Saul sent
him away and appointed him commander over 1,000
men, and David faithfully led his troops into battle.

14David continued to succeed in everything he did, for
the LORD was with him. 15When Saul recognized this, he
became even more afraid of him. 16But all Israel and Judah loved David because he was so successful at leading
his troops into battle.

DAVID MARRIES SAUL'S DAUGHTER

17One day Saul said to David, "I am ready to give you my
older daughter, Merab, as your wife. But first you must
prove yourself to be a real warrior by fighting the LORD's

17:52 As in some Greek manuscripts; Hebrew reads *a valley*. **18:6** The type of instrument represented by the word *cymbals* is uncertain.
18:10 Or *an evil spirit*.

battles." For Saul thought, "I'll send him out against the Philistines and let them kill him rather than doing it myself."
18"Who am I, and what is my family in Israel that I
should be the king's son-in-law?" David exclaimed. "My
father's family is nothing!" 19So* when the time came for
Saul to give his daughter Merab in marriage to David, he
gave her instead to Adriel, a man from Meholah.

POPULARITY 18:5-18

While Saul's popularity made him arrogant, David remained humble even when the entire nation praised him. Although David succeeded in almost everything he tried and became famous throughout the land, he refused to allow his popularity to go to his head. Being the "flavor of the month" can lead to an inflated sense of importance if a person isn't careful. Next time you do something cool, how will you react to praise? ■

20In the meantime, Saul's daughter Michal had fallen
in love with David, and Saul was delighted when he heard
about it. 21"Here's another chance to see him killed by the
Philistines!" Saul said to himself. But to David he said,
"Today you have a second chance to become my son-in-
law!"
22Then Saul told his men to say to David, "The king
really likes you, and so do we. Why don't you accept the
king's offer and become his son-in-law?"
23When Saul's men said these things to David, he replied, "How can a poor man from a humble family afford
the bride price for the daughter of a king?"
24When Saul's men reported this back to the king, 25he
told them, "Tell David that all I want for the bride price is
100 Philistine foreskins! Vengeance on my enemies is all
I really want." But what Saul had in mind was that David
would be killed in the fight.
26David was delighted to accept the offer. Before the
time limit expired, 27he and his men went out and
killed 200 Philistines. Then David fulfilled the king's
requirement by presenting all their foreskins to him.
So Saul gave his daughter Michal to David to be his
wife.
28When Saul realized that the LORD was with David
and how much his daughter Michal loved him, 29Saul became even more afraid of him, and he remained David's
enemy for the rest of his life.
30Every time the commanders of the Philistines attacked, David was more successful against them than all
the rest of Saul's officers. So David's name became very
famous.

19 SAUL TRIES TO KILL DAVID

Saul now urged his servants and his son Jonathan to
assassinate David. But Jonathan, because of his strong
affection for David, 2told him what his father was planning. "Tomorrow morning," he warned him, "you must
find a hiding place out in the fields. 3I'll ask my father to
go out there with me, and I'll talk to him about you. Then
I'll tell you everything I can find out."
4The next morning Jonathan spoke with his father
about David, saying many good things about him. "The
king must not sin against his servant David," Jonathan
said. "He's never done anything to harm you. He has always helped you in any way he could. 5Have you forgotten about the time he risked his life to kill the Philistine
giant and how the LORD brought a great victory to all Israel as a result? You were certainly happy about it then.
Why should you murder an innocent man like David?
There is no reason for it at all!"
6So Saul listened to Jonathan and vowed, "As surely as
the LORD lives, David will not be killed."
7Afterward Jonathan called David and told him what
had happened. Then he brought David to Saul, and David
served in the court as before.
8War broke out again after that, and David led his
troops against the Philistines. He attacked them with
such fury that they all ran away.
9But one day when Saul was sitting at home, with spear
in hand, the tormenting spirit* from the LORD suddenly
came upon him again. As David played his harp, 10Saul
hurled his spear at David. But David dodged out of the
way, and leaving the spear stuck in the wall, he fled and
escaped into the night.

MICHAL SAVES DAVID'S LIFE

11Then Saul sent troops to watch David's house. They
were told to kill David when he came out the next morning. But Michal, David's wife, warned him, "If you don't
escape tonight, you will be dead by morning." 12So she
helped him climb out through a window, and he fled and
escaped. 13Then she took an idol* and put it in his bed,
covered it with blankets, and put a cushion of goat's hair
at its head.
14When the troops came to arrest David, she told them
he was sick and couldn't get out of bed.
15But Saul sent the troops back to get David. He ordered, "Bring him to me in his bed so I can kill him!" 16But
when they came to carry David out, they discovered that
it was only an idol in the bed with a cushion of goat's hair
at its head.
17"Why have you betrayed me like this and let my enemy escape?" Saul demanded of Michal.
"I had to," Michal replied. "He threatened to kill me if I
didn't help him."
18So David escaped and went to Ramah to see Samuel,
and he told him all that Saul had done to him. Then Samuel took David with him to live at Naioth. 19When the report reached Saul that David was at Naioth in Ramah, 20he
sent troops to capture him. But when they arrived and
saw Samuel leading a group of prophets who were
prophesying, the Spirit of God came upon Saul's men,
and they also began to prophesy. 21When Saul heard
what had happened, he sent other troops, but they, too,
prophesied! The same thing happened a third time.

18:19 Or *But*. **19:9** Or *evil spirit*. **19:13** Hebrew *teraphim;* also in 19:16.

[22]Finally, Saul himself went to Ramah and arrived at the
great well in Secu. "Where are Samuel and David?" he
demanded.
"They are at Naioth in Ramah," someone told him.
[23]But on the way to Naioth in Ramah the Spirit of God
came even upon Saul, and he, too, began to prophesy all
the way to Naioth! [24]He tore off his clothes and lay naked
on the ground all day and all night, prophesying in the
presence of Samuel. The people who were watching exclaimed, "What? Is even Saul a prophet?"

GOD'S PROTECTION 19:23

Jonathan spoke up for David (19:4). Michal helped him escape (19:11-17). Samuel gave him a place to hide (19:18). The Spirit of God interrupted Saul's manhunt (19:23). Each of these events was a demonstration of how God protected David from Saul. In what ways has God protected you recently? ■

20

JONATHAN HELPS DAVID

David now fled from Naioth in Ramah and found Jonathan. "What have I done?" he exclaimed. "What is my
crime? How have I offended your father that he is so determined to kill me?"
[2]"That's not true!" Jonathan protested. "You're not going to die. He always tells me everything he's going to do,
even the little things. I know my father wouldn't hide
something like this from me. It just isn't so!"
[3]Then David took an oath before Jonathan and said,
"Your father knows perfectly well about our friendship,
so he has said to himself, 'I won't tell Jonathan—why
should I hurt him?' But I swear to you that I am only a step
away from death! I swear it by the LORD and by your own
soul!"
[4]"Tell me what I can do to help you," Jonathan
exclaimed.
[5]David replied, "Tomorrow we celebrate the new
moon festival. I've always eaten with the king on this occasion, but tomorrow I'll hide in the field and stay there
until the evening of the third day. [6]If your father asks
where I am, tell him I asked permission to go home to
Bethlehem for an annual family sacrifice. [7]If he says,
'Fine!' you will know all is well. But if he is angry and loses
his temper, you will know he is determined to kill me.
[8]Show me this loyalty as my sworn friend—for we made a
solemn pact before the LORD—or kill me yourself if I have
sinned against your father. But please don't betray me to
him!"
[9]"Never!" Jonathan exclaimed. "You know that if I had
the slightest notion my father was planning to kill you, I
would tell you at once."
[10]Then David asked, "How will I know whether or not
your father is angry?"
[11]"Come out to the field with me," Jonathan replied.
And they went out there together. [12]Then Jonathan told
David, "I promise by the LORD, the God of Israel, that by
this time tomorrow, or the next day at the latest, I will talk
to my father and let you know at once how he feels about
you. If he speaks favorably about you, I will let you know.
[13]But if he is angry and wants you killed, may the LORD
strike me and even kill me if I don't warn you so you can
escape and live. May the LORD be with you as he used to
be with my father. [14]And may you treat me with the faithful love of the LORD as long as I live. But if I die, [15]treat my
family with this faithful love, even when the LORD destroys all your enemies from the face of the earth."
[16]So Jonathan made a solemn pact with David,* saying,
"May the LORD destroy all your enemies!" [17]And Jonathan
made David reaffirm his vow of friendship again, for Jonathan loved David as he loved himself.
[18]Then Jonathan said, "Tomorrow we celebrate the
new moon festival. You will be missed when your place at
the table is empty. [19]The day after tomorrow, toward evening, go to the place where you hid before, and wait there
by the stone pile.* [20]I will come out and shoot three arrows to the side of the stone pile as though I were shooting at a target. [21]Then I will send a boy to bring the arrows
back. If you hear me tell him, 'They're on this side,' then
you will know, as surely as the LORD lives, that all is well,
and there is no trouble. [22]But if I tell him, 'Go farther—the
arrows are still ahead of you,' then it will mean that you
must leave immediately, for the LORD is sending you
away. [23]And may the LORD make us keep our promises to
each other, for he has witnessed them."
[24]So David hid himself in the field, and when the new
moon festival began, the king sat down to eat. [25]He sat at his
usual place against the wall, with Jonathan sitting opposite
him* and Abner beside him. But David's place was empty.
[26]Saul didn't say anything about it that day, for he said to
himself, "Something must have made David ceremonially
unclean." [27]But when David's place was empty again the
next day, Saul asked Jonathan, "Why hasn't the son of Jesse
been here for the meal either yesterday or today?"
[28]Jonathan replied, "David earnestly asked me if he
could go to Bethlehem. [29]He said, 'Please let me go, for we
are having a family sacrifice. My brother demanded that I
be there. So please let me get away to see my brothers.'
That's why he isn't here at the king's table."
[30]Saul boiled with rage at Jonathan. "You stupid son of
a whore!"* he swore at him. "Do you think I don't know
that you want him to be king in your place, shaming yourself and your mother? [31]As long as that son of Jesse is
alive, you'll never be king. Now go and get him so I can kill
him!"
[32]"But why should he be put to death?" Jonathan asked
his father. "What has he done?" [33]Then Saul hurled his
spear at Jonathan, intending to kill him. So at last Jonathan realized that his father was really determined to kill
David.
[34]Jonathan left the table in fierce anger and refused to
eat on that second day of the festival, for he was crushed
by his father's shameful behavior toward David.

20:16 Hebrew *with the house of David.* 20:19 Hebrew *the stone Ezel.* The meaning of the Hebrew is uncertain. 20:25 As in Greek version; Hebrew reads *with Jonathan standing.* 20:30 Hebrew *You son of a perverse and rebellious woman.*

[35]The next morning, as agreed, Jonathan went out into
the field and took a young boy with him to gather his arrows. [36]"Start running," he told the boy, "so you can find
the arrows as I shoot them." So the boy ran, and Jonathan
shot an arrow beyond him. [37]When the boy had almost
reached the arrow, Jonathan shouted, "The arrow is still
ahead of you. [38]Hurry, hurry, don't wait." So the boy
quickly gathered up the arrows and ran back to his master. [39]He, of course, suspected nothing; only Jonathan and
David understood the signal. [40]Then Jonathan gave his
bow and arrows to the boy and told him to take them
back to town.

[41]As soon as the boy was gone, David came out from
where he had been hiding near the stone pile.* Then David bowed three times to Jonathan with his face to the
ground. Both of them were in tears as they embraced
each other and said good-bye, especially David.

[42]At last Jonathan said to David, "Go in peace, for we have
sworn loyalty to each other in the LORD's name. The LORD is
the witness of a bond between us and our children forever." Then David left, and Jonathan returned to the town.*

21 DAVID RUNS FROM SAUL

1*David went to the town of Nob to see Ahimelech the
priest. Ahimelech trembled when he saw him. "Why are
you alone?" he asked. "Why is no one with you?"

[2]"The king has sent me on a private matter," David said.
"He told me not to tell anyone why I am here. I have told my
men where to meet me later. [3]Now, what is there to eat?
Give me five loaves of bread or anything else you have."

LYING 21:2

David lied to protect himself from Saul (21:10). Some may excuse this lie because David feared for his life. But nowhere in Scripture is David's lie condoned. In fact, his lie led to the deaths of 85 priests (22:9-23). The Bible makes it very clear that lying is wrong (Lev 19:11) and may lead to all sorts of harmful consequences. Is any lie worth that? ■

[4]"We don't have any regular bread," the priest replied.
"But there is the holy bread, which you can have if your
young men have not slept with any women recently."

[5]"Don't worry," David replied. "I never allow my men to
be with women when they are on a campaign. And since
they stay clean even on ordinary trips, how much more on
this one!"

[6]Since there was no other food available, the priest
gave him the holy bread—the Bread of the Presence that
was placed before the LORD in the Tabernacle. It had just
been replaced that day with fresh bread.

20:41 As in Greek version; Hebrew reads *near the south edge*. **20:42** This sentence is numbered 21:1 in Hebrew text. **21:1** Verses 21:1-15 are numbered 21:2-16 in Hebrew text.

JONATHAN

UPS:
- Brave, loyal, and a natural leader
- Closest friend David ever had
- Did not put his personal well-being ahead of those he loved
- Depended on God

STATS:
- Occupation: Military leader
- Relatives: Saul (father); Ahinoam (mother); Abinadab, Malchishua, and Ishbosheth (brothers); Merab and Michal (sisters); Mephibosheth (son)

BOTTOM LINE:

Loyalty is one of the strongest aspects of friendship.

An allegiance to God puts all other relationships in perspective.

Great friendships are costly.

Jonathan's story is told in 1 Sam 13–15; 18–20; 31. He is also mentioned in 2 Sam 9.

JONATHAN Loyalty is one of life's most costly qualities and is the most unselfish part of love. To be loyal, you cannot live only for yourself. Loyal people not only stand by their commitments, they are also willing to suffer for them. Jonathan is a shining example of loyalty. Sometimes he was forced to deal with a conflict between his loyalties to his father, Saul, and to his friend David. For Jonathan, truth always guided loyalty.

Jonathan found the source of truth in his relationship with God. He realized that no matter what, he must be loyal to him. Loyalty to God gave Jonathan the wisdom to deal effectively with the complicated situations in his life. He was loyal to Saul because Saul was his father and the king. He was loyal to David because David was his friend. But his loyalty to God helped him see the limits of his other relationships.

The conflicting demands of our relationships can be challenging to us as well. If we try to settle these conflicts only at the human level, we will constantly have to deal with a sense of betrayal. No other human can claim the loyalty that belongs to God. If we communicate to our friends that our number-one loyalty is to God and his truth, many of our choices will be much clearer. Do those closest to you know who has your greatest loyalty?

[7]Now Doeg the Edomite, Saul's chief herdsman, was
there that day, having been detained before the LORD.*
[8]David asked Ahimelech, "Do you have a spear or
sword? The king's business was so urgent that I didn't
even have time to grab a weapon!"
[9]"I only have the sword of Goliath the Philistine, whom
you killed in the valley of Elah," the priest replied. "It is
wrapped in a cloth behind the ephod. Take that if you
want it, for there is nothing else here."
"There is nothing like it!" David replied. "Give it to me!"
[10]So David escaped from Saul and went to King Achish
of Gath. [11]But the officers of Achish were unhappy about
his being there. "Isn't this David, the king of the land?"
they asked. "Isn't he the one the people honor with
dances, singing,

'Saul has killed his thousands,
and David his ten thousands'?"

[12]David heard these comments and was very afraid of
what King Achish of Gath might do to him. [13]So he pretended to be insane, scratching on doors and drooling
down his beard.
[14]Finally, King Achish said to his men, "Must you bring
me a madman? [15]We already have enough of them
around here! Why should I let someone like this be my
guest?"

22 DAVID AT THE CAVE OF ADULLAM

So David left Gath and escaped to the cave of Adullam.
Soon his brothers and all his other relatives joined him
there. [2]Then others began coming—men who were in
trouble or in debt or who were just discontented—until
David was the captain of about 400 men.
[3]Later David went to Mizpeh in Moab, where he asked
the king, "Please allow my father and mother to live here
with you until I know what God is going to do for me." [4]So
David's parents stayed in Moab with the king during the
entire time David was living in his stronghold.
[5]One day the prophet Gad told David, "Leave the
stronghold and return to the land of Judah." So David
went to the forest of Hereth.
[6]The news of his arrival in Judah soon reached Saul. At
the time, the king was sitting beneath the tamarisk tree
on the hill at Gibeah, holding his spear and surrounded
by his officers.
[7]"Listen here, you men of Benjamin!" Saul shouted to
his officers when he heard the news. "Has that son of Jesse promised every one of you fields and vineyards? Has
he promised to make you all generals and captains in his
army?* [8]Is that why you have conspired against me? For
not one of you told me when my own son made a solemn
pact with the son of Jesse. You're not even sorry for me.
Think of it! My own son—encouraging him to kill me, as
he is trying to do this very day!"
[9]Then Doeg the Edomite, who was standing there with
Saul's men, spoke up. "When I was at Nob," he said, "I saw
the son of Jesse talking to the priest, Ahimelech son of
Ahitub. [10]Ahimelech consulted the LORD for him. Then
he gave him food and the sword of Goliath the
Philistine."

THE SLAUGHTER OF THE PRIESTS

[11]King Saul immediately sent for Ahimelech and all his
family, who served as priests at Nob. [12]When they arrived, Saul shouted at him, "Listen to me, you son of Ahitub!"
"What is it, my king?" Ahimelech asked.
[13]"Why have you and the son of Jesse conspired
against me?" Saul demanded. "Why did you give him
food and a sword? Why have you consulted God for him?
Why have you encouraged him to kill me, as he is trying
to do this very day?"
[14]"But sir," Ahimelech replied, "is anyone among all
your servants as faithful as David, your son-in-law? Why,
he is the captain of your bodyguard and a highly honored
member of your household! [15]This was certainly not the
first time I had consulted God for him! May the king not
accuse me and my family in this matter, for I knew nothing at all of any plot against you."
[16]"You will surely die, Ahimelech, along with your entire family!" the king shouted. [17]And he ordered his bodyguards, "Kill these priests of the LORD, for they are allies
and conspirators with David! They knew he was running
away from me, but they didn't tell me!" But Saul's men refused to kill the LORD's priests.

GOOD WILL TRIUMPH 22:18-19

Why did God allow 85 innocent priests to be killed? Scripture does not give a specific answer to this question, but it gives some insight into the issue.

Serving God is not a guarantee that all will be well in this life. While God does not promise that good people will never be touched by the evil in this world, we can find comfort in his promise that ultimately all evil will be abolished. Those who remain faithful to God will experience a reward in the age to come (Matt 5:11-12; Rev 21:1-7; 22:1-21). ■

[18]Then the king said to Doeg, "You do it." So Doeg the
Edomite turned on them and killed them that day, eighty-
five priests in all, still wearing their priestly garments.
[19]Then he went to Nob, the town of the priests, and killed
the priests' families—men and women, children and babies—and all the cattle, donkeys, sheep, and goats.
[20]Only Abiathar, one of the sons of Ahimelech, escaped and fled to David. [21]When he told David that Saul
had killed the priests of the LORD, [22]David exclaimed, "I
knew it! When I saw Doeg the Edomite there that day, I
knew he was sure to tell Saul. Now I have caused the
death of all your father's family. [23]Stay here with me, and
don't be afraid. I will protect you with my own life, for the
same person wants to kill us both."

21:7 The meaning of the Hebrew is uncertain. 22:7 Hebrew *commanders of thousands and commanders of hundreds?*

23 DAVID PROTECTS THE TOWN OF KEILAH

One day news came to David that the Philistines were at Keilah stealing grain from the threshing floors. 2David asked the LORD, "Should I go and attack them?"

"Yes, go and save Keilah," the LORD told him.

DECISIONS 23:2

David asked God for advice *before* he took action. He listened to God's directions and then proceeded accordingly. Rather than trying to find God's will *after* the fact or having to ask God to undo the results of our hasty decisions, we should take time to discern God's will beforehand. We can hear him speak through the advice we receive from others, through his Word, and through the leading of his Spirit in our heart. ■

3But David's men said, "We're afraid even here in Judah. We certainly don't want to go to Keilah to fight the whole Philistine army!"

4So David asked the LORD again, and again the LORD replied, "Go down to Keilah, for I will help you conquer the Philistines."

5So David and his men went to Keilah. They slaughtered the Philistines and took all their livestock and rescued the people of Keilah. 6Now when Abiathar son of Ahimelech fled to David at Keilah, he brought the ephod with him.

7Saul soon learned that David was at Keilah. "Good!" he exclaimed. "We've got him now! God has handed him over to me, for he has trapped himself in a walled town!" 8So Saul mobilized his entire army to march to Keilah and besiege David and his men.

9But David learned of Saul's plan and told Abiathar the priest to bring the ephod and ask the LORD what he should do. 10Then David prayed, "O LORD, God of Israel, I have heard that Saul is planning to come and destroy Keilah because I am here. 11Will the leaders of Keilah betray me to him?* And will Saul actually come as I have heard? O LORD, God of Israel, please tell me."

And the LORD said, "He will come."

12Again David asked, "Will the leaders of Keilah betray me and my men to Saul?"

And the LORD replied, "Yes, they will betray you."

DAVID HIDES IN THE WILDERNESS

13So David and his men—about 600 of them now—left Keilah and began roaming the countryside. Word soon reached Saul that David had escaped, so he didn't go to Keilah after all. 14David now stayed in the strongholds of the wilderness and in the hill country of Ziph. Saul hunted him day after day, but God didn't let Saul find him.

15One day near Horesh, David received the news that Saul was on the way to Ziph to search for him and kill him. 16Jonathan went to find David and encouraged him to stay strong in his faith in God. 17"Don't be afraid," Jonathan reassured him. "My father will never find you! You are going to be the king of Israel, and I will be next to you, as my father, Saul, is well aware." 18So the two of them renewed their solemn pact before the LORD. Then Jonathan returned home, while David stayed at Horesh.

19But now the men of Ziph went to Saul in Gibeah and betrayed David to him. "We know where David is hiding," they said. "He is in the strongholds of Horesh on the hill of Hakilah, which is in the southern part of Jeshimon. 20Come down whenever you're ready, O king, and we will catch him and hand him over to you!"

21"The LORD bless you," Saul said. "At last someone is concerned about me! 22Go and check again to be sure of where he is staying and who has seen him there, for I know that he is very crafty. 23Discover his hiding places, and come back when you are sure. Then I'll go with you. And if he is in the area at all, I'll track him down, even if I have to search every hiding place in Judah!" 24So the men of Ziph returned home ahead of Saul.

Meanwhile, David and his men had moved into the wilderness of Maon in the Arabah Valley south of Jeshimon. 25When David heard that Saul and his men were searching for him, he went even farther into the wilderness to the great rock, and he remained there in the wilderness of Maon. But Saul kept after him in the wilderness.

26Saul and David were now on opposite sides of a mountain. Just as Saul and his men began to close in on David and his men, 27an urgent message reached Saul that the Philistines were raiding Israel again. 28So Saul quit chasing David and returned to fight the Philistines. Ever since that time, the place where David was camped has been called the Rock of Escape.* 29*David then went to live in the strongholds of En-gedi.

FRIENDS 23:16-18

David and Jonathan shared a deep friendship. They encouraged each other's faith in God and trusted each other with their deepest thoughts and closest confidences. These are the marks of true friendship. How do you encourage your friends in their faith? ■

24 DAVID SPARES SAUL'S LIFE

1*After Saul returned from fighting the Philistines, he was told that David had gone into the wilderness of En-gedi. 2So Saul chose 3,000 elite troops from all Israel and went to search for David and his men near the rocks of the wild goats.

3At the place where the road passes some sheepfolds, Saul went into a cave to relieve himself. But as it happened, David and his men were hiding farther back in that very cave!

23:11 Some manuscripts lack the first sentence of 23:11. **23:28** Hebrew *Sela-hammahlekoth.* **23:29** Verse 23:29 is numbered 24:1 in Hebrew text. **24:1** Verses 24:1-22 are numbered 24:2-23 in Hebrew text.

4"Now's your opportunity!" David's men whispered to him. "Today the LORD is telling you, 'I will certainly put your enemy into your power, to do with as you wish.'" So David crept forward and cut off a piece of the hem of Saul's robe.

5But then David's conscience began bothering him because he had cut Saul's robe. 6"The LORD knows I shouldn't have done that to my lord the king," he said to his men. "The LORD forbid that I should do this to my lord the king and attack the LORD's anointed one, for the LORD himself has chosen him." 7So David restrained his men and did not let them kill Saul.

RESPECT 24:5-7

David had great respect for Saul, even though Saul continually tried to kill him. Although Saul was in a state of rebellion against God, David still respected the position he held as God's anointed king.

Romans 13:1-7 reminds us that God placed the government and its leaders in power. We may not know why, but like David, we are to respect the positions and roles of those to whom God has given authority. There is one exception, however. Because God is our highest authority, we should not allow a leader to force us to violate God's law. ■

After Saul had left the cave and gone on his way, 8David came out and shouted after him, "My lord the king!" And when Saul looked around, David bowed low before him. 9Then he shouted to Saul, "Why do you listen to the people who say I am trying to harm you? 10This very day you can see with your own eyes it isn't true. For the LORD placed you at my mercy back there in the cave. Some of my men told me to kill you, but I spared you. For I said, 'I will never harm the king—he is the LORD's anointed one.' 11Look, my father, at what I have in my hand. It is a piece of the hem of your robe! I cut it off, but I didn't kill you. This proves that I am not trying to harm you and that I have not sinned against you, even though you have been hunting for me to kill me.

12"May the LORD judge between us. Perhaps the LORD will punish you for what you are trying to do to me, but I will never harm you. 13As that old proverb says, 'From evil people come evil deeds.' So you can be sure I will never harm you. 14Who is the king of Israel trying to catch anyway? Should he spend his time chasing one who is as worthless as a dead dog or a single flea? 15May the LORD therefore judge which of us is right and punish the guilty one. He is my advocate, and he will rescue me from your power!"

16When David had finished speaking, Saul called back, "Is that really you, my son David?" Then he began to cry. 17And he said to David, "You are a better man than I am, for you have repaid me good for evil. 18Yes, you have been amazingly kind to me today, for when the LORD put me in a place where you could have killed me, you didn't do it. 19Who else would let his enemy get away when he had him in his power? May the LORD reward you well for the kindness you have shown me today. 20And now I realize that you are surely going to be king, and that the kingdom of Israel will flourish under your rule. 21Now swear to me by the LORD that when that happens you will not kill my family and destroy my line of descendants!"

22So David promised this to Saul with an oath. Then Saul went home, but David and his men went back to their stronghold.

25 THE DEATH OF SAMUEL

Now Samuel died, and all Israel gathered for his funeral. They buried him at his house in Ramah.

NABAL ANGERS DAVID

Then David moved down to the wilderness of Maon.* 2There was a wealthy man from Maon who owned property near the town of Carmel. He had 3,000 sheep and 1,000 goats, and it was sheep-shearing time. 3This man's name was Nabal, and his wife, Abigail, was a sensible and beautiful woman. But Nabal, a descendant of Caleb, was crude and mean in all his dealings.

4When David heard that Nabal was shearing his sheep, 5he sent ten of his young men to Carmel with this message for Nabal: 6"Peace and prosperity to you, your family, and everything you own! 7I am told that it is sheep-shearing time. While your shepherds stayed among us near Carmel, we never harmed them, and nothing was ever stolen from them. 8Ask your own men, and they will tell you this is true. So would you be kind to us, since we have come at a time of celebration? Please share any provisions you might have on hand with us and with your friend David." 9David's young men gave this message to Nabal in David's name, and they waited for a reply.

10"Who is this fellow David?" Nabal sneered to the young men. "Who does this son of Jesse think he is? There are lots of servants these days who run away from their masters. 11Should I take my bread and my water and my meat that I've slaughtered for my shearers and give it to a band of outlaws who come from who knows where?"

12So David's young men returned and told him what Nabal had said. 13"Get your swords!" was David's reply as he strapped on his own. Then 400 men started off with David, and 200 remained behind to guard their equipment.

14Meanwhile, one of Nabal's servants went to Abigail and told her, "David sent messengers from the wilderness to greet our master, but he screamed insults at them. 15These men have been very good to us, and we never suffered any harm from them. Nothing was stolen from us the whole time they were with us. 16In fact, day and night they were like a wall of protection to us and the sheep. 17You need to know this and figure out what to do, for there is going to be trouble for our master and his whole family. He's so ill-tempered that no one can even talk to him!"

18Abigail wasted no time. She quickly gathered

25:1 As in Greek version (see also 25:2); Hebrew reads *Paran*.

200 loaves of bread, two wineskins full of wine, five
sheep that had been slaughtered, nearly a bushel* of
roasted grain, 100 clusters of raisins, and 200 fig cakes.
She packed them on donkeys 19and said to her servants,
"Go on ahead. I will follow you shortly." But she didn't tell
her husband Nabal what she was doing.
20As she was riding her donkey into a mountain ravine,
she saw David and his men coming toward her. 21David
had just been saying, "A lot of good it did to help this fellow. We protected his flocks in the wilderness, and nothing he owned was lost or stolen. But he has repaid me evil
for good. 22May God strike me and kill me* if even one
man of his household is still alive tomorrow morning!"

STOP AND LISTEN 25:24

After Nabal refused his request for food, David was in no mood to listen when he set out for Nabal's property (25:13, 21-22). Nevertheless, he stopped to hear what Abigail had to say. If he had ignored her, he would have been guilty of taking vengeance into his own hands. No matter how right we think we are, we must always be careful to stop and listen to what others have to say. The extra time and effort can save us much pain and trouble in the long run. ■

ABIGAIL INTERCEDES FOR NABAL

23When Abigail saw David, she quickly got off her donkey
and bowed low before him. 24She fell at his feet and said,
"I accept all blame in this matter, my lord. Please listen
to what I have to say. 25I know Nabal is a wicked and ill-
tempered man; please don't pay any attention to him. He
is a fool, just as his name suggests.* But I never even saw
the young men you sent.
26"Now, my lord, as surely as the LORD lives and you
yourself live, since the LORD has kept you from murdering and taking vengeance into your own hands, let all
your enemies and those who try to harm you be as cursed
as Nabal is. 27And here is a present that I, your servant,
have brought to you and your young men. 28Please forgive me if I have offended you in any way. The LORD will
surely reward you with a lasting dynasty, for you are
fighting the LORD's battles. And you have not done wrong
throughout your entire life.
29"Even when you are chased by those who seek to kill
you, your life is safe in the care of the LORD your God, secure in his treasure pouch! But the lives of your enemies
will disappear like stones shot from a sling! 30When the
LORD has done all he promised and has made you leader
of Israel, 31don't let this be a blemish on your record.
Then your conscience won't have to bear the staggering
burden of needless bloodshed and vengeance. And when
the LORD has done these great things for you, please remember me, your servant!"
32David replied to Abigail, "Praise the LORD, the God of
Israel, who has sent you to meet me today! 33Thank God
for your good sense! Bless you for keeping me from
murder and from carrying out vengeance with my own
hands. 34For I swear by the LORD, the God of Israel, who
has kept me from hurting you, that if you had not hurried
out to meet me, not one of Nabal's men would still be
alive tomorrow morning." 35Then David accepted her
present and told her, "Return home in peace. I have heard
what you said. We will not kill your husband."
36When Abigail arrived home, she found that Nabal
was throwing a big party and was celebrating like a king.
He was very drunk, so she didn't tell him anything about
her meeting with David until dawn the next day. 37In the
morning when Nabal was sober, his wife told him what
had happened. As a result he had a stroke,* and he lay
paralyzed on his bed like a stone. 38About ten days later,
the LORD struck him, and he died.

DAVID MARRIES ABIGAIL

39When David heard that Nabal was dead, he said, "Praise
the LORD, who has avenged the insult I received from Nabal and has kept me from doing it myself. Nabal has received the punishment for his sin." Then David sent
messengers to Abigail to ask her to become his wife.
40When the messengers arrived at Carmel, they told
Abigail, "David has sent us to take you back to marry
him."
41She bowed low to the ground and responded, "I, your
servant, would be happy to marry David. I would even be
willing to become a slave, washing the feet of his servants!" 42Quickly getting ready, she took along five of her
servant girls as attendants, mounted her donkey, and
went with David's messengers. And so she became his
wife. 43David also married Ahinoam from Jezreel, making both of them his wives. 44Saul, meanwhile, had given
his daughter Michal, David's wife, to a man from Gallim
named Palti son of Laish.

A CREATIVE IMPACT 26:1-17

David could have killed Saul and Abner and made a point. That action would have caused him to disobey God and set into motion unknown consequences. Instead, he took a water jug and a spear to show that he had had the opportunity to do evil, but chose not to do it. What are some creative, God-honoring ways you can make an impact in your school? Your neighborhood? ■

26 DAVID SPARES SAUL AGAIN

Now some men from Ziph came to Saul at Gibeah to tell
him, "David is hiding on the hill of Hakilah, which overlooks Jeshimon."
2So Saul took 3,000 of Israel's elite troops and went to
hunt him down in the wilderness of Ziph. 3Saul camped
along the road beside the hill of Hakilah, near Jeshimon,
where David was hiding. When David learned that Saul

25:18 Hebrew *5 seahs* [30 liters]. 25:22 As in Greek version; Hebrew reads *May God strike and kill the enemies of David.* 25:25 The name *Nabal* means "fool." 25:37 Hebrew *his heart failed him.*

had come after him into the wilderness, 4he sent out spies to verify the report of Saul's arrival.

5David slipped over to Saul's camp one night to look around. Saul and Abner son of Ner, the commander of his army, were sleeping inside a ring formed by the slumbering warriors. 6"Who will volunteer to go in there with me?" David asked Ahimelech the Hittite and Abishai son of Zeruiah, Joab's brother.

"I'll go with you," Abishai replied. 7So David and Abishai went right into Saul's camp and found him asleep, with his spear stuck in the ground beside his head. Abner and the soldiers were lying asleep around him.

> The LORD gives his own reward for doing good and for being loyal.
>
> *1 SAMUEL 26:23*

8"God has surely handed your enemy over to you this time!" Abishai whispered to David. "Let me pin him to the ground with one thrust of the spear; I won't need to strike twice!"

9"No!" David said. "Don't kill him. For who can remain innocent after attacking the LORD's anointed one? 10Surely the LORD will strike Saul down someday, or he will die of old age or in battle. 11The LORD forbid that I should kill the one he has anointed! But take his spear and that jug of water beside his head, and then let's get out of here!"

12So David took the spear and jug of water that were near Saul's head. Then he and Abishai got away without anyone seeing them or even waking up, because the LORD had put Saul's men into a deep sleep.

13David climbed the hill opposite the camp until he was at a safe distance. 14Then he shouted down to the soldiers and to Abner son of Ner, "Wake up, Abner!"

"Who is it?" Abner demanded.

15"Well, Abner, you're a great man, aren't you?" David taunted. "Where in all Israel is there anyone as mighty? So why haven't you guarded your master the king when someone came to kill him? 16This isn't good at all! I swear by the LORD that you and your men deserve to die, because you failed to protect your master, the LORD's anointed! Look around! Where are the king's spear and the jug of water that were beside his head?"

17Saul recognized David's voice and called out, "Is that you, my son David?"

And David replied, "Yes, my lord the king. 18Why are you chasing me? What have I done? What is my crime? 19But now let my lord the king listen to his servant. If the LORD has stirred you up against me, then let him accept my offering. But if this is simply a human scheme, then may those involved be cursed by the LORD. For they have driven me from my home, so I can no longer live among the LORD's people, and they have said, 'Go, worship pagan gods.' 20Must I die on foreign soil, far from the presence of the LORD? Why has the king of Israel come out to search for a single flea? Why does he hunt me down like a partridge on the mountains?"

21Then Saul confessed, "I have sinned. Come back home, my son, and I will no longer try to harm you, for you valued my life today. I have been a fool and very, very wrong."

22"Here is your spear, O king," David replied. "Let one of your young men come over and get it. 23The LORD gives his own reward for doing good and for being loyal, and I refused to kill you even when the LORD placed you in my power, for you are the LORD's anointed one. 24Now may the LORD value my life, even as I have valued yours today. May he rescue me from all my troubles."

25And Saul said to David, "Blessings on you, my son David. You will do many heroic deeds, and you will surely succeed." Then David went away, and Saul returned home.

27

DAVID AMONG THE PHILISTINES

But David kept thinking to himself, "Someday Saul is going to get me. The best thing I can do is escape to the Philistines. Then Saul will stop hunting for me in Israelite territory, and I will finally be safe."

2So David took his 600 men and went over and joined Achish son of Maoch, the king of Gath. 3David and his men and their families settled there with Achish at Gath. David brought his two wives along with him—Ahinoam from Jezreel and Abigail, Nabal's widow from Carmel. 4Word soon reached Saul that David had fled to Gath, so he stopped hunting for him.

5One day David said to Achish, "If it is all right with you, we would rather live in one of the country towns instead of here in the royal city."

6So Achish gave him the town of Ziklag (which still belongs to the kings of Judah to this day), 7and they lived there among the Philistines for a year and four months.

PRETENSE 27:10-12

Was David wrong in falsely reporting his activities to Achish? No doubt David was lying; however, he may have felt that lying was justified in a time of war against an enemy. The Philistines were still his enemies, but their territory was an excellent place to hide from Saul.

You may never have to face life on the run like David. But one question is still very important: Is your loyalty to God real or pretend? ■

8David and his men spent their time raiding the Geshurites, the Girzites, and the Amalekites—people who had lived near Shur, toward the land of Egypt, since ancient times. 9David did not leave one person alive in the villages he attacked. He took the sheep, goats, cattle, donkeys, camels, and clothing before returning home to see King Achish.

10"Where did you make your raid today?" Achish would ask.

And David would reply, "Against the south of Judah, the Jerahmeelites, and the Kenites."

11No one was left alive to come to Gath and tell where he had really been. This happened again and again while he was living among the Philistines. 12Achish believed David and thought to himself, "By now the people of Israel must hate him bitterly. Now he will have to stay here and serve me forever!"

28 SAUL CONSULTS A MEDIUM

About that time the Philistines mustered their armies for another war with Israel. King Achish told David, "You and your men will be expected to join me in battle."

2"Very well!" David agreed. "Now you will see for yourself what we can do."

Then Achish told David, "I will make you my personal bodyguard for life."

3Meanwhile, Samuel had died, and all Israel had mourned for him. He was buried in Ramah, his hometown. And Saul had banned from the land of Israel all mediums and those who consult the spirits of the dead.

4The Philistines set up their camp at Shunem, and Saul gathered all the army of Israel and camped at Gilboa. 5When Saul saw the vast Philistine army, he became frantic with fear. 6He asked the LORD what he should do, but the LORD refused to answer him, either by dreams or by sacred lots* or by the prophets. 7Saul then said to his advisers, "Find a woman who is a medium, so I can go and ask her what to do."

His advisers replied, "There is a medium at Endor."

8So Saul disguised himself by wearing ordinary clothing instead of his royal robes. Then he went to the woman's home at night, accompanied by two of his men.

ACTING ON WHAT'S RIGHT 28:3-25

Although Saul had banned all mediums and psychics from Israel, he turned to one in desperation. Likewise, we may make a great show of denouncing something that we know is wrong. Yet if our heart doesn't change, we may find ourselves doing what we said was wrong. Knowing what is right and condemning what is wrong does not take the place of *doing* what is right. ■

"I have to talk to a man who has died," he said. "Will you call up his spirit for me?"

9"Are you trying to get me killed?" the woman demanded. "You know that Saul has outlawed all the mediums and all who consult the spirits of the dead. Why are you setting a trap for me?"

10But Saul took an oath in the name of the LORD and promised, "As surely as the LORD lives, nothing bad will happen to you for doing this."

11Finally, the woman said, "Well, whose spirit do you want me to call up?"

"Call up Samuel," Saul replied.

12When the woman saw Samuel, she screamed, "You've deceived me! You are Saul!"

13"Don't be afraid!" the king told her. "What do you see?"

"I see a god* coming up out of the earth," she said.

14"What does he look like?" Saul asked.

"He is an old man wrapped in a robe," she replied. Saul realized it was Samuel, and he fell to the ground before him.

15"Why have you disturbed me by calling me back?" Samuel asked Saul.

"Because I am in deep trouble," Saul replied. "The Philistines are at war with me, and God has left me and won't reply by prophets or dreams. So I have called for you to tell me what to do."

DIRECTIONS 28:15

God did not answer Saul's appeals for direction because Saul had not followed God's previous directions. Like Saul, many people wonder why their prayers seem unanswered. But if they don't fulfill the responsibilities God has already given them, further guidance cannot be given. Tempted to ignore some previously given advice? Remember what happened to Saul! ■

16But Samuel replied, "Why ask me, since the LORD has left you and has become your enemy? 17The LORD has done just as he said he would. He has torn the kingdom from you and given it to your rival, David. 18The LORD has done this to you today because you refused to carry out his fierce anger against the Amalekites. 19What's more, the LORD will hand you and the army of Israel over to the Philistines tomorrow, and you and your sons will be here with me. The LORD will bring down the entire army of Israel in defeat."

20Saul fell full length on the ground, paralyzed with fright because of Samuel's words. He was also faint with hunger, for he had eaten nothing all day and all night.

21When the woman saw how distraught he was, she said, "Sir, I obeyed your command at the risk of my life. 22Now do what I say, and let me give you a little something to eat so you can regain your strength for the trip back."

23But Saul refused. The men who were with him also urged him to eat, so he finally yielded and got up from the ground and sat on the couch.

24The woman had been fattening a calf, so she hurried out and killed it. She took some flour, kneaded it into dough and baked unleavened bread. 25She brought the meal to Saul and his men, and they ate it. Then they went out into the night.

29 THE PHILISTINES REJECT DAVID

The entire Philistine army now mobilized at Aphek, and the Israelites camped at the spring in Jezreel. 2As the

28:6 Hebrew *by Urim*. 28:13 Or *gods*.

Philistine rulers were leading out their troops in groups of hundreds and thousands, David and his men marched at the rear with King Achish. 3But the Philistine commanders demanded, "What are these Hebrews doing here?"

And Achish told them, "This is David, the servant of King Saul of Israel. He's been with me for years, and I've never found a single fault in him from the day he arrived until today."

4But the Philistine commanders were angry. "Send him back to the town you've given him!" they demanded. "He can't go into the battle with us. What if he turns against us in battle and becomes our adversary? Is there any better way for him to reconcile himself with his master than by handing our heads over to him? 5Isn't this the same David about whom the women of Israel sing in their dances,

'Saul has killed his thousands,
and David his ten thousands'?"

6So Achish finally summoned David and said to him, "I swear by the LORD that you have been a trustworthy ally. I think you should go with me into battle, for I've never found a single flaw in you from the day you arrived until today. But the other Philistine rulers won't hear of it. 7Please don't upset them, but go back quietly."

8"What have I done to deserve this treatment?" David demanded. "What have you ever found in your servant, that I can't go and fight the enemies of my lord the king?"

9But Achish insisted, "As far as I'm concerned, you're as perfect as an angel of God. But the Philistine commanders are afraid to have you with them in the battle. 10Now get up early in the morning, and leave with your men as soon as it gets light."

11So David and his men headed back into the land of the Philistines, while the Philistine army went on to Jezreel.

SCAPEGOAT 30:1-9

Faced with the tragedy of losing their families, David's soldiers began to turn against him and even talked about killing him. Instead of planning a rescue, they looked for someone to blame. But David began looking for a solution rather than a scapegoat. When you're facing problems, will you look for a scapegoat or a solution? ■

30 DAVID DESTROYS THE AMALEKITES

Three days later, when David and his men arrived home at their town of Ziklag, they found that the Amalekites had made a raid into the Negev and Ziklag; they had crushed Ziklag and burned it to the ground. 2They had carried off the women and children and everyone else but without killing anyone.

3When David and his men saw the ruins and realized what had happened to their families, 4they wept until they could weep no more. 5David's two wives, Ahinoam from Jezreel and Abigail, the widow of Nabal from Carmel, were among those captured. 6David was now in great danger because all his men were very bitter about losing their sons and daughters, and they began to talk of stoning him. But David found strength in the LORD his God.

7Then he said to Abiathar the priest, "Bring me the ephod!" So Abiathar brought it. 8Then David asked the LORD, "Should I chase after this band of raiders? Will I catch them?"

And the LORD told him, "Yes, go after them. You will surely recover everything that was taken from you!"

9So David and his 600 men set out, and they came to the brook Besor. 10But 200 of the men were too exhausted to cross the brook, so David continued the pursuit with 400 men.

KINDNESS 30:11-15

The Amalekites cruelly left a servant to die, but David and his men treated the young man kindly. He returned their kindness by leading them to the enemy, the Amalekites. If you make a habit of treating those you meet with respect and dignity no matter how insignificant they may seem, you might find yourself helped in return. (Check out Luke 6:31—the "golden rule.") ■

11Along the way they found an Egyptian man in a field and brought him to David. They gave him some bread to eat and water to drink. 12They also gave him part of a fig cake and two clusters of raisins, for he hadn't had anything to eat or drink for three days and nights. Before long his strength returned.

13"To whom do you belong, and where do you come from?" David asked him.

"I am an Egyptian—the slave of an Amalekite," he replied. "My master abandoned me three days ago because I was sick. 14We were on our way back from raiding the Kerethites in the Negev, the territory of Judah, and the land of Caleb, and we had just burned Ziklag."

15"Will you lead me to this band of raiders?" David asked.

The young man replied, "If you take an oath in God's name that you will not kill me or give me back to my master, then I will guide you to them."

16So he led David to them, and they found the Amalekites spread out across the fields, eating and drinking and dancing with joy because of the vast amount of plunder they had taken from the Philistines and the land of Judah. 17David and his men rushed in among them and slaughtered them throughout that night and the entire next day until evening. None of the Amalekites escaped except 400 young men who fled on camels. 18David got back everything the Amalekites had taken, and he rescued his two wives. 19Nothing was missing: small or great, son or daughter, nor anything else that had been taken. David brought everything back. 20He also recovered all the flocks and herds, and his men drove them ahead of the other livestock. "This plunder belongs to David!" they said.

[21]Then David returned to the brook Besor and met up with the 200 men who had been left behind because they were too exhausted to go with him. They went out to meet David and his men, and David greeted them joyfully. [22]But some evil troublemakers among David's men said, "They didn't go with us, so they can't have any of the plunder we recovered. Give them their wives and children, and tell them to be gone."

[23]But David said, "No, my brothers! Don't be selfish with what the Lord has given us. He has kept us safe and helped us defeat the band of raiders that attacked us. [24]Who will listen when you talk like this? We share and share alike—those who go to battle and those who guard the equipment." [25]From then on David made this a decree and regulation for Israel, and it is still followed today.

[26]When he arrived at Ziklag, David sent part of the plunder to the elders of Judah, who were his friends. "Here is a present for you, taken from the Lord's enemies," he said.

[27]The gifts were sent to the people of the following towns David had visited: Bethel, Ramoth-negev, Jattir, [28]Aroer, Siphmoth, Eshtemoa, [29]Racal,* the towns of the Jerahmeelites, the towns of the Kenites, [30]Hormah, Borashan, Athach, [31]Hebron, and all the other places David and his men had visited.

CHARACTER 31:3-4

Saul was tall, handsome, strong, rich, and powerful. But these qualities did not make him someone to imitate. He was tall physically, but he was small in God's eyes. He was strong, but his lack of faith made him weak. In other words, he looked good on the outside, but not so good on the inside. A good character is worth more than a face that could launch one thousand *Teen People* magazine covers. Would you agree? ■

31 THE DEATH OF SAUL

Now the Philistines attacked Israel, and the men of Israel fled before them. Many were slaughtered on the slopes of Mount Gilboa. [2]The Philistines closed in on Saul and his sons, and they killed three of his sons—Jonathan, Abinadab, and Malkishua. [3]The fighting grew very fierce around Saul, and the Philistine archers caught up with him and wounded him severely.

[4]Saul groaned to his armor bearer, "Take your sword and kill me before these pagan Philistines come to run me through and taunt and torture me."

But his armor bearer was afraid and would not do it. So Saul took his own sword and fell on it. [5]When his armor bearer realized that Saul was dead, he fell on his own sword and died beside the king. [6]So Saul, his three sons, his armor bearer, and his troops all died together that same day.

OBEDIENCE 31:13

Saul's death was also the death of an ideal. Israel could no longer believe that having a king like the other nations would solve their problems. The real problem was not the form of government, but the wrong actions of the king. Like a brick, each obedient act is small in itself, but in time the acts pile up, building a huge wall of strong character—a great defense against temptation. Saul failed to build a wall of defense, but you don't have to. Have you added another brick lately? ■

[7]When the Israelites on the other side of the Jezreel Valley and beyond the Jordan saw that the Israelite army had fled and that Saul and his sons were dead, they abandoned their towns and fled. So the Philistines moved in and occupied their towns.

[8]The next day, when the Philistines went out to strip the dead, they found the bodies of Saul and his three sons on Mount Gilboa. [9]So they cut off Saul's head and stripped off his armor. Then they proclaimed the good news of Saul's death in their pagan temple and to the people throughout the land of Philistia. [10]They placed his armor in the temple of the Ashtoreths, and they fastened his body to the wall of the city of Beth-shan.

[11]But when the people of Jabesh-gilead heard what the Philistines had done to Saul, [12]all their mighty warriors traveled through the night to Beth-shan and took the bodies of Saul and his sons down from the wall. They brought them to Jabesh, where they burned the bodies. [13]Then they took their bones and buried them beneath the tamarisk tree at Jabesh, and they fasted for seven days.

30:29 Greek version reads *Carmel.*

2 SAMUEL

WHO DO YOU look up to? Your youth leader? The lead singer of your favorite band? We usually admire heroes/heroines—those rare individuals who seem to do extraordinary things. The problem is they all seem to fall off the pedestals we put them on.

That's the way it is with any human being. All of us make mistakes. But somehow we expect our heroes to be bigger than life—to be perfect in fact.

David was the essence of a hero: strong, brave, handsome, forceful, and committed. He was on top of the world—he was king, his enemies were defeated, and the people loved him. But David was human, too. At the height of his success, he blew it and tried to cover up one wrong with another and another (chapters 11–12).

With most modern celebrities, that would be the end of the story. But with David, there was more to the story. Recognizing his wrongdoing, he turned back to God and led the nation God's way. His comeback complete, he again proved himself to be a "man after [God's] own heart."

Think David's life is cool enough to pattern your life after? Yeah, he had it all—or seemed to. But the most important thing that he had was his desire to make things right with God. That's one characteristic worth imitating.

2 samuel

timeline

1375 B.C.
Judges begin to rule

1050
Saul becomes king

1010
Saul dies; David is king of Judah

1003
David becomes king of all Israel

997(?)
David and Bathsheba sin

991
Solomon born

980(?)
David's census

970
David dies; Solomon made king

930
The kingdom is divided

stats

PURPOSE: (1) To record the history of David's reign; (2) to demonstrate effective leadership under God; (3) to reveal that one person *can* make a difference; (4) to show the personal qualities that please God; (5) to depict David as an ideal leader of an imperfect kingdom; and (6) to foreshadow Christ, who will be the ideal leader of a new and perfect kingdom (chapter 7)

AUTHOR: Unknown. Some have suggested that Nathan's son Zabud may have been the author (1 Kings 4:5). The book also includes the writings of Nathan and Gad (1 Chron. 29:29).

DATE WRITTEN: 930 B.C.; written soon after David's reign, 1010–970 B.C.

SETTING: The land of Israel under David's rule

SPECIAL FEATURE: This book was named after the prophet who anointed David and guided him in godly living.

KEY points

KINGDOM GROWTH
Under David's leadership, Israel grew rapidly. Yet through all of the changes, he continued to seek God's wisdom. David's example encourages us to stick with God no matter how much growth or how many changes we experience.

JUSTICE
King David showed justice, mercy, and fairness to all. Although David was the most fair of all Israel's kings, he was still imperfect. His use of justice offered hope for a heavenly, ideal kingdom. This hope will never be satisfied until Christ, the Son of David, comes to rule in perfect justice forever.

CONSEQUENCES OF SIN
David's sin with Bathsheba had consequences that affected his family and the nation for generations. Sin creates a cycle of suffering that is not worth the fleeting pleasure or "rush" it seems to offer.

KEY PLACES IN 2 SAMUEL

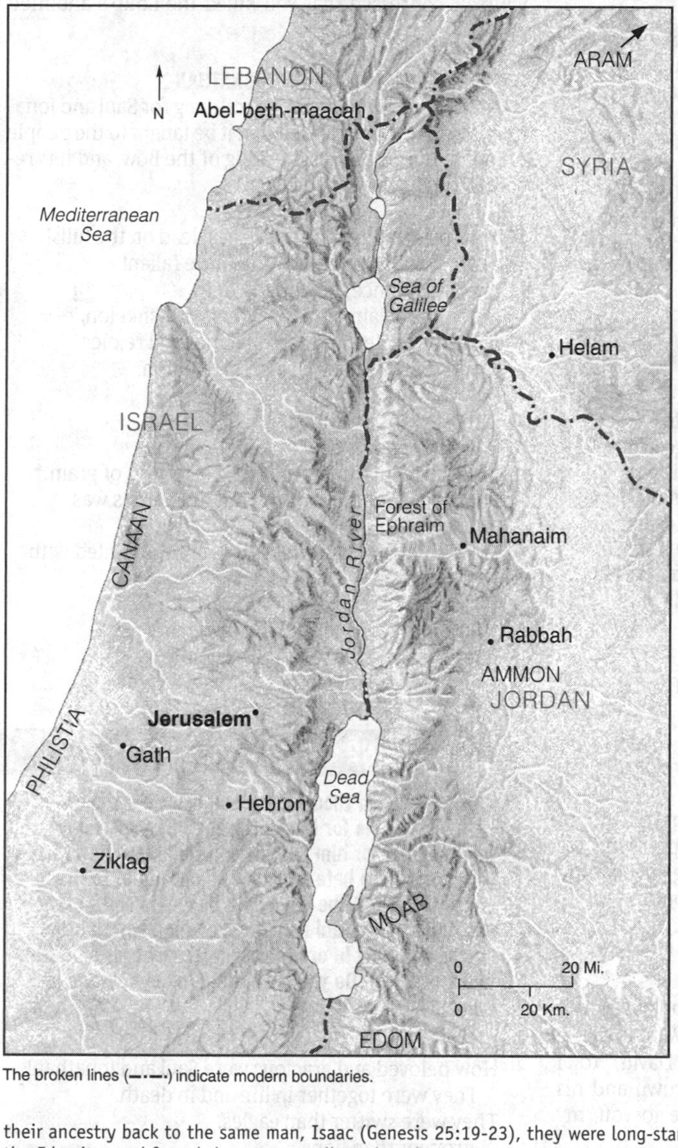

The broken lines (—·—) indicate modern boundaries.

• **HEBRON** After Saul's death, David moved from the Philistine city of Ziklag to Hebron, where the tribe of Judah crowned him king. But the rest of Israel's tribes backed Saul's son Ishbosheth, and crowned him king at Mahanaim. As a result, there was war between Judah and the rest of the tribes of Israel until Ishbosheth was assassinated. Then all of Israel pledged loyalty to David as their king (1:1–5:5).

• **JERUSALEM** One of David's first battles as king occurred at the fortress of Jerusalem. David and his troops took the city by surprise, and it became his capital. It was here that David brought the Ark of the Covenant and made a special covenant with God (5:6–7:29).

• **GATH** The Philistines were Israel's constant enemy, though they did give David sanctuary when he was hiding from Saul (1 Samuel 27). But when Saul died and David became king, the Philistines planned to defeat him. In a battle near Jerusalem, David and his troops routed the Philistines (5:17-25), but they were not completely subdued until David conquered Gath (8:1).

• **MOAB** During the time of the judges, Moab controlled many cities in Israel and demanded heavy taxes (Judges 3:12-30). David conquered Moab and, in turn, levied tribute from them (8:2).

• **EDOM** Though the Edomites and the Israelites traced their ancestry back to the same man, Isaac (Genesis 25:19-23), they were long-standing enemies. David defeated the Edomites and forced them to pay tribute (8:14).

• **RABBAH** The Ammonites insulted David's ambassadors and turned a peacemaking mission into angry warfare. The Ammonites called tens of thousands of mercenaries, but David defeated this alliance first at Helam, then at Rabbah, the capital city (9:1–12:31).

• **MAHANAIM** David had victory in the field, but problems at home. His son, Absalom, incited a rebellion and crowned himself king at Hebron. David and his men fled to Mahanaim. Acting on bad advice, Absalom mobilized his army to fight David (13:1–17:29).

• **FOREST OF EPHRAIM** The armies of Absalom and David fought in the forest of Ephraim. Absalom's hair got caught in a tree, and Joab, David's general, found and killed him. With Absalom's death, the rebellion died (18:1–19:43).

• **ABEL-BETH-MAACAH** A man named Sheba also incited a rebellion against David. He fled to Abel-beth-maacah, but Joab and a small troop besieged the city. The citizens of Abel killed Sheba themselves (20:1-26). David's victories laid the foundation for the peaceful reign of his son Solomon.

1

DAVID LEARNS OF SAUL'S DEATH

After the death of Saul, David returned from his victory
over the Amalekites and spent two days in Ziklag. 2On the
third day a man arrived from Saul's army camp. He had
torn his clothes and put dirt on his head to show that he
was in mourning. He fell to the ground before David in
deep respect.
3"Where have you come from?" David asked.
"I escaped from the Israelite camp," the man replied.
4"What happened?" David demanded. "Tell me how
the battle went."

GRIEF 1:1-12

David and his men were visibly shaken over Saul's death: "They mourned and wept and fasted all day" (1:12). These actions revealed their genuine sorrow over the loss of their king, their friend Jonathan, and the other soldiers of Israel who died that day. They were not ashamed to grieve. Today, expressing our emotions is considered by some to be a sign of weakness. Those who wish to appear strong try to hide their grief. But mourning can help us deal with our intense sorrow when a loved one dies. ■

The man replied, "Our entire army fled from the battle. Many of the men are dead, and Saul and his son Jonathan are also dead."
5"How do you know Saul and Jonathan are dead?" David demanded of the young man.
6The man answered, "I happened to be on Mount
Gilboa, and there was Saul leaning on his spear with the
enemy chariots and charioteers closing in on him.
7When he turned and saw me, he cried out for me to
come to him. 'How can I help?' I asked him.
8"He responded, 'Who are you?'
"'I am an Amalekite,' I told him.
9"Then he begged me, 'Come over here and put me out
of my misery, for I am in terrible pain and want to die.'
10"So I killed him," the Amalekite told David, "for I
knew he couldn't live. Then I took his crown and his
armband, and I have brought them here to you, my
lord."
11David and his men tore their clothes in sorrow when
they heard the news. 12They mourned and wept and
fasted all day for Saul and his son Jonathan, and for the
LORD's army and the nation of Israel, because they had
died by the sword that day.
13Then David said to the young man who had brought
the news, "Where are you from?"
And he replied, "I am a foreigner, an Amalekite, who
lives in your land."
14"Why were you not afraid to kill the LORD's anointed
one?" David asked.
15Then David said to one of his men, "Kill him!" So the
man thrust his sword into the Amalekite and killed him.
16"You have condemned yourself," David said, "for you
yourself confessed that you killed the LORD's anointed
one."

DAVID'S SONG FOR SAUL AND JONATHAN

17Then David composed a funeral song for Saul and Jonathan, 18and he commanded that it be taught to the people
of Judah. It is known as the Song of the Bow, and it is recorded in *The Book of Jashar*.*

19 Your pride and joy, O Israel, lies dead on the hills!
Oh, how the mighty heroes have fallen!
20 Don't announce the news in Gath,
don't proclaim it in the streets of Ashkelon,
or the daughters of the Philistines will rejoice
and the pagans will laugh in triumph.

21 O mountains of Gilboa,
let there be no dew or rain upon you,
nor fruitful fields producing offerings of grain.*
For there the shield of the mighty heroes was
defiled;
the shield of Saul will no longer be anointed with
oil.
22 The bow of Jonathan was powerful,
and the sword of Saul did its mighty work.
They shed the blood of their enemies
and pierced the bodies of mighty heroes.

SEEING GOOD INSTEAD OF EVIL 1:17-27

Even though Saul had caused a ton of trouble for David, David still composed a funeral song for him and his son Jonathan. David had every reason to hate Saul, yet he chose not to. He chose to look at the good Saul had done and to forget the times when Saul had attacked him. Laying aside hatred and hurt in order to show respect for an enemy takes courage. Do you have that kind of courage and respect? ■

23 How beloved and gracious were Saul and Jonathan!
They were together in life and in death.
They were swifter than eagles,
stronger than lions.
24 O women of Israel, weep for Saul,
for he dressed you in luxurious scarlet clothing,
in garments decorated with gold.

25 Oh, how the mighty heroes have fallen in battle!
Jonathan lies dead on the hills.
26 How I weep for you, my brother Jonathan!
Oh, how much I loved you!
And your love for me was deep,
deeper than the love of women!

27 Oh, how the mighty heroes have fallen!
Stripped of their weapons, they lie dead.

1:18 Or *The Book of the Upright*. **1:21** The meaning of the Hebrew is uncertain.

Highs and Lows of David's Life

The Bible calls David a man after God's own heart (Acts 13:22), but that didn't mean his life was free of troubles. David's life was full of highs and lows. Some of David's troubles were a result of his sins; some were a result of the sins of others. We can't always control our ups and downs, but we can trust God every day. We can be certain that he will help us through our trials, just as he helped David. In the end, he will reward us for our consistent faith.

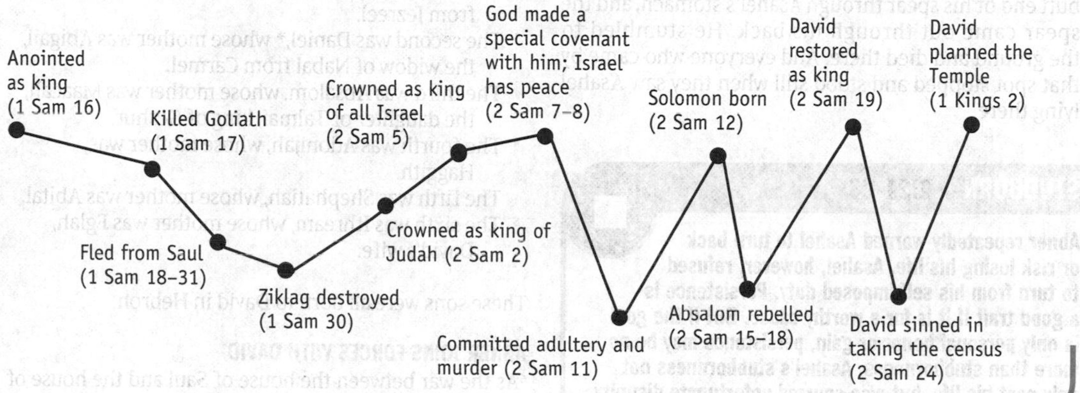

2

DAVID ANOINTED KING OF JUDAH

After this, David asked the LORD, "Should I move back to
one of the towns of Judah?"
"Yes," the LORD replied.
Then David asked, "Which town should I go to?"
"To Hebron," the LORD answered.
[2]David's two wives were Ahinoam from Jezreel and
Abigail, the widow of Nabal from Carmel. So David and
his wives [3]and his men and their families all moved to Judah, and they settled in the villages near Hebron. [4]Then
the men of Judah came to David and crowned him king
over the people of Judah.
When David heard that the men of Jabesh-gilead had
buried Saul, [5]he sent them this message: "May the LORD
bless you for being so loyal to your master Saul and giving
him a decent burial. [6]May the LORD be loyal to you in return and reward you with his unfailing love! And I, too,
will reward you for what you have done. [7]Now that Saul is
dead, I ask you to be my strong and loyal subjects like the
people of Judah, who have anointed me as their new
king."

ISHBOSHETH CROWNED KING OF ISRAEL

[8]But Abner son of Ner, the commander of Saul's army,
had already gone to Mahanaim with Saul's son Ishbosheth.* [9]There he proclaimed Ishbosheth king over Gilead, Jezreel, Ephraim, Benjamin, the land of the Ashurites,
and all the rest of Israel.
[10]Ishbosheth, Saul's son, was forty years old when he
became king, and he ruled from Mahanaim for two years.
Meanwhile, the people of Judah remained loyal to David.
[11]David made Hebron his capital, and he ruled as king of
Judah for seven and a half years.

WAR BETWEEN ISRAEL AND JUDAH

[12]One day Abner led Ishbosheth's troops from Mahanaim to Gibeon. [13]About the same time, Joab son of Zeruiah
led David's troops out and met them at the pool of Gibeon. The two groups sat down there, facing each other
from opposite sides of the pool.
[14]Then Abner suggested to Joab, "Let's have a few of
our warriors fight hand to hand here in front of us."
"All right," Joab agreed. [15]So twelve men were chosen
to fight from each side—twelve men of Benjamin representing Ishbosheth son of Saul, and twelve representing
David. [16]Each one grabbed his opponent by the hair and
thrust his sword into the other's side so that all of them
died. So this place at Gibeon has been known ever since
as the Field of Swords.*
[17]A fierce battle followed that day, and Abner and the
men of Israel were defeated by the forces of David.

THE DEATH OF ASAHEL

[18]Joab, Abishai, and Asahel—the three sons of Zeruiah—
were among David's forces that day. Asahel could run
like a gazelle, [19]and he began chasing Abner. He pursued
him relentlessly, not stopping for anything. [20]When

2:8 *Ishbosheth* is another name for Esh-baal. 2:16 Hebrew *Helkath-hazzurim*.

Abner looked back and saw him coming, he called out, "Is that you, Asahel?"

"Yes, it is," he replied.

21"Go fight someone else!" Abner warned. "Take on one of the younger men, and strip him of his weapons." But Asahel kept right on chasing Abner.

22Again Abner shouted to him, "Get away from here! I don't want to kill you. How could I ever face your brother Joab again?"

23But Asahel refused to turn back, so Abner thrust the butt end of his spear through Asahel's stomach, and the spear came out through his back. He stumbled to the ground and died there. And everyone who came by that spot stopped and stood still when they saw Asahel lying there.

STUBBORN 2:21-23

Abner repeatedly warned Asahel to turn back or risk losing his life. Asahel, however, refused to turn from his self-imposed duty. Persistence is a good trait if it is for a worthy cause. But if the goal is only personal honor or gain, persistence may be no more than stubbornness. Asahel's stubbornness not only cost his life, but also spurred unfortunate disunity in David's army for years to come (3:26-27; see also 1 Kings 2:28-35). Before you decide to pursue a goal, make sure it is worth your devotion. ■

24When Joab and Abishai found out what had happened, they set out after Abner. The sun was just going down as they arrived at the hill of Ammah near Giah, along the road to the wilderness of Gibeon. 25Abner's troops from the tribe of Benjamin regrouped there at the top of the hill to take a stand.

26Abner shouted down to Joab, "Must we always be killing each other? Don't you realize that bitterness is the only result? When will you call off your men from chasing their Israelite brothers?"

27Then Joab said, "God only knows what would have happened if you hadn't spoken, for we would have chased you all night if necessary." 28So Joab blew the ram's horn, and his men stopped chasing the troops of Israel.

29All that night Abner and his men retreated through the Jordan Valley.* They crossed the Jordan River, traveling all through the morning,* and didn't stop until they arrived at Mahanaim.

30Meanwhile, Joab and his men also returned home. When Joab counted his casualties, he discovered that only 19 men were missing in addition to Asahel. 31But 360 of Abner's men had been killed, all from the tribe of Benjamin. 32Joab and his men took Asahel's body to Bethlehem and buried him there in his father's tomb. Then they traveled all night and reached Hebron at daybreak.

3

That was the beginning of a long war between those who were loyal to Saul and those loyal to David. As time passed David became stronger and stronger, while Saul's dynasty became weaker and weaker.

DAVID'S SONS BORN IN HEBRON

2These are the sons who were born to David in Hebron:

The oldest was Amnon, whose mother was Ahinoam from Jezreel.
3 The second was Daniel,* whose mother was Abigail, the widow of Nabal from Carmel.
The third was Absalom, whose mother was Maacah, the daughter of Talmai, king of Geshur.
4 The fourth was Adonijah, whose mother was Haggith.
The fifth was Shephatiah, whose mother was Abital.
5 The sixth was Ithream, whose mother was Eglah, David's wife.

These sons were all born to David in Hebron.

ABNER JOINS FORCES WITH DAVID

6As the war between the house of Saul and the house of David went on, Abner became a powerful leader among those loyal to Saul. 7One day Ishbosheth,* Saul's son, accused Abner of sleeping with one of his father's concubines, a woman named Rizpah, daughter of Aiah.

STAND FIRM 3:7-11

Ishbosheth was right to speak out against Abner's behavior, but he didn't have the moral strength to maintain his authority (3:11). Lack of moral backbone became the root of Israel's troubles over the next four centuries. Taking a stand for what you believe requires courage and conviction. When you believe something is wrong, what will you do to avoid allowing yourself be talked out of your position? How will you firmly attack the wrong and uphold the right? ■

8Abner was furious. "Am I some Judean dog to be kicked around like this?" he shouted. "After all I have done for your father, Saul, and his family and friends by not handing you over to David, is this my reward—that you find fault with me about this woman? 9May God strike me and even kill me if I don't do everything I can to help David get what the LORD has promised him! 10I'm going to take Saul's kingdom and give it to David. I will establish the throne of David over Israel as well as Judah, all the way from Dan in the north to Beersheba in the south." 11Ishbosheth didn't dare say another word because he was afraid of what Abner might do.

2:29a Hebrew *the Arabah*. 2:29b Or *continued on through the Bithron*. The meaning of the Hebrew is uncertain. 3:3 As in parallel text at 1 Chr 3:1 (see also Greek version, which reads *Daluia*, and Dead Sea Scrolls, which read *Dan[iel]*); Hebrew reads *Kileab*. 3:7 *Ishbosheth* is another name for Esh-baal.

12Then Abner sent messengers to David, saying, "Doesn't
the entire land belong to you? Make a solemn pact with
me, and I will help turn over all of Israel to you."
13"All right," David replied, "but I will not negotiate
with you unless you bring back my wife Michal, Saul's
daughter, when you come."
14David then sent this message to Ishbosheth, Saul's
son: "Give me back my wife Michal, for I bought her with
the lives* of 100 Philistines."
15So Ishbosheth took Michal away from her husband,
Palti* son of Laish. 16Palti followed along behind her as
far as Bahurim, weeping as he went. Then Abner told
him, "Go back home!" So Palti returned.
17Meanwhile, Abner had consulted with the elders of
Israel. "For some time now," he told them, "you have
wanted to make David your king. 18Now is the time! For
the LORD has said, 'I have chosen David to save my people
Israel from the hands of the Philistines and from all their
other enemies.'" 19Abner also spoke with the men of Benjamin. Then he went to Hebron to tell David that all the
people of Israel and Benjamin had agreed to support
him.
20When Abner and twenty of his men came to Hebron,
David entertained them with a great feast. 21Then Abner
said to David, "Let me go and call an assembly of all Israel
to support my lord the king. They will make a covenant
with you to make you their king, and you will rule over
everything your heart desires." So David sent Abner
safely on his way.

JOAB MURDERS ABNER

22But just after David had sent Abner away in safety, Joab
and some of David's troops returned from a raid, bringing much plunder with them. 23When Joab arrived, he
was told that Abner had just been there visiting the king
and had been sent away in safety.
24Joab rushed to the king and demanded, "What have
you done? What do you mean by letting Abner get away?
25You know perfectly well that he came to spy on you and
find out everything you're doing!"
26Joab then left David and sent messengers to catch up
with Abner, asking him to return. They found him at the
well of Sirah and brought him back, though David knew
nothing about it. 27When Abner arrived back at Hebron,
Joab took him aside at the gateway as if to speak with him
privately. But then he stabbed Abner in the stomach and
killed him in revenge for killing his brother Asahel.
28When David heard about it, he declared, "I vow by
the LORD that I and my kingdom are forever innocent of
this crime against Abner son of Ner. 29Joab and his family
are the guilty ones. May the family of Joab be cursed in
every generation with a man who has open sores or leprosy* or who walks on crutches* or dies by the sword or
begs for food!"
30So Joab and his brother Abishai killed Abner because
Abner had killed their brother Asahel at the battle of
Gibeon.

DAVID MOURNS ABNER'S DEATH

31Then David said to Joab and all those who were with
him, "Tear your clothes and put on burlap. Mourn for Abner." And King David himself walked behind the procession to the grave. 32They buried Abner in Hebron, and the
king and all the people wept at his graveside. 33Then the
king sang this funeral song for Abner:

"Should Abner have died as fools die?
34 Your hands were not bound;
  your feet were not chained.
No, you were murdered—
  the victim of a wicked plot."

All the people wept again for Abner. 35David had refused to eat anything on the day of the funeral, and now
everyone begged him to eat. But David had made a vow,
saying, "May God strike me and even kill me if I eat anything before sundown."
36This pleased the people very much. In fact, everything the king did pleased them! 37So everyone in Judah
and all Israel understood that David was not responsible
for Abner's murder.
38Then King David said to his officials, "Don't you realize that a great commander has fallen today in Israel?
39And even though I am the anointed king, these two sons
of Zeruiah—Joab and Abishai—are too strong for me to
control. So may the LORD repay these evil men for their
evil deeds."

BE BOLD! 4:1-7

Ishbosheth was a man who took his courage from another man (Abner) rather than from God. When Abner died, Ishbosheth was left with nothing. In crisis and under pressure, he collapsed in fear. Fear can paralyze us, but faith and trust in God can overcome fear (2 Tim 1:6-8; Heb 13:6). If we trust in God, we will be free to respond boldly to the events around us. ■

4 THE MURDER OF ISHBOSHETH

When Ishbosheth,* Saul's son, heard about Abner's
death at Hebron, he lost all courage, and all Israel became
paralyzed with fear. 2Now there were two brothers, Baanah and Recab, who were captains of Ishbosheth's raiding parties. They were sons of Rimmon, a member of the
tribe of Benjamin who lived in Beeroth. The town of Beeroth is now part of Benjamin's territory 3because the
original people of Beeroth fled to Gittaim, where they still
live as foreigners.
4(Saul's son Jonathan had a son named Mephibosheth,*
who was crippled as a child. He was five years old when
the report came from Jezreel that Saul and Jonathan had

3:14 Hebrew *the foreskins.* 3:15 As in 1 Sam 25:44; Hebrew reads *Paltiel,* a variant spelling of Palti. 3:29a Or *or a contagious skin disease.* The Hebrew word used here can describe various skin diseases. 3:29b Or *who is effeminate;* Hebrew reads *who handles a spindle.*
4:1 *Ishbosheth* is another name for Esh-baal. 4:4 *Mephibosheth* is another name for Merib-baal.

been killed in battle. When the child's nurse heard the
news, she picked him up and fled. But as she hurried
away, she dropped him, and he became crippled.)
5One day Recab and Baanah, the sons of Rimmon from
Beeroth, went to Ishbosheth's house around noon as he
was taking his midday rest. 6The doorkeeper, who had
been sifting wheat, became drowsy and fell asleep. So Recab and Baanah slipped past her.* 7They went into the
house and found Ishbosheth sleeping on his bed. They
struck and killed him and cut off his head. Then, taking
his head with them, they fled across the Jordan Valley*
through the night. 8When they arrived at Hebron, they
presented Ishbosheth's head to David. "Look!" they exclaimed to the king. "Here is the head of Ishbosheth, the
son of your enemy Saul who tried to kill you. Today the
LORD has given my lord the king revenge on Saul and his
entire family!"
9But David said to Recab and Baanah, "The LORD, who
saves me from all my enemies, is my witness. 10Someone
once told me, 'Saul is dead,' thinking he was bringing me
good news. But I seized him and killed him at Ziklag. That's
the reward I gave him for his news! 11How much more
should I reward evil men who have killed an innocent man
in his own house and on his own bed? Shouldn't I hold you
responsible for his blood and rid the earth of you?"
12So David ordered his young men to kill them, and
they did. They cut off their hands and feet and hung their
bodies beside the pool in Hebron. Then they took Ishbosheth's head and buried it in Abner's tomb in Hebron.

PATIENCE 5:4-5

Although he had been promised the kingship many years earlier, David did not become king of all Israel until he was 37 years old (1 Sam 16:13). During those years, David had to wait patiently for the fulfillment of God's promise. If you feel pressured to achieve instant results and success, remember David's patience. Just as his time of waiting prepared him for this important task, a waiting period may help prepare you by strengthening your spiritual character. ■

5 DAVID BECOMES KING OF ALL ISRAEL

Then all the tribes of Israel went to David at Hebron and
told him, "We are your own flesh and blood. 2In the past,*
when Saul was our king, you were the one who really led
the forces of Israel. And the LORD told you, 'You will be
the shepherd of my people Israel. You will be Israel's
leader.'"
3So there at Hebron, King David made a covenant before the LORD with all the elders of Israel. And they
anointed him king of Israel.
4David was thirty years old when he began to reign, and
he reigned forty years in all. 5He had reigned over Judah
from Hebron for seven years and six months, and from
Jerusalem he reigned over all Israel and Judah for thirty-
three years.

DAVID CAPTURES JERUSALEM

6David then led his men to Jerusalem to fight against the
Jebusites, the original inhabitants of the land who were
living there. The Jebusites taunted David, saying, "You'll
never get in here! Even the blind and lame could keep you
out!" For the Jebusites thought they were safe. 7But David
captured the fortress of Zion, which is now called the City
of David.
8On the day of the attack, David said to his troops, "I
hate those 'lame' and 'blind' Jebusites.* Whoever attacks
them should strike by going into the city through the water tunnel.*" That is the origin of the saying, "The blind
and the lame may not enter the house."*
9So David made the fortress his home, and he called it
the City of David. He extended the city, starting at the
supporting terraces* and working inward. 10And David
became more and more powerful, because the LORD God
of Heaven's Armies was with him.
11Then King Hiram of Tyre sent messengers to David,
along with cedar timber and carpenters and stonemasons,
and they built David a palace. 12And David realized that the
LORD had confirmed him as king over Israel and had
blessed his kingdom for the sake of his people Israel.
13After moving from Hebron to Jerusalem, David married more concubines and wives, and they had more sons
and daughters. 14These are the names of David's sons
who were born in Jerusalem: Shammua, Shobab, Nathan,
Solomon, 15Ibhar, Elishua, Nepheg, Japhia, 16Elishama,
Eliada, and Eliphelet.

BATTLES 5:17-25

David fought his battles the way God instructed him. In each instance he (1) asked if he should fight or not; (2) followed instructions carefully; and (3) gave God the glory. We can err in our "battles" by ignoring these steps and instead (1) doing what we want without considering God's will; (2) doing things our way and ignoring advice in the Bible or from other wise people; and (3) taking the glory ourselves or giving it to someone else without acknowledging the help we received from God. Next time you find yourself in the middle of a battle, what will you do? ■

DAVID CONQUERS THE PHILISTINES

17When the Philistines heard that David had been
anointed king of Israel, they mobilized all their forces to
capture him. But David was told they were coming, so he
went into the stronghold. 18The Philistines arrived and
spread out across the valley of Rephaim. 19So David asked

4:6 As in Greek version; Hebrew reads *So they went into the house pretending to fetch wheat, but they stabbed him in the stomach. Then Recab and Baanah escaped.* 4:7 Hebrew *the Arabah.* 5:2 Or *For some time.* 5:8a Or *Those 'lame' and 'blind' Jebusites hate me.* 5:8b Or *with scaling hooks.* The meaning of the Hebrew is uncertain. 5:8c The meaning of this saying is uncertain. 5:9 Hebrew *the millo.* The meaning of the Hebrew is uncertain.

the LORD, "Should I go out to fight the Philistines? Will
you hand them over to me?"
The LORD replied to David, "Yes, go ahead. I will certainly hand them over to you."
20So David went to Baal-perazim and defeated the Philistines there. "The LORD did it!" David exclaimed. "He
burst through my enemies like a raging flood!" So he
named that place Baal-perazim (which means "the Lord
who bursts through"). 21The Philistines had abandoned
their idols there, so David and his men confiscated them.
22But after a while the Philistines returned and again
spread out across the valley of Rephaim. 23And again David asked the LORD what to do. "Do not attack them
straight on," the LORD replied. "Instead, circle around behind and attack them near the poplar* trees. 24When you
hear a sound like marching feet in the tops of the poplar
trees, be on the alert! That will be the signal that the LORD
is moving ahead of you to strike down the Philistine army."
25So David did what the LORD commanded, and he struck
down the Philistines all the way from Gibeon* to Gezer.

6 **MOVING THE ARK TO JERUSALEM**

Then David again gathered all the elite troops in Israel,
30,000 in all. 2He led them to Baalah of Judah* to bring
back the Ark of God, which bears the name of the LORD

5:23 Or *aspen,* or *balsam;* also in 5:24. The exact identification of this tree is uncertain. 5:25 As in Greek version (see also 1 Chr 14:16); Hebrew reads *Geba.* 6:2a *Baalah of Judah* is another name for Kiriath-jearim; compare 1 Chr 13:6.

UPS:
- Loved David and became his first wife
- Saved David's life
- Could think and act quickly when it was needed

DOWNS:
- Lied under pressure
- Allowed herself to become bitter over her circumstances
- In her unhappiness, hated David because of his love for God

STATS:
- Relatives: Saul and Ahinoam (parents); Abinadab, Jonathan, Malchishua (brothers); Merab (sister); David and Palti (husbands)

BOTTOM LINE:

We are not as responsible for what happens to us as we are for how we respond to our circumstances.

Disobedience to God almost always harms us as well as others.

Michal's story is told in 1 Sam 14:49-50; 18:20-29; 19:11-17; 25:44; 2 Sam 3:13-14; 6:16-23. She also is mentioned in 1 Chron 15:29.

MICHAL

Ever watch a romance movie where the couple vowed to love each other for all time? Sometimes what passes for "love" is little more than strong emotional attraction.

To Michal, King Saul's daughter, the courageous young David must have seemed like a dream come true. Her feelings for him gradually became obvious to others. Using this as an opportunity to get rid of his rival, Saul promised Michal's hand in marriage in exchange for David's success in the impossible mission of killing one hundred Philistines (1 Sam 18:21-25). But David was victorious. As a result, Saul had to allow Michal to marry David. David, meanwhile, became even more popular with the people.

Michal's love for David did not have time to be tested by the realities of marriage. Instead, she became involved in saving his life. Her quick thinking helped him escape, but the price was Saul's anger and Michal's separation from David (1 Sam 19:11-17). Her father gave her to another man, Palti, although David eventually took her back (1 Sam 25:44; 2 Sam 3:14-16).

Unlike her brother Jonathan, Michal did not have the kind of deep relationship with God that would have helped her come through the difficulties in her life. She could not share David's joyful worship of God when the stolen ark was returned (2 Sam 6:16-23). Instead, she expressed her bitterness and contempt for David. Sadly, Michal never bore David any children.

When the same faith in God is not shared by a couple, the one who could hold them together sometimes seems to come between them. Beyond feeling sorry for her, we need to see Michal as a person like us. How quickly and easily we become bitter when life takes unexpected turns. But bitterness cannot change the bad things that have happened. Instead, it makes a bad situation worse. On the other hand, a willingness to turn to God gives him the opportunity to bring good out of our difficulties. That willingness has two parts: asking God for his guidance, and looking for that guidance in his Word.

of Heaven's Armies,* who is enthroned between the cherubim. 3They placed the Ark of God on a new cart and brought it from Abinadab's house, which was on a hill. Uzzah and Ahio, Abinadab's sons, were guiding the cart as it left the house, 4carrying the Ark of God. Ahio walked in front of the Ark. 5David and all the people of Israel were celebrating before the LORD, singing songs* and playing all kinds of musical instruments—lyres, harps, tambourines, castanets, and cymbals.

6But when they arrived at the threshing floor of Nacon, the oxen stumbled, and Uzzah reached out his hand and steadied the Ark of God. 7Then the LORD's anger was aroused against Uzzah, and God struck him dead because of this.* So Uzzah died right there beside the Ark of God.

8David was angry because the LORD's anger had burst out against Uzzah. He named that place Perez-uzzah (which means "to burst out against Uzzah"), as it is still called today.

9David was now afraid of the LORD, and he asked, "How can I ever bring the Ark of the LORD back into my care?" 10So David decided not to move the Ark of the LORD into the City of David. Instead, he took it to the house of Obed-edom of Gath. 11The Ark of the LORD remained there in Obed-edom's house for three months, and the LORD blessed Obed-edom and his entire household.

12Then King David was told, "The LORD has blessed Obed-edom's household and everything he has because of the Ark of God." So David went there and brought the Ark of God from the house of Obed-edom to the City of David with a great celebration. 13After the men who were carrying the Ark of the LORD had gone six steps, David sacrificed a bull and a fattened calf. 14And David danced before the LORD with all his might, wearing a priestly garment.* 15So David and all the people of Israel brought up the Ark of the LORD with shouts of joy and the blowing of rams' horns.

MICHAL'S CONTEMPT FOR DAVID

16But as the Ark of the LORD entered the City of David, Michal, the daughter of Saul, looked down from her window. When she saw King David leaping and dancing before the LORD, she was filled with contempt for him.

17They brought the Ark of the LORD and set it in its place inside the special tent David had prepared for it. And David sacrificed burnt offerings and peace offerings to the LORD. 18When he had finished his sacrifices, David blessed the people in the name of the LORD of Heaven's Armies. 19Then he gave to every Israelite man and woman in the crowd a loaf of bread, a cake of dates,* and a cake of raisins. Then all the people returned to their homes.

20When David returned home to bless his own family, Michal, the daughter of Saul, came out to meet him. She said in disgust, "How distinguished the king of Israel looked today, shamelessly exposing himself to the servant girls like any vulgar person might do!"

21David retorted to Michal, "I was dancing before the LORD, who chose me above your father and all his family! He appointed me as the leader of Israel, the people of the LORD, so I celebrate before the LORD. 22Yes, and I am willing to look even more foolish than this, even to be humiliated in my own eyes! But those servant girls you mentioned will indeed think I am distinguished!" 23So Michal, the daughter of Saul, remained childless throughout her entire life.

7

THE LORD'S COVENANT PROMISE TO DAVID

When King David was settled in his palace and the LORD had given him rest from all the surrounding enemies, 2the king summoned Nathan the prophet. "Look," David said, "I am living in a beautiful cedar palace,* but the Ark of God is out there in a tent!"

3Nathan replied to the king, "Go ahead and do whatever you have in mind, for the LORD is with you."

4But that same night the LORD said to Nathan,

5"Go and tell my servant David, 'This is what the LORD has declared: Are you the one to build a house for me to live in? 6I have never lived in a house, from the day I brought the Israelites out of Egypt until this very day. I have always moved from one place to another with a tent and a Tabernacle as my dwelling. 7Yet no matter where I have gone with the Israelites, I have never once complained to Israel's tribal leaders, the shepherds of my people Israel. I have never asked them, "Why haven't you built me a beautiful cedar house?"'

WHEN GOD SAYS NO 7:1-16

David's request to build a temple was good, but God said no. This does not mean that God rejected David. In fact, God was planning to do something even greater in David's life than allowing him the prestige of building Israel's first temple. He promised that David's descendants would rule the kingdom forever. Although David's earthly dynasty ended four centuries later, Jesus Christ—a direct descendant of David—will be king forever (Acts 2:22-36).

Have you prayed with good intentions, only to have God say no? Realize that this is not rejection, but God's way of fulfilling a greater purpose in your life. ■

8"Now go and say to my servant David, 'This is what the LORD of Heaven's Armies has declared: I took you from tending sheep in the pasture and selected you to be the leader of my people Israel. 9I have been with you wherever you have gone, and I have destroyed all your enemies before your eyes. Now I will make your name as famous as anyone who has ever lived on the earth! 10And I will provide a homeland for my people Israel, planting them in a secure place where they will never be disturbed. Evil nations won't oppress them

6:2b Or *the Ark of God where the Name is proclaimed—the name of the LORD of Heaven's Armies.* **6:5** As in Greek version (see also 1 Chr 13:8); Hebrew reads *before the LORD with all manner of cypress trees.* **6:7** As in Dead Sea Scrolls; Masoretic Text reads *because of his irreverence.* **6:14** Hebrew *a linen ephod.* **6:19** Or *a portion of meat.* The meaning of the Hebrew is uncertain. **7:2** Hebrew *a house of cedar.*

as they've done in the past, 11starting from the time I
appointed judges to rule my people Israel. And I will
give you rest from all your enemies.
"'Furthermore, the LORD declares that he will make
a house for you—a dynasty of kings! 12For when you
die and are buried with your ancestors, I will raise up
one of your descendants, your own offspring, and I
will make his kingdom strong. 13He is the one who
will build a house—a temple—for my name. And I will
secure his royal throne forever. 14I will be his father,
and he will be my son. If he sins, I will correct and
discipline him with the rod, like any father would do.
15But my favor will not be taken from him as I took it
from Saul, whom I removed from your sight. 16Your
house and your kingdom will continue before me*
for all time, and your throne will be secure forever.'"

17So Nathan went back to David and told him everything
the LORD had said in this vision.

DAVID'S PRAYER OF THANKS

18Then King David went in and sat before the LORD and
prayed,

"Who am I, O Sovereign LORD, and what is my family,
that you have brought me this far? 19And now,
Sovereign LORD, in addition to everything else, you
speak of giving your servant a lasting
dynasty! Do you deal with everyone
this way, O Sovereign LORD?*
20"What more can I say to you?
You know what your servant is
really like, Sovereign LORD. 21Because
of your promise and according to
your will, you have done all these
great things and have made them
known to your servant.
22"How great you are, O Sovereign
LORD! There is no one like you. We
have never even heard of another
God like you! 23What other nation
on earth is like your people Israel?
What other nation, O God, have you
redeemed from slavery to be your own people? You
made a great name for yourself when you redeemed
your people from Egypt. You performed awesome
miracles and drove out the nations and gods that stood
in their way.* 24You made Israel your very own people
forever, and you, O LORD, became their God.
25"And now, O LORD God, I am your servant; do as
you have promised concerning me and my family.
Confirm it as a promise that will last forever. 26And
may your name be honored forever so that everyone
will say, 'The LORD of Heaven's Armies is God over
Israel!' And may the house of your servant David
continue before you forever.
27"O LORD of Heaven's Armies, God of Israel, I have
been bold enough to pray this prayer to you because you
have revealed all this to your servant, saying, 'I will build
a house for you—a dynasty of kings!' 28For you are God,
O Sovereign LORD. Your words are truth, and you have
promised these good things to your servant. 29And now,
may it please you to bless the house of your servant, so
that it may continue forever before you. For you have
spoken, and when you grant a blessing to your servant,
O Sovereign LORD, it is an eternal blessing!"

8

DAVID'S MILITARY VICTORIES

After this, David defeated and subdued the Philistines by
conquering Gath, their largest town.* 2David also conquered the land of Moab. He made the people lie down
on the ground in a row, and he measured them off in
groups with a length of rope. He measured off two
groups to be executed for every one group to be spared.
The Moabites who were spared became David's subjects
and paid him tribute money.
3David also destroyed the forces of Hadadezer son of
Rehob, king of Zobah, when Hadadezer marched out to
strengthen his control along the Euphrates River. 4David
captured 1,700 charioteers* and
20,000 foot soldiers. He crippled all
the chariot horses except enough for
100 chariots.
5When Arameans from Damascus
arrived to help King Hadadezer, David
killed 22,000 of them. 6Then he placed
several army garrisons in Damascus,
the Aramean capital, and the Arameans
became David's subjects and paid him
tribute money. So the LORD made David
victorious wherever he went.
7David brought the gold shields of
Hadadezer's officers to Jerusalem, 8along
with a large amount of bronze from Hadadezer's towns of Tebah* and Berothai.
9When King Toi of Hamath heard that David had destroyed the entire army of Hadadezer, 10he sent his son Joram to congratulate King David for his successful
campaign. Hadadezer and Toi had been enemies and were
often at war. Joram presented David with many gifts of silver, gold, and bronze.
11King David dedicated all these gifts to the LORD, as he
did with the silver and gold from the other nations he had
defeated—12from Edom,* Moab, Ammon, Philistia, and Amalek—and from Hadadezer son of Rehob, king of Zobah.
13So David became very famous. After his return he

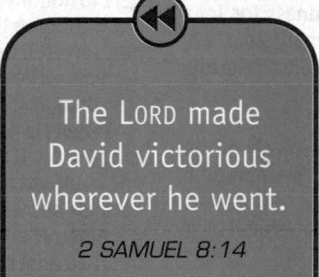

> The LORD made David victorious wherever he went.
>
> *2 SAMUEL 8:14*

7:16 As in Greek version and some Hebrew manuscripts; Masoretic Text reads *before you.* 7:19 Or *This is your instruction for all humanity, O Sovereign LORD.* 7:23 As in Greek version (see also 1 Chr 17:21); Hebrew reads *You made a great name for yourself and performed awesome miracles for your land. You did this in the sight of your people, whom you redeemed from Egypt, from nations and their gods.* 8:1 Hebrew *by conquering Metheg-ammah,* a name that means "the bridle," possibly referring to the size of the town or the tribute money taken from it. Compare 1 Chr 18:1. 8:4 Greek version reads *1,000 chariots and 7,000 charioteers;* compare 1 Chr 18:4. 8:8 As in some Greek manuscripts (see also 1 Chr 18:8); Hebrew reads *Betah.* 8:12 As in a few Hebrew manuscripts and Greek and Syriac versions (see also 8:14; 1 Chr 18:11); most Hebrew manuscripts read *Aram.*

destroyed 18,000 Edomites* in the Valley of Salt. 14He placed army garrisons throughout Edom, and all the Edomites became David's subjects. In fact, the LORD made David victorious wherever he went.

15So David reigned over all Israel and did what was just and right for all his people. 16Joab son of Zeruiah was commander of the army. Jehoshaphat son of Ahilud was the royal historian. 17Zadok son of Ahitub and Ahimelech son of Abiathar were the priests. Seraiah was the court secretary. 18Benaiah son of Jehoiada was captain of the king's bodyguard.* And David's sons served as priestly leaders.*

THE PUBLIC EYE 8:15

Everything David did pleased the people (3:36), not because he tried to please them, but because he tried to please God. Often those who try the hardest to become popular never make it. But the praise of people is not that important. Do you find yourself spending time trying to please others? Instead, strive to do what is right—and both God and people will respect your convictions. ■

9 DAVID'S KINDNESS TO MEPHIBOSHETH

One day David asked, "Is anyone in Saul's family still alive—anyone to whom I can show kindness for Jonathan's sake?" 2He summoned a man named Ziba, who had been one of Saul's servants. "Are you Ziba?" the king asked.

"Yes sir, I am," Ziba replied.

3The king then asked him, "Is anyone still alive from Saul's family? If so, I want to show God's kindness to them."

Ziba replied, "Yes, one of Jonathan's sons is still alive. He is crippled in both feet."

4"Where is he?" the king asked.

"In Lo-debar," Ziba told him, "at the home of Makir son of Ammiel."

5So David sent for him and brought him from Makir's home. 6His name was Mephibosheth*; he was Jonathan's son and Saul's grandson. When he came to David, he bowed low to the ground in deep respect. David said, "Greetings, Mephibosheth."

Mephibosheth replied, "I am your servant."

7"Don't be afraid!" David said. "I intend to show kindness to you because of my promise to your father, Jonathan. I will give you all the property that once belonged to your grandfather Saul, and you will eat here with me at the king's table!"

8Mephibosheth bowed respectfully and exclaimed, "Who is your servant, that you should show such kindness to a dead dog like me?"

9Then the king summoned Saul's servant Ziba and said, "I have given your master's grandson everything that belonged to Saul and his family. 10You and your sons and servants are to farm the land for him to produce food for your master's household.* But Mephibosheth, your master's grandson, will eat here at my table." (Ziba had fifteen sons and twenty servants.)

Ziba replied, 11"Yes, my lord the king; I am your servant, and I will do all that you have commanded." And from that time on, Mephibosheth ate regularly at David's table,* like one of the king's own sons.

12Mephibosheth had a young son named Mica. From then on, all the members of Ziba's household were Mephibosheth's servants. 13And Mephibosheth, who was crippled in both feet, lived in Jerusalem and ate regularly at the king's table.

10 DAVID DEFEATS THE AMMONITES

Some time after this, King Nahash* of the Ammonites died, and his son Hanun became king. 2David said, "I am going to show loyalty to Hanun just as his father, Nahash, was always loyal to me." So David sent ambassadors to express sympathy to Hanun about his father's death.

But when David's ambassadors arrived in the land of Ammon, 3the Ammonite commanders said to Hanun, their master, "Do you really think these men are coming here to honor your father? No! David has sent them to spy out the city so they can come in and conquer it!" 4So Hanun seized David's ambassadors and shaved off half of each man's beard, cut off their robes at the buttocks, and sent them back to David in shame.

5When David heard what had happened, he sent messengers to tell the men, "Stay at Jericho until your beards grow out, and then come back." For they felt deep shame because of their appearance.

6When the people of Ammon realized how seriously they had angered David, they sent and hired 20,000 Aramean foot soldiers from the lands of Beth-rehob and Zobah, 1,000 from the king of Maacah, and 12,000 from the land of Tob. 7When David heard about this, he sent Joab and all his warriors to fight them. 8The Ammonite troops came out and drew up their battle lines at the entrance of the city gate, while the Arameans from Zobah and Rehob and the men from Tob and Maacah positioned themselves to fight in the open fields.

9When Joab saw that he would have to fight on both the front and the rear, he chose some of Israel's elite troops and placed them under his personal command to fight the Arameans in the fields. 10He left the rest of the army under the command of his brother Abishai, who was to attack the Ammonites. 11"If the Arameans are too strong for me, then come over and help me," Joab told his brother. "And if the Ammonites are too strong for you, I will come and help you. 12Be courageous! Let us fight

8:13 As in a few Hebrew manuscripts and Greek and Syriac versions (see also 8:14; 1 Chr 18:12); most Hebrew manuscripts read *Arameans.* **8:18a** Hebrew *of the Kerethites and Pelethites.* **8:18b** Hebrew *David's sons were priests;* compare parallel text at 1 Chr 18:17. **9:6** *Mephibosheth* is another name for Merib-baal. **9:10** As in Greek version; Hebrew reads *your master's grandson.* **9:11** As in Greek version; Hebrew reads *my table.* **10:1** As in parallel text at 1 Chr 19:1; Hebrew reads *the king.*

bravely for our people and the cities of our God. May the
LORD's will be done."
[13]When Joab and his troops attacked, the Arameans
began to run away. [14]And when the Ammonites saw the
Arameans running, they ran from Abishai and retreated
into the city. After the battle was over, Joab returned to
Jerusalem.

BALANCE 10:12

There must be a balance between our actions and our faith in God. In this verse, Joab says, "Let us fight bravely for our people and the cities of our God." In other words, do what you can. Plan the battle strategy, use your mind to figure out the best techniques, and use your resources. But he also says, "May the LORD's will be done." He knew that the outcome was in God's hands. In the same way, we are to use our mind and our resources to obey God, while trusting God for the outcome. In what ways do your actions show this level of trust? ■

[15]The Arameans now realized that they were no match
for Israel. So when they regrouped, [16]they were joined by
additional Aramean troops summoned by Hadadezer
from the other side of the Euphrates River.* These
troops arrived at Helam under the command of Shobach,
the commander of Hadadezer's forces.
[17]When David heard what was happening, he mobilized all Israel, crossed the Jordan River, and led the army
to Helam. The Arameans positioned themselves in battle
formation and fought against David. [18]But again the Arameans fled from the Israelites. This time David's forces
killed 700 charioteers and 40,000 foot soldiers,* including Shobach, the commander of their army. [19]When all
the kings allied with Hadadezer saw that they had been
defeated by Israel, they surrendered to Israel and became
their subjects. After that, the Arameans were afraid to
help the Ammonites.

11

DAVID AND BATHSHEBA

In the spring of the year,* when kings normally go out to
war, David sent Joab and the Israelite army to fight the
Ammonites. They destroyed the Ammonite army and
laid siege to the city of Rabbah. However, David stayed
behind in Jerusalem.
[2]Late one afternoon, after his midday rest, David got
out of bed and was walking on the roof of the palace. As
he looked out over the city, he noticed a woman of unusual beauty taking a bath. [3]He sent someone to find out
who she was, and he was told, "She is Bathsheba, the
daughter of Eliam and the wife of Uriah the Hittite."
[4]Then David sent messengers to get her; and when she
came to the palace, he slept with her. She had just
completed the purification rites after having her menstrual period. Then she returned home. [5]Later, when
Bathsheba discovered that she was pregnant, she sent
David a message, saying, "I'm pregnant."
[6]Then David sent word to Joab: "Send me Uriah the
Hittite." So Joab sent him to David. [7]When Uriah arrived,
David asked him how Joab and the army were getting
along and how the war was progressing. [8]Then he told
Uriah, "Go on home and relax.*" David even sent a gift to
Uriah after he had left the palace. [9]But Uriah didn't go
home. He slept that night at the palace entrance with the
king's palace guard.
[10]When David heard that Uriah had not gone home, he
summoned him and asked, "What's the matter? Why
didn't you go home last night after being away for so
long?"
[11]Uriah replied, "The Ark and the armies of Israel and
Judah are living in tents,* and Joab and my master's men
are camping in the open fields. How could I go home to
wine and dine and sleep with my wife? I swear that I
would never do such a thing."
[12]"Well, stay here today," David told him, "and tomorrow you may return to the army." So Uriah stayed in Jerusalem that day and the next. [13]Then David invited him to
dinner and got him drunk. But even then he couldn't get
Uriah to go home to his wife. Again he slept at the palace
entrance with the king's palace guard.

TEMPTATION 11:1-4

As David gazed from his palace roof, he saw a beautiful woman taking a bath, and lust filled his heart. He should have left the roof and fled from the temptation. Instead, he went further by asking about Bathsheba. The results of letting temptation stay in his heart were devastating.

At the root of most temptation is a real need or desire that God can fill. To flee temptation: (1) Ask God in earnest prayer to help you stay away from people, places, and situations that offer temptation. (2) Memorize and meditate on portions of Scripture that combat your specific weaknesses. (3) Find another believer with whom you can openly share your temptations and call this person for help when temptation strikes. ■

DAVID ARRANGES FOR URIAH'S DEATH

[14]So the next morning David wrote a letter to Joab and
gave it to Uriah to deliver. [15]The letter instructed Joab,
"Station Uriah on the front lines where the battle is fiercest. Then pull back so that he will be killed." [16]So Joab assigned Uriah to a spot close to the city wall where he
knew the enemy's strongest men were fighting. [17]And
when the enemy soldiers came out of the city to fight,
Uriah the Hittite was killed along with several other Israelite soldiers.

10:16 Hebrew *the river*. 10:18 As in some Greek manuscripts (see also 1 Chr 19:18); Hebrew reads *charioteers*. 11:1 Hebrew *At the turn of the year*. The first day of the year in the ancient Hebrew lunar calendar occurred in March or April. 11:8 Hebrew *and wash your feet*, an expression that may also have a connotation of ritualistic washing. 11:11 Or *at Succoth*.

LIVING FOR THE MOMENT

All winter, 17-year-old Traci thought about only one thing—spring break.

"It's gonna be so great!" she told anyone who would listen. "I'm going with my three best friends and my older sister. I had to, like, beg my mom for a year to get her permission, but she finally said I could. Anyway, I cannot wait to leave behind all this crummy weather and get away from my mom. I'm serious. Anyway, in just a few weeks, I'll have it made—tons of rays, millions of guys, and no nosy mother!"

That was before. Now that spring break is history, Traci rarely talks about her trip. See, the minute Traci hit the beach, she forgot everything she believed in. She let herself get sucked up into the "forget-your-troubles-and-party-till-you-puke" mentality. And that attitude has left Traci with a lot of scars.

"Why didn't I listen? My friends and my sister kept telling me to chill. But I just blew them off and went out by myself. The third night I met these college guys at a pool party and started hanging out with them. We started drinking and stuff. The next thing I knew, I was waking up in a motel room . . . in bed with some guy I'd never seen before."

Ever know anyone who only lived for the moment? What were the consequences? For another look at the consequences of living for the moment, read 2 Samuel 11–12.

18 Then Joab sent a battle report to David. 19 He told his
messenger, "Report all the news of the battle to the king.
20 But he might get angry and ask, 'Why did the troops go
so close to the city? Didn't they know there would be
shooting from the walls? 21 Wasn't Abimelech son of
Gideon* killed at Thebez by a woman who threw a millstone down on him from the wall? Why would you get so
close to the wall?' Then tell him, 'Uriah the Hittite was
killed, too.'"

22 So the messenger went to Jerusalem and gave a complete report to David. 23 "The enemy came out against us
in the open fields," he said. "And as we chased them back
to the city gate, 24 the archers on the wall shot arrows at us.
Some of the king's men were killed, including Uriah the
Hittite."

25 "Well, tell Joab not to be discouraged," David said.
"The sword devours this one today and that one tomorrow! Fight harder next time, and conquer the city!"

26 When Uriah's wife heard that her husband was dead,
she mourned for him. 27 When the period of mourning
was over, David sent for her and brought her to the palace, and she became one of his wives. Then she gave birth
to a son. But the LORD was displeased with what David
had done.

12

NATHAN REBUKES DAVID

So the LORD sent Nathan the prophet to tell David this
story: "There were two men in a certain town. One was
rich, and one was poor. 2 The rich man owned a great
many sheep and cattle. 3 The poor man owned nothing
but one little lamb he had bought. He raised that little
lamb, and it grew up with his children. It ate from the
man's own plate and drank from his cup. He cuddled it in
his arms like a baby daughter. 4 One day a guest arrived at
the home of the rich man. But instead of killing an animal
from his own flock or herd, he took the poor man's lamb
and killed it and prepared it for his guest."

5 David was furious. "As surely as the LORD lives," he
vowed, "any man who would do such a thing deserves to
die! 6 He must repay four lambs to the poor man for the
one he stole and for having no pity."

7 Then Nathan said to David, "You are that man! The
LORD, the God of Israel, says: I anointed you king of Israel
and saved you from the power of Saul. 8 I gave you your
master's house and his wives and the kingdoms of Israel
and Judah. And if that had not been enough, I would have
given you much, much more. 9 Why, then, have you despised the word of the LORD and done this horrible deed?
For you have murdered Uriah the Hittite with the sword
of the Ammonites and stolen his wife. 10 From this time
on, your family will live by the sword because you have
despised me by taking Uriah's wife to be your own.

11 "This is what the LORD says: Because of what you have
done, I will cause your own household to rebel against
you. I will give your wives to another man before your
very eyes, and he will go to bed with them in public view.
12 You did it secretly, but I will make this happen to you
openly in the sight of all Israel."

CONFRONT 12:1-14

As a prophet, Nathan was required to confront sin, even the sin of a king. It took great courage, skill, and tact to speak to David in a way that would make him aware of his wrong actions. When you have to confront someone with unpleasant news, pray for courage, skill, and tact. How you present your message may be as important as what you say. ■

DAVID CONFESSES HIS GUILT

13 Then David confessed to Nathan, "I have sinned against
the LORD."

Nathan replied, "Yes, but the LORD has forgiven you,
and you won't die for this sin. 14 Nevertheless, because
you have shown utter contempt for the LORD* by doing
this, your child will die."

15 After Nathan returned to his home, the LORD sent a
deadly illness to the child of David and Uriah's wife. 16 David begged God to spare the child. He went without food
and lay all night on the bare ground. 17 The elders of his

11:21 Hebrew *son of Jerub-besheth.* Jerub-besheth is a variation on the name Jerub-baal, which is another name for Gideon; see Judg 6:32.
12:14 As in Dead Sea Scrolls; Masoretic Text reads *the LORD's enemies.*

household pleaded with him to get up and eat with them, but he refused.

18Then on the seventh day the child died. David's advisers were afraid to tell him. "He wouldn't listen to reason while the child was ill," they said. "What drastic thing will he do when we tell him the child is dead?"

19When David saw them whispering, he realized what had happened. "Is the child dead?" he asked.

"Yes," they replied, "he is dead."

20Then David got up from the ground, washed himself, put on lotions,* and changed his clothes. He went to the Tabernacle and worshiped the LORD. After that, he returned to the palace and was served food and ate.

21His advisers were amazed. "We don't understand you," they told him. "While the child was still living, you wept and refused to eat. But now that the child is dead, you have stopped your mourning and are eating again."

22David replied, "I fasted and wept while the child was alive, for I said, 'Perhaps the LORD will be gracious to me and let the child live.' 23But why should I fast when he is dead? Can I bring him back again? I will go to him one day, but he cannot return to me."

24Then David comforted Bathsheba, his wife, and slept with her. She became pregnant and gave birth to a son, and they named him Solomon. The LORD loved the child 25and sent word through Nathan the prophet that they should name him Jedidiah (which means "beloved of the LORD"), as the LORD had commanded.*

DAVID CAPTURES RABBAH

26Meanwhile, Joab was fighting against Rabbah, the capital of Ammon, and he captured the royal fortifications.* 27Joab sent messengers to tell David, "I have fought against Rabbah and captured its water supply.* 28Now bring the rest of the army and capture the city. Otherwise, I will capture it and get credit for the victory."

29So David gathered the rest of the army and went to Rabbah, and he fought against it and captured it. 30David removed the crown from the king's head,* and it was placed on his own head. The crown was made of gold and set with gems, and it weighed seventy-five pounds.* David took a vast amount of plunder from the city. 31He also made slaves of the people of Rabbah and forced them to labor with* saws, iron picks, and iron axes, and to work in the brick kilns.* That is how he dealt with the people of all the Ammonite towns. Then David and all the army returned to Jerusalem.

13 THE RAPE OF TAMAR

Now David's son Absalom had a beautiful sister named Tamar. And Amnon, her half brother, fell desperately in love with her. 2Amnon became so obsessed with Tamar that he became ill. She was a virgin, and Amnon thought he could never have her.

3But Amnon had a very crafty friend—his cousin Jonadab. He was the son of David's brother Shimea.* 4One day Jonadab said to Amnon, "What's the trouble?

12:20 Hebrew *anointed himself.* **12:25** As in Greek version; Hebrew reads *because of the LORD.* **12:26** Or *the royal city.* **12:27** Or *captured the city of water.* **12:30a** Or *from the head of Milcom* (as in Greek version). Milcom, also called Molech, was the god of the Ammonites. **12:30b** Hebrew *1 talent* [34 kilograms]. **12:31a** Or *He also brought out the people of Rabbah and put them under.* **12:31b** Or *and he made them pass through the brick kilns.* **13:3** Hebrew *Shimeah* (also in 13:32), a variant spelling of Shimea; compare 1 Chr 2:13.

ABSALOM

Know anyone who talks a good game, but seems to lack character? Absalom was that kind of person. Although he looked like he would make the perfect king, his good looks could not make up for a lack of integrity.

The old saying that the apple doesn't fall far from the tree is true about Absalom. He made some of the same mistakes that David made and often chose the wrong advice. He administered his own brand of justice for the rape of his sister, after watching his father's passive response. After running away and being invited back to the kingdom, he decided that he deserved to be king more than David.

While David's sins took him away from God and back again, Absalom allowed his wrongdoings to keep him away from God. He later was killed after trying to take the kingdom by force.

Tempted to rebel like Absalom? Maybe you feel like your parents hassle you and don't give you the freedom you think you deserve. Or, maybe you think you can make better decisions than they. If so, take a close at Absalom's life. Your life doesn't have to hold the same tragedy. You can turn back. God is waiting.

DOWNS:
- Avenged the rape of his sister Tamar by killing his half brother Amnon
- Plotted against his father to take away the throne of Israel
- Consistently listened to the wrong advice

STATS:
- Where: Hebron
- Occupation: Prince
- Relatives: David (father); Maacah (mother); Amnon, Chileab, Solomon, and others (brothers); Tamar (sister)
- Contemporaries: Nathan, Jonadab, Joab, Ahithophel, Hushai

BOTTOM LINE:

The sins of parents are often repeated and amplified in their children.

A smart man gets a lot of advice; a wise man evaluates the advice he gets.

Actions against God's plans will fail sooner or later.

Absalom's story is told in 2 Sam 3:3; 13–18.

Why should the son of a king look so dejected morning
after morning?"
So Amnon told him, "I am in love with Tamar, my
brother Absalom's sister."
5"Well," Jonadab said, "I'll tell you what to do. Go back
to bed and pretend you are ill. When your father comes
to see you, ask him to let Tamar come and prepare some
food for you. Tell him you'll feel better if she prepares it
as you watch and feeds you with her own hands."
6So Amnon lay down and pretended to be sick. And
when the king came to see him, Amnon asked him,
"Please let my sister Tamar come and cook my favorite
dish* as I watch. Then I can eat it from her own hands."
7So David agreed and sent Tamar to Amnon's house to
prepare some food for him.
8When Tamar arrived at Amnon's house, she went to
the place where he was lying down so he could watch her
mix some dough. Then she baked his favorite dish for
him. 9But when she set the serving tray before him, he refused to eat. "Everyone get out of here," Amnon told his
servants. So they all left.
10Then he said to Tamar, "Now bring the food into my
bedroom and feed it to me here." So Tamar took his favorite dish to him. 11But as she was feeding him, he
grabbed her and demanded, "Come to bed with me, my
darling sister."

LOVE VS. LUST 13:1-15

Love and lust are very different. After Amnon raped his half sister, his "love" turned to hate. Although he had claimed to be in love, he was actually overcome by lust. "Love is patient"; lust requires immediate sexual satisfaction. Love is "kind"; lust is harsh. Love "does not demand its own way"; lust does. (See 1 Cor 13:4-5.) In what ways do you show real love to the people in your life? ■

12"No, my brother!" she cried. "Don't be foolish! Don't
do this to me! Such wicked things aren't done in Israel.
13Where could I go in my shame? And you would be
called one of the greatest fools in Israel. Please, just speak
to the king about it, and he will let you marry me."
14But Amnon wouldn't listen to her, and since he was
stronger than she was, he raped her. 15Then suddenly
Amnon's love turned to hate, and he hated her even more
than he had loved her. "Get out of here!" he snarled at her.
16"No, no!" Tamar cried. "Sending me away now is
worse than what you've already done to me."
But Amnon wouldn't listen to her. 17He shouted for his
servant and demanded, "Throw this woman out, and lock
the door behind her!"
18So the servant put her out and locked the door behind
her. She was wearing a long, beautiful robe,* as was the
custom in those days for the king's virgin daughters. 19But
now Tamar tore her robe and put ashes on her head. And
then, with her face in her hands, she went away crying.
20Her brother Absalom saw her and asked, "Is it true
that Amnon has been with you? Well, my sister, keep
quiet for now, since he's your brother. Don't you worry
about it." So Tamar lived as a desolate woman in her
brother Absalom's house.
21When King David heard what had happened, he was
very angry.* 22And though Absalom never spoke to Amnon about this, he hated Amnon deeply because of what
he had done to his sister.

ABSALOM'S REVENGE ON AMNON

23Two years later, when Absalom's sheep were being
sheared at Baal-hazor near Ephraim, Absalom invited all
the king's sons to come to a feast. 24He went to the king
and said, "My sheep-shearers are now at work. Would the
king and his servants please come to celebrate the occasion with me?"
25The king replied, "No, my son. If we all came, we
would be too much of a burden on you." Absalom
pressed him, but the king would not come, though he
gave Absalom his blessing.
26"Well, then," Absalom said, "if you can't come, how
about sending my brother Amnon with us?"
"Why Amnon?" the king asked. 27But Absalom kept on
pressing the king until he finally agreed to let all his sons
attend, including Amnon. So Absalom prepared a feast
fit for a king.*
28Absalom told his men, "Wait until Amnon gets drunk;
then at my signal, kill him! Don't be afraid. I'm the one
who has given the command. Take courage and do it!"
29So at Absalom's signal they murdered Amnon. Then the
other sons of the king jumped on their mules and fled.
30As they were on the way back to Jerusalem, this report reached David: "Absalom has killed all the king's
sons; not one is left alive!" 31The king got up, tore his robe,
and threw himself on the ground. His advisers also tore
their clothes in horror and sorrow.
32But just then Jonadab, the son of David's brother
Shimea, arrived and said, "No, don't believe that all the
king's sons have been killed! It was only Amnon! Absalom
has been plotting this ever since Amnon raped his sister
Tamar. 33No, my lord the king, your sons aren't all dead! It
was only Amnon." 34Meanwhile Absalom escaped.
Then the watchman on the Jerusalem wall saw a great
crowd coming toward the city from the west. He ran to
tell the king, "I see a crowd of people coming from the
Horonaim road* along the side of the hill."
35"Look!" Jonadab told the king. "There they are now!
The king's sons are coming, just as I said."
36They soon arrived, weeping and sobbing, and the
king and all his servants wept bitterly with them. 37And
David mourned many days for his son Amnon.
Absalom fled to his grandfather, Talmai son of Ammihud, the king of Geshur. 38He stayed there in Geshur for

13:6 Or *a couple of cakes;* also in 13:8, 10. 13:18 Or *a robe with sleeves,* or *an ornamented robe.* The meaning of the Hebrew is uncertain. 13:21 Dead Sea Scrolls and Greek version add *But he did not punish his son Amnon, because he loved him, for he was his firstborn.* 13:27 As in Greek and Latin versions (compare also Dead Sea Scrolls); the Hebrew text omits this sentence. 13:34 As in Greek version; Hebrew reads *from the road behind him.*

ULTIMATE ISSUES

DATE RAPE

Tamar's experience in chapter 13 is little different from that of many women today. Studies indicate the horrifying fact that as many as one out of every six women has been or will be raped. Date rape is the most common form of sexual abuse. One in eight female college students will experience rape or attempted rape, usually from a date or acquaintance. Even men are not immune: at least one out of every ten victims of sexual assault is male.

Most experts agree that these frightening numbers may reflect only a fraction of the reality. Only about 39 percent of sexual assaults are reported.

What should you do if you've been a victim of sexual abuse?

First, understand you *are* a victim of a crime. You did not "ask for it." Don't allow guilt to cause you to take responsibility for someone else's poor decision. If you said no, no means no.

Second, realize that you are not alone and without resources. Talking about what happened helps break the power the incident has over you; not talking about it will keep you a victim forever. If you need help or information on counseling centers, contact the sexual assault hotline (1-800-656-HOPE) of RAINN (the Rape, Abuse & Incest National Network).

The best source of help is God himself. He alone is able to heal your damaged body, emotions, and spirit. Turn to God and let him make you whole again. He can do it.

If you are a guy who is trying to help a female friend or family member work through this shattering experience, try to avoid telling a rape victim she should "just get over it" or "get on with her life." Every woman who has been sexually violated wants to do just that, but it is impossible to "carry on" as though the rape never happened. Rape changes a woman's life. The inner anguish must be dealt with. Try to be patient, supportive, and loving.

If you have committed this sin, cry out to God for mercy and forgiveness, and seek counseling. God is waiting—and willing—to help you.

three years. 39And King David, now reconciled to Amnon's death, longed to be reunited with his son
Absalom.*

14 JOAB ARRANGES FOR ABSALOM'S RETURN

Joab realized how much the king longed to see Absalom.
2So he sent for a woman from Tekoa who had a reputation for great wisdom. He said to her, "Pretend you are in
mourning; wear mourning clothes and don't put on lotions.* Act like a woman who has been mourning for the
dead for a long time. 3Then go to the king and tell him the
story I am about to tell you." Then Joab told her what to
say.

4When the woman from Tekoa approached the king,
she bowed with her face to the ground in deep respect
and cried out, "O king! Help me!"

5"What's the trouble?" the king asked.

"Alas, I am a widow!" she replied. "My husband is dead.
6My two sons had a fight out in the field. And since no
one was there to stop it, one of them was killed. 7Now the
rest of the family is demanding, 'Let us have your son. We
will execute him for murdering his brother. He doesn't
deserve to inherit his family's property.' They want to extinguish the only coal I have left, and my husband's name
and family will disappear from the face of the earth."

8"Leave it to me," the king told her. "Go home, and I'll
see to it that no one touches him."

9"Oh, thank you, my lord the king," the woman from
Tekoa replied. "If you are criticized for helping me, let
the blame fall on me and on my father's house, and let the
king and his throne be innocent."

10"If anyone objects," the king said, "bring him to me. I
can assure you he will never complain again!"

11Then she said, "Please swear to me by the LORD your
God that you won't let anyone take vengeance against my
son. I want no more bloodshed."

"As surely as the LORD lives," he replied, "not a hair on
your son's head will be disturbed!"

12"Please allow me to ask one more thing of my lord the
king," she said.

"Go ahead and speak," he responded.

13:39 Or *no longer felt a need to go out after Absalom.* **14:2** Hebrew *don't anoint yourself with oil.*

13She replied, "Why don't you do as much for the people
of God as you have promised to do for me? You have convicted yourself in making this decision, because you have
refused to bring home your own banished son. 14All of us
must die eventually. Our lives are like water spilled out on
the ground, which cannot be gathered up again. But God
does not just sweep life away; instead, he devises ways to
bring us back when we have been separated from him.

INDECISIVE 14:28

David only made halfhearted efforts to raise his children. In 13:21-39, David did not punish Amnon for his crime, nor did he deal decisively with Absalom's murder of Amnon. As a result, Absalom ran away to live with other relatives. When David finally allowed Absalom back, he did not speak to him for two years. Such indecisiveness became David's undoing. When bad behavior is ignored, it will bring greater pain than if it is dealt with immediately. ■

15"I have come to plead with my lord the king because
people have threatened me. I said to myself, 'Perhaps the
king will listen to me 16and rescue us from those who
would cut us off from the inheritance* God has given us.
17Yes, my lord the king will give us peace of mind again.' I
know that you are like an angel of God in discerning good
from evil. May the LORD your God be with you."
18"I must know one thing," the king replied, "and tell
me the truth."
"Yes, my lord the king," she responded.
19"Did Joab put you up to this?"
And the woman replied, "My lord the king, how can I
deny it? Nobody can hide anything from you. Yes, Joab
sent me and told me what to say. 20He did it to place the
matter before you in a different light. But you are as wise
as an angel of God, and you understand everything that
happens among us!"
21So the king sent for Joab and told him, "All right, go
and bring back the young man Absalom."
22Joab bowed with his face to the ground in deep respect and said, "At last I know that I have gained your approval, my lord the king, for you have granted me this
request!"
23Then Joab went to Geshur and brought Absalom
back to Jerusalem. 24But the king gave this order: "Absalom may go to his own house, but he must never come
into my presence." So Absalom did not see the king.

ABSALOM RECONCILED TO DAVID

25Now Absalom was praised as the most handsome man
in all Israel. He was flawless from head to foot. 26He cut
his hair only once a year, and then only because it was so
heavy. When he weighed it out, it came to five pounds!*
27He had three sons and one daughter. His daughter's
name was Tamar, and she was very beautiful.
28Absalom lived in Jerusalem for two years, but he
never got to see the king. 29Then Absalom sent for Joab to
ask him to intercede for him, but Joab refused to come.
Absalom sent for him a second time, but again Joab refused to come. 30So Absalom said to his servants, "Go and
set fire to Joab's barley field, the field next to mine." So
they set his field on fire, as Absalom had commanded.
31Then Joab came to Absalom at his house and demanded, "Why did your servants set my field on fire?"
32And Absalom replied, "Because I wanted you to ask
the king why he brought me back from Geshur if he
didn't intend to see me. I might as well have stayed there.
Let me see the king; if he finds me guilty of anything, then
let him kill me."
33So Joab told the king what Absalom had said. Then at
last David summoned Absalom, who came and bowed
low before the king, and the king kissed him.

15

ABSALOM'S REBELLION

After this, Absalom bought a chariot and horses, and he
hired fifty bodyguards to run ahead of him. 2He got up
early every morning and went out to the gate of the city.
When people brought a case to the king for judgment,
Absalom would ask where in Israel they were from, and
they would tell him their tribe. 3Then Absalom would say,
"You've really got a strong case here! It's too bad the king
doesn't have anyone to hear it. 4I wish I were the judge.
Then everyone could bring their cases to me for judgment, and I would give them justice!"
5When people tried to bow before him, Absalom

14:16 Or *the property;* or *the people.* **14:26** Hebrew *200 shekels* [2.3 kilograms] *by the royal standard.*

What can I do when I'm ridiculed for who I am or for my belief in God?

People ridicule what they don't understand or what they wish they had themselves. David experienced this when his son Absalom tried to take his kingdom away (2 Sam 15).

Feeling the fire of opposition? Check out this advice from 1 Peter 3.

First, your best defense is a quiet offense: "Don't repay evil for evil. Don't retaliate with insults when people insult you. Instead, pay them back with a blessing. That is what God has called you to do, and he will bless you for it" (1 Pet 3:9).

Second, quietly trust yourself to Christ (1 Pet 3:15). You trusted Christ to be Lord of your life; now allow him to be Lord over your circumstances. God is trying to develop your character.

Third, be ready to explain your faith when the opportunities arise (1 Pet 3:15-16). Don't be afraid to admit that you don't have all the answers.

Even doing all of this still may not relieve the tension. But, "it is better to suffer for doing good, if that is what God wants, than to suffer for doing wrong!" (1 Pet 3:17).

wouldn't let them. Instead, he took them by the hand and kissed them. 6Absalom did this with everyone who came to the king for judgment, and so he stole the hearts of all the people of Israel.

7After four years,* Absalom said to the king, "Let me go to Hebron to offer a sacrifice to the LORD and fulfill a vow I made to him. 8For while your servant was at Geshur in Aram, I promised to sacrifice to the LORD in Hebron* if he would bring me back to Jerusalem."

9"All right," the king told him. "Go and fulfill your vow."

So Absalom went to Hebron. 10But while he was there, he sent secret messengers to all the tribes of Israel to stir up a rebellion against the king. "As soon as you hear the ram's horn," his message read, "you are to say, 'Absalom has been crowned king in Hebron.'" 11He took 200 men from Jerusalem with him as guests, but they knew nothing of his intentions. 12While Absalom was offering the sacrifices, he sent for Ahithophel, one of David's counselors who lived in Giloh. Soon many others also joined Absalom, and the conspiracy gained momentum.

COURAGE 15:14

Had David not escaped from Jerusalem, the resulting fight might have destroyed both him and the innocent inhabitants of the city. Some fights that we think are necessary may be costly and destructive to those around us. In such cases, it may be wise to back down and save the fight for another day—even if doing so hurts our pride. It takes courage to stand and fight, but it also takes courage to back down when you must for the sake of others. ■

DAVID ESCAPES FROM JERUSALEM

13A messenger soon arrived in Jerusalem to tell David, "All Israel has joined Absalom in a conspiracy against you!"

14"Then we must flee at once, or it will be too late!" David urged his men. "Hurry! If we get out of the city before Absalom arrives, both we and the city of Jerusalem will be spared from disaster."

15"We are with you," his advisers replied. "Do what you think is best."

16So the king and all his household set out at once. He left no one behind except ten of his concubines to look after the palace. 17The king and all his people set out on foot, pausing at the last house 18to let all the king's men move past to lead the way. There were 600 men from Gath who had come with David, along with the king's bodyguard.*

19Then the king turned and said to Ittai, a leader of the men from Gath, "Why are you coming with us? Go on back to King Absalom, for you are a guest in Israel, a foreigner in exile. 20You arrived only recently, and should I force you today to wander with us? I don't even know where we will go. Go on back and take your kinsmen with you, and may the LORD show you his unfailing love and faithfulness.*"

21But Ittai said to the king, "I vow by the LORD and by your own life that I will go wherever my lord the king goes, no matter what happens—whether it means life or death."

22David replied, "All right, come with us." So Ittai and all his men and their families went along.

23Everyone cried loudly as the king and his followers passed by. They crossed the Kidron Valley and then went out toward the wilderness.

24Zadok and all the Levites also came along, carrying the Ark of the Covenant of God. They set down the Ark of God, and Abiathar offered sacrifices* until everyone had passed out of the city.

25Then the king instructed Zadok to take the Ark of God back into the city. "If the LORD sees fit," David said, "he will bring me back to see the Ark and the Tabernacle* again. 26But if he is through with me, then let him do what seems best to him."

27The king also told Zadok the priest, "Look,* here is my plan. You and Abiathar* should return quietly to the city with your son Ahimaaz and Abiathar's son Jonathan. 28I will stop at the shallows of the Jordan River* and wait there for a report from you." 29So Zadok and Abiathar took the Ark of God back to the city and stayed there.

30David walked up the road to the Mount of Olives, weeping as he went. His head was covered and his feet were bare as a sign of mourning. And the people who were with him covered their heads and wept as they climbed the hill. 31When someone told David that his adviser Ahithophel was now backing Absalom, David prayed, "O LORD, let Ahithophel give Absalom foolish advice!"

32When David reached the summit of the Mount of Olives where people worshiped God, Hushai the Arkite was waiting there for him. Hushai had torn his clothing and put dirt on his head as a sign of mourning. 33But David told him, "If you go with me, you will only be a burden. 34Return to Jerusalem and tell Absalom, 'I will now be your adviser, O king, just as I was your father's adviser in the past.' Then you can frustrate and counter Ahithophel's advice. 35Zadok and Abiathar, the priests, will be there. Tell them about the plans being made in the king's palace, 36and they will send their sons Ahimaaz and Jonathan to tell me what is going on."

37So David's friend Hushai returned to Jerusalem, getting there just as Absalom arrived.

16 DAVID AND ZIBA

When David had gone a little beyond the summit of the Mount of Olives, Ziba, the servant of Mephibosheth,* was waiting there for him. He had two donkeys loaded with 200 loaves of bread, 100 clusters of raisins, 100 bunches of summer fruit, and a wineskin full of wine.

15:7 As in Greek and Syriac versions; Hebrew reads *forty years.* 15:8 As in some Greek manuscripts; Hebrew lacks *in Hebron.* 15:18 Hebrew *the Kerethites and Pelethites.* 15:20 As in Greek version; Hebrew reads *and may unfailing love and faithfulness go with you.* 15:24 Or *Abiathar went up.* 15:25 Hebrew *and his dwelling place.* 15:27a As in Greek version; Hebrew reads *Are you a seer?* or *Do you see?* 15:27b Hebrew lacks *and Abiathar;* compare 15:29. 15:28 Hebrew *at the crossing points of the wilderness.* 16:1 *Mephibosheth* is another name for Merib-baal.

2"What are these for?" the king asked Ziba.
Ziba replied, "The donkeys are for the king's people to
ride on, and the bread and summer fruit are for the
young men to eat. The wine is for those who become exhausted in the wilderness."
3"And where is Mephibosheth, Saul's grandson?" the
king asked him.
"He stayed in Jerusalem," Ziba replied. "He said, 'Today
I will get back the kingdom of my grandfather Saul.'"
4"In that case," the king told Ziba, "I give you everything Mephibosheth owns."
"I bow before you," Ziba replied. "May I always be
pleasing to you, my lord the king."

CHECK IT OUT 16:1-4

David believed Ziba's charge against Mephibosheth without checking into it. Ever been hasty to accept a rumor or someone's condemnation of another person? The wise person always checks his or her sources. ■

SHIMEI CURSES DAVID

5As King David came to Bahurim, a man came out of the
village cursing them. It was Shimei son of Gera, from the
same clan as Saul's family. 6He threw stones at the king
and the king's officers and all the mighty warriors who
surrounded him. 7"Get out of here, you murderer, you
scoundrel!" he shouted at David. 8"The LORD is paying
you back for all the bloodshed in Saul's clan. You stole his
throne, and now the LORD has given it to your son Absalom. At last you will taste some of your own medicine, for
you are a murderer!"
9"Why should this dead dog curse my lord the king?"
Abishai son of Zeruiah demanded. "Let me go over and
cut off his head!"
10"No!" the king said. "Who asked your opinion, you
sons of Zeruiah! If the LORD has told him to curse me,
who are you to stop him?"
11Then David said to Abishai and to all his servants,
"My own son is trying to kill me. Doesn't this relative of
Saul* have even more reason to do so? Leave him alone
and let him curse, for the LORD has told him to do it.
12And perhaps the LORD will see that I am being wronged
and will bless me because of these curses today." 13So David and his men continued down the road, and Shimei
kept pace with them on a nearby hillside, cursing as he
went and throwing stones at David and tossing dust into
the air.
14The king and all who were with him grew weary
along the way, so they rested when they reached the Jordan River.*

AHITHOPHEL ADVISES ABSALOM

15Meanwhile, Absalom and all the army of Israel arrived
at Jerusalem, accompanied by Ahithophel. 16When David's friend Hushai the Arkite arrived, he went immediately to see Absalom. "Long live the king!" he exclaimed.
"Long live the king!"
17"Is this the way you treat your friend David?" Absalom asked him. "Why aren't you with him?"
18"I'm here because I belong to the man who is chosen
by the LORD and by all the men of Israel," Hushai replied.
19"And anyway, why shouldn't I serve you? Just as I was
your father's adviser, now I will be your adviser!"
20Then Absalom turned to Ahithophel and asked him,
"What should I do next?"
21Ahithophel told him, "Go and sleep with your father's concubines, for he has left them here to look after
the palace. Then all Israel will know that you have insulted your father beyond hope of reconciliation, and
they will throw their support to you." 22So they set up a
tent on the palace roof where everyone could see it,
and Absalom went in and had sex with his father's
concubines.
23Absalom followed Ahithophel's advice, just as David
had done. For every word Ahithophel spoke seemed as
wise as though it had come directly from the mouth of
God.

17 Now Ahithophel urged Absalom, "Let me
choose 12,000 men to start out after David tonight. 2I
will catch up with him while he is weary and discouraged. He and his troops will panic, and everyone will
run away. Then I will kill only the king, 3and I will bring
all the people back to you as a bride returns to her husband. After all, it is only one man's life that you seek.*
Then you will be at peace with all the people." 4This
plan seemed good to Absalom and to all the elders of
Israel.

HUSHAI COUNTERS AHITHOPHEL'S ADVICE

5But then Absalom said, "Bring in Hushai the Arkite. Let's
see what he thinks about this." 6When Hushai arrived,
Absalom told him what Ahithophel had said. Then he
asked, "What is your opinion? Should we follow Ahithophel's advice? If not, what do you suggest?"
7"Well," Hushai replied to Absalom, "this time Ahithophel has made a mistake. 8You know your father and his
men; they are mighty warriors. Right now they are as enraged as a mother bear who has been robbed of her cubs.
And remember that your father is an experienced man of
war. He won't be spending the night among the troops.
9He has probably already hidden in some pit or cave. And
when he comes out and attacks and a few of your men
fall, there will be panic among your troops, and the word
will spread that Absalom's men are being slaughtered.
10Then even the bravest soldiers, though they have the
heart of a lion, will be paralyzed with fear. For all Israel
knows what a mighty warrior your father is and how courageous his men are.
11"I recommend that you mobilize the entire army of
Israel, bringing them from as far away as Dan in the north
and Beersheba in the south. That way you will have an

16:11 Hebrew *this Benjaminite.* **16:14** As in Greek version (see also 17:16); Hebrew reads *when they reached their destination.* **17:3** As in Greek version; Hebrew reads *like the return of all is the man whom you seek.*

army as numerous as the sand on the seashore. And I advise that you personally lead the troops. 12When we find David, we'll fall on him like dew that falls on the ground. Then neither he nor any of his men will be left alive. 13And if David were to escape into some town, you will have all Israel there at your command. Then we can take ropes and drag the walls of the town into the nearest valley until every stone is torn down."

VANITY 17:11

When Hushai appealed to Absalom through flattery, Absalom wound up trapped by his vanity. Hushai predicted great glory for Absalom if he personally led the entire army against David. "Pride goes before destruction" (Prov 16:18) is an appropriate comment on Absalom's ambitions. Tempted to let someone's flattery go to your head? Remember Absalom. ■

14Then Absalom and all the men of Israel said, "Hushai's advice is better than Ahithophel's." For the LORD had determined to defeat the counsel of Ahithophel, which really was the better plan, so that he could bring disaster on Absalom!

HUSHAI WARNS DAVID TO ESCAPE

15Hushai told Zadok and Abiathar, the priests, what Ahithophel had said to Absalom and the elders of Israel and what he himself had advised instead. 16"Quick!" he told them. "Find David and urge him not to stay at the shallows of the Jordan River* tonight. He must go across at once into the wilderness beyond. Otherwise he will die and his entire army with him."

17Jonathan and Ahimaaz had been staying at En-rogel so as not to be seen entering and leaving the city. Arrangements had been made for a servant girl to bring them the message they were to take to King David. 18But a boy spotted them at En-rogel, and he told Absalom about it. So they quickly escaped to Bahurim, where a man hid them down inside a well in his courtyard. 19The man's wife put a cloth over the top of the well and scattered grain on it to dry in the sun; so no one suspected they were there.

20When Absalom's men arrived, they asked her, "Have you seen Ahimaaz and Jonathan?"

The woman replied, "They were here, but they crossed over the brook." Absalom's men looked for them without success and returned to Jerusalem.

21Then the two men crawled out of the well and hurried on to King David. "Quick!" they told him, "cross the Jordan tonight!" And they told him how Ahithophel had advised that he be captured and killed. 22So David and all the people with him went across the Jordan River during the night, and they were all on the other bank before dawn.

23When Ahithophel realized that his advice had not been followed, he saddled his donkey, went to his hometown, set his affairs in order, and hanged himself. He died there and was buried in the family tomb.

24David soon arrived at Mahanaim. By now, Absalom had mobilized the entire army of Israel and was leading his troops across the Jordan River. 25Absalom had appointed Amasa as commander of his army, replacing Joab, who had been commander under David. (Amasa was Joab's cousin. His father was Jether,* an Ishmaelite.* His mother, Abigail daughter of Nahash, was the sister of Joab's mother, Zeruiah.) 26Absalom and the Israelite army set up camp in the land of Gilead.

27When David arrived at Mahanaim, he was warmly greeted by Shobi son of Nahash, who came from Rabbah of the Ammonites, and by Makir son of Ammiel from Lo-debar, and by Barzillai of Gilead from Rogelim. 28They brought sleeping mats, cooking pots, serving bowls, wheat and barley, flour and roasted grain, beans, lentils, 29honey, butter, sheep, goats, and cheese for David and those who were with him. For they said, "You must all be very hungry and tired and thirsty after your long march through the wilderness."

18 ABSALOM'S DEFEAT AND DEATH

David now mustered the men who were with him and appointed generals and captains* to lead them. 2He sent the troops out in three groups, placing one group under Joab, one under Joab's brother Abishai son of Zeruiah, and one under Ittai, the man from Gath. The king told his troops, "I am going out with you."

3But his men objected strongly. "You must not go," they urged. "If we have to turn and run—and even if half of us die—it will make no difference to Absalom's troops; they will be looking only for you. You are worth 10,000 of us,* and it is better that you stay here in the town and send help if we need it."

4"If you think that's the best plan, I'll do it," the king answered. So he stood alongside the gate of the town as all the troops marched out in groups of hundreds and of thousands.

5And the king gave this command to Joab, Abishai, and Ittai: "For my sake, deal gently with young Absalom." And all the troops heard the king give this order to his commanders.

6So the battle began in the forest of Ephraim, 7and the Israelite troops were beaten back by David's men. There was a great slaughter that day, and 20,000 men laid down their lives. 8The battle raged all across the countryside, and more men died because of the forest than were killed by the sword.

9During the battle, Absalom happened to come upon some of David's men. He tried to escape on his mule, but as he rode beneath the thick branches of a great tree, his hair* got caught in the tree. His mule kept going and left

17:16 Hebrew *at the crossing points of the wilderness.* **17:25a** Hebrew *Ithra,* a variant spelling of Jether. **17:25b** As in some Greek manuscripts (see also 1 Chr 2:17); Hebrew reads *an Israelite.* **18:1** Hebrew *appointed commanders of thousands and commanders of hundreds.* **18:3** As in two Hebrew manuscripts and some Greek and Latin manuscripts; most Hebrew manuscripts read *Now there are 10,000 like us.* **18:9** Hebrew *his head.*

him dangling in the air. 10 One of David's men saw what had happened and told Joab, "I saw Absalom dangling from a great tree."

11 "What?" Joab demanded. "You saw him there and didn't kill him? I would have rewarded you with ten pieces of silver* and a hero's belt!"

12 "I would not kill the king's son for even a thousand pieces of silver,*" the man replied to Joab. "We all heard the king say to you and Abishai and Ittai, 'For my sake, please spare young Absalom.' 13 And if I had betrayed the king by killing his son—and the king would certainly find out who did it—you yourself would be the first to abandon me."

14 "Enough of this nonsense," Joab said. Then he took three daggers and plunged them into Absalom's heart as he dangled, still alive, in the great tree. 15 Ten of Joab's young armor bearers then surrounded Absalom and killed him.

16 Then Joab blew the ram's horn, and his men returned from chasing the army of Israel. 17 They threw Absalom's body into a deep pit in the forest and piled a great heap of stones over it. And all Israel fled to their homes.

18 During his lifetime, Absalom had built a monument to himself in the King's Valley, for he said, "I have no son to carry on my name." He named the monument after himself, and it is known as Absalom's Monument to this day.

DAVID MOURNS ABSALOM'S DEATH

19 Then Zadok's son Ahimaaz said, "Let me run to the king with the good news that the LORD has rescued him from his enemies."

20 "No," Joab told him, "it wouldn't be good news to the king that his son is dead. You can be my messenger another time, but not today."

21 Then Joab said to a man from Ethiopia,* "Go tell the king what you have seen." The man bowed and ran off.

22 But Ahimaaz continued to plead with Joab, "Whatever happens, please let me go, too."

"Why should you go, my son?" Joab replied. "There will be no reward for your news."

23 "Yes, but let me go anyway," he begged.

Joab finally said, "All right, go ahead." So Ahimaaz took the less demanding route by way of the plain and ran to Mahanaim ahead of the Ethiopian.

24 While David was sitting between the inner and outer gates of the town, the watchman climbed to the roof of the gateway by the wall. As he looked, he saw a lone man running toward them. 25 He shouted the news down to David, and the king replied, "If he is alone, he has news."

As the messenger came closer, 26 the watchman saw another man running toward them. He shouted down, "Here comes another one!"

The king replied, "He also will have news."

27 "The first man runs like Ahimaaz son of Zadok," the watchman said.

"He is a good man and comes with good news," the king replied.

28 Then Ahimaaz cried out to the king, "Everything is all right!" He bowed before the king with his face to the ground and said, "Praise to the LORD your God, who has handed over the rebels who dared to stand against my lord the king."

29 "What about young Absalom?" the king demanded. "Is he all right?"

Ahimaaz replied, "When Joab told me to come, there was a lot of commotion. But I didn't know what was happening."

30 "Wait here," the king told him. So Ahimaaz stepped aside.

31 Then the man from Ethiopia arrived and said, "I have good news for my lord the king. Today the LORD has rescued you from all those who rebelled against you."

32 "What about young Absalom?" the king demanded. "Is he all right?"

And the Ethiopian replied, "May all of your enemies, my lord the king, both now and in the future, share the fate of that young man!"

33* The king was overcome with emotion. He went up to the room over the gateway and burst into tears. And as he went, he cried, "O my son Absalom! My son, my son Absalom! If only I had died instead of you! O Absalom, my son, my son."

GRACE UNDESERVED 18:33

Why was David so upset over the death of his rebel son? (1) David realized that he, in part, was responsible for Absalom's death. Nathan, the prophet, had said that because David had killed Uriah, the members of his household would rebel against him (12:11-12); (2) David was angry at Joab and his officers for killing Absalom against his wishes; (3) David truly loved his son and wanted to show mercy to him even though Absalom rebelled. Just as God bestows undeserved grace upon us when we rebel against him, David was gracious to Absalom. Is that how you are? ■

19

JOAB REBUKES THE KING

1* Word soon reached Joab that the king was weeping and mourning for Absalom. 2 As all the people heard of the king's deep grief for his son, the joy of that day's victory was turned into deep sadness. 3 They crept back into the town that day as though they were ashamed and had deserted in battle. 4 The king covered his face with his hands and kept on crying, "O my son Absalom! O Absalom, my son, my son!"

5 Then Joab went to the king's room and said to him, "We saved your life today and the lives of your sons, your daughters, and your wives and concubines. Yet you act

18:11 Hebrew *10 shekels of silver,* about 4 ounces or 114 grams in weight. 18:12 Hebrew *1,000 shekels,* about 25 pounds or 11.4 kilograms in weight. 18:21 Hebrew *from Cush;* similarly in 18:23, 31, 32. 18:33 Verse 18:33 is numbered 19:1 in Hebrew text. 19:1 Verses 19:1-43 are numbered 19:2-44 in Hebrew text.

like this, making us feel ashamed of ourselves. 6You seem
to love those who hate you and hate those who love you.
You have made it clear today that your commanders and
troops mean nothing to you. It seems that if Absalom had
lived and all of us had died, you would be pleased. 7Now
go out there and congratulate your troops, for I swear by
the LORD that if you don't go out, not a single one of them
will remain here tonight. Then you will be worse off than
ever before."
8So the king went out and took his seat at the town
gate, and as the news spread throughout the town that he
was there, everyone went to him.

Meanwhile, the Israelites who had supported Absalom
fled to their homes. 9And throughout all the tribes of Israel there was much discussion and argument going on.
The people were saying, "The king rescued us from our
enemies and saved us from the Philistines, but Absalom
chased him out of the country. 10Now Absalom, whom we
anointed to rule over us, is dead. Why not ask David to
come back and be our king again?"

THE CROWD 19:8-10

Just a few days before, Absalom had turned the hearts of Israel away from David. Here the people wanted David back as their king. Jesus would later experience this same kind of fickleness. (Compare Matt 21:1-11 with Matt 27:20-25.) How about you? Are you a the kind of person who seeks to please the crowd no matter what the cost? Since a crowd's approval never lasts for long, is pleasing them worth the cost? ■

11Then King David sent Zadok and Abiathar, the
priests, to say to the elders of Judah, "Why are you the last
ones to welcome back the king into his palace? For I have
heard that all Israel is ready. 12You are my relatives, my
own tribe, my own flesh and blood! So why are you the last
ones to welcome back the king?" 13And David told them to
tell Amasa, "Since you are my own flesh and blood, like
Joab, may God strike me and even kill me if I do not appoint you as commander of my army in his place."
14Then Amasa* convinced all the men of Judah, and
they responded unanimously. They sent word to the king,
"Return to us, and bring back all who are with you."

DAVID'S RETURN TO JERUSALEM

15So the king started back to Jerusalem. And when he arrived at the Jordan River, the people of Judah came to
Gilgal to meet him and escort him across the river.
16Shimei son of Gera, the man from Bahurim in Benjamin, hurried across with the men of Judah to welcome
King David. 17A thousand other men from the tribe of
Benjamin were with him, including Ziba, the chief servant of the house of Saul, and Ziba's fifteen sons and
twenty servants. They rushed down to the Jordan to meet
the king. 18They crossed the shallows of the Jordan to
bring the king's household across the river, helping him
in every way they could.

DAVID'S MERCY TO SHIMEI

As the king was about to cross the river, Shimei fell down
before him. 19"My lord the king, please forgive me," he
pleaded. "Forget the terrible thing your servant did when
you left Jerusalem. May the king put it out of his mind. 20I
know how much I sinned. That is why I have come here
today, the very first person in all Israel* to greet my lord
the king."
21Then Abishai son of Zeruiah said, "Shimei should
die, for he cursed the LORD's anointed king!"
22"Who asked your opinion, you sons of Zeruiah!" David exclaimed. "Why have you become my adversary* today? This is not a day for execution but for celebration!
Today I am once again the king of Israel!" 23Then, turning
to Shimei, David vowed, "Your life will be spared."

DAVID'S KINDNESS TO MEPHIBOSHETH

24Now Mephibosheth,* Saul's grandson, came down
from Jerusalem to meet the king. He had not cared for his
feet, trimmed his beard, or washed his clothes since the
day the king left Jerusalem. 25"Why didn't you come with
me, Mephibosheth?" the king asked him.
26Mephibosheth replied, "My lord the king, my servant
Ziba deceived me. I told him, 'Saddle my donkey* so I can
go with the king.' For as you know I am crippled. 27Ziba
has slandered me by saying that I refused to come. But I
know that my lord the king is like an angel of God, so do
what you think is best. 28All my relatives and I could expect only death from you, my lord, but instead you have
honored me by allowing me to eat at your own table!
What more can I ask?"
29"You've said enough," David replied. "I've decided
that you and Ziba will divide your land equally between
you."
30"Give him all of it," Mephibosheth said. "I am content
just to have you safely back again, my lord the king!"

DAVID'S KINDNESS TO BARZILLAI

31Barzillai of Gilead had come down from Rogelim to escort the king across the Jordan. 32He was very old, about
eighty, and very wealthy. He was the one who had provided food for the king during his stay in Mahanaim.
33"Come across with me and live in Jerusalem," the king
said to Barzillai. "I will take care of you there."
34"No," he replied, "I am far too old to go with the king
to Jerusalem. 35I am eighty years old today, and I can no
longer enjoy anything. Food and wine are no longer tasty,
and I cannot hear the singers as they sing. I would only be
a burden to my lord the king. 36Just to go across the Jordan River with the king is all the honor I need! 37Then let
me return again to die in my own town, where my father
and mother are buried. But here is your servant, my son
Kimham. Let him go with my lord the king and receive
whatever you want to give him."
38"Good," the king agreed. "Kimham will go with me,

19:14 As in Greek version; Hebrew reads *he*. **19:20** Hebrew *in the house of Joseph*. **19:22** Or *my prosecutor*. **19:24** *Mephibosheth* is another name for Merib-baal. **19:26** As in Greek, Syriac, and Latin versions; Hebrew reads *I will saddle a donkey for myself*.

and I will help him in any way you would like. And I will do for you anything you want." 39So all the people crossed the Jordan with the king. After David had blessed Barzillai and kissed him, Barzillai returned to his own home.

40The king then crossed over to Gilgal, taking Kimham with him. All the troops of Judah and half the troops of Israel escorted the king on his way.

AN ARGUMENT OVER THE KING

41But all the men of Israel complained to the king, "The men of Judah stole the king and didn't give us the honor of helping take you, your household, and all your men across the Jordan."

42The men of Judah replied, "The king is one of our own kinsmen. Why should this make you angry? We haven't eaten any of the king's food or received any special favors!"

43"But there are ten tribes in Israel," the others replied. "So we have ten times as much right to the king as you do. What right do you have to treat us with such contempt? Weren't we the first to speak of bringing him back to be our king again?" The argument continued back and forth, and the men of Judah spoke even more harshly than the men of Israel.

20

THE REVOLT OF SHEBA

There happened to be a troublemaker there named Sheba son of Bicri, a man from the tribe of Benjamin. Sheba blew a ram's horn and began to chant:

"Down with the dynasty of David!
 We have no interest in the son of Jesse.
Come on, you men of Israel,
 back to your homes!"

2So all the men of Israel deserted David and followed Sheba son of Bicri. But the men of Judah stayed with their king and escorted him from the Jordan River to Jerusalem.

3When David came to his palace in Jerusalem, he took the ten concubines he had left to look after the palace and placed them in seclusion. Their needs were provided for, but he no longer slept with them. So each of them lived like a widow until she died.

4Then the king told Amasa, "Mobilize the army of Judah within three days, and report back at that time." 5So Amasa went out to notify Judah, but it took him longer than the time he had been given.

6Then David said to Abishai, "Sheba son of Bicri is going to hurt us more than Absalom did. Quick, take my troops and chase after him before he gets into a fortified town where we can't reach him."

7So Abishai and Joab,* together with the king's bodyguard* and all the mighty warriors, set out from Jerusalem to go after Sheba. 8As they arrived at the great stone in Gibeon, Amasa met them. Joab was wearing his military tunic with a dagger strapped to his belt. As he stepped forward to greet Amasa, he slipped the dagger from its sheath.*

9"How are you, my cousin?" Joab said and took him by the beard with his right hand as though to kiss him. 10Amasa didn't notice the dagger in his left hand, and Joab stabbed him in the stomach with it so that his insides gushed out onto the ground. Joab did not need to strike again, and Amasa soon died. Joab and his brother Abishai left him lying there and continued after Sheba.

JUSTICE 20:7-10

Once again Joab's murderous treachery went unpunished, just as it did when he killed Abner (3:26-30). Eventually, however, justice caught up with him (1 Kings 2:28-35). It may seem that sin and treachery often go unpunished, but God's justice is not limited to this life's rewards. Are you worried that someone will get away with what he or she has done? "Don't worry about the wicked or envy those who do wrong. For like grass, they soon fade away. Like spring flowers, they soon wither" (Ps 37:1-2). ■

11One of Joab's young men shouted to Amasa's troops, "If you are for Joab and David, come and follow Joab." 12But Amasa lay in his blood in the middle of the road, and Joab's man saw that everyone was stopping to stare at him. So he pulled him off the road into a field and threw a cloak over him. 13With Amasa's body out of the way, everyone went on with Joab to capture Sheba son of Bicri.

14Meanwhile, Sheba traveled through all the tribes of Israel and eventually came to the town of Abel-beth-maacah. All the members of his own clan, the Bicrites,* assembled for battle and followed him into the town. 15When Joab's forces arrived, they attacked Abel-beth-maacah. They built a siege ramp against the town's fortifications and began battering down the wall. 16But a wise woman in the town called out to Joab, "Listen to me, Joab. Come over here so I can talk to you." 17As he approached, the woman asked, "Are you Joab?"

"I am," he replied.

So she said, "Listen carefully to your servant."

"I'm listening," he said.

18Then she continued, "There used to be a saying, 'If you want to settle an argument, ask advice at the town of Abel.' 19I am one who is peace loving and faithful in Israel. But you are destroying an important town in Israel.* Why do you want to devour what belongs to the LORD?"

20And Joab replied, "Believe me, I don't want to devour or destroy your town! 21That's not my purpose. All I want is a man named Sheba son of Bicri from the hill country of Ephraim, who has revolted against King David. If you hand over this one man to me, I will leave the town in peace."

"All right," the woman replied, "we will throw his head

20:7a Hebrew *So Joab's men.* **20:7b** Hebrew *the Kerethites and Pelethites;* also in 20:23. **20:8** Hebrew *As he stepped forward, it fell out.* **20:14** As in Greek and Latin versions; Hebrew reads *All the Berites.* **20:19** Hebrew *a town that is a mother in Israel.*

over the wall to you." 22Then the woman went to all the people with her wise advice, and they cut off Sheba's head and threw it out to Joab. So he blew the ram's horn and called his troops back from the attack. They all returned to their homes, and Joab returned to the king at Jerusalem.

SPEAK UP 20:16-22

Joab's men were on the brink of destroying the city of Abel-beth-maacah. Though women in that society were usually quiet in public, this woman spoke out. She stopped Joab's attack, not with weapons, but with wise words and a plan of action. Sometimes the courage to speak a few sensible words can prevent great disaster. ■

23Now Joab was the commander of the army of Israel. Benaiah son of Jehoiada was captain of the king's bodyguard. 24Adoniram* was in charge of the labor force. Jehoshaphat son of Ahilud was the royal historian. 25Sheva was the court secretary. Zadok and Abiathar were the priests. 26And Ira, a descendant of Jair, was David's personal priest.

21

DAVID AVENGES THE GIBEONITES

There was a famine during David's reign that lasted for three years, so David asked the LORD about it. And the LORD said, "The famine has come because Saul and his family are guilty of murdering the Gibeonites."

2So the king summoned the Gibeonites. They were not part of Israel but were all that was left of the nation of the Amorites. The people of Israel had sworn not to kill them, but Saul, in his zeal for Israel and Judah, had tried to wipe them out. 3David asked them, "What can I do for you? How can I make amends so that you will bless the LORD's people again?"

4"Well, money can't settle this matter between us and the family of Saul," the Gibeonites replied. "Neither can we demand the life of anyone in Israel."

"What can I do then?" David asked. "Just tell me and I will do it for you."

5Then they replied, "It was Saul who planned to destroy us, to keep us from having any place at all in the territory of Israel. 6So let seven of Saul's sons be handed over to us, and we will execute them before the LORD at Gibeon, on the mountain of the LORD.*"

"All right," the king said, "I will do it." 7The king spared Jonathan's son Mephibosheth,* who was Saul's grandson, because of the oath David and Jonathan had sworn before the LORD. 8But he gave them Saul's two sons Armoni and Mephibosheth, whose mother was Rizpah daughter of Aiah. He also gave them the five sons of Saul's daughter Merab,* the wife of Adriel son of Barzillai from Meholah. 9The men of Gibeon executed them on the mountain before the LORD. So all seven of them died together at the beginning of the barley harvest.

10Then Rizpah daughter of Aiah, the mother of two of the men, spread burlap on a rock and stayed there the entire harvest season. She prevented the scavenger birds from tearing at their bodies during the day and stopped wild animals from eating them at night. 11When David learned what Rizpah, Saul's concubine, had done, 12he went to the people of Jabesh-gilead and retrieved the bones of Saul and his son Jonathan. (When the Philistines had killed Saul and Jonathan on Mount Gilboa, the people of Jabesh-gilead stole their bodies from the public square of Beth-shan, where the Philistines had hung them.) 13So David obtained the bones of Saul and Jonathan, as well as the bones of the men the Gibeonites had executed.

14Then the king ordered that they bury the bones in the tomb of Kish, Saul's father, at the town of Zela in the land of Benjamin. After that, God ended the famine in the land.

BATTLES AGAINST PHILISTINE GIANTS

15Once again the Philistines were at war with Israel. And when David and his men were in the thick of battle, David became weak and exhausted. 16Ishbi-benob was a descendant of the giants*; his bronze spearhead weighed more than seven pounds,* and he was armed with a new sword. He had cornered David and was about to kill him. 17But Abishai son of Zeruiah came to David's rescue and killed the Philistine. Then David's men declared, "You are not going out to battle with us again! Why risk snuffing out the light of Israel?"

18After this, there was another battle against the Philistines at Gob. As they fought, Sibbecai from Hushah killed Saph, another descendant of the giants.

19During another battle at Gob, Elhanan son of Jair* from Bethlehem killed the brother of Goliath of Gath.* The handle of his spear was as thick as a weaver's beam!

20In another battle with the Philistines at Gath, they encountered a huge man with six fingers on each hand and six toes on each foot, twenty-four in all, who was also a descendant of the giants. 21But when he defied and taunted Israel, he was killed by Jonathan, the son of David's brother Shimea.*

22These four Philistines were descendants of the giants of Gath, but David and his warriors killed them.

22

DAVID'S SONG OF PRAISE

David sang this song to the LORD on the day the LORD rescued him from all his enemies and from Saul. 2He sang:

20:24 As in Greek version (see also 1 Kgs 4:6; 5:14); Hebrew reads *Adoram.* **21:6** As in Greek version (see also 21:9); Hebrew reads *at Gibeah of Saul, the chosen of the LORD.* **21:7** *Mephibosheth* is another name for Merib-baal. **21:8** As in a few Hebrew and Greek manuscripts and Syriac version (see also 1 Sam 18:19); most Hebrew manuscripts read *Michal.* **21:16a** As in Greek version; Hebrew reads *a descendant of the Rephaites;* also in 21:18, 20, 22. **21:16b** Hebrew *300 shekels* [3.4 kilograms]. **21:19a** As in parallel text at 1 Chr 20:5; Hebrew reads *son of Jaare-oregim.* **21:19b** As in parallel text at 1 Chr 20:5; Hebrew reads *killed Goliath of Gath.* **21:21** As in parallel text at 1 Chr 20:7; Hebrew reads *Shimei,* a variant spelling of Shimea.

keeping it real

I was at a summer camp in Florida. Our group wanted to go swimming in the Gulf of Mexico, but we couldn't because there was a hurricane off the coast at the time and the riptides and undertow were too strong.

After dinner I walked down to the beach to look for a hat I had lost. A guy in my group noticed four boys—I couldn't tell how old they were—about 100 feet out in the water. They started swimming, but one couldn't make it. He kept drifting farther out. The guy I was with ran into the water to save him. I stood on the shore for 10 seconds and then without thinking jumped in also.

When I was halfway to the boy, the guy from my group passed me; he couldn't make it so he had turned back. When I finally reached the boy, he was semiconscious. I grabbed him and tried to walk back to shore, but the water was over my head. I told the boy that every time there was a wave we would kick and try to ride it. I began to pray; I didn't know whether to just try to save my own life or hang onto the guy and keep trying to swim. I remembered 2 Samuel 22:17 and 2 Samuel 22:40 and kept on swimming. After five minutes I stopped swimming; I was able to stand up. Before long we were on the shore. I believe the only reason I made it was because God gave me the strength. I never saw the boy I rescued again.

—**Mike**

"The LORD is my rock, my fortress, and my
savior;
3 my God is my rock, in whom I find protection.
He is my shield, the power that saves me,
and my place of safety.
He is my refuge, my savior,
the one who saves me from violence.
4 I called on the LORD, who is worthy of praise,
and he saved me from my enemies.

5 "The waves of death overwhelmed me;
floods of destruction swept over me.
6 The grave* wrapped its ropes around me;
death laid a trap in my path.
7 But in my distress I cried out to the LORD;
yes, I cried to my God for help.
He heard me from his sanctuary;
my cry reached his ears.

8 "Then the earth quaked and trembled.
The foundations of the heavens shook;
they quaked because of his anger.
9 Smoke poured from his nostrils;
fierce flames leaped from his mouth.
Glowing coals blazed forth from him.
10 He opened the heavens and came down;
dark storm clouds were beneath his feet.
11 Mounted on a mighty angelic being,* he flew,
soaring* on the wings of the wind.
12 He shrouded himself in darkness,
veiling his approach with dense rain clouds.
13 A great brightness shone around him,
and burning coals* blazed forth.
14 The LORD thundered from heaven;
the voice of the Most High resounded.
15 He shot arrows and scattered his enemies;
his lightning flashed, and they were confused.
16 Then at the command of the LORD,
at the blast of his breath,
the bottom of the sea could be seen,
and the foundations of the earth were laid bare.

17 "He reached down from heaven and rescued me;
he drew me out of deep waters.
18 He rescued me from my powerful enemies,
from those who hated me and were too strong
for me.
19 They attacked me at a moment when I was in
distress,
but the LORD supported me.
20 He led me to a place of safety;
he rescued me because he delights in me.
21 The LORD rewarded me for doing right;
he restored me because of my innocence.

22:6 Hebrew *Sheol.* **22:11a** Hebrew *a cherub.* **22:11b** As in some Hebrew manuscripts (see also Ps 18:10); other Hebrew manuscripts read *appearing.* **22:13** Or *and lightning bolts.*

22 For I have kept the ways of the LORD;
I have not turned from my God to follow evil.
23 I have followed all his regulations;
I have never abandoned his decrees.
24 I am blameless before God;
I have kept myself from sin.

FORGIVEN 22:22-24

David was not saying that he had never sinned. Psalm 51 shows his tremendous anguish over his sin against Uriah and Bathsheba. But David understood God's faithfulness and wrote this song from God's perspective. He knew that God had made him clean again—"whiter than snow," (Ps 51:7) with a "clean heart" (Ps 51:10). Because of the death and resurrection of Jesus Christ, we also can be forgiven for anything we have done or will do wrong. Our guilt is replaced with his purity and forgiveness. ■

25 The LORD rewarded me for doing right.
He has seen my innocence.

26 "To the faithful you show yourself faithful;
to those with integrity you show integrity.
27 To the pure you show yourself pure,
but to the wicked you show yourself hostile.
28 You rescue the humble,
but your eyes watch the proud and humiliate them.
29 O LORD, you are my lamp.
The LORD lights up my darkness.
30 In your strength I can crush an army;
with my God I can scale any wall.

31 "God's way is perfect.
All the LORD's promises prove true.
He is a shield for all who look to him for
protection.
32 For who is God except the LORD?
Who but our God is a solid rock?
33 God is my strong fortress,
and he makes my way perfect.
34 He makes me as surefooted as a deer,
enabling me to stand on mountain heights.
35 He trains my hands for battle;
he strengthens my arm to draw a bronze bow.
36 You have given me your shield of victory;
your help* has made me great.
37 You have made a wide path for my feet
to keep them from slipping.

38 "I chased my enemies and destroyed them;
I did not stop until they were conquered.
39 I consumed them;
I struck them down so they did not get up;
they fell beneath my feet.
40 You have armed me with strength for the battle;
you have subdued my enemies under my feet.
41 You placed my foot on their necks.
I have destroyed all who hated me.
42 They looked for help, but no one came to their rescue.
They even cried to the LORD, but he refused
to answer.
43 I ground them as fine as the dust of the earth;
I trampled them* in the gutter like dirt.

44 "You gave me victory over my accusers.
You preserved me as the ruler over nations;
people I don't even know now serve me.
45 Foreign nations cringe before me;
as soon as they hear of me, they submit.
46 They all lose their courage
and come trembling* from their strongholds.

47 "The LORD lives! Praise to my Rock!
May God, the Rock of my salvation, be exalted!
48 He is the God who pays back those who harm me;
he brings down the nations under me
49 and delivers me from my enemies.
You hold me safe beyond the reach of my enemies;
you save me from violent opponents.
50 For this, O LORD, I will praise you among the nations;
I will sing praises to your name.
51 You give great victories to your king;
you show unfailing love to your anointed,
to David and all his descendants forever."

GOD'S MAN 22:51

Since the Israelites first entered the Promised Land under Joshua, they had struggled to drive out their enemies. At this time, after more than 400 years, Israel finally achieved peace. David had accomplished what no leader before him, judge or king, had done. His administration was run on the principle of dedication to God and to the well-being of the people. Yet David wasn't perfect. Despite his offenses, however, the Bible calls David a man after God's own heart (1 Sam 13:14; Acts 13:22). Is that the way your family and friends would describe you? ■

23 DAVID'S LAST WORDS

These are the last words of David:

"David, the son of Jesse, speaks—
David, the man who was raised up so high,
David, the man anointed by the God of Jacob,
David, the sweet psalmist of Israel.*

2 "The Spirit of the LORD speaks through me;
his words are upon my tongue.

22:36 As in Dead Sea Scrolls (see also Ps 18:35); Masoretic Text reads *your answering*. 22:43 As in Dead Sea Scrolls (see also Ps 18:42); Masoretic Text reads *I crushed and trampled them*. 22:46 As in parallel text at Ps 18:45; Hebrew reads *come girding themselves*. 23:1 Or *the favorite subject of the songs of Israel;* or *the favorite of the Strong One of Israel*.

3 The God of Israel spoke.
The Rock of Israel said to me:
'The one who rules righteously,
who rules in the fear of God,
4 is like the light of morning at sunrise,
like a morning without clouds,
like the gleaming of the sun
on new grass after rain.'

5 "Is it not my family God has chosen?
Yes, he has made an everlasting covenant with me.
His agreement is arranged and guaranteed in every detail.
He will ensure my safety and success.
6 But the godless are like thorns to be thrown away,
for they tear the hand that touches them.
7 One must use iron tools to chop them down;
they will be totally consumed by fire."

DAVID'S MIGHTIEST WARRIORS

8These are the names of David's mightiest warriors. The first was Jashobeam the Hacmonite,* who was leader of the Three*—the three mightiest warriors among David's men. He once used his spear to kill 800 enemy warriors in a single battle.*

9Next in rank among the Three was Eleazar son of Dodai, a descendant of Ahoah. Once Eleazar and David stood together against the Philistines when the entire Israelite army had fled. 10He killed Philistines until his
hand was too tired to lift his sword, and the LORD gave him a great victory that day. The rest of the army did not return until it was time to collect the plunder!

11Next in rank was Shammah son of Agee from Harar. One time the Philistines gathered at Lehi and attacked the Israelites in a field full of lentils. The Israelite army
fled, 12but Shammah* held his ground in the middle of
the field and beat back the Philistines. So the LORD brought about a great victory.

13Once during the harvest, when David was at the cave of Adullam, the Philistine army was camped in the valley of Rephaim. The Three (who were among the Thirty—an elite group among David's fighting men) went down to
meet him there. 14David was staying in the stronghold at
the time, and a Philistine detachment had occupied the town of Bethlehem.

15David remarked longingly to his men, "Oh, how I would love some of that good water from the well by
the gate in Bethlehem." 16So the Three broke through the
Philistine lines, drew some water from the well by the gate in Bethlehem, and brought it back to David. But he refused to drink it. Instead, he poured it out as an offering to the LORD. 17"The LORD forbid that I should drink
this!" he exclaimed. "This water is as precious as the blood of these men* who risked their lives to bring it to me." So David did not drink it. These are examples of the exploits of the Three.

POURED OUT 23:13-17

David's mighty men risked their lives to get water for their thirsty leader. David poured out the water as an offering to God because he was so moved by the sacrifice it represented. When Hebrews offered sacrifices, they never consumed the blood. It represented life, and they poured it out before God. David would not drink this water, which represented the lives of his soldiers. Instead, he offered it to God. What would you offer to God? ■

DAVID'S THIRTY MIGHTY MEN

18Abishai son of Zeruiah, the brother of Joab, was the leader of the Thirty.* He once used his spear to kill 300 enemy warriors in a single battle. It was by such feats
that he became as famous as the Three. 19Abishai was the
most famous of the Thirty* and was their commander, though he was not one of the Three.

20There was also Benaiah son of Jehoiada, a valiant warrior* from Kabzeel. He did many heroic deeds, which included killing two champions* of Moab. Another time, on a snowy day, he chased a lion down into a pit and killed it.
21Once, armed only with a club, he killed a great Egyptian
warrior who was armed with a spear. Benaiah wrenched the spear from the Egyptian's hand and killed him with it.
22Deeds like these made Benaiah as famous as the Three
mightiest warriors. 23He was more honored than the
other members of the Thirty, though he was not one of the Three. And David made him captain of his bodyguard.
24Other members of the Thirty included:

Asahel, Joab's brother;
Elhanan son of Dodo from Bethlehem;
25 Shammah from Harod;
Elika from Harod;
26 Helez from Pelon*;
Ira son of Ikkesh from Tekoa;
27 Abiezer from Anathoth;
Sibbecai* from Hushah;
28 Zalmon from Ahoah;
Maharai from Netophah;
29 Heled* son of Baanah from Netophah;
Ithai* son of Ribai from Gibeah (in the land of Benjamin);
30 Benaiah from Pirathon;
Hurai* from Nahale-gaash*;

23:8a As in parallel text at 1 Chr 11:11; Hebrew reads *Josheb-basshebeth the Tahkemonite.* **23:8b** As in Greek and Latin versions (see also 1 Chr 11:11); the meaning of the Hebrew is uncertain. **23:8c** As in some Greek manuscripts (see also 1 Chr 11:11); the meaning of the Hebrew is uncertain, though it might be rendered *the Three. It was Adino the Eznite who killed 800 men at one time.* **23:12** Hebrew *he.* **23:17** Hebrew *Shall I drink the blood of these men?* **23:18** As in a few Hebrew manuscripts and Syriac version; most Hebrew manuscripts read *the Three.* **23:19** As in Syriac version; Hebrew reads *the Three.* **23:20a** Or *son of Jehoiada, son of Ish-hai.* **23:20b** Or *two sons of Ariel.* **23:26** As in parallel text at 1 Chr 11:27 (see also 1 Chr 27:10); Hebrew reads *from Palti.* **23:27** As in some Greek manuscripts (see also 1 Chr 11:29); Hebrew reads *Mebunnai.* **23:29a** As in some Hebrew manuscripts (see also 1 Chr 11:30); most Hebrew manuscripts read *Heleb.* **23:29b** As in parallel text at 1 Chr 11:31; Hebrew reads *Ittai.* **23:30a** As in some Greek manuscripts (see also 1 Chr 11:32); Hebrew reads *Hiddai.* **23:30b** Or *from the ravines of Gaash.*

31 Abi-albon from Arabah;
Azmaveth from Bahurim;
32 Eliahba from Shaalbon;
the sons of Jashen;
33 Jonathan son of Shagee* from Harar;
Ahiam son of Sharar from Harar;
34 Eliphelet son of Ahasbai from Maacah;
Eliam son of Ahithophel from Giloh;
35 Hezro from Carmel;
Paarai from Arba;
36 Igal son of Nathan from Zobah;
Bani from Gad;
37 Zelek from Ammon;
Naharai from Beeroth, Joab's armor bearer;
38 Ira from Jattir;
Gareb from Jattir;
39 Uriah the Hittite.

There were thirty-seven in all.

24 DAVID TAKES A CENSUS

Once again the anger of the LORD burned against Israel,
and he caused David to harm them by taking a census.
"Go and count the people of Israel and Judah," the LORD
told him.
2So the king said to Joab and the commanders* of the
army, "Take a census of all the tribes of Israel—from Dan
in the north to Beersheba in the south—so I may know
how many people there are."
3But Joab replied to the king, "May the LORD your God
let you live to see a hundred times as many people as
there are now! But why, my lord the king, do you want to
do this?"
4But the king insisted that they take the census, so Joab
and the commanders of the army went out to count the
people of Israel. 5First they crossed the Jordan and
camped at Aroer, south of the town in the valley, in the direction of Gad. Then they went on to Jazer, 6then to Gilead in the land of Tahtim-hodshi* and to Dan-jaan and
around to Sidon. 7Then they came to the fortress of Tyre,
and all the towns of the Hivites and Canaanites. Finally,
they went south to Judah* as far as Beersheba.
8Having gone through the entire land for nine months
and twenty days, they returned to Jerusalem. 9Joab reported the number of people to the king. There were
800,000 capable warriors in Israel who could handle a
sword, and 500,000 in Judah.

23:33 As in parallel text at 1 Chr 11:34; Hebrew reads *Jonathan, Shammah;* some Greek manuscripts read *Jonathan son of Shammah.* **24:2** As in Greek version (see also 24:4 and 1 Chr 21:2); Hebrew reads *Joab the commander.* **24:6** Greek version reads *to Gilead and to Kadesh in the land of the Hittites.* **24:7** Or *they went to the Negev of Judah.*

DAVID'S MIGHTY MEN

As a kid, you might have played "Follow the Leader." But for many of us, that game blends into "real life" as we connect with the people in authority over us.

One way to understand David's success is to notice the kind of men who followed him. During the time he spent running from Saul, David built a fighting force of several hundred men. Some were relatives, others were outcasts of society. Many were in trouble with the law and probably seemed like gangbangers! But they all had at least one trait in common—complete devotion to David. He knew that he could count on them.

These guys were as close to superheroes as was humanly possible. Their achievements made them famous. Among these men were elite military groups like "the Thirty" and "the Three" (2 Sam 23:8-39).

Scripture gives the impression that these men were motivated to greatness by the qualities of their leader. David inspired them to achieve beyond their goals and meet their true potential. His effectiveness as a leader was clearly connected with his awareness of God's leading.

The leaders we follow and the causes to which we commit ourselves will affect our lives. Who are the leaders you follow? Your answer can help you decide whether or not they deserve your loyalty. Do you also recognize God's leading in your life? No one can lead you to excellence as your Creator can.

UPS:
- Very capable
- Shared many special skills
- Though frequently outnumbered, were consistently victorious
- Loyal to David

STATS:
- Where: They came from all over Israel (primarily Judah and Benjamin), and from some of the other surrounding nations as well
- Occupations: Various backgrounds—almost all were fugitives

BOTTOM LINE:

Greatness is often inspired by the quality and character of leadership.

Even a small force of able and loyal men can accomplish great feats.

Their stories are told in 1 Sam 22–27; 29–30; 2 Sam 1–5; 10–11; 15:12; 21:15-22; 23:8-39. They also are mentioned in 1 Chron 11–12.

DAVID'S MIGHTY MEN

JUDGMENT FOR DAVID'S SIN

10But after he had taken the census, David's conscience
began to bother him. And he said to the LORD, "I have
sinned greatly by taking this census. Please forgive my
guilt, LORD, for doing this foolish thing."
11The next morning the word of the LORD came to the
prophet Gad, who was David's seer. This was the message: 12"Go and say to David, 'This is what the LORD says: I
will give you three choices. Choose one of these punishments, and I will inflict it on you.'"
13So Gad came to David and asked him, "Will you choose
three* years of famine throughout your land, three months
of fleeing from your enemies, or three days of severe
plague throughout your land? Think this over and decide
what answer I should give the LORD who sent me."
14"I'm in a desperate situation!" David replied to Gad.
"But let us fall into the hands of the LORD, for his mercy is
great. Do not let me fall into human hands."
15So the LORD sent a plague upon Israel that morning,
and it lasted for three days.* A total of 70,000 people
died throughout the nation, from Dan in the north to Beersheba in the south. 16But as the angel was preparing to
destroy Jerusalem, the LORD relented and said to the
death angel, "Stop! That is enough!" At that moment the
angel of the LORD was by the threshing floor of Araunah
the Jebusite.
17When David saw the angel, he said to the LORD, "I am
the one who has sinned and done wrong! But these people
are as innocent as sheep—what have they done? Let your
anger fall against me and my family."

DAVID BUILDS AN ALTAR

18That day Gad came to David and said to him, "Go up and
build an altar to the LORD on the threshing floor of Araunah the Jebusite."
19So David went up to do what the LORD had commanded him. 20When Araunah saw the king and his men
coming toward him, he came and bowed before the king
with his face to the ground. 21"Why have you come, my
lord the king?" Araunah asked.

David replied, "I have come to buy your threshing floor
and to build an altar to the LORD there, so that he will stop
the plague."
22"Take it, my lord the king, and use it as you wish,"
Araunah said to David. "Here are oxen for the burnt offering, and you can use the threshing boards and ox
yokes for wood to build a fire on the altar. 23I will give it
all to you, Your Majesty, and may the LORD your God accept your sacrifice."
24But the king replied to Araunah, "No, I insist on buying it, for I will not present burnt offerings to the LORD my
God that have cost me nothing." So David paid him fifty
pieces of silver* for the threshing floor and the oxen.
25David built an altar there to the LORD and sacrificed
burnt offerings and peace offerings. And the LORD answered his prayer for the land, and the plague on Israel
was stopped.

24:13 As in Greek version (see also 1 Chr 21:12); Hebrew reads *seven.* **24:15** Hebrew *for the designated time.* **24:24** Hebrew *50 shekels of silver,* about 20 ounces or 570 grams in weight.

1 KINGS

HERE'S A QUICK QUIZ. What do you think of when you hear each of these names: Solomon . . . Elijah . . . Ahab . . . Jezebel . . . Nadab?

The usual response for Solomon would be "wisdom" or "the temple." For Elijah, you might answer, "prophet" or "defeated the Baal worshipers on the mountain." Ahab and Jezebel are usually thought of as evil. As for Nadab, the usual response is "Nadab, who?"

Whether good or evil, a person's reputation often remains long after his or her death.

First Kings tells the stories of many of the leaders of Israel. Some stories, like Solomon's, take several chapters to relate. Others, like Nadab, just take a line or two. But one choice line sums up his reputation: "He did what was evil in the LORD's sight and followed the example of his father, continuing the sins that Jeroboam had led Israel to commit" (15:26). That's some rep!

What would your friends and family say if they found your name in a similar quiz? What kind of a reputation are you building?

1 Kings

timeline

1010 B.C.
David becomes king

970
Solomon becomes king

959
Temple completed

930
The kingdom divides

925
Shishak invades Jerusalem

910
Asa becomes king of Judah

875
Elijah begins his ministry

874
Ahab becomes king of Israel

872
Jehoshaphat becomes king of Judah

857
Ben-hadad attacks Samaria

853
Ahab dies in battle

stats

PURPOSE: To contrast the lives of those who live for God with the lives of those who refuse to do so, using the history of the kings of Israel and Judah

AUTHOR: Unknown; possibly Jeremiah or a group of prophets

SETTING: The once great nation of Israel turns into a divided land, both physically and spiritually.

KEY PEOPLE: David, Solomon, Rehoboam, Jeroboam, Elijah, Ahab, Jezebel

SPECIAL FEATURE: The books of 1 and 2 Kings were one book originally.

KEY points

RULING THE RIGHT WAY

All the kings of Israel and Judah were told to obey God and to govern according to his laws. But their tendency to abandon God's Word and to worship other gods led to their downfall. Having authority doesn't make us immune to the consequences of ignoring God's rules.

THE TEMPLE

Solomon's Temple was a beautiful place of worship, prayer, and the presence of God. In the same way, the human heart is a place of worship, prayer, and the presence of God.

OTHER GODS

Although the Israelites had God's law and had experienced his presence among them, they soon looked for other gods to worship. Although God has given us many things also, many of us also find other gods (money, possessions, power) to worship.

PROPHETIC MESSAGE

Elijah had the responsibility to confront the king and the people of Israel about their disobedience to God. Today, God uses the Bible and the wise counsel of believers to warn us to keep to his way.

SEEK FORGIVENESS

Whenever the people of Israel owned up to their sin and returned to God, God heard their prayers and forgave them. We have the same assurance of forgiveness if we're willing to ask for it.

KEY PLACES IN 1 KINGS

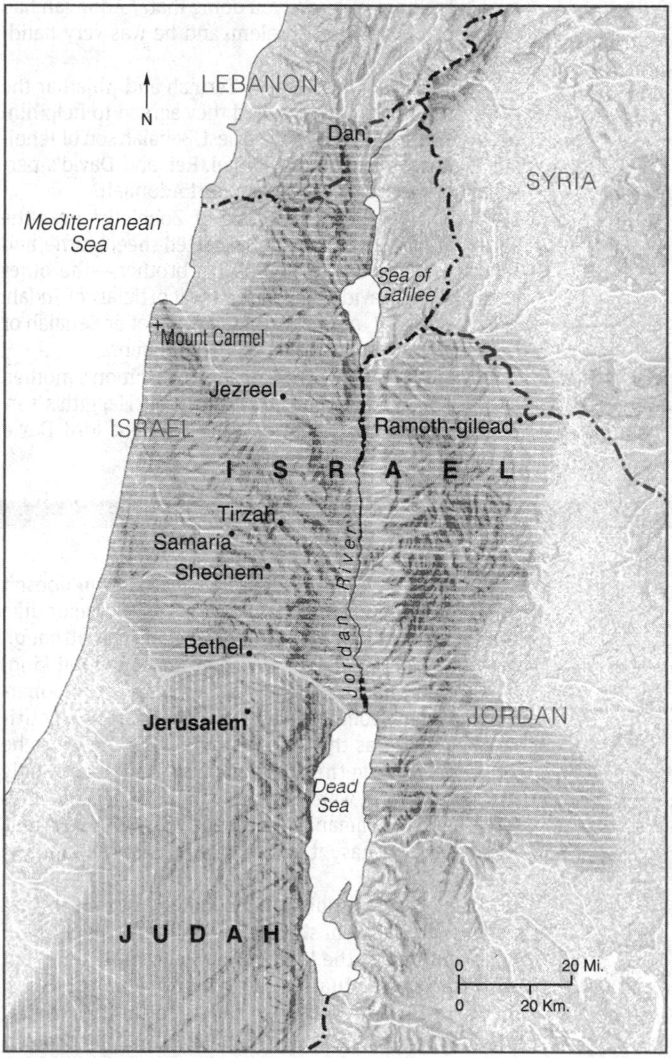

The broken lines (—·—) indicate modern boundaries.

David's son Solomon brought Israel into its golden age. His wealth and wisdom were acclaimed worldwide. But he ignored God in his later years (1:1–11:25).

• **SHECHEM** After Solomon's death, Israel assembled at Shechem to inaugurate his son Rehoboam. However, Rehoboam foolishly angered the people by threatening even higher taxes, which caused a revolt (11:26–12:19).

• **ISRAEL** Jeroboam, leader of the rebels, was made king of Israel, now called the northern kingdom. Jeroboam made Shechem his capital city (12:20,25).

• **JUDAH** Only the tribes of Judah and Benjamin remained loyal to Rehoboam. These two tribes became the southern kingdom. Rehoboam returned to Judah from Shechem and prepared to force the rebels into submission, but a prophet's message halted these plans (12:21-24).

• **JERUSALEM** Jerusalem was the capital city of Judah. Its Temple, built by Solomon, was the focal point of Jewish worship. This worried Jeroboam. How could he keep his people loyal if they were constantly going to Rehoboam's capital to worship (12:26-27)?

• **DAN** Jeroboam's solution was to set up his own worship centers. He had two calf idols made and proclaimed them to be Israel's gods. One was placed in Dan, and the people were told that they could go there instead of to Jerusalem to worship (12:28-29).

• **BETHEL** The other idol made at Jeroboam's command was placed in Bethel. The people of the northern kingdom had two convenient locations for worship in their own country. But their sin displeased God. Meanwhile, in Jerusalem, Rehoboam was also allowing idolatry to creep in. The two nations were constantly at war (12:29–15:26).

• **TIRZAH** Baasha became king of Israel after assassinating Nadab. He moved the capital from Shechem to Tirzah (15:27–16:22).

• **SAMARIA** Israel continued to gain and lose kings through plots, assassinations, and warfare. When Omri became king, he bought a hill on which he built a new capital city, Samaria. Omri's son, Ahab, became the most wicked king of Israel. His wife, Jezebel, worshiped Baal. Ahab erected a temple to Baal in Samaria (16:23-34).

• **MOUNT CARMEL** Great evil often brings great people who oppose it. Elijah challenged the prophets of Baal and Asherah at Mount Carmel, where he would prove that they were false prophets. There Elijah humiliated these prophets and then executed them (17:1–18:46).

• **JEZREEL** Elijah returned to Jezreel. But Queen Jezebel, furious at the execution of her prophets, vowed to kill Elijah. He ran for his life, but God cared for and encouraged him. During his travels, he anointed the future kings of Syria and Israel, as well as his own replacement, Elisha (19:1-21).

• **RAMOTH-GILEAD** The king of Syria declared war on Israel and was defeated in two battles. But the Syrians occupied Ramoth-gilead. Ahab and Jehoshaphat joined forces to recover the city. In this battle, Ahab was killed. Later, Jehoshaphat died (20:1–22:53).

1

DAVID IN HIS OLD AGE

King David was now very old, and no matter how many
blankets covered him, he could not keep warm. [2]So his
advisers told him, "Let us find a young virgin to wait on
you and look after you, my lord. She will lie in your arms
and keep you warm."
[3]So they searched throughout the land of Israel for a
beautiful girl, and they found Abishag from Shunem and
brought her to the king. [4]The girl was very beautiful, and
she looked after the king and took care of him. But the
king had no sexual relations with her.

ADONIJAH CLAIMS THE THRONE

[5]About that time David's son Adonijah, whose mother
was Haggith, began boasting, "I will make myself king."
So he provided himself with chariots and charioteers and
recruited fifty men to run in front of him. [6]Now his father, King David, had never disciplined him at any time,
even by asking, "Why are you doing that?" Adonijah had
been born next after Absalom, and he was very handsome.
[7]Adonijah took Joab son of Zeruiah and Abiathar the
priest into his confidence, and they agreed to help him
become king. [8]But Zadok the priest, Benaiah son of Jehoiada, Nathan the prophet, Shimei, Rei, and David's personal bodyguard refused to support Adonijah.
[9]Adonijah went to the Stone of Zoheleth* near the
spring of En-rogel, where he sacrificed sheep, cattle, and
fattened calves. He invited all his brothers—the other
sons of King David—and all the royal officials of Judah.
[10]But he did not invite Nathan the prophet or Benaiah or
the king's bodyguard or his brother Solomon.
[11]Then Nathan went to Bathsheba, Solomon's mother,
and asked her, "Haven't you heard that Haggith's son,
Adonijah, has made himself king, and our lord David

1:9 Or *to the Serpent's Stone;* Greek version supports reading *Zoheleth* as a proper name.

UPS:

- Third king of Israel, David's chosen heir
- The wisest man who ever lived
- Author of Ecclesiastes and Song of Songs, as well as many of the proverbs and some of the psalms
- Built God's Temple in Jerusalem

DOWNS:

- Sealed many foreign agreements by marrying women from enemy nations
- Allowed his wives to draw him away from God
- Taxed his people excessively and drafted them into a labor force

STATS:

- Where: Jerusalem
- Occupation: King of Israel
- Relatives: David (father); Bathsheba (mother); Absalom, Adonijah (brothers); Tamar (sister); Rehoboam (son); 700 wives and 300 concubines

BOTTOM LINE:

A truly effective leader not only leads in public but at home as well.

Knowing what actions are required of us means little if we don't have the will to perform those actions.

Solomon's story is told in 2 Sam 12:24-25; 1 Kings 1:10–11:43. He also is mentioned in 1 Chron 28–29; 2 Chron 1–9; Neh 13:26; Ps 72; and Matt 6:29; 12:42.

SOLOMON Got wisdom? Having wisdom doesn't help unless you use it. Early in his life, Solomon had the sense to realize his need for wisdom. But although he asked God to give him wisdom to be a good king, he showed poor judgment in his private life. He married a woman from an enemy nation as part of a political deal. She was the first of several hundred wives he married. In doing this, Solomon went against not only his father's last words (see 1 Kings 2:3-4), but also God's direct commands (see Deut 7:3-4). His actions remind us how easy it is to know what is right and yet not do it.

God's gift of wisdom to Solomon did not mean that he couldn't make mistakes. He had been given great opportunities as the king of God's chosen people, but with those opportunities came great responsibilities. Solomon took advantage of the opportunities, building a temple for God and a huge palace for himself. Yet he became infamous as a king who charged high taxes and overworked his people.

Little is mentioned in the Bible about the last decade of Solomon's reign. Ecclesiastes probably records his final reflections on life. In that book, we observe a man proving through bitter experience that finding meaning in life apart from God doesn't work. Real security and contentment are only found in a relationship with God.

The contentment we find in the opportunities and successes of this life is real, but temporary. The more we expect those feelings to last, the more quickly they are gone. Be sure to balance your pursuit of all the opportunities in life with keeping up with your responsibilities. Or, as Solomon put it, "Don't let the excitement of youth cause you to forget your Creator. Honor him in your youth before you grow old and say, 'Life is not pleasant anymore' " (Eccles 12:1).

doesn't even know about it? 12If you want to save your own life and the life of your son Solomon, follow my advice. 13Go at once to King David and say to him, 'My lord the king, didn't you make a vow and say to me, "Your son Solomon will surely be the next king and will sit on my throne"? Why then has Adonijah become king?' 14And while you are still talking with him, I will come and confirm everything you have said."

TAKE ACTION 1:5-14

When Nathan learned of Adonijah's conspiracy, he immediately tried to stop it. He knew the right course to take—that Solomon should be king—and moved quickly when he saw someone trying to block what was right. We often know what is right, but may not always act on it. Want to be a Nathan? Good intentions or angry feelings will only take you so far. Why not pray first, then take the action needed to correct the situation. ■

15So Bathsheba went into the king's bedroom. (He was very old now, and Abishag was taking care of him.) 16Bathsheba bowed down before the king.

"What can I do for you?" he asked her.

17She replied, "My lord, you made a vow before the LORD your God when you said to me, 'Your son Solomon will surely be the next king and will sit on my throne.' 18But instead, Adonijah has made himself king, and my lord the king does not even know about it. 19He has sacrificed many cattle, fattened calves, and sheep, and he has invited all the king's sons to attend the celebration. He also invited Abiathar the priest and Joab, the commander of the army. But he did not invite your servant Solomon. 20And now, my lord the king, all Israel is waiting for you to announce who will become king after you. 21If you do not act, my son Solomon and I will be treated as criminals as soon as my lord the king has died."

22While she was still speaking with the king, Nathan the prophet arrived. 23The king's officials told him, "Nathan the prophet is here to see you."

Nathan went in and bowed before the king with his face to the ground. 24Nathan asked, "My lord the king, have you decided that Adonijah will be the next king and that he will sit on your throne? 25Today he has sacrificed many cattle, fattened calves, and sheep, and he has invited all the king's sons to attend the celebration. He also invited the commanders of the army and Abiathar the priest. They are feasting and drinking with him and shouting, 'Long live King Adonijah!' 26But he did not invite me or Zadok the priest or Benaiah or your servant Solomon. 27Has my lord the king really done this without letting any of his officials know who should be the next king?"

DAVID MAKES SOLOMON KING

28King David responded, "Call Bathsheba!" So she came back in and stood before the king. 29And the king repeated his vow: "As surely as the LORD lives, who has rescued me from every danger, 30your son Solomon will be the next king and will sit on my throne this very day, just as I vowed to you before the LORD, the God of Israel."

31Then Bathsheba bowed down with her face to the ground before the king and exclaimed, "May my lord King David live forever!"

32Then King David ordered, "Call Zadok the priest, Nathan the prophet, and Benaiah son of Jehoiada." When they came into the king's presence, 33the king said to them, "Take Solomon and my officials down to Gihon Spring. Solomon is to ride on my own mule. 34There Zadok the priest and Nathan the prophet are to anoint him king over Israel. Blow the ram's horn and shout, 'Long live King Solomon!' 35Then escort him back here, and he will sit on my throne. He will succeed me as king, for I have appointed him to be ruler over Israel and Judah."

36"Amen!" Benaiah son of Jehoiada replied. "May the LORD, the God of my lord the king, decree that it happen. 37And may the LORD be with Solomon as he has been with you, my lord the king, and may he make Solomon's reign even greater than yours!"

38So Zadok the priest, Nathan the prophet, Benaiah son of Jehoiada, and the king's bodyguard* took Solomon down to Gihon Spring, with Solomon riding on King David's own mule. 39There Zadok the priest took the flask of olive oil from the sacred tent and anointed Solomon with the oil. Then they sounded the ram's horn and all the people shouted, "Long live King Solomon!" 40And all the people followed Solomon into Jerusalem, playing flutes and shouting for joy. The celebration was so joyous and noisy that the earth shook with the sound.

41Adonijah and his guests heard the celebrating and shouting just as they were finishing their banquet. When Joab heard the sound of the ram's horn, he asked, "What's going on? Why is the city in such an uproar?"

42And while he was still speaking, Jonathan son of Abiathar the priest arrived. "Come in," Adonijah said to him, "for you are a good man. You must have good news."

SEEK GOD FIRST 1:49-50

When Adonijah learned that his plans to usurp the throne of Israel had been exposed, he panicked and ran to the altar—the highest symbol of God's mercy and forgiveness. If Adonijah had first considered what God wanted, he might have avoided trouble. Do you check out what God has to say before you make plans or after? Unlike Adonijah, you don't have to learn the hard way. ■

43"Not at all!" Jonathan replied. "Our lord King David has just declared Solomon king! 44The king sent him down to Gihon Spring with Zadok the priest, Nathan the prophet, and Benaiah son of Jehoiada, protected by the king's bodyguard. They had him ride on the king's own mule, 45and Zadok and Nathan have anointed him at Gihon Spring as the new king. They have just returned,

1:38 Hebrew *the Kerethites and Pelethites;* also in 1:44.

The Appeal of Idols

On the surface, the lives of the kings don't make sense. How could they run to idolatry so fast when they had God's Word (at least some of it), the prophets, and the example of David? Below are some of the reasons for the enticement of idols. As societies change and evolve, they often throw out norms and values no longer considered necessary or acceptable. Believers must be careful not to follow society's example when it discards God's Word. When society does that, only godlessness and evil remain.

	POWER	PLEASURE	PASSION	PRAISE AND POPULARITY
THE APPEAL OF IDOLS	The people wanted freedom from the authority of both God and the priests. They wanted their religion to fit their lifestyle, not their lifestyle to fit their religion.	Idol worship exalted sensuality without responsibility or guilt. People acted out the vicious and sensuous personalities of the gods they worshiped, thus gaining approval for their degraded lives.	Humanity was reduced to little more than animals. The people did not have to be viewed as unique individuals but could be exploited sexually, politically, and economically.	The high and holy nature of God was replaced by gods who were more a reflection of human nature, thus more culturally suitable to the people. These gods no longer required sacrifice, just a token of appeasement.
MODERN PARALLEL	People do not want to answer to a greater authority. God wants us to have the Holy Spirit's power to help others instead of having power over others.	People defy pleasure, seeking it at the expense of everything else. God calls us to seek the kind of pleasure that leads to long-range rewards instead of seeking pleasure that leads to long-range disaster.	Like animals, people let physical drives and passions rule them. God calls us to redirect our passions to areas that build others up instead of seeking passion that exploits others.	Sacrifice is seen as a self-inflicted punishment, making no sense. Success is to be sought at all costs. God calls us to praise him and those who honor him instead of seeking praise for ourselves.

and the whole city is celebrating and rejoicing. That's
what all the noise is about. 46What's more, Solomon is
now sitting on the royal throne as king. 47And all the
royal officials have gone to King David and congratu-
lated him, saying, 'May your God make Solomon's fame
even greater than your own, and may Solomon's reign
be even greater than yours!' Then the king bowed his
head in worship as he lay in his bed, 48and he said,
'Praise the LORD, the God of Israel, who today has chosen
a successor to sit on my throne while I am still alive to
see it.'"

49Then all of Adonijah's guests jumped up in panic
from the banquet table and quickly scattered.
50Adonijah was afraid of Solomon, so he rushed to the
sacred tent and grabbed onto the horns of the altar.
51Word soon reached Solomon that Adonijah had
seized the horns of the altar in fear, and that he was
pleading, "Let King Solomon swear today that he will
not kill me!"

52Solomon replied, "If he proves himself to be loyal,
not a hair on his head will be touched. But if he makes
trouble, he will die." 53So King Solomon summoned
Adonijah, and they brought him down from the altar. He
came and bowed respectfully before King Solomon, who
dismissed him, saying, "Go on home."

2

DAVID'S FINAL INSTRUCTIONS TO SOLOMON

As the time of King David's death approached, he gave
this charge to his son Solomon:

2"I am going where everyone on earth must someday
go. Take courage and be a man. 3Observe the requirements of the LORD your God, and follow all his ways. Keep
the decrees, commands, regulations, and laws written in
the Law of Moses so that you will be successful in all you
do and wherever you go. 4If you do this, then the LORD
will keep the promise he made to me. He told me, 'If your
descendants live as they should and follow me faithfully
with all their heart and soul, one of them will always sit on
the throne of Israel.'

5"And there is something else. You know what Joab son
of Zeruiah did to me when he murdered my two army
commanders, Abner son of Ner and Amasa son of Jether.
He pretended that it was an act of war, but it was done in a
time of peace,* staining his belt and sandals with innocent blood.* 6Do with him what you think best, but don't
let him grow old and go to his grave in peace.*

7"Be kind to the sons of Barzillai of Gilead. Make them
permanent guests at your table, for they took care of me
when I fled from your brother Absalom.

2:5a Or *He murdered them during a time of peace as revenge for deaths they had caused in time of war.* 2:5b As in some Greek and Old Latin manuscripts; Hebrew reads *with the blood of war.* 2:6 Hebrew *don't let his white head go down to Sheol in peace.*

8“And remember Shimei son of Gera, the man from Bahurim in Benjamin. He cursed me with a terrible curse as I was fleeing to Mahanaim. When he came down to meet me at the Jordan River, I swore by the LORD that I would not kill him. 9But that oath does not make him innocent. You are a wise man, and you will know how to arrange a bloody death for him.*”

10Then David died and was buried with his Ancestors in the City of David. 11David had reigned over Israel for forty years, seven of them in Hebron and thirty-three in Jerusalem. 12Solomon became king and sat on the throne of David his father, and his kingdom was firmly established.

AN ALLIANCE WORTH MAKING **2:13-25**

This conspiracy to gain the throne of Israel was like an episode of *Survivor*. Adonijah tried to make an alliance with Solomon's mother. But Solomon knew that Adonijah wanted to use his mother to gain the throne for himself. Many people today try to form alliances to gain power or status. Consider your motives carefully before making alliances with others. If you want what God wants, you only need one ally—God. ■

SOLOMON ESTABLISHES HIS RULE

13One day Adonijah, whose mother was Haggith, came to see Bathsheba, Solomon's mother. “Have you come with peaceful intentions?” she asked him.

“Yes,” he said, “I come in peace. 14In fact, I have a favor to ask of you.”

“What is it?” she asked.

15He replied, “As you know, the kingdom was rightfully mine; all Israel wanted me to be the next king. But the tables were turned, and the kingdom went to my brother instead; for that is the way the LORD wanted it. 16So now I have just one favor to ask of you. Please don't turn me down.”

“What is it?” she asked.

17He replied, “Speak to King Solomon on my behalf, for I know he will do anything you request. Ask him to let me marry Abishag, the girl from Shunem.”

18“All right,” Bathsheba replied. “I will speak to the king for you.”

19So Bathsheba went to King Solomon to speak on Adonijah's behalf. The king rose from his throne to meet her, and he bowed down before her. When he sat down on his throne again, the king ordered that a throne be brought for his mother, and she sat at his right hand.

20“I have one small request to make of you,” she said. “I hope you won't turn me down.”

“What is it, my mother?” he asked. “You know I won't refuse you.”

21“Then let your brother Adonijah marry Abishag, the girl from Shunem,” she replied.

22“How can you possibly ask me to give Abishag to Adonijah?” King Solomon demanded. “You might as well ask me to give him the kingdom! You know that he is my older brother, and that he has Abiathar the priest and Joab son of Zeruiah on his side.”

23Then King Solomon made a vow before the LORD: “May God strike me and even kill me if Adonijah has not sealed his fate with this request. 24The LORD has confirmed me and placed me on the throne of my father, David; he has established my dynasty as he promised. So as surely as the LORD lives, Adonijah will die this very day!” 25So King Solomon ordered Benaiah son of Jehoiada to execute him, and Adonijah was put to death.

26Then the king said to Abiathar the priest, “Go back to your home in Anathoth. You deserve to die, but I will not kill you now, because you carried the Ark of the Sovereign LORD for David my father and you shared all his hardships.” 27So Solomon deposed Abiathar from his position as priest of the LORD, thereby fulfilling the prophecy the LORD had given at Shiloh concerning the descendants of Eli.

28Joab had not joined Absalom's earlier rebellion, but he had joined Adonijah's rebellion. So when Joab heard about Adonijah's death, he ran to the sacred tent of the LORD and grabbed onto the horns of the altar. 29When this was reported to King Solomon, he sent Benaiah son of Jehoiada to execute him.

30Benaiah went to the sacred tent of the LORD and said to Joab, “The king orders you to come out!”

But Joab answered, “No, I will die here.”

So Benaiah returned to the king and told him what Joab had said.

31“Do as he said,” the king replied. “Kill him there beside the altar and bury him. This will remove the guilt of Joab's senseless murders from me and from my father's family. 32The LORD will repay him* for the murders of two men who were more righteous and better than he. For my father knew nothing about the deaths of Abner son of Ner, commander of the army of Israel, and of Amasa son of Jether, commander of the army of Judah. 33May their blood be on Joab and his descendants forever, and may the LORD grant peace forever to David, his descendants, his dynasty, and his throne.”

34So Benaiah son of Jehoiada returned to the sacred tent and killed Joab, and he was buried at his home in the wilderness. 35Then the king appointed Benaiah to command the army in place of Joab, and he installed Zadok the priest to take the place of Abiathar.

36The king then sent for Shimei and told him, “Build a house here in Jerusalem and live there. But don't step outside the city to go anywhere else. 37On the day you so much as cross the Kidron Valley, you will surely die; and your blood will be on your own head.”

38Shimei replied, “Your sentence is fair; I will do whatever my lord the king commands.” So Shimei lived in Jerusalem for a long time.

39But three years later two of Shimei's slaves ran away to King Achish son of Maacah of Gath. When Shimei learned where they were, 40he saddled his donkey and

2:9 Hebrew *how to bring his white head down to Sheol in blood.* 2:32 Hebrew *will return his blood on his own head.*

went to Gath to search for them. When he found them,
he brought them back to Jerusalem.
41Solomon heard that Shimei had left Jerusalem and
had gone to Gath and returned. 42So the king sent for
Shimei and demanded, "Didn't I make you swear by the
LORD and warn you not to go anywhere else or you would
surely die? And you replied, 'The sentence is fair; I will do
as you say.' 43Then why haven't you kept your oath to the
LORD and obeyed my command?"
44The king also said to Shimei, "You certainly remember all the wicked things you did to my father, David. May
the LORD now bring that evil on your own head. 45But may
I, King Solomon, receive the LORD's blessings, and may
one of David's descendants always sit on this throne in
the presence of the LORD." 46Then, at the king's command, Benaiah son of Jehoiada took Shimei outside and
killed him.
So the kingdom was now firmly in Solomon's grip.

3 SOLOMON ASKS FOR WISDOM

Solomon made an alliance with Pharaoh, the king of
Egypt, and married one of his daughters. He brought her
to live in the City of David until he could finish building
his palace and the Temple of the LORD and the wall
around the city. 2At that time the people of Israel sacrificed their offerings at local places of worship, for a temple honoring the name of the LORD had not yet been built.
3Solomon loved the LORD and followed all the decrees
of his father, David, except that Solomon, too, offered
sacrifices and burned incense at the local places of
worship. 4The most important of these places of worship
was at Gibeon, so the king went there and sacrificed
1,000 burnt offerings. 5That night the LORD appeared to
Solomon in a dream, and God said, "What do you want?
Ask, and I will give it to you!"
6Solomon replied, "You showed faithful love to your
servant my father, David, because he was honest and true
and faithful to you. And you have continued your faithful
love to him today by giving him a son to sit on his throne.
7"Now, O LORD my God, you have made me king instead of my father, David, but I am like a little child who
doesn't know his way around. 8And here I am in the midst
of your own chosen people, a nation so great and numerous they cannot be counted! 9Give me an understanding
heart so that I can govern your people well and know the
difference between right and wrong. For who by himself
is able to govern this great people of yours?"
10The Lord was pleased that Solomon had asked for
wisdom. 11So God replied, "Because you have asked for
wisdom in governing my people with justice and have not
asked for a long life or wealth or the death of your enemies—12I will give you what you asked for! I will give you a
wise and understanding heart such as no one else has had
or ever will have! 13And I will also give you what you did
not ask for—riches and fame! No other king in all the
world will be compared to you for the rest of your life!
14And if you follow me and obey my decrees and my
commands as your father, David, did, I will give you a long
life."
15Then Solomon woke up and realized it had been a
dream. He returned to Jerusalem and stood before the
Ark of the LORD's Covenant, where he sacrificed burnt
offerings and peace offerings. Then he invited all his officials to a great banquet.

SOLOMON JUDGES WISELY

16Some time later two prostitutes came to the king to
have an argument settled. 17"Please, my lord," one of
them began, "this woman and I live in the same house. I
gave birth to a baby while she was with me in the house.
18Three days later this woman also had a baby. We were
alone; there were only two of us in the house.
19"But her baby died during the night when she rolled
over on it. 20Then she got up in the night and took my son
from beside me while I was asleep. She laid her dead
child in my arms and took mine to sleep beside her.
21And in the morning when I tried to nurse my son, he
was dead! But when I looked more closely in the morning
light, I saw that it wasn't my son at all."
22Then the other woman interrupted, "It certainly was
your son, and the living child is mine."
"No," the first woman said, "the living child is mine,
and the dead one is yours." And so they argued back and
forth before the king.
23Then the king said, "Let's get the facts straight. Both

With so many things out there that I want and so many things I know I need, how do I know what to pray for?

Many people find themselves overwhelmed by what to pray for. They approach God like he's a department store: so much to choose from, so little time to shop. Does that describe you?

God told Solomon that he would give him anything he wanted. All he had to do was ask for it. Solomon's choice showed that the gift had already been given—he asked for wisdom. God not only gave him wisdom he also added riches and honor as a bonus. (See 1 Kings 3:3-14.)

Still wondering what to ask God for? You could follow Solomon's example. Choose a request that will honor God and help others. You might pray for character qualities (like patience, self-control, gentleness) that will help you get along better with other people and will help point others toward Christ. Another example is praying for the health of someone who is sick (James 5:14-16).

When you have needs, however, you should never be afraid to ask God to meet them. He loves to answer the prayers of his children! (See Luke 11:9-13.) As you pray, however, just know that God has the right to answer whenever or however he chooses.

WISE GUY 3:5-9

When given a chance to have anything in the world, Solomon asked for wisdom to rule his people. God invites us to ask for wisdom and promises to give it. (See James 1:5.) Gaining wisdom isn't a guarantee that life will always be problem free, however. Having wisdom also doesn't mean that you automatically know everything. Actually, wisdom starts with the realization that God is the only one who truly knows all. (See Prov 1:7.) ■

of you claim the living child is yours, and each says that
the dead one belongs to the other. 24All right, bring me a
sword." So a sword was brought to the king.
25Then he said, "Cut the living child in two, and give
half to one woman and half to the other!"
26Then the woman who was the real mother of the living child, and who loved him very much, cried out, "Oh
no, my lord! Give her the child—please do not kill him!"
But the other woman said, "All right, he will be neither
yours nor mine; divide him between us!"
27Then the king said, "Do not kill the child, but give him
to the woman who wants him to live, for she is his
mother!"
28When all Israel heard the king's decision, the people
were in awe of the king, for they saw the wisdom God had
given him for rendering justice.

4

SOLOMON'S OFFICIALS AND GOVERNORS

King Solomon now ruled over all Israel, 2and these were
his high officials:

Azariah son of Zadok was the priest.
3 Elihoreph and Ahijah, the sons of Shisha, were court secretaries.
Jehoshaphat son of Ahilud was the royal historian.
4 Benaiah son of Jehoiada was commander of the army.
Zadok and Abiathar were priests.
5 Azariah son of Nathan was in charge of the district governors.
Zabud son of Nathan, a priest, was a trusted adviser to the king.
6 Ahishar was manager of the palace property.
Adoniram son of Abda was in charge of the labor force.

7Solomon also had twelve district governors who were
over all Israel. They were responsible for providing food
for the king's household. Each of them arranged provisions for one month of the year. 8These are the names of
the twelve governors:

Ben-hur, in the hill country of Ephraim.
9 Ben-deker, in Makaz, Shaalbim, Beth-shemesh, and Elon-bethhanan.
10 Ben-hesed, in Arubboth, including Socoh and all the land of Hepher.
11 Ben-abinadab, in all of Naphoth-dor.* (He was married to Taphath, one of Solomon's daughters.)
12 Baana son of Ahilud, in Taanach and Megiddo, all of Beth-shan* near Zarethan below Jezreel, and all the territory from Beth-shan to Abel-meholah and over to Jokmeam.
13 Ben-geber, in Ramoth-gilead, including the Towns of Jair (named for Jair of the tribe of Manasseh*) in Gilead, and in the Argob region of Bashan, including sixty large fortified towns with bronze bars on their gates.
14 Ahinadab son of Iddo, in Mahanaim.
15 Ahimaaz, in Naphtali. (He was married to Basemath, another of Solomon's daughters.)
16 Baana son of Hushai, in Asher and in Aloth.
17 Jehoshaphat son of Paruah, in Issachar.
18 Shimei son of Ela, in Benjamin.
19 Geber son of Uri, in the land of Gilead,* including the territories of King Sihon of the Amorites and King Og of Bashan.
There was also one governor over the land of Judah.*

SOLOMON'S PROSPERITY AND WISDOM

20The people of Judah and Israel were as numerous as the
sand on the seashore. They were very contented, with
plenty to eat and drink. 21*Solomon ruled over all the
kingdoms from the Euphrates River* in the north to the
land of the Philistines and the border of Egypt in the
south. The conquered peoples of those lands sent tribute
money to Solomon and continued to serve him throughout his lifetime.
22The daily food requirements for Solomon's palace
were 150 bushels of choice flour and 300 bushels of
meal*; 23also 10 oxen from the fattening pens, 20 pasture-fed cattle, 100 sheep or goats, as well as deer, gazelles,
roe deer, and choice poultry.*
24Solomon's dominion extended over all the kingdoms
west of the Euphrates River, from Tiphsah to Gaza. And
there was peace on all his borders. 25During the lifetime
of Solomon, all of Judah and Israel lived in peace and
safety. And from Dan in the north to Beersheba in the
south, each family had its own home and garden.*
26Solomon had 4,000* stalls for his chariot horses,
and he had 12,000 horses.*
27The district governors faithfully provided food for
King Solomon and his court; each made sure nothing was
lacking during the month assigned to him. 28They also
brought the necessary barley and straw for the royal
horses in the stables.

4:11 Hebrew *Naphath-dor,* a variant spelling of Naphoth-dor. 4:12 Hebrew *Beth-shean,* a variant spelling of Beth-shan; also in 4:12b. 4:13 Hebrew *Jair son of Manasseh;* compare 1 Chr 2:22. 4:19a Greek version reads *of Gad;* compare 4:13. 4:19b As in some Greek manuscripts; Hebrew lacks *of Judah.* The meaning of the Hebrew is uncertain. 4:21a Verses 4:21-34 are numbered 5:1-14 in Hebrew text. 4:21b Hebrew *the river;* also in 4:24. 4:22 Hebrew *30 cors* [5.5 kiloliters] *of choice flour and 60 cors* [11 kiloliters] *of meal.* 4:23 Or *and fattened geese.* 4:25 Hebrew *each family lived under its own grapevine and under its own fig tree.* 4:26a As in some Greek manuscripts (see also 2 Chr 9:25); Hebrew reads *40,000.* 4:26b Or *12,000 charioteers.*

29God gave Solomon very great wisdom and understanding, and knowledge as vast as the sands of the seashore. 30In fact, his wisdom exceeded that of all the wise men of the East and the wise men of Egypt. 31He was wiser than anyone else, including Ethan the Ezrahite and the sons of Mahol—Heman, Calcol, and Darda. His fame spread throughout all the surrounding nations. 32He composed some 3,000 proverbs and wrote 1,005 songs. 33He could speak with authority about all kinds of plants, from the great cedar of Lebanon to the tiny hyssop that grows from cracks in a wall. He could also speak about animals, birds, small creatures, and fish. 34And kings from every nation sent their ambassadors to listen to the wisdom of Solomon.

5 PREPARATIONS FOR BUILDING THE TEMPLE

1*King Hiram of Tyre had always been a loyal friend of David. When Hiram learned that David's son Solomon was the new king of Israel, he sent ambassadors to congratulate him.

2Then Solomon sent this message back to Hiram:

3"You know that my father, David, was not able to build a Temple to honor the name of the LORD his God because of the many wars waged against him by surrounding nations. He could not build until the LORD gave him victory over all his enemies. 4But now the LORD my God has given me peace on every side; I have no enemies, and all is well. 5So I am planning to build a Temple to honor the name of the LORD my God, just as he had instructed my father, David. For the LORD told him, 'Your son, whom I will place on your throne, will build the Temple to honor my name.'

6"Therefore, please command that cedars from Lebanon be cut for me. Let my men work alongside yours, and I will pay your men whatever wages you ask. As you know, there is no one among us who can cut timber like you Sidonians!"

7When Hiram received Solomon's message, he was very pleased and said, "Praise the LORD today for giving David a wise son to be king of the great nation of Israel." 8Then he sent this reply to Solomon:

"I have received your message, and I will supply all the cedar and cypress timber you need. 9My servants will bring the logs from the Lebanon mountains to the Mediterranean Sea* and make them into rafts and float them along the coast to whatever place you choose. Then we will break the rafts apart so you can carry the logs away. You can pay me by supplying me with food for my household."

10So Hiram supplied as much cedar and cypress timber as Solomon desired. 11In return, Solomon sent him an annual payment of 100,000 bushels* of wheat for his household and 110,000 gallons* of pure olive oil. 12So the LORD gave wisdom to Solomon, just as he had promised. And Hiram and Solomon made a formal alliance of peace.

FAMILY TIME 5:13-14

Solomon drafted three times the number of workers needed for the Temple project and arranged their schedules so they wouldn't have to be away from home for long periods of time. Solomon wisely recognized that family time was a top priority in the lives of his workers. Is spending time with your family one of your top priorities? ■

13Then King Solomon conscripted a labor force of 30,000 men from all Israel. 14He sent them to Lebanon in shifts, 10,000 every month, so that each man would be one month in Lebanon and two months at home. Adoniram was in charge of this labor force. 15Solomon also had 70,000 common laborers, 80,000 quarry workers in the hill country, 16and 3,600* foremen to supervise the work. 17At the king's command, they quarried large blocks of high-quality stone and shaped them to make the foundation of the Temple. 18Men from the city of Gebal helped Solomon's and Hiram's builders prepare the timber and stone for the Temple.

6 SOLOMON BUILDS THE TEMPLE

It was in midspring, in the month of Ziv,* during the fourth year of Solomon's reign, that he began to construct the Temple of the LORD. This was 480 years after the people of Israel were rescued from their slavery in the land of Egypt.

2The Temple that King Solomon built for the LORD was 90 feet long, 30 feet wide, and 45 feet high.* 3The entry room at the front of the Temple was 30 feet* wide, running across the entire width of the Temple. It projected outward 15 feet* from the front of the Temple. 4Solomon also made narrow recessed windows throughout the Temple.

5He built a complex of rooms against the outer walls of the Temple, all the way around the sides and rear of the building. 6The complex was three stories high, the bottom floor being 7½ feet wide, the second floor 9 feet wide, and the top floor 10½ feet wide.* The rooms were

5:1 Verses 5:1-18 are numbered 5:15-32 in Hebrew text. **5:9** Hebrew *the sea.* **5:11a** Hebrew *20,000 cors* [3,640 kiloliters]. **5:11b** As in Greek version, which reads *20,000 baths* [420 kiloliters] (see also 2 Chr 2:10); Hebrew reads *20 cors,* about 800 gallons or 3.6 kiloliters in volume. **5:16** As in some Greek manuscripts (see also 2 Chr 2:2, 18); Hebrew reads *3,300.* **6:1** Hebrew *It was in the month of Ziv, which is the second month.* This month of the ancient Hebrew lunar calendar usually occurs within the months of April and May. **6:2** Hebrew *60 cubits* [27.6 meters] *long, 20 cubits* [9.2 meters] *wide, and 30 cubits* [13.8 meters] *high.* **6:3a** Hebrew *20 cubits* [9.2 meters]; also in 6:16, 20. **6:3b** Hebrew *10 cubits* [4.6 meters]. **6:6** Hebrew *the bottom floor being 5 cubits* [2.3 meters] *wide, the second floor 6 cubits* [2.8 meters] *wide, and the top floor 7 cubits* [3.2 meters] *wide.*

connected to the walls of the Temple by beams resting on
ledges built out from the wall. So the beams were not inserted into the walls themselves.
7The stones used in the construction of the Temple
were finished at the quarry, so there was no sound of
hammer, ax, or any other iron tool at the building site.

RESPECT 6:7

The people's respect for God extended to every aspect of constructing the Temple. Not only were the best materials used, the sound of a hammer or any tool was not heard at the building site. Doing so required incredibly accurate measuring. Do you believe that God deserves this kind of respect? How do you show your respect for God? ■

8The entrance to the bottom floor* was on the south
side of the Temple. There were winding stairs going up to
the second floor, and another flight of stairs between the
second and third floors. 9After completing the Temple
structure, Solomon put in a ceiling made of cedar beams
and planks. 10As already stated, he built a complex of
rooms on three sides of the building, attached to the
Temple walls by cedar timbers. Each story of the complex was 7½ feet* high.
11Then the LORD gave this message to Solomon:
12"Concerning this Temple you are building, if you keep
all my decrees and regulations and obey all my commands, I will fulfill through you the promise I made to
your father, David. 13I will live among the Israelites and
will never abandon my people Israel."

THE TEMPLE'S INTERIOR

14So Solomon finished building the Temple. 15The entire
inside, from floor to ceiling, was paneled with wood. He
paneled the walls and ceilings with cedar, and he used
planks of cypress for the floors. 16He partitioned off an
inner sanctuary—the Most Holy Place—at the far end of
the Temple. It was 30 feet deep and was paneled with cedar from floor to ceiling. 17The main room of the Temple,
outside the Most Holy Place, was 60 feet* long. 18Cedar
paneling completely covered the stone walls throughout
the Temple, and the paneling was decorated with carvings of gourds and open flowers.
19He prepared the inner sanctuary at the far end of the
Temple, where the Ark of the LORD's Covenant would be
placed. 20This inner sanctuary was 30 feet long, 30 feet
wide, and 30 feet high. He overlaid the inside with solid
gold. He also overlaid the altar made of cedar.* 21Then
Solomon overlaid the rest of the Temple's interior with
solid gold, and he made gold chains to protect the
entrance* to the Most Holy Place. 22So he finished overlaying the entire Temple with gold, including the altar
that belonged to the Most Holy Place.
23He made two cherubim of wild olive* wood, each
15 feet* tall, and placed them in the inner sanctuary.
24The wingspan of each of the cherubim was 15 feet,
each wing being 7½ feet* long. 25The two cherubim were
identical in shape and size; 26each was 15 feet tall. 27He
placed them side by side in the inner sanctuary of the
Temple. Their outspread wings reached from wall to
wall, while their inner wings touched at the center of the
room. 28He overlaid the two cherubim with gold.
29He decorated all the walls of the inner sanctuary and
the main room with carvings of cherubim, palm trees,
and open flowers. 30He overlaid the floor in both rooms
with gold.
31For the entrance to the inner sanctuary, he made
double doors of wild olive wood with five-sided
doorposts.* 32These double doors were decorated with
carvings of cherubim, palm trees, and open flowers. The
doors, including the decorations of cherubim and palm
trees, were overlaid with gold.
33Then he made four-sided doorposts of wild olive
wood for the entrance to the Temple. 34There were two
folding doors of cypress wood, and each door was hinged
to fold back upon itself. 35These doors were decorated
with carvings of cherubim, palm trees, and open flowers—all overlaid evenly with gold.
36The walls of the inner courtyard were built so that
there was one layer of cedar beams between every three
layers of finished stone.
37The foundation of the LORD's Temple was laid in
midspring, in the month of Ziv,* during the fourth year of
Solomon's reign. 38The entire building was completed in
every detail by midautumn, in the month of Bul,* during
the eleventh year of his reign. So it took seven years to
build the Temple.

7

SOLOMON BUILDS HIS PALACE

Solomon also built a palace for himself, and it took him
thirteen years to complete the construction.
2One of Solomon's buildings was called the Palace of
the Forest of Lebanon. It was 150 feet long, 75 feet wide,
and 45 feet high.* There were four rows of cedar pillars,
and great cedar beams rested on the pillars. 3The hall had
a cedar roof. Above the beams on the pillars were forty-
five side rooms,* arranged in three tiers of fifteen each.
4On each end of the long hall were three rows of windows
facing each other. 5All the doorways and doorposts* had
rectangular frames and were arranged in sets of three,
facing each other.

6:8 As in Greek version; Hebrew reads *middle floor*. **6:10** Hebrew *5 cubits* [2.3 meters]. **6:17** Hebrew *40 cubits* [18.4 meters]. **6:20** Or *overlaid the altar with cedar*. The meaning of the Hebrew is uncertain. **6:21** Or *to draw curtains across*. The meaning of the Hebrew is uncertain. **6:23a** Or *pine;* Hebrew reads *oil tree;* also in 6:31, 33. **6:23b** Hebrew *10 cubits* [4.6 meters]; also in 6:24, 25. **6:24** Hebrew *5 cubits* [2.3 meters]. **6:31** The meaning of the Hebrew is uncertain. **6:37** Hebrew *was laid in the month of Ziv*. This month of the ancient Hebrew lunar calendar usually occurs within the months of April and May. **6:38** Hebrew *by the month of Bul, which is the eighth month*. This month of the ancient Hebrew lunar calendar usually occurs within the months of October and November. **7:2** Hebrew *100 cubits* [46 meters] *long, 50 cubits* [23 meters] *wide, and 30 cubits* [13.5 meters] *high*. **7:3** Or *45 rafters*, or *45 beams*, or *45 pillars*. The architectural details in 7:2-6 can be interpreted in many different ways. **7:5** Greek version reads *windows*.

[6]Solomon also built the Hall of Pillars, which was 75 feet long and 45 feet wide.* There was a porch in front, along with a canopy supported by pillars.

[7]Solomon also built the throne room, known as the Hall of Justice, where he sat to hear legal matters. It was paneled with cedar from floor to ceiling.* [8]Solomon's living quarters surrounded a courtyard behind this hall, and they were constructed the same way. He also built similar living quarters for Pharaoh's daughter, whom he had married.

[9]From foundation to eaves, all these buildings were built from huge blocks of high-quality stone, cut with saws and trimmed to exact measure on all sides. [10]Some of the huge foundation stones were 15 feet long, and some were 12 feet* long. [11]The blocks of high-quality stone used in the walls were also cut to measure, and cedar beams were also used. [12]The walls of the great courtyard were built so that there was one layer of cedar beams between every three layers of finished stone, just like the walls of the inner courtyard of the LORD's Temple with its entry room.

FURNISHINGS FOR THE TEMPLE

[13]King Solomon then asked for a man named Huram* to come from Tyre. [14]He was half Israelite, since his mother was a widow from the tribe of Naphtali, and his father had been a craftsman in bronze from Tyre. Huram was extremely skillful and talented in any work in bronze, and he came to do all the metal work for King Solomon.

[15]Huram cast two bronze pillars, each 27 feet tall and 18 feet in circumference.* [16]For the tops of the pillars he cast bronze capitals, each 7½ feet* tall. [17]Each capital was decorated with seven sets of latticework and interwoven chains. [18]He also encircled the latticework with two rows of pomegranates to decorate the capitals over the pillars. [19]The capitals on the columns inside the entry room were shaped like water lilies, and they were six feet* tall. [20]The capitals on the two pillars had 200 pomegranates in two rows around them, beside the rounded surface next to the latticework. [21]Huram set the pillars at the entrance of the Temple, one toward the south and one toward the north. He named the one on the south Jakin, and the one on the north Boaz.* [22]The capitals on the pillars were shaped like water lilies. And so the work on the pillars was finished.

[23]Then Huram cast a great round basin, 15 feet across from rim to rim, called the Sea. It was 7½ feet deep and about 45 feet in circumference.* [24]It was encircled just below its rim by two rows of decorative gourds. There were about six gourds per foot* all the way around, and they were cast as part of the basin.

[25]The Sea was placed on a base of twelve bronze oxen,* all facing outward. Three faced north, three faced west, three faced south, and three faced east, and the Sea rested on them. [26]The walls of the Sea were about three inches* thick, and its rim flared out like a cup and resembled a water lily blossom. It could hold about 11,000 gallons* of water.

[27]Huram also made ten bronze water carts, each 6 feet long, 6 feet wide, and 4½ feet tall.* [28]They were constructed with side panels braced with crossbars. [29]Both the panels and the crossbars were decorated with carved lions, oxen, and cherubim. Above and below the lions and oxen were wreath decorations. [30]Each of these carts had four bronze wheels and bronze axles. There were supporting posts for the bronze basins at the corners of the carts; these supports were decorated on each side with carvings of wreaths. [31]The top of each cart had a rounded frame for the basin. It projected 1½ feet* above the cart's top like a round pedestal, and its opening was 2¼ feet* across; it was decorated on the outside with carvings of wreaths. The panels of the carts were square, not round. [32]Under the panels were four wheels that were connected to axles that had been cast as one unit with the cart. The wheels were 2¼ feet in diameter [33]and were similar to chariot wheels. The axles, spokes, rims, and hubs were all cast from molten bronze.

[34]There were handles at each of the four corners of the carts, and these, too, were cast as one unit with the cart. [35]Around the top of each cart was a rim nine inches wide.* The corner supports and side panels were cast as one unit with the cart. [36]Carvings of cherubim, lions, and palm trees decorated the panels and corner supports wherever there was room, and there were wreaths all around. [37]All ten water carts were the same size and were made alike, for each was cast from the same mold.

WORSHIP ITEMS 7:38-46

Huram designed items of bronze for use in the Temple. Today's churches contain different items for worship: stained-glass windows, crosses, pulpits, hymnals, and Communion tables. While the instruments of worship may change, the purpose—to give honor and praise to God—never does. ■

[38]Huram also made ten smaller bronze basins, one for each cart. Each basin was six feet across and could hold 220 gallons* of water. [39]He set five water carts on the south side of the Temple and five on the north side. The great bronze basin called the Sea was placed near the southeast corner of the Temple. [40]He also made the necessary washbasins, shovels, and bowls.

7:6 Hebrew *50 cubits* [23 meters] *long and 30 cubits* [13.8 meters] *wide.* **7:7** As in Syriac version and Latin Vulgate; Hebrew reads *from floor to floor.* **7:10** Hebrew *10 cubits* [4.6 meters] . . . *8 cubits* [3.7 meters]. **7:13** Hebrew *Hiram* (also in 7:40, 45); compare 2 Chr 2:13. This is not the same person mentioned in 5:1. **7:15** Hebrew *18 cubits* [8.3 meters] *tall and 12 cubits* [5.5 meters] *in circumference.* **7:16** Hebrew *5 cubits* [2.3 meters]. **7:19** Hebrew *4 cubits* [1.8 meters]; also in 7:38. **7:21** *Jakin* probably means "he establishes"; *Boaz* probably means "in him is strength." **7:23** Hebrew *10 cubits* [4.6 meters] *across.* . . . *5 cubits* [2.3 meters] *deep and 30 cubits* [13.8 meters] *in circumference.* **7:24** Or *20 gourds per meter;* Hebrew reads *10 per cubit.* **7:25** Hebrew *12 oxen;* compare 2 Kgs 16:17, which specifies *bronze oxen.* **7:26a** Hebrew *a handbreadth* [8 centimeters]. **7:26b** Hebrew *2,000 baths* [42 kiloliters]. **7:27** Hebrew *4 cubits* [1.8 meters] *long, 4 cubits wide, and 3 cubits* [1.4 meters] *high.* **7:31a** Hebrew *a cubit* [46 centimeters]. **7:31b** Hebrew *1½ cubits* [69 centimeters]; also in 7:32. **7:35** Hebrew *half a cubit wide* [23 centimeters]. **7:38** Hebrew *40 baths* [840 liters].

So at last Huram completed everything King Solomon
had assigned him to make for the Temple of the LORD:

41 the two pillars;
the two bowl-shaped capitals on top of the pillars;
the two networks of interwoven chains that
decorated the capitals;
42 the 400 pomegranates that hung from the chains on
the capitals (two rows of pomegranates for each
of the chain networks that decorated the capitals
on top of the pillars);
43 the ten water carts holding the ten basins;
44 the Sea and the twelve oxen under it;
45 the ash buckets, the shovels, and the bowls.

Huram made all these things of burnished bronze for the
Temple of the LORD, just as King Solomon had directed.
46The king had them cast in clay molds in the Jordan Valley between Succoth and Zarethan. 47Solomon did not
weigh all these things because there were so many; the
weight of the bronze could not be measured.

48Solomon also made all the furnishings of the Temple
of the LORD:

the gold altar;
the gold table for the Bread of the Presence;
49 the lampstands of solid gold, five on the south and
five on the north, in front of the Most Holy Place;
the flower decorations, lamps, and tongs—all of gold;
50 the small bowls, lamp snuffers, bowls, dishes, and
incense burners—all of solid gold;
the doors for the entrances to the Most Holy Place
and the main room of the Temple, with their
fronts overlaid with gold.

51So King Solomon finished all his work on the Temple
of the LORD. Then he brought all the gifts his father, David, had dedicated—the silver, the gold, and the various
articles—and he stored them in the treasuries of the
LORD's Temple.

8

THE ARK BROUGHT TO THE TEMPLE

Solomon then summoned to Jerusalem the elders of Israel and all the heads of the tribes—the leaders of the ancestral families of the Israelites. They were to bring the
Ark of the LORD's Covenant to the Temple from its location in the City of David, also known as Zion. 2So all the
men of Israel assembled before King Solomon at the annual Festival of Shelters, which is held in early autumn in
the month of Ethanim.*

3When all the elders of Israel arrived, the priests
picked up the Ark. 4The priests and Levites brought up
the Ark of the LORD along with the special tent* and all
the sacred items that had been in it. 5There, before the
Ark, King Solomon and the entire community of Israel
sacrificed so many sheep, goats, and cattle that no one
could keep count!

6Then the priests carried the Ark of the LORD's Covenant
into the inner sanctuary of the Temple—the Most Holy
Place—and placed it beneath the wings of the cherubim.
7The cherubim spread their wings over the Ark, forming a
canopy over the Ark and its carrying poles. 8These poles
were so long that their ends could be seen from the Temple's main room—the Holy Place—but not from the outside.
They are still there to this day. 9Nothing was in the Ark except the two stone tablets that Moses had placed in it at
Mount Sinai,* where the LORD made a covenant with the
people of Israel when they left the land of Egypt.

10When the priests came out of the Holy Place, a thick
cloud filled the Temple of the LORD. 11The priests could
not continue their service because of the cloud, for the
glorious presence of the LORD filled the Temple.

SOLOMON PRAISES THE LORD

12Then Solomon prayed, "O LORD, you have said that you
would live in a thick cloud of darkness. 13Now I have built
a glorious Temple for you, a place where you can live forever!*"

14Then the king turned around to the entire community of Israel standing before him and gave this blessing:
15"Praise the LORD, the God of Israel, who has kept the
promise he made to my father, David. For he told my father, 16'From the day I brought my people Israel out of
Egypt, I have never chosen a city among any of the tribes
of Israel as the place where a Temple should be built to
honor my name. But I have chosen David to be king over
my people Israel.'"

17Then Solomon said, "My father, David, wanted to
build this Temple to honor the name of the LORD, the God
of Israel. 18But the LORD told him, 'You wanted to build
the Temple to honor my name. Your intention is good,
19but you are not the one to do it. One of your own sons
will build the Temple to honor me.'

20"And now the LORD has fulfilled the promise he
made, for I have become king in my father's place, and I
now sit on the throne of Israel, just as the LORD promised.
I have built this Temple to honor the name of the LORD,
the God of Israel. 21And I have prepared a place there for
the Ark, which contains the covenant that the LORD made
with our ancestors when he brought them out of Egypt."

SOLOMON'S PRAYER OF DEDICATION

22Then Solomon stood before the altar of the LORD in
front of the entire community of Israel. He lifted his
hands toward heaven, 23and he prayed,

"O LORD, God of Israel, there is no God like you in all
of heaven above or on the earth below. You keep your
covenant and show unfailing love to all who walk
before you in wholehearted devotion. 24You have
kept your promise to your servant David, my father.

8:2 Hebrew *at the festival in the month Ethanim, which is the seventh month.* The Festival of Shelters began on the fifteenth day of the seventh month of the ancient Hebrew lunar calendar. This day occurred in late September, October, or early November. **8:4** Hebrew *the Tent of Meeting;* i.e., the tent mentioned in 2 Sam 6:17 and 1 Chr 16:1. **8:9** Hebrew *at Horeb,* another name for Sinai. **8:13** Some Greek texts add the line *Is this not written in the Book of Jashar?*

You made that promise with your own mouth, and
with your own hands you have fulfilled it today.
25"And now, O LORD, God of Israel, carry out the
additional promise you made to your servant David,
my father. For you said to him, 'If your descendants
guard their behavior and faithfully follow me as you
have done, one of them will always sit on the throne
of Israel.' 26Now, O God of Israel, fulfill this promise
to your servant David, my father.
27"But will God really live on earth? Why, even the
highest heavens cannot contain you. How much less
this Temple I have built! 28Nevertheless, listen to my
prayer and my plea, O LORD my God. Hear the cry and
the prayer that your servant is making to you today.
29May you watch over this Temple night and day, this
place where you have said, 'My name will be there.'
May you always hear the prayers I make toward this
place. 30May you hear the humble and earnest
requests from me and your people Israel when we
pray toward this place. Yes, hear us from heaven
where you live, and when you hear, forgive.

GOD'S HOME 8:27

Solomon declared that even the highest heavens couldn't contain God. Although the heavens can't contain him, isn't it amazing that he's willing to take up residence in those who love him? If you're a believer, that includes you. What are you doing to welcome him home? ■

31"If someone wrongs another person and is
required to take an oath of innocence in front of your
altar in this Temple, 32then hear from heaven and
judge between your servants—the accuser and the
accused. Punish the guilty as they deserve. Acquit the
innocent because of their innocence.
33"If your people Israel are defeated by their
enemies because they have sinned against you, and
if they turn to you and acknowledge your name and
pray to you here in this Temple, 34then hear from
heaven and forgive the sin of your people Israel and
return them to this land you gave their ancestors.
35"If the skies are shut up and there is no rain
because your people have sinned against you, and if
they pray toward this Temple and acknowledge your
name and turn from their sins because you have
punished them, 36then hear from heaven and forgive
the sins of your servants, your people Israel. Teach
them to follow the right path, and send rain on your
land that you have given to your people as their
special possession.
37"If there is a famine in the land or a plague or
crop disease or attacks of locusts or caterpillars, or if
your people's enemies are in the land besieging their
towns—whatever disaster or disease there is—38and if
your people Israel pray about their troubles, raising
their hands toward this Temple, 39then hear from
heaven where you live, and forgive. Give your people
what their actions deserve, for you alone know each
human heart. 40Then they will fear you as long as they
live in the land you gave to our ancestors.
41"In the future, foreigners who do not belong to
your people Israel will hear of you. They will come
from distant lands because of your name, 42for they
will hear of your great name and your strong hand
and your powerful arm. And when they pray toward
this Temple, 43then hear from heaven where you live,
and grant what they ask of you. In this way, all the
people of the earth will come to know and fear you,
just as your own people Israel do. They, too, will know
that this Temple I have built honors your name.
44"If your people go out where you send them to
fight their enemies, and if they pray to the LORD by
turning toward this city you have chosen and toward
this Temple I have built to honor your name, 45then
hear their prayers from heaven and uphold their
cause.
46"If they sin against you—and who has never
sinned?—you might become angry with them and let
their enemies conquer them and take them captive to
their land far away or near. 47But in that land of exile,
they might turn to you in repentance and pray, 'We
have sinned, done evil, and acted wickedly.' 48If they
turn to you with their whole heart and soul in the land
of their enemies and pray toward the land you gave to
their ancestors—toward this city you have chosen, and
toward this Temple I have built to honor your name—
49then hear their prayers and their petition from
heaven where you live, and uphold their cause.
50Forgive your people who have sinned against you.
Forgive all the offenses they have committed against
you. Make their captors merciful to them, 51for they
are your people—your special possession—whom you
brought out of the iron-smelting furnace of Egypt.
52"May your eyes be open to my requests and to the
requests of your people Israel. May you hear and
answer them whenever they cry out to you. 53For
when you brought our ancestors out of Egypt,
O Sovereign LORD, you told your servant Moses that
you had set Israel apart from all the nations of the
earth to be your own special possession."

THE DEDICATION OF THE TEMPLE

54When Solomon finished making these prayers and petitions to the LORD, he stood up in front of the altar of the
LORD, where he had been kneeling with his hands raised
toward heaven. 55He stood and in a loud voice blessed the
entire congregation of Israel:
56"Praise the LORD who has given rest to his people Israel, just as he promised. Not one word has failed of all
the wonderful promises he gave through his servant
Moses. 57May the LORD our God be with us as he was with
our ancestors; may he never leave us or abandon us.
58May he give us the desire to do his will in everything and
to obey all the commands, decrees, and regulations that
he gave our ancestors. 59And may these words that I have
prayed in the presence of the LORD be before him constantly, day and night, so that the LORD our God may give

justice to me and to his people Israel, according to each day's needs. 60Then people all over the earth will know that the LORD alone is God and there is no other. 61And may you be completely faithful to the LORD our God. May you always obey his decrees and commands, just as you are doing today."

PRAYER REQUESTS 8:54-61

Solomon blessed the people and prayed for them. He asked for (1) God's continued presence among his people (8:57); (2) the desire to do God's will in everything (8:58, 61); (3) help with daily needs (8:59); (4) faithfulness (8:61); and (5) the spread of God's kingdom to the entire world (8:60). Are these requests also yours? ■

62Then the king and all Israel with him offered sacrifices to the LORD. 63Solomon offered to the LORD a peace offering of 22,000 cattle and 120,000 sheep and goats. And so the king and all the people of Israel dedicated the Temple of the LORD.

64That same day the king consecrated the central area of the courtyard in front of the LORD's Temple. He offered burnt offerings, grain offerings, and the fat of peace offerings there, because the bronze altar in the LORD's presence was too small to hold all the burnt offerings, grain offerings, and the fat of the peace offerings.

65Then Solomon and all Israel celebrated the Festival of Shelters* in the presence of the LORD our God. A large congregation had gathered from as far away as Lebo-hamath in the north and the Brook of Egypt in the south. The celebration went on for fourteen days in all—seven days for the dedication of the altar and seven days for the Festival of Shelters.* 66After the festival was over,* Solomon sent the people home. They blessed the king and went to their homes joyful and glad because the LORD had been good to his servant David and to his people Israel.

9 THE LORD'S RESPONSE TO SOLOMON

So Solomon finished building the Temple of the LORD, as well as the royal palace. He completed everything he had planned to do. 2Then the LORD appeared to Solomon a second time, as he had done before at Gibeon. 3The LORD said to him,

"I have heard your prayer and your petition. I have set this Temple apart to be holy—this place you have built where my name will be honored forever. I will always watch over it, for it is dear to my heart.

4"As for you, if you will follow me with integrity and godliness, as David your father did, obeying all my commands, decrees, and regulations, 5then I will establish the throne of your dynasty over Israel forever. For I made this promise to your father, David: 'One of your descendants will always sit on the throne of Israel.'

6"But if you or your descendants abandon me and disobey the commands and decrees I have given you, and if you serve and worship other gods, 7then I will uproot Israel from this land that I have given them. I will reject this Temple that I have made holy to honor my name. I will make Israel an object of mockery and ridicule among the nations. 8And though this Temple is impressive now, all who pass by will be appalled and will shake their heads in amazement. They will ask, 'Why did the LORD do such terrible things to this land and to this Temple?'

9"And the answer will be, 'Because his people abandoned the LORD their God, who brought their ancestors out of Egypt, and they worshiped other gods instead and bowed down to them. That is why the LORD has brought all these disasters on them.'"

SOLOMON'S AGREEMENT WITH HIRAM

10It took Solomon twenty years to build the LORD's Temple and his own royal palace. At the end of that time, 11he gave twenty towns in the land of Galilee to King Hiram of Tyre. (Hiram had previously provided all the cedar and cypress timber and gold that Solomon had requested.) 12But when Hiram came from Tyre to see the towns Solomon had given him, he was not at all pleased with them. 13"What kind of towns are these, my brother?" he asked. So Hiram called that area Cabul (which means "worthless"), as it is still known today. 14Nevertheless, Hiram paid* Solomon 9,000 pounds* of gold.

WHATEVER IT TAKES? 9:16

At this time, Israel and Egypt were the major powers in the area. During Solomon's reign, the Egyptian king captured the city of Gezer. To regain the city, Solomon married one of Pharaoh's daughters. Intermarriage among royal families was common, but was not endorsed by God (see Deut 7:3-4; 17:17). Like Solomon, are you willing to do whatever you have to do to get what you want, even if you have to do something wrong? Is any goal really worth that? ■

SOLOMON'S MANY ACHIEVEMENTS

15This is the account of the forced labor that King Solomon conscripted to build the LORD's Temple, the royal palace, the supporting terraces,* the wall of Jerusalem, and the cities of Hazor, Megiddo, and Gezer. 16(Pharaoh, the king of Egypt, had attacked and captured Gezer, killing the Canaanite population and burning it down. He gave the city to his daughter as a wedding gift when she married Solomon. 17So Solomon rebuilt the city of Gezer.) He also built up the towns of Lower Beth-horon,

8:65a Hebrew *the festival;* see note on 8:2. 8:65b Hebrew *seven days and seven days, fourteen days;* compare parallel text at 2 Chr 7:8-10. 8:66 Hebrew *On the eighth day,* probably referring to the day following the seven-day Festival of Shelters; compare parallel text at 2 Chr 7:9-10. 9:14a Or *For Hiram had paid.* 9:14b Hebrew *120 talents* [4,000 kilograms]. 9:15 Hebrew *the millo;* also in 9:24. The meaning of the Hebrew is uncertain.

18Baalath, and Tamar* in the wilderness within his land.
19He built towns as supply centers and constructed towns
where his chariots and horses* could be stationed. He
built everything he desired in Jerusalem and Lebanon
and throughout his entire realm.

20There were still some people living in the land who
were not Israelites, including Amorites, Hittites, Perizzites, Hivites, and Jebusites. 21These were descendants of
the nations whom the people of Israel had not completely destroyed.* So Solomon conscripted them for his
labor force, and they serve in the labor force to this day.
22But Solomon did not conscript any of the Israelites for
forced labor. Instead, he assigned them to serve as fighting men, government officials, officers and captains in
his army, commanders of his chariots, and charioteers.
23Solomon appointed 550 of them to supervise the people working on his various projects.

24Solomon moved his wife, Pharaoh's daughter, from
the City of David to the new palace he had built for her.
Then he constructed the supporting terraces.

25Three times each year Solomon presented burnt offerings and peace offerings on the altar he had built for
the LORD. He also burned incense to the LORD. And so he
finished the work of building the Temple.

26King Solomon also built a fleet of ships at Ezion-
geber, a port near Elath* in the land of Edom, along the
shore of the Red Sea.* 27Hiram sent experienced crews
of sailors to sail the ships with Solomon's men. 28They
sailed to Ophir and brought back to Solomon some sixteen tons* of gold.

10 VISIT OF THE QUEEN OF SHEBA

When the queen of Sheba heard of Solomon's fame,
which brought honor to the name of the LORD,* she came
to test him with hard questions. 2She arrived in Jerusalem
with a large group of attendants and a great caravan of
camels loaded with spices, large quantities of gold, and
precious jewels. When she met with Solomon, she talked
with him about everything she had on her mind. 3Solo-
mon had answers for all her questions; nothing was too
hard for the king to explain to her. 4When the queen of
Sheba realized how very wise Solomon was, and when
she saw the palace he had built, 5she was overwhelmed.
She was also amazed at the food on his tables, the organization of his officials and their splendid clothing, the
cup-bearers, and the burnt offerings Solomon made at
the Temple of the LORD.

6She exclaimed to the king, "Everything I heard in my
country about your achievements* and wisdom is true! 7I
didn't believe what was said until I arrived here and saw it
with my own eyes. In fact, I had not heard the half of it!
Your wisdom and prosperity are far beyond what I was
told. 8How happy your people* must be! What a privilege
for your officials to stand here day after day, listening to
your wisdom! 9Praise the LORD your God, who delights in
you and has placed you on the throne of Israel. Because
of the LORD's eternal love for Israel, he has made you king
so you can rule with justice and righteousness."

10Then she gave the king a gift of 9,000 pounds* of
gold, great quantities of spices, and precious jewels.
Never again were so many spices brought in as those the
queen of Sheba gave to King Solomon.

11(In addition, Hiram's ships brought gold from Ophir,
and they also brought rich cargoes of red sandalwood*
and precious jewels. 12The king used the sandalwood to
make railings for the Temple of the LORD and the royal
palace, and to construct lyres and harps for the musicians. Never before or since has there been such a supply
of sandalwood.)

13King Solomon gave the queen of Sheba whatever she
asked for, besides all the customary gifts he had so generously given. Then she and all her attendants returned to
their own land.

SOLOMON'S WEALTH AND SPLENDOR

14Each year Solomon received about 25 tons* of gold.
15This did not include the additional revenue he received
from merchants and traders, all the kings of Arabia, and
the governors of the land.

16King Solomon made 200 large shields of hammered
gold, each weighing more than fifteen pounds.* 17He also
made 300 smaller shields of hammered gold, each
weighing nearly four pounds.* The king placed these
shields in the Palace of the Forest of Lebanon.

18Then the king made a huge throne, decorated with
ivory and overlaid with fine gold. 19The throne had six
steps and a rounded back. There were armrests on both
sides of the seat, and the figure of a lion stood on each
side of the throne. 20There were also twelve other lions,
one standing on each end of the six steps. No other
throne in all the world could be compared with it!

21All of King Solomon's drinking cups were solid gold,
as were all the utensils in the Palace of the Forest of Lebanon. They were not made of silver, for silver was considered worthless in Solomon's day!

22The king had a fleet of trading ships* that sailed with
Hiram's fleet. Once every three years the ships returned,
loaded with gold, silver, ivory, apes, and peacocks.*

23So King Solomon became richer and wiser than any
other king on earth. 24People from every nation came to
consult him and to hear the wisdom God had given him.
25Year after year everyone who visited brought him gifts
of silver and gold, clothing, weapons, spices, horses, and
mules.

26Solomon built up a huge force of chariots and

9:18 An alternate reading in the Masoretic Text reads *Tadmor*. **9:19** Or *and charioteers*. **9:21** The Hebrew term used here refers to the complete consecration of things or people to the LORD, either by destroying them or by giving them as an offering. **9:26a** As in Greek version (see also 2 Kgs 14:22; 16:6); Hebrew reads *Eloth,* a variant spelling of Elath. **9:26b** Hebrew *sea of reeds*. **9:28** Hebrew *420 talents* [14 metric tons]. **10:1** Or *which was due to the name of the LORD*. The meaning of the Hebrew is uncertain. **10:6** Hebrew *your words*. **10:8** Greek and Syriac versions and Latin Vulgate read *your wives*. **10:10** Hebrew *120 talents* [4,000 kilograms]. **10:11** Hebrew *almug wood;* also in 10:12. **10:14** Hebrew *666 talents* [23 metric tons]. **10:16** Hebrew *600 shekels* [6.8 kilograms]. **10:17** Hebrew *3 minas* [1.8 kilograms]. **10:22a** Hebrew *fleet of ships of Tarshish*. **10:22b** Or *and baboons*.

horses.* He had 1,400 chariots and 12,000 horses. He
stationed some of them in the chariot cities and some
near him in Jerusalem. 27The king made silver as plentiful in Jerusalem as stone. And valuable cedar timber was
as common as the sycamore-fig trees that grow in the
foothills of Judah.* 28Solomon's horses were imported
from Egypt* and from Cilicia*; the king's traders acquired them from Cilicia at the standard price. 29At that
time chariots from Egypt could be purchased for
600 pieces of silver,* and horses for 150 pieces of silver.* They were then exported to the kings of the Hittites and the kings of Aram.

11 SOLOMON'S MANY WIVES

Now King Solomon loved many foreign women. Besides
Pharaoh's daughter, he married women from Moab, Ammon, Edom, Sidon, and from among the Hittites. 2The
Lord had clearly instructed the people of Israel, 'You
must not marry them, because they will turn your hearts
to their gods.' Yet Solomon insisted on loving them anyway. 3He had 700 wives of royal birth and 300 concubines. And in fact, they did turn his heart away from the
Lord.

4In Solomon's old age, they turned his heart to worship
other gods instead of being completely faithful to the
Lord his God, as his father, David, had been. 5Solomon
worshiped Ashtoreth, the goddess of the Sidonians, and
Molech,* the detestable god of the Ammonites. 6In this
way, Solomon did what was evil in the Lord's sight; he refused to follow the Lord completely, as his father, David,
had done.

KNOW IT AND APPLY IT 11:1-12

Although Solomon had clear instructions from God *not* to marry women from foreign nations (see Deut 7:3-4; 17:17), he chose to disregard God's commands. His wives led him away from God. This disobedience later led to the dividing of the kingdom. Unfortunately, disobedience is usually the catalyst for many problems today. God knows our human strengths and weaknesses, and his commands are always for our good. Knowing God's Word or even believing it isn't enough; we must follow it and apply it in all of our activities and decisions. ■

7On the Mount of Olives, east of Jerusalem,* he even
built a pagan shrine for Chemosh, the detestable god of
Moab, and another for Molech, the detestable god of the
Ammonites. 8Solomon built such shrines for all his foreign wives to use for burning incense and sacrificing to
their gods.

9The Lord was very angry with Solomon, for his heart
had turned away from the Lord, the God of Israel, who

DATING

Matt is so hot. I'm soooo thankful he's in my life. That's what Claire (who prefers to be called C. J.) says, even after over five months of going out with Matt. Here's the scoop on their relationship:

February—C. J. brought Matt to some youth group meetings and activities. He told her that her church friends were "OK." Maybe they could also hang out with his friends. (He never attended another youth group meeting.)

March—C. J. asked Matt to the spring youth retreat. He just smiled and said, "Hey, C. (he always calls her C.), that's not my thing. But if you decide to blow off that retreat, I can score us some tickets to the Amps's concert." (The Amps are only the hottest band ever.)

April—C. J. missed a couple more youth events in favor of partying with Matt and his friends.

May—C. J. slept with Matt for the first time. After all, they're "in love."

June—C. J. and her parents fought almost all month because she wouldn't break up with Matt.

July—C. J. has now gone 4½ months without reading her Bible. (She isn't even sure where it is.)

"Wait a minute!" you say. "Do Christian/non-Christian relationships always turn out bad? Haven't Christians fallen in love with non-Christians and led them to the Lord?" Yes. But that doesn't always happen. Healthy Christian/non-Christian dating situations are the exception—not the rule.

First Kings 11:1-13 shows how you can get burned through close relationships with those who don't share your values. Based on Solomon's experiences and 2 Corinthians 6:14, what advice would you have for your friends?

had appeared to him twice. 10He had warned Solomon
specifically about worshiping other gods, but Solomon
did not listen to the Lord's command. 11So now the Lord
said to him, "Since you have not kept my covenant and
have disobeyed my decrees, I will surely tear the kingdom
away from you and give it to one of your servants. 12But for
the sake of your father, David, I will not do this while you
are still alive. I will take the kingdom away from your son.
13And even so, I will not take away the entire kingdom; I
will let him be king of one tribe, for the sake of my servant
David and for the sake of Jerusalem, my chosen city."

SOLOMON'S ADVERSARIES

14Then the Lord raised up Hadad the Edomite, a member
of Edom's royal family, to be Solomon's adversary.
15Years before, David had defeated Edom. Joab, his army
commander, had stayed to bury some of the Israelite soldiers who had died in battle. While there, they killed

10:26 Or *charioteers;* also in 10:26b. **10:27** Hebrew *the Shephelah.* **10:28a** Possibly *Muzur,* a district near Cilicia; also in 10:29. **10:28b** Hebrew *Kue,* probably another name for Cilicia. **10:29a** Hebrew *600 shekels of silver,* about 15 pounds or 6.8 kilograms in weight. **10:29b** Hebrew *150 [shekels],* about 3.8 pounds or 1.7 kilograms in weight. **11:5** Hebrew *Milcom,* a variant spelling of Molech; also in 11:33. **11:7** Hebrew *On the mountain east of Jerusalem.*

every male in Edom. 16 Joab and the army of Israel had stayed there for six months, killing them.

17 But Hadad and a few of his father's royal officials escaped and headed for Egypt. (Hadad was just a boy at the time.) 18 They set out from Midian and went to Paran, where others joined them. Then they traveled to Egypt and went to Pharaoh, who gave them a home, food, and some land. 19 Pharaoh grew very fond of Hadad, and he gave him his wife's sister in marriage—the sister of Queen Tahpenes. 20 She bore him a son named Genubath. Tahpenes raised him* in Pharaoh's palace among Pharaoh's own sons.

21 When the news reached Hadad in Egypt that David and his commander Joab were both dead, he said to Pharaoh, "Let me return to my own country."

22 "Why?" Pharaoh asked him. "What do you lack here that makes you want to go home?"

"Nothing," he replied. "But even so, please let me return home."

23 God also raised up Rezon son of Eliada as Solomon's adversary. Rezon had fled from his master, King Hadadezer of Zobah, 24 and had become the leader of a gang of rebels. After David conquered Hadadezer, Rezon and his men fled to Damascus, where he became king. 25 Rezon was Israel's bitter adversary for the rest of Solomon's reign, and he made trouble, just as Hadad did. Rezon hated Israel intensely and continued to reign in Aram.

JEROBOAM REBELS AGAINST SOLOMON

26 Another rebel leader was Jeroboam son of Nebat, one of Solomon's own officials. He came from the town of Zeredah in Ephraim, and his mother was Zeruah, a widow.

27 This is the story behind his rebellion. Solomon was rebuilding the supporting terraces* and repairing the walls of the city of his father, David. 28 Jeroboam was a very capable young man, and when Solomon saw how industrious he was, he put him in charge of the labor force from the tribes of Ephraim and Manasseh, the descendants of Joseph.

29 One day as Jeroboam was leaving Jerusalem, the prophet Ahijah from Shiloh met him along the way. Ahijah was wearing a new cloak. The two of them were alone in a field, 30 and Ahijah took hold of the new cloak he was wearing and tore it into twelve pieces. 31 Then he said to Jeroboam, "Take ten of these pieces, for this is what the LORD, the God of Israel, says: 'I am about to tear the kingdom from the hand of Solomon, and I will give ten of the tribes to you! 32 But I will leave him one tribe for the sake of my servant David and for the sake of Jerusalem, which I have chosen out of all the tribes of Israel. 33 For Solomon has* abandoned me and worshiped Ashtoreth, the goddess of the Sidonians; Chemosh, the god of Moab; and Molech, the god of the Ammonites. He has not followed my ways and done what is pleasing in my sight. He has not obeyed my decrees and regulations as David his father did.

34 " 'But I will not take the entire kingdom from Solomon at this time. For the sake of my servant David, the one whom I chose and who obeyed my commands and decrees, I will keep Solomon as leader for the rest of his life. 35 But I will take the kingdom away from his son and give ten of the tribes to you. 36 His son will have one tribe so that the descendants of David my servant will continue to reign, shining like a lamp in Jerusalem, the city I have chosen to be the place for my name. 37 And I will place you on the throne of Israel, and you will rule over all that your heart desires. 38 If you listen to what I tell you and follow my ways and do whatever I consider to be right, and if you obey my decrees and commands, as my servant David did, then I will always be with you. I will establish an enduring dynasty for you as I did for David, and I will give Israel to you. 39 Because of Solomon's sin I will punish the descendants of David—though not forever.' "

40 Solomon tried to kill Jeroboam, but he fled to King Shishak of Egypt and stayed there until Solomon died.

SUMMARY OF SOLOMON'S REIGN

41 The rest of the events in Solomon's reign, including all his deeds and his wisdom, are recorded in *The Book of the Acts of Solomon.* 42 Solomon ruled in Jerusalem over all Israel for forty years. 43 When he died, he was buried in the City of David, named for his father. Then his son Rehoboam became the next king.

GOOD ADVICE 12:1-8

Rehoboam asked for advice, but didn't carefully evaluate that advice. If he had, he would have realized that the advice offered by the older men was wiser than that of his peers. Want some tips for evaluating advice? (1) Ask if it is realistic, workable, and consistent with the Bible. (2) Determine if the results of following the advice will be fair, make improvements, and give a positive solution or direction. (3) Seek counsel from those who are more experienced. Advice is helpful only if we evaluate it with God's standards in mind. ■

12

THE NORTHERN TRIBES REVOLT

Rehoboam went to Shechem, where all Israel had gathered to make him king. 2 When Jeroboam son of Nebat heard of this, he returned from Egypt,* for he had fled to Egypt to escape from King Solomon. 3 The leaders of Israel summoned him, and Jeroboam and the whole assembly of Israel went to speak with Rehoboam. 4 "Your father was a hard master," they said. "Lighten the harsh labor demands and heavy taxes that your father imposed on us. Then we will be your loyal subjects."

5 Rehoboam replied, "Give me three days to think this over. Then come back for my answer." So the people went away.

6 Then King Rehoboam discussed the matter with the older men who had counseled his father, Solomon.

11:20 As in Greek version; Hebrew reads *weaned him.* 11:27 Hebrew *the millo.* The meaning of the Hebrew is uncertain. 11:33 As in Greek, Syriac, and Latin Vulgate; Hebrew reads *For they have.* 12:2 As in Greek version and Latin Vulgate (see also 2 Chr 10:2); Hebrew reads *he lived in Egypt.*

"What is your advice?" he asked. "How should I answer these people?"

7The older counselors replied, "If you are willing to be a servant to these people today and give them a favorable answer, they will always be your loyal subjects."

8But Rehoboam rejected the advice of the older men and instead asked the opinion of the young men who had grown up with him and were now his advisers. 9"What is your advice?" he asked them. "How should I answer these people who want me to lighten the burdens imposed by my father?"

10The young men replied, "This is what you should tell those complainers who want a lighter burden: 'My little finger is thicker than my father's waist! 11Yes, my father laid heavy burdens on you, but I'm going to make them even heavier! My father beat you with whips, but I will beat you with scorpions!'"

12Three days later Jeroboam and all the people returned to hear Rehoboam's decision, just as the king had ordered. 13But Rehoboam spoke harshly to the people, for he rejected the advice of the older counselors 14and followed the counsel of his younger advisers. He told the people, "My father laid heavy burdens on you, but I'm going to make them even heavier! My father beat you with whips, but I will beat you with scorpions!"

15So the king paid no attention to the people. This turn of events was the will of the LORD, for it fulfilled the LORD's message to Jeroboam son of Nebat through the prophet Ahijah from Shiloh.

16When all Israel realized that the king had refused to listen to them, they responded,

"Down with the dynasty of David!
  We have no interest in the son of Jesse.
Back to your homes, O Israel!
  Look out for your own house, O David!"

So the people of Israel returned home. 17But Rehoboam continued to rule over the Israelites who lived in the towns of Judah.

18King Rehoboam sent Adoniram,* who was in charge of the labor force, to restore order, but the people of Israel stoned him to death. When this news reached King Rehoboam, he quickly jumped into his chariot and fled to Jerusalem. 19And to this day the northern tribes of Israel have refused to be ruled by a descendant of David.

20When the people of Israel learned of Jeroboam's return from Egypt, they called an assembly and made him king over all Israel. So only the tribe of Judah remained loyal to the family of David.

SHEMAIAH'S PROPHECY

21When Rehoboam arrived at Jerusalem, he mobilized the men of Judah and the tribe of Benjamin—180,000 select troops—to fight against the men of Israel and to restore the kingdom to himself.

22But God said to Shemaiah, the man of God, 23"Say to Rehoboam son of Solomon, king of Judah, and to all the people of Judah and Benjamin, and to the rest of the people, 24'This is what the LORD says: Do not fight against your relatives, the Israelites. Go back home, for what has happened is my doing!'" So they obeyed the message of the LORD and went home, as the LORD had commanded.

JEROBOAM MAKES GOLD CALVES

25Jeroboam then built up the city of Shechem in the hill country of Ephraim, and it became his capital. Later he went and built up the town of Peniel.*

26Jeroboam thought to himself, "Unless I am careful, the kingdom will return to the dynasty of David. 27When these people go to Jerusalem to offer sacrifices at the Temple of the LORD, they will again give their allegiance to King Rehoboam of Judah. They will kill me and make him their king instead."

28So on the advice of his counselors, the king made two gold calves. He said to the people,* "It is too much trouble for you to worship in Jerusalem. Look, Israel, these are the gods who brought you out of Egypt!"

DO WHAT'S RIGHT 12:28

Israelite males were required to travel to the Temple three times each year (see Deut 16:16). Jeroboam, however, set up his own worship centers and tried to convince the people of Israel to worship there. Those who obeyed Jeroboam disobeyed God. Likewise, some ideas, although practical, may lead you away from God. Are you willing to do what God wants no matter what the cost to you in time, energy, reputation, or resources? ■

29He placed these calf idols in Bethel and in Dan—at either end of his kingdom. 30But this became a great sin, for the people worshiped the idols, traveling as far north as Dan to worship the one there.

31Jeroboam also erected buildings at the pagan shrines and ordained priests from the common people—those who were not from the priestly tribe of Levi. 32And Jeroboam instituted a religious festival in Bethel, held on the fifteenth day of the eighth month,* in imitation of the annual Festival of Shelters in Judah. There at Bethel he himself offered sacrifices to the calves he had made, and he appointed priests for the pagan shrines he had made. 33So on the fifteenth day of the eighth month, a day that he himself had designated, Jeroboam offered sacrifices on the altar at Bethel. He instituted a religious festival for Israel, and he went up to the altar to burn incense.

13 A PROPHET DENOUNCES JEROBOAM

At the LORD's command, a man of God from Judah went to Bethel, arriving there just as Jeroboam was approaching the altar to burn incense. 2Then at the LORD's command,

12:18 As in some Greek manuscripts and Syriac version (see also 4:6; 5:14); Hebrew reads *Adoram*. **12:25** Hebrew *Penuel*, a variant spelling of Peniel. **12:28** Hebrew *to them*. **12:32** This day of the ancient Hebrew lunar calendar occurred in late October or early November, exactly one month after the annual Festival of Shelters in Judah (see Lev 23:34).

he shouted, "O altar, altar! This is what the LORD says: A child named Josiah will be born into the dynasty of David. On you he will sacrifice the priests from the pagan shrines who come here to burn incense, and human bones will be burned on you." 3That same day the man of God gave a sign to prove his message. He said, "The LORD has promised to give this sign: This altar will split apart, and its ashes will be poured out on the ground."

4When King Jeroboam heard the man of God speaking against the altar at Bethel, he pointed at him and shouted, "Seize that man!" But instantly the king's hand became paralyzed in that position, and he couldn't pull it back. 5At the same time a wide crack appeared in the altar, and the ashes poured out, just as the man of God had predicted in his message from the LORD.

6The king cried out to the man of God, "Please ask the LORD your God to restore my hand again!" So the man of God prayed to the LORD, and the king's hand was restored and he could move it again.

7Then the king said to the man of God, "Come to the palace with me and have something to eat, and I will give you a gift."

8But the man of God said to the king, "Even if you gave me half of everything you own, I would not go with you. I would not eat or drink anything in this place. 9For the LORD gave me this command: 'You must not eat or drink anything while you are there, and do not return to Judah by the same way you came.'" 10So he left Bethel and went home another way.

11As it happened, there was an old prophet living in Bethel, and his sons* came home and told him what the man of God had done in Bethel that day. They also told their father what the man had said to the king. 12The old prophet asked them, "Which way did he go?" So they showed their father* which road the man of God had taken. 13"Quick, saddle the donkey," the old man said. So they saddled the donkey for him, and he mounted it.

14Then he rode after the man of God and found him sitting under a great tree. The old prophet asked him, "Are you the man of God who came from Judah?"

"Yes, I am," he replied.

15Then he said to the man of God, "Come home with me and eat some food."

16"No, I cannot," he replied. "I am not allowed to eat or drink anything here in this place. 17For the LORD gave me this command: 'You must not eat or drink anything while you are there, and do not return to Judah by the same way you came.'"

18But the old prophet answered, "I am a prophet, too, just as you are. And an angel gave me this command from the LORD: 'Bring him home with you so he can have something to eat and drink.'" But the old man was lying to him. 19So they went back together, and the man of God ate and drank at the prophet's home.

20Then while they were sitting at the table, a command from the LORD came to the old prophet. 21He cried out to the man of God from Judah, "This is what the LORD says: You have defied the word of the LORD and have disobeyed the command the LORD your God gave you. 22You came back to this place and ate and drank where he told you not to eat or drink. Because of this, your body will not be buried in the grave of your ancestors."

23After the man of God had finished eating and drinking, the old prophet saddled his own donkey for him, 24and the man of God started off again. But as he was traveling along, a lion came out and killed him. His body lay there on the road, with the donkey and the lion standing beside it. 25People who passed by saw the body lying in the road and the lion standing beside it, and they went and reported it in Bethel, where the old prophet lived.

26When the prophet heard the report, he said, "It is the man of God who disobeyed the LORD's command. The LORD has fulfilled his word by causing the lion to attack and kill him."

27Then the prophet said to his sons, "Saddle a donkey for me." So they saddled a donkey, 28and he went out and found the body lying in the road. The donkey and lion were still standing there beside it, for the lion had not eaten the body nor attacked the donkey. 29So the prophet laid the body of the man of God on the donkey and took it back to the town to mourn over him and bury him. 30He laid the body in his own grave, crying out in grief, "Oh, my brother!"

31Afterward the prophet said to his sons, "When I die, bury me in the grave where the man of God is buried. Lay my bones beside his bones. 32For the message the LORD told him to proclaim against the altar in Bethel and against the pagan shrines in the towns of Samaria will certainly come true."

HARMFUL HEARSAY 13:1-32

This prophet had been given strict orders from God to avoid eating or drinking anything while on his mission (13:9). He died because he listened to a man who claimed to have a message from God. Which do you rely on: what your friends or others say or what you read in God's Word? Hearsay can be harmful! ■

33But even after this, Jeroboam did not turn from his evil ways. He continued to choose priests from the common people. He appointed anyone who wanted to become a priest for the pagan shrines. 34This became a great sin and resulted in the utter destruction of Jeroboam's dynasty from the face of the earth.

14 AHIJAH'S PROPHECY AGAINST JEROBOAM

At that time Jeroboam's son Abijah became very sick. 2So Jeroboam told his wife, "Disguise yourself so that no one will recognize you as my wife. Then go to the prophet Ahijah at Shiloh—the man who told me I would become king. 3Take him a gift of ten loaves of bread, some cakes, and a jar of honey, and ask him what will happen to the boy."

4So Jeroboam's wife went to Ahijah's home at Shiloh.

13:11 As in Greek version; Hebrew reads *son*. 13:12 As in Greek version; Hebrew reads *They had seen*.

He was an old man now and could no longer see. 5But the
Lord had told Ahijah, "Jeroboam's wife will come here,
pretending to be someone else. She will ask you about
her son, for he is very sick. Give her the answer I give you."

6So when Ahijah heard her footsteps at the door, he
called out, "Come in, wife of Jeroboam! Why are you pretending to be someone else?" Then he told her, "I have bad
news for you. 7Give your husband, Jeroboam, this message
from the Lord, the God of Israel: 'I promoted you from the
ranks of the common people and made you ruler over my
people Israel. 8I ripped the kingdom away from the family
of David and gave it to you. But you have not been like my
servant David, who obeyed my commands and followed
me with all his heart and always did whatever I wanted.
9You have done more evil than all who lived before you.
You have made other gods for yourself and have made me
furious with your gold calves. And since you have turned
your back on me, 10I will bring disaster on your dynasty
and will destroy every one of your male descendants, slave
and free alike, anywhere in Israel. I will burn up your royal
dynasty as one burns up trash until it is all gone. 11The
members of Jeroboam's family who die in the city will be
eaten by dogs, and those who die in the field will be eaten
by vultures. I, the Lord, have spoken.'"

12Then Ahijah said to Jeroboam's wife, "Go on home,
and when you enter the city, the child will die. 13All Israel
will mourn for him and bury him. He is the only member
of your family who will have a proper burial, for this child
is the only good thing that the Lord, the God of Israel,
sees in the entire family of Jeroboam.

14"In addition, the Lord will raise up a king over Israel
who will destroy the family of Jeroboam. This will happen
today, even now! 15Then the Lord will shake Israel like a
reed whipped about in a stream. He will uproot the people
of Israel from this good land that he gave their ancestors
and will scatter them beyond the Euphrates River,* for
they have angered the Lord with the Asherah poles they
have set up for worship. 16He will abandon Israel because
Jeroboam sinned and made Israel sin along with him."

17So Jeroboam's wife returned to Tirzah, and the child
died just as she walked through the door of her home.
18And all Israel buried him and mourned for him, as the
Lord had promised through the prophet Ahijah.

19The rest of the events in Jeroboam's reign, including
all his wars and how he ruled, are recorded in *The Book of
the History of the Kings of Israel*. 20Jeroboam reigned in
Israel twenty-two years. When Jeroboam died, his son
Nadab became the next king.

REHOBOAM RULES IN JUDAH

21Meanwhile, Rehoboam son of Solomon was king in Judah. He was forty-one years old when he became king,
and he reigned seventeen years in Jerusalem, the city the
Lord had chosen from among all the tribes of Israel as
the place to honor his name. Rehoboam's mother was
Naamah, an Ammonite woman.

22During Rehoboam's reign, the people of Judah did
what was evil in the Lord's sight, provoking his anger
with their sin, for it was even worse than that of their
ancestors. 23For they also built for themselves pagan
shrines and set up sacred pillars and Asherah poles on
every high hill and under every green tree. 24There were
even male and female shrine prostitutes throughout the
land. The people imitated the detestable practices of the
pagan nations the Lord had driven from the land ahead
of the Israelites.

25In the fifth year of King Rehoboam's reign, King Shishak of Egypt came up and attacked Jerusalem. 26He ransacked the treasuries of the Lord's Temple and the royal
palace; he stole everything, including all the gold shields
Solomon had made. 27King Rehoboam later replaced
them with bronze shields as substitutes, and he entrusted them to the care of the commanders of the guard
who protected the entrance to the royal palace.
28Whenever the king went to the Temple of the Lord, the
guards would also take the shields and then return them
to the guardroom.

ROBBED 14:25-26

When the people of Israel became spiritually corrupt (14:24), they lost everything a short time later. Just five years after Solomon died, foreign invaders raided the Temple and the palace. When we pay more attention to the "idols" of our lives (goals, money, relationships, status, possessions), we might find ourselves in the same boat as the people of Israel. ■

29The rest of the events in Rehoboam's reign and
everything he did are recorded in *The Book of the History
of the Kings of Judah*. 30There was constant war between
Rehoboam and Jeroboam. 31When Rehoboam died, he
was buried among his ancestors in the City of David. His
mother was Naamah, an Ammonite woman. Then his son
Abijam* became the next king.

15

ABIJAM RULES IN JUDAH

Abijam* began to rule over Judah in the eighteenth year of
Jeroboam's reign in Israel. 2He reigned in Jerusalem three
years. His mother was Maacah, the daughter of Absalom.*

3He committed the same sins as his father before him,
and he was not faithful to the Lord his God, as his ancestor David had been. 4But for David's sake, the Lord his
God allowed his descendants to continue ruling, shining
like a lamp, and he gave Abijam a son to rule after him in
Jerusalem. 5For David had done what was pleasing in the
Lord's sight and had obeyed the Lord's commands
throughout his life, except in the affair concerning Uriah
the Hittite.

6There was war between Abijam and Jeroboam*
throughout Abijam's reign. 7The rest of the events in
Abijam's reign and everything he did are recorded in

14:15 Hebrew *the river*. **14:31** Also known as *Abijah*. **15:1** Also known as *Abijah*. **15:2** Hebrew *Abishalom* (also in 15:10), a variant spelling of Absalom; compare 2 Chr 11:20. **15:6** As in a few Hebrew and Greek manuscripts; most Hebrew manuscripts read *between Rehoboam and Jeroboam*.

The Book of the History of the Kings of Judah. There was
constant war between Abijam and Jeroboam. 8When
Abijam died, he was buried in the City of David. Then his
son Asa became the next king.

ASA RULES IN JUDAH

9Asa began to rule over Judah in the twentieth year of Jeroboam's reign in Israel. 10He reigned in Jerusalem forty-
one years. His grandmother* was Maacah, the daughter
of Absalom.
11Asa did what was pleasing in the LORD's sight, as his
ancestor David had done. 12He banished the male and female shrine prostitutes from the land and got rid of all
the idols* his ancestors had made. 13He even deposed his
grandmother Maacah from her position as queen
mother because she had made an obscene Asherah pole.
He cut down her obscene pole and burned it in the Kidron Valley. 14Although the pagan shrines were not removed, Asa's heart remained completely faithful to the
LORD throughout his life. 15He brought into the Temple
of the LORD the silver and gold and the various items that
he and his father had dedicated.
16There was constant war between King Asa of Judah
and King Baasha of Israel. 17King Baasha of Israel invaded
Judah and fortified Ramah in order to prevent anyone
from entering or leaving King Asa's territory in Judah.
18Asa responded by removing all the silver and gold
that was left in the treasuries of the Temple of the LORD
and the royal palace. He sent it with some of his officials
to Ben-hadad son of Tabrimmon, son of Hezion, the king
of Aram, who was ruling in Damascus, along with this
message:

> 19"Let there be a treaty* between you and me like the
> one between your father and my father. See, I am
> sending you a gift of silver and gold. Break your
> treaty with King Baasha of Israel so that he will leave
> me alone."

20Ben-hadad agreed to King Asa's request and sent
the commanders of his army to attack the towns of Israel. They conquered the towns of Ijon, Dan, Abel-
beth-maacah, and all Kinnereth, and all the land of
Naphtali. 21As soon as Baasha of Israel heard what was
happening, he abandoned his project of fortifying Ramah and withdrew to Tirzah. 22Then King Asa sent an
order throughout Judah, requiring that everyone, without exception, help to carry away the building stones
and timbers that Baasha had been using to fortify Ramah. Asa used these materials to fortify the town of
Geba in Benjamin and the town of Mizpah.
23The rest of the events in Asa's reign—the extent of
his power, everything he did, and the names of the cities
he built—are recorded in *The Book of the History of the
Kings of Judah*. In his old age his feet became diseased.
24When Asa died, he was buried with his ancestors in the
City of David.
Then Jehoshaphat, Asa's son, became the next king.

NADAB RULES IN ISRAEL

25Nadab son of Jeroboam began to rule over Israel in the
second year of King Asa's reign in Judah. He reigned in
Israel two years. 26But he did what was evil in the LORD's
sight and followed the example of his father, continuing the sins that Jeroboam had led Israel to commit.
27Then Baasha son of Ahijah, from the tribe of Issachar, plotted against Nadab and assassinated him while
he and the Israelite army were laying siege to the Philistine town of Gibbethon. 28Baasha killed Nadab in the
third year of King Asa's reign in Judah, and he became the
next king of Israel.
29He immediately slaughtered all the descendants of
King Jeroboam, so that not one of the royal family was
left, just as the LORD had promised concerning Jeroboam
by the prophet Ahijah from Shiloh. 30This was done because Jeroboam had provoked the anger of the LORD, the
God of Israel, by the sins he had committed and the sins
he had led Israel to commit.
31The rest of the events in Nadab's reign and everything he did are recorded in *The Book of the History of
the Kings of Israel*.

BAASHA RULES IN ISRAEL

32There was constant war between King Asa of Judah and
King Baasha of Israel. 33Baasha son of Ahijah began to
rule over all Israel in the third year of King Asa's reign in
Judah. Baasha reigned in Tirzah twenty-four years. 34But
he did what was evil in the LORD's sight and followed the
example of Jeroboam, continuing the sins that Jeroboam
had led Israel to commit.

LEARNING FROM MISTAKES 16:1-7

Baasha did not learn from his ancestors' mistakes. So, God promised to destroy Baasha's family just as he destroyed Jeroboam's family when they sinned. What have you learned from your past or through the experiences of others? How will you avoid repeating their mistakes or mistakes you made in the past? ■

16

This message from the LORD was delivered to
King Baasha by the prophet Jehu son of Hanani: 2"I lifted
you out of the dust to make you ruler of my people Israel,
but you have followed the evil example of Jeroboam. You
have provoked my anger by causing my people Israel to
sin. 3So now I will destroy you and your family, just as I
destroyed the descendants of Jeroboam son of Nebat.
4The members of Baasha's family who die in the city will
be eaten by dogs, and those who die in the field will be
eaten by vultures."
5The rest of the events in Baasha's reign and the extent
of his power are recorded in *The Book of the History of
the Kings of Israel*. 6When Baasha died, he was buried in
Tirzah. Then his son Elah became the next king.

15:10 Or *The queen mother;* Hebrew reads *His mother* (also in 15:13); compare 15:2. 15:12 The Hebrew term (literally *round things*) probably alludes to dung. 15:19 As in Greek version; Hebrew reads *There is a treaty*.

7 The message from the LORD against Baasha and his
family came through the prophet Jehu son of Hanani. It
was delivered because Baasha had done what was evil in
the LORD's sight (just as the family of Jeroboam had
done), and also because Baasha had destroyed the family of Jeroboam. The LORD's anger was provoked by Baasha's sins.

ELAH RULES IN ISRAEL

8 Elah son of Baasha began to rule over Israel in the
twenty-sixth year of King Asa's reign in Judah. He
reigned in the city of Tirzah for two years.
9 Then Zimri, who commanded half of the royal chariots, made plans to kill him. One day in Tirzah, Elah was
getting drunk at the home of Arza, the supervisor of the
palace. 10 Zimri walked in and struck him down and killed
him. This happened in the twenty-seventh year of King
Asa's reign in Judah. Then Zimri became the next king.
11 Zimri immediately killed the entire royal family of
Baasha, leaving him not even a single male child. He even
destroyed distant relatives and friends. 12 So Zimri destroyed the dynasty of Baasha as the LORD had promised
through the prophet Jehu. 13 This happened because of all
the sins Baasha and his son Elah had committed, and because of the sins they led Israel to commit. They provoked the anger of the LORD, the God of Israel, with their
worthless idols.
14 The rest of the events in Elah's reign and everything
he did are recorded in *The Book of the History of the
Kings of Israel.*

ZIMRI RULES IN ISRAEL

15 Zimri began to rule over Israel in the twenty-seventh
year of King Asa's reign in Judah, but his reign in Tirzah
lasted only seven days. The army of Israel was then attacking the Philistine town of Gibbethon. 16 When they
heard that Zimri had committed treason and had assassinated the king, that very day they chose Omri, commander of the army, as the new king of Israel. 17 So Omri
led the entire army of Israel up from Gibbethon to attack
Tirzah, Israel's capital. 18 When Zimri saw that the city
had been taken, he went into the citadel of the palace and
burned it down over himself and died in the flames. 19 For
he, too, had done what was evil in the LORD's sight. He followed the example of Jeroboam in all the sins he had
committed and led Israel to commit.
20 The rest of the events in Zimri's reign and his conspiracy are recorded in *The Book of the History of the
Kings of Israel.*

OMRI RULES IN ISRAEL

21 But now the people of Israel were split into two factions. Half the people tried to make Tibni son of Ginath
their king, while the other half supported Omri. 22 But
Omri's supporters defeated the supporters of Tibni. So
Tibni was killed, and Omri became the next king.
23 Omri began to rule over Israel in the thirty-first year
of King Asa's reign in Judah. He reigned twelve years in
all, six of them in Tirzah. 24 Then Omri bought the hill
now known as Samaria from its owner, Shemer, for
150 pounds of silver.* He built a city on it and called the
city Samaria in honor of Shemer.

16:24 Hebrew *for 2 talents* [68 kilograms] *of silver.*

UPS:
- Eighth king of Israel
- Capable leader and military strategist

DOWNS:
- Considered the most evil of Israel's kings
- Married Jezebel, a woman from an enemy nation, and allowed her to promote Baal worship
- Desired land that belonged to another and allowed its owner to be killed

STATS:
- Where: Northern kingdom of Israel
- Occupation: King
- Relatives: Jezebel (wife); Omri (father); Ahaziah, Jehoram (sons)
- Contemporaries: Elijah, Naboth, Jehu, Ben-hadad, Jehoshaphat

BOTTOM LINE:
Selfishness, left unchecked, can lead to great evil.
Wise counsel is invaluable.

Ahab's story is told in 1 Kings 16:28–22:40. He also is mentioned in 2 Chron 18:1-34 and Mic 6:16.

AHAB

AHAB When someone gives you advice, what do you do? Do you consider it or ignore it? Ahab consistently chose the latter.

The kings of Israel and Judah, both good and evil, had prophets sent by God to advise, confront, and aid them. Elijah had been sent to Ahab with bad news: No rain would fall in Israel. Ahab refused to acknowledge that his disobedience to God had earned this consequence. Instead, he blamed Elijah for bringing the prophecies of judgment, rather than taking Elijah's advice and changing his ways.

Ahab was trapped by his own choices, and he was unwilling to take the right action. He took his wife's advice, listened only to the "prophets" who gave good news, and surrounded himself with people who encouraged him to do whatever he wanted. The wrong advice eventually led to his death.

Many of us, if we're honest, will admit to wanting someone to confirm our plans, rather than advising us to change them. But our plans aren't always right. That's why God encourages us to get advice from wise counselors. Who is a wise counselor? Someone who follows God's rules.

ULTIMATE ISSUES

THE PROPHETS

They step off the page like something out of a science fiction novel or a fantasy—wild individuals wearing strange clothes, seeing mind-boggling visions, hearing God's voice, and preaching a bone-chilling message: Repent or you will pay. Who were they? They were the prophets—the men and women God sent to the nation of Israel (and occasionally to other nations) as his spokespeople.

Elijah was chosen as a prophet during a rough time in Israel's history—during Ahab's term as king. Others, like Isaiah and Daniel, were powerful men in the life of the nation. They held important government positions or served as the king's advisers. Amos, on the other hand, was a shepherd and gardener.

The prophets were all unique and preached to the nation of Israel under a variety of circumstances. So, what did they have in common?

First, they were God's appointed speakers. While the priests spoke to God for the people, the prophets spoke to the people for God. Often they called on the people to stop doing wrong and return to God. Time after time their messages were ignored, and Israel suffered as a result.

Second, the prophets preached two kinds of messages: (1) a warning of the need to repent or (2) a message about future events.

Many people claimed to be prophets, and sometimes there was confusion over who to believe when the "prophets" disagreed. There were, however, tests used to determine who was or wasn't a true prophet.

- True prophets spoke whenever and whatever God told them to. They didn't dream up prophecies and oracles and then say they came from God. In other religions, pagan prophets constantly tried to manipulate their gods into doing what they wanted. That's what the prophets of Baal tried to do (18:26-29).
- Any prediction given about the future had to come true or the prophet was considered false. The Old Testament is filled with amazing predictions of events, sometimes many centuries into the future. An incredible number of them, especially those concerning Israel and the coming Messiah, have come true.

25But Omri did what was evil in the LORD's sight, even
more than any of the kings before him. 26He followed the
example of Jeroboam son of Nebat in all the sins he had
committed and led Israel to commit. The people provoked the anger of the LORD, the God of Israel, with their
worthless idols.
27The rest of the events in Omri's reign, the extent of
his power, and everything he did are recorded in *The
Book of the History of the Kings of Israel*. 28When Omri
died, he was buried in Samaria. Then his son Ahab became the next king.

AHAB RULES IN ISRAEL

29Ahab son of Omri began to rule over Israel in the thirty-
eighth year of King Asa's reign in Judah. He reigned in Samaria twenty-two years. 30But Ahab son of Omri did what
was evil in the LORD's sight, even more than any of the kings
before him. 31And as though it were not enough to follow
the example of Jeroboam, he married Jezebel, the daughter
of King Ethbaal of the Sidonians, and he began to bow
down in worship of Baal. 32First Ahab built a temple and an
altar for Baal in Samaria. 33Then he set up an Asherah pole.
He did more to provoke the anger of the LORD, the God of
Israel, than any of the other kings of Israel before him.
34It was during his reign that Hiel, a man from Bethel,
rebuilt Jericho. When he laid its foundations, it cost him
the life of his oldest son, Abiram. And when he completed it and set up its gates, it cost him the life of his
youngest son, Segub.* This all happened according to the
message from the LORD concerning Jericho spoken by
Joshua son of Nun.

17

ELIJAH FED BY RAVENS

Now Elijah, who was from Tishbe in Gilead, told King
Ahab, "As surely as the LORD, the God of Israel, lives—the

16:34 An ancient Hebrew scribal tradition reads *He killed his oldest son when he laid its foundations, and he killed his youngest son when he set up its gates.*

God I serve—there will be no dew or rain during the next
few years until I give the word!"
2Then the LORD said to Elijah, 3"Go to the east and hide
by Kerith Brook, near where it enters the Jordan River.
4Drink from the brook and eat what the ravens bring you,
for I have commanded them to bring you food."
5So Elijah did as the LORD told him and camped beside
Kerith Brook, east of the Jordan. 6The ravens brought
him bread and meat each morning and evening, and he
drank from the brook. 7But after a while the brook dried
up, for there was no rainfall anywhere in the land.

GOD PROVIDES 17:1-15

In a nation that was required by law to care for its prophets, it is ironic that God turned to ravens (unclean birds—see Lev 11:13-15) and a widow (a foreigner from Jezebel's home territory) to care for Elijah. God sometimes provides help where we least expect it and in ways that go beyond our narrow definitions or expectations. How has God provided for your needs lately? ■

THE WIDOW AT ZAREPHATH
8Then the LORD said to Elijah, 9"Go and live in the village
of Zarephath, near the city of Sidon. I have instructed a
widow there to feed you."
10So he went to Zarephath. As he arrived at the gates of
the village, he saw a widow gathering sticks, and he asked
her, "Would you please bring me a little water in a cup?"
11As she was going to get it, he called to her, "Bring me a
bite of bread, too."
12But she said, "I swear by the LORD your God that I
don't have a single piece of bread in the house. And I have
only a handful of flour left in the jar and a little cooking
oil in the bottom of the jug. I was just gathering a few
sticks to cook this last meal, and then my son and I will
die."
13But Elijah said to her, "Don't be afraid! Go ahead and
do just what you've said, but make a little bread for me
first. Then use what's left to prepare a meal for yourself
and your son. 14For this is what the LORD, the God of Israel, says: There will always be flour and olive oil left in your
containers until the time when the LORD sends rain and
the crops grow again!"
15So she did as Elijah said, and she and Elijah and her
son continued to eat for many days. 16There was always
enough flour and olive oil left in the containers, just as
the LORD had promised through Elijah.
17Some time later the woman's son became sick. He
grew worse and worse, and finally he died. 18Then she
said to Elijah, "O man of God, what have you done to me?
Have you come here to point out my sins and kill my
son?"
19But Elijah replied, "Give me your son." And he took
the child's body from her arms, carried him up the stairs
to the room where he was staying, and laid the body on
his bed. 20Then Elijah cried out to the LORD, "O LORD my

ELIJAH

Are you a comforter or a confronter? God made Elijah a confronter. He had to speak God's words to a king who often rejected his message. Elijah experienced depression and loneliness even though he worked for God.

In Elijah's life we really see the thrills of victory and the agonies of defeat. One huge victory was the defeat of the prophets of Baal. But the agony of defeat came through Elijah's depressed response to Jezebel's death threat. God used a gentle whisper to remind Elijah that he was still in control.

Elijah also had to learn that he wasn't alone. God reminded Elijah there were 7,000 others in Israel who were faithful.

Like Elijah, do you fear that you're the only one still faithful to God? God always has more plans and people than we know about.

UPS:
- The most famous and dramatic of Israel's prophets
- Predicted the beginning and end of a three-year drought
- Used by God to restore a dead child to his mother
- God's representative in a showdown with the priests of Baal and Asherah
- Appeared with Moses and Jesus during Jesus' transfiguration

DOWNS:
- Chose to work alone and paid for it through isolation
- Fled in fear from Jezebel when she threatened his life

STATS:
- Where: Gilead
- Occupation: Prophet
- Contemporaries: Ahab, Jezebel, Ahaziah, Obadiah, Jehu, Hazael

BOTTOM LINE:
We are never as alone as we may feel; God is always there.
God speaks more frequently in persistent whispers than in shouts.

Elijah's story is told in 1 Kings 17:1–2 Kings 2:11. He is also mentioned in 2 Chron 21:12-15; Mal 4:5-6; Matt 11:14; 16:14; 17:3-13; 27:47-49; Luke 1:17; 4:25-26; John 1:21-24; Rom 11:2-4; James 5:17-18.

Prophets—False and True

The false prophets were an obstacle to bringing God's word to the people. They would bring "messages" that contradicted the words of the true prophets. They gave messages that appealed to the people's sinful nature and comforted their fears. False prophets told people what they wanted to hear; true prophets told God's truth.

FALSE PROPHETS	TRUE PROPHETS
Worked for political purposes to benefit themselves	Worked for spiritual purposes to serve God and the people
Held positions of great wealth	Owned little or nothing
Gave false messages	Spoke only true messages
Spoke only what the people wanted to hear	Spoke only what God told them to say—no matter how unpopular

God, why have you brought tragedy to this widow who
has opened her home to me, causing her son to die?"
[21]And he stretched himself out over the child three
times and cried out to the LORD, "O LORD my God, please
let this child's life return to him." [22]The LORD heard Elijah's prayer, and the life of the child returned, and he revived! [23]Then Elijah brought him down from the upper
room and gave him to his mother. "Look!" he said. "Your
son is alive!"
[24]Then the woman told Elijah, "Now I know for sure
that you are a man of God, and that the LORD truly speaks
through you."

18 THE CONTEST ON MOUNT CARMEL

Later on, in the third year of the drought, the LORD said to
Elijah, "Go and present yourself to King Ahab. Tell him
that I will soon send rain!" [2]So Elijah went to appear before Ahab.

Meanwhile, the famine had become very severe in Samaria. [3]So Ahab summoned Obadiah, who was in charge of
the palace. (Obadiah was a devoted follower of the LORD.
[4]Once when Jezebel had tried to kill all the LORD's prophets, Obadiah had hidden 100 of them in two caves. He put
fifty prophets in each cave and supplied them with food
and water.) [5]Ahab said to Obadiah, "We must check every
spring and valley in the land to see if we can find enough
grass to save at least some of my horses and mules." [6]So
they divided the land between them. Ahab went one way by
himself, and Obadiah went another way by himself.
[7]As Obadiah was walking along, he suddenly saw Elijah
coming toward him. Obadiah recognized him at once
and bowed low to the ground before him. "Is it really you,
my lord Elijah?" he asked.
[8]"Yes, it is," Elijah replied. "Now go and tell your master, 'Elijah is here.'"
[9]"Oh, sir," Obadiah protested, "what harm have I done to
you that you are sending me to my death at the hands of
Ahab? [10]For I swear by the LORD your God that the king has
searched every nation and kingdom on earth from end to
end to find you. And each time he was told, 'Elijah isn't
here,' King Ahab forced the king of that nation to swear to
the truth of his claim. [11]And now you say, 'Go and tell your
master, "Elijah is here."' [12]But as soon as I leave you, the
Spirit of the LORD will carry you away to who knows where.
When Ahab comes and cannot find you, he will kill me. Yet
I have been a true servant of the LORD all my life. [13]Has no
one told you, my lord, about the time when Jezebel was trying to kill the LORD's prophets? I hid 100 of them in two
caves and supplied them with food and water. [14]And now
you say, 'Go and tell your master, "Elijah is here."' Sir, if I do
that, Ahab will certainly kill me."
[15]But Elijah said, "I swear by the LORD Almighty, in
whose presence I stand, that I will present myself to Ahab
this very day."
[16]So Obadiah went to tell Ahab that Elijah had come,
and Ahab went out to meet Elijah. [17]When Ahab saw him,
he exclaimed, "So, is it really you, you troublemaker of
Israel?"
[18]"I have made no trouble for Israel," Elijah replied.
"You and your family are the troublemakers, for you have
refused to obey the commands of the LORD and have
worshiped the images of Baal instead. [19]Now summon all
Israel to join me at Mount Carmel, along with the
450 prophets of Baal and the 400 prophets of Asherah
who are supported by Jezebel.*"
[20]So Ahab summoned all the people of Israel and the
prophets to Mount Carmel. [21]Then Elijah stood in front of
them and said, "How much longer will you waver, hobbling

18:19 Hebrew *who eat at Jezebel's table.*

between two opinions? If the LORD is God, follow him! But if Baal is God, then follow him!" But the people were completely silent.

MAKE A CHOICE 18:21

Elijah challenged the people of Israel to take a stand—to follow God or Baal. Why did so many people waver between the two choices? Perhaps some were not sure what to believe. Many, however, probably went along with the crowd and worshiped a god they thought they could see—a god represented by a statue. How like many of us today! We might worship a god we can see—a god of money, status, or possessions. But God offers us the same choice offered to the people of Israel: Will we worship him or an idol? What's your choice? ■

22Then Elijah said to them, "I am the only prophet of the LORD who is left, but Baal has 450 prophets. 23Now bring two bulls. The prophets of Baal may choose whichever one they wish and cut it into pieces and lay it on the wood of their altar, but without setting fire to it. I will prepare the other bull and lay it on the wood on the altar, but not set fire to it. 24Then call on the name of your god, and I will call on the name of the LORD. The god who answers by setting fire to the wood is the true God!" And all the people agreed.

25Then Elijah said to the prophets of Baal, "You go first, for there are many of you. Choose one of the bulls, and prepare it and call on the name of your god. But do not set fire to the wood."

26So they prepared one of the bulls and placed it on the altar. Then they called on the name of Baal from morning until noontime, shouting, "O Baal, answer us!" But there was no reply of any kind. Then they danced, hobbling around the altar they had made.

27About noontime Elijah began mocking them. "You'll have to shout louder," he scoffed, "for surely he is a god! Perhaps he is daydreaming, or is relieving himself.* Or maybe he is away on a trip, or is asleep and needs to be wakened!"

28So they shouted louder, and following their normal custom, they cut themselves with knives and swords until the blood gushed out. 29They raved all afternoon until the time of the evening sacrifice, but still there was no sound, no reply, no response.

30Then Elijah called to the people, "Come over here!" They all crowded around him as he repaired the altar of the LORD that had been torn down. 31He took twelve stones, one to represent each of the tribes of Israel,* 32and he used the stones to rebuild the altar in the name of the LORD. Then he dug a trench around the altar large enough to hold about three gallons.* 33He piled wood on the altar, cut the bull into pieces, and laid the pieces on the wood.

Then he said, "Fill four large jars with water, and pour the water over the offering and the wood."

34After they had done this, he said, "Do the same thing again!" And when they were finished, he said, "Now do it a third time!" So they did as he said, 35and the water ran around the altar and even filled the trench.

36At the usual time for offering the evening sacrifice, Elijah the prophet walked up to the altar and prayed, "O LORD, God of Abraham, Isaac, and Jacob,* prove today that you are God in Israel and that I am your servant. Prove that I have done all this at your command. 37O LORD, answer me! Answer me so these people will know that you, O LORD, are God and that you have brought them back to yourself."

38Immediately the fire of the LORD flashed down from heaven and burned up the young bull, the wood, the stones, and the dust. It even licked up all the water in the trench! 39And when all the people saw it, they fell face down on the ground and cried out, "The LORD—he is God! Yes, the LORD is God!"

GOD'S HELP 18:36-38

God answered Elijah's request by sending fire from heaven. He also promises to help us accomplish what he commands us to do. The proof may not be as dramatic in our life as in Elijah's, but God will make resources available to us in creative ways to accomplish his purposes. He might give us the wisdom to live a life that's pleasing to him, the courage to take a stand for truth, or the means to provide help for someone in need. Like Elijah, we can have faith that, whatever God commands us to do, he will provide what we need to carry it through. ■

40Then Elijah commanded, "Seize all the prophets of Baal. Don't let a single one escape!" So the people seized them all, and Elijah took them down to the Kishon Valley and killed them there.

ELIJAH PRAYS FOR RAIN

41Then Elijah said to Ahab, "Go get something to eat and drink, for I hear a mighty rainstorm coming!"

42So Ahab went to eat and drink. But Elijah climbed to the top of Mount Carmel and bowed low to the ground and prayed with his face between his knees.

43Then he said to his servant, "Go and look out toward the sea."

The servant went and looked, then returned to Elijah and said, "I didn't see anything."

Seven times Elijah told him to go and look. 44Finally the seventh time, his servant told him, "I saw a little cloud about the size of a man's hand rising from the sea."

Then Elijah shouted, "Hurry to Ahab and tell him, 'Climb into your chariot and go back home. If you don't hurry, the rain will stop you!'"

18:27 Or *is busy somewhere else, or is engaged in business.* 18:31 Hebrew *each of the tribes of the sons of Jacob to whom the LORD had said, "Your name will be Israel."* 18:32 Hebrew *2 seahs* [12 liters] *of seed.* 18:36 Hebrew *and Israel.* The names "Jacob" and "Israel" are often interchanged throughout the Old Testament, referring sometimes to the individual patriarch and sometimes to the nation.

[45]And soon the sky was black with clouds. A heavy wind brought a terrific rainstorm, and Ahab left quickly for Jezreel. [46]Then the LORD gave special strength to Elijah. He tucked his cloak into his belt* and ran ahead of Ahab's chariot all the way to the entrance of Jezreel.

19

ELIJAH FLEES TO SINAI

When Ahab got home, he told Jezebel everything Elijah had done, including the way he had killed all the prophets of Baal. [2]So Jezebel sent this message to Elijah: "May the gods strike me and even kill me if by this time tomorrow I have not killed you just as you killed them."

[3]Elijah was afraid and fled for his life. He went to Beersheba, a town in Judah, and he left his servant there. [4]Then he went on alone into the wilderness, traveling all day. He sat down under a solitary broom tree and prayed that he might die. "I have had enough, LORD," he said. "Take my life, for I am no better than my ancestors who have already died."

> **FROM A HIGH TO A LOW 19:3-4**
>
> **Elijah experienced the depths of fatigue and discouragement just after his two great spiritual victories: the defeat of the prophets of Baal and the answered prayer for rain. But God took care of him in practical ways. Often discouragement sets in after great spiritual experiences, especially those requiring physical effort or producing emotional excitement. When the blues hit after a great spiritual experience, remember that God's purpose for your life is not over yet. ■**

[5]Then he lay down and slept under the broom tree. But as he was sleeping, an angel touched him and told him, "Get up and eat!" [6]He looked around and there beside his head was some bread baked on hot stones and a jar of water! So he ate and drank and lay down again.

[7]Then the angel of the LORD came again and touched him and said, "Get up and eat some more, or the journey ahead will be too much for you."

[8]So he got up and ate and drank, and the food gave him enough strength to travel forty days and forty nights to Mount Sinai,* the mountain of God. [9]There he came to a cave, where he spent the night.

THE LORD SPEAKS TO ELIJAH

But the LORD said to him, "What are you doing here, Elijah?"

[10]Elijah replied, "I have zealously served the LORD God Almighty. But the people of Israel have broken their covenant with you, torn down your altars, and killed every one of your prophets. I am the only one left, and now they are trying to kill me, too."

[11]"Go out and stand before me on the mountain," the LORD told him. And as Elijah stood there, the LORD passed by, and a mighty windstorm hit the mountain. It was such a terrible blast that the rocks were torn loose, but the LORD was not in the wind. After the wind there was an earthquake, but the LORD was not in the earthquake. [12]And after the earthquake there was a fire, but the LORD was not in the fire. And after the fire there was the sound of a gentle whisper. [13]When Elijah heard it, he wrapped his face in his cloak and went out and stood at the entrance of the cave.

And a voice said, "What are you doing here, Elijah?"

> **WHISPERS 19:11-13**
>
> **Elijah knew that the gentle whisper was God's voice. He realized that God didn't reveal himself only in powerful, miraculous ways. Many of us look for God only at retreats, conferences, or through the powerful messages of leaders). Yet he often gently whispers in the quietness of a humbled heart. Are you listening for God? You might need to take a step back from the noise and activity of your busy life. His guidance may come when you least expect it. ■**

[14]He replied again, "I have zealously served the LORD God Almighty. But the people of Israel have broken their covenant with you, torn down your altars, and killed every one of your prophets. I am the only one left, and now they are trying to kill me, too."

[15]Then the LORD told him, "Go back the same way you came, and travel to the wilderness of Damascus. When you arrive there, anoint Hazael to be king of Aram. [16]Then anoint Jehu son of Nimshi to be king of Israel, and anoint Elisha son of Shaphat from the town of Abel-meholah to replace you as my prophet. [17]Anyone who escapes from Hazael will be killed by Jehu, and those who escape Jehu will be killed by Elisha! [18]Yet I will preserve 7,000 others in Israel who have never bowed down to Baal or kissed him!"

THE CALL OF ELISHA

[19]So Elijah went and found Elisha son of Shaphat plowing a field. There were twelve teams of oxen in the field, and Elisha was plowing with the twelfth team. Elijah went over to him and threw his cloak across his shoulders and then walked away. [20]Elisha left the oxen standing there, ran after Elijah, and said to him, "First let me go and kiss my father and mother good-bye, and then I will go with you!"

Elijah replied, "Go on back, but think about what I have done to you."

[21]So Elisha returned to his oxen and slaughtered them. He used the wood from the plow to build a fire to roast their flesh. He passed around the meat to the townspeople, and they all ate. Then he went with Elijah as his assistant.

20

BEN-HADAD ATTACKS SAMARIA

About that time King Ben-hadad of Aram mobilized his army, supported by the chariots and horses of thirty-two

18:46 Hebrew *He bound up his loins.* 19:8 Hebrew *to Horeb,* another name for Sinai.

allied kings. They went to besiege Samaria, the capital of
Israel, and launched attacks against it. 2Ben-hadad sent
messengers into the city to relay this
message to King Ahab of Israel: "This
is what Ben-hadad says: 3'Your silver
and gold are mine, and so are your
wives and the best of your children!'"
4"All right, my lord the king," Israel's
king replied. "All that I have is yours!"
5Soon Ben-hadad's messengers returned again and said, "This is what
Ben-hadad says: 'I have already demanded that you give me your silver,
gold, wives, and children. 6But about
this time tomorrow I will send my officials to search your palace and the
homes of your people. They will take
away everything you consider valuable!'"
7Then Ahab summoned all the elders of the land and said to them,
"Look how this man is stirring up trouble! I already
agreed with his demand that I give him my wives and
children and silver and gold."
8"Don't give in to any more demands," all the elders
and the people advised.
9So Ahab told the messengers from Ben-hadad, "Say
this to my lord the king: 'I will give you everything you
asked for the first time, but I cannot accept this last demand of yours.'" So the messengers returned to Ben-hadad
with that response.
10Then Ben-hadad sent this message to Ahab: "May the
gods strike me and even kill me if there remains enough
dust from Samaria to provide even a handful for each of
my soldiers."
11The king of Israel sent back this answer: "A warrior
putting on his sword for battle should not boast like a
warrior who has already won."
12Ahab's reply reached Ben-hadad and the other kings
as they were drinking in their tents.* "Prepare to attack!"
Ben-hadad commanded his officers. So they prepared to
attack the city.

> After the earthquake there was a fire, but the LORD was not in the fire. And after the fire there was the sound of a gentle whisper.
>
> 1 KINGS 19:12

AHAB'S VICTORY OVER BEN-HADAD

13Then a certain prophet came to see King Ahab of Israel
and told him, "This is what the LORD says: Do you see all
these enemy forces? Today I will hand them all over to
you. Then you will know that I am the LORD."
14Ahab asked, "How will he do it?"
And the prophet replied, "This is what the LORD says:
The troops of the provincial commanders will do it."
"Should we attack first?" Ahab asked.
"Yes," the prophet answered.
15So Ahab mustered the troops of the 232 provincial
commanders. Then he called out the rest of the army of
Israel, some 7,000 men. 16About noontime, as Ben-hadad
and the thirty-two allied kings were still in their tents
drinking themselves into a stupor, 17the troops of the
provincial commanders marched out of the city as the
first contingent.
As they approached, Ben-hadad's
scouts reported to him, "Some troops
are coming from Samaria."
18"Take them alive," Ben-hadad
commanded, "whether they have
come for peace or for war."
19But Ahab's provincial commanders and the entire army had now come
out to fight. 20Each Israelite soldier
killed his Aramean opponent, and
suddenly the entire Aramean army
panicked and fled. The Israelites
chased them, but King Ben-hadad and
a few of his charioteers escaped on
horses. 21However, the king of Israel
destroyed the other horses and chariots and slaughtered the Arameans.
22Afterward the prophet said to
King Ahab, "Get ready for another at-
tack. Begin making plans now, for the king of Aram will
come back next spring.*"

BEN-HADAD'S SECOND ATTACK

23After their defeat, Ben-hadad's officers said to him,
"The Israelite gods are gods of the hills; that is why they
won. But we can beat them easily on the plains. 24Only
this time replace the kings with field commanders!
25Recruit another army like the one you lost. Give us the
same number of horses, chariots, and men, and we will
fight against them on the plains. There's no doubt that we
will beat them." So King Ben-hadad did as they suggested.

A SECRET WEAPON 20:23

Since the days of Joshua, Israel's soldiers had a reputation for being superior fighters in the hills. Yet they were ineffective in the open plains and valleys, because they didn't use chariots in battle. This was the assessment of Ben-hadad's officers. What they didn't understand was that God was the one who made all of the difference in battle. When faced with emotional or spiritual battles, remember that victory doesn't come from how you fight, but from having God at your side. ■

26The following spring he called up the Aramean army
and marched out against Israel, this time at Aphek. 27Isra-
el then mustered its army, set up supply lines, and
marched out for battle. But the Israelite army looked like
two little flocks of goats in comparison to the vast Aramean forces that filled the countryside!
28Then the man of God went to the king of Israel and
said, "This is what the LORD says: The Arameans have
said, 'The LORD is a god of the hills and not of the plains.'

20:12 Or *in Succoth;* also in 20:16. **20:22** Hebrew *at the turn of the year;* similarly in 20:26. The first day of the year in the ancient Hebrew lunar calendar occurred in March or April.

So I will defeat this vast army for you. Then you will know that I am the LORD."

29The two armies camped opposite each other for seven days, and on the seventh day the battle began. The Israelites killed 100,000 Aramean foot soldiers in one day. 30The rest fled into the town of Aphek, but the wall fell on them and killed another 27,000. Ben-hadad fled into the town and hid in a secret room.

31Ben-hadad's officers said to him, "Sir, we have heard that the kings of Israel are merciful. So let's humble ourselves by wearing burlap around our waists and putting ropes on our heads, and surrender to the king of Israel. Then perhaps he will let you live."

32So they put on burlap and ropes, and they went to the king of Israel and begged, "Your servant Ben-hadad says, 'Please let me live!'"

The king of Israel responded, "Is he still alive? He is my brother!"

33The men took this as a good sign and quickly picked up on his words. "Yes," they said, "your brother Ben-hadad!"

"Go and get him," the king of Israel told them. And when Ben-hadad arrived, Ahab invited him up into his chariot.

34Ben-hadad told him, "I will give back the towns my father took from your father, and you may establish places of trade in Damascus, as my father did in Samaria."

Then Ahab said, "I will release you under these conditions." So they made a new treaty, and Ben-hadad was set free.

A PROPHET CONDEMNS AHAB

35Meanwhile, the LORD instructed one of the group of prophets to say to another man, "Hit me!" But the man refused to hit the prophet. 36Then the prophet told him, "Because you have not obeyed the voice of the LORD, a lion will kill you as soon as you leave me." And when he had gone, a lion did attack and kill him.

37Then the prophet turned to another man and said, "Hit me!" So he struck the prophet and wounded him.

38The prophet placed a bandage over his eyes to disguise himself and then waited beside the road for the king. 39As the king passed by, the prophet called out to him, "Sir, I was in the thick of battle, and suddenly a man brought me a prisoner. He said, 'Guard this man; if for any reason he gets away, you will either die or pay a fine of seventy-five pounds* of silver!' 40But while I was busy doing something else, the prisoner disappeared!"

"Well, it's your own fault," the king replied. "You have brought the judgment on yourself."

41Then the prophet quickly pulled the bandage from his eyes, and the king of Israel recognized him as one of the prophets. 42The prophet said to him, "This is what the LORD says: Because you have spared the man I said must be destroyed,* now you must die in his place, and your people will die instead of his people." 43So the king of Israel went home to Samaria angry and sullen.

21 NABOTH'S VINEYARD

Now there was a man named Naboth, from Jezreel, who owned a vineyard in Jezreel beside the palace of King Ahab of Samaria. 2One day Ahab said to Naboth, "Since your vineyard is so convenient to my palace, I would like to buy it to use as a vegetable garden. I will give you a better vineyard in exchange, or if you prefer, I will pay you for it."

3But Naboth replied, "The LORD forbid that I should give you the inheritance that was passed down by my ancestors."

4So Ahab went home angry and sullen because of Naboth's answer. The king went to bed with his face to the wall and refused to eat!

5"What's the matter?" his wife Jezebel asked him. "What's made you so upset that you're not eating?"

6"I asked Naboth to sell me his vineyard or trade it, but he refused!" Ahab told her.

7"Are you the king of Israel or not?" Jezebel demanded. "Get up and eat something, and don't worry about it. I'll get you Naboth's vineyard!"

8So she wrote letters in Ahab's name, sealed them with his seal, and sent them to the elders and other leaders of the town where Naboth lived. 9In her letters she commanded: "Call the citizens together for fasting and prayer, and give Naboth a place of honor. 10And then seat two scoundrels across from him who will accuse him of cursing God and the king. Then take him out and stone him to death."

11So the elders and other town leaders followed the instructions Jezebel had written in the letters. 12They called for a fast and put Naboth at a prominent place before the people. 13Then the two scoundrels came and sat down across from him. And they accused Naboth before all the people, saying, "He cursed God and the king." So he was dragged outside the town and stoned to death. 14The town leaders then sent word to Jezebel, "Naboth has been stoned to death."

15When Jezebel heard the news, she said to Ahab, "You know the vineyard Naboth wouldn't sell you? Well, you can have it now! He's dead!" 16So Ahab immediately went down to the vineyard of Naboth to claim it.

17But the LORD said to Elijah,* 18"Go down to meet King Ahab of Israel, who rules in Samaria. He will be at Naboth's vineyard in Jezreel, claiming it for himself. 19Give him this message: 'This is what the LORD says: Wasn't it enough that you killed Naboth? Must you rob him, too? Because you have done this, dogs will lick your blood at the very place where they licked the blood of Naboth!'"

20"So, my enemy, you have found me!" Ahab exclaimed to Elijah.

"Yes," Elijah answered, "I have come because you have sold yourself to what is evil in the LORD's sight. 21So now the LORD says, 'I will bring disaster on you and consume you. I will destroy every one of your male descendants,

20:39 Hebrew *1 talent* [34 kilograms]. **20:42** The Hebrew term used here refers to the complete consecration of things or people to the LORD, either by destroying them or by giving them as an offering. **21:17** Hebrew *Elijah the Tishbite;* also in 21:28.

slave and free alike, anywhere in Israel! [22]I am going to destroy your family as I did the family of Jeroboam son of Nebat and the family of Baasha son of Ahijah, for you have made me very angry and have led Israel into sin.'

[23]"And regarding Jezebel, the LORD says, 'Dogs will eat Jezebel's body at the plot of land in Jezreel.*'

[24]"The members of Ahab's family who die in the city will be eaten by dogs, and those who die in the field will be eaten by vultures."

[25](No one else so completely sold himself to what was evil in the LORD's sight as Ahab did under the influence of his wife Jezebel. [26]His worst outrage was worshiping idols* just as the Amorites had done—the people whom the LORD had driven out from the land ahead of the Israelites.)

[27]But when Ahab heard this message, he tore his clothing, dressed in burlap, and fasted. He even slept in burlap and went about in deep mourning.

[28]Then another message from the LORD came to Elijah: [29]"Do you see how Ahab has humbled himself before me? Because he has done this, I will not do what I promised during his lifetime. It will happen to his sons; I will destroy his dynasty."

NEVER TOO LATE 21:29

Ahab was more wicked than any other king of Israel (16:30; 21:25), but when he repented in deep humility, God took notice and reduced his punishment. The same Lord who was merciful to Ahab wants to be merciful to you. It's never too late to humble yourself, turn to God, and ask for forgiveness. ■

22

JEHOSHAPHAT AND AHAB

For three years there was no war between Aram and Israel. [2]Then during the third year, King Jehoshaphat of Judah went to visit King Ahab of Israel. [3]During the visit, the king of Israel said to his officials, "Do you realize that the town of Ramoth-gilead belongs to us? And yet we've done nothing to recapture it from the king of Aram!"

[4]Then he turned to Jehoshaphat and asked, "Will you join me in battle to recover Ramoth-gilead?"

Jehoshaphat replied to the king of Israel, "Why, of course! You and I are as one. My troops are your troops, and my horses are your horses." [5]Then Jehoshaphat added, "But first let's find out what the LORD says."

[6]So the king of Israel summoned the prophets, about 400 of them, and asked them, "Should I go to war against Ramoth-gilead, or should I hold back?"

They all replied, "Yes, go right ahead! The Lord will give the king victory."

[7]But Jehoshaphat asked, "Is there not also a prophet of the LORD here? We should ask him the same question."

[8]The king of Israel replied to Jehoshaphat, "There is one more man who could consult the LORD for us, but I hate him. He never prophesies anything but trouble for me! His name is Micaiah son of Imlah."

Jehoshaphat replied, "That's not the way a king should talk! Let's hear what he has to say."

[9]So the king of Israel called one of his officials and said, "Quick! Bring Micaiah son of Imlah."

MICAIAH PROPHESIES AGAINST AHAB

[10]King Ahab of Israel and King Jehoshaphat of Judah, dressed in their royal robes, were sitting on thrones at the threshing floor near the gate of Samaria. All of Ahab's prophets were prophesying there in front of them. [11]One of them, Zedekiah son of Kenaanah, made some iron horns and proclaimed, "This is what the LORD says: With these horns you will gore the Arameans to death!"

[12]All the other prophets agreed. "Yes," they said, "go up to Ramoth-gilead and be victorious, for the LORD will give the king victory!"

[13]Meanwhile, the messenger who went to get Micaiah said to him, "Look, all the prophets are promising victory for the king. Be sure that you agree with them and promise success."

[14]But Micaiah replied, "As surely as the LORD lives, I will say only what the LORD tells me to say."

[15]When Micaiah arrived before the king, Ahab asked him, "Micaiah, should we go to war against Ramoth-gilead, or should we hold back?"

Micaiah replied sarcastically, "Yes, go up and be victorious, for the LORD will give the king victory!"

[16]But the king replied sharply, "How many times must I demand that you speak only the truth to me when you speak for the LORD?"

[17]Then Micaiah told him, "In a vision I saw all Israel scattered on the mountains, like sheep without a shepherd. And the LORD said, 'Their master has been killed.* Send them home in peace.'"

[18]"Didn't I tell you?" the king of Israel exclaimed to Jehoshaphat. "He never prophesies anything but trouble for me."

[19]Then Micaiah continued, "Listen to what the LORD says! I saw the LORD sitting on his throne with all the armies of heaven around him, on his right and on his left. [20]And the LORD said, 'Who can entice Ahab to go into battle against Ramoth-gilead so he can be killed?'

"There were many suggestions, [21]and finally a spirit approached the LORD and said, 'I can do it!'

[22]"'How will you do this?' the LORD asked.

"And the spirit replied, 'I will go out and inspire all of Ahab's prophets to speak lies.'

"'You will succeed,' said the LORD. 'Go ahead and do it.'

[23]"So you see, the LORD has put a lying spirit in the mouths of all your prophets. For the LORD has pronounced your doom."

[24]Then Zedekiah son of Kenaanah walked up to Micaiah and slapped him across the face. "Since when did

21:23 As in several Hebrew manuscripts, Syriac, and Latin Vulgate (see also 2 Kgs 9:26, 36); most Hebrew manuscripts read *at the city wall.* 21:26 The Hebrew term (literally *round things*) probably alludes to dung. 22:17 Hebrew *These people have no master.*

the Spirit of the LORD leave me to speak to you?" he demanded.

25And Micaiah replied, "You will find out soon enough when you are trying to hide in some secret room!"

26"Arrest him!" the king of Israel ordered. "Take him back to Amon, the governor of the city, and to my son Joash. 27Give them this order from the king: 'Put this man in prison, and feed him nothing but bread and water until I return safely from the battle!'"

28But Micaiah replied, "If you return safely, it will mean that the LORD has not spoken through me!" Then he added to those standing around, "Everyone mark my words!"

A FUTILE ESCAPE 22:29-34

Ahab could not escape God's judgment. Ben-hadad, the king of Aram, sent his 32 charioteers with the sole purpose of killing Ahab. Thinking he could escape, Ahab tried a disguise; but a random shot struck him while the chariots chased the wrong king—Jehoshaphat. Sometimes people today try to escape reality by disguising themselves: acting differently, changing schools, moving to a new town. Yet no one can escape the consequences of wrong actions. ■

THE DEATH OF AHAB

29So King Ahab of Israel and King Jehoshaphat of Judah led their armies against Ramoth-gilead. 30The king of Israel said to Jehoshaphat, "As we go into battle, I will disguise myself so no one will recognize me, but you wear your royal robes." So the king of Israel disguised himself, and they went into battle.

31Meanwhile, the king of Aram had issued these orders to his thirty-two chariot commanders: "Attack only the king of Israel. Don't bother with anyone else!" 32So when the Aramean chariot commanders saw Jehoshaphat in his royal robes, they went after him. "There is the king of Israel!" they shouted. But when Jehoshaphat called out, 33the chariot commanders realized he was not the king of Israel, and they stopped chasing him.

34An Aramean soldier, however, randomly shot an arrow at the Israelite troops and hit the king of Israel between the joints of his armor. "Turn the horses* and get me out of here!" Ahab groaned to the driver of his chariot. "I'm badly wounded!"

35The battle raged all that day, and the king remained propped up in his chariot facing the Arameans. The blood from his wound ran down to the floor of his chariot, and as evening arrived he died. 36Just as the sun was setting, the cry ran through his troops: "We're done for! Run for your lives!"

37So the king died, and his body was taken to Samaria and buried there. 38Then his chariot was washed beside the pool of Samaria, and dogs came and licked his blood at the place where the prostitutes bathed,* just as the LORD had promised.

39The rest of the events in Ahab's reign and everything he did, including the story of the ivory palace and the towns he built, are recorded in *The Book of the History of the Kings of Israel.* 40So Ahab died, and his son Ahaziah became the next king.

JEHOSHAPHAT RULES IN JUDAH

41Jehoshaphat son of Asa began to rule over Judah in the fourth year of King Ahab's reign in Israel. 42Jehoshaphat was thirty-five years old when he became king, and he reigned in Jerusalem twenty-five years. His mother was Azubah, the daughter of Shilhi.

43Jehoshaphat was a good king, following the example of his father, Asa. He did what was pleasing in the LORD's sight. *During his reign, however, he failed to remove all the pagan shrines, and the people still offered sacrifices and burned incense there. 44Jehoshaphat also made peace with the king of Israel.

45The rest of the events in Jehoshaphat's reign, the extent of his power, and the wars he waged are recorded in *The Book of the History of the Kings of Judah.* 46He banished from the land the rest of the male and female shrine prostitutes, who still continued their practices from the days of his father, Asa.

47(There was no king in Edom at that time, only a deputy.)

48Jehoshaphat also built a fleet of trading ships* to sail to Ophir for gold. But the ships never set sail, for they met with disaster in their home port of Ezion-geber. 49At one time Ahaziah son of Ahab had proposed to Jehoshaphat, "Let my men sail with your men in the ships." But Jehoshaphat refused the request.

50When Jehoshaphat died, he was buried with his ancestors in the City of David. Then his son Jehoram became the next king.

ULTIMATELY DEFEATED 22:52-53

The book of 1 Kings began with a united nation under King David—the greatest king in Israel's history. However, it ends with a divided kingdom and the death of Ahab, the king with the worst reputation of all. What happened? The people stopped acknowledging God as their ultimate leader. Instead they conformed to the lifestyles of evil leaders. So, God allowed enemy nations to arise and defeat Israel and Judah as punishment for their sins. Failing to acknowledge God as the ultimate leader of our lives is the first step toward ultimate defeat. ■

AHAZIAH RULES IN ISRAEL

51Ahaziah son of Ahab began to rule over Israel in the seventeenth year of King Jehoshaphat's reign in Judah. He reigned in Samaria two years. 52But he did what was evil in the LORD's sight, following the example of his father and mother and the example of Jeroboam son of Nebat, who had led Israel to sin. 53He served Baal and worshiped him, provoking the anger of the LORD, the God of Israel, just as his father had done.

22:34 Hebrew *Turn your hand.* 22:38 Or *his blood, and the prostitutes bathed [in it];* or *his blood, and they washed his armor.* 22:43 Verses 22:43b-53 are numbered 22:44-54 in Hebrew text. 22:48 Hebrew *fleet of ships of Tarshish.*

2 KINGS

"HE USED TO BE COOL. But since he became class president, he thinks he owns the school!"

"We used to be friends. But she turned into a snob about a week after making cheerleader!"

Maybe you've heard, thought, or even spoken lines like that. It's amazing, isn't it, how some people change when they get a little power or an important position? Suddenly they're in the spotlight, and you're not good enough or popular enough or rich enough to be seen with them.

Lord Acton, a nineteenth-century scholar, put it this way: "Power tends to corrupt, and absolute power corrupts absolutely."

Of course, it doesn't always happen that way. Now and then someone who has made it to the top avoids being corrupted by power. But such people are the exceptions.

Second Kings tells about the leaders of the two nations of Israel and Judah. These kings could have led their people God's way. But of the 12 northern kings and the 16 southern kings recorded in 2 Kings, only two—Hezekiah and Josiah—are called "good."

Many people seek power, but fail to use it for good. If power were within your grasp—the power to influence others—what would you do with it?

2 kings

timeline

930 B.C.
The kingdom divides

848
Elijah's ministry transfers to Elisha

841
Jehu becomes king of Israel

835
Joash becomes king of Judah

793
Jeroboam II becomes king of Israel

760
Amos's ministry begins

753
Hosea's ministry begins

742
Micah's ministry begins

740
Isaiah's ministry begins

722
Israel (northern kingdom) falls

715
Hezekiah becomes king of Judah

640
Josiah becomes king of Judah

627
Jeremiah's ministry begins

605
First captivity of Judah—Daniel taken

597
Second captivity of Judah—Ezekiel taken

586
Judah (southern kingdom) falls

stats

PURPOSE: To demonstrate the consequences that await all who refuse to make God their true leader

AUTHOR: Unknown; possibly Jeremiah or a group of prophets

SETTING: The once united nation of Israel has been divided into two kingdoms, Israel and Judah, for over a century.

KEY PEOPLE: Elijah, Elisha, the woman from Shunem, Naaman, Jezebel, Jehu, Athaliah, Joash, Hezekiah, Sennacherib, Isaiah, Manasseh, Josiah, Jehoiakim, Zedekiah, Nebuchadnezzar

SPECIAL FEATURE: The 17 prophetic books at the end of the Old Testament give great insights into the time period of 2 Kings.

KEY points

A LONE VOICE

Elisha was a lone voice against the evil practices of the kings of Israel. Likewise we're called to take a stand against wrong, even if it means standing alone. Yet we're not really alone. God stands with us.

WORSHIPING IDOLS

Every evil king in both Israel and Judah encouraged the worship of idols. An idol is any idea, ability, possession, or person that we regard more highly than God. Idols today are power, money, physical attractiveness, and so on. Those who believe in God must resist the allure of these idols.

A CORRUPTING INFLUENCE

Only 20 percent of all of the kings of both kingdoms followed God. That means corrupt leaders had control of the kingdom for the majority of the time. Even if a leader chooses to disobey God, we're still responsible to obey him.

JUDGMENT

After repeated warnings to his people, God used enemy nations to punish his wrongdoing people. When we reject God's commands and purpose for our life, the consequences can be severe. But God offers forgiveness if we ask for it.

KEY PLACES IN 2 KINGS

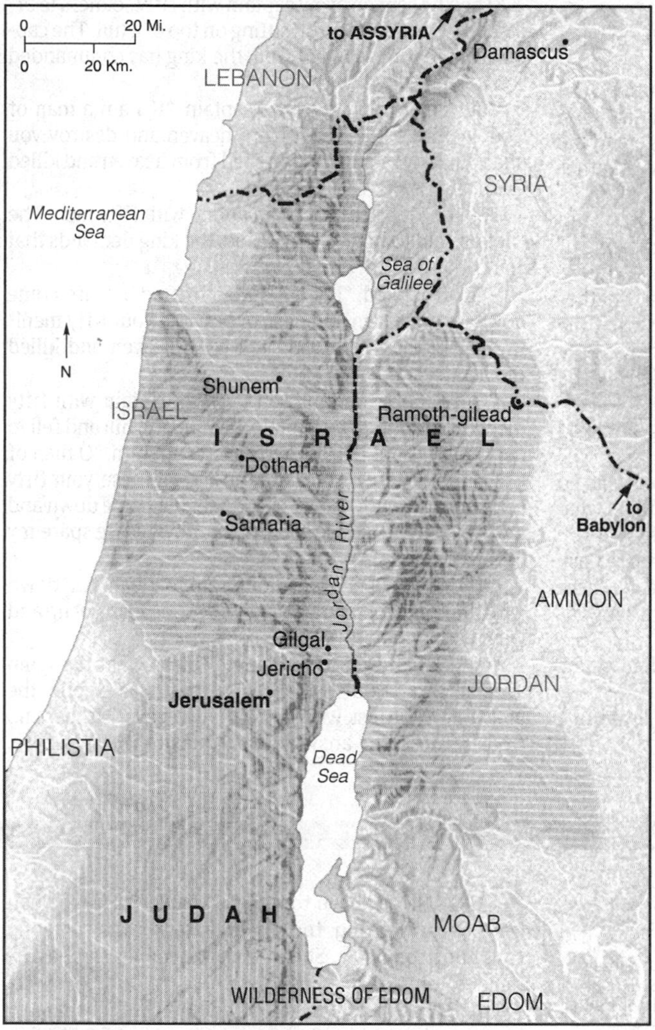

The broken lines (–·–·–) indicate modern boundaries.

The history of both Israel and Judah was greatly affected by the prophet Elisha's ministry. He served Israel for 50 years, fighting the idolatry of its kings and calling its people back to God.

- **JERICHO** Elijah's ministry had come to an end. He touched his cloak to the Jordan River, and he and Elisha crossed on dry land. Elijah was taken by God in a whirlwind, and Elisha returned alone with the cloak. The prophets in Jericho realized that Elisha was Elijah's replacement with Elijah's power (1:1–2:25).
- **WILDERNESS OF EDOM** The king of Moab rebelled against Israel, so the nations of Israel, Judah, and Edom decided to attack from the wilderness of Edom, but ran out of water. The kings consulted Elisha, who said that God would send both water and victory (3:1-27).
- **SHUNEM** Elisha cared for individuals and their needs. He helped a woman clear a debt by giving her a supply of olive oil to sell. For another family, in Shunem, he raised a son from the dead (4:1-37).
- **GILGAL** Elisha cared for the young prophets in Gilgal—he removed poison from a stew, miraculously fed everyone with a small amount of food, and even caused an ax head to float so someone could retrieve it. (4:38–6:7).
- **DOTHAN** Although he cured an Aramean commander's leprosy, Elisha was loyal to Israel. He knew the Aramean army's battle plans and kept Israel's king informed. The Aramean king tracked Elisha down in Dothan and surrounded the city, hoping to kill him. But Elisha prayed that the Arameans would be blinded—and they were! Then he led the blinded army into Samaria, Israel's capital city (6:8-23).
- **SAMARIA** The Arameans didn't learn their lesson. Later they besieged Samaria. Ironically, Israel's king thought it was Elisha's fault, but Elisha said food would be available in abundance the next day. True to Elisha's word, the Lord caused panic in the Aramean camp and the enemy ran, leaving their supplies to Samaria's starving people (6:24–7:20).
- **DAMASCUS** Despite Elisha's loyalty to Israel, he obeyed God and traveled to Damascus, the capital of Aram. King Ben-hadad was sick, and he sent Hazael to ask Elisha if he would recover. Elisha knew the king would die, and told this to Hazael. Hazael then murdered Ben-hadad, making himself king. Later Israel and Judah joined forces to fight this new Aramean threat (8:1-29).
- **RAMOTH-GILEAD** As Israel and Judah warred with Syria, Elisha sent a young prophet to Ramoth-gilead to anoint Jehu as Israel's next king. Jehu set out to destroy the wicked dynasties of Israel and Judah, killing Kings Joram and Ahaziah and wicked Queen Jezebel. He then destroyed King Ahab's family and all the Baal worshipers in Israel (9:1–11:1).
- **JERUSALEM** Power-hungry Athaliah became queen of Judah when her son Ahaziah was killed. She had all her grandsons killed except Joash, who was hidden by his aunt. Joash was crowned king at the age of seven and overthrew Athaliah. Meanwhile in Samaria, the Arameans continued to harass Israel. Israel's new king met with Elisha and was told that he would be victorious over Aram three times (11:2–13:19).

Following Elisha's death came a series of evil kings in Israel. Their idolatry and rejection of God caused their downfall. The Assyrian empire captured Samaria and took most of the Israelites into captivity (13:20–17:41). Jerusalem fell to the next world power, Babylon, and its people were taken captive (18:1–25:30).

1 ELIJAH CONFRONTS KING AHAZIAH

After King Ahab's death, the land of Moab rebelled against Israel.

2 One day Israel's new king, Ahaziah, fell through the latticework of an upper room at his palace in Samaria and was seriously injured. So he sent messengers to the temple of Baal-zebub, the god of Ekron, to ask whether he would recover.

3 But the angel of the LORD told Elijah, who was from Tishbe, "Go and confront the messengers of the king of Samaria and ask them, 'Is there no God in Israel? Why are you going to Baal-zebub, the god of Ekron, to ask whether the king will recover? 4 Now, therefore, this is what the LORD says: You will never leave the bed you are lying on; you will surely die.' " So Elijah went to deliver the message.

5 When the messengers returned to the king, he asked them, "Why have you returned so soon?"

6 They replied, "A man came up to us and told us to go back to the king and give him this message. 'This is what the LORD says: Is there no God in Israel? Why are you sending men to Baal-zebub, the god of Ekron, to ask whether you will recover? Therefore, because you have done this, you will never leave the bed you are lying on; you will surely die.' "

7 "What sort of man was he?" the king demanded. "What did he look like?"

8 They replied, "He was a hairy man,* and he wore a leather belt around his waist."

"Elijah from Tishbe!" the king exclaimed.

9 Then he sent an army captain with fifty soldiers to arrest him. They found him sitting on top of a hill. The captain said to him, "Man of God, the king has commanded you to come down with us."

10 But Elijah replied to the captain, "If I am a man of God, let fire come down from heaven and destroy you and your fifty men!" Then fire fell from heaven and killed them all.

11 So the king sent another captain with fifty men. The captain said to him, "Man of God, the king demands that you come down at once."

12 Elijah replied, "If I am a man of God, let fire come down from heaven and destroy you and your fifty men!" And again the fire of God fell from heaven and killed them all.

13 Once more the king sent a third captain with fifty men. But this time the captain went up the hill and fell to his knees before Elijah. He pleaded with him, "O man of God, please spare my life and the lives of these, your fifty servants. 14 See how the fire from heaven came down and destroyed the first two groups. But now please spare my life!"

15 Then the angel of the LORD said to Elijah, "Go down with him, and don't be afraid of him." So Elijah got up and went with him to the king.

16 And Elijah said to the king, "This is what the LORD says: Why did you send messengers to Baal-zebub, the god of Ekron, to ask whether you will recover? Is there no God in Israel to answer your question? Therefore,

1:8 Or *He was wearing clothing made of hair.*

ELISHA

UPS:
- Elijah's successor as a prophet of God
- Had a ministry that lasted over 50 years
- Had a major impact on four nations: Israel, Judah, Moab, and Syria
- A man of integrity who did not try to enrich himself at others' expense
- Did many miracles to help those in need

STATS:
- Where: From the tribe of Issachar, prophesied to northern kingdom
- Occupations: Farmer, prophet
- Relatives: Shaphat (father)
- Contemporaries: Elijah, Ahab, Jezebel, Jehu

BOTTOM LINE:
One measure of greatness is the willingness to serve the poor as well as the powerful.

An effective replacement not only learns from his or her master, but also builds upon his or her master's achievements.

Elisha's story is told in 1 Kings 19:16-21; 2 Kings 2:1–13:20. He is also mentioned in Luke 4:27.

ELISHA Ever have to replace someone? Maybe you were second string took over a task that someone could not complete. Some talented people can be difficult to replace.

Elijah was a tough act to follow. But Elisha had been handpicked by God as a replacement for the job of prophet. Elisha carefully observed Elijah's example in order to learn the knowledge and wisdom he needed for the work to which God had called him.

Though Elijah and Elisha were both prophets, each had his own style. Because Elijah did a good job of confronting evil and idol worship, Elisha was able to be a comforter. He showed people how much God cared. The Bible records eighteen encounters between Elisha and people who needed help.

Elisha saw more *in* life than most people because he recognized that with God there was more *to* life. He knew that all we are and have comes from God. The miracles done through Elisha put people in touch with the personal and all-powerful God. Elijah would have been proud of his replacement's work.

The person you will become and the work you will do are being shaped by the people you follow today. Are they worth following?

MIRACLES

ULTIMATE ISSUES

Fire from heaven . . . flaming chariots . . . dead people coming back to life . . . floating ax heads. When you read such stories in 2 Kings, do you sometimes feel as if you're being asked to believe the impossible?

Ever wonder whether or not miracles really happen?

First we need to define what a miracle is. A miracle is any observable event that breaks the normal laws of nature. This includes miracles of nature (the parting of the Red Sea in Exod 14); healings (Naaman in 2 Kings 5); and supernatural displays (appearances of angels or the writing on the wall in Dan 5). By definition, miracles take place by God's initiative, not a human being's. They aren't predictable. And that's one of the problems.

We tend to be skeptical of anything that cannot be photographed, documented, or otherwise objectively "proven." Often, our first response to accounts of something unusual is, "Right. Prove it." When no proof is offered, we are (often rightly) unconvinced.

The miracles in the Bible often were witnessed by more than one or two people. The plagues in Egypt were experienced by thousands of people. It's hard to fake that kind of testimony.

Another argument to consider is the logical one. If there is a God and he created the universe and set up the laws that govern it, why would it be inconsistent or unbelievable for him to bend or break the rules he made in the first place? The answer is simple: it's not. It is logical that the one who made natural law can act in ways that go beyond it.

Just as we believe in other world-changing events without the benefit of being there, so the biblical writers ask us to believe their testimonies of God's supernatural actions in human history. These writings are just one more way God demonstrates his sovereign control and his intense personal involvement in our lives.

because you have done this, you will never leave the bed
you are lying on; you will surely die."
17So Ahaziah died, just as the LORD had promised
through Elijah. Since Ahaziah did not have a son to succeed him, his brother Joram* became the next king. This
took place in the second year of the reign of Jehoram son
of Jehoshaphat, king of Judah.
18The rest of the events in Ahaziah's reign are recorded
in *The Book of the History of the Kings of Israel.*

2 **ELIJAH TAKEN INTO HEAVEN**

When the LORD was about to take Elijah up to heaven in a
whirlwind, Elijah and Elisha were traveling from Gilgal.
2And Elijah said to Elisha, "Stay here, for the LORD has told
me to go to Bethel."
But Elisha replied, "As surely as the LORD lives and you
yourself live, I will never leave you!" So they went down
together to Bethel.
3The group of prophets from Bethel came to Elisha
and asked him, "Did you know that the LORD is going to
take your master away from you today?"
"Of course I know," Elisha answered. "But be quiet
about it."
4Then Elijah said to Elisha, "Stay here, for the LORD has
told me to go to Jericho."
But Elisha replied again, "As surely as the LORD lives
and you yourself live, I will never leave you." So they went
on together to Jericho.
5Then the group of prophets from Jericho came to Elisha and asked him, "Did you know that the LORD is going
to take your master away from you today?"
"Of course I know," Elisha answered. "But be quiet
about it."
6Then Elijah said to Elisha, "Stay here, for the LORD has
told me to go to the Jordan River."
But again Elisha replied, "As surely as the LORD lives
and you yourself live, I will never leave you." So they went
on together.
7Fifty men from the group of prophets also went and
watched from a distance as Elijah and Elisha stopped beside the Jordan River. 8Then Elijah folded his cloak together and struck the water with it. The river divided, and
the two of them went across on dry ground!

1:17 Hebrew *Jehoram,* a variant spelling of Joram.

9When they came to the other side, Elijah said to Elisha, "Tell me what I can do for you before I am taken away."

And Elisha replied, "Please let me inherit a double share of your spirit and become your successor."

PURE MOTIVES 2:9

Elisha asked to become Elijah's successor. He literally asked Elijah for "a double share of your spirit." This was a bold request, but God granted it. Why? Because Elisha's motives were pure. His goal was not to be better or more powerful than Elijah, but to accomplish more for God. If our motives are pure, we don't have to be afraid to ask for big things from God. What's your request? ■

10"You have asked a difficult thing," Elijah replied. "If you see me when I am taken from you, then you will get your request. But if not, then you won't."

11As they were walking along and talking, suddenly a chariot of fire appeared, drawn by horses of fire. It drove between the two men, separating them, and Elijah was carried by a whirlwind into heaven.
12Elisha saw it and cried out, "My father! My father! I see the chariots and charioteers of Israel!" And as they disappeared from sight, Elisha tore his clothes in distress.

13Elisha picked up Elijah's cloak, which had fallen when he was taken up. Then Elisha returned to the bank of the Jordan River.
14He struck the water with Elijah's cloak and cried out, "Where is the LORD, the God of Elijah?" Then the river divided, and Elisha went across.

15When the group of prophets from Jericho saw from a distance what happened, they exclaimed, "Elijah's spirit rests upon Elisha!" And they went to meet him and bowed to the ground before him.
16"Sir," they said, "just say the word and fifty of our strongest men will search the wilderness for your master. Perhaps the Spirit of the LORD has left him on some mountain or in some valley."

"No," Elisha said, "don't send them."
17But they kept urging him until they shamed him into agreeing, and he finally said, "All right, send them." So fifty men searched for three days but did not find Elijah.
18Elisha was still at Jericho when they returned. "Didn't I tell you not to go?" he asked.

ELISHA'S FIRST MIRACLES

19One day the leaders of the town of Jericho visited Elisha. "We have a problem, my lord," they told him. "This town is located in pleasant surroundings, as you can see. But the water is bad, and the land is unproductive."

20Elisha said, "Bring me a new bowl with salt in it." So they brought it to him.
21Then he went out to the spring that supplied the town with water and threw the salt into it. And he said, "This is what the LORD says: I have purified this water. It will no longer cause death or infertility.*"
22And the water has remained pure ever since, just as Elisha said.

23Elisha left Jericho and went up to Bethel. As he was walking along the road, a group of boys from the town began mocking and making fun of him. "Go away, baldy!" they chanted. "Go away, baldy!"
24Elisha turned around and looked at them, and he cursed them in the name of the LORD. Then two bears came out of the woods and mauled forty-two of them.
25From there Elisha went to Mount Carmel and finally returned to Samaria.

ZERO-TOLERANCE 2:23-25

These boys made fun of Elisha and paid for it with their lives. Sound harsh? God had a reason for allowing this. He wanted to show a zero-tolerance policy toward anyone who dissed his messenger. Making fun of religious leaders has been a popular sport through the ages. Sometimes we express cynicism or disrespect toward leaders whom we feel "deserve" our contempt. Instead of mocking them, we could pray for them. True leaders, those who follow God, need to be heard with respect and encouraged in their ministry. ■

3 WAR BETWEEN ISRAEL AND MOAB

Ahab's son Joram* began to rule over Israel in the eighteenth year of King Jehoshaphat's reign in Judah. He reigned in Samaria twelve years.
2He did what was evil in the LORD's sight, but not to the same extent as his father and mother. He at least tore down the sacred pillar of Baal that his father had set up.
3Nevertheless, he continued in the sins that Jeroboam son of Nebat had committed and led the people of Israel to commit.

4King Mesha of Moab was a sheep breeder. He used to pay the king of Israel an annual tribute of 100,000 lambs and the wool of 100,000 rams.
5But after Ahab's death, the king of Moab rebelled against the king of Israel.
6So King Joram promptly mustered the army of Israel and marched from Samaria.
7On the way, he sent this message to King Jehoshaphat of Judah: "The king of Moab has rebelled against me. Will you join me in battle against him?"

And Jehoshaphat replied, "Why, of course! You and I are as one. My troops are your troops, and my horses are your horses."
8Then Jehoshaphat asked, "What route will we take?"

"We will attack from the wilderness of Edom," Joram replied.

9The king of Edom and his troops joined them, and all three armies traveled along a roundabout route through the wilderness for seven days. But there was no water for the men or their animals.

10"What should we do?" the king of Israel cried out. "The LORD has brought the three of us here to let the king of Moab defeat us."

11But King Jehoshaphat of Judah asked, "Is there no

2:21 Or *or make the land unproductive;* Hebrew reads *or barrenness.* 3:1 Hebrew *Jehoram,* a variant spelling of Joram; also in 3:6.

prophet of the LORD with us? If there is, we can ask the
LORD what to do through him."
One of King Joram's officers replied, "Elisha son
of Shaphat is here. He used to be Elijah's personal
assistant.*"
12 Jehoshaphat said, "Yes, the LORD speaks through
him." So the kings of Israel, Judah, and Edom went to consult with Elisha.
13 "Why are you coming to me?"* Elisha asked the king
of Israel. "Go to the pagan prophets of your father and
mother!"
But King Joram of Israel said, "No! For it was the LORD
who called us three kings here—only to be defeated by
the king of Moab!"
14 Elisha replied, "As surely as the LORD Almighty lives,
whom I serve, I wouldn't even bother with you except for
my respect for King Jehoshaphat of Judah. 15 Now bring
me someone who can play the harp."
While the harp was being played, the power* of the
LORD came upon Elisha, 16 and he said, "This is what the
LORD says: This dry valley will be filled with pools of water! 17 You will see neither wind nor rain, says the LORD,
but this valley will be filled with water. You will have
plenty for yourselves and your cattle and other animals.
18 But this is only a simple thing for the LORD, for he will
make you victorious over the army of Moab! 19 You will
conquer the best of their towns, even the fortified ones.
You will cut down all their good trees, stop up all their
springs, and ruin all their good land with stones."
20 The next day at about the time when the morning
sacrifice was offered, water suddenly appeared! It was
flowing from the direction of Edom, and soon there was
water everywhere.

FAITH DECLINE 3:1-20

Jehoshaphat's request for a "prophet of the LORD" (3:11) shows a decline in the worship of God in both Israel and Judah. The decline usually started in the heart of each person and worked its way out. If your heart could be examined, what would be found: a decline or a rise in worship? ■

21 Meanwhile, when the people of Moab heard about
the three armies marching against them, they mobilized
every man who was old enough to strap on a sword, and
they stationed themselves along their border. 22 But when
they got up the next morning, the sun was shining across
the water, making it appear red to the Moabites—like
blood. 23 "It's blood!" the Moabites exclaimed. "The three
armies must have attacked and killed each other! Let's go,
men of Moab, and collect the plunder!"
24 But when the Moabites arrived at the Israelite camp,
the army of Israel rushed out and attacked them until
they turned and ran. The army of Israel chased them
into the land of Moab, destroying everything as they
went.* 25 They destroyed the towns, covered their good
land with stones, stopped up all the springs, and cut
down all the good trees. Finally, only Kir-hareseth and
its stone walls were left, but men with slings surrounded
and attacked it.
26 When the king of Moab saw that he was losing the
battle, he led 700 of his swordsmen in a desperate attempt to break through the enemy lines near the king of
Edom, but they failed. 27 Then the king of Moab took his
oldest son, who would have been the next king, and sacrificed him as a burnt offering on the wall. So there was
great anger against Israel,* and the Israelites withdrew
and returned to their own land.

EMPTY JARS, FULL FAITH 4:1-7

The widow and her sons collected empty jars from their neighbors. The number of jars they gathered was an indication of their faith. God's provision was as large as their willingness to obey. How "full" is your faith? ■

4

ELISHA HELPS A POOR WIDOW

One day the widow of a member of the group of prophets
came to Elisha and cried out, "My husband who served
you is dead, and you know how he feared the LORD. But
now a creditor has come, threatening to take my two sons
as slaves."
2 "What can I do to help you?" Elisha asked. "Tell me,
what do you have in the house?"
"Nothing at all, except a flask of olive oil," she replied.
3 And Elisha said, "Borrow as many empty jars as you
can from your friends and neighbors. 4 Then go into your
house with your sons and shut the door behind you. Pour
olive oil from your flask into the jars, setting each one
aside when it is filled."
5 So she did as she was told. Her sons kept bringing jars
to her, and she filled one after another. 6 Soon every container was full to the brim!
"Bring me another jar," she said to one of her sons.
"There aren't any more!" he told her. And then the olive oil stopped flowing.
7 When she told the man of God what had happened,
he said to her, "Now sell the olive oil and pay your debts,
and you and your sons can live on what is left over."

ELISHA AND THE WOMAN FROM SHUNEM

8 One day Elisha went to the town of Shunem. A wealthy
woman lived there, and she urged him to come to her
home for a meal. After that, whenever he passed that way,
he would stop there for something to eat.
9 She said to her husband, "I am sure this man who
stops in from time to time is a holy man of God. 10 Let's
build a small room for him on the roof and furnish it with
a bed, a table, a chair, and a lamp. Then he will have a
place to stay whenever he comes by."

3:11 Hebrew *He used to pour water on the hands of Elijah.* 3:13 Hebrew *What is there in common between you and me?* 3:15 Hebrew *the hand.* 3:24 The meaning of the Hebrew is uncertain. 3:27 Or *So Israel's anger was great.* The meaning of the Hebrew is uncertain.

keeping it real

I've always been a leader in anything I'm involved in: class president, a member of the leadership team in our youth group, vice president of the Key Club. And I always assumed that leadership meant enjoying certain privileges: respect, being treated well, people listening to me when I made suggestions or comments, even a certain amount of special consideration when decisions were made.

Then I read 2 Kings, and saw how the different kinds of leaders affected their people. Good kings led their people in ways that pleased the Lord, and that resulted in them being blessed. Evil kings led their people into disaster and destruction. So much seemed to depend on the leaders!

One day not long after that, I read Matthew 20:25-28, and finally realized that my idea of leadership was all wrong. I usually thought only of myself; here Jesus was saying that leaders must be servants. After being in the habit of serving myself, it was difficult to serve, as Jesus said. Putting others first made leadership harder, not easier.

I talked about it with my youth leader. She encouraged me to look at a few other verses—Romans 5:3-4 and 8:18. These verses talk about how difficulties have a purpose: to strengthen our faith. Serving others doesn't come naturally, and sometimes it hurts to give up my own rights. But I'm finding that following Jesus' way is helping my faith to grow—and some people even think I'm a better leader! **—Amanda**

11One day Elisha returned to Shunem, and he went up
to this upper room to rest. 12He said to his servant Gehazi,
"Tell the woman from Shunem I want to speak to her."
When she appeared, 13Elisha said to Gehazi, "Tell her,
'We appreciate the kind concern you have shown us.
What can we do for you? Can we put in a good word for
you to the king or to the commander of the army?'"

"No," she replied, "my family takes good care of me."

14Later Elisha asked Gehazi, "What can we do for her?"

Gehazi replied, "She doesn't have a son, and her husband is an old man."

15"Call her back again," Elisha told him. When the
woman returned, Elisha said to her as she stood in the
doorway, 16"Next year at this time you will be holding a
son in your arms!"

"No, my lord!" she cried. "O man of God, don't deceive me and get my hopes up like that."

17But sure enough, the woman soon became pregnant.
And at that time the following year she had a son, just as Elisha had said.

18One day when her child was older, he went out to
help his father, who was working with the harvesters.
19Suddenly he cried out, "My head hurts! My head hurts!"

His father said to one of the servants, "Carry him home to his mother."

20So the servant took him home, and his mother held
him on her lap. But around noontime he died. 21She
carried him up and laid him on the bed of the man of
God, then shut the door and left him there. 22She sent a
message to her husband: "Send one of the servants and a
donkey so that I can hurry to the man of God and come
right back."

23"Why go today?" he asked. "It is neither a new moon festival nor a Sabbath."

But she said, "It will be all right."

24So she saddled the donkey and said to the servant,
"Hurry! Don't slow down unless I tell you to."

25As she approached the man of God at Mount Carmel,
Elisha saw her in the distance. He said to Gehazi, "Look,
the woman from Shunem is coming. 26Run out to meet
her and ask her, 'Is everything all right with you, your husband, and your child?'"

"Yes," the woman told Gehazi, "everything is fine."

27But when she came to the man of God at the mountain, she fell to the ground before him and caught hold of
his feet. Gehazi began to push her away, but the man of
God said, "Leave her alone. She is deeply troubled, but the
LORD has not told me what it is."

28Then she said, "Did I ask you for a son, my lord? And
didn't I say, 'Don't deceive me and get my hopes up'?"

29Then Elisha said to Gehazi, "Get ready to travel*; take
my staff and go! Don't talk to anyone along the way. Go
quickly and lay the staff on the child's face."

30But the boy's mother said, "As surely as the LORD lives

4:29 Hebrew *Bind up your loins.*

God or Idols

Why did people continually turn to idols instead of to God?

IDOLS WERE:	**GOD IS:**
Tangible	Intangible—no physical form
Morally similar—had human characteristics	Morally dissimilar—has divine characteristics
Comprehensible	Incomprehensible
Able to be manipulated	Not able to be manipulated
WORSHIPING IDOLS INVOLVED:	**WORSHIPING GOD INVOLVES:**
Materialism	Sacrifice
Sexual immorality	Purity and commitment
Doing whatever a person wanted	Doing what God wants
Focusing on self	Focusing on others

and you yourself live, I won't go home unless you go with
me." So Elisha returned with her.
31Gehazi hurried on ahead and laid the staff on the
child's face, but nothing happened. There was no sign of
life. He returned to meet Elisha and told him, "The child
is still dead."
32When Elisha arrived, the child was indeed dead, lying there on the prophet's bed. 33He went in alone and
shut the door behind him and prayed to the LORD. 34Then
he lay down on the child's body, placing his mouth on the
child's mouth, his eyes on the child's eyes, and his hands
on the child's hands. And as he stretched out on him, the
child's body began to grow warm again! 35Elisha got up,
walked back and forth across the room once, and then
stretched himself out again on the child. This time the
boy sneezed seven times and opened his eyes!
36Then Elisha summoned Gehazi. "Call the child's
mother!" he said. And when she came in, Elisha said,
"Here, take your son!" 37She fell at his feet and bowed before him, overwhelmed with gratitude. Then she took her
son in her arms and carried him downstairs.

MIRACLES DURING A FAMINE

38Elisha now returned to Gilgal, and there was a famine in
the land. One day as the group of prophets was seated before him, he said to his servant, "Put a large pot on the
fire, and make some stew for the rest of the group."
39One of the young men went out into the field to
gather herbs and came back with a pocketful of wild
gourds. He shredded them and put them into the pot
without realizing they were poisonous. 40Some of the
stew was served to the men. But after they had eaten a
bite or two they cried out, "Man of God, there's poison in
this stew!" So they would not eat it.
41Elisha said, "Bring me some flour." Then he threw it
into the pot and said, "Now it's all right; go ahead and eat."
And then it did not harm them.
42One day a man from Baal-shalishah brought the man
of God a sack of fresh grain and twenty loaves of barley
bread made from the first grain of his harvest. Elisha
said, "Give it to the people so they can eat."
43"What?" his servant exclaimed. "Feed a hundred
people with only this?"
But Elisha repeated, "Give it to the people so they can
eat, for this is what the LORD says: Everyone will eat, and
there will even be some left over!" 44And when they gave
it to the people, there was plenty for all and some left
over, just as the LORD had promised.

5

THE HEALING OF NAAMAN

The king of Aram had great admiration for Naaman, the
commander of his army, because through him the LORD
had given Aram great victories. But though Naaman was a
mighty warrior, he suffered from leprosy.*
2At this time Aramean raiders had invaded the land of
Israel, and among their captives was a young girl who had
been given to Naaman's wife as a maid. 3One day the girl
said to her mistress, "I wish my master would go to see
the prophet in Samaria. He would heal him of his
leprosy."
4So Naaman told the king what the young girl from
Israel had said. 5"Go and visit the prophet," the king of
Aram told him. "I will send a letter of introduction for
you to take to the king of Israel." So Naaman started out,
carrying as gifts 750 pounds of silver, 150 pounds of
gold,* and ten sets of clothing. 6The letter to the king of
Israel said: "With this letter I present my servant Naaman. I want you to heal him of his leprosy."
7When the king of Israel read the letter, he tore his
clothes in dismay and said, "This man sends me a leper to
heal! Am I God, that I can give life and take it away? I can
see that he's just trying to pick a fight with me."
8But when Elisha, the man of God, heard that the king
of Israel had torn his clothes in dismay, he sent this message to him: "Why are you so upset? Send Naaman to me,
and he will learn that there is a true prophet here in
Israel."
9So Naaman went with his horses and chariots and
waited at the door of Elisha's house. 10But Elisha sent a
messenger out to him with this message: "Go and wash
yourself seven times in the Jordan River. Then your skin
will be restored, and you will be healed of your leprosy."
11But Naaman became angry and stalked away. "I

5:1 Or *from a contagious skin disease*. The Hebrew word used here and throughout this passage can describe various skin diseases. 5:5 Hebrew *10 talents* [340 kilograms] *of silver, 6,000 shekels* [68 kilograms] *of gold*.

thought he would certainly come out to meet me!" he said. "I expected him to wave his hand over the leprosy and call on the name of the LORD his God and heal me! [12]Aren't the rivers of Damascus, the Abana and the Pharpar, better than any of the rivers of Israel? Why shouldn't I wash in them and be healed?" So Naaman turned and went away in a rage.

[13]But his officers tried to reason with him and said, "Sir,* if the prophet had told you to do something very difficult, wouldn't you have done it? So you should certainly obey him when he says simply, 'Go and wash and be cured!'" [14]So Naaman went down to the Jordan River and dipped himself seven times, as the man of God had instructed him. And his skin became as healthy as the skin of a young child's, and he was healed!

[15]Then Naaman and his entire party went back to find the man of God. They stood before him, and Naaman said, "Now I know that there is no God in all the world except in Israel. So please accept a gift from your servant."

HUMILITY 5:9-15

Naaman, a great hero, was outraged when Elisha treated him like an ordinary person. But he had to humble himself and obey Elisha's commands in order to be healed. Like Naaman, have you ever felt that one of God's rules was too embarrassing to follow? Obedience to God often begins with humility. It also involves loving God more than our pride. ■

[16]But Elisha replied, "As surely as the LORD lives, whom I serve, I will not accept any gifts." And though Naaman urged him to take the gift, Elisha refused.

[17]Then Naaman said, "All right, but please allow me to load two of my mules with earth from this place, and I will take it back home with me. From now on I will never again offer burnt offerings or sacrifices to any other god except the LORD. [18]However, may the LORD pardon me in this one thing: When my master the king goes into the temple of the god Rimmon to worship there and leans on my arm, may the LORD pardon me when I bow, too."

[19]"Go in peace," Elisha said. So Naaman started home again.

THE GREED OF GEHAZI

[20]But Gehazi, the servant of Elisha, the man of God, said to himself, "My master should not have let this Aramean get away without accepting any of his gifts. As surely as the LORD lives, I will chase after him and get something from him." [21]So Gehazi set off after Naaman.

When Naaman saw Gehazi running after him, he climbed down from his chariot and went to meet him. "Is everything all right?" Naaman asked.

[22]"Yes," Gehazi said, "but my master has sent me to tell you that two young prophets from the hill country of Ephraim have just arrived. He would like 75 pounds* of silver and two sets of clothing to give to them."

[23]"By all means, take twice as much* silver," Naaman insisted. He gave him two sets of clothing, tied up the money in two bags, and sent two of his servants to carry the gifts for Gehazi. [24]But when they arrived at the citadel,* Gehazi took the gifts from the servants and sent the men back. Then he went and hid the gifts inside the house.

GAIN OR GOD? 5:20-27

Gehazi saw a perfect opportunity to get rich by selfishly asking for the reward Elisha had refused. Although Gehazi had been a helpful servant, personal gain had become more important to him than serving God. True service is motivated by love for God and seeks no personal gain. Is that a good description of your motive for serving God? ■

[25]When he went in to his master, Elisha asked him, "Where have you been, Gehazi?"

"I haven't been anywhere," he replied.

[26]But Elisha asked him, "Don't you realize that I was there in spirit when Naaman stepped down from his chariot to meet you? Is this the time to receive money and clothing, olive groves and vineyards, sheep and cattle, and male and female servants? [27]Because you have done this, you and your descendants will suffer from Naaman's leprosy forever." When Gehazi left the room, he was covered with leprosy; his skin was white as snow.

6

THE FLOATING AX HEAD

One day the group of prophets came to Elisha and told him, "As you can see, this place where we meet with you is too small. [2]Let's go down to the Jordan River, where there are plenty of logs. There we can build a new place for us to meet."

"All right," he told them, "go ahead."

[3]"Please come with us," someone suggested.

"I will," he said. [4]So he went with them.

When they arrived at the Jordan, they began cutting down trees. [5]But as one of them was cutting a tree, his ax head fell into the river. "Oh, sir!" he cried. "It was a borrowed ax!"

[6]"Where did it fall?" the man of God asked. When he showed him the place, Elisha cut a stick and threw it into the water at that spot. Then the ax head floated to the surface. [7]"Grab it," Elisha said. And the man reached out and grabbed it.

ELISHA TRAPS THE ARAMEANS

[8]When the king of Aram was at war with Israel, he would confer with his officers and say, "We will mobilize our forces at such and such a place."

[9]But immediately Elisha, the man of God, would warn

5:13 Hebrew *My father*. 5:22 Hebrew *1 talent* [34 kilograms]. 5:23 Hebrew *take 2 talents* [68 kilograms]. 5:24 Hebrew *the Ophel*.

the king of Israel, "Do not go near that place, for the Arameans are planning to mobilize their troops there." 10So
the king of Israel would send word to the place indicated
by the man of God. Time and again Elisha warned the
king, so that he would be on the alert there.
11The king of Aram became very upset over this. He
called his officers together and demanded, "Which of
you is the traitor? Who has been informing the king of Israel of my plans?"
12"It's not us, my lord the king," one of the officers replied. "Elisha, the prophet in Israel, tells the king of Israel
even the words you speak in the privacy of your
bedroom!"
13"Go and find out where he is," the king commanded,
"so I can send troops to seize him."
And the report came back: "Elisha is at Dothan." 14So
one night the king of Aram sent a great army with many
chariots and horses to surround the city.
15When the servant of the man of God got up early the
next morning and went outside, there were troops,
horses, and chariots everywhere. "Oh, sir, what will we do
now?" the young man cried to Elisha.
16"Don't be afraid!" Elisha told him. "For there are
more on our side than on theirs!" 17Then Elisha prayed,
"O LORD, open his eyes and let him see!" The LORD opened
the young man's eyes, and when he looked up, he saw that
the hillside around Elisha was filled with horses and
chariots of fire.

HIDDEN RESOURCES 6:16-17

Elisha's servant was no longer afraid when he saw God's mighty heavenly army. Faith reveals that God is doing more for his people than we could ever realize through human understanding alone. When you face situations that seem overwhelming, God can give you the faith to see his plan in action. ■

18As the Aramean army advanced toward him, Elisha
prayed, "O LORD, please make them blind." So the LORD
struck them with blindness as Elisha had asked.
19Then Elisha went out and told them, "You have come
the wrong way! This isn't the right city! Follow me, and I
will take you to the man you are looking for." And he led
them to the city of Samaria.
20As soon as they had entered Samaria, Elisha prayed,
"O LORD, now open their eyes and let them see." So the
LORD opened their eyes, and they discovered that they
were in the middle of Samaria.
21When the king of Israel saw them, he shouted to Elisha, "My father, should I kill them? Should I kill them?"
22"Of course not!" Elisha replied. "Do we kill prisoners
of war? Give them food and drink and send them home
again to their master."
23So the king made a great feast for them and then sent
them home to their master. After that, the Aramean raiders stayed away from the land of Israel.

OUTSPOKEN

Sixteen-year-old David H. not only went to a youth retreat this past weekend (unbelievable), but he also said that he believed that Jesus died for him (major shock)! It's not a joke. David was dead serious.

Remember now, this is the same guy who was wasted for most of his whole freshman year. We're talking about the most outspoken enemy of the Christian students at Lanier High School.

At school on Monday, word quickly got around about David's surprising decision. When David's wild partying buds approached him to find out what really happened, David brushed them off, saying, "Hey, it's kind of private. I'd rather not talk about it now."

Puzzled, David's best friend, Randy, dropped by after school.

"C'mon, Dave," he urged. "What's really up?"

David froze. He knew he made the right decision at the retreat. He felt closer to God and peaceful inside. And yet he didn't want to be abused by his cynical, definitely non-Christian friends.

What do you think? Should he tell Randy what happened—and risk catching a lot of grief? Or should he just hope his friends find out the truth about God on their own?

Can you relate to David's fear of sharing the Good News? Read 2 Kings 6:24–7:11 (and take special note of 7:9). How would you handle the situation?

BEN-HADAD BESIEGES SAMARIA

24Some time later, however, King Ben-hadad of Aram
mustered his entire army and besieged Samaria. 25As a
result, there was a great famine in the city. The siege
lasted so long that a donkey's head sold for eighty pieces
of silver, and a cup of dove's dung sold for five pieces* of
silver.
26One day as the king of Israel was walking along the
wall of the city, a woman called to him, "Please help me,
my lord the king!"
27He answered, "If the LORD doesn't help you, what can
I do? I have neither food from the threshing floor nor
wine from the press to give you." 28But then the king
asked, "What is the matter?"
She replied, "This woman said to me: 'Come on, let's
eat your son today, then we will eat my son tomorrow.'
29So we cooked my son and ate him. Then the next day I
said to her, 'Kill your son so we can eat him,' but she has
hidden her son."
30When the king heard this, he tore his clothes in despair. And as the king walked along the wall, the people
could see that he was wearing burlap under his robe next
to his skin.* 31"May God strike me and even kill me if I

6:25 Hebrew *sold for 80 shekels* [2 pounds, or 0.9 kilograms] *of silver, and ¼ of a cab* [0.3 liters] *of dove's dung sold for 5 shekels* [2 ounces, or 57 grams]. *Dove's dung* may be a variety of wild vegetable. 6:30 As in Greek version; Hebrew reads *wearing burlap next to his skin from the house.*

don't separate Elisha's head from his shoulders this very
day," the king vowed.
32Elisha was sitting in his house with the elders of Israel when the king sent a messenger to summon him. But
before the messenger arrived, Elisha said to the elders, "A
murderer has sent a man to cut off my head. When he arrives, shut the door and keep him out. We will soon hear
his master's steps following him."
33While Elisha was still saying this, the messenger arrived. And the king* said, "All this misery is from the
LORD! Why should I wait for the LORD any longer?"

A FATAL FOCUS 7:1-2

The king's officer didn't believe Elisha's message concerning the end of the famine. Yet God's words came true anyway (7:14-16). Like the officer, we're sometimes preoccupied with problems instead of looking for the solutions that God offers. When a problem comes your way, will you focus on it or on God? ■

7

Elisha replied, "Listen to this message from the
LORD! This is what the LORD says: By this time tomorrow
in the markets of Samaria, five quarts of choice flour will
cost only one piece of silver,* and ten quarts of barley
grain will cost only one piece of silver.*"
2The officer assisting the king said to the man of God,
"That couldn't happen even if the LORD opened the windows of heaven!"
But Elisha replied, "You will see it happen with your
own eyes, but you won't be able to eat any of it!"

LEPERS VISIT THE ENEMY CAMP

3Now there were four men with leprosy* sitting at the entrance of the city gates. "Why should we sit here waiting
to die?" they asked each other. 4"We will starve if we stay
here, but with the famine in the city, we will starve if we
go back there. So we might as well go out and surrender
to the Aramean army. If they let us live, so much the
better. But if they kill us, we would have died anyway."
5So at twilight they set out for the camp of the Arameans. But when they came to the edge of the camp, no one
was there! 6For the Lord had caused the Aramean army to
hear the clatter of speeding chariots and the galloping of
horses and the sounds of a great army approaching. "The
king of Israel has hired the Hittites and Egyptians* to attack us!" they cried to one another. 7So they panicked and
ran into the night, abandoning their tents, horses, donkeys, and everything else, as they fled for their lives.
8When the lepers arrived at the edge of the camp, they
went into one tent after another, eating and drinking
wine; and they carried off silver and gold and clothing
and hid it. 9Finally, they said to each other, "This is not
right. This is a day of good news, and we aren't sharing it
with anyone! If we wait until morning, some calamity will
certainly fall upon us. Come on, let's go back and tell the
people at the palace."
10So they went back to the city and told the gatekeepers what had happened. "We went out to the Aramean camp," they said, "and no one was there! The horses
and donkeys were tethered and the tents were all in order, but there wasn't a single person around!" 11Then the
gatekeepers shouted the news to the people in the
palace.

ISRAEL PLUNDERS THE CAMP

12The king got out of bed in the middle of the night and
told his officers, "I know what has happened. The Arameans know we are starving, so they have left their camp
and have hidden in the fields. They are expecting us to
leave the city, and then they will take us alive and capture
the city."
13One of his officers replied, "We had better send out
scouts to check into this. Let them take five of the remaining horses. If something happens to them, it will
be no worse than if they stay here and die with the rest
of us."
14So two chariots with horses were prepared, and the
king sent scouts to see what had happened to the Aramean army. 15They went all the way to the Jordan River, following a trail of clothing and equipment that the

6:33 Hebrew *he.* **7:1a** Hebrew *1 seah* [6 liters] *of choice flour will cost 1 shekel* [0.4 ounces, or 11 grams]; also in 7:16, 18. **7:1b** Hebrew *2 seahs* [12 liters] *of barley grain will cost 1 shekel* [0.4 ounces, or 11 grams]; also in 7:16, 18. **7:3** Or *with a contagious skin disease.* The Hebrew word used here and throughout this passage can describe various skin diseases. **7:6** Possibly *and the people of Muzur,* a district near Cilicia.

Which is more important, living like a Christian or telling others what I believe about God?

Try to remember the best gift you ever received. What did you do after you opened it? More than likely, you called your best friend to tell him or her about it.

Forgiveness from sin is the greatest gift you will ever receive! It is impossible to keep quiet about it if you truly recognize how important this free gift really is.

Check out the story of the four men with leprosy who discovered the empty camp (2 Kings 7:3-15). All of their enemies were gone! They couldn't wait to share the good news with everyone.

The choice for the four men with leprosy—keeping their discovery a secret or telling others about it—probably was tough to make because their disease separated them from other people. But they didn't hesitate to make their choice.

Our sin is like leprosy. We cannot always tell its effects, but left unchecked, the "disease" gets progressively worse. But forgiveness is the antidote for this disease. Our response in thankfulness to God could cause us to tell all who will listen!

Arameans had thrown away in their mad rush to escape. The scouts returned and told the king about it. 16Then the people of Samaria rushed out and plundered the Aramean camp. So it was true that five quarts of choice flour were sold that day for one piece of silver, and ten quarts of barley grain were sold for one piece of silver, just as the LORD had promised. 17The king appointed his officer to control the traffic at the gate, but he was knocked down and trampled to death as the people rushed out.

So everything happened exactly as the man of God had predicted when the king came to his house. 18The man of God had said to the king, "By this time tomorrow in the markets of Samaria, five quarts of choice flour will cost one piece of silver, and ten quarts of barley grain will cost one piece of silver."

19The king's officer had replied, "That couldn't happen even if the LORD opened the windows of heaven!" And the man of God had said, "You will see it happen with your own eyes, but you won't be able to eat any of it!" 20And so it was, for the people trampled him to death at the gate!

8

THE WOMAN FROM SHUNEM RETURNS HOME

Elisha had told the woman whose son he had brought back to life, "Take your family and move to some other place, for the LORD has called for a famine on Israel that will last for seven years." 2So the woman did as the man of God instructed. She took her family and settled in the land of the Philistines for seven years.

3After the famine ended she returned from the land of the Philistines, and she went to see the king about getting back her house and land. 4As she came in, the king was talking with Gehazi, the servant of the man of God. The king had just said, "Tell me some stories about the great things Elisha has done." 5And Gehazi was telling the king about the time Elisha had brought a boy back to life. At that very moment, the mother of the boy walked in to make her appeal to the king about her house and land.

"Look, my lord the king!" Gehazi exclaimed. "Here is the woman now, and this is her son—the very one Elisha brought back to life!"

6"Is this true?" the king asked her. And she told him the story. So he directed one of his officials to see that everything she had lost was restored to her, including the value of any crops that had been harvested during her absence.

HAZAEL MURDERS BEN-HADAD

7Elisha went to Damascus, the capital of Aram, where King Ben-hadad lay sick. When someone told the king that the man of God had come, 8the king said to Hazael, "Take a gift to the man of God. Then tell him to ask the LORD, 'Will I recover from this illness?'"

9So Hazael loaded down forty camels with the finest products of Damascus as a gift for Elisha. He went to him and said, "Your servant Ben-hadad, the king of Aram, has sent me to ask, 'Will I recover from this illness?'"

10And Elisha replied, "Go and tell him, 'You will surely recover.' But actually the LORD has shown me that he will surely die!" 11Elisha stared at Hazael* with a fixed gaze until Hazael became uneasy.* Then the man of God started weeping.

12"What's the matter, my lord?" Hazael asked him.

Elisha replied, "I know the terrible things you will do to the people of Israel. You will burn their fortified cities, kill their young men with the sword, dash their little children to the ground, and rip open their pregnant women!"

13Hazael responded, "How could a nobody like me* ever accomplish such great things?"

Elisha answered, "The LORD has shown me that you are going to be the king of Aram."

14When Hazael left Elisha and went back, the king asked him, "What did Elisha tell you?"

And Hazael replied, "He told me that you will surely recover."

15But the next day Hazael took a blanket, soaked it in water, and held it over the king's face until he died. Then Hazael became the next king of Aram.

JEHORAM RULES IN JUDAH

16Jehoram son of King Jehoshaphat of Judah began to rule over Judah in the fifth year of the reign of Joram son of Ahab, king of Israel. 17Jehoram was thirty-two years old when he became king, and he reigned in Jerusalem eight years. 18But Jehoram followed the example of the kings of Israel and was as wicked as King Ahab, for he had married one of Ahab's daughters. So Jehoram did what was evil in the LORD's sight. 19But the LORD did not want to destroy Judah, for he had made a covenant with David and promised that his descendants would continue to rule, shining like a lamp forever.

20During Jehoram's reign, the Edomites revolted against Judah and crowned their own king. 21So Jehoram* went with all his chariots to attack the town of Zair.* The Edomites surrounded him and his chariot commanders, but he went out at night and attacked them* under cover of darkness. But Jehoram's army deserted him and fled to their homes. 22So Edom has been independent from Judah to this day. The town of Libnah also revolted about that same time.

23The rest of the events in Jehoram's reign and everything he did are recorded in *The Book of the History of the Kings of Judah.* 24When Jehoram died, he was buried with his ancestors in the City of David. Then his son Ahaziah became the next king.

AHAZIAH RULES IN JUDAH

25Ahaziah son of Jehoram began to rule over Judah in the twelfth year of the reign of Joram son of Ahab, king of Israel.

26Ahaziah was twenty-two years old when he became king, and he reigned in Jerusalem one year. His mother was Athaliah, a granddaughter of King Omri of Israel. 27Ahaziah followed the evil example of King Ahab's family. He did what was evil in the LORD's sight, just as Ahab's

8:11a Hebrew *He stared at him.* **8:11b** The meaning of the Hebrew is uncertain. **8:13** Hebrew *a dog.* **8:21a** Hebrew *Joram,* a variant spelling of Jehoram; also in 8:23, 24. **8:21b** Greek version reads *Seir.* **8:21c** Or *he went out and escaped.* The meaning of the Hebrew is uncertain.

family had done, for he was related by marriage to the
family of Ahab.
28Ahaziah joined Joram son of Ahab, the king of Israel,
in his war against King Hazael of Aram at Ramoth-gilead.
When the Arameans wounded King Joram in the battle,
29he returned to Jezreel to recover from the wounds he
had received at Ramoth.* Because Joram was wounded,
King Ahaziah of Judah went to Jezreel to visit him.

9

JEHU ANOINTED KING OF ISRAEL

Meanwhile, Elisha the prophet had summoned a member of the group of prophets. "Get ready to travel,"* he
told him, "and take this flask of olive oil with you. Go to
Ramoth-gilead, 2and find Jehu son of Jehoshaphat, son of
Nimshi. Call him into a private room away from his
friends, 3and pour the oil over his head. Say to him, 'This
is what the LORD says: I anoint you to be the king over Israel.' Then open the door and run for your life!"
4So the young prophet did as he was told and went to
Ramoth-gilead. 5When he arrived there, he found Jehu
sitting around with the other army officers. "I have a
message for you, Commander," he said.
"For which one of us?" Jehu asked.
"For you, Commander," he replied.
6So Jehu left the others and went into the house. Then
the young prophet poured the oil over Jehu's head and
said, "This is what the LORD, the God of Israel, says: I
anoint you king over the LORD's people, Israel. 7You are to
destroy the family of Ahab, your master. In this way, I will
avenge the murder of my prophets and all the LORD's servants who were killed by Jezebel. 8The entire family of
Ahab must be wiped out. I will destroy every one of his
male descendants, slave and free alike, anywhere in Israel. 9I will destroy the family of Ahab as I destroyed the
families of Jeroboam son of Nebat and of Baasha son of
Ahijah. 10Dogs will eat Ahab's wife Jezebel at the plot of
land in Jezreel, and no one will bury her." Then the young
prophet opened the door and ran.
11Jehu went back to his fellow officers, and one of
them asked him, "What did that madman want? Is everything all right?"
"You know how a man like that babbles on," Jehu
replied.
12"You're hiding something," they said. "Tell us."
So Jehu told them, "He said to me, 'This is what the
LORD says: I have anointed you to be king over Israel.'"
13Then they quickly spread out their cloaks on the bare
steps and blew the ram's horn, shouting, "Jehu is king!"

JEHU KILLS JORAM AND AHAZIAH

14So Jehu son of Jehoshaphat, son of Nimshi, led a conspiracy against King Joram. (Now Joram had been with
the army at Ramoth-gilead, defending Israel against the
forces of King Hazael of Aram. 15But King Joram* was
wounded in the fighting and returned to Jezreel to recover from his wounds.) So Jehu told the men with him,
"If you want me to be king, don't let anyone leave town
and go to Jezreel to report what we have done."
16Then Jehu got into a chariot and rode to Jezreel to
find King Joram, who was lying there wounded. King
Ahaziah of Judah was there, too, for he had gone to visit
him. 17The watchman on the tower of Jezreel saw Jehu
and his company approaching, so he shouted to Joram, "I
see a company of troops coming!"
"Send out a rider to ask if they are coming in peace,"
King Joram ordered.
18So a horseman went out to meet Jehu and said, "The
king wants to know if you are coming in peace."
Jehu replied, "What do you know about peace? Fall in
behind me!"
The watchman called out to the king, "The messenger
has met them, but he's not returning."
19So the king sent out a second horseman. He rode up
to them and said, "The king wants to know if you come in
peace."
Again Jehu answered, "What do you know about
peace? Fall in behind me!"

PEACE 9:18-19

The riders met Jehu and asked if he came in peace and friendship. But Jehu responded, "What do you know about peace?" Jehu scoffed, because he knew that the men represented a cruel king. Friendship and peace are genuine when they are rooted in a relationship with God. Is the friendship you offer genuine? ■

20The watchman exclaimed, "The messenger has met
them, but he isn't returning either! It must be Jehu son
of Nimshi, for he's driving like a madman."
21"Quick! Get my chariot ready!" King Joram commanded.
Then King Joram of Israel and King Ahaziah of Judah
rode out in their chariots to meet Jehu. They met him at
the plot of land that had belonged to Naboth of Jezreel.
22King Joram demanded, "Do you come in peace, Jehu?"
Jehu replied, "How can there be peace as long as the
idolatry and witchcraft of your mother, Jezebel, are all
around us?"
23Then King Joram turned the horses around* and
fled, shouting to King Ahaziah, "Treason, Ahaziah!" 24But
Jehu drew his bow and shot Joram between the shoulders. The arrow pierced his heart, and he sank down dead
in his chariot.
25Jehu said to Bidkar, his officer, "Throw him into the
plot of land that belonged to Naboth of Jezreel. Do you
remember when you and I were riding along behind his
father, Ahab? The LORD pronounced this message
against him: 26'I solemnly swear that I will repay him here
on this plot of land, says the LORD, for the murder of Naboth and his sons that I saw yesterday.' So throw him out
on Naboth's property, just as the LORD said."

8:29 Hebrew *Ramah,* a variant spelling of Ramoth. **9:1** Hebrew *Bind up your loins.* **9:15** Hebrew *Jehoram,* a variant spelling of Joram; also in 9:17, 21, 22, 23, 24. **9:23** Hebrew *turned his hands.*

27When King Ahaziah of Judah saw what was happening,
he fled along the road to Beth-haggan. Jehu rode after him,
shouting, "Shoot him, too!" So they shot Ahaziah in his chariot at the Ascent of Gur, near Ibleam. He was able to go on as
far as Megiddo, but he died there. 28His servants took him by
chariot to Jerusalem, where they buried him with his ancestors in the City of David. 29Ahaziah had become king over Judah in the eleventh year of the reign of Joram son of Ahab.

THE DEATH OF JEZEBEL

30When Jezebel, the queen mother, heard that Jehu had
come to Jezreel, she painted her eyelids and fixed her
hair and sat at a window. 31When Jehu entered the gate of
the palace, she shouted at him, "Have you come in peace,
you murderer? You're just like Zimri, who murdered his
master!"*

32Jehu looked up and saw her at the window and
shouted, "Who is on my side?" And two or three eunuchs
looked out at him. 33"Throw her down!" Jehu yelled. So
they threw her out the window, and her blood spattered
against the wall and on the horses. And Jehu trampled
her body under his horses' hooves.

34Then Jehu went into the palace and ate and drank.
Afterward he said, "Someone go and bury this cursed
woman, for she is the daughter of a king." 35But when
they went out to bury her, they found only her skull, her
feet, and her hands.

36When they returned and told Jehu, he stated, "This
fulfills the message from the LORD, which he spoke
through his servant Elijah from Tishbe: 'At the plot of
land in Jezreel, dogs will eat Jezebel's body. 37Her remains
will be scattered like dung on the plot of land in Jezreel,
so that no one will be able to recognize her.'"

10

JEHU KILLS AHAB'S FAMILY

Ahab had seventy sons living in the city of Samaria. So
Jehu wrote letters and sent them to Samaria, to the elders
and officials of the city,* and to the guardians of King
Ahab's sons. He said, 2"The king's sons are with you, and
you have at your disposal chariots, horses, a fortified city,
and weapons. As soon as you receive this letter, 3select
the best qualified of your master's sons to be your king,
and prepare to fight for Ahab's dynasty."

4But they were paralyzed with fear and said, "We've
seen that two kings couldn't stand against this man!
What can we do?"

5So the palace and city administrators, together with
the elders and the guardians of the king's sons, sent this
message to Jehu: "We are your servants and will do anything you tell us. We will not make anyone king; do whatever you think is best."

6Jehu responded with a second letter: "If you are on my
side and are going to obey me, bring the heads of your
master's sons to me at Jezreel by this time tomorrow."
Now the seventy sons of the king were being cared for by
the leaders of Samaria, where they had been raised since
childhood. 7When the letter arrived, the leaders killed all
seventy of the king's sons. They placed their heads in baskets and presented them to Jehu at Jezreel.

8A messenger went to Jehu and said, "They have
brought the heads of the king's sons."

So Jehu ordered, "Pile them in two heaps at the entrance of the city gate, and leave them there until
morning."

9In the morning he went out and spoke to the crowd
that had gathered around them. "You are not to blame,"
he told them. "I am the one who conspired against my
master and killed him. But who killed all these? 10You can
be sure that the message of the LORD that was spoken
concerning Ahab's family will not fail. The LORD declared
through his servant Elijah that this would happen."
11Then Jehu killed all who were left of Ahab's relatives living in Jezreel and all his important officials, his personal
friends, and his priests. So Ahab was left without a single
survivor.

12Then Jehu set out for Samaria. Along the way, while
he was at Beth-eked of the Shepherds, 13he met some relatives of King Ahaziah of Judah. "Who are you?" he asked
them.

And they replied, "We are relatives of King Ahaziah.
We are going to visit the sons of King Ahab and the sons
of the queen mother."

14"Take them alive!" Jehu shouted to his men. And they
captured all forty-two of them and killed them at the well
of Beth-eked. None of them escaped.

15When Jehu left there, he met Jehonadab son of Recab, who was coming to meet him. After they had greeted
each other, Jehu said to him, "Are you as loyal to me as I
am to you?"

"Yes, I am," Jehonadab replied.

"If you are," Jehu said, "then give me your hand." So Jehonadab put out his hand, and Jehu helped him into the
chariot. 16Then Jehu said, "Now come with me, and see
how devoted I am to the LORD." So Jehonadab rode along
with him.

17When Jehu arrived in Samaria, he killed everyone
who was left there from Ahab's family, just as the LORD
had promised through Elijah.

JEHU KILLS THE PRIESTS OF BAAL

18Then Jehu called a meeting of all the people of the city
and said to them, "Ahab's worship of Baal was nothing
compared to the way I will worship him! 19Therefore,
summon all the prophets and worshipers of Baal, and call
together all his priests. See to it that every one of them
comes, for I am going to offer a great sacrifice to Baal.
Anyone who fails to come will be put to death." But Jehu's
cunning plan was to destroy all the worshipers of Baal.

20Then Jehu ordered, "Prepare a solemn assembly to
worship Baal!" So they did. 21He sent messengers
throughout all Israel summoning those who worshiped
Baal. They all came—not a single one remained behind—
and they filled the temple of Baal from one end to the
other. 22And Jehu instructed the keeper of the wardrobe,

9:31 See 1 Kgs 16:9-10, where Zimri killed his master, King Elah. **10:1** As in some Greek manuscripts and Latin Vulgate (see also 10:6); Hebrew reads *of Jezreel*.

"Be sure that every worshiper of Baal wears one of these
robes." So robes were given to them.
23Then Jehu went into the temple of Baal with Jehonadab son of Recab. Jehu said to the worshipers of Baal,
"Make sure no one who worships the LORD is here—only
those who worship Baal." 24So they were all inside the
temple to offer sacrifices and burnt offerings. Now Jehu
had stationed eighty of his men outside the building and
had warned them, "If you let anyone escape, you will pay
for it with your own life."
25As soon as Jehu had finished sacrificing the burnt offering, he commanded his guards and officers, "Go in
and kill all of them. Don't let a single one escape!" So they
killed them all with their swords, and the guards and officers dragged their bodies outside.* Then Jehu's men
went into the innermost fortress* of the temple of Baal.
26They dragged out the sacred pillar* used in the worship
of Baal and burned it. 27They smashed the sacred pillar
and wrecked the temple of Baal, converting it into a public toilet, as it remains to this day.
28In this way, Jehu destroyed every trace of Baal worship from Israel. 29He did not, however, destroy the gold
calves at Bethel and Dan, with which Jeroboam son of Nebat had caused Israel to sin.
30Nonetheless the LORD said to Jehu, "You have done
well in following my instructions to destroy the family of
Ahab. Therefore, your descendants will be kings of Israel
down to the fourth generation." 31But Jehu did not obey
the Law of the LORD, the God of Israel, with all his heart.
He refused to turn from the sins that Jeroboam had led
Israel to commit.

LIP SERVICE 10:30-31

Jehu did much of what the Lord told him to, but did not fully obey him. He had become God's *instrument* for carrying out justice, rather than God's *servant.* As a result, Jehu gave only lip service to God while he worshiped the golden calves. In the same way, we can be very active in our work for God and still not give the heartfelt obedience he desires. Are you a servant or an instrument? ■

THE DEATH OF JEHU

32At about that time the LORD began to cut down the size
of Israel's territory. King Hazael conquered several sections of the country 33east of the Jordan River, including
all of Gilead, Gad, Reuben, and Manasseh. He conquered
the area from the town of Aroer by the Arnon Gorge to as
far north as Gilead and Bashan.
34The rest of the events in Jehu's reign—everything he
did and all his achievements—are recorded in *The Book
of the History of the Kings of Israel.*
35When Jehu died, he was buried in Samaria. Then his
son Jehoahaz became the next king. 36In all, Jehu reigned
over Israel from Samaria for twenty-eight years.

11

QUEEN ATHALIAH RULES IN JUDAH

When Athaliah, the mother of King Ahaziah of Judah,
learned that her son was dead, she began to destroy the
rest of the royal family. 2But Ahaziah's sister Jehosheba,
the daughter of King Jehoram,* took Ahaziah's infant
son, Joash, and stole him away from among the rest of the
king's children, who were about to be killed. She put Joash and his nurse in a bedroom to hide him from Athaliah, so the child was not murdered. 3Joash remained
hidden in the Temple of the LORD for six years while Athaliah ruled over the land.

REVOLT AGAINST ATHALIAH

4In the seventh year of Athaliah's reign, Jehoiada the
priest summoned the commanders, the Carite mercenaries, and the palace guards to come to the Temple of the
LORD. He made a solemn pact with them and made them
swear an oath of loyalty there in the LORD's Temple; then
he showed them the king's son.
5Jehoiada told them, "This is what you must do. A third
of you who are on duty on the Sabbath are to guard the
royal palace itself. 6Another third of you are to stand
guard at the Sur Gate. And the final third must stand
guard behind the palace guard. These three groups will
all guard the palace. 7The other two units who are off
duty on the Sabbath must stand guard for the king at the
LORD's Temple. 8Form a bodyguard around the king and
keep your weapons in hand. Kill anyone who tries to
break through. Stay with the king wherever he goes."
9So the commanders did everything as Jehoiada the
priest ordered. The commanders took charge of the men
reporting for duty that Sabbath, as well as those who were
going off duty. They brought them all to Jehoiada the
priest, 10and he supplied them with the spears and small
shields that had once belonged to King David and were
stored in the Temple of the LORD. 11The palace guards stationed themselves around the king, with their weapons
ready. They formed a line from the south side of the Temple around to the north side and all around the altar.
12Then Jehoiada brought out Joash, the king's son,
placed the crown on his head, and presented him with a
copy of God's laws.* They anointed him and proclaimed
him king, and everyone clapped their hands and shouted,
"Long live the king!"

THE DEATH OF ATHALIAH

13When Athaliah heard all the noise made by the palace
guards and the people, she hurried to the LORD's Temple
to see what was happening. 14When she arrived, she saw
the newly crowned king standing in his place of authority
by the pillar, as was the custom at times of coronation.
The commanders and trumpeters were surrounding
him, and people from all over the land were rejoicing and
blowing trumpets. When Athaliah saw all this, she tore
her clothes in despair and shouted, "Treason! Treason!"

10:25a Or *they left their bodies lying there;* or *they threw them out into the outermost court.* **10:25b** Hebrew *city.* **10:26** As in Greek and Syriac versions and Latin Vulgate; Hebrew reads *sacred pillars.* **11:2** Hebrew *Joram,* a variant spelling of Jehoram. **11:12** Or *a copy of the covenant.*

15Then Jehoiada the priest ordered the commanders who were in charge of the troops, "Take her to the soldiers in front of the Temple,* and kill anyone who tries to rescue her." For the priest had said, "She must not be killed in the Temple of the LORD." 16So they seized her and led her out to the gate where horses enter the palace grounds, and she was killed there.

JEHOIADA'S RELIGIOUS REFORMS

17Then Jehoiada made a covenant between the LORD and the king and the people that they would be the LORD's people. He also made a covenant between the king and the people. 18And all the people of the land went over to the temple of Baal and tore it down. They demolished the altars and smashed the idols to pieces, and they killed Mattan the priest of Baal in front of the altars.

Jehoiada the priest stationed guards at the Temple of the LORD. 19Then the commanders, the Carite mercenaries, the palace guards, and all the people of the land escorted the king from the Temple of the LORD. They went through the gate of the guards and into the palace, and the king took his seat on the royal throne. 20So all the people of the land rejoiced, and the city was peaceful because Athaliah had been killed at the king's palace.

21*Joash* was seven years old when he became king.

12

JOASH REPAIRS THE TEMPLE

1*Joash* began to rule over Judah in the seventh year of King Jehu's reign in Israel. He reigned in Jerusalem forty years. His mother was Zibiah from Beersheba. 2All his life Joash did what was pleasing in the LORD's sight because Jehoiada the priest instructed him. 3Yet even so, he did not destroy the pagan shrines, and the people still offered sacrifices and burned incense there.

A GOOD INFLUENCE 12:1-2

Jehoiada, the high priest, was a good influence over Joash, the young king of Judah. As long as Joash heeded Jehoiada's good instruction, he fulfilled God's plan for his life. Who offers you wise advice? Do you follow that advice? ■

4One day King Joash said to the priests, "Collect all the money brought as a sacred offering to the LORD's Temple, whether it is a regular assessment, a payment of vows, or a voluntary gift. 5Let the priests take some of that money to pay for whatever repairs are needed at the Temple."

6But by the twenty-third year of Joash's reign, the priests still had not repaired the Temple. 7So King Joash called for Jehoiada and the other priests and asked them, "Why haven't you repaired the Temple? Don't use any more money for your own needs. From now on, it must all be spent on Temple repairs." 8So the priests agreed not to accept any more money from the people, and they also agreed to let others take responsibility for repairing the Temple.

9Then Jehoiada the priest bored a hole in the lid of a large chest and set it on the right-hand side of the altar at the entrance of the Temple of the LORD. The priests guarding the entrance put all of the people's contributions into the chest. 10Whenever the chest became full, the court secretary and the high priest counted the money that had been brought to the LORD's Temple and put it into bags. 11Then they gave the money to the construction supervisors, who used it to pay the people working on the LORD's Temple—the carpenters, the builders, 12the masons, and the stonecutters. They also used the money to buy the timber and the finished stone needed for repairing the LORD's Temple, and they paid any other expenses related to the Temple's restoration.

EVALUATE ACTIONS 12:3

Like Jehu (see 10:30-31), Joash didn't go far enough in his plan to reform the nation, but he did a lot of good. When we aren't sure if we've gone far enough in correcting our actions, we can ask ourselves these questions: (1) Does the Bible prohibit this action? (2) Does this action take me away from loving, worshiping, or serving God? (3) Does it bring out the best in me, consistent with God's purpose? (4) Does it benefit other believers? ■

13The money brought to the Temple was not used for making silver bowls, lamp snuffers, basins, trumpets, or other articles of gold or silver for the Temple of the LORD. 14It was paid to the workmen, who used it for the Temple repairs. 15No accounting of this money was required from the construction supervisors, because they were honest and trustworthy men. 16However, the money that was contributed for guilt offerings and sin offerings was not brought into the LORD's Temple. It was given to the priests for their own use.

THE END OF JOASH'S REIGN

17About this time King Hazael of Aram went to war against Gath and captured it. Then he turned to attack Jerusalem. 18King Joash collected all the sacred objects that Jehoshaphat, Jehoram, and Ahaziah, the previous kings of Judah, had dedicated, along with what he himself had dedicated. He sent them all to Hazael, along with all the gold in the treasuries of the LORD's Temple and the royal palace. So Hazael called off his attack on Jerusalem.

19The rest of the events in Joash's reign and everything he did are recorded in *The Book of the History of the Kings of Judah.*

20Joash's officers plotted against him and assassinated him at Beth-millo on the road to Silla. 21The assassins were Jozacar* son of Shimeath and Jehozabad son of

11:15 Or *Bring her out from between the ranks;* or *Take her out of the Temple precincts.* The meaning of the Hebrew is uncertain. **11:21a** Verse 11:21 is numbered 12:1 in Hebrew text. **11:21b** Hebrew *Jehoash,* a variant spelling of Joash. **12:1a** Verses 12:1-21 are numbered 12:2-22 in Hebrew text. **12:1b** Hebrew *Jehoash,* a variant spelling of Joash; also in 12:2, 4, 6, 7, 18. **12:21** As in Greek and Syriac versions; Hebrew reads *Jozabad.*

Shomer—both trusted advisers. Joash was buried with his ancestors in the City of David. Then his son Amaziah became the next king.

13 JEHOAHAZ RULES IN ISRAEL

Jehoahaz son of Jehu began to rule over Israel in the twenty-third year of King Joash's reign in Judah. He
reigned in Samaria seventeen years. 2But he did what was
evil in the LORD's sight. He followed the example of Jeroboam son of Nebat, continuing the sins that Jeroboam
had led Israel to commit. 3So the LORD was very angry
with Israel, and he allowed King Hazael of Aram and his son Ben-hadad to defeat them repeatedly.

YES! 13:4-6

Although God rescued Israel from their enemies, they didn't stick with him for long. Pretty soon, they were back to worshiping idols. Saying no to wrong actions isn't enough; we must also say yes to a life of commitment to God. Have you said yes lately? ■

4Then Jehoahaz prayed for the LORD's help, and the LORD heard his prayer, for he could see how severely the
king of Aram was oppressing Israel. 5So the LORD pro-
vided someone to rescue the Israelites from the tyranny of the Arameans. Then Israel lived in safety again as they had in former days.

6But they continued to sin, following the evil example of Jeroboam. They also allowed the Asherah pole in Samaria to remain standing. 7Finally, Jehoahaz's army was
reduced to 50 charioteers, 10 chariots, and 10,000 foot soldiers. The king of Aram had killed the others, trampling them like dust under his feet.

8The rest of the events in Jehoahaz's reign—everything he did and the extent of his power—are recorded in *The Book of the History of the Kings of Israel.*
9When Jehoa-
haz died, he was buried in Samaria. Then his son Jehoash* became the next king.

JEHOASH RULES IN ISRAEL

10Jehoash son of Jehoahaz began to rule over Israel in the thirty-seventh year of King Joash's reign in Judah. He
reigned in Samaria sixteen years. 11But he did what was
evil in the LORD's sight. He refused to turn from the sins that Jeroboam son of Nebat had led Israel to commit.

12The rest of the events in Jehoash's reign and everything he did, including the extent of his power and his war with King Amaziah of Judah, are recorded in *The Book of the History of the Kings of Israel.*
13When Jehoash
died, he was buried in Samaria with the kings of Israel. Then his son Jeroboam II became the next king.

ELISHA'S FINAL PROPHECY

14When Elisha was in his last illness, King Jehoash of Israel visited him and wept over him. "My father! My father! I see the chariots and charioteers of Israel!" he cried.

15Elisha told him, "Get a bow and some arrows." And
the king did as he was told. 16Elisha told him, "Put your
hand on the bow," and Elisha laid his own hands on the king's hands.

17Then he commanded, "Open that eastern window," and he opened it. Then he said, "Shoot!" So he shot an arrow. Elisha proclaimed, "This is the LORD's arrow, an arrow of victory over Aram, for you will completely conquer the Arameans at Aphek."

18Then he said, "Now pick up the other arrows and strike them against the ground." So the king picked them
up and struck the ground three times. 19But the man of
God was angry with him. "You should have struck the ground five or six times!" he exclaimed. "Then you would have beaten Aram until it was entirely destroyed. Now you will be victorious only three times."

20Then Elisha died and was buried.

Groups of Moabite raiders used to invade the land
each spring. 21Once when some Israelites were burying a
man, they spied a band of these raiders. So they hastily threw the corpse into the tomb of Elisha and fled. But as soon as the body touched Elisha's bones, the dead man revived and jumped to his feet!

PARTIAL VICTORY 13:14-19

When Jehoash was told to strike the ground with arrows, he halfheartedly obeyed. As a result, Elisha told him that his victory over Aram would not be complete. Receiving the full benefits of God's plan for our life requires wholehearted obedience to God's commands. Want to fully experience the "full" life God offers? (See John 10:10.) Love him wholeheartedly. ■

22King Hazael of Aram had oppressed Israel during the
entire reign of King Jehoahaz. 23But the LORD was gra-
cious and merciful to the people of Israel, and they were not totally destroyed. He pitied them because of his covenant with Abraham, Isaac, and Jacob. And to this day he still has not completely destroyed them or banished them from his presence.

24King Hazael of Aram died, and his son Ben-hadad became the next king. 25Then Jehoash son of Jehoahaz re-
captured from Ben-hadad son of Hazael the towns that had been taken from Jehoash's father, Jehoahaz. Jehoash defeated Ben-hadad on three occasions, and he recovered the Israelite towns.

14 AMAZIAH RULES IN JUDAH

Amaziah son of Joash began to rule over Judah in the second year of the reign of King Jehoash* of Israel.
2Ama-
ziah was twenty-five years old when he became king, and he reigned in Jerusalem twenty-nine years. His mother
was Jehoaddin from Jerusalem. 3Amaziah did what was
pleasing in the LORD's sight, but not like his ancestor Da-

13:9 Hebrew *Joash,* a variant spelling of Jehoash; also in 13:10, 12, 13, 14, 25. 14:1 Hebrew *Joash,* a variant spelling of Jehoash; also in 14:13, 23, 27.

vid. Instead, he followed the example of his father, Joash.
4Amaziah did not destroy the pagan shrines, and the people still offered sacrifices and burned incense there.
5When Amaziah was well established as king, he executed the officials who had assassinated his father.
6However, he did not kill the children of the assassins, for
he obeyed the command of the LORD as written by Moses
in the Book of the Law: "Parents must not be put to death
for the sins of their children, nor children for the sins of
their parents. Those deserving to die must be put to
death for their own crimes."*
7Amaziah also killed 10,000 Edomites in the Valley of
Salt. He also conquered Sela and changed its name to Joktheel, as it is called to this day.

A WISE USE OF RESOURCES 14:23-28

Although Jeroboam II had no regard for God, Israel enjoyed power and prosperity under his warlike policies and skillful administration. Yet his administration ignored policies of justice and mercy. The rich people grew self-centered; the poor grew discouraged. Jesus once said that to those who are given much, much will be required (Luke 12:48). We have a responsibility to use our resources wisely and mercifully. ■

8One day Amaziah sent messengers with this challenge to Israel's king Jehoash, the son of Jehoahaz and
grandson of Jehu: "Come and meet me in battle!"*
9But King Jehoash of Israel replied to King Amaziah of
Judah with this story: "Out in the Lebanon mountains, a
thistle sent a message to a mighty cedar tree: 'Give your
daughter in marriage to my son.' But just then a wild animal of Lebanon came by and stepped on the thistle,
crushing it!
10"You have indeed defeated Edom, and you are very
proud of it. But be content with your victory and stay at
home! Why stir up trouble that will only bring disaster on
you and the people of Judah?"
11But Amaziah refused to listen, so King Jehoash of
Israel mobilized his army against King Amaziah of
Judah. The two armies drew up their battle lines at Beth-
shemesh in Judah. 12Judah was routed by the army of Israel, and its army scattered and fled for home. 13King
Jehoash of Israel captured Judah's king, Amaziah son of
Joash and grandson of Ahaziah, at Beth-shemesh. Then
he marched to Jerusalem, where he demolished
600 feet* of Jerusalem's wall, from the Ephraim Gate to
the Corner Gate. 14He carried off all the gold and silver
and all the articles from the Temple of the LORD. He also
seized the treasures from the royal palace, along with
hostages, and then returned to Samaria.
15The rest of the events in Jehoash's reign and everything he did, including the extent of his power and his
war with King Amaziah of Judah, are recorded in *The
Book of the History of the Kings of Israel.* 16When Jehoash
died, he was buried in Samaria with the kings of Israel.
And his son Jeroboam II became the next king.
17King Amaziah of Judah lived for fifteen years after
the death of King Jehoash of Israel. 18The rest of the
events in Amaziah's reign are recorded in *The Book of the
History of the Kings of Judah.*
19There was a conspiracy against Amaziah's life in Jerusalem, and he fled to Lachish. But his enemies sent assassins after him, and they killed him there. 20They
brought his body back to Jerusalem on a horse, and he
was buried with his ancestors in the City of David.
21All the people of Judah had crowned Amaziah's
sixteen-year-old son, Uzziah,* as king in place of his
father, Amaziah. 22After his father's death, Uzziah rebuilt the town of Elath and restored it to Judah.

JEROBOAM II RULES IN ISRAEL

23Jeroboam II, the son of Jehoash, began to rule over Israel in the fifteenth year of King Amaziah's reign in Judah.
Jeroboam reigned in Samaria forty-one years. 24He did
what was evil in the LORD's sight. He refused to turn from
the sins that Jeroboam son of Nebat had led Israel to
commit. 25Jeroboam II recovered the territories of Israel
between Lebo-hamath and the Dead Sea,* just as the
LORD, the God of Israel, had promised through Jonah son
of Amittai, the prophet from Gath-hepher.
26For the LORD saw the bitter suffering of everyone in
Israel, and that there was no one in Israel, slave or free, to
help them. 27And because the LORD had not said he would
blot out the name of Israel completely, he used Jeroboam
II, the son of Jehoash, to save them.
28The rest of the events in the reign of Jeroboam II and
everything he did—including the extent of his power, his
wars, and how he recovered for Israel both Damascus
and Hamath, which had belonged to Judah*—are recorded in *The Book of the History of the Kings of Israel.*
29When Jeroboam II died, he was buried in Samaria* with
the kings of Israel. Then his son Zechariah became the
next king.

THE BEST ROLE MODEL 15:1-5

Although Uzziah accomplished a great deal, he failed to destroy the centers of idol worship, just as his father (Amaziah) and grandfather (Joash) had failed to do. Although Uzziah's father and grandfather were basically good kings, they were poor models in some important areas. Looking for a good role model to imitate? You can't find a better one than Jesus. ■

15

UZZIAH RULES IN JUDAH

Uzziah* son of Amaziah began to rule over Judah in the
twenty-seventh year of the reign of King Jeroboam II of
Israel. 2He was sixteen years old when he became king,

14:6 Deut 24:16. 14:8 Hebrew *Come, let us look one another in the face.* 14:13 Hebrew *400 cubits* [180 meters]. 14:21 Hebrew *Azariah,* a variant spelling of Uzziah. 14:25 Hebrew *the sea of the Arabah.* 14:28 Or *to Yaudi.* The meaning of the Hebrew is uncertain. 14:29 As in some Greek manuscripts; Hebrew omits *in Samaria.* 15:1 Hebrew *Azariah,* a variant spelling of Uzziah; also in 15:6, 7, 8, 17, 23, 27.

and he reigned in Jerusalem fifty-two years. His mother
was Jecoliah from Jerusalem.
3He did what was pleasing in the LORD's sight, just as his
father, Amaziah, had done. 4But he did not destroy the pagan
shrines, and the people still offered sacrifices and burned
incense there. 5The LORD struck the king with leprosy,*
which lasted until the day he died. He lived in isolation in a
separate house. The king's son Jotham was put in charge of
the royal palace, and he governed the people of the land.
6The rest of the events in Uzziah's reign and everything he did are recorded in *The Book of the History of
the Kings of Judah.* 7When Uzziah died, he was buried
with his ancestors in the City of David. And his son Jotham became the next king.

ZECHARIAH RULES IN ISRAEL

8Zechariah son of Jeroboam II began to rule over Israel in
the thirty-eighth year of King Uzziah's reign in Judah. He
reigned in Samaria six months. 9Zechariah did what was
evil in the LORD's sight, as his ancestors had done. He refused to turn from the sins that Jeroboam son of Nebat
had led Israel to commit. 10Then Shallum son of Jabesh
conspired against Zechariah, assassinated him in public,* and became the next king.

INFLUENCE 15:8-9

Zechariah encouraged Israel (the northern kingdom) to disobey God by worshiping idols. The wrong things we do become doubly worse when we encourage others to disobey God. We are responsible for the way we influence others. What would your friends say about your influence over them? ■

11The rest of the events in Zechariah's reign are recorded in *The Book of the History of the Kings of Israel.*
12So the LORD's message to Jehu came true: "Your descendants will be kings of Israel down to the fourth
generation."

SHALLUM RULES IN ISRAEL

13Shallum son of Jabesh began to rule over Israel in the
thirty-ninth year of King Uzziah's reign in Judah. Shallum reigned in Samaria only one month. 14Then Menahem son of Gadi went to Samaria from Tirzah and
assassinated him, and he became the next king.
15The rest of the events in Shallum's reign, including
his conspiracy, are recorded in *The Book of the History of
the Kings of Israel.*

MENAHEM RULES IN ISRAEL

16At that time Menahem destroyed the town of Tappuah*
and all the surrounding countryside as far as Tirzah, because its citizens refused to surrender the town. He
killed the entire population and ripped open the pregnant women.
17Menahem son of Gadi began to rule over Israel in the
thirty-ninth year of King Uzziah's reign in Judah. He
reigned in Samaria ten years. 18But Menahem did what
was evil in the LORD's sight. During his entire reign, he refused to turn from the sins that Jeroboam son of Nebat
had led Israel to commit.
19Then King Tiglath-pileser* of Assyria invaded the
land. But Menahem paid him thirty-seven tons* of silver
to gain his support in tightening his grip on royal power.
20Menahem extorted the money from the rich of Israel,
demanding that each of them pay fifty pieces* of silver to
the king of Assyria. So the king of Assyria turned from attacking Israel and did not stay in the land.
21The rest of the events in Menahem's reign and everything he did are recorded in *The Book of the History of
the Kings of Israel.* 22When Menahem died, his son Pekahiah became the next king.

PEKAHIAH RULES IN ISRAEL

23Pekahiah son of Menahem began to rule over Israel in
the fiftieth year of King Uzziah's reign in Judah. He
reigned in Samaria two years. 24But Pekahiah did what
was evil in the LORD's sight. He refused to turn from the
sins that Jeroboam son of Nebat had led Israel to commit.
25Then Pekah son of Remaliah, the commander of
Pekahiah's army, conspired against him. With fifty men
from Gilead, Pekah assassinated the king, along with Argob and Arieh, in the citadel of the palace at Samaria.
And Pekah reigned in his place.
26The rest of the events in Pekahiah's reign and everything he did are recorded in *The Book of the History of
the Kings of Israel.*

PEKAH RULES IN ISRAEL

27Pekah son of Remaliah began to rule over Israel in the
fifty-second year of King Uzziah's reign in Judah. He
reigned in Samaria twenty years. 28But Pekah did what
was evil in the LORD's sight. He refused to turn from the
sins that Jeroboam son of Nebat had led Israel to commit.
29During Pekah's reign, King Tiglath-pileser of Assyria
attacked Israel again, and he captured the towns of Ijon,
Abel-beth-maacah, Janoah, Kedesh, and Hazor. He also
conquered the regions of Gilead, Galilee, and all of Naphtali, and he took the people to Assyria as captives. 30Then
Hoshea son of Elah conspired against Pekah and assassinated him. He began to rule over Israel in the twentieth
year of Jotham son of Uzziah.
31The rest of the events in Pekah's reign and everything
he did are recorded in *The Book of the History of the
Kings of Israel.*

JOTHAM RULES IN JUDAH

32Jotham son of Uzziah began to rule over Judah in the
second year of King Pekah's reign in Israel. 33He was
twenty-five years old when he became king, and he
reigned in Jerusalem sixteen years. His mother was Jerusha, the daughter of Zadok.

15:5 Or *with a contagious skin disease.* The Hebrew word used here and throughout this passage can describe various skin diseases. **15:10** Or *at Ibleam.* **15:16** As in some Greek manuscripts; other Greek manuscripts read *at Ibleam.* Hebrew reads *Tiphsah.* **15:19a** Hebrew *Pul,* another name for Tiglath-pileser. **15:19b** Hebrew *1,000 talents* [34 metric tons]. **15:20** Hebrew *50 shekels* [20 ounces, or 570 grams].

[34]Jotham did what was pleasing in the LORD's sight. He did everything his father, Uzziah, had done. [35]But he did not destroy the pagan shrines, and the people still offered sacrifices and burned incense there. He rebuilt the upper gate of the Temple of the LORD.

FIRST PRIORITY 15:34-35

Although Jotham was a decent king of Judah, he failed in a most critical area: He didn't destroy the pagan shrines where the people worshiped idols. Like Jotham, we may live a basically good life and yet miss doing what is most important. A lifetime of doing good is not enough if we make the crucial mistake of not fully obeying God. A true follower of God puts him first in all areas of life. That's what you do, right? ■

[36]The rest of the events in Jotham's reign and everything he did are recorded in *The Book of the History of the Kings of Judah.* [37]In those days the LORD began to send King Rezin of Aram and King Pekah of Israel to attack Judah. [38]When Jotham died, he was buried with his ancestors in the City of David. And his son Ahaz became the next king.

16 AHAZ RULES IN JUDAH

Ahaz son of Jotham began to rule over Judah in the seventeenth year of King Pekah's reign in Israel. [2]Ahaz was twenty years old when he became king, and he reigned in Jerusalem sixteen years. He did not do what was pleasing in the sight of the LORD his God, as his ancestor David had done. [3]Instead, he followed the example of the kings of Israel, even sacrificing his own son in the fire.* In this way, he followed the detestable practices of the pagan nations the LORD had driven from the land ahead of the Israelites. [4]He offered sacrifices and burned incense at the pagan shrines and on the hills and under every green tree.

[5]Then King Rezin of Aram and King Pekah of Israel came up to attack Jerusalem. They besieged Ahaz but could not conquer him. [6]At that time the king of Edom* recovered the town of Elath for Edom.* He drove out the people of Judah and sent Edomites* to live there, as they do to this day.

[7]King Ahaz sent messengers to King Tiglath-pileser of Assyria with this message: "I am your servant and your vassal.* Come up and rescue me from the attacking armies of Aram and Israel." [8]Then Ahaz took the silver and gold from the Temple of the LORD and the palace treasury and sent it as a payment to the Assyrian king. [9]So the king of Assyria attacked the Aramean capital of Damascus and led its population away as captives, resettling them in Kir. He also killed King Rezin.

[10]King Ahaz then went to Damascus to meet with King Tiglath-pileser of Assyria. While he was there, he took special note of the altar. Then he sent a model of the altar to Uriah the priest, along with its design in full detail. [11]Uriah followed the king's instructions and built an altar just like it, and it was ready before the king returned from Damascus. [12]When the king returned, he inspected the altar and made offerings on it. [13]He presented a burnt offering and a grain offering, he poured out a liquid offering, and he sprinkled the blood of peace offerings on the altar.

[14]Then King Ahaz removed the old bronze altar from its place in front of the LORD's Temple, between the entrance and the new altar, and placed it on the north side of the new altar. [15]He told Uriah the priest, "Use the new altar* for the morning sacrifices of burnt offering, the evening grain offering, the king's burnt offering and grain offering, and the burnt offerings of all the people, as well as their grain offerings and liquid offerings. Sprinkle the blood from all the burnt offerings and sacrifices on the new altar. The bronze altar will be for my personal use only." [16]Uriah the priest did just as King Ahaz commanded him.

BLATANT DISREGARD 16:1-16

Evil King Ahaz copied pagan religious customs, changed the Temple services, and used the Temple altar for his personal use. In so doing, he demonstrated a blatant disregard for God's commands. We condemn Ahaz for his action, but we do the same thing if we try to mold God's message to fit our preferences. God wants to be worshiped for who he is, not what we would like him to be. ■

[17]Then the king removed the side panels and basins from the portable water carts. He also removed the great bronze basin called the Sea from the backs of the bronze oxen and placed it on the stone pavement. [18]In deference to the king of Assyria, he also removed the canopy that had been constructed inside the palace for use on the Sabbath day,* as well as the king's outer entrance to the Temple of the LORD.

[19]The rest of the events in Ahaz's reign and everything he did are recorded in *The Book of the History of the Kings of Judah.* [20]When Ahaz died, he was buried with his ancestors in the City of David. Then his son Hezekiah became the next king.

17 HOSHEA RULES IN ISRAEL

Hoshea son of Elah began to rule over Israel in the twelfth year of King Ahaz's reign in Judah. He reigned in Samaria nine years. [2]He did what was evil in the LORD's sight, but not to the same extent as the kings of Israel who ruled before him.

[3]King Shalmaneser of Assyria attacked King Hoshea,

16:3 Or *even making his son pass through the fire.* **16:6a** As in Latin Vulgate; Hebrew reads *Rezin king of Aram.* **16:6b** As in Latin Vulgate; Hebrew reads *Aram.* **16:6c** As in Greek version, Latin Vulgate, and an alternate reading of the Masoretic Text; the other alternate reads *Arameans.* **16:7** Hebrew *your son.* **16:15** Hebrew *the great altar.* **16:18** The meaning of the Hebrew is uncertain.

so Hoshea was forced to pay heavy tribute to Assyria. 4But
Hoshea stopped paying the annual tribute and conspired
against the king of Assyria by asking King So of Egypt* to
help him shake free of Assyria's power. When the king of
Assyria discovered this treachery, he seized Hoshea and
put him in prison.

SAMARIA FALLS TO ASSYRIA

5Then the king of Assyria invaded the entire land, and for
three years he besieged the city of Samaria. 6Finally, in
the ninth year of King Hoshea's reign, Samaria fell, and
the people of Israel were exiled to Assyria. They were settled in colonies in Halah, along the banks of the Habor
River in Gozan, and in the cities of the Medes.

COPYING 17:7-17

The Lord judged the people of Israel because they copied the bad habits of the surrounding nations. We do the same when we follow the crowd, instead of obeying God. How do your actions show your willingness to imitate God? (See Eph 5:1.) ■

7This disaster came upon the people of Israel because
they worshiped other gods. They sinned against the LORD
their God, who had brought them safely out of Egypt and
had rescued them from the power of Pharaoh, the king of
Egypt. 8They had followed the practices of the pagan nations the LORD had driven from the land ahead of them,
as well as the practices the kings of Israel had introduced.
9The people of Israel had also secretly done many things
that were not pleasing to the LORD their God. They built
pagan shrines for themselves in all their towns, from the
smallest outpost to the largest walled city. 10They set up
sacred pillars and Asherah poles at the top of every hill
and under every green tree. 11They offered sacrifices on
all the hilltops, just like the nations the LORD had driven
from the land ahead of them. So the people of Israel had
done many evil things, arousing the LORD's anger. 12Yes,
they worshiped idols,* despite the LORD's specific and repeated warnings.

13Again and again the LORD had sent his prophets and
seers to warn both Israel and Judah: "Turn from all your
evil ways. Obey my commands and decrees—the entire
law that I commanded your ancestors to obey, and that I
gave you through my servants the prophets."

14But the Israelites would not listen. They were as stubborn as their ancestors who had refused to believe in the
LORD their God. 15They rejected his decrees and the covenant he had made with their ancestors, and they despised all his warnings. They worshiped worthless idols,
so they became worthless themselves. They followed the
example of the nations around them, disobeying the
LORD's command not to imitate them.

16They rejected all the commands of the LORD their
God and made two calves from metal. They set up an
Asherah pole and worshiped Baal and all the forces of
heaven. 17They even sacrificed their own sons and
daughters in the fire.* They consulted fortune-tellers
and practiced sorcery and sold themselves to evil, arousing the LORD's anger.

18Because the LORD was very angry with Israel, he
swept them away from his presence. Only the tribe of Judah remained in the land. 19But even the people of Judah
refused to obey the commands of the LORD their God, for
they followed the evil practices that Israel had introduced. 20The LORD rejected all the descendants of Israel.
He punished them by handing them over to their attackers until he had banished Israel from his presence.

21For when the LORD* tore Israel away from the kingdom of David, they chose Jeroboam son of Nebat as their
king. But Jeroboam drew Israel away from following the
LORD and made them commit a great sin. 22And the people of Israel persisted in all the evil ways of Jeroboam.
They did not turn from these sins 23until the LORD finally
swept them away from his presence, just as all his prophets had warned. So Israel was exiled from their land to
Assyria, where they remain to this day.

FOREIGNERS SETTLE IN ISRAEL

24The king of Assyria transported groups of people from
Babylon, Cuthah, Avva, Hamath, and Sepharvaim and resettled them in the towns of Samaria, replacing the people of Israel. They took possession of Samaria and lived
in its towns. 25But since these foreign settlers did not
worship the LORD when they first arrived, the LORD sent
lions among them, which killed some of them.

PART OF THE COLLECTION? 17:24-29

The new settlers in Israel worshiped God without giving up their pagan customs. They treated God as a good luck charm or like one of the gods in their collection. A similar attitude is common today. Many people claim to believe in God while refusing to give up attitudes and actions that displease God. God prefers to be first in a life, rather than used as a back-up plan. ■

26So a message was sent to the king of Assyria: "The
people you have sent to live in the towns of Samaria do
not know the religious customs of the God of the land. He
has sent lions among them to destroy them because they
have not worshiped him correctly."

27The king of Assyria then commanded, "Send one of
the exiled priests back to Samaria. Let him live there and
teach the new residents the religious customs of the God
of the land." 28So one of the priests who had been exiled
from Samaria returned to Bethel and taught the new residents how to worship the LORD.

29But these various groups of foreigners also continued to worship their own gods. In town after town where
they lived, they placed their idols at the pagan shrines

17:4 Or *by asking the king of Egypt at Sais.* 17:12 The Hebrew term (literally *round things*) probably alludes to dung. 17:17 Or *They even made their sons and daughters pass through the fire.* 17:21 Hebrew *he;* compare 1 Kgs 11:31-32.

that the people of Samaria had built. 30Those from Babylon worshiped idols of their god Succoth-benoth. Those
from Cuthah worshiped their god Nergal. And those
from Hamath worshiped Ashima. 31The Avvites worshiped their gods Nibhaz and Tartak. And the people
from Sepharvaim even burned their own children as sacrifices to their gods Adrammelech and Anammelech.
32These new residents worshiped the LORD, but they
also appointed from among themselves all sorts of people as priests to offer sacrifices at their places of worship.
33And though they worshiped the LORD, they continued
to follow their own gods according to the religious customs of the nations from which they came. 34And this is
still going on today. They continue to follow their former
practices instead of truly worshiping the LORD and
obeying the decrees, regulations, instructions, and commands he gave the descendants of Jacob, whose name he
changed to Israel.
35For the LORD had made a covenant with the descendants of Jacob and commanded them: "Do not worship
any other gods or bow before them or serve them or offer
sacrifices to them. 36But worship only the LORD, who
brought you out of Egypt with great strength and a powerful arm. Bow down to him alone, and offer sacrifices
only to him. 37Be careful at all times to obey the decrees,
regulations, instructions, and commands that he wrote
for you. You must not worship other gods. 38Do not forget the covenant I made with you, and do not worship
other gods. 39You must worship only the LORD your God.
He is the one who will rescue you from all your enemies."

HEZEKIAH

Think about your spiritual heritage. What have your parents or grandparents taught you about God? The people and kings of Judah had a rich past, filled with God's action, guidance, and commands. But with each passing generation, they forgot that God, who had cared for them in the past, also cared about the present and the future—and demanded their continued obedience. Hezekiah was one of the few kings of Judah who was constantly aware of God's acts in the past and his interest in the events of every day. The Bible describes him as a king who had a close relationship with God.

As a reformer, Hezekiah was most concerned with present obedience. Judah was filled with visual reminders of the people's lack of trust in God, and Hezekiah boldly cleaned house. Altars, idols, and temples built for false gods were destroyed. Not even the bronze serpent Moses had made in the wilderness (see Num 21:9) was spared—it had become an idol (2 Kings 18:4). The Temple in Jerusalem, whose doors had been nailed shut by Hezekiah's father, was cleaned and reopened. The Passover was celebrated once more as a national holiday, and there was revival in Judah.

Although he had a natural inclination to respond to present problems, Hezekiah wasn't concerned for the future. He took few actions to preserve the effects of his sweeping reforms. His successful efforts made him proud. His unwise display of wealth to the Babylonian delegation got Judah included on Babylon's "Nations to Conquer" list. When Isaiah told Hezekiah of the foolishness of this, the king answered by saying he was thankful that any evil consequences would be delayed until after he died. And the lives of three kings who followed him—Manasseh, Amon, and Josiah—were deeply affected by both Hezekiah's accomplishments *and* his weaknesses.

The past affects your decisions and actions today, and these, in turn, affect the future. Part of the success of your past will be measured by what you do with it now and how well you use it to prepare for the future.

UPS:
- Was the king of Judah who brought about civil and religious reforms
- Had a relationship with God
- Devoted to a powerful prayer life
- Arranged for the collection of many proverbs (see Prov 25:1)

DOWNS:
- Showed little interest or wisdom in planning for the future or in protecting the spiritual heritage he enjoyed
- Rashly showed his wealth to messengers from Babylon

STATS:
- Where: Jerusalem
- Occupation: Thirteenth king of Judah (the southern kingdom)
- Relatives: Ahaz (father); Abi (mother); Manasseh (son)
- Contemporaries: Isaiah, Hoshea, Micah, Sennacherib

BOTTOM LINE:

Sweeping reforms are short-lived when little action is taken to preserve them for the future.

Past obedience to God does not remove the possibility of present disobedience.

Complete dependence on God brings amazing results.

Hezekiah's story is told in 2 Kings 16:20; 18:1–20:21; 2 Chron 28:27–32:33; Isa 36:1–39:8. He also is mentioned in Prov 25:1; Isa 1:1; Jer 15:4; 26:18-19; Hos 1:1; Mic 1:1.

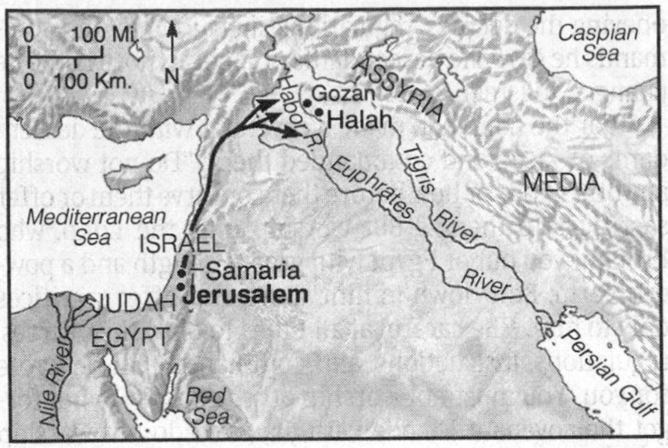

ISRAEL TAKEN CAPTIVE
Finally the sins of Israel's people caught up with them. God allowed Assyria to defeat and disperse the people. They were led into captivity, swallowed up by the mighty, evil Assyrian empire. Sin always brings discipline, and the consequences of that sin are sometimes irreversible.

40But the people would not listen and continued to follow their former practices. 41So while these new residents worshiped the LORD, they also worshiped their idols. And to this day their descendants do the same.

18 HEZEKIAH RULES IN JUDAH

Hezekiah son of Ahaz began to rule over Judah in the third year of King Hoshea's reign in Israel. 2He was twenty-five years old when he became king, and he reigned in Jerusalem twenty-nine years. His mother was Abijah,* the daughter of Zechariah. 3He did what was pleasing in the LORD's sight, just as his ancestor David had done. 4He removed the pagan shrines, smashed the sacred pillars, and cut down the Asherah poles. He broke up the bronze serpent that Moses had made, because the people of Israel had been offering sacrifices to it. The bronze serpent was called Nehushtan.*

5Hezekiah trusted in the LORD, the God of Israel. There was no one like him among all the kings of Judah, either before or after his time. 6He remained faithful to the LORD in everything, and he carefully obeyed all the commands the LORD had given Moses. 7So the LORD was with him, and Hezekiah was successful in everything he did. He revolted against the king of Assyria and refused to pay him tribute. 8He also conquered the Philistines as far distant as Gaza and its territory, from their smallest outpost to their largest walled city.

9During the fourth year of Hezekiah's reign, which was the seventh year of King Hoshea's reign in Israel, King Shalmaneser of Assyria attacked the city of Samaria and began a siege against it. 10Three years later, during the sixth year of King Hezekiah's reign and the ninth year of King Hoshea's reign in Israel, Samaria fell. 11At that time the king of Assyria exiled the Israelites to Assyria and placed them in colonies in Halah, along the banks of the Habor River in Gozan, and in the cities of the Medes. 12For they refused to listen to the LORD their God and obey him. Instead, they violated his covenant—all the laws that Moses the LORD's servant had commanded them to obey.

ASSYRIA INVADES JUDAH

13In the fourteenth year of King Hezekiah's reign,* King Sennacherib of Assyria came to attack the fortified towns of Judah and conquered them. 14King Hezekiah sent this message to the king of Assyria at Lachish: "I have done wrong. I will pay whatever tribute money you demand if you will only withdraw." The king of Assyria then demanded a settlement of more than eleven tons of silver and one ton of gold.* 15To gather this amount, King Hezekiah used all the silver stored in the Temple of the LORD and in the palace treasury. 16Hezekiah even stripped the gold from the doors of the LORD's Temple and from the doorposts he had overlaid with gold, and he gave it all to the Assyrian king.

17Nevertheless, the king of Assyria sent his commander in chief, his field commander, and his chief of staff* from Lachish with a huge army to confront King Hezekiah in Jerusalem. The Assyrians took up a position beside the aqueduct that feeds water into the upper pool, near the road leading to the field where cloth is washed.* 18They summoned King Hezekiah, but the king sent these officials to meet with them: Eliakim son of Hilkiah, the palace administrator; Shebna the court secretary; and Joah son of Asaph, the royal historian.

AN OBJECT OF WORSHIP 18:4

The bronze serpent had been made to cure the Israelites of a deadly plague (see Num 21:4-9). It demonstrated God's presence, power, and mercy. But when it became an object of worship instead of a reminder of *whom* to worship, Hezekiah was forced to destroy it. We must be careful that the things we use to aid our worship don't become objects of worship themselves. ■

SENNACHERIB THREATENS JERUSALEM

19Then the Assyrian king's chief of staff told them to give this message to Hezekiah:

"This is what the great king of Assyria says: What are you trusting in that makes you so confident? 20Do you think that mere words can substitute for military skill and strength? Who are you counting on, that you have rebelled against me? 21On Egypt? If you lean on Egypt, it will be like a reed that splinters beneath your weight and pierces your hand. Pharaoh, the king of Egypt, is completely unreliable!

22"But perhaps you will say to me, 'We are trusting in the LORD our God!' But isn't he the one who was insulted by Hezekiah? Didn't Hezekiah tear down his

18:2 As in parallel text at 2 Chr 29:1; Hebrew reads *Abi,* a variant spelling of Abijah. **18:4** *Nehushtan* sounds like the Hebrew terms that mean "snake," "bronze," and "unclean thing." **18:13** The fourteenth year of Hezekiah's reign was 701 B.C. **18:14** Hebrew *300 talents* [10 metric tons] *of silver and 30 talents* [1 metric ton] *of gold.* **18:17a** Or *the rabshakeh;* also in 18:19, 26, 27, 28, 37. **18:17b** Or *bleached.*

shrines and altars and make everyone in Judah and Jerusalem worship only at the altar here in Jerusalem?

23“I'll tell you what! Strike a bargain with my master, the king of Assyria. I will give you 2,000 horses if you can find that many men to ride on them! 24With your tiny army, how can you think of challenging even the weakest contingent of my master's troops, even with the help of Egypt's chariots and charioteers? 25What's more, do you think we have invaded your land without the LORD's direction? The LORD himself told us, ‘Attack this land and destroy it!’”

> Hezekiah trusted in the LORD, the God of Israel. There was no one like him.
>
> *2 KINGS 18:5*

26Then Eliakim son of Hilkiah, Shebna, and Joah said to the Assyrian chief of staff, “Please speak to us in Aramaic, for we understand it well. Don't speak in Hebrew,* for the people on the wall will hear.”

27But Sennacherib's chief of staff replied, “Do you think my master sent this message only to you and your master? He wants all the people to hear it, for when we put this city under siege, they will suffer along with you. They will be so hungry and thirsty that they will eat their own dung and drink their own urine.”

28Then the chief of staff stood and shouted in Hebrew to the people on the wall, “Listen to this message from the great king of Assyria! 29This is what the king says: Don't let Hezekiah deceive you. He will never be able to rescue you from my power. 30Don't let him fool you into trusting in the LORD by saying, ‘The LORD will surely rescue us. This city will never fall into the hands of the Assyrian king!’

31“Don't listen to Hezekiah! These are the terms the king of Assyria is offering: Make peace with me—open the gates and come out. Then each of you can continue eating from your own grapevine and fig tree and drinking from your own well. 32Then I will arrange to take you to another land like this one—a land of grain and new wine, bread and vineyards, olive groves and honey. Choose life instead of death!

“Don't listen to Hezekiah when he tries to mislead you by saying, ‘The LORD will rescue us!’ 33Have the gods of any other nations ever saved their people from the king of Assyria? 34What happened to the gods of Hamath and Arpad? And what about the gods of Sepharvaim, Hena, and Ivvah? Did any god rescue Samaria from my power? 35What god of any nation has ever been able to save its people from my power? So what makes you think that the LORD can rescue Jerusalem from me?”

36But the people were silent and did not utter a word because Hezekiah had commanded them, “Do not answer him.”

37Then Eliakim son of Hilkiah, the palace administrator; Shebna the court secretary; and Joah son of Asaph, the royal historian, went back to Hezekiah. They tore their clothes in despair, and they went in to see the king and told him what the Assyrian chief of staff had said.

19 HEZEKIAH SEEKS THE LORD'S HELP

When King Hezekiah heard their report, he tore his clothes and put on burlap and went into the Temple of the LORD. 2And he sent Eliakim the palace administrator, Shebna the court secretary, and the leading priests, all dressed in burlap, to the prophet Isaiah son of Amoz. 3They told him, “This is what King Hezekiah says: Today is a day of trouble, insults, and disgrace. It is like when a child is ready to be born, but the mother has no strength to deliver the baby. 4But perhaps the LORD your God has heard the Assyrian chief of staff,* sent by the king to defy the living God, and will punish him for his words. Oh, pray for those of us who are left!”

5After King Hezekiah's officials delivered the king's message to Isaiah, 6the prophet replied, “Say to your master, ‘This is what the LORD says: Do not be disturbed by this blasphemous speech against me from the Assyrian king's messengers. 7Listen! I myself will move against him,* and the king will receive a message that he is needed at home. So he will return to his land, where I will have him killed with a sword.’”

8Meanwhile, the Assyrian chief of staff left Jerusalem and went to consult the king of Assyria, who had left Lachish and was attacking Libnah.

9Soon afterward King Sennacherib received word that King Tirhakah of Ethiopia* was leading an army to fight against him. Before leaving to meet the attack, he sent messengers back to Hezekiah in Jerusalem with this message:

10“This message is for King Hezekiah of Judah. Don't let your God, in whom you trust, deceive you with promises that Jerusalem will not be captured by the king of Assyria. 11You know perfectly well what the kings of Assyria have done wherever they have gone. They have completely destroyed everyone who stood in their way! Why should you be any different? 12Have the gods of other nations rescued them—such nations as Gozan, Haran, Rezeph, and the people of Eden who were in Tel-assar? My predecessors destroyed them all! 13What happened to the king of Hamath and the king of Arpad? What happened to the kings of Sepharvaim, Hena, and Ivvah?”

14After Hezekiah received the letter from the messengers and read it, he went up to the LORD's Temple and spread it out before the LORD. 15And Hezekiah prayed this prayer before the LORD: “O LORD, God of Israel, you are enthroned between the mighty cherubim! You alone

18:26 Hebrew *in the dialect of Judah;* also in 18:28. **19:4** Or *the rabshakeh;* also in 19:8. **19:7** Hebrew *I will put a spirit in him.* **19:9** Hebrew *of Cush.*

are God of all the kingdoms of the earth. You alone created the heavens and the earth. 16Bend down, O LORD, and
listen! Open your eyes, O LORD, and see! Listen to Sennacherib's words of defiance against the living God.
17"It is true, LORD, that the kings of Assyria have destroyed all these nations. 18And they have thrown the
gods of these nations into the fire and burned them. But
of course the Assyrians could destroy them! They were
not gods at all—only idols of wood and stone shaped by
human hands. 19Now, O LORD our God, rescue us from his
power; then all the kingdoms of the earth will know that
you alone, O LORD, are God."

ISAIAH PREDICTS JUDAH'S DELIVERANCE

20Then Isaiah son of Amoz sent this message to Hezekiah: "This is what the LORD, the God of Israel, says: I have
heard your prayer about King Sennacherib of Assyria.
21And the LORD has spoken this word against him:

"The virgin daughter of Zion
despises you and laughs at you.
The daughter of Jerusalem
shakes her head in derision as you flee.

22 "Whom have you been defying and ridiculing?
Against whom did you raise your voice?
At whom did you look with such haughty eyes?
It was the Holy One of Israel!
23 By your messengers you have defied the Lord.
You have said, 'With my many chariots
I have conquered the highest mountains—
yes, the remotest peaks of Lebanon.
I have cut down its tallest cedars
and its finest cypress trees.
I have reached its farthest corners
and explored its deepest forests.
24 I have dug wells in many foreign lands
and refreshed myself with their water.
With the sole of my foot
I stopped up all the rivers of Egypt!'

25 "But have you not heard?
I decided this long ago.
Long ago I planned it,
and now I am making it happen.
I planned for you to crush fortified cities
into heaps of rubble.
26 That is why their people have so little power
and are so frightened and confused.
They are as weak as grass,
as easily trampled as tender green shoots.
They are like grass sprouting on a housetop,
scorched before it can grow lush and tall.

27 "But I know you well—
where you stay
and when you come and go.
I know the way you have raged against me.
28 And because of your raging against me
and your arrogance, which I have heard for myself,
I will put my hook in your nose
and my bit in your mouth.
I will make you return
by the same road on which you came."

29Then Isaiah said to Hezekiah, "Here is the proof that
what I say is true:

"This year you will eat only what grows up by itself,
and next year you will eat what springs up from
that.
But in the third year you will plant crops and harvest
them;
you will tend vineyards and eat their fruit.
30 And you who are left in Judah,
who have escaped the ravages of the siege,
will put roots down in your own soil
and will grow up and flourish.
31 For a remnant of my people will spread out from
Jerusalem,
a group of survivors from Mount Zion.
The passionate commitment of the LORD of Heaven's
Armies*
will make this happen!

PRAYER 19:1-37

Sennacherib, whose armies had captured the fortified cities of Judah, sent a message telling Hezekiah to surrender (18:13-35). Having realized that the situation was hopeless, Hezekiah asked God for help. God answered by defeating this seemingly invincible army. Is prayer your first response in a crisis? ■

32"And this is what the LORD says about the king of
Assyria:

"His armies will not enter Jerusalem.
They will not even shoot an arrow at it.
They will not march outside its gates with their
shields
nor build banks of earth against its walls.
33 The king will return to his own country
by the same road on which he came.
He will not enter this city,
says the LORD.
34 For my own honor and for the sake of my servant
David,
I will defend this city and protect it."

35That night the angel of the LORD went out to the Assyrian camp and killed 185,000 Assyrian soldiers. When
the surviving Assyrians* woke up the next morning, they
found corpses everywhere. 36Then King Sennacherib of

19:31 As in Greek and Syriac versions, Latin Vulgate, and an alternate reading of the Masoretic Text (see also Isa 37:32); the other alternate reads *the LORD*. **19:35** Hebrew *When they*.

Assyria broke camp and returned to his own land. He
went home to his capital of Nineveh and stayed there.
[37]One day while he was worshiping in the temple of his
god Nisroch, his sons* Adrammelech and Sharezer killed
him with their swords. They then escaped to the land of
Ararat, and another son, Esarhaddon, became the next
king of Assyria.

THE POWER OF ONE 20:1-11

Over a 100-year period of Judah's history (732-640 B.C.), Hezekiah was the only faithful king; but what a difference he made! Because of Hezekiah's faith and prayer, God healed him and saved his city from the Assyrians. You can make a difference, too, even if your faith puts you in the minority. Faith in the power of the one true God can bring about change in any situation. ■

20

HEZEKIAH'S SICKNESS AND RECOVERY

About that time Hezekiah became deathly ill, and the
prophet Isaiah son of Amoz went to visit him. He gave the
king this message: "This is what the LORD says: Set your
affairs in order, for you are going to die. You will not recover from this illness."
[2]When Hezekiah heard this, he turned his face to the
wall and prayed to the LORD, [3]"Remember, O LORD, how I
have always been faithful to you and have served you
single-mindedly, always doing what pleases you." Then
he broke down and wept bitterly.
[4]But before Isaiah had left the middle courtyard, this
message came to him from the LORD: [5]"Go back to Hezekiah, the leader of my people. Tell him, 'This is what the
LORD, the God of your ancestor David, says: I have heard
your prayer and seen your tears. I will heal you, and three
days from now you will get out of bed and go to the Temple of the LORD. [6]I will add fifteen years to your life, and
I will rescue you and this city from the king of Assyria. I
will defend this city for my own honor and for the sake
of my servant David.'"
[7]Then Isaiah said, "Make an ointment from figs." So
Hezekiah's servants spread the ointment over the boil,
and Hezekiah recovered!
[8]Meanwhile, Hezekiah had said to Isaiah, "What sign
will the LORD give to prove that he will heal me and that I
will go to the Temple of the LORD three days from now?"
[9]Isaiah replied, "This is the sign from the LORD to prove
that he will do as he promised. Would you like the
shadow on the sundial to go forward ten steps or backward ten steps?*"
[10]"The shadow always moves forward," Hezekiah replied, "so that would be easy. Make it go ten steps backward instead." [11]So Isaiah the prophet asked the LORD to
do this, and he caused the shadow to move ten steps
backward on the sundial* of Ahaz!

ENVOYS FROM BABYLON

[12]Soon after this, Merodach-baladan son of Baladan, king
of Babylon, sent Hezekiah his best wishes and a gift, for
he had heard that Hezekiah had been very sick. [13]Hezeki-
ah received the Babylonian envoys and showed them
everything in his treasure-houses—the silver, the gold,
the spices, and the aromatic oils. He also took them to see
his armory and showed them everything in his royal treasuries! There was nothing in his palace or kingdom that
Hezekiah did not show them.
[14]Then Isaiah the prophet went to King Hezekiah and
asked him, "What did those men want? Where were they
from?"
Hezekiah replied, "They came from the distant land of
Babylon."
[15]"What did they see in your palace?" Isaiah asked.
"They saw everything," Hezekiah replied. "I showed
them everything I own—all my royal treasuries."
[16]Then Isaiah said to Hezekiah, "Listen to this message
from the LORD: [17]The time is coming when everything in
your palace—all the treasures stored up by your ancestors until now—will be carried off to Babylon. Nothing
will be left, says the LORD. [18]Some of your very own sons
will be taken away into exile. They will become eunuchs
who will serve in the palace of Babylon's king."
[19]Then Hezekiah said to Isaiah, "This message you
have given me from the LORD is good." For the king was
thinking, "At least there will be peace and security during
my lifetime."
[20]The rest of the events in Hezekiah's reign, including
the extent of his power and how he built a pool and dug a
tunnel* to bring water into the city, are recorded in *The
Book of the History of the Kings of Judah.* [21]Hezekiah
died, and his son Manasseh became the next king.

OCCULT 21:1-18

Manasseh, the king of Judah, angered God by dabbling in the occult. His actions showed his disregard for God's laws (Lev 19:31; Deut 18:9-14). Today, many books, television shows, and games emphasize the "harmlessness" of consulting psychics or attending séances in order to discover the truth about the future. But dabbling in the occult is far from harmless. Want to be assured of a good future? Don't mess up in the present by doing what you know is wrong. ■

21

MANASSEH RULES IN JUDAH

Manasseh was twelve years old when he became king,
and he reigned in Jerusalem fifty-five years. His mother
was Hephzibah. [2]He did what was evil in the LORD's sight,
following the detestable practices of the pagan nations
that the LORD had driven from the land ahead of the Israelites. [3]He rebuilt the pagan shrines his father, Hezekiah,

19:37 As in Greek version and an alternate reading of the Masoretic Text (see also Isa 37:38); the other alternate reading lacks *his sons*.
20:9 Or *The shadow on the sundial has gone forward ten steps; do you want it to go backward ten steps?* **20:11** Hebrew *the steps*.
20:20 Hebrew *watercourse*.

had destroyed. He constructed altars for Baal and set up
an Asherah pole, just as King Ahab of Israel had done. He
also bowed before all the powers of the heavens and worshiped them.
4He built pagan altars in the Temple of the LORD, the
place where the LORD had said, "My name will remain in
Jerusalem forever." 5He built these altars for all the powers of the heavens in both courtyards of the LORD's Temple. 6Manasseh also sacrificed his own son in the fire.*
He practiced sorcery and divination, and he consulted
with mediums and psychics. He did much that was evil in
the LORD's sight, arousing his anger.
7Manasseh even made a carved image of Asherah and
set it up in the Temple, the very place where the LORD had
told David and his son Solomon: "My name will be honored forever in this Temple and in Jerusalem—the city I
have chosen from among all the tribes of Israel. 8If the Israelites will be careful to obey my commands—all the
laws my servant Moses gave them—I will not send them
into exile from this land that I gave their ancestors." 9But
the people refused to listen, and Manasseh led them to do
even more evil than the pagan nations that the LORD had
destroyed when the people of Israel entered the land.
10Then the LORD said through his servants the prophets:
11"King Manasseh of Judah has done many detestable
things. He is even more wicked than the Amorites, who
lived in this land before Israel. He has caused the people of
Judah to sin with his idols.* 12So this is what the LORD, the
God of Israel, says: I will bring such disaster on Jerusalem
and Judah that the ears of those who hear about it will tin-
gle with horror. 13I will judge Jerusalem by the same standard I used for Samaria and the same measure* I used for
the family of Ahab. I will wipe away the people of Jerusalem as one wipes a dish and turns it upside down. 14Then I
will reject even the remnant of my own people who are
left, and I will hand them over as plunder for their enemies. 15For they have done great evil in my sight and have
angered me ever since their ancestors came out of Egypt."
16Manasseh also murdered many innocent people until Jerusalem was filled from one end to the other with innocent blood. This was in addition to the sin that he
caused the people of Judah to commit, leading them to do
evil in the LORD's sight.
17The rest of the events in Manasseh's reign and everything he did, including the sins he committed, are recorded in *The Book of the History of the Kings of Judah*.
18When Manasseh died, he was buried in the palace garden, the garden of Uzza. Then his son Amon became the
next king.

21:6 Or *also made his son pass through the fire.* **21:11** The Hebrew term (literally *round things*) probably alludes to dung; also in 21:21. **21:13** Hebrew *the same plumb line I used for Samaria and the same plumb bob.*

JOSIAH

UPS:

- King of Judah
- Wanted to know God and obey him
- A reformer like his great-grandfather, Hezekiah
- Cleaned out the Temple and revived obedience to God's laws

DOWN:

- Became involved in a military conflict that he had been warned against

STATS:

- Where: Jerusalem
- Occupation: Sixteenth king of Judah, the southern kingdom
- Relatives: Amon (father); Jedidah (mother); Jehoahaz (son)
- Contemporaries: Jeremiah, Huldah, Hilkiah, Zephaniah

BOTTOM LINE:

God consistently responds to those who turn from their sins with a humble heart.

Even sweeping outward reforms are of little lasting value if there are no changes in people's lives.

Josiah's story is told in 2 Kings 21:24; 22:1–23:30; 2 Chron 33:25–35:27. He also is mentioned in Jer 1:3; 22:11, 15-16.

JOSIAH Think waaaayyy back to the time when you were eight. What were your responsibilities? Josiah had a huge one: he was king of Judah. Oh sure, he had advisers to help him. But he also had something else going for him: a close relationship with God, like that of his great-grandfather Hezekiah.

At a young age, Josiah became aware of the spiritual sickness in his land. In a sense, Josiah began his search for God by destroying and cleaning up whatever he found that didn't belong to the worship of the true God. Along the way, a scroll containing God's law was rediscovered in the Temple. For Josiah, the discovery of the scroll was better than finding a hidden treasure map.

As the scroll of God's law was read to Josiah, he was shocked, frightened, and humbled. He tried everything he could to help his people return to God. Although he changed many things, he couldn't change hearts. On the outside, the people cooperated with Josiah, but there were few changes on the inside.

How would you describe your relationship with God? Would you have to admit that you usually just "go along" with God like the people of Judah? Or are you, like Josiah, deeply humbled by God's Word and anxious to do what he wants? Humble obedience pleases God. Outside changes aren't enough. God wants to change lives inside and out.

AMON RULES IN JUDAH

19Amon was twenty-two years old when he became king,
and he reigned in Jerusalem two years. His mother was
Meshullemeth, the daughter of Haruz from Jotbah. 20He
did what was evil in the LORD's sight, just as his father,
Manasseh, had done. 21He followed the example of his
father, worshiping the same idols his father had worshiped. 22He abandoned the LORD, the God of his ancestors, and he refused to follow the LORD's ways.
23Then Amon's own officials conspired against him
and assassinated him in his palace. 24But the people of
the land killed all those who had conspired against King
Amon, and they made his son Josiah the next king.
25The rest of the events in Amon's reign and what he
did are recorded in *The Book of the History of the Kings of
Judah.* 26He was buried in his tomb in the garden of Uzza.
Then his son Josiah became the next king.

22 JOSIAH RULES IN JUDAH

Josiah was eight years old when he became king, and he
reigned in Jerusalem thirty-one years. His mother was
Jedidah, the daughter of Adaiah from Bozkath. 2He did
what was pleasing in the LORD's sight and followed the
example of his ancestor David. He did not turn away
from doing what was right.

FOUNDATION OF OBEDIENCE 22:1-2

In reading the biblical lists of kings, it is rare to find one who obeyed God completely. Josiah was such a person. For 18 years he reigned obediently; then, when he was 26, he began the reforms based on God's laws. You're never too young to begin learning the discipline of obedience. The foundation of obedience that you establish now can lead to greater responsibilities in your adulthood. ■

3In the eighteenth year of his reign, King Josiah sent
Shaphan son of Azaliah and grandson of Meshullam, the
court secretary, to the Temple of the LORD. He told him,
4"Go to Hilkiah the high priest and have him count the
money the gatekeepers have collected from the people at
the LORD's Temple. 5Entrust this money to the men assigned to supervise the Temple's restoration. Then they
can use it to pay workers to repair the Temple of the
LORD. 6They will need to hire carpenters, builders, and
masons. Also have them buy the timber and the finished
stone needed to repair the Temple. 7But don't require the
construction supervisors to keep account of the money
they receive, for they are honest and trustworthy men."

HILKIAH DISCOVERS GOD'S LAW

8Hilkiah the high priest said to Shaphan the court secretary, "I have found the Book of the Law in the LORD's
Temple!" Then Hilkiah gave the scroll to Shaphan, and
he read it.
9Shaphan went to the king and reported, "Your officials
have turned over the money collected at the Temple of
the LORD to the workers and supervisors at the Temple."
10Shaphan also told the king, "Hilkiah the priest has given
me a scroll." So Shaphan read it to the king.

SORROW OVER SIN 22:3-19

When Josiah realized how corrupt his nation had become, he tore his clothes and wept before God. Josiah used the customs of his day to show his sorrow over the nation's wrongdoing. We are unlikely to tear our clothing these days, but there are other ways to demonstrate our how sorry we are when we do wrong things. How do you show your sorrow? ■

11When the king heard what was written in the Book of
the Law, he tore his clothes in despair. 12Then he gave
these orders to Hilkiah the priest, Ahikam son of Shaphan, Acbor son of Micaiah, Shaphan the court secretary,
and Asaiah the king's personal adviser: 13"Go to the Temple and speak to the LORD for me and for the people and
for all Judah. Inquire about the words written in this
scroll that has been found. For the LORD's great anger is
burning against us because our ancestors have not
obeyed the words in this scroll. We have not been doing
everything it says we must do."
14So Hilkiah the priest, Ahikam, Acbor, Shaphan, and
Asaiah went to the New Quarter* of Jerusalem to consult
with the prophet Huldah. She was the wife of Shallum
son of Tikvah, son of Harhas, the keeper of the Temple
wardrobe.
15She said to them, "The LORD, the God of Israel, has
spoken! Go back and tell the man who sent you, 16'This is
what the LORD says: I am going to bring disaster on this
city* and its people. All the words written in the scroll
that the king of Judah has read will come true. 17For my
people have abandoned me and offered sacrifices to pagan gods, and I am very angry with them for everything
they have done. My anger will burn against this place, and
it will not be quenched.'
18"But go to the king of Judah who sent you to seek the
LORD and tell him: 'This is what the LORD, the God of Israel, says concerning the message you have just heard:
19You were sorry and humbled yourself before the LORD
when you heard what I said against this city and its people—that this land would be cursed and become desolate. You tore your clothing in despair and wept before
me in repentance. And I have indeed heard you, says the
LORD. 20So I will not send the promised disaster until after you have died and been buried in peace. You will not
see the disaster I am going to bring on this city.'"
So they took her message back to the king.

23 JOSIAH'S RELIGIOUS REFORMS

Then the king summoned all the elders of Judah and Jerusalem. 2And the king went up to the Temple of the
LORD with all the people of Judah and Jerusalem, along

22:14 Or *the Second Quarter*, a newer section of Jerusalem. Hebrew reads *the Mishneh*. 22:16 Hebrew *this place;* also in 22:19, 20.

with the priests and the prophets—all the people from the least to the greatest. There the king read to them the entire Book of the Covenant that had been found in the LORD's Temple. [3]The king took his place of authority beside the pillar and renewed the covenant in the LORD's presence. He pledged to obey the LORD by keeping all his commands, laws, and decrees with all his heart and soul. In this way, he confirmed all the terms of the covenant that were written in the scroll, and all the people pledged themselves to the covenant.

[4]Then the king instructed Hilkiah the high priest and the priests of the second rank and the Temple gatekeepers to remove from the LORD's Temple all the articles that were used to worship Baal, Asherah, and all the powers of the heavens. The king had all these things burned outside Jerusalem on the terraces of the Kidron Valley, and he carried the ashes away to Bethel. [5]He did away with the idolatrous priests, who had been appointed by the previous kings of Judah, for they had offered sacrifices at the pagan shrines throughout Judah and even in the vicinity of Jerusalem. They had also offered sacrifices to Baal, and to the sun, the moon, the constellations, and to all the powers of the heavens. [6]The king removed the Asherah pole from the LORD's Temple and took it outside Jerusalem to the Kidron Valley, where he burned it. Then he ground the ashes of the pole to dust and threw the dust over the graves of the people. [7]He also tore down the living quarters of the male and female shrine prostitutes that were inside the Temple of the LORD, where the women wove coverings for the Asherah pole.

JUST DO IT! 23:1-7

Josiah didn't just cry about his people's wrongdoing; he also took action. It is not enough to say we believe what is right; we must respond with action, doing what faith requires. This is what James meant when he said that "faith without good deeds is useless" (James 2:20). How active is your faith? ■

[8]Josiah brought to Jerusalem all the priests who were living in other towns of Judah. He also defiled the pagan shrines, where they had offered sacrifices—all the way from Geba to Beersheba. He destroyed the shrines at the entrance to the gate of Joshua, the governor of Jerusalem. This gate was located to the left of the city gate as one enters the city. [9]The priests who had served at the pagan shrines were not allowed* to serve at the LORD's altar in Jerusalem, but they were allowed to eat unleavened bread with the other priests.

[10]Then the king defiled the altar of Topheth in the valley of Ben-Hinnom, so no one could ever again use it to sacrifice a son or daughter in the fire* as an offering to Molech. [11]He removed from the entrance of the LORD's Temple the horse statues that the former kings of Judah had dedicated to the sun. They were near the quarters of Nathan-melech the eunuch, an officer of the court.* The king also burned the chariots dedicated to the sun.

[12]Josiah tore down the altars that the kings of Judah had built on the palace roof above the upper room of Ahaz. The king destroyed the altars that Manasseh had built in the two courtyards of the LORD's Temple. He smashed them to bits* and scattered the pieces in the Kidron Valley. [13]The king also desecrated the pagan shrines east of Jerusalem, to the south of the Mount of Corruption, where King Solomon of Israel had built shrines for Ashtoreth, the detestable goddess of the Sidonians; and for Chemosh, the detestable god of the Moabites; and for Molech,* the vile god of the Ammonites. [14]He smashed the sacred pillars and cut down the Asherah poles. Then he desecrated these places by scattering human bones over them.

[15]The king also tore down the altar at Bethel—the pagan shrine that Jeroboam son of Nebat had made when he caused Israel to sin. He burned down the shrine and ground it to dust, and he burned the Asherah pole. [16]Then Josiah turned around and noticed several tombs in the side of the hill. He ordered that the bones be brought out, and he burned them on the altar at Bethel to desecrate it. (This happened just as the LORD had promised through the man of God when Jeroboam stood beside the altar at the festival.)

Then Josiah turned and looked up at the tomb of the man of God* who had predicted these things. [17]"What is that monument over there?" Josiah asked.

And the people of the town told him, "It is the tomb of the man of God who came from Judah and predicted the very things that you have just done to the altar at Bethel!"

[18]Josiah replied, "Leave it alone. Don't disturb his bones." So they did not burn his bones or those of the old prophet from Samaria.

[19]Then Josiah demolished all the buildings at the pagan shrines in the towns of Samaria, just as he had done at Bethel. They had been built by the various kings of Israel and had made the LORD* very angry. [20]He executed the priests of the pagan shrines on their own altars, and he burned human bones on the altars to desecrate them. Finally, he returned to Jerusalem.

JOSIAH CELEBRATES PASSOVER

[21]King Josiah then issued this order to all the people: "You must celebrate the Passover to the LORD your God, as required in this Book of the Covenant." [22]There had not been a Passover celebration like that since the time when the judges ruled in Israel, nor throughout all the years of the kings of Israel and Judah. [23]This Passover was celebrated to the LORD in Jerusalem in the eighteenth year of King Josiah's reign.

[24]Josiah also got rid of the mediums and psychics, the household gods, the idols,* and every other kind of detestable practice, both in Jerusalem and throughout the

23:9 Hebrew *did not come up.* **23:10** Or *to make a son or daughter pass through the fire.* **23:11** The meaning of the Hebrew is uncertain. **23:12** Or *He quickly removed them.* **23:13** Hebrew *Milcom,* a variant spelling of Molech. **23:16** As in Greek version; Hebrew lacks *when Jeroboam stood beside the altar at the festival. Then Josiah turned and looked up at the tomb of the man of God.* **23:19** As in Greek and Syriac versions and Latin Vulgate; Hebrew lacks *the LORD.* **23:24** The Hebrew term (literally *round things*) probably alludes to dung.

land of Judah. He did this in obedience to the laws written in the scroll that Hilkiah the priest had found in the
LORD's Temple. 25Never before had there been a king like
Josiah, who turned to the LORD with all his heart and soul
and strength, obeying all the laws of Moses. And there
has never been a king like him since.
26Even so, the LORD was very angry with Judah because
of all the wicked things Manasseh had done to provoke
him. 27For the LORD said, "I will also banish Judah from
my presence just as I have banished Israel. And I will reject my chosen city of Jerusalem and the Temple where
my name was to be honored."
28The rest of the events in Josiah's reign and all his
deeds are recorded in *The Book of the History of the
Kings of Judah.*
29While Josiah was king, Pharaoh Neco, king of Egypt,
went to the Euphrates River to help the king of Assyria.
King Josiah and his army marched out to fight him,* but
King Neco* killed him when they met at Megiddo. 30Josi-
ah's officers took his body back in a chariot from Megiddo to Jerusalem and buried him in his own tomb. Then
the people of the land anointed Josiah's son Jehoahaz and
made him the next king.

JEHOAHAZ RULES IN JUDAH

31Jehoahaz was twenty-three years old when he became
king, and he reigned in Jerusalem three months. His
mother was Hamutal, the daughter of Jeremiah from Libnah. 32He did what was evil in the LORD's sight, just as his
ancestors had done.
33Pharaoh Neco put Jehoahaz in prison at Riblah in the
land of Hamath to prevent him from ruling* in Jerusalem. He also demanded that Judah pay 7,500 pounds of
silver and 75 pounds of gold* as tribute.

JEHOIAKIM RULES IN JUDAH

34Pharaoh Neco then installed Eliakim, another of Josiah's sons, to reign in place of his father, and he changed
Eliakim's name to Jehoiakim. Jehoahaz was taken to
Egypt as a prisoner, where he died.
35In order to get the silver and gold demanded as tribute by Pharaoh Neco, Jehoiakim collected a tax from the
people of Judah, requiring them to pay in proportion to
their wealth.
36Jehoiakim was twenty-five years old when he became king, and he reigned in Jerusalem eleven years. His
mother was Zebidah, the daughter of Pedaiah from Ru-
mah. 37He did what was evil in the LORD's sight, just as his
ancestors had done.

24

During Jehoiakim's reign, King Nebuchadnezzar of Babylon invaded the land of Judah. Jehoiakim
surrendered and paid him tribute for three years but
then rebelled. 2Then the LORD sent bands of Babylonian,*
Aramean, Moabite, and Ammonite raiders against Judah
to destroy it, just as the LORD had promised through his
prophets. 3These disasters happened to Judah because of

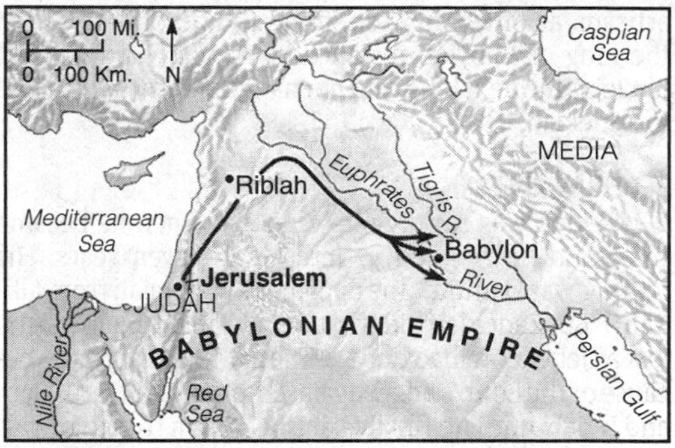

JUDAH EXILED
Evil permeated Judah, and God's anger flared against his rebellious people. Babylon conquered Assyria and became the new world power. The Babylonian army marched into Jerusalem, burned the Temple, tore down the city's massive walls, and carried off the people into captivity.

the LORD's command. He had decided to banish Judah
from his presence because of the many sins of Manasseh,
4who had filled Jerusalem with innocent blood. The LORD
would not forgive this.
5The rest of the events in Jehoiakim's reign and all his
deeds are recorded in *The Book of the History of the
Kings of Judah.* 6When Jehoiakim died, his son Jehoiachin became the next king.
7The king of Egypt did not venture out of his country
after that, for the king of Babylon captured the entire
area formerly claimed by Egypt—from the Brook of Egypt
to the Euphrates River.

JEHOIACHIN RULES IN JUDAH

8Jehoiachin was eighteen years old when he became king,
and he reigned in Jerusalem three months. His mother
was Nehushta, the daughter of Elnathan from Jerusalem.
9Jehoiachin did what was evil in the LORD's sight, just as
his father had done.
10During Jehoiachin's reign, the officers of King Nebuchadnezzar of Babylon came up against Jerusalem and
besieged it. 11Nebuchadnezzar himself arrived at the city
during the siege. 12Then King Jehoiachin, along with the
queen mother, his advisers, his commanders, and his officials, surrendered to the Babylonians.
In the eighth year of Nebuchadnezzar's reign, he took
Jehoiachin prisoner. 13As the LORD had said beforehand,
Nebuchadnezzar carried away all the treasures from the
LORD's Temple and the royal palace. He stripped away*
all the gold objects that King Solomon of Israel had
placed in the Temple. 14King Nebuchadnezzar took all of
Jerusalem captive, including all the commanders and the
best of the soldiers, craftsmen, and artisans—10,000 in
all. Only the poorest people were left in the land.
15Nebuchadnezzar led King Jehoiachin away as a captive to Babylon, along with the queen mother, his wives
and officials, and all Jerusalem's elite. 16He also exiled
7,000 of the best troops and 1,000 craftsmen and

23:29a Or *Josiah went out to meet him.* **23:29b** Hebrew *he.* **23:33a** The meaning of the Hebrew is uncertain. **23:33b** Hebrew *100 talents* [3,400 kilograms] *of silver and 1 talent* [34 kilograms] *of gold.* **24:2** Or *Chaldean.* **24:13** Or *He cut apart.*

artisans, all of whom were strong and fit for war. [17]Then the king of Babylon installed Mattaniah, Jehoiachin's* uncle, as the next king, and he changed Mattaniah's name to Zedekiah.

ZEDEKIAH RULES IN JUDAH

[18]Zedekiah was twenty-one years old when he became king, and he reigned in Jerusalem eleven years. His mother was Hamutal, the daughter of Jeremiah from Libnah. [19]But Zedekiah did what was evil in the LORD's sight, just as Jehoiakim had done. [20]These things happened because of the LORD's anger against the people of Jerusalem and Judah, until he finally banished them from his presence and sent them into exile.

THE FALL OF JERUSALEM

Zedekiah rebelled against the king of Babylon.

EARLY WARNINGS 25:1-21

Judah, like Israel (the northern kingdom), was unfaithful to God. So God, as he had warned, allowed the people of Judah to be exiled. The book of Lamentations records the prophet Jeremiah's sorrow at seeing Jerusalem destroyed. (See, for example, Lam 1:1-3.)

God will fulfill his promises and carry out his warnings. Have you received any warnings in your life lately? How will you respond to them? ■

25 So on January 15,* during the ninth year of Zedekiah's reign, King Nebuchadnezzar of Babylon led his entire army against Jerusalem. They surrounded the city and built siege ramps against its walls. [2]Jerusalem was kept under siege until the eleventh year of King Zedekiah's reign.

[3]By July 18 in the eleventh year of Zedekiah's reign,* the famine in the city had become very severe, and the last of the food was entirely gone. [4]Then a section of the city wall was broken down, and all the soldiers fled. Since the city was surrounded by the Babylonians,* they waited for nightfall. Then they slipped through the gate between the two walls behind the king's garden and headed toward the Jordan Valley.*

[5]But the Babylonian* troops chased the king and caught him on the plains of Jericho, for his men had all deserted him and scattered. [6]They took him to the king of Babylon at Riblah, where they pronounced judgment upon Zedekiah. [7]They made Zedekiah watch as they slaughtered his sons. Then they gouged out Zedekiah's eyes, bound him in bronze chains, and led him away to Babylon.

THE TEMPLE DESTROYED

[8]On August 14 of that year,* which was the nineteenth year of King Nebuchadnezzar's reign, Nebuzaradan, the captain of the guard and an official of the Babylonian king, arrived in Jerusalem. [9]He burned down the Temple of the LORD, the royal palace, and all the houses of Jerusalem. He destroyed all the important buildings* in the city. [10]Then he supervised the entire Babylonian army as they tore down the walls of Jerusalem on every side. [11]Nebuzaradan, the captain of the guard, then took as exiles the rest of the people who remained in the city, the defectors who had declared their allegiance to the king of Babylon, and the rest of the population. [12]But the captain of the guard allowed some of the poorest people to stay behind in Judah to care for the vineyards and fields.

[13]The Babylonians broke up the bronze pillars in front of the LORD's Temple, the bronze water carts, and the great bronze basin called the Sea, and they carried all the bronze away to Babylon. [14]They also took all the ash buckets, shovels, lamp snuffers, dishes, and all the other bronze articles used for making sacrifices at the Temple. [15]Nebuzaradan, the captain of the guard, also took the incense burners and basins, and all the other articles made of pure gold or silver.

[16]The weight of the bronze from the two pillars, the Sea, and the water carts was too great to be measured. These things had been made for the LORD's Temple in the days of King Solomon. [17]Each of the pillars was 27 feet* tall. The bronze capital on top of each pillar was 7½ feet* high and was decorated with a network of bronze pomegranates all the way around.

AN UNHAPPY ENDING 25:30

The book of 2 Kings opened with Elijah being carried to heaven—the destination awaiting those who follow God. But the book ends with the people of Judah being driven away from their land—the result of failing to follow God.

Second Kings is an illustration of what happens when disobedience becomes a way of life. An unhappy ending is a guarantee for those who adopt that lifestyle. Is any momentary thrill worth that? ■

[18]Nebuzaradan, the captain of the guard, took with him as prisoners Seraiah the high priest, Zephaniah the priest of the second rank, and the three chief gatekeepers. [19]And from among the people still hiding in the city, he took an officer who had been in charge of the Judean army; five of the king's personal advisers; the army commander's chief secretary, who was in charge of recruitment; and sixty other citizens. [20]Nebuzaradan, the captain of the guard, took them all to the king of Babylon

24:17 Hebrew *his.* **25:1** Hebrew *on the tenth day of the tenth month,* of the ancient Hebrew lunar calendar. A number of events in 2 Kings can be cross-checked with dates in surviving Babylonian records and related accurately to our modern calendar. This day was January 15, 588 B.C. **25:3** Hebrew *By the ninth day of the [fourth] month* [in the eleventh year of Zedekiah's reign] (compare Jer 52:6 and the note there). This day was July 18, 586 B.C.; also see note on 25:1. **25:4a** Or *the Chaldeans;* also in 25:13, 25, 26. **25:4b** Hebrew *the Arabah.* **25:5** Or *Chaldean;* also in 25:10, 24. **25:8** Hebrew *On the seventh day of the fifth month,* of the ancient Hebrew lunar calendar. This day was August 14, 586 B.C.; also see note on 25:1. **25:9** Or *destroyed the houses of all the important people.* **25:17a** Hebrew *18 cubits* [8.1 meters]. **25:17b** As in parallel texts at 1 Kgs 7:16, 2 Chr 3:15, and Jer 52:22, all of which read *5 cubits* [2.3 meters]; Hebrew reads *3 cubits,* which is 4.5 feet or 1.4 meters.

at Riblah. [21]And there at Riblah, in the land of Hamath, the king of Babylon had them all put to death. So the people of Judah were sent into exile from their land.

GEDALIAH GOVERNS IN JUDAH

[22]Then King Nebuchadnezzar appointed Gedaliah son of Ahikam and grandson of Shaphan as governor over the people he had left in Judah. [23]When all the army commanders and their men learned that the king of Babylon had appointed Gedaliah as governor, they went to see him at Mizpah. These included Ishmael son of Nethaniah, Johanan son of Kareah, Seraiah son of Tanhumeth the Netophathite, and Jezaniah* son of the Maacathite, and all their men.

[24]Gedaliah vowed to them that the Babylonian officials meant them no harm. "Don't be afraid of them. Live in the land and serve the king of Babylon, and all will go well for you," he promised.

[25]But in midautumn of that year,* Ishmael son of Nethaniah and grandson of Elishama, who was of the royal family, went to Mizpah with ten men and killed Gedaliah. He also killed all the Judeans and Babylonians who were with Gedaliah at Mizpah.

[26]Then all the people of Judah, from the least to the greatest, as well as the army commanders, fled in panic to Egypt, for they were afraid of what the Babylonians would do to them.

HOPE FOR ISRAEL'S ROYAL LINE

[27]In the thirty-seventh year of the exile of King Jehoiachin of Judah, Evil-merodach ascended to the Babylonian throne. He was kind to* Jehoiachin and released him from prison on April 2 of that year.* [28]He spoke kindly to Jehoiachin and gave him a higher place than all the other exiled kings in Babylon. [29]He supplied Jehoiachin with new clothes to replace his prison garb and allowed him to dine in the king's presence for the rest of his life. [30]So the Babylonian king gave him a regular food allowance as long as he lived.

25:23 As in parallel text at Jer 40:8; Hebrew reads *Jaazaniah*, a variant spelling of Jezaniah. **25:25** Hebrew *in the seventh month*, of the ancient Hebrew lunar calendar. This month occurred within the months of October and November 586 B.C.; also see note on 25:1. **25:27a** Hebrew *He raised the head of*. **25:27b** Hebrew *on the twenty-seventh day of the twelfth month*, of the ancient Hebrew lunar calendar. This day was April 2, 561 B.C.; also see note on 25:1.

1 CHRONICLES

1 chronicles

"THAT TEAM will be toast tonight!" The coach's voice booms over the PA in the packed gymnasium. With those words the student body begins to clap and yell wildly. Somewhere in the back a few people start chanting. Soon everyone is screaming in unison.

Pep rallies can draw a school together. And for those few moments, all differences are forgotten as the crowd focuses on the one objective—winning the game.

First Chronicles can be considered a written pep rally. Writing for the Jews who had returned to their homeland, the author attempts to form a sense of national conscience and awaken a sense of national pride and unity.

Beginning with Adam, 1 Chronicles relates the exciting history of Israel. By recalling the past, the author hoped to spur the Israelites on to a great future. But 1 Chronicles is more than a history lesson. It shows the spiritual strength of the nation. Only as the nation united in its worship of God could it regain the importance and vitality it once had.

We, too, have a great spiritual heritage that was passed on to us by the people in the Bible and in our families. As you read 1 Chronicles, why not commit to doing your part to pass on God's truth to the next generation.

timeline

1050 B.C.
Saul becomes king

1010
Saul dies; David becomes king of Judah

1003
David becomes king of all Israel

1000
David captures Jerusalem

997(?)
David captures Rabbah

980(?)
David's census

970
Solomon becomes king

930
The kingdom divides

stats

PURPOSE: To unify God's people, to trace the Davidic line, and to teach that genuine worship ought to be the center of individual and national life

AUTHOR: Ezra, according to Jewish tradition

TO WHOM WRITTEN: All Israel

DATE WRITTEN: Approximately 430 B.C.; recording events which occurred about 1000–960 B.C.

SETTING: First Chronicles parallels 2 Samuel and serves as a commentary on it. Written after the Exile from a priestly point of view, 1 Chronicles emphasizes the religious history of Judah and Israel.

KEY PLACES: Hebron, Jerusalem, the Temple

KEY points

A SPIRITUAL FOUNDATION
By retelling Israel's history in the family histories of the kings, the writer showed the spiritual foundation of the nation. The Bible provides a spiritual foundation upon which we can build our lives.

A PERFECT KING
Although the story of David's life and relationship with God showed that he was a great king, he was still imperfect. His descendant, Jesus Christ, is the only totally perfect king who will someday rule over all the earth.

AN ENCOURAGEMENT TO WORSHIP
David brought the Ark of the Covenant to the Tabernacle at Jerusalem to encourage the people to worship God. In the same way, we are to encourage each other to worship God.

KEY PLACES IN 1 CHRONICLES

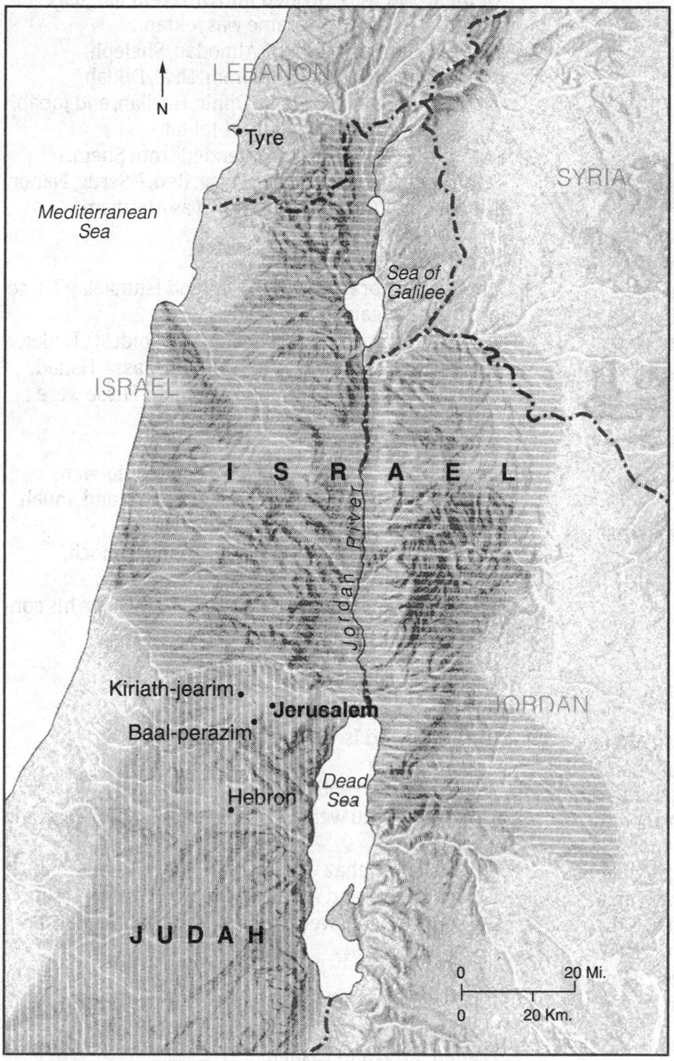

The broken lines (—·—·) indicate modern boundaries.

The genealogies of 1 Chronicles present an overview of Israel's history. The first nine chapters are filled with genealogies tracing the lineages of people from the Creation to the Exile in Babylon. Saul's death is recorded in chapter 10. Chapter 11 begins the history of David's reign over Israel.

• **HEBRON** Although David had been anointed king years earlier, his reign began when the leaders of Israel accepted him as king at Hebron (11:1-3).

• **JERUSALEM** David set out to complete the conquest of the land begun by Joshua. He attacked Jerusalem, captured it, and made it his capital (11:4–12:40).

• **KIRIATH-JEARIM** The Ark of the Covenant, which had been captured by the Philistines in battle and then returned (1 Samuel 4–6), was in safekeeping in Kiriath-jearim. David summoned all Israel to this city to join in bringing the Ark to Jerusalem. Unfortunately, it was not moved according to God's instructions, and as a result one man died. David left the Ark in the home of Obed-edom until he could discover how to transport it correctly (13:1-14).

• **TYRE** David did much building in Jerusalem. King Hiram of Tyre sent workers and supplies to help build David's palace. Cedar, abundant in the mountains north of Israel, was a valuable and hardy wood for the beautiful buildings in Jerusalem (14:1–17:27).

• **BAAL-PERAZIM** David was not very popular with the Philistines because he had slain Goliath, one of their greatest warriors (1 Samuel 17). When David began to rule over a united Israel, the Philistines set out to capture him. But David and his army attacked the Philistines at Baal-perazim as they approached Jerusalem. David's army defeated the mighty Philistines twice, causing all the surrounding nations to fear his power (14:11-17). After this battle, David moved the Ark to Jerusalem, this time in accordance with God's instructions for the transportation of the Ark. There was great celebration as the Ark was brought into Jerusalem (15:1–17:27). David spent the remainder of his life making preparations for the building of the Temple, a central place for the worship of God (18:1–29:30).

1

FROM ADAM TO NOAH'S SONS

The descendants of Adam were Seth, Enosh, 2Kenan,
Mahalalel, Jared, 3Enoch, Methuselah, Lamech, 4and
Noah.
The sons of Noah were* Shem, Ham, and Japheth.

A FAMILY HISTORY 1:1

The family histories of 1 Chronicles, beginning with this verse, demonstrate God's interest in nations and individuals. Although billions of people have lived since Adam, none is a stranger to God. He works through people to bring about his plans. These family histories can remind us of our place in God's plans and in his family. ■

DESCENDANTS OF JAPHETH

5The descendants of Japheth were Gomer, Magog,
Madai, Javan, Tubal, Meshech, and Tiras.
6The descendants of Gomer were Ashkenaz, Riphath,*
and Togarmah.
7The descendants of Javan were Elishah, Tarshish,
Kittim, and Rodanim.

DESCENDANTS OF HAM

8The descendants of Ham were Cush, Mizraim,* Put,
and Canaan.
9The descendants of Cush were Seba, Havilah, Sabtah,
Raamah, and Sabteca. The descendants of Raamah
were Sheba and Dedan. 10Cush was also the ancestor
of Nimrod, who was the first heroic warrior on earth.
11Mizraim was the ancestor of the Ludites, Anamites,
Lehabites, Naphtuhites, 12Pathrusites, Casluhites, and
the Caphtorites, from whom the Philistines came.*
13Canaan's oldest son was Sidon, the ancestor of the
Sidonians. Canaan was also the ancestor of the
Hittites, 14Jebusites, Amorites, Girgashites, 15Hivites,
Arkites, Sinites, 16Arvadites, Zemarites, and
Hamathites.

DESCENDANTS OF SHEM

17The descendants of Shem were Elam, Asshur,
Arphaxad, Lud, and Aram.
The descendants of Aram were* Uz, Hul, Gether, and
Mash.*
18Arphaxad was the father of Shelah.
Shelah was the father of Eber.
19Eber had two sons. The first was named Peleg (which
means "division"), for during his lifetime the people
of the world were divided into different language
groups. His brother's name was Joktan.
20Joktan was the ancestor of Almodad, Sheleph,
Hazarmaveth, Jerah, 21Hadoram, Uzal, Diklah,
22Obal,* Abimael, Sheba, 23Ophir, Havilah, and Jobab.
All these were descendants of Joktan.
24So this is the family line descended from Shem:
Arphaxad, Shelah,* 25Eber, Peleg, Reu, 26Serug, Nahor,
Terah, 27and Abram, later known as Abraham.

DESCENDANTS OF ABRAHAM

28The sons of Abraham were Isaac and Ishmael. 29These
are their genealogical records:
The sons of Ishmael were Nebaioth (the oldest), Kedar,
Adbeel, Mibsam, 30Mishma, Dumah, Massa, Hadad,
Tema, 31Jetur, Naphish, and Kedemah. These were
the sons of Ishmael.

32The sons of Keturah, Abraham's concubine, were
Zimran, Jokshan, Medan, Midian, Ishbak, and Shuah.
The sons of Jokshan were Sheba and Dedan.
33The sons of Midian were Ephah, Epher, Hanoch,
Abida, and Eldaah.
All these were descendants of Abraham through his concubine Keturah.

DESCENDANTS OF ISAAC

34Abraham was the father of Isaac. The sons of Isaac
were Esau and Israel.*

DESCENDANTS OF ESAU

35The sons of Esau were Eliphaz, Reuel, Jeush, Jalam, and
Korah.
36The sons of Eliphaz were Teman, Omar, Zepho,*
Gatam, Kenaz, and Amalek, who was born to Timna.*
37The sons of Reuel were Nahath, Zerah, Shammah, and
Mizzah.

ORIGINAL PEOPLES OF EDOM

38The sons of Seir were Lotan, Shobal, Zibeon, Anah,
Dishon, Ezer, and Dishan.
39The sons of Lotan were Hori and Heman.* Lotan's
sister was named Timna.
40The sons of Shobal were Alvan,* Manahath, Ebal,
Shepho,* and Onam.
The sons of Zibeon were Aiah and Anah.
41The son of Anah was Dishon.
The sons of Dishon were Hemdan,* Eshban, Ithran, and
Keran.

1:4 As in Greek version (see also Gen 5:3-32); Hebrew lacks *The sons of Noah were.* **1:6** As in some Hebrew manuscripts and Greek version (see also Gen 10:3); most Hebrew manuscripts read *Diphath.* **1:8** Or *Egypt;* also in 1:11. **1:12** Hebrew *Casluhites, from whom the Philistines came, Caphtorites.* See Jer 47:4; Amos 9:7. **1:17a** As in one Hebrew manuscript and some Greek manuscripts (see also Gen 10:23); most Hebrew manuscripts lack *The descendants of Aram were.* **1:17b** As in parallel text at Gen 10:23; Hebrew reads *and Meshech.* **1:22** As in some Hebrew manuscripts and Syriac version (see also Gen 10:28); most Hebrew manuscripts read *Ebal.* **1:24** Some Greek manuscripts read *Arphaxad, Cainan, Shelah.* See notes on Gen 10:24; 11:12-13. **1:34** *Israel* is the name that God gave to Jacob. **1:36a** As in many Hebrew manuscripts and a few Greek manuscripts (see also Gen 36:11); most Hebrew manuscripts read *Zephi.* **1:36b** As in some Greek manuscripts (see also Gen 36:12); Hebrew reads *Kenaz, Timna, and Amalek.* **1:39** As in parallel text at Gen 36:22; Hebrew reads *and Homam.* **1:40a** As in many Hebrew manuscripts and a few Greek manuscripts (see also Gen 36:23); most Hebrew manuscripts read *Alian.* **1:40b** As in some Hebrew manuscripts (see also Gen 36:23); most Hebrew manuscripts read *Shephi.* **1:41** As in many Hebrew manuscripts and some Greek manuscripts (see also Gen 36:26); most Hebrew manuscripts read *Hamran.*

42The sons of Ezer were Bilhan, Zaavan, and Akan.*
The sons of Dishan* were Uz and Aran.

RULERS OF EDOM

43These are the kings who ruled in Edom before there
were kings in Israel*:

Bela son of Beor, who ruled from his city of Dinhabah.
44When Bela died, Jobab son of Zerah from Bozrah
became king.
45When Jobab died, Husham from the land of the
Temanites became king.
46When Husham died, Hadad son of Bedad became king
and ruled from the city of Avith. He was the one who
destroyed the Midianite army in the land of Moab.
47When Hadad died, Samlah from the city of Masrekah
became king.
48When Samlah died, Shaul from the city of Rehoboth
on the river became king.
49When Shaul died, Baal-hanan son of Acbor became king.
50When Baal-hanan died, Hadad became king and ruled
from the city of Pau.* His wife was Mehetabel, the
daughter of Matred and granddaughter of Me-zahab.
51Then Hadad died.

The clan leaders of Edom were Timna, Alvah,* Jetheth,
52Oholibamah, Elah, Pinon, 53Kenaz, Teman, Mibzar,
54Magdiel, and Iram. These were the clan leaders of
Edom.

2 DESCENDANTS OF ISRAEL

The sons of Israel* were Reuben, Simeon, Levi, Judah,
Issachar, Zebulun, 2Dan, Joseph, Benjamin, Naphtali,
Gad, and Asher.

DESCENDANTS OF JUDAH

3Judah had three sons from Bathshua, a Canaanite
woman. Their names were Er, Onan, and Shelah. But
the LORD saw that the oldest son, Er, was a wicked

1:42a As in many Hebrew and Greek manuscripts (see also Gen 36:27); most Hebrew manuscripts read *Jaakan.* **1:42b** Hebrew *Dishon;* compare 1:38 and parallel text at Gen 36:28. **1:43** Or *before an Israelite king ruled over them.* **1:50** As in many Hebrew manuscripts, some Greek manuscripts, Syriac version, and Latin Vulgate (see also Gen 36:39); most Hebrew manuscripts read *Pai.* **1:51** As in parallel text at Gen 36:40; Hebrew reads *Aliah.* **2:1** *Israel* is the name that God gave to Jacob.

ISHMAEL

Have you ever wondered whether you were born into the wrong family? That question must have haunted Ishmael at times. He might have felt trapped in a conflict between two jealous women: Sarah and Hagar.

Sarah's impatience with God led to her decision to have a child through another woman. Since Hagar was a servant, she allowed herself to be used this way. But Hagar's pregnancy gave birth to strong feelings of superiority toward Sarah. Into this tense atmosphere Ishmael was born.

Much of what happened to Ishmael cannot be blamed on him. He was caught in a process much bigger than himself. But his actions showed that he chose to become part of the problem, not the solution. He chose to live in his circumstances instead of living above them.

The choice Ishmael had is one we all must make. There are circumstances over which we have no control (heredity, for instance), but there are others over which we do have control (our decisions). We all have inherited a nature that desires to do wrong. It can be partly controlled—but not overcome—by human effort. Ishmael's life is a picture of the mess we make when we don't try to change those things that we can change.

The God of the Bible has offered us a solution. His answer is not control, but a changed life freely given by God. To begin a changed life, trust God to forgive your sinful past, and to help you change your attitude toward him and others.

UPS:
- One of the first to experience circumcision—the physical sign of God's covenant
- Known for his ability as an archer and hunter
- Fathered twelve sons who became leaders of warrior tribes

DOWN:
- Failed to recognize the place of his half brother, Isaac, and mocked him

STATS:
- Where: Canaan and Egypt
- Occupations: Archer, hunter, warrior
- Relatives: Hagar and Abraham (parents); Isaac (half brother)

BOTTOM LINE:
God's plans even allow for people's mistakes.

Ishmael's story is told in Gen 16; 17:24-25; 21; 25:9-18. He also is mentioned in 1 Chron 1:28-31; Gal 4:29-30.

man, so he killed him. 4Later Judah had twin sons
from Tamar, his widowed daughter-in-law. Their
names were Perez and Zerah. So Judah had five sons
in all.

REPUTATION 2:3

This long genealogy provides names and insights into some of the people of Israel. For example, "The LORD saw that the oldest son, Er, was a wicked man, so he killed him." That's all we learn about Er's reputation. Someday each of us will be remembered based on our reputation. What you do now *does* matter. How would God summarize your life up to now? ■

5The sons of Perez were Hezron and Hamul.
6The sons of Zerah were Zimri, Ethan, Heman, Calcol,
and Darda*—five in all.
7 The son of Carmi (a descendant of Zimri) was Achan,*
who brought disaster on Israel by taking plunder that
had been set apart for the LORD.*
8The son of Ethan was Azariah.

FROM JUDAH'S GRANDSON HEZRON TO DAVID

9The sons of Hezron were Jerahmeel, Ram, and Caleb.*
10 Ram was the father of Amminadab.
Amminadab was the father of Nahshon, a leader
of Judah.
11 Nahshon was the father of Salmon.*
Salmon was the father of Boaz.
12 Boaz was the father of Obed.
Obed was the father of Jesse.
13Jesse's first son was Eliab, his second was Abinadab,
his third was Shimea, 14his fourth was Nethanel, his
fifth was Raddai, 15his sixth was Ozem, and his
seventh was David.
16Their sisters were named Zeruiah and Abigail.
Zeruiah had three sons named Abishai, Joab, and
Asahel. 17Abigail married a man named Jether, an
Ishmaelite, and they had a son named Amasa.

OTHER DESCENDANTS OF HEZRON

18Hezron's son Caleb had sons from his wife Azubah
and from Jerioth.* Her sons were named Jesher,
Shobab, and Ardon. 19After Azubah died, Caleb
married Ephrathah,* and they had a son named Hur.
20Hur was the father of Uri. Uri was the father of
Bezalel.
21When Hezron was sixty years old, he married Gilead's
sister, the daughter of Makir. They had a son named
Segub. 22Segub was the father of Jair, who ruled
twenty-three towns in the land of Gilead. 23(But
Geshur and Aram captured the Towns of Jair* and
also took Kenath and its sixty surrounding villages.)
All these were descendants of Makir, the father of
Gilead.
24Soon after Hezron died in the town of Caleb-
ephrathah, his wife Abijah gave birth to a son named
Ashhur (the father of* Tekoa).

DESCENDANTS OF HEZRON'S SON JERAHMEEL

25The sons of Jerahmeel, the oldest son of Hezron, were
Ram (the firstborn), Bunah, Oren, Ozem, and Ahijah.
26Jerahmeel had a second wife named Atarah. She
was the mother of Onam.
27The sons of Ram, the oldest son of Jerahmeel, were
Maaz, Jamin, and Eker.
28The sons of Onam were Shammai and Jada.
The sons of Shammai were Nadab and Abishur.
29The sons of Abishur and his wife Abihail were Ahban
and Molid.
30The sons of Nadab were Seled and Appaim. Seled died
without children, 31but Appaim had a son named Ishi.
The son of Ishi was Sheshan. Sheshan had a
descendant named Ahlai.
32The sons of Jada, Shammai's brother, were Jether and
Jonathan. Jether died without children, 33but
Jonathan had two sons named Peleth and Zaza.
These were all descendants of Jerahmeel.
34Sheshan had no sons, though he did have daughters.
He also had an Egyptian servant named Jarha.
35Sheshan gave one of his daughters to be the wife
of Jarha, and they had a son named Attai.
36 Attai was the father of Nathan.
Nathan was the father of Zabad.
37 Zabad was the father of Ephlal.
Ephlal was the father of Obed.
38 Obed was the father of Jehu.
Jehu was the father of Azariah.
39 Azariah was the father of Helez.
Helez was the father of Eleasah.
40 Eleasah was the father of Sismai.
Sismai was the father of Shallum.
41 Shallum was the father of Jekamiah.
Jekamiah was the father of Elishama.

DESCENDANTS OF HEZRON'S SON CALEB

42The descendants of Caleb, the brother of Jerahmeel,
included Mesha (the firstborn), who became the
father of Ziph. Caleb's descendants also included
the sons of Mareshah, the father of Hebron.*
43The sons of Hebron were Korah, Tappuah, Rekem,
and Shema. 44Shema was the father of Raham.
Raham was the father of Jorkeam. Rekem was the
father of Shammai. 45The son of Shammai was Maon.
Maon was the father of Beth-zur.
46Caleb's concubine Ephah gave birth to Haran, Moza,
and Gazez. Haran was the father of Gazez.

2:6 As in many Hebrew manuscripts, some Greek manuscripts, and Syriac version (see also 1 Kgs 4:31); Hebrew reads *Dara.* **2:7a** Hebrew *Achar;* compare Josh 7:1. *Achar* means "disaster." **2:7b** The Hebrew term used here refers to the complete consecration of things or people to the LORD, either by destroying them or by giving them as an offering. **2:9** Hebrew *Kelubai,* a variant spelling of Caleb; compare 2:18. **2:11** As in Greek version (see also Ruth 4:21); Hebrew reads *Salma.* **2:18** Or *Caleb had a daughter named Jerioth from his wife, Azubah.* The meaning of the Hebrew is uncertain. **2:19** Hebrew *Ephrath,* a variant spelling of Ephrathah; compare 2:50 and 4:4. **2:23** Or *captured Havvoth-jair.* **2:24** Or *the founder of;* also in 2:42, 45, 49. **2:42** Or *who founded Hebron.* The meaning of the Hebrew is uncertain.

47 The sons of Jahdai were Regem, Jotham, Geshan, Pelet,
Ephah, and Shaaph.
48 Another of Caleb's concubines, Maacah, gave birth to
Sheber and Tirhanah. 49 She also gave birth to Shaaph
(the father of Madmannah) and Sheva (the father of
Macbenah and Gibea). Caleb also had a daughter
named Acsah.
50 These were all descendants of Caleb.

DESCENDANTS OF CALEB'S SON HUR

The sons of Hur, the oldest son of Caleb's wife
Ephrathah, were Shobal (the founder of Kiriath-
jearim), 51 Salma (the founder of Bethlehem), and
Hareph (the founder of Beth-gader).
52 The descendants of Shobal (the founder of Kiriath-
jearim) were Haroeh, half the Manahathites, 53 and
the families of Kiriath-jearim—the Ithrites, Puthites,
Shumathites, and Mishraites, from whom came the
people of Zorah and Eshtaol.
54 The descendants of Salma were the people of
Bethlehem, the Netophathites, Atroth-beth-joab, the
other half of the Manahathites, the Zorites, 55 and the
families of scribes living at Jabez—the Tirathites,
Shimeathites, and Sucathites. All these were Kenites
who descended from Hammath, the father of the
family of Recab.*

3

DESCENDANTS OF DAVID

These are the sons of David who were born in Hebron:

The oldest was Amnon, whose mother was Ahinoam
from Jezreel.
The second was Daniel, whose mother was Abigail
from Carmel.
2 The third was Absalom, whose mother was Maacah,
the daughter of Talmai, king of Geshur.
The fourth was Adonijah, whose mother was
Haggith.
3 The fifth was Shephatiah, whose mother was Abital.
The sixth was Ithream, whose mother was Eglah,
David's wife.

4 These six sons were born to David in Hebron, where he
reigned seven and a half years.

Then David reigned another thirty-three years in Jerusalem. 5 The sons born to David in Jerusalem included
Shammua,* Shobab, Nathan, and Solomon. Their mother
was Bathsheba,* the daughter of Ammiel. 6 David also had
nine other sons: Ibhar, Elishua,* Elpelet,* 7 Nogah, Nepheg, Japhia, 8 Elishama, Eliada, and Eliphelet.
9 These were the sons of David, not including his sons
born to his concubines. Their sister was named Tamar.

DESCENDANTS OF SOLOMON

10 The descendants of Solomon were Rehoboam, Abijah,
Asa, Jehoshaphat, 11 Jehoram,* Ahaziah, Joash,
12 Amaziah, Uzziah,* Jotham, 13 Ahaz, Hezekiah,
Manasseh, 14 Amon, and Josiah.
15 The sons of Josiah were Johanan (the oldest),
Jehoiakim (the second), Zedekiah (the third), and
Jehoahaz* (the fourth).
16 The successors of Jehoiakim were his son Jehoiachin
and his brother Zedekiah.*

DESCENDANTS OF JEHOIACHIN

17 The sons of Jehoiachin,* who was taken prisoner by
the Babylonians, were Shealtiel, 18 Malkiram, Pedaiah,
Shenazzar, Jekamiah, Hoshama, and Nedabiah.
19 The sons of Pedaiah were Zerubbabel and Shimei.
The sons of Zerubbabel were Meshullam and Hananiah.
(Their sister was Shelomith.) 20 His five other sons
were Hashubah, Ohel, Berekiah, Hasadiah, and
Jushab-hesed.
21 The sons of Hananiah were Pelatiah and Jeshaiah.
Jeshaiah's son was Rephaiah. Rephaiah's son was
Arnan. Arnan's son was Obadiah. Obadiah's son was
Shecaniah.
22 The descendants of Shecaniah were Shemaiah and
his sons, Hattush, Igal, Bariah, Neariah, and Shaphat—
six in all.
23 The sons of Neariah were Elioenai, Hizkiah, and
Azrikam—three in all.
24 The sons of Elioenai were Hodaviah, Eliashib, Pelaiah,
Akkub, Johanan, Delaiah, and Anani—seven in all.

4

OTHER DESCENDANTS OF JUDAH

The descendants of Judah were Perez, Hezron, Carmi,
Hur, and Shobal.
2 Shobal's son Reaiah was the father of Jahath. Jahath
was the father of Ahumai and Lahad. These were the
families of the Zorathites.
3 The descendants of* Etam were Jezreel, Ishma, Idbash,
their sister Hazzelelponi, 4 Penuel (the father of*
Gedor), and Ezer (the father of Hushah). These were
the descendants of Hur (the firstborn of Ephrathah),
the ancestor of Bethlehem.
5 Ashhur (the father of Tekoa) had two wives, named
Helah and Naarah. 6 Naarah gave birth to Ahuzzam,
Hepher, Temeni, and Haahashtari. 7 Helah gave birth
to Zereth, Izhar, Ethnan, 8 and Koz, who became the
ancestor of Anub, Zobebah, and all the families of
Aharhel son of Harum.
9 There was a man named Jabez who was more
honorable than any of his brothers. His mother
named him Jabez* because his birth had been so

2:55 Or *the founder of Beth-recab.* 3:5a As in Syriac version (see also 14:4; 2 Sam 5:14); Hebrew reads *Shimea.* 3:5b Hebrew *Bathshua,* a variant spelling of Bathsheba. 3:6a As in some Hebrew and Greek manuscripts (see also 14:5-7 and 2 Sam 5:15); most Hebrew manuscripts read *Elishama.* 3:6b Hebrew *Eliphelet;* compare parallel text at 14:5-7. 3:11 Hebrew *Joram,* a variant spelling of Jehoram. 3:12 Hebrew *Azariah,* a variant spelling of Uzziah. 3:15 Hebrew *Shallum,* another name for Jehoahaz. 3:16 Hebrew *The sons of Jehoiakim were his son Jeconiah* [a variant spelling of Jehoiachin] *and his son Zedekiah.* 3:17 Hebrew *Jeconiah,* a variant spelling of Jehoiachin. 4:3 As in Greek version; Hebrew reads *father of.* The meaning of the Hebrew is uncertain. 4:4 Or *the founder of;* also in 4:5, 12, 14, 17, 18, and perhaps other instances where the text reads *the father of.* 4:9 *Jabez* sounds like a Hebrew word meaning "distress" or "pain."

painful. 10He was the one who prayed to the God of
Israel, "Oh, that you would bless me and expand my
territory! Please be with me in all that I do, and keep
me from all trouble and pain!" And God granted him
his request.

A MEMORABLE PRAYER 4:10

Jabez is remembered as "the one who prayed to the God of Israel." It is significant that he is remembered for a prayer rather than a heroic act. This is quite a contrast to what Er is remembered for (see note at 2:3). Jabez wasn't afraid to ask for something huge from God. His simple prayer has made a huge impact on our lives today, mainly because of God's response to it. Think back over your recent prayers. Could you imagine one of them having such an impact on a future generation? ■

11Kelub (the brother of Shuhah) was the father of
Mehir. Mehir was the father of Eshton. 12Eshton
was the father of Beth-rapha, Paseah, and Tehinnah.
Tehinnah was the father of Ir-nahash. These were
the descendants of Recah.
13The sons of Kenaz were Othniel and Seraiah. Othniel's
sons were Hathath and Meonothai.* 14Meonothai was
the father of Ophrah. Seraiah was the father of Joab,
the founder of the Valley of Craftsmen,* so called
because they were craftsmen.
15The sons of Caleb son of Jephunneh were Iru, Elah,
and Naam. The son of Elah was Kenaz.
16The sons of Jehallelel were Ziph, Ziphah, Tiria, and
Asarel.
17The sons of Ezrah were Jether, Mered, Epher, and
Jalon. One of Mered's wives became* the mother
of Miriam, Shammai, and Ishbah (the father of
Eshtemoa). 18He married a woman from Judah, who
became the mother of Jered (the father of Gedor),
Heber (the father of Soco), and Jekuthiel (the father
of Zanoah). Mered also married Bithia, a daughter
of Pharaoh, and she bore him children.
19Hodiah's wife was the sister of Naham. One of her
sons was the father of Keilah the Garmite, and
another was the father of Eshtemoa the Maacathite.
20The sons of Shimon were Amnon, Rinnah, Ben-hanan,
and Tilon.
The descendants of Ishi were Zoheth and Ben-zoheth.

DESCENDANTS OF JUDAH'S SON SHELAH

21Shelah was one of Judah's sons. The descendants of
Shelah were Er (the father of Lecah); Laadah (the
father of Mareshah); the families of linen workers at
Beth-ashbea; 22Jokim; the men of Cozeba; and Joash
and Saraph, who ruled over Moab and Jashubi-lehem.
These names all come from ancient records. 23They
were the pottery makers who lived in Netaim and
Gederah. They lived there and worked for the king.

DESCENDANTS OF SIMEON

24The sons of Simeon were Jemuel,* Jamin, Jarib,
Zohar,* and Shaul.
25The descendants of Shaul were Shallum, Mibsam, and
Mishma.
26The descendants of Mishma were Hammuel, Zaccur,
and Shimei.
27Shimei had sixteen sons and six daughters, but none
of his brothers had large families. So Simeon's tribe
never grew as large as the tribe of Judah.
28They lived in Beersheba, Moladah, Hazar-shual,
29Bilhah, Ezem, Tolad, 30Bethuel, Hormah, Ziklag,
31Beth-marcaboth, Hazar-susim, Beth-biri, and
Shaaraim. These towns were under their control
until the time of King David. 32Their descendants
also lived in Etam, Ain, Rimmon, Token, and
Ashan—five towns 33and their surrounding villages
as far away as Baalath.* This was their territory, and
these names are listed in their genealogical records.
34Other descendants of Simeon included Meshobab,
Jamlech, Joshah son of Amaziah, 35Joel, Jehu son of
Joshibiah, son of Seraiah, son of Asiel, 36Elioenai,
Jaakobah, Jeshohaiah, Asaiah, Adiel, Jesimiel, Benaiah,
37and Ziza son of Shiphi, son of Allon, son of Jedaiah,
son of Shimri, son of Shemaiah.

38These were the names of some of the leaders of Simeon's wealthy clans. Their families grew, 39and they traveled to the region of Gerar,* in the east part of the valley,
seeking pastureland for their flocks. 40They found lush
pastures there, and the land was quiet and peaceful.
Some of Ham's descendants had been living in that
region. 41But during the reign of King Hezekiah of Judah, these leaders of Simeon invaded the region and
completely destroyed* the homes of the descendants of
Ham and of the Meunites. No trace of them remains today. They killed everyone who lived there and took the
land for themselves, because they wanted its good
pastureland for their flocks. 42Five hundred of these invaders from the tribe of Simeon went to Mount Seir, led
by Pelatiah, Neariah, Rephaiah, and Uzziel—all sons of
Ishi. 43They destroyed the few Amalekites who had survived, and they have lived there ever since.

5 DESCENDANTS OF REUBEN

The oldest son of Israel* was Reuben. But since he dishonored his father by sleeping with one of his father's
concubines, his birthright was given to the sons of his
brother Joseph. For this reason, Reuben is not listed in
the genealogical records as the firstborn son. 2The descendants of Judah became the most powerful tribe and

4:13 As in some Greek manuscripts and Latin Vulgate; Hebrew lacks *and Meonothai.* 4:14 Or *Joab, the father of Ge-harashim.* 4:17 Or *Jether's wife became;* Hebrew reads *She became.* 4:24a As in Syriac version (see also Gen 46:10; Exod 6:15); Hebrew reads *Nemuel.* 4:24b As in parallel texts at Gen 46:10 and Exod 6:15; Hebrew reads *Zerah.* 4:33 As in some Greek manuscripts (see also Josh 19:8); Hebrew reads *Baal.* 4:39 As in Greek version; Hebrew reads *Gedor.* 4:41 The Hebrew term used here refers to the complete consecration of things or people to the LORD, either by destroying them or by giving them as an offering. 5:1 *Israel* is the name that God gave to Jacob.

provided a ruler for the nation,* but the birthright belonged to Joseph.

CONSEQUENCES 5:1

This record of Reuben's wrong shows the lasting consequences of sin. As the oldest son, Reuben would've inherited a double portion of his father's estate. But he lost everything because of one act. Every wrong action has consequences, either now or in the future. When temptation comes, consider the consequences. ■

3The sons of Reuben, the oldest son of Israel, were
Hanoch, Pallu, Hezron, and Carmi.
4The descendants of Joel were Shemaiah, Gog, Shimei,
5Micah, Reaiah, Baal, 6and Beerah. Beerah was the
leader of the Reubenites when they were taken into
captivity by King Tiglath-pileser* of Assyria.
7Beerah's* relatives are listed in their genealogical
records by their clans: Jeiel (the leader), Zechariah,
8and Bela son of Azaz, son of Shema, son of Joel.
The Reubenites lived in the area that stretches from
Aroer to Nebo and Baal-meon. 9And since they had so
many livestock in the land of Gilead, they spread east
toward the edge of the desert that stretches to the
Euphrates River.
10During the reign of Saul, the Reubenites defeated the
Hagrites in battle. Then they moved into the Hagrite
settlements all along the eastern edge of Gilead.

DESCENDANTS OF GAD

11Next to the Reubenites, the descendants of Gad lived
in the land of Bashan as far east as Salecah. 12Joel was
the leader in the land of Bashan, and Shapham was
second-in-command, followed by Janai and Shaphat.
13Their relatives, the leaders of seven other clans, were
Michael, Meshullam, Sheba, Jorai, Jacan, Zia, and
Eber. 14These were all descendants of Abihail son of
Huri, son of Jaroah, son of Gilead, son of Michael, son
of Jeshishai, son of Jahdo, son of Buz. 15Ahi son of
Abdiel, son of Guni, was the leader of their clans.

16The Gadite lived in the land of Gilead, in Bashan and
its villages, and throughout all the pasturelands of Sharon. 17All of these were listed in the genealogical records
during the days of King Jotham of Judah and King Jeroboam of Israel.

THE TRIBES EAST OF THE JORDAN

18There were 44,760 capable warriors in the armies of
Reuben, Gad, and the half-tribe of Manasseh. They were
all skilled in combat and armed with shields, swords, and
bows. 19They waged war against the Hagrites, the Jetur-
ites, the Naphishites, and the Nodabites. 20They cried out
to God during the battle, and he answered their prayer
because they trusted in him. So the Hagrites and all their
allies were defeated. 21The plunder taken from the
Hagrites included 50,000 camels, 250,000 sheep and
goats, 2,000 donkeys, and 100,000 captives. 22Many of
the Hagrites were killed in the battle because God was
fighting against them. The people of Reuben, Gad, and
Manasseh lived in their land until they were taken into
exile.

23The half-tribe of Manasseh was very large and
spread through the land from Bashan to Baal-hermon,
Senir, and Mount Hermon. 24These were the leaders of
their clans: Epher,* Ishi, Eliel, Azriel, Jeremiah, Hodaviah,
and Jahdiel. These men had a great reputation as mighty
warriors and leaders of their clans.

25But these tribes were unfaithful to the God of their
ancestors. They worshiped the gods of the nations that
God had destroyed. 26So the God of Israel caused King Pul
of Assyria (also known as Tiglath-pileser) to invade the
land and take away the people of Reuben, Gad, and the
half-tribe of Manasseh as captives. The Assyrians exiled
them to Halah, Habor, Hara, and the Gozan River, where
they remain to this day.

SUCCESSFUL FAILURES 5:23-26

As warriors and leaders, these men seemed successful. They were numerous and powerful. But they failed in the most important quality—putting God first in their lives. In a way, they were "successful failures." They followed the world's standard of success but not God's. Do your standards for success match God's standards or the world's? ■

6 THE PRIESTLY LINE

1*The sons of Levi were Gershon, Kohath, and Merari.
2The descendants of Kohath included Amram, Izhar,
Hebron, and Uzziel.
3The children of Amram were Aaron, Moses, and
Miriam.
The sons of Aaron were Nadab, Abihu, Eleazar, and
Ithamar.
4 Eleazar was the father of Phinehas.
Phinehas was the father of Abishua.
5 Abishua was the father of Bukki.
Bukki was the father of Uzzi.
6 Uzzi was the father of Zerahiah.
Zerahiah was the father of Meraioth.
7 Meraioth was the father of Amariah.
Amariah was the father of Ahitub.
8 Ahitub was the father of Zadok.
Zadok was the father of Ahimaaz.
9 Ahimaaz was the father of Azariah.
Azariah was the father of Johanan.
10 Johanan was the father of Azariah, the high priest
at the Temple* built by Solomon in Jerusalem.

5:2 Or *and from Judah came a prince.* **5:6** Hebrew *Tilgath-pilneser,* a variant spelling of Tiglath-pileser; also in 5:26. **5:7** Hebrew *His.* **5:24** As in Greek version and Latin Vulgate; Hebrew reads *and Epher.* **6:1** Verses 6:1-15 are numbered 5:27-41 in Hebrew text. **6:10** Hebrew *the house.*

11 Azariah was the father of Amariah.
Amariah was the father of Ahitub.
12 Ahitub was the father of Zadok.
Zadok was the father of Shallum.
13 Shallum was the father of Hilkiah.
Hilkiah was the father of Azariah.
14 Azariah was the father of Seraiah.
Seraiah was the father of Jehozadak, 15 who went into
exile when the LORD sent the people of Judah and
Jerusalem into captivity under Nebuchadnezzar.

THE LEVITE CLANS

16* The sons of Levi were Gershon,* Kohath, and Merari.
17 The descendants of Gershon included Libni and
Shimei.
18 The descendants of Kohath included Amram, Izhar,
Hebron, and Uzziel.
19 The descendants of Merari included Mahli and Mushi.

The following were the Levite clans, listed according to their ancestral descent:

20 The descendants of Gershon included Libni, Jahath,
Zimmah, 21 Joah, Iddo, Zerah, and Jeatherai.
22 The descendants of Kohath included Amminadab,
Korah, Assir, 23 Elkanah, Abiasaph,* Assir, 24 Tahath,
Uriel, Uzziah, and Shaul.
25 The descendants of Elkanah included Amasai,
Ahimoth, 26 Elkanah, Zophai, Nahath, 27 Eliab, Jeroham,
Elkanah, and Samuel.*
28 The sons of Samuel were Joel* (the older) and Abijah
(the second).
29 The descendants of Merari included Mahli, Libni,
Shimei, Uzzah, 30 Shimea, Haggiah, and Asaiah.

THE TEMPLE MUSICIANS

31 David assigned the following men to lead the music at
the house of the LORD after the Ark was placed there.
32 They ministered with music at the Tabernacle* until
Solomon built the Temple of the LORD in Jerusalem. They
carried out their work, following all the regulations
handed down to them. 33 These are the men who served,
along with their sons:

Heman the musician was from the clan of Kohath. His
genealogy was traced back through Joel, Samuel,
34 Elkanah, Jeroham, Eliel, Toah, 35 Zuph, Elkanah,
Mahath, Amasai, 36 Elkanah, Joel, Azariah, Zephaniah,
37 Tahath, Assir, Abiasaph, Korah, 38 Izhar, Kohath,
Levi, and Israel.*
39 Heman's first assistant was Asaph from the clan of
Gershon.* Asaph's genealogy was traced back
through Berekiah, Shimea, 40 Michael, Baaseiah,
Malkijah, 41 Ethni, Zerah, Adaiah, 42 Ethan, Zimmah,
Shimei, 43 Jahath, Gershon, and Levi.
44 Heman's second assistant was Ethan from the clan of
Merari. Ethan's genealogy was traced back through
Kishi, Abdi, Malluch, 45 Hashabiah, Amaziah, Hilkiah,
46 Amzi, Bani, Shemer, 47 Mahli, Mushi, Merari, and
Levi.

48 Their fellow Levites were appointed to various other
tasks in the Tabernacle, the house of God.

AARON'S DESCENDANTS

49 Only Aaron and his descendants served as priests. They
presented the offerings on the altar of burnt offering and
the altar of incense, and they performed all the other duties related to the Most Holy Place. They made atonement
for Israel by doing everything that Moses, the servant of
God, had commanded them.

SELECTIVE OR THOROUGH? 6:49

Aaron and his descendants strictly followed the details of worship commanded by God through Moses. They did not choose only those commands they *wanted* to obey. This is a sharp contrast to what happened to Uzzah when important details in handling the Ark of the Covenant were neglected (13:6-10). When it comes to obeying God's rules, are you selective or thorough? ■

50 The descendants of Aaron were Eleazar, Phinehas,
Abishua, 51 Bukki, Uzzi, Zerahiah, 52 Meraioth,
Amariah, Ahitub, 53 Zadok, and Ahimaaz.

TERRITORY FOR THE LEVITES

54 This is a record of the towns and territory assigned by
means of sacred lots to the descendants of Aaron, who
were from the clan of Kohath. 55 This territory included
Hebron and its surrounding pasturelands in Judah, 56 but
the fields and outlying areas belonging to the city were
given to Caleb son of Jephunneh. 57 So the descendants
of Aaron were given the following towns, each with its
pasturelands: Hebron (a city of refuge),* Libnah, Jattir,
Eshtemoa, 58 Holon,* Debir, 59 Ain,* Juttah,* and Beth-
shemesh. 60 And from the territory of Benjamin they
were given Gibeon,* Geba, Alemeth, and Anathoth, each
with its pasturelands. So thirteen towns were given to
the descendants of Aaron. 61 The remaining descendants
of Kohath received ten towns from the territory of the
half-tribe of Manasseh by means of sacred lots.
62 The descendants of Gershon received by sacred
lots thirteen towns from the territories of Issachar, Asher,

6:16a Verses 6:16-81 are numbered 6:1-66 in Hebrew text. **6:16b** Hebrew *Gershom,* a variant spelling of Gershon (see 6:1); also in 6:17, 20, 43, 62, 71. **6:23** Hebrew *Ebiasaph,* a variant spelling of Abiasaph (also in 6:37); compare parallel text at Exod 6:24. **6:27** As in some Greek manuscripts (see also 6:33-34); Hebrew lacks *and Samuel.* **6:28** As in some Greek manuscripts and the Syriac version (see also 6:33 and 1 Sam 8:2); Hebrew lacks *Joel.* **6:32** Hebrew *the Tabernacle, the Tent of Meeting.* **6:38** *Israel* is the name that God gave to Jacob. **6:39** Hebrew lacks *from the clan of Gershon;* see 6:43. **6:57** As in parallel text at Josh 21:13; Hebrew reads *were given the cities of refuge: Hebron, and the following towns, each with its pasturelands.* **6:58** As in parallel text at Josh 21:15; Hebrew reads *Hilen.* **6:59a** As in parallel text at Josh 21:16; Hebrew reads *Ashan.* **6:59b** As in Syriac version (see also Josh 21:16); Hebrew lacks *Juttah.* **6:60** As in parallel text at Josh 21:17; Hebrew lacks *Gibeon.*

Naphtali, and from the Bashan area of Manasseh, east of
the Jordan.
63 The descendants of Merari received by sacred lots
twelve towns from the territories of Reuben, Gad, and
Zebulun.
64 So the people of Israel assigned all these towns and
pasturelands to the Levites. 65 The towns in the territories
of Judah, Simeon, and Benjamin, mentioned above, were
assigned to them by means of sacred lots.
66 The descendants of Kohath were given the following
towns from the territory of Ephraim, each with its
pasturelands: 67 Shechem (a city of refuge in the hill country of Ephraim),* Gezer, 68 Jokmeam, Beth-horon, 69 Aijalon, and Gath-rimmon. 70 The remaining descendants of
Kohath were assigned the towns of Aner and Bileam
from the territory of the half-tribe of Manasseh, each
with its pasturelands.
71 The descendants of Gershon received the towns of
Golan (in Bashan) and Ashtaroth from the territory of the
half-tribe of Manasseh, each with its pasturelands.
72 From the territory of Issachar, they were given Kedesh,
Daberath, 73 Ramoth, and Anem, each with its pasturelands. 74 From the territory of Asher, they received Mashal,
Abdon, 75 Hukok, and Rehob, each with its pasturelands.
76 From the territory of Naphtali, they were given Kedesh
in Galilee, Hammon, and Kiriathaim, each with its
pasturelands.
77 The remaining descendants of Merari received the
towns of Jokneam, Kartah,* Rimmon,* and Tabor from
the territory of Zebulun, each with its pasturelands.
78 From the territory of Reuben, east of the Jordan River
opposite Jericho, they received Bezer (a desert town),
Jahaz,* 79 Kedemoth, and Mephaath, each with its
pasturelands. 80 And from the territory of Gad, they received Ramoth in Gilead, Mahanaim, 81 Heshbon, and
Jazer, each with its pasturelands.

7

DESCENDANTS OF ISSACHAR

The four sons of Issachar were Tola, Puah, Jashub, and
Shimron.
2 The sons of Tola were Uzzi, Rephaiah, Jeriel, Jahmai,
Ibsam, and Shemuel. Each of them was the leader of
an ancestral clan. At the time of King David, the total
number of mighty warriors listed in the records of
these clans was 22,600.
3 The son of Uzzi was Izrahiah. The sons of Izrahiah were
Michael, Obadiah, Joel, and Isshiah. These five became
the leaders of clans. 4 All of them had many wives and
many sons, so the total number of men available for
military service among their descendants was 36,000.
5 The total number of mighty warriors from all the clans
of the tribe of Issachar was 87,000. All of them were
listed in their genealogical records.

DESCENDANTS OF BENJAMIN

6 Three of Benjamin's sons were Bela, Beker, and Jediael.
7 The five sons of Bela were Ezbon, Uzzi, Uzziel,
Jerimoth, and Iri. Each of them was the leader of an
ancestral clan. The total number of mighty warriors
from these clans was 22,034, as listed in their
genealogical records.
8 The sons of Beker were Zemirah, Joash, Eliezer,
Elioenai, Omri, Jeremoth, Abijah, Anathoth, and
Alemeth. 9 Each of them was the leader of an
ancestral clan. The total number of mighty warriors
and leaders from these clans was 20,200, as listed in
their genealogical records.
10 The son of Jediael was Bilhan. The sons of Bilhan were
Jeush, Benjamin, Ehud, Kenaanah, Zethan, Tarshish,
and Ahishahar. 11 Each of them was the leader of an
ancestral clan. From these clans the total number of
mighty warriors ready for war was 17,200.
12 The sons of Ir were Shuppim and Huppim. Hushim
was the son of Aher.

DESCENDANTS OF NAPHTALI

13 The sons of Naphtali were Jahzeel,* Guni, Jezer, and
Shillem.* They were all descendants of Jacob's
concubine Bilhah.

DESCENDANTS OF MANASSEH

14 The descendants of Manasseh through his Aramean
concubine included Asriel. She also bore Makir, the
father of Gilead. 15 Makir found wives for* Huppim
and Shuppim. Makir had a sister named Maacah. One
of his descendants was Zelophehad, who had only
daughters.
16 Makir's wife, Maacah, gave birth to a son whom she
named Peresh. His brother's name was Sheresh. The
sons of Peresh were Ulam and Rakem. 17 The son of
Ulam was Bedan. All these were considered
Gileadites, descendants of Makir son of Manasseh.
18 Makir's sister Hammoleketh gave birth to Ishhod,
Abiezer, and Mahlah.
19 The sons of Shemida were Ahian, Shechem, Likhi, and
Aniam.

DESCENDANTS OF EPHRAIM

20 The descendants of Ephraim were Shuthelah, Bered,
Tahath, Eleadah, Tahath, 21 Zabad, Shuthelah, Ezer,
and Elead. These two were killed trying to steal
livestock from the local farmers near Gath. 22 Their
father, Ephraim, mourned for them a long time, and
his relatives came to comfort him. 23 Afterward
Ephraim slept with his wife, and she became
pregnant and gave birth to a son. Ephraim named
him Beriah* because of the tragedy his family had
suffered. 24 He had a daughter named Sheerah. She

6:66-67 As in parallel text at Josh 21:21. Hebrew text reads *were given the cities of refuge: Shechem in the hill country of Ephraim, and the following towns, each with its pasturelands.* **6:77a** As in Greek version (see also Josh 21:34); Hebrew lacks *Jokneam, Kartah.* **6:77b** As in Greek version (see also Josh 19:13); Hebrew reads *Rimmono.* **6:78** Hebrew *Jahzah,* a variant spelling of Jahaz. **7:13a** As in parallel text at Gen 46:24; Hebrew reads *Jahziel,* a variant spelling of Jahzeel. **7:13b** As in some Hebrew and Greek manuscripts (see also Gen 46:24; Num 26:49); most Hebrew manuscripts read *Shallum.* **7:15** Or *Makir took a wife from.* The meaning of the Hebrew is uncertain. **7:23** *Beriah* sounds like a Hebrew term meaning "tragedy" or "misfortune."

built the towns of Lower and Upper Beth-horon and
Uzzen-sheerah.
25 The descendants of Ephraim included Rephah,
Resheph, Telah, Tahan, 26 Ladan, Ammihud, Elishama,
27 Nun, and Joshua.

28 The descendants of Ephraim lived in the territory
that included Bethel and its surrounding towns to the
south, Naaran to the east, Gezer and its villages to the
west, and Shechem and its surrounding villages to
the north as far as Ayyah and its towns. 29 Along the
border of Manasseh were the towns of Beth-shan,*
Taanach, Megiddo, Dor, and their surrounding villages. The descendants of Joseph son of Israel* lived
in these towns.

DESCENDANTS OF ASHER

30 The sons of Asher were Imnah, Ishvah, Ishvi, and
Beriah. They had a sister named Serah.
31 The sons of Beriah were Heber and Malkiel (the father
of Birzaith).
32 The sons of Heber were Japhlet, Shomer, and Hotham.
They had a sister named Shua.
33 The sons of Japhlet were Pasach, Bimhal, and Ashvath.
34 The sons of Shomer were Ahi,* Rohgah, Hubbah, and
Aram.
35 The sons of his brother Helem* were Zophah, Imna,
Shelesh, and Amal.
36 The sons of Zophah were Suah, Harnepher, Shual,
Beri, Imrah, 37 Bezer, Hod, Shamma, Shilshah, Ithran,*
and Beera.
38 The sons of Jether were Jephunneh, Pispah, and Ara.
39 The sons of Ulla were Arah, Hanniel, and Rizia.
40 Each of these descendants of Asher was the head of an
ancestral clan. They were all select men—mighty warriors and outstanding leaders. The total number of men
available for military service was 26,000, as listed in their
genealogical records.

8

DESCENDANTS OF BENJAMIN

Benjamin's first son was Bela, the second was Ashbel,
the third was Aharah, 2 the fourth was Nohah, and the
fifth was Rapha.
3 The sons of Bela were Addar, Gera, Abihud,* 4 Abishua,
Naaman, Ahoah, 5 Gera, Shephuphan, and Huram.
6 The sons of Ehud, leaders of the clans living at Geba,
were exiled to Manahath. 7 Ehud's sons were Naaman,
Ahijah, and Gera. Gera, who led them into exile, was
the father of Uzza and Ahihud.*
8 After Shaharaim divorced his wives Hushim and Baara,
he had children in the land of Moab. 9 Hodesh, his
new wife, gave birth to Jobab, Zibia, Mesha, Malcam,
10 Jeuz, Sakia, and Mirmah. These sons all became the
leaders of clans.

DIVORCE? GOD SAYS NO 8:8-10

Divorce and polygamy are sometimes recorded in the Old Testament without critical comments. This does not mean that God takes them lightly. His opinion can be found in Malachi 2:15-16: "Guard your heart; remain loyal to the wife of your youth. 'For I hate divorce!' says the LORD, the God of Israel." Jesus later explained that although divorce was allowed, it was not God's will (see Matt 19:8). Based on the current high divorce rate, many think that God has changed his mind about divorce. But he hasn't. ■

11 Shaharaim's wife Hushim had already given birth
to Abitub and Elpaal. 12 The sons of Elpaal were
Eber, Misham, Shemed (who built the towns of
Ono and Lod and their nearby villages), 13 Beriah,
and Shema. They were the leaders of the clans
living in Aijalon, and they drove out the
inhabitants of Gath.
14 Ahio, Shashak, Jeremoth, 15 Zebadiah, Arad, Eder,
16 Michael, Ishpah, and Joha were the sons of Beriah.
17 Zebadiah, Meshullam, Hizki, Heber, 18 Ishmerai, Izliah,
and Jobab were the sons of Elpaal.
19 Jakim, Zicri, Zabdi, 20 Elienai, Zillethai, Eliel, 21 Adaiah,
Beraiah, and Shimrath were the sons of Shimei.
22 Ishpan, Eber, Eliel, 23 Abdon, Zicri, Hanan, 24 Hananiah,
Elam, Anthothijah, 25 Iphdeiah, and Penuel were the
sons of Shashak.
26 Shamsherai, Shehariah, Athaliah, 27 Jaareshiah, Elijah,
and Zicri were the sons of Jeroham.
28 These were the leaders of the ancestral clans; they were
listed in their genealogical records, and they all lived in
Jerusalem.

THE FAMILY OF SAUL

29 Jeiel* (the father of* Gibeon) lived in the town of
Gibeon. His wife's name was Maacah, 30 and his oldest
son was named Abdon. Jeiel's other sons were Zur,
Kish, Baal, Ner,* Nadab, 31 Gedor, Ahio, Zechariah,*
32 and Mikloth, who was the father of Shimeam.* All
these families lived near each other in Jerusalem.
33 Ner was the father of Kish.
Kish was the father of Saul.
Saul was the father of Jonathan, Malkishua,
Abinadab, and Esh-baal.
34 Jonathan was the father of Merib-baal.
Merib-baal was the father of Micah.
35 Micah was the father of Pithon, Melech, Tahrea,*
and Ahaz.

7:29a Hebrew *Beth-shean,* a variant spelling of Beth-shan. **7:29b** *Israel* is the name that God gave to Jacob. **7:34** Or *The sons of Shomer, his brother, were.* **7:35** Possibly another name for *Hotham;* compare 7:32. **7:37** Possibly another name for *Jether;* compare 7:38. **8:3** Possibly *Gera the father of Ehud;* compare 8:6. **8:7** Or *Gera, that is Heglam, was the father of Uzza and Ahihud.* **8:29a** As in some Greek manuscripts (see also 9:35); Hebrew lacks *Jeiel.* **8:29b** Or *the founder of.* **8:30** As in some Greek manuscripts (see also 9:36); Hebrew lacks *Ner.* **8:31** As in parallel text at 9:37; Hebrew reads *Zeker,*a variant spelling of Zechariah. **8:32** As in parallel text at 9:38; Hebrew reads *Shimeah,* a variant spelling of Shimeam. **8:35** As in parallel text at 9:41; Hebrew reads *Tarea,* a variant spelling of Tahrea.

36 Ahaz was the father of Jadah.*
Jadah was the father of Alemeth, Azmaveth, and Zimri.
Zimri was the father of Moza.
37 Moza was the father of Binea.
Binea was the father of Rephaiah.*
Rephaiah was the father of Eleasah.
Eleasah was the father of Azel.
38 Azel had six sons: Azrikam, Bokeru, Ishmael, Sheariah, Obadiah, and Hanan. These were the sons of Azel.
39 Azel's brother Eshek had three sons: the first was Ulam, the second was Jeush, and the third was
Eliphelet. 40 Ulam's sons were all mighty warriors and expert archers. They had many sons and grandsons—150 in all.

All these were descendants of Benjamin.

9 So all Israel was listed in the genealogical records in *The Book of the Kings of Israel.*

A MAJOR EFFECT 9:1

Although every person in Judah did not worship idols, the entire nation had been driven away from their homeland. Now they were allowed to return. The wrongdoings of a few can have a huge effect on everyone. Rather than think, *I'm not hurting anyone but me,* think of the impact one isolated incident can have on others. ■

THE RETURNING EXILES

The people of Judah were exiled to Babylon because they
were unfaithful to the LORD. 2 The first of the exiles to return to their property in their former towns were priests,
Levites, Temple servants, and other Israelites. 3 Some of
the people from the tribes of Judah, Benjamin, Ephraim, and Manasseh came and settled in Jerusalem.

4 One family that returned was that of Uthai son of Ammihud, son of Omri, son of Imri, son of Bani, a descendant of Perez son of Judah.
5 Others returned from the Shilonite clan, including Asaiah (the oldest) and his sons.
6 From the Zerahite clan, Jeuel returned with his relatives.
In all, 690 families from the tribe of Judah returned.

7 From the tribe of Benjamin came Sallu son of Meshullam, son of Hodaviah, son of Hassenuah;
8 Ibneiah son of Jeroham; Elah son of Uzzi, son of Micri; and Meshullam son of Shephatiah, son of Reuel, son of Ibnijah.
9 These men were all leaders of clans, and they were listed in their genealogical records. In all, 956 families from the tribe of Benjamin returned.

THE RETURNING PRIESTS

10 Among the priests who returned were Jedaiah,
Jehoiarib, Jakin, 11 Azariah son of Hilkiah, son of Meshullam, son of Zadok, son of Meraioth, son of Ahitub. Azariah was the chief officer of the house of God.
12 Other returning priests were Adaiah son of Jeroham, son of Pashhur, son of Malkijah, and Maasai son of Adiel, son of Jahzerah, son of Meshullam, son of Meshillemith, son of Immer.
13 In all, 1,760 priests returned. They were heads of clans and very able men. They were responsible for ministering at the house of God.

THE RETURNING LEVITES

14 The Levites who returned were Shemaiah son of Hasshub, son of Azrikam, son of Hashabiah, a
descendant of Merari; 15 Bakbakkar; Heresh; Galal;
Mattaniah son of Mica, son of Zicri, son of Asaph;
16 Obadiah son of Shemaiah, son of Galal, son of Jeduthun; and Berekiah son of Asa, son of Elkanah, who lived in the area of Netophah.
17 The gatekeepers who returned were Shallum, Akkub, Talmon, Ahiman, and their relatives. Shallum was
the chief gatekeeper. 18 Prior to this time, they were responsible for the King's Gate on the east side. These men served as gatekeepers for the camps
of the Levites. 19 Shallum was the son of Kore, a descendant of Abiasaph,* from the clan of Korah. He and his relatives, the Korahites, were responsible for guarding the entrance to the sanctuary, just as their ancestors had guarded the Tabernacle in the camp of the LORD.
20 Phinehas son of Eleazar had been in charge of the gatekeepers in earlier times, and the LORD
had been with him. 21 And later Zechariah son of Meshelemiah was responsible for guarding the entrance to the Tabernacle.*

22 In all, there were 212 gatekeepers in those days, and they were listed according to the genealogies in their villages. David and Samuel the seer had appointed their ancestors because they were reliable
men. 23 These gatekeepers and their descendants, by their divisions, were responsible for guarding the entrance to the house of the LORD when that house was
a tent. 24 The gatekeepers were stationed on all four
sides—east, west, north, and south. 25 Their relatives in the villages came regularly to share their duties for seven-day periods.
26 The four chief gatekeepers, all Levites, were trusted officials, for they were responsible for the rooms and
treasuries at the house of God. 27 They would spend the night around the house of God, since it was their duty to guard it and to open the gates every morning.
28 Some of the gatekeepers were assigned to care for the various articles used in worship. They checked them
in and out to avoid any loss. 29 Others were responsible

8:36 As in parallel text at 9:42; Hebrew reads *Jehoaddah,* a variant spelling of Jadah. 8:37 As in parallel text at 9:43; Hebrew reads *Raphah,* a variant spelling of Rephaiah. 9:19 Hebrew *Ebiasaph,* a variant spelling of Abiasaph; compare Exod 6:24. 9:21 Hebrew *Tent of Meeting.*

for the furnishings, the items in the sanctuary, and the
supplies, such as choice flour, wine, olive oil, frankincense, and spices. 30But it was the priests who blended
the spices. 31Mattithiah, a Levite and the oldest son of
Shallum the Korahite, was entrusted with baking the
bread used in the offerings. 32And some members of the
clan of Kohath were in charge of preparing the bread to
be set on the table each Sabbath day.

BE PREPARED 9:22-32

The priests and Levites put a lot of time and effort into worship. Not only did they perform rather complicated tasks (described in Lev 1–9), they also took care of many pieces of equipment. Their maintenance of the Tabernacle allowed the people to worship without worry. Think of the many people who work behind the scenes at your church. Their dedication allows you to worship without worry. The preparations they make also serve as a reminder to be prepared for worship. How do you prepare for worship? ■

33The musicians, all prominent Levites, lived at the
Temple. They were exempt from other responsibilities
since they were on duty at all hours. 34All these men lived
in Jerusalem. They were the heads of Levite families and
were listed as prominent leaders in their genealogical
records.

KING SAUL'S FAMILY TREE

35Jeiel (the father of* Gibeon) lived in the town of
Gibeon. His wife's name was Maacah, 36and his
oldest son was named Abdon. Jeiel's other sons
were Zur, Kish, Baal, Ner, Nadab, 37Gedor, Ahio,
Zechariah, and Mikloth. 38Mikloth was the father
of Shimeam. All these families lived near each other
in Jerusalem.

39 Ner was the father of Kish.
Kish was the father of Saul.
Saul was the father of Jonathan, Malkishua,
Abinadab, and Esh-baal.

40 Jonathan was the father of Merib-baal.
Merib-baal was the father of Micah.

41 The sons of Micah were Pithon, Melech, Tahrea,
and Ahaz.*

42 Ahaz was the father of Jadah.*
Jadah was the father of Alemeth, Azmaveth, and
Zimri.
Zimri was the father of Moza.

43 Moza was the father of Binea.
Binea's son was Rephaiah.
Rephaiah's son was Eleasah.
Eleasah's son was Azel.

44Azel had six sons, whose names were Azrikam,
Bokeru, Ishmael, Sheariah, Obadiah, and Hanan.
These were the sons of Azel.

10

THE DEATH OF KING SAUL

Now the Philistines attacked Israel, and the men of Israel
fled before them. Many were slaughtered on the slopes
of Mount Gilboa. 2The Philistines closed in on Saul and
his sons, and they killed three of his sons—Jonathan,
Abinadab, and Malkishua. 3The fighting grew very fierce
around Saul, and the Philistine archers caught up with
him and wounded him.

4Saul groaned to his armor bearer, "Take your sword
and kill me before these pagan Philistines come to taunt
and torture me."

But his armor bearer was afraid and would not do it. So
Saul took his own sword and fell on it. 5When his armor
bearer realized that Saul was dead, he fell on his own
sword and died. 6So Saul and his three sons died there together, bringing his dynasty to an end.

7When all the Israelites in the Jezreel Valley saw that
their army had fled and that Saul and his sons were dead,
they abandoned their towns and fled. So the Philistines
moved in and occupied their towns.

8The next day, when the Philistines went out to strip
the dead, they found the bodies of Saul and his sons on
Mount Gilboa. 9So they stripped off Saul's armor and cut
off his head. Then they proclaimed the good news of
Saul's death before their idols and to the people throughout the land of Philistia. 10They placed his armor in the
temple of their gods, and they fastened his head to the
temple of Dagon.

11But when everyone in Jabesh-gilead heard about
everything the Philistines had done to Saul, 12all their
mighty warriors brought the bodies of Saul and his sons
back to Jabesh. Then they buried their bones beneath the
great tree at Jabesh, and they fasted for seven days.

IN PURSUIT 10:13-14

Saul's unfaithfulness was both active and passive; he not only did wrong, he also *failed* to do right. He actively disobeyed by attempting murder, ignoring God's instructions, and seeking guidance from a witch. He passively disobeyed by neglecting to ask God for guidance as he ran the king-dom. Obedience, too, is both passive and active. It is not enough just to avoid what is wrong; we need to actively pursue what is right. Is that what you seek? ■

13So Saul died because he was unfaithful to the LORD.
He failed to obey the LORD's command, and he even consulted a medium 14instead of asking the LORD for guidance. So the LORD killed him and turned the kingdom
over to David son of Jesse.

11

DAVID BECOMES KING OF ALL ISRAEL

Then all Israel gathered before David at Hebron and told
him, "We are your own flesh and blood. 2In the past,*

9:35 Or *the founder of.* 9:41 As in Syriac version and Latin Vulgate (see also 8:35); Hebrew lacks *and Ahaz.* 9:42 As in some Hebrew manuscripts and Greek version (see also 8:36); Hebrew reads *Jarah.* 11:2 Or *For some time.*

even when Saul was king, you were the one who really led
the forces of Israel. And the LORD your God told you, 'You
will be the shepherd of my people Israel. You will be the
leader of my people Israel.'"
[3]So there at Hebron, David made a covenant before the
LORD with all the elders of Israel. And they anointed him
king of Israel, just as the LORD had promised through
Samuel.

FAME 11:9

King David's power and fame increased as a result of his consistent trust in God. In contrast, King Saul's power and fame decreased because he wanted all the credit for himself and ignored God (1 Sam 15:1-26; 1 Chron 10:13-14). Those who are concerned about building a name for themselves risk losing the very recognition they crave. Are you a David or a Saul? ■

DAVID CAPTURES JERUSALEM

[4]Then David and all Israel went to Jerusalem (or Jebus, as it
used to be called), where the Jebusites, the original inhabitants of the land, were living. [5]The people of Jebus taunted
David, saying, "You'll never get in here!" But David captured
the fortress of Zion, which is now called the City of David.
[6]David had said to his troops, "Whoever is first to attack
the Jebusites will become the commander of my armies!"
And Joab, the son of David's sister Zeruiah, was first to attack, so he became the commander of David's armies.
[7]David made the fortress his home, and that is why it is
called the City of David. [8]He extended the city from the
supporting terraces* to the surrounding area, while Joab
rebuilt the rest of Jerusalem. [9]And David became more
and more powerful, because the LORD of Heaven's Armies was with him.

DAVID'S MIGHTIEST WARRIORS

[10]These are the leaders of David's mighty warriors. Together with all Israel, they decided to make David their
king, just as the LORD had promised concerning Israel.
[11]Here is the record of David's mightiest warriors: The
first was Jashobeam the Hacmonite, who was leader of the
Three—the mightiest warriors among David's men.* He
once used his spear to kill 300 enemy warriors in a single
battle.
[12]Next in rank among the Three was Eleazar son of
Dodai,* a descendant of Ahoah. [13]He was with David in
the battle against the Philistines at Pas-dammim. The
battle took place in a field full of barley, and the Israelite
army fled. [14]But Eleazar and David* held their ground in
the middle of the field and beat back the Philistines. So
the LORD saved them by giving them a great victory.
[15]Once when David was at the rock near the cave of
Adullam, the Philistine army was camped in the valley of
Rephaim. The Three (who were among the Thirty—an
elite group among David's fighting men) went down to
meet him there. [16]David was staying in the stronghold at
the time, and a Philistine detachment had occupied the
town of Bethlehem.
[17]David remarked longingly to his men, "Oh, how I
would love some of that good water from the well by the
gate in Bethlehem." [18]So the Three broke through the Philistine lines, drew some water from the well by the gate in
Bethlehem, and brought it back to David. But David refused
to drink it. Instead, he poured it out as an offering to the
LORD. [19]"God forbid that I should drink this!" he exclaimed.
"This water is as precious as the blood of these men* who
risked their lives to bring it to me." So David did not drink
it. These are examples of the exploits of the Three.

DAVID'S THIRTY MIGHTY MEN

[20]Abishai, the brother of Joab, was the leader of the
Thirty.* He once used his spear to kill 300 enemy warriors in a single battle. It was by such feats that he became
as famous as the Three. [21]Abishai was the most famous of
the Thirty and was their commander, though he was not
one of the Three.
[22]There was also Benaiah son of Jehoiada, a valiant
warrior from Kabzeel. He did many heroic deeds, which
included killing two champions* of Moab. Another time,
on a snowy day, he chased a lion down into a pit and killed
it. [23]Once, armed only with a club, he killed an Egyptian
warrior who was 7½ feet* tall and whose spear was as
thick as a weaver's beam. Benaiah wrenched the spear
from the Egyptian's hand and killed him with it. [24]Deeds
like these made Benaiah as famous as the three mightiest
warriors. [25]He was more honored than the other members of the Thirty, though he was not one of the Three.
And David made him captain of his bodyguard.
[26]David's mighty warriors also included:

Asahel, Joab's brother;
Elhanan son of Dodo from Bethlehem;
27 Shammah from Harod;*
Helez from Pelon;
28 Ira son of Ikkesh from Tekoa;
Abiezer from Anathoth;
29 Sibbecai from Hushah;
Zalmon* from Ahoah;
30 Maharai from Netophah;
Heled son of Baanah from Netophah;
31 Ithai son of Ribai from Gibeah (in the land of Benjamin);
Benaiah from Pirathon;
32 Hurai from near Nahale-gaash*;
Abi-albon* from Arabah;

11:8 Hebrew *the millo.* The meaning of the Hebrew is uncertain. **11:11** As in some Greek manuscripts (see also 2 Sam 23:8); Hebrew reads *leader of the Thirty,* or *leader of the captains.* **11:12** As in parallel text at 2 Sam 23:9 (see also 1 Chr 27:4); Hebrew reads *Dodo,* a variant spelling of Dodai. **11:14** Hebrew *they.* **11:19** Hebrew *Shall I drink the lifeblood of these men?* **11:20** As in Syriac version; Hebrew reads *the Three;* also in 11:21. **11:22** Or *two sons of Ariel.* **11:23** Hebrew *5 cubits* [2.3 meters]. **11:27** As in parallel text at 2 Sam 23:25; Hebrew reads *Shammoth from Haror.* **11:29** As in parallel text at 2 Sam 23:28; Hebrew reads *Ilai.* **11:32a** Or *from the ravines of Gaash.* **11:32b** As in parallel text at 2 Sam 23:31; Hebrew reads *Abiel.*

33 Azmaveth from Bahurim*;
Eliahba from Shaalbon;
34 the sons of Jashen* from Gizon;
Jonathan son of Shagee from Harar;
35 Ahiam son of Sharar* from Harar;
Eliphal son of Ur;
36 Hepher from Mekerah;
Ahijah from Pelon;
37 Hezro from Carmel;
Paarai* son of Ezbai;
38 Joel, the brother of Nathan;
Mibhar son of Hagri;
39 Zelek from Ammon;
Naharai from Beeroth, Joab's armor bearer;
40 Ira from Jattir;
Gareb from Jattir;
41 Uriah the Hittite;
Zabad son of Ahlai;
42 Adina son of Shiza, the Reubenite leader who had thirty men with him;
43 Hanan son of Maacah;
Joshaphat from Mithna;
44 Uzzia from Ashtaroth;
Shama and Jeiel, the sons of Hotham, from Aroer;
45 Jediael son of Shimri;
Joha, his brother, from Tiz;
46 Eliel from Mahavah;
Jeribai and Joshaviah, the sons of Elnaam;
Ithmah from Moab;
47 Eliel and Obed;
Jaasiel from Zobah.*

12 WARRIORS JOIN DAVID'S ARMY

The following men joined David at Ziklag while he was
hiding from Saul son of Kish. They were among the warriors who fought beside David in battle. 2All of them were
expert archers, and they could shoot arrows or sling
stones with their left hand as well as their right. They
were all relatives of Saul from the tribe of Benjamin.
3Their leader was Ahiezer son of Shemaah from Gibeah;
his brother Joash was second-in-command. These were
the other warriors:

Jeziel and Pelet, sons of Azmaveth;
Beracah;
Jehu from Anathoth;
4 Ishmaiah from Gibeon, a famous warrior and leader among the Thirty;
*Jeremiah, Jahaziel, Johanan, and Jozabad from Gederah;
5 Eluzai, Jerimoth, Bealiah, Shemariah, and Shephatiah from Haruph;
6 Elkanah, Isshiah, Azarel, Joezer, and Jashobeam, who were Korahites;
7 Joelah and Zebadiah, sons of Jeroham from Gedor.

8Some brave and experienced warriors from the tribe
of Gad also defected to David while he was at the stronghold in the wilderness. They were expert with both shield
and spear, as fierce as lions and as swift as deer on the
mountains.

9 Ezer was their leader.
Obadiah was second.
Eliab was third.
10 Mishmannah was fourth.
Jeremiah was fifth.
11 Attai was sixth.
Eliel was seventh.
12 Johanan was eighth.
Elzabad was ninth.
13 Jeremiah was tenth.
Macbannai was eleventh.

14These warriors from Gad were army commanders.
The weakest among them could take on a hundred regular troops, and the strongest could take on a thousand!
15These were the men who crossed the Jordan River during its seasonal flooding at the beginning of the year and
drove out all the people living in the lowlands on both the
east and west banks.
16Others from Benjamin and Judah came to David at
the stronghold. 17David went out to meet them and said,
"If you have come in peace to help me, we are friends. But
if you have come to betray me to my enemies when I am
innocent, then may the God of our ancestors see it and
punish you."

HOLY SPIRIT 12:18

How did the Holy Spirit work in Old Testament times? When God chose a person to do a task, the Spirit would give that person the ability to do it. The Spirit gave Bezalel artistic ability (Exod 31:1-5), military prowess to Jephthah (Judg 11:29), and a word of prophecy to Zechariah (2 Chron 24:20). Here the Holy Spirit came upon Amasai, one of David's warriors. Beginning at Pentecost, however, the Spirit came upon all believers (Acts 2:1-21). That same Spirit is ready to equip you for any task. ■

18Then the Spirit came upon Amasai, the leader of the
Thirty, and he said,

"We are yours, David!
We are on your side, son of Jesse.
Peace and prosperity be with you,
and success to all who help you,
for your God is the one who helps you."

So David let them join him, and he made them officers
over his troops.
19Some men from Manasseh defected from the Israelite

11:33 As in parallel text at 2 Sam 23:31; Hebrew reads *Baharum.* **11:34** As in parallel text at 2 Sam 23:32; Hebrew reads *sons of Hashem.* **11:35** As in parallel text at 2 Sam 23:33; Hebrew reads *son of Sacar.* **11:37** As in parallel text at 2 Sam 23:35; Hebrew reads *Naarai.* **11:47** Or *the Mezobaite.* **12:4** Verses 12:4b-40 are numbered 12:5-41 in Hebrew text.

army and joined David when he set out with the Philistines to fight against Saul. But as it turned out, the Philistine rulers refused to let David and his men go with them.
After much discussion, they sent them back, for they
said, "It will cost us our heads if David switches loyalties
to Saul and turns against us."

[20]Here is a list of the men from Manasseh who defected to David as he was returning to Ziklag: Adnah,
Jozabad, Jediael, Michael, Jozabad, Elihu, and Zillethai.
Each commanded 1,000 troops from the tribe of Manasseh. [21]They helped David chase down bands of raiders, for they were all brave and able warriors who
became commanders in his army. [22]Day after day more
men joined David until he had a great army, like the
army of God.

[23]These are the numbers of armed warriors who
joined David at Hebron. They were all eager to see David
become king instead of Saul, just as the LORD had
promised.

[24]From the tribe of Judah, there were 6,800 warriors
armed with shields and spears.
[25]From the tribe of Simeon, there were 7,100 brave
warriors.
[26]From the tribe of Levi, there were 4,600 warriors.
[27]This included Jehoiada, leader of the family of
Aaron, who had 3,700 under his command. [28]This
also included Zadok, a brave young warrior, with
22 members of his family who were all officers.
[29]From the tribe of Benjamin, Saul's relatives, there were
3,000 warriors. Most of the men from Benjamin had
remained loyal to Saul until this time.
[30]From the tribe of Ephraim, there were 20,800 brave
warriors, each highly respected in his own clan.
[31]From the half-tribe of Manasseh west of the Jordan,
18,000 men were designated by name to help David
become king.
[32]From the tribe of Issachar, there were 200 leaders
of the tribe with their relatives. All these men
understood the signs of the times and knew the best
course for Israel to take.
[33]From the tribe of Zebulun, there were 50,000 skilled
warriors. They were fully armed and prepared for
battle and completely loyal to David.
[34]From the tribe of Naphtali, there were 1,000 officers
and 37,000 warriors armed with shields and spears.
[35]From the tribe of Dan, there were 28,600 warriors, all
prepared for battle.
[36]From the tribe of Asher, there were 40,000 trained
warriors, all prepared for battle.
[37]From the east side of the Jordan River—where the
tribes of Reuben and Gad and the half-tribe of
Manasseh lived—there were 120,000 troops armed
with every kind of weapon.

[38]All these men came in battle array to Hebron with the
single purpose of making David the king over all Israel. In
fact, everyone in Israel agreed that David should be their
king. [39]They feasted and drank with David for three days,
for preparations had been made by their relatives for
their arrival. [40]And people from as far away as Issachar,
Zebulun, and Naphtali brought food on donkeys, camels,
mules, and oxen. Vast supplies of flour, fig cakes, clusters
of raisins, wine, olive oil, cattle, sheep, and goats were
brought to the celebration. There was great joy throughout the land of Israel.

13 DAVID ATTEMPTS TO MOVE THE ARK

David consulted with all his officials, including the generals and captains of his army.* [2]Then he addressed the
entire assembly of Israel as follows: "If you approve and if
it is the will of the LORD our God, let us send messages to
all the Israelites throughout the land, including the
priests and Levites in their towns and pasturelands. Let
us invite them to come and join us. [3]It is time to bring
back the Ark of our God, for we neglected it during the
reign of Saul."

[4]The whole assembly agreed to this, for the people
could see it was the right thing to do. [5]So David summoned all Israel, from the Shihor Brook of Egypt in the
south all the way to the town of Lebo-hamath in the
north, to join in bringing the Ark of God from Kiriath-
jearim. [6]Then David and all Israel went to Baalah of Judah
(also called Kiriath-jearim) to bring back the Ark of God,
which bears the name* of the LORD who is enthroned between the cherubim. [7]They placed the Ark of God on a
new cart and brought it from Abinadab's house. Uzzah
and Ahio were guiding the cart. [8]David and all Israel were
celebrating before God with all their might, singing songs
and playing all kinds of musical instruments—lyres,
harps, tambourines, cymbals, and trumpets.

[9]But when they arrived at the threshing floor of Nacon,* the oxen stumbled, and Uzzah reached out his
hand to steady the Ark. [10]Then the LORD's anger was
aroused against Uzzah, and he struck him dead because
he had laid his hand on the Ark. So Uzzah died there in
the presence of God.

[11]David was angry because the LORD's anger had burst
out against Uzzah. He named that place Perez-uzzah
(which means "to burst out against Uzzah"), as it is still
called today.

[12]David was now afraid of God, and he asked, "How can
I ever bring the Ark of God back into my care?" [13]So David
did not move the Ark into the City of David. Instead, he
took it to the house of Obed-edom of Gath. [14]The Ark of
God remained there in Obed-edom's house for three
months, and the LORD blessed the household of Obed-
edom and everything he owned.

14 DAVID'S PALACE AND FAMILY

Then King Hiram of Tyre sent messengers to David, along
with cedar timber, and stonemasons and carpenters to
build him a palace. [2]And David realized that the LORD had

13:1 Hebrew *the commanders of thousands and of hundreds.* 13:6 Or *the Ark of God, where the Name is proclaimed—the name.* 13:9 As in parallel text at 2 Sam 6:6; Hebrew reads *Kidon.*

confirmed him as king over Israel and had greatly blessed his kingdom for the sake of his people Israel.

3Then David married more wives in Jerusalem, and they had more sons and daughters. 4These are the names of David's sons who were born in Jerusalem: Shammua, Shobab, Nathan, Solomon, 5Ibhar, Elishua, Elpelet, 6Nogah, Nepheg, Japhia, 7Elishama, Eliada,* and Eliphelet.

DAVID CONQUERS THE PHILISTINES

8When the Philistines heard that David had been anointed king over all Israel, they mobilized all their forces to capture him. But David was told they were coming, so he marched out to meet them. 9The Philistines arrived and made a raid in the valley of Rephaim. 10So David asked God, "Should I go out to fight the Philistines? Will you hand them over to me?"

The LORD replied, "Yes, go ahead. I will hand them over to you."

11So David and his troops went up to Baal-perazim and defeated the Philistines there. "God did it!" David exclaimed. "He used me to burst through my enemies like a raging flood!" So they named that place Baal-perazim (which means "the Lord who bursts through"). 12The Philistines had abandoned their gods there, so David gave orders to burn them.

> David realized that the LORD had confirmed him as king over Israel and had greatly blessed his kingdom for the sake of his people.
>
> *1 CHRONICLES 14:2*

ASK GOD FIRST 14:10

Before David went to battle, he first asked God for his opinion. When do you ask for God's help? Do you seek him firsthand or as a last resort? Too often we wait until we are in the middle of trouble before turning to God. By then the consequences of our actions are already unfolding. ■

13But after a while the Philistines returned and raided the valley again. 14And once again David asked God what to do. "Do not attack them straight on," God replied. "Instead, circle around behind and attack them near the poplar* trees. 15When you hear a sound like marching feet in the tops of the poplar trees, go out and attack! That will be the signal that God is moving ahead of you to strike down the Philistine army." 16So David did what God commanded, and they struck down the Philistine army all the way from Gibeon to Gezer.

17So David's fame spread everywhere, and the LORD caused all the nations to fear David.

15 PREPARING TO MOVE THE ARK

David now built several buildings for himself in the City of David. He also prepared a place for the Ark of God and set up a special tent for it. 2Then he commanded, "No one except the Levites may carry the Ark of God. The LORD has chosen them to carry the Ark of the LORD and to serve him forever."

3Then David summoned all Israel to Jerusalem to bring the Ark of the LORD to the place he had prepared for it. 4This is the number of the descendants of Aaron (the priests) and the Levites who were called together:

5From the clan of Kohath, 120, with Uriel as their leader.
6From the clan of Merari, 220, with Asaiah as their leader.
7From the clan of Gershon,* 130, with Joel as their leader.
8From the descendants of Elizaphan, 200, with Shemaiah as their leader.
9From the descendants of Hebron, 80, with Eliel as their leader.
10From the descendants of Uzziel, 112, with Amminadab as their leader.

11Then David summoned the priests, Zadok and Abiathar, and these Levite leaders: Uriel, Asaiah, Joel, Shemaiah, Eliel, and Amminadab. 12He said to them, "You are the leaders of the Levite families. You must purify yourselves and all your fellow Levites, so you can bring the Ark of the LORD, the God of Israel, to the place I have prepared for it. 13Because you Levites did not carry the Ark the first time, the anger of the LORD our God burst out against us. We failed to ask God how to move it properly." 14So the priests and the Levites purified themselves in order to bring the Ark of the LORD, the God of Israel, to Jerusalem. 15Then the Levites carried the Ark of God on their shoulders with its carrying poles, just as the LORD had instructed Moses.

EXACT INSTRUCTIONS 15:13-15

When David's first attempt to move the Ark failed (13:8-14), he learned an important lesson: always follow God's instructions precisely. This time David saw to it that the Levites carried the Ark as Numbers 4:5-15 instructed. We may not fully understand the reasons behind God's instructions, but we can choose to believe that his judgment is perfect. Is that what you believe? ■

16David also ordered the Levite leaders to appoint a choir of Levites who were singers and musicians to sing joyful songs to the accompaniment of harps, lyres, and cymbals. 17So the Levites appointed Heman son of Joel along with his fellow Levites: Asaph son of Berekiah, and Ethan son of Kushaiah from the clan of Merari. 18The following men were chosen as their assistants: Zechariah, Jaaziel,* Shemiramoth, Jehiel, Unni, Eliab, Benaiah,

14:7 Hebrew *Beeliada,* a variant spelling of Eliada; compare 3:8 and parallel text at 2 Sam 5:16. 14:14 Or *aspen,* or *balsam;* also in 14:15. The exact identification of this tree is uncertain. 15:7 Hebrew *Gershom,* a variant spelling of Gershon. 15:18 Or *Zechariah son of Jaaziel;* or *Zechariah, Ben, Jaaziel.*

Music in Bible Times

Paul clearly puts forth the Christian's view that things are not good or bad in and of themselves (see Rom 14 and 1 Cor 14:7-8, 26). The point always should be to worship the Lord or help others by means of the things of this world, including music. Music was created by God and can be returned to him in praise. Does the music you play or listen to have a negative impact upon your relationship with God or a positive one?

HIGHLIGHTS OF MUSICAL USE IN SCRIPTURE	REFERENCES
Jubal was the first musician	Genesis 4:21
Miriam and other women sang and danced to praise God	Exodus 15:1-21
The priest was to have bells on his robes	Exodus 28:34-35
Jericho fell to the sound of rams' horns	Joshua 6:4-20
Saul experienced the soothing effect of music	1 Samuel 16:14-23
The king's coronation was accompanied by music	1 Kings 1:39-40
David organized the use of music for worship	1 Chronicles 16:4-7
The Ark of the Covenant was accompanied by trumpeters	1 Chronicles 16:6
There were musicians for the king's court	Ecclesiastes 2:8
Everything was to be used by everyone to praise the Lord	Psalm 150
Jesus and the disciples sang a hymn	Matthew 26:30
Paul and Silas sang in jail	Acts 16:25
We are to sing to the Lord with thankful hearts	Colossians 3:16

In the New Testament, worship continued in the synagogues until the Christians became unwelcome there, so there was a rich musical heritage already established. The fact that music is mentioned less often in the New Testament does not mean it was less important.

Maaseiah, Mattithiah, Eliphelehu, Mikneiah, and the
gatekeepers—Obed-edom and Jeiel.
19The musicians Heman, Asaph, and Ethan were chosen to sound the bronze cymbals. 20Zechariah, Aziel, Shemiramoth, Jehiel, Unni, Eliab, Maaseiah, and Benaiah
were chosen to play the harps.* 21Mattithiah, Eliphelehu,
Mikneiah, Obed-edom, Jeiel, and Azaziah were chosen to
play the lyres.* 22Kenaniah, the head Levite, was chosen
as the choir leader because of his skill.
23Berekiah and Elkanah were chosen to guard* the
Ark. 24Shebaniah, Joshaphat, Nethanel, Amasai, Zechariah, Benaiah, and Eliezer—all of whom were priests—were
chosen to blow the trumpets as they marched in front of
the Ark of God. Obed-edom and Jehiah were chosen to
guard the Ark.

MOVING THE ARK TO JERUSALEM

25Then David and the elders of Israel and the generals of
the army* went to the house of Obed-edom to bring the
Ark of the LORD's Covenant up to Jerusalem with a great
celebration. 26And because God was clearly helping the
Levites as they carried the Ark of the LORD's Covenant,
they sacrificed seven bulls and seven rams.
27David was dressed in a robe of fine linen, as were all

15:20 Hebrew adds *according to Alamoth,* which is probably a musical term. The meaning of the Hebrew is uncertain. **15:21** Hebrew adds *according to the Sheminith,* which is probably a musical term. The meaning of the Hebrew is uncertain. **15:23** Hebrew *chosen as gatekeepers for;* also in 15:24. **15:25** Hebrew *the commanders of thousands.*

the Levites who carried the Ark, and also the singers, and
Kenaniah the choir leader. David was also wearing a priestly
garment.* 28So all Israel brought up the Ark of the LORD's
Covenant with shouts of joy, the blowing of rams' horns
and trumpets, the crashing of cymbals, and loud playing
on harps and lyres.

29But as the Ark of the LORD's Covenant entered the City
of David, Michal, the daughter of Saul, looked down from
her window. When she saw King David skipping about and
laughing with joy, she was filled with contempt for him.

16 They brought the Ark of God and placed it inside the special tent David had prepared for it. And they
presented burnt offerings and peace offerings to God.
2When he had finished his sacrifices, David blessed the
people in the name of the LORD. 3Then he gave to every
man and woman in all Israel a loaf of bread, a cake of
dates,* and a cake of raisins.

4David appointed the following Levites to lead the people in worship before the Ark of the LORD—to invoke his
blessings, to give thanks, and to praise the LORD, the God
of Israel. 5Asaph, the leader of this group, sounded the
cymbals. Second to him was Zechariah, followed by Jeiel,
Shemiramoth, Jehiel, Mattithiah, Eliab, Benaiah, Obed-
edom, and Jeiel. They played the harps and lyres. 6The
priests, Benaiah and Jahaziel, played the trumpets regularly before the Ark of God's Covenant.

DAVID'S SONG OF PRAISE

7On that day David gave to Asaph and his fellow Levites
this song of thanksgiving to the LORD:

8 Give thanks to the LORD and proclaim his greatness.
Let the whole world know what he has done.
9 Sing to him; yes, sing his praises.
Tell everyone about his wonderful deeds.
10 Exult in his holy name;
rejoice, you who worship the LORD.
11 Search for the LORD and for his strength;
continually seek him.
12 Remember the wonders he has performed,
his miracles, and the rulings he has given,
13 you children of his servant Israel,
you descendants of Jacob, his chosen ones.

14 He is the LORD our God.
His justice is seen throughout the land.
15 Remember his covenant forever—
the commitment he made to a thousand
generations.
16 This is the covenant he made with Abraham
and the oath he swore to Isaac.
17 He confirmed it to Jacob as a decree,
and to the people of Israel as a never-ending
covenant:
18 "I will give you the land of Canaan
as your special possession."
19 He said this when you were few in number,
a tiny group of strangers in Canaan.
20 They wandered from nation to nation,
from one kingdom to another.
21 Yet he did not let anyone oppress them.
He warned kings on their behalf:
22 "Do not touch my chosen people,
and do not hurt my prophets."

23 Let the whole earth sing to the LORD!
Each day proclaim the good news that he saves.
24 Publish his glorious deeds among the nations.
Tell everyone about the amazing things
he does.
25 Great is the LORD! He is most worthy of praise!
He is to be feared above all gods.
26 The gods of other nations are mere idols,
but the LORD made the heavens!
27 Honor and majesty surround him;
strength and joy fill his dwelling.

28 O nations of the world, recognize the LORD,
recognize that the LORD is glorious and strong.
29 Give to the LORD the glory he deserves!
Bring your offering and come into his presence.
Worship the LORD in all his holy splendor.
30 Let all the earth tremble before him.
The world stands firm and cannot be shaken.

31 Let the heavens be glad, and the earth rejoice!
Tell all the nations, "The LORD reigns!"
32 Let the sea and everything in it shout his praise!
Let the fields and their crops burst out with joy!
33 Let the trees of the forest rustle with praise,
for the LORD is coming to judge the earth.

34 Give thanks to the LORD, for he is good!
His faithful love endures forever.

THANK YOU 16:7-36

David used a psalm to express his gratitude to God. In that psalm he recalled what God had done for him and why God always deserved praise. Many of David's psalms (see the book of Psalms) have inspired generations of people to offer praise to God. How do you express thanks to God? ■

35 Cry out, "Save us, O God of our salvation!
Gather and rescue us from among the nations,
so we can thank your holy name
and rejoice and praise you."

36 Praise the LORD, the God of Israel,
who lives from everlasting to everlasting!

And all the people shouted "Amen!" and praised the
LORD.

15:27 Hebrew *a linen ephod.* 16:3 Or *a portion of meat.* The meaning of the Hebrew is uncertain.

WORSHIP AT JERUSALEM AND GIBEON

[37]David arranged for Asaph and his fellow Levites to serve regularly before the Ark of the LORD's Covenant, doing whatever needed to be done each day. [38]This group included Obed-edom (son of Jeduthun), Hosah, and sixty-eight other Levites as gatekeepers.

[39]Meanwhile, David stationed Zadok the priest and his fellow priests at the Tabernacle of the LORD at the place of worship in Gibeon, where they continued to minister before the LORD. [40]They sacrificed the regular burnt offerings to the LORD each morning and evening on the altar set aside for that purpose, obeying everything written in the Law of the LORD, as he had commanded Israel. [41]David also appointed Heman, Jeduthun, and the others chosen by name to give thanks to the LORD, for "his faithful love endures forever." [42]They used their trumpets, cymbals, and other instruments to accompany their songs of praise to God.* And the sons of Jeduthun were appointed as gatekeepers.

[43]Then all the people returned to their homes, and David turned and went home to bless his own family.

17

THE LORD'S COVENANT PROMISE TO DAVID

When David was settled in his palace, he summoned Nathan the prophet. "Look," David said, "I am living in a beautiful cedar palace,* but the Ark of the LORD's Covenant is out there under a tent!"

[2]Nathan replied to David, "Do whatever you have in mind, for God is with you."

[3]But that same night God said to Nathan,

[4]"Go and tell my servant David, 'This is what the LORD has declared: You are not the one to build a house for me to live in. [5]I have never lived in a house, from the day I brought the Israelites out of Egypt until this very day. My home has always been a tent, moving from one place to another in a Tabernacle. [6]Yet no matter where I have gone with the Israelites, I have never once complained to Israel's leaders,* the shepherds of my people. I have never asked them, "Why haven't you built me a beautiful cedar house?"'

[7]"Now go and say to my servant David, 'This is what the LORD of Heaven's Armies has declared: I took you from tending sheep in the pasture and selected you to be the leader of my people Israel. [8]I have been with you wherever you have gone, and I have destroyed all your enemies before your eyes. Now I will make your name as famous as anyone who has ever lived on the earth! [9]And I will provide a homeland for my people Israel, planting them in a secure place where they will never be disturbed. Evil nations won't oppress them as they've done in the past, [10]starting from the time I appointed judges to rule my people Israel. And I will defeat all your enemies.

"'Furthermore, I declare that the LORD will build a house for you—a dynasty of kings! [11]For when you die and join your ancestors, I will raise up one of your descendants, one of your sons, and I will make his kingdom strong. [12]He is the one who will build a house—a temple—for me. And I will secure his throne forever. [13]I will be his father, and he will be my son. I will never take my favor from him as I took it from the one who ruled before you. [14]I will confirm him as king over my house and my kingdom for all time, and his throne will be secure forever.'"

[15]So Nathan went back to David and told him everything the LORD had said in this vision.

A HUMBLE RESPONSE 17:16-27

When God said no to David's request to build a temple, David responded with humility, rather than resentment. He recognized that the true King, God, had a right to say yes or no to any request. What's your response when God says no? ■

DAVID'S PRAYER OF THANKS

[16]Then King David went in and sat before the LORD and prayed,

"Who am I, O LORD God, and what is my family, that you have brought me this far? [17]And now, O God, in addition to everything else, you speak of giving your servant a lasting dynasty! You speak as though I were someone very great,* O LORD God!

[18]"What more can I say to you about the way you have honored me? You know what your servant is really like. [19]For the sake of your servant, O LORD, and according to your will, you have done all these great things and have made them known.

[20]"O LORD, there is no one like you. We have never even heard of another God like you! [21]What other nation on earth is like your people Israel? What other nation, O God, have you redeemed from slavery to be your own people? You made a great name for yourself when you redeemed your people from Egypt. You performed awesome miracles and drove out the nations that stood in their way. [22]You chose Israel to be your very own people forever, and you, O LORD, became their God.

[23]"And now, O LORD, I am your servant; do as you have promised concerning me and my family. May it be a promise that will last forever. [24]And may your name be established and honored forever so that everyone will say, 'The LORD of Heaven's Armies, the God of Israel, is Israel's God!' And may the house of your servant David continue before you forever.

[25]"O my God, I have been bold enough to pray to you because you have revealed to your servant that you will build a house for him—a dynasty of kings! [26]For you are God, O LORD. And you have promised these good things to your servant.

16:42 Or *to accompany the sacred music;* or *to accompany singing to God.* **17:1** Hebrew *a house of cedar.* **17:6** As in Greek version (see also 2 Sam 7:7); Hebrew reads *judges.* **17:17** The meaning of the Hebrew is uncertain.

27And now, it has pleased you to bless the house of
your servant, so that it will continue forever before
you. For when you grant a blessing, O LORD, it is an
eternal blessing!"

18 DAVID'S MILITARY VICTORIES

After this, David defeated and subdued the Philistines by
conquering Gath and its surrounding towns. 2David also
conquered the land of Moab, and the Moabites who were
spared became David's subjects and paid him tribute
money.
3David also destroyed the forces of Hadadezer, king of
Zobah, as far as Hamath,* when Hadadezer marched out
to strengthen his control along the Euphrates River. 4Da-
vid captured 1,000 chariots, 7,000 charioteers, and
20,000 foot soldiers. He crippled all the chariot horses
except enough for 100 chariots.
5When Arameans from Damascus arrived to help King
Hadadezer, David killed 22,000 of them. 6Then he
placed several army garrisons* in Damascus, the Aramean capital, and the Arameans became David's subjects
and paid him tribute money. So the LORD made David victorious wherever he went.

GOD ON OUR SIDE 18:1-14

God helped David to be victorious over his enemies. In the same way, God promises to see us through the battles that we fight here on earth: battles over temptation, attitudes of the heart, and those against spiritual or physical enemies. As Paul once said, "If God is for us, who can ever be against us?" (Rom 8:31). ■

7David brought the gold shields of Hadadezer's officers to Jerusalem, 8along with a large amount of bronze
from Hadadezer's towns of Tebah* and Cun. Later Solomon melted the bronze and molded it into the great
bronze basin called the Sea, the pillars, and the various
bronze articles used at the Temple.
9When King Toi* of Hamath heard that David had destroyed the entire army of King Hadadezer of Zobah, 10he
sent his son Joram* to congratulate King David for his
successful campaign. Hadadezer and Toi had been enemies and were often at war. Joram presented David with
many gifts of gold, silver, and bronze.
11King David dedicated all these gifts to the LORD,
along with the silver and gold he had taken from the
other nations—from Edom, Moab, Ammon, Philistia, and
Amalek.
12Abishai son of Zeruiah destroyed 18,000 Edomites in
the Valley of Salt. 13He placed army garrisons in Edom,
and all the Edomites became David's subjects. In fact, the
LORD made David victorious wherever he went.
14So David reigned over all Israel and did what was just
and right for all his people. 15Joab son of Zeruiah was
commander of the army. Jehoshaphat son of Ahilud was
the royal historian. 16Zadok son of Ahitub and Ahimelech* son of Abiathar were the priests. Seraiah* was the
court secretary. 17Benaiah son of Jehoiada was captain of
the king's bodyguard.* And David's sons served as the
king's chief assistants.

19 DAVID DEFEATS THE AMMONITES

Some time after this, King Nahash of the Ammonites
died, and his son Hanun* became king. 2David said, "I am
going to show loyalty to Hanun because his father, Nahash, was always loyal to me." So David sent messengers
to express sympathy to Hanun about his father's death.
But when David's ambassadors arrived in the land of
Ammon, 3the Ammonite commanders said to Hanun,
"Do you really think these men are coming here to honor
your father? No! David has sent them to spy out the land
so they can come in and conquer it!" 4So Hanun seized
David's ambassadors and shaved them, cut off their
robes at the buttocks, and sent them back to David in
shame.
5When David heard what had happened to the men, he
sent messengers to tell them, "Stay at Jericho until your
beards grow out, and then come back." For they felt deep
shame because of their appearance.
6When the people of Ammon realized how seriously
they had angered David, Hanun and the Ammonites sent
75,000 pounds* of silver to hire chariots and charioteers
from Aram-naharaim, Aram-maacah, and Zobah. 7They
also hired 32,000 chariots and secured the support of the
king of Maacah and his army. These forces camped at
Medeba, where they were joined by the Ammonite troops
that Hanun had recruited from his own towns. 8When David heard about this, he sent Joab and all his warriors to
fight them. 9The Ammonite troops came out and drew up
their battle lines at the entrance of the city, while the other
kings positioned themselves to fight in the open fields.
10When Joab saw that he would have to fight on both
the front and the rear, he chose some of Israel's elite
troops and placed them under his personal command to
fight the Arameans in the fields. 11He left the rest of the
army under the command of his brother Abishai, who
was to attack the Ammonites. 12"If the Arameans are too
strong for me, then come over and help me," Joab told his
brother. "And if the Ammonites are too strong for you, I
will help you. 13Be courageous! Let us fight bravely for our
people and the cities of our God. May the LORD's will be
done."
14When Joab and his troops attacked, the Arameans
began to run away. 15And when the Ammonites saw the

18:3 The meaning of the Hebrew is uncertain. 18:6 As in Greek version and Latin Vulgate (see also 2 Sam 8:6); Hebrew lacks *several army garrisons*. 18:8 Hebrew reads *Tibhath*, a variant spelling of Tebah; compare parallel text at 2 Sam 8:8. 18:9 As in parallel text at 2 Sam 8:9; Hebrew reads *Tou;* also in 18:10. 18:10 As in parallel text at 2 Sam 8:10; Hebrew reads *Hadoram*, a variant spelling of Joram. 18:16a As in some Hebrew manuscripts, Syriac version, and Latin Vulgate (see also 2 Sam 8:17); most Hebrew manuscripts read *Abimelech*. 18:16b As in parallel text at 2 Sam 8:17; Hebrew reads *Shavsha*. 18:17 Hebrew *of the Kerethites and Pelethites*. 19:1 As in parallel text at 2 Sam 10:1; Hebrew lacks *Hanun*. 19:6 Hebrew *1,000 talents* [34,000 kilograms].

Arameans running, they also ran from Abishai and retreated into the city. Then Joab returned to Jerusalem.
16The Arameans now realized that they were no match
for Israel, so they sent messengers and summoned additional Aramean troops from the other side of the Euphrates River.* These troops were under the command of
Shobach,* the commander of Hadadezer's forces.
17When David heard what was happening, he mobilized all Israel, crossed the Jordan River, and positioned
his troops in battle formation. Then David engaged the
Arameans in battle, and they fought against him. 18But
again the Arameans fled from the Israelites. This time
David's forces killed 7,000 charioteers and 40,000 foot
soldiers, including Shobach, the commander of their
army. 19When Hadadezer's allies saw that they had been
defeated by Israel, they surrendered to David and became his subjects. After that, the Arameans were no longer willing to help the Ammonites.

20 DAVID CAPTURES RABBAH

In the spring of the year,* when kings normally go out to
war, Joab led the Israelite army in successful attacks
against the land of the Ammonites. In the process he laid
siege to the city of Rabbah. However, David stayed behind in Jerusalem.

SPRING INTO WAR 20:1

Why was spring the season when wars usually began? During the winter, opposing kings planned future conquests. Then, when the fair weather permitted it, their pent-up rage and energy broke forth into war. Are there "springs" in your life—times when you are most sensitive to the conflicts around you? You can "diffuse" them by confessing any fear, bitterness, or anger to God, allowing him to heal deal with it. ■

2When David arrived at Rabbah, he removed the crown
from the king's head,* and it was placed on his own head.
The crown was made of gold and set with gems, and he
found that it weighed seventy-five pounds.* David took a
vast amount of plunder from the city. 3He also made
slaves of the people of Rabbah and forced them to labor
with* saws, iron picks, and iron axes.* That is how David
dealt with the people of all the Ammonite towns. Then
David and all the army returned to Jerusalem.

BATTLES AGAINST PHILISTINE GIANTS

4After this, war broke out with the Philistines at Gezer. As
they fought, Sibbecai from Hushah killed Saph,* a descendant of the giants,* and so the Philistines were subdued.
5During another battle with the Philistines, Elhanan
son of Jair killed Lahmi, the brother of Goliath of Gath.
The handle of Lahmi's spear was as thick as a weaver's
beam!
6In another battle with the Philistines at Gath, they encountered a huge man with six fingers on each hand and
six toes on each foot, twenty-four in all, who was also a
descendant of the giants. 7But when he defied and
taunted Israel, he was killed by Jonathan, the son of David's brother Shimea.
8These Philistines were descendants of the giants of
Gath, but David and his warriors killed them.

21 DAVID TAKES A CENSUS

Satan rose up against Israel and caused David to take a
census of the people of Israel. 2So David said to Joab and
the commanders of the army, "Take a census of all the
people of Israel—from Beersheba in the south to Dan in
the north—and bring me a report so I may know how
many there are."
3But Joab replied, "May the LORD increase the number
of his people a hundred times over! But why, my lord the
king, do you want to do this? Are they not all your servants? Why must you cause Israel to sin?"
4But the king insisted that they take the census, so Joab
traveled throughout all Israel to count the people. Then
he returned to Jerusalem 5and reported the number of
people to David. There were 1,100,000 warriors in all Israel who could handle a sword, and 470,000 in Judah.
6But Joab did not include the tribes of Levi and Benjamin
in the census because he was so distressed at what the
king had made him do.

JUDGMENT FOR DAVID'S SIN

7God was very displeased with the census, and he punished Israel for it. 8Then David said to God, "I have sinned
greatly by taking this census. Please forgive my guilt for
doing this foolish thing."
9Then the LORD spoke to Gad, David's seer. This was
the message: 10"Go and say to David, 'This is what the
LORD says: I will give you three choices. Choose one of
these punishments, and I will inflict it on you.'"
11So Gad came to David and said, "These are the
choices the LORD has given you. 12You may choose three
years of famine, three months of destruction by the
sword of your enemies, or three days of severe plague as
the angel of the LORD brings devastation throughout the
land of Israel. Decide what answer I should give the LORD
who sent me."
13"I'm in a desperate situation!" David replied to Gad.
"But let me fall into the hands of the LORD, for his mercy
is very great. Do not let me fall into human hands."
14So the LORD sent a plague upon Israel, and 70,000
people died as a result. 15And God sent an angel to destroy Jerusalem. But just as the angel was preparing to destroy it, the LORD relented and said to the death angel,

19:16a Hebrew *the river.* **19:16b** As in parallel text at 2 Sam 10:16; Hebrew reads *Shophach;* also in 19:18. **20:1** Hebrew *At the turn of the year.* The first day of the year in the ancient Hebrew lunar calendar occurred in March or April. **20:2a** Or *from the head of Milcom* (as in Greek version and Latin Vulgate). Milcom, also called Molech, was the god of the Ammonites. **20:2b** Hebrew *1 talent* [34 kilograms]. **20:3a** Or *He also brought out the people of Rabbah and cut them with.* **20:3b** As in parallel text at 2 Sam 12:31; Hebrew reads *and saws.* **20:4a** As in parallel text at 2 Sam 21:18; Hebrew reads *Sippai.* **20:4b** Hebrew *descendant of the Rephaites;* also in 20:6, 8.

"Stop! That is enough!" At that moment the angel of the LORD was standing by the threshing floor of Araunah* the Jebusite.

16 David looked up and saw the angel of the LORD standing between heaven and earth with his sword drawn, reaching out over Jerusalem. So David and the leaders of Israel put on burlap to show their deep distress and fell face down on the ground. 17 And David said to God, "I am the one who called for the census! I am the one who has sinned and done wrong! But these people are as innocent as sheep—what have they done? O LORD my God, let your anger fall against me and my family, but do not destroy your people."

CLEANING HOUSE 21:1-16

When David realized his sin, he took full responsibility, admitted he was wrong, and asked God to forgive him. Many people want the "perks" of a relationship with God but not the hard stuff (owning up to a wrong done). But admitting is a necessary part of a relationship with God. It's like brushing your teeth or cleaning out your locker—you've got to do it regularly. ■

DAVID BUILDS AN ALTAR

18 Then the angel of the LORD told Gad to instruct David to go up and build an altar to the LORD on the threshing floor of Araunah the Jebusite. 19 So David went up to do what the LORD had commanded him through Gad. 20 Araunah, who was busy threshing wheat at the time, turned and saw the angel there. His four sons, who were with him, ran away and hid. 21 When Araunah saw David approaching, he left his threshing floor and bowed before David with his face to the ground.

22 David said to Araunah, "Let me buy this threshing floor from you at its full price. Then I will build an altar to the LORD there, so that he will stop the plague."

23 "Take it, my lord the king, and use it as you wish," Araunah said to David. "I will give the oxen for the burnt offerings, and the threshing boards for wood to build a fire on the altar, and the wheat for the grain offering. I will give it all to you."

24 But King David replied to Araunah, "No, I insist on buying it for the full price. I will not take what is yours and give it to the LORD. I will not present burnt offerings that have cost me nothing!" 25 So David gave Araunah 600 pieces of gold* in payment for the threshing floor.

26 David built an altar there to the LORD and sacrificed burnt offerings and peace offerings. And when David prayed, the LORD answered him by sending fire from heaven to burn up the offering on the altar. 27 Then the LORD spoke to the angel, who put the sword back into its sheath.

28 When David saw that the LORD had answered his prayer, he offered sacrifices there at Araunah's threshing floor. 29 At that time the Tabernacle of the LORD and the altar of burnt offering that Moses had made in the wilderness were located at the place of worship in Gibeon. 30 But David was not able to go there to inquire of God, because he was terrified by the drawn sword of the angel of the LORD.

22

Then David said, "This will be the location for the Temple of the LORD God and the place of the altar for Israel's burnt offerings!"

PREPARATIONS FOR THE TEMPLE

2 So David gave orders to call together the foreigners living in Israel, and he assigned them the task of preparing finished stone for building the Temple of God. 3 David provided large amounts of iron for the nails that would be needed for the doors in the gates and for the clamps, and he gave more bronze than could be weighed. 4 He also provided innumerable cedar logs, for the men of Tyre and Sidon had brought vast amounts of cedar to David.

5 David said, "My son Solomon is still young and inexperienced. And since the Temple to be built for the LORD must be a magnificent structure, famous and glorious throughout the world, I will begin making preparations for it now." So David collected vast amounts of building materials before his death.

6 Then David sent for his son Solomon and instructed him to build a Temple for the LORD, the God of Israel. 7 "My son, I wanted to build a Temple to honor the name of the LORD my God," David told him. 8 "But the LORD said to me, 'You have killed many men in the battles you have fought. And since you have shed so much blood in my sight, you will not be the one to build a Temple to honor my name. 9 But you will have a son who will be a man of peace. I will give him peace with his enemies in all the surrounding lands. His name will be Solomon,* and I will give peace and quiet to Israel during his reign. 10 He is the one who will build a Temple to honor my name. He will be my son, and I will be his father. And I will secure the throne of his kingdom over Israel forever.'

11 "Now, my son, may the LORD be with you and give you success as you follow his directions in building the Temple of the LORD your God. 12 And may the LORD give you wisdom and understanding, that you may obey the Law of the LORD your God as you rule over Israel. 13 For you will be successful if you carefully obey the decrees and regulations that the LORD gave to Israel through Moses. Be strong and courageous; do not be afraid or lose heart!

14 "I have worked hard to provide materials for building the Temple of the LORD—nearly 4,000 tons of gold, 40,000 tons of silver,* and so much iron and bronze that it cannot be weighed. I have also gathered timber and stone for the walls, though you may need to add more. 15 You have a large number of skilled stonemasons and carpenters and craftsmen of every kind. 16 You have expert goldsmiths and silversmiths and workers of bronze and iron. Now begin the work, and may the LORD be with you!"

21:15 As in parallel text at 2 Sam 24:16; Hebrew reads *Ornan,* another name for Araunah; also in 21:18-28. **21:25** Hebrew *600 shekels of gold,* about 15 pounds or 6.8 kilograms in weight. **22:9** *Solomon* sounds like and is probably derived from the Hebrew word for "peace." **22:14** Hebrew *100,000 talents* [3,400 metric tons] *of gold, 1,000,000 talents* [34,000 metric tons] *of silver.*

17Then David ordered all the leaders of Israel to assist
Solomon in this project. 18"The LORD your God is with
you," he declared. "He has given you peace with the surrounding nations. He has handed them over to me, and
they are now subject to the LORD and his people. 19Now
seek the LORD your God with all your heart and soul.
Build the sanctuary of the LORD God so that you can
bring the Ark of the LORD's Covenant and the holy vessels of God into the Temple built to honor the LORD's
name."

WHOLEHEARTEDLY 22:11-19

David wanted his son Solomon to understand the value of wholeheartedly obeying God. This kind of obedience involves using good judgment and having the right attitudes (strength, courage, and enthusiasm). Is that an accurate description of your dedication to God? ■

23 DUTIES OF THE LEVITES

When David was an old man, he appointed his son Solomon to be king over Israel. 2David summoned all the leaders of Israel, together with the priests and Levites. 3All the
Levites who were thirty years old or older were counted,
and the total came to 38,000. 4Then David said, "From all
the Levites, 24,000 will supervise the work at the Temple
of the LORD. Another 6,000 will serve as officials and
judges. 5Another 4,000 will work as gatekeepers, and
4,000 will praise the LORD with the musical instruments I
have made." 6Then David divided the Levites into divisions named after the clans descended from the three
sons of Levi—Gershon, Kohath, and Merari.

THE GERSHONITES

7The Gershonite family units were defined by their
lines of descent from Libni* and Shimei, the sons
of Gershon. 8Three of the descendants of Libni were
Jehiel (the family leader), Zetham, and Joel. 9These
were the leaders of the family of Libni.
Three of the descendants of Shimei were Shelomoth,
Haziel, and Haran. 10Four other descendants of
Shimei were Jahath, Ziza,* Jeush, and Beriah. 11Jahath
was the family leader, and Ziza was next. Jeush and
Beriah were counted as a single family because
neither had many sons.

THE KOHATHITES

12Four of the descendants of Kohath were Amram,
Izhar, Hebron, and Uzziel.
13The sons of Amram were Aaron and Moses. Aaron and
his descendants were set apart to dedicate the most
holy things, to offer sacrifices in the LORD's presence,
to serve the LORD, and to pronounce blessings in his
name forever.
14As for Moses, the man of God, his sons were
included with the tribe of Levi. 15The sons of Moses
were Gershom and Eliezer. 16The descendants of
Gershom included Shebuel, the family leader.
17Eliezer had only one son, Rehabiah, the family
leader. Rehabiah had numerous descendants.
18The descendants of Izhar included Shelomith, the
family leader.
19The descendants of Hebron included Jeriah (the
family leader), Amariah (the second), Jahaziel (the
third), and Jekameam (the fourth).
20The descendants of Uzziel included Micah (the family
leader) and Isshiah (the second).

THE MERARITES

21The descendants of Merari included Mahli and Mushi.
The sons of Mahli were Eleazar and Kish. 22Eleazar died
with no sons, only daughters. His daughters married
their cousins, the sons of Kish.
23Three of the descendants of Mushi were Mahli, Eder,
and Jerimoth.

24These were the descendants of Levi by clans, the
leaders of their family groups, registered carefully by
name. Each had to be twenty years old or older to qualify
for service in the house of the LORD. 25For David said,
"The LORD, the God of Israel, has given us peace, and he
will always live in Jerusalem. 26Now the Levites will no
longer need to carry the Tabernacle and its furnishings
from place to place." 27In accordance with David's final
instructions, all the Levites twenty years old or older were
registered for service.

28The work of the Levites was to assist the priests, the descendants of Aaron, as they served at the house of the LORD.
They also took care of the courtyards and side rooms,
helped perform the ceremonies of purification, and
served in many other ways in the house of God. 29They were
in charge of the sacred bread that was set out on the table,
the choice flour for the grain offerings, the wafers made
without yeast, the cakes cooked in olive oil, and the other
mixed breads. They were also responsible to check all the
weights and measures. 30And each morning and evening
they stood before the LORD to sing songs of thanks and
praise to him. 31They assisted with the burnt offerings that
were presented to the LORD on Sabbath days, at new moon
celebrations, and at all the appointed festivals. The required number of Levites served in the LORD's presence at
all times, following all the procedures they had been given.

32And so, under the supervision of the priests, the Levites watched over the Tabernacle and the Temple* and
faithfully carried out their duties of service at the house
of the LORD.

24 DUTIES OF THE PRIESTS

This is how Aaron's descendants, the priests, were divided
into groups for service. The sons of Aaron were Nadab,

23:7 Hebrew *Ladan* (also in 23:8, 9), a variant spelling of Libni; compare 6:17. 23:10 As in Greek version and Latin Vulgate (see also 23:11); Hebrew reads *Zina*. 23:32 Hebrew *the Tent of Meeting and the sanctuary*.

Abihu, Eleazar, and Ithamar. 2 But Nadab and Abihu died
before their father, and they had no sons. So only Eleazar
and Ithamar were left to carry on as priests.
3 With the help of Zadok, who was a descendant of Eleazar, and of Ahimelech, who was a descendant of Ithamar, David divided Aaron's descendants into groups
according to their various duties. 4 Eleazar's descendants
were divided into sixteen groups and Ithamar's into
eight, for there were more family leaders among the descendants of Eleazar.
5 All tasks were assigned to the various groups by
means of sacred lots so that no preference would be
shown, for there were many qualified officials serving
God in the sanctuary from among the descendants of
both Eleazar and Ithamar. 6 Shemaiah son of Nethanel, a
Levite, acted as secretary and wrote down the names and
assignments in the presence of the king, the officials, Zadok the priest, Ahimelech son of Abiathar, and the family
leaders of the priests and Levites. The descendants of Eleazar and Ithamar took turns casting lots.

7 The first lot fell to Jehoiarib.
The second lot fell to Jedaiah.
8 The third lot fell to Harim.
The fourth lot fell to Seorim.
9 The fifth lot fell to Malkijah.
The sixth lot fell to Mijamin.
10 The seventh lot fell to Hakkoz.
The eighth lot fell to Abijah.
11 The ninth lot fell to Jeshua.
The tenth lot fell to Shecaniah.
12 The eleventh lot fell to Eliashib.
The twelfth lot fell to Jakim.
13 The thirteenth lot fell to Huppah.
The fourteenth lot fell to Jeshebeab.
14 The fifteenth lot fell to Bilgah.
The sixteenth lot fell to Immer.
15 The seventeenth lot fell to Hezir.
The eighteenth lot fell to Happizzez.
16 The nineteenth lot fell to Pethahiah.
The twentieth lot fell to Jehezkel.
17 The twenty-first lot fell to Jakin.
The twenty-second lot fell to Gamul.
18 The twenty-third lot fell to Delaiah.
The twenty-fourth lot fell to Maaziah.

19 Each group carried out its appointed duties in the
house of the LORD according to the procedures established by their ancestor Aaron in obedience to the commands of the LORD, the God of Israel.

FAMILY LEADERS AMONG THE LEVITES

20 These were the other family leaders descended from
Levi:

From the descendants of Amram, the leader was
Shebuel.*
From the descendants of Shebuel, the leader was
Jehdeiah.
21 From the descendants of Rehabiah, the leader
was Isshiah.
22 From the descendants of Izhar, the leader was
Shelomith.*
From the descendants of Shelomith, the leader
was Jahath.
23 From the descendants of Hebron, Jeriah was the
leader,* Amariah was second, Jahaziel was third,
and Jekameam was fourth.
24 From the descendants of Uzziel, the leader was
Micah.
From the descendants of Micah, the leader was
Shamir, 25 along with Isshiah, the brother of
Micah.
From the descendants of Isshiah, the leader was
Zechariah.
26 From the descendants of Merari, the leaders were
Mahli and Mushi.
From the descendants of Jaaziah, the leader was
Beno.
27 From the descendants of Merari through Jaaziah,
the leaders were Beno, Shoham, Zaccur, and Ibri.
28 From the descendants of Mahli, the leader was
Eleazar, though he had no sons.
29 From the descendants of Kish, the leader was
Jerahmeel.
30 From the descendants of Mushi, the leaders were
Mahli, Eder, and Jerimoth.

These were the descendants of Levi in their various
families. 31 Like the descendants of Aaron, they were assigned to their duties by means of sacred lots, without regard to age or rank. Lots were drawn in the presence of
King David, Zadok, Ahimelech, and the family leaders of
the priests and the Levites.

25 DUTIES OF THE MUSICIANS

David and the army commanders then appointed men
from the families of Asaph, Heman, and Jeduthun to proclaim God's messages to the accompaniment of lyres,
harps, and cymbals. Here is a list of their names and their
work:

2 From the sons of Asaph, there were Zaccur, Joseph,
Nethaniah, and Asarelah. They worked under the
direction of their father, Asaph, who proclaimed
God's messages by the king's orders.
3 From the sons of Jeduthun, there were Gedaliah, Zeri,
Jeshaiah, Shimei,* Hashabiah, and Mattithiah, six in
all. They worked under the direction of their father,
Jeduthun, who proclaimed God's messages to the
accompaniment of the lyre, offering thanks and
praise to the LORD.
4 From the sons of Heman, there were Bukkiah,

24:20 Hebrew *Shubael* (also in 24:20b), a variant spelling of Shebuel; compare 23:16 and 26:24. 24:22 Hebrew *Shelomoth* (also in 24:22b), a variant spelling of Shelomith; compare 23:18. 24:23 Hebrew *From the descendants of Jeriah;* compare 23:19. 25:3 As in one Hebrew manuscript and some Greek manuscripts (see also 25:17); most Hebrew manuscripts lack *Shimei.*

Mattaniah, Uzziel, Shubael,* Jerimoth, Hananiah,
Hanani, Eliathah, Giddalti, Romamti-ezer,
Joshbekashah, Mallothi, Hothir, and Mahazioth. 5All
these were the sons of Heman, the king's seer, for
God had honored him with fourteen sons and three
daughters.

6All these men were under the direction of their fathers as they made music at the house of the LORD. Their
responsibilities included the playing of cymbals, harps,
and lyres at the house of God. Asaph, Jeduthun, and Heman reported directly to the king. 7They and their families were all trained in making music before the LORD,
and each of them—288 in all—was an accomplished musician. 8The musicians were appointed to their term of
service by means of sacred lots, without regard to
whether they were young or old, teacher or student.

PITCH IN 25:1-7

There were many ways to contribute to the worship in the Tabernacle. Some proclaimed God's messages (25:1), some led in prayer (25:3), and others played instruments and sang (25:6-7). Because God has given everyone an ability of some kind (see Rom 12:3-11; 1 Cor 12:12-31), everyone has a significant contribution to make in the church. How will you use your talents? ■

9 The first lot fell to Joseph of the Asaph clan and twelve of his sons and relatives.*
The second lot fell to Gedaliah and twelve of his sons and relatives.
10 The third lot fell to Zaccur and twelve of his sons and relatives.
11 The fourth lot fell to Zeri* and twelve of his sons and relatives.
12 The fifth lot fell to Nethaniah and twelve of his sons and relatives.
13 The sixth lot fell to Bukkiah and twelve of his sons and relatives.
14 The seventh lot fell to Asarelah* and twelve of his sons and relatives.
15 The eighth lot fell to Jeshaiah and twelve of his sons and relatives.
16 The ninth lot fell to Mattaniah and twelve of his sons and relatives.
17 The tenth lot fell to Shimei and twelve of his sons and relatives.
18 The eleventh lot fell to Uzziel* and twelve of his sons and relatives.
19 The twelfth lot fell to Hashabiah and twelve of his sons and relatives.
20 The thirteenth lot fell to Shubael and twelve of his sons and relatives.
21 The fourteenth lot fell to Mattithiah and twelve of his sons and relatives.
22 The fifteenth lot fell to Jerimoth* and twelve of his sons and relatives.
23 The sixteenth lot fell to Hananiah and twelve of his sons and relatives.
24 The seventeenth lot fell to Joshbekashah* and twelve of his sons and relatives.
25 The eighteenth lot fell to Hanani and twelve of his sons and relatives.
26 The nineteenth lot fell to Mallothi and twelve of his sons and relatives.
27 The twentieth lot fell to Eliathah and twelve of his sons and relatives.
28 The twenty-first lot fell to Hothir and twelve of his sons and relatives.
29 The twenty-second lot fell to Giddalti and twelve of his sons and relatives.
30 The twenty-third lot fell to Mahazioth and twelve of his sons and relatives.
31 The twenty-fourth lot fell to Romamti-ezer and twelve of his sons and relatives.

26

DUTIES OF THE GATEKEEPERS

These are the divisions of the gatekeepers:

From the Korahites, there was Meshelemiah son of
Kore, of the family of Abiasaph.* 2The sons of
Meshelemiah were Zechariah (the oldest), Jediael (the
second), Zebadiah (the third), Jathniel (the fourth),
3Elam (the fifth), Jehohanan (the sixth), and
Eliehoenai (the seventh).
4The sons of Obed-edom, also gatekeepers, were Shemaiah
(the oldest), Jehozabad (the second), Joah (the third),
Sacar (the fourth), Nethanel (the fifth), 5Ammiel (the
sixth), Issachar (the seventh), and Peullethai (the
eighth). God had richly blessed Obed-edom.

6Obed-edom's son Shemaiah had sons with great
ability who earned positions of great authority in the
clan. 7Their names were Othni, Rephael, Obed, and
Elzabad. Their relatives, Elihu and Semakiah, were
also very capable men.
8All of these descendants of Obed-edom, including
their sons and grandsons—sixty-two of them in all—
were very capable men, well qualified for their work.
9Meshelemiah's eighteen sons and relatives were also
very capable men.

10Hosah, of the Merari clan, appointed Shimri as the
leader among his sons, though he was not the oldest.
11His other sons included Hilkiah (the second),
Tebaliah (the third), and Zechariah (the fourth).
Hosah's sons and relatives, who served as
gatekeepers, numbered thirteen in all.

25:4 Hebrew *Shebuel,* a variant spelling of Shubael; compare 25:20. 25:9 As in Greek version; Hebrew lacks *and twelve of his sons and relatives.* 25:11 Hebrew *Izri,* a variant spelling of Zeri; compare 25:3. 25:14 Hebrew *Jesarelah,* a variant spelling of Asarelah; compare 25:2. 25:18 Hebrew *Azarel,* a variant spelling of Uzziel; compare 25:4. 25:22 Hebrew *Jeremoth,* a variant spelling of Jerimoth; compare 25:4. 25:24 Hebrew *Joshbekasha,* a variant spelling of Joshbekashah; compare 25:4. 26:1 As in Greek version (see also Exod 6:24); Hebrew reads *Asaph.*

12These divisions of the gatekeepers were named for
their family leaders, and like the other Levites, they
served at the house of the LORD. 13They were assigned by
families for guard duty at the various gates, without regard to age or training, for it was all decided by means of
sacred lots.
14The responsibility for the east gate went to Meshelemiah* and his group. The north gate was assigned to his
son Zechariah, a man of unusual wisdom. 15The south gate
went to Obed-edom, and his sons were put in charge of the
storehouse. 16Shuppim and Hosah were assigned the west
gate and the gateway leading up to the Temple.* Guard duties were divided evenly. 17Six Levites were assigned each
day to the east gate, four to the north gate, four to the south
gate, and two pairs at the storehouse. 18Six were assigned
each day to the west gate, four to the gateway leading up to
the Temple, and two to the courtyard.*
19These were the divisions of the gatekeepers from the
clans of Korah and Merari.

TREASURERS AND OTHER OFFICIALS

20Other Levites, led by Ahijah, were in charge of the treasuries of the house of God and the treasuries of the gifts
dedicated to the LORD. 21From the family of Libni* in the
clan of Gershon, Jehiel* was the leader. 22The sons of Jehiel, Zetham and his brother Joel, were in charge of the
treasuries of the house of the LORD.
23These are the leaders that descended from Amram,
Izhar, Hebron, and Uzziel:

JOYFUL GIVING 26:27

The spoils of war rightfully belonged to the victorious army. These soldiers, however, gave their portion of all the battle plunder to the Temple to express their dedication to God. Many times, we give out of obligation, rather than out of joy. Is your giving a matter of rejoicing rather than duty? ■

24From the clan of Amram, Shebuel was a descendant of
Gershom son of Moses. He was the chief officer of
the treasuries. 25His relatives through Eliezer were
Rehabiah, Jeshaiah, Joram, Zicri, and Shelomoth.
26Shelomoth and his relatives were in charge of the
treasuries containing the gifts that King David, the
family leaders, and the generals and captains* and
other officers of the army had dedicated to the LORD.
27These men dedicated some of the plunder they had
gained in battle to maintain the house of the LORD.
28Shelomoth* and his relatives also cared for the gifts
dedicated to the LORD by Samuel the seer, Saul son of
Kish, Abner son of Ner, and Joab son of Zeruiah. All
the other dedicated gifts were in their care, too.
29From the clan of Izhar came Kenaniah. He and his
sons were given administrative responsibilities* over
Israel as officials and judges.
30From the clan of Hebron came Hashabiah. He and his
relatives—1,700 capable men—were put in charge of
the Israelite lands west of the Jordan River. They
were responsible for all matters related to the things
of the LORD and the service of the king in that area.
31Also from the clan of Hebron came Jeriah,* who
was the leader of the Hebronites according to the
genealogical records. (In the fortieth year of David's
reign, a search was made in the records, and capable
men from the clan of Hebron were found at Jazer in
the land of Gilead.) 32There were 2,700 capable men
among the relatives of Jeriah. King David sent them
to the east side of the Jordan River and put them in
charge of the tribes of Reuben and Gad and the half-
tribe of Manasseh. They were responsible for all
matters related to God and to the king.

27

MILITARY COMMANDERS AND DIVISIONS

This is the list of Israelite generals and captains,* and
their officers, who served the king by supervising the
army divisions that were on duty each month of the year.
Each division served for one month and had 24,000
troops.

2Jashobeam son of Zabdiel was commander of the first
division of 24,000 troops, which was on duty during
the first month. 3He was a descendant of Perez and
was in charge of all the army officers for the first
month.
4Dodai, a descendant of Ahoah, was commander of the
second division of 24,000 troops, which was on duty
during the second month. Mikloth was his chief
officer.
5Benaiah son of Jehoiada the priest was commander of
the third division of 24,000 troops, which was on
duty during the third month. 6This was the Benaiah
who commanded David's elite military group known
as the Thirty. His son Ammizabad was his chief
officer.
7Asahel, the brother of Joab, was commander of the
fourth division of 24,000 troops, which was on duty
during the fourth month. Asahel was succeeded by
his son Zebadiah.
8Shammah* the Izrahite was commander of the fifth
division of 24,000 troops, which was on duty during
the fifth month.
9Ira son of Ikkesh from Tekoa was commander of the
sixth division of 24,000 troops, which was on duty
during the sixth month.
10Helez, a descendant of Ephraim from Pelon, was

26:14 Hebrew *Shelemiah,* a variant spelling of Meshelemiah; compare 26:2. **26:16** Or *the gate of Shalleketh on the upper road* (also in 26:18). The meaning of the Hebrew is uncertain. **26:18** Or *the colonnade.* The meaning of the Hebrew is uncertain. **26:21a** Hebrew *Ladan,* a variant spelling of Libni; compare 6:17. **26:21b** Hebrew *Jehieli* (also in 26:22), a variant spelling of Jehiel; compare 23:8. **26:26** Hebrew *the commanders of thousands and of hundreds.* **26:28** Hebrew *Shelomith,* a variant spelling of Shelomoth. **26:29** Or *were given outside work;* or *were given work away from the Temple area.* **26:31** Hebrew *Jerijah,* a variant spelling of Jeriah; compare 23:19. **27:1** Hebrew *commanders of thousands and of hundreds.* **27:8** Hebrew *Shamhuth,* a variant spelling of Shammah; compare 11:27 and 2 Sam 23:25.

commander of the seventh division of 24,000 troops, which was on duty during the seventh month.
11Sibbecai, a descendant of Zerah from Hushah, was commander of the eighth division of 24,000 troops, which was on duty during the eighth month.
12Abiezer from Anathoth in the territory of Benjamin was commander of the ninth division of 24,000 troops, which was on duty during the ninth month.
13Maharai, a descendant of Zerah from Netophah, was commander of the tenth division of 24,000 troops, which was on duty during the tenth month.
14Benaiah from Pirathon in Ephraim was commander of the eleventh division of 24,000 troops, which was on duty during the eleventh month.
15Heled,* a descendant of Othniel from Netophah, was commander of the twelfth division of 24,000 troops, which was on duty during the twelfth month.

LEADERS OF THE TRIBES

16The following were the tribes of Israel and their leaders:

	Tribe	*Leader*
	Reuben	Eliezer son of Zicri
	Simeon	Shephatiah son of Maacah
17	Levi	Hashabiah son of Kemuel
	Aaron (the priests)	Zadok
18	Judah	Elihu (a brother of David)
	Issachar	Omri son of Michael
19	Zebulun	Ishmaiah son of Obadiah
	Naphtali	Jeremoth son of Azriel
20	Ephraim	Hoshea son of Azaziah
	Manasseh (west)	Joel son of Pedaiah
21	Manasseh in Gilead (east)	Iddo son of Zechariah
	Benjamin	Jaasiel son of Abner
22	Dan	Azarel son of Jeroham

These were the leaders of the tribes of Israel.
23When David took his census, he did not count those
who were younger than twenty years of age, because the
LORD had promised to make the Israelites as numerous as
the stars in heaven. 24Joab son of Zeruiah began the census but never finished it because* the anger of God fell
on Israel. The total number was never recorded in King
David's official records.

OFFICIALS OF DAVID'S KINGDOM

25Azmaveth son of Adiel was in charge of the palace treasuries.
Jonathan son of Uzziah was in charge of the regional treasuries throughout the towns, villages, and fortresses of Israel.
26Ezri son of Kelub was in charge of the field workers who farmed the king's lands.
27Shimei from Ramah was in charge of the king's vineyards.
Zabdi from Shepham was responsible for the grapes and the supplies of wine.
28Baal-hanan from Geder was in charge of the king's olive groves and sycamore-fig trees in the foothills of Judah.*
Joash was responsible for the supplies of olive oil.
29Shitrai from Sharon was in charge of the cattle on the Sharon Plain.
Shaphat son of Adlai was responsible for the cattle in the valleys.
30Obil the Ishmaelite was in charge of the camels.
Jehdeiah from Meronoth was in charge of the donkeys.
31Jaziz the Hagrite was in charge of the king's flocks of sheep and goats.
All these officials were overseers of King David's property.

32Jonathan, David's uncle, was a wise counselor to the
king, a man of great insight, and a scribe. Jehiel the Hacmonite was responsible for teaching the king's sons.
33Ahithophel was the royal adviser. Hushai the Arkite was
the king's friend. 34Ahithophel was succeeded by Jehoiada son of Benaiah and by Abiathar. Joab was commander
of the king's army.

TAKE HIM SERIOUSLY 28:1-10

David encouraged Solomon to obey all of God's rules. He wanted Solomon to take God seriously. Maybe you don't have to run a country. But as you grow closer to adulthood, perhaps you're already considering the decisions you'll need to make for yourself. Like Solomon, are you willing to take God seriously? He's your best hope for the future. ■

28 DAVID'S INSTRUCTIONS TO SOLOMON

David summoned all the officials of Israel to Jerusalem—
the leaders of the tribes, the commanders of the army divisions, the other generals and captains,* the overseers of
the royal property and livestock, the palace officials, the
mighty men, and all the other brave warriors in the kingdom. 2David rose to his feet and said: "My brothers and
my people! It was my desire to build a temple where the
Ark of the LORD's Covenant, God's footstool, could rest
permanently. I made the necessary preparations for
building it, 3but God said to me, 'You must not build a
temple to honor my name, for you are a warrior and have
shed much blood.'
4"Yet the LORD, the God of Israel, has chosen me from
among all my father's family to be king over Israel forever. For he has chosen the tribe of Judah to rule, and
from among the families of Judah he chose my father's
family. And from among my father's sons the LORD was
pleased to make me king over all Israel. 5And from
among my sons—for the LORD has given me many—he
chose Solomon to succeed me on the throne of Israel and
to rule over the LORD's kingdom. 6He said to me, 'Your son
Solomon will build my Temple and its courtyards, for I

27:15 Hebrew *Heldai,* a variant spelling of Heled; compare 11:30 and 2 Sam 23:29. **27:24** Or *never finished it, and yet.* **27:28** Hebrew *the Shephelah.* **28:1** Hebrew *the commanders of thousands and commanders of hundreds.*

Principles to Live By

David gave his son Solomon principles to guide him through life (see 1 Chron 28:9-10). These same ideas are ones that any Christian can learn and follow.

1	2	3	4	5	6
Get to know God personally.	Learn God's commands and discover what he wants you to do.	Worship God with a clean heart.	Serve God with a willing mind.	Be faithful.	Don't become discouraged.

have chosen him as my son, and I will be his father. 7And
if he continues to obey my commands and regulations as
he does now, I will make his kingdom last forever.'
8"So now, with God as our witness, and in the sight of
all Israel—the LORD's assembly—I give you this charge. Be
careful to obey all the commands of the
LORD your God, so that you may continue to possess this good land and
leave it to your children as a permanent
inheritance.
9"And Solomon, my son, learn to
know the God of your ancestors intimately. Worship and serve him with
your whole heart and a willing mind.
For the LORD sees every heart and
knows every plan and thought. If you
seek him, you will find him. But if you
forsake him, he will reject you forever.
10So take this seriously. The LORD has
chosen you to build a Temple as his
sanctuary. Be strong, and do the work."
11Then David gave Solomon the plans for the Temple
and its surroundings, including the entry room, the storerooms, the upstairs rooms, the inner rooms, and the inner sanctuary—which was the place of atonement.
12David also gave Solomon all the plans he had in mind*
for the courtyards of the LORD's Temple, the outside
rooms, the treasuries, and the rooms for the gifts dedicated to the LORD. 13The king also gave Solomon the instructions concerning the work of the various divisions
of priests and Levites in the Temple of the LORD. And he
gave specifications for the items in the Temple that were
to be used for worship.
14David gave instructions regarding how much gold
and silver should be used to make the items needed for
service. 15He told Solomon the amount of gold needed for
the gold lampstands and lamps, and the amount of silver
for the silver lampstands and lamps, depending on how
each would be used. 16He designated the amount of gold
for the table on which the Bread of the Presence would be
placed and the amount of silver for other tables.

> If you seek him, you will find him.
>
> *1 CHRONICLES 28:9*

17David also designated the amount of gold for the
solid gold meat hooks used to handle the sacrificial meat
and for the basins, pitchers, and dishes, as well as the
amount of silver for every dish. 18He designated the
amount of refined gold for the altar of incense. Finally,
he gave him a plan for the LORD's
"chariot"—the gold cherubim* whose
wings were stretched out over the Ark
of the LORD's Covenant. 19"Every part
of this plan," David told Solomon, "was
given to me in writing from the hand
of the LORD.*"
20Then David continued, "Be strong
and courageous, and do the work.
Don't be afraid or discouraged, for the
LORD God, my God, is with you. He will
not fail you or forsake you. He will see
to it that all the work related to the
Temple of the LORD is finished correctly. 21The various divisions of
priests and Levites will serve in the
Temple of God. Others with skills of every kind will volunteer, and the officials and the entire nation are at your
command."

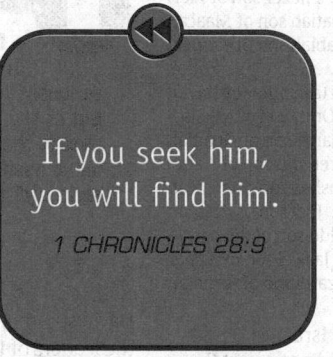

29 GIFTS FOR BUILDING THE TEMPLE

Then King David turned to the entire assembly and said,
"My son Solomon, whom God has clearly chosen as the
next king of Israel, is still young and inexperienced. The
work ahead of him is enormous, for the Temple he will
build is not for mere mortals—it is for the LORD God
himself! 2Using every resource at my command, I have
gathered as much as I could for building the Temple of
my God. Now there is enough gold, silver, bronze, iron,
and wood, as well as great quantities of onyx, other precious stones, costly jewels, and all kinds of fine stone and
marble.
3"And now, because of my devotion to the Temple of
my God, I am giving all of my own private treasures of gold
and silver to help in the construction. This is in addition to

28:12 Or *the plans of the spirit that was with him.* **28:18** Hebrew *for the gold cherub chariot.* **28:19** Or *was written under the direction of the LORD.*

the building materials I have already collected for his holy Temple. 4I am donating more than 112 tons of gold* from Ophir and 262 tons of refined silver* to be used for overlaying the walls of the buildings 5and for the other gold and silver work to be done by the craftsmen. Now then, who will follow my example and give offerings to the LORD today?"

6Then the family leaders, the leaders of the tribes of Israel, the generals and captains of the army,* and the king's administrative officers all gave willingly. 7For the construction of the Temple of God, they gave about 188 tons of gold,* 10,000 gold coins,* 375 tons of silver,* 675 tons of bronze,* and 3,750 tons of iron.* 8They also contributed numerous precious stones, which were deposited in the treasury of the house of the LORD under the care of Jehiel, a descendant of Gershon. 9The people rejoiced over the offerings, for they had given freely and wholeheartedly to the LORD, and King David was filled with joy.

DAVID'S PRAYER OF PRAISE

10Then David praised the LORD in the presence of the whole assembly:

"O LORD, the God of our ancestor Israel,* may you
be praised forever and ever! 11Yours, O LORD, is the
greatness, the power, the glory, the victory, and the
majesty. Everything in the heavens and on earth is
yours, O LORD, and this is your kingdom. We adore you
as the one who is over all things. 12Wealth and honor
come from you alone, for you rule over everything.
Power and might are in your hand, and at your
discretion people are made great and given strength.

13"O our God, we thank you and praise your
glorious name! 14But who am I, and who are my
people, that we could give anything to you?
Everything we have has come from you, and we give
you only what you first gave us! 15We are here for
only a moment, visitors and strangers in the land as
our ancestors were before us. Our days on earth are
like a passing shadow, gone so soon without a trace.

16"O LORD our God, even this material we have
gathered to build a Temple to honor your holy name
comes from you! It all belongs to you! 17I know, my
God, that you examine our hearts and rejoice when
you find integrity there. You know I have done all this
with good motives, and I have watched your people
offer their gifts willingly and joyously.

18"O LORD, the God of our ancestors Abraham,
Isaac, and Israel, make your people always want to
obey you. See to it that their love for you never
changes. 19Give my son Solomon the wholehearted
desire to obey all your commands, laws, and decrees,
and to do everything necessary to build this Temple,
for which I have made these preparations."

I just realized that I've been living off of the faith of my parents. How do I own my faith?

Living off of someone else's faith is like borrowing something from a friend. No matter what you borrow—a car, cell phone, clothes, CDs, or faith—it isn't yours and must be returned.

Solomon was challenged to "learn to know the God of your ancestors intimately" (1 Chron 28:9). In other words, he wasn't to settle for hearing how someone else trusted God. He needed to find out for himself.

During these years, your faith will be tested. Friends who do not believe in Christ may see nothing wrong with doing things that would cause your conscience to start screaming in protest. That's when you will have to make a choice: Will you go along with your friends or will you stand on what you believe? If your faith is strong (if it is yours and not your parents' or your youth leader's), no amount of pressure from friends will be able to blow you away. (See Matt 7:24-27.)

Consider taking these steps to help develop your faith. First, make sure you have asked Jesus Christ to forgive your sin and come into your life. Second, begin to ask questions about the Bible. God wants you to understand it as well as believe and obey it. Third, look for other Christians who are excited about developing their faith in God—people who do not want to settle for second best. What you learn from them can convince you that being a Christian is worth the work and is 100 percent right for you!

A DESIRE TO SERVE 29:19

David wanted Solomon to have a heart that desired, above all else, to serve God. Do you find it hard to do what God wants, or even harder to *want* to do it? God can give you a loyal heart that wants to do his will. If you trust Jesus as your Savior, this is already happening in you. Paul wrote, "God is working in you, giving you the desire and the power to do what pleases him" (Phil 2:13). ■

20Then David said to the whole assembly, "Give praise to the LORD your God!" And the entire assembly praised the LORD, the God of their ancestors, and they bowed low and knelt before the LORD and the king.

SOLOMON NAMED AS KING

21The next day they brought 1,000 bulls, 1,000 rams, and 1,000 male lambs as burnt offerings to the LORD. They

29:4a Hebrew *3,000 talents* [102 metric tons] *of gold.* **29:4b** Hebrew *7,000 talents* [238 metric tons] *of silver.* **29:6** Hebrew *the commanders of thousands and commanders of hundreds.* **29:7a** Hebrew *5,000 talents* [170 metric tons] *of gold.* **29:7b** Hebrew *10,000 darics* [a Persian coin] *of gold,* about 185 pounds or 84 kilograms in weight. **29:7c** Hebrew *10,000 talents* [340 metric tons] *of silver.* **29:7d** Hebrew *18,000 talents* [612 metric tons] *of bronze.* **29:7e** Hebrew *100,000 talents* [3,400 metric tons] *of iron.* **29:10** *Israel* is the name that God gave to Jacob.

also brought liquid offerings and many other sacrifices
on behalf of all Israel. 22They feasted and drank in the
LORD's presence with great joy that day.

And again they crowned David's son Solomon as their
new king. They anointed him before the LORD as their
leader, and they anointed Zadok as priest. 23So Solomon
took the throne of the LORD in place of his father, David, and
he succeeded in everything, and all Israel obeyed him. 24All
the officials, the warriors, and the sons of King David
pledged their loyalty to King Solomon. 25And the LORD exalted Solomon in the sight of all Israel, and he gave Solomon
greater royal splendor than any king in Israel before him.

SUMMARY OF DAVID'S REIGN

26So David son of Jesse reigned over all Israel. 27He
reigned over Israel for forty years, seven of them in Hebron and thirty-three in Jerusalem. 28He died at a ripe old
age, having enjoyed long life, wealth, and honor. Then his
son Solomon ruled in his place.

29All the events of King David's reign, from beginning
to end, are written in *The Record of Samuel the Seer, The
Record of Nathan the Prophet*, and *The Record of Gad the
Seer*. 30These accounts include the mighty deeds of his
reign and everything that happened to him and to Israel
and to all the surrounding kingdoms.

2 CHRONICLES

"YOU CAN'T USE the car for two weeks." "Detention for five days." "No parties for two weeks." "You're grounded for a week." "No cell phone for a month."

So, what do those statements have in common? They're punishments. Have you experienced one lately?

Many times during Israel's history, God sent messengers to the divided country's leaders threatening punishment for their disobedience. Each time, the leaders would beg for one more chance, but they never kept their promises. Finally God allowed them to be conquered by an army from Babylon and taken into captivity.

Second Chronicles was written after the return of some of the Jews from their exile. The author reminded these people of their forefathers' sin and its results. Only by truly submitting to God could Israel regain its strength as a nation. As God told Solomon, "If my people who are called by my name will humble themselves and pray and seek my face and turn from their wicked ways, I will hear from heaven and will forgive their sins and restore their land" (7:14).

Second Chronicles is a reminder for you, too. God never takes wrongdoing lightly. But he's always ready to forgive those who ask.

timeline

970 B.C.
Solomon becomes king

966–959
Temple built

930
The kingdom divides

910
Asa becomes king of Judah

872
Jehoshaphat becomes king of Judah

853
Ahab killed in battle

841
Athaliah seizes the throne

792
Uzziah becomes king of Judah

722
Israel (northern kingdom) falls

715
Hezekiah becomes king of Judah

701
Sennacherib taunts Hezekiah

640
Josiah becomes king

622
Book of the Law found

586
Judah (southern kingdom) falls

538
Cyrus's decree

stats

PURPOSE: To unify the nation around true worship of God by showing his standard for judging kings

AUTHOR: Ezra, according to Jewish tradition

TO WHOM WRITTEN: All Israel

DATE WRITTEN: Approximately 430 B.C.; recording events from Solomon's reign (970 B.C.) to Babylonian captivity (586 B.C.)

SETTING: Second Chronicles parallels and is commentary to 1 and 2 Kings.

KEY PEOPLE: Solomon, the queen of Sheba, Rehoboam, Asa, Jehoshaphat, Jehoram, Joash, Uzziah, Ahaz, Hezekiah, Manasseh, Josiah

KEY PLACES: Jerusalem, the Temple

SPECIAL FEATURES: Includes a detailed record of the Temple's construction

KEY points

TEMPLE
The Temple was the symbol of God's presence and the place set aside for worship and prayer. Although we attend church in a physical building, the human heart is the main center of God's presence today.

PEACE
While Solomon and his descendants were faithful to God, they experienced victory in battle, success in government, and peace with other nations. Peace was, and is, the result of loyalty to God and his law. Only God can bring true peace.

PRAYER
When the king and his people prayed for help against enemies, God responded. If we pray to God with humility, God will answer.

CHANGE FOR THE BETTER
Although idol worship and injustice were common, some kings led the people back to God and reformed their society. We can be instruments of change as we remind people of God's standards.

CONSEQUENCE OF CASUAL COMMITMENT
When the people of Israel refused to stop doing wrong, God allowed them to be conquered by their enemies. Our disobedience may not be as obvious as Israel's, but our commitment to God can be casual or phony. God wants his people to be fully committed to him.

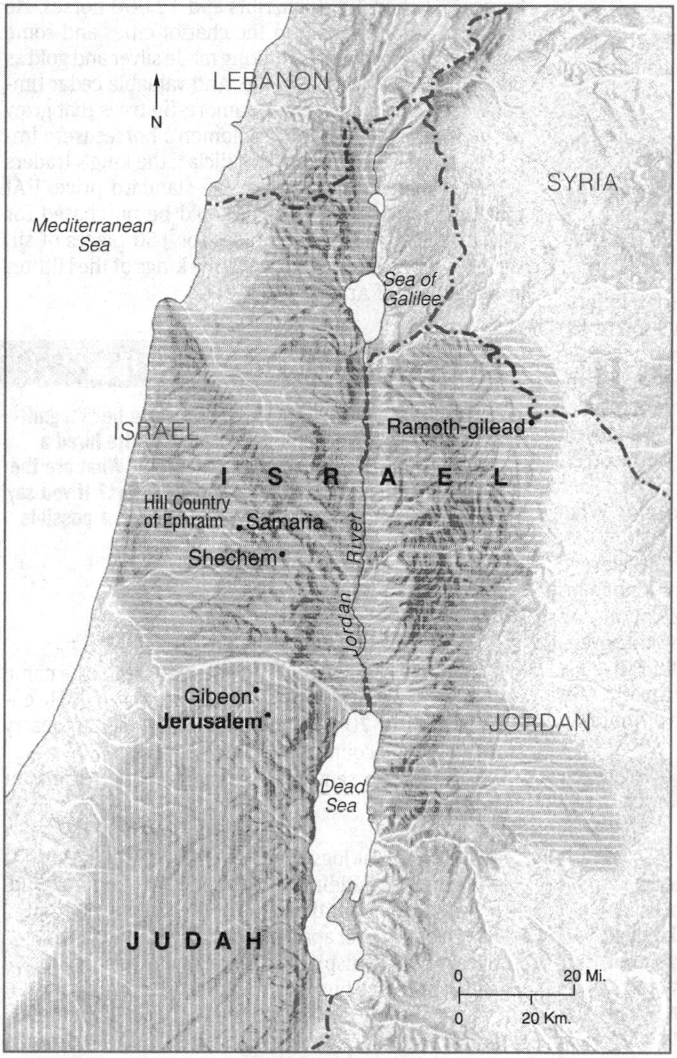

The broken lines (—·—) indicate modern boundaries.

KEY PLACES IN 2 CHRONICLES

• **GIBEON** David's son Solomon became king of Israel. He summoned the nation's leaders to a ceremony in Gibeon. Here God told Solomon to ask for whatever he desired. Solomon asked for wisdom and knowledge to rule Israel (1:1-12).

• **JERUSALEM** After the ceremony in Gibeon, Solomon returned to the capital city, Jerusalem. His reign began a golden age for Israel. Solomon implemented plans for the Temple that had been drawn up by his father, David. It was a magnificent construction. It symbolized Solomon's wealth and wisdom, which had become known worldwide (1:13–9:31).

• **SHECHEM** After Solomon's death, his son Rehoboam was ready to be crowned in Shechem. However, his promise of higher taxes and harder work for the people led to rebellion. Everyone but the tribes of Judah and Benjamin deserted Rehoboam and set up their own kingdom, called Israel, to the north. Rehoboam returned to Jerusalem as ruler over the southern kingdom, called Judah (10:1–12:16). The remainder of 2 Chronicles records the history of Judah.

• **HILL COUNTRY OF EPHRAIM** Abijah became the next king of Judah, and soon war broke out between Israel and Judah. When the armies of the two nations arrived for battle in the hill country of Ephraim, Israel had twice as many troops as Judah. It looked like Judah's defeat was certain. But they cried out to God, and God gave them victory over Israel. In their history as separate nations, Judah did have a few godly kings who instituted reforms and brought the people back to God. Israel, however, had a succession of only evil kings (13:1-22).

• **ARAM** Asa, a godly king, removed every trace of idol worship from Judah and renewed the people's covenant with God in Jerusalem. But King Baasha of Israel built a fortress to control traffic into Judah. Instead of looking to God for guidance, Asa took the silver and gold from the Temple and sent it to the king of Aram, in the region of modern Syria, requesting his help against King Baasha. As a result, God became angry with Judah (14:1–16:14).

• **SAMARIA** Although Jehoshaphat was a godly king, he allied himself with Israel's most evil king, Ahab. Ahab's capital was in Samaria. Ahab wanted help fighting for Ramoth-gilead. Jehoshaphat wanted advice, but rather than listening to God's prophet who had promised defeat, he joined Ahab in battle (17:1–18:27).

• **RAMOTH-GILEAD** The alliance with Israel against Ramoth-gilead ended in defeat and Ahab's death. Although shaken by his defeat, Jehoshaphat returned to Jerusalem and to God. But his son Jehoram was a wicked king, as was *his* son, Ahaziah. And history repeated itself. Ahaziah formed an alliance with Israel's King Jehoram (who had the same name as his brother) to do battle with the Arameans at Ramoth-gilead. This led to the death of both kings (18:28–22:9).

• **JERUSALEM** The rest of Judah's history recorded in 2 Chronicles centers on Jerusalem. Some kings caused Judah to sin by promoting idol worship. Others cleaned up the idol worship, reopened and restored the Temple, and, in the case of Josiah, tried to follow God's laws as they were written by Moses. In spite of the few good influences, a series of evil kings sent Judah into a downward spiral that ended with the Babylonian empire overrunning the country. The Temple was burned, the walls of the city were broken down, and the people were deported to Babylon.

1

SOLOMON ASKS FOR WISDOM

Solomon son of David took firm control of his kingdom, for the LORD his God was with him and made him very powerful.

[2]Solomon called together all the leaders of Israel—the generals and captains of the army,* the judges, and all the political and clan leaders. [3]Then he led the entire assembly to the place of worship in Gibeon, for God's Tabernacle* was located there. (This was the Tabernacle that Moses, the LORD's servant, had made in the wilderness.)

[4]David had already moved the Ark of God from Kiriath-jearim to the tent he had prepared for it in Jerusalem. [5]But the bronze altar made by Bezalel son of Uri and grandson of Hur was there* at Gibeon in front of the Tabernacle of the LORD. So Solomon and the people gathered in front of it to consult the LORD.* [6]There in front of the Tabernacle, Solomon went up to the bronze altar in the LORD's presence and sacrificed 1,000 burnt offerings on it.

[7]That night God appeared to Solomon and said, "What do you want? Ask, and I will give it to you!"

[8]Solomon replied to God, "You showed faithful love to David, my father, and now you have made me king in his place. [9]O LORD God, please continue to keep your promise to David my father, for you have made me king over a people as numerous as the dust of the earth! [10]Give me the wisdom and knowledge to lead them properly,* for who could possibly govern this great people of yours?"

PRIORITIES 1:11-13

Although Solomon could have asked for anything, he asked for wisdom to rule the nation. Because God approved of the way Solomon ordered his priorities, he gave him the wisdom he asked for *and* money to spare. Jesus also spoke about priorities. When we put God first, everything we need will be provided (Matt 6:33). This isn't a guarantee that we'll be wealthy and famous like Solomon. When we wisely put God first, the wisdom he gives us will enable us to live a rich, rewarding life. ■

[11]God said to Solomon, "Because your greatest desire is to help your people, and you did not ask for wealth, riches, fame, or even the death of your enemies or a long life, but rather you asked for wisdom and knowledge to properly govern my people—[12]I will certainly give you the wisdom and knowledge you requested. But I will also give you wealth, riches, and fame such as no other king has had before you or will ever have in the future!"

[13]Then Solomon returned to Jerusalem from the Tabernacle at the place of worship in Gibeon, and he reigned over Israel.

[14]Solomon built up a huge force of chariots and horses.* He had 1,400 chariots and 12,000 horses. He stationed some of them in the chariot cities and some near him in Jerusalem. [15]The king made silver and gold as plentiful in Jerusalem as stone. And valuable cedar timber was as common as the sycamore-fig trees that grow in the foothills of Judah.* [16]Solomon's horses were imported from Egypt* and from Cilicia*; the king's traders acquired them from Cilicia at the standard price. [17]At that time chariots from Egypt could be purchased for 600 pieces of silver,* and horses for 150 pieces of silver.* They were then exported to the kings of the Hittites and the kings of Aram.

PUT SOME EFFORT INTO IT 2:1-10

Solomon wanted the Temple to be "magnificent" to honor an awesome God. He hired a huge workforce to get the job done right. What are the activities into which you put the most effort? If you say that you trust God, every move you make is a possible reflection of your belief. ■

2

PREPARATIONS FOR BUILDING THE TEMPLE

[1]*Solomon decided to build a Temple to honor the name of the LORD, and also a royal palace for himself. [2]*He enlisted a force of 70,000 laborers, 80,000 men to quarry stone in the hill country, and 3,600 foremen.

[3]Solomon also sent this message to King Hiram* at Tyre:

"Send me cedar logs as you did for my father, David, when he was building his palace. [4]I am about to build a Temple to honor the name of the LORD my God. It will be a place set apart to burn fragrant incense before him, to display the special sacrificial bread, and to sacrifice burnt offerings each morning and evening, on the Sabbaths, at new moon celebrations, and at the other appointed festivals of the LORD our God. He has commanded Israel to do these things forever.

[5]"This must be a magnificent Temple because our God is greater than all other gods. [6]But who can really build him a worthy home? Not even the highest heavens can contain him! So who am I to consider building a Temple for him, except as a place to burn sacrifices to him?

[7]"So send me a master craftsman who can work with gold, silver, bronze, and iron, as well as with purple, scarlet, and blue cloth. He must be a skilled engraver who can work with the craftsmen of Judah and Jerusalem who were selected by my father, David.

1:2 Hebrew *the commanders of thousands and of hundreds.* **1:3** Hebrew *Tent of Meeting;* also in 1:6, 13. **1:5a** As in Greek version and Latin Vulgate, and some Hebrew manuscripts. Masoretic Text reads *he placed.* **1:5b** Hebrew *to consult him.* **1:10** Hebrew *to go out and come in before this people.* **1:14** Or *charioteers;* also in 1:14b. **1:15** Hebrew *the Shephelah.* **1:16a** Possibly *Muzur,* a district near Cilicia; also in 1:17. **1:16b** Hebrew *Kue,* probably another name for Cilicia. **1:17a** Hebrew *600 shekels of silver,* about 15 pounds or 6.8 kilograms in weight. **1:17b** Hebrew *150 shekels,* about 3.8 pounds or 1.7 kilograms in weight. **2:1** Verse 2:1 is numbered 1:18 in Hebrew text. **2:2** Verses 2:2-18 are numbered 2:1-17 in Hebrew text. **2:3** Hebrew *Huram,* a variant spelling of Hiram; also in 2:11.

8"Also send me cedar, cypress, and red sandalwood* logs from Lebanon, for I know that your men
are without equal at cutting timber in Lebanon. I will
send my men to help them. 9An immense amount
of timber will be needed, for the Temple I am going
to build will be very large and magnificent. 10In
payment for your woodcutters, I will send 100,000
bushels of crushed wheat, 100,000 bushels of
barley,* 110,000 gallons of wine, and 110,000
gallons of olive oil.*"

11King Hiram sent this letter of reply to Solomon:

"It is because the LORD loves his people that he has
made you their king! 12Praise the LORD, the God of
Israel, who made the heavens and the earth! He has
given King David a wise son, gifted with skill and
understanding, who will build a Temple for the LORD
and a royal palace for himself.

13"I am sending you a master craftsman named
Huram-abi, who is extremely talented. 14His mother
is from the tribe of Dan in Israel, and his father is
from Tyre. He is skillful at making things from gold,
silver, bronze, and iron, and he also works with stone
and wood. He can work with purple, blue, and scarlet
cloth and fine linen. He is also an engraver and can
follow any design given to him. He will work with
your craftsmen and those appointed by my lord
David, your father.

15"Send along the wheat, barley, olive oil, and wine
that my lord has mentioned. 16We will cut whatever
timber you need from the Lebanon mountains and
will float the logs in rafts down the coast of the
Mediterranean Sea* to Joppa. From there you can
transport the logs up to Jerusalem."

17Solomon took a census of all foreigners in the land of
Israel, like the census his father had taken, and he
counted 153,600. 18He assigned 70,000 of them as common laborers, 80,000 as quarry workers in the hill country, and 3,600 as foremen.

3 SOLOMON BUILDS THE TEMPLE

So Solomon began to build the Temple of the LORD in Jerusalem on Mount Moriah, where the LORD had appeared
to David, his father. The Temple was built on the threshing floor of Araunah* the Jebusite, the site that David had
selected. 2The construction began in midspring,* during
the fourth year of Solomon's reign.

3These are the dimensions Solomon used for the foundation of the Temple of God (using the old standard of
measurement).* It was 90 feet long and 30 feet wide.*
4The entry room at the front of the Temple was 30 feet*
wide, running across the entire width of the Temple, and
30 feet* high. He overlaid the inside with pure gold.

5He paneled the main room of the Temple with cypress wood, overlaid it with fine gold, and decorated it
with carvings of palm trees and chains. 6He decorated
the walls of the Temple with beautiful jewels and with
gold from the land of Parvaim. 7He overlaid the beams,
thresholds, walls, and doors throughout the Temple with
gold, and he carved figures of cherubim on the walls.

8He made the Most Holy Place 30 feet wide, corresponding to the width of the Temple, and 30 feet deep.
He overlaid its interior with 23 tons* of fine gold. 9The
gold nails that were used weighed 20 ounces* each. He
also overlaid the walls of the upper rooms with gold.

10He made two figures shaped like cherubim, overlaid
them with gold, and placed them in the Most Holy Place.
11The total wingspan of the two cherubim standing side
by side was 30 feet. One wing of the first figure was
7½ feet* long, and it touched the Temple wall. The other
wing, also 7½ feet long, touched one of the wings of the
second figure. 12In the same way, the second figure had
one wing 7½ feet long that touched the opposite wall.
The other wing, also 7½ feet long, touched the wing of
the first figure. 13So the wingspan of the two cherubim
side by side was 30 feet. They stood on their feet and
faced out toward the main room of the Temple.

14Across the entrance of the Most Holy Place he hung a
curtain made of fine linen, decorated with blue, purple,
and scarlet thread and embroidered with figures of
cherubim.

15For the front of the Temple, he made two pillars
that were 27 feet* tall, each topped by a capital extending upward another 7½ feet. 16He made a network of interwoven chains and used them to decorate the tops of
the pillars. He also made 100 decorative pomegranates
and attached them to the chains. 17Then he set up the
two pillars at the entrance of the Temple, one to the
south of the entrance and the other to the north. He
named the one on the south Jakin, and the one on the
north Boaz.*

4 FURNISHINGS FOR THE TEMPLE

Solomon* also made a bronze altar 30 feet long, 30 feet
wide, and 15 feet high.* 2Then he cast a great round basin,
15 feet across from rim to rim, called the Sea. It was

2:8 Or *juniper;* Hebrew reads *algum,* perhaps a variant spelling of *almug;* compare 9:10-11 and parallel text at 1 Kgs 10:11-12. 2:10a Hebrew *20,000 cors* [3,640 kiloliters] *of crushed wheat, 20,000 cors of barley.* 2:10b Hebrew *20,000 baths* [420 kiloliters] *of wine, and 20,000 baths of olive oil.* 2:16 Hebrew *the sea.* 3:1 Hebrew reads *Ornan,* a variant spelling of Araunah; compare 2 Sam 24:16. 3:2 Hebrew *on the second day of the second month.* This day of the ancient Hebrew lunar calendar occurred in April or May. 3:3a The "old standard of measurement" was a cubit equal to 18 inches [46 centimeters]. The new standard was a cubit of approximately 21 inches [53 centimeters]. 3:3b Hebrew *60 cubits* [27.6 meters] *long and 20 cubits* [9.2 meters] *wide.* 3:4a Hebrew *20 cubits* [9.2 meters]; also in 3:8, 11, 13. 3:4b As in some Greek and Syriac manuscripts, which read *20 cubits* [9.2 meters]; Hebrew reads *120 cubits,* which is 180 feet or 55 meters. 3:8 Hebrew *600 talents* [20.4 metric tons]. 3:9 Hebrew *50 shekels* [570 grams]. 3:11 Hebrew *5 cubits* [2.3 meters]; also in 3:11b, 12, 15. 3:15 As in Syriac version (see also 1 Kgs 7:15; 2 Kgs 25:17; Jer 52:21), which reads *18 cubits* [8.3 meters]; Hebrew reads *35 cubits,* which is 52.5 feet or 16.5 meters. 3:17 *Jakin* probably means "he establishes"; *Boaz* probably means "in him is strength." 4:1a Or *Huram-abi;* Hebrew reads *He.* 4:1b Hebrew *20 cubits* [9.2 meters] *long, 20 cubits wide, and 10 cubits* [4.6 meters] *high.*

Careful Obedience

Solomon and his workers carefully followed God's instructions (4:7). As a result, the Temple work was blessed by God and completed in every detail. Here are a few examples of (1) people in the Bible who did not carefully follow one of God's instructions and (2) the resulting consequences. It is not enough to obey God halfheartedly.

WHO	GOD'S INSTRUCTION	DISOBEDIENCE	RESULT
Adam and Eve	Don't eat fruit from the tree of the knowledge of good and evil (Gen 2:16-17)	Satan tempted them and they ate (Gen 3:1-6)	They were banished from the Garden of Eden; pain and death were inflicted on all humanity (Gen 3:24; Rom 5:12)
Nadab and Abihu	Fire for the sacrifice must come from the proper source (Lev 6:12-13)	They used a different kind of fire for their sacrifice (Lev 10:1)	They were struck dead (Lev 10:2)
Moses	"Speak to the rock over there, and it will pour out its water" (Num 20:8)	He spoke to the rock, but also struck it with his staff (Num 20:11)	He was not allowed to enter the Promised Land (Num 20:12)
Saul	Completely destroy the evil Amalekites (1 Sam 15:3)	He spared the king and kept some of the plunder (1 Sam 15:8-9)	God promised to end his reign (1 Sam 15:16-26)
Uzzah	Only a priest can touch the Tabernacle's furnishings and articles (Num 4:15)	He touched the Ark of the Covenant (2 Sam 6:6)	He died instantly (2 Sam 6:7)
Uzziah	Only the priests can offer incense in the Temple or Tabernacle sanctuary (Num 16:39-40; 18:7)	He entered the sanctuary in the Temple, where only priests were allowed to go (2 Chron 26:16-18)	He became a leper (2 Chron 26:19)

7½ feet deep and about 45 feet in circumference.* 3It was
encircled just below its rim by two rows of figures that resembled oxen. There were about six oxen per foot* all the
way around, and they were cast as part of the basin.
4The Sea was placed on a base of twelve bronze oxen,
all facing outward. Three faced north, three faced west,
three faced south, and three faced east, and the Sea
rested on them. 5The walls of the Sea were about three
inches* thick, and its rim flared out like a cup and resembled a water lily blossom. It could hold about 16,500 gallons* of water.
6He also made ten smaller basins for washing the utensils for the burnt offerings. He set five on the south side
and five on the north. But the priests washed themselves
in the Sea.
7He then cast ten gold lampstands according to the
specifications that had been given, and he put them in
the Temple. Five were placed against the south wall, and
five were placed against the north wall.
8He also built ten tables and placed them in the Temple,
five along the south wall and five along the north wall.
Then he molded 100 gold basins.
9He then built a courtyard for the priests, and also the
large outer courtyard. He made doors for the courtyard
entrances and overlaid them with bronze. 10The great
bronze basin called the Sea was placed near the southeast corner of the Temple.
11Huram-abi also made the necessary washbasins,
shovels, and bowls.

So at last Huram-abi completed everything King Solomon had assigned him to make for the Temple of God:

12 the two pillars;
the two bowl-shaped capitals on top of the pillars;
the two networks of interwoven chains that decorated the capitals;
13 the 400 pomegranates that hung from the chains on the capitals (two rows of pomegranates for each of the chain networks that decorated the capitals on top of the pillars);

4:2 Hebrew *10 cubits* [4.6 meters] *across . . . 5 cubits* [2.3 meters] *deep and 30 cubits* [13.8 meters] *in circumference.* **4:3** Or *20 oxen per meter;* Hebrew reads *10 per cubit.* **4:5a** Hebrew *a handbreadth* [8 centimeters]. **4:5b** Hebrew *3,000 baths* [63 kiloliters].

14 the water carts holding the basins;
15 the Sea and the twelve oxen under it;
16 the ash buckets, the shovels, the meat hooks, and all
the related articles.

Huram-abi made all these things of burnished bronze for
the Temple of the LORD, just as King Solomon had directed. 17The king had them cast in clay molds in the Jordan Valley between Succoth and Zarethan.* 18Solomon
used such great quantities of bronze that its weight could
not be determined.

19Solomon also made all the furnishings for the Temple of God:

the gold altar;
the tables for the Bread of the Presence;
20 the lampstands and their lamps of solid gold, to burn
in front of the Most Holy Place as prescribed;
21 the flower decorations, lamps, and tongs—all of the
purest gold;
22 the lamp snuffers, bowls, dishes, and incense
burners—all of solid gold;
the doors for the entrances to the Most Holy Place
and the main room of the Temple, overlaid with
gold.

5

So Solomon finished all his work on the Temple of
the LORD. Then he brought all the gifts his father, David,
had dedicated—the silver, the gold, and the various articles—and he stored them in the treasuries of the Temple
of God.

THE ARK BROUGHT TO THE TEMPLE

2Solomon then summoned to Jerusalem the elders of Israel and all the heads of tribes—the leaders of the ancestral families of Israel. They were to bring the Ark of the
LORD's Covenant to the Temple from its location in the
City of David, also known as Zion. 3So all the men of Israel
assembled before the king at the annual Festival of Shelters, which is held in early autumn.*

4When all the elders of Israel arrived, the Levites
picked up the Ark. 5The priests and Levites brought up
the Ark along with the special tent* and all the sacred
items that had been in it. 6There, before the Ark, King
Solomon and the entire community of Israel sacrificed
so many sheep, goats, and cattle that no one could keep
count!

7Then the priests carried the Ark of the LORD's Covenant into the inner sanctuary of the Temple—the Most
Holy Place—and placed it beneath the wings of the cherubim. 8The cherubim spread their wings over the Ark,
forming a canopy over the Ark and its carrying poles.
9These poles were so long that their ends could be seen
from the Temple's main room—the Holy Place*—but not
from the outside. They are still there to this day.
10Nothing was in the Ark except the two stone tablets that
Moses had placed in it at Mount Sinai,* where the LORD
made a covenant with the people of Israel when they left
Egypt.

11Then the priests left the Holy Place. All the priests
who were present had purified themselves, whether or
not they were on duty that day. 12And the Levites who
were musicians—Asaph, Heman, Jeduthun, and all their
sons and brothers—were dressed in fine linen robes and
stood at the east side of the altar playing cymbals, lyres,
and harps. They were joined by 120 priests who were
playing trumpets. 13The trumpeters and singers performed together in unison to praise and give thanks to
the LORD. Accompanied by trumpets, cymbals, and other
instruments, they raised their voices and praised the
LORD with these words:

"He is good!
His faithful love endures forever!"

At that moment a thick cloud filled the Temple of the
LORD. 14The priests could not continue their service because of the cloud, for the glorious presence of the LORD
filled the Temple of God.

ANY TIME IS RIGHT 5:2-14

Solomon ended the Temple project with the biggest worship service ever. The whole nation was invited to Jerusalem to celebrate the completion of the Temple. When you complete a task, is praise your first order of business? Praise isn't reserved for completing temples or other tasks that we think are "for" God. Any time is the right time to give God some praise. ■

6

SOLOMON PRAISES THE LORD

Then Solomon prayed, "O LORD, you have said that you
would live in a thick cloud of darkness. 2Now I have built a
glorious Temple for you, a place where you can live forever!"

3Then the king turned around to the entire community
of Israel standing before him and gave this blessing:
4"Praise the LORD, the God of Israel, who has kept the
promise he made to my father, David. For he told my father, 5'From the day I brought my people out of the land
of Egypt, I have never chosen a city among any of the
tribes of Israel as the place where a Temple should be
built to honor my name. Nor have I chosen a king to lead
my people Israel. 6But now I have chosen Jerusalem as the
place for my name to be honored, and I have chosen David to be king over my people Israel.'"

7Then Solomon said, "My father, David, wanted to
build this Temple to honor the name of the LORD, the God
of Israel. 8But the LORD told him, 'You wanted to build the

4:17 As in parallel text at 1 Kgs 7:46; Hebrew reads *Zeredah*. **5:3** Hebrew *at the festival that is in the seventh month.* The Festival of Shelters began on the fifteenth day of the seventh month of the ancient Hebrew lunar calendar. This day occurred in late September, October, or early November. **5:5** Hebrew *the Tent of Meeting;* i.e., the tent mentioned in 2 Sam 6:17 and 1 Chr 16:1. **5:9** As in parallel text at 1 Kgs 8:8; Hebrew reads *from the Ark in front of the Most Holy Place.* **5:10** Hebrew *Horeb*, another name for Sinai.

Temple to honor my name. Your intention is good, 9but
you are not the one to do it. One of your own sons will
build the Temple to honor me.'
10"And now the LORD has fulfilled the promise he
made, for I have become king in my father's place, and
now I sit on the throne of Israel, just as the LORD promised. I have built this Temple to honor the name of the
LORD, the God of Israel. 11There I have placed the Ark,
which contains the covenant that the LORD made with the
people of Israel."

SOLOMON'S PRAYER OF DEDICATION

12Then Solomon stood before the altar of the LORD in
front of the entire community of Israel, and he lifted his
hands in prayer. 13Now Solomon had made a bronze platform 7½ feet long, 7½ feet wide, and 4½ feet high* and
had placed it at the center of the Temple's outer courtyard. He stood on the platform, and then he knelt in front
of the entire community of Israel and lifted his hands toward heaven. 14He prayed,

"O LORD, God of Israel, there is no God like you in
all of heaven and earth. You keep your covenant
and show unfailing love to all who walk before you
in wholehearted devotion. 15You have kept your
promise to your servant David, my father. You made
that promise with your own mouth, and with your
own hands you have fulfilled it today.
16"And now, O LORD, God of Israel, carry out the
additional promise you made to your servant David,
my father. For you said to him, 'If your descendants
guard their behavior and faithfully follow my Law as
you have done, one of them will always sit on the
throne of Israel.' 17Now, O LORD, God of Israel, fulfill
this promise to your servant David.

AMAZING GRACE 6:18

Solomon was amazed that God was willing to live on earth—a planet he created. What's even more amazing is the fact that Jesus, the Son of God, chose to live on earth as a man. Some would call that amazing grace. What would you call it? ■

18"But will God really live on earth among people?
Why, even the highest heavens cannot contain
you. How much less this Temple I have built!
19Nevertheless, listen to my prayer and my plea,
O LORD my God. Hear the cry and the prayer that your
servant is making to you. 20May you watch over this
Temple day and night, this place where you have said
you would put your name. May you always hear the
prayers I make toward this place. 21May you hear the
humble and earnest requests from me and your
people Israel when we pray toward this place. Yes,
hear us from heaven where you live, and when you
hear, forgive.

FAR AWAY 6:21-39

In his prayer, Solomon acknowledged God's willingness to forgive his people when they admitted their wrongdoing. Have you ever felt far away from God—separated by personal problems and feelings of failure? Romans 8:38 mentions that "nothing can ever separate us from God's love." Why is that true? It's true because Jesus made forgiveness an open door you can always walk through. All you have to do is believe. ■

22"If someone wrongs another person and is
required to take an oath of innocence in front of
your altar at this Temple, 23then hear from heaven
and judge between your servants—the accuser and
the accused. Pay back the guilty as they deserve.
Acquit the innocent because of their innocence.
24"If your people Israel are defeated by their
enemies because they have sinned against you, and
if they turn back and acknowledge your name and
pray to you here in this Temple, 25then hear from
heaven and forgive the sin of your people Israel and
return them to this land you gave to them and to their
ancestors.
26"If the skies are shut up and there is no rain
because your people have sinned against you, and if
they pray toward this Temple and acknowledge your
name and turn from their sins because you have
punished them, 27then hear from heaven and forgive
the sins of your servants, your people Israel. Teach
them to follow the right path, and send rain on your
land that you have given to your people as their
special possession.
28"If there is a famine in the land or a plague or
crop disease or attacks of locusts or caterpillars, or
if your people's enemies are in the land besieging
their towns—whatever disaster or disease there is—
29and if your people Israel pray about their troubles
or sorrow, raising their hands toward this Temple,
30then hear from heaven where you live, and forgive.
Give your people what their actions deserve, for you
alone know each human heart. 31Then they will fear
you and walk in your ways as long as they live in the
land you gave to our ancestors.
32"In the future, foreigners who do not belong to
your people Israel will hear of you. They will come
from distant lands when they hear of your great
name and your strong hand and your powerful arm.
And when they pray toward this Temple, 33then hear
from heaven where you live, and grant what they ask
of you. In this way, all the people of the earth will
come to know and fear you, just as your own people
Israel do. They, too, will know that this Temple I have
built honors your name.
34"If your people go out where you send them to
fight their enemies, and if they pray to you by turning
toward this city you have chosen and toward this

6:13 Hebrew *5 cubits* [2.3 meters] *long, 5 cubits wide, and 3 cubits* [1.4 meters] *high.*

Temple I have built to honor your name, 35then hear
their prayers from heaven and uphold their cause.
36"If they sin against you—and who has never
sinned?—you might become angry with them and let
their enemies conquer them and take them captive to
a foreign land far away or near. 37But in that land of
exile, they might turn to you in repentance and pray,
'We have sinned, done evil, and acted wickedly.' 38If
they turn to you with their whole heart and soul in
the land of their captivity and pray toward the land
you gave to their ancestors—toward this city you have
chosen, and toward this Temple I have built to honor
your name—39then hear their prayers and their
petitions from heaven where you live, and uphold
their cause. Forgive your people who have sinned
against you.
40"O my God, may your eyes be open and your ears
attentive to all the prayers made to you in this place.

41 "And now arise, O LORD God, and enter your
resting place,
along with the Ark, the symbol of your power.
May your priests, O LORD God, be clothed with
salvation;
may your loyal servants rejoice in your
goodness.
42 O LORD God, do not reject the king you have
anointed.
Remember your unfailing love for your servant
David."

7 THE DEDICATION OF THE TEMPLE

When Solomon finished praying, fire flashed down
from heaven and burned up the burnt offerings and
sacrifices, and the glorious presence of the LORD filled
the Temple. 2The priests could not en-
ter the Temple of the LORD because
the glorious presence of the LORD
filled it. 3When all the people of Israel
saw the fire coming down and the glorious presence of the LORD filling the
Temple, they fell face down on the
ground and worshiped and praised
the LORD, saying,

"He is good!
His faithful love endures
forever!"

4Then the king and all the people offered sacrifices to the LORD. 5King Solomon offered a sacrifice of 22,000
cattle and 120,000 sheep and goats.
And so the king and all the people dedicated the Temple of God. 6The priests took their assigned positions, and so did the Levites who were singing,
"His faithful love endures forever!" They accompanied
the singing with music from the instruments King David
had made for praising the LORD. Across from the Levites,
the priests blew the trumpets, while all Israel stood.
7Solomon then consecrated the central area of the
courtyard in front of the LORD's Temple. He offered
burnt offerings and the fat of peace offerings there, because the bronze altar he had built could not hold all the
burnt offerings, grain offerings, and sacrificial fat.
8For the next seven days Solomon and all Israel celebrated the Festival of Shelters.* A large congregation had
gathered from as far away as Lebo-hamath in the north
and the Brook of Egypt in the south. 9On the eighth day
they had a closing ceremony, for they had celebrated the
dedication of the altar for seven days and the Festival of
Shelters for seven days. 10Then at the end of the celebration,* Solomon sent the people home. They were all joyful and glad because the LORD had been so good to David
and to Solomon and to his people Israel.

> **STEPS TO FORGIVENESS 7:12-22**
>
> **In chapter 6, Solomon asked God to forgive his people when they messed up. God answered with three conditions for forgiveness: (1) humble yourself by admitting what you did wrong, (2) ask God to forgive you, and (3) reject harmful habits. Owning up to a wrong is more than talk—it's changed behavior and a commitment to doing what's right. Are you committed? ■**

> If my people . . . will humble themselves . . . and turn from their wicked ways, I will . . . forgive their sins and restore their land.
>
> *2 CHRONICLES 7:14*

THE LORD'S RESPONSE TO SOLOMON

11So Solomon finished the Temple of the LORD, as well as
the royal palace. He completed everything he had
planned to do in the construction of the Temple and the
palace. 12Then one night the LORD ap-
peared to Solomon and said,

"I have heard your prayer and have
chosen this Temple as the place for
making sacrifices. 13At times I might
shut up the heavens so that no rain
falls, or command grasshoppers to
devour your crops, or send plagues
among you. 14Then if my people who
are called by my name will humble
themselves and pray and seek my
face and turn from their wicked ways,
I will hear from heaven and will
forgive their sins and restore their
land. 15My eyes will be open and my
ears attentive to every prayer made
in this place. 16For I have chosen this
Temple and set it apart to be holy—a
place where my name will be honored forever. I will
always watch over it, for it is dear to my heart.
17"As for you, if you faithfully follow me as David

7:8 Hebrew *the festival* (also in 7:9); see note on 5:3. **7:10** Hebrew *Then on the twenty-third day of the seventh month.* This day of the ancient Hebrew lunar calendar occurred in October or early November.

your father did, obeying all my commands, decrees,
and regulations, 18then I will establish the throne of
your dynasty. For I made this covenant with your
father, David, when I said, 'One of your descendants
will always rule over Israel.'
19"But if you or your descendants abandon me and
disobey the decrees and commands I have given you,
and if you serve and worship other gods, 20then I will
uproot the people from this land that I have given
them. I will reject this Temple that I have made
holy to honor my name. I will make it an object of
mockery and ridicule among the nations. 21And
though this Temple is impressive now, all who pass
by will be appalled. They will ask, 'Why did the LORD
do such terrible things to this land and to this
Temple?'
22"And the answer will be, 'Because his people
abandoned the LORD, the God of their ancestors, who
brought them out of Egypt, and they worshiped other
gods instead and bowed down to them. That is why
he has brought all these disasters on them.'"

8 SOLOMON'S MANY ACHIEVEMENTS

It took Solomon twenty years to build the LORD's Temple
and his own royal palace. At the end of that time, 2Solo-
mon turned his attention to rebuilding the towns that
King Hiram* had given him, and he settled Israelites in
them.
3Solomon also fought against the town of Hamath-
zobah and conquered it. 4He rebuilt Tadmor in the wilderness and built towns in the region of Hamath as
supply centers. 5He fortified the towns of Upper Beth-
horon and Lower Beth-horon, rebuilding their walls and
installing barred gates. 6He also rebuilt Baalath and other
supply centers and constructed towns where his chariots
and horses* could be stationed. He built everything he
desired in Jerusalem and Lebanon and throughout his
entire realm.
7There were still some people living in the land who
were not Israelites, including the Hittites, Amorites, Perizzites, Hivites, and Jebusites. 8These were descendants
of the nations whom the people of Israel had not destroyed. So Solomon conscripted them for his labor
force, and they serve in the labor force to this day. 9But
Solomon did not conscript any of the Israelites for his labor force. Instead, he assigned them to serve as fighting
men, officers in his army, commanders of his chariots,
and charioteers. 10King Solomon appointed 250 of them
to supervise the people.
11Solomon moved his wife, Pharaoh's daughter, from
the City of David to the new palace he had built for her.
He said, "My wife must not live in King David's palace, for
the Ark of the LORD has been there, and it is holy ground."
12Then Solomon presented burnt offerings to the
LORD on the altar he had built for him in front of the entry
room of the Temple. 13He offered the sacrifices for the
Sabbaths, the new moon festivals, and the three annual
festivals—the Passover celebration, the Festival of Harvest,* and the Festival of Shelters—as Moses had
commanded.
14In assigning the priests to their duties, Solomon followed the regulations of his father, David. He also assigned the Levites to lead the people in praise and to
assist the priests in their daily duties. And he assigned the
gatekeepers to their gates by their divisions, following
the commands of David, the man of God. 15Solomon did
not deviate in any way from David's commands concerning the priests and Levites and the treasuries.
16So Solomon made sure that all the work related
to building the Temple of the LORD was carried out,
from the day its foundation was laid to the day of its
completion.
17Later Solomon went to Ezion-geber and Elath,* ports
along the shore of the Red Sea* in the land of Edom. 18Hi-
ram sent him ships commanded by his own officers and
manned by experienced crews of sailors. These ships
sailed to Ophir with Solomon's men and brought back to
Solomon almost seventeen tons* of gold.

THE GOD BEHIND IT ALL 9:1-8

The queen of Sheba had heard about Solomon's wisdom, but she was overwhelmed when she saw for herself the proof of that wisdom. She could see the God behind Solomon's incredible wisdom and wealth. As people get to know you, do they catch a glimpse of the God behind you? Your life is your most powerful witness. ■

9 VISIT OF THE QUEEN OF SHEBA

When the queen of Sheba heard of Solomon's fame, she
came to Jerusalem to test him with hard questions. She
arrived with a large group of attendants and a great caravan of camels loaded with spices, large quantities of gold,
and precious jewels. When she met with Solomon, she
talked with him about everything she had on her mind.
2Solomon had answers for all her questions; nothing was
too hard for him to explain to her. 3When the queen of
Sheba realized how wise Solomon was, and when she saw
the palace he had built, 4she was overwhelmed. She was
also amazed at the food on his tables, the organization of
his officials and their splendid clothing, the cup-bearers
and their robes, and the burnt offerings Solomon made
at the Temple of the LORD.
5She exclaimed to the king, "Everything I heard in my
country about your achievements* and wisdom is true! 6I
didn't believe what was said until I arrived here and saw it
with my own eyes. In fact, I had not heard the half of your
great wisdom! It is far beyond what I was told. 7How happy
your people must be! What a privilege for your officials

8:2 Hebrew *Huram,* a variant spelling of Hiram; also in 8:18. **8:6** Or *and charioteers.* **8:13** Or *Festival of Weeks.* **8:17a** As in Greek version (see also 2 Kgs 14:22; 16:6); Hebrew reads *Eloth,* a variant spelling of Elath. **8:17b** As in parallel text at 1 Kgs 9:26; Hebrew reads *the sea.* **8:18** Hebrew *450 talents* [15.3 metric tons]. **9:5** Hebrew *your words.*

to stand here day after day, listening to your wisdom! 8 Praise the LORD your God, who delights in you and has placed you on the throne as king to rule for him. Because God loves Israel and desires this kingdom to last forever, he has made you king over them so you can rule with justice and righteousness."

9 Then she gave the king a gift of 9,000 pounds* of gold, great quantities of spices, and precious jewels. Never before had there been spices as fine as those the queen of Sheba gave to King Solomon.

10 (In addition, the crews of Hiram and Solomon brought gold from Ophir, and they also brought red sandalwood* and precious jewels. 11 The king used the sandalwood to make steps* for the Temple of the LORD and the royal palace, and to construct lyres and harps for the musicians. Never before had such beautiful things been seen in Judah.)

12 King Solomon gave the queen of Sheba whatever she asked for—gifts of greater value than the gifts she had given him. Then she and all her attendants returned to their own land.

SOLOMON'S WEALTH AND SPLENDOR

13 Each year Solomon received about 25 tons* of gold. 14 This did not include the additional revenue he received from merchants and traders. All the kings of Arabia and the governors of the provinces also brought gold and silver to Solomon.

15 King Solomon made 200 large shields of hammered gold, each weighing more than 15 pounds.* 16 He also made 300 smaller shields of hammered gold, each weighing more than 7½ pounds.* The king placed these shields in the Palace of the Forest of Lebanon.

17 Then the king made a huge throne, decorated with ivory and overlaid with pure gold. 18 The throne had six steps, with a footstool of gold. There were armrests on both sides of the seat, and the figure of a lion stood on each side of the throne. 19 There were also twelve other lions, one standing on each end of the six steps. No other throne in all the world could be compared with it!

20 All of King Solomon's drinking cups were solid gold, as were all the utensils in the Palace of the Forest of Lebanon. They were not made of silver, for silver was considered worthless in Solomon's day!

21 The king had a fleet of trading ships* manned by the sailors sent by Hiram.* Once every three years the ships returned, loaded with gold, silver, ivory, apes, and peacocks.*

22 So King Solomon became richer and wiser than any other king on earth. 23 Kings from every nation came to consult him and to hear the wisdom God had given him. 24 Year after year everyone who visited brought him gifts of silver and gold, clothing, weapons, spices, horses, and mules.

25 Solomon had 4,000 stalls for his horses and chariots, and he had 12,000 horses.* He stationed some of them in the chariot cities, and some near him in Jerusalem. 26 He ruled over all the kings from the Euphrates River* in the north to the land of the Philistines and the border of Egypt in the south. 27 The king made silver as plentiful in Jerusalem as stone. And valuable cedar timber was as common as the sycamore-fig trees that grow in the foothills of Judah.* 28 Solomon's horses were imported from Egypt* and many other countries.

SUMMARY OF SOLOMON'S REIGN

29 The rest of the events of Solomon's reign, from beginning to end, are recorded in *The Record of Nathan the Prophet,* and *The Prophecy of Ahijah from Shiloh,* and also in *The Visions of Iddo the Seer,* concerning Jeroboam son of Nebat. 30 Solomon ruled in Jerusalem over all Israel for forty years. 31 When he died, he was buried in the City of David, named for his father. Then his son Rehoboam became the next king.

PEERS 10:1-14

Rehoboam messed up when he followed his friends' advice, instead of that of the older advisers. Like Rehoboam, many live by the philosophy that *If I can't trust my friends, who can I trust?* Is that how you feel? But friends don't always see the big picture. The best advice often comes from people with the most experience. Are you willing to listen? ■

10 THE NORTHERN TRIBES REVOLT

Rehoboam went to Shechem, where all Israel had gathered to make him king. 2 When Jeroboam son of Nebat heard of this, he returned from Egypt, for he had fled to Egypt to escape from King Solomon. 3 The leaders of Israel summoned him, and Jeroboam and all Israel went to speak with Rehoboam. 4 "Your father was a hard master," they said. "Lighten the harsh labor demands and heavy taxes that your father imposed on us. Then we will be your loyal subjects."

5 Rehoboam replied, "Come back in three days for my answer." So the people went away.

6 Then King Rehoboam discussed the matter with the older men who had counseled his father, Solomon. "What is your advice?" he asked. "How should I answer these people?"

7 The older counselors replied, "If you are good to these people and do your best to please them and give them a favorable answer, they will always be your loyal subjects."

8 But Rehoboam rejected the advice of the older men and instead asked the opinion of the young men who had grown up with him and were now his advisers. 9 "What is your advice?" he asked them. "How should I answer these people who want me to lighten the burdens imposed by my father?"

9:9 Hebrew *120 talents* [4,000 kilograms]. 9:10 Hebrew *algum wood* (also in 9:11); perhaps a variant spelling of *almug*. Compare parallel text at 1 Kgs 10:11-12. 9:11 Or *gateways*. The meaning of the Hebrew is uncertain. 9:13 Hebrew *666 talents* [23 metric tons]. 9:15 Hebrew *600 shekels* [6.8 kilograms]. 9:16 Hebrew *300 shekels* [3.4 kilograms]. 9:21a Hebrew *fleet of ships that could sail to Tarshish*. 9:21b Hebrew *Huram*, a variant spelling of Hiram. 9:21c Or *and baboons*. 9:25 Or *12,000 charioteers*. 9:26 Hebrew *the river*. 9:27 Hebrew *the Shephelah*. 9:28 Possibly *Muzur*, a district near Cilicia.

10The young men replied, "This is what you should tell those complainers who want a lighter burden: 'My little finger is thicker than my father's waist! 11Yes, my father laid heavy burdens on you, but I'm going to make them even heavier! My father beat you with whips, but I will beat you with scorpions!'"

12Three days later Jeroboam and all the people returned to hear Rehoboam's decision, just as the king had ordered. 13But Rehoboam spoke harshly to them, for he rejected the advice of the older counselors 14and followed the counsel of his younger advisers. He told the people, "My father laid* heavy burdens on you, but I'm going to make them even heavier! My father beat you with whips, but I will beat you with scorpions!"

15So the king paid no attention to the people. This turn of events was the will of God, for it fulfilled the LORD's message to Jeroboam son of Nebat through the prophet Ahijah from Shiloh.

16When all Israel realized* that the king had refused to listen to them, they responded,

"Down with the dynasty of David!
  We have no interest in the son of Jesse.
Back to your homes, O Israel!
  Look out for your own house, O David!"

So all the people of Israel returned home. 17But Rehoboam continued to rule over the Israelites who lived in the towns of Judah.

18King Rehoboam sent Adoniram,* who was in charge of the labor force, to restore order, but the people of Israel stoned him to death. When this news reached King Rehoboam, he quickly jumped into his chariot and fled to Jerusalem. 19And to this day the northern tribes of Israel have refused to be ruled by a descendant of David.

11

SHEMAIAH'S PROPHECY

When Rehoboam arrived at Jerusalem, he mobilized the men of Judah and Benjamin—180,000 select troops—to fight against Israel and to restore the kingdom to himself.

2But the LORD said to Shemaiah, the man of God, 3"Say to Rehoboam son of Solomon, king of Judah, and to all the Israelites in Judah and Benjamin: 4'This is what the LORD says: Do not fight against your relatives. Go back home, for what has happened is my doing!'" So they obeyed the message of the LORD and did not fight against Jeroboam.

REHOBOAM FORTIFIES JUDAH

5Rehoboam remained in Jerusalem and fortified various towns for the defense of Judah. 6He built up Bethlehem, Etam, Tekoa, 7Beth-zur, Soco, Adullam, 8Gath, Mareshah, Ziph, 9Adoraim, Lachish, Azekah, 10Zorah, Aijalon, and Hebron. These became the fortified towns of Judah and Benjamin. 11Rehoboam strengthened their defenses and stationed commanders in them, and he stored supplies of food, olive oil, and wine. 12He also put shields and spears in these towns as a further safety measure. So only Judah and Benjamin remained under his control.

13But all the priests and Levites living among the northern tribes of Israel sided with Rehoboam. 14The Levites even abandoned their pasturelands and property and moved to Judah and Jerusalem, because Jeroboam and his sons would not allow them to serve the LORD as priests. 15Jeroboam appointed his own priests to serve at the pagan shrines, where they worshiped the goat and calf idols he had made. 16From all the tribes of Israel, those who sincerely wanted to worship the LORD, the God of Israel, followed the Levites to Jerusalem, where they could offer sacrifices to the LORD, the God of their ancestors. 17This strengthened the kingdom of Judah, and for three years they supported Rehoboam son of Solomon, for during those years they faithfully followed in the footsteps of David and Solomon.

REHOBOAM'S FAMILY

18Rehoboam married his cousin Mahalath, the daughter of David's son Jerimoth and of Abihail, the daughter of Eliab son of Jesse. 19Mahalath had three sons—Jeush, Shemariah, and Zaham.

20Later Rehoboam married another cousin, Maacah, the daughter of Absalom. Maacah gave birth to Abijah, Attai, Ziza, and Shelomith. 21Rehoboam loved Maacah more than any of his other wives and concubines. In all, he had eighteen wives and sixty concubines, and they gave birth to twenty-eight sons and sixty daughters.

22Rehoboam appointed Maacah's son Abijah as leader among the princes, making it clear that he would be the next king. 23Rehoboam also wisely gave responsibilities to his other sons and stationed some of them in the fortified towns throughout the land of Judah and Benjamin. He provided them with generous provisions, and he found many wives for them.

GOOD TIMES 12:1

At the height of his popularity and power, Rehoboam started to ignore God. Often it is more difficult to be a believer in good times than in bad. Tough times push us toward God; but success can make us feel self-sufficient and self-satisfied. When everything is going right, how will you guard your faith? ■

12

EGYPT INVADES JUDAH

But when Rehoboam was firmly established and strong, he abandoned the Law of the LORD, and all Israel followed him in this sin. 2Because they were unfaithful to the LORD, King Shishak of Egypt came up and attacked Jerusalem in the fifth year of King Rehoboam's reign. 3He came with 1,200 chariots, 60,000 horses,* and a count-

10:14 As in Greek version and many Hebrew manuscripts (see also 1 Kgs 12:14); Masoretic Text reads *I will lay.* **10:16** As in Syriac version, Latin Vulgate, and many Hebrew manuscripts (see also 1 Kgs 12:16); Masoretic Text lacks *realized.* **10:18** Hebrew *Hadoram,* a variant spelling of Adoniram; compare 1 Kgs 4:6; 5:14; 12:18. **12:3a** Or *charioteers,* or *horsemen.*

less army of foot soldiers, including Libyans, Sukkites, and Ethiopians.* 4Shishak conquered Judah's fortified towns and then advanced to attack Jerusalem.

5The prophet Shemaiah then met with Rehoboam and Judah's leaders, who had all fled to Jerusalem because of Shishak. Shemaiah told them, "This is what the LORD says: You have abandoned me, so I am abandoning you to Shishak."

6Then the leaders of Israel and the king humbled themselves and said, "The LORD is right in doing this to us!"

7When the LORD saw their change of heart, he gave this message to Shemaiah: "Since the people have humbled themselves, I will not completely destroy them and will soon give them some relief. I will not use Shishak to pour out my anger on Jerusalem. 8But they will become his subjects, so they will know the difference between serving me and serving earthly rulers."

9So King Shishak of Egypt came up and attacked Jerusalem. He ransacked the treasuries of the LORD's Temple and the royal palace; he stole everything, including all the gold shields Solomon had made. 10King Rehoboam later replaced them with bronze shields as substitutes, and he entrusted them to the care of the commanders of the guard who protected the entrance to the royal palace. 11Whenever the king went to the Temple of the LORD, the guards would also take the shields and then return them to the guardroom. 12Because Rehoboam humbled himself, the LORD's anger was turned away, and he did not destroy him completely. There were still some good things in the land of Judah.

SUMMARY OF REHOBOAM'S REIGN

13King Rehoboam firmly established himself in Jerusalem and continued to rule. He was forty-one years old when he became king, and he reigned seventeen years in Jerusalem, the city the LORD had chosen from among all the tribes of Israel as the place to honor his name. Rehoboam's mother was Naamah, a woman from Ammon. 14But he was an evil king, for he did not seek the LORD with all his heart.

15The rest of the events of Rehoboam's reign, from beginning to end, are recorded in *The Record of Shemaiah the Prophet* and *The Record of Iddo the Seer,* which are part of the genealogical record. Rehoboam and Jeroboam were continually at war with each other. 16When Rehoboam died, he was buried in the City of David. Then his son Abijah became the next king.

13 ABIJAH'S WAR WITH JEROBOAM

Abijah began to rule over Judah in the eighteenth year of Jeroboam's reign in Israel. 2He reigned in Jerusalem three years. His mother was Maacah,* the daughter of Uriel from Gibeah.

Then war broke out between Abijah and Jeroboam. 3Judah, led by King Abijah, fielded 400,000 select warriors, while Jeroboam mustered 800,000 select troops from Israel.

4When the army of Judah arrived in the hill country of Ephraim, Abijah stood on Mount Zemaraim and shouted to Jeroboam and all Israel: "Listen to me! 5Don't you realize that the LORD, the God of Israel, made a lasting covenant* with David, giving him and his descendants the throne of Israel forever? 6Yet Jeroboam son of Nebat, a mere servant of David's son Solomon, rebelled against his master. 7Then a whole gang of scoundrels joined him, defying Solomon's son Rehoboam when he was young and inexperienced and could not stand up to them.

8"Do you really think you can stand against the kingdom of the LORD that is led by the descendants of David? You may have a vast army, and you have those gold calves that Jeroboam made as your gods. 9But you have chased away the priests of the LORD (the descendants of Aaron) and the Levites, and you have appointed your own priests, just like the pagan nations. You let anyone become a priest these days! Whoever comes to be dedicated with a young bull and seven rams can become a priest of these so-called gods of yours!

10"But as for us, the LORD is our God, and we have not abandoned him. Only the descendants of Aaron serve the LORD as priests, and the Levites alone may help them in their work. 11They present burnt offerings and fragrant incense to the LORD every morning and evening. They place the Bread of the Presence on the holy table, and they light the gold lampstand every evening. We are following the instructions of the LORD our God, but you have abandoned him. 12So you see, God is with us. He is our leader. His priests blow their trumpets and lead us into battle against you. O people of Israel, do not fight against the LORD, the God of your ancestors, for you will not succeed!"

13Meanwhile, Jeroboam had secretly sent part of his army around behind the men of Judah to ambush them. 14When Judah realized that they were being attacked from the front and the rear, they cried out to the LORD for help. Then the priests blew the trumpets, 15and the men of Judah began to shout. At the sound of their battle cry, God defeated Jeroboam and all Israel and routed them before Abijah and the army of Judah.

16The Israelite army fled from Judah, and God handed them over to Judah in defeat. 17Abijah and his army inflicted heavy losses on them; 500,000 of Israel's select troops were killed that day. 18So Judah defeated Israel on that occasion because they trusted in the LORD, the God of their ancestors. 19Abijah and his army pursued Jeroboam's troops and captured some of his towns, including Bethel, Jeshanah, and Ephron, along with their surrounding villages.

20So Jeroboam of Israel never regained his power during Abijah's lifetime, and finally the LORD struck him down and he died. 21Meanwhile, Abijah of Judah grew more and more powerful. He married fourteen wives and had twenty-two sons and sixteen daughters.

22The rest of the events of Abijah's reign, including his words and deeds, are recorded in *The Commentary of Iddo the Prophet.*

12:3b Hebrew *and Cushites.* 13:2 As in most Greek manuscripts and Syriac version (see also 2 Chr 11:20-21; 1 Kgs 15:2); Hebrew reads *Micaiah,* a variant spelling of Maacah. 13:5 Hebrew *a covenant of salt.*

14

EARLY YEARS OF ASA'S REIGN

1*When Abijah died, he was buried in the City of David.
Then his son Asa became the next king. There was peace
in the land for ten years. 2*Asa did what was pleasing and
good in the sight of the LORD his God. 3He removed the
foreign altars and the pagan shrines. He smashed the sacred pillars and cut down the Asherah poles. 4He commanded the people of Judah to seek the LORD, the God of
their ancestors, and to obey his law and his commands.
5Asa also removed the pagan shrines, as well as the incense altars from every one of Judah's towns. So Asa's
kingdom enjoyed a period of peace. 6During those peaceful years, he was able to build up the fortified towns
throughout Judah. No one tried to make war against him
at this time, for the LORD was giving him rest from his enemies.

7Asa told the people of Judah, "Let us build towns and
fortify them with walls, towers, gates, and bars. The land
is still ours because we sought the LORD our God, and he
has given us peace on every side." So they went ahead
with these projects and brought them to completion.

8King Asa had an army of 300,000 warriors from the
tribe of Judah, armed with large shields and spears. He
also had an army of 280,000 warriors from the tribe of
Benjamin, armed with small shields and bows. Both armies were composed of well-trained fighting men.

BE PREPARED 14:1-8

King Asa chose to build up Judah's defenses during a time of peace. Times of peace are not just for resting. They allow us to prepare for times of trouble. The best decisions about what to do when temptations arise are made with a cool head, long before the heat of temptation is upon us. What are you doing now to build your defenses? ■

9Once an Ethiopian* named Zerah attacked Judah
with an army of 1,000,000 men* and 300 chariots. They
advanced to the town of Mareshah, 10so Asa deployed his
armies for battle in the valley north of Mareshah.*
11Then Asa cried out to the LORD his God, "O LORD, no one
but you can help the powerless against the mighty! Help
us, O LORD our God, for we trust in you alone. It is in your
name that we have come against this vast horde. O LORD,
you are our God; do not let mere men prevail against you!"

12So the LORD defeated the Ethiopians* in the presence of Asa and the army of Judah, and the enemy fled.
13Asa and his army pursued them as far as Gerar, and so
many Ethiopians fell that they were unable to rally. They
were destroyed by the LORD and his army, and the army
of Judah carried off a vast amount of plunder.

14While they were at Gerar, they attacked all the towns
in that area, and terror from the LORD came upon the
people there. As a result, a vast amount of plunder was
taken from these towns, too. 15They also attacked the
camps of herdsmen and captured many sheep, goats, and
camels before finally returning to Jerusalem.

15

ASA'S RELIGIOUS REFORMS

Then the Spirit of God came upon Azariah son of Oded,
2and he went out to meet King Asa as he was returning
from the battle. "Listen to me, Asa!" he shouted. "Listen,
all you people of Judah and Benjamin! The LORD will stay
with you as long as you stay with him! Whenever you seek
him, you will find him. But if you abandon him, he will
abandon you. 3For a long time Israel was without the true
God, without a priest to teach them, and without the Law
to instruct them. 4But whenever they were in trouble and
turned to the LORD, the God of Israel, and sought him out,
they found him.

5"During those dark times, it was not safe to travel.
Problems troubled the people of every land. 6Nation
fought against nation, and city against city, for God was
troubling them with every kind of problem. 7But as for
you, be strong and courageous, for your work will be
rewarded."

8When Asa heard this message from Azariah the
prophet,* he took courage and removed all the detestable idols from the land of Judah and Benjamin and in the
towns he had captured in the hill country of Ephraim.
And he repaired the altar of the LORD, which stood in
front of the entry room of the LORD's Temple.

9Then Asa called together all the people of Judah and
Benjamin, along with the people of Ephraim, Manasseh,
and Simeon who had settled among them. For many
from Israel had moved to Judah during Asa's reign when
they saw that the LORD his God was with him. 10The people gathered at Jerusalem in late spring,* during the fifteenth year of Asa's reign.

11On that day they sacrificed to the LORD 700 cattle
and 7,000 sheep and goats from the plunder they had
taken in the battle. 12Then they entered into a covenant to
seek the LORD, the God of their ancestors, with all their
heart and soul. 13They agreed that anyone who refused to
seek the LORD, the God of Israel, would be put to death—
whether young or old, man or woman. 14They shouted
out their oath of loyalty to the LORD with trumpets blaring and rams' horns sounding. 15All in Judah were happy
about this covenant, for they had entered into it with all
their heart. They earnestly sought after God, and they
found him. And the LORD gave them rest from their enemies on every side.

16King Asa even deposed his grandmother* Maacah
from her position as queen mother because she had
made an obscene Asherah pole. He cut down her obscene pole, broke it up, and burned it in the Kidron

14:1 Verse 14:1 is numbered 13:23 in the Hebrew text. **14:2** Verses 14:2-15 are numbered 14:1-14 in Hebrew text. **14:9a** Hebrew *a Cushite.* **14:9b** Or *an army of thousands and thousands;* Hebrew reads *an army of a thousand thousands.* **14:10** Or *in the Zephathah Valley near Mareshah.* **14:12** Hebrew *Cushites;* also in 14:13. **15:8** As in Syriac version and Latin Vulgate (see also 15:1); Hebrew reads *from Oded the prophet.* **15:10** Hebrew *in the third month.* This month of the ancient Hebrew lunar calendar usually occurs within the months of May and June. **15:16** Hebrew *his mother.*

Valley. 17 Although the pagan shrines were not removed
from Israel, Asa's heart remained completely faithful
throughout his life. 18 He brought into the Temple of God
the silver and gold and the various
items that he and his father had
dedicated.
19 So there was no more war until the
thirty-fifth year of Asa's reign.

16 FINAL YEARS OF ASA'S REIGN

In the thirty-sixth year of Asa's reign,
King Baasha of Israel invaded Judah and
fortified Ramah in order to prevent anyone from entering or leaving King Asa's
territory in Judah.
2 Asa responded by removing the silver and gold from the treasuries of the
Temple of the LORD and the royal palace. He sent it to King Ben-hadad of
Aram, who was ruling in Damascus,
along with this message:

3 "Let there be a treaty between you and me like the
one between your father and my father. See, I am
sending you silver and gold. Break your treaty with
King Baasha of Israel so that he will leave me alone."

4 Ben-hadad agreed to King Asa's request and sent
the commanders of his army to attack the towns of Israel. They conquered the towns of Ijon, Dan, Abel-beth-
maacah,* and all the store cities in Naphtali. 5 As soon as
Baasha of Israel heard what was happening, he abandoned
his project of fortifying Ramah and stopped all work on it.
6 Then King Asa called out all the men of Judah to carry
away the building stones and timbers that Baasha had
been using to fortify Ramah. Asa used these materials to
fortify the towns of Geba and Mizpah.

> The eyes of the LORD search the whole earth in order to strengthen those whose hearts are fully committed to him.
>
> *2 CHRONICLES 16:9*

THE TRUTH 16:1-10

Asa, the king of Judah, blew it when he chose to trust the king of Aram, rather than God. So, God sent a prophet—Hanani—with a message of woe for Asa. But Asa threw the prophet in jail. Ever know someone who reacted angrily when told the truth about a wrong he or she committed? How well do you accept the truth when you hear it? Jesus once said that the truth can make a person free (see John 8:32). But it has to be accepted before it can do that. ■

7 At that time Hanani the seer came to King Asa and
told him, "Because you have put your trust in the king of
Aram instead of in the LORD your God, you missed your
chance to destroy the army of the king of Aram. 8 Don't
you remember what happened to the Ethiopians* and
Libyans and their vast army, with all of their chariots and
charioteers?* At that time you relied on the LORD, and he
handed them over to you. 9 The eyes of the LORD search
the whole earth in order to strengthen those whose
hearts are fully committed to him.
What a fool you have been! From now
on you will be at war."
10 Asa became so angry with Hanani
for saying this that he threw him into
prison and put him in stocks. At that
time Asa also began to oppress some
of his people.

SUMMARY OF ASA'S REIGN

11 The rest of the events of Asa's reign,
from beginning to end, are recorded
in *The Book of the Kings of Judah and
Israel.* 12 In the thirty-ninth year of his
reign, Asa developed a serious foot
disease. Yet even with the severity of
his disease, he did not seek the LORD's
help but turned only to his physicians.
13 So he died in the forty-first year of
his reign. 14 He was buried in the tomb he had carved out
for himself in the City of David. He was laid on a bed perfumed with sweet spices and fragrant ointments, and the
people built a huge funeral fire in his honor.

17 JEHOSHAPHAT RULES IN JUDAH

Then Jehoshaphat, Asa's son, became the next king. He
strengthened Judah to stand against any attack from Israel. 2 He stationed troops in all the fortified towns of Judah, and he assigned additional garrisons to the land of
Judah and to the towns of Ephraim that his father, Asa,
had captured.
3 The LORD was with Jehoshaphat because he followed
the example of his father's early years* and did not worship the images of Baal. 4 He sought his father's God and
obeyed his commands instead of following the evil practices of the kingdom of Israel. 5 So the LORD established
Jehoshaphat's control over the kingdom of Judah. All the
people of Judah brought gifts to Jehoshaphat, so he became very wealthy and highly esteemed. 6 He was deeply
committed to* the ways of the LORD. He removed the pagan shrines and Asherah poles from Judah.
7 In the third year of his reign Jehoshaphat sent his officials to teach in all the towns of Judah. These officials included Ben-hail, Obadiah, Zechariah, Nethanel, and
Micaiah. 8 He sent Levites along with them, including
Shemaiah, Nethaniah, Zebadiah, Asahel, Shemiramoth,
Jehonathan, Adonijah, Tobijah, and Tob-adonijah. He
also sent out the priests Elishama and Jehoram. 9 They
took copies of the Book of the Law of the LORD and traveled around through all the towns of Judah, teaching the
people.
10 Then the fear of the LORD fell over all the surrounding kingdoms so that none of them wanted to declare war
on Jehoshaphat. 11 Some of the Philistines brought him

16:4 As in parallel text at 1 Kgs 15:20; Hebrew reads *Abel-maim*, a variant spelling of Abel-beth-maacah. **16:8a** Hebrew *Cushites.* **16:8b** Or *and horsemen?* **17:3** Some Hebrew manuscripts read *the example of his father, David.* **17:6** Hebrew *His heart was courageous in.*

gifts and silver as tribute, and the Arabs brought 7,700 rams and 7,700 male goats.

12So Jehoshaphat became more and more powerful and built fortresses and storage cities throughout Judah. 13He stored numerous supplies in Judah's towns and stationed an army of seasoned troops at Jerusalem. 14His army was enrolled according to ancestral clans.

From Judah there were 300,000 troops organized in units of 1,000, under the command of Adnah. 15Next in command was Jehohanan, who commanded 280,000 troops. 16Next was Amasiah son of Zicri, who volunteered for the LORD's service, with 200,000 troops under his command.
17From Benjamin there were 200,000 troops equipped with bows and shields. They were under the command of Eliada, a veteran soldier. 18Next in command was Jehozabad, who commanded 180,000 armed men.

19These were the troops stationed in Jerusalem to serve the king, besides those Jehoshaphat stationed in the fortified towns throughout Judah.

18 JEHOSHAPHAT AND AHAB

Jehoshaphat enjoyed great riches and high esteem, and he made an alliance with Ahab of Israel by having his son marry Ahab's daughter. 2A few years later he went to Samaria to visit Ahab, who prepared a great banquet for him and his officials. They butchered great numbers of sheep, goats, and cattle for the feast. Then Ahab enticed Jehoshaphat to join forces with him to recover Ramoth-gilead.

3"Will you go with me to Ramoth-gilead?" King Ahab of Israel asked King Jehoshaphat of Judah.

Jehoshaphat replied, "Why, of course! You and I are as one, and my troops are your troops. We will certainly join you in battle." 4Then Jehoshaphat added, "But first let's find out what the LORD says."

5So the king of Israel summoned the prophets, 400 of them, and asked them, "Should we go to war against Ramoth-gilead, or should I hold back?"

They all replied, "Yes, go right ahead! God will give the king victory."

6But Jehoshaphat asked, "Is there not also a prophet of the LORD here? We should ask him the same question."

7The king of Israel replied to Jehoshaphat, "There is one more man who could consult the LORD for us, but I hate him. He never prophesies anything but trouble for me! His name is Micaiah son of Imlah."

Jehoshaphat replied, "That's not the way a king should talk! Let's hear what he has to say."

8So the king of Israel called one of his officials and said, "Quick! Bring Micaiah son of Imlah."

JEHOSHAPHAT

UPS:
- A bold follower of God, he reminded the people of the early years with his father, Asa
- Carried out a national program of religious education
- Had many military victories
- Developed an extensive legal structure throughout the kingdom

DOWNS:
- Failed to recognize the long-term results of his decisions
- Did not completely destroy idol worship in the land
- Became entangled with evil King Ahab through alliances
- Became Ahaziah's business partner in a disastrous shipping venture

STATS:
- Where: Jerusalem
- Occupation: King of Judah
- Relatives: Asa (father); Azubah (mother); Jehoram (son); Athaliah (daughter-in-law)
- Contemporaries: Ahab, Jezebel, Micaiah, Ahaziah, Jehu

BOTTOM LINE:
God is pleased when his people are consistent in their relationship with him.

Jehoshaphat's story is told in 1 Kings 15:24; 22; and 2 Chron 17:1–21:1. He also is mentioned in 2 Kings 3:1-14 and Joel 3:2, 12.

JEHOSHAPHAT Are you a product of your environment? Some would argue that they are. "Yo, I grew up in the projects, man. I can't help it." Or, "I'm from a dysfunctional family."

Jehoshaphat seemed to be a product of his environment. His father, Asa, had served God for a while during his time as king of Judah. But he eventually forgot about God. Jehoshaphat didn't seem to want to make the same mistake. When in trouble, he turned to God right away. But in day-to-day plans and actions, Jehoshaphat forgot about God, just as his father did.

Jehoshaphat's story and those of other kings of Israel and Judah are examples of the need for God's help to rise above one's environment. We can only fall back on that excuse for so long. Sooner or later, a bigger life change is needed.

MICAIAH PROPHESIES AGAINST AHAB

9King Ahab of Israel and King Jehoshaphat of Judah,
dressed in their royal robes, were sitting on thrones at the
threshing floor near the gate of Samaria. All of Ahab's
prophets were prophesying there in front of them. 10One
of them, Zedekiah son of Kenaanah, made some iron
horns and proclaimed, "This is what the LORD says: With
these horns you will gore the Arameans to death!"

11All the other prophets agreed. "Yes," they said, "go up
to Ramoth-gilead and be victorious, for the LORD will give
the king victory!"

12Meanwhile, the messenger who went to get Micaiah
said to him, "Look, all the prophets are promising victory
for the king. Be sure that you agree with them and promise success."

13But Micaiah replied, "As surely as the LORD lives, I will
say only what my God says."

14When Micaiah arrived before the king, Ahab asked
him, "Micaiah, should we go to war against Ramoth-
gilead, or should I hold back?"

Micaiah replied sarcastically, "Yes, go up and be victorious, for you will have victory over them!"

15But the king replied sharply, "How many times must I
demand that you speak only the truth to me when you
speak for the LORD?"

GOD'S UNSTOPPABLE WILL 18:1-32

After Micaiah prophesied death for King Ahab (18:16, 27), Ahab disguised himself to fool the enemy. Although the disguise fooled the enemy, it didn't stop the prophecy from coming to pass. A random Aramean arrow found a crack in his armor and killed him. God's will is always fulfilled despite the defenses people try to erect. God can use anything, even an error, to bring his will to pass. That means we can trust him to work his plans and keep his promises, no matter what. ■

16Then Micaiah told him, "In a vision I saw all Israel
scattered on the mountains, like sheep without a shepherd. And the LORD said, 'Their master has been killed.*
Send them home in peace.'"

17"Didn't I tell you?" the king of Israel exclaimed to Jehoshaphat. "He never prophesies anything but trouble
for me."

18Then Micaiah continued, "Listen to what the LORD
says! I saw the LORD sitting on his throne with all the armies of heaven around him, on his right and on his left.
19And the LORD said, 'Who can entice King Ahab of Israel
to go into battle against Ramoth-gilead so he can be
killed?'

"There were many suggestions, 20and finally a spirit
approached the LORD and said, 'I can do it!'

"'How will you do this?' the LORD asked.

21"And the spirit replied, 'I will go out and inspire all of
Ahab's prophets to speak lies.'

"'You will succeed,' said the LORD. 'Go ahead and do it.'

22"So you see, the LORD has put a lying spirit in the
mouths of your prophets. For the LORD has pronounced
your doom."

23Then Zedekiah son of Kenaanah walked up to Micaiah and slapped him across the face. "Since when did the
Spirit of the LORD leave me to speak to you?" he
demanded.

24And Micaiah replied, "You will find out soon enough
when you are trying to hide in some secret room!"

25"Arrest him!" the king of Israel ordered. "Take him
back to Amon, the governor of the city, and to my son Joash. 26Give them this order from the king: 'Put this man in
prison, and feed him nothing but bread and water until I
return safely from the battle!'"

27But Micaiah replied, "If you return safely, it will mean
that the LORD has not spoken through me!" Then he
added to those standing around, "Everyone mark my
words!"

THE DEATH OF AHAB

28So King Ahab of Israel and King Jehoshaphat of Judah
led their armies against Ramoth-gilead. 29The king of Israel said to Jehoshaphat, "As we go into battle, I will disguise myself so no one will recognize me, but you wear
your royal robes." So the king of Israel disguised himself,
and they went into battle.

30Meanwhile, the king of Aram had issued these orders
to his chariot commanders: "Attack only the king of Israel! Don't bother with anyone else." 31So when the Aramean chariot commanders saw Jehoshaphat in his royal
robes, they went after him. "There is the king of Israel!"
they shouted. But Jehoshaphat called out, and the LORD
saved him. God helped him by turning the attackers
away from him. 32As soon as the chariot commanders realized he was not the king of Israel, they stopped chasing
him.

33An Aramean soldier, however, randomly shot an arrow at the Israelite troops and hit the king of Israel between the joints of his armor. "Turn the horses* and get
me out of here!" Ahab groaned to the driver of the chariot. "I'm badly wounded!"

34The battle raged all that day, and the king of Israel
propped himself up in his chariot facing the Arameans.
In the evening, just as the sun was setting, he died.

19 JEHOSHAPHAT APPOINTS JUDGES

When King Jehoshaphat of Judah arrived safely home in
Jerusalem, 2Jehu son of Hanani the seer went out to meet
him. "Why should you help the wicked and love those
who hate the LORD?" he asked the king. "Because of what
you have done, the LORD is very angry with you. 3Even so,
there is some good in you, for you have removed the
Asherah poles throughout the land, and you have committed yourself to seeking God."

4Jehoshaphat lived in Jerusalem, but he went out
among the people, traveling from Beersheba to the hill
country of Ephraim, encouraging the people to return to

18:16 Hebrew *These people have no master.* 18:33 Hebrew *Turn your hand.*

the LORD, the God of their ancestors. 5He appointed judges throughout the nation in all the fortified towns, 6and he said to them, "Always think carefully before pronouncing judgment. Remember that you do not judge to please people but to please the LORD. He will be with you when you render the verdict in each case. 7Fear the LORD and judge with integrity, for the LORD our God does not tolerate perverted justice, partiality, or the taking of bribes."

INTEGRITY 19:5-10

Jehoshaphat delegated some of his authority to a group of judges. His advice for the judges is helpful for all leaders: (1) Think carefully before you make a decision(19:6); (2) be fair (19:7); (3) act with integrity (19:9). How does a person act with integrity? The first step is to depend on God. Have you taken that first step? ■

8In Jerusalem, Jehoshaphat appointed some of the Levites and priests and clan leaders in Israel to serve as judges for cases involving the LORD's regulations and for civil disputes. 9These were his instructions to them: "You must always act in the fear of the LORD, with faithfulness and an undivided heart. 10Whenever a case comes to you from fellow citizens in an outlying town, whether a murder case or some other violation of God's laws, commands, decrees, or regulations, you must warn them not to sin against the LORD, so that he will not be angry with you and them. Do this and you will not be guilty.

11"Amariah the high priest will have final say in all cases involving the LORD. Zebadiah son of Ishmael, a leader from the tribe of Judah, will have final say in all civil cases. The Levites will assist you in making sure that justice is served. Take courage as you fulfill your duties, and may the LORD be with those who do what is right."

20

WAR WITH SURROUNDING NATIONS

After this, the armies of the Moabites, Ammonites, and some of the Meunites* declared war on Jehoshaphat. 2Messengers came and told Jehoshaphat, "A vast army from Edom* is marching against you from beyond the Dead Sea.* They are already at Hazazon-tamar." (This was another name for En-gedi.)

3Jehoshaphat was terrified by this news and begged the LORD for guidance. He also ordered everyone in Judah to begin fasting. 4So people from all the towns of Judah came to Jerusalem to seek the LORD's help.

5Jehoshaphat stood before the community of Judah and Jerusalem in front of the new courtyard at the Temple of the LORD. 6He prayed, "O LORD, God of our ancestors, you alone are the God who is in heaven. You are ruler of all the kingdoms of the earth. You are powerful and mighty; no one can stand against you! 7O our God, did you not drive out those who lived in this land when your people Israel arrived? And did you not give this land forever to the descendants of your friend Abraham? 8Your people settled here and built this Temple to honor your name. 9They said, 'Whenever we are faced with any calamity such as war,* plague, or famine, we can come to stand in your presence before this Temple where your name is honored. We can cry out to you to save us, and you will hear us and rescue us.'

10"And now see what the armies of Ammon, Moab, and Mount Seir are doing. You would not let our ancestors invade those nations when Israel left Egypt, so they went around them and did not destroy them. 11Now see how they reward us! For they have come to throw us out of your land, which you gave us as an inheritance. 12O our God, won't you stop them? We are powerless against this mighty army that is about to attack us. We do not know what to do, but we are looking to you for help."

13As all the men of Judah stood before the LORD with their little ones, wives, and children, 14the Spirit of the LORD came upon one of the men standing there. His name was Jahaziel son of Zechariah, son of Benaiah, son of Jeiel, son of Mattaniah, a Levite who was a descendant of Asaph.

15He said, "Listen, all you people of Judah and Jerusalem! Listen, King Jehoshaphat! This is what the LORD says: Do not be afraid! Don't be discouraged by this mighty army, for the battle is not yours, but God's. 16Tomorrow, march out against them. You will find them coming up through the ascent of Ziz at the end of the valley that opens into the wilderness of Jeruel. 17But you will not even need to fight. Take your positions; then stand still and watch the LORD's victory. He is with you, O people of Judah and Jerusalem. Do not be afraid or discouraged. Go out against them tomorrow, for the LORD is with you!"

BATTLES 20:1-15

When faced with an unstoppable enemy, Jehoshaphat turned to God. Through the prophet Jahaziel, God promised to fight for Judah. We may not fight an enemy army, but we daily battle temptation, pressure, and "mighty powers in this dark world, and against evil spirits in the heavenly places" (Eph 6:12). But God promises to fight for us. How do we let God fight for us? By asking him for help and by relying on his power to work through our fears and weaknesses. ■

18Then King Jehoshaphat bowed low with his face to the ground. And all the people of Judah and Jerusalem did the same, worshiping the LORD. 19Then the Levites from the clans of Kohath and Korah stood to praise the LORD, the God of Israel, with a very loud shout.

20Early the next morning the army of Judah went out into the wilderness of Tekoa. On the way Jehoshaphat stopped and said, "Listen to me, all you people of Judah

20:1 As in some Greek manuscripts (see also 26:7); Hebrew repeats *Ammonites.* **20:2a** As in one Hebrew manuscript; most Hebrew manuscripts and ancient versions read *Aram.* **20:2b** Hebrew *the sea.* **20:9** Or *sword of judgment;* or *sword, judgment.*

and Jerusalem! Believe in the LORD your God, and you will
be able to stand firm. Believe in his prophets, and you will
succeed."
21 After consulting the people, the king appointed singers to walk ahead of the army, singing to the LORD and
praising him for his holy splendor. This is what they sang:

"Give thanks to the LORD;
his faithful love endures forever!"

22 At the very moment they began to sing and give
praise, the LORD caused the armies of Ammon, Moab, and
Mount Seir to start fighting among themselves. 23 The armies of Moab and Ammon turned against their allies
from Mount Seir and killed every one of them. After they
had destroyed the army of Seir, they began attacking
each other. 24 So when the army of Judah arrived at the
lookout point in the wilderness, all they saw were dead
bodies lying on the ground as far as they could see. Not a
single one of the enemy had escaped.
25 King Jehoshaphat and his men went out to gather
the plunder. They found vast amounts of equipment,
clothing,* and other valuables—more than they could
carry. There was so much plunder that it took them
three days just to collect it all! 26 On the fourth day
they gathered in the Valley of Blessing,* which got its
name that day because the people praised and
thanked the LORD there. It is still called the Valley of
Blessing today.
27 Then all the men returned to Jerusalem, with Jehoshaphat leading them, overjoyed that the LORD had given
them victory over their enemies. 28 They marched into Jerusalem to the music of harps, lyres, and trumpets, and
they proceeded to the Temple of the LORD.
29 When all the surrounding kingdoms heard that the
LORD himself had fought against the enemies of Israel,
the fear of God came over them. 30 So Jehoshaphat's kingdom was at peace, for his God had given him rest on every
side.

SUMMARY OF JEHOSHAPHAT'S REIGN

31 So Jehoshaphat ruled over the land of Judah. He was
thirty-five years old when he became king, and he
reigned in Jerusalem twenty-five years. His mother was
Azubah, the daughter of Shilhi.
32 Jehoshaphat was a good king, following the ways of
his father, Asa. He did what was pleasing in the LORD's
sight. 33 During his reign, however, he failed to remove all
the pagan shrines, and the people never fully committed
themselves to follow the God of their ancestors.
34 The rest of the events of Jehoshaphat's reign, from
beginning to end, are recorded in *The Record of Jehu Son
of Hanani*, which is included in *The Book of the Kings of
Israel.*
35 Some time later King Jehoshaphat of Judah made an
alliance with King Ahaziah of Israel, who was very
wicked.* 36 Together they built a fleet of trading ships* at
the port of Ezion-geber. 37 Then Eliezer son of Dodavahu
from Mareshah prophesied against Jehoshaphat. He
said, "Because you have allied yourself with King Ahaziah, the LORD will destroy your work." So the ships met
with disaster and never put out to sea.*

21 JEHORAM RULES IN JUDAH

When Jehoshaphat died, he was buried with his ancestors in the City of David. Then his son Jehoram became
the next king.
2 Jehoram's brothers—the other sons of Jehoshaphat—
were Azariah, Jehiel, Zechariah, Azariahu, Michael, and
Shephatiah; all these were the sons of Jehoshaphat king
of Judah.* 3 Their father had given each of them valuable
gifts of silver, gold, and costly items, and also some of Judah's fortified towns. However, he designated Jehoram
as the next king because he was the oldest. 4 But when Jehoram had become solidly established as king, he killed
all his brothers and some of the other leaders of Judah.
5 Jehoram was thirty-two years old when he became
king, and he reigned in Jerusalem eight years. 6 But Jehoram followed the example of the kings of Israel and was

Church seems boring and confusing sometimes. Are all of the songs, readings, and rituals necessary?

Worshiping God keeps us connected to him. In worship we recognize God as the one who is in control and who has the power to change our circumstances and life. (See 2 Chron 20:20-22.)

Jehoshaphat discovered this fact very graphically as he sent the worshipers out with his army. As the worshipers were singing, God miraculously provided a victory!

Worship takes many forms. Most of the songs and readings come right from Scripture. If you concentrate on the meaning behind what is being sung or read, you will see that the words communicate very important facts about God.

Another purpose of worship is to encourage us to grow in our faith. It can encourage us to go out to face a world of collapsed morals.

Ephesians 5:19 was written during a time when Christians were put in prison for their faith. It says that believers should always sing "psalms and hymns and spiritual songs among yourselves, . . . making music to the Lord in your hearts." By doing what this verse talks about, believers were able to encourage each other as they reminded themselves of the faithfulness, goodness, and strength of God.

20:25 As in some Hebrew manuscripts and Latin Vulgate; most Hebrew manuscripts read *corpses*. **20:26** Hebrew *valley of Beracah*. **20:35** Or *who made him do what was wicked*. **20:36** Hebrew *fleet of ships that could go to Tarshish*. **20:37** Hebrew *never set sail for Tarshish*. **21:2** Hebrew *of Israel;* also in 21:4. The author of Chronicles sees Judah as representative of the true Israel. See also some Hebrew manuscripts, Greek and Syriac versions, and Latin Vulgate.

as wicked as King Ahab, for he had married one of Ahab's daughters. So Jehoram did what was evil in the LORD's sight. 7But the LORD did not want to destroy David's dynasty, for he had made a covenant with David and promised that his descendants would continue to rule, shining like a lamp forever.
8During Jehoram's reign, the Edomites revolted against Judah and crowned their own king. 9So Jehoram went out with his full army and all his chariots. The Edomites surrounded him and his chariot commanders, but he went out at night and attacked them* under cover of darkness. 10Even so, Edom has been independent from Judah to this day. The town of Libnah also revolted about that same time. All this happened because Jehoram had abandoned the LORD, the God of his ancestors. 11He had built pagan shrines in the hill country of Judah and had led the people of Jerusalem and Judah to give themselves to pagan gods and to go astray.

NOT INDIFFERENT 21:8-11

Jehoram "did what was evil in the LORD's sight" (21:6). Yet he wasn't killed in battle or by treachery; instead, he died by a lingering and painful disease (21:18-19). Worried that someone will get away with something he or she did wrong just as Jehoram seemed to? Sometimes God waits for just the right time to allow a person to reap the consequences of his or her actions. (See also Ps 37:1-2, 12-13.) ■

12Then Elijah the prophet wrote Jehoram this letter:

"This is what the LORD, the God of your ancestor David, says: You have not followed the good example of your father, Jehoshaphat, or your grandfather King Asa of Judah. 13Instead, you have been as evil as the kings of Israel. You have led the people of Jerusalem and Judah to worship idols, just as King Ahab did in Israel. And you have even killed your own brothers, men who were better than you. 14So now the LORD is about to strike you, your people, your children, your wives, and all that is yours with a heavy blow. 15You yourself will suffer with a severe intestinal disease that will get worse each day until your bowels come out."

16Then the LORD stirred up the Philistines and the Arabs, who lived near the Ethiopians,* to attack Jehoram. 17They marched against Judah, broke down its defenses, and carried away everything of value in the royal palace, including the king's sons and his wives. Only his youngest son, Ahaziah,* was spared.
18After all this, the LORD struck Jehoram with the severe intestinal disease. 19The disease grew worse and worse, and at the end of two years it caused his bowels to come out, and he died in agony. His people did not build a great funeral fire to honor him as they had done for his ancestors.
20Jehoram was thirty-two years old when he became king, and he reigned in Jerusalem eight years. No one was sorry when he died. They buried him in the City of David, but not in the royal cemetery.

22 AHAZIAH RULES IN JUDAH

Then the people of Jerusalem made Ahaziah, Jehoram's youngest son, their next king, since the marauding bands who came with the Arabs* had killed all the older sons. So Ahaziah son of Jehoram reigned as king of Judah.
2Ahaziah was twenty-two* years old when he became king, and he reigned in Jerusalem one year. His mother was Athaliah, a granddaughter of King Omri. 3Ahaziah also followed the evil example of King Ahab's family, for his mother encouraged him in doing wrong. 4He did what was evil in the LORD's sight, just as Ahab's family had done. They even became his advisers after the death of his father, and they led him to ruin.
5Following their evil advice, Ahaziah joined King Joram,* the son of King Ahab of Israel, in his war against King Hazael of Aram at Ramoth-gilead. When the Arameans wounded Joram in the battle, 6he returned to Jezreel to recover from the wounds he had received at Ramoth.* Because Joram was wounded, King Ahaziah* of Judah went to Jezreel to visit him.

GOOD ADVICE 22:4-5

Like Rehoboam before him (see 10:1-14), Ahaziah chose to listen to bad advice and paid for it with his life. A person who seeks advice needs to consider the source, then carefully weigh what is said. Looking for advice? You can use God's Word to "test everything that is said. Hold on to what is good" (1 Thess 5:21). ■

7But God had decided that this visit would be Ahaziah's downfall. While he was there, Ahaziah went out with Joram to meet Jehu son of Nimshi, whom the LORD had appointed to destroy the dynasty of Ahab.
8While Jehu was executing judgment against the family of Ahab, he happened to meet some of Judah's officials and Ahaziah's relatives* who were traveling with Ahaziah. So Jehu killed them all. 9Then Jehu's men searched for Ahaziah, and they found him hiding in the city of Samaria. They brought him to Jehu, who killed him. Ahaziah was given a decent burial because the people said, "He was the grandson of Jehoshaphat—a man who sought the LORD with all his heart." But none of the surviving members of Ahaziah's family was capable of ruling the kingdom.

21:9 Or *he went out and escaped.* The meaning of the Hebrew is uncertain. 21:16 Hebrew *the Cushites.* 21:17 Hebrew *Jehoahaz,* a variant spelling of Ahaziah; compare 22:1. 22:1 Or *marauding bands of Arabs.* 22:2 As in some Greek manuscripts and Syriac version (see also 2 Kgs 8:26); Hebrew reads *forty-two.* 22:5 Hebrew *Jehoram,* a variant spelling of Joram; also in 22:6, 7. 22:6a Hebrew *Ramah,* a variant spelling of Ramoth. 22:6b As in some Hebrew manuscripts, Greek and Syriac versions, and Latin Vulgate (see also 2 Kgs 8:29); most Hebrew manuscripts read *Azariah.* 22:8 As in Greek version (see also 2 Kgs 10:13); Hebrew reads *and sons of the brothers of Ahaziah.*

QUEEN ATHALIAH RULES IN JUDAH

10When Athaliah, the mother of King Ahaziah of Judah, learned that her son was dead, she began to destroy the rest of Judah's royal family. 11But Ahaziah's sister Jehosheba,* the daughter of King Jehoram, took Ahaziah's infant son, Joash, and stole him away from among the rest of the king's children, who were about to be killed. She put Joash and his nurse in a bedroom. In this way, Jehosheba, wife of Jehoiada the priest and sister of Ahaziah, hid the child so that Athaliah could not murder him. 12Joash remained hidden in the Temple of God for six years while Athaliah ruled over the land.

23 REVOLT AGAINST ATHALIAH

In the seventh year of Athaliah's reign, Jehoiada the priest decided to act. He summoned his courage and made a pact with five army commanders: Azariah son of Jeroham, Ishmael son of Jehohanan, Azariah son of Obed, Maaseiah son of Adaiah, and Elishaphat son of Zicri. 2These men traveled secretly throughout Judah and summoned the Levites and clan leaders in all the towns to come to Jerusalem. 3They all gathered at the Temple of God, where they made a solemn pact with Joash, the young king.

Jehoiada said to them, "Here is the king's son! The time has come for him to reign! The LORD has promised that a descendant of David will be our king. 4This is what you must do. When you priests and Levites come on duty on the Sabbath, a third of you will serve as gatekeepers. 5Another third will go over to the royal palace, and the final third will be at the Foundation Gate. Everyone else should stay in the courtyards of the LORD's Temple. 6Remember, only the priests and Levites on duty may enter the Temple of the LORD, for they are set apart as holy. The rest of the people must obey the LORD's instructions and stay outside. 7You Levites, form a bodyguard around the king and keep your weapons in hand. Kill anyone who tries to enter the Temple. Stay with the king wherever he goes."

8So the Levites and all the people of Judah did everything as Jehoiada the priest ordered. The commanders took charge of the men reporting for duty that Sabbath, as well as those who were going off duty. Jehoiada the priest did not let anyone go home after their shift ended. 9Then Jehoiada supplied the commanders with the spears and the large and small shields that had once belonged to King David and were stored in the Temple of God. 10He stationed all the people around the king, with their weapons ready. They formed a line from the south side of the Temple around to the north side and all around the altar.

11Then Jehoiada and his sons brought out Joash, the king's son, placed the crown on his head, and presented him with a copy of God's laws.* They anointed him and proclaimed him king, and everyone shouted, "Long live the king!"

THE DEATH OF ATHALIAH

12When Athaliah heard the noise of the people running and the shouts of praise to the king, she hurried to the LORD's Temple to see what was happening. 13When she arrived, she saw the newly crowned king standing in his place of authority by the pillar at the Temple entrance. The commanders and trumpeters were surrounding him, and people from all over the land were rejoicing and blowing trumpets. Singers with musical instruments were leading the people in a great celebration. When Athaliah saw all this, she tore her clothes in despair and shouted, "Treason! Treason!"

14Then Jehoiada the priest ordered the commanders who were in charge of the troops, "Take her to the soldiers in front of the Temple,* and kill anyone who tries to rescue her." For the priest had said, "She must not be killed in the Temple of the LORD." 15So they seized her and led her out to the entrance of the Horse Gate on the palace grounds, and they killed her there.

> **TAKE A STAND 23:1-11**
>
> **Although it could have cost him his life, Jehoiada gathered up his courage and did what was right, restoring the Temple worship and anointing the new king. There are times when we must correct a wrong or speak out for what is right. When such a situation arises, what will you do? ■**

JEHOIADA'S RELIGIOUS REFORMS

16Then Jehoiada made a covenant between himself and the king and the people that they would be the LORD's people. 17And all the people went over to the temple of Baal and tore it down. They demolished the altars and smashed the idols, and they killed Mattan the priest of Baal in front of the altars.

18Jehoiada now put the priests and Levites in charge of the Temple of the LORD, following all the directions given by David. He also commanded them to present burnt offerings to the LORD, as prescribed by the Law of Moses, and to sing and rejoice as David had instructed. 19He also stationed gatekeepers at the gates of the LORD's Temple to keep out those who for any reason were ceremonially unclean.

20Then the commanders, nobles, rulers, and all the people of the land escorted the king from the Temple of the LORD. They went through the upper gate and into the palace, and they seated the king on the royal throne. 21So all the people of the land rejoiced, and the city was peaceful because Athaliah had been killed.

24 JOASH REPAIRS THE TEMPLE

Joash was seven years old when he became king, and he reigned in Jerusalem forty years. His mother was Zibiah from Beersheba. 2Joash did what was pleasing in the LORD's sight throughout the lifetime of Jehoiada the priest. 3Jehoiada chose two wives for Joash, and he had sons and daughters.

4At one point Joash decided to repair and restore the

22:11 As in parallel text at 2 Kgs 11:2; Hebrew omits *Ahaziah's sister* and reads *Jehoshabeath* [a variant spelling of Jehosheba]. **23:11** Or *a copy of the covenant.* **23:14** Or *Bring her out from between the ranks;* or *Take her out of the Temple precincts.* The meaning of the Hebrew is uncertain.

Temple of the LORD. 5He summoned the priests and Levites and gave them these instructions: "Go to all the
towns of Judah and collect the required annual offerings,
so that we can repair the Temple of your God. Do not delay!" But the Levites did not act immediately.
6So the king called for Jehoiada the high priest and
asked him, "Why haven't you demanded that the Levites
go out and collect the Temple taxes from the towns of Judah and from Jerusalem? Moses, the servant of the LORD,
levied this tax on the community of Israel in order to
maintain the Tabernacle of the Covenant.*"
7Over the years the followers of wicked Athaliah had
broken into the Temple of God, and they had used all the
dedicated things from the Temple of the LORD to worship the images of Baal.
8So now the king ordered a chest to be made and set
outside the gate leading to the Temple of the LORD. 9Then
a proclamation was sent throughout Judah and Jerusalem, telling the people to bring to the LORD the tax that
Moses, the servant of God, had required of the Israelites
in the wilderness. 10This pleased all the leaders and the
people, and they gladly brought their money and filled
the chest with it.
11Whenever the chest became full, the Levites would
carry it to the king's officials. Then the court secretary
and an officer of the high priest would come and empty
the chest and take it back to the Temple again. This went
on day after day, and a large amount of money was collected. 12The king and Jehoiada gave the money to the
construction supervisors, who hired masons and
carpenters to restore the Temple of the LORD. They also
hired metalworkers, who made articles of iron and
bronze for the LORD's Temple.
13The men in charge of the renovation worked hard
and made steady progress. They restored the Temple of
God according to its original design and strengthened it.
14When all the repairs were finished, they brought the remaining money to the king and Jehoiada. It was used to
make various articles for the Temple of the LORD—articles for worship services and for burnt offerings, including ladles and other articles made of gold and silver. And
the burnt offerings were sacrificed continually in the
Temple of the LORD during the lifetime of Jehoiada the
priest.
15Jehoiada lived to a very old age, finally dying at 130.
16He was buried among the kings in the City of David, because he had done so much good in Judah* for God and
his Temple.

JEHOIADA'S REFORMS REVERSED

17But after Jehoiada's death, the leaders of Judah came
and bowed before King Joash and persuaded him to listen
to their advice. 18They decided to abandon the Temple of
the LORD, the God of their ancestors, and they worshiped
Asherah poles and idols instead! Because of this sin, divine anger fell on Judah and Jerusalem. 19Yet the LORD
sent prophets to bring them back to him. The prophets
warned them, but still the people would not listen.
20Then the Spirit of God came upon Zechariah son of
Jehoiada the priest. He stood before the people and said,

24:6 Hebrew *Tent of the Testimony*. **24:16** Hebrew *in Israel*. The author of Chronicles sees Judah as representative of the true Israel.

JOASH

UPS:
- Carried out extensive repairs on the Temple
- Was faithful to God as long as Jehoiada, a priest, lived

DOWNS:
- Allowed his people to continue worshiping idols
- Used the Temple treasures to bribe King Hazael of Syria
- Killed Jehoiada's son, Zechariah
- Allowed his advisers to lead the people away from God

STATS:
- Where: Jerusalem
- Occupation: King of Judah
- Relatives: Ahaziah (father); Zibiah (mother); Athaliah (grandmother); Jehosheba (aunt); Jehoiada (uncle); Amaziah (son); Zechariah (cousin)
- Contemporaries: Jehu, Hazael

BOTTOM LINE:
Even the best counsel is ineffective if it doesn't help us make wise decisions.
All of us are responsible for what we do.

Joash's story is told in 2 Kings 11:1–12:21 and 2 Chron 22:11–24:27.

JOASH Ever know someone who seems to have had it rough all of his or her life? Maybe you feel that life couldn't be more unfair if it tried.

Joash could've felt like that. Although he was a prince, his life was hardly easy. After his father (Ahaziah) was killed, his grandmother tried to kill Joash so that *she* could rule the kingdom. But an aunt and uncle (Jehosheba and Jehoiada) protected and raised him.

When Joash became king at age seven, Jehoiada made most of the decisions for him. Although Jehoiada was a good man, he never taught Joash how to be a good king. After Jehoiada died, however, Joash began to make a mess of his life and his kingdom. Joash had depended on Jehoiada, but never really learned to depend on Jehoiada's God.

Is God your parents' God or yours as well? Your view of life is usually affected by your view of God.

"This is what God says: Why do you disobey the LORD's commands and keep yourselves from prospering? You have abandoned the LORD, and now he has abandoned you!"

[21]Then the leaders plotted to kill Zechariah, and King Joash ordered that they stone him to death in the courtyard of the LORD's Temple. [22]That was how King Joash repaid Jehoiada for his loyalty—by killing his son. Zechariah's last words as he died were, "May the LORD see what they are doing and avenge my death!"

THE END OF JOASH'S REIGN

[23]In the spring of the year* the Aramean army marched against Joash. They invaded Judah and Jerusalem and killed all the leaders of the nation. Then they sent all the plunder back to their king in Damascus. [24]Although the Arameans attacked with only a small army, the LORD helped them conquer the much larger army of Judah. The people of Judah had abandoned the LORD, the God of their ancestors, so judgment was carried out against Joash.

[25]The Arameans withdrew, leaving Joash severely wounded. But his own officials plotted to kill him for murdering the son* of Jehoiada the priest. They assassinated him as he lay in bed. Then he was buried in the City of David, but not in the royal cemetery. [26]The assassins were Jozacar,* the son of an Ammonite woman named Shimeath, and Jehozabad, the son of a Moabite woman named Shomer.*

[27]The account of the sons of Joash, the prophecies about him, and the record of his restoration of the Temple of God are written in *The Commentary on the Book of the Kings*. His son Amaziah became the next king.

25

AMAZIAH RULES IN JUDAH

Amaziah was twenty-five years old when he became king, and he reigned in Jerusalem twenty-nine years. His mother was Jehoaddin* from Jerusalem. [2]Amaziah did what was pleasing in the LORD's sight, but not wholeheartedly.

[3]When Amaziah was well established as king, he executed the officials who had assassinated his father. [4]However, he did not kill the children of the assassins, for he obeyed the command of the LORD as written by Moses in the Book of the Law: "Parents must not be put to death for the sins of their children, nor children for the sins of their parents. Those deserving to die must be put to death for their own crimes."*

[5]Then Amaziah organized the army, assigning generals and captains* for all Judah and Benjamin. He took a census and found that he had an army of 300,000 select troops, twenty years old and older, all trained in the use of spear and shield. [6]He also paid about 7,500 pounds* of silver to hire 100,000 experienced fighting men from Israel.

[7]But a man of God came to him and said, "Your Majesty, do not hire troops from Israel, for the LORD is not with Israel. He will not help those people of Ephraim! [8]If you let them go with your troops into battle, you will be defeated by the enemy no matter how well you fight. God will overthrow you, for he has the power to help you or to trip you up."

[9]Amaziah asked the man of God, "But what about all that silver I paid to hire the army of Israel?"

The man of God replied, "The LORD is able to give you much more than this!" [10]So Amaziah discharged the hired troops and sent them back to Ephraim. This made them very angry with Judah, and they returned home in a great rage.

A COSTLY DECISION 25:5-10

Amaziah made a financial agreement with mercenaries, offering to pay them to fight for him (25:6). But before they could go to battle, Amaziah received the prophet's warning. Although sending the soldiers home with pay cost him plenty, Amaziah wisely realized that the money was not worth the ruin the alliance could cause. Sometimes we pay a price in order to do what's right. What would you have chosen to do? ■

[11]Then Amaziah summoned his courage and led his army to the Valley of Salt, where they killed 10,000 Edomite troops from Seir. [12]They captured another 10,000 and took them to the top of a cliff and threw them off, dashing them to pieces on the rocks below.

[13]Meanwhile, the hired troops that Amaziah had sent home raided several of the towns of Judah between Samaria and Beth-horon. They killed 3,000 people and carried off great quantities of plunder.

[14]When King Amaziah returned from slaughtering the Edomites, he brought with him idols taken from the people of Seir. He set them up as his own gods, bowed down in front of them, and offered sacrifices to them! [15]This made the LORD very angry, and he sent a prophet to ask, "Why do you turn to gods who could not even save their own people from you?"

[16]But the king interrupted him and said, "Since when have I made you the king's counselor? Be quiet now before I have you killed!"

So the prophet stopped with this warning: "I know that God has determined to destroy you because you have done this and have refused to accept my counsel."

[17]After consulting with his advisers, King Amaziah of Judah sent this challenge to Israel's king Jehoash,* the son of Jehoahaz and grandson of Jehu: "Come and meet me in battle!"*

24:23 Hebrew *At the turn of the year*. The first day of the year in the ancient Hebrew lunar calendar occurred in March or April. **24:25** As in Greek version and Latin Vulgate; Hebrew reads *sons*. **24:26a** As in parallel text at 2 Kgs 12:21; Hebrew reads *Zabad*. **24:26b** As in parallel text at 2 Kgs 12:21; Hebrew reads *Shimrith*, a variant spelling of Shomer. **25:1** As in parallel text at 2 Kgs 14:2; Hebrew reads *Jehoaddan*, a variant spelling of Jehoaddin. **25:4** Deut 24:16. **25:5** Hebrew *commanders of thousands and commanders of hundreds*. **25:6** Hebrew *100 talents* [3,400 kilograms]. **25:17a** Hebrew *Joash*, a variant spelling of Jehoash; also in 25:18, 21, 23, 25. **25:17b** Hebrew *Come, let us look one another in the face*.

18But King Jehoash of Israel replied to King Amaziah of Judah with this story: "Out in the Lebanon mountains, a thistle sent a message to a mighty cedar tree: 'Give your daughter in marriage to my son.' But just then a wild animal of Lebanon came by and stepped on the thistle, crushing it!

19"You are saying, 'I have defeated Edom,' and you are very proud of it. But my advice is to stay at home. Why stir up trouble that will only bring disaster on you and the people of Judah?"

20But Amaziah refused to listen, for God was determined to destroy him for turning to the gods of Edom. 21So King Jehoash of Israel mobilized his army against King Amaziah of Judah. The two armies drew up their battle lines at Beth-shemesh in Judah. 22Judah was routed by the army of Israel, and its army scattered and fled for home. 23King Jehoash of Israel captured Judah's king, Amaziah son of Joash and grandson of Ahaziah, at Beth-shemesh. Then he brought him to Jerusalem, where he demolished 600 feet* of Jerusalem's wall, from the Ephraim Gate to the Corner Gate. 24He carried off all the gold and silver and all the articles from the Temple of God that had been in the care of Obed-edom. He also seized the treasures of the royal palace, along with hostages, and then returned to Samaria.

25King Amaziah of Judah lived on for fifteen years after the death of King Jehoash of Israel. 26The rest of the events in Amaziah's reign, from beginning to end, are recorded in *The Book of the Kings of Judah and Israel.*

27After Amaziah turned away from the LORD, there was a conspiracy against his life in Jerusalem, and he fled to Lachish. But his enemies sent assassins after him, and they killed him there. 28They brought his body back on a horse, and he was buried with his ancestors in the City of David.*

26

UZZIAH RULES IN JUDAH

All the people of Judah had crowned Amaziah's sixteen-year-old son, Uzziah, as king in place of his father. 2After his father's death, Uzziah rebuilt the town of Elath* and restored it to Judah.

3Uzziah was sixteen years old when he became king, and he reigned in Jerusalem fifty-two years. His mother was Jecoliah from Jerusalem. 4He did what was pleasing in the LORD's sight, just as his father, Amaziah, had done. 5Uzziah sought God during the days of Zechariah, who taught him to fear God.* And as long as the king sought guidance from the LORD, God gave him success.

6Uzziah declared war on the Philistines and broke down the walls of Gath, Jabneh, and Ashdod. Then he built new towns in the Ashdod area and in other parts of Philistia. 7God helped him in his wars against the Philistines, his battles with the Arabs of Gur,* and his wars with the Meunites. 8The Meunites* paid annual tribute to him, and his fame spread even to Egypt, for he had become very powerful.

9Uzziah built fortified towers in Jerusalem at the Corner Gate, at the Valley Gate, and at the angle in the wall. 10He also constructed forts in the wilderness and dug many water cisterns, because he kept great herds of livestock in the foothills of Judah* and on the plains. He was also a man who loved the soil. He had many workers who cared for his farms and vineyards, both on the hillsides and in the fertile valleys.

11Uzziah had an army of well-trained warriors, ready to march into battle, unit by unit. This army had been mustered and organized by Jeiel, the secretary of the army, and his assistant, Maaseiah. They were under the direction of Hananiah, one of the king's officials. 12These regiments of mighty warriors were commanded by 2,600 clan leaders. 13The army consisted of 307,500 men, all elite troops. They were prepared to assist the king against any enemy.

14Uzziah provided the entire army with shields, spears, helmets, coats of mail, bows, and sling stones. 15And he built structures on the walls of Jerusalem, designed by experts to protect those who shot arrows and hurled large stones* from the towers and the corners of the wall. His fame spread far and wide, for the LORD gave him marvelous help, and he became very powerful.

THE PULL OF PRIDE 26:1-16

After God gave Uzziah great power as king of Judah, he became proud and corrupt. God hates pride. In fact, "pride goes before destruction, and haughtiness before a fall" (Prov 16:18). What do you have or want that sparks your pride? Talent? Money? Popularity? Power? Don't forget Proverbs 16:18. How will you give God credit for what you have? ■

UZZIAH'S SIN AND PUNISHMENT

16But when he had become powerful, he also became proud, which led to his downfall. He sinned against the LORD his God by entering the sanctuary of the LORD's Temple and personally burning incense on the incense altar. 17Azariah the high priest went in after him with eighty other priests of the LORD, all brave men. 18They confronted King Uzziah and said, "It is not for you, Uzziah, to burn incense to the LORD. That is the work of the priests alone, the descendants of Aaron who are set apart for this work. Get out of the sanctuary, for you have sinned. The LORD God will not honor you for this!"

19Uzziah, who was holding an incense burner, became furious. But as he was standing there raging at the priests before the incense altar in the LORD's Temple, leprosy* suddenly broke out on his forehead. 20When Azariah the high priest and all the other priests saw the leprosy, they

25:23 Hebrew *400 cubits* [180 meters]. **25:28** As in some Hebrew manuscripts and other ancient versions (see also 2 Kgs 14:20); most Hebrew manuscripts read *the city of Judah.* **26:2** As in Greek version (see also 2 Kgs 14:22; 16:6); Hebrew reads *Eloth,* a variant spelling of Elath. **26:5** As in Syriac and Greek versions; Hebrew reads *who instructed him in divine visions.* **26:7** As in Greek version; Hebrew reads *Gur-baal.* **26:8** As in Greek version; Hebrew reads *Ammonites.* Compare 26:7. **26:10** Hebrew *the Shephelah.* **26:15** Or *to shoot arrows and hurl large stones.* **26:19** Or *a contagious skin disease.* The Hebrew word used here and throughout this passage can describe various skin diseases.

ABORTION

ULTIMATE ISSUES

In 2 Chronicles 28:3, Ahaz earned God's anger because he sacrificed his children to idols. Yet this wasn't the last time that a parent would allow his or her children to be killed.

In 1973—ancient history—abortions became legal because of a Supreme Court case: *Roe v. Wade*. This decision sparked protests as well as cries of victory throughout the country for decades. But in 2003, the story took a surprising turn when "Jane Roe," the plaintiff in the case, requested that the Supreme Court's ruling be overturned. Having discovered the harmful effects of abortion, she regretted being part of the fight to legalize abortion.

If a person (a judge, a doctor, or a legislator) or a human institution (the Supreme Court or the Senate) makes a decision in this matter, there is always the potential for another person or institution to overturn that decision later on, as "Jane Roe" hopes. It has happened countless times. What is needed, it would seem, is a judgment or a ruling from a source higher than human opinion. That's why for many centuries Christians have turned to the Bible.

Since God gave life to all, it is a logical conclusion that no one should treat that life lightly. If we are God's "masterpiece" (see Eph 2:10), who has the right to tamper with or destroy the life of another? Yet, tragically, that is what happens on a daily basis. Abortion is used as a means of birth control, of removing an unwanted complication. For those who take seriously the sanctity of life as an expression of God's handiwork, this can be seen only as wrong.

There are a number of related topics (being made in the image of God, sexual morality, etc.) and Scripture passages (Exod 21:22-25; Lev 24:17-22; Jer 1:4-5) that are closely related to the abortion issue. Concerned Christians should think through their stand on the rights of the unborn in relation to these other issues and in light of the whole counsel of God, not just one passage.

rushed him out. And the king himself was eager to get out because the LORD had struck him. 21So King Uzziah had leprosy until the day he died. He lived in isolation in a separate house, for he was excluded from the Temple of the LORD. His son Jotham was put in charge of the royal palace, and he governed the people of the land.

22The rest of the events of Uzziah's reign, from beginning to end, are recorded by the prophet Isaiah son of Amoz. 23When Uzziah died, he was buried with his ancestors; his grave was in a nearby burial field belonging to the kings, for the people said, "He had leprosy." And his son Jotham became the next king.

27 JOTHAM RULES IN JUDAH

Jotham was twenty-five years old when he became king, and he reigned in Jerusalem sixteen years. His mother was Jerusha, the daughter of Zadok.

2Jotham did what was pleasing in the LORD's sight. He did everything his father, Uzziah, had done, except that Jotham did not sin by entering the Temple of the LORD. But the people continued in their corrupt ways.

3Jotham rebuilt the upper gate of the Temple of the LORD. He also did extensive rebuilding on the wall at the hill of Ophel. 4He built towns in the hill country of Judah and constructed fortresses and towers in the wooded areas. 5Jotham went to war against the Ammonites and conquered them. Over the next three years he received from them an annual tribute of 7,500 pounds* of silver, 50,000 bushels of wheat, and 50,000 bushels of barley.*

6King Jotham became powerful because he was careful to live in obedience to the LORD his God.

7The rest of the events of Jotham's reign, including all his wars and other activities, are recorded in *The Book of the Kings of Israel and Judah*. 8He was twenty-five years old when he became king, and he reigned in Jerusalem sixteen years. 9When Jotham died, he was buried in the City of David. And his son Ahaz became the next king.

28 AHAZ RULES IN JUDAH

Ahaz was twenty years old when he became king, and he reigned in Jerusalem sixteen years. He did not do what was pleasing in the sight of the LORD, as his ancestor David

27:5a Hebrew *100 talents* [3,400 kilograms]. **27:5b** Hebrew *10,000 cors* [1,820 kiloliters] *of wheat, and 10,000 cors of barley.*

had done. 2Instead, he followed the example of the kings
of Israel. He cast metal images for the worship of Baal.
3He offered sacrifices in the valley of Ben-Hinnom, even
sacrificing his own sons in the fire.* In this way, he followed the detestable practices of the pagan nations the
LORD had driven from the land ahead of the Israelites. 4He
offered sacrifices and burned incense at the pagan
shrines and on the hills and under every green tree.

5Because of all this, the LORD his God allowed the king
of Aram to defeat Ahaz and to exile large numbers of his
people to Damascus. The armies of the king of Israel also
defeated Ahaz and inflicted many casualties on his army.
6In a single day Pekah son of Remaliah, Israel's king,
killed 120,000 of Judah's troops, all of them experienced
warriors, because they had abandoned the LORD, the God
of their ancestors. 7Then Zicri, a warrior from Ephraim,
killed Maaseiah, the king's son; Azrikam, the king's palace commander; and Elkanah, the king's second-in-
command. 8The armies of Israel captured 200,000
women and children from Judah and seized tremendous
amounts of plunder, which they took back to Samaria.

9But a prophet of the LORD named Oded was there in
Samaria when the army of Israel returned home. He went
out to meet them and said, "The LORD, the God of your ancestors, was angry with Judah and let you defeat them.
But you have gone too far, killing them without mercy,
and all heaven is disturbed. 10And now you are planning
to make slaves of these people from Judah and Jerusalem. What about your own sins against the LORD your
God? 11Listen to me and return these prisoners you have
taken, for they are your own relatives. Watch out, because now the LORD's fierce anger has been turned
against you!"

12Then some of the leaders of Israel*—Azariah son of
Jehohanan, Berekiah son of Meshillemoth, Jehizkiah son
of Shallum, and Amasa son of Hadlai—agreed with this
and confronted the men returning from battle. 13"You
must not bring the prisoners here!" they declared. "We
cannot afford to add to our sins and guilt. Our guilt is already great, and the LORD's fierce anger is already turned
against Israel."

14So the warriors released the prisoners and handed
over the plunder in the sight of the leaders and all the
people. 15Then the four men just mentioned by name
came forward and distributed clothes from the plunder
to the prisoners who were naked. They provided clothing
and sandals to wear, gave them enough food and drink,
and dressed their wounds with olive oil. They put those
who were weak on donkeys and took all the prisoners
back to their own people in Jericho, the city of palms.
Then they returned to Samaria.

AHAZ CLOSES THE TEMPLE

16At that time King Ahaz of Judah asked the king of Assyria for help. 17The armies of Edom had again invaded
Judah and taken captives. 18And the Philistines had
raided towns located in the foothills of Judah* and in the

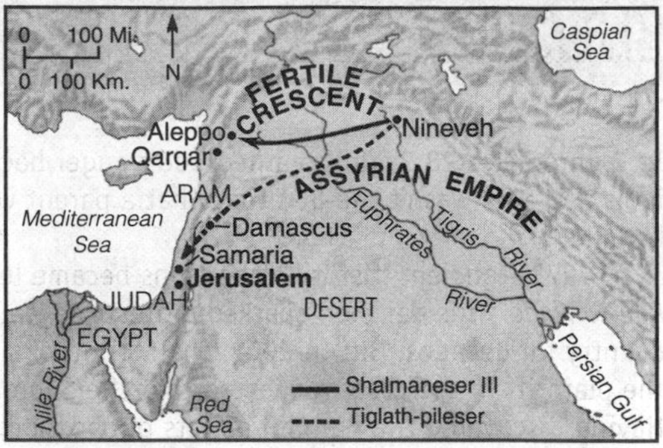

THE ASSYRIAN EMPIRE
The mighty Assyrian empire extended north from the Persian Gulf, across the Fertile Crescent, and south to Egypt. Shalmaneser III extended the empire toward the Mediterranean Sea by conquering cities as far west as Qarqar. Tiglath-pileser extended the empire south into Aram, Judah, and Philistia. It was Shalmaneser V who destroyed Samaria, Israel's capital.

Negev of Judah. They had already captured and occupied
Beth-shemesh, Aijalon, Gederoth, Soco with its villages,
Timnah with its villages, and Gimzo with its villages.
19The LORD was humbling Judah because of King Ahaz of
Judah,* for he had encouraged his people to sin and had
been utterly unfaithful to the LORD.

20So when King Tiglath-pileser* of Assyria arrived, he
attacked Ahaz instead of helping him. 21Ahaz took valuable items from the LORD's Temple, the royal palace, and
from the homes of his officials and gave them to the king
of Assyria as tribute. But this did not help him.

22Even during this time of trouble, King Ahaz continued to reject the LORD. 23He offered sacrifices to the gods
of Damascus who had defeated him, for he said, "Since
these gods helped the kings of Aram, they will help me,
too, if I sacrifice to them." But instead, they led to his ruin
and the ruin of all Judah.

24The king took the various articles from the Temple
of God and broke them into pieces. He shut the doors of
the LORD's Temple so that no one could worship there,
and he set up altars to pagan gods in every corner of Jerusalem. 25He made pagan shrines in all the towns of Judah
for offering sacrifices to other gods. In this way, he
aroused the anger of the LORD, the God of his ancestors.

26The rest of the events of Ahaz's reign and everything
he did, from beginning to end, are recorded in *The Book
of the Kings of Judah and Israel.* 27When Ahaz died, he
was buried in Jerusalem but not in the royal cemetery of
the kings of Judah. Then his son Hezekiah became the
next king.

29 HEZEKIAH RULES IN JUDAH

Hezekiah was twenty-five years old when he became the
king of Judah, and he reigned in Jerusalem twenty-nine
years. His mother was Abijah, the daughter of Zechariah.

28:3 Or *even making his sons pass through the fire.* **28:12** Hebrew *Ephraim,* referring to the northern kingdom of Israel. **28:18** Hebrew *the Shephelah.* **28:19** Hebrew *of Israel;* also in 28:23, 27. The author of Chronicles sees Judah as representative of the true Israel. See also some Hebrew manuscripts, Greek and Syriac versions, and Latin Vulgate. **28:20** Hebrew *Tilgath-pilneser,* a variant spelling of Tiglath-pileser.

2He did what was pleasing in the LORD's sight, just as his
ancestor David had done.

HEZEKIAH REOPENS THE TEMPLE

3In the very first month of the first year of his reign, Hezekiah reopened the doors of the Temple of the LORD and
repaired them. 4He summoned the priests and Levites to
meet him at the courtyard east of the Temple. 5He said to
them, "Listen to me, you Levites! Purify yourselves, and
purify the Temple of the LORD, the God of your ancestors.
Remove all the defiled things from the sanctuary. 6Our
ancestors were unfaithful and did what was evil in the
sight of the LORD our God. They abandoned the LORD and
his dwelling place; they turned their backs on him. 7They
also shut the doors to the Temple's entry room, and they
snuffed out the lamps. They stopped burning incense
and presenting burnt offerings at the sanctuary of the
God of Israel.

8"That is why the LORD's anger has fallen upon Judah
and Jerusalem. He has made them an object of dread,
horror, and ridicule, as you can see with your own eyes.
9Because of this, our fathers have been killed in battle,
and our sons and daughters and wives have been captured. 10But now I will make a covenant with the LORD, the
God of Israel, so that his fierce anger will turn away from
us. 11My sons, do not neglect your duties any longer! The
LORD has chosen you to stand in his presence, to minister
to him, and to lead the people in worship and present offerings to him."

BACK IN THE GAME 29:11

The Levites had been kept from their Temple duties by Ahaz (28:24). But Hezekiah called them back into service. Feeling inactive like the Levites due to pressure or responsibilities? If you're serious about getting back in the game, your "life coach"—God—will send opportunities your way. Then, like the Levites, be ready for action (29:12-15). ■

12Then these Levites got right to work:

From the clan of Kohath: Mahath son of Amasai and
Joel son of Azariah.
From the clan of Merari: Kish son of Abdi and
Azariah son of Jehallelel.
From the clan of Gershon: Joah son of Zimmah and
Eden son of Joah.
13 From the family of Elizaphan: Shimri and Jeiel.
From the family of Asaph: Zechariah and Mattaniah.
14 From the family of Heman: Jehiel and Shimei.
From the family of Jeduthun: Shemaiah and Uzziel.

15These men called together their fellow Levites, and
they all purified themselves. Then they began to cleanse
the Temple of the LORD, just as the king had commanded.
They were careful to follow all the LORD's instructions in
their work. 16The priests went into the sanctuary of the
Temple of the LORD to cleanse it, and they took out to the
Temple courtyard all the defiled things they found. From
there the Levites carted it all out to the Kidron Valley.
17They began the work in early spring, on the first day
of the new year,* and in eight days they had reached the
entry room of the LORD's Temple. Then they purified the
Temple of the LORD itself, which took another eight days.
So the entire task was completed in sixteen days.

THE TEMPLE REDEDICATION

18Then the Levites went to King Hezekiah and gave him
this report: "We have cleansed the entire Temple of the
LORD, the altar of burnt offering with all its utensils, and
the table of the Bread of the Presence with all its utensils.
19We have also recovered all the items discarded by King
Ahaz when he was unfaithful and closed the Temple.
They are now in front of the altar of the LORD, purified
and ready for use."

20Early the next morning King Hezekiah gathered the
city officials and went to the Temple of the LORD. 21They
brought seven bulls, seven rams, and seven male lambs as
a burnt offering, together with seven male goats as a sin
offering for the kingdom, for the Temple, and for Judah.
The king commanded the priests, who were descendants
of Aaron, to sacrifice the animals on the altar of the LORD.
22So they killed the bulls, and the priests took the blood
and sprinkled it on the altar. Next they killed the rams
and sprinkled their blood on the altar. And finally, they
did the same with the male lambs. 23The male goats for
the sin offering were then brought before the king and
the assembly of people, who laid their hands on them.
24The priests then killed the goats as a sin offering and
sprinkled their blood on the altar to make atonement for
the sins of all Israel. The king had specifically commanded that this burnt offering and sin offering should
be made for all Israel.

25King Hezekiah then stationed the Levites at the Temple of the LORD with cymbals, lyres, and harps. He obeyed
all the commands that the LORD had given to King David
through Gad, the king's seer, and the prophet Nathan.
26The Levites then took their positions around the Temple with the instruments of David, and the priests took
their positions with the trumpets.

27Then Hezekiah ordered that the burnt offering be
placed on the altar. As the burnt offering was presented,
songs of praise to the LORD were begun, accompanied by
the trumpets and other instruments of David, the former
king of Israel. 28The entire assembly worshiped the LORD as
the singers sang and the trumpets blew, until all the burnt
offerings were finished. 29Then the king and everyone with
him bowed down in worship. 30King Hezekiah and the officials ordered the Levites to praise the LORD with the
psalms written by David and by Asaph the seer. So they offered joyous praise and bowed down in worship.

31Then Hezekiah declared, "Now that you have consecrated yourselves to the LORD, bring your sacrifices and
thanksgiving offerings to the Temple of the LORD." So the
people brought their sacrifices and thanksgiving offerings, and all whose hearts were willing brought burnt

29:17 Hebrew *on the first day of the first month.* This day in the ancient Hebrew lunar calendar occurred in March or early April, 715 B.C.

offerings, too. 32The people brought to the LORD 70 bulls, 100 rams, and 200 male lambs for burnt offerings. 33They also brought 600 cattle and 3,000 sheep and goats as sacred offerings.

34But there were too few priests to prepare all the burnt offerings. So their relatives the Levites helped them until the work was finished and more priests had been purified, for the Levites had been more conscientious about purifying themselves than the priests had been. 35There was an abundance of burnt offerings, along with the usual liquid offerings, and a great deal of fat from the many peace offerings.

So the Temple of the LORD was restored to service. 36And Hezekiah and all the people rejoiced because of what God had done for the people, for everything had been accomplished so quickly.

30 PREPARATIONS FOR PASSOVER

King Hezekiah now sent word to all Israel and Judah, and he wrote letters of invitation to the people of Ephraim and Manasseh. He asked everyone to come to the Temple of the LORD at Jerusalem to celebrate the Passover of the LORD, the God of Israel. 2The king, his officials, and all the community of Jerusalem decided to celebrate Passover a month later than usual.* 3They were unable to celebrate it at the prescribed time because not enough priests could be purified by then, and the people had not yet assembled at Jerusalem.

4This plan for keeping the Passover seemed right to the king and all the people. 5So they sent a proclamation throughout all Israel, from Beersheba in the south to Dan in the north, inviting everyone to come to Jerusalem to celebrate the Passover of the LORD, the God of Israel. The people had not been celebrating it in great numbers as required in the Law.

6At the king's command, runners were sent throughout Israel and Judah. They carried letters that said:

> "O people of Israel, return to the LORD, the God of Abraham, Isaac, and Israel,* so that he will return to the few of us who have survived the conquest of the Assyrian kings. 7Do not be like your ancestors and relatives who abandoned the LORD, the God of their ancestors, and became an object of derision, as you yourselves can see. 8Do not be stubborn, as they were, but submit yourselves to the LORD. Come to his Temple, which he has set apart as holy forever. Worship the LORD your God so that his fierce anger will turn away from you.
>
> 9"For if you return to the LORD, your relatives and your children will be treated mercifully by their captors, and they will be able to return to this land. For the LORD your God is gracious and merciful. If you return to him, he will not continue to turn his face from you."

FIRST PLACE 30:1-9

Hezekiah was a king dedicated to God and to making his people right with God. In letters to the people of Judah and Israel, he urged everyone to return to God. He knew that his people could be stubborn in their refusal to let God run their lives. Running our own lives is one habit many of us like to hold on to. We might let God make a decision or two for us, while we make the majority of them. But God is an all-or-nothing God. Either he runs the whole show or we do. Who's running your show? ■

CELEBRATION OF PASSOVER

10The runners went from town to town throughout Ephraim and Manasseh and as far as the territory of Zebulun. But most of the people just laughed at the runners and made fun of them. 11However, some people from Asher, Manasseh, and Zebulun humbled themselves and went to Jerusalem.

12At the same time, God's hand was on the people in the land of Judah, giving them all one heart to obey the orders of the king and his officials, who were following the word of the LORD. 13So a huge crowd assembled at Jerusalem in midspring* to celebrate the Festival of Unleavened Bread. 14They set to work and removed the pagan altars from Jerusalem. They took away all the incense altars and threw them into the Kidron Valley.

15On the fourteenth day of the second month, one month later than usual,* the people slaughtered the Passover lamb. This shamed the priests and Levites, so they purified themselves and brought burnt offerings to the Temple of the LORD. 16Then they took their places at the Temple as prescribed in the Law of Moses, the man of God. The Levites brought the sacrificial blood to the priests, who then sprinkled it on the altar.

17Since many of the people had not purified themselves, the Levites had to slaughter their Passover lamb for them, to set them apart for the LORD. 18Most of those who came from Ephraim, Manasseh, Issachar, and Zebulun had not purified themselves. But King Hezekiah prayed for them, and they were allowed to eat the Passover meal anyway, even though this was contrary to the requirements of the Law. For Hezekiah said, "May the LORD, who is good, pardon those 19who decide to follow the LORD, the God of their ancestors, even though they are not properly cleansed for the ceremony." 20And the LORD listened to Hezekiah's prayer and healed the people.

21So the people of Israel who were present in Jerusalem joyously celebrated the Festival of Unleavened Bread for seven days. Each day the Levites and priests sang to the LORD, accompanied by loud instruments.* 22Hezekiah encouraged all the Levites regarding the skill they displayed as they served the LORD. The celebration continued for seven days. Peace offerings were

30:2 Hebrew *in the second month.* Passover was normally observed in the first month (of the ancient Hebrew lunar calendar). **30:6** *Israel* is the name that God gave to Jacob. **30:13** Hebrew *in the second month.* The second month of the ancient Hebrew lunar calendar usually occurs within the months of April and May. **30:15** Hebrew *On the fourteenth day of the second month.* Passover normally began on the fourteenth day of the first month (see Lev 23:5). **30:21** Or *sang to the LORD with all their strength.*

sacrificed, and the people gave thanks to the Lord, the God of their ancestors.

[23]The entire assembly then decided to continue the festival another seven days, so they celebrated joyfully for another week. [24]King Hezekiah gave the people 1,000 bulls and 7,000 sheep and goats for offerings, and the officials donated 1,000 bulls and 10,000 sheep and goats. Meanwhile, many more priests purified themselves.

[25]The entire assembly of Judah rejoiced, including the priests, the Levites, all who came from the land of Israel, the foreigners who came to the festival, and all those who lived in Judah. [26]There was great joy in the city, for Jerusalem had not seen a celebration like this one since the days of Solomon, King David's son. [27]Then the priests and Levites stood and blessed the people, and God heard their prayer from his holy dwelling in heaven.

31 HEZEKIAH'S RELIGIOUS REFORMS

When the festival ended, the Israelites who attended went to all the towns of Judah, Benjamin, Ephraim, and Manasseh, and they smashed all the sacred pillars, cut down the Asherah poles, and removed the pagan shrines and altars. After this, the Israelites returned to their own towns and homes.

[2]Hezekiah then organized the priests and Levites into divisions to offer the burnt offerings and peace offerings, and to worship and give thanks and praise to the Lord at the gates of the Temple. [3]The king also made a personal contribution of animals for the daily morning and evening burnt offerings, the weekly Sabbath festivals, the monthly new moon festivals, and the annual festivals as prescribed in the Law of the Lord. [4]In addition, he required the people in Jerusalem to bring a portion of their goods to the priests and Levites, so they could devote themselves fully to the Law of the Lord.

[5]The people of Israel responded immediately and generously by bringing the first of their crops and grain, new wine, olive oil, honey, and all the produce of their fields. They brought a large quantity—a tithe of all they produced. [6]The people who had moved to Judah from Israel, and the people of Judah themselves, brought in the tithes of their cattle, sheep, and goats and a tithe of the things that had been dedicated to the Lord their God, and they piled them up in great heaps. [7]They began piling them up in late spring, and the heaps continued to grow until early autumn.* [8]When Hezekiah and his officials came and saw these huge piles, they thanked the Lord and his people Israel!

[9]"Where did all this come from?" Hezekiah asked the priests and Levites.

[10]And Azariah the high priest, from the family of Zadok, replied, "Since the people began bringing their gifts to the Lord's Temple, we have had enough to eat and plenty to spare. The Lord has blessed his people, and all this is left over."

[11]Hezekiah ordered that storerooms be prepared in the Temple of the Lord. When this was done, [12]the people faithfully brought all the tithes and gifts to the Temple. Conaniah the Levite was put in charge, assisted by his brother Shimei. [13]The supervisors under them were Jehiel, Azaziah, Nahath, Asahel, Jerimoth, Jozabad, Eliel, Ismakiah, Mahath, and Benaiah. These appointments were made by King Hezekiah and Azariah, the chief official in the Temple of God.

GENEROSITY 31:4-12

Hezekiah reestablished the practice of tithing—giving the first portion of one's income—to the priests and Levites to allow them to serve God in the Temple. The people responded immediately and generously. God's work needs the support of his people. Does God receive the first portion of your income or your time? Generosity makes our giving delightful to God (2 Cor 8–9). How different the church would be today if all believers consistently followed this pattern. ■

[14]Kore son of Imnah the Levite, who was the gatekeeper at the East Gate, was put in charge of distributing the voluntary offerings given to God, the gifts, and the things that had been dedicated to the Lord. [15]His faithful assistants were Eden, Miniamin, Jeshua, Shemaiah, Amariah, and Shecaniah. They distributed the gifts among the families of priests in their towns by their divisions, dividing the gifts fairly among old and young alike. [16]They distributed the gifts to all males three years old or older, regardless of their place in the genealogical records. The distribution went to all who would come to the Lord's Temple to perform their daily duties according to their divisions. [17]They distributed gifts to the priests who were listed by their families in the genealogical records, and to the Levites twenty years old or older who were listed according to their jobs and their divisions. [18]Food allotments were also given to the families of all those listed in the genealogical records, including their little babies, wives, sons, and daughters. For they had all been faithful in purifying themselves.

[19]As for the priests, the descendants of Aaron, who were living in the open villages around the towns, men were appointed by name to distribute portions to every male among the priests and to all the Levites listed in the genealogical records.

[20]In this way, King Hezekiah handled the distribution throughout all Judah, doing what was pleasing and good in the sight of the Lord his God. [21]In all that he did in the service of the Temple of God and in his efforts to follow God's laws and commands, Hezekiah sought his God wholeheartedly. As a result, he was very successful.

31:7 Hebrew *in the third month . . . until the seventh month.* The third month of the ancient Hebrew lunar calendar usually occurs within the months of May and June; the seventh month usually occurs within September and October.

32 ASSYRIA INVADES JUDAH

After Hezekiah had faithfully carried out this work, King
Sennacherib of Assyria invaded Judah. He laid siege to
the fortified towns, giving orders for his army to break
through their walls. 2When Hezekiah realized that Sennacherib also intended to attack Jerusalem, 3he consulted with his officials and military advisers, and they
decided to stop the flow of the springs outside the city.
4They organized a huge work crew to stop the flow of the
springs, cutting off the brook that ran through the fields.
For they said, "Why should the kings of Assyria come
here and find plenty of water?"

TRUSTING GOD 32:1-8

When King Hezekiah was confronted with an Assyrian invasion, he made two important decisions. (1) He did everything he could to deal with the situation, and (2) he trusted God for the outcome. When you're faced with difficult or frightening situations, is this your pattern of action? ■

5Then Hezekiah worked hard at repairing all the broken sections of the wall, erecting towers, and constructing a second wall outside the first. He also reinforced the
supporting terraces* in the City of David and manufac-
tured large numbers of weapons and shields. 6He appointed military officers over the people and assembled
them before him in the square at the city gate. Then
Hezekiah encouraged them by saying: 7"Be strong and
courageous! Don't be afraid or discouraged because of
the king of Assyria or his mighty army, for there is a
power far greater on our side! 8He may have a great army,
but they are merely men. We have the LORD our God to
help us and to fight our battles for us!" Hezekiah's words
greatly encouraged the people.

32:5 Hebrew *the millo*. The meaning of the Hebrew is uncertain.

SENNACHERIB THREATENS JERUSALEM

9While King Sennacherib of Assyria was still besieging
the town of Lachish, he sent his officers to Jerusalem
with this message for Hezekiah and all the people in
the city:

10"This is what King Sennacherib of Assyria says:
What are you trusting in that makes you think you
can survive my siege of Jerusalem? 11Hezekiah has
said, 'The LORD our God will rescue us from the king
of Assyria.' Surely Hezekiah is misleading you,
sentencing you to death by famine and thirst! 12Don't
you realize that Hezekiah is the very person who
destroyed all the LORD's shrines and altars? He
commanded Judah and Jerusalem to worship only
at the altar at the Temple and to offer sacrifices on
it alone.
13"Surely you must realize what I and the other
kings of Assyria before me have done to all the
people of the earth! Were any of the gods of those
nations able to rescue their people from my power?
14Which of their gods was able to rescue its people
from the destructive power of my predecessors?

MANASSEH

UP:
- Humbly repented of his sins before God

DOWNS:
- Challenged God's authority and was defeated
- Reversed many of the positive effects of his father Hezekiah's rule
- Sacrificed his children to idols

STATS:
- Occupation: King of Judah
- Relatives: Hezekiah (father); Hephzibah (mother); Amon (son)

BOTTOM LINE:
Forgiveness is limited not by the amount of sin, but by our willingness to repent.

Manasseh's story is told in 2 Kings 21:1-18 and 2 Chron 32:33–33:20. He also is mentioned in Jer 15:4.

MANASSEH In your opinion what's the worst thing that a person could do? Got a list in mind? If you take a good look at Manasseh's life, you might find an action or two from your list. Manasseh made evil an art form.

Just how bad was this guy? Not only did he build altars dedicated to pagan gods in Solomon's Temple, he also sacrificed his children to them! He also had a few hobbies that angered God, namely sorcery, divination, and witchcraft. He also frequented the psychic hotline of the day.

But God showed justice to Manasseh by warning him, then allowing him to be conquered and captured.

Something amazing happened in response: Manasseh asked God to forgive his sins! When God said yes to his request, Manasseh was given a new start.

Still got that list in your head of the worse things that a person could do? Maybe your name's on that list as the doer of one of those terrible actions. If so, take a minute to reread Manasseh's story. God is still ready to forgive even the worst things that a person could do.

What makes you think your God can rescue you from me? 15Don't let Hezekiah deceive you! Don't let him fool you like this! I say it again—no god of any nation or kingdom has ever yet been able to rescue his people from me or my ancestors. How much less will your God rescue you from my power!"

16And Sennacherib's officers further mocked the LORD God and his servant Hezekiah, heaping insult upon insult. 17The king also sent letters scorning the LORD, the God of Israel. He wrote, "Just as the gods of all the other nations failed to rescue their people from my power, so the God of Hezekiah will also fail." 18The Assyrian officials who brought the letters shouted this in Hebrew* to the people gathered on the walls of the city, trying to terrify them so it would be easier to capture the city. 19These officers talked about the God of Jerusalem as though he were one of the pagan gods, made by human hands.

20Then King Hezekiah and the prophet Isaiah son of Amoz cried out in prayer to God in heaven. 21And the LORD sent an angel who destroyed the Assyrian army with all its commanders and officers. So Sennacherib was forced to return home in disgrace to his own land. And when he entered the temple of his god, some of his own sons killed him there with a sword.

22That is how the LORD rescued Hezekiah and the people of Jerusalem from King Sennacherib of Assyria and from all the others who threatened them. So there was peace throughout the land. 23From then on King Hezekiah became highly respected among all the surrounding nations, and many gifts for the LORD arrived at Jerusalem, with valuable presents for King Hezekiah, too.

HEZEKIAH'S SICKNESS AND RECOVERY

24About that time Hezekiah became deathly ill. He prayed to the LORD, who healed him and gave him a miraculous sign. 25But Hezekiah did not respond appropriately to the kindness shown him, and he became proud. So the LORD's anger came against him and against Judah and Jerusalem. 26Then Hezekiah humbled himself and repented of his pride, as did the people of Jerusalem. So the LORD's anger did not fall on them during Hezekiah's lifetime.

27Hezekiah was very wealthy and highly honored. He built special treasury buildings for his silver, gold, precious stones, and spices, and for his shields and other valuable items. 28He also constructed many storehouses for his grain, new wine, and olive oil; and he made many stalls for his cattle and pens for his flocks of sheep and goats. 29He built many towns and acquired vast flocks and herds, for God had given him great wealth. 30He blocked up the upper spring of Gihon and brought the water down through a tunnel to the west side of the City of David. And so he succeeded in everything he did.

31However, when ambassadors arrived from Babylon to ask about the remarkable events that had taken place in the land, God withdrew from Hezekiah in order to test him and to see what was really in his heart.

SUMMARY OF HEZEKIAH'S REIGN

32The rest of the events in Hezekiah's reign and his acts of devotion are recorded in *The Vision of the Prophet Isaiah Son of Amoz,* which is included in *The Book of the Kings of Judah and Israel.* 33When Hezekiah died, he was buried in the upper area of the royal cemetery, and all Judah and Jerusalem honored him at his death. And his son Manasseh became the next king.

BEYOND FORGIVENESS? 33:1-13

In the list of corrupt kings, Manasseh would rank near the top. His life is a catalog of evil deeds including idol worship, sacrificing his own children, and Temple desecration. But after being captured by the Assyrians, he asked God to forgive him for his wrongs. God forgave him. Even after reading that story, do you still doubt that anyone could forgive what you have done? Take heart—until death, no one is beyond God's forgiveness. ■

33

MANASSEH RULES IN JUDAH

Manasseh was twelve years old when he became king, and he reigned in Jerusalem fifty-five years. 2He did what was evil in the LORD's sight, following the detestable practices of the pagan nations that the LORD had driven from the land ahead of the Israelites. 3He rebuilt the pagan shrines his father, Hezekiah, had broken down. He constructed altars for the images of Baal and set up Asherah poles. He also bowed before all the powers of the heavens and worshiped them.

4He built pagan altars in the Temple of the LORD, the place where the LORD had said, "My name will remain in Jerusalem forever." 5He built these altars for all the powers of the heavens in both courtyards of the LORD's Temple. 6Manasseh also sacrificed his own sons in the fire* in the valley of Ben-Hinnom. He practiced sorcery, divination, and witchcraft, and he consulted with mediums and psychics. He did much that was evil in the LORD's sight, arousing his anger.

7Manasseh even took a carved idol he had made and set it up in God's Temple, the very place where God had told David and his son Solomon: "My name will be honored forever in this Temple and in Jerusalem—the city I have chosen from among all the tribes of Israel. 8If the Israelites will be careful to obey my commands—all the laws, decrees, and regulations given through Moses—I will not send them into exile from this land that I set aside for your ancestors." 9But Manasseh led the people of Judah and Jerusalem to do even more evil than the pagan nations that the LORD had destroyed when the people of Israel entered the land.

10The LORD spoke to Manasseh and his people, but they ignored all his warnings. 11So the LORD sent the commanders of the Assyrian armies, and they took Manasseh prisoner. They put a ring through his nose, bound him in

32:18 Hebrew *in the dialect of Judah.* **33:6** Or *also made his sons pass through the fire.*

bronze chains, and led him away to Babylon. 12But while
in deep distress, Manasseh sought the LORD his God and
sincerely humbled himself before the God of his ancestors. 13And when he prayed, the LORD listened to him and
was moved by his request. So the LORD brought Manasseh back to Jerusalem and to his kingdom. Then Manasseh finally realized that the LORD alone is God!
14After this Manasseh rebuilt the outer wall of the
City of David, from west of the Gihon Spring in the Kidron Valley to the Fish Gate, and continuing around the
hill of Ophel. He built the wall very high. And he stationed his military officers in all of the fortified towns
of Judah. 15Manasseh also removed the foreign gods
and the idol from the LORD's Temple. He tore down all
the altars he had built on the hill where the Temple
stood and all the altars that were in Jerusalem, and he
dumped them outside the city. 16Then he restored the
altar of the LORD and sacrificed peace offerings and
thanksgiving offerings on it. He also encouraged the
people of Judah to worship the LORD, the God of Israel.
17However, the people still sacrificed at the pagan
shrines, though only to the LORD their God.
18The rest of the events of Manasseh's reign, his prayer
to God, and the words the seers spoke to him in the name
of the LORD, the God of Israel, are recorded in *The Book of
the Kings of Israel.* 19Manasseh's prayer, the account of
the way God answered him, and an account of all his sins
and unfaithfulness are recorded in *The Record of the
Seers.** It includes a list of the locations where he built
pagan shrines and set up Asherah poles and idols before
he humbled himself and repented. 20When Manasseh
died, he was buried in his palace. Then his son Amon became the next king.

AMON RULES IN JUDAH

21Amon was twenty-two years old when he became king,
and he reigned in Jerusalem two years. 22He did what was
evil in the LORD's sight, just as his father, Manasseh, had
done. He worshiped and sacrificed to all the idols his father had made. 23But unlike his father, he did not humble
himself before the LORD. Instead, Amon sinned even
more.
24Then Amon's own officials conspired against him
and assassinated him in his palace. 25But the people of
the land killed all those who had conspired against King
Amon, and they made his son Josiah the next king.

34 JOSIAH RULES IN JUDAH

Josiah was eight years old when he became king, and he
reigned in Jerusalem thirty-one years. 2He did what was
pleasing in the LORD's sight and followed the example of
his ancestor David. He did not turn away from doing
what was right.
3During the eighth year of his reign, while he was still
young, Josiah began to seek the God of his ancestor David. Then in the twelfth year he began to purify Judah and
Jerusalem, destroying all the pagan shrines, the Asherah
poles, and the carved idols and cast images. 4He ordered
that the altars of Baal be demolished and that the incense
altars which stood above them be broken down. He also
made sure that the Asherah poles, the carved idols, and
the cast images were smashed and scattered over the
graves of those who had sacrificed to them. 5He burned
the bones of the pagan priests on their own altars, and so
he purified Judah and Jerusalem.

AMERICAN IDOLS

Tim normally uses anthropology class to snooze or do algebra homework. Not today. Mr. Mariano spent the hour talking about the religious beliefs of certain tribes indigenous to the rainforests of the Amazon. The discussion of human sacrifices and strange rituals had Tim paying extra special attention.

After school, he continued to rattle on about what he had heard. "Lindsey, can you believe people would actually worship a piece of wood or stone? Don't you think that's weird?"

"Like we're any better in this country?" Lindsey scoffed.

"What are you talking about?"

"We worship idols here, too."

"Aw, come on! Nobody worships statues or rocks around here."

"Well, no. But think about it. Think about the people who build their lives around the American dream—getting more stuff or a bigger house, gaining more status. Or think about the people who spend all of their time and money on sports or getting good grades, or—"

"Hey! What's wrong with sports?"

"Nothing . . . unless a sport takes over your whole life. Tim, anything that becomes more important than God is an idol."

Do you think Lindsey's right? Why or why not? Not sure? Check out the story of King Josiah in 2 Chronicles 34.

6He did the same thing in the towns of Manasseh,
Ephraim, and Simeon, even as far as Naphtali, and in the
regions* all around them. 7He destroyed the pagan altars
and the Asherah poles, and he crushed the idols into
dust. He cut down all the incense altars throughout the
land of Israel. Finally, he returned to Jerusalem.
8In the eighteenth year of his reign, after he had purified the land and the Temple, Josiah appointed Shaphan
son of Azaliah, Maaseiah the governor of Jerusalem, and
Joah son of Joahaz, the royal historian, to repair the Temple of the LORD his God. 9They gave Hilkiah the high
priest the money that had been collected by the Levites
who served as gatekeepers at the Temple of God. The gifts

33:19 Or *The Record of Hozai.* **34:6** As in Syriac version. Hebrew reads *in their temples,* or *in their ruins.* The meaning of the Hebrew is uncertain.

were brought by people from Manasseh, Ephraim, and
from all the remnant of Israel, as well as from all Judah,
Benjamin, and the people of Jerusalem.
10He entrusted the money to the men assigned to supervise the restoration of the LORD's Temple. Then they
paid the workers who did the repairs and renovation of
the Temple. 11They hired carpenters and builders, who
purchased finished stone for the walls and timber for the
rafters and beams. They restored what earlier kings of Judah had allowed to fall into ruin.
12The workers served faithfully under the leadership
of Jahath and Obadiah, Levites of the Merarite clan, and
Zechariah and Meshullam, Levites of the Kohathite clan.
Other Levites, all of whom were skilled musicians, 13were
put in charge of the laborers of the various trades. Still
others assisted as secretaries, officials, and gatekeepers.

HILKIAH DISCOVERS GOD'S LAW

14While they were bringing out the money collected at
the LORD's Temple, Hilkiah the priest found the Book of
the Law of the LORD that was written by Moses. 15Hilkiah
said to Shaphan the court secretary, "I have found the
Book of the Law in the LORD's Temple!" Then Hilkiah
gave the scroll to Shaphan.
16Shaphan took the scroll to the king and reported,
"Your officials are doing everything they were assigned to
do. 17The money that was collected at the Temple of the
LORD has been turned over to the supervisors and workmen." 18Shaphan also told the king, "Hilkiah the priest has
given me a scroll." So Shaphan read it to the king.
19When the king heard what was written in the Law, he
tore his clothes in despair. 20Then he gave these orders to
Hilkiah, Ahikam son of Shaphan, Acbor son of Micaiah,*
Shaphan the court secretary, and Asaiah the king's personal
adviser: 21"Go to the Temple and speak to the LORD for me
and for all the remnant of Israel and Judah. Inquire about
the words written in the scroll that has been found. For the
LORD's great anger has been poured out on us because our
ancestors have not obeyed the word of the LORD. We have
not been doing everything this scroll says we must do."
22So Hilkiah and the other men went to the New Quarter* of Jerusalem to consult with the prophet Huldah.
She was the wife of Shallum son of Tikvah, son of Harhas,* the keeper of the Temple wardrobe.
23She said to them, "The LORD, the God of Israel, has
spoken! Go back and tell the man who sent you, 24'This is
what the LORD says: I am going to bring disaster on this
city* and its people. All the curses written in the scroll
that was read to the king of Judah will come true. 25For
my people have abandoned me and offered sacrifices to
pagan gods, and I am very angry with them for everything
they have done. My anger will be poured out on this place,
and it will not be quenched.'
26"But go to the king of Judah who sent you to seek the
LORD and tell him: 'This is what the LORD, the God of Israel, says concerning the message you have just heard:
27You were sorry and humbled yourself before God when
you heard his words against this city and its people. You
humbled yourself and tore your clothing in despair and
wept before me in repentance. And I have indeed heard
you, says the LORD. 28So I will not send the promised disaster until after you have died and been buried in peace.
You yourself will not see the disaster I am going to bring
on this city and its people.'"
So they took her message back to the king.

JOSIAH'S RELIGIOUS REFORMS

29Then the king summoned all the elders of Judah and Jerusalem. 30And the king went up to the Temple of the
LORD with all the people of Judah and Jerusalem, along
with the priests and the Levites—all the people from the
greatest to the least. There the king read to them the entire Book of the Covenant that had been found in the
LORD's Temple. 31The king took his place of authority beside the pillar and renewed the covenant in the LORD's
presence. He pledged to obey the LORD by keeping all his
commands, laws, and decrees with all his heart and soul.
He promised to obey all the terms of the covenant that
were written in the scroll. 32And he required everyone in
Jerusalem and the people of Benjamin to make a similar
pledge. The people of Jerusalem did so, renewing their
covenant with God, the God of their ancestors.

GOTTA READ IT 34:31

When Josiah read the Book of the Law that Hilkiah discovered (34:14), he promised to follow God's commandments. There's not much difference between a book hidden in the Temple and a Bible hidden on the bookshelf. We can't know what God wants us to do if we don't read it. And reading God's Word isn't enough; we need to be willing to do what it says. Are you willing? ■

33So Josiah removed all detestable idols from the entire land of Israel and required everyone to worship the
LORD their God. And throughout the rest of his lifetime,
they did not turn away from the LORD, the God of their
ancestors.

35 JOSIAH CELEBRATES PASSOVER

Then Josiah announced that the Passover of the LORD
would be celebrated in Jerusalem, and so the Passover
lamb was slaughtered on the fourteenth day of the first
month.* 2Josiah also assigned the priests to their duties
and encouraged them in their work at the Temple of the
LORD. 3He issued this order to the Levites, who were to
teach all Israel and who had been set apart to serve the
LORD: "Put the holy Ark in the Temple that was built by
Solomon son of David, the king of Israel. You no longer
need to carry it back and forth on your shoulders. Now
spend your time serving the LORD your God and his people
Israel. 4Report for duty according to the family divisions

34:20 As in parallel text at 2 Kgs 22:12; Hebrew reads *Abdon son of Micah*. 34:22a Or *the Second Quarter*, a newer section of Jerusalem. Hebrew reads *the Mishneh*. 34:22b As in parallel text at 2 Kgs 22:14; Hebrew reads *son of Tokhath, son of Hasrah*. 34:24 Hebrew *this place;* also in 34:27, 28. 35:1 This day in the ancient Hebrew lunar calendar was April 5, 622 B.C.

of your ancestors, following the directions of King David
of Israel and the directions of his son Solomon.
5"Then stand in the sanctuary at the place appointed
for your family division and help the families assigned
to you as they bring their offerings to the Temple.
6Slaughter the Passover lambs, purify yourselves, and
prepare to help those who come. Follow all the directions
that the LORD gave through Moses."
7Then Josiah provided 30,000 lambs and young goats
for the people's Passover offerings, along with 3,000 cattle, all from the king's own flocks and herds. 8The king's
officials also made willing contributions to the people,
priests, and Levites. Hilkiah, Zechariah, and Jehiel, the
administrators of God's Temple, gave the priests 2,600
lambs and young goats and 300 cattle as Passover offerings. 9The Levite leaders—Conaniah and his brothers
Shemaiah and Nethanel, as well as Hashabiah, Jeiel, and
Jozabad—gave 5,000 lambs and young goats and
500 cattle to the Levites for their Passover offerings.
10When everything was ready for the Passover celebration, the priests and the Levites took their places, organized by their divisions, as the king had commanded.
11The Levites then slaughtered the Passover lambs and
presented the blood to the priests, who sprinkled the
blood on the altar while the Levites prepared the animals.
12They divided the burnt offerings among the people by
their family groups, so they could offer them to the LORD
as prescribed in the Book of Moses. They did the same
with the cattle. 13Then they roasted the Passover lambs as
prescribed; and they boiled the holy offerings in pots,
kettles, and pans, and brought them out quickly so the
people could eat them.
14Afterward the Levites prepared Passover offerings
for themselves and for the priests—the descendants of
Aaron—because the priests had been busy from morning
till night offering the burnt offerings and the fat portions. The Levites took responsibility for all these
preparations.
15The musicians, descendants of Asaph, were in their
assigned places, following the commands that had been
given by David, Asaph, Heman, and Jeduthun, the king's
seer. The gatekeepers guarded the gates and did not need
to leave their posts of duty, for their Passover offerings
were prepared for them by their fellow Levites.
16The entire ceremony for the LORD's Passover was completed that day. All the burnt offerings were sacrificed on
the altar of the LORD, as King Josiah had commanded. 17All
the Israelites present in Jerusalem celebrated Passover
and the Festival of Unleavened Bread for seven days.
18Never since the time of the prophet Samuel had there
been such a Passover. None of the kings of Israel had ever
kept a Passover as Josiah did, involving all the priests and
Levites, all the people of Jerusalem, and people from all
over Judah and Israel. 19This Passover celebration took
place in the eighteenth year of Josiah's reign.

JOSIAH DIES IN BATTLE

20After Josiah had finished restoring the Temple, King
Neco of Egypt led his army up from Egypt to do battle at

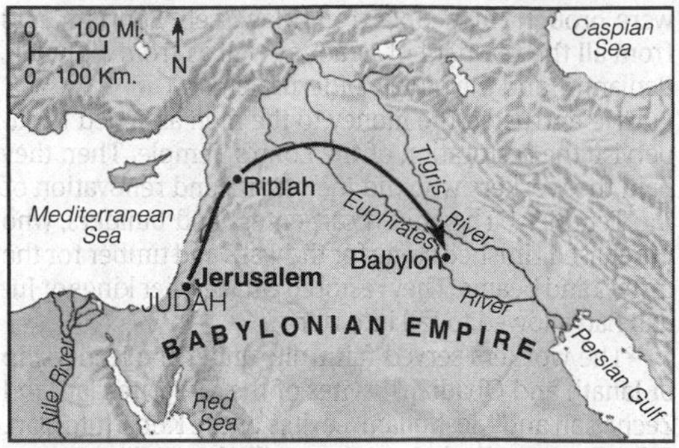

EXILE TO BABYLON

Despite Judah's few good kings and timely reforms, the people never truly changed. Their evil continued, and finally God used the Babylonian empire under Nebuchadnezzar to conquer Judah, destroy Jerusalem, and take the people captive to Babylon.

Carchemish on the Euphrates River, and Josiah and his
army marched out to fight him.* 21But King Neco sent
messengers to Josiah with this message:

> "What do you want with me, king of Judah? I have no quarrel with you today! I am on my way to fight another nation, and God has told me to hurry! Do not interfere with God, who is with me, or he will destroy you."

22But Josiah refused to listen to Neco, to whom God
had indeed spoken, and he would not turn back. Instead,
he disguised himself and led his army into battle on the
plain of Megiddo. 23But the enemy archers hit King Josiah with their arrows and wounded him. He cried out to
his men, "Take me from the battle, for I am badly
wounded!"
24So they lifted Josiah out of his chariot and placed
him in another chariot. Then they brought him back to
Jerusalem, where he died. He was buried there in the
royal cemetery. And all Judah and Jerusalem mourned
for him. 25The prophet Jeremiah composed funeral
songs for Josiah, and to this day choirs still sing these
sad songs about his death. These songs of sorrow have
become a tradition and are recorded in *The Book of
Laments*.
26The rest of the events of Josiah's reign and his acts
of devotion (carried out according to what was written
in the Law of the LORD), 27from beginning to end—all
are recorded in *The Book of the Kings of Israel and
Judah*.

36 JEHOAHAZ RULES IN JUDAH

Then the people of the land took Josiah's son Jehoahaz
and made him the next king in Jerusalem.
2Jehoahaz* was twenty-three years old when he became king, and he reigned in Jerusalem three months.
3Then he was deposed by the king of Egypt, who

35:20 Or *Josiah went out to meet him.* 36:2 Hebrew *Joahaz,* a variant spelling of Jehoahaz; also in 36:4.

BEYOND CURE 36:16

God continually warned the people of Judah about their wrongs and offered forgiveness. But the people constantly returned to their bad habits. Eventually the situation was beyond cure. Wondering why? After a time God allows people who constantly reject him to go their own way. (See Rom 1:18-32.) When that happens, judgment follows. As Romans 1:18 tell us, "God shows his anger from heaven against all sinful, wicked people who suppress the truth by their wickedness." Don't want that? Don't reject him. ■

demanded that Judah pay 7,500 pounds of silver and 75 pounds of gold* as tribute.

JEHOIAKIM RULES IN JUDAH

4The king of Egypt then installed Eliakim, the brother of
Jehoahaz, as the next king of Judah and Jerusalem, and he
changed Eliakim's name to Jehoiakim. Then Neco took
Jehoahaz to Egypt as a prisoner.
5Jehoiakim was twenty-five years old when he became
king, and he reigned in Jerusalem eleven years. He did
what was evil in the sight of the LORD his God.
6Then King Nebuchadnezzar of Babylon came to Jerusalem and captured it, and he bound Jehoiakim in bronze
chains and led him away to Babylon. 7Nebuchadnezzar
also took some of the treasures from the Temple of the
LORD, and he placed them in his palace* in Babylon.
8The rest of the events in Jehoiakim's reign, including
all the evil things he did and everything found against
him, are recorded in *The Book of the Kings of Israel and Judah*. Then his son Jehoiachin became the next king.

JEHOIACHIN RULES IN JUDAH

9Jehoiachin was eighteen* years old when he became
king, and he reigned in Jerusalem three months and ten
days. Jehoiachin did what was evil in the LORD's sight.
10In the spring of the year* King Nebuchadnezzar took
Jehoiachin to Babylon. Many treasures from the Temple
of the LORD were also taken to Babylon at that time. And
Nebuchadnezzar installed Jehoiachin's uncle,* Zedekiah, as the next king in Judah and Jerusalem.

ZEDEKIAH RULES IN JUDAH

11Zedekiah was twenty-one years old when he became
king, and he reigned in Jerusalem eleven years. 12He did
what was evil in the sight of the LORD his God, and he refused to humble himself when the prophet Jeremiah
spoke to him directly from the LORD. 13He also rebelled
against King Nebuchadnezzar, even though he had
taken an oath of loyalty in God's name. Zedekiah was a
hard and stubborn man, refusing to turn to the LORD, the
God of Israel.
14Likewise, all the leaders of the priests and the people
became more and more unfaithful. They followed all the
pagan practices of the surrounding nations, desecrating
the Temple of the LORD that had been consecrated in
Jerusalem.
15The LORD, the God of their ancestors, repeatedly sent
his prophets to warn them, for he had compassion on his
people and his Temple. 16But the people mocked these
messengers of God and despised their words. They
scoffed at the prophets until the LORD's anger could no
longer be restrained and nothing could be done.

THE FALL OF JERUSALEM

17So the LORD brought the king of Babylon against them.
The Babylonians* killed Judah's young men, even chasing after them into the Temple. They had no pity on the
people, killing both young men and young women, the
old and the infirm. God handed all of them over to Nebuchadnezzar. 18The king took home to Babylon all the articles, large and small, used in the Temple of God, and the
treasures from both the LORD's Temple and from the palace of the king and his officials. 19Then his army burned
the Temple of God, tore down the walls of Jerusalem,
burned all the palaces, and completely destroyed everything of value.* 20The few who survived were taken as exiles to Babylon, and they became servants to the king and
his sons until the kingdom of Persia came to power.
21So the message of the LORD spoken through Jeremiah was fulfilled. The land finally enjoyed its Sabbath rest,
lying desolate until the seventy years were fulfilled, just
as the prophet had said.

STRIPPED 36:22-23

Second Chronicles started off on a high note, with the people gladly worshiping in the newly built Temple. But after ignoring God, they found themselves stripped of everything and carried off to Babylon. Even though they lost it all, God was still with them. Like the people of Israel, are you feeling like you've been left with nothing? When everything in life seems stripped away from us, we also can be assured that God will never abandon us. ■

CYRUS ALLOWS THE EXILES TO RETURN

22In the first year of King Cyrus of Persia,* the LORD fulfilled the prophecy he had given through Jeremiah.* He
stirred the heart of Cyrus to put this proclamation in
writing and to send it throughout his kingdom:

23"This is what King Cyrus of Persia says:
"The LORD, the God of heaven, has given me all the kingdoms of the earth. He has appointed me to build him a Temple at Jerusalem, which is in Judah. Any of you who are the LORD's people may go there for this task. And may the LORD your God be with you!"

36:3 Hebrew *100 talents* [3,400 kilograms] *of silver and 1 talent* [34 kilograms] *of gold*. **36:7** Or *temple*. **36:9** As in one Hebrew manuscript, some Greek manuscripts, and Syriac version (see also 2 Kgs 24:8); most Hebrew manuscripts read *eight*. **36:10a** Hebrew *At the turn of the year*. The first day of this year in the ancient Hebrew lunar calendar was April 13, 597 B.C. **36:10b** As in parallel text at 2 Kgs 24:17; Hebrew reads *brother*, or *relative*. **36:17** Or *Chaldeans*. **36:19** Or *destroyed all the valuable articles from the Temple*. **36:22a** The first year of Cyrus's reign over Babylon was 538 B.C. **36:22b** See Jer 25:11-12; 29:10.

EZRA

EVER LOOK at someone who seems to have everything and think, *Man, he/she's got it made. What more could he/she want?* On the surface, that person's life seems perfect. But looks can be deceiving.

The same holds true in the life of the people of Israel. Years earlier, under Zerubbabel's leadership, some of the people from Israel had been given permission to leave Babylon and return to build the Temple. Although the returnees had met with some opposition, eventually they were successful. The Temple was completed and dedicated. Everything looked good on the outside.

But when Ezra, a priest and scribe, reached Jerusalem, he wept. The people *looked* obedient because they had rebuilt the Temple. Yet their lives were a mess. Ezra knew that they needed a spiritual tune-up. The book of Ezra shows his commitment to helping his people to make things right with God.

In need of a spiritual tune-up? As you read Ezra you can make Ezra's commitment yours.

timeline

586 B.C.
Jerusalem destroyed; exiles to Babylon

539
Babylon overthrown by Cyrus

538
Cyrus's decree to return

537
Exiles return to Jerusalem

536
Temple construction begins

530
Temple work halted

522
Darius becomes king of Persia

520
Temple work resumed; messages of Haggai, Zechariah given

516
Temple completed

458
Ezra comes to Jerusalem

445
Nehemiah comes to Jerusalem

stats

PURPOSE: To show God's faithfulness as he kept his promise to restore his people to their land

AUTHOR: Not stated, but probably Ezra

DATE WRITTEN: Around 450 B.C., recording events from about 538–450 B.C. (omitting 516–458 B.C.); possibly begun earlier in Babylon and finished in Jerusalem

SETTING: Ezra follows 2 Chronicles as a history of the Jews, recording their return to the Promised Land after their captivity.

KEY PEOPLE: Ezra, Cyrus, Zerubbabel, Haggai, Zechariah, Darius, Artaxerxes

KEY PLACES: Babylon, Jerusalem

SPECIAL FEATURES: Ezra and Nehemiah originally were one book in the Hebrew Bible and, with Esther, are considered the post-captivity historical books. The post-captivity prophetic books are Haggai, Zechariah, and Malachi. Haggai and Zechariah prophesied during the period of the reconstruction of Jerusalem.

KEY points

RESTORATION
By returning to the land of Israel from Babylon, the Jews showed their belief in God 's promise to restore them. God promises to forgive and restore us when we return to him.

OPPOSITION
Opposition came soon after the people of Israel built the altar and the Temple foundation was laid. Opposition always comes whenever anyone does anything for God. But God can overcome all opposition.

GOD'S WORD
When the people of Israel returned to their homeland, they also returned to the influence of God's Word. The Bible also can be a powerful influence on our lives.

1 CYRUS ALLOWS THE EXILES TO RETURN

In the first year of King Cyrus of Persia,* the LORD fulfilled the prophecy he had given through Jeremiah.* He
stirred the heart of Cyrus to put this proclamation in
writing and to send it throughout his kingdom:

CAPTIVES 1:1-7

King Cyrus of Persia allowed many of the people of Israel to return to their homeland. What he didn't realize, however, was that he was the means of fulfilling God's promise to return the people to their land. As Proverbs 21:1 says, "The king's heart is like a stream of water directed by the LORD; he guides it wherever he pleases." God's plans are never overthrown. Are you willing to trust that he will fulfill any promise he's made to you? ■

[2]"This is what King Cyrus of Persia says:
"The LORD, the God of heaven, has given me all the
kingdoms of the earth. He has appointed me to build
him a Temple at Jerusalem, which is in Judah. [3]Any of
you who are his people may go to Jerusalem in Judah
to rebuild this Temple of the LORD, the God of Israel,
who lives in Jerusalem. And may your God be with
you! [4]Wherever this Jewish remnant is found, let
their neighbors contribute toward their expenses by
giving them silver and gold, supplies for the journey,
and livestock, as well as a voluntary offering for the
Temple of God in Jerusalem."

[5]Then God stirred the hearts of the priests and Levites
and the leaders of the tribes of Judah and Benjamin to go
to Jerusalem to rebuild the Temple of the LORD. [6]And all
their neighbors assisted by giving them articles of silver
and gold, supplies for the journey, and livestock. They
gave them many valuable gifts in addition to all the voluntary offerings.
[7]King Cyrus himself brought out the articles that King
Nebuchadnezzar had taken from the LORD's Temple in
Jerusalem and had placed in the temple of his own gods.
[8]Cyrus directed Mithredath, the treasurer of Persia, to
count these items and present them to Sheshbazzar, the
leader of the exiles returning to Judah.* [9]This is a list of
the items that were returned:

	gold basins	30
	silver basins	1,000
	silver incense burners*	29
10	gold bowls	30
	silver bowls	410
	other items	1,000

[11]In all, there were 5,400 articles of gold and silver.
Sheshbazzar brought all of these along when the exiles
went from Babylon to Jerusalem.

2 EXILES WHO RETURNED WITH ZERUBBABEL

Here is the list of the Jewish exiles of the provinces who
returned from their captivity. King Nebuchadnezzar had
deported them to Babylon, but now they returned to Jerusalem and the other towns in Judah where they originally
lived. [2]Their leaders were Zerubbabel, Jeshua, Nehemiah,

1:1a The first year of Cyrus's reign over Babylon was 538 B.C. 1:1b See Jer 25:11-12; 29:10. 1:8 Hebrew *Sheshbazzar, the prince of Judah.* 1:9 The meaning of this Hebrew word is uncertain.

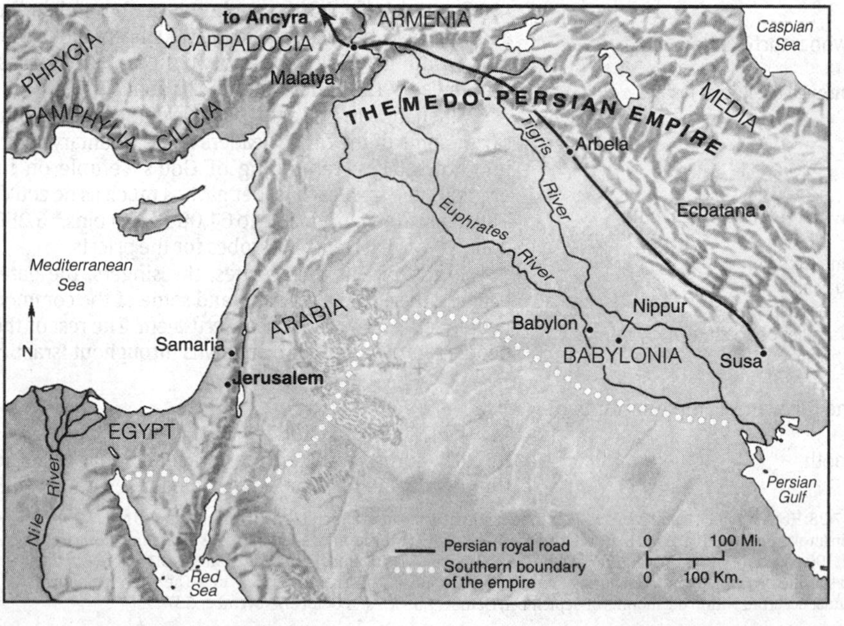

THE MEDO-PERSIAN EMPIRE
The Medo-Persian empire included the lands of Media and Persia, much of the area shown on this map and more. The Jewish exiles were concentrated in the area around Nippur in the Babylonian province. King Cyrus's decree, which allowed the Israelites to return to their homeland and rebuild the Temple, was discovered in the palace of Achmetha (also called Ecbatana).

Seraiah, Reelaiah, Mordecai, Bilshan, Mispar, Bigvai, Rehum, and Baanah.

This is the number of the men of Israel who returned from exile:

3 The family of Parosh ... 2,172
4 The family of Shephatiah ... 372
5 The family of Arah ... 775
6 The family of Pahath-moab (descendants of Jeshua and Joab) ... 2,812
7 The family of Elam ... 1,254
8 The family of Zattu ... 945
9 The family of Zaccai ... 760
10 The family of Bani ... 642
11 The family of Bebai ... 623
12 The family of Azgad ... 1,222
13 The family of Adonikam ... 666
14 The family of Bigvai ... 2,056
15 The family of Adin ... 454
16 The family of Ater (descendants of Hezekiah) ... 98
17 The family of Bezai ... 323
18 The family of Jorah ... 112
19 The family of Hashum ... 223
20 The family of Gibbar ... 95
21 The people of Bethlehem ... 123
22 The people of Netophah ... 56
23 The people of Anathoth ... 128
24 The people of Beth-azmaveth* ... 42
25 The people of Kiriath-jearim,* Kephirah, and Beeroth ... 743
26 The people of Ramah and Geba ... 621
27 The people of Micmash ... 122
28 The people of Bethel and Ai ... 223
29 The citizens of Nebo ... 52
30 The citizens of Magbish ... 156
31 The citizens of Elam ... 1,254
32 The citizens of Harim ... 320
33 The citizens of Lod, Hadid, and Ono ... 725
34 The citizens of Jericho ... 345
35 The citizens of Senaah ... 3,630

36These are the priests who returned from exile:

The family of Jedaiah (through the line of Jeshua) ... 973
37 The family of Immer ... 1,052
38 The family of Pashhur ... 1,247
39 The family of Harim ... 1,017

40These are the Levites who returned from exile:

The families of Jeshua and Kadmiel (descendants of Hodaviah) ... 74
41 The singers of the family of Asaph ... 128
42 The gatekeepers of the families of Shallum, Ater, Talmon, Akkub, Hatita, and Shobai ... 139

43The descendants of the following Temple servants returned from exile:

Ziha, Hasupha, Tabbaoth,
44 Keros, Siaha, Padon,
45 Lebanah, Hagabah, Akkub,
46 Hagab, Shalmai,* Hanan,
47 Giddel, Gahar, Reaiah,
48 Rezin, Nekoda, Gazzam,
49 Uzza, Paseah, Besai,
50 Asnah, Meunim, Nephusim,
51 Bakbuk, Hakupha, Harhur,
52 Bazluth, Mehida, Harsha,
53 Barkos, Sisera, Temah,
54 Neziah, and Hatipha.

55The descendants of these servants of King Solomon returned from exile:

Sotai, Hassophereth, Peruda,
56 Jaalah, Darkon, Giddel,
57 Shephatiah, Hattil, Pokereth-hazzebaim, and Ami.

58In all, the Temple servants and the descendants of Solomon's servants numbered 392.

59Another group returned at this time from the towns
of Tel-melah, Tel-harsha, Kerub, Addan, and Immer.
However, they could not prove that they or their families
were descendants of Israel. 60This group included the
families of Delaiah, Tobiah, and Nekoda—a total of
652 people.

61Three families of priests—Hobaiah, Hakkoz, and
Barzillai—also returned. (This Barzillai had married a
woman who was a descendant of Barzillai of Gilead, and
he had taken her family name.) 62They searched for their
names in the genealogical records, but they were not
found, so they were disqualified from serving as priests.
63The governor told them not to eat the priests' share of
food from the sacrifices until a priest could consult the
LORD about the matter by using the Urim and Thummim—the sacred lots.

64So a total of 42,360 people returned to Judah, 65in
addition to 7,337 servants and 200 singers, both men
and women. 66They took with them 736 horses,
245 mules, 67435 camels, and 6,720 donkeys.

68When they arrived at the Temple of the LORD in Jerusalem, some of the family leaders made voluntary offerings toward the rebuilding of God's Temple on its
original site, 69and each leader gave as much as he could.
The total of their gifts came to 61,000 gold coins,* 6,250
pounds* of silver, and 100 robes for the priests.

70So the priests, the Levites, the singers, the gatekeepers, the Temple servants, and some of the common people settled in villages near Jerusalem. The rest of the people returned to their own towns throughout Israel.

3 THE ALTAR IS REBUILT

In early autumn,* when the Israelites had settled in their towns, all the people assembled in Jerusalem with

2:24 As in parallel text at Neh 7:28; Hebrew reads *Azmaveth.* **2:25** As in some Hebrew manuscripts and Greek version (see also Neh 7:29); Hebrew reads *Kiriath-arim.* **2:46** As in an alternate reading of the Masoretic Text (see also Neh 7:48); the other alternate reads *Shamlai.* **2:69a** Hebrew *61,000 darics of gold,* about 1,100 pounds or 500 kilograms in weight. **2:69b** Hebrew *5,000 minas* [3,000 kilograms]. **3:1** Hebrew *in the seventh month.* The year is not specified, so it may have been during Cyrus's first year (538 B.C.) or second year (537 B.C.). The seventh month of the ancient Hebrew lunar calendar occurred within the months of September/October 538 B.C. and October/November 537 B.C.

a unified purpose. 2Then Jeshua son of Jehozadak* joined his fellow priests and Zerubbabel son of Shealtiel with his family in rebuilding the altar of the God of Israel. They wanted to sacrifice burnt offerings on it, as instructed in the Law of Moses, the man of God. 3Even though the people were afraid of the local residents, they rebuilt the altar at its old site. Then they began to sacrifice burnt offerings on the altar to the LORD each morning and evening.

4They celebrated the Festival of Shelters as prescribed in the Law, sacrificing the number of burnt offerings specified for each day of the festival. 5They also offered the regular burnt offerings and the offerings required for the new moon celebrations and the annual festivals as prescribed by the LORD. The people also gave voluntary offerings to the LORD. 6Fifteen days before the Festival of Shelters began,* the priests had begun to sacrifice burnt offerings to the LORD. This was even before they had started to lay the foundation of the LORD's Temple.

TIME TO PREPARE 3:1-8

The people of Israel spent months just *preparing* to build the Temple. During this time, the altar was built, materials were ordered and collected, and workers were hired. How much prep time do you take before doing a project? Most of us would rather do a job than prepare for it. Preparation time may not feel heroic or spiritual, but it is vital to any project you want to do well. ■

THE PEOPLE BEGIN TO REBUILD THE TEMPLE

7Then the people hired masons and carpenters and bought cedar logs from the people of Tyre and Sidon, paying them with food, wine, and olive oil. The logs were brought down from the Lebanon mountains and floated along the coast of the Mediterranean Sea* to Joppa, for King Cyrus had given permission for this.

8The construction of the Temple of God began in midspring,* during the second year after they arrived in Jerusalem. The work force was made up of everyone who had returned from exile, including Zerubbabel son of Shealtiel, Jeshua son of Jehozadak and his fellow priests, and all the Levites. The Levites who were twenty years old or older were put in charge of rebuilding the LORD's Temple. 9The workers at the Temple of God were supervised by Jeshua with his sons and relatives, and Kadmiel and his sons, all descendants of Hodaviah.* They were helped in this task by the Levites of the family of Henadad.

10When the builders completed the foundation of the LORD's Temple, the priests put on their robes and took their places to blow their trumpets. And the Levites, descendants of Asaph, clashed their cymbals to praise the LORD, just as King David had prescribed. 11With praise and thanks, they sang this song to the LORD:

"He is so good!
His faithful love for Israel endures forever!"

Then all the people gave a great shout, praising the LORD because the foundation of the LORD's Temple had been laid.

12But many of the older priests, Levites, and other leaders who had seen the first Temple wept aloud when they saw the new Temple's foundation. The others, however, were shouting for joy. 13The joyful shouting and weeping mingled together in a loud noise that could be heard far in the distance.

4 ENEMIES OPPOSE THE REBUILDING

The enemies of Judah and Benjamin heard that the exiles were rebuilding a Temple to the LORD, the God of Israel. 2So they approached Zerubbabel and the other leaders and said, "Let us build with you, for we worship your God just as you do. We have sacrificed to him ever since King Esarhaddon of Assyria brought us here."

3But Zerubbabel, Jeshua, and the other leaders of Israel replied, "You may have no part in this work. We alone will build the Temple for the LORD, the God of Israel, just as King Cyrus of Persia commanded us."

4Then the local residents tried to discourage and frighten the people of Judah to keep them from their work. 5They bribed agents to work against them and to frustrate their plans. This went on during the entire reign of King Cyrus of Persia and lasted until King Darius of Persia took the throne.*

SPIRITUAL TROUBLE 4:1-6

Enemies of the people of Israel interfered with the building project. In the same way, believers can expect opposition as they do God's work (2 Tim 3:12). The opposition may involve offers of friendships that only lead to distractions (4:2), attempts to discourage or intimidate (4:4-5), or unjust accusations (4:6). If you learn to expect opposition, you won't be stopped by it. Instead, you can trust God to overcome the obstacles. ■

LATER OPPOSITION UNDER XERXES AND ARTAXERXES

6Years later when Xerxes* began his reign, the enemies of Judah wrote a letter of accusation against the people of Judah and Jerusalem.

7Even later, during the reign of King Artaxerxes of Persia,* the enemies of Judah, led by Bishlam, Mithredath, and Tabeel, sent a letter to Artaxerxes in the Aramaic language, and it was translated for the king.

3:2 Hebrew *Jozadak,* a variant spelling of Jehozadak; also in 3:8. 3:6 Hebrew *On the first day of the seventh month.* This day in the ancient Hebrew lunar calendar occurred in September or October. The Festival of Shelters began on the fifteenth day of the seventh month. 3:7 Hebrew *the sea.* 3:8 Hebrew *in the second month.* This month in the ancient Hebrew lunar calendar occurred within the months of April and May 536 B.C. 3:9 Hebrew *sons of Judah* (i.e., *bene Yehudah*). *Bene* might also be read here as the proper name Binnui; *Yehudah* is probably another name for Hodaviah. Compare 2:40; Neh 7:43; 1 Esdras 5:58. 4:5 Darius reigned 521–486 B.C. 4:6 Hebrew *Ahasuerus,* another name for Xerxes. He reigned 486–465 B.C. 4:7 Artaxerxes reigned 465–424 B.C.

8*Rehum the governor and Shimshai the court secretary wrote the letter, telling King Artaxerxes about the
situation in Jerusalem. 9They greeted the king for all their
colleagues—the judges and local leaders, the people of
Tarpel, the Persians, the Babylonians, and the people of
Erech and Susa (that is, Elam). 10They also sent greetings
from the rest of the people whom the great and noble
Ashurbanipal* had deported and relocated in Samaria
and throughout the neighboring lands of the province
west of the Euphrates River.* 11This is a copy of their
letter:

"To King Artaxerxes, from your loyal subjects in the
province west of the Euphrates River.

12"The king should know that the Jews who came
here to Jerusalem from Babylon are rebuilding this
rebellious and evil city. They have already laid the
foundation and will soon finish its walls. 13And
the king should know that if this city is rebuilt and
its walls are completed, it will be much to your
disadvantage, for the Jews will then refuse to pay
their tribute, customs, and tolls to you.

14"Since we are your loyal subjects* and do not want
to see the king dishonored in this way, we have sent
the king this information. 15We suggest that a search
be made in your ancestors' records, where you will
discover what a rebellious city this has been in the
past. In fact, it was destroyed because of its long and
troublesome history of revolt against the kings and
countries who controlled it. 16We declare to the king
that if this city is rebuilt and its walls are completed,
the province west of the Euphrates River will be lost
to you."

17Then King Artaxerxes sent this reply:

"To Rehum the governor, Shimshai the court
secretary, and their colleagues living in Samaria
and throughout the province west of the Euphrates
River. Greetings.

18"The letter you sent has been translated and
read to me. 19I ordered a search of the records
and have found that Jerusalem has indeed been a
hotbed of insurrection against many kings. In fact,
rebellion and revolt are normal there! 20Powerful
kings have ruled over Jerusalem and the entire
province west of the Euphrates River, receiving
tribute, customs, and tolls. 21Therefore, issue
orders to have these men stop their work. That
city must not be rebuilt except at my express
command. 22Be diligent, and don't neglect this
matter, for we must not permit the situation to
harm the king's interests."

23When this letter from King Artaxerxes was read to
Rehum, Shimshai, and their colleagues, they hurried to
Jerusalem. Then, with a show of strength, they forced the
Jews to stop building.

THE REBUILDING RESUMES

24So the work on the Temple of God in Jerusalem had
stopped, and it remained at a standstill until the second
year of the reign of King Darius of Persia.*

5 At that time the prophets Haggai and Zechariah
son of Iddo prophesied to the Jews in Judah and Jerusalem. They prophesied in the name of the God of Israel
who was over them. 2Zerubbabel son of Shealtiel and
Jeshua son of Jehozadak* responded by starting again to
rebuild the Temple of God in Jerusalem. And the prophets of God were with them and helped them.

3But Tattenai, governor of the province west of the Euphrates River,* and Shethar-bozenai and their colleagues
soon arrived in Jerusalem and asked, "Who gave you permission to rebuild this Temple and restore this structure?" 4They also asked for the names of all the men
working on the Temple. 5But because their God was
watching over them, the leaders of the Jews were not prevented from building until a report was sent to Darius
and he returned his decision.

A BOLD RESPONSE 5:3-11

While rebuilding the Temple, the workers were confronted by the governor, who demanded to know who gave permission for their construction project (5:3). The people boldly replied, "We are the servants of the God of heaven and earth." They knew that God was on their side. Is this bold response your response when you face opposition? Like the people of Israel, you can be assured that God is on your side when you take a stand for what's right. ■

TATTENAI'S LETTER TO KING DARIUS

6This is a copy of the letter that Tattenai the governor,
Shethar-bozenai, and the other officials of the province
west of the Euphrates River sent to King Darius:

7"To King Darius. Greetings.

8"The king should know that we went to the
construction site of the Temple of the great God
in the province of Judah. It is being rebuilt with
specially prepared stones, and timber is being laid in
its walls. The work is going forward with great energy
and success.

9"We asked the leaders, 'Who gave you permission
to rebuild this Temple and restore this structure?'
10And we demanded their names so that we could tell
you who the leaders were.

11"This was their answer: 'We are the servants of the

4:8 The original text of 4:8–6:18 is in Aramaic. **4:10a** Aramaic *Osnappar,* another name for Ashurbanipal. **4:10b** Aramaic *the province beyond the river;* also in 4:11, 16, 17, 20. **4:14** Aramaic *Since we eat the salt of the palace.* **4:24** The second year of Darius's reign was 520 B.C. The narrative started in 4:1-5 is resumed at verse 24. **5:2** Aramaic *Jozadak,* a variant spelling of Jehozadak. **5:3** Aramaic *the province beyond the river;* also in 5:6.

God of heaven and earth, and we are rebuilding the Temple that was built here many years ago by a great king of Israel. [12]But because our ancestors angered the God of heaven, he abandoned them to King Nebuchadnezzar of Babylon,* who destroyed this Temple and exiled the people to Babylonia.
[13]However, King Cyrus of Babylon,* during the first year of his reign, issued a decree that the Temple of God should be rebuilt. [14]King Cyrus returned the gold and silver cups that Nebuchadnezzar had taken from the Temple of God in Jerusalem and had placed in the temple of Babylon. These cups were taken from that temple and presented to a man named Shesh-bazzar, whom King Cyrus appointed as governor of Judah.
[15]The king instructed him to return the cups to their place in Jerusalem and to rebuild the Temple of God there on its original site. [16]So this Shesh-bazzar came and laid the foundations of the Temple of God in Jerusalem. The people have been working on it ever since, though it is not yet completed.'

[17]"Therefore, if it pleases the king, we request that a search be made in the royal archives of Babylon to discover whether King Cyrus ever issued a decree to rebuild God's Temple in Jerusalem. And then let the king send us his decision in this matter."

6

DARIUS APPROVES THE REBUILDING

So King Darius issued orders that a search be made in the Babylonian archives, which were stored in the treasury.
[2]But it was at the fortress at Ecbatana in the province of Media that a scroll was found. This is what it said:

"Memorandum:

[3]"In the first year of King Cyrus's reign, a decree was sent out concerning the Temple of God at Jerusalem.

"Let the Temple be rebuilt on the site where Jews used to offer their sacrifices, using the original foundations. Its height will be ninety feet, and its width will be ninety feet.* [4]Every three layers of specially prepared stones will be topped by a layer of timber. All expenses will be paid by the royal treasury. [5]Furthermore, the gold and silver cups, which were taken to Babylon by Nebuchadnezzar from the Temple of God in Jerusalem, must be returned to Jerusalem and put back where they belong. Let them be taken back to the Temple of God."

[6]So King Darius sent this message:

"Now therefore, Tattenai, governor of the province west of the Euphrates River,* and Shethar-bozenai, and your colleagues and other officials west of the Euphrates River—stay away from there! [7]Do not disturb the construction of the Temple of God. Let it be rebuilt on its original site, and do not hinder the governor of Judah and the elders of the Jews in their work.

[8]"Moreover, I hereby decree that you are to help these elders of the Jews as they rebuild this Temple of God. You must pay the full construction costs, without delay, from my taxes collected in the province west of the Euphrates River so that the work will not be interrupted.

[9]"Give the priests in Jerusalem whatever is needed in the way of young bulls, rams, and male lambs for the burnt offerings presented to the God of heaven. And without fail, provide them with as much wheat, salt, wine, and olive oil as they need each day. [10]Then they will be able to offer acceptable sacrifices to the God of heaven and pray for the welfare of the king and his sons.

[11]"Those who violate this decree in any way will have a beam pulled from their house. Then they will be tied to it and flogged, and their house will be reduced to a pile of rubble.* [12]May the God who has chosen the city of Jerusalem as the place to honor his name destroy any king or nation that violates this command and destroys this Temple.

"I, Darius, have issued this decree. Let it be obeyed with all diligence."

TIMING 6:16-22

Feasting and celebration were on the menu at the great Temple dedication. But that also was the time when the priests and Levites "were divided into their various divisions to serve at the Temple." There is a time to celebrate and a time to work. Both, in their time, are proper and necessary when worshiping and serving God; and God is evident in both. ■

THE TEMPLE'S DEDICATION

[13]Tattenai, governor of the province west of the Euphrates River, and Shethar-bozenai and their colleagues complied at once with the command of King Darius. [14]So the Jewish elders continued their work, and they were greatly encouraged by the preaching of the prophets Haggai and Zechariah son of Iddo. The Temple was finally finished, as had been commanded by the God of Israel and decreed by Cyrus, Darius, and Artaxerxes, the kings of Persia. [15]The Temple was completed on March 12,* during the sixth year of King Darius's reign.
[16]The Temple of God was then dedicated with great joy by the people of Israel, the priests, the Levites, and the rest of the

5:12 Aramaic *Nebuchadnezzar the Chaldean.* **5:13** King Cyrus of Persia is here identified as the king of Babylon because Persia had conquered the Babylonian Empire. **6:3** Aramaic *Its height will be 60 cubits* [27.6 meters], *and its width will be 60 cubits.* It is commonly held that this verse should be emended to read: "Its height will be 30 cubits [45 feet, or 13.8 meters], its length will be 60 cubits [90 feet, or 27.6 meters], and its width will be 20 cubits [30 feet, or 9.2 meters]"; compare 1 Kgs 6:2. The emendation regarding the width is supported by the Syriac version. **6:6** Aramaic *the province beyond the river;* also in 6:6b, 8, 13. **6:11** Aramaic *a dunghill.* **6:15** Aramaic *on the third day of the month Adar,* of the ancient Hebrew lunar calendar. A number of events in Ezra can be cross-checked with dates in surviving Persian records and related accurately to our modern calendar. This day was March 12, 515 B.C.

people who had returned from exile.
17During the dedication ceremony for
the Temple of God, 100 young bulls,
200 rams, and 400 male lambs were
sacrificed. And 12 male goats were
presented as a sin offering for the
twelve tribes of Israel. 18Then the
priests and Levites were divided into
their various divisions to serve at the
Temple of God in Jerusalem, as prescribed in the Book of Moses.

> There was great joy throughout the land.
>
> EZRA 6:22

CELEBRATION OF PASSOVER

19On April 21* the returned exiles celebrated Passover. 20The priests and
Levites had purified themselves and were ceremonially
clean. So they slaughtered the Passover lamb for all the
returned exiles, for their fellow priests, and for themselves. 21The Passover meal was eaten by the people of
Israel who had returned from exile and by the others in
the land who had turned from their immoral customs
to worship the LORD, the God of Israel. 22Then they celebrated the Festival of Unleavened Bread for seven days.
There was great joy throughout the land because the
LORD had caused the king of Assyria* to be favorable to
them, so that he helped them to rebuild the Temple of
God, the God of Israel.

7 EZRA ARRIVES IN JERUSALEM

Many years later, during the reign of King Artaxerxes of
Persia,* there was a man named Ezra. He was the son* of
Seraiah, son of Azariah, son of Hilkiah, 2son of Shallum,
son of Zadok, son of Ahitub, 3son of Amariah, son of Azariah, son* of Meraioth, 4son of Zerahiah, son of Uzzi, son
of Bukki, 5son of Abishua, son of Phinehas, son of Eleazar, son of Aaron the high priest.* 6This Ezra was a scribe
who was well versed in the Law of Moses, which the
LORD, the God of Israel, had given to the people of Israel.
He came up to Jerusalem from Babylon, and the king
gave him everything he asked for, because the gracious
hand of the LORD his God was on him. 7Some of the people of Israel, as well as some of the priests, Levites, singers, gatekeepers, and Temple servants, traveled up to
Jerusalem with him in the seventh year of King Artaxerxes' reign.

8Ezra arrived in Jerusalem in August* of that year. 9He
had arranged to leave Babylon on April 8, the first day of
the new year,* and he arrived at Jerusalem on August 4,*
for the gracious hand of his God was on him. 10This was
because Ezra had determined to study and obey the Law
of the LORD and to teach those decrees and regulations to
the people of Israel.

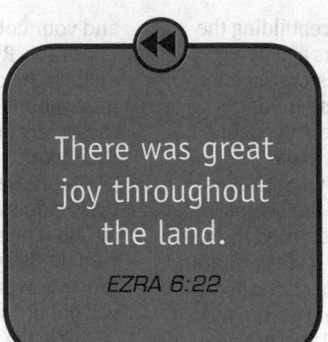

ARTAXERXES' LETTER TO EZRA

11King Artaxerxes had given a copy of
the following letter to Ezra, the priest
and scribe who studied and taught the
commands and decrees of the LORD to
Israel:

12*"From Artaxerxes, the king of
kings, to Ezra the priest, the
teacher of the law of the God of
heaven. Greetings.

13"I decree that any of the people
of Israel in my kingdom, including
the priests and Levites, may
volunteer to return to Jerusalem
with you. 14I and my council of seven hereby instruct
you to conduct an inquiry into the situation in Judah
and Jerusalem, based on your God's law, which is in
your hand. 15We also commission you to take with you
silver and gold, which we are freely presenting as an
offering to the God of Israel who lives in Jerusalem.

ABSOLUTES

See Miranda, the brown-haired girl sitting on the bench in front of the gym? Watch her for a few minutes. Though she seems pretty happy on the outside, on the inside she's seriously confused!

It all started two weeks ago when she attended an after-school debate on this resolution: "Resolved: Absolute standards for human behavior do not exist."

What Miranda first saw as an easy opportunity for some quick extra credit in forensics class has turned into a long and difficult inner debate. She's not sure what she thinks about anything . . . or even *how* to think about anything.

"The team arguing in favor of the resolution just about had me convinced," Miranda says, "but then the other team raised a lot of troubling questions in my mind.

"Even though the crowd ended up voting for the resolution, I'm not so sure. I mean, if there aren't any absolutes, then nothing makes sense. 'Right' and 'wrong' don't have meaning.

"There must be some standards that hold true for everyone. But once you get beyond murder and child abuse, I'm not sure what they are."

If you are looking for some standards to base your actions upon, check out what an Old Testament scribe named Ezra did. Read Ezra 7:10. Why is this good advice when you're searching for answers concerning right and wrong?

6:19 Hebrew *On the fourteenth day of the first month,* of the ancient Hebrew lunar calendar. This day was April 21, 515 B.C.; also see note on 6:15. **6:22** King Darius of Persia is here identified as the king of Assyria because Persia had conquered the Babylonian Empire, which included the earlier Assyrian Empire. **7:1a** Artaxerxes reigned 465–424 B.C. **7:1b** Or *descendant;* see 1 Chr 6:14. **7:3** Or *descendant;* see 1 Chr 6:6-10. **7:5** Or *the first priest.* **7:8** Hebrew *in the fifth month.* This month in the ancient Hebrew lunar calendar occurred within the months of August and September 458 B.C. **7:9a** Hebrew *on the first day of the first month,* of the ancient Hebrew lunar calendar. This day was April 8, 458 B.C.; also see note on 6:15. **7:9b** Hebrew *on the first day of the fifth month,* of the ancient Hebrew lunar calendar. This day was August 4, 458 B.C.; also see note on 6:15. **7:12** The original text of 7:12-26 is in Aramaic.

16"Furthermore, you are to take any silver and gold that you may obtain from the province of Babylon, as well as the voluntary offerings of the people and the priests that are presented for the Temple of their God in Jerusalem. 17These donations are to be used specifically for the purchase of bulls, rams, male lambs, and the appropriate grain offerings and liquid offerings, all of which will be offered on the altar of the Temple of your God in Jerusalem. 18Any silver and gold that is left over may be used in whatever way you and your colleagues feel is the will of your God.

19"But as for the cups we are entrusting to you for the service of the Temple of your God, deliver them all to the God of Jerusalem. 20If you need anything else for your God's Temple or for any similar needs, you may take it from the royal treasury.

21"I, Artaxerxes the king, hereby send this decree to all the treasurers in the province west of the Euphrates River*: 'You are to give Ezra, the priest and teacher of the law of the God of heaven, whatever he requests of you. 22You are to give him up to 7,500 pounds* of silver, 500 bushels* of wheat, 550 gallons of wine, 550 gallons of olive oil,* and an unlimited supply of salt. 23Be careful to provide whatever the God of heaven demands for his Temple, for why should we risk bringing God's anger against the realm of the king and his sons? 24I also decree that no priest, Levite, singer, gatekeeper, Temple servant, or other worker in this Temple of God will be required to pay tribute, customs, or tolls of any kind.'

SUPPORT FOR LEADERS 7:24

Why did Artaxerxes exempt Temple workers from paying taxes? He recognized that the priests and Levites filled an important role in society as spiritual leaders, so he freed them from paying taxes. When we give money to support the work of our local churches, we free our leaders and their staff to do what they're called to do. In what ways do you support your church leaders? ■

25"And you, Ezra, are to use the wisdom your God has given you to appoint magistrates and judges who know your God's laws to govern all the people in the province west of the Euphrates River. Teach the law to anyone who does not know it. 26Anyone who refuses to obey the law of your God and the law of the king will be punished immediately, either by death, banishment, confiscation of goods, or imprisonment."

EZRA PRAISES THE LORD

27Praise the LORD, the God of our ancestors, who made the king want to beautify the Temple of the LORD in Jerusalem! 28And praise him for demonstrating such unfailing love to me by honoring me before the king, his council, and all his mighty nobles! I felt encouraged because the gracious hand of the LORD my God was on me. And I gathered some of the leaders of Israel to return with me to Jerusalem.

8 EXILES WHO RETURNED WITH EZRA

Here is a list of the family leaders and the genealogies of those who came with me from Babylon during the reign of King Artaxerxes:

2 From the family of Phinehas: Gershom.
From the family of Ithamar: Daniel.
From the family of David: Hattush, 3a descendant of Shecaniah.
From the family of Parosh: Zechariah and 150 other men were registered.
4 From the family of Pahath-moab: Eliehoenai son of Zerahiah and 200 other men.
5 From the family of Zattu*: Shecaniah son of Jahaziel and 300 other men.
6 From the family of Adin: Ebed son of Jonathan and 50 other men.
7 From the family of Elam: Jeshaiah son of Athaliah and 70 other men.
8 From the family of Shephatiah: Zebadiah son of Michael and 80 other men.
9 From the family of Joab: Obadiah son of Jehiel and 218 other men.
10 From the family of Bani*: Shelomith son of Josiphiah and 160 other men.
11 From the family of Bebai: Zechariah son of Bebai and 28 other men.
12 From the family of Azgad: Johanan son of Hakkatan and 110 other men.
13 From the family of Adonikam, who came later*: Eliphelet, Jeuel, Shemaiah, and 60 other men.
14 From the family of Bigvai: Uthai, Zaccur,* and 70 other men.

EZRA'S JOURNEY TO JERUSALEM

15I assembled the exiles at the Ahava Canal, and we camped there for three days while I went over the lists of the people and the priests who had arrived. I found that not one Levite had volunteered to come along. 16So I sent for Eliezer, Ariel, Shemaiah, Elnathan, Jarib, Elnathan, Nathan, Zechariah, and Meshullam, who were leaders of the people. I also sent for Joiarib and Elnathan, who were men of discernment. 17I sent them to Iddo, the leader of the Levites at Casiphia, to ask him and his relatives and the Temple servants to send us ministers for the Temple of God at Jerusalem.

18Since the gracious hand of our God was on us, they sent us a man named Sherebiah, along with eighteen of

7:21 Aramaic *the province beyond the river;* also in 7:25. 7:22a Aramaic *100 talents* [3,400 kilograms]. 7:22b Aramaic *100 cors* [18.2 kiloliters]. 7:22c Aramaic *100 baths* [2.1 kiloliters] *of wine, 100 baths of olive oil.* 8:5 As in some Greek manuscripts (see also 1 Esdras 8:32); Hebrew lacks *Zattu.* 8:10 As in some Greek manuscripts (see also 1 Esdras 8:36); Hebrew lacks *Bani.* 8:13 Or *who were the last of his family.* 8:14 As in Greek and Syriac versions and an alternate reading of the Masoretic Text; the other alternate reads *Zabbud.*

his sons and brothers. He was a very astute man and a descendant of Mahli, who was a descendant of Levi son of Israel.* [19]They also sent Hashabiah, together with Jeshaiah from the descendants of Merari, and twenty of his sons and brothers, [20]and 220 Temple servants. The Temple servants were assistants to the Levites—a group of Temple workers first instituted by King David and his officials. They were all listed by name.

A DANGEROUS JOURNEY 8:15-36

Ezra and the people traveled approximately nine hundred or so miles on foot. The trip took them through dangerous territory and lasted about four months. They prayed that God would protect them and give them a good journey. We may never have to travel that far (on foot at least). But we still need guidance and protection. Have you asked God for either lately? ■

[21]And there by the Ahava Canal, I gave orders for all of us to fast and humble ourselves before our God. We prayed that he would give us a safe journey and protect us, our children, and our goods as we traveled. [22]For I was ashamed to ask the king for soldiers and horsemen* to accompany us and protect us from enemies along the way. After all, we had told the king, "Our God's hand of protection is on all who worship him, but his fierce anger rages against those who abandon him." [23]So we fasted and earnestly prayed that our God would take care of us, and he heard our prayer.

[24]I appointed twelve leaders of the priests—Sherebiah, Hashabiah, and ten other priests—[25]to be in charge of transporting the silver, the gold, the gold bowls, and the other items that the king, his council, his officials, and all the people of Israel had presented for the Temple of God. [26]I weighed the treasure as I gave it to them and found the totals to be as follows:

24 tons* of silver,
7,500 pounds* of silver articles,
7,500 pounds of gold,
27 20 gold bowls, equal in value to 1,000 gold coins,*
2 fine articles of polished bronze, as precious as gold.

[28]And I said to these priests, "You and these treasures have been set apart as holy to the LORD. This silver and gold is a voluntary offering to the LORD, the God of our ancestors. [29]Guard these treasures well until you present them to the leading priests, the Levites, and the leaders of Israel, who will weigh them at the storerooms of the LORD's Temple in Jerusalem." [30]So the priests and the Levites accepted the task of transporting these treasures of silver and gold to the Temple of our God in Jerusalem.

[31]We broke camp at the Ahava Canal on April 19* and started off to Jerusalem. And the gracious hand of our God protected us and saved us from enemies and bandits along the way. [32]So we arrived safely in Jerusalem, where we rested for three days.

[33]On the fourth day after our arrival, the silver, gold, and other valuables were weighed at the Temple of our God and entrusted to Meremoth son of Uriah the priest and to Eleazar son of Phinehas, along with Jozabad son of Jeshua and Noadiah son of Binnui—both of whom were Levites. [34]Everything was accounted for by number and weight, and the total weight was officially recorded.

[35]Then the exiles who had come out of captivity sacrificed burnt offerings to the God of Israel. They presented twelve bulls for all the people of Israel, as well as ninety-six rams and seventy-seven male lambs. They also offered twelve male goats as a sin offering. All this was given as a burnt offering to the LORD. [36]The king's decrees were delivered to his highest officers and the governors of the province west of the Euphrates River,* who then cooperated by supporting the people and the Temple of God.

MARRIAGE LAWS 9:1-15

Marriages between the people of Israel and the people of other nations were forbidden by law (see Deut 7:3-4). God knew that people from other nations would encourage his people to worship their gods. Although we're not forbidden to marry people from other nations today, problems occur when believers marry unbelievers. (See 2 Cor 6:14-15). Such marriages cannot have unity in the most important issue in life—commitment to God. If you're thinking that who you marry later on doesn't matter, think again! ■

9

EZRA'S PRAYER CONCERNING INTERMARRIAGE

When these things had been done, the Jewish leaders came to me and said, "Many of the people of Israel, and even some of the priests and Levites, have not kept themselves separate from the other peoples living in the land. They have taken up the detestable practices of the Canaanites, Hittites, Perizzites, Jebusites, Ammonites, Moabites, Egyptians, and Amorites. [2]For the men of Israel have married women from these people and have taken them as wives for their sons. So the holy race has become polluted by these mixed marriages. Worse yet, the leaders and officials have led the way in this outrage."

[3]When I heard this, I tore my cloak and my shirt, pulled hair from my head and beard, and sat down utterly shocked. [4]Then all who trembled at the words of the God of Israel came and sat with me because of this outrage committed by the returned exiles. And I sat there utterly appalled until the time of the evening sacrifice.

8:18 *Israel* is the name that God gave to Jacob. **8:22** Or *charioteers*. **8:26a** Hebrew *650 talents* [22 metric tons]. **8:26b** Hebrew *100 talents* [3,400 kilograms]; also in 8:26c. **8:27** Hebrew *1,000 darics*, about 19 pounds or 8.6 kilograms in weight. **8:31** Hebrew *on the twelfth day of the first month*, of the ancient Hebrew lunar calendar. This day was April 19, 458 B.C.; also see note on 6:15. **8:36** Hebrew *the province beyond the river*.

5At the time of the sacrifice, I stood up from where I
had sat in mourning with my clothes torn. I fell to my
knees and lifted my hands to the LORD my God. 6I prayed,

"O my God, I am utterly ashamed; I blush to lift up my
face to you. For our sins are piled higher than our
heads, and our guilt has reached to the heavens.
7From the days of our ancestors until now, we have
been steeped in sin. That is why we and our kings and
our priests have been at the mercy of the pagan kings
of the land. We have been killed, captured, robbed,
and disgraced, just as we are today.
8"But now we have been given a brief moment of
grace, for the LORD our God has allowed a few of us
to survive as a remnant. He has given us security in
this holy place. Our God has brightened our eyes and
granted us some relief from our slavery. 9For we
were slaves, but in his unfailing love our God did not
abandon us in our slavery. Instead, he caused the
kings of Persia to treat us favorably. He revived us so
we could rebuild the Temple of our God and repair
its ruins. He has given us a protective wall in Judah
and Jerusalem.
10"And now, O our God, what can we say after all
of this? For once again we have abandoned your
commands! 11Your servants the prophets warned us
when they said, 'The land you are entering to possess is
totally defiled by the detestable practices of the people
living there. From one end to the other, the land is filled
with corruption. 12Don't let your daughters marry their
sons! Don't take their daughters as wives for your sons.
Don't ever promote the peace and prosperity of those
nations. If you follow these instructions, you will be
strong and will enjoy the good things the land produces,
and you will leave this prosperity to your children
forever.'
13"Now we are being punished because of our
wickedness and our great guilt. But we have actually
been punished far less than we deserve, for you, our
God, have allowed some of us to survive as a remnant.
14But even so, we are again breaking your commands
and intermarrying with people who do these detestable
things. Won't your anger be enough to destroy us,
so that even this little remnant no longer survives?
15O LORD, God of Israel, you are just. We come before
you in our guilt as nothing but an escaped remnant,
though in such a condition none of us can stand in your
presence."

10 THE PEOPLE CONFESS THEIR SIN

While Ezra prayed and made this confession, weeping
and lying face down on the ground in front of the Temple
of God, a very large crowd of people from Israel—men,
women, and children—gathered and wept bitterly with
him. 2Then Shecaniah son of Jehiel, a descendant of
Elam, said to Ezra, "We have been unfaithful to our God,
for we have married these pagan women of the land. But
in spite of this there is hope for Israel. 3Let us now make
a covenant with our God to divorce our pagan wives and
to send them away with their children. We will follow
the advice given by you and by the others who respect the
commands of our God. Let it be done according to the
Law of God. 4Get up, for it is your duty to tell us how to
proceed in setting things straight. We are behind you, so
be strong and take action."

OBEDIENCE 10:1-3

The men who married women from other nations agreed to divorce their wives and send away their children. Sounds cruel, right? Yet this act was necessary to preserve Israel as a nation committed to God. So, the disobedient Israelites were forced to choose between two painful options: continue in these marriages and risk God's wrath or divorce their wives. Does this mean that God approves of divorce? No! Elsewhere in Scripture, God makes it clear that he hates divorce (Mal 2:15-16; Matt 19:8). Obeying God's commands can keep us from facing a no-win situation as the Israelites did here. ■

5So Ezra stood up and demanded that the leaders of
the priests and the Levites and all the people of Israel
swear that they would do as Shecaniah had said. And they
all swore a solemn oath. 6Then Ezra left the front of the
Temple of God and went to the room of Jehohanan son of
Eliashib. He spent the night* there without eating or
drinking anything. He was still in mourning because of
the unfaithfulness of the returned exiles.
7Then a proclamation was made throughout Judah and
Jerusalem that all the exiles should come to Jerusalem.
8Those who failed to come within three days would, if the
leaders and elders so decided, forfeit all their property
and be expelled from the assembly of the exiles.

FROM SORROW TO ACTION 10:1-11

Following Ezra's earnest prayer, the people owned up to their wrong actions and asked for help to make things right with God. Making things right doesn't just involve an apology. It also involves a change in attitude and actions. If you've blown it with God or with someone else, what are you going to do about it? ■

9Within three days, all the people of Judah and Benjamin had gathered in Jerusalem. This took place on December 19,* and all the people were sitting in the
square before the Temple of God. They were trembling
both because of the seriousness of the matter and because it was raining. 10Then Ezra the priest stood and
said to them: "You have committed a terrible sin. By

10:6 As in parallel text at 1 Esdras 9:2; Hebrew reads *He went.* **10:9** Hebrew *on the twentieth day of the ninth month,* of the ancient Hebrew lunar calendar. This day was December 19, 458 B.C.; also see note on 6:15.

marrying pagan women, you have increased Israel's guilt. 11So now confess your sin to the LORD, the God of your ancestors, and do what he demands. Separate yourselves from the people of the land and from these pagan women."

12Then the whole assembly raised their voices and answered, "Yes, you are right; we must do as you say!" 13Then they added, "This isn't something that can be done in a day or two, for many of us are involved in this extremely sinful affair. And this is the rainy season, so we cannot stay out here much longer. 14Let our leaders act on behalf of us all. Let everyone who has a pagan wife come at a scheduled time, accompanied by the leaders and judges of his city, so that the fierce anger of our God concerning this affair may be turned away from us."

15Only Jonathan son of Asahel and Jahzeiah son of Tikvah opposed this course of action, and they were supported by Meshullam and Shabbethai the Levite.

16So this was the plan they followed. Ezra selected leaders to represent their families, designating each of the representatives by name. On December 29,* the leaders sat down to investigate the matter. 17By March 27, the first day of the new year,* they had finished dealing with all the men who had married pagan wives.

THOSE GUILTY OF INTERMARRIAGE

18These are the priests who had married pagan wives:
From the family of Jeshua son of Jehozadak* and his brothers: Maaseiah, Eliezer, Jarib, and Gedaliah.
19They vowed to divorce their wives, and they each acknowledged their guilt by offering a ram as a guilt offering.
20From the family of Immer: Hanani and Zebadiah.
21From the family of Harim: Maaseiah, Elijah, Shemaiah, Jehiel, and Uzziah.
22From the family of Pashhur: Elioenai, Maaseiah, Ishmael, Nethanel, Jozabad, and Elasah.

23These are the Levites who were guilty: Jozabad, Shimei, Kelaiah (also called Kelita), Pethahiah, Judah, and Eliezer.

24This is the singer who was guilty: Eliashib.

These are the gatekeepers who were guilty: Shallum, Telem, and Uri.

25These are the other people of Israel who were guilty:
From the family of Parosh: Ramiah, Izziah, Malkijah, Mijamin, Eleazar, Hashabiah,* and Benaiah.
26From the family of Elam: Mattaniah, Zechariah, Jehiel, Abdi, Jeremoth, and Elijah.
27From the family of Zattu: Elioenai, Eliashib, Mattaniah, Jeremoth, Zabad, and Aziza.
28From the family of Bebai: Jehohanan, Hananiah, Zabbai, and Athlai.
29From the family of Bani: Meshullam, Malluch, Adaiah, Jashub, Sheal, and Jeremoth.
30From the family of Pahath-moab: Adna, Kelal, Benaiah, Maaseiah, Mattaniah, Bezalel, Binnui, and Manasseh.
31From the family of Harim: Eliezer, Ishijah, Malkijah, Shemaiah, Shimeon, 32Benjamin, Malluch, and Shemariah.
33From the family of Hashum: Mattenai, Mattattah, Zabad, Eliphelet, Jeremai, Manasseh, and Shimei.
34From the family of Bani: Maadai, Amram, Uel, 35Benaiah, Bedeiah, Keluhi, 36Vaniah, Meremoth, Eliashib, 37Mattaniah, Mattenai, and Jaasu.
38From the family of Binnui*: Shimei, 39Shelemiah, Nathan, Adaiah, 40Macnadebai, Shashai, Sharai, 41Azarel, Shelemiah, Shemariah, 42Shallum, Amariah, and Joseph.
43From the family of Nebo: Jeiel, Mattithiah, Zabad, Zebina, Jaddai, Joel, and Benaiah.

44Each of these men had a pagan wife, and some even had children by these wives.*

10:16 Hebrew *On the first day of the tenth month,* of the ancient Hebrew lunar calendar. This day was December 29, 458 B.C.; also see note on 6:15. **10:17** Hebrew *By the first day of the first month,* of the ancient Hebrew lunar calendar. This day was March 27, 457 B.C.; also see note on 6:15. **10:18** Hebrew *Jozadak,* a variant spelling of Jehozadak. **10:25** As in parallel text at 1 Esdras 9:26; Hebrew reads *Malkijah.* **10:37-38** As in Greek version; Hebrew reads *Jaasu, 38Bani, Binnui.* **10:44** Or *and they sent them away with their children.* The meaning of the Hebrew is uncertain.

NEHEMIAH

ARE YOU A LEADER? Maybe you're the one people count on the most for input ("Where do *you* think we should go this Friday?") or motivation to do a task ("Chavon really helps the team to focus."). But real leadership often is shown by the way you handle tough problems.

Nehemiah was a proven leader. He left a secure position in the government of Persia to return to his homeland and rebuild the walls of Jerusalem. He succeeded, too, despite incredible opposition.

Let's face it: The glory and the praise of leadership can seem pretty sweet. But how many of us want the difficulties that come with being a leader? Yet those whom God chooses to be leaders can be assured that he also will equip them for the job ahead. Think you've got what it takes to be a leader? The book of Nehemiah provides a picture of leadership in action. Do you see yourself in that picture?

nehemiah

timeline

586 B.C.
Jerusalem destroyed; exiles go to Babylon

537
First exiles return to Jerusalem

516
Temple completed

486
Ahasuerus (Xerxes I) becomes king of Persia

465
Artaxerxes I becomes king of Persia

458
Ezra comes to Jerusalem

445
Nehemiah comes to Jerusalem; wall completed

433
Nehemiah returns to Babylon

432
Nehemiah goes back to Jerusalem

430(?)
Malachi begins his ministry

stats

PURPOSE: Nehemiah is the last of the Old Testament historical books. It records the history of the third return to Jerusalem after captivity, telling how the walls were rebuilt and of the renewal in faith of the former exiles.

AUTHOR: Since much of the book is written in the first person, Nehemiah probably wrote the book, with Ezra serving as editor.

DATE WRITTEN: Approximately 445–432 B.C.

SETTING: Zerubbabel led the first return to Jerusalem in 537 B.C. In 458, Ezra led the second return. Finally, in 445, Nehemiah returned with the third group of exiles to rebuild the city walls.

KEY PEOPLE: Nehemiah, Ezra, Sanballat, Tobiah

KEY PLACE: Jerusalem

SPECIAL FEATURE: The book shows the fulfillment of the prophecies of Zechariah and Daniel concerning the rebuilding of Jerusalem's walls.

KEY points

VISION
God put the desire in Nehemiah's heart to rebuild the walls, giving him a vision for the work. Likewise, God can give us the vision and desire to work toward the building of his kingdom.

PRAYER
Nehemiah and Ezra responded to problems with prayer. When Nehemiah began his work he recognized the problem, prayed right away, and then acted on the problem. Prayer and action go hand-in-hand. Through prayer, God guides our preparation, teamwork, and efforts to carry out his will.

LEADERSHIP
Nehemiah used careful planning, teamwork, problem solving, and courage to get the work done. These same qualities are needed in leaders today.

PROBLEMS
After the work began, Nehemiah faced threats from enemies and the discouragement of his own workers. But he didn't give up. When problems arise, we must face them squarely and press on to complete God's work.

A COMPLETE CHANGE
Although God had enabled them to build the wall, the work wasn't complete until the people rebuilt their lives spiritually. Recognizing and admitting sin is not enough. Being serious about God must result in a changed life.

1
These are the memoirs of Nehemiah son of Hacaliah.

NEHEMIAH'S CONCERN FOR JERUSALEM

In late autumn, in the month of Kislev, in the twentieth
year of King Artaxerxes' reign,* I was at the fortress of
Susa. 2Hanani, one of my brothers, came to visit me with
some other men who had just arrived from Judah. I asked
them about the Jews who had returned there from captivity and about how things were going in Jerusalem.
3They said to me, "Things are not going well for those
who returned to the province of Judah. They are in great
trouble and disgrace. The wall of Jerusalem has been torn
down, and the gates have been destroyed by fire."

TAKE ACTION 1:4-11

Although Nehemiah was upset about the condition of Jerusalem, he didn't just brood about it. After his initial grief, he poured his heart out to God and looked for ways to improve the situation. Is that what you do when you're faced with a problem? Many of us, if we're honest, will admit that we might whine first ("Why me?") before any thought of action comes to mind. Asking God for help is the part of the equation that we sometimes leave out. But God can offer solutions we've never even dreamed of. Do you trust him enough to ask for his help? ■

4When I heard this, I sat down and wept. In fact, for
days I mourned, fasted, and prayed to the God of heaven.
5Then I said,

"O LORD, God of heaven, the great and awesome
God who keeps his covenant of unfailing love
with those who love him and obey his commands,
6listen to my prayer! Look down and see me
praying night and day for your people Israel.
I confess that we have sinned against you. Yes,
even my own family and I have sinned! 7We have
sinned terribly by not obeying the commands,
decrees, and regulations that you gave us through
your servant Moses.
8"Please remember what you told your servant
Moses: 'If you are unfaithful to me, I will scatter you
among the nations. 9But if you return to me and obey
my commands and live by them, then even if you are
exiled to the ends of the earth, I will bring you back
to the place I have chosen for my name to be
honored.'
10"The people you rescued by your great power and
strong hand are your servants. 11O Lord, please hear
my prayer! Listen to the prayers of those of us who
delight in honoring you. Please grant me success
today by making the king favorable to me.* Put it into
his heart to be kind to me."

In those days I was the king's cup-bearer.

HAVE NO FEAR! 2:3

Nehemiah wasn't ashamed to admit his fear; he just refused to be ruled by it. When we focus on our fears instead of on God, we can't accomplish much for him. Is fear keeping you from doing something for God? God is greater than our fears. Recognizing your fear is the first step in committing it to God. ■

2

NEHEMIAH GOES TO JERUSALEM

Early the following spring, in the month of Nisan,* during
the twentieth year of King Artaxerxes' reign, I was serving the king his wine. I had never before appeared sad in
his presence. 2So the king asked me, "Why are you looking so sad? You don't look sick to me. You must be deeply
troubled."
Then I was terrified, 3but I replied, "Long live the king!
How can I not be sad? For the city where my ancestors are
buried is in ruins, and the gates have been destroyed by
fire."
4The king asked, "Well, how can I help you?"
With a prayer to the God of heaven, 5I replied, "If it
please the king, and if you are pleased with me, your servant, send me to Judah to rebuild the city where my ancestors are buried."
6The king, with the queen sitting beside him, asked,
"How long will you be gone? When will you return?" After I told him how long I would be gone, the king agreed
to my request.
7I also said to the king, "If it please the king, let me have
letters addressed to the governors of the province west of
the Euphrates River,* instructing them to let me travel
safely through their territories on my way to Judah. 8And
please give me a letter addressed to Asaph, the manager
of the king's forest, instructing him to give me timber. I
will need it to make beams for the gates of the Temple
fortress, for the city walls, and for a house for myself."
And the king granted these requests, because the gracious hand of God was on me.
9When I came to the governors of the province west of
the Euphrates River, I delivered the king's letters to them.
The king, I should add, had sent along army officers and
horsemen* to protect me. 10But when Sanballat the Horonite and Tobiah the Ammonite official heard of my arrival, they were very displeased that someone had come
to help the people of Israel.

1:1 Hebrew *In the month of Kislev of the twentieth year.* A number of dates in the book of Nehemiah can be cross-checked with dates in surviving Persian records and related accurately to our modern calendar. This month of the ancient Hebrew lunar calendar occurred within the months of November and December 446 B.C. The *twentieth year* probably refers to the reign of King Artaxerxes I; compare 2:1; 5:14.
1:11 Hebrew *today in the sight of this man.* 2:1 Hebrew *In the month of Nisan.* This month of the ancient Hebrew lunar calendar occurred within the months of April and May 445 B.C. 2:7 Hebrew *the province beyond the river;* also in 2:9. 2:9 Or *charioteers.*

NEHEMIAH INSPECTS JERUSALEM'S WALL

11So I arrived in Jerusalem. Three days later, 12I slipped out during the night, taking only a few others with me. I had not told anyone about the plans God had put in my heart for Jerusalem. We took no pack animals with us except the donkey I was riding. 13After dark I went out through the Valley Gate, past the Jackal's Well,* and over to the Dung Gate to inspect the broken walls and burned gates. 14Then I went to the Fountain Gate and to the King's Pool, but my donkey couldn't get through the rubble. 15So, though it was still dark, I went up the Kidron Valley* instead, inspecting the wall before I turned back and entered again at the Valley Gate.

16The city officials did not know I had been out there or what I was doing, for I had not yet said anything to anyone about my plans. I had not yet spoken to the Jewish leaders—the priests, the nobles, the officials, or anyone else in the administration. 17But now I said to them, "You know very well what trouble we are in. Jerusalem lies in ruins, and its gates have been destroyed by fire. Let us rebuild the wall of Jerusalem and end this disgrace!" 18Then I told them about how the gracious hand of God had been on me, and about my conversation with the king.

They replied at once, "Yes, let's rebuild the wall!" So they began the good work.

SHARING THE VISION 2:16-18

Spiritual renewal often begins with one person's vision. Nehemiah had a vision, and shared it with enthusiasm, inspiring Jerusalem's leaders to rebuild the wall. Often God uses one person to express the vision and others to turn it into reality. When you inspire others, you put teamwork into action to accomplish God's goals. ■

19But when Sanballat, Tobiah, and Geshem the Arab heard of our plan, they scoffed contemptuously. "What are you doing? Are you rebelling against the king?" they asked.

20I replied, "The God of heaven will help us succeed. We, his servants, will start rebuilding this wall. But you have no share, legal right, or historic claim in Jerusalem."

3

REBUILDING THE WALL OF JERUSALEM

Then Eliashib the high priest and the other priests started to rebuild at the Sheep Gate. They dedicated it and set up its doors, building the wall as far as the Tower of the Hundred, which they dedicated, and the Tower of Hananel. 2People from the town of Jericho worked next to them, and beyond them was Zaccur son of Imri.

3The Fish Gate was built by the sons of Hassenaah. They laid the beams, set up its doors, and installed its bolts and bars. 4Meremoth son of Uriah and grandson of Hakkoz repaired the next section of wall. Beside him

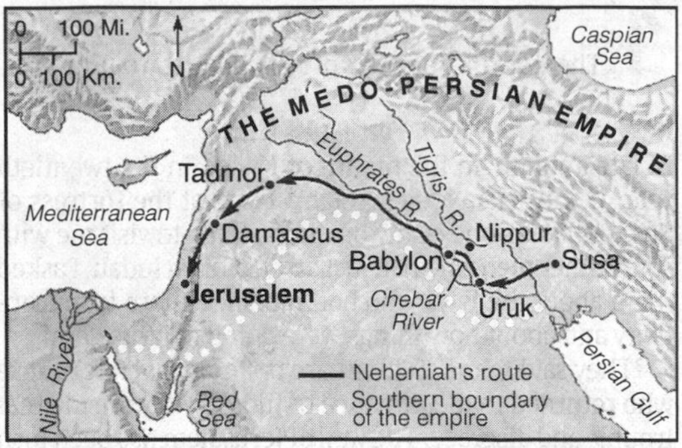

NEHEMIAH GOES TO JERUSALEM
Nehemiah worked in Susa as a personal assistant for the king of the vast Medo-Persian empire. When he heard that the rebuilding projects in Jerusalem were progressing slowly, he asked the king if he could go there to help his people complete the task of rebuilding their city's walls. The king agreed to let him go; so he left as soon as possible, traveling along much the same route Ezra had taken.

were Meshullam son of Berekiah and grandson of Meshezabel, and then Zadok son of Baana. 5Next were the people from Tekoa, though their leaders refused to work with the construction supervisors.

6The Old City Gate* was repaired by Joiada son of Paseah and Meshullam son of Besodeiah. They laid the beams, set up its doors, and installed its bolts and bars. 7Next to them were Melatiah from Gibeon, Jadon from Meronoth, people from Gibeon, and people from Mizpah, the headquarters of the governor of the province west of the Euphrates River.* 8Next was Uzziel son of Harhaiah, a goldsmith by trade, who also worked on the wall. Beyond him was Hananiah, a manufacturer of perfumes. They left out a section of Jerusalem as they built the Broad Wall.*

9Rephaiah son of Hur, the leader of half the district of Jerusalem, was next to them on the wall. 10Next Jedaiah son of Harumaph repaired the wall across from his own house, and next to him was Hattush son of Hashabneiah. 11Then came Malkijah son of Harim and Hasshub son of Pahath-moab, who repaired another section of the wall and the Tower of the Ovens. 12Shallum son of Hallohesh and his daughters repaired the next section. He was the leader of the other half of the district of Jerusalem.

13The Valley Gate was repaired by the people from Zanoah, led by Hanun. They set up its doors and installed its bolts and bars. They also repaired the 1,500 feet* of wall to the Dung Gate.

14The Dung Gate was repaired by Malkijah son of Recab, the leader of the Beth-hakkerem district. He rebuilt it, set up its doors, and installed its bolts and bars.

15The Fountain Gate was repaired by Shallum* son of Col-hozeh, the leader of the Mizpah district. He rebuilt it, roofed it, set up its doors, and installed its bolts and bars. Then he repaired the wall of the pool of Siloam* near the

2:13 Or *Serpent's Well.* 2:15 Hebrew *the valley.* 3:6 Or *The Mishneh Gate,* or *The Jeshanah Gate.* 3:7 Hebrew *the province beyond the river.* 3:8 Or *They fortified Jerusalem up to the Broad Wall.* 3:13 Hebrew *1,000 cubits* [450 meters]. 3:15a As in Syriac version; Hebrew reads *Shallun.* 3:15b Hebrew *pool of Shelah,* another name for the pool of Siloam.

king's garden, and he rebuilt the wall as far as the stairs that descend from the City of David. 16Next to him was Nehemiah son of Azbuk, the leader of half the district of Beth-zur. He rebuilt the wall from a place across from the tombs of David's family as far as the water reservoir and the House of the Warriors.

17Next to him, repairs were made by a group of Levites working under the supervision of Rehum son of Bani. Then came Hashabiah, the leader of half the district of Keilah, who supervised the building of the wall on behalf of his own district. 18Next down the line were his countrymen led by Binnui* son of Henadad, the leader of the other half of the district of Keilah.

19Next to them, Ezer son of Jeshua, the leader of Mizpah, repaired another section of wall across from the ascent to the armory near the angle in the wall. 20Next to him was Baruch son of Zabbai, who zealously repaired an additional section from the angle to the door of the house of Eliashib the high priest. 21Meremoth son of Uriah and grandson of Hakkoz rebuilt another section of the wall extending from the door of Eliashib's house to the end of the house.

22The next repairs were made by the priests from the surrounding region. 23After them, Benjamin and Hasshub repaired the section across from their house, and Azariah son of Maaseiah and grandson of Ananiah repaired the section across from his house. 24Next was Binnui son of Henadad, who rebuilt another section of the wall from Azariah's house to the angle and the corner. 25Palal son of Uzai carried on the work from a point opposite the angle and the tower that projects up from the king's upper house beside the court of the guard. Next to him were Pedaiah son of Parosh, 26with the Temple servants living on the hill of Ophel, who repaired the wall as far as a point across from the Water Gate to the east and the projecting tower. 27Then came the people of Tekoa, who repaired another section across from the great projecting tower and over to the wall of Ophel.

28Above the Horse Gate, the priests repaired the wall. Each one repaired the section immediately across from his own house. 29Next Zadok son of Immer also rebuilt the wall across from his own house, and beyond him was Shemaiah son of Shecaniah, the gatekeeper of the East Gate. 30Next Hananiah son of Shelemiah and Hanun, the sixth son of Zalaph, repaired another section, while Meshullam son of Berekiah rebuilt the wall across from where he lived. 31Malkijah, one of the goldsmiths, repaired the wall as far as the housing for the Temple servants and merchants, across from the Inspection Gate. Then he continued as far as the upper room at the corner. 32The other goldsmiths and merchants repaired the wall from that corner to the Sheep Gate.

4 ENEMIES OPPOSE THE REBUILDING

1*Sanballat was very angry when he learned that we were rebuilding the wall. He flew into a rage and mocked the Jews, 2saying in front of his friends and the Samarian army officers, "What does this bunch of poor, feeble Jews think they're doing? Do they think they can build the wall in a single day by just offering a few sacrifices?* Do they actually think they can make something of stones from a rubbish heap—and charred ones at that?"

3Tobiah the Ammonite, who was standing beside him, remarked, "That stone wall would collapse if even a fox walked along the top of it!"

OPPOSITION

At a church camp this summer, Tyson was challenged to start a Bible study at his school.

***Cool!* Tyson thought. So he started praying about it and, in time, became convinced that God wanted him to do it. And that's when all of the trouble started. Here are some of the highlights:**

- **The principal doesn't want to give him a room (even though Tyson keeps assuring him that the Bible study will not take place during school hours).**
- **No faculty members will agree to sponsor the group.**
- **A few Christian friends urge him to forget it.**
- **Some of Tyson's classmates have nicknamed him "Holy Roller" and "Jesus Freak."**
- **One huge senior (who's very anti-Christian) has been trying to pick a fight during P.E. class.**

With these obstacles, Tyson wonders whether starting that Bible study is worth it after all. Dumping the plan has started to sound good. Would you agree?

Read Nehemiah 4. The people of Israel were no strangers to opposition. They found plenty as they tried to rebuild the walls of Jerusalem. What would you say to Tyson, based on their experience?

4Then I prayed, "Hear us, our God, for we are being mocked. May their scoffing fall back on their own heads, and may they themselves become captives in a foreign land! 5Do not ignore their guilt. Do not blot out their sins, for they have provoked you to anger here in front of* the builders."

6At last the wall was completed to half its height around the entire city, for the people had worked with enthusiasm.

7*But when Sanballat and Tobiah and the Arabs, Ammonites, and Ashdodites heard that the work was going ahead and that the gaps in the wall of Jerusalem were being repaired, they were furious. 8They all made plans to come and fight against Jerusalem and throw us into confusion. 9But we prayed to our God and guarded the city day and night to protect ourselves.

10Then the people of Judah began to complain, "The workers are getting tired, and there is so much rubble to

3:18 As in a few Hebrew manuscripts, some Greek manuscripts, and Syriac version (see also 3:24; 10:9); most Hebrew manuscripts read *Bavvai.* **4:1** Verses 4:1-6 are numbered 3:33-38 in Hebrew text. **4:2** The meaning of the Hebrew is uncertain. **4:5** Or *for they have thrown insults in the face of.* **4:7** Verses 4:7-23 are numbered 4:1-17 in Hebrew text.

be moved. We will never be able to build the wall by
ourselves."
[11]Meanwhile, our enemies were saying, "Before they
know what's happening, we will swoop down on them
and kill them and end their work."
[12]The Jews who lived near the enemy came and told us
again and again, "They will come from all directions and
attack us!"* [13]So I placed armed guards behind the lowest
parts of the wall in the exposed areas. I stationed the people to stand guard by families, armed with swords, spears,
and bows.
[14]Then as I looked over the situation, I called together
the nobles and the rest of the people and said to them,
"Don't be afraid of the enemy! Remember the Lord, who
is great and glorious, and fight for your brothers, your
sons, your daughters, your wives, and your homes!"

A CURE FOR DISCOURAGEMENT 4:10-14

When the builders of the wall grew discouraged, Nehemiah reminded them of their goal and of God's protection. Feeling overwhelmed and discouraged by an assignment? The only cure for fatigue and discouragement is God. He can remind you of what you're working toward and give you the strength to do it. ■

[15]When our enemies heard that we knew of their plans
and that God had frustrated them, we all returned to our
work on the wall. [16]But from then on, only half my men
worked while the other half stood guard with spears,
shields, bows, and coats of mail. The leaders stationed
themselves behind the people of Judah [17]who were building the wall. The laborers carried on their work with one
hand supporting their load and one hand holding a
weapon. [18]All the builders had a sword belted to their
side. The trumpeter stayed with me to sound the alarm.
[19]Then I explained to the nobles and officials and all
the people, "The work is very spread out, and we are
widely separated from each other along the wall. [20]When
you hear the blast of the trumpet, rush to wherever it is
sounding. Then our God will fight for us!"
[21]We worked early and late, from sunrise to sunset.
And half the men were always on guard. [22]I also told
everyone living outside the walls to stay in Jerusalem.
That way they and their servants could help with guard
duty at night and work during the day. [23]During this
time, none of us—not I, nor my relatives, nor my servants, nor the guards who were with me—ever took off
our clothes. We carried our weapons with us at all times,
even when we went for water.*

5 NEHEMIAH DEFENDS THE OPPRESSED

About this time some of the men and their wives raised a
cry of protest against their fellow Jews. [2]They were saying, "We have such large families. We need more food to
survive."
[3]Others said, "We have mortgaged our fields, vineyards, and homes to get food during the famine."
[4]And others said, "We have had to borrow money on
our fields and vineyards to pay our taxes. [5]We belong to
the same family as those who are wealthy, and our children are just like theirs. Yet we must sell our children into
slavery just to get enough money to live. We have already
sold some of our daughters, and we are helpless to do anything about it, for our fields and vineyards are already
mortgaged to others."
[6]When I heard their complaints, I was very angry.
[7]After thinking it over, I spoke out against these nobles
and officials. I told them, "You are hurting your own relatives by charging interest when they borrow money!"
Then I called a public meeting to deal with the problem.
[8]At the meeting I said to them, "We are doing all we
can to redeem our Jewish relatives who have had to sell
themselves to pagan foreigners, but you are selling them
back into slavery again. How often must we redeem
them?" And they had nothing to say in their defense.
[9]Then I pressed further, "What you are doing is not
right! Should you not walk in the fear of our God in order
to avoid being mocked by enemy nations? [10]I myself, as
well as my brothers and my workers, have been lending
the people money and grain, but now let us stop this business of charging interest. [11]You must restore their fields,
vineyards, olive groves, and homes to them this very day.
And repay the interest you charged when you lent them
money, grain, new wine, and olive oil."
[12]They replied, "We will give back everything and demand nothing more from the people. We will do as you
say." Then I called the priests and made the nobles and
officials swear to do what they had promised.
[13]I shook out the folds of my robe and said, "If you fail
to keep your promise, may God shake you like this from
your homes and from your property!"
The whole assembly responded, "Amen," and they
praised the LORD. And the people did as they had promised.
[14]For the entire twelve years that I was governor of Judah—from the twentieth year to the thirty-second year of
the reign of King Artaxerxes*—neither I nor my officials
drew on our official food allowance. [15]The former governors, in contrast, had laid heavy burdens on the people, demanding a daily ration of food and wine, besides forty
pieces* of silver. Even their assistants took advantage of
the people. But because I feared God, I did not act that way.
[16]I also devoted myself to working on the wall and refused to acquire any land. And I required all my servants
to spend time working on the wall. [17]I asked for nothing,
even though I regularly fed 150 Jewish officials at my table, besides all the visitors from other lands! [18]The provisions I paid for each day included one ox, six choice
sheep or goats, and a large number of poultry. And every
ten days we needed a large supply of all kinds of wine. Yet
I refused to claim the governor's food allowance because
the people already carried a heavy burden.

4:12 The meaning of the Hebrew is uncertain. **4:23** Or *Each carried his weapon in his right hand.* Hebrew reads *Each his weapon the water.* The meaning of the Hebrew is uncertain. **5:14** That is, 445–433 B.C. **5:15** Hebrew *40 shekels* [1 pound, or 456 grams].

[19]Remember, O my God, all that I have done for these people, and bless me for it.

6 CONTINUED OPPOSITION TO REBUILDING

Sanballat, Tobiah, Geshem the Arab, and the rest of our enemies found out that I had finished rebuilding the wall and that no gaps remained—though we had not yet set up the doors in the gates. [2]So Sanballat and Geshem sent a message asking me to meet them at one of the villages* in the plain of Ono.

But I realized they were plotting to harm me, [3]so I replied by sending this message to them: "I am engaged in a great work, so I can't come. Why should I stop working to come and meet with you?"

[4]Four times they sent the same message, and each time I gave the same reply. [5]The fifth time, Sanballat's servant came with an open letter in his hand, [6]and this is what it said:

> "There is a rumor among the surounding nations, and Geshem* tells me it is true, that you and the Jews are planning to rebel and that is why you are building the wall. According to his reports, you plan to be their king. [7]He also reports that you have appointed prophets in Jerusalem to proclaim about you, 'Look! There is a king in Judah!'
>
> "You can be very sure that this report will get back to the king, so I suggest that you come and talk it over with me."

[8]I replied, "There is no truth in any part of your story. You are making up the whole thing."

[9]They were just trying to intimidate us, imagining that they could discourage us and stop the work. So I continued the work with even greater determination.*

COURAGE 6:10-13

When enemies threatened Nehemiah, he refused to give in to fear and flee to the Temple. Since Nehemiah wasn't a priest, he wasn't allowed to hide in the Temple (see Num 18:22). If he had run for his life, he would have undermined the courage he wanted to instill in the people.

Leaders often are targets for attacks nowadays. Maybe that's why Paul later encouraged believers to pray for those in authority (1 Tim 2:2). Have you developed that habit? ■

[10]Later I went to visit Shemaiah son of Delaiah and grandson of Mehetabel, who was confined to his home. He said, "Let us meet together inside the Temple of God and bolt the doors shut. Your enemies are coming to kill you tonight."

[11]But I replied, "Should someone in my position run from danger? Should someone in my position enter the Temple to save his life? No, I won't do it!" [12]I realized that God had not spoken to him, but that he had uttered this prophecy against me because Tobiah and Sanballat had hired him. [13]They were hoping to intimidate me and make me sin. Then they would be able to accuse and discredit me.

[14]Remember, O my God, all the evil things that Tobiah and Sanballat have done. And remember Noadiah the prophet and all the prophets like her who have tried to intimidate me.

THE BUILDERS COMPLETE THE WALL

[15]So on October 2* the wall was finished—just fifty-two days after we had begun. [16]When our enemies and the surrounding nations heard about it, they were frightened and humiliated. They realized this work had been done with the help of our God.

[17]During those fifty-two days, many letters went back and forth between Tobiah and the nobles of Judah. [18]For many in Judah had sworn allegiance to him because his father-in-law was Shecaniah son of Arah, and his son Jehohanan was married to the daughter of Meshullam son of Berekiah. [19]They kept telling me about Tobiah's good deeds, and then they told him everything I said. And Tobiah kept sending threatening letters to intimidate me.

PROJECT FOLLOW-UP 7:1-4

The wall was complete, but the work wasn't finished. Nehemiah assigned each family the task of protecting the section of wall next to their home. Ever been tempted to let your guard down and rest on past accomplishments after you've completed a large task? According to Nehemiah, you've still got work to do! Following through after a project is completed is as vital as doing the project itself. ■

7

After the wall was finished and I had set up the doors in the gates, the gatekeepers, singers, and Levites were appointed. [2]I gave the responsibility of governing Jerusalem to my brother Hanani, along with Hananiah, the commander of the fortress, for he was a faithful man who feared God more than most. [3]I said to them, "Do not leave the gates open during the hottest part of the day.* And even while the gatekeepers are on duty, have them shut and bar the doors. Appoint the residents of Jerusalem to act as guards, everyone on a regular watch. Some will serve at sentry posts and some in front of their own homes."

NEHEMIAH REGISTERS THE PEOPLE

[4]At that time the city was large and spacious, but the population was small, and none of the houses had been rebuilt. [5]So my God gave me the idea to call together all the

6:2 As in Greek version; Hebrew reads *at Kephirim.* 6:6 Hebrew *Gashmu,* a variant spelling of Geshem. 6:9 As in Greek version; Hebrew reads *But now to strengthen my hands.* 6:15 Hebrew *on the twenty-fifth day of the month Elul,* of the ancient Hebrew lunar calendar. This day was October 2, 445 B.C.; also see note on 1:1. 7:3 Or *Keep the gates of Jerusalem closed until the sun is hot.*

nobles and leaders of the city, along with the ordinary citizens, for registration. I had found the genealogical record of those who had first returned to Judah. This is what
was written there:

6 Here is the list of the Jewish exiles of the provinces
who returned from their captivity. King Nebuchadnezzar had deported them to Babylon, but now they
returned to Jerusalem and the other towns in Judah
where they originally lived. 7 Their leaders were
Zerubbabel, Jeshua, Nehemiah, Seraiah,* Reelaiah,*
Nahamani, Mordecai, Bilshan, Mispar,* Bigvai,
Rehum,* and Baanah.

This is the number of the men of Israel who returned from exile:

8 The family of Parosh . . . 2,172
9 The family of Shephatiah . . . 372
10 The family of Arah . . . 652
11 The family of Pahath-moab (descendants of Jeshua and Joab) . . . 2,818
12 The family of Elam . . . 1,254
13 The family of Zattu . . . 845
14 The family of Zaccai . . . 760
15 The family of Bani* . . . 648
16 The family of Bebai . . . 628
17 The family of Azgad . . . 2,322
18 The family of Adonikam . . . 667
19 The family of Bigvai . . . 2,067
20 The family of Adin . . . 655
21 The family of Ater (descendants of Hezekiah) . . . 98
22 The family of Hashum . . . 328
23 The family of Bezai . . . 324
24 The family of Jorah* . . . 112
25 The family of Gibbar* . . . 95
26 The people of Bethlehem and Netophah . . . 188
27 The people of Anathoth . . . 128
28 The people of Beth-azmaveth . . . 42
29 The people of Kiriath-jearim, Kephirah, and Beeroth . . . 743
30 The people of Ramah and Geba . . . 621
31 The people of Micmash . . . 122
32 The people of Bethel and Ai . . . 123
33 The people of Nebo . . . 52
34 The citizens of Elam . . . 1,254
35 The citizens of Harim . . . 320
36 The citizens of Jericho . . . 345
37 The citizens of Lod, Hadid, and Ono . . . 721
38 The citizens of Senaah . . . 3,930

39 These are the priests who returned from exile:
The family of Jedaiah (through the line of Jeshua) . . . 973
40 The family of Immer . . . 1,052
41 The family of Pashhur . . . 1,247
42 The family of Harim . . . 1,017

43 These are the Levites who returned from exile:
The families of Jeshua and Kadmiel (descendants of Hodaviah*) . . . 74
44 The singers of the family of Asaph . . . 148
45 The gatekeepers of the families of Shallum, Ater, Talmon, Akkub, Hatita, and Shobai . . . 138

46 The descendants of the following Temple servants returned from exile:
Ziha, Hasupha, Tabbaoth,
47 Keros, Siaha,* Padon,
48 Lebanah, Hagabah, Shalmai,
49 Hanan, Giddel, Gahar,
50 Reaiah, Rezin, Nekoda,
51 Gazzam, Uzza, Paseah,
52 Besai, Meunim, Nephusim,*
53 Bakbuk, Hakupha, Harhur,
54 Bazluth,* Mehida, Harsha,
55 Barkos, Sisera, Temah,
56 Neziah, and Hatipha.

57 The descendants of these servants of King Solomon returned from exile:
Sotai, Hassophereth, Peruda,*
58 Jaalah,* Darkon, Giddel,
59 Shephatiah, Hattil, Pokereth-hazzebaim, and Ami.*

60 In all, the Temple servants and the descendants of Solomon's servants numbered 392.

61 Another group returned at this time from the towns
of Tel-melah, Tel-harsha, Kerub, Addan,* and Immer.
However, they could not prove that they or their
families were descendants of Israel. 62 This group
included the families of Delaiah, Tobiah, and
Nekoda—a total of 642 people.
63 Three families of priests—Hobaiah, Hakkoz, and
Barzillai—also returned. (This Barzillai had married
a woman who was a descendant of Barzillai of Gilead,
and he had taken her family name.) 64 They searched
for their names in the genealogical records, but they
were not found, so they were disqualified from
serving as priests. 65 The governor told them not to eat
the priests' share of food from the sacrifices until a
priest could consult the LORD about the matter by
using the Urim and Thummim—the sacred lots.
66 So a total of 42,360 people returned to Judah,
67 in addition to 7,337 servants and 245 singers, both
men and women. 68 They took with them 736 horses,
245 mules,* 69 435 camels, and 6,720 donkeys.

7:7a As in parallel text at Ezra 2:2; Hebrew reads *Azariah.* **7:7b** As in parallel text at Ezra 2:2; Hebrew reads *Raamiah.* **7:7c** As in parallel text at Ezra 2:2; Hebrew reads *Mispereth.* **7:7d** As in parallel text at Ezra 2:2; Hebrew reads *Nehum.* **7:15** As in parallel text at Ezra 2:10; Hebrew reads *Binnui.* **7:24** As in parallel text at Ezra 2:18; Hebrew reads *Hariph.* **7:25** As in parallel text at Ezra 2:20; Hebrew reads *Gibeon.* **7:43** As in parallel text at Ezra 2:40; Hebrew reads *Hodevah.* **7:47** As in parallel text at Ezra 2:44; Hebrew reads *Sia.* **7:52** As in parallel text at Ezra 2:50; Hebrew reads *Nephushesim.* **7:54** As in parallel text at Ezra 2:52; Hebrew reads *Bazlith.* **7:57** As in parallel text at Ezra 2:55; Hebrew reads *Sotai, Sophereth, Perida.* **7:58** As in parallel text at Ezra 2:56; Hebrew reads *Jaala.* **7:59** As in parallel text at Ezra 2:57; Hebrew reads *Amon.* **7:61** As in parallel text at Ezra 2:59; Hebrew reads *Addon.* **7:68** As in some Hebrew manuscripts (see also Ezra 2:66); most Hebrew manuscripts lack this verse. Verses 7:69-73 are numbered 7:68-72 in Hebrew text.

70Some of the family leaders
gave gifts for the work. The
governor gave to the treasury
1,000 gold coins,* 50 gold basins,
and 530 robes for the priests.
71The other leaders gave to the
treasury a total of 20,000 gold
coins* and some 2,750 pounds*
of silver for the work. 72The rest of
the people gave 20,000 gold coins,
about 2,500 pounds* of silver, and
67 robes for the priests.
73So the priests, the Levites, the
gatekeepers, the singers, the
Temple servants, and some of the
common people settled near Jerusalem. The
rest of the people returned to their own towns
throughout Israel.

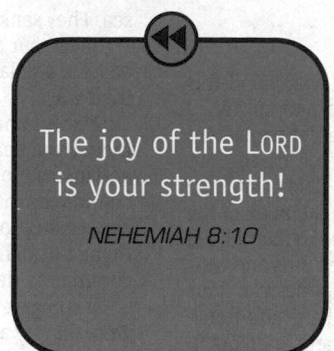

> The joy of the LORD is your strength!
>
> *NEHEMIAH 8:10*

8

EZRA READS THE LAW

In October,* when the Israelites had settled in their
towns, 8:1all the people assembled with a unified purpose
at the square just inside the Water Gate. They asked Ezra
the scribe to bring out the Book of the Law of Moses,
which the LORD had given for Israel to obey.
2So on October 8* Ezra the priest brought the Book of
the Law before the assembly, which included the men
and women and all the children old enough to understand. 3He faced the square just inside the Water Gate
from early morning until noon and read aloud to everyone who could understand. All the people listened
closely to the Book of the Law.
4Ezra the scribe stood on a high wooden platform
that had been made for the occasion. To his right stood
Mattithiah, Shema, Anaiah, Uriah, Hilkiah, and Maaseiah. To his left stood Pedaiah, Mishael, Malkijah, Hashum, Hashbaddanah, Zechariah, and Meshullam. 5Ezra
stood on the platform in full view of all the people.
When they saw him open the book, they all rose to their
feet.
6Then Ezra praised the LORD, the great God, and all the
people chanted, "Amen! Amen!" as they lifted their
hands. Then they bowed down and worshiped the LORD
with their faces to the ground.
7The Levites—Jeshua, Bani, Sherebiah, Jamin, Akkub,
Shabbethai, Hodiah, Maaseiah, Kelita, Azariah, Jozabad,
Hanan, and Pelaiah—then instructed the people in the
Law while everyone remained in their places. 8They read
from the Book of the Law of God and clearly explained
the meaning of what was being read, helping the people
understand each passage.
9Then Nehemiah the governor, Ezra the priest and
scribe, and the Levites who were interpreting for the
people said to them, "Don't mourn or
weep on such a day as this! For today is a
sacred day before the LORD your God."
For the people had all been weeping as
they listened to the words of the Law.
10And Nehemiah* continued, "Go
and celebrate with a feast of rich foods
and sweet drinks, and share gifts of
food with people who have nothing
prepared. This is a sacred day before
our Lord. Don't be dejected and sad, for
the joy of the LORD is your strength!"
11And the Levites, too, quieted the
people, telling them, "Hush! Don't
weep! For this is a sacred day." 12So the
people went away to eat and drink at a festive meal, to
share gifts of food, and to celebrate with great joy because they had heard God's words and understood them.

THE FESTIVAL OF SHELTERS

13On October 9* the family leaders of all the people, together with the priests and Levites, met with Ezra the
scribe to go over the Law in greater detail. 14As they studied the Law, they discovered that the LORD had commanded through Moses that the Israelites should live in
shelters during the festival to be held that month.* 15He
had said that a proclamation should be made throughout
their towns and in Jerusalem, telling the people to go to
the hills to get branches from olive, wild olive,* myrtle,
palm, and other leafy trees. They were to use these
branches to make shelters in which they would live during the festival, as prescribed in the Law.

ACT ON IT! 8:1-14

After Ezra read God's laws to the people, they studied them further and then acted upon them. A careful reading of a Scripture passage always calls for a response to these questions: "What should I *do* with this knowledge?" "How should my life change?" Action is the fruit of belief. ■

16So the people went out and cut branches and used
them to build shelters on the roofs of their houses, in
their courtyards, in the courtyards of God's Temple, or in
the squares just inside the Water Gate and the Ephraim
Gate. 17So everyone who had returned from captivity
lived in these shelters during the festival, and they were
all filled with great joy! The Israelites had not celebrated
like this since the days of Joshua* son of Nun.
18Ezra read from the Book of the Law of God on each of
the seven days of the festival. Then on the eighth day they
held a solemn assembly, as was required by law.

7:70 Hebrew *1,000 darics of gold,* about 19 pounds or 8.6 kilograms in weight. **7:71a** Hebrew *20,000 darics of gold,* about 375 pounds or 170 kilograms in weight; also in 7:72. **7:71b** Hebrew *2,200 minas* [1,300 kilograms]. **7:72** Hebrew *2,000 minas* [1,200 kilograms]. **7:73** Hebrew *in the seventh month.* This month of the ancient Hebrew lunar calendar occurred within the months of October and November 445 B.C. **8:2** Hebrew *on the first day of the seventh month,* of the ancient Hebrew lunar calendar. This day was October 8, 445 B.C.; also see note on 1:1. **8:10** Hebrew *he.* **8:13** Hebrew *On the second day,* of the seventh month of the ancient Hebrew lunar calendar. This day was October 9, 445 B.C.; also see notes on 1:1 and 8:2. **8:14** Hebrew *in the seventh month.* This month of the ancient Hebrew lunar calendar usually occurs within the months of September and October. See Lev 23:39-43. **8:15** Or *pine;* Hebrew reads *oil tree.* 8:17 Hebrew *Jeshua,* a variant spelling of Joshua.

9

THE PEOPLE CONFESS THEIR SINS

On October 31* the people assembled again, and this time they fasted and dressed in burlap and sprinkled dust on their heads. 2Those of Israelite descent separated themselves from all foreigners as they confessed their own sins and the sins of their ancestors. 3They remained standing in place for three hours* while the Book of the Law of the LORD their God was read aloud to them. Then for three more hours they confessed their sins and worshiped the LORD their God. 4The Levites—Jeshua, Bani, Kadmiel, Shebaniah, Bunni, Sherebiah, Bani, and Kenani—stood on the stairway of the Levites and cried out to the LORD their God with loud voices.

TRUTH HURTS 9:1-3

After hearing the word of God (see 8:18), the people of Israel admitted their wrongs to one another. As we study God's Word, God sometimes shows us attitudes and actions to change in our lives. That's why the Bible is considered "sharper than the sharpest two-edged sword" (Heb 4:12). The truth hurts sometimes. But Jesus promised that "the truth will set you free" (John 8:32). ■

5Then the leaders of the Levites—Jeshua, Kadmiel, Bani, Hashabneiah, Sherebiah, Hodiah, Shebaniah, and Pethahiah—called out to the people: "Stand up and praise the LORD your God, for he lives from everlasting to everlasting!" Then they prayed:

"May your glorious name be praised! May it be exalted above all blessing and praise!

6"You alone are the LORD. You made the skies and the heavens and all the stars. You made the earth and the seas and everything in them. You preserve them all, and the angels of heaven worship you.

7"You are the LORD God, who chose Abram and brought him from Ur of the Chaldeans and renamed him Abraham. 8When he had proved himself faithful, you made a covenant with him to give him and his descendants the land of the Canaanites, Hittites, Amorites, Perizzites, Jebusites, and Girgashites. And you have done what you promised, for you are always true to your word.

9"You saw the misery of our ancestors in Egypt, and you heard their cries from beside the Red Sea.* 10You displayed miraculous signs and wonders against Pharaoh, his officials, and all his people, for you knew how arrogantly they were treating our ancestors. You have a glorious reputation that has never been forgotten. 11You divided the sea for your people so they could walk through on dry land! And then you hurled their enemies into the depths of the sea. They sank like stones beneath the mighty waters. 12You led our ancestors by a pillar of cloud during the day and a pillar of fire at night so that they could find their way.

13"You came down at Mount Sinai and spoke to them from heaven. You gave them regulations and instructions that were just, and decrees and commands that were good. 14You instructed them concerning your holy Sabbath. And you commanded them, through Moses your servant, to obey all your commands, decrees, and instructions.

15"You gave them bread from heaven when they were hungry and water from the rock when they were thirsty. You commanded them to go and take possession of the land you had sworn to give them.

16"But our ancestors were proud and stubborn, and they paid no attention to your commands. 17They refused to obey and did not remember the miracles you had done for them. Instead, they became stubborn and appointed a leader to take them back to their slavery in Egypt! But you are a God of forgiveness, gracious and merciful, slow to become angry, and rich in unfailing love. You did not abandon them, 18even when they made an idol shaped like a calf and said, 'This is your god who brought you out of Egypt!' They committed terrible blasphemies.

19"But in your great mercy you did not abandon them to die in the wilderness. The pillar of cloud still led them forward by day, and the pillar of fire showed them the way through the night. 20You sent your good Spirit to instruct them, and you did not stop giving them manna from heaven or water for their thirst. 21For forty years you sustained them in the wilderness, and they lacked nothing. Their clothes did not wear out, and their feet did not swell!

22"Then you helped our ancestors conquer kingdoms and nations, and you placed your people in every corner of the land.* They took over the land of King Sihon of Heshbon and the land of King Og of Bashan. 23You made their descendants as numerous as the stars in the sky and brought them into the land you had promised to their ancestors.

24"They went in and took possession of the land. You subdued whole nations before them. Even the Canaanites, who inhabited the land, were powerless! Your people could deal with these nations and their kings as they pleased. 25Our ancestors captured fortified cities and fertile land. They took over houses full of good things, with cisterns already dug and vineyards and olive groves and fruit trees in abundance. So they ate until they were full and grew fat and enjoyed themselves in all your blessings.

26"But despite all this, they were disobedient and rebelled against you. They turned their backs on your Law, they killed your prophets who warned them to return to you, and they committed terrible

9:1 Hebrew *On the twenty-fourth day of that same month,* the seventh month of the ancient Hebrew lunar calendar. This day was October 31, 445 B.C.; also see notes on 1:1 and 8:2. 9:3 Hebrew *for a quarter of a day.* 9:9 Hebrew *sea of reeds.* 9:22 The meaning of the Hebrew is uncertain.

blasphemies. 27So you handed them over to their
enemies, who made them suffer. But in their time of
trouble they cried to you, and you heard them from
heaven. In your great mercy, you sent them liberators
who rescued them from their enemies.
28"But as soon as they were at peace, your people
again committed evil in your sight, and once more
you let their enemies conquer them. Yet whenever
your people turned and cried to you again for help,
you listened once more from heaven. In your
wonderful mercy, you rescued them many times!
29"You warned them to return to your Law, but they
became proud and obstinate and disobeyed your
commands. They did not follow your regulations,
by which people will find life if only they obey. They
stubbornly turned their backs on you and refused to
listen. 30In your love, you were patient with them for
many years. You sent your Spirit, who warned them
through the prophets. But still they wouldn't listen!
So once again you allowed the peoples of the land to
conquer them. 31But in your great mercy, you did not
destroy them completely or abandon them forever.
What a gracious and merciful God you are!
32"And now, our God, the great and mighty and
awesome God, who keeps his covenant of unfailing
love, do not let all the hardships we have suffered
seem insignificant to you. Great trouble has come
upon us and upon our kings and leaders and priests
and prophets and ancestors—all of your people—
from the days when the kings of Assyria first
triumphed over us until now. 33Every time you
punished us you were being just. We have sinned
greatly, and you gave us only what we deserved.
34Our kings, leaders, priests, and ancestors did not
obey your Law or listen to the warnings in your
commands and laws. 35Even while they had their
own kingdom, they did not serve you, though you
showered your goodness on them. You gave them
a large, fertile land, but they refused to turn from
their wickedness.
36"So now today we are slaves in the land of plenty
that you gave our ancestors for their enjoyment! We
are slaves here in this good land. 37The lush produce
of this land piles up in the hands of the kings whom
you have set over us because of our sins. They have
power over us and our livestock. We serve them at
their pleasure, and we are in great misery."

THE PEOPLE AGREE TO OBEY

38*The people responded, "In view of all this,* we are
making a solemn promise and putting it in writing. On
this sealed document are the names of our leaders and
Levites and priests."

10
1*The document was ratified and sealed with
the following names:

The governor:
Nehemiah son of Hacaliah, and also Zedekiah.
2The following priests:
Seraiah, Azariah, Jeremiah, 3Pashhur, Amariah,
Malkijah, 4Hattush, Shebaniah, Malluch, 5Harim,
Meremoth, Obadiah, 6Daniel, Ginnethon, Baruch,
7Meshullam, Abijah, Mijamin, 8Maaziah, Bilgai, and
Shemaiah. These were the priests.
9The following Levites:
Jeshua son of Azaniah, Binnui from the family
of Henadad, Kadmiel, 10and their fellow Levites:
Shebaniah, Hodiah, Kelita, Pelaiah, Hanan, 11Mica,
Rehob, Hashabiah, 12Zaccur, Sherebiah, Shebaniah,
13Hodiah, Bani, and Beninu.
14The following leaders:
Parosh, Pahath-moab, Elam, Zattu, Bani, 15Bunni,
Azgad, Bebai, 16Adonijah, Bigvai, Adin, 17Ater,
Hezekiah, Azzur, 18Hodiah, Hashum, Bezai, 19Hariph,
Anathoth, Nebai, 20Magpiash, Meshullam, Hezir,
21Meshezabel, Zadok, Jaddua, 22Pelatiah, Hanan,
Anaiah, 23Hoshea, Hananiah, Hasshub, 24Hallohesh,
Pilha, Shobek, 25Rehum, Hashabnah, Maaseiah,
26Ahiah, Hanan, Anan, 27Malluch, Harim, and Baanah.

COMMITTED 10:28-39

The wall was completed, and the covenant God made with his people in the days of Moses (see Deut 8) was restored. This covenant includes principles that are important for us today. Our relationship with God goes far beyond church attendance and regular quiet times. It affects our relationships (10:30), our time (10:31), and our resources (10:32-39). How committed are you? ■

THE VOW OF THE PEOPLE

28Then the rest of the people—the priests, Levites, gatekeepers, singers, Temple servants, and all who had separated themselves from the pagan people of the land in
order to obey the Law of God, together with their wives,
sons, daughters, and all who were old enough to understand—29joined their leaders and bound themselves with
an oath. They swore a curse on themselves if they failed
to obey the Law of God as issued by his servant Moses.
They solemnly promised to carefully follow all the commands, regulations, and decrees of the LORD our Lord:

30"We promise not to let our daughters marry the
pagan people of the land, and not to let our sons
marry their daughters.
31"We also promise that if the people of the land
should bring any merchandise or grain to be sold on
the Sabbath or on any other holy day, we will refuse
to buy it. Every seventh year we will let our land rest,
and we will cancel all debts owed to us.
32"In addition, we promise to obey the command to
pay the annual Temple tax of one-eighth of an ounce

9:38a Verse 9:38 is numbered 10:1 in Hebrew text. **9:38b** Or *In spite of all this.* **10:1** Verses 10:1-39 are numbered 10:2-40 in Hebrew text.

of silver* for the care of the Temple of our God.
33 This will provide for the Bread of the Presence;
for the regular grain offerings and burnt offerings;
for the offerings on the Sabbaths, the new moon
celebrations, and the annual festivals; for the holy
offerings; and for the sin offerings to make atonement for Israel. It will provide for everything
necessary for the work of the Temple of our God.

34 "We have cast sacred lots to determine when—
at regular times each year—the families of the priests,
Levites, and the common people should bring wood
to God's Temple to be burned on the altar of the LORD
our God, as is written in the Law.

35 "We promise to bring the first part of every
harvest to the LORD's Temple year after year—
whether it be a crop from the soil or from our fruit
trees. 36 We agree to give God our oldest sons and the
firstborn of all our herds and flocks, as prescribed
in the Law. We will present them to the priests who
minister in the Temple of our God. 37 We will store
the produce in the storerooms of the Temple of our
God. We will bring the best of our flour and other
grain offerings, the best of our fruit, and the best of
our new wine and olive oil. And we promise to bring
to the Levites a tenth of everything our land produces,
for it is the Levites who collect the tithes in all our
rural towns.

38 "A priest—a descendant of Aaron—will be with
the Levites as they receive these tithes. And a tenth
of all that is collected as tithes will be delivered by
the Levites to the Temple of our God and placed in
the storerooms. 39 The people and the Levites must
bring these offerings of grain, new wine, and olive
oil to the storerooms and place them in the sacred
containers near the ministering priests, the gatekeepers, and the singers.

"We promise together not to neglect the Temple
of our God."

11

THE PEOPLE OCCUPY JERUSALEM

The leaders of the people were living in Jerusalem, the
holy city. A tenth of the people from the other towns of
Judah and Benjamin were chosen by sacred lots to live
there, too, while the rest stayed where they were. 2 And
the people commended everyone who volunteered to resettle in Jerusalem.

3 Here is a list of the names of the provincial officials
who came to live in Jerusalem. (Most of the people,
priests, Levites, Temple servants, and descendants of Solomon's servants continued to live in their own homes in
the various towns of Judah, 4 but some of the people from
Judah and Benjamin resettled in Jerusalem.)

From the tribe of Judah:
Athaiah son of Uzziah, son of Zechariah, son of
Amariah, son of Shephatiah, son of Mahalalel, of the
family of Perez. 5 Also Maaseiah son of Baruch, son of
Col-hozeh, son of Hazaiah, son of Adaiah, son of
Joiarib, son of Zechariah, of the family of Shelah.*
6 There were 468 descendants of Perez who lived
in Jerusalem—all outstanding men.

7 From the tribe of Benjamin:
Sallu son of Meshullam, son of Joed, son of Pedaiah,
son of Kolaiah, son of Maaseiah, son of Ithiel, son of
Jeshaiah. 8 After him were Gabbai and Sallai and a
total of 928 relatives. 9 Their chief officer was Joel
son of Zicri, who was assisted by Judah son of
Hassenuah, second-in-command over the city.

10 From the priests:
Jedaiah son of Joiarib; Jakin; 11 and Seraiah son of
Hilkiah, son of Meshullam, son of Zadok, son of
Meraioth, son of Ahitub, the supervisor of the
Temple of God. 12 Also 822 of their associates, who
worked at the Temple. Also Adaiah son of Jeroham,
son of Pelaliah, son of Amzi, son of Zechariah, son
of Pashhur, son of Malkijah, 13 along with 242 of his
associates, who were heads of their families. Also
Amashsai son of Azarel, son of Ahzai, son of
Meshillemoth, son of Immer, 14 and 128 of his*
outstanding associates. Their chief officer was
Zabdiel son of Haggedolim.

15 From the Levites:
Shemaiah son of Hasshub, son of Azrikam, son of
Hashabiah, son of Bunni. 16 Also Shabbethai and
Jozabad, who were in charge of the work outside the
Temple of God. 17 Also Mattaniah son of Mica, son of
Zabdi, a descendant of Asaph, who led in thanksgiving
and prayer. Also Bakbukiah, who was Mattaniah's
assistant, and Abda son of Shammua, son of Galal,
son of Jeduthun. 18 In all, there were 284 Levites in
the holy city.

19 From the gatekeepers:
Akkub, Talmon, and 172 of their associates, who
guarded the gates.

20 The other priests, Levites, and the rest of the Israelites lived wherever their family inheritance was located
in any of the towns of Judah. 21 The Temple servants, however, whose leaders were Ziha and Gishpa, all lived on the
hill of Ophel.

22 The chief officer of the Levites in Jerusalem was Uzzi
son of Bani, son of Hashabiah, son of Mattaniah, son of
Mica, a descendant of Asaph, whose family served as
singers at God's Temple. 23 Their daily responsibilities
were carried out according to the terms of a royal
command.

24 Pethahiah son of Meshezabel, a descendant of Zerah
son of Judah, was the royal adviser in all matters of public
administration.

25 As for the surrounding villages with their open
fields, some of the people of Judah lived in Kiriath-arba
with its settlements, Dibon with its settlements, and
Jekabzeel with its villages. 26 They also lived in Jeshua,
Moladah, Beth-pelet, 27 Hazar-shual, Beersheba with its
settlements, 28 Ziklag, and Meconah with its settlements.

10:32 Hebrew *tax of ⅓ of a shekel* [4 grams]. **11:5** Hebrew *son of the Shilonite.* **11:14** As in Greek version; Hebrew reads *their.*

[29]They also lived in En-rimmon, Zorah, Jarmuth, [30]Zano-
ah, and Adullam with their surrounding villages. They also lived in Lachish with its nearby fields and Azekah with its surrounding villages. So the people of Judah were living all the way from Beersheba in the south to the valley of Hinnom.

[31]Some of the people of Benjamin lived at Geba, Micmash, Aija, and Bethel with its settlements. [32]They
also lived in Anathoth, Nob, Ananiah, [33]Hazor, Ramah,
Gittaim, [34]Hadid, Zeboim, Neballat, [35]Lod, Ono, and the
Valley of Craftsmen.* [36]Some of the Levites who lived in
Judah were sent to live with the tribe of Benjamin.

12

A HISTORY OF THE PRIESTS AND LEVITES

Here is the list of the priests and Levites who returned with Zerubbabel son of Shealtiel and Jeshua the high priest:

Seraiah, Jeremiah, Ezra,
2 Amariah, Malluch, Hattush,
3 Shecaniah, Harim,* Meremoth,
4 Iddo, Ginnethon,* Abijah,
5 Miniamin, Moadiah,* Bilgah,
6 Shemaiah, Joiarib, Jedaiah,
7 Sallu, Amok, Hilkiah, and Jedaiah.

These were the leaders of the priests and their associates in the days of Jeshua.

[8]The Levites who returned with them were Jeshua, Binnui, Kadmiel, Sherebiah, Judah, and Mattaniah, who with his associates was in charge of the songs of thanksgiving.
[9]Their associates, Bakbukiah and Unni, stood opposite them during the service.

10 Jeshua the high priest was the father of Joiakim.
Joiakim was the father of Eliashib.
Eliashib was the father of Joiada.
11 Joiada was the father of Johanan.*
Johanan was the father of Jaddua.

[12]Now when Joiakim was high priest, the family leaders of the priests were as follows:

Meraiah was leader of the family of Seraiah.
Hananiah was leader of the family of Jeremiah.
13 Meshullam was leader of the family of Ezra.
Jehohanan was leader of the family of Amariah.
14 Jonathan was leader of the family of Malluch.*
Joseph was leader of the family of Shecaniah.*
15 Adna was leader of the family of Harim.
Helkai was leader of the family of Meremoth.*
16 Zechariah was leader of the family of Iddo.
Meshullam was leader of the family of Ginnethon.
17 Zicri was leader of the family of Abijah.
There was also a* leader of the family of Miniamin.
Piltai was leader of the family of Moadiah.
18 Shammua was leader of the family of Bilgah.
Jehonathan was leader of the family of Shemaiah.
19 Mattenai was leader of the family of Joiarib.
Uzzi was leader of the family of Jedaiah.
20 Kallai was leader of the family of Sallu.*
Eber was leader of the family of Amok.
21 Hashabiah was leader of the family of Hilkiah.
Nethanel was leader of the family of Jedaiah.

[22]A record of the Levite families was kept during the years when Eliashib, Joiada, Johanan, and Jaddua served as high priest. Another record of the priests was kept
during the reign of Darius the Persian.* [23]A record of the
heads of the Levite families was kept in *The Book of History* down to the days of Johanan, the grandson* of Eliashib.

[24]These were the family leaders of the Levites: Hashabiah, Sherebiah, Jeshua, Binnui,* Kadmiel, and other associates, who stood opposite them during the ceremonies of praise and thanksgiving, one section responding to the other, as commanded by David, the man
of God. [25]This included Mattaniah, Bakbukiah, and
Obadiah.

Meshullam, Talmon, and Akkub were the gatekeepers
in charge of the storerooms at the gates. [26]These all served
in the days of Joiakim son of Jeshua, son of Jehozadak,* and in the days of Nehemiah the governor and of Ezra the priest and scribe.

DEDICATION OF JERUSALEM'S WALL

[27]For the dedication of the new wall of Jerusalem, the Levites throughout the land were asked to come to Jerusalem to assist in the ceremonies. They were to take part in the joyous occasion with their songs of thanksgiving and
with the music of cymbals, harps, and lyres. [28]The singers
were brought together from the region around Jerusalem
and from the villages of the Netophathites. [29]They also
came from Beth-gilgal and the rural areas near Geba and Azmaveth, for the singers had built their own settlements around Jerusalem. [30]The priests and Levites first
purified themselves; then they purified the people, the gates, and the wall.

[31]I led the leaders of Judah to the top of the wall and organized two large choirs to give thanks. One of the choirs proceeded southward* along the top of the wall to the
Dung Gate. [32]Hoshaiah and half the leaders of Judah
followed them, [33]along with Azariah, Ezra, Meshullam,
[34]Judah, Benjamin, Shemaiah, and Jeremiah. [35]Then

11:35 Or *and Ge-harashim.* **12:3** Hebrew *Rehum;* compare 7:42; 12:15; Ezra 2:39. **12:4** As in some Hebrew manuscripts and Latin Vulgate (see also 12:16); most Hebrew manuscripts read *Ginnethoi.* **12:5** Hebrew *Mijamin, Maadiah;* compare 12:17. **12:11** Hebrew *Jonathan;* compare 12:22. **12:14a** As in Greek version (see also 10:4; 12:2); Hebrew reads *Malluchi.* **12:14b** As in many Hebrew manuscripts, some Greek manuscripts, and Syriac version (see also 12:3); most Hebrew manuscripts read *Shebaniah.* **12:15** As in some Greek manuscripts (see also 12:3); Hebrew reads *Meraioth.* **12:17** Hebrew lacks the name of this family leader. **12:20** Hebrew *Sallai;* compare 12:7. **12:22** *Darius the Persian* is probably Darius II, who reigned 423–404 B.C., or possibly Darius III, who reigned 336–331 B.C. **12:23** Hebrew *son;* compare 12:10-11. **12:24** Hebrew *son of* (i.e., *ben*), which should probably be read here as the proper name Binnui; compare Ezra 3:9 and the note there. **12:26** Hebrew *Jozadak,* a variant spelling of Jehozadak. **12:31** Hebrew *to the right.*

came some priests who played trumpets, including Zechariah son of Jonathan, son of Shemaiah, son of Mattaniah, son of Micaiah, son of Zaccur, a descendant of Asaph. 36And Zechariah's colleagues were Shemaiah, Azarel, Milalai, Gilalai, Maai, Nethanel, Judah, and Hanani. They used the musical instruments prescribed by David, the man of God. Ezra the scribe led this procession. 37At the Fountain Gate they went straight up the steps on the ascent of the city wall toward the City of David. They passed the house of David and then proceeded to the Water Gate on the east.

38The second choir giving thanks went northward* around the other way to meet them. I followed them, together with the other half of the people, along the top of the wall past the Tower of the Ovens to the Broad Wall, 39then past the Ephraim Gate to the Old City Gate,* past the Fish Gate and the Tower of Hananel, and on to the Tower of the Hundred. Then we continued on to the Sheep Gate and stopped at the Guard Gate.

40The two choirs that were giving thanks then proceeded to the Temple of God, where they took their places. So did I, together with the group of leaders who were with me. 41We went together with the trumpet-playing priests—Eliakim, Maaseiah, Miniamin, Micaiah, Elioenai, Zechariah, and Hananiah—42and the singers—Maaseiah, Shemaiah, Eleazar, Uzzi, Jehohanan, Malkijah, Elam, and Ezer. They played and sang loudly under the direction of Jezrahiah the choir director.

TUNE IN 12:31-41

Music was an important part of the dedication of the city wall. It still is an important part of worship today. But sometimes, we tune out God and are more in the tune with the tune (how much we like a song). But praise is still a delight to God. He wants our full focus as we worship. Does he have your attention? ■

43Many sacrifices were offered on that joyous day, for God had given the people cause for great joy. The women and children also participated in the celebration, and the joy of the people of Jerusalem could be heard far away.

PROVISIONS FOR TEMPLE WORSHIP

44On that day men were appointed to be in charge of the storerooms for the offerings, the first part of the harvest, and the tithes. They were responsible to collect from the fields outside the towns the portions required by the Law for the priests and Levites. For all the people of Judah took joy in the priests and Levites and their work. 45They performed the service of their God and the service of purification, as commanded by David and his son Solomon, and so did the singers and the gatekeepers. 46The custom of having choir directors to lead the choirs in hymns of praise and thanksgiving to God began long ago in the days of David and Asaph. 47So now, in the days of Zerubbabel and of Nehemiah, all Israel brought a daily supply of food for the singers, the gatekeepers, and the Levites. The Levites, in turn, gave a portion of what they received to the priests, the descendants of Aaron.

13

NEHEMIAH'S VARIOUS REFORMS

On that same day, as the Book of Moses was being read to the people, the passage was found that said no Ammonite or Moabite should ever be permitted to enter the assembly of God.* 2For they had not provided the Israelites with food and water in the wilderness. Instead, they hired Balaam to curse them, though our God turned the curse into a blessing. 3When this passage of the Law was read, all those of foreign descent were immediately excluded from the assembly.

A BAD INFLUENCE? 13:1-3

"Those of foreign descent" refers to the Moabites and Ammonites, two enemies of Israel. They were not allowed in the Temple (see Deut 23:3-5). This rule wasn't about prejudice; it was to protect the people of Israel. They were easily led astray. In the same way, God warns believers to be wise about relationships (Prov 16:29; 24:1; 2 Tim 2:22). Think about the people who influence you the most. Do they bring out the best or the worst in you? ■

4Before this had happened, Eliashib the priest, who had been appointed as supervisor of the storerooms of the Temple of our God and who was also a relative of Tobiah, 5had converted a large storage room and placed it at Tobiah's disposal. The room had previously been used for storing the grain offerings, the frankincense, various articles for the Temple, and the tithes of grain, new wine, and olive oil (which were prescribed for the Levites, the singers, and the gatekeepers), as well as the offerings for the priests.

6I was not in Jerusalem at that time, for I had returned to King Artaxerxes of Babylon in the thirty-second year of his reign,* though I later asked his permission to return. 7When I arrived back in Jerusalem, I learned about Eliashib's evil deed in providing Tobiah with a room in the courtyards of the Temple of God. 8I became very upset and threw all of Tobiah's belongings out of the room. 9Then I demanded that the rooms be purified, and I brought back the articles for God's Temple, the grain offerings, and the frankincense.

10I also discovered that the Levites had not been given their prescribed portions of food, so they and the singers who were to conduct the worship services had all returned to work their fields. 11I immediately confronted the leaders and demanded, "Why has the Temple of God been neglected?" Then I called all the Levites back again and restored them to their proper duties. 12And once

12:38 Hebrew *to the left*. 12:39 Or *the Mishneh Gate*, or *the Jeshanah Gate*. 13:1 See Deut 23:3-6. 13:6 King Artaxerxes of Persia is here identified as the king of Babylon because Persia had conquered the Babylonian Empire. The thirty-second year of Artaxerxes was 433 B.C.

more all the people of Judah began bringing their
tithes of grain, new wine, and olive oil to the Temple
storerooms.
13 I assigned supervisors for the storerooms: Shelemiah the priest, Zadok the scribe, and Pedaiah, one of the
Levites. And I appointed Hanan son of Zaccur and grandson of Mattaniah as their assistant. These men had an excellent reputation, and it was their job to make honest
distributions to their fellow Levites.

14 Remember this good deed, O my God, and do not
forget all that I have faithfully done for the Temple of
my God and its services.

15 In those days I saw men of Judah treading out their
winepresses on the Sabbath. They were also bringing in
grain, loading it on donkeys, and bringing their wine,
grapes, figs, and all sorts of produce to Jerusalem to sell
on the Sabbath. So I rebuked them for selling their produce on that day. 16 Some men from Tyre, who lived in
Jerusalem, were bringing in fish and all kinds of merchandise. They were selling it on the Sabbath to the people of Judah—and in Jerusalem at that!
17 So I confronted the nobles of Judah. "Why are you
profaning the Sabbath in this evil way?" I asked. 18 "Wasn't
it just this sort of thing that your ancestors did that
caused our God to bring all this trouble upon us and our
city? Now you are bringing even more wrath upon Israel
by permitting the Sabbath to be desecrated in this way!"
19 Then I commanded that the gates of Jerusalem
should be shut as darkness fell every Friday evening,* not
to be opened until the Sabbath ended. I sent some of my
own servants to guard the gates so that no merchandise
could be brought in on the Sabbath day. 20 The merchants
and tradesmen with a variety of wares camped outside
Jerusalem once or twice. 21 But I spoke sharply to them
and said, "What are you doing out here, camping around
the wall? If you do this again, I will arrest you!" And that
was the last time they came on the Sabbath. 22 Then I
commanded the Levites to purify themselves and to
guard the gates in order to preserve the holiness of the
Sabbath.

Remember this good deed also, O my God! Have
compassion on me according to your great and
unfailing love.

23 About the same time I realized that some of the men
of Judah had married women from Ashdod, Ammon, and
Moab. 24 Furthermore, half their children spoke the language of Ashdod or of some other people and could not
speak the language of Judah at all. 25 So I confronted them
and called down curses on them. I beat some of them and
pulled out their hair. I made them swear in the name of
God that they would not let their children intermarry
with the pagan people of the land.
26 "Wasn't this exactly what led King Solomon of Israel
into sin?" I demanded. "There was no king from any nation who could compare to him, and God loved him and
made him king over all Israel. But even he was led into sin
by his foreign wives. 27 How could you even think of committing this sinful deed and acting unfaithfully toward
God by marrying foreign women?"
28 One of the sons of Joiada son of Eliashib the high
priest had married a daughter of Sanballat the Horonite,
so I banished him from my presence.

29 Remember them, O my God, for they have defiled
the priesthood and the solemn vows of the priests
and Levites.

30 So I purged out everything foreign and assigned
tasks to the priests and Levites, making certain that each
knew his work. 31 I also made sure that the supply of wood
for the altar and the first portions of the harvest were
brought at the proper times.

Remember this in my favor, O my God.

13:19 Hebrew *on the day before the Sabbath.*

OVERFLOWING WITH FANS, the gymnasium rocks with excitement. It's the crucial moment—the one anticipated all season—but joy mixes with fear and tension. Only one point behind, the team could find its season ending abruptly. But two seconds remain, and *their* player is at the free throw line. Cheers erupt as the ball swishes through the hoop. But then silence engulfs the stands as the player approaches the line for the second shot. Everything is on the line. But the shooter's training pays off. The basket is made, the game is won, and a hero is made. She came through when it counted.

In Persia, Esther similarly faced a crucial moment—but the stakes were the lives of thousands. As the queen, Esther, who also was a Jew, was the only one who could save them. She could make the difference. She could have looked for an easy way out. But Esther knew that God placed her in an influential position "for just such a time as this" (4:14). She seized the moment and took action, regardless of the consequences (4:16).

As you read Esther, consider your willingness to act for God if you had the opportunity. Remember, he placed you where you can make a difference "for just such a time as this."

esther

timeline

586 B.C.
Jerusalem destroyed; exiles go to Babylon

537
First exiles return to Jerusalem

516
Temple completed

486
Ahasuerus (Xerxes I) becomes king of Persia

479
Esther becomes queen

474
Haman's decree to destroy the Jews

473
First Feast of Purim

stats

PURPOSE: To demonstrate God's sovereignty and his concern for his people

AUTHOR: Unknown; possibly Mordecai (9:29). Some have suggested Ezra or Nehemiah because of the similarity of the writing style.

DATE WRITTEN: Approximately 483–471 B.C. (Esther became queen in 479 B.C.)

SETTING: Although Esther follows Nehemiah in the Bible, the events are about 30 years prior to those recorded in Nehemiah. The story is set in the Persian Empire with most of the action taking place in the king's palace in Susa, the Persian capital.

KEY PEOPLE: Esther, Mordecai, King Xerxes, Haman

KEY PLACE: The king's palace in Susa, Persia

SPECIAL FEATURES: Esther is one of only two books named for women. (Ruth is the other.) The book is unusual in that in the original version no name, title, or pronoun for God appears in it. This caused some early church leaders to question its inclusion in the Bible. But God's presence is clear throughout the book.

KEY points

RACISM
Haman was a descendant of King Agag, an enemy of the Jews. Lust for power and pride drove Haman to hate Mordecai, Esther's cousin. Racial hatred is always wrong. We must learn to see others the way that God does, rather than through the often cloudy lenses of our own cultural "glasses."

ACTION
Faced with death, Esther and Mordecai set aside their fear and took action. Believing that God is in control sometimes isn't enough; we also must courageously follow God's guidance.

RESCUE
The Feast of Purim symbolized God's rescue of the Jews from death. God is able to rescue us when we're in trouble.

WISDOM
Mordecai took steps to understand and work within the Persian law. Yet he did not compromise his integrity. Surviving in an unbelieving world takes great wisdom. We demonstrate wisdom by respecting what's true and good and by taking a stand against whatever is wrong.

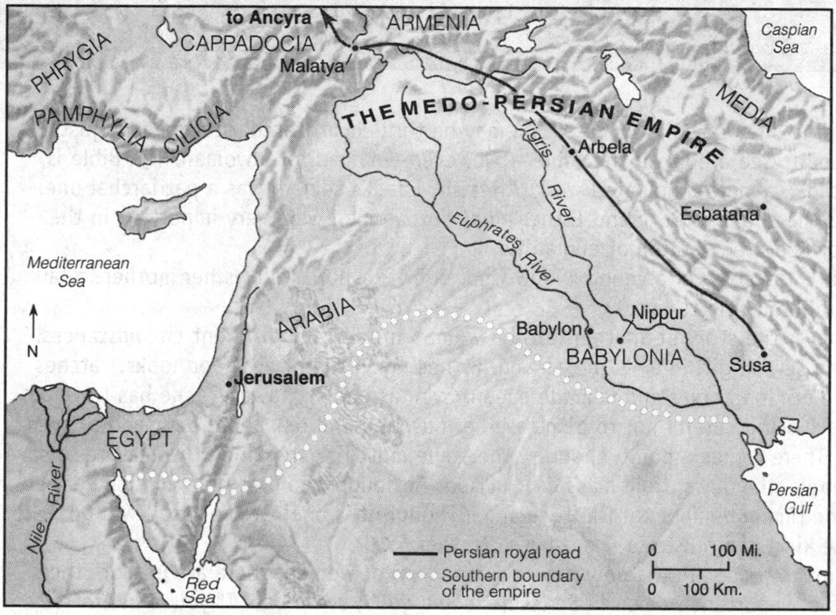

THE WORLD OF ESTHER'S DAY Esther lived in the capital of the vast Medo-Persian empire, which incorporated the provinces of Media and Persia, as well as the previous empires of Assyria and Babylon. Esther, a Jewess, was chosen by King Xerxes to be his queen. The story of how she saved her people takes place in the palace in Susa.

1

THE KING'S BANQUET
These events happened in the days of King Xerxes,* who
reigned over 127 provinces stretching from India to
Ethiopia.* 2At that time Xerxes ruled his empire from his
royal throne at the fortress of Susa. 3In the third year of
his reign, he gave a banquet for all his nobles and officials. He invited all the military officers of Persia and Media as well as the princes and nobles of the provinces.
4The celebration lasted 180 days—a tremendous display
of the opulent wealth of his empire and the pomp and
splendor of his majesty.
5When it was all over, the king gave a banquet for all
the people, from the greatest to the least, who were in the
fortress of Susa. It lasted for seven days and was held in
the courtyard of the palace garden. 6The courtyard was
beautifully decorated with white cotton curtains and
blue hangings, which were fastened with white linen
cords and purple ribbons to silver rings embedded in
marble pillars. Gold and silver couches stood on a mosaic
pavement of porphyry, marble, mother-of-pearl, and
other costly stones.
7Drinks were served in gold goblets of many designs,
and there was an abundance of royal wine, reflecting the
king's generosity. 8By edict of the king, no limits were
placed on the drinking, for the king had instructed all his
palace officials to serve each man as much as he wanted.
9At the same time, Queen Vashti gave a banquet for the
women in the royal palace of King Xerxes.

QUEEN VASHTI DEPOSED
10On the seventh day of the feast, when King Xerxes was
in high spirits because of the wine, he told the seven eunuchs who attended him—Mehuman, Biztha, Harbona,
Bigtha, Abagtha, Zethar, and Carcas—11to bring Queen
Vashti to him with the royal crown on her head. He
wanted the nobles and all the other men to gaze on her
beauty, for she was a very beautiful woman. 12But when
they conveyed the king's order to Queen Vashti, she refused to come. This made the king furious, and he
burned with anger.

DECISIONS 1:10-11

Xerxes made a rash decision—one that he later regretted (2:1). Poor decisions often are made on the impulse, when a person isn't thinking clearly. When do you make decisions: on the impulse or after careful thought? ■

13He immediately consulted with his wise advisers,
who knew all the Persian laws and customs, for he always
asked their advice. 14The names of these men were Car-
shena, Shethar, Admatha, Tarshish, Meres, Marsena, and
Memucan—seven nobles of Persia and Media. They met
with the king regularly and held the highest positions in
the empire.
15"What must be done to Queen Vashti?" the king demanded. "What penalty does the law provide for a queen
who refuses to obey the king's orders, properly sent
through his eunuchs?"
16Memucan answered the king and his nobles, "Queen
Vashti has wronged not only the king but also every noble
and citizen throughout your empire. 17Women everywhere will begin to despise their husbands when they
learn that Queen Vashti has refused to appear before the

1:1a Hebrew *Ahasuerus*, another name for Xerxes; also throughout the book of Esther. Xerxes reigned 486–465 B.C. 1:1b Hebrew *to Cush*.

WOMEN OF THE BIBLE

ULTIMATE ISSUES

Depending on your point of view, you may be thrilled, irritated, intrigued, or just surprised to see a book of the Bible—two, even—named for a woman. The Bible is, admittedly, a male-dominated work. After all, Israel's society was a patriarchal one. But, as the books of Ruth and Esther point out, women were very important in the story of God's redemption of humanity.

Ruth is the story of a young widow who, out of loyalty, follows her mother-in-law back to Bethlehem to live.

Esther is the story of another faithful woman in radically different circumstances. A young Jewish girl in exile in Babylon, Esther, by virtue of her good looks, catches the eye of King Xerxes and is made queen. Even as queen, however, she has to watch her step, being careful not to displease her husband and risk being banished or even killed. There comes a point, though, where she must risk the king's displeasure to save her people, the Jews, from mass destruction. Although afraid at first to stick her neck out, she finally decides to risk it, saying, "Though it is against the law, I will go in to see the king. If I must die, I must die" (Esther 4:16).

Although these are the only two books named for women, there are lots of other stories of important women in Scripture; some good, some bad. If you're interested, look at the accounts of Rahab (Joshua 2; 6); Deborah (Judges 4–5); Jezebel (1 Kings 16:31; 19; 21; 2 Kings 9:30-37); Mary and Martha (Luke 10:38-42); and, of course, Mary, Jesus' mother (Luke 1–2; John 19, etc.).

For a number of reasons, cultural and otherwise, most of the prominent characters in the Bible are men. But women play a vital role in the unfolding drama of both the Old and New Testaments, just as they do in God's work in the world today.

king. 18Before this day is out, the wives of all the king's
nobles throughout Persia and Media will hear what the
queen did and will start treating their husbands the same
way. There will be no end to their contempt and anger.

LORD IT OVER OR LOVE? 1:20-21

One way to rule a nation is to issue edicts that force people to obey the law. King Xerxes and his advisers responded this way. But in Matthew 20:25-26, Jesus spoke disfavorably over the way some leaders "lord it over the people beneath them." As believers, we're to act differently. God encourages us to treat each other with respect and love (1 Cor 13). How do you show your respect toward others? ■

19"So if it please the king, we suggest that you issue a
written decree, a law of the Persians and Medes that cannot be revoked. It should order that Queen Vashti be forever banished from the presence of King Xerxes, and
that the king should choose another queen more worthy
than she. 20When this decree is published throughout
the king's vast empire, husbands everywhere, whatever
their rank, will receive proper respect from their wives!"
21The king and his nobles thought this made good
sense, so he followed Memucan's counsel. 22He sent letters to all parts of the empire, to each province in its own
script and language, proclaiming that every man should
be the ruler of his own home and should say whatever he
pleases.*

2 ESTHER BECOMES QUEEN

But after Xerxes' anger had subsided, he began thinking
about Vashti and what she had done and the decree he
had made. 2So his personal attendants suggested, "Let us
search the empire to find beautiful young virgins for the
king. 3Let the king appoint agents in each province to
bring these beautiful young women into the royal harem
at the fortress of Susa. Hegai, the king's eunuch in charge
of the harem, will see that they are all given beauty treatments. 4After that, the young woman who most pleases
the king will be made queen instead of Vashti." This advice was very appealing to the king, so he put the plan into
effect.
5At that time there was a Jewish man in the fortress of
Susa whose name was Mordecai son of Jair. He was from
the tribe of Benjamin and was a descendant of Kish and
Shimei. 6His family* had been among those who, with
King Jehoiachin* of Judah, had been exiled from Jerusalem to Babylon by King Nebuchadnezzar. 7This man had

1:22 Or *and should speak in the language of his own people.* **2:6a** Hebrew *He.* **2:6b** Hebrew *Jeconiah,* a variant spelling of Jehoiachin.

How God Works in the World

God's will . . . What God wants done—he works through . . .

GOD'S ACTION	*Natural Order* God set into action through creation a normal working of his universe. He also revealed his expectations of people through his Word and people's consciences.	*Miracles* God breaks into the natural order to respond to the expressed needs of people.	*Providence* God overrules the natural order to accomplish an act that people may or may not have requested.
EXAMPLES FROM ESTHER	God gave Esther natural beauty.	God allowed Esther to speak to the king.	God allowed Mordecai to overhear a plot.
	Esther planned a way to save her people.	The people prayed and fasted.	Mordecai trusted God to accomplish what was impossible in human terms.

Our will . . . What we want done—we either . . .

ACTION WE CAN TAKE	*Plan* Can make plans based on the order and dependability of God's creation. Know and obey his words.	*Pray* Can ask God to intervene in certain affairs while realizing that our knowledge and perspective are limited.	*Trust & Obey* Can trust that God is in control even when the circumstances may not seem to indicate that he is.

Or . . .

MISTAKES WE CAN MAKE	*Disobey* Can violate the natural order, disobey God's commands.	*Demand* Can assume that we understand what is needed and expect God to agree and answer our prayers that way.	*Despair* Can assume God doesn't answer prayer or respond to our needs and live as though there is nothing but the natural order.

a very beautiful and lovely young cousin, Hadassah, who
was also called Esther. When her father and mother died,
Mordecai adopted her into his family and raised her as
his own daughter.
8As a result of the king's decree, Esther, along with
many other young women, was brought to the king's
harem at the fortress of Susa and placed in Hegai's care.
9Hegai was very impressed with Esther and treated her
kindly. He quickly ordered a special menu for her and
provided her with beauty treatments. He also assigned
her seven maids specially chosen from the king's palace,
and he moved her and her maids into the best place in the
harem.
10Esther had not told anyone of her nationality and
family background, because Mordecai had directed her
not to do so. 11Every day Mordecai would take a walk near
the courtyard of the harem to find out about Esther and
what was happening to her.
12Before each young woman was taken to the king's
bed, she was given the prescribed twelve months of
beauty treatments—six months with oil of myrrh, followed by six months with special perfumes and ointments.
13When it was time for her to go to the king's
palace, she was given her choice of whatever clothing or
jewelry she wanted to take from the harem. 14That evening she was taken to the king's private rooms, and the
next morning she was brought to the second harem,*
where the king's wives lived. There she would be under
the care of Shaashgaz, the king's eunuch in charge of the
concubines. She would never go to the king again unless
he had especially enjoyed her and requested her by
name.
15Esther was the daughter of Abihail, who was Mordecai's uncle. (Mordecai had adopted his younger cousin
Esther.) When it was Esther's turn to go to the king, she
accepted the advice of Hegai, the eunuch in charge of
the harem. She asked for nothing except what he suggested, and she was admired by everyone who saw her.

2:14 Or *to another part of the harem.*

[16]Esther was taken to King Xerxes at the royal palace in
early winter* of the seventh year of his reign. [17]And the
king loved Esther more than any of the other young
women. He was so delighted with her that he set the royal
crown on her head and declared her queen instead of
Vashti. [18]To celebrate the occasion, he gave a great banquet in Esther's honor for all his nobles and officials,
declaring a public holiday for the provinces and giving
generous gifts to everyone.

TAKING A STAND

Ryan's in a jam and none of his options are very appealing.

See, in just a few minutes, Ryan and Ben will be face to face with one of Mrs. Seal's infamous geometry exams. But Ben just announced, "Hey, Ryan! You've got to help me out, dude. I didn't have time to study last night. I don't know any of the theorems. So look, just write big, and when I tap you on the shoulder, lean to your left, OK?"

Lunch is almost over. The bell will be ringing any minute. Ryan's mind is racing:

"Do I let Ben copy off me just this once? But what if I get accused of cheating? I probably should tell him no now—before class starts. But then he'll tell everyone I wouldn't help him out, and I'll never hear the end of it. What am I gonna do?

"It ticks me off the way he uses people. . . . He should've studied, instead of being so lazy. Still, I don't want everybody thinking I'm a loser. Maybe I should—"

BBBBRRRIIIINNNNNGGGGG!!!

What would you do in Ryan's shoes?

Chapters 3 and 4 of the exciting book of Esther are about taking a stand for what is right, no matter what. Read about the young queen who made tough decisions when the stakes were—literally—life and death.

[19]Even after all the young women had been transferred
to the second harem* and Mordecai had become a palace
official,* [20]Esther continued to keep her family background and nationality a secret. She was still following
Mordecai's directions, just as she did when she lived in
his home.

MORDECAI'S LOYALTY TO THE KING

[21]One day as Mordecai was on duty at the king's gate, two
of the king's eunuchs, Bigthana* and Teresh—who were
guards at the door of the king's private quarters—became
angry at King Xerxes and plotted to assassinate him.
[22]But Mordecai heard about the plot and gave the information to Queen Esther. She then told the king about it
and gave Mordecai credit for the report. [23]When an investigation was made and Mordecai's story was found to
be true, the two men were impaled on a sharpened pole.
This was all recorded in *The Book of the History of King
Xerxes' Reign*.

3 HAMAN'S PLOT AGAINST THE JEWS

Some time later King Xerxes promoted Haman son of
Hammedatha the Agagite over all the other nobles, making him the most powerful official in the empire. [2]All the
king's officials would bow down before Haman to show
him respect whenever he passed by, for so the king had
commanded. But Mordecai refused to bow down or
show him respect.

CONVICTION 3:2

Mordecai's faith was based on conviction. He didn't first take a poll to determine the safest or most popular course of action; he had the courage to stand alone. Doing what's right is not always popular. But to obey God is more important than to obey people (see Acts 5:29). Would you agree? ■

[3]Then the palace officials at the king's gate asked Mordecai, "Why are you disobeying the king's command?"
[4]They spoke to him day after day, but still he refused to
comply with the order. So they spoke to Haman about
this to see if he would tolerate Mordecai's conduct, since
Mordecai had told them he was a Jew.
[5]When Haman saw that Mordecai would not bow
down or show him respect, he was filled with rage. [6]He
had learned of Mordecai's nationality, so he decided it
was not enough to lay hands on Mordecai alone. Instead,
he looked for a way to destroy all the Jews throughout the
entire empire of Xerxes.
[7]So in the month of April,* during the twelfth year of
King Xerxes' reign, lots were cast in Haman's presence
(the lots were called *purim*) to determine the best day and
month to take action. And the day selected was March 7,
nearly a year later.*
[8]Then Haman approached King Xerxes and said,
"There is a certain race of people scattered through all
the provinces of your empire who keep themselves separate from everyone else. Their laws are different from
those of any other people, and they refuse to obey the
laws of the king. So it is not in the king's interest to let
them live. [9]If it please the king, issue a decree that they be
destroyed, and I will give 10,000 large sacks* of silver to
the government administrators to be deposited in the
royal treasury."

2:16 Hebrew *in the tenth month, the month of Tebeth*. A number of dates in the book of Esther can be cross-checked with dates in surviving Persian records and related accurately to our modern calendar. This month of the ancient Hebrew lunar calendar occurred within the months of December 479 B.C. and January 478 B.C. **2:19a** The meaning of the Hebrew is uncertain. **2:19b** Hebrew *and Mordecai was sitting in the gate of the king*. **2:21** Hebrew *Bigthan;* compare 6:2. **3:7a** Hebrew *in the first month, the month of Nisan*. This month of the ancient Hebrew lunar calendar occurred within the months of April and May 474 B.C.; also see note on 2:16. **3:7b** As in Greek version, which reads *the thirteenth day of the twelfth month, the month of Adar* (see also 3:13). Hebrew reads *in the twelfth month*, of the ancient Hebrew lunar calendar. The date selected was March 7, 473 B.C.; also see note on 2:16. **3:9** Hebrew *10,000 talents*, about 375 tons or 340 metric tons in weight.

10The king agreed, confirming his decision by removing his signet ring from his finger and giving it to Haman
son of Hammedatha the Agagite, the enemy of the Jews.
11The king said, "The money and the people are both
yours to do with as you see fit."
12So on April 17* the king's secretaries were summoned, and a decree was written exactly as Haman dictated. It was sent to the king's highest officers, the
governors of the respective provinces, and the nobles
of each province in their own scripts and languages.
The decree was written in the name of King Xerxes and
sealed with the king's signet ring. 13Dispatches were
sent by swift messengers into all the provinces of the
empire, giving the order that all Jews—young and old,
including women and children—must be killed,
slaughtered, and annihilated on a single day. This was
scheduled to happen on March 7 of the next year.* The
property of the Jews would be given to those who killed
them.
14A copy of this decree was to be issued as law in every
province and proclaimed to all peoples, so that they
would be ready to do their duty on the appointed day.
15At the king's command, the decree went out by swift
messengers, and it was also proclaimed in the fortress of
Susa. Then the king and Haman sat down to drink, but
the city of Susa fell into confusion.

3:12 Hebrew *On the thirteenth day of the first month,* of the ancient Hebrew lunar calendar. This day was April 17, 474 B.C.; also see note on 2:16. 3:13 Hebrew *on the thirteenth day of the twelfth month, the month of Adar,* of the ancient Hebrew lunar calendar. The date selected was March 7, 473 B.C.; also see note on 2:16.

UPS:
- Won the heart of Persia's king
- Was a courageous and careful planner
- Open to advice and willing to act
- More concerned for others than for her own security

STATS:
- Where: Persian Empire
- Occupation: Queen of Persia
- Relatives: Mordecai (cousin); Xerxes (husband); Abihail (father)

BOTTOM LINE:

Serving God sometimes involves risking our own security.

God has a purpose for the situations in which he places us.

Courage, while often vital, does not replace careful planning.

Esther's story is told in the book of Esther.

ESTHER *Cinderella. Sleeping Beauty. Beauty and the Beast.* You could probably name a thousand fairy tales off the top of your head. Fairy tales are just entertaining stories you read when you were a kid. Surely this kind of thing couldn't happen in real life, right?

Wrong. The story of Esther is a fairy tale come true. You know the saga. A poor, beautiful, young woman catches the eye of and marries a king. You've seen that scenario a thousand times. But this is one fairy tale with some bite. Esther's story isn't just a romance. It's a story of survival—the survival of the people of Israel because of the courage of one woman.

Esther just happened to be in the right place at the right time. Although her beauty and character won her the notice of King Xerxes, God ultimately was the one who placed her in that position. When her cousin, Mordecai, told her of the plot to kill the Jews—her people—she had to risk her own security to help them. After all, her family heritage wasn't known. If the king disapproved of her request to appear before him, he could have sent her away or put her to death. (The former queen had been sent away in disgrace.)

Esther's story has a happy ending. Her quick thinking allowed her people to be saved and the villain of the story punished. And thus a new holiday—Purim—was born in honor of the risk-taking young queen who saved the lives of her people.

Ever wish that your life could be a fairy tale with a guaranteed happy ending? If you're a believer, you're in the same boat as Esther. You've caught the eye of the King of the Universe. The defeat of the villain of the story (Satan) has already been accomplished, because of the death and resurrection of this King. But even a guaranteed happy ending doesn't mean that you'll never have to take a risk for your faith. You might have to. Are you willing?

ESTHER

4

MORDECAI REQUESTS ESTHER'S HELP

When Mordecai learned about all that had been done, he tore his clothes, put on burlap and ashes, and went out into the city, crying with a loud and bitter wail. 2He went as far as the gate of the palace, for no one was allowed to enter the palace gate while wearing clothes of mourning. 3And as news of the king's decree reached all the provinces, there was great mourning among the Jews. They fasted, wept, and wailed, and many people lay in burlap and ashes.

4When Queen Esther's maids and eunuchs came and told her about Mordecai, she was deeply distressed. She sent clothing to him to replace the burlap, but he refused it. 5Then Esther sent for Hathach, one of the king's eunuchs who had been appointed as her attendant. She ordered him to go to Mordecai and find out what was troubling him and why he was in mourning. 6So Hathach went out to Mordecai in the square in front of the palace gate.

7Mordecai told him the whole story, including the exact amount of money Haman had promised to pay into the royal treasury for the destruction of the Jews. 8Mordecai gave Hathach a copy of the decree issued in Susa that called for the death of all Jews. He asked Hathach to show it to Esther and explain the situation to her. He also asked Hathach to direct her to go to the king to beg for mercy and plead for her people. 9So Hathach returned to Esther with Mordecai's message.

10Then Esther told Hathach to go back and relay this message to Mordecai: 11"All the king's officials and even the people in the provinces know that anyone who appears before the king in his inner court without being invited is doomed to die unless the king holds out his gold scepter. And the king has not called for me to come to him for thirty days." 12So Hathach* gave Esther's message to Mordecai.

13Mordecai sent this reply to Esther: "Don't think for a moment that because you're in the palace you will escape when all other Jews are killed. 14If you keep quiet at a time like this, deliverance and relief for the Jews will arise from some other place, but you and your relatives will die. Who knows if perhaps you were made queen for just such a time as this?"

15Then Esther sent this reply to Mordecai: 16"Go and gather together all the Jews of Susa and fast for me. Do not eat or drink for three days, night or day. My maids and I will do the same. And then, though it is against the law, I will go in to see the king. If I must die, I must die." 17So Mordecai went away and did everything as Esther had ordered him.

> If I must die,
> I must die.
>
> ESTHER 4:16

5

ESTHER'S REQUEST TO THE KING

On the third day of the fast, Esther put on her royal robes and entered the inner court of the palace, just across from the king's hall. The king was sitting on his royal throne, facing the entrance. 2When he saw Queen Esther standing there in the inner court, he welcomed her and held out the gold scepter to her. So Esther approached and touched the end of the scepter.

3Then the king asked her, "What do you want, Queen Esther? What is your request? I will give it to you, even if it is half the kingdom!"

4And Esther replied, "If it please the king, let the king and Haman come today to a banquet I have prepared for the king."

5The king turned to his attendants and said, "Tell Haman to come quickly to a banquet, as Esther has requested." So the king and Haman went to Esther's banquet.

6And while they were drinking wine, the king said to Esther, "Now tell me what you really want. What is your request? I will give it to you, even if it is half the kingdom!"

7Esther replied, "This is my request and deepest wish. 8If I have found favor with the king, and if it pleases the king to grant my request and do what I ask, please come with Haman tomorrow to the banquet I will prepare for you. Then I will explain what this is all about."

HAMAN'S PLAN TO KILL MORDECAI

9Haman was a happy man as he left the banquet! But when he saw Mordecai sitting at the palace gate, not standing up or trembling nervously before him, Haman became furious. 10However, he restrained himself and went on home.

Then Haman gathered together his friends and Zeresh, his wife, 11and boasted to them about his great wealth and his many children. He bragged about the honors the king had given him and how he had been promoted over all the other nobles and officials.

12Then Haman added, "And that's not all! Queen Esther invited only me and the king himself to the banquet she prepared for us. And she has invited me to dine with her and the king again tomorrow!" 13Then he added, "But this is all worth nothing as long as I see Mordecai the Jew just sitting there at the palace gate."

14So Haman's wife, Zeresh, and all his friends suggested, "Set up a sharpened pole that stands seventy-five feet* tall, and in the morning ask the king to impale Mordecai on it. When this is done, you can go on your merry way to the banquet with the king." This pleased Haman, and he ordered the pole set up.

6

THE KING HONORS MORDECAI

That night the king had trouble sleeping, so he ordered an attendant to bring the book of the history of his reign

4:12 As in Greek version; Hebrew reads *they*. 5:14 Hebrew *50 cubits* [22.5 meters].

so it could be read to him. 2In those records he discovered an account of how Mordecai had exposed the plot of Bigthana and Teresh, two of the eunuchs who guarded the door to the king's private quarters. They had plotted to assassinate King Xerxes.

3"What reward or recognition did we ever give Mordecai for this?" the king asked.

His attendants replied, "Nothing has been done for him."

4"Who is that in the outer court?" the king inquired. As it happened, Haman had just arrived in the outer court of the palace to ask the king to impale Mordecai on the pole he had prepared.

5So the attendants replied to the king, "Haman is out in the court."

"Bring him in," the king ordered. 6So Haman came in, and the king said, "What should I do to honor a man who truly pleases me?"

Haman thought to himself, "Whom would the king wish to honor more than me?" 7So he replied, "If the king wishes to honor someone, 8he should bring out one of the king's own royal robes, as well as a horse that the king himself has ridden—one with a royal emblem on its head. 9Let the robes and the horse be handed over to one of the king's most noble officials. And let him see that the man whom the king wishes to honor is dressed in the king's robes and led through the city square on the king's horse. Have the official shout as they go, 'This is what the king does for someone he wishes to honor!' "

10"Excellent!" the king said to Haman. "Quick! Take the robes and my horse, and do just as you have said for Mordecai the Jew, who sits at the gate of the palace. Leave out nothing you have suggested!"

BRAGGING 6:6-12

Just the night before (5:9-14), Haman had bragged about his position and the honor he was about to receive. Now he was humiliated and later marked for death (7:8-10). How quickly the course of life can change! Maybe that's why James 4:13-16 warns us to avoid bragging. Got a skill or something else you think is worth bragging about? What will you do instead of bragging? ■

11So Haman took the robes and put them on Mordecai, placed him on the king's own horse, and led him through the city square, shouting, "This is what the king does for someone he wishes to honor!" 12Afterward Mordecai returned to the palace gate, but Haman hurried home dejected and completely humiliated.

13When Haman told his wife, Zeresh, and all his friends what had happened, his wise advisers and his wife said, "Since Mordecai—this man who has humiliated you—is of Jewish birth, you will never succeed in your plans against him. It will be fatal to continue opposing him."

14While they were still talking, the king's eunuchs arrived and quickly took Haman to the banquet Esther had prepared.

7

THE KING EXECUTES HAMAN

So the king and Haman went to Queen Esther's banquet. 2On this second occasion, while they were drinking wine, the king again said to Esther, "Tell me what you want, Queen Esther. What is your request? I will give it to you, even if it is half the kingdom!"

3Queen Esther replied, "If I have found favor with the king, and if it pleases the king to grant my request, I ask that my life and the lives of my people will be spared. 4For my people and I have been sold to those who would kill, slaughter, and annihilate us. If we had merely been sold as slaves, I could remain quiet, for that would be too trivial a matter to warrant disturbing the king."

5"Who would do such a thing?" King Xerxes demanded. "Who would be so presumptuous as to touch you?"

6Esther replied, "This wicked Haman is our adversary and our enemy." Haman grew pale with fright before the king and queen. 7Then the king jumped to his feet in a rage and went out into the palace garden.

Haman, however, stayed behind to plead for his life with Queen Esther, for he knew that the king intended to kill him. 8In despair he fell on the couch where Queen Esther was reclining, just as the king was returning from the palace garden.

The king exclaimed, "Will he even assault the queen right here in the palace, before my very eyes?" And as soon as the king spoke, his attendants covered Haman's face, signaling his doom.

9Then Harbona, one of the king's eunuchs, said, "Haman has set up a sharpened pole that stands seventy-five feet* tall in his own courtyard. He intended to use it to impale Mordecai, the man who saved the king from assassination."

"Then impale Haman on it!" the king ordered. 10So they impaled Haman on the pole he had set up for Mordecai, and the king's anger subsided.

8

A DECREE TO HELP THE JEWS

On that same day King Xerxes gave the property of Haman, the enemy of the Jews, to Queen Esther. Then Mordecai was brought before the king, for Esther had told the king how they were related. 2The king took off his signet ring—which he had taken back from Haman—and gave it to Mordecai. And Esther appointed Mordecai to be in charge of Haman's property.

3Then Esther went again before the king, falling down at his feet and begging him with tears to stop the evil plot devised by Haman the Agagite against the Jews. 4Again the king held out the gold scepter to Esther. So she rose and stood before him.

5Esther said, "If it please the king, and if I have found favor with him, and if he thinks it is right, and if I am pleasing to him, let there be a decree that reverses the orders of Haman son of Hammedatha the Agagite, who ordered that Jews throughout all the king's provinces

7:9 Hebrew *50 cubits* [22.5 meters].

should be destroyed. 6For how can I endure to see my people and my family slaughtered and destroyed?"

7Then King Xerxes said to Queen Esther and Mordecai the Jew, "I have given Esther the property of Haman, and he has been impaled on a pole because he tried to destroy the Jews. 8Now go ahead and send a message to the Jews in the king's name, telling them whatever you want, and seal it with the king's signet ring. But remember that whatever has already been written in the king's name and sealed with his signet ring can never be revoked."

9So on June 25* the king's secretaries were summoned, and a decree was written exactly as Mordecai dictated. It was sent to the Jews and to the highest officers, the governors, and the nobles of all the 127 provinces stretching from India to Ethiopia.* The decree was written in the scripts and languages of all the peoples of the empire, including that of the Jews. 10The decree was written in the name of King Xerxes and sealed with the king's signet ring. Mordecai sent the dispatches by swift messengers, who rode fast horses especially bred for the king's service.

11The king's decree gave the Jews in every city authority to unite to defend their lives. They were allowed to kill, slaughter, and annihilate anyone of any nationality or province who might attack them or their children and wives, and to take the property of their enemies. 12The day chosen for this event throughout all the provinces of King Xerxes was March 7 of the next year.*

13A copy of this decree was to be issued as law in every province and proclaimed to all peoples, so that the Jews would be ready to take revenge on their enemies on the appointed day. 14So urged on by the king's command, the messengers rode out swiftly on fast horses bred for the king's service. The same decree was also proclaimed in the fortress of Susa.

THE PRICE OF HEROISM 8:15-17

Everyone wants to be a hero and receive praise, honor, and wealth. But few are willing to pay the price of heroism. Mordecai served the government faithfully for years, put up with Haman's hatred and oppression, and risked his life for his people. The price to be paid by God's heroes is long-term commitment. Are you ready and willing to pay the price? ■

15Then Mordecai left the king's presence, wearing the royal robe of blue and white, the great crown of gold, and an outer cloak of fine linen and purple. And the people of Susa celebrated the new decree. 16The Jews were filled with joy and gladness and were honored everywhere. 17In every province and city, wherever the king's decree arrived, the Jews rejoiced and had a great celebration and declared a public festival and holiday. And many of the people of the land became Jews themselves, for they feared what the Jews might do to them.

9 THE VICTORY OF THE JEWS

So on March 7* the two decrees of the king were put into effect. On that day, the enemies of the Jews had hoped to overpower them, but quite the opposite happened. It was the Jews who overpowered their enemies. 2The Jews gathered in their cities throughout all the king's provinces to attack anyone who tried to harm them. But no one could make a stand against them, for everyone was afraid of them. 3And all the nobles of the provinces, the highest officers, the governors, and the royal officials helped the Jews for fear of Mordecai. 4For Mordecai had been promoted in the king's palace, and his fame spread throughout all the provinces as he became more and more powerful.

5So the Jews went ahead on the appointed day and struck down their enemies with the sword. They killed and annihilated their enemies and did as they pleased with those who hated them. 6In the fortress of Susa itself, the Jews killed 500 men. 7They also killed Parshandatha, Dalphon, Aspatha, 8Poratha, Adalia, Aridatha, 9Parmashta, Arisai, Aridai, and Vaizatha—10the ten sons of Haman son of Hammedatha, the enemy of the Jews. But they did not take any plunder.

11That very day, when the king was informed of the number of people killed in the fortress of Susa, 12he called for Queen Esther. He said, "The Jews have killed 500 men in the fortress of Susa alone, as well as Haman's ten sons. If they have done that here, what has happened in the rest of the provinces? But now, what more do you want? It will be granted to you; tell me and I will do it."

13Esther responded, "If it please the king, give the Jews in Susa permission to do again tomorrow as they have done today, and let the bodies of Haman's ten sons be impaled on a pole."

14So the king agreed, and the decree was announced in Susa. And they impaled the bodies of Haman's ten sons. 15Then the Jews at Susa gathered together on March 8* and killed 300 more men, and again they took no plunder.

16Meanwhile, the other Jews throughout the king's provinces had gathered together to defend their lives. They gained relief from all their enemies, killing 75,000 of those who hated them. But they did not take any plunder. 17This was done throughout the provinces on March 7, and on March 8 they rested,* celebrating their victory with a day of feasting and gladness. 18(The Jews at Susa killed their enemies on March 7 and again on March 8, then rested on March 9,* making that their day

8:9a Hebrew *on the twenty-third day of the third month, the month of Sivan,* of the ancient Hebrew lunar calendar. This day was June 25, 474 B.C.; also see note on 2:16. **8:9b** Hebrew *to Cush.* **8:12** Hebrew *the thirteenth day of the twelfth month, the month of Adar,* of the ancient Hebrew lunar calendar. The date selected was March 7, 473 B.C.; also see note on 2:16. **9:1** Hebrew *on the thirteenth day of the twelfth month, the month of Adar,* of the ancient Hebrew lunar calendar. This day was March 7, 473 B.C.; also see note on 2:16. **9:15** Hebrew *the fourteenth day of the month of Adar,* of the Hebrew lunar calendar. This day was March 8, 473 B.C.; also see note on 2:16. **9:17** Hebrew *on the thirteenth day of the month of Adar, and on the fourteenth day they rested.* These days were March 7 and 8, 473 B.C.; also see note on 2:16. **9:18** Hebrew *killed their enemies on the thirteenth day and the fourteenth day, and then rested on the fifteenth day,* of the Hebrew month of Adar.

READY, WILLING, AND ABLE 9:29-31

Jewish women were expected to be quiet, to serve in the home, and to stay on the fringe of religious and political life. But Esther was a Jewish woman who broke through the cultural norms, stepping outside her expected role to risk her life to help God's people. Whatever your place in life, God can use you. Be open, available, and ready—God may use you to do what others are afraid even to consider. ■

of feasting and gladness.) 19So to this day, rural Jews living in remote villages celebrate an annual festival and
holiday on the appointed day in late winter,* when they
rejoice and send gifts of food to each other.

THE FESTIVAL OF PURIM

20Mordecai recorded these events and sent letters to the
Jews near and far, throughout all the provinces of King
Xerxes, 21calling on them to celebrate an annual festival
on these two days.* 22He told them to celebrate these
days with feasting and gladness and by giving gifts of
food to each other and presents to the poor. This would
commemorate a time when the Jews gained relief from
their enemies, when their sorrow was turned into gladness and their mourning into joy.

23So the Jews accepted Mordecai's proposal and
adopted this annual custom. 24Haman son of Hammedatha the Agagite, the enemy of the Jews, had plotted to
crush and destroy them on the date determined by casting lots (the lots were called *purim*). 25But when Esther
came before the king, he issued a decree causing
Haman's evil plot to backfire, and Haman and his sons
were impaled on a sharpened pole. 26That is why this celebration is called Purim, because it is the ancient word
for casting lots.

So because of Mordecai's letter and because of what
they had experienced, 27the Jews throughout the realm
agreed to inaugurate this tradition and to pass it on to
their descendants and to all who became Jews. They declared they would never fail to celebrate these two prescribed days at the appointed time each year. 28These
days would be remembered and kept from generation to
generation and celebrated by every family throughout
the provinces and cities of the empire. This Festival of
Purim would never cease to be celebrated among the
Jews, nor would the memory of what happened ever die
out among their descendants.

29Then Queen Esther, the daughter of Abihail, along
with Mordecai the Jew, wrote another letter putting the
queen's full authority behind Mordecai's letter to establish the Festival of Purim. 30Letters wishing peace and security were sent to the Jews throughout the 127 provinces
of the empire of Xerxes. 31These letters established the
Festival of Purim—an annual celebration of these days at
the appointed time, decreed by both Mordecai the Jew
and Queen Esther. (The people decided to observe this
festival, just as they had decided for themselves and their
descendants to establish the times of fasting and mourning.) 32So the command of Esther confirmed the practices
of Purim, and it was all written down in the records.

IN CONTROL 10:1-3

In the book of Esther, we clearly see God at work in the lives of individuals and in the affairs of a nation, even though he's not mentioned directly. Esther's story reminds us of the need to look for God's behind-the-scenes work in our lives. Even when it looks as if the world is in the hands of evil people, God is still in control, protecting those who belong to him. Do you trust him enough to let him tackle the most hopeless situation you face? ■

10
THE GREATNESS OF XERXES AND MORDECAI

King Xerxes imposed a tribute throughout his empire,
even to the distant coastlands. 2His great achievements
and the full account of the greatness of Mordecai, whom
the king had promoted, are recorded in *The Book of the*
History of the Kings of Media and Persia. 3Mordecai the
Jew became the prime minister, with authority next to
that of King Xerxes himself. He was very great among the
Jews, who held him in high esteem, because he continued
to work for the good of his people and to speak up for the
welfare of all their descendants.

9:19 Hebrew *on the fourteenth day of the month of Adar*. This day of the Hebrew lunar calendar occurs in February or March. **9:21** Hebrew *on the fourteenth and fifteenth days of Adar*, of the Hebrew lunar calendar.

"WHY ME, GOD?" Have you ever thought, whispered, or screamed that question? Maybe you've even thought that God was against you.

When hard times come, many of us are tempted to sing the blues. The why mes are one part of the chorus. Along with the why mes comes, at times, a loss of trust in God. *I did everything right, God,* someone might say. *Why have you let me down like this?*

Job loved God, and everything was going great in his life. He had money, land and possessions, and a large family. But one day his world fell apart. He lost everything . . . except his life, a bitter wife, and accusing "friends." As you might imagine, Job asked why. Why him? Why now? The book of Job tells this story, and it gives God's reply. And after God spoke, Job was silent.

Job is a book about success, tragedy, friends, and faith. As you read Job, allow God to begin changing your ideas about suffering. Learn to trust God even when you don't understand.

stats

PURPOSE: To demonstrate God's sovereignty and the meaning of true faith. It addresses the question, Why does God allow bad things happen to good people?

AUTHOR: Possibly Job. Some have suggested Moses, Solomon, or Elihu.

DATE WRITTEN: Unknown. Records events that probably occurred during the time of the patriarchs (approximately 2000–1800 B.C.)

SETTING: The land of Uz, probably located northeast of Palestine, near desert land between Damascus and the Euphrates River

KEY PEOPLE: Job, Job's wife (unnamed), Eliphaz the Temanite, Bildad the Shuhite, Zophar the Naamathite, Elihu the Buzite

SPECIAL FEATURES: Job is the first of the poetic books in the Hebrew Bible. Many consider it to be the oldest book in the Bible. The book gives us insights into the work of Satan. Ezekiel 14:14, 20 and James 5:11 mention Job as a historical character.

KEY points

SUFFERING

For Job, the greatest trial was not the pain or loss; it was his inability to understand why God allowed him to suffer. Many of us who suffer have the same question. Although we may not be able to understand fully the pain we experience, it can lead us to rediscover God. He's always present, even when we suffer.

TRUST

Satan tried to drive a wedge between Job and God by getting Job to doubt God's love and justice. When life seems unfair, we're sometimes tempted to believe that God is unfair. Like Job, we can choose to trust instead of doubt.

PRIDE

Job's friends thought they had all of the right answers concerning Job's suffering. But they were dead wrong. We must be careful not to judge others who are suffering, because we may fall into the same pit of pride.

1

PROLOGUE

There once was a man named Job who lived in the land of
Uz. He was blameless—a man of complete integrity. He
feared God and stayed away from evil. 2He had seven
sons and three daughters. 3He owned 7,000 sheep, 3,000
camels, 500 teams of oxen, and 500 female donkeys. He
also had many servants. He was, in fact, the richest person in that entire area.

WHY ME? 1:1

Job lost all he had through no fault of his own. As he struggled to understand why all this was happening to him, it became clear that he was not meant to know the reasons. He would have to face life with the answers and explanations held back. Only then would his faith fully develop. Like Job, you may not have the answers to why you suffer. But you can choose to trust God no matter what or choose to be frustrated and bitter. What will you choose? ■

4Job's sons would take turns preparing feasts in their
homes, and they would also invite their three sisters to
celebrate with them. 5When these celebrations ended—
sometimes after several days—Job would purify his children. He would get up early in the morning and offer a
burnt offering for each of them. For Job said to himself,
"Perhaps my children have sinned and have cursed God
in their hearts." This was Job's regular practice.

JOB'S FIRST TEST

6One day the members of the heavenly court* came to
present themselves before the LORD, and the Accuser, Satan,* came with them. 7"Where have you come from?"
the LORD asked Satan.

Satan answered the LORD, "I have been patrolling the
earth, watching everything that's going on."

8Then the LORD asked Satan, "Have you noticed my
servant Job? He is the finest man in all the earth. He is
blameless—a man of complete integrity. He fears God
and stays away from evil."

9Satan replied to the LORD, "Yes, but Job has good reason to fear God. 10You have always put a wall of protection around him and his home and his property. You have
made him prosper in everything he does. Look how rich
he is! 11But reach out and take away everything he has,
and he will surely curse you to your face!"

12"All right, you may test him," the LORD said to Satan. "Do
whatever you want with everything he possesses, but don't
harm him physically." So Satan left the LORD's presence.

13One day when Job's sons and daughters were feasting
at the oldest brother's house, 14a messenger arrived at
Job's home with this news: "Your oxen were plowing, with
the donkeys feeding beside them, 15when the Sabeans
raided us. They stole all the animals and killed all the
farmhands. I am the only one who escaped to tell you."

16While he was still speaking, another messenger arrived with this news: "The fire of God has fallen from
heaven and burned up your sheep and all the shepherds.
I am the only one who escaped to tell you."

17While he was still speaking, a third messenger arrived with this news: "Three bands of Chaldean raiders
have stolen your camels and killed your servants. I am the
only one who escaped to tell you."

18While he was still speaking, another messenger arrived with this news: "Your sons and daughters were
feasting in their oldest brother's home. 19Suddenly, a
powerful wind swept in from the wilderness and hit the
house on all sides. The house collapsed, and all your children are dead. I am the only one who escaped to tell you."

20Job stood up and tore his robe in grief. Then he
shaved his head and fell to the ground to worship. 21He
said,

"I came naked from my mother's womb,
  and I will be naked when I leave.
The LORD gave me what I had,
  and the LORD has taken it away.
Praise the name of the LORD!"

22In all of this, Job did not sin by blaming God.

A TIME TO GRIEVE 1:20-22

Job did not hide his overwhelming grief. This emotional display did not mean he had lost his faith in God; instead, it showed that he was human and that he loved his family. Often we try to hold back our emotions in an attempt to be stoic. Or, we fear that our friends can't handle such emotions. But God understands our need to grieve when bad things happen. And best of all, he's always willing to listen. ■

2

JOB'S SECOND TEST

One day the members of the heavenly court* came again
to present themselves before the LORD, and the Accuser,
Satan,* came with them. 2"Where have you come from?"
the LORD asked Satan.

Satan answered the LORD, "I have been patrolling the
earth, watching everything that's going on."

3Then the LORD asked Satan, "Have you noticed my servant Job? He is the finest man in all the earth. He is blameless—a man of complete integrity. He fears God and stays
away from evil. And he has maintained his integrity, even
though you urged me to harm him without cause."

4Satan replied to the LORD, "Skin for skin! A man will
give up everything he has to save his life. 5But reach out
and take away his health, and he will surely curse you to
your face!"

6"All right, do with him as you please," the LORD said to

1:6a Hebrew *the sons of God.* 1:6b Hebrew *and the satan;* similarly throughout this chapter. 2:1a Hebrew *the sons of God.* 2:1b Hebrew *and the satan;* similarly throughout this chapter.

Satan. "But spare his life." 7So Satan left the LORD's presence, and he struck Job with terrible boils from head to foot.

SILENT COMFORT 2:11-13

Why did Job's friends arrive and then just sit quietly? According to Jewish tradition, people who came to comfort someone in mourning were not to speak until the mourner spoke. Job's friends realized that his pain was too deep to be healed with mere words, so they said nothing. Often, we feel we must say something spiritual to a hurting friend. But silence often is the best response to another person's suffering. Want to help a grieving friend? Just be there for him or her. ■

8Job scraped his skin with a piece of broken pottery as he sat among the ashes. 9His wife said to him, "Are you still trying to maintain your integrity? Curse God and die."

10But Job replied, "You talk like a foolish woman. Should we accept only good things from the hand of God and never anything bad?" So in all this, Job said nothing wrong.

JOB'S THREE FRIENDS SHARE HIS ANGUISH

11When three of Job's friends heard of the tragedy he had suffered, they got together and traveled from their homes to comfort and console him. Their names were Eliphaz the Temanite, Bildad the Shuhite, and Zophar the Naamathite. 12When they saw Job from a distance, they scarcely recognized him. Wailing loudly, they tore their robes and threw dust into the air over their heads to show their grief. 13Then they sat on the ground with him for seven days and nights. No one said a word to Job, for they saw that his suffering was too great for words.

3

JOB'S FIRST SPEECH

At last Job spoke, and he cursed the day of his birth. 2He said:

3 "Let the day of my birth be erased,
and the night I was conceived.
4 Let that day be turned to darkness.
Let it be lost even to God on high,

JOB

UPS:
- A man of faith, patience, and endurance
- Known as a generous and caring person
- Very wealthy

DOWN:
- Allowed his suffering to overwhelm him and make him question God

STATS:
- Where: Land of Uz
- Occupation: Wealthy land and livestock owner
- Relatives: His wife and first ten children not named. Daughters from the second set of children: Jemimah, Keziah, Keren-happuch
- Contemporaries: Eliphaz, Bildad, Zophar, Elihu

BOTTOM LINE:
Knowing God is better than knowing the answers.
God is not arbitrary or uncaring.
Pain is not always punishment.

Job's story is told in the book of Job. He also is mentioned in Ezek 14:14, 20 and James 5:11.

JOB Think about the worst tragedy you've ever faced. The death of a parent. The breakup of your family due to divorce. The end of a treasured relationship. A terminal illness. The loss of all of your possessions. Now imagine all of that happening in *one day*.

Job faced a day of unbelievable sorrow as loss after loss occurred. As we read his story, our minds reel. *It wasn't supposed to happen that way,* we think. *Job was a good man.* Good things should happen to people who do good things, and bad things should happen to people who do bad things, right? It often works out that way—but not always. Job's life can teach us what God wants us to do when we don't understand what's happening to us.

When knowing *why* becomes important, we can use the letters of that word *why* to remind us of Job's lessons. Like Job, we need to *wait, hope,* and *yield.*

Waiting is hard. Our "instant" age has taught us to expect answers and help fast. Job wanted to know why. When God finally spoke, he didn't offer Job an answer. He showed Job that knowing God was better than knowing all of the answers.

That's why *hope* is important. When we remember that God loves us, that he has good plans for us, and that he is more powerful than any situation we might encounter, we have hope. Hope means we trust God even if we never find out why something happened.

Yielding means wanting to do whatever God wants. It means praying like this: "God, I'm willing to wait and hope, because you are my God." Are there some areas in your life that need this prayer?

How Suffering Affects Us

SUFFERING IS HELPFUL WHEN:	SUFFERING IS HARMFUL WHEN:
We turn to God for understanding, endurance, and deliverance	We become hardened and reject God
We ask important questions we might not take time to think about in our normal routine	We refuse to ask any questions and miss any lessons that might be good for us
We let it prepare us to identify with and comfort others who suffer	We allow it to make us self-centered and selfish
We are open to being helped by others who are obeying God	We withdraw from the help others can give
We realize we can identify with what Christ suffered on the cross for us	We accuse God of being unjust and perhaps lead others to reject him
We are sensitized to the amount of suffering in the world	We refuse to be open to any changes in our lives

and let no light shine on it.
5 Let the darkness and utter gloom claim that
day for its own.
Let a black cloud overshadow it,
and let the darkness terrify it.
6 Let that night be blotted off the calendar,
never again to be counted among the days
of the year,
never again to appear among the months.
7 Let that night be childless.
Let it have no joy.
8 Let those who are experts at cursing—
whose cursing could rouse Leviathan*—
curse that day.
9 Let its morning stars remain dark.
Let it hope for light, but in vain;
may it never see the morning light.
10 Curse that day for failing to shut my mother's womb,
for letting me be born to see all this trouble.

11 "Why wasn't I born dead?
Why didn't I die as I came from the womb?
12 Why was I laid on my mother's lap?
Why did she nurse me at her breasts?
13 Had I died at birth, I would now be at peace.
I would be asleep and at rest.
14 I would rest with the world's kings and prime
ministers,
whose great buildings now lie in ruins.
15 I would rest with princes, rich in gold,
whose palaces were filled with silver.
16 Why wasn't I buried like a stillborn child,
like a baby who never lives to see the light?
17 For in death the wicked cause no trouble,
and the weary are at rest.
18 Even captives are at ease in death,
with no guards to curse them.
19 Rich and poor are both there,
and the slave is free from his master.

20 "Oh, why give light to those in misery,
and life to those who are bitter?
21 They long for death, and it won't come.
They search for death more eagerly than
for hidden treasure.
22 They're filled with joy when they finally die,
and rejoice when they find the grave.
23 Why is life given to those with no future,
those God has surrounded with difficulties?
24 I cannot eat for sighing;
my groans pour out like water.
25 What I always feared has happened to me.
What I dreaded has come true.
26 I have no peace, no quietness.
I have no rest; only trouble comes."

4 ELIPHAZ'S FIRST RESPONSE TO JOB

Then Eliphaz the Temanite replied to Job:

2 "Will you be patient and let me say a word?
For who could keep from speaking out?

3 "In the past you have encouraged many people;
you have strengthened those who were weak.
4 Your words have supported those who were falling;

3:8 The identification of Leviathan is disputed, ranging from an earthly creature to a mythical sea monster in ancient literature.

you encouraged those with shaky
knees.
5 But now when trouble strikes, you
lose heart.
You are terrified when it touches
you.
6 Doesn't your reverence for God
give you confidence?
Doesn't your life of integrity give
you hope?

7 "Stop and think! Do the innocent die?
When have the upright been
destroyed?
8 My experience shows that those
who plant trouble
and cultivate evil will harvest the same.
9 A breath from God destroys them.
They vanish in a blast of his anger.
10 The lion roars and the wildcat snarls,
but the teeth of strong lions will be broken.
11 The fierce lion will starve for lack of prey,
and the cubs of the lioness will be scattered.

12 "This truth was given to me in secret,
as though whispered in my ear.
13 It came to me in a disturbing vision at night,
when people are in a deep sleep.
14 Fear gripped me,
and my bones trembled.
15 A spirit* swept past my face,
and my hair stood on end.*
16 The spirit stopped, but I couldn't see its shape.
There was a form before my eyes.
In the silence I heard a voice say,
17 'Can a mortal be innocent before God?
Can anyone be pure before the Creator?'

18 "If God does not trust his own angels
and has charged his messengers with foolishness,
19 how much less will he trust people made of clay!
They are made of dust, crushed as easily
as a moth.
20 They are alive in the morning but dead by evening,
gone forever without a trace.
21 Their tent-cords are pulled and the tent collapses,
and they die in ignorance.

5 ELIPHAZ'S RESPONSE CONTINUES

1 "Cry for help, but will anyone answer you?
Which of the angels* will help you?
2 Surely resentment destroys the fool,
and jealousy kills the simple.
3 I have seen that fools may be successful for
the moment,
but then comes sudden disaster.

> From six disasters he will rescue you; even in the seventh, he will keep you from evil.
>
> JOB 5:19

4 Their children are abandoned far
from help;
they are crushed in court with
no one to defend them.
5 The hungry devour their harvest,
even when it is guarded by
brambles.*
The thirsty pant after their wealth.
6 But evil does not spring from the
soil,
and trouble does not sprout
from the earth.
7 People are born for trouble
as readily as sparks fly up from
a fire.

8 "If I were you, I would go to God
and present my case to him.
9 He does great things too marvelous to understand.
He performs countless miracles.
10 He gives rain for the earth
and water for the fields.
11 He gives prosperity to the poor
and protects those who suffer.
12 He frustrates the plans of schemers
so the work of their hands will not succeed.
13 He traps the wise in their own cleverness
so their cunning schemes are thwarted.
14 They find it is dark in the daytime,
and they grope at noon as if it were night.
15 He rescues the poor from the cutting words
of the strong,
and rescues them from the clutches of
the powerful.
16 And so at last the poor have hope,
and the snapping jaws of the wicked are shut.

GOOD ADVICE 5:17

Eliphaz was right—being "corrected" by God when we do wrong is a blessing. His advice, however, did not apply to Job. As we know from the beginning of the book, Job's suffering was not a result of a wrong action on his part. Like Eliphaz, we sometimes give people excellent advice only to learn that it doesn't apply to them and is therefore not very helpful. Those who offer counsel from God's Word should take care to thoroughly understand a person's situation *before* giving advice. ■

17 "But consider the joy of those corrected by God!
Do not despise the discipline of the Almighty when
you sin.
18 For though he wounds, he also bandages.
He strikes, but his hands also heal.
19 From six disasters he will rescue you;
even in the seventh, he will keep you from evil.

4:15a Or *wind;* also in 4:16. **4:15b** Or *its wind sent shivers up my spine.* **5:1** Hebrew *the holy ones.* **5:5** The meaning of the Hebrew for this phrase is uncertain.

20 He will save you from death in time of famine,
from the power of the sword in time of war.
21 You will be safe from slander
and have no fear when destruction comes.
22 You will laugh at destruction and famine;
wild animals will not terrify you.
23 You will be at peace with the stones of the field,
and its wild animals will be at peace with you.
24 You will know that your home is safe.
When you survey your possessions, nothing
will be missing.
25 You will have many children;
your descendants will be as plentiful as grass!
26 You will go to the grave at a ripe old age,
like a sheaf of grain harvested at the proper time!

27 "We have studied life and found all this to be true.
Listen to my counsel, and apply it to yourself."

6

JOB'S SECOND SPEECH: A RESPONSE TO ELIPHAZ

Then Job spoke again:

2 "If my misery could be weighed
and my troubles be put on the scales,
3 they would outweigh all the sands of the sea.
That is why I spoke impulsively.
4 For the Almighty has struck me down with
his arrows.
Their poison infects my spirit.
God's terrors are lined up against me.
5 Don't I have a right to complain?
Don't wild donkeys bray when they find no grass,
and oxen bellow when they have no food?
6 Don't people complain about unsalted food?
Does anyone want the tasteless white of an egg?*
7 My appetite disappears when I look at it;
I gag at the thought of eating it!

STRUGGLES 6:8-13

In his grief, Job wanted to give in, to be freed from his discomfort, and to die. But God did not grant Job's request. He had a greater plan for him. When the going gets tough, are you tempted to give up? To trust God in the good times is commendable, but to trust him during the difficult times tests us to our limits and exercises our faith. In your struggles, large or small, are you willing to trust that God is in control as Romans 8:28 suggests? ■

8 "Oh, that I might have my request,
that God would grant my desire.
9 I wish he would crush me.
I wish he would reach out his hand and kill me.
10 At least I can take comfort in this:
Despite the pain,
I have not denied the words of the Holy One.
11 But I don't have the strength to endure.
I have nothing to live for.
12 Do I have the strength of a stone?
Is my body made of bronze?
13 No, I am utterly helpless,
without any chance of success.

14 "One should be kind to a fainting friend,
but you accuse me without any fear of
the Almighty.*
15 My brothers, you have proved as unreliable
as a seasonal brook
that overflows its banks in the spring
16 when it is swollen with ice and melting snow.
17 But when the hot weather arrives, the water
disappears.
The brook vanishes in the heat.
18 The caravans turn aside to be refreshed,
but there is nothing to drink, so they die.
19 The caravans from Tema search for this water;
the travelers from Sheba hope to find it.
20 They count on it but are disappointed.
When they arrive, their hopes are dashed.
21 You, too, have given no help.
You have seen my calamity, and you are afraid.
22 But why? Have I ever asked you for a gift?
Have I begged for anything of yours for myself?
23 Have I asked you to rescue me from my enemies,
or to save me from ruthless people?
24 Teach me, and I will keep quiet.
Show me what I have done wrong.
25 Honest words can be painful,
but what do your criticisms amount to?
26 Do you think your words are convincing
when you disregard my cry of desperation?
27 You would even send an orphan into slavery*
or sell a friend.
28 Look at me!
Would I lie to your face?
29 Stop assuming my guilt,
for I have done no wrong.
30 Do you think I am lying?
Don't I know the difference between right
and wrong?

7

1 "Is not all human life a struggle?
Our lives are like that of a hired hand,
2 like a worker who longs for the shade,
like a servant waiting to be paid.
3 I, too, have been assigned months of futility,
long and weary nights of misery.
4 Lying in bed, I think, 'When will it be morning?'
But the night drags on, and I toss till dawn.
5 My body is covered with maggots and scabs.
My skin breaks open, oozing with pus.

6:6 Or *the tasteless juice of the mallow plant?* **6:14** Or *friend, / or he might lose his fear of the Almighty.* **6:27** Hebrew *even gamble over an orphan.*

JOB CRIES OUT TO GOD

6 "My days fly faster than a weaver's shuttle.
They end without hope.
7 O God, remember that my life is but a breath,
and I will never again feel happiness.
8 You see me now, but not for long.
You will look for me, but I will be gone.
9 Just as a cloud dissipates and vanishes,
those who die* will not come back.
10 They are gone forever from their home—
never to be seen again.

11 "I cannot keep from speaking.
I must express my anguish.
My bitter soul must complain.
12 Am I a sea monster or a dragon
that you must place me under guard?
13 I think, 'My bed will comfort me,
and sleep will ease my misery,'
14 but then you shatter me with dreams
and terrify me with visions.
15 I would rather be strangled—
rather die than suffer like this.
16 I hate my life and don't want to go on living.
Oh, leave me alone for my few remaining days.

17 "What are people, that you should make
so much of us,
that you should think of us so often?
18 For you examine us every morning
and test us every moment.
19 Why won't you leave me alone,
at least long enough for me to swallow!
20 If I have sinned, what have I done to you,
O watcher of all humanity?
Why make me your target?
Am I a burden to you?
21 Why not just forgive my sin
and take away my guilt?
For soon I will lie down in the dust and die.
When you look for me, I will be gone."

8 BILDAD'S FIRST RESPONSE TO JOB

Then Bildad the Shuhite replied to Job:

2 "How long will you go on like this?
You sound like a blustering wind.
3 Does God twist justice?
Does the Almighty twist what is right?
4 Your children must have sinned against him,
so their punishment was well deserved.
5 But if you pray to God
and seek the favor of the Almighty,
6 and if you are pure and live with integrity,
he will surely rise up and restore your happy home.
7 And though you started with little,
you will end with much.

8 "Just ask the previous generation.
Pay attention to the experience of our ancestors.
9 For we were born but yesterday and know nothing.
Our days on earth are as fleeting as a shadow.
10 But those who came before us will teach you.
They will teach you the wisdom of old.

11 "Can papyrus reeds grow tall without a marsh?
Can marsh grass flourish without water?
12 While they are still flowering, not ready to be cut,
they begin to wither more quickly than grass.
13 The same happens to all who forget God.
The hopes of the godless evaporate.
14 Their confidence hangs by a thread.
They are leaning on a spider's web.
15 They cling to their home for security, but it
won't last.
They try to hold it tight, but it will not endure.

FEELING SECURE 8:14-15

Bildad wrongly assumed that Job failed to trust God for his security. Everyone has a need to feel secure. But sometimes our security is based on money, possessions, knowledge, or relationships. All of these are temporary. Only God can give lasting security. What have you trusted for your security? How lasting is it? A secure foundation with God keeps feelings of insecurity at bay. ■

16 The godless seem like a lush plant growing in
the sunshine,
its branches spreading across the garden.
17 Its roots grow down through a pile of stones;
it takes hold on a bed of rocks.
18 But when it is uprooted,
it's as though it never existed!
19 That's the end of its life,
and others spring up from the earth to replace it.

20 "But look, God will not reject a person of integrity,
nor will he lend a hand to the wicked.
21 He will once again fill your mouth with laughter
and your lips with shouts of joy.
22 Those who hate you will be clothed with shame,
and the home of the wicked will be destroyed."

9 JOB'S THIRD SPEECH: A RESPONSE TO BILDAD

Then Job spoke again:

2 "Yes, I know all this is true in principle.
But how can a person be declared innocent
in God's sight?
3 If someone wanted to take God to court,*
would it be possible to answer him even once
in a thousand times?

7:9 Hebrew *who go down to Sheol.* 9:3 Or *If God wanted to take someone to court.*

4 For God is so wise and so mighty.
Who has ever challenged him successfully?

5 "Without warning, he moves the mountains,
overturning them in his anger.
6 He shakes the earth from its place,
and its foundations tremble.
7 If he commands it, the sun won't rise
and the stars won't shine.
8 He alone has spread out the heavens
and marches on the waves of the sea.
9 He made all the stars—the Bear and Orion,
the Pleiades and the constellations of the
southern sky.
10 He does great things too marvelous to understand.
He performs countless miracles.

11 "Yet when he comes near, I cannot see him.
When he moves by, I do not see him go.
12 If he snatches someone in death, who can stop him?
Who dares to ask, 'What are you doing?'
13 And God does not restrain his anger.
Even the monsters of the sea* are crushed
beneath his feet.

14 "So who am I, that I should try to answer God
or even reason with him?
15 Even if I were right, I would have no defense.
I could only plead for mercy.
16 And even if I summoned him and he responded,
I'm not sure he would listen to me.
17 For he attacks me with a storm
and repeatedly wounds me without cause.
18 He will not let me catch my breath,
but fills me instead with bitter sorrows.
19 If it's a question of strength, he's the strong one.
If it's a matter of justice, who dares to summon
him to court?
20 Though I am innocent, my own mouth would
pronounce me guilty.
Though I am blameless, it* would prove me wicked.

21 "I am innocent,
but it makes no difference to me—
I despise my life.
22 Innocent or wicked, it is all the same to God.
That's why I say, 'He destroys both the blameless
and the wicked.'
23 When a plague* sweeps through,
he laughs at the death of the innocent.
24 The whole earth is in the hands of the wicked,
and God blinds the eyes of the judges.
If he's not the one who does it, who is?

25 "My life passes more swiftly than a runner.
It flees away without a glimpse of happiness.
26 It disappears like a swift papyrus boat,
like an eagle swooping down on its prey.
27 If I decided to forget my complaints,
to put away my sad face and be cheerful,
28 I would still dread all the pain,
for I know you will not find me innocent, O God.
29 Whatever happens, I will be found guilty.
So what's the use of trying?
30 Even if I were to wash myself with soap
and clean my hands with lye,
31 you would plunge me into a muddy ditch,
and my own filthy clothing would hate me.

32 "God is not a mortal like me,
so I cannot argue with him or take him to trial.
33 If only there were a mediator between us,
someone who could bring us together.
34 The mediator could make God stop beating me,
and I would no longer live in terror of his
punishment.
35 Then I could speak to him without fear,
but I cannot do that in my own strength.

10 JOB FRAMES HIS PLEA TO GOD

1 "I am disgusted with my life.
Let me complain freely.
My bitter soul must complain.

HOW UNFAIR! 10:1

Job complained to his friends about his misery. When life seems unfair, self-pity is a natural response. We might say, "Look what happened to me; how unfair it is!" But what we *really* mean is, "God is unfair." But hard times can help us mature in faith. When facing difficult situations, are you willing to ask, "What can I learn and how can I grow?" rather than "Who did this to me and how can I get out of it?" ■

2 I will say to God, 'Don't simply condemn me—
tell me the charge you are bringing against me.
3 What do you gain by oppressing me?
Why do you reject me, the work of your
own hands,
while smiling on the schemes of the wicked?
4 Are your eyes like those of a human?
Do you see things only as people see them?
5 Is your lifetime only as long as ours?
Is your life so short
6 that you must quickly probe for my guilt
and search for my sin?
7 Although you know I am not guilty,
no one can rescue me from your hands.

8 "'You formed me with your hands; you made me,
yet now you completely destroy me.
9 Remember that you made me from dust—
will you turn me back to dust so soon?

9:13 Hebrew *the helpers of Rahab*, the name of a mythical sea monster that represents chaos in ancient literature. **9:20** Or *he*.
9:23 Or *disaster*.

10 You guided my conception
and formed me in the womb.*
11 You clothed me with skin and flesh,
and you knit my bones and sinews together.
12 You gave me life and showed me your unfailing love.
My life was preserved by your care.

13 "'Yet your real motive—
your true intent—
14 was to watch me, and if I sinned,
you would not forgive my guilt.
15 If I am guilty, too bad for me;
and even if I'm innocent, I can't hold my head high,
because I am filled with shame and misery.
16 And if I hold my head high, you hunt me like a lion
and display your awesome power against me.
17 Again and again you witness against me.
You pour out your growing anger on me
and bring fresh armies against me.

18 "'Why, then, did you deliver me from my
mother's womb?
Why didn't you let me die at birth?
19 It would be as though I had never existed,
going directly from the womb to the grave.
20 I have only a few days left, so leave me alone,
that I may have a moment of comfort
21 before I leave—never to return—
for the land of darkness and utter gloom.
22 It is a land as dark as midnight,
a land of gloom and confusion,
where even the light is dark as midnight.'"

11 ZOPHAR'S FIRST RESPONSE TO JOB

Then Zophar the Naamathite replied to Job:

2 "Shouldn't someone answer this torrent of words?
Is a person proved innocent just by a lot of talking?
3 Should I remain silent while you babble on?
When you mock God, shouldn't someone make
you ashamed?
4 You claim, 'My beliefs are pure,'
and 'I am clean in the sight of God.'
5 If only God would speak;
if only he would tell you what he thinks!
6 If only he would tell you the secrets of wisdom,
for true wisdom is not a simple matter.
Listen! God is doubtless punishing you
far less than you deserve!

7 "Can you solve the mysteries of God?
Can you discover everything about the Almighty?
8 Such knowledge is higher than the heavens—
and who are you?
It is deeper than the underworld*—
what do you know?
9 It is broader than the earth
and wider than the sea.
10 If God comes and puts a person in prison
or calls the court to order, who can stop him?
11 For he knows those who are false,
and he takes note of all their sins.

NO HIDING FROM GOD 11:1-11

Zophar incorrectly assumed that Job was being punished because of hidden wrongdoings. Although his assumption was wrong, he explained quite accurately that God knows and sees everything. Ever think, *No one will ever know* in regard to something you've done? We can hide some wrongs from others, but we can do *nothing* without God knowing about it. Our lives are an open book to him. ■

12 An empty-headed person won't become wise
any more than a wild donkey can bear a
human child.*

13 "If only you would prepare your heart
and lift up your hands to him in prayer!
14 Get rid of your sins,
and leave all iniquity behind you.
15 Then your face will brighten with innocence.
You will be strong and free of fear.
16 You will forget your misery;
it will be like water flowing away.
17 Your life will be brighter than the noonday.
Even darkness will be as bright as morning.
18 Having hope will give you courage.
You will be protected and will rest in safety.
19 You will lie down unafraid,
and many will look to you for help.
20 But the wicked will be blinded.
They will have no escape.
Their only hope is death."

12 JOB'S FOURTH SPEECH: A RESPONSE TO ZOPHAR

Then Job spoke again:

2 "You people really know everything, don't you?
And when you die, wisdom will die with you!
3 Well, I know a few things myself—
and you're no better than I am.
Who doesn't know these things you've
been saying?
4 Yet my friends laugh at me,
for I call on God and expect an answer.
I am a just and blameless man,
yet they laugh at me.
5 People who are at ease mock those in trouble.
They give a push to people who are stumbling.

10:10 Hebrew *You poured me out like milk / and curdled me like cheese.* 11:8 Hebrew *than Sheol.* 11:12 Or *than a wild male donkey can bear a tame colt.*

6 But robbers are left in peace,
and those who provoke God live in safety—
though God keeps them in his power.

7 "Just ask the animals, and they will teach you.
Ask the birds of the sky, and they will tell you.
8 Speak to the earth, and it will instruct you.
Let the fish in the sea speak to you.
9 For they all know
that my disaster* has come from the hand
of the LORD.
10 For the life of every living thing is in his hand,
and the breath of every human being.
11 The ear tests the words it hears
just as the mouth distinguishes between foods.
12 Wisdom belongs to the aged,
and understanding to the old.

GUIDANCE 12:13-25

Job acknowledged that real wisdom comes from God. Many leaders brag about their intelligence and wisdom. But human wisdom is child's play compared to God's wisdom. His wisdom is 100 percent trustworthy. Who do you trust for advice? ■

13 "But true wisdom and power are found in God;
counsel and understanding are his.
14 What he destroys cannot be rebuilt.
When he puts someone in prison, there
is no escape.
15 If he holds back the rain, the earth becomes
a desert.
If he releases the waters, they flood the earth.
16 Yes, strength and wisdom are his;
deceivers and deceived are both in his power.
17 He leads counselors away, stripped of good
judgment;
wise judges become fools.
18 He removes the royal robe of kings.
They are led away with ropes around their waist.
19 He leads priests away, stripped of status;
he overthrows those with long years in power.
20 He silences the trusted adviser
and removes the insight of the elders.
21 He pours disgrace upon princes
and disarms the strong.

22 "He uncovers mysteries hidden in darkness;
he brings light to the deepest gloom.
23 He builds up nations, and he destroys them.
He expands nations, and he abandons them.
24 He strips kings of understanding
and leaves them wandering in a pathless
wasteland.
25 They grope in the darkness without a light.
He makes them stagger like drunkards.

13

JOB WANTS TO ARGUE HIS CASE WITH GOD

1 "Look, I have seen all this with my own eyes
and heard it with my own ears, and now
I understand.
2 I know as much as you do.
You are no better than I am.
3 As for me, I would speak directly to the Almighty.
I want to argue my case with God himself.
4 As for you, you smear me with lies.
As physicians, you are worthless quacks.
5 If only you could be silent!
That's the wisest thing you could do.
6 Listen to my charge;
pay attention to my arguments.

7 "Are you defending God with lies?
Do you make your dishonest arguments
for his sake?
8 Will you slant your testimony in his favor?
Will you argue God's case for him?
9 What will happen when he finds out what
you are doing?
Can you fool him as easily as you fool people?
10 No, you will be in trouble with him
if you secretly slant your testimony in his favor.
11 Doesn't his majesty terrify you?
Doesn't your fear of him overwhelm you?
12 Your platitudes are as valuable as ashes.
Your defense is as fragile as a clay pot.

13 "Be silent now and leave me alone.
Let me speak, and I will face the consequences.
14 Yes, I will take my life in my hands
and say what I really think.
15 God might kill me, but I have no other hope.
I am going to argue my case with him.
16 But this is what will save me—I am not godless.
If I were, I could not stand before him.

17 "Listen closely to what I am about to say.
Hear me out.
18 I have prepared my case;
I will be proved innocent.
19 Who can argue with me over this?
And if you prove me wrong, I will remain
silent and die.

JOB ASKS HOW HE HAS SINNED

20 "O God, grant me these two things,
and then I will be able to face you.
21 Remove your heavy hand from me,
and don't terrify me with your awesome
presence.
22 Now summon me, and I will answer!
Or let me speak to you, and you reply.
23 Tell me, what have I done wrong?
Show me my rebellion and my sin.

12:9 Hebrew *that this.*

24 Why do you turn away from me?
Why do you treat me as your enemy?
25 Would you terrify a leaf blown by the wind?
Would you chase dry straw?

26 "You write bitter accusations against me
and bring up all the sins of my youth.
27 You put my feet in stocks.
You examine all my paths.
You trace all my footprints.
28 I waste away like rotting wood,
like a moth-eaten coat.

14

1 "How frail is humanity!
How short is life, how full of trouble!
2 We blossom like a flower and then wither.
Like a passing shadow, we quickly disappear.
3 Must you keep an eye on such a frail creature
and demand an accounting from me?
4 Who can bring purity out of an impure person?
No one!
5 You have decided the length of our lives.
You know how many months we will live,
and we are not given a minute longer.
6 So leave us alone and let us rest!
We are like hired hands, so let us finish
our work in peace.

UNENDING LIFE 14:1-15

Although Job realized that life is brief and full of trouble, he held on to the hope of life after death. God's solution to an unfair world is to guarantee life with him forever. No matter how unfair your present world seems, God offers the hope of being in his presence forever. ■

7 "Even a tree has more hope!
If it is cut down, it will sprout again
and grow new branches.
8 Though its roots have grown old in the earth
and its stump decays,
9 at the scent of water it will bud
and sprout again like a new seedling.

10 "But when people die, their strength is gone.
They breathe their last, and then where are they?
11 As water evaporates from a lake
and a river disappears in drought,
12 people are laid to rest and do not rise again.
Until the heavens are no more, they will not wake up
nor be roused from their sleep.

13 "I wish you would hide me in the grave*
and forget me there until your anger has passed.
But mark your calendar to think of me again!
14 Can the dead live again?
If so, this would give me hope through all
my years of struggle,
and I would eagerly await the release of death.
15 You would call and I would answer,
and you would yearn for me, your handiwork.
16 For then you would guard my steps,
instead of watching for my sins.
17 My sins would be sealed in a pouch,
and you would cover my guilt.

18 "But instead, as mountains fall and crumble
and as rocks fall from a cliff,
19 as water wears away the stones
and floods wash away the soil,
so you destroy people's hope.
20 You always overpower them, and they pass
from the scene.
You disfigure them in death and send them away.
21 They never know if their children grow up in honor
or sink to insignificance.
22 They suffer painfully;
their life is full of trouble."

15

ELIPHAZ'S SECOND RESPONSE TO JOB

Then Eliphaz the Temanite replied:

2 "A wise man wouldn't answer with such empty talk!
You are nothing but a windbag.
3 The wise don't engage in empty chatter.
What good are such words?
4 Have you no fear of God,
no reverence for him?
5 Your sins are telling your mouth what to say.
Your words are based on clever deception.
6 Your own mouth condemns you, not I.
Your own lips testify against you.

7 "Were you the first person ever born?
Were you born before the hills were made?
8 Were you listening at God's secret council?
Do you have a monopoly on wisdom?
9 What do you know that we don't?
What do you understand that we do not?
10 On our side are aged, gray-haired men
much older than your father!

11 "Is God's comfort too little for you?
Is his gentle word not enough?
12 What has taken away your reason?
What has weakened your vision,*
13 that you turn against God
and say all these evil things?
14 Can any mortal be pure?
Can anyone born of a woman be just?
15 Look, God does not even trust the angels.*

14:13 Hebrew *in Sheol.* 15:12 Or *Why do your eyes flash with anger;* Hebrew reads *Why do your eyes blink.* 15:15 Hebrew *the holy ones.*

Even the heavens are not absolutely pure in
his sight.
16 How much less pure is a corrupt and sinful person
with a thirst for wickedness!

17 "If you will listen, I will show you.
I will answer you from my own experience.
18 And it is confirmed by the reports of wise men
who have heard the same thing from their
fathers—
19 from those to whom the land was given
long before any foreigners arrived.

20 "The wicked writhe in pain throughout their lives.
Years of trouble are stored up for the ruthless.
21 The sound of terror rings in their ears,
and even on good days they fear the attack
of the destroyer.
22 They dare not go out into the darkness
for fear they will be murdered.
23 They wander around, saying, 'Where can
I find bread?'*
They know their day of destruction is near.
24 That dark day terrifies them.
They live in distress and anguish,
like a king preparing for battle.
25 For they shake their fists at God,
defying the Almighty.
26 Holding their strong shields,
they defiantly charge against him.

27 "These wicked people are heavy and prosperous;
their waists bulge with fat.
28 But their cities will be ruined.
They will live in abandoned houses
that are ready to tumble down.
29 Their riches will not last,
and their wealth will not endure.
Their possessions will no longer spread across
the horizon.

30 "They will not escape the darkness.
The burning sun will wither their shoots,
and the breath of God will destroy them.
31 Let them no longer fool themselves by trusting in
empty riches,
for emptiness will be their only reward.
32 Like trees, they will be cut down in the prime
of life;
their branches will never again be green.
33 They will be like a vine whose grapes are harvested
too early,
like an olive tree that loses its blossoms before
the fruit can form.
34 For the godless are barren.
Their homes, enriched through bribery, will burn.
35 They conceive trouble and give birth to evil.
Their womb produces deceit."

16

JOB'S FIFTH SPEECH: A RESPONSE TO ELIPHAZ

Then Job spoke again:

2 "I have heard all this before.
What miserable comforters you are!
3 Won't you ever stop blowing hot air?
What makes you keep on talking?
4 I could say the same things if you were in my place.
I could spout off criticism and shake my head
at you.
5 But if it were me, I would encourage you.
I would try to take away your grief.
6 Instead, I suffer if I defend myself,
and I suffer no less if I refuse to speak.

COMFORTING 101 16:1-5

Instead of comforting Job, his friends blamed him for his suffering. Job began his reply to Eliphaz by calling him and his friends "miserable comforters" (vs. 2). Want to avoid that label as you offer comfort to someone in pain? Job offers some advice: (1) Don't talk just for the sake of talking; (2) don't give pat answers; (3) don't criticize; (4) put yourself in the other person's place; and (5) offer sincere help and encouragement. The best comforters are those who know something about suffering. ■

7 "O God, you have ground me down
and devastated my family.
8 As if to prove I have sinned, you've reduced me to
skin and bones.
My gaunt flesh testifies against me.
9 God hates me and angrily tears me apart.
He snaps his teeth at me
and pierces me with his eyes.
10 People jeer and laugh at me.
They slap my cheek in contempt.
A mob gathers against me.
11 God has handed me over to sinners.
He has tossed me into the hands of the wicked.

12 "I was living quietly until he shattered me.
He took me by the neck and broke me in pieces.
Then he set me up as his target,
13 and now his archers surround me.
His arrows pierce me without mercy.
The ground is wet with my blood.*
14 Again and again he smashes against me,
charging at me like a warrior.
15 I wear burlap to show my grief.
My pride lies in the dust.
16 My eyes are red with weeping;
dark shadows circle my eyes.
17 Yet I have done no wrong,
and my prayer is pure.

15:23 Greek version reads *He is appointed to be food for a vulture.* **16:13** Hebrew *my gall.*

SUFFERING AND EVIL

ULTIMATE ISSUES

Sooner or later, every Christian faces these questions: Why does God allow suffering and evil? Does God see what's going on here? Does he care? If so, why doesn't he intervene?

The book of Job addresses the question of suffering more than any portion of Scripture. Although God responds to Job's questions (chapters 38–41) with his longest unbroken speech in the Bible, he never tells Job why. He basically tells Job that as God he can do whatever he wants, and that's all the answer Job needs.

Big help, right?

The fact that God doesn't answer Job's question is somewhat disturbing. But the following perspectives may help when you are faced with suffering and evil.

- God didn't condemn Job for his questions. He just reminded Job whom he was talking to. It seems that why is a question we're free to ask, but God isn't bound to answer. Sometimes he will; sometimes he won't.
- We live in a fallen world. Bad stuff can and will happen.
- Being a Christian—or a "good person"—does not exempt you from pain and suffering. Jesus even guaranteed that we'll experience hard times (John 16:33). But we can be comforted: Jesus overcame suffering and we can, too. It's easy to serve God when life is sunny; the test is how we respond when the storm washes over us.
- Contrary to what a lot of Christians believe, God doesn't promise his children happiness. He's much more concerned with our holiness. Worthwhile things seldom, if ever, come without great cost. Following Jesus is no exception. That's why the Christian life sometimes involves pain and sacrifice.
- Finally, when nothing else helps, remember this: When you or someone you love suffers, no one hurts more than God. He's a good Father who hates to see his children hurt. He feels with us so genuinely that he got personally involved in our struggle—he became a man who suffered and died for us. So when you hurt, remember: You never cry alone. God knows and cares.

18 "O earth, do not conceal my blood.
Let it cry out on my behalf.
19 Even now my witness is in heaven.
My advocate is there on high.
20 My friends scorn me,
but I pour out my tears to God.
21 I need someone to mediate between
God and me,
as a person mediates between friends.
22 For soon I must go down that road
from which I will never return.

17 JOB CONTINUES TO DEFEND HIS INNOCENCE

1 "My spirit is crushed,
and my life is nearly snuffed out.
The grave is ready to receive me.
2 I am surrounded by mockers.
I watch how bitterly they taunt me.

3 "You must defend my innocence, O God,
since no one else will stand up for me.
4 You have closed their minds to understanding,
but do not let them triumph.
5 They betray their friends for their own advantage,
so let their children faint with hunger.

6 "God has made a mockery of me among
the people;
they spit in my face.
7 My eyes are swollen with weeping,
and I am but a shadow of my former self.
8 The virtuous are horrified when they see me.
The innocent rise up against the ungodly.

9 The righteous keep moving forward,
and those with clean hands become stronger
and stronger.

10 "As for all of you, come back with a better argument,
though I still won't find a wise man among you.
11 My days are over.
My hopes have disappeared.
My heart's desires are broken.
12 These men say that night is day;
they claim that the darkness is light.
13 What if I go to the grave*
and make my bed in darkness?
14 What if I call the grave my father,
and the maggot my mother or my sister?
15 Where then is my hope?
Can anyone find it?
16 No, my hope will go down with me to the grave.
We will rest together in the dust!"

18 BILDAD'S SECOND RESPONSE TO JOB

Then Bildad the Shuhite replied:

2 "How long before you stop talking?
Speak sense if you want us to answer!
3 Do you think we are mere animals?
Do you think we are stupid?
4 You may tear out your hair in anger,
but will that destroy the earth?
Will it make the rocks tremble?

5 "Surely the light of the wicked will be snuffed out.
The sparks of their fire will not glow.
6 The light in their tent will grow dark.
The lamp hanging above them will be quenched.
7 The confident stride of the wicked will be shortened.
Their own schemes will be their downfall.
8 The wicked walk into a net.
They fall into a pit.
9 A trap grabs them by the heel.
A snare holds them tight.
10 A noose lies hidden on the ground.
A rope is stretched across their path.

11 "Terrors surround the wicked
and trouble them at every step.
12 Hunger depletes their strength,
and calamity waits for them to stumble.
13 Disease eats their skin;
death devours their limbs.
14 They are torn from the security of their homes
and are brought down to the king of terrors.
15 The homes of the wicked will burn down;
burning sulfur rains on their houses.
16 Their roots will dry up,
and their branches will wither.
17 All memory of their existence will fade from
the earth,
No one will remember their names.
18 They will be thrust from light into darkness,
driven from the world.
19 They will have neither children nor grandchildren,
nor any survivor in the place where they lived.
20 People in the west are appalled at their fate;
people in the east are horrified.
21 They will say, 'This was the home of a wicked person,
the place of one who rejected God.'"

19 JOB'S SIXTH SPEECH: A RESPONSE TO BILDAD

Then Job spoke again:

2 "How long will you torture me?
How long will you try to crush me with
your words?
3 You have already insulted me ten times.
You should be ashamed of treating me so badly.
4 Even if I have sinned,
that is my concern, not yours.
5 You think you're better than I am,
using my humiliation as evidence of my sin.
6 But it is God who has wronged me,
capturing me in his net.*

7 "I cry out, 'Help!' but no one answers me.
I protest, but there is no justice.
8 God has blocked my way so I cannot move.
He has plunged my path into darkness.
9 He has stripped me of my honor
and removed the crown from my head.
10 He has demolished me on every side, and
I am finished.
He has uprooted my hope like a fallen tree.
11 His fury burns against me;
he counts me as an enemy.
12 His troops advance.
They build up roads to attack me.
They camp all around my tent.

13 "My relatives stay far away,
and my friends have turned against me.
14 My family is gone,
and my close friends have forgotten me.
15 My servants and maids consider me a stranger.
I am like a foreigner to them.
16 When I call my servant, he doesn't come;
I have to plead with him!
17 My breath is repulsive to my wife.
I am rejected by my own family.
18 Even young children despise me.
When I stand to speak, they turn their
backs on me.
19 My close friends detest me.
Those I loved have turned against me.

17:13 Hebrew *to Sheol;* also in 17:16. **19:6** Or *for I am like a city under siege.*

20 I have been reduced to skin and
bones
and have escaped death by the
skin of my teeth.

21 "Have mercy on me, my friends,
have mercy,
for the hand of God has
struck me.
22 Must you also persecute me, like
God does?
Haven't you chewed me up
enough?

23 "Oh, that my words could
be recorded.
Oh, that they could be inscribed on a monument,
24 carved with an iron chisel and filled with lead,
engraved forever in the rock.

25 "But as for me, I know that my Redeemer lives,
and he will stand upon the earth at last.
26 And after my body has decayed,
yet in my body I will see God*!
27 I will see him for myself.
Yes, I will see him with my own eyes.
I am overwhelmed at the thought!

28 "How dare you go on persecuting me,
saying, 'It's his own fault'?
29 You should fear punishment yourselves,
for your attitude deserves punishment.
Then you will know that there is indeed
a judgment."

I know that my Redeemer lives, and he will stand upon the earth at last.

JOB 19:25

20 ZOPHAR'S SECOND RESPONSE TO JOB

Then Zophar the Naamathite replied:

2 "I must reply
because I am greatly disturbed.
3 I've had to endure your insults,
but now my spirit prompts me to reply.

4 "Don't you realize that from the beginning of time,
ever since people were first placed on the earth,
5 the triumph of the wicked has been short lived
and the joy of the godless has been only
temporary?
6 Though the pride of the godless reaches to
the heavens
and their heads touch the clouds,
7 yet they will vanish forever,
thrown away like their own dung.
Those who knew them will ask,
'Where are they?'
8 They will fade like a dream and not be found.
They will vanish like a vision in the night.
9 Those who once saw them will see
them no more.
Their families will never see
them again.
10 Their children will beg from
the poor,
for they must give back their
stolen riches.
11 Though they are young,
their bones will lie in the dust.

12 "They enjoyed the sweet taste
of wickedness,
letting it melt under their
tongue.
13 They savored it,
holding it long in their mouths.
14 But suddenly the food in their bellies turns sour,
a poisonous venom in their stomach.
15 They will vomit the wealth they swallowed.
God won't let them keep it down.
16 They will suck the poison of cobras.
The viper will kill them.
17 They will never again enjoy streams of olive oil
or rivers of milk and honey.
18 They will give back everything they worked for.
Their wealth will bring them no joy.
19 For they oppressed the poor and left them
destitute.
They foreclosed on their homes.
20 They were always greedy and never satisfied.
Nothing remains of all the things they
dreamed about.
21 Nothing is left after they finish gorging themselves.
Therefore, their prosperity will not endure.

PAYBACK 20:1-7

Although Zophar was wrong in his assumptions about Job, he was right in his opinions about the final end of evil people. Ever been burned by someone who seemed to get away with hurting you? Maybe you've wondered if crime really *does* pay, especially when lying, stealing, and oppressing others brings temporary gain to those who practice them. But in the end, God's justice will prevail. (See Ps 37.) ■

22 "In the midst of plenty, they will run into trouble
and be overcome by misery.
23 May God give them a bellyful of trouble.
May God rain down his anger upon them.
24 When they try to escape an iron weapon,
a bronze-tipped arrow will pierce them.
25 The arrow is pulled from their back,
and the arrowhead glistens with blood.*
The terrors of death are upon them.
26 Their treasures will be thrown into deepest
darkness.

19:26 Or *without my body I will see God.* The meaning of the Hebrew is uncertain. **20:25** Hebrew *with gall.*

A wildfire will devour their goods,
consuming all they have left.
27 The heavens will reveal their guilt,
and the earth will testify against them.
28 A flood will sweep away their house.
God's anger will descend on them in torrents.
29 This is the reward that God gives the wicked.
It is the inheritance decreed by God."

21 JOB'S SEVENTH SPEECH: A RESPONSE TO ZOPHAR

Then Job spoke again:

2 "Listen closely to what I am saying.
That's one consolation you can give me.
3 Bear with me, and let me speak.
After I have spoken, you may resume mocking me.

4 "My complaint is with God, not with people.
I have good reason to be so impatient.
5 Look at me and be stunned.
Put your hand over your mouth in shock.
6 When I think about what I am saying, I shudder.
My body trembles.

7 "Why do the wicked prosper,
growing old and powerful?
8 They live to see their children grow up and
settle down,
and they enjoy their grandchildren.
9 Their homes are safe from every fear,
and God does not punish them.
10 Their bulls never fail to breed.
Their cows bear calves and never miscarry.
11 They let their children frisk about like lambs.
Their little ones skip and dance.
12 They sing with tambourine and harp.
They celebrate to the sound of the flute.
13 They spend their days in prosperity,
then go down to the grave* in peace.
14 And yet they say to God, 'Go away.
We want no part of you and your ways.
15 Who is the Almighty, and why should we obey him?
What good will it do us to pray?'
16 (They think their prosperity is of their own doing,
but I will have nothing to do with that kind
of thinking.)

17 "Yet the light of the wicked never seems
to be extinguished.
Do they ever have trouble?
Does God distribute sorrows to them in anger?
18 Are they driven before the wind like straw?
Are they carried away by the storm like chaff?
Not at all!

19 "'Well,' you say, 'at least God will punish
their children!'
But I say he should punish the ones who sin,
so that they understand his judgment.
20 Let them see their destruction with their own eyes.
Let them drink deeply of the anger of the Almighty.
21 For they will not care what happens to their family
after they are dead.

22 "But who can teach a lesson to God,
since he judges even the most powerful?

A RIGHT ATTITUDE 21:22

In the middle of Job's confusion about his suffering, he asked, "But who can teach God knowledge, since he judges even the most powerful?" He refused to allow his suffering to cause him to diss God. Can you say the same? Even if your struggles seem as great and difficult as Job's, your response will indicate your current attitude toward God. Rather than becoming angry with God, are you willing to continue to trust him, no matter what your circumstances may be? Although it's sometimes difficult to believe, God *is* in control. ■

23 One person dies in prosperity,
completely comfortable and secure,
24 the picture of good health,
vigorous and fit.
25 Another person dies in bitter poverty,
never having tasted the good life.
26 But both are buried in the same dust,
both eaten by the same maggots.

27 "Look, I know what you're thinking.
I know the schemes you plot against me.
28 You will tell me of rich and wicked people
whose houses have vanished because of their sins.
29 But ask those who have been around,
and they will tell you the truth.
30 Evil people are spared in times of calamity
and are allowed to escape disaster.
31 No one criticizes them openly
or pays them back for what they have done.
32 When they are carried to the grave,
an honor guard keeps watch at their tomb.
33 A great funeral procession goes to the cemetery.
Many pay their respects as the body is laid to rest,
and the earth gives sweet repose.

34 "How can your empty clichés comfort me?
All your explanations are lies!"

22 ELIPHAZ'S THIRD RESPONSE TO JOB

Then Eliphaz the Temanite replied:

2 "Can a person do anything to help God?
Can even a wise person be helpful to him?

21:13 Hebrew *to Sheol.*

3 Is it any advantage to the Almighty if you are
righteous?
Would it be any gain to him if you were perfect?
4 Is it because you're so pious that he accuses you
and brings judgment against you?
5 No, it's because of your wickedness!
There's no limit to your sins.

6 "For example, you must have lent money
to your friend
and demanded clothing as security.
Yes, you stripped him to the bone.
7 You must have refused water for the thirsty
and food for the hungry.
8 You probably think the land belongs to the powerful
and only the privileged have a right to it!
9 You must have sent widows away empty-handed
and crushed the hopes of orphans.
10 That is why you are surrounded by traps
and tremble from sudden fears.
11 That is why you cannot see in the darkness,
and waves of water cover you.

12 "God is so great—higher than the heavens,
higher than the farthest stars.
13 But you reply, 'That's why God can't see what
I am doing!
How can he judge through the thick darkness?
14 For thick clouds swirl about him, and he cannot
see us.
He is way up there, walking on the vault of heaven.'

15 "Will you continue on the old paths
where evil people have walked?
16 They were snatched away in the prime of life,
the foundations of their lives washed away.
17 For they said to God, 'Leave us alone!
What can the Almighty do to us?'
18 Yet he was the one who filled their homes with
good things,
so I will have nothing to do with that kind
of thinking.

19 "The righteous will be happy to see the wicked
destroyed,
and the innocent will laugh in contempt.
20 They will say, 'See how our enemies have
been destroyed.
The last of them have been consumed in the fire.'

21 "Submit to God, and you will have peace;
then things will go well for you.
22 Listen to his instructions,
and store them in your heart.
23 If you return to the Almighty, you will be restored—
so clean up your life.
24 If you give up your lust for money
and throw your precious gold into the river,
25 the Almighty himself will be your treasure.
He will be your precious silver!

26 "Then you will take delight in the Almighty
and look up to God.
27 You will pray to him, and he will hear you,
and you will fulfill your vows to him.
28 You will succeed in whatever you choose to do,
and light will shine on the road ahead of you.
29 If people are in trouble and you say, 'Help them,'
God will save them.
30 Even sinners will be rescued;
they will be rescued because your hands are pure."

23 JOB'S EIGHTH SPEECH: A RESPONSE TO ELIPHAZ

Then Job spoke again:

2 "My complaint today is still a bitter one,
and I try hard not to groan aloud.
3 If only I knew where to find God,
I would go to his court.
4 I would lay out my case
and present my arguments.
5 Then I would listen to his reply
and understand what he says to me.
6 Would he use his great power to argue with me?
No, he would give me a fair hearing.
7 Honest people can reason with him,
so I would be forever acquitted by my judge.
8 I go east, but he is not there.
I go west, but I cannot find him.
9 I do not see him in the north, for he is hidden.
I look to the south, but he is concealed.

DEEP PURPOSES 23:8-14

Job wavered back and forth, first proclaiming loyalty to God and then expressing his terror of him. His friends' words and his own suspicions undermined his confidence in God. When hard times come, we sometimes blame God or think he's punishing us. But God's purposes go deeper than our ability to grasp what's really happening. While that might sound like a pat answer, it is the same answer God gave Job in chapters 38–41. Often we cannot know, or are not meant to know, why God allows us to suffer until later. ■

10 "But he knows where I am going.
And when he tests me, I will come out as pure
as gold.
11 For I have stayed on God's paths;
I have followed his ways and not turned aside.
12 I have not departed from his commands,
but have treasured his words more than
daily food.
13 But once he has made his decision, who can change
his mind?
Whatever he wants to do, he does.
14 So he will do to me whatever he has planned.
He controls my destiny.

15 No wonder I am so terrified in his presence.
When I think of it, terror grips me.
16 God has made me sick at heart;
the Almighty has terrified me.
17 Darkness is all around me;
thick, impenetrable darkness is everywhere.

24 JOB ASKS WHY THE WICKED ARE NOT PUNISHED

1 "Why doesn't the Almighty bring the wicked
to judgment?
Why must the godly wait for him in vain?
2 Evil people steal land by moving the boundary
markers.
They steal livestock and put them in their
own pastures.
3 They take the orphan's donkey
and demand the widow's ox as security for a loan.
4 The poor are pushed off the path;
the needy must hide together for safety.
5 Like wild donkeys in the wilderness,
the poor must spend all their time looking
for food,
searching even in the desert for food for
their children.
6 They harvest a field they do not own,
and they glean in the vineyards of the wicked.
7 All night they lie naked in the cold,
without clothing or covering.
8 They are soaked by mountain showers,
and they huddle against the rocks for want
of a home.

9 "The wicked snatch a widow's child from her breast,
taking the baby as security for a loan.
10 The poor must go about naked, without any clothing.
They harvest food for others while they themselves
are starving.
11 They press out olive oil without being allowed
to taste it,
and they tread in the winepress as they suffer
from thirst.
12 The groans of the dying rise from the city,
and the wounded cry for help,
yet God ignores their moaning.

13 "Wicked people rebel against the light.
They refuse to acknowledge its ways
or stay in its paths.
14 The murderer rises in the early dawn
to kill the poor and needy;
at night he is a thief.
15 The adulterer waits for the twilight,
saying, 'No one will see me then.'
He hides his face so no one will know him.
16 Thieves break into houses at night
and sleep in the daytime.
They are not acquainted with the light.
17 The black night is their morning.
They ally themselves with the terrors of the darkness.

18 "But they disappear like foam down a river.
Everything they own is cursed,
and they are afraid to enter their own vineyards.
19 The grave* consumes sinners
just as drought and heat consume snow.
20 Their own mothers will forget them.
Maggots will find them sweet to eat.
No one will remember them.
Wicked people are broken like a tree in the storm.
21 They cheat the woman who has no son to help her.
They refuse to help the needy widow.

22 "God, in his power, drags away the rich.
They may rise high, but they have no assurance
of life.
23 They may be allowed to live in security,
but God is always watching them.
24 And though they are great now,
in a moment they will be gone like all others,
cut off like heads of grain.
25 Can anyone claim otherwise?
Who can prove me wrong?"

25 BILDAD'S THIRD RESPONSE TO JOB

Then Bildad the Shuhite replied:

2 "God is powerful and dreadful.
He enforces peace in the heavens.
3 Who is able to count his heavenly army?
Doesn't his light shine on all the earth?
4 How can a mortal be innocent before God?
Can anyone born of a woman be pure?
5 God is more glorious than the moon;
he shines brighter than the stars.
6 In comparison, people are maggots;
we mortals are mere worms."

GREATER RESULTS 26:1-4

With great sarcasm, Job attacked his friends' comments. Their explanations failed to bring any relief because they were unable to turn their knowledge into helpful counsel. When dealing with people, loving and understanding them is more important than analyzing them or giving advice. Compassion produces greater results than criticism or blame. ■

26 JOB'S NINTH SPEECH: A RESPONSE TO BILDAD

Then Job spoke again:

2 "How you have helped the powerless!
How you have saved the weak!

24:19 Hebrew *Sheol.*

3 How you have enlightened my stupidity!
What wise advice you have offered!
4 Where have you gotten all these wise sayings?
Whose spirit speaks through you?

5 "The dead tremble—
those who live beneath the waters.
6 The underworld* is naked in God's presence.
The place of destruction* is uncovered.
7 God stretches the northern sky over empty space
and hangs the earth on nothing.
8 He wraps the rain in his thick clouds,
and the clouds don't burst with the weight.
9 He covers the face of the moon,*
shrouding it with his clouds.
10 He created the horizon when he separated
the waters;
he set the boundary between day and night.
11 The foundations of heaven tremble;
they shudder at his rebuke.
12 By his power the sea grew calm.
By his skill he crushed the great sea monster.*
13 His Spirit made the heavens beautiful,
and his power pierced the gliding serpent.
14 These are just the beginning of all that he does,
merely a whisper of his power.
Who, then, can comprehend the thunder
of his power?"

CLEAR CONSCIENCE 27:1-6

In the face of his friends' accusations, Job declared that his conscience was clear. Only right living can cause a person to have a clear conscience. Like Job, we can't claim perfect lives, but we *can* claim forgiven lives. When we confess our wrongs to God, we are forgiven and can live our lives with clear consciences (1 John 1:9). ■

27 JOB'S FINAL SPEECH

Job continued speaking:

2 "I vow by the living God, who has taken away
my rights,
by the Almighty who has embittered my soul—
3 As long as I live,
while I have breath from God,
4 my lips will speak no evil,
and my tongue will speak no lies.
5 I will never concede that you are right;
I will defend my integrity until I die.
6 I will maintain my innocence without wavering.
My conscience is clear for as long as I live.

7 "May my enemy be punished like the wicked,
my adversary like those who do evil.
8 For what hope do the godless have when God
cuts them off
and takes away their life?
9 Will God listen to their cry
when trouble comes upon them?
10 Can they take delight in the Almighty?
Can they call to God at any time?
11 I will teach you about God's power.
I will not conceal anything concerning
the Almighty.
12 But you have seen all this,
yet you say all these useless things to me.

13 "This is what the wicked will receive from God;
this is their inheritance from the Almighty.
14 They may have many children,
but the children will die in war or starve to death.
15 Those who survive will die of a plague,
and not even their widows will mourn them.

16 "Evil people may have piles of money
and may store away mounds of clothing.
17 But the righteous will wear that clothing,
and the innocent will divide that money.
18 The wicked build houses as fragile as a spider's web,*
as flimsy as a shelter made of branches.
19 The wicked go to bed rich
but wake to find that all their wealth is gone.
20 Terror overwhelms them like a flood,
and they are blown away in the storms of the night.
21 The east wind carries them away, and they are gone.
It sweeps them away.
22 It whirls down on them without mercy.
They struggle to flee from its power.
23 But everyone jeers at them
and mocks them.

28 JOB SPEAKS OF WISDOM AND UNDERSTANDING

1 "People know where to mine silver
and how to refine gold.
2 They know where to dig iron from the earth
and how to smelt copper from rock.
3 They know how to shine light in the darkness
and explore the farthest regions of the earth
as they search in the dark for ore.
4 They sink a mine shaft into the earth
far from where anyone lives.
They descend on ropes, swinging back and forth.
5 Food is grown on the earth above,
but down below, the earth is melted as by fire.
6 Here the rocks contain precious lapis lazuli,
and the dust contains gold.
7 These are treasures no bird of prey can see,
no falcon's eye observe.
8 No wild animal has walked upon these treasures;
no lion has ever set his paw there.

26:6a Hebrew *Sheol.* **26:6b** Hebrew *Abaddon.* **26:9** Or *covers his throne.* **26:12** Hebrew *Rahab,* the name of a mythical sea monster that represents chaos in ancient literature. **27:18** As in Greek and Syriac versions (see also 8:14); Hebrew reads *a moth.*

9 People know how to tear apart flinty rocks
and overturn the roots of mountains.
10 They cut tunnels in the rocks
and uncover precious stones.
11 They dam up the trickling streams
and bring to light the hidden treasures.

12 "But do people know where to find wisdom?
Where can they find understanding?
13 No one knows where to find it,
for it is not found among the living.
14 'It is not here,' says the ocean.
'Nor is it here,' says the sea.
15 It cannot be bought with gold.
It cannot be purchased with silver.
16 It's worth more than all the gold of Ophir,
greater than precious onyx or lapis lazuli.
17 Wisdom is more valuable than gold and crystal.
It cannot be purchased with jewels mounted
in fine gold.
18 Coral and jasper are worthless in trying to get it.
The price of wisdom is far above rubies.
19 Precious peridot from Ethiopia* cannot be
exchanged for it.
It's worth more than the purest gold.

WISE WITHOUT GOD? 28:1-28

Job knew that the search for wisdom began and ended with God. Even the greatest scientists, on their own, are at a loss to discover wisdom for their daily lives. God is the true source of wisdom. True wisdom is having God's perspective on life. Do you have his perspective? ■

20 "But do people know where to find wisdom?
Where can they find understanding?
21 It is hidden from the eyes of all humanity.
Even the sharp-eyed birds in the sky cannot
discover it.
22 Destruction* and Death say,
'We've heard only rumors of where wisdom
can be found.'

23 "God alone understands the way to wisdom;
he knows where it can be found,
24 for he looks throughout the whole earth
and sees everything under the heavens.
25 He decided how hard the winds should blow
and how much rain should fall.
26 He made the laws for the rain
and laid out a path for the lightning.
27 Then he saw wisdom and evaluated it.
He set it in place and examined it thoroughly.
28 And this is what he says to all humanity:
'The fear of the Lord is true wisdom;
to forsake evil is real understanding.'"

29 JOB SPEAKS OF HIS FORMER BLESSINGS

Job continued speaking:

2 "I long for the years gone by
when God took care of me,
3 when he lit up the way before me
and I walked safely through the darkness.
4 When I was in my prime,
God's friendship was felt in my home.
5 The Almighty was still with me,
and my children were around me.
6 My cows produced milk in abundance,
and my groves poured out streams of olive oil.

7 "Those were the days when I went to the city gate
and took my place among the honored leaders.
8 The young stepped aside when they saw me,
and even the aged rose in respect at my coming.
9 The princes stood in silence
and put their hands over their mouths.
10 The highest officials of the city stood quietly,
holding their tongues in respect.

11 "All who heard me praised me.
All who saw me spoke well of me.
12 For I assisted the poor in their need
and the orphans who required help.
13 I helped those without hope, and they blessed me.
And I caused the widows' hearts to sing for joy.
14 Everything I did was honest.
Righteousness covered me like a robe,
and I wore justice like a turban.
15 I served as eyes for the blind
and feet for the lame.
16 I was a father to the poor
and assisted strangers who needed help.
17 I broke the jaws of godless oppressors
and plucked their victims from their teeth.

18 "I thought, 'Surely I will die surrounded by my family
after a long, good life.*
19 For I am like a tree whose roots reach the water,
whose branches are refreshed with the dew.
20 New honors are constantly bestowed on me,
and my strength is continually renewed.'

21 "Everyone listened to my advice.
They were silent as they waited for me to speak.
22 And after I spoke, they had nothing to add,
for my counsel satisfied them.
23 They longed for me to speak as people long for rain.
They drank my words like a refreshing spring rain.
24 When they were discouraged, I smiled at them.
My look of approval was precious to them.
25 Like a chief, I told them what to do.
I lived like a king among his troops
and comforted those who mourned.

28:19 Hebrew *from Cush.* **28:22** Hebrew *Abaddon.* **29:18** Hebrew *after I have counted my days like sand.*

30 JOB SPEAKS OF HIS ANGUISH

1 "But now I am mocked by people younger than I,
by young men whose fathers are not worthy to
run with my sheepdogs.
2 A lot of good they are to me—
those worn-out wretches!
3 They are gaunt with hunger
and flee to the deserts,
to desolate and gloomy wastelands.
4 They pluck wild greens from among the bushes
and eat from the roots of broom trees.
5 They are driven from human society,
and people shout at them as if they were thieves.
6 So now they live in frightening ravines,
in caves and among the rocks.
7 They sound like animals howling among the bushes,
huddled together beneath the nettles.
8 They are nameless fools,
outcasts from society.

9 "And now they mock me with vulgar songs!
They taunt me!
10 They despise me and won't come near me,
except to spit in my face.
11 For God has cut my bowstring.
He has humbled me,
so they have thrown off all restraint.
12 These outcasts oppose me to my face.
They send me sprawling
and lay traps in my path.
13 They block my road
and do everything they can to destroy me.
They know I have no one to help me.
14 They come at me from all directions.
They jump on me when I am down.
15 I live in terror now.
My honor has blown away in the wind,
and my prosperity has vanished like a cloud.

16 "And now my life seeps away.
Depression haunts my days.
17 At night my bones are filled with pain,
which gnaws at me relentlessly.
18 With a strong hand, God grabs my shirt.
He grips me by the collar of my coat.
19 He has thrown me into the mud.
I'm nothing more than dust and ashes.

20 "I cry to you, O God, but you don't answer.
I stand before you, but you don't even look.
21 You have become cruel toward me.
You use your power to persecute me.
22 You throw me into the whirlwind
and destroy me in the storm.
23 And I know you are sending me to my death—
the destination of all who live.

24 "Surely no one would turn against the needy
when they cry for help in their trouble.
25 Did I not weep for those in trouble?
Was I not deeply grieved for the needy?
26 So I looked for good, but evil came instead.
I waited for the light, but darkness fell.
27 My heart is troubled and restless.
Days of suffering torment me.
28 I walk in gloom, without sunlight.
I stand in the public square and cry for help.
29 Instead, I am considered a brother to jackals
and a companion to owls.
30 My skin has turned dark,
and my bones burn with fever.
31 My harp plays sad music,
and my flute accompanies those who weep.

31 JOB'S FINAL PROTEST OF INNOCENCE

1 "I made a covenant with my eyes
not to look with lust at a young woman.
2 For what has God above chosen for us?
What is our inheritance from the Almighty
on high?
3 Isn't it calamity for the wicked
and misfortune for those who do evil?
4 Doesn't he see everything I do
and every step I take?

5 "Have I lied to anyone
or deceived anyone?
6 Let God weigh me on the scales of justice,
for he knows my integrity.
7 If I have strayed from his pathway,
or if my heart has lusted for what my eyes
have seen,
or if I am guilty of any other sin,
8 then let someone else eat the crops I have planted.
Let all that I have planted be uprooted.

9 "If my heart has been seduced by a woman,
or if I have lusted for my neighbor's wife,
10 then let my wife belong to* another man;
let other men sleep with her.
11 For lust is a shameful sin,
a crime that should be punished.
12 It is a fire that burns all the way to hell.*
It would wipe out everything I own.

13 "If I have been unfair to my male or female servants
when they brought their complaints to me,
14 how could I face God?
What could I say when he questioned me?
15 For God created both me and my servants.
He created us both in the womb.

16 "Have I refused to help the poor,
or crushed the hopes of widows?

31:10 Hebrew *grind for.* **31:12** Hebrew *to Abaddon.*

PORNOGRAPHY

Jared's problem started three years ago while surfing the Net with some friends. As they looked for a game site, they suddenly stumbled across a porn site. Jared was 12.

Pretty soon, Jared and his friends had moved on to downloading pictures. None of their parents suspected a thing, since one of Jared's friends had his own laptop—and no firewalls.

After a while, Jared's friends moved on to other things. But by then, Jared was hooked on porn. At first he didn't think much about it. *I'm not really hurting anyone*, he decided. *It's just a little harmless fun.* Yet he kept wanting to see more and more.

Not only did Jared's obsession bring him great frustration (because pornography is such a lie), but it also caused him unbelievable guilt. He couldn't even glance at a woman without mentally undressing her. And no matter how hard he tried, he couldn't get the dirty images out of his mind. Not only that, Christ's warning about lust (Matt 5:28) haunted him.

Finally he realized, *I've got a problem. But I can't handle it on my own.* After talking with his parents, he decided to talk to Jeff, his youth leader. After praying with him, Jeff got Jared into a good Bible study. Jeff also helped Jared to find a prayer partner who would pray with him each week and hold him accountable for his Internet visits.

By the way, Jared doesn't surf the Net much any more.

Pornography addiction is one hard habit to break. Check out the insight in Job 31:1. Could you claim this promise for yourself?

17 Have I been stingy with my food
and refused to share it with orphans?
18 No, from childhood I have cared for orphans
like a father,
and all my life I have cared for widows.
19 Whenever I saw the homeless without clothes
and the needy with nothing to wear,
20 did they not praise me
for providing wool clothing to keep them warm?

21 "If I raised my hand against an orphan,
knowing the judges would take my side,
22 then let my shoulder be wrenched out of place!
Let my arm be torn from its socket!
23 That would be better than facing God's judgment.
For if the majesty of God opposes me, what hope
is there?

24 "Have I put my trust in money
or felt secure because of my gold?
25 Have I gloated about my wealth
and all that I own?
26 "Have I looked at the sun shining in the skies,
or the moon walking down its silver pathway,
27 and been secretly enticed in my heart
to throw kisses at them in worship?
28 If so, I should be punished by the judges,
for it would mean I had denied the God of heaven.

29 "Have I ever rejoiced when disaster struck my
enemies,
or become excited when harm came their way?
30 No, I have never sinned by cursing anyone
or by asking for revenge.

31 "My servants have never said,
'He let others go hungry.'
32 I have never turned away a stranger
but have opened my doors to everyone.

33 "Have I tried to hide my sins like other people do,
concealing my guilt in my heart?
34 Have I feared the crowd
or the contempt of the masses,
so that I kept quiet and stayed indoors?

35 "If only someone would listen to me!
Look, I will sign my name to my defense.
Let the Almighty answer me.
Let my accuser write out the charges against me.
36 I would face the accusation proudly.
I would wear it like a crown.
37 For I would tell him exactly what I have done.
I would come before him like a prince.

38 "If my land accuses me
and all its furrows cry out together,
39 or if I have stolen its crops
or murdered its owners,
40 then let thistles grow on that land instead of wheat,
and weeds instead of barley."

Job's words are ended.

32 ELIHU RESPONDS TO JOB'S FRIENDS

Job's three friends refused to reply further to him because he kept insisting on his innocence.
2Then Elihu son of Barakel the Buzite, of the clan of
Ram, became angry. He was angry because Job refused to
admit that he had sinned and that God was right in punishing him. 3He was also angry with Job's three friends,
for they made God* appear to be wrong by their inability
to answer Job's arguments. 4Elihu had waited for the others to speak to Job because they were older than he. 5But
when he saw that they had no further reply, he spoke out
angrily. 6Elihu son of Barakel the Buzite said,

"I am young and you are old,
so I held back from telling you what I think.

32:3 As in ancient Hebrew scribal tradition; the Masoretic Text reads *Job*.

7 I thought, 'Those who are older should speak,
for wisdom comes with age.'
8 But there is a spirit* within people,
the breath of the Almighty within them,
that makes them intelligent.
9 Sometimes the elders are not wise.
Sometimes the aged do not understand justice.
10 So listen to me,
and let me tell you what I think.

11 "I have waited all this time,
listening very carefully to your arguments,
listening to you grope for words.
12 I have listened,
but not one of you has refuted Job
or answered his arguments.
13 And don't tell me, 'He is too wise for us.
Only God can convince him.'
14 If Job had been arguing with me,
I would not answer with your kind of logic!
15 You sit there baffled,
with nothing more to say.
16 Should I continue to wait, now that you are silent?
Must I also remain silent?
17 No, I will say my piece.
I will speak my mind.
18 For I am full of pent-up words,
and the spirit within me urges me on.
19 I am like a cask of wine without a vent,
like a new wineskin ready to burst!
20 I must speak to find relief,
so let me give my answers.
21 I won't play favorites
or try to flatter anyone.
22 For if I tried flattery,
my Creator would soon destroy me.

33 ELIHU PRESENTS HIS CASE AGAINST JOB

1 "Listen to my words, Job;
pay attention to what I have to say.
2 Now that I have begun to speak,
let me continue.
3 I speak with all sincerity;
I speak the truth.
4 For the Spirit of God has made me,
and the breath of the Almighty gives me life.
5 Answer me, if you can;
make your case and take your stand.
6 Look, you and I both belong to God.
I, too, was formed from clay.
7 So you don't need to be afraid of me.
I won't come down hard on you.

8 "You have spoken in my hearing,
and I have heard your very words.
9 You said, 'I am pure; I am without sin;
I am innocent; I have no guilt.
10 God is picking a quarrel with me,
and he considers me his enemy.
11 He puts my feet in the stocks
and watches my every move.'

12 "But you are wrong, and I will show you why.
For God is greater than any human being.
13 So why are you bringing a charge against him?
Why say he does not respond to people's
complaints?
14 For God speaks again and again,
though people do not recognize it.
15 He speaks in dreams, in visions of the night,
when deep sleep falls on people
as they lie in their beds.
16 He whispers in their ears
and terrifies them with warnings.
17 He makes them turn from doing wrong;
he keeps them from pride.
18 He protects them from the grave,
from crossing over the river of death.

19 "Or God disciplines people with pain
on their sickbeds,
with ceaseless aching in their bones.
20 They lose their appetite
for even the most delicious food.
21 Their flesh wastes away,
and their bones stick out.
22 They are at death's door;
the angels of death wait for them.

23 "But if an angel from heaven appears—
a special messenger to intercede for a person
and declare that he is upright—
24 he will be gracious and say,
'Rescue him from the grave,
for I have found a ransom for his life.'
25 Then his body will become as healthy as a child's,
firm and youthful again.
26 When he prays to God,
he will be accepted.
And God will receive him with joy
and restore him to good standing.
27 He will declare to his friends,
'I sinned and twisted the truth,
but it was not worth it.*
28 God rescued me from the grave,
and now my life is filled with light.'

29 "Yes, God does these things
again and again for people.
30 He rescues them from the grave
so they may enjoy the light of life.
31 Mark this well, Job. Listen to me,
for I have more to say.
32 But if you have anything to say, go ahead.
Speak, for I am anxious to see you justified.

32:8 Or *Spirit;* also in 32:18. **33:27** Greek version reads *but he* [God] *did not punish me as my sin deserved.*

33 But if not, then listen to me.
Keep silent and I will teach you wisdom!"

34 ELIHU ACCUSES JOB OF ARROGANCE

Then Elihu said:

2 "Listen to me, you wise men.
Pay attention, you who have knowledge.
3 Job said, 'The ear tests the words it hears
just as the mouth distinguishes between foods.'
4 So let us discern for ourselves what is right;
let us learn together what is good.
5 For Job also said, 'I am innocent,
but God has taken away my rights.
6 I am innocent, but they call me a liar.
My suffering is incurable, though I have
not sinned.'

7 "Tell me, has there ever been a man like Job,
with his thirst for irreverent talk?
8 He chooses evil people as companions.
He spends his time with wicked men.
9 He has even said, 'Why waste time
trying to please God?'

10 "Listen to me, you who have understanding.
Everyone knows that God doesn't sin!
The Almighty can do no wrong.
11 He repays people according to their deeds.
He treats people as they deserve.
12 Truly, God will not do wrong.
The Almighty will not twist justice.
13 Did someone else put the world in his care?
Who set the whole world in place?
14 If God were to take back his spirit
and withdraw his breath,
15 all life would cease,
and humanity would turn again to dust.

16 "Now listen to me if you are wise.
Pay attention to what I say.
17 Could God govern if he hated justice?
Are you going to condemn the almighty judge?
18 For he says to kings, 'You are wicked,'
and to nobles, 'You are unjust.'
19 He doesn't care how great a person may be,
and he pays no more attention to the rich than
to the poor.
He made them all.
20 In a moment they die.
In the middle of the night they pass away;
the mighty are removed without human hand.

21 "For God watches how people live;
he sees everything they do.
22 No darkness is thick enough
to hide the wicked from his eyes.
23 We don't set the time
when we will come before God in judgment.
24 He brings the mighty to ruin without asking anyone,
and he sets up others in their place.
25 He knows what they do,
and in the night he overturns and destroys them.
26 He strikes them down because they are wicked,
doing it openly for all to see.
27 For they turned away from following him.
They have no respect for any of his ways.
28 They cause the poor to cry out, catching God's
attention.
He hears the cries of the needy.
29 But if he chooses to remain quiet,
who can criticize him?
When he hides his face, no one can find him,
whether an individual or a nation.
30 He prevents the godless from ruling
so they cannot be a snare to the people.

31 "Why don't people say to God, 'I have sinned,
but I will sin no more'?
32 Or 'I don't know what evil I have done—tell me.
If I have done wrong, I will stop at once'?

33 "Must God tailor his justice to your demands?
But you have rejected him!
The choice is yours, not mine.
Go ahead, share your wisdom with us.
34 After all, bright people will tell me,
and wise people will hear me say,
35 'Job speaks out of ignorance;
his words lack insight.'
36 Job, you deserve the maximum penalty
for the wicked way you have talked.
37 For you have added rebellion to your sin;
you show no respect,
and you speak many angry words against God."

35 ELIHU REMINDS JOB OF GOD'S JUSTICE

Then Elihu said:

2 "Do you think it is right for you to claim,
'I am righteous before God'?
3 For you also ask, 'What's in it for me?
What's the use of living a righteous life?'

4 "I will answer you
and all your friends, too.
5 Look up into the sky,
and see the clouds high above you.
6 If you sin, how does that affect God?
Even if you sin again and again,
what effect will it have on him?
7 If you are good, is this some great gift to him?
What could you possibly give him?
8 No, your sins affect only people like yourself,
and your good deeds also affect only humans.

9 "People cry out when they are oppressed.
They groan beneath the power of the mighty.
10 Yet they don't ask, 'Where is God my Creator,
the one who gives songs in the night?
11 Where is the one who makes us smarter than
the animals
and wiser than the birds of the sky?'
12 And when they cry out, God does not answer
because of their pride.
13 But it is wrong to say God doesn't listen,
to say the Almighty isn't concerned.
14 You say you can't see him,
but he will bring justice if you will only wait.*
15 You say he does not respond to sinners with anger
and is not greatly concerned about wickedness.*
16 But you are talking nonsense, Job.
You have spoken like a fool."

36

Elihu continued speaking:

2 "Let me go on, and I will show you the truth.
For I have not finished defending God!
3 I will present profound arguments
for the righteousness of my Creator.
4 I am telling you nothing but the truth,
for I am a man of great knowledge.

5 "God is mighty, but he does not despise anyone!
He is mighty in both power and
understanding.
6 He does not let the wicked live
but gives justice to the afflicted.
7 He never takes his eyes off the innocent,
but he sets them on thrones with kings
and exalts them forever.
8 If they are bound in chains
and caught up in a web of trouble,
9 he shows them the reason.
He shows them their sins of pride.
10 He gets their attention
and commands that they turn from evil.

11 "If they listen and obey God,
they will be blessed with prosperity throughout
their lives.
All their years will be pleasant.
12 But if they refuse to listen to him,
they will be killed by the sword*
and die from lack of understanding.
13 For the godless are full of resentment.
Even when he punishes them,
they refuse to cry out to him for help.
14 They die when they are young,
after wasting their lives in immoral living.
15 But by means of their suffering, he rescues
those who suffer.
For he gets their attention through adversity.

16 "God is leading you away from danger, Job,
to a place free from distress.
He is setting your table with the best food.
17 But you are obsessed with whether the godless
will be judged.
Don't worry, judgment and justice will be upheld.
18 But watch out, or you may be seduced by wealth.*
Don't let yourself be bribed into sin.
19 Could all your wealth*
or all your mighty efforts
keep you from distress?
20 Do not long for the cover of night,
for that is when people will be destroyed.*
21 Be on guard! Turn back from evil,
for God sent this suffering
to keep you from a life of evil.

ELIHU REMINDS JOB OF GOD'S POWER

22 "Look, God is all-powerful.
Who is a teacher like him?
23 No one can tell him what to do,
or say to him, 'You have done wrong.'
24 Instead, glorify his mighty works,
singing songs of praise.
25 Everyone has seen these things,
though only from a distance.

NEVER ENOUGH KNOWLEDGE 36:26

One theme in the poetic literature of the Bible is that we cannot know God completely. This doesn't mean that we can't have any knowledge about God, because the Bible is full of details about who God is, how we can know him, and how we can have an eternal relationship with him. What it means is that we can never know enough to answer all of life's questions (Eccles 3:11), to predict our own future, or to manipulate God for our own ends. Life sometimes inspires more questions than answers. But God provides fresh insights into life's dilemmas. (See 37:19-24.) ■

26 "Look, God is greater than we can understand.
His years cannot be counted.
27 He draws up the water vapor
and then distills it into rain.
28 The rain pours down from the clouds,
and everyone benefits.
29 Who can understand the spreading of the clouds
and the thunder that rolls forth from heaven?
30 See how he spreads the lightning around him
and how it lights up the depths of the sea.

35:13-14 These verses can also be translated as follows: 13*Indeed, God doesn't listen to their empty plea; / the Almighty is not concerned. /* 14*How much less will he listen when you say you don't see him, / and that your case is before him and you're waiting for justice.* **35:15** As in Greek and Latin versions; the meaning of this Hebrew word is uncertain. **36:12** Or *they will cross the river* [of death]. **36:18** Or *But don't let your anger lead you to mockery.* **36:19** Or *Could all your cries for help.* **36:16-20** The meaning of the Hebrew in this passage is uncertain.

31 By these mighty acts he nourishes* the people,
giving them food in abundance.
32 He fills his hands with lightning bolts
and hurls each at its target.
33 The thunder announces his presence;
the storm announces his indignant anger.*

37

1 "My heart pounds as I think of this.
It trembles within me.
2 Listen carefully to the thunder of God's voice
as it rolls from his mouth.
3 It rolls across the heavens,
and his lightning flashes in every direction.
4 Then comes the roaring of the thunder—
the tremendous voice of his majesty.
He does not restrain it when he speaks.
5 God's voice is glorious in the thunder.
We can't even imagine the greatness of his power.

6 "He directs the snow to fall on the earth
and tells the rain to pour down.
7 Then everyone stops working
so they can watch his power.
8 The wild animals take cover
and stay inside their dens.
9 The stormy wind comes from its chamber,
and the driving winds bring the cold.
10 God's breath sends the ice,
freezing wide expanses of water.
11 He loads the clouds with moisture,
and they flash with his lightning.
12 The clouds churn about at his direction.
They do whatever he commands throughout
the earth.
13 He makes these things happen either to punish
people
or to show his unfailing love.

14 "Pay attention to this, Job.
Stop and consider the wonderful miracles
of God!
15 Do you know how God controls the storm
and causes the lightning to flash from his clouds?
16 Do you understand how he moves the clouds
with wonderful perfection and skill?
17 When you are sweltering in your clothes
and the south wind dies down and everything
is still,
18 he makes the skies reflect the heat like
a bronze mirror.
Can you do that?

19 "So teach the rest of us what to say to God.
We are too ignorant to make our own arguments.
20 Should God be notified that I want to speak?
Can people even speak when they are confused?*
21 We cannot look at the sun,
for it shines brightly in the sky
when the wind clears away the clouds.
22 So also, golden splendor comes from the mountain
of God.*
He is clothed in dazzling splendor.
23 We cannot imagine the power of the Almighty;
but even though he is just and righteous,
he does not destroy us.
24 No wonder people everywhere fear him.
All who are wise show him reverence."

38

THE LORD CHALLENGES JOB

Then the LORD answered Job from the whirlwind:

2 "Who is this that questions my wisdom
with such ignorant words?
3 Brace yourself like a man,
because I have some questions for you,
and you must answer them.

ALL ABOUT GOD 38:1

God didn't answer any of Job's questions. They weren't the heart of the issue. Instead, God used Job's ignorance of the earth's natural order to reveal his ignorance of God's moral order. If Job didn't understand the workings of God's physical creation, how could he possibly understand God's mind and character? Only God has that understanding. Our only option is to submit to his authority and care. ■

4 "Where were you when I laid the foundations
of the earth?
Tell me, if you know so much.
5 Who determined its dimensions
and stretched out the surveying line?
6 What supports its foundations,
and who laid its cornerstone
7 as the morning stars sang together
and all the angels* shouted for joy?

8 "Who kept the sea inside its boundaries
as it burst from the womb,
9 and as I clothed it with clouds
and wrapped it in thick darkness?
10 For I locked it behind barred gates,
limiting its shores.
11 I said, 'This far and no farther will you come.
Here your proud waves must stop!'

12 "Have you ever commanded the morning
to appear
and caused the dawn to rise in the east?

36:31 Or *he governs.* 36:33 Or *even the cattle know when a storm is coming.* The meaning of the Hebrew is uncertain. 37:20 Or *speak without being swallowed up?* 37:22 Or *from the north;* or *from the abode.* 38:7 Hebrew *the sons of God.*

13 Have you made daylight spread to the ends
of the earth,
to bring an end to the night's wickedness?
14 As the light approaches,
the earth takes shape like clay pressed beneath
a seal;
it is robed in brilliant colors.*
15 The light disturbs the wicked
and stops the arm that is raised in violence.

16 "Have you explored the springs from which
the seas come?
Have you explored their depths?
17 Do you know where the gates of death are located?
Have you seen the gates of utter gloom?
18 Do you realize the extent of the earth?
Tell me about it if you know!

19 "Where does light come from,
and where does darkness go?
20 Can you take each to its home?
Do you know how to get there?
21 But of course you know all this!
For you were born before it was all created,
and you are so very experienced!

22 "Have you visited the storehouses of the snow
or seen the storehouses of hail?
23 (I have reserved them as weapons for the time
of trouble,
for the day of battle and war.)
24 Where is the path to the source of light?
Where is the home of the east wind?

25 "Who created a channel for the torrents of rain?
Who laid out the path for the lightning?
26 Who makes the rain fall on barren land,
in a desert where no one lives?
27 Who sends rain to satisfy the parched ground
and make the tender grass spring up?

28 "Does the rain have a father?
Who gives birth to the dew?
29 Who is the mother of the ice?
Who gives birth to the frost from the heavens?
30 For the water turns to ice as hard as rock,
and the surface of the water freezes.

31 "Can you direct the movement of the stars—
binding the cluster of the Pleiades
or loosening the cords of Orion?
32 Can you direct the sequence of the seasons
or guide the Bear with her cubs across the heavens?
33 Do you know the laws of the universe?
Can you use them to regulate the earth?

34 "Can you shout to the clouds
and make it rain?

38:14 Or *its features stand out like folds in a robe.*

35 Can you make lightning appear
and cause it to strike as you direct?
36 Who gives intuition to the heart
and instinct to the mind?
37 Who is wise enough to count all the clouds?
Who can tilt the water jars of heaven
38 when the parched ground is dry
and the soil has hardened into clods?

39 "Can you stalk prey for a lioness
and satisfy the young lions' appetites
40 as they lie in their dens
or crouch in the thicket?
41 Who provides food for the ravens
when their young cry out to God
and wander about in hunger?

39

THE LORD'S CHALLENGE CONTINUES

1 "Do you know when the wild goats give birth?
Have you watched as deer are born in the wild?
2 Do you know how many months they carry
their young?
Are you aware of the time of their delivery?
3 They crouch down to give birth to their young
and deliver their offspring.
4 Their young grow up in the open fields,
then leave home and never return.

5 "Who gives the wild donkey its freedom?
Who untied its ropes?
6 I have placed it in the wilderness;
its home is the wasteland.
7 It hates the noise of the city
and has no driver to shout at it.
8 The mountains are its pastureland,
where it searches for every blade of grass.

9 "Will the wild ox consent to being tamed?
Will it spend the night in your stall?
10 Can you hitch a wild ox to a plow?
Will it plow a field for you?
11 Given its strength, can you trust it?
Can you leave and trust the ox to do your work?
12 Can you rely on it to bring home your grain
and deliver it to your threshing floor?

13 "The ostrich flaps her wings grandly,
but they are no match for the feathers of the stork.
14 She lays her eggs on top of the earth,
letting them be warmed in the dust.
15 She doesn't worry that a foot might crush them
or a wild animal might destroy them.
16 She is harsh toward her young,
as if they were not her own.
She doesn't care if they die.
17 For God has deprived her of wisdom.
He has given her no understanding.

[18] But whenever she jumps up to run,
she passes the swiftest horse with its rider.

[19] "Have you given the horse its strength
or clothed its neck with a flowing mane?
[20] Did you give it the ability to leap like a locust?
Its majestic snorting is terrifying!
[21] It paws the earth and rejoices in its strength
when it charges out to battle.
[22] It laughs at fear and is unafraid.
It does not run from the sword.
[23] The arrows rattle against it,
and the spear and javelin flash.
[24] It paws the ground fiercely
and rushes forward into battle when
the ram's horn blows.
[25] It snorts at the sound of the horn.
It senses the battle in the distance.
It quivers at the captain's commands and
the noise of battle.

[26] "Is it your wisdom that makes the hawk soar
and spread its wings toward the south?
[27] Is it at your command that the eagle rises
to the heights to make its nest?
[28] It lives on the cliffs,
making its home on a distant, rocky crag.
[29] From there it hunts its prey,
keeping watch with piercing eyes.
[30] Its young gulp down blood.
Where there's a carcass, there you'll find it."

40

Then the LORD said to Job,

[2] "Do you still want to argue with the Almighty?
You are God's critic, but do you have the answers?"

JOB RESPONDS TO THE LORD

[3]Then Job replied to the LORD,

[4] "I am nothing—how could I ever find the answers?
I will cover my mouth with my hand.
[5] I have said too much already.
I have nothing more to say."

THE LORD CHALLENGES JOB AGAIN

[6]Then the LORD answered Job from the whirlwind:

[7] "Brace yourself like a man,
because I have some questions for you,
and you must answer them.

[8] "Will you discredit my justice
and condemn me just to prove you are right?
[9] Are you as strong as God?
Can you thunder with a voice like his?
[10] All right, put on your glory and splendor,
your honor and majesty.
[11] Give vent to your anger.
Let it overflow against the proud.
[12] Humiliate the proud with a glance;
walk on the wicked where they stand.
[13] Bury them in the dust.
Imprison them in the world of the dead.
[14] Then even I would praise you,
for your own strength would save you.

[15] "Take a look at Behemoth,*
which I made, just as I made you.
It eats grass like an ox.
[16] See its powerful loins
and the muscles of its belly.
[17] Its tail is as strong as a cedar.
The sinews of its thighs are knit
tightly together.
[18] Its bones are tubes of bronze.
Its limbs are bars of iron.
[19] It is a prime example of God's handiwork,
and only its Creator can threaten it.
[20] The mountains offer it their best food,
where all the wild animals play.
[21] It lies under the lotus plants,*
hidden by the reeds in the marsh.
[22] The lotus plants give it shade
among the willows beside the stream.
[23] It is not disturbed by the raging river,
not concerned when the swelling Jordan rushes
around it.
[24] No one can catch it off guard
or put a ring in its nose and lead it away.

ARGUING WITH GOD 40:1-5

Job realized the futility of arguing with God. In what ways do you argue with God? Do you demand answers when things don't go your way, when you get cut from a team, when someone close to you is ill or dies, when money is tight, when you fail, or when unexpected changes occur? The next time you are tempted to complain to God, consider how much he loves you and remember Job's reaction when he had his chance to speak. Are you willing to give God a chance to reveal his greater purposes for you? His plans may unfold over the course of your life and not at any given moment. ■

41

THE LORD'S CHALLENGE CONTINUES

[1]*"Can you catch Leviathan* with a hook
or put a noose around its jaw?
[2] Can you tie it with a rope through the nose
or pierce its jaw with a spike?

40:15 The identification of Behemoth is disputed, ranging from an earthly creature to a mythical sea monster in ancient literature. **40:21** Or *bramble bushes;* also in 40:22. **41:1a** Verses 41:1-8 are numbered 40:25-32 in Hebrew text. **41:1b** The identification of Leviathan is disputed, ranging from an earthly creature to a mythical sea monster in ancient literature.

3 Will it beg you for mercy
or implore you for pity?
4 Will it agree to work for you,
to be your slave for life?
5 Can you make it a pet like a bird,
or give it to your little girls to play with?
6 Will merchants try to buy it
to sell it in their shops?
7 Will its hide be hurt by spears
or its head by a harpoon?
8 If you lay a hand on it,
you will certainly remember the battle that follows.
You won't try that again!
9*No, it is useless to try to capture it.
The hunter who attempts it will be knocked down.
10 And since no one dares to disturb it,
who then can stand up to me?
11 Who has given me anything that I need to pay back?
Everything under heaven is mine.

12 "I want to emphasize Leviathan's limbs
and its enormous strength and graceful form.
13 Who can strip off its hide,
and who can penetrate its double layer of armor?*
14 Who could pry open its jaws?
For its teeth are terrible!
15 Its scales are like rows of shields
tightly sealed together.
16 They are so close together
that no air can get between them.
17 Each scale sticks tight to the next.
They interlock and cannot be penetrated.

18 "When it sneezes, it flashes light!
Its eyes are like the red of dawn.
19 Lightning leaps from its mouth;
flames of fire flash out.
20 Smoke streams from its nostrils
like steam from a pot heated over burning rushes.
21 Its breath would kindle coals,
for flames shoot from its mouth.

22 "The tremendous strength in Leviathan's neck
strikes terror wherever it goes.
23 Its flesh is hard and firm
and cannot be penetrated.
24 Its heart is hard as rock,
hard as a millstone.
25 When it rises, the mighty are afraid,
gripped by terror.
26 No sword can stop it,
no spear, dart, or javelin.
27 Iron is nothing but straw to that creature,
and bronze is like rotten wood.
28 Arrows cannot make it flee.
Stones shot from a sling are like bits of grass.
29 Clubs are like a blade of grass,
and it laughs at the swish of javelins.
30 Its belly is covered with scales as sharp as glass.
It plows up the ground as it drags through
the mud.

31 "Leviathan makes the water boil with its commotion.
It stirs the depths like a pot of ointment.
32 The water glistens in its wake,
making the sea look white.
33 Nothing on earth is its equal,
no other creature so fearless.
34 Of all the creatures, it is the proudest.
It is the king of beasts."

42 JOB RESPONDS TO THE LORD

Then Job replied to the LORD:

2 "I know that you can do anything,
and no one can stop you.
3 You asked, 'Who is this that questions my wisdom
with such ignorance?'
It is I—and I was talking about things I knew
nothing about,
things far too wonderful for me.
4 You said, 'Listen and I will speak!
I have some questions for you,
and you must answer them.'
5 I had only heard about you before,
but now I have seen you with my own eyes.
6 I take back everything I said,
and I sit in dust and ashes to show my repentance."

UNANSWERED QUESTIONS 42:1-6

Throughout the book, Job's friends demanded that he admit what he did wrong and ask for forgiveness. Although Job made things right with God, his repentance was not the kind called for by his friends. Instead, he repented of his attitude and acknowledged God's great power and perfect justice. Like Job, we can't know the reasons for everything that happens. Thus we often must choose between anger and trust. Will you trust God with your unanswered questions? ■

CONCLUSION: THE LORD BLESSES JOB

7After the LORD had finished speaking to Job, he said to
Eliphaz the Temanite: "I am angry with you and your
two friends, for you have not spoken accurately about
me, as my servant Job has. 8So take seven bulls and seven
rams and go to my servant Job and offer a burnt offering
for yourselves. My servant Job will pray for you, and I
will accept his prayer on your behalf. I will not treat you
as you deserve, for you have not spoken accurately
about me, as my servant Job has." 9So Eliphaz the Temanite, Bildad the Shuhite, and Zophar the Naamathite
did as the LORD commanded them, and the LORD accepted Job's prayer.

41:9 Verses 41:9-34 are numbered 41:1-26 in Hebrew text. **41:13** As in Greek version; Hebrew reads *its bridle?*

WILLING TO FORGIVE 42:7-10

After receiving much criticism, Job was still able to pray for his three friends. Forgiving someone who wrongly accused you of something you didn't do can be difficult, but Job did it. During New Testament times, Jesus advised his followers to offer forgiveness to those who wronged them. (See Matt 6:14-15; 18:35.) Are you willing? ■

10When Job prayed for his friends, the LORD restored
his fortunes. In fact, the LORD gave him twice as much
as before! 11Then all his brothers, sisters, and former
friends came and feasted with him in his home. And they
consoled him and comforted him because of all the trials
the LORD had brought against him. And each of them
brought him a gift of money* and a gold ring.
12So the LORD blessed Job in the second half of his life
even more than in the beginning. For now he had
14,000 sheep, 6,000 camels, 1,000 teams of oxen, and
1,000 female donkeys. 13He also gave Job seven more
sons and three more daughters. 14He named his first
daughter Jemimah, the second Keziah, and the third
Keren-happuch. 15In all the land no women were as
lovely as the daughters of Job. And their father put them
into his will along with their brothers.
16Job lived 140 years after that, living to see four generations of his children and grandchildren. 17Then he
died, an old man who had lived a long, full life.

42:11 Hebrew *a kesitah;* the value or weight of the kesitah is no longer known.

PSALMS

EMOTIONS. WE EXPERIENCE countless feelings every day, ranging from exuberant joy to deep grief. We feel pain, anger, confusion, or joy depending on what happens on any given day.

The book of Psalms is about emotions. Anger, confusion, joy, pain, humility, bewilderment, contentment—and all are directed toward God. God created us with emotions, and he knows they will be part of our walk with him.

Many people read the book of Psalms because of its honesty. Rather than ignoring the "negative" emotions or condemning them as sinful, the writers faced their feelings and continued to talk with God.

Psalms also is loved because of the clear picture of God it presents. Our emotions change constantly, but God is constant. While we fret, worry, and shout about injustice, God remains calm. When we come to him, embarrassed because of something we did wrong, he doesn't express surprise or anger. Psalms reminds us that God is exalted, the Creator and Ruler of the world, and worthy of worship.

How are you feeling today? Angry? Afraid? Frustrated? Or are you joyful, happy, and excited? Read Psalms and express yourself honestly to God.

stats

PURPOSE: To provide a collection of songs expressing praise, thanksgiving, and confession to God

AUTHORS: David wrote 73 psalms; Asaph wrote 12; the descendants of Korah wrote 10; Solomon wrote 2; Heman (with the descendants of Korah), Ethan, and Moses each wrote 1. Although 51 psalms are anonymous, the New Testament ascribes two of the anonymous psalms—Psalms 2 and 95—to David. (See Acts 4:25; Heb 4:7.)

DATE WRITTEN: Between the time of Moses (around 1440 B.C.) and the Babylonian captivity (586 B.C.)

SETTING: For the most part, the psalms were not intended to be narrations of historical events. However, they often parallel events in history, such as David's flight from Saul (Ps 18) and his sin with Bathsheba (Ps 51).

KEY PERSON: David

KEY PLACE: God's holy Temple

SPECIAL FEATURES: Although Psalms has a unified plan, each psalm can be read and understood alone. Psalms is probably the most widely read book of the Bible, because it is easy to relate to the writers' emotions.

KEY points

PRAISE
Psalms are songs of praise to God as our Creator, Savior, and provider. Reading Psalms can encourage us to praise him.

GOD'S POWER
God is all-powerful, and always in control of every situation. Believing in God's power can overcome the despair of any pain or trial.

FORGIVENESS
Many psalms are intense prayers asking God for forgiveness. Because God forgives us, we can pray to him honestly and directly. When we receive God's forgiveness, we move from being separated from him to being close to him, from feeling guilty to feeling loved.

GRATITUDE
God protects, guides, forgives, and provides everything we need. When we realize how much we benefit from knowing God, we can fully express our thanks to him.

TRUST
God's faithfulness and justice has been proven throughout history. Knowing him intimately drives away doubt, fear, and loneliness.

BOOK ONE (Psalms 1–41)

1

1 Oh, the joys of those who do not
follow the advice of the wicked,
or stand around with sinners,
or join in with mockers.
2 But they delight in the law of the LORD,
meditating on it day and night.
3 They are like trees planted along the riverbank,
bearing fruit each season.
Their leaves never wither,
and they prosper in all they do.

FRIENDSHIP

As senior year begins, Chelsea decides that, as God is her witness, she would never be unpopular again. She suffered through that for three years. This is her time to shine.

One of the key ingredients of popularity is having the right friends. And so far, Chelsea has started to make the right friends—thanks to the fact that she was cast in a popular TV commercial over the summer. (That's a long story.)

Who are the right friends? Well, there's Jack, the star player on the basketball team. Everybody knows him. Even the lunchroom ladies mention his name at least once a day. And then there's Lauren. Her dad's company was mentioned in *Fortune* magazine and *People*.

And let's not forget Tyler. His parties are legendary around the school.

There are just two teensy problems with having these friends: They don't like Chelsea's other friends. In fact, they think Chelsea should dump her friends and hang with them and their friends totally. Also, they have the habit of making decisions that are against Chelsea's beliefs. You see, Chelsea is a Christian. None of her new friends are.

They're quick to give her all kinds of advice—how to dress, what colleges to apply to, what music to listen to. Chelsea considers herself so "lucky" to have such caring friends—even if she doesn't always agree with them.

What would you do in this situation? Do friends really affect the direction of your life? Read Psalm 1, noting especially the first verse.

4 But not the wicked!
They are like worthless chaff, scattered
by the wind.
5 They will be condemned at the time
of judgment.
Sinners will have no place among the godly.
6 For the LORD watches over the path of the godly,
but the path of the wicked leads to destruction.

2

1 Why are the nations so angry?
Why do they waste their time with futile plans?
2 The kings of the earth prepare for battle;
the rulers plot together
against the LORD
and against his anointed one.
3 "Let us break their chains," they cry,
"and free ourselves from slavery to God."

FREEDOM 2:3

Some people think they can experience freedom away from God and his rules. Ever feel that way? Yet we all serve somebody or something, whether a person in authority, the wishes of friends, or our own desires. Just as a fish is not free when it leaves the water and a tree is not free when it leaves the soil, we aren't really free if we try to live our lives without God. The one sure route to freedom is wholeheartedly serving God the Creator. He can set you free to be the person he created you to be. ■

4 But the one who rules in heaven laughs.
The Lord scoffs at them.
5 Then in anger he rebukes them,
terrifying them with his fierce fury.
6 For the Lord declares, "I have placed my chosen
king on the throne
in Jerusalem,* on my holy mountain."

7 The king proclaims the LORD's decree:
"The LORD said to me, 'You are my son.*
Today I have become your Father.*
8 Only ask, and I will give you the nations as your
inheritance,
the whole earth as your possession.
9 You will break* them with an iron rod
and smash them like clay pots.'"

10 Now then, you kings, act wisely!
Be warned, you rulers of the earth!
11 Serve the LORD with reverent fear,
and rejoice with trembling.
12 Submit to God's royal son,* or he will become angry,
and you will be destroyed in the midst of all
your activities—
for his anger flares up in an instant.
But what joy for all who take refuge in him!

3

A psalm of David, regarding the time David fled from his son Absalom.

1 O LORD, I have so many enemies;
so many are against me.

2:6 Hebrew *on Zion.* **2:7a** Or *Son;* also in 2:12. **2:7b** Or *Today I reveal you as my son.* **2:9** Greek version reads *rule.* Compare Rev 2:27.
2:12 The meaning of the Hebrew is uncertain.

Reasons to Read Psalms

God's Word was written to be studied, understood, and applied, and the book of Psalms lends itself most directly to application. We may turn to Psalms looking for something, but sooner or later we will meet Someone. As we read and memorize Psalms, we will discover how much they are already part of us. They put our deepest hurts, longings, thoughts, and prayers into words. They gently push us toward being what God designed us to be—people who love and live for him.

To find comfort
Psalm 23

To learn a new prayer
Psalm 136

To meet God intimately
Psalm 103

To learn a new song
Psalm 92

To understand why you should read the Bible
Psalm 119

To know that God is in control
Psalm 146

To give praise to God
Psalm 145

To understand yourself more clearly
Psalm 8

To be forgiven for your sins
Psalm 51

To know how to come to God each day
Psalm 5

To feel worthwhile
Psalm 139

To give thanks to God
Psalm 136

To know why you should worship God
Psalm 104

To please God
Psalm 15

---

2 So many are saying,
"God will never rescue him!" *Interlude**
3 But you, O LORD, are a shield around me;
you are my glory, the one who holds my head high.
4 I cried out to the LORD,
and he answered me from his holy mountain. *Interlude*

5 I lay down and slept,
yet I woke up in safety,
for the LORD was watching over me.
6 I am not afraid of ten thousand enemies
who surround me on every side.

7 Arise, O LORD!
Rescue me, my God!
Slap all my enemies in the face!
Shatter the teeth of the wicked!
8 Victory comes from you, O LORD.
May you bless your people. *Interlude*

4

For the choir director: A psalm of David, to be accompanied by stringed instruments.

1 Answer me when I call to you,
O God who declares me innocent.
Free me from my troubles.
Have mercy on me and hear my prayer.

2 How long will you people ruin my reputation?
How long will you make groundless accusations?
How long will you continue your lies? *Interlude*
3 You can be sure of this:
The LORD set apart the godly for himself.
The LORD will answer when I call to him.

HE ALWAYS LISTENS 4:1-3

David knew God heard his prayers and would answer him. Ever doubt that God listens to your prayers? Sometimes we fear that God will ignore us because we've messed up somehow. But God is still willing to listen to us. When you feel that your prayers are bouncing off the ceiling, remember that God loves you. He hears and answers. ■

4 Don't sin by letting anger control you.
Think about it overnight and remain silent. *Interlude*
5 Offer sacrifices in the right spirit,
and trust the LORD.

6 Many people say, "Who will show us better times?"
Let your face smile on us, LORD.
7 You have given me greater joy
than those who have abundant harvests of grain and new wine.
8 In peace I will lie down and sleep,
for you alone, O LORD, will keep me safe.

3:2 Hebrew *Selah.* The meaning of this word is uncertain, though it is probably a musical or literary term. It is rendered *Interlude* throughout the Psalms.

keeping it real

There was a time a couple of years ago when I was really down on myself and very confused. I couldn't do anything to make myself feel better. So, I prayed about it.

One night I opened my Bible looking for help. I leafed through Psalms, remembering that a Christian friend had once told me that whenever he felt bad, reading Psalms helped.

Psalm 6 sort of jumped off the page at me—especially verse 3: "I am sick at heart. How long, O LORD, until you restore me?" That's how I felt—totally distressed. I read and reread that psalm. It spoke straight to my heart, and it showed me that God was there for me, as always.

Now whenever I'm in doubt about God's love and care, I turn to that psalm. It reminds me that God is always there and that he will lead me through any dark time I experience, just as he did on the night when I first read Psalm 6. —**Jenna**

5

For the choir director: A psalm of David, to be accompanied by the flute.

1 O LORD, hear me as I pray;
pay attention to my groaning.
2 Listen to my cry for help, my King and my God,
for I pray to no one but you.
3 Listen to my voice in the morning, LORD.
Each morning I bring my requests to you and
wait expectantly.

4 O God, you take no pleasure in wickedness;
you cannot tolerate the sins of the wicked.
5 Therefore, the proud may not stand in your
presence,
for you hate all who do evil.
6 You will destroy those who tell lies.
The LORD detests murderers and deceivers.

7 Because of your unfailing love, I can enter
your house;
I will worship at your Temple with deepest awe.
8 Lead me in the right path, O LORD,
or my enemies will conquer me.
Make your way plain for me to follow.

9 My enemies cannot speak a truthful word.
Their deepest desire is to destroy others.
Their talk is foul, like the stench from an open grave.
Their tongues are filled with flattery.*
10 O God, declare them guilty.
Let them be caught in their own traps.
Drive them away because of their many sins,
for they have rebelled against you.

11 But let all who take refuge in you rejoice;
let them sing joyful praises forever.
Spread your protection over them,
that all who love your name may be filled
with joy.
12 For you bless the godly, O LORD;
you surround them with your shield of love.

6

*For the choir director: A psalm of David, to be accompanied by an eight-stringed instrument.**

1 O LORD, don't rebuke me in your anger
or discipline me in your rage.
2 Have compassion on me, LORD, for I am weak.
Heal me, LORD, for my bones are in agony.
3 I am sick at heart.
How long, O LORD, until you restore me?

4 Return, O LORD, and rescue me.
Save me because of your unfailing love.
5 For the dead do not remember you.
Who can praise you from the grave?*

6 I am worn out from sobbing.
All night I flood my bed with weeping,
drenching it with my tears.
7 My vision is blurred by grief;
my eyes are worn out because of all
my enemies.

5:9 Greek version reads *with lies.* Compare Rom 3:12. **6:TITLE** Hebrew *with stringed instruments; according to the sheminith.*
6:5 Hebrew *from Sheol?*

8 Go away, all you who do evil,
for the LORD has heard my weeping.
9 The LORD has heard my plea;
the LORD will answer my prayer.
10 May all my enemies be disgraced and terrified.
May they suddenly turn back in shame.

7

A psalm of David, which he sang to the LORD concerning Cush of the tribe of Benjamin.

1 I come to you for protection, O LORD my God.
Save me from my persecutors—rescue me!
2 If you don't, they will maul me like a lion,
tearing me to pieces with no one to rescue me.
3 O LORD my God, if I have done wrong
or am guilty of injustice,
4 if I have betrayed a friend
or plundered my enemy without cause,
5 then let my enemies capture me.
Let them trample me into the ground
and drag my honor in the dust. *Interlude*

6 Arise, O LORD, in anger!
Stand up against the fury of my enemies!
Wake up, my God, and bring justice!

REVENGE 7:1-6

Have you ever been falsely accused by someone and wanted revenge? David wrote this psalm when he was falsely accused of trying to kill King Saul to gain the throne (1 Sam 24:9-11). Instead of seeking revenge, David cried out to God for justice. The proper response to false accusations is prayer, not revenge. God says, "I will take revenge; I will pay them back" (Deut 32:35; see also Rom 12:19). Instead of striking back, ask God to right your wrong and restore your reputation. ■

7 Gather the nations before you.
Rule over them from on high.
8 The LORD judges the nations.
Declare me righteous, O LORD,
for I am innocent, O Most High!
9 End the evil of those who are wicked,
and defend the righteous.
For you look deep within the mind and heart,
O righteous God.

10 God is my shield,
saving those whose hearts are true and right.
11 God is an honest judge.
He is angry with the wicked every day.
12 If a person does not repent,
God* will sharpen his sword;
he will bend and string his bow.
13 He will prepare his deadly weapons
and shoot his flaming arrows.

14 The wicked conceive evil;
they are pregnant with trouble
and give birth to lies.
15 They dig a deep pit to trap others,
then fall into it themselves.
16 The trouble they make for others backfires on them.
The violence they plan falls on their own heads.

17 I will thank the LORD because he is just;
I will sing praise to the name of the LORD Most High.

8

*For the choir director: A psalm of David, to be accompanied by a stringed instrument.**

1 O LORD, our Lord, your majestic name fills the earth!
Your glory is higher than the heavens.
2 You have taught children and infants
to tell of your strength,*
silencing your enemies
and all who oppose you.

3 When I look at the night sky and see the work
of your fingers—
the moon and the stars you set in place—
4 what are mere mortals that you should think about them,
human beings that you should care for them?*
5 Yet you made them only a little lower than God*
and crowned them* with glory and honor.
6 You gave them charge of everything you made,
putting all things under their authority—
7 the flocks and the herds
and all the wild animals,
8 the birds in the sky, the fish in the sea,
and everything that swims the ocean currents.

9 O LORD, our Lord, your majestic name fills the earth!

9

For the choir director: A psalm of David, to be sung to the tune "Death of the Son."

1 I will praise you, LORD, with all my heart;
I will tell of all the marvelous things you have done.
2 I will be filled with joy because of you.
I will sing praises to your name, O Most High.

3 My enemies retreated;
they staggered and died when you appeared.
4 For you have judged in my favor;
from your throne you have judged with fairness.

7:12 Hebrew *he.* 8:TITLE Hebrew *according to the gittith.* 8:2 Greek version reads *to give you praise.* Compare Matt 21:16. 8:4 Hebrew *what is man that you should think of him, / the son of man that you should care for him?* 8:5a Or *Yet you made them only a little lower than the angels;* Hebrew reads *Yet you made him* [i.e., man] *a little lower than Elohim.* 8:5b Hebrew *him* [i.e., man]; similarly in 8:6.

MADE IN THE IMAGE OF GOD

ULTIMATE ISSUES

Got a coin handy? Good. Whose face is on it? More than likely, you're looking at the image of a former president or a well-known woman from history (Susan B. Anthony or Sacagawea). If you check out a set of stamps (the non-flag kind), you might see the image of another well-known person from history.

Imagine having millions of coins or stamps bearing your image. (Unfortunately, you have to be dead before you can appear on either.) Although God has never been on a stamp or a coin, millions of people bear his image. According to Psalm 8, we were made in his image. We're "stamped" with his likeness. This doesn't mean that we have his chin or his eyebrows. We have his characteristics.

It's easy to believe this truth when we think about kind, attractive, thoughtful people. But it's just as true of the murderer on death row or the terrorist who bombs airports. We're God's image-bearers not because we're good but because he created us.

When you're confronted by people who seem to exist only to make your life unpleasant—the classmate who majors in being obnoxious, the relative who constantly criticizes you, the teacher who takes pleasure in humiliating you—remember: that person was made in God's image just as you were. Regardless of our habit of wrongdoing, we are all of great value to God.

5 You have rebuked the nations and destroyed the wicked;
you have erased their names forever.
6 The enemy is finished, in endless ruins;
the cities you uprooted are now forgotten.

7 But the LORD reigns forever,
executing judgment from his throne.
8 He will judge the world with justice
and rule the nations with fairness.
9 The LORD is a shelter for the oppressed,
a refuge in times of trouble.
10 Those who know your name trust in you,
for you, O LORD, do not abandon those who
search for you.

11 Sing praises to the LORD who reigns in Jerusalem.*
Tell the world about his unforgettable deeds.
12 For he who avenges murder cares for the helpless.
He does not ignore the cries of those who suffer.

13 LORD, have mercy on me.
See how my enemies torment me.
Snatch me back from the jaws of death.
14 Save me so I can praise you publicly at
Jerusalem's gates,
so I can rejoice that you have rescued me.

15 The nations have fallen into the pit they dug for
others.
Their own feet have been caught in the trap
they set.
16 The LORD is known for his justice.
The wicked are trapped by their own deeds.
*Quiet Interlude**

17 The wicked will go down to the grave.*
This is the fate of all the nations who ignore God.
18 But the needy will not be ignored forever;
the hopes of the poor will not always be crushed.

19 Arise, O LORD!
Do not let mere mortals defy you!
Judge the nations!
20 Make them tremble in fear, O LORD.
Let the nations know they are merely human.
Interlude

9:11 Hebrew *Zion;* also in 9:14. **9:16** Hebrew *Higgaion Selah.* The meaning of this phrase is uncertain. **9:17** Hebrew *to Sheol.*

10

1 O LORD, why do you stand so far away?
Why do you hide when I am in trouble?
2 The wicked arrogantly hunt down the poor.
Let them be caught in the evil they plan for others.

KEEP ON PRAYING 10:1

To the psalmist, God seemed far away. "Why do you hide when I am in trouble?" he asked God. But though he had honest doubts, he didn't stop praying. He also didn't assume that God no longer cared. Would you have the same reaction in a moment of doubt? During those times when you feel alone or forgotten are you willing to stick with God? ■

3 For they brag about their evil desires;
they praise the greedy and curse the LORD.

4 The wicked are too proud to seek God.
They seem to think that God is dead.
5 Yet they succeed in everything they do.
They do not see your punishment
awaiting them.
They sneer at all their enemies.
6 They think, "Nothing bad will ever happen to us!
We will be free of trouble forever!"

7 Their mouths are full of cursing, lies, and threats.*
Trouble and evil are on the tips of their tongues.
8 They lurk in ambush in the villages,
waiting to murder innocent people.
They are always searching for helpless victims.
9 Like lions crouched in hiding,
they wait to pounce on the helpless.
Like hunters they capture the helpless
and drag them away in nets.
10 Their helpless victims are crushed;
they fall beneath the strength of the wicked.
11 The wicked think, "God isn't watching us!
He has closed his eyes and won't even see
what we do!"

12 Arise, O LORD!
Punish the wicked, O God!
Do not ignore the helpless!
13 Why do the wicked get away with despising God?
They think, "God will never call us to account."
14 But you see the trouble and grief they cause.
You take note of it and punish them.
The helpless put their trust in you.
You defend the orphans.

15 Break the arms of these wicked, evil people!
Go after them until the last one is destroyed.
16 The LORD is king forever and ever!
The godless nations will vanish from the land.
17 LORD, you know the hopes of the helpless.
Surely you will hear their cries and comfort them.
18 You will bring justice to the orphans and the
oppressed,
so mere people can no longer terrify them.

11

For the choir director: A psalm of David.

1 I trust in the LORD for protection.
So why do you say to me,
"Fly like a bird to the mountains for safety!
2 The wicked are stringing their bows
and fitting their arrows on the bowstrings.
They shoot from the shadows
at those whose hearts are right.
3 The foundations of law and order have collapsed.
What can the righteous do?"

4 But the LORD is in his holy Temple;
the LORD still rules from heaven.
He watches everyone closely,
examining every person on earth.
5 The LORD examines both the righteous and the wicked.
He hates those who love violence.
6 He will rain down blazing coals and burning sulfur
on the wicked,
punishing them with scorching winds.
7 For the righteous LORD loves justice.
The virtuous will see his face.

LYING LIPS 12:2-4

We may be tempted to believe that lies are relatively harmless, even useful at times. But God doesn't ignore deceit, flattery, or boasting. Each action originates from an attitude expressed in our speech. The tongue can be our greatest enemy because, though small, it can do great damage (James 3:2-12). ■

12

*For the choir director: A psalm of David, to be accompanied by an eight-stringed instrument.**

1 Help, O LORD, for the godly are fast disappearing!
The faithful have vanished from the earth!
2 Neighbors lie to each other,
speaking with flattering lips and deceitful hearts.
3 May the LORD cut off their flattering lips
and silence their boastful tongues.
4 They say, "We will lie to our hearts' content.
Our lips are our own—who can stop us?"

5 The LORD replies, "I have seen violence done
to the helpless,
and I have heard the groans of the poor.

10:7 Greek version reads *cursing and bitterness*. Compare Rom 3:14. 12:TITLE Hebrew *according to the sheminith*.

keeping it real

I couldn't get out of my mind what my friend had told me. She said that when she was eight years old, her oldest brother sexually abused her—more than once.

This really bothered me for a long time. I felt angry, mainly at God. I just couldn't understand it. How could God let such a terrible thing happen to such a wonderful person? Why hadn't he done anything to stop it—like have the phone ring, or someone come to the door, or someone come home? Anything!

One day I was reading in the Psalms and came across Psalm 13. I saw that the psalmist was angry at God, too—he was actually complaining to God! That gave me the freedom to spill out my heart to God. I told God all my bitter and confused thoughts concerning what happened to my friend. I cried. I even lashed out at God. And the result of telling God what was on my mind and my heart was an incredible peace. Psalm 13 showed me that God always wants to hear what's on my mind, even when I'm angry with him. In the end, I found that God is there for me—even if I don't always understand all his ways.

—**Eric**

Now I will rise up to rescue them,
as they have longed for me to do."
6 The LORD's promises are pure,
like silver refined in a furnace,
purified seven times over.
7 Therefore, LORD, we know you will protect
the oppressed,
preserving them forever from this lying
generation,
8 even though the wicked strut about,
and evil is praised throughout the land.

13 *For the choir director: A psalm of David.*

1 O LORD, how long will you forget me? Forever?
How long will you look the other way?
2 How long must I struggle with anguish in
my soul,
with sorrow in my heart every day?
How long will my enemy have the
upper hand?

3 Turn and answer me, O LORD my God!
Restore the sparkle to my eyes, or I will die.
4 Don't let my enemies gloat, saying, "We have
defeated him!"
Don't let them rejoice at my downfall.

5 But I trust in your unfailing love.
I will rejoice because you have rescued me.
6 I will sing to the LORD
because he is good to me.

14 *For the choir director: A psalm of David.*

1 Only fools say in their hearts,
"There is no God."
They are corrupt, and their actions are evil;
not one of them does good!

2 The LORD looks down from heaven
on the entire human race;
he looks to see if anyone is truly wise,
if anyone seeks God.

Does God always forgive? Could I possibly do something that he wouldn't forgive? Why or why not?

The incident that caused King David to pray the prayer in Psalm 51 is found in 2 Samuel 11. David not only committed adultery, but he had the woman's husband murdered so he could marry her! But when confronted with his wrongdoing a year after those events (2 Sam 12), David sincerely wanted to change. He asked God to forgive him and to renew their relationship once again. Although David really blew it, God forgave him.

It has been said that the only sin God cannot forgive is the one we have not confessed. God is always willing to forgive those who admit their mistakes and who genuinely try not to repeat them.

Where to Get Help in the Book of Psalms

WHEN YOU FEEL . . .

Afraid 3, 4, 27, 46, 49, 56, 91, 118
Alone 9, 10, 12, 13, 27, 40, 43
"Burned Out" 6, 63
Cheated 41
Confused 10, 12, 73
Depressed 27, 34, 42, 43, 88, 143
Distressed 13, 25, 31, 40, 107
Elated 19, 96
Guilty 19, 32, 38, 51
Hateful 11
Impatient 13, 27, 37, 40
Insecure 3, 5, 12, 91
Insulted 41, 70
Jealous 37
Like Quitting 29, 43, 145
Lost 23, 139
Overwhelmed 25, 69, 142
Penitent/Sorry 32, 51, 66
Proud 14, 30, 49
Purposeless 14, 25, 39, 49, 90
Sad 13
Self-confident 24
Tense 4
Thankful 118, 136, 138
Threatened 3, 11, 17
Tired/Weak 6, 13, 18, 28, 29, 40, 86
Trapped 7, 17, 42, 88, 142
Unimportant 8, 90, 139
Vengeful 3, 7, 109
Worried 37
Worshipful 8, 19, 27, 29, 150

WHEN YOU'RE FACING . . .

Atheists 10, 14, 19, 52, 53, 115
Competition 133
Criticism 35, 56, 120
Danger 11
Death 6, 71, 90
Decisions 1, 119
Discrimination 54
Doubts 34, 37, 94
Evil people 10, 35, 36, 49, 52, 109, 140
Enemies 3, 25, 35, 41, 56, 59
Handicap/Illness 6, 139
Heresy 14
Hypocrisy 26, 28, 40, 50
Lies 5, 12, 120
Old Age 71, 92
Persecution 1, 3, 7, 56
Poverty 9, 10, 12
Punishment 6, 38, 39
Slander/Insults 7, 15, 35, 43, 120
Slaughter 6, 46, 83
Sorrow 23, 34
Success 18, 112, 127, 128
Temptation 38, 141
Troubles 34, 55, 86, 102, 142, 145
Verbal Cruelty 35, 120

WHEN YOU WANT . . .

Acceptance 139
Answers 4, 17
Confidence 46, 71
Courage 11, 42
Fellowship with God 5, 16, 25, 27, 37, 133
Forgiveness 32, 38, 40, 51, 69, 86, 103, 130
Friendship 16
Godliness 15, 25
Guidance 1, 5, 15, 19, 25, 32, 48
Healing 6, 41
Hope 16, 17, 18, 23, 27
Humility 19, 147
Illumination 19
Integrity 24, 25
Joy 9, 16, 28, 126
Justice 2, 7, 14, 26, 37, 49, 58, 82
Knowledge 2, 8, 18, 19, 25, 29, 97, 103
Leadership 72
Miracles 60, 111
Money 15, 16, 17, 49
Peace 3, 4
Perspective 2, 11
Prayer 5, 17, 27, 61
Protection 3, 4, 7, 16, 17, 18, 23, 27, 31, 91, 121, 125
Provision 23
Rest 23, 27
Salvation 26, 37, 49, 126
Stability 11, 33, 46
Vindication 9, 14, 28, 35, 109
Wisdom 1, 16, 19, 64, 111

3 But no, all have turned away;
all have become corrupt.*
No one does good,
not a single one!

4 Will those who do evil never learn?
They eat up my people like bread
and wouldn't think of praying to the LORD.
5 Terror will grip them,
for God is with those who obey him.
6 The wicked frustrate the plans of the oppressed,
but the LORD will protect his people.

14:3 Greek version reads *have become useless.* Compare Rom 3:12.

7 Who will come from Mount Zion to rescue Israel?
When the LORD restores his people,
Jacob will shout with joy, and Israel will rejoice.

15

A psalm of David.

1 Who may worship in your sanctuary, LORD?
Who may enter your presence on your holy hill?
2 Those who lead blameless lives and do what
is right,
speaking the truth from sincere hearts.

3 Those who refuse to gossip
or harm their neighbors
or speak evil of their friends.
4 Those who despise flagrant sinners,
and honor the faithful followers of the LORD,
and keep their promises even when it hurts.
5 Those who lend money without charging interest,
and who cannot be bribed to lie about the
innocent.
Such people will stand firm forever.

16

A psalm of David.

1 Keep me safe, O God,
for I have come to you for refuge.

2 I said to the LORD, "You are my Master!
Every good thing I have comes from you."
3 The godly people in the land
are my true heroes!
I take pleasure in them!
4 Troubles multiply for those who chase after
other gods.
I will not take part in their sacrifices of blood
or even speak the names of their gods.

5 LORD, you alone are my inheritance, my cup
of blessing.
You guard all that is mine.
6 The land you have given me is a pleasant land.
What a wonderful inheritance!

7 I will bless the LORD who guides me;
even at night my heart instructs me.
8 I know the LORD is always with me.
I will not be shaken, for he is right beside me.

9 No wonder my heart is glad, and I rejoice.*
My body rests in safety.
10 For you will not leave my soul among the dead*
or allow your holy one* to rot in the grave.
11 You will show me the way of life,
granting me the joy of your presence
and the pleasures of living with you forever.*

17

A prayer of David.

1 O LORD, hear my plea for justice.
Listen to my cry for help.
Pay attention to my prayer,
for it comes from honest lips.
2 Declare me innocent,
for you see those who do right.
3 You have tested my thoughts and examined my
heart in the night.
You have scrutinized me and found
nothing wrong.
I am determined not to sin in what I say.
4 I have followed your commands,
which keep me from following cruel and
evil people.
5 My steps have stayed on your path;
I have not wavered from following you.

6 I am praying to you because I know you will answer,
O God.
Bend down and listen as I pray.
7 Show me your unfailing love in wonderful ways.
By your mighty power you rescue
those who seek refuge from their enemies.
8 Guard me as you would guard your own eyes.*
Hide me in the shadow of your wings.
9 Protect me from wicked people who attack me,
from murderous enemies who surround me.
10 They are without pity.
Listen to their boasting!
11 They track me down and surround me,
watching for the chance to throw me to
the ground.
12 They are like hungry lions, eager to tear me apart—
like young lions hiding in ambush.

13 Arise, O LORD!
Stand against them, and bring them to their knees!
Rescue me from the wicked with your sword!
14 By the power of your hand, O LORD,
destroy those who look to this world for
their reward.
But satisfy the hunger of your treasured ones.
May their children have plenty,
leaving an inheritance for their descendants.
15 Because I am righteous, I will see you.
When I awake, I will see you face to face and
be satisfied.

18

For the choir director: A psalm of David, the servant of the LORD. He sang this song to the LORD on the day the LORD rescued him from all his enemies and from Saul. He sang:

1 I love you, LORD;
you are my strength.
2 The LORD is my rock, my fortress, and my savior;
my God is my rock, in whom I find protection.
He is my shield, the power that saves me,
and my place of safety.
3 I called on the LORD, who is worthy of praise,
and he saved me from my enemies.

16:9 Greek version reads *and my tongue shouts his praises.* Compare Acts 2:26. **16:10a** Hebrew *in Sheol.* **16:10b** Or *your Holy One.*
16:11 Greek version reads *You have shown me the way of life, / and you will fill me with the joy of your presence.* Compare Acts 2:28.
17:8 Hebrew *as the pupil of your eye.*

4 The ropes of death entangled me;
floods of destruction swept over me.
5 The grave* wrapped its ropes around me;
death laid a trap in my path.
6 But in my distress I cried out to the LORD;
yes, I prayed to my God for help.
He heard me from his sanctuary;
my cry to him reached his ears.

7 Then the earth quaked and trembled.
The foundations of the mountains shook;
they quaked because of his anger.

SHIELD 18:30

Ever hear someone say that belief in God is a crutch for weak people? Although David was a mighty warrior who fought with highly trained soldiers, he still knew that only God could protect him. God is indeed a shield to protect us when we are too weak to face certain problems by ourselves. He strengthens, protects, and guides us. ■

8 Smoke poured from his nostrils;
fierce flames leaped from his mouth.
Glowing coals blazed forth from him.
9 He opened the heavens and came down;
dark storm clouds were beneath his feet.
10 Mounted on a mighty angelic being,* he flew,
soaring on the wings of the wind.
11 He shrouded himself in darkness,
veiling his approach with dark rain clouds.
12 Thick clouds shielded the brightness around him
and rained down hail and burning coals.*
13 The LORD thundered from heaven;
the voice of the Most High resounded
amid the hail and burning coals.
14 He shot his arrows and scattered his enemies;
his lightning flashed, and they were greatly
confused.
15 Then at your command, O LORD,
at the blast of your breath,
the bottom of the sea could be seen,
and the foundations of the earth were laid bare.

16 He reached down from heaven and rescued me;
he drew me out of deep waters.
17 He rescued me from my powerful enemies,
from those who hated me and were too strong
for me.
18 They attacked me at a moment when I was
in distress,
but the LORD supported me.
19 He led me to a place of safety;
he rescued me because he delights in me.
20 The LORD rewarded me for doing right;
he restored me because of my innocence.

21 For I have kept the ways of the LORD;
I have not turned from my God to follow evil.
22 I have followed all his regulations;
I have never abandoned his decrees.
23 I am blameless before God;
I have kept myself from sin.
24 The LORD rewarded me for doing right.
He has seen my innocence.

25 To the faithful you show yourself faithful;
to those with integrity you show integrity.
26 To the pure you show yourself pure,
but to the wicked you show yourself hostile.
27 You rescue the humble,
but you humiliate the proud.
28 You light a lamp for me.
The LORD, my God, lights up my darkness.
29 In your strength I can crush an army;
with my God I can scale any wall.

30 God's way is perfect.
All the LORD's promises prove true.
He is a shield for all who look to him for protection.
31 For who is God except the LORD?
Who but our God is a solid rock?
32 God arms me with strength,
and he makes my way perfect.
33 He makes me as surefooted as a deer,
enabling me to stand on mountain heights.
34 He trains my hands for battle;
he strengthens my arm to draw a bronze bow.
35 You have given me your shield of victory.
Your right hand supports me;
your help has made me great.
36 You have made a wide path for my feet
to keep them from slipping.

HIS GENTLENESS 18:35

David offers an interesting twist to the concept of greatness by admitting that God's gentleness made him great. Our society believes that greatness is attained through a combination of opportunity, talent, and aggressiveness. But Jesus once described himself as "gentle at heart" (Matt 11:29). True greatness comes from living according to God's laws and standards and recognizing that all we have comes from the gentleness of God's mercy. ■

37 I chased my enemies and caught them;
I did not stop until they were conquered.
38 I struck them down so they could not get up;
they fell beneath my feet.
39 You have armed me with strength for the battle;
you have subdued my enemies under my feet.
40 You placed my foot on their necks.
I have destroyed all who hated me.
41 They called for help, but no one came to their rescue.

18:5 Hebrew *Sheol.* **18:10** Hebrew *a cherub.* **18:12** Or *and lightning bolts;* also in 18:13.

They even cried to the LORD, but he refused
to answer.
42 I ground them as fine as dust in the wind.
I swept them into the gutter like dirt.
43 You gave me victory over my accusers.
You appointed me ruler over nations;
people I don't even know now serve me.
44 As soon as they hear of me, they submit;
foreign nations cringe before me.
45 They all lose their courage
and come trembling from their strongholds.

46 The LORD lives! Praise to my Rock!
May the God of my salvation be exalted!
47 He is the God who pays back those who harm me;
he subdues the nations under me
48 and rescues me from my enemies.
You hold me safe beyond the reach of my enemies;
you save me from violent opponents.
49 For this, O LORD, I will praise you among the nations;
I will sing praises to your name.
50 You give great victories to your king;
you show unfailing love to your anointed,
to David and all his descendants forever.

19

For the choir director: A psalm of David.

1 The heavens proclaim the glory of God.
The skies display his craftsmanship.
2 Day after day they continue to speak;
night after night they make him known.
3 They speak without a sound or word;
their voice is never heard.*
4 Yet their message has gone
throughout the earth,
and their words to all the world.

God has made a home in the
heavens for the sun.
5 It bursts forth like a radiant
bridegroom after his
wedding.
It rejoices like a great athlete
eager to run the race.
6 The sun rises at one end of
the heavens
and follows its course to the
other end.
Nothing can hide from its heat.

7 The instructions of the LORD are perfect,
reviving the soul.
The decrees of the LORD are trustworthy,
making wise the simple.
8 The commandments of the LORD are right,
bringing joy to the heart.
The commands of the LORD are clear,
giving insight for living.
9 Reverence for the LORD is pure,
lasting forever.
The laws of the LORD are true;
each one is fair.
10 They are more desirable than gold,
even the finest gold.
They are sweeter than honey,
even honey dripping from the comb.
11 They are a warning to your servant,
a great reward for those who obey them.

12 How can I know all the sins lurking in my heart?
Cleanse me from these hidden faults.
13 Keep your servant from deliberate sins!
Don't let them control me.
Then I will be free of guilt
and innocent of great sin.

14 May the words of my mouth
and the meditation of my heart
be pleasing to you,
O LORD, my rock and my redeemer.

> The heavens proclaim the glory of God. The skies display his craftsmanship.
>
> PSALM 19:1

20

For the choir director: A psalm of David.

1 In times of trouble, may the LORD answer your cry.
May the name of the God of Jacob keep you safe
from all harm.
2 May he send you help from his sanctuary
and strengthen you from Jerusalem.*
3 May he remember all your gifts
and look favorably on your burnt
offerings. *Interlude*
4 May he grant your heart's desires
and make all your plans succeed.
5 May we shout for joy when we
hear of your victory
and raise a victory banner in the
name of our God.
May the LORD answer all your
prayers.

6 Now I know that the LORD rescues
his anointed king.
He will answer him from his
holy heaven
and rescue him by his great
power.
7 Some nations boast of their chariots
and horses,
but we boast in the name of the LORD
our God.
8 Those nations will fall down and collapse,
but we will rise up and stand firm.

9 Give victory to our king, O LORD!
Answer our cry for help.

19:3 Or *There is no speech or language where their voice is not heard.* **20:2** Hebrew *Zion.*

21 *For the choir director: A psalm of David.*

1 How the king rejoices in your strength, O Lord!
He shouts with joy because you give him victory.
2 For you have given him his heart's desire;
you have withheld nothing he requested. *Interlude*

3 You welcomed him back with success and prosperity.
You placed a crown of finest gold on his head.
4 He asked you to preserve his life,
and you granted his request.
The days of his life stretch on forever.
5 Your victory brings him great honor,
and you have clothed him with splendor and majesty.
6 You have endowed him with eternal blessings
and given him the joy of your presence.
7 For the king trusts in the Lord.
The unfailing love of the Most High will keep him from stumbling.

8 You will capture all your enemies.
Your strong right hand will seize all who hate you.
9 You will throw them in a flaming furnace
when you appear.
The Lord will consume them in his anger;
fire will devour them.
10 You will wipe their children from the face of the earth;
they will never have descendants.
11 Although they plot against you,
their evil schemes will never succeed.
12 For they will turn and run
when they see your arrows aimed at them.
13 Rise up, O Lord, in all your power.
With music and singing we celebrate your mighty acts.

22 *For the choir director: A psalm of David, to be sung to the tune "Doe of the Dawn."*

1 My God, my God, why have you abandoned me?
Why are you so far away when I groan for help?
2 Every day I call to you, my God, but you do not answer.
Every night you hear my voice, but I find no relief.

3 Yet you are holy,
enthroned on the praises of Israel.
4 Our ancestors trusted in you,
and you rescued them.
5 They cried out to you and were saved.
They trusted in you and were never disgraced.
6 But I am a worm and not a man.
I am scorned and despised by all!
7 Everyone who sees me mocks me.
They sneer and shake their heads, saying,
8 "Is this the one who relies on the Lord?
Then let the Lord save him!
If the Lord loves him so much,
let the Lord rescue him!"

9 Yet you brought me safely from my mother's womb
and led me to trust you at my mother's breast.
10 I was thrust into your arms at my birth.
You have been my God from the moment I was born.

11 Do not stay so far from me,
for trouble is near,
and no one else can help me.
12 My enemies surround me like a herd of bulls;
fierce bulls of Bashan have hemmed me in!
13 Like lions they open their jaws against me,
roaring and tearing into their prey.
14 My life is poured out like water,
and all my bones are out of joint.
My heart is like wax,
melting within me.
15 My strength has dried up like sunbaked clay.
My tongue sticks to the roof of my mouth.
You have laid me in the dust and left me for dead.
16 My enemies surround me like a pack of dogs;
an evil gang closes in on me.
They have pierced my hands and feet.
17 I can count all my bones.
My enemies stare at me and gloat.
18 They divide my garments among themselves
and throw dice* for my clothing.

19 O Lord, do not stay far away!
You are my strength; come quickly to my aid!
20 Save me from the sword;
spare my precious life from these dogs.
21 Snatch me from the lion's jaws
and from the horns of these wild oxen.

22 I will proclaim your name to my brothers and sisters.*
I will praise you among your assembled people.
23 Praise the Lord, all you who fear him!
Honor him, all you descendants of Jacob!
Show him reverence, all you descendants of Israel!
24 For he has not ignored or belittled the suffering of the needy.
He has not turned his back on them,
but has listened to their cries for help.
25 I will praise you in the great assembly.
I will fulfill my vows in the presence of those who worship you.

22:18 Hebrew *cast lots.* **22:22** Hebrew *my brothers.*

26 The poor will eat and be satisfied.
All who seek the LORD will praise him.
Their hearts will rejoice with everlasting joy.
27 The whole earth will acknowledge the LORD and
return to him.
All the families of the nations will bow down
before him.
28 For royal power belongs to the LORD.
He rules all the nations.
29 Let the rich of the earth feast and worship.
Bow before him, all who are mortal,
all whose lives will end as dust.
30 Our children will also serve him.
Future generations will hear about the wonders
of the Lord.
31 His righteous acts will be told to those not
yet born.
They will hear about everything he has done.

BEST INTERESTS 23:1-3

David compares God's concern for his people to that of a shepherd. When we allow God to guide us, we experience peace and contentment. Our Shepherd knows the "green meadows" and "peaceful streams" that will renew us. We will reach these places only by sticking close to him like a sheep would to a shepherd. How close are you? ■

23
A psalm of David.

1 The LORD is my shepherd;
I have all that I need.
2 He lets me rest in green meadows;
he leads me beside peaceful streams.
3 He renews my strength.
He guides me along right paths,
bringing honor to his name.
4 Even when I walk
through the darkest valley,*
I will not be afraid,
for you are close beside me.
Your rod and your staff
protect and comfort me.
5 You prepare a feast for me
in the presence of my enemies.
You honor me by anointing my
head with oil.
My cup overflows with
blessings.
6 Surely your goodness and
unfailing love will pursue me
all the days of my life,
and I will live in the house of the LORD
forever.

The LORD is my shepherd; I have all that I need.

PSALM 23:1

24
A psalm of David.

1 The earth is the LORD's, and everything in it.
The world and all its people belong to him.
2 For he laid the earth's foundation on the seas
and built it on the ocean depths.

3 Who may climb the mountain of the LORD?
Who may stand in his holy place?
4 Only those whose hands and hearts are pure,
who do not worship idols
and never tell lies.
5 They will receive the LORD's blessing
and have a right relationship with God their savior.
6 Such people may seek you
and worship in your presence, O God
of Jacob. *Interlude*

7 Open up, ancient gates!
Open up, ancient doors,
and let the King of glory enter.
8 Who is the King of glory?
The LORD, strong and mighty;
the LORD, invincible in battle.
9 Open up, ancient gates!
Open up, ancient doors,
and let the King of glory enter.
10 Who is the King of glory?
The LORD of Heaven's Armies—
he is the King of glory. *Interlude*

25*
A psalm of David.

1 O LORD, I give my life to you.
2 I trust in you, my God!
Do not let me be disgraced,
or let my enemies rejoice in my defeat.
3 No one who trusts in you will ever
be disgraced,
but disgrace comes to those who
try to deceive others.
4 Show me the right path, O LORD;
point out the road for me
to follow.
5 Lead me by your truth and
teach me,
for you are the God who
saves me.
All day long I put my hope in you.
6 Remember, O LORD, your
compassion and unfailing
love,
which you have shown from long ages past.
7 Do not remember the rebellious sins of my youth.
Remember me in the light of your unfailing love,
for you are merciful, O LORD.

23:4 Or *the dark valley of death.* 25 This psalm is a Hebrew acrostic poem; each verse begins with a successive letter of the Hebrew alphabet.

8 The LORD is good and does what is right;
he shows the proper path to those who go astray.
9 He leads the humble in doing right,
teaching them his way.
10 The LORD leads with unfailing love and
faithfulness
all who keep his covenant and obey his demands.

ENEMIES 25:2

David asked God to keep his enemies from overcoming him because they opposed what God stood for. Seventy-two psalms—almost half the book—speak about enemies. Enemies are those who not only oppose us, but also oppose God's way of living. A less tangible enemy can be a temptation like money, success, prestige, or lust. And our greatest enemy is Satan. Although these enemies may seem huge, they're no match for God. Is that your view as well? ■

11 For the honor of your name, O LORD,
forgive my many, many sins.
12 Who are those who fear the LORD?
He will show them the path they should choose.
13 They will live in prosperity,
and their children will inherit the land.
14 The LORD is a friend to those who fear him.
He teaches them his covenant.
15 My eyes are always on the LORD,
for he rescues me from the traps of my enemies.

16 Turn to me and have mercy,
for I am alone and in deep distress.
17 My problems go from bad to worse.
Oh, save me from them all!
18 Feel my pain and see my trouble.
Forgive all my sins.
19 See how many enemies I have
and how viciously they hate me!
20 Protect me! Rescue my life from them!
Do not let me be disgraced, for in you I
take refuge.
21 May integrity and honesty protect me,
for I put my hope in you.

22 O God, ransom Israel
from all its troubles.

26

A psalm of David.

1 Declare me innocent, O LORD,
for I have acted with integrity;
I have trusted in the LORD without wavering.
2 Put me on trial, LORD, and cross-examine me.
Test my motives and my heart.
3 For I am always aware of your unfailing love,
and I have lived according to your truth.
4 I do not spend time with liars
or go along with hypocrites.
5 I hate the gatherings of those who do evil,
and I refuse to join in with the wicked.
6 I wash my hands to declare my innocence.
I come to your altar, O LORD,
7 singing a song of thanksgiving
and telling of all your wonders.
8 I love your sanctuary, LORD,
the place where your glorious presence dwells.

9 Don't let me suffer the fate of sinners.
Don't condemn me along with murderers.
10 Their hands are dirty with evil schemes,
and they constantly take bribes.
11 But I am not like that; I live with integrity.
So redeem me and show me mercy.
12 Now I stand on solid ground,
and I will publicly praise the LORD.

27

A psalm of David.

1 The LORD is my light and my salvation—
so why should I be afraid?
The LORD is my fortress, protecting me from danger,
so why should I tremble?
2 When evil people come to devour me,
when my enemies and foes attack me,
they will stumble and fall.
3 Though a mighty army surrounds me,
my heart will not be afraid.
Even if I am attacked,
I will remain confident.

ALREADY PREPARED 27:1-14

David sought God's guidance every day. So, when troubles came his way, he was already prepared to handle any test. We often run to God when we are experiencing difficulties. Many of our problems could be avoided or handled far more easily by constantly relying on God's help and direction. Do you seek God daily or only during emergencies? ■

4 The one thing I ask of the LORD—
the thing I seek most—
is to live in the house of the LORD all the days
of my life,
delighting in the LORD's perfections
and meditating in his Temple.
5 For he will conceal me there when troubles come;
he will hide me in his sanctuary.
He will place me out of reach on a high rock.
6 Then I will hold my head high
above my enemies who surround me.
At his sanctuary I will offer sacrifices with
shouts of joy,
singing and praising the LORD with music.

7 Hear me as I pray, O LORD.
Be merciful and answer me!
8 My heart has heard you say, "Come and talk with me."
And my heart responds, "LORD, I am coming."
9 Do not turn your back on me.
Do not reject your servant in anger.
You have always been my helper.
Don't leave me now; don't abandon me,
O God of my salvation!
10 Even if my father and mother abandon me,
the LORD will hold me close.

11 Teach me how to live, O LORD.
Lead me along the right path,
for my enemies are waiting for me.
12 Do not let me fall into their hands.
For they accuse me of things I've never done;
with every breath they threaten me with violence.
13 Yet I am confident I will see the LORD's goodness
while I am here in the land of the living.

14 Wait patiently for the LORD.
Be brave and courageous.
Yes, wait patiently for the LORD.

28

A psalm of David.

1 I pray to you, O LORD, my rock.
Do not turn a deaf ear to me.
For if you are silent,
I might as well give up and die.
2 Listen to my prayer for mercy
as I cry out to you for help,
as I lift my hands toward your holy sanctuary.

FAKE FRIENDSHIP 28:3-5

As king of Israel David may have met many who pretended friendship for selfish reasons. David knew God would punish them accordingly, but he prayed that their punishment would come swiftly. It's easy to pretend friendship. Deceitful people often pretend to be kind or offer a false sort of friendship to gain their own ends. True believers live honest lives before God and others. They don't offer friendship only for what they can get out of it. How would your friends describe the friendship you offer? ■

3 Do not drag me away with the wicked—
with those who do evil—
those who speak friendly words to their neighbors
while planning evil in their hearts.
4 Give them the punishment they so richly deserve!
Measure it out in proportion to their wickedness.
Pay them back for all their evil deeds!
Give them a taste of what they have done to others.
5 They care nothing for what the LORD has done
or for what his hands have made.
So he will tear them down,
and they will never be rebuilt!

6 Praise the LORD!
For he has heard my cry for mercy.
7 The LORD is my strength and shield.
I trust him with all my heart.
He helps me, and my heart is filled with joy.
I burst out in songs of thanksgiving.

8 The LORD gives his people strength.
He is a safe fortress for his anointed king.
9 Save your people!
Bless Israel, your special possession.*
Lead them like a shepherd,
and carry them in your arms forever.

29

A psalm of David.

1 Honor the LORD, you heavenly beings*;
honor the LORD for his glory and strength.
2 Honor the LORD for the glory of his name.
Worship the LORD in the splendor of his holiness.

3 The voice of the LORD echoes above the sea.
The God of glory thunders.
The LORD thunders over the mighty sea.
4 The voice of the LORD is powerful;
the voice of the LORD is majestic.
5 The voice of the LORD splits the mighty cedars;
the LORD shatters the cedars of Lebanon.
6 He makes Lebanon's mountains skip like a calf;
he makes Mount Hermon* leap like a young wild ox.
7 The voice of the LORD strikes
with bolts of lightning.
8 The voice of the LORD makes the barren wilderness quake;
the LORD shakes the wilderness of Kadesh.
9 The voice of the LORD twists mighty oaks*
and strips the forests bare.
In his Temple everyone shouts, "Glory!"

10 The LORD rules over the floodwaters.
The LORD reigns as king forever.
11 The LORD gives his people strength.
The LORD blesses them with peace.

28:9 Hebrew *Bless your inheritance.* 29:1 Hebrew *you sons of God.* 29:6 Hebrew *Sirion,* another name for Mount Hermon.
29:9 Or *causes the deer to writhe in labor.*

30

A psalm of David. A song for the dedication of the Temple.

1 I will exalt you, LORD, for you rescued me.
You refused to let my enemies triumph over me.
2 O LORD my God, I cried to you for help,
and you restored my health.
3 You brought me up from the grave,* O LORD.
You kept me from falling into the pit of death.

4 Sing to the LORD, all you godly ones!
Praise his holy name.
5 For his anger lasts only a moment,
but his favor lasts a lifetime!
Weeping may last through the night,
but joy comes with the morning.

6 When I was prosperous, I said,
"Nothing can stop me now!"
7 Your favor, O LORD, made me as secure as a mountain.
Then you turned away from me, and I was shattered.

FALSE SECURITY 30:6-7

Wealth and power had made David feel invincible. Although he knew that both came from God, he felt a certain pride in them. Wealth, power, and fame can have an intoxicating effect on people, making them feel self-reliant and independent from God. But this is a false security that is shattered easily. Feeling secure because of what you have (popularity; money; high GPA)? Don't be fooled by the false security of prosperity or status. Unlike God, these won't last forever. ■

8 I cried out to you, O LORD.
I begged the Lord for mercy, saying,
9 "What will you gain if I die,
if I sink into the grave?
Can my dust praise you?
Can it tell of your faithfulness?
10 Hear me, LORD, and have mercy on me.
Help me, O LORD."

11 You have turned my mourning into joyful dancing.
You have taken away my clothes of mourning and
clothed me with joy,
12 that I might sing praises to you and not be silent.
O LORD my God, I will give you thanks forever!

31

For the choir director: A psalm of David.

1 O LORD, I have come to you for protection;
don't let me be disgraced.
Save me, for you do what is right.
2 Turn your ear to listen to me;
rescue me quickly.
Be my rock of protection,
a fortress where I will be safe.
3 You are my rock and my fortress.
For the honor of your name, lead me out
of this danger.
4 Pull me from the trap my enemies set for me,
for I find protection in you alone.
5 I entrust my spirit into your hand.
Rescue me, LORD, for you are a faithful God.

6 I hate those who worship worthless idols.
I trust in the LORD.
7 I will be glad and rejoice in your unfailing love,
for you have seen my troubles,
and you care about the anguish of my soul.
8 You have not handed me over to my enemies
but have set me in a safe place.

9 Have mercy on me, LORD, for I am in distress.
Tears blur my eyes.
My body and soul are withering away.
10 I am dying from grief;
my years are shortened by sadness.
Sin has drained my strength;
I am wasting away from within.
11 I am scorned by all my enemies
and despised by my neighbors—
even my friends are afraid to come near me.
When they see me on the street,
they run the other way.
12 I am ignored as if I were dead,
as if I were a broken pot.
13 I have heard the many rumors about me,
and I am surrounded by terror.
My enemies conspire against me,
plotting to take my life.

14 But I am trusting you, O LORD,
saying, "You are my God!"
15 My future is in your hands.
Rescue me from those who hunt me
down relentlessly.
16 Let your favor shine on your servant.
In your unfailing love, rescue me.
17 Don't let me be disgraced, O LORD,
for I call out to you for help.
Let the wicked be disgraced;
let them lie silent in the grave.*
18 Silence their lying lips—
those proud and arrogant lips that accuse the godly.

19 How great is the goodness
you have stored up for those who fear you.
You lavish it on those who come to you for
protection,
blessing them before the watching world.

30:3 Hebrew *from Sheol.* 31:17 Hebrew *in Sheol.*

20 You hide them in the shelter of your presence,
safe from those who conspire against them.
You shelter them in your presence,
far from accusing tongues.

21 Praise the LORD,
for he has shown me the wonders of his
unfailing love.
He kept me safe when my city was under attack.
22 In panic I cried out,
"I am cut off from the LORD!"
But you heard my cry for mercy
and answered my call for help.

23 Love the LORD, all you godly ones!
For the LORD protects those who are loyal to him,
but he harshly punishes the arrogant.
24 So be strong and courageous,
all you who put your hope in the LORD!

32

A psalm of David.*

1 Oh, what joy for those
whose disobedience is forgiven,
whose sin is put out of sight!
2 Yes, what joy for those
whose record the LORD has cleared of guilt,*
whose lives are lived in complete honesty!
3 When I refused to confess my sin,
my body wasted away,
and I groaned all day long.
4 Day and night your hand of discipline was heavy
on me.
My strength evaporated like water in the summer
heat. *Interlude*

5 Finally, I confessed all my sins to you
and stopped trying to hide my guilt.
I said to myself, "I will confess my rebellion to the
LORD."
And you forgave me! All my guilt is gone. *Interlude*

6 Therefore, let all the godly pray to you while there
is still time,
that they may not drown in the floodwaters
of judgment.
7 For you are my hiding place;
you protect me from trouble.
You surround me with songs of victory. *Interlude*

8 The LORD says, "I will guide you along the best
pathway for your life.
I will advise you and watch over you.
9 Do not be like a senseless horse or mule
that needs a bit and bridle to keep it under
control."

10 Many sorrows come to the wicked,
but unfailing love surrounds those who trust
the LORD.
11 So rejoice in the LORD and be glad, all you who
obey him!
Shout for joy, all you whose hearts are pure!

33

1 Let the godly sing for joy to the LORD;
it is fitting for the pure to praise him.
2 Praise the LORD with melodies on the lyre;
make music for him on the ten-stringed harp.
3 Sing a new song of praise to him;
play skillfully on the harp, and sing with joy.
4 For the word of the LORD holds true,
and we can trust everything he does.

IN GOD WE TRUST? 33:4

A person's words are measured by the quality of his or her character. If your friends trust what you say, it is because they trust you. If you trust what God says, it is because you trust him to be the God he claims to be. If you doubt his words, you doubt the integrity of God himself. Would you, like the psalmist, say, "We can trust everything he does"? ■

5 He loves whatever is just and good;
the unfailing love of the LORD fills the earth.

6 The LORD merely spoke,
and the heavens were created.
He breathed the word,
and all the stars were born.
7 He assigned the sea its boundaries
and locked the oceans in vast reservoirs.
8 Let the whole world fear the LORD,
and let everyone stand in awe of him.
9 For when he spoke, the world began!
It appeared at his command.

10 The LORD frustrates the plans of the nations
and thwarts all their schemes.
11 But the LORD's plans stand firm forever;
his intentions can never be shaken.

12 What joy for the nation whose God is the LORD,
whose people he has chosen as his inheritance.

13 The LORD looks down from heaven
and sees the whole human race.
14 From his throne he observes
all who live on the earth.
15 He made their hearts,
so he understands everything they do.
16 The best-equipped army cannot save a king,
nor is great strength enough to save a warrior.

32:TITLE Hebrew *maskil.* This may be a literary or musical term. 32:2 Greek version reads *of sin.* Compare Rom 4:7.

keeping it real

There are two Scriptures that help me daily. Because I suffer from Chronic Fatigue Syndrome (Epstein-Barr Virus), I am always tired and often in pain. Psalm 34 reminds me that I can rely on God constantly for every ounce of strength I need. It also reminds me that God hears the cry of those who trust him.

Jeremiah 29:11 is my source of hope for the future. It reminds me that my constant worry about college and about ever getting over my illness is totally unnecessary; everything that happens is part of God's plan for my life. His plan is for good, not disaster, and he intends to give me a future and a hope. He truly will take care of everything as I trust him.

I have memorized these passages, and I remind myself of the words whenever I need to—which is almost every day! They are a great source of comfort to me.

—Anita

17 Don't count on your warhorse to give you victory—
for all its strength, it cannot save you.

18 But the LORD watches over those who fear him,
those who rely on his unfailing love.
19 He rescues them from death
and keeps them alive in times of famine.

20 We put our hope in the LORD.
He is our help and our shield.
21 In him our hearts rejoice,
for we trust in his holy name.
22 Let your unfailing love surround us, LORD,
for our hope is in you alone.

34*

A psalm of David, regarding the time he pretended to be insane in front of Abimelech, who sent him away.

1 I will praise the LORD at all times.
I will constantly speak his praises.
2 I will boast only in the LORD;
let all who are helpless take heart.
3 Come, let us tell of the LORD's greatness;
let us exalt his name together.

4 I prayed to the LORD, and he answered me.
He freed me from all my fears.
5 Those who look to him for help will be radiant
with joy;
no shadow of shame will darken their faces.
6 In my desperation I prayed, and the LORD listened;
he saved me from all my troubles.
7 For the angel of the LORD is a guard;
he surrounds and defends all who fear him.

8 Taste and see that the LORD is good.
Oh, the joys of those who take refuge in him!
9 Fear the LORD, you his godly people,
for those who fear him will have all they need.
10 Even strong young lions sometimes go hungry,
but those who trust in the LORD will lack no
good thing.

ALL WE NEED 34:9-10

"Those who fear him will have all they need." This is not a blanket promise that all Christians will be rich. After all, many Christians face unbearable poverty and hardship. It reflects David's belief in God's goodness—all those who call upon God will be answered, sometimes in unexpected ways. In what unusual ways have you seen God act in your life? How do these experiences help you to trust him in other situations? ■

11 Come, my children, and listen to me,
and I will teach you to fear the LORD.
12 Does anyone want to live a life
that is long and prosperous?
13 Then keep your tongue from speaking evil
and your lips from telling lies!
14 Turn away from evil and do good.
Search for peace, and work to maintain it.

15 The eyes of the LORD watch over those who do right;
his ears are open to their cries for help.

34 This psalm is a Hebrew acrostic poem; each verse begins with a successive letter of the Hebrew alphabet.

16 But the LORD turns his face against those who
do evil;
he will erase their memory from the earth.
17 The LORD hears his people when they call to him
for help.
He rescues them from all their troubles.
18 The LORD is close to the brokenhearted;
he rescues those whose spirits are crushed.

19 The righteous person faces many troubles,
but the LORD comes to the rescue each time.
20 For the LORD protects the bones of the righteous;
not one of them is broken!

21 Calamity will surely overtake the wicked,
and those who hate the righteous will be punished.
22 But the LORD will redeem those who serve him.
No one who takes refuge in him will
be condemned.

35

A psalm of David.

1 O LORD, oppose those who oppose me.
Fight those who fight against me.
2 Put on your armor, and take up your shield.
Prepare for battle, and come to my aid.
3 Lift up your spear and javelin
against those who pursue me.
Let me hear you say,
"I will give you victory!"
4 Bring shame and disgrace on those trying to kill me;
turn them back and humiliate those who want
to harm me.
5 Blow them away like chaff in the wind—
a wind sent by the angel of the LORD.
6 Make their path dark and slippery,
with the angel of the LORD pursuing them.
7 I did them no wrong, but they laid a trap for me.
I did them no wrong, but they dug a pit to catch me.
8 So let sudden ruin come upon them!
Let them be caught in the trap they set for me!
Let them be destroyed in the pit they dug for me.

9 Then I will rejoice in the LORD.
I will be glad because he rescues me.
10 With every bone in my body I will praise him:
"LORD, who can compare with you?
Who else rescues the helpless from the strong?
Who else protects the helpless and poor from
those who rob them?"

11 Malicious witnesses testify against me.
They accuse me of crimes I know nothing about.
12 They repay me evil for good.
I am sick with despair.
13 Yet when they were ill, I grieved for them.
I denied myself by fasting for them,
but my prayers returned unanswered.
14 I was sad, as though they were my friends or family,
as if I were grieving for my own mother.
15 But they are glad now that I am in trouble;
they gleefully join together against me.
I am attacked by people I don't even know;
they slander me constantly.
16 They mock me and call me names;
they snarl at me.

17 How long, O Lord, will you look on and do nothing?
Rescue me from their fierce attacks.
Protect my life from these lions!
18 Then I will thank you in front of the great assembly.
I will praise you before all the people.
19 Don't let my treacherous enemies rejoice over
my defeat.
Don't let those who hate me without cause gloat
over my sorrow.
20 They don't talk of peace;
they plot against innocent people who mind their
own business.
21 They shout, "Aha! Aha!
With our own eyes we saw him do it!"

22 O LORD, you know all about this.
Do not stay silent.
Do not abandon me now, O Lord.
23 Wake up! Rise to my defense!
Take up my case, my God and my Lord.
24 Declare me not guilty, O LORD my God, for you
give justice.
Don't let my enemies laugh about me in
my troubles.
25 Don't let them say, "Look, we got what we wanted!
Now we will eat him alive!"

26 May those who rejoice at my troubles
be humiliated and disgraced.
May those who triumph over me
be covered with shame and dishonor.
27 But give great joy to those who came to my defense.
Let them continually say, "Great is the LORD,
who delights in blessing his servant with peace!"
28 Then I will proclaim your justice,
and I will praise you all day long.

36

For the choir director: A psalm of David, the servant of the LORD.

1 Sin whispers to the wicked, deep within their hearts.
They have no fear of God at all.
2 In their blind conceit,
they cannot see how wicked they really are.
3 Everything they say is crooked and deceitful.
They refuse to act wisely or do good.
4 They lie awake at night, hatching sinful plots.
Their actions are never good.
They make no attempt to turn from evil.

5 Your unfailing love, O LORD, is as vast as the heavens;
your faithfulness reaches beyond the clouds.
6 Your righteousness is like the mighty mountains,
your justice like the ocean depths.
You care for people and animals alike, O LORD.
7 How precious is your unfailing love, O God!
All humanity finds shelter
in the shadow of your wings.
8 You feed them from the abundance of your own house,
letting them drink from your river of delights.
9 For you are the fountain of life,
the light by which we see.

10 Pour out your unfailing love on those who love you;
give justice to those with honest hearts.
11 Don't let the proud trample me
or the wicked push me around.
12 Look! Those who do evil have fallen!
They are thrown down, never to rise again.

37*

A psalm of David.

1 Don't worry about the wicked
or envy those who do wrong.
2 For like grass, they soon fade away.
Like spring flowers, they soon wither.

3 Trust in the LORD and do good.
Then you will live safely in the land and prosper.
4 Take delight in the LORD,
and he will give you your heart's desires.

5 Commit everything you do to the LORD.
Trust him, and he will help you.
6 He will make your innocence radiate like the dawn,
and the justice of your cause will shine like the noonday sun.

7 Be still in the presence of the LORD,
and wait patiently for him to act.
Don't worry about evil people who prosper
or fret about their wicked schemes.

8 Stop being angry!
Turn from your rage!
Do not lose your temper—
it only leads to harm.
9 For the wicked will be destroyed,
but those who trust in the LORD will possess the land.

10 Soon the wicked will disappear.
Though you look for them, they will be gone.
11 The lowly will possess the land
and will live in peace and prosperity.

12 The wicked plot against the godly;
they snarl at them in defiance.
13 But the Lord just laughs,
for he sees their day of judgment coming.

14 The wicked draw their swords
and string their bows
to kill the poor and the oppressed,
to slaughter those who do right.

SHORT-/LONG-TERM REWARDS 37:1-40

Like David, have you ever worried when people seem to gain by their evil acts while kind people suffer? Maybe you're wondering what the advantage of being good is when you see bad behavior rewarded. The rewards of those who do evil are in the short term while those who stick with God have long-term rewards. In other words, they're getting theirs now, you'll get most of yours later. An eternal reward awaits you, but only eternal destruction awaits evil. ■

15 But their swords will stab their own hearts,
and their bows will be broken.

16 It is better to be godly and have little
than to be evil and rich.
17 For the strength of the wicked will be shattered,
but the LORD takes care of the godly.

18 Day by day the LORD takes care of the innocent,
and they will receive an inheritance that lasts forever.
19 They will not be disgraced in hard times;
even in famine they will have more than enough.

20 But the wicked will die.
The LORD's enemies are like flowers in a field—
they will disappear like smoke.

21 The wicked borrow and never repay,
but the godly are generous givers.
22 Those the LORD blesses will possess the land,
but those he curses will die.

23 The LORD directs the steps of the godly.
He delights in every detail of their lives.
24 Though they stumble, they will never fall,
for the LORD holds them by the hand.

25 Once I was young, and now I am old.
Yet I have never seen the godly abandoned
or their children begging for bread.
26 The godly always give generous loans to others,
and their children are a blessing.

27 Turn from evil and do good,
and you will live in the land forever.

37 This psalm is a Hebrew acrostic poem; each stanza begins with a successive letter of the Hebrew alphabet.

28 For the LORD loves justice,
and he will never abandon the godly.

He will keep them safe forever,
but the children of the wicked will die.
29 The godly will possess the land
and will live there forever.

30 The godly offer good counsel;
they teach right from wrong.
31 They have made God's law their own,
so they will never slip from his path.

32 The wicked wait in ambush for the godly,
looking for an excuse to kill them.
33 But the LORD will not let the wicked succeed
or let the godly be condemned when they are
put on trial.

34 Put your hope in the LORD.
Travel steadily along his path.
He will honor you by giving you the land.
You will see the wicked destroyed.

35 I have seen wicked and ruthless people
flourishing like a tree in its native soil.
36 But when I looked again, they were gone!
Though I searched for them, I could not find them!

37 Look at those who are honest and good,
for a wonderful future awaits those who love peace.
38 But the rebellious will be destroyed;
they have no future.

39 The LORD rescues the godly;
he is their fortress in times of trouble.
40 The LORD helps them,
rescuing them from the wicked.
He saves them,
and they find shelter in him.

38

A psalm of David, asking God to remember him.

1 O LORD, don't rebuke me in your anger
or discipline me in your rage!
2 Your arrows have struck deep,
and your blows are crushing me.
3 Because of your anger, my whole body is sick;
my health is broken because of my sins.
4 My guilt overwhelms me—
it is a burden too heavy to bear.
5 My wounds fester and stink
because of my foolish sins.
6 I am bent over and racked with pain.
All day long I walk around filled with grief.
7 A raging fever burns within me,
and my health is broken.
8 I am exhausted and completely crushed.
My groans come from an anguished heart.

9 You know what I long for, Lord;
you hear my every sigh.
10 My heart beats wildly, my strength fails,
and I am going blind.
11 My loved ones and friends stay away, fearing
my disease.
Even my own family stands at a distance.
12 Meanwhile, my enemies lay traps to kill me.
Those who wish me harm make plans to ruin me.
All day long they plan their treachery.

13 But I am deaf to all their threats.
I am silent before them as one who cannot speak.
14 I choose to hear nothing,
and I make no reply.
15 For I am waiting for you, O LORD.
You must answer for me, O Lord my God.
16 I prayed, "Don't let my enemies gloat over me
or rejoice at my downfall."

17 I am on the verge of collapse,
facing constant pain.
18 But I confess my sins;
I am deeply sorry for what I have done.
19 I have many aggressive enemies;
they hate me without reason.
20 They repay me evil for good
and oppose me for pursuing good.
21 Do not abandon me, O LORD.
Do not stand at a distance, my God.
22 Come quickly to help me,
O Lord my savior.

39

For Jeduthun, the choir director: A psalm of David.

1 I said to myself, "I will watch what I do
and not sin in what I say.
I will hold my tongue
when the ungodly are around me."
2 But as I stood there in silence—
not even speaking of good things—
the turmoil within me grew worse.
3 The more I thought about it,
the hotter I got,
igniting a fire of words:
4 "LORD, remind me how brief my time on earth
will be.
Remind me that my days are numbered—
how fleeting my life is.
5 You have made my life no longer than the width
of my hand.
My entire lifetime is just a moment to you;
at best, each of us is but a breath." *Interlude*

DON'T PUT IT OFF 39:4

David acknowledged the brevity of life. Life seems short no matter how long we live. Maybe that's why procrastination is such a thief of time. We put off telling people how much they matter to us. We put off doing that research paper until the day before it's due. Some of us realize too late how short life is. But David's warning about the shortness of life is antidote to the virus of procrastination. Are there decisions or other important things that you're putting off? Life is short. What are you doing to do? ■

6 We are merely moving shadows,
and all our busy rushing ends in nothing.
We heap up wealth,
not knowing who will spend it.
7 And so, Lord, where do I put my hope?
My only hope is in you.
8 Rescue me from my rebellion.
Do not let fools mock me.
9 I am silent before you; I won't say a word,
for my punishment is from you.
10 But please stop striking me!
I am exhausted by the blows from your hand.
11 When you discipline us for our sins,
you consume like a moth what is precious to us.
Each of us is but a breath. *Interlude*

12 Hear my prayer, O LORD!
Listen to my cries for help!
Don't ignore my tears.
For I am your guest—
a traveler passing through,
as my ancestors were before me.
13 Leave me alone so I can smile again
before I am gone and exist no more.

40

For the choir director: A psalm of David.

1 I waited patiently for the LORD to help me,
and he turned to me and heard my cry.
2 He lifted me out of the pit of despair,
out of the mud and the mire.
He set my feet on solid ground
and steadied me as I walked along.
3 He has given me a new song to sing,
a hymn of praise to our God.
Many will see what he has done and be amazed.
They will put their trust in the LORD.

4 Oh, the joys of those who trust the LORD,
who have no confidence in the proud
or in those who worship idols.
5 O LORD my God, you have performed many
wonders for us.
Your plans for us are too numerous to list.
You have no equal.
If I tried to recite all your wonderful deeds,
I would never come to the end of them.

6 You take no delight in sacrifices or offerings.
Now that you have made me listen, I finally
understand*—
you don't require burnt offerings or sin offerings.
7 Then I said, "Look, I have come.
As is written about me in the Scriptures:
8 I take joy in doing your will, my God,
for your instructions are written on my heart."

9 I have told all your people about your justice.
I have not been afraid to speak out,
as you, O LORD, well know.
10 I have not kept the good news of your justice hidden
in my heart;
I have talked about your faithfulness and
saving power.
I have told everyone in the great assembly
of your unfailing love and faithfulness.

11 LORD, don't hold back your tender mercies from me.
Let your unfailing love and faithfulness always
protect me.
12 For troubles surround me—
too many to count!
My sins pile up so high
I can't see my way out.
They outnumber the hairs on my head.
I have lost all courage.

13 Please, LORD, rescue me!
Come quickly, LORD, and help me.
14 May those who try to destroy me
be humiliated and put to shame.
May those who take delight in my trouble
be turned back in disgrace.
15 Let them be horrified by their shame,
for they said, "Aha! We've got him now!"

16 But may all who search for you
be filled with joy and gladness in you.
May those who love your salvation
repeatedly shout, "The LORD is great!"
17 As for me, since I am poor and needy,
let the Lord keep me in his thoughts.
You are my helper and my savior.
O my God, do not delay.

41

For the choir director: A psalm of David.

1 Oh, the joys of those who are kind to the poor!
The LORD rescues them when they are in trouble.
2 The LORD protects them

40:6 Greek text reads *You have given me a body*. Compare Heb 10:5.

and keeps them alive.
He gives them prosperity in the land
and rescues them from their enemies.
3 The LORD nurses them when they are sick
and restores them to health.

4 "O LORD," I prayed, "have mercy on me.
Heal me, for I have sinned against you."
5 But my enemies say nothing but evil about me.
"How soon will he die and be forgotten?" they ask.
6 They visit me as if they were my friends,
but all the while they gather gossip,
and when they leave, they spread it everywhere.
7 All who hate me whisper about me,
imagining the worst.
8 "He has some fatal disease," they say.
"He will never get out of that bed!"
9 Even my best friend, the one I trusted completely,
the one who shared my food, has turned
against me.

10 LORD, have mercy on me.
Make me well again, so I can pay them back!
11 I know you are pleased with me,
for you have not let my enemies triumph over me.
12 You have preserved my life because I am innocent;
you have brought me into your presence forever.

13 Praise the LORD, the God of Israel,
who lives from everlasting to everlasting.
Amen and amen!

BOOK TWO (Psalms 42–72)

42

For the choir director: A psalm of the descendants of Korah.*

1 As the deer longs for streams of water,
so I long for you, O God.
2 I thirst for God, the living God.
When can I go and stand before him?
3 Day and night I have only tears for food,
while my enemies continually taunt me, saying,
"Where is this God of yours?"

4 My heart is breaking
as I remember how it used to be:
I walked among the crowds of worshipers,
leading a great procession to the house of God,
singing for joy and giving thanks
amid the sound of a great celebration!

5 Why am I discouraged?
Why is my heart so sad?
I will put my hope in God!
I will praise him again—
my Savior and 6my God!

Now I am deeply discouraged,
but I will remember you—
even from distant Mount Hermon, the source of
the Jordan,
from the land of Mount Mizar.
7 I hear the tumult of the raging seas
as your waves and surging tides sweep over me.
8 But each day the LORD pours his unfailing love
upon me,
and through each night I sing his songs,
praying to God who gives me life.

9 "O God my rock," I cry,
"Why have you forgotten me?
Why must I wander around in grief,
oppressed by my enemies?"
10 Their taunts break my bones.
They scoff, "Where is this God of yours?"

DEPRESSION 42:1-11

After being carried away from Jerusalem by an invading army, the psalmist was understandably depressed. Many of us can relate to feelings of depression. One cure for the blues is to think about what God has done in the past for his people. That's why this psalm is an antidepressant. It's a sure cure for the blues. ■

11 Why am I discouraged?
Why is my heart so sad?
I will put my hope in God!
I will praise him again—
my Savior and my God!

43

1 Declare me innocent, O God!
Defend me against these ungodly people.
Rescue me from these unjust liars.
2 For you are God, my only safe haven.
Why have you tossed me aside?
Why must I wander around in grief,
oppressed by my enemies?
3 Send out your light and your truth;
let them guide me.
Let them lead me to your holy mountain,
to the place where you live.
4 There I will go to the altar of God,
to God—the source of all my joy.
I will praise you with my harp,
O God, my God!

5 Why am I discouraged?
Why is my heart so sad?
I will put my hope in God!
I will praise him again—
my Savior and my God!

42:TITLE Hebrew *maskil*. This may be a literary or musical term.

44

For the choir director: A psalm of the descendants of Korah.*

1 O God, we have heard it with our own ears—
our ancestors have told us
of all you did in their day,
in days long ago:
2 You drove out the pagan nations by your power
and gave all the land to our ancestors.
You crushed their enemies
and set our ancestors free.
3 They did not conquer the land with their swords;
it was not their own strong arm that gave them victory.
It was your right hand and strong arm
and the blinding light from your face that helped them,
for you loved them.

4 You are my King and my God.
You command victories for Israel.*
5 Only by your power can we push back our enemies;
only in your name can we trample our foes.
6 I do not trust in my bow;
I do not count on my sword to save me.
7 You are the one who gives us victory over our enemies;
you disgrace those who hate us.
8 O God, we give glory to you all day long
and constantly praise your name. *Interlude*

9 But now you have tossed us aside in dishonor.
You no longer lead our armies to battle.
10 You make us retreat from our enemies
and allow those who hate us to plunder our land.
11 You have butchered us like sheep
and scattered us among the nations.
12 You sold your precious people for a pittance,
making nothing on the sale.
13 You let our neighbors mock us.
We are an object of scorn and derision to those around us.
14 You have made us the butt of their jokes;
they shake their heads at us in scorn.
15 We can't escape the constant humiliation;
shame is written across our faces.
16 All we hear are the taunts of our mockers.
All we see are our vengeful enemies.

17 All this has happened though we have not forgotten you.
We have not violated your covenant.
18 Our hearts have not deserted you.
We have not strayed from your path.
19 Yet you have crushed us in the jackal's desert home.
You have covered us with darkness and death.
20 If we had forgotten the name of our God
or spread our hands in prayer to foreign gods,
21 God would surely have known it,
for he knows the secrets of every heart.
22 But for your sake we are killed every day;
we are being slaughtered like sheep.

CONSTANT LOVE 44:22-26

After a defeat by Israel's enemies, the writer cried to God to save his people by his constant love. When you're in trouble, what truths do you hold on to? Like the psalmist, you can hold on to the fact that God's love will never change. Nothing can separate us from God's love, not even death (see Rom 8:36-39). ■

23 Wake up, O Lord! Why do you sleep?
Get up! Do not reject us forever.
24 Why do you look the other way?
Why do you ignore our suffering and oppression?
25 We collapse in the dust,
lying face down in the dirt.
26 Rise up! Help us!
Ransom us because of your unfailing love.

45

For the choir director: A love song to be sung to the tune "Lilies." A psalm of the descendants of Korah.*

1 Beautiful words stir my heart.
I will recite a lovely poem about the king,
for my tongue is like the pen of a skillful poet.

2 You are the most handsome of all.
Gracious words stream from your lips.
God himself has blessed you forever.
3 Put on your sword, O mighty warrior!
You are so glorious, so majestic!
4 In your majesty, ride out to victory,
defending truth, humility, and justice.
Go forth to perform awe-inspiring deeds!
5 Your arrows are sharp, piercing your enemies' hearts.
The nations fall beneath your feet.

6 Your throne, O God,* endures forever and ever.
You rule with a scepter of justice.
7 You love justice and hate evil.
Therefore God, your God, has anointed you,
pouring out the oil of joy on you more than on anyone else.
8 Myrrh, aloes, and cassia perfume your robes.
In ivory palaces the music of strings entertains you.
9 Kings' daughters are among your noble women.

44:TITLE Hebrew *maskil.* This may be a literary or musical term. **44:4** Hebrew *for Jacob.* The names "Jacob" and "Israel" are often interchanged throughout the Old Testament, referring sometimes to the individual patriarch and sometimes to the nation. **45:TITLE** Hebrew *maskil.* This may be a literary or musical term. **45:6** Or *Your divine throne.*

keeping it real

Everything was going wrong in my life. My parents were getting a divorce. My boyfriend broke up with me. I couldn't concentrate in school, so my grades started going down.

My faith was affected, too . I couldn't understand why God allowed all this to happen to me. When I prayed, I felt like I was talking to myself. I guess I was mad at God, blaming him in my heart for the things that were happening.

I tried to read the Bible anyway, even though I was struggling spiritually. One day I read Psalm 46. Verse 10 really made me stop and think. This verse seemed to say, "Stop looking at your problems and look at me. Look at who I am." I realized God was in charge—he knew exactly what he was doing and had a purpose in mind for what I was going through. I just needed to accept it and believe he is a loving God who would never deliberately hurt me.

That changed my perspective. Instead of blaming God, I asked him to help me through my struggles. And he has. Things are still rough sometimes, but now I know that God is for me, and he will work things out for good. As Romans 8:31 says, "If God is for us, who can ever be against us?" **—Jodi**

At your right side stands the queen,
wearing jewelry of finest gold from Ophir!

10 Listen to me, O royal daughter; take to heart
what I say.
Forget your people and your family far away.
11 For your royal husband delights in your beauty;
honor him, for he is your lord.
12 The princess of Tyre* will shower you with gifts.
The wealthy will beg your favor.
13 The bride, a princess, looks glorious
in her golden gown.
14 In her beautiful robes, she is led to the king,
accompanied by her bridesmaids.
15 What a joyful and enthusiastic procession
as they enter the king's palace!

16 Your sons will become kings like their father.
You will make them rulers over many lands.
17 I will bring honor to your name in every generation.
Therefore, the nations will praise you forever
and ever.

46

*For the choir director: A song of the descendants of Korah, to be sung by soprano voices.**

1 God is our refuge and strength,
always ready to help in times of trouble.
2 So we will not fear when earthquakes come
and the mountains crumble into the sea.
3 Let the oceans roar and foam.
Let the mountains tremble as the waters
surge! *Interlude*

CONFIDENCE 46:1-3

Even in the face of utter destruction, the psalmist expressed a quiet confidence in God's ability to save him. The fear of mountains or cities suddenly crumbling because of a nuclear blast haunts many people today. Facing destruction or terrorism without fear seems impossible. Yet the Bible is clear: God is our eternal refuge, even in the face of total destruction. Like the psalmist would you confidently say, "We will not fear" even if the world seems to crumble around you? ■

4 A river brings joy to the city of our God,
the sacred home of the Most High.
5 God dwells in that city; it cannot be destroyed.
From the very break of day, God will protect it.
6 The nations are in chaos,
and their kingdoms crumble!
God's voice thunders,
and the earth melts!
7 The LORD of Heaven's Armies is here among us;
the God of Israel* is our fortress. *Interlude*

45:12 Hebrew *The daughter of Tyre.* 46:TITLE Hebrew *according to alamoth.* 46:7 Hebrew *of Jacob;* also in 46:11. See note on 44:4.

8 Come, see the glorious works of the LORD:
See how he brings destruction upon the world.
9 He causes wars to end throughout the earth.
He breaks the bow and snaps the spear;
he burns the shields with fire.

10 "Be still, and know that I am God!
I will be honored by every nation.
I will be honored throughout the world."

11 The LORD of Heaven's Armies is here among us;
the God of Israel is our fortress. *Interlude*

47

For the choir director: A psalm of the descendants of Korah.

1 Come, everyone! Clap your hands!
Shout to God with joyful praise!
2 For the LORD Most High is awesome.
He is the great King of all the earth.
3 He subdues the nations before us,
putting our enemies beneath our feet.
4 He chose the Promised Land as our inheritance,
the proud possession of Jacob's descendants,
whom he loves. *Interlude*

5 God has ascended with a mighty shout.
The LORD has ascended with trumpets blaring.
6 Sing praises to God, sing praises;
sing praises to our King, sing praises!
7 For God is the King over all the earth.
Praise him with a psalm!
8 God reigns above the nations,
sitting on his holy throne.
9 The rulers of the world have gathered together
with the people of the God of Abraham.
For all the kings of the earth belong to God.
He is highly honored everywhere.

48

A song. A psalm of the descendants of Korah.

1 How great is the LORD,
how deserving of praise,
in the city of our God,
which sits on his holy mountain!
2 It is high and magnificent;
the whole earth rejoices to see it!
Mount Zion, the holy mountain,*
is the city of the great King!
3 God himself is in Jerusalem's towers,
revealing himself as its defender.

4 The kings of the earth joined forces
and advanced against the city.
5 But when they saw it, they were stunned;
they were terrified and ran away.
6 They were gripped with terror
and writhed in pain like a woman in labor.
7 You destroyed them like the mighty ships
of Tarshish
shattered by a powerful east wind.

8 We had heard of the city's glory,
but now we have seen it ourselves—
the city of the LORD of Heaven's Armies.
It is the city of our God;
he will make it safe forever. *Interlude*

9 O God, we meditate on your unfailing love
as we worship in your Temple.
10 As your name deserves, O God,
you will be praised to the ends of the earth.
Your strong right hand is filled with victory.
11 Let the people on Mount Zion rejoice.
Let all the towns of Judah be glad
because of your justice.

12 Go, inspect the city of Jerusalem.*
Walk around and count the many towers.
13 Take note of the fortified walls,
and tour all the citadels,
that you may describe them
to future generations.
14 For that is what God is like.
He is our God forever and ever,
and he will guide us until we die.

THE GUIDE 48:14

We often pray for God's guidance as we struggle with decisions. What we need is both guidance and a guide—a map that gives us landmarks and directions and a constant companion who has an intimate knowledge of the way. A guide can also make sure that we interpret the map correctly. The Bible is just such a map, and God is a constant companion and guide. Is he yours? ■

49

For the choir director: A psalm of the descendants of Korah.

1 Listen to this, all you people!
Pay attention, everyone in the world!
2 High and low,
rich and poor—listen!
3 For my words are wise,
and my thoughts are filled with insight.
4 I listen carefully to many proverbs
and solve riddles with inspiration from a harp.

5 Why should I fear when trouble comes,
when enemies surround me?

48:2 Or *Mount Zion, in the far north;* Hebrew reads *Mount Zion, the heights of Zaphon.* 48:12 Hebrew *Zion.*

6 They trust in their wealth
and boast of great riches.
7 Yet they cannot redeem themselves from death*
by paying a ransom to God.
8 Redemption does not come so easily,
for no one can ever pay enough
9 to live forever
and never see the grave.

10 Those who are wise must finally die,
just like the foolish and senseless,
leaving all their wealth behind.
11 The grave is their eternal home,
where they will stay forever.
They may name their estates after themselves,
12 but their fame will not last.
They will die, just like animals.
13 This is the fate of fools,
though they are remembered as
being wise.* *Interlude*

14 Like sheep, they are led to the grave,*
where death will be their shepherd.
In the morning the godly will rule over them.
Their bodies will rot in the grave,
far from their grand estates.
15 But as for me, God will redeem my life.
He will snatch me from the power of
the grave. *Interlude*

16 So don't be dismayed when the wicked grow rich
and their homes become ever more splendid.
17 For when they die, they take nothing with them.
Their wealth will not follow them into the grave.
18 In this life they consider themselves fortunate
and are applauded for their success.
19 But they will die like all before them
and never again see the light of day.
20 People who boast of their wealth don't understand;
they will die, just like animals.

50

A psalm of Asaph.

1 The LORD, the Mighty One, is God,
and he has spoken;
he has summoned all humanity
from where the sun rises to where it sets.
2 From Mount Zion, the perfection of beauty,
God shines in glorious radiance.
3 Our God approaches,
and he is not silent.
Fire devours everything in his way,
and a great storm rages around him.
4 He calls on the heavens above and earth below
to witness the judgment of his people.
5 "Bring my faithful people to me—
those who made a covenant with me by
giving sacrifices."
6 Then let the heavens proclaim his justice,
for God himself will be the judge. *Interlude*

7 "O my people, listen as I speak.
Here are my charges against you, O Israel:
I am God, your God!
8 I have no complaint about your sacrifices
or the burnt offerings you constantly offer.
9 But I do not need the bulls from your barns
or the goats from your pens.
10 For all the animals of the forest are mine,
and I own the cattle on a thousand hills.
11 I know every bird on the mountains,
and all the animals of the field are mine.
12 If I were hungry, I would not tell you,
for all the world is mine and everything in it.
13 Do I eat the meat of bulls?
Do I drink the blood of goats?
14 Make thankfulness your sacrifice to God,
and keep the vows you made to the Most High.
15 Then call on me when you are in trouble,
and I will rescue you,
and you will give me glory."

16 But God says to the wicked:
"Why bother reciting my decrees
and pretending to obey my covenant?
17 For you refuse my discipline
and treat my words like trash.
18 When you see thieves, you approve of them,
and you spend your time with adulterers.
19 Your mouth is filled with wickedness,
and your tongue is full of lies.
20 You sit around and slander your brother—
your own mother's son.
21 While you did all this, I remained silent,
and you thought I didn't care.
But now I will rebuke you,
listing all my charges against you.
22 Repent, all of you who forget me,
or I will tear you apart,
and no one will help you.
23 But giving thanks is a sacrifice that truly
honors me.
If you keep to my path,
I will reveal to you the salvation of God."

51

For the choir director: A psalm of David, regarding the time Nathan the prophet came to him after David had committed adultery with Bathsheba.

1 Have mercy on me, O God,
because of your unfailing love.
Because of your great compassion,
blot out the stain of my sins.

49:7 Or *no one can redeem the life of another.* **49:13** The meaning of the Hebrew is uncertain. **49:14** Hebrew *Sheol;* also in 49:14b, 15.

2 Wash me clean from my guilt.
Purify me from my sin.
3 For I recognize my rebellion;
it haunts me day and night.
4 Against you, and you alone, have I sinned;
I have done what is evil in your sight.
You will be proved right in what you say,
and your judgment against me is just.*
5 For I was born a sinner—
yes, from the moment my mother conceived me.
6 But you desire honesty from the womb,*
teaching me wisdom even there.

7 Purify me from my sins,* and I will be clean;
wash me, and I will be whiter than snow.
8 Oh, give me back my joy again;
you have broken me—
now let me rejoice.
9 Don't keep looking at my sins.
Remove the stain of my guilt.
10 Create in me a clean heart, O God.
Renew a loyal spirit within me.

AN ISOLATED INCIDENT? 51:4

David admitted that he hurt God when he did wrong. When someone steals, murders, or lies, he or she hurts someone else. According to the world's standards, sex between two consenting adults is acceptable because nobody gets hurt. But people *do* get hurt. In David's case, a man was murdered and a baby died. When we blow it, we hurt ourselves, God, and others. Makes you want to think before you act, doesn't it? ■

11 Do not banish me from your presence,
and don't take your Holy Spirit* from me.

12 Restore to me the joy of your salvation,
and make me willing to obey you.
13 Then I will teach your ways to rebels,
and they will return to you.
14 Forgive me for shedding blood, O God who saves;
then I will joyfully sing of your forgiveness.
15 Unseal my lips, O Lord,
that my mouth may praise you.

16 You do not desire a sacrifice, or I would offer one.
You do not want a burnt offering.
17 The sacrifice you desire is a broken spirit.
You will not reject a broken and repentant heart,
O God.
18 Look with favor on Zion and help her;
rebuild the walls of Jerusalem.
19 Then you will be pleased with sacrifices offered in
the right spirit—
with burnt offerings and whole burnt offerings.
Then bulls will again be sacrificed on your altar.

Does God get tired of hearing about our troubles? I get frustrated when I struggle with the same problems over and over.

When we get into trouble, one of the first things many of us do is complain about it. Complaining means that we aren't happy with what's going on around us and we think that by telling others we want something to change, it will happen.

There's a big difference between an honest discussion of a problem and complaining about it. As you read the Psalms, you can see that David and some of the other psalmists tell God all about their troubles. (See Pss 5, 6, 10, 13, and 88, for example.) They hold nothing back. Although this may seem like complaining, it actually is a very honest way to pray.

The motivation behind our complaining is the key issue. Sometimes we complain about our problems because we want attention from others. But sometimes we complain or ask God for help because we have made wrong choices that have gotten us into trouble. Our natural response is to ask God to get us out of it. Although God always listens to us, he knows that the solution is not found in his coming to the rescue. Some troubles are best solved by being humble and admitting we are wrong.

But if trouble comes from people or situations that are beyond our control, God is not only quick to hear, but also quick to answer. Either he will provide the internal resources necessary to handle the problem (for example, see Phil 4:7 or 1 Cor 10:13). God never gets tired of hearing us and coming to our rescue if we need his help.

52

For the choir director: A psalm of David, regarding the time Doeg the Edomite said to Saul, "David has gone to see Ahimelech."*

1 Why do you boast about your crimes, great warrior?
Don't you realize God's justice continues forever?
2 All day long you plot destruction.
Your tongue cuts like a sharp razor;
you're an expert at telling lies.
3 You love evil more than good
and lies more than truth. *Interlude*

4 You love to destroy others with your words,
you liar!
5 But God will strike you down once and for all.
He will pull you from your home
and uproot you from the land of
the living. *Interlude*

51:4 Greek version reads *and you will win your case in court.* Compare Rom 3:4. **51:6** Or *from the heart;* Hebrew reads *in the inward parts.* **51:7** Hebrew *Purify me with the hyssop branch.* **51:11** Or *your spirit of holiness.* **52:TITLE** Hebrew *maskil.* This may be a literary or musical term.

6 The righteous will see it and be amazed.
They will laugh and say,
7 "Look what happens to mighty warriors
who do not trust in God.
They trust their wealth instead
and grow more and more bold in their
wickedness."

8 But I am like an olive tree, thriving in the house
of God.
I will always trust in God's unfailing love.
9 I will praise you forever, O God,
for what you have done.
I will trust in your good name
in the presence of your faithful people.

53

For the choir director: A meditation; a psalm of David.*

1 Only fools say in their hearts,
"There is no God."
They are corrupt, and their actions are evil;
not one of them does good!

FOOLS 53:1

Echoing the message of Psalm 14, David proclaimed that "only fools say in their hearts, 'There is no God.'" People may say there is no God in order to hide what they do, to have an excuse to continue doing what they're doing, and/or to ignore the Judge and avoid the judgment. A "fool" is not necessarily lacking intelligence; many atheists have some serious IQs. They believe that Christians are foolish in their beliefs. But according to God, fools are people who reject God, the only one who can save them. What's your response? ■

2 God looks down from heaven
on the entire human race;
he looks to see if anyone is truly wise,
if anyone seeks God.
3 But no, all have turned away;
all have become corrupt.*
No one does good,
not a single one!

4 Will those who do evil never learn?
They eat up my people like bread
and wouldn't think of praying to God.
5 Terror will grip them,
terror like they have never known before.
God will scatter the bones of your enemies.
You will put them to shame, for God has
rejected them.

6 Who will come from Mount Zion to rescue Israel?
When God restores his people,
Jacob will shout with joy, and Israel will rejoice.

54

For the choir director: A psalm of David, regarding the time the Ziphites came and said to Saul, "We know where David is hiding." To be accompanied by stringed instruments.*

1 Come with great power, O God, and rescue me!
Defend me with your might.
2 Listen to my prayer, O God.
Pay attention to my plea.
3 For strangers are attacking me;
violent people are trying to kill me.
They care nothing for God. *Interlude*

4 But God is my helper.
The Lord keeps me alive!
5 May the evil plans of my enemies be turned
against them.
Do as you promised and put an end to them.

6 I will sacrifice a voluntary offering to you;
I will praise your name, O LORD,
for it is good.
7 For you have rescued me from my troubles
and helped me to triumph over my enemies.

55

For the choir director: A psalm of David, to be accompanied by stringed instruments.*

1 Listen to my prayer, O God.
Do not ignore my cry for help!
2 Please listen and answer me,
for I am overwhelmed by my troubles.
3 My enemies shout at me,
making loud and wicked threats.
They bring trouble on me
and angrily hunt me down.

4 My heart pounds in my chest.
The terror of death assaults me.
5 Fear and trembling overwhelm me,
and I can't stop shaking.
6 Oh, that I had wings like a dove;
then I would fly away and rest!
7 I would fly far away
to the quiet of the wilderness. *Interlude*
8 How quickly I would escape—
far from this wild storm of hatred.

9 Confuse them, Lord, and frustrate their plans,
for I see violence and conflict in the city.

53:TITLE Hebrew *maskil.* This may be a literary or musical term. 53:3 Greek version reads *have become useless.* Compare Rom 3:12.
54:TITLE Hebrew *maskil.* This may be a literary or musical term. 55:TITLE Hebrew *maskil.* This may be a literary or musical term.

10 Its walls are patrolled day and night against
invaders,
but the real danger is wickedness within the city.
11 Everything is falling apart;
threats and cheating are rampant in the streets.

12 It is not an enemy who taunts me—
I could bear that.
It is not my foes who so arrogantly insult me—
I could have hidden from them.
13 Instead, it is you—my equal,
my companion and close friend.
14 What good fellowship we once enjoyed
as we walked together to the house of God.

REAL FRIENDS 55:12-14

Nothing hurts as much as a wound from a friend. Real friends, however, stick by you in times of trouble and offer love, acceptance, and understanding. There will be times when friends lovingly confront us, but their motive will be to help. Would your friends describe you as faithful or fickle? ■

15 Let death stalk my enemies;
let the grave* swallow them alive,
for evil makes its home within them.

16 But I will call on God,
and the LORD will rescue me.
17 Morning, noon, and night
I cry out in my distress,
and the LORD hears my voice.
18 He ransoms me and keeps me safe
from the battle waged against me,
though many still oppose me.
19 God, who has ruled forever,
will hear me and humble them. *Interlude*
For my enemies refuse to change their ways;
they do not fear God.

20 As for my companion, he betrayed his friends;
he broke his promises.
21 His words are as smooth as butter,
but in his heart is war.
His words are as soothing as lotion,
but underneath are daggers!

22 Give your burdens to the LORD,
and he will take care of you.
He will not permit the godly to slip and fall.

23 But you, O God, will send the wicked
down to the pit of destruction.
Murderers and liars will die young,
but I am trusting you to save me.

56

For the choir director: A psalm of David, regarding the time the Philistines seized him in Gath. To be sung to the tune "Dove on Distant Oaks."

1 O God, have mercy on me,
for people are hounding me.
My foes attack me all day long.
2 I am constantly hounded by those who
slander me,
and many are boldly attacking me.
3 But when I am afraid,
I will put my trust in you.
4 I praise God for what he has promised.
I trust in God, so why should I be afraid?
What can mere mortals do to me?

5 They are always twisting what I say;
they spend their days plotting to harm me.
6 They come together to spy on me—
watching my every step, eager to kill me.
7 Don't let them get away with their wickedness;
in your anger, O God, bring them down.

8 You keep track of all my sorrows.*
You have collected all my tears in your bottle.
You have recorded each one in your book.

9 My enemies will retreat when I call to you for help.
This I know: God is on my side!
10 I praise God for what he has promised;
Yes, I praise the LORD for what he has promised.
11 I trust in God, so why should I be afraid?
What can mere mortals do to me?

12 I will fulfill my vows to you, O God,
and will offer a sacrifice of thanks for your help.
13 For you have rescued me from death;
you have kept my feet from slipping.
So now I can walk in your presence, O God,
in your life-giving light.

57

For the choir director: A psalm of David, regarding the time he fled from Saul and went into the cave. To be sung to the tune "Do Not Destroy!"

1 Have mercy on me, O God, have mercy!
I look to you for protection.
I will hide beneath the shadow of your wings
until the danger passes by.
2 I cry out to God Most High,*
to God who will fulfill his purpose for me.
3 He will send help from heaven to rescue me,
disgracing those who hound me. *Interlude*
My God will send forth his unfailing love and
faithfulness.

55:15 Hebrew *let Sheol.* 56:8 Or *my wanderings.* 57:2 Hebrew *El-Elyon.*

keeping it real

I'll never forget the day my father collapsed and was rushed to the hospital. The doctor told my mother and me that he'd suffered a severe heart attack and was now teetering between life and death; it could go either way. I was really scared! Standing with my mother by his bed, I prayed harder than I'd ever prayed before. I didn't want to lose my dad! I asked God for a promise from his Word. The verse he brought to mind is Psalm 57:1: "Have mercy on me, O God, have mercy! I look to you for protection. I will hide beneath the shadow of your wings until the danger passes by."

Through that verse, I knew that whatever happened, God would take care of my mom and me. I was to leave everything absolutely in God's hands and trust him for the outcome.

That's what I did. And I discovered that God is faithful: My father did recover. God has continued to use Dad in marvelous ways to bring others to trust in Christ. And I learned something invaluable about trusting God and leaving everything in his hands when I'm facing life's storms.

—David

4 I am surrounded by fierce lions
who greedily devour human prey—
whose teeth pierce like spears and arrows,
and whose tongues cut like swords.

5 Be exalted, O God, above the highest heavens!
May your glory shine over all the earth.

6 My enemies have set a trap for me.
I am weary from distress.
They have dug a deep pit in my path,
but they themselves have fallen into it. *Interlude*

7 My heart is confident in you, O God;
my heart is confident.
No wonder I can sing your praises!
8 Wake up, my heart!
Wake up, O lyre and harp!
I will wake the dawn with my song.
9 I will thank you, Lord, among all the people.
I will sing your praises among the nations.
10 For your unfailing love is as high as the heavens.
Your faithfulness reaches to the clouds.

11 Be exalted, O God, above the highest heavens.
May your glory shine over all the earth.

58

For the choir director: A psalm of David, to be sung to the tune "Do Not Destroy!"

1 Justice—do you rulers* know the meaning of the word?
Do you judge the people fairly?
2 No! You plot injustice in your hearts.
You spread violence throughout the land.
3 These wicked people are born sinners;
even from birth they have lied and gone their own way.
4 They spit venom like deadly snakes;
they are like cobras that refuse to listen,
5 ignoring the tunes of the snake charmers,
no matter how skillfully they play.

6 Break off their fangs, O God!
Smash the jaws of these lions, O LORD!
7 May they disappear like water into thirsty ground.
Make their weapons useless in their hands.*
8 May they be like snails that dissolve into slime,
like a stillborn child who will never see the sun.
9 God will sweep them away, both young and old,
faster than a pot heats over burning thorns.

10 The godly will rejoice when they see injustice avenged.
They will wash their feet in the blood of the wicked.
11 Then at last everyone will say,
"There truly is a reward for those who live for God;
surely there is a God who judges justly here on earth."

59

For the choir director: A psalm of David, regarding the time Saul sent soldiers to watch David's house in order to kill him. To be sung to the tune "Do Not Destroy!"

58:1 Or *you gods.* **58:7** Or *Let them be trodden down and wither like grass.* The meaning of the Hebrew is uncertain.

1 Rescue me from my enemies, O God.
Protect me from those who have come
to destroy me.
2 Rescue me from these criminals;
save me from these murderers.
3 They have set an ambush for me.
Fierce enemies are out there waiting, LORD,
though I have not sinned or offended them.
4 I have done nothing wrong,
yet they prepare to attack me.
Wake up! See what is happening and help me!
5 O LORD God of Heaven's Armies, the God of Israel,
wake up and punish those hostile nations.
Show no mercy to wicked traitors. *Interlude*

6 They come out at night,
snarling like vicious dogs
as they prowl the streets.
7 Listen to the filth that comes from their mouths;
their words cut like swords.
"After all, who can hear us?" they sneer.
8 But LORD, you laugh at them.
You scoff at all the hostile nations.
9 You are my strength; I wait for you to rescue me,
for you, O God, are my fortress.
10 In his unfailing love, my God will stand with me.
He will let me look down in triumph on all
my enemies.

UNCHANGING 59:1-11

While David was hunted by enemies, changes occurred daily as he ran from place to place. But David knew that he could count on God for stability even in the midst of constant change. Ever feel like your life is in a constant state of change? One thing won't ever change: God's love for you. Like David, you can count on that. ■

11 Don't kill them, for my people soon forget
such lessons;
stagger them with your power, and bring them
to their knees,
O Lord our shield.
12 Because of the sinful things they say,
because of the evil that is on their lips,
let them be captured by their pride,
their curses, and their lies.
13 Destroy them in your anger!
Wipe them out completely!
Then the whole world will know
that God reigns in Israel.* *Interlude*

14 My enemies come out at night,
snarling like vicious dogs
as they prowl the streets.
15 They scavenge for food
but go to sleep unsatisfied.*
16 But as for me, I will sing about your power.
Each morning I will sing with joy about your
unfailing love.
For you have been my refuge,
a place of safety when I am in distress.
17 O my Strength, to you I sing praises,
for you, O God, are my refuge,
the God who shows me unfailing love.

60

For the choir director: A psalm of David useful for teaching, regarding the time David fought Aram-naharaim and Aram-zobah, and Joab returned and killed 12,000 Edomites in the Valley of Salt. To be sung to the tune "Lily of the Testimony."

1 You have rejected us, O God, and broken our
defenses.
You have been angry with us; now restore us
to your favor.
2 You have shaken our land and split it open.
Seal the cracks, for the land trembles.
3 You have been very hard on us,
making us drink wine that sent us reeling.
4 But you have raised a banner for those who
fear you—
a rallying point in the face of attack. *Interlude*

5 Now rescue your beloved people.
Answer and save us by your power.
6 God has promised this by his holiness*:
"I will divide up Shechem with joy.
I will measure out the valley of Succoth.
7 Gilead is mine,
and Manasseh, too.
Ephraim, my helmet, will produce my warriors,
and Judah, my scepter, will produce my kings.
8 But Moab, my washbasin, will become my servant,
and I will wipe my feet on Edom
and shout in triumph over Philistia."

9 Who will bring me into the fortified city?
Who will bring me victory over Edom?
10 Have you rejected us, O God?
Will you no longer march with our armies?
11 Oh, please help us against our enemies,
for all human help is useless.
12 With God's help we will do mighty things,
for he will trample down our foes.

61

For the choir director: A psalm of David, to be accompanied by stringed instruments.

1 O God, listen to my cry!
Hear my prayer!
2 From the ends of the earth,
I cry to you for help

59:13 Hebrew *in Jacob*. See note on 44:4. **59:15** Or *and growl if they don't get enough.* **60:6** Or *in his sanctuary.*

when my heart is overwhelmed.
Lead me to the towering rock of safety,
3 for you are my safe refuge,
a fortress where my enemies cannot reach me.
4 Let me live forever in your sanctuary,
safe beneath the shelter of your wings! *Interlude*

5 For you have heard my vows, O God.
You have given me an inheritance reserved for
those who fear your name.
6 Add many years to the life of the king!
May his years span the generations!
7 May he reign under God's protection forever.
May your unfailing love and faithfulness watch
over him.
8 Then I will sing praises to your name forever
as I fulfill my vows each day.

A COMMITMENT TO PRAISE 61:8

David continually praised God through both the good and difficult times of his life. His commitment to praise God every day showed his respect for God. Do you have the same commitment to praise? How do you show your respect for God?

62

For Jeduthun, the choir director: A psalm of David.

1 I wait quietly before God,
for my victory comes from him.
2 He alone is my rock and my salvation,
my fortress where I will never be shaken.

3 So many enemies against one man—
all of them trying to kill me.
To them I'm just a broken-down wall
or a tottering fence.
4 They plan to topple me from my high position.
They delight in telling lies about me.
They praise me to my face
but curse me in their hearts. *Interlude*

5 Let all that I am wait quietly before God,
for my hope is in him.
6 He alone is my rock and my salvation,
my fortress where I will not be shaken.
7 My victory and honor come from God alone.
He is my refuge, a rock where no enemy can
reach me.
8 O my people, trust in him at all times.
Pour out your heart to him,
for God is our refuge. *Interlude*

9 Common people are as worthless as a puff
of wind,
and the powerful are not what they appear to be.
If you weigh them on the scales,
together they are lighter than a breath of air.

10 Don't make your living by extortion
or put your hope in stealing.
And if your wealth increases,
don't make it the center of your life.

11 God has spoken plainly,
and I have heard it many times:
Power, O God, belongs to you;
12 unfailing love, O Lord, is yours.
Surely you repay all people
according to what they have done.

63

A psalm of David, regarding a time when David was in the wilderness of Judah.

1 O God, you are my God;
I earnestly search for you.
My soul thirsts for you;
my whole body longs for you
in this parched and weary land
where there is no water.
2 I have seen you in your sanctuary
and gazed upon your power and glory.
3 Your unfailing love is better than life itself;
how I praise you!
4 I will praise you as long as I live,
lifting up my hands to you in prayer.
5 You satisfy me more than the richest feast.
I will praise you with songs of joy.

6 I lie awake thinking of you,
meditating on you through the night.
7 Because you are my helper,
I sing for joy in the shadow of your wings.
8 I cling to you;
your strong right hand holds me securely.

9 But those plotting to destroy me will come
to ruin.
They will go down into the depths of the earth.
10 They will die by the sword
and become the food of jackals.
11 But the king will rejoice in God.
All who trust in him will praise him,
while liars will be silenced.

64

For the choir director: A psalm of David.

1 O God, listen to my complaint.
Protect my life from my enemies' threats.
2 Hide me from the plots of this evil mob,
from this gang of wrongdoers.
3 They sharpen their tongues like swords
and aim their bitter words like arrows.

4 They shoot from ambush at the innocent,
attacking suddenly and fearlessly.
5 They encourage each other to do evil
and plan how to set their traps in secret.
"Who will ever notice?" they ask.
6 As they plot their crimes, they say,
"We have devised the perfect plan!"
Yes, the human heart and mind are cunning.

7 But God himself will shoot them with his arrows,
suddenly striking them down.
8 Their own tongues will ruin them,
and all who see them will shake their heads in scorn.
9 Then everyone will be afraid;
they will proclaim the mighty acts of God
and realize all the amazing things he does.
10 The godly will rejoice in the LORD
and find shelter in him.
And those who do what is right
will praise him.

65

For the choir director: A song. A psalm of David.

1 What mighty praise, O God,
belongs to you in Zion.
We will fulfill our vows to you,
2 for you answer our prayers.
All of us must come to you.
3 Though we are overwhelmed by our sins,
you forgive them all.
4 What joy for those you choose to bring near,
those who live in your holy courts.
What festivities await us
inside your holy Temple.

5 You faithfully answer our prayers with awesome deeds,
O God our savior.
You are the hope of everyone on earth,
even those who sail on distant seas.
6 You formed the mountains by your power
and armed yourself with mighty strength.
7 You quieted the raging oceans
with their pounding waves
and silenced the shouting of the nations.
8 Those who live at the ends of the earth
stand in awe of your wonders.
From where the sun rises to where it sets,
you inspire shouts of joy.

9 You take care of the earth and water it,
making it rich and fertile.
The river of God has plenty of water;
it provides a bountiful harvest of grain,
for you have ordered it so.
10 You drench the plowed ground with rain,
melting the clods and leveling the ridges.
You soften the earth with showers
and bless its abundant crops.
11 You crown the year with a bountiful harvest;
even the hard pathways overflow with
abundance.
12 The grasslands of the wilderness become a
lush pasture,
and the hillsides blossom with joy.
13 The meadows are clothed with flocks of sheep,
and the valleys are carpeted with grain.
They all shout and sing for joy!

66

For the choir director: A song. A psalm.

1 Shout joyful praises to God, all the earth!
2 Sing about the glory of his name!
Tell the world how glorious he is.
3 Say to God, "How awesome are your deeds!
Your enemies cringe before your mighty power.
4 Everything on earth will worship you;
they will sing your praises,
shouting your name in glorious songs." *Interlude*

5 Come and see what our God has done,
what awesome miracles he performs for people!
6 He made a dry path through the Red Sea,*
and his people went across on foot.
There we rejoiced in him.
7 For by his great power he rules forever.
He watches every movement of the nations;
let no rebel rise in defiance. *Interlude*

A PROMISE REMEMBERED 66:13-15

People sometimes make bargains with God, saying, "If you heal me (or get me out of this mess), I'll obey you for the rest of my life." Soon after they recover, however, the vow is often forgotten and the old lifestyle resumes. This writer remembered his promise and fulfilled it. God always keeps his promises and wants us to follow his example. How careful are you to follow through on whatever you promise to do? ■

8 Let the whole world bless our God
and loudly sing his praises.
9 Our lives are in his hands,
and he keeps our feet from stumbling.
10 You have tested us, O God;
you have purified us like silver.
11 You captured us in your net
and laid the burden of slavery on our backs.
12 Then you put a leader over us.*
We went through fire and flood,
but you brought us to a place of great abundance.

13 Now I come to your Temple with burnt offerings
to fulfill the vows I made to you—

66:6 Hebrew *the sea.* **66:12** Or *You made people ride over our heads.*

14 yes, the sacred vows that I made
when I was in deep trouble.
15 That is why I am sacrificing burnt offerings to you—
the best of my rams as a pleasing aroma,
and a sacrifice of bulls and male goats. *Interlude*

16 Come and listen, all you who fear God,
and I will tell you what he did for me.
17 For I cried out to him for help,
praising him as I spoke.
18 If I had not confessed the sin in my heart,
the Lord would not have listened.
19 But God did listen!
He paid attention to my prayer.
20 Praise God, who did not ignore my prayer
or withdraw his unfailing love from me.

67

For the choir director: A song. A psalm, to be accompanied by stringed instruments.

1 May God be merciful and bless us.
May his face smile with favor on us. *Interlude*

2 May your ways be known throughout the earth,
your saving power among people everywhere.
3 May the nations praise you, O God.
Yes, may all the nations praise you.
4 Let the whole world sing for joy,
because you govern the nations with justice
and guide the people of the whole world. *Interlude*

5 May the nations praise you, O God.
Yes, may all the nations praise you.
6 Then the earth will yield its harvests,
and God, our God, will richly bless us.
7 Yes, God will bless us,
and people all over the world will fear him.

68

For the choir director: A song. A psalm of David.

1 Rise up, O God, and scatter your enemies.
Let those who hate God run for their lives.
2 Blow them away like smoke.
Melt them like wax in a fire.
Let the wicked perish in the presence of God.
3 But let the godly rejoice.
Let them be glad in God's presence.
Let them be filled with joy.
4 Sing praises to God and to his name!
Sing loud praises to him who rides the clouds.
His name is the LORD—
rejoice in his presence!

5 Father to the fatherless, defender of widows—
this is God, whose dwelling is holy.
6 God places the lonely in families;
he sets the prisoners free and gives them joy.
But he makes the rebellious live in a sun-scorched land.

7 O God, when you led your people out from Egypt,
when you marched through the dry wasteland, *Interlude*
8 the earth trembled, and the heavens poured down rain
before you, the God of Sinai,
before God, the God of Israel.
9 You sent abundant rain, O God,
to refresh the weary land.
10 There your people finally settled,
and with a bountiful harvest, O God,
you provided for your needy people.

11 The Lord gives the word,
and a great army* brings the good news.
12 Enemy kings and their armies flee,
while the women of Israel divide the plunder.
13 Even those who lived among the sheepfolds found treasures—
doves with wings of silver
and feathers of gold.
14 The Almighty scattered the enemy kings
like a blowing snowstorm on Mount Zalmon.

15 The mountains of Bashan are majestic,
with many peaks stretching high into the sky.
16 Why do you look with envy, O rugged mountains,
at Mount Zion, where God has chosen to live,
where the LORD himself will live forever?

17 Surrounded by unnumbered thousands of chariots,
the Lord came from Mount Sinai into his sanctuary.
18 When you ascended to the heights,
you led a crowd of captives.
You received gifts from the people,
even from those who rebelled against you.
Now the LORD God will live among us there.

19 Praise the Lord; praise God our savior!
For each day he carries us in his arms. *Interlude*
20 Our God is a God who saves!
The Sovereign LORD rescues us from death.

21 But God will smash the heads of his enemies,
crushing the skulls of those who love their guilty ways.
22 The Lord says, "I will bring my enemies down from Bashan;
I will bring them up from the depths of the sea.
23 You, my people, will wash your feet in their blood,
and even your dogs will get their share!"

68:11 Or *a host of women.*

24 Your procession has come into view, O God—
the procession of my God and King as he goes into
the sanctuary.
25 Singers are in front, musicians behind;
between them are young women playing
tambourines.
26 Praise God, all you people of Israel;
praise the LORD, the source of Israel's life.
27 Look, the little tribe of Benjamin leads the way.
Then comes a great throng of rulers from Judah
and all the rulers of Zebulun and Naphtali.

28 Summon your might, O God.
Display your power, O God, as you have in the past.
29 The kings of the earth are bringing tribute
to your Temple in Jerusalem.
30 Rebuke these enemy nations—
these wild animals lurking in the reeds,
this herd of bulls among the weaker calves.
Make them bring bars of silver in humble tribute.
Scatter the nations that delight in war.
31 Let Egypt come with gifts of precious metals*;
let Ethiopia* bow in submission to God.
32 Sing to God, you kingdoms of the earth.
Sing praises to the Lord. *Interlude*
33 Sing to the one who rides across the ancient heavens,
his mighty voice thundering from the sky.
34 Tell everyone about God's power.
His majesty shines down on Israel;
his strength is mighty in the heavens.
35 God is awesome in his sanctuary.
The God of Israel gives power and strength
to his people.

Praise be to God!

69

For the choir director: A psalm of David, to be sung to the tune "Lilies."

1 Save me, O God,
for the floodwaters are up to my neck.
2 Deeper and deeper I sink into the mire;
I can't find a foothold.
I am in deep water,
and the floods overwhelm me.
3 I am exhausted from crying for help;
my throat is parched.
My eyes are swollen with weeping,
waiting for my God to help me.
4 Those who hate me without cause
outnumber the hairs on my head.
Many enemies try to destroy me with lies,
demanding that I give back what I didn't steal.

5 O God, you know how foolish I am;
my sins cannot be hidden from you.
6 Don't let those who trust in you be ashamed because
of me,
O Sovereign LORD of Heaven's Armies.
Don't let me cause them to be humiliated,
O God of Israel.
7 For I endure insults for your sake;
humiliation is written all over my face.
8 Even my own brothers pretend they don't know me;
they treat me like a stranger.

9 Passion for your house has consumed me,
and the insults of those who insult you have
fallen on me.
10 When I weep and fast,
they scoff at me.
11 When I dress in burlap to show sorrow,
they make fun of me.
12 I am the favorite topic of town gossip,
and all the drunks sing about me.

13 But I keep praying to you, LORD,
hoping this time you will show me favor.
In your unfailing love, O God,
answer my prayer with your sure salvation.
14 Rescue me from the mud;
don't let me sink any deeper!
Save me from those who hate me,
and pull me from these deep waters.
15 Don't let the floods overwhelm me,
or the deep waters swallow me,
or the pit of death devour me.

16 Answer my prayers, O LORD,
for your unfailing love is wonderful.
Take care of me,
for your mercy is so plentiful.
17 Don't hide from your servant;
answer me quickly, for I am in deep trouble!
18 Come and redeem me;
free me from my enemies.

19 You know of my shame, scorn, and disgrace.
You see all that my enemies are doing.
20 Their insults have broken my heart,
and I am in despair.
If only one person would show some pity;
if only one would turn and comfort me.
21 But instead, they give me poison* for food;
they offer me sour wine for my thirst.

22 Let the bountiful table set before them become
a snare
and their prosperity become a trap.*
23 Let their eyes go blind so they cannot see,
and make their bodies shake continually.*
24 Pour out your fury on them;
consume them with your burning anger.

68:31a Or *of rich cloth.* **68:31b** Hebrew *Cush.* **69:21** Or *gall.* **69:22** Greek version reads *Let their bountiful table set before them become a snare, / a trap that makes them think all is well. / Let their blessings cause them to stumble, / and let them get what they deserve.* Compare Rom 11:9. **69:23** Greek version reads *and let their backs be bent forever.* Compare Rom 11:10.

25 Let their homes become desolate
and their tents be deserted.
26 To the one you have punished, they add insult
to injury;
they add to the pain of those you have hurt.
27 Pile their sins up high,
and don't let them go free.
28 Erase their names from the Book of Life;
don't let them be counted among the righteous.

29 I am suffering and in pain.
Rescue me, O God, by your saving power.
30 Then I will praise God's name with singing,
and I will honor him with thanksgiving.
31 For this will please the LORD more than
sacrificing cattle,
more than presenting a bull with its horns
and hooves.
32 The humble will see their God at work and be glad.
Let all who seek God's help be encouraged.
33 For the LORD hears the cries of the needy;
he does not despise his imprisoned people.

34 Praise him, O heaven and earth,
the seas and all that move in them.
35 For God will save Jerusalem*
and rebuild the towns of Judah.
His people will live there
and settle in their own land.
36 The descendants of those who obey him will
inherit the land,
and those who love him will live there in safety.

PANIC 70:1-4

This short psalm was David's plea for God to rush to his aid. Yet even in this moment of panic, praise was not forgotten. Often our prayers are filled with requests for others and ourselves. Consequently, we forget to thank God for what he has done or to worship him for who he is. Adding a praise "postscript" to a prayer is important because it helps us remember who God is. How much of a priority is praise in your prayers? ■

70

For the choir director: A psalm of David, asking God to remember him.

1 Please, God, rescue me!
Come quickly, LORD, and help me.
2 May those who try to kill me
be humiliated and put to shame.
May those who take delight in my trouble
be turned back in disgrace.
3 Let them be horrified by their shame,
for they said, "Aha! We've got him now!"
4 But may all who search for you
be filled with joy and gladness in you.
May those who love your salvation
repeatedly shout, "God is great!"
5 But as for me, I am poor and needy;
please hurry to my aid, O God.
You are my helper and my savior;
O LORD, do not delay.

71

1 O LORD, I have come to you for protection;
don't let me be disgraced.
2 Save me and rescue me,
for you do what is right.
Turn your ear to listen to me,
and set me free.
3 Be my rock of safety
where I can always hide.
Give the order to save me,
for you are my rock and my fortress.
4 My God, rescue me from the power of the wicked,
from the clutches of cruel oppressors.
5 O Lord, you alone are my hope.
I've trusted you, O LORD, from childhood.
6 Yes, you have been with me from birth;
from my mother's womb you have cared for me.
No wonder I am always praising you!

7 My life is an example to many,
because you have been my strength and
protection.
8 That is why I can never stop praising you;
I declare your glory all day long.
9 And now, in my old age, don't set me aside.
Don't abandon me when my strength is failing.
10 For my enemies are whispering against me.
They are plotting together to kill me.
11 They say, "God has abandoned him.
Let's go and get him,
for no one will help him now."

12 O God, don't stay away.
My God, please hurry to help me.
13 Bring disgrace and destruction on my accusers.
Humiliate and shame those who want to harm me.
14 But I will keep on hoping for your help;
I will praise you more and more.
15 I will tell everyone about your righteousness.
All day long I will proclaim your saving power,
though I am not skilled with words.*
16 I will praise your mighty deeds, O Sovereign LORD.
I will tell everyone that you alone are just.
17 O God, you have taught me from my earliest childhood,
and I constantly tell others about the wonderful
things you do.
18 Now that I am old and gray,
do not abandon me, O God.

69:35 Hebrew *Zion.* 71:15 Or *though I cannot count it.*

Let me proclaim your power to this new generation,
your mighty miracles to all who come after me.
19 Your righteousness, O God, reaches to the highest heavens.
You have done such wonderful things.
Who can compare with you, O God?
20 You have allowed me to suffer much hardship,
but you will restore me to life again
and lift me up from the depths of the earth.
21 You will restore me to even greater honor
and comfort me once again.

22 Then I will praise you with music on the harp,
because you are faithful to your promises,
O my God.
I will sing praises to you with a lyre,
O Holy One of Israel.
23 I will shout for joy and sing your praises,
for you have ransomed me.
24 I will tell about your righteous deeds
all day long,
for everyone who tried to hurt me
has been shamed and humiliated.

72

A psalm of Solomon.

1 Give your love of justice to the king, O God,
and righteousness to the king's son.
2 Help him judge your people in the right way;
let the poor always be treated fairly.
3 May the mountains yield prosperity for all,
and may the hills be fruitful.
4 Help him to defend the poor,
to rescue the children of the needy,
and to crush their oppressors.
5 May they fear you as long as the sun shines,
as long as the moon remains in the sky.
Yes, forever!

6 May the king's rule be refreshing like spring rain on freshly cut grass,
like the showers that water the earth.
7 May all the godly flourish during his reign.
May there be abundant prosperity until the moon is no more.
8 May he reign from sea to sea,
and from the Euphrates River* to the ends of the earth.
9 Desert nomads will bow before him;
his enemies will fall before him in the dust.
10 The western kings of Tarshish and other distant lands
will bring him tribute.
The eastern kings of Sheba and Seba
will bring him gifts.
11 All kings will bow before him,
and all nations will serve him.
12 He will rescue the poor when they cry to him;
he will help the oppressed, who have no one to defend them.
13 He feels pity for the weak and the needy,
and he will rescue them.
14 He will redeem them from oppression
and violence,
for their lives are precious to him.

REACHING OUT 72:12-14

Solomon acknowledged God's concern for the poor and those who are mistreated. God encourages us to show the same compassion. What are you doing to reach out with God's love to the poor, weak, and needy in the world? ■

15 Long live the king!
May the gold of Sheba be given to him.
May the people always pray for him
and bless him all day long.
16 May there be abundant grain throughout the land,
flourishing even on the hilltops.
May the fruit trees flourish like the trees of Lebanon,
and may the people thrive like grass in a field.
17 May the king's name endure forever;
may it continue as long as the sun shines.
May all nations be blessed through him
and bring him praise.

18 Praise the LORD God, the God of Israel,
who alone does such wonderful things.
19 Praise his glorious name forever!
Let the whole earth be filled with his glory.
Amen and amen!

20 (This ends the prayers of David son of Jesse.)

BOOK THREE (Psalms 73–89)

73

A psalm of Asaph.

1 Truly God is good to Israel,
to those whose hearts are pure.
2 But as for me, I almost lost my footing.
My feet were slipping, and I was almost gone.
3 For I envied the proud
when I saw them prosper despite their wickedness.
4 They seem to live such painless lives;
their bodies are so healthy and strong.
5 They don't have troubles like other people;
they're not plagued with problems like everyone else.
6 They wear pride like a jeweled necklace
and clothe themselves with cruelty.

72:8 Hebrew *the river*.

DOWN IN THE DUMPS

ULTIMATE ISSUES

In the book (and the soon-to-be-released movie) *Prozac Nation: Young and Depressed in America,* the author (Elizabeth Wurtzel), describes her experiences with chronic depression.

Unfortunately, depression is an experience common to many people. Life can be terribly unfair, terribly tragic. That's why many people like Elizabeth have sought relief from antidepressants like Prozac.

There are those who feel that being a Christian makes you somehow immune to depression. If you happen to fall into the pit of despair, well, you're not very "spiritual" are you? Such judgments add a load of guilt to a person who is already miserable.

For those who struggle with feelings of depression, there's good news and bad news. The bad news is that such feelings are a fact of life in this broken world. Some disappointments or tragedies can leave a person depressed. Now the good news: You are not alone. As Psalm 73 (and many other passages) clearly shows, even God's chosen people experience anxiety, despair, and darkness in their soul. If Psalm 73 doesn't convince you, check out Elijah's story (1 Kings 19) and Jesus' experience in Gethsemane. Matthew 26 speaks of Jesus' soul being "crushed with grief to the point of death" (v. 38).

Obviously, depression that lasts for a long time indicates a need for counseling; but there is nothing unusual or unspiritual about "walking through the dark valley" from time to time.

So when you are caught in one of those unpleasant times, don't add guilt to your load. Just trust that God knows what's up and will help you through this.

7 These fat cats have everything
their hearts could ever wish for!
8 They scoff and speak only evil;
in their pride they seek to crush others.
9 They boast against the very heavens,
and their words strut throughout the earth.
10 And so the people are dismayed and confused,
drinking in all their words.
11 "What does God know?" they ask.
"Does the Most High even know what's
happening?"
12 Look at these wicked people—
enjoying a life of ease while their riches
multiply.

13 Did I keep my heart pure for nothing?
Did I keep myself innocent for no reason?
14 I get nothing but trouble all day long;
every morning brings me pain.

15 If I had really spoken this way to others,
I would have been a traitor to your people.
16 So I tried to understand why the wicked prosper.
But what a difficult task it is!
17 Then I went into your sanctuary, O God,
and I finally understood the destiny of
the wicked.

18 Truly, you put them on a slippery path
and send them sliding over the cliff
to destruction.
19 In an instant they are destroyed,
completely swept away by terrors.
20 When you arise, O Lord,
you will laugh at their silly ideas
as a person laughs at dreams in the morning.

21 Then I realized that my heart was bitter,
and I was all torn up inside.
22 I was so foolish and ignorant—
I must have seemed like a senseless animal
to you.
23 Yet I still belong to you;
you hold my right hand.
24 You guide me with your counsel,
leading me to a glorious destiny.
25 Whom have I in heaven but you?
I desire you more than anything on earth.
26 My health may fail, and my spirit may
grow weak,
but God remains the strength of my heart;
he is mine forever.

27 Those who desert him will perish,
for you destroy those who abandon you.

INJUSTICE

"It isn't fair!" Joy sobs. "I go to church, read my Bible, pray every day, try to tell my friends about God—everything! But does it do any good? No way! My life is still the worst. My family is awful, I'm so out of shape, I never get asked out, I have only two friends, and I can't even pass pre-calc! You'd think God would at least reward me a little bit.

"On the other hand, Renita has it made! All the guys think she's so hot. She goes out every weekend. She makes straight A's without even trying. Her family is rich—I mean, how many other kids get their own MX-5 Miata? She never has any problems. Her life is totally perfect . . . and get this: She's not even a Christian! In fact, she couldn't care less about God.

"It doesn't make any sense. Why do I get hassled for doing what's right, and she gets rewarded for doing whatever she wants whenever she wants? You know what I'm saying?

"Doesn't God see what's going on? Doesn't he care? I'm serious . . . there is absolutely no justice in this world. I might as well live by my own rules for all the good it does me."

Ever wonder why some non-Christians seem to have perfect lives, while so many of God's people struggle and have lives full of pain? A follower of God named Asaph once asked some of the very same questions. Psalm 73 describes the answers he found.

28 But as for me, how good it is to be near God!
I have made the Sovereign LORD my shelter,
and I will tell everyone about the wonderful
things you do.

74

A psalm of Asaph.*

1 O God, why have you rejected us so long?
Why is your anger so intense against the sheep
of your own pasture?
2 Remember that we are the people you chose
long ago,
the tribe you redeemed as your own special
possession!
And remember Jerusalem,* your home here
on earth.
3 Walk through the awful ruins of the city;
see how the enemy has destroyed your sanctuary.

4 There your enemies shouted their victorious
battle cries;
there they set up their battle standards.
5 They swung their axes
like woodcutters in a forest.
6 With axes and picks,
they smashed the carved paneling.
7 They burned your sanctuary to the ground.
They defiled the place that bears your name.
8 Then they thought, "Let's destroy everything!"
So they burned down all the places where God
was worshiped.

9 We no longer see your miraculous signs.
All the prophets are gone,
and no one can tell us when it will end.
10 How long, O God, will you allow our enemies
to insult you?
Will you let them dishonor your name forever?
11 Why do you hold back your strong right hand?
Unleash your powerful fist and destroy them.

12 You, O God, are my king from ages past,
bringing salvation to the earth.
13 You split the sea by your strength
and smashed the heads of the sea monsters.
14 You crushed the heads of Leviathan*
and let the desert animals eat him.
15 You caused the springs and streams to gush forth,
and you dried up rivers that never run dry.
16 Both day and night belong to you;
you made the starlight* and the sun.
17 You set the boundaries of the earth,
and you made both summer and winter.

18 See how these enemies insult you, LORD.
A foolish nation has dishonored your name.
19 Don't let these wild beasts destroy your turtledoves.
Don't forget your suffering people forever.

TRACES OF GOD 74:1-8

When enemy armies defeated Israel, they destroyed Jerusalem, trying to wipe out every trace of God. This has often been the response of people who hate God. Today many continually try to erase all traces of God from our society and in our schools. Yet the strongest traces of God can be found in the lives of believers. Is that true of you? How do your actions show "traces of God"? ■

20 Remember your covenant promises,
for the land is full of darkness and violence!
21 Don't let the downtrodden be humiliated again.
Instead, let the poor and needy praise
your name.

22 Arise, O God, and defend your cause.
Remember how these fools insult you all
day long.
23 Don't overlook what your enemies have said
or their growing uproar.

74:TITLE Hebrew *maskil.* This may be a literary or musical term. **74:2** Hebrew *Mount Zion.* **74:14** The identification of Leviathan is disputed, ranging from an earthly creature to a mythical sea monster in ancient literature. **74:16** Or *moon;* Hebrew reads *light.*

75

For the choir director: A psalm of Asaph. A song to be sung to the tune "Do Not Destroy!"

1 We thank you, O God!
We give thanks because you are near.
People everywhere tell of your wonderful deeds.

GOD'S TIMING 75:2

God's time frame is a mystery to most of us. Sometimes he seems to move much too slowly. We want everything *now*, not recognizing that God usually comes at just the right time. Think about the last time God came through for you. Are you willing to trust that his timing is just right for you? ■

2 God says, "At the time I have planned,
I will bring justice against the wicked.
3 When the earth quakes and its people live in turmoil,
I am the one who keeps its foundations firm. *Interlude*

4 "I warned the proud, 'Stop your boasting!'
I told the wicked, 'Don't raise your fists!
5 Don't raise your fists in defiance at the heavens
or speak with such arrogance.'"
6 For no one on earth—from east or west,
or even from the wilderness—
should raise a defiant fist.*
7 It is God alone who judges;
he decides who will rise and who will fall.
8 For the LORD holds a cup in his hand
that is full of foaming wine mixed with spices.
He pours out the wine in judgment,
and all the wicked must drink it,
draining it to the dregs.

9 But as for me, I will always proclaim what God has done;
I will sing praises to the God of Jacob.
10 For God says, "I will break the strength of the wicked,
but I will increase the power of the godly."

76

For the choir director: A psalm of Asaph. A song to be accompanied by stringed instruments.

1 God is honored in Judah;
his name is great in Israel.
2 Jerusalem* is where he lives;
Mount Zion is his home.
3 There he has broken the fiery arrows of the enemy,
the shields and swords and weapons of war. *Interlude*

4 You are glorious and more majestic
than the everlasting mountains.*
5 Our boldest enemies have been plundered.
They lie before us in the sleep of death.
No warrior could lift a hand against us.
6 At the blast of your breath, O God of Jacob,
their horses and chariots lay still.

7 No wonder you are greatly feared!
Who can stand before you when your anger explodes?
8 From heaven you sentenced your enemies;
the earth trembled and stood silent before you.
9 You stand up to judge those who do evil, O God,
and to rescue the oppressed of the earth. *Interlude*
10 Human defiance only enhances your glory,
for you use it as a weapon.*

11 Make vows to the LORD your God, and keep them.
Let everyone bring tribute to the Awesome One.
12 For he breaks the pride of princes,
and the kings of the earth fear him.

77

For Jeduthun, the choir director: A psalm of Asaph.

1 I cry out to God; yes, I shout.
Oh, that God would listen to me!
2 When I was in deep trouble,
I searched for the Lord.
All night long I prayed, with hands lifted toward heaven,
but my soul was not comforted.
3 I think of God, and I moan,
overwhelmed with longing for his help. *Interlude*

4 You don't let me sleep.
I am too distressed even to pray!
5 I think of the good old days,
long since ended,
6 when my nights were filled with joyful songs.
I search my soul and ponder the difference now.
7 Has the Lord rejected me forever?
Will he never again be kind to me?
8 Is his unfailing love gone forever?
Have his promises permanently failed?
9 Has God forgotten to be gracious?
Has he slammed the door on his compassion? *Interlude*

10 And I said, "This is my fate;
the Most High has turned his hand against me."
11 But then I recall all you have done, O LORD;
I remember your wonderful deeds of long ago.
12 They are constantly in my thoughts.
I cannot stop thinking about your mighty works.

75:6 Hebrew *should lift*. 76:2 Hebrew *Salem,* another name for Jerusalem. 76:4 As in Greek version; Hebrew reads *than mountains filled with beasts of prey*. 76:10 The meaning of the Hebrew is uncertain.

13 O God, your ways are holy.
Is there any god as mighty as you?
14 You are the God of great wonders!
You demonstrate your awesome power among
the nations.
15 By your strong arm, you redeemed your people,
the descendants of Jacob and Joseph. *Interlude*

16 When the Red Sea* saw you, O God,
its waters looked and trembled!
The sea quaked to its very depths.
17 The clouds poured down rain;
the thunder rumbled in the sky.
Your arrows of lightning flashed.
18 Your thunder roared from the whirlwind;
the lightning lit up the world!
The earth trembled and shook.
19 Your road led through the sea,
your pathway through the mighty waters—
a pathway no one knew was there!
20 You led your people along that road like a flock
of sheep,
with Moses and Aaron as their shepherds.

78

A psalm of Asaph.*

1 O my people, listen to my instructions.
Open your ears to what I am saying,
2 for I will speak to you in a parable.
I will teach you hidden lessons from our past—
3 stories we have heard and known,
stories our ancestors handed down to us.
4 We will not hide these truths from our children;
we will tell the next generation
about the glorious deeds of the LORD,
about his power and his mighty wonders.
5 For he issued his laws to Jacob;
he gave his instructions to Israel.
He commanded our ancestors
to teach them to their children,
6 so the next generation might know them—
even the children not yet born—
and they in turn will teach their own children.
7 So each generation should set its hope anew on God,
not forgetting his glorious miracles
and obeying his commands.
8 Then they will not be like their ancestors—
stubborn, rebellious, and unfaithful,
refusing to give their hearts to God.

9 The warriors of Ephraim, though armed with bows,
turned their backs and fled on the day of battle.
10 They did not keep God's covenant
and refused to live by his instructions.
11 They forgot what he had done—
the great wonders he had shown them,
12 the miracles he did for their ancestors
on the plain of Zoan in the land of Egypt.
13 For he divided the sea and led them through,
making the water stand up like walls!
14 In the daytime he led them by a cloud,
and all night by a pillar of fire.
15 He split open the rocks in the wilderness
to give them water, as from a gushing spring.
16 He made streams pour from the rock,
making the waters flow down like a river!

ALL TALK, NO ACTION 78:1-72

Over and over the people of Israel promised that they would follow God; yet they turned away from him again and again. The problem was that they followed God with words and not with their hearts. Talk is cheap. God wants our words and actions to match. Do yours? ■

17 Yet they kept on sinning against him,
rebelling against the Most High in the desert.
18 They stubbornly tested God in their hearts,
demanding the foods they craved.
19 They even spoke against God himself, saying,
"God can't give us food in the wilderness.
20 Yes, he can strike a rock so water gushes out,
but he can't give his people bread and meat."
21 When the LORD heard them, he was furious.
The fire of his wrath burned against Jacob.
Yes, his anger rose against Israel,
22 for they did not believe God
or trust him to care for them.
23 But he commanded the skies to open;
he opened the doors of heaven.
24 He rained down manna for them to eat;
he gave them bread from heaven.
25 They ate the food of angels!
God gave them all they could hold.
26 He released the east wind in the heavens
and guided the south wind by his mighty power.
27 He rained down meat as thick as dust—
birds as plentiful as the sand on the seashore!
28 He caused the birds to fall within their camp
and all around their tents.
29 The people ate their fill.
He gave them what they craved.
30 But before they satisfied their craving,
while the meat was yet in their mouths,
31 the anger of God rose against them,
and he killed their strongest men.
He struck down the finest of Israel's young men.

32 But in spite of this, the people kept sinning.
Despite his wonders, they refused to trust him.
33 So he ended their lives in failure,
their years in terror.
34 When God began killing them,
they finally sought him.

77:16 Hebrew *the waters.* **78:TITLE** Hebrew *maskil.* This may be a literary or musical term.

They repented and took God seriously.
35 Then they remembered that God was their rock,
that God Most High* was their redeemer.
36 But all they gave him was lip service;
they lied to him with their tongues.
37 Their hearts were not loyal to him.
They did not keep his covenant.
38 Yet he was merciful and forgave their sins
and did not destroy them all.
Many times he held back his anger
and did not unleash his fury!
39 For he remembered that they were merely mortal,
gone like a breath of wind that never returns.

40 Oh, how often they rebelled against him in
the wilderness
and grieved his heart in that dry wasteland.
41 Again and again they tested God's patience
and provoked the Holy One of Israel.
42 They did not remember his power
and how he rescued them from their enemies.
43 They did not remember his miraculous signs
in Egypt,
his wonders on the plain of Zoan.
44 For he turned their rivers into blood,
so no one could drink from the streams.
45 He sent vast swarms of flies to consume them
and hordes of frogs to ruin them.
46 He gave their crops to caterpillars;
their harvest was consumed by locusts.
47 He destroyed their grapevines with hail
and shattered their sycamore-figs with sleet.
48 He abandoned their cattle to the hail,
their livestock to bolts of lightning.
49 He loosed on them his fierce anger—
all his fury, rage, and hostility.
He dispatched against them
a band of destroying angels.
50 He turned his anger against them;
he did not spare the Egyptians' lives
but ravaged them with the plague.
51 He killed the oldest son in each Egyptian family,
the flower of youth throughout the land
of Egypt.*
52 But he led his own people like a flock of sheep,
guiding them safely through the wilderness.
53 He kept them safe so they were not afraid;
but the sea covered their enemies.
54 He brought them to the border of his holy land,
to this land of hills he had won for them.
55 He drove out the nations before them;
he gave them their inheritance by lot.
He settled the tribes of Israel into their homes.

56 But they kept testing and rebelling against God
Most High.
They did not obey his laws.
57 They turned back and were as faithless as
their parents.
They were as undependable as a crooked bow.
58 They angered God by building shrines to other gods;
they made him jealous with their idols.
59 When God heard them, he was very angry,
and he completely rejected Israel.
60 Then he abandoned his dwelling at Shiloh,
the Tabernacle where he had lived among
the people.
61 He allowed the Ark of his might to be captured;
he surrendered his glory into enemy hands.
62 He gave his people over to be butchered by
the sword,
because he was so angry with his own people—
his special possession.
63 Their young men were killed by fire;
their young women died before singing their
wedding songs.
64 Their priests were slaughtered,
and their widows could not mourn their deaths.

65 Then the Lord rose up as though waking from sleep,
like a warrior aroused from a drunken stupor.
66 He routed his enemies
and sent them to eternal shame.
67 But he rejected Joseph's descendants;
he did not choose the tribe of Ephraim.
68 He chose instead the tribe of Judah,
and Mount Zion, which he loved.
69 There he built his sanctuary as high as the heavens,
as solid and enduring as the earth.
70 He chose his servant David,
calling him from the sheep pens.

BASIC TRAINING 78:71-72

Although David had assumed the throne of Israel when this psalm was written, he was called a shepherd and not a king. Shepherding, a common profession in biblical times, was a highly responsible job. The flocks were completely dependent upon shepherds for guidance, provision, and protection. David had spent his early years as a shepherd (1 Sam 16:10-11). Being a shepherd trained him for the responsibilities God had in store for him. When he was ready, God took him from caring for sheep to caring for Israel, God's people. God is shaping you right now for future responsibilities. Maybe you can't see how doing those same dull chores day after day can shape you for a cool purpose. But God can. ■

71 He took David from tending the ewes and lambs
and made him the shepherd of Jacob's
descendants—
God's own people, Israel.
72 He cared for them with a true heart
and led them with skillful hands.

78:35 Hebrew *El-Elyon.* **78:51** Hebrew *in the tents of Ham.*

79

A psalm of Asaph.

1 O God, pagan nations have conquered your land,
your special possession.
They have defiled your holy Temple
and made Jerusalem a heap of ruins.
2 They have left the bodies of your servants
as food for the birds of heaven.
The flesh of your godly ones
has become food for the wild animals.
3 Blood has flowed like water all around Jerusalem;
no one is left to bury the dead.
4 We are mocked by our neighbors,
an object of scorn and derision to those around us.

5 O LORD, how long will you be angry with us?
Forever?
How long will your jealousy burn like fire?
6 Pour out your wrath on the nations that refuse to
acknowledge you—
on kingdoms that do not call upon your name.
7 For they have devoured your people Israel,*
making the land a desolate wilderness.
8 Do not hold us guilty for the sins of our ancestors!
Let your compassion quickly meet our needs,
for we are on the brink of despair.

BE PREPARED 79:10

The psalmist acknowledged how enemies mocked the beliefs of Israel. Throughout the ages, Christians have endured terrible treatment because of their faith. Some have given up their faith, because the persecution seemed too great. If you're a Christian, you can expect to face persecution. As Jesus said, "Here on earth you will have many trials and sorrows. But take heart, because I have overcome the world" (John 16:33). His words are a warning to be prepared. ■

9 Help us, O God of our salvation!
Help us for the glory of your name.
Save us and forgive our sins
for the honor of your name.
10 Why should pagan nations be allowed to scoff,
asking, "Where is their God?"
Show us your vengeance against the nations,
for they have spilled the blood of your servants.
11 Listen to the moaning of the prisoners.
Demonstrate your great power by saving those
condemned to die.

12 O Lord, pay back our neighbors seven times
for the scorn they have hurled at you.
13 Then we your people, the sheep of your pasture,
will thank you forever and ever,
praising your greatness from generation
to generation.

80

For the choir director: A psalm of Asaph, to be sung to the tune "Lilies of the Covenant."

1 Please listen, O Shepherd of Israel,
you who lead Joseph's descendants like a flock.
O God, enthroned above the cherubim,
display your radiant glory
2 to Ephraim, Benjamin, and Manasseh.
Show us your mighty power.
Come to rescue us!

3 Turn us again to yourself, O God.
Make your face shine down upon us.
Only then will we be saved.
4 O LORD God of Heaven's Armies,
how long will you be angry with our prayers?
5 You have fed us with sorrow
and made us drink tears by the bucketful.
6 You have made us the scorn* of neighboring nations.
Our enemies treat us as a joke.

7 Turn us again to yourself, O God of Heaven's Armies.
Make your face shine down upon us.
Only then will we be saved.
8 You brought us from Egypt like a grapevine;
you drove away the pagan nations and transplanted
us into your land.
9 You cleared the ground for us,
and we took root and filled the land.
10 Our shade covered the mountains;
our branches covered the mighty cedars.
11 We spread our branches west to the
Mediterranean Sea;
our shoots spread east to the Euphrates River.*
12 But now, why have you broken down our walls
so that all who pass by may steal our fruit?
13 The wild boar from the forest devours it,
and the wild animals feed on it.

14 Come back, we beg you, O God of Heaven's Armies.
Look down from heaven and see our plight.
Take care of this grapevine
15 that you yourself have planted,
this son you have raised for yourself.
16 For we are chopped up and burned by our enemies.
May they perish at the sight of your frown.
17 Strengthen the man you love,
the son of your choice.
18 Then we will never abandon you again.
Revive us so we can call on your name once more.

19 Turn us again to yourself, O LORD God of
Heaven's Armies.

79:7 Hebrew *devoured Jacob*. See note on 44:4. 80:6 As in Syriac version; Hebrew reads *the strife*. 80:11 Hebrew *west to the sea, . . . east to the river*.

Make your face shine down upon us.
Only then will we be saved.

81

*For the choir director: A psalm of Asaph, to be accompanied by a stringed instrument.**

1 Sing praises to God, our strength.
Sing to the God of Jacob.
2 Sing! Beat the tambourine.
Play the sweet lyre and the harp.
3 Blow the ram's horn at new moon,
and again at full moon to call a festival!
4 For this is required by the decrees of Israel;
it is a regulation of the God of Jacob.
5 He made it a law for Israel*
when he attacked Egypt to set us free.

HOLIDAYS 81:1-5

Israel's sacred feasts were times of celebration to remind the nation of God's amazing help throughout the years. Thanksgiving, Christmas, and Easter are times of celebration for our nation. But for many, those holidays have little meaning beyond presents, food, and football. Yet each holiday presents an opportunity to worship God for what he's done for us—especially for sending his Son to die for us. As each holiday approaches, how will you acknowledge the spiritual significance of the day? ■

I heard an unknown voice say,
6 "Now I will take the load from your shoulders;
I will free your hands from their heavy tasks.
7 You cried to me in trouble, and I saved you;
I answered out of the thundercloud
and tested your faith when there was no water
at Meriah. *Interlude*

8 "Listen to me, O my people, while I give you stern
warnings.
O Israel, if you would only listen to me!
9 You must never have a foreign god;
you must not bow down before a false god.
10 For it was I, the LORD your God,
who rescued you from the land of Egypt.
Open your mouth wide, and I will fill it with
good things.

11 "But no, my people wouldn't listen.
Israel did not want me around.
12 So I let them follow their own stubborn desires,
living according to their own ideas.
13 Oh, that my people would listen to me!
Oh, that Israel would follow me, walking in
my paths!
14 How quickly I would then subdue their enemies!
How soon my hands would be upon their foes!
15 Those who hate the LORD would cringe before him;
they would be doomed forever.
16 But I would feed you with the finest wheat.
I would satisfy you with wild honey from
the rock."

82

A psalm of Asaph.

1 God presides over heaven's court;
he pronounces judgment on the heavenly beings:
2 "How long will you hand down unjust decisions
by favoring the wicked? *Interlude*

3 "Give justice to the poor and the orphan;
uphold the rights of the oppressed and the
destitute.
4 Rescue the poor and helpless;
deliver them from the grasp of evil people.
5 But these oppressors know nothing;
they are so ignorant!
They wander about in darkness,
while the whole world is shaken to the core.
6 I say, 'You are gods;
you are all children of the Most High.
7 But you will die like mere mortals
and fall like every other ruler.'"

8 Rise up, O God, and judge the earth,
for all the nations belong to you.

83

A song. A psalm of Asaph.

1 O God, do not be silent!
Do not be deaf.
Do not be quiet, O God.
2 Don't you hear the uproar of your enemies?
Don't you see that your arrogant enemies are
rising up?
3 They devise crafty schemes against your people;
they conspire against your precious ones.
4 "Come," they say, "let us wipe out Israel as a nation.
We will destroy the very memory of
its existence."
5 Yes, this was their unanimous decision.
They signed a treaty as allies against you—
6 these Edomites and Ishmaelites;
Moabites and Hagrites;
7 Gebalites, Ammonites, and Amalekites;
and people from Philistia and Tyre.
8 Assyria has joined them, too,
and is allied with the descendants of Lot. *Interlude*

9 Do to them as you did to the Midianites
and as you did to Sisera and Jabin at the
Kishon River.

81:TITLE Hebrew *according to the gittith.* 81:5 Hebrew *for Joseph.*

10 They were destroyed at Endor,
and their decaying corpses fertilized the soil.
11 Let their mighty nobles die as Oreb and Zeeb did.
Let all their princes die like Zebah and Zalmunna,
12 for they said, "Let us seize for our own use
these pasturelands of God!"
13 O my God, scatter them like tumbleweed,
like chaff before the wind!
14 As a fire burns a forest
and as a flame sets mountains ablaze,
15 chase them with your fierce storm;
terrify them with your tempest.
16 Utterly disgrace them
until they submit to your name, O LORD.
17 Let them be ashamed and terrified forever.
Let them die in disgrace.
18 Then they will learn that you alone are called
the LORD,
that you alone are the Most High,
supreme over all the earth.

BLOWN AWAY 83:1-18

Surrounding Judah were enemy nations that sought its downfall. Asaph prayed that God would blow these nations away like chaff before the wind until, in their defeat, they recognized the greatness of God. Sometimes we must be defeated before we turn to God for help. Wouldn't it be better to seek the Lord in times of prosperity than to wait until his judgment is upon us? ■

84

*For the choir director: A psalm of the descendants of Korah, to be accompanied by a stringed instrument.**

1 How lovely is your dwelling place,
O LORD of Heaven's Armies.
2 I long, yes, I faint with longing
to enter the courts of the LORD.
With my whole being, body and soul,
I will shout joyfully to the living God.
3 Even the sparrow finds a home,
and the swallow builds her nest and raises
her young
at a place near your altar,
O LORD of Heaven's Armies, my King and my God!
4 What joy for those who can live in your house,
always singing your praises. *Interlude*

5 What joy for those whose strength comes from
the LORD,
who have set their minds on a pilgrimage
to Jerusalem.
6 When they walk through the Valley of Weeping,*
it will become a place of refreshing springs.
The autumn rains will clothe it with blessings.
7 They will continue to grow stronger,
and each of them will appear before God
in Jerusalem.*

8 O LORD God of Heaven's Armies, hear my prayer.
Listen, O God of Jacob. *Interlude*

9 O God, look with favor upon the king, our shield!
Show favor to the one you have anointed.

10 A single day in your courts
is better than a thousand anywhere else!
I would rather be a gatekeeper in the house
of my God
than live the good life in the homes of the wicked.
11 For the LORD God is our sun and our shield.
He gives us grace and glory.
The LORD will withhold no good thing
from those who do what is right.
12 O LORD of Heaven's Armies,
what joy for those who trust in you.

85

For the choir director: A psalm of the descendants of Korah.

1 LORD, you poured out blessings on your land!
You restored the fortunes of Israel.*
2 You forgave the guilt of your people—
yes, you covered all their sins. *Interlude*
3 You held back your fury.
You kept back your blazing anger.

4 Now restore us again, O God of our salvation.
Put aside your anger against us once more.
5 Will you be angry with us always?
Will you prolong your wrath to all generations?
6 Won't you revive us again,
so your people can rejoice in you?
7 Show us your unfailing love, O LORD,
and grant us your salvation.

8 I listen carefully to what God the LORD is saying,
for he speaks peace to his faithful people.
But let them not return to their foolish ways.
9 Surely his salvation is near to those who fear him,
so our land will be filled with his glory.

10 Unfailing love and truth have met together.
Righteousness and peace have kissed!
11 Truth springs up from the earth,
and righteousness smiles down from heaven.
12 Yes, the LORD pours down his blessings.
Our land will yield its bountiful harvest.
13 Righteousness goes as a herald before him,
preparing the way for his steps.

84:TITLE Hebrew *according to the gittith.* 84:6 Or *Valley of Poplars;* Hebrew reads *valley of Baca.* 84:7 Hebrew *Zion.* 85:1 Hebrew *of Jacob.* See note on 44:4.

86 *A prayer of David.*

1 Bend down, O LORD, and hear my prayer;
answer me, for I need your help.
2 Protect me, for I am devoted to you.
Save me, for I serve you and trust you.
You are my God.
3 Be merciful to me, O Lord,
for I am calling on you constantly.
4 Give me happiness, O Lord,
for I give myself to you.
5 O Lord, you are so good, so ready to forgive,
so full of unfailing love for all who ask for
your help.
6 Listen closely to my prayer, O LORD;
hear my urgent cry.
7 I will call to you whenever I'm in trouble,
and you will answer me.

8 No pagan god is like you, O Lord.
None can do what you do!
9 All the nations you made
will come and bow before you, Lord;
they will praise your holy name.
10 For you are great and perform wonderful deeds.
You alone are God.

WHOLEHEARTED 86:11-12

Praising God with all our heart means appreciating him and honoring him in all areas of life. If we're wholehearted about our relationship with God, then our work, other relationships, use of money, and desires will be in keeping with his will. ■

11 Teach me your ways, O LORD,
that I may live according to your truth!
Grant me purity of heart,
so that I may honor you.
12 With all my heart I will praise you, O Lord my God.
I will give glory to your name forever,
13 for your love for me is very great.
You have rescued me from the depths of death.*

14 O God, insolent people rise up against me;
a violent gang is trying to kill me.
You mean nothing to them.
15 But you, O Lord,
are a God of compassion and mercy,
slow to get angry
and filled with unfailing love and faithfulness.
16 Look down and have mercy on me.
Give your strength to your servant;
save me, the son of your servant.
17 Send me a sign of your favor.
Then those who hate me will be put to shame,
for you, O LORD, help and comfort me.

87 *A song. A psalm of the descendants of Korah.*

1 On the holy mountain
stands the city founded by the LORD.
2 He loves the city of Jerusalem
more than any other city in Israel.*
3 O city of God,
what glorious things are said of you! *Interlude*

4 I will count Egypt* and Babylon among those who
know me—
also Philistia and Tyre, and even distant Ethiopia.*
They have all become citizens of Jerusalem!
5 Regarding Jerusalem* it will be said,
"Everyone enjoys the rights of citizenship there."
And the Most High will personally bless this city.
6 When the LORD registers the nations, he will say,
"They have all become citizens of Jerusalem."
Interlude

7 The people will play flutes* and sing,
"The source of my life springs from Jerusalem!"

88 *For the choir director: A psalm of the descendants of Korah. A song to be sung to the tune "The Suffering of Affliction." A psalm* of Heman the Ezrahite.*

1 O LORD, God of my salvation,
I cry out to you by day.
I come to you at night.
2 Now hear my prayer;
listen to my cry.
3 For my life is full of troubles,
and death* draws near.
4 I am as good as dead,
like a strong man with no strength left.
5 They have left me among the dead,
and I lie like a corpse in a grave.
I am forgotten,
cut off from your care.
6 You have thrown me into the lowest pit,
into the darkest depths.
7 Your anger weighs me down;
with wave after wave you have engulfed me.
Interlude

8 You have driven my friends away
by making me repulsive to them.
I am in a trap with no way of escape.

86:13 Hebrew *of Sheol.* **87:2** Hebrew *He loves the gates of Zion more than all the dwellings of Jacob.* See note on 44:4. **87:4a** Hebrew *Rahab,* the name of a mythical sea monster that represents chaos in ancient literature. The name is used here as a poetic name for Egypt. **87:4b** Hebrew *Cush.* **87:5** Hebrew *Zion.* **87:7** Or *will dance.* **88:TITLE** Hebrew *maskil.* This may be a literary or musical term. **88:3** Hebrew *Sheol.*

9 My eyes are blinded by my tears.
Each day I beg for your help, O LORD;
I lift my hands to you for mercy.
10 Are your wonderful deeds of any use to the dead?
Do the dead rise up and praise you? *Interlude*
11 Can those in the grave declare your unfailing love?
Can they proclaim your faithfulness in the place of destruction?*
12 Can the darkness speak of your wonderful deeds?
Can anyone in the land of forgetfulness talk about your righteousness?
13 O LORD, I cry out to you.
I will keep on pleading day by day.
14 O LORD, why do you reject me?
Why do you turn your face from me?

15 I have been sick and close to death since my youth.
I stand helpless and desperate before your terrors.
16 Your fierce anger has overwhelmed me.
Your terrors have paralyzed me.
17 They swirl around me like floodwaters all day long.
They have engulfed me completely.
18 You have taken away my companions and loved ones.
Darkness is my closest friend.

89

A psalm of Ethan the Ezrahite.*

1 I will sing of the LORD's unfailing love forever!
Young and old will hear of your faithfulness.
2 Your unfailing love will last forever.
Your faithfulness is as enduring as the heavens.

3 The LORD said, "I have made a covenant with David, my chosen servant.
I have sworn this oath to him:
4 'I will establish your descendants as kings forever;
they will sit on your throne from now until eternity.'" *Interlude*
5 All heaven will praise your great wonders, LORD;
myriads of angels will praise you for your faithfulness.
6 For who in all of heaven can compare with the LORD?
What mightiest angel is anything like the LORD?
7 The highest angelic powers stand in awe of God.
He is far more awesome than all who surround his throne.
8 O LORD God of Heaven's Armies!
Where is there anyone as mighty as you, O LORD?
You are entirely faithful.

9 You rule the oceans.
You subdue their storm-tossed waves.
10 You crushed the great sea monster.*
You scattered your enemies with your mighty arm.
11 The heavens are yours, and the earth is yours;
everything in the world is yours—you created it all.
12 You created north and south.
Mount Tabor and Mount Hermon praise your name.
13 Powerful is your arm!
Strong is your hand!
Your right hand is lifted high in glorious strength.
14 Righteousness and justice are the foundation of your throne.
Unfailing love and truth walk before you as attendants.
15 Happy are those who hear the joyful call to worship,
for they will walk in the light of your presence, LORD.

HIS REPRESENTATIVES 89:14-15

God's throne is pictured with a foundation of righteousness and justice. These describe fundamental aspects of the way God deals with people. As God's representatives, we have the responsibility of treating people the same way that God treats them. Would a friend or family member describe your actions as righteous, fair, or loving? ■

16 They rejoice all day long in your wonderful reputation.
They exult in your righteousness.
17 You are their glorious strength.
It pleases you to make us strong.
18 Yes, our protection comes from the LORD,
and he, the Holy One of Israel, has given us our king.

19 Long ago you spoke in a vision to your faithful people.
You said, "I have raised up a warrior.
I have selected him from the common people to be king.
20 I have found my servant David.
I have anointed him with my holy oil.
21 I will steady him with my hand;
with my powerful arm I will make him strong.
22 His enemies will not defeat him,
nor will the wicked overpower him.
23 I will beat down his adversaries before him
and destroy those who hate him.
24 My faithfulness and unfailing love will be with him,
and by my authority he will grow in power.
25 I will extend his rule over the sea,
his dominion over the rivers.
26 And he will call out to me, 'You are my Father,
my God, and the Rock of my salvation.'

88:11 Hebrew *in Abaddon?* **89:TITLE** Hebrew *maskil.* This may be a literary or musical term. **89:10** Hebrew *Rahab,* the name of a mythical sea monster that represents chaos in ancient literature.

27 I will make him my firstborn son,
the mightiest king on earth.
28 I will love him and be kind to him forever;
my covenant with him will never end.
29 I will preserve an heir for him;
his throne will be as endless as the days of heaven.
30 But if his descendants forsake my instructions
and fail to obey my regulations,
31 if they do not obey my decrees
and fail to keep my commands,
32 then I will punish their sin with the rod,
and their disobedience with beating.
33 But I will never stop loving him
nor fail to keep my promise to him.
34 No, I will not break my covenant;
I will not take back a single word I said.
35 I have sworn an oath to David,
and in my holiness I cannot lie:
36 His dynasty will go on forever;
his kingdom will endure as the sun.
37 It will be as eternal as the moon,
my faithful witness in the sky!" *Interlude*

38 But now you have rejected him and cast him off.
You are angry with your anointed king.
39 You have renounced your covenant with him;
you have thrown his crown in the dust.
40 You have broken down the walls protecting him
and ruined every fort defending him.
41 Everyone who comes along has robbed him,
and he has become a joke to his neighbors.
42 You have strengthened his enemies
and made them all rejoice.
43 You have made his sword useless
and refused to help him in battle.
44 You have ended his splendor
and overturned his throne.
45 You have made him old before his time
and publicly disgraced him. *Interlude*

46 O LORD, how long will this go on?
Will you hide yourself forever?
How long will your anger burn like fire?
47 Remember how short my life is,
how empty and futile this human existence!
48 No one can live forever; all will die.
No one can escape the power of the grave.*
Interlude

49 Lord, where is your unfailing love?
You promised it to David with a faithful pledge.
50 Consider, Lord, how your servants are disgraced!
I carry in my heart the insults of so many people.
51 Your enemies have mocked me, O LORD;
they mock your anointed king wherever he goes.

52 Praise the LORD forever!
Amen and amen!

89:48 Hebrew *of Sheol.*

BOOK FOUR (Psalms 90–106)

90

A prayer of Moses, the man of God.

1 Lord, through all the generations
you have been our home!
2 Before the mountains were born,
before you gave birth to the earth and the world,
from beginning to end, you are God.

3 You turn people back to dust, saying,
"Return to dust, you mortals!"
4 For you, a thousand years are as a passing day,
as brief as a few night hours.
5 You sweep people away like dreams that disappear.
They are like grass that springs up in the morning.
6 In the morning it blooms and flourishes,
but by evening it is dry and withered.
7 We wither beneath your anger;
we are overwhelmed by your fury.
8 You spread out our sins before you—
our secret sins—and you see them all.
9 We live our lives beneath your wrath,
ending our years with a groan.

10 Seventy years are given to us!
Some even live to eighty.
But even the best years are filled with pain and
trouble;
soon they disappear, and we fly away.
11 Who can comprehend the power of your anger?
Your wrath is as awesome as the fear you deserve.
12 Teach us to realize the brevity of life,
so that we may grow in wisdom.

13 O LORD, come back to us!
How long will you delay?
Take pity on your servants!
14 Satisfy us each morning with your unfailing love,
so we may sing for joy to the end of our lives.
15 Give us gladness in proportion to our former misery!
Replace the evil years with good.
16 Let us, your servants, see you work again;
let our children see your glory.
17 And may the Lord our God show us his approval
and make our efforts successful.
Yes, make our efforts successful!

91

1 Those who live in the shelter of the
Most High
will find rest in the shadow of the Almighty.
2 This I declare about the LORD:
He alone is my refuge, my place of safety;
he is my God, and I trust him.
3 For he will rescue you from every trap
and protect you from deadly disease.
4 He will cover you with his feathers.

He will shelter you with his wings.
His faithful promises are your armor and protection.
5 Do not be afraid of the terrors of the night,
nor the arrow that flies in the day.
6 Do not dread the disease that stalks in darkness,
nor the disaster that strikes at midday.
7 Though a thousand fall at your side,
though ten thousand are dying around you,
these evils will not touch you.
8 Just open your eyes,
and see how the wicked are punished.

A SHELTER 91:1-16

When bad weather strikes, everyone immediately heads for shelter. When hard times come, the psalmist encourages everyone to head to shelter—God. The protection he offers is tailor made to fit any kind of trouble. Is God your first option for shelter when trouble comes? ■

9 If you make the LORD your refuge,
if you make the Most High your shelter,
10 no evil will conquer you;
no plague will come near your home.
11 For he will order his angels
to protect you wherever you go.
12 They will hold you up with their hands
so you won't even hurt your foot on a stone.
13 You will trample upon lions and cobras;
you will crush fierce lions and serpents under your feet!

14 The LORD says, "I will rescue those who love me.
I will protect those who trust in my name.
15 When they call on me, I will answer;
I will be with them in trouble.
I will rescue and honor them.
16 I will reward them with a long life
and give them my salvation."

92

A psalm. A song to be sung on the Sabbath Day.

1 It is good to give thanks to the LORD,
to sing praises to the Most High.
2 It is good to proclaim your unfailing love in the morning,
your faithfulness in the evening,
3 accompanied by the ten-stringed harp
and the melody of the lyre.

4 You thrill me, LORD, with all you have done for me!
I sing for joy because of what you have done.
5 O LORD, what great works you do!
And how deep are your thoughts.
6 Only a simpleton would not know,
and only a fool would not understand this:
7 Though the wicked sprout like weeds
and evildoers flourish,
they will be destroyed forever.
8 But you, O LORD, will be exalted forever.
9 Your enemies, LORD, will surely perish;
all evildoers will be scattered.
10 But you have made me as strong as a wild ox.
You have anointed me with the finest oil.
11 My eyes have seen the downfall of my enemies;
my ears have heard the defeat of my wicked opponents.
12 But the godly will flourish like palm trees
and grow strong like the cedars of Lebanon.
13 For they are transplanted to the LORD's own house.
They flourish in the courts of our God.
14 Even in old age they will still produce fruit;
they will remain vital and green.
15 They will declare, "The LORD is just!
He is my rock!
There is no evil in him!"

A LIFE OF HONORING GOD 92:14-15

A person can honor God his or her entire life. There are many faithful older people who have much to teach others based on their long relationship with God. Are you willing to listen? ■

93

1 The LORD is king! He is robed in majesty.
Indeed, the LORD is robed in majesty and armed with strength.
The world stands firm
and cannot be shaken.

2 Your throne, O LORD, has stood from time immemorial.
You yourself are from the everlasting past.
3 The floods have risen up, O LORD.
The floods have roared like thunder;
the floods have lifted their pounding waves.
4 But mightier than the violent raging of the seas,
mightier than the breakers on the shore—
the LORD above is mightier than these!
5 Your royal laws cannot be changed.
Your reign, O LORD, is holy forever and ever.

94

1 O LORD, the God of vengeance,
O God of vengeance, let your glorious justice shine forth!
2 Arise, O judge of the earth.
Give the proud what they deserve.
3 How long, O LORD?
How long will the wicked be allowed to gloat?

4 How long will they speak with arrogance?
How long will these evil people boast?
5 They crush your people, LORD,
hurting those you claim as your own.
6 They kill widows and foreigners
and murder orphans.
7 "The LORD isn't looking," they say,
"and besides, the God of Israel* doesn't care."

8 Think again, you fools!
When will you finally catch on?
9 Is he deaf—the one who made your ears?
Is he blind—the one who formed your eyes?
10 He punishes the nations—won't he also punish you?
He knows everything—doesn't he also know what
you are doing?
11 The LORD knows people's thoughts;
he knows they are worthless!

12 Joyful are those you discipline, LORD,
those you teach with your instructions.
13 You give them relief from troubled times
until a pit is dug to capture the wicked.
14 The LORD will not reject his people;
he will not abandon his special possession.
15 Judgment will again be founded on justice,
and those with virtuous hearts will pursue it.

16 Who will protect me from the wicked?
Who will stand up for me against evildoers?
17 Unless the LORD had helped me,
I would soon have settled in the silence of the grave.
18 I cried out, "I am slipping!"
but your unfailing love, O LORD, supported me.
19 When doubts filled my mind,
your comfort gave me renewed hope and cheer.

20 Can unjust leaders claim that God is on their side—
leaders whose decrees permit injustice?
21 They gang up against the righteous
and condemn the innocent to death.
22 But the LORD is my fortress;
my God is the mighty rock where I hide.
23 God will turn the sins of evil people back on them.
He will destroy them for their sins.
The LORD our God will destroy them.

95

1 Come, let us sing to the LORD!
Let us shout joyfully to the Rock of our salvation.
2 Let us come to him with thanksgiving.
Let us sing psalms of praise to him.
3 For the LORD is a great God,
a great King above all gods.
4 He holds in his hands the depths of the earth
and the mightiest mountains.
5 The sea belongs to him, for he made it.
His hands formed the dry land, too.

6 Come, let us worship and bow down.
Let us kneel before the LORD our maker,
7 for he is our God.
We are the people he watches over,
the flock under his care.

If only you would listen to his voice today!
8 The LORD says, "Don't harden your hearts as Israel
did at Meribah,
as they did at Massah in the wilderness.
9 For there your ancestors tested and tried my
patience,
even though they saw everything I did.
10 For forty years I was angry with them, and I said,
'They are a people whose hearts turn away
from me.
They refuse to do what I tell them.'
11 So in my anger I took an oath:
'They will never enter my place of rest.'"

96

1 Sing a new song to the LORD!
Let the whole earth sing to the LORD!
2 Sing to the LORD; praise his name.
Each day proclaim the good news that he saves.
3 Publish his glorious deeds among the nations.
Tell everyone about the amazing things
he does.
4 Great is the LORD! He is most worthy of praise!
He is to be feared above all gods.
5 The gods of other nations are mere idols,
but the LORD made the heavens!
6 Honor and majesty surround him;
strength and beauty fill his sanctuary.

7 O nations of the world, recognize the LORD;
recognize that the LORD is glorious and strong.
8 Give to the LORD the glory he deserves!
Bring your offering and come into his courts.
9 Worship the LORD in all his holy splendor.
Let all the earth tremble before him.
10 Tell all the nations, "The LORD reigns!"
The world stands firm and cannot be shaken.
He will judge all peoples fairly.

11 Let the heavens be glad, and the earth rejoice!
Let the sea and everything in it shout his praise!
12 Let the fields and their crops burst out with joy!
Let the trees of the forest rustle with praise
13 before the LORD, for he is coming!
He is coming to judge the earth.
He will judge the world with justice,
and the nations with his truth.

97

1 The LORD is king!
Let the earth rejoice!
Let the farthest coastlands be glad.

94:7 Hebrew *of Jacob.* See note on 44:4.

2 Dark clouds surround him.
Righteousness and justice are the foundation of his throne.
3 Fire spreads ahead of him
and burns up all his foes.
4 His lightning flashes out across the world.
The earth sees and trembles.
5 The mountains melt like wax before the LORD,
before the Lord of all the earth.
6 The heavens proclaim his righteousness;
every nation sees his glory.
7 Those who worship idols are disgraced—
all who brag about their worthless gods—
for every god must bow to him.
8 Jerusalem* has heard and rejoiced,
and all the towns of Judah are glad
because of your justice, O LORD!
9 For you, O LORD, are supreme over all the earth;
you are exalted far above all gods.

10 You who love the LORD, hate evil!
He protects the lives of his godly people
and rescues them from the power of the wicked.

WANTING WHAT HE WANTS 97:10

A sincere desire to please God will result in an alignment of your desires with God's desires. You will love what God loves and hate what God hates. If you do not despise the actions of people who take advantage of others, if you admire people who look out only for themselves, or if you envy those who get ahead using any means to accomplish their ends, then your primary desire in life is out of alignment with God's desires. In need of a realignment? Just by acknowledging your need, you're halfway there! ■

11 Light shines on the godly,
and joy on those whose hearts are right.
12 May all who are godly rejoice in the LORD
and praise his holy name!

98

A psalm.

1 Sing a new song to the LORD,
for he has done wonderful deeds.
His right hand has won a mighty victory;
his holy arm has shown his saving power!
2 The LORD has announced his victory
and has revealed his righteousness to every nation!
3 He has remembered his promise to love and be faithful to Israel.
The ends of the earth have seen the victory of our God.
4 Shout to the LORD, all the earth;
break out in praise and sing for joy!
5 Sing your praise to the LORD with the harp,
with the harp and melodious song,
6 with trumpets and the sound of the ram's horn.
Make a joyful symphony before the LORD, the King!

7 Let the sea and everything in it shout his praise!
Let the earth and all living things join in.
8 Let the rivers clap their hands in glee!
Let the hills sing out their songs of joy
9 before the LORD.
For the LORD is coming to judge the earth.
He will judge the world with justice,
and the nations with fairness.

FAMILY NAME 99:3

God's name symbolizes his nature and his reputation. Unfortunately, the name of God is often misused or treated lightly by those who don't understand its significance. How can you honor God's name by your words and your life? ■

99

1 The LORD is king!
Let the nations tremble!
He sits on his throne between the cherubim.
Let the whole earth quake!
2 The LORD sits in majesty in Jerusalem,*
exalted above all the nations.
3 Let them praise your great and awesome name.
Your name is holy!
4 Mighty King, lover of justice,
you have established fairness.
You have acted with justice
and righteousness throughout Israel.*
5 Exalt the LORD our God!
Bow low before his feet, for he is holy!

6 Moses and Aaron were among his priests;
Samuel also called on his name.
They cried to the LORD for help,
and he answered them.
7 He spoke to Israel from the pillar of cloud,
and they followed the laws and decrees he gave them.
8 O LORD our God, you answered them.
You were a forgiving God to them,
but you punished them when they went wrong.

9 Exalt the LORD our God,
and worship at his holy mountain in Jerusalem,
for the LORD our God is holy!

97:8 Hebrew *Zion*. 99:2 Hebrew *Zion*. 99:4 Hebrew *Jacob*. See note on 44:4.

100

A psalm of thanksgiving.

1 Shout with joy to the LORD, all the
earth!
2 Worship the LORD with gladness.
Come before him, singing
with joy.
3 Acknowledge that the LORD is God!
He made us, and we are his.
We are his people, the sheep of
his pasture.
4 Enter his gates with thanksgiving;
go into his courts with praise.
Give thanks to him and praise
his name.
5 For the LORD is good.
His unfailing love continues
forever,
and his faithfulness continues to
each generation.

> Enter his gates with thanksgiving; go into his courts with praise. Give thanks to him and praise his name.
> PSALM 100:4

101

A psalm of David.

1 I will sing of your love and justice, LORD.
I will praise you with songs.
2 I will be careful to live a blameless life—
when will you come to help me?
I will lead a life of integrity
in my own home.
3 I will refuse to look at
anything vile and vulgar.
I hate all who deal crookedly;
I will have nothing to do with them.
4 I will reject perverse ideas
and stay away from every evil.
5 I will not tolerate people who slander their
neighbors.
I will not endure conceit and pride.

6 I will search for faithful people
to be my companions.
Only those who are above reproach
will be allowed to serve me.
7 I will not allow deceivers to serve in my house,
and liars will not stay in my presence.
8 My daily task will be to ferret out the wicked
and free the city of the LORD from their grip.

102

A prayer of one overwhelmed with trouble, pouring out problems before the LORD.

1 LORD, hear my prayer!
Listen to my plea!
2 Don't turn away from me
in my time of distress.
Bend down to listen,
and answer me quickly when I call to you.
3 For my days disappear like smoke,
and my bones burn like red-hot coals.
4 My heart is sick, withered like grass,
and I have lost my appetite.
5 Because of my groaning,
I am reduced to skin and bones.
6 I am like an owl in the desert,
like a little owl in a far-off
wilderness.
7 I lie awake,
lonely as a solitary bird on the
roof.
8 My enemies taunt me day
after day.
They mock and curse me.
9 I eat ashes for food.
My tears run down into my drink
10 because of your anger and wrath.
For you have picked me up and
thrown me out.
11 My life passes as swiftly as the evening shadows.
I am withering away like grass.

12 But you, O LORD, will sit on your throne forever.
Your fame will endure to every generation.
13 You will arise and have mercy on Jerusalem*—
and now is the time to pity her,
now is the time you promised to help.
14 For your people love every stone in her walls
and cherish even the dust in her streets.
15 Then the nations will tremble before the LORD.
The kings of the earth will tremble before his glory.
16 For the LORD will rebuild Jerusalem.
He will appear in his glory.
17 He will listen to the prayers of the destitute.
He will not reject their pleas.

18 Let this be recorded for future generations,
so that a people not yet born will praise
the LORD.
19 Tell them the LORD looked down
from his heavenly sanctuary.
He looked down to earth from heaven
20 to hear the groans of the prisoners,
to release those condemned to die.
21 And so the LORD's fame will be celebrated in Zion,
his praises in Jerusalem,
22 when multitudes gather together
and kingdoms come to worship the LORD.

23 He broke my strength in midlife,
cutting short my days.
24 But I cried to him, "O my God, who lives forever,
don't take my life while I am so young!
25 Long ago you laid the foundation of the earth
and made the heavens with your hands.

102:13 Hebrew *Zion;* also in 102:16.

26 They will perish, but you remain forever;
they will wear out like old clothing.
You will change them like a garment
and discard them.
27 But you are always the same;
you will live forever.
28 The children of your people
will live in security.
Their children's children
will thrive in your presence."

103

A psalm of David.

1 Let all that I am praise the LORD;
with my whole heart, I will praise his holy name.
2 Let all that I am praise the LORD;
may I never forget the good things he does for me.
3 He forgives all my sins
and heals all my diseases.

PRAISE LIST 103:3-18

David praised God for his glorious acts. Here's his list of reasons to praise God: for his love, forgiveness, salvation, kindness, mercy, justice, patience, and tenderness. We receive all of these freely, without having to earn any of them. No matter how difficult your life seems, there's always something for which you can be grateful. When you feel as though you have nothing for which to praise God, read David's list. ■

4 He redeems me from death
and crowns me with love and tender mercies.
5 He fills my life with good things.
My youth is renewed like the eagle's!

6 The LORD gives righteousness
and justice to all who are treated unfairly.

7 He revealed his character to Moses
and his deeds to the people of Israel.
8 The LORD is compassionate and merciful,
slow to get angry and filled with unfailing love.
9 He will not constantly accuse us,
nor remain angry forever.
10 He does not punish us for all our sins;
he does not deal harshly with us, as we deserve.
11 For his unfailing love toward those who fear him
is as great as the height of the heavens above
the earth.
12 He has removed our sins as far from us
as the east is from the west.
13 The LORD is like a father to his children,
tender and compassionate to those who
fear him.
14 For he knows how weak we are;
he remembers we are only dust.
15 Our days on earth are like grass;
like wildflowers, we bloom and die.
16 The wind blows, and we are gone—
as though we had never been here.
17 But the love of the LORD remains forever
with those who fear him.
His salvation extends to the children's children
18 of those who are faithful to his covenant,
of those who obey his commandments!

19 The LORD has made the heavens his throne;
from there he rules over everything.

20 Praise the LORD, you angels,
you mighty ones who carry out his plans,
listening for each of his commands.
21 Yes, praise the LORD, you armies of angels
who serve him and do his will!
22 Praise the LORD, everything he has created,
everything in all his kingdom.

Let all that I am praise the LORD.

104

1 Let all that I am praise the LORD.

O LORD my God, how great you are!
You are robed with honor and majesty.
2 You are dressed in a robe of light.
You stretch out the starry curtain of the heavens;
3 you lay out the rafters of your home in the
rain clouds.
You make the clouds your chariot;
you ride upon the wings of the wind.
4 The winds are your messengers;
flames of fire are your servants.*

5 You placed the world on its foundation
so it would never be moved.
6 You clothed the earth with floods of water,
water that covered even the mountains.
7 At your command, the water fled;
at the sound of your thunder, it hurried away.
8 Mountains rose and valleys sank
to the levels you decreed.
9 Then you set a firm boundary for the seas,
so they would never again cover the earth.

10 You make springs pour water into the ravines,
so streams gush down from the mountains.
11 They provide water for all the animals,
and the wild donkeys quench their thirst.
12 The birds nest beside the streams
and sing among the branches of the trees.
13 You send rain on the mountains from your
heavenly home,

104:4 Greek version reads *He sends his angels like the winds, / his servants like flames of fire*. Compare Heb 1:7.

and you fill the earth with the fruit of
your labor.
14 You cause grass to grow for the livestock
and plants for people to use.
You allow them to produce food from the earth—
15 wine to make them glad,
olive oil to soothe their skin,
and bread to give them strength.
16 The trees of the LORD are well cared for—
the cedars of Lebanon that he planted.
17 There the birds make their nests,
and the storks make their homes in
the cypresses.
18 High in the mountains live the wild goats,
and the rocks form a refuge for the hyraxes.*

19 You made the moon to mark the seasons,
and the sun knows when to set.
20 You send the darkness, and it becomes night,
when all the forest animals prowl about.
21 Then the young lions roar for their prey,
stalking the food provided by God.
22 At dawn they slink back
into their dens to rest.
23 Then people go off to their work,
where they labor until evening.

A RICH VARIETY 104:24

The earth is filled with an amazing variety of plants and creatures. Such a variety reveals the rich creativity, goodness, and wisdom of God. As you observe your surroundings, what's the first thing you notice? Take a fresh look at people, seeing each one as his unique creation, each with his or her own special talents, abilities, and gifts. Like the psalmist, you'll probably be inspired to praise God. ■

24 O LORD, what a variety of things you have made!
In wisdom you have made them all.
The earth is full of your creatures.
25 Here is the ocean, vast and wide,
teeming with life of every kind,
both large and small.
26 See the ships sailing along,
and Leviathan,* which you made to play
in the sea.

27 They all depend on you
to give them food as they need it.
28 When you supply it, they gather it.
You open your hand to feed them,
and they are richly satisfied.
29 But if you turn away from them, they panic.
When you take away their breath,
they die and turn again to dust.
30 When you give them your breath,* life is created,
and you renew the face of the earth.

31 May the glory of the LORD continue forever!
The LORD takes pleasure in all he has made!
32 The earth trembles at his glance;
the mountains smoke at his touch.

33 I will sing to the LORD as long as I live.
I will praise my God to my last breath!
34 May all my thoughts be pleasing to him,
for I rejoice in the LORD.
35 Let all sinners vanish from the face of the earth;
let the wicked disappear forever.

Let all that I am praise the LORD.

Praise the LORD!

105

1 Give thanks to the LORD and proclaim
his greatness.
Let the whole world know what he has done.
2 Sing to him; yes, sing his praises.
Tell everyone about his wonderful deeds.
3 Exult in his holy name;
rejoice, you who worship the LORD.
4 Search for the LORD and for his strength;
continually seek him.
5 Remember the wonders he has performed,
his miracles, and the rulings he has given,
6 you children of his servant Abraham,
you descendants of Jacob, his chosen ones.

KEEP SEARCHING 105:1-5

If God seems far away, keep searching for him. God rewards "those who sincerely seek him" (Heb 11:6). Jesus promised, "Keep on seeking, and you will find" (Matt 7:7). David suggested a valuable way to search out God—become familiar with the way he helped his people in the past. The Bible records the history of God's people. In searching its pages we will discover a loving God who is waiting for us to find him. ■

7 He is the LORD our God.
His justice is seen throughout the land.
8 He always stands by his covenant—
the commitment he made to a thousand
generations.
9 This is the covenant he made with Abraham
and the oath he swore to Isaac.
10 He confirmed it to Jacob as a decree,
and to the people of Israel as a never-ending
covenant:

104:18 Or *coneys*, or *rock badgers*. **104:26** The identification of Leviathan is disputed, ranging from an earthly creature to a mythical sea monster in ancient literature. **104:30** Or *When you send your Spirit*.

11 "I will give you the land of Canaan
as your special possession."

12 He said this when they were few in number,
a tiny group of strangers in Canaan.
13 They wandered from nation to nation,
from one kingdom to another.
14 Yet he did not let anyone oppress them.
He warned kings on their behalf:
15 "Do not touch my chosen people,
and do not hurt my prophets."

16 He called for a famine on the land of Canaan,
cutting off its food supply.
17 Then he sent someone to Egypt ahead of them—
Joseph, who was sold as a slave.
18 They bruised his feet with fetters
and placed his neck in an iron collar.
19 Until the time came to fulfill his dreams,*
the LORD tested Joseph's character.
20 Then Pharaoh sent for him and set him free;
the ruler of the nation opened his prison door.
21 Joseph was put in charge of all the king's household;
he became ruler over all the king's possessions.
22 He could instruct the king's aides as he pleased
and teach the king's advisers.

23 Then Israel arrived in Egypt;
Jacob lived as a foreigner in the land of Ham.
24 And the LORD multiplied the people of Israel
until they became too mighty for their enemies.
25 Then he turned the Egyptians against the Israelites,
and they plotted against the LORD's servants.

26 But the LORD sent his servant Moses,
along with Aaron, whom he had chosen.
27 They performed miraculous signs among
the Egyptians,
and wonders in the land of Ham.
28 The LORD blanketed Egypt in darkness,
for they had defied his commands to let his
people go.
29 He turned their water into blood,
poisoning all the fish.
30 Then frogs overran the land
and even invaded the king's bedrooms.
31 When the LORD spoke, flies descended on
the Egyptians,
and gnats swarmed across Egypt.
32 He sent them hail instead of rain,
and lightning flashed over the land.
33 He ruined their grapevines and fig trees
and shattered all the trees.
34 He spoke, and hordes of locusts came—
young locusts beyond number.
35 They ate up everything green in the land,
destroying all the crops in their fields.
36 Then he killed the oldest son in each Egyptian
home,
the pride and joy of each family.

37 The LORD brought his people out of Egypt, loaded
with silver and gold;
and not one among the tribes of Israel even
stumbled.
38 Egypt was glad when they were gone,
for they feared them greatly.
39 The LORD spread a cloud above them as a covering
and gave them a great fire to light the darkness.
40 They asked for meat, and he sent them quail;
he satisfied their hunger with manna—bread
from heaven.
41 He split open a rock, and water gushed out
to form a river through the dry wasteland.
42 For he remembered his sacred promise
to his servant Abraham.
43 So he brought his people out of Egypt with joy,
his chosen ones with rejoicing.
44 He gave his people the lands of pagan nations,
and they harvested crops that others had planted.
45 All this happened so they would follow his decrees
and obey his instructions.

Praise the LORD!

106

1 Praise the LORD!

Give thanks to the LORD, for he is good!
His faithful love endures forever.
2 Who can list the glorious miracles of the LORD?
Who can ever praise him enough?
3 There is joy for those who deal justly with others
and always do what is right.

4 Remember me, LORD, when you show favor to
your people;
come near and rescue me.
5 Let me share in the prosperity of your chosen ones.
Let me rejoice in the joy of your people;
let me praise you with those who are
your heritage.

6 Like our ancestors, we have sinned.
We have done wrong! We have acted wickedly!
7 Our ancestors in Egypt
were not impressed by the LORD's miraculous
deeds.
They soon forgot his many acts of kindness to them.
Instead, they rebelled against him at the Red Sea.*
8 Even so, he saved them—
to defend the honor of his name
and to demonstrate his mighty power.
9 He commanded the Red Sea* to dry up.
He led Israel across the sea as if it were a desert.

105:19 Hebrew *his word.* **106:7** Hebrew *at the sea, the sea of reeds.* **106:9** Hebrew *sea of reeds;* also in 106:22.

10 So he rescued them from their enemies
and redeemed them from their foes.
11 Then the water returned and covered
their enemies;
not one of them survived.
12 Then his people believed his promises.
Then they sang his praise.

13 Yet how quickly they forgot what he had done!
They wouldn't wait for his counsel!
14 In the wilderness their desires ran wild,
testing God's patience in that dry wasteland.
15 So he gave them what they asked for,
but he sent a plague along with it.
16 The people in the camp were jealous of Moses
and envious of Aaron, the LORD's holy priest.
17 Because of this, the earth opened up;
it swallowed Dathan
and buried Abiram and the other rebels.
18 Fire fell upon their followers;
a flame consumed the wicked.

19 The people made a calf at Mount Sinai*;
they bowed before an image made of gold.
20 They traded their glorious God
for a statue of a grass-eating bull.
21 They forgot God, their savior,
who had done such great things in Egypt—
22 such wonderful things in the land of Ham,
such awesome deeds at the Red Sea.
23 So he declared he would destroy them.
But Moses, his chosen one, stepped between the
LORD and the people.
He begged him to turn from his anger and not
destroy them.

24 The people refused to enter the pleasant land,
for they wouldn't believe his promise to care
for them.
25 Instead, they grumbled in their tents
and refused to obey the LORD.
26 Therefore, he solemnly swore
that he would kill them in the wilderness,
27 that he would scatter their descendants among
the nations,
exiling them to distant lands.

28 Then our ancestors joined in the worship of Baal
at Peor;
they even ate sacrifices offered to the dead!
29 They angered the LORD with all these things,
so a plague broke out among them.
30 But Phinehas had the courage to intervene,
and the plague was stopped.
31 So he has been regarded as a righteous man
ever since that time.

32 At Meribah, too, they angered the LORD,
causing Moses serious trouble.
33 They made Moses angry,*
and he spoke foolishly.

34 Israel failed to destroy the nations in the land,
as the LORD had commanded them.
35 Instead, they mingled among the pagans
and adopted their evil customs.
36 They worshiped their idols,
which led to their downfall.
37 They even sacrificed their sons
and their daughters to the demons.
38 They shed innocent blood,
the blood of their sons and daughters.
By sacrificing them to the idols of Canaan,
they polluted the land with murder.
39 They defiled themselves by their evil deeds,
and their love of idols was adultery in the
LORD's sight.

TROUBLES 106:40-42

God allowed trouble to come to the Israelites to help them. Some of our troubles can be helpful because they (1) humble us, (2) allow us to experience more of God's faithfulness, (3) make us more dependent upon God, (4) encourage us to submit to God's purpose for our life, and (5) make us more compassionate to others in trouble. Of course, believing that hard times can be helpful doesn't come naturally! But as Romans 8:28 states, "God causes everything to work together for the good of those who love God and are called according to his purpose for them." ■

40 That is why the LORD's anger burned against his people,
and he abhorred his own special possession.
41 He handed them over to pagan nations,
and they were ruled by those who hated them.
42 Their enemies crushed them
and brought them under their cruel power.
43 Again and again he rescued them,
but they chose to rebel against him,
and they were finally destroyed by their sin.
44 Even so, he pitied them in their distress
and listened to their cries.
45 He remembered his covenant with them
and relented because of his unfailing love.
46 He even caused their captors
to treat them with kindness.

47 Save us, O LORD our God!
Gather us back from among the nations,
so we can thank your holy name
and rejoice and praise you.

48 Praise the LORD, the God of Israel,
who lives from everlasting to everlasting!
Let all the people say, "Amen!"

Praise the LORD!

106:19 Hebrew *at Horeb,* another name for Sinai. 106:33 Hebrew *They embittered his spirit.*

Book Five (Psalms 107–150)

107

1 Give thanks to the Lord, for he is good!
His faithful love endures forever.
2 Has the Lord redeemed you? Then speak out!
Tell others he has redeemed you from your
enemies.
3 For he has gathered the exiles from many lands,
from east and west,
from north and south.

4 Some wandered in the wilderness,
lost and homeless.
5 Hungry and thirsty,
they nearly died.
6 "Lord, help!" they cried in their trouble,
and he rescued them from their distress.
7 He led them straight to safety,
to a city where they could live.
8 Let them praise the Lord for his great love
and for the wonderful things he has done
for them.
9 For he satisfies the thirsty
and fills the hungry with good things.

10 Some sat in darkness and deepest gloom,
imprisoned in iron chains of misery.
11 They rebelled against the words of God,
scorning the counsel of the Most High.
12 That is why he broke them with hard labor;
they fell, and no one was there to help them.
13 "Lord, help!" they cried in their trouble,
and he saved them from their distress.
14 He led them from the darkness and deepest gloom;
he snapped their chains.
15 Let them praise the Lord for his great love
and for the wonderful things he has done
for them.
16 For he broke down their prison gates of bronze;
he cut apart their bars of iron.

17 Some were fools; they rebelled
and suffered for their sins.
18 They couldn't stand the thought of food,
and they were knocking on death's door.
19 "Lord, help!" they cried in their trouble,
and he saved them from their distress.
20 He sent out his word and healed them,
snatching them from the door of death.
21 Let them praise the Lord for his great love
and for the wonderful things he has done
for them.
22 Let them offer sacrifices of thanksgiving
and sing joyfully about his glorious acts.

23 Some went off to sea in ships,
plying the trade routes of the world.
24 They, too, observed the Lord's power in action,
his impressive works on the deepest seas.
25 He spoke, and the winds rose,
stirring up the waves.
26 Their ships were tossed to the heavens
and plunged again to the depths;
the sailors cringed in terror.
27 They reeled and staggered like drunkards
and were at their wits' end.
28 "Lord, help!" they cried in their trouble,
and he saved them from their distress.
29 He calmed the storm to a whisper
and stilled the waves.
30 What a blessing was that stillness
as he brought them safely into harbor!
31 Let them praise the Lord for his great love
and for the wonderful things he has done
for them.
32 Let them exalt him publicly before the congregation
and before the leaders of the nation.

33 He changes rivers into deserts,
and springs of water into dry, thirsty land.
34 He turns the fruitful land into salty wastelands,
because of the wickedness of those who
live there.
35 But he also turns deserts into pools of water,
the dry land into springs of water.
36 He brings the hungry to settle there
and to build their cities.
37 They sow their fields, plant their vineyards,
and harvest their bumper crops.
38 How he blesses them!
They raise large families there,
and their herds of livestock increase.

39 When they decrease in number and become
impoverished
through oppression, trouble, and sorrow,
40 the Lord pours contempt on their princes,
causing them to wander in trackless wastelands.
41 But he rescues the poor from trouble
and increases their families like flocks of sheep.
42 The godly will see these things and be glad,
while the wicked are struck silent.
43 Those who are wise will take all this to heart;
they will see in our history the faithful love
of the Lord.

108

A song. A psalm of David.

1 My heart is confident in you, O God;
no wonder I can sing your praises with all
my heart!
2 Wake up, lyre and harp!
I will wake the dawn with my song.
3 I will thank you, Lord, among all the people.
I will sing your praises among the nations.
4 For your unfailing love is higher than the heavens.
Your faithfulness reaches to the clouds.

5 Be exalted, O God, above the highest heavens.
May your glory shine over all the earth.
6 Now rescue your beloved people.
Answer and save us by your power.
7 God has promised this by his holiness*:
"I will divide up Shechem with joy.
I will measure out the valley of Succoth.
8 Gilead is mine,
and Manasseh, too.
Ephraim, my helmet, will produce my warriors,
and Judah, my scepter, will produce my kings.
9 But Moab, my washbasin, will become my servant,
and I will wipe my feet on Edom
and shout in triumph over Philistia."

10 Who will bring me into the fortified city?
Who will bring me victory over Edom?
11 Have you rejected us, O God?
Will you no longer march with our armies?
12 Oh, please help us against our enemies,
for all human help is useless.
13 With God's help we will do mighty things,
for he will trample down our foes.

BEYOND SURVIVAL 108:12-13

David prayed not just for rescue, but for victory. Ever pray for just enough strength to make it through a stressful situation? With God's help we can claim more than just survival, we can claim victory! Look for ways God can use your distress as an opportunity to show his mighty power. ■

109

For the choir director: A psalm of David.

1 O God, whom I praise,
don't stand silent and aloof
2 while the wicked slander me
and tell lies about me.
3 They surround me with hateful words
and fight against me for no reason.
4 I love them, but they try to destroy me with accusations
even as I am praying for them!
5 They repay evil for good,
and hatred for my love.

6 They say,* "Get an evil person to turn against him.
Send an accuser to bring him to trial.
7 When his case comes up for judgment,
let him be pronounced guilty.
Count his prayers as sins.
8 Let his years be few;
let someone else take his position.
9 May his children become fatherless,
and his wife a widow.
10 May his children wander as beggars
and be driven from their ruined homes.
11 May creditors seize his entire estate,
and strangers take all he has earned.
12 Let no one be kind to him;
let no one pity his fatherless children.
13 May all his offspring die.
May his family name be blotted out in a single generation.
14 May the LORD never forget the sins of his fathers;
may his mother's sins never be erased from the record.
15 May the LORD always remember these sins,
and may his name disappear from human memory.
16 For he refused all kindness to others;
he persecuted the poor and needy,
and he hounded the brokenhearted to death.
17 He loved to curse others;
now you curse him.
He never blessed others;
now don't you bless him.
18 Cursing is as natural to him as his clothing,
or the water he drinks,
or the rich food he eats.
19 Now may his curses return and cling to him like clothing;
may they be tied around him like a belt."

20 May those curses become the LORD's punishment
for my accusers who speak evil of me.
21 But deal well with me, O Sovereign LORD,
for the sake of your own reputation!
Rescue me
because you are so faithful and good.
22 For I am poor and needy,
and my heart is full of pain.
23 I am fading like a shadow at dusk;
I am brushed off like a locust.
24 My knees are weak from fasting,
and I am skin and bones.
25 I am a joke to people everywhere;
when they see me, they shake their heads in scorn.

26 Help me, O LORD my God!
Save me because of your unfailing love.
27 Let them see that this is your doing,
that you yourself have done it, LORD.
28 Then let them curse me if they like,
but you will bless me!
When they attack me, they will be disgraced!
But I, your servant, will go right on rejoicing!
29 May my accusers be clothed with disgrace;
may their humiliation cover them like a cloak.
30 But I will give repeated thanks to the LORD,
praising him to everyone.

108:7 Or *in his sanctuary.* 109:6 Hebrew lacks *They say.*

31 For he stands beside the needy,
ready to save them from those who
condemn them.

110

A psalm of David.

1 The LORD said to my Lord,
"Sit in the place of honor at my right hand
until I humble your enemies,
making them a footstool under your feet."
2 The LORD will extend your powerful kingdom
from Jerusalem*;
you will rule over your enemies.
3 When you go to war,
your people will serve you willingly.
You are arrayed in holy garments,
and your strength will be renewed each day
like the morning dew.

ON THE FENCE? 110:1-7

This psalm shows God's promise of sending the Messiah. Both the Old and New Testaments proclaim the characteristics of the Savior. The New Testament clearly shows that Jesus is the promised Savior. Many people have a vague belief in God, but refuse to accept Jesus as anything more than a great human teacher. But the Bible does not allow that option. Are you on or off the fence concerning your beliefs about Jesus? Do you believe that he's God or just a great teacher? ■

4 The LORD has taken an oath and will not break
his vow:
"You are a priest forever in the order of
Melchizedek."

5 The Lord stands at your right hand to protect you.
He will strike down many kings when his anger
erupts.
6 He will punish the nations
and fill their lands with corpses;
he will shatter heads over the whole earth.
7 But he himself will be refreshed from brooks along
the way.
He will be victorious.

111*

1 Praise the LORD!

I will thank the LORD with all my heart
as I meet with his godly people.
2 How amazing are the deeds of the LORD!
All who delight in him should ponder them.
3 Everything he does reveals his glory and majesty.
His righteousness never fails.
4 He causes us to remember his wonderful works.
How gracious and merciful is our LORD!
5 He gives food to those who fear him;
he always remembers his covenant.
6 He has shown his great power to his people
by giving them the lands of other nations.

FEARLESS 112:1, 7-8

We all want to live without fear. We admire people who face dangers and overcome them. The psalmist teaches us that *fear* of God can lead to a *fearless* life. To fear God means to respect him. When we trust God completely to take care of us, we will find that our other fears—even of death itself—will subside. ■

7 All he does is just and good,
and all his commandments are trustworthy.
8 They are forever true,
to be obeyed faithfully and with integrity.
9 He has paid a full ransom for his people.
He has guaranteed his covenant with
them forever.
What a holy, awe-inspiring name he has!
10 Fear of the LORD is the foundation of true wisdom.
All who obey his commandments will grow
in wisdom.

Praise him forever!

112*

1 Praise the LORD!

How joyful are those who fear the LORD
and delight in obeying his commands.
2 Their children will be successful everywhere;
an entire generation of godly people will
be blessed.
3 They themselves will be wealthy,
and their good deeds will last forever.
4 Light shines in the darkness for the godly.
They are generous, compassionate, and righteous.
5 Good comes to those who lend money generously
and conduct their business fairly.
6 Such people will not be overcome by evil.
Those who are righteous will be long remembered.
7 They do not fear bad news;
they confidently trust the LORD to care for them.
8 They are confident and fearless
and can face their foes triumphantly.
9 They share freely and give generously to those
in need.
Their good deeds will be remembered forever.
They will have influence and honor.

110:2 Hebrew *Zion*. **111** This psalm is a Hebrew acrostic poem; after the introductory note of praise, each line begins with a successive letter of the Hebrew alphabet. **112** This psalm is a Hebrew acrostic poem; after the introductory note of praise, each line begins with a successive letter of the Hebrew alphabet.

10 The wicked will see this and be infuriated.
They will grind their teeth in anger;
they will slink away, their hopes thwarted.

113

1 Praise the LORD!

Yes, give praise, O servants of the LORD.
Praise the name of the LORD!
2 Blessed be the name of the LORD
now and forever.
3 Everywhere—from east to west—
praise the name of the LORD.
4 For the LORD is high above the nations;
his glory is higher than the heavens.

5 Who can be compared with the LORD our God,
who is enthroned on high?
6 He stoops to look down
on heaven and on earth.
7 He lifts the poor from the dust
and the needy from the garbage dump.
8 He sets them among princes,
even the princes of his own people!
9 He gives the childless woman a family,
making her a happy mother.

Praise the LORD!

114

1 When the Israelites escaped from Egypt—
when the family of Jacob left that foreign land—
2 the land of Judah became God's sanctuary,
and Israel became his kingdom.

3 The Red Sea* saw them coming and hurried out of their way!
The water of the Jordan River turned away.
4 The mountains skipped like rams,
the hills like lambs!
5 What's wrong, Red Sea, that made you hurry out of their way?
What happened, Jordan River, that you turned away?
6 Why, mountains, did you skip like rams?
Why, hills, like lambs?

7 Tremble, O earth, at the presence of the Lord,
at the presence of the God of Jacob.
8 He turned the rock into a pool of water;
yes, a spring of water flowed from solid rock.

115

1 Not to us, O LORD, not to us,
but to your name goes all the glory
for your unfailing love and faithfulness.
2 Why let the nations say,
"Where is their God?"
3 Our God is in the heavens,
and he does as he wishes.
4 Their idols are merely things of silver and gold,
shaped by human hands.
5 They have mouths but cannot speak,
and eyes but cannot see.
6 They have ears but cannot hear,
and noses but cannot smell.
7 They have hands but cannot feel,
and feet but cannot walk,
and throats but cannot make a sound.
8 And those who make idols are just like them,
as are all who trust in them.

9 O Israel, trust the LORD!
He is your helper and your shield.
10 O priests, descendants of Aaron, trust the LORD!
He is your helper and your shield.
11 All you who fear the LORD, trust the LORD!
He is your helper and your shield.

THINKING OF YOU 115:12

"The LORD remembers us" says the psalm writer. What a fantastic truth! There are many times when we feel isolated and abandoned, even by God. In reality, he sees, understands, and is thinking about us. When depressed or struggling, be encouraged that God keeps you in his thoughts. If he thinks about you, surely his help is near. ■

12 The LORD remembers us and will bless us.
He will bless the people of Israel
and bless the priests, the descendants of Aaron.
13 He will bless those who fear the LORD,
both great and lowly.

14 May the LORD richly bless
both you and your children.
15 May you be blessed by the LORD,
who made heaven and earth.
16 The heavens belong to the LORD,
but he has given the earth to all humanity.
17 The dead cannot sing praises to the LORD,
for they have gone into the silence of the grave.
18 But we can praise the LORD
both now and forever!

Praise the LORD!

116

1 I love the LORD because he hears my voice
and my prayer for mercy.
2 Because he bends down to listen,
I will pray as long as I have breath!
3 Death wrapped its ropes around me;

114:3 Hebrew *the sea;* also in 114:5.

the terrors of the grave* overtook me.
I saw only trouble and sorrow.
4 Then I called on the name of the LORD:
"Please, LORD, save me!"
5 How kind the LORD is! How good he is!
So merciful, this God of ours!
6 The LORD protects those of childlike faith;
I was facing death, and he saved me.
7 Let my soul be at rest again,
for the LORD has been good to me.
8 He has saved me from death,
my eyes from tears,
my feet from stumbling.
9 And so I walk in the LORD's presence
as I live here on earth!
10 I believed in you, so I said,
"I am deeply troubled, LORD."
11 In my anxiety I cried out to you,
"These people are all liars!"
12 What can I offer the LORD
for all he has done for me?
13 I will lift up the cup of salvation
and praise the LORD's name for saving me.
14 I will keep my promises to the LORD
in the presence of all his people.
15 The LORD cares deeply
when his loved ones die.
16 O LORD, I am your servant;
yes, I am your servant, born into your household;
you have freed me from my chains.
17 I will offer you a sacrifice of thanksgiving
and call on the name of the LORD.
18 I will fulfill my vows to the LORD
in the presence of all his people—
19 in the house of the LORD
in the heart of Jerusalem.

Praise the LORD!

117

1 Praise the LORD, all you nations.
Praise him, all you people of the earth.
2 For he loves us with unfailing love;
the LORD's faithfulness endures forever.

Praise the LORD!

118

1 Give thanks to the LORD, for he is good!
His faithful love endures forever.

2 Let all Israel repeat:
"His faithful love endures forever."
3 Let Aaron's descendants, the priests, repeat:
"His faithful love endures forever."
4 Let all who fear the LORD repeat:
"His faithful love endures forever."
5 In my distress I prayed to the LORD,
and the LORD answered me and set me free.
6 The LORD is for me, so I will have no fear.
What can mere people do to me?
7 Yes, the LORD is for me; he will help me.
I will look in triumph at those who hate me.
8 It is better to take refuge in the LORD
than to trust in people.
9 It is better to take refuge in the LORD
than to trust in princes.

10 Though hostile nations surrounded me,
I destroyed them all with the authority of
the LORD.
11 Yes, they surrounded and attacked me,
but I destroyed them all with the authority
of the LORD.
12 They swarmed around me like bees;
they blazed against me like a crackling fire.
But I destroyed them all with the authority
of the LORD.
13 My enemies did their best to kill me,
but the LORD rescued me.
14 The LORD is my strength and my song;
he has given me victory.
15 Songs of joy and victory are sung in the camp
of the godly.
The strong right arm of the LORD has done
glorious things!
16 The strong right arm of the LORD is raised
in triumph.
The strong right arm of the LORD has done
glorious things!
17 I will not die; instead, I will live
to tell what the LORD has done.
18 The LORD has punished me severely,
but he did not let me die.

19 Open for me the gates where the righteous enter,
and I will go in and thank the LORD.
20 These gates lead to the presence of the LORD,
and the godly enter there.
21 I thank you for answering my prayer
and giving me victory!

22 The stone that the builders rejected
has now become the cornerstone.
23 This is the LORD's doing,
and it is wonderful to see.
24 This is the day the LORD has made.
We will rejoice and be glad in it.
25 Please, LORD, please save us.
Please, LORD, please give us success.
26 Bless the one who comes in the name of the LORD.
We bless you from the house of the LORD.
27 The LORD is God, shining upon us.
Take the sacrifice and bind it with cords
on the altar.

116:3 Hebrew *of Sheol.*

28 You are my God, and I will praise you!
You are my God, and I will exalt you!

29 Give thanks to the LORD, for he is good!
His faithful love endures forever.

119

Aleph*

1 Joyful are people of integrity,
who follow the instructions of the LORD.
2 Joyful are those who obey his laws
and search for him with all their hearts.
3 They do not compromise with evil,
and they walk only in his paths.
4 You have charged us
to keep your commandments carefully.
5 Oh, that my actions would consistently
reflect your decrees!
6 Then I will not be ashamed
when I compare my life with your commands.
7 As I learn your righteous regulations,
I will thank you by living as I should!
8 I will obey your decrees.
Please don't give up on me!

RULES 119:12-18

Most of us don't like rules because we think they keep us from doing what we want. So it may seem strange to hear the psalmist talk of rejoicing in God's laws as much as in riches (119:14). But God's laws were given to free us to be all he wants us to be. They restrict us from doing those things that will cripple us and keep us from being our best. God's laws are guidelines to help us follow in his path and not wander onto paths that would lead to destruction. ■

Beth

9 How can a young person stay pure?
By obeying your word.
10 I have tried hard to find you—
don't let me wander from your commands.
11 I have hidden your word in my heart,
that I might not sin against you.
12 I praise you, O LORD;
teach me your decrees.
13 I have recited aloud
all the regulations you have given us.
14 I have rejoiced in your laws
as much as in riches.
15 I will study your commandments
and reflect on your ways.
16 I will delight in your decrees
and not forget your word.

Gimel

17 Be good to your servant,
that I may live and obey your word.
18 Open my eyes to see
the wonderful truths in your instructions.
19 I am only a foreigner in the land.
Don't hide your commands from me!
20 I am always overwhelmed
with a desire for your regulations.
21 You rebuke the arrogant;
those who wander from your commands are
cursed.
22 Don't let them scorn and insult me,
for I have obeyed your laws.
23 Even princes sit and speak against me,
but I will meditate on your decrees.
24 Your laws please me;
they give me wise advice.

Daleth

25 I lie in the dust;
revive me by your word.
26 I told you my plans, and you answered.
Now teach me your decrees.
27 Help me understand the meaning of your
commandments,
and I will meditate on your wonderful deeds.
28 I weep with sorrow;
encourage me by your word.
29 Keep me from lying to myself;
give me the privilege of knowing your instructions.
30 I have chosen to be faithful;
I have determined to live by your regulations.
31 I cling to your laws.
LORD, don't let me be put to shame!
32 I will pursue your commands,
for you expand my understanding.

He

33 Teach me your decrees, O LORD;
I will keep them to the end.
34 Give me understanding and I will obey your
instructions;
I will put them into practice with all my heart.
35 Make me walk along the path of your commands,
for that is where my happiness is found.
36 Give me an eagerness for your laws
rather than a love for money!
37 Turn my eyes from worthless things,
and give me life through your word.*
38 Reassure me of your promise,
made to those who fear you.
39 Help me abandon my shameful ways;
for your regulations are good.
40 I long to obey your commandments!
Renew my life with your goodness.

119 This psalm is a Hebrew acrostic poem; there are twenty-two stanzas, one for each successive letter of the Hebrew alphabet. Each of the eight verses within each stanza begins with the Hebrew letter named in its heading. 119:37 Some manuscripts read *in your ways.*

Waw

41 LORD, give me your unfailing love,
the salvation that you promised me.
42 Then I can answer those who taunt me,
for I trust in your word.
43 Do not snatch your word of truth from me,
for your regulations are my only hope.
44 I will keep on obeying your instructions
forever and ever.
45 I will walk in freedom,
for I have devoted myself to your commandments.
46 I will speak to kings about your laws,
and I will not be ashamed.
47 How I delight in your commands!
How I love them!
48 I honor and love your commands.
I meditate on your decrees.

Zayin

49 Remember your promise to me;
it is my only hope.
50 Your promise revives me;
it comforts me in all my troubles.
51 The proud hold me in utter contempt,
but I do not turn away from your instructions.
52 I meditate on your age-old regulations;
O LORD, they comfort me.
53 I become furious with the wicked,
because they reject your instructions.
54 Your decrees have been the theme of my songs
wherever I have lived.
55 I reflect at night on who you are, O LORD;
therefore, I obey your instructions.
56 This is how I spend my life:
obeying your commandments.

Heth

57 LORD, you are mine!
I promise to obey your words!
58 With all my heart I want your blessings.
Be merciful as you promised.
59 I pondered the direction of my life,
and I turned to follow your laws.
60 I will hurry, without delay,
to obey your commands.
61 Evil people try to drag me into sin,
but I am firmly anchored to your instructions.
62 I rise at midnight to thank you
for your just regulations.
63 I am a friend to anyone who fears you—
anyone who obeys your commandments.
64 O LORD, your unfailing love fills the earth;
teach me your decrees.

Teth

65 You have done many good things for me, LORD,
just as you promised.
66 I believe in your commands;
now teach me good judgment and knowledge.
67 I used to wander off until you disciplined me;
but now I closely follow your word.
68 You are good and do only good;
teach me your decrees.
69 Arrogant people smear me with lies,
but in truth I obey your commandments with
all my heart.
70 Their hearts are dull and stupid,
but I delight in your instructions.
71 My suffering was good for me,
for it taught me to pay attention to your decrees.
72 Your instructions are more valuable to me
than millions in gold and silver.

Yodh

73 You made me; you created me.
Now give me the sense to follow your commands.
74 May all who fear you find in me a cause for joy,
for I have put my hope in your word.
75 I know, O LORD, that your regulations are fair;
you disciplined me because I needed it.
76 Now let your unfailing love comfort me,
just as you promised me, your servant.
77 Surround me with your tender mercies so I may live,
for your instructions are my delight.
78 Bring disgrace upon the arrogant people who lied
about me;
meanwhile, I will concentrate on your
commandments.
79 Let me be united with all who fear you,
with those who know your laws.
80 May I be blameless in keeping your decrees;
then I will never be ashamed.

Kaph

81 I am worn out waiting for your rescue,
but I have put my hope in your word.
82 My eyes are straining to see your promises
come true.
When will you comfort me?
83 I am shriveled like a wineskin in the smoke,
but I have not forgotten to obey your decrees.
84 How long must I wait?
When will you punish those who persecute me?
85 These arrogant people who hate your instructions
have dug deep pits to trap me.
86 All your commands are trustworthy.
Protect me from those who hunt me down
without cause.
87 They almost finished me off,
but I refused to abandon your commandments.
88 In your unfailing love, spare my life;
then I can continue to obey your laws.

Lamedh

89 Your eternal word, O LORD,
stands firm in heaven.
90 Your faithfulness extends to every generation,
as enduring as the earth you created.
91 Your regulations remain true to this day,
for everything serves your plans.

92 If your instructions hadn't sustained me with joy,
I would have died in my misery.
93 I will never forget your commandments,
for by them you give me life.
94 I am yours; rescue me!
For I have worked hard at obeying your
commandments.
95 Though the wicked hide along the way to kill me,
I will quietly keep my mind on your laws.
96 Even perfection has its limits,
but your commands have no limit.

Mem

97 Oh, how I love your instructions!
I think about them all day long.
98 Your commands make me wiser than my enemies,
for they are my constant guide.
99 Yes, I have more insight than my teachers,
for I am always thinking of your laws.
100 I am even wiser than my elders,
for I have kept your commandments.
101 I have refused to walk on any evil path,
so that I may remain obedient to your word.
102 I haven't turned away from your regulations,
for you have taught me well.
103 How sweet your words taste to me;
they are sweeter than honey.
104 Your commandments give me understanding;
no wonder I hate every false way of life.

Nun

105 Your word is a lamp to guide my feet
and a light for my path.
106 I've promised it once, and I'll promise it again:
I will obey your righteous regulations.
107 I have suffered much, O LORD;
restore my life again as you promised.
108 LORD, accept my offering of praise,
and teach me your regulations.
109 My life constantly hangs in the balance,
but I will not stop obeying your instructions.
110 The wicked have set their traps for me,
but I will not turn from your commandments.
111 Your laws are my treasure;
they are my heart's delight.
112 I am determined to keep your decrees
to the very end.

Samekh

113 I hate those with divided loyalties,
but I love your instructions.
114 You are my refuge and my shield;
your word is my source of hope.
115 Get out of my life, you evil-minded people,
for I intend to obey the commands of my God.
116 LORD, sustain me as you promised, that I may live!
Do not let my hope be crushed.
117 Sustain me, and I will be rescued;
then I will meditate continually on your decrees.
118 But you have rejected all who stray from
your decrees.
They are only fooling themselves.
119 You skim off the wicked of the earth like scum;
no wonder I love to obey your laws!
120 I tremble in fear of you;
I stand in awe of your regulations.

MEDICINE FOR LIFE 119:125

Faith comes alive at the points where we apply Scripture to our life. The Bible is similar to medicine—it goes to work when it is applied to the areas where it is most needed. As you read the Bible, be on the alert for lessons, commands, or examples that you can apply to situations in your life. ■

Ayin

121 Don't leave me to the mercy of my enemies,
for I have done what is just and right.
122 Please guarantee a blessing for me.
Don't let the arrogant oppress me!
123 My eyes strain to see your rescue,
to see the truth of your promise fulfilled.
124 I am your servant; deal with me in unfailing love,
and teach me your decrees.
125 Give discernment to me, your servant;
then I will understand your laws.
126 LORD, it is time for you to act,
for these evil people have violated your
instructions.
127 Truly, I love your commands
more than gold, even the finest gold.
128 Each of your commandments is right.
That is why I hate every false way.

Pe

129 Your laws are wonderful.
No wonder I obey them!
130 The teaching of your word gives light,
so even the simple can understand.
131 I pant with expectation,
longing for your commands.
132 Come and show me your mercy,
as you do for all who love your name.
133 Guide my steps by your word,
so I will not be overcome by evil.
134 Ransom me from the oppression of evil people;
then I can obey your commandments.
135 Look upon me with love;
teach me your decrees.
136 Rivers of tears gush from my eyes
because people disobey your instructions.

Tsadhe

137 O LORD, you are righteous,
and your regulations are fair.
138 Your laws are perfect
and completely trustworthy.

139 I am overwhelmed with indignation,
for my enemies have disregarded your words.
140 Your promises have been thoroughly tested;
that is why I love them so much.
141 I am insignificant and despised,
but I don't forget your commandments.
142 Your justice is eternal,
and your instructions are perfectly true.
143 As pressure and stress bear down on me,
I find joy in your commands.
144 Your laws are always right;
help me to understand them so I may live.

Qoph
145 I pray with all my heart; answer me, LORD!
I will obey your decrees.
146 I cry out to you; rescue me,
that I may obey your laws.
147 I rise early, before the sun is up;
I cry out for help and put my
hope in your words.
148 I stay awake through the night,
thinking about your promise.
149 In your faithful love, O LORD, hear
my cry;
let me be revived by following
your regulations.
150 Lawless people are coming to
attack me;
they live far from your
instructions.
151 But you are near, O LORD,
and all your commands are true.
152 I have known from my earliest days
that your laws will last forever.

Resh
153 Look upon my suffering and rescue me,
for I have not forgotten your instructions.
154 Argue my case; take my side!
Protect my life as you promised.
155 The wicked are far from rescue,
for they do not bother with your decrees.
156 LORD, how great is your mercy;
let me be revived by following your regulations.
157 Many persecute and trouble me,
yet I have not swerved from your laws.
158 Seeing these traitors makes me sick at heart,
because they care nothing for your word.
159 See how I love your commandments, LORD.
Give back my life because of your
unfailing love.
160 The very essence of your words is truth;
all your just regulations will stand forever.

Shin
161 Powerful people harass me without cause,
but my heart trembles only at your word.
162 I rejoice in your word
like one who discovers a great treasure.

> He will not let you stumble; the one who watches over you will not slumber.
>
> *PSALM 121:3*

163 I hate and abhor all falsehood,
but I love your instructions.
164 I will praise you seven times a day
because all your regulations are just.
165 Those who love your instructions have
great peace
and do not stumble.
166 I long for your rescue, LORD,
so I have obeyed your commands.
167 I have obeyed your laws,
for I love them very much.
168 Yes, I obey your commandments and laws
because you know everything I do.

Taw
169 O LORD, listen to my cry;
give me the discerning mind you promised.
170 Listen to my prayer;
rescue me as you promised.
171 Let praise flow from my lips,
for you have taught me your
decrees.
172 Let my tongue sing about your
word,
for all your commands are
right.
173 Give me a helping hand,
for I have chosen to follow your
commandments.
174 O LORD, I have longed for your
rescue,
and your instructions are my
delight.
175 Let me live so I can praise you,
and may your regulations help me.
176 I have wandered away like a lost sheep;
come and find me,
for I have not forgotten your commands.

120

A song for pilgrims ascending to Jerusalem.

1 I took my troubles to the LORD;
I cried out to him, and he answered
my prayer.
2 Rescue me, O LORD, from liars
and from all deceitful people.
3 O deceptive tongue, what will God do to you?
How will he increase your punishment?
4 You will be pierced with sharp arrows
and burned with glowing coals.

5 How I suffer in far-off Meshech.
It pains me to live in distant Kedar.
6 I am tired of living
among people who hate peace.
7 I search for peace;
but when I speak of peace, they want war!

121 A song for pilgrims ascending to Jerusalem.

1 I look up to the mountains—
does my help come from there?
2 My help comes from the LORD,
who made heaven and earth!

3 He will not let you stumble;
the one who watches over you will not slumber.
4 Indeed, he who watches over Israel
never slumbers or sleeps.

5 The LORD himself watches over you!
The LORD stands beside you as your
protective shade.
6 The sun will not harm you by day,
nor the moon at night.

7 The LORD keeps you from all harm
and watches over your life.
8 The LORD keeps watch over you as you
come and go,
both now and forever.

122 A song for pilgrims ascending to Jerusalem. A psalm of David.

1 I was glad when they said to me,
"Let us go to the house of the LORD."
2 And now here we are,
standing inside your gates, O Jerusalem.
3 Jerusalem is a well-built city;
its seamless walls cannot be breached.
4 All the tribes of Israel—the LORD's people—
make their pilgrimage here.
They come to give thanks to the name of the LORD,
as the law requires of Israel.
5 Here stand the thrones where judgment is given,
the thrones of the dynasty of David.

PRAYING FOR OTHERS 122:6-9

The psalmist was not praying for his own peace and prosperity, but for his fellow citizens of Jerusalem. Prayer on behalf of others is usually unselfish. So, are you ready to pray for someone today? ■

6 Pray for peace in Jerusalem.
May all who love this city prosper.
7 O Jerusalem, may there be peace within your walls
and prosperity in your palaces.
8 For the sake of my family and friends, I will say,
"May you have peace."
9 For the sake of the house of the LORD our God,
I will seek what is best for you, O Jerusalem.

123 A song for pilgrims ascending to Jerusalem.

1 I lift my eyes to you,
O God, enthroned in heaven.
2 We keep looking to the LORD our God for
his mercy,
just as servants keep their eyes on their master,
as a slave girl watches her mistress for the
slightest signal.
3 Have mercy on us, LORD, have mercy,
for we have had our fill of contempt.
4 We have had more than our fill of the scoffing
of the proud
and the contempt of the arrogant.

124 A song for pilgrims ascending to Jerusalem. A psalm of David.

1 What if the LORD had not been on our side?
Let all Israel repeat:
2 What if the LORD had not been on our side
when people attacked us?
3 They would have swallowed us alive
in their burning anger.
4 The waters would have engulfed us;
a torrent would have overwhelmed us.
5 Yes, the raging waters of their fury
would have overwhelmed our very lives.

6 Praise the LORD,
who did not let their teeth tear us apart!
7 We escaped like a bird from a hunter's trap.
The trap is broken, and we are free!
8 Our help is from the LORD,
who made heaven and earth.

125 A song for pilgrims ascending to Jerusalem.

1 Those who trust in the LORD are as secure as
Mount Zion;
they will not be defeated but will endure forever.
2 Just as the mountains surround Jerusalem,
so the LORD surrounds his people, both now and
forever.
3 The wicked will not rule the land of the godly,
for then the godly might be tempted to
do wrong.
4 O LORD, do good to those who are good,
whose hearts are in tune with you.
5 But banish those who turn to crooked ways,
O LORD.
Take them away with those who do evil.

May Israel have peace!

126 *A song for pilgrims ascending to Jerusalem.*

1 When the LORD brought back his exiles to Jerusalem,*
it was like a dream!
2 We were filled with laughter,
and we sang for joy.
And the other nations said,
"What amazing things the LORD has done
for them."
3 Yes, the LORD has done amazing things for us!
What joy!

4 Restore our fortunes, LORD,
as streams renew the desert.
5 Those who plant in tears
will harvest with shouts of joy.
6 They weep as they go to plant their seed,
but they sing as they return with the harvest.

127 *A song for pilgrims ascending to Jerusalem. A psalm of Solomon.*

1 Unless the LORD builds a house,
the work of the builders is wasted.
Unless the LORD protects a city,
guarding it with sentries will do no good.
2 It is useless for you to work so hard
from early morning until late at night,
anxiously working for food to eat;
for God gives rest to his loved ones.

GOD'S FOUNDATION 127:1

Families establish homes and sentries guard cities, but both of these activities are futile unless God does the work. A family without God can never experience the true sense of community that God brings to relationships. Are your relationships built on the foundation God established? ■

3 Children are a gift from the LORD;
they are a reward from him.
4 Children born to a young man
are like arrows in a warrior's hands.
5 How joyful is the man whose quiver is full of them!
He will not be put to shame when he confronts
his accusers at the city gates.

128 *A song for pilgrims ascending to Jerusalem.*

1 How joyful are those who fear the LORD—
all who follow his ways!
2 You will enjoy the fruit of your labor.
How joyful and prosperous you will be!
3 Your wife will be like a fruitful grapevine,
flourishing within your home.
Your children will be like vigorous young olive trees
as they sit around your table.
4 That is the LORD's blessing
for those who fear him.

5 May the LORD continually bless you from Zion.
May you see Jerusalem prosper as long
as you live.
6 May you live to enjoy your grandchildren.
May Israel have peace!

129 *A song for pilgrims ascending to Jerusalem.*

1 From my earliest youth my enemies have
persecuted me.
Let all Israel repeat this:
2 From my earliest youth my enemies have
persecuted me,
but they have never defeated me.
3 My back is covered with cuts,
as if a farmer had plowed long furrows.
4 But the LORD is good;
he has cut me free from the ropes of the ungodly.

5 May all who hate Jerusalem*
be turned back in shameful defeat.
6 May they be as useless as grass on a rooftop,
turning yellow when only half grown,
7 ignored by the harvester,
despised by the binder.
8 And may those who pass by
refuse to give them this blessing:
"The LORD bless you;
we bless you in the LORD's name."

130 *A song for pilgrims ascending to Jerusalem.*

1 From the depths of despair, O LORD,
I call for your help.
2 Hear my cry, O Lord.
Pay attention to my prayer.

3 LORD, if you kept a record of our sins,
who, O Lord, could ever survive?
4 But you offer forgiveness,
that we might learn to fear you.

5 I am counting on the LORD;
yes, I am counting on him.
I have put my hope in his word.

126:1 Hebrew *Zion*. **129:5** Hebrew *Zion*.

6 I long for the Lord
more than sentries long for the dawn,
yes, more than sentries long for the dawn.

7 O Israel, hope in the LORD;
for with the LORD there is unfailing love.
His redemption overflows.
8 He himself will redeem Israel
from every kind of sin.

131 *A song for pilgrims ascending to Jerusalem. A psalm of David.*

1 LORD, my heart is not proud;
my eyes are not haughty.
I don't concern myself with matters too great
or too awesome for me to grasp.
2 Instead, I have calmed and quieted myself,
like a weaned child who no longer cries for its mother's milk.
Yes, like a weaned child is my soul within me.

3 O Israel, put your hope in the LORD—
now and always.

132 *A song for pilgrims ascending to Jerusalem.*

1 LORD, remember David
and all that he suffered.
2 He made a solemn promise to the LORD.
He vowed to the Mighty One of Israel,*
3 "I will not go home;
I will not let myself rest.
4 I will not let my eyes sleep
nor close my eyelids in slumber
5 until I find a place to build a house for the LORD,
a sanctuary for the Mighty One of Israel."

6 We heard that the Ark was in Ephrathah;
then we found it in the distant countryside of Jaar.
7 Let us go to the sanctuary of the LORD;
let us worship at the footstool of his throne.
8 Arise, O LORD, and enter your resting place,
along with the Ark, the symbol of your power.
9 May your priests be clothed in godliness;
may your loyal servants sing for joy.
10 For the sake of your servant David,
do not reject the king you have anointed.
11 The LORD swore an oath to David
with a promise he will never take back:
"I will place one of your descendants
on your throne.
12 If your descendants obey the terms of my covenant
and the laws that I teach them,
then your royal line
will continue forever and ever."

13 For the LORD has chosen Jerusalem*;
he has desired it for his home.
14 "This is my resting place forever," he said.
"I will live here, for this is the home I desired.
15 I will bless this city and make it prosperous;
I will satisfy its poor with food.
16 I will clothe its priests with godliness;
its faithful servants will sing for joy.
17 Here I will increase the power of David;
my anointed one will be a light for my people.
18 I will clothe his enemies with shame,
but he will be a glorious king."

133 *A song for pilgrims ascending to Jerusalem. A psalm of David.*

1 How wonderful and pleasant it is
when brothers live together in harmony!
2 For harmony is as precious as the anointing oil
that was poured over Aaron's head,
that ran down his beard
and onto the border of his robe.
3 Harmony is as refreshing as the dew from Mount Hermon
that falls on the mountains of Zion.
And there the LORD has pronounced his blessing,
even life everlasting.

134 *A song for pilgrims ascending to Jerusalem.*

1 Oh, praise the LORD, all you servants of the LORD,
you who serve at night in the house of the LORD.
2 Lift up holy hands in prayer,
and praise the LORD.

3 May the LORD, who made heaven and earth,
bless you from Jerusalem.*

135

1 Praise the LORD!

Praise the name of the LORD!
Praise him, you who serve the LORD,
2 you who serve in the house of the LORD,
in the courts of the house of our God.

3 Praise the LORD, for the LORD is good;
celebrate his lovely name with music.
4 For the LORD has chosen Jacob for himself,
Israel for his own special treasure.

132:2 Hebrew *of Jacob;* also in 132:5. See note on 44:4. 132:13 Hebrew *Zion.* 134:3 Hebrew *Zion.*

5 I know the greatness of the LORD—
that our Lord is greater than any other god.
6 The LORD does whatever pleases him
throughout all heaven and earth,
and on the seas and in their depths.
7 He causes the clouds to rise over the whole earth.
He sends the lightning with the rain
and releases the wind from his storehouses.

8 He destroyed the firstborn in each Egyptian home,
both people and animals.
9 He performed miraculous signs and wonders
in Egypt
against Pharaoh and all his people.
10 He struck down great nations
and slaughtered mighty kings—
11 Sihon king of the Amorites,
Og king of Bashan,
and all the kings of Canaan.
12 He gave their land as an inheritance,
a special possession to his people Israel.

13 Your name, O LORD, endures forever;
your fame, O LORD, is known to every generation.
14 For the LORD will give justice to his people
and have compassion on his servants.

15 The idols of the nations are merely things of silver
and gold,
shaped by human hands.
16 They have mouths but cannot speak,
and eyes but cannot see.
17 They have ears but cannot hear,
and noses but cannot smell.
18 And those who make idols are just like them,
as are all who trust in them.

19 O Israel, praise the LORD!
O priests—descendants of Aaron—praise the LORD!
20 O Levites, praise the LORD!
All you who fear the LORD, praise the LORD!
21 The LORD be praised from Zion,
for he lives here in Jerusalem.

Praise the LORD!

136

1 Give thanks to the LORD, for he is good!
His faithful love endures forever.
2 Give thanks to the God of gods.
His faithful love endures forever.
3 Give thanks to the Lord of lords.
His faithful love endures forever.

4 Give thanks to him who alone does mighty miracles.
His faithful love endures forever.
5 Give thanks to him who made the heavens so skillfully.
His faithful love endures forever.
6 Give thanks to him who placed the earth among
the waters.
His faithful love endures forever.
7 Give thanks to him who made the heavenly lights—
His faithful love endures forever.
8 the sun to rule the day,
His faithful love endures forever.
9 and the moon and stars to rule the night.
His faithful love endures forever.

10 Give thanks to him who killed the firstborn
of Egypt.
His faithful love endures forever.
11 He brought Israel out of Egypt.
His faithful love endures forever.
12 He acted with a strong hand and powerful arm.
His faithful love endures forever.
13 Give thanks to him who parted the Red Sea.*
His faithful love endures forever.
14 He led Israel safely through,
His faithful love endures forever.
15 but he hurled Pharaoh and his army into the Red Sea.
His faithful love endures forever.
16 Give thanks to him who led his people through the
wilderness.
His faithful love endures forever.

17 Give thanks to him who struck down mighty kings.
His faithful love endures forever.
18 He killed powerful kings—
His faithful love endures forever.
19 Sihon king of the Amorites,
His faithful love endures forever.
20 and Og king of Bashan.
His faithful love endures forever.
21 God gave the land of these kings as an inheritance—
His faithful love endures forever.
22 a special possession to his servant Israel.
His faithful love endures forever.

23 He remembered us in our weakness.
His faithful love endures forever.
24 He saved us from our enemies.
His faithful love endures forever.
25 He gives food to every living thing.
His faithful love endures forever.
26 Give thanks to the God of heaven.
His faithful love endures forever.

137

1 Beside the rivers of Babylon, we sat
and wept
as we thought of Jerusalem.*
2 We put away our harps,
hanging them on the branches of poplar trees.
3 For our captors demanded a song from us.
Our tormentors insisted on a joyful hymn:
"Sing us one of those songs of Jerusalem!"

136:13 Hebrew *sea of reeds;* also in 136:15. **137:1** Hebrew *Zion;* also in 137:3.

4 But how can we sing the songs of the LORD
while in a pagan land?

5 If I forget you, O Jerusalem,
let my right hand forget how to play the harp.
6 May my tongue stick to the roof of my mouth
if I fail to remember you,
if I don't make Jerusalem my greatest joy.

7 O LORD, remember what the Edomites did
on the day the armies of Babylon captured
Jerusalem.
"Destroy it!" they yelled.
"Level it to the ground!"
8 O Babylon, you will be destroyed.
Happy is the one who pays you back
for what you have done to us.
9 Happy is the one who takes your babies
and smashes them against the rocks!

138

A psalm of David.

1 I give you thanks, O LORD, with all my heart;
I will sing your praises before the gods.
2 I bow before your holy Temple as I worship.
I praise your name for your unfailing love
and faithfulness;
for your promises are backed
by all the honor of your name.
3 As soon as I pray, you answer me;
you encourage me by giving me strength.

PLANS 138:8

David counted on God's plan for his life. Each of us makes plans for our future. We work hard to see those dreams come true. But to truly make the most of life, we must include God's plans in our plans. He alone knows what is best for us. How willing are you to submit your plans and dreams to God? ■

4 Every king in all the earth will thank you, LORD,
for all of them will hear your words.
5 Yes, they will sing about the LORD's ways,
for the glory of the LORD is very great.
6 Though the LORD is great, he cares for
the humble,
but he keeps his distance from the proud.

7 Though I am surrounded by troubles,
you will protect me from the anger of
my enemies.
You reach out your hand,
and the power of your right hand saves me.
8 The LORD will work out his plans for my life—
for your faithful love, O LORD, endures forever.
Don't abandon me, for you made me.

139

For the choir director: A psalm of David.

1 O LORD, you have examined my heart
and know everything about me.
2 You know when I sit down or stand up.
You know my thoughts even when I'm far away.
3 You see me when I travel
and when I rest at home.
You know everything I do.

ABORTION

"Sarah, maybe you made a mistake—or maybe the test is wrong."

"I don't think so. . . . Oh, Kris, what am I gonna do?" The tears begin to roll down Sarah's face. "I'm pregnant!"

Kris hugs her friend. "Look, don't panic. Everything's gonna work out. My sister will help us. She knows about this clinic. The doctors are good, and nobody else has to find out."

Sarah is shocked. "You mean an abortion?"

"Well, do you have any better ideas? C'mon, Sarah, you're only 17. What are you gonna do with a kid? And what would you tell your mom?"

"I don't know . . . I'm so confused." Sarah sighs, wiping her eyes on her sleeve. "What would you do? I mean, could you kill your own baby?"

"What do you mean, 'kill'? It's just a bunch of cells! It's not a person yet. If you were six or seven months pregnant, I'd tell you not to do it. But you're probably only about five weeks along. I don't see what else you can do."

"You really think it's right?"

"Well, let's just say I don't think it's wrong."

Sarah sighs again. "Well, how soon can you call your sister?"

Kris picks up the phone. "I bet she's at her dorm right now."

Is abortion really the safe route? When do you think life begins? To gain some perspective on this issue, see Psalm 139:13-18.

4 You know what I am going to say
even before I say it, LORD.
5 You go before me and follow me.
You place your hand of blessing on my head.
6 Such knowledge is too wonderful for me,
too great for me to understand!

7 I can never escape from your Spirit!
I can never get away from your presence!
8 If I go up to heaven, you are there;
if I go down to the grave,* you are there.

139:8 Hebrew *to Sheol.*

keeping it real

I had an unusual, frightening experience at the beginning of my sophomore year: I ate an apple that some disturbed person had tampered with. It wasn't poisonous—not like it would have killed me—but it did make me pretty sick. Most of all, the experience scared me. For about a year and a half, I wouldn't eat anything unless I shared it with someone, or someone else tried a bite first and was okay.

Finally, I talked to my youth leader about my fear. She encouraged me to read Psalm 140, and to realize that God was there to help and protect me—no matter what! Then she pointed out that God didn't want me to give in to a spirit of fear, and she showed me 2 Timothy 1:7. That verse became very meaningful to me. I memorized it and reminded myself of it over and over, until eventually I began to believe that most people could be trusted, that most people weren't out to hurt me.

I'm so glad God used the Psalms and 2 Timothy to remind me that he cares for me.

—Melinda

9 If I ride the wings of the morning,
if I dwell by the farthest oceans,
10 even there your hand will guide me,
and your strength will support me.
11 I could ask the darkness to hide me
and the light around me to become night—
12 but even in darkness I cannot hide from you.
To you the night shines as bright as day.
Darkness and light are the same to you.

13 You made all the delicate, inner parts of my body
and knit me together in my mother's womb.
14 Thank you for making me so wonderfully complex!
Your workmanship is marvelous—how well
I know it.
15 You watched me as I was being formed in utter
seclusion,
as I was woven together in the dark of the womb.
16 You saw me before I was born.
Every day of my life was recorded in your book.
Every moment was laid out
before a single day had passed.

17 How precious are your thoughts about me,* O God.
They cannot be numbered!
18 I can't even count them;
they outnumber the grains of sand!
And when I wake up,
you are still with me!

19 O God, if only you would destroy the wicked!
Get out of my life, you murderers!
20 They blaspheme you;
your enemies misuse your name.
21 O LORD, shouldn't I hate those who hate you?
Shouldn't I despise those who oppose you?
22 Yes, I hate them with total hatred,
for your enemies are my enemies.

23 Search me, O God, and know my heart;
test me and know my anxious thoughts.
24 Point out anything in me that offends you,
and lead me along the path of everlasting life.

140

For the choir director: A psalm of David.

1 O LORD, rescue me from evil people.
Protect me from those who are violent,
2 those who plot evil in their hearts
and stir up trouble all day long.
3 Their tongues sting like a snake;
the venom of a viper drips from
their lips. *Interlude*

4 O LORD, keep me out of the hands of the wicked.
Protect me from those who are violent,
for they are plotting against me.
5 The proud have set a trap to catch me;
they have stretched out a net;
they have placed traps all along the way. *Interlude*

6 I said to the LORD, "You are my God!"
Listen, O LORD, to my cries for mercy!

139:17 Or *How precious to me are your thoughts.*

7 O Sovereign LORD, the strong one who
rescued me,
you protected me on the day of battle.
8 LORD, do not let evil people have their way.
Do not let their evil schemes succeed,
or they will become proud. *Interlude*

9 Let my enemies be destroyed
by the very evil they have planned for me.
10 Let burning coals fall down on their heads.
Let them be thrown into the fire
or into watery pits from which they
can't escape.
11 Don't let liars prosper here in our land.
Cause great disasters to fall on the violent.

12 But I know the LORD will help those they
persecute;
he will give justice to the poor.
13 Surely righteous people are praising your name;
the godly will live in your presence.

141

A psalm of David.

1 O LORD, I am calling to you. Please hurry!
Listen when I cry to you for help!
2 Accept my prayer as incense offered to you,
and my upraised hands as an evening
offering.

3 Take control of what I say, O LORD,
and guard my lips.
4 Don't let me drift toward evil
or take part in acts of wickedness.
Don't let me share in the delicacies
of those who do wrong.

5 Let the godly strike me!
It will be a kindness!
If they correct me, it is soothing medicine.
Don't let me refuse it.

But I pray constantly
against the wicked and their deeds.
6 When their leaders are thrown down from
a cliff,
the wicked will listen to my words and find
them true.
7 Like rocks brought up by a plow,
the bones of the wicked will lie scattered
without burial.*

8 I look to you for help, O Sovereign LORD.
You are my refuge; don't let them kill me.
9 Keep me from the traps they have set for me,
from the snares of those who do wrong.
10 Let the wicked fall into their own nets,
but let me escape.

142

A psalm of David, regarding his experience in the cave. A prayer.*

1 I cry out to the LORD;
I plead for the LORD's mercy.
2 I pour out my complaints before him
and tell him all my troubles.
3 When I am overwhelmed,
you alone know the way I should turn.
Wherever I go,
my enemies have set traps for me.
4 I look for someone to come and help me,
but no one gives me a passing thought!
No one will help me;
no one cares a bit what happens to me.
5 Then I pray to you, O LORD.
I say, "You are my place of refuge.
You are all I really want in life.
6 Hear my cry,
for I am very low.
Rescue me from my persecutors,
for they are too strong for me.
7 Bring me out of prison
so I can thank you.
The godly will crowd around me,
for you are good to me."

143

A psalm of David.

1 Hear my prayer, O LORD;
listen to my plea!
Answer me because you are faithful
and righteous.
2 Don't put your servant on trial,
for no one is innocent before you.
3 My enemy has chased me.
He has knocked me to the ground
and forces me to live in darkness like those
in the grave.
4 I am losing all hope;
I am paralyzed with fear.
5 I remember the days of old.
I ponder all your great works
and think about what you have done.
6 I lift my hands to you in prayer.
I thirst for you as parched land thirsts
for rain. *Interlude*

7 Come quickly, LORD, and answer me,
for my depression deepens.
Don't turn away from me,
or I will die.
8 Let me hear of your unfailing love each morning,
for I am trusting you.
Show me where to walk,
for I give myself to you.

141:7 Hebrew *scattered at the mouth of Sheol.* **142:TITLE** Hebrew *maskil.* This may be a literary or musical term.

9 Rescue me from my enemies, LORD;
I run to you to hide me.
10 Teach me to do your will,
for you are my God.
May your gracious Spirit lead me forward
on a firm footing.
11 For the glory of your name, O LORD, preserve
my life.
Because of your faithfulness, bring me out
of this distress.
12 In your unfailing love, silence all my enemies
and destroy all my foes,
for I am your servant.

144

A psalm of David.

1 Praise the LORD, who is my rock.
He trains my hands for war
and gives my fingers skill for battle.
2 He is my loving ally and my fortress,
my tower of safety, my rescuer.
He is my shield, and I take refuge in him.
He makes the nations* submit to me.

3 O LORD, what are human beings that you should
notice them,
mere mortals that you should think about them?
4 For they are like a breath of air;
their days are like a passing shadow.

5 Open the heavens, LORD, and come down.
Touch the mountains so they billow smoke.
6 Hurl your lightning bolts and scatter your enemies!
Shoot your arrows and confuse them!
7 Reach down from heaven and rescue me;
rescue me from deep waters,
from the power of my enemies.
8 Their mouths are full of lies;
they swear to tell the truth, but they lie instead.

9 I will sing a new song to you, O God!
I will sing your praises with a ten-stringed harp.
10 For you grant victory to kings!
You rescued your servant David from the
fatal sword.
11 Save me!
Rescue me from the power of my enemies.
Their mouths are full of lies;
they swear to tell the truth, but they lie instead.

12 May our sons flourish in their youth
like well-nurtured plants.
May our daughters be like graceful pillars,
carved to beautify a palace.
13 May our barns be filled
with crops of every kind.
May the flocks in our fields multiply by the
thousands,
even tens of thousands,
14 and may our oxen be loaded down with produce.
May there be no enemy breaking through our walls,
no going into captivity,
no cries of alarm in our town squares.
15 Yes, joyful are those who live like this!
Joyful indeed are those whose God is the LORD.

145*

A psalm of praise of David.

1 I will exalt you, my God and King,
and praise your name forever and ever.
2 I will praise you every day;
yes, I will praise you forever.
3 Great is the LORD! He is most worthy of praise!
No one can measure his greatness.

4 Let each generation tell its children of your
mighty acts;
let them proclaim your power.
5 I will meditate* on your majestic, glorious splendor
and your wonderful miracles.
6 Your awe-inspiring deeds will be on every tongue;
I will proclaim your greatness.
7 Everyone will share the story of your wonderful
goodness;
they will sing with joy about your righteousness.

8 The LORD is merciful and compassionate,
slow to get angry and filled with unfailing love.
9 The LORD is good to everyone.
He showers compassion on all his creation.
10 All of your works will thank you, LORD,
and your faithful followers will praise you.
11 They will speak of the glory of your kingdom;
they will give examples of your power.
12 They will tell about your mighty deeds
and about the majesty and glory of your reign.
13 For your kingdom is an everlasting kingdom.
You rule throughout all generations.

The LORD always keeps his promises;
he is gracious in all he does.*
14 The LORD helps the fallen
and lifts those bent beneath their loads.
15 The eyes of all look to you in hope;
you give them their food as they need it.
16 When you open your hand,
you satisfy the hunger and thirst of every
living thing.
17 The LORD is righteous in everything he does;
he is filled with kindness.
18 The LORD is close to all who call on him,
yes, to all who call on him in truth.

144:2 Some manuscripts read *my people*. **145** This psalm is a Hebrew acrostic poem; each verse (including 13b) begins with a successive letter of the Hebrew alphabet. **145:5** Some manuscripts read *They will speak*. **145:13** The last two lines of 145:13 are not found in many of the ancient manuscripts.

19 He grants the desires of those who fear him;
he hears their cries for help and rescues them.
20 The LORD protects all those who love him,
but he destroys the wicked.

21 I will praise the LORD,
and may everyone on earth bless his holy name
forever and ever.

146

1 Praise the LORD!

Let all that I am praise the LORD.
2 I will praise the LORD as long as I live.
I will sing praises to my God with my dying breath.

3 Don't put your confidence in powerful people;
there is no help for you there.
4 When they breathe their last, they return to
the earth,
and all their plans die with them.
5 But joyful are those who have the God of Israel*
as their helper,
whose hope is in the LORD their God.
6 He made heaven and earth,
the sea, and everything in them.
He keeps every promise forever.
7 He gives justice to the oppressed
and food to the hungry.
The LORD frees the prisoners.
8 The LORD opens the eyes of the blind.
The LORD lifts up those who are weighed down.
The LORD loves the godly.
9 The LORD protects the foreigners among us.
He cares for the orphans and widows,
but he frustrates the plans of the wicked.

10 The LORD will reign forever.
He will be your God, O Jerusalem,* throughout
the generations.

Praise the LORD!

147

1 Praise the LORD!

How good to sing praises to our God!
How delightful and how fitting!
2 The LORD is rebuilding Jerusalem
and bringing the exiles back to Israel.
3 He heals the brokenhearted
and bandages their wounds.
4 He counts the stars
and calls them all by name.
5 How great is our Lord! His power is absolute!
His understanding is beyond comprehension!
6 The LORD supports the humble,
but he brings the wicked down into the dust.

7 Sing out your thanks to the LORD;
sing praises to our God with a harp.
8 He covers the heavens with clouds,
provides rain for the earth,
and makes the grass grow in mountain
pastures.
9 He gives food to the wild animals
and feeds the young ravens when they cry.
10 He takes no pleasure in the strength of a horse
or in human might.
11 No, the LORD's delight is in those who fear him,
those who put their hope in his unfailing love.

12 Glorify the LORD, O Jerusalem!
Praise your God, O Zion!
13 For he has strengthened the bars of your gates
and blessed your children within your walls.
14 He sends peace across your nation
and satisfies your hunger with the finest wheat.
15 He sends his orders to the world—
how swiftly his word flies!
16 He sends the snow like white wool;
he scatters frost upon the ground like ashes.
17 He hurls the hail like stones.*
Who can stand against his freezing cold?
18 Then, at his command, it all melts.
He sends his winds, and the ice thaws.
19 He has revealed his words to Jacob,
his decrees and regulations to Israel.
20 He has not done this for any other nation;
they do not know his regulations.

Praise the LORD!

148

1 Praise the LORD!

Praise the LORD from the heavens!
Praise him from the skies!
2 Praise him, all his angels!
Praise him, all the armies of heaven!
3 Praise him, sun and moon!
Praise him, all you twinkling stars!
4 Praise him, skies above!
Praise him, vapors high above the clouds!
5 Let every created thing give praise to the LORD,
for he issued his command, and they came
into being.
6 He set them in place forever and ever.
His decree will never be revoked.

7 Praise the LORD from the earth,
you creatures of the ocean depths,
8 fire and hail, snow and clouds,*
wind and weather that obey him,
9 mountains and all hills,
fruit trees and all cedars,
10 wild animals and all livestock,

146:5 Hebrew *of Jacob*. See note on 44:4. **146:10** Hebrew *Zion*. **147:17** Hebrew *like bread crumbs*. **148:8** Or *mist*, or *smoke*.

small scurrying animals and birds,
11 kings of the earth and all people,
rulers and judges of the earth,
12 young men and young women,
old men and children.

13 Let them all praise the name of the LORD.
For his name is very great;
his glory towers over the earth and heaven!
14 He has made his people strong,
honoring his faithful ones—
the people of Israel who are close to him.

Praise the LORD!

PRAISE YOUR WAY 149:3-5

Although the Bible invites us to praise God, we often aren't sure how to go about it. Here, several ways are suggested: with your voice, in music, in your actions. Which way is your favorite way to offer praise? ■

149

1 Praise the LORD!

Sing to the LORD a new song.
Sing his praises in the assembly of the faithful.

2 O Israel, rejoice in your Maker.
O people of Jerusalem,* exult in your King.
3 Praise his name with dancing,
accompanied by tambourine and harp.
4 For the LORD delights in his people;
he crowns the humble with victory.
5 Let the faithful rejoice that he honors them.
Let them sing for joy as they lie on their beds.

6 Let the praises of God be in their mouths,
and a sharp sword in their hands—
7 to execute vengeance on the nations
and punishment on the peoples,
8 to bind their kings with shackles
and their leaders with iron chains,
9 to execute the judgment written against them.
This is the glorious privilege of his
faithful ones.

Praise the LORD!

150

1 Praise the LORD!

Praise God in his sanctuary;
praise him in his mighty heaven!
2 Praise him for his mighty works;
praise his unequaled greatness!
3 Praise him with a blast of the ram's horn;
praise him with the lyre and harp!
4 Praise him with the tambourine and dancing;
praise him with strings and flutes!
5 Praise him with a clash of cymbals;
praise him with loud clanging cymbals.
6 Let everything that breathes sing praises
to the LORD!

Praise the LORD!

149:2 Hebrew *Zion*.

PROVERBS

proverbs

WHAT DO YOU think you need to get by in life? Your good looks or sparkling personality? A good bank account? Friends in high places? Incredible grades? You probably have a list of "needs." But is wisdom on your list?

Many people confuse wisdom with intelligence. Wisdom is an intelligence of a different sort. According to the American Heritage Dictionary, it means "having understanding or discernment of what is true, right, or lasting; exhibiting common sense." In other words, it is the ability to make good (wise) decisions.

Proverbs was written by Solomon, the king who asked for and received wisdom from God. (See 1 Kings 3.) In this book he provides proverbs—wise sayings—about money, marriage, family life, discipline, friends, laziness, speech, relationships, temptation, and leadership. Solomon's purpose was "to teach people wisdom and discipline, to help them understand the insights of the wise . . . to teach people to live disciplined and successful lives, to help them do what is right, just, and fair" (1:2-3).

Proverbs is a book of answers—answers to our questions about life. There are many areas where most of us would like to have more wisdom. In what areas could you use more wisdom?

stats

PURPOSE: To teach people how to be understanding, just, and fair in everything they do

AUTHOR: Solomon wrote most of this book; Agur and Lemuel contributed some of the later sections.

DATE WRITTEN: Solomon wrote and compiled most of these proverbs early in his reign.

SETTING: The book of Proverbs reflects the poetic style of the era.

SPECIAL FEATURES: The book uses varied literary forms: poems, brief parables, pointed questions, and couplets. Other literary devices include antithesis, comparison, and personification.

KEY points

WISDOM
God wants his people to be wise. He helps us gain wisdom through the rules and advice in the Bible and through making right decisions.

RELATIONSHIPS
Proverbs gives us advice for developing our relationships with friends, family members, and co-workers. To relate to people, we need consistency, sensitivity, and discipline.

WISE WORDS
What we say shows our real attitude toward others. To be wise in our speech we need to use self-control. What we say affects others.

SUCCESS
Although people work very hard for money and fame, God considers a good reputation, faith, and obedience to be the true measures of success. A successful relationship with God counts for eternity. Everything else is only temporary.

1 THE PURPOSE OF PROVERBS

These are the proverbs of Solomon, David's son, king of Israel.

2 Their purpose is to teach people wisdom and
discipline,
to help them understand the insights of the wise.
3 Their purpose is to teach people to live disciplined
and successful lives,
to help them do what is right, just, and fair.
4 These proverbs will give insight to the simple,
knowledge and discernment to the young.

5 Let the wise listen to these proverbs and become
even wiser.
Let those with understanding receive guidance
6 by exploring the meaning in these proverbs and
parables,
the words of the wise and their riddles.

7 Fear of the LORD is the foundation of true
knowledge,
but fools despise wisdom and discipline.

A FATHER'S EXHORTATION: ACQUIRE WISDOM

8 My child,* listen when your father corrects you.
Don't neglect your mother's instruction.
9 What you learn from them will crown you
with grace
and be a chain of honor around your neck.

10 My child, if sinners entice you,
turn your back on them!
11 They may say, "Come and join us.
Let's hide and kill someone!
Just for fun, let's ambush the innocent!
12 Let's swallow them alive, like the grave*;
let's swallow them whole, like those who go down
to the pit of death.
13 Think of the great things we'll get!
We'll fill our houses with all the stuff we take.
14 Come, throw in your lot with us;
we'll all share the loot."

15 My child, don't go along with them!
Stay far away from their paths.
16 They rush to commit evil deeds.
They hurry to commit murder.
17 If a bird sees a trap being set,
it knows to stay away.
18 But these people set an ambush for themselves;
they are trying to get themselves killed.
19 Such is the fate of all who are greedy for money;
it robs them of life.

WISDOM SHOUTS IN THE STREETS

20 Wisdom shouts in the streets.
She cries out in the public square.
21 She calls to the crowds along the main street,
to those gathered in front of the city gate:
22 "How long, you simpletons,
will you insist on being simpleminded?
How long will you mockers relish your mocking?
How long will you fools hate knowledge?
23 Come and listen to my counsel.
I'll share my heart with you
and make you wise.

24 "I called you so often, but you wouldn't come.
I reached out to you, but you paid no attention.
25 You ignored my advice
and rejected the correction I offered.
26 So I will laugh when you are in trouble!
I will mock you when disaster overtakes you—
27 when calamity overtakes you like a storm,
when disaster engulfs you like a cyclone,
and anguish and distress overwhelm you.

28 "When they cry for help, I will not answer.
Though they anxiously search for me, they
will not find me.
29 For they hated knowledge
and chose not to fear the LORD.

1:8 Hebrew *My son;* also in 1:10, 15. **1:12** Hebrew *like Sheol.*

Some of my friends try to pressure me into doing things that I know are wrong. I've given in lots of times. (I feel doubly guilty, since I'm a Christian.) How do I withstand the pressure?

Too often we hide our real character, hoping to be liked by someone or by a group. We want the acceptance of others. That's why sooner or later everyone is tempted to bend his or her rules or beliefs in order for someone to like him/her. Maybe you can relate to this all too well. But God wants to provide the inner muscle you'll need to combat the outer pressure you feel. Ask him to give you the courage and strength to say no and for the ability to stand by what you believe.

He also wants to teach you what to do. Remember when your mom or dad helped you learn a task or skill? They didn't just tell you to do it, they showed you how.

God shows us how to act through the teachings and stories in the Bible. For example, Proverbs 1:10 provides advice on resisting those who do wrong. Also, commands like "Don't copy the behavior and customs of this world, but let God transform you into a new person by changing the way you think" (Rom 12:2) are a reminder of God's willingness to change you. You can't change your friends or anyone else. But you can definitely change your reaction to temptation.

30 They rejected my advice
and paid no attention when I corrected them.
31 Therefore, they must eat the bitter fruit of living
their own way,
choking on their own schemes.
32 For simpletons turn away from me—to death.
Fools are destroyed by their own complacency.
33 But all who listen to me will live in peace,
untroubled by fear of harm."

2 THE BENEFITS OF WISDOM

1 My child,* listen to what I say,
and treasure my commands.
2 Tune your ears to wisdom,
and concentrate on understanding.
3 Cry out for insight,
and ask for understanding.
4 Search for them as you would for silver;
seek them like hidden treasures.
5 Then you will understand what it means to fear
the LORD,
and you will gain knowledge of God.
6 For the LORD grants wisdom!
From his mouth come knowledge and
understanding.
7 He grants a treasure of common sense to the honest.
He is a shield to those who walk with integrity.
8 He guards the paths of the just
and protects those who are faithful to him.

CHOICES 2:9-10

Wisdom isn't developed all at once. It comes through a constant process of growth. Some aspects of wisdom might seem to develop faster than others. For example, some people seem to have more insight than discretion; others have more knowledge than common sense. But the source of wisdom is still God. Want to be wise? Start at the source. ■

9 Then you will understand what is right, just,
and fair,
and you will find the right way to go.
10 For wisdom will enter your heart,
and knowledge will fill you with joy.
11 Wise choices will watch over you.
Understanding will keep you safe.

12 Wisdom will save you from evil people,
from those whose words are twisted.
13 These men turn from the right way
to walk down dark paths.
14 They take pleasure in doing wrong,
and they enjoy the twisted ways of evil.
15 Their actions are crooked,
and their ways are wrong.

16 Wisdom will save you from the immoral woman,
from the seductive words of the promiscuous
woman.
17 She has abandoned her husband
and ignores the covenant she made before God.
18 Entering her house leads to death;
it is the road to the grave.*
19 The man who visits her is doomed.
He will never reach the paths of life.

20 Follow the steps of good men instead,
and stay on the paths of the righteous.
21 For only the godly will live in the land,
and those with integrity will remain in it.
22 But the wicked will be removed from the land,
and the treacherous will be uprooted.

3 TRUSTING IN THE LORD

1 My child,* never forget the things I have
taught you.
Store my commands in your heart.
2 If you do this, you will live many years,
and your life will be satisfying.
3 Never let loyalty and kindness leave you!
Tie them around your neck as a reminder.
Write them deep within your heart.
4 Then you will find favor with both God and people,
and you will earn a good reputation.

5 Trust in the LORD with all your heart;
do not depend on your own understanding.
6 Seek his will in all you do,
and he will show you which path to take.

7 Don't be impressed with your own wisdom.
Instead, fear the LORD and turn away from evil.
8 Then you will have healing for your body
and strength for your bones.

9 Honor the LORD with your wealth
and with the best part of everything you produce.
10 Then he will fill your barns with grain,
and your vats will overflow with good wine.

11 My child, don't reject the LORD's discipline,
and don't be upset when he corrects you.
12 For the LORD corrects those he loves,
just as a father corrects a child in whom
he delights.*

13 Joyful is the person who finds wisdom,
the one who gains understanding.
14 For wisdom is more profitable than silver,
and her wages are better than gold.
15 Wisdom is more precious than rubies;
nothing you desire can compare with her.

2:1 Hebrew *My son.* 2:18 Hebrew *to the spirits of the dead.* 3:1 Hebrew *My son;* also in 3:11, 21. 3:12 Greek version reads *And he punishes those he accepts as his children.* Compare Heb 12:6.

16 She offers you long life in her right hand,
and riches and honor in her left.
17 She will guide you down delightful paths;
all her ways are satisfying.
18 Wisdom is a tree of life to those who
embrace her;
happy are those who hold her tightly.

19 By wisdom the LORD founded the earth;
by understanding he created the heavens.
20 By his knowledge the deep fountains
of the earth burst forth,
and the dew settles beneath the
night sky.

21 My child, don't lose sight of
common sense and
discernment.
Hang on to them,
22 for they will refresh your soul.
They are like jewels on a
necklace.
23 They keep you safe on your way,
and your feet will not stumble.
24 You can go to bed without fear;
you will lie down and sleep
soundly.
25 You need not be afraid of sudden
disaster
or the destruction that comes upon the wicked,
26 for the LORD is your security.
He will keep your foot from being caught
in a trap.

27 Do not withhold good from those who deserve it
when it's in your power to help them.
28 If you can help your neighbor now, don't say,
"Come back tomorrow, and then I'll help you."

29 Don't plot harm against your neighbor,
for those who live nearby trust you.
30 Don't pick a fight without reason,
when no one has done you harm.

31 Don't envy violent people
or copy their ways.
32 Such wicked people are detestable to the LORD,
but he offers his friendship to the godly.

33 The LORD curses the house of the wicked,
but he blesses the home of the upright.

34 The LORD mocks the mockers
but is gracious to the humble.*

35 The wise inherit honor,
but fools are put to shame!

Trust in the LORD with all your heart; . . . Seek his will in all you do, and he will show you which path to take.

PROVERBS 3:5-6

4

A FATHER'S WISE ADVICE

1 My children,* listen when your father
corrects you.
Pay attention and learn good judgment,
2 for I am giving you good guidance.
Don't turn away from my instructions.
3 For I, too, was once my father's son,
tenderly loved as my mother's only child.

4 My father taught me,
"Take my words to heart.
Follow my commands, and you
will live.
5 Get wisdom; develop good
judgment.
Don't forget my words or turn
away from them.
6 Don't turn your back on wisdom,
for she will protect you.
Love her, and she will guard you.
7 Getting wisdom is the wisest thing
you can do!
And whatever else you do,
develop good judgment.
8 If you prize wisdom, she will make
you great.
Embrace her, and she will honor
you.
9 She will place a lovely wreath on your head;
she will present you with a beautiful crown."

10 My child,* listen to me and do as I say,
and you will have a long, good life.
11 I will teach you wisdom's ways
and lead you in straight paths.
12 When you walk, you won't be held back;
when you run, you won't stumble.
13 Take hold of my instructions; don't let them go.
Guard them, for they are the key to life.

14 Don't do as the wicked do,
and don't follow the path of evildoers.
15 Don't even think about it; don't go that way.
Turn away and keep moving.
16 For evil people can't sleep until they've done their
evil deed for the day.
They can't rest until they've caused someone
to stumble.
17 They eat the food of wickedness
and drink the wine of violence!

18 The way of the righteous is like the first gleam
of dawn,
which shines ever brighter until the full light of day.
19 But the way of the wicked is like total darkness.
They have no idea what they are stumbling over.

3:34 Greek version reads *The LORD opposes the proud / but favors the humble.* Compare Jas 4:6; 1 Pet 5:5. **4:1** Hebrew *My sons.*
4:10 Hebrew *My son;* also in 4:20.

20 My child, pay attention to what I say.
Listen carefully to my words.
21 Don't lose sight of them.
Let them penetrate deep into your heart,
22 for they bring life to those who find them,
and healing to their whole body.

GUARD YOUR HEART 4:23-27

According to Solomon, the wise person guards his or her heart. Our heart dictates to a great extent how we live because we always find time to do what we enjoy. So, how do we guard our heart? By concentrating on those desires that will keep us on the right path. This will involve discipline and a commitment to God's purposes. It will also mean watching out for detours that lead to temptation. ■

23 Guard your heart above all else,
for it determines the course of your life.

24 Avoid all perverse talk;
stay away from corrupt speech.

25 Look straight ahead,
and fix your eyes on what lies before you.
26 Mark out a straight path for your feet;
stay on the safe path.
27 Don't get sidetracked;
keep your feet from following evil.

5 AVOID IMMORAL WOMEN

1 My son, pay attention to my wisdom;
listen carefully to my wise counsel.
2 Then you will show discernment,
and your lips will express what you've learned.
3 For the lips of an immoral woman are as sweet as honey,
and her mouth is smoother than oil.
4 But in the end she is as bitter as poison,
as dangerous as a double-edged sword.
5 Her feet go down to death;
her steps lead straight to the grave.*
6 For she cares nothing about the path to life.
She staggers down a crooked trail and doesn't realize it.

7 So now, my sons, listen to me.
Never stray from what I am about to say:
8 Stay away from her!
Don't go near the door of her house!
9 If you do, you will lose your honor
and will lose to merciless people all you have achieved.
10 Strangers will consume your wealth,
and someone else will enjoy the fruit of your labor.
11 In the end you will groan in anguish
when disease consumes your body.
12 You will say, "How I hated discipline!
If only I had not ignored all the warnings!
13 Oh, why didn't I listen to my teachers?
Why didn't I pay attention to my instructors?
14 I have come to the brink of utter ruin,
and now I must face public disgrace."

15 Drink water from your own well—
share your love only with your wife.*
16 Why spill the water of your springs in the streets,
having sex with just anyone?*
17 You should reserve it for yourselves.
Never share it with strangers.

18 Let your wife be a fountain of blessing for you.
Rejoice in the wife of your youth.
19 She is a loving deer, a graceful doe.
Let her breasts satisfy you always.
May you always be captivated by her love.
20 Why be captivated, my son, by an immoral woman,
or fondle the breasts of a promiscuous woman?

21 For the LORD sees clearly what a man does,
examining every path he takes.
22 An evil man is held captive by his own sins;
they are ropes that catch and hold him.
23 He will die for lack of self-control;
he will be lost because of his great foolishness.

6 LESSONS FOR DAILY LIFE

1 My child,* if you have put up security for a friend's debt
or agreed to guarantee the debt of a stranger—
2 if you have trapped yourself by your agreement
and are caught by what you said—
3 follow my advice and save yourself,
for you have placed yourself at your friend's mercy.
Now swallow your pride;
go and beg to have your name erased.
4 Don't put it off; do it now!
Don't rest until you do.
5 Save yourself like a gazelle escaping from a hunter,
like a bird fleeing from a net.

6 Take a lesson from the ants, you lazybones.
Learn from their ways and become wise!
7 Though they have no prince
or governor or ruler to make them work,
8 they labor hard all summer,
gathering food for the winter.
9 But you, lazybones, how long will you sleep?
When will you wake up?

5:5 Hebrew *to Sheol.* 5:15 Hebrew *Drink water from your own cistern, / flowing water from your own well.* 5:16 Hebrew *Why spill your springs in the streets, / your streams in the city squares?* 6:1 Hebrew *My son.*

keeping it real

I've had this problem with procrastination and laziness. Basically, I just don't make an effort with things that bore me (like school or chores my parents want me to do). One day, as I was reading along in Proverbs 6:6-11, which describes what a lazy person is like, I knew that it was talking about me! Those verses taught me that putting things off isn't just a bad habit, it's a sin that can lead to some pretty bad consequences. This passage helped motivate me to quit sitting around and to take some action even if I don't feel like it.

—John

10 A little extra sleep, a little more slumber,
a little folding of the hands to rest—
11 then poverty will pounce on you like a bandit;
scarcity will attack you like an armed robber.

12 What are worthless and wicked people like?
They are constant liars,
13 signaling their deceit with a wink of the eye,
a nudge of the foot, or the wiggle of fingers.
14 Their perverted hearts plot evil,
and they constantly stir up trouble.
15 But they will be destroyed suddenly,
broken in an instant beyond all hope of healing.

16 There are six things the LORD hates—
no, seven things he detests:
17 haughty eyes,
a lying tongue,
hands that kill the innocent,
18 a heart that plots evil,
feet that race to do wrong,
19 a false witness who pours out lies,
a person who sows discord in a family.

LISTEN UP! 6:20-24

"My son, obey your father's commands, and don't neglect your mother's instruction" (6:20). Have you ever had a parent give this advice? Yet many of us turn a deaf ear to a parent's advice at times. But the wise person can gain wisdom by seeking the advice of a godly parent or other older adults.

20 My son, obey your father's commands,
and don't neglect your mother's instruction.
21 Keep their words always in your heart.
Tie them around your neck.
22 When you walk, their counsel will lead you.
When you sleep, they will protect you.
When you wake up, they will advise you.
23 For their command is a lamp
and their instruction a light;
their corrective discipline
is the way to life.
24 It will keep you from the immoral woman,
from the smooth tongue of a promiscuous woman.
25 Don't lust for her beauty.
Don't let her coy glances seduce you.
26 For a prostitute will bring you to poverty,*
but sleeping with another man's wife will cost you
your life.
27 Can a man scoop a flame into his lap
and not have his clothes catch on fire?
28 Can he walk on hot coals
and not blister his feet?
29 So it is with the man who sleeps with another
man's wife.
He who embraces her will not go unpunished.

30 Excuses might be found for a thief
who steals because he is starving.
31 But if he is caught, he must pay back seven times
what he stole,
even if he has to sell everything in his house.
32 But the man who commits adultery is an utter fool,
for he destroys himself.
33 He will be wounded and disgraced.
His shame will never be erased.
34 For the woman's jealous husband will be furious,
and he will show no mercy when he takes revenge.
35 He will accept no compensation,
nor be satisfied with a payoff of any size.

7 ANOTHER WARNING ABOUT IMMORAL WOMEN

1 Follow my advice, my son;
always treasure my commands.
2 Obey my commands and live!
Guard my instructions as you guard your
own eyes.*

6:26 Hebrew *to a loaf of bread.* 7:2 Hebrew *as the pupil of your eye.*

Strategy for Effective Living

BEGINS WITH	REQUIRES	REQUIRES	RESULTS IN
GOD'S WISDOM	MORAL APPLICATION	PRACTICAL APPLICATION	EFFECTIVE LIVING
Respecting and appreciating who God is. Reverence and awe in recognizing the almighty God.	Trusting in God and his Word. Allowing his Word to speak to us personally. Being willing to obey.	Acting on God's direction in daily devotions.	Experiencing what God does with our obedience.

3 Tie them on your fingers as a reminder.
Write them deep within your heart.

4 Love wisdom like a sister;
make insight a beloved member of your family.
5 Let them protect you from an affair with an immoral woman,
from listening to the flattery of a promiscuous woman.
6 While I was at the window of my house,
looking through the curtain,
7 I saw some naive young men,
and one in particular who lacked common sense.
8 He was crossing the street near the house of an immoral woman,
strolling down the path by her house.
9 It was at twilight, in the evening,
as deep darkness fell.
10 The woman approached him,
seductively dressed and sly of heart.
11 She was the brash, rebellious type,
never content to stay at home.
12 She is often in the streets and markets,
soliciting at every corner.
13 She threw her arms around him and kissed him,
and with a brazen look she said,
14 "I've just made my peace offerings
and fulfilled my vows.
15 You're the one I was looking for!
I came out to find you, and here you are!
16 My bed is spread with beautiful blankets,
with colored sheets of Egyptian linen.
17 I've perfumed my bed
with myrrh, aloes, and cinnamon.
18 Come, let's drink our fill of love until morning.
Let's enjoy each other's caresses,
19 for my husband is not home.
He's away on a long trip.
20 He has taken a wallet full of money with him
and won't return until later this month.*"

21 So she seduced him with her pretty speech
and enticed him with her flattery.
22 He followed her at once,
like an ox going to the slaughter.
He was like a stag caught in a trap,
23 awaiting the arrow that would pierce its heart.
He was like a bird flying into a snare,
little knowing it would cost him his life.

24 So listen to me, my sons,
and pay attention to my words.
25 Don't let your hearts stray away toward her.
Don't wander down her wayward path.
26 For she has been the ruin of many;
many men have been her victims.
27 Her house is the road to the grave.*
Her bedroom is the den of death.

8 WISDOM CALLS FOR A HEARING

1 Listen as Wisdom calls out!
Hear as understanding raises her voice!
2 On the hilltop along the road,
she takes her stand at the crossroads.
3 By the gates at the entrance to the town,
on the road leading in, she cries aloud,
4 "I call to you, to all of you!
I raise my voice to all people.
5 You simple people, use good judgment.
You foolish people, show some understanding.
6 Listen to me! For I have important things to tell you.
Everything I say is right,
7 for I speak the truth
and detest every kind of deception.
8 My advice is wholesome.
There is nothing devious or crooked in it.
9 My words are plain to anyone with understanding,
clear to those with knowledge.
10 Choose my instruction rather than silver,
and knowledge rather than pure gold.
11 For wisdom is far more valuable than rubies.
Nothing you desire can compare with it.

12 "I, Wisdom, live together with good judgment.
I know where to discover knowledge and discernment.

7:20 Hebrew *until the moon is full.* 7:27 Hebrew *to Sheol.*

13 All who fear the LORD will hate evil.
Therefore, I hate pride and arrogance,
corruption and perverse speech.
14 Common sense and success belong to me.
Insight and strength are mine.
15 Because of me, kings reign,
and rulers make just decrees.
16 Rulers lead with my help,
and nobles make righteous judgments.

17 "I love all who love me.
Those who search will surely find me.
18 I have riches and honor,
as well as enduring wealth and justice.
19 My gifts are better than gold, even the purest gold,
my wages better than sterling silver!
20 I walk in righteousness,
in paths of justice.
21 Those who love me inherit wealth.
I will fill their treasuries.

22 "The LORD formed me from the beginning,
before he created anything else.
23 I was appointed in ages past,
at the very first, before the earth began.
24 I was born before the oceans were created,
before the springs bubbled forth their waters.
25 Before the mountains were formed,
before the hills, I was born—
26 before he had made the earth and fields
and the first handfuls of soil.
27 I was there when he established the heavens,
when he drew the horizon on the oceans.
28 I was there when he set the clouds above,
when he established springs deep in the earth.
29 I was there when he set the limits of the seas,
so they would not spread beyond
their boundaries.
And when he marked off the earth's
foundations,
30 I was the architect at his side.
I was his constant delight,
rejoicing always in his presence.
31 And how happy I was with the world he created;
how I rejoiced with the human family!

32 "And so, my children,* listen to me,
for all who follow my ways are joyful.
33 Listen to my instruction and be wise.
Don't ignore it.
34 Joyful are those who listen to me,
watching for me daily at my gates,
waiting for me outside my home!
35 For whoever finds me finds life
and receives favor from the LORD.
36 But those who miss me injure themselves.
All who hate me love death."

9

1 Wisdom has built her house;
she has carved its seven columns.
2 She has prepared a great banquet,
mixed the wines, and set the table.
3 She has sent her servants to invite everyone to come.
She calls out from the heights overlooking the city.
4 "Come in with me," she urges the simple.
To those who lack good judgment, she says,
5 "Come, eat my food,
and drink the wine I have mixed.
6 Leave your simple ways behind, and begin to live;
learn to use good judgment."

7 Anyone who rebukes a mocker will get an insult in
return.
Anyone who corrects the wicked will get hurt.
8 So don't bother correcting mockers;
they will only hate you.
But correct the wise,
and they will love you.
9 Instruct the wise,
and they will be even wiser.
Teach the righteous,
and they will learn even more.

10 Fear of the LORD is the foundation of wisdom.
Knowledge of the Holy One results in good
judgment.

11 Wisdom will multiply your days
and add years to your life.
12 If you become wise, you will be the one to benefit.
If you scorn wisdom, you will be the one to suffer.

STOLEN FOOD 9:1-17

There's something hypnotic and intoxicating about some wrongdoings. That's why many people put aside all thought of wisdom's banquet (9:1-6) in order to eat the stolen food of foolishness (9:5, 17). Before reaching for forbidden fruit, take a long look at what happens to those who eat it. ■

FOLLY CALLS FOR A HEARING

13 The woman named Folly is brash.
She is ignorant and doesn't know it.
14 She sits in her doorway
on the heights overlooking the city.
15 She calls out to men going by
who are minding their own business.
16 "Come in with me," she urges the simple.
To those who lack good judgment, she says,
17 "Stolen water is refreshing;
food eaten in secret tastes the best!"
18 But little do they know that the dead are there.
Her guests are in the depths of the grave.*

8:32 Hebrew *my sons.* 9:18 Hebrew *in Sheol.*

10 THE PROVERBS OF SOLOMON

The proverbs of Solomon:

A wise child* brings joy to a father;
a foolish child brings grief to a mother.

2 Tainted wealth has no lasting value,
but right living can save your life.

3 The LORD will not let the godly go hungry,
but he refuses to satisfy the craving of the wicked.

4 Lazy people are soon poor;
hard workers get rich.

5 A wise youth harvests in the summer,
but one who sleeps during harvest is a disgrace.

WASTED TIME 10:4-5

Every day has 24 hours filled with opportunities to grow, serve, and be productive. It's so easy to waste time, letting life slip from our grasp. Yet we can choose to use time in a productive way. How will you use your time? ■

6 The godly are showered with blessings;
the words of the wicked conceal violent intentions.

7 We have happy memories of the godly,
but the name of a wicked person rots away.

8 The wise are glad to be instructed,
but babbling fools fall flat on their faces.

9 People with integrity walk safely,
but those who follow crooked paths will slip and fall.

10 People who wink at wrong cause trouble,
but a bold reproof promotes peace.*

11 The words of the godly are a life-giving fountain;
the words of the wicked conceal violent intentions.

12 Hatred stirs up quarrels,
but love makes up for all offenses.

13 Wise words come from the lips of people with understanding,
but those lacking sense will be beaten with a rod.

14 Wise people treasure knowledge,
but the babbling of a fool invites disaster.

15 The wealth of the rich is their fortress;
the poverty of the poor is their destruction.

16 The earnings of the godly enhance their lives,
but evil people squander their money on sin.

17 People who accept discipline are on the pathway to life,
but those who ignore correction will go astray.

18 Hiding hatred makes you a liar;
slandering others makes you a fool.

19 Too much talk leads to sin.
Be sensible and keep your mouth shut.

20 The words of the godly are like sterling silver;
the heart of a fool is worthless.

21 The words of the godly encourage many,
but fools are destroyed by their lack of common sense.

22 The blessing of the LORD makes a person rich,
and he adds no sorrow with it.

23 Doing wrong is fun for a fool,
but living wisely brings pleasure to the sensible.

24 The fears of the wicked will be fulfilled;
the hopes of the godly will be granted.

25 When the storms of life come, the wicked are whirled away,
but the godly have a lasting foundation.

26 Lazy people irritate their employers,
like vinegar to the teeth or smoke in the eyes.

27 Fear of the LORD lengthens one's life,
but the years of the wicked are cut short.

28 The hopes of the godly result in happiness,
but the expectations of the wicked come to nothing.

29 The way of the LORD is a stronghold to those with integrity,
but it destroys the wicked.

30 The godly will never be disturbed,
but the wicked will be removed from the land.

31 The mouth of the godly person gives wise advice,
but the tongue that deceives will be cut off.

32 The lips of the godly speak helpful words,
but the mouth of the wicked speaks perverse words.

10:1 Hebrew *son;* also in 10:1b. 10:10 As in Greek version; Hebrew reads *but babbling fools fall flat on their faces.*

11

1 The Lord detests the use of dishonest
scales,
but he delights in accurate weights.

2 Pride leads to disgrace,
but with humility comes wisdom.

CHEATING

When it comes to ditching schoolwork, Ben's always been the man with the plan. Check this out:

- **Through the Internet Ben found a company that sells term papers. For thirty bucks and an hour's worth of editing, he can turn in a top-notch report on almost any subject.**
- **He gets his friends to divide the daily pre-calc assignments. In study hall they each spend about 15 minutes doing a part of the homework (instead of an hour or more doing the whole thing by themselves). Ben makes photocopies of the pages on his family's scanner/copier for everyone, and passes them out first thing in the morning.**
- **Ben has never read an assigned book for language arts. Between the movie versions and CliffsNotes™, he can always fake it.**
- **Two of his teachers use the exact same tests from last year. Ben bought old copies from two college freshmen.**
- **He has a programmable watch that can store up to 100 facts and dates. On exam days, the watch gets a mean workout!**
- **Ben laughs at how stupid his teachers are and at how many people get away with cheating.**

Do you ever feel like cheating? Check out Proverbs 11:1 to see what God thinks about it.

3 Honesty guides good people;
dishonesty destroys treacherous people.

4 Riches won't help on the day of judgment,
but right living can save you from death.

5 The godly are directed by honesty;
the wicked fall beneath their load of sin.

6 The godliness of good people rescues them;
the ambition of treacherous people traps them.

7 When the wicked die, their hopes die with them,
for they rely on their own feeble strength.

8 The godly are rescued from trouble,
and it falls on the wicked instead.

9 With their words, the godless destroy their friends,
but knowledge will rescue the righteous.

10 The whole city celebrates when the godly succeed;
they shout for joy when the wicked die.

11 Upright citizens are good for a city and make
it prosper,
but the talk of the wicked tears it apart.

12 It is foolish to belittle one's neighbor;
a sensible person keeps quiet.

13 A gossip goes around telling secrets,
but those who are trustworthy can keep
a confidence.

14 Without wise leadership, a nation falls;
there is safety in having many advisers.

15 There's danger in putting up security for
a stranger's debt;
it's safer not to guarantee another person's debt.

16 A gracious woman gains respect,
but ruthless men gain only wealth.

17 Your kindness will reward you,
but your cruelty will destroy you.

18 Evil people get rich for the moment,
but the reward of the godly will last.

19 Godly people find life;
evil people find death.

20 The Lord detests people with crooked hearts,
but he delights in those with integrity.

21 Evil people will surely be punished,
but the children of the godly will go free.

22 A beautiful woman who lacks discretion
is like a gold ring in a pig's snout.

23 The godly can look forward to a reward,
while the wicked can expect only judgment.

24 Give freely and become more wealthy;
be stingy and lose everything.

25 The generous will prosper;
those who refresh others will themselves
be refreshed.

26 People curse those who hoard their grain,
but they bless the one who sells in time of need.

27 If you search for good, you will find favor;
but if you search for evil, it will find you!

28 Trust in your money and down you go!
But the godly flourish like leaves in spring.

29 Those who bring trouble on their families inherit
the wind.
The fool will be a servant to the wise.

30 The seeds of good deeds become a tree of life;
a wise person wins friends.*

31 If the righteous are rewarded here on earth,
what will happen to wicked sinners?*

REWARDS AND PUNISHMENT 11:31

Contrary to popular opinion, no one will ever completely get away with a wrongdoing. Ultimately, the faithful are rewarded for their faith while those who do evil acts are punished. (See also 1 Pet 4:17-18.) Tempted to think that what you do doesn't matter? News flash: it does. ■

12

1 To learn, you must love discipline;
it is stupid to hate correction.

2 The LORD approves of those who are good,
but he condemns those who plan wickedness.

3 Wickedness never brings stability,
but the godly have deep roots.

4 A worthy wife is a crown for her husband,
but a disgraceful woman is like cancer in
his bones.

5 The plans of the godly are just;
the advice of the wicked is treacherous.

6 The words of the wicked are like a murderous
ambush,
but the words of the godly save lives.

7 The wicked die and disappear,
but the family of the godly stands firm.

8 A sensible person wins admiration,
but a warped mind is despised.

9 Better to be an ordinary person with a servant
than to be self-important but have no food.

10 The godly care for their animals,
but the wicked are always cruel.

11 A hard worker has plenty of food,
but a person who chases fantasies has
no sense.

12 Thieves are jealous of each other's loot,
but the godly are well rooted and bear their
own fruit.

13 The wicked are trapped by their own words,
but the godly escape such trouble.

14 Wise words bring many benefits,
and hard work brings rewards.

15 Fools think their own way is right,
but the wise listen to others.

16 A fool is quick-tempered,
but a wise person stays calm when
insulted.

KEEP YOUR COOL 12:16

When someone insults you, do you immediately think of an insult in return? Many of us do. But this solves nothing and only encourages trouble. That's why the psalmist suggests that a better reaction is to "stay calm" and answer slowly and quietly. Your positive response can achieve positive results. ■

17 An honest witness tells the truth;
a false witness tells lies.

18 Some people make cutting remarks,
but the words of the wise bring healing.

19 Truthful words stand the test of time,
but lies are soon exposed.

20 Deceit fills hearts that are plotting evil;
joy fills hearts that are planning peace!

21 No harm comes to the godly,
but the wicked have their fill of trouble.

22 The LORD detests lying lips,
but he delights in those who tell the truth.

23 The wise don't make a show of their
knowledge,
but fools broadcast their foolishness.

24 Work hard and become a leader;
be lazy and become a slave.

25 Worry weighs a person down;
an encouraging word cheers a person up.

26 The godly give good advice to their friends;*
the wicked lead them astray.

11:30 Or *and those who win souls are wise.* **11:31** Greek version reads *If the righteous are barely saved, / what will happen to godless sinners?* Compare 1 Pet 4:18. **12:26** Or *The godly are cautious in friendship;* or *The godly are freed from evil.* The meaning of the Hebrew is uncertain.

How God Is Described in Proverbs

Proverbs is a book about wise living. It often focuses on a person's response and attitude toward God, who is the source of wisdom. And a number of proverbs point out aspects of God's character. Knowing God helps us on the way to wisdom.

GOD . . .
Is aware of all that happens—15:3
Knows all people—15:11; 16:2; 21:2
Is the maker of all things—16:4
Controls all things—16:33; 21:30
Is a strong fortress—18:10
Rescues good people from danger—11:8, 21
Rewards the godly—11:31
Blesses good people, condemns the wicked—12:2
Delights in our prayers—15:8, 29
Loves those who obey him—11:27; 15:9-10; 16:20; 22:12
Cares for poor, sick, and widows—15:25; 22:22-23
Purifies hearts—17:3
Hates evil—17:5; 21:27; 28:9

OUR RESPONSE SHOULD BE . . .
To reverence God—10:27; 14:26-27; 15:16; 16:6; 19:23; 28:14
To obey God's Word—13:13; 19:16
To please God—16:7; 20:12; 21:3
To trust God—22:17-19; 29:25

27 Lazy people don't even cook the game they catch,
but the diligent make use of everything they find.

28 The way of the godly leads to life;
that path does not lead to death.

13

1 A wise child accepts a parent's discipline;*
a mocker refuses to listen to correction.

2 Wise words will win you a good meal,
but treacherous people have an appetite for violence.

3 Those who control their tongue will have a long life;
opening your mouth can ruin everything.

4 Lazy people want much but get little,
but those who work hard will prosper.

5 The godly hate lies;
the wicked cause shame and disgrace.

6 Godliness guards the path of the blameless,
but the evil are misled by sin.

7 Some who are poor pretend to be rich;
others who are rich pretend to be poor.

8 The rich can pay a ransom for their lives,
but the poor won't even get threatened.

9 The life of the godly is full of light and joy,
but the light of the wicked will be snuffed out.

10 Pride leads to conflict;
those who take advice are wise.

11 Wealth from get-rich-quick schemes quickly disappears;
wealth from hard work grows over time.

12 Hope deferred makes the heart sick,
but a dream fulfilled is a tree of life.

13 People who despise advice are asking for trouble;
those who respect a command will succeed.

14 The instruction of the wise is like a life-giving fountain;
those who accept it avoid the snares of death.

15 A person with good sense is respected;
a treacherous person is headed for destruction.*

16 Wise people think before they act;
fools don't—and even brag about their foolishness.

17 An unreliable messenger stumbles into trouble,
but a reliable messenger brings healing.

18 If you ignore criticism, you will end in poverty and disgrace;
if you accept correction, you will be honored.

19 It is pleasant to see dreams come true,
but fools refuse to turn from evil to attain them.

20 Walk with the wise and become wise;
associate with fools and get in trouble.

21 Trouble chases sinners,
while blessings reward the righteous.

22 Good people leave an inheritance to their grandchildren,
but the sinner's wealth passes to the godly.

23 A poor person's farm may produce much food,
but injustice sweeps it all away.

24 Those who spare the rod of discipline hate their children.

13:1 Hebrew *A wise son accepts his father's discipline.* **13:15** As in Greek version; Hebrew reads *the way of the treacherous is lasting.*

Those who love their children care enough to
discipline them.

25 The godly eat to their hearts' content,
but the belly of the wicked goes hungry.

14

1 A wise woman builds her home,
but a foolish woman tears it down with her
own hands.

2 Those who follow the right path fear the LORD;
those who take the wrong path despise him.

3 A fool's proud talk becomes a rod that beats him,
but the words of the wise keep them safe.

4 Without oxen a stable stays clean,
but you need a strong ox for a large harvest.

5 An honest witness does not lie;
a false witness breathes lies.

6 A mocker seeks wisdom and never finds it,
but knowledge comes easily to those
with understanding.

7 Stay away from fools,
for you won't find knowledge on their lips.

8 The prudent understand where they are going,
but fools deceive themselves.

9 Fools make fun of guilt,
but the godly acknowledge it and seek
reconciliation.

MAKE THINGS RIGHT 14:9

Siblings argue. Husbands and wives part ways. People continue to hold on to past bitterness. But God wants his people to forgive each other. When you know you have wronged someone, are you willing to own up to it or to ask yourself, "How can I make things right with this person?" ■

10 Each heart knows its own bitterness,
and no one else can fully share its joy.

11 The house of the wicked will be destroyed,
but the tent of the godly will flourish.

12 There is a path before each person that
seems right,
but it ends in death.

13 Laughter can conceal a heavy heart,
but when the laughter ends, the grief remains.

14 Backsliders get what they deserve;
good people receive their reward.

15 Only simpletons believe everything they're told!
The prudent carefully consider their steps.

16 The wise are cautious* and avoid danger;
fools plunge ahead with reckless confidence.

17 Short-tempered people do foolish things,
and schemers are hated.

18 Simpletons are clothed with foolishness,*
but the prudent are crowned with knowledge.

19 Evil people will bow before good people;
the wicked will bow at the gates of the godly.

20 The poor are despised even by their neighbors,
while the rich have many "friends."

21 It is a sin to belittle one's neighbor;
blessed are those who help the poor.

22 If you plan to do evil, you will be lost;
if you plan to do good, you will receive unfailing
love and faithfulness.

23 Work brings profit,
but mere talk leads to poverty!

24 Wealth is a crown for the wise;
the effort of fools yields only foolishness.

25 A truthful witness saves lives,
but a false witness is a traitor.

26 Those who fear the LORD are secure;
he will be a refuge for their children.

27 Fear of the LORD is a life-giving fountain;
it offers escape from the snares of death.

28 A growing population is a king's glory;
a prince without subjects has nothing.

29 People with understanding control their anger;
a hot temper shows great foolishness.

30 A peaceful heart leads to a healthy body;
jealousy is like cancer in the bones.

31 Those who oppress the poor insult their Maker,
but helping the poor honors him.

32 The wicked are crushed by disaster,
but the godly have a refuge when they die.

14:16 Hebrew *The wise fear.* **14:18** Or *inherit foolishness.*

[33] Wisdom is enshrined in an understanding heart;
wisdom is not* found among fools.

[34] Godliness makes a nation great,
but sin is a disgrace to any people.

[35] A king rejoices in wise servants
but is angry with those who disgrace him.

15

[1] A gentle answer deflects anger,
but harsh words make tempers flare.

[2] The tongue of the wise makes knowledge appealing,
but the mouth of a fool belches out foolishness.

[3] The LORD is watching everywhere,
keeping his eye on both the evil and the good.

[4] Gentle words are a tree of life;
a deceitful tongue crushes the spirit.

[5] Only a fool despises a parent's* discipline;
whoever learns from correction is wise.

[6] There is treasure in the house of the godly,
but the earnings of the wicked bring trouble.

[7] The lips of the wise give good advice;
the heart of a fool has none to give.

[8] The LORD detests the sacrifice of the wicked,
but he delights in the prayers of the upright.

[9] The LORD detests the way of the wicked,
but he loves those who pursue godliness.

[10] Whoever abandons the right path will be severely disciplined;
whoever hates correction will die.

[11] Even Death and Destruction* hold no secrets from the LORD.
How much more does he know the human heart!

[12] Mockers hate to be corrected,
so they stay away from the wise.

[13] A glad heart makes a happy face;
a broken heart crushes the spirit.

[14] A wise person is hungry for knowledge,
while the fool feeds on trash.

> A gentle answer deflects anger, but harsh words make tempers flare.
>
> *PROVERBS 15:1*

[15] For the despondent, every day brings trouble;
for the happy heart, life is a continual feast.

[16] Better to have little, with fear for the LORD,
than to have great treasure and inner turmoil.

[17] A bowl of vegetables with someone you love
is better than steak with someone you hate.

[18] A hot-tempered person starts fights;
a cool-tempered person stops them.

[19] A lazy person's way is blocked with briers,
but the path of the upright is an open highway.

[20] Sensible children bring joy to their father;
foolish children despise their mother.

[21] Foolishness brings joy to those with no sense;
a sensible person stays on the right path.

[22] Plans go wrong for lack of advice;
many advisers bring success.

[23] Everyone enjoys a fitting reply;
it is wonderful to say the right thing at the right time!

A QUIET RESPONSE 15:1

Have you ever tried to argue in a whisper? It's hard to argue with someone who insists on answering softly. On the other hand, a rising voice almost always triggers an angry response. Want to seek peace instead of arguing? A quiet response is your best choice. ■

[24] The path of life leads upward for the wise;
they leave the grave* behind.

[25] The LORD tears down the house of the proud,
but he protects the property of widows.

[26] The LORD detests evil plans,
but he delights in pure words.

[27] Greed brings grief to the whole family,
but those who hate bribes will live.

[28] The heart of the godly thinks carefully before speaking;
the mouth of the wicked overflows with evil words.

14:33 As in Greek and Syriac versions; Hebrew lacks *not*. 15:5 Hebrew *father's*. 15:11 Hebrew *Sheol and Abaddon*. 15:24 Hebrew *Sheol*.

29 The LORD is far from the wicked,
but he hears the prayers of the righteous.

30 A cheerful look brings joy to the heart;
good news makes for good health.

31 If you listen to constructive criticism,
you will be at home among the wise.

32 If you reject discipline, you only harm yourself;
but if you listen to correction, you grow in
understanding.

33 Fear of the LORD teaches wisdom;
humility precedes honor.

16 1 We can make our own plans,
but the LORD gives the right answer.

2 People may be pure in their own eyes,
but the LORD examines their motives.

3 Commit your actions to the LORD,
and your plans will succeed.

4 The LORD has made everything for his own purposes,
even the wicked for a day of disaster.

5 The LORD detests the proud;
they will surely be punished.

6 Unfailing love and faithfulness make atonement
for sin.
By fearing the LORD, people avoid evil.

7 When people's lives please the LORD,
even their enemies are at peace with them.

8 Better to have little, with godliness,
than to be rich and dishonest.

9 We can make our plans,
but the LORD determines our steps.

10 The king speaks with divine wisdom;
he must never judge unfairly.

11 The LORD demands accurate scales and balances;
he sets the standards for fairness.

12 A king detests wrongdoing,
for his rule is built on justice.

13 The king is pleased with words from righteous lips;
he loves those who speak honestly.

14 The anger of the king is a deadly threat;
the wise will try to appease it.

15 When the king smiles, there is life;
his favor refreshes like a spring rain.

16 How much better to get wisdom than gold,
and good judgment than silver!

17 The path of the virtuous leads away from evil;
whoever follows that path is safe.

18 Pride goes before destruction,
and haughtiness before a fall.

19 Better to live humbly with the poor
than to share plunder with the proud.

20 Those who listen to instruction will prosper;
those who trust the LORD will be joyful.

21 The wise are known for their understanding,
and pleasant words are persuasive.

22 Discretion is a life-giving fountain to those who
possess it,
but discipline is wasted on fools.

23 From a wise mind comes wise speech;
the words of the wise are persuasive.

24 Kind words are like honey—
sweet to the soul and healthy for the body.

25 There is a path before each person that
seems right,
but it ends in death.

26 It is good for workers to have an appetite;
an empty stomach drives them on.

27 Scoundrels create trouble;
their words are a destructive blaze.

28 A troublemaker plants seeds of strife;
gossip separates the best of friends.

29 Violent people mislead their companions,
leading them down a harmful path.

30 With narrowed eyes, people plot evil;
with a smirk, they plan their mischief.

31 Gray hair is a crown of glory;
it is gained by living a godly life.

32 Better to be patient than powerful;
better to have self-control than to conquer
a city.

33 We may throw the dice,*
but the LORD determines how they fall.

16:33 Hebrew *We may cast lots.*

17

1 Better a dry crust eaten in peace
than a house filled with feasting—and conflict.

2 A wise servant will rule over the master's
disgraceful son
and will share the inheritance of the master's
children.

3 Fire tests the purity of silver and gold,
but the LORD tests the heart.

4 Wrongdoers eagerly listen to gossip;
liars pay close attention to slander.

5 Those who mock the poor insult their Maker;
those who rejoice at the misfortune of others
will be punished.

A MAJOR INSULT 17:5

Few acts are as cruel as making fun of those who are less fortunate, but many people do it because it makes them feel good to be better off or more successful than someone else. But God takes personally any insults leveled at the poor, the weak, those who are different, or anyone who is an easy target. Making fun of them is the same as making fun of him. Want to be wise? Avoid this. ■

6 Grandchildren are the crowning glory of the aged;
parents* are the pride of their children.

7 Eloquent words are not fitting for a fool;
even less are lies fitting for a ruler.

8 A bribe is like a lucky charm;
whoever gives one will prosper!

9 Love prospers when a fault is forgiven,
but dwelling on it separates close friends.

10 A single rebuke does more for a person of
understanding
than a hundred lashes on the back of a fool.

11 Evil people are eager for rebellion,
but they will be severely punished.

12 It is safer to meet a bear robbed of her cubs
than to confront a fool caught in foolishness.

13 If you repay good with evil,
evil will never leave your house.

14 Starting a quarrel is like opening a floodgate,
so stop before a dispute breaks out.

15 Acquitting the guilty and condemning the innocent—
both are detestable to the LORD.

16 It is senseless to pay tuition to educate a fool,
since he has no heart for learning.

17 A friend is always loyal,
and a brother is born to help in time of need.

18 It's poor judgment to guarantee another
person's debt
or put up security for a friend.

19 Anyone who loves to quarrel loves sin;
anyone who trusts in high walls invites disaster.

20 The crooked heart will not prosper;
the lying tongue tumbles into trouble.

21 It is painful to be the parent of a fool;
there is no joy for the father of a rebel.

22 A cheerful heart is good medicine,
but a broken spirit saps a person's strength.

23 The wicked take secret bribes
to pervert the course of justice.

24 Sensible people keep their eyes glued on wisdom,
but a fool's eyes wander to the ends of the earth.

25 Foolish children* bring grief to their father
and bitterness to the one who gave them birth.

26 It is wrong to punish the godly for being good
or to flog leaders for being honest.

27 A truly wise person uses few words;
a person with understanding is even-tempered.

28 Even fools are thought wise when they keep silent;
with their mouths shut, they seem intelligent.

18

1 Unfriendly people care only about
themselves;
they lash out at common sense.

2 Fools have no interest in understanding;
they only want to air their own opinions.

3 Doing wrong leads to disgrace,
and scandalous behavior brings contempt.

4 Wise words are like deep waters;
wisdom flows from the wise like a
bubbling brook.

17:6 Hebrew *fathers.* 17:25 Hebrew *A foolish son.*

5 It is not right to acquit the guilty
or deny justice to the innocent.

6 Fools' words get them into constant quarrels;
they are asking for a beating.

7 The mouths of fools are their ruin;
they trap themselves with their lips.

8 Rumors are dainty morsels
that sink deep into one's heart.

9 A lazy person is as bad as
someone who destroys things.

10 The name of the LORD is a strong fortress;
the godly run to him and are safe.

11 The rich think of their wealth as a strong defense;
they imagine it to be a high wall of safety.

12 Haughtiness goes before destruction;
humility precedes honor.

13 Spouting off before listening to the facts
is both shameful and foolish.

14 The human spirit can endure a sick body,
but who can bear a crushed spirit?

15 Intelligent people are always ready to learn.
Their ears are open for
knowledge.

16 Giving a gift can open doors;
it gives access to important
people!

17 The first to speak in court sounds
right—
until the cross-examination
begins.

18 Flipping a coin* can end arguments;
it settles disputes between
powerful opponents.

19 An offended friend is harder to win back than a
fortified city.
Arguments separate friends like a gate locked
with bars.

20 Wise words satisfy like a good meal;
the right words bring satisfaction.

21 The tongue can bring death or life;
those who love to talk will reap the consequences.

22 The man who finds a wife finds a treasure,
and he receives favor from the LORD.

23 The poor plead for mercy;
the rich answer with insults.

24 There are "friends" who destroy each other,
but a real friend sticks closer than a brother.

TRUE FRIENDSHIP 18:24

Many people today feel isolated from others. Ever feel that way? Being in a crowd might make you more aware of your isolation. Lonely people don't need to hear "Have a nice day." They need friends who will stick close, listen, care, and offer help when it is needed—in good and bad times. It is better to have one such friend than dozens of superficial acquaintances. Instead of wishing you could find a true friend, why not seek to become one yourself. There are people who need your friendship. Ask God to reveal them to you, and then take on the challenge of being a true friend.

19

1 Better to be poor and honest
than to be dishonest and a fool.

2 Enthusiasm without knowledge is no good;
haste makes mistakes.

3 People ruin their lives by their own foolishness
and then are angry at the LORD.

4 Wealth makes many "friends";
poverty drives them all away.

5 A false witness will not go
unpunished,
nor will a liar escape.

6 Many seek favors from a ruler;
everyone is the friend of a
person who gives gifts!

7 The relatives of the poor despise
them;
how much more will their
friends avoid them!
Though the poor plead with them,
their friends are gone.

8 To acquire wisdom is to love oneself;
people who cherish understanding will prosper.

9 A false witness will not go unpunished,
and a liar will be destroyed.

10 It isn't right for a fool to live in luxury
or for a slave to rule over princes!

11 Sensible people control their temper;
they earn respect by overlooking wrongs.

> There are "friends" who destroy each other, but a real friend sticks closer than a brother.
> *PROVERBS 18:24*

18:18 Hebrew *Casting lots.*

12 The king's anger is like a lion's roar,
but his favor is like dew on the grass.

13 A foolish child* is a calamity to a father;
a quarrelsome wife is as annoying as constant dripping.

14 Fathers can give their sons an inheritance of houses and wealth,
but only the LORD can give an understanding wife.

15 Lazy people sleep soundly,
but idleness leaves them hungry.

16 Keep the commandments and keep your life;
despising them leads to death.

17 If you help the poor, you are lending to the LORD—
and he will repay you!

18 Discipline your children while there is hope.
Otherwise you will ruin their lives.

19 Hot-tempered people must pay the penalty.
If you rescue them once, you will have to do it again.

20 Get all the advice and instruction you can,
so you will be wise the rest of your life.

21 You can make many plans,
but the LORD's purpose will prevail.

INNER BEAUTY 19:22

Many people spend tons of money trying to improve the way they look outside. Unfortunately, they sometimes neglect their inner appearance. Inwardly, you can be as attractive as you want to be. You can have kindness, for example, in any amount you choose. Or, as this verse suggests, you can be loyal. You can control your most important asset: the attractiveness of your character. ■

22 Loyalty makes a person attractive.
It is better to be poor than dishonest.

23 Fear of the LORD leads to life,
bringing security and protection from harm.

24 Lazy people take food in their hand
but don't even lift it to their mouth.

To acquire wisdom is to love oneself; people who cherish understanding will prosper.

PROVERBS 19:8

25 If you punish a mocker, the simpleminded will learn a lesson;
if you correct the wise, they will be all the wiser.

26 Children who mistreat their father or chase away their mother
are an embarrassment and a public disgrace.

27 If you stop listening to instruction, my child,
you will turn your back on knowledge.

28 A corrupt witness makes a mockery of justice;
the mouth of the wicked gulps down evil.

29 Punishment is made for mockers,
and the backs of fools are made to be beaten.

20

1 Wine produces mockers; alcohol leads to brawls.
Those led astray by drink cannot be wise.

2 The king's fury is like a lion's roar;
to rouse his anger is to risk your life.

3 Avoiding a fight is a mark of honor;
only fools insist on quarreling.

4 Those too lazy to plow in the right season
will have no food at the harvest.

5 Though good advice lies deep within the heart,
a person with understanding will draw it out.

6 Many will say they are loyal friends,
but who can find one who is truly reliable?

7 The godly walk with integrity;
blessed are their children who follow them.

8 When a king sits in judgment, he weighs all the evidence,
distinguishing the bad from the good.

9 Who can say, "I have cleansed my heart;
I am pure and free from sin"?

10 False weights and unequal measures*—
the LORD detests double standards of every kind.

11 Even children are known by the way they act,
whether their conduct is pure, and whether it is right.

19:13 Hebrew *son;* also in 19:27. 20:10 Hebrew *A stone and a stone, an ephah and an ephah.*

12 Ears to hear and eyes to see—
both are gifts from the LORD.

13 If you love sleep, you will end in poverty.
Keep your eyes open, and there will be plenty to eat!

14 The buyer haggles over the price, saying, "It's worthless,"
then brags about getting a bargain!

15 Wise words are more valuable
than much gold and many rubies.

16 Get security from someone who guarantees a stranger's debt.
Get a deposit if he does it for foreigners.*

17 Stolen bread tastes sweet,
but it turns to gravel in the mouth.

18 Plans succeed through good counsel;
don't go to war without wise advice.

19 A gossip goes around telling secrets,
so don't hang around with chatterers.

20 If you insult your father or mother,
your light will be snuffed out in total darkness.

21 An inheritance obtained too early in life
is not a blessing in the end.

22 Don't say, "I will get even for this wrong."
Wait for the LORD to handle the matter.

23 The LORD detests double standards;
he is not pleased by dishonest scales.

24 The LORD directs our steps,
so why try to understand everything along the way?

25 Don't trap yourself by making a rash promise to God
and only later counting the cost.

26 A wise king scatters the wicked like wheat,
then runs his threshing wheel over them.

27 The LORD's light penetrates the human spirit,*
exposing every hidden motive.

28 Unfailing love and faithfulness protect the king;
his throne is made secure through love.

29 The glory of the young is their strength;
the gray hair of experience is the splendor of the old.

30 Physical punishment cleanses away evil;*
such discipline purifies the heart.

21

1 The king's heart is like a stream of water directed by the LORD;
he guides it wherever he pleases.

2 People may be right in their own eyes,
but the LORD examines their heart.

MOTIVES 21:2

People can find an excuse for doing almost anything, but God looks behind the excuse to the motives of the heart. We often have to make difficult choices in areas of life where the right action is hard to discern. A good first step to making such a decision is to identify our motives. For example, are we serving others in order to gain attention? Identifying our motives can help us avoid phony actions. ■

3 The LORD is more pleased when we do what is right and just
than when we offer him sacrifices.

4 Haughty eyes, a proud heart,
and evil actions are all sin.

5 Good planning and hard work lead to prosperity,
but hasty shortcuts lead to poverty.

6 Wealth created by a lying tongue
is a vanishing mist and a deadly trap.*

7 The violence of the wicked sweeps them away,
because they refuse to do what is just.

8 The guilty walk a crooked path;
the innocent travel a straight road.

9 It's better to live alone in the corner of an attic
than with a quarrelsome wife in a lovely home.

10 Evil people desire evil;
their neighbors get no mercy from them.

11 If you punish a mocker, the simpleminded become wise;
if you instruct the wise, they will be all the wiser.

12 The Righteous One* knows what is going on in the homes of the wicked;
he will bring disaster on them.

13 Those who shut their ears to the cries of the poor
will be ignored in their own time of need.

20:16 An alternate reading in the Hebrew text is *for a promiscuous woman.* **20:27** Or *The human spirit is the LORD's light.* **20:30** The meaning of the Hebrew is uncertain. **21:6** As in Greek version; Hebrew reads *mist for those who seek death.* **21:12** Or *The righteous man.*

14 A secret gift calms anger;
a bribe under the table pacifies fury.

15 Justice is a joy to the godly,
but it terrifies evildoers.

16 The person who strays from common sense
will end up in the company of the dead.

17 Those who love pleasure become poor;
those who love wine and luxury will never be rich.

18 The wicked are punished in place of the godly,
and traitors in place of the honest.

19 It's better to live alone in the desert
than with a quarrelsome, complaining wife.

20 The wise have wealth and luxury,
but fools spend whatever they get.

21 Whoever pursues righteousness and unfailing love
will find life, righteousness, and honor.

22 The wise conquer the city of the strong
and level the fortress in which they trust.

23 Watch your tongue and keep your mouth shut,
and you will stay out of trouble.

24 Mockers are proud and haughty;
they act with boundless arrogance.

25 Despite their desires, the lazy will come to ruin,
for their hands refuse to work.

26 Some people are always greedy for more,
but the godly love to give!

27 The sacrifice of an evil person is detestable,
especially when it is offered with wrong motives.

28 A false witness will be cut off,
but a credible witness will be allowed to speak.

29 The wicked bluff their way through,
but the virtuous think before they act.

30 No human wisdom or understanding or plan
can stand against the LORD.

31 The horse is prepared for the day of battle,
but the victory belongs to the LORD.

22

1 Choose a good reputation over great riches;
being held in high esteem is better than silver or gold.

2 The rich and poor have this in common:
The LORD made them both.

3 A prudent person foresees danger and takes precautions.
The simpleton goes blindly on and suffers the consequences.

4 True humility and fear of the LORD
lead to riches, honor, and long life.

5 Corrupt people walk a thorny, treacherous road;
whoever values life will avoid it.

6 Direct your children onto the right path,
and when they are older, they will not leave it.

7 Just as the rich rule the poor,
so the borrower is servant to the lender.

8 Those who plant injustice will harvest disaster,
and their reign of terror will come to an end.*

9 Blessed are those who are generous,
because they feed the poor.

10 Throw out the mocker, and fighting goes, too.
Quarrels and insults will disappear.

11 Whoever loves a pure heart and gracious speech
will have the king as a friend.

12 The LORD preserves those with knowledge,
but he ruins the plans of the treacherous.

13 The lazy person claims, "There's a lion out there!
If I go outside, I might be killed!"

14 The mouth of an immoral woman is a dangerous trap;
those who make the LORD angry will fall into it.

15 A youngster's heart is filled with foolishness,
but physical discipline will drive it far away.

16 A person who gets ahead by oppressing the poor
or by showering gifts on the rich will end in poverty.

SAYINGS OF THE WISE

17 Listen to the words of the wise;
apply your heart to my instruction.
18 For it is good to keep these sayings in your heart
and always ready on your lips.
19 I am teaching you today—yes, you—
so you will trust in the LORD.
20 I have written thirty sayings* for you,
filled with advice and knowledge.

22:8 The Greek version includes an additional proverb: *God blesses a man who gives cheerfully, / but his worthless deeds will come to an end.* Compare 2 Cor 9:7. **22:20** Or *excellent sayings;* the meaning of the Hebrew is uncertain.

21 In this way, you may know the truth
and take an accurate report to those who
sent you.

22 Don't rob the poor just because you can,
or exploit the needy in court.
23 For the LORD is their defender.
He will ruin anyone who ruins them.

CHOOSING FRIENDS 22:24-25

People tend to become like those around them. Even the negative characteristics sometimes rub off. The Bible exhorts us to be cautious in our choice of friends. When it comes to your friends, how choosy are you? ■

24 Don't befriend angry people
or associate with hot-tempered people,
25 or you will learn to be like them
and endanger your soul.

26 Don't agree to guarantee another person's debt
or put up security for someone else.
27 If you can't pay it,
even your bed will be snatched from under you.

28 Don't cheat your neighbor by moving the ancient
boundary markers
set up by previous generations.

29 Do you see any truly competent workers?
They will serve kings
rather than working for ordinary people.

23

1 While dining with a ruler,
pay attention to what is put before you.
2 If you are a big eater,
put a knife to your throat;
3 don't desire all the delicacies,
for he might be trying to trick you.

4 Don't wear yourself out trying to get rich.
Be wise enough to know when to quit.
5 In the blink of an eye wealth disappears,
for it will sprout wings
and fly away like an eagle.

6 Don't eat with people who are stingy;
don't desire their delicacies.
7 They are always thinking about how much
it costs.*
"Eat and drink," they say, but they don't mean it.
8 You will throw up what little you've eaten,
and your compliments will be wasted.

9 Don't waste your breath on fools,
for they will despise the wisest advice.

10 Don't cheat your neighbor by moving the ancient
boundary markers;
don't take the land of defenseless orphans.
11 For their Redeemer* is strong;
he himself will bring their charges against you.

12 Commit yourself to instruction;
listen carefully to words of knowledge.

13 Don't fail to discipline your children.
They won't die if you spank them.
14 Physical discipline
may well save them from death.*

15 My child,* if your heart is wise,
my own heart will rejoice!
16 Everything in me will celebrate
when you speak what is right.

17 Don't envy sinners,
but always continue to fear the LORD.
18 You will be rewarded for this;
your hope will not be disappointed.

19 My child, listen and be wise:
Keep your heart on the right course.
20 Do not carouse with drunkards
or feast with gluttons,
21 for they are on their way to poverty,
and too much sleep clothes them in rags.

22 Listen to your father, who gave you life,
and don't despise your mother when she is old.
23 Get the truth and never sell it;
also get wisdom, discipline, and good judgment.
24 The father of godly children has cause for joy.
What a pleasure to have children who are wise.*
25 So give your father and mother joy!
May she who gave you birth be happy.

26 O my son, give me your heart.
May your eyes take delight in following my ways.
27 A prostitute is a dangerous trap;
a promiscuous woman is as dangerous as falling
into a narrow well.
28 She hides and waits like a robber,
eager to make more men unfaithful.

29 Who has anguish? Who has sorrow?
Who is always fighting? Who is always
complaining?
Who has unnecessary bruises? Who has
bloodshot eyes?
30 It is the one who spends long hours in the taverns,
trying out new drinks.

23:7 The meaning of the Hebrew is uncertain. 23:11 Or *redeemer.* 23:14 Hebrew *from Sheol.* 23:15 Hebrew *My son;* also in 23:19. 23:24 Hebrew *to have a wise son.*

DRINKING

The first time 13-year-old Paul drank with his friends, Mario and Antoine, it was kind of exciting. With the help of a college student, the three guys managed to get a six-pack—two beers each. It wasn't enough to get smashed, but it was enough to get a slight buzz. Sipping slowly as they sat around a campfire, the boys laughed for several hours. The next day Mario suggested, "We should do this more often!"

So each weekend they played the game, always coming up with a new scheme to acquire alcohol. Once they stumbled upon a block party where there were three "unguarded" kegs just sitting there. Another time they swiped a bottle of vodka from a neighbor's liquor cabinet. Another time a high school senior bought them some tequila and showed them how to shoot it.

Every now and then one of the guys would overdo it and end up with a mean hangover. But they never got caught. It didn't affect their grades at school since they only did it on weekends. Yeah, they thought everything was cool.

How do you feel about alcohol? Read Proverbs 23:29-35 for a good portrait of what drink can do.

31 Don't gaze at the wine, seeing how red it is,
how it sparkles in the cup, how smoothly
it goes down.
32 For in the end it bites like a poisonous snake;
it stings like a viper.
33 You will see hallucinations,
and you will say crazy things.
34 You will stagger like a sailor tossed at sea,
clinging to a swaying mast.
35 And you will say, "They hit me, but I didn't feel it.
I didn't even know it when they beat me up.
When will I wake up
so I can look for another drink?"

24

1 Don't envy evil people
or desire their company.
2 For their hearts plot violence,
and their words always stir up trouble.

3 A house is built by wisdom
and becomes strong through good sense.
4 Through knowledge its rooms are filled
with all sorts of precious riches and valuables.

5 The wise are mightier than the strong,*
and those with knowledge grow stronger
and stronger.
6 So don't go to war without wise guidance;
victory depends on having many advisers.
7 Wisdom is too lofty for fools.
Among leaders at the city gate, they have
nothing to say.

8 A person who plans evil
will get a reputation as a troublemaker.
9 The schemes of a fool are sinful;
everyone detests a mocker.

10 If you fail under pressure,
your strength is too small.

11 Rescue those who are unjustly sentenced to die;
save them as they stagger to their death.
12 Don't excuse yourself by saying, "Look, we
didn't know."
For God understands all hearts, and he sees you.
He who guards your soul knows you knew.
He will repay all people as their actions deserve.

13 My child,* eat honey, for it is good,
and the honeycomb is sweet to the taste.
14 In the same way, wisdom is sweet to your soul.
If you find it, you will have a bright future,
and your hopes will not be cut short.

15 Don't wait in ambush at the home of the godly,
and don't raid the house where the godly live.
16 The godly may trip seven times, but they will get
up again.
But one disaster is enough to overthrow
the wicked.

THE STING OF DRINKING 23:29-35

Some people drink in order to seem cool. Others might drink to find relief from their problems. But the "comfort" of alcohol is only temporary. Real relief comes from dealing with the cause of anguish and sorrow, and turning to God for peace. Getting drunk leads to more problems. As this passage states, "in the end it bites like a poisonous snake; it stings like a viper" (23:32). ■

17 Don't rejoice when your enemies fall;
don't be happy when they stumble.
18 For the LORD will be displeased with you
and will turn his anger away from them.

19 Don't fret because of evildoers;
don't envy the wicked.
20 For evil people have no future;
the light of the wicked will be snuffed out.

21 My child, fear the LORD and the king.
Don't associate with rebels,
22 for disaster will hit them suddenly.

24:5 As in Greek version; Hebrew reads *A wise man is strength.* **24:13** Hebrew *My son;* also in 24:21.

Who knows what punishment will come
from the LORD and the king?

MORE SAYINGS OF THE WISE

23 Here are some further sayings of the wise:

It is wrong to show favoritism when passing
judgment.
24 A judge who says to the wicked, "You are innocent,"
will be cursed by many people and denounced by
the nations.
25 But it will go well for those who convict the guilty;
rich blessings will be showered on them.

26 An honest answer
is like a kiss of friendship.

27 Do your planning and prepare your fields
before building your house.

28 Don't testify against your neighbors without cause;
don't lie about them.
29 And don't say, "Now I can pay them back for what
they've done to me!
I'll get even with them!"

30 I walked by the field of a lazy person,
the vineyard of one with no common sense.
31 I saw that it was overgrown with nettles.
It was covered with weeds,
and its walls were broken down.
32 Then, as I looked and thought about it,
I learned this lesson:
33 A little extra sleep, a little more slumber,
a little folding of the hands to rest—
34 then poverty will pounce on you like a bandit;
scarcity will attack you like an armed robber.

25 MORE PROVERBS OF SOLOMON

These are more proverbs of Solomon, collected by the advisers of King Hezekiah of Judah.

2 It is God's privilege to conceal things
and the king's privilege to discover them.

3 No one can comprehend the height of heaven,
the depth of the earth,
or all that goes on in the king's mind!

4 Remove the impurities from silver,
and the sterling will be ready for the silversmith.
5 Remove the wicked from the king's court,
and his reign will be made secure by justice.

6 Don't demand an audience with the king
or push for a place among the great.
7 It's better to wait for an invitation to the head table
than to be sent away in public disgrace.
Just because you've seen something,
8 don't be in a hurry to go to court.
For what will you do in the end
if your neighbor deals you a shameful defeat?

9 When arguing with your neighbor,
don't betray another person's secret.
10 Others may accuse you of gossip,
and you will never regain your good reputation.

11 Timely advice is lovely,
like golden apples in a silver basket.

12 To one who listens, valid criticism
is like a gold earring or other gold jewelry.

13 Trustworthy messengers refresh like snow in summer.
They revive the spirit of their employer.

14 A person who promises a gift but doesn't give it
is like clouds and wind that bring no rain.

15 Patience can persuade a prince,
and soft speech can break bones.

16 Do you like honey?
Don't eat too much, or it will make you sick!

17 Don't visit your neighbors too often,
or you will wear out your welcome.

LYING 25:18

The effects of lying can be as permanent as those of a stab wound. Yet sometimes, we don't call our actions lies. Instead, we might pass on information or "stretch the truth" a little. A lie by any other name is still a lie. The next time you are tempted to pass on a bit of gossip, imagine yourself striking the victim of your remarks with a sword. This image may shock you into silence. ■

18 Telling lies about others
is as harmful as hitting them with an ax,
wounding them with a sword,
or shooting them with a sharp arrow.

19 Putting confidence in an unreliable person in times
of trouble
is like chewing with a broken tooth or walking on
a lame foot.

20 Singing cheerful songs to a person with a heavy heart
is like taking someone's coat in cold weather
or pouring vinegar in a wound.*

21 If your enemies are hungry, give them food to eat.
If they are thirsty, give them water to drink.

25:20 As in Greek version; Hebrew reads *pouring vinegar on soda.*

22 You will heap burning coals of shame on their heads,
and the LORD will reward you.

23 As surely as a north wind brings rain,
so a gossiping tongue causes anger!

24 It's better to live alone in the corner of an attic
than with a quarrelsome wife in a lovely home.

25 Good news from far away
is like cold water to the thirsty.

26 If the godly give in to the wicked,
it's like polluting a fountain or muddying a spring.

27 It's not good to eat too much honey,
and it's not good to seek honors for yourself.

28 A person without self-control
is like a city with broken-down walls.

26

1 Honor is no more associated with fools
than snow with summer or rain with harvest.

2 Like a fluttering sparrow or a darting swallow,
an undeserved curse will not land on its intended victim.

3 Guide a horse with a whip, a donkey with a bridle,
and a fool with a rod to his back!

4 Don't answer the foolish arguments of fools,
or you will become as foolish as they are.

5 Be sure to answer the foolish arguments of fools,
or they will become wise in their own estimation.

6 Trusting a fool to convey a message
is like cutting off one's feet or drinking poison!

7 A proverb in the mouth of a fool
is as useless as a paralyzed leg.

8 Honoring a fool
is as foolish as tying a stone to a slingshot.

9 A proverb in the mouth of a fool
is like a thorny branch brandished by a drunk.

10 An employer who hires a fool or a bystander
is like an archer who shoots at random.

11 As a dog returns to its vomit,
so a fool repeats his foolishness.

12 There is more hope for fools
than for people who think they are wise.

13 The lazy person claims, "There's a lion on the road!
Yes, I'm sure there's a lion out there!"

14 As a door swings back and forth on its hinges,
so the lazy person turns over in bed.

15 Lazy people take food in their hand
but don't even lift it to their mouth.

LAZINESS 26:13-16

If a person is not willing to work, he or she can find endless excuses to avoid it. But laziness is more dangerous than a fierce lion. The less you do, the less you want to do, and the more useless you become. Overcoming laziness or procrastination can be achieved by these small steps toward change: (1) Set a concrete, realistic goal; (2) figure out the steps needed to reach it; and (3) pray for strength and persistence. ■

16 Lazy people consider themselves smarter
than seven wise counselors.

17 Interfering in someone else's argument
is as foolish as yanking a dog's ears.

18 Just as damaging
as a madman shooting a deadly weapon
19 is someone who lies to a friend
and then says, "I was only joking."

20 Fire goes out without wood,
and quarrels disappear when gossip stops.

21 A quarrelsome person starts fights
as easily as hot embers light charcoal or fire lights wood.

22 Rumors are dainty morsels
that sink deep into one's heart.

23 Smooth* words may hide a wicked heart,
just as a pretty glaze covers a clay pot.

24 People may cover their hatred with pleasant words,
but they're deceiving you.
25 They pretend to be kind, but don't believe them.
Their hearts are full of many evils.*
26 While their hatred may be concealed by trickery,
their wrongdoing will be exposed in public.

27 If you set a trap for others,
you will get caught in it yourself.
If you roll a boulder down on others,
it will crush you instead.

26:23 As in Greek version; Hebrew reads *Burning*. **26:25** Hebrew *seven evils*.

28 A lying tongue hates its victims,
and flattering words cause ruin.

27

1 Don't brag about tomorrow,
since you don't know what the day will bring.

2 Let someone else praise you, not your own mouth—
a stranger, not your own lips.

3 A stone is heavy and sand is weighty,
but the resentment caused by a fool is even heavier.

4 Anger is cruel, and wrath is like a flood,
but jealousy is even more dangerous.

5 An open rebuke
is better than hidden love!

6 Wounds from a sincere friend
are better than many kisses from an enemy.

7 A person who is full refuses honey,
but even bitter food tastes sweet to the hungry.

8 A person who strays from home
is like a bird that strays from its nest.

9 The heartfelt counsel of a friend
is as sweet as perfume and incense.

10 Never abandon a friend—
either yours or your father's.
When disaster strikes, you won't have to ask your brother for assistance.
It's better to go to a neighbor than to a brother who lives far away.

11 Be wise, my child,* and make my heart glad.
Then I will be able to answer my critics.

12 A prudent person foresees danger and takes precautions.
The simpleton goes blindly on and suffers the consequences.

13 Get security from someone who guarantees a stranger's debt.
Get a deposit if he does it for foreigners.*

14 A loud and cheerful greeting early in the morning
will be taken as a curse!

15 A quarrelsome wife is as annoying
as constant dripping on a rainy day.

16 Stopping her complaints is like trying to stop the wind
or trying to hold something with greased hands.

NAGGING 27:15-16

People nag because they think they're not getting through to the person to whom they're talking. Yet nagging sometimes hinders communication more than it helps. When tempted to engage in this destructive habit, stop and examine your motives. Are you more concerned about yourself—about getting your way or being right—than about the person you are "helping"? If you truly are concerned about other people, here is a more effective way to get through to them: Surprise them with words of love and patience. See what happens. ■

17 As iron sharpens iron,
so a friend sharpens a friend.

18 As workers who tend a fig tree are allowed to eat the fruit,
so workers who protect their employer's interests will be rewarded.

19 As a face is reflected in water,
so the heart reflects the real person.

20 Just as Death and Destruction* are never satisfied,
so human desire is never satisfied.

21 Fire tests the purity of silver and gold,
but a person is tested by being praised.*

22 You cannot separate fools from their foolishness,
even though you grind them like grain with mortar and pestle.

23 Know the state of your flocks,
and put your heart into caring for your herds,
24 for riches don't last forever,
and the crown might not be passed to the next generation.
25 After the hay is harvested and the new crop appears
and the mountain grasses are gathered in,
26 your sheep will provide wool for clothing,
and your goats will provide the price of a field.
27 And you will have enough goats' milk for yourself,
your family, and your servant girls.

28

1 The wicked run away when no one is chasing them,
but the godly are as bold as lions.

27:11 Hebrew *my son.* **27:13** As in Greek and Latin versions (see also 20:16); Hebrew reads *for a promiscuous woman.* **27:20** Hebrew *Sheol and Abaddon.* **27:21** Or *by flattery.*

[2] When there is moral rot within a nation, its
government topples easily.
But wise and knowledgeable leaders bring stability.

[3] A poor person who oppresses the poor
is like a pounding rain that destroys the crops.

[4] To reject the law is to praise the wicked;
to obey the law is to fight them.

[5] Evil people don't understand justice,
but those who follow the LORD understand
completely.

[6] Better to be poor and honest
than to be dishonest and rich.

[7] Young people who obey the law are wise;
those with wild friends bring shame to their
parents.*

[8] Income from charging high interest rates
will end up in the pocket of someone who is kind
to the poor.

[9] God detests the prayers
of a person who ignores the law.

INTENTIONS 28:9

God does not listen to our prayers if we intend to go back to what we did wrong as soon as we get off our knees. If we want to forsake our sin and follow him, however, he willingly listens—no matter how bad our wrongdoing has been. What closes his ears is not the depth of our sin, but the shallowness of our "repentance." ■

[10] Those who lead good people along an evil path
will fall into their own trap,
but the honest will inherit good things.

[11] Rich people may think they are wise,
but a poor person with discernment can see right
through them.

[12] When the godly succeed, everyone is glad.
When the wicked take charge, people go into
hiding.

[13] People who conceal their sins will not prosper,
but if they confess and turn from them, they will
receive mercy.

[14] Blessed are those who fear to do wrong,*
but the stubborn are headed for serious trouble.

[15] A wicked ruler is as dangerous to the poor
as a roaring lion or an attacking bear.

[16] A ruler with no understanding will oppress his
people,
but one who hates corruption will have a long life.

[17] A murderer's tormented conscience will drive him
into the grave.
Don't protect him!

[18] The blameless will be rescued from harm,
but the crooked will be suddenly destroyed.

[19] A hard worker has plenty of food,
but a person who chases fantasies ends up
in poverty.

[20] The trustworthy person will get a rich reward,
but a person who wants quick riches will get into
trouble.

[21] Showing partiality is never good,
yet some will do wrong for a mere piece of bread.

[22] Greedy people try to get rich quick
but don't realize they're headed for poverty.

[23] In the end, people appreciate honest criticism
far more than flattery.

[24] Anyone who steals from his father and mother
and says, "What's wrong with that?"
is no better than a murderer.

[25] Greed causes fighting;
trusting the LORD leads to prosperity.

[26] Those who trust their own insight are foolish,
but anyone who walks in wisdom is safe.

[27] Whoever gives to the poor will lack nothing,
but those who close their eyes to poverty will
be cursed.

[28] When the wicked take charge, people go
into hiding.
When the wicked meet disaster, the
godly flourish.

29

[1] Whoever stubbornly refuses to accept
criticism
will suddenly be destroyed beyond recovery.

[2] When the godly are in authority, the people rejoice.
But when the wicked are in power, they groan.

[3] The man who loves wisdom brings joy to his father,
but if he hangs around with prostitutes, his wealth
is wasted.

28:7 Hebrew *their father.* **28:14** Or *those who fear the LORD;* Hebrew reads *those who fear.*

keeping it real

I went to England with a missions group to do street evangelism right after I graduated from high school. Once I got out on the street, supposedly ready to talk to someone, I froze. I was struck with fear and couldn't say a word.

It really bothered me. That evening I looked up "fear" in a concordance, and read through several Scriptures. The verse that helped me most was Proverbs 29:25: "Fearing people is a dangerous trap, but trusting the LORD means safety." I realized that I had fallen into Satan's trap because I was afraid of people—what they would think of me, even what they might do to me—if I tried to share the gospel. I vowed that I would trust God.

The next day I was still nervous. So, I asked God to keep me from falling into the trap of fear and to help me know what to say. Things went much better. As I trusted God to help and protect me during that missions trip, I grew more and more bold in sharing my faith. I actually came to enjoy it! But I might have stayed stuck in fear if I hadn't found that verse and really applied it to my situation. **—Kristen**

4 A just king gives stability to his nation,
but one who demands bribes destroys it.

5 To flatter friends
is to lay a trap for their feet.

6 Evil people are trapped by sin,
but the righteous escape, shouting for joy.

7 The godly care about the rights of the poor;
the wicked don't care at all.

8 Mockers can get a whole town agitated,
but the wise will calm anger.

9 If a wise person takes a fool to court,
there will be ranting and ridicule but no
satisfaction.

10 The bloodthirsty hate blameless people,
but the upright seek to help them.*

11 Fools vent their anger,
but the wise quietly hold it back.

12 If a ruler pays attention to liars,
all his advisers will be wicked.

13 The poor and the oppressor have this in common—
the LORD gives sight to the eyes of both.

14 If a king judges the poor fairly,
his throne will last forever.

15 To discipline a child produces wisdom,
but a mother is disgraced by an undisciplined child.

16 When the wicked are in authority, sin flourishes,
but the godly will live to see their downfall.

17 Discipline your children, and they will give you peace
of mind
and will make your heart glad.

18 When people do not accept divine guidance, they
run wild.
But whoever obeys the law is joyful.

19 Words alone will not discipline a servant;
the words may be understood, but they are
not heeded.

20 There is more hope for a fool
than for someone who speaks without thinking.

21 A servant pampered from childhood
will become a rebel.

22 An angry person starts fights;
a hot-tempered person commits all kinds of sin.

23 Pride ends in humiliation,
while humility brings honor.

24 If you assist a thief, you only hurt yourself.
You are sworn to tell the truth, but you dare
not testify.

29:10 Or *The bloodthirsty hate blameless people, / and they seek to kill the upright*; Hebrew reads *The bloodthirsty hate blameless people; / as for the upright, they seek their life.*

[25] Fearing people is a dangerous trap,
but trusting the LORD means safety.

[26] Many seek the ruler's favor,
but justice comes from the LORD.

[27] The righteous despise the unjust;
the wicked despise the godly.

30 THE SAYINGS OF AGUR

The sayings of Agur son of Jakeh contain this message.*

I am weary, O God;
I am weary and worn out, O God.*
[2] I am too stupid to be human,
and I lack common sense.
[3] I have not mastered human wisdom,
nor do I know the Holy One.

[4] Who but God goes up to heaven and comes back down?
Who holds the wind in his fists?
Who wraps up the oceans in his cloak?
Who has created the whole wide world?
What is his name—and his son's name?
Tell me if you know!

[5] Every word of God proves true.
He is a shield to all who come to him for protection.
[6] Do not add to his words,
or he may rebuke you and expose you as a liar.

[7] O God, I beg two favors from you;
let me have them before I die.
[8] First, help me never to tell a lie.
Second, give me neither poverty nor riches!
Give me just enough to satisfy my needs.
[9] For if I grow rich, I may deny you and say, "Who is the LORD?"
And if I am too poor, I may steal and thus insult God's holy name.

[10] Never slander a worker to the employer,
or the person will curse you, and you will pay for it.

[11] Some people curse their father
and do not thank their mother.
[12] They are pure in their own eyes,
but they are filthy and unwashed.
[13] They look proudly around,
casting disdainful glances.
[14] They have teeth like swords
and fangs like knives.
They devour the poor from the earth
and the needy from among humanity.

[15] The leech has two suckers
that cry out, "More, more!"*

There are three things that are never satisfied—
no, four that never say, "Enough!":
[16] the grave,*
the barren womb,
the thirsty desert,
the blazing fire.

[17] The eye that mocks a father
and despises a mother's instructions
will be plucked out by ravens of the valley
and eaten by vultures.

[18] There are three things that amaze me—
no, four things that I don't understand:
[19] how an eagle glides through the sky,
how a snake slithers on a rock,
how a ship navigates the ocean,
how a man loves a woman.

[20] An adulterous woman consumes a man,
then wipes her mouth and says, "What's wrong with that?"

[21] There are three things that make the earth tremble—
no, four it cannot endure:
[22] a slave who becomes a king,
an overbearing fool who prospers,
[23] a bitter woman who finally gets a husband,
a servant girl who supplants her mistress.

[24] There are four things on earth that are small but unusually wise:
[25] Ants—they aren't strong,
but they store up food all summer.
[26] Hyraxes*—they aren't powerful,
but they make their homes among the rocks.
[27] Locusts—they have no king,
but they march in formation.
[28] Lizards—they are easy to catch,
but they are found even in kings' palaces.

[29] There are three things that walk with stately stride—
no, four that strut about:
[30] the lion, king of animals, who won't turn aside for anything,
[31] the strutting rooster,
the male goat,
a king as he leads his army.

[32] If you have been a fool by being proud or plotting evil,
cover your mouth in shame.

[33] As the beating of cream yields butter
and striking the nose causes bleeding,
so stirring up anger causes quarrels.

30:1a Or *son of Jakeh from Massa;* or *son of Jakeh, an oracle.* **30:1b** The Hebrew can also be translated *The man declares this to Ithiel, / to Ithiel and to Ucal.* **30:15** Hebrew *two daughters who cry out, "Give, give!"* **30:16** Hebrew *Sheol.* **30:26** Or *Coneys,* or *Rock badgers.*

ULTIMATE ISSUES

HOT OR NOT?

Catch the recent show *Are You Hot? The Search for America's Sexiest People*? Several contestants were put on display and judged on whether they were hot or not.

Most of us have our own ideas of who's hot or who's not. Looks play a key role in who ranks as hot. Most of our views come from being bombarded daily by images of actors and supermodels who have made the "hot" list.

Next to looks, we might think that having a great personality is another key contributor to the hottie sweepstakes. Can't be Miss America? Maybe you can settle for Miss Congeniality.

But there's a spiritual part of you that makes you more than a mass of oxygen-absorbing molecules, glands, and hormones. If you belong to Christ, that spiritual part of you has been reborn and is connected to God. (For more on this, see John 3; Romans 3; Galatians 5:16-26; Ephesians 2:1-10.)

So, while looks and personality might gain someone admiration in our society, they don't count for much with God. Want to know what does? Spiritual maturity. Proverbs 31:10-31 provides a vivid picture of a spiritually mature woman. She's strong, intelligent, industrious, compassionate, wise: "She is clothed with strength and dignity (v. 25)." (When you get right down to it, that's a good description of a godly man, too.)

Sure, good looks are great. But everyone eventually grows old, gets wrinkles, and adds a few pounds. That's why a relationship based on looks or personality is doomed to failure. Don't believe it? Check out the average Hollywood marriage. The only cement that can bond two people together for life is mutual commitment to God and to each other.

So, instead of wondering whether you're hot or not, consider whether you're hot—on fire for God—or not.

That's one question he'd rather have you answer.

31 THE SAYINGS OF KING LEMUEL

The sayings of King Lemuel contain this message,* which his mother taught him.

2 O my son, O son of my womb,
O son of my vows,
3 do not waste your strength on women,
on those who ruin kings.

4 It is not for kings, O Lemuel, to guzzle wine.
Rulers should not crave alcohol.
5 For if they drink, they may forget the law
and not give justice to the oppressed.
6 Alcohol is for the dying,
and wine for those in bitter distress.
7 Let them drink to forget their poverty
and remember their troubles no more.

8 Speak up for those who cannot speak
for themselves;
ensure justice for those being crushed.
9 Yes, speak up for the poor and helpless,
and see that they get justice.

A WIFE OF NOBLE CHARACTER

10*Who can find a virtuous and capable wife?
She is more precious than rubies.
11 Her husband can trust her,
and she will greatly enrich his life.
12 She brings him good, not harm,
all the days of her life.

13 She finds wool and flax
and busily spins it.
14 She is like a merchant's ship,
bringing her food from afar.
15 She gets up before dawn to prepare breakfast
for her household
and plan the day's work for her servant girls.

16 She goes to inspect a field and buys it;
with her earnings she plants a vineyard.
17 She is energetic and strong,
a hard worker.

31:1 Or *of Lemuel, king of Massa;* or *of King Lemuel, an oracle.* **31:10** Verses 10-31 comprise a Hebrew acrostic poem; each verse begins with a successive letter of the Hebrew alphabet.

AN IDEAL WOMAN 31:10-31

Proverbs has a lot to say about women. How fitting that the book ends with a picture of a woman of strong character, great wisdom, many skills, and great compassion.

Some people have the mistaken idea that the ideal woman in the Bible is shy and totally domestic. Not so! This woman is an excellent wife and mother. She also is a manufacturer, importer, manager, realtor, farmer, seamstress, upholsterer, and merchant. Her strength and dignity do not come from her amazing achievements, however. They are a result of her reverence for God. In our society where physical appearance counts for so much, it may surprise us to realize that her appearance is never mentioned. Her attractiveness comes entirely from her character. How does this description of her character inspire you? ■

18 She makes sure her dealings are profitable;
her lamp burns late into the night.

19 Her hands are busy spinning thread,
her fingers twisting fiber.
20 She extends a helping hand to the poor
and opens her arms to the needy.
21 She has no fear of winter for her household,
for everyone has warm* clothes.

31:21 As in Greek and Latin versions; Hebrew reads *scarlet*.

22 She makes her own bedspreads.
She dresses in fine linen and
purple gowns.
23 Her husband is well known at the city gates,
where he sits with the other civic leaders.
24 She makes belted linen garments
and sashes to sell to the merchants.

25 She is clothed with strength and dignity,
and she laughs without fear of the future.
26 When she speaks, her words are wise,
and she gives instructions with kindness.
27 She carefully watches everything in her
household
and suffers nothing from laziness.

28 Her children stand and bless her.
Her husband praises her:
29 "There are many virtuous and capable women
in the world,
but you surpass them all!"

30 Charm is deceptive, and beauty does
not last;
but a woman who fears the LORD will be
greatly praised.
31 Reward her for all she has done.
Let her deeds publicly declare her praise.

ECCLESIASTES

"DO WHAT YOU wanna do, as long as you're true to yourself." "All I wanna do is have some fun." You've probably heard expressions like that, or even know people who follow their own rules in life. This philosophy isn't new. In fact, essentially the same message appears in the Bible.

Centuries ago, King Solomon wrote "People should eat and drink and enjoy the fruits of their labor, for these are gifts from God" (Eccles 3:13). Solomon knew what he was talking about. He had spent a lifetime experiencing and analyzing everything the world had to offer. Homes, servants, parties, money, music, sex—Solomon had done it all. His conclusion? Life is short, boring, and empty, so enjoy pleasure while you can!

"Wait a minute," you might interrupt. "You mean one of the Bible writers says that life is meaningless, so we should just party and do what we want?"

Yes—but there's a catch. Solomon says that to really enjoy life, we need to keep God right at the center. (See Eccles 12:1-7.) Without God, people merely exist, moving from the excitement of youth to the bitterness of old age. But with God, we can enjoy each moment, relationship, and experience along the way.

Read Ecclesiastes—and then have a real party!

ecclesiastes

stats

PURPOSE: To spare future generations the bitterness of learning through their own experience that life is meaningless apart from God

AUTHOR: Solomon, although no passages mention him by name

TO WHOM WRITTEN: Solomon's subjects in particular, and all people in general

DATE WRITTEN: Probably around 935 B.C., late in Solomon's life

SETTING: Solomon looks back on his life, much of which was lived apart from God.

KEY points

SEARCHING

Solomon searched for satisfaction almost as though he conducted a scientific experiment. As he gained pleasure, wealth, and success, he discovered that life without God was meaningless. Like Solomon, our search for meaning ultimately will end with the same conclusion.

WORK

Solomon tried to shake people's confidence in their own efforts, abilities, and wisdom. He did this to direct them to faith in God as the only sound basis for living. Without God, there is no lasting reward or benefit in hard work.

LIFE AND DEATH

The reality of aging and dying reminds us of the end to come, when God will judge each person's life. Because life is so short, we need a wisdom greater than this world can offer. We need the wisdom of God. If we listen to him, we will be spared from the bitterness of a meaningless life.

IS THERE MEANING TO LIFE?

ULTIMATE ISSUES

What do you do when you're bored? A recent Associated Press News Service story mentioned the recreational choice of two teens. Having used the video game *Grand Theft Auto* as "a means of escaping the monotony of teenage life," they decided to act it out by shooting at cars. They wound up killing one person and injuring others.

Some choices reveal a sad lack of meaning to a life. Many people wonder whether or not their lives have a purpose. Can you relate? If so, the book of Ecclesiastes was written for you.

The message of Ecclesiastes is brutally straightforward. The writer, Solomon, tells us that he has tried everything life has to offer—wine, women, and song (the ancient equivalent of sex, drugs, and alternative rock). His conclusion is this: "Fear God and obey his commands, for this is everyone's duty" (12:13). In other words, God gives meaning to our lives. No God, no meaning.

Think of it this way: Without God, you are just a bunch of molecules thrown together by chance. If there is no God, you came from—and are headed toward—impersonal nothingness. Any attempt at finding purpose is utterly doomed to failure. You might just as well be a lizard, or a rock, or *nothing at all* . . . if there is no God.

Sounds pretty bleak, doesn't it? It *is* bleak, if we subtract God from the equation. This belief that there is no God and therefore no meaning is what has driven many, including some of the greatest minds in history, to despair, alcoholism, and even suicide.

The good news is: There *is* something more. We don't have to run pointlessly after illusions like a slightly more sophisticated version of a hamster on a treadmill. There is a God who created you, knows you by name, loves you, and wants you to know him intimately. He gives meaning to life as he calls us to follow him in his grand adventure.

If you're searching for meaning, follow the writer of Ecclesiastes to its source: a lifelong, personal encounter with God.

1 These are the words of the Teacher,* King David's son, who ruled in Jerusalem.

EVERYTHING IS MEANINGLESS

2"Everything is meaningless," says the Teacher, "completely meaningless!"

3What do people get for all their hard work under the sun? 4Generations come and generations go, but the earth never changes. 5The sun rises and the sun sets, then hurries around to rise again. 6The wind blows south, and then turns north. Around and around it goes, blowing in circles. 7Rivers run into the sea, but the sea is never full. Then the water returns again to the rivers and flows out again to the sea. 8Everything is wearisome beyond description. No matter how much we see, we are never satisfied. No matter how much we hear, we are not content.

9History merely repeats itself. It has all been done before. Nothing under the sun is truly new. 10Sometimes people say, "Here is something new!" But actually it is old; nothing is ever truly new. 11We don't remember what happened in the past, and in future generations, no one will remember what we are doing now.

THE TEACHER SPEAKS: THE FUTILITY OF WISDOM

12I, the Teacher, was king of Israel, and I lived in Jerusalem. 13I devoted myself to search for understanding and to explore by wisdom everything being done under heaven. I soon discovered that God has dealt a tragic existence to the human race. 14I observed everything going on under the sun, and really, it is all meaningless—like chasing the wind.

THE MEANING OF LIFE 1:8-11

Solomon expressed his weariness and discontentment with life. Many people feel restless and dissatisfied. They wonder if their lives have a purpose. In this book, Solomon tests our faith, challenging us to find true and lasting meaning in God alone. Have you taken a hard look at your life lately? Does it seem filled with purpose or is it a daily drudgery? If it is the latter, perhaps God is challenging you to rethink your direction in life. ■

15 What is wrong cannot be made right.
What is missing cannot be recovered.

1:1 Hebrew *Qoheleth;* this term is rendered "the Teacher" throughout this book.

keeping it real

When I graduated from junior high school, I was popular and had good grades and stuff. I had everything going for me. During the summer before senior high school, though, I realized things would be different. Most of my friends wouldn't be going to the same high school with me. I'd have to start over.

I decided to live it up that summer. I partied with my friends and had a blast. But in between these times I felt depressed. I was living for the moment. Somehow that felt lonely.

One day I was flipping through the Bible, y'know, just messing around, and decided to read the book of Ecclesiastes. The whole book really spoke to me. Here was a dude I could identify with. He, too, seemed to be living for the moment and found it just as empty as I did! One verse especially expressed my feelings: "But as I looked at everything I had worked so hard to accomplish, it was all so meaningless—like chasing the wind. There was nothing really worthwhile anywhere." (2:11). My whole summer to that point had been consumed with pleasure—chasing the wind.

Although that verse may sound depressing, it actually made me feel better. Here was someone who knew how I was feeling, and expressed it perfectly.

After reading Ecclesiastes, I realized how futile it is to strive after material possessions, money, fame, and even popularity. They are all temporary. But what God gives us (love, joy, and other stuff) is more permanent. —Rick

16I said to myself, "Look, I am wiser than any of the
kings who ruled in Jerusalem before me. I have greater
wisdom and knowledge than any of them." 17So I set out
to learn everything from wisdom to madness and folly.
But I learned firsthand that pursuing all this is like chasing the wind.

18 The greater my wisdom, the greater my grief.
To increase knowledge only increases sorrow.

2 THE FUTILITY OF PLEASURE

I said to myself, "Come on, let's try pleasure. Let's look for
the 'good things' in life." But I found that this, too, was
meaningless. 2So I said, "Laughter is silly. What good
does it do to seek pleasure?" 3After much thought, I decided to cheer myself with wine. And while still seeking
wisdom, I clutched at foolishness. In this way, I tried to
experience the only happiness most people find during
their brief life in this world.

4I also tried to find meaning by building huge homes
for myself and by planting beautiful vineyards. 5I made
gardens and parks, filling them with all kinds of fruit
trees. 6I built reservoirs to collect the water to irrigate my
many flourishing groves. 7I bought slaves, both men and
women, and others were born into my household. I also
owned large herds and flocks, more than any of the kings
who had lived in Jerusalem before me. 8I collected great
sums of silver and gold, the treasure of many kings and
provinces. I hired wonderful singers, both men and
women, and had many beautiful concubines. I had everything a man could desire!

9So I became greater than all who had lived in Jerusalem before me, and my wisdom never failed me.
10Anything I wanted, I would take. I denied myself no
pleasure. I even found great pleasure in hard work, a reward for all my labors. 11But as I looked at everything I
had worked so hard to accomplish, it was all so meaningless—like chasing the wind. There was nothing really
worthwhile anywhere.

THE WISE AND THE FOOLISH

12So I decided to compare wisdom with foolishness and
madness (for who can do this better than I, the king?*).
13I thought, "Wisdom is better than foolishness, just
as light is better than darkness. 14For the wise can see
where they are going, but fools walk in the dark." Yet I
saw that the wise and the foolish share the same fate.
15Both will die. So I said to myself, "Since I will end up
the same as the fool, what's the value of all my wisdom?
This is all so meaningless!" 16For the wise and the foolish both die. The wise will not be remembered any lon-

2:12 The meaning of the Hebrew is uncertain.

ger than the fool. In the days to come, both will be
forgotten.
17So I came to hate life because everything done here
under the sun is so troubling. Everything is meaningless—like chasing the wind.

THE FUTILITY OF WORK

18I came to hate all my hard work here on earth, for I must
leave to others everything I have earned. 19And who can
tell whether my successors will be wise or foolish? Yet
they will control everything I have gained by my skill and
hard work under the sun. How meaningless! 20So I gave
up in despair, questioning the value of all my hard work
in this world.
21Some people work wisely with knowledge and skill,
then must leave the fruit of their efforts to someone who
hasn't worked for it. This, too, is meaningless, a great
tragedy. 22So what do people get in this life for all their
hard work and anxiety? 23Their days of labor are filled
with pain and grief; even at night their minds cannot rest.
It is all meaningless.

AN ENDLESS PARTY? 2:24-26

Is Solomon recommending that we party until we drop? No, he is encouraging us to take pleasure in what we're doing now and to enjoy life, because it comes from God's hand. True enjoyment in life comes only as we follow God's guidelines for living. Those who really know how to enjoy life are the ones who consider each day to be a gift from God, thanking him for it and serving him in it. That's what you do, right? ■

24So I decided there is nothing better than to enjoy
food and drink and to find satisfaction in work. Then I
realized that these pleasures are from the hand of God.
25For who can eat or enjoy anything apart from him?*
26God gives wisdom, knowledge, and joy to those who
please him. But if a sinner becomes wealthy, God takes
the wealth away and gives it to those who please him.
This, too, is meaningless—like chasing the wind.

3

A TIME FOR EVERYTHING

1 For everything there is a season,
a time for every activity under heaven.
2 A time to be born and a time to die.
A time to plant and a time to harvest.
3 A time to kill and a time to heal.
A time to tear down and a time to build up.
4 A time to cry and a time to laugh.
A time to grieve and a time to dance.
5 A time to scatter stones and a time to gather stones.
A time to embrace and a time to turn away.
6 A time to search and a time to quit searching.
A time to keep and a time to throw away.
7 A time to tear and a time to mend.
A time to be quiet and a time to speak.
8 A time to love and a time to hate.
A time for war and a time for peace.

9What do people really get for all their hard work? 10I
have seen the burden God has placed on us all. 11Yet God
has made everything beautiful for its own time. He has
planted eternity in the human heart, but even so, people
cannot see the whole scope of God's work from beginning to end. 12So I concluded there is nothing better than
to be happy and enjoy ourselves as long as we can. 13And
people should eat and drink and enjoy the fruits of their
labor, for these are gifts from God.
14And I know that whatever God does is final. Nothing
can be added to it or taken from it. God's purpose is that people should fear him. 15What is happening now has happened before, and what will happen in the future has
happened before, because God makes the same things
happen over and over again.

THE INJUSTICES OF LIFE

16I also noticed that under the sun there is evil in the
courtroom. Yes, even the courts of law are corrupt! 17I
said to myself, "In due season God will judge everyone,
both good and bad, for all their deeds."
18I also thought about the human condition—how God
proves to people that they are like animals. 19For people
and animals share the same fate—both breathe* and both
must die. So people have no real advantage over the animals. How meaningless! 20Both go to the same place—they
came from dust and they return to dust. 21For who can
prove that the human spirit goes up and the spirit of animals goes down into the earth? 22So I saw that there is nothing better for people than to be happy in their work. That is
why we are here! No one will bring us back from death to
enjoy life after we die.

4

Again, I observed all the oppression that takes
place under the sun. I saw the tears of the oppressed, with
no one to comfort them. The oppressors have great
power, and their victims are helpless. 2So I concluded
that the dead are better off than the living. 3But most fortunate of all are those who are not yet born. For they have
not seen all the evil that is done under the sun.
4Then I observed that most people are motivated to
success because they envy their neighbors. But this, too,
is meaningless—like chasing the wind.

5 "Fools fold their idle hands,
leading them to ruin."

6And yet,

"Better to have one handful with quietness
than two handfuls with hard work
and chasing the wind."

2:25 As in Greek and Syriac versions; Hebrew reads *apart from me?* 3:19 Or *both have the same spirit.*

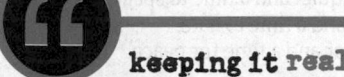

keeping it real

I really wanted to grow in my walk with God, so I vowed that I would have a quiet time every night. For a while everything went very well. I felt I understood what I read, and as I tried to apply the Bible to my daily life, I began to see changes in myself. That excited me.

But then I went through a period of time when I didn't seem to be getting anything out of the Bible. But then, for some reason, one night I started reading Ecclesiastes. I felt stressed—in a rush to get to my homework done so I could get to bed at a decent hour. When I came across chapter 5, verses 1-7, I suddenly woke up! I remembered that I had vowed to spend time with God every day and that it was **God** I was treating so rudely by rushing through my time with him. My attitude was all wrong. Having a quiet time wasn't like some chore I had to do; it was a privilege to meet with the awesome God of the universe! I asked God to forgive me for my attitude and thanked him for speaking to me through his Word.

—Kelsey

THE ADVANTAGES OF COMPANIONSHIP

7I observed yet another example of something meaningless under the sun. 8This is the case of a man who is all alone, without a child or a brother, yet who works hard to gain as much wealth as he can. But then he asks himself, "Who am I working for? Why am I giving up so much pleasure now?" It is all so meaningless and depressing.

9Two people are better off than one, for they can help each other succeed. 10If one person falls, the other can reach out and help. But someone who falls alone is in real trouble. 11Likewise, two people lying close together can keep each other warm. But how can one be warm alone? 12A person standing alone can be attacked and defeated, but two can stand back-to-back and conquer. Three are even better, for a triple-braided cord is not easily broken.

THE FUTILITY OF POLITICAL POWER

13It is better to be a poor but wise youth than an old and foolish king who refuses all advice. 14Such a youth could rise from poverty and succeed. He might even become king, though he has been in prison. 15But then everyone rushes to the side of yet another youth* who replaces him. 16Endless crowds stand around him,* but then another generation grows up and rejects him, too. So it is all meaningless—like chasing the wind.

5

APPROACHING GOD WITH CARE

1*As you enter the house of God, keep your ears open and your mouth shut. It is evil to make mindless offerings to God. 2*Don't make rash promises, and don't be hasty in bringing matters before God. After all, God is in heaven, and you are here on earth. So let your words be few.

3 Too much activity gives you restless dreams; too many words make you a fool.

4When you make a promise to God, don't delay in following through, for God takes no pleasure in fools. Keep all the promises you make to him. 5It is better to say nothing than to make a promise and not keep it. 6Don't let your mouth make you sin. And don't defend yourself by telling the Temple messenger that the promise you made was a mistake. That would make God angry, and he might wipe out everything you have achieved.

7Talk is cheap, like daydreams and other useless activities. Fear God instead.

THE FUTILITY OF WEALTH

8Don't be surprised if you see a poor person being oppressed by the powerful and if justice is being miscarried throughout the land. For every official is under orders from higher up, and matters of justice get lost in red tape and bureaucracy. 9Even the king milks the land for his own profit!*

10Those who love money will never have enough. How meaningless to think that wealth brings true happiness! 11The more you have, the more people come to help you spend it. So what good is wealth—except perhaps to watch it slip through your fingers!

12People who work hard sleep well, whether they eat little or much. But the rich seldom get a good night's sleep.

13There is another serious problem I have seen under the sun. Hoarding riches harms the saver. 14Money is put into risky investments that turn sour, and everything is lost. In the end, there is nothing left to pass on to one's

4:15 Hebrew *the second youth.* **4:16** Hebrew *There is no end to all the people, to all those who are before them.* **5:1** Verse 5:1 is numbered 4:17 in Hebrew text. **5:2** Verses 5:2-20 are numbered 5:1-19 in Hebrew text. **5:9** The meaning of the Hebrew in verses 8 and 9 is uncertain.

children. [15]We all come to the end of our lives as naked and empty-handed as on the day we were born. We can't take our riches with us.

[16]And this, too, is a very serious problem. People leave this world no better off than when they came. All their hard work is for nothing—like working for the wind. [17]Throughout their lives, they live under a cloud—frustrated, discouraged, and angry.

[18]Even so, I have noticed one thing, at least, that is good. It is good for people to eat, drink, and enjoy their work under the sun during the short life God has given them, and to accept their lot in life. [19]And it is a good thing to receive wealth from God and the good health to enjoy it. To enjoy your work and accept your lot in life—this is indeed a gift from God. [20]God keeps such people so busy enjoying life that they take no time to brood over the past.

6 There is another serious tragedy I have seen under the sun, and it weighs heavily on humanity. [2]God gives some people great wealth and honor and everything they could ever want, but then he doesn't give them the chance to enjoy these things. They die, and someone else, even a stranger, ends up enjoying their wealth! This is meaningless—a sickening tragedy.

[3]A man might have a hundred children and live to be very old. But if he finds no satisfaction in life and doesn't even get a decent burial, it would have been better for him to be born dead. [4]His birth would have been meaningless, and he would have ended in darkness. He wouldn't even have had a name, [5]and he would never have seen the sun or known of its existence. Yet he would have had more peace than in growing up to be an unhappy man. [6]He might live a thousand years twice over but still not find contentment. And since he must die like everyone else—well, what's the use?

[7]All people spend their lives scratching for food, but they never seem to have enough. [8]So are wise people really better off than fools? Do poor people gain anything by being wise and knowing how to act in front of others?

[9]Enjoy what you have rather than desiring what you don't have. Just dreaming about nice things is meaningless—like chasing the wind.

THE FUTURE—DETERMINED AND UNKNOWN

[10]Everything has already been decided. It was known long ago what each person would be. So there's no use arguing with God about your destiny.

[11]The more words you speak, the less they mean. So what good are they?

[12]In the few days of our meaningless lives, who knows how our days can best be spent? Our lives are like a shadow. Who can tell what will happen on this earth after we are gone?

7 WISDOM FOR LIFE

1 A good reputation is more valuable than costly
perfume.
And the day you die is better than the day you are
born.
2 Better to spend your time at funerals than at parties.
After all, everyone dies—
so the living should take this to heart.
3 Sorrow is better than laughter,
for sadness has a refining influence on us.
4 A wise person thinks a lot about death,
while a fool thinks only about having
a good time.

5 Better to be criticized by a wise person
than to be praised by a fool.
6 A fool's laughter is quickly gone,
like thorns crackling in a fire.
This also is meaningless.

7 Extortion turns wise people into fools,
and bribes corrupt the heart.

FLATTERY 7:5-6

Have you ever been paid a compliment when you knew it was inappropriate or merely an attempt to flatter you? Some people would rather feel good than know the truth. Too often, pleasant compliments are valued above helpful information. Solomon reminds us that facing honest criticism is far better than wallowing in the compliments of fools. (See also Prov 27:6.) ■

8 Finishing is better than starting.
Patience is better than pride.

9 Control your temper,
for anger labels you a fool.

10 Don't long for "the good old days."
This is not wise.

11 Wisdom is even better when you have money.
Both are a benefit as you go through life.
12 Wisdom and money can get you almost anything,
but only wisdom can save your life.

13 Accept the way God does things,
for who can straighten what he has
made crooked?
14 Enjoy prosperity while you can,
but when hard times strike, realize that both come
from God.
Remember that nothing is certain in this life.

THE LIMITS OF HUMAN WISDOM

[15]I have seen everything in this meaningless life, including the death of good young people and the long life of wicked people. [16]So don't be too good or too wise! Why destroy yourself? [17]On the other hand, don't be too wicked either. Don't be a fool! Why die before your time?

18 Pay attention to these instructions, for anyone who fears God will avoid both extremes.*

19 One wise person is stronger than ten leading citizens of a town!

20 Not a single person on earth is always good and never sins.

21 Don't eavesdrop on others—you may hear your servant curse you. 22 For you know how often you yourself have cursed others.

23 I have always tried my best to let wisdom guide my thoughts and actions. I said to myself, "I am determined to be wise." But it didn't work. 24 Wisdom is always distant and difficult to find. 25 I searched everywhere, determined to find wisdom and to understand the reason for things. I was determined to prove to myself that wickedness is stupid and that foolishness is madness.

26 I discovered that a seductive woman* is a trap more bitter than death. Her passion is a snare, and her soft hands are chains. Those who are pleasing to God will escape her, but sinners will be caught in her snare.

27 "This is my conclusion," says the Teacher. "I discovered this after looking at the matter from every possible angle. 28 Though I have searched repeatedly, I have not found what I was looking for. Only one out of a thousand men is virtuous, but not one woman! 29 But I did find this: God created people to be virtuous, but they have each turned to follow their own downward path."

8

1 How wonderful to be wise,
to analyze and interpret things.
Wisdom lights up a person's face,
softening its harshness.

OBEDIENCE TO THE KING

2 Obey the king since you vowed to God that you would. 3 Don't try to avoid doing your duty, and don't stand with those who plot evil, for the king can do whatever he wants. 4 His command is backed by great power. No one can resist or question it. 5 Those who obey him will not be punished. Those who are wise will find a time and a way to do what is right, 6 for there is a time and a way for everything, even when a person is in trouble.

7 Indeed, how can people avoid what they don't know is going to happen? 8 None of us can hold back our spirit from departing. None of us has the power to prevent the day of our death. There is no escaping that obligation, that dark battle. And in the face of death, wickedness will certainly not rescue the wicked.

THE WICKED AND THE RIGHTEOUS

9 I have thought deeply about all that goes on here under the sun, where people have the power to hurt each other. 10 I have seen wicked people buried with honor. Yet they were the very ones who frequented the Temple and are now praised* in the same city where they committed their crimes! This, too, is meaningless. 11 When a crime is not punished quickly, people feel it is safe to do wrong. 12 But even though a person sins a hundred times and still lives a long time, I know that those who fear God will be better off. 13 The wicked will not prosper, for they do not fear God. Their days will never grow long like the evening shadows.

CONSEQUENCES 8:11

Like Solomon, have you ever noticed others doing the same wrong thing that they saw someone else get away with? Unfortunately, doing what someone else did wrong is easier when we don't see that person suffer consequences immediately. But God knows every wrong we commit. One day we *will* have to answer for everything we have done (12:14). ■

14 And this is not all that is meaningless in our world. In this life, good people are often treated as though they were wicked, and wicked people are often treated as though they were good. This is so meaningless!

15 So I recommend having fun, because there is nothing better for people in this world than to eat, drink, and enjoy life. That way they will experience some happiness along with all the hard work God gives them under the sun.

16 In my search for wisdom and in my observation of people's burdens here on earth, I discovered that there is ceaseless activity, day and night. 17 I realized that no one can discover everything God is doing under the sun. Not even the wisest people discover everything, no matter what they claim.

9

DEATH COMES TO ALL

This, too, I carefully explored: Even though the actions of godly and wise people are in God's hands, no one knows whether God will show them favor. 2 The same destiny ultimately awaits everyone, whether righteous or wicked, good or bad,* ceremonially clean or unclean, religious or irreligious. Good people receive the same treatment as sinners, and people who make promises to God are treated like people who don't.

3 It seems so tragic that everyone under the sun suffers the same fate. That is why people are not more careful to be good. Instead, they choose their own mad course, for they have no hope. There is nothing ahead but death anyway. 4 There is hope only for the living. As they say, "It's better to be a live dog than a dead lion!"

5 The living at least know they will die, but the dead know nothing. They have no further reward, nor are they remembered. 6 Whatever they did in their lifetime—loving, hating, envying—is all long gone. They no longer play a part in anything here on earth. 7 So go ahead. Eat your food with joy, and drink your wine with a happy heart, for God approves of this! 8 Wear fine clothes, with a splash of cologne!

7:18 Or *will follow them both.* **7:26** Hebrew *a woman.* **8:10** As in some Hebrew manuscripts and Greek version; many Hebrew manuscripts read *and are forgotten.* **9:2** As in Greek and Syriac versions and Latin Vulgate; Hebrew lacks *or bad.*

keeping it real

One time, my best friend and I had an argument and stopped speaking to each other. I was bummed for a while over some of the things she said to me. I wasn't going to let her get away with treating me like she had!

Then I came across two verses: Ecclesiastes 10:12, "Wise words bring approval, but fools are destroyed by their own words" and 1 Peter 4:8, "Most important of all, continue to show deep love for each other, for love covers a multitude of sins." As I read these verses over and over, whatever we had argued about became less and less important. Maintaining a friendship with someone who also knew God's love became very important. I also realized that there were some faults in **me** that needed her forgiveness.

I didn't waste any time. I called my friend on the phone, read her the passages, and told her I was sorry for letting something petty come between us. She cried a little and said she was so glad I had called, and that she didn't feel right either about us fighting.

I'm really thankful that God helped me to work things out with my friend.

—Amanda

9Live happily with the woman you love through all the
meaningless days of life that God has given you under the
sun. The wife God gives you is your reward for all your
earthly toil. 10Whatever you do, do well. For when you go
to the grave,* there will be no work or planning or knowledge or wisdom.

11I have observed something else under the sun. The
fastest runner doesn't always win the race, and the strongest warrior doesn't always win the battle. The wise
sometimes go hungry, and the skillful are not necessarily
wealthy. And those who are educated don't always lead
successful lives. It is all decided by chance, by being in
the right place at the right time.

12People can never predict when hard times might
come. Like fish in a net or birds in a trap, people are
caught by sudden tragedy.

THOUGHTS ON WISDOM AND FOLLY

13Here is another bit of wisdom that has impressed me as
I have watched the way our world works. 14There was a
small town with only a few people, and a great king came
with his army and besieged it. 15A poor, wise man knew
how to save the town, and so it was rescued. But afterward no one thought to thank him. 16So even though wisdom is better than strength, those who are wise will be
despised if they are poor. What they say will not be appreciated for long.

17 Better to hear the quiet words of a wise person
than the shouts of a foolish king.
18 Better to have wisdom than weapons of war,
but one sinner can destroy much that is good.

9:10 Hebrew *to Sheol.*

10

1 As dead flies cause even a bottle of perfume
to stink,
so a little foolishness spoils great wisdom and honor.

2 A wise person chooses the right road;
a fool takes the wrong one.

3 You can identify fools
just by the way they walk down the street!

4 If your boss is angry at you, don't quit!
A quiet spirit can overcome even great mistakes.

THE IRONIES OF LIFE

5There is another evil I have seen under the sun. Kings
and rulers make a grave mistake 6when they give great
authority to foolish people and low positions to people of
proven worth. 7I have even seen servants riding horseback like princes—and princes walking like servants!

8 When you dig a well,
you might fall in.
When you demolish an old wall,
you could be bitten by a snake.
9 When you work in a quarry,
stones might fall and crush you.
When you chop wood,
there is danger with each stroke of your ax.

10 Using a dull ax requires great strength,
so sharpen the blade.

That's the value of wisdom;
it helps you succeed.

11 If a snake bites before you charm it,
what's the use of being a snake charmer?

12 Wise words bring approval,
but fools are destroyed by their own words.

13 Fools base their thoughts on foolish assumptions,
so their conclusions will be wicked madness;
14 they chatter on and on.

No one really knows what is going to happen;
no one can predict the future.

15 Fools are so exhausted by a little work
that they can't even find their way home.

16 What sorrow for the land ruled by a servant,*
the land whose leaders feast in the morning.
17 Happy is the land whose king is a noble leader
and whose leaders feast at the proper time
to gain strength for their work, not to get drunk.

18 Laziness leads to a sagging roof;
idleness leads to a leaky house.

MONEY MATTERS 10:19

Many people believe that money is the answer to all their problems. But just as the effects of alcohol are only temporary, the soothing effect of the last purchase soon wears off. Although some verses in the Bible mention the necessity of money for survival, others warn against the love of money (see Matt 6:24; 1 Tim 6:10; Heb 13:5). The love of money is a problem because we trust it—rather than God—to solve our problems. Those who pursue money's empty promises will discover one day that they are spiritually bankrupt. ■

19 A party gives laughter,
wine gives happiness,
and money gives everything!

20 Never make light of the king, even in
your thoughts.
And don't make fun of the powerful, even in
your own bedroom.
For a little bird might deliver your message
and tell them what you said.

11 THE UNCERTAINTIES OF LIFE

1 Send your grain across the seas,
and in time, profits will flow back to you.*
2 But divide your investments among many places,*
for you do not know what risks might lie ahead.

3 When clouds are heavy, the rains come down.
Whether a tree falls north or south, it stays where
it falls.

4 Farmers who wait for perfect weather never plant.
If they watch every cloud, they never harvest.

5 Just as you cannot understand the path of the wind or
the mystery of a tiny baby growing in its mother's
womb,* so you cannot understand the activity of God,
who does all things.
6 Plant your seed in the morning and keep busy all afternoon, for you don't know if profit will come from one
activity or another—or maybe both.

10:16 Or *a child.* **11:1** Or *Give generously, / for your gifts will return to you later.* Hebrew reads *Throw your bread on the waters, / for after many days you will find it again.* **11:2** Hebrew *among seven or even eight.* **11:5** Some manuscripts read *Just as you cannot understand how breath comes to a tiny baby in its mother's womb.*

I recently became a Christian, but I'm afraid I'll miss out on a lot of fun during my teenage years. Can't I wait until later to live for Christ? Why or why not?

A speaker once related a dream he'd had involving demons who tried to think of ways to stop people from accepting Christ.

The ideas they came up with included the usual ones: drugs, sexual temptations, intellectualism, money, fame, status, etc.

All of these strategies were tried, but they weren't very effective.

Finally, one demon suggested a plan that surprised everyone. "Let's tell people that believing the Bible and following Christ are the right things to do; and tell them that being a committed believer is the only way to live life. But," he concluded, "tell them to do it *tomorrow!*"

This delaying tactic works like Novocain. It numbs people and keeps them from turning to the truth when they hear it.

We are creatures of habit. We've learned almost everything—reading, writing, math, speech—by doing the same thing over and over. Our thoughts about God are the same way. Believing we can play now and get committed later fulfills Satan's strategy.

Thought patterns become habits; habits become beliefs; beliefs become actions; and actions determine our eternity!

You may be afraid you'll miss out on the fun, but those "good times" don't last. Ecclesiastes 11:9–12:8 makes it clear that to live life to the fullest, we must follow God—not in fear that he wants to take away our fun, but in faith that he wants to make our life into something wonderful.

Life begins the moment we realize that the world doesn't revolve around us, but around God, who made the world and all that is in it.

ADVICE FOR YOUNG AND OLD

7 Light is sweet; how pleasant to see a
new day dawning.
8 When people live to be very old, let
them rejoice in every day of life. But let
them also remember there will be
many dark days. Everything still to
come is meaningless.
9 Young people,* it's wonderful to be
young! Enjoy every minute of it. Do
everything you want to do; take it all in.
But remember that you must give an account to God for everything you do. 10 So
refuse to worry, and keep your body
healthy. But remember that youth, with
a whole life before you, is meaningless.

> Fear God and obey his commands, for this is everyone's duty. God will judge us for everything we do, including every secret thing. . . .
>
> *ECCLESIASTES 12:13-14*

12 Don't let the excitement of youth cause you to
forget your Creator. Honor him in your youth before you
grow old and say, "Life is not pleasant anymore."
2 Remember him before the light of the sun, moon, and
stars is dim to your old eyes, and rain clouds continually
darken your sky. 3 Remember him before your legs—the
guards of your house—start to tremble; and before your
shoulders—the strong men—stoop. Remember him before your teeth—your few remaining servants—stop
grinding; and before your eyes—the women looking
through the windows—see dimly.
4 Remember him before the door to life's opportunities is closed and the sound of work fades. Now you rise
at the first chirping of the birds, but then all their sounds
will grow faint.
5 Remember him before you become fearful of falling
and worry about danger in the streets; before your hair
turns white like an almond tree in bloom, and you drag
along without energy like a dying grasshopper, and the
caperberry no longer inspires sexual desire. Remember
him before you near the grave, your everlasting home,
when the mourners will weep at your funeral.
6 Yes, remember your Creator now while you are
young, before the silver cord of life snaps and the
golden bowl is broken. Don't wait un-
til the water jar is smashed at the
spring and the pulley is broken at the
well. 7 For then the dust will return to
the earth, and the spirit will return to
God who gave it.

CONCLUDING THOUGHTS ABOUT THE TEACHER

8 "Everything is meaningless," says the
Teacher, "completely meaningless."
9 Keep this in mind: The Teacher
was considered wise, and he taught
the people everything he knew. He listened carefully to many proverbs,
studying and classifying them. 10 The
Teacher sought to find just the right
words to express truths clearly.*
11 The words of the wise are like cattle prods—painful
but helpful. Their collected sayings are like a nail-studded
stick with which a shepherd* drives the sheep.

SOLOMON'S ADVICE 12:1-14

Solomon presents his antidotes for the two main ailments presented in this book: those who lack purpose and direction in life should respect God and follow his principles for living; those who think life is unfair should remember that God will review every person's life to determine how he or she has responded to him. Have you committed your life to him, both present and future? Does your life measure up to his standards? ■

12 But, my child,* let me give you some further advice:
Be careful, for writing books is endless, and much study
wears you out.
13 That's the whole story. Here now is my final conclusion: Fear God and obey his commands, for this is everyone's duty. 14 God will judge us for everything we do,
including every secret thing, whether good or bad.

11:9 Hebrew *Young man.* **12:10** Or *sought to write what was upright and true.* **12:11** Or *one shepherd.* **12:12** Hebrew *my son.*

SONG OF SONGS

song of songs

CHECK OUT SOME of the songs on the Billboard Hot 100, and you'll probably find a mix of I-gotta-have-you-now lyrics. Or glance at the steadily growing list of reality TV shows or reruns of primetime soaps like *Sex in the City* and you'll find stories of "instant love" or a "paint-by-the-numbers" view of relationships. The message comes through loud and clear: "Love is a formula, lust is in, and marriage isn't necessary for a couple to experience sex."

That's not what God had in mind for love, sex, or marriage. Sex is meant to be an exciting, fulfilling physical union of a man and a woman who are protected by the commitment of marriage—not an act of conquest. Love is meant to be a self-giving action, not a self-centered emotion.

Nowhere are the true meanings of love and sex more beautifully portrayed than in the Song of Songs. Here we get an intimate glimpse into the relationship between the king (Solomon) and his bride. Love, sex, and marriage are celebrated in the context of living the way God designed us to live.

Confused about the messages you hear about love and marriage? The Song of Songs may have the answers you need.

stats

PURPOSE: To tell of the love between a bridegroom (King Solomon) and his bride, to affirm the value of marriage, and to picture God's love for his people

AUTHOR: Solomon

DATE WRITTEN: Probably early in Solomon's reign

SETTING: Israel—the bride's garden and the king's palace

KEY PEOPLE: King Solomon, his chosen bride, and the daughters of Jerusalem

KEY points

COMMITMENT
Solomon and his bride celebrated their commitment to each other. The decision to commit yourself to your spouse alone is one that needs to be maintained daily. But it can begin even before marriage as you flee from sexual temptation.

SEX
God wants sex to be a product of the love and commitment of two married people rather than lust. God is glorified by sex within a godly marriage—sex that is for mutual pleasure, not selfish enjoyment.

BEAUTY
The two lovers praise the beauty they see in each other. The language they use shows the spontaneity and mystery of love. The love one feels for a husband or wife reveals that person's inner beauty—qualities that keep love alive.

PROBLEMS
Over time, feelings of loneliness, indifference, and isolation came between Solomon and his bride. During those times, love grew cold and barriers arose. Through careful communication, lovers can be reconciled, a commitment renewed, and romance refreshed.

1

This is Solomon's song of songs, more wonderful than any other.

*Young Woman**

2 Kiss me and kiss me again,
for your love is sweeter than wine.
3 How fragrant your cologne;
your name is like its spreading fragrance.
No wonder all the young women love you!
4 Take me with you; come, let's run!
The king has brought me into his bedroom.

Young Women of Jerusalem

How happy we are for you, O king.
We praise your love even more than wine.

Young Woman

How right they are to adore you.

5 I am dark but beautiful,
O women of Jerusalem—
dark as the tents of Kedar,
dark as the curtains of Solomon's tents.
6 Don't stare at me because I am dark—
the sun has darkened my skin.
My brothers were angry with me;
they forced me to care for their vineyards,
so I couldn't care for myself—my own vineyard.

7 Tell me, my love, where are you leading your flock today?
Where will you rest your sheep at noon?
For why should I wander like a prostitute*
among your friends and their flocks?

Young Man

8 If you don't know, O most beautiful woman,
follow the trail of my flock,
and graze your young goats by the shepherds' tents.
9 You are as exciting, my darling,
as a mare among Pharaoh's stallions.
10 How lovely are your cheeks;
your earrings set them afire!
How lovely is your neck,
enhanced by a string of jewels.
11 We will make for you earrings of gold
and beads of silver.

Young Woman

12 The king is lying on his couch,
enchanted by the fragrance of my perfume.
13 My lover is like a sachet of myrrh
lying between my breasts.
14 He is like a bouquet of sweet henna blossoms
from the vineyards of En-gedi.

Young Man

15 How beautiful you are, my darling,
how beautiful!
Your eyes are like doves.

Young Woman

16 You are so handsome, my love,
pleasing beyond words!
The soft grass is our bed;
17 fragrant cedar branches are the beams of our house,
and pleasant smelling firs are the rafters.

2

Young Woman

1 I am the spring crocus blooming on the Sharon Plain,*
the lily of the valley.

Young Man

2 Like a lily among thistles
is my darling among young women.

Young Woman

3 Like the finest apple tree in the orchard
is my lover among other young men.
I sit in his delightful shade
and taste his delicious fruit.
4 He escorts me to the banquet hall;
it's obvious how much he loves me.
5 Strengthen me with raisin cakes,
refresh me with apples,
for I am weak with love.
6 His left arm is under my head,
and his right arm embraces me.

OVERPOWERED 2:7; 3:5

Feelings of love can create intimacy that overpowers reason. Ever feel like that? Many couples too often are in a hurry to develop an intimate relationship based on their strong feelings. But feelings aren't enough to support a lasting relationship. This verse encourages us to avoid forcing romance lest the feelings of love grow faster than the commitment needed to make love last. Want to be wise? Wait for feelings of love and commitment to develop together. ■

7 Promise me, O women of Jerusalem,
by the gazelles and wild deer,
not to awaken love until the time is right.*

8 Ah, I hear my lover coming!
He is leaping over the mountains,
bounding over the hills.
9 My lover is like a swift gazelle
or a young stag.

1:1 The headings identifying the speakers are not in the original text, though the Hebrew usually gives clues by means of the gender of the person speaking. 1:7 Hebrew *like a veiled woman.* 2:1 Traditionally rendered *I am the rose of Sharon.* Sharon Plain is a region in the coastal plain of Palestine. 2:7 Or *not to awaken love until it is ready.*

Look, there he is behind the wall,
looking through the window,
peering into the room.

10 My lover said to me,
"Rise up, my darling!
Come away with me, my fair one!
11 Look, the winter is past,
and the rains are over and gone.
12 The flowers are springing up,
the season of singing birds* has come,
and the cooing of turtledoves fills the air.
13 The fig trees are forming young fruit,
and the fragrant grapevines are blossoming.
Rise up, my darling!
Come away with me, my fair one!"

Young Man

14 My dove is hiding behind the rocks,
behind an outcrop on the cliff.
Let me see your face;
let me hear your voice.
For your voice is pleasant,
and your face is lovely.

Young Women of Jerusalem

15 Catch all the foxes,
those little foxes,
before they ruin the vineyard of love,
for the grapevines are blossoming!

Young Woman

16 My lover is mine, and I am his.
He browses among the lilies.
17 Before the dawn breezes blow
and the night shadows flee,
return to me, my love, like a gazelle
or a young stag on the rugged mountains.*

3

Young Woman

1 One night as I lay in bed, I yearned for my lover.
I yearned for him, but he did not come.
2 So I said to myself, "I will get up and roam the city,
searching in all its streets and squares.
I will search for the one I love."
So I searched everywhere but did not find him.
3 The watchmen stopped me as they made
their rounds,
and I asked, "Have you seen the one I love?"
4 Then scarcely had I left them
when I found my love!
I caught and held him tightly,
then I brought him to my mother's house,
into my mother's bed, where I had
been conceived.
5 Promise me, O women of Jerusalem,
by the gazelles and wild deer,
not to awaken love until the time is right.*

Young Women of Jerusalem

6 Who is this sweeping in from the wilderness
like a cloud of smoke?
Who is it, fragrant with myrrh and frankincense
and every kind of spice?
7 Look, it is Solomon's carriage,
surrounded by sixty heroic men,
the best of Israel's soldiers.
8 They are all skilled swordsmen,
experienced warriors.
Each wears a sword on his thigh,
ready to defend the king against an attack
in the night.
9 King Solomon's carriage is built
of wood imported from Lebanon.
10 Its posts are silver,
its canopy gold;
its cushions are purple.
It was decorated with love
by the young women of Jerusalem.

Young Woman

11 Come out to see King Solomon,
young women of Jerusalem.*
He wears the crown his mother gave him on his
wedding day,
his most joyous day.

4

Young Man

1 You are beautiful, my darling,
beautiful beyond words.
Your eyes are like doves
behind your veil.
Your hair falls in waves,
like a flock of goats winding down the slopes
of Gilead.
2 Your teeth are as white as sheep,
recently shorn and freshly washed.
Your smile is flawless,
each tooth matched with its twin.*
3 Your lips are like scarlet ribbon;
your mouth is inviting.
Your cheeks are like rosy pomegranates
behind your veil.
4 Your neck is as beautiful as the tower of David,
jeweled with the shields of a thousand heroes.
5 Your breasts are like two fawns,
twin fawns of a gazelle grazing among the lilies.
6 Before the dawn breezes blow
and the night shadows flee,
I will hurry to the mountain of myrrh
and to the hill of frankincense.

2:12 Or *the season of pruning vines.* 2:17 Or *on the hills of Bether.* 3:5 Or *not to awaken love until it is ready.* 3:11 Hebrew *of Zion.*
4:2 Hebrew *Not one is missing; each has a twin.*

7 You are altogether beautiful, my darling,
beautiful in every way.

8 Come with me from Lebanon, my bride,
come with me from Lebanon.
Come down* from Mount Amana,
from the peaks of Senir and Hermon,
where the lions have their dens
and leopards live among the hills.

9 You have captured my heart,
my treasure,* my bride.
You hold it hostage with one glance of your eyes,
with a single jewel of your necklace.
10 Your love delights me,
my treasure, my bride.
Your love is better than wine,
your perfume more fragrant than spices.
11 Your lips are as sweet as nectar, my bride.
Honey and milk are under your tongue.
Your clothes are scented
like the cedars of Lebanon.

WHY WAIT? 4:12

In comparing his bride to a private garden, Solomon praised her virginity. On many talk shows, sitcoms, and in magazines, many people see their virginity as something they need to get rid of as soon as possible. Yet abstinence has always been God's plan for unmarried people—and with good reason. Sex without marriage is cheap. It cannot compare with the joy of giving yourself completely to the one who is totally committed to you. ■

12 You are my private garden, my treasure,
my bride,
a secluded spring, a hidden fountain.
13 Your thighs shelter a paradise of pomegranates
with rare spices—
henna with nard,
14 nard and saffron,
fragrant calamus and cinnamon,
with all the trees of frankincense, myrrh,
and aloes,
and every other lovely spice.
15 You are a garden fountain,
a well of fresh water
streaming down from Lebanon's mountains.

Young Woman

16 Awake, north wind!
Rise up, south wind!
Blow on my garden
and spread its fragrance all around.
Come into your garden, my love;
taste its finest fruits.

5

Young Man

1 I have entered my garden, my treasure,*
my bride!
I gather myrrh with my spices
and eat honeycomb with my honey.
I drink wine with my milk.

Young Women of Jerusalem

Oh, lover and beloved, eat and drink!
Yes, drink deeply of your love!

Young Woman

2 I slept, but my heart was awake,
when I heard my lover knocking and calling:
"Open to me, my treasure, my darling,
my dove, my perfect one.
My head is drenched with dew,
my hair with the dampness of the night."

3 But I responded,
"I have taken off my robe.
Should I get dressed again?
I have washed my feet.
Should I get them soiled?"

4 My lover tried to unlatch the door,
and my heart thrilled within me.
5 I jumped up to open the door for my love,
and my hands dripped with perfume.
My fingers dripped with lovely myrrh
as I pulled back the bolt.
6 I opened to my lover,
but he was gone!
My heart sank.
I searched for him
but could not find him anywhere.
I called to him,
but there was no reply.
7 The night watchmen found me
as they made their rounds.
They beat and bruised me
and stripped off my veil,
those watchmen on the walls.

8 Make this promise, O women of Jerusalem—
If you find my lover,
tell him I am weak with love.

Young Women of Jerusalem

9 Why is your lover better than all others,
O woman of rare beauty?
What makes your lover so special
that we must promise this?

Young Woman

10 My lover is dark and dazzling,
better than ten thousand others!

4:8 Or *Look down.* 4:9 Hebrew *my sister;* also in 4:10, 12. 5:1 Hebrew *my sister;* also in 5:2.

11 His head is finest gold,
his wavy hair is black as a raven.
12 His eyes sparkle like doves
beside springs of water;
they are set like jewels
washed in milk.
13 His cheeks are like gardens of spices
giving off fragrance.
His lips are like lilies,
perfumed with myrrh.
14 His arms are like rounded bars of gold,
set with beryl.
His body is like bright ivory,
glowing with lapis lazuli.
15 His legs are like marble pillars
set in sockets of finest gold.
His posture is stately,
like the noble cedars of Lebanon.
16 His mouth is sweetness itself;
he is desirable in every way.
Such, O women of Jerusalem,
is my lover, my friend.

6

Young Women of Jerusalem

1 Where has your lover gone,
O woman of rare beauty?
Which way did he turn
so we can help you find him?

Young Woman

2 My lover has gone down to his garden,
to his spice beds,
to browse in the gardens
and gather the lilies.
3 I am my lover's, and my lover is mine.
He browses among the lilies.

Young Man

4 You are beautiful, my darling,
like the lovely city of Tirzah.
Yes, as beautiful as Jerusalem,
as majestic as an army with
billowing banners.
5 Turn your eyes away,
for they overpower me.
Your hair falls in waves,
like a flock of goats winding down the slopes
of Gilead.
6 Your teeth are as white as sheep
that are freshly washed.
Your smile is flawless,
each tooth matched with its twin.*
7 Your cheeks are like rosy pomegranates
behind your veil.
8 Even among sixty queens
and eighty concubines
and countless young women,
9 I would still choose my dove, my perfect one—
the favorite of her mother,
dearly loved by the one who bore her.
The young women see her and praise her;
even queens and royal concubines sing her praises:
10 "Who is this, arising like the dawn,
as fair as the moon,
as bright as the sun,
as majestic as an army with billowing banners?"

11 I went down to the grove of walnut trees
and out to the valley to see the new spring growth,
to see whether the grapevines had budded
or the pomegranates were in bloom.
12 Before I realized it,
I found myself in the royal chariot with
my beloved.*

Young Women of Jerusalem

13*Return, return to us, O maid of Shulam.
Come back, come back, that we may see you again.

Young Man

Why do you stare at this young woman of Shulam,
as she moves so gracefully between two lines
of dancers?*

MORE LOVE 7:1-13

Solomon and his bride confidently expressed their love for each other. When marriage partners are secure in their love and relationship, they find the freedom to initiate and enjoy acts of love. In your dating relationships, have you ever doubted God's plan for sex? Many people have. Don't accept anything less than the kind of love he wants for you: the secure, freeing love that you will find only in marriage. ■

7

1*How beautiful are your sandaled feet,
O queenly maiden.
Your rounded thighs are like jewels,
the work of a skilled craftsman.
2 Your navel is perfectly formed
like a goblet filled with mixed wine.
Between your thighs lies a mound of wheat
bordered with lilies.
3 Your breasts are like two fawns,
twin fawns of a gazelle.
4 Your neck is as beautiful as an ivory tower.
Your eyes are like the sparkling pools in Heshbon
by the gate of Bath-rabbim.

6:6 Hebrew *Not one is missing; each has a twin.* 6:12 Or *among the royal chariots of my people,* or *among the chariots of Amminadab.* The meaning of the Hebrew is uncertain. 6:13a Verse 6:13 is numbered 7:1 in Hebrew text. 6:13b Or *as you would at the movements of two armies?* or *as you would at the dance of Mahanaim?* The meaning of the Hebrew is uncertain. 7:1 Verses 7:1-13 are numbered 7:2-14 in Hebrew text.

THE REAL TRUTH ABOUT SEX

"Your rounded thighs are like jewels, the work of a skilled craftsman. Your navel is perfectly formed." Where would you expect to find this kind of writing? A steamy romance novel? The Internet? How about your local Bible—namely Song of Songs 7:1-2?

Song of Songs provides a frank and poetic view of sex. Sex *is* God's invention—not Hollywood's or the average music video producer. So, what can we conclude from this?

- Sex is *good.* Unfortunately, some have treated this aspect of God's creation as if it were shameful or to be avoided. But God created sex, and he created us as sexual creatures; therefore, sex is good.
- Sex is *powerful.* Of all the ways people have of expressing themselves to one another, sex is the most powerful. It involves a person's total being. When sex is kept in its proper context—marriage—it is a powerful vehicle for good, for bringing a husband and wife together as one. Unfortunately, when sex is expressed before or outside of marriage, it can be powerfully destructive.

Think of it like this: Would you give a six-year-old the keys to a new Ferrari and send him or her out to drive it in the Grand Prix? No way, right? A six-year-old isn't physically, mentally, or emotionally prepared to handle the car or the course. Get the picture?

- Sex is *made for marriage.* Period. Sex is such an explosive force between two people that it must be expressed in an environment of love, support, and commitment. Especially commitment. That's what is missing in sex outside of marriage—commitment. Sex is 100 percent physical commitment. Unless there is 100 percent emotional, financial, social, and spiritual commitment, the relationship will be unbalanced and will probably collapse, leading to pain, anger, shame, and much more. Those who decide to become sexually involved in spite of God's instructions shouldn't be surprised when, like our young Ferrari driver, they crash and burn.

Sex, as the Song of Songs says so beautifully, is God's idea. If you follow his leading—including waiting until marriage to have sex—you'll experience one of God's greatest gifts in a way that is fulfilling to you and pleasing to him.

Your nose is as fine as the tower of Lebanon
overlooking Damascus.
5 Your head is as majestic as Mount Carmel,
and the sheen of your hair radiates royalty.
The king is held captive by its tresses.
6 Oh, how beautiful you are!
How pleasing, my love, how full of delights!
7 You are slender like a palm tree,
and your breasts are like its clusters of fruit.
8 I said, "I will climb the palm tree
and take hold of its fruit."
May your breasts be like grape clusters,
and the fragrance of your breath like apples.
9 May your kisses be as exciting as the best wine,
flowing gently over lips and teeth.*

Young Woman
10 I am my lover's,
and he claims me as his own.
11 Come, my love, let us go out to the fields
and spend the night among the
wildflowers.*
12 Let us get up early and go to the vineyards
to see if the grapevines have budded,
if the blossoms have opened,
and if the pomegranates have bloomed.
There I will give you my love.
13 There the mandrakes give off their fragrance,
and the finest fruits are at our door,
new delights as well as old,
which I have saved for you, my lover.

7:9 As in Greek and Syriac versions and Latin Vulgate; Hebrew reads *over lips of sleepers.* **7:11** Or *in the villages.*

8

Young Woman

1 Oh, I wish you were my brother,
who nursed at my mother's breasts.
Then I could kiss you no matter who was watching,
and no one would criticize me.
2 I would bring you to my childhood home,
and there you would teach me.*
I would give you spiced wine to drink,
my sweet pomegranate wine.
3 Your left arm would be under my head,
and your right arm would embrace me.

4 Promise me, O women of Jerusalem,
not to awaken love until the time is right.*

Young Women of Jerusalem

5 Who is this sweeping in from the desert,
leaning on her lover?

PRICELESS LOVE 8:6-7

In this final description of their love, the bride includes some of its significant characteristics. (See also 1 Cor 13.) Love is as strong as death; it cannot be killed by time or disaster; and it cannot be bought for any price because it is freely given. Love is priceless—even the richest king cannot buy it. It must be accepted as a gift from God and then shared within the guidelines God provides. ■

Young Woman

I aroused you under the apple tree,
where your mother gave you birth,
where in great pain she delivered you.
6 Place me like a seal over your heart,
like a seal on your arm.
For love is as strong as death,
its jealousy* as enduring as the grave.*
Love flashes like fire,
the brightest kind of flame.
7 Many waters cannot quench love,
nor can rivers drown it.
If a man tried to buy love
with all his wealth,
his offer would be utterly scorned.

The Young Woman's Brothers

8 We have a little sister
too young to have breasts.
What will we do for our sister
if someone asks to marry her?
9 If she is a virgin, like a wall,
we will protect her with a silver tower.
But if she is promiscuous, like a swinging door,
we will block her door with a cedar bar.

Young Woman

10 I was a virgin, like a wall;
now my breasts are like towers.
When my lover looks at me,
he is delighted with what he sees.

11 Solomon has a vineyard at Baal-hamon,
which he leases out to tenant farmers.
Each of them pays a thousand pieces of silver*
for harvesting its fruit.
12 But my vineyard is mine to give,
and Solomon need not pay a thousand pieces
of silver.
But I will give two hundred pieces
to those who care for its vines.

Young Man

13 O my darling, lingering in the gardens,
your companions are fortunate to hear
your voice.
Let me hear it, too!

Young Woman

14 Come away, my love! Be like a gazelle
or a young stag on the mountains of spices.

8:2 Or *there she will teach me;* or *there she bore me.* **8:4** Or *not to awaken love until it is ready.* **8:6a** Or *its passion.* **8:6b** Hebrew *as Sheol.* **8:11** Hebrew *1,000 shekels of silver.*

isaiah

MATT WALKED to the front of the room on rubber legs. He turned to face the class. Blood rushed to his head; his heart raced. He pulled out his note cards with sweaty hands and began to speak.

Stage fright. We know it all too well. According to many studies, the greatest fear most people have is doing what Matt did—giving a speech.

If you think that's tough, imagine being a prophet like Isaiah. Public speaking meant you would have to give messages that the people wouldn't want to hear. As a prophet, you would have to speak God's judgment. And you would have to confront kings—men who could have you put to death on a whim. Sometimes, you would have to act out your messages. Not fun; yet true prophets spoke out for God, regardless of how they felt.

The book bearing Isaiah's name is the first of the major prophetic books in the Bible. This book has often been called a "little Bible," since it has 66 chapters. Among these chapters are some of the most well known prophecies concerning the coming Messiah. As you read the book of Isaiah, may it encourage you to faithfully take God's message wherever he might send you.

timeline

760 B.C.
Amos becomes a prophet

753
Hosea becomes a prophet

742
Micah becomes a prophet

740
Isaiah becomes a prophet

735
Ahaz becomes king of Judah

732
Hoshea becomes king of Israel

722
Israel falls to the Assyrians

715
Hezekiah becomes king of Judah

701
Sennacherib surrounds Jerusalem

697
Manasseh becomes king of Judah

681
Isaiah's ministry ends

640
Josiah becomes king of Judah

stats

PURPOSE: To call Judah back to God and to tell of God's salvation through the Messiah

AUTHOR: Isaiah, son of Amoz

DATE WRITTEN: Since the events of chapters 1–39 occurred during Isaiah's ministry, these chapters probably were written about 700 B.C. Chapters 40–66, however, may have been written near the end of Isaiah's life—about 681 B.C.

SETTING: Jerusalem

KEY PEOPLE: Isaiah; his two sons Shear-Jashub and Maher-Shalal-Hash-Baz

SPECIAL FEATURES: The book of Isaiah contains both prose and poetry and uses personification (attributing personal qualities to inanimate objects). Also, many of the prophecies in Isaiah contain predictions that foretell both a soon-to-occur event and a distant, future event at the same time.

KEY points

HOLINESS
God's moral perfection stands in contrast to evil people and nations. Because he is without sin, he alone can help us when we mess up.

PUNISHMENT
God promised to punish Israel and other nations for their wrongdoings. Likewise, we won't be shielded from the consequences of our wrongdoing if we boldly choose to disobey God.

SALVATION/MESSIAH
The Savior's perfect sacrifice, his servant life, and his coming kingdom all are foretold by Isaiah. Through Christ, the promise of redemption and restoration are fulfilled.

HOPE
God promises comfort, deliverance, and restoration in his future kingdom. No matter how bleak our current situation, or how evil the world becomes, we have the hope that God will keep his promises.

1 These are the visions that Isaiah son of Amoz saw concerning Judah and Jerusalem. He saw these visions during the years when Uzziah, Jotham, Ahaz, and Hezekiah were kings of Judah.*

A MESSAGE FOR REBELLIOUS JUDAH

2 Listen, O heavens! Pay attention, earth!
This is what the LORD says:
"The children I raised and cared for
have rebelled against me.
3 Even an ox knows its owner,
and a donkey recognizes its master's care—
but Israel doesn't know its master.
My people don't recognize my care for them."
4 Oh, what a sinful nation they are—
loaded down with a burden of guilt.
They are evil people,
corrupt children who have rejected the LORD.
They have despised the Holy One of Israel
and turned their backs on him.

ISOLATED 1:1-9

As long as the people of Judah continued to do wrong things, they isolated themselves from God's help. (See also 54:6-8.) Have you ever felt separated from God because of something you've done? The only sure cure for this kind of isolation is to own up to what you've done and admit that you want to change (see Isa 1:16-19; 1 John 1:9). Are you willing? ■

5 Why do you continue to invite punishment?
Must you rebel forever?
Your head is injured,
and your heart is sick.
6 You are battered from head to foot—
covered with bruises, welts, and
infected wounds—
without any soothing ointments or bandages.
7 Your country lies in ruins,
and your towns are burned.
Foreigners plunder your fields before your eyes
and destroy everything they see.
8 Beautiful Jerusalem* stands abandoned
like a watchman's shelter in a vineyard,
like a lean-to in a cucumber field after the harvest,
like a helpless city under siege.
9 If the LORD of Heaven's Armies
had not spared a few of us,*
we would have been wiped out like Sodom,
destroyed like Gomorrah.

10 Listen to the LORD, you leaders of "Sodom."
Listen to the law of our God, people
of "Gomorrah."
11 "What makes you think I want all your sacrifices?"
says the LORD.
"I am sick of your burnt offerings of rams
and the fat of fattened cattle.
I get no pleasure from the blood
of bulls and lambs and goats.
12 When you come to worship me,
who asked you to parade through my courts with
all your ceremony?
13 Stop bringing me your meaningless gifts;
the incense of your offerings disgusts me!
As for your celebrations of the new moon and
the Sabbath
and your special days for fasting—
they are all sinful and false.
I want no more of your pious meetings.
14 I hate your new moon celebrations and your
annual festivals.
They are a burden to me. I cannot stand them!
15 When you lift up your hands in prayer, I will
not look.
Though you offer many prayers, I will not listen,
for your hands are covered with the blood of
innocent victims.
16 Wash yourselves and be clean!
Get your sins out of my sight.
Give up your evil ways.
17 Learn to do good.
Seek justice.
Help the oppressed.
Defend the cause of orphans.
Fight for the rights of widows.

STAINS 1:18

Some stains are virtually impossible to remove from clothing. The "stain" of sin seems equally permanent. But God can remove it from our lives just as he promised to do for the Israelites. All we have to do is ask (see Ps 51:1-10). ■

18 "Come now, let's settle this,"
says the LORD.
"Though your sins are like scarlet,
I will make them as white as snow.
Though they are red like crimson,
I will make them as white as wool.
19 If you will only obey me,
you will have plenty to eat.
20 But if you turn away and refuse to listen,
you will be devoured by the sword of
your enemies.
I, the LORD, have spoken!"

UNFAITHFUL JERUSALEM

21 See how Jerusalem, once so faithful,
has become a prostitute.

1:1 These kings reigned from 792 to 686 B.C. 1:8 Hebrew *The daughter of Zion.* 1:9 Greek version reads *a few of our children.* Compare Rom 9:29.

Isaiah

SERVED AS A PROPHET TO JUDAH FROM 740 TO 681 B.C.

Climate of the times	Society was in a great upheaval. Under King Ahaz and King Manasseh the people reverted to idolatry, and there was even child sacrifice.
Main message	Although judgment from other nations was inevitable, the people could still have a special relationship with God.
Importance of message	Sometimes we must suffer judgment and discipline before we are restored to God.
Contemporary prophets	Hosea (753–715) Micah (742–687)

Once the home of justice and righteousness,
she is now filled with murderers.
22 Once like pure silver,
you have become like worthless slag.
Once so pure,
you are now like watered-down wine.
23 Your leaders are rebels,
the companions of thieves.
All of them love bribes
and demand payoffs,
but they refuse to defend the cause of orphans
or fight for the rights of widows.

24 Therefore, the Lord, the LORD of Heaven's Armies,
the Mighty One of Israel, says,
"I will take revenge on my enemies
and pay back my foes!
25 I will raise my fist against you.
I will melt you down and skim off your slag.
I will remove all your impurities.
26 Then I will give you good judges again
and wise counselors like you used to have.
Then Jerusalem will again be called the Home of Justice
and the Faithful City."

27 Zion will be restored by justice;
those who repent will be revived by righteousness.
28 But rebels and sinners will be completely destroyed,
and those who desert the LORD will be consumed.

29 You will be ashamed of your idol worship
in groves of sacred oaks.
You will blush because you worshiped
in gardens dedicated to idols.
30 You will be like a great tree with withered leaves,
like a garden without water.
31 The strongest among you will disappear like straw;
their evil deeds will be the spark that sets it on fire.
They and their evil works will burn up together,
and no one will be able to put out the fire.

2

THE LORD'S FUTURE REIGN

This is a vision that Isaiah son of Amoz saw concerning Judah and Jerusalem:

2 In the last days, the mountain of the LORD's house
will be the highest of all—
the most important place on earth.
It will be raised above the other hills,
and people from all over the world will stream there to worship.
3 People from many nations will come and say,
"Come, let us go up to the mountain of the LORD,
to the house of Jacob's God.
There he will teach us his ways,
and we will walk in his paths."
For the LORD's teaching will go out from Zion;
his word will go out from Jerusalem.
4 The LORD will mediate between nations
and will settle international disputes.
They will hammer their swords into plowshares
and their spears into pruning hooks.
Nation will no longer fight against nation,
nor train for war anymore.

A WARNING OF JUDGMENT

5 Come, descendants of Jacob,
let us walk in the light of the LORD!
6 For the LORD has rejected his people,
the descendants of Jacob,
because they have filled their land with practices from the East
and with sorcerers, as the Philistines do.
They have made alliances with pagans.
7 Israel is full of silver and gold;
there is no end to its treasures.

Their land is full of warhorses;
there is no end to its chariots.
8 Their land is full of idols;
the people worship things they have made
with their own hands.
9 So now they will be humbled,
and all will be brought low—
do not forgive them.
10 Crawl into caves in the rocks.
Hide in the dust
from the terror of the LORD
and the glory of his majesty.
11 Human pride will be brought down,
and human arrogance will be humbled.
Only the LORD will be exalted
on that day of judgment.

12 For the LORD of Heaven's Armies
has a day of reckoning.
He will punish the proud and mighty
and bring down everything that is exalted.
13 He will cut down the tall cedars of Lebanon
and all the mighty oaks of Bashan.
14 He will level all the high mountains
and all the lofty hills.
15 He will break down every high tower
and every fortified wall.
16 He will destroy all the great trading ships*
and every magnificent vessel.
17 Human pride will be humbled,
and human arrogance will be brought down.
Only the LORD will be exalted
on that day of judgment.

RELIABLE 2:22

Isaiah warned the people of Judah to stop putting all of their trust in other people. Often we trust our fellow humans instead of trusting the all-knowing God. But only God is completely reliable. ■

18 Idols will completely disappear.
19 When the LORD rises to shake the earth,
his enemies will crawl into holes in the ground.
They will hide in caves in the rocks
from the terror of the LORD
and the glory of his majesty.
20 On that day of judgment they will abandon the gold
and silver idols
they made for themselves to worship.
They will leave their gods to the rodents
and bats,
21 while they crawl away into caverns
and hide among the jagged rocks in the cliffs.
They will try to escape the terror of the LORD
and the glory of his majesty
as he rises to shake the earth.
22 Don't put your trust in mere humans.
They are as frail as breath.
What good are they?

3 JUDGMENT AGAINST JUDAH

1 The Lord, the LORD of Heaven's Armies,
will take away from Jerusalem and Judah
everything they depend on:
every bit of bread
and every drop of water,
2 all their heroes and soldiers,
judges and prophets,
fortune-tellers and elders,
3 army officers and high officials,
advisers, skilled craftsmen, and astrologers.

4 I will make boys their leaders,
and toddlers their rulers.
5 People will oppress each other—
man against man,
neighbor against neighbor.
Young people will insult their elders,
and vulgar people will sneer at the honorable.

6 In those days a man will say to his brother,
"Since you have a coat, you be our leader!
Take charge of this heap of ruins!"
7 But he will reply,
"No! I can't help.
I don't have any extra food or clothes.
Don't put me in charge!"

8 For Jerusalem will stumble,
and Judah will fall,
because they speak out against the LORD and refuse
to obey him.
They provoke him to his face.
9 The very look on their faces gives them away.
They display their sin like the people of Sodom
and don't even try to hide it.
They are doomed!
They have brought destruction upon themselves.

10 Tell the godly that all will be well for them.
They will enjoy the rich reward they have earned!
11 But the wicked are doomed,
for they will get exactly what they deserve.

12 Childish leaders oppress my people,
and women rule over them.
O my people, your leaders mislead you;
they send you down the wrong road.

13 The LORD takes his place in court
and presents his case against his people!
14 The LORD comes forward to pronounce judgment
on the elders and rulers of his people:
"You have ruined Israel, my vineyard.

2:16 Hebrew *every ship of Tarshish.*

Your houses are filled with things stolen from
the poor.
15 How dare you crush my people,
grinding the faces of the poor into the dust?"
demands the Lord, the LORD of Heaven's Armies.

A WARNING TO JERUSALEM

16 The LORD says, "Beautiful Zion* is haughty:
craning her elegant neck,
flirting with her eyes,
walking with dainty steps,
tinkling her ankle bracelets.
17 So the Lord will send scabs on her head;
the LORD will make beautiful Zion bald."

SELF-CENTERED THINKING 3:16-26

The women of Judah had placed their emphasis on clothing and jewelry rather than on God. They thought only of themselves instead of the mistreated poor people around them (3:14-15). (Remind you of anyone you know?) Does this mean that God has a problem with clothing and jewelry? No. But self-centered thinking of any kind disturbs him. How observant are you about the needs of those around you? ■

18 On that day of judgment
the Lord will strip away everything that makes
her beautiful:
ornaments, headbands, crescent necklaces,
19 earrings, bracelets, and veils;
20 scarves, ankle bracelets, sashes,
perfumes, and charms;
21 rings, jewels,
22 party clothes, gowns, capes, and purses;
23 mirrors, fine linen garments,
head ornaments, and shawls.

24 Instead of smelling of sweet perfume, she
will stink.
She will wear a rope for a sash,
and her elegant hair will fall out.
She will wear rough burlap instead of rich robes.
Shame will replace her beauty.*
25 The men of the city will be killed with the sword,
and her warriors will die in battle.
26 The gates of Zion will weep and mourn.
The city will be like a ravaged woman,
huddled on the ground.

4 In that day so few men will be left that seven women will fight for each man, saying, "Let us all marry you! We will provide our own food and clothing. Only let us take your name so we won't be mocked as old maids."

A PROMISE OF RESTORATION

2 But in that day, the branch* of the LORD
will be beautiful and glorious;
the fruit of the land will be the pride and glory
of all who survive in Israel.
3 All who remain in Zion
will be a holy people—
those who survive the destruction of Jerusalem
and are recorded among the living.
4 The Lord will wash the filth from
beautiful Zion*
and cleanse Jerusalem of its bloodstains
with the hot breath of fiery judgment.
5 Then the LORD will provide shade for Mount Zion
and all who assemble there.
He will provide a canopy of cloud during the day
and smoke and flaming fire at night,
covering the glorious land.
6 It will be a shelter from daytime heat
and a hiding place from storms and rain.

5

A SONG ABOUT THE LORD'S VINEYARD

1 Now I will sing for the one I love
a song about his vineyard:
My beloved had a vineyard
on a rich and fertile hill.
2 He plowed the land, cleared its stones,
and planted it with the best vines.
In the middle he built a watchtower
and carved a winepress in the nearby rocks.
Then he waited for a harvest of sweet grapes,
but the grapes that grew were bitter.

3 Now, you people of Jerusalem and Judah,
you judge between me and my vineyard.
4 What more could I have done for my vineyard
that I have not already done?
When I expected sweet grapes,
why did my vineyard give me bitter grapes?

5 Now let me tell you
what I will do to my vineyard:
I will tear down its hedges
and let it be destroyed.
I will break down its walls
and let the animals trample it.
6 I will make it a wild place
where the vines are not pruned and the ground
is not hoed,
a place overgrown with briers and thorns.
I will command the clouds
to drop no rain on it.

7 The nation of Israel is the vineyard of the LORD
of Heaven's Armies.
The people of Judah are his pleasant garden.

3:16 Or *The women of Zion* (with corresponding changes to plural forms through verse 24); Hebrew reads *The daughters of Zion;* also in 3:17. 3:24 As in Dead Sea Scrolls; Masoretic Text reads *robes / because instead of beauty.* 4:2 Or *the Branch.* 4:4 Or *from the women of Zion;* Hebrew reads *from the daughters of Zion.*

He expected a crop of justice,
but instead he found oppression.
He expected to find righteousness,
but instead he heard cries of violence.

JUDAH'S GUILT AND JUDGMENT

8 What sorrow for you who buy up house after house
and field after field,
until everyone is evicted and you live alone in
the land.
9 But I have heard the LORD of Heaven's Armies
swear a solemn oath:
"Many houses will stand deserted;
even beautiful mansions will be empty.
10 Ten acres* of vineyard will not produce even six
gallons* of wine.
Ten baskets of seed will yield only one basket*
of grain."

HUMAN IDOLS 5:1-13

God planned to punish the people of Israel by sending them into exile. The nation's heroes—the great and honored among them—would suffer the same humiliation as the common people. Why? Because they lived by their own values rather than God's. God wanted the people of Israel to see that their human idols fall. Many of today's heroes in TV, movies, and books are idolized because of their ability to live as they please. Are your heroes those who defy God, or those who defy the world in order to serve God? ■

11 What sorrow for those who get up early in
the morning
looking for a drink of alcohol
and spend long evenings drinking wine
to make themselves flaming drunk.
12 They furnish wine and lovely music at their
grand parties—
lyre and harp, tambourine and flute—
but they never think about the LORD
or notice what he is doing.
13 So my people will go into exile far away
because they do not know me.
Those who are great and honored will starve,
and the common people will die of thirst.
14 The grave* is licking its lips in anticipation,
opening its mouth wide.
The great and the lowly
and all the drunken mob will be swallowed up.
15 Humanity will be destroyed, and people
brought down;
even the arrogant will lower their eyes in humiliation.
16 But the LORD of Heaven's Armies will be exalted
by his justice.
The holiness of God will be displayed by
his righteousness.
17 In that day lambs will find good pastures,
and fattened sheep and young goats* will feed
among the ruins.

18 What sorrow for those who drag their sins
behind them
with ropes made of lies,
who drag wickedness behind them like a cart!
19 They even mock God and say,
"Hurry up and do something!
We want to see what you can do.
Let the Holy One of Israel carry out his plan,
for we want to know what it is."

20 What sorrow for those who say
that evil is good and good is evil,
that dark is light and light is dark,
that bitter is sweet and sweet is bitter.
21 What sorrow for those who are wise in their own eyes
and think themselves so clever.
22 What sorrow for those who are heroes at
drinking wine
and boast about all the alcohol they can hold.
23 They take bribes to let the wicked go free,
and they punish the innocent.

24 Therefore, just as fire licks up stubble
and dry grass shrivels in the flame,
so their roots will rot
and their flowers wither.
For they have rejected the law of the LORD of
Heaven's Armies;
they have despised the word of the Holy One
of Israel.
25 That is why the LORD's anger burns against
his people,
and why he has raised his fist to crush them.
The mountains tremble,
and the corpses of his people litter the streets
like garbage.
But even then the LORD's anger is not satisfied.
His fist is still poised to strike!

26 He will send a signal to distant nations far away
and whistle to those at the ends of the earth.
They will come racing toward Jerusalem.
27 They will not get tired or stumble.
They will not stop for rest or sleep.
Not a belt will be loose,
not a sandal strap broken.
28 Their arrows will be sharp
and their bows ready for battle.
Sparks will fly from their horses' hooves,
and the wheels of their chariots will spin like
a whirlwind.

5:10a Hebrew *A ten yoke,* that is, the area of land plowed by ten teams of oxen in one day. **5:10b** Hebrew *a bath* [21 liters]. **5:10c** Hebrew *A homer* [5 bushels or 182 liters] *of seed will yield only an ephah* [20 quarts or 22 liters]. **5:14** Hebrew *Sheol.* **5:17** As in Greek version; Hebrew reads *and strangers.*

ULTIMATE ISSUES

SO, WHAT'S GOD REALLY LIKE?

Is there really a God? If so, what's he really like? Have you been asked those questions lately? Maybe you've *asked* those questions yourself because of conflicting information you've heard.

In the sixth chapter of Isaiah, the prophet describes a vision of God. Obviously, he was convinced that God existed! So, what is God like?

We can know what God is like by looking at the names given for him in Scripture. Each name—Elohim, Adonai, El Shaddai, Yahweh (or Jehovah), Abba—reveals an aspect of God's character.

Yet there are some aspects of God's character that are mysterious. For example, God has always existed. (See Ps 90:2.) That's mind-boggling.

Another mysterious element of God's character is the fact that he never changes (see Mal 3:6). He is the same yesterday, today, and forever (see Heb 13:8). In other words, he is forever consistent.

Still another is the fact that God is infinite—limitless. This infinity is expressed in different ways. In regard to *time,* God is eternal; he always was, is, and will be. In regard to *space,* he is omnipresent, or everywhere at once. No corner of the universe lacks his presence. In regard to *power,* he is omnipotent, or all-powerful. God can do anything that is consistent with his character. In regard to *knowledge,* he is omniscient, or all-knowing. There is nothing and no one that God does not know completely. He knows everything about you.

We can comprehend many of God's characteristics because he shares them with us to some degree. These include the abilities to think, to love, to make wise choices, to communicate, to work, and so on. Though God's ability in these areas is light-years beyond ours, he has given us some capacity to resemble him in certain areas. Remember, we are made in the image of God.

There are many different ideas and belief systems centered around the question, Who is God? Christianity is based on the confident assertion that the real God, the God of Isaiah and of the Bible, has revealed himself to us, and we can know him.

29 They will roar like lions,
like the strongest of lions.
Growling, they will pounce on their victims and
carry them off,
and no one will be there to rescue them.
30 They will roar over their victims on that day
of destruction
like the roaring of the sea.
If someone looks across the land,
only darkness and distress will be seen;
even the light will be darkened by clouds.

6 ISAIAH'S CLEANSING AND CALL

It was in the year King Uzziah died* that I saw the Lord.
He was sitting on a lofty throne, and the train of his robe
filled the Temple. 2 Attending him were mighty seraphim,
each having six wings. With two wings they covered their
faces, with two they covered their feet, and with two they
flew. 3 They were calling out to each other,

"Holy, holy, holy is the LORD of Heaven's Armies!
The whole earth is filled with his glory!"

4 Their voices shook the Temple to its foundations, and
the entire building was filled with smoke.
5 Then I said, "It's all over! I am doomed, for I am a sinful man. I have filthy lips, and I live among a people with
filthy lips. Yet I have seen the King, the LORD of Heaven's
Armies."
6 Then one of the seraphim flew to me with a burning
coal he had taken from the altar with a pair of tongs. 7 He
touched my lips with it and said, "See, this coal has
touched your lips. Now your guilt is removed, and your
sins are forgiven."
8 Then I heard the Lord asking, "Whom should I send as
a messenger to this people? Who will go for us?"
I said, "Here I am. Send me."
9 And he said, "Yes, go, and say to this people,

'Listen carefully, but do not understand.
Watch closely, but learn nothing.'

6:1 King Uzziah died in 740 B.C.

10 Harden the hearts of these people.
  Plug their ears and shut their eyes.
That way, they will not see with their eyes,
  nor hear with their ears,
nor understand with their hearts
  and turn to me for healing."*

GREATNESS 6:1-7

Isaiah's lofty view of God in 6:1-4 gives us a sense of God's greatness, mystery, and power. Isaiah's recognition of his sinfulness reminds us that none of us is without fault. When we recognize how great God is, and how desperately we need his forgiveness, we will be energized to do his work. How does your concept of the greatness of God measure up to Isaiah's? ■

11Then I said, "Lord, how long will this go on?"
And he replied,

"Until their towns are empty,
  their houses are deserted,
  and the whole country is a wasteland;
12 until the LORD has sent everyone away,
  and the entire land of Israel lies deserted.
13 If even a tenth—a remnant—survive,
  it will be invaded again and burned.
But as a terebinth or oak tree leaves a stump when
    it is cut down,
  so Israel's stump will be a holy seed."

7

A MESSAGE FOR AHAZ

When Ahaz, son of Jotham and grandson of Uzziah, was
king of Judah, King Rezin of Syria* and Pekah son of
Remaliah, the king of Israel, set out to attack Jerusalem.
However, they were unable to carry out their plan.
2The news had come to the royal court of Judah: "Syria
is allied with Israel* against us!" So the hearts of the king
and his people trembled with fear, like trees shaking in a
storm.
3Then the LORD said to Isaiah, "Take your son Shear-
jashub* and go out to meet King Ahaz. You will find him
at the end of the aqueduct that feeds water into the upper
pool, near the road leading to the field where cloth is
washed.* 4Tell him to stop worrying. Tell him he doesn't
need to fear the fierce anger of those two burned-out
embers, King Rezin of Syria and Pekah son of Remaliah.
5Yes, the kings of Syria and Israel are plotting against
him, saying, 6'We will attack Judah and capture it for
ourselves. Then we will install the son of Tabeel as Judah's king.' 7But this is what the Sovereign LORD says:

"This invasion will never happen;
  it will never take place;
8 for Syria is no stronger than its capital, Damascus,
  and Damascus is no stronger than its king, Rezin.
As for Israel, within sixty-five years
  it will be crushed and completely destroyed.
9 Israel is no stronger than its capital, Samaria,
  and Samaria is no stronger than its king, Pekah
    son of Remaliah.
Unless your faith is firm,
  I cannot make you stand firm."

THE SIGN OF IMMANUEL

10Later, the LORD sent this message to King Ahaz: 11"Ask
the LORD your God for a sign of confirmation, Ahaz.
Make it as difficult as you want—as high as heaven or as
deep as the place of the dead.*"
12But the king refused. "No," he said, "I will not test the
LORD like that."
13Then Isaiah said, "Listen well, you royal family of
David! Isn't it enough to exhaust human patience? Must
you exhaust the patience of my God as well? 14All right
then, the Lord himself will give you the sign. Look! The
virgin* will conceive a child! She will give birth to a son
and will call him Immanuel (which means 'God is with
us'). 15By the time this child is old enough to choose
what is right and reject what is wrong, he will be eating
yogurt* and honey. 16For before the child is that old, the
lands of the two kings you fear so much will both be
deserted.
17"Then the LORD will bring things on you, your nation, and your family unlike anything since Israel broke
away from Judah. He will bring the king of Assyria upon
you!"
18In that day the LORD will whistle for the army of
southern Egypt and for the army of Assyria. They will
swarm around you like flies and bees. 19They will come
in vast hordes and settle in the fertile areas and also in
the desolate valleys, caves, and thorny places. 20In that
day the Lord will hire a "razor" from beyond the Euphrates River*—the king of Assyria—and use it to shave off
everything: your land, your crops, and your people.*
21In that day a farmer will be fortunate to have a cow
and two sheep or goats left. 22Nevertheless, there will be
enough milk for everyone because so few people will be
left in the land. They will eat their fill of yogurt and
honey. 23In that day the lush vineyards, now worth
1,000 pieces of silver,* will become patches of briers
and thorns. 24The entire land will become a vast ex-
panse of briers and thorns, a hunting ground overrun by

6:9-10 Greek version reads *And he said, "Go and say to this people, / 'When you hear what I say, you will not understand. / When you see what I do, you will not comprehend.' / For the hearts of these people are hardened, / and their ears cannot hear, and they have closed their eyes— / so their eyes cannot see, / and their ears cannot hear, / and their hearts cannot understand, / and they cannot turn to me and let me heal them."* Compare Matt 13:14-15; Mark 4:12; Luke 8:10; Acts 28:26-27. **7:1** Hebrew *Aram;* also in 7:2, 4, 5, 8. **7:2** Hebrew *Ephraim,* referring to the northern kingdom of Israel; also in 7:5, 8, 9, 17. **7:3a** *Shear-jashub* means "A remnant will return." **7:3b** Or *bleached.* **7:11** Hebrew *as deep as Sheol.* **7:14** Or *young woman.* **7:15** Or *curds;* also in 7:22. **7:20a** Hebrew *the river.* **7:20b** Hebrew *shave off the head, the hair of the legs, and the beard.* **7:23** Hebrew *1,000 shekels of silver,* about 25 pounds or 11.4 kilograms in weight.

keeping it real

I became a Christian in seventh grade, but had trouble really living like one. I was good at putting people down, for one thing. And I swore a lot. But probably the biggest weakness I had was partying.

When someone asked me to go to a party, it was like I couldn't say no. Then when I got there, if there was drinking, I couldn't resist. I tried to resist a couple of times, but people would ask why I wasn't having a beer. Once I even tried to tell them it was because I was a Christian. I shouldn't have said that. They joked about my being too "holy" for them, and I felt so bad I gave in and even drank too much that night. After that, I was afraid to say anything about my faith because I thought it would be worse if I said something and then didn't act at all like a Christian.

Still, I read my Bible. And I started going to youth group in our church. That helped me change some, but I continued to feel like a hypocrite.

One day I was reading in Isaiah, and for some reason Isaiah 7:9 leaped out at me. It said, "Unless your faith is firm, I cannot make you stand firm." I had been praying that God would make me a stronger Christian. This verse seemed to be saying to me that I needed to choose to stand firm rather than give in to pressure.

Reading that verse was a turning point for me. I decided that I had to learn more about my faith and God's promises, and more about how God's Holy Spirit worked in my life. I spent more time with my church friends and less with my school friends. At first that was difficult, but it later turned out to be easier than I thought. The youth group often had things planned for the weekend, so when someone invited me to a party, I could honestly say I had other plans. I'm still struggling with saying no to my friends, but it's less of a struggle now. The more I learn about God, the more I see how he works in me through his Holy Spirit; and the more I believe God, the more he really does protect me. **—Jason**

wildlife. 25No one will go to the fertile hillsides where
the gardens once grew, for briers and thorns will cover
them. Cattle, sheep, and goats will graze there.

8

THE COMING ASSYRIAN INVASION

Then the LORD said to me, "Make a large signboard and
clearly write this name on it: Maher-shalal-hash-baz.*" 2I
asked Uriah the priest and Zechariah son of Jeberekiah,
both known as honest men, to witness my doing this.
3Then I slept with my wife, and she became pregnant
and gave birth to a son. And the LORD said, "Call him
Maher-shalal-hash-baz. 4For before this child is old
enough to say 'Papa' or 'Mama,' the king of Assyria will
carry away both the abundance of Damascus and the
riches of Samaria."
5Then the LORD spoke to me again and said, 6"My care
for the people of Judah is like the gently flowing waters of
Shiloah, but they have rejected it. They are rejoicing over
what will happen to* King Rezin and King Pekah.*
7Therefore, the Lord will overwhelm them with a mighty
flood from the Euphrates River*—the king of Assyria and
all his glory. This flood will overflow all its channels 8and
sweep into Judah until it is chin deep. It will spread its
wings, submerging your land from one end to the other,
O Immanuel.

9 "Huddle together, you nations, and be terrified.
Listen, all you distant lands.
Prepare for battle, but you will be crushed!
Yes, prepare for battle, but you will be crushed!
10 Call your councils of war, but they will be worthless.
Develop your strategies, but they will
not succeed.
For God is with us!*"

A CALL TO TRUST THE LORD

11The LORD has given me a strong warning not to think
like everyone else does. He said,

12 "Don't call everything a conspiracy, like they do,
and don't live in dread of what frightens them.

8:1 *Maher-shalal-hash-baz* means "Swift to plunder and quick to carry away." 8:6a Or *They are rejoicing because of.* 8:6b Hebrew *and the son of Remaliah.* 8:7 Hebrew *the river.* 8:10 Hebrew *Immanuel!*

[13] Make the LORD of Heaven's Armies holy
in your life.
He is the one you should fear.
He is the one who should make you tremble.
[14] He will keep you safe.
But to Israel and Judah
he will be a stone that makes people stumble,
a rock that makes them fall.
And for the people of Jerusalem
he will be a trap and a snare.
[15] Many will stumble and fall,
never to rise again.
They will be snared and captured."

CHOICES 8:5-15

Because the people of Judah rejected God's gentle care in favor of seeking help from other nations, God planned to punish them. Here we see two distinct attributes of God—his love and his wrath. Continually ignoring God's love and guidance often leads us into trouble, which invites his wrath. We must recognize the consequences of our choices. God seeks to protect us from bad choices, but he still gives us the freedom to make them. ■

[16] Preserve the teaching of God;
entrust his instructions to those who follow me.
[17] I will wait for the LORD,
who has turned away from the descendants
of Jacob.
I will put my hope in him.

[18]I and the children the LORD has given me serve as
signs and warnings to Israel from the LORD of Heaven's
Armies who dwells in his Temple on Mount Zion.
[19]Someone may say to you, "Let's ask the mediums and
those who consult the spirits of the dead. With their
whisperings and mutterings, they will tell us what to do."
But shouldn't people ask God for guidance? Should the
living seek guidance from the dead?
[20]Look to God's instructions and teachings! People
who contradict his word are completely in the dark.
[21]They will go from one place to another, weary and hungry. And because they are hungry, they will rage and
curse their king and their God. They will look up to
heaven [22]and down at the earth, but wherever they look,
there will be trouble and anguish and dark despair. They
will be thrown out into the darkness.

9 HOPE IN THE MESSIAH

[1]*Nevertheless, that time of darkness and despair will
not go on forever. The land of Zebulun and Naphtali will
be humbled, but there will be a time in the future when
Galilee of the Gentiles, which lies along the road that
runs between the Jordan and the sea, will be filled with
glory.

[2]*The people who walk in darkness
will see a great light.
For those who live in a land of deep darkness,*
a light will shine.
[3] You will enlarge the nation of Israel,
and its people will rejoice.
They will rejoice before you
as people rejoice at the harvest
and like warriors dividing the plunder.
[4] For you will break the yoke of their slavery
and lift the heavy burden from their shoulders.
You will break the oppressor's rod,
just as you did when you destroyed the army
of Midian.
[5] The boots of the warrior
and the uniforms bloodstained by war
will all be burned.
They will be fuel for the fire.

[6] For a child is born to us,
a son is given to us.
The government will rest on his shoulders.
And he will be called:
Wonderful Counselor,* Mighty God,
Everlasting Father, Prince of Peace.
[7] His government and its peace
will never end.
He will rule with fairness and justice from the throne
of his ancestor David
for all eternity.
The passionate commitment of the LORD of
Heaven's Armies
will make this happen!

BLAME 8:21-22

After rejecting God's plan for their lives, the people of Judah blamed him for their trials. People continually blame God for their self-induced problems. How do you respond to the unpleasant consequences of poor choices? Where do you fix the blame? If you've been tempted to blame God in the past, consider the ways you can grow even through when you fail. ■

THE LORD'S ANGER AGAINST ISRAEL

[8] The Lord has spoken out against Jacob;
his judgment has fallen upon Israel.
[9] And the people of Israel* and Samaria,
who spoke with such pride and arrogance,
will soon know it.
[10] They said, "We will replace the broken bricks of our
ruins with finished stone,

9:1 Verse 9:1 is numbered 8:23 in Hebrew text. **9:2a** Verses 9:2-21 are numbered 9:1-20 in Hebrew text. **9:2b** Greek version reads *a land where death casts its shadow.* Compare Matt 4:16. **9:6** Or *Wonderful, Counselor.* **9:9** Hebrew *of Ephraim,* referring to the northern kingdom of Israel.

Names for Messiah

ISAIAH USES FIVE NAMES TO DESCRIBE THE MESSIAH (9:6). THESE NAMES HAVE SPECIAL MEANING TO US.

WONDERFUL	COUNSELOR	MIGHTY GOD	EVERLASTING FATHER	PRINCE OF PEACE
He is exceptional, distinguished, and without peers.	He gives the right advice.	He is God himself.	He is timeless; he is God our Father.	His government is one of justice and peace.

and replant the felled sycamore-fig trees
with cedars."
11 But the LORD will bring Rezin's enemies against Israel
and stir up all their foes.
12 The Syrians* from the east and the Philistines from
the west
will bare their fangs and devour Israel.
But even then the LORD's anger will not be satisfied.
His fist is still poised to strike.

THE PROBLEM OF PRIDE 9:8-10

Israel was called arrogant for saying, in essence, "We've faced a temporary setback, but by our own strength we will rebuild our city." Though God made Israel a nation and gave them the land they occupied, the people trusted themselves rather than God. Too often we take pride in our accomplishments or possessions, forgetting that God has given us every ability we have. We become proud of our status as Christians. God is not pleased with *any* pride or attitudes of self-sufficiency. Tempted to think you're all that? Watch out! ■

13 For after all this punishment, the people will still
not repent.
They will not seek the LORD of Heaven's Armies.
14 Therefore, in a single day the LORD will destroy both
the head and the tail,
the noble palm branch and the lowly reed.
15 The leaders of Israel are the head,
and the lying prophets are the tail.
16 For the leaders of the people have misled them.
They have led them down the path
of destruction.
17 That is why the Lord takes no pleasure in the
young men
and shows no mercy even to the widows
and orphans.
For they are all wicked hypocrites,
and they all speak foolishness.
But even then the LORD's anger will not
be satisfied.
His fist is still poised to strike.

18 This wickedness is like a brushfire.
It burns not only briers and thorns
but also sets the forests ablaze.
Its burning sends up clouds of smoke.
19 The land will be blackened
by the fury of the LORD of Heaven's Armies.
The people will be fuel for the fire,
and no one will spare even his own brother.
20 They will attack their neighbor on the right
but will still be hungry.
They will devour their neighbor on the left
but will not be satisfied.
In the end they will even eat their own children.*
21 Manasseh will feed on Ephraim,
Ephraim will feed on Manasseh,
and both will devour Judah.
But even then the LORD's anger will not be satisfied.
His fist is still poised to strike.

10

1 What sorrow awaits the unjust judges
and those who issue unfair laws.
2 They deprive the poor of justice
and deny the rights of the needy among my people.
They prey on widows
and take advantage of orphans.
3 What will you do when I punish you,
when I send disaster upon you from a distant land?
To whom will you turn for help?
Where will your treasures be safe?
4 You will stumble along as prisoners
or lie among the dead.
But even then the LORD's anger will not be satisfied.
His fist is still poised to strike.

JUDGMENT AGAINST ASSYRIA

5 "What sorrow awaits Assyria, the rod of my anger.
I use it as a club to express my anger.
6 I am sending Assyria against a godless nation,
against a people with whom I am angry.
Assyria will plunder them,
trampling them like dirt beneath its feet.
7 But the king of Assyria will not understand that
he is my tool;
his mind does not work that way.

9:12 Hebrew *Arameans*. 9:20 Or *eat their own arms*.

His plan is simply to destroy,
to cut down nation after nation.
8 He will say,
'Each of my princes will soon be a king.
9 We destroyed Calno just as we did Carchemish.
Hamath fell before us as Arpad did.
And we destroyed Samaria just as we
did Damascus.
10 Yes, we have finished off many a kingdom
whose gods were greater than those in Jerusalem
and Samaria.
11 So we will defeat Jerusalem and her gods,
just as we destroyed Samaria with hers.'"

12After the Lord has used the king of Assyria to accomplish his purposes on Mount Zion and in Jerusalem, he
will turn against the king of Assyria and punish him—for
he is proud and arrogant. 13He boasts,

"By my own powerful arm I have done this.
With my own shrewd wisdom I planned it.
I have broken down the defenses of nations
and carried off their treasures.
I have knocked down their kings like a bull.
14 I have robbed their nests of riches
and gathered up kingdoms as a farmer
gathers eggs.
No one can even flap a wing against me
or utter a peep of protest."

15 But can the ax boast greater power than the person
who uses it?
Is the saw greater than the person who saws?
Can a rod strike unless a hand moves it?
Can a wooden cane walk by itself?
16 Therefore, the Lord, the LORD of Heaven's Armies,
will send a plague among Assyria's proud troops,
and a flaming fire will consume its glory.
17 The LORD, the Light of Israel, will be a fire;
the Holy One will be a flame.
He will devour the thorns and briers with fire,
burning up the enemy in a single night.
18 The LORD will consume Assyria's glory
like a fire consumes a forest in a fruitful land;
it will waste away like sick people in a plague.
19 Of all that glorious forest, only a few trees
will survive—
so few that a child could count them!

HOPE FOR THE LORD'S PEOPLE

20 In that day the remnant left in Israel,
the survivors in the house of Jacob,
will no longer depend on allies
who seek to destroy them.
But they will faithfully trust the LORD,
the Holy One of Israel.
21 A remnant will return;*
yes, the remnant of Jacob will return to the
Mighty God.
22 But though the people of Israel are as numerous
as the sand of the seashore,
only a remnant of them will return.
The LORD has rightly decided to destroy
his people.
23 Yes, the Lord, the LORD of Heaven's Armies,
has already decided to destroy the entire land.*

THE REMNANT 10:20-22

Those who remained faithful to God despite the horrors of the promised enemy invasion were called the remnant. The key to being a part of the remnant was *faith.* Being a descendant of Abraham, living in the Promised Land, having trusted God at one time—none of these characteristics were good enough. Are you relying on your Christian heritage, the rituals of worship, or past experiences to put you in a right relationship with God? The key to being set apart by God is faith in him. ■

24So this is what the Lord, the LORD of Heaven's Armies, says: "O my people in Zion, do not be afraid of the
Assyrians when they oppress you with rod and club as
the Egyptians did long ago. 25In a little while my anger
against you will end, and then my anger will rise up to
destroy them." 26The LORD of Heaven's Armies will lash
them with his whip, as he did when Gideon triumphed
over the Midianites at the rock of Oreb, or when the
LORD's staff was raised to drown the Egyptian army in
the sea.

27 In that day the LORD will end the bondage of
his people.
He will break the yoke of slavery
and lift it from their shoulders.*

28 Look, the Assyrians are now at Aiath.
They are passing through Migron
and are storing their equipment at Micmash.
29 They are crossing the pass
and are camping at Geba.
Fear strikes the town of Ramah.
All the people of Gibeah, the hometown of Saul,
are running for their lives.
30 Scream in terror,
you people of Gallim!
Shout out a warning to Laishah.
Oh, poor Anathoth!
31 There go the people of Madmenah, all fleeing.
The citizens of Gebim are trying to hide.
32 The enemy stops at Nob for the rest of that day.
He shakes his fist at beautiful Mount Zion, the
mountain of Jerusalem.

10:21 Hebrew *Shear-jashub;* see 7:3; 8:18. 10:22-23 Greek version reads *only a remnant of them will be saved. / For he will carry out his sentence quickly and with finality and righteousness; / for God will carry out his sentence upon all the world with finality.* Compare Rom 9:27-28. 10:27 As in Greek version; Hebrew reads *The yoke will be broken, / for you have grown so fat.*

33 But look! The Lord, the LORD of Heaven's Armies,
will chop down the mighty tree of Assyria with
great power!
He will cut down the proud.
That lofty tree will be brought down.
34 He will cut down the forest trees with an ax.
Lebanon will fall to the Mighty One.*

11 A BRANCH FROM DAVID'S LINE

1 Out of the stump of David's family* will grow
a shoot—
yes, a new Branch bearing fruit from the old root.
2 And the Spirit of the LORD will rest on him—
the Spirit of wisdom and understanding,
the Spirit of counsel and might,
the Spirit of knowledge and the fear of the LORD.
3 He will delight in obeying the LORD.
He will not judge by appearance
nor make a decision based on hearsay.
4 He will give justice to the poor
and make fair decisions for the exploited.
The earth will shake at the force of his word,
and one breath from his mouth will destroy
the wicked.
5 He will wear righteousness like a belt
and truth like an undergarment.

FAIR TREATMENT 11:1-5

Isaiah prophesied about a perfect leader who would judge everyone fairly. We all long for fair treatment from others, but do we give it? We hate being judged based on appearance, false evidence, or hearsay. But we can be quick to judge others using those same criteria. Only Christ—the promised perfect leader—is totally fair. And only as he governs our hearts can we learn to be as fair in our treatment of others as we expect them to be with us. (See also Luke 6:31.) ■

6 In that day the wolf and the lamb will live together;
the leopard will lie down with the baby goat.
The calf and the yearling will be safe with the lion,
and a little child will lead them all.
7 The cow will graze near the bear.
The cub and the calf will lie down together.
The lion will eat hay like a cow.
8 The baby will play safely near the hole of a cobra.
Yes, a little child will put its hand in a nest of
deadly snakes without harm.
9 Nothing will hurt or destroy in all my holy mountain,
for as the waters fill the sea,
so the earth will be filled with people who know
the LORD.
10 In that day the heir to David's throne*
will be a banner of salvation to all the world.
The nations will rally to him,
and the land where he lives will be a glorious
place.*
11 In that day the Lord will reach out his hand
a second time
to bring back the remnant of his people—
those who remain in Assyria and northern Egypt;
in southern Egypt, Ethiopia,* and Elam;
in Babylonia,* Hamath, and all the distant
coastlands.
12 He will raise a flag among the nations
and assemble the exiles of Israel.
He will gather the scattered people of Judah
from the ends of the earth.
13 Then at last the jealousy between Israel* and Judah
will end.
They will not be rivals anymore.
14 They will join forces to swoop down on Philistia
to the west.
Together they will attack and plunder the nations
to the east.
They will occupy the lands of Edom and Moab,
and Ammon will obey them.
15 The LORD will make a dry path through the gulf of
the Red Sea.*
He will wave his hand over the Euphrates River,*
sending a mighty wind to divide it into seven streams
so it can easily be crossed on foot.
16 He will make a highway for the remnant of
his people,
the remnant coming from Assyria,
just as he did for Israel long ago
when they returned from Egypt.

12 SONGS OF PRAISE FOR SALVATION

1 In that day you will sing:
"I will praise you, O LORD!
You were angry with me, but not any more.
Now you comfort me.
2 See, God has come to save me.
I will trust in him and not be afraid.
The LORD GOD is my strength and my song;
he has given me victory."

3 With joy you will drink deeply
from the fountain of salvation!
4 In that wonderful day you will sing:
"Thank the LORD! Praise his name!
Tell the nations what he has done.
Let them know how mighty he is!
5 Sing to the LORD, for he has done wonderful things.

10:34 Or *with an ax / as even the mighty trees of Lebanon fall.* **11:1** Hebrew *the stump of the line of Jesse.* Jesse was King David's father. **11:10a** Hebrew *the root of Jesse.* **11:10b** Greek version reads *In that day the heir to David's throne* [literally *the root of Jesse*] *will come, / and he will rule over the Gentiles. / They will place their hopes on him.* Compare Rom 15:12. **11:11a** Hebrew *in Pathros, Cush.* **11:11b** Hebrew *in Shinar.* **11:13** Hebrew *Ephraim,* referring to the northern kingdom of Israel. **11:15a** Hebrew *will destroy the tongue of the sea of Egypt.* **11:15b** Hebrew *the river.*

Make known his praise around the world.
6 Let all the people of Jerusalem* shout his praise
with joy!
For great is the Holy One of Israel who lives
among you."

13 A MESSAGE ABOUT BABYLON

Isaiah son of Amoz received this message concerning the destruction of Babylon:

2 "Raise a signal flag on a bare hilltop.
Call up an army against Babylon.
Wave your hand to encourage them
as they march into the palaces of the high
and mighty.
3 I, the LORD, have dedicated these soldiers for
this task.
Yes, I have called mighty warriors to express
my anger,
and they will rejoice when I am exalted."

4 Hear the noise on the mountains!
Listen, as the vast armies march!
It is the noise and shouting of many nations.
The LORD of Heaven's Armies has called this
army together.
5 They come from distant countries,
from beyond the farthest horizons.
They are the LORD's weapons to carry out his anger.
With them he will destroy the whole land.

6 Scream in terror, for the day of the LORD
has arrived—
the time for the Almighty to destroy.
7 Every arm is paralyzed with fear.
Every heart melts,
8 and people are terrified.
Pangs of anguish grip them,
like those of a woman in labor.
They look helplessly at one another,
their faces aflame with fear.

9 For see, the day of the LORD is coming—
the terrible day of his fury and fierce anger.
The land will be made desolate,
and all the sinners destroyed with it.
10 The heavens will be black above them;
the stars will give no light.
The sun will be dark when it rises,
and the moon will provide no light.

11 "I, the LORD, will punish the world for its evil
and the wicked for their sin.
I will crush the arrogance of the proud
and humble the pride of the mighty.
12 I will make people scarcer than gold—
more rare than the fine gold of Ophir.
13 For I will shake the heavens.
The earth will move from its place
when the LORD of Heaven's Armies displays his wrath
in the day of his fierce anger."

14 Everyone in Babylon will run about like a
hunted gazelle,
like sheep without a shepherd.
They will try to find their own people
and flee to their own land.
15 Anyone who is captured will be cut down—
run through with a sword.
16 Their little children will be dashed to death before
their eyes.
Their homes will be sacked, and their wives
will be raped.

17 "Look, I will stir up the Medes against Babylon.
They cannot be tempted by silver
or bribed with gold.
18 The attacking armies will shoot down the young men
with arrows.
They will have no mercy on helpless babies
and will show no compassion for children."

19 Babylon, the most glorious of kingdoms,
the flower of Chaldean pride,
will be devastated like Sodom and Gomorrah
when God destroyed them.
20 Babylon will never be inhabited again.
It will remain empty for generation
after generation.
Nomads will refuse to camp there,
and shepherds will not bed down their sheep.
21 Desert animals will move into the ruined city,
and the houses will be haunted by
howling creatures.
Owls will live among the ruins,
and wild goats will go there to dance.
22 Hyenas will howl in its fortresses,
and jackals will make dens in its luxurious palaces.
Babylon's days are numbered;
its time of destruction will soon arrive.

14 A TAUNT FOR BABYLON'S KING

But the LORD will have mercy on the descendants of Jacob. He will choose Israel as his special people once again. He will bring them back to settle once again in their own land. And people from many different nations will come and join them there and unite with the people of Israel.* 2The nations of the world will help the LORD's people to return, and those who come to live in their land will serve them. Those who captured Israel will themselves be captured, and Israel will rule over its enemies.
3In that wonderful day when the LORD gives his people

12:6 Hebrew *Zion.* **14:1** Hebrew *the house of Jacob.* The names "Jacob" and "Israel" are often interchanged throughout the Old Testament, referring sometimes to the individual patriarch and sometimes to the nation.

rest from sorrow and fear, from slavery and chains, [4]you
will taunt the king of Babylon. You will say,

"The mighty man has been destroyed.
Yes, your insolence* is ended.
5 For the LORD has crushed your wicked power
and broken your evil rule.
6 You struck the people with endless blows of rage
and held the nations in your angry grip
with unrelenting tyranny.
7 But finally the earth is at rest and quiet.
Now it can sing again!
8 Even the trees of the forest—
the cypress trees and the cedars of Lebanon—
sing out this joyous song:
'Since you have been cut down,
no one will come now to cut us down!'

POWER FAILURE 14:1-6

God permitted Babylon to have power for a purpose—to chastise his wayward people. (See 13:1-22.) When that purpose ended, so did the power. Earthly power is temporary. If you don't believe that, consider the ex-politicians you read about in the news. Is your confidence in human power or in God? Only God's power is everlasting. ■

9 "In the place of the dead* there is excitement
over your arrival.
The spirits of world leaders and mighty kings
long dead
stand up to see you.
10 With one voice they all cry out,
'Now you are as weak as we are!
11 Your might and power were buried with you.*
The sound of the harp in your palace
has ceased.
Now maggots are your sheet,
and worms your blanket.'

12 "How you are fallen from heaven,
O shining star, son of the morning!
You have been thrown down to the earth,
you who destroyed the nations of the world.
13 For you said to yourself,
'I will ascend to heaven and set my throne above
God's stars.
I will preside on the mountain of the gods
far away in the north.*
14 I will climb to the highest heavens
and be like the Most High.'
15 Instead, you will be brought down to the place
of the dead,
down to its lowest depths.
16 Everyone there will stare at you and ask,
'Can this be the one who shook the earth
and made the kingdoms of the world tremble?
17 Is this the one who destroyed the world
and made it into a wasteland?
Is this the king who demolished the world's
greatest cities
and had no mercy on his prisoners?'

18 "The kings of the nations lie in stately glory,
each in his own tomb,
19 but you will be thrown out of your grave
like a worthless branch.
Like a corpse trampled underfoot,
you will be dumped into a mass grave
with those killed in battle.
You will descend to the pit.
20 You will not be given a proper burial,
for you have destroyed your nation
and slaughtered your people.
The descendants of such an evil person
will never again receive honor.
21 Kill this man's children!
Let them die because of their father's sins!
They must not rise and conquer the earth,
filling the world with their cities."

22 This is what the LORD of Heaven's Armies says:
"I, myself, have risen against Babylon!
I will destroy its children and its children's children,"
says the LORD.
23 "I will make Babylon a desolate place of owls,
filled with swamps and marshes.
I will sweep the land with the broom of destruction.
I, the LORD of Heaven's Armies, have spoken!"

A MESSAGE ABOUT ASSYRIA

[24]The LORD of Heaven's Armies has sworn this oath:

"It will all happen as I have planned.
It will be as I have decided.
25 I will break the Assyrians when they are in Israel;
I will trample them on my mountains.
My people will no longer be their slaves
nor bow down under their heavy loads.
26 I have a plan for the whole earth,
a hand of judgment upon all the nations.
27 The LORD of Heaven's Armies has spoken—
who can change his plans?
When his hand is raised,
who can stop him?"

A MESSAGE ABOUT PHILISTIA

[28]This message came to me the year King Ahaz died:*

29 Do not rejoice, you Philistines,
that the rod that struck you is broken—
that the king who attacked you is dead.

14:4 As in Dead Sea Scrolls; the meaning of the Masoretic Text is uncertain. **14:9** Hebrew *Sheol;* also in 14:15. **14:11** Hebrew *were brought down to Sheol.* **14:13** Or *on the heights of Zaphon.* **14:28** King Ahaz died in 715 B.C.

For from that snake a more poisonous snake
will be born,
a fiery serpent to destroy you!
30 I will feed the poor in my pasture;
the needy will lie down in peace.
But as for you, I will wipe you out with famine
and destroy the few who remain.
31 Wail at the gates! Weep in the cities!
Melt with fear, you Philistines!
A powerful army comes like smoke from the north.
Each soldier rushes forward eager to fight.

32What should we tell the Philistine messengers? Tell them,

"The LORD has built Jerusalem*;
its walls will give refuge to his oppressed people."

THE ENEMY 15:1-9

Ever know someone who seemed to constantly make trouble for you or someone else? The nation of Moab was like that. They invaded Israel (Judg 3:12-14) and fought against the armies of Saul (1 Sam 14:47) and David (2 Sam 8:2, 11-12). They were like mosquitoes—persistently annoying. But Isaiah prophesied that Moab would be punished for its harsh treatment of Israel. If you've despaired over the persistence of an enemy, consider the example of Moab. Sooner or later, God will bring all evil to an end. ■

15 A MESSAGE ABOUT MOAB

This message came to me concerning Moab:

In one night the town of Ar will be leveled,
and the city of Kir will be destroyed.
2 Your people will go to their temple in Dibon to mourn.
They will go to their sacred shrines to weep.
They will wail for the fate of Nebo and Medeba,
shaving their heads in sorrow and cutting off
their beards.
3 They will wear burlap as they wander the streets.
From every home and public square will come the
sound of wailing.
4 The people of Heshbon and Elealeh will cry out;
their voices will be heard as far away as Jahaz!
The bravest warriors of Moab will cry out in
utter terror.
They will be helpless with fear.

5 My heart weeps for Moab.
Its people flee to Zoar and Eglath-shelishiyah.
Weeping, they climb the road to Luhith.
Their cries of distress can be heard all along the
road to Horonaim.
6 Even the waters of Nimrim are dried up!
The grassy banks are scorched.
The tender plants are gone;
nothing green remains.
7 The people grab their possessions
and carry them across the Ravine of Willows.
8 A cry of distress echoes through the land of Moab
from one end to the other—
from Eglaim to Beer-elim.
9 The stream near Dibon* runs red with blood,
but I am still not finished with Dibon!
Lions will hunt down the survivors—
both those who try to escape
and those who remain behind.

16

1 Send lambs from Sela as tribute
to the ruler of the land.
Send them through the desert
to the mountain of beautiful Zion.
2 The women of Moab are left like homeless birds
at the shallow crossings of the Arnon River.
3 "Help us," they cry.
"Defend us against our enemies.
Protect us from their relentless attack.
Do not betray us now that we have escaped.
4 Let our refugees stay among you.
Hide them from our enemies until the terror
is past."

When oppression and destruction have ended
and enemy raiders have disappeared,
5 then God will establish one of David's descendants
as king.
He will rule with mercy and truth.
He will always do what is just
and be eager to do what is right.

6 We have heard about proud Moab—
about its pride and arrogance and rage.
But all that boasting has disappeared.
7 The entire land of Moab weeps.
Yes, everyone in Moab mourns
for the cakes of raisins from Kir-hareseth.
They are all gone now.
8 The farms of Heshbon are abandoned;
the vineyards at Sibmah are deserted.
The rulers of the nations have broken down Moab—
that beautiful grapevine.
Its tendrils spread north as far as the town of Jazer
and trailed eastward into the wilderness.
Its shoots reached so far west
that they crossed over the Dead Sea.*

9 So now I weep for Jazer and the vineyards
of Sibmah;
my tears will flow for Heshbon and Elealeh.

14:32 Hebrew *Zion*. **15:9** As in Dead Sea Scrolls, some Greek manuscripts, and Latin Vulgate; Masoretic Text reads *Dimon;* also in 15:9b.
16:8 Hebrew *the sea*.

There are no more shouts of joy
over your summer fruits and harvest.
10 Gone now is the gladness,
gone the joy of harvest.
There will be no singing in the vineyards,
no more happy shouts,
no treading of grapes in the winepresses.
I have ended all their harvest joys.
11 My heart's cry for Moab is like a lament on a harp.
I am filled with anguish for Kir-hareseth.*
12 The people of Moab will worship at their pagan shrines,
but it will do them no good.
They will cry to the gods in their temples,
but no one will be able to save them.

13The LORD has already said these things about Moab
in the past. 14But now the LORD says, "Within three years,
counting each day,* the glory of Moab will be ended.
From its great population, only a few of its people will be
left alive."

17 A MESSAGE ABOUT DAMASCUS AND ISRAEL

This message came to me concerning Damascus:

"Look, the city of Damascus will disappear!
It will become a heap of ruins.
2 The towns of Aroer will be deserted.
Flocks will graze in the streets and lie down
undisturbed,
with no one to chase them away.
3 The fortified towns of Israel* will also be destroyed,
and the royal power of Damascus will end.
All that remains of Syria*
will share the fate of Israel's departed glory,"
declares the LORD of Heaven's Armies.

4 "In that day Israel's* glory will grow dim;
its robust body will waste away.
5 The whole land will look like a grainfield
after the harvesters have gathered the grain.
It will be desolate,
like the fields in the valley of Rephaim after
the harvest.
6 Only a few of its people will be left,
like stray olives left on a tree after the harvest.
Only two or three remain in the highest branches,
four or five scattered here and there on the limbs,"
declares the LORD, the God of Israel.

7 Then at last the people will look to their Creator
and turn their eyes to the Holy One of Israel.
8 They will no longer look to their idols for help
or worship what their own hands have made.
They will never again bow down to their Asherah poles
or worship at the pagan shrines they have built.

9 Their largest cities will be like a deserted forest,
like the land the Hivites and Amorites abandoned*
when the Israelites came here so long ago.
It will be utterly desolate.
10 Why? Because you have turned from the God who
can save you.
You have forgotten the Rock who can hide you.
So you may plant the finest grapevines
and import the most expensive seedlings.
11 They may sprout on the day you set them out;
yes, they may blossom on the very morning you
plant them,
but you will never pick any grapes from them.
Your only harvest will be a load of grief and
unrelieved pain.

12 Listen! The armies of many nations
roar like the roaring of the sea.
Hear the thunder of the mighty forces
as they rush forward like thundering waves.
13 But though they thunder like breakers on a beach,
God will silence them, and they will run away.
They will flee like chaff scattered by the wind,
like a tumbleweed whirling before a storm.
14 In the evening Israel waits in terror,
but by dawn its enemies are dead.
This is the just reward of those who plunder us,
a fitting end for those who destroy us.

18 A MESSAGE ABOUT ETHIOPIA

1 Listen, Ethiopia*—land of fluttering sails*
that lies at the headwaters of the Nile,
2 that sends ambassadors
in swift boats down the river.

Go, swift messengers!
Take a message to a tall, smooth-skinned people,
who are feared far and wide
for their conquests and destruction,
and whose land is divided by rivers.

3 All you people of the world,
everyone who lives on the earth—
when I raise my battle flag on the mountain, look!
When I blow the ram's horn, listen!
4 For the LORD has told me this:
"I will watch quietly from my dwelling place—
as quietly as the heat rises on a summer day,
or as the morning dew forms during the harvest."
5 Even before you begin your attack,
while your plans are ripening like grapes,
the LORD will cut off your new growth with
pruning shears.
He will snip off and discard your spreading
branches.

16:11 Hebrew *Kir-heres,* a variant spelling of Kir-hareseth. **16:14** Hebrew *Within three years, as a servant bound by contract would count them.* **17:3a** Hebrew *of Ephraim,* referring to the northern kingdom of Israel. **17:3b** Hebrew *Aram.* **17:4** Hebrew *Jacob's.* See note on 14:1. **17:9** As in Greek version; Hebrew reads *like places of the wood and the highest bough.* **18:1a** Hebrew *Cush.* **18:1b** Or *land of many locusts;* Hebrew reads *land of whirring wings.*

6 Your mighty army will be left dead in the fields
for the mountain vultures and wild animals.
The vultures will tear at the corpses all summer.
The wild animals will gnaw at the bones all winter.

7 At that time the LORD of Heaven's Armies will
receive gifts
from this land divided by rivers,
from this tall, smooth-skinned people,
who are feared far and wide for their conquests
and destruction.
They will bring the gifts to Jerusalem,*
where the LORD of Heaven's Armies dwells.

19 A MESSAGE ABOUT EGYPT

This message came to me concerning Egypt:

Look! The LORD is advancing against Egypt,
riding on a swift cloud.
The idols of Egypt tremble.
The hearts of the Egyptians melt with fear.

2 "I will make Egyptian fight against Egyptian—
brother against brother,
neighbor against neighbor,
city against city,
province against province.
3 The Egyptians will lose heart,
and I will confuse their plans.
They will plead with their idols for wisdom
and call on spirits, mediums, and those who
consult the spirits of the dead.
4 I will hand Egypt over
to a hard, cruel master.
A fierce king will rule them,"
says the Lord, the LORD of Heaven's Armies.

5 The waters of the Nile will fail to rise and flood
the fields.
The riverbed will be parched and dry.
6 The canals of the Nile will dry up,
and the streams of Egypt will stink
with rotting reeds and rushes.
7 All the greenery along the riverbank
and all the crops along the river
will dry up and blow away.
8 The fishermen will lament for lack of work.
Those who cast hooks into the Nile will groan,
and those who use nets will lose heart.
9 There will be no flax for the harvesters,
no thread for the weavers.
10 They will be in despair,
and all the workers will be sick at heart.

11 What fools are the officials of Zoan!
Their best counsel to the king of Egypt is stupid
and wrong.
Will they still boast to Pharaoh of their wisdom?
Will they dare brag about all their wise ancestors?
12 Where are your wise counselors, Pharaoh?
Let them tell you what God plans,
what the LORD of Heaven's Armies is going
to do to Egypt.
13 The officials of Zoan are fools,
and the officials of Memphis* are deluded.
The leaders of the people
have led Egypt astray.
14 The LORD has sent a spirit of foolishness on them,
so all their suggestions are wrong.
They cause Egypt to stagger
like a drunk in his vomit.
15 There is nothing Egypt can do.
All are helpless—
the head and the tail,
the noble palm branch and the lowly reed.

UNITY 19:21-25

Isaiah prophesied that at some future time, the people of Egypt and Assyria would unite and turn to God. That prophecy probably sounded utterly impossible to the people of Israel. After all, Egypt and Assyria were bitter enemies. Yet Jesus breaks down every barrier that threatens relationships. In Christ, people and nations who are poles apart politically will bow at his feet as brothers and sisters. Is there someone you can't imagine ever getting along with? Believe in the Barrier Breaker—Jesus. ■

16In that day the Egyptians will be as weak as women.
They will cower in fear beneath the upraised fist of the
LORD of Heaven's Armies. 17Just to speak the name of Israel will terrorize them, for the LORD of Heaven's Armies
has laid out his plans against them.
18In that day five of Egypt's cities will follow the LORD
of Heaven's Armies. They will even begin to speak Hebrew, the language of Canaan. One of these cities will be
Heliopolis, the City of the Sun.*
19In that day there will be an altar to the LORD in the
heart of Egypt, and there will be a monument to the LORD
at its border. 20It will be a sign and a witness that the LORD
of Heaven's Armies is worshiped in the land of Egypt.
When the people cry to the LORD for help against those
who oppress them, he will send them a savior who will
rescue them. 21The LORD will make himself known to the
Egyptians. Yes, they will know the LORD and will give their
sacrifices and offerings to him. They will make a vow to
the LORD and will keep it. 22The LORD will strike Egypt, and
then he will bring healing. For the Egyptians will turn to
the LORD, and he will listen to their pleas and heal them.
23In that day Egypt and Assyria will be connected by a
highway. The Egyptians and Assyrians will move freely
between their lands, and they will both worship God.
24And Israel will be their ally. The three will be together,
and Israel will be a blessing to them. 25For the LORD of

18:7 Hebrew *to Mount Zion.* **19:13** Hebrew *Noph.* **19:18** Or *will be the City of Destruction.*

Heaven's Armies will say, "Blessed be Egypt, my people.
Blessed be Assyria, the land I have made. Blessed be Israel, my special possession!"

20 A MESSAGE ABOUT EGYPT AND ETHIOPIA

In the year when King Sargon of Assyria sent his commander in chief to capture the Philistine city of Ashdod,*
2the LORD told Isaiah son of Amoz, "Take off the burlap
you have been wearing, and remove your sandals." Isaiah
did as he was told and walked around naked and barefoot.
3Then the LORD said, "My servant Isaiah has been walking around naked and barefoot for the last three years.
This is a sign—a symbol of the terrible troubles I will
bring upon Egypt and Ethiopia.* 4For the king of Assyria
will take away the Egyptians and Ethiopians* as prisoners. He will make them walk naked and barefoot, both
young and old, their buttocks bared, to the shame of
Egypt. 5Then the Philistines will be thrown into panic, for
they counted on the power of Ethiopia and boasted of
their allies in Egypt! 6They will say, 'If this can happen to
Egypt, what chance do we have? We were counting on
Egypt to protect us from the king of Assyria.'"

21 A MESSAGE ABOUT BABYLON

This message came to me concerning Babylon—the desert by the sea*:

Disaster is roaring down on you from the desert,
like a whirlwind sweeping in from the Negev.
2 I see a terrifying vision:
I see the betrayer betraying,
the destroyer destroying.
Go ahead, you Elamites and Medes,
attack and lay siege.
I will make an end
to all the groaning Babylon caused.
3 My stomach aches and burns with pain.
Sharp pangs of anguish are upon me,
like those of a woman in labor.
I grow faint when I hear what God is planning;
I am too afraid to look.
4 My mind reels and my heart races.
I longed for evening to come,
but now I am terrified of the dark.

5 Look! They are preparing a great feast.
They are spreading rugs for people to sit on.
Everyone is eating and drinking.
But quick! Grab your shields and prepare for battle.
You are being attacked!

6 Meanwhile, the Lord said to me,
"Put a watchman on the city wall.
Let him shout out what he sees.
7 He should look for chariots
drawn by pairs of horses,
and for riders on donkeys and camels.
Let the watchman be fully alert."

8 Then the watchman* called out,
"Day after day I have stood on the watchtower,
my lord.
Night after night I have remained at my post.
9 Now at last—look!
Here comes a man in a chariot
with a pair of horses!"
Then the watchman said,
"Babylon is fallen, fallen!
All the idols of Babylon
lie broken on the ground!"
10 O my people, threshed and winnowed,
I have told you everything the LORD of Heaven's
Armies has said,
everything the God of Israel has told me.

A MESSAGE ABOUT EDOM

11This message came to me concerning Edom*:

Someone from Edom* keeps calling to me,
"Watchman, how much longer until morning?
When will the night be over?"
12 The watchman replies,
"Morning is coming, but night will soon return.
If you wish to ask again, then come back and ask."

A MESSAGE ABOUT ARABIA

13This message came to me concerning Arabia:

O caravans from Dedan,
hide in the deserts of Arabia.
14 O people of Tema,
bring water to these thirsty people,
food to these weary refugees.
15 They have fled from the sword,
from the drawn sword,
from the bent bow
and the terrors of battle.

16The Lord said to me, "Within a year, counting each
day,* all the glory of Kedar will come to an end. 17Only a
few of its courageous archers will survive. I, the LORD, the
God of Israel, have spoken!"

22 A MESSAGE ABOUT JERUSALEM

This message came to me concerning Jerusalem—the Valley of Vision*:

What is happening?
Why is everyone running to the rooftops?

20:1 Ashdod was captured by Assyria in 711 B.C. **20:3** Hebrew *Cush;* also in 20:5. **20:4** Hebrew *Cushites.* **21:1** Hebrew *concerning the desert by the sea.* **21:8** As in Dead Sea Scrolls and Syriac version; Masoretic Text reads *a lion.* **21:11a** Hebrew *Dumah,* which means "silence" or "stillness." It is a wordplay on the word *Edom.* **21:11b** Hebrew *Seir,* another name for Edom. **21:16** Hebrew *Within a year, as a servant bound by contract would count it.* Some ancient manuscripts read *Within three years,* as in 16:14. **22:1** Hebrew *concerning the Valley of Vision.*

2 The whole city is in a terrible uproar.
What do I see in this reveling city?
Bodies are lying everywhere,
killed not in battle but by famine and disease.
3 All your leaders have fled.
They surrendered without resistance.
The people tried to slip away,
but they were captured, too.
4 That's why I said, "Leave me alone to weep;
do not try to comfort me.
Let me cry for my people
as I watch them being destroyed."

CONSEQUENCES 22:4

Isaiah mourned because of the punishment his people experienced due to their rebellion against God. Sometimes people we care for ignore our attempts to help them. We feel helpless as we watch them suffer the consequences of actions we tried to stop. Is someone you know experiencing the consequences of wrong actions? There's one thing you can do: Pray for God's mercy. ■

5 Oh, what a day of crushing defeat!
What a day of confusion and terror
brought by the Lord, the LORD of Heaven's Armies,
upon the Valley of Vision!
The walls of Jerusalem have been broken,
and cries of death echo from the mountainsides.
6 Elamites are the archers,
with their chariots and charioteers.
The men of Kir hold up the shields.
7 Chariots fill your beautiful valleys,
and charioteers storm your gates.
8 Judah's defenses have been stripped away.
You run to the armory* for your weapons.
9 You inspect the breaks in the walls
of Jerusalem.*
You store up water in the lower pool.
10 You survey the houses and tear some down
for stone to strengthen the walls.
11 Between the city walls, you build a reservoir
for water from the old pool.
But you never ask for help from the One who
did all this.
You never considered the One who planned
this long ago.

12 At that time the Lord, the LORD of Heaven's
Armies,
called you to weep and mourn.
He told you to shave your heads in sorrow for
your sins
and to wear clothes of burlap to show your
remorse.
13 But instead, you dance and play;
you slaughter cattle and kill sheep.
You feast on meat and drink wine.
You say, "Let's feast and drink,
for tomorrow we die!"

HOPE 22:13-14

The people of Israel said, "Let's feast and drink" (22:13), because they had given up hope. Today, we see people giving up hope as well. There are two common responses to hopelessness: despair and self-indulgence. But neither response is helpful. A more helpful response is to turn to God and trust in his promises. ■

14The LORD of Heaven's Armies has revealed this to me:
"Till the day you die, you will never be forgiven for this
sin." That is the judgment of the Lord, the LORD of
Heaven's Armies.

A MESSAGE FOR SHEBNA

15This is what the Lord, the LORD of Heaven's Armies, said
to me: "Confront Shebna, the palace administrator, and
give him this message:

16 "Who do you think you are,
and what are you doing here,
building a beautiful tomb for yourself—
a monument high up in the rock?
17 For the LORD is about to hurl you away,
mighty man.
He is going to grab you,
18 crumple you into a ball,
and toss you away into a distant, barren land.
There you will die,
and your glorious chariots will be broken
and useless.
You are a disgrace to your master!

19"Yes, I will drive you out of office," says the LORD. "I
will pull you down from your high position. 20And then I
will call my servant Eliakim son of Hilkiah to replace you.
21I will dress him in your royal robes and will give him
your title and your authority. And he will be a father to
the people of Jerusalem and Judah. 22I will give him the
key to the house of David—the highest position in the
royal court. When he opens doors, no one will be able to
close them; when he closes doors, no one will be able to
open them. 23He will bring honor to his family name, for I
will drive him firmly in place like a nail in the wall. 24They
will give him great responsibility, and he will bring honor
to even the lowliest members of his family.*"
25But the LORD of Heaven's Armies also says: "The time
will come when I will pull out the nail that seemed so
firm. It will come out and fall to the ground. Everything it
supports will fall with it. I, the LORD, have spoken!"

22:8 Hebrew *to the House of the Forest;* see 1 Kgs 7:2-5. 22:9 Hebrew *the city of David.* 22:24 Hebrew *They will hang on him all the glory of his father's house: its offspring and offshoots, all its lesser vessels, from the bowls to all the jars.*

23 A MESSAGE ABOUT TYRE

This message came to me concerning Tyre:

Weep, O ships of Tarshish,
for the harbor and houses of Tyre are gone!
The rumors you heard in Cyprus*
are all true.
2 Mourn in silence, you people of the coast
and you merchants of Sidon.
Your traders crossed the sea,
3 sailing over deep waters.
They brought you grain from Egypt*
and harvests from along the Nile.
You were the marketplace of the world.

4 But now you are put to shame, city of Sidon,
for Tyre, the fortress of the sea, says,
"Now I am childless;
I have no sons or daughters."
5 When Egypt hears the news about Tyre,
there will be great sorrow.
6 Send word now to Tarshish!
Wail, you people who live in distant lands!
7 Is this silent ruin all that is left of your once
joyous city?
What a long history was yours!
Think of all the colonists you sent to
distant places.

8 Who has brought this disaster on Tyre,
that great creator of kingdoms?
Her traders were all princes,
her merchants were nobles.
9 The LORD of Heaven's Armies has done it
to destroy your pride
and bring low all earth's nobility.
10 Come, people of Tarshish,
sweep over the land like the flooding Nile,
for Tyre is defenseless.*
11 The LORD held out his hand over the sea
and shook the kingdoms of the earth.
He has spoken out against Phoenicia,*
ordering that her fortresses be destroyed.
12 He says, "Never again will you rejoice,
O daughter of Sidon, for you have been crushed.
Even if you flee to Cyprus,
you will find no rest."
13 Look at the land of Babylonia*—
the people of that land are gone!
The Assyrians have handed Babylon over
to the wild animals of the desert.
They have built siege ramps against its walls,
torn down its palaces,
and turned it to a heap of rubble.

14 Wail, O ships of Tarshish,
for your harbor is destroyed!

15 For seventy years, the length of a king's life, Tyre will
be forgotten. But then the city will come back to life as in
the song about the prostitute:

16 Take a harp and walk the streets,
you forgotten harlot.
Make sweet melody and sing your songs
so you will be remembered again.

17 Yes, after seventy years the LORD will revive Tyre. But
she will be no different than she was before. She will
again be a prostitute to all kingdoms around the world.
18 But in the end her profits will be given to the LORD. Her
wealth will not be hoarded but will provide good food
and fine clothing for the LORD's priests.

DETER DETERIORATION 24:1-13

The land of Israel was a reflection of the consequences of Israel's rebellion. Crops withered or wouldn't grow. Today we see the results of sin in our own land—pollution, crime, poverty, and more. Sin affects every aspect of society so extensively that even those faithful to God suffer. Yet believers can slow our society's deterioration by their examples of faithfulness toward God and others. Are you ready to make a difference? ■

24 DESTRUCTION OF THE EARTH

1 Look! The LORD is about to destroy the earth
and make it a vast wasteland.
He devastates the surface of the earth
and scatters the people.
2 Priests and laypeople,
servants and masters,
maids and mistresses,
buyers and sellers,
lenders and borrowers,
bankers and debtors—none will be spared.
3 The earth will be completely emptied
and looted.
The LORD has spoken!

4 The earth mourns and dries up,
and the crops waste away and wither.
Even the greatest people on earth waste away.
5 The earth suffers for the sins of its people,
for they have twisted God's instructions,
violated his laws,
and broken his everlasting covenant.
6 Therefore, a curse consumes the earth.
Its people must pay the price for their sin.

23:1 Hebrew *Kittim;* also in 23:12. 23:3 Hebrew *from Shihor,* a branch of the Nile River. 23:10 The meaning of the Hebrew in this verse is uncertain. 23:11 Hebrew *Canaan.* 23:13 Or *Chaldea.*

They are destroyed by fire,
and only a few are left alive.
7 The grapevines waste away,
and there is no new wine.
All the merrymakers sigh and mourn.
8 The cheerful sound of tambourines is stilled;
the happy cries of celebration are heard no more.
The melodious chords of the harp are silent.
9 Gone are the joys of wine and song;
alcoholic drink turns bitter in the mouth.
10 The city writhes in chaos;
every home is locked to keep out intruders.
11 Mobs gather in the streets, crying out for wine.
Joy has turned to gloom.
Gladness has been banished from the land.
12 The city is left in ruins,
its gates battered down.
13 Throughout the earth the story is the same—
only a remnant is left,
like the stray olives left on the tree
or the few grapes left on the vine after harvest.

14 But all who are left shout and sing for joy.
Those in the west praise the LORD's majesty.
15 In eastern lands, give glory to the LORD.
In the lands beyond the sea, praise the name of the LORD, the God of Israel.
16 We hear songs of praise from the ends of the earth,
songs that give glory to the Righteous One!

But my heart is heavy with grief.
Weep for me, for I wither away.
Deceit still prevails,
and treachery is everywhere.
17 Terror and traps and snares will be your lot,
you people of the earth.
18 Those who flee in terror will fall into a trap,
and those who escape the trap will be caught in a snare.

Destruction falls like rain from the heavens;
the foundations of the earth shake.
19 The earth has broken up.
It has utterly collapsed;
it is violently shaken.
20 The earth staggers like a drunk.
It trembles like a tent in a storm.
It falls and will not rise again,
for the guilt of its rebellion is very heavy.

21 In that day the LORD will punish the gods in the heavens
and the proud rulers of the nations on earth.
22 They will be rounded up and put in prison.
They will be shut up in prison
and will finally be punished.
23 Then the glory of the moon will wane,
and the brightness of the sun will fade,
for the LORD of Heaven's Armies will rule on Mount Zion.
He will rule in great glory in Jerusalem,
in the sight of all the leaders of his people.

25 PRAISE FOR JUDGMENT AND SALVATION

1 O LORD, I will honor and praise your name,
for you are my God.
You do such wonderful things!
You planned them long ago,
and now you have accomplished them.
2 You turn mighty cities into heaps of ruins.
Cities with strong walls are turned to rubble.
Beautiful palaces in distant lands disappear
and will never be rebuilt.
3 Therefore, strong nations will declare your glory;
ruthless nations will fear you.

4 But you are a tower of refuge to the poor, O LORD,
a tower of refuge to the needy in distress.
You are a refuge from the storm
and a shelter from the heat.
For the oppressive acts of ruthless people
are like a storm beating against a wall,
5 or like the relentless heat of the desert.
But you silence the roar of foreign nations.
As the shade of a cloud cools relentless heat,
so the boastful songs of ruthless people are stilled.

6 In Jerusalem,* the LORD of Heaven's Armies
will spread a wonderful feast
for all the people of the world.
It will be a delicious banquet
with clear, well-aged wine and choice meat.
7 There he will remove the cloud of gloom,
the shadow of death that hangs over the earth.
8 He will swallow up death forever!*
The Sovereign LORD will wipe away all tears.
He will remove forever all insults and mockery
against his land and people.
The LORD has spoken!

9 In that day the people will proclaim,
"This is our God!
We trusted in him, and he saved us!
This is the LORD, in whom we trusted.
Let us rejoice in the salvation he brings!"
10 For the LORD's hand of blessing will rest on Jerusalem.
But Moab will be crushed.
It will be like straw trampled down and left to rot.
11 God will push down Moab's people
as a swimmer pushes down water with his hands.
He will end their pride
and all their evil works.
12 The high walls of Moab will be demolished.
They will be brought down to the ground,
down into the dust.

25:6 Hebrew *On this mountain;* also in 25:10. **25:8** Greek version reads *Death is swallowed up in victory.* Compare 1 Cor 15:54.

26 A SONG OF PRAISE TO THE LORD

In that day, everyone in the land of Judah will sing this song:

Our city is strong!
We are surrounded by the walls
of God's salvation.
2 Open the gates to all who are
righteous;
allow the faithful to enter.
3 You will keep in perfect peace
all who trust in you,
all whose thoughts are fixed on you!
4 Trust in the LORD always,
for the LORD GOD is the eternal Rock.
5 He humbles the proud
and brings down the arrogant city.
He brings it down to the dust.
6 The poor and oppressed trample it underfoot,
and the needy walk all over it.

You will keep in perfect peace all who trust in you, all whose thoughts are fixed on you!

ISAIAH 26:3

FIX YOUR EYES 26:3

Here's an experiment for you: Try not to think about rabbits. Ready? Go. You're thinking of them, aren't you? Essentially this is Isaiah's message. (No, not rabbits. Forget about them.) Whatever you "fix" your mind on affects your life. If you're fixated on problems, you'll be filled with fear. If you focus on God, as Isaiah suggests, you will be kept "in perfect peace." (Check out Phil 4:8 also.) Okay. You can stop thinking about rabbits now. ■

7 But for those who are righteous,
the way is not steep and rough.
You are a God who does what is right,
and you smooth out the path ahead of them.
8 LORD, we show our trust in you by obeying
your laws;
our heart's desire is to glorify your name.
9 All night long I search for you;
in the morning I earnestly seek for God.
For only when you come to judge the earth
will people learn what is right.
10 Your kindness to the wicked
does not make them do good.
Although others do right, the wicked keep
doing wrong
and take no notice of the LORD's majesty.
11 O LORD, they pay no attention to your upraised fist.
Show them your eagerness to defend
your people.
Then they will be ashamed.
Let your fire consume your enemies.
12 LORD, you will grant us peace;
all we have accomplished is
really from you.
13 O LORD our God, others have
ruled us,
but you alone are the one
we worship.
14 Those we served before are dead
and gone.
Their departed spirits will
never return!
You attacked them and
destroyed them,
and they are long forgotten.
15 O LORD, you have made our
nation great;
yes, you have made us great.
You have extended our borders,
and we give you the glory!
16 LORD, in distress we searched for you.
We prayed beneath the burden of your discipline.
17 Just as a pregnant woman
writhes and cries out in pain as she gives birth,
so were we in your presence, LORD.
18 We, too, writhe in agony,
but nothing comes of our suffering.
We have not given salvation to the earth,
nor brought life into the world.
19 But those who die in the LORD will live;
their bodies will rise again!
Those who sleep in the earth
will rise up and sing for joy!
For your life-giving light will fall like dew
on your people in the place of the dead!

RESTORATION FOR ISRAEL

20 Go home, my people,
and lock your doors!
Hide yourselves for a little while
until the LORD's anger has passed.
21 Look! The LORD is coming from heaven
to punish the people of the earth for their sins.
The earth will no longer hide those who have
been killed.
They will be brought out for all to see.

27

In that day the LORD will take his terrible, swift sword and punish Leviathan,* the swiftly moving serpent, the coiling, writhing serpent. He will kill the dragon of the sea.

2 "In that day,
sing about the fruitful vineyard.
3 I, the LORD, will watch over it,
watering it carefully.
Day and night I will watch so no one can harm it.

27:1 The identification of Leviathan is disputed, ranging from an earthly creature to a mythical sea monster in ancient literature.

4 My anger will be gone.
If I find briers and thorns growing,
I will attack them;
I will burn them up—
5 unless they turn to me for help.
Let them make peace with me;
yes, let them make peace with me."
6 The time is coming when Jacob's descendants
will take root.
Israel will bud and blossom
and fill the whole earth with fruit!

7 Has the LORD struck Israel
as he struck her enemies?
Has he punished her
as he punished them?
8 No, but he exiled Israel to call her to account.
She was exiled from her land
as though blown away in a storm from the east.
9 The LORD did this to purge Israel's* wickedness,
to take away all her sin.
As a result, all the pagan altars will be crushed to dust.
No Asherah pole or pagan shrine will be
left standing.
10 The fortified towns will be silent and empty,
the houses abandoned, the streets overgrown
with weeds.
Calves will graze there,
chewing on twigs and branches.
11 The people are like the dead branches of a tree,
broken off and used for kindling beneath the
cooking pots.
Israel is a foolish and stupid nation,
for its people have turned away from God.
Therefore, the one who made them
will show them no pity or mercy.

12Yet the time will come when the LORD will gather
them together like handpicked grain. One by one he will
gather them—from the Euphrates River* in the east to
the Brook of Egypt in the west. 13In that day the great
trumpet will sound. Many who were dying in exile in Assyria and Egypt will return to Jerusalem to worship the
LORD on his holy mountain.

28 A MESSAGE ABOUT SAMARIA

1 What sorrow awaits the proud city of Samaria—
the glorious crown of the drunks of Israel.*
It sits at the head of a fertile valley,
but its glorious beauty will fade like a flower.
It is the pride of a people
brought down by wine.
2 For the Lord will send a mighty army against it.
Like a mighty hailstorm and a torrential rain,
they will burst upon it like a surging flood
and smash it to the ground.
3 The proud city of Samaria—
the glorious crown of the drunks of Israel*—
will be trampled beneath its enemies' feet.
4 It sits at the head of a fertile valley,
but its glorious beauty will fade like a flower.
Whoever sees it will snatch it up,
as an early fig is quickly picked and eaten.

5 Then at last the LORD of Heaven's Armies
will himself be Israel's glorious crown.
He will be the pride and joy
of the remnant of his people.
6 He will give a longing for justice
to their judges.
He will give great courage
to their warriors who stand at the gates.

AGAIN AND AGAIN 28:1-13

God used repetition and simple words to get his messages through to the people. Do you find that God has to teach you the same lessons over and over? The simplicity of God's message can be a stumbling block for some (28:9-10), leading them to think it must have little value. But some of the simplest messages (for example, Jesus loves you) can have a profound impact. What messages have you heard again and again? Maybe it's time you listened. ■

7 Now, however, Israel is led by drunks
who reel with wine and stagger with alcohol.
The priests and prophets stagger
with alcohol
and lose themselves in wine.
They reel when they see visions
and stagger as they render decisions.
8 Their tables are covered with vomit;
filth is everywhere.
9 "Who does the LORD think we are?" they ask.
"Why does he speak to us like this?
Are we little children,
just recently weaned?
10 He tells us everything over and over—
one line at a time,
one line at a time,
a little here,
and a little there!"

11 So now God will have to speak to his people
through foreign oppressors who speak a
strange language!
12 God has told his people,
"Here is a place of rest;
let the weary rest here.
This is a place of quiet rest."
But they would not listen.

27:9 Hebrew *Jacob's*. See note on 14:1. 27:12 Hebrew *the river*. 28:1 Hebrew *What sorrow awaits the crowning glory of the drunks of Ephraim*, referring to Samaria, capital of the northern kingdom of Israel. 28:3 Hebrew *The crowning glory of the drunks of Ephraim*; see note on 28:1.

[13] So the LORD will spell out his message
for them again,
one line at a time,
one line at a time,
a little here,
and a little there,
so that they will stumble and fall.
They will be injured, trapped, and captured.

[14] Therefore, listen to this message from the LORD,
you scoffing rulers in Jerusalem.
[15] You boast, "We have struck a bargain to cheat death
and have made a deal to dodge the grave.*
The coming destruction can never touch us,
for we have built a strong refuge made of lies
and deception."

[16] Therefore, this is what the Sovereign LORD says:
"Look! I am placing a foundation stone
in Jerusalem,*
a firm and tested stone.
It is a precious cornerstone that is safe to build on.
Whoever believes need never be shaken.*
[17] I will test you with the measuring line of justice
and the plumb line of righteousness.
Since your refuge is made of lies,
a hailstorm will knock it down.
Since it is made of deception,
a flood will sweep it away.
[18] I will cancel the bargain you made to cheat death,
and I will overturn your deal to dodge the grave.
When the terrible enemy sweeps through,
you will be trampled into the ground.
[19] Again and again that flood will come,
morning after morning,
day and night,
until you are carried away."

This message will bring terror to your people.
[20] The bed you have made is too short to lie on.
The blankets are too narrow to cover you.
[21] The LORD will come as he did against the Philistines
at Mount Perazim
and against the Amorites at Gibeon.
He will come to do a strange thing;
he will come to do an unusual deed:
[22] For the Lord, the LORD of Heaven's Armies,
has plainly said that he is determined to crush
the whole land.
So scoff no more,
or your punishment will be even greater.

[23] Listen to me;
listen, and pay close attention.
[24] Does a farmer always plow and never sow?
Is he forever cultivating the soil and
never planting?
[25] Does he not finally plant his seeds—
black cumin, cumin, wheat, barley, and
emmer wheat—
each in its proper way,
and each in its proper place?
[26] The farmer knows just what to do,
for God has given him understanding.
[27] A heavy sledge is never used to thresh black cumin;
rather, it is beaten with a light stick.
A threshing wheel is never rolled on cumin;
instead, it is beaten lightly with a flail.
[28] Grain for bread is easily crushed,
so he doesn't keep on pounding it.
He threshes it under the wheels of a cart,
but he doesn't pulverize it.
[29] The LORD of Heaven's Armies is a wonderful teacher,
and he gives the farmer great wisdom.

29 A MESSAGE ABOUT JERUSALEM

[1] "What sorrow awaits Ariel,* the City of David.
Year after year you celebrate your feasts.
[2] Yet I will bring disaster upon you,
and there will be much weeping and sorrow.
For Jerusalem will become what her name
Ariel means—
an altar covered with blood.
[3] I will be your enemy,
surrounding Jerusalem and attacking its walls.
I will build siege towers
and destroy it.
[4] Then deep from the earth you will speak;
from low in the dust your words will come.
Your voice will whisper from the ground
like a ghost conjured up from the grave.

[5] "But suddenly, your ruthless enemies will be crushed
like the finest of dust.
Your many attackers will be driven away
like chaff before the wind.
Suddenly, in an instant,
[6] I, the LORD of Heaven's Armies, will act for you
with thunder and earthquake and great noise,
with whirlwind and storm and consuming fire.
[7] All the nations fighting against Jerusalem*
will vanish like a dream!
Those who are attacking her walls
will vanish like a vision in the night.
[8] A hungry person dreams of eating
but wakes up still hungry.
A thirsty person dreams of drinking
but is still faint from thirst when morning comes.
So it will be with your enemies,
with those who attack Mount Zion."
[9] Are you amazed and incredulous?
Don't you believe it?

28:15 Hebrew *Sheol;* also in 28:18. **28:16a** Hebrew *in Zion.* **28:16b** Greek version reads *Look! I am placing a stone in the foundation of Jerusalem* [literally *Zion*], */ a precious cornerstone for its foundation, chosen for great honor. / Anyone who trusts in him will never be disgraced.* Compare Rom 9:33; 1 Pet 2:6. **29:1** *Ariel* sounds like a Hebrew term that means "hearth" or "altar." **29:7** Hebrew *Ariel.*

Then go ahead and be blind.
You are stupid, but not from wine!
You stagger, but not from liquor!
10 For the LORD has poured out on you a spirit of deep sleep.
He has closed the eyes of your prophets and visionaries.

11All the future events in this vision are like a sealed book to them. When you give it to those who can read, they will say, "We can't read it because it is sealed."
12When you give it to those who cannot read, they will say, "We don't know how to read."

13 And so the Lord says,
"These people say they are mine.
They honor me with their lips,
but their hearts are far from me.
And their worship of me
is nothing but man-made rules learned by rote.*
14 Because of this, I will once again astound these hypocrites
with amazing wonders.
The wisdom of the wise will pass away,
and the intelligence of the intelligent will disappear."

HYPOCRISY 29:13-14

Isaiah condemned the people of Judah for being hypocrites. They claimed to belong to God. Yet because they were disobedient and merely went through the motions, God punished them. Religion had become routine instead of real. That's why Jesus quoted this passage (Matt 15:8-9; Mark 7:6-7) when he spoke to the Pharisees, the religious leaders of his day. Like the Pharisees, we fall into the same pit of hypocrisy when worship becomes ritualistic, rather than sincere. But God wants people to worship him with sincerity. Is that your desire as well? ■

15 What sorrow awaits those who try to hide their plans from the LORD,
who do their evil deeds in the dark!
"The LORD can't see us," they say.
"He doesn't know what's going on!"
16 How foolish can you be?
He is the Potter, and he is certainly greater than you, the clay!
Should the created thing say of the one who made it,
"He didn't make me"?
Does a jar ever say,
"The potter who made me is stupid"?

17 Soon—and it will not be very long—
the forests of Lebanon will become a fertile field,
and the fertile field will yield bountiful crops.

HIDING 29:15-16

The people of Jerusalem tried to hide their plans from God. They thought God couldn't see them and didn't know what was happening. It's strange that so many people think they can hide from God. In Psalm 139 we learn that God has examined us and knows everything about us. Would you be embarrassed if your best friends knew your personal thoughts? Remember that God knows all of them. ■

18 In that day the deaf will hear words read from a book,
and the blind will see through the gloom and darkness.
19 The humble will be filled with fresh joy from the LORD.
The poor will rejoice in the Holy One of Israel.
20 The scoffer will be gone,
the arrogant will disappear,
and those who plot evil will be killed.
21 Those who convict the innocent
by their false testimony will disappear.
A similar fate awaits those who use trickery to pervert justice
and who tell lies to destroy the innocent.

22That is why the LORD, who redeemed Abraham, says to the people of Israel,*

"My people will no longer be ashamed
or turn pale with fear.
23 For when they see their many children
and all the blessings I have given them,
they will recognize the holiness of the Holy One of Israel.
They will stand in awe of the God of Jacob.
24 Then the wayward will gain understanding,
and complainers will accept instruction.

30 JUDAH'S WORTHLESS TREATY WITH EGYPT

1 "What sorrow awaits my rebellious children,"
says the LORD.
"You make plans that are contrary to mine.
You make alliances not directed by my Spirit,
thus piling up your sins.
2 For without consulting me,
you have gone down to Egypt for help.
You have put your trust in Pharaoh's protection.
You have tried to hide in his shade.
3 But by trusting Pharaoh, you will be humiliated,
and by depending on him, you will be disgraced.
4 For though his power extends to Zoan
and his officials have arrived in Hanes,
5 all who trust in him will be ashamed.
He will not help you.
Instead, he will disgrace you."

29:13 Greek version reads *Their worship is a farce, / for they teach man-made ideas as commands from God*. Compare Mark 7:7.
29:22 Hebrew *of Jacob*. See note on 14:1.

Alliances Today

Isaiah warned Judah not to ally with Egypt (30:1-7; 31:1-3). He knew that trust in any nation or military might was futile. Judah's only hope was to trust in God. Although we don't consciously put our hope for deliverance in political alliances in quite the same way, we often put our hope in other forces.

GOVERNMENT	SCIENCE	EDUCATION	FINANCIAL SYSTEMS	MEDICAL CARE
We rely on government legislation to protect the moral decisions we want made, but legislation cannot change people's hearts.	We enjoy the benefits of science and technology. We look to scientific predictions and analysis before we look to the Bible.	We act as though education and degrees can guarantee our future and success without considering what God plans for our future.	We place our faith in financial "security," making as much money as we can for ourselves and forgetting that, while being wise with our money, we must trust God for our needs.	We regard medicine as the way to prolong life and preserve its quality—quite apart from faith and moral living.

6This message came to me concerning the animals in the Negev:

The caravan moves slowly
across the terrible desert to Egypt—
donkeys weighed down with riches
and camels loaded with treasure—
all to pay for Egypt's protection.
They travel through the wilderness,
a place of lionesses and lions,
a place where vipers and poisonous snakes live.
All this, and Egypt will give you nothing in return.
7 Egypt's promises are worthless!
Therefore, I call her Rahab—
the Harmless Dragon.*

A WARNING FOR REBELLIOUS JUDAH

8 Now go and write down these words.
Write them in a book.
They will stand until the end of time
as a witness
9 that these people are stubborn rebels
who refuse to pay attention to the LORD's instructions.
10 They tell the seers,
"Stop seeing visions!"
They tell the prophets,
"Don't tell us what is right.
Tell us nice things.
Tell us lies.
11 Forget all this gloom.
Get off your narrow path.
Stop telling us about your
'Holy One of Israel.'"

12This is the reply of the Holy One of Israel:

"Because you despise what I tell you
and trust instead in oppression and lies,
13 calamity will come upon you suddenly—
like a bulging wall that bursts and falls.
In an instant it will collapse
and come crashing down.
14 You will be smashed like a piece of pottery—
shattered so completely that
there won't be a piece big enough
to carry coals from a fireplace
or a little water from the well."

15 This is what the Sovereign LORD,
the Holy One of Israel, says:
"Only in returning to me
and resting in me will you be saved.
In quietness and confidence is your strength.
But you would have none of it.
16 You said, 'No, we will get our help from Egypt.
They will give us swift horses for riding into battle.'
But the only swiftness you are going to see
is the swiftness of your enemies chasing you!
17 One of them will chase a thousand of you.
Five of them will make all of you flee.
You will be left like a lonely flagpole on a hill
or a tattered banner on a distant mountaintop."

BLESSINGS FOR THE LORD'S PEOPLE

18 So the LORD must wait for you to come to him
so he can show you his love and compassion.
For the LORD is a faithful God.
Blessed are those who wait for his help.

30:7 Hebrew *Rahab who sits still.* Rahab is the name of a mythical sea monster that represents chaos in ancient literature. The name is used here as a poetic name for Egypt.

19 O people of Zion, who live in Jerusalem,
you will weep no more.
He will be gracious if you ask for help.
He will surely respond to the sound of your cries.
20 Though the Lord gave you adversity for food
and suffering for drink,
he will still be with you to teach you.
You will see your teacher with your own eyes.
21 Your own ears will hear him.
Right behind you a voice will say,
"This is the way you should go,"
whether to the right or to the left.
22 Then you will destroy all your silver idols
and your precious gold images.
You will throw them out like filthy rags,
saying to them, "Good riddance!"

23Then the LORD will bless you with rain at planting
time. There will be wonderful harvests and plenty of
pastureland for your livestock. 24The oxen and donkeys that till the ground will eat good grain, its chaff
blown away by the wind. 25In that day, when your enemies are slaughtered and the towers fall, there will be
streams of water flowing down every mountain and
hill. 26The moon will be as bright as the sun, and the
sun will be seven times brighter—like the light of seven
days in one! So it will be when the LORD begins to heal
his people and cure the wounds he gave them.

27 Look! The LORD is coming from far away,
burning with anger,
surrounded by thick, rising smoke.
His lips are filled with fury;
his words consume like fire.
28 His hot breath pours out like a flood
up to the neck of his enemies.
He will sift out the proud nations for destruction.
He will bridle them and lead them away to ruin.

29 But the people of God will sing a song of joy,
like the songs at the holy festivals.
You will be filled with joy,
as when a flutist leads a group of pilgrims
to Jerusalem, the mountain of the LORD—
to the Rock of Israel.
30 And the LORD will make his majestic voice heard.
He will display the strength of his mighty arm.
It will descend with devouring flames,
with cloudbursts, thunderstorms, and huge hailstones.
31 At the LORD's command, the Assyrians will
be shattered.
He will strike them down with his royal scepter.
32 And as the LORD strikes them with his rod of
punishment,
his people will celebrate with tambourines
and harps.
Lifting his mighty arm, he will fight the Assyrians.
33 Topheth—the place of burning—
has long been ready for the Assyrian king;
the pyre is piled high with wood.
The breath of the LORD, like fire from a volcano,
will set it ablaze.

31

THE FUTILITY OF RELYING ON EGYPT

1 What sorrow awaits those who look to Egypt for help,
trusting their horses, chariots, and charioteers
and depending on the strength of human armies
instead of looking to the LORD,
the Holy One of Israel.
2 In his wisdom, the LORD will send great disaster;
he will not change his mind.
He will rise against the wicked
and against their helpers.
3 For these Egyptians are mere humans, not God!
Their horses are puny flesh, not mighty spirits!
When the LORD raises his fist against them,
those who help will stumble,
and those being helped will fall.
They will all fall down and die together.

4But this is what the LORD has told me:

"When a strong young lion
stands growling over a sheep it has killed,
it is not frightened by the shouts and noise
of a whole crowd of shepherds.
In the same way, the LORD of Heaven's Armies
will come down and fight on Mount Zion.
5 The LORD of Heaven's Armies will hover over
Jerusalem
and protect it like a bird protecting its nest.
He will defend and save the city;
he will pass over it and rescue it."

IDOLS 31:7

Someday the people of Israel would throw their idols away, recognizing that they were nothing but wood or stone. Today, idols such as money, fame, or success seem harder to throw away. Instead of contributing to our spiritual development, they rob us of our thoughts, time, energy, and devotion to God. At first they seem exciting and promise to take us places, but in the end we will find that we have become their slaves. What idols, if any, do you need to throw away? ■

6Though you are such wicked rebels, my people, come
and return to the LORD. 7I know the glorious day will
come when each of you will throw away the gold idols
and silver images your sinful hands have made.

8 "The Assyrians will be destroyed,
but not by the swords of men.
The sword of God will strike them,
and they will panic and flee.
The strong young Assyrians
will be taken away as captives.

[9] Even the strongest will quake with terror,
and princes will flee when they see your
battle flags,"
says the LORD, whose fire burns in Zion,
whose flame blazes from Jerusalem.

32 ISRAEL'S ULTIMATE DELIVERANCE

[1] Look, a righteous king is coming!
And honest princes will rule under him.
[2] Each one will be like a shelter from the wind
and a refuge from the storm,
like streams of water in the desert
and the shadow of a great rock in a parched land.
[3] Then everyone who has eyes will be able to see
the truth,
and everyone who has ears will be able to hear it.
[4] Even the hotheads will be full of sense and
understanding.
Those who stammer will speak out plainly.
[5] In that day ungodly fools will not be heroes.
Scoundrels will not be respected.
[6] For fools speak foolishness
and make evil plans.
They practice ungodliness
and spread false teachings about the LORD.
They deprive the hungry of food
and give no water to the thirsty.
[7] The smooth tricks of scoundrels are evil.
They plot crooked schemes.
They lie to convict the poor,
even when the cause of the poor is just.
[8] But generous people plan to do what is generous,
and they stand firm in their generosity.

AT EASE 32:9-13

The people turned their backs on God and concentrated on their own best interests. This warning was not just to the women of Israel, but it applied to all who chose to concentrate on their own comfort, little knowing that an enemy approached. Wealth and luxury bring false security, lulling us into thinking all is well. Yet disaster could lurk around the corner. By abandoning God's purpose for our life, we also abandon his help. Are you at ease or at work for his Kingdom? ■

[9] Listen, you women who lie around in ease.
Listen to me, you who are so smug.
[10] In a short time—just a little more than a year—
you careless ones will suddenly begin to care.
For your fruit crops will fail,
and the harvest will never take place.
[11] Tremble, you women of ease;
throw off your complacency.
Strip off your pretty clothes,
and put on burlap to show your grief.
[12] Beat your breasts in sorrow for your bountiful farms
and your fruitful grapevines.
[13] For your land will be overgrown with thorns
and briers.
Your joyful homes and happy towns will be gone.
[14] The palace and the city will be deserted,
and busy towns will be empty.
Wild donkeys will frolic and flocks will graze
in the empty forts* and watchtowers
[15] until at last the Spirit is poured out
on us from heaven.
Then the wilderness will become a fertile field,
and the fertile field will yield bountiful crops.

PROMISES 33:1

The Assyrians continually broke their promises, but demanded that others keep theirs. Does that sound familiar? Maybe you know someone who recently broke a promise. Maybe that someone was you. (Be honest.) Broken promises shatter trust and destroy relationships. Are you willing to exercise the same fairness with others that you demand for yourself? ■

[16] Justice will rule in the wilderness
and righteousness in the fertile field.
[17] And this righteousness will bring peace.
Yes, it will bring quietness and confidence
forever.
[18] My people will live in safety, quietly at home.
They will be at rest.
[19] Even if the forest should be destroyed
and the city torn down,
[20] the LORD will greatly bless his people.
Wherever they plant seed, bountiful crops will
spring up.
Their cattle and donkeys will graze freely.

33 A MESSAGE ABOUT ASSYRIA

[1] What sorrow awaits you Assyrians, who have
destroyed others*
but have never been destroyed yourselves.
You betray others,
but you have never been betrayed.
When you are done destroying,
you will be destroyed.
When you are done betraying,
you will be betrayed.
[2] But LORD, be merciful to us,
for we have waited for you.
Be our strong arm each day
and our salvation in times of trouble.

32:14 Hebrew *the Ophel.* 33:1 Hebrew *What sorrow awaits you, O destroyer.* The Hebrew text does not specifically name Assyria as the object of the prophecy in this chapter.

3 The enemy runs at the sound of your voice.
When you stand up, the nations flee!
4 Just as caterpillars and locusts strip the fields
and vines,
so the fallen army of Assyria will be stripped!

5 Though the LORD is very great and lives in heaven,
he will make Jerusalem* his home of justice
and righteousness.
6 In that day he will be your sure foundation,
providing a rich store of salvation, wisdom,
and knowledge.
The fear of the LORD will be your treasure.

7 But now your brave warriors weep in public.
Your ambassadors of peace cry in bitter
disappointment.
8 Your roads are deserted;
no one travels them anymore.
The Assyrians have broken their peace treaty
and care nothing for the promises they made
before witnesses.*
They have no respect for anyone.
9 The land of Israel wilts in mourning.
Lebanon withers with shame.
The plain of Sharon is now a wilderness.
Bashan and Carmel have been plundered.

10 But the LORD says: "Now I will stand up.
Now I will show my power and might.
11 You Assyrians produce nothing but dry grass
and stubble.
Your own breath will turn to fire and consume you.
12 Your people will be burned up completely,
like thornbushes cut down and tossed in a fire.
13 Listen to what I have done, you nations far away!
And you that are near, acknowledge my might!"
14 The sinners in Jerusalem shake with fear.
Terror seizes the godless.
"Who can live with this devouring fire?" they cry.
"Who can survive this all-consuming fire?"
15 Those who are honest and fair,
who refuse to profit by fraud,
who stay far away from bribes,
who refuse to listen to those who plot murder,
who shut their eyes to all enticement
to do wrong—
16 these are the ones who will dwell on high.
The rocks of the mountains will be their fortress.
Food will be supplied to them,
and they will have water in abundance.

17 Your eyes will see the king in all his splendor,
and you will see a land that stretches into
the distance.
18 You will think back to this time of terror, asking,
"Where are the Assyrian officers
who counted our towers?
Where are the bookkeepers
who recorded the plunder taken from our
fallen city?"
19 You will no longer see these fierce, violent people
with their strange, unknown language.

20 Instead, you will see Zion as a place of holy festivals.
You will see Jerusalem, a city quiet and secure.
It will be like a tent whose ropes are taught
and whose stakes are firmly fixed.
21 The LORD will be our Mighty One.
He will be like a wide river of protection
that no enemy can cross,
that no enemy ship can sail upon.
22 For the LORD is our judge,
our lawgiver, and our king.
He will care for us and save us.
23 The enemies' sails hang loose
on broken masts with useless tackle.
Their treasure will be divided by the people of God.
Even the lame will take their share!
24 The people of Israel will no longer say,
"We are sick and helpless,"
for the LORD will forgive their sins.

34 A MESSAGE FOR THE NATIONS

1 Come here and listen, O nations of the earth.
Let the world and everything in it hear my words.
2 For the LORD is enraged against the nations.
His fury is against all their armies.
He will completely destroy* them,
dooming them to slaughter.
3 Their dead will be left unburied,
and the stench of rotting bodies will fill the land.
The mountains will flow with their blood.
4 The heavens above will melt away
and disappear like a rolled-up scroll.
The stars will fall from the sky
like withered leaves from a grapevine,
or shriveled figs from a fig tree.

5 And when my sword has finished its work in
the heavens,
it will fall upon Edom,
the nation I have marked for destruction.
6 The sword of the LORD is drenched with blood
and covered with fat—
with the blood of lambs and goats,
with the fat of rams prepared for sacrifice.
Yes, the LORD will offer a sacrifice in the city
of Bozrah.
He will make a mighty slaughter in Edom.
7 Even men as strong as wild oxen will die—
the young men alongside the veterans.

33:5 Hebrew *Zion;* also in 33:14. 33:8 As in Dead Sea Scrolls; Masoretic Text reads *care nothing for the cities.* 34:2 The Hebrew term used here refers to the complete consecration of things or people to the LORD, either by destroying them or by giving them as an offering; similarly in 34:5.

The land will be soaked with blood
and the soil enriched with fat.
8 For it is the day of the LORD's revenge,
the year when Edom will be paid back for all
it did to Israel.*
9 The streams of Edom will be filled with
burning pitch,
and the ground will be covered with fire.
10 This judgment on Edom will never end;
the smoke of its burning will rise forever.
The land will lie deserted from generation
to generation.
No one will live there anymore.
11 It will be haunted by the desert owl and the
screech owl,
the great owl and the raven.*
For God will measure that land carefully;
he will measure it for chaos and destruction.
12 It will be called the Land of Nothing,
and all its nobles will soon be gone.*
13 Thorns will overrun its palaces;
nettles and thistles will grow in its forts.
The ruins will become a haunt for jackals
and a home for owls.
14 Desert animals will mingle there with hyenas,
their howls filling the night.
Wild goats will bleat at one another among the ruins,
and night creatures* will come there to rest.
15 There the owl will make her nest and lay her eggs.
She will hatch her young and cover them with
her wings.
And the buzzards will come,
each one with its mate.

16 Search the book of the LORD,
and see what he will do.
Not one of these birds and animals will be missing,
and none will lack a mate,
for the LORD has promised this.
His Spirit will make it all come true.
17 He has surveyed and divided the land
and deeded it over to those creatures.
They will possess it forever,
from generation to generation.

35

HOPE FOR RESTORATION

1 Even the wilderness and desert will be glad in
those days.
The wasteland will rejoice and blossom with
spring crocuses.
2 Yes, there will be an abundance of flowers
and singing and joy!
The deserts will become as green as the mountains
of Lebanon,
as lovely as Mount Carmel or the plain of Sharon.
There the LORD will display his glory,
the splendor of our God.
3 With this news, strengthen those who have
tired hands,
and encourage those who have weak knees.
4 Say to those with fearful hearts,
"Be strong, and do not fear,
for your God is coming to destroy your enemies.
He is coming to save you."
5 And when he comes, he will open the eyes of
the blind
and unplug the ears of the deaf.
6 The lame will leap like a deer,
and those who cannot speak will sing for joy!
Springs will gush forth in the wilderness,
and streams will water the wasteland.
7 The parched ground will become a pool,
and springs of water will satisfy the
thirsty land.
Marsh grass and reeds and rushes will flourish
where desert jackals once lived.

VISIONS 35:1-10

In chapters 1–34, Isaiah delivered a message of judgment on all nations, including the divided nation of Israel, for rejecting God. Although there were glimpses of relief and restoration for the remnant of faithful believers, the climate of wrath, fury, judgment, and destruction prevailed. Now Isaiah breaks through with a vision of beauty and encouragement. God is just as complete in his mercy as he is severe in his judgment. God's complete moral perfection is revealed by his hatred of all sin, and this leads to judgment. This same moral perfection is revealed in his love for all he has created. We can trust that God's judgment will always be balanced by his love. ■

8 And a great road will go through that once
deserted land.
It will be named the Highway of Holiness.
Evil-minded people will never travel on it.
It will be only for those who walk in God's ways;
fools will never walk there.
9 Lions will not lurk along its course,
nor any other ferocious beasts.
There will be no other dangers.
Only the redeemed will walk on it.
10 Those who have been ransomed by the LORD
will return.
They will enter Jerusalem* singing,
crowned with everlasting joy.
Sorrow and mourning will disappear,
and they will be filled with joy and gladness.

34:8 Hebrew *to Zion.* 34:11 The identification of some of these birds is uncertain. 34:12 The meaning of the Hebrew is uncertain. 34:14 Hebrew *Lilith,* possibly a reference to a mythical demon of the night. 35:10 Hebrew *Zion.*

36 ASSYRIA INVADES JUDAH

In the fourteenth year of King Hezekiah's reign,* King Sennacherib of Assyria came to attack the fortified towns of Judah and conquered them. [2]Then the king of Assyria sent his chief of staff* from Lachish with a huge army to confront King Hezekiah in Jerusalem. The Assyrians took up a position beside the aqueduct that feeds water into the upper pool, near the road leading to the field where cloth is washed.*

[3]These are the officials who went out to meet with them: Eliakim son of Hilkiah, the palace administrator; Shebna the court secretary; and Joah son of Asaph, the royal historian.

SENNACHERIB THREATENS JERUSALEM

[4]Then the Assyrian king's chief of staff told them to give this message to Hezekiah:

"This is what the great king of Assyria says: What are you trusting in that makes you so confident? [5]Do you think that mere words can substitute for military skill and strength? Who are you counting on, that you have rebelled against me? [6]On Egypt? If you lean on Egypt, it will be like a reed that splinters beneath your weight and pierces your hand. Pharaoh, the king of Egypt, is completely unreliable!

DECEIT 36:7

The representative of the Assyrian king claimed that Hezekiah insulted God by tearing down his altars in the hills and making the people worship in Jerusalem. Either the Assyrians didn't understand how God was worshiped, or they wanted to deceive the people into thinking they had angered God. In the same way, Satan tries to confuse or deceive us. People don't necessarily need to be sinful to be ineffective for God; they need only be confused about what God wants. A careful study of God's Word can help us avoid Satan's deceit. ■

[7]"But perhaps you will say to me, 'We are trusting in the LORD our God!' But isn't he the one who was insulted by Hezekiah? Didn't Hezekiah tear down his shrines and altars and make everyone in Judah and Jerusalem worship only at the altar here in Jerusalem?

[8]"I'll tell you what! Strike a bargain with my master, the king of Assyria. I will give you 2,000 horses if you can find that many men to ride on them! [9]With your tiny army, how can you think of challenging even the weakest contingent of my master's troops, even with the help of Egypt's chariots and charioteers? [10]What's more, do you think we have invaded your land without the LORD's direction? The LORD himself told us, 'Attack this land and destroy it!'"

[11]Then Eliakim, Shebna, and Joah said to the Assyrian chief of staff, "Please speak to us in Aramaic, for we understand it well. Don't speak in Hebrew,* for the people on the wall will hear."

[12]But Sennacherib's chief of staff replied, "Do you think my master sent this message only to you and your master? He wants all the people to hear it, for when we put this city under siege, they will suffer along with you. They will be so hungry and thirsty that they will eat their own dung and drink their own urine."

[13]Then the chief of staff stood and shouted in Hebrew to the people on the wall, "Listen to this message from the great king of Assyria! [14]This is what the king says: Don't let Hezekiah deceive you. He will never be able to rescue you. [15]Don't let him fool you into trusting in the LORD by saying, 'The LORD will surely rescue us. This city will never fall into the hands of the Assyrian king!'

[16]"Don't listen to Hezekiah! These are the terms the king of Assyria is offering: Make peace with me—open the gates and come out. Then each of you can continue eating from your own grapevine and fig tree and drinking from your own well. [17]Then I will arrange to take you to another land like this one—a land of grain and new wine, bread and vineyards.

[18]"Don't let Hezekiah mislead you by saying, 'The LORD will rescue us!' Have the gods of any other nations ever saved their people from the king of Assyria? [19]What happened to the gods of Hamath and Arpad? And what about the gods of Sepharvaim? Did any god rescue Samaria from my power? [20]What god of any nation has ever been able to save its people from my power? So what makes you think that the LORD can rescue Jerusalem from me?"

[21]But the people were silent and did not utter a word because Hezekiah had commanded them, "Do not answer him."

[22]Then Eliakim son of Hilkiah, the palace administrator; Shebna the court secretary; and Joah son of Asaph, the royal historian, went back to Hezekiah. They tore their clothes in despair, and they went in to see the king and told him what the Assyrian chief of staff had said.

37 HEZEKIAH SEEKS THE LORD'S HELP

When King Hezekiah heard their report, he tore his clothes and put on burlap and went into the Temple of the LORD. [2]And he sent Eliakim the palace administrator, Shebna the court secretary, and the leading priests, all dressed in burlap, to the prophet Isaiah son of Amoz. [3]They told him, "This is what King Hezekiah says: Today is a day of trouble, insults, and disgrace. It is like when a child is ready to be born, but the mother has no strength to deliver the baby. [4]But perhaps the LORD your God has heard the Assyrian chief of staff,* sent by the king to defy the living God, and will punish him for his words. Oh, pray for those of us who are left!"

[5]After King Hezekiah's officials delivered the king's message to Isaiah, [6]the prophet replied, "Say to your

36:1 The fourteenth year of Hezekiah's reign was 701 B.C. 36:2a Or *the rabshakeh;* also in 36:4, 11, 12, 22. 36:2b Or *bleached.* 36:11 Hebrew *in the dialect of Judah;* also in 36:13. 37:4 Or *the rabshakeh;* also in 37:8.

master, 'This is what the LORD says: Do not be disturbed by
this blasphemous speech against me from the Assyrian
king's messengers. 7 Listen! I myself will move against
him,* and the king will receive a message that he is
needed at home. So he will return to his land, where I will
have him killed with a sword.'"

8 Meanwhile, the Assyrian chief of staff left Jerusalem
and went to consult the king of Assyria, who had left Lachish and was attacking Libnah.

9 Soon afterward King Sennacherib received word that
King Tirhakah of Ethiopia* was leading an army to fight
against him. Before leaving to meet the attack, he sent
messengers back to Hezekiah in Jerusalem with this
message:

10 "This message is for King Hezekiah of Judah. Don't
let your God, in whom you trust, deceive you with
promises that Jerusalem will not be captured by the
king of Assyria. 11 You know perfectly well what the
kings of Assyria have done wherever they have gone.
They have completely destroyed everyone who stood
in their way! Why should you be any different?
12 Have the gods of other nations rescued them—such
nations as Gozan, Haran, Rezeph, and the people
of Eden who were in Tel-assar? My predecessors
destroyed them all! 13 What happened to the king of
Hamath and the king of Arpad? What happened to
the kings of Sepharvaim, Hena, and Ivvah?"

THE ANSWER 37:8-10

Although the answer to Hezekiah's prayer was already in motion, Hezekiah wasn't aware of it. He persisted in prayer and faith even though he couldn't see the answer coming. Sometimes, we can't see the answer to our prayers right away. Still, our task is to ask in faith and wait. ■

14 After Hezekiah received the letter from the messengers and read it, he went up to the LORD's Temple
and spread it out before the LORD. 15 And Hezekiah
prayed this prayer before the LORD: 16 "O LORD of
Heaven's Armies, God of Israel, you are enthroned between the mighty cherubim! You alone are God of all the
kingdoms of the earth. You alone created the heavens
and the earth. 17 Bend down, O LORD, and listen! Open
your eyes, O LORD, and see! Listen to Sennacherib's
words of defiance against the living God.

18 "It is true, LORD, that the kings of Assyria have destroyed all these nations. 19 And they have thrown the
gods of these nations into the fire and burned them. But
of course the Assyrians could destroy them! They were
not gods at all—only idols of wood and stone shaped by
human hands. 20 Now, O LORD our God, rescue us from his
power; then all the kingdoms of the earth will know that
you alone, O LORD, are God.*"

ISAIAH PREDICTS JUDAH'S DELIVERANCE

21 Then Isaiah son of Amoz sent this message to Hezekiah: "This is what the LORD, the God of Israel, says: Because
you prayed about King Sennacherib of Assyria, 22 the
LORD has spoken this word against him:

"The virgin daughter of Zion
  despises you and laughs at you.
The daughter of Jerusalem
  shakes her head in derision as you flee.

23 "Whom have you been defying and ridiculing?
  Against whom did you raise your voice?
At whom did you look with such haughty eyes?
  It was the Holy One of Israel!
24 By your messengers you have defied the Lord.
  You have said, 'With my many chariots
I have conquered the highest mountains—
  yes, the remotest peaks of Lebanon.
I have cut down its tallest cedars
  and its finest cypress trees.
I have reached its farthest heights
  and explored its deepest forests.
25 I have dug wells in many foreign lands*
  and refreshed myself with their water.
With the sole of my foot,
  I stopped up all the rivers of Egypt!'

26 "But have you not heard?
  I decided this long ago.
Long ago I planned it,
  and now I am making it happen.
I planned for you to crush fortified cities
  into heaps of rubble.
27 That is why their people have so little power
  and are so frightened and confused.
They are as weak as grass,
  as easily trampled as tender green shoots.
They are like grass sprouting on a housetop,
  scorched* before it can grow lush and tall.

28 "But I know you well—
  where you stay
and when you come and go.
  I know the way you have raged against me.
29 And because of your raging against me
  and your arrogance, which I have heard for myself,
I will put my hook in your nose
  and my bit in your mouth.
I will make you return
  by the same road on which you came."

30 Then Isaiah said to Hezekiah, "Here is the proof that
what I say is true:

"This year you will eat only what grows up by itself,
  and next year you will eat what springs up from that.

37:7 Hebrew *I will put a spirit in him.* 37:9 Hebrew *of Cush.* 37:20 As in Dead Sea Scrolls (see also 2 Kgs 19:19); Masoretic Text reads *you alone are the LORD.* 37:25 As in Dead Sea Scrolls (see also 2 Kgs 19:24); Masoretic Text lacks *in many foreign lands.* 37:27 As in Dead Sea Scrolls and some Greek manuscripts (see also 2 Kgs 19:26); most Hebrew manuscripts read *like a terraced field.*

But in the third year you will plant crops and
harvest them;
you will tend vineyards and eat their fruit.
31 And you who are left in Judah,
who have escaped the ravages of the siege,
will put roots down in your own soil
and grow up and flourish.
32 For a remnant of my people will spread out
from Jerusalem,
a group of survivors from Mount Zion.
The passionate commitment of the LORD of
Heaven's Armies
will make this happen!

33"And this is what the LORD says about the king of
Assyria:

"'His armies will not enter Jerusalem.
They will not even shoot an arrow at it.
They will not march outside its gates with
their shields
nor build banks of earth against its walls.
34 The king will return to his own country
by the same road on which he came.
He will not enter this city,'
says the LORD.
35 'For my own honor and for the sake of my
servant David,
I will defend this city and protect it.'"

36That night the angel of the LORD went out to the Assyrian camp and killed 185,000 Assyrian soldiers. When
the surviving Assyrians* woke up the next morning, they
found corpses everywhere. 37Then King Sennacherib of
Assyria broke camp and returned to his own land. He
went home to his capital of Nineveh and stayed there.
38One day while he was worshiping in the temple of his
god Nisroch, his sons Adrammelech and Sharezer killed
him with their swords. They then escaped to the land of
Ararat, and another son, Esarhaddon, became the next
king of Assyria.

38

HEZEKIAH'S SICKNESS AND RECOVERY

About that time Hezekiah became deathly ill, and the
prophet Isaiah son of Amoz went to visit him. He gave the
king this message: "This is what the LORD says: 'Set your
affairs in order, for you are going to die. You will not recover from this illness.'"
2When Hezekiah heard this, he turned his face to the
wall and prayed to the LORD, 3"Remember, O LORD, how I
have always been faithful to you and have served you single-
mindedly, always doing what pleases you." Then he broke
down and wept bitterly.
4Then this message came to Isaiah from the LORD: 5"Go
back to Hezekiah and tell him, 'This is what the LORD, the
God of your ancestor David, says: I have heard your
prayer and seen your tears. I will add fifteen years to your
life, 6and I will rescue you and this city from the king of
Assyria. Yes, I will defend this city.
7"'And this is the sign from the LORD to prove that he
will do as he promised: 8I will cause the sun's shadow to
move ten steps backward on the sundial* of Ahaz!'" So
the shadow on the sundial moved backward ten steps.

RADICAL CHANGE 38:1-8

When Isaiah told Hezekiah of his impending death, Hezekiah immediately turned to God. God responded to Hezekiah's prayer, allowing him to live another 15 years. In response to fervent prayer, God may change the course of our life, too. So, what's your prayer? ■

HEZEKIAH'S POEM OF PRAISE

9When King Hezekiah was well again, he wrote this
poem:

10 I said, "In the prime of my life,
must I now enter the place of the dead?*
Am I to be robbed of the rest of my years?"
11 I said, "Never again will I see the LORD GOD
while still in the land of the living.
Never again will I see my friends
or be with those who live in this world.
12 My life has been blown away
like a shepherd's tent in a storm.
It has been cut short,
as when a weaver cuts cloth from a loom.
Suddenly, my life was over.
13 I waited patiently all night,
but I was torn apart as though by lions.
Suddenly, my life was over.
14 Delirious, I chattered like a swallow or a crane,
and then I moaned like a mourning dove.
My eyes grew tired of looking to heaven for help.
I am in trouble, Lord. Help me!"

15 But what could I say?
For he himself sent this sickness.
Now I will walk humbly throughout my years
because of this anguish I have felt.
16 Lord, your discipline is good,
for it leads to life and health.
You restore my health
and allow me to live!
17 Yes, this anguish was good for me,
for you have rescued me from death
and forgiven all my sins.
18 For the dead* cannot praise you;
they cannot raise their voices in praise.
Those who go down to the grave
can no longer hope in your faithfulness.
19 Only the living can praise you as I do today.
Each generation tells of your faithfulness
to the next.

37:36 Hebrew *When they.* 38:8 Hebrew *the steps.* 38:10 Hebrew *enter the gates of Sheol?* 38:18 Hebrew *Sheol.*

20 Think of it—the LORD is ready to heal me!
I will sing his praises with instruments
every day of my life
in the Temple of the LORD.

21 Isaiah had said to Hezekiah's servants, "Make an ointment from figs and spread it over the boil, and Hezekiah will recover."

22 And Hezekiah had asked, "What sign will prove that I will go to the Temple of the LORD?"

39 ENVOYS FROM BABYLON

Soon after this, Merodach-baladan son of Baladan, king of
Babylon, sent Hezekiah his best wishes and a gift. He had
heard that Hezekiah had been very sick and that he had recovered. 2 Hezekiah was delighted with the Babylonian envoys and showed them everything in his treasure-houses—
the silver, the gold, the spices, and the aromatic oils. He also
took them to see his armory and showed them everything
in his royal treasuries! There was nothing in his palace or
kingdom that Hezekiah did not show them.
3 Then Isaiah the prophet went to King Hezekiah and
asked him, "What did those men want? Where were they
from?"

Hezekiah replied, "They came from the distant land of Babylon."

4 "What did they see in your palace?" asked Isaiah.

"They saw everything," Hezekiah replied. "I showed them everything I own—all my royal treasuries."

GOD AT WORK 39:8

Hezekiah worked hard throughout his reign to stamp out idol worship and to purify the worship of the true God at the Temple in Jerusalem. Nevertheless, he knew his kingdom was not completely pure. Only God's miraculous interventions preserved Judah from its enemies. Many times we're tempted to grumble about what we think God isn't doing, instead of thanking him for what he is doing. How is God at work around you? Have you thanked him lately? ■

5 Then Isaiah said to Hezekiah, "Listen to this message
from the LORD of Heaven's Armies: 6 'The time is coming
when everything in your palace—all the treasures stored
up by your ancestors until now—will be carried off to
Babylon. Nothing will be left,' says the LORD. 7 'Some of
your very own sons will be taken away into exile. They
will become eunuchs who will serve in the palace of Babylon's king.'"
8 Then Hezekiah said to Isaiah, "This message you have
given me from the LORD is good." For the king was thinking, "At least there will be peace and security during my
lifetime."

40 COMFORT FOR GOD'S PEOPLE

1 "Comfort, comfort my people,"
says your God.
2 "Speak tenderly to Jerusalem.
Tell her that her sad days are gone
and her sins are pardoned.
Yes, the LORD has punished her twice over
for all her sins."

COMFORT 40:1

God's people still had 100 years of trouble before Jerusalem would fall. After that would come 70 years of exile. So God told Isaiah to comfort Jerusalem. When your life seems to be falling apart, ask God to comfort you. You may not escape hard times, but you can find God's comfort during them. ■

3 Listen! It's the voice of someone shouting,
"Clear the way through the wilderness
for the LORD!
Make a straight highway through the wasteland
for our God!
4 Fill in the valleys,
and level the mountains and hills.
Straighten the curves,
and smooth out the rough places.
5 Then the glory of the LORD will be revealed,
and all people will see it together.
The LORD has spoken!"*

6 A voice said, "Shout!"
I asked, "What should I shout?"

"Shout that people are like the grass.
Their beauty fades as quickly
as the flowers in a field.
7 The grass withers and the flowers fade
beneath the breath of the LORD.
And so it is with people.
8 The grass withers and the flowers fade,
but the word of our God stands forever."

9 O Zion, messenger of good news,
shout from the mountaintops!
Shout it louder, O Jerusalem.*
Shout, and do not be afraid.
Tell the towns of Judah,
"Your God is coming!"
10 Yes, the Sovereign LORD is coming in power.
He will rule with a powerful arm.
See, he brings his reward with him
as he comes.

40:3-5 Greek version reads *He is a voice shouting in the wilderness, / "Prepare the way for the LORD's coming! / Clear a road for our God! / Fill in the valleys, / and level the mountains and hills. / And then the glory of the LORD will be revealed, / and all people will see the salvation sent from God. / The LORD has spoken!"* Compare Matt 3:3; Mark 1:3; Luke 3:4-6. 40:9 Or *O messenger of good news, shout to Zion from the mountaintops! Shout it louder to Jerusalem.*

11 He will feed his flock like a shepherd.
He will carry the lambs in his arms,
holding them close to his heart.
He will gently lead the mother sheep with
their young.

THE LORD HAS NO EQUAL

12 Who else has held the oceans in his hand?
Who has measured off the heavens with
his fingers?
Who else knows the weight of the earth
or has weighed the mountains and hills
on a scale?
13 Who is able to advise the Spirit of the LORD?*
Who knows enough to give him advice or
teach him?
14 Has the LORD ever needed anyone's advice?
Does he need instruction about what is good?
Did someone teach him what is right
or show him the path of justice?

15 No, for all the nations of the world
are but a drop in the bucket.
They are nothing more
than dust on the scales.
He picks up the whole earth
as though it were a grain of sand.
16 All the wood in Lebanon's forests
and all Lebanon's animals would not be enough
to make a burnt offering worthy of our God.
17 The nations of the world are worth nothing to him.
In his eyes they count for less than nothing—
mere emptiness and froth.

18 To whom can you compare God?
What image can you find to resemble him?
19 Can he be compared to an idol formed in a mold,
overlaid with gold, and decorated with
silver chains?
20 Or if people are too poor for that,
they might at least choose wood that won't decay
and a skilled craftsman
to carve an image that won't fall down!

21 Haven't you heard? Don't you understand?
Are you deaf to the words of God—
the words he gave before the world began?
Are you so ignorant?
22 God sits above the circle of the earth.
The people below seem like grasshoppers to him!
He spreads out the heavens like a curtain
and makes his tent from them.
23 He judges the great people of the world
and brings them all to nothing.
24 They hardly get started, barely taking root,
when he blows on them and they wither.
The wind carries them off like chaff.

25 "To whom will you compare me?
Who is my equal?" asks the Holy One.

26 Look up into the heavens.
Who created all the stars?
He brings them out like an army, one after another,
calling each by its name.
Because of his great power and incomparable
strength,
not a single one is missing.
27 O Jacob, how can you say the LORD does not see
your troubles?
O Israel, how can you say God ignores your rights?
28 Have you never heard?
Have you never understood?
The LORD is the everlasting God,
the Creator of all the earth.
He never grows weak or weary.
No one can measure the depths of his
understanding.
29 He gives power to the weak
and strength to the powerless.
30 Even youths will become weak and tired,
and young men will fall in exhaustion.
31 But those who trust in the LORD will find
new strength.
They will soar high on wings like eagles.
They will run and not grow weary.
They will walk and not faint.

STRENGTH 40:29-31

Even the strongest people get tired at times, but God's power and strength never diminish. He is never too busy to help and listen. His strength is our source of strength. When you feel all of life crushing you and you can't go another step, remember that you can ask God to renew your strength. ■

41 GOD'S HELP FOR ISRAEL

1 "Listen in silence before me, you lands beyond
the sea.
Bring your strongest arguments.
Come now and speak.
The court is ready for your case.

2 "Who has stirred up this king from the east,
rightly calling him to God's service?
Who gives this man victory over many nations
and permits him to trample their kings underfoot?
With his sword, he reduces armies to dust.
With his bow, he scatters them like chaff before
the wind.
3 He chases them away and goes on safely,
though he is walking over unfamiliar ground.

40:13 Greek version reads *Who can know the LORD's thoughts?* Compare Rom 11:34; 1 Cor 2:16.

keeping it real

I recently switched schools. In my old school, I knew everyone. In this new, much larger school, I knew no one. The situation forced me to depend on God. I knew that I really needed God's help and guidance to make it through those first few months.

During this time, I memorized Isaiah 41:10 and Philippians 4:13. Whenever I felt unnoticed or afraid to talk to someone, I would repeat these verses to myself. I remembered that God was with me, he will strengthen me, and that he has already won the victory for me. These two verses became a lifeline for me. —Amie

4 Who has done such mighty deeds,
summoning each new generation from the beginning of time?
It is I, the LORD, the First and the Last.
I alone am he."

THE FUTURE 41:4

Each generation gets caught up in its own problems, but God's plan embraces all generations. When your great-grandparents lived, God worked personally in the lives of his people. When your great-grandchildren live, God will still work personally in the lives of his people. He is the only One who sees as clearly a hundred years from now as he saw a hundred years ago. When you are concerned about the future, talk with God—he knows the generations of the future as well as he knows the generations of the past. ■

5 The lands beyond the sea watch in fear.
Remote lands tremble and mobilize for war.
6 The idol makers encourage one another,
saying to each other, "Be strong!"
7 The carver encourages the goldsmith,
and the molder helps at the anvil.
"Good," they say. "It's coming along fine."
Carefully they join the parts together,
then fasten the thing in place so it won't fall over.

8 "But as for you, Israel my servant,
Jacob my chosen one,
descended from Abraham my friend,
9 I have called you back from the ends of the earth,
saying, 'You are my servant.'
For I have chosen you
and will not throw you away.
10 Don't be afraid, for I am with you.
Don't be discouraged, for I am your God.
I will strengthen you and help you.
I will hold you up with my victorious right hand.

11 "See, all your angry enemies lie there,
confused and humiliated.
Anyone who opposes you will die
and come to nothing.
12 You will look in vain
for those who tried to conquer you.
Those who attack you
will come to nothing.
13 For I hold you by your right hand—
I, the LORD your God.
And I say to you,
'Don't be afraid. I am here to help you.
14 Though you are a lowly worm, O Jacob,
don't be afraid, people of Israel, for I will help you.
I am the LORD, your Redeemer.
I am the Holy One of Israel.'
15 You will be a new threshing instrument
with many sharp teeth.
You will tear your enemies apart,
making chaff of mountains.
16 You will toss them into the air,
and the wind will blow them all away;
a whirlwind will scatter them.
Then you will rejoice in the LORD.
You will glory in the Holy One of Israel.

17 "When the poor and needy search for water and there is none,
and their tongues are parched from thirst,
then I, the LORD, will answer them.
I, the God of Israel, will never abandon them.
18 I will open up rivers for them on the high plateaus.
I will give them fountains of water in the valleys.
I will fill the desert with pools of water.
Rivers fed by springs will flow across the parched ground.
19 I will plant trees in the barren desert—
cedar, acacia, myrtle, olive, cypress, fir, and pine.
20 I am doing this so all who see this miracle
will understand what it means—
that it is the LORD who has done this,
the Holy One of Israel who created it.

21 "Present the case for your idols,"
says the LORD.
"Let them show what they can do,"
says the King of Israel.*
22 "Let them try to tell us what happened long ago
so that we may consider the evidence.
Or let them tell us what the future holds,
so we can know what's going to happen.
23 Yes, tell us what will occur in the days ahead.
Then we will know you are gods.
In fact, do anything—good or bad!
Do something that will amaze and frighten us.
24 But no! You are less than nothing and can do
nothing at all.
Those who choose you pollute themselves.

25 "But I have stirred up a leader who will come from
the north.
I have called him by name from the east.
I will give him victory over kings and princes.
He will trample them as a potter treads on clay.

26 "Who told you from the beginning
that this would happen?
Who predicted this,
making you admit that he was right?
No one said a word!
27 I was the first to tell Zion,
'Look! Help is on the way!'*
I will send Jerusalem a messenger with good news.
28 Not one of your idols told you this.
Not one gave any answer when I asked.
29 See, they are all foolish, worthless things.
All your idols are as empty as the wind.

42

THE LORD'S CHOSEN SERVANT

1 "Look at my servant, whom I strengthen.
He is my chosen one, who pleases me.
I have put my Spirit upon him.
He will bring justice to the nations.
2 He will not shout
or raise his voice in public.
3 He will not crush the weakest reed
or put out a flickering candle.
He will bring justice to all who have been wronged.
4 He will not falter or lose heart
until justice prevails throughout the earth.
Even distant lands beyond the sea will wait for
his instruction.*"

5 God, the LORD, created the heavens and stretched
them out.
He created the earth and everything in it.
He gives breath to everyone,
life to everyone who walks the earth.
And it is he who says,
6 "I, the LORD, have called you to demonstrate my
righteousness.
I will take you by the hand and guard you,
and I will give you to my people, Israel,
as a symbol of my covenant with them.
And you will be a light to guide the nations.
7 You will open the eyes of the blind.
You will free the captives from prison,
releasing those who sit in dark dungeons.

8 "I am the LORD; that is my name!
I will not give my glory to anyone else,
nor share my praise with carved idols.
9 Everything I prophesied has come true,
and now I will prophesy again.
I will tell you the future before it happens."

A SONG OF PRAISE TO THE LORD

10 Sing a new song to the LORD!
Sing his praises from the ends of the earth!
Sing, all you who sail the seas,
all you who live in distant coastlands.
11 Join in the chorus, you desert towns;
let the villages of Kedar rejoice!
Let the people of Sela sing for joy;
shout praises from the mountaintops!
12 Let the whole world glorify the LORD;
let it sing his praise.
13 The LORD will march forth like a mighty hero;
he will come out like a warrior, full of fury.
He will shout his battle cry
and crush all his enemies.

14 He will say, "I have long been silent;
yes, I have restrained myself.
But now, like a woman in labor,
I will cry and groan and pant.
15 I will level the mountains and hills
and blight all their greenery.
I will turn the rivers into dry land
and will dry up all the pools.
16 I will lead blind Israel down a new path,
guiding them along an unfamiliar way.
I will brighten the darkness before them
and smooth out the road ahead of them.
Yes, I will indeed do these things;
I will not forsake them.
17 But those who trust in idols,
who say, 'You are our gods,'
will be turned away in shame.

ISRAEL'S FAILURE TO LISTEN AND SEE

18 "Listen, you who are deaf!
Look and see, you blind!
19 Who is as blind as my own people, my servant?
Who is as deaf as my messenger?
Who is as blind as my chosen people,
the servant of the LORD?

41:21 Hebrew *the King of Jacob*. See note on 14:1. **41:27** Or *'Look! They are coming home.'* **42:4** Greek version reads *And his name will be the hope of all the world*. Compare Matt 12:21.

20 You see and recognize what is right
but refuse to act on it.
You hear with your ears,
but you don't really listen."
21 Because he is righteous,
the LORD has exalted his glorious law.
22 But his own people have been robbed and plundered,
enslaved, imprisoned, and trapped.
They are fair game for anyone
and have no one to protect them,
no one to take them back home.

23 Who will hear these lessons from the past
and see the ruin that awaits you in the future?
24 Who allowed Israel to be robbed and hurt?
It was the LORD, against whom we sinned,
for the people would not walk in his path,
nor would they obey his law.
25 Therefore, he poured out his fury on them
and destroyed them in battle.
They were enveloped in flames,
but they still refused to understand.
They were consumed by fire,
but they did not learn their lesson.

43

THE SAVIOR OF ISRAEL

1 But now, O Jacob, listen to the LORD who created you.
O Israel, the one who formed you says,
"Do not be afraid, for I have ransomed you.
I have called you by name; you are mine.
2 When you go through deep waters,
I will be with you.
When you go through rivers of difficulty,
you will not drown.
When you walk through the fire of oppression,
you will not be burned up;
the flames will not consume you.
3 For I am the LORD, your God,
the Holy One of Israel, your Savior.
I gave Egypt as a ransom for your freedom;
I gave Ethiopia* and Seba in your place.
4 Others were given in exchange for you.
I traded their lives for yours
because you are precious to me.
You are honored, and I love you.

5 "Do not be afraid, for I am with you.
I will gather you and your children from east
and west.
6 I will say to the north and south,
'Bring my sons and daughters back to Israel
from the distant corners of the earth.
7 Bring all who claim me as their God,
for I have made them for my glory.
It was I who created them.'"
8 Bring out the people who have eyes but are blind,
who have ears but are deaf.
9 Gather the nations together!
Assemble the peoples of the world!
Which of their idols has ever foretold such things?
Which can predict what will happen tomorrow?
Where are the witnesses of such predictions?
Who can verify that they spoke the truth?

GOD THROUGH YOUR EYES 43:10-11

Israel's task was to be a witness, telling the world who God is and what he has done. Believers today share the responsibility of being God's witnesses. How do your words and example reveal to others what God is like? Although they can't see God directly, they can see him reflected in you. ■

10 "But you are my witnesses, O Israel!" says the LORD.
"You are my servant.
You have been chosen to know me, believe in me,
and understand that I alone am God.
There is no other God—
there never has been, and there never will be.
11 I, yes I, am the LORD,
and there is no other Savior.
12 First I predicted your rescue,
then I saved you and proclaimed it to the world.
No foreign god has ever done this.
You are witnesses that I am the only God,"
says the LORD.
13 "From eternity to eternity I am God.
No one can snatch anyone out of my hand.
No one can undo what I have done."

THE LORD'S PROMISE OF VICTORY

14This is what the LORD says—your Redeemer, the Holy
One of Israel:

"For your sakes I will send an army against Babylon,
forcing the Babylonians* to flee in those ships they
are so proud of.
15 I am the LORD, your Holy One,
Israel's Creator and King.
16 I am the LORD, who opened a way through
the waters,
making a dry path through the sea.
17 I called forth the mighty army of Egypt
with all its chariots and horses.
I drew them beneath the waves, and they drowned,
their lives snuffed out like a smoldering
candlewick.

18 "But forget all that—
it is nothing compared to what I am going to do.
19 For I am about to do something new.
See, I have already begun! Do you not see it?

43:3 Hebrew *Cush*. 43:14 Or *Chaldeans*.

Today's Idolatry

God asks, "Who but a fool would make his own god—an idol that cannot help him one bit!" (44:10). We think of idols as statues of wood or stone, but in reality an idol is anything natural that is given sacred value and power. If your answer to any of the following questions is anyone other than God, you need to check out who you are ultimately worshiping.

Who created me? Whom do I ultimately trust? To whom do I look for security and happiness? To whom do I look for ultimate truth? Who is in charge of my future?

I will make a pathway through the wilderness.
I will create rivers in the dry wasteland.
20 The wild animals in the fields will thank me,
the jackals and owls, too,
for giving them water in the desert.
Yes, I will make rivers in the dry wasteland
so my chosen people can be refreshed.
21 I have made Israel for myself,
and they will someday honor me before the whole world.

22 "But, dear family of Jacob, you refuse to ask for my help.
You have grown tired of me, O Israel!
23 You have not brought me sheep or goats for burnt offerings.
You have not honored me with sacrifices,
though I have not burdened and wearied you
with requests for grain offerings and frankincense.
24 You have not brought me fragrant calamus
or pleased me with the fat from sacrifices.
Instead, you have burdened me with your sins
and wearied me with your faults.

25 "I—yes, I alone—will blot out your sins for my own sake
and will never think of them again.
26 Let us review the situation together,
and you can present your case to prove your innocence.
27 From the very beginning, your first ancestor sinned against me;
all your leaders broke my laws.
28 That is why I have disgraced your priests;
I have decreed complete destruction* for Jacob
and shame for Israel.

44
1 "But now, listen to me, Jacob my servant,
Israel my chosen one.
2 The LORD who made you and helps you says:
Do not be afraid, O Jacob, my servant,
O dear Israel,* my chosen one.
3 For I will pour out water to quench your thirst
and to irrigate your parched fields.
And I will pour out my Spirit on your descendants,
and my blessing on your children.
4 They will thrive like watered grass,
like willows on a riverbank.
5 Some will proudly claim, 'I belong to the LORD.'
Others will say, 'I am a descendant of Jacob.'
Some will write the LORD's name on their hands
and will take the name of Israel as their own."

THE FOOLISHNESS OF IDOLS

6 This is what the LORD says—Israel's King and Redeemer,
the LORD of Heaven's Armies:

"I am the First and the Last;
there is no other God.
7 Who is like me?
Let him step forward and prove to you his power.
Let him do as I have done since ancient times
when I established a people and explained its future.
8 Do not tremble; do not be afraid.
Did I not proclaim my purposes for you long ago?
You are my witnesses—is there any other God?
No! There is no other Rock—not one!"

9 How foolish are those who manufacture idols.
These prized objects are really worthless.
The people who worship idols don't know this,
so they are all put to shame.
10 Who but a fool would make his own god—
an idol that cannot help him one bit?
11 All who worship idols will be disgraced
along with all these craftsmen—mere humans—
who claim they can make a god.
They may all stand together,
but they will stand in terror and shame.

43:28 The Hebrew term used here refers to the complete consecration of things or people to the LORD, either by destroying them or by giving them as an offering. 44:2 Hebrew *Jeshurun*, a term of endearment for Israel.

[12] The blacksmith stands at his forge to make
a sharp tool,
pounding and shaping it with all his might.
His work makes him hungry and weak.
It makes him thirsty and faint.
[13] Then the wood-carver measures a block of wood
and draws a pattern on it.
He works with chisel and plane
and carves it into a human figure.
He gives it human beauty
and puts it in a little shrine.
[14] He cuts down cedars;
he selects the cypress and the oak;
he plants the pine in the forest
to be nourished by the rain.
[15] Then he uses part of the wood to make a fire.
With it he warms himself and bakes his bread.
Then—yes, it's true—he takes the rest of it
and makes himself a god to worship!
He makes an idol
and bows down in front of it!
[16] He burns part of the tree to roast his meat
and to keep himself warm.
He says, "Ah, that fire feels good."
[17] Then he takes what's left
and makes his god: a carved idol!
He falls down in front of it,
worshiping and praying to it.
"Rescue me!" he says.
"You are my god!"

[18] Such stupidity and ignorance!
Their eyes are closed, and they cannot see.
Their minds are shut, and they cannot think.
[19] The person who made the idol never stops to reflect,
"Why, it's just a block of wood!
I burned half of it for heat
and used it to bake my bread and roast my meat.
How can the rest of it be a god?
Should I bow down to worship a piece of wood?"
[20] The poor, deluded fool feeds on ashes.
He trusts something that can't help him at all.
Yet he cannot bring himself to ask,
"Is this idol that I'm holding in my hand a lie?"

RESTORATION FOR JERUSALEM

[21] "Pay attention, O Jacob,
for you are my servant, O Israel.
I, the LORD, made you,
and I will not forget you.
[22] I have swept away your sins like a cloud.
I have scattered your offenses like the morning mist.
Oh, return to me,
for I have paid the price to set you free."

[23] Sing, O heavens, for the LORD has done this
wondrous thing.
Shout for joy, O depths of the earth!
Break into song,
O mountains and forests and every tree!
For the LORD has redeemed Jacob
and is glorified in Israel.

[24] This is what the LORD says—
your Redeemer and Creator:
"I am the LORD, who made all things.
I alone stretched out the heavens.
Who was with me
when I made the earth?
[25] I expose the false prophets as liars
and make fools of fortune-tellers.
I cause the wise to give bad advice,
thus proving them to be fools.
[26] But I carry out the predictions of my prophets!
By them I say to Jerusalem, 'People will live
here again,'
and to the towns of Judah, 'You will be rebuilt;
I will restore all your ruins!'
[27] When I speak to the rivers and say, 'Dry up!'
they will be dry.
[28] When I say of Cyrus, 'He is my shepherd,'
he will certainly do as I say.
He will command, 'Rebuild Jerusalem';
he will say, 'Restore the Temple.'"

PROPHECIES 44:28

Isaiah, who lived from about 740 to 681 B.C., called Cyrus by name almost 150 years before he ruled (559–530 B.C.)! Later historians said that Cyrus read this prophecy and was so moved that he carried it out. Isaiah also had predicted the fall of Jerusalem more than 100 years before it happened (586 B.C.), and the rebuilding of the Temple about 200 years before it happened. Obviously these prophecies came from a God who knows the future. Knowing this, are you willing to let him have your biggest concerns? ■

45 CYRUS, THE LORD'S CHOSEN ONE

[1] This is what the LORD says to Cyrus, his anointed one,
whose right hand he will empower.
Before him, mighty kings will be paralyzed with fear.
Their fortress gates will be opened,
never to shut again.
[2] This is what the LORD says:

"I will go before you, Cyrus,
and level the mountains.*
I will smash down gates of bronze
and cut through bars of iron.
[3] And I will give you treasures hidden in the darkness—
secret riches.
I will do this so you may know that I am the LORD,
the God of Israel, the one who calls you by name.

45:2 As in Dead Sea Scrolls and Greek version; Masoretic Text reads *the swellings*.

4 "And why have I called you for this work?
Why did I call you by name when you did not know me?
It is for the sake of Jacob my servant,
Israel my chosen one.
5 I am the LORD;
there is no other God.
I have equipped you for battle,
though you don't even know me,
6 so all the world from east to west
will know there is no other God.
I am the LORD, and there is no other.
7 I create the light and make the darkness.
I send good times and bad times.
I, the LORD, am the one who does these things.

BAD TIMES 45:7

God tells us that he sends the good times and the bad. Our life is sprinkled with both types of experiences, and both are needed for us to grow spiritually. We might complain to God about the bad and forget to thank him for the good. But the good or the bad experiences can build up our trust in God. ■

8 "Open up, O heavens,
and pour out your righteousness.
Let the earth open wide
so salvation and righteousness can sprout up together.
I, the LORD, created them.

9 "What sorrow awaits those who argue with their Creator.
Does a clay pot argue with its maker?
Does the clay dispute with the one who shapes it, saying,
'Stop, you're doing it wrong!'
Does the pot exclaim,
'How clumsy can you be?'
10 How terrible it would be if a newborn baby said to its father,
'Why was I born?'
or if it said to its mother,
'Why did you make me this way?'"

11 This is what the LORD says—
the Holy One of Israel and your Creator:
"Do you question what I do for my children?
Do you give me orders about the work of my hands?
12 I am the one who made the earth
and created people to live on it.
With my hands I stretched out the heavens.
All the stars are at my command.
13 I will raise up Cyrus to fulfill my righteous purpose,
and I will guide his actions.
He will restore my city and free my captive people—
without seeking a reward!
I, the LORD of Heaven's Armies, have spoken!"

FUTURE CONVERSION OF GENTILES

14 This is what the LORD says:

"You will rule the Egyptians,
the Ethiopians,* and the Sabeans.
They will come to you with all their merchandise,
and it will all be yours.
They will follow you as prisoners in chains.
They will fall to their knees in front of you and say,
'God is with you, and he is the only God.
There is no other.'"

15 Truly, O God of Israel, our Savior,
you work in mysterious ways.
16 All craftsmen who make idols will be humiliated.
They will all be disgraced together.
17 But the LORD will save the people of Israel
with eternal salvation.
Throughout everlasting ages,
they will never again be humiliated and disgraced.

18 For the LORD is God,
and he created the heavens and earth
and put everything in place.
He made the world to be lived in,
not to be a place of empty chaos.
"I am the LORD," he says,
"and there is no other.
19 I publicly proclaim bold promises.
I do not whisper obscurities in some dark corner.
I would not have told the people of Israel*
to seek me
if I could not be found.
I, the LORD, speak only what is true
and declare only what is right.

20 "Gather together and come,
you fugitives from surrounding nations.
What fools they are who carry around their wooden idols
and pray to gods that cannot save!
21 Consult together, argue your case.
Get together and decide what to say.
Who made these things known so long ago?
What idol ever told you they would happen?
Was it not I, the LORD?
For there is no other God but me,
a righteous God and Savior.
There is none but me.
22 Let all the world look to me for salvation!
For I am God; there is no other.
23 I have sworn by my own name;
I have spoken the truth,
and I will never go back on my word:

45:14 Hebrew *Cushites*. 45:19 Hebrew *of Jacob*. See note on 14:1.

keeping it real

When my family moved from Mexico to the United States, everything familiar to me was gone. I had to learn a new language, adjust to totally different ways of doing things, and make friends with people who seemed to have grown up on a different planet rather than in a different country. I was very, very lonely for a long time.

I turned often to the Bible. So many verses were meaningful to me. But Isaiah 46:4 especially helped because it spoke of God's tender care and how he would be with me always, even when I'm old. I would imagine God right there with me in this strange school, and I'd talk to him in my heart, telling him how I felt. It was a great comfort to know that he was right there with me and that he cared. I knew he heard my prayers and understood—and I could speak to him in Spanish! This experience has brought me closer to God as I depend on him every day for the understanding and help I need to make this adjustment.

—Julio

Every knee will bend to me,
and every tongue will confess allegiance to me.*"
24 The people will declare,
"The LORD is the source of all my righteousness
and strength."
And all who were angry with him
will come to him and be ashamed.
25 In the LORD all the generations of Israel will
be justified,
and in him they will boast.

46 BABYLON'S FALSE GODS

1 Bel and Nebo, the gods of Babylon,
bow as they are lowered to the ground.
They are being hauled away on ox carts.
The poor beasts stagger under the weight.
2 Both the idols and their owners are bowed down.
The gods cannot protect the people,
and the people cannot protect the gods.
They go off into captivity together.

3 "Listen to me, descendants of Jacob,
all you who remain in Israel.
I have cared for you since you were born.
Yes, I carried you before you were born.
4 I will be your God throughout your lifetime—
until your hair is white with age.
I made you, and I will care for you.
I will carry you along and save you.

5 "To whom will you compare me?
Who is my equal?
6 Some people pour out their silver and gold
and hire a craftsman to make a god from it.
Then they bow down and worship it!
7 They carry it around on their shoulders,
and when they set it down, it stays there.
It can't even move!
And when someone prays to it, there is no answer.
It can't rescue anyone from trouble.

8 "Do not forget this! Keep it in mind!
Remember this, you guilty ones.
9 Remember the things I have done in the past.
For I alone am God!
I am God, and there is none like me.
10 Only I can tell you the future
before it even happens.
Everything I plan will come to pass,
for I do whatever I wish.
11 I will call a swift bird of prey from the east—
a leader from a distant land to come and
do my bidding.
I have said what I would do,
and I will do it.

12 "Listen to me, you stubborn people
who are so far from doing right.
13 For I am ready to set things right,
not in the distant future, but right now!
I am ready to save Jerusalem*
and show my glory to Israel.

47 PREDICTION OF BABYLON'S FALL

1 "Come down, virgin daughter of Babylon, and sit in
the dust.

45:23 Hebrew *will confess;* Greek version reads *will confess and give praise to God.* Compare Rom 14:11. **46:13** Hebrew *Zion.*

For your days of sitting on a throne have ended.
O daughter of Babylonia,* never again will you be
the lovely princess, tender and delicate.
2 Take heavy millstones and grind flour.
Remove your veil, and strip off your robe.
Expose yourself to public view.
3 You will be naked and burdened with shame.
I will take vengeance against you without pity."

4 Our Redeemer, whose name is the LORD of
Heaven's Armies,
is the Holy One of Israel.

5 "O beautiful Babylon, sit now in darkness
and silence.
Never again will you be known as the queen
of kingdoms.
6 For I was angry with my chosen people
and punished them by letting them fall into
your hands.
But you, Babylon, showed them no mercy.
You oppressed even the elderly.
7 You said, 'I will reign forever as queen of
the world!'
You did not reflect on your actions
or think about their consequences.

8 "Listen to this, you pleasure-loving kingdom,
living at ease and feeling secure.
You say, 'I am the only one, and there is no other.
I will never be a widow or lose my children.'
9 Well, both these things will come upon you
in a moment:
widowhood and the loss of your children.
Yes, these calamities will come upon you,
despite all your witchcraft and magic.

POWER 47:1-9

Caught up in the pursuit of power and pleasure, Babylon believed in its own greatness and claimed to be the *only* power on earth. But Isaiah predicted the fall of this seemingly invincible nation, just as he prophesied about the destruction of other nations. Only God is truly invincible. Does he have your complete trust? ■

10 "You felt secure in your wickedness.
'No one sees me,' you said.
But your 'wisdom' and 'knowledge' have led
you astray,
and you said, 'I am the only one, and there is
no other.'
11 So disaster will overtake you,
and you won't be able to charm it away.
Calamity will fall upon you,
and you won't be able to buy your way out.
A catastrophe will strike you suddenly,
one for which you are not prepared.

12 "Now use your magical charms!
Use the spells you have worked at all these years!
Maybe they will do you some good.
Maybe they can make someone afraid of you.
13 All the advice you receive has made you tired.
Where are all your astrologers,
those stargazers who make predictions each month?
Let them stand up and save you from what the
future holds.
14 But they are like straw burning in a fire;
they cannot save themselves from the flame.
You will get no help from them at all;
their hearth is no place to sit for warmth.
15 And all your friends,
those with whom you've done business
since childhood,
will go their own ways,
turning a deaf ear to your cries.

48 GOD'S STUBBORN PEOPLE

1 "Listen to me, O family of Jacob,
you who are called by the name of Israel
and born into the family of Judah.

47:1 Or *Chaldea;* also in 47:5.

What's so wrong about horoscopes? They're just harmless entertainment, right?

Many activities that seem harmless unfortunately lead to more harmful activities like those of the occult.

The Bible mentions several examples of occult activity among the people of Israel and other nations. When King Saul of Israel wanted information about an upcoming battle, he consulted someone who claimed to be able to speak to the dead (see 1 Sam 28). Other passages deal with astrology, divination, wizards, and sorcery (see Deut 18:10-14; 2 Chron 33:6; Isa 47:12-15; Dan 2:1-2; Acts 8:9-13; 16:16-19). God always condemned these activities.

If Satan can get people to take in evil small doses at a time, eventually they may become desensitized and not recognize that they are being fed something that will dull their interest in God.

Satan would never get anyone to follow him if he revealed all of his evil at once. Instead, he slowly gives us small doses of evil until we're so desensitized to it that it seems a normal part of life.

This is the strategy: to capture our mind through one small compromise into darkness after another.

Our best defense is to know the truth of the Word of God, so we can discern when we are being tempted by evil. God knows it is real. And Jesus came to destroy the works of the devil. Remember, "the Spirit who lives in you is greater than the spirit who lives in the world" (1 John 4:4).

Listen, you who take oaths in the name of the LORD
and call on the God of Israel.
You don't keep your promises,
2 even though you call yourself the holy city
and talk about depending on the God of Israel,
whose name is the LORD of Heaven's Armies.
3 Long ago I told you what was going to happen.
Then suddenly I took action,
and all my predictions came true.
4 For I know how stubborn and obstinate you are.
Your necks are as unbending as iron.
Your heads are as hard as bronze.
5 That is why I told you what would happen;
I told you beforehand what I was going to do.
Then you could never say, 'My idols did it.
My wooden image and metal god commanded
it to happen!'
6 You have heard my predictions and seen
them fulfilled,
but you refuse to admit it.
Now I will tell you new things,
secrets you have not yet heard.
7 They are brand new, not things from the past.
So you cannot say, 'We knew that all the time!'

8 "Yes, I will tell you of things that are entirely new,
things you never heard of before.
For I know so well what traitors you are.
You have been rebels from birth.
9 Yet for my own sake and for the honor of
my name,
I will hold back my anger and not wipe you out.
10 I have refined you, but not as silver is refined.
Rather, I have refined you in the furnace
of suffering.
11 I will rescue you for my sake—
yes, for my own sake!
I will not let my reputation be tarnished,
and I will not share my glory with idols!

FREEDOM FROM BABYLON

12 "Listen to me, O family of Jacob,
Israel my chosen one!
I alone am God,
the First and the Last.
13 It was my hand that laid the foundations of
the earth,
my right hand that spread out the heavens above.
When I call out the stars,
they all appear in order."

14 Have any of your idols ever told you this?
Come, all of you, and listen:
The LORD has chosen Cyrus as his ally.
He will use him to put an end to the empire
of Babylon
and to destroy the Babylonian* armies.
15 "I have said it: I am calling Cyrus!
I will send him on this errand and will help
him succeed.
16 Come closer, and listen to this.
From the beginning I have told you plainly what
would happen."

And now the Sovereign LORD and his Spirit
have sent me with this message.
17 This is what the LORD says—
your Redeemer, the Holy One of Israel:
"I am the LORD your God,
who teaches you what is good for you
and leads you along the paths you should follow.
18 Oh, that you had listened to my commands!
Then you would have had peace flowing like
a gentle river
and righteousness rolling over you like waves
in the sea.
19 Your descendants would have been like the sands
along the seashore—
too many to count!
There would have been no need for your destruction,
or for cutting off your family name."

20 Yet even now, be free from your captivity!
Leave Babylon and the Babylonians.*
Sing out this message!
Shout it to the ends of the earth!
The LORD has redeemed his servants,
the people of Israel.*
21 They were not thirsty
when he led them through the desert.
He divided the rock,
and water gushed out for them to drink.
22 "But there is no peace for the wicked,"
says the LORD.

49 THE LORD'S SERVANT COMMISSIONED

1 Listen to me, all you in distant lands!
Pay attention, you who are far away!
The LORD called me before my birth;
from within the womb he called me by name.
2 He made my words of judgment as sharp
as a sword.
He has hidden me in the shadow of his hand.
I am like a sharp arrow in his quiver.

3 He said to me, "You are my servant, Israel,
and you will bring me glory."

4 I replied, "But my work seems so useless!
I have spent my strength for nothing and
to no purpose.
Yet I leave it all in the LORD's hand;
I will trust God for my reward."

48:14 Or *Chaldean.* **48:20a** Or *the Chaldeans.* **48:20b** Hebrew *his servant, Jacob.* See note on 14:1.

5 And now the LORD speaks—
the one who formed me in my mother's womb
to be his servant,
who commissioned me to bring Israel back to him.
The LORD has honored me,
and my God has given me strength.
6 He says, "You will do more than restore the people
of Israel to me.
I will make you a light to the Gentiles,
and you will bring my salvation to the ends
of the earth."

7 The LORD, the Redeemer
and Holy One of Israel,
says to the one who is despised and rejected
by the nations,
to the one who is the servant of rulers:
"Kings will stand at attention when you pass by.
Princes will also bow low
because of the LORD, the faithful one,
the Holy One of Israel, who has chosen you."

PROMISES OF ISRAEL'S RESTORATION

8 This is what the LORD says:

"At just the right time, I will respond to you.*
On the day of salvation I will help you.
I will protect you and give you to the people
as my covenant with them.
Through you I will reestablish the land of Israel
and assign it to its own people again.
9 I will say to the prisoners, 'Come out in freedom,'
and to those in darkness, 'Come into the light.'
They will be my sheep, grazing in green pastures
and on hills that were previously bare.
10 They will neither hunger nor thirst.
The searing sun will not reach them anymore.
For the LORD in his mercy will lead them;
he will lead them beside cool waters.
11 And I will make my mountains into level paths
for them.
The highways will be raised above the valleys.
12 See, my people will return from far away,
from lands to the north and west,
and from as far south as Egypt.*"

13 Sing for joy, O heavens!
Rejoice, O earth!
Burst into song, O mountains!
For the LORD has comforted his people
and will have compassion on them in their suffering.

14 Yet Jerusalem* says, "The LORD has deserted us;
the Lord has forgotten us."

15 "Never! Can a mother forget her nursing child?
Can she feel no love for the child she has borne?

DESERTED 49:14-15

Isaiah prophesied that the people of Israel would feel deserted by God after their land was invaded. Isaiah pointed out that God would never leave them, just as a mother wouldn't leave her little child. Yet hard times can make us feel unloved or abandoned. But this passage in Isaiah is a good reminder that God will never forsake us. (See also Heb 13:5.) ■

But even if that were possible,
I would not forget you!
16 See, I have written your name on the palms of
my hands.
Always in my mind is a picture of Jerusalem's walls
in ruins.
17 Soon your descendants will come back,
and all who are trying to destroy you will go away.
18 Look around you and see,
for all your children will come back to you.
As surely as I live," says the LORD,
"they will be like jewels or bridal ornaments for
you to display.

19 "Even the most desolate parts of your
abandoned land
will soon be crowded with your people.
Your enemies who enslaved you
will be far away.
20 The generations born in exile will return and say,
'We need more room! It's crowded here!'
21 Then you will think to yourself,
'Who has given me all these descendants?
For most of my children were killed,
and the rest were carried away into exile.
I was left here all alone.
Where did all these people come from?
Who bore these children?
Who raised them for me?'"

22 This is what the Sovereign LORD says:
"See, I will give a signal to the godless nations.
They will carry your little sons back to you
in their arms;
they will bring your daughters on their shoulders.
23 Kings and queens will serve you
and care for all your needs.
They will bow to the earth before you
and lick the dust from your feet.
Then you will know that I am the LORD.
Those who trust in me will never be put to shame."

24 Who can snatch the plunder of war from the hands
of a warrior?
Who can demand that a tyrant* let his captives go?

49:8 Greek version reads *I heard you.* Compare 2 Cor 6:2. **49:12** As in Dead Sea Scrolls, which read *from the region of Aswan,* which is in southern Egypt. Masoretic Text reads *from the region of Sinim.* **49:14** Hebrew *Zion.* **49:24** As in Dead Sea Scrolls, Syriac version, and Latin Vulgate (also see 49:25); Masoretic Text reads *a righteous person.*

25 But the LORD says,
"The captives of warriors will be released,
and the plunder of tyrants will be retrieved.
For I will fight those who fight you,
and I will save your children.
26 I will feed your enemies with their own flesh.
They will be drunk with rivers of their own blood.
All the world will know that I, the LORD,
am your Savior and your Redeemer,
the Mighty One of Israel.*"

50

This is what the LORD says:

"Was your mother sent away because I divorced her?
Did I sell you as slaves to my creditors?
No, you were sold because of your sins.
And your mother, too, was taken because
of your sins.
2 Why was no one there when I came?
Why didn't anyone answer when I called?
Is it because I have no power to rescue?
No, that is not the reason!
For I can speak to the sea and make it dry up!
I can turn rivers into deserts covered with
dying fish.
3 I dress the skies in darkness,
covering them with clothes of mourning."

THE LORD'S OBEDIENT SERVANT

4 The Sovereign LORD has given me his words of wisdom,
so that I know how to comfort the weary.
Morning by morning he wakens me
and opens my understanding to his will.
5 The Sovereign LORD has spoken to me,
and I have listened.
I have not rebelled or turned away.
6 I offered my back to those who beat me
and my cheeks to those who pulled out my beard.
I did not hide my face
from mockery and spitting.

7 Because the Sovereign LORD helps me,
I will not be disgraced.
Therefore, I have set my face like a stone,
determined to do his will.
And I know that I will not be put to shame.
8 He who gives me justice is near.
Who will dare to bring charges against me now?
Where are my accusers?
Let them appear!
9 See, the Sovereign LORD is on my side!
Who will declare me guilty?
All my enemies will be destroyed
like old clothes that have been eaten by moths!

10 Who among you fears the LORD
and obeys his servant?
If you are walking in darkness,
without a ray of light,
trust in the LORD
and rely on your God.
11 But watch out, you who live in your own light
and warm yourselves by your own fires.
This is the reward you will receive from me:
You will soon fall down in great torment.

51

A CALL TO TRUST THE LORD

1 "Listen to me, all who hope for deliverance—
all who seek the LORD!
Consider the rock from which you were cut,
the quarry from which you were mined.
2 Yes, think about Abraham, your ancestor,
and Sarah, who gave birth to your nation.
Abraham was only one man when I called him.
But when I blessed him, he became a great nation."

3 The LORD will comfort Israel* again
and have pity on her ruins.
Her desert will blossom like Eden,
her barren wilderness like the garden of the LORD.
Joy and gladness will be found there.
Songs of thanksgiving will fill the air.

RIDICULED 51:7

Isaiah encouraged those who served God to discern right from wrong and to follow God's laws. He also gave them hope when they faced people's scorn or slander because of their faith. We need not fear when people ridicule us for our faith because God is with us and truth will prevail. If people make fun of you or dislike you because you believe in God, remember that they are not against you personally, but against God. He'll deal with them. ■

4 "Listen to me, my people.
Hear me, Israel,
for my law will be proclaimed,
and my justice will become a light to the nations.
5 My mercy and justice are coming soon.
My salvation is on the way.
My strong arm will bring justice to the nations.
All distant lands will look to me
and wait in hope for my powerful arm.
6 Look up to the skies above,
and gaze down on the earth below.
For the skies will disappear like smoke,
and the earth will wear out like a piece of clothing.
The people of the earth will die like flies,
but my salvation lasts forever.
My righteous rule will never end!

7 "Listen to me, you who know right from wrong,
you who cherish my law in your hearts.

49:26 Hebrew *of Jacob*. See note on 14:1. **51:3** Hebrew *Zion;* also in 51:16.

Do not be afraid of people's scorn,
nor fear their insults.
8 For the moth will devour them as it devours clothing.
The worm will eat at them as it eats wool.
But my righteousness will last forever.
My salvation will continue from generation
to generation."

9 Wake up, wake up, O LORD! Clothe yourself
with strength!
Flex your mighty right arm!
Rouse yourself as in the days of old
when you slew Egypt, the dragon of the Nile.*
10 Are you not the same today,
the one who dried up the sea,
making a path of escape through the depths
so that your people could cross over?
11 Those who have been ransomed by the LORD
will return.
They will enter Jerusalem* singing,
crowned with everlasting joy.
Sorrow and mourning will disappear,
and they will be filled with joy and gladness.

12 "I, yes I, am the one who comforts you.
So why are you afraid of mere humans,
who wither like the grass and disappear?
13 Yet you have forgotten the LORD, your Creator,
the one who stretched out the sky like a canopy
and laid the foundations of the earth.
Will you remain in constant dread of human
oppressors?
Will you continue to fear the anger of your enemies?
Where is their fury and anger now?
It is gone!
14 Soon all you captives will be released!
Imprisonment, starvation, and death will not
be your fate!
15 For I am the LORD your God,
who stirs up the sea, causing its waves to roar.
My name is the LORD of Heaven's Armies.
16 And I have put my words in your mouth
and hidden you safely in my hand.
I stretched out* the sky like a canopy
and laid the foundations of the earth.
I am the one who says to Israel,
'You are my people!'"

17 Wake up, wake up, O Jerusalem!
You have drunk the cup of the LORD's fury.
You have drunk the cup of terror,
tipping out its last drops.
18 Not one of your children is left alive
to take your hand and guide you.
19 These two calamities have fallen on you:
desolation and destruction, famine and war.
And who is left to sympathize with you?
Who is left to comfort you?*
20 For your children have fainted and lie in the streets,
helpless as antelopes caught in a net.
The LORD has poured out his fury;
God has rebuked them.

21 But now listen to this, you afflicted ones
who sit in a drunken stupor,
though not from drinking wine.
22 This is what the Sovereign LORD,
your God and Defender, says:
"See, I have taken the terrible cup from your hands.
You will drink no more of my fury.
23 Instead, I will hand that cup to your tormentors,
those who said, 'We will trample you into
the dust
and walk on your backs.'"

52

DELIVERANCE FOR JERUSALEM

1 Wake up, wake up, O Zion!
Clothe yourself with strength.
Put on your beautiful clothes, O holy city
of Jerusalem,
for unclean and godless people will enter your
gates no longer.
2 Rise from the dust, O Jerusalem.
Sit in a place of honor.
Remove the chains of slavery from your neck,
O captive daughter of Zion.
3 For this is what the LORD says:
"When I sold you into exile,
I received no payment.
Now I can redeem you
without having to pay for you."

HE'S IN CONTROL 52:1-12

The servant, as the term is used here, is the Messiah—Jesus. This prophecy occurred hundreds of years before Jesus arrived and is one among many in the book of Isaiah. (See also 7:14; 9:6-7; 42:1-4.) Think of the coordination necessary to bring everything to pass! This just goes to show the incredible control God has over everything. Yet for all of his control, he never forces himself into someone's life. He waits to be invited. Does he have control over your life? ■

4This is what the Sovereign LORD says: "Long ago my
people chose to live in Egypt. Now they are oppressed by
Assyria. 5What is this?" asks the LORD. "Why are my people enslaved again? Those who rule them shout in exulta-
tion. My name is blasphemed all day long.* 6But I will
reveal my name to my people, and they will come to know

51:9 Hebrew *You slew Rahab; you pierced the dragon.* Rahab is the name of a mythical sea monster that represents chaos in ancient literature. The name is used here as a poetic name for Egypt. 51:11 Hebrew *Zion.* 51:16 As in Syriac version (see also 51:13); Hebrew reads *planted.* 51:19 As in Dead Sea Scrolls and Greek, Latin, and Syriac versions; Masoretic Text reads *How can I comfort you?* 52:5 Greek version reads *The Gentiles continually blaspheme my name because of you.* Compare Rom 2:24.

its power. Then at last they will recognize that I am the one who speaks to them."

7 How beautiful on the mountains
are the feet of the messenger who brings good news,
the good news of peace and salvation,
the news that the God of Israel* reigns!
8 The watchmen shout and sing with joy,
for before their very eyes
they see the LORD returning
to Jerusalem.*
9 Let the ruins of Jerusalem break
into joyful song,
for the LORD has comforted
his people.
He has redeemed Jerusalem.
10 The LORD has demonstrated his
holy power
before the eyes of all the nations.
All the ends of the earth will see
the victory of our God.

11 Get out! Get out and leave your
captivity,
where everything you touch
is unclean.
Get out of there and purify yourselves,
you who carry home the sacred objects
of the LORD.
12 You will not leave in a hurry,
running for your lives.
For the LORD will go ahead of you;
yes, the God of Israel will protect you from behind.

THE LORD'S SUFFERING SERVANT

13 See, my servant will prosper;
he will be highly exalted.
14 But many were amazed when they saw him.*
His face was so disfigured he seemed
hardly human,
and from his appearance, one would scarcely know
he was a man.
15 And he will startle* many nations.
Kings will stand speechless in his presence.
For they will see what they had not been told;
they will understand what they had not
heard about.*

53

1 Who has believed our message?
To whom has the LORD revealed his powerful arm?
2 My servant grew up in the LORD's presence like a
tender green shoot,
like a root in dry ground.
There was nothing beautiful or majestic about
his appearance,
nothing to attract us to him.
3 He was despised and rejected—
a man of sorrows, acquainted with deepest grief.
We turned our backs on him and looked the
other way.
He was despised, and we did not care.

> But he was pierced for our rebellion, crushed for our sins. He was beaten so we could be whole. He was whipped so we could be healed.
>
> ISAIAH 53:5

4 Yet it was our weaknesses
he carried;
it was our sorrows* that weighed
him down.
And we thought his troubles were
a punishment from God,
a punishment for his own sins!
5 But he was pierced for our
rebellion,
crushed for our sins.
He was beaten so we could be whole.
He was whipped so we could
be healed.
6 All of us, like sheep, have
strayed away.
We have left God's paths to
follow our own.
Yet the LORD laid on him
the sins of us all.

7 He was oppressed and treated harshly,
yet he never said a word.
He was led like a lamb to the slaughter.
And as a sheep is silent before the shearers,
he did not open his mouth.
8 Unjustly condemned,
he was led away.*
No one cared that he died without descendants,
that his life was cut short in midstream.*
But he was struck down
for the rebellion of my people.
9 He had done no wrong
and had never deceived anyone.
But he was buried like a criminal;
he was put in a rich man's grave.

10 But it was the LORD's good plan to crush him
and cause him grief.
Yet when his life is made an offering for sin,
he will have many descendants.
He will enjoy a long life,
and the LORD's good plan will prosper in his hands.
11 When he sees all that is accomplished by his anguish,
he will be satisfied.
And because of his experience,
my righteous servant will make it possible

52:7 Hebrew *of Zion.* 52:8 Hebrew *to Zion.* 52:14 As in Syriac version; Hebrew reads *you.* 52:15a Or *cleanse.* 52:15b Greek version reads *Those who have never been told about him will see, / and those who have never heard of him will understand.* Compare Rom 15:21. 53:4 Or *Yet it was our sicknesses he carried; / it was our diseases.* 53:8a Greek version reads *He was humiliated and received no justice.* Compare Acts 8:33. 53:8b Or *As for his contemporaries, / who cared that his life was cut short in midstream?* Greek version reads *Who can speak of his descendants? / For his life was taken from the earth.* Compare Acts 8:33.

for many to be counted righteous,
for he will bear all their sins.
12 I will give him the honors of a victorious soldier,
because he exposed himself to death.
He was counted among the rebels.
He bore the sins of many and interceded
for rebels.

54 FUTURE GLORY FOR JERUSALEM

1 "Sing, O childless woman,
you who have never given birth!
Break into loud and joyful song, O Jerusalem,
you who have never been in labor.
For the desolate woman now has more children
than the woman who lives with her husband,"
says the LORD.
2 "Enlarge your house; build an addition.
Spread out your home, and spare no expense!
3 For you will soon be bursting at the seams.
Your descendants will occupy other nations
and resettle the ruined cities.

4 "Fear not; you will no longer live in shame.
Don't be afraid; there is no more disgrace for you.
You will no longer remember the shame of
your youth
and the sorrows of widowhood.
5 For your Creator will be your husband;
the LORD of Heaven's Armies is his name!
He is your Redeemer, the Holy One of Israel,
the God of all the earth.
6 For the LORD has called you back from your grief—
as though you were a young wife abandoned
by her husband,"
says your God.
7 "For a brief moment I abandoned you,
but with great compassion I will take you back.
8 In a burst of anger I turned my face away for
a little while.
But with everlasting love I will have compassion
on you,"
says the LORD, your Redeemer.

9 "Just as I swore in the time of Noah
that I would never again let a flood cover
the earth,
so now I swear
that I will never again be angry and punish you.
10 For the mountains may move
and the hills disappear,
but even then my faithful love for you will remain.
My covenant of blessing will never be broken,"
says the LORD, who has mercy on you.

11 "O storm-battered city,
troubled and desolate!
I will rebuild you with precious jewels
and make your foundations from lapis lazuli.
12 I will make your towers of sparkling rubies,
your gates of shining gems,
and your walls of precious stones.
13 I will teach all your children,
and they will enjoy great peace.
14 You will be secure under a government that is just
and fair.
Your enemies will stay far away.
You will live in peace,
and terror will not come near.
15 If any nation comes to fight you,
it is not because I sent them.
Whoever attacks you will go down in defeat.

16 "I have created the blacksmith
who fans the coals beneath the forge
and makes the weapons of destruction.
And I have created the armies that destroy.
17 But in that coming day
no weapon turned against you will succeed.
You will silence every voice
raised up to accuse you.
These benefits are enjoyed by the servants
of the LORD;
their vindication will come from me.
I, the LORD, have spoken!

55 INVITATION TO THE LORD'S SALVATION

1 "Is anyone thirsty?
Come and drink—
even if you have no money!
Come, take your choice of wine or milk—
it's all free!
2 Why spend your money on food that does not give
you strength?
Why pay for food that does you no good?
Listen to me, and you will eat what is good.
You will enjoy the finest food.

3 "Come to me with your ears wide open.
Listen, and you will find life.
I will make an everlasting covenant with you.
I will give you all the unfailing love I promised
to David.
4 See how I used him to display my power among
the peoples.
I made him a leader among the nations.
5 You also will command nations you do not know,
and peoples unknown to you will come running
to obey,
because I, the LORD your God,
the Holy One of Israel, have made you glorious."

6 Seek the LORD while you can find him.
Call on him now while he is near.
7 Let the wicked change their ways
and banish the very thought of doing wrong.

Let them turn to the LORD that he may have mercy
on them.
Yes, turn to our God, for he will forgive generously.

8 "My thoughts are nothing like your thoughts," says
the LORD.
"And my ways are far beyond anything you
could imagine.
9 For just as the heavens are higher than the earth,
so my ways are higher than your ways
and my thoughts higher than your thoughts.

CALL NOW 55:6

Isaiah encouraged the people of Israel to call upon the Lord while he was near. Sometimes, we might think that God has moved away from us. Often the truth is that we're the ones who have drifted away. We do that when we decide to go our own way, rather than his. But God is always close by and will hear us whenever we call, even if we're not sure he'll listen. Feeling far away? Don't be afraid to call now! ■

10 "The rain and snow come down from the heavens
and stay on the ground to water the earth.
They cause the grain to grow,
producing seed for the farmer
and bread for the hungry.
11 It is the same with my word.
I send it out, and it always produces fruit.
It will accomplish all I want it to,
and it will prosper everywhere I send it.
12 You will live in joy and peace.
The mountains and hills will burst into song,
and the trees of the field will clap their hands!
13 Where once there were thorns, cypress trees will grow.
Where nettles grew, myrtles will sprout up.
These events will bring great honor to the
LORD's name;
they will be an everlasting sign of his power
and love."

56 BLESSINGS FOR ALL NATIONS

This is what the LORD says:

"Be just and fair to all.
Do what is right and good,
for I am coming soon to rescue you
and to display my righteousness among you.
2 Blessed are all those
who are careful to do this.
Blessed are those who honor my Sabbath days of rest
and keep themselves from doing wrong.

3 "Don't let foreigners who commit themselves to the
LORD say,
'The LORD will never let me be part of his people.'
And don't let the eunuchs say,
'I'm a dried-up tree with no children and
no future.'
4 For this is what the LORD says:
I will bless those eunuchs
who keep my Sabbath days holy
and who choose to do what pleases me
and commit their lives to me.
5 I will give them—within the walls of my house—
a memorial and a name
far greater than sons and daughters could give.
For the name I give them is an everlasting one.
It will never disappear!

6 "I will also bless the foreigners who commit
themselves to the LORD,
who serve him and love his name,
who worship him and do not desecrate the Sabbath
day of rest,
and who hold fast to my covenant.
7 I will bring them to my holy mountain of Jerusalem
and will fill them with joy in my house of prayer.
I will accept their burnt offerings and sacrifices,
because my Temple will be called a house of prayer
for all nations.
8 For the Sovereign LORD,
who brings back the outcasts of Israel, says:
I will bring others, too,
besides my people Israel."

SINFUL LEADERS CONDEMNED

9 Come, wild animals of the field!
Come, wild animals of the forest!
Come and devour my people!
10 For the leaders of my people—
the LORD's watchmen, his shepherds—
are blind and ignorant.
They are like silent watchdogs
that give no warning when danger comes.
They love to lie around, sleeping and dreaming.
11 Like greedy dogs, they are never satisfied.
They are ignorant shepherds,
all following their own path
and intent on personal gain.
12 "Come," they say, "let's get some wine and have
a party.
Let's all get drunk.
Then tomorrow we'll do it again
and have an even bigger party!"

57

1 Good people pass away;
the godly often die before their time.
But no one seems to care or wonder why.
No one seems to understand
that God is protecting them from the evil
to come.
2 For those who follow godly paths
will rest in peace when they die.

IDOLATROUS WORSHIP CONDEMNED

3 "But you—come here, you witches' children,
you offspring of adulterers and prostitutes!
4 Whom do you mock,
making faces and sticking out your tongues?
You children of sinners and liars!
5 You worship your idols with great passion
beneath the oaks and under every green tree.
You sacrifice your children down in the valleys,
among the jagged rocks in the cliffs.
6 Your gods are the smooth stones in the valleys.
You worship them with liquid offerings and
grain offerings.
They, not I, are your inheritance.
Do you think all this makes me happy?
7 You have committed adultery on every high mountain.
There you have worshiped idols
and have been unfaithful to me.
8 You have put pagan symbols
on your doorposts and behind your doors.
You have left me
and climbed into bed with these detestable gods.
You have committed yourselves to them.
You love to look at their naked bodies.
9 You have given olive oil to Molech*
with many gifts of perfume.
You have traveled far,
even into the world of the dead,*
to find new gods to love.
10 You grew weary in your search,
but you never gave up.
Desire gave you renewed strength,
and you did not grow weary.

GOOD DEEDS 57:12-13

Isaiah warned the idol worshipers of Judah that their attempts at right living wouldn't save them any more than their weak, worthless idols could. We cannot be saved through good deeds because our best deeds aren't good enough to outweigh the bad things we've done. (See also Isa 64:6.) Salvation is a gift from God. (See also Eph 2:10.) Like any gift, we can either accept it or reject it. So, your choice is . . . ? ■

11 "Are you afraid of these idols?
Do they terrify you?
Is that why you have lied to me
and forgotten me and my words?
Is it because of my long silence
that you no longer fear me?
12 Now I will expose your so-called good deeds.
None of them will help you.
13 Let's see if your idols can save you
when you cry to them for help.
Why, a puff of wind can knock them down!
If you just breathe on them, they fall over!
But whoever trusts in me will inherit the land
and possess my holy mountain."

GOD FORGIVES THE REPENTANT

14 God says, "Rebuild the road!
Clear away the rocks and stones
so my people can return from captivity."
15 The high and lofty one who lives in eternity,
the Holy One, says this:
"I live in the high and holy place
with those whose spirits are contrite and humble.
I restore the crushed spirit of the humble
and revive the courage of those with
repentant hearts.
16 For I will not fight against you forever;
I will not always be angry.
If I were, all people would pass away—
all the souls I have made.
17 I was angry,
so I punished these greedy people.
I withdrew from them,
but they kept going on their own stubborn way.
18 I have seen what they do,
but I will heal them anyway!
I will lead them.
I will comfort those who mourn,
19 bringing words of praise to their lips.
May they have abundant peace, both near and far,"
says the LORD, who heals them.
20 "But those who still reject me are like the restless sea,
which is never still
but continually churns up mud and dirt.
21 There is no peace for the wicked,"
says my God.

58 TRUE AND FALSE WORSHIP

1 "Shout with the voice of a trumpet blast.
Shout aloud! Don't be timid.
Tell my people Israel* of their sins!
2 Yet they act so pious!
They come to the Temple every day
and seem delighted to learn all about me.
They act like a righteous nation
that would never abandon the laws of its God.
They ask me to take action on their behalf,
pretending they want to be near me.
3 'We have fasted before you!' they say.
'Why aren't you impressed?
We have been very hard on ourselves,
and you don't even notice it!'

"I will tell you why!" I respond.
"It's because you are fasting to please yourselves.
Even while you fast,
you keep oppressing your workers.
4 What good is fasting
when you keep on fighting and quarreling?

57:9a Or *to the king*. 57:9b Hebrew *into Sheol*. 58:1 Hebrew *Jacob*. See note on 14:1.

This kind of fasting
will never get you anywhere with me.
5 You humble yourselves
by going through the motions of penance,
bowing your heads
like reeds bending in the wind.
You dress in burlap
and cover yourselves with ashes.
Is this what you call fasting?
Do you really think this will please the LORD?

6 "No, this is the kind of fasting I want:
Free those who are wrongly imprisoned;
lighten the burden of those who work for you.
Let the oppressed go free,
and remove the chains that bind people.
7 Share your food with the hungry,
and give shelter to the homeless.
Give clothes to those who need them,
and do not hide from relatives who need
your help.

TRUE WORSHIP 58:1-14

Isaiah warned the people against hypocritical actions. He wanted them to know that true worship was more than religious ritual, going to the Temple every day, and listening to Scripture readings. It involved authenticity and an honest confession of wrongdoing. But having a genuine compassion for the poor, the helpless, and the oppressed was also an aspect of worship. That's still the case today. How "true" is your worship of God? ■

8 "Then your salvation will come like the dawn,
and your wounds will quickly heal.
Your godliness will lead you forward,
and the glory of the LORD will protect you
from behind.
9 Then when you call, the LORD will answer.
'Yes, I am here,' he will quickly reply.

"Remove the heavy yoke of oppression.
Stop pointing your finger and spreading
vicious rumors!
10 Feed the hungry,
and help those in trouble.
Then your light will shine out from the darkness,
and the darkness around you will be as bright
as noon.
11 The LORD will guide you continually,
giving you water when you are dry
and restoring your strength.
You will be like a well-watered garden,
like an ever-flowing spring.
12 Some of you will rebuild the deserted ruins
of your cities.
Then you will be known as a rebuilder of walls
and a restorer of homes.

13 "Keep the Sabbath day holy.
Don't pursue your own interests on that day,
but enjoy the Sabbath
and speak of it with delight as the LORD's holy day.
Honor the Sabbath in everything you do on that day,
and don't follow your own desires or talk idly.
14 Then the LORD will be your delight.
I will give you great honor
and satisfy you with the inheritance I promised to
your ancestor Jacob.
I, the LORD, have spoken!"

59 WARNINGS AGAINST SIN

1 Listen! The LORD's arm is not too weak to
save you,
nor is his ear too deaf to hear you call.
2 It's your sins that have cut you off from God.
Because of your sins, he has turned away
and will not listen anymore.
3 Your hands are the hands of murderers,
and your fingers are filthy with sin.
Your lips are full of lies,
and your mouth spews corruption.

4 No one cares about being fair and honest.
The people's lawsuits are based on lies.
They conceive evil deeds
and then give birth to sin.
5 They hatch deadly snakes
and weave spiders' webs.
Whoever falls into their webs will die,
and there's danger even in getting near them.
6 Their webs can't be made into clothing,
and nothing they do is productive.
All their activity is filled with sin,
and violence is their trademark.
7 Their feet run to do evil,
and they rush to commit murder.
They think only about sinning.
Misery and destruction always follow them.
8 They don't know where to find peace
or what it means to be just and good.
They have mapped out crooked roads,
and no one who follows them knows a
moment's peace.

9 So there is no justice among us,
and we know nothing about right living.
We look for light but find only darkness.
We look for bright skies but walk in gloom.
10 We grope like the blind along a wall,
feeling our way like people without eyes.
Even at brightest noontime,
we stumble as though it were dark.
Among the living,
we are like the dead.
11 We growl like hungry bears;
we moan like mournful doves.

We look for justice, but it never comes.
We look for rescue, but it is far away from us.
12 For our sins are piled up before God
and testify against us.
Yes, we know what sinners we are.
13 We know we have rebelled and have denied the LORD.
We have turned our backs on our God.
We know how unfair and oppressive we have been,
carefully planning our deceitful lies.
14 Our courts oppose the righteous,
and justice is nowhere to be found.
Truth stumbles in the streets,
and honesty has been outlawed.
15 Yes, truth is gone,
and anyone who renounces evil is attacked.

The LORD looked and was displeased
to find there was no justice.
16 He was amazed to see that no one intervened
to help the oppressed.
So he himself stepped in to save them with his
strong arm,
and his justice sustained him.
17 He put on righteousness as his body armor
and placed the helmet of salvation on his head.
He clothed himself with a robe of vengeance
and wrapped himself in a cloak of divine passion.
18 He will repay his enemies for their evil deeds.
His fury will fall on his foes.
He will pay them back even to the ends of
the earth.
19 In the west, people will respect the name of the LORD;
in the east, they will glorify him.
For he will come like a raging flood tide
driven by the breath of the LORD.*

20 "The Redeemer will come to Jerusalem
to buy back those in Israel
who have turned from their sins,"*
says the LORD.

21 "And this is my covenant with them," says the LORD. "My Spirit will not leave them, and neither will these words I have given you. They will be on your lips and on the lips of your children and your children's children forever. I, the LORD, have spoken!

60

FUTURE GLORY FOR JERUSALEM

1 "Arise, Jerusalem! Let your light shine for all to see.
For the glory of the LORD rises to shine on you.
2 Darkness as black as night covers all the nations of
the earth,
but the glory of the LORD rises and appears
over you.
3 All nations will come to your light;
mighty kings will come to see your radiance.

4 "Look and see, for everyone is coming home!
Your sons are coming from distant lands;
your little daughters will be carried home.
5 Your eyes will shine,
and your heart will thrill with joy,
for merchants from around the world will come
to you.
They will bring you the wealth of many lands.
6 Vast caravans of camels will converge on you,
the camels of Midian and Ephah.
The people of Sheba will bring gold and
frankincense
and will come worshiping the LORD.
7 The flocks of Kedar will be given to you,
and the rams of Nebaioth will be brought for
my altars.
I will accept their offerings,
and I will make my Temple glorious.

8 "And what do I see flying like clouds to Israel,
like doves to their nests?
9 They are ships from the ends of the earth,
from lands that trust in me,
led by the great ships of Tarshish.
They are bringing the people of Israel home from
far away,
carrying their silver and gold.
They will honor the LORD your God,
the Holy One of Israel,
for he has filled you with splendor.

PATIENCE 60:1-22

What are you longing for these days? As we read these promises of a future period, we long for their fulfillment. But we must patiently wait for God's timing. God is in control of history, and he weaves all of our lives together into his plan. ■

10 "Foreigners will come to rebuild your towns,
and their kings will serve you.
For though I have destroyed you in my anger,
I will now have mercy on you through my grace.
11 Your gates will stay open around the clock
to receive the wealth of many lands.
The kings of the world will be led as captives
in a victory procession.
12 For the nations that refuse to serve you
will be destroyed.

13 "The glory of Lebanon will be yours—
the forests of cypress, fir, and pine—
to beautify my sanctuary.
My Temple will be glorious!
14 The descendants of your tormentors
will come and bow before you.

59:19 Or *When the enemy comes like a raging flood tide, / the Spirit of the LORD will drive him back.* **59:20** Hebrew *The Redeemer will come to Zion / to buy back those in Jacob / who have turned from their sins.* Greek version reads *The one who rescues will come on behalf of Zion, / and he will turn Jacob away from ungodliness.* Compare Rom 11:26.

Those who despised you
will kiss your feet.
They will call you the City of the LORD,
and Zion of the Holy One of Israel.

15 "Though you were once despised and hated,
with no one traveling through you,
I will make you beautiful forever,
a joy to all generations.
16 Powerful kings and mighty nations
will satisfy your every need,
as though you were a child
nursing at the breast of a queen.
You will know at last that I, the LORD,
am your Savior and your Redeemer,
the Mighty One of Israel.*
17 I will exchange your bronze for gold,
your iron for silver,
your wood for bronze,
and your stones for iron.
I will make peace your leader
and righteousness your ruler.
18 Violence will disappear from your land;
the desolation and destruction of war will end.
Salvation will surround you like city walls,
and praise will be on the lips of all who
enter there.

19 "No longer will you need the sun to shine by day,
nor the moon to give its light by night,
for the LORD your God will be your everlasting light,
and your God will be your glory.
20 Your sun will never set;
your moon will not go down.
For the LORD will be your everlasting light.
Your days of mourning will come to an end.
21 All your people will be righteous.
They will possess their land forever,
for I will plant them there with my own hands
in order to bring myself glory.
22 The smallest family will become a thousand people,
and the tiniest group will become a mighty nation.
At the right time, I, the LORD, will make
it happen."

61

GOOD NEWS FOR THE OPPRESSED

1 The Spirit of the Sovereign LORD is upon me,
for the LORD has anointed me
to bring good news to the poor.
He has sent me to comfort the brokenhearted
and to proclaim that captives will be released
and prisoners will be freed.*
2 He has sent me to tell those who mourn
that the time of the LORD's favor has come,*
and with it, the day of God's anger against
their enemies.
3 To all who mourn in Israel,*
he will give a crown of beauty for ashes,
a joyous blessing instead of mourning,
festive praise instead of despair.
In their righteousness, they will be like great oaks
that the LORD has planted for his own glory.

JUSTICE FOR THE SUFFERING 61:1-3

Isaiah assured the people of Judah that a Savior would someday make things right for his suffering people. Centuries after Isaiah, Jesus quoted this very passage (see Luke 4:16-22) as a sign that he had come to fulfill this passage. Some periods of suffering seem to go on forever. We long for relief, but also for justice when we're treated unjustly. Wondering when God will make things right for you? He may not act as quickly as we would like him to act. But he's never late. ■

4 They will rebuild the ancient ruins,
repairing cities destroyed long ago.
They will revive them,
though they have been deserted for many
generations.
5 Foreigners will be your servants.
They will feed your flocks
and plow your fields
and tend your vineyards.
6 You will be called priests of the LORD,
ministers of our God.
You will feed on the treasures of the nations
and boast in their riches.
7 Instead of shame and dishonor,
you will enjoy a double share of honor.
You will possess a double portion of prosperity in
your land,
and everlasting joy will be yours.

8 "For I, the LORD, love justice.
I hate robbery and wrongdoing.
I will faithfully reward my people for their suffering
and make an everlasting covenant with them.
9 Their descendants will be recognized
and honored among the nations.
Everyone will realize that they are a people
the LORD has blessed."

10 I am overwhelmed with joy in the LORD my God!
For he has dressed me with the clothing
of salvation
and draped me in a robe of righteousness.
I am like a bridegroom in his wedding suit
or a bride with her jewels.
11 The Sovereign LORD will show his justice to the
nations of the world.
Everyone will praise him!

60:16 Hebrew *of Jacob*. See note on 14:1. 61:1 Greek version reads *and the blind will see*. Compare Luke 4:18. 61:2 Or *to proclaim the acceptable year of the LORD*. 61:3 Hebrew *in Zion*.

His righteousness will be like a garden in
early spring,
with plants springing up everywhere.

62 ISAIAH'S PRAYER FOR JERUSALEM

1 Because I love Zion,
I will not keep still.
Because my heart yearns for Jerusalem,
I cannot remain silent.
I will not stop praying for her
until her righteousness shines like the dawn,
and her salvation blazes like a burning torch.
2 The nations will see your righteousness.
World leaders will be blinded by your glory.
And you will be given a new name
by the LORD's own mouth.
3 The LORD will hold you in his hand for
all to see—
a splendid crown in the hand of God.
4 Never again will you be called "The Forsaken City"*
or "The Desolate Land."*
Your new name will be "The City of God's Delight"*
and "The Bride of God,"*
for the LORD delights in you
and will claim you as his bride.
5 Your children will commit themselves to you,
O Jerusalem,
just as a young man commits himself to
his bride.
Then God will rejoice over you
as a bridegroom rejoices over his bride.

DETERMINATION 62:1-7

Isaiah's zeal for his country and his desire to see the work of salvation completed caused him to pray continually, hoping that Israel would be saved. What are you most determined to do? Get into a good college? Break a sports record? Become valedictorian? Do you share Isaiah's determination to see God's will done? When we pray, "May your Kingdom come soon. May your will be done on earth, as it is in heaven" (Matt 6:10), we're saying, in a sense, "Go for it God—whatever you want to do." How much zeal do you have in regard to praying for others and doing other work for the Kingdom? ■

6 O Jerusalem, I have posted watchmen on
your walls;
they will pray day and night, continually.
Take no rest, all you who pray to the LORD.
7 Give the LORD no rest until he completes
his work,
until he makes Jerusalem the pride of
the earth.
8 The LORD has sworn to Jerusalem by his
own strength:
"I will never again hand you over to
your enemies.
Never again will foreign warriors come
and take away your grain and new wine.
9 You raised the grain, and you will eat it,
praising the LORD.
Within the courtyards of the Temple,
you yourselves will drink the wine you
have pressed."

10 Go out through the gates!
Prepare the highway for my people to return!
Smooth out the road; pull out the boulders;
raise a flag for all the nations to see.
11 The LORD has sent this message to every land:
"Tell the people of Israel,*
'Look, your Savior is coming.
See, he brings his reward with him as he comes.'"
12 They will be called "The Holy People"
and "The People Redeemed by the LORD."
And Jerusalem will be known as "The
Desirable Place"
and "The City No Longer Forsaken."

63 JUDGMENT AGAINST THE LORD'S ENEMIES

1 Who is this who comes from Edom,
from the city of Bozrah,
with his clothing stained red?
Who is this in royal robes,
marching in his great strength?

"It is I, the LORD, announcing your salvation!
It is I, the LORD, who has the power to save!"

2 Why are your clothes so red,
as if you have been treading out grapes?

3 "I have been treading the winepress alone;
no one was there to help me.
In my anger I have trampled my enemies
as if they were grapes.
In my fury I have trampled my foes.
Their blood has stained my clothes.
4 For the time has come for me to avenge
my people,
to ransom them from their oppressors.
5 I was amazed to see that no one intervened
to help the oppressed.
So I myself stepped in to save them with my
strong arm,
and my wrath sustained me.
6 I crushed the nations in my anger
and made them stagger and fall to the ground,
spilling their blood upon the earth."

62:4a Hebrew *Azubah*, which means "forsaken." **62:4b** Hebrew *Shemamah*, which means "desolate." **62:4c** Hebrew *Hephzibah*, which means "my delight is in her." **62:4d** Hebrew *Beulah*, which means "married." **62:11** Hebrew *Tell the daughter of Zion.*

PRAISE FOR DELIVERANCE

7 I will tell of the LORD's unfailing love.
I will praise the LORD for all he has done.
I will rejoice in his great goodness to Israel,
which he has granted according to his mercy
and love.
8 He said, "They are my very own people.
Surely they will not betray me again."
And he became their Savior.
9 In all their suffering he also suffered,
and he personally* rescued them.
In his love and mercy he redeemed them.
He lifted them up and carried them
through all the years.
10 But they rebelled against him
and grieved his Holy Spirit.
So he became their enemy
and fought against them.

11 Then they remembered those days of old
when Moses led his people out of Egypt.
They cried out, "Where is the one who brought Israel
through the sea,
with Moses as their shepherd?
Where is the one who sent his Holy Spirit
to be among his people?
12 Where is the one whose power was displayed
when Moses lifted up his hand—
the one who divided the sea before them,
making himself famous forever?
13 Where is the one who led them through the bottom
of the sea?
They were like fine stallions
racing through the desert, never stumbling.
14 As with cattle going down into a peaceful valley,
the Spirit of the LORD gave them rest.
You led your people, LORD,
and gained a magnificent reputation."

PRAYER FOR MERCY AND PARDON

15 LORD, look down from heaven;
look from your holy, glorious home, and see us.
Where is the passion and the might
you used to show on our behalf?
Where are your mercy and compassion now?
16 Surely you are still our Father!
Even if Abraham and Jacob* would disown us,
LORD, you would still be our Father.
You are our Redeemer from ages past.
17 LORD, why have you allowed us to turn from
your path?
Why have you given us stubborn hearts so we no
longer fear you?
Return and help us, for we are your servants,
the tribes that are your special possession.
18 How briefly your holy people possessed your
holy place,
and now our enemies have destroyed it.
19 Sometimes it seems as though we never belonged
to you,
as though we had never been known as your people.

64

1* Oh, that you would burst from the
heavens and come down!
How the mountains would quake in
your presence!
2* As fire causes wood to burn
and water to boil,
your coming would make the nations tremble.
Then your enemies would learn the reason for
your fame!
3 When you came down long ago,
you did awesome deeds beyond our highest
expectations.
And oh, how the mountains quaked!
4 For since the world began,
no ear has heard,
and no eye has seen a God like you,
who works for those who wait for him!
5 You welcome those who gladly do good,
who follow godly ways.
But you have been very angry with us,
for we are not godly.
We are constant sinners;
how can people like us be saved?
6 We are all infected and impure with sin.
When we display our righteous deeds,
they are nothing but filthy rags.
Like autumn leaves, we wither and fall,
and our sins sweep us away like the wind.
7 Yet no one calls on your name
or pleads with you for mercy.
Therefore, you have turned away from us
and turned us over* to our sins.
8 And yet, O LORD, you are our Father.
We are the clay, and you are the potter.
We all are formed by your hand.
9 Don't be so angry with us, LORD.
Please don't remember our sins forever.
Look at us, we pray,
and see that we are all your people.
10 Your holy cities are destroyed.
Zion is a wilderness;
yes, Jerusalem is a desolate ruin.
11 The holy and beautiful Temple
where our ancestors praised you
has been burned down,
and all the things of beauty are destroyed.
12 After all this, LORD, must you still refuse
to help us?
Will you continue to be silent and
punish us?

63:9 Hebrew *and the angel of his presence.* 63:16 Hebrew *Israel.* See note on 14:1. 64:1 Verse 64:1 is numbered 63:20 in Hebrew text. 64:2 Verses 64:2-12 are numbered 64:1-11 in Hebrew text. 64:7 As in Greek, Syriac, and Aramaic versions; Hebrew reads *melted us.*

65 JUDGMENT AND FINAL SALVATION

The LORD says,

"I was ready to respond, but no one asked for help.
I was ready to be found, but no one was looking for me.
I said, 'Here I am, here I am!'
to a nation that did not call on my name.*
2 All day long I opened my arms to a rebellious people.*
But they follow their own evil paths
and their own crooked schemes.
3 All day long they insult me to my face
by worshiping idols in their sacred gardens.
They burn incense on pagan altars.
4 At night they go out among the graves,
worshiping the dead.
They eat the flesh of pigs
and make stews with other forbidden foods.
5 Yet they say to each other,
'Don't come too close or you will defile me!
I am holier than you!'
These people are a stench in my nostrils,
an acrid smell that never goes away.

6 "Look, my decree is written out* in front of me:
I will not stand silent;
I will repay them in full!
Yes, I will repay them—
7 both for their own sins
and for those of their ancestors,"
says the LORD.
"For they also burned incense on the mountains
and insulted me on the hills.
I will pay them back in full!

8 "But I will not destroy them all,"
says the LORD.
"For just as good grapes are found among a cluster of bad ones
(and someone will say, 'Don't throw them all away—
some of those grapes are good!'),
so I will not destroy all Israel.
For I still have true servants there.
9 I will preserve a remnant of the people of Israel*
and of Judah to possess my land.
Those I choose will inherit it,
and my servants will live there.
10 The plain of Sharon will again be filled with flocks
for my people who have searched for me,
and the valley of Achor will be a place to pasture herds.

11 "But because the rest of you have forsaken the LORD
and have forgotten his Temple,
and because you have prepared feasts to honor the god of Fate
and have offered mixed wine to the god of Destiny,
12 now I will 'destine' you for the sword.
All of you will bow down before the executioner.
For when I called, you did not answer.
When I spoke, you did not listen.
You deliberately sinned—before my very eyes—
and chose to do what you know I despise."

13 Therefore, this is what the Sovereign LORD says:
"My servants will eat,
but you will starve.
My servants will drink,
but you will be thirsty.
My servants will rejoice,
but you will be sad and ashamed.
14 My servants will sing for joy,
but you will cry in sorrow and despair.
15 Your name will be a curse word among my people,
for the Sovereign LORD will destroy you
and will call his true servants by another name.
16 All who invoke a blessing or take an oath
will do so by the God of truth.
For I will put aside my anger
and forget the evil of earlier days.

17 "Look! I am creating new heavens and a new earth,
and no one will even think about the old ones anymore.
18 Be glad; rejoice forever in my creation!
And look! I will create Jerusalem as a place of happiness.
Her people will be a source of joy.
19 I will rejoice over Jerusalem
and delight in my people.
And the sound of weeping and crying
will be heard in it no more.

20 "No longer will babies die when only a few days old.
No longer will adults die before they have lived a full life.
No longer will people be considered old at one hundred!
Only the cursed will die that young!
21 In those days people will live in the houses they build
and eat the fruit of their own vineyards.
22 Unlike the past, invaders will not take their houses
and confiscate their vineyards.
For my people will live as long as trees,
and my chosen ones will have time to enjoy their hard-won gains.
23 They will not work in vain,

65:1 Or *to a nation that did not bear my name.* 65:1-2 Greek version reads *I was found by people who were not looking for me. / I showed myself to those who were not asking for me. / All day long I opened my arms to them, / but they were disobedient and rebellious.* Compare Rom 10:20. 65:6 Or *their sins are written out;* Hebrew reads *it stands written.* 65:9 Hebrew *remnant of Jacob.* See note on 14:1.

and their children will not be doomed
to misfortune.
For they are people blessed by the LORD,
and their children, too, will be blessed.
24 I will answer them before they even call to me.
While they are still talking about their needs,
I will go ahead and answer their prayers!
25 The wolf and the lamb will feed together.
The lion will eat hay like a cow.
But the snakes will eat dust.
In those days no one will be hurt or destroyed
on my holy mountain.
I, the LORD, have spoken!"

66

This is what the LORD says:

"Heaven is my throne,
and the earth is my footstool.
Could you build me a temple as good as that?
Could you build me such a resting place?
2 My hands have made both heaven and earth;
they and everything in them are mine.*
I, the LORD, have spoken!

"I will bless those who have humble and
contrite hearts,
who tremble at my word.
3 But those who choose their own ways—
delighting in their detestable sins—
will not have their offerings accepted.
When such people sacrifice a bull,
it is no more acceptable than a human sacrifice.
When they sacrifice a lamb,
it's as though they had sacrificed a dog!
When they bring an offering of grain,
they might as well offer the blood of a pig.
When they burn frankincense,
it's as if they had blessed an idol.
4 I will send them great trouble—
all the things they feared.
For when I called, they did not answer.
When I spoke, they did not listen.
They deliberately sinned before my very eyes
and chose to do what they know I despise."

5 Hear this message from the LORD,
all you who tremble at his words:
"Your own people hate you
and throw you out for being loyal to my name.
'Let the LORD be honored!' they scoff.
'Be joyful in him!'
But they will be put to shame.
6 What is all the commotion in the city?
What is that terrible noise from the Temple?
It is the voice of the LORD
taking vengeance against his enemies.

7 "Before the birth pains even begin,
Jerusalem gives birth to a son.
8 Who has ever seen anything as strange as this?
Who ever heard of such a thing?
Has a nation ever been born in a single day?
Has a country ever come forth in a mere moment?
But by the time Jerusalem's* birth pains begin,
her children will be born.
9 Would I ever bring this nation to the point of birth
and then not deliver it?" asks the LORD.
"No! I would never keep this nation from being born,"
says your God.

10 "Rejoice with Jerusalem!
Be glad with her, all you who love her
and all you who mourn for her.
11 Drink deeply of her glory
even as an infant drinks at its mother's
comforting breasts."
12 This is what the LORD says:
"I will give Jerusalem a river of peace and prosperity.
The wealth of the nations will flow to her.
Her children will be nursed at her breasts,
carried in her arms, and held on her lap.
13 I will comfort you there in Jerusalem
as a mother comforts her child."

DRAMA 66:22-24

Isaiah brings his book to a close with great drama. For the faithless, there is a sobering portrayal of judgment. For the faithful, there is a glorious picture of a future rich reward—"As surely as my new heavens and earth will remain, so will you always be my people, with a name that will never disappear." Is that what you're looking forward to? Your faithfulness now can assure that bright future. ■

14 When you see these things, your heart will rejoice.
You will flourish like the grass!
Everyone will see the LORD's hand of blessing on his
servants—
and his anger against his enemies.
15 See, the LORD is coming with fire,
and his swift chariots roar like a whirlwind.
He will bring punishment with the fury of his anger
and the flaming fire of his hot rebuke.
16 The LORD will punish the world by fire
and by his sword.
He will judge the earth,
and many will be killed by him.

17"Those who 'consecrate' and 'purify' themselves in a sacred garden with its idol in the center—feasting on pork and rats and other detestable meats—will come to a terrible end," says the LORD.

66:2 As in Greek, Latin, and Syriac versions; Hebrew reads *these things are.* 66:8 Hebrew *Zion's.*

[18]"I can see what they are doing, and I know what they
are thinking. So I will gather all nations and peoples together, and they will see my glory. [19]I will perform a sign
among them. And I will send those who survive to be
messengers to the nations—to Tarshish, to the Libyans*
and Lydians* (who are famous as archers), to Tubal and
Greece,* and to all the lands beyond the sea that have not
heard of my fame or seen my glory. There they will declare my glory to the nations. [20]They will bring the remnant of your people back from every nation. They will
bring them to my holy mountain in Jerusalem as an offering to the LORD. They will ride on horses, in chariots and
wagons, and on mules and camels," says the LORD. [21]"And
I will appoint some of them to be my priests and Levites. I,
the LORD, have spoken!

[22] "As surely as my new heavens and earth
will remain,
so will you always be my people,
with a name that will never disappear,"
says the LORD.
[23] "All humanity will come to worship me
from week to week
and from month to month.
[24] And as they go out, they will see
the dead bodies of those who have rebelled
against me.
For the worms that devour them will never die,
and the fire that burns them will never go out.
All who pass by
will view them with utter horror."

66:19a As in some Greek manuscripts, which read *Put* [that is, *Libya*]; Hebrew reads *Pul.* **66:19b** Hebrew *Lud.* **66:19c** Hebrew *Javan.*

WHEN WAS THE last time you cried?

Tears can seem embarrassing and awkward—even a sign of weakness. When we were young, tears came easily over a broken toy, a skinned knee, and other assorted real or imagined hurts. As we grew older, we learned to hide our feelings, especially our sadness. We tried to look tough or put on a happy face. Yet tears allow us see what affects people deeply.

Jeremiah is called the weeping prophet. In his books (Jeremiah and Lamentations), it seems as though all he did was cry. But Jeremiah's tears didn't stem from immaturity, self-centeredness, or weakness. Jeremiah cried because God planned to punish his beloved nation because of their long history of rebellion. An enemy nation would invade their land, destroy it, and take the people away. He tried to help the people of Israel see the need to return to God, but they wouldn't listen. So he cried.

What brings tears to your eyes? Have you ever cried over the consequences of someone's poor choice? A heart filled with compassion can't help but cry over the trouble in the world. Is that the kind of heart you have?

timeline

640 B.C.
Zephaniah becomes a prophet

627
Jeremiah becomes a prophet

612
Habakkuk becomes a prophet

609
King Josiah killed in battle

605
Daniel taken captive

597
Ezekiel taken captive

593
Ezekiel begins to prophesy in Babylon

586
Judah falls; Jerusalem destroyed; Jeremiah's ministry ends

537
First exiles return to Judah

stats

PURPOSE: To urge God's people to turn from their sins and to turn back to God

AUTHOR: Jeremiah

TO WHOM WRITTEN: Judah (the southern kingdom) and its capital Jerusalem

DATE WRITTEN: During Jeremiah's ministry, approximately 627–586 B.C.

SETTING: Jeremiah ministered during the reigns of Judah's last five kings—Josiah, Jehoahaz, Jehoiakim, Jehoiachin (Coniah), and Zedekiah. The nation was conquered by Babylon in 586 B.C. (see 2 Kings 21–25). Zephaniah preceded Jeremiah; Habakkuk was his contemporary.

KEY PEOPLE: Judah's kings (listed above), Baruch, Ebed-melech, King Nebuchadnezzar, the Recabites

KEY PLACES: Anathoth, Jerusalem, Ramah, Egypt

SPECIAL FEATURES: The book of Jeremiah is a combination of history, poetry, and biography. Jeremiah often used symbolism to communicate his message.

KEY points

SIN
Judah's deterioration and disaster stemmed from their disobedience to God. When we refuse to listen to God's warnings and go our own way, we invite disaster.

PUNISHMENT
The people of Judah had only themselves to blame for their suffering. Likewise, we must answer to God for how we live.

FAITHFUL TO FULFILL
God brought the prophecies of Micah, Isaiah, and Zephaniah to pass according to his timetable. God is faithful to fulfill his promises.

HOPE
Jeremiah predicted that after the nation's destruction, God would send the Messiah who would lead them into a new future, a new covenant, and a new day of hope. God still renews hope with the promise of eternal life.

FAITHFUL SERVICE
Jeremiah served God faithfully for over 40 years. The people ignored, rejected, and persecuted him, yet he did not fail. People's acceptance or rejection of us is not the measure of our success. God's approval is our standard for service.

1

These are the words of Jeremiah son of Hilkiah,
one of the priests from the town of Anathoth in the
land of Benjamin. 2The LORD first gave messages to Jeremiah during the thirteenth year of the reign of Josiah
son of Amon, king of Judah.* 3The LORD's messages
continued throughout the reign of King Jehoiakim, Josiah's son, until the eleventh year of the reign of King
Zedekiah, another of Josiah's sons. In August* of that
eleventh year the people of Jerusalem were taken away
as captives.

JEREMIAH'S CALL AND FIRST VISIONS

4The LORD gave me this message:

5 "I knew you before I formed you in your
mother's womb.
Before you were born I set you apart
and appointed you as my prophet to the nations."

6"O Sovereign LORD," I said, "I can't speak for you! I'm
too young!"
7The LORD replied, "Don't say, 'I'm too young,' for you
must go wherever I send you and say whatever I tell
you. 8And don't be afraid of the people, for I will be with
you and will protect you. I, the LORD, have spoken!" 9Then
the LORD reached out and touched my mouth and said,

TOO YOUNG TO SERVE? 1:1-8

Jeremiah tried to use his youth as an excuse to avoid being God's spokesman. But God overruled any excuse that he came up with. Have you ever thought that your age exempted you from doing anything for God? Maybe you've thought that you could wait until after you've finished college to get serious about God. Knowing that God doesn't accept the age excuse, how does that change your view of what you can do for God? ■

"Look, I have put my words in your mouth!
10 Today I appoint you to stand up
against nations and kingdoms.
Some you must uproot and tear down,
destroy and overthrow.
Others you must build up
and plant."

11Then the LORD said to me, "Look, Jeremiah! What do
you see?"
And I replied, "I see a branch from an almond tree."
12And the LORD said, "That's right, and it means that I
am watching,* and I will certainly carry out all my plans."
13Then the LORD spoke to me again and asked, "What
do you see now?"
And I replied, "I see a pot of boiling water, spilling
from the north."
14"Yes," the LORD said, "for terror from the north will
boil out on the people of this land. 15Listen! I am calling
the armies of the kingdoms of the north to come to Jerusalem. I, the LORD, have spoken!

"They will set their thrones
at the gates of the city.
They will attack its walls
and all the other towns of Judah.
16 I will pronounce judgment
on my people for all their evil—
for deserting me and burning incense to other gods.
Yes, they worship idols made with their own hands!

STAY TRUE 1:16; 2:1-3

The people of Israel obeyed God initially but failed to be faithful to their commitment. Think about how you feel when someone fails to keep a promise. Yet some of us are distracted at times from our commitment to God. Other relationships and commitments take first priority. God takes seriously any vows of commitment made to him. Are you just as serious about your commitment to him? ■

17 "Get up and prepare for action.
Go out and tell them everything I tell you to say.
Do not be afraid of them,
or I will make you look foolish in front of them.
18 For see, today I have made you strong
like a fortified city that cannot be captured,
like an iron pillar or a bronze wall.
You will stand against the whole land—
the kings, officials, priests, and people of Judah.
19 They will fight you, but they will fail.
For I am with you, and I will take care of you.
I, the LORD, have spoken!"

2

THE LORD'S CASE AGAINST HIS PEOPLE

The LORD gave me another message. He said, 2"Go and
shout this message to Jerusalem. This is what the LORD
says:

"I remember how eager you were to please me
as a young bride long ago,
how you loved me and followed me
even through the barren wilderness.
3 In those days Israel was holy to the LORD,
the first of his children.*
All who harmed his people were declared guilty,
and disaster fell on them.
I, the LORD, have spoken!"

1:2 The thirteenth year of Josiah's reign was 627 B.C. 1:3 Hebrew *In the fifth month,* of the ancient Hebrew lunar calendar. A number of events in Jeremiah can be cross-checked with dates in surviving Babylonian records and related accurately to our modern calendar. The fifth month in the eleventh year of Zedekiah's reign occurred within the months of August and September 586 B.C. Also see 52:12 and the note there. 1:12 The Hebrew word for "watching" *(shoqed)* sounds like the word for "almond tree" *(shaqed).* 2:3 Hebrew *the firstfruits of his harvest.*

4 Listen to the word of the LORD, people of Jacob—all you families of Israel!
5 This is what the LORD says:

"What did your ancestors find
wrong with me
that led them to stray so far
from me?
They worshiped worthless idols,
only to become worthless
themselves.
6 They did not ask, 'Where is the LORD
who brought us safely out
of Egypt
and led us through the barren
wilderness—
a land of deserts and pits,
a land of drought and death,
where no one lives or even travels?'
7 "And when I brought you into a fruitful land
to enjoy its bounty and goodness,
you defiled my land and
corrupted the possession I had promised you.
8 The priests did not ask,
'Where is the LORD?'
Those who taught my word ignored me,
the rulers turned against me,
and the prophets spoke in the name of Baal,
wasting their time on worthless idols.
9 Therefore, I will bring my case against you,"
says the LORD.
"I will even bring charges against your
children's children
in the years to come.
10 "Go west and look in the land of Cyprus*;
go east and search through the land of Kedar.
Has anyone ever heard of anything
as strange as this?
11 Has any nation ever traded its gods for new ones,
even though they are not gods at all?
Yet my people have exchanged their glorious God*
for worthless idols!
12 The heavens are shocked at such a thing
and shrink back in horror and dismay,"
says the LORD.
13 "For my people have done two evil things:
They have abandoned me—
the fountain of living water.
And they have dug for themselves cracked cisterns
that can hold no water at all!

THE RESULTS OF ISRAEL'S SIN

14 "Why has Israel become a slave?
Why has he been carried away as plunder?
15 Strong lions have roared against him,
and the land has been destroyed.
The towns are now in ruins,
and no one lives in them
anymore.
16 Egyptians, marching from their
cities of Memphis* and
Tahpanhes,
have destroyed Israel's glory
and power.
17 And you have brought this upon
yourselves
by rebelling against the LORD
your God,
even though he was leading you
on the way!

18 "What have you gained by your
alliances with Egypt
and your covenants with Assyria?
What good to you are the streams of the Nile*
or the waters of the Euphrates River?*
19 Your wickedness will bring its own punishment.
Your turning from me will shame you.
You will see what an evil, bitter thing it is
to abandon the LORD your God and not to fear him.
I, the Lord, the LORD of Heaven's Armies, have spoken!

You will see what an evil, bitter thing it is to abandon the LORD your God and not to fear him.

JEREMIAH 2:19

CRACKED CISTERNS 2:13

Who would set aside a sparkling fountain of water for a cistern, a pit that collected rainwater? God used Jeremiah to remind the Israelites that they had turned from him, the fountain of living water, to idols. Not only that, the cisterns they chose were cracked and empty. Today's "cracked cisterns" are money, power/status, other relationships, popularity—the list goes on. Are you clinging to any of these? None can compare with God's promise of living water (see John 4:10). Have you taken a drink of it lately? ■

20 "Long ago I broke the yoke that oppressed you
and tore away the chains of your slavery,
but still you said,
'I will not serve you.'
On every hill and under every green tree,
you have prostituted yourselves by bowing down
to idols.
21 But I was the one who planted you,
choosing a vine of the purest stock—the very best.
How did you grow into this corrupt wild vine?
22 No amount of soap or lye can make you clean.
I still see the stain of your guilt.
I, the Sovereign LORD, have spoken!

ISRAEL, AN UNFAITHFUL WIFE

23 "You say, 'That's not true!
I haven't worshiped the images of Baal!'

2:10 Hebrew *Kittim.* 2:11 Hebrew *their glory.* 2:16 Hebrew *Noph.* 2:18a Hebrew *of Shihor,* a branch of the Nile River. 2:18b Hebrew *the river?*

But how can you say that?
Go and look in any valley in the land!
Face the awful sins you have done.
You are like a restless female camel
desperately searching for a mate.
24 You are like a wild donkey,
sniffing the wind at mating time.
Who can restrain her lust?
Those who desire her don't need to search,
for she goes running to them!
25 When will you stop running?
When will you stop panting after other gods?
But you say, 'Save your breath.
I'm in love with these foreign gods,
and I can't stop loving them now!'

26 "Israel is like a thief
who feels shame only when he gets caught.
They, their kings, officials, priests, and prophets—
all are alike in this.
27 To an image carved from a piece of wood they say,
'You are my father.'
To an idol chiseled from a block of stone they say,
'You are my mother.'
They turn their backs on me,
but in times of trouble they cry out to me,
'Come and save us!'
28 But why not call on these gods you have made?
When trouble comes, let them save you if they can!
For you have as many gods
as there are towns in Judah.
29 Why do you accuse me of doing wrong?
You are the ones who have rebelled,"
says the LORD.
30 "I have punished your children,
but they did not respond to my discipline.
You yourselves have killed your prophets
as a lion kills its prey.

31 "O my people, listen to the words of the LORD!
Have I been like a desert to Israel?
Have I been to them a land of darkness?
Why then do my people say, 'At last we are free
from God!
We don't need him anymore!'
32 Does a young woman forget her jewelry?
Does a bride hide her wedding dress?
Yet for years on end
my people have forgotten me.

33 "How you plot and scheme to win your lovers.
Even an experienced prostitute could learn
from you!
34 Your clothing is stained with the blood of the
innocent and the poor,
though you didn't catch them breaking into
your houses!
35 And yet you say,
'I have done nothing wrong.
Surely God isn't angry with me!'
But now I will punish you severely
because you claim you have not sinned.
36 First here, then there—
you flit from one ally to another asking for help.
But your new friends in Egypt will let you down,
just as Assyria did before.
37 In despair, you will be led into exile
with your hands on your heads,
for the LORD has rejected the nations you trust.
They will not help you at all.

DOWNPLAY IT? 3:1-5

The people of Israel tried to minimize their wrongs. When we know we've done something wrong, we want to downplay the error by saying, "It wasn't that bad!" In that way, we relieve some of the guilt we feel. But if we view every wrong attitude and action as a serious offense to God, we'll begin to understand what living for God is all about. Is there an action in your life that you've written off as too small to worry about? God wants us to confess every wrong and turn from it. ■

3

1 "If a man divorces a woman
and she goes and marries someone else,
he will not take her back again,
for that would surely corrupt the land.
But you have prostituted yourself with many lovers,
so why are you trying to come back to me?"
says the LORD.
2 "Look at the shrines on every hilltop.
Is there any place you have not been defiled
by your adultery with other gods?
You sit like a prostitute beside the road waiting
for a customer.
You sit alone like a nomad in the desert.
You have polluted the land with your prostitution
and your wickedness.
3 That's why even the spring rains have failed.
For you are a brazen prostitute and
completely shameless.
4 Yet you say to me,
'Father, you have been my guide since
my youth.
5 Surely you won't be angry forever!
Surely you can forget about it!'
So you talk,
but you keep on doing all the evil you can."

JUDAH FOLLOWS ISRAEL'S EXAMPLE

6During the reign of King Josiah, the LORD said to me,
"Have you seen what fickle Israel has done? Like a wife
who commits adultery, Israel has worshiped other gods
on every hill and under every green tree. 7I thought, 'After
she has done all this, she will return to me.' But she did
not return, and her faithless sister Judah saw this. 8She

Jeremiah

Served as a prophet to Judah from 627 B.C. until the Exile in 586 B.C.

CLIMATE OF THE TIMES	Society was deteriorating economically, politically, spiritually. Wars and captivity threatened the people. God's Word was outlawed.
MAIN MESSAGE	Repentance from sin would postpone Judah's coming judgment at the hands of Babylon.
IMPORTANCE OF MESSAGE	Repentance is one of the greatest needs in our immoral world. God's promises to the faithful shine brightly by bringing hope for tomorrow and strength for today.
CONTEMPORARY PROPHETS	Habakkuk (612–589) Zephaniah (640–621)

saw that I divorced faithless Israel because of her adultery. But that treacherous sister Judah had no fear, and
now she, too, has left me and given herself to prostitution. 9Israel treated it all so lightly—she thought nothing
of committing adultery by worshiping idols made of
wood and stone. So now the land has been polluted. 10But
despite all this, her faithless sister Judah has never sincerely returned to me. She has only pretended to be
sorry. I, the LORD, have spoken!"

HOPE FOR WAYWARD ISRAEL

11Then the LORD said to me, "Even faithless Israel is less
guilty than treacherous Judah! 12Therefore, go and give
this message to Israel.* This is what the LORD says:

"O Israel, my faithless people,
come home to me again,
for I am merciful.
I will not be angry with you forever.
13 Only acknowledge your guilt.
Admit that you rebelled against the LORD your God
and committed adultery against him
by worshiping idols under every green tree.
Confess that you refused to listen to my voice.
I, the LORD, have spoken!

14 "Return home, you wayward children,"
says the LORD,
"for I am your master.
I will bring you back to the land of Israel*—
one from this town and two from that family—
from wherever you are scattered.
15 And I will give you shepherds after my own heart,
who will guide you with knowledge and
understanding.

16"And when your land is once more filled with people," says the LORD, "you will no longer wish for 'the
good old days' when you possessed the Ark of the LORD's
Covenant. You will not miss those days or even remember them, and there will be no need to rebuild the Ark.
17In that day Jerusalem will be known as 'The Throne of
the LORD.' All nations will come there to honor the LORD.
They will no longer stubbornly follow their own evil desires. 18In those days the people of Judah and Israel will
return together from exile in the north. They will return
to the land I gave their ancestors as an inheritance
forever.

19 "I thought to myself,
'I would love to treat you as my own children!'
I wanted nothing more than to give you this
beautiful land—
the finest possession in the world.
I looked forward to your calling me 'Father,'
and I wanted you never to turn from me.
20 But you have been unfaithful to me, you people
of Israel!
You have been like a faithless wife who leaves
her husband.
I, the LORD, have spoken."

21 Voices are heard high on the windswept mountains,
the weeping and pleading of Israel's people.
For they have chosen crooked paths
and have forgotten the LORD their God.

22 "My wayward children," says the LORD,
"come back to me, and I will heal your
wayward hearts."

"Yes, we're coming," the people reply,
"for you are the LORD our God.
23 Our worship of idols on the hills
and our religious orgies on the mountains
are a delusion.
Only in the LORD our God
will Israel ever find salvation.

3:12 Hebrew *toward the north.* 3:14 Hebrew *to Zion.*

24 From childhood we have watched
as everything our ancestors worked for—
their flocks and herds, their sons and daughters—
was squandered on a delusion.
25 Let us now lie down in shame
and cover ourselves with dishonor,
for we and our ancestors have sinned
against the LORD our God.
From our childhood to this day
we have never obeyed him."

4

1 "O Israel," says the LORD,
"if you wanted to return to me, you could.
You could throw away your detestable idols
and stray away no more.
2 Then when you swear by my name, saying,
'As surely as the LORD lives,'
you could do so
with truth, justice, and righteousness.
Then you would be a blessing to the nations
of the world,
and all people would come and praise my name."

COMING JUDGMENT AGAINST JUDAH

3This is what the LORD says to the people of Judah and
Jerusalem:

"Plow up the hard ground of your hearts!
Do not waste your good seed among thorns.
4 O people of Judah and Jerusalem,
surrender your pride and power.
Change your hearts before the LORD,*
or my anger will burn like an unquenchable fire
because of all your sins.

5 "Shout to Judah, and broadcast to Jerusalem!
Tell them to sound the alarm throughout the land:
'Run for your lives!
Flee to the fortified cities!'
6 Raise a signal flag as a warning for Jerusalem*:
'Flee now! Do not delay!'
For I am bringing terrible destruction upon you
from the north."

7 A lion stalks from its den,
a destroyer of nations.
It has left its lair and is headed your way.
It's going to devastate your land!
Your towns will lie in ruins,
with no one living in them anymore.
8 So put on clothes of mourning
and weep with broken hearts,
for the fierce anger of the LORD
is still upon us.

9 "In that day," says the LORD,
"the king and the officials will tremble in fear.
The priests will be struck with horror,
and the prophets will be appalled."
10 Then I said, "O Sovereign LORD,
the people have been deceived by what you said,
for you promised peace for Jerusalem.
But the sword is held at their throats!"

11 The time is coming when the LORD will say
to the people of Jerusalem,
"My dear people, a burning wind is blowing in from
the desert,
and it's not a gentle breeze useful for winnowing
grain.
12 It is a roaring blast sent by me!
Now I will pronounce your destruction!"

13 Our enemy rushes down on us like storm clouds!
His chariots are like whirlwinds.
His horses are swifter than eagles.
How terrible it will be, for we are doomed!
14 O Jerusalem, cleanse your heart
that you may be saved.
How long will you harbor
your evil thoughts?
15 Your destruction has been announced
from Dan and the hill country of Ephraim.

16 "Warn the surrounding nations
and announce this to Jerusalem:
The enemy is coming from a distant land,
raising a battle cry against the towns of Judah.
17 They surround Jerusalem like watchmen around
a field,
for my people have rebelled against me,"
says the LORD.
18 "Your own actions have brought this upon you.
This punishment is bitter, piercing you to
the heart!"

JEREMIAH WEEPS FOR HIS PEOPLE

19 My heart, my heart—I writhe in pain!
My heart pounds within me! I cannot be still.
For I have heard the blast of enemy trumpets
and the roar of their battle cries.
20 Waves of destruction roll over the land,
until it lies in complete desolation.
Suddenly my tents are destroyed;
in a moment my shelters are crushed.
21 How long must I see the battle flags
and hear the trumpets of war?

22 "My people are foolish
and do not know me," says the LORD.
"They are stupid children
who have no understanding.
They are clever enough at doing wrong,
but they have no idea how to do right!"

4:4 Hebrew *Circumcise yourselves to the LORD, and take away the foreskins of your heart.* **4:6** Hebrew *Zion.*

JEREMIAH'S VISION OF COMING DISASTER

23 I looked at the earth, and it was empty and formless.
I looked at the heavens, and there was no light.
24 I looked at the mountains and hills,
and they trembled and shook.
25 I looked, and all the people were gone.
All the birds of the sky had flown away.
26 I looked, and the fertile fields had become
a wilderness.
The towns lay in ruins,
crushed by the LORD's fierce anger.

27 This is what the LORD says:
"The whole land will be ruined,
but I will not destroy it completely.
28 The earth will mourn
and the heavens will be draped in black
because of my decree against my people.
I have made up my mind and will not change it."

29 At the noise of charioteers and archers,
the people flee in terror.
They hide in the bushes
and run for the mountains.
All the towns have been abandoned—
not a person remains!
30 What are you doing,
you who have been plundered?
Why do you dress up in beautiful clothing
and put on gold jewelry?
Why do you brighten your eyes with mascara?
Your primping will do you no good!
The allies who were your lovers
despise you and seek to kill you.

31 I hear a cry, like that of a woman in labor,
the groans of a woman giving birth to her
first child.
It is beautiful Jerusalem*
gasping for breath and crying out,
"Help! I'm being murdered!"

5 THE SINS OF JUDAH

1 "Run up and down every street in Jerusalem," says
the LORD.
"Look high and low; search throughout the city!
If you can find even one just and honest person,
I will not destroy the city.
2 But even when they are under oath,
saying, 'As surely as the LORD lives,'
they are still telling lies!"

3 LORD, you are searching for honesty.
You struck your people,
but they paid no attention.
You crushed them,
but they refused to be corrected.
They are determined, with faces set like stone;
they have refused to repent.

4 Then I said, "But what can we expect from the poor?
They are ignorant.
They don't know the ways of the LORD.
They don't understand God's laws.
5 So I will go and speak to their leaders.
Surely they know the ways of the LORD
and understand God's laws."
But the leaders, too, as one man,
had thrown off God's yoke
and broken his chains.
6 So now a lion from the forest will attack them;
a wolf from the desert will pounce on them.
A leopard will lurk near their towns,
tearing apart any who dare to venture out.
For their rebellion is great,
and their sins are many.

7 "How can I pardon you?
For even your children have turned from me.
They have sworn by gods that are not gods at all!
I fed my people until they were full.
But they thanked me by committing adultery
and lining up at the brothels.
8 They are well-fed, lusty stallions,
each neighing for his neighbor's wife.
9 Should I not punish them for this?" says the LORD.
"Should I not avenge myself against such a nation?

10 "Go down the rows of the vineyards and destroy
the grapevines,
leaving a scattered few alive.
Strip the branches from the vines,
for these people do not belong to the LORD.
11 The people of Israel and Judah
are full of treachery against me,"
says the LORD.
12 "They have lied about the LORD
and said, 'He won't bother us!
No disasters will come upon us.
There will be no war or famine.
13 God's prophets are all windbags
who don't really speak for him.
Let their predictions of disaster fall
on themselves!'"

14 Therefore, this is what the LORD God of Heaven's Armies says:

"Because the people are talking like this,
my messages will flame out of your mouth
and burn the people like kindling wood.
15 O Israel, I will bring a distant nation against you,"
says the LORD.
"It is a mighty nation,
an ancient nation,

4:31 Hebrew *the daughter of Zion.*

a people whose language you do not know,
whose speech you cannot understand.
16 Their weapons are deadly;
their warriors are mighty.
17 They will devour the food of your harvest;
they will devour your sons and daughters.
They will devour your flocks and herds;
they will devour your grapes and figs.
And they will destroy your fortified towns,
which you think are so safe.

18"Yet even in those days I will not blot you out completely," says the LORD. 19"And when your people ask,
'Why did the LORD our God do all this to us?' you must reply, 'You rejected him and gave yourselves to foreign
gods in your own land. Now you will serve foreigners in a
land that is not your own.'

RESPECT 5:20-24

The people of the divided nation of Israel had lost their awe of God. God had to strip away the things that Israel had grown to respect more than him. For many people today, respect for God isn't a priority. Some even have the attitude that God has yet to do something to *earn* their respect. Does God have your respect? If so, how do your actions reveal your level of respect? ■

A WARNING FOR GOD'S PEOPLE

20 "Make this announcement to Israel,*
and say this to Judah:
21 Listen, you foolish and senseless people,
with eyes that do not see
and ears that do not hear.
22 Have you no respect for me?
Why don't you tremble in my presence?
I, the LORD, define the ocean's sandy shoreline
as an everlasting boundary that the waters
cannot cross.
The waves may toss and roar,
but they can never pass the boundaries I set.
23 But my people have stubborn and rebellious
hearts.
They have turned away and abandoned me.
24 They do not say from the heart,
'Let us live in awe of the LORD our God,
for he gives us rain each spring and fall,
assuring us of a harvest when the time is right.'
25 Your wickedness has deprived you of these
wonderful blessings.
Your sin has robbed you of all these good things.

26 "Among my people are wicked men
who lie in wait for victims like a hunter hiding
in a blind.
They continually set traps
to catch people.
27 Like a cage filled with birds,
their homes are filled with evil plots.
And now they are great and rich.
28 They are fat and sleek,
and there is no limit to their wicked deeds.
They refuse to provide justice to orphans
and deny the rights of the poor.
29 Should I not punish them for this?" says the LORD.
"Should I not avenge myself against such a nation?
30 A horrible and shocking thing
has happened in this land—
31 the prophets give false prophecies,
and the priests rule with an iron hand.
Worse yet, my people like it that way!
But what will you do when the end comes?

6 JERUSALEM'S LAST WARNING

1 "Run for your lives, you people of Benjamin!
Get out of Jerusalem!
Sound the alarm in Tekoa!
Send up a signal at Beth-hakkerem!
A powerful army is coming from the north,
coming with disaster and destruction.
2 O Jerusalem,* you are my beautiful and
delicate daughter—
but I will destroy you!
3 Enemies will surround you, like shepherds camped
around the city.
Each chooses a place for his troops to devour.
4 They shout, 'Prepare for battle!
Attack at noon!'
'No, it's too late; the day is fading,
and the evening shadows are falling.'
5 'Well then, let's attack at night
and destroy her palaces!'"

6 This is what the LORD of Heaven's Armies says:
"Cut down the trees for battering rams.
Build siege ramps against the walls of Jerusalem.
This is the city to be punished,
for she is wicked through and through.
7 She spouts evil like a fountain.
Her streets echo with the sounds of violence
and destruction.
I always see her sickness and sores.
8 Listen to this warning, Jerusalem,
or I will turn from you in disgust.
Listen, or I will turn you into a heap of ruins,
a land where no one lives."

9 This is what the LORD of Heaven's Armies says:
"Even the few who remain in Israel
will be picked over again,
as when a harvester checks each vine a second time
to pick the grapes that were missed."

5:20 Hebrew *to the house of Jacob.* The names "Jacob" and "Israel" are often interchanged throughout the Old Testament, referring sometimes to the individual patriarch and sometimes to the nation. 6:2 Hebrew *Daughter of Zion.*

ISRAEL'S CONSTANT REBELLION

10 To whom can I give warning?
Who will listen when I speak?
Their ears are closed,
and they cannot hear.
They scorn the word of the LORD.
They don't want to listen at all.
11 So now I am filled with the LORD's fury.
Yes, I am tired of holding it in!

SAY IT ANYWAY 6:10-11

Jeremiah's job as prophet was to remind the people of Judah to obey God, even though they didn't want to listen to him. Being obedient wasn't very exciting to them. Does that sound familiar? Maybe you've heard people say that being a Christian doesn't seem "fun." As unsettling as people's responses might be, God still wants us to share his truth. Are you just as determined to say it anyway? ■

"I will pour out my fury on children playing
in the streets
and on gatherings of young men,
on husbands and wives
and on those who are old and gray.
12 Their homes will be turned over to their enemies,
as will their fields and their wives.
For I will raise my powerful fist
against the people of this land,"
says the LORD.
13 "From the least to the greatest,
their lives are ruled by greed.
From prophets to priests,
they are all frauds.
14 They offer superficial treatments
for my people's mortal wound.
They give assurances of peace
when there is no peace.
15 Are they ashamed of their disgusting actions?
Not at all—they don't even know how to blush!
Therefore, they will lie among the slaughtered.
They will be brought down when I
punish them,"
says the LORD.

ISRAEL REJECTS THE LORD'S WAY

16 This is what the LORD says:
"Stop at the crossroads and look around.
Ask for the old, godly way, and walk in it.
Travel its path, and you will find rest for your souls.
But you reply, 'No, that's not the road we want!'
17 I posted watchmen over you who said,
'Listen for the sound of the alarm.'
But you replied,
'No! We won't pay attention!'
18 "Therefore, listen to this, all you nations.
Take note of my people's situation.
19 Listen, all the earth!
I will bring disaster on my people.
It is the fruit of their own schemes,
because they refuse to listen to me.
They have rejected my word.
20 There's no use offering me sweet frankincense
from Sheba.
Keep your fragrant calamus imported from
distant lands!
I will not accept your burnt offerings.
Your sacrifices have no pleasing aroma
for me."
21 Therefore, this is what the LORD says:
"I will put obstacles in my people's path.
Fathers and sons will both fall over them.
Neighbors and friends will die together."

AN INVASION FROM THE NORTH

22 This is what the LORD says:
"Look! A great army coming from the north!
A great nation is rising against you from
far-off lands.
23 They are armed with bows and spears.
They are cruel and show no mercy.
They sound like a roaring sea
as they ride forward on horses.
They are coming in battle formation,
planning to destroy you, beautiful Jerusalem.*"

24 We have heard reports about the enemy,
and we wring our hands in fright.
Pangs of anguish have gripped us,
like those of a woman in labor.
25 Don't go out to the fields!
Don't travel on the roads!
The enemy's sword is everywhere
and terrorizes us at every turn!
26 Oh, my people, dress yourselves in burlap
and sit among the ashes.
Mourn and weep bitterly, as for the loss of an
only son.
For suddenly the destroying armies will be
upon you!

27 "Jeremiah, I have made you a tester of metals,*
that you may determine the quality of
my people.
28 They are the worst kind of rebel,
full of slander.
They are as hard as bronze and iron,
and they lead others into corruption.
29 The bellows fiercely fan the flames
to burn out the corruption.
But it does not purify them,
for the wickedness remains.

6:23 Hebrew *daughter of Zion.* 6:27 As in Greek version; Hebrew reads *of metals in my people a fortress.*

30 I will label them ‘Rejected Silver,’
for I, the LORD, am discarding them.”

7

JEREMIAH SPEAKS AT THE TEMPLE

The LORD gave another message to Jeremiah. He said,
2“Go to the entrance of the LORD’s Temple, and give this
message to the people: ‘O Judah, listen to this message
from the LORD! Listen to it, all of you who worship here!
3This is what the LORD of Heaven’s Armies, the God of Israel, says:

“‘Even now, if you quit your evil ways, I will let you stay
in your own land. 4But don’t be fooled by those who
promise you safety simply because the LORD’s Temple is
here. They chant, “The LORD’s Temple is here! The LORD’s
Temple is here!” 5But I will be merciful only if you stop
your evil thoughts and deeds and start treating each
other with justice; 6only if you stop exploiting foreigners,
orphans, and widows; only if you stop your murdering;
and only if you stop harming yourselves by worshiping
idols. 7Then I will let you stay in this land that I gave to
your ancestors to keep forever.

8“‘Don’t be fooled into thinking that you will never suffer because the Temple is here. It’s a lie! 9Do you really
think you can steal, murder, commit adultery, lie, and
burn incense to Baal and all those other new gods of
yours, 10and then come here and stand before me in my
Temple and chant, “We are safe!”—only to go right back
to all those evils again? 11Don’t you yourselves admit that
this Temple, which bears my name, has become a den of
thieves? Surely I see all the evil going on there. I, the LORD,
have spoken!

AN EMPTY RITUAL 7:1-8

The people of Judah thought that their Temple attendance would keep them from being punished by God. They were “religious,” rather than committed to God. We can easily fall into this trap if we go through the motions of attending church or youth group without a real heart connection. Sometimes, we even think that God demands us to participate in these activities regardless of how we feel. But empty rituals never impress God. He desires a true heart connection with his people. Does he have a connection to your heart or to your head? ■

12“‘Go now to the place at Shiloh where I once put the
Tabernacle that bore my name. See what I did there because of all the wickedness of my people, the Israelites.
13While you were doing these wicked things, says the
LORD, I spoke to you about it repeatedly, but you would
not listen. I called out to you, but you refused to answer.
14So just as I destroyed Shiloh, I will now destroy this
Temple that bears my name, this Temple that you trust in
for help, this place that I gave to you and your ancestors.
15And I will send you out of my sight into exile, just as I
did your relatives, the people of Israel.*’

JUDAH’S PERSISTENT IDOLATRY

16“Pray no more for these people, Jeremiah. Do not weep
or pray for them, and don’t beg me to help them, for I will
not listen to you. 17Don’t you see what they are doing
throughout the towns of Judah and in the streets of Jerusalem? 18No wonder I am so angry! Watch how the children gather wood and the fathers build sacrificial fires.
See how the women knead dough and make cakes to offer to the Queen of Heaven. And they pour out liquid offerings to their other idol gods! 19Am I the one they are
hurting?” asks the LORD. “Most of all, they hurt themselves, to their own shame.”

20So this is what the Sovereign LORD says: “I will pour
out my terrible fury on this place. Its people, animals,
trees, and crops will be consumed by the unquenchable
fire of my anger.”

STAY CONNECTED 7:19

This verse answers the question, “Who gets hurt when we turn away from God?” We do! Separating oneself from God is like keeping a green plant away from sunlight or water, or cutting off its food supply. God is our only source of spiritual strength. Want to keep spiritually alive? Stay connected to the source. (See also John 15:1-8.) ■

21This is what the LORD of Heaven’s Armies, the God of
Israel, says: “Take your burnt offerings and your other
sacrifices and eat them yourselves! 22When I led your ancestors out of Egypt, it was not burnt offerings and sacrifices I wanted from them. 23This is what I told them:
‘Obey me, and I will be your God, and you will be my people. Do everything as I say, and all will be well!’

24“But my people would not listen to me. They kept doing whatever they wanted, following the stubborn desires of their evil hearts. They went backward instead of
forward. 25From the day your ancestors left Egypt until
now, I have continued to send my servants, the prophets—day in and day out. 26But my people have not listened
to me or even tried to hear. They have been stubborn and
sinful—even worse than their ancestors.

27“Tell them all this, but do not expect them to listen.
Shout out your warnings, but do not expect them to respond. 28Say to them, ‘This is the nation whose people
will not obey the LORD their God and who refuse to be
taught. Truth has vanished from among them; it is no
longer heard on their lips. 29Shave your head in mourning, and weep alone on the mountains. For the LORD has
rejected and forsaken this generation that has provoked
his fury.’

THE VALLEY OF SLAUGHTER

30“The people of Judah have sinned before my very eyes,”
says the LORD. “They have set up their abominable idols

7:15 Hebrew *of Ephraim,* referring to the northern kingdom of Israel.

right in the Temple that bears my name, defiling it.
31They have built pagan shrines at Topheth, the garbage dump in the valley of Ben-Hinnom, and there they burn their sons and daughters in the fire. I have never commanded such a horrible deed; it never even crossed my mind to command such a thing!
32So beware, for the time is coming," says the LORD, "when that garbage dump will no longer be called Topheth or the valley of Ben-Hinnom, but the Valley of Slaughter. They will bury the bodies in Topheth until there is no more room for them.
33The bodies of my people will be food for the vultures and wild animals, and no one will be left to scare them away.
34I will put an end to the happy singing and laughter in the streets of Jerusalem. The joyful voices of bridegrooms and brides will no longer be heard in the towns of Judah. The land will lie in complete desolation.

8 "In that day," says the LORD, "the enemy will break open the graves of the kings and officials of Judah, and the graves of the priests, prophets, and common people of Jerusalem.
2They will spread out their bones on the ground before the sun, moon, and stars—the gods my people have loved, served, and worshiped. Their bones will not be gathered up again or buried but will be scattered on the ground like manure.
3And the people of this evil nation who survive will wish to die rather than live where I will send them. I, the LORD of Heaven's Armies, have spoken!

DECEPTION BY FALSE PROPHETS

4"Jeremiah, say to the people, 'This is what the LORD says:

"'When people fall down, don't they get up again?
When they discover they're on the wrong road,
don't they turn back?
5 Then why do these people stay on their self-destructive path?
Why do the people of Jerusalem refuse to turn back?
They cling tightly to their lies
and will not turn around.
6 I listen to their conversations
and don't hear a word of truth.
Is anyone sorry for doing wrong?
Does anyone say, "What a terrible thing
I have done"?
No! All are running down the path of sin
as swiftly as a horse galloping into battle!
7 Even the stork that flies across the sky
knows the time of her migration,
as do the turtledove, the swallow, and the crane.*
They all return at the proper time each year.
But not my people!
They do not know the LORD's laws.

8 "'How can you say, "We are wise because we have the
word of the LORD,"
when your teachers have twisted it by writing lies?
9 These wise teachers will fall
into the trap of their own foolishness,
for they have rejected the word of the LORD.
Are they so wise after all?
10 I will give their wives to others
and their farms to strangers.
From the least to the greatest,
their lives are ruled by greed.
Yes, even my prophets and priests are like that.
They are all frauds.
11 They offer superficial treatments
for my people's mortal wound.
They give assurances of peace
when there is no peace.
12 Are they ashamed of these disgusting actions?
Not at all—they don't even know how to blush!
Therefore, they will lie among the slaughtered.
They will be brought down when I punish them,
says the LORD.
13 I will surely consume them.
There will be no more harvests of figs and grapes.
Their fruit trees will all die.
Whatever I gave them will soon be gone.
I, the LORD, have spoken!'

BEWARE 8:8-13

The prophets and priests were giving false assurances rather than correction. How can we correct a fault or turn from a sin if our leaders tell us that all is well? Beware of people who are always agreeable. At best, they give you no help; at worst, they may be trying to manipulate you. Your best defense is to know the truth for yourself. ■

14 "Then the people will say,
'Why should we wait here to die?
Come, let's go to the fortified towns and die there.
For the LORD our God has decreed
our destruction
and has given us a cup of poison to drink
because we sinned against the LORD.
15 We hoped for peace, but no peace came.
We hoped for a time of healing, but found
only terror.'

16 "The snorting of the enemies' warhorses can
be heard
all the way from the land of Dan in the north!
The neighing of their stallions makes the whole
land tremble.
They are coming to devour the land and
everything in it—
cities and people alike.
17 I will send these enemy troops among you
like poisonous snakes you cannot charm.
They will bite you, and you will die.
I, the Lord, have spoken!"

8:7 The identification of some of these birds is uncertain.

JEREMIAH WEEPS FOR SINFUL JUDAH

18 My grief is beyond healing;
my heart is broken.
19 Listen to the weeping of my people;
it can be heard all across the land.
"Has the LORD abandoned Jerusalem?*" the people ask.
"Is her King no longer there?"
"Oh, why have they provoked my anger with their carved idols
and their worthless foreign gods?" says the LORD.

20 "The harvest is finished,
and the summer is gone," the people cry,
"yet we are not saved!"

21 I hurt with the hurt of my people.
I mourn and am overcome with grief.
22 Is there no medicine in Gilead?
Is there no physician there?
Why is there no healing
for the wounds of my people?

SO MOVED 8:18-22

These verses provide a vivid picture of Jeremiah's emotions as he watched his people reject God. How often do we respond this way for friends and neighbors who reject God? Only when we have Jeremiah's kind of concern will we be moved to help. ■

9

1*If only my head were a pool of water
and my eyes a fountain of tears,
I would weep day and night
for all my people who have been slaughtered.
2*Oh, that I could go away and forget my people
and live in a travelers' shack in the desert.
For they are all adulterers—
a pack of treacherous liars.

JUDGMENT FOR DISOBEDIENCE

3 "My people bend their tongues like bows
to shoot out lies.
They refuse to stand up for the truth.
They only go from bad to worse.
They do not know me,"
says the LORD.

4 "Beware of your neighbor!
Don't even trust your brother!
For brother takes advantage of brother,
and friend slanders friend.
5 They all fool and defraud each other;
no one tells the truth.
With practiced tongues they tell lies;
they wear themselves out with all their sinning.
6 They pile lie upon lie
and utterly refuse to acknowledge me,"
says the LORD.

7 Therefore, this is what the LORD of Heaven's Armies says:
"See, I will melt them down in a crucible
and test them like metal.
What else can I do with my people?*
8 For their tongues shoot lies like poisoned arrows.
They speak friendly words to their neighbors
while scheming in their heart to kill them.
9 Should I not punish them for this?" says the LORD.
"Should I not avenge myself against such a nation?"

10 I will weep for the mountains
and wail for the wilderness pastures.
For they are desolate and empty of life;
the lowing of cattle is heard no more;
the birds and wild animals have all fled.

11 "I will make Jerusalem into a heap of ruins," says the LORD.
"It will be a place haunted by jackals.
The towns of Judah will be ghost towns,
with no one living in them."

12Who is wise enough to understand all this? Who has
been instructed by the LORD and can explain it to others?
Why has the land been so ruined that no one dares to
travel through it?
13The LORD replies, "This has happened because my
people have abandoned my instructions; they have refused to obey what I said. 14Instead, they have stubbornly
followed their own desires and worshiped the images of
Baal, as their ancestors taught them. 15So now, this is
what the LORD of Heaven's Armies, the God of Israel, says:
Look! I will feed them with bitterness and give them poison to drink. 16I will scatter them around the world, in
places they and their ancestors never heard of, and even
there I will chase them with the sword until I have destroyed them completely."

WEEPING IN JERUSALEM

17 This is what the LORD of Heaven's Armies says:
"Consider all this, and call for the mourners.
Send for the women who mourn at funerals.
18 Quick! Begin your weeping!
Let the tears flow from your eyes.
19 Hear the people of Jerusalem* crying in despair,
'We are ruined! We are completely humiliated!
We must leave our land,
because our homes have been torn down.'"

20 Listen, you women, to the words of the LORD;
open your ears to what he has to say.

8:19 Hebrew *Zion?* **9:1** Verse 9:1 is numbered 8:23 in Hebrew text. **9:2** Verses 9:2-26 are numbered 9:1-25 in Hebrew text. **9:7** Hebrew *with the daughter of my people?* Greek version reads *with the evil daughter of my people?* **9:19** Hebrew *Zion.*

Teach your daughters to wail;
teach one another how to lament.
21 For death has crept in through our windows
and has entered our mansions.
It has killed off the flower of our youth:
Children no longer play in the streets,
and young men no longer gather in the squares.

22 This is what the LORD says:
"Bodies will be scattered across the fields like clumps
of manure,
like bundles of grain after the harvest.
No one will be left to bury them."

PRIORITIES

In August, some guys from Adams High are sitting around discussing their summers:

Brandon: "Get this—my dad is paying me twelve bucks an hour to make deliveries! Counting that and my afternoon lawn business, I'm gonna clear $4,500 easy!"

Devin: "That's great, but money ain't gonna help you block on the football field. I've been in the gym every day. So far, I've increased my bench press from 200 to 250 pounds! I'll be all-district this year."

Alejandro: "Too bad you didn't work on your brain muscle! I've had the best of all possible summers. I've biked most of the summer, I earned a little money, I hung out and had a blast, and I just got back from computer camp—"

Brandon (laughing): "Computer camp?! Dude, you're kidding!"

Alejandro: "Hey, laugh all you want. We'll see who's laughing next spring when I get a scholarship to Princeton or Harvard, and you're stuck at some junior college."

Devin: "Not likely, bro! What about you, Josiah? Didn't you just go on some church trip?"

Josiah's kind of embarrassed. He did just return from a mission trip to Mexico. It was incredible, but compared to making tons of money, building the perfect athletic body, or getting a scholarship, it doesn't seem like much. Or does it?

Can you relate to Josiah's feelings?

What does this scene show us about priorities? See Jeremiah 9:23-24 for a clear look at what really matters.

23 This is what the LORD says:
"Don't let the wise boast in their wisdom,
or the powerful boast in their power,
or the rich boast in their riches.
24 But those who wish to boast
should boast in this alone:
that they truly know me and understand that
I am the LORD
who demonstrates unfailing love
and who brings justice and righteousness
to the earth,
and that I delight in these things.
I, the LORD, have spoken!

25"A time is coming," says the LORD, "when I will punish
all those who are circumcised in body but not in spirit—
26the Egyptians, Edomites, Ammonites, Moabites, the people who live in the desert in remote places,* and yes, even
the people of Judah. And like all these pagan nations, the
people of Israel also have uncircumcised hearts."

STAR CHARTS 10:1-5

Everyone would like to know the future. Decisions would be easier, failures avoided, and success assured. The people of Judah tried to figure out the future by reading signs in the sky (like horoscopes). Jeremiah's response applies today: God made the stars that people consult. God, who promises to guide you, knows your future and will be with you all the way. Don't trust the stars; trust the One who made them. ■

10 IDOLATRY BRINGS DESTRUCTION

Hear the word that the LORD speaks to you, O Israel! 2This
is what the LORD says:

"Do not act like the other nations,
who try to read their future in the stars.
Do not be afraid of their predictions,
even though other nations are terrified by them.
3 Their ways are futile and foolish.
They cut down a tree, and a craftsman carves
an idol.
4 They decorate it with gold and silver
and then fasten it securely with hammer and nails
so it won't fall over.
5 Their gods are like
helpless scarecrows in a cucumber field!
They cannot speak,
and they need to be carried because they
cannot walk.
Do not be afraid of such gods,
for they can neither harm you nor do you any good."

6 LORD, there is no one like you!
For you are great, and your name is full of power.
7 Who would not fear you, O King of nations?
That title belongs to you alone!
Among all the wise people of the earth
and in all the kingdoms of the world,
there is no one like you.

8 People who worship idols are stupid and foolish.
The things they worship are made of wood!

9:26 Or *in the desert and clip the corners of their hair.*

9 They bring beaten sheets of silver from Tarshish
and gold from Uphaz,
and they give these materials to skillful craftsmen
who make their idols.
Then they dress these gods in royal blue and
purple robes
made by expert tailors.
10 But the LORD is the only true God.
He is the living God and the everlasting King!
The whole earth trembles at his anger.
The nations cannot stand up to his wrath.

11Say this to those who worship other gods: "Your so-called gods, who did not make the heavens and earth, will vanish from the earth and from under the heavens."*

12 But God made the earth by his power,
and he preserves it by his wisdom.
With his own understanding
he stretched out the heavens.
13 When he speaks in the thunder,
the heavens roar with rain.
He causes the clouds to rise over the earth.
He sends the lightning with the rain
and releases the wind from his storehouses.
14 The whole human race is foolish and has no
knowledge!
The craftsmen are disgraced by the idols
they make,
for their carefully shaped works are a fraud.
These idols have no breath or power.
15 Idols are worthless; they are ridiculous lies!
On the day of reckoning they will all be
destroyed.
16 But the God of Israel* is no idol!
He is the Creator of everything that exists,
including Israel, his own special possession.
The LORD of Heaven's Armies is his name!

THE COMING DESTRUCTION

17 Pack your bags and prepare to leave;
the siege is about to begin.
18 For this is what the LORD says:
"Suddenly, I will fling out
all you who live in this land.
I will pour great troubles upon you,
and at last you will feel my anger."

19 My wound is severe,
and my grief is great.
My sickness is incurable,
but I must bear it.
20 My home is gone,
and no one is left to help me rebuild it.
My children have been taken away,
and I will never see them again.
21 The shepherds of my people have lost their senses.
They no longer seek wisdom from the LORD.
Therefore, they fail completely,
and their flocks are scattered.
22 Listen! Hear the terrifying roar of great armies
as they roll down from the north.
The towns of Judah will be destroyed
and become a haunt for jackals.

JEREMIAH'S PRAYER

23 I know, LORD, that our lives are not our own.
We are not able to plan our own course.
24 So correct me, LORD, but please be gentle.
Do not correct me in anger, for I would die.
25 Pour out your wrath on the nations that refuse to
acknowledge you—
on the peoples that do not call upon your name.
For they have devoured your people Israel*;
they have devoured and consumed them,
making the land a desolate wilderness.

11

JUDAH'S BROKEN COVENANT

The LORD gave another message to Jeremiah. He said,
2"Remind the people of Judah and Jerusalem about the
terms of my covenant with them. 3Say to them, 'This is
what the LORD, the God of Israel, says: Cursed is anyone
who does not obey the terms of my covenant! 4For I said
to your ancestors when I brought them out of the iron-
smelting furnace of Egypt, "If you obey me and do whatever I command you, then you will be my people, and I
will be your God." 5I said this so I could keep my promise
to your ancestors to give you a land flowing with milk and
honey—the land you live in today.'"

Then I replied, "Amen, LORD! May it be so."

6Then the LORD said, "Broadcast this message in the
streets of Jerusalem. Go from town to town throughout
the land and say, 'Remember the ancient covenant, and
do everything it requires. 7For I solemnly warned your
ancestors when I brought them out of Egypt, "Obey me!" I
have repeated this warning over and over to this day, 8but
your ancestors did not listen or even pay attention. Instead, they stubbornly followed their own evil desires.
And because they refused to obey, I brought upon them
all the curses described in this covenant.'"

9Again the LORD spoke to me and said, "I have discovered a conspiracy against me among the people of Judah
and Jerusalem. 10They have returned to the sins of their
forefathers. They have refused to listen to me and are
worshiping other gods. Israel and Judah have both
broken the covenant I made with their ancestors.
11Therefore, this is what the LORD says: I am going to
bring calamity upon them, and they will not escape.
Though they beg for mercy, I will not listen to their cries.
12Then the people of Judah and Jerusalem will pray to
their idols and burn incense before them. But the idols
will not save them when disaster strikes! 13Look now,
people of Judah; you have as many gods as you have
towns. You have as many altars of shame—altars for

10:11 The original text of this verse is in Aramaic. 10:16 Hebrew *the Portion of Jacob*. See note on 5:20. 10:25 Hebrew *devoured Jacob*. See note on 5:20.

ULTIMATE ISSUES

MODERN-DAY IDOLS

A drunken orgy around a golden calf . . . the latest sports car . . . offering sacrifices to Baal . . . teens screaming their adoration of their favorite band at a concert . . .

What do these scenes have in common? They all represent forms of idol worship.

"Wait a minute," you say. "The golden calf and Baal are definitely idols. But why bring up a car and a concert?"

Glad you asked. An idol is *anything* we desire above God and his will for our lives. Ouch!

Idols in Jeremiah's day were statues representing pagan gods. Idolatry comes in more subtle forms these days. Instead of a golden calf, we're enticed by a "golden"—or platinum—credit card. Instead of Baal, we "worship" rock stars, imitating their lifestyles. So, is having a credit card or liking a band wrong? Of course not. The problem comes in loving things (or people) more than we love God.

So, why is idolatry so bad?

First, worshiping a false god (anything that comes before the *real* God is a *false* god) degrades us. It makes us less than what we are intended to be. We are made in the image of God, with the opportunity through Christ to know him and, in some ways, to be like him. When we worship an idol—a lesser god—we aim much lower and, all too often, hit our target.

Second, idolatry often is subtle and hard to detect. Think about your latest crush or one you used to have. (OK—one you wish you had.) Maybe you wanted to hang out with him or her all of the time—more than with anyone else. But some relationships involve an unhealthy dependence; the couple puts each other before God. This can be disastrous for a relationship with each other and with God.

Finally, idol worship steals from God. Nobody with functional brain cells would knowingly do that. When we love someone or something else more than God, we rob him of the worship and loyalty that rightly belong only to him. (See Exod 20:4-5.)

Idolatry has a way of creeping in and destroying parts of your life, just as cancer destroys parts of your body. That's why it needs a radical cure, just as cancer does. What's that radical cure? Give up the idol.

burning incense to your god Baal—as there are streets in Jerusalem.

14"Pray no more for these people, Jeremiah. Do not weep or pray for them, for I will not listen to them when they cry out to me in distress.

15 "What right do my beloved people have to come
to my Temple,
when they have done so many immoral things?
Can their vows and sacrifices prevent their
destruction?
They actually rejoice in doing evil!
16 I, the LORD, once called them a thriving olive tree,
beautiful to see and full of good fruit.
But now I have sent the fury of their enemies
to burn them with fire,
leaving them charred and broken.

17"I, the LORD of Heaven's Armies, who planted this olive tree, have ordered it destroyed. For the people of Israel and Judah have done evil, arousing my anger by burning incense to Baal."

A PLOT AGAINST JEREMIAH

18Then the LORD told me about the plots my enemies were making against me. 19I was like a lamb being led to the slaughter. I had no idea that they were planning to kill me! "Let's destroy this man and all his words," they said. "Let's cut him down, so his name will be forgotten forever."

20 O LORD of Heaven's Armies,
you make righteous judgments,
and you examine the deepest thoughts and secrets.
Let me see your vengeance against them,
for I have committed my cause to you.

21This is what the LORD says about the men of Anathoth who wanted me dead. They had said, "We will kill you if you do not stop prophesying in the LORD's name."

[22]So this is what the LORD of Heaven's Armies says about them: "I will punish them! Their young men will die in battle, and their boys and girls will starve to death. [23]Not one of these plotters from Anathoth will survive, for I will bring disaster upon them when their time of punishment comes."

12 JEREMIAH QUESTIONS THE LORD'S JUSTICE

1 LORD, you always give me justice
when I bring a case before you.
So let me bring you this complaint:
Why are the wicked so prosperous?
Why are evil people so happy?
2 You have planted them,
and they have taken root and prospered.
Your name is on their lips,
but you are far from their hearts.
3 But as for me, LORD, you know my heart.
You see me and test my thoughts.
Drag these people away like sheep to be butchered!
Set them aside to be slaughtered!

4 How long must this land mourn?
Even the grass in the fields has withered.
The wild animals and birds have disappeared
because of the evil in the land.
For the people have said,
"The LORD doesn't see what's ahead for us!"

TOUGH TIMES 12:1-6

Life was difficult for Jeremiah despite his love for and obedience to God. When he asked God for relief, God's reply in effect was, "If you think this is bad, how are you going to cope when life gets really tough?" Not all of God's answers to prayer are easy to accept. Any Christian who has experienced war, grief, or a serious illness knows this. But we are to be committed to God even when the going gets tough, or when he doesn't answer our prayers with immediate relief. Would you agree? ■

THE LORD'S REPLY TO JEREMIAH

5 "If racing against mere men makes you tired,
how will you race against horses?
If you stumble and fall on open ground,
what will you do in the thickets near the Jordan?
6 Even your brothers, members of your own family,
have turned against you.
They plot and raise complaints against you.
Do not trust them,
no matter how pleasantly they speak.

7 "I have abandoned my people, my special possession.
I have surrendered my dearest ones to their
enemies.
8 My chosen people have roared at me like a lion
of the forest,
so I have treated them with contempt.
9 My chosen people act like speckled vultures,*
but they themselves are surrounded by vultures.
Bring on the wild animals to pick their
corpses clean!

10 "Many rulers have ravaged my vineyard,
trampling down the vines
and turning all its beauty into a barren wilderness.
11 They have made it an empty wasteland;
I hear its mournful cry.
The whole land is desolate,
and no one even cares.
12 On all the bare hilltops,
destroying armies can be seen.
The sword of the LORD devours people
from one end of the nation to the other.
No one will escape!
13 My people have planted wheat
but are harvesting thorns.
They have worn themselves out,
but it has done them no good.
They will harvest a crop of shame
because of the fierce anger of the LORD."

A MESSAGE FOR ISRAEL'S NEIGHBORS

[14]Now this is what the LORD says: "I will uproot from their
land all the evil nations reaching out for the possession I
gave my people Israel. And I will uproot Judah from
among them. [15]But afterward I will return and have compassion on all of them. I will bring them home to their
own lands again, each nation to its own possession. [16]And
if these nations truly learn the ways of my people, and if
they learn to swear by my name, saying, 'As surely as the
LORD lives' (just as they taught my people to swear by the
name of Baal), then they will be given a place among my
people. [17]But any nation who refuses to obey me will be
uprooted and destroyed. I, the LORD, have spoken!"

13 JEREMIAH'S LINEN LOINCLOTH

This is what the LORD said to me: "Go and buy a linen loincloth and put it on, but do not wash it." [2]So I bought the
loincloth as the LORD directed me, and I put it on.

[3]Then the LORD gave me another message: [4]"Take the
linen loincloth you are wearing, and go to the Euphrates
River.* Hide it there in a hole in the rocks." [5]So I went and
hid it by the Euphrates as the LORD had instructed me.

[6]A long time afterward the LORD said to me, "Go back
to the Euphrates and get the loincloth I told you to hide
there." [7]So I went to the Euphrates and dug it out of the
hole where I had hidden it. But now it was rotting and
falling apart. The loincloth was good for nothing.

[8]Then I received this message from the LORD: [9]"This is
what the LORD says: This shows how I will rot away the
pride of Judah and Jerusalem. [10]These wicked people

12:9 Or *speckled hyenas.* 13:4 Hebrew *Perath;* also in 13:5, 6, 7.

refuse to listen to me. They stubbornly follow their own desires and worship other gods. Therefore, they will become like this loincloth—good for nothing! [11]As a loincloth clings to a man's waist, so I created Judah and Israel to cling to me, says the LORD. They were to be my people, my pride, my glory—an honor to my name. But they would not listen to me.

USELESS 13:1-11

Actions speak louder than words. Jeremiah often used vivid object lessons to arouse the people's curiosity and get his point across. The linen belt represented Judah. Although the people had once been close to God, their pride made them as useless as Jeremiah's belt. How do you think God would describe your actions lately? Useful? Useless? If you want to be useful or even more so, actions speak louder than words. ■

[12]"So tell them, 'This is what the LORD, the God of Israel,
says: May all your jars be filled with wine.' And they will
reply, 'Of course! Jars are made to be filled with wine!'
[13]"Then tell them, 'No, this is what the LORD means: I
will fill everyone in this land with drunkenness—from
the king sitting on David's throne to the priests and the
prophets, right down to the common people of Jerusalem. [14]I will smash them against each other, even parents
against children, says the LORD. I will not let my pity or
mercy or compassion keep me from destroying them.'"

A WARNING AGAINST PRIDE

15 Listen and pay attention!
Do not be arrogant, for the LORD has spoken.
16 Give glory to the LORD your God
before it is too late.
Acknowledge him before he brings darkness
upon you,
causing you to stumble and fall on the darkening
mountains.
For then, when you look for light,
you will find only terrible darkness and gloom.
17 And if you still refuse to listen,
I will weep alone because of your pride.
My eyes will overflow with tears,
because the LORD's flock will be led away into exile.

18 Say to the king and his mother,
"Come down from your thrones
and sit in the dust,
for your glorious crowns
will soon be snatched from your heads."
19 The towns of the Negev will close their gates,
and no one will be able to open them.
The people of Judah will be taken away as captives.
All will be carried into exile.

20 Open up your eyes and see
the armies marching down from the north!
Where is your flock—
your beautiful flock—
that he gave you to care for?
21 What will you say when the LORD takes the allies
you have cultivated
and appoints them as your rulers?
Pangs of anguish will grip you,
like those of a woman in labor!
22 You may ask yourself,
"Why is all this happening to me?"
It is because of your many sins!
That is why you have been stripped
and raped by invading armies.
23 Can an Ethiopian* change the color of his skin?
Can a leopard take away its spots?
Neither can you start doing good,
for you have always done evil.

24 "I will scatter you like chaff
that is blown away by the desert winds.
25 This is your allotment,
the portion I have assigned to you,"
says the LORD,
"for you have forgotten me,
putting your trust in false gods.
26 I myself will strip you
and expose you to shame.
27 I have seen your adultery and lust,
and your disgusting idol worship out in the fields
and on the hills.
What sorrow awaits you, Jerusalem!
How long before you are pure?"

14 JUDAH'S TERRIBLE DROUGHT

This message came to Jeremiah from the LORD, explaining why he was holding back the rain:

2 "Judah wilts;
commerce at the city gates grinds to a halt.
All the people sit on the ground in mourning,
and a great cry rises from Jerusalem.
3 The nobles send servants to get water,
but all the wells are dry.
The servants return with empty pitchers,
confused and desperate,
covering their heads in grief.
4 The ground is parched
and cracked for lack of rain.
The farmers are deeply troubled;
they, too, cover their heads.
5 Even the doe abandons her newborn fawn
because there is no grass in the field.
6 The wild donkeys stand on the bare hills
panting like thirsty jackals.
They strain their eyes looking for grass,
but there is none to be found."

13:23 Hebrew *a Cushite.*

7 The people say, "Our wickedness has caught up
with us, LORD,
but help us for the sake of your own reputation.
We have turned away from you
and sinned against you again and again.
8 O Hope of Israel, our Savior in times of trouble,
why are you like a stranger to us?
Why are you like a traveler passing through the land,
stopping only for the night?
9 Are you also confused?
Is our champion helpless to save us?
You are right here among us, LORD.
We are known as your people.
Please don't abandon us now!"

10 So this is what the LORD says to his people:
"You love to wander far from me
and do not restrain yourselves.
Therefore, I will no longer accept you as my people.
Now I will remember all your wickedness
and will punish you for your sins."

HIS WILL OR YOURS? 14:11-12

Because of the continual false repentance of the people of Judah, God turned deaf ears to their cries. He left them to wallow in the mess of their own making. God will allow only so much rebellion to take place before he tells a person, "*Your* will be done." Although he is infinitely patient, he doesn't force anyone to obey him. Do you want his will or your will to be done? ■

THE LORD FORBIDS JEREMIAH TO INTERCEDE

11Then the LORD said to me, "Do not pray for these people
anymore. 12When they fast, I will pay no attention. When
they present their burnt offerings and grain offerings to
me, I will not accept them. Instead, I will devour them
with war, famine, and disease."
13Then I said, "O Sovereign LORD, their prophets are
telling them, 'All is well—no war or famine will come. The
LORD will surely send you peace.'"
14Then the LORD said, "These prophets are telling lies
in my name. I did not send them or tell them to speak.
I did not give them any messages. They prophesy of visions and revelations they have never seen or heard. They
speak foolishness made up in their own lying hearts.
15Therefore, this is what the LORD says: I will punish these
lying prophets, for they have spoken in my name even
though I never sent them. They say that no war or famine
will come, but they themselves will die by war and famine! 16As for the people to whom they prophesy—their
bodies will be thrown out into the streets of Jerusalem,
victims of famine and war. There will be no one left to
bury them. Husbands, wives, sons, and daughters—all
will be gone. For I will pour out their own wickedness on
them. 17Now, Jeremiah, say this to them:

"Night and day my eyes overflow with tears.
I cannot stop weeping,
for my virgin daughter—my precious people—
has been struck down
and lies mortally wounded.
18 If I go out into the fields,
I see the bodies of people slaughtered by the enemy.
If I walk the city streets,
I see people who have died of starvation.
The prophets and priests continue with their work,
but they don't know what they're doing."

A PRAYER FOR HEALING

19 LORD, have you completely rejected Judah?
Do you really hate Jerusalem?*
Why have you wounded us past all hope of healing?
We hoped for peace, but no peace came.
We hoped for a time of healing, but found
only terror.
20 LORD, we confess our wickedness
and that of our ancestors, too.
We all have sinned against you.
21 For the sake of your reputation, LORD, do not
abandon us.
Do not disgrace your own glorious throne.
Please remember us,
and do not break your covenant with us.

22 Can any of the worthless foreign gods send us rain?
Does it fall from the sky by itself?
No, you are the one, O LORD our God!
Only you can do such things.
So we will wait for you to help us.

15 JUDAH'S INEVITABLE DOOM

Then the LORD said to me, "Even if Moses and Samuel
stood before me pleading for these people, I wouldn't
help them. Away with them! Get them out of my sight!
2And if they say to you, 'But where can we go?' tell them,
'This is what the LORD says:

"'Those who are destined for death, to death;
those who are destined for war, to war;
those who are destined for famine, to famine;
those who are destined for captivity, to captivity.'

3"I will send four kinds of destroyers against them,"
says the LORD. "I will send the sword to kill, the dogs to
drag away, the vultures to devour, and the wild animals to
finish up what is left. 4Because of the wicked things Manasseh son of Hezekiah, king of Judah, did in Jerusalem, I
will make my people an object of horror to all the kingdoms of the earth.

5 "Who will feel sorry for you, Jerusalem?
Who will weep for you?
Who will even bother to ask how you are?

14:19 Hebrew *Zion?*

6 You have abandoned me
and turned your back on me,"
says the LORD.
"Therefore, I will raise my fist to destroy you.
I am tired of always giving you another chance.
7 I will winnow you like grain at the gates of
your cities
and take away the children you hold dear.
I will destroy my own people,
because they refuse to change their evil ways.
8 There will be more widows
than the grains of sand on the seashore.
At noontime I will bring a destroyer
against the mothers of young men.
I will cause anguish and terror
to come upon them suddenly.
9 The mother of seven grows faint and gasps
for breath;
her sun has gone down while it is still day.
She sits childless now,
disgraced and humiliated.
And I will hand over those who are left
to be killed by the enemy.
I, the LORD, have spoken!"

JEREMIAH'S COMPLAINT

10Then I said,

"What sorrow is mine, my mother.
Oh, that I had died at birth!
I am hated everywhere I go.
I am neither a lender who threatens to foreclose
nor a borrower who refuses to pay—
yet they all curse me."

11The LORD replied,

"I will take care of you, Jeremiah.
Your enemies will ask you to plead on their behalf
in times of trouble and distress.
12 Can a man break a bar of iron from the north,
or a bar of bronze?
13 At no cost to them,
I will hand over your wealth and treasures
as plunder to your enemies,
for sin runs rampant in your land.
14 I will tell your enemies to take you
as captives to a foreign land.
For my anger blazes like a fire
that will burn forever.*"

15Then I said,

"LORD, you know what's happening to me.
Please step in and help me. Punish my
persecutors!
Please give me time; don't let me die young.
It's for your sake that I am suffering.
16 When I discovered your words, I devoured them.
They are my joy and my heart's delight,
for I bear your name,
O LORD God of Heaven's Armies.
17 I never joined the people in their merry feasts.
I sat alone because your hand was on me.
I was filled with indignation at their sins.
18 Why then does my suffering continue?
Why is my wound so incurable?
Your help seems as uncertain as a seasonal brook,
like a spring that has gone dry."

19This is how the LORD responds:

"If you return to me, I will restore you
so you can continue to serve me.
If you speak good words rather than worthless ones,
you will be my spokesman.
You must influence them;
do not let them influence you!
20 They will fight against you like an attacking army,
but I will make you as secure as a fortified wall
of bronze.
They will not conquer you,
for I am with you to protect and rescue you.
I, the LORD, have spoken!
21 Yes, I will certainly keep you safe from these
wicked men.
I will rescue you from their cruel hands."

16 INFLUENCE 15:17-21

Jeremiah accused God of not helping him when he really needed it. Jeremiah had taken his eyes off God's purposes and was feeling sorry for himself. He was angry, hurt, and afraid. In response, God didn't get angry at Jeremiah; he answered by reminding Jeremiah of his promise—"You will be my spokesman." So, what does that tell us? Namely: (1) we can reveal our deepest thoughts to God; (2) God expects us to trust no matter what; and (3) we are here to influence others for God. ■

16

JEREMIAH FORBIDDEN TO MARRY

The LORD gave me another message. He said, 2"Do not get married or have children in this place. 3For this is what the LORD says about the children born here in this city and about their mothers and fathers: 4They will die from terrible diseases. No one will mourn for them or bury them, and they will lie scattered on the ground like manure. They will die from war and famine, and their bodies will be food for the vultures and wild animals."

JUDAH'S COMING PUNISHMENT

5This is what the LORD says: "Do not go to funerals to
mourn and show sympathy for these people, for I have

15:14 As in some Hebrew manuscripts (see also 17:4); most Hebrew manuscripts read *will burn against you.*

removed my protection and peace from them. I have
taken away my unfailing love and my mercy. 6 Both the
great and the lowly will die in this land. No one will bury
them or mourn for them. Their friends will not cut
themselves in sorrow or shave their heads in sadness.
7 No one will offer a meal to comfort those who mourn
for the dead—not even at the death of a mother or father. No one will send a cup of wine to console them.

8 "And do not go to their feasts and parties. Do not eat
and drink with them at all. 9 For this is what the LORD of
Heaven's Armies, the God of Israel, says: In your own lifetime, before your very eyes, I will put an end to the happy singing and laughter in this land. The joyful voices of bridegrooms and brides will no longer be heard.

10 "When you tell the people all these things, they will ask, 'Why has the LORD decreed such terrible things against us? What have we done to deserve such treatment? What is our sin against the LORD our God?'

11 "Then you will give them the LORD's reply: 'It is because your ancestors were unfaithful to me. They worshiped other gods and served them. They abandoned
me and did not obey my word. 12 And you are even worse
than your ancestors! You stubbornly follow your own
evil desires and refuse to listen to me. 13 So I will throw
you out of this land and send you into a foreign land where you and your ancestors have never been. There you can worship idols day and night—and I will grant you no favors!'

HIDE AND SEEK 16:17

Small children think that if they can't see you, then you can't see them. The people of Judah may have wished that hiding from God was as simple as closing their eyes. Although they closed their eyes to their wrongs, everything was revealed to God. Ever been tempted to play hide and seek with God, thinking that maybe he won't notice a certain action? News flash: He knows everything. You already knew that, right? So, instead of hiding, why not seek him? ■

HOPE DESPITE THE DISASTER

14 "But the time is coming," says the LORD, "when people who are taking an oath will no longer say, 'As surely as the LORD lives, who rescued the people of Israel from the land
of Egypt.' 15 Instead, they will say, 'As surely as the LORD
lives, who brought the people of Israel back to their own land from the land of the north and from all the countries to which he had exiled them.' For I will bring them back to this land that I gave their ancestors.

16 "But now I am sending for many fishermen who will catch them," says the LORD. "I am sending for hunters who will hunt them down in the mountains, hills, and
caves. 17 I am watching them closely, and I see every sin.
They cannot hope to hide from me. 18 I will double their
punishment for all their sins, because they have defiled my land with lifeless images of their detestable gods and have filled my territory with their evil deeds."

JEREMIAH'S PRAYER OF CONFIDENCE

19 LORD, you are my strength and fortress,
my refuge in the day of trouble!
Nations from around the world
will come to you and say,
"Our ancestors left us a foolish heritage,
for they worshiped worthless idols.
20 Can people make their own gods?
These are not real gods at all!"

21 The LORD says,
"Now I will show them my power;
now I will show them my might.
At last they will know and understand
that I am the LORD.

17

JUDAH'S SIN AND PUNISHMENT

1 "The sin of Judah
is inscribed with an iron chisel—
engraved with a diamond point on their stony hearts
and on the corners of their altars.
2 Even their children go to worship
at their pagan altars and Asherah poles,
beneath every green tree
and on every high hill.
3 So I will hand over my holy mountain—
along with all your wealth and treasures
and your pagan shrines—
as plunder to your enemies,
for sin runs rampant in your land.
4 The wonderful possession I have reserved for you
will slip from your hands.
I will tell your enemies to take you
as captives to a foreign land.
For my anger blazes like a fire
that will burn forever."

WISDOM FROM THE LORD

5 This is what the LORD says:
"Cursed are those who put their trust in
mere humans,
who rely on human strength
and turn their hearts away from the LORD.
6 They are like stunted shrubs in the desert,
with no hope for the future.
They will live in the barren wilderness,
in an uninhabited salty land.

7 "But blessed are those who trust in the LORD
and have made the LORD their hope and
confidence.
8 They are like trees planted along a riverbank,
with roots that reach deep into the water.
Such trees are not bothered by the heat
or worried by long months of drought.
Their leaves stay green,
and they never stop producing fruit.

9 "The human heart is the most deceitful of all things,
and desperately wicked.
Who really knows how bad it is?
10 But I, the LORD, search all hearts
and examine secret motives.
I give all people their due rewards,
according to what their actions deserve."

JEREMIAH'S TRUST IN THE LORD

11 Like a partridge that hatches eggs she has not laid,
so are those who get their wealth by unjust means.
At midlife they will lose their riches;
in the end, they will become poor old fools.
12 But we worship at your throne—
eternal, high, and glorious!
13 O LORD, the hope of Israel,
all who turn away from you will be disgraced.
They will be buried in the dust of the earth,
for they have abandoned the LORD, the fountain
of living water.

14 O LORD, if you heal me, I will be truly healed;
if you save me, I will be truly saved.
My praises are for you alone!
15 People scoff at me and say,
"What is this 'message from the LORD' you talk about?
Why don't your predictions come true?"

I've done some pretty awful things in my life. How could God forgive me for what I've done?

Recognizing that you've done wrong is 90 percent of the battle.

Usually people who build up years of wrong actions also have built a shell around their hearts. This shell protects them from feeling guilty about what they've done. As the shell gets harder and thicker, they continue in a downward spiral, doing more and more wrong things.

Jeremiah looked at the human tendency to sin and came to this conclusion: "The human heart is the most deceitful of all things, and desperately wicked. Who really knows how bad it is?" (Jer 17:9).

As you'll notice, this passage doesn't say that some people's hearts are more wicked than others. All of us have the potential for destructive actions.

But there's good news. Check out Isaiah 1:18: "'Come now, let's settle this,' says the LORD. 'Though your sins are like scarlet, I will make them as white as snow. Though they are red like crimson, I will make them as white as wool.'"

God isn't shocked by anything you've done. He's willing to forgive you if you let him.

So, don't give up—give in . . . to God. Ask him to forgive you and help you start over.

16 LORD, I have not abandoned my job
as a shepherd for your people.
I have not urged you to send disaster.
You have heard everything I've said.
17 LORD, don't terrorize me!
You alone are my hope in the day of disaster.
18 Bring shame and dismay on all who persecute me,
but don't let me experience shame and dismay.
Bring a day of terror on them.
Yes, bring double destruction upon them!

OBSERVING THE SABBATH

19 This is what the LORD said to me: "Go and stand in the
gates of Jerusalem, first in the gate where the king goes in
and out, and then in each of the other gates.
20 Say to all the
people, 'Listen to this message from the LORD, you kings
of Judah and all you people of Judah and everyone living
in Jerusalem.
21 This is what the LORD says: Listen to my
warning! Stop carrying on your trade at Jerusalem's gates
on the Sabbath day.
22 Do not do your work on the Sabbath,
but make it a holy day. I gave this command to your ancestors,
23 but they did not listen or obey. They stubbornly refused
to pay attention or accept my discipline.
24 "'But if you obey me, says the LORD, and do not carry
on your trade at the gates or work on the Sabbath day, and
if you keep it holy,
25 then kings and their officials will go
in and out of these gates forever. There will always be a
descendant of David sitting on the throne here in Jerusalem.
Kings and their officials will always ride in and out
among the people of Judah in chariots and on horses, and
this city will remain forever.
26 And from all around Jerusalem,
from the towns of Judah and Benjamin, from the
western foothills* and the hill country and the Negev, the
people will come with their burnt offerings and sacrifices.
They will bring their grain offerings, frankincense,
and thanksgiving offerings to the LORD's Temple.
27 "'But if you do not listen to me and refuse to keep the
Sabbath holy, and if on the Sabbath day you bring loads
of merchandise through the gates of Jerusalem just as on
other days, then I will set fire to these gates. The fire will
spread to the palaces, and no one will be able to put out
the roaring flames.'"

18

THE POTTER AND THE CLAY

The LORD gave another message to Jeremiah. He said,
2 "Go down to the potter's shop, and I will speak to you
there."
3 So I did as he told me and found the potter working
at his wheel.
4 But the jar he was making did not turn
out as he had hoped, so he crushed it into a lump of clay
again and started over.
5 Then the LORD gave me this message:
6 "O Israel, can I
not do to you as this potter has done to his clay? As the clay
is in the potter's hand, so are you in my hand.
7 If I announce
that a certain nation or kingdom is to be uprooted,
torn down, and destroyed,
8 but then that nation
renounces its evil ways, I will not destroy it as I had
planned.
9 And if I announce that I will plant and build up a

17:26 Hebrew *the Shephelah.*

certain nation or kingdom, 10 but then that nation turns to
evil and refuses to obey me, I will not bless it as I said I
would.

11 "Therefore, Jeremiah, go and warn all Judah and Jerusalem. Say to them, 'This is what the LORD says: I am
planning disaster for you instead of good. So turn from
your evil ways, each of you, and do what is right.'"

12 But the people replied, "Don't waste your breath. We
will continue to live as we want to, stubbornly following
our own evil desires."

13 So this is what the LORD says:

"Has anyone ever heard of such a thing,
even among the pagan nations?
My virgin daughter Israel
has done something terrible!

14 Does the snow ever disappear from the
mountaintops of Lebanon?
Do the cold streams flowing from those distant
mountains ever run dry?

15 But my people are not so reliable, for they have
deserted me;
they burn incense to worthless idols.
They have stumbled off the ancient highways
and walk in muddy paths.

16 Therefore, their land will become desolate,
a monument to their stupidity.
All who pass by will be astonished
and will shake their heads in amazement.

17 I will scatter my people before their enemies
as the east wind scatters dust.
And in all their trouble I will turn my back on them
and refuse to notice their distress."

OPPOSITION 18:18

Jeremiah's words and actions challenged the people of Judah's social and moral behavior. So, they spread false rumors about him to shut him up. Have you ever been mistreated because you've told people about God? Many people have been so discouraged by persecution that they gave up even speaking about God. God never promised to keep his faithful servants from experiencing persecution. But he does promise that he will be with them and will give them strength to endure (2 Cor 1:3-7). Knowing this, are you willing to persevere even through persecution? ■

A PLOT AGAINST JEREMIAH

18 Then the people said, "Come on, let's plot a way to stop
Jeremiah. We have plenty of priests and wise men and
prophets. We don't need him to teach the word and give
us advice and prophecies. Let's spread rumors about him
and ignore what he says."

19 LORD, hear me and help me!
Listen to what my enemies are saying.

20 Should they repay evil for good?
They have dug a pit to kill me,
though I pleaded for them
and tried to protect them from your anger.

21 So let their children starve!
Let them die by the sword!
Let their wives become childless widows.
Let their old men die in a plague,
and let their young men be killed in battle!

22 Let screaming be heard from their homes
as warriors come suddenly upon them.
For they have dug a pit for me
and have hidden traps along my path.

23 LORD, you know all about their murderous plots
against me.
Don't forgive their crimes and blot out their sins.
Let them die before you.
Deal with them in your anger.

19 JEREMIAH'S SHATTERED JAR

This is what the LORD said to me: "Go and buy a clay jar.
Then ask some of the leaders of the people and of the
priests to follow you. 2 Go out through the Gate of Broken
Pots to the garbage dump in the valley of Ben-Hinnom, and
give them this message. 3 Say to them, 'Listen to this message from the LORD, you kings of Judah and citizens of Jerusalem! This is what the LORD of Heaven's Armies, the God
of Israel, says: I will bring a terrible disaster on this place,
and the ears of those who hear about it will ring!

4 "'For Israel has forsaken me and turned this valley
into a place of wickedness. The people burn incense to
foreign gods—idols never before acknowledged by this
generation, by their ancestors, or by the kings of Judah.
And they have filled this place with the blood of innocent
children. 5 They have built pagan shrines to Baal, and
there they burn their sons as sacrifices to Baal. I have
never commanded such a horrible deed; it never even
crossed my mind to command such a thing! 6 So beware,
for the time is coming, says the LORD, when this garbage
dump will no longer be called Topheth or the valley of
Ben-Hinnom, but the Valley of Slaughter.

7 "'For I will upset the careful plans of Judah and Jerusalem. I will allow the people to be slaughtered by invading armies, and I will leave their dead bodies as food for
the vultures and wild animals. 8 I will reduce Jerusalem to
ruins, making it a monument to their stupidity. All who
pass by will be astonished and will gasp at the destruction
they see there. 9 I will see to it that your enemies lay siege
to the city until all the food is gone. Then those trapped
inside will eat their own sons and daughters and friends.
They will be driven to utter despair.'

10 "As these men watch you, Jeremiah, smash the jar you
brought. 11 Then say to them, 'This is what the LORD of
Heaven's Armies says: As this jar lies shattered, so I will
shatter the people of Judah and Jerusalem beyond all
hope of repair. They will bury the bodies here in Topheth,
the garbage dump, until there is no more room for them.
12 This is what I will do to this place and its people, says the
LORD. I will cause this city to become defiled like Topheth.
13 Yes, all the houses in Jerusalem, including the palace of

ULTIMATE ISSUES

SUICIDE

"I curse the day I was born! . . . Why was I ever born? My entire life has been filled with trouble, sorrow, and shame."

This doesn't sound like one of God's greatest prophets. Yet it is! It's Jeremiah, pouring his heart out to God (see Jer 20:14, 18), wishing he'd never been born.

Have you ever felt this kind of despair? Problems like broken relationships, misunderstandings, abuse, or changes in family life (for example, divorce) can trigger feelings of despair or helplessness. For some, though, these feelings become so intense that death seems more desirable than life.

Statistics show that suicide is the second or third leading cause of death among American teens. Everyone occasionally faces despair, but why does one person struggle through while another ends his life? The critical factor is loss of hope.

A suicidal person looks at his or her problems and says, "I am powerless to change things. What's more, I have no hope that things will get better."

So what do you do when you—or someone you care about—decide you simply want to end it all?

First, remember you're not alone. Everyone has felt that way. If others can deal with it, you can, too.

Second, don't believe the lie that your circumstances will never change. They can. Sometimes all you need is time.

Third, know the danger signals that indicate someone might be considering suicide: withdrawal; decreased academic performance; drug abuse; approaching the anniversary date of a significant loss or death; previous suicide attempts; family history of suicide; preoccupation with death and/or talk of suicide. If you or a friend are experiencing one or more of these signals, get help from someone you can trust. You might also contact the National Suicide Hotline: 1-800-SUICIDE—(1-800-784-2433).

Finally, remember, even if it seems no one else cares about you and your pain, God cares. You can trust him with your deepest fears or sorrows.

Judah's kings, will become like Topheth—all the houses
where you burned incense on the rooftops to your star
gods, and where liquid offerings were poured out to your
idols.'"
14 Then Jeremiah returned from Topheth, the garbage
dump where he had delivered this message, and he
stopped in front of the Temple of the LORD. He said to the
people there, 15 "This is what the LORD of Heaven's Armies,
the God of Israel, says: 'I will bring disaster upon
this city and its surrounding towns as I promised, because
you have stubbornly refused to listen to me.'"

20

JEREMIAH AND PASHHUR

Now Pashhur son of Immer, the priest in charge of the
Temple of the LORD, heard what Jeremiah was prophesying.
2 So he arrested Jeremiah the prophet and had him
whipped and put in stocks at the Benjamin Gate of the
LORD's Temple.
3 The next day, when Pashhur finally released him, Jeremiah
said, "Pashhur, the LORD has changed your name.
From now on you are to be called 'The Man Who Lives in
Terror.'* 4 For this is what the LORD says: 'I will send terror
upon you and all your friends, and you will watch as they
are slaughtered by the swords of the enemy. I will hand
the people of Judah over to the king of Babylon. He will
take them captive to Babylon or run them through with
the sword. 5 And I will let your enemies plunder Jerusalem.
All the famed treasures of the city—the precious
jewels and gold and silver of your kings—will be carried
off to Babylon. 6 As for you, Pashhur, you and all your
household will go as captives to Babylon. There you will
die and be buried, you and all your friends to whom you
prophesied that everything would be all right.'"

JEREMIAH'S COMPLAINT

7 O LORD, you misled me,
and I allowed myself to be misled.
You are stronger than I am,
and you overpowered me.
Now I am mocked every day;
everyone laughs at me.

20:3 Hebrew *Magor-missabib,* which means "surrounded by terror"; also in 20:10.

TAKE TRUTH TO HEART 20:1-3

Pashhur heard Jeremiah's words and, because of his guilt, locked Jeremiah up instead of taking his message to heart and acting on it. The truth sometimes stings, but our reaction to the truth shows what we are made of. Pashhur's actions proved that he didn't value truth. How do you react to truth? ■

8 When I speak, the words burst out.
"Violence and destruction!" I shout.
So these messages from the LORD
have made me a household joke.
9 But if I say I'll never mention the LORD
or speak in his name,
his word burns in my heart like a fire.
It's like a fire in my bones!
I am worn out trying to hold it in!
I can't do it!
10 I have heard the many rumors about me.
They call me "The Man Who Lives in Terror."
They threaten, "If you say anything, we will
report it."
Even my old friends are watching me,
waiting for a fatal slip.
"He will trap himself," they say,
"and then we will get our revenge on him."

11 But the LORD stands beside me like a great warrior.
Before him my persecutors will stumble.
They cannot defeat me.
They will fail and be thoroughly humiliated.
Their dishonor will never be forgotten.
12 O LORD of Heaven's Armies,
you test those who are righteous,
and you examine the deepest thoughts
and secrets.
Let me see your vengeance against them,
for I have committed my cause to you.
13 Sing to the LORD!
Praise the LORD!
For though I was poor and needy,
he rescued me from my oppressors.

14 Yet I curse the day I was born!
May no one celebrate the day of my birth.
15 I curse the messenger who told my father,
"Good news—you have a son!"
16 Let him be destroyed like the cities of old
that the LORD overthrew without mercy.
Terrify him all day long with battle shouts,
17 because he did not kill me at birth.
Oh, that I had died in my mother's womb,
that her body had been my grave!
18 Why was I ever born?
My entire life has been filled
with trouble, sorrow, and shame.

21

NO DELIVERANCE FROM BABYLON

The LORD spoke through Jeremiah when King Zedekiah
sent Pashhur son of Malkijah and Zephaniah son of Maaseiah, the priest, to speak with him. They begged Jeremiah,
2"Please speak to the LORD for us and ask him to help
us. King Nebuchadnezzar* of Babylon is attacking Judah.
Perhaps the LORD will be gracious and do a mighty miracle as he has done in the past. Perhaps he will force Nebuchadnezzar to withdraw his armies."
3Jeremiah replied, "Go back to King Zedekiah and tell
him, 4'This is what the LORD, the God of Israel, says: I will
make your weapons useless against the king of Babylon
and the Babylonians* who are outside your walls attacking
you. In fact, I will bring your enemies right into the heart of
this city. 5I myself will fight against you with a strong hand
and a powerful arm, for I am very angry. You have made me
furious! 6I will send a terrible plague upon this city, and
both people and animals will die. 7And after all that, says
the LORD, I will hand over King Zedekiah, his staff, and
everyone else in the city who survives the disease, war, and
famine. I will hand them over to King Nebuchadnezzar of
Babylon and to their other enemies. He will slaughter them
and show them no mercy, pity, or compassion.'
8"Tell all the people, 'This is what the LORD says: Take
your choice of life or death! 9Everyone who stays in Jerusalem will die from war, famine, or disease, but those who
go out and surrender to the Babylonians will live. Their reward will be life! 10For I have decided to bring disaster and
not good upon this city, says the LORD. It will be handed
over to the king of Babylon, and he will reduce it to ashes.'

JUDGMENT ON JUDAH'S KINGS

11"Say to the royal family of Judah, 'Listen to this message
from the LORD! 12This is what the LORD says to the dynasty
of David:

"'Give justice each morning to the people you judge!
Help those who have been robbed;
rescue them from their oppressors.
Otherwise, my anger will burn like an
unquenchable fire
because of all your sins.
13 I will personally fight against the people in Jerusalem,
that mighty fortress—
the people who boast, "No one can touch us here.
No one can break in here."
14 And I myself will punish you for your sinfulness,
says the LORD.
I will light a fire in your forests
that will burn up everything around you.'"

22

A MESSAGE FOR JUDAH'S KINGS

This is what the LORD said to me: "Go over and speak directly to the king of Judah. Say to him, 2'Listen to this
message from the LORD, you king of Judah, sitting on David's throne. Let your attendants and your people listen,

21:2 Hebrew *Nebuchadrezzar,* a variant spelling of Nebuchadnezzar; also in 21:7. 21:4 Or *Chaldeans;* also in 21:9.

too. [3]This is what the LORD says: Be fair-minded and just.
Do what is right! Help those who have been robbed; rescue them from their oppressors. Quit your evil deeds! Do
not mistreat foreigners, orphans, and widows. Stop murdering the innocent! [4]If you obey me, there will always be
a descendant of David sitting on the throne here in Jerusalem. The king will ride through the palace gates in
chariots and on horses, with his parade of attendants and
subjects. [5]But if you refuse to pay attention to this warning, I swear by my own name, says the LORD, that this palace will become a pile of rubble.'"

A MESSAGE ABOUT THE PALACE

[6]Now this is what the LORD says concerning Judah's royal
palace:

"I love you as much as fruitful Gilead
 and the green forests of Lebanon.
But I will turn you into a desert,
 with no one living within your walls.
7 I will call for wreckers,
 who will bring out their tools to dismantle you.
They will tear out all your fine cedar beams
 and throw them on the fire.

[8]"People from many nations will pass by the ruins of
this city and say to one another, 'Why did the LORD destroy such a great city?' [9]And the answer will be, 'Because
they violated their covenant with the LORD their God by
worshiping other gods.'"

A MESSAGE ABOUT JEHOAHAZ

10 Do not weep for the dead king or mourn his loss.
 Instead, weep for the captive king being led away!
 For he will never return to see his native
 land again.

[11]For this is what the LORD says about Jehoahaz,* who
succeeded his father, King Josiah, and was taken away as
a captive: "He will never return. [12]He will die in a distant
land and will never again see his own country."

A MESSAGE ABOUT JEHOIAKIM

13 And the LORD says, "What sorrow awaits Jehoiakim,*
 who builds his palace with forced labor.*
He builds injustice into its walls,
 for he makes his neighbors work for nothing.
 He does not pay them for their labor.
14 He says, 'I will build a magnificent palace
 with huge rooms and many windows.
I will panel it throughout with fragrant cedar
 and paint it a lovely red.'
15 But a beautiful cedar palace does not make
 a great king!
 Your father, Josiah, also had plenty to eat
 and drink.
But he was just and right in all his dealings.
 That is why God blessed him.
16 He gave justice and help to the poor and needy,
 and everything went well for him.
Isn't that what it means to know me?"
 says the LORD.
17 "But you! You have eyes only for greed and
 dishonesty!
You murder the innocent,
 oppress the poor, and reign ruthlessly."

YOUR OWN FAITH 22:15-16

King Jehoiakim's father, Josiah, had been faithful to God. Unfortunately, Jehoiakim was unfaithful. He refused to follow his father's example of faith. Are you relying on the father of your fathers? Faith cannot be inherited from parents or grandparents like money can. We must have our own faith in God. ■

[18]Therefore, this is what the LORD says about Jehoiakim,
son of King Josiah:

"The people will not mourn for him, crying to
 one another,
 'Alas, my brother! Alas, my sister!'
His subjects will not mourn for him, crying,
 'Alas, our master is dead! Alas, his splendor is gone!'
19 He will be buried like a dead donkey—
 dragged out of Jerusalem and dumped outside
 the gates!
20 Weep for your allies in Lebanon.
 Shout for them in Bashan.
Search for them in the regions east of the river.*
 See, they are all destroyed.
 Not one is left to help you.
21 I warned you when you were prosperous,
 but you replied, 'Don't bother me.'
You have been that way since childhood—
 you simply will not obey me!
22 And now the wind will blow away your allies.
 All your friends will be taken away as captives.
 Surely then you will see your wickedness and
 be ashamed.
23 It may be nice to live in a beautiful palace
 paneled with wood from the cedars of Lebanon,
but soon you will groan with pangs of anguish—
 anguish like that of a woman in labor.

A MESSAGE FOR JEHOIACHIN

[24]"As surely as I live," says the LORD, "I will abandon you,
Jehoiachin* son of Jehoiakim, king of Judah. Even if you
were the signet ring on my right hand, I would pull
you off. [25]I will hand you over to those who seek to kill
you, those you so desperately fear—to King Nebuchadnezzar* of Babylon and the mighty Babylonian* army. [26]I
will expel you and your mother from this land, and you

22:11 Hebrew *Shallum*, another name for Jehoahaz. **22:13a** The brother and successor of the exiled Jehoahaz. See 22:18. **22:13b** Hebrew *by unrighteousness*. **22:20** Or *in Abarim*. **22:24** Hebrew *Coniah*, a variant spelling of Jehoiachin; also 22:28. **22:25a** Hebrew *Nebuchadrezzar*, a variant spelling of Nebuchadnezzar. **22:25b** Or *Chaldean*.

will die in a foreign country, not in your native land. 27You will never again return to the land you yearn for.

28 "Why is this man Jehoiachin like a discarded,
broken jar?
Why are he and his children to be exiled
to a foreign land?
29 O earth, earth, earth!
Listen to this message from the LORD!
30 This is what the LORD says:
'Let the record show that this man Jehoiachin
was childless.
He is a failure,
for none of his children will succeed him
on the throne of David
to rule over Judah.'

23 THE RIGHTEOUS DESCENDANT

"What sorrow awaits the leaders of my people—the shepherds of my sheep—for they have destroyed and scattered the very ones they were expected to care for," says the LORD.
2Therefore, this is what the LORD, the God of Israel, says to these shepherds: "Instead of caring for my flock and leading them to safety, you have deserted them and driven them to destruction. Now I will pour out judgment on you for the evil you have done to them. 3But I will gather together the remnant of my flock from the countries where I have driven them. I will bring them back to their own sheepfold, and they will be fruitful and increase in number. 4Then I will appoint responsible shepherds who will care for them, and they will never be afraid again. Not a single one will be lost or missing. I, the LORD, have spoken!

5 "For the time is coming,"
says the LORD,
"when I will raise up a righteous descendant*
from King David's line.
He will be a King who rules with wisdom.
He will do what is just and right throughout
the land.
6 And this will be his name:
'The LORD Is Our Righteousness.'*
In that day Judah will be saved,
and Israel will live in safety.

7"In that day," says the LORD, "when people are taking an oath, they will no longer say, 'As surely as the LORD lives, who rescued the people of Israel from the land of Egypt.'
8Instead, they will say, 'As surely as the LORD lives, who brought the people of Israel back to their own land from the land of the north and from all the countries to which he had exiled them.' Then they will live in their own land."

JUDGMENT ON FALSE PROPHETS

9 My heart is broken because of the false prophets,
and my bones tremble.
I stagger like a drunkard,
like someone overcome by wine,
because of the holy words
the LORD has spoken against them.
10 For the land is full of adultery,
and it lies under a curse.
The land itself is in mourning—
its wilderness pastures are dried up.
For they all do evil
and abuse what power they have.

11 "Even the priests and prophets
are ungodly, wicked men.
I have seen their despicable acts
right here in my own Temple,"
says the LORD.
12 "Therefore, the paths they take
will become slippery.
They will be chased through the dark,
and there they will fall.
For I will bring disaster upon them
at the time fixed for their punishment.
I, the LORD, have spoken!

CORRUPTION 23:9-14

How did the nation become so corrupt? A major factor was false prophecy. The false prophets were very popular, because they made the people of Judah believe that all was well. By contrast, Jeremiah's message from God was unpopular because it showed the people how bad their actions were. Check out these three characteristics of false prophets: (1) They fail to speak God's messages or they water the messages down to make them more "acceptable." (2) They encourage their listeners, often subtly, to disobey God. (3) They tend to be arrogant and self-serving, appealing to the desires of their audience instead of being true to God's Word. Don't be fooled. ■

13 "I saw that the prophets of Samaria were terribly evil,
for they prophesied in the name of Baal
and led my people of Israel into sin.
14 But now I see that the prophets of Jerusalem are
even worse!
They commit adultery and love dishonesty.
They encourage those who are doing evil
so that no one turns away from their sins.
These prophets are as wicked
as the people of Sodom and Gomorrah once were."

15Therefore, this is what the LORD of Heaven's Armies says concerning the prophets:

"I will feed them with bitterness
and give them poison to drink.
For it is because of Jerusalem's prophets
that wickedness has filled this land."

23:5 Hebrew *a righteous branch.* 23:6 Hebrew *Yahweh Tsidqenu.*

16This is what the LORD of Heaven's Armies says to his
people:

"Do not listen to these prophets when they prophesy
to you,
filling you with futile hopes.
They are making up everything they say.
They do not speak for the LORD!
17 They keep saying to those who despise my word,
'Don't worry! The LORD says you will have peace!'
And to those who stubbornly follow their own desires,
they say, 'No harm will come your way!'

18 "Have any of these prophets been in the
LORD's presence
to hear what he is really saying?
Has even one of them cared enough to listen?
19 Look! The LORD's anger bursts out like a storm,
a whirlwind that swirls down on the heads
of the wicked.
20 The anger of the LORD will not diminish
until it has finished all he has planned.
In the days to come
you will understand all this very clearly.

21 "I have not sent these prophets,
yet they run around claiming to speak for me.
I have given them no message,
yet they go on prophesying.
22 If they had stood before me and listened to me,
they would have spoken my words,
and they would have turned my people
from their evil ways and deeds.
23 Am I a God who is only close at hand?" says the LORD.
"No, I am far away at the same time.
24 Can anyone hide from me in a secret place?
Am I not everywhere in all the heavens and earth?"
says the LORD.

25"I have heard these prophets say, 'Listen to the dream
I had from God last night.' And then they proceed to tell
lies in my name. 26How long will this go on? If they are
prophets, they are prophets of deceit, inventing everything they say. 27By telling these false dreams, they are
trying to get my people to forget me, just as their ancestors did by worshiping the idols of Baal.

28 "Let these false prophets tell their dreams,
but let my true messengers faithfully proclaim
my every word.
There is a difference between straw and grain!
29 Does not my word burn like fire?"
says the LORD.
"Is it not like a mighty hammer
that smashes a rock to pieces?

30"Therefore," says the LORD, "I am against these
prophets who steal messages from each other and claim
they are from me. 31I am against these smooth-tongued
prophets who say, 'This prophecy is from the LORD!' 32I
am against these false prophets. Their imaginary dreams
are flagrant lies that lead my people into sin. I did not
send or appoint them, and they have no message at all for
my people. I, the LORD have spoken!

FALSE PROPHECIES AND FALSE PROPHETS

33"Suppose one of the people or one of the prophets or
priests asks you, 'What prophecy has the LORD burdened
you with now?' You must reply, 'You are the burden!* The
LORD says he will abandon you!'

34"If any prophet, priest, or anyone else says, 'I have a
prophecy from the LORD,' I will punish that person along
with his entire family. 35You should keep asking each
other, 'What is the LORD's answer?' or 'What is the LORD
saying?' 36But stop using this phrase, 'prophecy from the
LORD.' For people are using it to give authority to their
own ideas, turning upside down the words of our God,
the living God, the LORD of Heaven's Armies.

37"This is what you should say to the prophets: 'What is
the LORD's answer?' or 'What is the LORD saying?' 38But
suppose they respond, 'This is a prophecy from the
LORD!' Then you should say, 'This is what the LORD says:
Because you have used this phrase, "prophecy from the
LORD," even though I warned you not to use it, 39I will forget you completely. I will expel you from my presence,
along with this city that I gave to you and your ancestors.
40And I will make you an object of ridicule, and your
name will be infamous throughout the ages.'"

THE BLESSING OF TROUBLE 24:1-10

The good figs represented the exiles to Babylon—not because they were good, but because the captivity would cause them to turn back to God. The bad figs represented those who remained in Judah or ran away to Egypt. Trouble can be a blessing if it makes us stronger, while prosperity can be a curse if it entices us away from God. God can use any event of your life to help you grow stronger and closer to him. ■

24 GOOD AND BAD FIGS

After King Nebuchadnezzar* of Babylon exiled Jehoiachin* son of Jehoiakim, king of Judah, to Babylon along
with the officials of Judah and all the craftsmen and artisans, the LORD gave me this vision. I saw two baskets of
figs placed in front of the LORD's Temple in Jerusalem.
2One basket was filled with fresh, ripe figs, while the
other was filled with bad figs that were too rotten to eat.
3Then the LORD said to me, "What do you see,
Jeremiah?"

I replied, "Figs, some very good and some very bad, too
rotten to eat."

4Then the LORD gave me this message: 5"This is what
the LORD, the God of Israel, says: The good figs represent

23:33 As in Greek version and Latin Vulgate; Hebrew reads *What burden?*
24:1b Hebrew *Jeconiah,* a variant spelling of Jehoiachin.
24:1a Hebrew *Nebuchadrezzar,* a variant spelling of Nebuchadnezzar.

the exiles I sent from Judah to the land of the Babylonians.* 6I will watch over and care for them, and I will
bring them back here again. I will build them up and not
tear them down. I will plant them and not uproot them. 7I
will give them hearts that recognize me as the LORD. They
will be my people, and I will be their God, for they will return to me wholeheartedly.
8"But the bad figs," the LORD said, "represent King Zedekiah of Judah, his officials, all the people left in Jerusalem, and those who live in Egypt. I will treat them like bad
figs, too rotten to eat. 9I will make them an object of horror and a symbol of evil to every nation on earth. They will
be disgraced and mocked, taunted and cursed, wherever
I scatter them. 10And I will send war, famine, and disease
until they have vanished from the land of Israel, which I
gave to them and their ancestors."

DON'T QUIT! 25:1-6

Imagine preaching the same message for 23 years and continually being rejected! Even though he was rejected, Jeremiah continued to proclaim the same message: "Turn from the evil road you are traveling and from the evil things you are doing." God is even more faithful to us. He never stops loving us, even when we reject him. Are you that faithful? ■

25

SEVENTY YEARS OF CAPTIVITY

This message for all the people of Judah came to Jeremiah from the LORD during the fourth year of Jehoiakim's
reign over Judah.* This was the year when King Nebuchadnezzar* of Babylon began his reign.
2Jeremiah the prophet said to all the people in Judah
and Jerusalem, 3"For the past twenty-three years—from
the thirteenth year of the reign of Josiah son of Amon,*
king of Judah, until now—the LORD has been giving me
his messages. I have faithfully passed them on to you, but
you have not listened.
4"Again and again the LORD has sent you his servants,
the prophets, but you have not listened or even paid attention. 5Each time the message was this: 'Turn from the
evil road you are traveling and from the evil things you
are doing. Only then will I let you live in this land that the
LORD gave to you and your ancestors forever. 6Do not provoke my anger by worshiping idols you made with your
own hands. Then I will not harm you.'
7"But you would not listen to me," says the LORD. "You
made me furious by worshiping idols you made with your
own hands, bringing on yourselves all the disasters you
now suffer. 8And now the LORD of Heaven's Armies says:
Because you have not listened to me, 9I will gather together all the armies of the north under King Nebuchadnezzar of Babylon, whom I have appointed as my deputy.
I will bring them all against this land and its people and
against the surrounding nations. I will completely
destroy* you and make you an object of horror and contempt and a ruin forever. 10I will take away your happy
singing and laughter. The joyful voices of bridegrooms
and brides will no longer be heard. Your millstones will
fall silent, and the lights in your homes will go out. 11This
entire land will become a desolate wasteland. Israel and
her neighboring lands will serve the king of Babylon for
seventy years.
12"Then, after the seventy years of captivity are over, I
will punish the king of Babylon and his people for their
sins," says the LORD. "I will make the country of the Babylonians* a wasteland forever. 13I will bring upon them
all the terrors I have promised in this book—all the penal-
ties announced by Jeremiah against the nations. 14Many
nations and great kings will enslave the Babylonians, just
as they enslaved my people. I will punish them in proportion to the suffering they cause my people."

THE CUP OF THE LORD'S ANGER

15This is what the LORD, the God of Israel, said to me:
"Take from my hand this cup filled to the brim with my
anger, and make all the nations to whom I send you drink
from it. 16When they drink from it, they will stagger,
crazed by the warfare I will send against them."
17So I took the cup of anger from the LORD and made
all the nations drink from it—every nation to which the
LORD sent me. 18I went to Jerusalem and the other towns
of Judah, and their kings and officials drank from the
cup. From that day until this, they have been a desolate
ruin, an object of horror, contempt, and cursing. 19I gave
the cup to Pharaoh, king of Egypt, his attendants, his officials, and all his people, 20along with all the foreigners living in that land. I also gave it to all the kings of the land of
Uz and the kings of the Philistine cities of Ashkelon,
Gaza, Ekron, and what remains of Ashdod. 21Then I gave
the cup to the nations of Edom, Moab, and Ammon, 22and
the kings of Tyre and Sidon, and the kings of the regions
across the sea. 23I gave it to Dedan, Tema, and Buz, and to
the people who live in distant places.* 24I gave it to the
kings of Arabia, the kings of the nomadic tribes of the
desert, 25and to the kings of Zimri, Elam, and Media.
26And I gave it to the kings of the northern countries, far
and near, one after the other—all the kingdoms of the
world. And finally, the king of Babylon* himself drank
from the cup of the LORD's anger.
27Then the LORD said to me, "Now tell them, 'This is
what the LORD of Heaven's Armies, the God of Israel, says:
Drink from this cup of my anger. Get drunk and vomit;
fall to rise no more, for I am sending terrible wars against
you.' 28And if they refuse to accept the cup, tell them, 'The
LORD of Heaven's Armies says: You have no choice but to
drink from it. 29I have begun to punish Jerusalem, the city
that bears my name. Now should I let you go unpunished? No, you will not escape disaster. I will call for war

24:5 Or *Chaldeans.* 25:1a The fourth year of Jehoiakim's reign and the accession year of Nebuchadnezzar's reign was 605 B.C. 25:1b Hebrew *Nebuchadrezzar,* a variant spelling of Nebuchadnezzar; also in 25:9. 25:3 The thirteenth year of Josiah's reign was 627 B.C. 25:9 The Hebrew term used here refers to the complete consecration of things or people to the LORD, either by destroying them or by giving them as an offering. 25:12 Or *Chaldeans.* 25:23 Or *who clip the corners of their hair.* 25:26 Hebrew *of Sheshach,* a code name for Babylon.

against all the nations of the earth. I, the LORD of Heaven's
Armies, have spoken!'

30"Now prophesy all these things, and say to them,

"'The LORD will roar against his own land
from his holy dwelling in heaven.
He will shout like those who tread grapes;
he will shout against everyone on earth.
31 His cry of judgment will reach the ends of the earth,
for the LORD will bring his case against all
the nations.
He will judge all the people of the earth,
slaughtering the wicked with the sword.
I, the LORD, have spoken!'"

32 This is what the LORD of Heaven's Armies says:
"Look! Disaster will fall upon nation after nation!
A great whirlwind of fury is rising
from the most distant corners of the earth!"

33In that day those the LORD has slaughtered will fill
the earth from one end to the other. No one will mourn
for them or gather up their bodies to bury them. They will
be scattered on the ground like manure.

34 Weep and moan, you evil shepherds!
Roll in the dust, you leaders of the flock!
The time of your slaughter has arrived;
you will fall and shatter like a fragile vase.
35 You will find no place to hide;
there will be no way to escape.
36 Listen to the frantic cries of the shepherds.
The leaders of the flock are wailing in despair,
for the LORD is ruining their pastures.
37 Peaceful meadows will be turned into a wasteland
by the LORD's fierce anger.
38 He has left his den like a strong lion seeking its prey,
and their land will be made desolate
by the sword of the enemy
and the LORD's fierce anger.

26 JEREMIAH'S ESCAPE FROM DEATH

This message came to Jeremiah from the LORD early in
the reign of Jehoiakim son of Josiah,* king of Judah.
2"This is what the LORD says: Stand in the courtyard in
front of the Temple of the LORD, and make an announcement to the people who have come there to worship from
all over Judah. Give them my entire message; include
every word. 3Perhaps they will listen and turn from their
evil ways. Then I will change my mind about the disaster I
am ready to pour out on them because of their sins.

4"Say to them, 'This is what the LORD says: If you will
not listen to me and obey my word I have given you, 5and
if you will not listen to my servants, the prophets—for I
sent them again and again to warn you, but you would not
listen to them—6then I will destroy this Temple as I
destroyed Shiloh, the place where the Tabernacle was
located. And I will make Jerusalem an object of cursing in
every nation on earth.'"

7The priests, the prophets, and all the people listened
to Jeremiah as he spoke in front of the LORD's Temple.
8But when Jeremiah had finished his message, saying
everything the LORD had told him to say, the priests and
prophets and all the people at the Temple mobbed him.
"Kill him!" they shouted. 9"What right do you have to
prophesy in the LORD's name that this Temple will be destroyed like Shiloh? What do you mean, saying that Jerusalem will be destroyed and left with no inhabitants?"
And all the people threatened him as he stood in front of
the Temple.

10When the officials of Judah heard what was happening, they rushed over from the palace and sat down at the
New Gate of the Temple to hold court. 11The priests and
prophets presented their accusations to the officials and
the people. "This man should die!" they said. "You have
heard with your own ears what a traitor he is, for he has
prophesied against this city."

12Then Jeremiah spoke to the officials and the people
in his own defense. "The LORD sent me to prophesy
against this Temple and this city," he said. "The LORD gave
me every word that I have spoken. 13But if you stop your
sinning and begin to obey the LORD your God, he will
change his mind about this disaster that he has announced against you. 14As for me, I am in your hands—do
with me as you think best. 15But if you kill me, rest assured
that you will be killing an innocent man! The responsibility for such a deed will lie on you, on this city, and on every
person living in it. For it is absolutely true that the LORD
sent me to speak every word you have heard."

16Then the officials and the people said to the priests
and prophets, "This man does not deserve the death sentence, for he has spoken to us in the name of the LORD our
God."

17Then some of the wise old men stood and spoke to all
the people assembled there. 18They said, "Remember
when Micah of Moresheth prophesied during the reign
of King Hezekiah of Judah. He told the people of Judah,

'This is what the LORD of Heaven's Armies says:
Mount Zion will be plowed like an open field;
Jerusalem will be reduced to ruins!
A thicket will grow on the heights
where the Temple now stands.'*

19But did King Hezekiah and the people kill him for saying this? No, they turned from their sins and worshiped
the LORD. They begged him for mercy. Then the LORD
changed his mind about the terrible disaster he had pronounced against them. So we are about to do ourselves
great harm."

20At this time Uriah son of Shemaiah from Kiriath-
jearim was also prophesying for the LORD. And he predicted the same terrible disaster against the city and nation as Jeremiah did. 21When King Jehoiakim and the
army officers and officials heard what he was saying, the

26:1 The first year of Jehoiakim's reign was 608 B.C. **26:18** Mic 3:12.

king sent someone to kill him. But Uriah heard about the plan and escaped in fear to Egypt. 22Then King Jehoiakim sent Elnathan son of Acbor to Egypt along with several other men to capture Uriah. 23They took him prisoner and brought him back to King Jehoiakim. The king then killed Uriah with a sword and had him buried in an unmarked grave.

24Nevertheless, Ahikam son of Shaphan stood up for Jeremiah and persuaded the court not to turn him over to the mob to be killed.

27 JEREMIAH WEARS AN OX YOKE

This message came to Jeremiah from the LORD early in the reign of Zedekiah* son of Josiah, king of Judah.

2This is what the LORD said to me: "Make a yoke, and fasten it on your neck with leather thongs. 3Then send messages to the kings of Edom, Moab, Ammon, Tyre, and Sidon through their ambassadors who have come to see King Zedekiah in Jerusalem. 4Give them this message for their masters: 'This is what the LORD of Heaven's Armies, the God of Israel, says: 5With my great strength and powerful arm I made the earth and all its people and every animal. I can give these things of mine to anyone I choose. 6Now I will give your countries to King Nebuchadnezzar of Babylon, who is my servant. I have put everything, even the wild animals, under his control. 7All the nations will serve him, his son, and his grandson until his time is up. Then many nations and great kings will conquer and rule over Babylon. 8So you must submit to Babylon's king and serve him; put your neck under Babylon's yoke! I will punish any nation that refuses to be his slave, says the LORD. I will send war, famine, and disease upon that nation until Babylon has conquered it.

9"'Do not listen to your false prophets, fortune-tellers, interpreters of dreams, mediums, and sorcerers who say, "The king of Babylon will not conquer you." 10They are all liars, and their lies will lead to your being driven out of your land. I will drive you out and send you far away to die. 11But the people of any nation that submits to the king of Babylon will be allowed to stay in their own country to farm the land as usual. I, the LORD, have spoken!'"

12Then I repeated this same message to King Zedekiah of Judah. "If you want to live, submit to the yoke of the king of Babylon and his people. 13Why do you insist on dying—you and your people? Why should you choose war, famine, and disease, which the LORD will bring against every nation that refuses to submit to Babylon's king? 14Do not listen to the false prophets who keep telling you, 'The king of Babylon will not conquer you.' They are liars. 15This is what the LORD says: 'I have not sent these prophets! They are telling you lies in my name, so I will drive you from this land. You will all die—you and all these prophets, too.'"

16Then I spoke to the priests and the people and said, "This is what the LORD says: 'Do not listen to your prophets who claim that soon the gold articles taken from my Temple will be returned from Babylon. It is all a lie! 17Do not listen to them. Surrender to the king of Babylon, and you will live. Why should this whole city be destroyed? 18If they really are prophets and speak the LORD's messages, let them pray to the LORD of Heaven's Armies. Let them pray that the articles remaining in the LORD's Temple and in the king's palace and in the palaces of Jerusalem will not be carried away to Babylon!'

THE TRUTH HURTS 28:1-17

Jeremiah spoke the truth, but was unpopular. Hananiah spoke lies, but his deceitful words brought false hope and comfort to the people. God had already outlined the marks of a true prophet: The predictions always came true and never contradicted previous revelations (Deut 13; 18:15-22; Jer 23:9-14). Even though Jeremiah's predictions came true, the people still preferred to listen to comforting lies rather than painful truth. Which would you prefer: a comforting lie or a painful truth? Are you open to God's words to you, even if you don't particularly like what he has to say? ■

19"For the LORD of Heaven's Armies has spoken about the pillars in front of the Temple, the great bronze basin called the Sea, the water carts, and all the other ceremonial articles. 20King Nebuchadnezzar of Babylon left them here when he exiled Jehoiachin* son of Jehoiakim, king of Judah, to Babylon, along with all the other nobles of Judah and Jerusalem. 21Yes, this is what the LORD of Heaven's Armies, the God of Israel, says about the precious things still in the Temple and in the palace of Judah's king: 22'They will all be carried away to Babylon and will stay there until I send for them,' says the LORD. 'Then I will bring them back to Jerusalem again.'"

28 JEREMIAH CONDEMNS HANANIAH

One day in late summer* of that same year—the fourth year of the reign of Zedekiah, king of Judah—Hananiah son of Azzur, a prophet from Gibeon, addressed me publicly in the Temple while all the priests and people listened. He said, 2"This is what the LORD of Heaven's Armies, the God of Israel, says: 'I will remove the yoke of the king of Babylon from your necks. 3Within two years I will bring back all the Temple treasures that King Nebuchadnezzar carried off to Babylon. 4And I will bring back Jehoiachin* son of Jehoiakim, king of Judah, and all the other captives that were taken to Babylon. I will surely break the yoke that the king of Babylon has put on your necks. I, the LORD, have spoken!'"

5Jeremiah responded to Hananiah as they stood in

27:1 As in some Hebrew manuscripts and Syriac version (see also 27:3, 12); most Hebrew manuscripts read *Jehoiakim.* **27:20** Hebrew *Jeconiah,* a variant spelling of Jehoiachin. **28:1** Hebrew *In the fifth month,* of the ancient Hebrew lunar calendar. The fifth month in the fourth year of Zedekiah's reign occurred within the months of August and September 593 B.C. Also see note on 1:3. **28:4** Hebrew *Jeconiah,* a variant spelling of Jehoiachin.

front of all the priests and people at the
Temple. 6He said, "Amen! May your
prophecies come true! I hope the LORD
does everything you say. I hope he does
bring back from Babylon the treasures
of this Temple and all the captives. 7But
listen now to the solemn words I speak
to you in the presence of all these people. 8The ancient prophets who preceded you and me spoke against many
nations, always warning of war, disaster, and disease. 9So a prophet who pre-
dicts peace must show he is right. Only
when his predictions come true can we
know that he is really from the LORD."
10Then Hananiah the prophet took
the yoke off Jeremiah's neck and broke
it in pieces. 11And Hananiah said again
to the crowd that had gathered, "This is what the LORD
says: 'Just as this yoke has been broken, within two years I
will break the yoke of oppression from all the nations
now subject to King Nebuchadnezzar of Babylon.'" With
that, Jeremiah left the Temple area.
12Soon after this confrontation with Hananiah, the
LORD gave this message to Jeremiah: 13"Go and tell Hananiah, 'This is what the LORD says: You have broken a
wooden yoke, but you have replaced it with a yoke of iron.
14The LORD of Heaven's Armies, the God of Israel, says: I
have put a yoke of iron on the necks of all these nations,
forcing them into slavery under King Nebuchadnezzar
of Babylon. I have put everything, even the wild animals,
under his control.'"
15Then Jeremiah the prophet said to Hananiah, "Listen,
Hananiah! The LORD has not sent you, but the people believe your lies. 16Therefore, this is what the LORD says:
'You must die. Your life will end this very year because
you have rebelled against the LORD.'"
17Two months later* the prophet Hananiah died.

29 A LETTER TO THE EXILES

Jeremiah wrote a letter from Jerusalem to the elders,
priests, prophets, and all the people who had been exiled
to Babylon by King Nebuchadnezzar. 2This was after
King Jehoiachin,* the queen mother, the court officials,
the other officials of Judah, and all the craftsmen and artisans had been deported from Jerusalem. 3He sent the
letter with Elasah son of Shaphan and Gemariah son of
Hilkiah when they went to Babylon as King Zedekiah's
ambassadors to Nebuchadnezzar. This is what Jeremiah's letter said:

4This is what the LORD of Heaven's Armies, the God of
Israel, says to all the captives he has exiled to Babylon
from Jerusalem: 5"Build homes, and plan to stay.
Plant gardens, and eat the food they produce. 6Marry
and have children. Then find spouses for them so
that you may have many grandchildren. Multiply! Do
not dwindle away! 7And work for the peace and
prosperity of the city where I sent
you into exile. Pray to the LORD for it,
for its welfare will determine your
welfare."
8This is what the LORD of Heaven's
Armies, the God of Israel, says: "Do
not let your prophets and fortune-
tellers who are with you in the land
of Babylon trick you. Do not listen to
their dreams, 9because they are
telling you lies in my name. I have
not sent them," says the LORD.
10This is what the LORD says: "You
will be in Babylon for seventy years.
But then I will come and do for you
all the good things I have promised,
and I will bring you home again.
11For I know the plans I have for
you," says the LORD. "They are plans for good and not
for disaster, to give you a future and a hope. 12In
those days when you pray, I will listen. 13If you look
for me wholeheartedly, you will find me. 14I will be
found by you," says the LORD. "I will end your
captivity and restore your fortunes. I will gather you

"For I know the plans I have for you," says the LORD. "They are plans for good and not for disaster, to give you a future and a hope."

JEREMIAH 29:11

28:17 Hebrew *In the seventh month of that same year*. See 28:1 and the note there. 29:2 Hebrew *Jeconiah*, a variant spelling of Jehoiachin.

I'm afraid to give my whole life to God because I think he'll tell me to do something I don't want to do. What happens if I hold back part of my life from God?

Imagine going out for the basketball team and telling the coach that you only want to practice, not to play in the games. How do you think your coach or teammates would react?

Undoubtedly they would be a little put off by your attitude. After all, if you're going to be on the team, you should play in the games.

Unfortunately, many people have that attitude about their relationship with God. They want it on their terms—with all the benefits and no hassles.

A relationship with God requires a full commitment like that in any good relationship. God wants your whole life so he can make something extraordinary out of it.

His goal isn't to make you miserable. Just take a look at Jeremiah 29:11. "'For I know the plans I have for you,' says the LORD. 'They are plans for good and not for disaster, to give you a future and a hope.'"

So what does that mean? It means that God has good plans for your life. He knows you better than anyone else does and knows what will fulfill you the most in life. If you choose any other direction, you'll be settling for second best. Please don't.

out of the nations where I sent you and will bring you
home again to your own land."

15 You claim that the LORD has raised up prophets for
you in Babylon. 16 But this is what the LORD says about
the king who sits on David's throne and all those still
living here in Jerusalem—your relatives who were not
exiled to Babylon. 17 This is what the LORD of Heaven's
Armies says: "I will send war, famine, and disease upon
them and make them like bad figs, too rotten to eat.
18 Yes, I will pursue them with war, famine, and disease,
and I will scatter them around the world. In every nation
where I send them, I will make them an object of
damnation, horror, contempt, and mockery. 19 For they
refuse to listen to me, though I have spoken to them
repeatedly through the prophets I sent. And you who
are in exile have not listened either," says the LORD.

20 Therefore, listen to this message from the LORD, all
you captives there in Babylon. 21 This is what the LORD
of Heaven's Armies, the God of Israel, says about your
prophets—Ahab son of Kolaiah and Zedekiah son of
Maaseiah—who are telling you lies in my name: "I will
turn them over to Nebuchadnezzar* for execution
before your eyes. 22 Their terrible fate will become
proverbial, so that the Judean exiles will curse someone
by saying, 'May the LORD make you like Zedekiah and
Ahab, whom the king of Babylon burned alive!' 23 For
these men have done terrible things among my people.
They have committed adultery with their neighbors'
wives and have lied in my name, saying things I did
not command. I am a witness to this. I, the LORD,
have spoken."

A MESSAGE FOR SHEMAIAH

24 The LORD sent this message to Shemaiah the Nehelamite in Babylon: 25 "This is what the LORD of Heaven's Armies, the God of Israel, says: You wrote a letter on your
own authority to Zephaniah son of Maaseiah, the priest,
and you sent copies to the other priests and people in
Jerusalem. You wrote to Zephaniah,

26 "The LORD has appointed you to replace Jehoiada as
the priest in charge of the house of the LORD. You are
responsible to put into stocks and neck irons any crazy
man who claims to be a prophet. 27 So why have you
done nothing to stop Jeremiah from Anathoth, who
pretends to be a prophet among you? 28 Jeremiah sent a
letter here to Babylon, predicting that our captivity will
be a long one. He said, 'Build homes, and plan to stay.
Plant gardens, and eat the food they produce.'"

29 But when Zephaniah the priest received Shemaiah's
letter, he took it to Jeremiah and read it to him. 30 Then the
LORD gave this message to Jeremiah: 31 "Send an open letter to all the exiles in Babylon. Tell them, 'This is what the
LORD says concerning Shemaiah the Nehelamite: Since
he has prophesied to you when I did not send him and
has tricked you into believing his lies, 32 I will punish him
and his family. None of his descendants will see the good
things I will do for my people, for he has incited you to
rebel against me. I, the LORD, have spoken!'"

30 PROMISES OF DELIVERANCE

The LORD gave another message to Jeremiah. He said,
2 "This is what the LORD, the God of Israel, says: Write
down for the record everything I have said to you, Jeremiah. 3 For the time is coming when I will restore the fortunes of my people of Israel and Judah. I will bring them
home to this land that I gave to their ancestors, and they
will possess it again. I, the LORD, have spoken!"

4 This is the message the LORD gave concerning Israel
and Judah. 5 This is what the LORD says:

"I hear cries of fear;
there is terror and no peace.
6 Now let me ask you a question:
Do men give birth to babies?
Then why do they stand there, ashen-faced,
hands pressed against their sides
like a woman in labor?
7 In all history there has never been such a time
of terror.
It will be a time of trouble for my people Israel.*
Yet in the end they will be saved!
8 For in that day,"
says the LORD of Heaven's Armies,
"I will break the yoke from their necks
and snap their chains.
Foreigners will no longer be their masters.
9 For my people will serve the LORD their God
and their king descended from David—
the king I will raise up for them.

10 "So do not be afraid, Jacob, my servant;
do not be dismayed, Israel,"
says the LORD.
"For I will bring you home again from distant lands,
and your children will return from their exile.
Israel will return to a life of peace and quiet,
and no one will terrorize them.
11 For I am with you and will save you,"
says the LORD.
"I will completely destroy the nations where I have
scattered you,
but I will not completely destroy you.
I will discipline you, but with justice;
I cannot let you go unpunished."

12 This is what the LORD says:
"Your injury is incurable—
a terrible wound.
13 There is no one to help you
or to bind up your injury.
No medicine can heal you.
14 All your lovers—your allies—have left you
and do not care about you anymore.

29:21 Hebrew *Nebuchadrezzar*, a variant spelling of Nebuchadnezzar. 30:7 Hebrew *Jacob;* also in 30:10b, 18. See note on 5:20.

I have wounded you cruelly,
as though I were your enemy.
For your sins are many,
and your guilt is great.
15 Why do you protest your punishment—
this wound that has no cure?
I have had to punish you
because your sins are many
and your guilt is great.

16 "But all who devour you will be devoured,
and all your enemies will be sent into exile.
All who plunder you will be plundered,
and all who attack you will be attacked.
17 I will give you back your health
and heal your wounds," says the LORD.
"For you are called an outcast—
'Jerusalem* for whom no one cares.'"

18 This is what the LORD says:
"When I bring Israel home again from captivity
and restore their fortunes,
Jerusalem will be rebuilt on its ruins,
and the palace reconstructed as before.
19 There will be joy and songs of thanksgiving,
and I will multiply my people, not diminish them;
I will honor them, not despise them.
20 Their children will prosper as they did long ago.
I will establish them as a nation before me,
and I will punish anyone who hurts them.
21 They will have their own ruler again,
and he will come from their own people.
I will invite him to approach me," says the LORD,
"for who would dare to come unless invited?
22 You will be my people,
and I will be your God."

23 Look! The LORD's anger bursts out like a storm,
a driving wind that swirls down on the heads
of the wicked.
24 The fierce anger of the LORD will not diminish
until it has finished all he has planned.
In the days to come
you will understand all this.

31

HOPE FOR RESTORATION

"In that day," says the LORD, "I will be the God of all the
families of Israel, and they will be my people. 2This is
what the LORD says:

"Those who survive the coming destruction
will find blessings even in the barren land,
for I will give rest to the people of Israel."

3 Long ago the LORD said to Israel:
"I have loved you, my people, with an everlasting love.
With unfailing love I have drawn you to myself.

MAGNIFICENT LOVE 31:3

God reaches toward his people with kindness motivated by deep and everlasting love. God is eager to do the best for his people if they will only let him. After many words of warning about sin, this reminder of God's magnificent love is refreshing. We may often think of God with dread or fear; but if we look carefully, we can see him lovingly drawing us toward himself. ■

4 I will rebuild you, my virgin Israel.
You will again be happy
and dance merrily with your tambourines.
5 Again you will plant your vineyards on the mountains
of Samaria
and eat from your own gardens there.
6 The day will come when watchmen will shout
from the hill country of Ephraim,
'Come, let us go up to Jerusalem*
to worship the LORD our God.'"

7 Now this is what the LORD says:
"Sing with joy for Israel.*
Shout for the greatest of nations!
Shout out with praise and joy:
'Save your people, O LORD,
the remnant of Israel!'
8 For I will bring them from the north
and from the distant corners of the earth.
I will not forget the blind and lame,
the expectant mothers and women in labor.
A great company will return!
9 Tears of joy will stream down their faces,
and I will lead them home with great care.
They will walk beside quiet streams
and on smooth paths where they will not stumble.
For I am Israel's father,
and Ephraim is my oldest child.

10 "Listen to this message from the LORD,
you nations of the world;
proclaim it in distant coastlands:
The LORD, who scattered his people,
will gather them and watch over them
as a shepherd does his flock.
11 For the LORD has redeemed Israel
from those too strong for them.
12 They will come home and sing songs of joy on the
heights of Jerusalem.
They will be radiant because of the LORD's
good gifts—
the abundant crops of grain, new wine, and olive oil,
and the healthy flocks and herds.
Their life will be like a watered garden,
and all their sorrows will be gone.
13 The young women will dance for joy,

30:17 Hebrew *Zion*. **31:6** Hebrew *Zion;* also in 31:12. **31:7** Hebrew *Jacob;* also in 31:11. See note on 5:20.

and the men—old and young—will join in the
celebration.
I will turn their mourning into joy.
I will comfort them and exchange their sorrow for
rejoicing.
14 The priests will enjoy abundance,
and my people will feast on my good gifts.
I, the LORD, have spoken!"

RACHEL'S SADNESS TURNS TO JOY

15 This is what the LORD says:

"A cry is heard in Ramah—
deep anguish and bitter weeping.
Rachel weeps for her children,
refusing to be comforted—
for her children are gone."

16 But now this is what the LORD says:
"Do not weep any longer,
for I will reward you," says the LORD.
"Your children will come back to you
from the distant land of the enemy.
17 There is hope for your future," says the LORD.
"Your children will come again to their own land.
18 I have heard Israel* saying,
'You disciplined me severely,
like a calf that needs training for the yoke.
Turn me again to you and restore me,
for you alone are the LORD my God.
19 I turned away from God,
but then I was sorry.
I kicked myself for my stupidity!
I was thoroughly ashamed of all I did in my
younger days.'

20 "Is not Israel still my son,
my darling child?" says the LORD.
"I often have to punish him,
but I still love him.
That's why I long for him
and surely will have mercy on him.
21 Set up road signs;
put up guideposts.
Mark well the path
by which you came.
Come back again, my virgin Israel;
return to your towns here.
22 How long will you wander,
my wayward daughter?
For the LORD will cause something new to happen—
Israel will embrace her God.*"

23 This is what the LORD of Heaven's Armies, the God of
Israel, says: "When I bring them back from captivity, the
people of Judah and its towns will again say, 'The LORD
bless you, O righteous home, O holy mountain!' 24 Townspeople and farmers and shepherds alike will live together
in peace and happiness. 25 For I have given rest to the
weary and joy to the sorrowing."

26 At this, I woke up and looked around. My sleep had
been very sweet.

27 "The day is coming," says the LORD, "when I will
greatly increase the human population and the number
of animals here in Israel and Judah. 28 In the past I deliberately uprooted and tore down this nation. I overthrew it,
destroyed it, and brought disaster upon it. But in the future I will just as deliberately plant it and build it up. I, the
LORD, have spoken!

29 "The people will no longer quote this proverb:

'The parents have eaten sour grapes,
but their children's mouths pucker at the taste.'

30 All people will die for their own sins—those who eat the
sour grapes will be the ones whose mouths will pucker.

31 "The day is coming," says the LORD, "when I will make
a new covenant with the people of Israel and Judah. 32 This
covenant will not be like the one I made with their ancestors when I took them by the hand and brought them out
of the land of Egypt. They broke that covenant, though I
loved them as a husband loves his wife," says the LORD.

REVOLUTION 31:33

The old covenant, broken by the people, would be replaced by a new covenant. The foundation of this new covenant is the promised Messiah. It's revolutionary, involving not only Israel, but also the Gentiles. It also involves a personal relationship with God, with his laws inscribed on the human heart instead of on stone tablets. Jeremiah looked forward to the day when the Messiah would come to establish this covenant. This covenant is already established through Christ (see Heb 8:6). He makes a relationship with God possible. Is this an offer you've accepted? ■

33 "But this is the new covenant I will make with the people of Israel on that day," says the LORD. "I will put my instructions deep within them, and I will write them on
their hearts. I will be their God, and they will be my people. 34 And they will not need to teach their neighbors, nor
will they need to teach their relatives, saying, 'You should
know the LORD.' For everyone, from the least to the greatest, will know me already," says the LORD. "And I will forgive their wickedness, and I will never again remember
their sins."

35 It is the LORD who provides the sun to light the day
and the moon and stars to light the night,
and who stirs the sea into roaring waves.
His name is the LORD of Heaven's Armies,
and this is what he says:
36 "I am as likely to reject my people Israel
as I am to abolish the laws of nature!"

31:18 Hebrew *Ephraim,* referring to the northern kingdom of Israel; also in 31:20. **31:22** Hebrew *a woman will court a suitor.*

37 This is what the LORD says:
"Just as the heavens cannot be measured
and the foundations of the earth cannot
be explored,
so I will not consider casting them away
for the evil they have done.
I, the LORD, have spoken!

38"The day is coming," says the LORD, "when all Jerusalem will be rebuilt for me, from the Tower of Hananel to the Corner Gate. 39A measuring line will be
stretched out over the hill of Gareb and across to Goah.
40And the entire area—including the graveyard and ash
dump in the valley, and all the fields out to the Kidron
Valley on the east as far as the Horse Gate—will be holy
to the LORD. The city will never again be captured or
destroyed."

32 JEREMIAH'S LAND PURCHASE

The following message came to Jeremiah from the LORD
in the tenth year of the reign of Zedekiah,* king of Judah.
This was also the eighteenth year of the reign of King
Nebuchadnezzar.* 2Jerusalem was then under siege
from the Babylonian army, and Jeremiah was imprisoned in the courtyard of the guard in the royal palace.
3King Zedekiah had put him there, asking why he kept
giving this prophecy: "This is what the LORD says: 'I am
about to hand this city over to the king of Babylon, and
he will take it. 4King Zedekiah will be captured by the
Babylonians* and taken to meet the king of Babylon face
to face. 5He will take Zedekiah to Babylon, and I will deal
with him there,' says the LORD. 'If you fight against the
Babylonians, you will never succeed.'"

TRUST 32:6-12

Trust doesn't come easy. It wasn't easy for Jeremiah to buy land already captured by the enemy. But he trusted God. It wasn't easy for David to think that he would become king, even after he was anointed. But he trusted God (1 Sam 16–30). It wasn't easy for Moses to believe that he and his people would escape Egypt, even after God spoke to him from a burning bush. But he trusted God (Exod 3:1–4:20). How about you? You can choose to trust or choose to doubt. ■

6At that time the LORD sent me a message. He said,
7"Your cousin Hanamel son of Shallum will come and say
to you, 'Buy my field at Anathoth. By law you have the
right to buy it before it is offered to anyone else.'"

8Then, just as the LORD had said he would, my cousin
Hanamel came and visited me in the prison. He said,
"Please buy my field at Anathoth in the land of Benjamin.
By law you have the right to buy it before it is offered to
anyone else, so buy it for yourself." Then I knew that the
message I had heard was from the LORD.

9So I bought the field at Anathoth, paying Hanamel
seventeen pieces* of silver for it. 10I signed and sealed
the deed of purchase before witnesses, weighed out the
silver, and paid him. 11Then I took the sealed deed and
an unsealed copy of the deed, which contained the
terms and conditions of the purchase, 12and I handed
them to Baruch son of Neriah and grandson of Mahseiah. I did all this in the presence of my cousin Hanamel,
the witnesses who had signed the deed, and all the men
of Judah who were there in the courtyard of the
guardhouse.

13Then I said to Baruch as they all listened, 14"This is
what the LORD of Heaven's Armies, the God of Israel, says:
'Take both this sealed deed and the unsealed copy, and
put them into a pottery jar to preserve them for a long
time.' 15For this is what the LORD of Heaven's Armies, the
God of Israel, says: 'Someday people will again own property here in this land and will buy and sell houses and
vineyards and fields.'"

JEREMIAH'S PRAYER

16Then after I had given the papers to Baruch, I prayed to
the LORD:

17"O Sovereign LORD! You made the heavens and earth
by your strong hand and powerful arm. Nothing is too
hard for you! 18You show unfailing love to thousands,
but you also bring the consequences of one generation's
sin upon the next. You are the great and powerful God,
the LORD of Heaven's Armies. 19You have all wisdom and
do great and mighty miracles. You see the conduct of all
people, and you give them what they deserve. 20You
performed miraculous signs and wonders in the land
of Egypt—things still remembered to this day! And you
have continued to do great miracles in Israel and all
around the world. You have made your name famous
to this day.

21"You brought Israel out of Egypt with mighty
signs and wonders, with a strong hand and powerful
arm, and with overwhelming terror. 22You gave the
people of Israel this land that you had promised their
ancestors long before—a land flowing with milk and
honey. 23Our ancestors came and conquered it and
lived in it, but they refused to obey you or follow your
word. They have not done anything you commanded.
That is why you have sent this terrible disaster upon
them.

24"See how the siege ramps have been built against
the city walls! Through war, famine, and disease, the
city will be handed over to the Babylonians, who will
conquer it. Everything has happened just as you said.
25And yet, O Sovereign LORD, you have told me to buy
the field—paying good money for it before these
witnesses—even though the city will soon be handed
over to the Babylonians."

32:1a The tenth year of Zedekiah's reign and the eighteenth year of Nebuchadnezzar's reign was 587 B.C. **32:1b** Hebrew *Nebuchadrezzar*, a variant spelling of Nebuchadnezzar; also in 32:28. **32:4** Or *Chaldeans;* also in 32:5, 24, 25, 28, 29, 43. **32:9** Hebrew *17 shekels*, about 7 ounces or 194 grams in weight.

A PREDICTION OF JERUSALEM'S FALL

26Then this message came to Jeremiah from the LORD:
27"I am the LORD, the God of all the peoples of the world.
Is anything too hard for me? 28Therefore, this is what the
LORD says: I will hand this city over to the Babylonians
and to Nebuchadnezzar, king of Babylon, and he will capture it. 29The Babylonians outside the walls will come in
and set fire to the city. They will burn down all these
houses where the people provoked my anger by burning
incense to Baal on the rooftops and by pouring out liquid
offerings to other gods. 30Israel and Judah have done
nothing but wrong since their earliest days. They have infuriated me with all their evil deeds," says the LORD.
31"From the time this city was built until now, it has done
nothing but anger me, so I am determined to get rid of it.
32"The sins of Israel and Judah—the sins of the people
of Jerusalem, the kings, the officials, the priests, and the
prophets—have stirred up my anger. 33My people have
turned their backs on me and have refused to return.
Even though I diligently taught them, they would not receive instruction or obey. 34They have set up their abominable idols right in my own Temple, defiling it. 35They
have built pagan shrines to Baal in the valley of Ben-
Hinnom, and there they sacrifice their sons and daughters to Molech. I have never commanded such a horrible
deed; it never even crossed my mind to command such a
thing. What an incredible evil, causing Judah to sin so
greatly!

A PROMISE OF RESTORATION

36"Now I want to say something more about this city. You
have been saying, 'It will fall to the king of Babylon
through war, famine, and disease.' But this is what the
LORD, the God of Israel, says: 37I will certainly bring my
people back again from all the countries where I will
scatter them in my fury. I will bring them back to this very
city and let them live in peace and safety. 38They will be
my people, and I will be their God. 39And I will give them
one heart and one purpose: to worship me forever, for
their own good and for the good of all their descendants.
40And I will make an everlasting covenant with them: I
will never stop doing good for them. I will put a desire in
their hearts to worship me, and they will never leave me.
41I will find joy doing good for them and will faithfully
and wholeheartedly replant them in this land.
42"This is what the LORD says: Just as I have brought all
these calamities on them, so I will do all the good I have
promised them. 43Fields will again be bought and sold in
this land about which you now say, 'It has been ravaged
by the Babylonians, a desolate land where people and
animals have all disappeared.' 44Yes, fields will once
again be bought and sold—deeds signed and sealed and
witnessed—in the land of Benjamin and here in Jerusalem, in the towns of Judah and in the hill country, in the
foothills of Judah* and in the Negev, too. For someday I
will restore prosperity to them. I, the LORD, have
spoken!"

33

PROMISES OF PEACE AND PROSPERITY

While Jeremiah was still confined in the courtyard of the
guard, the LORD gave him this second message: 2"This is
what the LORD says—the LORD who made the earth, who
formed and established it, whose name is the LORD: 3Ask
me and I will tell you remarkable secrets you do not know
about things to come. 4For this is what the LORD, the God
of Israel, says: You have torn down the houses of this city
and even the king's palace to get materials to strengthen
the walls against the siege ramps and swords of the enemy. 5You expect to fight the Babylonians,* but the men
of this city are already as good as dead, for I have determined to destroy them in my terrible anger. I have abandoned them because of all their wickedness.
6"Nevertheless, the time will come when I will heal Jerusalem's wounds and give it prosperity and true peace.
7I will restore the fortunes of Judah and Israel and rebuild their towns. 8I will cleanse them of their sins
against me and forgive all their sins of rebellion. 9Then
this city will bring me joy, glory, and honor before all the
nations of the earth! The people of the world will see all
the good I do for my people, and they will tremble with
awe at the peace and prosperity I provide for them.
10"This is what the LORD says: You have said, 'This is a
desolate land where people and animals have all disappeared.' Yet in the empty streets of Jerusalem and Judah's other towns, there will be heard once more 11the
sounds of joy and laughter. The joyful voices of bridegrooms and brides will be heard again, along with the joyous songs of people bringing thanksgiving offerings to
the LORD. They will sing,

'Give thanks to the LORD of Heaven's Armies,
for the LORD is good.
His faithful love endures forever!'

For I will restore the prosperity of this land to what it was
in the past, says the LORD.
12"This is what the LORD of Heaven's Armies says: This
land—though it is now desolate and has no people and
animals—will once more have pastures where shepherds
can lead their flocks. 13Once again shepherds will count
their flocks in the towns of the hill country, the foothills
of Judah,* the Negev, the land of Benjamin, the vicinity
of Jerusalem, and all the towns of Judah. I, the LORD,
have spoken!
14"The day will come, says the LORD, when I will do for
Israel and Judah all the good things I have promised
them.

15 "In those days and at that time
I will raise up a righteous descendant* from
King David's line.
He will do what is just and right throughout
the land.
16 In that day Judah will be saved,
and Jerusalem will live in safety.

32:44 Hebrew *the Shephelah.* 33:5 Or *Chaldeans.* 33:13 Hebrew *the Shephelah.* 33:15 Hebrew *a righteous branch.*

And this will be its name:
'The LORD Is Our Righteousness.'*

17For this is what the LORD says: David will have a descendant sitting on the throne of Israel forever. 18And there will always be Levitical priests to offer burnt offerings and grain offerings and sacrifices to me."

19Then this message came to Jeremiah from the LORD: 20"This is what the LORD says: If you can break my covenant with the day and the night so that one does not follow the other, 21only then will my covenant with my servant David be broken. Only then will he no longer have a descendant to reign on his throne. The same is true for my covenant with the Levitical priests who minister before me. 22And as the stars of the sky cannot be counted and the sand on the seashore cannot be measured, so I will multiply the descendants of my servant David and the Levites who minister before me."

23The LORD gave another message to Jeremiah. He said, 24"Have you noticed what people are saying?—'The LORD chose Judah and Israel and then abandoned them!' They are sneering and saying that Israel is not worthy to be counted as a nation. 25But this is what the LORD says: I would no more reject my people than I would change my laws that govern night and day, earth and sky. 26I will never abandon the descendants of Jacob or David, my servant, or change the plan that David's descendants will rule the descendants of Abraham, Isaac, and Jacob. Instead, I will restore them to their land and have mercy on them."

34

A WARNING FOR ZEDEKIAH

King Nebuchadnezzar of Babylon came with all the armies from the kingdoms he ruled, and he fought against Jerusalem and the towns of Judah. At that time this message came to Jeremiah from the LORD: 2"Go to King Zedekiah of Judah, and tell him, 'This is what the LORD, the God of Israel, says: I am about to hand this city over to the king of Babylon, and he will burn it down. 3You will not escape his grasp but will be captured and taken to meet the king of Babylon face to face. Then you will be exiled to Babylon.

4"'But listen to this promise from the LORD, O Zedekiah, king of Judah. This is what the LORD says: You will not be killed in war 5but will die peacefully. People will burn incense in your memory, just as they did for your ancestors, the kings who preceded you. They will mourn for you, crying, "Alas, our master is dead!" This I have decreed, says the LORD.'"

6So Jeremiah the prophet delivered the message to King Zedekiah of Judah. 7At this time the Babylonian army was besieging Jerusalem, Lachish, and Azekah—the only fortified cities of Judah not yet captured.

FREEDOM FOR HEBREW SLAVES

8This message came to Jeremiah from the LORD after King Zedekiah made a covenant with the people, proclaiming freedom for the slaves. 9He had ordered all the people to free their Hebrew slaves—both men and women. No one was to keep a fellow Judean in bondage. 10The officials and all the people had obeyed the king's command, 11but later they changed their minds. They took back the men and women they had freed, forcing them to be slaves again.

12So the LORD gave them this message through Jeremiah: 13"This is what the LORD, the God of Israel, says: I made a covenant with your ancestors long ago when I rescued them from their slavery in Egypt. 14I told them that every Hebrew slave must be freed after serving six years. But your ancestors paid no attention to me. 15Recently you repented and did what was right, following my command. You freed your slaves and made a solemn covenant with me in the Temple that bears my name. 16But now you have shrugged off your oath and defiled my name by taking back the men and women you had freed, forcing them to be slaves once again.

17"Therefore, this is what the LORD says: Since you have not obeyed me by setting your countrymen free, I will set you free to be destroyed by war, disease, and famine. You will be an object of horror to all the nations of the earth. 18Because you have broken the terms of our covenant, I will cut you apart just as you cut apart the calf when you walked between its halves to solemnize your vows. 19Yes, I will cut you apart, whether you are officials of Judah or Jerusalem, court officials, priests, or common people—for you have broken your oath. 20I will give you to your enemies, and they will kill you. Your bodies will be food for the vultures and wild animals.

21"I will hand over King Zedekiah of Judah and his officials to the army of the king of Babylon. And although Babylon's king has left Jerusalem for a while, 22I will call the Babylonian armies back again. They will fight against this city and will capture it and burn it down. I will see to it that all the towns of Judah are destroyed, with no one living there."

35

THE FAITHFUL RECABITES

This is the message the LORD gave Jeremiah when Jehoiakim son of Josiah was king of Judah: 2"Go to the settlement where the families of the Recabites live, and invite them to the LORD's Temple. Take them into one of the inner rooms, and offer them some wine."

3So I went to see Jaazaniah son of Jeremiah and grandson of Habazziniah and all his brothers and sons—representing all the Recabite families. 4I took them to the Temple, and we went into the room assigned to the sons of Hanan son of Igdaliah, a man of God. This room was located next to the one used by the Temple officials, directly above the room of Maaseiah son of Shallum, the Temple gatekeeper.

5I set cups and jugs of wine before them and invited them to have a drink, 6but they refused. "No," they said, "we don't drink wine, because our ancestor Jehonadab* son of Recab gave us this command: 'You and your descendants must never drink wine. 7And do not build houses or plant crops or vineyards, but always live in tents. If you follow

33:16 Hebrew *Yahweh Tsidqenu*. **35:6** Hebrew *Jonadab*, a variant spelling of Jehonadab; also in 35:10, 14, 16, 18, 19. See 2 Kgs 10:15.

these commands, you will live long, good lives in the land.' 8 So we have obeyed him in all these things. We have never had a drink of wine to this day, nor have our wives, our sons, or our daughters. 9 We haven't built houses or owned vineyards or farms or planted crops. 10 We have lived in tents and have fully obeyed all the commands of Jehonadab, our ancestor. 11 But when King Nebuchadnezzar* of Babylon attacked this country, we were afraid of the Babylonian and Syrian* armies. So we decided to move to Jerusalem. That is why we are here."

12 Then the LORD gave this message to Jeremiah: 13 "This is what the LORD of Heaven's Armies, the God of Israel, says: Go and say to the people in Judah and Jerusalem, 'Come and learn a lesson about how to obey me. 14 The Recabites do not drink wine to this day because their ancestor Jehonadab told them not to. But I have spoken to you again and again, and you refuse to obey me. 15 Time after time I sent you prophets, who told you, "Turn from your wicked ways, and start doing things right. Stop worshiping other gods so that you might live in peace here in the land I have given to you and your ancestors." But you would not listen to me or obey me. 16 The descendants of Jehonadab son of Recab have obeyed their ancestor completely, but you have refused to listen to me.'

WHY OBEY? 35:1-17

Consider the contrast between the Recabites and the other Israelites: (1) The Recabites kept their vows to a fallible human leader; Israel broke their covenant with their infallible divine Leader. (2) Jehonadab told his family once not to drink and they didn't; God continually commanded Israel to turn from sin and they refused. (3) The Recabites obeyed laws dealing with temporal issues; Israel disobeyed God's laws dealing with eternal issues. (4) The Recabites would be rewarded; Israel would be punished. Often we observe customs because of tradition. But God's Word is eternal. Isn't it worth believing and obeying? ■

17 "Therefore, this is what the LORD God of Heaven's Armies, the God of Israel, says: 'Because you refuse to listen or answer when I call, I will send upon Judah and Jerusalem all the disasters I have threatened.'"

18 Then Jeremiah turned to the Recabites and said, "This is what the LORD of Heaven's Armies, the God of Israel, says: 'You have obeyed your ancestor Jehonadab in every respect, following all his instructions.' 19 Therefore, this is what the LORD of Heaven's Armies, the God of Israel, says: 'Jehonadab son of Recab will always have descendants who serve me.'"

36 BARUCH READS THE LORD'S MESSAGES

During the fourth year that Jehoiakim son of Josiah was king in Judah,* the LORD gave this message to Jeremiah: 2 "Get a scroll, and write down all my messages against Israel, Judah, and the other nations. Begin with the first message back in the days of Josiah, and write down every message, right up to the present time. 3 Perhaps the people of Judah will repent when they hear again all the terrible things I have planned for them. Then I will be able to forgive their sins and wrongdoings."

4 So Jeremiah sent for Baruch son of Neriah, and as Jeremiah dictated all the prophecies that the LORD had given him, Baruch wrote them on a scroll. 5 Then Jeremiah said to Baruch, "I am a prisoner here and unable to go to the Temple. 6 So you go to the Temple on the next day of fasting, and read the messages from the LORD that I have had you write on this scroll. Read them so the people who are there from all over Judah will hear them. 7 Perhaps even yet they will turn from their evil ways and ask the LORD's forgiveness before it is too late. For the LORD has threatened them with his terrible anger."

FASTING TO FOCUS 36:9

Days of fasting often were called at times of national emergency. At such times, the people abstained from eating food and concentrated on prayer and worship. Fasting is one of the spiritual disciplines—a way to deny self and concentrate on God. It is also a time of preparation. Moses fasted for 40 days while God talked with him on Mt. Sinai (Exod 24:18). Jesus fasted 40 days at the beginning of his ministry (Matt 4:1-2). In what ways do you deny self in order to focus on God? ■

8 Baruch did as Jeremiah told him and read these messages from the LORD to the people at the Temple. 9 He did this on a day of sacred fasting held in late autumn,* during the fifth year of the reign of Jehoiakim son of Josiah. People from all over Judah had come to Jerusalem to attend the services at the Temple on that day. 10 Baruch read Jeremiah's words on the scroll to all the people. He stood in front of the Temple room of Gemariah, son of Shaphan the secretary. This room was just off the upper courtyard of the Temple, near the New Gate entrance.

11 When Micaiah son of Gemariah and grandson of Shaphan heard the messages from the LORD, 12 he went down to the secretary's room in the palace where the administrative officials were meeting. Elishama the secretary was there, along with Delaiah son of Shemaiah, Elnathan son of Acbor, Gemariah son of Shaphan, Zedekiah son of Hananiah, and all the other officials. 13 When Micaiah told them about the messages Baruch was reading to the people, 14 the officials sent Jehudi son of Nethaniah, grandson of Shelemiah and great-grandson of Cushi, to ask Baruch to come and read the messages to them, too. So Baruch took the scroll and went to them. 15 "Sit down and read the scroll to us," the officials said, and Baruch did as they requested.

35:11a Hebrew *Nebuchadrezzar,* a variant spelling of Nebuchadnezzar. **35:11b** Or *Chaldean and Aramean.* **36:1** The fourth year of Jehoiakim's reign was 605 B.C. **36:9** Hebrew *in the ninth month,* of the ancient Hebrew lunar calendar (also in 36:22). The ninth month in the fifth year of Jehoiakim's reign occurred within the months of November and December 604 B.C. Also see note on 1:3.

16When they heard all the messages, they looked at one another in alarm. "We must tell the king what we have heard," they said to Baruch. 17"But first, tell us how you got these messages. Did they come directly from Jeremiah?"
18So Baruch explained, "Jeremiah dictated them, and I wrote them down in ink, word for word, on this scroll."
19"You and Jeremiah should both hide," the officials told Baruch. "Don't tell anyone where you are!" 20Then the officials left the scroll for safekeeping in the room of Elishama the secretary and went to tell the king what had happened.

GOD'S WORD 36:21-32

Although King Jehoiakim burned Jeremiah's scroll, he couldn't destroy God's Word. Today many people try to put God's Word aside, or say that it contains errors and cannot be trusted. People may reject God's Word, but they cannot destroy it. God's Word will stand forever (Ps 119:89). ■

KING JEHOIAKIM BURNS THE SCROLL

21The king sent Jehudi to get the scroll. Jehudi brought it from Elishama's room and read it to the king as all his officials stood by. 22It was late autumn, and the king was in a winterized part of the palace, sitting in front of a fire to keep warm. 23Each time Jehudi finished reading three or four columns, the king took a knife and cut off that section of the scroll. He then threw it into the fire, section by section, until the whole scroll was burned up. 24Neither the king nor his attendants showed any signs of fear or repentance at what they heard. 25Even when Elnathan, Delaiah, and Gemariah begged the king not to burn the scroll, he wouldn't listen.
26Then the king commanded his son Jerahmeel, Seraiah son of Azriel, and Shelemiah son of Abdeel to arrest Baruch and Jeremiah. But the LORD had hidden them.

JEREMIAH REWRITES THE SCROLL

27After the king had burned the scroll on which Baruch had written Jeremiah's words, the LORD gave Jeremiah another message. He said, 28"Get another scroll, and write everything again just as you did on the scroll King Jehoiakim burned. 29Then say to the king, 'This is what the LORD says: You burned the scroll because it said the king of Babylon would destroy this land and empty it of people and animals. 30Now this is what the LORD says about King Jehoiakim of Judah: He will have no heirs to sit on the throne of David. His dead body will be thrown out to lie unburied—exposed to the heat of the day and the frost of the night. 31I will punish him and his family and his attendants for their sins. I will pour out on them and on all the people of Jerusalem and Judah all the disasters I promised, for they would not listen to my warnings.'"
32So Jeremiah took another scroll and dictated again to his secretary, Baruch. He wrote everything that had been on the scroll King Jehoiakim had burned in the fire. Only this time he added much more!

37 ZEDEKIAH CALLS FOR JEREMIAH

Zedekiah son of Josiah succeeded Jehoiachin* son of Jehoiakim as the king of Judah. He was appointed by King Nebuchadnezzar* of Babylon. 2But neither King Zedekiah nor his attendants nor the people who were left in the land listened to what the LORD said through Jeremiah.
3Nevertheless, King Zedekiah sent Jehucal son of Shelemiah, and Zephaniah the priest, son of Maaseiah, to ask Jeremiah, "Please pray to the LORD our God for us." 4Jeremiah had not yet been imprisoned, so he could come and go among the people as he pleased.
5At this time the army of Pharaoh Hophra* of Egypt appeared at the southern border of Judah. When the Babylonian* army heard about it, they withdrew from their siege of Jerusalem.
6Then the LORD gave this message to Jeremiah: 7"This is what the LORD, the God of Israel, says: The king of Judah sent you to ask me what is going to happen. Tell him, 'Pharaoh's army is about to return to Egypt, though he came here to help you. 8Then the Babylonians* will come back and capture this city and burn it to the ground.'
9"This is what the LORD says: Do not fool yourselves into thinking that the Babylonians are gone for good. They aren't! 10Even if you were to destroy the entire Babylonian army, leaving only a handful of wounded survivors, they would still stagger from their tents and burn this city to the ground!"

JEREMIAH IS IMPRISONED

11When the Babylonian army left Jerusalem because of Pharaoh's approaching army, 12Jeremiah started to leave the city on his way to the territory of Benjamin, to claim his share of the property among his relatives there.*
13But as he was walking through the Benjamin Gate, a sentry arrested him and said, "You are defecting to the Babylonians!" The sentry making the arrest was Irijah son of Shelemiah, grandson of Hananiah.
14"That's not true!" Jeremiah protested. "I had no intention of doing any such thing." But Irijah wouldn't listen, and he took Jeremiah before the officials. 15They were furious with Jeremiah and had him flogged and imprisoned in the house of Jonathan the secretary. Jonathan's house had been converted into a prison. 16Jeremiah was put into a dungeon cell, where he remained for many days.
17Later King Zedekiah secretly requested that Jeremiah come to the palace, where the king asked him, "Do you have any messages from the LORD?"
"Yes, I do!" said Jeremiah. "You will be defeated by the king of Babylon."
18Then Jeremiah asked the king, "What crime have I committed? What have I done against you, your attendants, or the people that I should be imprisoned like this?

37:1a Hebrew *Coniah*, a variant spelling of Jehoiachin. **37:1b** Hebrew *Nebuchadrezzar*, a variant spelling of Nebuchadnezzar. **37:5a** Hebrew *army of Pharaoh;* see 44:30. **37:5b** Or *Chaldean;* also in 37:10, 11. **37:8** Or *Chaldeans;* also in 37:9, 13. **37:12** Hebrew *to separate from there in the midst of the people.*

19Where are your prophets now who told you the king of Babylon would not attack you or this land? 20Listen, my lord the king, I beg you. Don't send me back to the dungeon in the house of Jonathan the secretary, for I will die there."

21So King Zedekiah commanded that Jeremiah not be returned to the dungeon. Instead, he was imprisoned in the courtyard of the guard in the royal palace. The king also commanded that Jeremiah be given a loaf of fresh bread every day as long as there was any left in the city. So Jeremiah was put in the palace prison.

38

JEREMIAH IN A CISTERN

Now Shephatiah son of Mattan, Gedaliah son of Pashhur, Jehucal* son of Shelemiah, and Pashhur son of Malkijah heard what Jeremiah had been telling the people. He had been saying, 2"This is what the LORD says: 'Everyone who stays in Jerusalem will die from war, famine, or disease, but those who surrender to the Babylonians* will live. Their reward will be life. They will live!' 3The LORD also says: 'The city of Jerusalem will certainly be handed over to the army of the king of Babylon, who will capture it.'"

4So these officials went to the king and said, "Sir, this man must die! That kind of talk will undermine the morale of the few fighting men we have left, as well as that of all the people. This man is a traitor!"

5King Zedekiah agreed. "All right," he said. "Do as you like. I can't stop you."

6So the officials took Jeremiah from his cell and lowered him by ropes into an empty cistern in the prison yard. It belonged to Malkijah, a member of the royal family. There was no water in the cistern, but there was a thick layer of mud at the bottom, and Jeremiah sank down into it.

THE COURAGE TO STAND ALONE 38:9-13

Ebed-melech feared God more than man. He alone among the palace officials stood up against the murder plot. His obedience could have cost him his life. Because he risked his life to save Jeremiah, he was spared when Jerusalem fell (39:15-18). Would you do the same? Standing alone can be difficult. But God willingly provides the courage to do what's right. Just ask him for it. ■

7But Ebed-melech the Ethiopian,* an important court official, heard that Jeremiah was in the cistern. At that time the king was holding court at the Benjamin Gate, 8so Ebed-melech rushed from the palace to speak with him. 9"My lord the king," he said, "these men have done a very evil thing in putting Jeremiah the prophet into the cistern. He will soon die of hunger, for almost all the bread in the city is gone."

10So the king told Ebed-melech, "Take thirty of my men with you, and pull Jeremiah out of the cistern before he dies."

11So Ebed-melech took the men with him and went to a room in the palace beneath the treasury, where he found some old rags and discarded clothing. He carried these to the cistern and lowered them to Jeremiah on a rope. 12Ebed-melech called down to Jeremiah, "Put these rags under your armpits to protect you from the ropes." Then when Jeremiah was ready, 13they pulled him out. So Jeremiah was returned to the courtyard of the guard—the palace prison—where he remained.

ZEDEKIAH QUESTIONS JEREMIAH

14One day King Zedekiah sent for Jeremiah and had him brought to the third entrance of the LORD's Temple. "I want to ask you something," the king said. "And don't try to hide the truth."

15Jeremiah said, "If I tell you the truth, you will kill me. And if I give you advice, you won't listen to me anyway."

16So King Zedekiah secretly promised him, "As surely as the LORD our Creator lives, I will not kill you or hand you over to the men who want you dead."

17Then Jeremiah said to Zedekiah, "This is what the LORD God of Heaven's Armies, the God of Israel, says: 'If you surrender to the Babylonian officers, you and your family will live, and the city will not be burned down. 18But if you refuse to surrender, you will not escape! This city will be handed over to the Babylonians, and they will burn it to the ground.'"

19"But I am afraid to surrender," the king said, "for the Babylonians may hand me over to the Judeans who have defected to them. And who knows what they will do to me!"

20Jeremiah replied, "You won't be handed over to them if you choose to obey the LORD. Your life will be spared, and all will go well for you. 21But if you refuse to surrender, this is what the LORD has revealed to me: 22All the women left in your palace will be brought out and given to the officers of the Babylonian army. Then the women will taunt you, saying,

'What fine friends you have!
 They have betrayed and misled you.
When your feet sank in the mud,
 they left you to your fate!'

23All your wives and children will be led out to the Babylonians, and you will not escape. You will be seized by the king of Babylon, and this city will be burned down."

24Then Zedekiah said to Jeremiah, "Don't tell anyone you told me this, or you will die! 25My officials may hear that I spoke to you, and they may say, 'Tell us what you and the king were talking about. If you don't tell us, we will kill you.' 26If this happens, just tell them you begged me not to send you back to Jonathan's dungeon, for fear you would die there."

27Sure enough, it wasn't long before the king's officials came to Jeremiah and asked him why the king had called for him. But Jeremiah followed the king's instructions, and they left without finding out the truth. No one had

38:1 Hebrew *Jucal,* a variant spelling of Jehucal; see 37:3. **38:2** Or *Chaldeans;* also in 38:18, 19, 23. **38:7** Hebrew *the Cushite.*

overheard the conversation between Jeremiah and the king. [28]And Jeremiah remained a prisoner in the courtyard of the guard until the day Jerusalem was captured.

39

THE FALL OF JERUSALEM

In January* of the ninth year of King Zedekiah's reign, King Nebuchadnezzar* came with his army to besiege Jerusalem. [2]Two and a half years later, on July 18* in the eleventh year of Zedekiah's reign, the Babylonians broke through the wall, and the city fell. [3]All the officers of the Babylonian army came in and sat in triumph at the Middle Gate: Nergal-sharezer of Samgar, and Nebo-sarsekim,* a chief officer, and Nergal-sharezer, the king's adviser, and all the other officers.

[4]When King Zedekiah and all the soldiers saw that the Babylonians had broken into the city, they fled. They waited for nightfall and then slipped through the gate between the two walls behind the king's garden and headed toward the Jordan Valley.*

[5]But the Babylonian* troops chased the king and caught him on the plains of Jericho. They took him to King Nebuchadnezzar of Babylon, who was at Riblah in the land of Hamath. There the king of Babylon pronounced judgment upon Zedekiah. [6]He made Zedekiah watch as they slaughtered his sons and all the nobles of Judah. [7]Then they gouged out Zedekiah's eyes, bound him in bronze chains, and led him away to Babylon.

[8]Meanwhile, the Babylonians burned Jerusalem, including the palace, and tore down the walls of the city. [9]Then Nebuzaradan, the captain of the guard, sent to Babylon the rest of the people who remained in the city as well as those who had defected to him. [10]But Nebuzaradan left a few of the poorest people in Judah, and he assigned them vineyards and fields to care for.

JEREMIAH REMAINS IN JUDAH

[11]King Nebuchadnezzar had told Nebuzaradan, the captain of the guard, to find Jeremiah. [12]"See that he isn't hurt," he said. "Look after him well, and give him anything he wants." [13]So Nebuzaradan, the captain of the guard; Nebushazban, a chief officer; Nergal-sharezer, the king's adviser; and the other officers of Babylon's king [14]sent messengers to bring Jeremiah out of the prison. They put him under the care of Gedaliah son of Ahikam and grandson of Shaphan, who took him back to his home. So Jeremiah stayed in Judah among his own people.

[15]The LORD had given the following message to Jeremiah while he was still in prison: [16]"Say to Ebed-melech the Ethiopian,* 'This is what the LORD of Heaven's Armies, the God of Israel, says: I will do to this city everything I have threatened. I will send disaster, not prosperity. You will see its destruction, [17]but I will rescue you from those you fear so much. [18]Because you trusted me, I will give you your life as a reward. I will rescue you and keep you safe. I, the LORD, have spoken!'"

40

The LORD gave a message to Jeremiah after Nebuzaradan, the captain of the guard, had released him at Ramah. He had found Jeremiah bound in chains among all the other captives of Jerusalem and Judah who were being sent to exile in Babylon.

[2]The captain of the guard called for Jeremiah and said, "The LORD your God has brought this disaster on this land, [3]just as he said he would. For these people have sinned against the LORD and disobeyed him. That is why it happened. [4]But I am going to take off your chains and let you go. If you want to come with me to Babylon, you are welcome. I will see that you are well cared for. But if you don't want to come, you may stay here. The whole land is before you—go wherever you like. [5]If you decide to stay, then return to Gedaliah son of Ahikam and grandson of Shaphan. He has been appointed governor of Judah by the king of Babylon. Stay there with the people he rules. But it's up to you; go wherever you like."

KNOW HIM 40:1-3

The Babylonian captain, who did not know God, acknowledged that God had given the Babylonians victory. Many people recognize that God exists and does miracles, yet they fail to have a relationship with him. Do you know God or know about him? There's a big difference! ■

Then Nebuzaradan, the captain of the guard, gave Jeremiah some food and money and let him go. [6]So Jeremiah returned to Gedaliah son of Ahikam at Mizpah, and he lived in Judah with the few who were still left in the land.

GEDALIAH GOVERNS IN JUDAH

[7]The leaders of the Judean guerrilla bands in the countryside heard that the king of Babylon had appointed Gedaliah son of Ahikam as governor over the poor people who were left behind in Judah—the men, women, and children who hadn't been exiled to Babylon. [8]So they went to see Gedaliah at Mizpah. These included: Ishmael son of Nethaniah, Johanan and Jonathan sons of Kareah, Seraiah son of Tanhumeth, the sons of Ephai the Netophathite, Jezaniah son of the Maacathite, and all their men.

[9]Gedaliah vowed to them that the Babylonians* meant them no harm. "Don't be afraid to serve them. Live in the land and serve the king of Babylon, and all will go well for you," he promised. [10]"As for me, I will stay at Mizpah to represent you before the Babylonians who come to meet with us. Settle in the towns you have taken, and live off

39:1a Hebrew *in the tenth month,* of the ancient Hebrew lunar calendar. A number of events in Jeremiah can be cross-checked with dates in surviving Babylonian records and related accurately to our modern calendar. This event occurred on January 15, 588 B.C.; see 52:4a and the note there. **39:1b** Hebrew *Nebuchadrezzar,* a variant spelling of Nebuchadnezzar; also in 39:11. **39:2** Hebrew *On the ninth day of the fourth month.* This day was July 18, 586 B.C.; also see note on 39:1a. **39:3** Or *Nergal-sharezer, Samgar-nebo, Sarsekim.* **39:4** Hebrew *the Arabah.* **39:5** Or *Chaldean;* similarly in 39:8. **39:16** Hebrew *the Cushite.* **40:9** Or *Chaldeans;* also in 40:10.

the land. Harvest the grapes and summer fruits and
olives, and store them away."
11When the Judeans in Moab, Ammon, Edom, and the
other nearby countries heard that the king of Babylon
had left a few people in Judah and that Gedaliah was the
governor, 12they began to return to Judah from the places
to which they had fled. They stopped at Mizpah to meet
with Gedaliah and then went into the Judean countryside
to gather a great harvest of grapes and other crops.

A PLOT AGAINST GEDALIAH

13Soon after this, Johanan son of Kareah and the other
guerrilla leaders came to Gedaliah at Mizpah. 14They said
to him, "Did you know that Baalis, king of Ammon, has
sent Ishmael son of Nethaniah to assassinate you?" But
Gedaliah refused to believe them.
15Later Johanan had a private conference with Gedaliah and volunteered to kill Ishmael secretly. "Why should
we let him come and murder you?" Johanan asked.
"What will happen then to the Judeans who have returned? Why should the few of us who are still left be
scattered and lost?"
16But Gedaliah said to Johanan, "I forbid you to do any
such thing, for you are lying about Ishmael."

41 THE MURDER OF GEDALIAH

But in midautumn,* Ishmael son of Nethaniah and
grandson of Elishama, who was a member of the royal
family and had been one of the king's high officials, went
to Mizpah with ten men to meet Gedaliah. While they
were eating together, 2Ishmael and his ten men suddenly
jumped up, drew their swords, and killed Gedaliah,
whom the king of Babylon had appointed governor. 3Ish-
mael also killed all the Judeans and the Babylonian* soldiers who were with Gedaliah at Mizpah.
4The next day, before anyone had heard about Gedaliah's murder, 5eighty men arrived from Shechem, Shiloh,
and Samaria to worship at the Temple of the LORD. They
had shaved off their beards, torn their clothes, and cut
themselves, and had brought along grain offerings and
frankincense. 6Ishmael left Mizpah to meet them, weeping as he went. When he reached them, he said, "Oh,
come and see what has happened to Gedaliah!"
7But as soon as they were all inside the town, Ishmael
and his men killed all but ten of them and threw their
bodies into a cistern. 8The other ten had talked Ishmael
into letting them go by promising to bring him their
stores of wheat, barley, olive oil, and honey that they had
hidden away. 9The cistern where Ishmael dumped the
bodies of the men he murdered was the large one dug by
King Asa when he fortified Mizpah to protect himself
against King Baasha of Israel. Ishmael son of Nethaniah
filled it with corpses.
10Then Ishmael made captives of the king's daughters
and the other people who had been left under Gedaliah's
care in Mizpah by Nebuzaradan, the captain of the guard.
Taking them with him, he started back toward the land of
Ammon.
11But when Johanan son of Kareah and the other guerrilla leaders heard about Ishmael's crimes, 12they took all
their men and set out to stop him. They caught up with
him at the large pool near Gibeon. 13The people Ishmael
had captured shouted for joy when they saw Johanan and
the other guerrilla leaders. 14And all the captives from
Mizpah escaped and began to help Johanan. 15Meanwhile,
Ishmael and eight of his men escaped from Johanan into
the land of Ammon.
16Then Johanan son of Kareah and the other guerrilla
leaders took all the people they had rescued in Gibeon—
the soldiers, women, children, and court officials* whom
Ishmael had captured after he killed Gedaliah. 17They
took them all to the village of Geruth-kimham near Bethlehem, where they prepared to leave for Egypt. 18They
were afraid of what the Babylonians* would do when
they heard that Ishmael had killed Gedaliah, the governor
appointed by the Babylonian king.

42 WARNING TO STAY IN JUDAH

Then all the guerrilla leaders, including Johanan son of
Kareah and Jezaniah* son of Hoshaiah, and all the people, from the least to the greatest, approached 2Jeremiah
the prophet. They said, "Please pray to the LORD your God
for us. As you can see, we are only a tiny remnant compared to what we were before. 3Pray that the LORD your
God will show us what to do and where to go."
4"All right," Jeremiah replied. "I will pray to the LORD
your God, as you have asked, and I will tell you everything
he says. I will hide nothing from you."
5Then they said to Jeremiah, "May the LORD your God
be a faithful witness against us if we refuse to obey whatever he tells us to do! 6Whether we like it or not, we will
obey the LORD our God to whom we are sending you with
our plea. For if we obey him, everything will turn out well
for us."
7Ten days later the LORD gave his reply to Jeremiah. 8So
he called for Johanan son of Kareah and the other guerrilla leaders, and for all the people, from the least to the
greatest. 9He said to them, "You sent me to the LORD, the
God of Israel, with your request, and this is his reply:
10'Stay here in this land. If you do, I will build you up and
not tear you down; I will plant you and not uproot you. For
I am sorry about all the punishment I have had to bring
upon you. 11Do not fear the king of Babylon anymore,'
says the LORD. 'For I am with you and will save you and
rescue you from his power. 12I will be merciful to you by
making him kind, so he will let you stay here in your land.'
13"But if you refuse to obey the LORD your God, and if
you say, 'We will not stay here; 14instead, we will go to
Egypt where we will be free from war, the call to arms,
and hunger,' 15then hear the LORD's message to the remnant of Judah. This is what the LORD of Heaven's Armies,
the God of Israel, says: 'If you are determined to go to

41:1 Hebrew *in the seventh month,* of the ancient Hebrew lunar calendar. This month occurred within the months of October and November 586 B.C.; also see note on 39:1a. **41:3** Or *Chaldean.* **41:16** Or *eunuchs.* **41:18** Or *Chaldeans.* **42:1** Greek version reads *Azariah;* compare 43:2.

Egypt and live there, 16the very war and famine you fear will catch up to you, and you will die there. 17That is the fate awaiting every one of you who insists on going to live in Egypt. Yes, you will die from war, famine, and disease. None of you will escape the disaster I will bring upon you there.'

18"This is what the LORD of Heaven's Armies, the God of Israel, says: 'Just as my anger and fury have been poured out on the people of Jerusalem, so they will be poured out on you when you enter Egypt. You will be an object of damnation, horror, cursing, and mockery. And you will never see your homeland again.'

19"Listen, you remnant of Judah. The LORD has told you: 'Do not go to Egypt!' Don't forget this warning I have given you today. 20For you were not being honest when you sent me to pray to the LORD your God for you. You said, 'Just tell us what the LORD our God says, and we will do it!' 21And today I have told you exactly what he said, but you will not obey the LORD your God any better now than you have in the past. 22So you can be sure that you will die from war, famine, and disease in Egypt, where you insist on going."

43

JEREMIAH TAKEN TO EGYPT

When Jeremiah had finished giving this message from the LORD their God to all the people, 2Azariah son of Hoshaiah and Johanan son of Kareah and all the other proud men said to Jeremiah, "You lie! The LORD our God hasn't forbidden us to go to Egypt! 3Baruch son of Neriah has convinced you to say this, because he wants us to stay here and be killed by the Babylonians* or be carried off into exile."

4So Johanan and the other guerrilla leaders and all the people refused to obey the LORD's command to stay in Judah. 5Johanan and the other leaders took with them all the people who had returned from the nearby countries to which they had fled. 6In the crowd were men, women, and children, the king's daughters, and all those whom Nebuzaradan, the captain of the guard, had left with Gedaliah. The prophet Jeremiah and Baruch were also included. 7The people refused to obey the voice of the LORD and went to Egypt, going as far as the city of Tahpanhes.

8Then at Tahpanhes, the LORD gave another message to Jeremiah. He said, 9"While the people of Judah are watching, take some large rocks and bury them under the pavement stones at the entrance of Pharaoh's palace here in Tahpanhes. 10Then say to the people of Judah, 'This is what the LORD of Heaven's Armies, the God of Israel, says: I will certainly bring my servant Nebuchadnezzar,* king of Babylon, here to Egypt. I will set his throne over these stones that I have hidden. He will spread his royal canopy over them. 11And when he comes, he will destroy the land of Egypt. He will bring death to those destined for death, captivity to those destined for captivity, and war to those destined for war. 12He will set fire to the temples of Egypt's gods; he will burn the temples and carry the idols away as plunder. He will pick clean the land of Egypt as a shepherd picks fleas from his cloak. And he himself will leave unharmed. 13He will break down the sacred pillars standing in the temple of the sun* in Egypt, and he will burn down the temples of Egypt's gods.'"

44

JUDGMENT FOR IDOLATRY

This is the message Jeremiah received concerning the Judeans living in northern Egypt in the cities of Migdol, Tahpanhes, and Memphis,* and in southern Egypt* as well: 2"This is what the LORD of Heaven's Armies, the God of Israel, says: You saw the calamity I brought on Jerusalem and all the towns of Judah. They now lie deserted and in ruins. 3They provoked my anger with all their wickedness. They burned incense and worshiped other gods—gods that neither they nor you nor any of your ancestors had ever even known.

4"Again and again I sent my servants, the prophets, to plead with them, 'Don't do these horrible things that I hate so much.' 5But my people would not listen or turn back from their wicked ways. They kept on burning incense to these gods. 6And so my fury boiled over and fell like fire on the towns of Judah and into the streets of Jerusalem, and they are still a desolate ruin today.

REPEATING 44:9-10

The people of Judah failed to learn from mistakes made in the past. Your past is your school of experience. Mistakes are to be learned from, rather than ignored. When you don't learn from a mistake, you risk repeating it. Let your past mistakes point you to God's way. ■

7"And now the LORD God of Heaven's Armies, the God of Israel, asks you: Why are you destroying yourselves? For not one of you will survive—not a man, woman, or child among you who has come here from Judah, not even the babies in your arms. 8Why provoke my anger by burning incense to the idols you have made here in Egypt? You will only destroy yourselves and make yourselves an object of cursing and mockery for all the nations of the earth. 9Have you forgotten the sins of your ancestors, the sins of the kings and queens of Judah, and the sins you and your wives committed in Judah and Jerusalem? 10To this very hour you have shown no remorse or reverence. No one has chosen to follow my word and the decrees I gave to you and your ancestors before you.

11"Therefore, this is what the LORD of Heaven's Armies, the God of Israel, says: I am determined to destroy every one of you! 12I will take this remnant of Judah—those who were determined to come here and live in Egypt—and I will consume them. They will fall here in Egypt, killed by war and famine. All will die, from the least to the greatest. They will be an object of damnation, horror, cursing, and

43:3 Or *Chaldeans.* **43:10** Hebrew *Nebuchadrezzar,* a variant spelling of Nebuchadnezzar. **43:13** Or *in Heliopolis.* **44:1a** Hebrew *Noph.* **44:1b** Hebrew *in Pathros.* **44:15** Hebrew *in Egypt, in Pathros.*

mockery. [13]I will punish them in Egypt just as I punished them in Jerusalem, by war, famine, and disease. [14]Of that remnant who fled to Egypt, hoping someday to return to Judah, there will be no survivors. Even though they long to return home, only a handful will do so."

CHANGE OF ATTITUDE AND ACTION 44:14

Through Jeremiah, God warned the people of Judah not to go to Egypt. But they ignored him. Only those who repented of going to Egypt and returned to their own land would escape judgment. God wanted both a change of attitude and some action. The same goes for us when we mess up. All we have to do is (1) admit we have rebelled against God, (2) turn from whatever we've done wrong, and (3) seek to live as God instructs in his Word. ■

[15]Then all the women present and all the men who knew that their wives had burned incense to idols—a great crowd of all the Judeans living in northern Egypt and southern Egypt*—answered Jeremiah, [16]"We will not listen to your messages from the LORD! [17]We will do whatever we want. We will burn incense and pour out liquid offerings to the Queen of Heaven just as much as we like—just as we, and our ancestors, and our kings and officials have always done in the towns of Judah and in the streets of Jerusalem. For in those days we had plenty to eat, and we were well off and had no troubles! [18]But ever since we quit burning incense to the Queen of Heaven and stopped worshiping her with liquid offerings, we have been in great trouble and have been dying from war and famine."

[19]"Besides," the women added, "do you suppose that we were burning incense and pouring out liquid offerings to the Queen of Heaven, and making cakes marked with her image, without our husbands knowing it and helping us? Of course not!"

[20]Then Jeremiah said to all of them, men and women alike, who had given him that answer, [21]"Do you think the LORD did not know that you and your ancestors, your kings and officials, and all the people were burning incense to idols in the towns of Judah and in the streets of Jerusalem? [22]It was because the LORD could no longer bear all the disgusting things you were doing that he made your land an object of cursing—a desolate ruin without inhabitants—as it is today. [23]All these terrible things happened to you because you have burned incense to idols and sinned against the LORD. You have refused to obey him and have not followed his instructions, his decrees, and his laws."

[24]Then Jeremiah said to them all, including the women, "Listen to this message from the LORD, all you citizens of Judah who live in Egypt. [25]This is what the LORD of Heaven's Armies, the God of Israel, says: 'You and your wives have said, "We will keep our promises to burn incense and pour out liquid offerings to the Queen of Heaven," and you have proved by your actions that you meant it. So go ahead and carry out your promises and vows to her!'

[26]"But listen to this message from the LORD, all you Judeans now living in Egypt: 'I have sworn by my great name,' says the LORD, 'that my name will no longer be spoken by any of the Judeans in the land of Egypt. None of you may invoke my name or use this oath: "As surely as the Sovereign LORD lives." [27]For I will watch over you to bring you disaster and not good. Everyone from Judah who is now living in Egypt will suffer war and famine until all of you are dead. [28]Only a small number will escape death and return to Judah from Egypt. Then all those who came to Egypt will find out whose words are true—mine or theirs!

[29]"'And this is the proof I give you,' says the LORD, 'that all I have threatened will happen to you and that I will punish you here.' [30]This is what the LORD says: 'I will turn Pharaoh Hophra, king of Egypt, over to his enemies who want to kill him, just as I turned King Zedekiah of Judah over to King Nebuchadnezzar* of Babylon.'"

45 A MESSAGE FOR BARUCH

The prophet Jeremiah gave a message to Baruch son of Neriah in the fourth year of the reign of Jehoiakim son of Josiah,* after Baruch had written down everything Jeremiah had dictated to him. He said, [2]"This is what the LORD, the God of Israel, says to you, Baruch: [3]You have said, 'I am overwhelmed with trouble! Haven't I had enough pain already? And now the LORD has added more! I am worn out from sighing and can find no rest.'

[4]"Baruch, this is what the LORD says: 'I will destroy this nation that I built. I will uproot what I planted. [5]Are you seeking great things for yourself? Don't do it! I will bring great disaster upon all these people; but I will give you your life as a reward wherever you go. I, the LORD, have spoken!'"

46 MESSAGES FOR THE NATIONS

The following messages were given to Jeremiah the prophet from the LORD concerning foreign nations.

MESSAGES ABOUT EGYPT

[2]This message concerning Egypt was given in the fourth year of the reign of Jehoiakim son of Josiah, the king of Judah, on the occasion of the battle of Carchemish* when Pharaoh Neco, king of Egypt, and his army were defeated beside the Euphrates River by King Nebuchadnezzar* of Babylon.

3 "Prepare your shields,
and advance into battle!
4 Harness the horses,
and mount the stallions.
Take your positions.
Put on your helmets.

44:30 Hebrew *Nebuchadrezzar,* a variant spelling of Nebuchadnezzar. **45:1** The fourth year of Jehoiakim's reign was 605 B.C. **46:2a** This event occurred in 605 B.C., during the fourth year of Jehoiakim's reign (according to the calendar system in which the new year begins in the spring). **46:2b** Hebrew *Nebuchadrezzar,* a variant spelling of Nebuchadnezzar; also in 46:13, 26.

Sharpen your spears,
and prepare your armor.
5 But what do I see?
The Egyptian army flees in terror.
The bravest of its fighting men run
without a backward glance.
They are terrorized at every turn,"
says the LORD.
6 "The swiftest runners cannot flee;
the mightiest warriors cannot escape.
By the Euphrates River to the north,
they stumble and fall.

7 "Who is this, rising like the Nile at floodtime,
overflowing all the land?
8 It is the Egyptian army,
overflowing all the land,
boasting that it will cover the earth like a flood,
destroying cities and their people.
9 Charge, you horses and chariots;
attack, you mighty warriors of Egypt!
Come, all you allies from Ethiopia, Libya, and Lydia*
who are skilled with the shield and bow!
10 For this is the day of the Lord, the LORD of
Heaven's Armies,
a day of vengeance on his enemies.
The sword will devour until it is satisfied,
yes, until it is drunk with your blood!
The Lord, the LORD of Heaven's Armies, will receive
a sacrifice today
in the north country beside the Euphrates River.

11 "Go up to Gilead to get medicine,
O virgin daughter of Egypt!
But your many treatments
will bring you no healing.
12 The nations have heard of your shame.
The earth is filled with your cries of despair.
Your mightiest warriors will run into each other
and fall down together."

13 Then the LORD gave the prophet Jeremiah this message about King Nebuchadnezzar's plans to attack Egypt.

14 "Shout it out in Egypt!
Publish it in the cities of Migdol, Memphis,*
and Tahpanhes!
Mobilize for battle,
for the sword will devour everyone around you.
15 Why have your warriors fallen?
They cannot stand, for the LORD has knocked
them down.
16 They stumble and fall over each other
and say among themselves,
'Come, let's go back to our people,
to the land of our birth.
Let's get away from the sword of the enemy!'
17 There they will say,
'Pharaoh, the king of Egypt, is a loudmouth
who missed his opportunity!'
18 "As surely as I live," says the King,
whose name is the LORD of Heaven's Armies,
"one is coming against Egypt
who is as tall as Mount Tabor,
or as Mount Carmel by the sea!
19 Pack up! Get ready to leave for exile,
you citizens of Egypt!
The city of Memphis will be destroyed,
without a single inhabitant.
20 Egypt is as sleek as a beautiful young cow,
but a horsefly from the north is on its way!
21 Egypt's mercenaries have become like
fattened calves.
They, too, will turn and run,
for it is a day of great disaster for Egypt,
a time of great punishment.
22 Egypt flees, silent as a serpent gliding away.
The invading army marches in;
they come against her with axes like woodsmen.
23 They will cut down her people like trees,"
says the LORD,
"for they are more numerous than locusts.
24 Egypt will be humiliated;
she will be handed over to people from
the north."

ALL ABOUT GOD 46:1-28

In this chapter, we gain several insights about God and his plan for this world. (1) Although God chose Israel for a special purpose, he loves all people and wants them to come to him. (2) God is holy and will not tolerate sin. (3) God's judgments are not based on prejudice and a desire for revenge, but on fairness and justice. (4) God does not delight in judgment, but in salvation. (5) God is impartial—he judges everyone by the same standard. How do these insights affect your view of God? ■

25 The LORD of Heaven's Armies, the God of Israel, says:
"I will punish Amon, the god of Thebes,* and all the other
gods of Egypt. I will punish its rulers and Pharaoh, too,
and all who trust in him. 26 I will hand them over to those
who want them killed—to King Nebuchadnezzar of Babylon and his army. But afterward the land will recover
from the ravages of war. I, the LORD, have spoken!

27 "But do not be afraid, Jacob, my servant;
do not be dismayed, Israel.
For I will bring you home again from distant lands,
and your children will return from their exile.
Israel* will return to a life of peace and quiet,
and no one will terrorize them.
28 Do not be afraid, Jacob, my servant,
for I am with you," says the LORD.

46:9 Hebrew *from Cush, Put, and Lud.* 46:14 Hebrew *Noph;* also in 46:19. 46:25 Hebrew *of No.* 46:27 Hebrew *Jacob.* See note on 5:20.

"I will completely destroy the nations to which I have
exiled you,
but I will not completely destroy you.
I will discipline you, but with justice;
I cannot let you go unpunished."

47 A MESSAGE ABOUT PHILISTIA

This is the LORD's message to the prophet Jeremiah concerning the Philistines of Gaza, before it was captured by the Egyptian army. 2This is what the LORD says:

"A flood is coming from the north
to overflow the land.
It will destroy the land and everything in it—
cities and people alike.
People will scream in terror,
and everyone in the land will wail.
3 Hear the clatter of stallions' hooves
and the rumble of wheels as the chariots rush by.
Terrified fathers run madly,
without a backward glance at their helpless children.

4 "The time has come for the Philistines to be
destroyed,
along with their allies from Tyre and Sidon.
Yes, the LORD is destroying the remnant of the
Philistines,
those colonists from the island of Crete.*
5 Gaza will be humiliated, its head shaved bald;
Ashkelon will lie silent.
You remnant from the Mediterranean coast,*
how long will you lament and mourn?

6 "Now, O sword of the LORD,
when will you be at rest again?
Go back into your sheath;
rest and be still.

7 "But how can it be still
when the LORD has sent it on a mission?
For the city of Ashkelon
and the people living along the sea
must be destroyed."

48 A MESSAGE ABOUT MOAB

This message was given concerning Moab. This is what the LORD of Heaven's Armies, the God of Israel, says:

"What sorrow awaits the city of Nebo;
it will soon lie in ruins.
The city of Kiriathaim will be humiliated
and captured;
the fortress will be humiliated and broken down.
2 No one will ever brag about Moab again,
for in Heshbon there is a plot to destroy her.
'Come,' they say, 'we will cut her off from being
a nation.'
The town of Madmen,* too, will be silenced;
the sword will follow you there.
3 Listen to the cries from Horonaim,
cries of devastation and great destruction.
4 All Moab is destroyed.
Her little ones will cry out.*
5 Her refugees weep bitterly,
climbing the slope to Luhith.
They cry out in terror,
descending the slope to Horonaim.
6 Flee for your lives!
Hide* in the wilderness!
7 Because you have trusted in your wealth and skill,
you will be taken captive.
Your god Chemosh, with his priests and officials,
will be hauled off to distant lands!

8 "All the towns will be destroyed,
and no one will escape—
either on the plateaus or in the valleys,
for the LORD has spoken.
9 Oh, that Moab had wings
so she could fly away,*
for her towns will be left empty,
with no one living in them.
10 Cursed are those who refuse to do the LORD's work,
who hold back their swords from shedding blood!

11 "From his earliest history, Moab has lived in peace,
never going into exile.
He is like wine that has been allowed to settle.
He has not been poured from flask to flask,
and he is now fragrant and smooth.
12 But the time is coming soon," says the LORD,
"when I will send men to pour him from his jar.
They will pour him out,
then shatter the jar!
13 At last Moab will be ashamed of his idol Chemosh,
as the people of Israel were ashamed of their gold
calf at Bethel.*

14 "You used to boast, 'We are heroes,
mighty men of war.'
15 But now Moab and his towns will be destroyed.
His most promising youth are doomed to slaughter,"
says the King, whose name is the LORD of
Heaven's Armies.
16 "Destruction is coming fast for Moab;
calamity threatens ominously.
17 You friends of Moab,
weep for him and cry!
See how the strong scepter is broken,
how the beautiful staff is shattered!

47:4 Hebrew *from Caphtor.* **47:5** Hebrew *the plain.* **48:2** *Madmen* sounds like the Hebrew word for "silence"; it should not be confused with the English word *madmen.* **48:4** Greek version reads *Her cries are heard as far away as Zoar.* **48:6** Or *Hide like a wild donkey;* or *Hide like a juniper shrub;* or *Be like* [the town of] *Aroer.* The meaning of the Hebrew is uncertain. **48:9** Or *Put salt on Moab, / for she will be laid waste.* **48:13** Hebrew *ashamed when they trusted in Bethel.*

18 "Come down from your glory
and sit in the dust, you people of Dibon,
for those who destroy Moab will shatter Dibon, too.
They will tear down all your towers.
19 You people of Aroer,
stand beside the road and watch.
Shout to those who flee from Moab,
'What has happened there?'

20 "And the reply comes back,
'Moab lies in ruins, disgraced;
weep and wail!
Tell it by the banks of the Arnon River:
Moab has been destroyed!'
21 Judgment has been poured out on the towns
of the plateau—
on Holon and Jahaz* and Mephaath,
22 on Dibon and Nebo and Beth-diblathaim,
23 on Kiriathaim and Beth-gamul and Beth-meon,
24 on Kerioth and Bozrah—
all the towns of Moab, far and near.

25 "The strength of Moab has ended.
His arm has been broken," says the LORD.
26 "Let him stagger and fall like a drunkard,
for he has rebelled against the LORD.
Moab will wallow in his own vomit,
ridiculed by all.
27 Did you not ridicule the people of Israel?
Were they caught in the company of thieves
that you should despise them as you do?

28 "You people of Moab,
flee from your towns and live in the caves.
Hide like doves that nest
in the clefts of the rocks.
29 We have all heard of the pride of Moab,
for his pride is very great.
We know of his lofty pride,
his arrogance, and his haughty heart.
30 I know about his insolence,"
says the LORD,
"but his boasts are empty—
as empty as his deeds.
31 So now I wail for Moab;
yes, I will mourn for Moab.
My heart is broken for the men of Kir-hareseth.*

32 "You people of Sibmah, rich in vineyards,
I will weep for you even more than I did for Jazer.
Your spreading vines once reached as far as the
Dead Sea,*
but the destroyer has stripped you bare!
He has harvested your grapes and summer fruits.
33 Joy and gladness are gone from fruitful Moab.
The presses yield no wine.
No one treads the grapes with shouts of joy.
There is shouting, yes, but not of joy.

DON'T PUSH IT 48:1–49:38

God is loving, merciful, and kind. But he is also just. Eventually he will judge and punish those who do wrong. Check out God's words in the prophecies of Jeremiah as he speaks to the Moabites who trusted in their military might (48:1-47), the Ammonites who trusted in their wealth (49:1-6), the Edomites who trusted in their wisdom and secure location (49:7-22), and others. Yet many times people think they can "push their luck" by ignoring God until they're ready to be serious about him. The warnings in Jeremiah are a chilling reminder of the folly of playing with God. ■

34"Instead, their awful cries of terror can be heard
from Heshbon clear across to Elealeh and Jahaz; from
Zoar all the way to Horonaim and Eglath-shelishiyah.
Even the waters of Nimrim are dried up now.
35"I will put an end to Moab," says the LORD, "for the
people offer sacrifices at the pagan shrines and burn incense to their false gods. 36My heart moans like a flute for
Moab and Kir-hareseth, for all their wealth has disappeared. 37The people shave their heads and beards in
mourning. They slash their hands and put on clothes
made of burlap. 38There is crying and sorrow in every
Moabite home and on every street. For I have smashed
Moab like an old, unwanted jar. 39How it is shattered!
Hear the wailing! See the shame of Moab! It has become
an object of ridicule, an example of ruin to all its
neighbors."
40This is what the LORD says:

"Look! The enemy swoops down like an eagle,
spreading his wings over Moab.
41 Its cities will fall,
and its strongholds will be seized.
Even the mightiest warriors will be in anguish
like a woman in labor.
42 Moab will no longer be a nation,
for it has boasted against the LORD.

43 "Terror and traps and snares will be your lot,
O Moab," says the LORD.
44 "Those who flee in terror will fall into a trap,
and those who escape the trap will step
into a snare.
I will see to it that you do not get away,
for the time of your judgment has come,"
says the LORD.
45 "The people flee as far as Heshbon
but are unable to go on.
For a fire comes from Heshbon,
King Sihon's ancient home,
to devour the entire land
with all its rebellious people.

48:21 Hebrew *Jahzah,* a variant spelling of Jahaz. **48:31** Hebrew *Kir-heres,* a variant spelling of Kir-hareseth; also in 48:36. **48:32** Hebrew *the sea of Jazer.*

46 "O Moab, they weep for you!
The people of the god Chemosh are destroyed!
Your sons and your daughters
have been taken away as captives.
47 But I will restore the fortunes of Moab
in days to come.
I, the LORD, have spoken!"

This is the end of Jeremiah's prophecy concerning Moab.

49

A MESSAGE ABOUT AMMON

This message was given concerning the Ammonites. This is what the LORD says:

"Are there no descendants of Israel
to inherit the land of Gad?
Why are you, who worship Molech,*
living in its towns?
2 In the days to come," says the LORD,
"I will sound the battle cry against your city
of Rabbah.
It will become a desolate heap of ruins,
and the neighboring towns will be burned.
Then Israel will take back the land
you took from her," says the LORD.

3 "Cry out, O Heshbon,
for the town of Ai is destroyed.
Weep, O people of Rabbah!
Put on your clothes of mourning.
Weep and wail, hiding in the hedges,
for your god Molech, with his priests and officials,
will be hauled off to distant lands.
4 You are proud of your fertile valleys,
but they will soon be ruined.
You trusted in your wealth,
you rebellious daughter,
and thought no one could ever harm you.
5 But look! I will bring terror upon you,"
says the Lord, the LORD of Heaven's Armies.
"Your neighbors will chase you from your land,
and no one will help your exiles as they flee.
6 But I will restore the fortunes of the Ammonites
in days to come.
I, the LORD, have spoken."

MESSAGES ABOUT EDOM

7This message was given concerning Edom. This is what the LORD of Heaven's Armies says:

"Is there no wisdom in Teman?
Is no one left to give wise counsel?
8 Turn and flee!
Hide in deep caves, you people of Dedan!
For when I bring disaster on Edom,*
I will punish you, too!
9 Those who harvest grapes
always leave a few for the poor.
If thieves came at night,
they would not take everything.
10 But I will strip bare the land of Edom,
and there will be no place left to hide.
Its children, its brothers, and its neighbors
will all be destroyed,
and Edom itself will be no more.
11 But I will protect the orphans who remain
among you.
Your widows, too, can depend on me for help."

12And this is what the LORD says: "If the innocent must
suffer, how much more must you! You will not go unpunished! You must drink this cup of judgment! 13For I have
sworn by my own name," says the LORD, "that Bozrah will
become an object of horror and a heap of ruins; it will be
mocked and cursed. All its towns and villages will be desolate forever."

14 I have heard a message from the LORD
that an ambassador was sent to the nations to say,
"Form a coalition against Edom,
and prepare for battle!"

15 The LORD says to Edom,
"I will cut you down to size among the nations.
You will be despised by all.
16 You have been deceived
by the fear you inspire in others
and by your own pride.
You live in a rock fortress
and control the mountain heights.
But even if you make your nest among the peaks
with the eagles,
I will bring you crashing down,"
says the LORD.

17 "Edom will be an object of horror.
All who pass by will be appalled
and will gasp at the destruction they see there.
18 It will be like the destruction of Sodom and
Gomorrah
and their neighboring towns," says the LORD.
"No one will live there;
no one will inhabit it.
19 I will come like a lion from the thickets of the Jordan,
leaping on the sheep in the pasture.
I will chase Edom from its land,
and I will appoint the leader of my choice.
For who is like me, and who can challenge me?
What ruler can oppose my will?"

20 Listen to the LORD's plans against Edom
and the people of Teman.
Even the little children will be dragged off like sheep,
and their homes will be destroyed.

49:1 Hebrew *Malcam,* a variant spelling of Molech; also in 49:3. **49:8** Hebrew *Esau;* also in 49:10.

21 The earth will shake with the noise of Edom's fall,
and its cry of despair will be heard all the way to
the Red Sea.*
22 Look! The enemy swoops down like an eagle,
spreading his wings over Bozrah.
Even the mightiest warriors will be in anguish
like a woman in labor.

A MESSAGE ABOUT DAMASCUS

23 This message was given concerning Damascus. This is what the LORD says:

"The towns of Hamath and Arpad are struck
with fear,
for they have heard the news of their
destruction.
Their hearts are troubled
like a wild sea in a raging storm.
24 Damascus has become feeble,
and all her people turn to flee.
Fear, anguish, and pain have gripped her
as they grip a woman in labor.
25 That famous city, a city of joy,
will be forsaken!
26 Her young men will fall in the streets and die.
Her soldiers will all be killed,"
says the LORD of Heaven's Armies.
27 "And I will set fire to the walls of Damascus
that will burn up the palaces of Ben-hadad."

A MESSAGE ABOUT KEDAR AND HAZOR

28 This message was given concerning Kedar and the kingdoms of Hazor, which were attacked by King Nebuchadnezzar* of Babylon. This is what the LORD says:

"Advance against Kedar!
Destroy the warriors from the East!
29 Their flocks and tents will be captured,
and their household goods and camels will
be taken away.
Everywhere shouts of panic will be heard:
'We are terrorized at every turn!'
30 Run for your lives," says the LORD.
"Hide yourselves in deep caves, you people
of Hazor,
for King Nebuchadnezzar of Babylon has plotted
against you
and is preparing to destroy you.

31 "Go up and attack that complacent nation,"
says the LORD.
"Its people live alone in the desert
without walls or gates.
32 Their camels and other livestock will all be yours.
I will scatter to the winds these people
who live in remote places.*
I will bring calamity upon them
from every direction," says the LORD.
33 "Hazor will be inhabited by jackals,
and it will be desolate forever.
No one will live there;
no one will inhabit it."

A MESSAGE ABOUT ELAM

34 This message concerning Elam came to the prophet Jeremiah from the LORD at the beginning of the reign of King Zedekiah of Judah. 35 This is what the LORD of Heaven's Armies says:

"I will destroy the archers of Elam—
the best of their forces.
36 I will bring enemies from all directions,
and I will scatter the people of Elam to the
four winds.
They will be exiled to countries around the world.
37 I myself will go with Elam's enemies to shatter it.
In my fierce anger, I will bring great disaster
upon the people of Elam," says the LORD.
"Their enemies will chase them with the sword
until I have destroyed them completely.
38 I will set my throne in Elam," says the LORD,
"and I will destroy its king and officials.
39 But I will restore the fortunes of Elam
in days to come.
I, the LORD, have spoken!"

A POWERFUL PAWN 50:1-3

Babylon is another name for the nation of the Chaldeans. At the height of its power, this empire seemed unbeatable. Yet this powerful nation was just a pawn. When Babylon had finished serving God's purpose of punishing Judah for her sins, it would be punished and crushed for its own. Babylon was destroyed in 539 B.C. by the Medo-Persians (see Dan 5). Only God has real, lasting power. Would you agree?

50

A MESSAGE ABOUT BABYLON

The LORD gave Jeremiah the prophet this message concerning Babylon and the land of the Babylonians.* 2 This is what the LORD says:

"Tell the whole world,
and keep nothing back.
Raise a signal flag
to tell everyone that Babylon will fall!
Her images and idols* will be shattered.
Her gods Bel and Marduk will be utterly disgraced.
3 For a nation will attack her from the north
and bring such destruction that no one will live
there again.
Everything will be gone;
both people and animals will flee.

49:21 Hebrew *sea of reeds.* **49:28** Hebrew *Nebuchadrezzar,* a variant spelling of Nebuchadnezzar; also in 49:30. **49:32** Or *who clip the corners of their hair.* **50:1** Or *Chaldeans;* also in 50:8, 25, 35, 45. **50:2** The Hebrew term (literally *round things*) probably alludes to dung.

HOPE FOR ISRAEL AND JUDAH

4 "In those coming days,"
says the LORD,
"the people of Israel will return home
together with the people of Judah.
They will come weeping
and seeking the LORD their God.
5 They will ask the way to Jerusalem*
and will start back home again.
They will bind themselves to the LORD
with an eternal covenant that will never be forgotten.

6 "My people have been lost sheep.
Their shepherds have led them astray
and turned them loose in the mountains.
They have lost their way
and can't remember how to get back to the
sheepfold.
7 All who found them devoured them.
Their enemies said,
'We did nothing wrong in attacking them,
for they sinned against the LORD,
their true place of rest,
and the hope of their ancestors.'

8 "But now, flee from Babylon!
Leave the land of the Babylonians.
Like male goats at the head of the flock,
lead my people home again.
9 For I am raising up an army
of great nations from the north.
They will join forces to attack Babylon,
and she will be captured.
The enemies' arrows will go straight to the mark;
they will not miss!
10 Babylonia* will be looted
until the attackers are glutted with loot.
I, the LORD, have spoken!

BABYLON'S SURE FALL

11 "You rejoice and are glad,
you who plundered my chosen people.
You frisk about like a calf in a meadow
and neigh like a stallion.
12 But your homeland* will be overwhelmed
with shame and disgrace.
You will become the least of nations—
a wilderness, a dry and desolate land.
13 Because of the LORD's anger,
Babylon will become a deserted wasteland.
All who pass by will be horrified
and will gasp at the destruction they see there.

14 "Yes, prepare to attack Babylon,
all you surrounding nations.
Let your archers shoot at her; spare no arrows.
For she has sinned against the LORD.
15 Shout war cries against her from every side.
Look! She surrenders!
Her walls have fallen.
It is the LORD's vengeance,
so take vengeance on her.
Do to her as she has done to others!
16 Take from Babylon all those who plant crops;
send all the harvesters away.
Because of the sword of the enemy,
everyone will run away and rush back to their
own lands.

HOPE FOR GOD'S PEOPLE

17 "The Israelites are like sheep
that have been scattered by lions.
First the king of Assyria ate them up.
Then King Nebuchadnezzar* of Babylon cracked
their bones."
18 Therefore, this is what the LORD of Heaven's Armies,
the God of Israel, says:
"Now I will punish the king of Babylon and his land,
just as I punished the king of Assyria.
19 And I will bring Israel home again to its own land,
to feed in the fields of Carmel and Bashan,
and to be satisfied once more
in the hill country of Ephraim and Gilead.
20 In those days," says the LORD,
"no sin will be found in Israel or in Judah,
for I will forgive the remnant I preserve.

THE LORD'S JUDGMENT ON BABYLON

21 "Go up, my warriors, against the land
of Merathaim
and against the people of Pekod.
Pursue, kill, and completely destroy* them,
as I have commanded you," says the LORD.
22 "Let the battle cry be heard in the land,
a shout of great destruction.
23 Babylon, the mightiest hammer in all the earth,
lies broken and shattered.
Babylon is desolate among the nations!
24 Listen, Babylon, for I have set a trap for you.
You are caught, for you have fought against
the LORD.
25 The LORD has opened his armory
and brought out weapons to vent his fury.
The terror that falls upon the Babylonians
will be the work of the Sovereign LORD of
Heaven's Armies.
26 Yes, come against her from distant lands.
Break open her granaries.
Crush her walls and houses into heaps of rubble.
Destroy her completely, and leave nothing!
27 Destroy even her young bulls—
it will be terrible for them, too!
Slaughter them all!
For Babylon's day of reckoning has come.

50:5 Hebrew *Zion;* also in 50:28. **50:10** Or *Chaldea.* **50:12** Hebrew *your mother.* **50:17** Hebrew *Nebuchadrezzar,* a variant spelling of Nebuchadnezzar. **50:21** The Hebrew term used here refers to the complete consecration of things or people to the LORD, either by destroying them or by giving them as an offering.

28 Listen to the people who have escaped from Babylon,
as they tell in Jerusalem
how the LORD our God has taken vengeance
against those who destroyed his Temple.

29 "Send out a call for archers to come to Babylon.
Surround the city so none can escape.
Do to her as she has done to others,
for she has defied the LORD, the Holy One of Israel.
30 Her young men will fall in the streets and die.
Her soldiers will all be killed,"
says the LORD.

31 "See, I am your enemy, you arrogant people,"
says the Lord, the LORD of Heaven's Armies.
"Your day of reckoning has arrived—
the day when I will punish you.
32 O land of arrogance, you will stumble and fall,
and no one will raise you up.
For I will light a fire in the cities of Babylon
that will burn up everything around them."

33 This is what the LORD of Heaven's Armies says:
"The people of Israel and Judah have been wronged.
Their captors hold them and refuse to let them go.
34 But the one who redeems them is strong.
His name is the LORD of Heaven's Armies.
He will defend them
and give them rest again in Israel.
But for the people of Babylon
there will be no rest!

35 "The sword of destruction will strike the
Babylonians,"
says the LORD.
"It will strike the people of Babylon—
her officials and wise men, too.
36 The sword will strike her wise counselors,
and they will become fools.
The sword will strike her mightiest warriors,
and panic will seize them.
37 The sword will strike her horses and chariots
and her allies from other lands,
and they will all become like women.
The sword will strike her treasures,
and they all will be plundered.
38 The sword will even strike her water supply,
causing it to dry up.
And why? Because the whole land is filled with idols,
and the people are madly in love with them.

39 "Soon Babylon will be inhabited by desert animals
and hyenas.
It will be a home for owls.
Never again will people live there;
it will lie desolate forever.
40 I will destroy it as I* destroyed Sodom and Gomorrah
and their neighboring towns," says the LORD.
"No one will live there;
no one will inhabit it.

41 "Look! A great army is coming from the north.
A great nation and many kings
are rising against you from far-off lands.
42 They are armed with bows and spears.
They are cruel and show no mercy.
As they ride forward on horses,
they sound like a roaring sea.
They are coming in battle formation,
planning to destroy you, Babylon.
43 The king of Babylon has heard reports about
the enemy,
and he is weak with fright.
Pangs of anguish have gripped him,
like those of a woman in labor.

44 "I will come like a lion from the thickets of
the Jordan,
leaping on the sheep in the pasture.
I will chase Babylon from its land,
and I will appoint the leader of my choice.
For who is like me, and who can challenge me?
What ruler can oppose my will?"

45 Listen to the LORD's plans against Babylon
and the land of the Babylonians.
Even the little children will be dragged off like sheep,
and their homes will be destroyed.
46 The earth will shake with the shout, "Babylon has
been taken!"
and its cry of despair will be heard around
the world.

51

1 This is what the LORD says:
"I will stir up a destroyer against Babylon
and the people of Babylonia.*
2 Foreigners will come and winnow her,
blowing her away as chaff.
They will come from every side
to rise against her in her day of trouble.
3 Don't let the archers put on their armor
or draw their bows.
Don't spare even her best soldiers!
Let her army be completely destroyed.*
4 They will fall dead in the land of the Babylonians,*
slashed to death in her streets.
5 For the LORD of Heaven's Armies
has not abandoned Israel and Judah.
He is still their God,
even though their land was filled with sin
against the Holy One of Israel."

6 Flee from Babylon! Save yourselves!
Don't get trapped in her punishment!

50:40 Hebrew *as God.* **51:1** Hebrew *of Leb-kamai,* a code name for Babylonia. **51:3** The Hebrew term used here refers to the complete consecration of things or people to the LORD, either by destroying them or by giving them as an offering. **51:4** Or *Chaldeans;* also in 51:54.

It is the LORD's time for vengeance;
he will repay her in full.
7 Babylon has been a gold cup in the LORD's hands,
a cup that made the whole earth drunk.
The nations drank Babylon's wine,
and it drove them all mad.
8 But suddenly Babylon, too, has fallen.
Weep for her.
Give her medicine.
Perhaps she can yet be healed.
9 We would have helped her if we could,
but nothing can save her now.
Let her go; abandon her.
Return now to your own land.
For her punishment reaches to the heavens;
it is so great it cannot be measured.
10 The LORD has vindicated us.
Come, let us announce in Jerusalem*
everything the LORD our God has done.

11 Sharpen the arrows!
Lift up the shields!*
For the LORD has inspired the kings of the Medes
to march against Babylon and destroy her.
This is his vengeance against those
who desecrated his Temple.
12 Raise the battle flag against Babylon!
Reinforce the guard and station the watchmen.
Prepare an ambush,
for the LORD will fulfill all his plans
against Babylon.
13 You are a city by a great river,
a great center of commerce,
but your end has come.
The thread of your life is cut.
14 The LORD of Heaven's Armies has taken this vow
and has sworn to it by his own name:
"Your cities will be filled with enemies,
like fields swarming with locusts,
and they will shout in triumph over you."

A HYMN OF PRAISE TO THE LORD

15 The LORD made the earth by his power,
and he preserves it by his wisdom.
With his own understanding
he stretched out the heavens.
16 When he speaks in the thunder,
the heavens are filled with water.
He causes the clouds to rise over the earth.
He sends the lightning with the rain
and releases the wind from his storehouses.

17 The whole human race is foolish and has
no knowledge!
The craftsmen are disgraced by the idols
they make,
for their carefully shaped works are a fraud.
These idols have no breath or power.
18 Idols are worthless; they are ridiculous lies!
On the day of reckoning they will all
be destroyed.
19 But the God of Israel* is no idol!
He is the Creator of everything that exists,
including his people, his own special possession.
The LORD of Heaven's Armies is his name!

BABYLON'S GREAT PUNISHMENT

20 "You* are my battle-ax and sword,"
says the LORD.
"With you I will shatter nations
and destroy many kingdoms.
21 With you I will shatter armies—
destroying the horse and rider,
the chariot and charioteer.
22 With you I will shatter men and women,
old people and children,
young men and maidens.
23 With you I will shatter shepherds and flocks,
farmers and oxen,
captains and officers.

24 "I will repay Babylon
and the people of Babylonia*
for all the wrong they have done
to my people in Jerusalem," says the LORD.

25 "Look, O mighty mountain, destroyer of the earth!
I am your enemy," says the LORD.
"I will raise my fist against you,
to knock you down from the heights.
When I am finished,
you will be nothing but a heap of burnt rubble.
26 You will be desolate forever.
Even your stones will never again be used
for building.
You will be completely wiped out,"
says the LORD.

27 Raise a signal flag to the nations.
Sound the battle cry!
Mobilize them all against Babylon.
Prepare them to fight against her!
Bring out the armies of Ararat, Minni, and Ashkenaz.
Appoint a commander,
and bring a multitude of horses like
swarming locusts!
28 Bring against her the armies of the nations—
led by the kings of the Medes
and all their captains and officers.

29 The earth trembles and writhes in pain,
for everything the LORD has planned against
Babylon stands unchanged.
Babylon will be left desolate without a single
inhabitant.
30 Her mightiest warriors no longer fight.

51:10 Hebrew *Zion;* also in 51:24. **51:11** Greek version reads *Fill up the quivers.* **51:19** Hebrew *the Portion of Jacob.* See note on 5:20. **51:20** Possibly Cyrus, whom God used to conquer Babylon. Compare Isa 44:28; 45:1. **51:24** Or *Chaldea;* also in 51:35.

They stay in their barracks, their courage gone.
They have become like women.
The invaders have burned the houses
and broken down the city gates.
31 The news is passed from one runner
to the next
as the messengers hurry to tell the king
that his city has been captured.
32 All the escape routes are blocked.
The marshes have been set aflame,
and the army is in a panic.

33 This is what the LORD of Heaven's Armies,
the God of Israel, says:
"Babylon is like wheat on a threshing floor,
about to be trampled.
In just a little while
her harvest will begin."

34 "King Nebuchadnezzar* of Babylon has eaten
and crushed us
and drained us of strength.
He has swallowed us like a great monster
and filled his belly with our riches.
He has thrown us out of our own country.
35 Make Babylon suffer as she made us suffer,"
say the people of Zion.
"Make the people of Babylonia pay for spilling
our blood,"
says Jerusalem.

THE LORD'S VENGEANCE ON BABYLON

36 This is what the LORD says to Jerusalem:

"I will be your lawyer to plead your case,
and I will avenge you.
I will dry up her river,
as well as her springs,
37 and Babylon will become a heap of ruins,
haunted by jackals.
She will be an object of horror and contempt,
a place where no one lives.
38 Her people will roar together like strong lions.
They will growl like lion cubs.
39 And while they lie inflamed with all their wine,
I will prepare a different kind of feast
for them.
I will make them drink until they fall asleep,
and they will never wake up again,"
says the LORD.
40 "I will bring them down
like lambs to the slaughter,
like rams and goats to be sacrificed.

41 "How Babylon* is fallen—
great Babylon, praised throughout the earth!
Now she has become an object of horror
among the nations.
42 The sea has risen over Babylon;
she is covered by its crashing waves.
43 Her cities now lie in ruins;
she is a dry wasteland
where no one lives or even passes by.
44 And I will punish Bel, the god of Babylon,
and make him vomit up all he has eaten.
The nations will no longer come and worship him.
The wall of Babylon has fallen!

A MESSAGE FOR THE EXILES

45 "Come out, my people, flee from Babylon.
Save yourselves! Run from the LORD's fierce anger.
46 But do not panic; don't be afraid
when you hear the first rumor of
approaching forces.
For rumors will keep coming year by year.
Violence will erupt in the land
as the leaders fight against each other.
47 For the time is surely coming
when I will punish this great city and all her idols.
Her whole land will be disgraced,
and her dead will lie in the streets.
48 Then the heavens and earth will rejoice,
for out of the north will come destroying armies
against Babylon," says the LORD.
49 "Just as Babylon killed the people of Israel
and others throughout the world,
so must her people be killed.
50 Get out, all you who have escaped the sword!
Do not stand and watch—flee while you can!
Remember the LORD, though you are in
a far-off land,
and think about your home in Jerusalem."

51 "We are ashamed," the people say.
"We are insulted and disgraced
because the LORD's Temple
has been defiled by foreigners."

52 "Yes," says the LORD, "but the time is coming
when I will destroy Babylon's idols.
The groans of her wounded people
will be heard throughout the land.
53 Though Babylon reaches as high as the heavens
and makes her fortifications incredibly strong,
I will still send enemies to plunder her.
I, the LORD, have spoken!

BABYLON'S COMPLETE DESTRUCTION

54 "Listen! Hear the cry of Babylon,
the sound of great destruction from the land
of the Babylonians.
55 For the LORD is destroying Babylon.
He will silence her loud voice.
Waves of enemies pound against her;
the noise of battle rings through the city.
56 Destroying armies come against Babylon.

51:34 Hebrew *Nebuchadrezzar*, a variant spelling of Nebuchadnezzar. **51:41** Hebrew *Sheshach*, a code name for Babylon.

Her mighty men are captured,
and their weapons break in their hands.
For the LORD is a God who gives just punishment;
he always repays in full.
57 I will make her officials and wise men drunk,
along with her captains, officers, and warriors.
They will fall asleep
and never wake up again!"
says the King, whose name is
the LORD of Heaven's Armies.

58 This is what the LORD of Heaven's Armies says:
"The thick walls of Babylon will be leveled to
the ground,
and her massive gates will be burned.
The builders from many lands have worked in vain,
for their work will be destroyed by fire!"

JUDGMENT 51:60-64

In Jeremiah's last message, we find again the twin themes of God's sovereignty and his judgment. Babylon had been allowed to torment the people of Israel, but here Babylon itself will be judged. Although God brings good out of evil, he doesn't allow evil to remain unpunished. (Check out Ps 37 also.) ■

JEREMIAH'S MESSAGE SENT TO BABYLON

59The prophet Jeremiah gave this message to Seraiah son
of Neriah and grandson of Mahseiah, a staff officer,
when Seraiah went to Babylon with King Zedekiah of Judah. This was during the fourth year of Zedekiah's
reign.* 60Jeremiah had recorded on a scroll all the terrible disasters that would soon come upon Babylon—all
the words written here. 61He said to Seraiah, "When you
get to Babylon, read aloud everything on this scroll.
62Then say, 'LORD, you have said that you will destroy Babylon so that neither people nor animals will remain here.
She will lie empty and abandoned forever.' 63When you
have finished reading the scroll, tie it to a stone and
throw it into the Euphrates River. 64Then say, 'In this
same way Babylon and her people will sink, never again to
rise, because of the disasters I will bring upon her.'"
This is the end of Jeremiah's messages.

52

THE FALL OF JERUSALEM

Zedekiah was twenty-one years old when he became
king, and he reigned in Jerusalem eleven years. His
mother was Hamutal, the daughter of Jeremiah from Libnah. 2But Zedekiah did what was evil in the LORD's sight,
just as Jehoiakim had done. 3These things happened because of the LORD's anger against the people of Jerusalem
and Judah, until he finally banished them from his presence and sent them into exile.
Zedekiah rebelled against the king of Babylon. 4So on
January 15,* during the ninth year of Zedekiah's reign,
King Nebuchadnezzar* of Babylon led his entire army
against Jerusalem. They surrounded the city and built
siege ramps against its walls. 5Jerusalem was kept under
siege until the eleventh year of King Zedekiah's reign.
6By July 18 in the eleventh year of Zedekiah's reign,*
the famine in the city had become very severe, and the
last of the food was entirely gone. 7Then a section of the
city wall was broken down, and all the soldiers fled. Since
the city was surrounded by the Babylonians,* they waited
for nightfall. Then they slipped through the gate between
the two walls behind the king's garden and headed toward the Jordan Valley.*
8But the Babylonian troops chased King Zedekiah and
caught him on the plains of Jericho, for his men had all
deserted him and scattered. 9They took him to the king
of Babylon at Riblah in the land of Hamath. There the
king of Babylon pronounced judgment upon Zedekiah.
10He made Zedekiah watch as they slaughtered his sons
and all the other officials of Judah. 11Then they gouged
out Zedekiah's eyes, bound him in bronze chains, and led
him away to Babylon. Zedekiah remained there in prison
until the day of his death.

THE TEMPLE DESTROYED

12On August 17 of that year,* which was the nineteenth
year of King Nebuchadnezzar's reign, Nebuzaradan, the
captain of the guard and an official of the Babylonian
king, arrived in Jerusalem. 13He burned down the Temple
of the LORD, the royal palace, and all the houses of Jerusalem. He destroyed all the important buildings* in the
city. 14Then he supervised the entire Babylonian* army as
they tore down the walls of Jerusalem on every side.
15Nebuzaradan, the captain of the guard, then took as exiles some of the poorest of the people, the rest of the people who remained in the city, the defectors who had
declared their allegiance to the king of Babylon, and the
rest of the craftsmen. 16But Nebuzaradan allowed some
of the poorest people to stay behind in Judah to care for
the vineyards and fields.
17The Babylonians broke up the bronze pillars in front
of the LORD's Temple, the bronze water carts, and the
great bronze basin called the Sea, and they carried all the
bronze away to Babylon. 18They also took all the ash
buckets, shovels, lamp snuffers, basins, dishes, and all the
other bronze articles used for making sacrifices at the
Temple. 19Nebuzaradan, the captain of the guard, also
took the small bowls, incense burners, basins, pots, lampstands, dishes, bowls used for liquid offerings, and all the
other articles made of pure gold or silver.
20The weight of the bronze from the two pillars, the Sea

51:59 The fourth year of Zedekiah's reign was 593 B.C. **52:4a** Hebrew *on the tenth day of the tenth month,* of the ancient Hebrew lunar calendar. A number of events in Jeremiah can be cross-checked with dates in surviving Babylonian records and related accurately to our modern calendar. This day was January 15, 588 B.C. **52:4b** Hebrew *Nebuchadrezzar,* a variant spelling of Nebuchadnezzar; also in 52:12, 28, 29, 30. **52:6** Hebrew *By the ninth day of the fourth month* [in the eleventh year of Zedekiah's reign]. This day was July 18, 586 B.C.; also see note on 52:4a. **52:7a** Or *the Chaldeans;* similarly in 52:8, 17. **52:7b** Hebrew *the Arabah.* **52:12** Hebrew *On the tenth day of the fifth month,* of the ancient Hebrew lunar calendar. This day was August 17, 586 B.C.; also see note on 52:4a. **52:13** Or *destroyed the houses of all the important people.* **52:14** Or *Chaldean.*

with the twelve bronze oxen beneath it, and the water
carts was too great to be measured. These things had been
made for the LORD's Temple in the days of King Solomon.
21Each of the pillars was 27 feet tall and 18 feet in circumference.* They were hollow, with walls 3 inches thick.*
22The bronze capital on top of each pillar was 7½ feet*
high and was decorated with a network of bronze pomegranates all the way around. 23There were 96 pomegranates on the sides, and a total of 100 on the network
around the top.
24Nebuzaradan, the captain of the guard, took with
him as prisoners Seraiah the high priest, Zephaniah the
priest of the second rank, and the three chief gatekeepers. 25And from among the people still hiding in the
city, he took an officer who had been in charge of the Judean army; seven of the king's personal advisers; the
army commander's chief secretary, who was in charge of
recruitment; and sixty other citizens. 26Nebuzaradan, the
captain of the guard, took them all to the king of Babylon
at Riblah. 27And there at Riblah, in the land of Hamath,
the king of Babylon had them all put to death. So the people of Judah were sent into exile from their land.
28The number of captives taken to Babylon in the seventh year of Nebuchadnezzar's reign* was 3,023. 29Then
in Nebuchadnezzar's eighteenth year* he took 832 more.
30In Nebuchadnezzar's twenty-third year* he sent Nebuzaradan, the captain of the guard, who took 745 more—a
total of 4,600 captives in all.

GOD'S VIEW OF SUCCESS 52:34

In the world's eyes, Jeremiah looked like a total failure. He had no money, family, or friends. For over 40 years, he prophesied about the destruction of the nation, the capital city, and the Temple, but the political and religious leaders neither accepted nor followed his advice. The people of Judah ignored him. Yet to God, he was a huge success. God measures our success with the yardsticks of obedience, faithfulness, and righteousness. If you are faithfully doing the work God gives you, you are successful in his eyes. ■

HOPE FOR ISRAEL'S ROYAL LINE

31In the thirty-seventh year of the exile of King Jehoiachin of Judah, Evil-merodach ascended to the Babylonian
throne. He was kind to* Jehoiachin and released him
from prison on March 31 of that year.* 32He spoke kindly
to Jehoiachin and gave him a higher place than all the
other exiled kings in Babylon. 33He supplied Jehoiachin
with new clothes to replace his prison garb and allowed
him to dine in the king's presence for the rest of his life.
34So the Babylonian king gave him a regular food allowance as long as he lived. This continued until the day of
his death.

52:21a Hebrew *18 cubits* [8.1 meters] *tall and 12 cubits* [5.4 meters] *in circumference*. 52:21b Hebrew *4 fingers thick* [8 centimeters]. 52:22 Hebrew *5 cubits* [2.3 meters]. 52:28 This exile in the seventh year of Nebuchadnezzar's reign occurred in 597 B.C. 52:29 This exile in the eighteenth year of Nebuchadnezzar's reign occurred in 586 B.C. 52:30 This exile in the twenty-third year of Nebuchadnezzar's reign occurred in 581 B.C. 52:31a Hebrew *He raised the head of*. 52:31b Hebrew *on the twenty-fifth day of the twelfth month*, of the ancient lunar Hebrew calendar. This day was March 31, 561 B.C.; also see note on 52:4a.

LAMENTATIONS

WHAT BREAKS your heart? Losing a game? Saying good-bye? Being dumped or ignored? These are emotional experiences, and worthy of tears. But would you shed a tear over injustice, poverty, war, famine, or for people who don't know God?

Jeremiah would. As a prophet of God, he couldn't help seeing the mess people made of their lives as they disobeyed God. He cared about them and he cared about God. Seeing their sorrow and the destruction they had earned because of their choices made him weep. But he did more than just cry. He talked to God on their behalf.

As you read Lamentations, think about the people in your area or in other parts of the world. What breaks your heart about their situations? What will you do to help?

Lamentations

stats

PURPOSE: To teach people that to disobey God is to invite disaster and to show that God suffers when his people suffer

AUTHOR: Jeremiah

TO WHOM WRITTEN: The nation of Judah and believers everywhere

DATE WRITTEN: Soon after the fall of Jerusalem in 586 B.C.

SETTING: Babylon destroyed Jerusalem and captured the people of Judah.

KEY PEOPLE: Jeremiah; the people of Judah

KEY PLACE: Jerusalem

SPECIAL FEATURES: Three strands of Hebrew thought meet in Lamentations—prophecy, ritual, and wisdom. Lamentations is written in the rhythm and style of ancient Jewish funeral songs or chants. It contains five poems in five chapters.

KEY points

SIN'S CONSEQUENCES

Lamentations is a requiem—sad funeral song—for Jerusalem, the great capital city of the Jews. The Temple had been destroyed, the king was gone, and the people were in exile. This chilling reminder of the consequences of wrong actions also is an invitation to make things right with God.

GOD'S MERCY

God's compassion was at work even though the Israelites suffered in captivity. When we mess up and suffer the consequences, God's mercy seems like a pipe dream. But he never forgets his people nor lets them suffer forever.

HOPE

The fact that God spared the lives of the people of Judah offered them hope for better days. In the same way, Christ's death for us, his resurrection, and promise to return provides the hope of a better life—eternal life with God.

1*

SORROW IN JERUSALEM

1 Jerusalem, once so full of people,
is now deserted.
She who was once great among the nations
now sits alone like a widow.
Once the queen of all the earth,
she is now a slave.

TRUE FREEDOM 1:1-14

The people of Judah's captivity to wrongdoing led to their physical captivity. As with any addiction, the sin cycle grows gradually. Before we know it, we can't help doing wrong. Freedom from sin's captivity comes only from God. He gives us the freedom, not to do anything we want, but to do what he knows is best for us. Strange as it may seem, true freedom comes in obeying God—following his guidance so that we can receive his best. ■

2 She sobs through the night;
tears stream down her cheeks.
Among all her lovers,
there is no one left to comfort her.
All her friends have betrayed her
and become her enemies.

3 Judah has been led away into captivity,
oppressed with cruel slavery.
She lives among foreign nations
and has no place of rest.
Her enemies have chased her down,
and she has nowhere to turn.

4 The roads to Jerusalem* are in mourning,
for crowds no longer come to celebrate
the festivals.
The city gates are silent,
her priests groan,
her young women are crying—
how bitter is her fate!

5 Her oppressors have become her masters,
and her enemies prosper,
for the LORD has punished Jerusalem
for her many sins.
Her children have been captured
and taken away to distant lands.

6 All the majesty of beautiful Jerusalem*
has been stripped away.
Her princes are like starving deer
searching for pasture.
They are too weak to run
from the pursuing enemy.

7 In the midst of her sadness and wandering,
Jerusalem remembers her ancient splendor.
But now she has fallen to her enemy,
and there is no one to help her.
Her enemy struck her down
and laughed as she fell.

8 Jerusalem has sinned greatly,
so she has been tossed away like a filthy rag.
All who once honored her now despise her,
for they have seen her stripped naked
and humiliated.
All she can do is groan
and hide her face.

9 She defiled herself with immorality
and gave no thought to her future.
Now she lies in the gutter
with no one to lift her out.
"LORD, see my misery," she cries.
"The enemy has triumphed."

ADVICE

Sitting on an uncomfortable bench in the visitor's area at a large juvenile correctional facility, Claudius can't help feeling down. He claws unconsciously at the handcuffs that bite into his bony wrists.

Who would imagine that this 14-year-old, former *A*-student is a convicted felon—with a rap sheet that includes car theft and armed robbery?

"I knew better," Claudius mutters to himself. "Grandma was right. I should've listened. But I kept messing up, letting my friends tell me what to do. And, well, here I am.

"I ask God to forgive me every day, but I don't know if it does any good. I just don't know. . . ."

The conversation continues for another twenty minutes. At last the guards come in and usher Claudius away. *Clang!*—just like that, the steel doors slam shut. Claudius disappears from view.

Jeremiah's diary—the book of Lamentations—is a similarly sad story of what happens when people neglect and/or reject the Lord. His advice brought life; the advice and example of other nations brought trouble.

Despite the book of Job's generally depressing tone, there is a wonderful note of hope in 3:19-26. Check it out. What would you tell Claudius about this passage or about seeking the right sources for advice?

10 The enemy has plundered her completely,
taking every precious thing she owns.
She has seen foreigners violate her sacred Temple,
the place the LORD had forbidden them to enter.

1 Each of the first four chapters of this book is an acrostic, laid out in the order of the Hebrew alphabet. The first word of each verse begins with a successive Hebrew letter. Chapters 1, 2, and 4 have one verse for each of the 22 Hebrew letters. Chapter 3 contains 22 stanzas of three verses each. Though chapter 5 has 22 verses, it is not an acrostic. 1:4 Hebrew *Zion;* also in 1:17. 1:6 Hebrew *of the daughter of Zion.*

11 Her people groan as they search for bread.
They have sold their treasures for food to stay alive.
"O LORD, look," she mourns,
"and see how I am despised.

12 "Does it mean nothing to you, all you who pass by?
Look around and see if there is any suffering
like mine,
which the LORD brought on me
when he erupted in fierce anger.

13 "He has sent fire from heaven that burns in my bones.
He has placed a trap in my path and turned
me back.
He has left me devastated,
racked with sickness all day long.

14 "He wove my sins into ropes
to hitch me to a yoke of captivity.
The Lord sapped my strength and turned me over
to my enemies;
I am helpless in their hands.

15 "The Lord has treated my mighty men
with contempt.
At his command a great army has come
to crush my young warriors.
The Lord has trampled his beloved city*
like grapes are trampled in a winepress.

16 "For all these things I weep;
tears flow down my cheeks.
No one is here to comfort me;
any who might encourage me are far away.
My children have no future,
for the enemy has conquered us."

17 Jerusalem reaches out for help,
but no one comforts her.
Regarding his people Israel,*
the LORD has said,
"Let their neighbors be their enemies!
Let them be thrown away like a filthy rag!"

18 "The LORD is right," Jerusalem says,
"for I rebelled against him.
Listen, people everywhere;
look upon my anguish and despair,
for my sons and daughters
have been taken captive to distant lands.

19 "I begged my allies for help,
but they betrayed me.
My priests and leaders
starved to death in the city,
even as they searched for food
to save their lives.

WEAK ALLIES 1:19

The allies of the people of Judah could not come to their aid. Like Judah, they failed to seek God. Though these allies appeared strong, they were actually weak, because God was not with them. Dependable assistance can come only from an ally whose power is from God. When you need advice or other help, whom do you depend on? Do your allies have God's seal of approval? ■

20 "LORD, see my anguish!
My heart is broken
and my soul despairs,
for I have rebelled against you.
In the streets the sword kills,
and at home there is only death.

21 "Others heard my groans,
but no one turned to comfort me.
When my enemies heard about my troubles,
they were happy to see what you had done.
Oh, bring the day you promised,
when they will suffer as I have suffered.

22 "Look at all their evil deeds, LORD.
Punish them,
as you have punished me
for all my sins.
My groans are many,
and I am sick at heart."

2

GOD'S ANGER AT SIN

1 The Lord in his anger
has cast a dark shadow over beautiful
Jerusalem.*
The fairest of Israel's cities lies in the dust,
thrown down from the heights of heaven.
In his day of great anger,
the Lord has shown no mercy even to
his Temple.*

2 Without mercy the Lord has destroyed
every home in Israel.*
In his anger he has broken down
the fortress walls of beautiful Jerusalem.*
He has brought them to the ground,
dishonoring the kingdom and its rulers.

3 All the strength of Israel
vanishes beneath his fierce anger.
The Lord has withdrawn his protection
as the enemy attacks.
He consumes the whole land of Israel
like a raging fire.

1:15 Hebrew *the virgin daughter of Judah.* **1:17** Hebrew *Jacob.* The names "Jacob" and "Israel" are often interchanged throughout the Old Testament, referring sometimes to the individual patriarch and sometimes to the nation. **2:1a** Hebrew *the daughter of Zion;* also in 2:8, 10, 18. **2:1b** Hebrew *his footstool.* **2:2a** Hebrew *Jacob;* also in 2:3b. See note on 1:17. **2:2b** Hebrew *the daughter of Judah;* also in 2:5.

4 He bends his bow against his people,
as though he were their enemy.
His strength is used against them
to kill their finest youth.
His fury is poured out like fire
on beautiful Jerusalem.*

5 Yes, the Lord has vanquished Israel
like an enemy.
He has destroyed her palaces
and demolished her fortresses.
He has brought unending sorrow and tears
upon beautiful Jerusalem.

6 He has broken down his Temple
as though it were merely a garden shelter.
The LORD has blotted out all memory
of the holy festivals and Sabbath days.
Kings and priests fall together
before his fierce anger.

7 The Lord has rejected his own altar;
he despises his own sanctuary.
He has given Jerusalem's palaces
to her enemies.
They shout in the LORD's Temple
as though it were a day of celebration.

TRUE WORSHIP 2:1-7

Although the people of Judah had a beautiful Temple, their rejection of God made their worship a lie. *Where* we worship is not so important to God as *how* we worship. A church may be beautiful, but if its people don't sincerely follow God, it decays from within. When you worship, do you mean the words you say? How do your actions show that you worship God wholeheartedly? ■

8 The LORD was determined
to destroy the walls of beautiful Jerusalem.
He made careful plans for their destruction,
then did what he had planned.
Therefore, the ramparts and walls
have fallen down before him.

9 Jerusalem's gates have sunk into the ground.
He has smashed their locks and bars.
Her kings and princes have been exiled
to distant lands;
her law has ceased to exist.
Her prophets receive
no more visions from the LORD.

10 The leaders of beautiful Jerusalem
sit on the ground in silence.
They are clothed in burlap
and throw dust on their heads.
The young women of Jerusalem
hang their heads in shame.

11 I have cried until the tears no longer come;
my heart is broken.
My spirit is poured out in agony
as I see the desperate plight of my people.
Little children and tiny babies
are fainting and dying in the streets.

12 They cry out to their mothers,
"We need food and drink!"
Their lives ebb away in the streets
like the life of a warrior wounded in battle.
They gasp for life
as they collapse in their mothers' arms.

13 What can I say about you?
Who has ever seen such sorrow?
O daughter of Jerusalem,
to what can I compare your anguish?
O virgin daughter of Zion,
how can I comfort you?
For your wound is as deep as the sea.
Who can heal you?

14 Your prophets have said
so many foolish things, false to the core.
They did not save you from exile
by pointing out your sins.
Instead, they painted false pictures,
filling you with false hope.

15 All who pass by jeer at you.
They scoff and insult beautiful Jerusalem,* saying,
"Is this the city called 'Most Beautiful in All
the World'
and 'Joy of All the Earth'?"

16 All your enemies mock you.
They scoff and snarl and say,
"We have destroyed her at last!
We have long waited for this day,
and it is finally here!"

17 But it is the LORD who did just as he planned.
He has fulfilled the promises of disaster
he made long ago.
He has destroyed Jerusalem without mercy.
He has caused her enemies to gloat over her
and has given them power over her.

18 Cry aloud* before the Lord,
O walls of beautiful Jerusalem!
Let your tears flow like a river
day and night.
Give yourselves no rest;
give your eyes no relief.

2:4 Hebrew *on the tent of the daughter of Zion.* 2:15 Hebrew *the daughter of Jerusalem.* 2:18 Hebrew *Their heart cried.*

keeping it real

I had blown it again—my parents and I had another major disagreement. I ran to my room, slammed the door, and threw myself on the bed. Then I burst into tears, thinking, **They're so unfair!**

After I had cried for a while, I thought about our fight. I still thought my parents were wrong, but I also had to admit that I'd said some pretty ugly things. The more I thought about it, the more I realized I needed to apologize.

It took me a couple of hours. Finally I came out and apologized for some of the hurtful things I had said. My mother's response was, "You think it's that easy? Just say you're sorry, and everything's OK? Well, it doesn't work that way."

I just turned and went back to my room and cried some more. I had said I was sorry, and I was. Why couldn't they just forgive me?

The next morning, still feeling bad, I picked up my Bible. I remembered reading a passage from a strange book in the Old Testament—Lamentations. "Yet I still dare to hope when I remember this: The faithful love of the LORD never ends! . . . Great is his faithfulness; his mercies begin afresh each morning" (3:21-23).

So, I realized that even if my parents didn't forgive me, God did. He knew I was sincere, and would help me do better. And even if I didn't, he'd love me. His compassion would be there for me tomorrow, just like the sun coming up to warm me. **—Lydia**

19 Rise during the night and cry out.
Pour out your hearts like water to the Lord.
Lift up your hands to him in prayer,
pleading for your children,
for in every street
they are faint with hunger.

20 "O LORD, think about this!
Should you treat your own people this way?
Should mothers eat their own children,
those they once bounced on their knees?
Should priests and prophets be killed
within the Lord's Temple?

21 "See them lying in the streets—
young and old,
boys and girls,
killed by the swords of the enemy.
You have killed them in your anger,
slaughtering them without mercy.

22 "You have invited terrors from all around,
as though you were calling them to a day
of feasting.
In the day of the LORD's anger,
no one has escaped or survived.
The enemy has killed all the children
whom I carried and raised."

3 HOPE IN THE LORD'S FAITHFULNESS

1 I am the one who has seen the afflictions
that come from the rod of the LORD's anger.
2 He has led me into darkness,
shutting out all light.
3 He has turned his hand against me
again and again, all day long.

4 He has made my skin and flesh grow old.
He has broken my bones.
5 He has besieged and surrounded me
with anguish and distress.
6 He has buried me in a dark place,
like those long dead.

7 He has walled me in, and I cannot escape.
He has bound me in heavy chains.
8 And though I cry and shout,
he has shut out my prayers.
9 He has blocked my way with a high stone wall;
he has made my road crooked.

10 He has hidden like a bear or a lion,
waiting to attack me.
11 He has dragged me off the path and torn
me in pieces,
leaving me helpless and devastated.

12 He has drawn his bow
and made me the target for his arrows.

13 He shot his arrows
deep into my heart.
14 My own people laugh at me.
All day long they sing their mocking songs.
15 He has filled me with bitterness
and given me a bitter cup of sorrow to drink.

16 He has made me chew on gravel.
He has rolled me in the dust.
17 Peace has been stripped away,
and I have forgotten what prosperity is.
18 I cry out, "My splendor is gone!
Everything I had hoped for from the LORD is lost!"

19 The thought of my suffering and homelessness
is bitter beyond words.*
20 I will never forget this awful time,
as I grieve over my loss.
21 Yet I still dare to hope
when I remember this:

22 The faithful love of the LORD never ends!*
His mercies never cease.
23 Great is his faithfulness;
his mercies begin afresh each morning.
24 I say to myself, "The LORD is my inheritance;
therefore, I will hope in him!"

GRACE 3:19-23

Jeremiah saw one ray of hope in Judah's sad situation: *The undeserved love of the LORD* never ends (3:21)! Even when we mess up, God willingly responds with help when we ask. God offers love and forgiveness even when we don't deserve it. That's "grace": *G*od's *r*iches *a*t *C*hrist's *e*xpense. Need some? Don't be afraid to ask. ■

25 The LORD is good to those who depend on him,
to those who search for him.
26 So it is good to wait quietly
for salvation from the LORD.
27 And it is good for people to submit at an early age
to the yoke of his discipline:

28 Let them sit alone in silence
beneath the LORD's demands.
29 Let them lie face down in the dust,
for there may be hope at last.
30 Let them turn the other cheek to those who
strike them
and accept the insults of their enemies.

31 For no one is abandoned
by the Lord forever.
32 Though he brings grief, he also shows compassion
because of the greatness of his unfailing love.
33 For he does not enjoy hurting people
or causing them sorrow.

SUBMIT 3:25-33

To "submit . . . to the yoke of his discipline" means to accept God's correction. It sometimes means letting go of your anger or disappointment because of your circumstances and paying attention to what God wants to teach you. Some attitudes of learning involve (1) humility, (2) self-control in the face of adversity, and (3) confident patience. God has several long-term and short-term lessons for you right now. Are you willing to learn? ■

34 If people crush underfoot
all the prisoners of the land,
35 if they deprive others of their rights
in defiance of the Most High,
36 if they twist justice in the courts—
doesn't the Lord see all these things?

37 Who can command things to happen
without the Lord's permission?
38 Does not the Most High
send both calamity and good?
39 Then why should we, mere humans, complain
when we are punished for our sins?

40 Instead, let us test and examine our ways.
Let us turn back to the LORD.
41 Let us lift our hearts and hands
to God in heaven and say,
42 "We have sinned and rebelled,
and you have not forgiven us.

43 "You have engulfed us with your anger, chased us down,
and slaughtered us without mercy.
44 You have hidden yourself in a cloud
so our prayers cannot reach you.
45 You have discarded us as refuse and garbage
among the nations.

46 "All our enemies
have spoken out against us.
47 We are filled with fear,
for we are trapped, devastated, and ruined."
48 Tears stream from my eyes
because of the destruction of my people!

49 My tears flow endlessly;
they will not stop
50 until the LORD looks down
from heaven and sees.
51 My heart is breaking
over the fate of all the women of Jerusalem.

3:19 Or *is wormwood and gall.* 3:22 As in Syriac version; Hebrew reads *of the LORD keeps us from destruction.*

52 My enemies, whom I have never harmed,
hunted me down like a bird.
53 They threw me into a pit
and dropped stones on me.
54 The water rose over my head,
and I cried out, "This is the end!"

55 But I called on your name, LORD,
from deep within the pit.
56 You heard me when I cried, "Listen to my pleading!
Hear my cry for help!"
57 Yes, you came when I called;
you told me, "Do not fear."

58 Lord, you are my lawyer! Plead my case!
For you have redeemed my life.
59 You have seen the wrong they have done
to me, LORD.
Be my judge, and prove me right.
60 You have seen the vengeful plots
my enemies have laid against me.

61 LORD, you have heard the vile names they call me.
You know all about the plans they have made.
62 My enemies whisper and mutter
as they plot against me all day long.
63 Look at them! Whether they sit or stand,
I am the object of their mocking songs.

64 Pay them back, LORD,
for all the evil they have done.
65 Give them hard and stubborn hearts,
and then let your curse fall on them!
66 Chase them down in your anger,
destroying them beneath the LORD's heavens.

4 GOD'S ANGER SATISFIED

1 How the gold has lost its luster!
Even the finest gold has become dull.
The sacred gemstones
lie scattered in the streets!

2 See how the precious children of Jerusalem,*
worth their weight in fine gold,
are now treated like pots of clay
made by a common potter.

3 Even the jackals feed their young,
but not my people Israel.
They ignore their children's cries,
like ostriches in the desert.

4 The parched tongues of their little ones
stick to the roofs of their mouths in thirst.
The children cry for bread,
but no one has any to give them.

5 The people who once ate the richest foods
now beg in the streets for anything they
can get.
Those who once wore the finest clothes
now search the garbage dumps for food.

6 The guilt* of my people
is greater than that of Sodom,
where utter disaster struck in a moment
and no hand offered help.

7 Our princes once glowed with health—
brighter than snow, whiter than milk.
Their faces were as ruddy as rubies,
their appearance like fine jewels.*
8 But now their faces are blacker than soot.
No one recognizes them in the streets.
Their skin sticks to their bones;
it is as dry and hard as wood.

9 Those killed by the sword are better off
than those who die of hunger.
Starving, they waste away
for lack of food from the fields.

10 Tenderhearted women
have cooked their own children.
They have eaten them
to survive the siege.

11 But now the anger of the LORD is satisfied.
His fierce anger has been poured out.
He started a fire in Jerusalem*
that burned the city to its foundations.

BANKRUPT 4:1-22

This chapter provides a view of Jerusalem before and after the siege. The people of Judah had been prosperous before, now they were poor. What they didn't realize was that they were spiritually poor when they were wealthy. How is your spiritual bank account these days? Are you spiritually rich or overdrawn? ■

12 Not a king in all the earth—
no one in all the world—
would have believed that an enemy
could march through the gates of Jerusalem.

13 Yet it happened because of the sins of her prophets
and the sins of her priests,
who defiled the city
by shedding innocent blood.

14 They wandered blindly
through the streets,

4:2 Hebrew *precious sons of Zion.* 4:6 Or *punishment.* 4:7 Hebrew *like lapis lazuli.* 4:11 Hebrew *in Zion.*

so defiled by blood
that no one dared touch them.

15 "Get away!" the people shouted at them.
"You're defiled! Don't touch us!"
So they fled to distant lands
and wandered among foreign nations,
but none would let them stay.

16 The LORD himself has scattered them,
and he no longer helps them.
People show no respect for the priests
and no longer honor the leaders.

17 We looked in vain for our allies
to come and save us,
but we were looking to nations
that could not help us.

18 We couldn't go into the streets
without danger to our lives.
Our end was near; our days were numbered.
We were doomed!

19 Our enemies were swifter than eagles in flight.
If we fled to the mountains, they found us.
If we hid in the wilderness,
they were waiting for us there.

20 Our king—the LORD's anointed, the very life
of our nation—
was caught in their snares.
We had thought that his shadow
would protect us against any nation on earth!

21 Are you rejoicing in the land of Uz,
O people of Edom?
But you, too, must drink from the cup of the
LORD's anger.
You, too, will be stripped naked in your
drunkenness.

22 O beautiful Jerusalem,* your punishment will end;
you will soon return from exile.
But Edom, your punishment is just beginning;
soon your many sins will be exposed.

5 PRAYER FOR RESTORATION

1 LORD, remember what has happened to us.
See how we have been disgraced!
2 Our inheritance has been turned over to strangers,
our homes to foreigners.
3 We are orphaned and fatherless.
Our mothers are widowed.
4 We have to pay for water to drink,
and even firewood is expensive.
5 Those who pursue us are at our heels;
we are exhausted but are given no rest.
6 We submitted to Egypt and Assyria
to get enough food to survive.
7 Our ancestors sinned, but they have died—
and we are suffering the punishment
they deserved!

THE PROMISE OF RESTORATION 5:1-22

The book of Lamentations is a portrait of the suffering experienced by the people of Judah as a consequence for sin. Every material goal they had lived for disappeared. Even though God allowed them to go through pain, he did not abandon them. He promised to restore them if they returned to him. He promises to do the same for us when we seek him. ■

8 Slaves have now become our masters;
there is no one left to rescue us.
9 We hunt for food at the risk of our lives,
for violence rules the countryside.
10 The famine has blackened our skin
as though baked in an oven.
11 Our enemies rape the women in Jerusalem*
and the young girls in all the towns of Judah.
12 Our princes are being hanged by their thumbs,
and our elders are treated with contempt.
13 Young men are led away to work at millstones,
and boys stagger under heavy loads of wood.
14 The elders no longer sit in the city gates;
the young men no longer dance and sing.
15 Joy has left our hearts;
our dancing has turned to mourning.
16 The garlands have* fallen from our heads.
Weep for us because we have sinned.
17 Our hearts are sick and weary,
and our eyes grow dim with tears.
18 For Jerusalem* is empty and desolate,
a place haunted by jackals.

19 But LORD, you remain the same forever!
Your throne continues from generation
to generation.
20 Why do you continue to forget us?
Why have you abandoned us for so long?
21 Restore us, O LORD, and bring us back to you again!
Give us back the joys we once had!
22 Or have you utterly rejected us?
Are you angry with us still?

4:22 Hebrew *O daughter of Zion.* **5:11** Hebrew *in Zion.* **5:16** Or *The crown has.* **5:18** Hebrew *Mount Zion.*

EZEKIEL

"CHILL," Andrew said. "I'm my dad's favorite."

Andrew's dad had gone out of town—leaving his brand new convertible—that Andrew was not allowed to drive—in the garage.

The drive to the movie was great. Girls honked and guys drooled. Andrew and his friends loved it.

After the movie, they headed to the car. It was late, and the parking lot was no longer full. But they were shocked to find wires dangling from where the stereo used to be. Andrew had forgotten to put the top up or turn on the alarm!

"What are we gonna do?" One of his friends asked.

Andrew smiled weakly. "Hey, dad's favorite, no problem!"

Israel reacted like Andrew. They thought they could get away with anything. Ezekiel was written to captive Jews in Babylon. They were "God's favorites." Surely Jerusalem would not be harmed, and they would return home very soon. Ezekiel, God's prophet to the exiled people of Judah, corrected their thinking. They were captives in Babylon because they had disobeyed God. Though they were his chosen people, God could not overlook sin.

Ezekiel reminds us of the consequences of our actions. But thanks to Jesus, we can escape the judgment that we all deserve. Have you taken this escape route?

ezekiel

timeline

627 B.C.
Jeremiah becomes a prophet to Judah

605
Daniel taken captive to Babylon

597
Ezekiel taken captive to Babylon

593
Ezekiel becomes a prophet to exiles

586
Judah falls; Jerusalem destroyed

571
Ezekiel's ministry ends

539
Babylon overthrown by Cyrus

537
First exiles return to Judah

stats

PURPOSE: To announce God's judgment; to foretell the salvation of God's people

AUTHOR: Ezekiel—the son of Buzi, a Zadokite priest

TO WHOM WRITTEN: The Jews in captivity in Babylon and God's people everywhere

DATE WRITTEN: Approximately 571 B.C.

SETTING: While Jeremiah ministered to the people still in Judah, Ezekiel prophesied to those already exiled in Babylon after the defeat of Jehoiachin. He was among the captives taken there in 597 B.C.

KEY PEOPLE: Ezekiel, Israel's leaders, Ezekiel's wife, Nebuchadnezzar, the "prince"

KEY PLACES: Jerusalem, Babylon, and Egypt

KEY points

RESPONSIBILITY
Ezekiel warned the exiles of Israel that not only was the nation responsible for sin, each individual also was responsible. In the same way, each of us is responsible for the wrong things we do.

RESTORATION
Ezekiel comforted the people with God's promise to restore them to their land. When life seems bleak for us, we can choose to focus on God's promises of restoration, peace, and eternal life with him.

ROGUE SHEPHERDS
Ezekiel condemned the unfaithful priests and leaders ("shepherds") who led the people astray. By contrast, Ezekiel was a caring shepherd as he warned the people about their sin. A good leader does whatever is necessary to care for the people under his or her charge.

REAL WORSHIP
Although God's holy presence had left the Temple, one day he would return and restore true worship. We, too, can look forward to the fulfillment of God's promises under the future rule of the Savior. The faithful followers will be brought back to perfect fellowship with God and with one another. But we can prepare for that today by walking closely with God.

1 A VISION OF LIVING BEINGS

On July 31* of my thirtieth year,* while I was with the
Judean exiles beside the Kebar River in Babylon, the heavens were opened and I saw visions of God. 2This happened during the fifth year of King Jehoiachin's captivity.
3(The LORD gave this message to Ezekiel son of Buzi, a
priest, beside the Kebar River in the land of the Babylonians,* and he felt the hand of the LORD take hold of him.)

CONFRONT

Chad's been hearing rumors about his friend Seth for a couple of weeks now—rumors like: "You should've seen Seth at Becca's party last weekend! Man, he was wasted!"

"I heard Seth popped X (Ecstasy) at a party the other day. I thought Seth used to be religious. He sure has changed!" Chad had heard some of these rumors before.

Tonight some of Chad's worst fears were confirmed. Driving through the school parking lot after a game, Chad happened to see Seth and Will, another guy from school, sitting in the back of a pick-up truck, taking tequila shots. Chad didn't stop, so he doesn't know whether or not Seth saw him.

Chad is concerned, but also confused. Here's his childhood friend starting to run with a pretty wild crowd. It seems Seth is headed for major-league trouble. Chad ponders what to do: "Should I talk to Seth or just keep my mouth shut? I mean, I want to do what's right. But if I speak up, Seth'll just laugh at me. Besides, who am I to tell him how to live?"

Do you agree or disagree with Chad? Why? When friends head for trouble, we have a God-given responsibility to pull them aside and help them get back on track. The question isn't how they may or may not respond—that's irrelevant. The real question is whether or not we love them enough to do what's right and confront them.

Well? Do you?

Check out Ezekiel 2:3-7. What do you think God is saying to you?

4As I looked, I saw a great storm coming from the
north, driving before it a huge cloud that flashed with
lightning and shone with brilliant light. There was fire inside the cloud, and in the middle of the fire glowed something like gleaming amber.* 5From the center of the
cloud came four living beings that looked human,
6except that each had four faces and four wings. 7Their
legs were straight, and their feet had hooves like those of
a calf and shone like burnished bronze. 8Under each of
their four wings I could see human hands. So each of the
four beings had four faces and four wings. 9The wings of
each living being touched the wings of the beings beside
it. Each one moved straight forward in any direction
without turning around.

IN AWE 1:1-28

A bright light, a dazzling fire—that's what the glory of the Lord looked like to Ezekiel. He fell to the ground, overwhelmed by the holiness of God and his own sinfulness and insignificance. Eventually every person will kneel before God, either out of awe and gratitude for his mercy or out of fear of his judgment. Based on the way you're living today, how will you respond? ■

10Each had a human face in the front, the face of a lion
on the right side, the face of an ox on the left side, and the
face of an eagle at the back. 11Each had two pairs of out-
stretched wings—one pair stretched out to touch the
wings of the living beings on either side of it, and the
other pair covered its body. 12They went in whatever direction the spirit chose, and they moved straight forward
in any direction without turning around.
13The living beings looked like bright coals of fire or
brilliant torches, and lightning seemed to flash back and
forth among them. 14And the living beings darted to and
fro like flashes of lightning.
15As I looked at these beings, I saw four wheels touching the ground beside them, one wheel belonging to each.
16The wheels sparkled as if made of beryl. All four wheels
looked alike and were made the same; each wheel had a
second wheel turning crosswise within it. 17The beings
could move in any of the four directions they faced, without turning as they moved. 18The rims of the four wheels
were tall and frightening, and they were covered with eyes
all around.
19When the living beings moved, the wheels moved
with them. When they flew upward, the wheels went up,
too. 20The spirit of the living beings was in the wheels. So
wherever the spirit went, the wheels and the living beings
also went. 21When the beings moved, the wheels moved.
When the beings stopped, the wheels stopped. When the
beings flew upward, the wheels rose up, for the spirit of
the living beings was in the wheels.
22Spread out above them was a surface like the sky, glittering like crystal. 23Beneath this surface the wings of
each living being stretched out to touch the others' wings,
and each had two wings covering its body. 24As they flew,
their wings sounded to me like waves crashing against the
shore or like the voice of the Almighty* or like the shouting of a mighty army. When they stopped, they let down
their wings. 25As they stood with wings lowered, a voice
spoke from beyond the crystal surface above them.
26Above this surface was something that looked like a

1:1a Hebrew *On the fifth day of the fourth month,* of the ancient Hebrew lunar calendar. A number of dates in Ezekiel can be cross-checked with dates in surviving Babylonian records and related accurately to our modern calendar. This event occurred on July 31, 593 B.C. **1:1b** Or *in the thirtieth year*. **1:3** Or *Chaldeans*. **1:4** Or *like burnished metal;* also in 1:27. **1:24** Hebrew *Shaddai*.

throne made of blue lapis lazuli. And on this throne high above was a figure whose appearance resembled a man. 27From what appeared to be his waist up, he looked like gleaming amber, flickering like a fire. And from his waist down, he looked like a burning flame, shining with splendor. 28All around him was a glowing halo, like a rainbow shining in the clouds on a rainy day. This is what the glory of the LORD looked like to me. When I saw it, I fell face down on the ground, and I heard someone's voice speaking to me.

2

EZEKIEL'S CALL AND COMMISSION

"Stand up, son of man," said the voice. "I want to speak with you." 2The Spirit came into me as he spoke, and he set me on my feet. I listened carefully to his words. 3"Son of man," he said, "I am sending you to the nation of Israel, a rebellious nation that has rebelled against me. They and their ancestors have been rebelling against me to this very day. 4They are a stubborn and hard-hearted people. But I am sending you to say to them, 'This is what the Sovereign LORD says!' 5And whether they listen or refuse to listen—for remember, they are rebels—at least they will know they have had a prophet among them.

TOUGH TALK 2:1-8

Ezekiel was given the difficult responsibility of presenting God's messages to people who wouldn't listen to him. Sometimes we also are called to share our faith with people who may react the same way the exiles did. Just as God told Ezekiel not to give up, he tells us not give up, too. Instead, we are to tell the Good News whether people listen or not (see 2 Tim 4:2). Are you willing? ■

6"Son of man, do not fear them or their words. Don't be afraid even though their threats surround you like nettles and briers and stinging scorpions. Do not be dismayed by their dark scowls, even though they are rebels. 7You must give them my messages whether they listen or not. But they won't listen, for they are completely rebellious! 8Son of man, listen to what I say to you. Do not join them in their rebellion. Open your mouth, and eat what I give you."

9Then I looked and saw a hand reaching out to me. It held a scroll, 10which he unrolled. And I saw that both sides were covered with funeral songs, words of sorrow, and pronouncements of doom.

3

The voice said to me, "Son of man, eat what I am giving you—eat this scroll! Then go and give its message to the people of Israel." 2So I opened my mouth, and he fed me the scroll. 3"Fill your stomach with this," he said. And when I ate it, it tasted as sweet as honey in my mouth.

4Then he said, "Son of man, go to the people of Israel and give them my messages. 5I am not sending you to a foreign people whose language you cannot understand. 6No, I am not sending you to people with strange and difficult speech. If I did, they would listen! 7But the people of Israel won't listen to you any more than they listen to me! For the whole lot of them are hard-hearted and stubborn. 8But look, I have made you as obstinate and hard-hearted as they are. 9I have made your forehead as hard as the hardest rock! So don't be afraid of them or fear their angry looks, even though they are rebels."

10Then he added, "Son of man, let all my words sink deep into your own heart first. Listen to them carefully for yourself. 11Then go to your people in exile and say to them, 'This is what the Sovereign LORD says!' Do this whether they listen to you or not."

12Then the Spirit lifted me up, and I heard a loud rumbling sound behind me. (May the glory of the LORD be praised in his place!)* 13It was the sound of the wings of the living beings as they brushed against each other and the rumbling of their wheels beneath them.

14The Spirit lifted me up and took me away. I went in bitterness and turmoil, but the LORD's hold on me was strong. 15Then I came to the colony of Judean exiles in Tel-abib, beside the Kebar River. I was overwhelmed and sat among them for seven days.

A WATCHMAN FOR ISRAEL

16After seven days the LORD gave me a message. He said, 17"Son of man, I have appointed you as a watchman for Israel. Whenever you receive a message from me, warn people immediately. 18If I warn the wicked, saying, 'You are under the penalty of death,' but you fail to deliver the warning, they will die in their sins. And I will hold you responsible for their deaths. 19If you warn them and they refuse to repent and keep on sinning, they will die in their sins. But you will have saved yourself because you obeyed me.

20"If righteous people turn away from their righteous behavior and ignore the obstacles I put in their way, they will die. And if you do not warn them, they will die in their sins. None of their righteous acts will be remembered, and I will hold you responsible for their deaths. 21But if you warn righteous people not to sin and they listen to you and do not sin, they will live, and you will have saved yourself, too."

22Then the LORD took hold of me and said, "Get up and go out into the valley, and I will speak to you there." 23So I got up and went, and there I saw the glory of the LORD, just as I had seen in my first vision by the Kebar River. And I fell face down on the ground.

24Then the Spirit came into me and set me on my feet. He spoke to me and said, "Go to your house and shut yourself in. 25There, son of man, you will be tied with ropes so you cannot go out among the people. 26And I will make your tongue stick to the roof of your mouth so that you will be speechless and unable to rebuke them, for

3:12 A possible reading for this verse is *Then the Spirit lifted me up, and as the glory of the LORD rose from its place, I heard a loud rumbling sound behind me.*

they are rebels. [27]But when I give you a message, I will loosen your tongue and let you speak. Then you will say to them, 'This is what the Sovereign LORD says!' Those who choose to listen will listen, but those who refuse will refuse, for they are rebels.

4 A SIGN OF THE COMING SIEGE

"And now, son of man, take a large clay brick and set it down in front of you. Then draw a map of the city of Jerusalem on it. [2]Show the city under siege. Build a wall around it so no one can escape. Set up the enemy camp, and surround the city with siege ramps and battering rams. [3]Then take an iron griddle and place it between you and the city. Turn toward the city and demonstrate how harsh the siege will be against Jerusalem. This will be a warning to the people of Israel.

DETAILS 4:1-17

Ezekiel dramatically performed the siege and fall of Jerusalem before the actual events happened. God gave Ezekiel specific instructions about what to say and how to say it. Each detail had a special meaning. These days, some of the details of God's Word are ignored. Ever notice that? Some might think these details don't really matter. Like Ezekiel, are you willing to obey God completely, even down to the smallest detail? ■

[4]"Now lie on your left side and place the sins of Israel on yourself. You are to bear their sins for the number of days you lie there on your side. [5]I am requiring you to bear Israel's sins for 390 days—one day for each year of their sin. [6]After that, turn over and lie on your right side for 40 days—one day for each year of Judah's sin.

[7]"Meanwhile, keep staring at the siege of Jerusalem. Lie there with your arm bared and prophesy her destruction. [8]I will tie you up with ropes so you won't be able to turn from side to side until the days of your siege have been completed.

[9]"Now go and get some wheat, barley, beans, lentils, millet, and emmer wheat, and mix them together in a storage jar. Use them to make bread for yourself during the 390 days you will be lying on your side. [10]Ration this out to yourself, eight ounces* of food for each day, and eat it at set times. [11]Then measure out a jar* of water for each day, and drink it at set times. [12]Prepare and eat this food as you would barley cakes. While all the people are watching, bake it over a fire using dried human dung as fuel and then eat the bread." [13]Then the LORD said, "This is how Israel will eat defiled bread in the Gentile lands to which I will banish them!"

[14]Then I said, "O Sovereign LORD, must I be defiled by using human dung? For I have never been defiled before. From the time I was a child until now I have never eaten any animal that died of sickness or was killed by other animals. I have never eaten any meat forbidden by the law."

[15]"All right," the LORD said. "You may bake your bread with cow dung instead of human dung." [16]Then he told me, "Son of man, I will make food very scarce in Jerusalem. It will be weighed out with great care and eaten fearfully. The water will be rationed out drop by drop, and the people will drink it with dismay. [17]Lacking food and water, people will look at one another in terror, and they will waste away under their punishment.

5 A SIGN OF THE COMING JUDGMENT

"Son of man, take a sharp sword and use it as a razor to shave your head and beard. Use a scale to weigh the hair into three equal parts. [2]Place a third of it at the center of your map of Jerusalem. After acting out the siege, burn it there. Scatter another third across your map and chop it with a sword. Scatter the last third to the wind, for I will scatter my people with the sword. [3]Keep just a bit of the hair and tie it up in your robe. [4]Then take some of these hairs out and throw them into the fire, burning them up. A fire will then spread from this remnant and destroy all of Israel.

[5]"This is what the Sovereign LORD says: This is an illustration of what will happen to Jerusalem. I placed her at the center of the nations, [6]but she has rebelled against my regulations and decrees and has been even more wicked than the surrounding nations. She has refused to obey the regulations and decrees I gave her to follow.

FOLLOW THROUGH 5:1-13

Have you ever seen a parent try to discipline a child by saying, "If you do that one more time . . ."? If the parent never follows through on his or her threat, the child learns not to listen. Empty threats backfire. God planned to punish the Israelites for their wrong actions. The people learned the hard way that God always follows through on his word. Too many people ignore God's warnings that he will punish sin. But what God threatens, he does. What will you do to avoid learning this truth the hard way? ■

[7]"Therefore, this is what the Sovereign LORD says: You people have behaved worse than your neighbors and have refused to obey my decrees and regulations. You have not even lived up to the standards of the nations around you. [8]Therefore, I myself, the Sovereign LORD, am now your enemy. I will punish you publicly while all the nations watch. [9]Because of your detestable idols, I will punish you like I have never punished anyone before or ever will again. [10]Parents will eat their own children, and children will eat their parents. I will punish you and scatter to the winds the few who survive.

[11]"As surely as I live, says the Sovereign LORD, I will cut you off completely. I will show you no pity at all because you have defiled my Temple with your vile images and detestable sins. [12]A third of your people will die in the city from disease and famine. A third of them will be

4:10 Hebrew *20 shekels* [228 grams]. **4:11** Hebrew *1/6 of a hin* [about 1 pint or 0.6 liters].

slaughtered by the enemy outside the city walls. And I will scatter a third to the winds, chasing them with my sword. 13Then at last my anger will be spent, and I will be satisfied. And when my fury against them has subsided, all Israel will know that I, the LORD, have spoken to them in my jealous anger.

14"So I will turn you into a ruin, a mockery in the eyes of the surrounding nations and to all who pass by. 15You will become an object of mockery and taunting and horror. You will be a warning to all the nations around you. They will see what happens when the LORD punishes a nation in anger and rebukes it, says the LORD.

16"I will shower you with the deadly arrows of famine to destroy you. The famine will become more and more severe until every crumb of food is gone. 17And along with the famine, wild animals will attack you and rob you of your children. Disease and war will stalk your land, and I will bring the sword of the enemy against you. I, the LORD, have spoken!"

6

JUDGMENT AGAINST ISRAEL'S MOUNTAINS

Again a message came to me from the LORD: 2"Son of man, turn and face the mountains of Israel and prophesy against them. 3Proclaim this message from the Sovereign LORD against the mountains of Israel. This is what the Sovereign LORD says to the mountains and hills and to the ravines and valleys: I am about to bring war upon you, and I will smash your pagan shrines. 4All your altars will be demolished, and your places of worship will be destroyed. I will kill your people in front of your idols.* 5I will lay your corpses in front of your idols and scatter your bones around your altars. 6Wherever you live there will be desolation, and I will destroy your pagan shrines. Your altars will be demolished, your idols will be smashed, your places of worship will be torn down, and all the religious objects you have made will be destroyed. 7The place will be littered with corpses, and you will know that I alone am the LORD.

8"But I will let a few of my people escape destruction, and they will be scattered among the nations of the world. 9Then when they are exiled among the nations, they will remember me. They will recognize how hurt I am by their unfaithful hearts and lustful eyes that long for their idols. Then at last they will hate themselves for all their detestable sins. 10They will know that I alone am the LORD and that I was serious when I said I would bring this calamity on them.

11"This is what the Sovereign LORD says: Clap your hands in horror, and stamp your feet. Cry out because of all the detestable sins the people of Israel have committed. Now they are going to die from war and famine and disease. 12Disease will strike down those who are far away in exile. War will destroy those who are nearby. And anyone who survives will be killed by famine. So at last I will spend my fury on them. 13They will know that I am the LORD when their dead lie scattered among their idols and altars on every hill and mountain and under every green tree and every great shade tree—the places where they offered sacrifices to their idols. 14I will crush them and make their cities desolate from the wilderness in the south to Riblah* in the north. Then they will know that I am the LORD."

ONE AND ONLY 6:7-14

The phrase "then they will know that I am the LORD" (or a variation on this phrase) occurs about 70 times in the book of Ezekiel. God used the punishment method to remind the exiled people of Israel and Judah that he was the only God. Many people in Ezekiel's day worshiped man-made idols. Today money, sex, and power have become idols for many. God sometimes uses the difficulties of a person's life to remind him or her that he alone is God. Is he your only God? ■

7

THE COMING OF THE END

Then this message came to me from the LORD: 2"Son of man, this is what the Sovereign LORD says to Israel:

"The end is here!
Wherever you look—
east, west, north, or south—
your land is finished.
3 No hope remains,
for I will unleash my anger against you.
I will call you to account
for all your detestable sins.
4 I will turn my eyes away and show no pity.
I will repay you for all your detestable sins.
Then you will know that I am the LORD.

5 "This is what the Sovereign LORD says:
Disaster after disaster
is coming your way!
6 The end has come.
It has finally arrived.
Your final doom is waiting!
7 O people of Israel, the day of your destruction
is dawning.
The time has come; the day of trouble is near.
Shouts of anguish will be heard on the mountains,
not shouts of joy.
8 Soon I will pour out my fury on you
and unleash my anger against you.
I will call you to account
for all your detestable sins.
9 I will turn my eyes away and show no pity.
I will repay you for all your detestable sins.
Then you will know that it is I, the LORD,
who is striking the blow.

6:4 The Hebrew term (literally *round things*) probably alludes to dung; also in 6:5, 6, 9, 13. 6:14 As in some Hebrew manuscripts; most Hebrew manuscripts read *Diblah*.

10 "The day of judgment is here;
your destruction awaits!
The people's wickedness and pride
have blossomed to full flower.
11 Their violence has grown into a rod
that will beat them for their wickedness.
None of these proud and wicked people will survive.
All their wealth and prestige will be swept away.
12 Yes, the time has come;
the day is here!
Buyers should not rejoice over bargains,
nor sellers grieve over losses,
for all of them will fall
under my terrible anger.
13 Even if the merchants survive,
they will never return to their business.
For what God has said applies to everyone—
it will not be changed!
Not one person whose life is twisted by sin
will ever recover.

THE DESOLATION OF ISRAEL

14 "The trumpet calls Israel's army to mobilize,
but no one listens,
for my fury is against them all.
15 There is war outside the city
and disease and famine within.
Those outside the city walls
will be killed by enemy swords.
Those inside the city
will die of famine and disease.
16 The survivors who escape to the mountains
will moan like doves, weeping for their sins.
17 Their hands will hang limp,
their knees will be weak as water.
18 They will dress themselves in burlap;
horror and shame will cover them.
They will shave their heads
in sorrow and remorse.

MONEY 7:19

Ezekiel prophesied that hard times would make money seem worthless. Money wouldn't buy them out of trouble. Have you ever thought of money as the ultimate deliverance from whatever problems you face? Many people do. It can pay for a lot of things. But it can also cause trouble if it stands between a person and God. That's why the apostle Paul later wrote that the love of money—not money itself—is the real problem (see 1 Tim 6:10). How ironic that we use wealth—a gift of God—to buy things that separate us from him. Is God your true source of satisfaction, or is money? ■

19 "They will throw their money in the streets,
tossing it out like worthless trash.
Their silver and gold won't save them
on that day of the LORD's anger.
It will neither satisfy nor feed them,
for their greed can only trip them up.
20 They were proud of their beautiful jewelry
and used it to make detestable idols and
vile images.
Therefore, I will make all their wealth
disgusting to them.
21 I will give it as plunder to foreigners,
to the most wicked of nations,
and they will defile it.
22 I will turn my eyes from them
as these robbers invade and defile my
treasured land.

23 "Prepare chains for my people,
for the land is bloodied by terrible crimes.
Jerusalem is filled with violence.
24 I will bring the most ruthless of nations
to occupy their homes.
I will break down their proud fortresses
and defile their sanctuaries.
25 Terror and trembling will overcome my people.
They will look for peace but not find it.
26 Calamity will follow calamity;
rumor will follow rumor.
They will look in vain
for a vision from the prophets.
They will receive no teaching from the priests
and no counsel from the leaders.
27 The king and the prince will stand helpless,
weeping in despair,
and the people's hands
will tremble with fear.
I will bring on them
the evil they have done to others,
and they will receive the punishment
they so richly deserve.
Then they will know that I am the LORD."

8 IDOLATRY IN THE TEMPLE

Then on September 17,* during the sixth year of King Jehoiachin's captivity, while the leaders of Judah were in
my home, the Sovereign LORD took hold of me. 2I saw a
figure that appeared to be a man. From what appeared to
be his waist down, he looked like a burning flame. From
the waist up he looked like gleaming amber.* 3He
reached out what seemed to be a hand and took me by
the hair. Then the Spirit lifted me up into the sky and
transported me to Jerusalem in a vision from God. I was
taken to the north gate of the inner courtyard of the Temple, where there is a large idol that has made the LORD
very jealous. 4Suddenly, the glory of the God of Israel was
there, just as I had seen it before in the valley.
5Then the LORD said to me, "Son of man, look toward
the north." So I looked, and there to the north, beside the

8:1 Hebrew *on the fifth day of the sixth month,* of the ancient Hebrew lunar calendar. This event occurred on September 17, 592 B.C.; also see note on 1:1. 8:2 Or *like burnished metal.*

entrance to the gate near the altar, stood the idol that had made the LORD so jealous.

6"Son of man," he said, "do you see what they are doing? Do you see the detestable sins the people of Israel are committing to drive me from my Temple? But come, and you will see even more detestable sins than these!" 7Then he brought me to the door of the Temple courtyard, where I could see a hole in the wall. 8He said to me, "Now, son of man, dig into the wall." So I dug into the wall and found a hidden doorway.

AN OPEN BOOK 8:6

In scene after scene, God revealed to Ezekiel the moral downfall of the people of Judah. God's Spirit works with us in a similar way, convicting us of the wrong things we do. Our lives are like an open book to him. How comfortable would you feel if God revealed what's on the pages of your life today? ■

9"Go in," he said, "and see the wicked and detestable sins they are committing in there!" 10So I went in and saw the walls engraved with all kinds of crawling animals and detestable creatures. I also saw the various idols* worshiped by the people of Israel. 11Seventy leaders of Israel were standing there with Jaazaniah son of Shaphan in the center. Each of them held an incense burner, from which a cloud of incense rose above their heads.

12Then the LORD said to me, "Son of man, have you seen what the leaders of Israel are doing with their idols in dark rooms? They are saying, 'The LORD doesn't see us; he has deserted our land!'" 13Then the LORD added, "Come, and I will show you even more detestable sins than these!"

14He brought me to the north gate of the LORD's Temple, and some women were sitting there, weeping for the god Tammuz. 15"Have you seen this?" he asked. "But I will show you even more detestable sins than these!"

16Then he brought me into the inner courtyard of the LORD's Temple. At the entrance to the sanctuary, between the entry room and the bronze altar, there were about twenty-five men with their backs to the sanctuary of the LORD. They were facing east, bowing low to the ground, worshiping the sun!

17"Have you seen this, son of man?" he asked. "Is it nothing to the people of Judah that they commit these detestable sins, leading the whole nation into violence, thumbing their noses at me, and provoking my anger? 18Therefore, I will respond in fury. I will neither pity nor spare them. And though they cry for mercy, I will not listen."

9 THE SLAUGHTER OF IDOLATERS

Then the LORD thundered, "Bring on the men appointed to punish the city! Tell them to bring their weapons with them!" 2Six men soon appeared from the upper gate that faces north, each carrying a deadly weapon in his hand. With them was a man dressed in linen, who carried a writer's case at his side. They all went into the Temple courtyard and stood beside the bronze altar.

3Then the glory of the God of Israel rose up from between the cherubim, where it had rested, and moved to the entrance of the Temple. And the LORD called to the man dressed in linen who was carrying the writer's case. 4He said to him, "Walk through the streets of Jerusalem and put a mark on the foreheads of all who weep and sigh because of the detestable sins being committed in their city."

5Then I heard the LORD say to the other men, "Follow him through the city and kill everyone whose forehead is not marked. Show no mercy; have no pity! 6Kill them all—old and young, girls and women and little children. But do not touch anyone with the mark. Begin right here at the Temple." So they began by killing the seventy leaders.

7"Defile the Temple!" the LORD commanded. "Fill its courtyards with corpses. Go!" So they went and began killing throughout the city.

8While they were out killing, I was all alone. I fell face down on the ground and cried out, "O Sovereign LORD! Will your fury against Jerusalem wipe out everyone left in Israel?"

9Then he said to me, "The sins of the people of Israel and Judah are very, very great. The entire land is full of murder; the city is filled with injustice. They are saying, 'The LORD doesn't see it! The LORD has abandoned the land!' 10So I will not spare them or have any pity on them. I will fully repay them for all they have done."

NO EXCUSE 9:9-10

The people of Israel and Judah claimed that God had gone away and no longer cared what they did. Many people today rely on convenient explanations in order to continue wrong actions: "It doesn't matter." "Everybody's doing it." Or, "Nobody will ever know." Have you heard these excuses? Have you used them yourself? Yet rationalizing can't erase the consequences of wrongdoing. ■

11Then the man in linen clothing, who carried the writer's case, reported back and said, "I have done as you commanded."

10 THE LORD'S GLORY LEAVES THE TEMPLE

In my vision I saw what appeared to be a throne of blue lapis lazuli above the crystal surface over the heads of the cherubim. 2Then the LORD spoke to the man in linen clothing and said, "Go between the whirling wheels beneath the cherubim, and take a handful of burning coals and scatter them over the city." He did this as I watched.

3The cherubim were standing at the south end of the Temple when the man went in, and the cloud of glory filled the inner courtyard. 4Then the glory of the LORD

8:10 The Hebrew term (literally *round things*) probably alludes to dung.

rose up from above the cherubim and went over to the door of the Temple. The Temple was filled with this cloud of glory, and the courtyard glowed brightly with the glory of the LORD. 5The moving wings of the cherubim sounded like the voice of God Almighty* and could be heard even in the outer courtyard.

6The LORD said to the man in linen clothing, "Go between the cherubim and take some burning coals from between the wheels." So the man went in and stood beside one of the wheels. 7Then one of the cherubim reached out his hand and took some live coals from the fire burning among them. He put the coals into the hands of the man in linen clothing, and the man took them and went out. 8(All the cherubim had what looked like human hands under their wings.)

9I looked, and each of the four cherubim had a wheel beside him, and the wheels sparkled like beryl. 10All four wheels looked alike and were made the same; each wheel had a second wheel turning crosswise within it. 11The cherubim could move in any of the four directions they faced, without turning as they moved. They went straight in the direction they faced, never turning aside. 12Both the cherubim and the wheels were covered with eyes. The cherubim had eyes all over their bodies, including their hands, their backs, and their wings. 13I heard someone refer to the wheels as "the whirling wheels." 14Each of the four cherubim had four faces: the first was the face of an ox,* the second was a human face, the third was the face of a lion, and the fourth was the face of an eagle.

15Then the cherubim rose upward. These were the same living beings I had seen beside the Kebar River. 16When the cherubim moved, the wheels moved with them. When they lifted their wings to fly, the wheels stayed beside them. 17When the cherubim stopped, the wheels stopped. When they flew upward, the wheels rose up, for the spirit of the living beings was in the wheels.

18Then the glory of the LORD moved out from the door of the Temple and hovered above the cherubim. 19And as I watched, the cherubim flew with their wheels to the east gate of the LORD's Temple. And the glory of the God of Israel hovered above them.

20These were the same living beings I had seen beneath the God of Israel when I was by the Kebar River. I knew they were cherubim, 21for each had four faces and four wings and what looked like human hands under their wings. 22And their faces were just like the faces of the beings I had seen at the Kebar, and they traveled straight ahead, just as the others had.

11

JUDGMENT ON ISRAEL'S LEADERS

Then the Spirit lifted me and brought me to the east gateway of the LORD's Temple, where I saw twenty-five prominent men of the city. Among them were Jaazaniah son of Azzur and Pelatiah son of Benaiah, who were leaders among the people.

2The Spirit said to me, "Son of man, these are the men who are planning evil and giving wicked counsel in this city. 3They say to the people, 'Is it not a good time to build houses? This city is like an iron pot. We are safe inside it like meat in a pot.*' 4Therefore, son of man, prophesy against them loudly and clearly."

5Then the Spirit of the LORD came upon me, and he told me to say, "This is what the LORD says to the people of Israel: I know what you are saying, for I know every thought that comes into your minds. 6You have murdered many in this city and filled its streets with the dead.

7"Therefore, this is what the Sovereign LORD says: This city is an iron pot all right, but the pieces of meat are the victims of your injustice. As for you, I will soon drag you from this pot. 8I will bring on you the sword of war you so greatly fear, says the Sovereign LORD. 9I will drive you out of Jerusalem and hand you over to foreigners, who will carry out my judgments against you. 10You will be slaughtered all the way to the borders of Israel. I will execute judgment on you, and you will know that I am the LORD. 11No, this city will not be an iron pot for you, and you will not be like meat safe inside it. I will judge you even to the borders of Israel, 12and you will know that I am the LORD. For you have refused to obey my decrees and regulations; instead, you have copied the standards of the nations around you."

CONSEQUENCES 11:1-12

From the time they entered the Promised Land (see Joshua), the Israelites were warned not to copy the customs and religious practices of other nations. Disobeying this command always led to trouble—then and now. Following the crowd might save you the hassle of being ridiculed and might even make you popular temporarily. But it won't save you from the consequences of wrong. Is anything (popularity, a relationship with the person of your dreams, money) worth the price of your soul? (See Matt 16:26.) ■

13While I was still prophesying, Pelatiah son of Benaiah suddenly died. Then I fell face down on the ground and cried out, "O Sovereign LORD, are you going to kill everyone in Israel?"

HOPE FOR EXILED ISRAEL

14Then this message came to me from the LORD: 15"Son of man, the people still left in Jerusalem are talking about you and your relatives and all the people of Israel who are in exile. They are saying, 'Those people are far away from the LORD, so now he has given their land to us!'

16"Therefore, tell the exiles, 'This is what the Sovereign LORD says: Although I have scattered you in the countries of the world, I will be a sanctuary to you during your time in exile. 17I, the Sovereign LORD, will gather you back from the nations where you have been scattered, and I will give you the land of Israel once again.'

18"When the people return to their homeland, they will remove every trace of their vile images and detestable idols. 19And I will give them singleness of heart and put a

10:5 Hebrew *El-Shaddai*. 10:14 Hebrew *the face of a cherub;* compare 1:10. 11:3 Hebrew *This city is the pot, and we are the meat.*

new spirit within them. I will take away their stony, stubborn heart and give them a tender, responsive heart,* 20so they will obey my decrees and regulations. Then they will truly be my people, and I will be their God. 21But as for those who long for vile images and detestable idols, I will repay them fully for their sins. I, the Sovereign LORD, have spoken!"

THE LORD'S GLORY LEAVES JERUSALEM

22Then the cherubim lifted their wings and rose into the air with their wheels beside them, and the glory of the God of Israel hovered above them. 23Then the glory of the LORD went up from the city and stopped above the mountain to the east.

24Afterward the Spirit of God carried me back again to Babylonia,* to the people in exile there. And so ended the vision of my visit to Jerusalem. 25And I told the exiles everything the LORD had shown me.

12 SIGNS OF THE COMING EXILE

Again a message came to me from the LORD: 2"Son of man, you live among rebels who have eyes but refuse to see. They have ears but refuse to hear. For they are a rebellious people.

3"So now, son of man, pretend you are being sent into exile. Pack the few items an exile could carry, and leave your home to go somewhere else. Do this right in front of the people so they can see you. For perhaps they will pay attention to this, even though they are such rebels. 4Bring your baggage outside during the day so they can watch you. Then in the evening, as they are watching, leave your house as captives do when they begin a long march to distant lands. 5Dig a hole through the wall while they are watching and go out through it. 6As they watch, lift your pack to your shoulders and walk away into the night. Cover your face so you cannot see the land you are leaving. For I have made you a sign for the people of Israel."

7So I did as I was told. In broad daylight I brought my pack outside, filled with the things I might carry into exile. Then in the evening while the people looked on, I dug through the wall with my hands and went out into the night with my pack on my shoulder.

8The next morning this message came to me from the LORD: 9"Son of man, these rebels, the people of Israel, have asked you what all this means. 10Say to them, 'This is what the Sovereign LORD says: These actions contain a message for King Zedekiah in Jerusalem* and for all the people of Israel.' 11Explain that your actions are a sign to show what will soon happen to them, for they will be driven into exile as captives.

12"Even Zedekiah will leave Jerusalem at night through a hole in the wall, taking only what he can carry with him. He will cover his face, and his eyes will not see the land he is leaving. 13Then I will throw my net over him and capture him in my snare. I will bring him to Babylon, the land of the Babylonians,* though he will never see it, and he will die there. 14I will scatter his servants and warriors to the four winds and send the sword after them. 15And when I scatter them among the nations, they will know that I am the LORD. 16But I will spare a few of them from death by war, famine, or disease, so they can confess all their detestable sins to their captors. Then they will know that I am the LORD."

17Then this message came to me from the LORD: 18"Son of man, tremble as you eat your food. Shake with fear as you drink your water. 19Tell the people, 'This is what the Sovereign LORD says concerning those living in Israel and Jerusalem: They will eat their food with trembling and sip their water in despair, for their land will be stripped bare because of their violence. 20The cities will be destroyed and the farmland made desolate. Then you will know that I am the LORD.'"

A NEW PROVERB FOR ISRAEL

21Again a message came to me from the LORD: 22"Son of man, you've heard that proverb they quote in Israel: 'Time passes, and prophecies come to nothing.' 23Tell the people, 'This is what the Sovereign LORD says: I will put an end to this proverb, and you will soon stop quoting it.' Now give them this new proverb to replace the old one: 'The time has come for every prophecy to be fulfilled!'

24"There will be no more false visions and flattering predictions in Israel. 25For I am the LORD! If I say it, it will happen. There will be no more delays, you rebels of Israel. I will fulfill my threat of destruction in your own lifetime. I, the Sovereign LORD, have spoken!"

26Then this message came to me from the LORD: 27"Son of man, the people of Israel are saying, 'He's talking about the distant future. His visions won't come true for a long, long time.' 28Therefore, tell them, 'This is what the Sovereign LORD says: No more delay! I will now do everything I have threatened. I, the Sovereign LORD, have spoken!'"

OUT OF TIME 12:21-28

These two short messages were warnings that God's words would come true—*soon!* Less than six years later, Jerusalem was destroyed. Ever think that you or someone you know has plenty of time to make things right with God? Judgment can sometimes come swiftly. Before you know it, you may be out of time. ■

13 JUDGMENT AGAINST FALSE PROPHETS

Then this message came to me from the LORD: 2"Son of man, prophesy against the false prophets of Israel who are inventing their own prophecies. Say to them, 'Listen to the word of the LORD. 3This is what the Sovereign LORD says: What sorrow awaits the false prophets who are following their own imaginations and have seen nothing at all!'

11:19 Hebrew *a heart of flesh.* **11:24** Or *Chaldea.* **12:10** Hebrew *the prince in Jerusalem;* similarly in 12:12. **12:13** Or *Chaldeans.*

A COMFORTABLE LIE 13:1-3

The false prophets had a large following because they comforted the people and approved of their actions even while they were sinning. Lies often are attractive, and liars may have large followings. Today, for example, some leaders assure us that God wants everyone to have health and material success. This is comforting, but is it true? God's own Son did not have an easy life on earth. He didn't even have a home (Matt 8:20)! Are the messages you believe consistent with what God teaches in his Word? ■

4"O people of Israel, these prophets of yours are like
jackals digging in the ruins. 5They have done nothing to
repair the breaks in the walls around the nation. They
have not helped it to stand firm in battle on the day of the
LORD. 6Instead, they have told lies and made false predictions. They say, 'This message is from the LORD,' even
though the LORD never sent them. And yet they expect
him to fulfill their prophecies! 7Can your visions be anything but false if you claim, 'This message is from the
LORD,' when I have not even spoken to you?
8"Therefore, this is what the Sovereign LORD says: Because what you say is false and your visions are a lie, I will
stand against you, says the Sovereign LORD. 9I will raise
my fist against all the prophets who see false visions and
make lying predictions, and they will be banished from
the community of Israel. I will blot their names from Israel's record books, and they will never again set foot in
their own land. Then you will know that I am the Sovereign LORD.
10"This will happen because these evil prophets deceive my people by saying, 'All is peaceful' when there is
no peace at all! It's as if the people have built a flimsy wall,
and these prophets are trying to reinforce it by covering
it with whitewash! 11Tell these whitewashers that their
wall will soon fall down. A heavy rainstorm will undermine it; great hailstones and mighty winds will knock it
down. 12And when the wall falls, the people will cry out,
'What happened to your whitewash?'
13"Therefore, this is what the Sovereign LORD says: I
will sweep away your whitewashed wall with a storm of
indignation, with a great flood of anger, and with hailstones of fury. 14I will break down your wall right to its
foundation, and when it falls, it will crush you. Then you
will know that I am the LORD. 15At last my anger against
the wall and those who covered it with whitewash will be
satisfied. Then I will say to you: 'The wall and those who
whitewashed it are both gone. 16They were lying prophets who claimed peace would come to Jerusalem when
there was no peace. I, the Sovereign LORD, have spoken!'

JUDGMENT AGAINST FALSE WOMEN PROPHETS

17"Now, son of man, speak out against the women who
prophesy from their own imaginations. 18This is what the
Sovereign LORD says: What sorrow awaits you women
who are ensnaring the souls of my people, young and old
alike. You tie magic charms on their wrists and furnish
them with magic veils. Do you think you can trap others
without bringing destruction on yourselves? 19You bring
shame on me among my people for a few handfuls of
barley or a piece of bread. By lying to my people who love
to listen to lies, you kill those who should not die, and you
promise life to those who should not live.
20"This is what the Sovereign LORD says: I am against
all your magic charms, which you use to ensnare my
people like birds. I will tear them from your arms, setting my people free like birds set free from a cage. 21I
will tear off the magic veils and save my people from
your grasp. They will no longer be your victims. Then
you will know that I am the LORD. 22You have discouraged the righteous with your lies, but I didn't want them
to be sad. And you have encouraged the wicked by
promising them life, even though they continue in their
sins. 23Because of all this, you will no longer talk of seeing visions that you never saw, nor will you make predictions. For I will rescue my people from your grasp.
Then you will know that I am the LORD."

14 THE IDOLATRY OF ISRAEL'S LEADERS

Then some of the leaders of Israel visited me, and while
they were sitting with me, 2this message came to me from
the LORD: 3"Son of man, these leaders have set up idols*
in their hearts. They have embraced things that will make
them fall into sin. Why should I listen to their requests?
4Tell them, 'This is what the Sovereign LORD says: The
people of Israel have set up idols in their hearts and fallen
into sin, and then they go to a prophet asking for a message. So I, the LORD, will give them the kind of answer
their great idolatry deserves. 5I will do this to capture the
minds and hearts of all my people who have turned from
me to worship their detestable idols.'

A FEW GOOD PEOPLE 14:6-11

The nation of Judah, though eager to accept the messages of false prophets, considered the presence of a few godly people in the nation an insurance policy against disaster. But merely having godly people around didn't prevent the nation from being destroyed. In the same way, the godliness of a pastor or friends will not protect us from the consequences of our own wrong actions. Each person is responsible for his or her own relationship with God. How are *you* living? ■

6"Therefore, tell the people of Israel, 'This is what the
Sovereign LORD says: Repent and turn away from your
idols, and stop all your detestable sins. 7I, the LORD, will
answer all those, both Israelites and foreigners, who reject me and set up idols in their hearts and so fall into sin,
and who then come to a prophet asking for my advice. 8I
will turn against such people and make a terrible

14:3 The Hebrew term (literally *round things*) probably alludes to dung; also in 14:4, 5, 6, 7.

example of them, eliminating them from among my people. Then you will know that I am the LORD.

9“‘And if a prophet is deceived into giving a message, it is because I, the LORD, have deceived that prophet. I will lift my fist against such prophets and cut them off from the community of Israel. 10False prophets and those who seek their guidance will all be punished for their sins. 11In this way, the people of Israel will learn not to stray from me, polluting themselves with sin. They will be my people, and I will be their God. I, the Sovereign LORD, have spoken!’”

THE CERTAINTY OF THE LORD'S JUDGMENT

12Then this message came to me from the LORD: 13“Son of man, suppose the people of a country were to sin against me, and I lifted my fist to crush them, cutting off their food supply and sending a famine to destroy both people and animals. 14Even if Noah, Daniel, and Job were there, their righteousness would save no one but themselves, says the Sovereign LORD.

15“Or suppose I were to send wild animals to invade the country, kill the people, and make the land too desolate and dangerous to pass through. 16As surely as I live, says the Sovereign LORD, even if those three men were there, they wouldn't be able to save their own sons or daughters. They alone would be saved, but the land would be made desolate.

17“Or suppose I were to bring war against the land, and I sent enemy armies to destroy both people and animals. 18As surely as I live, says the Sovereign LORD, even if those three men were there, they wouldn't be able to save their own sons or daughters. They alone would be saved.

19“Or suppose I were to pour out my fury by sending an epidemic into the land, and the disease killed people and animals alike. 20As surely as I live, says the Sovereign LORD, even if Noah, Daniel, and Job were there, they wouldn't be able to save their own sons or daughters. They alone would be saved by their righteousness.

21“Now this is what the Sovereign LORD says: How terrible it will be when all four of these dreadful punishments fall upon Jerusalem—war, famine, wild animals, and disease—destroying all her people and animals. 22Yet there will be survivors, and they will come here to join you as exiles in Babylon. You will see with your own eyes how wicked they are, and then you will feel better about what I have done to Jerusalem. 23When you meet them and see their behavior, you will understand that these things are not being done to Israel without cause. I, the Sovereign LORD, have spoken!”

15 JERUSALEM—A USELESS VINE

Then this message came to me from the LORD: 2“Son of man, how does a grapevine compare to a tree? Is a vine's wood as useful as the wood of a tree? 3Can its wood be used for making things, like pegs to hang up pots and pans? 4No, it can only be used for fuel, and even as fuel, it burns too quickly. 5Vines are useless both before and after being put into the fire!

6“And this is what the Sovereign LORD says: The people of Jerusalem are like grapevines growing among the trees of the forest. Since they are useless, I have thrown them on the fire to be burned. 7And I will see to it that if they escape from one fire, they will fall into another. When I turn against them, you will know that I am the LORD. 8And I will make the land desolate because my people have been unfaithful to me. I, the Sovereign LORD, have spoken!”

USELESS 15:1-8

The messages given to Ezekiel in chapters 15 through 17 provided further evidence that God was going to destroy Jerusalem. The first message was about a grapevine, useless at first and even more useless after being burned. Since the people of Jerusalem were useless to God because of their idol worship, they would be destroyed and their cities burned. (See also Jer 13:1-11.) All of that could have been prevented with regular spiritual checkups. Just as a physical checkup is necessary for good health, a spiritual checkup is necessary for spiritual health. You can do that by regularly communicating with God and keeping a clean slate with him (see 1 John 1:9). Are you spiritually healthy? (See also Phil 1:1-8.) ■

16 JERUSALEM—AN UNFAITHFUL WIFE

Then another message came to me from the LORD: 2“Son of man, confront Jerusalem with her detestable sins. 3Give her this message from the Sovereign LORD: You are nothing but a Canaanite! Your father was an Amorite and your mother a Hittite. 4On the day you were born, no one cared about you. Your umbilical cord was not cut, and you were never washed, rubbed with salt, and wrapped in cloth. 5No one had the slightest interest in you; no one pitied you or cared for you. On the day you were born, you were unwanted, dumped in a field and left to die.

6“But I came by and saw you there, helplessly kicking about in your own blood. As you lay there, I said, ‘Live!’ 7And I helped you to thrive like a plant in the field. You grew up and became a beautiful jewel. Your breasts became full, and your body hair grew, but you were still naked. 8And when I passed by again, I saw that you were old enough for love. So I wrapped my cloak around you to cover your nakedness and declared my marriage vows. I made a covenant with you, says the Sovereign LORD, and you became mine.

9“Then I bathed you and washed off your blood, and I rubbed fragrant oils into your skin. 10I gave you expensive clothing of fine linen and silk, beautifully embroidered, and sandals made of fine goatskin leather. 11I gave you lovely jewelry, bracelets, beautiful necklaces, 12a ring for your nose, earrings for your ears, and a lovely crown for your head. 13And so you were adorned with gold and silver. Your clothes were made of fine linen and were beautifully embroidered. You ate the finest foods—

choice flour, honey, and olive oil—and became more beautiful than ever. You looked like a queen, and so you were! 14Your fame soon spread throughout the world because of your beauty. I dressed you in my splendor and perfected your beauty, says the Sovereign LORD.

SPECIAL PRIVILEGES 16:8-14

The people of Israel were God's chosen people—the nation through whom his message of salvation would be communicated to the entire world. Israel had been privileged as a nation. But their resources and advantages became sources of pride that eventually destroyed them. Ever know someone who allowed his or her advantages (looks, money, grades, whatever) to go to his/her head? Pride always leads to a fall (Prov 16:18). ■

15"But you thought your fame and beauty were your own. So you gave yourself as a prostitute to every man who came along. Your beauty was theirs for the asking. 16You used the lovely things I gave you to make shrines for idols, where you played the prostitute. Unbelievable! How could such a thing ever happen? 17You took the very jewels and gold and silver ornaments I had given you and made statues of men and worshiped them. This is adultery against me! 18You used the beautifully embroidered clothes I gave you to dress your idols. Then you used my special oil and my incense to worship them. 19Imagine it! You set before them as a sacrifice the choice flour, olive oil, and honey I had given you, says the Sovereign LORD.

20"Then you took your sons and daughters—the children you had borne to me—and sacrificed them to your gods. Was your prostitution not enough? 21Must you also slaughter my children by sacrificing them to idols? 22In all your years of adultery and detestable sin, you have not once remembered the days long ago when you lay naked in a field, kicking about in your own blood.

23"What sorrow awaits you, says the Sovereign LORD. In addition to all your other wickedness, 24you built a pagan shrine and put altars to idols in every town square. 25On every street corner you defiled your beauty, offering your body to every passerby in an endless stream of prostitution. 26Then you added lustful Egypt to your lovers, provoking my anger with your increasing promiscuity. 27That is why I struck you with my fist and reduced your boundaries. I handed you over to your enemies, the Philistines, and even they were shocked by your lewd conduct. 28You have prostituted yourself with the Assyrians, too. It seems you can never find enough new lovers! And after your prostitution there, you still were not satisfied. 29You added to your lovers by embracing Babylonia,* the land of merchants, but you still weren't satisfied.

30"What a sick heart you have, says the Sovereign LORD, to do such things as these, acting like a shameless prostitute. 31You build your pagan shrines on every street corner and your altars to idols in every square. In fact, you have been worse than a prostitute, so eager for sin that you have not even demanded payment. 32Yes, you are an adulterous wife who takes in strangers instead of her own husband. 33Prostitutes charge for their services—but not you! You give gifts to your lovers, bribing them to come and have sex with you. 34So you are the opposite of other prostitutes. You pay your lovers instead of their paying you!

JUDGMENT ON JERUSALEM'S PROSTITUTION

35"Therefore, you prostitute, listen to this message from the LORD! 36This is what the Sovereign LORD says: Because you have poured out your lust and exposed yourself in prostitution to all your lovers, and because you have worshiped detestable idols,* and because you have slaughtered your children as sacrifices to your gods, 37this is what I am going to do. I will gather together all your allies—the lovers with whom you have sinned, both those you loved and those you hated—and I will strip you naked in front of them so they can stare at you. 38I will punish you for your murder and adultery. I will cover you with blood in my jealous fury. 39Then I will give you to these many nations who are your lovers, and they will destroy you. They will knock down your pagan shrines and the

16:29 Or *Chaldea.* **16:36** The Hebrew term (literally *round things*) probably alludes to dung.

I feel like I keep blowing it with God. What can I do to make things right?

Until about age 25, we grow physically. After that, we start to die. Fortunately, it usually takes another 50 to 60 years to complete the dying process!

Our spiritual life goes through a living-and-dying process, too. It either grows or it gradually dies. It can't remain at the same level.

When you recognize that you've messed up, you're already at the beginning stage of spiritual growth.

The second stage is discovering what caused you to "die" spiritually. God confronted his people continually about this. Speaking through Ezekiel, he showed them that idols had taken God's place in their hearts (see Ezek 14:1-11).

Is there an "idol" (sports or other leisure activities, a relationship, money and possessions) in your life—something you love more than God? If so, are you willing to give up the idol and be straight with God? (see 1 John 1:9).

The third stage is the one that many Christians forget—finding someone to hold us accountable. You need someone to encourage you, to ask tough questions, to kick you in the pants when you need it, and to pray for you. This could be a friend who has a real desire to grow spiritually. It could be a Christian adult whom you like and respect—or anyone who is genuinely concerned for you and won't give up on you. Need a friend like that? Just ask God to supply one.

altars to your idols. They will strip you and take your
beautiful jewels, leaving you stark naked. 40They will
band together in a mob to stone you and cut you up with
swords. 41They will burn your homes and punish you in
front of many women. I will stop your prostitution and
end your payments to your many lovers.
42"Then at last my fury against you will be spent, and
my jealous anger will subside. I will be calm and will not
be angry with you anymore. 43But first, because you have
not remembered your youth but have angered me by doing all these evil things, I will fully repay you for all of your
sins, says the Sovereign LORD. For you have added lewd
acts to all your detestable sins. 44Everyone who makes up
proverbs will say of you, 'Like mother, like daughter.'
45For your mother loathed her husband and her children,
and so do you. And you are exactly like your sisters, for
they despised their husbands and their children. Truly
your mother was a Hittite and your father an Amorite.
46"Your older sister was Samaria, who lived with her
daughters in the north. Your younger sister was Sodom,
who lived with her daughters in the south. 47But you have
not merely sinned as they did. You quickly surpassed
them in corruption. 48As surely as I live, says the Sovereign LORD, Sodom and her daughters were never as
wicked as you and your daughters. 49Sodom's sins were
pride, gluttony, and laziness, while the poor and needy
suffered outside her door. 50She was proud and committed detestable sins, so I wiped her out, as you have seen.*
51"Even Samaria did not commit half your sins. You
have done far more detestable things than your sisters
ever did. They seem righteous compared to you. 52Shame
on you! Your sins are so terrible that you make your sisters seem righteous, even virtuous.

NOT AS BAD? 16:46-58

The people of Judah might have believed they weren't as bad as the people of Sodom (see Gen 19) or of Samaria (the northern kingdom of Israel). But God cured them of that delusion. Nowadays, we might think we're better than those who murder, steal, or commit sexual sins. But we forget about sins like pride, lying, and ignoring the needy (see Rev 3:14-22). These sins may not seem as "bad" as the others to us. Yet all sin is equal in God's eyes. ■

53"But someday I will restore the fortunes of Sodom
and Samaria, and I will restore you, too. 54Then you will be
truly ashamed of everything you have done, for your sins
make them feel good in comparison. 55Yes, your sisters,
Sodom and Samaria, and all their people will be restored,
and at that time you also will be restored. 56In your proud
days you held Sodom in contempt. 57But now your
greater wickedness has been exposed to all the world,
and you are the one who is scorned—by Edom* and all
her neighbors and by Philistia. 58This is your punishment
for all your lewdness and detestable sins, says the LORD.
59"Now this is what the Sovereign LORD says: I will give
you what you deserve, for you have taken your solemn
vows lightly by breaking your covenant. 60Yet I will remember the covenant I made with you when you were
young, and I will establish an everlasting covenant with
you. 61Then you will remember with shame all the evil you
have done. I will make your sisters, Samaria and Sodom, to
be your daughters, even though they are not part of our
covenant. 62And I will reaffirm my covenant with you, and
you will know that I am the LORD. 63You will remember
your sins and cover your mouth in silent shame when I
forgive you of all that you have done. I, the Sovereign
LORD, have spoken!"

GOD'S MESSENGERS 17:1-8

The first eagle in this chapter represents King Nebuchadnezzar of Babylon (see 17:12), who appointed or "planted" Zedekiah as king in Jerusalem. Zedekiah rebelled against this arrangement and tried to join with Egypt, the second eagle, to battle Babylon. In Babylon, as Ezekiel described these events, Jeremiah (a prophet in Judah) also warned Zedekiah not to form this alliance (Jer 2:36-37). Though miles apart, the prophets had the same message, because both spoke for God. God still directs his chosen spokespeople to speak his truth all around the world. Are you willing to speak for God? ■

17 A STORY OF TWO EAGLES

Then this message came to me from the LORD: 2"Son of
man, give this riddle, and tell this story to the people of Israel. 3Give them this message from the Sovereign LORD:

"A great eagle with broad wings and long feathers,
covered with many-colored plumage,
came to Lebanon.
He seized the top of a cedar tree
4 and plucked off its highest branch.
He carried it away to a city filled with merchants.
He planted it in a city of traders.
5 He also took a seedling from the land
and planted it in fertile soil.
He placed it beside a broad river,
where it could grow like a willow tree.
6 It took root there and
grew into a low, spreading vine.
Its branches turned up toward the eagle,
and its roots grew down into the ground.
It produced strong branches
and put out shoots.
7 But then another great eagle came
with broad wings and full plumage.
So the vine now sent its roots and branches
toward him for water,
8 even though it was already planted in good soil
and had plenty of water

16:50 As in a few Hebrew manuscripts and Greek version; Masoretic Text reads *as I have seen.* 16:57 Many ancient manuscripts read *Aram.*

so it could grow into a splendid vine
and produce rich leaves and luscious fruit.

9 "So now the Sovereign LORD asks:
Will this vine grow and prosper?
No! I will pull it up, roots and all!
I will cut off its fruit
and let its leaves wither and die.
I will pull it up easily
without a strong arm or a large army.
10 But when the vine is transplanted,
will it thrive?
No, it will wither away
when the east wind blows against it.
It will die in the same good soil
where it had grown so well."

THE RIDDLE EXPLAINED

11 Then this message came to me from the LORD: 12 "Say to
these rebels of Israel: Don't you understand the meaning
of this riddle of the eagles? The king of Babylon came to
Jerusalem, took away her king and princes, and brought
them to Babylon. 13 He made a treaty with a member of
the royal family and forced him to take an oath of loyalty.
He also exiled Israel's most influential leaders, 14 so Israel
would not become strong again and revolt. Only by keeping her treaty with Babylon could Israel survive.
15 "Nevertheless, this man of Israel's royal family rebelled against Babylon, sending ambassadors to Egypt to
request a great army and many horses. Can Israel break
her sworn treaties like that and get away with it? 16 No! For
as surely as I live, says the Sovereign LORD, the king of Israel will die in Babylon, the land of the king who put him
in power and whose treaty he disregarded and broke.
17 Pharaoh and all his mighty army will fail to help Israel
when the king of Babylon lays siege to Jerusalem again
and destroys many lives. 18 For the king of Israel disregarded his treaty and broke it after swearing to obey;
therefore, he will not escape.
19 "So this is what the Sovereign LORD says: As surely as I
live, I will punish him for breaking my covenant and disregarding the solemn oath he made in my name. 20 I will
throw my net over him and capture him in my snare. I will
bring him to Babylon and put him on trial for this treason
against me. 21 And all his best warriors* will be killed in
battle, and those who survive will be scattered to the four
winds. Then you will know that I, the LORD, have spoken.
22 "This is what the Sovereign LORD says: I will take a
branch from the top of a tall cedar, and I will plant it on
the top of Israel's highest mountain. 23 It will become a
majestic cedar, sending forth its branches and producing
seed. Birds of every sort will nest in it, finding shelter in
the shade of its branches. 24 And all the trees will know
that it is I, the LORD, who cuts the tall tree down and
makes the short tree grow tall. It is I who makes the green
tree wither and gives the dead tree new life. I, the LORD,
have spoken, and I will do what I said!"

18

THE JUSTICE OF A RIGHTEOUS GOD

Then another message came to me from the LORD: 2 "Why
do you quote this proverb concerning the land of Israel:
'The parents have eaten sour grapes, but their children's
mouths pucker at the taste'? 3 As surely as I live, says the
Sovereign LORD, you will not quote this proverb anymore
in Israel. 4 For all people are mine to judge—both parents
and children alike. And this is my rule: The person who
sins is the one who will die.
5 "Suppose a certain man is righteous and does what is
just and right. 6 He does not feast in the mountains before
Israel's idols* or worship them. He does not commit
adultery or have intercourse with a woman during her
menstrual period. 7 He is a merciful creditor, not keeping
the items given as security by poor debtors. He does not
rob the poor but instead gives food to the hungry and
provides clothes for the needy. 8 He grants loans without
interest, stays away from injustice, is honest and fair
when judging others, 9 and faithfully obeys my decrees
and regulations. Anyone who does these things is just
and will surely live, says the Sovereign LORD.
10 "But suppose that man has a son who grows up to be a
robber or murderer and refuses to do what is right. 11 And
that son does all the evil things his father would never
do—he worships idols on the mountains, commits adultery, 12 oppresses the poor and helpless, steals from debtors by refusing to let them redeem their security,
worships idols, commits detestable sins, 13 and lends
money at excessive interest. Should such a sinful person
live? No! He must die and must take full blame.

TRADITIONS 18:14-18

Family traditions were very important to the Jews, but God made it clear that people should not follow the tradition of wrongdoing. Although your family is a powerful influence in your life, your actions are not determined by the past behavior of family members. Worried about being the product of your environment? You can choose to start a new tradition of closely following God. ■

14 "But suppose that sinful son, in turn, has a son who
sees his father's wickedness and decides against that
kind of life. 15 This son refuses to worship idols on the
mountains and does not commit adultery. 16 He does not
exploit the poor, but instead is fair to debtors and does
not rob them. He gives food to the hungry and provides
clothes for the needy. 17 He helps the poor, does not lend
money at interest, and obeys all my regulations and decrees. Such a person will not die because of his father's
sins; he will surely live. 18 But the father will die for his
many sins—for being cruel, robbing people, and doing
what was clearly wrong among his people.
19 "'What?' you ask. 'Doesn't the child pay for the parent's

17:21 Or *his fleeing warriors*. The meaning of the Hebrew is uncertain.

18:6 The Hebrew term (literally *round things*) probably alludes to dung; also in 18:12, 15.

sins?' No! For if the child does what is just and right and keeps my decrees, that child will surely live. [20]The person who sins is the one who will die. The child will not be punished for the parent's sins, and the parent will not be punished for the child's sins. Righteous people will be rewarded for their own righteous behavior, and wicked people will be punished for their own wickedness. [21]But if wicked people turn away from all their sins and begin to obey my decrees and do what is just and right, they will surely live and not die. [22]All their past sins will be forgotten, and they will live because of the righteous things they have done.

[23]"Do you think that I like to see wicked people die? says the Sovereign LORD. Of course not! I want them to turn from their wicked ways and live. [24]However, if righteous people turn from their righteous behavior and start doing sinful things and act like other sinners, should they be allowed to live? No, of course not! All their righteous acts will be forgotten, and they will die for their sins.

[25]"Yet you say, 'The Lord isn't doing what's right!' Listen to me, O people of Israel. Am I the one not doing what's right, or is it you? [26]When righteous people turn from their righteous behavior and start doing sinful things, they will die for it. Yes, they will die because of their sinful deeds. [27]And if wicked people turn from their wickedness, obey the law, and do what is just and right, they will save their lives. [28]They will live because they thought it over and decided to turn from their sins. Such people will not die. [29]And yet the people of Israel keep saying, 'The Lord isn't doing what's right!' O people of Israel, it is you who are not doing what's right, not I.

UNFAIR? 18:25-32

The exiled people of Israel accused God of being unjust by punishing them. A typical response to punishment is to say, "That's not fair!" Ever think that? In reality, God is fair, but *we* have broken the rules. God doesn't have to live up to our ideas of fairness; instead, we must live up to his. Looking for loopholes in God's law? Why not commit to enforce it instead? ■

[30]"Therefore, I will judge each of you, O people of Israel, according to your actions, says the Sovereign LORD. Repent, and turn from your sins. Don't let them destroy you! [31]Put all your rebellion behind you, and find yourselves a new heart and a new spirit. For why should you die, O people of Israel? [32]I don't want you to die, says the Sovereign LORD. Turn back and live!

19 A FUNERAL SONG FOR ISRAEL'S KINGS

"Sing this funeral song for the princes of Israel:

2 "What is your mother?
A lioness among lions!
She lay down among the young lions
and reared her cubs.
3 She raised one of her cubs
to become a strong young lion.
He learned to hunt and devour prey,
and he became a man-eater.
4 Then the nations heard about him,
and he was trapped in their pit.
They led him away with hooks
to the land of Egypt.

5 "When the lioness saw
that her hopes for him were gone,
she took another of her cubs
and taught him to be a strong young lion.
6 He prowled among the other lions
and stood out among them in his strength.
He learned to hunt and devour prey,
and he, too, became a man-eater.
7 He demolished fortresses*
and destroyed their towns and cities.
Their farms were desolated,
and their crops were destroyed.
The land and its people trembled in fear
when they heard him roar.
8 Then the armies of the nations attacked him,
surrounding him from every direction.
They threw a net over him
and captured him in their pit.
9 With hooks, they dragged him into a cage
and brought him before the king of Babylon.
They held him in captivity,
so his voice could never again be heard
on the mountains of Israel.

10 "Your mother was like a vine
planted by the water's edge.
It had lush, green foliage
because of the abundant water.

TRUE POWER 19:11-14

Not even the political and military might of Judah's kings could save the nation. Like branches of a vine, they would be cut off and uprooted by "the desert wind"—the Babylonian army (19:12). What do you depend on most? Physical strength? Intelligence? Financial status? Popularity? Nothing can stand against the true power—or judgment—of almighty God. ■

11 Its branches became strong—
strong enough to be a ruler's scepter.
It grew very tall,
towering above all others.
It stood out because of its height
and its many lush branches.
12 But the vine was uprooted in fury
and thrown down to the ground.

19:7 As in Greek version; Hebrew reads *He knew widows.*

The desert wind dried up its fruit
and tore off its strong branches,
so that it withered
and was destroyed by fire.
13 Now the vine is transplanted to the wilderness,
where the ground is hard and dry.
14 A fire has burst out from its branches
and devoured its fruit.
Its remaining limbs are not
strong enough to be a ruler's scepter.
"This is a funeral song, and it will be used in a funeral."

20 THE REBELLION OF ISRAEL

On August 14,* during the seventh year of King Jehoiachin's captivity, some of the leaders of Israel came to request a message from the LORD. They sat down in front of
me to wait for his reply. 2Then this message came to me
from the LORD: 3"Son of man, tell the leaders of Israel,
'This is what the Sovereign LORD says: How dare you
come to ask me for a message? As surely as I live, says the
Sovereign LORD, I will tell you nothing!'

4"Son of man, bring charges against them and condemn them. Make them realize how detestable the sins
of their ancestors really were. 5Give them this message
from the Sovereign LORD: When I chose Israel—when I
revealed myself to the descendants of Jacob in Egypt—I
took a solemn oath that I, the LORD, would be their God.
6I took a solemn oath that day that I would bring them
out of Egypt to a land I had discovered and explored for
them—a good land, a land flowing with milk and honey,
the best of all lands anywhere. 7Then I said to them,
'Each of you, get rid of the vile images you are so obsessed with. Do not defile yourselves with the idols* of
Egypt, for I am the LORD your God.'

8"But they rebelled against me and would not listen.
They did not get rid of the vile images they were obsessed
with, or forsake the idols of Egypt. Then I threatened to
pour out my fury on them to satisfy my anger while they
were still in Egypt. 9But I didn't do it, for I acted to protect
the honor of my name. I would not allow shame to be
brought on my name among the surrounding nations
who saw me reveal myself by bringing the Israelites out
of Egypt. 10So I brought them out of Egypt and led them
into the wilderness. 11There I gave them my decrees and
regulations so they could find life by keeping them.
12And I gave them my Sabbath days of rest as a sign between them and me. It was to remind them that I am the
LORD, who had set them apart to be holy.

13"But the people of Israel rebelled against me, and they
refused to obey my decrees there in the wilderness. They
wouldn't obey my regulations even though obedience
would have given them life. They also violated my Sabbath days. So I threatened to pour out my fury on them,
and I made plans to utterly consume them in the wilderness. 14But again I held back in order to protect the honor
of my name before the nations who had seen my power in
bringing Israel out of Egypt. 15But I took a solemn oath
against them in the wilderness. I swore I would not bring
them into the land I had given them, a land flowing with
milk and honey, the most beautiful place on earth. 16For
they had rejected my regulations, refused to follow my
decrees, and violated my Sabbath days. Their hearts were
given to their idols. 17Nevertheless, I took pity on them
and held back from destroying them in the wilderness.

18"Then I warned their children not to follow in their
parents' footsteps, defiling themselves with their idols.
19'I am the LORD your God,' I told them. 'Follow my decrees, pay attention to my regulations, 20and keep my
Sabbath days holy, for they are a sign to remind you that I
am the LORD your God.'

21"But their children, too, rebelled against me. They refused to keep my decrees and follow my regulations,
even though obedience would have given them life. And
they also violated my Sabbath days. So again I threatened
to pour out my fury on them in the wilderness. 22Never-
theless, I withdrew my judgment against them to protect
the honor of my name before the nations that had seen
my power in bringing them out of Egypt. 23But I took a
solemn oath against them in the wilderness. I swore I
would scatter them among all the nations 24because they
did not obey my regulations. They scorned my decrees by
violating my Sabbath days and longing for the idols of
their ancestors. 25I gave them over to worthless decrees
and regulations that would not lead to life. 26I let them
pollute themselves* with the very gifts I had given them,
and I allowed them to give their firstborn children as
offerings to their gods—so I might devastate them and
remind them that I alone am the LORD.

JUDGMENT AND RESTORATION

27"Therefore, son of man, give the people of Israel this
message from the Sovereign LORD: Your ancestors continued to blaspheme and betray me, 28for when I brought
them into the land I had promised them, they offered
sacrifices on every high hill and under every green tree
they saw! They roused my fury as they offered up sacrifices to their gods. They brought their perfumes and incense and poured out their liquid offerings to them. 29I
said to them, 'What is this high place where you are going?' (This kind of pagan shrine has been called Bamah—
'high place'—ever since.)

30"Therefore, give the people of Israel this message
from the Sovereign LORD: Do you plan to pollute yourselves just as your ancestors did? Do you intend to keep
prostituting yourselves by worshiping vile images? 31For
when you offer gifts to them and give your little children
to be burned as sacrifices,* you continue to pollute yourselves with idols to this day. Should I allow you to ask for a
message from me, O people of Israel? As surely as I live,
says the Sovereign LORD, I will tell you nothing.

32"You say, 'We want to be like the nations all around
us, who serve idols of wood and stone.' But what you have

20:1 Hebrew *In the fifth month, on the tenth day,* of the ancient Hebrew lunar calendar. This day was August 14, 591 B.C.; also see note on 1:1. **20:7** The Hebrew term (literally *round things*) probably alludes to dung; also in 20:8, 16, 18, 24, 31, 39. **20:25-26** Or *I gave them worthless decrees and regulations. . . . I polluted them.* **20:31** Or *and make your little children pass through the fire.*

in mind will never happen. 33As surely as I live, says the
Sovereign LORD, I will rule over you with an iron fist in
great anger and with awesome power. 34And in anger I
will reach out with my strong hand and powerful arm,
and I will bring you back* from the lands where you are
scattered. 35I will bring you into the wilderness of the nations, and there I will judge you face to face. 36I will judge
you there just as I did your ancestors in the wilderness after bringing them out of Egypt, says the Sovereign LORD.
37I will examine you carefully and hold you to the terms
of the covenant. 38I will purge you of all those who rebel
and revolt against me. I will bring them out of the countries where they are in exile, but they will never enter the
land of Israel. Then you will know that I am the LORD.

POLLUTION 20:30-38

God told the people of Israel that worshiping idols made them polluted. Water containing contaminants is polluted. Likewise, our lives are polluted when we accept the contaminants—immoral values—of this world. If we love money, we become greedy. If we lust, we become sexually immoral. Remaining pure in a polluted world is difficult, to say the least. But a heart filled with God's Holy Spirit leaves little room for pollution (see Titus 1:15-16). ■

39"As for you, O people of Israel, this is what the Sovereign LORD says: Go right ahead and worship your
idols, but sooner or later you will obey me and will stop
bringing shame on my holy name by worshiping idols.
40For on my holy mountain, the great mountain of Israel, says the Sovereign LORD, the people of Israel will
someday worship me, and I will accept them. There I
will require that you bring me all your offerings and
choice gifts and sacrifices. 41When I bring you home
from exile, you will be like a pleasing sacrifice to me.
And I will display my holiness through you as all the nations watch. 42Then when I have brought you home to
the land I promised with a solemn oath to give to your
ancestors, you will know that I am the LORD. 43You will
look back on all the ways you defiled yourselves and
will hate yourselves because of the evil you have done.
44You will know that I am the LORD, O people of Israel,
when I have honored my name by treating you mercifully in spite of your wickedness. I, the Sovereign LORD,
have spoken!"

JUDGMENT AGAINST THE NEGEV

45*Then this message came to me from the LORD: 46"Son
of man, turn and face the south* and speak out against it;
prophesy against the brushlands of the Negev. 47Tell the
southern wilderness, 'This is what the Sovereign LORD
says: Hear the word of the LORD! I will set you on fire, and
every tree, both green and dry, will be burned. The terrible
flames will not be quenched and will scorch everything
from south to north. 48And everyone in the world will see
that I, the LORD, have set this fire. It will not be put out.'"
49Then I said, "O Sovereign LORD, they are saying of me,
'He only talks in riddles!'"

21

THE LORD'S SWORD OF JUDGMENT

1*Then this message came to me from the LORD: 2"Son of
man, turn and face Jerusalem and prophesy against Israel
and her sanctuaries. 3Tell her, 'This is what the LORD says:
I am your enemy, O Israel, and I am about to unsheath my
sword to destroy your people—the righteous and the
wicked alike. 4Yes, I will cut off both the righteous and
the wicked! I will draw my sword against everyone in the
land from south to north. 5Everyone in the world will
know that I am the LORD. My sword is in my hand, and it
will not return to its sheath until its work is finished.'
6"Son of man, groan before the people! Groan before
them with bitter anguish and a broken heart. 7When they
ask why you are groaning, tell them, 'I groan because of
the terrifying news I have heard. When it comes true, the
boldest heart will melt with fear; all strength will disappear. Every spirit will faint; strong knees will become
as weak as water. And the Sovereign LORD says: It is coming! It's on its way!'"
8Then the LORD said to me, 9"Son of man, give the people this message from the LORD:

"A sword, a sword
  is being sharpened and polished.
10 It is sharpened for terrible slaughter
  and polished to flash like lightning!
Now will you laugh?
  Those far stronger than you have fallen beneath
  its power!*
11 Yes, the sword is now being sharpened and polished;
  it is being prepared for the executioner.

12 "Son of man, cry out and wail;
  pound your thighs in anguish,
for that sword will slaughter my people and
  their leaders—
  everyone will die!
13 It will put them all to the test.
  What chance do they have?*
  says the Sovereign LORD.

14 "Son of man, prophesy to them
  and clap your hands.
Then take the sword and brandish it twice,
  even three times,
to symbolize the great massacre,
  the great massacre facing them on every side.
15 Let their hearts melt with terror,
  for the sword glitters at every gate.
It flashes like lightning
  and is polished for slaughter!

20:34 Greek version reads *I will welcome you.* Compare 2 Cor 6:17. 20:45 Verses 20:45-49 are numbered 21:1-5 in Hebrew text.
20:46 Hebrew *toward Teman.* 21:1 Verses 21:1-32 are numbered 21:6-37 in Hebrew text. 21:10 The meaning of the Hebrew is uncertain.
21:13 The meaning of the Hebrew is uncertain.

16 O sword, slash to the right,
then slash to the left,
wherever you will,
wherever you want.
17 I, too, will clap my hands,
and I will satisfy my fury.
I, the LORD, have spoken!"

OMENS FOR BABYLON'S KING

18Then this message came to me from the LORD: 19"Son of man, make a map and trace two routes on it for the sword of Babylon's king to follow. Put a signpost on the road that comes out of Babylon where the road forks into two—20one road going to Ammon and its capital, Rabbah, and the other to Judah and fortified Jerusalem. 21The king of Babylon now stands at the fork, uncertain whether to attack Jerusalem or Rabbah. He calls his magicians to look for omens. They cast lots by shaking arrows from the quiver. They inspect the livers of animal sacrifices. 22The omen in his right hand says, 'Jerusalem!' With battering rams his soldiers will go against the gates, shouting for the kill. They will put up siege towers and build ramps against the walls. 23The people of Jerusalem will think it is a false omen, because of their treaty with the Babylonians. But the king of Babylon will remind the people of their rebellion. Then he will attack and capture them.

IN THE FIRE 21:1-23

The short message in 20:45-48 introduces the four messages in chapter 21 about the judgments that would come upon Jerusalem. The city would be destroyed because it was corrupted or spiritually unclean. According to Jewish law, unclean objects were to be passed through fire in order to purify them (see Num 31:21-23; Job 23:10; Ps 66:10; Prov 17:3). God's judgment is designed to purify; destruction often is a necessary part of that process. Hard times and discipline are the "fire" God uses to purify. Feeling the heat? Can you, like Job, say with confidence, "[God] knows where I am going. And when he tests me, I will come out as pure as gold" (Job 23:10)? ■

24"Therefore, this is what the Sovereign LORD says: Again and again you remind me of your sin and your guilt. You don't even try to hide it! In everything you do, your sins are obvious for all to see. So now the time of your punishment has come!

25"O you corrupt and wicked prince of Israel, your final day of reckoning is here! 26This is what the Sovereign LORD says:

"Take off your jeweled crown,
for the old order changes.
Now the lowly will be exalted,
and the mighty will be brought down.
27 Destruction! Destruction!
I will surely destroy the kingdom.
And it will not be restored until the one appears
who has the right to judge it.
Then I will hand it over to him.

A MESSAGE FOR THE AMMONITES

28"And now, son of man, prophesy concerning the Ammonites and their mockery. Give them this message from the Sovereign LORD:

"A sword, a sword
is drawn for your slaughter.
It is polished to destroy,
flashing like lightning!
29 Your prophets have given false visions,
and your fortune-tellers have told lies.
The sword will fall on the necks of the wicked
for whom the day of final reckoning has come.
30 "Now return the sword to its sheath,
for in your own country,
the land of your birth,
I will pass judgment upon you.
31 I will pour out my fury on you
and blow on you with the fire of my anger.
I will hand you over to cruel men
who are skilled in destruction.
32 You will be fuel for the fire,
and your blood will be spilled in your own land.
You will be utterly wiped out,
your memory lost to history,
for I, the LORD, have spoken!"

22 THE SINS OF JERUSALEM

Now this message came to me from the LORD: 2"Son of man, are you ready to judge Jerusalem? Are you ready to judge this city of murderers? Publicly denounce her detestable sins, 3and give her this message from the Sovereign LORD: O city of murderers, doomed and damned—city of idols,* filthy and foul—4you are guilty because of the blood you have shed. You are defiled because of the idols you have made. Your day of destruction has come! You have reached the end of your years. I will make you an object of mockery throughout the world. 5O infamous city, filled with confusion, you will be mocked by people far and near.

6"Every leader in Israel who lives within your walls is bent on murder. 7Fathers and mothers are treated with contempt. Foreigners are forced to pay for protection. Orphans and widows are wronged and oppressed among you. 8You despise my holy things and violate my Sabbath days of rest. 9People accuse others falsely and send them to their death. You are filled with idol worshipers and people who do obscene things. 10Men sleep with their fathers' wives and have intercourse with women who are menstruating. 11Within your walls live men who commit adultery with their neighbors' wives, who defile their daughters-in-law, or who rape their own sisters. 12There

22:3 The Hebrew term (literally *round things*) probably alludes to dung; also in 22:4.

are hired murderers, loan racketeers, and extortioners everywhere. They never even think of me and my commands, says the Sovereign LORD.

13"But now I clap my hands in indignation over your dishonest gain and bloodshed. 14How strong and courageous will you be in my day of reckoning? I, the LORD, have spoken, and I will do what I said. 15I will scatter you among the nations and purge you of your wickedness. 16And when I have been dishonored among the nations because of you,* you will know that I am the LORD."

THE LORD'S REFINING FURNACE

17Then this message came to me from the LORD: 18"Son of man, the people of Israel are the worthless slag that remains after silver is smelted. They are the dross that is left over—a useless mixture of copper, tin, iron, and lead. 19So tell them, 'This is what the Sovereign LORD says: Because you are all worthless slag, I will bring you to my crucible in Jerusalem. 20Just as copper, iron, lead, and tin are melted down in a furnace, I will melt you down in the heat of my fury. 21I will gather you together and blow the fire of my anger upon you, 22and you will melt like silver in fierce heat. Then you will know that I, the LORD, have poured out my fury on you.'"

THE SINS OF ISRAEL'S LEADERS

23Again a message came to me from the LORD: 24"Son of man, give the people of Israel this message: In the day of my indignation, you will be like a polluted land, a land without rain. 25Your princes* plot conspiracies just as lions stalk their prey. They devour innocent people, seizing treasures and extorting wealth. They make many widows in the land. 26Your priests have violated my instructions and defiled my holy things. They make no distinction between what is holy and what is not. And they do not teach my people the difference between what is ceremonially clean and unclean. They disregard my Sabbath days so that I am dishonored among them. 27Your leaders are like wolves who tear apart their victims. They actually destroy people's lives for money! 28And your prophets cover up for them by announcing false visions and making lying predictions. They say, 'My message is from the Sovereign LORD,' when the LORD hasn't spoken a single word to them. 29Even common people oppress the poor, rob the needy, and deprive foreigners of justice.

30"I looked for someone who might rebuild the wall of righteousness that guards the land. I searched for someone to stand in the gap in the wall so I wouldn't have to destroy the land, but I found no one. 31So now I will pour out my fury on them, consuming them with the fire of my anger. I will heap on their heads the full penalty for all their sins. I, the Sovereign LORD, have spoken!"

23 THE ADULTERY OF TWO SISTERS

This message came to me from the LORD: 2"Son of man, once there were two sisters who were daughters of the same mother. 3They became prostitutes in Egypt. Even as young girls, they allowed men to fondle their breasts. 4The older girl was named Oholah, and her sister was Oholibah. I married them, and they bore me sons and daughters. I am speaking of Samaria and Jerusalem, for Oholah is Samaria and Oholibah is Jerusalem.

5"Then Oholah lusted after other lovers instead of me, and she gave her love to the Assyrian officers. 6They were all attractive young men, captains and commanders dressed in handsome blue, charioteers driving their horses. 7And so she prostituted herself with the most desirable men of Assyria, worshiping their idols* and defiling herself. 8For when she left Egypt, she did not leave her spirit of prostitution behind. She was still as lewd as in her youth, when the Egyptians slept with her, fondled her breasts, and used her as a prostitute.

9"And so I handed her over to her Assyrian lovers, whom she desired so much. 10They stripped her, took away her children as their slaves, and then killed her. After she received her punishment, her reputation was known to every woman in the land.

11"Yet even though Oholibah saw what had happened to Oholah, her sister, she followed right in her footsteps. And she was even more depraved, abandoning herself to her lust and prostitution. 12She fawned over all the Assyrian officers—those captains and commanders in handsome uniforms, those charioteers driving their horses—all of them attractive young men. 13I saw the way she was going, defiling herself just like her older sister.

14"Then she carried her prostitution even further. She fell in love with pictures that were painted on a wall—pictures of Babylonian* military officers, outfitted in striking red uniforms. 15Handsome belts encircled their waists, and flowing turbans crowned their heads. They were dressed like chariot officers from the land of Babylonia.* 16When she saw these paintings, she longed to give herself to them, so she sent messengers to Babylonia to invite them to come to her. 17So they came and committed adultery with her, defiling her in the bed of love. After being defiled, however, she rejected them in disgust.

18"In the same way, I became disgusted with Oholibah and rejected her, just as I had rejected her sister, because she flaunted herself before them and gave herself to satisfy their lusts. 19Yet she turned to even greater prostitution, remembering her youth when she was a prostitute in Egypt. 20She lusted after lovers with genitals as large as a donkey's and emissions like those of a horse. 21And so, Oholibah, you relived your former days as a young girl in Egypt, when you first allowed your breasts to be fondled.

THE LORD'S JUDGMENT OF OHOLIBAH

22"Therefore, Oholibah, this is what the Sovereign LORD says: I will send your lovers against you from every direction—those very nations from which you turned away in disgust. 23For the Babylonians will come with all the Chaldeans from Pekod and Shoa and Koa. And all the Assyrians will come with them—handsome young cap-

22:16 Or *when you have been dishonored among the nations.* 22:25 As in Greek version; Hebrew reads *prophets.* 23:7 The Hebrew term (literally *round things*) probably alludes to dung; also in 23:30, 37, 39, 49. 23:14 Or *Chaldean.* 23:15 Or *Chaldea;* also in 23:16.

tains, commanders, chariot officers, and other high-
ranking officers, all riding their horses. 24They will all
come against you from the north* with chariots, wagons,
and a great army prepared for attack. They will take up
positions on every side, surrounding you with men
armed with shields and helmets. And I will hand you
over to them for punishment so they can do with you as
they please. 25I will turn my jealous anger against you,
and they will deal harshly with you. They will cut off your
nose and ears, and any survivors will then be slaughtered
by the sword. Your children will be taken away as captives, and everything that is left will be burned. 26They
will strip you of your beautiful clothes and jewels. 27In
this way, I will put a stop to the lewdness and prostitution
you brought from Egypt. You will never again cast longing eyes on those things or fondly remember your time
in Egypt.

28"For this is what the Sovereign LORD says: I will surely
hand you over to your enemies, to those you loathe, those
you rejected. 29They will treat you with hatred and rob
you of all you own, leaving you stark naked. The shame of
your prostitution will be exposed to all the world. 30You
brought all this on yourself by prostituting yourself to
other nations, defiling yourself with all their idols.
31Because you have followed in your sister's footsteps, I
will force you to drink the same cup of terror she drank.

32"Yes, this is what the Sovereign LORD says:

"You will drink from your sister's cup of terror,
 a cup that is large and deep.
It is filled to the brim
 with scorn and derision.
33 Drunkenness and anguish will fill you,
 for your cup is filled to the brim with distress
  and desolation,
 the same cup your sister Samaria drank.
34 You will drain that cup of terror
 to the very bottom.
Then you will smash it to pieces
 and beat your breast in anguish.
I, the Sovereign LORD, have spoken!

35"And because you have forgotten me and turned
your back on me, this is what the Sovereign LORD says:
You must bear the consequences of all your lewdness
and prostitution."

THE LORD'S JUDGMENT ON BOTH SISTERS

36The LORD said to me, "Son of man, you must accuse
Oholah and Oholibah of all their detestable sins. 37They
have committed both adultery and murder—adultery by
worshiping idols and murder by burning as sacrifices the
children they bore to me. 38Furthermore, they have defiled my Temple and violated my Sabbath day! 39On the
very day that they sacrificed their children to their idols,
they boldly came into my Temple to worship! They came
in and defiled my house.

40"You sisters sent messengers to distant lands to get

DOUBLE-MINDED 23:36-39

The Israelites sacrificed their own children to idols and then sacrificed to the Lord on the same day. But God called them on their double-mindedness. As James 1:6 says, "A person with divided loyalty is as unsettled as a wave of the sea that is blown and tossed by the wind." We cannot praise God and willfully do wrong things at the same time! That would be like telling your crush that he or she's your one and only, but then going on a date with someone else. As Joshua once told the people of Israel, "Choose today whom you will serve" (Josh 24:15). ■

men. Then when they arrived, you bathed yourselves,
painted your eyelids, and put on your finest jewels for
them. 41You sat with them on a beautifully embroidered
couch and put my incense and my special oil on a table
that was spread before you. 42From your room came the
sound of many men carousing. They were lustful men and
drunkards* from the wilderness, who put bracelets on
your wrists and beautiful crowns on your heads. 43Then I
said, 'If they really want to have sex with worn-out prostitutes like these, let them!' 44And that is what they did.
They had sex with Oholah and Oholibah, these shameless
prostitutes. 45But righteous people will judge these sister
cities for what they really are—adulterers and murderers.

46"Now this is what the Sovereign LORD says: Bring an
army against them and hand them over to be terrorized
and plundered. 47For their enemies will stone them and
kill them with swords. They will butcher their sons and
daughters and burn their homes. 48In this way, I will put
an end to lewdness and idolatry in the land, and my judgment will be a warning to others not to follow their
wicked example. 49You will be fully repaid for all your
prostitution—your worship of idols. Yes, you will suffer
the full penalty. Then you will know that I am the Sovereign LORD."

24

THE SIGN OF THE COOKING POT

On January 15,* during the ninth year of King Jehoiachin's captivity, this message came to me from the LORD:
2"Son of man, write down today's date, because on this
very day the king of Babylon is beginning his attack
against Jerusalem. 3Then give these rebels an illustration
with this message from the Sovereign LORD:

"Put a pot on the fire,
 and pour in some water.
4 Fill it with choice pieces of meat—
 the rump and the shoulder
 and all the most tender cuts.
5 Use only the best sheep from the flock,
 and heap fuel on the fire beneath the pot.
Bring the pot to a boil,
 and cook the bones along with the meat.

23:24 As in Greek version; the meaning of the Hebrew is uncertain. 23:42 Or *Sabeans*. 24:1 Hebrew *On the tenth day of the tenth month*, of the ancient Hebrew lunar calendar. This event occurred on January 15, 588 B.C.; also see note on 1:1.

6 "Now this is what the Sovereign LORD says:
What sorrow awaits Jerusalem,
the city of murderers!
She is a cooking pot
whose corruption can't be cleaned out.
Take the meat out in random order,
for no piece is better than another.
7 For the blood of her murders
is splashed on the rocks.
It isn't even spilled on the ground,
where the dust could cover it!
8 So I will splash her blood on a rock
for all to see,
an expression of my anger
and vengeance against her.

9 "This is what the Sovereign LORD says:
What sorrow awaits Jerusalem,
the city of murderers!
I myself will pile up the fuel beneath her.
10 Yes, heap on the wood!
Let the fire roar to make the pot boil.
Cook the meat with many spices,
and afterward burn the bones.
11 Now set the empty pot on the coals.
Heat it red hot!
Burn away the filth and corruption.
12 But it's hopeless;
the corruption can't be cleaned out.
So throw it into the fire.
13 Your impurity is your lewdness
and the corruption of your idolatry.
I tried to cleanse you,
but you refused.
So now you will remain in your filth
until my fury against you has been satisfied.

14"I, the LORD, have spoken! The time has come, and I
won't hold back. I will not change my mind, and I will
have no pity on you. You will be judged on the basis of all
your wicked actions, says the Sovereign LORD."

THE DEATH OF EZEKIEL'S WIFE

15Then this message came to me from the LORD: 16"Son of
man, with one blow I will take away your dearest treasure.
Yet you must not show any sorrow at her death. Do not
weep; let there be no tears. 17Groan silently, but let there
be no wailing at her grave. Do not uncover your head or
take off your sandals. Do not perform the usual rituals of
mourning or accept any food brought to you by consoling
friends."

18So I proclaimed this to the people the next morning,
and in the evening my wife died. The next morning I did
everything I had been told to do. 19Then the people asked,
"What does all this mean? What are you trying to tell us?"

20So I said to them, "A message came to me from the
LORD, 21and I was told to give this message to the people of
Israel. This is what the Sovereign LORD says: I will defile my
Temple, the source of your security and pride, the place
your heart delights in. Your sons and daughters whom you
left behind in Judea will be slaughtered by the sword.
22Then you will do as Ezekiel has done. You will not mourn
in public or console yourselves by eating the food brought
by friends. 23Your heads will remain covered, and your sandals will not be taken off. You will not mourn or weep, but
you will waste away because of your sins. You will mourn
privately for all the evil you have done. 24Ezekiel is an example for you; you will do just as he has done. And when that
time comes, you will know that I am the LORD."

25Then the LORD said to me, "Son of man, on the day I
take away their stronghold—their joy and glory, their
heart's desire, their dearest treasure—I will also take
away their sons and daughters. 26And on that day a survivor from Jerusalem will come to you in Babylon and tell
you what has happened. 27And when he arrives, your
voice will suddenly return so you can talk to him, and you
will be a symbol for these people. Then they will know
that I am the LORD."

THE AGONY OF OBEDIENCE 24:15-27

Although Ezekiel's wife died, God told him not to do the usual public mourning (loud crying, putting dust on the head, wearing sackcloth). Instead, he was to be silent to mirror the grief Israel would go through when Jerusalem was destroyed. Ezekiel was obedient even in the face of agonizing grief. Would you have done the same? Many times, we slip into disobedience mode when obedience seems too difficult. But "too difficult" is an excuse, really. When the going gets tough, are you willing to keep going in obedience? ■

25 A MESSAGE FOR AMMON

Then this message came to me from the LORD: 2"Son of man,
turn and face the land of Ammon and prophesy against its
people. 3Give the Ammonites this message from the Sovereign LORD: Hear the word of the Sovereign LORD! Because
you cheered when my Temple was defiled, mocked Israel in
her desolation, and laughed at Judah as she went away into
exile, 4I will allow nomads from the eastern deserts to overrun your country. They will set up their camps among you
and pitch their tents on your land. They will harvest all your
fruit and drink the milk from your livestock. 5And I will turn
the city of Rabbah into a pasture for camels, and all the land
of the Ammonites into a resting place for sheep and goats.
Then you will know that I am the LORD.

6"This is what the Sovereign LORD says: Because you
clapped and danced and cheered with glee at the destruction of my people, 7I will raise my fist of judgment
against you. I will give you as plunder to many nations. I
will cut you off from being a nation and destroy you completely. Then you will know that I am the LORD.

A MESSAGE FOR MOAB

8"This is what the Sovereign LORD says: Because the people of Moab have said that Judah is just like all the other

nations, 9I will open up their eastern flank and wipe out
their glorious frontier towns—Beth-jeshimoth, Baal-
meon, and Kiriathaim. 10And I will hand Moab over to
nomads from the eastern deserts, just as I handed over
Ammon. Yes, the Ammonites will no longer be counted
among the nations. 11In the same way, I will bring my
judgment down on the Moabites. Then they will know
that I am the LORD.

A MESSAGE FOR EDOM

12"This is what the Sovereign LORD says: The people of
Edom have sinned greatly by avenging themselves
against the people of Judah. 13Therefore, says the Sovereign LORD, I will raise my fist of judgment against Edom. I
will wipe out its people and animals with the sword. I will
make a wasteland of everything from Teman to Dedan.
14I will accomplish this by the hand of my people of Israel. They will carry out my vengeance with anger, and
Edom will know that this vengeance is from me. I, the
Sovereign LORD, have spoken!

A MESSAGE FOR PHILISTIA

15"This is what the Sovereign LORD says: The people of
Philistia have acted against Judah out of bitter revenge
and long-standing contempt. 16Therefore, this is what
the Sovereign LORD says: I will raise my fist of judgment
against the land of the Philistines. I will wipe out the Kerethites and utterly destroy the people who live by the sea.
17I will execute terrible vengeance against them to punish them for what they have done. And when I have inflicted my revenge, they will know that I am the LORD."

26 A MESSAGE FOR TYRE

On February 3, during the twelfth year of King Jehoiachin's captivity,* this message came to me from the
LORD: 2"Son of man, Tyre has rejoiced over the fall of Jerusalem, saying, 'Ha! She who was the gateway to the rich
trade routes to the east has been broken, and I am the
heir! Because she has been made desolate, I will become
wealthy!'

3"Therefore, this is what the Sovereign LORD says: I am
your enemy, O Tyre, and I will bring many nations against
you, like the waves of the sea crashing against your shoreline. 4They will destroy the walls of Tyre and tear down its
towers. I will scrape away its soil and make it a bare rock!
5It will be just a rock in the sea, a place for fishermen to
spread their nets, for I have spoken, says the Sovereign
LORD. Tyre will become the prey of many nations, 6and its
mainland villages will be destroyed by the sword. Then
they will know that I am the LORD.

7"This is what the Sovereign LORD says: From the north
I will bring King Nebuchadnezzar* of Babylon against
Tyre. He is king of kings and brings his horses, chariots,
charioteers, and great army. 8First he will destroy your
mainland villages. Then he will attack you by building a
siege wall, constructing a ramp, and raising a roof of
shields against you. 9He will pound your walls with battering rams and demolish your towers with sledge-
hammers. 10The hooves of his horses will choke the city
with dust, and the noise of the charioteers and chariot
wheels will shake your walls as they storm through your
broken gates. 11His horsemen will trample through every
street in the city. They will butcher your people, and your
strong pillars will topple.

12"They will plunder all your riches and merchandise
and break down your walls. They will destroy your lovely
homes and dump your stones and timbers and even your
dust into the sea. 13I will stop the music of your songs. No
more will the sound of harps be heard among your people. 14I will make your island a bare rock, a place for
fishermen to spread their nets. You will never be rebuilt,
for I, the LORD, have spoken. Yes, the Sovereign LORD has
spoken!

HE MEANS WHAT HE SAYS 26:1-14

Through Ezekiel, God declared that Tyre would be destroyed and never rebuilt. After a 15-year siege, Nebuchadnezzar couldn't conquer the part of Tyre located on the island. Consequently, certain aspects of the description in 26:12-14 actually go beyond the damage done to Tyre by Nebuchadnezzar and predict what would happen to the island settlement later during the conquests of Alexander the Great. Alexander threw the rubble of the mainland city into the sea until it made a bridge to the island. Today, the island city is still a pile of rubble—a testimony to God's judgment.

What God says will happen *will* happen. He doesn't take pleasure in destruction. He would much rather save than destroy. This is why he often warned people what would happen if they chose to disobey. How seriously do you take God's warnings? ■

THE EFFECT OF TYRE'S DESTRUCTION

15"This is what the Sovereign LORD says to Tyre: The
whole coastline will tremble at the sound of your fall, as
the screams of the wounded echo in the continuing
slaughter. 16All the seaport rulers will step down from
their thrones and take off their royal robes and beautiful
clothing. They will sit on the ground trembling with horror at your destruction. 17Then they will wail for you,
singing this funeral song:

"O famous island city,
once ruler of the sea,
how you have been destroyed!
Your people, with their naval power,
once spread fear around the world.
18 Now the coastlands tremble at your fall.
The islands are dismayed as you disappear.

26:1 Hebrew *In the eleventh year, on the first day of the month,* of the ancient Hebrew lunar calendar year. Since an element is missing in the date formula here, scholars have reconstructed this probable reading: *In the eleventh [month of the twelfth] year, on the first day of the month.* This reading would put this message on February 3, 585 B.C.; also see note on 1:1. 26:7 Hebrew *Nebuchadrezzar,* a variant spelling of Nebuchadnezzar.

19"This is what the Sovereign LORD says: I will make
Tyre an uninhabited ruin, like many others. I will bury
you beneath the terrible waves of enemy attack. Great
seas will swallow you. 20I will send you to the pit to join
those who descended there long ago. Your city will lie in
ruins, buried beneath the earth, like those in the pit who
have entered the world of the dead. You will have no
place of respect here in the land of the living. 21I will
bring you to a terrible end, and you will exist no more.
You will be looked for, but you will never again be found.
I, the Sovereign LORD, have spoken!"

27

THE END OF TYRE'S GLORY

Then this message came to me from the LORD: 2"Son of
man, sing a funeral song for Tyre, 3that mighty gateway to
the sea, the trading center of the world. Give Tyre this
message from the Sovereign LORD:

"You boasted, O Tyre,
'My beauty is perfect!'
4 You extended your boundaries into the sea.
Your builders made your beauty perfect.
5 You were like a great ship
built of the finest cypress from Senir.*
They took a cedar from Lebanon
to make a mast for you.
6 They carved your oars
from the oaks of Bashan.
Your deck of pine from the coasts of Cyprus*
was inlaid with ivory.
7 Your sails were made of Egypt's finest linen,
and they flew as a banner above you.
You stood beneath blue and purple awnings
made bright with dyes from the coasts of Elishah.
8 Your oarsmen came from Sidon and Arvad;
your helmsmen were skilled men from
Tyre itself.
9 Wise old craftsmen from Gebal did the caulking.
Ships from every land came with goods to barter
for your trade.

10"Men from distant Persia, Lydia, and Libya* served in
your great army. They hung their shields and helmets on
your walls, giving you great honor. 11Men from Arvad and
Helech stood on your walls. Your towers were manned by
men from Gammad. Their shields hung on your walls,
completing your beauty.

12"Tarshish sent merchants to buy your wares in exchange for silver, iron, tin, and lead. 13Merchants from
Greece,* Tubal, and Meshech brought slaves and articles
of bronze to trade with you.

14"From Togarmah came riding horses, chariot horses,
and mules, all in exchange for your goods. 15Merchants
came to you from Dedan.* Numerous coastlands were
your captive markets; they brought payment in ivory
tusks and ebony wood.

16"Syria* sent merchants to buy your rich variety of
goods. They traded turquoise, purple dyes, embroidery,
fine linen, and jewelry of coral and rubies. 17Judah and Israel traded for your wares, offering wheat from Minnith,
figs,* honey, olive oil, and balm.

18"Damascus sent merchants to buy your rich variety
of goods, bringing wine from Helbon and white wool
from Zahar. 19Greeks from Uzal* came to trade for your
merchandise. Wrought iron, cassia, and fragrant calamus were bartered for your wares.

20"Dedan sent merchants to trade their expensive saddle blankets with you. 21The Arabians and the princes of
Kedar sent merchants to trade lambs and rams and male
goats in exchange for your goods. 22The merchants of
Sheba and Raamah came with all kinds of spices, jewels,
and gold in exchange for your wares.

23"Haran, Canneh, Eden, Sheba, Asshur, and Kilmad
came with their merchandise, too. 24They brought choice
fabrics to trade—blue cloth, embroidery, and multi-
colored carpets rolled up and bound with cords. 25The
ships of Tarshish were your ocean caravans. Your island
warehouse was filled to the brim!

THE DESTRUCTION OF TYRE

26 "But look! Your oarsmen
have taken you into stormy seas!
A mighty eastern gale
has wrecked you in the heart of the sea!
27 Everything is lost—
your riches and wares,
your sailors and pilots,
your ship builders, merchants, and warriors.
On the day of your ruin,
everyone on board sinks into the depths of the sea.
28 Your cities by the sea tremble
as your pilots cry out in terror.
29 All the oarsmen abandon their ships;
the sailors and pilots on shore come to stand
on the beach.
30 They cry aloud over you
and weep bitterly.
They throw dust on their heads
and roll in ashes.
31 They shave their heads in grief for you
and dress themselves in burlap.
They weep for you with bitter anguish
and deep mourning.
32 As they wail and mourn over you,
they sing this sad funeral song:
'Was there ever such a city as Tyre,
now silent at the bottom of the sea?
33 The merchandise you traded
satisfied the desires of many nations.
Kings at the ends of the earth
were enriched by your trade.
34 Now you are a wrecked ship,
broken at the bottom of the sea.

27:5 Or *Hermon*. 27:6 Hebrew *Kittim*. 27:10 Hebrew *Paras, Lud, and Put*. 27:13 Hebrew *Javan*. 27:15 Greek version reads *Rhodes*. 27:16 Hebrew *Aram;* some manuscripts read *Edom*. 27:17 The meaning of the Hebrew is uncertain. 27:19 Hebrew *Vedan and Javan from Uzal*. The meaning of the Hebrew is uncertain.

All your merchandise and crew
have gone down with you.
35 All who live along the coastlands
are appalled at your terrible fate.
Their kings are filled with horror
and look on with twisted faces.
36 The merchants among the nations
shake their heads at the sight of you,*
for you have come to a horrible end
and will exist no more.'"

28 A MESSAGE FOR TYRE'S KING

Then this message came to me from the LORD: 2"Son of man, give the prince of Tyre this message from the Sovereign LORD:

"In your great pride you claim, 'I am a god!
I sit on a divine throne in the heart of the sea.'
But you are only a man and not a god,
though you boast that you are a god.
3 You regard yourself as wiser than Daniel
and think no secret is hidden from you.
4 With your wisdom and understanding you have
amassed great wealth—
gold and silver for your treasuries.
5 Yes, your wisdom has made you very rich,
and your riches have made you very proud.

6 "Therefore, this is what the Sovereign LORD says:
Because you think you are as wise as a god,
7 I will now bring against you a foreign army,
the terror of the nations.
They will draw their swords against your
marvelous wisdom
and defile your splendor!
8 They will bring you down to the pit,
and you will die in the heart of the sea,
pierced with many wounds.
9 Will you then boast, 'I am a god!'
to those who kill you?
To them you will be no god
but merely a man!
10 You will die like an outcast*
at the hands of foreigners.
I, the Sovereign LORD, have spoken!"

11Then this further message came to me from the LORD: 12"Son of man, sing this funeral song for the king of Tyre. Give him this message from the Sovereign LORD:

"You were the model of perfection,
full of wisdom and exquisite in beauty.
13 You were in Eden,
the garden of God.
Your clothing was adorned with every precious stone*—
red carnelian, pale-green peridot, white moonstone,
blue-green beryl, onyx, green jasper,
blue lapis lazuli, turquoise, and emerald—
all beautifully crafted for you
and set in the finest gold.
They were given to you
on the day you were created.
14 I ordained and anointed you
as the mighty angelic guardian.*
You had access to the holy mountain of God
and walked among the stones of fire.

15 "You were blameless in all you did
from the day you were created
until the day evil was found in you.
16 Your rich commerce led you to violence,
and you sinned.
So I banished you in disgrace
from the mountain of God.
I expelled you, O mighty guardian,
from your place among the stones of fire.
17 Your heart was filled with pride
because of all your beauty.
Your wisdom was corrupted
by your love of splendor.
So I threw you to the ground
and exposed you to the curious gaze of kings.
18 You defiled your sanctuaries
with your many sins and your dishonest trade.
So I brought fire out from within you,
and it consumed you.
I reduced you to ashes on the ground
in the sight of all who were watching.
19 All who knew you are appalled at your fate.
You have come to a terrible end,
and you will exist no more."

A MESSAGE FOR SIDON

20Then another message came to me from the LORD: 21"Son of man, turn and face the city of Sidon and prophesy against it. 22Give the people of Sidon this message from the Sovereign LORD:

"I am your enemy, O Sidon,
and I will reveal my glory by what I do to you.
When I bring judgment against you
and reveal my holiness among you,
everyone watching will know
that I am the LORD.
23 I will send a plague against you,
and blood will be spilled in your streets.
The attack will come from every direction,
and your people will lie slaughtered within your walls.
Then everyone will know
that I am the LORD.
24 No longer will Israel's scornful neighbors
prick and tear at her like briers and thorns.
For then they will know
that I am the Sovereign LORD.

27:36 Hebrew *hiss at you.* 28:10 Hebrew *will die the death of the uncircumcised.* 28:13 The identification of some of these gemstones is uncertain. 28:14 Hebrew *guardian cherub;* similarly in 28:16.

RESTORATION FOR ISRAEL

25"This is what the Sovereign LORD says: The people of Israel will again live in their own land, the land I gave my servant Jacob. For I will gather them from the distant lands where I have scattered them. I will reveal to the nations of the world my holiness among my people. 26They will live safely in Israel and build homes and plant vineyards. And when I punish the neighboring nations that treated them with contempt, they will know that I am the LORD their God."

THE PROMISE REMAINS 28:24-26

The promise that God's people will live in complete safety has yet to be fulfilled. Although many Jews were allowed to return from exile under Zerubbabel, Ezra, and Nehemiah, and the political nation is restored today, the inhabitants do not yet "live safely in Israel" (28:26). Therefore, this promise will have its ultimate fulfillment when Christ sets up his eternal Kingdom. God is into long-range planning. Are you willing to trust his plans for your life? ■

29 A MESSAGE FOR EGYPT

On January 7,* during the tenth year of King Jehoiachin's captivity, this message came to me from the LORD: 2"Son of man, turn and face Egypt and prophesy against Pharaoh the king and all the people of Egypt. 3Give them this message from the Sovereign LORD:

"I am your enemy, O Pharaoh, king of Egypt—
you great monster, lurking in the streams
of the Nile.
For you have said, 'The Nile River is mine;
I made it for myself.'
4 I will put hooks in your jaws
and drag you out on the land
with fish sticking to your scales.
5 I will leave you and all your fish
stranded in the wilderness to die.
You will lie unburied on the open ground,
for I have given you as food to the wild animals
and birds.
6 All the people of Egypt will know that I am the LORD,
for to Israel you were just a staff made of reeds.
7 When Israel leaned on you,
you splintered and broke
and stabbed her in the armpit.
When she put her weight on you, you gave way,
and her back was thrown out of joint.

8"Therefore, this is what the Sovereign LORD says: I will bring an army against you, O Egypt, and destroy both people and animals. 9The land of Egypt will become a desolate wasteland, and the Egyptians will know that I am the LORD.

"Because you said, 'The Nile River is mine; I made it,' 10I
am now the enemy of both you and your river. I will make the land of Egypt a totally desolate wasteland, from Migdol to Aswan, as far south as the border of Ethiopia.*
11For forty years not a soul will pass that way, neither people nor animals. It will be completely uninhabited. 12I will
make Egypt desolate, and it will be surrounded by other desolate nations. Its cities will be empty and desolate for forty years, surrounded by other ruined cities. I will scatter the Egyptians to distant lands.

CREDIT WHERE CREDIT IS DUE 29:9-12

The Nile River was Egypt's pride and joy, a life-giving river cutting through the middle of the desert. Rather than thanking God, however, Egypt declared, "The Nile is mine!" We do the same when we say, "I owe all of my success to me, myself, and I." Of course, we have put forth a lot of hard effort, but God supplied us with the resources, abilities, and opportunities to make it happen. Tempted to pat yourself on the back? Why not give God some praise instead? ■

13"But this is what the Sovereign LORD also says: At the end of the forty years I will bring the Egyptians home again from the nations to which they have been scattered.
14I will restore the prosperity of Egypt and bring its people back to the land of Pathros in southern Egypt from which they came. But Egypt will remain an unimportant, minor kingdom. 15It will be the lowliest of all the nations, never again great enough to rise above its neighbors.

16"Then Israel will no longer be tempted to trust in Egypt for help. Egypt's shattered condition will remind Israel of how sinful she was to trust Egypt in earlier days. Then Israel will know that I am the Sovereign LORD."

NEBUCHADNEZZAR TO CONQUER EGYPT

17On April 26, the first day of the new year,* during the twenty-seventh year of King Jehoiachin's captivity, this message came to me from the LORD: 18"Son of man, the army of King Nebuchadnezzar* of Babylon fought so hard against Tyre that the warriors' heads were rubbed bare and their shoulders were raw and blistered. Yet Nebuchadnezzar and his army won no plunder to compensate them for all their work. 19Therefore, this is what
the Sovereign LORD says: I will give the land of Egypt to Nebuchadnezzar, king of Babylon. He will carry off its wealth, plundering everything it has so he can pay his army. 20Yes, I have given him the land of Egypt as a reward
for his work, says the Sovereign LORD, because he was working for me when he destroyed Tyre.

21"And the day will come when I will cause the ancient

29:1 Hebrew *On the twelfth day of the tenth month,* of the ancient Hebrew lunar calendar. This event occurred on January 7, 587 B.C.; also see note on 1:1. 29:10 Hebrew *from Migdol to Syene as far as the border of Cush.* 29:17 Hebrew *On the first day of the first month,* of the ancient Hebrew lunar calendar. This event occurred on April 26, 571 B.C.; also see note on 1:1. 29:18 Hebrew *Nebuchadrezzar,* a variant spelling of Nebuchadnezzar; also in 29:19.

glory of Israel to revive,* and then, Ezekiel, your words will be respected. Then they will know that I am the LORD."

30 A SAD DAY FOR EGYPT

This is another message that came to me from the LORD:
2"Son of man, prophesy and give this message from the Sovereign LORD:

"Weep and wail
for that day,
3 for the terrible day is almost here—
the day of the LORD!
It is a day of clouds and gloom,
a day of despair for the nations.
4 A sword will come against Egypt,
and those who are slaughtered will cover
the ground.
Its wealth will be carried away
and its foundations destroyed.
The land of Ethiopia* will be ravished.
5 Ethiopia, Libya, Lydia, all Arabia,*
and all their other allies
will be destroyed in that war.

6 "For this is what the LORD says:
All of Egypt's allies will fall,
and the pride of her power will end.
From Migdol to Aswan*
they will be slaughtered by the sword,
says the Sovereign LORD.
7 Egypt will be desolate,
surrounded by desolate nations,
and its cities will be in ruins,
surrounded by other ruined cities.
8 And the people of Egypt will know that I am
the LORD
when I have set Egypt on fire
and destroyed all their allies.
9 At that time I will send swift messengers in ships
to terrify the complacent Ethiopians.
Great panic will come upon them
on that day of Egypt's certain destruction.
Watch for it!
It is sure to come!

10 "For this is what the Sovereign LORD says:
By the power of King Nebuchadnezzar* of Babylon,
I will destroy the hordes of Egypt.
11 He and his armies—the most ruthless of all—
will be sent to demolish the land.
They will make war against Egypt
until slaughtered Egyptians cover the ground.
12 I will dry up the Nile River
and sell the land to wicked men.
I will destroy the land of Egypt and everything in it
by the hands of foreigners.
I, the LORD, have spoken!

13 "This is what the Sovereign LORD says:
I will smash the idols* of Egypt
and the images at Memphis.*
There will be no rulers left in Egypt;
terror will sweep the land.
14 I will destroy southern Egypt,*
set fire to Zoan,
and bring judgment against Thebes.*
15 I will pour out my fury on Pelusium,*
the strongest fortress of Egypt,
and I will stamp out
the hordes of Thebes.
16 Yes, I will set fire to all Egypt!
Pelusium will be racked with pain;
Thebes will be torn apart;
Memphis will live in constant terror.
17 The young men of Heliopolis and Bubastis* will
die in battle,
and the women* will be taken away as slaves.
18 When I come to break the proud strength of Egypt,
it will be a dark day for Tahpanhes, too.
A dark cloud will cover Tahpanhes,
and its daughters will be led away as captives.
19 And so I will greatly punish Egypt,
and they will know that I am the LORD."

RUMORS OF WAR 30:20-26

God ended Egypt's military superiority and passed the torch to Babylon. God allows nations to rise to power to accomplish a particular purpose, often beyond our immediate understanding. Sometimes wars happen as a result. But rumors of war or ongoing wars can sometimes inspire fear. Yet God is still in control. Besides praying for your military and government leaders, you could pray that God's greater purpose will be carried out "on earth, as it is in heaven" (Matt 6:10). ■

THE BROKEN ARMS OF PHARAOH

20On April 29,* during the eleventh year of King Jehoiachin's captivity, this message came to me from the LORD:
21"Son of man, I have broken the arm of Pharaoh, the king
of Egypt. His arm has not been put in a cast so that it may
heal. Neither has it been bound up with a splint to make it
strong enough to hold a sword. 22Therefore, this is what
the Sovereign LORD says: I am the enemy of Pharaoh, the
king of Egypt! I will break both of his arms—the good arm

29:21 Hebrew *I will cause a horn to sprout for the house of Israel.* 30:4 Hebrew *Cush;* similarly in 30:9. 30:5 Hebrew *Cush, Put, Lud, all Arabia, Cub. Cub* is otherwise unknown and may be another spelling for *Lub* (Libya). 30:6 Hebrew *to Syene.* 30:10 Hebrew *Nebuchadrezzar,* a variant spelling of Nebuchadnezzar. 30:13a The Hebrew term (literally *round things*) probably alludes to dung. 30:13b Hebrew *Noph;* also in 30:16. 30:14a Hebrew *Pathros.* 30:14b Hebrew *No;* also in 30:15, 16. 30:15 Hebrew *Sin;* also in 30:16. 30:17a Hebrew *of Awen and Pi-beseth.* 30:17b Or *and her cities.* 30:20 Hebrew *On the seventh day of the first month,* of the ancient Hebrew lunar calendar. This event occurred on April 29, 587 B.C.; also see note on 1:1.

along with the broken one—and I will make his sword
clatter to the ground. 23 I will scatter the Egyptians to
many lands throughout the world. 24 I will strengthen the
arms of Babylon's king and put my sword in his hand. But
I will break the arms of Pharaoh, king of Egypt, and he
will lie there mortally wounded, groaning in pain. 25 I will
strengthen the arms of the king of Babylon, while the
arms of Pharaoh fall useless to his sides. And when I put
my sword in the hand of Babylon's king and he brings it
against the land of Egypt, Egypt will know that I am the
LORD. 26 I will scatter the Egyptians among the nations,
dispersing them throughout the earth. Then they will
know that I am the LORD."

31 EGYPT COMPARED TO FALLEN ASSYRIA

On June 21,* during the eleventh year of King Jehoiachin's captivity, this message came to me from the LORD:
2 "Son of man, give this message to Pharaoh, king of Egypt,
and all his hordes:

"To whom would you compare your greatness?
3 You are like mighty Assyria,
which was once like a cedar of Lebanon,
with beautiful branches that cast deep forest shade
and with its top high among the clouds.
4 Deep springs watered it
and helped it to grow tall and luxuriant.
The water flowed around it like a river,
streaming to all the trees nearby.
5 This great tree towered high,
higher than all the other trees around it.
It prospered and grew long thick branches
because of all the water at its roots.
6 The birds nested in its branches,
and in its shade all the wild animals gave birth.
All the great nations of the world
lived in its shadow.
7 It was strong and beautiful,
with wide-spreading branches,
for its roots went deep
into abundant water.
8 No other cedar in the garden of God
could rival it.
No cypress had branches to equal it;
no plane tree had boughs to compare.
No tree in the garden of God
came close to it in beauty.
9 Because I made this tree so beautiful,
and gave it such magnificent foliage,
it was the envy of all the other trees of Eden,
the garden of God.

10 "Therefore, this is what the Sovereign LORD says: Because Egypt* became proud and arrogant, and because it
set itself so high above the others, with its top reaching to
the clouds, 11 I will hand it over to a mighty nation that will
destroy it as its wickedness deserves. I have already discarded it. 12 A foreign army—the terror of the nations—
has cut it down and left it fallen on the ground. Its
branches are scattered across the mountains and valleys
and ravines of the land. All those who lived in its shadow
have gone away and left it lying there.

THE CRASH 31:1-18

Ezekiel compared Egypt to Assyria, calling Assyria a great cedar tree that had crashed to the ground. The fall of the mighty nation of Assyria was to be an example to the Egyptians of what would happen to them. Just like Assyria, Egypt took pride in her strength and beauty. Someday, however, Egypt would come crashing down just like Assyria. Nothing—not even a great society with magnificent culture and military power—lasts apart from God. Even a person with a bank account the size of Fort Knox or supermodel looks can crash and burn if God is ignored. In what do you trust? ■

13 "The birds roost on its fallen trunk,
and the wild animals lie among its branches.
14 Let the tree of no other nation
proudly exult in its own prosperity,
though it be higher than the clouds
and it be watered from the depths.
For all are doomed to die,
to go down to the depths of the earth.
They will land in the pit
along with everyone else on earth.

15 "This is what the Sovereign LORD says: When Assyria
went down to the grave,* I made the deep springs mourn. I
stopped its rivers and dried up its abundant water. I clothed
Lebanon in black and caused the trees of the field to wilt. 16 I
made the nations shake with fear at the sound of its fall, for
I sent it down to the grave with all the others who descend to
the pit. And all the other proud trees of Eden, the most
beautiful and the best of Lebanon, the ones whose roots
went deep into the water, took comfort to find it there with
them in the depths of the earth. 17 Its allies, too, were all destroyed and had passed away. They had gone down to the
grave—all those nations that had lived in its shade.
18 "O Egypt, to which of the trees of Eden will you compare your strength and glory? You, too, will be brought
down to the depths with all these other nations. You will
lie there among the outcasts* who have died by the
sword. This will be the fate of Pharaoh and all his hordes.
I, the Sovereign LORD, have spoken!"

32 A WARNING FOR PHARAOH

On March 3,* during the twelfth year of King Jehoiachin's captivity, this message came to me from the LORD:

31:1 Hebrew *On the first day of the third month,* of the ancient Hebrew lunar calendar. This event occurred on June 21, 587 B.C.; also see note on 1:1. 31:10 Hebrew *you.* 31:15 Hebrew *to Sheol;* also in 31:16, 17. 31:18 Hebrew *among the uncircumcised.* 32:1 Hebrew *On the first day of the twelfth month,* of the ancient Hebrew lunar calendar. This event occurred on March 3, 585 B.C.; also see note on 1:1.

WHO'S IN CHARGE?

Many Christians throw around terms like *free will* and *sovereignty*. *Free will,* of course is freedom of choice. But *sovereignty* means that God ultimately is in control of everything. So, is free will really possible?

The idea that God is in control goes against our notions of fairness and individual choice. And yet, we draw strength and comfort from the belief that God is running the universe. Which is right? Is God truly sovereign—is he calling the shots—or are people free and ultimately responsible for making their own decisions, even those that have eternal consequences?

This question has perplexed people for thousands of years. It raises itself here, in the account of Pharaoh in Ezekiel 32. It came up in the story of another Pharaoh, too (Exod 3–15). Before he allowed Pharaoh to rise to power, did God know that Pharaoh would sin? Did God simply allow Pharaoh to follow his own course of action? These questions might lead some to think *If God is truly and completely sovereign, then I have no real freedom, and I'm just a puppet. But if I'm truly free to do whatever I want, then God isn't really in control of the universe.*

What's really true?

The greatest minds of history have wrestled with this issue, and quite frankly, it remains as impenetrable today as ever. So if you were hoping this article would resolve it, you're going to be disappointed. But we can leave you with one answer: It is a *mystery*.

Sovereignty, responsibility, free will . . . and *mystery*. The Bible teaches them all. The modern American mind balks at accepting two truths that seem to be contradictory. But when you think about it, it makes sense that God is bigger than our minds—big enough to encompass what seems to us to be paradoxical.

If someone asks you whether you believe in God's sovereignty or human freedom, the best answer is yes.

2"Son of man, mourn for Pharaoh, king of Egypt, and give
him this message:

"You think of yourself as a strong young lion among
the nations,
but you are really just a sea monster,
heaving around in your own rivers,
stirring up mud with your feet.
3 Therefore, this is what the Sovereign LORD says:
I will send many people
to catch you in my net
and haul you out of the water.
4 I will leave you stranded on the land to die.
All the birds of the heavens will land on you,
and the wild animals of the whole earth
will gorge themselves on you.
5 I will scatter your flesh on the hills
and fill the valleys with your bones.
6 I will drench the earth with your gushing blood
all the way to the mountains,
filling the ravines to the brim.
7 When I blot you out,
I will veil the heavens and darken the stars.
I will cover the sun with a cloud,
and the moon will not give you its light.
8 I will darken the bright stars overhead
and cover your land in darkness.
I, the Sovereign LORD, have spoken!

9"I will disturb many hearts when I bring news of
your downfall to distant nations you have never seen.
10Yes, I will shock many lands, and their kings will be
terrified at your fate. They will shudder in fear for
their lives as I brandish my sword before them on the
day of your fall. 11For this is what the Sovereign LORD
says:

"The sword of the king of Babylon
will come against you.
12 I will destroy your hordes with the swords of
mighty warriors—
the terror of the nations.
They will shatter the pride of Egypt,
and all its hordes will be destroyed.
13 I will destroy all your flocks and herds
that graze beside the streams.

Never again will people or animals
muddy those waters with their feet.
14 Then I will let the waters of Egypt become
calm again,
and they will flow as smoothly as olive oil,
says the Sovereign LORD.
15 And when I destroy Egypt
and strip you of everything you own
and strike down all your people,
then you will know that I am the LORD.
16 Yes, this is the funeral song
they will sing for Egypt.
Let all the nations mourn.
Let them mourn for Egypt and its hordes.
I, the Sovereign LORD, have spoken!"

EGYPT FALLS INTO THE PIT

17 On March 17,* during the twelfth year, another message came to me from the LORD: 18 "Son of man, weep for
the hordes of Egypt and for the other mighty nations.*
For I will send them down to the world below in company
with those who descend to the pit. 19 Say to them,

'O Egypt, are you lovelier than the other nations?
No! So go down to the pit and lie there among the
outcasts.*'

20 The Egyptians will fall with the many who have died by
the sword, for the sword is drawn against them. Egypt
and its hordes will be dragged away to their judgment.
21 Down in the grave* mighty leaders will mockingly welcome Egypt and its allies, saying, 'They have come down;
they lie among the outcasts, hordes slaughtered by the
sword.'

LIFE AFTER DEATH 32:17-21

The Hebrews believed in an existence beyond the grave for all people, good and bad, in "the world below." Ezekiel's message assumed that other nations had already been sent "to the pit" (32:19), and that Egypt would soon follow. The Egyptians had a preoccupation with the afterlife. After all, the pyramids were built solely to ensure the pharaohs' comfort in the next life. Such human attempts are foolish. God alone controls what happens after death. But we can decide where we want to spend eternity: in heaven with God or in hell. What will you decide? ■

22 "Assyria lies there surrounded by the graves of its
army, those who were slaughtered by the sword. 23 Their
graves are in the depths of the pit, and they are surrounded by their allies. They struck terror in the hearts of
people everywhere, but now they have been slaughtered
by the sword.
24 "Elam lies there surrounded by the graves of all its
hordes, those who were slaughtered by the sword. They
struck terror in the hearts of people everywhere, but now
they have descended as outcasts to the world below. Now
they lie in the pit and share the shame of those who have
gone before them. 25 They have a resting place among the
slaughtered, surrounded by the graves of all their hordes.
Yes, they terrorized the nations while they lived, but now
they lie in shame with others in the pit, all of them outcasts, slaughtered by the sword.
26 "Meshech and Tubal are there, surrounded by the
graves of all their hordes. They once struck terror in the
hearts of people everywhere. But now they are outcasts,
all slaughtered by the sword. 27 They are not buried in
honor like their fallen heroes, who went down to the
grave* with their weapons—their shields covering their
bodies* and their swords beneath their heads. Their guilt
rests upon them because they brought terror to everyone
while they were still alive.
28 "You too, Egypt, will lie crushed and broken among
the outcasts, all slaughtered by the sword.
29 "Edom is there with its kings and princes. Mighty as
they were, they also lie among those slaughtered by the
sword, with the outcasts who have gone down to the pit.
30 "All the princes of the north and the Sidonians are
there with others who have died. Once a terror, they have
been put to shame. They lie there as outcasts with others
who were slaughtered by the sword. They share the
shame of all who have descended to the pit.
31 "When Pharaoh and his entire army arrive, he will
take comfort that he is not alone in having his hordes
killed, says the Sovereign LORD. 32 Although I have caused
his terror to fall upon all the living, Pharaoh and his
hordes will lie there among the outcasts who were
slaughtered by the sword. I, the Sovereign LORD, have
spoken!"

33 EZEKIEL AS ISRAEL'S WATCHMAN

Once again a message came to me from the LORD: 2 "Son
of man, give your people this message: 'When I bring an
army against a country, the people of that land choose
one of their own to be a watchman. 3 When the watchman sees the enemy coming, he sounds the alarm to
warn the people. 4 Then if those who hear the alarm refuse to take action, it is their own fault if they die. 5 They
heard the alarm but ignored it, so the responsibility is
theirs. If they had listened to the warning, they could
have saved their lives. 6 But if the watchman sees the enemy coming and doesn't sound the alarm to warn the
people, he is responsible for their captivity. They will die
in their sins, but I will hold the watchman responsible
for their deaths.'

32:17 Hebrew *On the fifteenth day of the month,* presumably in the twelfth month of the ancient Hebrew lunar calendar (see 32:1). This would put this message at the end of King Jehoiachin's twelfth year of captivity, on March 17, 585 B.C.; also see note on 1:1. Greek version reads *On the fifteenth day of the first month,* which would put this message on April 27, 586 B.C., at the beginning of Jehoiachin's twelfth year. **32:18** The meaning of the Hebrew is uncertain. **32:19** Hebrew *the uncircumcised;* also in 32:21, 24, 25, 26, 28, 29, 30, 32. **32:21** Hebrew *in Sheol.* **32:27a** Hebrew *to Sheol.* **32:27b** The meaning of the Hebrew is uncertain.

FAITHFUL 33:1-6

This chapter shows a new direction for Ezekiel's prophecies. Up to this point, he had pronounced judgment on Judah (chapters 1–24) and the surrounding nations (25–32). After Jerusalem fell, his messages of doom turned to messages of hope for God's people (33–48). Previously God appointed Ezekiel to be a watchman, warning the nation of coming judgment (see 3:16-21). Here God appointed him to be a watchman again, to preach a message of hope. (See 34:11-16, 22-31; 36:8-38.) There are still warnings (33:23–34:10, 17-21; 36:1-7), but these are part of the larger picture of hope.

God warns and comforts us today through the Bible and through messengers he appoints. Most of us, if we're honest, would say that we prefer his words of comfort, rather than his warnings. But both are needed. But are both *heeded* in your life? How willing are you to be a watchman—someone who warns people about spiritual issues? ■

[7]"Now, son of man, I am making you a watchman for
the people of Israel. Therefore, listen to what I say and
warn them for me. [8]If I announce that some wicked people are sure to die and you fail to tell them to change their
ways, then they will die in their sins, and I will hold you responsible for their deaths. [9]But if you warn them to repent and they don't repent, they will die in their sins, but
you will have saved yourself.

THE WATCHMAN'S MESSAGE

[10]"Son of man, give the people of Israel this message: You
are saying, 'Our sins are heavy upon us; we are wasting
away! How can we survive?' [11]As surely as I live, says the
Sovereign LORD, I take no pleasure in the death of wicked
people. I only want them to turn from their wicked ways
so they can live. Turn! Turn from your wickedness,
O people of Israel! Why should you die?
[12]"Son of man, give your people this message: The
righteous behavior of righteous people will not save
them if they turn to sin, nor will the wicked behavior of
wicked people destroy them if they repent and turn
from their sins. [13]When I tell righteous people that they
will live, but then they sin, expecting their past righteousness to save them, then none of their righteous
acts will be remembered. I will destroy them for their
sins. [14]And suppose I tell some wicked people that they
will surely die, but then they turn from their sins and do
what is just and right. [15]For instance, they might give
back a debtor's security, return what they have stolen,
and obey my life-giving laws, no longer doing what is
evil. If they do this, then they will surely live and not die.
[16]None of their past sins will be brought up again, for
they have done what is just and right, and they will
surely live.
[17]"Your people are saying, 'The Lord isn't doing what's
right,' but it is they who are not doing what's right. [18]For
again I say, when righteous people turn away from their
righteous behavior and turn to evil, they will die. [19]But if
wicked people turn from their wickedness and do what is
just and right, they will live. [20]O people of Israel, you are
saying, 'The Lord isn't doing what's right.' But I judge
each of you according to your deeds."

FACE IT 33:10-12

The exiles were discouraged by their past sins. They felt heavy guilt for living in rebellion against God for so many years. This was an important turning point. Elsewhere in Ezekiel the people had refused to admit their wrongs. But God assured them of forgiveness if they were willing to change. God *wants* everyone to turn to him. He looks at what we are and will become, not what we have been. God gives every person the opportunity to turn to him. Desperately seeking change? You know where to turn. ■

EXPLANATION OF JERUSALEM'S FALL

[21]On January 8,* during the twelfth year of our captivity, a
survivor from Jerusalem came to me and said, "The city
has fallen!" [22]The previous evening the LORD had taken
hold of me and given me back my voice. So I was able to
speak when this man arrived the next morning.
[23]Then this message came to me from the LORD: [24]"Son
of man, the scattered remnants of Judah living among the
ruined cities keep saying, 'Abraham was only one man,
yet he gained possession of the entire land. We are many;
surely the land has been given to us as a possession.' [25]So
tell these people, 'This is what the Sovereign LORD says:
You eat meat with blood in it, you worship idols,* and you
murder the innocent. Do you really think the land should
be yours? [26]Murderers! Idolaters! Adulterers! Should the
land belong to you?'
[27]"Say to them, 'This is what the Sovereign LORD says:
As surely as I live, those living in the ruins will die by the
sword. And I will send wild animals to eat those living in
the open fields. Those hiding in the forts and caves will
die of disease. [28]I will completely destroy the land and demolish her pride. Her arrogant power will come to an
end. The mountains of Israel will be so desolate that no
one will even travel through them. [29]When I have completely destroyed the land because of their detestable
sins, then they will know that I am the LORD.'
[30]"Son of man, your people talk about you in their
houses and whisper about you at the doors. They say to
each other, 'Come on, let's go hear the prophet tell us
what the LORD is saying!' [31]So my people come pretending to be sincere and sit before you. They listen to your
words, but they have no intention of doing what you say.
Their mouths are full of lustful words, and their hearts
seek only after money. [32]You are very entertaining to

33:21 Hebrew *On the fifth day of the tenth month,* of the ancient Hebrew lunar calendar. This event occurred on January 8, 585 B.C.; also see note on 1:1. 33:25 The Hebrew term (literally *round things*) probably alludes to dung.

them, like someone who sings love songs with a beautiful voice or plays fine music on an instrument. They hear what you say, but they don't act on it! 33But when all these terrible things happen to them—as they certainly will—then they will know a prophet has been among them."

IGNORED 33:30-32

Even though the exiles ignored Ezekiel's messages, he kept delivering them anyway. When people make fun of you because of your faith or fail to take your advice, don't give up. You cannot make others accept your message; you can only be faithful in delivering it. ■

34

THE SHEPHERDS OF ISRAEL

Then this message came to me from the LORD: 2"Son of man, prophesy against the shepherds, the leaders of Israel. Give them this message from the Sovereign LORD: What sorrow awaits you shepherds who feed yourselves instead of your flocks. Shouldn't shepherds feed their sheep? 3You drink the milk, wear the wool, and butcher the best animals, but you let your flocks starve. 4You have not taken care of the weak. You have not tended the sick or bound up the injured. You have not gone looking for those who have wandered away and are lost. Instead, you have ruled them with harshness and cruelty. 5So my sheep have been scattered without a shepherd, and they are easy prey for any wild animal. 6They have wandered through all the mountains and all the hills, across the face of the earth, yet no one has gone to search for them.

7"Therefore, you shepherds, hear the word of the LORD: 8As surely as I live, says the Sovereign LORD, you abandoned my flock and left them to be attacked by every wild animal. And though you were my shepherds, you didn't search for my sheep when they were lost. You took care of yourselves and left the sheep to starve. 9Therefore, you shepherds, hear the word of the LORD. 10This is what the Sovereign LORD says: I now consider these shepherds my enemies, and I will hold them responsible for what has happened to my flock. I will take away their right to feed the flock, and I will stop them from feeding themselves. I will rescue my flock from their mouths; the sheep will no longer be their prey.

THE GOOD SHEPHERD

11"For this is what the Sovereign LORD says: I myself will search and find my sheep. 12I will be like a shepherd looking for his scattered flock. I will find my sheep and rescue them from all the places where they were scattered on that dark and cloudy day. 13I will bring them back home to their own land of Israel from among the peoples and nations. I will feed them on the mountains of Israel and by the rivers and in all the places where people live. 14Yes, I will give them good pastureland on the high hills of Israel. There they will lie down in pleasant places and feed in the lush pastures of the hills. 15I myself will tend my sheep and give them a place to lie down in peace, says the Sovereign LORD. 16I will search for my lost ones who strayed away, and I will bring them safely home again. I will bandage the injured and strengthen the weak. But I will destroy those who are fat and powerful. I will feed them, yes—feed them justice!

GOOD AND BAD SHEPHERDS 34:1-16

God had hard words for the leaders of the people of Israel. He was angry because these leaders (the shepherds) didn't take care of his people (the sheep). The shepherds' actions (34:2-4) were just the opposite of God's (34:11-16; see also Ps 23).

A good spiritual leader points his or her "flock" toward God. Yet, in the New Testament, Jesus gives a warning to would-be spiritual leaders. "If you cause one of these little ones who trusts in me to fall into sin, it would be better for you to be thrown into the sea with a large millstone hung around your neck" (Mark 9:42). You don't have to be a minister to be in a position of leadership. You're a leader anytime you work or hang out with anyone younger. How will you care for your "flock"? ■

17"And as for you, my flock, this is what the Sovereign LORD says to his people: I will judge between one animal of the flock and another, separating the sheep from the goats. 18Isn't it enough for you to keep the best of the pastures for yourselves? Must you also trample down the rest? Isn't it enough for you to drink clear water for yourselves? Must you also muddy the rest with your feet? 19Why must my flock eat what you have trampled down and drink water you have fouled?

20"Therefore, this is what the Sovereign LORD says: I will surely judge between the fat sheep and the scrawny sheep. 21For you fat sheep pushed and butted and crowded my sick and hungry flock until you scattered them to distant lands. 22So I will rescue my flock, and they will no longer be abused. I will judge between one animal of the flock and another. 23And I will set over them one shepherd, my servant David. He will feed them and be a shepherd to them. 24And I, the LORD, will be their God, and my servant David will be a prince among my people. I, the LORD, have spoken!

THE LORD'S COVENANT OF PEACE

25"I will make a covenant of peace with my people and drive away the dangerous animals from the land. Then they will be able to camp safely in the wildest places and sleep in the woods without fear. 26I will bless my people and their homes around my holy hill. And in the proper season I will send the showers they need. There will be showers of blessing. 27The orchards and fields of my people will yield bumper crops, and everyone will live in safety. When I have broken their chains of slavery and rescued them from those who enslaved them, then they will know that I am the LORD. 28They will no longer be prey for other nations, and wild animals will no longer devour them. They will live in safety, and no one will frighten them.

Ezekiel

Served as a prophet to the exiles in Babylon from 593 to 571 B.C.

Climate of the times	Ezekiel and his people are taken to Babylon as captives. The Jews become foreigners in a strange land ruled by an authoritarian government.
Main message	God allowed the nation of Judah to be destroyed because of the people's sins, but there was still hope—God promised to restore the land to those who remained faithful to him.
Importance of message	God never forgets those who faithfully seek to obey him. They have a glorious future ahead.
Contemporary prophets	Daniel (605–536) Habakkuk (612–588) Jeremiah (627–586)

29"And I will make their land famous for its crops, so
my people will never again suffer from famines or the insults of foreign nations. 30In this way, they will know that
I, the LORD their God, am with them. And they will know
that they, the people of Israel, are my people, says the Sovereign LORD. 31You are my flock, the sheep of my pasture.
You are my people, and I am your God. I, the Sovereign
LORD, have spoken!"

SYMBOLS OF PRIDE 35:1-9

Ezekiel prophesied not only against the people of Edom, but also against their mountains and land. Mountains, usually symbols of strength and power, represented the pride of a nation who thought it could get away with evil. We have different symbols of pride nowadays. We take pride in our possessions or in being known as cool or popular. But neither money nor status can make a person invincible. What symbols of pride have you noticed around you? Are there any you've noticed in your own life? Anyone who takes a stand against God won't find a strong shelter in status or possessions. ■

35 A MESSAGE FOR EDOM

Again a message came to me from the LORD: 2"Son of
man, turn and face Mount Seir, and prophesy against its
people. 3Give them this message from the Sovereign
LORD:

"I am your enemy, O Mount Seir,
and I will raise my fist against you
to destroy you completely.
4 I will demolish your cities
and make you desolate.
Then you will know that I am the LORD.

5"Your eternal hatred for the people of Israel led you
to butcher them when they were helpless, when I had already punished them for all their sins. 6As surely as I
live, says the Sovereign LORD, since you show no distaste
for blood, I will give you a bloodbath of your own. Your
turn has come! 7I will make Mount Seir utterly desolate,
killing off all who try to escape and any who return. 8I
will fill your mountains with the dead. Your hills, your
valleys, and your ravines will be filled with people
slaughtered by the sword. 9I will make you desolate forever. Your cities will never be rebuilt. Then you will
know that I am the LORD.

10"For you said, 'The lands of Israel and Judah will be
ours. We will take possession of them. What do we care
that the LORD is there!' 11Therefore, as surely as I live,
says the Sovereign LORD, I will pay back your angry
deeds with my own. I will punish you for all your acts of
anger, envy, and hatred. And I will make myself known
to Israel* by what I do to you. 12Then you will know that
I, the LORD, have heard every contemptuous word you
spoke against the mountains of Israel. For you said,
'They are desolate; they have been given to us as food to
eat!' 13In saying that, you boasted proudly against me,
and I have heard it all!

14"This is what the Sovereign LORD says: The whole
world will rejoice when I make you desolate. 15You rejoiced at the desolation of Israel's territory. Now I will rejoice at yours! You will be wiped out, you people of Mount
Seir and all who live in Edom! Then you will know that I
am the LORD.

35:11 Hebrew *to them;* Greek version reads *to you.*

36 RESTORATION FOR ISRAEL

"Son of man, prophesy to Israel's mountains. Give them this message: O mountains of Israel, hear the word of the LORD! 2This is what the Sovereign LORD says: Your enemies have taunted you, saying, 'Aha! Now the ancient heights belong to us!' 3Therefore, son of man, give the mountains of Israel this message from the Sovereign LORD: Your enemies have attacked you from all directions, making you the property of many nations and the object of much mocking and slander. 4Therefore, O mountains of Israel, hear the word of the Sovereign LORD. He speaks to the hills and mountains, ravines and valleys, and to ruined wastes and long-deserted cities that have been destroyed and mocked by the surrounding nations. 5This is what the Sovereign LORD says: My jealous anger burns against these nations, especially Edom, because they have shown utter contempt for me by gleefully taking my land for themselves as plunder.

6"Therefore, prophesy to the hills and mountains, the ravines and valleys of Israel. This is what the Sovereign LORD says: I am furious that you have suffered shame before the surrounding nations. 7Therefore, this is what the Sovereign LORD says: I have taken a solemn oath that those nations will soon have their own shame to endure.

8"But the mountains of Israel will produce heavy crops of fruit for my people—for they will be coming home again soon! 9See, I care about you, and I will pay attention to you. Your ground will be plowed and your crops planted. 10I will greatly increase the population of Israel, and the ruined cities will be rebuilt and filled with people. 11I will increase not only the people, but also your animals. O mountains of Israel, I will bring people to live on you once again. I will make you even more prosperous than you were before. Then you will know that I am the LORD. 12I will cause my people to walk on you once again, and you will be their territory. You will never again rob them of their children.

13"This is what the Sovereign LORD says: The other nations taunt you, saying, 'Israel is a land that devours its own people and robs them of their children!' 14But you will never again devour your people or rob them of their children, says the Sovereign LORD. 15I will not let you hear those other nations insult you, and you will no longer be mocked by them. You will not be a land that causes its nation to fall, says the Sovereign LORD."

> I will give you a new heart, and . . . a new spirit. . . . I will take out your stony, stubborn heart and give you a tender, responsive heart.
>
> EZEKIEL 36:26

16Then this further message came to me from the LORD: 17"Son of man, when the people of Israel were living in their own land, they defiled it by the evil way they lived. To me their conduct was as unclean as a woman's menstrual cloth. 18They polluted the land with murder and the worship of idols,* so I poured out my fury on them. 19I scattered them to many lands to punish them for the evil way they had lived. 20But when they were scattered among the nations, they brought shame on my holy name. For the nations said, 'These are the people of the LORD, but he couldn't keep them safe in his own land!' 21Then I was concerned for my holy name, on which my people brought shame among the nations.

THE HONOR OF HIS NAME 36:16-24

Why did God want to protect his holy name—his reputation? To allow his people to be destroyed by their enemies would lead other nations to believe their nonexistent gods were victorious (Isa 48:11). Yet the people of Israel had the responsibility to represent God properly to the rest of the world. Believers today have that same responsibility. What would people learn about God by watching you? ■

22"Therefore, give the people of Israel this message from the Sovereign LORD: I am bringing you back, but not because you deserve it. I am doing it to protect my holy name, on which you brought shame while you were scattered among the nations. 23I will show how holy my great name is—the name on which you brought shame among the nations. And when I reveal my holiness through you before their very eyes, says the Sovereign LORD, then the nations will know that I am the LORD. 24For I will gather you up from all the nations and bring you home again to your land.

25"Then I will sprinkle clean water on you, and you will be clean. Your filth will be washed away, and you will no longer worship idols. 26And I will give you a new heart, and I will put a new spirit in you. I will take out your stony, stubborn heart and give you a tender, responsive heart.* 27And I will put my Spirit in you so that you will follow my decrees and be careful to obey my regulations.

28"And you will live in Israel, the land I gave your ancestors long ago. You will be my people, and I will be your God. 29I will cleanse you of your filthy behavior. I will give you good crops of grain, and I will send no more famines on the land. 30I will give you great harvests from your fruit trees and fields, and never again will the surrounding nations be able to scoff at your land for its famines. 31Then you will remember your past sins and despise yourselves for all the detestable things you did. 32But remember, says the Sovereign LORD, I am not doing this because you deserve it. O my people of Israel, you should be utterly ashamed of all you have done!

33"This is what the Sovereign LORD says: When I cleanse

36:18 The Hebrew term (literally *round things*) probably alludes to dung; also in 36:25. 36:26 Hebrew *a heart of flesh.*

you from your sins, I will repopulate your cities, and the ruins will be rebuilt. 34The fields that used to lie empty and desolate in plain view of everyone will again be farmed. 35And when I bring you back, people will say, 'This former wasteland is now like the Garden of Eden! The abandoned and ruined cities now have strong walls and are filled with people!' 36Then the surrounding nations that survive will know that I, the LORD, have rebuilt the ruins and replanted the wasteland. For I, the LORD, have spoken, and I will do what I say.

37"This is what the Sovereign LORD says: I am ready to hear Israel's prayers and to increase their numbers like a flock. 38They will be as numerous as the sacred flocks that fill Jerusalem's streets at the time of her festivals. The ruined cities will be crowded with people once more, and everyone will know that I am the LORD."

37

A VALLEY OF DRY BONES

The LORD took hold of me, and I was carried away by the Spirit of the LORD to a valley filled with bones. 2He led me all around among the bones that covered the valley floor. They were scattered everywhere across the ground and were completely dried out. 3Then he asked me, "Son of man, can these bones become living people again?"

"O Sovereign LORD," I replied, "you alone know the answer to that."

4Then he said to me, "Speak a prophetic message to these bones and say, 'Dry bones, listen to the word of the LORD! 5This is what the Sovereign LORD says: Look! I am going to put breath into you and make you live again! 6I will put flesh and muscles on you and cover you with skin. I will put breath into you, and you will come to life. Then you will know that I am the LORD.'"

7So I spoke this message, just as he told me. Suddenly as I spoke, there was a rattling noise all across the valley. The bones of each body came together and attached themselves as complete skeletons. 8Then as I watched, muscles and flesh formed over the bones. Then skin formed to cover their bodies, but they still had no breath in them.

9Then he said to me, "Speak a prophetic message to the winds, son of man. Speak a prophetic message and say, 'This is what the Sovereign LORD says: Come, O breath, from the four winds! Breathe into these dead bodies so they may live again.'"

10So I spoke the message as he commanded me, and breath came into their bodies. They all came to life and stood up on their feet—a great army.

11Then he said to me, "Son of man, these bones represent the people of Israel. They are saying, 'We have become old, dry bones—all hope is gone. Our nation is finished.' 12Therefore, prophesy to them and say, 'This is what the Sovereign LORD says: O my people, I will open your graves of exile and cause you to rise again. Then I will bring you back to the land of Israel. 13When this happens, O my people, you will know that I am the LORD. 14I will put my Spirit in you, and you will live again and return home to your own land. Then you will know that I, the LORD, have spoken, and I have done what I said. Yes, the LORD has spoken!'"

DRIED UP 37:1-14

The dry bones represented the people's spiritually dead condition. At some point or other, every Christian will probably feel spiritually dry. Sometimes this dryness is due to doubt. At other times, dryness is a result of wrong actions that haven't been confessed. But just as God promised to restore his nation, he can restore anyone, no matter how dry or dead that person may feel. Rather than give up, pray for God to restore you or someone else you know. ■

REUNION OF ISRAEL AND JUDAH

15Again a message came to me from the LORD: 16"Son of man, take a piece of wood and carve on it these words: 'This represents Judah and its allied tribes.' Then take another piece and carve these words on it: 'This represents Ephraim and the northern tribes of Israel.'* 17Now hold them together in your hand as if they were one piece of wood. 18When your people ask you what your actions mean, 19say to them, 'This is what the Sovereign LORD says: I will take Ephraim and the northern tribes and join them to Judah. I will make them one piece of wood in my hand.'

20"Then hold out the pieces of wood you have inscribed, so the people can see them. 21And give them this message from the Sovereign LORD: I will gather the people of Israel from among the nations. I will bring them home to their own land from the places where they have been scattered. 22I will unify them into one nation on the mountains of Israel. One king will rule them all; no longer will they be divided into two nations or into two kingdoms. 23They will never again pollute themselves with their idols* and vile images and rebellion, for I will save them from their sinful backsliding. I will cleanse them. Then they will truly be my people, and I will be their God.

24"My servant David will be their king, and they will have only one shepherd. They will obey my regulations and be careful to keep my decrees. 25They will live in the land I gave my servant Jacob, the land where their ancestors lived. They and their children and their grandchildren after them will live there forever, generation after generation. And my servant David will be their prince forever. 26And I will make a covenant of peace with them, an everlasting covenant. I will give them their land and increase their numbers,* and I will put my Temple among them forever. 27I will make my home among them. I will be their God, and they will be my people. 28And when my Temple is among them forever, the nations will know that I am the LORD, who makes Israel holy."

37:16 Hebrew *This is Ephraim's wood, representing Joseph and all the house of Israel.* 37:23 The Hebrew term (literally *round things*) probably alludes to dung. 37:26 Hebrew reads *I will give them and increase their numbers;* Greek version omits the entire phrase.

38 A MESSAGE FOR GOG

This is another message that came to me from the LORD: 2"Son of man, turn and face Gog of the land of Magog, the prince who rules over the nations of Meshech and Tubal, and prophesy against him. 3Give him this message from the Sovereign LORD: Gog, I am your enemy! 4I will turn you around and put hooks in your jaws to lead you out with your whole army—your horses and charioteers in full armor and a great horde armed with shields and swords. 5Persia, Ethiopia, and Libya* will join you, too, with all their weapons. 6Gomer and all its armies will also join you, along with the armies of Beth-togarmah from the distant north, and many others.

7"Get ready; be prepared! Keep all the armies around you mobilized, and take command of them. 8A long time from now you will be called into action. In the distant future you will swoop down on the land of Israel, which will be enjoying peace after recovering from war and after its people have returned from many lands to the mountains of Israel. 9You and all your allies—a vast and awesome army—will roll down on them like a storm and cover the land like a cloud.

10"This is what the Sovereign LORD says: At that time evil thoughts will come to your mind, and you will devise a wicked scheme. 11You will say, 'Israel is an unprotected land filled with unwalled villages! I will march against her and destroy these people who live in such confidence! 12I will go to those formerly desolate cities that are now filled with people who have returned from exile in many nations. I will capture vast amounts of plunder, for the people are rich with livestock and other possessions now. They think the whole world revolves around them!' 13But Sheba and Dedan and the merchants of Tarshish will ask, 'Do you really think the armies you have gathered can rob them of silver and gold? Do you think you can drive away their livestock and seize their goods and carry off plunder?'

14"Therefore, son of man, prophesy against Gog. Give him this message from the Sovereign LORD: When my people are living in peace in their land, then you will rouse yourself.* 15You will come from your homeland in the distant north with your vast cavalry and your mighty army, 16and you will attack my people Israel, covering their land like a cloud. At that time in the distant future, I will bring you against my land as everyone watches, and my holiness will be displayed by what happens to you, Gog. Then all the nations will know that I am the LORD.

17"This is what the Sovereign LORD asks: Are you the one I was talking about long ago, when I announced through Israel's prophets that in the future I would bring you against my people? 18But this is what the Sovereign LORD says: When Gog invades the land of Israel, my fury will boil over! 19In my jealousy and blazing anger, I promise a mighty shaking in the land of Israel on that day. 20All living things—the fish in the sea, the birds of the sky, the animals of the field, the small animals that scurry along the ground, and all the people on earth—will quake in terror at my presence. Mountains will be thrown down; cliffs will crumble; walls will fall to the earth. 21I will summon the sword against you on all the hills of Israel, says the Sovereign LORD. Your men will turn their swords against each other. 22I will punish you and your armies with disease and bloodshed; I will send torrential rain, hailstones, fire, and burning sulfur! 23In this way, I will show my greatness and holiness, and I will make myself known to all the nations of the world. Then they will know that I am the LORD.

A SURE WIN 38:18; 39:1-16

In this passage, two themes are intertwined: God's total victory over his enemies and the need to purify the land to make it holy. After the final battle, teams will give proper burial to the bodies of the dead enemies so that the land may be cleansed. The message for us is an exciting one: With God on our side, we are assured of an ultimate victory over any foe (see also Zeph 3:14-17; Rom 8:35-37). ■

39 THE SLAUGHTER OF GOG'S HORDES

"Son of man, prophesy against Gog. Give him this message from the Sovereign LORD: I am your enemy, O Gog, ruler of the nations of Meshech and Tubal. 2I will turn you around and drive you toward the mountains of Israel, bringing you from the distant north. 3I will knock the bow from your left hand and the arrows from your right hand, and I will leave you helpless. 4You and your army and your allies will all die on the mountains. I will feed you to the vultures and wild animals. 5You will fall in the open fields, for I have spoken, says the Sovereign LORD. 6And I will rain down fire on Magog and on all your allies who live safely on the coasts. Then they will know that I am the LORD.

7"In this way, I will make known my holy name among my people of Israel. I will not let anyone bring shame on it. And the nations, too, will know that I am the LORD, the Holy One of Israel. 8That day of judgment will come, says the Sovereign LORD. Everything will happen just as I have declared it.

9"Then the people in the towns of Israel will go out and pick up your small and large shields, bows and arrows, javelins and spears, and they will use them for fuel. There will be enough to last them seven years! 10They won't need to cut wood from the fields or forests, for these weapons will give them all the fuel they need. They will plunder those who planned to plunder them, and they will rob those who planned to rob them, says the Sovereign LORD.

11"And I will make a vast graveyard for Gog and his hordes in the Valley of the Travelers, east of the Dead Sea.* It will block the way of those who travel there, and they will change the name of the place to the Valley of Gog's Hordes. 12It will take seven months for the people

38:5 Hebrew *Paras, Cush, and Put.* 38:14 As in Greek version; Hebrew reads *then you will know.* 39:11 Hebrew *the sea.*

Old and New Covenants

OLD COVENANT	NEW COVENANT
Placed upon stone	*Placed upon people's hearts*
Based on the law	*Based on desire to love and serve God*
Must be taught	*Known by all*
Legal relationship with God	*Personal relationship with God*

of Israel to bury the bodies and cleanse the land. 13Every-
one in Israel will help, for it will be a glorious victory for
Israel when I demonstrate my glory on that day, says the
Sovereign LORD.
14"After seven months, teams of men will be appointed
to search the land for skeletons to bury, so the land will
be made clean again. 15Whenever bones are found, a
marker will be set up so the burial crews will take them to
be buried in the Valley of Gog's Hordes. 16(There will be a
town there named Hamonah, which means 'horde.') And
so the land will finally be cleansed.
17"And now, son of man, this is what the Sovereign
LORD says: Call all the birds and wild animals. Say to them:
Gather together for my great sacrificial feast. Come from
far and near to the mountains of Israel, and there eat
flesh and drink blood! 18Eat the flesh of mighty men and
drink the blood of princes as though they were rams,
lambs, goats, and bulls—all fattened animals from Bashan! 19Gorge yourselves with flesh until you are glutted;
drink blood until you are drunk. This is the sacrificial
feast I have prepared for you. 20Feast at my banquet table—feast on horses and charioteers, on mighty men and
all kinds of valiant warriors, says the Sovereign LORD.
21"In this way, I will demonstrate my glory to the nations. Everyone will see the punishment I have inflicted
on them and the power of my fist when I strike. 22And
from that time on the people of Israel will know that I am
the LORD their God. 23The nations will then know why Israel was sent away to exile—it was punishment for sin, for
they were unfaithful to their God. Therefore, I turned
away from them and let their enemies destroy them. 24I
turned my face away and punished them because of their
defilement and their sins.

RESTORATION FOR GOD'S PEOPLE

25"So now, this is what the Sovereign LORD says: I will end
the captivity of my people*; I will have mercy on all Israel,
for I jealously guard my holy reputation! 26They will accept responsibility for their past shame and unfaithfulness after they come home to live in peace in their own
land, with no one to bother them. 27When I bring them
home from the lands of their enemies, I will display my
holiness among them for all the nations to see. 28Then my
people will know that I am the LORD their God, because I
sent them away to exile and brought them home again. I
will leave none of my people behind. 29And I will never
again turn my face from them, for I will pour out my
Spirit upon the people of Israel. I, the Sovereign LORD,
have spoken!"

40

THE NEW TEMPLE AREA

On April 28,* during the twenty-fifth year of our captivity—fourteen years after the fall of Jerusalem—the LORD
took hold of me. 2In a vision from God he took me to the
land of Israel and set me down on a very high mountain.
From there I could see toward the south what appeared
to be a city. 3As he brought me nearer, I saw a man whose
face shone like bronze standing beside a gateway entrance. He was holding in his hand a linen measuring
cord and a measuring rod.
4He said to me, "Son of man, watch and listen. Pay close
attention to everything I show you. You have been
brought here so I can show you many things. Then you
will return to the people of Israel and tell them everything you have seen."

THE EAST GATEWAY

5I could see a wall completely surrounding the Temple
area. The man took a measuring rod that was 10½ feet*
long and measured the wall, and the wall was 10½ feet*
thick and 10½ feet high.
6Then he went over to the eastern gateway. He climbed
the steps and measured the threshold of the gateway; it
was 10½ feet front to back.* 7There were guard alcoves
on each side built into the gateway passage. Each of these
alcoves was 10½ feet square, with a distance between
them of 8¾ feet* along the passage wall. The gateway's

39:25 Hebrew *of Jacob.* **40:1** Hebrew *At the beginning of the year, on the tenth day of the month,* of the ancient Hebrew lunar calendar. This event occurred on April 28, 573 B.C.; also see note on 1:1. **40:5a** Hebrew *6 long cubits* [3.2 meters], *each being a cubit* [18 inches or 45 centimeters] *and a handbreadth* [3 inches or 8 centimeters] *in length.* **40:5b** Hebrew *1 rod* [3.2 meters]; also in 40:5c, 7. **40:6** As in Greek version, which reads *1 rod* [3.2 meters] *deep;* Hebrew reads *1 rod deep, and 1 threshold, 1 rod deep.* **40:7** Hebrew *5 cubits* [2.7 meters]; also in 40:48.

inner threshold, which led to the entry room at the inner end of the gateway passage, was 10½ feet front to back. [8]He also measured the entry room of the gateway.* [9]It was 14 feet* across, with supporting columns 3½ feet* thick. This entry room was at the inner end of the gateway structure, facing toward the Temple.

[10]There were three guard alcoves on each side of the gateway passage. Each had the same measurements, and the dividing walls separating them were also identical. [11]The man measured the gateway entrance, which was 17½ feet* wide at the opening and 22¾ feet* wide in the gateway passage. [12]In front of each of the guard alcoves was a 21-inch* curb. The alcoves themselves were 10½ feet* on each side.

[13]Then he measured the entire width of the gateway, measuring the distance between the back walls of facing guard alcoves; this distance was 43¾ feet.* [14]He measured the dividing walls all along the inside of the gateway up to the entry room of the gateway; this distance was 105 feet.* [15]The full length of the gateway passage was 87½ feet* from one end to the other. [16]There were recessed windows that narrowed inward through the walls of the guard alcoves and their dividing walls. There were also windows in the entry room. The surfaces of the dividing walls were decorated with carved palm trees.

THE OUTER COURTYARD

[17]Then the man brought me through the gateway into the outer courtyard of the Temple. A stone pavement ran along the walls of the courtyard, and thirty rooms were built against the walls, opening onto the pavement. [18]This pavement flanked the gates and extended out from the walls into the courtyard the same distance as the gateway entrance. This was the lower pavement. [19]Then the man measured across the Temple's outer courtyard between the outer and inner gateways; the distance was 175 feet.*

THE NORTH GATEWAY

[20]The man measured the gateway on the north just like the one on the east. [21]Here, too, there were three guard alcoves on each side, with dividing walls and an entry room. All the measurements matched those of the east gateway. The gateway passage was 87½ feet long and 43¾ feet wide between the back walls of facing guard alcoves. [22]The windows, the entry room, and the palm tree decorations were identical to those in the east gateway. There were seven steps leading up to the gateway entrance, and the entry room was at the inner end of the gateway passage. [23]Here on the north side, just as on the east, there was another gateway leading to the Temple's inner courtyard directly opposite this outer gateway. The distance between the two gateways was 175 feet.

THE SOUTH GATEWAY

[24]Then the man took me around to the south gateway and measured its various parts, and they were exactly the same as in the others. [25]It had windows along the walls as the others did, and there was an entry room where the gateway passage opened into the outer courtyard. And like the others, the gateway passage was 87½ feet long and 43¾ feet wide between the back walls of facing guard alcoves. [26]This gateway also had a stairway of seven steps leading up to it, and an entry room at the inner end, and palm tree decorations along the dividing walls. [27]And here again, directly opposite the outer gateway, was another gateway that led into the inner courtyard. The distance between the two gateways was 175 feet.

RESTORED DREAMS 40:1–42:20

Ezekiel saw a vision of a restored Temple. After hearing about the destruction of the Temple, this vision probably comforted the grieving people of Israel. If you've ever suffered the loss of a dream, you can probably understand their need for hope. But sometimes God has something even bigger in mind for his people. Ezekiel saw a Temple more beautiful than the one that had been destroyed. Are you hoping that God will restore a dream you once had? Maybe he has something bigger in mind for you. ■

GATEWAYS TO THE INNER COURTYARD

[28]Then the man took me to the south gateway leading into the inner courtyard. He measured it, and it had the same measurements as the other gateways. [29]Its guard alcoves, dividing walls, and entry room were the same size as those in the others. It also had windows along its walls and in the entry room. And like the others, the gateway passage was 87½ feet long and 43¾ feet wide. [30](The entry rooms of the gateways leading into the inner courtyard were 14 feet* across and 43¾ feet wide.) [31]The entry room to the south gateway faced into the outer courtyard. It had palm tree decorations on its columns, and there were eight steps leading to its entrance.

[32]Then he took me to the east gateway leading to the inner courtyard. He measured it, and it had the same measurements as the other gateways. [33]Its guard alcoves, dividing walls, and entry room were the same size as those of the others, and there were windows along the walls and in the entry room. The gateway passage measured 87½ feet long and 43¾ feet wide. [34]Its entry room faced into the outer courtyard. It had palm tree decorations on its columns, and there were eight steps leading to its entrance.

[35]Then he took me around to the north gateway leading

40:8 Many Hebrew manuscripts add *which faced inward toward the Temple; it was 1 rod* [10.5 feet or 3.2 meters] *deep. [9]Then he measured the entry room of the gateway.* **40:9a** Hebrew *8 cubits* [4.2 meters]. **40:9b** Hebrew *2 cubits* [1.1 meters]. **40:11a** Hebrew *10 cubits* [5.3 meters]. **40:11b** Hebrew *13 cubits* [6.9 meters]. **40:12a** Hebrew *1 cubit* [53 centimeters]. **40:12b** Hebrew *6 cubits* [3.2 meters]. **40:13** Hebrew *25 cubits* [13.3 meters]; also in 40:21, 25, 29, 30, 33, 36. **40:14** Hebrew *60 cubits* [31.8 meters]. The meaning of the Hebrew in this verse is uncertain. **40:15** Hebrew *50 cubits* [26.5 meters]; also in 40:21, 25, 29, 33, 36. **40:19** Hebrew *100 cubits* [53 meters]; also in 40:23, 27, 47. **40:30** As in 40:9, which reads *8 cubits* [14 feet or 4.2 meters]; here the Hebrew reads *5 cubits* [8¾ feet or 2.7 meters]. Some Hebrew manuscripts and the Greek version omit this entire verse.

to the inner courtyard. He measured it, and it had the same measurements as the other gateways. 36The guard alcoves, dividing walls, and entry room of this gateway had the same measurements as in the others and the same window arrangements. The gateway passage measured 87½ feet long and 43¾ feet wide. 37Its entry room faced into the outer courtyard, and it had palm tree decorations on the columns. There were eight steps leading to its entrance.

ROOMS FOR PREPARING SACRIFICES

38A door led from the entry room of one of the inner gateways into a side room, where the meat for sacrifices was washed. 39On each side of this entry room were two tables, where the sacrificial animals were slaughtered for the burnt offerings, sin offerings, and guilt offerings. 40Outside the entry room, on each side of the stairs going up to the north entrance, were two more tables. 41So there were eight tables in all—four inside and four outside—where the sacrifices were cut up and prepared. 42There were also four tables of finished stone for preparation of the burnt offerings, each 31½ inches square and 21 inches high.* On these tables were placed the butchering knives and other implements for slaughtering the sacrificial animals. 43There were hooks, each 3 inches* long, fastened to the foyer walls. The sacrificial meat was laid on the tables.

AN ACCEPTABLE SACRIFICE 40:38-43

The washing of the sacrifices was done according to the standards of preparation established in Leviticus 1:6-9. This washing was part of the process of presenting an acceptable sacrifice to God. An "acceptable sacrifice" was one that honored God. What is there in your life that you would like to present as a sacrifice to God? ■

ROOMS FOR THE PRIESTS

44Inside the inner courtyard were two rooms,* one beside the north gateway, facing south, and the other beside the south* gateway, facing north. 45And the man said to me, "The room beside the north inner gate is for the priests who supervise the Temple maintenance. 46The room beside the south inner gate is for the priests in charge of the altar—the descendants of Zadok—for they alone of all the Levites may approach the LORD to minister to him."

THE INNER COURTYARD AND TEMPLE

47Then the man measured the inner courtyard, and it was a square, 175 feet wide and 175 feet across. The altar stood in the courtyard in front of the Temple. 48Then he brought me to the entry room of the Temple. He measured the walls on either side of the opening to the entry room, and they were 8¾ feet thick. The entrance itself was 24½ feet* wide, and the walls on each side of the entrance were an additional 5¼ feet* long. 49The entry room was 35 feet* wide and 21 feet* deep. There were ten steps leading up to it, with a column on each side.

41

After that, the man brought me into the sanctuary of the Temple. He measured the walls on either side of its doorway, and they were 10½ feet* thick. 2The doorway was 17½ feet* wide, and the walls on each side of it were 8¾ feet* long. The sanctuary itself was 70 feet long and 35 feet wide.*

3Then he went beyond the sanctuary into the inner room. He measured the walls on either side of its entrance, and they were 3½ feet* thick. The entrance was 10½ feet wide, and the walls on each side of the entrance were 12¼ feet* long. 4The inner room of the sanctuary was 35 feet* long and 35 feet wide. "This," he told me, "is the Most Holy Place."

5Then he measured the wall of the Temple, and it was 10½ feet thick. There was a row of rooms along the outside wall; each room was 7 feet* wide. 6These side rooms were built in three levels, one above the other, with thirty rooms on each level. The supports for these side rooms rested on exterior ledges on the Temple wall; they did not extend into the wall. 7Each level was wider than the one below it, corresponding to the narrowing of the Temple wall as it rose higher. A stairway led up from the bottom level through the middle level to the top level.

8I saw that the Temple was built on a terrace, which provided a foundation for the side rooms. This terrace was 10½ feet* high. 9The outer wall of the Temple's side rooms was 8¾ feet thick. This left an open area between these side rooms 10and the row of rooms along the outer wall of the inner courtyard. This open area was 35 feet wide, and it went all the way around the Temple. 11Two doors opened from the side rooms into the terrace yard, which was 8¾ feet wide. One door faced north and the other south.

12A large building stood on the west, facing the Temple courtyard. It was 122½ feet wide and 157½ feet long, and its walls were 8¾ feet* thick. 13Then the man measured the Temple, and it was 175 feet* long. The courtyard around the building, including its walls, was an additional 175 feet in length. 14The inner courtyard to the east of the Temple was also 175 feet wide. 15The building to the west, including its two walls, was also 175 feet wide.

40:42 Hebrew *1½ cubits* [80 centimeters] *long and 1½ cubits wide and 1 cubit* [53 centimeters] *high.* **40:43** Hebrew *a handbreadth* [8 centimeters]. **40:44a** As in Greek version; Hebrew reads *rooms for singers.* **40:44b** As in Greek version; Hebrew reads *east.* **40:48a** Hebrew *14 cubits* [7.4 meters]. **40:48b** Hebrew *3 cubits* [1.6 meters]. **40:49a** Hebrew *20 cubits* [10.6 meters]. **40:49b** As in Greek version, which reads *12 cubits* [21 feet or 6.4 meters]; Hebrew reads *11 cubits* [19¼ feet or 5.8 meters]. **41:1** Hebrew *6 cubits* [3.2 meters]; also in 41:3, 5. **41:2a** Hebrew *10 cubits* [5.3 meters]. **41:2b** Hebrew *5 cubits* [2.7 meters]; also in 41:9, 11. **41:2c** Hebrew *40 cubits* [21.2 meters] *long and 20 cubits* [10.6 meters] *wide.* **41:3a** Hebrew *2 cubits* [1.1 meters]. **41:3b** Hebrew *7 cubits* [3.7 meters]. **41:4** Hebrew *20 cubits* [10.6 meters]; also in 41:4b, 10. **41:5** Hebrew *4 cubits* [2.1 meters]. **41:8** Hebrew *1 rod, 6 cubits* [3.2 meters]. **41:12** Hebrew *70 cubits* [37.1 meters] *wide and 90 cubits* [47.7 meters] *long, and its walls were 5 cubits* [2.7 meters] *thick.* **41:13** Hebrew *100 cubits* [53 meters]; also in 41:13b, 14, 15.

The sanctuary, the inner room, and the entry room
of the Temple 16were all paneled with wood, as were
the frames of the recessed windows. The inner walls of
the Temple were paneled with wood above and below the
windows. 17The space above the door leading into the inner room, and its walls inside and out, were also paneled.
18All the walls were decorated with carvings of cherubim,
each with two faces, and there was a carving of a palm
tree between each of the cherubim. 19One face—that of a
man—looked toward the palm tree on one side. The
other face—that of a young lion—looked toward the palm
tree on the other side. The figures were carved all along
the inside of the Temple, 20from the floor to the top of the
walls, including the outer wall of the sanctuary.

21There were square columns at the entrance to the
sanctuary, and the ones at the entrance of the Most Holy
Place were similar. 22There was an altar made of wood,
5¼ feet high and 3½ feet across.* Its corners, base, and
sides were all made of wood. "This," the man told me, "is
the table that stands in the LORD's presence."

23Both the sanctuary and the Most Holy Place had double doorways, 24each with two swinging doors. 25The
doors leading into the sanctuary were decorated with
carved cherubim and palm trees, just as on the walls. And
there was a wooden roof at the front of the entry room to
the Temple. 26On both sides of the entry room were recessed windows decorated with carved palm trees. The
side rooms along the outside wall also had roofs.

THE MOST HOLY PLACE 41:1-26

The Most Holy Place was the innermost room in the Temple (Exod 26:33-34). This was where the Ark of the Covenant was kept and where God's glory was said to dwell. Guess where the Most Holy Place is today. You—if you've acknowledged that Jesus is your Savior. How do your actions reveal God's glory (the Holy Spirit) within you? ■

42

ROOMS FOR THE PRIESTS

Then the man led me out of the Temple courtyard by way
of the north gateway. We entered the outer courtyard
and came to a group of rooms against the north wall of
the inner courtyard. 2This structure, whose entrance
opened toward the north, was 175 feet long and 87½
feet wide.* 3One block of rooms overlooked the 35-foot*
width of the inner courtyard. Another block of rooms
looked out onto the pavement of the outer courtyard.
The two blocks were built three levels high and stood
across from each other. 4Between the two blocks of
rooms ran a walkway 17½ feet* wide. It extended the entire 175 feet* of the complex, and all the doors faced
north. 5Each of the two upper levels of rooms was nar-
rower than the one beneath it because the upper levels
had to allow space for walkways in front of them. 6Since
there were three levels and they did not have supporting
columns as in the courtyards, each of the upper levels
was set back from the level beneath it. 7There was an
outer wall that separated the rooms from the outer courtyard; it was 87½ feet* long. 8This wall added length to the
outer block of rooms, which extended for only 87½ feet,
while the inner block—the rooms toward the Temple—
extended for 175 feet. 9There was an eastern entrance
from the outer courtyard to these rooms.

10On the south* side of the Temple there were two
blocks of rooms just south of the inner courtyard between the Temple and the outer courtyard. These rooms
were arranged just like the rooms on the north. 11There
was a walkway between the two blocks of rooms just like
the complex on the north side of the Temple. This complex of rooms was the same length and width as the other
one, and it had the same entrances and doors. The dimensions of each were identical. 12So there was an entrance in the wall facing the doors of the inner block of
rooms, and another on the east at the end of the interior
walkway.

13Then the man told me, "These rooms that overlook
the Temple from the north and south are holy. Here the
priests who offer sacrifices to the LORD will eat the most
holy offerings. And because these rooms are holy, they
will be used to store the sacred offerings—the grain offerings, sin offerings, and guilt offerings. 14When the
priests leave the sanctuary, they must not go directly to
the outer courtyard. They must first take off the clothes
they wore while ministering, because these clothes are
holy. They must put on other clothes before entering the
parts of the building complex open to the public."

15When the man had finished measuring the inside of
the Temple area, he led me out through the east gateway
to measure the entire perimeter. 16He measured the east
side with his measuring rod, and it was 875 feet long.*
17Then he measured the north side, and it was also
875 feet. 18The south side was also 875 feet, 19and the
west side was also 875 feet. 20So the area was 875 feet on
each side with a wall all around it to separate what was
holy from what was common.

43

THE LORD'S GLORY RETURNS

After this, the man brought me back around to the east
gateway. 2Suddenly, the glory of the God of Israel appeared from the east. The sound of his coming was like
the roar of rushing waters, and the whole landscape
shone with his glory. 3This vision was just like the others I
had seen, first by the Kebar River and then when he came
to destroy Jerusalem. I fell face down on the ground.
4And the glory of the LORD came into the Temple through
the east gateway.

5Then the Spirit took me up and brought me into the
inner courtyard, and the glory of the LORD filled the

41:22 Hebrew *3 cubits* [1.6 meters] *high and 2 cubits* [1.1 meters] *across.* 42:2 Hebrew *100 cubits* [53 meters] *long and 50 cubits* [26.5 meters] *wide.* 42:3 Hebrew *20 cubits* [10.6 meters]. 42:4a Hebrew *10 cubits* [5.3 meters]. 42:4b Hebrew *100 cubits* [53 meters]; also in 42:8. 42:7 Hebrew *50 cubits* [26.5 meters]; also in 42:8. 42:10 As in Greek version; Hebrew reads *east.* 42:16 As in 45:2 and in Greek version at 42:17, which reads *500 cubits* [265 meters]; Hebrew reads *500 rods* [5,250 feet or 1,590 meters]; similarly in 42:17, 18, 19, 20.

Temple. 6And I heard someone speaking to me from within the Temple, while the man who had been measuring stood beside me. 7The LORD said to me, "Son of man, this is the place of my throne and the place where I will rest my feet. I will live here forever among the people of Israel. They and their kings will not defile my holy name any longer by their adulterous worship of other gods or by honoring the relics of their kings who have died. 8They put their idol altars right next to mine with only a wall between them and me. They defiled my holy name by such detestable sin, so I consumed them in my anger. 9Now let them stop worshiping other gods and honoring the relics of their kings, and I will live among them forever.

RETURNING GLORY 43:1-9

Ezekiel saw a vision of God's glory returning to the Temple—the ultimate sign of blessing for a nation. When we've blown it spiritually, we can't imagine God wanting to remain with us. Ever feel this way? Maybe you've wondered whether God plans to leave you forever because of something you did or said. But check out verse 7 again: "This is the place of my throne and the place where I will rest my feet. I will live here forever." If he won't give up on you, should you give up on him? ■

10"Son of man, describe to the people of Israel the Temple I have shown you, so they will be ashamed of all their sins. Let them study its plan, 11and they will be ashamed* of what they have done. Describe to them all the specifications of the Temple—including its entrances and exits—and everything else about it. Tell them about its decrees and laws. Write down all these specifications and decrees as they watch so they will be sure to remember and follow them. 12And this is the basic law of the Temple: absolute holiness! The entire top of the mountain where the Temple is built is holy. Yes, this is the basic law of the Temple.

THE ALTAR

13"These are the measurements of the altar*: There is a gutter all around the altar 21 inches deep and 21 inches wide,* with a curb 9 inches* wide around its edge. And this is the height* of the altar: 14From the gutter the altar rises 3½ feet* to a lower ledge that surrounds the altar and is 21 inches* wide. From the lower ledge the altar rises 7 feet* to the upper ledge that is also 21 inches wide. 15The top of the altar, the hearth, rises another 7 feet higher, with a horn rising up from each of the four corners. 16The top of the altar is square, measuring 21 feet by 21 feet.* 17The upper ledge also forms a square, measuring 24½ feet by 24½ feet,* with a 21-inch gutter and a 10½-inch curb* all around the edge. There are steps going up the east side of the altar."

18Then he said to me, "Son of man, this is what the Sovereign LORD says: These will be the regulations for the burning of offerings and the sprinkling of blood when the altar is built. 19At that time, the Levitical priests of the family of Zadok, who minister before me, are to be given a young bull for a sin offering, says the Sovereign LORD. 20You will take some of its blood and smear it on the four horns of the altar, the four corners of the upper ledge, and the curb that runs around that ledge. This will cleanse and make atonement for the altar. 21Then take the young bull for the sin offering and burn it at the appointed place outside the Temple area.

22"On the second day, sacrifice as a sin offering a young male goat that has no physical defects. Then cleanse and make atonement for the altar again, just as you did with the young bull. 23When you have finished the cleansing ceremony, offer another young bull that has no defects and a perfect ram from the flock. 24You are to present them to the LORD, and the priests are to sprinkle salt on them and offer them as a burnt offering to the LORD.

25"Every day for seven days a male goat, a young bull, and a ram from the flock will be sacrificed as a sin offering. None of these animals may have physical defects of any kind. 26Do this each day for seven days to cleanse and make atonement for the altar, thus setting it apart for holy use. 27On the eighth day, and on each day afterward, the priests will sacrifice on the altar the burnt offerings and peace offerings of the people. Then I will accept you. I, the Sovereign LORD, have spoken!"

44 THE PRINCE, LEVITES, AND PRIESTS

Then the man brought me back to the east gateway in the outer wall of the Temple area, but it was closed. 2And the LORD said to me, "This gate must remain closed; it will never again be opened. No one will ever open it and pass through, for the LORD, the God of Israel, has entered here. Therefore, it must always remain shut. 3Only the prince himself may sit inside this gateway to feast in the LORD's presence. But he may come and go only through the entry room of the gateway."

4Then the man brought me through the north gateway to the front of the Temple. I looked and saw that the glory of the LORD filled the Temple of the LORD, and I fell face down on the ground.

5And the LORD said to me, "Son of man, take careful notice. Use your eyes and ears, and listen to everything I tell you about the regulations concerning the LORD's Temple. Take careful note of the procedures for using the Temple's entrances and exits. 6And give these rebels, the people of Israel, this message from the Sovereign

43:11 As in Greek version; Hebrew reads *if they are ashamed.* 43:13a Hebrew *measurements of the altar in long cubits, each being a cubit* [18 inches or 45 centimeters] *and a handbreadth* [3 inches or 8 centimeters] *in length.* 43:13b Hebrew *a cubit* [53 centimeters] *deep and a cubit wide.* 43:13c Hebrew *1 span* [23 centimeters]. 43:13d As in Greek version; Hebrew reads *base.* 43:14a Hebrew *2 cubits* [1.1 meters]. 43:14b Hebrew *1 cubit* [53 centimeters]; also in 43:14d. 43:14c Hebrew *4 cubits* [2.1 meters]; also in 43:15. 43:16 Hebrew *12 cubits* [6.4 meters] *long and 12 cubits wide.* 43:17a Hebrew *14 cubits* [7.4 meters] *long and 14 cubits wide.* 43:17b Hebrew *a gutter of 1 cubit* [53 centimeters] *and a curb of ½ a cubit* [27 centimeters].

LORD: O people of Israel, enough of your detestable sins! [7]You have brought uncircumcised foreigners into my sanctuary—people who have no heart for God. In this way, you defiled my Temple even as you offered me my food, the fat and blood of sacrifices. In addition to all your other detestable sins, you have broken my covenant. [8]Instead of safeguarding my sacred rituals, you have hired foreigners to take charge of my sanctuary.

[9]"So this is what the Sovereign LORD says: No foreigners, including those who live among the people of Israel, will enter my sanctuary if they have not been circumcised and have not surrendered themselves to the LORD. [10]And the men of the tribe of Levi who abandoned me when Israel strayed away from me to worship idols* must bear the consequences of their unfaithfulness. [11]They may still be Temple guards and gatekeepers, and they may slaughter the animals brought for burnt offerings and be present to help the people. [12]But they encouraged my people to worship idols, causing Israel to fall into deep sin. So I have taken a solemn oath that they must bear the consequences for their sins, says the Sovereign LORD. [13]They may not approach me to minister as priests. They may not touch any of my holy things or the holy offerings, for they must bear the shame of all the detestable sins they have committed. [14]They are to serve as the Temple caretakers, taking charge of the maintenance work and performing general duties.

[15]"However, the Levitical priests of the family of Zadok continued to minister faithfully in the Temple when Israel abandoned me for idols. These men will serve as my ministers. They will stand in my presence and offer the fat and blood of the sacrifices, says the Sovereign LORD. [16]They alone will enter my sanctuary and approach my table to serve me. They will fulfill all my requirements.

[17]"When they enter the gateway to the inner courtyard, they must wear only linen clothing. They must wear no wool while on duty in the inner courtyard or in the Temple itself. [18]They must wear linen turbans and linen undergarments. They must not wear anything that would cause them to perspire. [19]When they return to the outer courtyard where the people are, they must take off the clothes they wear while ministering to me. They must leave them in the sacred rooms and put on other clothes so they do not endanger anyone by transmitting holiness to them through this clothing.

[20]"They must neither shave their heads nor let their hair grow too long. Instead, they must trim it regularly. [21]The priests must not drink wine before entering the inner courtyard. [22]They may choose their wives only from among the virgins of Israel or the widows of the priests. They may not marry other widows or divorced women. [23]They will teach my people the difference between what is holy and what is common, what is ceremonially clean and unclean.

[24]"They will serve as judges to resolve any disagreements among my people. Their decisions must be based on my regulations. And the priests themselves must obey my instructions and decrees at all the sacred festivals, and see to it that the Sabbaths are set apart as holy days.

[25]"A priest must not defile himself by being in the presence of a dead person unless it is his father, mother, child, brother, or unmarried sister. In such cases it is permitted. [26] Even then, he can return to his Temple duties only after being ceremonially cleansed and then waiting for seven days. [27]The first day he returns to work and enters the inner courtyard and the sanctuary, he must offer a sin offering for himself, says the Sovereign LORD.

[28]"The priests will not have any property or possession of land, for I alone am their special possession. [29]Their food will come from the gifts and sacrifices brought to the Temple by the people—the grain offerings, the sin offerings, and the guilt offerings. Whatever anyone sets apart* for the LORD will belong to the priests. [30]The first of the ripe fruits and all the gifts brought to the LORD will go to the priests. The first samples of each grain harvest and the first of your flour must also be given to the priests so the LORD will bless your homes. [31]The priests may not eat meat from any bird or animal that dies a natural death or that dies after being attacked by another animal.

45

DIVISION OF THE LAND

"When you divide the land among the tribes of Israel, you must set aside a section for the LORD as his holy portion. This piece of land will be 8⅓ miles long and 6⅔ miles wide.* The entire area will be holy. [2]A section of this land, measuring 875 feet by 875 feet,* will be set aside for the Temple. An additional strip of land 87½ feet* wide is to be left empty all around it. [3]Within the larger sacred area, measure out a portion of land 8⅓ miles long and 3⅓ miles wide.* Within it the sanctuary of the Most Holy Place will be located. [4]This area will be holy, set aside for the priests who minister to the LORD in the sanctuary. They will use it for their homes, and my Temple will be located within it. [5]The strip of sacred land next to it, also 8⅓ miles long and 3⅓ miles wide, will be a living area for the Levites who work at the Temple. It will be their possession and a place for their towns.*

[6]"Adjacent to the larger sacred area will be a section of land 8⅓ miles long and 1⅔ miles wide.* This will be set aside for a city where anyone in Israel can live.

[7]"Two special sections of land will be set apart for the prince. One section will share a border with the east side of the sacred lands and city, and the second section will share a border on the west side. Then the far eastern and

44:10 The Hebrew term (literally *round things*) probably alludes to dung; also in 44:12. **44:29** The Hebrew term used here refers to the complete consecration of things or people to the LORD, either by destroying them or by giving them as an offering. **45:1** Reflecting the Greek version, which reads *25,000 cubits* [13.3 kilometers] *long and 20,000 cubits* [10.6 kilometers] *wide;* Hebrew reads *25,000 cubits long and 10,000 cubits* [3⅓ miles or 5.3 kilometers] *wide.* Compare 45:3, 5; 48:9. **45:2a** Hebrew *500 cubits* [265 meters] *by 500 cubits, a square.* **45:2b** Hebrew *50 cubits* [26.5 meters]. **45:3** Hebrew *25,000 cubits* [13.3 kilometers] *long and 10,000 cubits* [5.3 kilometers] *wide;* also in 45:5. **45:5** As in Greek version; Hebrew reads *They will have as their possession 20 rooms.* **45:6** Hebrew *25,000 cubits* [13.3 kilometers] *long and 5,000 cubits* [2.65 kilometers] *wide.*

western borders of the prince's lands will line up with the eastern and western boundaries of the tribal areas. 8These sections of land will be the prince's allotment. Then my princes will no longer oppress and rob my people; they will assign the rest of the land to the people, giving an allotment to each tribe.

RULES FOR THE PRINCES

9"For this is what the Sovereign LORD says: Enough, you princes of Israel! Stop your violence and oppression and do what is just and right. Quit robbing and cheating my people out of their land. Stop expelling them from their homes, says the Sovereign LORD. 10Use only honest weights and scales and honest measures, both dry and liquid.* 11The homer* will be your standard unit for measuring volume. The ephah and the bath* will each measure one-tenth of a homer. 12The standard unit for weight will be the silver shekel.* One shekel will consist of twenty gerahs, and sixty shekels will be equal to one mina.*

HONESTY 45:7-12

Greed and extortion were two of the major social sins of the nation during this time (see also Amos 5:7-13). In the new economy there would be plenty of land for the "princes" (45:7-8) and no longer any basis for greed. Therefore, the princes and the people were commanded to be fair and honest, especially in business transactions. Are *fair* and *honest* two words that describe you? ■

SPECIAL OFFERINGS AND CELEBRATIONS

13"You must give this tax to the prince: one bushel of wheat or barley for every 60* you harvest, 14one percent of your olive oil,* 15and one sheep or goat for every 200 in your flocks in Israel. These will be the grain offerings, burnt offerings, and peace offerings that will make atonement for the people who bring them, says the Sovereign LORD. 16All the people of Israel must join in bringing these offerings to the prince. 17The prince will be required to provide offerings that are given at the religious festivals, the new moon celebrations, the Sabbath days, and all other similar occasions. He will provide the sin offerings, burnt offerings, grain offerings, liquid offerings, and peace offerings to purify the people of Israel, making them right with the LORD.*

18"This is what the Sovereign LORD says: In early spring, on the first day of each new year,* sacrifice a young bull with no defects to purify the Temple. 19The priest will take blood from this sin offering and put it on the doorposts of the Temple, the four corners of the upper ledge of the altar, and the gateposts at the entrance to the inner courtyard. 20Do this also on the seventh day of the new year for anyone who has sinned through error or ignorance. In this way, you will purify* the Temple.

21"On the fourteenth day of the first month,* you must celebrate the Passover. This festival will last for seven days. The bread you eat during that time must be made without yeast. 22On the day of Passover the prince will provide a young bull as a sin offering for himself and the people of Israel. 23On each of the seven days of the feast he will prepare a burnt offering to the LORD, consisting of seven young bulls and seven rams without defects. A male goat will also be given each day for a sin offering. 24The prince will provide a basket of flour as a grain offering and a gallon of olive oil* with each young bull and ram.

25"During the seven days of the Festival of Shelters, which occurs every year in early autumn,* the prince will provide these same sacrifices for the sin offering, the burnt offering, and the grain offering, along with the required olive oil.

46

"This is what the Sovereign LORD says: The east gateway of the inner courtyard will be closed during the six workdays each week, but it will be open on Sabbath days and the days of new moon celebrations. 2The prince will enter the entry room of the gateway from the outside. Then he will stand by the gatepost while the priest offers his burnt offering and peace offering. He will bow down in worship inside the gateway passage and then go back out the way he came. The gateway will not be closed until evening. 3The common people will bow down and worship the LORD in front of this gateway on Sabbath days and the days of new moon celebrations.

4"Each Sabbath day the prince will present to the LORD a burnt offering of six lambs and one ram, all with no defects. 5He will present a grain offering of a basket of choice flour to go with the ram and whatever amount of flour he chooses to go with each lamb, and he is to offer one gallon of olive oil* for each basket of flour. 6At the new moon celebrations, he will bring one young bull, six lambs, and one ram, all with no defects. 7With the young bull he must bring a basket of choice flour for a grain offering. With the ram he must bring another basket of flour. And with each lamb he is to bring whatever amount of flour he chooses to give. With each basket of flour he must offer one gallon of olive oil.

8"The prince must enter the gateway through the entry

45:10 Hebrew *use honest scales, an honest ephah, and an honest bath.* **45:11a** The *homer* measures about 40 gallons or 182 liters. **45:11b** The *ephah* is a dry measure; the *bath* is a liquid measure. **45:12a** The *shekel* weighs about 0.4 ounces or 11 grams. **45:12b** Elsewhere the *mina* is equated to 50 shekels. **45:13** Hebrew *⅙ of an ephah from each homer of wheat and ⅙ of an ephah from each homer of barley.* **45:14** Hebrew *the portion of oil, measured by the bath, is 1/10 of a bath from each cor, which consists of 10 baths or 1 homer, for 10 baths are equivalent to a homer.* **45:17** Or *to make atonement for the people of Israel.* **45:18** Hebrew *On the first day of the first month,* of the Hebrew calendar. This day in the ancient Hebrew lunar calendar occurred in March or April. **45:20** Or *will make atonement for.* **45:21** This day in the ancient Hebrew lunar calendar occurred in late March, April, or early May. **45:24** Hebrew *an ephah* [20 quarts or 22 liters] *of flour . . . and a hin* [3.8 liters] *of olive oil.* **45:25** Hebrew *the festival which begins on the fifteenth day of the seventh month* (see Lev 23:34). This day in the ancient Hebrew lunar calendar occurred in late September, October, or early November. **46:5** Hebrew *an ephah* [20 quarts or 22 liters] *of choice flour . . . a hin* [3.8 liters] *of olive oil;* similarly in 46:7, 11.

room, and he must leave the same way. [9]But when the
people come in through the north gateway to worship
the LORD during the religious festivals, they must leave by
the south gateway. And those who entered through the
south gateway must leave by the north gateway. They
must never leave by the same gateway they came in, but
must always use the opposite gateway. [10]The prince will
enter and leave with the people on these occasions.

RHYTHM 46:1-15

Ezekiel continues to describe various aspects of daily worship. While allowing for diversity in worship, God prescribed order and continuity. This provided a healthy rhythm to the spiritual life of his people. Just as the goal of exercise is to maintain a healthy heart rhythm, the goal of keeping spiritually fit is to maintain a healthy spiritual rhythm. What's your spiritual routine? Do you set aside time with God each day? each week? each month? What do you need to do to maintain a healthy spiritual rhythm? ■

[11]"So at the special feasts and sacred festivals, the
grain offering will be a basket of choice flour with each
young bull, another basket of flour with each ram, and as
much flour as the prince chooses to give with each lamb.
Give one gallon of olive oil with each basket of flour.
[12]When the prince offers a voluntary burnt offering or
peace offering to the LORD, the east gateway to the inner
courtyard will be opened for him, and he will offer his
sacrifices as he does on Sabbath days. Then he will leave,
and the gateway will be shut behind him.

[13]"Each morning you must sacrifice a one-year-old
lamb with no defects as a burnt offering to the LORD.
[14]With the lamb, a grain offering must also be given to
the LORD—about three quarts of flour with a third of a
gallon of olive oil* to moisten the choice flour. This will
be a permanent law for you. [15]The lamb, the grain offering, and the olive oil must be given as a daily sacrifice
every morning without fail.

[16]"This is what the Sovereign LORD says: If the prince
gives a gift of land to one of his sons as his inheritance, it
will belong to him and his descendants forever. [17]But if
the prince gives a gift of land from his inheritance to one
of his servants, the servant may keep it only until the Year
of Jubilee, which comes every fiftieth year.* At that time
the land will return to the prince. But when the prince
gives gifts to his sons, those gifts will be permanent.
[18]And the prince may never take anyone's property by
force. If he gives property to his sons, it must be from his
own land, for I do not want any of my people unjustly
evicted from their property."

THE TEMPLE KITCHENS

[19]In my vision, the man brought me through the entrance
beside the gateway and led me to the sacred rooms assigned to the priests, which faced toward the north. He
showed me a place at the extreme west end of these
rooms. [20]He explained, "This is where the priests will
cook the meat from the guilt offerings and sin offerings
and bake the flour from the grain offerings into bread.
They will do it here to avoid carrying the sacrifices
through the outer courtyard and endangering the people
by transmitting holiness to them."

[21]Then he brought me back to the outer courtyard
and led me to each of its four corners. In each corner I
saw an enclosure. [22]Each of these enclosures was
70 feet long and 52½ feet wide,* surrounded by walls.
[23]Along the inside of these walls was a ledge of stone
with fireplaces under the ledge all the way around.
[24]The man said to me, "These are the kitchens to be
used by the Temple assistants to boil the sacrifices offered by the people."

47

THE RIVER OF HEALING

In my vision, the man brought me back to the entrance of
the Temple. There I saw a stream flowing east from beneath the door of the Temple and passing to the right of
the altar on its south side. [2]The man brought me outside the
wall through the north gateway and led me around to the
eastern entrance. There I could see the water flowing out
through the south side of the east gateway.

[3]Measuring as he went, he took me along the stream
for 1,750 feet* and then led me across. The water was up
to my ankles. [4]He measured off another 1,750 feet and
led me across again. This time the water was up to my
knees. After another 1,750 feet, it was up to my waist.
[5]Then he measured another 1,750 feet, and the river was
too deep to walk across. It was deep enough to swim in,
but too deep to walk through.

HEALING RIVER 47:1-12

This river (or stream) is similar to the river mentioned in Revelation 22:1-2, both of which are associated with the river in the Garden of Eden (see Gen 2:10). It is a gentle, safe river that expands as it flows and brings life to all it touches. This is one of the images the Bible gives us of heaven: health and well-being for all who love God. When you or someone you know faces illness or other undeserved suffering, may this picture of God's healing power comfort you. ■

[6]He asked me, "Have you been watching, son of man?"
Then he led me back along the riverbank. [7]When I returned, I was surprised by the sight of many trees growing on both sides of the river. [8]Then he said to me, "This
river flows east through the desert into the valley of the
Dead Sea.* The waters of this stream will make the salty
waters of the Dead Sea fresh and pure. [9]There will be

46:14 Hebrew *⅙ of an ephah* [3.7 liters] *of flour with ⅓ of a hin* [1.3 liters] *of olive oil.* **46:17** Hebrew *until the Year of Release;* see Lev 25:8-17. **46:22** Hebrew *40 cubits* [21.2 meters] *long and 30 cubits* [15.9 meters] *wide.* **47:3** Hebrew *1,000 cubits* [530 meters]; also in 47:4, 5. **47:8** Hebrew *the sea.*

swarms of living things wherever the water of this river
flows. Fish will abound in the Dead Sea, for its waters will
become fresh. Life will flourish wherever this water
flows. [10]Fishermen will stand along the shores of the
Dead Sea. All the way from En-gedi to En-eglaim, the
shores will be covered with nets drying in the sun. Fish of
every kind will fill the Dead Sea, just as they fill the Mediterranean.* [11]But the marshes and swamps will not be
purified; they will still be salty. [12]Fruit trees of all kinds
will grow along both sides of the river. The leaves of these
trees will never turn brown and fall, and there will always
be fruit on their branches. There will be a new crop every
month, for they are watered by the river flowing from the
Temple. The fruit will be for food and the leaves for
healing."

BOUNDARIES FOR THE LAND

[13]This is what the Sovereign LORD says: "Divide the land in
this way for the twelve tribes of Israel: The descendants
of Joseph will be given two shares of land.* [14]Otherwise
each tribe will receive an equal share. I took a solemn
oath and swore that I would give this land to your ancestors, and it will now come to you as your possession.

[15]"These are the boundaries of the land: The
northern border will run from the Mediterranean
toward Hethlon, then on through Lebo-hamath to
Zedad; [16]then it will run to Berothah and Sibraim,
which are on the border between Damascus and
Hamath, and finally to Hazer-hatticon, on the border
of Hauran. [17]So the northern border will run from the
Mediterranean to Hazar-enan, on the border between
Hamath to the north and Damascus to the south.

[18]"The eastern border starts at a point between
Hauran and Damascus and runs south along the
Jordan River between Israel and Gilead, past the
Dead Sea* and as far south as Tamar.* This will
be the eastern border.

[19]"The southern border will go west from Tamar
to the waters of Meribah at Kadesh* and then follow
the course of the Brook of Egypt to the
Mediterranean. This will be the southern border.

[20]"On the west side, the Mediterranean itself will
be your border from the southern border to the point
where the northern border begins, opposite Lebo-
hamath.

[21]"Divide the land within these boundaries among the
tribes of Israel. [22]Distribute the land as an allotment for
yourselves and for the foreigners who have joined you
and are raising their families among you. They will be
like native-born Israelites to you and will receive an allotment among the tribes. [23]These foreigners are to be given
land within the territory of the tribe with whom they now
live. I, the Sovereign LORD, have spoken!

48

DIVISION OF THE LAND

"Here is the list of the tribes of Israel and the territory
each is to receive. The territory of Dan is in the extreme
north. Its boundary line follows the Hethlon road to
Lebo-hamath and then runs on to Hazar-enan on the border of Damascus, with Hamath to the north. Dan's territory extends all the way across the land of Israel from
east to west.

THE PRESENCE 48:1-35

The book of Ezekiel begins by describing the holiness of God, which Israel had ignored. As a result, God's presence had departed from the Temple, the city, and the people. The book ends with a detailed vision of the new Temple, the new city, and the new people—all demonstrating God's holiness.

The concept of a holy God might seem prehistoric in the face of changing technology and constantly evolving ideas of right and wrong. Yet God never changes. He still wants his people to follow his ways, even if those ways clash with society's. Are you willing? ■

[2]"Asher's territory lies south of Dan's and also extends
from east to west. [3]Naphtali's land lies south of Asher's,
also extending from east to west. [4]Then comes Manasseh
south of Naphtali, and its territory also extends from east
to west. [5]South of Manasseh is Ephraim, [6]and then Reuben, [7]and then Judah, all of whose boundaries extend
from east to west.

[8]"South of Judah is the land set aside for a special purpose. It will be 8⅓ miles* wide and will extend as far east
and west as the tribal territories, with the Temple at the
center.

[9]"The area set aside for the LORD's Temple will be 8⅓
miles long and 6⅔ miles wide.* [10]For the priests there
will be a strip of land measuring 8⅓ miles long by 3⅓
miles wide,* with the LORD's Temple at the center. [11]This
area is set aside for the ordained priests, the descendants
of Zadok who served me faithfully and did not go astray
with the people of Israel and the rest of the Levites. [12]It
will be their special portion when the land is distributed,
the most sacred land of all. Next to the priests' territory
will lie the land where the other Levites will live.

[13]"The land allotted to the Levites will be the same size
and shape as that belonging to the priests—8⅓ miles long
and 3⅓ miles wide. Together these portions of land will
measure 8⅓ miles long by 6⅔ miles wide.* [14]None of this
special land may ever be sold or traded or used by others,
for it belongs to the LORD; it is set apart as holy.

[15]"An additional strip of land 8⅓ miles long by 1⅔ miles

47:10 Hebrew *the great sea;* also in 47:15, 17, 19, 20. **47:13** It was important to retain twelve portions of land. Since Levi had no portion, the descendants of Joseph's sons, Ephraim and Manasseh, received land as two tribes. **47:18a** Hebrew *the eastern sea.* **47:18b** As in Greek version; Hebrew reads *you will measure.* **47:19** Hebrew *waters of Meribath-kadesh.* **48:8** Hebrew *25,000 cubits* [13.3 kilometers]. **48:9** Reflecting one Greek manuscript and the Greek reading in 45:1: *25,000 cubits* [13.3 kilometers] *long and 20,000 cubits* [10.6 kilometers] *wide;* Hebrew reads *25,000 cubits long and 10,000 cubits* [3⅓ miles or 5.3 kilometers] *wide.* Similarly in 48:13b. Compare 45:1-5; 48:10-13. **48:10** Hebrew *25,000 cubits* [13.3 kilometers] *long by 10,000 cubits* [5.3 kilometers] *wide;* also in 48:13a. **48:13** See note on 48:9.

wide,* south of the sacred Temple area, will be allotted for public use—homes, pasturelands, and common lands, with a city at the center. 16The city will measure 1½ miles* on each side—north, south, east, and west. 17Open lands will surround the city for 150 yards* in every direction. 18Outside the city there will be a farming area that stretches 3⅓ miles to the east and 3⅓ miles to the west* along the border of the sacred area. This farmland will produce food for the people working in the city. 19Those who come from the various tribes to work in the city may farm it. 20This entire area—including the sacred lands and the city—is a square that measures 8⅓ miles* on each side.

21"The areas that remain, to the east and to the west of the sacred lands and the city, will belong to the prince. Each of these areas will be 8⅓ miles wide, extending in opposite directions to the eastern and western borders of Israel, with the sacred lands and the sanctuary of the Temple in the center. 22So the prince's land will include everything between the territories allotted to Judah and Benjamin, except for the areas set aside for the sacred lands and the city.

23"These are the territories allotted to the rest of the tribes. Benjamin's territory lies just south of the prince's lands, and it extends across the entire land of Israel from east to west. 24South of Benjamin's territory lies that of Simeon, also extending across the land from east to west. 25Next is the territory of Issachar with the same eastern and western boundaries.

26"Then comes the territory of Zebulun, which also extends across the land from east to west. 27The territory of Gad is just south of Zebulun with the same borders to the east and west. 28The southern border of Gad runs from Tamar to the waters of Meribah at Kadesh* and then follows the Brook of Egypt to the Mediterranean.*

29"These are the allotments that will be set aside for each tribe's exclusive possession. I, the Sovereign LORD, have spoken!

THE GATES OF THE CITY

30"These will be the exits to the city: On the north wall, which is 1½ miles long, 31there will be three gates, each one named after a tribe of Israel. The first will be named for Reuben, the second for Judah, and the third for Levi. 32On the east wall, also 1½ miles long, the gates will be named for Joseph, Benjamin, and Dan. 33The south wall, also 1½ miles long, will have gates named for Simeon, Issachar, and Zebulun. 34And on the west wall, also 1½ miles long, the gates will be named for Gad, Asher, and Naphtali.

35"The distance around the entire city will be 6 miles.* And from that day the name of the city will be 'The LORD Is There.'*"

48:15 Hebrew *25,000 cubits* [13.3 kilometers] *long by 5,000 cubits* [2.65 kilometers] *wide.* **48:16** Hebrew *4,500 cubits* [2.4 kilometers]; also in 48:30, 32, 33, 34. **48:17** Hebrew *250 cubits* [133 meters]. **48:18** Hebrew *10,000 cubits* [5.3 kilometers] *to the east and 10,000 cubits to the west.* **48:20** Hebrew *25,000 cubits* [13.3 kilometers]; also in 48:21. **48:28a** Hebrew *waters of Meribath-kadesh.* **48:28b** Hebrew *the great sea.* **48:35a** Hebrew *18,000 cubits* [9.6 kilometers]. **48:35b** Hebrew *Yahweh Shammah.*

DANIEL

COURAGE IS . . . risking injury to help a friend . . . doing what's right against all odds . . . standing for the truth despite the consequences . . . living for God no matter what.

Daniel had courage. While living in a foreign land, he stood for what he believed and did what was right despite incredible pressure from society, from peers, and from the government.

Courage was Daniel's trademark throughout his life and through the reigns of four kings. He boldly interpreted dreams, rejected royal food and drink, and publicly lived his faith.

God still needs men and women of courage and faith. What kinds of risks or pressures do you face? How do you avoid giving in to the temptation to conform or to turn away from God?

As you read the book of Daniel, take note of any impressions you gain of the man who refused to give in or give up. Is this the kind of courage you have?

daniel

timeline

612 B.C.
Habakkuk becomes a prophet to Judah

609
Jehoiakim becomes king of Judah

605
Daniel taken captive to Babylon

600?
Daniel becomes a Babylonian official; fiery furnace

597
Nebuchadnezzar takes more captives

593
Ezekiel becomes a prophet to exiles

586
Judah falls; Jerusalem is destroyed; Jeremiah's ministry ends

562
Nebuchadnezzar dies

553
Daniel's first vision

539
Babylon overthrown; Daniel thrown to lions

538
First exiles return to Judah

536
Daniel's ministry ends

stats

PURPOSE: To give a historical account of the faithful Jews who lived in captivity and to show how God is in control of heaven and earth

AUTHOR: Daniel

TO WHOM WRITTEN: The captives in Babylon and God's people everywhere

DATE WRITTEN: Approximately 535 B.C., recording events that occurred from about 605 to 535 B.C.

SETTING: Daniel had been taken captive and deported to Babylon by Nebuchadnezzar in 605 B.C. There he served in the government for about 60 years during the reigns of Nebuchadnezzar, Belshazzar, Darius, and Cyrus.

KEY PEOPLE: Daniel, Nebuchadnezzar, Shadrach, Meshach, Abednego, Belshazzar, Darius

KEY PLACES: Nebuchadnezzar's palace, the fiery furnace, Belshazzar's banquet, the den of lions

SPECIAL FEATURES: Daniel's apocalyptic visions (chapters 7–12, which include information about the coming Messiah) provide a glimpse of God's plan for the ages.

KEY points

GOD'S CONTROL
God is the behind-the-scenes power behind world events. Although nations compete for world control now, one day Christ will rule.

UNCOMPROMISING
Daniel and his three friends refused to give in to pressures from an ungodly society. Like Daniel and his friends, we can choose to avoid compromising, no matter what the consequences.

PERSEVERANCE
For many decades Daniel persevered in his role of godly leader to many kings. He was truthful, persistent in prayer, and humble. Persistence in prayer can help us hold fast to our commitment to God.

GOD'S FAITHFULNESS
God's faithfulness could be seen as he rescued Daniel from enemies. Therefore, we can trust God to take us through any trial.

1

DANIEL IN NEBUCHADNEZZAR'S COURT

During the third year of King Jehoiakim's reign in Judah,* King Nebuchadnezzar of Babylon came to Jerusalem and besieged it. [2]The LORD gave him victory over King Jehoiakim of Judah and permitted him to take some of the sacred objects from the Temple of God. So Nebuchadnezzar took them back to the land of Babylonia* and placed them in the treasure-house of his god.

[3]Then the king ordered Ashpenaz, his chief of staff, to bring to the palace some of the young men of Judah's royal family and other noble families, who had been brought to Babylon as captives. [4]"Select only strong, healthy, and good-looking young men," he said. "Make sure they are well versed in every branch of learning, are gifted with knowledge and good judgment, and are suited to serve in the royal palace. Train these young men in the language and literature of Babylon.*" [5]The king assigned them a daily ration of food and wine from his own kitchens. They were to be trained for three years, and then they would enter the royal service.

WHERE DO YOU STAND? 1:1-8

Resisting temptation can be easier if you've thought through your convictions well before the temptation arises. Since Daniel and his friends made their decision to be faithful to the laws God established (see Lev 11) before they were faced with the king's delicacies, they didn't hesitate to stick with their convictions. Sometimes we get into trouble because we failed to decide where to draw the line beforehand. Before such situations arise, make a decision about your beliefs. Then, when temptation comes, you'll be ready. ■

[6]Daniel, Hananiah, Mishael, and Azariah were four of the young men chosen, all from the tribe of Judah. [7]The chief of staff renamed them with these Babylonian names:

Daniel was called Belteshazzar.
Hananiah was called Shadrach.
Mishael was called Meshach.
Azariah was called Abednego.

[8]But Daniel was determined not to defile himself by eating the food and wine given to them by the king. He asked the chief of staff for permission not to eat these unacceptable foods. [9]Now God had given the chief of staff both respect and affection for Daniel. [10]But he responded, "I am afraid of my lord the king, who has ordered that you eat this food and wine. If you become pale and thin compared to the other youths your age, I am afraid the king will have me beheaded."

[11]Daniel spoke with the attendant who had been appointed by the chief of staff to look after Daniel,

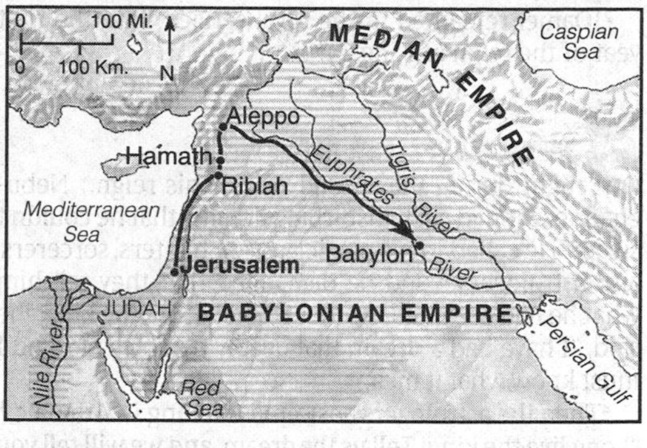

TAKEN TO BABYLON
Daniel, as a captive of Babylonian soldiers, faced a long and difficult march to a new land. The five-hundred-mile trek, mostly under harsh conditions, certainly tested Daniel's faith in God.

Hananiah, Mishael, and Azariah. [12]"Please test us for ten days on a diet of vegetables and water," Daniel said. [13]"At the end of the ten days, see how we look compared to the other young men who are eating the king's food. Then make your decision in light of what you see." [14]The attendant agreed to Daniel's suggestion and tested them for ten days.

[15]At the end of the ten days, Daniel and his three friends looked healthier and better nourished than the young men who had been eating the food assigned by the king. [16]So after that, the attendant fed them only vegetables instead of the food and wine provided for the others.

[17]God gave these four young men an unusual aptitude for understanding every aspect of literature and wisdom. And God gave Daniel the special ability to interpret the meanings of visions and dreams.

CULTURE CLASH? 1:17

Daniel and his friends learned all they could about their new culture so they could do their work with excellence. But while they learned, they remained faithful to God. So, does this mean you have to totally ignore pop culture and become a hermit? No. What you know about culture can aid in accomplishing God's purpose. We who follow God are free to be leaders in our culture. But God wants to be first in our lives. ■

[18]When the training period ordered by the king was completed, the chief of staff brought all the young men to King Nebuchadnezzar. [19]The king talked with them, and no one impressed him as much as Daniel, Hananiah, Mishael, and Azariah. So they entered the royal service. [20]Whenever the king consulted them in any matter requiring wisdom and balanced judgment, he found them ten times more capable than any of the magicians and enchanters in his entire kingdom.

1:1 This event occurred in 605 B.C., during the third year of Jehoiakim's reign (according to the calendar system in which the new year begins in the spring). 1:2 Hebrew *the land of Shinar*. 1:4 Or *of the Chaldeans*.

21 Daniel remained in the royal service until the first
year of the reign of King Cyrus.*

2 NEBUCHADNEZZAR'S DREAM

One night during the second year of his reign,* Nebuchadnezzar had such disturbing dreams that he couldn't
sleep. 2 He called in his magicians, enchanters, sorcerers,
and astrologers,* and he demanded that they tell him
what he had dreamed. As they stood before the king, 3 he
said, "I have had a dream that deeply troubles me, and I
must know what it means."
4 Then the astrologers answered the king in Aramaic,*
"Long live the king! Tell us the dream, and we will tell you
what it means."
5 But the king said to the astrologers, "I am serious
about this. If you don't tell me what my dream was and
what it means, you will be torn limb from limb, and your
houses will be turned into heaps of rubble! 6 But if you tell
me what I dreamed and what the dream means, I will give
you many wonderful gifts and honors. Just tell me the
dream and what it means!"
7 They said again, "Please, Your Majesty. Tell us the
dream, and we will tell you what it means."
8 The king replied, "I know what you are doing! You're
stalling for time because you know I am serious when I
say, 9 'If you don't tell me the dream, you are doomed.' So
you have conspired to tell me lies, hoping I will change
my mind. But tell me the dream, and then I'll know that
you can tell me what it means."

DOING THE IMPOSSIBLE 2:10-11

King Nebuchadnezzar's astrologers told him that no one could know the dreams of another person. But Daniel was able to explain the meaning of the king's dream because God worked through him. In daily life, we face many apparently impossible situations that would be hopeless if we had to handle them with limited human strength alone. But God specializes in the impossible. ■

10 The astrologers replied to the king, "No one on
earth can tell the king his dream! And no king, however
great and powerful, has ever asked such a thing of any
magician, enchanter, or astrologer! 11 The king's demand is impossible. No one except the gods can tell
you your dream, and they do not live here among
people."
12 The king was furious when he heard this, and he ordered that all the wise men of Babylon be executed.

1:21 Cyrus began his reign (over Babylon) in 539 B.C. **2:1** The second year of Nebuchadnezzar's reign was 603 B.C. **2:2** Or *Chaldeans;* also in 2:4, 5, 10. **2:4** The original text from this point through chapter 7 is in Aramaic.

DANIEL

UPS

- Remained true to his faith even though he was taken from his home at an early age
- Served as a counselor to two Babylonian kings and two Medo-Persian kings
- Was a man of prayer and a statesman with the gift of prophecy

STATS

- Where: Judah and the courts of Babylon and Persia
- Occupation: A captive of Israel who became a counselor of kings
- Contemporaries: Hananiah (Shadrach), Mishael (Meshach), Azariah (Abednego), Nebuchadnezzar, Belshazzar, Darius, Cyrus

BOTTOM LINE:

Wise words and actions often earn long-term respect.

God never promised to keep his people from hard times. He does promise to be with us as we go through hard times.

God has the power to deliver his people even from the worst situations.

Daniel's story is told in the book of Daniel. He also is mentioned in Matt 24:15.

DANIEL Have you ever noticed how often life's biggest mistakes begin with this thought: *I'd better do this because everybody else is doing it*? Sometimes we cave to the pressures to be like everyone else, simply to save face.

Even as a young man, Daniel refused to compromise. Instead, he held on to the habits and convictions that came from studying God's Word. Pleasing God was more important to Daniel than pleasing anyone else.

Daniel's convictions weren't just beliefs; they created positive actions in his life. For instance, he ate carefully and lived prayerfully. His position gave him all-you-can-eat privileges at the king's table, but Daniel chose a simpler menu—a choice that proved to be healthier.

While Daniel cut back on food (Dan 1), he cut loose on prayer. He felt comfortable talking to God because he did it all the time. Even lions couldn't come between him and his habit of prayer (Dan 6).

Where do your habits come from? What happens to your convictions when the pressure is on? Like Daniel, is prayer your lifeline? Notice, though, that prayer may not keep you from "lions' dens" like hard times. Rather, prayer will keep you in touch with God even in the middle of problems or pain!

Daniel

Served as a prophet to the exiles in Babylon from 605 to 536 B.C.

Climate of the times	The people of Judah were captives in a strange land, feeling hopeless.
Main message	God is sovereign over all of human history, past, present, and future.
Importance of message	We should spend less time wondering when future events will happen and more time learning how we should live now.
Contemporary prophets	Jeremiah (627–586) Habakkuk (612–588)

[13]And because of the king's decree, men were sent to find and kill Daniel and his friends.

[14]When Arioch, the commander of the king's guard, came to kill them, Daniel handled the situation with wisdom and discretion. [15]He asked Arioch, "Why has the king issued such a harsh decree?" So Arioch told him all that had happened. [16]Daniel went at once to see the king and requested more time to tell the king what the dream meant.

[17]Then Daniel went home and told his friends Hananiah, Mishael, and Azariah what had happened. [18]He urged them to ask the God of heaven to show them his mercy by telling them the secret, so they would not be executed along with the other wise men of Babylon. [19]That night the secret was revealed to Daniel in a vision. Then Daniel praised the God of heaven. [20]He said,

"Praise the name of God forever and ever,
for he has all wisdom and power.
21 He controls the course of world events;
he removes kings and sets up other kings.
He gives wisdom to the wise
and knowledge to the scholars.
22 He reveals deep and mysterious things
and knows what lies hidden in darkness,
though he is surrounded by light.
23 I thank and praise you, God of my ancestors,
for you have given me wisdom and strength.
You have told me what we asked of you
and revealed to us what the king demanded."

DANIEL INTERPRETS THE DREAM

[24]Then Daniel went in to see Arioch, whom the king had ordered to execute the wise men of Babylon. Daniel said to him, "Don't kill the wise men. Take me to the king, and I will tell him the meaning of his dream."

[25]Arioch quickly took Daniel to the king and said, "I have found one of the captives from Judah who will tell the king the meaning of his dream!"

[26]The king said to Daniel (also known as Belteshazzar), "Is this true? Can you tell me what my dream was and what it means?"

[27]Daniel replied, "There are no wise men, enchanters, magicians, or fortune-tellers who can reveal the king's secret. [28]But there is a God in heaven who reveals secrets, and he has shown King Nebuchadnezzar what will happen in the future. Now I will tell you your dream and the visions you saw as you lay on your bed.

[29]"While Your Majesty was sleeping, you dreamed about coming events. He who reveals secrets has shown you what is going to happen. [30]And it is not because I am wiser than anyone else that I know the secret of your dream, but because God wants you to understand what was in your heart.

[31]"In your vision, Your Majesty, you saw standing before you a huge, shining statue of a man. It was a frightening sight. [32]The head of the statue was made of fine gold. Its chest and arms were silver, its belly and thighs were bronze, [33]its legs were iron, and its feet were a combination of iron and baked clay. [34]As you watched, a rock was cut from a mountain, but not by human hands. It struck the feet of iron and clay, smashing them to bits. [35]The whole statue was crushed into small pieces of iron, clay, bronze, silver, and gold. Then the wind blew them away without a trace, like chaff on a threshing floor. But the rock that knocked the statue down became a great mountain that covered the whole earth.

[36]"That was the dream. Now we will tell the king what it means. [37]Your Majesty, you are the greatest of kings. The God of heaven has given you sovereignty, power, strength, and honor. [38]He has made you the ruler over all the inhabited world and has put even the wild animals and birds under your control. You are the head of gold.

[39]"But after your kingdom comes to an end, another kingdom, inferior to yours, will rise to take your place. After that kingdom has fallen, yet a third kingdom, represented by bronze, will rise to rule the world. [40]Following that kingdom, there will be a fourth one, as strong as iron. That kingdom will smash and crush all previous empires, just as iron smashes and crushes everything it strikes. [41]The feet and toes you saw were a combination of iron

and baked clay, showing that this kingdom will be divided. Like iron mixed with clay, it will have some of the
strength of iron. 42But while some parts of it will be as
strong as iron, other parts will be as weak as clay. 43This
mixture of iron and clay also shows that these kingdoms
will try to strengthen themselves by forming alliances
with each other through intermarriage. But they will not
hold together, just as iron and clay do not mix.
44"During the reigns of those kings, the God of heaven
will set up a kingdom that will never be destroyed or conquered. It will crush all these kingdoms into nothingness,
and it will stand forever. 45That is the meaning of the rock
cut from the mountain, though not by human hands, that
crushed to pieces the statue of iron, bronze, clay, silver,
and gold. The great God was showing the king what will
happen in the future. The dream is true, and its meaning
is certain."

NEBUCHADNEZZAR REWARDS DANIEL

46Then King Nebuchadnezzar threw himself down before Daniel and worshiped him, and he commanded his
people to offer sacrifices and burn sweet incense before
him. 47The king said to Daniel, "Truly, your God is the
greatest of gods, the Lord over kings, a revealer of mysteries, for you have been able to reveal this secret."
48Then the king appointed Daniel to a high position
and gave him many valuable gifts. He made Daniel ruler
over the whole province of Babylon, as well as chief over
all his wise men. 49At Daniel's request, the king appointed
Shadrach, Meshach, and Abednego to be in charge of all
the affairs of the province of Babylon, while Daniel remained in the king's court.

3 NEBUCHADNEZZAR'S GOLD STATUE

King Nebuchadnezzar made a gold statue ninety feet tall
and nine feet wide* and set it up on the plain of Dura in
the province of Babylon. 2Then he sent messages to the
high officers, officials, governors, advisers, treasurers,
judges, magistrates, and all the provincial officials to
come to the dedication of the statue he had set up. 3So all
these officials* came and stood before the statue King
Nebuchadnezzar had set up.
4Then a herald shouted out, "People of all races and nations and languages, listen to the king's command!
5When you hear the sound of the horn, flute, zither, lyre,

3:1 Aramaic *60 cubits* [27 meters] *tall and 6 cubits* [2.7 meters] *wide.* **3:3** Aramaic *the high officers, officials, governors, advisers, treasurers, judges, magistrates, and all the provincial officials.*

SHADRACH, MESHACH, & ABEDNEGO

UPS:

- Like Daniel, refused to break the dietary laws of their people
- Shared a friendship that stood the tests of hardship, success, wealth, and threats of death
- Would not compromise their convictions even in the face of death

STATS:

- Where: Babylon
- Occupations: King's servants and counselors
- Contemporaries: Daniel (Belteshazzar), Nebuchadnezzar

BOTTOM LINE:

A real friend shares your convictions and is willing to take a stand with you when the going gets tough.

God can be trusted even when we can't predict the outcome of a trial.

The story of Shadrach (Hananiah), Meshach (Mishael), and Abednego (Azariah) is told in the book of Daniel.

SHADRACH, MESHACH, & ABEDNEGO

Have you ever wound up too close to a fire that suddenly sent out flames? If so, you know how powerful and frightening fire can be. But would you willingly walk into a blast furnace to prove your faith in God? Daniel's friends Shadrach, Meshach, and Abednego did.

Along with Daniel and the other people of Jerusalem, these three young Jewish men were taken into captivity by the Babylonians in 605 B.C. and forced to serve in the court of an enemy king, Nebuchadnezzar.

Although the king obviously respected and admired his young Hebrew servants, he just as clearly did not understand the depth of their relationship with the One True God.

If you read Daniel 3, you know the story. Shadrach, Meshach, and Abednego refused to bow to a statue Nebuchadnezzar had ordered to be built. Disobedience meant a trip to the fiery furnace. They preferred to face the fire rather than offend God by worshiping a statue. Now that's putting your faith on the line!

Shadrach, Meshach, and Abednego were three friends who probably encouraged each other to stick with God. They were a living example of Proverbs 27:17: "As iron sharpens iron, so a friend sharpens a friend." What also helped their friendship was a fourth friend: God. Do you have friends like that—friends who will encourage you to avoid compromising, even at the cost of your reputation?

harp, pipes, and other musical instruments,* bow to the
ground to worship King Nebuchadnezzar's gold statue.
6Anyone who refuses to obey will immediately be thrown
into a blazing furnace."
7So at the sound of the musical instruments,* all the
people, whatever their race or nation or language, bowed
to the ground and worshiped the gold statue that King
Nebuchadnezzar had set up.
8But some of the astrologers* went to the king and informed on the Jews. 9They said to King Nebuchadnezzar,
"Long live the king! 10You issued a decree requiring all the
people to bow down and worship the gold statue when
they hear the sound of the horn, flute, zither, lyre, harp,
pipes, and other musical instruments. 11That decree also
states that those who refuse to obey must be thrown into
a blazing furnace. 12But there are some Jews—Shadrach,
Meshach, and Abednego—whom you have put in charge
of the province of Babylon. They pay no attention to you,
Your Majesty. They refuse to serve your gods and do not
worship the gold statue you have set up."

STAND OUT 3:12

Why didn't Shadrach, Meshach, and Abednego just bow to the image and tell God that they didn't mean it? They had determined never to worship an idol, and they courageously took their stand. As a result, they were condemned to be executed. They didn't know whether or not they would be rescued from the fire; all they knew was that they wouldn't disobey God. Are you ready to take a stand for God no matter what? When you stand for God, you will stand out. Taking a stand is painful sometimes and doesn't always have a happy ending. Like Shadrach, Meshach, and Abednego, are you prepared to say, "If he rescues me, or if he doesn't, I will serve only God"? ■

13Then Nebuchadnezzar flew into a rage and ordered
that Shadrach, Meshach, and Abednego be brought before him. When they were brought in, 14Nebuchadnezzar
said to them, "Is it true, Shadrach, Meshach, and Abednego, that you refuse to serve my gods or to worship the
gold statue I have set up? 15I will give you one more
chance to bow down and worship the statue I have made
when you hear the sound of the musical instruments.*
But if you refuse, you will be thrown immediately into the
blazing furnace. And then what god will be able to rescue
you from my power?"
16Shadrach, Meshach, and Abednego replied, "O Nebuchadnezzar, we do not need to defend ourselves before
you. 17If we are thrown into the blazing furnace, the God
whom we serve is able to save us. He will rescue us from
your power, Your Majesty. 18But even if he doesn't, we
want to make it clear to you, Your Majesty, that we will
never serve your gods or worship the gold statue you have
set up."

FRIENDSHIP

Kennedy, Lola, and Montana are inseparable. Find one and you'll find the other two. Besides a lot of laughs and six years' worth of great memories, the three-way friendship has helped keep the girls on track with God all through high school. Whenever one of them has struggled in her faith, the other two have been there to pick her up. For instance:

- **When Lola began dating a non-Christian, the other two girls confronted her and convinced her that she was making a mistake.**
- **When Montana's parents split up one winter and Montana wondered if God really cared, Kennedy and Lola showered their hurting friend with love.**
- **When Kennedy got so involved in extracurricular school activities one semester that she quit coming to Bible study, the other girls practically dragged her back into the fold!**
- **When none of them were asked to the prom because of their stand against alcohol, they all dressed up and went to dinner instead.**

Without such a strong Christ-centered friendship, these teens might have wandered away from God when the pressure got too intense. However, because they had a friendship like this to lean on, they all were able to have a huge impact for Christ!

Do you have close Christian friends who constantly challenge you to grow in Christ? Read in Daniel 3 about three godly guys who braved some serious heat together.

THE BLAZING FURNACE

19Nebuchadnezzar was so furious with Shadrach, Meshach, and Abednego that his face became distorted with
rage. He commanded that the furnace be heated seven
times hotter than usual. 20Then he ordered some of the
strongest men of his army to bind Shadrach, Meshach,
and Abednego and throw them into the blazing furnace.
21So they tied them up and threw them into the furnace,
fully dressed in their pants, turbans, robes, and other garments. 22And because the king, in his anger, had demanded such a hot fire in the furnace, the flames killed
the soldiers as they threw the three men in. 23So Shadrach, Meshach, and Abednego, securely tied, fell into
the roaring flames.
24But suddenly, Nebuchadnezzar jumped up in amazement and exclaimed to his advisers, "Didn't we tie up
three men and throw them into the furnace?"
"Yes, Your Majesty, we certainly did," they replied.
25"Look!" Nebuchadnezzar shouted. "I see four men,
unbound, walking around in the fire unharmed! And the
fourth looks like a god*!"

3:5 The identification of some of these musical instruments is uncertain. 3:7 Aramaic *the horn, flute, zither, lyre, harp, and other musical instruments.* 3:8 Aramaic *Chaldeans.* 3:15 Aramaic *the horn, flute, zither, lyre, harp, pipes, and other musical instruments.* 3:25 Aramaic *like a son of the gods.*

26Then Nebuchadnezzar came as close as he could to the door of the flaming furnace and shouted: "Shadrach, Meshach, and Abednego, servants of the Most High God, come out! Come here!"

So Shadrach, Meshach, and Abednego stepped out of the fire. 27Then the high officers, officials, governors, and advisers crowded around them and saw that the fire had not touched them. Not a hair on their heads was singed, and their clothing was not scorched. They didn't even smell of smoke!

28Then Nebuchadnezzar said, "Praise to the God of Shadrach, Meshach, and Abednego! He sent his angel to rescue his servants who trusted in him. They defied the king's command and were willing to die rather than serve or worship any god except their own God. 29Therefore, I make this decree: If any people, whatever their race or nation or language, speak a word against the God of Shadrach, Meshach, and Abednego, they will be torn limb from limb, and their houses will be turned into heaps of rubble. There is no other god who can rescue like this!"

30Then the king promoted Shadrach, Meshach, and Abednego to even higher positions in the province of Babylon.

4 NEBUCHADNEZZAR'S DREAM ABOUT A TREE

1*King Nebuchadnezzar sent this message to the people of every race and nation and language throughout the world:

"Peace and prosperity to you!

2"I want you all to know about the miraculous signs and wonders the Most High God has performed for me.

3 How great are his signs,
how powerful his wonders!
His kingdom will last forever,
his rule through all generations.

4*"I, Nebuchadnezzar, was living in my palace in comfort and prosperity. 5But one night I had a dream that frightened me; I saw visions that terrified me as I lay in my bed. 6So I issued an order calling in all the wise men of Babylon, so they could tell me what my dream meant. 7When all the magicians, enchanters, astrologers,* and fortune-tellers came in, I told them the dream, but they could not tell me what it meant.
8At last Daniel came in before me, and I told him the dream. (He was named Belteshazzar after my god, and the spirit of the holy gods is in him.)

9"I said to him, 'Belteshazzar, chief of the magicians, I know that the spirit of the holy gods is in you and that no mystery is too great for you to solve. Now tell me what my dream means.

10"'While I was lying in my bed, this is what I dreamed. I saw a large tree in the middle of the earth. 11The tree grew very tall and strong, reaching high into the heavens for all the world to see. 12It had fresh green leaves, and it was loaded with fruit for all to eat. Wild animals lived in its shade, and birds nested in its branches. All the world was fed from this tree.

13"'Then as I lay there dreaming, I saw a messenger,* a holy one, coming down from heaven. 14The messenger shouted,

"Cut down the tree and lop off its branches!
Shake off its leaves and scatter its fruit!
Chase the wild animals from its shade
and the birds from its branches.
15 But leave the stump and the roots in the ground,
bound with a band of iron and bronze
and surrounded by tender grass.
Now let him be drenched with the dew of heaven,
and let him live with the wild animals among
the plants of the field.
16 For seven periods of time,
let him have the mind of a wild animal
instead of the mind of a human.
17 For this has been decreed by the messengers*;
it is commanded by the holy ones,
so that everyone may know
that the Most High rules over the kingdoms
of the world.
He gives them to anyone he chooses—
even to the lowliest of people."

18"'Belteshazzar, that was the dream that I, King Nebuchadnezzar, had. Now tell me what it means, for none of the wise men of my kingdom can do so. But you can tell me because the spirit of the holy gods is in you.'

HARD TO FORGIVE 4:19

When Daniel learned the meaning of Nebuchadnezzar's dream, he was stunned. How could he be so deeply grieved at the fate of Nebuchadnezzar—the king who was responsible for the destruction of his home and the captivity of his people? One word: *forgiveness*. Often when we have been wronged by someone, we find it difficult to forget the past. We may even be glad if that person suffers. Forgiving people means putting the past behind us. Can you love someone who has hurt you? Ask God to help you forgive, forget, and love. God may use you in an extraordinary way in that person's life! ■

DANIEL EXPLAINS THE DREAM

19"Upon hearing this, Daniel (also known as Belteshazzar) was overcome for a time, frightened by the meaning of the dream. Then the king said to him, 'Belteshazzar, don't be alarmed by the dream and what it means.'

4:1 Verses 4:1-3 are numbered 3:31-33 in Aramaic text. **4:4** Verses 4:4-37 are numbered 4:1-34 in Aramaic text. **4:7** Or *Chaldeans.* **4:13** Aramaic *a watcher;* also in 4:23. **4:17** Aramaic *the watchers.*

"Belteshazzar replied, 'I wish the events
foreshadowed in this dream would happen to your
enemies, my lord, and not to you! 20The tree you saw
was growing very tall and strong, reaching high into
the heavens for all the world to see. 21It had fresh
green leaves and was loaded with fruit for all to eat.
Wild animals lived in its shade, and birds nested in
its branches. 22That tree, Your Majesty, is you. For you
have grown strong and great; your greatness reaches
up to heaven, and your rule to the ends of the earth.

23"'Then you saw a messenger, a holy one, coming
down from heaven and saying, "Cut down the tree
and destroy it. But leave the stump and the roots in
the ground, bound with a band of iron and bronze
and surrounded by tender grass. Let him be
drenched with the dew of heaven. Let him live with
the animals of the field for seven periods of time."

24"'This is what the dream means, Your Majesty,
and what the Most High has declared will happen to
my lord the king. 25You will be driven from human
society, and you will live in the fields with the wild
animals. You will eat grass like a cow, and you will
be drenched with the dew of heaven. Seven periods
of time will pass while you live this way, until you
learn that the Most High rules over the kingdoms
of the world and gives them to anyone he chooses.
26But the stump and roots of the tree were left in
the ground. This means that you will receive your
kingdom back again when you have learned that
heaven rules.

27"'King Nebuchadnezzar, please accept my advice.
Stop sinning and do what is right. Break from your
wicked past and be merciful to the poor. Perhaps
then you will continue to prosper.'

THE DREAM'S FULFILLMENT

28"But all these things did happen to King
Nebuchadnezzar. 29Twelve months later he was
taking a walk on the flat roof of the royal palace in
Babylon. 30As he looked out across the city, he said,
'Look at this great city of Babylon! By my own mighty
power, I have built this beautiful city as my royal
residence to display my majestic splendor.'

31"While these words were still in his mouth, a voice
called down from heaven, 'O King Nebuchadnezzar,
this message is for you! You are no longer ruler of this
kingdom. 32You will be driven from human society.
You will live in the fields with the wild animals, and
you will eat grass like a cow. Seven periods of time will
pass while you live this way, until you learn that the
Most High rules over the kingdoms of the world and
gives them to anyone he chooses.'

33"That same hour the judgment was fulfilled, and
Nebuchadnezzar was driven from human society.
He ate grass like a cow, and he was drenched with the
dew of heaven. He lived this way until his hair was as
long as eagles' feathers and his nails were like birds'
claws.

NEBUCHADNEZZAR PRAISES GOD

34"After this time had passed, I, Nebuchadnezzar,
looked up to heaven. My sanity returned, and I
praised and worshiped the Most High and honored
the one who lives forever.

His rule is everlasting,
and his kingdom is eternal.
35 All the people of the earth
are nothing compared to him.
He does as he pleases
among the angels of heaven
and among the people of the earth.
No one can stop him or say to him,
'What do you mean by doing these things?'

36"When my sanity returned to me, so did my
honor and glory and kingdom. My advisers and
nobles sought me out, and I was restored as head of
my kingdom, with even greater honor than before.

37"Now I, Nebuchadnezzar, praise and glorify and
honor the King of heaven. All his acts are just and
true, and he is able to humble the proud."

ACKNOWLEDGE GOD 4:1-37

In 2:47, Nebuchadnezzar acknowledged that God revealed dreams to Daniel. In 3:28-29, he praised the God who delivered the three Hebrews. Despite Nebuchadnezzar's recognition of God's power, in 4:30 we see that he still did not acknowledge God as his own ruler. What about you? Is God just a great God who performs miracles? Or, is he a great God whom you trust as your ruler? ■

5 THE WRITING ON THE WALL

Many years later King Belshazzar gave a great feast for
1,000 of his nobles, and he drank wine with them.
2While Belshazzar was drinking the wine, he gave orders
to bring in the gold and silver cups that his predecessor,*
Nebuchadnezzar, had taken from the Temple in Jerusalem. He wanted to drink from them with his nobles, his
wives, and his concubines. 3So they brought these gold
cups taken from the Temple, the house of God in Jerusalem, and the king and his nobles, his wives, and his concubines drank from them. 4While they drank from them
they praised their idols made of gold, silver, bronze, iron,
wood, and stone.

5Suddenly, they saw the fingers of a human hand writing on the plaster wall of the king's palace, near the lampstand. The king himself saw the hand as it wrote, 6and his
face turned pale with fright. His knees knocked together
in fear and his legs gave way beneath him.

7The king shouted for the enchanters, astrologers,*
and fortune-tellers to be brought before him. He said to
these wise men of Babylon, "Whoever can read this

5:2 Aramaic *father;* also in 5:11, 13, 18. 5:7 Or *Chaldeans;* also in 5:11.

writing and tell me what it means will be dressed in purple robes of royal honor and will have a gold chain placed around his neck. He will become the third highest ruler in the kingdom!"

8But when all the king's wise men had come in, none of them could read the writing or tell him what it meant. 9So the king grew even more alarmed, and his face turned pale. His nobles, too, were shaken.

UNBIASED 5:1-17

The king offered Daniel beautiful gifts and great power if he would explain the writing on the wall. Daniel, however, refused them. He wanted the king to know that the interpretation of his dream was unbiased. Delivering a hard message from God isn't easy, especially when you have to talk to someone who has authority over you. Like Daniel, you may be in a position to confront something about a wrongdoing. Will their influence sway you or will God's? ■

10But when the queen mother heard what was happening, she hurried to the banquet hall. She said to Belshazzar, "Long live the king! Don't be so pale and frightened. 11There is a man in your kingdom who has within him the spirit of the holy gods. During Nebuchadnezzar's reign, this man was found to have insight, understanding, and wisdom like that of the gods. Your predecessor, the king—your predecessor King Nebuchadnezzar—made him chief over all the magicians, enchanters, astrologers, and fortune-tellers of Babylon. 12This man Daniel, whom the king named Belteshazzar, has exceptional ability and is filled with divine knowledge and understanding. He can interpret dreams, explain riddles, and solve difficult problems. Call for Daniel, and he will tell you what the writing means."

DANIEL EXPLAINS THE WRITING

13So Daniel was brought in before the king. The king asked him, "Are you Daniel, one of the exiles brought from Judah by my predecessor, King Nebuchadnezzar? 14I have heard that you have the spirit of the gods within you and that you are filled with insight, understanding, and wisdom. 15My wise men and enchanters have tried to read the words on the wall and tell me their meaning, but they cannot do it. 16I am told that you can give interpretations and solve difficult problems. If you can read these words and tell me their meaning, you will be clothed in purple robes of royal honor, and you will have a gold chain placed around your neck. You will become the third highest ruler in the kingdom."

17Daniel answered the king, "Keep your gifts or give them to someone else, but I will tell you what the writing means. 18Your Majesty, the Most High God gave sovereignty, majesty, glory, and honor to your predecessor, Nebuchadnezzar. 19He made him so great that people of all races and nations and languages trembled before him in fear. He killed those he wanted to kill and spared those he wanted to spare. He honored those he wanted to honor and disgraced those he wanted to disgrace. 20But when his heart and mind were puffed up with arrogance, he was brought down from his royal throne and stripped of his glory. 21He was driven from human society. He was given the mind of a wild animal, and he lived among the wild donkeys. He ate grass like a cow, and he was drenched with the dew of heaven, until he learned that the Most High God rules over the kingdoms of the world and appoints anyone he desires to rule over them.

22"You are his successor,* O Belshazzar, and you knew all this, yet you have not humbled yourself. 23For you have proudly defied the Lord of heaven and have had these cups from his Temple brought before you. You and your nobles and your wives and concubines have been drinking wine from them while praising gods of silver, gold, bronze, iron, wood, and stone—gods that neither see nor hear nor know anything at all. But you have not honored the God who gives you the breath of life and controls your destiny! 24So God has sent this hand to write this message.

25"This is the message that was written: MENE, MENE, TEKEL, and PARSIN. 26This is what these words mean:

Mene means 'numbered'—God has numbered the days of your reign and has brought it to an end.

27 *Tekel* means 'weighed'—you have been weighed on the balances and have not measured up.

28 *Parsin** means 'divided'—your kingdom has been divided and given to the Medes and Persians."

DO IT NOW 5:25-27

Belshazzar probably thought that his kingdom would last a lot longer than it did. But God ended it that night. God's time of judgment comes for all people. Yet many people believe that they have plenty of time to make things right with God. "I'll do it tomorrow," they say. Know anyone like that? The time to make things right is now. ■

29Then at Belshazzar's command, Daniel was dressed in purple robes, a gold chain was hung around his neck, and he was proclaimed the third highest ruler in the kingdom.

30That very night Belshazzar, the Babylonian* king, was killed.*

31*And Darius the Mede took over the kingdom at the age of sixty-two.

6 DANIEL IN THE LIONS' DEN

1*Darius the Mede decided to divide the kingdom into 120 provinces, and he appointed a high officer to rule over each province. 2The king also chose Daniel and two others as administrators to supervise the high officers

5:22 Aramaic *son.* 5:28 Aramaic *Peres,* the singular of *Parsin.* 5:30a Or *Chaldean.* 5:30b The Persians and Medes conquered Babylon in October 539 B.C. 5:31 Verse 5:31 is numbered 6:1 in Aramaic text. 6:1 Verses 6:1-28 are numbered 6:2-29 in Aramaic text.

and protect the king's interests. [3]Daniel soon proved
himself more capable than all the other administrators
and high officers. Because of Daniel's great ability, the
king made plans to place him over the entire empire.

RESPECT 6:1-3

At this time, Daniel was in his eighties and was one of Darius's top three administrators. Yet Daniel was a cut above all of the other workers. Thus, Daniel earned the king's respect. One of the best ways to influence non-Christian employers is to work hard. Are you gainfully employed? How do you represent God to your employer? ■

[4]Then the other administrators and high officers began searching for some fault in the way Daniel was handling government affairs, but they couldn't find anything
to criticize or condemn. He was faithful, always responsible, and completely trustworthy. [5]So they concluded,
"Our only chance of finding grounds for accusing Daniel
will be in connection with the rules of his religion."
[6]So the administrators and high officers went to the
king and said, "Long live King Darius! [7]We are all in
agreement—we administrators, officials, high officers,
advisers, and governors—that the king should make a law
that will be strictly enforced. Give orders that for the next
thirty days any person who prays to anyone, divine or human—except to you, Your Majesty—will be thrown into
the den of lions. [8]And now, Your Majesty, issue and sign
this law so it cannot be changed, an official law of the
Medes and Persians that cannot be revoked." [9]So King
Darius signed the law.
[10]But when Daniel learned that the law had been
signed, he went home and knelt down as usual in his upstairs room, with its windows open toward Jerusalem. He
prayed three times a day, just as he had always done, giving thanks to his God. [11]Then the officials went together
to Daniel's house and found him praying and asking for
God's help. [12]So they went straight to the king and reminded him about his law. "Did you not sign a law that
for the next thirty days any person who prays to anyone,
divine or human—except to you, Your Majesty—will be
thrown into the den of lions?"
"Yes," the king replied, "that decision stands; it is an official law of the Medes and Persians that cannot be
revoked."
[13]Then they told the king, "That man Daniel, one of the
captives from Judah, is ignoring you and your law. He still
prays to his God three times a day."
[14]Hearing this, the king was deeply troubled, and he
tried to think of a way to save Daniel. He spent the rest of
the day looking for a way to get Daniel out of this
predicament.
[15]In the evening the men went together to the king and
said, "Your Majesty, you know that according to the law of
the Medes and the Persians, no law that the king signs can
be changed."
[16]So at last the king gave orders for Daniel to be
arrested and thrown into the den of lions. The king said
to him, "May your God, whom you serve so faithfully, rescue you."
[17]A stone was brought and placed over the mouth of
the den. The king sealed the stone with his own royal seal
and the seals of his nobles, so that no one could rescue
Daniel. [18]Then the king returned to his palace and spent
the night fasting. He refused his usual entertainment and
couldn't sleep at all that night.
[19]Very early the next morning, the king got up and hurried out to the lions' den. [20]When he got there, he called
out in anguish, "Daniel, servant of the living God! Was
your God, whom you serve so faithfully, able to rescue
you from the lions?"
[21]Daniel answered, "Long live the king! [22]My God sent
his angel to shut the lions' mouths so that they would not
hurt me, for I have been found innocent in his sight. And
I have not wronged you, Your Majesty."
[23]The king was overjoyed and ordered that Daniel be
lifted from the den. Not a scratch was found on him, for
he had trusted in his God.
[24]Then the king gave orders to arrest the men who had
maliciously accused Daniel. He had them thrown into the
lions' den, along with their wives and children. The lions
leaped on them and tore them apart before they even hit
the floor of the den.
[25]Then King Darius sent this message to the people of
every race and nation and language throughout the
world:

Christians are really persecuted at my school. I've even heard some teachers speak critically of Christians. Is there a way to avoid compromising and not be thought of as . . . well . . . a freak?

Jesus once said, "No one can serve two masters" (Matt 6:24). He was talking about God and money. But the same truth—you can only serve one master—applies here.

Sometimes God's desires and those approved by society are as different as night and day. Daniel and his friends understood that. When they were taken to Babylon as teens, they were plunged into a new culture. It was like being in a new school in a new town. Since they were handpicked to work for the king, the temptation to compromise probably was a daily occurrence. Yet they risked their lives to avoid compromising. (See Dan 1, 3, 6.) They valued God more than they valued their reputations or even their lives.

Instead of wondering how you can avoid looking like a "freak" or how you can be accepted by those around you and still be a Christian, why not ask God to give you the courage to please him, no matter what?

"Peace and prosperity to you!

26"I decree that everyone throughout my kingdom
should tremble with fear before the God of Daniel.

For he is the living God,
and he will endure forever.
His kingdom will never be destroyed,
and his rule will never end.
27 He rescues and saves his people;
he performs miraculous signs and wonders
in the heavens and on earth.
He has rescued Daniel
from the power of the lions."

28So Daniel prospered during the reign of Darius and the reign of Cyrus the Persian.*

A FAITHFUL WITNESS 6:25-27

Nebuchadnezzar learned about God through the faithfulness of Daniel and his friends (chaps. 2–3). Here Darius also was convinced of God's power after God rescued his faithful servant. Although Daniel was captive in a strange land, his devotion to God was a testimony to powerful rulers. If you find yourself in new surroundings, are you willing to talk about God's power in your life? ■

7

DANIEL'S VISION OF FOUR BEASTS

Earlier, during the first year of King Belshazzar's reign in Babylon,* Daniel had a dream and saw visions as he lay in his bed. He wrote down the dream, and this is what he saw.

2In my vision that night, I, Daniel, saw a great storm churning the surface of a great sea, with strong winds blowing from every direction. 3Then four huge beasts came up out of the water, each different from the others.

4The first beast was like a lion with eagles' wings. As I watched, its wings were pulled off, and it was left standing with its two hind feet on the ground, like a human being. And it was given a human mind.

5Then I saw a second beast, and it looked like a bear. It was rearing up on one side, and it had three ribs in its mouth between its teeth. And I heard a voice saying to it, "Get up! Devour the flesh of many people!"

6Then the third of these strange beasts appeared, and it looked like a leopard. It had four bird's wings on its back, and it had four heads. Great authority was given to this beast.

7Then in my vision that night, I saw a fourth beast—terrifying, dreadful, and very strong. It devoured and crushed its victims with huge iron teeth and trampled their remains beneath its feet. It was different from any of the other beasts, and it had ten horns.

8As I was looking at the horns, suddenly another small horn appeared among them. Three of the first horns were torn out by the roots to make room for it. This little horn had eyes like human eyes and a mouth that was boasting arrogantly.

9 I watched as thrones were put in place
and the Ancient One* sat down to judge.
His clothing was as white as snow,
his hair like purest wool.
He sat on a fiery throne
with wheels of blazing fire,
10 and a river of fire was pouring out,
flowing from his presence.
Millions of angels ministered to him;
many millions stood to attend him.
Then the court began its session,
and the books were opened.

JUDGMENT DAY 7:9-10

Daniel saw a vision of God judging millions of people as they stood before his throne. Someday, we'll all be judged by God for our actions. If God were to judge your life today, what would he say about it? If the thought of God's judgment is too scary, just think: You can change that right now. Wondering how? Take the keys of your life and hand them over to Jesus. Let him "drive" from now on. Feel better? ■

11I continued to watch because I could hear the little horn's boastful speech. I kept watching until the fourth beast was killed and its body was destroyed by fire. 12The other three beasts had their authority taken from them, but they were allowed to live a while longer.*

13As my vision continued that night, I saw someone like a son of man* coming with the clouds of heaven. He approached the Ancient One and was led into his presence. 14He was given authority, honor, and sovereignty over all the nations of the world, so that people of every race and nation and language would obey him. His rule is eternal—it will never end. His kingdom will never be destroyed.

THE VISION IS EXPLAINED

15I, Daniel, was troubled by all I had seen, and my visions terrified me. 16So I approached one of those standing beside the throne and asked him what it all meant. He explained it to me like this: 17"These four huge beasts represent four kingdoms that will arise from the earth. 18But in the end, the holy people of the Most High will be given the kingdom, and they will rule forever and ever."

19Then I wanted to know the true meaning of the fourth beast, the one so different from the others and so terrifying. It had devoured and crushed its victims with iron teeth and bronze claws, trampling their remains

6:28 Or *of Darius, that is, the reign of Cyrus the Persian.* **7:1** The first year of Belshazzar's reign (who was co-regent with his father, Nabonidus) was 556 B.C. (or perhaps as late as 553 B.C.). **7:9** Aramaic *an Ancient of Days;* also in 7:13, 22. **7:12** Aramaic *for a season and a time.* **7:13** Or *like a Son of Man.*

beneath its feet. 20I also asked about the ten horns on the
fourth beast's head and the little horn that came up afterward and destroyed three of the other horns. This horn
had seemed greater than the others, and it had human
eyes and a mouth that was boasting arrogantly. 21As I
watched, this horn was waging war against God's holy
people and was defeating them, 22until the Ancient
One—the Most High—came and judged in favor of his
holy people. Then the time arrived for the holy people to
take over the kingdom.

A MYSTERY 7:1-15

If you feel as Daniel did about these prophecies—troubled (7:15)—recognize with him that these events have yet to come to pass. Some prophecies are mysteries that God has chosen not to fully reveal at this time. We may or may not know the whole story in this life. Yet there are some mysteries that the Bible describes (how God is three, yet one), which we may never fully understand. Are you content to believe, even if you don't fully understand? ■

23Then he said to me, "This fourth beast is the fourth
world power that will rule the earth. It will be different
from all the others. It will devour the whole world, trampling and crushing everything in its path. 24Its ten horns
are ten kings who will rule that empire. Then another
king will arise, different from the other ten, who will subdue three of them. 25He will defy the Most High and oppress the holy people of the Most High. He will try to
change their sacred festivals and laws, and they will be
placed under his control for a time, times, and half a time.
26"But then the court will pass judgment, and all his
power will be taken away and completely destroyed.
27Then the sovereignty, power, and greatness of all the
kingdoms under heaven will be given to the holy people
of the Most High. His kingdom will last forever, and all
rulers will serve and obey him."
28That was the end of the vision. I, Daniel, was terrified
by my thoughts and my face was pale with fear, but I kept
these things to myself.

8

DANIEL'S VISION OF A RAM AND GOAT

1*During the third year of King Belshazzar's reign, I, Daniel, saw another vision, following the one that had already
appeared to me. 2In this vision I was at the fortress of
Susa, in the province of Elam, standing beside the Ulai
River.*
3As I looked up, I saw a ram with two long horns standing beside the river.* One of the horns was longer than
the other, even though it had grown later than the other
one. 4The ram butted everything out of his way to the
west, to the north, and to the south, and no one could
stand against him or help his victims. He did as he
pleased and became very great.
5While I was watching, suddenly a male goat appeared
from the west, crossing the land so swiftly that he didn't
even touch the ground. This goat, which had one very
large horn between its eyes, 6headed toward the two-
horned ram that I had seen standing beside the river,
rushing at him in a rage. 7The goat charged furiously at
the ram and struck him, breaking off both his horns. Now
the ram was helpless, and the goat knocked him down
and trampled him. No one could rescue the ram from the
goat's power.
8The goat became very powerful. But at the height of
his power, his large horn was broken off. In the large
horn's place grew four prominent horns pointing in the
four directions of the earth. 9Then from one of the prominent horns came a small horn whose power grew very
great. It extended toward the south and the east and toward the glorious land of Israel. 10Its power reached to
the heavens, where it attacked the heavenly army, throwing some of the heavenly beings and some of the stars to
the ground and trampling them. 11It even challenged the
Commander of heaven's army by canceling the daily
sacrifices offered to him and by destroying his Temple.
12The army of heaven was restrained from responding
to this rebellion. So the daily sacrifice was halted, and
truth was overthrown. The horn succeeded in everything it did.*
13Then I heard two holy ones talking to each other.
One of them asked, "How long will the events of this vision last? How long will the rebellion that causes desecration stop the daily sacrifices? How long will the Temple
and heaven's army be trampled on?"
14The other replied, "It will take 2,300 evenings
and mornings; then the Temple will be made right
again."

GABRIEL EXPLAINS THE VISION

15As I, Daniel, was trying to understand the meaning of
this vision, someone who looked like a man stood in front
of me. 16And I heard a human voice calling out from the
Ulai River, "Gabriel, tell this man the meaning of his
vision."
17As Gabriel approached the place where I was standing, I became so terrified that I fell with my face to the
ground. "Son of man," he said, "you must understand that
the events you have seen in your vision relate to the time
of the end."
18While he was speaking, I fainted and lay there with
my face to the ground. But Gabriel roused me with a
touch and helped me to my feet.
19Then he said, "I am here to tell you what will happen
later in the time of wrath. What you have seen pertains to
the very end of time. 20The two-horned ram represents
the kings of Media and Persia. 21The shaggy male goat
represents the king of Greece,* and the large horn between his eyes represents the first king of the Greek Empire. 22The four prominent horns that replaced the one
large horn show that the Greek Empire will break into
four kingdoms, but none as great as the first.

8:1 The original text from this point through chapter 12 is in Hebrew. See note at 2:4. 8:2 Or *the Ulai Gate;* also in 8:16. 8:3 Or *the gate;* also in 8:6. 8:11-12 The meaning of the Hebrew for these verses is uncertain. 8:21 Hebrew *of Javan.*

23“At the end of their rule, when their sin is at its
height, a fierce king, a master of intrigue, will rise to
power. 24He will become very strong, but not by his own
power. He will cause a shocking amount of destruction
and succeed in everything he does. He will destroy powerful leaders and devastate the holy people. 25He will be a
master of deception and will become arrogant; he will
destroy many without warning. He will even take on the
Prince of princes in battle, but he will be broken, though
not by human power.

INVINCIBLE 8:23-25

Daniel saw a vision of a battle between the “Prince of princes” (God) and “a master of intrigue.” The master of intrigue was a seemingly invincible human ruler whom God defeated long after Daniel’s death. Only God can truly be called invincible. Does this invincible God—the God who can defeat even the greatest evil—have your trust? ■

26“This vision about the 2,300 evenings and mornings* is true. But none of these things will happen for a
long time, so keep this vision a secret.”
27Then I, Daniel, was overcome and lay sick for several
days. Afterward I got up and performed my duties for the
king, but I was greatly troubled by the vision and could
not understand it.

9 DANIEL’S PRAYER FOR HIS PEOPLE

It was the first year of the reign of Darius the Mede, the
son of Ahasuerus, who became king of the Babylonians.*
2During the first year of his reign, I, Daniel, learned from
reading the word of the LORD, as revealed to Jeremiah the
prophet, that Jerusalem must lie desolate for seventy
years.* 3So I turned to the LORD God and pleaded with
him in prayer and fasting. I also wore rough burlap and
sprinkled myself with ashes.
4I prayed to the LORD my God and confessed:

“O Lord, you are a great and awesome God! You
always fulfill your covenant and keep your promises
of unfailing love to those who love you and obey your
commands. 5But we have sinned and done wrong.
We have rebelled against you and scorned your
commands and regulations. 6We have refused to
listen to your servants the prophets, who spoke on
your authority to our kings and princes and ancestors
and to all the people of the land.
7“Lord, you are in the right; but as you see, our
faces are covered with shame. This is true of all of us,
including the people of Judah and Jerusalem and all
Israel, scattered near and far, wherever you have
driven us because of our disloyalty to you. 8O LORD,
we and our kings, princes, and ancestors are covered
with shame because we have sinned against you. 9But
the Lord our God is merciful and forgiving, even
though we have rebelled against him. 10We have not
obeyed the LORD our God, for we have not followed
the instructions he gave us through his servants the
prophets. 11All Israel has disobeyed your instruction
and turned away, refusing to listen to your voice.
“So now the solemn curses and judgments written
in the Law of Moses, the servant of God, have been
poured down on us because of our sin. 12You have
kept your word and done to us and our rulers exactly
as you warned. Never has there been such a disaster
as happened in Jerusalem. 13Every curse written
against us in the Law of Moses has come true. Yet we
have refused to seek mercy from the LORD our God
by turning from our sins and recognizing his truth.
14Therefore, the LORD has brought upon us the
disaster he prepared. The LORD our God was right
to do all of these things, for we did not obey him.
15“O Lord our God, you brought lasting honor to
your name by rescuing your people from Egypt in
a great display of power. But we have sinned and
are full of wickedness. 16In view of all your faithful
mercies, Lord, please turn your furious anger away
from your city Jerusalem, your holy mountain. All the
neighboring nations mock Jerusalem and your people
because of our sins and the sins of our ancestors.
17“O our God, hear your servant’s prayer! Listen as
I plead. For your own sake, Lord, smile again on your
desolate sanctuary.
18“O my God, lean down and listen to me. Open
your eyes and see our despair. See how your city—the
city that bears your name—lies in ruins. We make
this plea, not because we deserve help, but because of
your mercy.
19“O Lord, hear. O Lord, forgive. O Lord, listen and
act! For your own sake, do not delay, O my God, for
your people and your city bear your name.”

GOD-CENTERED PRAYER 9:1-19

Daniel prayed, fasted, confessed his sins, and pleaded that God would reveal his will. His openness and faith that God would answer pleased God. Most of us, if we were honest, would admit that our prayers are more of a laundry list than communication that honors God. When you pray, how open are you to honoring God and seeing his will done? Daniel’s prayer can inspire you to make your communication God-centered rather than you-centered. ■

GABRIEL’S MESSAGE ABOUT THE ANOINTED ONE

20I went on praying and confessing my sin and the sin of
my people, pleading with the LORD my God for Jerusalem,
his holy mountain. 21As I was praying, Gabriel, whom I
had seen in the earlier vision, came swiftly to me at the
time of the evening sacrifice. 22He explained to me, “Daniel, I have come here to give you insight and understanding. 23The moment you began praying, a command

8:26 Hebrew *about the evenings and mornings;* compare 8:14. 9:1 Or *the Chaldeans.* 9:2 See Jer 25:11-12; 29:10.

was given. And now I am here to tell you what it was, for
you are very precious to God. Listen carefully so that you
can understand the meaning of your vision.
24"A period of seventy sets of seven* has been decreed
for your people and your holy city to finish their rebellion, to put an end to their sin, to atone for their guilt, to
bring in everlasting righteousness, to confirm the prophetic vision, and to anoint the Most Holy Place.* 25Now
listen and understand! Seven sets of seven plus sixty-two
sets of seven* will pass from the time the command is
given to rebuild Jerusalem until a ruler—the Anointed
One*—comes. Jerusalem will be rebuilt with streets and
strong defenses,* despite the perilous times.
26"After this period of sixty-two sets of seven,* the
Anointed One will be killed, appearing to have accomplished nothing, and a ruler will arise whose armies will
destroy the city and the Temple. The end will come with
a flood, and war and its miseries are decreed from that
time to the very end. 27The ruler will make a treaty with
the people for a period of one set of seven,* but after
half this time, he will put an end to the sacrifices and offerings. And as a climax to all his terrible deeds,* he will
set up a sacrilegious object that causes desecration,*
until the fate decreed for this defiler is finally poured
out on him."

10 DANIEL'S VISION OF A MESSENGER

In the third year of the reign of King Cyrus of Persia,*
Daniel (also known as Belteshazzar) had another vision.
He understood that the vision concerned events certain
to happen in the future—times of war and great hardship.
2When this vision came to me, I, Daniel, had been in
mourning for three whole weeks. 3All that time I had
eaten no rich food. No meat or wine crossed my lips, and I
used no fragrant lotions until those three weeks had
passed.
4On April 23,* as I was standing on the bank of the
great Tigris River, 5I looked up and saw a man dressed in
linen clothing, with a belt of pure gold around his waist.
6His body looked like a precious gem. His face flashed
like lightning, and his eyes flamed like torches. His arms
and feet shone like polished bronze, and his voice roared
like a vast multitude of people.
7Only I, Daniel, saw this vision. The men with me saw
nothing, but they were suddenly terrified and ran away to
hide. 8So I was left there all alone to see this amazing vision. My strength left me, my face grew deathly pale, and
I felt very weak. 9Then I heard the man speak, and when I
heard the sound of his voice, I fainted and lay there with
my face to the ground.
10Just then a hand touched me and lifted me, still trembling, to my hands and knees. 11And the man said to me,
"Daniel, you are very precious to God, so listen carefully
to what I have to say to you. Stand up, for I have been sent
to you." When he said this to me, I stood up, still
trembling.
12Then he said, "Don't be afraid, Daniel. Since the
first day you began to pray for understanding and to
humble yourself before your God, your request has
been heard in heaven. I have come in answer to your
prayer. 13But for twenty-one days the spirit prince* of
the kingdom of Persia blocked my way. Then Michael,
one of the archangels,* came to help me, and I left him
there with the spirit prince of the kingdom of Persia.*
14Now I am here to explain what will happen to your
people in the future, for this vision concerns a time yet
to come."
15While he was speaking to me, I looked down at the
ground, unable to say a word. 16Then the one who looked
like a man* touched my lips, and I opened my mouth and
began to speak. I said to the one standing in front of me,
"I am filled with anguish because of the vision I have
seen, my lord, and I am very weak. 17How can someone
like me, your servant, talk to you, my lord? My strength is
gone, and I can hardly breathe."
18Then the one who looked like a man touched me
again, and I felt my strength returning. 19"Don't be
afraid," he said, "for you are very precious to God. Peace!
Be encouraged! Be strong!"
As he spoke these words to me, I suddenly felt stronger
and said to him, "Please speak to me, my lord, for you
have strengthened me."

HIS STRENGTH 10:10-19

Daniel was frightened by this vision, but the messenger's hand calmed his fears; Daniel felt weak, but the messenger's words strengthened him. God can heal us when we are hurt, provide peace when we are troubled, and strengthen us when we are weak. All we have to do is ask. ■

20He replied, "Do you know why I have come? Soon I
must return to fight against the spirit prince of the kingdom of Persia, and after that the spirit prince of the kingdom of Greece* will come. 21Meanwhile, I will tell you
what is written in the Book of Truth. (No one helps me
against these spirit princes except Michael, your spirit
prince.* 11:1I have been standing beside Michael* to support and strengthen him since the first year of the reign
of Darius the Mede.)

9:24a Hebrew *seventy sevens.* **9:24b** Or *the Most Holy One.* **9:25a** Hebrew *Seven sevens plus sixty-two sevens.* **9:25b** Or *an anointed one;* similarly in 9:26. Hebrew reads *a messiah.* **9:25c** Or *and a moat,* or *and trenches.* **9:26** Hebrew *After sixty-two sevens.* **9:27a** Hebrew *for one seven.* **9:27b** Hebrew *And on the wing of abominations;* the meaning of the Hebrew is uncertain. **9:27c** Hebrew *an abomination of desolation.* **10:1** The third year of Cyrus's reign was 536 B.C. **10:4** Hebrew *On the twenty-fourth day of the first month,* of the ancient Hebrew lunar calendar. This date in the book of Daniel can be cross-checked with dates in surviving Persian records and can be related accurately to our modern calendar. This event occurred on April 23, 536 B.C. **10:13a** Hebrew *the prince;* also in 10:13c, 20. **10:13b** Hebrew *the chief princes.* **10:13c** As in one Greek version; Hebrew reads *and I was left there with the kings of Persia.* The meaning of the Hebrew is uncertain. **10:16** As in most manuscripts of the Masoretic Text; one manuscript of the Masoretic Text and one Greek version read *Then something that looked like a human hand.* **10:20** Hebrew *of Javan.* **10:21** Hebrew *against these except Michael, your prince.* **11:1** Hebrew *him.*

11 KINGS OF THE SOUTH AND NORTH

2"Now then, I will reveal the truth to you. Three more Persian kings will reign, to be succeeded by a fourth, far
richer than the others. He will use his wealth to stir up
everyone to fight against the kingdom of Greece.*
3"Then a mighty king will rise to power who will rule
with great authority and accomplish everything he sets
out to do. 4But at the height of his power, his kingdom
will be broken apart and divided into four parts. It will
not be ruled by the king's descendants, nor will the kingdom hold the authority it once had. For his empire will be
uprooted and given to others.
5"The king of the south will increase in power, but one
of his own officials will become more powerful than he
and will rule his kingdom with great strength.
6"Some years later an alliance will be formed between
the king of the north and the king of the south. The
daughter of the king of the south will be given in marriage
to the king of the north to secure the alliance, but she will
lose her influence over him, and so will her father. She
will be abandoned along with her supporters. 7But when
one of her relatives* becomes king of the south, he will
raise an army and enter the fortress of the king of the
north and defeat him. 8When he returns to Egypt, he will
carry back their idols with him, along with priceless articles of gold and silver. For some years afterward he will
leave the king of the north alone.
9"Later the king of the north will invade the realm of
the king of the south but will soon return to his own land.
10However, the sons of the king of the north will assemble a mighty army that will advance like a flood and carry
the battle as far as the enemy's fortress.
11"Then, in a rage, the king of the south will rally
against the vast forces assembled by the king of the north
and will defeat them. 12After the enemy army is swept
away, the king of the south will be filled with pride and
will execute many thousands of his enemies. But his success will be short lived.
13"A few years later the king of the north will return
with a fully equipped army far greater than before. 14At
that time there will be a general uprising against the king
of the south. Violent men among your own people will
join them in fulfillment of this vision, but they will not
succeed. 15Then the king of the north will come and lay
siege to a fortified city and capture it. The best troops of
the south will not be able to stand in the face of the
onslaught.
16"The king of the north will march onward unop-
posed; none will be able to stop him. He will pause in the
glorious land of Israel,* intent on destroying it. 17He will
make plans to come with the might of his entire kingdom
and will form an alliance with the king of the south. He
will give him a daughter in marriage in order to overthrow the kingdom from within, but his plan will fail.
18"After this, he will turn his attention to the coastland
and conquer many cities. But a commander from
another land will put an end to his insolence and cause
him to retreat in shame. 19He will take refuge in his own
fortresses but will stumble and fall and be seen no more.
20"His successor will send out a tax collector to maintain the royal splendor. But after a very brief reign, he will
die, though not from anger or in battle.
21"The next to come to power will be a despicable man
who is not in line for royal succession. He will slip in
when least expected and take over the kingdom by flattery and intrigue. 22Before him great armies will be swept
away, including a covenant prince. 23With deceitful
promises, he will make various alliances. He will become
strong despite having only a handful of followers.
24Without warning he will enter the richest areas of the
land. Then he will distribute among his followers the
plunder and wealth of the rich—something his predecessors had never done. He will plot the overthrow of
strongholds, but this will last for only a short while.
25"Then he will stir up his courage and raise a great
army against the king of the south. The king of the south
will go to battle with a mighty army, but to no avail, for
there will be plots against him. 26His own household will
cause his downfall. His army will be swept away, and
many will be killed. 27Seeking nothing but each other's
harm, these kings will plot against each other at the conference table, attempting to deceive each other. But it
will make no difference, for the end will come at the appointed time.
28"The king of the north will then return home with
great riches. On the way he will set himself against the
people of the holy covenant, doing much damage before
continuing his journey.
29"Then at the appointed time he will once again invade the south, but this time the result will be different.
30For warships from western coastlands* will scare him
off, and he will withdraw and return home. But he will
vent his anger against the people of the holy covenant
and reward those who forsake the covenant.

GET READY 11:33-35

Trying times remind us of our weaknesses and inability to cope. We reach out for answers, for leadership, for clear direction. God's Word begins to interest even those who, in better times, would never look at it. We who are believers can prepare ourselves for the opportunities God provides to share God's Word in needy times. We also can prepare ourselves for persecution and rejection as we teach God's Word. Are you prepared? ■

31"His army will take over the Temple fortress, pollute
the sanctuary, put a stop to the daily sacrifices, and set up
the sacrilegious object that causes desecration.* 32He will
flatter and win over those who have violated the covenant. But the people who know their God will be strong
and will resist him.

11:2 Hebrew *of Javan.* **11:7** Hebrew *a branch from her roots.* **11:16** Hebrew *the glorious land.* **11:30** Hebrew *from Kittim.*
11:31 Hebrew *the abomination of desolation.*

33“Wise leaders will give instruction to many, but these teachers will die by fire and sword, or they will be jailed and robbed. 34During these persecutions, little help will arrive, and many who join them will not be sincere. 35And some of the wise will fall victim to persecution. In this way, they will be refined and cleansed and made pure until the time of the end, for the appointed time is still to come.

36“The king will do as he pleases, exalting himself and claiming to be greater than every god, even blaspheming the God of gods. He will succeed, but only until the time of wrath is completed. For what has been determined will surely take place. 37He will have no respect for the gods of his ancestors, or for the god loved by women, or for any other god, for he will boast that he is greater than them all. 38Instead of these, he will worship the god of fortresses—a god his ancestors never knew—and lavish on him gold, silver, precious stones, and expensive gifts. 39Claiming this foreign god's help, he will attack the strongest fortresses. He will honor those who submit to him, appointing them to positions of authority and dividing the land among them as their reward.*

40“Then at the time of the end, the king of the south will attack the king of the north. The king of the north will storm out with chariots, charioteers, and a vast navy. He will invade various lands and sweep through them like a flood. 41He will enter the glorious land of Israel,* and many nations will fall, but Moab, Edom, and the best part of Ammon will escape. 42He will conquer many countries, and even Egypt will not escape. 43He will gain control over the gold, silver, and treasures of Egypt, and the Libyans and Ethiopians* will be his servants.

44“But then news from the east and the north will alarm him, and he will set out in great anger to destroy and obliterate many. 45He will stop between the glorious holy mountain and the sea and will pitch his royal tents. But while he is there, his time will suddenly run out, and no one will help him.

12 THE TIME OF THE END

“At that time Michael, the archangel* who stands guard over your nation, will arise. Then there will be a time of anguish greater than any since nations first came into existence. But at that time every one of your people whose name is written in the book will be rescued. 2Many of those whose bodies lie dead and buried will rise up, some to everlasting life and some to shame and everlasting disgrace. 3Those who are wise will shine as bright as the sky, and those who lead many to righteousness will shine like the stars forever. 4But you, Daniel, keep this prophecy a secret; seal up the book until the time of the end, when many will rush here and there, and knowledge will increase.”

5Then I, Daniel, looked and saw two others standing on opposite banks of the river. 6One of them asked the man dressed in linen, who was now standing above the river, “How long will it be until these shocking events are over?”

7The man dressed in linen, who was standing above the river, raised both his hands toward heaven and took a solemn oath by the One who lives forever, saying, “It will go on for a time, times, and half a time. When the shattering of the holy people has finally come to an end, all these things will have happened.”

8I heard what he said, but I did not understand what he meant. So I asked, “How will all this finally end, my lord?”

9But he said, “Go now, Daniel, for what I have said is kept secret and sealed until the time of the end. 10Many will be purified, cleansed, and refined by these trials. But the wicked will continue in their wickedness, and none of them will understand. Only those who are wise will know what it means.

11“From the time the daily sacrifice is stopped and the sacrilegious object that causes desecration* is set up to be worshiped, there will be 1,290 days. 12And blessed are those who wait and remain until the end of the 1,335 days!

> Those who are wise will shine as bright as the sky, and those who lead many to righteousness will shine like the stars forever.
>
> *DANIEL 12:3*

A LEGACY OF FAITHFULNESS 12:13

Daniel stands tall in the gallery of God's remarkable servants. He was born of royal heritage and taken into captivity when young. Despite all this, Daniel remained faithful to God in the land of his captivity. God chose Daniel to record events of his life and significant events concerning the future. As an old man, having always been faithful to God, Daniel was assured by God that he would be resurrected from the dead and receive his portion in God's eternal kingdom.

Consider your own “spiritual resume.” How are you adding to your legacy of faithfulness? Faithfulness to God has a rich reward, not necessarily in this life, but most certainly in the life to come. ■

13“As for you, go your way until the end. You will rest, and then at the end of the days, you will rise again to receive the inheritance set aside for you.”

11:39 Or *at a price.* **11:41** Hebrew *the glorious land.* **11:43** Hebrew *Cushites.* **12:1** Hebrew *the great prince.* **12:11** Hebrew *the abomination of desolation.*

"OH," SHE WHISPERED. "I love you, too!" Together the reunited lovers rode off into the sunset.

Isn't love wonderful? We've grown up believing love is a cure-all; someday we'll meet "Mr. Right" or "Miss Perfect." He or she will be totally hot of course. He or she also will be free of emotional baggage. Is that your dream of love?

Hosea is a book about love, but with an unusual twist. Hosea was a prophet who was told to marry Gomer. But far from being "Miss Perfect," Gomer was a prostitute. In fact, after they were married, she was unfaithful to Hosea. But God told him to marry her anyway, knowing that she would be unfaithful.

The book of Hosea is a love story: Hosea and Gomer's and also that of God and his people, who were unfaithful like Gomer.

As you read this story, you'll learn a lot about God and what he expects of his followers. But look for yourself in the story, too. Are you like Hosea? Gomer? Israel?

hosea

timeline

793 B.C.
Jeroboam II becomes king of Israel

760
Amos becomes a prophet

753
Hosea becomes a prophet; King Zechariah of Israel is killed

752
King Shallum of Israel is killed

743
Tiglath-pileser III invades Israel

742
Micah becomes a prophet to Judah

740
Isaiah becomes a prophet to Judah

722
Israel (northern kingdom) falls

715
Hosea's ministry ends

stats

PURPOSE: To illustrate God's love for his sinful people

AUTHOR: Hosea, son of Beeri ("Hosea" means "salvation.")

TO WHOM WRITTEN: Israel (the northern kingdom) and God's people everywhere

DATE WRITTEN: Approximately 715 B.C., recording events from about 753 to 715 B.C.

SETTING: Hosea began his ministry during the end of the prosperous but morally declining reign of Jeroboam II of Israel. (The rich prospered by oppressing the poor.) Hosea prophesied until shortly after the fall of Samaria in 722 B.C.

KEY PEOPLE: Hosea, Gomer, their three children

KEY PLACES: The northern kingdom (Israel), Samaria, Ephraim

SPECIAL FEATURES: Hosea employs many images from daily life. God is depicted as a husband, father, lion, leopard, she-bear, dew, rain, moth, and others. Israel is pictured as a wife, sick person, grapevine, grapes, early fig, olive tree, woman in labor, oven, morning mist, chaff, and smoke, to name a few.

KEY points

A NATION'S SIN
Just as Hosea's wife, Gomer, was unfaithful to him, so the nation of Israel had been spiritually unfaithful to God. The temptations in this world (power, popularity, pleasure, or money) can lure us toward spiritual unfaithfulness. God wants his people to remain faithful to him.

GOD'S JUDGMENT
Because Judah turned away from God, the nation experienced a devastating invasion and exile. Wrong actions still result in terrible consequences. Some may not happen right away.

GOD'S LOVE
Just as Hosea went after his unfaithful wife to bring her back, so God pursues us with his unchanging and undying love.

RESTORATION
God encouraged and restored those who repented. There's forgiveness and restoration for all who turn back to God.

1

1 The LORD gave this message to Hosea son of Beeri
during the years when Uzziah, Jotham, Ahaz, and Hezekiah were kings of Judah, and Jeroboam son of Jehoash*
was king of Israel.

HOSEA'S WIFE AND CHILDREN

2 When the LORD first began speaking to Israel through
Hosea, he said to him, "Go and marry a prostitute,* so that
some of her children will be conceived in prostitution.
This will illustrate how Israel has acted like a prostitute
by turning against the LORD and worshiping other gods."
3 So Hosea married Gomer, the daughter of Diblaim,
and she became pregnant and gave Hosea a son. 4 And the
LORD said, "Name the child Jezreel, for I am about to punish King Jehu's dynasty to avenge the murders he committed at Jezreel. In fact, I will bring an end to Israel's
independence. 5 I will break its military power in the Jezreel Valley."

A DIFFICULT TASK 1:1-3

It's hard to imagine Hosea's feelings when God told him to marry a woman who would be unfaithful to him. Although such a marriage was far from ideal, Hosea still obeyed. Other prophets like Jeremiah and Ezekiel also faced some difficult tasks. If God asks you to do something difficult, how will you respond? Will you obey him, trusting that he who knows everything has a special purpose for his request? Will you be satisfied with the knowledge that the pain involved in obedience may benefit those you serve, and not you personally? ■

6 Soon Gomer became pregnant again and gave birth to
a daughter. And the LORD said to Hosea, "Name your
daughter Lo-ruhamah—'Not loved'—for I will no longer
show love to the people of Israel or forgive them. 7 But I
will show love to the people of Judah. I will free them
from their enemies—not with weapons and armies or
horses and charioteers, but by my power as the LORD
their God."
8 After Gomer had weaned Lo-ruhamah, she again became pregnant and gave birth to a second son. 9 And the
LORD said, "Name him Lo-ammi—'Not my people'—for
Israel is not my people, and I am not their God.
10 *"Yet the time will come when Israel's people will be
like the sands of the seashore—too many to count! Then, at
the place where they were told, 'You are not my people,' it
will be said, 'You are children of the living God.' 11 Then the
people of Judah and Israel will unite together. They will
choose one leader for themselves, and they will return
from exile together. What a day that will be—the day of Jezreel*—when God will again plant his people in his land.
2:1 *"In that day you will call your brothers Ammi—'My
people.' And you will call your sisters Ruhamah—'The
ones I love.'

2

CHARGES AGAINST AN UNFAITHFUL WIFE

2 "But now bring charges against Israel—
your mother—
for she is no longer my wife,
and I am no longer her husband.
Tell her to remove the prostitute's makeup from
her face
and the clothing that exposes her breasts.
3 Otherwise, I will strip her as naked
as she was on the day she was born.
I will leave her to die of thirst,
as in a dry and barren wilderness.
4 And I will not love her children,
for they were conceived in prostitution.
5 Their mother is a shameless prostitute
and became pregnant in a shameful way.
She said, 'I'll run after other lovers
and sell myself to them for food and water,
for clothing of wool and linen,
and for olive oil and drinks.'
6 "For this reason I will fence her in with thornbushes.
I will block her path with a wall
to make her lose her way.
7 When she runs after her lovers,
she won't be able to catch them.
She will search for them
but not find them.
Then she will think,
'I might as well return to my husband,
for I was better off with him than I am now.'
8 She doesn't realize it was I who gave her
everything she has—
the grain, the new wine, the olive oil;
I even gave her silver and gold.
But she gave all my gifts to Baal.

SIGNS OF SUCCESS 2:8

Material possessions are signs of success in most societies. Although Israel was a wealthy nation at this time, the people didn't recognize God as the Giver of blessings. They used their possessions irresponsibly as they worshiped other gods. How do you use your possessions? How could you honor God with your resources? ■

9 "But now I will take back the ripened grain
and new wine
I generously provided each harvest season.
I will take away the wool and linen clothing
I gave her to cover her nakedness.
10 I will strip her naked in public,
while all her lovers look on.
No one will be able
to rescue her from my hands.

1:1 Hebrew *Joash,* a variant spelling of Jehoash. 1:2 Or *a promiscuous woman.* 1:10 Verses 1:10-11 are numbered 2:1-2 in Hebrew text.
1:11 *Jezreel* means "God plants." 2:1 Verses 2:1-23 are numbered 2:3-25 in Hebrew text.

ADULTERY

Marianna still can't believe the news. Her mom has decided to leave their family to live with someone she claims to have fallen in love with. One day she seemed fine. On the next—boom! She's packing and telling their family that she can no longer live a lie.

A lie?* Marianna wonders. *Was her marriage to Dad a lie? . . . I still don't believe it. I think there must be some mistake.

Yet, there are the suitcases by the door. Her father had asked—demanded, actually—that Marianna's mom leave. Not that she was reluctant to do so . . .

"You can come with me if you like," her mom says. But her words are like a knife through Marianna's heart. She doesn't want her mom to go. But she doesn't want to leave her dad either—or her friends.

Can you imagine how Marianna feels as the awfulness of adultery plays out in her life? But how many Christians are guilty of spiritual adultery? We claim to belong to God while we flirt with the world and spend most of our time in other pursuits. Imagine how rejected God must feel!

Don't just imagine it. Read the startling book of Hosea for an intimate look at how unfaithfulness hurts God's heart. Chapter 2 is especially expressive as it depicts God as a wounded lover who desperately wants his people to return to him.

11 I will put an end to her annual festivals,
her new moon celebrations, and her
Sabbath days—
all her appointed festivals.
12 I will destroy her grapevines and fig trees,
things she claims her lovers gave her.
I will let them grow into tangled thickets,
where only wild animals will eat the fruit.
13 I will punish her for all those times
when she burned incense to her images of Baal,
when she put on her earrings and jewels
and went out to look for her lovers
but forgot all about me,"
says the LORD.

THE LORD'S LOVE FOR UNFAITHFUL ISRAEL

14 "But then I will win her back once again.
I will lead her into the desert
and speak tenderly to her there.
15 I will return her vineyards to her
and transform the Valley of Trouble* into
a gateway of hope.
She will give herself to me there,
as she did long ago when she was young,
when I freed her from her captivity in Egypt.
16 When that day comes," says the LORD,
"you will call me 'my husband'
instead of 'my master.'*
17 O Israel, I will wipe the many names of Baal
from your lips,
and you will never mention them again.
18 On that day I will make a covenant
with all the wild animals and the birds
of the sky
and the animals that scurry along the ground
so they will not harm you.
I will remove all weapons of war from the land,
all swords and bows,
so you can live unafraid
in peace and safety.
19 I will make you my wife forever,
showing you righteousness and justice,
unfailing love and compassion.
20 I will be faithful to you and make you mine,
and you will finally know me as the LORD.

21 "In that day, I will answer,"
says the LORD.
"I will answer the sky as it pleads for clouds.
And the sky will answer the earth with rain.
22 Then the earth will answer the thirsty cries
of the grain, the grapevines, and the
olive trees.
And they in turn will answer,
'Jezreel'—'God plants!'
23 At that time I will plant a crop of Israelites
and raise them for myself.
I will show love
to those I called 'Not loved.'*
And to those I called 'Not my people,'*
I will say, 'Now you are my people.'
And they will reply, 'You are our God!'"

ABSENT AND ISOLATED 3:1-5

After this passage, Gomer is no longer mentioned by Hosea. Gomer's absence and isolation are signs of how God will deal with the constantly rebellious northern kingdom (5:6-15). The consequences of rebellion can be high. If God were ever to withdraw his love and mercy, we would be without hope. Is any act of rebellion worth that? ■

3 HOSEA'S WIFE IS REDEEMED

Then the LORD said to me, "Go and love your wife again, even though she* commits adultery with another lover. This will illustrate that the LORD still loves Israel, even though the people have turned to other gods and love to worship them.*"
2So I bought her back for fifteen pieces of silver* and

2:15 Hebrew *valley of Achor.* 2:16 Hebrew *'my baal.'* 2:23a Hebrew *Lo-ruhamah;* see 1:6. 2:23b Hebrew *Lo-ammi;* see 1:9. 3:1a Or *Go and love a woman who.* 3:1b Hebrew *love their raisin cakes.* 3:2a Hebrew *15 shekels of silver,* about 6 ounces or 171 grams in weight.

Hosea

Served as a prophet to Israel (the northern kingdom) from 753 to 715 B.C. *Climate of the times*	Israel's last six kings were especially wicked; they promoted heavy taxes, oppression of the poor, idol worship, and total disregard for God. Israel was subjected to Assyria and was forced to pay tribute, which robbed its few remaining resources.
Main message	The people of Israel had sinned against God as an adulterous woman sins against her husband. They were sure to be judged for living in total disregard for God and fellow humans. Hosea saw the nation fail to Assyria in 722 B.C.
Importance of message	When we sin, we sever our relationship with God, which breaks our commitment to him. While all must answer to God for their sins, those who seek God's forgiveness are spared eternal judgment.
Contemporary prophets	Jonah (793–753) Amos (760–750) Micah (742–687) Isaiah (740–681)

five bushels of barley and a measure of wine.* 3Then I
said to her, "You must live in my house for many days and
stop your prostitution. During this time, you will not have
sexual relations with anyone, not even with me.*"
4This shows that Israel will go a long time without a
king or prince, and without sacrifices, sacred pillars,
priests,* or even idols! 5But afterward the people will return and devote themselves to the LORD their God and to
David's descendant, their king.* In the last days, they will
tremble in awe of the LORD and of his goodness.

4

THE LORD'S CASE AGAINST ISRAEL

1 Hear the word of the LORD, O people of Israel!
The LORD has brought charges against you, saying:
"There is no faithfulness, no kindness,
no knowledge of God in your land.
2 You make vows and break them;
you kill and steal and commit adultery.
There is violence everywhere—
one murder after another.
3 That is why your land is in mourning,
and everyone is wasting away.
Even the wild animals, the birds of the sky,
and the fish of the sea are disappearing.

4 "Don't point your finger at someone else
and try to pass the blame!
My complaint, you priests,
is with you.*
5 So you will stumble in broad daylight,
and your false prophets will fall with you
in the night.
And I will destroy Israel, your mother.
6 My people are being destroyed
because they don't know me.
Since you priests refuse to know me,
I refuse to recognize you as my priests.
Since you have forgotten the laws of your God,
I will forget to bless your children.
7 The more priests there are,
the more they sin against me.
They have exchanged the glory of God
for the shame of idols.*

8 "When the people bring their sin offerings, the
priests get fed.
So the priests are glad when the people sin!
9 'And what the priests do, the people also do.'
So now I will punish both priests and people
for their wicked deeds.

3:2b As in Greek version, which reads *a homer of barley and a measure of wine;* Hebrew reads *a homer* [5 bushels or 182 liters] *of barley and a lethech* [2.5 bushels or 91 liters] *of barley.* 3:3 Or *and I will live with you.* 3:4 Hebrew *ephod,* the vest worn by the priest. 3:5 Hebrew *to David their king.* 4:4 Hebrew *Your people are like those with a complaint against the priests.* 4:7 As in Syriac version and an ancient Hebrew tradition; Masoretic Text reads *I will turn their glory into shame.*

10 They will eat and still be hungry.
They will play the prostitute and gain nothing from it,
for they have deserted the LORD
11 to worship other gods.

"Wine has robbed my people
of their understanding.
12 They ask a piece of wood for advice!
They think a stick can tell them the future!
Longing after idols
has made them foolish.
They have played the prostitute,
serving other gods and deserting their God.
13 They offer sacrifices to idols on the mountaintops.
They go up into the hills to burn incense
in the pleasant shade of oaks, poplars, and terebinth trees.

"That is why your daughters turn to prostitution,
and your daughters-in-law commit adultery.
14 But why should I punish them
for their prostitution and adultery?
For your men are doing the same thing,
sinning with whores and shrine prostitutes.
O foolish people! You refuse to understand,
so you will be destroyed.

15 "Though you, Israel, are a prostitute,
may Judah avoid such guilt.
Do not join the false worship at Gilgal or Beth-aven,*
even though they take oaths there in the LORD's name.
16 Israel is stubborn,
like a stubborn heifer.
So should the LORD feed her
like a lamb in a lush pasture?
17 Leave Israel* alone,
because she is married to idolatry.
18 When the rulers of Israel finish their drinking,
off they go to find some prostitutes.
They love shame more than honor.*
19 So a mighty wind will sweep them away.
Their sacrifices to idols will bring them shame.

5 THE FAILURE OF ISRAEL'S LEADERS

1 "Hear this, you priests.
Pay attention, you leaders of Israel.
Listen, you members of the royal family.
Judgment has been handed down against you.
For you have led the people into a snare
by worshiping the idols at Mizpah and Tabor.
2 You have dug a deep pit to trap them at Acacia Grove.*
But I will settle with you for what you have done.
3 I know what you are like, O Ephraim.
You cannot hide yourself from me, O Israel.
You have left me as a prostitute leaves her husband;
you are utterly defiled.
4 Your deeds won't let you return to your God.
You are a prostitute through and through,
and you do not know the LORD.

A DIET OF DISOBEDIENCE 5:4

Hosea confronted the leaders of Israel about their habit of wrongdoing. Their actions kept them from returning to God. A constant diet of disobedience hardens a person's heart and builds a solid path away from God. Each sin makes the next one easier to commit. But even this hard habit can begin to be broken by just three words, "Help me, God." Know anyone who needs to say those words? Do you need to say them? ■

5 "The arrogance of Israel testifies against her;
Israel and Ephraim will stumble under their load of guilt.
Judah, too, will fall with them.
6 When they come with their flocks and herds
to offer sacrifices to the LORD,
they will not find him,
because he has withdrawn from them.
7 They have betrayed the honor of the LORD,
bearing children that are not his.
Now their false religion will devour them
along with their wealth.*

8 "Sound the alarm in Gibeah!
Blow the trumpet in Ramah!
Raise the battle cry in Beth-aven*!
Lead on into battle, O warriors of Benjamin!
9 One thing is certain, Israel*:
On your day of punishment,
you will become a heap of rubble.

10 "The leaders of Judah have become like thieves.*
So I will pour my anger on them like a waterfall.
11 The people of Israel will be crushed and broken by my judgment
because they are determined to worship idols.*
12 I will destroy Israel as a moth consumes wool.
I will make Judah as weak as rotten wood.

4:15 *Beth-aven* means "house of wickedness"; it is being used as another name for Bethel, which means "house of God." **4:17** Hebrew *Ephraim,* referring to the northern kingdom of Israel. **4:18** As in Greek version; the meaning of the Hebrew is uncertain. **5:2** Hebrew *at Shittim.* The meaning of the Hebrew for this sentence is uncertain. **5:7** The meaning of the Hebrew is uncertain. **5:8** *Beth-aven* means "house of wickedness"; it is being used as another name for Bethel, which means "house of God." **5:9** Hebrew *Ephraim,* referring to the northern kingdom of Israel; also in 5:11, 12, 13, 14. **5:10** Hebrew *like those who move a boundary marker.* **5:11** Or *determined to follow human commands.* The meaning of the Hebrew is uncertain.

[13] "When Israel and Judah saw how
sick they were,
Israel turned to Assyria—
to the great king there—
but he could neither help nor
cure them.
[14] I will be like a lion to Israel,
like a strong young lion to Judah.
I will tear them to pieces!
I will carry them off,
and no one will be left to
rescue them.
[15] Then I will return to my place
until they admit their guilt and
turn to me.
For as soon as trouble comes,
they will earnestly search
for me."

Oh, that we might know the LORD! . . . He will respond to us as surely as the arrival of dawn or the coming of rains in early spring.

HOSEA 6:3

6 A CALL TO REPENTANCE

[1] "Come, let us return to the LORD.
He has torn us to pieces;
now he will heal us.
He has injured us;
now he will bandage our wounds.
[2] In just a short time he will restore us,
so that we may live in his presence.
[3] Oh, that we might know the LORD!
Let us press on to know him.
He will respond to us as surely as the arrival of dawn
or the coming of rains in early spring."

REAL REGRET 6:1-3

Ever hear someone say, "I'm sorry," but know that person didn't mean those words? The people of Israel claimed to be sorry about the wrong things they did. Yet they didn't seem to understand or regret what they did. Basically, they apologized to stop God from punishing them. In a sense they were saying, "I'm sorry we were caught." Repentance is more than just saying, "I'm sorry." It involves a desire to change. ■

[4] "O Israel* and Judah,
what should I do with you?" asks the LORD.
"For your love vanishes like the morning mist
and disappears like dew in the sunlight.
[5] I sent my prophets to cut you to pieces—
to slaughter you with my words,
with judgments as inescapable as light.
[6] I want you to show love,*
not offer sacrifices.
I want you to know me*
more than I want burnt offerings.
[7] But like Adam,* you broke my covenant
and betrayed my trust.
[8] "Gilead is a city of sinners,
tracked with footprints of blood.
[9] Priests form bands of robbers,
waiting in ambush for their
victims.
They murder travelers along the
road to Shechem
and practice every kind of sin.
[10] Yes, I have seen something
horrible in Ephraim and Israel:
My people are defiled by
prostituting themselves with
other gods!
[11] "O Judah, a harvest of punishment
is also waiting for you,
though I wanted to restore the
fortunes of my people.

7 ISRAEL'S LOVE FOR WICKEDNESS

[1] "I want to heal Israel,* but its sins are too great.
Samaria is filled with liars.
Thieves are on the inside
and bandits on the outside!
[2] Its people don't realize
that I am watching them.
Their sinful deeds are all around them,
and I see them all.

[3] "The people entertain the king with their wickedness,
and the princes laugh at their lies.
[4] They are all adulterers,
always aflame with lust.
They are like an oven that is kept hot
while the baker is kneading the dough.
[5] On royal holidays, the princes get drunk with wine,
carousing with those who mock them.
[6] Their hearts are like an oven
blazing with intrigue.
Their plot smolders* through the night,
and in the morning it breaks out like a raging fire.
[7] Burning like an oven,
they consume their leaders.
They kill their kings one after another,
and no one cries to me for help.

[8] "The people of Israel mingle with godless foreigners,
making themselves as worthless as a
half-baked cake!
[9] Worshiping foreign gods has sapped their strength,
but they don't even know it.
Their hair is gray,
but they don't realize they're old and weak.
[10] Their arrogance testifies against them,
yet they don't return to the LORD their God
or even try to find him.

6:4 Hebrew *Ephraim,* referring to the northern kingdom of Israel. **6:6a** Greek version reads *to show mercy.* Compare Matt 9:13; 12:7. **6:6b** Hebrew *to know God.* **6:7** Or *But at Adam.* **7:1** Hebrew *Ephraim,* referring to the northern kingdom of Israel; also in 7:8, 11. **7:6** Hebrew *Their baker sleeps.*

11 "The people of Israel have become like silly,
witless doves,
first calling to Egypt, then flying to Assyria
for help.
12 But as they fly about,
I will throw my net over them
and bring them down like a bird from the sky.
I will punish them for all the evil they do.*

13 "What sorrow awaits those who have deserted me!
Let them die, for they have rebelled against me.
I wanted to redeem them,
but they have told lies about me.
14 They do not cry out to me with sincere hearts.
Instead, they sit on their couches and wail.
They cut themselves,* begging foreign gods for grain
and new wine,
and they turn away from me.
15 I trained them and made them strong,
yet now they plot evil against me.
16 They look everywhere except to the Most High.
They are as useless as a crooked bow.
Their leaders will be killed by their enemies
because of their insolence toward me.
Then the people of Egypt
will laugh at them.

8 ISRAEL HARVESTS THE WHIRLWIND

1 "Sound the alarm!
The enemy descends like an eagle on the people
of the LORD,
for they have broken my covenant
and revolted against my law.
2 Now Israel pleads with me,
'Help us, for you are our God!'
3 But it is too late.
The people of Israel have rejected what is good,
and now their enemies will chase after them.
4 The people have appointed kings without
my consent,
and princes without my knowledge.
By making idols for themselves from their silver
and gold,
they have brought about their own destruction.

5 "O Samaria, I reject this calf—
this idol you have made.
My fury burns against you.
How long will you be incapable of innocence?
6 This calf you worship, O Israel,
was crafted by your own hands!
It is not God!
Therefore, it must be smashed to bits.

7 "They have planted the wind
and will harvest the whirlwind.
The stalks of grain wither
and produce nothing to eat.
And even if there is any grain,
foreigners will eat it.
8 The people of Israel have been swallowed up;
they lie among the nations like an old
discarded pot.
9 Like a wild donkey looking for a mate,
they have gone up to Assyria.
The people of Israel* have sold themselves—
sold themselves to many lovers.
10 But though they have sold themselves to
many allies,
I will now gather them together for judgment.
Then they will writhe
under the burden of the great king.

APPLYING THE WORD 8:11-12

The Israelites applied God's laws to others but not to themselves. It's easy to listen to a sermon or read a Bible passage and think of other people who need this message. But applying God's Word to our own lives seems harder, mainly because doing so involves humility most of the time. As you think of others who might benefit from what you've heard or read, check to see if the same application might fit you, too. ■

11 "Israel has built many altars to take away sin,
but these very altars became places for sinning!
12 Even though I gave them all my laws,
they act as if those laws don't apply to them.
13 The people of Israel love their rituals of sacrifice,
but to me their sacrifices are all meaningless.
I will hold my people accountable for their sins,
and I will punish them.
They will return to Egypt.
14 Israel has forgotten its Maker and built great palaces,
and Judah has fortified its cities.
Therefore, I will send down fire on their cities
and will burn up their fortresses."

9 HOSEA ANNOUNCES ISRAEL'S PUNISHMENT

1 O people of Israel,
do not rejoice as other nations do.
For you have been unfaithful to your God,
hiring yourselves out like prostitutes,
worshiping other gods on every threshing floor.
2 So now your harvests will be too small to feed you.
There will be no grapes for making new wine.
3 You may no longer stay here in the LORD's land.
Instead, you will return to Egypt,
and in Assyria you will eat food
that is ceremonially unclean.

7:12 Hebrew *I will punish them because of what was reported against them in the assembly.* 7:14 As in Greek version; Hebrew reads *They gather together.* 8:9 Hebrew *Ephraim,* referring to the northern kingdom of Israel; also in 8:11.

4 There you will make no offerings of wine to the LORD.
None of your sacrifices there will please him.
They will be unclean, like food touched by a person
in mourning.
All who present such sacrifices will be defiled.
They may eat this food themselves,
but they may not offer it to the LORD.
5 What then will you do on festival days?
How will you observe the LORD's festivals?
6 Even if you escape destruction from Assyria,
Egypt will conquer you, and Memphis* will
bury you.
Nettles will take over your treasures of silver;
thistles will invade your ruined homes.

7 The time of Israel's punishment has come;
the day of payment is here.
Soon Israel will know this all too well.
Because of your great sin and hostility,
you say, "The prophets are crazy
and the inspired men are fools!"
8 The prophet is a watchman over Israel* for my God,
yet traps are laid for him wherever he goes.
He faces hostility even in the house of God.
9 The things my people do are as depraved
as what they did in Gibeah long ago.
God will not forget.
He will surely punish them for their sins.

YOU ARE WHAT YOU WORSHIP 9:10

Back in Numbers 22–24, Balaam, a prophet, was hired by King Balak of Moab to curse the Israelites. The Moabites enticed the Israelites into sexual sin and the worship of the Moabite god, Baal-peor. (See Num 25:3.) Before long, the people of Israel became as corrupt as the Moabites. People can take on the characteristics of whatever or whomever they love or worship. What do you worship? Are you becoming more like God, or are you becoming more like someone or something else? ■

10 The LORD says, "O Israel, when I first found you,
it was like finding fresh grapes in the desert.
When I saw your ancestors,
it was like seeing the first ripe figs of the season.
But then they deserted me for Baal-peor,
giving themselves to that shameful idol.
Soon they became vile,
as vile as the god they worshiped.
11 The glory of Israel will fly away like a bird,
for your children will not be born
or grow in the womb
or even be conceived.
12 Even if you do have children who grow up,
I will take them from you.
It will be a terrible day when I turn away
and leave you alone.
13 I have watched Israel become as beautiful as Tyre.
But now Israel will bring out her children
for slaughter."

14 O LORD, what should I request for your people?
I will ask for wombs that don't give birth
and breasts that give no milk.

15 The LORD says, "All their wickedness began at Gilgal;
there I began to hate them.
I will drive them from my land
because of their evil actions.
I will love them no more
because all their leaders are rebels.
16 The people of Israel are struck down.
Their roots are dried up,
and they will bear no more fruit.
And if they give birth,
I will slaughter their beloved children."

17 My God will reject the people of Israel
because they will not listen or obey.
They will be wanderers,
homeless among the nations.

MORE AND MORE STUFF? 10:1

Israel prospered under Jeroboam II, gaining military and economic strength. But the more prosperous the nation became, the more the people spent on sacrifices to idols. Are we any different nowadays? We want more and more stuff: more CDs and DVDs, a better car, a faster computer, a cooler cell phone. Now, God isn't against material possessions. He grieves when people live only to acquire more and more stuff. As you prosper, consider where your money is going. Is it being used for God's purposes or your own? ■

10 THE LORD'S JUDGMENT AGAINST ISRAEL

1 How prosperous Israel is—
a luxuriant vine loaded with fruit.
But the richer the people get,
the more pagan altars they build.
The more bountiful their harvests,
the more beautiful their sacred pillars.
2 The hearts of the people are fickle;
they are guilty and must be punished.
The LORD will break down their altars
and smash their sacred pillars.
3 Then they will say, "We have no king
because we didn't fear the LORD.
But even if we had a king,
what could he do for us anyway?"
4 They spout empty words
and make covenants they don't intend
to keep.

9:6 Memphis was the capital of northern Egypt. 9:8 Hebrew *Ephraim*, referring to the northern kingdom of Israel; also in 9:11, 13, 16.

So injustice springs up among them
like poisonous weeds in a farmer's field.
5 The people of Samaria tremble in fear
for what might happen to their calf idol
at Beth-aven.*
The people mourn and the priests wail,
because its glory will be stripped away.*
6 This idol will be carted away to Assyria,
a gift to the great king there.
Ephraim will be ridiculed and Israel will be shamed,
because its people have trusted in this idol.
7 Samaria and its king will be cut off;
they will float away like driftwood on an
ocean wave.
8 And the pagan shrines of Aven,* the place of Israel's
sin, will crumble.
Thorns and thistles will grow up around
their altars.
They will beg the mountains, "Bury us!"
and plead with the hills, "Fall on us!"

9 The LORD says, "O Israel, ever since Gibeah,
there has been only sin and more sin!
You have made no progress whatsoever.
Was it not right that the wicked men of Gibeah
were attacked?
10 Now whenever it fits my plan,
I will attack you, too.
I will call out the armies of the nations
to punish you for your multiplied sins.

11 "Israel* is like a trained heifer treading out
the grain—
an easy job she loves.
But I will put a heavy yoke on her tender neck.
I will force Judah to pull the plow
and Israel* to break up the hard ground.
12 I said, 'Plant the good seeds of righteousness,
and you will harvest a crop of love.
Plow up the hard ground of your hearts,
for now is the time to seek the LORD,
that he may come
and shower righteousness upon you.'

13 "But you have cultivated wickedness
and harvested a thriving crop of sins.
You have eaten the fruit of lies—
trusting in your military might,
believing that great armies
could make your nation safe.
14 Now the terrors of war
will rise among your people.
All your fortifications will fall,
just as when Shalman destroyed Beth-arbel.
Even mothers and children
were dashed to death there.
15 You will share that fate, Bethel,
because of your great wickedness.
When the day of judgment dawns,
the king of Israel will be completely destroyed.

11 THE LORD'S LOVE FOR ISRAEL

1 "When Israel was a child, I loved him,
and I called my son out of Egypt.
2 But the more I* called to him,
the farther he moved from me,
offering sacrifices to the images of Baal
and burning incense to idols.
3 I myself taught Israel* how to walk,
leading him along by the hand.
But he doesn't know or even care
that it was I who took care of him.
4 I led Israel along
with my ropes of kindness and love.
I lifted the yoke from his neck,
and I myself stooped to feed him.

5 "But since my people refuse to return to me,
they will return to Egypt
and will be forced to serve Assyria.
6 War will swirl through their cities;
their enemies will crash through their gates.
They will destroy them,
trapping them in their own evil plans.
7 For my people are determined to desert me.
They call me the Most High,
but they don't truly honor me.

8 "Oh, how can I give you up, Israel?
How can I let you go?
How can I destroy you like Admah
or demolish you like Zeboiim?
My heart is torn within me,
and my compassion overflows.
9 No, I will not unleash my fierce anger.
I will not completely destroy Israel,
for I am God and not a mere mortal.
I am the Holy One living among you,
and I will not come to destroy.
10 For someday the people will follow me.
I, the LORD, will roar like a lion.
And when I roar,
my people will return trembling from the west.
11 Like a flock of birds, they will come from Egypt.
Trembling like doves, they will return
from Assyria.
And I will bring them home again,"
says the LORD.

10:5a *Beth-aven* means "house of wickedness"; it is being used as another name for Bethel, which means "house of God." **10:5b** Or *because it will be taken away into exile.* **10:8** *Aven* is a reference to Beth-aven; see 10:5a and the note there. **10:11a** Hebrew *Ephraim,* referring to the northern kingdom of Israel. **10:11b** Hebrew *Jacob.* The names "Jacob" and "Israel" are often interchanged throughout the Old Testament, referring sometimes to the individual patriarch and sometimes to the nation. **11:2** As in Greek version; Hebrew reads *they.* **11:3** Hebrew *Ephraim,* referring to the northern kingdom of Israel; also in 11:8, 9, 12.

CHARGES AGAINST ISRAEL AND JUDAH

12*Israel surrounds me with lies and deceit,
but Judah still obeys God
and is faithful to the Holy One.*

12

1* The people of Israel* feed on the wind;
they chase after the east wind all day long.
They pile up lies and violence;
they are making an alliance with Assyria
while sending olive oil to buy support from Egypt.

2 Now the LORD is bringing charges against Judah.
He is about to punish Jacob* for all his
deceitful ways,
and pay him back for all he has done.
3 Even in the womb,
Jacob struggled with his brother;
when he became a man,
he even fought with God.
4 Yes, he wrestled with the angel and won.
He wept and pleaded for a blessing from him.
There at Bethel he met God face to face,
and God spoke to him*—
5 the LORD God of Heaven's Armies,
the LORD is his name!
6 So now, come back to your God.
Act with love and justice,
and always depend on him.

7 But no, the people are like crafty merchants
selling from dishonest scales—
they love to cheat.
8 Israel boasts, "I am rich!
I've made a fortune all by myself!
No one has caught me cheating!
My record is spotless!"

REMEMBER 12:1-10

Israel took credit for its own success. Many successful people and nations do the same today. Because they have all they want, they don't feel a need for God. If you find yourself taking credit for all of your accomplishments, remember that all your opportunities, abilities, and resources come from God—and that you hold them in sacred trust for him. ■

9 "But I am the LORD your God,
who rescued you from slavery in Egypt.
And I will make you live in tents again,
as you do each year at the Festival of Shelters.*
10 I sent my prophets to warn you
with many visions and parables."

11 But the people of Gilead are worthless
because of their idol worship.
And in Gilgal, too, they sacrifice bulls;
their altars are lined up like the heaps of stone
along the edges of a plowed field.

12 Jacob fled to the land of Aram,
and there he* earned a wife by tending sheep.
13 Then by a prophet
the LORD brought Jacob's descendants* out
of Egypt;
and by that prophet
they were protected.
14 But the people of Israel
have bitterly provoked the LORD,
so their Lord will now sentence them to death
in payment for their sins.

13

THE LORD'S ANGER AGAINST ISRAEL

1 When the tribe of Ephraim spoke,
the people shook with fear,
for that tribe was important in Israel.
But the people of Ephraim sinned by
worshiping Baal
and thus sealed their destruction.

11:12a Verse 11:12 is numbered 12:1 in Hebrew text. **11:12b** Or *and Judah is unruly against God, the faithful Holy One*. The meaning of the Hebrew is uncertain. **12:1a** Verses 12:1-14 are numbered 12:2-15 in Hebrew text. **12:1b** Hebrew *Ephraim*, referring to the northern kingdom of Israel; also in 12:8, 14. **12:2** *Jacob* sounds like the Hebrew word for "deceiver." **12:4** As in Greek and Syriac versions; Hebrew reads *to us*. **12:9** Hebrew *as in the days of your appointed feast*. **12:12** Hebrew *Israel*. See note on 10:11b. **12:13** Hebrew *brought Israel*. See note on 10:11b.

How can I share my faith in Christ with my friends if they don't feel a need to know him?

Rarely will people want a relationship with someone whom they feel they don't need. The Bible is filled with stories of people who have actively rejected God, who felt no need for him because their lives were going so well. In Hosea 13:6, God confronted the people of Israel—his chosen people—for doing that very thing.

You can't make someone need God, but here are some things you can do:

First, be ready to help your friends when they do have needs. Keep the friendship bridges strong so they will come to you for help. Then you can point them to Christ. Seek the help of a mature Christian friend for advice on how to do this best.

Second, look for people who are hurt already and share the Good News with them. Be sensitive when you do this. Don't make it sound as though you have all the answers, or as if having a relationship with God means you'll never go through bad times. Simply share how God has helped you, and what he means in your life.

Third, watch out for your own heart. The Bible warns us that some things can distract us from God: "There is a path before each person that seems right, but it ends in death" (Prov 14:12).

The Symbolic Nature of Marriage

While the prophet Hosea lived out his message regarding Israel's relationship with God, other prophets also used the symbol of marriage to describe God's love for his people.

HOSEA AND GOMER	GOD AND ISRAEL
God said to Hosea: "Go and marry a prostitute, so that some of her children will be conceived in prostitution. This will illustrate how Israel has acted like a prostitute by turning against the LORD and worshiping other gods." So Hosea married Gomer, the daughter of Diblaim, and she became pregnant and gave Hosea a son. *Hosea 1:2-3*	*God said to Israel through Ezekiel:* "I wrapped my cloak around you . . . and declared my marriage vows. I made a covenant with you, says the Sovereign LORD, and you became mine." *Ezekiel 16:8* *God said to Israel through Jeremiah:* "I remember how eager you were to please me as a young bride long ago, how you loved me and followed me even through the barren wilderness." *Jeremiah 2:2*
Then [Hosea] said to [Gomer, his wife], "You must live in my house for many days and stop your prostitution. During this time, you will not have sexual relations with anyone, not even with me." This shows that Israel will go a long time without a king or prince, and without sacrifices, sacred pillars, priests, or even idols! *Hosea 3:3-4*	*God said to Israel through Jeremiah:* "How can I pardon you? For even your children have turned from me. They have sworn by gods that are not gods at all! I fed my people until they were full. But they thanked me by committing adultery and lining up at the brothels." *Jeremiah 5:7* *God said to Israel through Ezekiel:* "You thought your fame and beauty were your own. So you gave yourself as a prostitute to every man who came along. Your beauty was theirs for the asking." *Ezekiel 16:15*
God said to Hosea: "Go and love your wife again, even though she commits adultery with another lover. This will illustrate that the LORD still loves Israel, even though the people have turned to other gods and love to worship them." *Hosea 3:1*	*God said to Israel through Jeremiah:* "O Israel, my faithless people, come home to me again, for I am merciful. I will not be angry with you forever. Only acknowledge your guilt. Admit that you rebelled against the LORD your God and committed adultery against him by worshiping idols under every green tree. . . . Return home . . . for I am your master." *Jeremiah 3:12-14*
God said to Hosea: "Afterward the people will return and devote themselves to the LORD their God and to David's descendant, their king. In the last days, they will tremble in awe of the LORD and of his goodness." *Hosea 3:5*	*God said to Israel through Ezekiel:* "I will remember the covenant I made with you when you were young, and I will establish an everlasting covenant with you." *Ezekiel 16:60*

2 Now they continue to sin by making silver idols,
images shaped skillfully with human hands.
"Sacrifice to these," they cry,
"and kiss the calf idols!"
3 Therefore, they will disappear like the
morning mist,
like dew in the morning sun,
like chaff blown by the wind,
like smoke from a chimney.

4 "I have been the LORD your God
ever since I brought you out of Egypt.
You must acknowledge no God but me,
for there is no other savior.
5 I took care of you in the wilderness,
in that dry and thirsty land.
6 But when you had eaten and were satisfied,
you became proud and forgot me.
7 So now I will attack you like a lion,
like a leopard that lurks along the road.
8 Like a bear whose cubs have been taken away,
I will tear out your heart.
I will devour you like a hungry lioness
and mangle you like a wild animal.

9 "You are about to be destroyed, O Israel—
yes, by me, your only helper.
10 Now where is* your king?
Let him save you!
Where are all the leaders of the land,
the king and the officials you demanded of me?
11 In my anger I gave you kings,
and in my fury I took them away.

12 "Ephraim's guilt has been collected,
and his sin has been stored up for punishment.
13 Pain has come to the people
like the pain of childbirth,
but they are like a child
who resists being born.
The moment of birth has arrived,
but they stay in the womb!

14 "Should I ransom them from the grave*?
Should I redeem them from death?
O death, bring on your terrors!
O grave, bring on your plagues!*
For I will not take pity on them.
15 Ephraim was the most fruitful of all his brothers,
but the east wind—a blast from the LORD—
will arise in the desert.
All their flowing springs will run dry,
and all their wells will disappear.
Every precious thing they own
will be plundered and carried away.
16 The people of Samaria
must bear the consequences of their guilt
because they rebelled against their God.
They will be killed by an invading army,
their little ones dashed to death against
the ground,
their pregnant women ripped open by swords."

RESTORED 14:1-2

The people could return to God by asking him to forgive them and turn their lives around. The same is true for us: we can pray Hosea's prayer and know our sins are forgiven because Christ paid the penalty for them on the cross (John 3:16). Forgiveness begins when we admit our need for it. We cannot save ourselves; our only hope is in God's mercy. Is that what you believe? ■

14 HEALING FOR THE REPENTANT

1 Return, O Israel, to the LORD your God,
for your sins have brought you down.
2 Bring your confessions, and return to the LORD.
Say to him,
"Forgive all our sins and graciously receive us,
so that we may offer you our praises.
3 Assyria cannot save us,
nor can our warhorses.
Never again will we say to the idols we have made,
'You are our gods.'
No, in you alone
do the orphans find mercy."

NEVER-FAILING 14:4

God declared his boundless love to Israel. When our will is weak and our conscience is burdened with a load of guilt, we can remind ourselves that God offers forgiveness and boundless love. When friends and family desert us or don't understand us, when we are tired of being good, God's love knows no bounds. When we can't see the way or hear God's voice, when we lack courage to go on, when our shortcomings or an awareness of our messed-up lives overwhelms us, God's love knows no bounds. Regardless of how things seem or even how you feel, you can rely on this truth: God's love knows *no bounds*. ■

4 The LORD says,
"Then I will heal you of your faithlessness;
my love will know no bounds,
for my anger will be gone forever.
5 I will be to Israel
like a refreshing dew from heaven.
Israel will blossom like the lily;
it will send roots deep into the soil
like the cedars in Lebanon.
6 Its branches will spread out like beautiful
olive trees,
as fragrant as the cedars of Lebanon.
7 My people will again live under my shade.
They will flourish like grain and blossom
like grapevines.
They will be as fragrant as the wines
of Lebanon.

8 "O Israel,* stay away from idols!
I am the one who answers your prayers and
cares for you.
I am like a tree that is always green;
all your fruit comes from me."

9 Let those who are wise understand
these things.
Let those with discernment listen carefully.
The paths of the LORD are true and right,
and righteous people live by walking in them.
But in those paths sinners stumble and fall.

13:10 As in Greek and Syriac versions and Latin Vulgate; Hebrew reads *I will be*. **13:14a** Hebrew *Sheol;* also in 13:14b. **13:14b** Greek version reads *O death, where is your punishment? / O grave* [Hades], *where is your sting?* Compare 1 Cor 15:55. **14:8** Hebrew *Ephraim,* referring to the northern kingdom of Israel.

"OKAY, PEOPLE," Mr. Ortiz said, "your final papers are due. Anyone who fails to hand in a paper will receive a zero for 25 percent of this quarter's grade."

Akiko considered Mr. Ortiz to be a good teacher. She expected to get an A or a B in his class. But her paper wasn't ready. She'd meant to finish it last weekend, but didn't get around to it. Maybe if she talked to him. . . .

Akiko walked up to Mr. Ortiz's desk. "Mr. Ortiz," she began, "I know what you said about the paper being due, but I've been really busy. Can I hand it in next week?"

Mr. Ortiz frowned as he answered. "Akiko, you're one of my better students, but two months ago I told the class there would be only a few acceptable reasons for a late paper. I can't extend the deadline for you. I'm sorry."

The book of Joel also is about a deadline, one for Judah to turn back to God. Joel called this deadline "the day of the LORD," (see 1:15). The people of Judah had forgotten about God and were living their own way. Joel reminded them that those who ignored God would one day face God's wrath.

The book of Joel reminds us that a day will come when God judges the actions of all people. What do you think he'll say about your life?

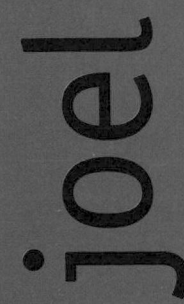

joel

timeline

853 B.C.
King Ahab dies in battle

848
Elisha becomes a prophet

841
Jehu becomes king of Israel; Athaliah seizes Judah's throne

835
Joel becomes a prophet; Joash becomes king of Judah

814
Jehoahaz becomes king of Israel

798
Jehoash becomes king of Israel

796?
Joel's ministry ends

793
Jonah becomes a prophet; Jeroboam II becomes king of Israel

stats

PURPOSE: To warn Judah of God's impending judgment because of their sins and to urge them to turn back to God

AUTHOR: Joel son of Pethuel

TO WHOM WRITTEN: The people of Judah, the southern kingdom, and God's people everywhere

DATE WRITTEN: Probably during the time Joel prophesied, from about 835 to 796 B.C.

SETTING: The people of Judah had become prosperous and complacent. They took God for granted as they indulged in idol worship. Joel warned them that this kind of lifestyle would inevitably bring down God's judgment.

KEY PEOPLE: Joel, the people of Judah

KEY PLACE: Jerusalem

KEY points

PUNISHMENT

Joel warned Judah of the coming "day of the LORD"—God's judgment for wrongdoing. All of us are accountable to God for our actions. One day he will judge both good and bad actions accordingly.

FORGIVENESS

God offered to restore his people to a proper relationship with him. He offers the same forgiveness today. As long as life endures on earth, it's never too late to ask for God's forgiveness.

THE HOLY SPIRIT

Joel predicted the time when God would pour out his Holy Spirit on all people. The Holy Spirit confirms God's love for us and convicts us when we do wrong.

1

The LORD gave this message to Joel son of Pethuel.

MOURNING OVER THE LOCUST PLAGUE

2 Hear this, you leaders of the people.
Listen, all who live in the land.
In all your history,
has anything like this happened before?
3 Tell your children about it in the years to come,
and let your children tell their children.
Pass the story down from generation
to generation.
4 After the cutting locusts finished eating the crops,
the swarming locusts took what was left!
After them came the hopping locusts,
and then the stripping locusts,* too!

WAKE-UP CALL 1:1-5

The people of Judah had become apathetic about their wrong actions. Joel wanted them to wake up before "the day of the LORD" (1:15) occurred. Otherwise, everything would be destroyed—even the grapes and wine that caused their drunkenness. Our times of peace and prosperity can lull us into thinking that everything's cool. The only way to know that everything's cool is to check in with God regularly. If you stick with God (see John 15), you'll be cool with him. ■

5 Wake up, you drunkards, and weep!
Wail, all you wine-drinkers!
All the grapes are ruined,
and all your sweet wine is gone.
6 A vast army of locusts* has invaded my land,
a terrible army too numerous to count.
Its teeth are like lions' teeth,
its fangs like those of a lioness.
7 It has destroyed my grapevines
and ruined my fig trees,
stripping their bark and destroying it,
leaving the branches white and bare.

8 Weep like a bride dressed in black,
mourning the death of her husband.
9 For there is no grain or wine
to offer at the Temple of the LORD.
So the priests are in mourning.
The ministers of the LORD are weeping.
10 The fields are ruined,
the land is stripped bare.
The grain is destroyed,
the grapes have shriveled,
and the olive oil is gone.

11 Despair, all you farmers!
Wail, all you vine growers!
Weep, because the wheat and barley—
all the crops of the field—are ruined.
12 The grapevines have dried up,
and the fig trees have withered.
The pomegranate trees, palm trees, and apple trees—
all the fruit trees—have dried up.
And the people's joy has dried up with them.

13 Dress yourselves in burlap and weep, you priests!
Wail, you who serve before the altar!
Come, spend the night in burlap,
you ministers of my God.
For there is no grain or wine
to offer at the Temple of your God.
14 Announce a time of fasting;
call the people together for a solemn meeting.
Bring the leaders
and all the people of the land
into the Temple of the LORD your God,
and cry out to him there.
15 The day of the LORD is near,
the day when destruction comes from
the Almighty.
How terrible that day will be!

16 Our food disappears before our very eyes.
No joyful celebrations are held in the house
of our God.
17 The seeds die in the parched ground,
and the grain crops fail.
The barns stand empty,
and granaries are abandoned.
18 How the animals moan with hunger!
The herds of cattle wander about confused,
because they have no pasture.
The flocks of sheep and goats bleat in misery.

19 LORD, help us!
The fire has consumed the wilderness pastures,
and flames have burned up all the trees.
20 Even the wild animals cry out to you
because the streams have dried up,
and fire has consumed the wilderness pastures.

2

LOCUSTS INVADE LIKE AN ARMY

1 Sound the alarm in Jerusalem*!
Raise the battle cry on my holy mountain!
Let everyone tremble in fear
because the day of the LORD is upon us.
2 It is a day of darkness and gloom,
a day of thick clouds and deep blackness.
Suddenly, like dawn spreading across
the mountains,
a great and mighty army appears.
Nothing like it has been seen before
or will ever be seen again.

1:4 The precise identification of the four kinds of locusts mentioned here is uncertain. 1:6 Hebrew *A nation.* 2:1 Hebrew *Zion;* also in 2:15, 23.

Joel

Served as a prophet to Judah from 835 to 796 B.C.	*Climate of the times*	Wicked Queen Athaliah seized power in a bloody coup but was overthrown after a few years. Joash was crowned king, but he was only seven years old and in great need of spiritual guidance. Joash followed God in his early years, then turned away from him.
	Main message	A plague of locusts had come to discipline the nation. Joel called the people to turn back to God before an even greater judgment occurred.
	Importance of message	God judges all people for their sins but is merciful and offers eternal salvation to those who turn to him in repentance.
	Contemporary prophets	Elisha (848–797) Jonah (793–753)

3 Fire burns in front of them,
and flames follow after them.
Ahead of them the land lies
as beautiful as the Garden of Eden.
Behind them is nothing but desolation;
not one thing escapes.
4 They look like horses;
they charge forward like warhorses.*
5 Look at them as they leap along the mountaintops.
Listen to the noise they make—like the rumbling of chariots,
like the roar of fire sweeping across a field of stubble,
or like a mighty army moving into battle.

6 Fear grips all the people;
every face grows pale with terror.
7 The attackers march like warriors
and scale city walls like soldiers.
Straight forward they march,
never breaking rank.
8 They never jostle each other;
each moves in exactly the right position.
They break through defenses
without missing a step.
9 They swarm over the city
and run along its walls.
They enter all the houses,
climbing like thieves through the windows.
10 The earth quakes as they advance,
and the heavens tremble.
The sun and moon grow dark,
and the stars no longer shine.

11 The LORD is at the head of the column.
He leads them with a shout.
This is his mighty army,
and they follow his orders.
The day of the LORD is an awesome, terrible thing.
Who can possibly survive?

A CALL TO REPENTANCE

12 That is why the LORD says,
"Turn to me now, while there is time.
Give me your hearts.
Come with fasting, weeping, and mourning.
13 Don't tear your clothing in your grief,
but tear your hearts instead."
Return to the LORD your God,
for he is merciful and compassionate,
slow to get angry and filled with unfailing love.
He is eager to relent and not punish.
14 Who knows? Perhaps he will give you a reprieve,
sending you a blessing instead of this curse.
Perhaps you will be able to offer grain and wine
to the LORD your God as before.

15 Blow the ram's horn in Jerusalem!
Announce a time of fasting;
call the people together
for a solemn meeting.
16 Gather all the people—
the elders, the children, and even the babies.
Call the bridegroom from his quarters
and the bride from her private room.
17 Let the priests, who minister in the LORD's presence,
stand and weep between the entry room to the Temple and the altar.
Let them pray, "Spare your people, LORD!
Don't let your special possession become an object of mockery.

2:4 Or *like charioteers.*

Don't let them become a joke for
unbelieving foreigners
who say,
'Has the God of Israel left
them?'"

THE LORD'S PROMISE OF RESTORATION

18 Then the LORD will pity his people
and jealously guard the honor of
his land.
19 The LORD will reply,
"Look! I am sending you grain and
new wine and olive oil,
enough to satisfy your needs.
You will no longer be an object
of mockery
among the surrounding nations.
20 I will drive away these armies from
the north.
I will send them into the parched wastelands.
Those in the front will be driven into the
Dead Sea,
and those at the rear into the Mediterranean.*
The stench of their rotting bodies will rise over
the land."

Surely the LORD has done great things!
21 Don't be afraid, my people.
Be glad now and rejoice,
for the LORD has done great things.
22 Don't be afraid, you animals of the field,
for the wilderness pastures will soon be green.
The trees will again be filled with fruit;
fig trees and grapevines will be loaded down
once more.
23 Rejoice, you people of Jerusalem!
Rejoice in the LORD your God!
For the rain he sends demonstrates his faithfulness.
Once more the autumn rains will come,
as well as the rains of spring.
24 The threshing floors will again be piled high
with grain,
and the presses will overflow with new wine and
olive oil.

25 The LORD says, "I will give you back what you lost
to the swarming locusts, the hopping locusts,
the stripping locusts, and the cutting locusts.*
It was I who sent this great destroying army
against you.
26 Once again you will have all the food you want,
and you will praise the LORD your God,
who does these miracles for you.
Never again will my people be disgraced.
27 Then you will know that I am among my
people Israel,
that I am the LORD your God, and there
is no other.
Never again will my people be disgraced.

I will pour out my Spirit upon all people. Your sons and daughters will prophesy. Your old men will dream dreams, and your young men will see visions.

JOEL 2:28

THE LORD'S PROMISE OF HIS SPIRIT

28*"Then, after doing all those things,
I will pour out my Spirit upon
all people.
Your sons and daughters will
prophesy.
Your old men will dream
dreams,
and your young men will
see visions.
29 In those days I will pour out
my Spirit
even on servants—men and
women alike.
30 And I will cause wonders in the
heavens and on the earth—
blood and fire and columns
of smoke.
31 The sun will become dark,
and the moon will turn blood red
before that great and terrible* day of the
LORD arrives.
32 But everyone who calls on the name of the LORD
will be saved,
for some on Mount Zion in Jerusalem will escape,
just as the LORD has said.
These will be among the survivors
whom the LORD has called.

2:20 Hebrew *into the eastern sea, . . . into the western sea.* 2:25 The precise identification of the four kinds of locusts mentioned here is uncertain. 2:28 Verses 2:28-32 are numbered 3:1-5 in Hebrew text. 2:31 Greek version reads *glorious.*

I wish God would do more miracles in my life. Why don't amazing things happen more often?

Ever wonder this? Miracles and "amazing things" are great. Still, the best miracle God could ever perform in any life is the miracle of salvation.

Maybe the real question is, What kind of miracles do you want God to do in your life? Do you want him to give you *A*'s in subjects you haven't studied for? Let you score the winning touchdown? Perform some healing to "prove" he's there? If so, you'll be disappointed. He doesn't "perform" just to prove he exists. He would rather that people have faith in what the Bible says about him (that he, in fact, exists).

God promised his followers that he would perform wonderful things through them (see Joel 2:28-32). And you'll find that the most exciting miracles are when God uses you to lead someone else to him. Those miracles are better; they lead to something eternal!

So ask God to use you to perform the greatest miracle of all—to lead someone to Christ.

3 JUDGMENT AGAINST ENEMY NATIONS

1*"At the time of those events," says the LORD,
"when I restore the prosperity of Judah and Jerusalem,
2 I will gather the armies of the world
into the valley of Jehoshaphat.*
There I will judge them
for harming my people, my special possession,
for scattering my people among the nations,
and for dividing up my land.
3 They threw dice* to decide which of my people
would be their slaves.
They traded boys to obtain prostitutes
and sold girls for enough wine to get drunk.

4"What do you have against me, Tyre and Sidon and
you cities of Philistia? Are you trying to take revenge on
me? If you are, then watch out! I will strike swiftly and pay
you back for everything you have done. 5You have taken
my silver and gold and all my precious treasures, and
have carried them off to your pagan temples. 6You have
sold the people of Judah and Jerusalem to the Greeks,* so
they could take them far from their homeland.
7"But I will bring them back from all the places to which
you sold them, and I will pay you back for everything you
have done. 8I will sell your sons and daughters to the people of Judah, and they will sell them to the people of Arabia,* a nation far away. I, the LORD, have spoken!"

9 Say to the nations far and wide:
"Get ready for war!
Call out your best warriors.
Let all your fighting men advance for the attack.
10 Hammer your plowshares into swords
and your pruning hooks into spears.
Train even your weaklings to be warriors.
11 Come quickly, all you nations everywhere.
Gather together in the valley."

And now, O LORD, call out your warriors!

12 "Let the nations be called to arms.
Let them march to the valley of Jehoshaphat.
There I, the LORD, will sit
to pronounce judgment on them all.
13 Swing the sickle,
for the harvest is ripe.*
Come, tread the grapes,
for the winepress is full.
The storage vats are overflowing
with the wickedness of these people."

14 Thousands upon thousands are waiting in the
valley of decision.
There the day of the LORD will soon arrive.
15 The sun and moon will grow dark,
and the stars will no longer shine.

FOR REAL 3:14

Joel described the multitudes waiting in the "valley of decision" (the valley of Jehoshaphat of 3:2, 12). This is a description of judgment. Everyone who has ever lived will face judgment. Look around you. See your friends, those with whom you work and live. Have they received God's forgiveness? Have they been warned about sin's consequences? If we really understood the severity of God's final judgment on the lost, we wouldn't want anyone to face that. ■

16 The LORD's voice will roar from Zion
and thunder from Jerusalem,
and the heavens and the earth will shake.
But the LORD will be a refuge for his people,
a strong fortress for the people of Israel.

BLESSINGS FOR GOD'S PEOPLE

17 "Then you will know that I, the LORD your God,
live in Zion, my holy mountain.
Jerusalem will be holy forever,
and foreign armies will never conquer her again.
18 In that day the mountains will drip with sweet wine,
and the hills will flow with milk.
Water will fill the streambeds of Judah,
and a fountain will burst forth from the
LORD's Temple,
watering the arid valley of acacias.*
19 But Egypt will become a wasteland
and Edom will become a wilderness,
because they attacked the people of Judah
and killed innocent people in their land.

NOT TOO LATE 3:21

The book of Joel began with a prophecy about the destruction of the land and ended with a prophecy about its restoration. The prophet began by stressing the need for repentance and ended with the promise of forgiveness that repentance brings. Joel was trying to convince the people to wake up (1:5), get rid of their complacency, and realize the danger of living apart from God. His message to us is that there is still time; anyone who calls on God's name can be saved (2:12-14, 32). Those who do this will enjoy the blessings mentioned in Joel's prophecy; those who refuse to turn to God will face destruction at some point. Is God's forgiveness an offer you've accepted? If you haven't, it's not too late. ■

20 "But Judah will be filled with people forever,
and Jerusalem will endure through all generations.
21 I will pardon my people's crimes,
which I have not yet pardoned;
and I, the LORD, will make my home
in Jerusalem* with my people."

3:1 Verses 3:1-21 are numbered 4:1-21 in Hebrew text. **3:2** *Jehoshaphat* means "the LORD judges." **3:3** Hebrew *They cast lots.* **3:6** Hebrew *to the peoples of Javan.* **3:8** Hebrew *to the Sabeans.* **3:13** Greek version reads *for the harvest time has come.* Compare Mark 4:29. **3:18** Hebrew *valley of Shittim.* **3:21** Hebrew *Zion.*

AMOS

WHAT MAKES your blood boil? Social injustice? Someone taking your stuff without asking? Failing a test?

Many people would agree that social injustice would really get under their skin. We all have a sense of fairness. We want to see justice done, especially when a bully is involved. But how many of us would willingly charge into battle against an oppressor if doing so took us out of our comfort zone or caused us to lose status, a job, or even our lives? We want to see justice done—but at little cost to ourselves.

God has always had a passion for justice. As God's spokesman, Amos had the responsibility of speaking a message to the people of Judah. They had become complacent. Life was good for some. But for others—the oppressed—life wasn't so good. God was outraged at the wealthier citizens' lack of compassion for the poor. Through Amos, he warned them that injustice would reap a harvest of judgment. God didn't utter a warning idly. But he first wanted to give his people the opportunity to change.

When was the last time you felt a sense of outrage on someone else's behalf? As you read Amos, perhaps you'll consider the plight of those around you. Who knows? Maybe you'll be the catalyst for change in your community.

timeline

793 B.C.
Jeroboam II becomes king of Israel

760
Amos becomes a prophet to Israel

753
Hosea becomes a prophet to Israel

752
King Shallum of Israel is assassinated

750
Amos's ministry ends

740
Isaiah becomes a prophet to Judah

stats

PURPOSE: To show God's judgment on Israel, the northern kingdom, for their idolatry and oppression of the poor

AUTHOR: Amos

TO WHOM WRITTEN: Israel, the northern kingdom, and God's people everywhere

DATE WRITTEN: Probably during the reigns of Jeroboam II of Israel and Uzziah of Judah (about 760 to 750 B.C)

SETTING: The wealthy people of Israel were complacent in their oppression of the poor. Soon, however, Israel would be conquered by Assyria, and the rich would become slaves.

KEY PEOPLE: Amos, Amaziah, Jeroboam II

KEY PLACES: Bethel, Samaria

KEY points

JUDGMENT
Through Amos, God announced that he would judge Judah and the surrounding nations. Someday, God will judge all people for their actions.

OPPRESSION
The wealthy and powerful people of Samaria, the capital of Israel, had become prosperous, greedy, and indifferent toward the poor. God never tolerates injustice. He wants his people to take a stand against injustice and to care for those in need.

PHONY RELIGION
Although many people in Israel and Judah had abandoned real faith in God, they still pretended to be religious. Merely participating in a ritual falls short of true faith. This leads to religion without relationship. God wants sincere obedience and commitment.

1

This message was given to Amos, a shepherd from the town of Tekoa in Judah. He received this message in visions two years before the earthquake, when Uzziah was king of Judah and Jeroboam II, the son of Jehoash,* was king of Israel.

WORK 1:1

All day long Amos took care of sheep—not a particularly "spiritual" job. Yet this ordinary man was chosen to do something extraordinary. Your job may not cause you to feel spiritual or successful; yet it can be a vital work if you are in the place God wants you to be. God can work through you to do extraordinary things, no matter how ordinary your occupation. ■

2This is what he saw and heard:

"The LORD's voice will roar from Zion
and thunder from Jerusalem!
The lush pastures of the shepherds will
dry up;
the grass on Mount Carmel will wither and die."

GOD'S JUDGMENT ON ISRAEL'S NEIGHBORS

3This is what the LORD says:

"The people of Damascus have sinned again
and again,*
and I will not let them go unpunished!
They beat down my people in Gilead
as grain is threshed with iron sledges.
4 So I will send down fire on King Hazael's palace,
and the fortresses of King Ben-hadad will
be destroyed.
5 I will break down the gates of Damascus
and slaughter the people in the valley of Aven.
I will destroy the ruler in Beth-eden,
and the people of Aram will go as captives to Kir,"
says the LORD.

6This is what the LORD says:

"The people of Gaza have sinned again
and again,
and I will not let them go unpunished!
They sent whole villages into exile,
selling them as slaves to Edom.
7 So I will send down fire on the walls of Gaza,
and all its fortresses will be destroyed.
8 I will slaughter the people of Ashdod
and destroy the king of Ashkelon.
Then I will turn to attack Ekron,
and the few Philistines still left will be killed,"
says the Sovereign LORD.

9This is what the LORD says:

"The people of Tyre have sinned again and again,
and I will not let them go unpunished!
They broke their treaty of brotherhood with Israel,
selling whole villages as slaves to Edom.
10 So I will send down fire on the walls of Tyre,
and all its fortresses will be destroyed."

11This is what the LORD says:

"The people of Edom have sinned again and again,
and I will not let them go unpunished!
They chased down their relatives, the Israelites,
with swords,
showing them no mercy.
In their rage, they slashed them continually
and were unrelenting in their anger.
12 So I will send down fire on Teman,
and the fortresses of Bozrah will be destroyed."

13This is what the LORD says:

"The people of Ammon have sinned again
and again,
and I will not let them go unpunished!
When they attacked Gilead to extend their borders,
they ripped open pregnant women with
their swords.
14 So I will send down fire on the walls of Rabbah,
and all its fortresses will be destroyed.
The battle will come upon them with shouts,
like a whirlwind in a mighty storm.
15 And their king* and his princes will go into
exile together,"
says the LORD.

2

This is what the LORD says:

"The people of Moab have sinned again and again,*
and I will not let them go unpunished!
They desecrated the bones of Edom's king,
burning them to ashes.
2 So I will send down fire on the land of Moab,
and all the fortresses in Kerioth will be destroyed.
The people will fall in the noise of battle,
as the warriors shout and the ram's horn sounds.
3 And I will destroy their king
and slaughter all their princes,"
says the LORD.

GOD'S JUDGMENT ON JUDAH AND ISRAEL

4This is what the LORD says:

"The people of Judah have sinned again and again,
and I will not let them go unpunished!

1:1 Hebrew *Joash,* a variant spelling of Jehoash. 1:3 Hebrew *have committed three sins, even four;* also in 1:6, 9, 11, 13. 1:15 Hebrew *malcam,* possibly referring to their god Molech. 2:1 Hebrew *have committed three sins, even four;* also in 2:4, 6.

They have rejected the instruction of the LORD,
refusing to obey his decrees.
They have been led astray by the same lies
that deceived their ancestors.
5 So I will send down fire on Judah,
and all the fortresses of Jerusalem will
be destroyed."

6 This is what the LORD says:

"The people of Israel have sinned again and again,
and I will not let them go unpunished!
They sell honorable people for silver
and poor people for a pair of sandals.
7 They trample helpless people in the dust
and shove the oppressed out of the way.
Both father and son sleep with the same woman,
corrupting my holy name.
8 At their religious festivals,
they lounge in clothing their debtors put up
as security.
In the house of their god,
they drink wine bought with unjust fines.

9 "But as my people watched,
I destroyed the Amorites,
though they were as tall as cedars
and as strong as oaks.
I destroyed the fruit on their branches
and dug out their roots.
10 It was I who rescued you from Egypt
and led you through the desert for forty years,
so you could possess the land of the Amorites.
11 I chose some of your sons to be prophets
and others to be Nazirites.
Can you deny this, my people of Israel?"
asks the LORD.
12 "But you caused the Nazirites to sin by making them
drink wine,
and you commanded the prophets, 'Shut up!'

13 "So I will make you groan
like a wagon loaded down with sheaves of grain.
14 Your fastest runners will not get away.
The strongest among you will become weak.
Even mighty warriors will be unable to
save themselves.
15 The archers will not stand their ground.
The swiftest runners won't be fast enough to escape.
Even those riding horses won't be able to
save themselves.
16 On that day the most courageous of your fighting men
will drop their weapons and run for their lives,"
says the LORD.

3 Listen to this message that the LORD has spoken
against you, O people of Israel and Judah—against the entire family I rescued from Egypt:

2 "From among all the families on the earth,
I have been intimate with you alone.
That is why I must punish you
for all your sins."

WITNESSES AGAINST GUILTY ISRAEL

3 Can two people walk together
without agreeing on the direction?
4 Does a lion ever roar in a thicket
without first finding a victim?
Does a young lion growl in its den
without first catching its prey?
5 Does a bird ever get caught in a trap
that has no bait?
Does a trap spring shut
when there's nothing to catch?
6 When the ram's horn blows a warning,
shouldn't the people be alarmed?
Does disaster come to a city
unless the LORD has planned it?

Why do some people seem to get away with stuff? Are there really consequences to what we do?

At the dentist, Novocain deadens the nerves in our mouth so we won't feel the drill. Repeated sin deadens the conscience, so the person no longer feels guilty about wrong behavior. But whether a person feels guilty or not, sin *does* have consequences. Some are immediate, like when the teacher catches you cheating on a test and gives you an *F*. Other consequences may be delayed.

The prophet Amos told the people of Israel what would happen if they didn't shape up (see Amos 2:6-16): They would be conquered. Though his predictions didn't immediately come to pass, they did prove to be right after many years. The Israelites were conquered by the Assyrians and were dragged away from their land.

Without a doubt, the Bible is clear about what will eventually happen to those who act contrary to God's plan: "Don't be misled—you cannot mock the justice of God. You will always harvest what you plant. Those who live only to satisfy their own sinful nature will harvest decay and death from that sinful nature. But those who live to please the Spirit will harvest everlasting life from the Spirit" (Gal 6:7-8).

If we "sow" bad actions, we'll reap that kind of fruit. If we sow good things and genuinely try to follow God's instructions, God will use us, and we'll reap a wonderful harvest.

Yet we sometimes tire of always trying to be good—especially when there's so much bad around us. That's when we have to remember God's promise of the eventual harvest: "Let's not get tired of doing what is good. At just the right time we will reap a harvest of blessing if we don't give up" (Gal 6:9).

Amos

Served as a prophet to Israel (the northern kingdom) from 760 to 750 B.C.	*Climate of the times*	Israel was enjoying prosperity and peace. But this had caused it to become a selfish, materialistic society. Those who were well off ignored the needs of those less fortunate. The people were self-centered and indifferent toward God.
	Main message	Amos spoke against those who exploited or ignored the needy.
	Importance of message	Believing in God is more than a personal matter. God calls all believers to work against injustices in society and to aid those less fortunate.
	Contemporary prophets	Jonah (793–753) Hosea (753–715)

7 Indeed, the Sovereign LORD never does anything
until he reveals his plans to his servants
the prophets.

8 The lion has roared—
so who isn't frightened?
The Sovereign LORD has spoken—
so who can refuse to proclaim his message?
9 Announce this to the leaders of Philistia*
and to the great ones of Egypt:
"Take your seats now on the hills around Samaria,
and witness the chaos and oppression
in Israel."

10 "My people have forgotten how to do right,"
says the LORD.
"Their fortresses are filled with wealth
taken by theft and violence.
11 Therefore," says the Sovereign LORD,
"an enemy is coming!
He will surround them and shatter their defenses.
Then he will plunder all their fortresses."

12This is what the LORD says:

"A shepherd who tries to rescue a sheep from
a lion's mouth
will recover only two legs or a piece of an ear.
So it will be for the Israelites in Samaria lying on
luxurious beds,
and for the people of Damascus reclining
on couches.*

13"Now listen to this, and announce it throughout all
Israel,*" says the Lord, the LORD God of Heaven's Armies.

14 "On the very day I punish Israel for its sins,
I will destroy the pagan altars at Bethel.
The horns of the altar will be cut off
and fall to the ground.
15 And I will destroy the beautiful homes of the wealthy—
their winter mansions and their summer
houses, too—
all their palaces filled with ivory,"
says the LORD.

MOOOVED TO HELP? 4:1-3

Israel's wealthy women were compared to the cows of Bashan—they were pampered, sleek, and well fed (see Ps 22:12). These women selfishly pushed their husbands to oppress the helpless in order to finance their lavish lifestyle. Their behavior "udderly" outraged God. Amos warned them that their time of prosperity would soon be over. Instead of being complacent, God wants us to be moooved to help. Are you? ■

4 ISRAEL'S FAILURE TO LEARN

1 Listen to me, you fat cows*
living in Samaria,
you women who oppress the poor
and crush the needy,
and who are always calling to your husbands,
"Bring us another drink!"
2 The Sovereign LORD has sworn this by
his holiness:
"The time will come when you will be led away
with hooks in your noses.

3:9 Hebrew *Ashdod.* 3:12 Or *So it will be when the Israelites in Samaria are rescued / with only a broken bed and a tattered pillow.* 3:13 Hebrew *the house of Jacob.* The names "Jacob" and "Israel" are often interchanged throughout the Old Testament, referring sometimes to the individual patriarch and sometimes to the nation. 4:1 Hebrew *you cows of Bashan.*

ULTIMATE ISSUES

DO THE RIGHT THING

Justice. You can't read more than a chapter or two in any of the Minor Prophets without a cry for justice leaping off the pages. Not that it is a minor theme found only in these books. God has sewn a broad thread of compassion for the oppressed throughout the tapestry of the Bible. But here in the books of the minor prophets, it becomes a central theme.

Check out Amos 5:24: "I want to see a mighty flood of justice, an endless river of righteous living."

Over and over, God told Israel that they were not to be like the other nations; they were to hold to a higher standard. The other nations took advantage of the poor, allowing the wealthy and powerful to grow fat off of their labor. God wanted his people to treat the less fortunate with compassion and fairness. In Proverbs 14:31, God even goes so far as to identify with the poor: "Those who oppress the poor insult their Maker, but helping the poor honors him."

Other nations considered widows, orphans, and foreigners as second-class citizens. But in Israel, these individuals were to be treated with dignity. "This is what the LORD of Heaven's Armies says: Judge fairly, and show mercy and kindness to one another. Do not oppress widows, orphans, foreigners, and the poor. And do not scheme against each other" (Zech 7:9-10).

We are confronted today with many opportunities to do the right thing. The plight of the homeless, the distress of our inner cities, the suffering of the hungry, questions of racial and economic fairness, the struggle for peace—these and countless other issues cry out for people of courage, compassion, and conviction to stand strong for justice in Jesus' name. God is vitally concerned for the widow, the orphan, the Somali Bantu refugee, the crack-addicted baby—anyone who suffers and needs help.

Are you?

Every last one of you will be dragged away
 like a fish on a hook!
3 You will be led out through the ruins of the wall;
 you will be thrown from your fortresses,*"
 says the LORD.

4 "Go ahead and offer sacrifices to the idols
  at Bethel.
 Keep on disobeying at Gilgal.
Offer sacrifices each morning,
 and bring your tithes every three days.
5 Present your bread made with yeast
 as an offering of thanksgiving.
Then give your extra voluntary offerings
 so you can brag about it everywhere!
This is the kind of thing you Israelites
  love to do,"
 says the Sovereign LORD.

6 "I brought hunger to every city
 and famine to every town.
But still you would not return to me,"
 says the LORD.

7 "I kept the rain from falling
 when your crops needed it the most.
I sent rain on one town
 but withheld it from another.
Rain fell on one field,
 while another field withered away.
8 People staggered from town to town looking
  for water,
 but there was never enough.
But still you would not return to me,"
 says the LORD.

9 "I struck your farms and vineyards with blight
  and mildew.
 Locusts devoured all your fig and olive trees.
But still you would not return to me,"
 says the LORD.

10 "I sent plagues on you
 like the plagues I sent on Egypt long ago.
I killed your young men in war
 and led all your horses away.*
 The stench of death filled the air!

4:3 Or *thrown out toward Harmon,* possibly a reference to Mount Hermon. 4:10 Or *and slaughtered your captured horses.*

But still you would not return to me,"
says the LORD.

11 "I destroyed some of your cities,
as I destroyed* Sodom and Gomorrah.
Those of you who survived
were like charred sticks pulled from a fire.
But still you would not return to me,"
says the LORD.

12 "Therefore, I will bring upon you all the disasters
I have announced.
Prepare to meet your God in judgment, you people
of Israel!"

13 For the LORD is the one who shaped the mountains,
stirs up the winds, and reveals his thoughts
to mankind.
He turns the light of dawn into darkness
and treads on the heights of the earth.
The LORD God of Heaven's Armies is his name!

5 A CALL TO REPENTANCE

Listen, you people of Israel! Listen to this funeral song I am singing:

2 "The virgin Israel has fallen,
never to rise again!
She lies abandoned on the ground,
with no one to help her up."

3The Sovereign LORD says:

"When a city sends a thousand men to battle,
only a hundred will return.
When a town sends a hundred,
only ten will come back alive."

4Now this is what the LORD says to the family of Israel:

"Come back to me and live!
5 Don't worship at the pagan altars at Bethel;
don't go to the shrines at Gilgal or Beersheba.
For the people of Gilgal will be dragged off into exile,
and the people of Bethel will be reduced
to nothing."
6 Come back to the LORD and live!
Otherwise, he will roar through Israel* like a fire,
devouring you completely.
Your gods in Bethel
won't be able to quench the flames.
7 You twist justice, making it a bitter pill for
the oppressed.
You treat the righteous like dirt.

8 It is the LORD who created the stars,
the Pleiades and Orion.
He turns darkness into morning
and day into night.
He draws up water from the oceans
and pours it down as rain on the land.
The LORD is his name!
9 With blinding speed and power he destroys
the strong,
crushing all their defenses.

10 How you hate honest judges!
How you despise people who tell the truth!
11 You trample the poor,
stealing their grain through taxes and
unfair rent.
Therefore, though you build beautiful
stone houses,
you will never live in them.
Though you plant lush vineyards,
you will never drink wine from them.
12 For I know the vast number of your sins
and the depth of your rebellions.
You oppress good people by taking bribes
and deprive the poor of justice in the courts.
13 So those who are smart keep their mouths shut,
for it is an evil time.

FREELY GIVE 5:10-12

Why does God put so much emphasis on the way we treat the poor? How we treat the rich or those of equal status too often reflects what we hope to get from them. But since the poor can give us nothing, how we treat them reflects our true character. Do you, like Christ, give without thought of gain? (See Matt 5:43-48.) ■

14 Do what is good and run from evil
so that you may live!
Then the LORD God of Heaven's Armies will be
your helper,
just as you have claimed.
15 Hate evil and love what is good;
turn your courts into true halls of justice.
Perhaps even yet the LORD God of
Heaven's Armies
will have mercy on the remnant of his people.*

16Therefore, this is what the Lord, the LORD God of Heaven's Armies, says:

"There will be crying in all the public squares
and mourning in every street.
Call for the farmers to weep with you,
and summon professional mourners to wail.
17 There will be wailing in every vineyard,
for I will destroy them all,"
says the LORD.

4:11 Hebrew *as when God destroyed.* 5:6 Hebrew *the house of Joseph.* 5:15 Hebrew *the remnant of Joseph.*

WARNING OF COMING JUDGMENT

18 What sorrow awaits you who say,
"If only the day of the LORD
were here!"
You have no idea what you are
wishing for.
That day will bring darkness,
not light.
19 In that day you will be like a man
who runs from a lion—
only to meet a bear.
Escaping from the bear, he leans
his hand against a wall in
his house—
and he's bitten by a snake.
20 Yes, the day of the LORD will be dark and hopeless,
without a ray of joy or hope.

21 "I hate all your show and pretense—
the hypocrisy of your religious festivals and
solemn assemblies.
22 I will not accept your burnt offerings and
grain offerings.
I won't even notice all your choice peace offerings.
23 Away with your noisy hymns of praise!
I will not listen to the music of your harps.
24 Instead, I want to see a mighty flood of justice,
an endless river of righteous living.

25"Was it to me you were bringing sacrifices and offerings during the forty years in the wilderness, Israel? 26No,
you served your pagan gods—Sakkuth your king god and
Kaiwan your star god—the images you made for yourselves. 27So I will send you into exile, to a land east of Damascus,*" says the LORD, whose name is the God of
Heaven's Armies.

I want to see a mighty flood of justice, an endless river of righteous living.

AMOS 5:24

6

1 What sorrow awaits you who lounge in luxury in
Jerusalem,*
and you who feel secure in Samaria!
You are famous and popular in Israel,
and people go to you for help.
2 But go over to Calneh
and see what happened there.
Then go to the great city of Hamath
and down to the Philistine city of Gath.
You are no better than they were,
and look at how they were destroyed.
3 You push away every thought of coming disaster,
but your actions only bring the day of
judgment closer.
4 How terrible for you who sprawl on ivory beds
and lounge on your couches,
eating the meat of tender lambs from the flock
and of choice calves fattened in the stall.
5 You sing trivial songs to the sound of the harp
and fancy yourselves to be great
musicians like David.
6 You drink wine by the bowlful
and perfume yourselves with
fragrant lotions.
You care nothing about the ruin
of your nation.*
7 Therefore, you will be the first to
be led away as captives.
Suddenly, all your parties
will end.

8The Sovereign LORD has sworn by his
own name, and this is what he, the
LORD God of Heaven's Armies, says:

"I despise the arrogance of Israel,*
and I hate their fortresses.
I will give this city
and everything in it to their enemies."

COMPLACENCY

When Deena joined the youth group at her church three years ago, exciting events were always taking place. One semester, some of the teens served in a local retirement home. During Deena's sophomore year, the group developed an ongoing outreach to homeless people. Each summer at least 30 or 40 teens went on some sort of short-term missions trip.

Nowadays things are different. Most of the older crowd has gone on to college. And for whatever reason, the younger teens in the group only seem to come to "fun" activities—parties, volleyball games, etc. Deena is concerned that youth group is becoming more of a social club than a place of ministry.

During sharing time at youth group, she expresses her concerns, telling the group that she misses the commitment to ministry, and sharing stories of the real joy and fun the group had experienced in the past through serving others.

The group's reaction ranges from glares, to whispers, to yawns. One girl approaches Deena after the meeting and says, "Who do you think you are? You act like you're so spiritual. What's wrong with having fun?"

Like Deena, the prophet Amos had the unpleasant task of lighting a spiritual fire under complacent people. Read Amos 5:21–6:9 and ask yourself: Am I more like Amos . . . or the people he addressed?

(9If there are ten men left in one house, they will all die.
10And when a relative who is responsible to dispose of
the dead* goes into the house to carry out the bodies, he
will ask the last survivor, "Is anyone else with you?" When

5:26-27 Greek version reads *No, you carried your pagan gods—the shrine of Molech, the star of your god Rephan, and the images you made for yourselves. So I will send you into exile, to a land east of Damascus.* Compare Acts 7:43. **6:1** Hebrew *in Zion.* **6:6** Hebrew *of Joseph.* **6:8** Hebrew *Jacob.* See note on 3:13. **6:10** Or *to burn the dead.* The meaning of the Hebrew is uncertain.

the person begins to swear, "No, by . . . ," he will interrupt
and say, "Stop! Don't even mention the name of the
LORD.")

11 When the LORD gives the command,
homes both great and small will be smashed
to pieces.

12 Can horses gallop over boulders?
Can oxen be used to plow them?
But that's how foolish you are when you turn justice
into poison
and the sweet fruit of righteousness
into bitterness.
13 And you brag about your conquest of Lo-debar.*
You boast, "Didn't we take Karnaim* by our
own strength?"
14 "O people of Israel, I am about to bring an enemy
nation against you,"
says the LORD God of Heaven's Armies.
"They will oppress you throughout your land—
from Lebo-hamath in the north
to the Arabah Valley in the south."

7

A VISION OF LOCUSTS

The Sovereign LORD showed me a vision. I saw him preparing to send a vast swarm of locusts over the land. This
was after the king's share had been harvested from the
fields and as the main crop was coming up. 2 In my vision
the locusts ate every green plant in sight. Then I said,
"O Sovereign LORD, please forgive us or we will not survive, for Israel* is so small."
3 So the LORD relented from this plan. "I will not do it,"
he said.

PRAYER POWER 7:1-9

Twice Amos was shown a vision of Israel's impending punishment. His immediate response was to pray that God would spare Israel. Is that your prayer for this nation? Prayer is a powerful privilege, one not to be wasted. ■

A VISION OF FIRE

4 Then the Sovereign LORD showed me another vision. I
saw him preparing to punish his people with a great fire.
The fire had burned up the depths of the sea and was devouring the entire land. 5 Then I said, "O Sovereign LORD,
please stop or we will not survive, for Israel is so small."
6 Then the LORD relented from this plan, too. "I will not
do that either," said the Sovereign LORD.

A VISION OF A PLUMB LINE

7 Then he showed me another vision. I saw the Lord standing beside a wall that had been built using a plumb line.
He was using a plumb line to see if it was still straight.
8 And the LORD said to me, "Amos, what do you see?"
I answered, "A plumb line."
And the Lord replied, "I will test my people with this
plumb line. I will no longer ignore all their sins. 9 The pagan shrines of your ancestors* will be ruined, and the
temples of Israel will be destroyed; I will bring the dynasty of King Jeroboam to a sudden end."

AMOS AND AMAZIAH

10 Then Amaziah, the priest of Bethel, sent a message to
Jeroboam, king of Israel: "Amos is hatching a plot against
you right here on your very doorstep! What he is saying is
intolerable. 11 He is saying, 'Jeroboam will soon be killed,
and the people of Israel will be sent away into exile.'"
12 Then Amaziah sent orders to Amos: "Get out of here,
you prophet! Go on back to the land of Judah, and earn
your living by prophesying there! 13 Don't bother us with
your prophecies here in Bethel. This is the king's sanctuary and the national place of worship!"
14 But Amos replied, "I'm not a professional prophet,
and I was never trained to be one.* I'm just a shepherd,
and I take care of sycamore-fig trees. 15 But the LORD
called me away from my flock and told me, 'Go and
prophesy to my people in Israel.' 16 Now then, listen to this
message from the LORD:

"You say,
'Don't prophesy against Israel.
Stop preaching against my people.*'
17 But this is what the LORD says:
'Your wife will become a prostitute in this city,
and your sons and daughters will be killed.
Your land will be divided up,
and you yourself will die in a foreign land.
And the people of Israel will certainly become
captives in exile,
far from their homeland.'"

8

A VISION OF RIPE FRUIT

Then the Sovereign LORD showed me another vision. In it
I saw a basket filled with ripe fruit. 2 "What do you see,
Amos?" he asked.
I replied, "A basket full of ripe fruit."
Then the LORD said, "Like this fruit, Israel is ripe for
punishment! I will not delay their punishment again. 3 In
that day the singing in the Temple will turn to wailing.
Dead bodies will be scattered everywhere. They will be
carried out of the city in silence. I, the Sovereign LORD,
have spoken!"

4 Listen to this, you who rob the poor
and trample down the needy!
5 You can't wait for the Sabbath day to be over
and the religious festivals to end
so you can get back to cheating the helpless.

6:13a *Lo-debar* means "nothing." 6:13b *Karnaim* means "horns," a term that symbolizes strength. 7:2 Hebrew *Jacob;* also in 7:5. See note on 3:13. 7:9 Hebrew *of Isaac.* 7:14 Or *I'm not a prophet nor the son of a prophet.* 7:16 Hebrew *against the house of Isaac.*

You measure out grain with dishonest measures
and cheat the buyer with dishonest scales.*
6 And you mix the grain you sell
with chaff swept from the floor.
Then you enslave poor people
for one piece of silver or a pair of sandals.

7 Now the LORD has sworn this oath
by his own name, the Pride of Israel*:
"I will never forget
the wicked things you have done!
8 The earth will tremble for your deeds,
and everyone will mourn.
The ground will rise like the Nile River
at floodtime;
it will heave up, then sink again.

9 "In that day," says the Sovereign LORD,
"I will make the sun go down at noon
and darken the earth while it is still day.
10 I will turn your celebrations into times
of mourning
and your singing into weeping.
You will wear funeral clothes
and shave your heads to show your sorrow—
as if your only son had died.
How very bitter that day will be!

AN APPETITE FOR ANSWERS 8:11-14

The people had no appetite for God's messages when prophets like Amos delivered them. Because of their apathy, God announced that he would take away even the opportunity to hear his word. We have God's Word, the Bible, but many people still look everywhere for answers to life's problems—everywhere *except* in Scripture. Does that describe anyone you know? You can help them by directing them to the Bible, showing them the parts that speak to their special needs and questions. God's Word is available to us. Our challenge is to point people toward it. ■

11 "The time is surely coming," says the Sovereign LORD,
"when I will send a famine on the land—
not a famine of bread or water
but of hearing the words of the LORD.
12 People will stagger from sea to sea
and wander from border to border*
searching for the word of the LORD,
but they will not find it.
13 Beautiful girls and strong young men
will grow faint in that day,
thirsting for the LORD's word.
14 And those who swear by the shameful idols of
Samaria—
who take oaths in the name of the god of Dan
and make vows in the name of the god of
Beersheba*—
they will all fall down,
never to rise again."

9

A VISION OF GOD AT THE ALTAR

Then I saw a vision of the Lord standing beside the altar. He said,

SIGN OF LOVE 9:8

Amos assured the Israelites that God would not "completely destroy" Israel. In other words, the punishment would not be permanent or total. God wants to redeem, not punish. But when punishment is necessary, he doesn't withhold it. Like a loving father, God disciplines those he loves in order to correct them. If he disciplines you, are you willing to accept it as a sign of his love? ■

"Strike the tops of the Temple columns,
so that the foundation will shake.
Bring down the roof
on the heads of the people below.
I will kill with the sword those who survive.
No one will escape!

2 "Even if they dig down to the place of the dead,*
I will reach down and pull them up.
Even if they climb up into the heavens,
I will bring them down.
3 Even if they hide at the very top of Mount Carmel,
I will search them out and capture them.
Even if they hide at the bottom of the ocean,
I will send the sea serpent after them to
bite them.
4 Even if their enemies drive them into exile,
I will command the sword to kill them there.
I am determined to bring disaster upon them
and not to help them."

5 The Lord, the LORD of Heaven's Armies,
touches the land and it melts,
and all its people mourn.
The ground rises like the Nile River at floodtime,
and then it sinks again.
6 The LORD's home reaches up to the heavens,
while its foundation is on the earth.
He draws up water from the oceans
and pours it down as rain on the land.
The LORD is his name!

7 "Are you Israelites more important to me
than the Ethiopians?*" asks the LORD.
"I brought Israel out of Egypt,

8:5 Hebrew *You make the ephah* [a unit for measuring grain] *small and the shekel* [a unit of weight] *great, and you deal falsely by using deceitful balances.* 8:7 Hebrew *the pride of Jacob.* See note on 3:13. 8:12 Hebrew *from north to east.* 8:14 Hebrew *the way of Beersheba.* 9:2 Hebrew *to Sheol.* 9:7a Hebrew *the Cushites?*

but I also brought the Philistines from Crete*
and led the Arameans out of Kir.

8 "I, the Sovereign LORD,
am watching this sinful nation of Israel.
I will destroy it
from the face of the earth.
But I will never completely destroy the family
of Israel,*"
says the LORD.
9 "For I will give the command
and will shake Israel along with the other nations
as grain is shaken in a sieve,
yet not one true kernel will be lost.
10 But all the sinners will die by the sword—
all those who say, 'Nothing bad will happen to us.'

A PROMISE OF RESTORATION

11 "In that day I will restore the fallen house* of David.
I will repair its damaged walls.
From the ruins I will rebuild it
and restore its former glory.
12 And Israel will possess what is left of Edom
and all the nations I have called to be mine.*"
The LORD has spoken,
and he will do these things.

13 "The time will come," says the LORD,
"when the grain and grapes will grow faster
than they can be harvested.

WARNINGS 9:13-15

The Jews of Amos's day had lost sight of God's love for them. The rich were carefree and comfortable—and refused to help others in need. They observed their religious rituals in hopes of appeasing God; yet they didn't truly love him. Amos announced God's warnings of destruction for their wrong actions. Therefore, we must not assume that going to church and being good is enough. God expects our belief in him to penetrate all areas of our lives and conduct. May Amos's words inspire us to live faithfully as God would have us live. ■

Then the terraced vineyards on the hills
of Israel
will drip with sweet wine!
14 I will bring my exiled people of Israel
back from distant lands,
and they will rebuild their ruined cities
and live in them again.
They will plant vineyards and gardens;
they will eat their crops and drink their wine.
15 I will firmly plant them there
in their own land.
They will never again be uprooted
from the land I have given them,"
says the LORD your God.

9:7b Hebrew *Caphtor.* **9:8** Hebrew *the house of Jacob.* See note on 3:13. **9:11a** Or *kingdom;* Hebrew reads *tent.* **9:11b-12** Greek version reads *and restore its former glory, / so that the rest of humanity, including the Gentiles — / all those I have called to be mine — might seek me.* Compare Acts 15:16-17.

OBADIAH

EVER PLAY "Good News, Bad News"? Sure you have. Deliver a message and you're in the game.

Most of life includes both good news and bad news. Some positive aspects have a downside. For example, you finally get your driver's license, but your parents want you to drive your younger brother everywhere. Some negative elements have a "silver lining." For example, you have to take pre-calculus in summer school, but one of the best teachers in the city has volunteered to teach the class.

The books in the Bible written by the prophets (Isaiah—Malachi) have good and bad news. The bad news was that Jerusalem would be destroyed and its people taken away as captives. The good news was that God would someday bring his people back and restore Israel's glory.

But one prophetical book is unique: It has no good news. That book is Obadiah. Written about Edom (a nearby nation), the prophet graphically describes the utter ruin that was about to come. Why? Because Edom had rejoiced when Israel was taken captive.

God loves his children. He'll protect his children and will deal harshly with those who attempt to hurt them.

As you read Obadiah, perhaps you'll be mindful of God's watchful concern for your life.

obadiah

stats

PURPOSE: To show that God judges those who have harmed his people

AUTHOR: Obadiah. Little is known about him. His name means "servant of the LORD" or "worshiper of Jehovah."

TO WHOM WRITTEN: The Edomites, the Jews in Judah, and God's people everywhere

DATE WRITTEN: Possibly during the reign of Jehoram in Judah, 853–841 B.C., or possibly during Jeremiah's ministry, 627–586 B.C.

SETTING: Historically, the people of Edom had constantly harassed the Jews. Prior to the time this book was written, they had participated in attacks against Judah. The exact historical context of Obadiah's prophecy is difficult to identify. It certainly comes after the division of Israel into the northern and southern kingdoms (930 B.C.), but it could belong hundreds of years later after Nebuchadnezzar's conquest of Judah in 586 B.C.

KEY PEOPLE: The Edomites

KEY PLACES: Edom, Jerusalem

KEY points

JUSTICE

Obadiah predicted that God would destroy Edom for their treachery in helping Babylon invade Judah. This story reminds us that God will judge and fiercely punish all who harm his people.

PRIDE

Because of their seemingly invincible rock fortress, the Edomites were proud and self-confident. But God caused their nation to disappear from the face of the earth. Likewise, any nation that trusts in power, wealth, technology, or wisdom more than in God will be brought down. No one can escape God's justice.

This is the vision that the Sovereign LORD revealed to Obadiah concerning the land of Edom.

EDOM'S JUDGMENT ANNOUNCED

We have heard a message from the LORD
that an ambassador was sent to the nations to say,
"Get ready, everyone!
Let's assemble our armies and attack Edom!"

2 The LORD says to Edom,
"I will cut you down to size among the nations;
you will be greatly despised.
3 You have been deceived by your own pride
because you live in a rock fortress
and make your home high in the mountains.
'Who can ever reach us way up here?'
you ask boastfully.
4 But even if you soar as high as eagles
and build your nest among the stars,
I will bring you crashing down,"
says the LORD.

TRUE SECURITY 1:3

The Edomites were proud of their might and land. But God warned them that they would be "cut . . . down to size" (1:2). Is your security in objects, people, or your own abilities? Possessions, people, and some abilities can disappear in a moment. God, however, never changes. Only he is the source of true security. Is he your source? ■

5 "If thieves came at night and robbed you
(what a disaster awaits you!),
they would not take everything.
Those who harvest grapes
always leave a few for the poor.
But your enemies will wipe you out completely!
6 Every nook and cranny of Edom*
will be searched and looted.
Every treasure will be found and taken.

7 "All your allies will turn against you.
They will help to chase you from your land.
They will promise you peace
while plotting to deceive and destroy you.
Your trusted friends will set traps for you,
and you won't even know about it.
8 At that time not a single wise person
will be left in the whole land of Edom,"
says the LORD.
"For on the mountains of Edom
I will destroy everyone who has understanding.
9 The mightiest warriors of Teman
will be terrified,
and everyone on the mountains of Edom
will be cut down in the slaughter.

REASONS FOR EDOM'S PUNISHMENT

10 "Because of the violence you did
to your close relatives in Israel,*
you will be filled with shame
and destroyed forever.
11 When they were invaded,
you stood aloof, refusing to help them.
Foreign invaders carried off their wealth
and cast lots to divide up Jerusalem,
but you acted like one of Israel's enemies.

ARROGANCE

Henderson Heights is a basketball community. Between the two high schools there are at least a dozen good basketball players. Then there is Kyle. Kyle is something special. He'll be able to play collegiate ball anywhere he wants. Some people think that he might have the skills to play in the NBA.

Kyle's 21 points-per-game scoring average is the good news. The bad news is his arrogance. Kyle talks a steady stream of trash out on the court. Not only does he like to run up the score on his opponents, but he often goes out of his way to humiliate whoever happens to be guarding him. Even his own teammates sometimes get embarrassed by Kyle's showboat antics.

Last night Kyle came crashing back to reality. His team lost a game they were supposed to win easily. Kyle was ejected late in the game for questioning a referee's call. He scored a grand total of seven points. And there were three college scouts in the stands.

See what happened when a whole nation [Edom] had an arrogant attitude. Read Obadiah 1:2-10.

12 "You should not have gloated
when they exiled your relatives to distant lands.
You should not have rejoiced
when the people of Judah suffered
such misfortune.
You should not have spoken arrogantly
in that terrible time of trouble.
13 You should not have plundered the land of Israel
when they were suffering such calamity.
You should not have gloated over their destruction
when they were suffering such calamity.
You should not have seized their wealth
when they were suffering such calamity.
14 You should not have stood at the crossroads,
killing those who tried to escape.
You should not have captured the survivors
and handed them over in their terrible time
of trouble.

6 Hebrew *Esau;* also in 8b, 9, 18, 19, 21. 10 Hebrew *your brother Jacob.* The names "Jacob" and "Israel" are often interchanged throughout the Old Testament, referring sometimes to the individual patriarch and sometimes to the nation.

Obadiah

Served as a prophet to Judah about 853 B.C.

Climate of the times	Edom was a constant thorn in Judah's side. It often participated in attacks initiated by other enemies.
Main message	God will judge Edom for its evil actions toward God's people.
Importance of message	Just as Edom was destroyed and disappeared as a nation, so God will destroy proud and wicked people.
Contemporary prophets	Elijah (875–848) Micaiah (865–853) Jehu (855–840?)

EDOM DESTROYED, ISRAEL RESTORED

15 "The day is near when I, the LORD,
will judge all godless nations!
As you have done to Israel,
so it will be done to you.
All your evil deeds
will fall back on your own heads.
16 Just as you swallowed up
my people
on my holy mountain,
so you and the surrounding
nations
will swallow the punishment
I pour out on you.
Yes, all you nations will drink
and stagger
and disappear from history.

17 "But Jerusalem* will become a
refuge for those who escape;
it will be a holy place.
And the people of Israel* will
come back
to reclaim their inheritance.
18 The people of Israel will be a raging fire,
and Edom a field of dry stubble.
The descendants of Joseph will be a flame
roaring across the field, devouring everything.
There will be no survivors in Edom.
I, the LORD, have spoken!

When they were invaded, you stood aloof, refusing to help them. . . . You should not have spoken arrogantly. . . .

OBADIAH 11-12

19 "Then my people living in the Negev
will occupy the mountains
of Edom.
Those living in the foothills of Judah*
will possess the Philistine plains
and take over the fields of
Ephraim and Samaria.
And the people of Benjamin
will occupy the land of Gilead.
20 The exiles of Israel will return to
their land
and occupy the Phoenician coast
as far north as Zarephath.
The captives from Jerusalem
exiled in the north*
will return home and resettle the
towns of the Negev.
21 Those who have been rescued* will go up to* Mount
Zion in Jerusalem
to rule over the mountains of Edom.
And the LORD himself will be king!"

17a Hebrew *Mount Zion.* **17b** Hebrew *house of Jacob;* also in 18. See note on 10. **19** Hebrew *the Shephelah.* **20** Hebrew *in Sepharad.* **21a** As in Greek and Syriac versions; Hebrew reads *Rescuers.* **21b** Or *from.*

JONAH

"DON'T GET MAD, get even." We've all heard or said that. Movies reflect the "get even" idea. We watch and cheer as the victim evens the score and the villains get what they deserve. We often live that way, too, sometimes without even knowing it. We do or say things to get back at those whom we think have offended us.

Jonah was like that. He's famous for being swallowed by a "great fish," but he ended up in that fish because of his "get even" attitude.

God told Jonah to go to Assyria (Israel's greatest enemy) and warn the people of Nineveh (the capital) to change their ways or face destruction. Because Jonah thought Assyria *should* be destroyed (and he was afraid to go there), he ran in the other direction—straight into the fish. Finally, after Jonah cried out to God and was rescued, he preached God's message in Nineveh.

"Don't get mad, get even." Fortunately, God doesn't work that way. Instead, God is "a merciful and compassionate God, slow to get angry and filled with unfailing love" (4:2). He wants our attitude to reflect these qualities also. Does yours?

jonah

timeline

793 B.C.
Jeroboam II becomes king; Jonah becomes a prophet

792
Uzziah becomes king of Judah

783
Shalmaneser IV becomes king of Assyria

772
Ashur-dan III becomes king of Assyria

760
Amos becomes a prophet

759?
Jonah preaches to Nineveh

754
Ashur-nirari V becomes king of Assyria

753
Jonah's ministry ends

722
Israel falls to Assyria

stats

PURPOSE: To show the extent of God's grace—the message of salvation is for *all* people

AUTHOR: Jonah, son of Amittai

TO WHOM WRITTEN: Israel and God's people everywhere

DATE WRITTEN: Approximately 785 to 760 B.C.

SETTING: Jonah preceded Amos and ministered under Jeroboam II, Israel's most powerful king (793–753 B.C., see 2 Kings 14:23-25). Assyria was Israel's greatest enemy; Israel was conquered by them in 722 B.C. Nineveh's repentance must have been short-lived.

KEY PEOPLE: Jonah, the ship's captain and crew

KEY PLACES: Joppa, Nineveh

SPECIAL FEATURES: This book is different from the other prophetic books because it centers on the prophet, not his prophecies. Only one verse summarizes Jonah's message to Nineveh (3:4). The book of Jonah is a historical narrative. Jesus also mentioned the story of Jonah as a picture of his death and resurrection (Matt 12:38-41).

KEY points

GOD'S SOVEREIGNTY
Jonah tried to run, but couldn't hide from God. Through Jonah's experience, we can understand how saying no to God can lead to disaster. Saying yes, however, can bring new understanding of God and his purposes for us and for the world.

MISSIONARY MESSAGE
God had given Jonah a purpose—to preach to the great Assyrian city of Nineveh. God wants his people to proclaim his love in words and actions to the whole world.

GOD'S COMPASSION
Although the Assyrians didn't deserve it, God spared them when they repented. God loves each of us, even when we fail him. His love also transcends cultural backgrounds, races, or denominations.

Miracles in the Book of Jonah

God caused a great storm 1:4	God arranged for a great fish to swallow Jonah 1:17	God ordered the fish to spit up Jonah 2:10	God made a plant to shade Jonah 4:6	God prepared a worm to eat the plant 4:7	God ordered a scorching wind to blow on Jonah 4:8

1

JONAH RUNS FROM THE LORD

The Lord gave this message to Jonah son of Amittai: 2"Get up and go to the great city of Nineveh. Announce my judgment against it because I have seen how wicked its people are."

3But Jonah got up and went in the opposite direction to get away from the Lord. He went down to the port of Joppa, where he found a ship leaving for Tarshish. He bought a ticket and went on board, hoping to escape from the Lord by sailing to Tarshish.

RUNNING AWAY 1:1-3

Jonah knew that God had a job for him, but he didn't want to do it. When God gives us directions through his Word, sometimes we run in fear, claiming that God is asking too much. Has that been your experience? Instead of running, are you willing to trust that when God asks you to do a task, he has your best interests at heart? ■

4But the Lord hurled a powerful wind over the sea, causing a violent storm that threatened to break the ship apart. 5Fearing for their lives, the desperate sailors shouted to their gods for help and threw the cargo overboard to lighten the ship.

But all this time Jonah was sound asleep down in the hold. 6So the captain went down after him. "How can you sleep at a time like this?" he shouted. "Get up and pray to your god! Maybe he will pay attention to us and spare our lives."

7Then the crew cast lots to see which of them had offended the gods and caused the terrible storm. When they did this, the lots identified Jonah as the culprit. 8"Why has this awful storm come down on us?" they demanded. "Who are you? What is your line of work? What country are you from? What is your nationality?"

9Jonah answered, "I am a Hebrew, and I worship the Lord, the God of heaven, who made the sea and the land."

10The sailors were terrified when they heard this, for he had already told them he was running away from the Lord. "Oh, why did you do it?" they groaned. 11And since the storm was getting worse all the time, they asked him, "What should we do to you to stop this storm?"

12"Throw me into the sea," Jonah said, "and it will become calm again. I know that this terrible storm is all my fault."

13Instead, the sailors rowed even harder to get the ship to the land. But the stormy sea was too violent for them, and they couldn't make it. 14Then they cried out to the Lord, Jonah's God. "O Lord," they pleaded, "don't make us die for this man's sin. And don't hold us responsible for his death. O Lord, you have sent this storm upon him for your own good reasons."

15Then the sailors picked Jonah up and threw him into the raging sea, and the storm stopped at once! 16The sailors were awestruck by the Lord's great power, and they offered him a sacrifice and vowed to serve him.

17*Now the Lord had arranged for a great fish to swallow Jonah. And Jonah was inside the fish for three days and three nights.

IN THE HOT SEAT 2:1-10

While inside the fish, Jonah prayed, asking God to forgive him. Sometimes God places us in the hot seat (a hard place) in order to gain our obedience. While we're there, two choices are before us: to ask for help or to be angry or resentful toward God. Jonah chose the first one. Which will you choose? ■

2

JONAH'S PRAYER

1*Then Jonah prayed to the Lord his God from inside the fish. 2He said,

"I cried out to the Lord in my great trouble,
  and he answered me.
I called to you from the land of the dead,*
  and Lord, you heard me!
3 You threw me into the ocean depths,
  and I sank down to the heart of the sea.
The mighty waters engulfed me;
  I was buried beneath your wild and stormy waves.
4 Then I said, 'O Lord, you have driven me from
    your presence.
  Yet I will look once more toward your
    holy Temple.'

1:17 Verse 1:17 is numbered 2:1 in Hebrew text. **2:1** Verses 2:1-10 are numbered 2:2-11 in Hebrew text. **2:2** Hebrew *from Sheol.*

Jonah

Served as a prophet to Israel and Assyria from 793 to 753 B.C.

Climate of the times	While Nineveh was the most important city in Assyria and would soon become the capital of the huge Assyrian empire, it also was a very wicked city.
Main message	Jonah, who hated the powerful and wicked Assyrians, was called by God to warn the Assyrians that they would receive judgment if they did not repent.
Importance of message	Jonah didn't want to go to Nineveh, so he tried to run from God. But God has ways of teaching us to obey and follow him. When Jonah finally did preach, the people repented and God withheld his judgment. Even the most wicked will be saved if they truly repent of their sins and turn to God.
Contemporary prophets	Joel (853–796?) Amos (760–750)

5 "I sank beneath the waves,
and the waters closed over me.
Seaweed wrapped itself around my head.
6 I sank down to the very roots of the mountains.
I was imprisoned in the earth,
whose gates lock shut forever.
But you, O LORD my God,
snatched me from the jaws of death!
7 As my life was slipping away,
I remembered the LORD.
And my earnest prayer went out to you
in your holy Temple.
8 Those who worship false gods
turn their backs on all God's mercies.
9 But I will offer sacrifices to you with songs of praise,
and I will fulfill all my vows.
For my salvation comes from the LORD alone."

10Then the LORD ordered the fish to spit Jonah out onto the beach.

3 JONAH GOES TO NINEVEH

Then the LORD spoke to Jonah a second time: 2"Get up and go to the great city of Nineveh, and deliver the message I have given you."

3This time Jonah obeyed the LORD's command and
went to Nineveh, a city so large that it took three days to
see it all.* 4On the day Jonah entered the city, he shouted
to the crowds: "Forty days from now Nineveh will be destroyed!" 5The people of Nineveh believed God's message, and from the greatest to the least, they declared a fast and put on burlap to show their sorrow.

6When the king of Nineveh heard what Jonah was saying, he stepped down from his throne and took off his royal robes. He dressed himself in burlap and sat on a heap of ashes. 7Then the king and his nobles sent this decree throughout the city:

"No one, not even the animals from your herds and flocks, may eat or drink anything at all. 8People and animals alike must wear garments of mourning, and everyone must pray earnestly to God. They must turn from their evil ways and stop all their violence. 9Who can tell? Perhaps even yet God will change his mind and hold back his fierce anger from destroying us."

10When God saw what they had done and how they had put a stop to their evil ways, he changed his mind and did not carry out the destruction he had threatened.

UNDESERVING 4:1-2

Jonah revealed the reason for his reluctance to go to Nineveh (1:3): He wanted the Ninevites destroyed, not forgiven. Jonah didn't understand that the God of Israel is also the God of the world. Is there someone to whom you're reluctant to extend forgiveness? Maybe this is someone you think is undeserving of it. News flash: None of us deserves to be forgiven by God. But he's willing to forgive us anyway. Are you? ■

4 JONAH'S ANGER AT THE LORD'S MERCY

This change of plans greatly upset Jonah, and he became very angry. 2So he complained to the LORD about it: "Didn't

3:3 Hebrew *a great city to God, of three days' journey.*

I say before I left home that you would do this, LORD? That is why I ran away to Tarshish! I knew that you are a merciful and compassionate God, slow to get angry and filled with unfailing love. You are eager to turn back from
destroying people. 3Just kill me now, LORD! I'd rather be dead than alive if what I predicted will not happen."
4The LORD replied, "Is it right for you to be angry about this?"
5Then Jonah went out to the east side of the city and made a shelter to sit under as he waited to see what would
happen to the city. 6And the LORD God arranged for a leafy plant to grow there, and soon it spread its broad leaves over Jonah's head, shading him from the sun. This eased his discomfort, and Jonah was very grateful for the plant.

SPIRITUALLY SENSITIVE 4:9

Jonah was angry at the death of the plant, but not over Nineveh's plight. Most of us have cried at the death of a pet or when an object with sentimental value is broken. But have we cried over a friend who does not know God? It's easy to be more sensitive to our own interests than to the spiritual needs of people around us. The best way to start being sensitive is to find out what the needs are. So, what *are* the needs of the people in your area? What will you do about them? ■

7But God also arranged for a worm! The next morning at dawn the worm ate through the stem of the plant so
that it withered away. 8And as the sun grew hot, God arranged for a scorching east wind to blow on Jonah. The sun beat down on his head until he grew faint and wished to die. "Death is certainly better than living like this!" he exclaimed.

ATTITUDES

Stephanie's favorite TV show is a hot new drama, *Manhattan Nights*. It's really not new—just a shameless rip-off of other nighttime dramas.

Tonight Stephanie is dying to find out if Heather is pregnant with Dade's child. But just as the show gets underway, the local TV station breaks in with a special report about a natural gas explosion in a nearby community.

"At least 12 people are known to be dead and another 17 are en route to area hospitals," the shaken reporter explains, as fires rage out of control behind him. "Nine others are still missing."

"Great!" Stephanie yells. "Because of this *stupid* fire, I'm gonna miss my show! Why can't they wait until the regular newscast to report all this junk?"

Stephanie picks up the phone and dials her friend Ashley. "Can you *believe* they're doing this?" she says.

What's your opinion of Stephanie's attitude? Is she right to think this way? Why or why not?

While you're thinking, check out Jonah 3–4. What advice would you have for Stephanie, based on Jonah's experiences?

9Then God said to Jonah, "Is it right for you to be angry because the plant died?"
"Yes," Jonah retorted, "even angry enough to die!"
10Then the LORD said, "You feel sorry about the plant, though you did nothing to put it there. It came quickly and died quickly. 11But Nineveh has more than
120,000 people living in spiritual darkness,* not to mention all the animals. Shouldn't I feel sorry for such a great city?"

4:11 Hebrew *people who don't know their right hand from their left.*

TODAY, AT 2 A.M., our country officially surrendered. Generals from both sides agreed to end the bloodshed, provided we hand over all munitions. Morale is low. The question is, "How could we have been overrun?"

Imagine reading that in your newspaper or on the Internet. What a terrible thought! Yet it happened to both Israel (northern tribes) and Judah (southern tribes). They couldn't see how they could have been defeated. They were God's chosen people. He rescued them from slavery and defeated nations to give them their homeland.

Although God had been faithful to his people, neither Israel nor Judah had been faithful to God. Micah wrote, "Why is this happening? Because of the rebellion of Israel—yes, the sins of the whole nation" (1:5). Israel and Judah were being judged for their sins. The people worshiped idols they had made. Many "sold" prophecies to make money. The rich harassed the poor. God was going to punish them all, because no one was without guilt.

God's standards haven't changed. One day, he will judge the actions of all people.

As you read Micah, remember that we as individuals and as a nation are responsible before God for the way we live. Are you faithful to him?

micah

timeline

753 B.C
Hosea becomes a prophet

750
Jotham becomes king of Judah

743
Tiglath-pileser III invades Israel

742
Micah becomes a prophet; Pekahiah becomes king

740
Isaiah becomes a prophet

735
Ahaz becomes king of Judah

722
Israel (the northern kingdom) falls

715
Hosea's ministry ends; Hezekiah becomes king of Judah

701
Sennacherib surrounds Jerusalem

687
Micah's ministry ends

stats

PURPOSE: To warn God's people that judgment is coming and to offer forgiveness to those who seek it

AUTHOR: Micah, a native of Moresheth, near Gath, about 20 miles southwest of Jerusalem

TO WHOM WRITTEN: The people of Israel (the northern kingdom) and of Judah (the southern kingdom)

DATE WRITTEN: Possibly during the reigns of Jotham, Ahaz, and Hezekiah (742–687 B.C.)

SETTING: The political situation is described in 2 Kings 15–20 and 2 Chronicles 26–30. Micah was a contemporary of Isaiah and Hosea.

KEY PLACES: Samaria, Jerusalem, and Bethlehem

KEY points

FAKE FAITH
God said that he would judge the false prophets, dishonest leaders, and selfish priests in Israel and Judah. While they publicly carried out religious ceremonies, they privately sought to gain money and influence. God desires the sincere worship of people publicly and privately.

OPPRESSION
The upper classes oppressed and exploited the poor. Yet no one spoke out against such behavior. Nowadays, we sometimes ignore those who are needy and oppressed, or silently condone the actions of those who oppress them. Sharing God's love includes meeting the needs of those who are rejected and neglected by society.

PLEASING GOD
Micah preached that God delighted in faith that produced fairness, love to others, and obedience to him. You can please God by showing these qualities at home, school, or in your neighborhood.

Micah

Served as a prophet to Judah from 742 to 687 B.C. *Climate of the times*	King Ahaz set up heathen idols in the Temple and finally nailed the Temple door shut. Four different nations harassed Judah. When Hezekiah became king, the nation began a slow road to recovery and economic strength. Hezekiah probably heeded much of Micah's advice.
Main message	Predicted the fall of both the northern kingdom of Israel and the southern kingdom of Judah. Through his disciplining the people, God was actually showing how much he cared for them. Hezekiah's good reign helped postpone Judah's punishment.
Importance of message	Choosing to live a life apart from God is making a commitment to sin. Sin leads to judgment and death. God alone shows us the way to eternal peace. His discipline often keeps us on the right path.
Contemporary prophets	Hosea (753–715) Isaiah (740–681)

1 The LORD gave this message to Micah of Moresheth during the years when Jotham, Ahaz, and Hezekiah were kings of Judah. The visions he saw concerned both Samaria and Jerusalem.

GRIEF OVER SAMARIA AND JERUSALEM

2 Attention! Let all the people of the
world listen!
Let the earth and everything in it hear.
The Sovereign LORD is making accusations
against you;
the LORD speaks from his holy Temple.
3 Look! The LORD is coming!
He leaves his throne in heaven
and tramples the heights of the earth.
4 The mountains melt beneath his feet
and flow into the valleys
like wax in a fire,
like water pouring down a hill.
5 And why is this happening?
Because of the rebellion of Israel*—
yes, the sins of the whole nation.
Who is to blame for Israel's rebellion?
Samaria, its capital city!
Where is the center of idolatry in
Judah?
In Jerusalem, its capital!

6 "So I, the LORD, will make the city of Samaria
a heap of ruins.
Her streets will be plowed up
for planting vineyards.
I will roll the stones of her walls into the valley below,
exposing her foundations.
7 All her carved images will be smashed.
All her sacred treasures will be burned.
These things were bought with the money
earned by her prostitution,
and they will now be carried away
to pay prostitutes elsewhere."

8 Therefore, I will mourn and lament.
I will walk around barefoot and naked.
I will howl like a jackal
and moan like an owl.
9 For my people's wound
is too deep to heal.
It has reached into Judah,
even to the gates of Jerusalem.

10 Don't tell our enemies in Gath*;
don't weep at all.
You people in Beth-leaphrah,*
roll in the dust to show your despair.
11 You people in Shaphir,*
go as captives into exile—naked and
ashamed.

1:5 Hebrew *Jacob;* also in 1:5b. The names "Jacob" and "Israel" are often interchanged throughout the Old Testament, referring sometimes to the individual patriarch and sometimes to the nation. **1:10a** *Gath* sounds like the Hebrew term for "tell." **1:10b** *Beth-leaphrah* means "house of dust." **1:11a** *Shaphir* means "pleasant."

The people of Zaanan*
dare not come outside their walls.
The people of Beth-ezel* mourn,
for their house has no support.
12 The people of Maroth* anxiously wait for relief,
but only bitterness awaits them
as the LORD's judgment reaches
even to the gates of Jerusalem.

13 Harness your chariot horses and flee,
you people of Lachish.*
You were the first city in Judah
to follow Israel in her rebellion,
and you led Jerusalem* into sin.
14 Send farewell gifts to Moresheth-gath*;
there is no hope of saving it.
The town of Aczib*
has deceived the kings of Israel.
15 O people of Mareshah,*
I will bring a conqueror to capture your town.
And the leaders* of Israel
will go to Adullam.

FOLLOW ME? 1:13

The people of Lachish (a fortress city in Judah) influenced many to follow their bad example. You probably have heard or know people who do the same thing today. Everyone has the opportunity to influence others for good or bad. Regardless of whether or not you consider yourself a leader, your actions and words also are observed by others more than you suspect. They may choose to follow your example, whether you know it or not. So, what kind of example are you setting? ■

16 Oh, people of Judah, shave your heads in sorrow,
for the children you love will be snatched away.
Make yourselves as bald as a vulture,
for your little ones will be exiled to
distant lands.

2 JUDGMENT AGAINST WEALTHY OPPRESSORS

1 What sorrow awaits you who lie awake at night,
thinking up evil plans.
You rise at dawn and hurry to carry them out,
simply because you have the power to do so.
2 When you want a piece of land,
you find a way to seize it.
When you want someone's house,
you take it by fraud and violence.
You cheat a man of his property,
stealing his family's inheritance.

IN YOUR DREAMS 2:1-2

Micah spoke out against those who planned evil deeds at night and rose at dawn to carry them out. A person's thoughts reflect his character. Evil thoughts lead to evil deeds as surely as morning follows night. What do you think about as you lie down to sleep? Is Hebrews 10:24—"Let us think of ways to motivate one another to acts of love and good works"—your motto? ■

3 But this is what the LORD says:
"I will reward your evil with evil;
you won't be able to pull your neck out
of the noose.
You will no longer walk around proudly,
for it will be a terrible time."

4 In that day your enemies will make fun of you
by singing this song of despair about you:
"We are finished,
completely ruined!
God has confiscated our land,
taking it from us.
He has given our fields
to those who betrayed us.*"
5 Others will set your boundaries then,
and the LORD's people will have no say
in how the land is divided.

TRUE AND FALSE PROPHETS

6 "Don't say such things,"
the people respond.*
"Don't prophesy like that.
Such disasters will never come our way!"

7 Should you talk that way, O family of Israel?*
Will the LORD's Spirit have patience with
such behavior?
If you would do what is right,
you would find my words comforting.
8 Yet to this very hour
my people rise against me like an enemy!
You steal the shirts right off the backs
of those who trusted you,
making them as ragged as men
returning from battle.
9 You have evicted women from their pleasant homes
and forever stripped their children of all that God
would give them.
10 Up! Begone!
This is no longer your land and home,
for you have filled it with sin
and ruined it completely.

1:11b *Zaanan* sounds like the Hebrew term for "come out." 1:11c *Beth-ezel* means "adjoining house." 1:12 *Maroth* sounds like the Hebrew term for "bitter." 1:13a *Lachish* sounds like the Hebrew term for "team of horses." 1:13b Hebrew *the daughter of Zion.* 1:14a *Moresheth* sounds like the Hebrew term for "gift" or "dowry." 1:14b *Aczib* means "deception." 1:15a *Mareshah* sounds like the Hebrew term for "conqueror." 1:15b Hebrew *the glory.* 2:4 Or *to those who took us captive.* 2:6 Or *the prophets respond;* Hebrew reads *they prophesy.* 2:7 Hebrew *O house of Jacob?* See note on 1:5a.

11 Suppose a prophet full of lies would say to you,
"I'll preach to you the joys of wine and alcohol!"
That's just the kind of prophet you would like!

HOPE FOR RESTORATION

12 "Someday, O Israel, I will gather you;
I will gather the remnant who are left.
I will bring you together again like sheep in a pen,
like a flock in its pasture.
Yes, your land will again
be filled with noisy crowds!
13 Your leader will break out
and lead you out of exile,
out through the gates of the enemy cities,
back to your own land.
Your king will lead you;
the LORD himself will guide you."

3 JUDGMENT AGAINST ISRAEL'S LEADERS

1 I said, "Listen, you leaders of Israel!
You are supposed to know right from wrong,
2 but you are the very ones
who hate good and love evil.
You skin my people alive
and tear the flesh from their bones.
3 Yes, you eat my people's flesh,
strip off their skin,
and break their bones.
You chop them up
like meat for the cooking pot.
4 Then you beg the LORD for help in times of trouble!
Do you really expect him to answer?
After all the evil you have done,
he won't even look at you!"

5 This is what the LORD says:
"You false prophets are leading my people astray!
You promise peace for those who give you food,
but you declare war on those who refuse to feed you.
6 Now the night will close around you,
cutting off all your visions.
Darkness will cover you,
putting an end to your predictions.
The sun will set for you prophets,
and your day will come to an end.
7 Then you seers will be put to shame,
and you fortune-tellers will be disgraced.
And you will cover your faces
because there is no answer from God."

8 But as for me, I am filled with power—
with the Spirit of the LORD.
I am filled with justice and strength
to boldly declare Israel's sin and rebellion.
9 Listen to me, you leaders of Israel!
You hate justice and twist all that is right.
10 You are building Jerusalem
on a foundation of murder and corruption.
11 You rulers make decisions based on bribes;
you priests teach God's laws only for a price;
you prophets won't prophesy unless you are paid.
Yet all of you claim to depend on the LORD.
"No harm can come to us," you say,
"for the LORD is here among us."
12 Because of you, Mount Zion will be plowed like
an open field;
Jerusalem will be reduced to ruins!
A thicket will grow on the heights
where the Temple now stands.

SPIRIT POWER 3:8

Micah admitted that the Spirit of the Lord gave him power to speak. Our power comes from the same source. Jesus told his followers that they would receive power to witness about him when the Holy Spirit came to them (Acts 1:8). Has fear kept you from speaking out for God? If you're a believer, you've got a built-in ally—the Holy Spirit. As Jesus said, "He will teach you everything and will remind you of everything I have told you" (John 14:26). ■

4 THE LORD'S FUTURE REIGN

1 In the last days, the mountain of the LORD's house
will be the highest of all—
the most important place on earth.
It will be raised above the other hills,
and people from all over the world will stream
there to worship.
2 People from many nations will come and say,
"Come, let us go up to the mountain of the LORD,
to the house of Jacob's God.
There he will teach us his ways,
and we will walk in his paths."
For the LORD's teaching will go out from Zion;
his word will go out from Jerusalem.
3 The LORD will mediate between peoples
and will settle disputes between strong nations
far away.
They will hammer their swords into plowshares
and their spears into pruning hooks.
Nation will no longer fight against nation,
nor train for war anymore.
4 Everyone will live in peace and prosperity,
enjoying their own grapevines and fig trees,
for there will be nothing to fear.
The LORD of Heaven's Armies
has made this promise!
5 Though the nations around us follow their idols,
we will follow the LORD our God forever
and ever.

ISRAEL'S RETURN FROM EXILE

6 "In that coming day," says the LORD,
"I will gather together those who are lame,

keeping it real

It wasn't easy being a Christian at my high school. One time, several of the more popular girls were putting down another girl, Nicole, for being a Christian. I didn't think it was right to remain silent, so I said, "So what if she's a Christian? I am, too. Why does that bother you?"

"Because it's weird," one of them said. "I mean, you don't fool around with guys, you don't drink—you must lead a pretty boring life." They all laughed.

"Why don't you try it yourself and see how boring it is," I said. They just laughed and made fun of me.

A few days later, when I was walking down the hall, one of the girls from that group called out, "What are you gonna do for fun today, Krista? Gonna pray on your knees for a couple of hours?" Her friends laughed. Other people just looked at me. I felt like a complete loser.

One day, Nicole told me to read Micah 4:6-13. I did, and it helped me a lot. It reminded me that even though these kids who rejected me were considered "cool" by the school, they weren't cool in God's eyes. This passage helped take away the pain of being rejected, because I stood up for someone else and for my beliefs. —**Krista**

those who have been exiles,
and those whom I have filled with grief.
7 Those who are weak will survive as a remnant;
those who were exiles will become a
strong nation.
Then I, the LORD, will rule from Jerusalem*
as their king forever."
8 As for you, Jerusalem,
the citadel of God's people,*
your royal might and power
will come back to you again.
The kingship will be restored
to my precious Jerusalem.

9 But why are you now screaming in terror?
Have you no king to lead you?
Have your wise people all died?
Pain has gripped you like a woman in childbirth.
10 Writhe and groan like a woman in labor,
you people of Jerusalem,*
for now you must leave this city
to live in the open country.
You will soon be sent in exile
to distant Babylon.
But the LORD will rescue you there;
he will redeem you from the grip of
your enemies.
11 Now many nations have gathered against you.
"Let her be desecrated," they say.
"Let us see the destruction of Jerusalem.*"
12 But they do not know the LORD's thoughts
or understand his plan.
These nations don't know
that he is gathering them together
to be beaten and trampled
like sheaves of grain on a threshing floor.
13 "Rise up and crush the nations, O Jerusalem!"*
says the LORD.
"For I will give you iron horns and bronze hooves,
so you can trample many nations to pieces.
You will present their stolen riches to the LORD,
their wealth to the LORD of all the earth."

5 1*Mobilize! Marshal your troops!
The enemy is laying siege to Jerusalem.
They will strike Israel's leader
in the face with a rod.

A RULER FROM BETHLEHEM

2*But you, O Bethlehem Ephrathah,
are only a small village among all the people of Judah.
Yet a ruler of Israel will come from you,
one whose origins are from the distant past.

4:7 Hebrew *Mount Zion.* 4:8 Hebrew *As for you, Migdal-eder, / the Ophel of the daughter of Zion.* 4:10 Hebrew *O daughter of Zion.* 4:11 Hebrew *of Zion.* 4:13 Hebrew *"Rise up and thresh, O daughter of Zion."* 5:1 Verse 5:1 is numbered 4:14 in Hebrew text. 5:2 Verses 5:2-15 are numbered 5:1-14 in Hebrew text.

BORN IN BETHLEHEM 5:2

Micah pinpointed the birthplace of Jesus hundreds of years before Jesus was born. Yet the promised Savior, who was to be born through David's family line, already existed: his "origins are from the distant past." Although eternal, he entered human history as the man Jesus of Nazareth. This prophecy and others in the Old Testament (Isa 7:14; 9:6) concerning the Savior show God's control over the events of human history. They also show his faithfulness. Knowing that God is faithful to keep his promises, are you willing to trust him with your life? ■

3 The people of Israel will be abandoned to
their enemies
until the woman in labor gives birth.
Then at last his fellow countrymen
will return from exile to their own land.
4 And he will stand to lead his flock with the
LORD's strength,
in the majesty of the name of the LORD
his God.
Then his people will live there undisturbed,
for he will be highly honored around the world.
5 And he will be the source of peace.

When the Assyrians invade our land
and break through our defenses,
we will appoint seven rulers to watch over us,
eight princes to lead us.
6 They will rule Assyria with drawn swords
and enter the gates of the land of Nimrod.
He will rescue us from the Assyrians
when they pour over the borders to invade
our land.

THE REMNANT PURIFIED

7 Then the remnant left in Israel*
will take their place among the nations.
They will be like dew sent by the LORD
or like rain falling on the grass,
which no one can hold back
and no one can restrain.
8 The remnant left in Israel
will take their place among the nations.
They will be like a lion among the animals of
the forest,
like a strong young lion among flocks of sheep
and goats,
pouncing and tearing as they go
with no rescuer in sight.
9 The people of Israel will stand up to their foes,
and all their enemies will be wiped out.

10 "In that day," says the LORD,
"I will slaughter your horses
and destroy your chariots.
11 I will tear down your walls
and demolish your defenses.
12 I will put an end to all witchcraft,
and there will be no more fortune-tellers.
13 I will destroy all your idols and sacred pillars,
so you will never again worship the work of your
own hands.
14 I will abolish your idol shrines with their
Asherah poles
and destroy your pagan cities.
15 I will pour out my vengeance
on all the nations that refuse to obey me."

6 THE LORD'S CASE AGAINST ISRAEL

Listen to what the LORD is saying:

"Stand up and state your case against me.
Let the mountains and hills be called to witness
your complaints.
2 And now, O mountains,
listen to the LORD's complaint!
He has a case against his people.
He will bring charges against Israel.

3 "O my people, what have I done to you?
What have I done to make you tired of me?
Answer me!
4 For I brought you out of Egypt
and redeemed you from slavery.
I sent Moses, Aaron, and Miriam to help you.
5 Don't you remember, my people,
how King Balak of Moab tried to have you cursed
and how Balaam son of Beor blessed
you instead?
And remember your journey from Acacia Grove*
to Gilgal,
when I, the LORD, did everything I could
to teach you about my faithfulness."

6 What can we bring to the LORD?
What kind of offerings should we give him?
Should we bow before God
with offerings of yearling calves?
7 Should we offer him thousands of rams
and ten thousand rivers of olive oil?
Should we sacrifice our firstborn children
to pay for our sins?

8 No, O people, the LORD has told you what
is good,
and this is what he requires of you:
to do what is right, to love mercy,
and to walk humbly with your God.

ISRAEL'S GUILT AND PUNISHMENT

9 Fear the LORD if you are wise!
His voice calls to everyone in Jerusalem:

5:7 Hebrew *in Jacob;* also in 5:8. See note on 1:5a. 6:5 Hebrew *Shittim.*

"The armies of destruction are coming;
the LORD is sending them.*
10 What shall I say about the homes of the wicked
filled with treasures gained by cheating?
What about the disgusting practice
of measuring out grain with dishonest measures?*
11 How can I tolerate your merchants
who use dishonest scales and weights?
12 The rich among you have become wealthy
through extortion and violence.
Your citizens are so used to lying
that their tongues can no longer tell the truth.

13 "Therefore, I will wound you!
I will bring you to ruin for all your sins.
14 You will eat but never have enough.
Your hunger pangs and emptiness will remain.
And though you try to save your money,
it will come to nothing in the end.
You will save a little,
but I will give it to those who conquer you.
15 You will plant crops
but not harvest them.
You will press your olives
but not get enough oil to anoint yourselves.
You will trample the grapes
but get no juice to make your wine.
16 You keep only the laws of evil King Omri;
you follow only the example of wicked King Ahab!
Therefore, I will make an example of you,
bringing you to complete ruin.
You will be treated with contempt,
mocked by all who see you."

EVERYBODY'S DOING IT? 7:1-4

Micah couldn't find a godly or fair-minded person anywhere in the land. Ever share that feeling of despair? When wrong actions are rationalized and we see Christians compromising, we can understand Micah's feelings. Sadly, too often we convince ourselves that wrong actions are okay, especially when "everyone else is doing it." But our standards for behavior come from God, not society. Are his standards yours? ■

7 MISERY TURNED TO HOPE

1 How miserable I am!
I feel like the fruit picker after the harvest
who can find nothing to eat.
Not a cluster of grapes or a single early fig
can be found to satisfy my hunger.
2 The godly people have all disappeared;
not one honest person is left on the earth.
They are all murderers,
setting traps even for their own brothers.
3 Both their hands are equally skilled at doing evil!
Officials and judges alike demand bribes.
The people with influence get what they want,
and together they scheme to twist justice.
4 Even the best of them is like a brier;
the most honest is as dangerous as a hedge of thorns.
But your judgment day is coming swiftly now.
Your time of punishment is here, a time
of confusion.
5 Don't trust anyone—
not your best friend or even your wife!
6 For the son despises his father.
The daughter defies her mother.
The daughter-in-law defies her mother-in-law.
Your enemies are right in your own household!

HONESTY

Terrance needs some new basketball shoes. He's got the perfect pair all picked out—a brand that the best dunkers in the NBA wear. Problem is, the shoes cost well over $150.

A few other guys in the neighborhood already have the shoes. One guy who deals drugs has three pairs. Another teen stole some from a locker at school. A third shoplifted his pair. Terrance really wants these new basketball shoes, but he would never do something illegal or dishonest to get them . . . or would he?

This afternoon, a guy from the neighborhood, who is the assistant manager of a downtown shoe store, came up with a foolproof plan. By marking certain shoes defective, he can cut the price, then cover it all up by juggling some figures.

"It's cool," a friend tells Terrance. "The store makes money, you get your shoes cheap, and you're not stealing."

Terrance thinks long and hard, then decides that the friend's plan is wrong. "It's hard to walk away from such a good deal," Terrance says, "but those shoes aren't worth doing something dishonest."

Meanwhile all his friends are taking advantage of the store's "defective" merchandise.

How would you have handled this situation? Read Micah 7:1-4. Do you think Terrance might be feeling the way the prophet Micah felt? Why or why not?

7 As for me, I look to the LORD for help.
I wait confidently for God to save me,
and my God will certainly hear me.
8 Do not gloat over me, my enemies!
For though I fall, I will rise again.
Though I sit in darkness,
the LORD will be my light.
9 I will be patient as the LORD punishes me,
for I have sinned against him.

6:9 Hebrew *"Listen to the rod. / Who appointed it?"* **6:10** Hebrew *of using the short ephah?* The ephah was a unit for measuring grain.

But after that, he will take up
my case
and give me justice for all I have
suffered from my enemies.
The LORD will bring me into
the light,
and I will see his righteousness.
10 Then my enemies will see that the
LORD is on my side.
They will be ashamed that they
taunted me, saying,
"So where is the LORD—
that God of yours?"
With my own eyes I will see
their downfall;
they will be trampled like mud in the streets.

All the nations of the world will stand amazed at what the LORD will do for you.

MICAH 7:16

11 In that day, Israel, your cities will be rebuilt,
and your borders will be extended.
12 People from many lands will come and honor you—
from Assyria all the way to the towns of Egypt,
from Egypt all the way to the Euphrates River,*
and from distant seas and mountains.
13 But the land* will become empty and desolate
because of the wickedness of those who live there.

MERCY 7:18-20

The book of Micah ends with a message of mercy. God delights in showing mercy. He doesn't forgive grudgingly; he's truly glad when we admit that we need his help to change. He offers forgiveness to all who come back to him. Is that the kind of mercy you offer to those who wrong you? ■

THE LORD'S COMPASSION ON ISRAEL

14 O LORD, protect your people with your
shepherd's staff;
lead your flock, your special possession.
Though they live alone in a thicket
on the heights of Mount
Carmel,*
let them graze in the fertile
pastures of Bashan and Gilead
as they did long ago.

15 "Yes," says the LORD,
"I will do mighty miracles
for you,
like those I did when I rescued you
from slavery in Egypt."

16 All the nations of the world will
stand amazed
at what the LORD will do for you.
They will be embarrassed
at their feeble power.
They will cover their mouths in silent awe,
deaf to everything around them.
17 Like snakes crawling from their holes,
they will come out to meet the LORD our God.
They will fear him greatly,
trembling in terror at his presence.

18 Where is another God like you,
who pardons the guilt of the remnant,
overlooking the sins of his special people?
You will not stay angry with your
people forever,
because you delight in showing
unfailing love.
19 Once again you will have compassion on us.
You will trample our sins under your feet
and throw them into the depths of
the ocean!
20 You will show us your faithfulness and
unfailing love
as you promised to our ancestors Abraham
and Jacob long ago.

7:12 Hebrew *the river.* **7:13** Or *earth.* **7:14** Or *surrounded by a fruitful land.*

NAHUM

OH NO, thought Cullen, *we're gonna lose again. "The Enforcer" is on their side.* "The Enforcer" was Jamie, the best athlete in the school. His team always won.

Cullen usually rejoiced when his gym class played football—except when Jamie was on the other team. Cullen was good, but Jamie was great. He could out*everything* anyone.

Nineveh, the Assyrian capital, was like "The Enforcer." Not one nation had been able to stand against them. They had overthrown Israel (northern kingdom); now their sights were on Judah. The people of Judah were afraid.

Through Nahum, God brought words of comfort to Judah and words of doom to Assyria. Nahum said, "The LORD is a jealous God. . . . He takes revenge on all who oppose him and continues to rage against his enemies!" (1:2). God told Judah, "Now I will break the yoke of bondage from your neck and tear off the chains of Assyrian oppression" (1:13). But God told Assyria, "I am your enemy! . . . Your chariots will soon go up in smoke. Your young men will be killed in battle. Never again will you plunder conquered nations" (2:13).

Such is the end of those who oppose the Lord and hurt his people. God loves his children and will protect them—at all costs. As you read Nahum, may this promise encourage you.

timeline

697 B.C.
Manasseh becomes king of Judah

669
Ashurbanipal becomes king of Assyria

663
The fall of Thebes; Nahum becomes a prophet

640
Josiah becomes king of Judah; Zephaniah becomes a prophet

627
Jeremiah becomes a prophet

612
Nineveh falls

609
Assyria completely conquered

605
Babylonians win battle of Carchemish

586
Judah falls to Babylon

stats

PURPOSE: To pronounce God's judgment on Assyria and to comfort Judah with this truth

AUTHOR: Nahum

TO WHOM WRITTEN: The people of Nineveh and Judah

DATE WRITTEN: Sometime during Nahum's prophetic ministry (probably between 663 and 612 B.C.)

SETTING: This particular prophecy takes place after the fall of Thebes in 663 B.C. (see 3:8-10).

KEY PLACE: Nineveh, the capital of Assyria

KEY points

INVINCIBLE
Although Assyria was the leading military power in the world, God would completely destroy this "invincible" nation. Only God is truly invincible. He has supreme power.

GOD RULES
God rules over all the earth, even over those who don't acknowledge him. God is all-powerful—no one can thwart his plans. If you're impressed by or afraid of any weapons, armies, or powerful people, remember that God alone can truly rescue you from fear or oppression.

1 This message concerning Nineveh came as a vision to Nahum, who lived in Elkosh.

VENGEANCE

Rich is mad—and rightly so. Before baseball practice yesterday, he confided in teammates Tony and Paul about his secret crush—Danielle—and how he wished he could get up the nerve to ask her out.

Not only did Rich's confidants take that information, twist it, and spread embarrassing rumors all over the locker room, but Tony went home last night and called Danielle to ask her out!

All day Rich has wanted to punch Tony out cold, or at the very least, knock his head off in practice that afternoon. He's been daydreaming of ways to get even. Mixed in with his rage is also a measure of hurt. *I thought those guys were my friends,* he tells himself over and over.

But at baseball practice, Rich doesn't react at all. He doesn't yell or throw punches. He even passes up several prime opportunities to get back at Tony and Paul with cheap shots and blindsides.

"Just because they were jerks doesn't mean I have to be one, too," he tells a surprised friend later.

When people wrong us, it's natural to want to take revenge. But, like Rich, we can resist that powerful urge to get even!

Yet there is One who claims the right to take revenge. Check out Nahum 1:2-8. While you're at it, read Leviticus 19:18 and Deuteronomy 32:35. Why do you think revenge is off-limits for us but not for God?

THE LORD'S ANGER AGAINST NINEVEH

2 The LORD is a jealous God,
filled with vengeance and rage.
He takes revenge on all who oppose him
and continues to rage against his enemies!
3 The LORD is slow to get angry, but his power is great,
and he never lets the guilty go unpunished.
He displays his power in the whirlwind and the storm.
The billowing clouds are the dust beneath his feet.
4 At his command the oceans dry up,
and the rivers disappear.
The lush pastures of Bashan and Carmel fade,
and the green forests of Lebanon wither.
5 In his presence the mountains quake,
and the hills melt away;
the earth trembles,
and its people are destroyed.
6 Who can stand before his fierce anger?
Who can survive his burning fury?
His rage blazes forth like fire,
and the mountains crumble to dust in his presence.
7 The LORD is good,
a strong refuge when trouble comes.
He is close to those who trust in him.
8 But he will sweep away his enemies
in an overwhelming flood.
He will pursue his foes
into the darkness of night.

TIME'S UP 1:1-8

Although God is slow to get angry, when he's ready to punish, even the earth trembles. Often people become angry with God because they think he is powerless over the evil in the world. They don't realize that because God is slow to anger, he gives people the opportunity to seek his forgiveness. But judgment *will* come. God won't allow evil to go unpunished forever. When people wonder why God doesn't punish evil immediately, you can remind them of the above truth. One day, God will call a time-out on evil. ■

9 Why are you scheming against the LORD?
He will destroy you with one blow;
he won't need to strike twice!
10 His enemies, tangled like thornbushes
and staggering like drunks,
will be burned up like dry stubble in a field.
11 Who is this wicked counselor of yours
who plots evil against the LORD?

12 This is what the LORD says:
"Though the Assyrians have many allies,
they will be destroyed and disappear.
O my people, I have punished you before,
but I will not punish you again.
13 Now I will break the yoke of bondage from your neck
and tear off the chains of Assyrian oppression."

14 And this is what the LORD says concerning the Assyrians in Nineveh:
"You will have no more children to carry on your name.
I will destroy all the idols in the temples of your gods.
I am preparing a grave for you
because you are despicable!"

15* Look! A messenger is coming over the mountains
with good news!
He is bringing a message of peace.
Celebrate your festivals, O people of Judah,
and fulfill all your vows,
for your wicked enemies will never invade your land again.
They will be completely destroyed!

1:15 Verse 1:15 is numbered 2:1 in Hebrew text.

2 THE FALL OF NINEVEH

1*Your enemy is coming to crush you, Nineveh.
Man the ramparts! Watch the roads!
Prepare your defenses! Call out your forces!

2 Even though the destroyer has destroyed Judah,
the LORD will restore its honor.
Israel's vine has been stripped of branches,
but he will restore its splendor.

3 Shields flash red in the sunlight!
See the scarlet uniforms of the valiant troops!
Watch as their glittering chariots move into position,
with a forest of spears waving above them.
4 The chariots race recklessly along the streets
and rush wildly through the squares.
They flash like firelight
and move as swiftly as lightning.
5 The king shouts to his officers;
they stumble in their haste,
rushing to the walls to set up their defenses.
6 The river gates have been torn open!
The palace is about to collapse!
7 Nineveh's exile has been decreed,
and all the servant girls mourn its capture.
They moan like doves
and beat their breasts in sorrow.
8 Nineveh is like a leaking water reservoir!
The people are slipping away.
"Stop, stop!" someone shouts,
but no one even looks back.
9 Loot the silver!
Plunder the gold!
There's no end to Nineveh's treasures—
its vast, uncounted wealth.
10 Soon the city is plundered, empty, and ruined.
Hearts melt and knees shake.
The people stand aghast,
their faces pale and trembling.

11 Where now is that great Nineveh,
that den filled with young lions?
It was a place where people—like lions and
their cubs—
walked freely and without fear.
12 The lion tore up meat for his cubs
and strangled prey for his mate.
He filled his den with prey,
his caverns with his plunder.

13 "I am your enemy!"
says the LORD of Heaven's Armies.
"Your chariots will soon go up in smoke.
Your young men* will be killed in battle.
Never again will you plunder conquered nations.
The voices of your proud messengers will be
heard no more."

TAKE A STAND 2:1-3:1

The major source of the Assyrians' wealth was what they stole from other nations. The Assyrians took the food of people they conquered to maintain their own luxurious standard of living. They deprived others to supply their excesses. Does that sound familiar? God wants his people to take a stand against any injustice they find. What are you willing to do in this fight for justice? ■

3 THE LORD'S JUDGMENT AGAINST NINEVEH

1 What sorrow awaits Nineveh,
the city of murder and lies!
She is crammed with wealth
and is never without victims.
2 Hear the crack of whips,
the rumble of wheels!
Horses' hooves pound,
and chariots clatter wildly.
3 See the flashing swords and glittering spears
as the charioteers charge past!
There are countless casualties,
heaps of bodies—
so many bodies that
people stumble over them.
4 All this because Nineveh,
the beautiful and faithless city,
mistress of deadly charms,
enticed the nations with her beauty.
She taught them all her magic,
enchanting people everywhere.

5 "I am your enemy!"
says the LORD of Heaven's Armies.
"And now I will lift your skirts
and show all the earth your nakedness and shame.
6 I will cover you with filth
and show the world how vile you really are.
7 All who see you will shrink back and say,
'Nineveh lies in ruins.
Where are the mourners?'
Does anyone regret your destruction?"

8 Are you any better than the city of Thebes,*
situated on the Nile River, surrounded by water?
She was protected by the river on all sides,
walled in by water.
9 Ethiopia* and the land of Egypt
gave unlimited assistance.
The nations of Put and Libya
were among her allies.
10 Yet Thebes fell,
and her people were led away as captives.
Her babies were dashed to death
against the stones of the streets.

2:1 Verses 2:1-13 are numbered 2:2-14 in Hebrew text. **2:13** Hebrew *young lions.* **3:8** Hebrew *No-amon;* also in 3:10. **3:9** Hebrew *Cush.*

Nahum

Served as a prophet to Judah and Assyria from 663 to 654 B.C.	*Climate of the times*	Manasseh, one of Judah's most wicked kings, ruled the land. He openly defied God and persecuted God's people. Assyria, the world power at that time, made Judah one of its vassal states. The people of Judah wanted to be like the Assyrians, who seemed to have all the power and possessions they wanted.
	Main message	The mighty empire of Assyria, the oppressors of God's people, would tumble soon.
	Importance of message	Those who do evil and oppress others will one day meet a bitter end.
	Contemporary prophet	Zephaniah (640–621)

Soldiers threw dice* to get Egyptian officers as servants.
All their leaders were bound in chains.

11 And you, Nineveh, will also stagger like a drunkard.
You will hide for fear of the attacking enemy.
12 All your fortresses will fall.
They will be devoured like the ripe figs
that fall into the mouths
of those who shake the trees.
13 Your troops will be as weak
and helpless as women.
The gates of your land will be opened wide
to the enemy
and set on fire and burned.
14 Get ready for the siege!
Store up water!
Strengthen the defenses!
Go into the pits to trample clay,
and pack it into molds,
making bricks to repair the walls.

15 But the fire will devour you;
the sword will cut you down.
The enemy will consume you like locusts,
devouring everything they see.
There will be no escape,
even if you multiply like swarming locusts.
16 Your merchants have multiplied
until they outnumber the stars.
But like a swarm of locusts,
they strip the land and fly away.
17 Your guards* and officials are also like
swarming locusts
that crowd together in the hedges on a cold day.
But like locusts that fly away when the sun
comes up,
all of them will fly away and disappear.

18 Your shepherds are asleep, O Assyrian king;
your princes lie dead in the dust.
Your people are scattered across the mountains
with no one to gather them together.
19 There is no healing for your wound;
your injury is fatal.
All who hear of your destruction
will clap their hands for joy.
Where can anyone be found
who has not suffered from your continual
cruelty?

3:10 Hebrew *They cast lots.* **3:17** Or *princes.*

HABAKKUK

habakkuk

EMMA SAT in Sunday school that week, hoping to get some questions answered. Each week the class had discussed questions that seemed to have no easy answers: If God is so good, why is there suffering in the world? If God controls everything, how can we truly have free will?

But Emma had her own question. As the room settled, Emma raised her hand. She began, "Why does it seem like those who try to live the way Jesus would want them to are so often abused by those who don't care how they live? Doesn't God care? It doesn't seem fair!"

Many centuries ago, Habakkuk had similar thoughts. He looked over his own country, Judah, and saw that wherever he looked there was "destruction and violence. . . . The wicked far outnumber the righteous" (1:3-4). He questioned God's concern for the people who really tried to please God. Those who did evil always got the upper hand.

God answered Habakkuk enough to satisfy his concerns. Habakkuk was inspired to reply, "I have heard all about you, LORD. I am filled with awe. . . . help us again. . . . And in your anger, remember your mercy" (3:2).

As you read this book, take note of God's answer. It may surprise you. And then, like Habakkuk, you can resolve to trust God to care for you.

timeline

627 B.C.
Jeremiah becomes a prophet

612
Habakkuk becomes a prophet

609
King Josiah dies in battle

605
Daniel taken captive to Babylon

597
Ezekiel a captive in Babylon; Zedekiah becomes king

588
Habakkuk's ministry ends

586
Fall of Judah; Jerusalem destroyed

stats

PURPOSE: To show that God is still in control of the world despite the apparent triumph of evil

AUTHOR: Habakkuk

TO WHOM WRITTEN: Judah (the southern kingdom) and God's people everywhere

DATE WRITTEN: Between 612 and 588 B.C.

SETTING: Babylon was becoming the dominant world power. Judah would soon feel Babylon's destructive force.

KEY PEOPLE: Habakkuk, the Chaldeans (Babylonians)

KEY PLACE: Judah

KEY points

STRUGGLE AND DOUBT

When Habakkuk cried out for answers in his time of struggle, God answered him with words of hope. God wants us to come to him with our struggles and doubts.

GOD'S SOVEREIGNTY

God planned to use the Babylonians to punish his people. He would also punish the Babylonians after they had fulfilled his purpose. God is still in control of this world, despite the apparent triumph of evil. One day he will rule the whole earth with perfect justice.

HOPE

Habakkuk ended his book on a note of hope as he praised God for strengthening him. We also can have confidence that God loves us and provides strength when we're weak.

1

This is the message that the prophet Habakkuk received in a vision.

HABAKKUK'S COMPLAINT

2 How long, O LORD, must I call for help?
But you do not listen!
"Violence is everywhere!" I cry,
but you do not come to save.
3 Must I forever see these evil deeds?
Why must I watch all this misery?
Wherever I look,
I see destruction and violence.
I am surrounded by people
who love to argue and fight.
4 The law has become paralyzed,
and there is no justice in the courts.
The wicked far outnumber the righteous,
so that justice has become perverted.

WAIT FOR IT 1:1–2:3

Habakkuk complained vigorously to God about the evil he noticed. Like Habakkuk, Christians often feel angry and discouraged as they observe the injustices that take place. Can you relate? God's answer to his prophet is the same answer he would give us: "If it [the unfolding of God's plans] seems slow in coming, wait patiently, for it will surely take place" (2:3). It isn't easy to be patient, but it helps to remember that God hates sin even more than we do. Trusting God fully means trusting him even when we don't understand why events occur as they do. ■

THE LORD'S REPLY

5The LORD replied,

"Look around at the nations;
look and be amazed!*
For I am doing something in your own day,
something you wouldn't believe
even if someone told you about it.
6 I am raising up the Babylonians,*
a cruel and violent people.
They will march across the world
and conquer other lands.
7 They are notorious for their cruelty
and do whatever they like.
8 Their horses are swifter than cheetahs*
and fiercer than wolves at dusk.
Their charioteers charge from far away.
Like eagles, they swoop down to devour their prey.

9 "On they come, all bent on violence.
Their hordes advance like a desert wind,
sweeping captives ahead of them like sand.
10 They scoff at kings and princes
and scorn all their fortresses.
They simply pile ramps of earth
against their walls and capture them!
11 They sweep past like the wind
and are gone.
But they are deeply guilty,
for their own strength is their god."

HABAKKUK'S SECOND COMPLAINT

12 O LORD my God, my Holy One, you who are eternal—
surely you do not plan to wipe us out?
O LORD, our Rock, you have sent these Babylonians
to correct us,
to punish us for our many sins.
13 But you are pure and cannot stand the sight of evil.
Will you wink at their treachery?
Should you be silent while the wicked
swallow up people more righteous than they?
14 Are we only fish to be caught and killed?
Are we only sea creatures that have no leader?
15 Must we be strung up on their hooks
and caught in their nets while they rejoice
and celebrate?
16 Then they will worship their nets
and burn incense in front of them.
"These nets are the gods who have made us rich!"
they will claim.
17 Will you let them get away with this forever?
Will they succeed forever in their heartless conquests?

LIVE BY FAITH 2:4

The just (righteous) live by their faith and trust in God. This verse has inspired countless Christians. Paul refers to it in Romans 1:17 and quotes it in Galatians 3:11. The writer of Hebrews quotes it in 10:38, just before the famous chapter on faith. And it is helpful to all Christians who live through difficult times. Those who live by faith believe that God directs all things according to his purposes. Is that your belief? ■

2

1 I will climb up to my watchtower
and stand at my guardpost.
There I will wait to see what the LORD says
and how he* will answer my complaint.

THE LORD'S SECOND REPLY

2Then the LORD said to me,

"Write my answer plainly on tablets,
so that a runner can carry the correct message
to others.
3 This vision is for a future time.
It describes the end, and it will be fulfilled.

1:5 Greek version reads *Look you mockers; / look and be amazed and die.* Compare Acts 13:41. 1:6 Or *Chaldeans.* 1:8 Or *leopards.*
2:1 As in Syriac version; Hebrew reads *I.*

Habakkuk

Served as a prophet to Judah from 612 to 588 B.C.	*Climate of the times*	Judah's last four kings were wicked men who rejected God and oppressed their own people. Babylon invaded Judah twice before finally destroying it in 586. It was a time of fear, oppression, persecution, lawlessness, and immorality.
	Main message	Habakkuk couldn't understand why God seemed to do nothing about the wickedness in society. Then he realized that faith in God alone would supply the answers to his questions.
	Importance of message	Instead of questioning the ways of God, we should realize that he is totally just, and we should have faith that he is in control and that one day evil will be utterly destroyed.
	Contemporary prophets	Jeremiah (627–586) Daniel (605–536) Ezekiel (593–571)

If it seems slow in coming, wait patiently,
for it will surely take place.
It will not be delayed.

4 "Look at the proud!
They trust in themselves, and
their lives are crooked.
But the righteous will live by their
faithfulness to God.*
5 Wealth* is treacherous,
and the arrogant are never
at rest.
They open their mouths as wide
as the grave,*
and like death, they are never
satisfied.
In their greed they have gathered
up many nations
and swallowed many peoples.

6 "But soon their captives will
taunt them.
They will mock them, saying,
'What sorrow awaits you thieves!
Now you will get what you deserve!
You've become rich by extortion,
but how much longer can this go on?'
7 Suddenly, your debtors will take action.
They will turn on you and take all
you have,
while you stand trembling and helpless.
8 Because you have plundered many nations;
now all the survivors will plunder you.
You committed murder throughout
the countryside
and filled the towns with violence.

9 "What sorrow awaits you who
build big houses
with money gained dishonestly!
You believe your wealth will buy
security,
putting your family's nest
beyond the reach of danger.
10 But by the murders you
committed,
you have shamed your name and
forfeited your lives.
11 The very stones in the walls cry out
against you,
and the beams in the ceilings
echo the complaint.

12 "What sorrow awaits you who build cities
with money gained through murder and corruption!
13 Has not the LORD of Heaven's Armies promised
that the wealth of nations will turn to ashes?
They work so hard,
but all in vain!
14 For as the waters fill the sea,
the earth will be filled with an awareness
of the glory of the LORD.

For as the waters fill the sea, the earth will be filled with an awareness of the glory of the LORD.
HABAKKUK 2:14

2:3b-4 Greek version reads *If the vision is delayed, wait patiently, / for it will surely come and not delay. / ⁴I will take no pleasure in anyone who turns away. / But the righteous person will live by my faith.* Compare Rom 1:17; Gal 3:11; Heb 10:37-38. **2:5a** As in Dead Sea Scroll 1QpHab; other Hebrew manuscripts read *Wine.* **2:5b** Hebrew *as Sheol.*

15 "What sorrow awaits you who make your
neighbors drunk!
You force your cup on them
so you can gloat over their shameful nakedness.
16 But soon it will be your turn to be disgraced.
Come, drink and be exposed!
Drink from the cup of the LORD's judgment,
and all your glory will be turned to shame.
17 You cut down the forests of Lebanon.
Now you will be cut down.
You destroyed the wild animals,
so now their terror will be yours.
You committed murder throughout the countryside
and filled the towns with violence.

18 "What good is an idol carved by man,
or a cast image that deceives you?
How foolish to trust in your own creation—
a god that can't even talk!
19 What sorrow awaits you who say to wooden idols,
'Wake up and save us!'
To speechless stone images you say,
'Rise up and teach us!'
Can an idol tell you what to do?
They may be overlaid with gold and silver,
but they are lifeless inside.
20 But the LORD is in his holy Temple.
Let all the earth be silent before him."

3 HABAKKUK'S PRAYER

This prayer was sung by the prophet Habakkuk*:

2 I have heard all about you, LORD.
I am filled with awe by your amazing works.
In this time of our deep need,
help us again as you did in years gone by.
And in your anger,
remember your mercy.

3 I see God moving across the deserts from Edom,*
the Holy One coming from Mount Paran.*
His brilliant splendor fills the heavens,
and the earth is filled with his praise.
4 His coming is as brilliant as the sunrise.
Rays of light flash from his hands,
where his awesome power is hidden.
5 Pestilence marches before him;
plague follows close behind.
6 When he stops, the earth shakes.
When he looks, the nations tremble.
He shatters the everlasting mountains
and levels the eternal hills.
He is the Eternal One!
7 I see the people of Cushan in distress,
and the nation of Midian trembling in terror.
8 Was it in anger, LORD, that you struck the rivers
and parted the sea?
Were you displeased with them?
No, you were sending your chariots
of salvation!
9 You brandished your bow
and your quiver of arrows.
You split open the earth with flowing rivers.
10 The mountains watched and trembled.
Onward swept the raging waters.
The mighty deep cried out,
lifting its hands to the LORD.
11 The sun and moon stood still in the sky
as your brilliant arrows flew
and your glittering spear flashed.

HARD TIMES

When people drive past the Hunter house, they almost always shake their heads and say: "I just don't understand why one family has had to undergo so much grief."

"I know. They've had one crisis after another."

"How do Sheila and her mom keep going? I don't know what I'd do if I were either one of them."

Exaggerations? Not at all.

- **Shane, the youngest son, committed suicide two years ago.**
- **Mr. Hunter had hepatitis, strokes, and serious back problems. He died suddenly last spring.**
- **The family has faced serious financial problems.**
- **Shannon, the 18-year-old daughter, has been rebellious and promiscuous. She just moved in with an older, married man.**

How *do* Sheila, the youngest daughter, and her mom keep going? Well, Sheila relies on her faith in God—a faith her mom has. Both cling to the promise that somehow, some way, God is in control. And in the dark and lonely nights of their ordeal, they hope that God will one day restore their shattered family.

Habakkuk tackles the tough issue of "Where is God when my world is falling apart?" The situation facing the ancient Hebrew prophet was very different from the problems above—and probably from yours—but the words of 3:17-19 give hope to all who hurt.

12 You marched across the land in anger
and trampled the nations in your fury.
13 You went out to rescue your chosen people,
to save your anointed ones.
You crushed the heads of the wicked
and stripped their bones from head to toe.
14 With his own weapons,
you destroyed the chief of those

3:1 Hebrew adds *according to shigionoth,* probably indicating the musical setting for the prayer. **3:3a** Hebrew *Teman.* **3:3b** Hebrew adds *selah;* also in 3:9, 13. The meaning of this Hebrew term is uncertain; it is probably a musical or literary term.

AMAZING STRENGTH 3:17-19

Crop failure and the death of animals would devastate Judah. But Habakkuk affirmed that even in the midst of starvation, he would still rejoice in the Lord. Habakkuk's feelings were not controlled by the events around him, but by faith in God's ability to give him strength. When nothing seems to make sense, and when troubles seem more than you can handle, what do you usually focus on—your difficulties or his deity? Like Habakkuk will you choose to rely on God? ■

CONFIDENCE 3:19

Habakkuk had asked God why evil people prosper while the righteous suffer. God's answer: In the long run, they don't. Habakkuk saw his own limitations in contrast to God's unlimited control of the world's events. God still maintains that control. We cannot see all that God is doing or will do. But we can be assured that he is God and will do what is right. Do you believe that? ■

who rushed out like a whirlwind,
thinking Israel would be easy prey.
15 You trampled the sea with your horses,
and the mighty waters piled high.

16 I trembled inside when I heard this;
my lips quivered with fear.
My legs gave way beneath me,*
and I shook in terror.
I will wait quietly for the coming day
when disaster will strike the people who invade us.
17 Even though the fig trees have no blossoms,
and there are no grapes on the vines;
even though the olive crop fails,
and the fields lie empty and barren;
even though the flocks die in the fields,
and the cattle barns are empty,
18 yet I will rejoice in the LORD!
I will be joyful in the God of my salvation!
19 The Sovereign LORD is my strength!
He makes me as surefooted as a deer,*
able to tread upon the heights.

(For the choir director: This prayer is to be accompanied by stringed instruments.)

3:16 Hebrew *Decay entered my bones.* **3:19** Or *He gives me the speed of a deer.*

ZEPHANIAH

IT WAS THE day grades were to be handed out and parent/teacher meetings. No classes were held, but appointments were set between students, parents, homeroom teachers, and the most recent grade slips. What a deadly mix!

Most students hated the idea, especially those who were not doing well in school. It was one thing to get bad grades, but quite another to sit with three adults and talk about them. Parents were known to react poorly. Teachers could get emotional, too. Even students who were doing well in school sometimes were reprimanded.

When the school paper wrote an article about this day (affectionately termed "Death Day"), the reactions were varied. However, most of the student body agreed with one student who was quoted as saying, "I don't think Judgment Day could be any worse!"

Well, Judgment Day will be much worse! Zephaniah tells us about it in his book. Like "Death Day," it will be a day of reckoning—a time of terrible wrath and punishment. Ironically, it also will be a time of mercy.

As you read Zephaniah, perhaps you'll confront any fears you have about Judgment Day. If you're a believer, this is one day you won't have to fear. Isn't that comforting?

zephaniah

timeline

640 B.C.
Zephaniah becomes a prophet; Josiah becomes king of Judah

627
Jeremiah becomes a prophet

622
Book of the Law found in the Temple

621
Zephaniah's ministry ends

609
Josiah dies in battle

605
First captives taken to Babylon

597
Babylon's second attack on Judah

586
Judah (the southern kingdom) falls

stats

PURPOSE: To shake the people of Judah out of their complacency and urge them to return to God

AUTHOR: Zephaniah

TO WHOM WRITTEN: Judah and all nations

DATE WRITTEN: Probably near the end of Zephaniah's ministry (640–621 B.C.), when King Josiah's great reforms began

SETTING: King Josiah of Judah attempted to reverse the evil trends set by the two previous kings—Manasseh and Amon. (See 2 Kings 21–23.) Josiah was able to extend his influence, because no other strong nation dominated the world at that time. (Assyria rapidly declined.) Zephaniah's prophecy may have been the motivating factor in Josiah's reform. Zephaniah was a contemporary of Jeremiah.

KEY PLACE: Jerusalem

KEY points

DAY OF JUDGMENT
Destruction was coming because the people of Judah worshiped idols instead of God. God's warning was a strong hint for them to return to him. Likewise, God warns of a coming worldwide time of judgment. Those who trust in Jesus will not have to fear this judgment.

INDIFFERENCE TO GOD
God's demands for righteous living seemed irrelevant to the people of Judah, whose security and wealth made them complacent. Complacency is a trap we can avoid by admitting our dependence on God, rather than on our resources.

DAY OF JOY
The day of judgment will also be a day of joy. God will restore his people and give them hope. God promises to restore us whenever we confess our wrongs and seek his forgiveness.

1

The LORD gave this message to Zephaniah when Josiah son of Amon was king of Judah. Zephaniah was the son of Cushi, son of Gedaliah, son of Amariah, son of Hezekiah.

SHORTSIGHTED 1:1-18

The people of Judah were clearly warned by the highest authority of all—God. But they refused to listen, either because they doubted God's prophet (and thus did not believe the message was from God), or because they doubted God himself (and thus did not believe he would do what he said). Now that we have the whole Bible, we can see how shortsighted they were. The people of Judah were conquered by their enemies, just as Zephaniah prophesied. But we're equally shortsighted if we ignore the warnings in the Bible. ■

COMING JUDGMENT AGAINST JUDAH

2 "I will sweep away everything
from the face of the earth," says the LORD.
3 "I will sweep away people and animals alike.
I will sweep away the birds of the sky and the fish in the sea.
I will reduce the wicked to heaps of rubble,*
and I will wipe humanity from the face of the earth," says the LORD.
4 "I will crush Judah and Jerusalem with my fist
and destroy every last trace of their Baal worship.
I will put an end to all the idolatrous priests,
so that even the memory of them will disappear.
5 For they go up to their roofs
and bow down to the sun, moon, and stars.
They claim to follow the LORD,
but then they worship Molech,* too.
6 And I will destroy those who used to worship me
but now no longer do.
They no longer ask for the LORD's guidance
or seek my blessings."

7 Stand in silence in the presence of the Sovereign LORD,
for the awesome day of the LORD's judgment is near.
The LORD has prepared his people for a great slaughter
and has chosen their executioners.*
8 "On that day of judgment,"
says the LORD,
"I will punish the leaders and princes of Judah
and all those following pagan customs.
9 Yes, I will punish those who participate in pagan worship ceremonies,
and those who fill their masters' houses with violence and deceit.

10 "On that day," says the LORD,
"a cry of alarm will come from the Fish Gate
and echo throughout the New Quarter of the city.*
And a great crash will sound from the hills.
11 Wail in sorrow, all you who live in the market area,
for all the merchants and traders will be destroyed.

12 "I will search with lanterns in Jerusalem's darkest corners
to punish those who sit complacent in their sins.
They think the LORD will do nothing to them,
either good or bad.
13 So their property will be plundered,
their homes will be ransacked.
They will build new homes
but never live in them.
They will plant vineyards
but never drink wine from them.

JUDGMENT

The people of the Bible Church sit in shocked silence as the guest preacher delivers his thundering message of moral decay and imminent judgment.

Point by point, he describes how "our nation has turned its back on God." He cites court decisions, humanistic trends, disturbing statistics, and alarming examples of Christians who are being persecuted for their faith.

Afterwards, Nate, Sam, and Ayisha are discussing the service over a large pepperoni pizza.

"Do you think that preacher was right?" Nate asks.

Ayisha shrugs. "Yeah, maybe."

"So you think this nation is gonna be judged by God?" Sam asks.

"Probably so," Ayisha replies.

"But can't we do anything?" Nate queries.

Ayisha shrugs again. "I guess if there was a nationwide revival or something like that, maybe God would hold back."

Sam snorts. "What're the odds of a revival?"

Ayisha sighs. "I dunno. Who knows what might happen if all the Christians in just our town would really get right with God?"

Have you ever wondered that about your city? Around 635 B.C. Zephaniah prophesied judgment on the nation of Judah. Read about the only alternative to national (as well as personal) disaster in 1:14–2:3.

14 "That terrible day of the LORD is near.
Swiftly it comes—
a day of bitter tears,
a day when even strong men will cry out.

1:3 The meaning of the Hebrew is uncertain. 1:5 Hebrew *Malcam*, a variant spelling of Molech; or it could possibly mean *their king*. 1:7 Hebrew *has prepared a sacrifice and sanctified his guests*. 1:10 Or *the Second Quarter*, a newer section of Jerusalem. Hebrew reads *the Mishneh*.

15 It will be a day when the LORD's
anger is poured out—
a day of terrible distress and
anguish,
a day of ruin and desolation,
a day of darkness and gloom,
a day of clouds and blackness,
16 a day of trumpet calls and battle
cries.
Down go the walled cities
and the strongest battlements!

17 "Because you have sinned against
the LORD,
I will make you grope around like
the blind.
Your blood will be poured into the dust,
and your bodies will lie rotting on the ground."

18 Your silver and gold will not save you
on that day of the LORD's anger.
For the whole land will be devoured
by the fire of his jealousy.
He will make a terrifying end
of all the people on earth.*

Seek the LORD, all who are humble, and follow his commands. Seek to do what is right and to live humbly.

ZEPHANIAH 2:3

2

A CALL TO REPENTANCE

1 Gather together—yes, gather together,
you shameless nation.
2 Gather before judgment begins,
before your time to repent is blown away
like chaff.
Act now, before the fierce fury of the LORD falls
and the terrible day of the LORD's anger begins.
3 Seek the LORD, all who are humble,
and follow his commands.
Seek to do what is right
and to live humbly.
Perhaps even yet the LORD will protect you—
protect you from his anger on that day
of destruction.

JUDGMENT AGAINST PHILISTIA

4 Gaza and Ashkelon will be abandoned,
Ashdod and Ekron torn down.
5 And what sorrow awaits you Philistines*
who live along the coast and in the land of Canaan,
for this judgment is against you, too!
The LORD will destroy you
until not one of you is left.
6 The Philistine coast will become a wilderness
pasture,
a place of shepherd camps
and enclosures for sheep and goats.
7 The remnant of the tribe of Judah will pasture there.
They will rest at night in the abandoned houses
in Ashkelon.
For the LORD their God will visit his
people in kindness
and restore their prosperity
again.

JUDGMENT AGAINST MOAB AND AMMON

8 "I have heard the taunts of
the Moabites
and the insults of the
Ammonites,
mocking my people
and invading their borders.
9 Now, as surely as I live,"
says the LORD of Heaven's
Armies, the God of Israel,
"Moab and Ammon will
be destroyed—
destroyed as completely as Sodom and Gomorrah.
Their land will become a place of stinging nettles,
salt pits, and eternal desolation.
The remnant of my people will plunder them
and take their land."

10 They will receive the wages of their pride,
for they have scoffed at the people of the LORD of
Heaven's Armies.
11 The LORD will terrify them
as he destroys all the gods in the land.
Then nations around the world will worship
the LORD,
each in their own land.

COUNT ON IT 2:7

Although God promised that Judah would be destroyed, he also promised to save a remnant. In this way, he kept his original covenant to preserve Abraham's descendants (Gen 17:4-8; see also Jer 4:27). God is holy and can't allow sin to continue; yet he also keeps his promises. Feeling the heat of hard times? You can still count on this promise from God: "I will never fail you. I will never abandon you" (Heb 13:5). ■

JUDGMENT AGAINST ETHIOPIA AND ASSYRIA

12 "You Ethiopians* will also be slaughtered
by my sword," says the LORD.

13 And the LORD will strike the lands of the north with
his fist,
destroying the land of Assyria.
He will make its great capital, Nineveh, a desolate
wasteland,
parched like a desert.
14 The proud city will become a pasture for flocks
and herds,
and all sorts of wild animals will settle there.

1:18 Or *the people living in the land.* 2:5 Hebrew *Kerethites.* 2:12 Hebrew *Cushites.*

Zephaniah

Served as a prophet to Judah from 640 to 621 B.C.	*Climate of the times*	Josiah was the last good king in Judah. His bold attempts to reform the nation and turn it back to God were probably influenced by Zephaniah.
	Main message	A day will come when God, as Judge, will severely punish all nations. But after judgment, he will show mercy to all who have been faithful to him.
	Importance of message	We will all be judged for our disobedience to God—but if we remain faithful to him, he will show us mercy.
	Contemporary prophet	Jeremiah (627–586)

The desert owl and screech owl will roost on its
ruined columns,
their calls echoing through the gaping windows.
Rubble will block all the doorways,
and the cedar paneling will be exposed to
the weather.
15 This is the boisterous city,
once so secure.
"I am the greatest!" it boasted.
"No other city can compare with me!"
But now, look how it has become an utter ruin,
a haven for wild animals.
Everyone passing by will laugh in derision
and shake a defiant fist.

CLOSED EARS 3:1-2

The people of Judah had become too proud to listen to God's correction. Do you know people who refuse to listen when someone disagrees with their opinions? Those who are proud often refuse to listen to anything that contradicts their opinion. Some listen with closed ears to the spiritual advice of others or spiritual advice from the Bible. But God has a way of opening closed ears. Sometimes he has to do it the hard way—through hard times. How willing are you to listen to spiritual advice? Does God have to get your attention the hard way? ■

3 JERUSALEM'S REBELLION AND REDEMPTION

1 What sorrow awaits rebellious, polluted Jerusalem,
the city of violence and crime!
2 No one can tell it anything;
it refuses all correction.
It does not trust in the LORD
or draw near to its God.

3 Its leaders are like roaring lions
hunting for their victims.
Its judges are like ravenous wolves at evening time,
who by dawn have left no trace of their prey.
4 Its prophets are arrogant liars seeking their
own gain.
Its priests defile the Temple by disobeying
God's instructions.
5 But the LORD is still there in the city,
and he does no wrong.
Day by day he hands down justice,
and he does not fail.
But the wicked know no shame.

6 "I have wiped out many nations,
devastating their fortress walls and towers.
Their streets are now deserted;
their cities lie in silent ruin.
There are no survivors—
none at all.
7 I thought, 'Surely they will have reverence for me now!
Surely they will listen to my warnings.
Then I won't need to strike again,
destroying their homes.'
But no, they get up early
to continue their evil deeds.
8 Therefore, be patient," says the LORD.
"Soon I will stand and accuse these evil nations.
For I have decided to gather the kingdoms of the earth
and pour out my fiercest anger and fury on them.
All the earth will be devoured
by the fire of my jealousy.

9 "Then I will purify the speech of all people,
so that everyone can worship the LORD together.
10 My scattered people who live beyond the rivers
of Ethiopia*
will come to present their offerings.

3:10 Hebrew *Cush.*

11 On that day you will no longer need to
be ashamed,
for you will no longer be rebels against me.
I will remove all proud and arrogant people from
among you.
There will be no more haughtiness on my
holy mountain.
12 Those who are left will be the lowly and humble,
for it is they who trust in the name of the LORD.
13 The remnant of Israel will do no wrong;
they will never tell lies or deceive one another.
They will eat and sleep in safety,
and no one will make them afraid."

OPPOSED TO PRIDE 3:12

God is opposed to the pride of every generation. But as Zephaniah prophesied, the lowly and humble, both physically and spiritually, will be blessed because they trust in God. The message of humility is echoed throughout the Bible. (See Prov 3:34; James 4:6; 1 Pet 5:5.) Is it one you live by? ■

14 Sing, O daughter of Zion;
shout aloud, O Israel!
Be glad and rejoice with all your heart,
O daughter of Jerusalem!
15 For the LORD will remove his hand of judgment
and will disperse the armies of your enemy.
And the LORD himself, the King of Israel,
will live among you!
At last your troubles will be over,
and you will never again fear disaster.
16 On that day the announcement to Jerusalem
will be,
"Cheer up, Zion! Don't be afraid!
17 For the LORD your God is living among you.
He is a mighty savior.
He will take delight in you with gladness.
With his love, he will calm all your fears.*
He will rejoice over you with joyful songs."

18 "I will gather you who mourn for the appointed
festivals;
you will be disgraced no more.*
19 And I will deal severely with all who have
oppressed you.
I will save the weak and helpless ones;
I will bring together
those who were chased away.
I will give glory and fame to my former exiles,
wherever they have been mocked and shamed.
20 On that day I will gather you together
and bring you home again.
I will give you a good name, a name of distinction,
among all the nations of the earth,
as I restore your fortunes before their very eyes.
I, the LORD, have spoken!"

3:17 Or *He will be silent in his love.* Greek and Syriac versions read *He will renew you with his love.* 3:18 The meaning of the Hebrew for this verse is uncertain.

HAGGAI

BJORN AND OMAR are camping—in Omar's huge backyard. You can barely see the house from their tent.

On "camping nights" Bjorn and Omar usually talk. In the past, it was girls, but they've discussed other subjects.

"Omar," Bjorn asks, "if you had to give up everything but one thing in your life, what would you keep?" Bjorn is not very serious most of the time, but he is now.

"I'd have to give up everything?" Omar responds.

"All but one. What's most important to you?"

Omar thinks for a few seconds before answering. "I can narrow it down to three. I would keep my family and friends, Cassandra (the girl he likes), and my wheels."

"What about God?" Bjorn questions. "You would give him up for Cassandra?"

"Oh," laughs Omar, "I didn't even think about God."

The Jews, who had returned from captivity, were like Omar—they'd forgotten about God. They had let him slip from their life. So God sent Haggai, a prophet, to remind them of what was really important in life.

God refuses to be forgotten. He wants top priority in our lives. As you read the book of Haggai, notice how God blesses those who make him number one. Is he number one in your life?

timeline

605 B.C.
Daniel taken to Babylon

597
Ezekiel taken to Babylon

586
Jerusalem falls

539
Babylon overthrown by Cyrus

538
Cyrus's decree allowing the exiles to return

537
Exiles return to Jerusalem

536
Temple construction begins

530
Temple work halted

520
Haggai, Zechariah become prophets; Temple work resumed

516
Temple completed

458
Ezra comes to Jerusalem

445
Nehemiah comes to Jerusalem

stats

PURPOSE: To encourage the returning exiles to complete the rebuilding of the Temple

AUTHOR: Haggai

TO WHOM WRITTEN: The people living in Jerusalem and those who had returned from exile

DATE WRITTEN: 520 B.C.

SETTING: The Temple in Jerusalem had been destroyed in 586 B.C. Cyrus allowed the Jews to return to their homeland and rebuild their Temple in 538 B.C. They began the work, but were unable to complete it. During the ministry of Haggai and Zechariah, the Temple was completed (520–515 B.C.).

KEY PEOPLE: Haggai, Zerubbabel, Joshua

KEY PLACE: Jerusalem

SPECIAL FEATURES: Haggai was the first of the postexilic prophets. The other two were Zechariah and Malachi. The literary style of this book is simple and direct.

KEY points

RIGHT PRIORITIES

God had given the formerly captive people of Israel the task of finishing the Temple in Jerusalem. But after 15 years, they still had not completed it. It's easy to make other activities more important than doing God's work. But God wants following his commands to be a high priority in his people's lives.

GOD'S ENCOURAGEMENT

Haggai encouraged the people as they worked, assuring them of the presence of the Holy Spirit, of final victory, and the future reign of the Messiah. If God gives you a task, he will help you complete it. His resources are infinite.

1 A CALL TO REBUILD THE TEMPLE

On August 29* of the second year of King Darius's reign,
the LORD gave a message through the prophet Haggai to
Zerubbabel son of Shealtiel, governor of Judah, and to
Jeshua* son of Jehozadak, the high priest.

PRIORITIES 1:1-9

The people of Judah had rebuilt their homes upon returning to Jerusalem. Yet the Temple—the house of God—was still in ruins. Haggai reminded them that their priorities were mixed up. Sometimes our priorities (work, family, and God's work) are mixed up. Friends, possessions, and fun may rank higher on our list of importance than God. What is most important to you? Where does God rank? ■

[2]"This is what the LORD of Heaven's Armies says: The
people are saying, 'The time has not yet come to rebuild
the house of the LORD.'"
[3]Then the LORD sent this message through the prophet
Haggai: [4]"Why are you living in luxurious houses while
my house lies in ruins? [5]This is what the LORD of Heaven's
Armies says: Look at what's happening to you! [6]You have
planted much but harvest little. You eat but are not satisfied. You drink but are still thirsty. You put on clothes but
cannot keep warm. Your wages disappear as though you
were putting them in pockets filled with holes!
[7]"This is what the LORD of Heaven's Armies says: Look
at what's happening to you! [8]Now go up into the hills,
bring down timber, and rebuild my house. Then I will
take pleasure in it and be honored, says the LORD. [9]You
hoped for rich harvests, but they were poor. And when
you brought your harvest home, I blew it away. Why? Because my house lies in ruins, says the
LORD of Heaven's Armies, while all of
you are busy building your own fine
houses. [10]It's because of you that the
heavens withhold the dew and the
earth produces no crops. [11]I have
called for a drought on your fields and
hills—a drought to wither the grain
and grapes and olive trees and all your
other crops, a drought to starve you
and your livestock and to ruin everything you have worked so hard to get."

> Why are you living in luxurious houses while my house lies in ruins?
>
> *HAGGAI 1:4*

OBEDIENCE TO GOD'S CALL

[12]Then Zerubbabel son of Shealtiel,
and Jeshua son of Jehozadak, the high priest, and the
whole remnant of God's people began to obey the message from the LORD their God. When they heard the
words of the prophet Haggai, whom the LORD their God
had sent, the people feared the LORD. [13]Then Haggai, the
LORD's messenger, gave the people this message from the
LORD: "I am with you, says the LORD!"
[14]So the LORD sparked the enthusiasm of Zerubbabel son of Shealtiel,
governor of Judah, and the enthusiasm
of Jeshua son of Jehozadak, the high
priest, and the enthusiasm of the
whole remnant of God's people. They
began to work on the house of their
God, the LORD of Heaven's Armies, [15]on
September 21* of the second year of
King Darius's reign.

SATISFACTION

With nothing more demanding to do than catch rays at the Fairfield Swim Club in early August, 15-year-old Gabrielle is bored silly. She had looked forward to summer ever since the first winter storm. Her plans had involved sleeping late, hanging out with friends, and just doing whatever she wanted.

Now here she sits, frustrated and unsatisfied. She's been involved in a ton of things in the last two months; yet summer hasn't been nearly as exciting as she'd imagined it would be. *Something's missing,* she thinks as she sips her diet Coke and watches the clouds form shapes against the crystal blue sky.

Gabrielle picks up her cell phone and sighs. *Oh well. Guess I'll call Drina and see if she's as bored as me.*

Two thousand miles away, 14-year-old Greg is drenched in sweat. Along with nineteen other teens from his youth group, he's helping to build a church in a poor village near the Texas/Mexico border. It's backbreaking work; yet Greg and his friends are having a blast serving God and the community.

What a paradox! When we chase after satisfaction, we inevitably find frustration. When we stop trying to find personal fulfillment and give our life away in service to God, we find indescribable joy. See Haggai 1 for another example of this truth. Based on this passage, what advice would you have for Gabrielle?

2 THE NEW TEMPLE'S DIMINISHED SPLENDOR

Then on October 17 of that same
year,* the LORD sent another message through the
prophet Haggai. [2]"Say this to Zerubbabel son of Shealtiel,
governor of Judah, and to Jeshua* son of Jehozadak, the

1:1a Hebrew *On the first day of the sixth month,* of the ancient Hebrew lunar calendar. A number of dates in Haggai can be cross-checked with dates in surviving Persian records and related accurately to our modern calendar. This event occurred on August 29, 520 B.C. **1:1b** Hebrew *Joshua,* a variant spelling of Jeshua; also in 1:12, 14. **1:15** Hebrew *on the twenty-fourth day of the sixth month,* of the ancient Hebrew lunar calendar. This event occurred on September 21, 520 B.C.; also see note on 1:1a. **2:1** Hebrew *on the twenty-first day of the seventh month,* of the ancient Hebrew lunar calendar. This event (in the second year of Darius's reign) occurred on October 17, 520 B.C.; also see note on 1:1a. **2:2** Hebrew *Joshua,* a variant spelling of Jeshua; also in 2:4.

high priest, and to the remnant of God's people there in
the land: 3'Does anyone remember this house—this Temple—in its former splendor? How, in comparison, does it
look to you now? It must seem like nothing at all! 4But
now the LORD says: Be strong, Zerubbabel. Be strong,
Jeshua son of Jehozadak, the high priest. Be strong, all
you people still left in the land. And now get to work, for I
am with you, says the LORD of Heaven's Armies. 5My
Spirit remains among you, just as I promised when you
came out of Egypt. So do not be afraid.'
6"For this is what the LORD of Heaven's Armies says: In
just a little while I will again shake the heavens and the
earth, the oceans and the dry land. 7I will shake all the nations, and the treasures of all the nations will be brought
to this Temple. I will fill this place with glory, says the
LORD of Heaven's Armies. 8The silver is mine, and the gold
is mine, says the LORD of Heaven's Armies. 9The future
glory of this Temple will be greater than its past glory, says
the LORD of Heaven's Armies. And in this place I will bring
peace. I, the LORD of Heaven's Armies, have spoken!"

FREE FORGIVENESS 2:10-14

Now that the people were beginning to obey God, he promised to bless them. But they needed to understand that performing activities in the Temple wouldn't earn them God's forgiveness or make them right with him. Their repentance and acceptance of his forgiveness made them right with God. Many times, we think that giving money or doing something nice for someone can somehow erase the wrong things we've done and thereby earn God's forgiveness. Or, we think we're somehow good on our own. Wrong. As Isaiah said, "When we display our righteous deeds, they are nothing but filthy rags" (64:6). Forgiveness is a free gift from God already paid for by Jesus. Is that a gift you've accepted? ■

BLESSINGS PROMISED FOR OBEDIENCE

10On December 18* of the second year of King Darius's
reign, the LORD sent this message to the prophet Haggai:
11"This is what the LORD of Heaven's Armies says. Ask the
priests this question about the law: 12'If one of you is carrying some meat from a holy sacrifice in his robes and his
robe happens to brush against some bread or stew, wine or
olive oil, or any other kind of food, will it also become
holy?'"
The priests replied, "No."
13Then Haggai asked, "If someone becomes ceremonially unclean by touching a dead person and then touches
any of these foods, will the food be defiled?"
And the priests answered, "Yes."
14Then Haggai responded, "That is how it is with this
people and this nation, says the LORD. Everything they
do and everything they offer is defiled by their sin.
15Look at what was happening to you before you began
to lay the foundation of the LORD's Temple. 16When
you hoped for a twenty-bushel crop, you harvested
only ten. When you expected to draw fifty gallons
from the winepress, you found only twenty. 17I sent
blight and mildew and hail to destroy everything you
worked so hard to produce. Even so, you refused to return to me, says the LORD.
18"Think about this eighteenth day of December, the
day* when the foundation of the LORD's Temple was laid.
Think carefully. 19I am giving you a promise now while
the seed is still in the barn.* You have not yet harvested
your grain, and your grapevines, fig trees, pomegranates,
and olive trees have not yet produced their crops. But
from this day onward I will bless you."

CHOSEN 2:23

God ended his message to Zerubbabel with this tremendous affirmation: "I have [specially] chosen you." Such a proclamation is ours as well. God chose each of us (Eph 1:4). This truth can help us see our value in God's eyes and motivate us to work for him. When you feel down, remind yourself, "God has chosen me!" ■

PROMISES FOR ZERUBBABEL

20On that same day, December 18,* the LORD sent this
second message to Haggai: 21"Tell Zerubbabel, the governor of Judah, that I am about to shake the heavens and the
earth. 22I will overthrow royal thrones and destroy the
power of foreign kingdoms. I will overturn their chariots
and riders. The horses will fall, and their riders will kill
each other.
23"But when this happens, says the LORD of Heaven's
Armies, I will honor you, Zerubbabel son of Shealtiel, my
servant. I will make you like a signet ring on my finger,
says the LORD, for I have chosen you. I, the LORD of
Heaven's Armies, have spoken!"

2:10 Hebrew *On the twenty-fourth day of the ninth month,* of the ancient Hebrew lunar calendar (similarly in 2:18). This event occurred on December 18, 520 B.C.; also see note on 1:1a. **2:18** Or *On this eighteenth day of December, think about the day.* **2:19** Hebrew *Is the seed yet in the barn?* **2:20** Hebrew *On the twenty-fourth day of the [ninth] month;* see note on 2:10.

ZECHARIAH

EVER WONDER about the future? Almost everyone wants to know what the future holds. Some people fear the future, wondering what evils lurk around the corner. Their fear might drive them to consult fortune-tellers, astrologers, and other future-telling charlatans who make a living providing personal prophecies.

But tomorrow's story is known only by God and by those special messengers, the prophets, to whom he has revealed a chapter or two. A prophet's job was to proclaim the word of the Lord, point out wrongdoings and their consequences, and direct men and women to God.

Nestled here among the Minor Prophets (the books starting with Hosea) is the book of Zechariah. As one of God's spokesmen, Zechariah preached to the small group of Jews who had returned to Judah to rebuild the Temple and the nation. Zechariah encouraged them, but his message went far beyond that. Zechariah gave a spectacular and graphic prophecy of the Messiah, the promised deliverer of Israel, and the only hope for humankind.

God knows and controls the future. We may never see a moment ahead, but we can be secure if we trust him. Read Zechariah and strengthen your faith in God. He alone is your hope and security.

zechariah

timeline

538 B.C.
Cyrus's decree allowing the exiles to return

537
Exiles return to Jerusalem

536
Temple construction begins

530
Temple work halted

520
Haggai, Zechariah become prophets; Temple work resumed

516
Temple completed

458
Ezra comes to Jerusalem

445
Nehemiah comes to Jerusalem

stats

PURPOSE: To give hope to God's people by revealing God's future deliverance through the Messiah

AUTHOR: Zechariah

TO WHOM WRITTEN: The Jews in Jerusalem who had returned from their captivity in Babylon and to God's people everywhere

DATE WRITTEN: Chapters 1–8 were written about 520 to 518 B.C. Chapters 9–14 were written around 480 B.C.

KEY PEOPLE: Zerubbabel, Joshua

KEY PLACE: Jerusalem

SPECIAL FEATURES: This book is the most apocalyptic and messianic of all the Minor Prophets.

KEY points

GOD'S JEALOUSY

Disobedience was the root of Judah's problems. God was jealous ("zealous") for his people's devotion. Likewise, God wants our complete loyalty.

REBUILDING THE TEMPLE

The Jews were home from exile, but the Temple was not yet rebuilt. Zechariah encouraged them to get moving on the rebuilding. God would both protect his workmen and also empower them by his Holy Spirit to complete the rebuilding. God will empower us to do whatever we're assigned to do.

THE COMING KING

Zechariah prophesied that the Messiah would come someday to rescue people from sin and to reign as King. Jesus already has fulfilled the first part of the prophecy. Someday, he will return to earth as a victorious King to usher in peace throughout the world.

GOD'S PROTECTION

Zechariah prophesied future times of trouble. But God would protect his people. God cares for his people and will deliver them from all who oppress them.

1

A CALL TO RETURN TO THE LORD

In November* of the second year of King Darius's reign,
the LORD gave this message to the prophet Zechariah son
of Berekiah and grandson of Iddo:
2"I, the LORD, was very angry with your ancestors.
3Therefore, say to the people, 'This is what the LORD of
Heaven's Armies says: Return to me, and I will return to
you, says the LORD of Heaven's Armies.' 4Don't be like
your ancestors who would not listen or pay attention
when the earlier prophets said to them, 'This is what the
LORD of Heaven's Armies says: Turn from your evil ways,
and stop all your evil practices.'

THE CHOICE IS YOURS 1:2-3

The familiar phrase "Like father, like son" implies that children turn out like their parents. But God warned Israel *not* to be like their fathers who disobeyed him and reaped the consequences—his judgment. We are responsible before God for our actions. We aren't trapped by our heredity or environment. We can choose to follow God or go our own way. What's your choice? ■

5"Where are your ancestors now? They and the prophets are long dead. 6But everything I said through my servants the prophets happened to your ancestors, just as I
said. As a result, they repented and said, 'We have received what we deserved from the LORD of Heaven's Armies. He has done what he said he would do.'"

A MAN AMONG THE MYRTLE TREES

7Three months later, on February 15,* the LORD sent another message to the prophet Zechariah son of Berekiah
and grandson of Iddo.
8In a vision during the night, I saw a man sitting on a
red horse that was standing among some myrtle trees in a
small valley. Behind him were riders on red, brown, and
white horses. 9I asked the angel who was talking with me,
"My lord, what do these horses mean?"
"I will show you," the angel replied.
10The rider standing among the myrtle trees then explained, "They are the ones the LORD has sent out to patrol the earth."
11Then the other riders reported to the angel of the
LORD, who was standing among the myrtle trees, "We have
been patrolling the earth, and the whole earth is at peace."
12Upon hearing this, the angel of the LORD prayed this
prayer: "O LORD of Heaven's Armies, for seventy years
now you have been angry with Jerusalem and the towns
of Judah. How long until you again show mercy to them?"
13And the LORD spoke kind and comforting words to the
angel who talked with me.
14Then the angel said to me, "Shout this message for all
to hear: 'This is what the LORD of Heaven's Armies says:
My love for Jerusalem and Mount Zion is passionate and
strong. 15But I am very angry with the other nations that
are now enjoying peace and security. I was only a little angry with my people, but the nations inflicted harm on
them far beyond my intentions.
16" 'Therefore, this is what the LORD says: I have returned to show mercy to Jerusalem. My Temple will be
rebuilt, says the LORD of Heaven's Armies, and measurements will be taken for the reconstruction of Jerusalem.*'
17"Say this also: 'This is what the LORD of Heaven's Armies says: The towns of Israel will again overflow with
prosperity, and the LORD will again comfort Zion and
choose Jerusalem as his own.'"

TURN BACK 1:12-17

God's people had endured 70 years of exile as a punishment for hundreds of years of wrongdoing. But here God spoke words of comfort and kindness. He promised that their Temple would be rebuilt. Ever worry that the hard times you're going through will last forever? Maybe you've thought that God is angry because of something you did in the past and is bent on ruining your life forever. The same encouragement that God offered to his people is there for you—just for the asking. ■

FOUR HORNS AND FOUR BLACKSMITHS

18*Then I looked up and saw four animal horns. 19"What
are these?" I asked the angel who was talking with me.
He replied, "These horns represent the nations that
scattered Judah, Israel, and Jerusalem."
20Then the LORD showed me four blacksmiths.
21"What are these men coming to do?" I asked.
The angel replied, "These four horns—these nations—
scattered and humbled Judah. Now these blacksmiths
have come to terrify those nations and throw them down
and destroy them."

2

FUTURE PROSPERITY OF JERUSALEM

1*When I looked again, I saw a man with a measuring line
in his hand. 2"Where are you going?" I asked.
He replied, "I am going to measure Jerusalem, to see
how wide and how long it is."
3Then the angel who was with me went to meet a second angel who was coming toward him. 4The other angel
said, "Hurry, and say to that young man, 'Jerusalem will
someday be so full of people and livestock that there
won't be room enough for everyone! Many will live outside the city walls. 5Then I, myself, will be a protective

1:1 Hebrew *In the eighth month.* A number of dates in Zechariah can be cross-checked with dates in surviving Persian records and related accurately to our modern calendar. This month of the ancient Hebrew lunar calendar occurred within the months of October and November 520 B.C. 1:7 Hebrew *On the twenty-fourth day of the eleventh month, the month of Shebat, in the second year of Darius.* This event occurred on February 15, 519 B.C.; also see note on 1:1. 1:16 Hebrew *and the measuring line will be stretched out over Jerusalem.* 1:18 Verses 1:18-21 are numbered 2:1-4 in Hebrew text. 2:1 Verses 2:1-13 are numbered 2:5-17 in Hebrew text.

wall of fire around Jerusalem, says the LORD. And I will be the glory inside the city!'"

THE EXILES ARE CALLED HOME

6The LORD says, "Come away! Flee from Babylon in the land of the north, for I have scattered you to the four winds. 7Come away, people of Zion, you who are exiled in Babylon!"

8After a period of glory, the LORD of Heaven's Armies sent me* against the nations who plundered you. For he said, "Anyone who harms you harms my most precious possession.* 9I will raise my fist to crush them, and their own slaves will plunder them." Then you will know that the LORD of Heaven's Armies has sent me.

HELPING GOD 2:8-9

God expressed his love for his people. Believers are precious to God (Ps 116:15); they're his children (Ps 103:13). Treating any believer unkindly is the same as treating God that way. As Jesus told his disciples, when we help others we're really helping him; when we neglect them we neglect him (Matt 25:34-46). How are you helping God by helping others? ■

10The LORD says, "Shout and rejoice, O beautiful Jerusalem,* for I am coming to live among you. 11Many nations will join themselves to the LORD on that day, and they, too, will be my people. I will live among you, and you will know that the LORD of Heaven's Armies sent me to you. 12The land of Judah will be the LORD's special possession in the holy land, and he will once again choose Jerusalem to be his own city. 13Be silent before the LORD, all humanity, for he is springing into action from his holy dwelling."

3 CLEANSING FOR THE HIGH PRIEST

Then the angel showed me Jeshua* the high priest standing before the angel of the LORD. The Accuser, Satan,* was there at the angel's right hand, making accusations against Jeshua. 2And the LORD said to Satan, "I, the LORD, reject your accusations, Satan. Yes, the LORD, who has chosen Jerusalem, rebukes you. This man is like a burning stick that has been snatched from the fire."

3Jeshua's clothing was filthy as he stood there before the angel. 4So the angel said to the others standing there, "Take off his filthy clothes." And turning to Jeshua he said, "See, I have taken away your sins, and now I am giving you these fine new clothes."

5Then I said, "They should also place a clean turban on his head." So they put a clean priestly turban on his head and dressed him in new clothes while the angel of the LORD stood by.

6Then the angel of the LORD spoke very solemnly to Jeshua and said, 7"This is what the LORD of Heaven's Armies says: If you follow my ways and carefully serve me, then you will be given authority over my Temple and its courtyards. I will let you walk among these others standing here.

8"Listen to me, O Jeshua the high priest, and all you other priests. You are symbols of things to come. Soon I am going to bring my servant, the Branch. 9Now look at the jewel I have set before Jeshua, a single stone with seven facets.* I will engrave an inscription on it, says the LORD of Heaven's Armies, and I will remove the sins of this land in a single day.

10"And on that day, says the LORD of Heaven's Armies, each of you will invite your neighbor to sit with you peacefully under your own grapevine and fig tree."

> It is not by force nor by strength, but by my Spirit, says the LORD of Heaven's Armies.
>
> *ZECHARIAH 4:6*

BY HIS SPIRIT 4:6

Many people believe that to survive in this world a person must be strong and aggressive. But God says, "It is not by force nor by strength, but by my Spirit." The key words are "by my Spirit." It is *only* through God's Spirit that anything of lasting value is accomplished. The returned exiles were indeed weak—harassed by their enemies, tired, discouraged, and poor. But they had God on their side! Where is the bulk of your trust? In your own strength or abilities? In God? ■

4 A LAMPSTAND AND TWO OLIVE TREES

Then the angel who had been talking with me returned and woke me, as though I had been asleep. 2"What do you see now?" he asked.

I answered, "I see a solid gold lampstand with a bowl of oil on top of it. Around the bowl are seven lamps, each having seven spouts with wicks. 3And I see two olive trees, one on each side of the bowl." 4Then I asked the angel, "What are these, my lord? What do they mean?"

5"Don't you know?" the angel asked.

"No, my lord," I replied.

6Then he said to me, "This is what the LORD says to Zerubbabel: It is not by force nor by strength, but by my Spirit, says the LORD of Heaven's Armies. 7Nothing, not even a mighty mountain, will stand in Zerubbabel's way; it will become a level plain before him! And when Zerubbabel sets the final stone of the Temple in place, the people will shout: 'May God bless it! May God bless it!'*"

2:8a The meaning of the Hebrew is uncertain. **2:8b** Hebrew *Anyone who touches you touches the pupil of his eye.* **2:10** Hebrew *O daughter of Zion.* **3:1a** Hebrew *Joshua,* a variant spelling of Jeshua; also in 3:3, 4, 6, 8, 9. **3:1b** Hebrew *The satan;* similarly in 3:2. **3:9** Hebrew *seven eyes.* **4:7** Hebrew *'Grace, grace to it.'*

[8]Then another message came to me from the LORD: [9]"Zerubbabel is the one who laid the foundation of this Temple, and he will complete it. Then you will know that the LORD of Heaven's Armies has sent me. [10]Do not despise these small beginnings, for the LORD rejoices to see the work begin, to see the plumb line in Zerubbabel's hand."

(The seven lamps* represent the eyes of the LORD that search all around the world.)

[11]Then I asked the angel, "What are these two olive trees on each side of the lampstand, [12]and what are the two olive branches that pour out golden oil through two gold tubes?"

[13]"Don't you know?" he asked.

"No, my lord," I replied.

[14]Then he said to me, "They represent the two heavenly beings who stand in the court of the Lord of all the earth."

5 A FLYING SCROLL

I looked up again and saw a scroll flying through the air.

[2]"What do you see?" the angel asked.

"I see a flying scroll," I replied. "It appears to be about 30 feet long and 15 feet wide.*"

[3]Then he said to me, "This scroll contains the curse that is going out over the entire land. One side of the scroll says that those who steal will be banished from the land; the other side says that those who swear falsely will be banished from the land. [4]And this is what the LORD of Heaven's Armies says: I am sending this curse into the house of every thief and into the house of everyone who swears falsely using my name. And my curse will remain in that house and completely destroy it—even its timbers and stones."

WIPED OUT 5:5-11

Zechariah saw a vision of wickedness (as represented by the woman in 5:8) being taken away from Israel. One day, that vision will come true. During Christ's future reign, all sin will be eliminated. People will live in safety and security. He has already removed sin's power and penalty by his death on the cross. When we trust him to forgive us, he gives us the power to live a life that's pleasing to him. ■

A WOMAN IN A BASKET

[5]Then the angel who was talking with me came forward and said, "Look up and see what's coming."

[6]"What is it?" I asked.

He replied, "It is a basket for measuring grain,* and it's filled with the sins* of everyone throughout the land."

[7]Then the heavy lead cover was lifted off the basket, and there was a woman sitting inside it. [8]The angel said, "The woman's name is Wickedness," and he pushed her back into the basket and closed the heavy lid again.

[9]Then I looked up and saw two women flying toward us, gliding on the wind. They had wings like a stork, and they picked up the basket and flew into the sky.

[10]"Where are they taking the basket?" I asked the angel.

[11]He replied, "To the land of Babylonia,* where they will build a temple for the basket. And when the temple is ready, they will set the basket there on its pedestal."

6 FOUR CHARIOTS

Then I looked up again and saw four chariots coming from between two bronze mountains. [2]The first chariot was pulled by red horses, the second by black horses, [3]the third by white horses, and the fourth by powerful dappled-gray horses. [4]"And what are these, my lord?" I asked the angel who was talking with me.

[5]The angel replied, "These are the four spirits* of heaven who stand before the Lord of all the earth. They are going out to do his work. [6]The chariot with black horses is going north, the chariot with white horses is going west,* and the chariot with dappled-gray horses is going south."

[7]The powerful horses were eager to set out to patrol the earth. And the LORD said, "Go and patrol the earth!" So they left at once on their patrol.

[8]Then the LORD summoned me and said, "Look, those who went north have vented the anger of my Spirit* there in the land of the north."

THE CROWNING OF JESHUA

[9]Then I received another message from the LORD: [10]"Heldai, Tobijah, and Jedaiah will bring gifts of silver and gold from the Jews exiled in Babylon. As soon as they arrive, meet them at the home of Josiah son of Zephaniah. [11]Accept their gifts, and make a crown* from the silver and gold. Then put the crown on the head of Jeshua* son of Jehozadak, the high priest. [12]Tell him, 'This is what the LORD of Heaven's Armies says: Here is the man called the Branch. He will branch out from where he is and build the Temple of the LORD. [13]Yes, he will build the Temple of the LORD. Then he will receive royal honor and will rule as king from his throne. He will also serve as priest from his throne,* and there will be perfect harmony between his two roles.'

[14]"The crown will be a memorial in the Temple of the LORD to honor those who gave it—Heldai,* Tobijah, Jedaiah, and Josiah* son of Zephaniah."

[15]People will come from distant lands to rebuild the Temple of the LORD. And when this happens, you will know that my messages have been from the LORD of Heaven's Armies. All this will happen if you carefully obey what the LORD your God says.

4:10 Or *The seven facets* (see 3:9); Hebrew reads *These seven.* **5:2** Hebrew *20 cubits* [9 meters] *long and 10 cubits* [4.5 meters] *wide.* **5:6a** Hebrew *an ephah* [20 quarts or 22 liters]; also in 5:7, 8, 9, 10, 11. **5:6b** As in Greek version; Hebrew reads *the appearance.* **5:11** Hebrew *the land of Shinar.* **6:5** Or *the four winds.* **6:6** Hebrew *is going after them.* **6:8** Hebrew *have given my Spirit rest.* **6:11a** As in Greek and Syriac versions; Hebrew reads *crowns.* **6:11b** Hebrew *Joshua,* a variant spelling of Jeshua. **6:13** Or *There will be a priest by his throne.* **6:14a** As in Syriac version (compare 6:10); Hebrew reads *Helem.* **6:14b** As in Syriac version (compare 6:10); Hebrew reads *Hen.*

7

A CALL TO JUSTICE AND MERCY

On December 7* of the fourth year of King Darius's
reign, another message came to Zechariah from the
LORD. 2The people of Bethel had sent Sharezer and Regemmelech,* along with their attendants, to seek the
LORD's favor. 3They were to ask this question of the
prophets and the priests at the Temple of the LORD of
Heaven's Armies: "Should we continue to mourn and fast
each summer on the anniversary of the Temple's destruction,* as we have done for so many years?"

4The LORD of Heaven's Armies sent me this message in
reply: 5"Say to all your people and your priests, 'During
these seventy years of exile, when you fasted and
mourned in the summer and in early autumn,* was it
really for me that you were fasting? 6And even now in
your holy festivals, aren't you eating and drinking just to
please yourselves? 7Isn't this the same message the LORD
proclaimed through the prophets in years past when Jerusalem and the towns of Judah were bustling with people, and the Negev and the foothills of Judah* were well
populated?'"

JUSTICE

Chris has a twisted sense of fairness. Case in point: When a convenience store clerk gives him change for $20 instead of $10 (it's her first day on the job; she's a little nervous), he never says a word. He eagerly pockets the extra bucks. "She shouldn't have been so stupid," he decides.

Later, while keeping score for an intramural basketball game, Chris gives his favorite team three extra points. *Hey, they deserve it,* he justifies to himself.

But Chris isn't amused when he's treated wrongly. You see, he's just been docked an hour's pay just for being a measly five minutes late for work because of a wreck on the expressway!

"That's not fair!" he whines.

Like Chris, we're quick to complain whenever we feel as though we've been treated unfairly. But check out Zechariah 7:8-14. Is this your idea of fairness? What would you say to Chris based on this passage?

8Then this message came to Zechariah from the LORD:
9"This is what the LORD of Heaven's Armies says: Judge
fairly, and show mercy and kindness to one another. 10Do
not oppress widows, orphans, foreigners, and the poor.
And do not scheme against each other.

11"Your ancestors refused to listen to this message.
They stubbornly turned away and put their fingers in
their ears to keep from hearing. 12They made their hearts
as hard as stone, so they could not hear the instructions
or the messages that the LORD of Heaven's Armies had
sent them by his Spirit through the earlier prophets. That
is why the LORD of Heaven's Armies was so angry with
them.

13"Since they refused to listen when I called to them, I
would not listen when they called to me, says the LORD
of Heaven's Armies. 14As with a whirlwind, I scattered
them among the distant nations, where they lived as
strangers. Their land became so desolate that no one
even traveled through it. They turned their pleasant
land into a desert."

8

PROMISED BLESSINGS FOR JERUSALEM

Then another message came to me from the LORD of
Heaven's Armies: 2"This is what the LORD of Heaven's Armies says: My love for Mount Zion is passionate and
strong; I am consumed with passion for Jerusalem!

3"And now the LORD says: I am returning to Mount
Zion, and I will live in Jerusalem. Then Jerusalem will be
called the Faithful City; the mountain of the LORD of
Heaven's Armies will be called the Holy Mountain.

4"This is what the LORD of Heaven's Armies says: Once
again old men and women will walk Jerusalem's streets
with their canes and will sit together in the city squares.
5And the streets of the city will be filled with boys and
girls at play.

6"This is what the LORD of Heaven's Armies says: All
this may seem impossible to you now, a small remnant of
God's people. But is it impossible for me? says the LORD
of Heaven's Armies.

7"This is what the LORD of Heaven's Armies says: You
can be sure that I will rescue my people from the east and
from the west. 8I will bring them home again to live safely
in Jerusalem. They will be my people, and I will be faithful
and just toward them as their God.

9"This is what the LORD of Heaven's Armies says: Be
strong and finish the task! Ever since the laying of the
foundation of the Temple of the LORD of Heaven's Armies, you have heard what the prophets have been saying
about completing the building. 10Before the work on the
Temple began, there were no jobs and no money to hire
people or animals. No traveler was safe from the enemy,
for there were enemies on all sides. I had turned everyone against each other.

11"But now I will not treat the remnant of my people as I
treated them before, says the LORD of Heaven's Armies.
12For I am planting seeds of peace and prosperity among
you. The grapevines will be heavy with fruit. The earth will
produce its crops, and the heavens will release the dew.
Once more I will cause the remnant in Judah and Israel to

7:1 Hebrew *On the fourth day of the ninth month, the month of Kislev,* of the ancient Hebrew lunar calendar. This event occurred on December 7, 518 B.C.; also see note on 1:1. 7:2 Or *Bethel-sharezer had sent Regemmelech.* 7:3 Hebrew *mourn and fast in the fifth month.* The Temple had been destroyed in the fifth month of the ancient Hebrew lunar calendar (August 586 B.C.); see 2 Kgs 25:8. 7:5 Hebrew *fasted and mourned in the fifth and seventh months.* The fifth month of the ancient Hebrew lunar calendar usually occurs within the months of July and August. The seventh month usually occurs within the months of September and October; both the Day of Atonement and the Festival of Shelters were celebrated in the seventh month. 7:7 Hebrew *the Shephelah.*

Zechariah

Served as a prophet to Judah about 520 B.C., after the return from exile.

Climate of the times	The exiles had returned from captivity to rebuild their Temple. But work on the Temple had stalled, and the people were neglecting their service to God.
Main message	Zechariah, like Haggai, encouraged the people to finish rebuilding the Temple. His visions gave the people hope. He told the people of a future King who one day would establish an eternal kingdom.
Importance of message	Even in times of discouragement and despair, God is working out his plan. God protects and guides us; we must trust and follow him.
Contemporary prophet	Haggai (about 520 B.C.)

inherit these blessings. 13Among the other nations, Judah
and Israel became symbols of a cursed nation. But no longer! Now I will rescue you and make you both a symbol
and a source of blessing. So don't be afraid. Be strong, and
get on with rebuilding the Temple!
14"For this is what the LORD of Heaven's Armies says: I
was determined to punish you when your ancestors angered me, and I did not change my mind, says the LORD of
Heaven's Armies. 15But now I am determined to bless Jerusalem and the people of Judah. So don't be afraid. 16But
this is what you must do: Tell the truth to each other. Render verdicts in your courts that are just and that lead to
peace. 17Don't scheme against each other. Stop your love
of telling lies that you swear are the truth. I hate all these
things, says the LORD."
18Here is another message that came to me from the
LORD of Heaven's Armies. 19"This is what the LORD of
Heaven's Armies says: The traditional fasts and times of
mourning you have kept in early summer, midsummer,
autumn, and winter* are now ended. They will become
festivals of joy and celebration for the people of Judah.
So love truth and peace.
20"This is what the LORD of Heaven's Armies says: People from nations and cities around the world will travel to
Jerusalem. 21The people of one city will say to the people
of another, 'Come with us to Jerusalem to ask the LORD to
bless us. Let's worship the LORD of Heaven's Armies. I'm
determined to go.' 22Many peoples and powerful nations
will come to Jerusalem to seek the LORD of Heaven's Armies and to ask for his blessing.
23"This is what the LORD of Heaven's Armies says: In
those days ten men from different nations and languages
of the world will clutch at the sleeve of one Jew. And they
will say, 'Please let us walk with you, for we have heard
that God is with you.'"

9

JUDGMENT AGAINST ISRAEL'S ENEMIES

This is the message* from the LORD against the land of Aram* and the city of Damascus, for the eyes of humanity, including all the tribes of Israel, are on the LORD.

2 Doom is certain for Hamath,
  near Damascus,
and for the cities of Tyre and Sidon,
  though they are so clever.
3 Tyre has built a strong fortress
  and has made silver and gold
  as plentiful as dust in the streets!
4 But now the Lord will strip away Tyre's possessions
  and hurl its fortifications into the sea,
  and it will be burned to the ground.
5 The city of Ashkelon will see Tyre fall
  and will be filled with fear.
Gaza will shake with terror,
  as will Ekron, for their hopes will be dashed.
Gaza's king will be killed,
  and Ashkelon will be deserted.
6 Foreigners will occupy the city of Ashdod.
  I will destroy the pride of the Philistines.
7 I will grab the bloody meat from their mouths
  and snatch the detestable sacrifices from
    their teeth.
Then the surviving Philistines will worship our God
  and become like a clan in Judah.*
The Philistines of Ekron will join my people,
  as the ancient Jebusites once did.
8 I will guard my Temple
  and protect it from invading armies.
I am watching closely to ensure

8:19 Hebrew *in the fourth, fifth, seventh, and tenth months.* The fourth month of the ancient Hebrew lunar calendar usually occurs within the months of June and July. The fifth month usually occurs within the months of July and August. The seventh month usually occurs within the months of September and October. The tenth month usually occurs within the months of December and January. **9:1a** Hebrew *An Oracle: The message.* **9:1b** Hebrew *land of Hadrach.* **9:7** Hebrew *and will become a leader in Judah.*

that no more foreign oppressors overrun my
people's land.

ZION'S COMING KING

9 Rejoice, O people of Zion!*
Shout in triumph, O people of Jerusalem!
Look, your king is coming to you.
He is righteous and victorious,*
yet he is humble, riding on a donkey—
riding on a donkey's colt.
10 I will remove the battle chariots from Israel*
and the warhorses from Jerusalem.
I will destroy all the weapons used in battle,
and your king will bring peace to the nations.
His realm will stretch from sea to sea
and from the Euphrates River* to the ends of
the earth.*
11 Because of the covenant I made with you,
sealed with blood,
I will free your prisoners
from death in a waterless dungeon.
12 Come back to the place of safety,
all you prisoners who still have hope!
I promise this very day
that I will repay two blessings for each of
your troubles.
13 Judah is my bow,
and Israel is my arrow.
Jerusalem* is my sword,
and like a warrior, I will brandish it against
the Greeks.*

PREDICTIONS 9:9

Jesus' triumphal entry into Jerusalem (Matt 21:1-11) is predicted here—more than 500 years before the event happened. Just as this prophecy was fulfilled when Jesus came to earth, so the prophecies of his second coming are certain to come true. Are you ready for his return? ■

14 The LORD will appear above his people;
his arrows will fly like lightning!
The Sovereign LORD will sound the ram's horn
and attack like a whirlwind from the
southern desert.
15 The LORD of Heaven's Armies will protect his people,
and they will defeat their enemies by hurling
great stones.
They will shout in battle as though drunk with wine.
They will be filled with blood like a bowl,
drenched with blood like the corners of the altar.
16 On that day the LORD their God will rescue his people,
just as a shepherd rescues his sheep.
They will sparkle in his land
like jewels in a crown.
17 How wonderful and beautiful they will be!
The young men will thrive on abundant grain,
and the young women will flourish on new wine.

10 THE LORD WILL RESTORE HIS PEOPLE

1 Ask the LORD for rain in the spring,
for he makes the storm clouds.
And he will send showers of rain
so every field becomes a lush pasture.
2 Household gods give worthless advice,
fortune-tellers predict only lies,
and interpreters of dreams pronounce
falsehoods that give no comfort.
So my people are wandering like lost sheep;
they are attacked because they have no shepherd.

FOOLISH TRUST 10:2

God warned the people not to trust in fortune-tellers or interpreters of dreams. Ever been tempted to consult a psychic or read a horoscope? Maybe you haven't, but some have. Psychic hotlines are big business. And many magazines, newspapers, and Internet sites carry horoscopes. People either want to know what's going to happen in the future or hope to find some direction for their lives in the present. Sadly, there are some who place their trust in just a few lines of text written on the page of a magazine. If you want to place your trust in a few lines of text, check out the promise in Proverbs 3:5-6. ■

3 "My anger burns against your shepherds,
and I will punish these leaders.*
For the LORD of Heaven's Armies has arrived
to look after Judah, his flock.
He will make them strong and glorious,
like a proud warhorse in battle.
4 From Judah will come the cornerstone,
the tent peg,
the bow for battle,
and all the rulers.
5 They will be like mighty warriors in battle,
trampling their enemies in the mud under
their feet.
Since the LORD is with them as they fight,
they will overthrow even the enemy's horsemen.
6 "I will strengthen Judah and save Israel*;
I will restore them because of my compassion.
It will be as though I had never rejected them,
for I am the LORD their God, who will hear
their cries.
7 The people of Israel* will become like
mighty warriors,
and their hearts will be made happy as if by wine.

9:9a Hebrew *O daughter of Zion!* 9:9b Hebrew *and is being vindicated.* 9:10a Hebrew *Ephraim,* referring to the northern kingdom of Israel; also in 9:13. 9:10b Hebrew *the river.* 9:10c Or *the end of the land.* 9:13a Hebrew *Zion.* 9:13b Hebrew *the sons of Javan.* 10:3 Or *these male goats.* 10:6 Hebrew *save the house of Joseph.* 10:7 Hebrew *of Ephraim.*

Their children, too, will see it and be glad;
their hearts will rejoice in the LORD.
8 When I whistle to them, they will come running,
for I have redeemed them.
From the few who are left,
they will grow as numerous as they were before.
9 Though I have scattered them like seeds among
the nations,
they will still remember me in distant lands.
They and their children will survive
and return again to Israel.
10 I will bring them back from Egypt
and gather them from Assyria.
I will resettle them in Gilead and Lebanon
until there is no more room for them all.
11 They will pass safely through the sea of distress,*
for the waves of the sea will be held back,
and the waters of the Nile will dry up.
The pride of Assyria will be crushed,
and the rule of Egypt will end.
12 By my power* I will make my people strong,
and by my authority they will go wherever
they wish.
I, the LORD, have spoken!"

SHEPHERDING THE SHEEP 10:3–11:17

Zechariah prophesied against the leaders of Israel who failed to care for the people under their care. He also predicted that the coming Savior—the good shepherd (John 10:11)—would be rejected by his own people. It is a great tragedy for God's people when their leaders fail to care for them adequately. God holds leaders particularly accountable for the condition of his people. The New Testament tells believers, "Not many of you should become teachers in the church, for we who teach will be judged more strictly" (James 3:1). If God puts you in a position of leadership, remember that it is also a place of great responsibility. ■

11 [1] Open your doors, Lebanon,
so that fire may devour your cedar forests.
2 Weep, you cypress trees, for all the ruined cedars;
the most majestic ones have fallen.
Weep, you oaks of Bashan,
for the thick forests have been cut down.
3 Listen to the wailing of the shepherds,
for their rich pastures are destroyed.
Hear the young lions roaring,
for their thickets in the Jordan Valley are ruined.

THE GOOD AND EVIL SHEPHERDS

4This is what the LORD my God says: "Go and care for the
flock that is intended for slaughter. 5The buyers slaughter their sheep without remorse. The sellers say, 'Praise
the LORD! Now I'm rich!' Even the shepherds have no
compassion for them. 6Likewise, I will no longer have pity
on the people of the land," says the LORD. "I will let them
fall into each other's hands and into the hands of their
king. They will turn the land into a wilderness, and I will
not rescue them."
7So I cared for the flock intended for slaughter—the
flock that was oppressed. Then I took two shepherd's
staffs and named one Favor and the other Union. 8I got
rid of their three evil shepherds in a single month.
But I became impatient with these sheep, and they
hated me, too. 9So I told them, "I won't be your shepherd
any longer. If you die, you die. If you are killed, you are
killed. And let those who remain devour each other!"
10Then I took my staff called Favor and cut it in two,
showing that I had revoked the covenant I had made with
all the nations. 11That was the end of my covenant with
them. The suffering flock was watching me, and they
knew that the LORD was speaking through my actions.
12And I said to them, "If you like, give me my wages,
whatever I am worth; but only if you want to." So they
counted out for my wages thirty pieces of silver.
13And the LORD said to me, "Throw it to the potter*"—
this magnificent sum at which they valued me! So I took
the thirty coins and threw them to the potter in the Temple of the LORD.
14Then I took my other staff, Union, and cut it in two,
showing that the bond of unity between Judah and Israel
was broken.
15Then the LORD said to me, "Go again and play the part
of a worthless shepherd. 16This illustrates how I will give
this nation a shepherd who will not care for those who
are dying, nor look after the young,* nor heal the injured,
nor feed the healthy. Instead, this shepherd will eat the
meat of the fattest sheep and tear off their hooves.

17 "What sorrow awaits this worthless shepherd
who abandons the flock!
The sword will cut his arm
and pierce his right eye.
His arm will become useless,
and his right eye completely blind."

12 **FUTURE DELIVERANCE FOR JERUSALEM**

This* message concerning the fate of Israel came from
the LORD: "This message is from the LORD, who stretched
out the heavens, laid the foundations of the earth, and
formed the human spirit. 2I will make Jerusalem like an
intoxicating drink that makes the nearby nations stagger
when they send their armies to besiege Jerusalem and Judah. 3On that day I will make Jerusalem an immovable
rock. All the nations will gather against it to try to move it,
but they will only hurt themselves.
4"On that day," says the LORD, "I will cause every horse
to panic and every rider to lose his nerve. I will watch over
the people of Judah, but I will blind all the horses of their

10:11 Or *the sea of Egypt,* referring to the Red Sea. **10:12** Hebrew *In the LORD.* **11:13** Syriac version reads *into the treasury;* also in 11:13b. Compare Matt 27:6-10. **11:16** Or *the scattered.* **12:1** Hebrew *An Oracle: This.*

enemies. 5And the clans of Judah will say to themselves, 'The people of Jerusalem have found strength in the LORD of Heaven's Armies, their God.'

A GREAT DAY! 12:1-5

This prophecy speaks of a great future battle against Jerusalem. Some say this battle is Armageddon—the last great battle on earth. Those who go against God's people will not prevail forever. One day all evil will be abolished once and for all. What do you think the world will be like without it? ■

6"On that day I will make the clans of Judah like a flame that sets a woodpile ablaze or like a burning torch among sheaves of grain. They will burn up all the neighboring nations right and left, while the people living in Jerusalem remain secure.
7"The LORD will give victory to the rest of Judah first, before Jerusalem, so that the people of Jerusalem and the royal line of David will not have greater honor than the rest of Judah. 8On that day the LORD will defend the people of Jerusalem; the weakest among them will be as mighty as King David! And the royal descendants will be like God, like the angel of the LORD who goes before them! 9For on that day I will begin to destroy all the nations that come against Jerusalem.
10"Then I will pour out a spirit* of grace and prayer on the family of David and on the people of Jerusalem. They will look on me whom they have pierced and mourn for him as for an only son. They will grieve bitterly for him as for a firstborn son who has died. 11The sorrow and mourning in Jerusalem on that day will be like the great mourning for Hadad-rimmon in the valley of Megiddo.
12"All Israel will mourn, each clan by itself, and with the husbands separate from their wives. The family clan of David will mourn alone, as will the clan of Nathan, 13the clan of Levi, and the clan of Shimei. 14Each of the surviving clans from Judah will mourn separately, and with the husbands separate from their wives.

13 A FOUNTAIN OF CLEANSING

"On that day a fountain will be opened for the dynasty of David and for the people of Jerusalem, a fountain to cleanse them from all their sins and impurity.
2"And on that day," says the LORD of Heaven's Armies, "I will erase idol worship throughout the land, so that even the names of the idols will be forgotten. I will remove from the land both the false prophets and the spirit of impurity that came with them. 3If anyone continues to prophesy, his own father and mother will tell him, 'You must die, for you have prophesied lies in the name of the LORD.' And as he prophesies, his own father and mother will stab him.
4"On that day people will be ashamed to claim the prophetic gift. No one will pretend to be a prophet by wearing prophet's clothes. 5He will say, 'I'm no prophet; I'm a farmer. I began working for a farmer as a boy.' 6And if someone asks, 'Then what about those wounds on your chest?*' he will say, 'I was wounded at my friends' house!'

THE SCATTERING OF THE SHEEP

7 "Awake, O sword, against my shepherd,
the man who is my partner,"
says the LORD of Heaven's Armies.
"Strike down the shepherd,
and the sheep will be scattered,
and I will turn against the lambs.
8 Two-thirds of the people in the land
will be cut off and die," says the LORD.
"But one-third will be left in the land.
9 I will bring that group through the fire
and make them pure.
I will refine them like silver
and purify them like gold.
They will call on my name,
and I will answer them.
I will say, 'These are my people,'
and they will say, 'The LORD is our God.'"

ANY MOMENT 14:1-10

Zechariah warned the people of the coming "day of the LORD." Days of judgment are mentioned in a number of Old Testament passages. (See Isa 13:6; Joel 1:15; 2:1; Mal 4:1.) One day, the ultimate day of judgment will take place. Jesus will return as the king and as the judge of all people. (See also Mark 13.) What if you knew exactly when this day of judgment would happen? What, if anything, would you do differently? ■

14 THE LORD WILL RULE THE EARTH

Watch, for the day of the LORD is coming when your possessions will be plundered right in front of you! 2I will gather all the nations to fight against Jerusalem. The city will be taken, the houses looted, and the women raped. Half the population will be taken into captivity, and the rest will be left among the ruins of the city.
3Then the LORD will go out to fight against those nations, as he has fought in times past. 4On that day his feet will stand on the Mount of Olives, east of Jerusalem. And the Mount of Olives will split apart, making a wide valley running from east to west. Half the mountain will move toward the north and half toward the south. 5You will flee through this valley, for it will reach across to Azal.* Yes, you will flee as you did from the earthquake in the days of King Uzziah of Judah. Then the LORD my God will come, and all his holy ones with him.*
6On that day the sources of light will no longer shine,*
7yet there will be continuous day! Only the LORD knows

12:10 Or *the Spirit*. 13:6 Hebrew *wounds between your hands?* 14:5a The meaning of the Hebrew is uncertain. 14:5b As in Greek version; Hebrew reads *with you*. 14:6 Hebrew *there will be no light, no cold or frost*. The meaning of the Hebrew is uncertain.

how this could happen. There will be no normal day and night, for at evening time it will still be light.

[8]On that day life-giving waters will flow out from Jerusalem, half toward the Dead Sea and half toward the Mediterranean,* flowing continuously in both summer and winter.

[9]And the LORD will be king over all the earth. On that day there will be one LORD—his name alone will be worshiped.

PROPHECY PANORAMA 14:21

Zechariah spoke to a people who endured hardships. They were harassed by neighbors and were discouraged over their small numbers and seemingly inadequate Temple. Consequently, their worship lacked energy and sincerity. Still God declared, "My love for Jerusalem and Mount Zion is passionate and strong" (1:14). He promised to restore their land, their city, and their Temple. Like other prophets, Zechariah blended prophecies of the present, near future, and the final days into one sweeping panorama. Through his message we learn that our hope is found in God, who IS in complete control of the world. ■

[10]All the land from Geba, north of Judah, to Rimmon, south of Jerusalem, will become one vast plain. But Jerusalem will be raised up in its original place and will be inhabited all the way from the Benjamin Gate over to the site of the old gate, then to the Corner Gate, and from the Tower of Hananel to the king's winepresses. [11]And Jerusalem will be filled, safe at last, never again to be cursed and destroyed.

[12]And the LORD will send a plague on all the nations that fought against Jerusalem. Their people will become like walking corpses, their flesh rotting away. Their eyes will rot in their sockets, and their tongues will rot in their mouths. [13]On that day they will be terrified, stricken by the LORD with great panic. They will fight their neighbors hand to hand. [14]Judah, too, will be fighting at Jerusalem. The wealth of all the neighboring nations will be captured—great quantities of gold and silver and fine clothing. [15]This same plague will strike the horses, mules, camels, donkeys, and all the other animals in the enemy camps.

[16]In the end, the enemies of Jerusalem who survive the plague will go up to Jerusalem each year to worship the King, the LORD of Heaven's Armies, and to celebrate the Festival of Shelters. [17]Any nation in the world that refuses to come to Jerusalem to worship the King, the LORD of Heaven's Armies, will have no rain. [18]If the people of Egypt refuse to attend the festival, the LORD will punish them with the same plague that he sends on the other nations who refuse to go. [19]Egypt and the other nations will all be punished if they don't go to celebrate the Festival of Shelters.

[20]On that day even the harness bells of the horses will be inscribed with these words: HOLY TO THE LORD. And the cooking pots in the Temple of the LORD will be as sacred as the basins used beside the altar. [21]In fact, every cooking pot in Jerusalem and Judah will be holy to the LORD of Heaven's Armies. All who come to worship will be free to use any of these pots to boil their sacrifices. And on that day there will no longer be traders* in the Temple of the LORD of Heaven's Armies.

14:8 Hebrew *half toward the eastern sea and half toward the western sea.* **14:21** Hebrew *Canaanites.*

MALACHI

"MOM, SHE DID it again!" Sierra screamed "Mom!"

Sierra had a little sister, Caitlin. Although five-year-old Caitlin was really cute, she never seemed to listen.

Because their house was small, Sierra and Caitlin shared a room . . . and a closet. Caitlin had been told to keep out of Sierra's clothes. Yet Caitlin was often found in the bedroom surrounded by Sierra's clothes. Lectures hadn't helped; neither had time-outs. Nothing seemed to deter Caitlin from playing in Sierra's clothes.

God had warned his people repeatedly that he would punish them if they did not stop sinning. When they refused to change, God punished them. Israel was taken into captivity, and some years later so was Judah.

Then God brought his people back. He forgave them and offered them a fresh start. Had they learned?

No, they hadn't. God's people, rather than learn from the mistakes of their ancestors, chose to repeat their actions. Because they hadn't learned, Malachi came to warn them that God was watching—and he cared.

As you read Malachi, consider the lessons you've learned the hard way over the years. Is there still something you need to learn?

malachi

timeline

586 B.C.
Jerusalem is destroyed

537
First exiles return to Jerusalem

536
Temple construction begins

520
Haggai, Zechariah become prophets

516
Temple completed

479
Esther becomes queen of Persia

465
Artaxerxes I becomes king of Persia

458
Ezra comes to Jerusalem

445
Nehemiah comes to Jerusalem

430
Malachi becomes a prophet

stats

PURPOSE: To confront the people with their sins and to restore their relationship with God

AUTHOR: Malachi

TO WHOM WRITTEN: The Jews in Jerusalem and God's people everywhere

DATE WRITTEN: About 430 B.C.

SETTING: Malachi, Haggai, and Zechariah were postexilic prophets to Judah (the southern kingdom). Haggai and Zechariah rebuked the people for their failure to rebuild the Temple. Malachi confronted them with their neglect of the Temple and their false and profane worship.

KEY PEOPLE: Malachi, the priests

KEY PLACE: Jerusalem, the Temple

SPECIAL FEATURES: Malachi's literary style displays a continual use of questions asked by God and his people (for example, see 3:7-8).

KEY points

REAL LOVE
Malachi pointed out the hypocrisy of Israel's "love" for God. God hates hypocrisy and careless living. This kind of living denies him the relationship he wants to have with us. What we give and how we live reflects the sincerity of our love for God.

THE PRIESTS' SINS
Malachi singled out the priests for condemnation. They knew what God required, yet they had a casual attitude toward worshiping God and meeting his standards. We all are leaders in some capacity. Neglect and insensitivity are acts of disobedience. God wants leaders who are faithful and sincere.

THE PEOPLE'S SINS
The people had not learned from their exile, nor had they listened to the prophets. Men were callously divorcing their faithful wives to marry younger women from other nations. God deserves our total honor, respect, and faithfulness.

THE LORD'S COMING
Malachi prophesied about the coming Messiah. The Messiah's purpose was, and is, to lead the people to the realization of all their fondest hopes. The day of his final coming will be a day of comfort and healing for a faithful few, and a day of judgment for those who reject him.

1 This is the message* that the LORD gave to Israel
through the prophet Malachi.*

THE LORD'S LOVE FOR ISRAEL

2"I have always loved you," says the LORD.
But you retort, "Really? How have you loved us?"
And the LORD replies, "This is how I showed my love
for you: I loved your ancestor Jacob, 3but I rejected his
brother, Esau, and devastated his hill country. I turned
Esau's inheritance into a desert for jackals."
4Esau's descendants in Edom may say, "We have been
shattered, but we will rebuild the ruins."
But the LORD of Heaven's Armies replies, "They may
try to rebuild, but I will demolish them again. Their
country will be known as 'The Land of Wickedness,' and
their people will be called 'The People with Whom the
LORD Is Forever Angry.' 5When you see the destruction
for yourselves, you will say, 'Truly, the LORD's greatness
reaches far beyond Israel's borders!'"

HALF-HEARTED WORSHIP

Last Sunday, Brian and Joseph fidgeted their way through the morning worship service, mumbled their way through the songs, daydreamed their way through the prayers, and played games on their cell phones while the pastor delivered his message. In short, they went through the motions of worshiping God, but they never actually thought about the one they were in church to honor.

That same Sunday afternoon, Brian and Joseph headed to the mall to catch a new flick filled with car races, chases, and other action. For two hours they were mesmerized, and they emerged into the bright sunlight enthusiastically buzzing about what they had just witnessed on the screen.

Bored with God in the morning . . . enthralled with Hollywood in the afternoon. That's how Brian and Joseph spent last Sunday.

So, what do Brian and Joseph's Sunday activities tell you about where their hearts are?

Read Malachi 1:6-14 to find out what God thinks about half-hearted devotion. What would you say to Brian and Joseph?

UNWORTHY SACRIFICES

6The LORD of Heaven's Armies says to the priests: "A son
honors his father, and a servant respects his master. If I
am your father and master, where are the honor and respect I deserve? You have shown contempt for my name!
"But you ask, 'How have we ever shown contempt for
your name?'

LEFTOVERS 1:6-14

God accused Israel of dishonoring him by offering imperfect sacrifices. If we give God only our leftover time, money, and energy, we repeat the same sin as these worshipers who didn't want to bring anything valuable to God. What we give to God reflects our attitude toward him. What have you given lately? ■

7"You have shown contempt by offering defiled sacrifices on my altar.
"Then you ask, 'How have we defiled the sacrifices?*'
"You defile them by saying the altar of the LORD deserves no respect. 8When you give blind animals as sacrifices, isn't that wrong? And isn't it wrong to offer animals
that are crippled and diseased? Try giving gifts like that
to your governor, and see how pleased he is!" says the
LORD of Heaven's Armies.
9"Go ahead, beg God to be merciful to you! But when
you bring that kind of offering, why should he show you
any favor at all?" asks the LORD of Heaven's Armies.
10"How I wish one of you would shut the Temple doors
so that these worthless sacrifices could not be offered! I
am not pleased with you," says the LORD of Heaven's Armies, "and I will not accept your offerings. 11But my name
is honored* by people of other nations from morning till
night. All around the world they offer* sweet incense and
pure offerings in honor of my name. For my name is
great among the nations," says the LORD of Heaven's
Armies.

CHOSEN 1:11

A theme that occurs throughout the Old Testament is affirmed in this book—"My name is honored by people of other nations. . . . My name is great among the nations." God planned to save and bless the world through his chosen people—the nation of Israel. Today God's chosen people include all who believe in Jesus—Jews and Gentiles. Does that include you? In what ways are you bringing honor to his name? ■

12"But you dishonor my name with your actions. By
bringing contemptible food, you are saying it's all right to
defile the Lord's table. 13You say, 'It's too hard to serve the
LORD,' and you turn up your noses at my commands," says
the LORD of Heaven's Armies. "Think of it! Animals that
are stolen and crippled and sick are being presented as
offerings! Should I accept from you such offerings as
these?" asks the LORD.
14"Cursed is the cheat who promises to give a fine ram
from his flock but then sacrifices a defective one to the
Lord. For I am a great king," says the LORD of Heaven's Armies, "and my name is feared among the nations!

1:1a Hebrew *An Oracle: The message.* **1:1b** *Malachi* means "my messenger." **1:7** As in Greek version; Hebrew reads *defiled you?* **1:11a** Or *will be honored.* **1:11b** Or *will offer.*

ULTIMATE ISSUES

DIVORCE

We all know how prevalent divorce is in our society today. Maybe you're no stranger to the trauma of divorce. Once divorce was considered a social stigma—sort of a "Scarlet Letter" for our time. Now it's so commonplace that we barely even react to the news that another couple is calling it quits.

Before we discuss divorce, let's consider a couple of basic truths about marriage. First, marriage was God's idea. At the beginning of human history, God declared, "It is not good for the man to be alone. I will make a helper who is just right for him" (Gen 2:18). God made Adam and Eve to be husband and wife—one man for one woman—thereby setting the parameters for marriage. Jesus added his stamp of approval by performing his first miracle at a wedding (John 2).

Divorce, however, is man's invention. When asked why Moses allowed divorce, Jesus replied: "Moses permitted divorce only as a concession to your hard hearts, but it was not what God had originally intended" (Matt 19:8). Divorce was never "Plan A."

God knows that we will make mistakes; we will "fall short of God's glorious standard" (Rom 3:23). Our fallen nature affects every area of our lives, including marriage. So God has allowed for divorce in some situations. (For more on the specifics of "biblical divorce," see Matt 19 and 1 Cor 7.) Even so, a divorce is always painful and damaging. That's why, in Malachi 2:16, God says, "I hate divorce!"

If the thought of divorce makes you slightly hesitant about marriage—*good*. That is a healthy hesitation to have. If a fuller understanding of the awesome implications of "two are united into one" (see Gen 2:24) causes you to approach the altar with prayer, respect for the holiness of marriage, and a godly perspective on the marriage covenant—great! Marriage is a high calling and should be treated as such. An attitude of "Oh well, if it doesn't work out, there's always divorce" is a formula for marital meltdown.

2

A WARNING TO THE PRIESTS

"Listen, you priests—this command is for you! 2Listen to
me and make up your minds to honor my name," says the
LORD of Heaven's Armies, "or I will bring a terrible curse
against you. I will curse even the blessings you receive.
Indeed, I have already cursed them, because you have not
taken my warning to heart. 3I will punish your descendants and splatter your faces with the manure from your
festival sacrifices, and I will throw you on the manure
pile. 4Then at last you will know it was I who sent you this
warning so that my covenant with the Levites can continue," says the LORD of Heaven's Armies.
5"The purpose of my covenant with the Levites was to
bring life and peace, and that is what I gave them. This required reverence from them, and they greatly revered me
and stood in awe of my name. 6They passed on to the people the truth of the instructions they received from me.
They did not lie or cheat; they walked with me, living
good and righteous lives, and they turned many from
lives of sin.
7"The words of a priest's lips should preserve
knowledge of God, and people should go to him for instruction, for the priest is the messenger of the LORD of
Heaven's Armies. 8But you priests have left God's paths.
Your instructions have caused many to stumble into sin.
You have corrupted the covenant I made with the Levites," says the LORD of Heaven's Armies. 9"So I have
made you despised and humiliated in the eyes of all the
people. For you have not obeyed me but have shown favoritism in the way you carry out my instructions."

A CALL TO FAITHFULNESS

10Are we not all children of the same Father? Are we not
all created by the same God? Then why do we betray each
other, violating the covenant of our ancestors?
11Judah has been unfaithful, and a detestable thing has
been done in Israel and in Jerusalem. The men of Judah
have defiled the LORD's beloved sanctuary by marrying
women who worship idols. 12May the LORD cut off from
the nation of Israel* every last man who has done this and
yet brings an offering to the LORD of Heaven's Armies.
13Here is another thing you do. You cover the LORD's altar with tears, weeping and groaning because he pays no

2:12 Hebrew *from the tents of Jacob*. The names "Jacob" and "Israel" are often interchanged throughout the Old Testament, referring sometimes to the individual patriarch and sometimes to the nation.

attention to your offerings and doesn't accept them with pleasure. 14You cry out, "Why doesn't the LORD accept my worship?" I'll tell you why! Because the LORD witnessed the vows you and your wife made when you were young. But you have been unfaithful to her, though she remained your faithful partner, the wife of your marriage vows.

15Didn't the LORD make you one with your wife? In body and spirit you are his.* And what does he want? Godly children from your union. So guard your heart; remain loyal to the wife of your youth. 16"For I hate divorce!" says the LORD, the God of Israel. "To divorce your wife is to overwhelm her with cruelty,*" says the LORD of Heaven's Armies. "So guard your heart; do not be unfaithful to your wife."

17You have wearied the LORD with your words.

"How have we wearied him?" you ask.

You have wearied him by saying that all who do evil are good in the LORD's sight, and he is pleased with them. You have wearied him by asking, "Where is the God of justice?"

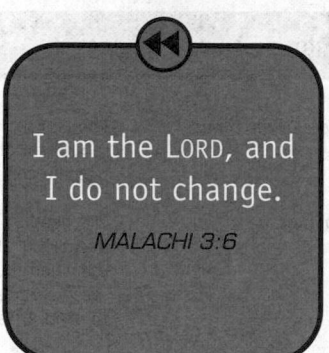

3 THE COMING DAY OF JUDGMENT

"Look! I am sending my messenger, and he will prepare the way before me. Then the Lord you are seeking will suddenly come to his Temple. The messenger of the covenant, whom you look for so eagerly, is surely coming," says the LORD of Heaven's Armies.

2"But who will be able to endure it when he comes? Who will be able to stand and face him when he appears? For he will be like a blazing fire that refines metal, or like a strong soap that bleaches clothes. 3He will sit like a refiner of silver, burning away the dross. He will purify the Levites, refining them like gold and silver, so that they may once again offer acceptable sacrifices to the LORD. 4Then once more the LORD will accept the offerings brought to him by the people of Judah and Jerusalem, as he did in the past.

5"At that time I will put you on trial. I am eager to witness against all sorcerers and adulterers and liars. I will speak against those who cheat employees of their wages, who oppress widows and orphans, or who deprive the foreigners living among you of justice, for these people do not fear me," says the LORD of Heaven's Armies.

A CALL TO REPENTANCE

6"I am the LORD, and I do not change. That is why you descendants of Jacob are not already destroyed. 7Ever since the days of your ancestors, you have scorned my decrees and failed to obey them. Now return to me, and I will return to you," says the LORD of Heaven's Armies.

"But you ask, 'How can we return when we have never gone away?'

8"Should people cheat God? Yet you have cheated me!

"But you ask, 'What do you mean? When did we ever cheat you?'

"You have cheated me of the tithes and offerings due to me. 9You are under a curse, for your whole nation has been cheating me. 10Bring all the tithes into the storehouse so there will be enough food in my Temple. If you do," says the LORD of Heaven's Armies, "I will open the windows of heaven for you. I will pour out a blessing so great you won't have enough room to take it in! Try it! Put me to the test! 11Your crops will be abundant, for I will

2:15 Or *Didn't the one LORD make us and preserve our life and breath?* or *Didn't the one LORD make her, both flesh and spirit?* The meaning of the Hebrew is uncertain. 2:16 Hebrew *to cover one's garment with violence.*

I am the LORD, and I do not change.

MALACHI 3:6

HOLDING BACK 3:6-12

Malachi urged the people not to hold back their gifts (tithes) to the priests. Tithing began during Moses' time (see Lev 27:30-34; Deut 14:22-25). The Levites received some of the tithes because they couldn't own land (Num 18:20-21). But during Malachi's day, since the tithes weren't used to support God's workers, the Levites had to go to work. God has given us everything. When we refuse to return to him a part of what he has given, we rob him. What are you willing to give to help advance God's kingdom? ■

I barely have any money. Does God really expect me to give what little I have to the church?

In Malachi 3:8-10, God warned that refusing to give him tithes and offerings was actually stealing from him!

So, why should God care? After all, he doesn't need our money. He owns everything! But he knows what an idol money can be.

Maybe that's why Jesus talked about money more than he talked about anything else. (See, for example, Matt 6:19-24.) He knew that the love of money (rather than money itself) leads to all sorts of problems (see 1 Tim 6:10).

The best way to keep from idolizing money is to learn the joy of giving it away. Some people do this by tithing: taking 10 percent of their income right off the top and giving it to their local church or in support of a missionary. Others give by supporting a child overseas.

Remember, it doesn't matter how much you give. What matters is your attitude when you give. See Luke 21:1-4 and 2 Corinthians 9:6-11.

Malachi

Served as a prophet to Judah about 430 B.C. He was the last of the Old Testament prophets.

Climate of the times	The city of Jerusalem and the Temple had been rebuilt for almost a century, but the people had become complacent in their worship of God.
Main message	The people's relationship with God was broken because of their sin, and they would soon be punished. But the few who repented would receive God's blessing, illustrated in his promise to send a Messiah.
Importance of message	Hypocrisy, neglecting God, and careless living have devastating consequences. Service and worship of God must be the primary focus of our life, both now and in eternity.
Contemporary prophets	None

guard them from insects and disease.* Your grapes will
not fall from the vine before they are ripe," says the LORD
of Heaven's Armies. 12"Then all nations will call you
blessed, for your land will be such a delight," says the
LORD of Heaven's Armies.

13"You have said terrible things about me," says the
LORD.

"But you say, 'What do you mean? What have we said
against you?'

14"You have said, 'What's the use of serving God? What
have we gained by obeying his commands or by trying to
show the LORD of Heaven's Armies that we are sorry for
our sins? 15From now on we will call the arrogant blessed.
For those who do evil get rich, and those who dare God to
punish them suffer no harm.'"

THE LORD'S PROMISE OF MERCY

16Then those who feared the LORD spoke with each other,
and the LORD listened to what they said. In his presence, a
scroll of remembrance was written to record the names
of those who feared him and always thought about the
honor of his name.

17"They will be my people," says the LORD of Heaven's
Armies. "On the day when I act in judgment, they will be
my own special treasure. I will spare them as a father
spares an obedient child. 18Then you will again see the
difference between the righteous and the wicked, between those who serve God and those who do not."

4

THE COMING DAY OF JUDGMENT

1*The LORD of Heaven's Armies says, "The day of judgment is coming, burning like a furnace. On that day the
arrogant and the wicked will be burned up like straw.
They will be consumed—roots, branches, and all.

2"But for you who fear my name, the Sun of Righteousness will rise with healing in his wings.* And you will go
free, leaping with joy like calves let out to pasture. 3On the
day when I act, you will tread upon the wicked as if they
were dust under your feet," says the LORD of Heaven's
Armies.

4"Remember to obey the Law of Moses, my servant—all
the decrees and regulations that I gave him on Mount
Sinai* for all Israel.

COST OF COMMITMENT 4:4

Malachi gives us practical guidelines about commitment to God. God deserves the best we have to offer (1:7-14). We must be willing to change any wrong attitudes or ways of living (2:1-2), make family a priority (2:13-16), to submit to God's refining process (3:3), give of our resources (3:8-12), and put pride aside (3:13-15). Such a commitment to God demands great sacrifice on our part. Is this a sacrifice you're prepared to make? ■

5"Look, I am sending you the prophet Elijah before
the great and dreadful day of the LORD arrives. 6His
preaching will turn the hearts of fathers to their children, and the hearts of children to their fathers. Otherwise I will come and strike the land with a curse."

3:11 Hebrew *from the devourer*. 4:1 Verses 4:1-6 are numbered 3:19-24 in Hebrew text. 4:2 Or *the sun of righteousness will rise with healing in its wings*. 4:4 Hebrew *Horeb*, another name for Sinai.

new testament

WHO WOULD YOU put on a list of the most influential people of all time? Think beyond celebrities. We're talking about the real "heavyweights" of history.

Maybe your list might feature leaders both good and bad: Julius Caesar, Karl Marx, Martin Luther King, Jr. Or, maybe your list includes people who helped advance science and technology: Marie Curie, George Washington Carver, Albert Einstein.

Those people—and many others—deserve to be on such a list. But the one person who changed the world more than anyone is Jesus. Naming a first-century evangelist "the most influential person of all time" probably won't sit well with some people. They may prefer to put him on a list of influential "religious" figures. But here's why Jesus Christ cannot be ignored:

Two thousand years ago, Jesus of Nazareth launched a spiritual revolution that continues today. He has been the motivation behind more songs, sermons, and acts of charity, and is the object of more affection than all of the other great figures of history combined. And don't forget the millions of lives that have been transformed.

See for yourself how Jesus succeeded in turning ancient Israel on its ear. And he still rocks the planet.

matthew

timeline

37 B.C.
Herod the Great begins to rule

6/5 B.C.
Jesus is born

5/4 B.C.
Escape to Egypt

4 B.C.
Herod the Great dies

4/3 B.C.
Return to Nazareth

A.D. 6
Judea becomes a Roman province

6/7
Jesus visits Temple as a boy

14
Tiberius Caesar becomes emperor

26
Pontius Pilate appointed governor

26/27
Jesus begins his ministry

28
Jesus chooses 12 disciples

29
Jesus feeds 5,000

30
Jesus is crucified, rises again, and ascends

stats

PURPOSE: To prove that Jesus is the Messiah, the eternal King

AUTHOR: Matthew (Levi)

TO WHOM WRITTEN: Especially for the Jews

DATE WRITTEN: Probably between A.D. 60 and 65

SETTING: Matthew was a Jewish tax collector who became one of Jesus' disciples. This Gospel forms the connecting link between the Old and New Testaments because of its emphasis on the fulfillment of prophecy.

KEY PEOPLE: Jesus, Mary, Joseph, John the Baptist, Jesus' disciples, religious leaders, Caiaphas, Pilate, Mary Magdalene

KEY PLACES: Bethlehem, Jerusalem, Capernaum, Galilee, Judea

KEY points

EXPECTATIONS ABOUT THE SAVIOR
Jesus was the Messiah, the deliverer for whom the Jews had waited for centuries. When he came, however, many failed to accept him, because he didn't meet their expectations of a deliverer. Likewise, we can fail to accept Jesus as our deliverer, because of our expectations or agendas. God wants us to accept him as he is.

THE KINGDOM OF GOD
Jesus preached about the Kingdom of God, and how people could belong to it through a process of spiritual rebirth. We can belong to this kingdom now through faith in Jesus.

TEACHINGS
Jesus taught the people using sermons, illustrations, and parables. He showed the true ingredients of faith and how to guard against an ineffective and hypocritical life. As we follow the radical lifestyle described in his teachings, we prepare for life in his Kingdom.

KEY PLACES IN MATTHEW

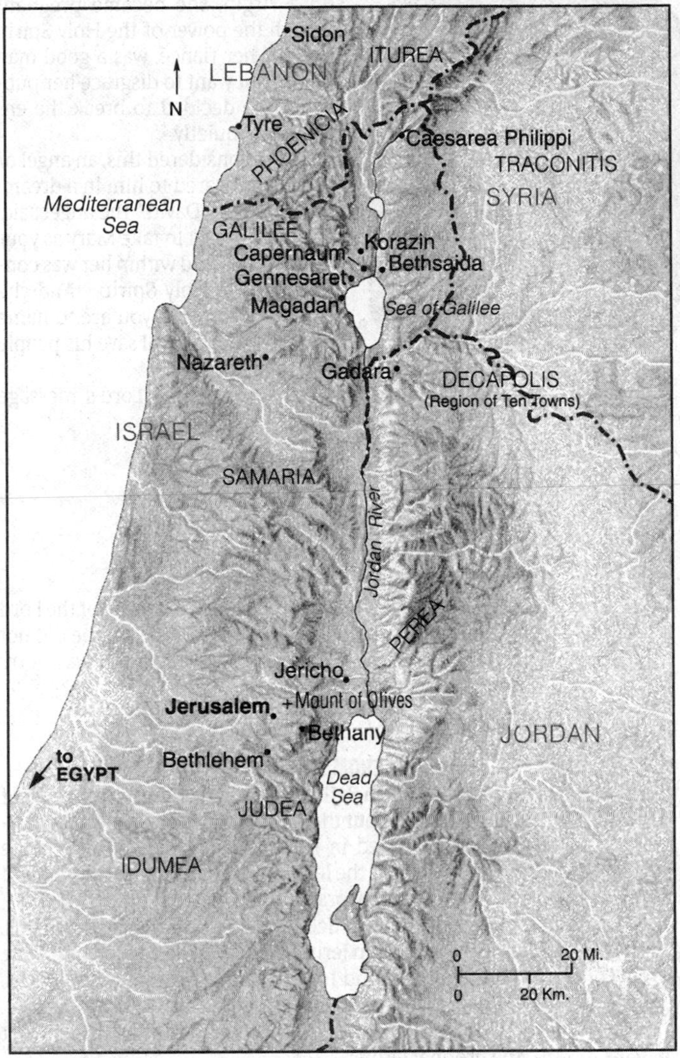

The broken lines (–··–) indicate modern boundaries.

Jesus' earthly story begins in the town of Bethlehem in the Roman province of Judea (2:1). A threat to kill the infant King led Joseph to take his family to Egypt (2:14). When they returned, God led them to settle in Nazareth in Galilee (2:22-23). At about age 30, Jesus was baptized in the Jordan River (3:13) and was tempted by Satan in the Judean wilderness (4:1). He set up his base of operations in Capernaum (4:12-13) and from there ministered throughout Israel, telling parables, teaching about the Kingdom, and healing the sick. He traveled to the country of the Gergesenes and healed two demon-possessed men (8:28-34); fed over 5,000 people with five small loaves of bread and two fish on the shores of Galilee near Bethsaida (14:13-21); healed the sick in Gennesaret (14:34-36); ministered to the Gentiles in Tyre and Sidon (15:21-28); visited Caesarea Philippi, where Peter declared him to be the Messiah (16:13-20); and taught in Perea, across the Jordan (19:1). As he set out on his last visit to Jerusalem, he told the disciples what would happen to him there (20:17-19). He spent some time in Jericho (20:29), then stayed in Bethany at night as he went back and forth into Jerusalem during his last week (21:17). In Jerusalem he would be crucified, but he would rise again.

1

THE ANCESTORS OF JESUS THE MESSIAH

This is a record of the ancestors of Jesus the Messiah, a descendant of David* and of Abraham:

2 Abraham was the father of Isaac.
Isaac was the father of Jacob.
Jacob was the father of Judah and his brothers.
3 Judah was the father of Perez and Zerah (whose mother was Tamar).
Perez was the father of Hezron.
Hezron was the father of Ram.*
4 Ram was the father of Amminadab.
Amminadab was the father of Nahshon.
Nahshon was the father of Salmon.
5 Salmon was the father of Boaz (whose mother was Rahab).
Boaz was the father of Obed (whose mother was Ruth).
Obed was the father of Jesse.
6 Jesse was the father of King David.
David was the father of Solomon (whose mother was Bathsheba, the widow of Uriah).

1:1 Greek *Jesus the Messiah, son of David.* 1:3 Greek *Aram*, a variant spelling of Ram; also in 1:4. See 1 Chr 2:9-10.

> And she will have a son, and you are to name him Jesus, for he will save his people from their sins.
>
> MATTHEW 1:21

7 Solomon was the father
of Rehoboam.
Rehoboam was the father
of Abijah.
Abijah was the father of Asa.*
8 Asa was the father of
Jehoshaphat.
Jehoshaphat was the father
of Jehoram.*
Jehoram was the father* of Uzziah.
9 Uzziah was the father of Jotham.
Jotham was the father of Ahaz.
Ahaz was the father of Hezekiah.
10 Hezekiah was the father
of Manasseh.
Manasseh was the father of Amon.*
Amon was the father of Josiah.
11 Josiah was the father of Jehoiachin* and his brothers
(born at the time of the exile to Babylon).
12 After the Babylonian exile:
Jehoiachin was the father of Shealtiel.
Shealtiel was the father of Zerubbabel.
13 Zerubbabel was the father of Abiud.
Abiud was the father of Eliakim.
Eliakim was the father of Azor.
14 Azor was the father of Zadok.
Zadok was the father of Akim.
Akim was the father of Eliud.
15 Eliud was the father of Eleazar.
Eleazar was the father of Matthan.
Matthan was the father of Jacob.
16 Jacob was the father of Joseph, the husband of Mary.
Mary gave birth to Jesus, who is called the Messiah.

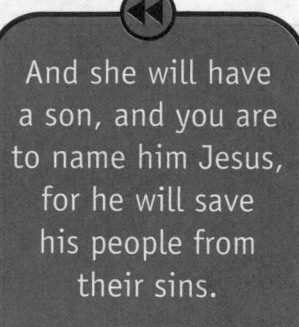

ORDINARY AND EXTRAORDINARY 1:1-17

The first 17 verses of Matthew are almost a "phone book" (minus the numbers) of names. Jesus' ancestors had different experiences and personalities. Some were well known for their faith (Abraham, Isaac, Ruth, and David). Many were ordinary (Hezron, Ram, and Akim). Others had bad reputations (Manasseh and Abijah). God's work has never been limited by human failures. He works through ordinary people to accomplish extraordinary things. What has he accomplished through you? ■

17All those listed above include fourteen generations from Abraham to David, fourteen from David to the Babylonian exile, and fourteen from the Babylonian exile to the Messiah.

THE BIRTH OF JESUS THE MESSIAH

18This is how Jesus the Messiah was born. His mother,
Mary, was engaged to be married to Joseph. But before
the marriage took place, while she was
still a virgin, she became pregnant
through the power of the Holy Spirit.
19Joseph, her fiancé, was a good man
and did not want to disgrace her publicly, so he decided to break the engagement* quietly.
20As he considered this, an angel of
the Lord appeared to him in a dream.
"Joseph, son of David," the angel said,
"do not be afraid to take Mary as your
wife. For the child within her was conceived by the Holy Spirit. 21And she
will have a son, and you are to name
him Jesus,* for he will save his people
from their sins."
22All of this occurred to fulfill the Lord's message
through his prophet:

23 "Look! The virgin will conceive a child!
She will give birth to a son,
and they will call him Immanuel,*
which means 'God is with us.'"

24When Joseph woke up, he did as the angel of the Lord
commanded and took Mary as his wife. 25But he did not
have sexual relations with her until her son was born.
And Joseph named him Jesus.

2 VISITORS FROM THE EAST

Jesus was born in Bethlehem in Judea, during the reign of
King Herod. About that time some wise men* from eastern lands arrived in Jerusalem, asking, 2"Where is the
newborn king of the Jews? We saw his star as it rose,* and
we have come to worship him."
3King Herod was deeply disturbed when he heard this,
as was everyone in Jerusalem. 4He called a meeting of the
leading priests and teachers of religious law and asked,
"Where is the Messiah supposed to be born?"
5"In Bethlehem in Judea," they said, "for this is what
the prophet wrote:

6 'And you, O Bethlehem in the land of Judah,
are not least among the ruling cities* of Judah,
for a ruler will come from you
who will be the shepherd for my people Israel.'*"

7Then Herod called for a private meeting with the wise
men, and he learned from them the time when the star
first appeared. 8Then he told them, "Go to Bethlehem and
search carefully for the child. And when you find him,
come back and tell me so that I can go and worship him,
too!"
9After this interview the wise men went their way. And

1:7 Greek *Asaph,* a variant spelling of Asa; also in 1:8. See 1 Chr 3:10. **1:8a** Greek *Joram,* a variant spelling of Jehoram; also in 1:8b. See 1 Kgs 22:50 and note at 1 Chr 3:11. **1:8b** Or *ancestor;* also in 1:11. **1:10** Greek *Amos,* a variant spelling of Amon; also in 1:10b. See 1 Chr 3:14. **1:11** Greek *Jeconiah,* a variant spelling of Jehoiachin; also in 1:12. See 2 Kgs 24:6 and note at 1 Chr 3:16. **1:19** Greek *to divorce her.* **1:21** *Jesus* means "The LORD saves." **1:23** Isa 7:14; 8:8, 10 (Greek version). **2:1** Or *royal astrologers;* Greek reads *magi;* also in 2:7, 16. **2:2** Or *star in the east.* **2:6a** Greek *the rulers.* **2:6b** Mic 5:2; 2 Sam 5:2.

the star they had seen in the east guided them to Bethlehem. It went ahead of them and stopped over the place
where the child was. [10]When they saw the star, they were
filled with joy! [11]They entered the house and saw the
child with his mother, Mary, and they bowed down and
worshiped him. Then they opened their treasure chests
and gave him gifts of gold, frankincense, and myrrh.
[12]When it was time to leave, they returned to their own
country by another route, for God had warned them in a
dream not to return to Herod.

THE ESCAPE TO EGYPT

[13]After the wise men were gone, an angel of the Lord appeared to Joseph in a dream. "Get up! Flee to Egypt with
the child and his mother," the angel said. "Stay there until
I tell you to return, because Herod is going to search for
the child to kill him."
[14]That night Joseph left for Egypt with the child and
Mary, his mother, [15]and they stayed there until Herod's
death. This fulfilled what the Lord had spoken through
the prophet: "I called my Son out of Egypt."*
[16]Herod was furious when he realized that the wise
men had outwitted him. He sent soldiers to kill all the
boys in and around Bethlehem who were two years old
and under, based on the wise men's report of the star's
first appearance. [17]Herod's brutal action fulfilled what
God had spoken through the prophet Jeremiah:

[18] "A cry was heard in Ramah—
weeping and great mourning.
Rachel weeps for her children,
refusing to be comforted,
for they are dead."*

UNSTOPPABLE 2:1-18

When told about the newborn King, Herod devised a cruel plan in order to keep his throne (2:16-18). This sad event was prophesied in Jeremiah 31:15.

But God protected his Son. Herod couldn't stop God's plan. No one could. This fact is no less true today. Yet because of the evil they see around them, many people fear that God is in the middle of a power outage of some kind. Is that your belief? The plans of a sovereign God—a God still in control—cannot be stopped. ■

THE RETURN TO NAZARETH

[19]When Herod died, an angel of the Lord appeared in a
dream to Joseph in Egypt. [20]"Get up!" the angel said.
"Take the child and his mother back to the land of Israel,
because those who were trying to kill the child are dead."
[21]So Joseph got up and returned to the land of Israel
with Jesus and his mother. [22]But when he learned that the
new ruler of Judea was Herod's son Archelaus, he was
afraid to go there. Then, after being warned in a dream,
he left for the region of Galilee. [23]So the family went and
lived in a town called Nazareth. This fulfilled what the
prophets had said: "He will be called a Nazarene."

3

JOHN THE BAPTIST PREPARES THE WAY

In those days John the Baptist came to the Judean wilderness and began preaching. His message was, [2]"Repent of
your sins and turn to God, for the Kingdom of Heaven is
near.*" [3]The prophet Isaiah was speaking about John
when he said,

"He is a voice shouting in the wilderness,
'Prepare the way for the LORD's coming!
Clear the road for him!'"*

PROVE IT 3:1-8

According to John the Baptist, actions speak louder than words. As he told the people of Israel, "Prove by the way you live that you have repented of your sins and turned to God" (3:8). God looks beyond our words and "Christian" activities (going to church; reading the Bible; giving money) to see if our life backs up our words. Do your actions agree with your words? ■

[4]John's clothes were woven from coarse camel hair,
and he wore a leather belt around his waist. For food he
ate locusts and wild honey. [5]People from Jerusalem and
from all of Judea and all over the Jordan Valley went out
to see and hear John. [6]And when they confessed their
sins, he baptized them in the Jordan River.
[7]But when he saw many Pharisees and Sadducees coming to watch him baptize,* he denounced them. "You
brood of snakes!" he exclaimed. "Who warned you to flee
God's coming wrath? [8]Prove by the way you live that you
have repented of your sins and turned to God. [9]Don't just
say to each other, 'We're safe, for we are descendants of
Abraham.' That means nothing, for I tell you, God can create children of Abraham from these very stones. [10]Even
now the ax of God's judgment is poised, ready to sever the
roots of the trees. Yes, every tree that does not produce
good fruit will be chopped down and thrown into the fire.
[11]"I baptize with* water those who repent of their sins
and turn to God. But someone is coming soon who is
greater than I am—so much greater that I'm not worthy
even to be his slave and carry his sandals. He will baptize
you with the Holy Spirit and with fire.* [12]He is ready to
separate the chaff from the wheat with his winnowing
fork. Then he will clean up the threshing area, gathering
the wheat into his barn but burning the chaff with never-
ending fire."

THE BAPTISM OF JESUS

[13]Then Jesus went from Galilee to the Jordan River to be
baptized by John. [14]But John tried to talk him out of it. "I

2:15 Hos 11:1. **2:18** Jer 31:15. **3:2** Or *has come,* or *is coming soon.* **3:3** Isa 40:3 (Greek version). **3:7** Or *coming to be baptized.* **3:11a** Or *in.*
3:11b Or *in the Holy Spirit and in fire.*

The Pharisees and Sadducees

The Pharisees and Sadducees were the two major religious groups in Israel at the time of Christ. The Pharisees were more religiously minded, while the Sadducees were more politically minded. Although the groups disliked and distrusted each other, they became allies in their common hatred for Jesus.

PHARISEES

Positive Characteristics
- Were committed to obeying all of God's Word
- Were admired by the common people for their apparent piety
- Believed in a bodily resurrection and eternal life
- Believed in angels and demons

Negative Characteristics
- Behaved as though their own religious rules were just as important as God's rules for living
- Were often hypocritical, forcing others to try to live up to standards they themselves could not live up to
- Believed that salvation came from perfect obedience to the law and was not based on forgiveness of sins
- Became so obsessed with obeying their legal interpretations in every detail that they completely ignored God's message of mercy and grace
- Were more concerned with appearing to be good than with obeying God

SADDUCEES

Positive Characteristics
- Believed God's Word was limited to the first five books of the Bible: Genesis through Deuteronomy
- Were more practically minded than the Pharisees

Negative Characteristics
- Relied on logic while placing little importance on faith
- Did not believe all the Old Testament was God's Word
- Did not believe in a bodily resurrection or eternal life
- Did not believe in angels or demons
- Were often willing to compromise their values with the Romans and others in order to maintain their status and influential positions

am the one who needs to be baptized by you," he said, "so why are you coming to me?"
15But Jesus said, "It should be done, for we must carry out all that God requires.*" So John agreed to baptize him.

INTEGRITY 3:11-15

Put yourself in John's shoes. Your work is going well; people are taking notice. But you know your work is to prepare people's hearts for someone else—the coming Savior (3:11; John 1:27-36). Now Jesus has arrived, and with him comes the real test of your integrity. Will you be able to turn your followers over to him? John passed the test by publicly baptizing Jesus. Soon he would say, "He must become greater and greater, and I must become less and less" (John 3:30). Are you willing to say the same? ■

16After his baptism, as Jesus came up out of the water,
the heavens were opened* and he saw the Spirit of God
descending like a dove and settling on him. 17And a voice
from heaven said, "This is my dearly loved Son, who
brings me great joy."

4

THE TEMPTATION OF JESUS

Then Jesus was led by the Spirit into the wilderness to be
tempted there by the devil. 2For forty days and forty
nights he fasted and became very hungry.
3During that time the devil* came and said to him, "If
you are the Son of God, tell these stones to become loaves
of bread."
4But Jesus told him, "No! The Scriptures say,

'People do not live by bread alone,
but by every word that comes from the mouth
of God.'*"

5Then the devil took him to the holy city, Jerusalem, to
the highest point of the Temple, 6and said, "If you are the
Son of God, jump off! For the Scriptures say,

'He will order his angels to protect you.
And they will hold you up with their hands
so you won't even hurt your foot on a stone.'*"

7Jesus responded, "The Scriptures also say, 'You must
not test the LORD your God.'*"
8Next the devil took him to the peak of a very high

3:15 Or *for we must fulfill all righteousness.* 3:16 Some manuscripts read *opened to him.* 4:3 Greek *the tempter.* 4:4 Deut 8:3. 4:6 Ps 91:11-12. 4:7 Deut 6:16.

mountain and showed him all the kingdoms of the world
and their glory. [9]"I will give it all to you," he said, "if you
will kneel down and worship me."
[10]"Get out of here, Satan," Jesus told him. "For the
Scriptures say,

'You must worship the LORD your God
and serve only him.'*"

[11]Then the devil went away, and angels came and took
care of Jesus.

THE MINISTRY OF JESUS BEGINS

[12]When Jesus heard that John had been arrested, he left
Judea and returned to Galilee. [13]He went first to Nazareth, then left there and moved to Capernaum, beside the
Sea of Galilee, in the region of Zebulun and Naphtali.
[14]This fulfilled what God said through the prophet Isaiah:

[15] "In the land of Zebulun and of Naphtali,
beside the sea, beyond the Jordan River,
in Galilee where so many Gentiles live,
[16] the people who sat in darkness
have seen a great light.
And for those who lived in the land where death
casts its shadow,
a light has shined."*

[17]From then on Jesus began to preach, "Repent of your
sins and turn to God, for the Kingdom of Heaven is
near.*"

THE FIRST DISCIPLES

[18]One day as Jesus was walking along the shore of the Sea
of Galilee, he saw two brothers—Simon, also called Peter,
and Andrew—throwing a net into the water, for they
fished for a living. [19]Jesus called out to them, "Come, follow me, and I will show you how to fish for people!" [20]And
they left their nets at once and followed him.
[21]A little farther up the shore he saw two other brothers, James and John, sitting in a boat with their father,
Zebedee, repairing their nets. And he called them to
come, too. [22]They immediately followed him, leaving the
boat and their father behind.

CROWDS FOLLOW JESUS

[23]Jesus traveled throughout the region of Galilee, teaching in the synagogues and announcing the Good News
about the Kingdom. And he healed every kind of disease and illness. [24]News about him spread as far as Syria, and people soon began bringing to him all who were
sick. And whatever their sickness or disease, or if they
were demon possessed or epileptic or paralyzed—he
healed them all. [25]Large crowds followed him wherever
he went—people from Galilee, the Ten Towns,* Jerusalem, from all over Judea, and from east of the Jordan
River.

5 THE SERMON ON THE MOUNT

One day as he saw the crowds gathering, Jesus went up on
the mountainside and sat down. His disciples gathered
around him, [2]and he began to teach them.

A "BLESSED" LIFE 5:1-12

Jesus began his sermon with words that seem to contradict each other. After all, no one would think that someone facing persecution or death was "blessed"—in favor with God. But God's way of living usually contradicts the world's. He wants his people to give when others take, to love when others hate, to help when others abuse. Is his way your way? ■

THE BEATITUDES

[3] "God blesses those who are poor and realize their
need for him,*
for the Kingdom of Heaven is theirs.
[4] God blesses those who mourn,
for they will be comforted.
[5] God blesses those who are humble,
for they will inherit the whole earth.
[6] God blesses those who hunger and thirst for justice,*
for they will be satisfied.
[7] God blesses those who are merciful,
for they will be shown mercy.
[8] God blesses those whose hearts are pure,
for they will see God.
[9] God blesses those who work for peace,
for they will be called the children of God.
[10] God blesses those who are persecuted for doing right,
for the Kingdom of Heaven is theirs.

[11]"God blesses you when people mock you and persecute you and lie about you* and say all sorts of evil things
against you because you are my followers. [12]Be happy
about it! Be very glad! For a great reward awaits you in
heaven. And remember, the ancient prophets were persecuted in the same way.

TEACHING ABOUT SALT AND LIGHT

[13]"You are the salt of the earth. But what good is salt if it
has lost its flavor? Can you make it salty again? It will be
thrown out and trampled underfoot as worthless.
[14]"You are the light of the world—like a city on a hilltop
that cannot be hidden. [15]No one lights a lamp and then
puts it under a basket. Instead, a lamp is placed on a
stand, where it gives light to everyone in the house. [16]In
the same way, let your good deeds shine out for all to see,
so that everyone will praise your heavenly Father.

TEACHING ABOUT THE LAW

[17]"Don't misunderstand why I have come. I did not
come to abolish the law of Moses or the writings of the

4:10 Deut 6:13. **4:15-16** Isa 9:1-2 (Greek version). **4:17** Or *has come,* or *is coming soon.* **4:25** Greek *Decapolis.* **5:3** Greek *poor in spirit.* **5:6** Or *for righteousness.* **5:11** Some manuscripts omit *and lie about you.*

prophets. No, I came to accomplish their purpose. 18 I tell you the truth, until heaven and earth disappear, not even the smallest detail of God's law will disappear until its purpose is achieved. 19 So if you ignore the least commandment and teach others to do the same, you will be called the least in the Kingdom of Heaven. But anyone who obeys God's laws and teaches them will be called great in the Kingdom of Heaven.

20 "But I warn you—unless your righteousness is better than the righteousness of the teachers of religious law and the Pharisees, you will never enter the Kingdom of Heaven!

ANGER MANAGEMENT 5:21-22

Jesus spoke about the wrongs that result from anger. Everyone would agree that murder is wrong. But anger? No way. Yet anger in this case refers to uncontrolled anger. This type of anger can lead to violence, emotional hurt, increased mental stress, and other destructive results.

Does this mean that anger is wrong? If you believe that, check out Jesus' actions in John 2:13-16 or the advice of Ephesians 4:26. The wise person practices self-control over thoughts and actions. (See 2 Cor 10:5; Gal 5:22-23; 2 Pet 1:6.) Get control of anger before it controls you. ■

TEACHING ABOUT ANGER

21 "You have heard that our ancestors were told, 'You must not murder. If you commit murder, you are subject to judgment.'* 22 But I say, if you are even angry with someone,* you are subject to judgment! If you call someone an idiot,* you are in danger of being brought before the court. And if you curse someone,* you are in danger of the fires of hell.*

23 "So if you are presenting a sacrifice* at the altar in the Temple and you suddenly remember that someone has something against you, 24 leave your sacrifice there at the altar. Go and be reconciled to that person. Then come and offer your sacrifice to God.

25 "When you are on the way to court with your adversary, settle your differences quickly. Otherwise, your accuser may hand you over to the judge, who will hand you over to an officer, and you will be thrown into prison. 26 And if that happens, you surely won't be free again until you have paid the last penny.*

TEACHING ABOUT ADULTERY

27 "You have heard the commandment that says, 'You must not commit adultery.'* 28 But I say, anyone who even looks at a woman with lust has already committed adultery with her in his heart. 29 So if your eye—even your good eye*—causes you to lust, gouge it out and throw it away. It is better for you to lose one part of your body than for your whole body to be thrown into hell. 30 And if your hand—even your stronger hand*—causes you to sin, cut it off and throw it away. It is better for you to lose one part of your body than for your whole body to be thrown into hell.

TEACHING ABOUT DIVORCE

31 "You have heard the law that says, 'A man can divorce his wife by merely giving her a written notice of divorce.'* 32 But I say that a man who divorces his wife, unless she has been unfaithful, causes her to commit adultery. And anyone who marries a divorced woman also commits adultery.

TEACHING ABOUT VOWS

33 "You have also heard that our ancestors were told, 'You must not break your vows; you must carry out the vows you make to the LORD.'* 34 But I say, do not make any vows! Do not say, 'By heaven!' because heaven is God's throne. 35 And do not say, 'By the earth!' because the earth is his footstool. And do not say, 'By Jerusalem!' for Jerusalem is the city of the great King. 36 Do not even say, 'By my head!' for you can't turn one hair white or black. 37 Just say a simple, 'Yes, I will,' or 'No, I won't.' Anything beyond this is from the evil one.

TEACHING ABOUT REVENGE

38 "You have heard the law that says the punishment must match the injury: 'An eye for an eye, and a tooth for a

5:21 Exod 20:13; Deut 5:17. **5:22a** Some manuscripts add *without cause*. **5:22b** Greek uses an Aramaic term of contempt: *If you say to your brother, 'Raca.'* **5:22c** Greek *if you say, 'You fool.'* **5:22d** Greek *Gehenna;* also in 5:29, 30. **5:23** Greek *gift;* also in 5:24. **5:26** Greek *the last kodrantes* [i.e., quadrans]. **5:27** Exod 20:14; Deut 5:18. **5:29** Greek *your right eye.* **5:30** Greek *your right hand.* **5:31** Deut 24:1. **5:33** Num 30:2.

Why should we bother to learn anything about the Old Testament? Isn't the New Testament more important? Why or why not?

It's not that one is more important than the other. Instead, it's a question of timing.

Imagine being six years old (hey, just play along) and your parents sitting you down and telling you all of the rules about driving a car. Not only would you have tuned them out after about two minutes, but ten years later, when it came time to drive (like, now, you might be thinking), you wouldn't have remembered anything they said.

In other words, timing is everything.

The Old Testament is a reminder of a constant problem we all have—the urge to do wrong. The Law was given in response to that urge. But no one was able to follow the Law perfectly. That's why the Old Testament drops hints about the Savior to come. Though the Old Testament was written from about 1450 to 430 B.C., it predicted minute details about the life of Jesus!

In Matthew 5:17, Jesus said he came to fulfill the law, not to abolish it. And that's what the Old Testament is all about, Charlie Brown.

keeping it real

Who would've thought that during a soccer game I would apply Matthew 5:38-39 in a very real way?

I was captain of our soccer team. The other team was really out for blood—elbowing, kicking. The refs never saw any of it. My team started taking matters into their own hands.

One time I was passed the ball and managed to have a clear break—only one person stood in my way. But she decided to play rough. So, instead of scoring, I was injured and taken out of the game. I was angry, but I started praying about it.

By halftime the other girls on my team were really down. But I told them not to seek revenge—not to take the attitude of "an eye for an eye," but to "offer the other cheek" as Matthew 5:39 says. In other words, to play fair. I told them that's what I planned to do.

I went back into the game and made sure I played clean. My team followed my example. I scored two goals late in the game and our team tied, 2-2.

The most important thing to me wasn't the score of that game, though. It was the fact that playing clean really was better. I think the whole team learned something that day. I know I did.

—Suzi

tooth.'* 39But I say, do not resist an evil person! If someone
slaps you on the right cheek, offer the other cheek also.
40If you are sued in court and your shirt is taken from you,
give your coat, too. 41If a soldier demands that you carry
his gear for a mile,* carry it two miles. 42Give to those who
ask, and don't turn away from those who want to borrow.

TEACHING ABOUT LOVE FOR ENEMIES

43"You have heard the law that says, 'Love your neighbor'*
and hate your enemy. 44But I say, love your enemies!*
Pray for those who persecute you! 45In that way, you will
be acting as true children of your Father in heaven. For he
gives his sunlight to both the evil and the good, and he
sends rain on the just and the unjust alike. 46If you love
only those who love you, what reward is there for that?
Even corrupt tax collectors do that much. 47If you are
kind only to your friends,* how are you different from
anyone else? Even pagans do that. 48But you are to be perfect, even as your Father in heaven is perfect.

6 TEACHING ABOUT GIVING TO THE NEEDY

"Watch out! Don't do your good deeds publicly, to be admired by others, for you will lose the reward from your
Father in heaven. 2When you give to someone in need,
don't do as the hypocrites do—blowing trumpets in the
synagogues and streets to call attention to their acts of
charity! I tell you the truth, they have received all the reward they will ever get. 3But when you give to someone in
need, don't let your left hand know what your right hand
is doing. 4Give your gifts in private, and your Father, who
sees everything, will reward you.

MEANINGLESS REPETITION 6:7-8

Jesus warned his followers against meaningless repetition in prayer. Meaningless repetition is not the same as persistence in prayer. Jesus encourages *persistent* prayer. But some people think that repeating the same words over and over ("O God hear me; hear me, O God") will ensure that God will hear them. But God promises to listen to the prayers of his people (2 Chron 7:14; Jer 29:12). We can never pray too much if our prayers are honest and sincere. Before you start to pray, make sure you mean what you say. ■

TEACHING ABOUT PRAYER AND FASTING

5"When you pray, don't be like the hypocrites who love to
pray publicly on street corners and in the synagogues
where everyone can see them. I tell you the truth, that is
all the reward they will ever get. 6But when you pray, go
away by yourself, shut the door behind you, and pray to
your Father in private. Then your Father, who sees everything, will reward you.
7"When you pray, don't babble on and on as people of
other religions do. They think their prayers are answered
merely by repeating their words again and again. 8Don't

5:38 Greek *the law that says: 'An eye for an eye and a tooth for a tooth.'* Exod 21:24; Lev 24:20; Deut 19:21. **5:41** Greek *milion* [4,854 feet or 1,478 meters]. **5:43** Lev 19:18. **5:44** Some manuscripts add *Bless those who curse you. Do good to those who hate you.* Compare Luke 6:27-28. **5:47** Greek *your brothers.*

Seven Reasons Not To Worry

1	2	3	4	5	6	7
The same God who created life in you can be trusted with the details of your life. 6:25	Worrying about the future hampers your efforts for today. 6:26	Worrying is more harmful than helpful. 6:27	God does not ignore those who depend on him. 6:28-30	Worry shows a lack of faith and understanding of God. 6:31-32	There are real challenges God wants us to pursue, and worrying keeps us from them. 6:33	Living one day at a time keeps us from being consumed with worry. 6:34

be like them, for your Father knows exactly what you
need even before you ask him! [9]Pray like this:

Our Father in heaven,
may your name be kept holy.
10 May your Kingdom come soon.
May your will be done on earth,
as it is in heaven.
11 Give us today the food we need,*
12 and forgive us our sins,
as we have forgiven those who sin against us.
13 And don't let us yield to temptation,*
but rescue us from the evil one.*

[14]"If you forgive those who sin against you, your heavenly Father will forgive you. [15]But if you refuse to forgive
others, your Father will not forgive your sins.
[16]"And when you fast, don't make it obvious, as the
hypocrites do, for they try to look miserable and dishev-
eled so people will admire them for their fasting. I tell
you the truth, that is the only reward they will ever get.
[17]But when you fast, comb your hair and wash your face.
[18]Then no one will notice that you are fasting, except your
Father, who knows what you do in private. And your Father, who sees everything, will reward you.

TEACHING ABOUT MONEY AND POSSESSIONS

[19]"Don't store up treasures here on earth, where moths
eat them and rust destroys them, and where thieves
break in and steal. [20]Store your treasures in heaven,
where moths and rust cannot destroy, and thieves do not
break in and steal. [21]Wherever your treasure is, there the
desires of your heart will also be.
[22]"Your eye is a lamp that provides light for your body.
When your eye is good, your whole body is filled with
light. [23]But when your eye is bad, your whole body is filled
with darkness. And if the light you think you have is actually darkness, how deep that darkness is!
[24]"No one can serve two masters. For you will hate one
and love the other; you will be devoted to one and despise
the other. You cannot serve both God and money.
[25]"That is why I tell you not to worry about everyday
life—whether you have enough food and drink, or
enough clothes to wear. Isn't life more than food, and
your body more than clothing? [26]Look at the birds. They
don't plant or harvest or store food in barns, for your
heavenly Father feeds them. And aren't you far more
valuable to him than they are? [27]Can all your worries add
a single moment to your life?

BODY IMAGE WORRIES

Freedom (her parents' name choice, not hers) tries on outfit after outfit. There's nothing in her closet to make her thighs look less huge than she believes they are. Honestly, some days she wishes that she could be homeschooled. Trying to find just the perfect outfit every day is sheer agony!

"Mom!" Freedom calls. "I need some new clothes!"

"I didn't hear that!" her mom replies.

Freedom gives an exasperated sigh. "Mother! I said—"

"I *know* what you said, Freedom. I'm *choosing* to ignore it. You spend too much on clothes as it is."

She doesn't get it,* Freedom decides. *Just because she was born in the dark ages, she can't imagine what it's like to go to school every day with huge thighs and absolutely nothing to wear. Ugh! I feel like such a freak.

What's up with Freedom? Ever felt like this? How could a passage like Matthew 6:25-34 help?

[28]"And why worry about your clothing? Look at the
lilies of the field and how they grow. They don't work or
make their clothing, [29]yet Solomon in all his glory was not
dressed as beautifully as they are. [30]And if God cares so
wonderfully for wildflowers that are here today and
thrown into the fire tomorrow, he will certainly care for
you. Why do you have so little faith?
[31]"So don't worry about these things, saying, 'What will

6:11 Or *Give us today our food for the day;* or *Give us today our food for tomorrow.* **6:13a** Or *And keep us from being tested.* **6:13b** Or *from evil.* Some manuscripts add *For yours is the kingdom and the power and the glory forever. Amen.*

keeping it real

I used to struggle a lot with doubt. Was God real? Did he really care about me? Is the Bible relevant? Then someone challenged me to apply a passage from the Bible every day for two weeks and see if that made any difference. So, I did. I read some of the psalms and found that they were wonderfully relevant.

When I came across Jesus' words in Matthew 7:24-27, I realized that only through obeying and applying God's Word can we know he's real. His Word is the only solid thing we have to build our lives on. The Matthew passage, and my two-week experiment, motivated me to try to live out what I read more and more every day. **—Laura**

we eat? What will we drink? What will we wear?' 32These
things dominate the thoughts of unbelievers, but your
heavenly Father already knows all your needs. 33Seek the
Kingdom of God* above all else, and live righteously, and
he will give you everything you need.
34"So don't worry about tomorrow, for tomorrow
will bring its own worries. Today's trouble is enough
for today.

7

DO NOT JUDGE OTHERS

"Do not judge others, and you will not be judged. 2For you
will be treated as you treat others.* The standard you use
in judging is the standard by which you
will be judged.*
3"And why worry about a speck in
your friend's eye* when you have a log
in your own? 4How can you think of
saying to your friend,* 'Let me help you
get rid of that speck in your eye,' when
you can't see past the log in your own
eye? 5Hypocrite! First get rid of the log
in your own eye; then you will see well
enough to deal with the speck in your
friend's eye.
6"Don't waste what is holy on people
who are unholy.* Don't throw your
pearls to pigs! They will trample the
pearls, then turn and attack you.

> Anyone who listens to my teaching and follows it is wise, like a person who builds a house on solid rock.
>
> *MATTHEW 7:24*

EFFECTIVE PRAYER

7"Keep on asking, and you will receive what you ask for.
Keep on seeking, and you will find. Keep on knocking,
and the door will be opened to you. 8For everyone who
asks, receives. Everyone who seeks, finds. And to everyone who knocks, the door will be opened.
9"You parents—if your children ask for a loaf of bread,
do you give them a stone instead? 10Or if they ask for a
fish, do you give them a snake? Of course not! 11So if you
sinful people know how to give good gifts to your children, how much more will your heavenly Father give
good gifts to those who ask him.

THE GOLDEN RULE

12"Do to others whatever you would like them to do to
you. This is the essence of all that is taught in the law and
the prophets.

THE NARROW GATE

13"You can enter God's Kingdom only through the narrow
gate. The highway to hell* is broad, and its gate is wide
for the many who choose that way. 14But the gateway to
life is very narrow and the road is difficult, and only a few ever find it.

THE TREE AND ITS FRUIT

15"Beware of false prophets who come
disguised as harmless sheep but are
really vicious wolves. 16You can identify
them by their fruit, that is, by the way
they act. Can you pick grapes from
thornbushes, or figs from thistles? 17A
good tree produces good fruit, and a bad
tree produces bad fruit. 18A good tree
can't produce bad fruit, and a bad tree
can't produce good fruit. 19So every
tree that does not produce good fruit is
chopped down and thrown into the fire.
20Yes, just as you can identify a tree by its
fruit, so you can identify people by their actions.

TRUE DISCIPLES

21"Not everyone who calls out to me, 'Lord! Lord!' will enter the Kingdom of Heaven. Only those who actually do
the will of my Father in heaven will enter. 22On judgment
day many will say to me, 'Lord! Lord! We prophesied in
your name and cast out demons in your name and performed many miracles in your name.' 23But I will reply, 'I

6:33 Some manuscripts do not include *of God*. **7:2a** Or *For God will judge you as you judge others*. **7:2b** Or *The measure you give will be the measure you get back*. **7:3** Greek *your brother's eye*; also in 7:5. **7:4** Greek *your brother*. **7:6** Greek *Don't give the sacred to dogs*. **7:13** Greek *The road that leads to destruction*.

never knew you. Get away from me, you who break God's laws.'

BUILDING ON A SOLID FOUNDATION

24"Anyone who listens to my teaching and follows it is wise, like a person who builds a house on solid rock. 25Though the rain comes in torrents and the floodwaters rise and the winds beat against that house, it won't collapse because it is built on bedrock. 26But anyone who hears my teaching and doesn't obey it is foolish, like a person who builds a house on sand. 27When the rains and floods come and the winds beat against that house, it will collapse with a mighty crash."

28When Jesus had finished saying these things, the crowds were amazed at his teaching, 29for he taught with real authority—quite unlike their teachers of religious law.

8

JESUS HEALS A MAN WITH LEPROSY

Large crowds followed Jesus as he came down the mountainside. 2Suddenly, a man with leprosy approached him and knelt before him. "Lord," the man said, "if you are willing, you can heal me and make me clean."

3Jesus reached out and touched him. "I am willing," he said. "Be healed!" And instantly the leprosy disappeared. 4Then Jesus said to him, "Don't tell anyone about this. Instead, go to the priest and let him examine you. Take along the offering required in the law of Moses for those who have been healed of leprosy.* This will be a public testimony that you have been cleansed."

A GOOD WAY TO HEAVEN 8:10-12

The people of Israel thought that their good works would earn them a life in heaven. But after talking with a centurion, Jesus told the crowd that many of them would be excluded from the Kingdom of God because of their lack of faith in him. Like the Jews, many people today believe that their good actions will get them to heaven. But only faith in Jesus will. Are you relying on your good works or good decisions to earn a place in heaven? The best decision you can make is to trust that Jesus is your only ticket there. ■

THE FAITH OF A ROMAN OFFICER

5When Jesus returned to Capernaum, a Roman officer* came and pleaded with him, 6"Lord, my young servant* lies in bed, paralyzed and in terrible pain."

7Jesus said, "I will come and heal him."

8But the officer said, "Lord, I am not worthy to have you come into my home. Just say the word from where you are, and my servant will be healed. 9I know this because I am under the authority of my superior officers, and I have authority over my soldiers. I only need to say, 'Go,' and they go, or 'Come,' and they come. And if I say to my slaves, 'Do this,' they do it."

10When Jesus heard this, he was amazed. Turning to those who were following him, he said, "I tell you the truth, I haven't seen faith like this in all Israel! 11And I tell you this, that many Gentiles will come from all over the world—from east and west—and sit down with Abraham, Isaac, and Jacob at the feast in the Kingdom of Heaven. 12But many Israelites—those for whom the Kingdom was prepared—will be thrown into outer darkness, where there will be weeping and gnashing of teeth."

13Then Jesus said to the Roman officer, "Go back home. Because you believed, it has happened." And the young servant was healed that same hour.

JESUS HEALS MANY PEOPLE

14When Jesus arrived at Peter's house, Peter's mother-in-law was sick in bed with a high fever. 15But when Jesus touched her hand, the fever left her. Then she got up and prepared a meal for him.

16That evening many demon-possessed people were brought to Jesus. He cast out the evil spirits with a simple command, and he healed all the sick. 17This fulfilled the word of the Lord through the prophet Isaiah, who said,

> "He took our sicknesses
> and removed our diseases."*

COUNT THE COST 8:19-20

Following Jesus is not always easy or comfortable. Often it means great cost and sacrifice, with no earthly rewards or security. For example, Jesus didn't have a place to call home. Following Jesus may cost you friendships, your reputation, or treasured habits. But while the costs of being a disciple may be high, the benefits last for eternity. Are you wiling to pay the price? ■

THE COST OF FOLLOWING JESUS

18When Jesus saw the crowd around him, he instructed his disciples to cross to the other side of the lake.

19Then one of the teachers of religious law said to him, "Teacher, I will follow you wherever you go."

20But Jesus replied, "Foxes have dens to live in, and birds have nests, but the Son of Man* has no place even to lay his head."

21Another of his disciples said, "Lord, first let me return home and bury my father."

22But Jesus told him, "Follow me now. Let the spiritually dead bury their own dead.*"

JESUS CALMS THE STORM

23Then Jesus got into the boat and started across the lake with his disciples. 24Suddenly, a fierce storm struck the lake, with waves breaking into the boat. But Jesus was sleeping. 25The disciples went and woke him up, shouting, "Lord, save us! We're going to drown!"

26Jesus responded, "Why are you afraid? You have so

8:4 See Lev 14:2-32. **8:5** Greek *a centurion;* similarly in 8:8, 13. **8:6** Or *child;* also in 8:13. **8:17** Isa 53:4. **8:20** "Son of Man" is a title Jesus used for himself. **8:22** Greek *Let the dead bury their own dead.*

little faith!" Then he got up and rebuked the wind and
waves, and suddenly there was a great calm.
27The disciples were amazed. "Who is this man?" they
asked. "Even the winds and waves obey him!"

JESUS HEALS TWO DEMON-POSSESSED MEN

28When Jesus arrived on the other side of the lake, in the
region of the Gadarenes,* two men who were possessed
by demons met him. They lived in a cemetery and were so
violent that no one could go through that area.
29They began screaming at him, "Why are you interfering with us, Son of God? Have you come here to torture us
before God's appointed time?"
30There happened to be a large herd of pigs feeding in
the distance. 31So the demons begged, "If you cast us out,
send us into that herd of pigs."
32"All right, go!" Jesus commanded them. So the demons came out of the men and entered the pigs, and the
whole herd plunged down the steep hillside into the lake
and drowned in the water.
33The herdsmen fled to the nearby town, telling
everyone what happened to the demon-possessed men.
34Then the entire town came out to meet Jesus, but they
begged him to go away and leave them alone.

9 JESUS HEALS A PARALYZED MAN

Jesus climbed into a boat and went back across the lake
to his own town. 2Some people brought to him a paralyzed man on a mat. Seeing their faith, Jesus said to the
paralyzed man, "Be encouraged, my child! Your sins are
forgiven."
3But some of the teachers of religious law said to themselves, "That's blasphemy! Does he think he's God?"
4Jesus knew* what they were thinking, so he asked
them, "Why do you have such evil thoughts in your
hearts? 5Is it easier to say 'Your sins are forgiven,' or
'Stand up and walk'? 6So I will prove to you that the Son of
Man* has the authority on earth to forgive sins." Then
Jesus turned to the paralyzed man and said, "Stand up,
pick up your mat, and go home!"
7And the man jumped up and went home! 8Fear swept

8:28 Other manuscripts read *Gerasenes;* still others read *Gergesenes.* Compare Mark 5:1; Luke 8:26. 9:4 Some manuscripts read *saw.* 9:6 "Son of Man" is a title Jesus used for himself.

UPS:
- Responded immediately to Jesus' call to be his disciple
- Invited many friends to his home to meet Jesus
- Compiled the Gospel of Matthew
- Clarified for his Jewish audience Jesus' fulfillment of Old Testament prophecies

STATS:
- Where: Capernaum
- Occupation: Tax collector, disciple of Jesus
- Relatives: Alphaeus (father)
- Contemporaries: Jesus, Pilate, Herod, other disciples

BOTTOM LINE:

Jesus consistently accepted people from every level of society.

God has the power to change any life for the better.

One sign of faith in Jesus is the desire to tell others about him.

Matthew's story is told in the Gospels. He also is mentioned in Acts 1:13.

MATTHEW Ever wonder whether someone with a bad reputation could ever really change? Being a tax collector for the Romans had earned Matthew a bad rep. Now Jesus undoubtedly knew about Matthew's reputation; yet he called him anyway. (See Matt 9:9-13.)

Matthew's life totally changed when he decided to follow Jesus. First, he not only belonged to a new group (Jesus' disciples); he belonged to the Son of God. For a despised tax collector, that change must have been wonderful! Second, Jesus gave Matthew a new purpose for his skills. When he followed Jesus, the only tool from his past job that he carried with him was a writing tool. From the beginning, God had made him a record keeper. Jesus' call eventually allowed him to put his skills to their finest work. Matthew was a keen observer, and he must have mentally recorded what he saw going on around him. The Gospel that bears his name came as a result.

Matthew's experience reminds us that we're each a work in progress. Sometimes God trusts us with skills and abilities before we know what to do with them. He has made us each capable of being his servant. When we trust him to help us use what he's given us, we begin a life of real adventure.

Matthew couldn't have known beforehand that God would use the very skills he had sharpened as a tax collector to record the greatest story ever lived. And God has no less meaningful a purpose for each of us. Have you recognized Jesus saying to you, "Follow me"? What has been your response?

through the crowd as they saw this happen. And they
praised God for sending a man with such great
authority.*

JESUS CALLS MATTHEW

9As Jesus was walking along, he saw a man named Matthew sitting at his tax collector's booth. "Follow me and
be my disciple," Jesus said to him. So Matthew got up and
followed him.

10Later, Matthew invited Jesus and his disciples to his
home as dinner guests, along with many tax collectors
and other disreputable sinners. 11But when the Pharisees
saw this, they asked his disciples, "Why does your teacher
eat with such scum?*"

12When Jesus heard this, he said, "Healthy people don't
need a doctor—sick people do." 13Then he added, "Now
go and learn the meaning of this Scripture: 'I want you to
show mercy, not offer sacrifices.'* For I have come to call
not those who think they are righteous, but those who
know they are sinners."

CONCERN FOR ALL 9:9-13

The Pharisees thought Jesus' association with tax collectors was the perfect opportunity to trap him. They were more concerned with criticism than encouragement and with their own appearance of holiness than in helping people. But God is concerned for all people, including those labeled as "losers" in society. Is there someone you've labeled as undeserving of help or unworthy to hear the Good News? According to God, no one is too low—or too "good," for that matter—to experience his forgiveness. ■

A DISCUSSION ABOUT FASTING

14One day the disciples of John the Baptist came to Jesus
and asked him, "Why don't your disciples fast* like we do
and the Pharisees do?"

15Jesus replied, "Do wedding guests mourn while celebrating with the groom? Of course not. But someday the
groom will be taken away from them, and then they will
fast.

16"Besides, who would patch old clothing with new
cloth? For the new patch would shrink and rip away from
the old cloth, leaving an even bigger tear than before.

17"And no one puts new wine into old wineskins. For
the old skins would burst from the pressure, spilling the
wine and ruining the skins. New wine is stored in new
wineskins so that both are preserved."

JESUS HEALS IN RESPONSE TO FAITH

18As Jesus was saying this, the leader of a synagogue came
and knelt before him. "My daughter has just died," he
said, "but you can bring her back to life again if you just
come and lay your hand on her."

19So Jesus and his disciples got up and went with him.
20Just then a woman who had suffered for twelve years
with constant bleeding came up behind him. She
touched the fringe of his robe, 21for she thought, "If I can
just touch his robe, I will be healed."

22Jesus turned around, and when he saw her he said,
"Daughter, be encouraged! Your faith has made you
well." And the woman was healed at that moment.

23When Jesus arrived at the official's home, he saw the
noisy crowd and heard the funeral music. 24"Get out!" he
told them. "The girl isn't dead; she's only asleep." But the
crowd laughed at him. 25After the crowd was put outside,
however, Jesus went in and took the girl by the hand, and
she stood up! 26The report of this miracle swept through
the entire countryside.

JESUS HEALS THE BLIND

27After Jesus left the girl's home, two blind men followed
along behind him, shouting, "Son of David, have mercy
on us!"

28They went right into the house where he was staying,
and Jesus asked them, "Do you believe I can make you see?"
"Yes, Lord," they told him, "we do."

29Then he touched their eyes and said, "Because of
your faith, it will happen." 30Then their eyes were opened,
and they could see! Jesus sternly warned them, "Don't tell
anyone about this." 31But instead, they went out and
spread his fame all over the region.

32When they left, a demon-possessed man who
couldn't speak was brought to Jesus. 33So Jesus cast out
the demon, and then the man began to speak. The crowds
were amazed. "Nothing like this has ever happened in Israel!" they exclaimed.

34But the Pharisees said, "He can cast out demons because he is empowered by the prince of demons."

TESTING 9:27-31

Jesus didn't respond immediately to the blind men's pleas. He waited to see how earnest they were. Not everyone who says he or she wants help really wants it badly enough to do something about it. Jesus may have waited and questioned these men to make their desire and faith stronger. If you believe that God is too slow in answering your prayers, consider the fact that he could be testing you as he did the blind men. Do you believe that God can help you? Do you *really* want his help? ■

THE NEED FOR WORKERS

35Jesus traveled through all the towns and villages of that
area, teaching in the synagogues and announcing the
Good News about the Kingdom. And he healed every
kind of disease and illness. 36When he saw the crowds, he
had compassion on them because they were confused
and helpless, like sheep without a shepherd. 37He said to
his disciples, "The harvest is great, but the workers are
few. 38So pray to the Lord who is in charge of the harvest;
ask him to send more workers into his fields."

9:8 Greek *for giving such authority to human beings.* **9:11** Greek *with tax collectors and sinners?* **9:13** Hos 6:6 (Greek version). **9:14** Some manuscripts read *fast often.*

10 JESUS SENDS OUT THE TWELVE APOSTLES

Jesus called his twelve disciples together and gave them
authority to cast out evil* spirits and to heal every kind of
disease and illness. 2 Here are the names of the twelve
apostles:

first, Simon (also called Peter),
then Andrew (Peter's brother),
James (son of Zebedee),
John (James's brother),
3 Philip,
Bartholomew,
Thomas,
Matthew (the tax collector),
James (son of Alphaeus),
Thaddaeus,*
4 Simon (the zealot*),
Judas Iscariot (who later betrayed him).

5 Jesus sent out the twelve apostles with these instructions: "Don't go to the Gentiles or the Samaritans, 6 but
only to the people of Israel—God's lost sheep. 7 Go and announce to them that the Kingdom of Heaven is near.*
8 Heal the sick, raise the dead, cure those with leprosy, and
cast out demons. Give as freely as you have received!

9 "Don't take any money in your money belts—no gold,
silver, or even copper coins. 10 Don't carry a traveler's bag
with a change of clothes and sandals or even a walking
stick. Don't hesitate to accept hospitality, because those
who work deserve to be fed.

11 "Whenever you enter a city or village, search for a
worthy person and stay in his home until you leave town.
12 When you enter the home, give it your blessing. 13 If it
turns out to be a worthy home, let your blessing stand; if it
is not, take back the blessing. 14 If any household or town
refuses to welcome you or listen to your message, shake
its dust from your feet as you leave. 15 I tell you the truth,
the wicked cities of Sodom and Gomorrah will be better
off than such a town on the judgment day.

16 "Look, I am sending you out as sheep among wolves.
So be as shrewd as snakes and harmless as doves. 17 But
beware! For you will be handed over to the courts and will
be flogged with whips in the synagogues. 18 You will stand
trial before governors and kings because you are my followers. But this will be your opportunity to tell the rulers
and other unbelievers about me.* 19 When you are arrested, don't worry about how to respond or what to say.
God will give you the right words at the right time. 20 For it
is not you who will be speaking—it will be the Spirit of
your Father speaking through you.

21 "A brother will betray his brother to death, a father
will betray his own child, and children will rebel against
their parents and cause them to be killed. 22 And all nations will hate you because you are my followers.* But
everyone who endures to the end will be saved. 23 When
you are persecuted in one town, flee to the next. I tell you
the truth, the Son of Man* will return before you have
reached all the towns of Israel.

24 "Students* are not greater than their teacher, and
slaves are not greater than their master. 25 Students are to
be like their teacher, and slaves are to be like their master. And since I, the master of the household, have been
called the prince of demons,* the members of my household will be called by even worse names!

26 "But don't be afraid of those who threaten you. For
the time is coming when everything that is covered will
be revealed, and all that is secret will be made known to
all. 27 What I tell you now in the darkness, shout abroad
when daybreak comes. What I whisper in your ear, shout
from the housetops for all to hear!

28 "Don't be afraid of those who want to kill your body;
they cannot touch your soul. Fear only God, who can destroy both soul and body in hell.* 29 What is the price of
two sparrows—one copper coin*? But not a single sparrow can fall to the ground without your Father knowing
it. 30 And the very hairs on your head are all numbered.
31 So don't be afraid; you are more valuable to God than a
whole flock of sparrows.

10:1 Greek *unclean.* **10:3** Other manuscripts read *Lebbaeus;* still others read *Lebbaeus who is called Thaddaeus.* **10:4** Greek *the Cananean,* an Aramaic term for Jewish nationalists. **10:7** Or *has come,* or *is coming soon.* **10:18** Or *But this will be your testimony against the rulers and other unbelievers.* **10:22** Greek *on account of my name.* **10:23** "Son of Man" is a title Jesus used for himself. **10:24** Or *Disciples.* **10:25** Greek *Beelzeboul;* other manuscripts read *Beezeboul;* Latin version reads *Beelzebub.* **10:28** Greek *Gehenna.* **10:29** Greek *one assarion* [i.e., one "as," a Roman coin equal to 1/16 of a denarius].

I'm the only Christian in my family. My parents think my faith is a big joke. How can I get them to take me seriously?

There are many difficult sayings of Jesus in the New Testament. Matthew 10:34-39 is one of the toughest. What does Jesus mean when he says, "Your enemies will be right in your own household" (Matt 10:36)?

Jesus is not telling us to disobey parents or to try to cause problems at home. He simply means that a person with different goals and values may cause division in a household. Rarely will the only Christian in a household go unchallenged.

The best course of action is to avoid trying to "make" your parents see anything. Instead, just live your life in obedience to them as the Bible commands: "'Honor your father and mother.' This is the first commandment with a promise: If you honor your father and mother, 'things will go well for you, and you will have a long life on the earth'" (Eph 6:2-3).

Is it your job to make your parents change? Nope. Only the Holy Spirit can do that. Check it out: "When he comes, he will convict the world of its sin, and of God's righteousness, and of the coming judgment" (John 16:8). You are simply to be God's representative in your home. Maybe someday you'll have the joy of seeing your family turn to Christ.

VALUABLE 10:29-31

Jesus said that God cares for the sparrows' every need. You are far more valuable to God than these little birds. Your worth was proven by the fact that God sent his only Son to die for you (John 3:16). Because God places such value on you, you need never fear personal threats or difficult trials. But don't think that because you're valuable to God, he will take away all of your troubles (see 10:16). Instead, he tests you to see how well you hold up under the hassles of everyday life. Those who stand up for Christ in spite of their troubles will receive great rewards (see 5:11-12). ■

32"Everyone who acknowledges me publicly here on
earth, I will also acknowledge before my Father in
heaven. 33But everyone who denies me here on earth, I
will also deny before my Father in heaven.
34"Don't imagine that I came to bring peace to the
earth! I came not to bring peace, but a sword.

35 'I have come to set a man against his father,
a daughter against her mother,
and a daughter-in-law against her mother-in-law.
36 Your enemies will be right in your own
household!'*

37"If you love your father or mother more than you love
me, you are not worthy of being mine; or if you love your
son or daughter more than me, you are not worthy of being mine. 38If you refuse to take up your cross and follow
me, you are not worthy of being mine. 39If you cling to
your life, you will lose it; but if you give up your life for
me, you will find it.
40"Anyone who receives you receives me, and anyone
who receives me receives the Father who sent me. 41If
you receive a prophet as one who speaks for God,* you
will be given the same reward as a prophet. And if you receive righteous people because of their righteousness,
you will be given a reward like theirs. 42And if you give
even a cup of cold water to one of the least of my followers, you will surely be rewarded."

11

JESUS AND JOHN THE BAPTIST

When Jesus had finished giving these instructions to his
twelve disciples, he went out to teach and preach in
towns throughout the region.
2John the Baptist, who was in prison, heard about all
the things the Messiah was doing. So he sent his disciples
to ask Jesus, 3"Are you the Messiah we've been expecting,* or should we keep looking for someone else?"
4Jesus told them, "Go back to John and tell him what
you have heard and seen—5the blind see, the lame walk,
the lepers are cured, the deaf hear, the dead are raised to
life, and the Good News is being preached to the poor.
6And tell him, 'God blesses those who do not turn away
because of me.*'"
7As John's disciples were leaving, Jesus began talking
about him to the crowds. "What kind of man did you go
into the wilderness to see? Was he a weak reed, swayed
by every breath of wind? 8Or were you expecting to see a
man dressed in expensive clothes? No, people with expensive clothes live in palaces. 9Were you looking for a
prophet? Yes, and he is more than a prophet. 10John is the
man to whom the Scriptures refer when they say,

'Look, I am sending my messenger ahead of you,
and he will prepare your way before you.'*

DOUBTS 11:1-6

As John sat in prison, he felt some doubts about whether Jesus really was the Savior. Jesus answered John's doubts by reminding him of the acts that revealed his identity: healing the sick, raising the dead, and preaching the gospel to the poor. With so much evidence, Jesus' identity was obvious. Do you share John's doubt? Look at the evidence in Scripture and in your life. When you doubt, don't turn away from Christ, turn *to* him. ■

11"I tell you the truth, of all who have ever lived, none is
greater than John the Baptist. Yet even the least person in
the Kingdom of Heaven is greater than he is! 12And from
the time John the Baptist began preaching until now, the
Kingdom of Heaven has been forcefully advancing,* and
violent people are attacking it. 13For before John came, all
the prophets and the law of Moses looked forward to this
present time. 14And if you are willing to accept what I say,
he is Elijah, the one the prophets said would come.*
15Anyone with ears to hear should listen and understand!
16"To what can I compare this generation? It is like
children playing a game in the public square. They complain to their friends,

17 'We played wedding songs,
and you didn't dance,
so we played funeral songs,
and you didn't mourn.'

18For John didn't spend his time eating and drinking, and
you say, 'He's possessed by a demon.' 19The Son of Man,*
on the other hand, feasts and drinks, and you say, 'He's a
glutton and a drunkard, and a friend of tax collectors and
other sinners!' But wisdom is shown to be right by its results."

JUDGMENT FOR THE UNBELIEVERS

20Then Jesus began to denounce the towns where he had
done so many of his miracles, because they hadn't re-

10:35-36 Mic 7:6. **10:41** Greek *receive a prophet in the name of a prophet.* **11:3** Greek *Are you the one who is coming?* **11:6** Or *who are not offended by me.* **11:10** Mal 3:1. **11:12** Or *the Kingdom of Heaven has suffered from violence.* **11:14** See Mal 4:5. **11:19** "Son of Man" is a title Jesus used for himself.

pented of their sins and turned to God. 21"What sorrow awaits you, Korazin and Bethsaida! For if the miracles I did in you had been done in wicked Tyre and Sidon, their people would have repented of their sins long ago, clothing themselves in burlap and throwing ashes on their heads to show their remorse. 22I tell you, Tyre and Sidon will be better off on judgment day than you.

23"And you people of Capernaum, will you be honored in heaven? No, you will go down to the place of the dead.* For if the miracles I did for you had been done in wicked Sodom, it would still be here today. 24I tell you, even Sodom will be better off on judgment day than you."

STRESS

Check out Teronda's schedule on her PDA for Tuesday alone. Aside from classes, this is what her day is like:

Tuesday: Meet w/ Jenna B4 homeroom

After school: Practice violin; drive Ronnie 2 his friend's as a favor 4 Mom; go 2 Shannon's to help her w/ algebra; study for test

Almost makes you tired just reading that list, huh? But this is a typical day for Teronda. On a "slow day" she might only have two activities to rush to after school. One of those activities is an after school job. She hopes to save money for college.

Now, most people would describe Teronda as cheerful, dependable, and quietly cool. But lately, her friends would also add "irritable" to that list of characteristics. Lately, she always seems irritable.

Even Teronda would agree with that assessment. She wonders why she's so tired all of the time. If only she didn't have so much to do! But everyone depends on her. What else can she do?

Stress is the frustration you feel when you have a lot to do and only a little time to do it. It's also the frustration of trying to live up to everyone else's expectations.

Feeling stressed like Teronda? Check out Matthew 11:28-30. Based on this passage, what advice would you offer Teronda or yourself?

JESUS' PRAYER OF THANKSGIVING

25At that time Jesus prayed this prayer: "O Father, Lord of heaven and earth, thank you for hiding these things from those who think themselves wise and clever, and for revealing them to the childlike. 26Yes, Father, it pleased you to do it this way!

27"My Father has entrusted everything to me. No one truly knows the Son except the Father, and no one truly knows the Father except the Son and those to whom the Son chooses to reveal him."

28Then Jesus said, "Come to me, all of you who are weary and carry heavy burdens, and I will give you rest. 29Take my yoke upon you. Let me teach you, because I am humble and gentle at heart, and you will find rest for your souls. 30For my yoke is easy to bear, and the burden I give you is light."

12

A DISCUSSION ABOUT THE SABBATH

At about that time Jesus was walking through some grainfields on the Sabbath. His disciples were hungry, so they began breaking off some heads of grain and eating them. 2But some Pharisees saw them do it and protested, "Look, your disciples are breaking the law by harvesting grain on the Sabbath."

3Jesus said to them, "Haven't you read in the Scriptures what David did when he and his companions were hungry? 4He went into the house of God, and he and his companions broke the law by eating the sacred loaves of bread that only the priests are allowed to eat. 5And haven't you read in the law of Moses that the priests on duty in the Temple may work on the Sabbath? 6I tell you, there is one here who is even greater than the Temple! 7But you would not have condemned my innocent disciples if you knew the meaning of this Scripture: 'I want you to show mercy, not offer sacrifices.'* 8For the Son of Man* is Lord, even over the Sabbath!"

JESUS HEALS ON THE SABBATH

9Then Jesus went over to their synagogue, 10where he noticed a man with a deformed hand. The Pharisees asked Jesus, "Does the law permit a person to work by healing on the Sabbath?" (They were hoping he would say yes, so they could bring charges against him.)

11And he answered, "If you had a sheep that fell into a well on the Sabbath, wouldn't you work to pull it out? Of course you would. 12And how much more valuable is a person than a sheep! Yes, the law permits a person to do good on the Sabbath."

13Then he said to the man, "Hold out your hand." So the man held out his hand, and it was restored, just like the other one! 14Then the Pharisees called a meeting to plot how to kill Jesus.

JESUS, GOD'S CHOSEN SERVANT

15But Jesus knew what they were planning. So he left that area, and many people followed him. He healed all the sick among them, 16but he warned them not to reveal who he was. 17This fulfilled the prophecy of Isaiah concerning him:

18 "Look at my Servant, whom I have chosen.
He is my Beloved, who pleases me.
I will put my Spirit upon him,
and he will proclaim justice to the nations.
19 He will not fight or shout
or raise his voice in public.
20 He will not crush the weakest reed
or put out a flickering candle.
Finally he will cause justice to be victorious.
21 And his name will be the hope
of all the world."*

11:23 Greek *to Hades.* 12:7 Hos 6:6 (Greek version). 12:8 "Son of Man" is a title Jesus used for himself. 12:18-21 Isa 42:1-4 (Greek version for 42:4).

JESUS AND THE PRINCE OF DEMONS

22Then a demon-possessed man, who was blind and couldn't speak, was brought to Jesus. He healed the man so that he could both speak and see. 23The crowd was amazed and asked, "Could it be that Jesus is the Son of David, the Messiah?"

24But when the Pharisees heard about the miracle, they said, "No wonder he can cast out demons. He gets his power from Satan,* the prince of demons."

25Jesus knew their thoughts and replied, "Any kingdom divided by civil war is doomed. A town or family splintered by feuding will fall apart. 26And if Satan is casting out Satan, he is divided and fighting against himself. His own kingdom will not survive. 27And if I am empowered by Satan, what about your own exorcists? They cast out demons, too, so they will condemn you for what you have said. 28But if I am casting out demons by the Spirit of God, then the Kingdom of God has arrived among you. 29For who is powerful enough to enter the house of a strong man like Satan and plunder his goods? Only someone even stronger—someone who could tie him up and then plunder his house.

30"Anyone who isn't with me opposes me, and anyone who isn't working with me is actually working against me.

31"So I tell you, every sin and blasphemy can be forgiven—except blasphemy against the Holy Spirit, which will never be forgiven. 32Anyone who speaks against the Son of Man can be forgiven, but anyone who speaks against the Holy Spirit will never be forgiven, either in this world or in the world to come.

33"A tree is identified by its fruit. If a tree is good, its fruit will be good. If a tree is bad, its fruit will be bad. 34You brood of snakes! How could evil men like you speak what is good and right? For whatever is in your heart determines what you say. 35A good person produces good things from the treasury of a good heart, and an evil person produces evil things from the treasury of an evil heart. 36And I tell you this, you must give an account on judgment day for every idle word you speak. 37The words you say will either acquit you or condemn you."

THE SIGN OF JONAH

38One day some teachers of religious law and Pharisees came to Jesus and said, "Teacher, we want you to show us a miraculous sign to prove your authority."

39But Jesus replied, "Only an evil, adulterous generation would demand a miraculous sign; but the only sign I will give them is the sign of the prophet Jonah. 40For as Jonah was in the belly of the great fish for three days and three nights, so will the Son of Man be in the heart of the earth for three days and three nights.

41"The people of Nineveh will stand up against this generation on judgment day and condemn it, for they repented of their sins at the preaching of Jonah. Now someone greater than Jonah is here—but you refuse to repent. 42The queen of Sheba* will also stand up against this generation on judgment day and condemn it, for she came from a distant land to hear the wisdom of Solomon. Now someone greater than Solomon is here—but you refuse to listen.

SHOW ME THE MIRACLE! 12:38-42

The Pharisees wanted Jesus to prove his identity as Savior by showing them a miracle. But Jesus knew that the Pharisees didn't believe in him; more miracles wouldn't change their minds. Like the Pharisees and a certain athlete from the old 1996 movie *Jerry Maguire*, many people have thought, *God needs to show me the miracle in order for me to believe!* But Jesus' death, resurrection, and ascension—plus the Bible and stories of believers around the world—all point to Jesus as the Savior. Instead of looking for additional evidence or miracles, are you willing to accept what God has already given and move forward? He may use your life as evidence to reach another person. ■

43"When an evil* spirit leaves a person, it goes into the desert, seeking rest but finding none. 44Then it says, 'I will return to the person I came from.' So it returns and finds its former home empty, swept, and in order. 45Then the spirit finds seven other spirits more evil than itself, and they all enter the person and live there. And so that person is worse off than before. That will be the experience of this evil generation."

THE TRUE FAMILY OF JESUS

46As Jesus was speaking to the crowd, his mother and brothers stood outside, asking to speak to him. 47Someone told Jesus, "Your mother and your brothers are outside, and they want to speak to you."*

48Jesus asked, "Who is my mother? Who are my brothers?" 49Then he pointed to his disciples and said, "Look, these are my mother and brothers. 50Anyone who does the will of my Father in heaven is my brother and sister and mother!"

13

PARABLE OF THE FARMER SCATTERING SEED

Later that same day Jesus left the house and sat beside the lake. 2A large crowd soon gathered around him, so he got into a boat. Then he sat there and taught as the people stood on the shore. 3He told many stories in the form of parables, such as this one:

"Listen! A farmer went out to plant some seeds. 4As he scattered them across his field, some seeds fell on a footpath, and the birds came and ate them. 5Other seeds fell on shallow soil with underlying rock. The seeds sprouted quickly because the soil was shallow. 6But the plants soon wilted under the hot sun, and since they didn't have deep roots, they died. 7Other seeds fell among thorns that grew up and choked out the tender plants. 8Still other

12:24 Greek *Beelzeboul;* also in 12:27. Other manuscripts read *Beezeboul;* Latin version reads *Beelzebub.* **12:42** Greek *The queen of the south.* **12:43** Greek *unclean.* **12:47** Some manuscripts do not include verse 47. Compare Mark 3:32 and Luke 8:20.

seeds fell on fertile soil, and they produced a crop that was thirty, sixty, and even a hundred times as much as had been planted! [9]Anyone with ears to hear should listen and understand."

SOWING SEEDS 13:1-23

Although the farmer in this parable sowed good seed, not all of his sowing brought a high yield. Ever wonder whether the "good seed" you've planted by telling someone about Jesus will ever sprout? Don't be discouraged if no one seems to be listening to you as you faithfully talk about or teach the Word. Belief doesn't come through a formula. Rather, it is a miracle of God's Holy Spirit as he uses your words to move others to come to him. ■

[10]His disciples came and asked him, "Why do you use parables when you talk to the people?"

[11]He replied, "You are permitted to understand the secrets* of the Kingdom of Heaven, but others are not. [12]To those who listen to my teaching, more understanding will be given, and they will have an abundance of knowledge. But for those who are not listening, even what little understanding they have will be taken away from them. [13]That is why I use these parables,

For they look, but they don't really see.
They hear, but they don't really listen or understand.

[14]This fulfills the prophecy of Isaiah that says,

'When you hear what I say,
you will not understand.
When you see what I do,
you will not comprehend.
[15] For the hearts of these people are hardened,
and their ears cannot hear,
and they have closed their eyes—
so their eyes cannot see,
and their ears cannot hear,
and their hearts cannot understand,
and they cannot turn to me
and let me heal them.'*

[16]"But blessed are your eyes, because they see; and your ears, because they hear. [17]I tell you the truth, many prophets and righteous people longed to see what you see, but they didn't see it. And they longed to hear what you hear, but they didn't hear it.

[18]"Now listen to the explanation of the parable about the farmer planting seeds: [19]The seed that fell on the footpath represents those who hear the message about the Kingdom and don't understand it. Then the evil one comes and snatches away the seed that was planted in their hearts. [20]The seed on the rocky soil represents those who hear the message and immediately receive it with joy. [21]But since they don't have deep roots, they don't last long. They fall away as soon as they have problems or are persecuted for believing God's word. [22]The seed that fell among the thorns represents those who hear God's word, but all too quickly the message is crowded out by the worries of this life and the lure of wealth, so no fruit is produced. [23]The seed that fell on good soil represents those who truly hear and understand God's word and produce a harvest of thirty, sixty, or even a hundred times as much as had been planted!"

RESPONSES 13:23

The four types of soil represent the different responses we can have to God's message. We respond differently because we are in different states of readiness. Some people are hardened, others are shallow. Distracting cares contaminate some, while some are receptive. What's your response to the Good News? ■

PARABLE OF THE WHEAT AND WEEDS

[24]Here is another story Jesus told: "The Kingdom of Heaven is like a farmer who planted good seed in his field. [25]But that night as the workers slept, his enemy came and planted weeds among the wheat, then slipped away. [26]When the crop began to grow and produce grain, the weeds also grew.

[27]"The farmer's workers went to him and said, 'Sir, the field where you planted that good seed is full of weeds! Where did they come from?'

[28]"'An enemy has done this!' the farmer exclaimed.

"'Should we pull out the weeds?' they asked.

[29]"'No,' he replied, 'you'll uproot the wheat if you do. [30]Let both grow together until the harvest. Then I will tell the harvesters to sort out the weeds, tie them into bundles, and burn them, and to put the wheat in the barn.'"

PARABLE OF THE MUSTARD SEED

[31]Here is another illustration Jesus used: "The Kingdom of Heaven is like a mustard seed planted in a field. [32]It is the smallest of all seeds, but it becomes the largest of garden plants; it grows into a tree, and birds come and make nests in its branches."

PARABLE OF THE YEAST

[33]Jesus also used this illustration: "The Kingdom of Heaven is like the yeast a woman used in making bread. Even though she put only a little yeast in three measures of flour, it permeated every part of the dough."

[34]Jesus always used stories and illustrations like these when speaking to the crowds. In fact, he never spoke to them without using such parables. [35]This fulfilled what God had spoken through the prophet:

"I will speak to you in parables.
I will explain things hidden since the creation
of the world.*"

13:11 Greek *the mysteries.* 13:14-15 Isa 6:9-10 (Greek version). 13:35 Some manuscripts do not include *of the world.* Ps 78:2.

PARABLE OF THE WHEAT AND WEEDS EXPLAINED

36Then, leaving the crowds outside, Jesus went into the house. His disciples said, "Please explain to us the story of the weeds in the field."

37Jesus replied, "The Son of Man* is the farmer who plants the good seed. 38The field is the world, and the good seed represents the people of the Kingdom. The weeds are the people who belong to the evil one. 39The enemy who planted the weeds among the wheat is the devil. The harvest is the end of the world,* and the harvesters are the angels.

40"Just as the weeds are sorted out and burned in the fire, so it will be at the end of the world. 41The Son of Man will send his angels, and they will remove from his Kingdom everything that causes sin and all who do evil. 42And the angels will throw them into the fiery furnace, where there will be weeping and gnashing of teeth. 43Then the righteous will shine like the sun in their Father's Kingdom. Anyone with ears to hear should listen and understand!

PARABLES OF THE HIDDEN TREASURE AND THE PEARL

44"The Kingdom of Heaven is like a treasure that a man discovered hidden in a field. In his excitement, he hid it again and sold everything he owned to get enough money to buy the field.

45"Again, the Kingdom of Heaven is like a merchant on the lookout for choice pearls. 46When he discovered a pearl of great value, he sold everything he owned and bought it!

PARABLE OF THE FISHING NET

47"Again, the Kingdom of Heaven is like a fishing net that was thrown into the water and caught fish of every kind. 48When the net was full, they dragged it up onto the shore, sat down, and sorted the good fish into crates, but threw the bad ones away. 49That is the way it will be at the end of the world. The angels will come and separate the wicked people from the righteous, 50throwing the wicked into the fiery furnace, where there will be weeping and gnashing of teeth. 51Do you understand all these things?"

"Yes," they said, "we do."

52Then he added, "Every teacher of religious law who becomes a disciple in the Kingdom of Heaven is like a homeowner who brings from his storeroom new gems of truth as well as old."

JESUS REJECTED AT NAZARETH

53When Jesus had finished telling these stories and illustrations, he left that part of the country. 54He returned to Nazareth, his hometown. When he taught there in the synagogue, everyone was amazed and said, "Where does he get this wisdom and the power to do miracles?" 55Then they scoffed, "He's just the carpenter's son, and we know Mary, his mother, and his brothers—James, Joseph,* Simon, and Judas. 56All his sisters live right here among us. Where did he learn all these things?" 57And they were deeply offended and refused to believe in him.

Then Jesus told them, "A prophet is honored everywhere except in his own hometown and among his own family." 58And so he did only a few miracles there because of their unbelief.

14

THE DEATH OF JOHN THE BAPTIST

When Herod Antipas, the ruler of Galilee,* heard about Jesus, 2he said to his advisers, "This must be John the Baptist raised from the dead! That is why he can do such miracles."

3For Herod had arrested and imprisoned John as a favor to his wife Herodias (the former wife of Herod's brother Philip). 4John had been telling Herod, "It is against God's law for you to marry her." 5Herod wanted to kill John, but he was afraid of a riot, because all the people believed John was a prophet.

6But at a birthday party for Herod, Herodias's daughter performed a dance that greatly pleased him, 7so he promised with a vow to give her anything she wanted. 8At her mother's urging, the girl said, "I want the head of John the Baptist on a tray!" 9Then the king regretted what he had said; but because of the vow he had made in front of his guests, he issued the necessary orders. 10So John was beheaded in the prison, 11and his head was brought on a tray and given to the girl, who took it to her mother. 12Later, John's disciples came for his body and buried it. Then they went and told Jesus what had happened.

GIVING IN 14:1-12

Although Herod didn't want to kill John the Baptist, he gave the order to avoid being embarrassed in front of his guests. Many of us say we would never make a similar decision. Yet, how often do we go along with what everyone else is doing just to avoid the "loser" label? Hanging on to your integrity might cost you some popularity points. But in the long run you'll win far more than you lose. ■

JESUS FEEDS FIVE THOUSAND

13As soon as Jesus heard the news, he left in a boat to a remote area to be alone. But the crowds heard where he was headed and followed on foot from many towns. 14Jesus saw the huge crowd as he stepped from the boat, and he had compassion on them and healed their sick.

15That evening the disciples came to him and said, "This is a remote place, and it's already getting late. Send the crowds away so they can go to the villages and buy food for themselves."

16But Jesus said, "That isn't necessary—you feed them."

17"But we have only five loaves of bread and two fish!" they answered.

18"Bring them here," he said. 19Then he told the people to sit down on the grass. Jesus took the five loaves and two fish, looked up toward heaven, and blessed them.

13:37 "Son of Man" is a title Jesus used for himself. **13:39** Or *the age;* also in 13:40, 49. **13:55** Other manuscripts read *Joses;* still others read *John.* **14:1** Greek *Herod the tetrarch.* Herod Antipas was a son of King Herod and was ruler over Galilee.

Then, breaking the loaves into pieces, he gave the bread to the disciples, who distributed it to the people. 20They all ate as much as they wanted, and afterward, the disciples picked up twelve baskets of leftovers. 21About 5,000 men were fed that day, in addition to all the women and children!

JESUS WALKS ON WATER

22Immediately after this, Jesus insisted that his disciples get back into the boat and cross to the other side of the lake, while he sent the people home. 23After sending them home, he went up into the hills by himself to pray. Night fell while he was there alone.

24Meanwhile, the disciples were in trouble far away from land, for a strong wind had risen, and they were fighting heavy waves. 25About three o'clock in the morning* Jesus came toward them, walking on the water. 26When the disciples saw him walking on the water, they were terrified. In their fear, they cried out, "It's a ghost!"

27But Jesus spoke to them at once. "Don't be afraid," he said. "Take courage. I am here!*"

28Then Peter called to him, "Lord, if it's really you, tell me to come to you, walking on the water."

29"Yes, come," Jesus said.

So Peter went over the side of the boat and walked on the water toward Jesus. 30But when he saw the strong* wind and the waves, he was terrified and began to sink. "Save me, Lord!" he shouted.

31Jesus immediately reached out and grabbed him. "You have so little faith," Jesus said. "Why did you doubt me?"

32When they climbed back into the boat, the wind stopped. 33Then the disciples worshiped him. "You really are the Son of God!" they exclaimed.

WALK OR SINK? 14:28-33

Peter started to sink because he took his eyes off Jesus and focused on the high waves around him. His faith wavered when he realized what he was doing. We may not walk on water, but we do walk through tough situations. If we focus on the waves of difficult circumstances around us without looking to Christ for help, we too may despair and sink. What tough situations are you facing now? Where is your focus: on the situation or on Jesus? ■

34After they had crossed the lake, they landed at Gennesaret. 35When the people recognized Jesus, the news of his arrival spread quickly throughout the whole area, and soon people were bringing all their sick to be healed. 36They begged him to let the sick touch at least the fringe of his robe, and all who touched him were healed.

15 JESUS TEACHES ABOUT INNER PURITY

Some Pharisees and teachers of religious law now arrived from Jerusalem to see Jesus. They asked him, 2"Why do your disciples disobey our age-old tradition? For they ignore our tradition of ceremonial hand washing before they eat."

3Jesus replied, "And why do you, by your traditions, violate the direct commandments of God? 4For instance, God says, 'Honor your father and mother,'* and 'Anyone who speaks disrespectfully of father or mother must be put to death.'* 5But you say it is all right for people to say to their parents, 'Sorry, I can't help you. For I have vowed to give to God what I would have given to you.' 6In this way, you say they don't need to honor their parents.* And so you cancel the word of God for the sake of your own tradition. 7You hypocrites! Isaiah was right when he prophesied about you, for he wrote,

8 'These people honor me with their lips,
but their hearts are far from me.
9 Their worship is a farce,
for they teach man-made ideas as commands
from God.'*"

10Then Jesus called to the crowd to come and hear. "Listen," he said, "and try to understand. 11It's not what goes into your mouth that defiles you; you are defiled by the words that come out of your mouth."

12Then the disciples came to him and asked, "Do you realize you offended the Pharisees by what you just said?"

13Jesus replied, "Every plant not planted by my heavenly Father will be uprooted, 14so ignore them. They are blind guides leading the blind, and if one blind person guides another, they will both fall into a ditch."

15Then Peter said to Jesus, "Explain to us the parable that says people aren't defiled by what they eat."

16"Don't you understand yet?" Jesus asked. 17"Anything you eat passes through the stomach and then goes into the sewer. 18But the words you speak come from the heart—that's what defiles you. 19For from the heart come evil thoughts, murder, adultery, all sexual immorality, theft, lying, and slander. 20These are what defile you. Eating with unwashed hands will never defile you."

THE FAITH OF A GENTILE WOMAN

21Then Jesus left Galilee and went north to the region of Tyre and Sidon. 22A Gentile* woman who lived there came to him, pleading, "Have mercy on me, O Lord, Son of David! For my daughter is possessed by a demon that torments her severely."

23But Jesus gave her no reply, not even a word. Then his disciples urged him to send her away. "Tell her to go away," they said. "She is bothering us with all her begging."

14:25 Greek *In the fourth watch of the night.* **14:27** Or *The 'I Am' is here;* Greek reads *I am.* See Exod 3:14. **14:30** Some manuscripts do not include *strong.* **15:4a** Exod 20:12; Deut 5:16. **15:4b** Exod 21:17 (Greek version); Lev 20:9 (Greek version). **15:6** Greek *their father;* other manuscripts read *their father or their mother.* **15:8-9** Isa 29:13 (Greek version). **15:22** Greek *Canaanite.*

[24]Then Jesus said to the woman, "I was sent only to help God's lost sheep—the people of Israel."

[25]But she came and worshiped him, pleading again, "Lord, help me!"

[26]Jesus responded, "It isn't right to take food from the children and throw it to the dogs."

[27]She replied, "That's true, Lord, but even dogs are allowed to eat the scraps that fall beneath their masters' table."

[28]"Dear woman," Jesus said to her, "your faith is great. Your request is granted." And her daughter was instantly healed.

MEETING THE NEEDS 15:21-28

The disciples responded without compassion for the woman. Ever respond that way when someone threatens to inconvenience you with a need? Many of us, if we're honest, would say yes. It's possible to become so occupied with spiritual matters that we miss real spiritual needs right around us. What are the needs of the people around you? How willing are you to meet those needs, even if doing so means stepping out of your comfort zone? ■

JESUS HEALS MANY PEOPLE

[29]Jesus returned to the Sea of Galilee and climbed a hill and sat down. [30]A vast crowd brought to him people who were lame, blind, crippled, those who couldn't speak, and many others. They laid them before Jesus, and he healed them all. [31]The crowd was amazed! Those who hadn't been able to speak were talking, the crippled were made well, the lame were walking, and the blind could see again! And they praised the God of Israel.

JESUS FEEDS FOUR THOUSAND

[32]Then Jesus called his disciples and told them, "I feel sorry for these people. They have been here with me for three days, and they have nothing left to eat. I don't want to send them away hungry, or they will faint along the way."

[33]The disciples replied, "Where would we get enough food here in the wilderness for such a huge crowd?"

[34]Jesus asked, "How much bread do you have?"

They replied, "Seven loaves, and a few small fish."

[35]So Jesus told all the people to sit down on the ground. [36]Then he took the seven loaves and the fish, thanked God for them, and broke them into pieces. He gave them to the disciples, who distributed the food to the crowd.

[37]They all ate as much as they wanted. Afterward, the disciples picked up seven large baskets of leftover food. [38]There were 4,000 men who were fed that day, in addition to all the women and children. [39]Then Jesus sent the people home, and he got into a boat and crossed over to the region of Magadan.

16

LEADERS DEMAND A MIRACULOUS SIGN

One day the Pharisees and Sadducees came to test Jesus, demanding that he show them a miraculous sign from heaven to prove his authority.

[2]He replied, "You know the saying, 'Red sky at night means fair weather tomorrow; [3]red sky in the morning means foul weather all day.' You know how to interpret the weather signs in the sky, but you don't know how to interpret the signs of the times!* [4]Only an evil, adulterous generation would demand a miraculous sign, but the only sign I will give them is the sign of the prophet Jonah.*" Then Jesus left them and went away.

YEAST OF THE PHARISEES AND SADDUCEES

[5]Later, after they crossed to the other side of the lake, the disciples discovered they had forgotten to bring any bread. [6]"Watch out!" Jesus warned them. "Beware of the yeast of the Pharisees and Sadducees."

[7]At this they began to argue with each other because they hadn't brought any bread. [8]Jesus knew what they were saying, so he said, "You have so little faith! Why are you arguing with each other about having no bread? [9]Don't you understand even yet? Don't you remember the 5,000 I fed with five loaves, and the baskets of leftovers you picked up? [10]Or the 4,000 I fed with seven loaves, and the large baskets of leftovers you picked up? [11]Why can't you understand that I'm not talking about bread? So again I say, 'Beware of the yeast of the Pharisees and Sadducees.'"

[12]Then at last they understood that he wasn't speaking about the yeast in bread, but about the deceptive teaching of the Pharisees and Sadducees.

PETER'S DECLARATION ABOUT JESUS

[13]When Jesus came to the region of Caesarea Philippi, he asked his disciples, "Who do people say that the Son of Man is?"*

[14]"Well," they replied, "some say John the Baptist, some say Elijah, and others say Jeremiah or one of the other prophets."

[15]Then he asked them, "But who do you say I am?"

[16]Simon Peter answered, "You are the Messiah,* the Son of the living God."

[17]Jesus replied, "You are blessed, Simon son of John,* because my Father in heaven has revealed this to you. You did not learn this from any human being. [18]Now I say to you that you are Peter (which means 'rock'),* and upon this rock I will build my church, and all the powers of hell* will not conquer it. [19]And I will give you the keys of the Kingdom of Heaven. Whatever you forbid* on earth will be forbidden in heaven, and whatever you permit* on earth will be permitted in heaven."

[20]Then he sternly warned the disciples not to tell anyone that he was the Messiah.

16:2-3 Several manuscripts do not include any of the words in 16:2-3 after *He replied.* **16:4** Greek *the sign of Jonah.* **16:13** "Son of Man" is a title Jesus used for himself. **16:16** Or *the Christ. Messiah* (a Hebrew term) and *Christ* (a Greek term) both mean "the anointed one." **16:17** Greek *Simon bar-Jonah;* see John 1:42; 21:15-17. **16:18a** Greek *that you are Peter.* **16:18b** Greek *and the gates of Hades.* **16:19a** Or *bind,* or *lock.* **16:19b** Or *loose,* or *open.*

WHAT'S THE DEAL ABOUT JESUS?

ULTIMATE ISSUES

Ever try to hold water in a sieve? Trying to understand God can seem as impossible as trying to hold water in a sieve. Just when you think you've got him all figured out, whoops. You discover "holes" in your theories.

God communicated with humans in many ways in the past through conversations with Adam and Eve, the covenant sign of the rainbow, a burning bush and columns of fire and smoke, his Law, and various miracles and visions. Still, as powerful and meaningful as all of those things were, they were only a hint of the reality behind them. That's why God saved the best way of revealing himself for last. He became one of us—the man called Jesus. He came with a nickname: Immanuel, which means "God is with us" (Matt 1:23).

But Jesus was not what people expected. Even the Jewish authorities—the people who claimed to know more about God than anyone—were totally unprepared for the way God came. They expected the promised Messiah to be a strong political and military leader, one who would free his people from Rome. Instead, the Messiah was a "suffering servant" (Isa 53), proclaiming a kingdom that was not of this world.

Like so many others, the Jews were very confused as to who Jesus really was. Jesus himself knew that even his closest followers felt that uncertainty. He asked them point-blank: "Who do you say I am?" Peter's response to this question, given in Matthew 16:16, was simple, direct, and tremendously powerful: "The Messiah, the Son of the living God."

Peter's answer, simple though it was, set off shock waves that rippled through history. If Jesus was—and is—indeed the Messiah, the Son of the living God, then God had entered into human history in a way he had never done before. Life on this planet could never be the same again.

The same question Jesus asked his disciples confronts each of us today: Who do you say Jesus is?

JESUS PREDICTS HIS DEATH

21From then on Jesus* began to tell his disciples plainly
that it was necessary for him to go to Jerusalem, and that
he would suffer many terrible things at the hands of the
elders, the leading priests, and the teachers of religious
law. He would be killed, but on the third day he would be
raised from the dead.

22But Peter took him aside and began to reprimand
him* for saying such things. "Heaven forbid, Lord," he
said. "This will never happen to you!"

23Jesus turned to Peter and said, "Get away from me,
Satan! You are a dangerous trap to me. You are seeing
things merely from a human point of view, not from
God's."

24Then Jesus said to his disciples, "If any of you wants
to be my follower, you must turn from your selfish ways,
take up your cross, and follow me. 25If you try to hang on
to your life, you will lose it. But if you give up your life for
my sake, you will save it. 26And what do you benefit if you
gain the whole world but lose your own soul?* Is anything
worth more than your soul? 27For the Son of Man will
come with his angels in the glory of his Father and will
judge all people according to their deeds. 28And I tell you
the truth, some standing here right now will not die before they see the Son of Man coming in his Kingdom."

HARMLESS ADVICE? 16:21-22

Peter, Jesus' friend and devoted follower who had just eloquently proclaimed his Lord's true identity as the Christ (16:13-16), sought to protect Jesus from the suffering Jesus had to face. Great temptation can come from those who love us and seek to protect us from something we must experience. Be wary when a friend says, "This will never happen to you!" (16:22). Although his or her motive is to prevent harm, this advice might cause more harm than good. ■

17 THE TRANSFIGURATION

Six days later Jesus took Peter and the two brothers,
James and John, and led them up a high mountain to be
alone. 2As the men watched, Jesus' appearance was

16:21 Some manuscripts read *Jesus the Messiah.* 16:22 Or *began to correct him.* 16:26 Or *your self?* also in 16:26b.

transformed so that his face shone like the sun, and his clothes became as white as light. 3Suddenly, Moses and Elijah appeared and began talking with Jesus.

4Peter exclaimed, "Lord, it's wonderful for us to be here! If you want, I'll make three shelters as memorials*—one for you, one for Moses, and one for Elijah."

5But even as he spoke, a bright cloud overshadowed them, and a voice from the cloud said, "This is my dearly loved Son, who brings me great joy. Listen to him." 6The disciples were terrified and fell face down on the ground.

7Then Jesus came over and touched them. "Get up," he said. "Don't be afraid." 8And when they looked up, Moses and Elijah were gone, and they saw only Jesus.

9As they went back down the mountain, Jesus commanded them, "Don't tell anyone what you have seen until the Son of Man* has been raised from the dead."

10Then his disciples asked him, "Why do the teachers of religious law insist that Elijah must return before the Messiah comes?*"

11Jesus replied, "Elijah is indeed coming first to get everything ready. 12But I tell you, Elijah has already come, but he wasn't recognized, and they chose to abuse him. And in the same way they will also make the Son of Man suffer." 13Then the disciples realized he was talking about John the Baptist.

JESUS HEALS A DEMON-POSSESSED BOY

14At the foot of the mountain, a large crowd was waiting for them. A man came and knelt before Jesus and said, 15"Lord, have mercy on my son. He has seizures and suffers terribly. He often falls into the fire or into the water. 16So I brought him to your disciples, but they couldn't heal him."

17Jesus said, "You faithless and corrupt people! How long must I be with you? How long must I put up with you? Bring the boy here to me." 18Then Jesus rebuked the demon in the boy, and it left him. From that moment the boy was well.

19Afterward the disciples asked Jesus privately, "Why couldn't we cast out that demon?"

20"You don't have enough faith," Jesus told them. "I tell you the truth, if you had faith even as small as a mustard seed, you could say to this mountain, 'Move from here to there,' and it would move. Nothing would be impossible.*"

JESUS AGAIN PREDICTS HIS DEATH

22After they gathered again in Galilee, Jesus told them, "The Son of Man is going to be betrayed into the hands of his enemies. 23He will be killed, but on the third day he will be raised from the dead." And the disciples were filled with grief.

PAYMENT OF THE TEMPLE TAX

24On their arrival in Capernaum, the collectors of the Temple tax* came to Peter and asked him, "Doesn't your teacher pay the Temple tax?"

25"Yes, he does," Peter replied. Then he went into the house.

But before he had a chance to speak, Jesus asked him, "What do you think, Peter?* Do kings tax their own people or the people they have conquered?*"

26"They tax the people they have conquered," Peter replied.

"Well, then," Jesus said, "the citizens are free! 27However, we don't want to offend them, so go down to the lake and throw in a line. Open the mouth of the first fish you catch, and you will find a large silver coin.* Take it and pay the tax for both of us."

18 THE GREATEST IN THE KINGDOM

About that time the disciples came to Jesus and asked, "Who is greatest in the Kingdom of Heaven?"

2Jesus called a little child to him and put the child among them. 3Then he said, "I tell you the truth, unless you turn from your sins and become like little children, you will never get into the Kingdom of Heaven. 4So anyone who becomes as humble as this little child is the greatest in the Kingdom of Heaven.

5"And anyone who welcomes a little child like this on my behalf* is welcoming me. 6But if you cause one of these little ones who trusts in me to fall into sin, it would be better for you to have a large millstone tied around your neck and be drowned in the depths of the sea.

7"What sorrow awaits the world, because it tempts people to sin. Temptations are inevitable, but what sorrow awaits the person who does the tempting. 8So if your hand or foot causes you to sin, cut it off and throw it away. It's better to enter eternal life with only one hand or one foot than to be thrown into eternal fire with both of your hands and feet. 9And if your eye causes you to sin, gouge it out and throw it away. It's better to enter eternal life with only one eye than to have two eyes and be thrown into the fire of hell.*

10"Beware that you don't look down on any of these little ones. For I tell you that in heaven their angels are always in the presence of my heavenly Father.*

PARABLE OF THE LOST SHEEP

12"If a man has a hundred sheep and one of them wanders away, what will he do? Won't he leave the ninety-nine others on the hills and go out to search for the one that is lost? 13And if he finds it, I tell you the truth, he will rejoice over it more than over the ninety-nine that didn't wander away! 14In the same way, it is not my heavenly Father's will that even one of these little ones should perish.

CORRECTING ANOTHER BELIEVER

15"If another believer* sins against you,* go privately and point out the offense. If the other person listens and confesses it, you have won that person back. 16But if you are

17:4 Greek *three tabernacles.* **17:9** "Son of Man" is a title Jesus used for himself. **17:10** Greek *that Elijah must come first?* **17:20** Some manuscripts add verse 21, *But this kind of demon won't leave except by prayer and fasting.* Compare Mark 9:29. **17:24** Greek *the two-drachma [tax];* also in 17:24b. See Exod 30:13-16; Neh 10:32-33. **17:25a** Greek *Simon?* **17:25b** Greek *their sons or others?* **17:27** Greek *a stater* [a Greek coin equivalent to four drachmas]. **18:5** Greek *in my name.* **18:9** Greek *the Gehenna of fire.* **18:10** Some manuscripts add verse 11, *And the Son of Man came to save those who are lost.* Compare Luke 19:10. **18:15a** Greek *If your brother.* **18:15b** Some manuscripts do not include *against you.*

unsuccessful, take one or two others with you and go
back again, so that everything you say may be confirmed
by two or three witnesses. 17If the person still refuses to
listen, take your case to the church. Then if he or she
won't accept the church's decision, treat that person as a
pagan or a corrupt tax collector.

18"I tell you the truth, whatever you forbid* on earth
will be forbidden in heaven, and whatever you permit*
on earth will be permitted in heaven.

19"I also tell you this: If two of you agree here on earth
concerning anything you ask, my Father in heaven will do
it for you. 20For where two or three gather together as my
followers,* I am there among them."

ALWAYS OPEN? 18:21-33

The rabbis taught that Jews should forgive those who offend them up to three times. Peter, in trying to be especially generous, asked Jesus if forgiving someone for the same offense seven (the "perfect" number) times was good enough. But Jesus' reply (18:22) was a hint that forgiveness was to be offered always. When it comes to forgiving others, are you like a convenience store—open 24/7—or like a store with limited hours? ■

PARABLE OF THE UNFORGIVING DEBTOR

21Then Peter came to him and asked, "Lord, how often
should I forgive someone* who sins against me? Seven
times?"

22"No, not seven times," Jesus replied, "but seventy
times seven!*

23"Therefore, the Kingdom of Heaven can be compared to a king who decided to bring his accounts up to
date with servants who had borrowed money from him.
24In the process, one of his debtors was brought in who
owed him millions of dollars.* 25He couldn't pay, so his
master ordered that he be sold—along with his wife, his
children, and everything he owned—to pay the debt.

26"But the man fell down before his master and begged
him, 'Please, be patient with me, and I will pay it all.'
27Then his master was filled with pity for him, and he released him and forgave his debt.

28"But when the man left the king, he went to a fellow
servant who owed him a few thousand dollars.* He
grabbed him by the throat and demanded instant payment.

29"His fellow servant fell down before him and begged
for a little more time. 'Be patient with me, and I will pay it,'
he pleaded. 30But his creditor wouldn't wait. He had the
man arrested and put in prison until the debt could be
paid in full.

31"When some of the other servants saw this, they were
very upset. They went to the king and told him everything
that had happened. 32Then the king called in the man he
had forgiven and said, 'You evil servant! I forgave you that
tremendous debt because you pleaded with me.
33Shouldn't you have mercy on your fellow servant, just as I
had mercy on you?' 34Then the angry king sent the man to
prison to be tortured until he had paid his entire debt.

35"That's what my heavenly Father will do to you if you
refuse to forgive your brothers and sisters* from your
heart."

19 DISCUSSION ABOUT DIVORCE AND MARRIAGE

When Jesus had finished saying these things, he left Galilee and went down to the region of Judea east of the Jordan River. 2Large crowds followed him there, and he
healed their sick.

3Some Pharisees came and tried to trap him with this
question: "Should a man be allowed to divorce his wife
for just any reason?"

4"Haven't you read the Scriptures?" Jesus replied.
"They record that from the beginning 'God made them
male and female.'* 5And he said, 'This explains why a
man leaves his father and mother and is joined to his
wife, and the two are united into one.'* 6Since they are no
longer two but one, let no one split apart what God has
joined together."

7"Then why did Moses say in the law that a man could
give his wife a written notice of divorce and send her
away?"* they asked.

8Jesus replied, "Moses permitted divorce only as a concession to your hard hearts, but it was not what God had
originally intended. 9And I tell you this, whoever divorces
his wife and marries someone else commits adultery—
unless his wife has been unfaithful.*"

10Jesus' disciples then said to him, "If this is the case, it
is better not to marry!"

11"Not everyone can accept this statement," Jesus said.
"Only those whom God helps. 12Some are born as eunuchs, some have been made eunuchs by others, and
some choose not to marry* for the sake of the Kingdom
of Heaven. Let anyone accept this who can."

JESUS BLESSES THE CHILDREN

13One day some parents brought their children to Jesus
so he could lay his hands on them and pray for them. But
the disciples scolded the parents for bothering him.

14But Jesus said, "Let the children come to me. Don't
stop them! For the Kingdom of Heaven belongs to those
who are like these children." 15And he placed his hands
on their heads and blessed them before he left.

THE RICH MAN

16Someone came to Jesus with this question: "Teacher,*
what good deed must I do to have eternal life?"

17"Why ask me about what is good?" Jesus replied.
"There is only One who is good. But to answer your

18:18a Or *bind*, or *lock*. 18:18b Or *loose*, or *open*. 18:20 Greek *gather together in my name*. 18:21 Greek *my brother*. 18:22 Or *seventy-seven times*. 18:24 Greek *10,000 talents* [375 tons or 340 metric tons of silver]. 18:28 Greek *100 denarii*. A denarius was equivalent to a laborer's full day's wage. 18:35 Greek *your brother*. 19:4 Gen 1:27; 5:2. 19:5 Gen 2:24. 19:7 See Deut 24:1. 19:9 Some manuscripts add *And anyone who marries a divorced woman commits adultery*. Compare Matt 5:32. 19:12 Greek *and some make themselves eunuchs*. 19:16 Some manuscripts read *Good Teacher*.

question—if you want to receive eternal life, keep* the commandments."

18"Which ones?" the man asked.

And Jesus replied: " 'You must not murder. You must not commit adultery. You must not steal. You must not testify falsely. 19Honor your father and mother. Love your neighbor as yourself.'*"

20"I've obeyed all these commandments," the young man replied. "What else must I do?"

21Jesus told him, "If you want to be perfect, go and sell all your possessions and give the money to the poor, and you will have treasure in heaven. Then come, follow me."

22But when the young man heard this, he went away sad, for he had many possessions.

23Then Jesus said to his disciples, "I tell you the truth, it is very hard for a rich person to enter the Kingdom of Heaven. 24I'll say it again—it is easier for a camel to go through the eye of a needle than for a rich person to enter the Kingdom of God!"

25The disciples were astounded. "Then who in the world can be saved?" they asked.

26Jesus looked at them intently and said, "Humanly speaking, it is impossible. But with God everything is possible."

27Then Peter said to him, "We've given up everything to follow you. What will we get?"

28Jesus replied, "I assure you that when the world is made new* and the Son of Man* sits upon his glorious throne, you who have been my followers will also sit on twelve thrones, judging the twelve tribes of Israel. 29And everyone who has given up houses or brothers or sisters or father or mother or children or property, for my sake, will receive a hundred times as much in return and will inherit eternal life. 30But many who are the greatest now will be least important then, and those who seem least important now will be the greatest then.*

20

PARABLE OF THE VINEYARD WORKERS

"For the Kingdom of Heaven is like the landowner who went out early one morning to hire workers for his vineyard. 2He agreed to pay the normal daily wage* and sent them out to work.

3"At nine o'clock in the morning he was passing through the marketplace and saw some people standing around doing nothing. 4So he hired them, telling them he would pay them whatever was right at the end of the day. 5So they went to work in the vineyard. At noon and again at three o'clock he did the same thing.

6"At five o'clock that afternoon he was in town again and saw some more people standing around. He asked them, 'Why haven't you been working today?'

7"They replied, 'Because no one hired us.'

"The landowner told them, 'Then go out and join the others in my vineyard.'

8"That evening he told the foreman to call the workers in and pay them, beginning with the last workers first. 9When those hired at five o'clock were paid, each received a full day's wage. 10When those hired first came to get their pay, they assumed they would receive more. But they, too, were paid a day's wage. 11When they received their pay, they protested to the owner, 12'Those people worked only one hour, and yet you've paid them just as much as you paid us who worked all day in the scorching heat.'

13"He answered one of them, 'Friend, I haven't been unfair! Didn't you agree to work all day for the usual wage? 14Take your money and go. I wanted to pay this last worker the same as you. 15Is it against the law for me to do what I want with my money? Should you be jealous because I am kind to others?'

16"So those who are last now will be first then, and those who are first will be last."

GOD'S GENEROSITY 20:1-15

The parable of the vineyard is a story about *grace*—God's generosity. Those who trust Jesus will get the same reward—eternal life with him—regardless of whether they turn to him early in life or in their last moments of life. (See, for example, the story of the thief on the cross—Luke 23:40-43. This, however, is *not* an invitation to wait until the last minute to make up your mind about Jesus. After all, no one knows when the last minute of life will take place.) God is generous to all. Are you cool with that? ■

JESUS AGAIN PREDICTS HIS DEATH

17As Jesus was going up to Jerusalem, he took the twelve disciples aside privately and told them what was going to happen to him. 18"Listen," he said, "we're going up to Jerusalem, where the Son of Man* will be betrayed to the leading priests and the teachers of religious law. They will sentence him to die. 19Then they will hand him over to the Romans* to be mocked, flogged with a whip, and crucified. But on the third day he will be raised from the dead."

JESUS TEACHES ABOUT SERVING OTHERS

20Then the mother of James and John, the sons of Zebedee, came to Jesus with her sons. She knelt respectfully to ask a favor. 21"What is your request?" he asked.

She replied, "In your Kingdom, please let my two sons sit in places of honor next to you, one on your right and the other on your left."

22But Jesus answered by saying to them, "You don't know what you are asking! Are you able to drink from the bitter cup of suffering I am about to drink?"

"Oh yes," they replied, "we are able!"

23Jesus told them, "You will indeed drink from my bitter cup. But I have no right to say who will sit on my right

19:17 Some manuscripts read *continue to keep.* **19:18-19** Exod 20:12-16; Deut 5:16-20; Lev 19:18. **19:28a** Or *in the regeneration.* **19:28b** "Son of Man" is a title Jesus used for himself. **19:30** Greek *But many who are first will be last; and the last, first.* **20:2** Greek *a denarius,* the payment for a full day's labor; similarly in 20:9, 10, 13. **20:18** "Son of Man" is a title Jesus used for himself. **20:19** Greek *the Gentiles.*

or my left. My Father has prepared those places for the
ones he has chosen."
24When the ten other disciples heard what James and
John had asked, they were indignant. 25But Jesus called
them together and said, "You know that the rulers in this
world lord it over their people, and officials flaunt their
authority over those under them. 26But among you it will
be different. Whoever wants to be a leader among you
must be your servant, 27and whoever wants to be first
among you must become your slave. 28For even the Son of
Man came not to be served but to serve others and to give
his life as a ransom for many."

JESUS HEALS TWO BLIND MEN

29As Jesus and the disciples left the town of Jericho, a
large crowd followed behind. 30Two blind men were sitting beside the road. When they heard that Jesus was
coming that way, they began shouting, "Lord, Son of David, have mercy on us!"
31"Be quiet!" the crowd yelled at them.
But they only shouted louder, "Lord, Son of David, have
mercy on us!"
32When Jesus heard them, he stopped and called,
"What do you want me to do for you?"
33"Lord," they said, "we want to see!" 34Jesus felt sorry
for them and touched their eyes. Instantly they could see!
Then they followed him.

21

JESUS' TRIUMPHANT ENTRY

As Jesus and the disciples approached Jerusalem, they
came to the town of Bethphage on the Mount of Olives.
Jesus sent two of them on ahead. 2"Go into the village
over there," he said. "As soon as you enter it, you will see a
donkey tied there, with its colt beside it. Untie them and
bring them to me. 3If anyone asks what you are doing, just
say, 'The Lord needs them,' and he will immediately let
you take them."
4This took place to fulfill the prophecy that said,

5 "Tell the people of Israel,*
'Look, your King is coming to you.
He is humble, riding on a donkey—
riding on a donkey's colt.'"*

6The two disciples did as Jesus commanded. 7They
brought the donkey and the colt to him and threw their
garments over the colt, and he sat on it.*
8Most of the crowd spread their garments on the road
ahead of him, and others cut branches from the trees and
spread them on the road. 9Jesus was in the center of the
procession, and the people all around him were shouting,

"Praise God* for the Son of David!
Blessings on the one who comes in the name
of the LORD!
Praise God in highest heaven!"*

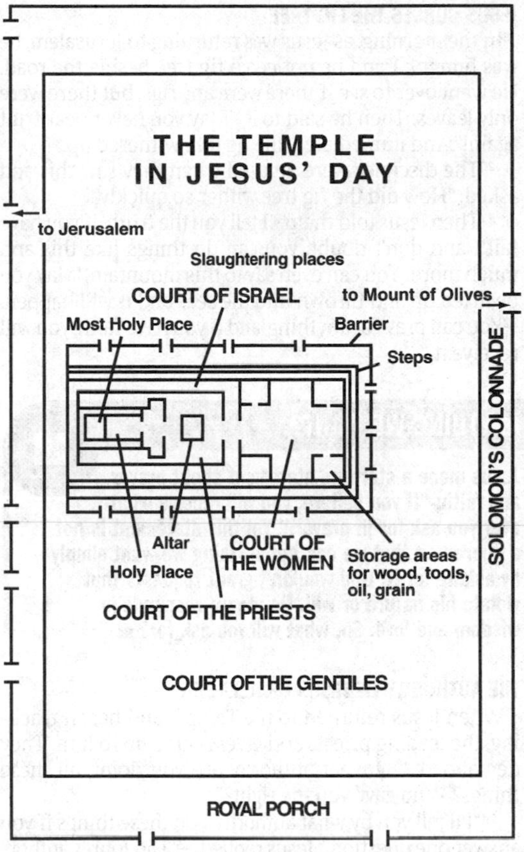

10The entire city of Jerusalem was in an uproar as he
entered. "Who is this?" they asked.
11And the crowds replied, "It's Jesus, the prophet from
Nazareth in Galilee."

JESUS CLEARS THE TEMPLE

12Jesus entered the Temple and began to drive out all the
people buying and selling animals for sacrifice. He
knocked over the tables of the money changers and the
chairs of those selling doves. 13He said to them, "The
Scriptures declare, 'My Temple will be called a house of
prayer,' but you have turned it into a den of thieves!"*
14The blind and the lame came to him in the Temple,
and he healed them. 15The leading priests and the teachers of religious law saw these wonderful miracles and
heard even the children in the Temple shouting, "Praise
God for the Son of David."
But the leaders were indignant. 16They asked Jesus,
"Do you hear what these children are saying?"
"Yes," Jesus replied. "Haven't you ever read the Scriptures? For they say, 'You have taught children and infants
to give you praise.'*" 17Then he returned to Bethany,
where he stayed overnight.

21:5a Greek *Tell the daughter of Zion.* Isa 62:11. **21:5b** Zech 9:9. **21:7** Greek *over them, and he sat on them.* **21:9a** Greek *Hosanna,* an exclamation of praise that literally means "save now"; also in 21:9b, 15. **21:9b** Pss 118:25-26; 148:1. **21:13** Isa 56:7; Jer 7:11. **21:16** Ps 8:2.

JESUS CURSES THE FIG TREE

18In the morning, as Jesus was returning to Jerusalem, he
was hungry, 19and he noticed a fig tree beside the road.
He went over to see if there were any figs, but there were
only leaves. Then he said to it, "May you never bear fruit
again!" And immediately the fig tree withered up.
20The disciples were amazed when they saw this and
asked, "How did the fig tree wither so quickly?"
21Then Jesus told them, "I tell you the truth, if you have
faith and don't doubt, you can do things like this and
much more. You can even say to this mountain, 'May you
be lifted up and thrown into the sea,' and it will happen.
22You can pray for anything, and if you have faith, you will
receive it."

ANYTHING WE WANT? 21:21-22

Jesus made a startling statement about prayer and faith: "If you believe, you will receive whatever you ask for in prayer." Yet this statement is not a guarantee that we can get anything we want simply by asking for it. God wouldn't grant requests that violate his nature or will. He always responds in wisdom and love. So, what will you ask for? ■

THE AUTHORITY OF JESUS CHALLENGED

23When Jesus returned to the Temple and began teaching, the leading priests and elders came up to him. They
demanded, "By what authority are you doing all these
things? Who gave you the right?"
24"I'll tell you by what authority I do these things if you
answer one question," Jesus replied. 25"Did John's authority to baptize come from heaven, or was it merely human?"

They talked it over among themselves. "If we say it was
from heaven, he will ask us why we didn't believe John.
26But if we say it was merely human, we'll be mobbed because the people believe John was a prophet." 27So they
finally replied, "We don't know."

And Jesus responded, "Then I won't tell you by what
authority I do these things.

PARABLE OF THE TWO SONS

28"But what do you think about this? A man with two sons
told the older boy, 'Son, go out and work in the vineyard
today.' 29The son answered, 'No, I won't go,' but later he
changed his mind and went anyway. 30Then the father
told the other son, 'You go,' and he said, 'Yes, sir, I will.'
But he didn't go.
31"Which of the two obeyed his father?"

They replied, "The first."*

Then Jesus explained his meaning: "I tell you the truth,
corrupt tax collectors and prostitutes will get into the
Kingdom of God before you do. 32For John the Baptist
came and showed you the right way to live, but you didn't
believe him, while tax collectors and prostitutes did. And
even when you saw this happening, you refused to believe him and repent of your sins.

FAKING IT 21:28-32

In Jesus' parable, the son who said he would obey but didn't represented the leaders of Israel. Although they claimed to be obedient to God, their actions didn't match their words. They thought they were better than the tax collectors and other "sinners."

God always knows when a person is being phony. All of the "good" behavior in the world (perfect attendance at youth group; Bible reading; helping out in homeless shelters) can't hide a heart that's cold toward God. Feel like you're faking it sometimes? Relax. God doesn't expect you to fake being on fire for him. He just wants you to admit that your flame is a little low. Only he can turn up the flame once more. ■

PARABLE OF THE EVIL FARMERS

33"Now listen to another story. A certain landowner
planted a vineyard, built a wall around it, dug a pit for
pressing out the grape juice, and built a lookout tower.
Then he leased the vineyard to tenant farmers and
moved to another country. 34At the time of the grape harvest, he sent his servants to collect his share of the crop.
35But the farmers grabbed his servants, beat one, killed
one, and stoned another. 36So the landowner sent a larger
group of his servants to collect for him, but the results
were the same.
37"Finally, the owner sent his son, thinking, 'Surely they
will respect my son.'
38"But when the tenant farmers saw his son coming,
they said to one another, 'Here comes the heir to this estate. Come on, let's kill him and get the estate for ourselves!' 39So they grabbed him, dragged him out of the
vineyard, and murdered him.
40"When the owner of the vineyard returns," Jesus
asked, "what do you think he will do to those farmers?"
41The religious leaders replied, "He will put the wicked
men to a horrible death and lease the vineyard to others
who will give him his share of the crop after each
harvest."
42Then Jesus asked them, "Didn't you ever read this in
the Scriptures?

'The stone that the builders rejected
has now become the cornerstone.
This is the LORD's doing,
and it is wonderful to see.'*

43I tell you, the Kingdom of God will be taken away from
you and given to a nation that will produce the proper
fruit. 44Anyone who stumbles over that stone will be broken to pieces, and it will crush anyone it falls on.*"

21:29-31 Other manuscripts read *"The second."* In still other manuscripts the first son says "Yes" but does nothing, the second son says "No" but then repents and goes, and the answer to Jesus' question is that the second son obeyed his father. **21:42** Ps 118:22-23. **21:44** This verse is omitted in some early manuscripts. Compare Luke 20:18.

45When the leading priests and Pharisees heard this
parable, they realized he was telling the story against
them—they were the wicked farmers. 46They wanted to
arrest him, but they were afraid of the crowds, who considered Jesus to be a prophet.

22

PARABLE OF THE GREAT FEAST

Jesus also told them other parables. He said, 2"The Kingdom of Heaven can be illustrated by the story of a king
who prepared a great wedding feast for his son. 3When
the banquet was ready, he sent his servants to notify
those who were invited. But they all refused to come!
4"So he sent other servants to tell them, 'The feast has
been prepared. The bulls and fattened cattle have been
killed, and everything is ready. Come to the banquet!'
5But the guests he had invited ignored them and went
their own way, one to his farm, another to his business.
6Others seized his messengers and insulted them and
killed them.
7"The king was furious, and he sent out his army to destroy the murderers and burn their town. 8And he said to
his servants, 'The wedding feast is ready, and the guests I
invited aren't worthy of the honor. 9Now go out to the
street corners and invite everyone you see.' 10So the servants brought in everyone they could find, good and bad
alike, and the banquet hall was filled with guests.
11"But when the king came in to meet the guests, he noticed a man who wasn't wearing the proper clothes for a
wedding. 12'Friend,' he asked, 'how is it that you are here
without wedding clothes?' But the man had no reply.
13Then the king said to his aides, 'Bind his hands and feet
and throw him into the outer darkness, where there will
be weeping and gnashing of teeth.'
14"For many are called, but few are chosen."

YOU'RE INVITED 22:1-14

In this culture, two invitations were expected when wedding banquets were given. The first invitation invited the guests to attend; the second announced that the feast was about to begin. Here the king—God—invited his guests three times. But each time they refused to come. God wants us to join him at his banquet, which will last for eternity. That's why he sends us invitations again and again. Have you accepted his invitation? ■

TAXES FOR CAESAR

15Then the Pharisees met together to plot how to trap
Jesus into saying something for which he could be arrested. 16They sent some of their disciples, along with the
supporters of Herod, to meet with him. "Teacher," they
said, "we know how honest you are. You teach the way of
God truthfully. You are impartial and don't play favorites.
17Now tell us what you think about this: Is it right to pay
taxes to Caesar or not?"
18But Jesus knew their evil motives. "You hypocrites!"
he said. "Why are you trying to trap me? 19Here, show me
the coin used for the tax." When they handed him a Roman coin,* 20he asked, "Whose picture and title are
stamped on it?"
21"Caesar's," they replied.
"Well, then," he said, "give to Caesar what belongs to
Caesar, and give to God what belongs to God."
22His reply amazed them, and they went away.

LIFE AFTER DEATH 22:23-33

The Sadducees asked Jesus what marriage would be like in eternity. But Jesus knew that their question was more about eternity than it was about marriage. They didn't believe in life after death. Many people today share that opinion. Maybe you've heard people say things like "The one who dies with the most toys wins!" or "Might as well live it up now, 'cause when you die, that's it!" Jesus would respond to both views with the same words he spoke to the Sadducees: "Your mistake is that you don't know the Scriptures." Do you? ■

DISCUSSION ABOUT RESURRECTION

23That same day Jesus was approached by some Sadducees—religious leaders who say there is no resurrection
from the dead. They posed this question: 24"Teacher,
Moses said, 'If a man dies without children, his brother
should marry the widow and have a child who will carry
on the brother's name.'* 25Well, suppose there were
seven brothers. The oldest one married and then died
without children, so his brother married the widow. 26But
the second brother also died, and the third brother married her. This continued with all seven of them. 27Last of
all, the woman also died. 28So tell us, whose wife will she
be in the resurrection? For all seven were married to her."
29Jesus replied, "Your mistake is that you don't know
the Scriptures, and you don't know the power of God.
30For when the dead rise, they will neither marry nor be
given in marriage. In this respect they will be like the angels in heaven.
31"But now, as to whether there will be a resurrection
of the dead—haven't you ever read about this in the
Scriptures? Long after Abraham, Isaac, and Jacob had
died, God said,* 32I am the God of Abraham, the God of
Isaac, and the God of Jacob.'* So he is the God of the living, not the dead."
33When the crowds heard him, they were astounded at
his teaching.

THE MOST IMPORTANT COMMANDMENT

34But when the Pharisees heard that he had silenced the
Sadducees with his reply, they met together to question
him again. 35One of them, an expert in religious law, tried
to trap him with this question: 36"Teacher, which is the
most important commandment in the law of Moses?"
37Jesus replied, " 'You must love the LORD your God
with all your heart, all your soul, and all your mind.'*

22:19 Greek *a denarius.* 22:24 Deut 25:5-6. 22:31 Greek *read about this? God said.* 22:32 Exod 3:6. 22:37 Deut 6:5.

38 This is the first and greatest commandment. 39 A second is equally important: 'Love your neighbor as yourself.'* 40 The entire law and all the demands of the prophets are based on these two commandments."

WHOSE SON IS THE MESSIAH?

41 Then, surrounded by the Pharisees, Jesus asked them a question: 42 "What do you think about the Messiah? Whose son is he?"

They replied, "He is the son of David."

43 Jesus responded, "Then why does David, speaking under the inspiration of the Spirit, call the Messiah 'my Lord'? For David said,

44 'The LORD said to my Lord,
Sit in the place of honor at my right hand
until I humble your enemies beneath your feet.'*

45 Since David called the Messiah 'my Lord,' how can the Messiah be his son?"

46 No one could answer him. And after that, no one dared to ask him any more questions.

23

JESUS CRITICIZES THE RELIGIOUS LEADERS

Then Jesus said to the crowds and to his disciples, 2 "The teachers of religious law and the Pharisees are the official interpreters of the law of Moses.* 3 So practice and obey whatever they tell you, but don't follow their example. For they don't practice what they teach. 4 They crush people with unbearable religious demands and never lift a finger to ease the burden.

5 "Everything they do is for show. On their arms they wear extra wide prayer boxes with Scripture verses inside, and they wear robes with extra long tassels.* 6 And they love to sit at the head table at banquets and in the seats of honor in the synagogues. 7 They love to receive respectful greetings as they walk in the marketplaces, and to be called 'Rabbi.'*

8 "Don't let anyone call you 'Rabbi,' for you have only one teacher, and all of you are equal as brothers and sisters.* 9 And don't address anyone here on earth as 'Father,' for only God in heaven is your spiritual Father. 10 And don't let anyone call you 'Teacher,' for you have only one teacher, the Messiah. 11 The greatest among you must be a servant. 12 But those who exalt themselves will be humbled, and those who humble themselves will be exalted.

13 "What sorrow awaits you teachers of religious law and you Pharisees. Hypocrites! For you shut the door of the Kingdom of Heaven in people's faces. You won't go in yourselves, and you don't let others enter either.*

15 "What sorrow awaits you teachers of religious law and you Pharisees. Hypocrites! For you cross land and sea to make one convert, and then you turn that person into twice the child of hell* you yourselves are!

16 "Blind guides! What sorrow awaits you! For you say that it means nothing to swear 'by God's Temple,' but that it is binding to swear 'by the gold in the Temple.' 17 Blind fools! Which is more important—the gold or the Temple that makes the gold sacred? 18 And you say that to swear 'by the altar' is not binding, but to swear 'by the gifts on the altar' is binding. 19 How blind! For which is more important—the gift on the altar or the altar that makes the gift sacred? 20 When you swear 'by the altar,' you are swearing by it and by everything on it. 21 And when you swear 'by the Temple,' you are swearing by it and by God, who lives in it. 22 And when you swear 'by heaven,' you are swearing by the throne of God and by God, who sits on the throne.

23 "What sorrow awaits you teachers of religious law and you Pharisees. Hypocrites! For you are careful to tithe even the tiniest income from your herb gardens,* but you ignore the more important aspects of the law—justice, mercy, and faith. You should tithe, yes, but do not neglect the more important things. 24 Blind guides! You strain your water so you won't accidentally swallow a gnat, but you swallow a camel!*

25 "What sorrow awaits you teachers of religious law and you Pharisees. Hypocrites! For you are so careful to clean the outside of the cup and the dish, but inside you are filthy—full of greed and self-indulgence! 26 You blind Pharisee! First wash the inside of the cup and the dish,* and then the outside will become clean, too.

27 "What sorrow awaits you teachers of religious law and you Pharisees. Hypocrites! For you are like whitewashed tombs—beautiful on the outside but filled on the inside with dead people's bones and all sorts of impurity. 28 Outwardly you look like righteous people, but inwardly your hearts are filled with hypocrisy and lawlessness.

29 "What sorrow awaits you teachers of religious law and you Pharisees. Hypocrites! For you build tombs for the prophets your ancestors killed, and you decorate the monuments of the godly people your ancestors destroyed. 30 Then you say, 'If we had lived in the days of our ancestors, we would never have joined them in killing the prophets.'

31 "But in saying that, you testify against yourselves that you are indeed the descendants of those who murdered the prophets. 32 Go ahead and finish what your ancestors started. 33 Snakes! Sons of vipers! How will you escape the judgment of hell?

34 "Therefore, I am sending you prophets and wise men and teachers of religious law. But you will kill some by crucifixion, and you will flog others with whips in your synagogues, chasing them from city to city. 35 As a result, you will be held responsible for the murder of all godly people of all time—from the murder of righteous Abel to the murder of Zechariah son of Barachiah, whom you killed in the Temple between the sanctuary and the altar.

22:39 Lev 19:18. **22:44** Ps 110:1. **23:2** Greek *and the Pharisees sit in the seat of Moses.* **23:5** Greek *They enlarge their phylacteries and lengthen their tassels.* **23:7** *Rabbi,* from Aramaic, means "master" or "teacher." **23:8** Greek *brothers.* **23:13** Some manuscripts add verse 14, *What sorrow awaits you teachers of religious law and you Pharisees. Hypocrites! You shamelessly cheat widows out of their property and then pretend to be pious by making long prayers in public. Because of this, you will be severely punished.* Compare Mark 12:40 and Luke 20:47. **23:15** Greek *of Gehenna;* also in 23:33. **23:23** Greek *tithe the mint, the dill, and the cumin.* **23:24** See Lev 11:4, 23, where gnats and camels are both forbidden as food. **23:26** Some manuscripts do not include *and the dish.*

[36]I tell you the truth, this judgment will fall on this very generation.

JESUS GRIEVES OVER JERUSALEM

[37]"O Jerusalem, Jerusalem, the city that kills the prophets and stones God's messengers! How often I have wanted to gather your children together as a hen protects her chicks beneath her wings, but you wouldn't let me. [38]And now, look, your house is abandoned and desolate.* [39]For I tell you this, you will never see me again until you say, 'Blessings on the one who comes in the name of the LORD!'*"

24

JESUS FORETELLS THE FUTURE

As Jesus was leaving the Temple grounds, his disciples pointed out to him the various Temple buildings. [2]But he responded, "Do you see all these buildings? I tell you the truth, they will be completely demolished. Not one stone will be left on top of another!"

[3]Later, Jesus sat on the Mount of Olives. His disciples came to him privately and said, "Tell us, when will all this happen? What sign will signal your return and the end of the world?*"

FRAUDS 24:11, 23-26

Jesus warned the disciples that in the end times false prophets would spring up in the land and fool many people. The Old Testament frequently mentioned false prophets (see 2 Kings 3:13; Isa 44:25; Jer 23:16-17; Ezek 13:1-3; Mic 3:5-7; Zech 13:2-3). These prophets claimed to receive messages from God, but really spoke for themselves.

Nowadays, many people claim to speak for God. But not all have been sent by God. So, how can you tell a false prophet from a true one? A true prophet's words always agree with Scriptures. Check out 2 Corinthians 4:2; 1 John 4:1-4. ■

[4]Jesus told them, "Don't let anyone mislead you, [5]for many will come in my name, claiming, 'I am the Messiah.' They will deceive many. [6]And you will hear of wars and threats of wars, but don't panic. Yes, these things must take place, but the end won't follow immediately. [7]Nation will go to war against nation, and kingdom against kingdom. There will be famines and earthquakes in many parts of the world. [8]But all this is only the first of the birth pains, with more to come.

[9]"Then you will be arrested, persecuted, and killed. You will be hated all over the world because you are my followers.* [10]And many will turn away from me and betray and hate each other. [11]And many false prophets will appear and will deceive many people. [12]Sin will be rampant everywhere, and the love of many will grow cold. [13]But the one who endures to the end will be saved. [14]And the Good News about the Kingdom will be preached throughout the whole world, so that all nations* will hear it; and then the end will come.

[15]"The day is coming when you will see what Daniel the prophet spoke about—the sacrilegious object that causes desecration* standing in the Holy Place." (Reader, pay attention!) [16]"Then those in Judea must flee to the hills. [17]A person out on the deck of a roof must not go down into the house to pack. [18]A person out in the field must not return even to get a coat. [19]How terrible it will be for pregnant women and for nursing mothers in those days. [20]And pray that your flight will not be in winter or on the Sabbath. [21]For there will be greater anguish than at any time since the world began. And it will never be so great again. [22]In fact, unless that time of calamity is shortened, not a single person will survive. But it will be shortened for the sake of God's chosen ones.

[23]"Then if anyone tells you, 'Look, here is the Messiah,' or 'There he is,' don't believe it. [24]For false messiahs and false prophets will rise up and perform great signs and wonders so as to deceive, if possible, even God's chosen ones. [25]See, I have warned you about this ahead of time.

[26]"So if someone tells you, 'Look, the Messiah is out in the desert,' don't bother to go and look. Or, 'Look, he is hiding here,' don't believe it! [27]For as the lightning flashes in the east and shines to the west, so it will be when the Son of Man* comes. [28]Just as the gathering of vultures shows there is a carcass nearby, so these signs indicate that the end is near.*

[29]"Immediately after the anguish of those days,

the sun will be darkened,
  the moon will give no light,
the stars will fall from the sky,
  and the powers in the heavens will be shaken.*

[30]And then at last, the sign that the Son of Man is coming will appear in the heavens, and there will be deep mourning among all the peoples of the earth. And they will see the Son of Man coming on the clouds of heaven with power and great glory.* [31]And he will send out his angels with the mighty blast of a trumpet, and they will gather his chosen ones from all over the world*—from the farthest ends of the earth and heaven.

[32]"Now learn a lesson from the fig tree. When its branches bud and its leaves begin to sprout, you know that summer is near. [33]In the same way, when you see all these things, you can know his return is very near, right at the door. [34]I tell you the truth, this generation* will not pass from the scene until all these things take place. [35]Heaven and earth will disappear, but my words will never disappear.

[36]"However, no one knows the day or hour when these things will happen, not even the angels in heaven or the Son himself.* Only the Father knows.

23:38 Some manuscripts do not include *and desolate*. **23:39** Ps 118:26. **24:3** Or *the age?* **24:9** Greek *on account of my name*. **24:14** Or *all peoples*. **24:15** Greek *the abomination of desolation*. See Dan 9:27; 11:31; 12:11. **24:27** "Son of Man" is a title Jesus used for himself. **24:28** Greek *Wherever the carcass is, the vultures gather*. **24:29** See Isa 13:10; 34:4; Joel 2:10. **24:30** See Dan 7:13. **24:31** Greek *from the four winds*. **24:34** Or *this age*, or *this nation*. **24:36** Some manuscripts do not include *or the Son himself*.

37"When the Son of Man returns, it will be like it was in Noah's day. 38In those days before the flood, the people were enjoying banquets and parties and weddings right up to the time Noah entered his boat. 39People didn't realize what was going to happen until the flood came and swept them all away. That is the way it will be when the Son of Man comes.

40"Two men will be working together in the field; one will be taken, the other left. 41Two women will be grinding flour at the mill; one will be taken, the other left.

42"So you, too, must keep watch! For you don't know what day your Lord is coming. 43Understand this: If a homeowner knew exactly when a burglar was coming, he would keep watch and not permit his house to be broken into. 44You also must be ready all the time, for the Son of Man will come when least expected.

45"A faithful, sensible servant is one to whom the master can give the responsibility of managing his other household servants and feeding them. 46If the master returns and finds that the servant has done a good job, there will be a reward. 47I tell you the truth, the master will put that servant in charge of all he owns. 48But what if the servant is evil and thinks, 'My master won't be back for a while,' 49and he begins beating the other servants, partying, and getting drunk? 50The master will return unannounced and unexpected, 51and he will cut the servant to pieces and assign him a place with the hypocrites. In that place there will be weeping and gnashing of teeth.

25

PARABLE OF THE TEN BRIDESMAIDS

"Then the Kingdom of Heaven will be like ten bridesmaids* who took their lamps and went to meet the bridegroom. 2Five of them were foolish, and five were wise. 3The five who were foolish didn't take enough olive oil for their lamps, 4but the other five were wise enough to take along extra oil. 5When the bridegroom was delayed, they all became drowsy and fell asleep.

6"At midnight they were roused by the shout, 'Look, the bridegroom is coming! Come out and meet him!'

7"All the bridesmaids got up and prepared their lamps. 8Then the five foolish ones asked the others, 'Please give us some of your oil because our lamps are going out.'

9"But the others replied, 'We don't have enough for all of us. Go to a shop and buy some for yourselves.'

10"But while they were gone to buy oil, the bridegroom came. Then those who were ready went in with him to the marriage feast, and the door was locked. 11Later, when the other five bridesmaids returned, they stood outside, calling, 'Lord! Lord! Open the door for us!'

12"But he called back, 'Believe me, I don't know you!'

13"So you, too, must keep watch! For you do not know the day or hour of my return.

PARABLE OF THE THREE SERVANTS

14"Again, the Kingdom of Heaven can be illustrated by the story of a man going on a long trip. He called together his servants and entrusted his money to them while he was gone. 15He gave five bags of silver* to one, two bags of silver to another, and one bag of silver to the last—dividing it in proportion to their abilities. He then left on his trip.

USE WHAT YOU'VE GOT 25:11-30

The master divided the money among his servants according to their abilities. No one received more or less money than he could handle. The money in this story represents any kind of resource we're given. God gives us time, abilities, and other resources to invest wisely until he returns. The issue is not how much we have, but what we do with what we have. What will you do with your resources? ■

16"The servant who received the five bags of silver began to invest the money and earned five more. 17The servant with two bags of silver also went to work and earned two more. 18But the servant who received the one bag of silver dug a hole in the ground and hid the master's money.

19"After a long time their master returned from his trip and called them to give an account of how they had used his money. 20The servant to whom he had entrusted the five bags of silver came forward with five more and said, 'Master, you gave me five bags of silver to invest, and I have earned five more.'

21"The master was full of praise. 'Well done, my good and faithful servant. You have been faithful in handling this small amount, so now I will give you many more responsibilities. Let's celebrate together!'*

22"The servant who had received the two bags of silver came forward and said, 'Master, you gave me two bags of silver to invest, and I have earned two more.'

23"The master said, 'Well done, my good and faithful servant. You have been faithful in handling this small amount, so now I will give you many more responsibilities. Let's celebrate together!'

24"Then the servant with the one bag of silver came and said, 'Master, I knew you were a harsh man, harvesting crops you didn't plant and gathering crops you didn't cultivate. 25I was afraid I would lose your money, so I hid it in the earth. Look, here is your money back.'

26"But the master replied, 'You wicked and lazy servant! If you knew I harvested crops I didn't plant and gathered crops I didn't cultivate, 27why didn't you deposit my money in the bank? At least I could have gotten some interest on it.'

28"Then he ordered, 'Take the money from this servant, and give it to the one with the ten bags of silver. 29To those who use well what they are given, even more will be given, and they will have an abundance. But from those who do nothing, even what little they have will be taken away. 30Now throw this useless servant into outer darkness, where there will be weeping and gnashing of teeth.'

25:1 Or *virgins;* also in 25:7, 11. **25:15** Greek *talents;* also throughout the story. A talent is equal to 75 pounds or 34 kilograms. **25:21** Greek *Enter into the joy of your master* [or *your Lord*]; also in 25:23.

THE FINAL JUDGMENT

31"But when the Son of Man* comes in his glory, and all the angels with him, then he will sit upon his glorious throne. 32All the nations* will be gathered in his presence, and he will separate the people as a shepherd separates the sheep from the goats. 33He will place the sheep at his right hand and the goats at his left.

34"Then the King will say to those on his right, 'Come, you who are blessed by my Father, inherit the Kingdom prepared for you from the creation of the world. 35For I was hungry, and you fed me. I was thirsty, and you gave me a drink. I was a stranger, and you invited me into your home. 36I was naked, and you gave me clothing. I was sick, and you cared for me. I was in prison, and you visited me.'

37"Then these righteous ones will reply, 'Lord, when did we ever see you hungry and feed you? Or thirsty and give you something to drink? 38Or a stranger and show you hospitality? Or naked and give you clothing? 39When did we ever see you sick or in prison and visit you?'

40"And the King will say, 'I tell you the truth, when you did it to one of the least of these my brothers and sisters,* you were doing it to me!'

41"Then the King will turn to those on the left and say, 'Away with you, you cursed ones, into the eternal fire prepared for the devil and his demons.* 42For I was hungry, and you didn't feed me. I was thirsty, and you didn't give me a drink. 43I was a stranger, and you didn't invite me into your home. I was naked, and you didn't give me clothing. I was sick and in prison, and you didn't visit me.'

44"Then they will reply, 'Lord, when did we ever see you hungry or thirsty or a stranger or naked or sick or in prison, and not help you?'

45"And he will answer, 'I tell you the truth, when you refused to help the least of these my brothers and sisters, you were refusing to help me.'

46"And they will go away into eternal punishment, but the righteous will go into eternal life."

SEPARATING GOOD FROM BAD 25:31-46

God will separate his obedient followers (the sheep) from pretenders and unbelievers (the goats). What we do for others demonstrates what we really think about Jesus' words to us—feed the hungry, give the homeless a place to stay, visit the sick. How well do your actions separate you from pretenders and unbelievers? ■

26

THE PLOT TO KILL JESUS

When Jesus had finished saying all these things, he said to his disciples, 2"As you know, Passover begins in two days, and the Son of Man* will be handed over to be crucified."

3At that same time the leading priests and elders were meeting at the residence of Caiaphas, the high priest, 4plotting how to capture Jesus secretly and kill him. 5"But not during the Passover celebration," they agreed, "or the people may riot."

JESUS ANOINTED AT BETHANY

6Meanwhile, Jesus was in Bethany at the home of Simon, a man who had previously had leprosy. 7While he was eating,* a woman came in with a beautiful alabaster jar of expensive perfume and poured it over his head.

8The disciples were indignant when they saw this. "What a waste!" they said. 9"It could have been sold for a high price and the money given to the poor."

10But Jesus, aware of this, replied, "Why criticize this woman for doing such a good thing to me? 11You will always have the poor among you, but you will not always have me. 12She has poured this perfume on me to prepare my body for burial. 13I tell you the truth, wherever the Good News is preached throughout the world, this woman's deed will be remembered and discussed."

JUDAS AGREES TO BETRAY JESUS

14Then Judas Iscariot, one of the twelve disciples, went to the leading priests 15and asked, "How much will you pay me to betray Jesus to you?" And they gave him thirty pieces of silver. 16From that time on, Judas began looking for an opportunity to betray Jesus.

THE LAST SUPPER

17On the first day of the Festival of Unleavened Bread, the disciples came to Jesus and asked, "Where do you want us to prepare the Passover meal for you?"

18"As you go into the city," he told them, "you will see a certain man. Tell him, 'The Teacher says: My time has come, and I will eat the Passover meal with my disciples at your house.'" 19So the disciples did as Jesus told them and prepared the Passover meal there.

20When it was evening, Jesus sat down at the table* with the twelve disciples.* 21While they were eating, he said, "I tell you the truth, one of you will betray me."

22Greatly distressed, each one asked in turn, "Am I the one, Lord?"

23He replied, "One of you who has just eaten from this bowl with me will betray me. 24For the Son of Man must die, as the Scriptures declared long ago. But how terrible it will be for the one who betrays him. It would be far better for that man if he had never been born!"

25Judas, the one who would betray him, also asked, "Rabbi, am I the one?"

And Jesus told him, "You have said it."

26As they were eating, Jesus took some bread and blessed it. Then he broke it in pieces and gave it to the disciples, saying, "Take this and eat it, for this is my body."

27And he took a cup of wine and gave thanks to God for it. He gave it to them and said, "Each of you drink from it, 28for this is my blood, which confirms the covenant* between God and his people. It is poured out as a sacrifice

25:31 "Son of Man" is a title Jesus used for himself. 25:32 Or *peoples.* 25:40 Greek *my brothers.* 25:41 Greek *his angels.* 26:2 "Son of Man" is a title Jesus used for himself. 26:7 Or *reclining.* 26:20a Or *Jesus reclined.* 26:20b Some manuscripts read *the Twelve.* 26:28 Some manuscripts read *the new covenant.*

to forgive the sins of many. 29 Mark my words—I will not drink wine again until the day I drink it new with you in my Father's Kingdom."

30 Then they sang a hymn and went out to the Mount of Olives.

JESUS PREDICTS PETER'S DENIAL

31 On the way, Jesus told them, "Tonight all of you will desert me. For the Scriptures say,

> 'God will strike* the Shepherd,
> and the sheep of the flock will be scattered.'

32 But after I have been raised from the dead, I will go ahead of you to Galilee and meet you there."

33 Peter declared, "Even if everyone else deserts you, I will never desert you."

34 Jesus replied, "I tell you the truth, Peter—this very night, before the rooster crows, you will deny three times that you even know me."

35 "No!" Peter insisted. "Even if I have to die with you, I will never deny you!" And all the other disciples vowed the same.

JESUS PRAYS IN GETHSEMANE

36 Then Jesus went with them to the olive grove called Gethsemane, and he said, "Sit here while I go over there to pray." 37 He took Peter and Zebedee's two sons, James and John, and he became anguished and distressed. 38 He told them, "My soul is crushed with grief to the point of death. Stay here and keep watch with me."

39 He went on a little farther and bowed with his face to the ground, praying, "My Father! If it is possible, let this cup of suffering be taken away from me. Yet I want your will to be done, not mine."

ALERT 26:40

Jesus used Peter's drowsiness to warn him about the kinds of temptation he would soon face (see 26:69-75). The way to overcome temptation is to be alert to it and pray. Because temptation strikes where we are most vulnerable, we can't resist it alone. Prayer is essential because God's strength can shore up our defenses and defeat Satan's power. (Check out 1 Cor 10:13; Eph 6:10-18.) Are you alert? ■

40 Then he returned to the disciples and found them asleep. He said to Peter, "Couldn't you watch with me even one hour? 41 Keep watch and pray, so that you will not give in to temptation. For the spirit is willing, but the body is weak!"

42 Then Jesus left them a second time and prayed, "My Father! If this cup cannot be taken away* unless I drink it, your will be done." 43 When he returned to them again, he found them sleeping, for they couldn't keep their eyes open.

44 So he went to pray a third time, saying the same things again. 45 Then he came to the disciples and said, "Go ahead and sleep. Have your rest. But look—the time has come. The Son of Man is betrayed into the hands of sinners. 46 Up, let's be going. Look, my betrayer is here!"

JESUS IS BETRAYED AND ARRESTED

47 And even as Jesus said this, Judas, one of the twelve disciples, arrived with a crowd of men armed with swords and clubs. They had been sent by the leading priests and elders of the people. 48 The traitor, Judas, had given them a prearranged signal: "You will know which one to arrest when I greet him with a kiss." 49 So Judas came straight to Jesus. "Greetings, Rabbi!" he exclaimed and gave him the kiss.

50 Jesus said, "My friend, go ahead and do what you have come for."

Then the others grabbed Jesus and arrested him. 51 But one of the men with Jesus pulled out his sword and struck the high priest's slave, slashing off his ear.

52 "Put away your sword," Jesus told him. "Those who use the sword will die by the sword. 53 Don't you realize that I could ask my Father for thousands* of angels to protect us, and he would send them instantly? 54 But if I did, how would the Scriptures be fulfilled that describe what must happen now?"

55 Then Jesus said to the crowd, "Am I some dangerous revolutionary, that you come with swords and clubs to arrest me? Why didn't you arrest me in the Temple? I was there teaching every day. 56 But this is all happening to fulfill the words of the prophets as recorded in the Scriptures." At that point, all the disciples deserted him and fled.

JESUS BEFORE THE COUNCIL

57 Then the people who had arrested Jesus led him to the home of Caiaphas, the high priest, where the teachers of religious law and the elders had gathered. 58 Meanwhile, Peter followed him at a distance and came to the high priest's courtyard. He went in and sat with the guards and waited to see how it would all end.

59 Inside, the leading priests and the entire high council* were trying to find witnesses who would lie about Jesus, so they could put him to death. 60 But even though they found many who agreed to give false witness, they could not use anyone's testimony. Finally, two men came forward 61 who declared, "This man said, 'I am able to destroy the Temple of God and rebuild it in three days.'"

62 Then the high priest stood up and said to Jesus, "Well, aren't you going to answer these charges? What do you have to say for yourself?" 63 But Jesus remained silent. Then the high priest said to him, "I demand in the name of the living God—tell us if you are the Messiah, the Son of God."

64 Jesus replied, "You have said it. And in the future you will see the Son of Man seated in the place of power at God's right hand* and coming on the clouds of heaven."*

26:31 Greek *I will strike.* Zech 13:7. **26:42** Greek *If this cannot pass.* **26:53** Greek *twelve legions.* **26:59** Greek *the Sanhedrin.* **26:64a** Greek *seated at the right hand of the power.* See Ps 110:1. **26:64b** See Dan 7:13.

65Then the high priest tore his clothing to show his horror and said, "Blasphemy! Why do we need other witnesses? You have all heard his blasphemy. 66What is your verdict?"

"Guilty!" they shouted. "He deserves to die!"

67Then they began to spit in Jesus' face and beat him with their fists. And some slapped him, 68jeering, "Prophesy to us, you Messiah! Who hit you that time?"

PETER DENIES JESUS

69Meanwhile, Peter was sitting outside in the courtyard. A servant girl came over and said to him, "You were one of those with Jesus the Galilean."

70But Peter denied it in front of everyone. "I don't know what you're talking about," he said.

71Later, out by the gate, another servant girl noticed him and said to those standing around, "This man was with Jesus of Nazareth.*"

72Again Peter denied it, this time with an oath. "I don't even know the man," he said.

73A little later some of the other bystanders came over to Peter and said, "You must be one of them; we can tell by your Galilean accent."

74Peter swore, "A curse on me if I'm lying—I don't know the man!" And immediately the rooster crowed.

75Suddenly, Jesus' words flashed through Peter's mind: "Before the rooster crows, you will deny three times that you even know me." And he went away, weeping bitterly.

DENIAL 26:69-75

When asked about the disciple with whom they most identify, most people would say Peter. And this is the passage that clinches it for them. As Jesus predicted (see 26:31-35), Peter denied him not once, but three times. Before his denial, Peter never could have imagined that he would do something so hurtful. Like Peter, have you ever denied that you could ever deny Jesus? Those of us who claim to be immune from denial are in denial. ■

27

JUDAS HANGS HIMSELF

Very early in the morning the leading priests and the elders met again to lay plans for putting Jesus to death. 2Then they bound him, led him away, and took him to Pilate, the Roman governor.

3When Judas, who had betrayed him, realized that Jesus had been condemned to die, he was filled with remorse. So he took the thirty pieces of silver back to the leading priests and the elders. 4"I have sinned," he declared, "for I have betrayed an innocent man."

"What do we care?" they retorted. "That's your problem."

5Then Judas threw the silver coins down in the Temple and went out and hanged himself.

6The leading priests picked up the coins. "It wouldn't be right to put this money in the Temple treasury," they said, "since it was payment for murder."* 7After some discussion they finally decided to buy the potter's field, and they made it into a cemetery for foreigners. 8That is why the field is still called the Field of Blood. 9This fulfilled the prophecy of Jeremiah that says,

"They took* the thirty pieces of silver—
the price at which he was valued by the people of Israel,
10 and purchased the potter's field,
as the LORD directed.*"

JESUS' TRIAL BEFORE PILATE

11Now Jesus was standing before Pilate, the Roman governor. "Are you the king of the Jews?" the governor asked him.

Jesus replied, "You have said it."

12But when the leading priests and the elders made their accusations against him, Jesus remained silent. 13"Don't you hear all these charges they are bringing against you?" Pilate demanded. 14But Jesus made no response to any of the charges, much to the governor's surprise.

15Now it was the governor's custom each year during the Passover celebration to release one prisoner to the crowd—anyone they wanted. 16This year there was a notorious prisoner, a man named Barabbas.* 17As the crowds gathered before Pilate's house that morning, he asked them, "Which one do you want me to release to you—Barabbas, or Jesus who is called the Messiah?" 18(He knew very well that the religious leaders had arrested Jesus out of envy.)

19Just then, as Pilate was sitting on the judgment seat, his wife sent him this message: "Leave that innocent man alone. I suffered through a terrible nightmare about him last night."

20Meanwhile, the leading priests and the elders persuaded the crowd to ask for Barabbas to be released and for Jesus to be put to death. 21So the governor asked again, "Which of these two do you want me to release to you?"

The crowd shouted back, "Barabbas!"

22Pilate responded, "Then what should I do with Jesus who is called the Messiah?"

They shouted back, "Crucify him!"

23"Why?" Pilate demanded. "What crime has he committed?"

But the mob roared even louder, "Crucify him!"

24Pilate saw that he wasn't getting anywhere and that a riot was developing. So he sent for a bowl of water and washed his hands before the crowd, saying, "I am innocent of this man's blood. The responsibility is yours!"

25And all the people yelled back, "We will take responsibility for his death—we and our children!"*

26So Pilate released Barabbas to them. He ordered Jesus flogged with a lead-tipped whip, then turned him over to the Roman soldiers to be crucified.

26:71 Or *Jesus the Nazarene*. 27:6 Greek *since it is the price for blood*. 27:9 Or *I took*. 27:9-10 Greek *as the LORD directed me*. Zech 11:12-13; Jer 32:6-9. 27:16 Some manuscripts read *Jesus Barabbas;* also in 27:17. 27:25 Greek *"His blood be on us and on our children."*

SEPARATION 27:46

Jesus' expression of agony is a quote of the first line of Psalm 22. Because Jesus died for every wrongdoing ever committed, he experienced what no one has yet experienced—complete separation from God. *This* was what Jesus dreaded as he prayed in the garden (26:39). The physical agony was horrible, but even worse was the period of spiritual separation from God. Although we may feel far away from God, we still have access to him. Jesus suffered so that we would never have to experience eternal separation from God. ■

THE SOLDIERS MOCK JESUS

27 Some of the governor's soldiers took Jesus into their headquarters* and called out the entire regiment. 28 They stripped him and put a scarlet robe on him. 29 They wove thorn branches into a crown and put it on his head, and they placed a reed stick in his right hand as a scepter. Then they knelt before him in mockery and taunted, "Hail! King of the Jews!" 30 And they spit on him and grabbed the stick and struck him on the head with it. 31 When they were finally tired of mocking him, they took off the robe and put his own clothes on him again. Then they led him away to be crucified.

THE CRUCIFIXION

32 Along the way, they came across a man named Simon, who was from Cyrene,* and the soldiers forced him to carry Jesus' cross. 33 And they went out to a place called Golgotha (which means "Place of the Skull"). 34 The soldiers gave him wine mixed with bitter gall, but when he had tasted it, he refused to drink it.

35 After they had nailed him to the cross, the soldiers gambled for his clothes by throwing dice.* 36 Then they sat around and kept guard as he hung there. 37 A sign was fastened to the cross above Jesus' head, announcing the charge against him. It read: "This is Jesus, the King of the Jews." 38 Two revolutionaries* were crucified with him, one on his right and one on his left.

39 The people passing by shouted abuse, shaking their heads in mockery. 40 "Look at you now!" they yelled at him. "You said you were going to destroy the Temple and rebuild it in three days. Well then, if you are the Son of God, save yourself and come down from the cross!"

41 The leading priests, the teachers of religious law, and the elders also mocked Jesus. 42 "He saved others," they scoffed, "but he can't save himself! So he is the King of Israel, is he? Let him come down from the cross right now, and we will believe in him! 43 He trusted God, so let God rescue him now if he wants him! For he said, 'I am the Son of God.'" 44 Even the revolutionaries who were crucified with him ridiculed him in the same way.

THE DEATH OF JESUS

45 At noon, darkness fell across the whole land until three o'clock. 46 At about three o'clock, Jesus called out with a loud voice, *"Eli, Eli,* lema sabachthani?"* which means "My God, my God, why have you abandoned me?"*

47 Some of the bystanders misunderstood and thought he was calling for the prophet Elijah. 48 One of them ran and filled a sponge with sour wine, holding it up to him on a reed stick so he could drink. 49 But the rest said, "Wait! Let's see whether Elijah comes to save him."*

50 Then Jesus shouted out again, and he released his spirit. 51 At that moment the curtain in the sanctuary of the Temple was torn in two, from top to bottom. The earth shook, rocks split apart, 52 and tombs opened. The bodies of many godly men and women who had died were raised from the dead. 53 They left the cemetery after Jesus' resurrection, went into the holy city of Jerusalem, and appeared to many people.

54 The Roman officer* and the other soldiers at the crucifixion were terrified by the earthquake and all that had happened. They said, "This man truly was the Son of God!"

55 And many women who had come from Galilee with Jesus to care for him were watching from a distance. 56 Among them were Mary Magdalene, Mary (the mother of James and Joseph), and the mother of James and John, the sons of Zebedee.

THE BURIAL OF JESUS

57 As evening approached, Joseph, a rich man from Arimathea who had become a follower of Jesus, 58 went to Pilate and asked for Jesus' body. And Pilate issued an order to release it to him. 59 Joseph took the body and wrapped it in a long sheet of clean linen cloth. 60 He placed it in his own new tomb, which had been carved out of the rock. Then he rolled a great stone across the entrance and left. 61 Both Mary Magdalene and the other Mary were sitting across from the tomb and watching.

THE GUARD AT THE TOMB

62 The next day, on the Sabbath,* the leading priests and Pharisees went to see Pilate. 63 They told him, "Sir, we remember what that deceiver once said while he was still alive: 'After three days I will rise from the dead.' 64 So we request that you seal the tomb until the third day. This will prevent his disciples from coming and stealing his body and then telling everyone he was raised from the dead! If that happens, we'll be worse off than we were at first."

65 Pilate replied, "Take guards and secure it the best you can." 66 So they sealed the tomb and posted guards to protect it.

27:27 Or *into the Praetorium.* 27:32 *Cyrene* was a city in northern Africa. 27:35 Greek *by casting lots.* A few late manuscripts add *This fulfilled the word of the prophet: "They divided my garments among themselves and cast lots for my robe."* See Ps 22:18. 27:38 Or *criminals;* also in 27:44. 27:46a Some manuscripts read *Eloi, Eloi.* 27:46b Ps 22:1. 27:49 Some manuscripts add *And another took a spear and pierced his side, and out flowed water and blood.* Compare John 19:34. 27:54 Greek *The centurion.* 27:62 Or *On the next day, which is after the Preparation.*

28 THE RESURRECTION

Early on Sunday morning,* as the new day was dawning,
Mary Magdalene and the other Mary went out to visit the
tomb.

CHOICES 28:1-15

Jesus' resurrection caused a great stir in Jerusalem. A group of women moved quickly through the streets, looking for the disciples to tell them the amazing news that Jesus was alive. At the same time, a group of religious leaders tried to cover up the Resurrection. The same two choices exist today: to believe that Jesus rose from the dead, or to be closed to the truth—denying it, ignoring it, or trying to explain it away. What's your choice? ■

2Suddenly there was a great earthquake! For an angel
of the Lord came down from heaven, rolled aside the
stone, and sat on it. 3His face shone like lightning, and his
clothing was as white as snow. 4The guards shook with
fear when they saw him, and they fell into a dead faint.

5Then the angel spoke to the women. "Don't be afraid!"
he said. "I know you are looking for Jesus, who was crucified. 6He isn't here! He is risen from the dead, just as he
said would happen. Come, see where his body was lying.
7And now, go quickly and tell his disciples that he has
risen from the dead, and he is going ahead of you to Galilee. You will see him there. Remember what I have told
you."

8The women ran quickly from the tomb. They were
very frightened but also filled with great joy, and they
rushed to give the disciples the angel's message. 9And as
they went, Jesus met them and greeted them. And they
ran to him, grasped his feet, and worshiped him. 10Then
Jesus said to them, "Don't be afraid! Go tell my brothers to
leave for Galilee, and they will see me there."

THE REPORT OF THE GUARD

11As the women were on their way, some of the guards
went into the city and told the leading priests what had
happened. 12A meeting with the elders was called, and
they decided to give the soldiers a large bribe. 13They told
the soldiers, "You must say, 'Jesus' disciples came during
the night while we were sleeping, and they stole his body.'
14If the governor hears about it, we'll stand up for you so
you won't get in trouble." 15So the guards accepted the
bribe and said what they were told to say. Their story
spread widely among the Jews, and they still tell it today.

COMMISSIONED 28:18-20

Jesus left the disciples with these last words of instruction: They were to make more disciples. Best of all, he promised to be with them always. Whereas in previous missions Jesus had sent his disciples only to the Jews (10:5-6), their mission from now on would be worldwide.

The disciples' mission also is ours. We are to go—whether it is next door or to another country—and make disciples. Making disciples is not an option—it is a command to all who call Jesus Lord. As we obey, we have comfort in the knowledge that Jesus is always with us. ■

THE GREAT COMMISSION

16Then the eleven disciples left for Galilee, going to the
mountain where Jesus had told them to go. 17When they
saw him, they worshiped him—but some of them
doubted!

18Jesus came and told his disciples, "I have been given
all authority in heaven and on earth. 19Therefore, go and
make disciples of all the nations,* baptizing them in the
name of the Father and the Son and the Holy Spirit.
20Teach these new disciples to obey all the commands I
have given you. And be sure of this: I am with you always,
even to the end of the age."

28:1 Greek *After the Sabbath, on the first day of the week.* **28:19** Or *all peoples.*

MARK

HAS THIS EVER happened to you?

Friends invite you to a critically acclaimed movie.

"It's supposed to be great," they insist. "You'll like it."

So you go—with high expectations. Only the movie isn't great. As far as excitement goes, this particular film ranks right up there with reading the phone book.

You keep thinking, *This has got to get better. Surely there's a car chase, special effects, or some sort of surprise plot twist.* But nothing happens. The most adventurous moment of the film comes at the end when two of the actors go to a fancy French restaurant and eat snails. It's gross, but at least they're finally doing something.

When you leave the theater you vow, "Never again!"

Guess what? You don't have to spend your time with phone-book action! Instead, you can read one of the most exciting books in existence! This book!

You name it, and the Gospel of Mark has it—demons, death, and amazing special effects (miracles), surrounded by an atmosphere of intrigue, jealousy, controversy, and murder. This book is an action-packed biography of the most influential person in the history of the world.

Go for it! And when you're done, you will vow, "Never again . . . never again will I think of the Bible as boring!"

mark

timeline

37 B.C.
Herod the Great begins to rule

6/5 B.C.
Jesus is born

5/4 B.C.
Escape to Egypt

4 B.C.
Herod the Great dies

4/3 B.C.
Return to Nazareth

A.D. 6/7
Jesus visits Temple as a boy

14
Tiberius Caesar becomes emperor

26
John's ministry begins

26/27
Jesus begins his ministry

28
Jesus chooses 12 disciples

29
Jesus feeds 5,000

30
Jesus is crucified, rises again, and ascends

stats

PURPOSE: To present Jesus' person, work, and teachings

AUTHOR: John Mark. He accompanied Paul on his first missionary journey (Acts 12:25).

TO WHOM WRITTEN: The Christians in Rome, where Mark wrote the Gospel, and believers everywhere

DATE WRITTEN: Between A.D. 55 and 65

SETTING: The Roman Empire, with its common language and excellent transportation and communication systems, was ripe to hear Jesus' message.

KEY PEOPLE: Jesus, the twelve disciples, Pilate, the Jewish religious leaders

KEY PLACES: Capernaum, Nazareth, Caesarea Philippi, Jericho, Bethany, Mount of Olives, Jerusalem, Golgotha

SPECIAL FEATURES: Mark was the first Gospel written. The other Gospels quote all but 31 verses of Mark. Mark records more miracles than does any other Gospel.

KEY points

MIRACLES
Mark records more of Jesus' miracles than his sermons. Jesus was clearly a man of power and action, not just words. His example encourages us to be people of faith and action.

SPREADING THE GOSPEL
Jesus directed his public ministry to the Jews first. But as he prepared to the leave the Earth, he commissioned the disciples to preach the Gospel everywhere. Jesus' message of faith and forgiveness is for the whole world—not just a particular church, neighborhood, or nation. Like the disciples, we are called to take the message everywhere.

RESURRECTION
When Jesus rose from the dead, he proved that he was God, that he could forgive sin, and that he has the power to change a life. By trusting in Christ for forgiveness, we can begin a new life with him.

KEY PLACES IN MARK

The broken lines (—·—) indicate modern boundaries.

Of the four Gospels, Mark's narrative is the most chronological—most of the stories are positioned in the order they actually occurred. Though the shortest of the four, the Gospel of Mark contains the most events; it is action packed. Most of this action centers in Galilee, where Jesus began his ministry. Capernaum served as his base of operation (1:21; 2:1; 9:33), from which he would go out to cities like Bethsaida—where he healed a blind man (8:22-26); Gennesaret—where he performed many healings (6:53-56); Tyre and Sidon (to the far north)—where he cured many, cast out demons, and met the Syro-Phoenician woman (7:24-30); and Caesarea Philippi—where Peter declared him to be the Messiah (8:27-29). After his ministry in Galilee and the surrounding regions, Jesus headed south for Jerusalem (10:1). Before going there, Jesus told his disciples three times that he would be crucified there and then come back to life (8:31; 9:31; 10:33-34).

1

JOHN THE BAPTIST PREPARES THE WAY

This is the Good News about Jesus the Messiah, the Son of
God.* It began 2just as the prophet Isaiah had written:

"Look, I am sending my messenger ahead
of you,
and he will prepare your way.*
3 He is a voice shouting in the wilderness,
'Prepare the way for the LORD's coming!
Clear the road for him!'*"

4This messenger was John the Baptist. He was in the wilderness and preached that people should be baptized to
show that they had repented of their sins and turned to
God to be forgiven. 5All of Judea, including all the people
of Jerusalem, went out to see and hear John. And when
they confessed their sins, he baptized them in the Jordan
River. 6His clothes were woven from coarse camel hair,
and he wore a leather belt around his waist. For food he
ate locusts and wild honey.
7John announced: "Someone is coming soon who is
greater than I am—so much greater that I'm not even

1:1 Some manuscripts do not include *the Son of God*. **1:2** Mal 3:1. **1:3** Isa 40:3 (Greek version).

worthy to stoop down like a slave and untie the straps of his sandals. 8I baptize you with* water, but he will baptize you with the Holy Spirit!"

THE BAPTISM AND TEMPTATION OF JESUS

9One day Jesus came from Nazareth in Galilee, and John baptized him in the Jordan River. 10As Jesus came up out of the water, he saw the heavens splitting apart and the Holy Spirit descending on him* like a dove. 11And a voice from heaven said, "You are my dearly loved Son, and you bring me great joy."

12The Spirit then compelled Jesus to go into the wilderness, 13where he was tempted by Satan for forty days. He was out among the wild animals, and angels took care of him.

14Later on, after John was arrested, Jesus went into Galilee, where he preached God's Good News.* 15"The time promised by God has come at last!" he announced. "The Kingdom of God is near! Repent of your sins and believe the Good News!"

THE FIRST DISCIPLES

16One day as Jesus was walking along the shore of the Sea of Galilee, he saw Simon* and his brother Andrew throwing a net into the water, for they fished for a living. 17Jesus called out to them, "Come, follow me, and I will show you how to fish for people!" 18And they left their nets at once and followed him.

19A little farther up the shore Jesus saw Zebedee's sons, James and John, in a boat repairing their nets. 20He called them at once, and they also followed him, leaving their father, Zebedee, in the boat with the hired men.

JESUS CASTS OUT AN EVIL SPIRIT

21Jesus and his companions went to the town of Capernaum. When the Sabbath day came, he went into the synagogue and began to teach. 22The people were amazed at his teaching, for he taught with real authority—quite unlike the teachers of religious law.

23Suddenly, a man in the synagogue who was possessed by an evil* spirit began shouting, 24"Why are you interfering with us, Jesus of Nazareth? Have you come to destroy us? I know who you are—the Holy One sent from God!"

25Jesus cut him short. "Be quiet! Come out of the man," he ordered. 26At that, the evil spirit screamed, threw the man into a convulsion, and then came out of him.

27Amazement gripped the audience, and they began to discuss what had happened. "What sort of new teaching is this?" they asked excitedly. "It has such authority! Even evil spirits obey his orders!" 28The news about Jesus spread quickly throughout the entire region of Galilee.

JESUS HEALS MANY PEOPLE

29After Jesus left the synagogue with James and John, they went to Simon and Andrew's home. 30Now Simon's mother-in-law was sick in bed with a high fever. They told Jesus about her right away. 31So he went to her bedside, took her by the hand, and helped her sit up. Then the fever left her, and she prepared a meal for them.

32That evening after sunset, many sick and demon-possessed people were brought to Jesus. 33The whole town gathered at the door to watch. 34So Jesus healed many people who were sick with various diseases, and he cast out many demons. But because the demons knew who he was, he did not allow them to speak.

JESUS PREACHES IN GALILEE

35Before daybreak the next morning, Jesus got up and went out to an isolated place to pray. 36Later Simon and the others went out to find him. 37When they found him, they said, "Everyone is looking for you."

38But Jesus replied, "We must go on to other towns as well, and I will preach to them, too. That is why I came." 39So he traveled throughout the region of Galilee, preaching in the synagogues and casting out demons.

THE PRIORITY OF PRAYER 1:35

Jesus started his day with prayer. He considered his communication with his Father a necessary part of his day—one that he couldn't do without. How do you start your day? What are some activities you can't do without each day? We usually find the time to do whatever we really want to do. Is communicating with God a priority for you? ■

JESUS HEALS A MAN WITH LEPROSY

40A man with leprosy came and knelt in front of Jesus, begging to be healed. "If you are willing, you can heal me and make me clean," he said.

41Moved with compassion,* Jesus reached out and touched him. "I am willing," he said. "Be healed!" 42Instantly the leprosy disappeared, and the man was healed. 43Then Jesus sent him on his way with a stern warning: 44"Don't tell anyone about this. Instead, go to the priest and let him examine you. Take along the offering required in the law of Moses for those who have been healed of leprosy.* This will be a public testimony that you have been cleansed."

45But the man went and spread the word, proclaiming to everyone what had happened. As a result, large crowds soon surrounded Jesus, and he couldn't publicly enter a town anywhere. He had to stay out in the secluded places, but people from everywhere kept coming to him.

2

JESUS HEALS A PARALYZED MAN

When Jesus returned to Capernaum several days later, the news spread quickly that he was back home. 2Soon the house where he was staying was so packed with visitors that there was no more room, even outside the door. While he was preaching God's word to them, 3four men

1:8 Or *in;* also in 1:8b. 1:10 Or *toward him,* or *into him.* 1:14 Some manuscripts read *the Good News of the Kingdom of God.* 1:16 *Simon* is called "Peter" in 3:16 and thereafter. 1:23 Greek *unclean;* also in 1:26, 27. 1:41 Some manuscripts read *Moved with anger.* 1:44 See Lev 14:2-32.

arrived carrying a paralyzed man on a mat. [4]They couldn't bring him to Jesus because of the crowd, so they dug a hole through the roof above his head. Then they lowered the man on his mat, right down in front of Jesus. [5]Seeing their faith, Jesus said to the paralyzed man, "My child, your sins are forgiven."

[6]But some of the teachers of religious law who were sitting there thought to themselves, [7]"What is he saying? This is blasphemy! Only God can forgive sins!"

[8]Jesus knew immediately what they were thinking, so he asked them, "Why do you question this in your hearts? [9]Is it easier to say to the paralyzed man 'Your sins are forgiven,' or 'Stand up, pick up your mat, and walk'? [10]So I will prove to you that the Son of Man* has the authority on earth to forgive sins." Then Jesus turned to the paralyzed man and said, [11]"Stand up, pick up your mat, and go home!"

I partied a lot in clubs and stuff before I became a Christian. Should I give that up? Why or why not?

Let's talk about motive for a minute. Some people party simply to get drunk, take drugs, and pick up the opposite sex. Others party to be seen with cool people. Is that your motive? Maybe being with certain people made you feel accepted and even popular. But what if their acceptance comes with a price (for example, take a little X [ecstasy], have a few drinks)? Motive is key.

Now, let's talk about Jesus for a second. Jesus went to parties, and was, in fact, the life of the party! But his motives were entirely different from the ones described above. He went to show people that he accepted them, to communicate truth about the character of God, and to celebrate life (see Mark 2:13-17; John 2:1-11).

Should you do the same? Perhaps, but here are a few questions to consider:

- Have you grown sufficiently in your faith that you will not be tempted when pressured to drink (or whatever)?
- Do you know someone who will go with you, so you can encourage each other to stay clean?
- Are you going as a light or as a hammer? That is, do you genuinely want to be a light in darkness (Matt 5:14-15), or do you want to pound on people to feel good about your "moral" lifestyle?
- Would you cause someone you've been talking to about Jesus to stumble (see 1 Cor 10:32-33) in the assumption that you probably were pressured to drink simply because you were present?
- Would you have to lie to someone (your parents or a guardian) about what'll happen at the party in order to go? If so, the advice of Romans 13:13 is for you. Need more advice? Check out Galatians 5:19-21.

[12]And the man jumped up, grabbed his mat, and walked out through the stunned onlookers. They were all amazed and praised God, exclaiming, "We've never seen anything like this before!"

SOMEONE YOU SHOULD KNOW 2:14-17

On the day that Levi (also known as Matthew—see Matt 9:9-13) met Jesus, he held a meeting at his house to introduce his friends to Jesus. His excitement and gratitude toward Jesus were obvious. He didn't worry about whether his friends would laugh at him or reject him because of his new faith in Jesus. He just wanted them to know Jesus. Is that what you want? How eager are you to introduce others to Jesus? ■

JESUS CALLS LEVI (MATTHEW)

[13]Then Jesus went out to the lakeshore again and taught the crowds that were coming to him. [14]As he walked along, he saw Levi son of Alphaeus sitting at his tax collector's booth. "Follow me and be my disciple," Jesus said to him. So Levi got up and followed him.

[15]Later, Levi invited Jesus and his disciples to his home as dinner guests, along with many tax collectors and other disreputable sinners. (There were many people of this kind among Jesus' followers.) [16]But when the teachers of religious law who were Pharisees* saw him eating with tax collectors and other sinners, they asked his disciples, "Why does he eat with such scum?*"

[17]When Jesus heard this, he told them, "Healthy people don't need a doctor—sick people do. I have come to call not those who think they are righteous, but those who know they are sinners."

A DISCUSSION ABOUT FASTING

[18]Once when John's disciples and the Pharisees were fasting, some people came to Jesus and asked, "Why don't your disciples fast like John's disciples and the Pharisees do?"

[19]Jesus replied, "Do wedding guests fast while celebrating with the groom? Of course not. They can't fast while the groom is with them. [20]But someday the groom will be taken away from them, and then they will fast.

[21]"Besides, who would patch old clothing with new cloth? For the new patch would shrink and rip away from the old cloth, leaving an even bigger tear than before.

[22]"And no one puts new wine into old wineskins. For the wine would burst the wineskins, and the wine and the skins would both be lost. New wine calls for new wineskins."

A DISCUSSION ABOUT THE SABBATH

[23]One Sabbath day as Jesus was walking through some grainfields, his disciples began breaking off heads of grain to eat. [24]But the Pharisees said to Jesus, "Look, why are they breaking the law by harvesting grain on the Sabbath?"

2:10 "Son of Man" is a title Jesus used for himself. 2:16a Greek *the scribes of the Pharisees.* 2:16b Greek *with tax collectors and sinners?*

25Jesus said to them, "Haven't you ever read in the
Scriptures what David did when he and his companions
were hungry? 26He went into the house of God (during
the days when Abiathar was high priest) and broke the
law by eating the sacred loaves of bread that only the
priests are allowed to eat. He also gave some to his companions."
27Then Jesus said to them, "The Sabbath was made to
meet the needs of people, and not people to meet the requirements of the Sabbath. 28So the Son of Man is Lord,
even over the Sabbath!"

3 JESUS HEALS ON THE SABBATH

Jesus went into the synagogue again and noticed a man
with a deformed hand. 2Since it was the Sabbath, Jesus'
enemies watched him closely. If he healed the man's
hand, they planned to accuse him of working on the
Sabbath.
3Jesus said to the man with the deformed hand, "Come
and stand in front of everyone." 4Then he turned to his
critics and asked, "Does the law permit good deeds on the
Sabbath, or is it a day for doing evil? Is this a day to save
life or to destroy it?" But they wouldn't answer him.
5He looked around at them angrily and was deeply
saddened by their hard hearts. Then he said to the man,
"Hold out your hand." So the man held out his hand, and
it was restored! 6At once the Pharisees went away and
met with the supporters of Herod to plot how to kill
Jesus.

USEFUL ANGER 3:1-6

Jesus was angry about the Pharisees' callous attitude toward a man with a crippled hand. What makes you angry? Anger itself isn't wrong. But too often anger is expressed in selfish and harmful ways. By contrast, Jesus expressed his anger by correcting a problem—healing the man's hand. How will you use your anger to find constructive solutions to a problem? ■

CROWDS FOLLOW JESUS

7Jesus went out to the lake with his disciples, and a large
crowd followed him. They came from all over Galilee, Judea, 8Jerusalem, Idumea, from east of the Jordan River,
and even from as far north as Tyre and Sidon. The news
about his miracles had spread far and wide, and vast
numbers of people came to see him.
9Jesus instructed his disciples to have a boat ready so
the crowd would not crush him. 10He had healed many
people that day, so all the sick people eagerly pushed forward to touch him. 11And whenever those possessed by
evil* spirits caught sight of him, the spirits would throw
them to the ground in front of him shrieking, "You are
the Son of God!" 12But Jesus sternly commanded the spirits not to reveal who he was.

JESUS CHOOSES THE TWELVE APOSTLES

13Afterward Jesus went up on a mountain and called out
the ones he wanted to go with him. And they came to
him. 14Then he appointed twelve of them and called
them his apostles.* They were to accompany him, and he
would send them out to preach, 15giving them authority
to cast out demons. 16These are the twelve he chose:

Simon (whom he named Peter),
17 James and John (the sons of Zebedee, but Jesus
nicknamed them "Sons of Thunder"*),
18 Andrew,
Philip,
Bartholomew,
Matthew,
Thomas,
James (son of Alphaeus),
Thaddaeus,
Simon (the zealot*),
19 Judas Iscariot (who later betrayed him).

JESUS AND THE PRINCE OF DEMONS

20One time Jesus entered a house, and the crowds began
to gather again. Soon he and his disciples couldn't even
find time to eat. 21When his family heard what was happening, they tried to take him away. "He's out of his
mind," they said.
22But the teachers of religious law who had arrived
from Jerusalem said, "He's possessed by Satan,* the
prince of demons. That's where he gets the power to cast
out demons."
23Jesus called them over and responded with an illustration. "How can Satan cast out Satan?" he asked. 24"A
kingdom divided by civil war will collapse. 25Similarly, a
family splintered by feuding will fall apart. 26And if Satan
is divided and fights against himself, how can he stand?
He would never survive. 27Let me illustrate this further.
Who is powerful enough to enter the house of a strong
man like Satan and plunder his goods? Only someone
even stronger—someone who could tie him up and then
plunder his house.
28"I tell you the truth, all sin and blasphemy can be forgiven, 29but anyone who blasphemes the Holy Spirit will
never be forgiven. This is a sin with eternal consequences." 30He told them this because they were saying,
"He's possessed by an evil spirit."

THE TRUE FAMILY OF JESUS

31Then Jesus' mother and brothers came to see him. They
stood outside and sent word for him to come out and talk
with them. 32There was a crowd sitting around Jesus, and
someone said, "Your mother and your brothers* are outside asking for you."
33Jesus replied, "Who is my mother? Who are my
brothers?" 34Then he looked at those around him and
said, "Look, these are my mother and brothers. 35Anyone
who does God's will is my brother and sister and mother."

3:11 Greek *unclean;* also in 3:30. 3:14 Some manuscripts do not include *and called them his apostles.* 3:17 Greek *whom he named Boanerges, which means Sons of Thunder.* 3:18 Greek *the Cananean,* an Aramaic term for Jewish nationalists. 3:22 Greek *Beelzeboul;* other manuscripts read *Beezeboul;* Latin version reads *Beelzebub.* 3:32 Some manuscripts add *and sisters.*

4 PARABLE OF THE FARMER SCATTERING SEED

Once again Jesus began teaching by the lakeshore. A
very large crowd soon gathered around him, so he
got into a boat. Then he sat in the boat while all the
people remained on the shore. 2He taught them by
telling many stories in the form of parables, such as
this one:
3"Listen! A farmer went out to plant some seed. 4As he
scattered it across his field, some of the seed fell on a
footpath, and the birds came and ate it. 5Other seed fell
on shallow soil with underlying rock. The seed sprouted
quickly because the soil was shallow. 6But the plant soon
wilted under the hot sun, and since it didn't have deep
roots, it died. 7Other seed fell among thorns that grew up
and choked out the tender plants so they produced no
grain. 8Still other seeds fell on fertile soil, and they
sprouted, grew, and produced a crop that was thirty,
sixty, and even a hundred times as much as had been
planted!" 9Then he said, "Anyone with ears to hear
should listen and understand."
10Later, when Jesus was alone with the twelve disciples
and with the others who were gathered around, they
asked him what the parables meant.

READY OR NOT? 4:1-12

The disciples didn't understand Jesus' parable. Some people don't understand God's truth because they're not ready for it. God reveals truth to people who will do something about it.

Many people hesitate to tell others about God, because they think they have to make them believe. But only God can help a person to understand truth and act on it. Is there someone you've been meaning to talk to about God? Why not start with prayer first? You might ask the Holy Spirit to help that person be ready to receive the truth. ■

JUDAS ISCARIOT

Suppose you knew ahead of time that a friend would later betray you. Would you still let him or her hang out with you?

Jesus would.

It's easy to forget that Jesus chose Judas to be his disciple. (See Mark 3:19.) We may also miss the point that while Judas betrayed Jesus, all of the disciples abandoned him (Mark 14:50).

The disciples, including Judas, all had the wrong idea of Jesus' mission on earth. They expected Jesus to rescue them from Roman tyranny. But when he kept talking about dying, they probably all felt a mixture of anger, fear, and disappointment.

We don't know exactly why Judas betrayed Jesus. But we can see that Judas let his own desires become so important that Satan was able to control him.

He tried to undo the evil he had done by returning the money to the priests (Matt 27:3-5), but it was too late. How sad that Judas ended his life in despair without ever experiencing the forgiveness God could have supplied even to him.

In betraying Jesus, Judas made the greatest mistake in history. But just the fact that Jesus knew Judas would betray him doesn't mean that Judas was a puppet of God's will. Judas made the choice. God knew what that choice would be and made it part of the plan.

Judas's life reminds us to think deeply about our commitment to God. Are we serious about following God or just faking it? We can choose disobedience and death, or we can choose repentance, forgiveness, hope, and eternal life. Judas's betrayal sent Jesus to the cross to guarantee that second choice, our only chance. Will we accept Christ's free gift, or—like Judas—betray him?

UPS:
- Chosen as one of the 12 disciples; the only non-Galilean
- Kept the money bag for the expenses of the group
- Recognized the evil in his betrayal of Jesus

DOWNS:
- Was greedy (John 12:6)
- Betrayed Jesus
- Committed suicide instead of seeking forgiveness

STATS:
- Where: probably from the town of Kerioth
- Occupation: disciple of Jesus
- Relatives: Simon (father)
- Contemporaries: Jesus, Pilate, Herod, the other 11 disciples

BOTTOM LINE:

Evil plans and motives leave us open to being used by Satan for even greater evil.

The consequences of evil are so devastating that even small lies and little wrongdoings have serious results.

God's plan and purposes are worked out even in the worst possible events.

Judas's story is told in the Gospels. He also is mentioned in Acts 1:17-19.

JUDAS ISCARIOT

11He replied, "You are permitted to understand the secret* of the Kingdom of God. But I use parables for everything I say to outsiders, 12so that the Scriptures might be
fulfilled:

'When they see what I do,
they will learn nothing.
When they hear what I say,
they will not understand.
Otherwise, they will turn to me
and be forgiven.'*"

13Then Jesus said to them, "If you can't understand the
meaning of this parable, how will you understand all the
other parables? 14The farmer plants seed by taking God's
word to others. 15The seed that fell on the footpath represents those who hear the message, only to have Satan
come at once and take it away. 16The seed on the rocky
soil represents those who hear the message and immediately receive it with joy. 17But since they don't have deep
roots, they don't last long. They fall away as soon as they
have problems or are persecuted for believing God's
word. 18The seed that fell among the thorns represents
others who hear God's word, 19but all too quickly the
message is crowded out by the worries of this life, the
lure of wealth, and the desire for other things, so no fruit
is produced. 20And the seed that fell on good soil represents those who hear and accept God's word and produce
a harvest of thirty, sixty, or even a hundred times as much
as had been planted!"

RESPONSES 4:14-20

The four soils represent four different ways people respond to God's Word. Usually we think Jesus was talking about four different kinds of people, but he may also have been talking about (1) different times or phases in a person's life, or (2) how we willingly receive God's message in some areas of our life and resist it in others. For example, you may be open to God where your future is concerned, but closed about the way you spend your money. What will you do to make every area of your life like the "good soil" mentioned in this passage? ■

PARABLE OF THE LAMP

21Then Jesus asked them, "Would anyone light a lamp
and then put it under a basket or under a bed? Of course
not! A lamp is placed on a stand, where its light will shine.
22For everything that is hidden will eventually be brought
into the open, and every secret will be brought to light.
23Anyone with ears to hear should listen and understand."

24Then he added, "Pay close attention to what you hear.
The closer you listen, the more understanding you will be
given*—and you will receive even more. 25To those who
listen to my teaching, more understanding will be given.
But for those who are not listening, even what little
understanding they have will be taken away from them."

PARABLE OF THE GROWING SEED

26Jesus also said, "The Kingdom of God is like a farmer
who scatters seed on the ground. 27Night and day, while
he's asleep or awake, the seed sprouts and grows, but he
does not understand how it happens. 28The earth produces the crops on its own. First a leaf blade pushes
through, then the heads of wheat are formed, and finally
the grain ripens. 29And as soon as the grain is ready, the
farmer comes and harvests it with a sickle, for the harvest
time has come."

PARABLE OF THE MUSTARD SEED

30Jesus said, "How can I describe the Kingdom of God?
What story should I use to illustrate it? 31It is like a mustard
seed planted in the ground. It is the smallest of all seeds,
32but it becomes the largest of all garden plants; it grows
long branches, and birds can make nests in its shade."

33Jesus used many similar stories and illustrations to
teach the people as much as they could understand. 34In
fact, in his public ministry he never taught without using
parables; but afterward, when he was alone with his disciples, he explained everything to them.

JESUS CALMS THE STORM

35As evening came, Jesus said to his disciples, "Let's cross
to the other side of the lake." 36So they took Jesus in the
boat and started out, leaving the crowds behind (although other boats followed). 37But soon a fierce storm
came up. High waves were breaking into the boat, and it
began to fill with water.

38Jesus was sleeping at the back of the boat with his
head on a cushion. The disciples woke him up, shouting,
"Teacher, don't you care that we're going to drown?"

39When Jesus woke up, he rebuked the wind and said
to the waves, "Silence! Be still!" Suddenly the wind
stopped, and there was a great calm. 40Then he asked
them, "Why are you afraid? Do you still have no faith?"

41The disciples were absolutely terrified. "Who is this
man?" they asked each other. "Even the wind and waves
obey him!"

5

JESUS HEALS A DEMON-POSSESSED MAN

So they arrived at the other side of the lake, in the region
of the Gerasenes.* 2When Jesus climbed out of the boat, a
man possessed by an evil* spirit came out from a cemetery to meet him. 3This man lived among the burial caves
and could no longer be restrained, even with a chain.
4Whenever he was put into chains and shackles—as he often
was—he snapped the chains from his wrists and smashed
the shackles. No one was strong enough to subdue him.
5Day and night he wandered among the burial caves and in
the hills, howling and cutting himself with sharp stones.

6When Jesus was still some distance away, the man

4:11 Greek *mystery*. 4:12 Isa 6:9-10 (Greek version). 4:24 Or *The measure you give will be the measure you get back.* 5:1 Other manuscripts read *Gadarenes;* still others read *Gergesenes.* See Matt 8:28; Luke 8:26. 5:2 Greek *unclean;* also in 5:8, 13.

saw him, ran to meet him, and bowed low before him. 7With a shriek, he screamed, "Why are you interfering with me, Jesus, Son of the Most High God? In the name of God, I beg you, don't torture me!" 8For Jesus had already said to the spirit, "Come out of the man, you evil spirit."

9Then Jesus demanded, "What is your name?"

And he replied, "My name is Legion, because there are many of us inside this man." 10Then the evil spirits begged him again and again not to send them to some distant place.

11There happened to be a large herd of pigs feeding on the hillside nearby. 12"Send us into those pigs," the spirits begged. "Let us enter them."

13So Jesus gave them permission. The evil spirits came out of the man and entered the pigs, and the entire herd of 2,000 pigs plunged down the steep hillside into the lake and drowned in the water.

14The herdsmen fled to the nearby town and the surrounding countryside, spreading the news as they ran. People rushed out to see what had happened. 15A crowd soon gathered around Jesus, and they saw the man who had been possessed by the legion of demons. He was sitting there fully clothed and perfectly sane, and they were all afraid. 16Then those who had seen what happened told the others about the demon-possessed man and the pigs. 17And the crowd began pleading with Jesus to go away and leave them alone.

18As Jesus was getting into the boat, the man who had been demon possessed begged to go with him. 19But Jesus said, "No, go home to your family, and tell them everything the Lord has done for you and how merciful he has been." 20So the man started off to visit the Ten Towns* of that region and began to proclaim the great things Jesus had done for him; and everyone was amazed at what he told them.

> Go home to your family, and tell them everything the Lord has done for you and how merciful he has been.
>
> *MARK 5:19*

JESUS HEALS IN RESPONSE TO FAITH

21Jesus got into the boat again and went back to the other side of the lake, where a large crowd gathered around him on the shore. 22Then a leader of the local synagogue, whose name was Jairus, arrived. When he saw Jesus, he fell at his feet, 23pleading fervently with him. "My little daughter is dying," he said. "Please come and lay your hands on her; heal her so she can live."

24Jesus went with him, and all the people followed, crowding around him. 25A woman in the crowd had suffered for twelve years with constant bleeding. 26She had suffered a great deal from many doctors, and over the years she had spent everything she had to pay them, but she had gotten no better. In fact, she had gotten worse. 27She had heard about Jesus, so she came up behind him through the crowd and touched his robe. 28For she thought to herself, "If I can just touch his robe, I will be healed." 29Immediately the bleeding stopped, and she could feel in her body that she had been healed of her terrible condition.

30Jesus realized at once that healing power had gone out from him, so he turned around in the crowd and asked, "Who touched my robe?"

31His disciples said to him, "Look at this crowd pressing around you. How can you ask, 'Who touched me?'"

32But he kept on looking around to see who had done it. 33Then the frightened woman, trembling at the realization of what had happened to her, came and fell to her knees in front of him and told him what she had done. 34And he said to her, "Daughter, your faith has made you well. Go in peace. Your suffering is over."

35While he was still speaking to her, messengers arrived from the home of Jairus, the leader of the synagogue. They told him, "Your daughter is dead. There's no use troubling the Teacher now."

5:20 Greek *Decapolis.*

How can I let others know I'm a Christian if I'm terrified that they'll laugh at me or ask a question I can't answer?

Some life changes are so obvious, others take notice right away. In Mark 5:1-20, Jesus changed the life of a demon-possessed man. He sent the now demon-free man back home to tell his family and friends what happened. But the change in him was obvious.

When a person becomes a Christian, the results are usually obvious. The people in your life can remember what your life was like before you met Christ. In the days ahead, they'll see how you live out that change. But being Christlike takes courage.

The Bible is filled with examples of people who faced the choice of either being courageous or letting their fears tell them how to act. For example, in Exodus 3, God had just finished speaking with Moses through a burning bush. Although this was an incredible miracle, Exodus 4 relates how Moses was afraid people wouldn't believe that God had actually spoken to him! He had to choose between giving in to his fears or facing them head on. Eventually, Moses chose to draw courage from God to complete the task God had given him.

As people observe the way you live, they may have questions. But you're not expected to have all of the answers. Your responsibility is only to share what God has done for you and what you have learned—not to be the Bible expert. If you don't know the answer, you can always say, "That's a good question. Can I find out the answer and get back with you later?"

Your changed life may have a much greater impact on those with whom you have relational bridges already built than a stranger who may speak more eloquently!

36 But Jesus overheard* them and said to Jairus, "Don't be afraid. Just have faith."

37 Then Jesus stopped the crowd and wouldn't let anyone go with him except Peter, James, and John (the brother of James). 38 When they came to the home of the synagogue leader, Jesus saw much commotion and weeping and wailing. 39 He went inside and asked, "Why all this commotion and weeping? The child isn't dead; she's only asleep."

40 The crowd laughed at him. But he made them all leave, and he took the girl's father and mother and his three disciples into the room where the girl was lying. 41 Holding her hand, he said to her, *"Talitha koum,"* which means "Little girl, get up!" 42 And the girl, who was twelve years old, immediately stood up and walked around! They were overwhelmed and totally amazed. 43 Jesus gave them strict orders not to tell anyone what had happened, and then he told them to give her something to eat.

6

JESUS REJECTED AT NAZARETH

Jesus left that part of the country and returned with his disciples to Nazareth, his hometown. 2 The next Sabbath he began teaching in the synagogue, and many who heard him were amazed. They asked, "Where did he get all this wisdom and the power to perform such miracles?" 3 Then they scoffed, "He's just a carpenter, the son of Mary* and the brother of James, Joseph,* Judas, and Simon. And his sisters live right here among us." They were deeply offended and refused to believe in him.

4 Then Jesus told them, "A prophet is honored everywhere except in his own hometown and among his relatives and his own family." 5 And because of their unbelief, he couldn't do any miracles among them except to place his hands on a few sick people and heal them. 6 And he was amazed at their unbelief.

FAMILIARITY 6:1-6

The old saying, "Familiarity breeds contempt" is true in this case. Although Jesus taught effectively and wisely, the people of his hometown saw him as only a carpenter. They rejected his authority because he grew up in their town. Ever have that reaction to someone? Sometimes, we reject the truth because we don't like or respect the source of it. But God's truth often comes in ways we don't expect. He might speak through a small child or through someone we've known forever. Are you open to his truth in whatever form it takes? ■

JESUS SENDS OUT THE TWELVE DISCIPLES

Then Jesus went from village to village, teaching the people. 7 And he called his twelve disciples together and began sending them out two by two, giving them authority to cast out evil* spirits. 8 He told them to take nothing for their journey except a walking stick—no food, no traveler's bag, no money.* 9 He allowed them to wear sandals but not to take a change of clothes.

10 "Wherever you go," he said, "stay in the same house until you leave town. 11 But if any place refuses to welcome you or listen to you, shake its dust from your feet as you leave to show that you have abandoned those people to their fate."

12 So the disciples went out, telling everyone they met to repent of their sins and turn to God. 13 And they cast out many demons and healed many sick people, anointing them with olive oil.

TEAMWORK 6:7

The disciples were sent out in pairs. Individually they could have reached more areas of the country, but this was not Jesus' plan. One advantage in traveling in pairs was that they could strengthen and encourage each other, especially when they faced rejection. Likewise, God sometimes meets some of our needs through others. How has teamwork aided you as you worked to build God's Kingdom? ■

THE DEATH OF JOHN THE BAPTIST

14 Herod Antipas, the king, soon heard about Jesus, because everyone was talking about him. Some were saying,* "This must be John the Baptist raised from the dead. That is why he can do such miracles." 15 Others said, "He's the prophet Elijah." Still others said, "He's a prophet like the other great prophets of the past."

16 When Herod heard about Jesus, he said, "John, the man I beheaded, has come back from the dead."

17 For Herod had sent soldiers to arrest and imprison John as a favor to Herodias. She had been his brother Philip's wife, but Herod had married her. 18 John had been telling Herod, "It is against God's law for you to marry your brother's wife." 19 So Herodias bore a grudge against John and wanted to kill him. But without Herod's approval she was powerless, 20 for Herod respected John; and knowing that he was a good and holy man, he protected him. Herod was greatly disturbed whenever he talked with John, but even so, he liked to listen to him.

21 Herodias's chance finally came on Herod's birthday. He gave a party for his high government officials, army officers, and the leading citizens of Galilee. 22 Then his daughter, also named Herodias,* came in and performed a dance that greatly pleased Herod and his guests. "Ask me for anything you like," the king said to the girl, "and I will give it to you." 23 He even vowed, "I will give you whatever you ask, up to half my kingdom!"

24 She went out and asked her mother, "What should I ask for?"

Her mother told her, "Ask for the head of John the Baptist!"

25 So the girl hurried back to the king and told him, "I want the head of John the Baptist, right now, on a tray!"

26 Then the king deeply regretted what he had said; but

5:36 Or *ignored.* 6:3a Some manuscripts read *He's just the son of the carpenter and of Mary.* 6:3b Most manuscripts read *Joses;* see Matt 13:55. 6:7 Greek *unclean.* 6:8 Greek *no copper coins in their money belts.* 6:14 Some manuscripts read *He was saying.* 6:22 Some manuscripts read *the daughter of Herodias herself.*

because of the vows he had made in front of his guests, he couldn't refuse her. 27So he immediately sent an executioner to the prison to cut off John's head and bring it to him. The soldier beheaded John in the prison, 28brought his head on a tray, and gave it to the girl, who took it to her mother. 29When John's disciples heard what had happened, they came to get his body and buried it in a tomb.

JESUS FEEDS FIVE THOUSAND

30The apostles returned to Jesus from their ministry tour and told him all they had done and taught. 31Then Jesus said, "Let's go off by ourselves to a quiet place and rest awhile." He said this because there were so many people coming and going that Jesus and his apostles didn't even have time to eat.

32So they left by boat for a quiet place, where they could be alone. 33But many people recognized them and saw them leaving, and people from many towns ran ahead along the shore and got there ahead of them. 34Jesus saw the huge crowd as he stepped from the boat, and he had compassion on them because they were like sheep without a shepherd. So he began teaching them many things.

35Late in the afternoon his disciples came to him and said, "This is a remote place, and it's already getting late. 36Send the crowds away so they can go to the nearby farms and villages and buy something to eat."

37But Jesus said, "You feed them."

"With what?" they asked. "We'd have to work for months to earn enough money* to buy food for all these people!"

38"How much bread do you have?" he asked. "Go and find out."

They came back and reported, "We have five loaves of bread and two fish."

39Then Jesus told the disciples to have the people sit down in groups on the green grass. 40So they sat down in groups of fifty or a hundred.

41Jesus took the five loaves and two fish, looked up toward heaven, and blessed them. Then, breaking the loaves into pieces, he kept giving the bread to the disciples so they could distribute it to the people. He also divided the fish for everyone to share. 42They all ate as much as they wanted, 43and afterward, the disciples picked up twelve baskets of leftover bread and fish. 44A total of 5,000 men and their families were fed from those loaves!

JESUS WALKS ON WATER

45Immediately after this, Jesus insisted that his disciples get back into the boat and head across the lake to Bethsaida, while he sent the people home. 46After telling everyone good-bye, he went up into the hills by himself to pray.

47Late that night, the disciples were in their boat in the middle of the lake, and Jesus was alone on land. 48He saw that they were in serious trouble, rowing hard and struggling against the wind and waves. About three o'clock in the morning* Jesus came toward them, walking on the water. He intended to go past them, 49but when they saw him walking on the water, they cried out in terror, thinking he was a ghost. 50They were all terrified when they saw him.

But Jesus spoke to them at once. "Don't be afraid," he said. "Take courage! I am here!*" 51Then he climbed into the boat, and the wind stopped. They were totally amazed, 52for they still didn't understand the significance of the miracle of the loaves. Their hearts were too hard to take it in.

53After they had crossed the lake, they landed at Gennesaret. They brought the boat to shore 54and climbed out. The people recognized Jesus at once, 55and they ran throughout the whole area, carrying sick people on mats to wherever they heard he was. 56Wherever he went—in villages, cities, or the countryside—they brought the sick out to the marketplaces. They begged him to let the sick touch at least the fringe of his robe, and all who touched him were healed.

MONEY MATTERS 7:1-11

The Pharisees used God as an excuse to avoid helping their families, especially their parents. They thought putting money in the Temple treasury was more important than helping their needy parents. But Jesus exposed their hypocrisy by reminding them of specific laws (see Exod 20:12 and Lev 25:35-43).

Sometimes we have the opposite problem. We would rather use our money to buy gifts for friends and family than to give it in church or to help others. But helping those in need is one of the most important ways to honor God. How will you use your money to honor God? ■

7

JESUS TEACHES ABOUT INNER PURITY

One day some Pharisees and teachers of religious law arrived from Jerusalem to see Jesus. 2They noticed that some of his disciples failed to follow the Jewish ritual of hand washing before eating. 3(The Jews, especially the Pharisees, do not eat until they have poured water over their cupped hands,* as required by their ancient traditions. 4Similarly, they don't eat anything from the market until they immerse their hands* in water. This is but one of many traditions they have clung to—such as their ceremonial washing of cups, pitchers, and kettles.*)

5So the Pharisees and teachers of religious law asked him, "Why don't your disciples follow our age-old tradition? They eat without first performing the hand-washing ceremony."

6Jesus replied, "You hypocrites! Isaiah was right when he prophesied about you, for he wrote,

6:37 Greek *It would take 200 denarii.* A denarius was equivalent to a laborer's full day's wage. 6:48 Greek *About the fourth watch of the night.* 6:50 Or *The 'I AM' is here;* Greek reads *I am.* See Exod 3:14. 7:3 Greek *have washed with the fist.* 7:4a Some manuscripts read *sprinkle themselves.* 7:4b Some manuscripts add *and dining couches.*

'These people honor me with their lips,
but their hearts are far from me.
7 Their worship is a farce,
for they teach man-made ideas as commands
from God.'*

8For you ignore God's law and substitute your own tradition."
9Then he said, "You skillfully sidestep God's law in order to hold on to your own tradition. 10For instance,
Moses gave you this law from God: 'Honor your father
and mother,'* and 'Anyone who speaks disrespectfully of
father or mother must be put to death.'* 11But you say it is
all right for people to say to their parents, 'Sorry, I can't
help you. For I have vowed to give to God what I would
have given to you.'* 12In this way, you let them disregard
their needy parents. 13And so you cancel the word of God
in order to hand down your own tradition. And this is
only one example among many others."
14Then Jesus called to the crowd to come and hear. "All
of you listen," he said, "and try to understand. 15It's not
what goes into your body that defiles you; you are defiled
by what comes from your heart.*"
17Then Jesus went into a house to get away from the
crowd, and his disciples asked him what he meant by
the parable he had just used. 18"Don't you understand either?" he asked. "Can't you see that the food you put into
your body cannot defile you? 19Food doesn't go into your
heart, but only passes through the stomach and then goes
into the sewer." (By saying this, he declared that every
kind of food is acceptable in God's eyes.)
20And then he added, "It is what comes from inside
that defiles you. 21For from within, out of a person's
heart, come evil thoughts, sexual immorality, theft, murder, 22adultery, greed, wickedness, deceit, lustful desires,
envy, slander, pride, and foolishness. 23All these vile
things come from within; they are what defile you."

THE FAITH OF A GENTILE WOMAN

24Then Jesus left Galilee and went north to the region of
Tyre.* He didn't want anyone to know which house he
was staying in, but he couldn't keep it a secret. 25Right
away a woman who had heard about him came and fell
at his feet. Her little girl was possessed by an evil* spirit,
26and she begged him to cast out the demon from her
daughter.
Since she was a Gentile, born in Syrian Phoenicia,
27Jesus told her, "First I should feed the children—my
own family, the Jews.* It isn't right to take food from the
children and throw it to the dogs."
28She replied, "That's true, Lord, but even the dogs
under the table are allowed to eat the scraps from the
children's plates."
29"Good answer!" he said. "Now go home, for the
demon has left your daughter." 30And when she arrived
home, she found her little girl lying quietly in bed, and
the demon was gone.

JESUS HEALS A DEAF MAN

31Jesus left Tyre and went up to Sidon before going back
to the Sea of Galilee and the region of the Ten Towns.*
32A deaf man with a speech impediment was brought to
him, and the people begged Jesus to lay his hands on the
man to heal him.
33Jesus led him away from the crowd so they could be
alone. He put his fingers into the man's ears. Then, spitting on his own fingers, he touched the man's tongue.
34Looking up to heaven, he sighed and said, *"Ephphatha,"*
which means, "Be opened!" 35Instantly the man could
hear perfectly, and his tongue was freed so he could
speak plainly!
36Jesus told the crowd not to tell anyone, but the more
he told them not to, the more they spread the news.
37They were completely amazed and said again and
again, "Everything he does is wonderful. He even makes
the deaf to hear and gives speech to those who cannot
speak."

8

JESUS FEEDS FOUR THOUSAND

About this time another large crowd had gathered, and the
people ran out of food again. Jesus called his disciples and
told them, 2"I feel sorry for these people. They have been
here with me for three days, and they have nothing left to
eat. 3If I send them home hungry, they will faint along the
way. For some of them have come a long distance."

HE KNOWS 8:1-3

Do you ever feel that God is so busy with important concerns that he can't possibly be aware of your needs? Just as Jesus was concerned about a large crowd's need for food, he is concerned about our daily needs. After all, he's the one who said, "Your heavenly Father already knows all your needs" (Matt 6:32). Do you have concerns that you think would not interest God? There is no concern too large for him to handle, and no need too small to escape his interest. ■

4His disciples replied, "How are we supposed to find
enough food to feed them out here in the wilderness?"
5Jesus asked, "How much bread do you have?"
"Seven loaves," they replied.
6So Jesus told all the people to sit down on the ground.
Then he took the seven loaves, thanked God for them,
and broke them into pieces. He gave them to his disciples, who distributed the bread to the crowd. 7A few
small fish were found, too, so Jesus also blessed these and
told the disciples to distribute them.

7:7 Isa 29:13 (Greek version). 7:10a Exod 20:12; Deut 5:16. 7:10b Exod 21:17 (Greek version); Lev 20:9 (Greek version). 7:11 Greek *'What I would have given to you is Corban' (that is, a gift).* 7:15 Some manuscripts add verse 16, *Anyone with ears to hear should listen and understand.* Compare 4:9, 23. 7:24 Some manuscripts add *and Sidon.* 7:25 Greek *unclean.* 7:27 Greek *Let the children eat first.* 7:31 Greek *Decapolis.*

8They ate as much as they wanted. Afterward, the disciples picked up seven large baskets of leftover food.
9There were about 4,000 people in the crowd that day,
and Jesus sent them home after they had eaten. 10Immedi-
ately after this, he got into a boat with his disciples and
crossed over to the region of Dalmanutha.

PHARISEES DEMAND A MIRACULOUS SIGN

11When the Pharisees heard that Jesus had arrived, they
came and started to argue with him. Testing him, they
demanded that he show them a miraculous sign from
heaven to prove his authority.
12When he heard this, he sighed deeply in his spirit
and said, "Why do these people keep demanding a miraculous sign? I tell you the truth, I will not give this generation any such sign." 13So he got back into the boat and left
them, and he crossed to the other side of the lake.

YEAST OF THE PHARISEES AND HEROD

14But the disciples had forgotten to bring any food. They
had only one loaf of bread with them in the boat. 15As
they were crossing the lake, Jesus warned them, "Watch
out! Beware of the yeast of the Pharisees and of Herod."
16At this they began to argue with each other because
they hadn't brought any bread. 17Jesus knew what they
were saying, so he said, "Why are you arguing about having no bread? Don't you know or understand even yet?
Are your hearts too hard to take it in? 18You have eyes—
can't you see? You have ears—can't you hear?* Don't you
remember anything at all? 19When I fed the 5,000 with
five loaves of bread, how many baskets of leftovers did
you pick up afterward?"
"Twelve," they said.
20"And when I fed the 4,000 with seven loaves, how
many large baskets of leftovers did you pick up?"
"Seven," they said.
21"Don't you understand yet?" he asked them.

JESUS HEALS A BLIND MAN

22When they arrived at Bethsaida, some people brought a
blind man to Jesus, and they begged him to touch the
man and heal him. 23Jesus took the blind man by the hand
and led him out of the village. Then, spitting on the man's
eyes, he laid his hands on him and asked, "Can you see
anything now?"
24The man looked around. "Yes," he said, "I see people,
but I can't see them very clearly. They look like trees
walking around."
25Then Jesus placed his hands on the man's eyes again,
and his eyes were opened. His sight was completely restored, and he could see everything clearly. 26Jesus sent
him away, saying, "Don't go back into the village on your
way home."

PETER'S DECLARATION ABOUT JESUS

27Jesus and his disciples left Galilee and went up to the
villages near Caesarea Philippi. As they were walking
along, he asked them, "Who do people say I am?"
28"Well," they replied, "some say John the Baptist,
some say Elijah, and others say you are one of the other
prophets."
29Then he asked them, "But who do you say I am?"
Peter replied, "You are the Messiah.*"
30But Jesus warned them not to tell anyone about him.

> **WHAT'S YOUR OPINION? 8:27-29**
>
> **Jesus asked the disciples who others thought he was; then he focused on them: "Who do you say I am?" Knowing what others say about Jesus isn't enough; you must accept the truth about him for yourself. Who do you say that he is?** ■

JESUS PREDICTS HIS DEATH

31Then Jesus began to tell them that the Son of Man*
must suffer many terrible things and be rejected by the
elders, the leading priests, and the teachers of religious
law. He would be killed, but three days later he would rise
from the dead. 32As he talked about this openly with his
disciples, Peter took him aside and began to reprimand
him for saying such things.*
33Jesus turned around and looked at his disciples, then
reprimanded Peter. "Get away from me, Satan!" he said.
"You are seeing things merely from a human point of
view, not from God's."
34Then, calling the crowd to join his disciples, he said,
"If any of you wants to be my follower, you must turn
from your selfish ways, take up your cross, and follow me.
35If you try to hang on to your life, you will lose it. But if
you give up your life for my sake and for the sake of the
Good News, you will save it. 36And what do you benefit if
you gain the whole world but lose your own soul?* 37Is
anything worth more than your soul? 38If anyone is
ashamed of me and my message in these adulterous and
sinful days, the Son of Man will be ashamed of that person when he returns in the glory of his Father with the
holy angels."

9 Jesus went on to say, "I tell you the truth, some
standing here right now will not die before they see the
Kingdom of God arrive in great power!"

THE TRANSFIGURATION

2Six days later Jesus took Peter, James, and John, and led
them up a high mountain to be alone. As the men
watched, Jesus' appearance was transformed, 3and his
clothes became dazzling white, far whiter than any
earthly bleach could ever make them. 4Then Elijah and
Moses appeared and began talking with Jesus.
5Peter exclaimed, "Rabbi, it's wonderful for us to be
here! Let's make three shelters as memorials*—one for
you, one for Moses, and one for Elijah." 6He said this

8:18 Jer 5:21. **8:29** Or *the Christ. Messiah* (a Hebrew term) and *Christ* (a Greek term) both mean "the anointed one." **8:31** "Son of Man" is a title Jesus used for himself. **8:32** Or *began to correct him.* **8:36** Or *your self?* also in 8:37. **9:5** Greek *three tabernacles.*

because he didn't really know what else to say, for they were all terrified.

7Then a cloud overshadowed them, and a voice from the cloud said, "This is my dearly loved Son. Listen to him." 8Suddenly, when they looked around, Moses and Elijah were gone, and they saw only Jesus with them.

YOUR PRAYER, GOD'S POWER 9:23

Jesus' words don't mean that we can automatically obtain anything we want if we just think positively. Jesus meant that anything is *possible* with faith because nothing is too difficult for God. (See Gen 18:14; Luke 1:37.) This is not a teaching on how to pray as much as a statement about God's power to overcome obstacles. Although we won't receive everything we pray for as if by magic, with faith we can have everything we need to serve God. ■

9As they went back down the mountain, he told them not to tell anyone what they had seen until the Son of Man* had risen from the dead. 10So they kept it to themselves, but they often asked each other what he meant by "rising from the dead."

11Then they asked him, "Why do the teachers of religious law insist that Elijah must return before the Messiah comes?*"

12Jesus responded, "Elijah is indeed coming first to get everything ready. Yet why do the Scriptures say that the Son of Man must suffer greatly and be treated with utter contempt? 13But I tell you, Elijah has already come, and they chose to abuse him, just as the Scriptures predicted."

JESUS HEALS A DEMON-POSSESSED BOY

14When they returned to the other disciples, they saw a large crowd surrounding them, and some teachers of religious law were arguing with them. 15When the crowd saw Jesus, they were overwhelmed with awe, and they ran to greet him.

16"What is all this arguing about?" Jesus asked.

17One of the men in the crowd spoke up and said, "Teacher, I brought my son so you could heal him. He is possessed by an evil spirit that won't let him talk. 18And whenever this spirit seizes him, it throws him violently to the ground. Then he foams at the mouth and grinds his teeth and becomes rigid.* So I asked your disciples to cast out the evil spirit, but they couldn't do it."

19Jesus said to them,* "You faithless people! How long must I be with you? How long must I put up with you? Bring the boy to me."

20So they brought the boy. But when the evil spirit saw Jesus, it threw the child into a violent convulsion, and he fell to the ground, writhing and foaming at the mouth.

21"How long has this been happening?" Jesus asked the boy's father.

He replied, "Since he was a little boy. 22The spirit often throws him into the fire or into water, trying to kill him. Have mercy on us and help us, if you can."

23"What do you mean, 'If I can'?" Jesus asked. "Anything is possible if a person believes."

24The father instantly cried out, "I do believe, but help me overcome my unbelief!"

25When Jesus saw that the crowd of onlookers was growing, he rebuked the evil* spirit. "Listen, you spirit that makes this boy unable to hear and speak," he said. "I command you to come out of this child and never enter him again!"

26Then the spirit screamed and threw the boy into another violent convulsion and left him. The boy appeared to be dead. A murmur ran through the crowd as people said, "He's dead." 27But Jesus took him by the hand and helped him to his feet, and he stood up.

28Afterward, when Jesus was alone in the house with his disciples, they asked him, "Why couldn't we cast out that evil spirit?"

29Jesus replied, "This kind can be cast out only by prayer.*"

SUCCESS

You've heard of *A Tale of Two Cities* by Charles Dickens, right? Call this "A Tale of Two Sisters." Elisa, a senior, has a 4.0 grade-point average and is practically guaranteed a scholarship. She is president of her class and is both captain and number one seed on the girls' tennis team. She also dates Miguel, the hottest guy at school. Together they were voted by their class as "the couple most likely to succeed." Elisa's ambition? To be the next Jennifer Lopez and possibly marry Miguel—but not necessarily in that order.

If Elisa represents "the best of times," then to many, Alita, a sophomore, probably embodies "the worst of times." She struggles in school, making mostly Cs. She is not especially popular, nor is she very athletic. No, the truth is that Alita is painfully shy and sort of average looking. She's not going out with anyone (not yet anyway) nor has she been voted into office or had predictions of greatness bestowed upon her. Most of her free time goes to serving as a Big Sister to two kids in a housing project in her town. Her goal in life? To be a social worker.

Do you know anyone like Elisa? Like Alita? Which girl do you think is the most successful? By what standards does our society judge success and failure? What does Jesus say in Mark 9:33-37? Do you agree? Why or why not?

JESUS AGAIN PREDICTS HIS DEATH

30Leaving that region, they traveled through Galilee. Jesus didn't want anyone to know he was there, 31for he wanted to spend more time with his disciples and teach them. He said to them, "The Son of Man is going to be betrayed into

9:9 "Son of Man" is a title Jesus used for himself. **9:11** Greek *that Elijah must come first?* **9:18** Or *becomes weak.* **9:19** Or *said to his disciples.* **9:25** Greek *unclean.* **9:29** Some manuscripts read *by prayer and fasting.*

keeping it real

In my school, people are popular only if they have the right looks, the right clothes, live in a certain neighborhood, play on the football team or are a cheerleader, or date a football player or a cheerleader. The lines are pretty clearly drawn. And I'm on the other side of every one of those lines.

For a while it really bothered me. But when I tried to break into one of the cliques at school, I found myself acting phony. I wanted people to like me.

Then, slowly, my viewpoint changed when my youth group studied the book of Mark. I really related to the disciples in chapters 9 and 10. They were trying to see who was more popular with Jesus, who would be considered the greatest. And Jesus said, "Many who are the greatest now will be least important then (in the world to come), and those who seem least important now will be the greatest then" (Mark 10:31).

I realized that it didn't really matter whether kids in my school thought I was great; what matters is what God thinks of me. To please him, I have to stop being phony and try to be friends with all kinds of people.

I've started doing that. Now I have lots of friends. Although I'm not one of the "popular" people, I'm okay with that. I know I'm popular with the one person whose opinion really matters—God. —Marita

the hands of his enemies. He will be killed, but three days
later he will rise from the dead." 32They didn't understand what he was saying, however, and they were afraid
to ask him what he meant.

THE GREATEST IN THE KINGDOM

33After they arrived at Capernaum and settled in a house,
Jesus asked his disciples, "What were you discussing out
on the road?" 34But they didn't answer, because they had
been arguing about which of them was the greatest. 35He
sat down, called the twelve disciples over to him, and said,
"Whoever wants to be first must take last place and be
the servant of everyone else."
36Then he put a little child among them. Taking the
child in his arms, he said to them, 37"Anyone who welcomes a little child like this on my behalf* welcomes me,
and anyone who welcomes me welcomes not only me but
also my Father who sent me."

USING THE NAME OF JESUS

38John said to Jesus, "Teacher, we saw someone using
your name to cast out demons, but we told him to stop because he wasn't in our group."
39"Don't stop him!" Jesus said. "No one who performs a
miracle in my name will soon be able to speak evil of me.
40Anyone who is not against us is for us. 41If anyone gives
you even a cup of water because you belong to the Messiah, I tell you the truth, that person will surely be rewarded.

CUT IT OUT 9:43-48

Jesus used startling language to stress the importance of ridding our lives of bad habits. Giving up a relationship, job, or habit that causes you to disobey God may seem just as painful as cutting off a hand. What, if anything, are you willing to give up if God asks it of you? ■

42"But if you cause one of these little ones who trusts in
me to fall into sin, it would be better for you to be thrown
into the sea with a large millstone hung around your
neck. 43If your hand causes you to sin, cut it off. It's better
to enter eternal life with only one hand than to go into the
unquenchable fires of hell* with two hands.* 45If your
foot causes you to sin, cut it off. It's better to enter eternal
life with only one foot than to be thrown into hell with
two feet.* 47And if your eye causes you to sin, gouge it out.
It's better to enter the Kingdom of God with only one eye
than to have two eyes and be thrown into hell, 48'where
the maggots never die and the fire never goes out.'*

9:37 Greek *in my name.* **9:43a** Greek *Gehenna;* also in 9:45, 47. **9:43b** Some manuscripts add verse 44, *'where the maggots never die and the fire never goes out.'* See 9:48. **9:45** Some manuscripts add verse 46, *'where the maggots never die and the fire never goes out.'* See 9:48. **9:48** Isa 66:24.

49 "For everyone will be tested with fire.* 50 Salt is good for seasoning. But if it loses its flavor, how do you make it salty again? You must have the qualities of salt among yourselves and live in peace with each other."

10

DISCUSSION ABOUT DIVORCE AND MARRIAGE

Then Jesus left Capernaum and went down to the region of Judea and into the area east of the Jordan River. Once again crowds gathered around him, and as usual he was teaching them.

2 Some Pharisees came and tried to trap him with this question: "Should a man be allowed to divorce his wife?"

3 Jesus answered them with a question: "What did Moses say in the law about divorce?"

4 "Well, he permitted it," they replied. "He said a man can give his wife a written notice of divorce and send her away."*

5 But Jesus responded, "He wrote this commandment only as a concession to your hard hearts. 6 But 'God made them male and female'* from the beginning of creation. 7 'This explains why a man leaves his father and mother and is joined to his wife,* 8 and the two are united into one.'* Since they are no longer two but one, 9 let no one split apart what God has joined together."

10 Later, when he was alone with his disciples in the house, they brought up the subject again. 11 He told them, "Whoever divorces his wife and marries someone else commits adultery against her. 12 And if a woman divorces her husband and marries someone else, she commits adultery."

JESUS BLESSES THE CHILDREN

13 One day some parents brought their children to Jesus so he could touch and bless them. But the disciples scolded the parents for bothering him.

14 When Jesus saw what was happening, he was angry with his disciples. He said to them, "Let the children come to me. Don't stop them! For the Kingdom of God belongs to those who are like these children. 15 I tell you the truth, anyone who doesn't receive the Kingdom of God like a child will never enter it." 16 Then he took the children in his arms and placed his hands on their heads and blessed them.

THE RICH MAN

17 As Jesus was starting out on his way to Jerusalem, a man came running up to him, knelt down, and asked, "Good Teacher, what must I do to inherit eternal life?"

18 "Why do you call me good?" Jesus asked. "Only God is truly good. 19 But to answer your question, you know the commandments: 'You must not murder. You must not commit adultery. You must not steal. You must not testify falsely. You must not cheat anyone. Honor your father and mother.'*"

20 "Teacher," the man replied, "I've obeyed all these commandments since I was young."

21 Looking at the man, Jesus felt genuine love for him. "There is still one thing you haven't done," he told him. "Go and sell all your possessions and give the money to the poor, and you will have treasure in heaven. Then come, follow me."

22 At this the man's face fell, and he went away sad, for he had many possessions.

23 Jesus looked around and said to his disciples, "How hard it is for the rich to enter the Kingdom of God!" 24 This amazed them. But Jesus said again, "Dear children, it is very hard* to enter the Kingdom of God. 25 In fact, it is easier for a camel to go through the eye of a needle than for a rich person to enter the Kingdom of God!"

BARRIERS 10:17-23

This young man wanted to be sure he would get eternal life, so he asked what he could *do.* Jesus lovingly addressed him with a challenge that brought out his true motives: "Sell all your possessions and give the money to the poor." Here was the barrier that could keep this man out of the Kingdom: his love of money. Ironically, his attitude kept him from keeping the first commandment—to let nothing be more important than God (Exod 20:3). He came to Jesus wondering what he could do; he left seeing what he was unable to do. What barriers, if any, are keeping you from turning your life completely over to Jesus? ■

26 The disciples were astounded. "Then who in the world can be saved?" they asked.

27 Jesus looked at them intently and said, "Humanly speaking, it is impossible. But not with God. Everything is possible with God."

28 Then Peter began to speak up. "We've given up everything to follow you," he said.

29 "Yes," Jesus replied, "and I assure you that everyone who has given up house or brothers or sisters or mother or father or children or property, for my sake and for the Good News, 30 will receive now in return a hundred times as many houses, brothers, sisters, mothers, children, and property—along with persecution. And in the world to come that person will have eternal life. 31 But many who are the greatest now will be least important then, and those who seem least important now will be the greatest then.*"

JESUS AGAIN PREDICTS HIS DEATH

32 They were now on the way up to Jerusalem, and Jesus was walking ahead of them. The disciples were filled with awe, and the people following behind were overwhelmed with fear. Taking the twelve disciples aside, Jesus once more began to describe everything that was about to happen to him. 33 "Listen," he said, "we're going up to Jerusalem, where the Son of Man* will be betrayed to the leading priests and the teachers of religious law. They will

9:49 Greek *salted with fire;* other manuscripts add *and every sacrifice will be salted with salt.* **10:4** See Deut 24:1. **10:6** Gen 1:27; 5:2. **10:7** Some manuscripts do not include *and is joined to his wife.* **10:7-8** Gen 2:24. **10:19** Exod 20:12-16; Deut 5:16-20. **10:24** Some manuscripts read *very hard for those who trust in riches.* **10:31** Greek *But many who are first will be last; and the last, first.* **10:33a** "Son of Man" is a title Jesus used for himself.

sentence him to die and hand him over to the Romans.* 34They will mock him, spit on him, flog him with a whip, and kill him, but after three days he will rise again."

JESUS TEACHES ABOUT SERVING OTHERS

35Then James and John, the sons of Zebedee, came over and spoke to him. "Teacher," they said, "we want you to do us a favor."

36"What is your request?" he asked.

37They replied, "When you sit on your glorious throne, we want to sit in places of honor next to you, one on your right and the other on your left."

38But Jesus said to them, "You don't know what you are asking! Are you able to drink from the bitter cup of suffering I am about to drink? Are you able to be baptized with the baptism of suffering I must be baptized with?"

39"Oh yes," they replied, "we are able!"

Then Jesus told them, "You will indeed drink from my bitter cup and be baptized with my baptism of suffering. 40But I have no right to say who will sit on my right or my left. God has prepared those places for the ones he has chosen."

41When the ten other disciples heard what James and John had asked, they were indignant. 42So Jesus called them together and said, "You know that the rulers in this world lord it over their people, and officials flaunt their authority over those under them. 43But among you it will be different. Whoever wants to be a leader among you must be your servant, 44and whoever wants to be first among you must be the slave of everyone else. 45For even the Son of Man came not to be served but to serve others and to give his life as a ransom for many."

JESUS HEALS BLIND BARTIMAEUS

46Then they reached Jericho, and as Jesus and his disciples left town, a large crowd followed him. A blind beggar named Bartimaeus (son of Timaeus) was sitting beside the road. 47When Bartimaeus heard that Jesus of Nazareth was nearby, he began to shout, "Jesus, Son of David, have mercy on me!"

48"Be quiet!" many of the people yelled at him.

But he only shouted louder, "Son of David, have mercy on me!"

49When Jesus heard him, he stopped and said, "Tell him to come here."

So they called the blind man. "Cheer up," they said. "Come on, he's calling you!" 50Bartimaeus threw aside his coat, jumped up, and came to Jesus.

51"What do you want me to do for you?" Jesus asked.

"My rabbi,*" the blind man said, "I want to see!"

52And Jesus said to him, "Go, for your faith has healed you." Instantly the man could see, and he followed Jesus down the road.*

11 JESUS' TRIUMPHANT ENTRY

As Jesus and his disciples approached Jerusalem, they came to the towns of Bethphage and Bethany on the Mount of Olives. Jesus sent two of them on ahead. 2"Go into that village over there," he told them. "As soon as you enter it, you will see a young donkey tied there that no one has ever ridden. Untie it and bring it here. 3If anyone asks, 'What are you doing?' just say, 'The Lord needs it and will return it soon.'"

4The two disciples left and found the colt standing in the street, tied outside the front door. 5As they were untying it, some bystanders demanded, "What are you doing, untying that colt?" 6They said what Jesus had told them to say, and they were permitted to take it. 7Then they brought the colt to Jesus and threw their garments over it, and he sat on it.

8Many in the crowd spread their garments on the road ahead of him, and others spread leafy branches they had cut in the fields. 9Jesus was in the center of the procession, and the people all around him were shouting,

"Praise God!*
  Blessings on the one who comes in the name
    of the LORD!
10 Blessings on the coming Kingdom of our
    ancestor David!
  Praise God in highest heaven!"*

11So Jesus came to Jerusalem and went into the Temple. After looking around carefully at everything, he left because it was late in the afternoon. Then he returned to Bethany with the twelve disciples.

JESUS CURSES THE FIG TREE

12The next morning as they were leaving Bethany, Jesus was hungry. 13He noticed a fig tree in full leaf a little way off, so he went over to see if he could find any figs. But there were only leaves because it was too early in the season for fruit. 14Then Jesus said to the tree, "May no one ever eat your fruit again!" And the disciples heard him say it.

JESUS CLEARS THE TEMPLE

15When they arrived back in Jerusalem, Jesus entered the Temple and began to drive out the people buying and selling animals for sacrifices. He knocked over the tables of the money changers and the chairs of those selling doves, 16and he stopped everyone from using the Temple as a marketplace.* 17He said to them, "The Scriptures declare, 'My Temple will be called a house of prayer for all nations,' but you have turned it into a den of thieves."*

18When the leading priests and teachers of religious law heard what Jesus had done, they began planning how to kill him. But they were afraid of him because the people were so amazed at his teaching.

19That evening Jesus and the disciples left* the city.

20The next morning as they passed by the fig tree he had cursed, the disciples noticed it had withered from the roots up. 21Peter remembered what Jesus had said to the tree on the previous day and exclaimed, "Look, Rabbi! The fig tree you cursed has withered and died!"

10:33b Greek *the Gentiles.* **10:51** Greek uses the Hebrew term *Rabboni.* **10:52** Or *on the way.* **11:9** Greek *Hosanna,* an exclamation of praise that literally means "save now"; also in 11:10. **11:9-10** Pss 118:25-26; 148:1. **11:16** Or *from carrying merchandise through the Temple.* **11:17** Isa 56:7; Jer 7:11. **11:19** Greek *they left;* other manuscripts read *he left.*

What Jesus Said about Love

In Mark 12:28, a religious teacher asked Jesus which one of all the commandments was the most important to follow. Jesus mentioned two commandments, one from Deuteronomy 6:5, the other from Leviticus 19:18. Both had to do with love. Why is love so important? Jesus said that all of the commandments were given for two simple reasons—to help us love God and love others as we should.

What Else Did Jesus Say about Love?

God loves us. . . . John 3:16

We are to love God. . . . Matthew 22:37

Because God loves us, he cares for us. . . . Matthew 6:25-34

God wants everyone to know how much he loves them. . . . John 17:23

God loves even those who hate him, we are to do the same. . . . Matthew 5:43-47; Luke 6:35

God seeks out even those most alienated from him. . . .Luke 15

God must be your first love. . . . Matthew 6:24; 10:37

You love God when you obey him. . . . John 14:21; 15:10

God loves Jesus, his Son. . . . John 5:20; 10:17

Jesus loves God. . . . John 14:31

Those who refuse Jesus don’t have God’s love. . . . John 5:41-44

Jesus loves us just as God loves Jesus. . . . John 15:9

Jesus proved his love for us by dying on the cross so that we could live eternally with him. . . . John 3:14-15; 15:13-14

The love between God and Jesus is the perfect example of how we are to love others. . . . John 17:21-26

We are to love one another (John 13:34-35) and demonstrate that love. . . . Matthew 5:40-42; 10:42

We are not to love the praise of men (John 12:43), selfish recognition (Matthew 23:6), earthly belongings (Luke 16:19-31), or anything more than God. . . . Luke 16:13

Jesus’ love extends to each individual. . . . John 10:11-15; Mark 10:21

Jesus wants us to love him through both the good and difficult times. . . . Matthew 26:31-35

Jesus wants our love to be genuine. . . . John 21:15-17

22Then Jesus said to the disciples, “Have faith in
God. 23I tell you the truth, you can say to this mountain, ‘May you be lifted up and thrown into the sea,’
and it will happen. But you must really believe it will
happen and have no doubt in your heart. 24I tell you,
you can pray for anything, and if you believe that
you’ve received it, it will be yours. 25But when you are
praying, first forgive anyone you are holding a grudge
against, so that your Father in heaven will forgive your
sins, too.*”

THE AUTHORITY OF JESUS CHALLENGED

27Again they entered Jerusalem. As Jesus was walking
through the Temple area, the leading priests, the teachers of religious law, and the elders came up to him. 28They
demanded, “By what authority are you doing all these
things? Who gave you the right to do them?”
29“I’ll tell you by what authority I do these things if you
answer one question,” Jesus replied. 30“Did John’s authority
to baptize come from heaven, or was it merely human? Answer me!”
31They talked it over among themselves. “If we say it
was from heaven, he will ask why we didn’t believe John.
32But do we dare say it was merely human?” For they were
afraid of what the people would do, because everyone believed that John was a prophet. 33So they finally replied,
“We don’t know.”
And Jesus responded, “Then I won’t tell you by what
authority I do these things.”

12 PARABLE OF THE EVIL FARMERS

Then Jesus began teaching them with stories: “A man
planted a vineyard. He built a wall around it, dug a pit
for pressing out the grape juice, and built a lookout
tower. Then he leased the vineyard to tenant farmers

11:25 Some manuscripts add verse 26, *But if you refuse to forgive, your Father in heaven will not forgive your sins.* Compare Matt 6:15.

and moved to another country. 2At the time of the grape
harvest, he sent one of his servants to collect his share of
the crop. 3But the farmers grabbed the servant, beat him
up, and sent him back empty-handed. 4The owner then
sent another servant, but they insulted him and beat
him over the head. 5The next servant he sent was
killed. Others he sent were either beaten or killed,
6until there was only one left—his son whom he loved
dearly. The owner finally sent him, thinking, 'Surely
they will respect my son.'
7"But the tenant farmers said to one another, 'Here
comes the heir to this estate. Let's kill him and get the estate for ourselves!' 8So they grabbed him and murdered
him and threw his body out of the vineyard.
9"What do you suppose the owner of the vineyard will
do?" Jesus asked. "I'll tell you—he will come and kill those
farmers and lease the vineyard to others. 10Didn't you
ever read this in the Scriptures?

'The stone that the builders rejected
has now become the cornerstone.
11 This is the LORD's doing,
and it is wonderful to see.'*"

IMAGE 12:12-27

The Pharisees and Herodians (a group of Jewish leaders who tried to keep on the Romans' good side) thought they had the perfect question to trap Jesus. But Jesus answered wisely, once again exposing their self-interest and wrong motives. Jesus said that the coin bearing the emperor's image should be given to the emperor. But whatever bears God's image—our life—belongs to God. Are you giving God all that's rightfully his? ■

12The religious leaders* wanted to arrest Jesus because they realized he was telling the story against
them—they were the wicked farmers. But they were
afraid of the crowd, so they left him and went away.

TAXES FOR CAESAR

13Later the leaders sent some Pharisees and supporters of
Herod to trap Jesus into saying something for which he
could be arrested. 14"Teacher," they said, "we know how
honest you are. You are impartial and don't play favorites. You teach the way of God truthfully. Now tell us—is
it right to pay taxes to Caesar or not? 15Should we pay
them, or shouldn't we?"
Jesus saw through their hypocrisy and said, "Why are
you trying to trap me? Show me a Roman coin,* and I'll
tell you." 16When they handed it to him, he asked,
"Whose picture and title are stamped on it?"
"Caesar's," they replied.
17"Well, then," Jesus said, "give to Caesar what belongs
to Caesar, and give to God what belongs to God."
His reply completely amazed them.

DISCUSSION ABOUT RESURRECTION

18Then Jesus was approached by some Sadducees—religious leaders who say there is no resurrection from the
dead. They posed this question: 19"Teacher, Moses gave
us a law that if a man dies, leaving a wife without children,
his brother should marry the widow and have a child who
will carry on the brother's name.* 20Well, suppose there
were seven brothers. The oldest one married and then
died without children. 21So the second brother married
the widow, but he also died without children. Then the
third brother married her. 22This continued with all
seven of them, and still there were no children. Last of all,
the woman also died. 23So tell us, whose wife will she be
in the resurrection? For all seven were married to her."
24Jesus replied, "Your mistake is that you don't know
the Scriptures, and you don't know the power of God.
25For when the dead rise, they will neither marry nor be
given in marriage. In this respect they will be like the angels in heaven.
26"But now, as to whether the dead will be raised—
haven't you ever read about this in the writings of Moses,
in the story of the burning bush? Long after Abraham,
Isaac, and Jacob had died, God said to Moses,* 'I am the
God of Abraham, the God of Isaac, and the God of Jacob.'*
27So he is the God of the living, not the dead. You have
made a serious error."

THE MOST IMPORTANT COMMANDMENT

28One of the teachers of religious law was standing there
listening to the debate. He realized that Jesus had answered well, so he asked, "Of all the commandments,
which is the most important?"

TWO SIMPLE RULES 12:29-34

God's laws can be reduced to two simple rules for life: love God and love others. These commands are from the Old Testament (Deut 6:5; Lev 19:18). When you love God completely and care for others as you care for yourself, then you have fulfilled the intent of the Ten Commandments and the other Old Testament laws. According to Jesus, these two rules summarize all God's laws. Do they rule your thoughts, decisions, and actions? ■

29Jesus replied, "The most important commandment is
this: 'Listen, O Israel! The LORD our God is the one and
only LORD. 30And you must love the LORD your God with
all your heart, all your soul, all your mind, and all your
strength.'* 31The second is equally important: 'Love your
neighbor as yourself.'* No other commandment is
greater than these."
32The teacher of religious law replied, "Well said,
Teacher. You have spoken the truth by saying that there
is only one God and no other. 33And I know it is important
to love him with all my heart and all my understanding
and all my strength, and to love my neighbor as myself.

12:10-11 Ps 118:22-23. **12:12** Greek *They.* **12:15** Greek *a denarius.* **12:19** See Deut 25:5-6. **12:26a** Greek *in the story of the bush? God said to him.* **12:26b** Exod 3:6. **12:29-30** Deut 6:4-5. **12:31** Lev 19:18.

This is more important than to offer all of the burnt offerings and sacrifices required in the law."

34 Realizing how much the man understood, Jesus said to him, "You are not far from the Kingdom of God." And after that, no one dared to ask him any more questions.

WHOSE SON IS THE MESSIAH?

35 Later, as Jesus was teaching the people in the Temple, he asked, "Why do the teachers of religious law claim that the Messiah is the son of David? 36 For David himself, speaking under the inspiration of the Holy Spirit, said,

'The LORD said to my Lord,
Sit in the place of honor at my right hand
until I humble your enemies beneath your feet.'*

37 Since David himself called the Messiah 'my Lord,' how can the Messiah be his son?" The large crowd listened to him with great delight.

38 Jesus also taught: "Beware of these teachers of religious law! For they like to parade around in flowing robes and receive respectful greetings as they walk in the marketplaces. 39 And how they love the seats of honor in the synagogues and the head table at banquets. 40 Yet they shamelessly cheat widows out of their property and then pretend to be pious by making long prayers in public. Because of this, they will be more severely punished."

THE WIDOW'S OFFERING

41 Jesus sat down near the collection box in the Temple and watched as the crowds dropped in their money. Many rich people put in large amounts. 42 Then a poor widow came and dropped in two small coins.*

43 Jesus called his disciples to him and said, "I tell you the truth, this poor widow has given more than all the others who are making contributions. 44 For they gave a tiny part of their surplus, but she, poor as she is, has given everything she had to live on."

13

JESUS FORETELLS THE FUTURE

As Jesus was leaving the Temple that day, one of his disciples said, "Teacher, look at these magnificent buildings! Look at the impressive stones in the walls."

2 Jesus replied, "Yes, look at these great buildings. But they will be completely demolished. Not one stone will be left on top of another!"

3 Later, Jesus sat on the Mount of Olives across the valley from the Temple. Peter, James, John, and Andrew came to him privately and asked him, 4 "Tell us, when will all this happen? What sign will show us that these things are about to be fulfilled?"

5 Jesus replied, "Don't let anyone mislead you, 6 for many will come in my name, claiming, 'I am the Messiah.'* They will deceive many. 7 And you will hear of wars and threats of wars, but don't panic. Yes, these things must take place, but the end won't follow immediately. 8 Nation will go to war against nation, and kingdom against kingdom. There will be earthquakes in many parts of the world, as well as famines. But this is only the first of the birth pains, with more to come.

9 "When these things begin to happen, watch out! You will be handed over to the local councils and beaten in the synagogues. You will stand trial before governors and kings because you are my followers. But this will be your opportunity to tell them about me.* 10 For the Good News must first be preached to all nations.* 11 But when you are arrested and stand trial, don't worry in advance about what to say. Just say what God tells you at that time, for it is not you who will be speaking, but the Holy Spirit.

12 "A brother will betray his brother to death, a father will betray his own child, and children will rebel against their parents and cause them to be killed. 13 And everyone will hate you because you are my followers.* But the one who endures to the end will be saved.

PERSECUTION 13:9-13

As the first-century church began to grow, most of the disciples experienced the kind of persecution Jesus described in this passage. Later, he promised that Christians could expect trouble of this kind (John 16:33). A quick look at a newspaper will show you that many Christians in other parts of the world daily face hardships. Although you might not experience persecution now, you might face it someday. Are you prepared to take a stand for Christ, even if doing so means trouble for you? ■

14 "The day is coming when you will see the sacrilegious object that causes desecration* standing where he* should not be." (Reader, pay attention!) "Then those in Judea must flee to the hills. 15 A person out on the deck of a roof must not go down into the house to pack. 16 A person out in the field must not return even to get a coat. 17 How terrible it will be for pregnant women and for nursing mothers in those days. 18 And pray that your flight will not be in winter. 19 For there will be greater anguish in those days than at any time since God created the world. And it will never be so great again. 20 In fact, unless the Lord shortens that time of calamity, not a single person will survive. But for the sake of his chosen ones he has shortened those days.

21 "Then if anyone tells you, 'Look, here is the Messiah,' or 'There he is,' don't believe it. 22 For false messiahs and false prophets will rise up and perform signs and wonders so as to deceive, if possible, even God's chosen ones. 23 Watch out! I have warned you about this ahead of time!

24 "At that time, after the anguish of those days,

the sun will be darkened,
the moon will give no light,

12:36 Ps 110:1. **12:42** Greek *two lepta, which is a kodrantes* [i.e., a quadrans]. **13:6** Greek *claiming, 'I am.'* **13:9** Or *But this will be your testimony against them.* **13:10** Or *all peoples.* **13:13** Greek *on account of my name.* **13:14a** Greek *the abomination of desolation.* See Dan 9:27; 11:31; 12:11. **13:14b** Or *it.*

25 the stars will fall from the sky,
and the powers in the heavens will be shaken.*

26 Then everyone will see the Son of Man* coming on the
clouds with great power and glory.* 27 And he will send
out his angels to gather his chosen ones from all over the
world*—from the farthest ends of the earth and heaven.
28 "Now learn a lesson from the fig tree. When its
branches bud and its leaves begin to sprout, you know
that summer is near. 29 In the same way, when you see all
these things taking place, you can know that his return is
very near, right at the door. 30 I tell you the truth, this generation* will not pass from the scene before all these
things take place. 31 Heaven and earth will disappear, but
my words will never disappear.
32 "However, no one knows the day or hour when these
things will happen, not even the angels in heaven or the Son
himself. Only the Father knows. 33 And since you don't
know when that time will come, be on guard! Stay alert*!
34 "The coming of the Son of Man can be illustrated by
the story of a man going on a long trip. When he left
home, he gave each of his slaves instructions about the
work they were to do, and he told the gatekeeper to
watch for his return. 35 You, too, must keep watch! For
you don't know when the master of the household will
return—in the evening, at midnight, before dawn, or at
daybreak. 36 Don't let him find you sleeping when he arrives without warning. 37 I say to you what I say to everyone: Watch for him!"

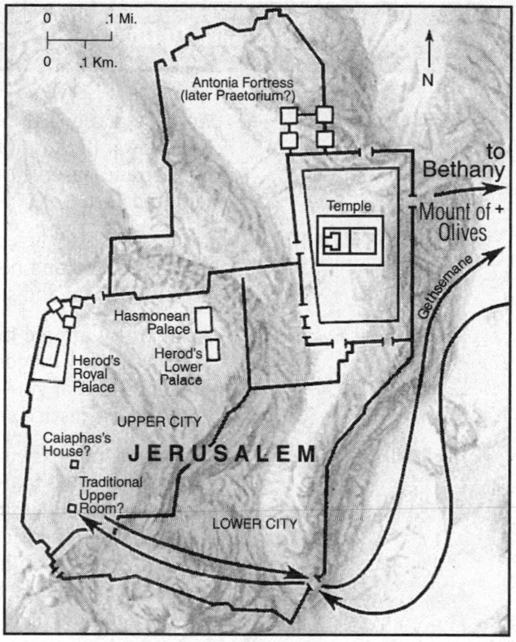

UPPER ROOM AND GETHSEMANE
Jesus and the disciples ate the traditional Passover meal in an upper room in the city and then went to the Mount of Olives into a garden called Gethsemane. In the cool of the evening, Jesus prayed for strength to face the trial and suffering ahead.

HIGHEST LOVE 14:1-9

By his statements, Jesus didn't imply that we should neglect the poor or be indifferent to them. He simply praised Mary for her unselfish act of worship. The essence of worshiping Christ is to regard him with utmost love, respect, and devotion and to be willing to sacrifice to him what is most precious. Is that the kind of love you have for him? ■

14

JESUS ANOINTED AT BETHANY

It was now two days before Passover and the Festival of Unleavened Bread. The leading priests and the teachers of religious law were still looking for an opportunity to capture
Jesus secretly and kill him. 2 "But not during the Passover
celebration," they agreed, "or the people may riot."
3 Meanwhile, Jesus was in Bethany at the home of Simon, a man who had previously had leprosy. While he was
eating,* a woman came in with a beautiful alabaster jar of
expensive perfume made from essence of nard. She
broke open the jar and poured the perfume over his head.
4 Some of those at the table were indignant. "Why
waste such expensive perfume?" they asked. 5 "It could
have been sold for a year's wages* and the money given to
the poor!" So they scolded her harshly.
6 But Jesus replied, "Leave her alone. Why criticize her
for doing such a good thing to me? 7 You will always have
the poor among you, and you can help them whenever
you want to. But you will not always have me. 8 She has
done what she could and has anointed my body for burial
ahead of time. 9 I tell you the truth, wherever the Good
News is preached throughout the world, this woman's
deed will be remembered and discussed."

JUDAS AGREES TO BETRAY JESUS

10 Then Judas Iscariot, one of the twelve disciples, went to
the leading priests to arrange to betray Jesus to them.
11 They were delighted when they heard why he had
come, and they promised to give him money. So he began
looking for an opportunity to betray Jesus.

THE LAST SUPPER

12 On the first day of the Festival of Unleavened Bread,
when the Passover lamb is sacrificed, Jesus' disciples
asked him, "Where do you want us to go to prepare the
Passover meal for you?"
13 So Jesus sent two of them into Jerusalem with these
instructions: "As you go into the city, a man carrying a
pitcher of water will meet you. Follow him. 14 At the house
he enters, say to the owner, 'The Teacher asks: Where is
the guest room where I can eat the Passover meal with my
disciples?' 15 He will take you upstairs to a large room that

13:24-25 See Isa 13:10; 34:4; Joel 2:10. 13:26a "Son of Man" is a title Jesus used for himself. 13:26b See Dan 7:13. 13:27 Greek *from the four winds.* 13:30 Or *this age,* or *this nation.* 13:33 Some manuscripts add *and pray.* 14:3 Or *reclining.* 14:5 Greek *for 300 denarii.* A denarius was equivalent to a laborer's full day's wage.

Why Did Jesus Have To Die?

THE PROBLEM We have all done things that are wrong, and we have failed to obey God's laws. Because of this, we have been separated from God our Creator and deserve death. By ourselves we can do nothing to become reunited with God.

WHY JESUS COULD HELP Jesus was not only a man, he was God's unique Son. Because Jesus never disobeyed God and never sinned, only he can bridge the gap between the sinless God and sinful humanity.

THE SOLUTION Jesus freely offered his life for us, dying on the cross in our place, taking all our wrongdoing upon himself, and saving us from the consequences of sin—including God's judgment and death. God in his love and his justice sent Jesus to take our place.

THE RESULTS Jesus took our past, present, and future sins upon himself so that we could have new life. Because all our wrongdoing is forgiven, we are reconciled to God. Furthermore, Jesus' resurrection from the dead is the proof that his sacrifice on the cross in our place was acceptable to God, and his resurrection has become the source of new life for those who believe that Jesus is the Son of God. All who believe in him may have new life and live it in union with him.

is already set up. That is where you should prepare our
meal." 16So the two disciples went into the city and found
everything just as Jesus had said, and they prepared the
Passover meal there.
17In the evening Jesus arrived with the twelve disciples.*
18As they were at the table* eating, Jesus said, "I tell you the
truth, one of you eating with me here will betray me."
19Greatly distressed, each one asked in turn, "Am I the one?"
20He replied, "It is one of you twelve who is eating from
this bowl with me. 21For the Son of Man* must die, as the
Scriptures declared long ago. But how terrible it will be
for the one who betrays him. It would be far better for
that man if he had never been born!"
22As they were eating, Jesus took some bread and
blessed it. Then he broke it in pieces and gave it to the
disciples, saying, "Take it, for this is my body."
23And he took a cup of wine and gave thanks to God for it.
He gave it to them, and they all drank from it. 24And he said
to them, "This is my blood, which confirms the covenant*
between God and his people. It is poured out as a sacrifice
for many. 25I tell you the truth, I will not drink wine again until the day I drink it new in the Kingdom of God."
26Then they sang a hymn and went out to the Mount of
Olives.

JESUS PREDICTS PETER'S DENIAL

27On the way, Jesus told them, "All of you will desert me.
For the Scriptures say,

'God will strike* the Shepherd,
and the sheep will be scattered.'

28But after I am raised from the dead, I will go ahead of
you to Galilee and meet you there."
29Peter said to him, "Even if everyone else deserts you, I
never will."
30Jesus replied, "I tell you the truth, Peter—this very
night, before the rooster crows twice, you will deny three
times that you even know me."
31"No!" Peter declared emphatically. "Even if I have to
die with you, I will never deny you!" And all the others
vowed the same.

JESUS PRAYS IN GETHSEMANE

32They went to the olive grove called Gethsemane, and Jesus
said, "Sit here while I go and pray." 33He took Peter, James,
and John with him, and he became deeply troubled and distressed. 34He told them, "My soul is crushed with grief to the
point of death. Stay here and keep watch with me."
35He went on a little farther and fell to the ground. He
prayed that, if it were possible, the awful hour awaiting him
might pass him by. 36"Abba, Father,"* he cried out, "everything is possible for you. Please take this cup of suffering
away from me. Yet I want your will to be done, not mine."
37Then he returned and found the disciples asleep. He
said to Peter, "Simon, are you asleep? Couldn't you watch
with me even one hour? 38Keep watch and pray, so that
you will not give in to temptation. For the spirit is willing,
but the body is weak."
39Then Jesus left them again and prayed the same
prayer as before. 40When he returned to them again, he
found them sleeping, for they couldn't keep their eyes
open. And they didn't know what to say.

14:17 Greek *the Twelve.* **14:18** Or *As they reclined.* **14:21** "Son of Man" is a title Jesus used for himself. **14:24** Some manuscripts read *the new covenant.* **14:27** Greek *I will strike.* Zech 13:7. **14:36** *Abba* is an Aramaic term for "father."

41When he returned to them the third time, he said, "Go ahead and sleep. Have your rest. But no—the time has come. The Son of Man is betrayed into the hands of sinners. 42Up, let's be going. Look, my betrayer is here!"

JESUS IS BETRAYED AND ARRESTED

43And immediately, even as Jesus said this, Judas, one of the twelve disciples, arrived with a crowd of men armed with swords and clubs. They had been sent by the leading priests, the teachers of religious law, and the elders. 44The traitor, Judas, had given them a prearranged signal: "You will know which one to arrest when I greet him with a kiss. Then you can take him away under guard." 45As soon as they arrived, Judas walked up to Jesus. "Rabbi!" he exclaimed, and gave him the kiss.

46Then the others grabbed Jesus and arrested him. 47But one of the men with Jesus pulled out his sword and struck the high priest's slave, slashing off his ear.

48Jesus asked them, "Am I some dangerous revolutionary, that you come with swords and clubs to arrest me? 49Why didn't you arrest me in the Temple? I was there among you teaching every day. But these things are happening to fulfill what the Scriptures say about me."

50Then all his disciples deserted him and ran away. 51One young man following behind was clothed only in a long linen shirt. When the mob tried to grab him, 52he slipped out of his shirt and ran away naked.

JESUS BEFORE THE COUNCIL

53They took Jesus to the high priest's home where the leading priests, the elders, and the teachers of religious law had gathered. 54Meanwhile, Peter followed him at a distance and went right into the high priest's courtyard. There he sat with the guards, warming himself by the fire.

ALL TO BLAME 14:55-72

The Jewish Sanhedrin are easy targets for our anger because of their injustice in condemning Jesus. Yet Peter and the rest of the disciples also contributed to Jesus' pain by deserting him and denying him (14:50, 66-72). We might shake our heads at their actions, thinking that we would never do such a thing. But how many of us deny Jesus by keeping silent about our Christianity or going along with actions that are contrary to God's Word? Every wrong thing we do is a denial of Jesus. Tempted to point the finger at someone who messed up? A pointing finger usually winds up pointing back at you. ■

55Inside, the leading priests and the entire high council* were trying to find evidence against Jesus, so they could put him to death. But they couldn't find any. 56Many false witnesses spoke against him, but they contradicted each other. 57Finally, some men stood up and gave this false testimony: 58"We heard him say, 'I will destroy this Temple made with human hands, and in three

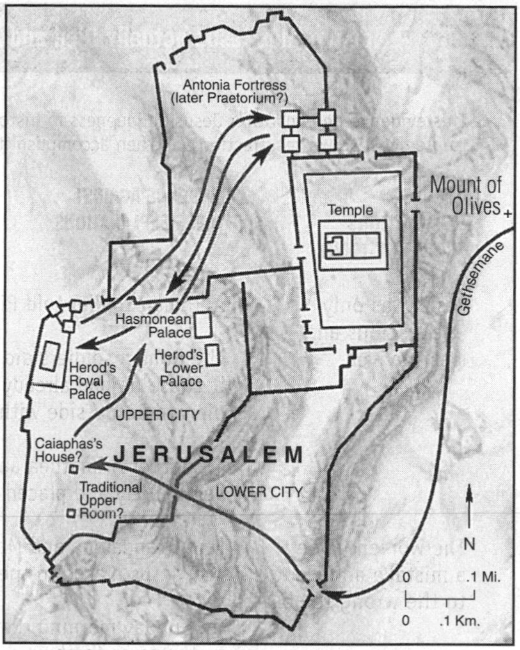

JESUS' TRIAL

From Gethsemane, Jesus' trial began at the home of Caiaphas, the high priest. He was then taken to Pilate, the Roman governor. Luke records that Pilate sent him to Herod, who was in Jerusalem—presumably in one of his two palaces (Luke 23:5-12). Herod sent him back to Pilate, who sentenced him to be crucified.

days I will build another, made without human hands.'" 59But even then they didn't get their stories straight!

60Then the high priest stood up before the others and asked Jesus, "Well, aren't you going to answer these charges? What do you have to say for yourself?" 61But Jesus was silent and made no reply. Then the high priest asked him, "Are you the Messiah, the Son of the Blessed One?"

62Jesus said, "I AM.* And you will see the Son of Man seated in the place of power at God's right hand* and coming on the clouds of heaven.*"

63Then the high priest tore his clothing to show his horror and said, "Why do we need other witnesses? 64You have all heard his blasphemy. What is your verdict?"

"Guilty!" they all cried. "He deserves to die!"

65Then some of them began to spit at him, and they blindfolded him and beat him with their fists. "Prophesy to us," they jeered. And the guards slapped him as they took him away.

PETER DENIES JESUS

66Meanwhile, Peter was in the courtyard below. One of the servant girls who worked for the high priest came by 67and noticed Peter warming himself at the fire. She

14:55 Greek *the Sanhedrin.* 14:62a Or *The 'I AM' is here;* or *I am the LORD.* See Exod 3:14. 14:62b Greek *at the right hand of the power.* See Ps 110:1. 14:62c See Dan 7:13.

Evidence that Jesus actually Died and Arose

This evidence demonstrates Jesus' uniqueness in history and proves that he is God's Son. No one else was able to predict his own resurrection and then accomplish it.

PROPOSED EXPLANATIONS FOR EMPTY TOMB	EVIDENCE AGAINST THESE EXPLANATIONS	REFERENCES
Jesus was only unconscious and later revived	A Roman soldier told Pilate Jesus was dead.	Mark 15:44-45
	The Roman soldiers did not break Jesus' legs because he had already died, and one of them pierced Jesus' side with a spear.	John 19:32-34
	Joseph of Arimathea and Nicodemus wrapped Jesus' body and placed it in the tomb.	John 19:38-40
The women made a mistake and went to the wrong tomb.	Mary Magdalene and Mary the mother of Jesus saw Jesus placed in the tomb.	Matthew 27:59-61 Mark 15:47 Luke 23:55
	On Sunday morning, Peter and John also went to the same tomb.	John 20:3-9
Unknown thieves stole Jesus' body.	The tomb was sealed and guarded by Roman soldiers.	Matthew 27:65-66
The disciples stole Jesus' body	The disciples were ready to die for their faith. Stealing Jesus' body would have been admitting their faith was meaningless.	Acts 12:2
	The tomb was guarded and sealed.	Matthew 27:65-66
The religious leaders stole Jesus' body to secure it.	If the religious leaders had taken Jesus' body, they would have produced it to stop the rumors of his resurrection.	None

looked at him closely and said, "You were one of those
with Jesus of Nazareth.*"
68 But Peter denied it. "I don't know what you're talking
about," he said, and he went out into the entryway. Just
then, a rooster crowed.*
69 When the servant girl saw him standing there, she
began telling the others, "This man is definitely one of
them!" 70 But Peter denied it again.
A little later some of the other bystanders confronted
Peter and said, "You must be one of them, because you
are a Galilean."
71 Peter swore, "A curse on me if I'm lying—I don't
know this man you're talking about!" 72 And immediately
the rooster crowed the second time.
Suddenly, Jesus' words flashed through Peter's mind:
"Before the rooster crows twice, you will deny three times
that you even know me." And he broke down and wept.

15

JESUS' TRIAL BEFORE PILATE

Very early in the morning the leading priests, the elders,
and the teachers of religious law—the entire high council*—met to discuss their next step. They bound Jesus,
led him away, and took him to Pilate, the Roman governor.
2 Pilate asked Jesus, "Are you the king of the Jews?"
Jesus replied, "You have said it."
3 Then the leading priests kept accusing him of many
crimes, 4 and Pilate asked him, "Aren't you going to answer them? What about all these charges they are bringing against you?" 5 But Jesus said nothing, much to Pilate's
surprise.
6 Now it was the governor's custom each year during
the Passover celebration to release one prisoner—anyone
the people requested. 7 One of the prisoners at that time

14:67 Or *Jesus the Nazarene.* **14:68** Some manuscripts do not include *Just then, a rooster crowed.* **15:1** Greek *the Sanhedrin;* also in 15:43.

was Barabbas, a revolutionary who had committed murder in an uprising. [8]The crowd went to Pilate and asked
him to release a prisoner as usual.
[9]"Would you like me to release to you this 'King of the
Jews'?" Pilate asked. [10](For he realized by now that the
leading priests had arrested Jesus out of envy.) [11]But at
this point the leading priests stirred up the crowd to demand the release of Barabbas instead of Jesus. [12]Pilate
asked them, "Then what should I do with this man you
call the king of the Jews?"
[13]They shouted back, "Crucify him!"
[14]"Why?" Pilate demanded. "What crime has he
committed?"
But the mob roared even louder, "Crucify him!"
[15]So to pacify the crowd, Pilate released Barabbas to
them. He ordered Jesus flogged with a lead-tipped whip,
then turned him over to the Roman soldiers to be
crucified.

THE RIGHT THING 15:15

Although Jesus was innocent according to Roman law, Pilate caved in under political pressure. He abandoned what he knew was right in his struggle to give a decision that would please everyone and keep himself safe. When we ignore God's statements of right and wrong and make decisions based on our audience, we compromise. God promises to honor those who do what's right—not those who make everyone happy. ■

THE SOLDIERS MOCK JESUS

[16]The soldiers took Jesus into the courtyard of the governor's headquarters (called the Praetorium) and called out
the entire regiment. [17]They dressed him in a purple robe,
and they wove thorn branches into a crown and put it on
his head. [18]Then they saluted him and taunted, "Hail! King
of the Jews!" [19]And they struck him on the head with a
reed stick, spit on him, and dropped to their knees in
mock worship. [20]When they were finally tired of mocking
him, they took off the purple robe and put his own clothes
on him again. Then they led him away to be crucified.

THE CRUCIFIXION

[21]A passerby named Simon, who was from Cyrene,* was
coming in from the countryside just then, and the soldiers forced him to carry Jesus' cross. (Simon was the father of Alexander and Rufus.) [22]And they brought Jesus
to a place called Golgotha (which means "Place of the
Skull"). [23]They offered him wine drugged with myrrh, but
he refused it.
[24]Then the soldiers nailed him to the cross. They divided his clothes and threw dice* to decide who would
get each piece. [25]It was nine o'clock in the morning when
they crucified him. [26]A sign was fastened to the cross, announcing the charge against him. It read, "The King of

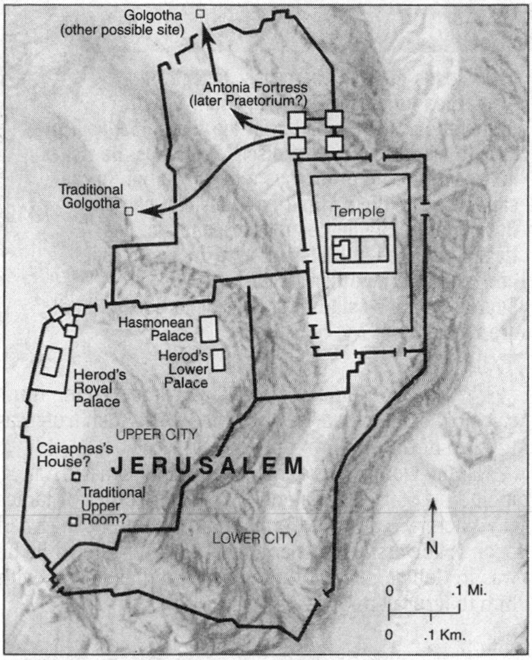

JESUS' ROUTE TO GOLGOTHA
After being sentenced by Pilate, Jesus was taken from the Praetorium to a place outside the city, Golgotha, for crucifixion.

the Jews." [27]Two revolutionaries* were crucified with
him, one on his right and one on his left.*
[29]The people passing by shouted abuse, shaking their
heads in mockery. "Ha! Look at you now!" they yelled at
him. "You said you were going to destroy the Temple and
rebuild it in three days. [30]Well then, save yourself and
come down from the cross!"
[31]The leading priests and teachers of religious law also
mocked Jesus. "He saved others," they scoffed, "but he
can't save himself! [32]Let this Messiah, this King of Israel,
come down from the cross so we can see it and believe
him!" Even the men who were crucified with Jesus ridiculed him.

THE DEATH OF JESUS

[33]At noon, darkness fell across the whole land until three
o'clock. [34]Then at three o'clock Jesus called out with a
loud voice, *"Eloi, Eloi, lema sabachthani?"* which means
"My God, my God, why have you abandoned me?"*
[35]Some of the bystanders misunderstood and thought
he was calling for the prophet Elijah. [36]One of them ran
and filled a sponge with sour wine, holding it up to him
on a reed stick so he could drink. "Wait!" he said. "Let's
see whether Elijah comes to take him down!"
[37]Then Jesus uttered another loud cry and breathed his
last. [38]And the curtain in the sanctuary of the Temple was
torn in two, from top to bottom.

15:21 *Cyrene* was a city in northern Africa. **15:24** Greek *cast lots.* See Ps 22:18. **15:27a** Or *Two criminals.* **15:27b** Some manuscripts add verse 28, *And the Scripture was fulfilled that said, "He was counted among those who were rebels."* See Isa 53:12; also compare Luke 22:37. **15:34** Ps 22:1.

RISKY BUSINESS 15:42-43

After Jesus died on the cross, Joseph of Arimathea buried his body in a new tomb. Although he was a member of the Jewish Sanhedrin, Joseph also was a secret disciple of Jesus. He risked his reputation to give Jesus a proper burial. In the same way, taking a stand for Jesus can be risky. But consider the outcome of Joseph's actions. He's mentioned in Bibles all over the world. But how many of the other members of the Jewish Supreme Court (aside from Nicodemus—see John 3) are remembered? ■

39 When the Roman officer* who stood facing him* saw how he had died, he exclaimed, "This man truly was the Son of God!"

40 Some women were there, watching from a distance, including Mary Magdalene, Mary (the mother of James the younger and of Joseph*), and Salome. 41 They had been followers of Jesus and had cared for him while he was in Galilee. Many other women who had come with him to Jerusalem were also there.

OPPORTUNITIES 15:40-16:8

The women at the tomb could do very little. They couldn't speak before the Sanhedrin in Jesus' defense; they couldn't appeal to Pilate; they couldn't stand against the crowds; and they couldn't overpower the Roman guards. But they did what they could. They stayed at the cross when the disciples had fled; they followed Jesus' body to its tomb; and they prepared spices for his body. Because they used the opportunities they had, they were the first to witness the Resurrection. God blessed their devotion and diligence. What opportunities has God given you to tell others about him? ■

THE BURIAL OF JESUS

42 This all happened on Friday, the day of preparation,* the day before the Sabbath. As evening approached, 43 Joseph of Arimathea took a risk and went to Pilate and asked for Jesus' body. (Joseph was an honored member of the high council, and he was waiting for the Kingdom of God to come.) 44 Pilate couldn't believe that Jesus was already dead, so he called for the Roman officer and asked if he had died yet. 45 The officer confirmed that Jesus was dead, so Pilate told Joseph he could have the body. 46 Joseph bought a long sheet of linen cloth. Then he took Jesus' body down from the cross, wrapped it in the cloth, and laid it in a tomb that had been carved out of the rock. Then he rolled a stone in front of the entrance. 47 Mary Magdalene and Mary the mother of Joseph saw where Jesus' body was laid.

16 THE RESURRECTION

Saturday evening, when the Sabbath ended, Mary Magdalene, Mary the mother of James, and Salome went out and purchased burial spices so they could anoint Jesus' body. 2 Very early on Sunday morning,* just at sunrise, they went to the tomb. 3 On the way they were asking each other, "Who will roll away the stone for us from the entrance to the tomb?" 4 But as they arrived, they looked up and saw that the stone, which was very large, had already been rolled aside.

5 When they entered the tomb, they saw a young man clothed in a white robe sitting on the right side. The women were shocked, 6 but the angel said, "Don't be alarmed. You are looking for Jesus of Nazareth,* who was crucified. He isn't here! He is risen from the dead! Look, this is where they laid his body. 7 Now go and tell his disciples, including Peter, that Jesus is going ahead of you to Galilee. You will see him there, just as he told you before he died."

8 The women fled from the tomb, trembling and bewildered, and they said nothing to anyone because they were too frightened.*

[*Shorter Ending of Mark*]

Then they briefly reported all this to Peter and his companions. Afterward Jesus himself sent them out from east to west with the sacred and unfailing message of salvation that gives eternal life. Amen.

[*Longer Ending of Mark*]

9 After Jesus rose from the dead early on Sunday morning, the first person who saw him was Mary Magdalene, the woman from whom he had cast out seven demons. 10 She went to the disciples, who were grieving and weeping, and told them what had happened. 11 But when she told them that Jesus was alive and she had seen him, they didn't believe her.

YOU'VE GOT THE POWER 16:15

The risen Jesus gave his disciples a mission: Make more disciples. Their mission is also the mission of believers today. Have you ever believed that you lack the skill or determination to do anything for God? Through the Holy Spirit, you've got the power. How will you use it? ■

12 Afterward he appeared in a different form to two of his followers who were walking from Jerusalem into the country. 13 They rushed back to tell the others, but no one believed them.

14 Still later he appeared to the eleven disciples as they were eating together. He rebuked them for their stubborn

15:39a Greek *the centurion;* similarly in 15:44, 45. **15:39b** Some manuscripts add *heard his cry and.* **15:40** Greek *Joses;* also in 15:47. See Matt 27:56. **15:42** Greek *It was the day of preparation.* **16:2** Greek *on the first day of the week;* also in 16:9. **16:6** Or *Jesus the Nazarene.* **16:8** The most reliable early manuscripts of the Gospel of Mark end at verse 8. Other manuscripts include various endings to the Gospel. A few include both the "shorter ending" and the "longer ending." The majority of manuscripts include the "longer ending" immediately after verse 8.

THE RESURRECTION

ULTIMATE ISSUES

Think about a time when you felt at your lowest point. Got that fixed in your mind? Then you can imagine what must have been going through the disciples' minds as they witnessed (or heard about) the crucifixion of their Master. They had hoped that Jesus was the Messiah who would lead Israel to freedom from the Romans. But now he was dead. All of their hopes and expectations died with him.

If that were the end of the story, you would never have heard of Jesus or Christianity. Jesus' followers would have disappeared like the followers of dozens of other would-be Messiahs. Also, you wouldn't be holding this book in your hands, reading it as countless millions of others have, basing your life on its principles.

But Jesus' death was not the end. It was only the beginning. As Mark 16 tells us, Jesus didn't stay dead. On an otherwise ordinary Sunday morning, he rose from the dead!

Some of us have a tendency to take the Resurrection for granted, especially after hearing the story 50 times. But we need to remember that people didn't vacate their graveyards 2,000 years ago in Palestine any more than they do today. Dead people stayed dead—with one major exception. And that exception, the resurrection of Jesus, has made all the difference in eternity for countless Christians.

When the first-century Christians, including the disciples, were called upon to defend their faith in Jesus as Messiah, they didn't point to his great moral teachings or his miracles. They pointed to one rock-solid proof: his death and resurrection. Because Jesus really came back from death, it stands to reason that the rest of what he told us is true: he is the way to the Father; anyone who puts his or her faith in Christ can live forever with him in heaven.

unbelief because they refused to believe those who had
seen him after he had been raised from the dead.*
15And then he told them, "Go into all the world and
preach the Good News to everyone. 16Anyone who believes and is baptized will be saved. But anyone who refuses to believe will be condemned. 17These miraculous
signs will accompany those who believe: They will cast
out demons in my name, and they will speak in new languages.* 18They will be able to handle snakes with safety,
and if they drink anything poisonous, it won't hurt them.
They will be able to place their hands on the sick, and
they will be healed."
19When the Lord Jesus had finished talking with them,
he was taken up into heaven and sat down in the place of
honor at God's right hand. 20And the disciples went
everywhere and preached, and the Lord worked through
them, confirming what they said by many miraculous
signs.

16:14 Some early manuscripts add: *And they excused themselves, saying, "This age of lawlessness and unbelief is under Satan, who does not permit God's truth and power to conquer the evil [unclean] spirits. Therefore, reveal your justice now." This is what they said to Christ. And Christ replied to them, "The period of years of Satan's power has been fulfilled, but other dreadful things will happen soon. And I was handed over to death for those who have sinned, so that they may return to the truth and sin no more, and so they may inherit the spiritual, incorruptible, and righteous glory in heaven."* **16:17** Or *new tongues;* some manuscripts omit *new.*

LUKE

THEY WERE two kids in love. In fact, they were *engaged*. And they had big plans, big dreams. Then the roof caved in. M. found out she was pregnant. J. was hurt, confused, and ticked. After all, he knew *he* wasn't the father. There was only one thing to do: call off the wedding.

But weird things started happening. M. claimed she'd been visited by a real-life angel, and that she'd been made pregnant by the Spirit of God!

Then J. started seeing angels! Surely it was all a dream . . . until the angel said, "Hey, J., don't break off the engagement! The child inside M. really *is* the Savior of the world." Soon M. could no longer hide her pregnancy. Rumors flew. M. and J. purposely kept a low profile. Together they wondered what it would be like.

Did M. realize that her little baby would incite a king to slaughter thousands of infants? Did J. know that the child would perform astounding miracles? Did these two realize their precious boy would die in a brutal manner?

Even if they *were* able to grasp any of that, did they truly believe that their murdered son would come back to life?

Does this sound like a weird soap opera? You can read about M. & J. and their son—mainly about their son—in the following pages. The story is the Gospel of Luke.

Luke

timeline

37 B.C.
Herod the Great begins to rule

6/5 B.C.
Jesus is born

5/4 B.C.
Escape to Egypt

4 B.C.
Herod the Great dies

4/3 B.C.
Return to Nazareth

A.D. 6/7
Jesus visits Temple as a boy

14
Tiberius Caesar becomes emperor

26
John's ministry begins

26/27
Jesus begins his ministry

28
Jesus chooses 12 disciples

29
Jesus feeds 5,000

30
Jesus is crucified, rises again, and ascends

stats

PURPOSE: To present an accurate account of the life of Christ and to present Christ as the perfect man and Savior

AUTHOR: Luke—a Greek doctor (Col 4:14) who became a believer. He is the only known Gentile author in the New Testament. He was a close friend and companion of Paul. He also wrote the book of Acts.

TO WHOM WRITTEN: Theophilus ("lover of God"), Gentiles, and people everywhere

DATE WRITTEN: About A.D. 60

SETTING: Luke wrote from Caesarea or from Rome.

KEY PEOPLE: Jesus, Elizabeth, Zechariah, John the Baptist, Mary, the disciples, Herod the Great, Pilate, Mary Magdalene

KEY PLACES: Bethlehem, Galilee, Judea, Jerusalem

KEY points

THE PERFECT MAN, THE PERFECT SACRIFICE
Jesus lived as the perfect man and provided a perfect sacrifice for sin. Jesus is uniquely qualified to offer forgiveness to all who believe.

HISTORY
Luke placed great emphasis on dates and details, connecting Jesus to events and people in history. Luke's devotion to accuracy gives us confidence in the reliability of the history of Jesus' life.

CARING FOR PEOPLE
Jesus was deeply interested in people and relationships. Jesus' love for people inspires us to show the same concern for others.

HOLY SPIRIT
The Holy Spirit was present at Jesus' birth, baptism, ministry, and resurrection. As a perfect example for us, Jesus lived in dependence on the Holy Spirit. The Holy Spirit is given to enable people to live for Christ. By faith we can have the Holy Spirit's presence and power to witness and to serve.

KEY PLACES IN LUKE

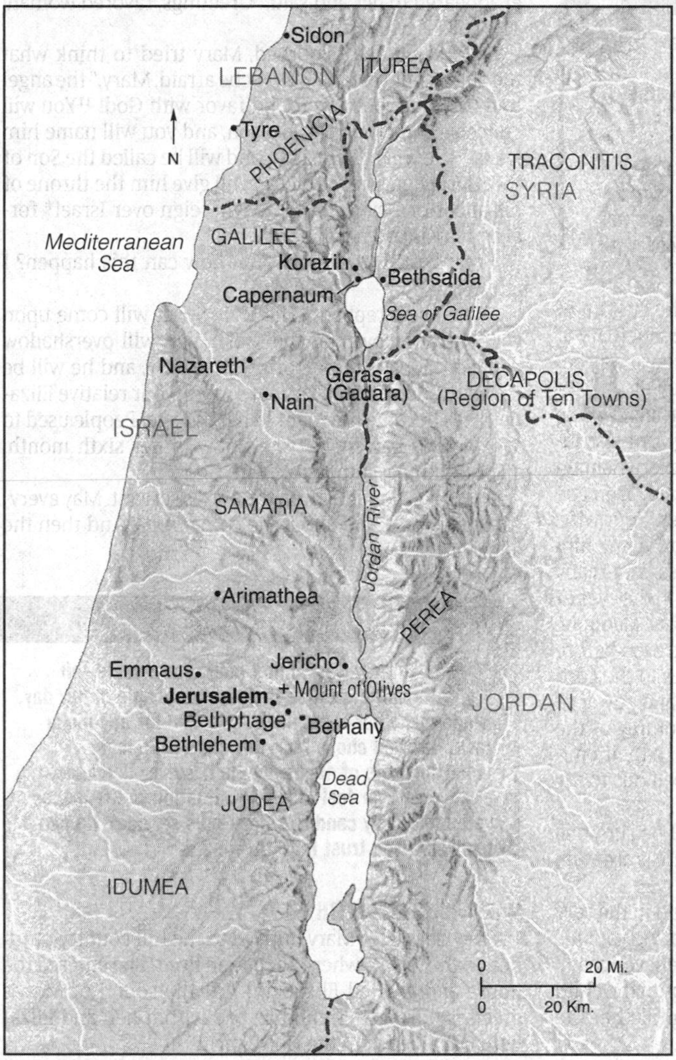

The broken lines (—·—) indicate modern boundaries.

Luke begins his account in the Temple in Jerusalem, giving us the background for the birth of John the Baptist, and then moves on to the city of Nazareth and the story of Mary, chosen to be Jesus' mother (1:26-38). As a result of Caesar's call for a census, Mary and Joseph had to travel to Bethlehem, where Jesus was born in fulfillment of prophecy (2:1-20). Jesus grew up in Nazareth and began his earthly ministry by being baptized by John (3:21-22) and tempted by Satan (4:1-13). Much of his ministry focused on Galilee—he set up his "home" in Capernaum (4:31), and from there he taught throughout the region (8:1-3). Later he visited the Gadarene country, where he healed a demon-possessed man from Gadara (8:36-39). He fed more than 5,000 people with one lunch on the shores of the Sea of Galilee near Bethsaida (9:10-17). Jesus traveled to Jerusalem for the major feasts and enjoyed visiting friends in nearby Bethany (10:38-42). He healed 10 men with leprosy on the border between Galilee and Samaria (17:11) and helped a dishonest tax collector in Jericho turn his life around (19:1-10). The little villages of Bethphage and Bethany on the Mount of Olives were Jesus' resting places during his last days on earth. He was crucified outside Jerusalem's walls, but he would rise again. Two people on the road leading to Emmaus were among the first to see the resurrected Christ (24:13-34).

1

INTRODUCTION

1 Many people have set out to write accounts about the
events that have been fulfilled among us. 2They used the
eyewitness reports circulating among us from the early
disciples.* 3Having carefully investigated everything
from the beginning, I also have decided to write a careful account for you, most honorable Theophilus, 4so you
can be certain of the truth of everything you were
taught.

THE BIRTH OF JOHN THE BAPTIST FORETOLD

5When Herod was king of Judea, there was a Jewish priest
named Zechariah. He was a member of the priestly order
of Abijah, and his wife, Elizabeth, was also from the
priestly line of Aaron. 6Zechariah and Elizabeth were
righteous in God's eyes, careful to obey all of the Lord's
commandments and regulations. 7They had no children
because Elizabeth was unable to conceive, and they were
both very old.
8One day Zechariah was serving God in the Temple, for

1:2 Greek *from those who from the beginning were servants of the word.*

ALL CHECKED OUT 1:1-3

As a medical doctor, Luke knew the importance of a thorough checkup. He used his skills in observation and analysis to do a complete investigation of the stories about Jesus. His diagnosis? The gospel of Jesus Christ is true! You can read Luke's account of Jesus' life with confidence that it was written by a clear thinker and a thoughtful researcher. Is that the kind of researcher you are? How thorough have you been in your investigation of the truth of the Gospel? ■

his order was on duty that week. 9As was the custom of
the priests, he was chosen by lot to enter the sanctuary of
the Lord and burn incense. 10While the incense was being burned, a great crowd stood outside, praying.
11While Zechariah was in the sanctuary, an angel of the
Lord appeared to him, standing to the right of the incense altar. 12Zechariah was shaken and overwhelmed
with fear when he saw him. 13But the angel said, "Don't be
afraid, Zechariah! God has heard your prayer. Your wife,
Elizabeth, will give you a son, and you are to name him
John. 14You will have great joy and gladness, and many
will rejoice at his birth, 15for he will be great in the eyes of
the Lord. He must never touch wine or other alcoholic
drinks. He will be filled with the Holy Spirit, even before
his birth.* 16And he will turn many Israelites to the Lord
their God. 17He will be a man with the spirit and power of
Elijah. He will prepare the people for the coming of the
Lord. He will turn the hearts of the fathers to their children,* and he will cause those who are rebellious to accept the wisdom of the godly."
18Zechariah said to the angel, "How can I be sure this
will happen? I'm an old man now, and my wife is also well
along in years."
19Then the angel said, "I am Gabriel! I stand in the very
presence of God. It was he who sent me to bring you this
good news! 20But now, since you didn't believe what I
said, you will be silent and unable to speak until the child
is born. For my words will certainly be fulfilled at the
proper time."
21Meanwhile, the people were waiting for Zechariah to
come out of the sanctuary, wondering why he was taking
so long. 22When he finally did come out, he couldn't
speak to them. Then they realized from his gestures and
his silence that he must have seen a vision in the
sanctuary.
23When Zechariah's week of service in the Temple was
over, he returned home. 24Soon afterward his wife, Elizabeth, became pregnant and went into seclusion for five
months. 25"How kind the Lord is!" she exclaimed. "He has
taken away my disgrace of having no children."

THE BIRTH OF JESUS FORETOLD

26In the sixth month of Elizabeth's pregnancy, God sent
the angel Gabriel to Nazareth, a village in Galilee, 27to a
virgin named Mary. She was engaged to be married to a
man named Joseph, a descendant of King David. 28Gabri-
el appeared to her and said, "Greetings, favored woman!
The Lord is with you!*"
29Confused and disturbed, Mary tried to think what
the angel could mean. 30"Don't be afraid, Mary," the angel
told her, "for you have found favor with God! 31You will
conceive and give birth to a son, and you will name him
Jesus. 32He will be very great and will be called the Son of
the Most High. The Lord God will give him the throne of
his ancestor David. 33And he will reign over Israel* forever; his Kingdom will never end!"
34Mary asked the angel, "But how can this happen? I
am a virgin."
35The angel replied, "The Holy Spirit will come upon
you, and the power of the Most High will overshadow
you. So the baby to be born will be holy, and he will be
called the Son of God. 36What's more, your relative Elizabeth has become pregnant in her old age! People used to
say she was barren, but she's now in her sixth month.
37For nothing is impossible with God.*"
38Mary responded, "I am the Lord's servant. May everything you have said about me come true." And then the
angel left her.

UNLIKELY 1:26-55

Mary was young, poor, and female—all characteristics that, to the people of her day, would make her seem useless to God for any major task. But God chose Mary for one of the most important acts of obedience he has ever demanded of anyone. Ever feel that your situation in life makes you an unlikely candidate for God's service? He can use you if you trust him. Do you? ■

MARY VISITS ELIZABETH

39A few days later Mary hurried to the hill country of Judea, to the town 40where Zechariah lived. She entered the
house and greeted Elizabeth. 41At the sound of Mary's
greeting, Elizabeth's child leaped within her, and Elizabeth was filled with the Holy Spirit.
42Elizabeth gave a glad cry and exclaimed to Mary,
"God has blessed you above all women, and your child
is blessed. 43Why am I so honored, that the mother of
my Lord should visit me? 44When I heard your greeting, the baby in my womb jumped for joy. 45You are
blessed because you believed that the Lord would do
what he said."

THE MAGNIFICAT: MARY'S SONG OF PRAISE

46Mary responded,

"Oh, how my soul praises the Lord.
47 How my spirit rejoices in God my Savior!
48 For he took notice of his lowly servant girl,
and from now on all generations will call
me blessed.

1:15 Or *even from birth.* 1:17 See Mal 4:5-6. 1:28 Some manuscripts add *Blessed are you among women.* 1:33 Greek *over the house of Jacob.* 1:37 Some manuscripts read *For the word of God will never fail.*

49 For the Mighty One is holy,
and he has done great things for me.
50 He shows mercy from generation to generation
to all who fear him.
51 His mighty arm has done tremendous things!
He has scattered the proud and haughty ones.
52 He has brought down princes from their thrones
and exalted the humble.
53 He has filled the hungry with good things
and sent the rich away with empty hands.
54 He has helped his servant Israel
and remembered to be merciful.
55 For he made this promise to our ancestors,
to Abraham and his children forever."

56Mary stayed with Elizabeth about three months and
then went back to her own home.

THE BIRTH OF JOHN THE BAPTIST

57When it was time for Elizabeth's baby to be born, she
gave birth to a son. 58And when her neighbors and relatives heard that the Lord had been very merciful to her,
everyone rejoiced with her.

59When the baby was eight days old, they all came for
the circumcision ceremony. They wanted to name him
Zechariah, after his father. 60But Elizabeth said, "No! His
name is John!"

61"What?" they exclaimed. "There is no one in all your
family by that name." 62So they used gestures to ask the
baby's father what he wanted to name him. 63He motioned for a writing tablet, and to everyone's surprise he
wrote, "His name is John." 64Instantly Zechariah could
speak again, and he began praising God.

65Awe fell upon the whole neighborhood, and the news
of what had happened spread throughout the Judean hills.
66Everyone who heard about it reflected on these events
and asked, "What will this child turn out to be?" For the
hand of the Lord was surely upon him in a special way.

ZECHARIAH'S PROPHECY

67Then his father, Zechariah, was filled with the Holy
Spirit and gave this prophecy:

UPS:
- The mother of Jesus, the Messiah
- The one human who was with Jesus from birth to death
- Willing to be available to God
- Knew and applied God's Word

STATS:
- Where: Nazareth, Bethlehem
- Relatives: Joseph (husband); Zechariah and Elizabeth (relatives); Jesus, James, Joseph, Judas, Simon, plus daughters (children)

BOTTOM LINE:

God's plans involve extraordinary events in the lives of ordinary people.

A person's character is revealed by his or her response to the unexpected.

Mary's story is told throughout the Gospels. She is also mentioned in Acts 1:14.

MARY

When was the last time you heard teen pregnancy described as a good thing? In Mary's case, it was. Mary of Nazareth had been uniquely chosen to be the mother of the Son of God.

Until Gabriel's surprise visit, Mary's life was going well. She had recently become engaged to a local carpenter, Joseph, and was anticipating married life. But God also had other plans for her.

Angels don't usually make appointments before visiting. They just show up. The angel greeted Mary as if she were the winner of a contest she had never entered. But Mary found the angel's greeting puzzling and his presence frightening. What she heard next was the news almost every woman in Israel hoped to hear—that her child would be the Messiah, God's promised Savior. Mary didn't doubt the message, nor did she worry about how her pregnancy would look to others. She just wondered how she could be pregnant without the involvement of a man. Gabriel told her that the baby would be God's Son.

Mary's answer was one that God waits to hear from every person: "I am the Lord's servant. May everything you have said about me come true" (Luke 1:38). Later, her song of joy to Elizabeth shows us how well Mary knew God. Her thoughts were filled with his words from the Old Testament (1:46-55).

But later, after Jesus was taken to the Temple to be dedicated to God, a man name Simeon had words for Mary concerning the future: "And a sword will pierce your very soul" (Luke 2:35).

We can imagine that even if she had known all that she would suffer as Jesus' mother, Mary would have given the same response. Is your life as available to be used by God as Mary's was?

68 "Praise the Lord, the God of Israel,
because he has visited and redeemed his people.
69 He has sent us a mighty Savior*
from the royal line of his servant David,
70 just as he promised
through his holy prophets long ago.
71 Now we will be saved from our enemies
and from all who hate us.
72 He has been merciful to our ancestors
by remembering his sacred covenant—
73 the covenant he swore with an oath
to our ancestor Abraham.
74 We have been rescued from our enemies
so we can serve God without fear,
75 in holiness and righteousness
for as long as we live.

76 "And you, my little son,
will be called the prophet of the Most High,
because you will prepare the way for the Lord.
77 You will tell his people how to find salvation
through forgiveness of their sins.
78 Because of God's tender mercy,
the morning light from heaven is about to break
upon us,*
79 to give light to those who sit in darkness and in the
shadow of death,
and to guide us to the path of peace."

80John grew up and became strong in spirit. And he
lived in the wilderness until he began his public ministry
to Israel.

2

THE BIRTH OF JESUS

At that time the Roman emperor, Augustus, decreed that
a census should be taken throughout the Roman Empire.
2(This was the first census taken when Quirinius was governor of Syria.) 3All returned to their own ancestral towns
to register for this census. 4And because Joseph was a descendant of King David, he had to go to Bethlehem in Judea, David's ancient home. He traveled there from the
village of Nazareth in Galilee. 5He took with him Mary, his
fiancée, who was now obviously pregnant.
6And while they were there, the time came for her baby
to be born. 7She gave birth to her first child, a son. She
wrapped him snugly in strips of cloth and laid him in a
manger, because there was no lodging available for
them.

THE SHEPHERDS AND ANGELS

8That night there were shepherds staying in the fields
nearby, guarding their flocks of sheep. 9Suddenly, an angel of the Lord appeared among them, and the radiance
of the Lord's glory surrounded them. They were terrified,
10but the angel reassured them. "Don't be afraid!" he said.
"I bring you good news that will bring great joy to all people. 11The Savior—yes, the Messiah, the Lord—has been
born today in Bethlehem, the city of David! 12And you will
recognize him by this sign: You will find a baby wrapped
snugly in strips of cloth, lying in a manger."
13Suddenly, the angel was joined by a vast host of
others—the armies of heaven—praising God and saying,

14 "Glory to God in highest heaven,
and peace on earth to those with whom God
is pleased."

15When the angels had returned to heaven, the shepherds said to each other, "Let's go to Bethlehem! Let's see
this thing that has happened, which the Lord has told us
about."
16They hurried to the village and found Mary and Joseph. And there was the baby, lying in the manger. 17After
seeing him, the shepherds told everyone what had happened and what the angel had said to them about this
child. 18All who heard the shepherds' story were astonished, 19but Mary kept all these things in her heart and
thought about them often. 20The shepherds went back to
their flocks, glorifying and praising God for all they had
heard and seen. It was just as the angel had told them.

JESUS IS PRESENTED IN THE TEMPLE

21Eight days later, when the baby was circumcised, he was
named Jesus, the name given him by the angel even before he was conceived.
22Then it was time for their purification offering, as required by the law of Moses after the birth of a child; so his
parents took him to Jerusalem to present him to the Lord.
23The law of the Lord says, "If a woman's first child is a
boy, he must be dedicated to the LORD."* 24So they offered the sacrifice required in the law of the Lord—
"either a pair of turtledoves or two young pigeons."*

WISDOM OF THE AGES 2:25-38

Although Simeon and Anna were very old, they still hoped to see the Messiah. Led by the Holy Spirit, they were among the first to proclaim the arrival of the Savior. Since elders were respected in the Jewish culture, Simeon's and Anna's prophecies carried extra weight. The opposite happens in our society. The opinions of youth often carry more weight (particularly with advertisers) than those of senior citizens. Think about the older people in your life or in your area. What have you learned from them? How can you encourage them through your friendship? You might be surprised at what you can teach each other! ■

THE PROPHECY OF SIMEON

25At that time there was a man in Jerusalem named Simeon. He was righteous and devout and was eagerly waiting
for the Messiah to come and rescue Israel. The Holy
Spirit was upon him 26and had revealed to him that he

1:69 Greek *has raised up a horn of salvation for us.* **1:78** Or *the Morning Light from Heaven is about to visit us.* **2:23** Exod 13:2. **2:24** Lev 12:8.

would not die until he had seen the Lord's Messiah. 27That day the Spirit led him to the Temple. So when Mary and Joseph came to present the baby Jesus to the Lord as the law required, 28Simeon was there. He took the child in his arms and praised God, saying,

29 "Sovereign Lord, now let your servant die in peace,
as you have promised.
30 I have seen your salvation,
31 which you have prepared for all people.
32 He is a light to reveal God to the nations,
and he is the glory of your people Israel!"

33Jesus' parents were amazed at what was being said about him. 34Then Simeon blessed them, and he said to Mary, the baby's mother, "This child is destined to cause many in Israel to fall, but he will be a joy to many others. He has been sent as a sign from God, but many will oppose him. 35As a result, the deepest thoughts of many hearts will be revealed. And a sword will pierce your very soul."

THE PROPHECY OF ANNA

36Anna, a prophet, was also there in the Temple. She was the daughter of Phanuel from the tribe of Asher, and she was very old. Her husband died when they had been married only seven years. 37Then she lived as a widow to the age of eighty-four.* She never left the Temple but stayed there day and night, worshiping God with fasting and prayer. 38She came along just as Simeon was talking with Mary and Joseph, and she began praising God. She talked about the child to everyone who had been waiting expectantly for God to rescue Jerusalem.

39When Jesus' parents had fulfilled all the requirements of the law of the Lord, they returned home to Nazareth in Galilee. 40There the child grew up healthy and strong. He was filled with wisdom, and God's favor was on him.

JESUS SPEAKS WITH THE TEACHERS

41Every year Jesus' parents went to Jerusalem for the Passover festival. 42When Jesus was twelve years old, they attended the festival as usual. 43After the celebration was over, they started home to Nazareth, but Jesus stayed behind in Jerusalem. His parents didn't miss him at first, 44because they assumed he was among the other travelers. But when he didn't show up that evening, they started looking for him among their relatives and friends.

45When they couldn't find him, they went back to Jerusalem to search for him there. 46Three days later they finally discovered him in the Temple, sitting among the religious teachers, listening to them and asking questions. 47All who heard him were amazed at his understanding and his answers.

48His parents didn't know what to think. "Son," his mother said to him, "why have you done this to us? Your father and I have been frantic, searching for you everywhere."

49"But why did you need to search?" he asked. "Didn't you know that I must be in my Father's house?"* 50But they didn't understand what he meant.

51Then he returned to Nazareth with them and was obedient to them. And his mother stored all these things in her heart.

52Jesus grew in wisdom and in stature and in favor with God and all the people.

GRIT AND SUBMIT? 2:46-52

This is the first hint that Jesus realized he was God's Son. Even though Jesus knew his real Father, he didn't reject his earthly parents. Jesus went back to Nazareth with them and lived under their authority for another 18 years. Do you find yourself grumbling about your parents' authority sometimes? Consider this: The Son of God submitted to the authority of his parents. How do you show by your actions that you're willing to submit? ■

3

JOHN THE BAPTIST PREPARES THE WAY

It was now the fifteenth year of the reign of Tiberius, the Roman emperor. Pontius Pilate was governor over Judea; Herod Antipas was ruler* over Galilee; his brother Philip was ruler* over Iturea and Traconitis; Lysanias was ruler over Abilene. 2Annas and Caiaphas were the high priests. At this time a message from God came to John son of Zechariah, who was living in the wilderness. 3Then John went from place to place on both sides of the Jordan River, preaching that people should be baptized to show that they had repented of their sins and turned to God to be forgiven. 4Isaiah had spoken of John when he said,

"He is a voice shouting in the wilderness,
'Prepare the way for the LORD's coming!
Clear the road for him!
5 The valleys will be filled,
and the mountains and hills made level.
The curves will be straightened,
and the rough places made smooth.
6 And then all people will see
the salvation sent from God.'"*

7When the crowds came to John for baptism, he said, "You brood of snakes! Who warned you to flee God's coming wrath? 8Prove by the way you live that you have repented of your sins and turned to God. Don't just say to each other, 'We're safe, for we are descendants of Abraham.' That means nothing, for I tell you, God can create children of Abraham from these very stones. 9Even now the ax of God's judgment is poised, ready to sever the

2:37 Or *She had been a widow for eighty-four years.* **2:49** Or *"Didn't you realize that I should be involved with my Father's affairs?"*
3:1a Greek *Herod was tetrarch.* Herod Antipas was a son of King Herod. **3:1b** Greek *tetrarch;* also in 3:1c. **3:4-6** Isa 40:3-5 (Greek version).

roots of the trees. Yes, every tree that does not produce good fruit will be chopped down and thrown into the fire.”

> **ON YOUR OWN 3:7-9**
>
> **The religious leaders relied more on their family line than on their faith. They thought being descendants of Abraham automatically made them right with God. Many people today think that having parents who are Christians automatically makes them Christians, too. But a relationship with God isn't handed down from parents to children. Everyone has to have his or her own relationship with God. As the old saying goes, God has *children*—not *grandchildren.* Are you relying on the faith of your family or your own?** ■

10 The crowds asked, “What should we do?”
11 John replied, “If you have two shirts, give one to the
poor. If you have food, share it with those who are
hungry.”
12 Even corrupt tax collectors came to be baptized and
asked, “Teacher, what should we do?”
13 He replied, “Collect no more taxes than the government requires.”
14 “What should we do?” asked some soldiers.
John replied, “Don't extort money or make false accusations. And be content with your pay.”
15 Everyone was expecting the Messiah to come soon,
and they were eager to know whether John might be the
Messiah. 16 John answered their questions by saying, “I
baptize you with* water; but someone is coming soon
who is greater than I am—so much greater that I'm not
even worthy to be his slave and untie the straps of his sandals. He will baptize you with the Holy Spirit and with
fire.* 17 He is ready to separate the chaff from the wheat
with his winnowing fork. Then he will clean up the
threshing area, gathering the wheat into his barn but
burning the chaff with never-ending fire.” 18 John used
many such warnings as he announced the Good News to
the people.
19 John also publicly criticized Herod Antipas, the ruler
of Galilee,* for marrying Herodias, his brother's wife, and
for many other wrongs he had done. 20 So Herod put John
in prison, adding this sin to his many others.

THE BAPTISM OF JESUS

21 One day when the crowds were being baptized, Jesus
himself was baptized. As he was praying, the heavens
opened, 22 and the Holy Spirit, in bodily form, descended
on him like a dove. And a voice from heaven said, “You
are my dearly loved Son, and you bring me great joy.*”

THE ANCESTORS OF JESUS

23 Jesus was about thirty years old when he began his public ministry.

Jesus was known as the son of Joseph.
Joseph was the son of Heli.

> **TIMING 3:23**
>
> **Imagine the Savior of the world driving nails in some small-town carpenter's shop until he was 30 years old! Jesus patiently trusted the Father's timing for his life and ministry. Do you have the same level of trust? If you're a believer, God wants some say in your decisions. Waiting on his timing means letting go of your right to run your life or even your desire to run ahead of God.** ■

24 Heli was the son of Matthat.
Matthat was the son of Levi.
Levi was the son of Melki.
Melki was the son of Jannai.
Jannai was the son of Joseph.
25 Joseph was the son of Mattathias.
Mattathias was the son of Amos.
Amos was the son of Nahum.
Nahum was the son of Esli.
Esli was the son of Naggai.
26 Naggai was the son of Maath.
Maath was the son of Mattathias.
Mattathias was the son of Semein.
Semein was the son of Josech.
Josech was the son of Joda.
27 Joda was the son of Joanan.
Joanan was the son of Rhesa.
Rhesa was the son of Zerubbabel.
Zerubbabel was the son of Shealtiel.
Shealtiel was the son of Neri.
28 Neri was the son of Melki.
Melki was the son of Addi.
Addi was the son of Cosam.
Cosam was the son of Elmadam.
Elmadam was the son of Er.
29 Er was the son of Joshua.
Joshua was the son of Eliezer.
Eliezer was the son of Jorim.
Jorim was the son of Matthat.
Matthat was the son of Levi.
30 Levi was the son of Simeon.
Simeon was the son of Judah.
Judah was the son of Joseph.
Joseph was the son of Jonam.
Jonam was the son of Eliakim.
31 Eliakim was the son of Melea.
Melea was the son of Menna.
Menna was the son of Mattatha.
Mattatha was the son of Nathan.
Nathan was the son of David.
32 David was the son of Jesse.
Jesse was the son of Obed.
Obed was the son of Boaz.

3:16a Or *in.* 3:16b Or *in the Holy Spirit and in fire.* 3:19 Greek *Herod the tetrarch.* 3:22 Some manuscripts read *my Son, and today I have become your Father.*

Boaz was the son of Salmon.*
Salmon was the son of Nahshon.
33 Nahshon was the son of Amminadab.
Amminadab was the son of Admin.
Admin was the son of Arni.*
Arni was the son of Hezron.
Hezron was the son of Perez.
Perez was the son of Judah.
34 Judah was the son of Jacob.
Jacob was the son of Isaac.
Isaac was the son of Abraham.
Abraham was the son of Terah.
Terah was the son of Nahor.
35 Nahor was the son of Serug.
Serug was the son of Reu.
Reu was the son of Peleg.
Peleg was the son of Eber.
Eber was the son of Shelah.
36 Shelah was the son of Cainan.
Cainan was the son of Arphaxad.
Arphaxad was the son of Shem.
Shem was the son of Noah.
Noah was the son of Lamech.
37 Lamech was the son of Methuselah.
Methuselah was the son of Enoch.
Enoch was the son of Jared.
Jared was the son of Mahalalel.
Mahalalel was the son of Kenan.
38 Kenan was the son of Enosh.*
Enosh was the son of Seth.
Seth was the son of Adam.
Adam was the son of God.

VULNERABLE 4:1-13

Jesus' defeat of Satan during his period of temptation was decisive but not final. Throughout his ministry, Jesus would confront Satan in many forms. Too often we see temptation as a once-and-for-all proposition. In reality, we need to be constantly on guard against the devil's ongoing attacks. What tempts you the most right now? How are you preparing to withstand it? ■

4 THE TEMPTATION OF JESUS

Then Jesus, full of the Holy Spirit, returned from the Jordan River. He was led by the Spirit in the wilderness,*
2where he was tempted by the devil for forty days. Jesus
ate nothing all that time and became very hungry.
3Then the devil said to him, "If you are the Son of God,
tell this stone to become a loaf of bread."
4But Jesus told him, "No! The Scriptures say, 'People do
not live by bread alone.'*"
5Then the devil took him up and revealed to him all the
kingdoms of the world in a moment of time. 6"I will give
you the glory of these kingdoms and authority over them,"
the devil said, "because they are mine to give to anyone I
please. 7I will give it all to you if you will worship me."
8Jesus replied, "The Scriptures say,

'You must worship the LORD your God
and serve only him.'*"

9Then the devil took him to Jerusalem, to the highest
point of the Temple, and said, "If you are the Son of God,
jump off! 10For the Scriptures say,

'He will order his angels to protect and guard you.
11 And they will hold you up with their hands
so you won't even hurt your foot on a stone.'*"

12Jesus responded, "The Scriptures also say, 'You must
not test the LORD your God.'*"
13When the devil had finished tempting Jesus, he left
him until the next opportunity came.

JESUS REJECTED AT NAZARETH

14Then Jesus returned to Galilee, filled with the Holy
Spirit's power. Reports about him spread quickly
through the whole region. 15He taught regularly in their
synagogues and was praised by everyone.

BE EXPECTANT 4:16-19

On an otherwise ordinary day in the synagogue, something extraordinary happened. A passage Jesus read in a synagogue—from Isaiah 61—happened to be one that proclaimed his mission. Jesus declared that he was the one who had come to set his people free—just as the passage said.

God longs to speak to his people. But many times, we don't look for him to speak to us or to act. Our ears are tuned elsewhere. Or, we expect him to speak to us in a certain way. Want to hear from God? Be expectant. Watch and wait. ■

16When he came to the village of Nazareth, his boy-
hood home, he went as usual to the synagogue on the
Sabbath and stood up to read the Scriptures. 17The scroll
of Isaiah the prophet was handed to him. He unrolled the
scroll and found the place where this was written:

18 "The Spirit of the LORD is upon me,
for he has anointed me to bring Good News to the poor.
He has sent me to proclaim that captives will be released,
that the blind will see,
that the oppressed will be set free,
19 and that the time of the LORD's favor has come.*"

3:32 Greek *Sala,* a variant spelling of Salmon; also in 3:32b. See Ruth 4:22. **3:33** Some manuscripts read *Amminadab was the son of Aram. Arni* and *Aram* are alternate spellings of Ram. See 1 Chr 2:9-10. **3:38** Greek *Enos,* a variant spelling of Enosh; also in 3:38b. See Gen 5:6. **4:1** Some manuscripts read *into the wilderness.* **4:4** Deut 8:3. **4:8** Deut 6:13. **4:10-11** Ps 91:11-12. **4:12** Deut 6:16. **4:18-19** Or *and to proclaim the acceptable year of the LORD.* Isa 61:1-2 (Greek version); 58:6.

20He rolled up the scroll, handed it back to the attendant,
and sat down. All eyes in the synagogue looked at him intently. 21Then he began to speak to them. "The Scripture
you've just heard has been fulfilled this very day!"
22Everyone spoke well of him and was amazed by the
gracious words that came from his lips. "How can this
be?" they asked. "Isn't this Joseph's son?"
23Then he said, "You will undoubtedly quote me this
proverb: 'Physician, heal yourself'—meaning, 'Do miracles here in your hometown like those you did in Capernaum.' 24But I tell you the truth, no prophet is accepted in
his own hometown.
25"Certainly there were many needy widows in Israel in
Elijah's time, when the heavens were closed for three and
a half years, and a severe famine devastated the land.
26Yet Elijah was not sent to any of them. He was sent instead to a foreigner—a widow of Zarephath in the land of
Sidon. 27And there were many lepers in Israel in the time
of the prophet Elisha, but the only one healed was Naaman, a Syrian."
28When they heard this, the people in the synagogue
were furious. 29Jumping up, they mobbed him and forced
him to the edge of the hill on which the town was built.
They intended to push him over the cliff, 30but he passed
right through the crowd and went on his way.

JESUS CASTS OUT A DEMON

31Then Jesus went to Capernaum, a town in Galilee, and
taught there in the synagogue every Sabbath day. 32There,
too, the people were amazed at his teaching, for he spoke
with authority.
33Once when he was in the synagogue, a man possessed by a demon—an evil* spirit—began shouting at
Jesus, 34"Go away! Why are you interfering with us, Jesus
of Nazareth? Have you come to destroy us? I know who
you are—the Holy One sent from God!"
35Jesus cut him short. "Be quiet!
Come out of the man," he ordered. At
that, the demon threw the man to the
floor as the crowd watched; then it
came out of him without hurting him
further.
36Amazed, the people exclaimed,
"What authority and power this man's
words possess! Even evil spirits obey
him, and they flee at his command!"
37The news about Jesus spread through
every village in the entire region.

JESUS HEALS MANY PEOPLE

38After leaving the synagogue that day,
Jesus went to Simon's home, where he
found Simon's mother-in-law very sick
with a high fever. "Please heal her,"
everyone begged. 39Standing at her bedside, he rebuked
the fever, and it left her. And she got up at once and prepared a meal for them.
40As the sun went down that evening, people throughout
the village brought sick family members to Jesus. No matter
what their diseases were, the touch of his hand healed every
one. 41Many were possessed by demons; and the demons
came out at his command, shouting, "You are the Son of
God!" But because they knew he was the Messiah, he rebuked them and refused to let them speak.

JESUS CONTINUES TO PREACH

42Early the next morning Jesus went out to an isolated
place. The crowds searched everywhere for him, and
when they finally found him, they begged him not to
leave them. 43But he replied, "I must
preach the Good News of the Kingdom of God in other towns, too, because that is why I was sent." 44So he
continued to travel around, preaching
in synagogues throughout Judea.*

> The Spirit of the LORD is upon me, for he has anointed me to bring Good News to the poor. . . . The time of the LORD's favor has come.
>
> LUKE 4:18-19

5 THE FIRST DISCIPLES

1One day as Jesus was preaching on the
shore of the Sea of Galilee,* great
crowds pressed in on him to listen to
the word of God. 2He noticed two
empty boats at the water's edge, for
the fishermen had left them and were
washing their nets. 3Stepping into one
of the boats, Jesus asked Simon,* its
owner, to push it out into the water. So
he sat in the boat and taught the
crowds from there.
4When he had finished speaking, he said to Simon,
"Now go out where it is deeper, and let down your nets to
catch some fish."

Jesus and Forgiveness

Jesus not only taught frequently about forgiveness, he also demonstrated his own willingness to forgive. Here are several examples that should help us recognize his willingness to forgive us also.

JESUS FORGAVE . . .

the paralyzed man lowered on a mat through the roof . . . Luke 5:17-26

the woman caught in adultery . . . John 8:3-11

the woman who anointed his feet with oil . . . Luke 7:47-50

Peter, for denying he knew Jesus . . . John 18:15-18, 25-27; 21:15-19

the criminal on the cross . . . Luke 23:39-43

the people who crucified him . . . Luke 23:34

4:33 Greek *unclean;* also in 4:36. 4:44 Some manuscripts read *Galilee.* 5:1 Greek *Lake Gennesaret,* another name for the Sea of Galilee.
5:3 *Simon* is called "Peter" in 6:14 and thereafter.

5"Master," Simon replied, "we worked hard all last night and didn't catch a thing. But if you say so, I'll let the nets down again." 6And this time their nets were so full of fish they began to tear! 7A shout for help brought their partners in the other boat, and soon both boats were filled with fish and on the verge of sinking.

8When Simon Peter realized what had happened, he fell to his knees before Jesus and said, "Oh, Lord, please leave me—I'm too much of a sinner to be around you." 9For he was awestruck by the number of fish they had caught, as were the others with him. 10His partners, James and John, the sons of Zebedee, were also amazed.

Jesus replied to Simon, "Don't be afraid! From now on you'll be fishing for people!" 11And as soon as they landed, they left everything and followed Jesus.

JESUS HEALS A MAN WITH LEPROSY

12In one of the villages, Jesus met a man with an advanced case of leprosy. When the man saw Jesus, he bowed with his face to the ground, begging to be healed. "Lord," he said, "if you are willing, you can heal me and make me clean."

13Jesus reached out and touched him. "I am willing," he said. "Be healed!" And instantly the leprosy disappeared.

5:14 See Lev 14:2-32.

14Then Jesus instructed him not to tell anyone what had happened. He said, "Go to the priest and let him examine you. Take along the offering required in the law of Moses for those who have been healed of leprosy.* This will be a public testimony that you have been cleansed."

15But despite Jesus' instructions, the report of his power spread even faster, and vast crowds came to hear him preach and to be healed of their diseases. 16But Jesus often withdrew to the wilderness for prayer.

JESUS HEALS A PARALYZED MAN

17One day while Jesus was teaching, some Pharisees and teachers of religious law were sitting nearby. (It seemed that these men showed up from every village in all Galilee and Judea, as well as from Jerusalem.) And the Lord's healing power was strongly with Jesus.

18Some men came carrying a paralyzed man on a sleeping mat. They tried to take him inside to Jesus, 19but they couldn't reach him because of the crowd. So they went up to the roof and took off some tiles. Then they lowered the sick man on his mat down into the crowd, right in front of Jesus. 20Seeing their faith, Jesus said to the man, "Young man, your sins are forgiven."

JAMES

UPS:
- One of the 12 disciples
- One of a special inner circle of three with Peter and John
- First of the 12 disciples to be killed for his faith

DOWN:
- Two outbursts indicate a struggle with his temper (Luke 9:54) and selfishness (Mark 10:37)

STATS:
- Where: Galilee
- Occupations: Fisherman, disciple
- Relatives: Zebedee (father); Salome (mother); John (brother)
- Contemporaries: Jesus, Pilate, Herod, the other 11 disciples

BOTTOM LINE:
Many of Jesus' followers do not consider the loss of life too heavy a price to pay for following him.

James's story is told in the Gospels. He is also mentioned in Acts 1:13 and 12:2.

JAMES Who are your closest friends? Jesus hung out the most with three of his 12 disciples: Peter, James, and James's brother John. Later, each played a key role among the first Christians. Peter became a great speaker. John became a great writer. But James became the first of the 12 disciples to die for his faith.

James was older than his brother, John. Zebedee, their father, owned a fishing business where they worked along with Peter and Andrew, who also became a disciple of Jesus. While Peter, Andrew, and John spent some time with John the Baptist, James stayed with the boats and nets. Later, when Jesus chose them to be his disciples, James was as eager as his partners to follow.

James understood that Jesus was worth following. But like all of the disciples, James had a limited view of Jesus' purpose. He hoped Jesus would start an earthly kingdom that would overthrow Rome and restore the nation of Israel. When that kingdom was established, he hoped to have a special position in it. But when Jesus died and rose from the grave, James finally understood Jesus' purpose—to provide new life for all.

Many years after Jesus' return to heaven, James was arrested and put to death. (See Acts 12:1-2.) He was willing to die because he knew that Jesus had conquered death. And he realized that death was only the doorway to eternal life.

Jesus promised eternal life to those willing to trust him. If we believe this promise, he'll give us the courage to stand for him even during dangerous times.

21 But the Pharisees and teachers of religious law said to themselves, "Who does he think he is? That's blasphemy! Only God can forgive sins!"

22 Jesus knew what they were thinking, so he asked them, "Why do you question this in your hearts? 23 Is it easier to say 'Your sins are forgiven,' or 'Stand up and walk'? 24 So I will prove to you that the Son of Man* has the authority on earth to forgive sins." Then Jesus turned to the paralyzed man and said, "Stand up, pick up your mat, and go home!"

25 And immediately, as everyone watched, the man jumped up, picked up his mat, and went home praising God. 26 Everyone was gripped with great wonder and awe, and they praised God, exclaiming, "We have seen amazing things today!"

BRING YOUR FRIENDS 5:17-25

Jesus responded to the faith of four men by healing their paralyzed friend. For better or for worse, our faith affects others. Although we can't make another person a Christian, we can do much through our words and actions to encourage him or her to respond positively. Like the four friends, you have a chance to bring your friends to Jesus. So, how 'bout it? You might be amazed at how God responds to your faith. ■

JESUS CALLS LEVI (MATTHEW)

27 Later, as Jesus left the town, he saw a tax collector named Levi sitting at his tax collector's booth. "Follow me and be my disciple," Jesus said to him. 28 So Levi got up, left everything, and followed him.

29 Later, Levi held a banquet in his home with Jesus as the guest of honor. Many of Levi's fellow tax collectors and other guests also ate with them. 30 But the Pharisees and their teachers of religious law complained bitterly to Jesus' disciples, "Why do you eat and drink with such scum?*"

31 Jesus answered them, "Healthy people don't need a doctor—sick people do. 32 I have come to call not those who think they are righteous, but those who know they are sinners and need to repent."

A DISCUSSION ABOUT FASTING

33 One day some people said to Jesus, "John the Baptist's disciples fast and pray regularly, and so do the disciples of the Pharisees. Why are your disciples always eating and drinking?"

34 Jesus responded, "Do wedding guests fast while celebrating with the groom? Of course not. 35 But someday the groom will be taken away from them, and then they will fast."

36 Then Jesus gave them this illustration: "No one tears a piece of cloth from a new garment and uses it to patch an old garment. For then the new garment would be ruined, and the new patch wouldn't even match the old garment.

37 "And no one puts new wine into old wineskins. For the new wine would burst the wineskins, spilling the wine and ruining the skins. 38 New wine must be stored in new wineskins. 39 But no one who drinks the old wine seems to want the new wine. 'The old is just fine,' they say."

6

A DISCUSSION ABOUT THE SABBATH

One Sabbath day as Jesus was walking through some grainfields, his disciples broke off heads of grain, rubbed off the husks in their hands, and ate the grain. 2 But some Pharisees said, "Why are you breaking the law by harvesting grain on the Sabbath?"

3 Jesus replied, "Haven't you read in the Scriptures what David did when he and his companions were hungry? 4 He went into the house of God and broke the law by eating the sacred loaves of bread that only the priests can eat. He also gave some to his companions." 5 And Jesus added, "The Son of Man* is Lord, even over the Sabbath."

JESUS HEALS ON THE SABBATH

6 On another Sabbath day, a man with a deformed right hand was in the synagogue while Jesus was teaching. 7 The teachers of religious law and the Pharisees watched Jesus closely. If he healed the man's hand, they planned to accuse him of working on the Sabbath.

8 But Jesus knew their thoughts. He said to the man with the deformed hand, "Come and stand in front of everyone." So the man came forward. 9 Then Jesus said to his critics, "I have a question for you. Does the law permit good deeds on the Sabbath, or is it a day for doing evil? Is this a day to save life or to destroy it?"

10 He looked around at them one by one and then said to the man, "Hold out your hand." So the man held out his hand, and it was restored! 11 At this, the enemies of Jesus were wild with rage and began to discuss what to do with him.

QUALIFIED 6:13-16

Jesus chose ordinary men—not superheroes or famous people—to be his disciples. Do you think your pastor or a famous evangelist somehow has "secret powers" that you somehow lack, thereby disqualifying you to serve God? Guess what. God still calls "ordinary" people to build his church. Alone we may feel unqualified to serve Christ well. But with the help of the Holy Spirit we can serve God in any way. Ready to serve? ■

JESUS CHOOSES THE TWELVE APOSTLES

12 One day soon afterward Jesus went up on a mountain to pray, and he prayed to God all night. 13 At daybreak he called together all of his disciples and chose twelve of them to be apostles. Here are their names:

14 Simon (whom he named Peter),
Andrew (Peter's brother),

5:24 "Son of Man" is a title Jesus used for himself. 5:30 Greek *with tax collectors and sinners?* 6:5 "Son of Man" is a title Jesus used for himself.

James,
John,
Philip,
Bartholomew,
15 Matthew,
Thomas,
James (son of Alphaeus),
Simon (who was called the zealot),
16 Judas (son of James),
Judas Iscariot (who later betrayed him).

CROWDS FOLLOW JESUS

17When they came down from the mountain, the disciples stood with Jesus on a large, level area, surrounded by
many of his followers and by the crowds. There were
people from all over Judea and from Jerusalem and from
as far north as the seacoasts of Tyre and Sidon. 18They
had come to hear him and to be healed of their diseases;
and those troubled by evil* spirits were healed. 19Every-
one tried to touch him, because healing power went out
from him, and he healed everyone.

THE BEATITUDES

20Then Jesus turned to his disciples and said,

"God blesses you who are poor,
for the Kingdom of God is yours.
21 God blesses you who are hungry now,
for you will be satisfied.
God blesses you who weep now,
for in due time you will laugh.

22What blessings await you when people hate you and ex-
clude you and mock you and curse you as evil because
you follow the Son of Man. 23When that happens, be
happy! Yes, leap for joy! For a great reward awaits you in
heaven. And remember, their ancestors treated the ancient prophets that same way.

SORROWS FORETOLD

24 "What sorrow awaits you who are rich,
for you have your only happiness now.
25 What sorrow awaits you who are fat and
prosperous now,
for a time of awful hunger awaits you.
What sorrow awaits you who laugh now,
for your laughing will turn to mourning
and sorrow.
26 What sorrow awaits you who are praised by
the crowds,
for their ancestors also praised false prophets.

LOVE FOR ENEMIES

27"But to you who are willing to listen, I say, love your enemies! Do good to those who hate you. 28Bless those who
curse you. Pray for those who hurt you. 29If someone
slaps you on one cheek, offer the other cheek also. If
someone demands your coat, offer your shirt also. 30Give
to anyone who asks; and when things are taken away
from you, don't try to get them back. 31Do to others as you
would like them to do to you.

32"If you love only those who love you, why should you
get credit for that? Even sinners love those who love
them! 33And if you do good only to those who do good to
you, why should you get credit? Even sinners do that
much! 34And if you lend money only to those who can repay you, why should you get credit? Even sinners will lend
to other sinners for a full return.

35"Love your enemies! Do good to them. Lend to them
without expecting to be repaid. Then your reward from
heaven will be very great, and you will truly be acting as
children of the Most High, for he is kind to those who are
unthankful and wicked. 36You must be compassionate,
just as your Father is compassionate.

TOUGH LOVE 6:27-36

The Jews hated the Romans, because the Romans oppressed them. But Jesus told them to love these enemies. What's your immediate reaction to Jesus' words? Many turned away from him because of these words. But Jesus wasn't talking about having affection for enemies; he was talking about an act of the will.

Loving our enemies means acting in their best interests. You can't "fall into" this kind of love—it takes a conscious effort. But mainly, you need the help of God.

Jesus loved the whole world, even though the world rebelled against God. He asks us to follow his example by loving our enemies. Will you? ■

DO NOT JUDGE OTHERS

37"Do not judge others, and you will not be judged. Do not
condemn others, or it will all come back against you. Forgive others, and you will be forgiven. 38Give, and you will
receive. Your gift will return to you in full—pressed
down, shaken together to make room for more, running
over, and poured into your lap. The amount you give will
determine the amount you get back.*"

39Then Jesus gave the following illustration: "Can one
blind person lead another? Won't they both fall into a
ditch? 40Students* are not greater than their teacher. But
the student who is fully trained will become like the
teacher.

41"And why worry about a speck in your friend's eye*
when you have a log in your own? 42How can you think of
saying, 'Friend,* let me help you get rid of that speck in
your eye,' when you can't see past the log in your own eye?
Hypocrite! First get rid of the log in your own eye; then
you will see well enough to deal with the speck in your
friend's eye.

THE TREE AND ITS FRUIT

43"A good tree can't produce bad fruit, and a bad tree
can't produce good fruit. 44A tree is identified by its fruit.

6:18 Greek *unclean.* 6:38 Or *The measure you give will be the measure you get back.* 6:40 Or *Disciples.* 6:41 Greek *your brother's eye;* also in 6:42. 6:42 Greek *Brother.*

keeping it real

Even before I became a Christian, the Bible amazed me. I remember being floored the first time I read Luke 6:27-38. That's the passage about loving your enemies. I wondered, **How could anyone act like that?** A year later, just before my freshman year in high school, I found out for myself.

In shop class, I decided to make a small bookcase for my mother for Christmas. I worked on it a lot in my spare time and finally left it in the finishing room, which was always locked.

After school, when I went back to get the bookcase, it was gone. The shop teacher did some investigating and finally discovered that a dude named Andy had stolen it. "We've had problems with Andy before," Mr. Petrako said. "Andy needs to learn a lesson. I've arranged to have him meet you after school to return your bookshelf." That's all he said, but I knew what he meant.

I didn't need any encouragement to "teach Andy a lesson." I was furious. And since I was a football player, y'know, kinda big, I wouldn't have any trouble beating someone up.

I waited for Andy, psyching myself up to face my enemy. Finally he walked in.

Something happened to me when I saw him. I had expected someone tough, but what I saw was just a boy, smaller and younger than me, who was obviously afraid. When I saw Andy's scared face, all the hate just leaked out of me.

Andy said, "Here's your bookshelf. I'm sorry." I had no words for him. I growled something, took the bookcase, and left.

That night I felt very confused. What happened? What took away my hate? As I thought about these things, I remembered the passage in Luke. I read it again: "Love your enemies. . . . When things are taken away from you, don't try to get them back" (6:27-30).

I felt like God was asking me to respond to what I read. But how? Suddenly I knew. I went to school early the next morning and started work on an identical bookcase. For four days straight I stayed as long as shop was open.

When the bookcase was finished, I had Andy meet me after school in an empty shop class. I said, "Andy, I want to give you this. It's a gift from me to you, and from me to Jesus. I'd never be able to do this if it weren't for him."

That's all I could say then. I didn't know how to share my faith. All I knew was that Jesus had touched my life and I wanted Andy to know.

Well, after that I got to know Andy. Seeing his family situation (they were broke), I understood him better. I invited him to youth group on Thursday afternoons. When there was a retreat and Andy couldn't afford to go, my friends and I scraped up enough money for him. And at that retreat, Andy became a Christian.

It's hard to know who was more excited about God right then, me or Andy.

—Daniel

Figs are never gathered from thornbushes, and grapes are not picked from bramble bushes. 45A good person produces good things from the treasury of a good heart, and an evil person produces evil things from the treasury of an evil heart. What you say flows from what is in your heart.

BUILDING ON A SOLID FOUNDATION

46"So why do you keep calling me 'Lord, Lord!' when you don't do what I say? 47I will show you what it's like when someone comes to me, listens to my teaching, and then follows it. 48It is like a person building a house who digs deep and lays the foundation on solid rock. When the floodwaters rise and break against that house, it stands firm because it is well built. 49But anyone who hears and doesn't obey is like a person who builds a house without a foundation. When the floods sweep down against that house, it will collapse into a heap of ruins."

7

THE FAITH OF A ROMAN OFFICER

When Jesus had finished saying all this to the people, he returned to Capernaum. 2At that time the highly valued slave of a Roman officer* was sick and near death. 3When the officer heard about Jesus, he sent some respected Jewish elders to ask him to come and heal his slave. 4So they earnestly begged Jesus to help the man. "If anyone deserves your help, he does," they said, 5"for he loves the Jewish people and even built a synagogue for us."

6So Jesus went with them. But just before they arrived at the house, the officer sent some friends to say, "Lord, don't trouble yourself by coming to my home, for I am not worthy of such an honor. 7I am not even worthy to come and meet you. Just say the word from where you are, and my servant will be healed. 8I know this because I am under the authority of my superior officers, and I have authority over my soldiers. I only need to say, 'Go,' and they go, or 'Come,' and they come. And if I say to my slaves, 'Do this,' they do it."

9When Jesus heard this, he was amazed. Turning to the crowd that was following him, he said, "I tell you, I haven't seen faith like this in all Israel!" 10And when the officer's friends returned to his house, they found the slave completely healed.

JESUS RAISES A WIDOW'S SON

11Soon afterward Jesus went with his disciples to the village of Nain, and a large crowd followed him. 12A funeral procession was coming out as he approached the village gate. The young man who had died was a widow's only son, and a large crowd from the village was with her. 13When the Lord saw her, his heart overflowed with compassion. "Don't cry!" he said. 14Then he walked over to the coffin and touched it, and the bearers stopped. "Young man," he said, "I tell you, get up." 15Then the dead boy sat up and began to talk! And Jesus gave him back to his mother.

16Great fear swept the crowd, and they praised God, saying, "A mighty prophet has risen among us," and "God has visited his people today." 17And the news about Jesus spread throughout Judea and the surrounding countryside.

JESUS AND JOHN THE BAPTIST

18The disciples of John the Baptist told John about everything Jesus was doing. So John called for two of his disciples, 19and he sent them to the Lord to ask him, "Are you the Messiah we've been expecting,* or should we keep looking for someone else?"

20John's two disciples found Jesus and said to him, "John the Baptist sent us to ask, 'Are you the Messiah we've been expecting, or should we keep looking for someone else?'"

21At that very time, Jesus cured many people of their diseases, illnesses, and evil spirits, and he restored sight to many who were blind. 22Then he told John's disciples, "Go back to John and tell him what you have seen and heard—the blind see, the lame walk, the lepers are cured, the deaf hear, the dead are raised to life, and the Good News is being preached to the poor. 23And tell him, 'God blesses those who do not turn away because of me.*'"

24After John's disciples left, Jesus began talking about him to the crowds. "What kind of man did you go into the wilderness to see? Was he a weak reed, swayed by every breath of wind? 25Or were you expecting to see a man dressed in expensive clothes? No, people who wear beautiful clothes and live in luxury are found in palaces. 26Were you looking for a prophet? Yes, and he is more than a prophet. 27John is the man to whom the Scriptures refer when they say,

QUESTIONS 7:18-35

While imprisoned, John's discouragement led him to wonder whether or not Jesus really was the Messiah. (See also Matt 11:1-19.) John's doubts were natural, and Jesus didn't condemn him for them. Instead, Jesus responded in a way that John would understand by explaining that he had in fact accomplished the things the Messiah was supposed to accomplish.

God can also handle our doubts. In fact, he welcomes our sincere questions. What questions, if any, do you have? Do you really want to know the answers? ■

'Look, I am sending my messenger ahead of you,
and he will prepare your way before you.'*

28I tell you, of all who have ever lived, none is greater than John. Yet even the least person in the Kingdom of God is greater than he is!"

29When they heard this, all the people—even the tax collectors—agreed that God's way was right,* for they had been baptized by John. 30But the Pharisees and experts in religious law rejected God's plan for them, for they had refused John's baptism.

31"To what can I compare the people of this generation?" Jesus asked. "How can I describe them? 32They are like children playing a game in the public square. They complain to their friends,

'We played wedding songs,
and you didn't dance,
so we played funeral songs,
and you didn't weep.'

33For John the Baptist didn't spend his time eating bread or drinking wine, and you say, 'He's possessed by a

7:2 Greek *a centurion;* similarly in 7:6. 7:19 Greek *Are you the one who is coming?* Also in 7:20. 7:23 Or *who are not offended by me.* 7:27 Mal 3:1. 7:29 Or *praised God for his justice.*

demon.' 34The Son of Man,* on the other hand, feasts and drinks, and you say, 'He's a glutton and a drunkard, and a friend of tax collectors and other sinners!' 35But wisdom is shown to be right by the lives of those who follow it.*"

JESUS ANOINTED BY A SINFUL WOMAN

36One of the Pharisees asked Jesus to have dinner with him, so Jesus went to his home and sat down to eat.* 37When a certain immoral woman from that city heard he was eating there, she brought a beautiful alabaster jar filled with expensive perfume. 38Then she knelt behind him at his feet, weeping. Her tears fell on his feet, and she wiped them off with her hair. Then she kept kissing his feet and putting perfume on them.

39When the Pharisee who had invited him saw this, he said to himself, "If this man were a prophet, he would know what kind of woman is touching him. She's a sinner!"

40Then Jesus answered his thoughts. "Simon," he said to the Pharisee, "I have something to say to you."

"Go ahead, Teacher," Simon replied.

41Then Jesus told him this story: "A man loaned money to two people—500 pieces of silver* to one and 50 pieces to the other. 42But neither of them could repay him, so he kindly forgave them both, canceling their debts. Who do you suppose loved him more after that?"

43Simon answered, "I suppose the one for whom he canceled the larger debt."

"That's right," Jesus said. 44Then he turned to the woman and said to Simon, "Look at this woman kneeling here. When I entered your home, you didn't offer me water to wash the dust from my feet, but she has washed them with her tears and wiped them with her hair. 45You didn't greet me with a kiss, but from the time I first came in, she has not stopped kissing my feet. 46You neglected the courtesy of olive oil to anoint my head, but she has anointed my feet with rare perfume.

47"I tell you, her sins—and they are many—have been forgiven, so she has shown me much love. But a person who is forgiven little shows only little love." 48Then Jesus said to the woman, "Your sins are forgiven."

49The men at the table said among themselves, "Who is this man, that he goes around forgiving sins?"

50And Jesus said to the woman, "Your faith has saved you; go in peace."

8

WOMEN WHO FOLLOWED JESUS

Soon afterward Jesus began a tour of the nearby towns and villages, preaching and announcing the Good News about the Kingdom of God. He took his twelve disciples with him, 2along with some women who had been cured of evil spirits and diseases. Among them were Mary Magdalene, from whom he had cast out seven demons; 3Joanna, the wife of Chuza, Herod's business manager; Susanna; and many others who were contributing their own resources to support Jesus and his disciples.

PARABLE OF THE FARMER SCATTERING SEED

4One day Jesus told a story in the form of a parable to a large crowd that had gathered from many towns to hear him: 5"A farmer went out to plant his seed. As he scattered it across his field, some seed fell on a footpath, where it was stepped on, and the birds ate it. 6Other seed fell among rocks. It began to grow, but the plant soon wilted and died for lack of moisture. 7Other seed fell among thorns that grew up with it and choked out the tender plants. 8Still other seed fell on fertile soil. This seed grew and produced a crop that was a hundred times as much as had been planted!" When he had said this, he called out, "Anyone with ears to hear should listen and understand."

9His disciples asked him what this parable meant. 10He replied, "You are permitted to understand the secrets* of the Kingdom of God. But I use parables to teach the others so that the Scriptures might be fulfilled:

'When they look, they won't really see.
When they hear, they won't understand.'*

11"This is the meaning of the parable: The seed is God's word. 12The seeds that fell on the footpath represent those who hear the message, only to have the devil come and take it away from their hearts and prevent them from believing and being saved. 13The seeds on the rocky soil represent those who hear the message and receive it with joy. But since they don't have deep roots, they believe for a while, then they fall away when they face temptation. 14The seeds that fell among the thorns represent those who hear the message, but all too quickly the message is crowded out by the cares and riches and pleasures of this life. And so they never grow into maturity. 15And the seeds that fell on the good soil represent honest, good-hearted people who hear God's word, cling to it, and patiently produce a huge harvest.

PARABLE OF THE LAMP

16"No one lights a lamp and then covers it with a bowl or hides it under a bed. A lamp is placed on a stand, where its light can be seen by all who enter the house. 17For all that is secret will eventually be brought into the open, and everything that is concealed will be brought to light and made known to all.

18"So pay attention to how you hear. To those who listen to my teaching, more understanding will be given. But for those who are not listening, even what they think they understand will be taken away from them."

THE TRUE FAMILY OF JESUS

19Then Jesus' mother and brothers came to see him, but they couldn't get to him because of the crowd. 20Someone told Jesus, "Your mother and your brothers are outside, and they want to see you."

21Jesus replied, "My mother and my brothers are all those who hear God's word and obey it."

7:34 "Son of Man" is a title Jesus used for himself. 7:35 Or *But wisdom is justified by all her children.* 7:36 Or *and reclined.* 7:41 Greek *500 denarii.* A denarius was equivalent to a laborer's full day's wage. 8:10a Greek *mysteries.* 8:10b Isa 6:9 (Greek version).

JESUS CALMS THE STORM

[22]One day Jesus said to his disciples, "Let's cross to the other side of the lake." So they got into a boat and started out. [23]As they sailed across, Jesus settled down for a nap. But soon a fierce storm came down on the lake. The boat was filling with water, and they were in real danger.

[24]The disciples went and woke him up, shouting, "Master, Master, we're going to drown!"

When Jesus woke up, he rebuked the wind and the raging waves. Suddenly the storm stopped and all was calm. [25]Then he asked them, "Where is your faith?"

The disciples were terrified and amazed. "Who is this man?" they asked each other. "When he gives a command, even the wind and waves obey him!"

PIGS OR PEOPLE? 8:26-37

When the demon-possessed pigs drowned, the herdsmen complained about their loss of money. But can pigs and money compare with a human life? A man had been freed from the devil's power, but the villagers thought only about the money they lost when the pigs drowned.

Throughout history many wars have been fought to protect economic interests. Much injustice and oppression, both at home and abroad, is the direct result of some individual's or company's goal to get rich. What's your goal? How do you show by your actions that you value people over "pigs" (money, possessions, etc.)? ■

JESUS HEALS A DEMON-POSSESSED MAN

[26]So they arrived in the region of the Gerasenes,* across the lake from Galilee. [27]As Jesus was climbing out of the boat, a man who was possessed by demons came out to meet him. For a long time he had been homeless and naked, living in a cemetery outside the town.

[28]As soon as he saw Jesus, he shrieked and fell down in front of him. Then he screamed, "Why are you interfering with me, Jesus, Son of the Most High God? Please, I beg you, don't torture me!" [29]For Jesus had already commanded the evil* spirit to come out of him. This spirit had often taken control of the man. Even when he was placed under guard and put in chains and shackles, he simply broke them and rushed out into the wilderness, completely under the demon's power.

[30]Jesus demanded, "What is your name?"

"Legion," he replied, for he was filled with many demons. [31]The demons kept begging Jesus not to send them into the bottomless pit.*

[32]There happened to be a large herd of pigs feeding on the hillside nearby, and the demons begged him to let them enter into the pigs.

So Jesus gave them permission. [33]Then the demons came out of the man and entered the pigs, and the entire herd plunged down the steep hillside into the lake and drowned.

[34]When the herdsmen saw it, they fled to the nearby town and the surrounding countryside, spreading the news as they ran. [35]People rushed out to see what had happened. A crowd soon gathered around Jesus, and they saw the man who had been freed from the demons. He was sitting at Jesus' feet, fully clothed and perfectly sane, and they were all afraid. [36]Then those who had seen what happened told the others how the demon-possessed man had been healed. [37]And all the people in the region of the Gerasenes begged Jesus to go away and leave them alone, for a great wave of fear swept over them.

So Jesus returned to the boat and left, crossing back to the other side of the lake. [38]The man who had been freed from the demons begged to go with him. But Jesus sent him home, saying, [39]"No, go back to your family, and tell them everything God has done for you." So he went all through the town proclaiming the great things Jesus had done for him.

JESUS HEALS IN RESPONSE TO FAITH

[40]On the other side of the lake the crowds welcomed Jesus, because they had been waiting for him. [41]Then a man named Jairus, a leader of the local synagogue, came and fell at Jesus' feet, pleading with him to come home with him. [42]His only daughter,* who was about twelve years old, was dying.

As Jesus went with him, he was surrounded by the crowds. [43]A woman in the crowd had suffered for twelve years with constant bleeding,* and she could find no cure. [44]Coming up behind Jesus, she touched the fringe of his robe. Immediately, the bleeding stopped.

[45]"Who touched me?" Jesus asked.

Everyone denied it, and Peter said, "Master, this whole crowd is pressing up against you."

[46]But Jesus said, "Someone deliberately touched me, for I felt healing power go out from me." [47]When the woman realized that she could not stay hidden, she began to tremble and fell to her knees in front of him. The whole crowd heard her explain why she had touched him and that she had been immediately healed. [48]"Daughter," he said to her, "your faith has made you well. Go in peace."

[49]While he was still speaking to her, a messenger arrived from the home of Jairus, the leader of the synagogue. He told him, "Your daughter is dead. There's no use troubling the Teacher now."

[50]But when Jesus heard what had happened, he said to Jairus, "Don't be afraid. Just have faith, and she will be healed."

[51]When they arrived at the house, Jesus wouldn't let anyone go in with him except Peter, John, James, and the little girl's father and mother. [52]The house was filled with people weeping and wailing, but he said, "Stop the weeping! She isn't dead; she's only asleep."

[53]But the crowd laughed at him because they all knew she had died. [54]Then Jesus took her by the hand and said in a loud voice, "My child, get up!" [55]And at that moment her life* returned, and she immediately stood up! Then Jesus told them to give her something to eat. [56]Her parents

8:26 Other manuscripts read *Gadarenes;* still others read *Gergesenes;* also in 8:37. See Matt 8:28; Mark 5:1. **8:29** Greek *unclean.* **8:31** Or *the abyss,* or *the underworld.* **8:42** Or *His only child, a daughter.* **8:43** Some manuscripts add *having spent everything she had on doctors.* **8:55** Or *her spirit.*

were overwhelmed, but Jesus insisted that they not tell anyone what had happened.

9

JESUS SENDS OUT THE TWELVE DISCIPLES

One day Jesus called together his twelve disciples* and gave them power and authority to cast out all demons and to heal all diseases. 2Then he sent them out to tell everyone about the Kingdom of God and to heal the sick. 3"Take nothing for your journey," he instructed them. "Don't take a walking stick, a traveler's bag, food, money,* or even a change of clothes. 4Wherever you go, stay in the same house until you leave town. 5And if a town refuses to welcome you, shake its dust from your feet as you leave to show that you have abandoned those people to their fate."

6So they began their circuit of the villages, preaching the Good News and healing the sick.

HEROD'S CONFUSION

7When Herod Antipas, the ruler of Galilee,* heard about everything Jesus was doing, he was puzzled. Some were saying that John the Baptist had been raised from the dead. 8Others thought Jesus was Elijah or one of the other prophets risen from the dead.

9"I beheaded John," Herod said, "so who is this man about whom I hear such stories?" And he kept trying to see him.

JESUS FEEDS FIVE THOUSAND

10When the apostles returned, they told Jesus everything they had done. Then he slipped quietly away with them toward the town of Bethsaida. 11But the crowds found out where he was going, and they followed him. He welcomed them and taught them about the Kingdom of God, and he healed those who were sick.

12Late in the afternoon the twelve disciples came to him and said, "Send the crowds away to the nearby villages and farms, so they can find food and lodging for the night. There is nothing to eat here in this remote place."

13But Jesus said, "You feed them."

"But we have only five loaves of bread and two fish," they answered. "Or are you expecting us to go and buy enough food for this whole crowd?" 14For there were about 5,000 men there.

Jesus replied, "Tell them to sit down in groups of about fifty each." 15So the people all sat down. 16Jesus took the five loaves and two fish, looked up toward heaven, and blessed them. Then, breaking the loaves into pieces, he kept giving the bread and fish to the disciples so they could distribute it to the people. 17They all ate as much as they wanted, and afterward, the disciples picked up twelve baskets of leftovers!

PETER'S DECLARATION ABOUT JESUS

18One day Jesus left the crowds to pray alone. Only his disciples were with him, and he asked them, "Who do people say I am?"

19"Well," they replied, "some say John the Baptist, some say Elijah, and others say you are one of the other ancient prophets risen from the dead."

20Then he asked them, "But who do you say I am?"

Peter replied, "You are the Messiah* sent from God!"

TROUBLEMAKER OR SON OF GOD? 9:7, 20

People couldn't accept Jesus for who he was, so they tried to come up with other answers. Many thought he was John the Baptist (see Matt 14:1-12) or another prophet come back to life. Some suggested he was Elijah, the great prophet who did not die but was taken to heaven in a whirlwind (2 Kings 2:1-11). Few found the correct answer, as Peter did (9:20).

Many today find it no easier to accept Jesus as the fully human yet fully divine Son of God. They seek alternate explanations: he was a great prophet, a radical political leader, a self-deceived troublemaker. None of these explanations can account for Jesus' miracles or, especially, his glorious resurrection. In the end, the attempts to explain Jesus away are far more difficult to believe than the truth.

Who do you say that Jesus is? ■

JESUS PREDICTS HIS DEATH

21Jesus warned his disciples not to tell anyone who he was. 22"The Son of Man* must suffer many terrible things," he said. "He will be rejected by the elders, the leading priests, and the teachers of religious law. He will be killed, but on the third day he will be raised from the dead."

23Then he said to the crowd, "If any of you wants to be my follower, you must turn from your selfish ways, take up your cross daily, and follow me. 24If you try to hang on to your life, you will lose it. But if you give up your life for my sake, you will save it. 25And what do you benefit if you gain the whole world but are yourself lost or destroyed? 26If anyone is ashamed of me and my message, the Son of Man will be ashamed of that person when he returns in his glory and in the glory of the Father and the holy angels. 27I tell you the truth, some standing here right now will not die before they see the Kingdom of God."

THE TRANSFIGURATION

28About eight days later Jesus took Peter, John, and James up on a mountain to pray. 29And as he was praying, the appearance of his face was transformed, and his clothes became dazzling white. 30Suddenly, two men, Moses and Elijah, appeared and began talking with Jesus. 31They were glorious to see. And they were speaking about his exodus from this world, which was about to be fulfilled in Jerusalem.

32Peter and the others had fallen asleep. When they woke up, they saw Jesus' glory and the two men standing with him. 33As Moses and Elijah were starting to leave,

9:1 Greek *the Twelve;* other manuscripts read *the twelve apostles.* 9:3 Or *silver coins.* 9:7 Greek *Herod the tetrarch.* Herod Antipas was a son of King Herod and was ruler over Galilee. 9:20 Or *the Christ. Messiah* (a Hebrew term) and *Christ* (a Greek term) both mean "the anointed one." 9:22 "Son of Man" is a title Jesus used for himself.

Peter, not even knowing what he was saying, blurted out, "Master, it's wonderful for us to be here! Let's make three shelters as memorials*—one for you, one for Moses, and one for Elijah." 34But even as he was saying this, a cloud overshadowed them, and terror gripped them as the cloud covered them.

35Then a voice from the cloud said, "This is my Son, my Chosen One.* Listen to him." 36When the voice finished, Jesus was there alone. They didn't tell anyone at that time what they had seen.

RETREAT AND RETURN 9:28-36

Peter, James, and John had such an amazing time with Jesus up on a mountain, they didn't want to leave. Ever been to a youth retreat or had a time with God that was so cool you didn't want it to end? Being away from the reality and problems of our daily life can seem inviting. But we can't stay "up on a mountain" forever. Instead of becoming spiritual giants, we would soon become giants of self-centeredness. We need times of retreat and renewal, but only so we can return to help build up our family and friends. Our faith must make sense off the mountain as well as on it. ■

JESUS HEALS A DEMON-POSSESSED BOY

37The next day, after they had come down the mountain, a large crowd met Jesus. 38A man in the crowd called out to him, "Teacher, I beg you to look at my son, my only child. 39An evil spirit keeps seizing him, making him scream. It throws him into convulsions so that he foams at the mouth. It batters him and hardly ever leaves him alone. 40I begged your disciples to cast out the spirit, but they couldn't do it."

41Jesus said, "You faithless and corrupt people! How long must I be with you and put up with you?" Then he said to the man, "Bring your son here."

42As the boy came forward, the demon knocked him to the ground and threw him into a violent convulsion. But Jesus rebuked the evil* spirit and healed the boy. Then he gave him back to his father. 43Awe gripped the people as they saw this majestic display of God's power.

JESUS AGAIN PREDICTS HIS DEATH

While everyone was marveling at everything he was doing, Jesus said to his disciples, 44"Listen to me and remember what I say. The Son of Man is going to be betrayed into the hands of his enemies." 45But they didn't know what he meant. Its significance was hidden from them, so they couldn't understand it, and they were afraid to ask him about it.

THE GREATEST IN THE KINGDOM

46Then his disciples began arguing about which of them was the greatest. 47But Jesus knew their thoughts, so he brought a little child to his side. 48Then he said to them, "Anyone who welcomes a little child like this on my behalf* welcomes me, and anyone who welcomes me also welcomes my Father who sent me. Whoever is the least among you is the greatest."

USING THE NAME OF JESUS

49John said to Jesus, "Master, we saw someone using your name to cast out demons, but we told him to stop because he isn't in our group."

50But Jesus said, "Don't stop him! Anyone who is not against you is for you."

OPPOSITION FROM SAMARITANS

51As the time drew near for him to ascend to heaven, Jesus resolutely set out for Jerusalem. 52He sent messengers ahead to a Samaritan village to prepare for his arrival. 53But the people of the village did not welcome Jesus because he was on his way to Jerusalem. 54When James and John saw this, they said to Jesus, "Lord, should we call down fire from heaven to burn them up*?" 55But Jesus turned and rebuked them.* 56So they went on to another village.

THE COST OF FOLLOWING JESUS

57As they were walking along, someone said to Jesus, "I will follow you wherever you go."

58But Jesus replied, "Foxes have dens to live in, and birds have nests, but the Son of Man has no place even to lay his head."

59He said to another person, "Come, follow me."

The man agreed, but he said, "Lord, first let me return home and bury my father."

60But Jesus told him, "Let the spiritually dead bury their own dead!* Your duty is to go and preach about the Kingdom of God."

61Another said, "Yes, Lord, I will follow you, but first let me say good-bye to my family."

62But Jesus told him, "Anyone who puts a hand to the plow and then looks back is not fit for the Kingdom of God."

10 JESUS SENDS OUT HIS DISCIPLES

The Lord now chose seventy-two* other disciples and sent them ahead in pairs to all the towns and places he planned to visit. 2These were his instructions to them: "The harvest is great, but the workers are few. So pray to the Lord who is in charge of the harvest; ask him to send more workers into his fields. 3Now go, and remember that I am sending you out as lambs among wolves. 4Don't take any money with you, nor a traveler's bag, nor an extra pair of sandals. And don't stop to greet anyone on the road.

5"Whenever you enter someone's home, first say, 'May God's peace be on this house.' 6If those who live there are peaceful, the blessing will stand; if they are not, the

9:33 Greek *three tabernacles.* 9:35 Some manuscripts read *This is my dearly loved Son.* 9:42 Greek *unclean.* 9:48 Greek *in my name.* 9:54 Some manuscripts add *as Elijah did.* 9:55 Some manuscripts add an expanded conclusion to verse 55 and an additional sentence in verse 56: *And he said, "You don't realize what your hearts are like. 56For the Son of Man has not come to destroy people's lives, but to save them."* 9:60 Greek *Let the dead bury their own dead.* 10:1 Some manuscripts read *seventy;* also in 10:17.

blessing will return to you. 7Don't move around from
home to home. Stay in one place, eating and drinking
what they provide. Don't hesitate to accept hospitality,
because those who work deserve their pay.
8"If you enter a town and it welcomes you, eat whatever
is set before you. 9Heal the sick, and tell them, 'The Kingdom of God is near you now.' 10But if a town refuses to
welcome you, go out into its streets and say, 11'We wipe
even the dust of your town from our feet to show that we
have abandoned you to your fate. And know this—the
Kingdom of God is near!' 12I assure you, even wicked Sodom will be better off than such a town on judgment day.

ENEMIES

The situation: Madison is driving home from Starbucks on a stormy night. As she rounds a curve in the road, she sees someone walking along the side in the mud. It's Ginny. A hundred yards up the road, Madison sees Ginny's car in the ditch.

Should she stop and help?

Maybe that seems like a stupid question, but consider . . .

The background: Last year, Ginny always went out of her way to make Madison feel like an absolute loser. She's made some really rude remarks about Madison—behind her back. Not only that, Ginny absolutely humiliated Madison at a pep rally—right in front of everyone! The two haven't spoken since. When they're in the same room, everyone can feel the tension.

The solution:

Read Luke 10:25-37. Based on this passage, what do you think Madison should do? Why?

13"What sorrow awaits you, Korazin and Bethsaida!
For if the miracles I did in you had been done in wicked
Tyre and Sidon, their people would have repented of
their sins long ago, clothing themselves in burlap and
throwing ashes on their heads to show their remorse.
14Yes, Tyre and Sidon will be better off on judgment day
than you. 15And you people of Capernaum, will you be
honored in heaven? No, you will go down to the place of
the dead.*"
16Then he said to the disciples, "Anyone who accepts
your message is also accepting me. And anyone who rejects you is rejecting me. And anyone who rejects me is
rejecting God, who sent me."
17When the seventy-two disciples returned, they joyfully reported to him, "Lord, even the demons obey us
when we use your name!"
18"Yes," he told them, "I saw Satan fall from heaven like
lightning! 19Look, I have given you authority over all the
power of the enemy, and you can walk among snakes and
scorpions and crush them. Nothing will injure you. 20But
don't rejoice because evil spirits obey you; rejoice because your names are registered in heaven."

JESUS' PRAYER OF THANKSGIVING

21At that same time Jesus was filled with the joy of the
Holy Spirit, and he said, "O Father, Lord of heaven and
earth, thank you for hiding these things from those
who think themselves wise and clever, and for revealing them to the childlike. Yes, Father, it pleased you to
do it this way.
22"My Father has entrusted everything to me. No one
truly knows the Son except the Father, and no one truly
knows the Father except the Son and those to whom the
Son chooses to reveal him."
23Then when they were alone, he turned to the disciples and said, "Blessed are the eyes that see what you have
seen. 24I tell you, many prophets and kings longed to see
what you see, but they didn't see it. And they longed to
hear what you hear, but they didn't hear it."

THE MOST IMPORTANT COMMANDMENT

25One day an expert in religious law stood up to test Jesus
by asking him this question: "Teacher, what should I do
to inherit eternal life?"
26Jesus replied, "What does the law of Moses say? How
do you read it?"
27The man answered, " 'You must love the LORD your
God with all your heart, all your soul, all your strength, and
all your mind.' And, 'Love your neighbor as yourself.' "*
28"Right!" Jesus told him. "Do this and you will live!"
29The man wanted to justify his actions, so he asked
Jesus, "And who is my neighbor?"

PARABLE OF THE GOOD SAMARITAN

30Jesus replied with a story: "A Jewish man was traveling
on a trip from Jerusalem to Jericho, and he was attacked
by bandits. They stripped him of his clothes, beat him up,
and left him half dead beside the road.
31"By chance a priest came along. But when he saw the
man lying there, he crossed to the other side of the road
and passed him by. 32A Temple assistant* walked over
and looked at him lying there, but he also passed by on
the other side.

A GOOD NEIGHBOR 10:27-37

The parable of the good Samaritan teaches us three principles about loving our neighbors: (1) lack of love is often easy to justify; (2) our neighbor is anyone of any race or social background who is in need; and (3) loving someone means acting to meet that person's need. Wherever you live, there are needy people close by. To whom will you be "a good Samaritan"? ■

33"Then a despised Samaritan came along, and when he
saw the man, he felt compassion for him. 34Going over to
him, the Samaritan soothed his wounds with olive oil and
wine and bandaged them. Then he put the man on his
own donkey and took him to an inn, where he took care
of him. 35The next day he handed the innkeeper two silver

10:15 Greek *to Hades.* 10:27 Deut 6:5; Lev 19:18. 10:32 Greek *A Levite.*

A Collection of Attitudes

The needs of others bring out various attitudes in us. Jesus used the story of the good but despised Samaritan (Luke 10:30-37) to make clear what attitude was acceptable to him. If we are honest, we often will find ourselves in the place of the lawyer, needing to learn again who our neighbor is. Note these different attitudes toward the wounded man.

To the **LAWYER**, the wounded man was a subject to discuss.

To **JESUS**, all of them—and all of us—were worth dying for.

To the **INNKEEPER**, the wounded man was a customer to serve for a fee.

To the **BANDITS**, the wounded man was someone to use and exploit.

To the **RELIGIOUS MEN**, the wounded man was a problem to be avoided.

To the **SAMARITAN**, the wounded man was a human being worth being cared for and loved.

coins,* telling him, 'Take care of this man. If his bill runs higher than this, I'll pay you the next time I'm here.'

36"Now which of these three would you say was a neighbor to the man who was attacked by bandits?" Jesus asked.

37The man replied, "The one who showed him mercy." Then Jesus said, "Yes, now go and do the same."

JESUS VISITS MARTHA AND MARY

38As Jesus and the disciples continued on their way to Jerusalem, they came to a certain village where a woman named Martha welcomed him into her home. 39Her sister, Mary, sat at the Lord's feet, listening to what he taught. 40But Martha was distracted by the big dinner she was preparing. She came to Jesus and said, "Lord, doesn't it seem unfair to you that my sister just sits here while I do all the work? Tell her to come and help me."

41But the Lord said to her, "My dear Martha, you are worried and upset over all these details! 42There is only one thing worth being concerned about. Mary has discovered it, and it will not be taken away from her."

11 TEACHING ABOUT PRAYER

Once Jesus was in a certain place praying. As he finished, one of his disciples came to him and said, "Lord, teach us to pray, just as John taught his disciples."

2Jesus said, "This is how you should pray:*

"Father, may your name be kept holy.
May your Kingdom come soon.
3 Give us each day the food we need,*
4 and forgive us our sins,
as we forgive those who sin against us.
And don't let us yield to temptation.*"

TEMPTATION 11:4

In this verse Jesus is not implying that God leads us into temptation. He is simply asking for deliverance from Satan and his deceit. All Christians struggle with temptation. Sometimes a temptation is so subtle we don't even realize what's happening to us. God promised that he won't allow us to be tempted beyond our endurance (1 Cor 10:13). God can help you recognize temptation and overcome it. ■

5Then, teaching them more about prayer, he used this story: "Suppose you went to a friend's house at midnight, wanting to borrow three loaves of bread. You say to him, 6'A friend of mine has just arrived for a visit, and I have nothing for him to eat.' 7And suppose he calls out from his bedroom, 'Don't bother me. The door is locked for the night, and my family and I are all in bed. I can't help you.' 8But I tell you this—though he won't do it for friendship's sake, if you keep knocking long enough, he will get up and give you whatever you need because of your shameless persistence.*

9"And so I tell you, keep on asking, and you will receive what you ask for. Keep on seeking, and you will find. Keep on knocking, and the door will be opened to you. 10For everyone who asks, receives. Everyone who seeks, finds. And to everyone who knocks, the door will be opened.

10:35 Greek *two denarii.* A denarius was equivalent to a laborer's full day's wage. **11:2** Some manuscripts add additional phrases from the Lord's Prayer as it reads in Matt 6:9-13. **11:3** Or *Give us each day our food for the day;* or *Give us each day our food for tomorrow.* **11:4** Or *And keep us from being tested.* **11:8** Or *in order to avoid shame, or so his reputation won't be damaged.*

11"You fathers—if your children ask* for a fish, do you give them a snake instead? 12Or if they ask for an egg, do you give them a scorpion? Of course not! 13So if you sinful people know how to give good gifts to your children, how much more will your heavenly Father give the Holy Spirit to those who ask him."

> For everyone who asks, receives. Everyone who seeks, finds. And to everyone who knocks, the door will be opened.
>
> *LUKE 11:10*

JESUS AND THE PRINCE OF DEMONS

14One day Jesus cast out a demon from a man who couldn't speak, and when the demon was gone, the man began to speak. The crowds were amazed, 15but some of them said, "No wonder he can cast out demons. He gets his power from Satan,* the prince of demons." 16Others, trying to test Jesus, demanded that he show them a miraculous sign from heaven to prove his authority.

17He knew their thoughts, so he said, "Any kingdom divided by civil war is doomed. A family splintered by feuding will fall apart. 18You say I am empowered by Satan. But if Satan is divided and fighting against himself, how can his kingdom survive? 19And if I am empowered by Satan, what about your own exorcists? They cast out demons, too, so they will condemn you for what you have said. 20But if I am casting out demons by the power of God,* then the Kingdom of God has arrived among you. 21For when a strong man like Satan is fully armed and guards his palace, his possessions are safe—22until someone even stronger attacks and overpowers him, strips him of his weapons, and carries off his belongings.

FOR OR AGAINST? 11:23

Jesus' statement, "Anyone who isn't working with me is actually working against me," goes along with a statement he'd made earlier: "Anyone who is not against you is for you" (9:50). People who are neutral toward Christians are actually helping them more than hurting them, because they aren't setting up barriers. But no one can remain neutral forever. Sooner or later everyone must choose. If you aren't actively for Christ, you are against him. What's your choice? ■

23"Anyone who isn't with me opposes me, and anyone who isn't working with me is actually working against me.

24"When an evil* spirit leaves a person, it goes into the desert, searching for rest. But when it finds none, it says, 'I will return to the person I came from.' 25So it returns and finds that its former home is all swept and in order. 26Then the spirit finds seven other spirits more evil than itself, and they all enter the person and live there. And so that person is worse off than before."

27As he was speaking, a woman in the crowd called out, "God bless your mother—the womb from which you came, and the breasts that nursed you!"

28Jesus replied, "But even more blessed are all who hear the word of God and put it into practice."

THE SIGN OF JONAH

29As the crowd pressed in on Jesus, he said, "This evil generation keeps asking me to show them a miraculous sign. But the only sign I will give them is the sign of Jonah. 30What happened to him was a sign to the people of Nineveh that God had sent him. What happens to the Son of Man* will be a sign to these people that he was sent by God.

31"The queen of Sheba* will stand up against this generation on judgment day and condemn it, for she came from a distant land to hear the wisdom of Solomon. Now someone greater than Solomon is here—but you refuse to listen. 32The people of Nineveh will also stand up against this generation on judgment day and condemn it, for they repented of their sins at the preaching of Jonah. Now someone greater than Jonah is here—but you refuse to repent.

RECEIVING THE LIGHT

33"No one lights a lamp and then hides it or puts it under a basket.* Instead, a lamp is placed on a stand, where its light can be seen by all who enter the house.

34"Your eye is a lamp that provides light for your body. When your eye is good, your whole body is filled with light. But when it is bad, your body is filled with darkness. 35Make sure that the light you think you have is not actually darkness. 36If you are filled with light, with no dark corners, then your whole life will be radiant, as though a floodlight were filling you with light."

JESUS CRITICIZES THE RELIGIOUS LEADERS

37As Jesus was speaking, one of the Pharisees invited him home for a meal. So he went in and took his place at the table.* 38His host was amazed to see that he sat down to eat without first performing the hand-washing ceremony required by Jewish custom. 39Then the Lord said to him, "You Pharisees are so careful to clean the outside of the cup and the dish, but inside you are filthy—full of greed and wickedness! 40Fools! Didn't God make the inside as well as the outside? 41So clean the inside by giving gifts to the poor, and you will be clean all over.

42"What sorrow awaits you Pharisees! For you are careful to tithe even the tiniest income from your herb gardens,* but you ignore justice and the love of God. You should tithe, yes, but do not neglect the more important things.

11:11 Some manuscripts add *for bread, do you give them a stone? Or [if they ask].* 11:15 Greek *Beelzeboul;* also in 11:18, 19. Other manuscripts read *Beezeboul;* Latin version reads *Beelzebub.* 11:20 Greek *by the finger of God.* 11:24 Greek *unclean.* 11:30 "Son of Man" is a title Jesus used for himself. 11:31 Greek *The queen of the south.* 11:33 Some manuscripts omit *or puts it under a basket.* 11:37 Or *and reclined.* 11:42 Greek *tithe the mint, the rue, and every herb.*

43"What sorrow awaits you Pharisees! For you love to sit in the seats of honor in the synagogues and receive respectful greetings as you walk in the marketplaces. 44Yes, what sorrow awaits you! For you are like hidden graves in a field. People walk over them without knowing the corruption they are stepping on."

45"Teacher," said an expert in religious law, "you have insulted us, too, in what you just said."

46"Yes," said Jesus, "what sorrow also awaits you experts in religious law! For you crush people with unbearable religious demands, and you never lift a finger to ease the burden. 47What sorrow awaits you! For you build monuments for the prophets your own ancestors killed long ago. 48But in fact, you stand as witnesses who agree with what your ancestors did. They killed the prophets, and you join in their crime by building the monuments! 49This is what God in his wisdom said about you:* 'I will send prophets and apostles to them, but they will kill some and persecute the others.'

50"As a result, this generation will be held responsible for the murder of all God's prophets from the creation of the world—51from the murder of Abel to the murder of Zechariah, who was killed between the altar and the sanctuary. Yes, it will certainly be charged against this generation.

52"What sorrow awaits you experts in religious law! For you remove the key to knowledge from the people. You don't enter the Kingdom yourselves, and you prevent others from entering."

53As Jesus was leaving, the teachers of religious law and the Pharisees became hostile and tried to provoke him with many questions. 54They wanted to trap him into saying something they could use against him.

MOTIVES 11:37-54

Jesus had harsh words for the Pharisees, because they (1) washed their hands but not their hearts, (2) remembered to tithe but forgot justice, (3) loved people's praise, (4) made impossible religious demands, and (5) didn't accept the truth about Jesus and prevented others from believing it. They wrongly focused on outward appearances and ignored the condition of their hearts. We do the same when our service is motivated by a desire to be seen rather than from a pure heart and love for others. Others may be fooled, but God isn't. What motivates you to serve others? ■

12

A WARNING AGAINST HYPOCRISY

Meanwhile, the crowds grew until thousands were milling about and stepping on each other. Jesus turned first to his disciples and warned them, "Beware of the yeast of the Pharisees—their hypocrisy. 2The time is coming when everything that is covered up will be revealed, and all that is secret will be made known to all. 3Whatever you have said in the dark will be heard in the light, and what you have whispered behind closed doors will be shouted from the housetops for all to hear!

4"Dear friends, don't be afraid of those who want to kill your body; they cannot do any more to you after that. 5But I'll tell you whom to fear. Fear God, who has the power to kill you and then throw you into hell.* Yes, he's the one to fear.

6"What is the price of five sparrows—two copper coins*? Yet God does not forget a single one of them. 7And the very hairs on your head are all numbered. So don't be afraid; you are more valuable to God than a whole flock of sparrows.

8"I tell you the truth, everyone who acknowledges me publicly here on earth, the Son of Man* will also acknowledge in the presence of God's angels. 9But anyone who denies me here on earth will be denied before God's angels. 10Anyone who speaks against the Son of Man can be forgiven, but anyone who blasphemes the Holy Spirit will not be forgiven.

REAL VALUE 12:11-21

When asked to give advice on how an estate should be split, Jesus gave a different answer than was expected: "Life is not measured by how much you own" (12:15). The parable he told (12:16-20) emphasized his point. Sadly, we often measure our worth or success by how much money or stuff we have. But as Jesus warned, a person with lots of stuff who lacks a relationship with God is poor indeed. Tempted to measure your life by your stuff? Don't. ■

11"And when you are brought to trial in the synagogues and before rulers and authorities, don't worry about how to defend yourself or what to say, 12for the Holy Spirit will teach you at that time what needs to be said."

PARABLE OF THE RICH FOOL

13Then someone called from the crowd, "Teacher, please tell my brother to divide our father's estate with me."

14Jesus replied, "Friend, who made me a judge over you to decide such things as that?" 15Then he said, "Beware! Guard against every kind of greed. Life is not measured by how much you own."

16Then he told them a story: "A rich man had a fertile farm that produced fine crops. 17He said to himself, 'What should I do? I don't have room for all my crops.' 18Then he said, 'I know! I'll tear down my barns and build bigger ones. Then I'll have room enough to store all my wheat and other goods. 19And I'll sit back and say to myself, "My friend, you have enough stored away for years to come. Now take it easy! Eat, drink, and be merry!"'

20"But God said to him, 'You fool! You will die this very night. Then who will get everything you worked for?'

21"Yes, a person is a fool to store up earthly wealth but not have a rich relationship with God."

11:49 Greek *Therefore, the wisdom of God said.* 12:5 Greek *Gehenna.* 12:6 Greek *two assaria* [Roman coins equal to 1/16 of a denarius]. 12:8 "Son of Man" is a title Jesus used for himself.

TEACHING ABOUT MONEY AND POSSESSIONS

22Then, turning to his disciples, Jesus said, "That is why I tell you not to worry about everyday life—whether you have enough food to eat or enough clothes to wear. 23For life is more than food, and your body more than clothing. 24Look at the ravens. They don't plant or harvest or store food in barns, for God feeds them. And you are far more valuable to him than any birds! 25Can all your worries add a single moment to your life? 26And if worry can't accomplish a little thing like that, what's the use of worrying over bigger things?

27"Look at the lilies and how they grow. They don't work or make their clothing, yet Solomon in all his glory was not dressed as beautifully as they are. 28And if God cares so wonderfully for flowers that are here today and thrown into the fire tomorrow, he will certainly care for you. Why do you have so little faith?

29"And don't be concerned about what to eat and what to drink. Don't worry about such things. 30These things dominate the thoughts of unbelievers all over the world, but your Father already knows your needs. 31Seek the Kingdom of God above all else, and he will give you everything you need.

32"So don't be afraid, little flock. For it gives your Father great happiness to give you the Kingdom.

33"Sell your possessions and give to those in need. This will store up treasure for you in heaven! And the purses of heaven never get old or develop holes. Your treasure will be safe; no thief can steal it and no moth can destroy it. 34Wherever your treasure is, there the desires of your heart will also be.

BE READY FOR THE LORD'S COMING

35"Be dressed for service and keep your lamps burning, 36as though you were waiting for your master to return from the wedding feast. Then you will be ready to open the door and let him in the moment he arrives and knocks. 37The servants who are ready and waiting for his return will be rewarded. I tell you the truth, he himself will seat them, put on an apron, and serve them as they sit and eat! 38He may come in the middle of the night or just before dawn.* But whenever he comes, he will reward the servants who are ready.

39"Understand this: If a homeowner knew exactly when a burglar was coming, he would not permit his house to be broken into. 40You also must be ready all the time, for the Son of Man will come when least expected."

41Peter asked, "Lord, is that illustration just for us or for everyone?"

42And the Lord replied, "A faithful, sensible servant is one to whom the master can give the responsibility of managing his other household servants and feeding them. 43If the master returns and finds that the servant has done a good job, there will be a reward. 44I tell you the truth, the master will put that servant in charge of all he owns. 45But what if the servant thinks, 'My master won't be back for a while,' and he begins beating the other servants, partying, and getting drunk? 46The master will return unannounced and unexpected, and he will cut the servant in pieces and banish him with the unfaithful.

47"And a servant who knows what the master wants, but isn't prepared and doesn't carry out those instructions, will be severely punished. 48But someone who does not know, and then does something wrong, will be punished only lightly. When someone has been given much, much will be required in return; and when someone has been entrusted with much, even more will be required.

JESUS CAUSES DIVISION

49"I have come to set the world on fire, and I wish it were already burning! 50I have a terrible baptism of suffering ahead of me, and I am under a heavy burden until it is accomplished. 51Do you think I have come to bring peace to the earth? No, I have come to divide people against each other! 52From now on families will be split apart, three in favor of me, and two against—or two in favor and three against.

53 'Father will be divided against son
and son against father;
mother against daughter
and daughter against mother;
and mother-in-law against daughter-in-law
and daughter-in-law against
mother-in-law.'*"

DIVIDED LOYALTIES 12:51-53

Jesus revealed that his coming often results in conflict. There is no middle ground with Jesus. Close groups can be torn apart when some choose to follow him and others refuse to do so. Loyalties must be declared and commitments made, sometimes to the severing of other relationships. Life is easiest when a whole family believes in Christ; yet this often is not the case. Are you willing to risk your family's disapproval (if necessary) to take a stand for Jesus? ■

54Then Jesus turned to the crowd and said, "When you see clouds beginning to form in the west, you say, 'Here comes a shower.' And you are right. 55When the south wind blows, you say, 'Today will be a scorcher.' And it is. 56You fools! You know how to interpret the weather signs of the earth and sky, but you don't know how to interpret the present times.

57"Why can't you decide for yourselves what is right? 58When you are on the way to court with your accuser, try to settle the matter before you get there. Otherwise, your accuser may drag you before the judge, who will hand you over to an officer, who will throw you into prison. 59And if that happens, you won't be free again until you have paid the very last penny.*"

12:38 Greek *in the second or third watch.* **12:53** Mic 7:6. **12:59** Greek *last lepton* [the smallest Jewish coin].

13

A CALL TO REPENTANCE

About this time Jesus was informed that Pilate had murdered some people from Galilee as they were offering sacrifices at the Temple. 2"Do you think those Galileans were worse sinners than all the other people from Galilee?" Jesus asked. "Is that why they suffered? 3Not at all! And you will perish, too, unless you repent of your sins and turn to God. 4And what about the eighteen people who died when the tower in Siloam fell on them? Were they the worst sinners in Jerusalem? 5No, and I tell you again that unless you repent, you will perish, too."

PARABLE OF THE BARREN FIG TREE

6Then Jesus told this story: "A man planted a fig tree in his garden and came again and again to see if there was any fruit on it, but he was always disappointed. 7Finally, he said to his gardener, 'I've waited three years, and there hasn't been a single fig! Cut it down. It's just taking up space in the garden.'

8"The gardener answered, 'Sir, give it one more chance. Leave it another year, and I'll give it special attention and plenty of fertilizer. 9If we get figs next year, fine. If not, then you can cut it down.'"

JESUS HEALS ON THE SABBATH

10One Sabbath day as Jesus was teaching in a synagogue, 11he saw a woman who had been crippled by an evil spirit. She had been bent double for eighteen years and was unable to stand up straight. 12When Jesus saw her, he called her over and said, "Dear woman, you are healed of your sickness!" 13Then he touched her, and instantly she could stand straight. How she praised God!

14But the leader in charge of the synagogue was indignant that Jesus had healed her on the Sabbath day. "There are six days of the week for working," he said to the crowd. "Come on those days to be healed, not on the Sabbath."

15But the Lord replied, "You hypocrites! Each of you works on the Sabbath day! Don't you untie your ox or your donkey from its stall on the Sabbath and lead it out for water? 16This dear woman, a daughter of Abraham, has been held in bondage by Satan for eighteen years. Isn't it right that she be released, even on the Sabbath?"

17This shamed his enemies, but all the people rejoiced at the wonderful things he did.

PARABLE OF THE MUSTARD SEED

18Then Jesus said, "What is the Kingdom of God like? How can I illustrate it? 19It is like a tiny mustard seed that a man planted in a garden; it grows and becomes a tree, and the birds make nests in its branches."

PARABLE OF THE YEAST

20He also asked, "What else is the Kingdom of God like? 21It is like the yeast a woman used in making bread. Even though she put only a little yeast in three measures of flour, it permeated every part of the dough."

THE NARROW DOOR

22Jesus went through the towns and villages, teaching as he went, always pressing on toward Jerusalem. 23Someone asked him, "Lord, will only a few be saved?"

He replied, 24"Work hard to enter the narrow door to God's Kingdom, for many will try to enter but will fail. 25When the master of the house has locked the door, it will be too late. You will stand outside knocking and pleading, 'Lord, open the door for us!' But he will reply, 'I don't know you or where you come from.' 26Then you will say, 'But we ate and drank with you, and you taught in our streets.' 27And he will reply, 'I tell you, I don't know you or where you come from. Get away from me, all you who do evil.'

28"There will be weeping and gnashing of teeth, for you will see Abraham, Isaac, Jacob, and all the prophets in the Kingdom of God, but you will be thrown out. 29And people will come from all over the world—from east and west, north and south—to take their places in the Kingdom of God. 30And note this: Some who seem least important now will be the greatest then, and some who are the greatest now will be least important then.*"

NARROW-MINDED 13:22-30

Maybe you've heard people talk about how "narrow-minded" Christians are. Well, they're right. Jesus declared that the way to heaven is narrow. In John 14:6, he talked more about this "narrow" way: he is the only way to heaven. For many, this narrow view is a stumbling block. They want more options. But those that seek other options will find the door to heaven closed to them (see 12:25). Want to get there? Jesus is your only option. ■

JESUS GRIEVES OVER JERUSALEM

31At that time some Pharisees said to him, "Get away from here if you want to live! Herod Antipas wants to kill you!"

32Jesus replied, "Go tell that fox that I will keep on casting out demons and healing people today and tomorrow; and the third day I will accomplish my purpose. 33Yes, today, tomorrow, and the next day I must proceed on my way. For it wouldn't do for a prophet of God to be killed except in Jerusalem!

34"O Jerusalem, Jerusalem, the city that kills the prophets and stones God's messengers! How often I have wanted to gather your children together as a hen protects her chicks beneath her wings, but you wouldn't let me. 35And now, look, your house is abandoned. And you will never see me again until you say, 'Blessings on the one who comes in the name of the LORD!'*"

14

JESUS HEALS ON THE SABBATH

One Sabbath day Jesus went to eat dinner in the home of a leader of the Pharisees, and the people were watching him closely. 2There was a man there whose arms and legs

13:30 Greek *Some are last who will be first, and some are first who will be last.* **13:35** Ps 118:26.

were swollen.* 3Jesus asked the Pharisees and experts in religious law, "Is it permitted in the law to heal people on the Sabbath day, or not?" 4When they refused to answer, Jesus touched the sick man and healed him and sent him away. 5Then he turned to them and said, "Which of you doesn't work on the Sabbath? If your son* or your cow falls into a pit, don't you rush to get him out?" 6Again they could not answer.

JESUS TEACHES ABOUT HUMILITY

7When Jesus noticed that all who had come to the dinner were trying to sit in the seats of honor near the head of the table, he gave them this advice: 8"When you are invited to a wedding feast, don't sit in the seat of honor. What if someone who is more distinguished than you has also been invited? 9The host will come and say, 'Give this person your seat.' Then you will be embarrassed, and you will have to take whatever seat is left at the foot of the table!

10"Instead, take the lowest place at the foot of the table. Then when your host sees you, he will come and say, 'Friend, we have a better place for you!' Then you will be honored in front of all the other guests. 11For those who exalt themselves will be humbled, and those who humble themselves will be exalted."

HOW LOW WILL YOU GO? 14:7-11

Jesus advised people not to rush for the best seats at a feast. Instead, he suggested, "Take the lowest place." In other words, go the humble route. Now, that advice is contrary to the "Look out for number one" philosophy. Taking the lowest place might involve helping someone less fortunate without making an announcement about doing so; letting someone else have the best seat in the movie theater, instead of racing to get it; or even giving up something you want in order to let someone else have it. How "low" will you go? ■

12Then he turned to his host. "When you put on a luncheon or a banquet," he said, "don't invite your friends, brothers, relatives, and rich neighbors. For they will invite you back, and that will be your only reward. 13Instead, invite the poor, the crippled, the lame, and the blind. 14Then at the resurrection of the righteous, God will reward you for inviting those who could not repay you."

PARABLE OF THE GREAT FEAST

15Hearing this, a man sitting at the table with Jesus exclaimed, "What a blessing it will be to attend a banquet* in the Kingdom of God!"

16Jesus replied with this story: "A man prepared a great feast and sent out many invitations. 17When the banquet was ready, he sent his servant to tell the guests, 'Come, the banquet is ready.' 18But they all began making excuses. One said, 'I have just bought a field and must inspect it. Please excuse me.' 19Another said, 'I have just bought five pairs of oxen, and I want to try them out. Please excuse me.' 20Another said, 'I now have a wife, so I can't come.'

21"The servant returned and told his master what they had said. His master was furious and said, 'Go quickly into the streets and alleys of the town and invite the poor, the crippled, the blind, and the lame.' 22After the servant had done this, he reported, 'There is still room for more.' 23So his master said, 'Go out into the country lanes and behind the hedges and urge anyone you find to come, so that the house will be full. 24For none of those I first invited will get even the smallest taste of my banquet.'"

SALTY 14:34-35

Salt can lose its flavor. When it gets wet and then dries, nothing is left but a tasteless residue. When Christians blend into the world to avoid the cost of standing for Christ, they're like salt without flavor. Just as salt flavors and preserves food, Christians preserve the good in the world, keep it from spoiling, and bring new flavor to life. This requires planning, willing sacrifice, and unswerving commitment to Christ's Kingdom. Being "salty" isn't always easy. However, if a Christian fails in this function, he or she fails to represent Christ in the world. How salty are you? ■

THE COST OF BEING A DISCIPLE

25A large crowd was following Jesus. He turned around and said to them, 26"If you want to be my disciple, you must hate everyone else by comparison—your father and mother, wife and children, brothers and sisters—yes, even your own life. Otherwise, you cannot be my disciple. 27And if you do not carry your own cross and follow me, you cannot be my disciple.

28"But don't begin until you count the cost. For who would begin construction of a building without first calculating the cost to see if there is enough money to finish it? 29Otherwise, you might complete only the foundation before running out of money, and then everyone would laugh at you. 30They would say, 'There's the person who started that building and couldn't afford to finish it!'

31"Or what king would go to war against another king without first sitting down with his counselors to discuss whether his army of 10,000 could defeat the 20,000 soldiers marching against him? 32And if he can't, he will send a delegation to discuss terms of peace while the enemy is still far away. 33So you cannot become my disciple without giving up everything you own.

34"Salt is good for seasoning. But if it loses its flavor, how do you make it salty again? 35Flavorless salt is good neither for the soil nor for the manure pile. It is thrown away. Anyone with ears to hear should listen and understand!"

14:2 Or *who had dropsy.* 14:5 Some manuscripts read *donkey.* 14:15 Greek *to eat bread.*

keeping it real

My mother and I sometimes had difficulty getting along. Often we would argue, sometimes over the stupidest things. After our fights, I'd feel real bad, but I didn't know what to do about it. I felt it was all her fault; she just didn't understand me; she was being totally unreasonable; etc.

Then I read the parable of the lost son (Luke 15:11-32). And I began to realize that the younger son felt he had every right to take his inheritance and go off on his own. But it didn't get him anywhere. He finally decided to go back home. But his father didn't say "I told you so" or anything like that. Instead, he gave him a big welcome.

I got to thinking about my attitude toward my mom. I had to admit that I probably was at fault at least some of the time. As hard as it was, I had to apologize when I was wrong and ask forgiveness. (It was probably really hard for the lost son, too.)

I sat down and went over the past several arguments that weren't really resolved and wrote down the specifics on where I was wrong. Then I prayed hard that I could swallow my pride and ask my mom to forgive me.

I finally did. And my mom reacted very much like the father in the story; she was very forgiving. Since then, I've tried to concentrate more on my attitude than on my mom's. And, amazingly, we argue less. But even when we do argue, and I fall into the old patterns, I know that God will forgive me when I ask for it. (So does Mom—usually.)

—Taylor

15

PARABLE OF THE LOST SHEEP

Tax collectors and other notorious sinners often came to
listen to Jesus teach. 2This made the Pharisees and teachers of religious law complain that he was associating with
such sinful people—even eating with them!
3So Jesus told them this story: 4"If a man has a hundred
sheep and one of them gets lost, what will he do? Won't
he leave the ninety-nine others in the wilderness and go
to search for the one that is lost until he finds it? 5And
when he has found it, he will joyfully carry it home on his
shoulders. 6When he arrives, he will call together his
friends and neighbors, saying, 'Rejoice with me because I
have found my lost sheep.' 7In the same way, there is
more joy in heaven over one lost sinner who repents and
returns to God than over ninety-nine others who are righteous and haven't strayed away!

PARABLE OF THE LOST COIN

8"Or suppose a woman has ten silver coins* and loses
one. Won't she light a lamp and sweep the entire house
and search carefully until she finds it? 9And when she
finds it, she will call in her friends and neighbors and say,
'Rejoice with me because I have found my lost coin.' 10In
the same way, there is joy in the presence of God's angels
when even one sinner repents."

PARABLE OF THE LOST SON

11To illustrate the point further, Jesus told them this
story: "A man had two sons. 12The younger son told his father, 'I want my share of your estate now before you die.'
So his father agreed to divide his wealth between his
sons.
13"A few days later this younger son packed all his belongings and moved to a distant land, and there he
wasted all his money in wild living. 14About the time his
money ran out, a great famine swept over the land, and he
began to starve. 15He persuaded a local farmer to hire
him, and the man sent him into his fields to feed the pigs.
16The young man became so hungry that even the pods
he was feeding the pigs looked good to him. But no one
gave him anything.
17"When he finally came to his senses, he said to himself, 'At home even the hired servants have food enough
to spare, and here I am dying of hunger! 18I will go home
to my father and say, "Father, I have sinned against both
heaven and you, 19and I am no longer worthy of being
called your son. Please take me on as a hired servant." '
20"So he returned home to his father. And while he was
still a long way off, his father saw him coming. Filled with
love and compassion, he ran to his son, embraced him,
and kissed him. 21His son said to him, 'Father, I have sinned

15:8 Greek *ten drachmas*. A drachma was the equivalent of a full day's wage.

against both heaven and you, and I am no longer worthy of being called your son.*'

22"But his father said to the servants, 'Quick! Bring the finest robe in the house and put it on him. Get a ring for his finger and sandals for his feet. 23And kill the calf we have been fattening. We must celebrate with a feast, 24for this son of mine was dead and has now returned to life. He was lost, but now he is found.' So the party began.

25"Meanwhile, the older son was in the fields working. When he returned home, he heard music and dancing in the house, 26and he asked one of the servants what was going on. 27'Your brother is back,' he was told, 'and your father has killed the fattened calf. We are celebrating because of his safe return.'

28"The older brother was angry and wouldn't go in. His father came out and begged him, 29but he replied, 'All these years I've slaved for you and never once refused to do a single thing you told me to. And in all that time you never gave me even one young goat for a feast with my friends. 30Yet when this son of yours comes back after squandering your money on prostitutes, you celebrate by killing the fattened calf!'

31"His father said to him, 'Look, dear son, you have always stayed by me, and everything I have is yours. 32We had to celebrate this happy day. For your brother was dead and has come back to life! He was lost, but now he is found!'"

A FORGIVING RESPONSE 15:11-32

In the story of the lost son, there is a contrast between the response of the father and that of the older brother (see 15:20-30). The father was forgiving and overjoyed. The brother was unforgiving and bitter. The father forgave because he was joyful, and the son refused to forgive because he was bitter. In fact, the older son didn't think his brother *deserved* forgiveness.

We sometimes base our decision to forgive someone on whether or not he or she deserves it. But lack of forgiveness reflects more on the attitude of the person who refuses to offer it than on the person who needs it. Which response will you choose when someone seeks your forgiveness? ■

16

PARABLE OF THE SHREWD MANAGER

Jesus told this story to his disciples: "There was a certain rich man who had a manager handling his affairs. One day a report came that the manager was wasting his employer's money. 2So the employer called him in and said, 'What's this I hear about you? Get your report in order, because you are going to be fired.'

3"The manager thought to himself, 'Now what? My boss has fired me. I don't have the strength to dig ditches, and I'm too proud to beg. 4Ah, I know how to ensure that I'll have plenty of friends who will give me a home when I am fired.'

5"So he invited each person who owed money to his employer to come and discuss the situation. He asked the first one, 'How much do you owe him?' 6The man replied, 'I owe him 800 gallons of olive oil.' So the manager told him, 'Take the bill and quickly change it to 400 gallons.*'

7"'And how much do you owe my employer?' he asked the next man. 'I owe him 1,000 bushels of wheat,' was the reply. 'Here,' the manager said, 'take the bill and change it to 800 bushels.*'

8"The rich man had to admire the dishonest rascal for being so shrewd. And it is true that the children of this world are more shrewd in dealing with the world around them than are the children of the light. 9Here's the lesson: Use your worldly resources to benefit others and make friends. Then, when your earthly possessions are gone, they will welcome you to an eternal home.*

10"If you are faithful in little things, you will be faithful in large ones. But if you are dishonest in little things, you won't be honest with greater responsibilities. 11And if you are untrustworthy about worldly wealth, who will trust you with the true riches of heaven? 12And if you are not faithful with other people's things, why should you be trusted with things of your own?

13"No one can serve two masters. For you will hate one and love the other; you will be devoted to one and despise the other. You cannot serve both God and money."

14The Pharisees, who dearly loved their money, heard all this and scoffed at him. 15Then he said to them, "You like to appear righteous in public, but God knows your hearts. What this world honors is detestable in the sight of God.

16"Until John the Baptist, the law of Moses and the messages of the prophets were your guides. But now the Good News of the Kingdom of God is preached, and everyone is eager to get in.* 17But that doesn't mean that the law has lost its force. It is easier for heaven and earth to disappear than for the smallest point of God's law to be overturned.

DIVORCE 16:18

With today's high divorce rate, have you ever found yourself wondering whether God has changed his mind about divorce? Most religious leaders of Jesus' day permitted a man to divorce his wife for nearly any reason. Jesus' words about divorce (see also Matt 19:10) went beyond Moses' (Deut 24:1-4). Jesus says in unmistakable terms that marriage is a lifetime commitment. Is that your view of marriage? ■

18"For example, a man who divorces his wife and marries someone else commits adultery. And anyone who marries a woman divorced from her husband commits adultery."

15:21 Some manuscripts add *Please take me on as a hired servant.* 16:6 Greek *100 baths . . . 50 [baths].* 16:7 Greek *100 korous . . . 80 [korous].* 16:9 Or *you will be welcomed into eternal homes.* 16:16 Or *everyone is urged to enter in.*

PARABLE OF THE RICH MAN AND LAZARUS

19Jesus said, "There was a certain rich man who was
splendidly clothed in purple and fine linen and who lived
each day in luxury. 20At his gate lay a poor man named
Lazarus who was covered with sores. 21As Lazarus lay
there longing for scraps from the rich man's table, the
dogs would come and lick his open sores.
22"Finally, the poor man died and was carried by the
angels to be with Abraham.* The rich man also died and
was buried, 23and his soul went to the place of the dead.*
There, in torment, he saw Abraham in the far distance
with Lazarus at his side.
24"The rich man shouted, 'Father Abraham, have some
pity! Send Lazarus over here to dip the tip of his finger in
water and cool my tongue. I am in anguish in these
flames.'
25"But Abraham said to him, 'Son, remember that during your lifetime you had everything you wanted, and
Lazarus had nothing. So now he is here being comforted,
and you are in anguish. 26And besides, there is a great
chasm separating us. No one can cross over to you from
here, and no one can cross over to us from there.'
27"Then the rich man said, 'Please, Father Abraham, at
least send him to my father's home. 28For I have five
brothers, and I want him to warn them so they don't end
up in this place of torment.'
29"But Abraham said, 'Moses and the prophets have
warned them. Your brothers can read what they wrote.'
30"The rich man replied, 'No, Father Abraham! But if
someone is sent to them from the dead, then they will repent of their sins and turn to God.'
31"But Abraham said, 'If they won't listen to Moses and
the prophets, they won't listen even if someone rises
from the dead.'"

LOVE AND TRUTH 17:3-4

To "rebuke" or "confront" someone does not mean pointing out every fault that person has. It means caring enough to bring wrongdoing to a person's attention with the purpose of restoring him or her to God and to fellow humans. When you feel you must rebuke another Christian for something he or she did wrong, check your attitude first. Will you, like Ephesians 4:15 says, "speak the truth in love"? ■

17

TEACHINGS ABOUT FORGIVENESS AND FAITH

One day Jesus said to his disciples, "There will always be
temptations to sin, but what sorrow awaits the person
who does the tempting! 2It would be better to be thrown
into the sea with a millstone hung around your neck than
to cause one of these little ones to fall into sin. 3So watch
yourselves!
"If another believer* sins, rebuke that person; then if
there is repentance, forgive. 4Even if that person wrongs
you seven times a day and each time turns again and asks
forgiveness, you must forgive."
5The apostles said to the Lord, "Show us how to increase our faith."
6The Lord answered, "If you had faith even as small as a
mustard seed, you could say to this mulberry tree, 'May
you be uprooted and thrown into the sea,' and it would
obey you!
7"When a servant comes in from plowing or taking
care of sheep, does his master say, 'Come in and eat with
me'? 8No, he says, 'Prepare my meal, put on your apron,
and serve me while I eat. Then you can eat later.' 9And
does the master thank the servant for doing what he was
told to do? Of course not. 10In the same way, when you
obey me you should say, 'We are unworthy servants who
have simply done our duty.'"

TEN HEALED OF LEPROSY

11As Jesus continued on toward Jerusalem, he reached
the border between Galilee and Samaria. 12As he entered
a village there, ten lepers stood at a distance, 13crying out,
"Jesus, Master, have mercy on us!"
14He looked at them and said, "Go show yourselves to
the priests."* And as they went, they were cleansed of
their leprosy.
15One of them, when he saw that he was healed, came
back to Jesus, shouting, "Praise God!" 16He fell to the
ground at Jesus' feet, thanking him for what he had done.
This man was a Samaritan.
17Jesus asked, "Didn't I heal ten men? Where are the
other nine? 18Has no one returned to give glory to God except this foreigner?" 19And Jesus said to the man, "Stand
up and go. Your faith has healed you.*"

THE COMING OF THE KINGDOM

20One day the Pharisees asked Jesus, "When will the
Kingdom of God come?"
Jesus replied, "The Kingdom of God can't be detected
by visible signs.* 21You won't be able to say, 'Here it is!' or
'It's over there!' For the Kingdom of God is already among
you.*"
22Then he said to his disciples, "The time is coming
when you will long to see the day when the Son of Man
returns,* but you won't see it. 23People will tell you,
'Look, there is the Son of Man,' or 'Here he is,' but don't
go out and follow them. 24For as the lightning flashes
and lights up the sky from one end to the other, so it will
be on the day when the Son of Man comes. 25But first the
Son of Man must suffer terribly* and be rejected by this
generation.
26"When the Son of Man returns, it will be like it was in
Noah's day. 27In those days, the people enjoyed banquets
and parties and weddings right up to the time Noah entered his boat and the flood came and destroyed them all.
28"And the world will be as it was in the days of Lot.
People went about their daily business—eating and
drinking, buying and selling, farming and building—

16:22 Greek *into Abraham's bosom.* **16:23** Greek *to Hades.* **17:3** Greek *If your brother.* **17:14** See Lev 14:2-32. **17:19** Or *Your faith has saved you.* **17:20** Or *by your speculations.* **17:21** Or *is within you,* or *is in your grasp.* **17:22** Or *long for even one day with the Son of Man.* "Son of Man" is a title Jesus used for himself. **17:25** Or *suffer many things.*

29until the morning Lot left Sodom. Then fire and burning sulfur rained down from heaven and destroyed them
all. 30Yes, it will be 'business as usual' right up to the day
when the Son of Man is revealed. 31On that day a person
out on the deck of a roof must not go down into the house
to pack. A person out in the field must not return home.
32Remember what happened to Lot's wife! 33If you cling
to your life, you will lose it, and if you let your life go, you
will save it. 34That night two people will be asleep in one
bed; one will be taken, the other left. 35Two women will
be grinding flour together at the mill; one will be taken,
the other left.*"

37"Where will this happen, Lord?"* the disciples
asked.

Jesus replied, "Just as the gathering of vultures shows
there is a carcass nearby, so these signs indicate that the
end is near."*

18

PARABLE OF THE PERSISTENT WIDOW

One day Jesus told his disciples a story to show that they
should always pray and never give up. 2"There was a judge
in a certain city," he said, "who neither feared God nor
cared about people. 3A widow of that city came to him repeatedly, saying, 'Give me justice in this dispute with my
enemy.' 4The judge ignored her for a while, but finally he
said to himself, 'I don't fear God or care about people,
5but this woman is driving me crazy. I'm going to see that
she gets justice, because she is wearing me out with her
constant requests!'"

6Then the Lord said, "Learn a lesson from this unjust
judge. 7Even he rendered a just decision in the end. So
don't you think God will surely give justice to his chosen
people who cry out to him day and night? Will he keep
putting them off? 8I tell you, he will grant justice to them
quickly! But when the Son of Man* returns, how many
will he find on the earth who have faith?"

PARABLE OF THE PHARISEE AND TAX COLLECTOR

9Then Jesus told this story to some who had great confidence in their own righteousness and scorned everyone
else: 10"Two men went to the Temple to pray. One was a
Pharisee, and the other was a despised tax collector.
11The Pharisee stood by himself and prayed this prayer*:
'I thank you, God, that I am not a sinner like everyone else.
For I don't cheat, I don't sin, and I don't commit adultery.
I'm certainly not like that tax collector! 12I fast twice a
week, and I give you a tenth of my income.'

13"But the tax collector stood at a distance and dared
not even lift his eyes to heaven as he prayed. Instead, he
beat his chest in sorrow, saying, 'O God, be merciful to
me, for I am a sinner.' 14I tell you, this sinner, not the Pharisee, returned home justified before God. For those who
exalt themselves will be humbled, and those who humble
themselves will be exalted."

JESUS BLESSES THE CHILDREN

15One day some parents brought their little children to
Jesus so he could touch and bless them. But when the disciples saw this, they scolded the parents for bothering
him.

16Then Jesus called for the children and said to the disciples, "Let the children come to me. Don't stop them! For
the Kingdom of God belongs to those who are like these
children. 17I tell you the truth, anyone who doesn't receive the Kingdom of God like a child will never enter it."

THE RICH MAN

18Once a religious leader asked Jesus this question: "Good
Teacher, what should I do to inherit eternal life?"

19"Why do you call me good?" Jesus asked him. "Only
God is truly good. 20But to answer your question, you

17:35 Some manuscripts add verse 36, *Two men will be working in the field; one will be taken, the other left.* Compare Matt 24:40. **17:37a** Greek *"Where, Lord?"* **17:37b** Greek *"Wherever the carcass is, the vultures gather."* **18:8** "Son of Man" is a title Jesus used for himself. **18:11** Some manuscripts read *stood and prayed this prayer to himself.*

I've always been taught to be self-reliant and to take credit for what I've done. Is being proud about your accomplishments wrong? Why or why not?

Have you ever known someone who thought he was so good in sports that he rarely listened to the coach? Although all coaches love to have players with great natural ability, most would settle for those with a few skills who are teachable. An athlete is much easier to mold than to motivate.

Being totally self-reliant is sort of like an athlete allowing the coach to give him advice only when he wants it. Before too long the athlete will start to deteriorate in talent. That's why advice from a coach is needed.

Taking the credit for everything we do is called pride. There is a good type of pride that comes from doing something well. Perhaps we've worked hard at something that turned out great. We feel good about ourselves—that's okay. The problem comes when we take all the credit. That's the wrong kind of pride.

God wants us to recognize that he gave us our life and our talents. This shows humility and a deep respect for God.

The Pharisee in Jesus' parable (Luke 18:9-14) is a perfect example of someone with the wrong kind of pride. He was proud of his "holy" life. Although he acted like he was talking to God, he was really just talking to himself.

On the flip side is the tax collector. He had nothing to be proud of, especially as it related to his relationship with God. In humility, he asked God for mercy.

If we go through life with an I-can-make-it-by-myself attitude, we're really saying to God, "I don't really need you after all." But God wants us to depend on him.

A CHILDLIKE FAITH 18:15-17

It was customary for parents to bring their children to a rabbi for a blessing. The disciples, however, thought the children were unworthy of the Master's time. But Jesus welcomed them because little children have the kind of faith needed to enter God's Kingdom. Is that the kind of faith you have? ■

know the commandments: 'You must not commit adultery. You must not murder. You must not steal. You must
not testify falsely. Honor your father and mother.'*"
21The man replied, "I've obeyed all these commandments since I was young."
22When Jesus heard his answer, he said, "There is still
one thing you haven't done. Sell all your possessions and
give the money to the poor, and you will have treasure in
heaven. Then come, follow me."
23But when the man heard this he became very sad, for
he was very rich.
24When Jesus saw this,* he said, "How hard it is for the
rich to enter the Kingdom of God! 25In fact, it is easier for
a camel to go through the eye of a needle than for a rich
person to enter the Kingdom of God!"
26Those who heard this said, "Then who in the world
can be saved?"
27He replied, "What is impossible for people is possible with God."
28Peter said, "We've left our homes to follow you."
29"Yes," Jesus replied, "and I assure you that everyone
who has given up house or wife or brothers or parents or
children, for the sake of the Kingdom of God, 30will be repaid many times over in this life, and will have eternal life
in the world to come."

GIVE AND GAIN 18:26-30

Peter and the other disciples had paid a high price to follow Jesus. But Jesus reminded Peter that following him has its benefits as well as its sacrifices. Are you worried about what you have to give up in order to say yes to God? Any believer who has had to give up something to follow Christ will be paid back in this life as well as in the next. Whatever you give, you'll gain. Convinced? ■

JESUS AGAIN PREDICTS HIS DEATH

31Taking the twelve disciples aside, Jesus said, "Listen,
we're going up to Jerusalem, where all the predictions of
the prophets concerning the Son of Man will come true.
32He will be handed over to the Romans,* and he will be
mocked, treated shamefully, and spit upon. 33They will
flog him with a whip and kill him, but on the third day he
will rise again."
34But they didn't understand any of this. The significance of his words was hidden from them, and they failed
to grasp what he was talking about.

JESUS HEALS A BLIND BEGGAR

35As Jesus approached Jericho, a blind beggar was sitting
beside the road. 36When he heard the noise of a crowd
going past, he asked what was happening. 37They told
him that Jesus the Nazarene* was going by. 38So he began
shouting, "Jesus, Son of David, have mercy on me!"
39"Be quiet!" the people in front yelled at him.
But he only shouted louder, "Son of David, have mercy
on me!"
40When Jesus heard him, he stopped and ordered that
the man be brought to him. As the man came near, Jesus
asked him, 41"What do you want me to do for you?"
"Lord," he said, "I want to see!"
42And Jesus said, "All right, receive your sight! Your
faith has healed you." 43Instantly the man could see, and
he followed Jesus, praising God. And all who saw it
praised God, too.

19

JESUS AND ZACCHAEUS

Jesus entered Jericho and made his way through the
town. 2There was a man there named Zacchaeus. He was
the chief tax collector in the region, and he had become
very rich. 3He tried to get a look at Jesus, but he was too
short to see over the crowd. 4So he ran ahead and climbed
a sycamore-fig tree beside the road, for Jesus was going
to pass that way.
5When Jesus came by, he looked up at Zacchaeus and
called him by name. "Zacchaeus!" he said. "Quick, come
down! I must be a guest in your home today."
6Zacchaeus quickly climbed down and took Jesus to
his house in great excitement and joy. 7But the people
were displeased. "He has gone to be the guest of a notorious sinner," they grumbled.
8Meanwhile, Zacchaeus stood before the Lord and
said, "I will give half my wealth to the poor, Lord, and if I
have cheated people on their taxes, I will give them back
four times as much!"
9Jesus responded, "Salvation has come to this home today, for this man has shown himself to be a true son of
Abraham. 10For the Son of Man* came to seek and save
those who are lost."

PARABLE OF THE TEN SERVANTS

11The crowd was listening to everything Jesus said. And
because he was nearing Jerusalem, he told them a story to
correct the impression that the Kingdom of God would
begin right away. 12He said, "A nobleman was called away
to a distant empire to be crowned king and then return.
13Before he left, he called together ten of his servants and
divided among them ten pounds of silver,* saying, 'Invest
this for me while I am gone.' 14But his people hated him
and sent a delegation after him to say, 'We do not want
him to be our king.'

18:20 Exod 20:12-16; Deut 5:16-20. **18:24** Some manuscripts read *When Jesus saw how sad the man was.* **18:32** Greek *the Gentiles.* **18:37** Or *Jesus of Nazareth.* **19:10** "Son of Man" is a title Jesus used for himself. **19:13** Greek *ten minas;* one mina was worth about three months' wages.

15"After he was crowned king, he returned and called
in the servants to whom he had given the money. He
wanted to find out what their profits were. 16The first
servant reported, 'Master, I invested your money and
made ten times the original amount!'

UNPOPULAR 19:1-10

Tax collectors were among the most unpopular people in Israel. Jews who chose to work for Rome were considered traitors. Besides, it was common knowledge that tax collectors made themselves rich by gouging their fellow Jews. No wonder the crowds were displeased when Jesus went home with the tax collector Zacchaeus. But Jesus' love caused Zacchaeus to change. Who are the "Zacchaeuses" at your school or in your neighborhood? How can you, like Jesus, reach out to the "lost"? ■

17"'Well done!' the king exclaimed. 'You are a good servant. You have been faithful with the little I entrusted to
you, so you will be governor of ten cities as your reward.'
18"The next servant reported, 'Master, I invested your
money and made five times the original amount.'
19"'Well done!' the king said. 'You will be governor over
five cities.'
20"But the third servant brought back only the original
amount of money and said, 'Master, I hid your money and
kept it safe. 21I was afraid because you are a hard man to
deal with, taking what isn't yours and harvesting crops
you didn't plant.'
22"'You wicked servant!' the king roared. 'Your own
words condemn you. If you knew that I'm a hard man
who takes what isn't mine and harvests crops I didn't
plant, 23why didn't you deposit my money in the bank? At
least I could have gotten some interest on it.'
24"Then, turning to the others standing nearby, the
king ordered, 'Take the money from this servant, and give
it to the one who has ten pounds.'
25"'But, master,' they said, 'he already has ten pounds!'
26"'Yes,' the king replied, 'and to those who use well
what they are given, even more will be given. But from
those who do nothing, even what little they have will be
taken away. 27And as for these enemies of mine who
didn't want me to be their king—bring them in and execute them right here in front of me.'"

JESUS' TRIUMPHANT ENTRY

28After telling this story, Jesus went on toward Jerusalem,
walking ahead of his disciples. 29As he came to the towns
of Bethphage and Bethany on the Mount of Olives, he
sent two disciples ahead. 30"Go into that village over
there," he told them. "As you enter it, you will see a young
donkey tied there that no one has ever ridden. Untie it
and bring it here. 31If anyone asks, 'Why are you untying
that colt?' just say, 'The Lord needs it.'"
32So they went and found the colt, just as Jesus had
said. 33And sure enough, as they were untying it, the owners asked them, "Why are you untying that colt?"
34And the disciples simply replied, "The Lord needs it."
35So they brought the colt to Jesus and threw their garments over it for him to ride on.
36As he rode along, the crowds spread out their garments on the road ahead of him. 37When he reached the
place where the road started down the Mount of Olives,
all of his followers began to shout and sing as they walked
along, praising God for all the wonderful miracles they
had seen.

38 "Blessings on the King who comes in the name
of the LORD!
Peace in heaven, and glory in highest heaven!"*

39But some of the Pharisees among the crowd said,
"Teacher, rebuke your followers for saying things like
that!"
40He replied, "If they kept quiet, the stones along the
road would burst into cheers!"

JESUS WEEPS OVER JERUSALEM

41But as he came closer to Jerusalem and saw the city
ahead, he began to weep. 42"How I wish today that you of
all people would understand the way to peace. But now it
is too late, and peace is hidden from your eyes. 43Before
long your enemies will build ramparts against your walls
and encircle you and close in on you from every side.
44They will crush you into the ground, and your children
with you. Your enemies will not leave a single stone in
place, because you did not accept your opportunity for
salvation."

JESUS CLEARS THE TEMPLE

45Then Jesus entered the Temple and began to drive out
the people selling animals for sacrifices. 46He said to
them, "The Scriptures declare, 'My Temple will be a
house of prayer,' but you have turned it into a den of
thieves."*
47After that, he taught daily in the Temple, but the
leading priests, the teachers of religious law, and the
other leaders of the people began planning how to kill
him. 48But they could think of nothing, because all the
people hung on every word he said.

20 THE AUTHORITY OF JESUS CHALLENGED

One day as Jesus was teaching the people and preaching
the Good News in the Temple, the leading priests, the
teachers of religious law, and the elders came up to him.
2They demanded, "By what authority are you doing all
these things? Who gave you the right?"
3"Let me ask you a question first," he replied. 4"Did
John's authority to baptize come from heaven, or was it
merely human?"
5They talked it over among themselves. "If we say it
was from heaven, he will ask why we didn't believe John.

19:38 Pss 118:26; 148:1. **19:46** Isa 56:7; Jer 7:11.

6But if we say it was merely human, the people will stone us because they are convinced John was a prophet." 7So they finally replied that they didn't know.

8And Jesus responded, "Then I won't tell you by what authority I do these things."

PARABLE OF THE EVIL FARMERS

9Now Jesus turned to the people again and told them this story: "A man planted a vineyard, leased it to tenant farmers, and moved to another country to live for several years. 10At the time of the grape harvest, he sent one of his servants to collect his share of the crop. But the farmers attacked the servant, beat him up, and sent him back empty-handed. 11So the owner sent another servant, but they also insulted him, beat him up, and sent him away empty-handed. 12A third man was sent, and they wounded him and chased him away.

13"'What will I do?' the owner asked himself. 'I know! I'll send my cherished son. Surely they will respect him.'

14"But when the tenant farmers saw his son, they said to each other, 'Here comes the heir to this estate. Let's kill him and get the estate for ourselves!' 15So they dragged him out of the vineyard and murdered him.

"What do you suppose the owner of the vineyard will do to them?" Jesus asked. 16"I'll tell you—he will come and kill those farmers and lease the vineyard to others."

"How terrible that such a thing should ever happen," his listeners protested.

17Jesus looked at them and said, "Then what does this Scripture mean?

'The stone that the builders rejected
  has now become the cornerstone.'*

18Everyone who stumbles over that stone will be broken to pieces, and it will crush anyone it falls on."

19The teachers of religious law and the leading priests wanted to arrest Jesus immediately because they realized he was telling the story against them—they were the wicked farmers. But they were afraid of the people's reaction.

TAXES FOR CAESAR

20Watching for their opportunity, the leaders sent spies pretending to be honest men. They tried to get Jesus to say something that could be reported to the Roman governor so he would arrest Jesus. 21"Teacher," they said, "we know that you speak and teach what is right and are not influenced by what others think. You teach the way of God truthfully. 22Now tell us—is it right for us to pay taxes to Caesar or not?"

23He saw through their trickery and said, 24"Show me a Roman coin.* Whose picture and title are stamped on it?"

"Caesar's," they replied.

25"Well then," he said, "give to Caesar what belongs to Caesar, and give to God what belongs to God."

26So they failed to trap him by what he said in front of the people. Instead, they were amazed by his answer, and they became silent.

DISCUSSION ABOUT RESURRECTION

27Then Jesus was approached by some Sadducees—religious leaders who say there is no resurrection from the dead. 28They posed this question: "Teacher, Moses gave us a law that if a man dies, leaving a wife but no children, his brother should marry the widow and have a child who will carry on the brother's name.* 29Well, suppose there were seven brothers. The oldest one married and then died without children. 30So the second brother married the widow, but he also died. 31Then the third brother married her. This continued with all seven of them, who died without children. 32Finally, the woman also died. 33So tell us, whose wife will she be in the resurrection? For all seven were married to her!"

34Jesus replied, "Marriage is for people here on earth. 35But in the age to come, those worthy of being raised from the dead will neither marry nor be given in marriage. 36And they will never die again. In this respect they will be like angels. They are children of God and children of the resurrection.

37"But now, as to whether the dead will be raised—even Moses proved this when he wrote about the burning bush. Long after Abraham, Isaac, and Jacob had died, he referred to the Lord* as 'the God of Abraham, the God of Isaac, and the God of Jacob.'* 38So he is the God of the living, not the dead, for they are all alive to him."

39"Well said, Teacher!" remarked some of the teachers of religious law who were standing there. 40And then no one dared to ask him any more questions.

WHOSE SON IS THE MESSIAH?

41Then Jesus presented them with a question. "Why is it," he asked, "that the Messiah is said to be the son of David? 42For David himself wrote in the book of Psalms:

'The LORD said to my Lord,
  Sit in the place of honor at my right hand
43 until I humble your enemies,
  making them a footstool under your feet.'*

44Since David called the Messiah 'Lord,' how can the Messiah be his son?"

DUTY 20:20-26

Jesus turned his enemies' attempt to trap him into a powerful lesson: God's followers have legitimate obligations to both God and the government. But keeping our priorities straight is important. When the two authorities conflict, our duty to God always comes before our duty to the government. ■

20:17 Ps 118:22. **20:24** Greek *a denarius.* **20:28** See Deut 25:5-6. **20:37a** Greek *when he wrote about the bush. He referred to the Lord.* **20:37b** Exod 3:6. **20:42-43** Ps 110:1.

45Then, with the crowds listening, he turned to his
disciples and said, 46"Beware of these teachers of religious law! For they like to parade around in flowing
robes and love to receive respectful greetings as they
walk in the marketplaces. And how they love the seats of
honor in the synagogues and the head table at banquets.
47Yet they shamelessly cheat widows out of their property and then pretend to be pious by making long
prayers in public. Because of this, they will be severely
punished."

GIVING

The hot topic at Thurgood Marshall High School is what Kyla Whitfield will do with the huge inheritance she's getting as a result of her grandfather's death last week.

"How much do you think she'll end up getting?" Alexis asks.

"Millions, I guess," her friend Harmony replies.

"Kyla gets it all?"

"No, I think she'll have to split it with three other relatives. But everyone will wind up loaded."

"I think I know what I'd do if I had a boatload of money!"

"What would you do?"

"Spend most of it."

"On what?"

Alexis counts the items with her fingers as she speaks. "I would buy clothes; CDs; DVDs; a cool car; a new computer; a trip around the world; a flat-screen, high-definition TV for my room; the latest games software; tuition at the best college in the world—whatever I wanted."

"What about giving?"

"What about it?"

"Would you give any of it away? You know, to other people, to your church, to charity?"

"Are you serious?"

That's a common response to the suggestion of giving. Unfortunately, even many Christians are that way.

What would you do if you were Kyla? What's your view of giving? Need a shot in the arm about giving? See Luke 21:1-4.

21

THE WIDOW'S OFFERING

While Jesus was in the Temple, he watched the rich people dropping their gifts in the collection box. 2Then a
poor widow came by and dropped in two small coins.*
3"I tell you the truth," Jesus said, "this poor widow has
given more than all the rest of them. 4For they have given
a tiny part of their surplus, but she, poor as she is, has
given everything she has."

JESUS FORETELLS THE FUTURE

5Some of his disciples began talking about the majestic
stonework of the Temple and the memorial decorations
on the walls. But Jesus said, 6"The time is coming when all
these things will be completely demolished. Not one
stone will be left on top of another!"
7"Teacher," they asked, "when will all this happen?
What sign will show us that these things are about to take
place?"
8He replied, "Don't let anyone mislead you, for many
will come in my name, claiming, 'I am the Messiah,'* and
saying, 'The time has come!' But don't believe them. 9And
when you hear of wars and insurrections, don't panic.
Yes, these things must take place first, but the end won't
follow immediately." 10Then he added, "Nation will go to
war against nation, and kingdom against kingdom.
11There will be great earthquakes, and there will be famines and plagues in many lands, and there will be terrifying things and great miraculous signs from heaven.
12"But before all this occurs, there will be a time of
great persecution. You will be dragged into synagogues
and prisons, and you will stand trial before kings and governors because you are my followers. 13But this will be
your opportunity to tell them about me.* 14So don't worry
in advance about how to answer the charges against you,
15for I will give you the right words and such wisdom that
none of your opponents will be able to reply or refute
you! 16Even those closest to you—your parents, brothers,
relatives, and friends—will betray you. They will even kill
some of you. 17And everyone will hate you because you
are my followers.* 18But not a hair of your head will perish! 19By standing firm, you will win your souls.

TROUBLE 21:12-19

Jesus warned his followers to expect persecution. Christians of every age have had to face this possibility. Yet even when we feel completely abandoned, the Holy Spirit stays with us. He will comfort us, protect us, and give us the words we need to defend our faith. (See John 14:26; 16:7-15; Heb 13:5-6.) ■

20"And when you see Jerusalem surrounded by armies,
then you will know that the time of its destruction has arrived. 21Then those in Judea must flee to the hills. Those
in Jerusalem must get out, and those out in the country
should not return to the city. 22For those will be days of
God's vengeance, and the prophetic words of the Scriptures will be fulfilled. 23How terrible it will be for pregnant women and for nursing mothers in those days. For
there will be disaster in the land and great anger against
this people. 24They will be killed by the sword or sent
away as captives to all the nations of the world. And Jerusalem will be trampled down by the Gentiles until the
period of the Gentiles comes to an end.
25"And there will be strange signs in the sun, moon,

21:2 Greek *two lepta* [the smallest of Jewish coins]. 21:8 Greek *claiming, 'I am.'* 21:13 Or *This will be your testimony against them.* 21:17 Greek *on account of my name.*

and stars. And here on earth the nations will be in turmoil, perplexed by the roaring seas and strange tides.
26People will be terrified at what they see coming upon
the earth, for the powers in the heavens will be shaken.
27Then everyone will see the Son of Man* coming on a
cloud with power and great glory.* 28So when all these
things begin to happen, stand and look up, for your salvation is near!"

29Then he gave them this illustration: "Notice the fig
tree, or any other tree. 30When the leaves come out, you
know without being told that summer is near. 31In the
same way, when you see all these things taking place, you
can know that the Kingdom of God is near. 32I tell you the
truth, this generation will not pass from the scene until
all these things have taken place. 33Heaven and earth will
disappear, but my words will never disappear.

34"Watch out! Don't let your hearts be dulled by carousing and drunkenness, and by the worries of this life.
Don't let that day catch you unaware, 35like a trap. For
that day will come upon everyone living on the earth.
36Keep alert at all times. And pray that you might be
strong enough to escape these coming horrors and stand
before the Son of Man."

37Every day Jesus went to the Temple to teach, and each
evening he returned to spend the night on the Mount of
Olives. 38The crowds gathered at the Temple early each
morning to hear him.

22

JUDAS AGREES TO BETRAY JESUS

The Festival of Unleavened Bread, which is also called
Passover, was approaching. 2The leading priests and
teachers of religious law were plotting how to kill Jesus,
but they were afraid of the people's reaction.

3Then Satan entered into Judas Iscariot, who was one
of the twelve disciples, 4and he went to the leading priests
and captains of the Temple guard to discuss the best way
to betray Jesus to them. 5They were delighted, and they
promised to give him money. 6So he agreed and began
looking for an opportunity to betray Jesus so they could
arrest him when the crowds weren't around.

THE LAST SUPPER

7Now the Festival of Unleavened Bread arrived, when the
Passover lamb is sacrificed. 8Jesus sent Peter and John
ahead and said, "Go and prepare the Passover meal, so we
can eat it together."

9"Where do you want us to prepare it?" they asked him.

10He replied, "As soon as you enter Jerusalem, a man
carrying a pitcher of water will meet you. Follow him. At
the house he enters, 11say to the owner, 'The Teacher
asks: Where is the guest room where I can eat the Passover meal with my disciples?' 12He will take you upstairs
to a large room that is already set up. That is where you
should prepare our meal." 13They went off to the city and
found everything just as Jesus had said, and they prepared the Passover meal there.

14When the time came, Jesus and the apostles sat
down together at the table.* 15Jesus said, "I have been
very eager to eat this Passover meal with you before my
suffering begins. 16For I tell you now that I won't eat this
meal again until its meaning is fulfilled in the Kingdom
of God."

17Then he took a cup of wine and gave thanks to God
for it. Then he said, "Take this and share it among yourselves. 18For I will not drink wine again until the Kingdom
of God has come."

19He took some bread and gave thanks to God for it. Then
he broke it in pieces and gave it to the disciples, saying, "This
is my body, which is given for you. Do this to remember me."
20After supper he took another cup of wine and said,
"This cup is the new covenant between God and his people—an agreement confirmed with my blood, which is
poured out as a sacrifice for you.*

21"But here at this table, sitting among us as a friend, is
the man who will betray me. 22For it has been determined
that the Son of Man* must die. But what sorrow awaits
the one who betrays him." 23The disciples began to ask
each other which of them would ever do such a thing.

24Then they began to argue among themselves about
who would be the greatest among them. 25Jesus told
them, "In this world the kings and great men lord it over
their people, yet they are called 'friends of the people.'
26But among you it will be different. Those who are the
greatest among you should take the lowest rank, and the
leader should be like a servant. 27Who is more important,
the one who sits at the table or the one who serves? The
one who sits at the table, of course. But not here! For I am
among you as one who serves.

ALL WRAPPED UP 22:24

Although the most important events in human history (Jesus' death and resurrection) were about to take place, the disciples were too focused on arguing about their prestige in the Kingdom! Looking back, we say, "This was no time to worry about status." But the disciples, wrapped up in their own concerns, didn't perceive what Jesus had been trying to tell them about his approaching death and resurrection. What are your major concerns today? Five years from now will these worries look petty and inappropriate? What can you choose to focus on instead? ■

28"You have stayed with me in my time of trial. 29And
just as my Father has granted me a Kingdom, I now grant
you the right 30to eat and drink at my table in my Kingdom. And you will sit on thrones, judging the twelve
tribes of Israel.

JESUS PREDICTS PETER'S DENIAL

31"Simon, Simon, Satan has asked to sift each of you like
wheat. 32But I have pleaded in prayer for you, Simon, that

21:27a "Son of Man" is a title Jesus used for himself. **21:27b** See Dan 7:13. **22:14** Or *reclined together*. **22:19-20** Some manuscripts omit 22:19b-20, *which is given for you . . . which is poured out as a sacrifice for you.* **22:22** "Son of Man" is a title Jesus used for himself.

your faith should not fail. So when you have repented and turned to me again, strengthen your brothers."

33Peter said, "Lord, I am ready to go to prison with you, and even to die with you."

34But Jesus said, "Peter, let me tell you something. Before the rooster crows tomorrow morning, you will deny three times that you even know me."

35Then Jesus asked them, "When I sent you out to preach the Good News and you did not have money, a traveler's bag, or extra clothing, did you need anything?"

"No," they replied.

36"But now," he said, "take your money and a traveler's bag. And if you don't have a sword, sell your cloak and buy one! 37For the time has come for this prophecy about me to be fulfilled: 'He was counted among the rebels.'* Yes, everything written about me by the prophets will come true."

38"Look, Lord," they replied, "we have two swords among us."

"That's enough," he said.

JESUS PRAYS ON THE MOUNT OF OLIVES

39Then, accompanied by the disciples, Jesus left the upstairs room and went as usual to the Mount of Olives. 40There he told them, "Pray that you will not give in to temptation."

41He walked away, about a stone's throw, and knelt down and prayed, 42"Father, if you are willing, please take this cup of suffering away from me. Yet I want your will to be done, not mine." 43Then an angel from heaven appeared and strengthened him. 44He prayed more fervently, and he was in such agony of spirit that his sweat fell to the ground like great drops of blood.*

45At last he stood up again and returned to the disciples, only to find them asleep, exhausted from grief. 46"Why are you sleeping?" he asked them. "Get up and pray, so that you will not give in to temptation."

JESUS IS BETRAYED AND ARRESTED

47But even as Jesus said this, a crowd approached, led by Judas, one of the twelve disciples. Judas walked over to Jesus to greet him with a kiss. 48But Jesus said, "Judas, would you betray the Son of Man with a kiss?"

49When the other disciples saw what was about to happen, they exclaimed, "Lord, should we fight? We brought the swords!" 50And one of them struck at the high priest's slave, slashing off his right ear.

51But Jesus said, "No more of this." And he touched the man's ear and healed him.

52Then Jesus spoke to the leading priests, the captains of the Temple guard, and the elders who had come for him. "Am I some dangerous revolutionary," he asked, "that you come with swords and clubs to arrest me? 53Why didn't you arrest me in the Temple? I was there every day. But this is your moment, the time when the power of darkness reigns."

PETER DENIES JESUS

54So they arrested him and led him to the high priest's home. And Peter followed at a distance. 55The guards lit a fire in the middle of the courtyard and sat around it, and Peter joined them there. 56A servant girl noticed him in the firelight and began staring at him. Finally she said, "This man was one of Jesus' followers!"

57But Peter denied it. "Woman," he said, "I don't even know him!"

58After a while someone else looked at him and said, "You must be one of them!"

"No, man, I'm not!" Peter retorted.

59About an hour later someone else insisted, "This must be one of them, because he is a Galilean, too."

60But Peter said, "Man, I don't know what you are talking about." And immediately, while he was still speaking, the rooster crowed.

61At that moment the Lord turned and looked at Peter. Suddenly, the Lord's words flashed through Peter's mind: "Before the rooster crows tomorrow morning, you will deny three times that you even know me." 62And Peter left the courtyard, weeping bitterly.

A BITTER FAILURE 22:62

Peter wept bitterly after realizing that he had denied his Lord. Although Peter had said he would *never* deny Christ (Matt 26:35), he went against all he had boldly promised.

Like Peter, have you ever been afraid that God will never use you again because you've blown it somehow? After his failure Peter learned much that would help him in the leadership responsibilities he soon would assume. So can you. ■

63The guards in charge of Jesus began mocking and beating him. 64They blindfolded him and said, "Prophesy to us! Who hit you that time?" 65And they hurled all sorts of terrible insults at him.

JESUS BEFORE THE COUNCIL

66At daybreak all the elders of the people assembled, including the leading priests and the teachers of religious law. Jesus was led before this high council,* 67and they said, "Tell us, are you the Messiah?"

But he replied, "If I tell you, you won't believe me. 68And if I ask you a question, you won't answer. 69But from now on the Son of Man will be seated in the place of power at God's right hand.*"

70They all shouted, "So, are you claiming to be the Son of God?"

And he replied, "You say that I am."

71"Why do we need other witnesses?" they said. "We ourselves heard him say it."

23 JESUS' TRIAL BEFORE PILATE

Then the entire council took Jesus to Pilate, the Roman governor. 2They began to state their case: "This man has been leading our people astray by telling them not to pay

22:37 Isa 53:12. **22:43-44** Verses 43 and 44 are not included in many ancient manuscripts. **22:66** Greek *before their Sanhedrin.* **22:69** See Ps 110:1.

WHY THE CROSS?

ULTIMATE ISSUES

A youth pastor explained to a group of junior highers how Jesus' death enabled God to forgive each of them.

"It's personal," he said. "Jesus didn't just die for people in general. He died for you."

When he paused to let the impact of the statement sink in, one seventh-grade girl suddenly blurted out, "So?"

"So?" That seventh grader's response is sadly representative of how many people think today. We know Jesus died on a cross for us; we just don't see the connection between that event 2,000 years ago and our lives today.

What is the cross about? Why did Jesus have to die such a horrible death?

First, he died to solve a big problem. All humans have broken God's laws (Rom 3:23) and have earned the punishment for that—death (Rom 6:23). But Jesus stepped into the picture 2,000 years ago to take that punishment himself.

God took the wrath we deserve and poured it out on Jesus on the cross. In some ways, it is beyond human understanding. Jesus took upon himself all of our wrong actions—every mean, dishonest, disgusting thought or action. Second Corinthians 5:21 tells us, "For God made Christ, who never sinned, to be the offering for our sin, so that we could be made right with God through Christ."

That's the second fact you need to know. Jesus took your place on the cross. Take it personally.

How the death of one perfect man pays for the wrong actions of everyone who ever lived is still a mystery. Still, though we may not understand it, it is the only way to peace with God and eternal life. It's fitting that God took the cross of Christ—the single darkest hour in the history of humanity—and turned it into the way to save all people. That's the kind of God the Bible talks about—a God who loves you so much he would even die on a cross for you.

their taxes to the Roman government and by claiming he
is the Messiah, a king."
3So Pilate asked him, "Are you the king of the Jews?"
Jesus replied, "You have said it."
4Pilate turned to the leading priests and to the crowd
and said, "I find nothing wrong with this man!"
5Then they became insistent. "But he is causing riots
by his teaching wherever he goes—all over Judea, from
Galilee to Jerusalem!"
6"Oh, is he a Galilean?" Pilate asked. 7When they said
that he was, Pilate sent him to Herod Antipas, because
Galilee was under Herod's jurisdiction, and Herod happened to be in Jerusalem at the time.
8Herod was delighted at the opportunity to see Jesus,
because he had heard about him and had been hoping
for a long time to see him perform a miracle. 9He asked
Jesus question after question, but Jesus refused to answer. 10Meanwhile, the leading priests and the teachers
of religious law stood there shouting their accusations.
11Then Herod and his soldiers began mocking and ridiculing Jesus. Finally, they put a royal robe on him and sent
him back to Pilate. 12(Herod and Pilate, who had been enemies before, became friends that day.)
13Then Pilate called together the leading priests and
other religious leaders, along with the people, 14and he
announced his verdict. "You brought this man to me, accusing him of leading a revolt. I have examined him thoroughly on this point in your presence and find him
innocent. 15Herod came to the same conclusion and sent
him back to us. Nothing this man has done calls for the
death penalty. 16So I will have him flogged, and then I will
release him."*
18Then a mighty roar rose from the crowd, and with
one voice they shouted, "Kill him, and release Barabbas to
us!" 19(Barabbas was in prison for taking part in an insurrection in Jerusalem against the government, and for
murder.) 20Pilate argued with them, because he wanted to
release Jesus. 21But they kept shouting, "Crucify him! Crucify him!"
22For the third time he demanded, "Why? What crime
has he committed? I have found no reason to sentence
him to death. So I will have him flogged, and then I will
release him."
23But the mob shouted louder and louder, demanding
that Jesus be crucified, and their voices prevailed. 24So Pilate sentenced Jesus to die as they demanded. 25As they

23:16 Some manuscripts add verse 17, *Now it was necessary for him to release one prisoner to them during the Passover celebration.* Compare Matt 27:15; Mark 15:6; John 18:39.

had requested, he released Barabbas, the man in prison for insurrection and murder. But he turned Jesus over to them to do as they wished.

THE CRUCIFIXION

26 As they led Jesus away, a man named Simon, who was from Cyrene,* happened to be coming in from the countryside. The soldiers seized him and put the cross on him and made him carry it behind Jesus. 27 A large crowd trailed behind, including many grief-stricken women. 28 But Jesus turned and said to them, "Daughters of Jerusalem, don't weep for me, but weep for yourselves and for your children. 29 For the days are coming when they will say, 'Fortunate indeed are the women who are childless, the wombs that have not borne a child and the breasts that have never nursed.' 30 People will beg the mountains, 'Fall on us,' and plead with the hills, 'Bury us.'* 31 For if these things are done when the tree is green, what will happen when it is dry?*"

32 Two others, both criminals, were led out to be executed with him. 33 When they came to a place called The Skull,* they nailed him to the cross. And the criminals were also crucified—one on his right and one on his left.

34 Jesus said, "Father, forgive them, for they don't know what they are doing."* And the soldiers gambled for his clothes by throwing dice.*

AN OFFER OF FORGIVENESS 23:34

Jesus asked God to forgive the people who were putting him to death—Jewish leaders, Roman politicians and soldiers, bystanders. God answered that prayer by opening up the way of salvation even to the people who put him to death. That includes us. Because of the wrong things we've done, we've all played a part in putting Jesus to death. The Good News is that God is gracious. He still offers forgiveness through his Son. Have you taken him up on his offer? ■

35 The crowd watched and the leaders scoffed. "He saved others," they said, "let him save himself if he is really God's Messiah, the Chosen One." 36 The soldiers mocked him, too, by offering him a drink of sour wine. 37 They called out to him, "If you are the King of the Jews, save yourself!" 38 A sign was fastened to the cross above him with these words: "This is the King of the Jews."

39 One of the criminals hanging beside him scoffed, "So you're the Messiah, are you? Prove it by saving yourself—and us, too, while you're at it!"

40 But the other criminal protested, "Don't you fear God even when you have been sentenced to die? 41 We deserve to die for our crimes, but this man hasn't done anything wrong." 42 Then he said, "Jesus, remember me when you come into your Kingdom."

43 And Jesus replied, "I assure you, today you will be with me in paradise."

NOT TOO LATE 23:39-43

As one of the criminals next to Jesus was about to die, he turned to Jesus for forgiveness. This shows that it's never too late to turn to God. Even in his misery, Jesus had mercy on the man who decided to believe in him. Our life is much more useful and fulfilling if we turn to God early, but even those who turn to him at the very last moment will be with God in his Kingdom. (But don't use this as an excuse to wait until the last moment to turn to him! If you know the truth, why wait?) ■

THE DEATH OF JESUS

44 By this time it was noon, and darkness fell across the whole land until three o'clock. 45 The light from the sun was gone. And suddenly, the curtain in the sanctuary of the Temple was torn down the middle. 46 Then Jesus shouted, "Father, I entrust my spirit into your hands!"* And with those words he breathed his last.

47 When the Roman officer* overseeing the execution saw what had happened, he worshiped God and said, "Surely this man was innocent.*" 48 And when all the crowd that came to see the crucifixion saw what had happened, they went home in deep sorrow.* 49 But Jesus' friends, including the women who had followed him from Galilee, stood at a distance watching.

THE BURIAL OF JESUS

50 Now there was a good and righteous man named Joseph. He was a member of the Jewish high council, 51 but he had not agreed with the decision and actions of the other religious leaders. He was from the town of Arimathea in Judea, and he was waiting for the Kingdom of God to come. 52 He went to Pilate and asked for Jesus' body. 53 Then he took the body down from the cross and wrapped it in a long sheet of linen cloth and laid it in a new tomb that had been carved out of rock. 54 This was done late on Friday afternoon, the day of preparation,* as the Sabbath was about to begin.

55 As his body was taken away, the women from Galilee followed and saw the tomb where his body was placed. 56 Then they went home and prepared spices and ointments to anoint his body. But by the time they were finished the Sabbath had begun, so they rested as required by the law.

24 THE RESURRECTION

But very early on Sunday morning* the women went to the tomb, taking the spices they had prepared. 2 They found that the stone had been rolled away from the en-

23:26 *Cyrene* was a city in northern Africa. 23:30 Hos 10:8. 23:31 Or *If these things are done to me, the living tree, what will happen to you, the dry tree?* 23:33 Sometimes rendered *Calvary,* which comes from the Latin word for "skull." 23:34a This sentence is not included in many ancient manuscripts. 23:34b Greek *by casting lots.* See Ps 22:18. 23:46 Ps 31:5. 23:47a Greek *the centurion.* 23:47b Or *righteous.* 23:48 Greek *went home beating their breasts.* 23:54 Greek *It was the day of preparation.* 24:1 Greek *But on the first day of the week, very early in the morning.*

Jesus and the Ten Commandments

THE TEN COMMANDMENTS SAID . . .	JESUS SAID . . .
You must not have any other god but me. *Exodus 20:3*	You must worship the LORD your God and serve only him. *Matthew 4:10*
You must not make for yourself an idol of any kind or an image of anything in the heavens or on the earth or in the sea. *Exodus 20:4*	No one can serve two masters. *Luke 16:13*
You must not misuse the name of the LORD your God. The LORD will not let you go unpunished if you misuse his name. *Exodus 20:7*	Do not make any vows! Do not say, "By heaven!" because heaven is God's throne. *Matthew 5:34*
Remember to observe the Sabbath day by keeping it holy. *Exodus 20:8*	The Sabbath was made to meet the needs of people, and not people to meet the requirements of the Sabbath. So the Son of Man is Lord, even over the Sabbath! *Mark 2:27-28*
Honor your father and mother. Then you will live a long, full life in the land the LORD your God is giving you. *Exodus 20:12*	If you love your father or mother more than you love me, you are not worthy of being mine; or if you love your son or daughter more than me, you are not worthy of being mine. *Matthew 10:37*
You must not murder. *Exodus 20:13*	If you are even angry with someone, you are subject to judgment! If you call someone an idiot, you are in danger of being brought before the court. And if you curse someone, you are in danger of the fires of hell. *Matthew 5:22*
You must not commit adultery. *Exodus 20:14*	Anyone who even looks at a woman with lust has already committed adultery with her in his heart. *Matthew 5:28*
You must not steal. *Exodus 20:15*	If you are sued in court and your shirt is taken from you, give your coat, too. *Matthew 5:40*
You must not testify falsely against your neighbor. *Exodus 20:16*	You must give an account on judgment day for every idle word you speak. The words you say will either acquit you or condemn you. *Matthew 12:36-37*
You must not covet your neighbor's house. You must not covet your neighbor's wife, male or female servant, ox or donkey, or anything else that belongs to your neighbor. *Exodus 20:17*	Guard against every kind of greed. Life is not measured by how much you own. *Luke 12:15*

trance. 3So they went in, but they didn't find the body of
the Lord Jesus. 4As they stood there puzzled, two men
suddenly appeared to them, clothed in dazzling robes.
5The women were terrified and bowed with their faces
to the ground. Then the men asked, "Why are you looking
among the dead for someone who is alive? 6He isn't here!
He is risen from the dead! Remember what he told you
back in Galilee, 7that the Son of Man* must be betrayed
into the hands of sinful men and be crucified, and that he
would rise again on the third day."
8Then they remembered that he had said this. 9So
they rushed back from the tomb to tell his eleven
disciples—and everyone else—what had happened. 10It
was Mary Magdalene, Joanna, Mary the mother of
James, and several other women who told the apostles
what had happened. 11But the story sounded like nonsense to the men, so they didn't believe it. 12However,
Peter jumped up and ran to the tomb to look. Stooping,
he peered in and saw the empty linen wrappings; then
he went home again, wondering what had happened.

THE WALK TO EMMAUS

13That same day two of Jesus' followers were walking to
the village of Emmaus, seven miles* from Jerusalem.

24:7 "Son of Man" is a title Jesus used for himself. **24:13** Greek *60 stadia* [11.1 kilometers].

14As they walked along they were talking about everything that had happened. 15As they talked and discussed
these things, Jesus himself suddenly came and began
walking with them. 16But God kept them from recognizing him.
17He asked them, "What are you discussing so intently
as you walk along?"
They stopped short, sadness written across their faces.
18Then one of them, Cleopas, replied, "You must be the
only person in Jerusalem who hasn't heard about all the
things that have happened there the last few days."
19"What things?" Jesus asked.
"The things that happened to Jesus, the man from Nazareth," they said. "He was a prophet who did powerful
miracles, and he was a mighty teacher in the eyes of God
and all the people. 20But our leading priests and other religious leaders handed him over to be condemned to
death, and they crucified him. 21We had hoped he was
the Messiah who had come to rescue Israel. This all happened three days ago.
22"Then some women from our group of his followers
were at his tomb early this morning, and they came back
with an amazing report. 23They said his body was missing, and they had seen angels who told them Jesus is alive!
24Some of our men ran out to see, and sure enough, his
body was gone, just as the women had said."
25Then Jesus said to them, "You foolish people! You
find it so hard to believe all that the prophets wrote in the
Scriptures. 26Wasn't it clearly predicted that the Messiah
would have to suffer all these things before entering his
glory?" 27Then Jesus took them through the writings of
Moses and all the prophets, explaining from all the Scriptures the things concerning himself.
28By this time they were nearing Emmaus and the end
of their journey. Jesus acted as if he were going on, 29but
they begged him, "Stay the night with us, since it is getting late." So he went home with them. 30As they sat down
to eat,* he took the bread and blessed it. Then he broke it
and gave it to them. 31Suddenly, their eyes were opened,
and they recognized him. And at that moment he
disappeared!
32They said to each other, "Didn't our hearts burn
within us as he talked with us on the road and explained
the Scriptures to us?" 33And within the hour they were on
their way back to Jerusalem. There they found the eleven
disciples and the others who had gathered with them,
34who said, "The Lord has really risen! He appeared to
Peter.*"

JESUS APPEARS TO THE DISCIPLES

35Then the two from Emmaus told their story of how
Jesus had appeared to them as they were walking along
the road, and how they had recognized him as he was
breaking the bread. 36And just as they were telling about
it, Jesus himself was suddenly standing there among
them. "Peace be with you," he said. 37But the whole group
was startled and frightened, thinking they were seeing a
ghost!
38"Why are you frightened?" he asked. "Why are your
hearts filled with doubt? 39Look at my hands. Look at my
feet. You can see that it's really me. Touch me and make
sure that I am not a ghost, because ghosts don't have bodies, as you see that I do." 40As he spoke, he showed them
his hands and his feet.
41Still they stood there in disbelief, filled with joy and
wonder. Then he asked them, "Do you have anything here
to eat?" 42They gave him a piece of broiled fish, 43and he
ate it as they watched.

INSIGHT 24:45

There were two instances where Jesus helped his disciples understand Scriptures: while on the road to Emmaus (24:13-33) and in this instance. The Holy Spirit provides this kind of help when we study the Bible. Have you ever wondered how to understand a difficult Bible passage? Besides reading surrounding passages, asking other people, and consulting reference works, you can pray that the Holy Spirit will open your mind to understand, giving you the needed insight to put God's Word into action in your life. ■

44Then he said, "When I was with you before, I told you
that everything written about me in the law of Moses and
the prophets and in the Psalms must be fulfilled." 45Then
he opened their minds to understand the Scriptures.
46And he said, "Yes, it was written long ago that the Messiah would suffer and die and rise from the dead on the
third day. 47It was also written that this message would be
proclaimed in the authority of his name to all the nations,* beginning in Jerusalem: 'There is forgiveness of sins
for all who repent.' 48You are witnesses of all these things.
49"And now I will send the Holy Spirit, just as my Father
promised. But stay here in the city until the Holy Spirit
comes and fills you with power from heaven."

THE ASCENSION

50Then Jesus led them to Bethany, and lifting his hands to
heaven, he blessed them. 51While he was blessing them, he
left them and was taken up to heaven.* 52So they worshiped
him and then returned to Jerusalem filled with great joy.
53And they spent all of their time in the Temple, praising God.

24:30 Or *As they reclined.* 24:34 Greek *Simon.* 24:47 Or *all peoples.* 24:51 Some manuscripts do not include *and was taken up to heaven.*

QUESTIONS. Life is full of 'em. There are . . .

Dumb questions: "If the plural of goose is geese, shouldn't the plural of moose be meese?"

Mysterious questions: "Um, if God can do anything, can he make a rock so big that even *he* couldn't lift it?"

Serious questions: "If God really cares about us, why does he allow evil in the world?"

"What gives my life meaning?"

Even people who don't (or won't) openly discuss serious issues have ideas about where to find happiness or fulfillment. For example, Cameron's formula for fulfillment includes partying and an active sex life. Ilsa thinks she'll find it in a 4.0 GPA. Sebastian is banking on athletic ability. Nana's relying on beauty and bucks.

Nagging questions: "If the pursuit of sex, academic or athletic achievement, or money really makes people happy, why are so many people who pursue these things so unhappy?"

"Why don't more people consider what Jesus had to say about the ingredients of a purpose-filled life?"

Personal questions: "Have *you* ever really thought about Jesus' teachings in the Gospel of John?"

"What are you waiting for?"

timeline

37 B.C.
Herod the Great begins to rule

6/5 B.C.
Jesus is born

5/4 B.C.
Escape to Egypt

4 B.C.
Herod the Great dies

4/3 B.C.
Return to Nazareth

A.D. 6
Judea becomes a Roman province

14
Tiberius Caesar becomes emperor

26
Pontius Pilate appointed governor

26/27
Jesus begins his ministry

27
Jesus and Nicodemus

28
Jesus chooses 12 disciples

29
Jesus feeds 5,000

30
Jesus is crucified, rises again, and ascends

stats

PURPOSE: To prove conclusively that Jesus is the Son of God and that all who believe in him will have eternal life

AUTHOR: The apostle John (the son of Zebedee) who also was known as a "Son of Thunder" along with his brother James

TO WHOM WRITTEN: New Christians and seeking non-Christians

DATE WRITTEN: Probably between A.D. 85 and 90

SETTING: Written after the destruction of Jerusalem in A.D. 70 and before John's exile to the island of Patmos

KEY PEOPLE: Jesus, John the Baptist, the disciples, Mary, Martha, Lazarus, Jesus' mother (Mary), Pilate, Mary Magdalene

KEY PLACES: Judean countryside, Samaria, Galilee, Bethany, Jerusalem

KEY points

ETERNAL LIFE

Because Jesus is God, he can offer eternal life—unending life—to us. This personal, eternal relationship with him begins now and will continue after our lives end here on Earth.

SIGNS OF LIFE

John records specific signs or miracles that prove Jesus' identity as the promised Savior. These signs encourage us to believe in him. When we believe in Jesus and commit our lives to him, he empowers us to build his Kingdom.

HOLY SPIRIT

Jesus told his disciples that after he went back to heaven, the Holy Spirit would come. The Holy Spirit would guide and comfort all believers. The Holy Spirit draws us to Jesus in faith.

RESURRECTION

On the third day after Jesus died, he rose from the dead. This reality changed the disciples from frightened deserters to dynamic leaders in the new church. We can experience the same change (from fear to freedom) and look forward to living with Christ forever.

KEY PLACES IN JOHN

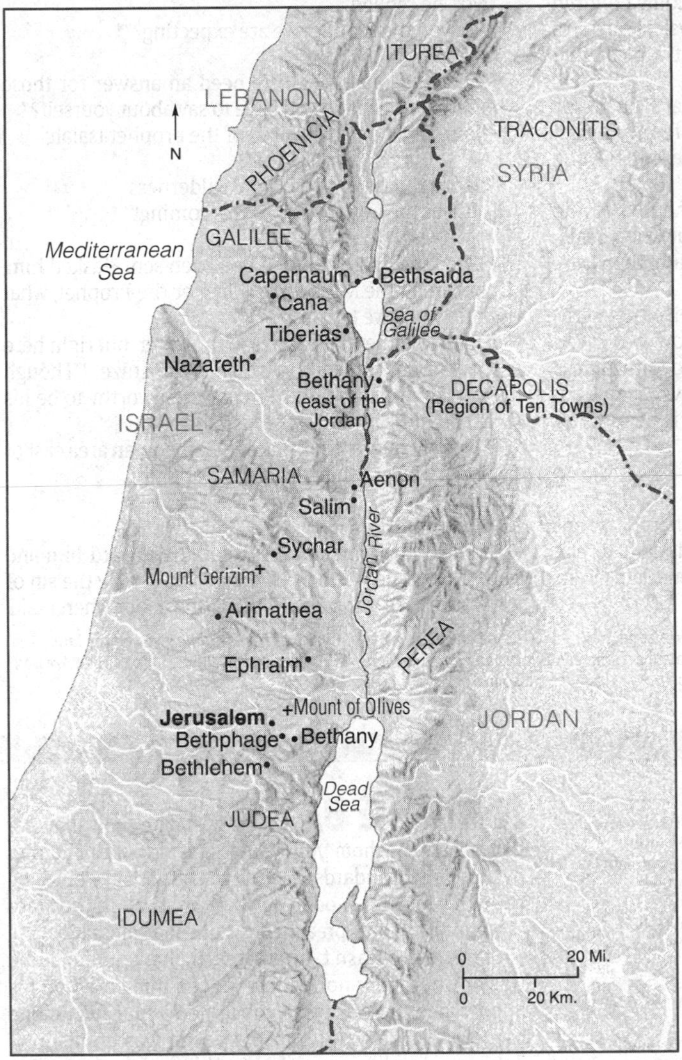

The broken lines (—·—) indicate modern boundaries.

John's story begins as John the Baptist ministers near Bethany beyond the Jordan (1:28). Jesus also begins his ministry, talking to some of the men who would later become his 12 disciples. Jesus' ministry in Galilee began with a visit to a wedding in Cana (2:1-11). Then he went to Capernaum, which became his new home (2:12). He journeyed to Jerusalem for the special feasts (2:13) and there met with Nicodemus, a religious leader (3:1-21). When he left Judea, he traveled through Samaria and ministered to the Samaritans (4:1-42). Jesus did miracles in Galilee (4:46-54), Judea, and Jerusalem (5:1-15). We follow him as he fed 5,000 near Bethsaida beside the Sea of Galilee (Sea of Tiberias) (6:1-15), walked on the water to his frightened disciples (6:16-21), preached throughout Galilee (7:1), returned to Jerusalem (7:10), preached beyond the Jordan in Perea (10:40), raised Lazarus from the dead in Bethany (11:1-44), and finally entered Jerusalem for the last time to celebrate the Passover with his disciples and give them key teachings about what was to come and how they should act. His last hours before his crucifixion were spent in the city (13–17), in the Garden of Gethsemane (18:1-11), and finally in various buildings in Jerusalem during his trial (18:12-16). He would be crucified, but he would rise again as he had promised.

1

PROLOGUE: CHRIST, THE ETERNAL WORD

1 In the beginning the Word already existed.
The Word was with God,
and the Word was God.
2 He existed in the beginning with God.
3 God created everything through him,
and nothing was created except through him.
4 The Word gave life to everything that was created,*
and his life brought light to everyone.
5 The light shines in the darkness,
and the darkness can never extinguish it.*

6God sent a man, John the Baptist,* 7to tell about the
light so that everyone might believe because of his testimony. 8John himself was not the light; he was simply a witness to tell about the light. 9The one who is the true light,
who gives light to everyone, was coming into the world.
10He came into the very world he created, but the
world didn't recognize him. 11He came to his own people,

1:3-4 Or *and nothing that was created was created except through him. The Word gave life to everything.* 1:5 Or *and the darkness has not understood it.* 1:6 Greek *a man named John.*

and even they rejected him. 12But to all who believed him
and accepted him, he gave the right to become children
of God. 13They are reborn—not with a physical birth resulting from human passion or plan, but a birth that
comes from God.

14So the Word became human* and made his home
among us. He was full of unfailing love and faithfulness.*
And we have seen his glory, the glory of the Father's one
and only Son.

15John testified about him when he shouted to the
crowds, "This is the one I was talking about when I said,
'Someone is coming after me who is far greater than I am,
for he existed long before me.'"

16From his abundance we have all received one gracious blessing after another.* 17For the law was given
through Moses, but God's unfailing love and faithfulness
came through Jesus Christ. 18No one has ever seen God.
But the unique One, who is himself God,* is near to the
Father's heart. He has revealed God to us.

THE TESTIMONY OF JOHN THE BAPTIST

19This was John's testimony when the Jewish leaders sent
priests and Temple assistants* from Jerusalem to ask
John, "Who are you?" 20He came right out and said, "I am
not the Messiah."

21"Well then, who are you?" they asked. "Are you Elijah?"
"No," he replied.
"Are you the Prophet we are expecting?"*
"No."

22"Then who are you? We need an answer for those
who sent us. What do you have to say about yourself?"
23John replied in the words of the prophet Isaiah:

"I am a voice shouting in the wilderness,
'Clear the way for the LORD's coming!'"*

24Then the Pharisees who had been sent 25asked him,
"If you aren't the Messiah or Elijah or the Prophet, what
right do you have to baptize?"

26John told them, "I baptize with* water, but right here
in the crowd is someone you do not recognize. 27Though
his ministry follows mine, I'm not even worthy to be his
slave and untie the straps of his sandal."

28This encounter took place in Bethany, an area east of
the Jordan River, where John was baptizing.

JESUS, THE LAMB OF GOD

29The next day John saw Jesus coming toward him and
said, "Look! The Lamb of God who takes away the sin of
the world! 30He is the one I was talking about when I said,

1:14a Greek *became flesh.* **1:14b** Or *grace and truth;* also in 1:17. **1:16** Or *received the grace of Christ rather than the grace of the law;* Greek reads *received grace upon grace.* **1:18** Some manuscripts read *But the one and only Son.* **1:19** Greek *and Levites.* **1:21** Greek *Are you the Prophet?* See Deut 18:15, 18; Mal 4:5-6. **1:23** Isa 40:3. **1:26** Or *in;* also in 1:31, 33.

JOHN THE BAPTIST

UPS:
- The God-appointed messenger who announced the arrival of Jesus
- A preacher who encouraged people to make things right with God
- A fearless confronter
- Was known for his remarkable and uncompromising lifestyle

STATS:
- Where: Judea
- Occupation: Prophet
- Relatives: Zechariah (father); Elizabeth (mother); Jesus (distant cousin perhaps—see Luke 1:36)
- Contemporaries: Herod, Herodias

BOTTOM LINE:

God doesn't guarantee an easy or safe life to those who serve him.

Doing what God desires is the greatest possible life investment.

Standing for the truth might make you feel alone. But you aren't really alone—God is with you.

John's story is told in all four Gospels. His message and arrival are predicted in Isa 40:3 and Mal 4:5-6. He also is mentioned in Acts 1:5, 22; 10:37; 11:16; 13:24-25; 18:25; 19:3-4.

JOHN THE BAPTIST Maybe you have a list of people whom you would consider odd. Judging by today's standards, John the Baptist would be called . . . well . . . odd. He wore unusual clothes, ate strange food, and preached an unusual message.

John really wasn't interested in how "unique" he was or whether or not people judged him based on his appearance. He was more concerned about his unique role: to tell the world that the Savior was on his way. John was totally committed to this purpose.

This wild-looking man stood face to face with people and told them to change their ways. He knew that the best way to get ready for the Savior was to be deeply sorry for the wrong choices they had made.

Not only that, John didn't try to hog the spotlight once Jesus arrived. When some of his disciples complained that Jesus seemed more popular than John, John replied, "He must become greater and greater, and I must become less and less" (John 3:30).

John's message still applies today. We also need to prepare for the Savior's arrival in our lives (through the Holy Spirit) by first admitting that we need a Savior. Once we admit that need, we can choose to allow Jesus to become "greater and greater" in our lives—to be the one who calls the shots. Like John, is that your choice?

keeping it real

It was an incredible weekend. A twister hit my town, and suddenly our house was ruined, my wrist was broken, and I lost my best friend.

I didn't know what to do. I felt depressed, then angry, then cheated. In all the confusion of adjusting to these disasters, I finally decided to open the Bible.

I started reading the Gospel of John. And as I thought about Jesus and all he gave up in heaven to live among us on earth, my attitude started to change. I thought about verses 10-12 in the first chapter—how Jesus wasn't respected by the very people he came to help. If anybody had the right to feel self-pity, he did! But Jesus did everything for love.

The first 27 verses of chapter 1 opened my eyes to God's faithfulness and love. They made me realize that God would stand by me even through this terrible time. I turned everything over to God and discovered a joy that was as incredible as everything that had happened to me in that one terrible weekend.

The following weeks were the happiest I'd ever felt, even though I still had to deal with the sorrow over losing my friend and our home. I found that the love of God was so much more real. It gave me strength. **—Hailey**

'A man is coming after me who is far greater than I am,
for he existed long before me.' 31I did not recognize him
as the Messiah, but I have been baptizing with water so
that he might be revealed to Israel."

HUMILITY 1:30

Although John the Baptist was a well-known preacher and attracted large crowds, he was content for Jesus to take the higher place. (See also John 3:27-36.) This is true humility, the basis for greatness in anything we do for God. When you are content to do what God wants you to do and let Jesus be honored for it, God will do great things through you. ■

32Then John testified, "I saw the Holy Spirit descending like a dove from heaven and resting upon him. 33I
didn't know he was the one, but when God sent me to
baptize with water, he told me, 'The one on whom you see
the Spirit descend and rest is the one who will baptize
with the Holy Spirit.' 34I saw this happen to Jesus, so I testify that he is the Chosen One of God.*"

THE FIRST DISCIPLES

35The following day John was again standing with two of
his disciples. 36As Jesus walked by, John looked at him
and declared, "Look! There is the Lamb of God!" 37When
John's two disciples heard this, they followed Jesus.
38Jesus looked around and saw them following. "What
do you want?" he asked them.

They replied, "Rabbi" (which means "Teacher"),
"where are you staying?"
39"Come and see," he said. It was about four o'clock in
the afternoon when they went with him to the place
where he was staying, and they remained with him the
rest of the day.
40Andrew, Simon Peter's brother, was one of these
men who heard what John said and then followed Jesus.
41Andrew went to find his brother, Simon, and told him,
"We have found the Messiah" (which means "Christ"*).
42Then Andrew brought Simon to meet Jesus. Looking
intently at Simon, Jesus said, "Your name is Simon, son of
John—but you will be called Cephas" (which means
"Peter"*).
43The next day Jesus decided to go to Galilee. He found
Philip and said to him, "Come, follow me." 44Philip was
from Bethsaida, Andrew and Peter's hometown.
45Philip went to look for Nathanael and told him, "We
have found the very person Moses* and the prophets wrote
about! His name is Jesus, the son of Joseph from Nazareth."
46"Nazareth!" exclaimed Nathanael. "Can anything
good come from Nazareth?"
"Come and see for yourself," Philip replied.
47As they approached, Jesus said, "Now here is a genuine son of Israel—a man of complete integrity."
48"How do you know about me?" Nathanael asked.
Jesus replied, "I could see you under the fig tree before
Philip found you."
49Then Nathanael exclaimed, "Rabbi, you are the Son
of God—the King of Israel!"

1:34 Some manuscripts read *the Son of God*. **1:41** *Messiah* (a Hebrew term) and *Christ* (a Greek term) both mean "the anointed one." **1:42** The names *Cephas* (from Aramaic) and *Peter* (from Greek) both mean "rock." **1:45** Greek *Moses in the law*.

50 Jesus asked him, "Do you believe this just because I told you I had seen you under the fig tree? You will see greater things than this." 51 Then he said, "I tell you the truth, you will all see heaven open and the angels of God going up and down on the Son of Man, the one who is the stairway between heaven and earth.*"

2

THE WEDDING AT CANA

The next day* there was a wedding celebration in the village of Cana in Galilee. Jesus' mother was there, 2 and Jesus and his disciples were also invited to the celebration. 3 The wine supply ran out during the festivities, so Jesus' mother told him, "They have no more wine."

4 "Dear woman, that's not our problem," Jesus replied. "My time has not yet come."

5 But his mother told the servants, "Do whatever he tells you."

6 Standing nearby were six stone water jars, used for Jewish ceremonial washing. Each could hold twenty to thirty gallons.* 7 Jesus told the servants, "Fill the jars with water." When the jars had been filled, 8 he said, "Now dip some out, and take it to the master of ceremonies." So the servants followed his instructions.

9 When the master of ceremonies tasted the water that was now wine, not knowing where it had come from (though, of course, the servants knew), he called the bridegroom over. 10 "A host always serves the best wine first," he said. "Then, when everyone has had a lot to drink, he brings out the less expensive wine. But you have kept the best until now!"

11 This miraculous sign at Cana in Galilee was the first time Jesus revealed his glory. And his disciples believed in him.

12 After the wedding he went to Capernaum for a few days with his mother, his brothers, and his disciples.

ANGER 2:15-16

Jesus obviously was angry with the merchants who conducted business in the Temple. Although there is a difference between uncontrolled rage and righteous indignation, both are called anger. How we use the powerful emotion of anger makes all the difference. Jesus used his anger for good instead of evil. Feeling angry? How can you use your anger to bring about positive changes? ■

JESUS CLEARS THE TEMPLE

13 It was nearly time for the Jewish Passover celebration, so Jesus went to Jerusalem. 14 In the Temple area he saw merchants selling cattle, sheep, and doves for sacrifices; he also saw dealers at tables exchanging foreign money. 15 Jesus made a whip from some ropes and chased them all out of the Temple. He drove out the sheep and cattle, scattered the money changers' coins over the floor, and turned over their tables. 16 Then, going over to the people who sold doves, he told them, "Get these things out of here. Stop turning my Father's house into a marketplace!"

17 Then his disciples remembered this prophecy from the Scriptures: "Passion for God's house will consume me."*

18 But the Jewish leaders demanded, "What are you doing? If God gave you authority to do this, show us a miraculous sign to prove it."

19 "All right," Jesus replied. "Destroy this temple, and in three days I will raise it up."

20 "What!" they exclaimed. "It has taken forty-six years to build this Temple, and you can rebuild it in three days?" 21 But when Jesus said "this temple," he meant his own body. 22 After he was raised from the dead, his disciples remembered he had said this, and they believed both the Scriptures and what Jesus had said.

JESUS AND NICODEMUS

23 Because of the miraculous signs Jesus did in Jerusalem at the Passover celebration, many began to trust in him. 24 But Jesus didn't trust them, because he knew human nature. 25 No one needed to tell him what mankind is really like.

3

There was a man named Nicodemus, a Jewish religious leader who was a Pharisee. 2 After dark one evening, he came to speak with Jesus. "Rabbi," he said, "we all know that God has sent you to teach us. Your miraculous signs are evidence that God is with you."

3 Jesus replied, "I tell you the truth, unless you are born again,* you cannot see the Kingdom of God."

4 "What do you mean?" exclaimed Nicodemus. "How can an old man go back into his mother's womb and be born again?"

GOD WITH US 3:6

Jesus explained to Nicodemus that the Holy Spirit is involved in the spiritual rebirth of each person. Who is the Holy Spirit? God is three persons in one—the Father, the Son, and the Holy Spirit. In Old Testament days, the Holy Spirit gave specific individuals power for specific purposes. But Jesus promised that the Holy Spirit would come to live permanently among believers (John 14:16-26; 16:7-8; see also 1 Cor 6:19-20; 12:13; Heb 13:5-6). After Pentecost (Acts 2), Jesus' promise came true. If you're a believer, you're never alone. The Holy Spirit is with you. ■

5 Jesus replied, "I assure you, no one can enter the Kingdom of God without being born of water and the Spirit.* 6 Humans can reproduce only human life, but the Holy Spirit gives birth to spiritual life.* 7 So don't be surprised

1:51 Greek *going up and down on the Son of Man;* see Gen 28:10-17. "Son of Man" is a title Jesus used for himself. 2:1 Greek *On the third day;* see 1:35, 43. 2:6 Greek *2 or 3 measures* [75 to 113 liters]. 2:17 Or *"Concern for God's house will be my undoing."* Ps 69:9. 3:3 Or *born from above;* also in 3:7. 3:5 Or *and spirit.* The Greek word for *Spirit* can also be translated *wind;* see 3:8. 3:6 Greek *what is born of the Spirit is spirit.*

when I say, 'You* must be born again.'
8 The wind blows wherever it wants.
Just as you can hear the wind but can't
tell where it comes from or where it is
going, so you can't explain how people
are born of the Spirit."
9 "How are these things possible?"
Nicodemus asked.
10 Jesus replied, "You are a respected
Jewish teacher, and yet you don't
understand these things? 11 I assure
you, we tell you what we know and
have seen, and yet you won't believe
our testimony. 12 But if you don't believe me when I tell you about earthly
things, how can you possibly believe if
I tell you about heavenly things? 13 No
one has ever gone to heaven and returned. But the Son of Man* has come down from
heaven. 14 And as Moses lifted up the bronze snake on a
pole in the wilderness, so the Son of Man must be lifted
up, 15 so that everyone who believes in him will have eternal life.*
16 "For God loved the world so much that he gave his
one and only Son, so that everyone who believes in him
will not perish but have eternal life. 17 God sent his Son
into the world not to judge the world, but to save the
world through him.
18 "There is no judgment against anyone who believes
in him. But anyone who does not believe in him has already been judged for not believing in God's one and only
Son. 19 And the judgment is based on this fact: God's light
came into the world, but people loved the darkness more
than the light, for their actions were evil. 20 All who do evil
hate the light and refuse to go near it for fear their sins
will be exposed. 21 But those who do what is right come to
the light so others can see that they are doing what God
wants.*"

> For God loved the world so much that he gave his one and only Son, so that everyone who believes in him will not perish but have eternal life.
>
> *JOHN 3:16*

JOHN THE BAPTIST EXALTS JESUS

22 Then Jesus and his disciples left Jerusalem and went
into the Judean countryside. Jesus spent some time with
them there, baptizing people.
23 At this time John the Baptist was baptizing at Aenon,
near Salim, because there was plenty of water there; and
people kept coming to him for baptism. 24 (This was before John was thrown into prison.) 25 A debate broke out
between John's disciples and a certain Jew* over ceremonial cleansing. 26 So John's disciples came to him and said,
"Rabbi, the man you met on the other side of the Jordan
River, the one you identified as the Messiah, is also baptizing people. And everybody is going to him instead of
coming to us."
27 John replied, "No one can receive anything unless
God gives it from heaven. 28 You yourselves know how
plainly I told you, 'I am not the Messiah. I am only here to
prepare the way for him.' 29 It is the
bridegroom who marries the bride,
and the best man is simply glad to
stand with him and hear his vows.
Therefore, I am filled with joy at his
success. 30 He must become greater
and greater, and I must become less
and less.
31 "He has come from above and is
greater than anyone else. We are of the
earth, and we speak of earthly things,
but he has come from heaven and is
greater than anyone else.* 32 He testifies about what he has seen and heard,
but how few believe what he tells them!
33 Anyone who accepts his testimony
can affirm that God is true. 34 For he is
sent by God. He speaks God's words,
for God gives him the Spirit without limit. 35 The Father
loves his Son and has put everything into his hands. 36 And
anyone who believes in God's Son has eternal life. Anyone
who doesn't obey the Son will never experience eternal
life but remains under God's angry judgment."

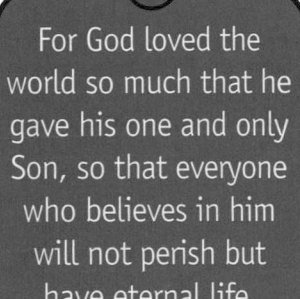

4 JESUS AND THE SAMARITAN WOMAN

Jesus* knew the Pharisees had heard that he was baptizing and making more disciples than John 2 (though Jesus
himself didn't baptize them—his disciples did). 3 So he
left Judea and returned to Galilee.
4 He had to go through Samaria on the way. 5 Eventually
he came to the Samaritan village of Sychar, near the field
that Jacob gave to his son Joseph. 6 Jacob's well was there;
and Jesus, tired from the long walk, sat wearily beside the
well about noontime. 7 Soon a Samaritan woman came to
draw water, and Jesus said to her, "Please give me a
drink." 8 He was alone at the time because his disciples
had gone into the village to buy some food.

CROSSING THE BARRIERS 4:7-9

This woman (1) was a Samaritan, a person of mixed heritage whom the Jews normally avoided; (2) had a bad reputation; and (3) was in a public place. No respectable Jewish man would talk to a woman under such circumstances. But Jesus didn't let these excuses stop him from talking to the woman. Would you have done the same? Is there someone you normally avoid for various reasons? Like Jesus, are you prepared to cross all barriers to share the Good News? ■

9 The woman was surprised, for Jews refuse to have
anything to do with Samaritans.* She said to Jesus, "You
are a Jew, and I am a Samaritan woman. Why are you asking me for a drink?"

3:7 The Greek word for *you* is plural; also in 3:12. 3:13 Some manuscripts add *who lives in heaven*. "Son of Man" is a title Jesus used for himself. 3:15 Or *everyone who believes will have eternal life in him*. 3:21 Or *can see God at work in what he is doing*. 3:25 Some manuscripts read *some Jews*. 3:31 Some manuscripts omit *and is greater than anyone else*. 4:1 Some manuscripts read *The Lord*. 4:9 Some manuscripts omit this sentence.

10Jesus replied, "If you only knew the gift God has for
you and who you are speaking to, you would ask me, and I
would give you living water."
11"But sir, you don't have a rope or a bucket," she said,
"and this well is very deep. Where would you get this living water? 12And besides, do you think you're greater
than our ancestor Jacob, who gave us this well? How can
you offer better water than he and his sons and his animals enjoyed?"

PREJUDICE

Ever think that prejudice is just related to race? If so, meet Jocelyn. She answers to Lyn, Jo, and Jay Bee, depending on her mood. Everybody thinks she's cool, and not because she plays the drums in her own band. She's also an excellent volleyball player, loves hanging out with her friends, and has more school spirit than anyone else at her high school.

So, what's the deal with Jocelyn? Check this out.

"No," Jocelyn says firmly. "I can't hang out with Brandi. She's *so* not cool. When I asked if she heard the latest cut from the Flea Bites' CD, I could tell she'd never heard of them. I was like, 'Where have you been for the last six months?' Who hasn't heard of the Flea Bites?"

"So, you're really not coming over tonight?" her friend Jessica asks. "I thought you said you wanted to hang out."

"With *you*, yes, with Brandi, no. I mean, Jess, why'd you invite her? Look at her clothes. Everybody at school thinks she's a complete loser."

"So, you're *really* not coming?"

"You already asked me that, Jess. I just can't. Sorry. Guess I'll see you at youth group on Thursday."

Check out John 4:1-42. The Jews treated the Samaritans the same way. Based on this passage, how should you treat others?

13Jesus replied, "Anyone who drinks this water will
soon become thirsty again. 14But those who drink the water I give will never be thirsty again. It becomes a fresh,
bubbling spring within them, giving them eternal life."
15"Please, sir," the woman said, "give me this water!
Then I'll never be thirsty again, and I won't have to come
here to get water."
16"Go and get your husband," Jesus told her.
17"I don't have a husband," the woman replied.
Jesus said, "You're right! You don't have a husband—
18for you have had five husbands, and you aren't even
married to the man you're living with now. You certainly
spoke the truth!"
19"Sir," the woman said, "you must be a prophet. 20So
tell me, why is it that you Jews insist that Jerusalem is
the only place of worship, while we Samaritans claim
it is here at Mount Gerizim,* where our ancestors
worshiped?"
21Jesus replied, "Believe me, dear woman, the time is
coming when it will no longer matter whether you worship the Father on this mountain or in Jerusalem. 22You
Samaritans know very little about the one you worship,
while we Jews know all about him, for salvation comes
through the Jews. 23But the time is coming—indeed it's
here now—when true worshipers will worship the Father
in spirit and in truth. The Father is looking for those who
will worship him that way. 24For God is Spirit, so those
who worship him must worship in spirit and in truth."
25The woman said, "I know the Messiah is coming—the
one who is called Christ. When he comes, he will explain
everything to us."
26Then Jesus told her, "I Am the Messiah!"*
27Just then his disciples came back. They were
shocked to find him talking to a woman, but none of
them had the nerve to ask, "What do you want with her?"
or "Why are you talking to her?" 28The woman left her
water jar beside the well and ran back to the village, telling everyone, 29"Come and see a man who told me everything I ever did! Could he possibly be the Messiah?" 30So
the people came streaming from the village to see him.
31Meanwhile, the disciples were urging Jesus, "Rabbi,
eat something."
32But Jesus replied, "I have a kind of food you know
nothing about."
33"Did someone bring him food while we were gone?"
the disciples asked each other.
34Then Jesus explained: "My nourishment comes from
doing the will of God, who sent me, and from finishing
his work. 35You know the saying, 'Four months between
planting and harvest.' But I say, wake up and look around.
The fields are already ripe* for harvest. 36The harvesters
are paid good wages, and the fruit they harvest is people
brought to eternal life. What joy awaits both the planter
and the harvester alike! 37You know the saying, 'One
plants and another harvests.' And it's true. 38I sent you to
harvest where you didn't plant; others had already done
the work, and now you will get to gather the harvest."

MANY SAMARITANS BELIEVE

39Many Samaritans from the village believed in Jesus because the woman had said, "He told me everything I ever
did!" 40When they came out to see him, they begged him
to stay in their village. So he stayed for two days, 41long
enough for many more to hear his message and believe.
42Then they said to the woman, "Now we believe, not just
because of what you told us, but because we have heard
him ourselves. Now we know that he is indeed the Savior
of the world."

JESUS HEALS AN OFFICIAL'S SON

43At the end of the two days, Jesus went on to Galilee. 44He
himself had said that a prophet is not honored in his own
hometown. 45Yet the Galileans welcomed him, for they

4:20 Greek *on this mountain.* 4:26 Or *"The 'I Am' is here"*; or *"I am the Lord"*; Greek reads *"I am, the one speaking to you."* See Exod 3:14.
4:35 Greek *white.*

had been in Jerusalem at the Passover celebration and
had seen everything he did there.
46As he traveled through Galilee, he came to Cana,
where he had turned the water into wine. There was a
government official in nearby Capernaum whose son
was very sick. 47When he heard that Jesus had come from
Judea to Galilee, he went and begged Jesus to come to
Capernaum to heal his son, who was about to die.
48Jesus asked, "Will you never believe in me unless you
see miraculous signs and wonders?"
49The official pleaded, "Lord, please come now before
my little boy dies."
50Then Jesus told him, "Go back home. Your son will
live!" And the man believed what Jesus said and started
home.
51While the man was on his way, some of his servants
met him with the news that his son was alive and well.
52He asked them when the boy had begun to get better,
and they replied, "Yesterday afternoon at one o'clock his
fever suddenly disappeared!" 53Then the father realized
that that was the very time Jesus had told him, "Your son
will live." And he and his entire household believed in
Jesus. 54This was the second miraculous sign Jesus did in
Galilee after coming from Judea.

AN ACTIVE BELIEF 4:46-54

This nobleman not only believed that Jesus could heal, he demonstrated his faith in Jesus by returning home. Saying that we believe Jesus can take care of our problems isn't enough. We need to act as if we believe that he can. When you pray about a need or problem, do your actions show that you believe Jesus can do what he says? ■

5 JESUS HEALS A LAME MAN

Afterward Jesus returned to Jerusalem for one of the Jewish holy days. 2Inside the city, near the Sheep Gate, was
the pool of Bethesda,* with five covered porches.
3Crowds of sick people—blind, lame, or paralyzed—lay
on the porches.* 5One of the men lying there had been
sick for thirty-eight years. 6When Jesus saw him and
knew he had been ill for a long time, he asked him,
"Would you like to get well?"
7"I can't, sir," the sick man said, "for I have no one to
put me into the pool when the water bubbles up. Someone else always gets there ahead of me."
8Jesus told him, "Stand up, pick up your mat, and walk!"
9Instantly, the man was healed! He rolled up his sleeping mat and began walking! But this miracle happened on
the Sabbath, 10so the Jewish leaders objected. They said to
the man who was cured, "You can't work on the Sabbath!
The law doesn't allow you to carry that sleeping mat!"
11But he replied, "The man who healed me told me,
'Pick up your mat and walk.'"

TRAPPED 5:6

Jesus' question to a sick man, "Would you like to get well?" might have seemed strange. Of course he would want to get well . . . . wouldn't he? But after 38 years, this man's problem had become a way of life. He had no hope of ever being healed and no desire to help himself. Ever feel trapped like that? Many have. Unfortunately, a loss of hope has led some people to abandon their faith. But God wants his people to keep on asking (Matt 7:7) and be willing to stick with him (John 15:4-8). Are you willing? ■

12"Who said such a thing as that?" they demanded.
13The man didn't know, for Jesus had disappeared into
the crowd. 14But afterward Jesus found him in the Temple and told him, "Now you are well; so stop sinning, or
something even worse may happen to you." 15Then the
man went and told the Jewish leaders that it was Jesus
who had healed him.

JESUS CLAIMS TO BE THE SON OF GOD

16So the Jewish leaders began harassing* Jesus for breaking the Sabbath rules. 17But Jesus replied, "My Father is
always working, and so am I." 18So the Jewish leaders
tried all the harder to find a way to kill him. For he not
only broke the Sabbath, he called God his Father, thereby
making himself equal with God.
19So Jesus explained, "I tell you the truth, the Son can
do nothing by himself. He does only what he sees the Father doing. Whatever the Father does, the Son also does.
20For the Father loves the Son and shows him everything
he is doing. In fact, the Father will show him how to do
even greater works than healing this man. Then you will
truly be astonished. 21For just as the Father gives life to
those he raises from the dead, so the Son gives life to anyone he wants. 22In addition, the Father judges no one. Instead, he has given the Son absolute authority to judge,
23so that everyone will honor the Son, just as they honor
the Father. Anyone who does not honor the Son is certainly not honoring the Father who sent him.
24"I tell you the truth, those who listen to my message
and believe in God who sent me have eternal life. They
will never be condemned for their sins, but they have
already passed from death into life.
25"And I assure you that the time is coming, indeed it's
here now, when the dead will hear my voice—the voice of
the Son of God. And those who listen will live. 26The Father has life in himself, and he has granted that same life-
giving power to his Son. 27And he has given him authority
to judge everyone because he is the Son of Man.* 28Don't
be so surprised! Indeed, the time is coming when all the
dead in their graves will hear the voice of God's Son, 29and
they will rise again. Those who have done good will rise to
experience eternal life, and those who have continued in
evil will rise to experience judgment. 30I can do nothing

5:2 Other manuscripts read *Beth-zatha;* still others read *Bethsaida.* 5:3 Some manuscripts add an expanded conclusion to verse 3 and all of verse 4: *waiting for a certain movement of the water, 4for an angel of the Lord came from time to time and stirred up the water. And the first person to step in after the water was stirred was healed of whatever disease he had.* 5:16 Or *persecuting.* 5:27 "Son of Man" is a title Jesus used for himself.

JUST LIKE HIM 5:19-23

Jesus told a crowd of people that he did whatever he saw the Father do. In other words, he imitated the Father's actions. Many of us imitate the actions of our parents. For example, some of us play a musical instrument or have the ability to fix cars, because our parents have done so or encouraged us to do so. But Jesus' example encourages us to imitate the actions of another parent—the heavenly Father. The questions "What would Jesus do?" and "What would Jesus have me do?" can help us make the right choices. Is imitating the Father a priority of yours? ■

on my own. I judge as God tells me. Therefore, my judgment is just, because I carry out the will of the one who sent me, not my own will.

WITNESSES TO JESUS

31"If I were to testify on my own behalf, my testimony would not be valid. 32But someone else is also testifying about me, and I assure you that everything he says about me is true. 33In fact, you sent investigators to listen to John the Baptist, and his testimony about me was true. 34Of course, I have no need of human witnesses, but I say these things so you might be saved. 35John was like a burning and shining lamp, and you were excited for a while about his message. 36But I have a greater witness than John—my teachings and my miracles. The Father gave me these works to accomplish, and they prove that he sent me. 37And the Father who sent me has testified about me himself. You have never heard his voice or seen him face to face, 38and you do not have his message in your hearts, because you do not believe me—the one he sent to you.

39"You search the Scriptures because you think they give you eternal life. But the Scriptures point to me! 40Yet you refuse to come to me to receive this life.

41"Your approval means nothing to me, 42because I know you don't have God's love within you. 43For I have come to you in my Father's name, and you have rejected me. Yet if others come in their own name, you gladly welcome them. 44No wonder you can't believe! For you gladly honor each other, but you don't care about the honor that comes from the one who alone is God.*

45"Yet it isn't I who will accuse you before the Father. Moses will accuse you! Yes, Moses, in whom you put your hopes. 46If you really believed Moses, you would believe me, because he wrote about me. 47But since you don't believe what he wrote, how will you believe what I say?"

6

JESUS FEEDS FIVE THOUSAND

After this, Jesus crossed over to the far side of the Sea of Galilee, also known as the Sea of Tiberias. 2A huge crowd kept following him wherever he went, because they saw his miraculous signs as he healed the sick. 3Then Jesus climbed a hill and sat down with his disciples around him. 4(It was nearly time for the Jewish Passover celebration.) 5Jesus soon saw a huge crowd of people coming to look for him. Turning to Philip, he asked, "Where can we buy bread to feed all these people?" 6He was testing Philip, for he already knew what he was going to do.

7Philip replied, "Even if we worked for months, we wouldn't have enough money* to feed them!"

8Then Andrew, Simon Peter's brother, spoke up. 9"There's a young boy here with five barley loaves and two fish. But what good is that with this huge crowd?"

RESOURCES 6:8-9

The disciples are contrasted with the boy who offered his lunch to help feed the crowd. While the disciples offered little but doubt, the boy gave what little he had. But God can turn a little into a lot. What will you offer to God (time, talents, resources)? ■

10"Tell everyone to sit down," Jesus said. So they all sat down on the grassy slopes. (The men alone numbered about 5,000.) 11Then Jesus took the loaves, gave thanks to God, and distributed them to the people. Afterward he did the same with the fish. And they all ate as much as they wanted. 12After everyone was full, Jesus told his disciples, "Now gather the leftovers, so that nothing is wasted." 13So they picked up the pieces and filled twelve baskets with scraps left by the people who had eaten from the five barley loaves.

14When the people saw him* do this miraculous sign, they exclaimed, "Surely, he is the Prophet we have been expecting!"* 15When Jesus saw that they were ready to force him to be their king, he slipped away into the hills by himself.

JESUS WALKS ON WATER

16That evening Jesus' disciples went down to the shore to wait for him. 17But as darkness fell and Jesus still hadn't come back, they got into the boat and headed across the lake toward Capernaum. 18Soon a gale swept down upon them, and the sea grew very rough. 19They had rowed three or four miles* when suddenly they saw Jesus walking on the water toward the boat. They were terrified, 20but he called out to them, "Don't be afraid. I am here!*" 21Then they were eager to let him in the boat, and immediately they arrived at their destination!

JESUS, THE BREAD OF LIFE

22The next day the crowd that had stayed on the far shore saw that the disciples had taken the only boat, and they realized Jesus had not gone with them. 23Several boats from Tiberias landed near the place where the Lord had

5:44 Some manuscripts read *from the only One*. **6:7** Greek *Two hundred denarii would not be enough.* A denarius was equivalent to a laborer's full day's wage. **6:14a** Some manuscripts read *Jesus*. **6:14b** See Deut 18:15, 18; Mal 4:5-6. **6:19** Greek *25 or 30 stadia* [4.6 or 5.5 kilometers]. **6:20** Or *The 'I AM' is here;* Greek reads *I am.* See Exod 3:14.

blessed the bread and the people had eaten. [24]So when the crowd saw that neither Jesus nor his disciples were there, they got into the boats and went across to Capernaum to look for him. [25]They found him on the other side of the lake and asked, "Rabbi, when did you get here?"

[26]Jesus replied, "I tell you the truth, you want to be with me because I fed you, not because you understood the miraculous signs. [27]But don't be so concerned about perishable things like food. Spend your energy seeking the eternal life that the Son of Man* can give you. For God the Father has given me the seal of his approval."

THE WAY 6:26

Jesus knew that many of the people who followed him did so only because he fed them miraculously. Yet they weren't "hungry" for the truth. True believers follow Jesus simply because they know his way is the way to live. Is that why you follow him? ■

[28]They replied, "We want to perform God's works, too. What should we do?"

[29]Jesus told them, "This is the only work God wants from you: Believe in the one he has sent."

[30]They answered, "Show us a miraculous sign if you want us to believe in you. What can you do? [31]After all, our ancestors ate manna while they journeyed through the wilderness! The Scriptures say, 'Moses gave them bread from heaven to eat.'*"

[32]Jesus said, "I tell you the truth, Moses didn't give you bread from heaven. My Father did. And now he offers you the true bread from heaven. [33]The true bread of God is the one who comes down from heaven and gives life to the world."

[34]"Sir," they said, "give us that bread every day."

[35]Jesus replied, "I am the bread of life. Whoever comes to me will never be hungry again. Whoever believes in me will never be thirsty. [36]But you haven't believed in me even though you have seen me. [37]However, those the Father has given me will come to me, and I will never reject them. [38]For I have come down from heaven to do the will of God who sent me, not to do my own will. [39]And this is the will of God, that I should not lose even one of all those he has given me, but that I should raise them up at the last day. [40]For it is my Father's will that all who see his Son and believe in him should have eternal life. I will raise them up at the last day."

[41]Then the people* began to murmur in disagreement because he had said, "I am the bread that came down from heaven." [42]They said, "Isn't this Jesus, the son of Joseph? We know his father and mother. How can he say, 'I came down from heaven'?"

[43]But Jesus replied, "Stop complaining about what I said. [44]For no one can come to me unless the Father who sent me draws them to me, and at the last day I will raise them up. [45]As it is written in the Scriptures,* 'They will all be taught by God.' Everyone who listens to the Father and learns from him comes to me. [46](Not that anyone has ever seen the Father; only I, who was sent from God, have seen him.)

[47]"I tell you the truth, anyone who believes has eternal life. [48]Yes, I am the bread of life! [49]Your ancestors ate manna in the wilderness, but they all died. [50]Anyone who eats the bread from heaven, however, will never die. [51]I am the living bread that came down from heaven. Anyone who eats this bread will live forever; and this bread, which I will offer so the world may live, is my flesh."

[52]Then the people began arguing with each other about what he meant. "How can this man give us his flesh to eat?" they asked.

[53]So Jesus said again, "I tell you the truth, unless you eat the flesh of the Son of Man and drink his blood, you cannot have eternal life within you. [54]But anyone who eats my flesh and drinks my blood has eternal life, and I will raise that person at the last day. [55]For my flesh is true food, and my blood is true drink. [56]Anyone who eats my flesh and drinks my blood remains in me, and I in him. [57]I live because of the living Father who sent me; in the same way, anyone who feeds on me will live because of me. [58]I am the true bread that came down from heaven. Anyone who eats this bread will not die as your ancestors did (even though they ate the manna) but will live forever."

[59]He said these things while he was teaching in the synagogue in Capernaum.

MANY DISCIPLES DESERT JESUS

[60]Many of his disciples said, "This is very hard to understand. How can anyone accept it?"

[61]Jesus was aware that his disciples were complaining, so he said to them, "Does this offend you? [62]Then what will you think if you see the Son of Man ascend to heaven again? [63]The Spirit alone gives eternal life. Human effort accomplishes nothing. And the very words I have spoken to you are spirit and life. [64]But some of you do not believe me." (For Jesus knew from the beginning which ones didn't believe, and he knew who would betray him.) [65]Then he said, "That is why I said that people can't come to me unless the Father gives them to me."

[66]At this point many of his disciples turned away and deserted him. [67]Then Jesus turned to the Twelve and asked, "Are you also going to leave?"

[68]Simon Peter replied, "Lord, to whom would we go? You have the words that give eternal life. [69]We believe, and we know you are the Holy One of God.*"

[70]Then Jesus said, "I chose the twelve of you, but one is a devil." [71]He was speaking of Judas, son of Simon Iscariot, one of the Twelve, who would later betray him.

7

JESUS AND HIS BROTHERS

After this, Jesus traveled around Galilee. He wanted to stay out of Judea, where the Jewish leaders were plotting his death. [2]But soon it was time for the Jewish Festival of

6:27 "Son of Man" is a title Jesus used for himself. **6:31** Exod 16:4; Ps 78:24. **6:41** Greek *Jewish people;* also in 6:52. **6:45** Greek *in the prophets.* Isa 54:13. **6:69** Other manuscripts read *you are the Christ, the Holy One of God;* still others read *you are the Christ, the Son of God;* and still others read *you are the Christ, the Son of the living God.*

THE SOURCE 6:67-68

After many of Jesus' followers deserted him, Jesus asked the 12 disciples if they also planned to leave. Peter responded, "Lord, to whom would we go? You have the words that give eternal life." In his straightforward way, Peter answered for all of us—there *is* no other way. Jesus alone gives life. Yet people search everywhere, hoping to find "life" or fulfillment through many sources (relationships, money, achievements, drugs). But none of these will provide that elusive fulfillment. Who or what is your source of life? ■

Shelters, 3and Jesus' brothers said to him, "Leave here and go to Judea, where your followers can see your miracles! 4You can't become famous if you hide like this! If you can do such wonderful things, show yourself to the world!" 5For even his brothers didn't believe in him.

6Jesus replied, "Now is not the right time for me to go, but you can go anytime. 7The world can't hate you, but it does hate me because I accuse it of doing evil. 8You go on. I'm not going* to this festival, because my time has not yet come." 9After saying these things, Jesus remained in Galilee.

JESUS TEACHES OPENLY AT THE TEMPLE

10But after his brothers left for the festival, Jesus also went, though secretly, staying out of public view. 11The Jewish leaders tried to find him at the festival and kept asking if anyone had seen him. 12There was a lot of grumbling about him among the crowds. Some argued, "He's a good man," but others said, "He's nothing but a fraud who deceives the people." 13But no one had the courage to speak favorably about him in public, for they were afraid of getting in trouble with the Jewish leaders.

14Then, midway through the festival, Jesus went up to the Temple and began to teach. 15The people* were surprised when they heard him. "How does he know so much when he hasn't been trained?" they asked.

16So Jesus told them, "My message is not my own; it comes from God who sent me. 17Anyone who wants to do the will of God will know whether my teaching is from God or is merely my own. 18Those who speak for themselves want glory only for themselves, but a person who seeks to honor the one who sent him speaks truth, not lies. 19Moses gave you the law, but none of you obeys it! In fact, you are trying to kill me."

20The crowd replied, "You're demon possessed! Who's trying to kill you?"

21Jesus replied, "I did one miracle on the Sabbath, and you were amazed. 22But you work on the Sabbath, too, when you obey Moses' law of circumcision. (Actually, this tradition of circumcision began with the patriarchs, long before the law of Moses.) 23For if the correct time for circumcising your son falls on the Sabbath, you go ahead and do it so as not to break the law of Moses. So why should you be angry with me for healing a man on the Sabbath? 24Look beneath the surface so you can judge correctly."

IS JESUS THE MESSIAH?

25Some of the people who lived in Jerusalem started to ask each other, "Isn't this the man they are trying to kill? 26But here he is, speaking in public, and they say nothing to him. Could our leaders possibly believe that he is the Messiah? 27But how could he be? For we know where this man comes from. When the Messiah comes, he will simply appear; no one will know where he comes from."

28While Jesus was teaching in the Temple, he called out, "Yes, you know me, and you know where I come from. But I'm not here on my own. The one who sent me is true, and you don't know him. 29But I know him because I come from him, and he sent me to you." 30Then the leaders tried to arrest him; but no one laid a hand on him, because his time* had not yet come.

31Many among the crowds at the Temple believed in him. "After all," they said, "would you expect the Messiah to do more miraculous signs than this man has done?"

32When the Pharisees heard that the crowds were whispering such things, they and the leading priests sent Temple guards to arrest Jesus. 33But Jesus told them, "I will be with you only a little longer. Then I will return to the one who sent me. 34You will search for me but not find me. And you cannot go where I am going."

35The Jewish leaders were puzzled by this statement. "Where is he planning to go?" they asked. "Is he thinking of leaving the country and going to the Jews in other lands?* Maybe he will even teach the Greeks! 36What does he mean when he says, 'You will search for me but not find me,' and 'You cannot go where I am going'?"

DON'T JUMP! 7:37-43

A crowd of people were divided in their reactions to Jesus. Some believed, others were hostile, and others disqualified Jesus as the Messiah because he was from Nazareth rather than Bethlehem as prophesied in Micah 5:2. (Yet he *was* born in Bethlehem; see Luke 2:1-7.) If they had looked more carefully or searched the Scriptures, they wouldn't have jumped to the wrong conclusions. What conclusions have you come to about Jesus? Are you willing to keep searching for answers if you're not sure what to believe? ■

JESUS PROMISES LIVING WATER

37On the last day, the climax of the festival, Jesus stood and shouted to the crowds, "Anyone who is thirsty may come to me! 38Anyone who believes in me may come and drink! For the Scriptures declare, 'Rivers of living water will flow from his heart.'"* 39(When he said "living water," he was speaking of the Spirit, who would be given to

7:8 Some manuscripts read *not yet going.* 7:15 Greek *Jewish people.* 7:30 Greek *his hour.* 7:35 Or *the Jews who live among the Greeks?* 7:37-38 Or *"Let anyone who is thirsty come to me and drink. 38For the Scriptures declare, 'Rivers of living water will flow from the heart of anyone who believes in me.'"*

everyone believing in him. But the Spirit had not yet been given,* because Jesus had not yet entered into his glory.)

DIVISION AND UNBELIEF

40When the crowds heard him say this, some of them declared, "Surely this man is the Prophet we've been expecting."* 41Others said, "He is the Messiah." Still others said, "But he can't be! Will the Messiah come from Galilee? 42For the Scriptures clearly state that the Messiah will be born of the royal line of David, in Bethlehem, the village where King David was born."* 43So the crowd was divided about him. 44Some even wanted him arrested, but no one laid a hand on him.

45When the Temple guards returned without having arrested Jesus, the leading priests and Pharisees demanded, "Why didn't you bring him in?"

46"We have never heard anyone speak like this!" the guards responded.

47"Have you been led astray, too?" the Pharisees mocked. 48"Is there a single one of us rulers or Pharisees who believes in him? 49This foolish crowd follows him, but they are ignorant of the law. God's curse is on them!"

50Then Nicodemus, the leader who had met with Jesus earlier, spoke up. 51"Is it legal to convict a man before he is given a hearing?" he asked.

52They replied, "Are you from Galilee, too? Search the Scriptures and see for yourself—no prophet ever comes* from Galilee!"

[*The most ancient Greek manuscripts do not include John 7:53–8:11.*]

53Then the meeting broke up, and everybody went home.

8

A WOMAN CAUGHT IN ADULTERY

Jesus returned to the Mount of Olives, 2but early the next morning he was back again at the Temple. A crowd soon gathered, and he sat down and taught them. 3As he was speaking, the teachers of religious law and the Pharisees brought a woman who had been caught in the act of adultery. They put her in front of the crowd.

4"Teacher," they said to Jesus, "this woman was caught in the act of adultery. 5The law of Moses says to stone her. What do you say?"

6They were trying to trap him into saying something they could use against him, but Jesus stooped down and wrote in the dust with his finger. 7They kept demanding an answer, so he stood up again and said, "All right, but let the one who has never sinned throw the first stone!" 8Then he stooped down again and wrote in the dust.

9When the accusers heard this, they slipped away one by one, beginning with the oldest, until only Jesus was left in the middle of the crowd with the woman. 10Then Jesus stood up again and said to the woman, "Where are your accusers? Didn't even one of them condemn you?"

JUDGE NOT 8:9

Jesus refused to condemn a woman caught in adultery. By this action, Jesus wasn't saying, "Adultery's okay. Go for it!" (See Exod 20:14.) Actually, he reacted to the hypocrisy of the Pharisees who wanted to condemn the woman.

Judging someone else is always easier than judging our own actions. During his sermon on the mount, Jesus' warning to "judge not" included this advice: "Why worry about a speck in your friend's eye when you have a log in your own? How can you think of saying to your friend, 'Let me help you get rid of that speck in your eye,' when you can't see past the log in your own eye? Hypocrite! First get rid of the log in your own eye; then you will see well enough to deal with the speck in your friend's eye" (Matt 7:3-5). Tempted to judge someone else? Judge not. ■

11"No, Lord," she said.

And Jesus said, "Neither do I. Go and sin no more."

JESUS, THE LIGHT OF THE WORLD

12Jesus spoke to the people once more and said, "I am the light of the world. If you follow me, you won't have to walk in darkness, because you will have the light that leads to life."

13The Pharisees replied, "You are making those claims about yourself! Such testimony is not valid."

14Jesus told them, "These claims are valid even though I make them about myself. For I know where I came from and where I am going, but you don't know this about me. 15You judge me by human standards, but I do not judge anyone. 16And if I did, my judgment would be correct in every respect because I am not alone. The Father* who sent me is with me. 17Your own law says that if two people agree about something, their witness is accepted as fact.* 18I am one witness, and my Father who sent me is the other."

19"Where is your father?" they asked.

Jesus answered, "Since you don't know who I am, you don't know who my Father is. If you knew me, you would also know my Father." 20Jesus made these statements while he was teaching in the section of the Temple known as the Treasury. But he was not arrested, because his time* had not yet come.

THE UNBELIEVING PEOPLE WARNED

21Later Jesus said to them again, "I am going away. You will search for me but will die in your sin. You cannot come where I am going."

22The people* asked, "Is he planning to commit suicide? What does he mean, 'You cannot come where I am going'?"

23Jesus continued, "You are from below; I am from above. You belong to this world; I do not. 24That is why I

7:39 Some manuscripts read *But as yet there was no Spirit.* Still others read *But as yet there was no Holy Spirit.* **7:40** See Deut 18:15, 18; Mal 4:5-6. **7:42** See Mic 5:2. **7:52** Some manuscripts read *the prophet does not come.* **8:16** Some manuscripts read *The One.* **8:17** See Deut 19:15. **8:20** Greek *his hour.* **8:22** Greek *Jewish people;* also in 8:31, 48, 52, 57.

said that you will die in your sins; for unless you believe
that I AM who I claim to be,* you will die in your sins."
25"Who are you?" they demanded.
Jesus replied, "The one I have always claimed to be.* 26I
have much to say about you and much to condemn, but I
won't. For I say only what I have heard from the one who
sent me, and he is completely truthful." 27But they still
didn't understand that he was talking about his Father.
28So Jesus said, "When you have lifted up the Son of Man
on the cross, then you will understand that I AM he.* I do
nothing on my own but say only what the Father taught me.
29And the one who sent me is with me—he has not deserted
me. For I always do what pleases him." 30Then many who
heard him say these things believed in him.

JESUS AND ABRAHAM

31Jesus said to the people who believed in him, "You are truly
my disciples if you remain faithful to my teachings. 32And
you will know the truth, and the truth will set you free."
33"But we are descendants of Abraham," they said.
"We have never been slaves to anyone. What do you
mean, 'You will be set free'?"
34Jesus replied, "I tell you the truth, everyone who sins is
a slave of sin. 35A slave is not a permanent member of the
family, but a son is part of the family forever. 36So if the Son
sets you free, you are truly free. 37Yes, I realize that you are
descendants of Abraham. And yet some of you are trying to
kill me because there's no room in your hearts for my message. 38I am telling you what I saw when I was with my Father. But you are following the advice of your father."

FREE 8:32-36

Jesus spoke of the freedom he offered. What's your idea of freedom? Having wheels that can take you wherever you want to go? Being able to make your own choices? But some choices aren't good. In fact, making their own choices caused trouble for Adam and Eve. (See Gen 3.) Consequently, we were all born with a desire to do wrong. That's why Jesus said, "Everyone who sins is a slave of sin" (8:34). But the freedom Jesus offers is the freedom to choose *not* to do wrong. Are you free? ■

39"Our father is Abraham!" they declared.
"No," Jesus replied, "for if you were really the children
of Abraham, you would follow his example.* 40Instead,
you are trying to kill me because I told you the truth,
which I heard from God. Abraham never did such a thing.
41No, you are imitating your real father."
They replied, "We aren't illegitimate children! God
himself is our true Father."
42Jesus told them, "If God were your Father, you would
love me, because I have come to you from God. I am not
here on my own, but he sent me. 43Why can't you understand what I am saying? It's because you can't even hear
me! 44For you are the children of your father the devil, and
you love to do the evil things he does. He was a murderer
from the beginning. He has always hated the truth, because
there is no truth in him. When he lies, it is consistent with
his character; for he is a liar and the father of lies. 45So
when I tell the truth, you just naturally don't believe me!
46Which of you can truthfully accuse me of sin? And since I
am telling you the truth, why don't you believe me?
47Anyone who belongs to God listens gladly to the words of
God. But you don't listen because you don't belong to God."
48The people retorted, "You Samaritan devil! Didn't we
say all along that you were possessed by a demon?"
49"No," Jesus said, "I have no demon in me. For I honor
my Father—and you dishonor me. 50And though I have no
wish to glorify myself, God is going to glorify me. He is
the true judge. 51I tell you the truth, anyone who obeys my
teaching will never die!"
52The people said, "Now we know you are possessed by
a demon. Even Abraham and the prophets died, but you
say, 'Anyone who obeys my teaching will never die!' 53Are
you greater than our father Abraham? He died, and so did
the prophets. Who do you think you are?"
54Jesus answered, "If I want glory for myself, it doesn't
count. But it is my Father who will glorify me. You say, 'He is
our God,*' 55but you don't even know him. I know him. If I
said otherwise, I would be as great a liar as you! But I do know
him and obey him. 56Your father Abraham rejoiced as he
looked forward to my coming. He saw it and was glad."
57The people said, "You aren't even fifty years old. How
can you say you have seen Abraham?*"
58Jesus answered, "I tell you the truth, before Abraham
was even born, I AM!*" 59At that point they picked up
stones to throw at him. But Jesus was hidden from them
and left the Temple.

SUFFERING 9:1-3

A common belief in Jewish culture was that hardships were punishments for the wrong things a person did. But through the healing of the man born blind, Jesus revealed that some hardships were allowed as a means to glorify God.

We live in a world where innocent people sometimes suffer. Regardless of the reasons for our suffering, Jesus has the power to help us deal with it. When hard times come, instead of asking "Why did this happen to me?" or "What did I do wrong?" consider asking God to strengthen you and offer you a deeper perspective on what's at stake. ■

9

JESUS HEALS A MAN BORN BLIND

As Jesus was walking along, he saw a man who had been
blind from birth. 2"Rabbi," his disciples asked him, "why
was this man born blind? Was it because of his own sins
or his parents' sins?"

8:24 Greek *unless you believe that I am.* See Exod 3:14. 8:25 Or *Why do I speak to you at all?* 8:28 Greek *When you have lifted up the Son of Man, then you will know that I am.* "Son of Man" is a title Jesus used for himself. 8:39 Some manuscripts read *if you are really the children of Abraham, follow his example.* 8:54 Some manuscripts read *your God.* 8:57 Some manuscripts read *How can you say Abraham has seen you?* 8:58 Or *before Abraham was even born, I have always been alive;* Greek reads *before Abraham was, I am.* See Exod 3:14.

³"It was not because of his sins or his parents' sins," Jesus answered. "This happened so the power of God could be seen in him. ⁴We must quickly carry out the tasks assigned us by the one who sent us.* The night is coming, and then no one can work. ⁵But while I am here in the world, I am the light of the world."

⁶Then he spit on the ground, made mud with the saliva, and spread the mud over the blind man's eyes. ⁷He told him, "Go wash yourself in the pool of Siloam" (Siloam means "sent"). So the man went and washed and came back seeing!

⁸His neighbors and others who knew him as a blind beggar asked each other, "Isn't this the man who used to sit and beg?" ⁹Some said he was, and others said, "No, he just looks like him!"

But the beggar kept saying, "Yes, I am the same one!"

¹⁰They asked, "Who healed you? What happened?"

¹¹He told them, "The man they call Jesus made mud and spread it over my eyes and told me, 'Go to the pool of Siloam and wash yourself.' So I went and washed, and now I can see!"

¹²"Where is he now?" they asked.

"I don't know," he replied.

¹³Then they took the man who had been blind to the Pharisees, ¹⁴because it was on the Sabbath that Jesus had made the mud and healed him. ¹⁵The Pharisees asked the man all about it. So he told them, "He put the mud over my eyes, and when I washed it away, I could see!"

¹⁶Some of the Pharisees said, "This man Jesus is not from God, for he is working on the Sabbath." Others said, "But how could an ordinary sinner do such miraculous signs?" So there was a deep division of opinion among them.

¹⁷Then the Pharisees again questioned the man who had been blind and demanded, "What's your opinion about this man who healed you?"

The man replied, "I think he must be a prophet."

¹⁸The Jewish leaders still refused to believe the man had been blind and could now see, so they called in his parents. ¹⁹They asked them, "Is this your son? Was he born blind? If so, how can he now see?"

²⁰His parents replied, "We know this is our son and that he was born blind, ²¹but we don't know how he can see or who healed him. Ask him. He is old enough to speak for himself." ²²His parents said this because they were afraid of the Jewish leaders, who had announced that anyone saying Jesus was the Messiah would be expelled from the synagogue. ²³That's why they said, "He is old enough. Ask him."

²⁴So for the second time they called in the man who had been blind and told him, "God should get the glory for this,* because we know this man Jesus is a sinner."

²⁵"I don't know whether he is a sinner," the man replied. "But I know this: I was blind, and now I can see!"

²⁶"But what did he do?" they asked. "How did he heal you?"

²⁷"Look!" the man exclaimed. "I told you once. Didn't you listen? Why do you want to hear it again? Do you want to become his disciples, too?"

²⁸Then they cursed him and said, "You are his disciple, but we are disciples of Moses! ²⁹We know God spoke to Moses, but we don't even know where this man comes from."

³⁰"Why, that's very strange!" the man replied. "He healed my eyes, and yet you don't know where he comes from? ³¹We know that God doesn't listen to sinners, but he is ready to hear those who worship him and do his will. ³²Ever since the world began, no one has been able to open the eyes of someone born blind. ³³If this man were not from God, he couldn't have done it."

³⁴"You were born a total sinner!" they answered. "Are you trying to teach us?" And they threw him out of the synagogue.

PERSECUTION 9:28-34

Because of his faith in Jesus, the man who had been born blind was thrown out of the synagogue. Jesus later told his disciples to expect this kind of persecution (John 16:1-4, 33). If you're a follower of Jesus, you can expect to face some kind of persecution. Does that sound horrible? Maybe that's why Jesus also promised, "I have told you all this so that you may have peace in me. Here on earth you will have many trials and sorrows. But take heart, because I have overcome the world" (16:33). ■

SPIRITUAL BLINDNESS

³⁵When Jesus heard what had happened, he found the man and asked, "Do you believe in the Son of Man?*"

³⁶The man answered, "Who is he, sir? I want to believe in him."

³⁷"You have seen him," Jesus said, "and he is speaking to you!"

³⁸"Yes, Lord, I believe!" the man said. And he worshiped Jesus.

³⁹Then Jesus told him,* "I entered this world to render judgment—to give sight to the blind and to show those who think they see* that they are blind."

⁴⁰Some Pharisees who were standing nearby heard him and asked, "Are you saying we're blind?"

⁴¹"If you were blind, you wouldn't be guilty," Jesus replied. "But you remain guilty because you claim you can see.

10 THE GOOD SHEPHERD AND HIS SHEEP

"I tell you the truth, anyone who sneaks over the wall of a sheepfold, rather than going through the gate, must surely be a thief and a robber! ²But the one who enters through the gate is the shepherd of the sheep. ³The gatekeeper

9:4 Other manuscripts read *I must quickly carry out the tasks assigned me by the one who sent me;* still others read *We must quickly carry out the tasks assigned us by the one who sent me.* 9:24 Or *Give glory to God, not to Jesus;* Greek reads *Give glory to God.* 9:35 Some manuscripts read *the Son of God?* "Son of Man" is a title Jesus used for himself. 9:38-39a Some manuscripts do not include *"Yes, Lord, I believe!" the man said. And he worshiped Jesus. Then Jesus told him.* 9:39b Greek *those who see.*

opens the gate for him, and the sheep recognize his voice
and come to him. He calls his own sheep by name and
leads them out. 4After he has gathered his own flock, he
walks ahead of them, and they follow him because they
know his voice. 5They won't follow a stranger; they will
run from him because they don't know his voice."
6Those who heard Jesus use this illustration didn't
understand what he meant, 7so he explained it to them: "I
tell you the truth, I am the gate for the sheep. 8All who
came before me* were thieves and robbers. But the true
sheep did not listen to them. 9Yes, I am the gate. Those
who come in through me will be saved.* They will come
and go freely and will find good pastures. 10The thief's
purpose is to steal and kill and destroy. My purpose is to
give them a rich and satisfying life.
11"I am the good shepherd. The good shepherd sacrifices his life for the sheep. 12A hired hand will run when
he sees a wolf coming. He will abandon the sheep because they don't belong to him and he isn't their shepherd. And so the wolf attacks them and scatters the flock.
13The hired hand runs away because he's working only
for the money and doesn't really care about the sheep.
14"I am the good shepherd; I know my own sheep, and
they know me, 15just as my Father knows me and I know
the Father. So I sacrifice my life for the sheep. 16I have
other sheep, too, that are not in this sheepfold. I must
bring them also. They will listen to my voice, and there
will be one flock with one shepherd.
17"The Father loves me because I sacrifice my life so I
may take it back again. 18No one can take my life from
me. I sacrifice it voluntarily. For I have the authority to lay
it down when I want to and also to take it up again. For
this is what my Father has commanded."
19When he said these things, the people* were again divided in their opinions about him. 20Some said, "He's
demon possessed and out of his mind. Why listen to a
man like that?" 21Others said, "This doesn't sound like a
man possessed by a demon! Can a demon open the eyes
of the blind?"

SPIRITUAL BLINDNESS 10:24-29

These leaders waited for the evidence *they* thought would convince them that Jesus was the Savior God promised to send. Thus they couldn't accept the truth Jesus offered. Spiritual blindness like this still keeps people away from Jesus. They want him on their own terms—not his. Know anyone like that? Are you like that? There's only one cure for spiritual blindness: a sincere desire to believe. ■

JESUS CLAIMS TO BE THE SON OF GOD

22It was now winter, and Jesus was in Jerusalem at the
time of Hanukkah, the Festival of Dedication. 23He was in
the Temple, walking through the section known as Solomon's Colonnade. 24The people surrounded him and
asked, "How long are you going to keep us in suspense? If
you are the Messiah, tell us plainly."
25Jesus replied, "I have already told you, and you don't
believe me. The proof is the work I do in my Father's
name. 26But you don't believe me because you are not my
sheep. 27My sheep listen to my voice; I know them, and
they follow me. 28I give them eternal life, and they will
never perish. No one can snatch them away from me,
29for my Father has given them to me, and he is more
powerful than anyone else.* No one can snatch them
from the Father's hand. 30The Father and I are one."
31Once again the people picked up stones to kill him.
32Jesus said, "At my Father's direction I have done many
good works. For which one are you going to stone me?"
33They replied, "We're stoning you not for any good
work, but for blasphemy! You, a mere man, claim to be
God."
34Jesus replied, "It is written in your own Scriptures*
that God said to certain leaders of the people, 'I say, you
are gods!'* 35And you know that the Scriptures cannot be

10:8 Some manuscripts do not include *before me.* **10:9** Or *will find safety.* **10:19** Greek *Jewish people;* also in 10:24, 31. **10:29** Other manuscripts read *for what my Father has given me is more powerful than anything;* still others read *for regarding that which my Father has given me, he is greater than all.* **10:34a** Greek *your own law.* **10:34b** Ps 82:6.

If God is a God of love, why does he allow evil and death in the world?

When Jesus's friend Lazarus died (John 11), Jesus cried. Even though he was the Son of God and could raise Lazarus to life, Jesus was always aware of the agony humans faced because of death and evil.

So, why are evil and death allowed in the world? Ages ago, after losing a war with the angels of God, a group of fallen angels—led by Satan—left heaven (see Jude 6) and made earth their kingdom. They still exist and have only one purpose—to destroy. But their evil provides a contrast to the love and mercy of God, who allows people the freedom to choose between good and evil.

As a result of believing the lie of Satan, Adam and Eve disobeyed God in the Garden of Eden and were separated from him. (You know the story.) This incident also set in motion the life cycle, which ends in death and caused everyone to be born "spiritually dead."

Jesus' angry words to the Pharisees in John 8:44 show the result of spiritual death: "You are the children of your father the devil, and you love to do the evil things he does. He was a murderer from the beginning. He has always hated the truth, because there is no truth in him. When he lies, it is consistent with his character; for he is a liar and the father of lies."

But there's good news: Jesus' death on the cross provides the antidote for spiritual death. Although all of us eventually will die, a second life—eternal life—will begin.

So, although evil and death continue, God can use any situation for good (Rom 8:28). He loves you and wants to work out his purposes in your life.

altered. So if those people who received God's message
were called 'gods,' 36why do you call it blasphemy when I
say, 'I am the Son of God'? After all, the Father set me apart
and sent me into the world. 37Don't believe me unless I
carry out my Father's work. 38But if I do his work, believe
in the evidence of the miraculous works I have done, even
if you don't believe me. Then you will know and understand that the Father is in me, and I am in the Father."
39Once again they tried to arrest him, but he got away
and left them. 40He went beyond the Jordan River near
the place where John was first baptizing and stayed there
awhile. 41And many followed him. "John didn't perform
miraculous signs," they remarked to one another, "but
everything he said about this man has come true." 42And
many who were there believed in Jesus.

11 THE RAISING OF LAZARUS

A man named Lazarus was sick. He lived in Bethany with
his sisters, Mary and Martha. 2This is the Mary who later
poured the expensive perfume on the Lord's feet and
wiped them with her hair.* Her brother, Lazarus, was
sick. 3So the two sisters sent a message to Jesus telling
him, "Lord, your dear friend is very sick."
4But when Jesus heard about it he said, "Lazarus's sickness will not end in death. No, it happened for the glory
of God so that the Son of God will receive glory from
this." 5So although Jesus loved Martha, Mary, and Lazarus, 6he stayed where he was for the next two days.
7Finally, he said to his disciples, "Let's go back to Judea."
8But his disciples objected. "Rabbi," they said, "only a
few days ago the people* in Judea were trying to stone
you. Are you going there again?"
9Jesus replied, "There are twelve hours of daylight
every day. During the day people can walk safely. They
can see because they have the light of this world. 10But at
night there is danger of stumbling because they have no
light." 11Then he said, "Our friend Lazarus has fallen
asleep, but now I will go and wake him up."
12The disciples said, "Lord, if he is sleeping, he will soon

11:2 This incident is recorded in chapter 12. 11:8 Greek *Jewish people;* also in 11:19, 31, 33, 36, 45, 54.

UPS:
- Known as hospitable homeowners
- Friends of Jesus
- Had a strong desire to do everything right (Martha)
- Had a deep concern for people's feelings (Mary)

DOWNS:
- Expected others to agree with her priorities (Martha)
- Overly concerned with details (Martha)
- Tended toward self-pity when her efforts were not recognized (Martha)
- Allowed others to do the work (Mary)
- Tended to respond, rather than prepare (Mary)

STATS:
- Where: Bethany
- Relative: Lazarus (brother)

BOTTOM LINE:
Getting caught up in details can make us forget the main reasons for our actions.
There is a proper time to listen to Jesus and a proper time to work for him.

Mary and Martha's story is told in Luke 10:38-42 and John 11:1–12:8.

MARY & MARTHA Are you the kind of person who loves to have people hang out at your house? Hospitality is an art. Making sure a guest is welcomed and well fed requires creativity, organization, and teamwork. Mary and Martha's ability to accomplish these tasks makes them the best sister hospitality team in the Bible.

For Mary, hospitality meant giving more attention to the guest himself than to his needs. She was more interested in her guest's words than in how clean her house was or what time dinner was served. She let her sister Martha take care of those details. Mary was mainly a "responder." She prepared little, but participated a lot.

Unlike her sister, Martha worried about details. She wished to please, to serve, to do the right thing. Perhaps she was the oldest and felt responsible. So, she tried too hard to have everything perfect. Mary's lack of cooperation bothered Martha so much that she finally asked Jesus to tell Mary to help. Jesus gently pointed out that Mary was actually doing her part.

Each sister had her own lesson to learn. Mary needed to learn that action often is appropriate and necessary. The fact that she later anointed Jesus' feet (John 12:2-8) shows that she probably learned that lesson.

Martha learned that obedient service often goes unnoticed. The last time she appears in the Gospels she is again serving a meal to Jesus and the disciples—this time without complaint (John 12:2).

There may be times when you feel like Mary or Martha. How will you determine the "one thing worth being concerned about" (serving others or spending time with Jesus)?

MARY & MARTHA

RIGHT ON TIME 11:5-7

Although Jesus knew that Lazarus was dying, he didn't rush over to help, as Mary and Martha requested. His delay had a specific purpose—one that Mary and Martha didn't understand. Likewise, God's timing, especially his delays, may make us think he plans to ignore us or that he won't answer the way we want. But he will meet all of our needs (see Phil 4:19) according to his perfect schedule and purpose (see Gal 4:4). Like David, can you say "I waited patiently for the Lord to help me"? If so, like David, you might also say, "He turned to me and heard my cry" (Ps 40:1). ■

get better!" 13They thought Jesus meant Lazarus was simply sleeping, but Jesus meant Lazarus had died.

14So he told them plainly, "Lazarus is dead. 15And for your sakes, I'm glad I wasn't there, for now you will really believe. Come, let's go see him."

16Thomas, nicknamed the Twin,* said to his fellow disciples, "Let's go, too—and die with Jesus."

17When Jesus arrived at Bethany, he was told that Lazarus had already been in his grave for four days. 18Bethany was only a few miles* down the road from Jerusalem, 19and many of the people had come to console Martha and Mary in their loss. 20When Martha got word that Jesus was coming, she went to meet him. But Mary stayed in the house. 21Martha said to Jesus, "Lord, if only you had been here, my brother would not have died. 22But even now I know that God will give you whatever you ask."

23Jesus told her, "Your brother will rise again."

24"Yes," Martha said, "he will rise when everyone else rises, at the last day."

25Jesus told her, "I am the resurrection and the life.* Anyone who believes in me will live, even after dying. 26Everyone who lives in me and believes in me will never ever die. Do you believe this, Martha?"

27"Yes, Lord," she told him. "I have always believed you are the Messiah, the Son of God, the one who has come into the world from God." 28Then she returned to Mary. She called Mary aside from the mourners and told her, "The Teacher is here and wants to see you." 29So Mary immediately went to him.

30Jesus had stayed outside the village, at the place where Martha met him. 31When the people who were at the house consoling Mary saw her leave so hastily, they assumed she was going to Lazarus's grave to weep. So they followed her there. 32When Mary arrived and saw Jesus, she fell at his feet and said, "Lord, if only you had been here, my brother would not have died."

33When Jesus saw her weeping and saw the other people wailing with her, a deep anger welled up within him,* and he was deeply troubled. 34"Where have you put him?" he asked them.

They told him, "Lord, come and see." 35Then Jesus wept. 36The people who were standing nearby said, "See how much he loved him!" 37But some said, "This man healed a blind man. Couldn't he have kept Lazarus from dying?"

38Jesus was still angry as he arrived at the tomb, a cave with a stone rolled across its entrance. 39"Roll the stone aside," Jesus told them.

But Martha, the dead man's sister, protested, "Lord, he has been dead for four days. The smell will be terrible."

40Jesus responded, "Didn't I tell you that you would see God's glory if you believe?" 41So they rolled the stone aside. Then Jesus looked up to heaven and said, "Father, thank you for hearing me. 42You always hear me, but I said it out loud for the sake of all these people standing here, so that they will believe you sent me." 43Then Jesus shouted, "Lazarus, come out!" 44And the dead man came out, his hands and feet bound in graveclothes, his face wrapped in a headcloth. Jesus told them, "Unwrap him and let him go!"

HE CARES 11:33-38

Through this passage, John reveals a God who cares. This contrasts with the Greek concept of God that was popular in John's day—a God with no emotions and no messy involvement with humans. Here we see many of Jesus' emotions—compassion, indignation, sorrow, even frustration. Jesus often expressed deep emotion. Knowing that, are you willing to express your deepest emotions to him? ■

THE PLOT TO KILL JESUS

45Many of the people who were with Mary believed in Jesus when they saw this happen. 46But some went to the Pharisees and told them what Jesus had done. 47Then the leading priests and Pharisees called the high council* together. "What are we going to do?" they asked each other. "This man certainly performs many miraculous signs. 48If we allow him to go on like this, soon everyone will believe in him. Then the Roman army will come and destroy both our Temple* and our nation."

49Caiaphas, who was high priest at that time,* said, "You don't know what you're talking about! 50You don't realize that it's better for you that one man should die for the people than for the whole nation to be destroyed."

51He did not say this on his own; as high priest at that time he was led to prophesy that Jesus would die for the entire nation. 52And not only for that nation, but to bring together and unite all the children of God scattered around the world.

53So from that time on, the Jewish leaders began to plot Jesus' death. 54As a result, Jesus stopped his public ministry among the people and left Jerusalem. He went to a place near the wilderness, to the village of Ephraim, and stayed there with his disciples.

55It was now almost time for the Jewish Passover celebration, and many people from all over the country

11:16 Greek *Thomas, who was called Didymus.* **11:18** Greek *was about 15 stadia* [about 2.8 kilometers]. **11:25** Some manuscripts do not include *and the life.* **11:33** Or *he was angry in his spirit.* **11:47** Greek *the Sanhedrin.* **11:48** Or *our position;* Greek reads *our place.* **11:49** Greek *that year;* also in 11:51.

arrived in Jerusalem several days early so they could go
through the purification ceremony before Passover began. 56They kept looking for Jesus, but as they stood
around in the Temple, they said to each other, "What
do you think? He won't come for Passover, will he?"
57Meanwhile, the leading priests and Pharisees had
publicly ordered that anyone seeing Jesus must report it immediately so they could arrest him.

12

JESUS ANOINTED AT BETHANY

Six days before the Passover celebration began, Jesus arrived in Bethany, the home of Lazarus—the man he had
raised from the dead. 2A dinner was prepared in Jesus'
honor. Martha served, and Lazarus was among those who
ate* with him. 3Then Mary took a twelve-ounce jar* of
expensive perfume made from essence of nard, and she
anointed Jesus' feet with it, wiping his feet with her hair.
The house was filled with the fragrance.
4But Judas Iscariot, the disciple who would soon betray
him, said, 5"That perfume was worth a year's wages.* It
should have been sold and the money given to the poor."
6Not that he cared for the poor—he was a thief, and since
he was in charge of the disciples' money, he often stole
some for himself.
7Jesus replied, "Leave her alone. She did this in preparation for my burial. 8You will always have the poor
among you, but you will not always have me."
9When all the people* heard of Jesus' arrival, they flocked
to see him and also to see Lazarus, the man Jesus had raised
from the dead. 10Then the leading priests decided to kill Lazarus, too, 11for it was because of him that many of the people
had deserted them* and believed in Jesus.

JESUS' TRIUMPHANT ENTRY

12The next day, the news that Jesus was on the way to Jerusalem swept through the city. A large crowd of Passover visitors 13took palm branches and went down the
road to meet him. They shouted,

"Praise God!*
Blessings on the one who comes in the name
of the LORD!
Hail to the King of Israel!"*

14Jesus found a young donkey and rode on it, fulfilling the
prophecy that said:

15 "Don't be afraid, people of Jerusalem.*
Look, your King is coming,
riding on a donkey's colt."*

16His disciples didn't understand at the time that this
was a fulfillment of prophecy. But after Jesus entered
into his glory, they remembered what had happened

LOOK BACK 12:12-16

Although they traveled with Jesus for three years, the disciples didn't always understand him. After his resurrection, Jesus' words and actions made more sense to the disciples. For example, they later understood how Jesus' entry into Jerusalem on the back of a donkey colt was one of the ways he fulfilled Scripture (see Zech 9:9).

Think back over the events of your life. How has God led you to this point? As you grow older, you probably will look back and see God's involvement even more clearly than you do now. ■

and realized that these things had been written about
him.
17Many in the crowd had seen Jesus call Lazarus from
the tomb, raising him from the dead, and they were telling others* about it. 18That was the reason so many went
out to meet him—because they had heard about this miraculous sign. 19Then the Pharisees said to each other,
"There's nothing we can do. Look, everyone* has gone
after him!"

JESUS PREDICTS HIS DEATH

20Some Greeks who had come to Jerusalem for the Passover celebration 21paid a visit to Philip, who was from
Bethsaida in Galilee. They said, "Sir, we want to meet
Jesus." 22Philip told Andrew about it, and they went together to ask Jesus.
23Jesus replied, "Now the time has come for the Son of
Man* to enter into his glory. 24I tell you the truth, unless a
kernel of wheat is planted in the soil and dies, it remains
alone. But its death will produce many new kernels—a
plentiful harvest of new lives. 25Those who love their life
in this world will lose it. Those who care nothing for their
life in this world will keep it for eternity. 26Anyone who
wants to be my disciple must follow me, because my servants must be where I am. And the Father will honor anyone who serves me.
27"Now my soul is deeply troubled. Should I pray, 'Father, save me from this hour'? But this is the very reason I
came! 28Father, bring glory to your name."
Then a voice spoke from heaven, saying, "I have already brought glory to my name, and I will do so again."
29When the crowd heard the voice, some thought it was
thunder, while others declared an angel had spoken to
him.
30Then Jesus told them, "The voice was for your benefit,
not mine. 31The time for judging this world has come,
when Satan, the ruler of this world, will be cast out. 32And
when I am lifted up from the earth, I will draw everyone to
myself." 33He said this to indicate how he was going to die.
34The crowd responded, "We understood from Scripture* that the Messiah would live forever. How can you

12:2 Or *who reclined.* **12:3** Greek *took 1 litra* [327 grams]. **12:5** Greek *worth 300 denarii.* A denarius was equivalent to a laborer's full day's wage. **12:9** Greek *Jewish people;* also in 12:11. **12:11** Or *had deserted their traditions;* Greek reads *had deserted.* **12:13a** Greek *Hosanna,* an exclamation of praise adapted from a Hebrew expression that means "save now." **12:13b** Ps 118:25-26; Zeph 3:15. **12:15a** Greek *daughter of Zion.* **12:15b** Zech 9:9. **12:17** Greek *were testifying.* **12:19** Greek *the world.* **12:23** "Son of Man" is a title Jesus used for himself. **12:34** Greek *from the law.*

say the Son of Man will die? Just who is this Son of Man,
anyway?"
35Jesus replied, "My light will shine for you just a little
longer. Walk in the light while you can, so the darkness
will not overtake you. Those who walk in the darkness
cannot see where they are going. 36Put your trust in the
light while there is still time; then you will become children of the light."
After saying these things, Jesus went away and was
hidden from them.

THE UNBELIEF OF THE PEOPLE

37But despite all the miraculous signs Jesus had done,
most of the people still did not believe in him. 38This is
exactly what Isaiah the prophet had predicted:

"LORD, who has believed our message?
To whom has the LORD revealed his
powerful arm?"*

REACH OUT 12:37-38

Although Jesus had performed many miracles, most people still didn't believe in him. Likewise, many today refuse to believe despite all that God does. Have you ever felt discouraged because a friend refused to believe even when you've shared your faith with him or her? You aren't responsible for your friend's lack of faith. After all, you can't make a person believe. Even God doesn't force faith on people. All you can do is reach out in faith and pray that God will reveal himself in a way that leads to belief. ■

39But the people couldn't believe, for as Isaiah also said,

40 "The Lord has blinded their eyes
and hardened their hearts—
so that their eyes cannot see,
and their hearts cannot understand,
and they cannot turn to me
and have me heal them."*

41Isaiah was referring to Jesus when he said this, because
he saw the future and spoke of the Messiah's glory.
42Many people did believe in him, however, including
some of the Jewish leaders. But they wouldn't admit it for
fear that the Pharisees would expel them from the synagogue. 43For they loved human praise more than the
praise of God.
44Jesus shouted to the crowds, "If you trust me, you are
trusting not only me, but also God who sent me. 45For
when you see me, you are seeing the one who sent me. 46I
have come as a light to shine in this dark world, so that all
who put their trust in me will no longer remain in the
dark. 47I will not judge those who hear me but don't obey
me, for I have come to save the world and not to judge it.
48But all who reject me and my message will be judged on
the day of judgment by the truth I have spoken. 49I don't
speak on my own authority. The Father who sent me has
commanded me what to say and how to say it. 50And I
know his commands lead to eternal life; so I say whatever
the Father tells me to say."

13 JESUS WASHES HIS DISCIPLES' FEET

Before the Passover celebration, Jesus knew that his hour
had come to leave this world and return to his Father. He
had loved his disciples during his ministry on earth, and
now he loved them to the very end.* 2It was time for supper, and the devil had already prompted Judas,* son of Simon Iscariot, to betray Jesus. 3Jesus knew that the Father
had given him authority over everything and that he had
come from God and would return to God. 4So he got up
from the table, took off his robe, wrapped a towel around
his waist, 5and poured water into a basin. Then he began
to wash the disciples' feet, drying them with the towel he
had around him.
6When Jesus came to Simon Peter, Peter said to him,
"Lord, are you going to wash my feet?"
7Jesus replied, "You don't understand now what I am
doing, but someday you will."
8"No," Peter protested, "you will never ever wash my
feet!"
Jesus replied, "Unless I wash you, you won't belong to
me."
9Simon Peter exclaimed, "Then wash my hands and
head as well, Lord, not just my feet!"
10Jesus replied, "A person who has bathed all over does
not need to wash, except for the feet,* to be entirely
clean. And you disciples are clean, but not all of you."
11For Jesus knew who would betray him. That is what he
meant when he said, "Not all of you are clean."
12After washing their feet, he put on his robe again and
sat down and asked, "Do you understand what I was doing? 13You call me 'Teacher' and 'Lord,' and you are right,
because that's what I am. 14And since I, your Lord and
Teacher, have washed your feet, you ought to wash each
other's feet. 15I have given you an example to follow. Do
as I have done to you. 16I tell you the truth, slaves are not
greater than their master. Nor is the messenger more important than the one who sends the message. 17Now that
you know these things, God will bless you for doing them.

JESUS PREDICTS HIS BETRAYAL

18"I am not saying these things to all of you; I know the
ones I have chosen. But this fulfills the Scripture that
says, 'The one who eats my food has turned against me.'*
19I tell you this beforehand, so that when it happens you
will believe that I AM the Messiah.* 20I tell you the truth,
anyone who welcomes my messenger is welcoming me,
and anyone who welcomes me is welcoming the Father
who sent me."

12:38 Isa 53:1. **12:40** Isa 6:10. **13:1** Or *he showed them the full extent of his love.* **13:2** Or *the devil had already intended for Judas.*
13:10 Some manuscripts do not include *except for the feet.* **13:18** Ps 41:9. **13:19** Or *that the 'I AM' has come;* or *that I am the LORD;* Greek reads *that I am.* See Exod 3:14.

21Now Jesus was deeply troubled,* and he exclaimed,
"I tell you the truth, one of you will betray me!"
22The disciples looked at each other, wondering whom
he could mean. 23The disciple Jesus loved was sitting next
to Jesus at the table.* 24Simon Peter motioned to him to
ask, "Who's he talking about?" 25So that disciple leaned
over to Jesus and asked, "Lord, who is it?"
26Jesus responded, "It is the one to
whom I give the bread I dip in the bowl."
And when he had dipped it, he gave it to
Judas, son of Simon Iscariot. 27When Judas had eaten the bread, Satan entered
into him. Then Jesus told him, "Hurry
and do what you're going to do." 28None
of the others at the table knew what
Jesus meant. 29Since Judas was their
treasurer, some thought Jesus was telling him to go and pay for the food or to
give some money to the poor. 30So Judas
left at once, going out into the night.

> Jesus told him, "I am the way, the truth, and the life. No one can come to the Father except through me."
>
> JOHN 14:6

JESUS PREDICTS PETER'S DENIAL

31As soon as Judas left the room, Jesus
said, "The time has come for the Son of
Man* to enter into his glory, and God will be glorified because of him. 32And since God receives glory because of
the Son,* he will soon give glory to the Son. 33Dear children, I will be with you only a little longer. And as I told
the Jewish leaders, you will search for me, but you can't
come where I am going. 34So now I am giving you a new
commandment: Love each other. Just as I have loved you,
you should love each other. 35Your love for one another
will prove to the world that you are my disciples."

ACTIVE LOVE 13:34-35

Jesus told his disciples to love each other. Real love isn't warm fuzzies—it's an attitude that reveals itself in action. How can we love others as Christ loves us? By helping when it's not convenient, by giving when it hurts, by devoting energy to others' welfare rather than our own without complaining or seeking recognition for what we do. (See 1 Cor 13.) Although showing love isn't always easy, the impact is always noticeable. Is this the kind of love you show? ■

36Simon Peter asked, "Lord, where are you going?"
And Jesus replied, "You can't go with me now, but you
will follow me later."
37"But why can't I come now, Lord?" he asked. "I'm
ready to die for you."
38Jesus answered, "Die for me? I tell you the truth,
Peter—before the rooster crows tomorrow morning,
you will deny three times that you even know me.

14 JESUS, THE WAY TO THE FATHER

"Don't let your hearts be troubled. Trust in God, and trust
also in me. 2There is more than enough room in my Father's home.* If this were not so, would I have told you
that I am going to prepare a place for you?* 3When everything is ready, I will come and get you,
so that you will always be with me
where I am. 4And you know the way to
where I am going."
5"No, we don't know, Lord," Thomas
said. "We have no idea where you are
going, so how can we know the way?"
6Jesus told him, "I am the way, the
truth, and the life. No one can come to
the Father except through me. 7If you
had really known me, you would know
who my Father is.* From now on, you
do know him and have seen him!"
8Philip said, "Lord, show us the Father, and we will be satisfied."
9Jesus replied, "Have I been with you
all this time, Philip, and yet you still
don't know who I am? Anyone who has
seen me has seen the Father! So why are you asking me to
show him to you? 10Don't you believe that I am in the Father and the Father is in me? The words I speak are not
my own, but my Father who lives in me does his work
through me. 11Just believe that I am in the Father and the
Father is in me. Or at least believe because of the work
you have seen me do.
12"I tell you the truth, anyone who believes in me will
do the same works I have done, and even greater works,
because I am going to be with the Father. 13You can ask
for anything in my name, and I will do it, so that the Son
can bring glory to the Father. 14Yes, ask me for anything
in my name, and I will do it!

JESUS PROMISES THE HOLY SPIRIT

15"If you love me, obey* my commandments. 16And I will
ask the Father, and he will give you another Advocate,*
who will never leave you. 17He is the Holy Spirit, who
leads into all truth. The world cannot receive him, because it isn't looking for him and doesn't recognize him.
But you know him, because he lives with you now and
later will be in you.* 18No, I will not abandon you as orphans—I will come to you. 19Soon the world will no longer see me, but you will see me. Since I live, you also will
live. 20When I am raised to life again, you will know that I
am in my Father, and you are in me, and I am in you.
21Those who accept my commandments and obey them
are the ones who love me. And because they love me, my
Father will love them. And I will love them and reveal myself to each of them."

13:21 Greek *was troubled in his spirit.* **13:23** Greek *was reclining on Jesus' bosom.* The "disciple Jesus loved" was probably John. **13:31** "Son of Man" is a title Jesus used for himself. **13:32** Some manuscripts omit *And since God receives glory because of the Son.* **14:2a** Or *There are many rooms in my Father's house.* **14:2b** Or *If this were not so, I would have told you that I am going to prepare a place for you.* Some manuscripts read *If this were not so, I would have told you. I am going to prepare a place for you.* **14:7** Some manuscripts read *If you have really known me, you will know who my Father is.* **14:15** Other manuscripts read *you will obey;* still others read *you should obey.* **14:16** Or *Comforter,* or *Encourager,* or *Counselor.* Greek reads *Paraclete;* also in 14:26. **14:17** Some manuscripts read *and is in you.*

keeping it real

One day I came home from school only to find a note saying that my mother had been rushed to the hospital! I called the hospital and discovered that she had a blood clot in her leg and would have to be hospitalized for a while.

Suddenly our household was thrown into chaos. Nothing seemed normal without Mom. Plus I was worried that the blood clot could lead to something serious.

Through this time, I read the Bible a lot. I memorized John 14:27: "I am leaving you with a gift—peace of mind and heart. And the peace I give is a gift the world cannot give. So don't be troubled or afraid." These words of Jesus' helped me not to freak out. Instead I gave the situation to God and trusted him to see me through it. Every time I started to worry, I repeated this verse to myself and felt calmer. Jesus understood what I was going through. Not only that, he was in control! The more I concentrated on this, the more peace I felt. It was strange to feel so peaceful even when there was plenty I could worry about. But I just kept reminding myself of this verse. It helped me get through that difficult time.

—Zoë

22Judas (not Judas Iscariot, but the other disciple with that name) said to him, "Lord, why are you going to reveal yourself only to us and not to the world at large?"

23Jesus replied, "All who love me will do what I say. My Father will love them, and we will come and make our home with each of them. 24Anyone who doesn't love me will not obey me. And remember, my words are not my own. What I am telling you is from the Father who sent me. 25I am telling you these things now while I am still with you. 26But when the Father sends the Advocate as my representative—that is, the Holy Spirit—he will teach you everything and will remind you of everything I have told you.

ACCURATE ACCOUNTS 14:26

Jesus promised the disciples that the Holy Spirit would help them remember what they had learned from Jesus. This promise underscores the validity of the Gospels, as well as the rest of the New Testament. The disciples were eyewitnesses of Jesus' life and teachings. The Holy Spirit helped them remember Jesus' words without taking away their individual perspective. We can be confident that the Gospels are accurate records of what Jesus taught and did (see also 1 Cor 2:10-16). How thoroughly have you investigated these records? ■

27"I am leaving you with a gift—peace of mind and heart. And the peace I give is a gift the world cannot give. So don't be troubled or afraid. 28Remember what I told you: I am going away, but I will come back to you again. If you really loved me, you would be happy that I am going to the Father, who is greater than I am. 29I have told you these things before they happen so that when they do happen, you will believe.

30"I don't have much more time to talk to you, because the ruler of this world approaches. He has no power over me, 31but I will do what the Father requires of me, so that the world will know that I love the Father. Come, let's be going.

15 JESUS, THE TRUE VINE

"I am the true grapevine, and my Father is the gardener. 2He cuts off every branch of mine that doesn't produce fruit, and he prunes the branches that do bear fruit so they will produce even more. 3You have already been pruned and purified by the message I have given you. 4Remain in me, and I will remain in you. For a branch cannot produce fruit if it is severed from the vine, and you cannot be fruitful unless you remain in me.

5"Yes, I am the vine; you are the branches. Those who remain in me, and I in them, will produce much fruit. For apart from me you can do nothing. 6Anyone who does not remain in me is thrown away like a useless branch and withers. Such branches are gathered into a pile to be burned. 7But if you remain in me and my words remain in you, you may ask for anything you want, and it will be granted! 8When you produce much fruit, you are my true disciples. This brings great glory to my Father.

9"I have loved you even as the Father has loved me. Remain in my love. 10When you obey my commandments, you remain in my love, just as I obey my Father's commandments and remain in his love. 11I have told you these things so that you will be filled with my joy. Yes, your joy will overflow! 12This is my commandment: Love each other in the same way I have loved you. 13There is no greater love than to lay down one's life for one's friends. 14You are my friends if you do what I command. 15I no longer call you slaves, because a master doesn't confide in his slaves. Now you are my friends, since I have told you everything the Father told me. 16You didn't choose me. I chose you. I appointed you to go and produce lasting fruit, so that the Father will give you whatever you ask for, using my name. 17This is my command: Love each other.

THE WORLD'S HATRED

18"If the world hates you, remember that it hated me first. 19The world would love you as one of its own if you belonged to it, but you are no longer part of the world. I chose you to come out of the world, so it hates you. 20Do you remember what I told you? 'A slave is not greater than the master.' Since they persecuted me, naturally they will persecute you. And if they had listened to me, they would listen to you. 21They will do all this to you because of me, for they have rejected the One who sent me. 22They would not be guilty if I had not come and spoken to them. But now they have no excuse for their sin. 23Anyone who hates me also hates my Father. 24If I hadn't done such miraculous signs among them that no one else could do, they would not be guilty. But as it is, they have seen everything I did, yet they still hate me and my Father. 25This fulfills what is written in their Scriptures*: 'They hated me without cause.'

26"But I will send you the Advocate*—the Spirit of truth. He will come to you from the Father and will testify all about me. 27And you must also testify about me because you have been with me from the beginning of my ministry.

16

"I have told you these things so that you won't abandon your faith. 2For you will be expelled from the synagogues, and the time is coming when those who kill you will think they are doing a holy service for God. 3This is because they have never known the Father or me. 4Yes, I'm telling you these things now, so that when they happen, you will remember my warning. I didn't tell you earlier because I was going to be with you for a while longer.

THE WORK OF THE HOLY SPIRIT

5"But now I am going away to the One who sent me, and not one of you is asking where I am going. 6Instead, you grieve because of what I've told you. 7But in fact, it is best for you that I go away, because if I don't, the Advocate* won't come. If I do go away, then I will send him to you. 8And when he comes, he will convict the world of its sin, and of God's righteousness, and of the coming judgment. 9The world's sin is that it refuses to believe in me. 10Righteousness is available because I go to the Father, and you will see me no more. 11Judgment will come because the ruler of this world has already been judged.

12"There is so much more I want to tell you, but you can't bear it now. 13When the Spirit of truth comes, he will guide you into all truth. He will not speak on his own but will tell you what he has heard. He will tell you about the future. 14He will bring me glory by telling you whatever he receives from me. 15All that belongs to the Father is mine; this is why I said, 'The Spirit will tell you whatever he receives from me.'

SADNESS WILL BE TURNED TO JOY

16"In a little while you won't see me anymore. But a little while after that, you will see me again."

LAST-MINUTE WARNINGS 16:1-16

In his last moments with his disciples, Jesus (1) warned them about further persecution, (2) told them where he was going, when he was leaving, and why, and (3) assured them they wouldn't be left alone—the Holy Spirit would come to stay with them. Although Jesus knew what lay ahead, he didn't want their faith shaken or destroyed. Likewise, God wants you to know that you aren't alone in the world. You have the Holy Spirit to comfort you, teach you truth, and help you. ■

17Some of the disciples asked each other, "What does he mean when he says, 'In a little while you won't see me, but then you will see me,' and 'I am going to the Father'? 18And what does he mean by 'a little while'? We don't understand."

19Jesus realized they wanted to ask him about it, so he said, "Are you asking yourselves what I meant? I said in a little while you won't see me, but a little while after that you will see me again. 20I tell you the truth, you will weep and mourn over what is going to happen to me, but the world will rejoice. You will grieve, but your grief will suddenly turn to wonderful joy. 21It will be like a woman suffering the pains of labor. When her child is born, her anguish gives way to joy because she has brought a new baby into the world. 22So you have sorrow now, but I will see you again; then you will rejoice, and no one can rob you of that joy. 23At that time you won't need to ask me for anything. I tell you the truth, you will ask the Father directly, and he will grant your request because you use my name. 24You haven't done this before. Ask, using my name, and you will receive, and you will have abundant joy.

25"I have spoken of these matters in figures of speech, but soon I will stop speaking figuratively and will tell you plainly all about the Father. 26Then you will ask in my name. I'm not saying I will ask the Father on your behalf, 27for the Father himself loves you dearly because you love me and believe that I came from God.* 28Yes, I came from the Father into the world, and now I will leave the world and return to the Father."

29Then his disciples said, "At last you are speaking plainly and not figuratively. 30Now we understand that

15:25 Greek *in their law.* Pss 35:19; 69:4. **15:26** Or *Comforter,* or *Encourager,* or *Counselor.* Greek reads *Paraclete.* **16:7** Or *Comforter,* or *Encourager,* or *Counselor.* Greek reads *Paraclete.* **16:27** Some manuscripts read *from the Father.*

you know everything, and there's no need to question you. From this we believe that you came from God."

31Jesus asked, "Do you finally believe? 32But the time is coming—indeed it's here now—when you will be scattered, each one going his own way, leaving me alone. Yet I am not alone because the Father is with me. 33I have told you all this so that you may have peace in me. Here on earth you will have many trials and sorrows. But take heart, because I have overcome the world."

17 THE PRAYER OF JESUS

After saying all these things, Jesus looked up to heaven and said, "Father, the hour has come. Glorify your Son so he can give glory back to you. 2For you have given him authority over everyone. He gives eternal life to each one you have given him. 3And this is the way to have eternal life—to know you, the only true God, and Jesus Christ, the one you sent to earth. 4I brought glory to you here on earth by completing the work you gave me to do. 5Now, Father, bring me into the glory we shared before the world began.

6"I have revealed you* to the ones you gave me from this world. They were always yours. You gave them to me, and they have kept your word. 7Now they know that everything I have is a gift from you, 8for I have passed on to them the message you gave me. They accepted it and know that I came from you, and they believe you sent me.

9"My prayer is not for the world, but for those you have given me, because they belong to you. 10All who are mine belong to you, and you have given them to me, so they bring me glory. 11Now I am departing from the world; they are staying in this world, but I am coming to you. Holy Father, you have given me your name;* now protect them by the power of your name so that they will be united just as we are. 12During my time here, I protected them by the power of the name you gave me.* I guarded them so that not one was lost, except the one headed for destruction, as the Scriptures foretold.

13"Now I am coming to you. I told them many things while I was with them in this world so they would be filled with my joy. 14I have given them your word. And the world hates them because they do not belong to the world, just as I do not belong to the world. 15I'm not asking you to take them out of the world, but to keep them safe from the evil one. 16They do not belong to this world any more than I do. 17Make them holy by your truth; teach them your word, which is truth. 18Just as you sent me into the world, I am sending them into the world. 19And I give myself as a holy sacrifice for them so they can be made holy by your truth.

20"I am praying not only for these disciples but also for all who will ever believe in me through their message. 21I pray that they will all be one, just as you and I are one—as you are in me, Father, and I am in you. And may they be in us so that the world will believe you sent me.

22"I have given them the glory you gave me, so they may

THE WORLD: *IN* IT BUT NOT *OF* IT 17:17-18

Jesus didn't ask God to take believers *out* of the world (17:18), but instead to use them *in* the world. In the same way, we're called to be salt and light (Matt 5:13-16)—to reveal the light of Jesus to a dark world. Yet some of us, if we're honest, would say that we have no trouble blending into the world. In fact, we blend in so well, no one can distinguish our actions from those of non-Christians! If so, perhaps we could make Jesus' prayer ours: "Make [us] holy by your truth; teach [us] your word, which is truth" (17:17). ■

be one as we are one. 23I am in them and you are in me. May they experience such perfect unity that the world will know that you sent me and that you love them as much as you love me. 24Father, I want these whom you have given me to be with me where I am. Then they can see all the glory you gave me because you loved me even before the world began!

25"O righteous Father, the world doesn't know you, but I do; and these disciples know you sent me. 26I have revealed you to them, and I will continue to do so. Then your love for me will be in them, and I will be in them."

18 JESUS IS BETRAYED AND ARRESTED

After saying these things, Jesus crossed the Kidron Valley with his disciples and entered a grove of olive trees. 2Judas, the betrayer, knew this place, because Jesus had often gone there with his disciples. 3The leading priests and Pharisees had given Judas a contingent of Roman soldiers and Temple guards to accompany him. Now with blazing torches, lanterns, and weapons, they arrived at the olive grove.

4Jesus fully realized all that was going to happen to him, so he stepped forward to meet them. "Who are you looking for?" he asked.

5"Jesus the Nazarene,"* they replied.

"I AM he,"* Jesus said. (Judas, who betrayed him, was standing with them.) 6As Jesus said "I AM he," they all drew back and fell to the ground! 7Once more he asked them, "Who are you looking for?"

And again they replied, "Jesus the Nazarene."

8"I told you that I AM he," Jesus said. "And since I am the one you want, let these others go." 9He did this to fulfill his own statement: "I did not lose a single one of those you have given me."*

10Then Simon Peter drew a sword and slashed off the right ear of Malchus, the high priest's slave. 11But Jesus said to Peter, "Put your sword back into its sheath. Shall I not drink from the cup of suffering the Father has given me?"

JESUS AT THE HIGH PRIEST'S HOUSE

12So the soldiers, their commanding officer, and the Temple guards arrested Jesus and tied him up. 13First they took

17:6 Greek *have revealed your name;* also in 17:26. **17:11** Some manuscripts read *you have given me these [disciples].* **17:12** Some manuscripts read *I protected those you gave me, by the power of your name.* **18:5a** Or *Jesus of Nazareth;* also in 18:7. **18:5b** Or *"The 'I AM' is here"*; or *"I am the LORD"*; Greek reads *I am;* also in 18:6, 8. See Exod 3:14. **18:9** See John 6:39 and 17:12.

him to Annas, the father-in-law of Caiaphas, the high priest at that time.* 14Caiaphas was the one who had told the other Jewish leaders, "It's better that one man should die for the people."

PETER'S FIRST DENIAL

15Simon Peter followed Jesus, as did another of the disciples. That other disciple was acquainted with the high priest, so he was allowed to enter the high priest's courtyard with Jesus. 16Peter had to stay outside the gate. Then the disciple who knew the high priest spoke to the woman watching at the gate, and she let Peter in. 17The woman asked Peter, "You're not one of that man's disciples, are you?"

"No," he said, "I am not."

18Because it was cold, the household servants and the guards had made a charcoal fire. They stood around it, warming themselves, and Peter stood with them, warming himself.

THE HIGH PRIEST QUESTIONS JESUS

19Inside, the high priest began asking Jesus about his followers and what he had been teaching them. 20Jesus replied, "Everyone knows what I teach. I have preached regularly in the synagogues and the Temple, where the people* gather. I have not spoken in secret. 21Why are you asking me this question? Ask those who heard me. They know what I said."

22Then one of the Temple guards standing nearby slapped Jesus across the face. "Is that the way to answer the high priest?" he demanded.

23Jesus replied, "If I said anything wrong, you must prove it. But if I'm speaking the truth, why are you beating me?"

24Then Annas bound Jesus and sent him to Caiaphas, the high priest.

PETER'S SECOND AND THIRD DENIALS

25Meanwhile, as Simon Peter was standing by the fire warming himself, they asked him again, "You're not one of his disciples, are you?"

He denied it, saying, "No, I am not."

26But one of the household slaves of the high priest, a relative of the man whose ear Peter had cut off, asked, "Didn't I see you out there in the olive grove with Jesus?" 27Again Peter denied it. And immediately a rooster crowed.

JESUS' TRIAL BEFORE PILATE

28Jesus' trial before Caiaphas ended in the early hours of the morning. Then he was taken to the headquarters of the Roman governor.* His accusers didn't go inside because it would defile them, and they wouldn't be allowed to celebrate the Passover. 29So Pilate, the governor, went out to them and asked, "What is your charge against this man?"

30"We wouldn't have handed him over to you if he weren't a criminal!" they retorted.

31"Then take him away and judge him by your own law," Pilate told them.

"Only the Romans are permitted to execute someone," the Jewish leaders replied. 32(This fulfilled Jesus' prediction about the way he would die.*)

33Then Pilate went back into his headquarters and called for Jesus to be brought to him. "Are you the king of the Jews?" he asked him.

34Jesus replied, "Is this your own question, or did others tell you about me?"

35"Am I a Jew?" Pilate retorted. "Your own people and their leading priests brought you to me for trial. Why? What have you done?"

36Jesus answered, "My Kingdom is not an earthly kingdom. If it were, my followers would fight to keep me from being handed over to the Jewish leaders. But my Kingdom is not of this world."

37Pilate said, "So you are a king?"

Jesus responded, "You say I am a king. Actually, I was born and came into the world to testify to the truth. All who love the truth recognize that what I say is true."

38"What is truth?" Pilate asked. Then he went out again to the people and told them, "He is not guilty of any crime. 39But you have a custom of asking me to release one prisoner each year at Passover. Would you like me to release this 'King of the Jews'?"

40But they shouted back, "No! Not this man. We want Barabbas!" (Barabbas was a revolutionary.)

19

JESUS SENTENCED TO DEATH

Then Pilate had Jesus flogged with a lead-tipped whip. 2The soldiers wove a crown of thorns and put it on his head, and they put a purple robe on him. 3"Hail! King of the Jews!" they mocked, as they slapped him across the face.

4Pilate went outside again and said to the people, "I am going to bring him out to you now, but understand clearly that I find him not guilty." 5Then Jesus came out wearing the crown of thorns and the purple robe. And Pilate said, "Look, here is the man!"

6When they saw him, the leading priests and Temple guards began shouting, "Crucify him! Crucify him!"

"Take him yourselves and crucify him," Pilate said. "I find him not guilty."

7The Jewish leaders replied, "By our law he ought to die because he called himself the Son of God."

8When Pilate heard this, he was more frightened than ever. 9He took Jesus back into the headquarters* again and asked him, "Where are you from?" But Jesus gave no answer. 10"Why don't you talk to me?" Pilate demanded. "Don't you realize that I have the power to release you or crucify you?"

11Then Jesus said, "You would have no power over me at all unless it were given to you from above. So the one who handed me over to you has the greater sin."

12Then Pilate tried to release him, but the Jewish leaders

18:13 Greek *that year.* **18:20** Greek *Jewish people;* also in 18:38. **18:28** Greek *to the Praetorium;* also in 18:33. **18:32** See John 12:32-33. **19:9** Greek *the Praetorium.*

shouted, "If you release this man, you are no 'friend of
Caesar.'* Anyone who declares himself a king is a rebel
against Caesar."
13When they said this, Pilate brought Jesus out to them
again. Then Pilate sat down on the judgment seat on the
platform that is called the Stone Pavement (in Hebrew,
Gabbatha). 14It was now about noon on the day of preparation for the Passover. And Pilate said to the people,*
"Look, here is your king!"
15"Away with him," they yelled. "Away with him! Crucify him!"
"What? Crucify your king?" Pilate asked.
"We have no king but Caesar," the leading priests
shouted back.
16Then Pilate turned Jesus over to them to be crucified.

THE CRUCIFIXION

So they took Jesus away. 17Carrying the cross by himself,
he went to the place called Place of the Skull (in Hebrew,
Golgotha). 18There they nailed him to the cross. Two others were crucified with him, one on either side, with Jesus
between them. 19And Pilate posted a sign over him that
read, "Jesus of Nazareth,* the King of the Jews." 20The
place where Jesus was crucified was near the city, and the
sign was written in Hebrew, Latin, and Greek, so that many
people could read it.
21Then the leading priests objected and said to Pilate,
"Change it from 'The King of the Jews' to 'He said, I am
King of the Jews.'"
22Pilate replied, "No, what I have written, I have written."
23When the soldiers had crucified Jesus, they divided
his clothes among the four of them. They also took his
robe, but it was seamless, woven in one piece from top to
bottom. 24So they said, "Rather than tearing it apart, let's
throw dice* for it." This fulfilled the Scripture that says,
"They divided my garments among themselves and
threw dice for my clothing."* So that is what they did.

FAMILY 19:25-27

Even while dying on the cross, Jesus was concerned about his mother. He instructed John to take care of Mary. What do you do to show your love for your family? ■

25Standing near the cross were Jesus' mother, and his
mother's sister, Mary (the wife of Clopas), and Mary Magdalene. 26When Jesus saw his mother standing there beside the disciple he loved, he said to her, "Dear woman,
here is your son." 27And he said to this disciple, "Here is
your mother." And from then on this disciple took her
into his home.

THE DEATH OF JESUS

28Jesus knew that his mission was now finished, and to
fulfill Scripture he said, "I am thirsty."* 29A jar of sour
wine was sitting there, so they soaked a sponge in it, put it
on a hyssop branch, and held it up to his lips. 30When
Jesus had tasted it, he said, "It is finished!" Then he
bowed his head and released his spirit.
31It was the day of preparation, and the Jewish leaders
didn't want the bodies hanging there the next day, which
was the Sabbath (and a very special Sabbath, because it
was the Passover). So they asked Pilate to hasten their
deaths by ordering that their legs be broken. Then their
bodies could be taken down. 32So the soldiers came and
broke the legs of the two men crucified with Jesus. 33But
when they came to Jesus, they saw that he was already
dead, so they didn't break his legs. 34One of the soldiers,
however, pierced his side with a spear, and immediately
blood and water flowed out. 35(This report is from an eyewitness giving an accurate account. He speaks the truth
so that you also can believe.*) 36These things happened in
fulfillment of the Scriptures that say, "Not one of his
bones will be broken,"* 37and "They will look on the one
they pierced."*

THE BURIAL OF JESUS

38Afterward Joseph of Arimathea, who had been a secret
disciple of Jesus (because he feared the Jewish leaders),
asked Pilate for permission to take down Jesus' body.
When Pilate gave permission, Joseph came and took the
body away. 39With him came Nicodemus, the man who
had come to Jesus at night. He brought seventy-five
pounds* of perfumed ointment made from myrrh and
aloes. 40Following Jewish burial custom, they wrapped
Jesus' body with the spices in long sheets of linen cloth.
41The place of crucifixion was near a garden, where there
was a new tomb, never used before. 42And so, because it
was the day of preparation for the Jewish Passover* and
since the tomb was close at hand, they laid Jesus there.

20 THE RESURRECTION

Early on Sunday morning,* while it was still dark, Mary
Magdalene came to the tomb and found that the stone
had been rolled away from the entrance. 2She ran and
found Simon Peter and the other disciple, the one whom
Jesus loved. She said, "They have taken the Lord's body out
of the tomb, and we don't know where they have put him!"
3Peter and the other disciple started out for the tomb.
4They were both running, but the other disciple outran
Peter and reached the tomb first. 5He stooped and looked
in and saw the linen wrappings lying there, but he didn't
go in. 6Then Simon Peter arrived and went inside. He also
noticed the linen wrappings lying there, 7while the cloth
that had covered Jesus' head was folded up and lying
apart from the other wrappings. 8Then the disciple who
had reached the tomb first also went in, and he saw and
believed—9for until then they still hadn't understood the
Scriptures that said Jesus must rise from the dead.
10Then they went home.

19:12 "Friend of Caesar" is a technical term that refers to an ally of the emperor. **19:14** Greek *Jewish people;* also in 19:20. **19:19** Or *Jesus the Nazarene.* **19:24a** Greek *cast lots.* **19:24b** Ps 22:18. **19:28** See Pss 22:15; 69:21. **19:35** Some manuscripts read *can continue to believe.* **19:36** Exod 12:46; Num 9:12; Ps 34:20. **19:37** Zech 12:10. **19:39** Greek *100 litras* [32.7 kilograms]. **19:42** Greek *because of the Jewish day of preparation.* **20:1** Greek *On the first day of the week.*

Jesus' Appearances after His Resurrection

The truth of Christianity rests heavily on the Resurrection. If Jesus rose from the grave, who saw him? How trustworthy were the witnesses? Those who claimed to have seen the risen Jesus went on to turn the world upside down. Most of them also died for being followers of Christ. People rarely die for halfhearted belief. There are people who saw Jesus risen from the grave:

Mary Magdalene	Mark 16:9-11; John 20:10-18
The other women at the tomb	Matthew 28:8-10
Peter in Jerusalem	Luke 24:34; 1 Corinthians 15:5
The two travelers on the road	Mark 16:12-13; Luke 24:13-35
Ten disciples behind closed doors	Mark 16:14; Luke 24:36-43; John 20:19-25
All the disciples, with Thomas (excluding Judas Iscariot)	John 20:26-31; 1 Corinthians 15:5
Seven disciples while fishing	John 21:1-14
Eleven disciples on the mountain	Matthew 28:16-20
A crowd of more than five hundred	1 Corinthians 15:6
Jesus' brother James	1 Corinthians 15:7
Those who watched Jesus ascend into heaven	Luke 24:44-49; Acts 1:3-8

JESUS APPEARS TO MARY MAGDALENE

11Mary was standing outside the tomb crying, and as she
wept, she stooped and looked in. 12She saw two white-
robed angels, one sitting at the head and the other at the foot of the place where the body of Jesus had been lying.
13"Dear woman, why are you crying?" the angels asked her.

"Because they have taken away my Lord," she replied, "and I don't know where they have put him."

14She turned to leave and saw someone standing there.
It was Jesus, but she didn't recognize him. 15"Dear
woman, why are you crying?" Jesus asked her. "Who are you looking for?"

She thought he was the gardener. "Sir," she said, "if you have taken him away, tell me where you have put him, and I will go and get him."

16"Mary!" Jesus said.

She turned to him and cried out, "Rabboni!" (which is Hebrew for "Teacher").

17"Don't cling to me," Jesus said, "for I haven't yet ascended to the Father. But go find my brothers and tell them, 'I am ascending to my Father and your Father, to my God and your God.'"

18Mary Magdalene found the disciples and told them, "I have seen the Lord!" Then she gave them his message.

JESUS APPEARS TO HIS DISCIPLES

19That Sunday evening* the disciples were meeting behind locked doors because they were afraid of the Jewish leaders. Suddenly, Jesus was standing there among them! "Peace be with you," he said. 20As he spoke, he showed
them the wounds in his hands and his side. They were
filled with joy when they saw the Lord! 21Again he said,
"Peace be with you. As the Father has sent me, so I am sending you." 22Then he breathed on them and said, "Receive the Holy Spirit. 23If you forgive anyone's sins, they
are forgiven. If you do not forgive them, they are not forgiven."

PROOF 20:29-31

Some people think they would believe in Jesus if they could see something miraculous. But Jesus says we're blessed if we believe without seeing. We have all the proof we need in the words of the Bible and the testimony of believers. How has this proof influenced your faith? ■

JESUS APPEARS TO THOMAS

24One of the twelve disciples, Thomas (nicknamed the Twin),* was not with the others when Jesus came. 25They
told him, "We have seen the Lord!"

But he replied, "I won't believe it unless I see the nail wounds in his hands, put my fingers into them, and place my hand into the wound in his side."

26Eight days later the disciples were together again, and this time Thomas was with them. The doors were locked; but suddenly, as before, Jesus was standing among them. "Peace be with you," he said. 27Then he said

20:19 Greek *In the evening of that day, the first day of the week.* **20:24** Greek *Thomas, who was called Didymus.*

to Thomas, "Put your finger here, and look at my hands.
Put your hand into the wound in my side. Don't be faithless any longer. Believe!"
28"My Lord and my God!" Thomas exclaimed.
29Then Jesus told him, "You believe because you have
seen me. Blessed are those who believe without seeing
me."

PURPOSE OF THE BOOK

30The disciples saw Jesus do many other miraculous
signs in addition to the ones recorded in this book.
31But these are written so that you may continue to believe* that Jesus is the Messiah, the Son of God, and that
by believing in him you will have life by the power of his
name.

21 EPILOGUE: JESUS APPEARS TO SEVEN DISCIPLES

Later, Jesus appeared again to the disciples beside the Sea
of Galilee.* This is how it happened. 2Several of the disciples were there—Simon Peter, Thomas (nicknamed the
Twin),* Nathanael from Cana in Galilee, the sons of Zebedee, and two other disciples.
3Simon Peter said, "I'm going fishing."
"We'll come, too," they all said. So they went out in the
boat, but they caught nothing all night.
4At dawn Jesus was standing on the beach, but the disciples couldn't see who he was. 5He called out, "Fellows,*
have you caught any fish?"
"No," they replied.

20:31 Some manuscripts read *that you may believe.* **21:1** Greek *Sea of Tiberias,* another name for the Sea of Galilee. **21:2** Greek *Thomas, who was called Didymus.* **21:5** Greek *Children.*

THOMAS

UPS:

- One of Jesus' 12 disciples
- Had a great capacity for intensity, both in doubt and belief
- Was a loyal and honest man

DOWNS:

- Along with the others, abandoned Jesus after his arrest
- Refused to believe the others' claims to have seen the risen Jesus
- Struggled with a pessimistic outlook

STATS:

- Where: Galilee, Judea, Samaria
- Occupation: Disciple of Jesus
- Contemporaries: Jesus, other disciples, Herod, Pilate

BOTTOM LINE:

Jesus doesn't condemn doubts that are honest and directed toward belief.

Doubting out loud is better than disbelieving in silence.

Thomas's story is told in the Gospels. He is also mentioned in Acts 1:13.

THOMAS What are you known for? Being cool? Being a troublemaker? Inspiring others? Throughout the ages, Thomas mainly has been known for doubting the resurrection of Jesus. Yet Thomas expressed doubt because he wanted to know the truth.

Although the Bible doesn't tell us much about Thomas, the brief glimpses of his life are consistent. He tried hard to be faithful to what he knew, even though faithfulness seemed costly. For example, when it was clear to everyone that Jesus' life would be in danger if he went to Jerusalem, only Thomas put into words what the other disciples probably felt: "Let's go, too—and die with Jesus" (John 11:16). But even though he expressed this fear, he didn't hesitate to follow Jesus.

We don't know why Thomas was missing the first time Jesus appeared to the disciples after the Resurrection (see John 20:19-24). Whatever the reason, Thomas was reluctant to believe that Jesus was alive (20:25). Even 10 friends couldn't change his mind! But Jesus' appearance soon changed his doubts to belief (20:28-29).

We can doubt without living a doubting way of life. Doubts help us clarify what we believe. They also encourage us to ask good questions, seek answers, and push for decisions. But doubt was never meant to be a permanent condition. Doubt is one foot lifted, poised to step forward or back. There is no motion until the foot comes down.

When you experience doubt, take encouragement from Thomas. He didn't remain doubtful. Instead, he allowed Jesus to help him toward belief. Take encouragement also from the fact that countless other followers of Christ have struggled with doubts. The answers God gave them may be of great help. Don't settle into doubt—move beyond it to decision and belief.

6Then he said, "Throw out your net on the right-hand side of the boat, and you'll get some!" So they did, and they couldn't haul in the net because there were so many fish in it.

7Then the disciple Jesus loved said to Peter, "It's the Lord!" When Simon Peter heard that it was the Lord, he put on his tunic (for he had stripped for work), jumped into the water, and headed to shore. 8The others stayed with the boat and pulled the loaded net to the shore, for they were only about a hundred yards* from shore. 9When they got there, they found breakfast waiting for them—fish cooking over a charcoal fire, and some bread.

10"Bring some of the fish you've just caught," Jesus said. 11So Simon Peter went aboard and dragged the net to the shore. There were 153 large fish, and yet the net hadn't torn.

12"Now come and have some breakfast!" Jesus said. None of the disciples dared to ask him, "Who are you?" They knew it was the Lord. 13Then Jesus served them the bread and the fish. 14This was the third time Jesus had appeared to his disciples since he had been raised from the dead.

15After breakfast Jesus asked Simon Peter, "Simon son of John, do you love me more than these?*"

"Yes, Lord," Peter replied, "you know I love you."

"Then feed my lambs," Jesus told him.

16Jesus repeated the question: "Simon son of John, do you love me?"

"Yes, Lord," Peter said, "you know I love you."

"Then take care of my sheep," Jesus said.

17A third time he asked him, "Simon son of John, do you love me?"

Peter was hurt that Jesus asked the question a third time. He said, "Lord, you know everything. You know that I love you."

Jesus said, "Then feed my sheep.

18"I tell you the truth, when you were young, you were able to do as you liked; you dressed yourself and went wherever you wanted to go. But when you are old, you will stretch out your hands, and others* will dress you and take you where you don't want to go." 19Jesus said this to let him know by what kind of death he would glorify God. Then Jesus told him, "Follow me."

20Peter turned around and saw behind them the disciple Jesus loved—the one who had leaned over to Jesus during supper and asked, "Lord, who will betray you?" 21Peter asked Jesus, "What about him, Lord?"

22Jesus replied, "If I want him to remain alive until I return, what is that to you? As for you, follow me." 23So the rumor spread among the community of believers* that this disciple wouldn't die. But that isn't what Jesus said at all. He only said, "If I want him to remain alive until I return, what is that to you?"

24This disciple is the one who testifies to these events and has recorded them here. And we know that his account of these things is accurate.

25Jesus also did many other things. If they were all written down, I suppose the whole world could not contain the books that would be written.

21:8 Greek *200 cubits* [90 meters]. **21:15** Or *more than these others do?* **21:18** Some manuscripts read *and another one.* **21:23** Greek *the brothers.*

After I became a Christian I was told to start reading the Bible. But where do I start?

Unfortunately, at no place in the Bible does it say, "Start here," and then, "Read this next." Consequently, we need help. Consider these suggestions:

Check out the Gospels to get to know Jesus. John tells us that he wrote his book "so that you may continue to believe that Jesus is the Messiah, the Son of God, and that by believing in him you will have life by the power of his name" (John 20:31).

Next, start reading through some of the letters that Paul, Peter, and John wrote. (Paul wrote most of the letters in the New Testament.)

Try Proverbs next. You can read one chapter a day and finish the book in a month.

After this, read books like Genesis, Exodus, Daniel, and Jonah. They offer stories of real people whose problems weren't all that different from yours.

Many people read through the Bible in a year. By reading the whole Bible, you can see how God's plan came about over the centuries.

ASSEMBLE NINE very different people:

- The class clown who makes everything funny
- The heir with the expensive cell phone and car
- The "gangsta" wannabes who look with contempt on anyone who's not down with their music
- The brainiac who just built her own computer system
- The big football player who loves to bash quarterbacks
- The student whose "achievements" read like a sleazy novel
- The school druggie who's not exactly headed for a career in molecular biology
- The campus philosopher/political activist who *loves* to argue and *hates* shallow people
- The shy kid who, for whatever reasons, never fits in

Now, give this diverse crowd a simple task to do . . . together. What do you think would happen?

Even if you could get them all in the same room, they'd *never* complete the task—they'd probably produce chaos!

So, how do we explain the first-century church? How did several hundred radically different people accomplish the mammoth project of taking Jesus' story all over the world? How did they handle conflicts? What kept them going?

If you'd like the answers to those questions, dive into the book of Acts.

timeline

A.D. 30
Jesus crucified; Pentecost; church begun

35
Stephen martyred; Paul's conversion

38
Paul returns to Tarsus

43
Barnabas goes to find Paul

44
James martyred; Peter in prison

46–48
Paul's first missionary journey

50
Jerusalem council

50–52
Paul's second missionary journey

53–57
Paul's third missionary journey

54
Nero becomes emperor

57–59
Paul imprisoned in Caesarea

59
Paul's voyage to Rome

62
Paul released from prison

67?
Paul martyred

70
Rome destroys Jerusalem

stats

PURPOSE: To give an accurate account of the birth and growth of the Christian church

AUTHOR: Luke

TO WHOM WRITTEN: Theophilus ("lover of God") and people everywhere

DATE WRITTEN: Between A.D. 63 and 70

SETTING: Acts is the link between Christ's life and the life of the church

KEY PEOPLE: Peter, John, James, Stephen, Philip, Paul, Barnabas, Cornelius, James (Jesus' brother), Timothy, Lydia, Silas, Titus, Apollos, Agabus, Ananias, Felix, Festus, Agrippa, Luke

KEY PLACES: Jerusalem, Samaria, Lydda, Joppa, Antioch in Syria, Cyprus, Antioch in Pisidia, Iconium, Lystra, Derbe, Philippi, Thessalonica, Berea, Athens, Corinth, Ephesus, Caesarea, Malta, Rome

KEY points

CHURCH BEGINNINGS
The community of believers were unified by faith in the risen Christ. Through faith in Jesus and in the power of the Holy Spirit, the church can be a vibrant agent for change in the world.

HOLY SPIRIT
The disciples were empowered by the Holy Spirit, the Counselor sent by Jesus. By faith, any believer can experience the Holy Spirit's power to serve God.

WITNESSING
Peter, John, Philip, Paul, Barnabas, and thousands more boldly told others about their faith in Christ. Their lives encourage us to pass on the truth of Christ to the world.

OPPOSITION
Although the first-century Christians experienced persecution, this opposition was a catalyst for the spread of Christianity. God can work through any obstacle to accomplish his purposes.

KEY PLACES IN ACTS

Modern names and boundaries are shown in gray.

The apostle Paul, whose missionary journeys fill much of this book, traveled tremendous distances as he tirelessly spread the gospel across much of the Roman Empire. His combined trips, by land and ship, total more than 13,000 airline miles, to say nothing of the circuitous land routes he walked and climbed.

- **JUDEA** Jesus ascended to heaven from the Mount of Olives outside Jerusalem, and his followers returned to the city to await the infilling of the Holy Spirit, which occurred at Pentecost. Peter gave a powerful sermon that was heard by Jews from across the empire. The Jerusalem church grew, but Stephen was martyred for his faith by Jewish leaders who did not believe in Jesus (1:1–7:59).
- **SAMARIA** After Stephen's death, persecution of Christians intensified, but it caused the believers to leave Jerusalem and spread the gospel to other cities in the empire. Philip took the gospel into Samaria and even to a man from Ethiopia (8:1-40).
- **SYRIA** Paul began his story as a persecutor of Christians, only to be met by Jesus himself on the road to Damascus. He became a believer, but his new faith caused opposition, so he returned to Tarsus, his home, for safety. Barnabas sought out Paul in Tarsus and brought him to the church in Antioch in Syria, where they worked together. Meanwhile, Peter had received a vision that led him to Caesarea, where he presented the gospel to a Gentile family, who became believers (9:1–12:25).
- **CYPRUS AND GALATIA** Paul and Barnabas were dedicated by the church in Antioch in Syria for God's work of spreading the gospel to other cities. They set off on their first missionary journey through Cyprus and Galatia (13:1–14:28).
- **JERUSALEM** Controversy between Jewish Christians and Gentile Christians over the matter of keeping the law led to a special council, with delegates from the churches in Antioch and Jerusalem meeting in Jerusalem. Together they resolved the conflict, and the news was taken back to Antioch (15:1-35).
- **MACEDONIA** Barnabas traveled to Cyprus while Paul took a second missionary journey. He revisited the churches in Galatia and headed toward Ephesus, but the Holy Spirit said no. He then turned north toward Bithynia and Pontus, but again was told not to go. He then received the "Macedonian call" and followed the Spirit's direction to the cities in Macedonia (15:36–17:14).
- **ACHAIA** Paul traveled from Macedonia to Athens and Corinth in Achaia, then traveled by ship to Ephesus before returning to Caesarea, Jerusalem, and finally back to Antioch (17:15–18:22).
- **EPHESUS** Paul's third missionary journey took him back through Cilicia and Galatia, this time straight to Ephesus in Asia. He visited other cities in Asia before going back to Macedonia and Achaia. He returned to Jerusalem by ship, despite knowing that arrest awaited him there (18:23–23:30).
- **CAESAREA** Paul was arrested in Jerusalem and taken to Antipatris, then on to Caesarea under Roman guard. Paul always took advantage of any opportunity to share the gospel, and he did so before many Gentile leaders. But because Paul appealed to Caesar, he began the long journey to Rome (23:31–26:32).
- **ROME** After storms, layovers in Crete, and a shipwreck on the island of Malta, Paul arrived in Sicily, and finally Italy, where he traveled by land, under guard, to his long-awaited destination, Rome, the capital of the empire (27:1–28:31).

1

THE PROMISE OF THE HOLY SPIRIT

In my first book* I told you, Theophilus, about everything Jesus began to do
and teach 2until the day he was taken
up to heaven after giving his chosen
apostles further instructions through
the Holy Spirit. 3During the forty days
after his crucifixion, he appeared to
the apostles from time to time, and he
proved to them in many ways that he
was actually alive. And he talked to
them about the Kingdom of God.
4Once when he was eating with
them, he commanded them, "Do not
leave Jerusalem until the Father sends
you the gift he promised, as I told you before. 5John baptized with* water, but in just a few days you will be baptized with the Holy Spirit."

> But you will receive power when the Holy Spirit comes upon you. And you will be my witnesses. . . .
>
> ACTS 1:8

PROMISES, PROMISES 1:4

Just before he left the earth, Jesus reminded the disciples of the promise he made to send the Holy Spirit. (See John 14:26.) The repetition of a promise of God was an indicator of the importance of the promise and the seriousness God attached to it. This was Jesus' way of saying, "Hey, this is definitely going to happen." You can check out Acts 2 to see that it did.

The Bible also mentions several promises of Jesus' second coming. (See Matt 24:30-31; 1 Cor 15:23; 1 Thess 4:16-17; Rev 22:20.) Since the promise to send the Holy Spirit was kept, you can count on Jesus to keep this one. So, do you? ■

THE ASCENSION OF JESUS

6So when the apostles were with Jesus, they kept asking
him, "Lord, has the time come for you to free Israel and
restore our kingdom?"
7He replied, "The Father alone has the authority to set
those dates and times, and they are not for you to know.
8But you will receive power when the Holy Spirit comes
upon you. And you will be my witnesses, telling people
about me everywhere—in Jerusalem, throughout Judea,
in Samaria, and to the ends of the earth."
9After saying this, he was taken up into a cloud while
they were watching, and they could no longer see him.
10As they strained to see him rising into heaven, two
white-robed men suddenly stood among them. 11"Men of
Galilee," they said, "why are you standing here staring
into heaven? Jesus has been taken from you into heaven,
but someday he will return from heaven in the same way
you saw him go!"

MATTHIAS REPLACES JUDAS

12Then the apostles returned to Jerusalem from the
Mount of Olives, a distance of half a mile.* 13When they
arrived, they went to the upstairs
room of the house where they were
staying.
Here are the names of those who
were present: Peter, John, James, Andrew, Philip, Thomas, Bartholomew,
Matthew, James (son of Alphaeus), Simon (the Zealot), and Judas (son of
James). 14They all met together and
were constantly united in prayer,
along with Mary the mother of Jesus,
several other women, and the brothers of Jesus.
15During this time, when about
120 believers* were together in one
place, Peter stood up and addressed
them. 16"Brothers," he said, "the Scriptures had to be fulfilled concerning Judas, who guided those who arrested
Jesus. This was predicted long ago by the Holy Spirit,
speaking through King David. 17Judas was one of us and
shared in the ministry with us."
18(Judas had bought a field with the money he received
for his treachery. Falling headfirst there, his body split
open, spilling out all his intestines. 19The news of his
death spread to all the people of Jerusalem, and they gave
the place the Aramaic name *Akeldama,* which means
"Field of Blood.")
20Peter continued, "This was written in the book of
Psalms, where it says, 'Let his home become desolate,
with no one living in it.' It also says, 'Let someone else take
his position.'*
21"So now we must choose a replacement for Judas
from among the men who were with us the entire time
we were traveling with the Lord Jesus—22from the time
he was baptized by John until the day he was taken from
us. Whoever is chosen will join us as a witness of Jesus'
resurrection."

CHOOSE WELL 1:21-22

The apostles had to choose a replacement for Judas Iscariot. They outlined specific criteria for making the choice. When the "finalists" had been chosen, the apostles prayed, asking God to guide the selection process. In that way, they knew they had chosen well. What is your usual way of making decisions? Is the apostles' decision-making process your way to make decisions? ■

23So they nominated two men: Joseph called Barsabbas (also known as Justus) and Matthias. 24Then they all
prayed, "O Lord, you know every heart. Show us which
of these men you have chosen 25as an apostle to replace
Judas in this ministry, for he has deserted us and gone
where he belongs." 26Then they cast lots, and Matthias
was selected to become an apostle with the other
eleven.

1:1 The reference is to the Gospel of Luke. **1:5** Or *in;* also in 1:5b. **1:12** Greek *a Sabbath day's journey.* **1:15** Greek *brothers.* **1:20** Pss 69:25; 109:8.

THE 411 ON THE HOLY SPIRIT

ULTIMATE ISSUES

You may know someone who seems to have three personalities (the real one, the phony one, and the really phony one). But have you ever seen three people who represented one person? Historically, Christians have believed that God exists in three persons: the Father, Son, and Holy Spirit. How this works, no one knows. This is one of the mysteries that the Bible mentions.

If we were to take a poll, we might find that the Holy Spirit is probably the least understood of the three. So just who is the Holy Spirit? What does he do?

- First of all, the New Testament always refers to the Holy Spirit as "he," not "it." The Spirit is personal, not merely a "force" or instrument. He has an intellect, feelings, will, and other personal characteristics.
- Second, the Holy Spirit is not in any way inferior to the Father or the Son. He is equal to them. One of the clearest statements of this reality is found in Matthew 28:19, where Jesus tells the disciples: "Go and make disciples of all the nations, baptizing them in the name of the Father and the Son and the Holy Spirit."
- Third, the Spirit acts in many powerful ways. Here are just a few: he unifies believers and helps them grow and serve others (1 Cor 12:4-11; Eph 4:1-16; 5:22-25); he gives new life (John 3:5-8); he helps us own up to what we've done and to change (John 16:8); he reminds us of the truth of Jesus as the Savior (John 14:26 and 16:13-14); he prays for us (Rom 8:26); he is present in *all* Christians (Rom 8:9-11; 1 Cor 6:19-20). His arrival in Acts 2 completely changed the lives of all of the believers.

Jesus described the Holy Spirit as the "Counselor" (John 15:26). Unlike a high school guidance counselor, the Holy Spirit is with you 24/7. He is your unseen adviser—one who will never steer you wrong.

2

THE HOLY SPIRIT COMES

On the day of Pentecost* all the believers were meeting together in one place. 2Suddenly, there was a sound from heaven like the roaring of a mighty windstorm, and it filled the house where they were sitting. 3Then, what looked like flames or tongues of fire appeared and settled on each of them. 4And everyone present was filled with the Holy Spirit and began speaking in other languages,* as the Holy Spirit gave them this ability.

5At that time there were devout Jews from every nation living in Jerusalem. 6When they heard the loud noise, everyone came running, and they were bewildered to hear their own languages being spoken by the believers.

7They were completely amazed. "How can this be?" they exclaimed. "These people are all from Galilee, 8and yet we hear them speaking in our own native languages! 9Here we are—Parthians, Medes, Elamites, people from Mesopotamia, Judea, Cappadocia, Pontus, the province of Asia, 10Phrygia, Pamphylia, Egypt, and the areas of Libya around Cyrene, visitors from Rome 11(both Jews and converts to Judaism), Cretans, and Arabs. And we all hear these people speaking in our own languages about the wonderful things God has done!" 12They stood there amazed and perplexed. "What can this mean?" they asked each other.

13But others in the crowd ridiculed them, saying, "They're just drunk, that's all!"

PETER PREACHES TO THE CROWD

14Then Peter stepped forward with the eleven other apostles and shouted to the crowd, "Listen carefully, all of you, fellow Jews and residents of Jerusalem! Make no mistake about this. 15These people are not drunk, as some of you are assuming. Nine o'clock in the morning is much too early for that. 16No, what you see was predicted long ago by the prophet Joel:

17 'In the last days,' God says,
'I will pour out my Spirit upon all people.
Your sons and daughters will prophesy.
Your young men will see visions,
and your old men will dream dreams.

2:1 The Festival of Pentecost came 50 days after Passover (when Jesus was crucified). 2:4 Or *in other tongues.*

18 In those days I will pour out my Spirit
even on my servants—men and women alike—
and they will prophesy.
19 And I will cause wonders in the heavens above
and signs on the earth below—
blood and fire and clouds of smoke.
20 The sun will become dark,
and the moon will turn blood red
before that great and glorious day of the
LORD arrives.
21 But everyone who calls on the name of the LORD
will be saved.'*

22"People of Israel, listen! God publicly endorsed
Jesus the Nazarene* by doing powerful miracles, wonders, and signs through him, as you well know. 23But God
knew what would happen, and his prearranged plan was
carried out when Jesus was betrayed. With the help of
lawless Gentiles, you nailed him to a cross and killed
him. 24But God released him from the horrors of death
and raised him back to life, for death could not keep
him in its grip. 25King David said this about him:

'I see that the LORD is always with me.
I will not be shaken, for he is right beside me.
26 No wonder my heart is glad,
and my tongue shouts his praises!
My body rests in hope.
27 For you will not leave my soul among the dead*
or allow your Holy One to rot in the grave.
28 You have shown me the way of life,
and you will fill me with the joy of your presence.'*

29"Dear brothers, think about this! You can be sure that
the patriarch David wasn't referring to himself, for he
died and was buried, and his tomb is still here among us.
30But he was a prophet, and he knew God had promised
with an oath that one of David's own descendants would
sit on his throne. 31David was looking into the future and
speaking of the Messiah's resurrection. He was saying
that God would not leave him among the dead or allow
his body to rot in the grave.
32"God raised Jesus from the dead, and we are all witnesses of this. 33Now he is exalted to the place of highest
honor in heaven, at God's right hand. And the Father, as
he had promised, gave him the Holy Spirit to pour out
upon us, just as you see and hear today. 34For David himself never ascended into heaven, yet he said,

'The LORD said to my Lord,
"Sit in the place of honor at my right hand
35 until I humble your enemies,
making them a footstool under your feet."'*

36"So let everyone in Israel know for certain that God
has made this Jesus, whom you crucified, to be both Lord
and Messiah!"

37Peter's words pierced their hearts, and they said to
him and to the other apostles, "Brothers, what should we
do?"
38Peter replied, "Each of you must repent of your sins
and turn to God, and be baptized in the name of Jesus
Christ for the forgiveness of your sins. Then you will receive the gift of the Holy Spirit. 39This promise is to you,
and to your children, and even to the Gentiles*—all who
have been called by the Lord our God." 40Then Peter continued preaching for a long time, strongly urging all his
listeners, "Save yourselves from this crooked
generation!"
41Those who believed what Peter said were baptized
and added to the church that day—about 3,000 in all.

THE BELIEVERS FORM A COMMUNITY

42All the believers devoted themselves to the apostles'
teaching, and to fellowship, and to sharing in meals (including the Lord's Supper*), and to prayer.
43A deep sense of awe came over them all, and the
apostles performed many miraculous signs and wonders. 44And all the believers met together in one place
and shared everything they had. 45They sold their property and possessions and shared the money with those in
need. 46They worshiped together at the Temple each day,
met in homes for the Lord's Supper, and shared their
meals with great joy and generosity*—47all the while
praising God and enjoying the goodwill of all the people.
And each day the Lord added to their fellowship those
who were being saved.

WE'RE IN THIS TOGETHER 2:44-47

Recognizing the other believers as brothers and sisters in the family of God, the Christians in Jerusalem shared all they had so that all could benefit from God's blessings. Sometimes having lots of money and possessions can tempt people to isolate themselves from others, each enjoying his or her own little piece of the world. But as part of God's spiritual family, we have a responsibility to help one another in every way possible. God's family works best when its members work together. ■

3 PETER HEALS A CRIPPLED BEGGAR

Peter and John went to the Temple one afternoon to take
part in the three o'clock prayer service. 2As they approached the Temple, a man lame from birth was being
carried in. Each day he was put beside the Temple gate,
the one called the Beautiful Gate, so he could beg from
the people going into the Temple. 3When he saw Peter
and John about to enter, he asked them for some money.
4Peter and John looked at him intently, and Peter said,
"Look at us!" 5The lame man looked at them eagerly, expecting some money. 6But Peter said, "I don't have any

2:17-21 Joel 2:28-32. **2:22** Or *Jesus of Nazareth.* **2:27** Greek *in Hades;* also in 2:31. **2:25-28** Ps 16:8-11 (Greek version). **2:34-35** Ps 110:1. **2:39** Or *and to people far in the future;* Greek reads *and to those far away.* **2:42** Greek *the breaking of bread;* also in 2:46. **2:46** Or *and sincere hearts.*

Unsung Heroes in Acts

When we think of the success of the early church, we often think of the work of the apostles. But the church could have died if it hadn't been for the "unsung" heroes, the men and women who through some small but committed act moved the church forward.

Hero	*Reference*	*Heroic Action*
LAME BEGGAR	3:9-10	After his healing, he praised God. With the crowds gathering to see what happened, Peter used the opportunity to tell many about Jesus.
FIVE DEACONS	6:2-5	Everyone knows Stephen, and many people know Philip, but there were five other men chosen to be deacons. They not only laid the foundation for service in the church, but their hard work gave the apostles more time to preach the gospel.
ANANIAS	9:10-19	He had the responsibility of being the first to demonstrate Christ's love to Saul (Paul) after his conversion.
CORNELIUS	10:30-35	His example showed Peter that the gospel was for all people, Jews and Gentiles.
RHODA	12:13-15	Her persistence brought Peter inside Mary's home, where he would be safe.
JAMES	15:13-21	He took command of the Jerusalem council and had the courage and discernment to make a decision that would affect literally millions of Christians over many generations.
LYDIA	16:13-15	She opened her home to Paul, from which he led many to Christ and founded a church in Philippi.
JASON	17:5-9	He risked his life for the gospel by allowing Paul to stay in his home. He stood up for what was true and right, even though he faced persecution for it.
PAUL'S NEPHEW	23:16-24	He saved Paul's life by telling officials of a plot to murder Paul.
JULIUS	27:1, 43	He spared Paul's life when the other soldiers wanted to kill him.

silver or gold for you. But I'll give you what I have. In the
name of Jesus Christ the Nazarene,* get up and* walk!"

BETTER 3:1-8

The lame beggar asked for something that would have offered him temporary help—money. Instead, Peter gave him something much better and longer lasting—the use of his legs. Often our requests are for items that will help us temporarily. But God always has the big picture in mind when he answers our prayers. When we ask God for help, he may say, "I've got something even better for you." Are you willing to trust that he knows what's best? ■

7Then Peter took the lame man by the right hand and
helped him up. And as he did, the man's feet and ankles
were instantly healed and strengthened. 8He jumped up,
stood on his feet, and began to walk! Then, walking, leaping, and praising God, he went into the Temple with them.

9All the people saw him walking and heard him praising God. 10When they realized he was the lame beggar
they had seen so often at the Beautiful Gate, they were
absolutely astounded! 11They all rushed out in amazement to Solomon's Colonnade, where the man was holding tightly to Peter and John.

PETER PREACHES IN THE TEMPLE

12Peter saw his opportunity and addressed the crowd.
"People of Israel," he said, "what is so surprising about
this? And why stare at us as though we had made this man
walk by our own power or godliness? 13For it is the God
of Abraham, Isaac, and Jacob—the God of all our ancestors—who has brought glory to his servant Jesus by doing
this. This is the same Jesus whom you handed over and
rejected before Pilate, despite Pilate's decision to release
him. 14You rejected this holy, righteous one and instead
demanded the release of a murderer. 15You killed the author of life, but God raised him from the dead. And we
are witnesses of this fact!

16"Through faith in the name of Jesus, this man was

3:6a Or *Jesus Christ of Nazareth.* **3:6b** Some manuscripts omit *get up and.*

keeping it real

It's hard for me to talk to people about God, y'know? I haven't memorized a lot of verses. I'm still working my way through the Bible. It's easy to tell myself that I can wait until I know more.

But when I read Acts 4:13, I realized I was kidding myself. The verse talks about the boldness of Peter and John. The Jewish council noticed that they were uneducated and nonprofessionals. Still, they knew Jesus. That's when I realized I didn't have to know the whole Bible or go to seminary to be able to share my faith. The main thing is to know Jesus and share what I know with other people. **Kenneth**

healed—and you know how crippled he was before. Faith
in Jesus' name has healed him before your very eyes.
17"Friends,* I realize that what you and your leaders
did to Jesus was done in ignorance. 18But God was fulfilling what all the prophets had foretold about the Messiah—that he must suffer these things. 19Now repent of
your sins and turn to God, so that your sins may be wiped
away. 20Then times of refreshment will come from the
presence of the Lord, and he will again send you Jesus,
your appointed Messiah. 21For he must remain in heaven
until the time for the final restoration of all things, as God
promised long ago through his holy prophets. 22Moses
said, 'The LORD your God will raise up for you a Prophet
like me from among your own people. Listen carefully to
everything he tells you.'* 23Then Moses said, 'Anyone
who will not listen to that Prophet will be completely cut
off from God's people.'*

REFRESHED 3:19

Peter advised the crowd to change their ways. When we turn from a bad habit (for example, lying, stealing—you know what we mean) and agree to change, God promises not only to wipe away that mark against us, but also to bring spiritual refreshment. Breaking a bad habit may seem painful at first. But God will give you a better way. As Hosea promised, "Let us press on to know him. He will respond to us as surely as the arrival of dawn or the coming of rains in early spring" (Hos 6:3). Do you feel a need to be refreshed? ■

24"Starting with Samuel, every prophet spoke about
what is happening today. 25You are the children of those
prophets, and you are included in the covenant God
promised to your ancestors. For God said to Abraham,
'Through your descendants* all the families on earth will
be blessed.' 26When God raised up his servant, Jesus, he
sent him first to you people of Israel, to bless you by turning each of you back from your sinful ways."

4 PETER AND JOHN BEFORE THE COUNCIL

While Peter and John were speaking to the people, they
were confronted by the priests, the captain of the Temple guard, and some of the Sadducees. 2These leaders
were very disturbed that Peter and John were teaching
the people that through Jesus there is a resurrection of
the dead. 3They arrested them and, since it was already
evening, put them in jail until morning. 4But many of the
people who heard their message believed it, so the number of believers now totaled about 5,000 men, not
counting women and children.*
5The next day the council of all the rulers and elders
and teachers of religious law met in Jerusalem. 6Annas
the high priest was there, along with Caiaphas, John,
Alexander, and other relatives of the high priest. 7They
brought in the two disciples and demanded, "By what
power, or in whose name, have you done this?"
8Then Peter, filled with the Holy Spirit, said to them,
"Rulers and elders of our people, 9are we being questioned today because we've done a good deed for a crippled man? Do you want to know how he was healed? 10Let
me clearly state to all of you and to all the people of Israel
that he was healed by the powerful name of Jesus Christ
the Nazarene,* the man you crucified but whom God
raised from the dead. 11For Jesus is the one referred to in
the Scriptures, where it says,

'The stone that you builders rejected
has now become the cornerstone.'*

12There is salvation in no one else! God has given no other
name under heaven by which we must be saved."
13The members of the council were amazed when they
saw the boldness of Peter and John, for they could see
that they were ordinary men with no special training in

3:17 Greek *Brothers.* **3:22** Deut 18:15. **3:23** Deut 18:19; Lev 23:29. **3:25** Greek *your seed;* see Gen 12:3; 22:18. **4:4** Greek *5,000 adult males.* **4:10** Or *Jesus Christ of Nazareth.* **4:11** Ps 118:22.

the Scriptures. They also recognized them as men who
had been with Jesus. 14But since they could see the man
who had been healed standing right there among them,
there was nothing the council could say. 15So they ordered Peter and John out of the council chamber* and
conferred among themselves.
16"What should we do with these men?" they asked
each other. "We can't deny that they have performed a
miraculous sign, and everybody in Jerusalem knows
about it. 17But to keep them from spreading their propa-
ganda any further, we must warn them not to speak to
anyone in Jesus' name again." 18So they called the apostles back in and commanded them never again to speak
or teach in the name of Jesus.
19But Peter and John replied, "Do you think God wants
us to obey you rather than him? 20We cannot stop telling
about everything we have seen and heard."
21The council then threatened them further, but they
finally let them go because they didn't know how to punish them without starting a riot. For everyone was praising God 22for this miraculous sign—the healing of a man
who had been lame for more than forty years.

STRENGTH 4:24-30

Notice how the believers prayed. (1) They praised God, (2) told God their problem, and (3) asked for his help. They didn't ask God to remove the problem. Instead, they asked for help to deal with it. God doesn't always remove problems from our lives. Many times he just provides the strength to deal with them. ■

THE BELIEVERS PRAY FOR COURAGE
23As soon as they were freed, Peter and John returned to
the other believers and told them what the leading
priests and elders had said. 24When they heard the report, all the believers lifted their voices together in prayer
to God: "O Sovereign Lord, Creator of heaven and earth,
the sea, and everything in them—25you spoke long ago by
the Holy Spirit through our ancestor David, your servant,
saying,

'Why were the nations so angry?
Why did they waste their time with futile plans?
26 The kings of the earth prepared for battle;
the rulers gathered together
against the LORD
and against his Messiah.'*

27"In fact, this has happened here in this very city! For
Herod Antipas, Pontius Pilate the governor, the Gentiles,
and the people of Israel were all united against Jesus,
your holy servant, whom you anointed. 28But everything
they did was determined beforehand according to your
will. 29And now, O Lord, hear their threats, and give us,
your servants, great boldness in preaching your word.
30Stretch out your hand with healing power; may
miraculous signs and wonders be done through the
name of your holy servant Jesus."
31After this prayer, the meeting place shook, and they
were all filled with the Holy Spirit. Then they preached
the word of God with boldness.

THE BELIEVERS SHARE THEIR POSSESSIONS
32All the believers were united in heart and mind. And
they felt that what they owned was not their own, so they
shared everything they had. 33The apostles testified
powerfully to the resurrection of the Lord Jesus, and
God's great blessing was upon them all. 34There were no
needy people among them, because those who owned
land or houses would sell them 35and bring the money to
the apostles to give to those in need.
36For instance, there was Joseph, the one the apostles
nicknamed Barnabas (which means "Son of Encouragement"). He was from the tribe of Levi and came from the
island of Cyprus. 37He sold a field he owned and brought
the money to the apostles.

5

ANANIAS AND SAPPHIRA
But there was a certain man named Ananias who, with his
wife, Sapphira, sold some property. 2He brought part of
the money to the apostles, claiming it was the full
amount. With his wife's consent, he kept the rest.
3Then Peter said, "Ananias, why have you let Satan fill
your heart? You lied to the Holy Spirit, and you kept some
of the money for yourself. 4The property was yours to sell
or not sell, as you wished. And after selling it, the money
was also yours to give away. How could you do a thing like
this? You weren't lying to us but to God!"
5As soon as Ananias heard these words, he fell to the
floor and died. Everyone who heard about it was terrified. 6Then some young men got up, wrapped him in a
sheet, and took him out and buried him.
7About three hours later his wife came in, not knowing
what had happened. 8Peter asked her, "Was this the price
you and your husband received for your land?"
"Yes," she replied, "that was the price."
9And Peter said, "How could the two of you even think
of conspiring to test the Spirit of the Lord like this? The
young men who buried your husband are just outside the
door, and they will carry you out, too."
10Instantly, she fell to the floor and died. When the
young men came in and saw that she was dead, they carried her out and buried her beside her husband. 11Great
fear gripped the entire church and everyone else who
heard what had happened.

THE APOSTLES HEAL MANY
12The apostles were performing many miraculous signs
and wonders among the people. And all the believers
were meeting regularly at the Temple in the area known
as Solomon's Colonnade. 13But no one else dared to join
them, even though all the people had high regard for
them. 14Yet more and more people believed and were

4:15 Greek *the Sanhedrin.* **4:25-26** Or *his anointed one;* or *his Christ.* Ps 2:1-2.

brought to the Lord—crowds of both men and women.
15As a result of the apostles' work, sick people were
brought out into the streets on beds and mats so that
Peter's shadow might fall across some of them as he went
by. 16Crowds came from the villages around Jerusalem,
bringing their sick and those possessed by evil* spirits,
and they were all healed.

THE APOSTLES MEET OPPOSITION

17The high priest and his officials, who were Sadducees,
were filled with jealousy. 18They arrested the apostles
and put them in the public jail. 19But an angel of the Lord
came at night, opened the gates of the jail, and brought
them out. Then he told them, 20"Go to the Temple and
give the people this message of life!"

21So at daybreak the apostles entered the Temple, as
they were told, and immediately began teaching.

When the high priest and his officials arrived, they
convened the high council*—the full assembly of the
elders of Israel. Then they sent for the apostles to be
brought from the jail for trial. 22But when the Temple
guards went to the jail, the men were gone. So they returned to the council and reported, 23"The jail was securely locked, with the guards standing outside, but
when we opened the gates, no one was there!"

THIS MEANS WAR 5:17-21

The high priest and other leaders reacted negatively to the apostles' bold preaching and miracles. Negative reactions like these can remind us that we're in a war. As Ephesians 6:12 says, "We are not fighting against flesh-and-blood enemies, but against evil rulers and authorities of the unseen world, against mighty powers in this dark world, and against evil spirits in the heavenly places." When you share your faith, you might experience what the apostles experienced. "But take heart," Jesus said, "because I have overcome the world" (John 16:33). ■

24When the captain of the Temple guard and the leading priests heard this, they were perplexed, wondering
where it would all end. 25Then someone arrived with startling news: "The men you put in jail are standing in the
Temple, teaching the people!"

26The captain went with his Temple guards and arrested the apostles, but without violence, for they were
afraid the people would stone them. 27Then they brought
the apostles before the high council, where the high
priest confronted them. 28"Didn't we tell you never again
to teach in this man's name?" he demanded. "Instead, you
have filled all Jerusalem with your teaching about him,
and you want to make us responsible for his death!"

29But Peter and the apostles replied, "We must obey
God rather than any human authority. 30The God of our
ancestors raised Jesus from the dead after you killed him
by hanging him on a cross.* 31Then God put him in the
place of honor at his right hand as Prince and Savior. He
did this so the people of Israel would repent of their sins
and be forgiven. 32We are witnesses of these things and
so is the Holy Spirit, who is given by God to those who
obey him."

33When they heard this, the high council was furious
and decided to kill them. 34But one member, a Pharisee
named Gamaliel, who was an expert in religious law and
respected by all the people, stood up and ordered that the
men be sent outside the council chamber for a while.
35Then he said to his colleagues, "Men of Israel, take care
what you are planning to do to these men! 36Some time
ago there was that fellow Theudas, who pretended to be
someone great. About 400 others joined him, but he was
killed, and all his followers went their various ways. The
whole movement came to nothing. 37After him, at the
time of the census, there was Judas of Galilee. He got people to follow him, but he was killed, too, and all his followers were scattered.

38"So my advice is, leave these men alone. Let them go.
If they are planning and doing these things merely on
their own, it will soon be overthrown. 39But if it is from
God, you will not be able to overthrow them. You may
even find yourselves fighting against God!"

40The others accepted his advice. They called in the
apostles and had them flogged. Then they ordered them
never again to speak in the name of Jesus, and they let
them go.

41The apostles left the high council rejoicing that God
had counted them worthy to suffer disgrace for the name
of Jesus.* 42And every day, in the Temple and from house
to house, they continued to teach and preach this message: "Jesus is the Messiah."

6

SEVEN MEN CHOSEN TO SERVE

But as the believers* rapidly multiplied, there were rum-
blings of discontent. The Greek-speaking believers complained about the Hebrew-speaking believers, saying
that their widows were being discriminated against in
the daily distribution of food.

2So the Twelve called a meeting of all the believers.
They said, "We apostles should spend our time teaching
the word of God, not running a food program. 3And so,
brothers, select seven men who are well respected and
are full of the Spirit and wisdom. We will give them this
responsibility. 4Then we apostles can spend our time in
prayer and teaching the word."

5Everyone liked this idea, and they chose the following:
Stephen (a man full of faith and the Holy Spirit), Philip,
Procorus, Nicanor, Timon, Parmenas, and Nicolas of Antioch (an earlier convert to the Jewish faith). 6These seven
were presented to the apostles, who prayed for them as
they laid their hands on them.

7So God's message continued to spread. The number
of believers greatly increased in Jerusalem, and many of
the Jewish priests were converted, too.

5:16 Greek *unclean.* **5:21** Greek *Sanhedrin;* also in 5:27, 41. **5:30** Greek *on a tree.* **5:41** Greek *for the name.* **6:1** Greek *disciples;* also in 6:2, 7.

THE WAVE 6:7

The gospel spread like ripples on a pond where, from a single center, each wave touched the next, spreading wider and farther. The gospel still spreads this way today. You don't have to change the world single-handedly. Being part of the wave, touching those around you, is enough. They in turn will touch others until all have felt the movement. Are you part of the wave? ■

STEPHEN IS ARRESTED

8 Stephen, a man full of God's grace and power, performed amazing miracles and signs among the people.
9 But one day some men from the Synagogue of Freed
Slaves, as it was called, started to debate with him. They
were Jews from Cyrene, Alexandria, Cilicia, and the province of Asia. 10 None of them could stand against the wisdom and the Spirit with which Stephen spoke.
11 So they persuaded some men to lie about Stephen,
saying, "We heard him blaspheme Moses, and even God."
12 This roused the people, the elders, and the teachers of
religious law. So they arrested Stephen and brought him
before the high council.*
13 The lying witnesses said, "This man is always speaking against the holy Temple and against the law of Moses.
14 We have heard him say that this Jesus of Nazareth* will
destroy the Temple and change the customs Moses
handed down to us."
15 At this point everyone in the high council stared at
Stephen, because his face became as bright as an angel's.

7

STEPHEN ADDRESSES THE COUNCIL

Then the high priest asked Stephen, "Are these accusations true?"
2 This was Stephen's reply: "Brothers and fathers, listen
to me. Our glorious God appeared to our ancestor Abraham in Mesopotamia before he settled in Haran.* 3 God
told him, 'Leave your native land and your relatives, and
come into the land that I will show you.'* 4 So Abraham
left the land of the Chaldeans and lived in Haran until his
father died. Then God brought him here to the land
where you now live.
5 "But God gave him no inheritance here, not even one
square foot of land. God did promise, however, that eventually the whole land would belong to Abraham and his
descendants—even though he had no children yet. 6 God

6:12 Greek *Sanhedrin;* also in 6:15. 6:14 Or *Jesus the Nazarene.* 7:2 *Mesopotamia* was the region now called Iraq. *Haran* was a city in what is now called Syria. 7:3 Gen 12:1.

UPS:
- One of seven leaders chosen to supervise food distribution to the needy in the early church
- Known for his spiritual qualities of faith, wisdom, grace, and power, and for the Spirit's presence in his life
- Outstanding leader, teacher, and debater
- The first to be martyred for his faith

STATS:
- Occupation: Deacon
- Contemporaries: Paul, Caiaphas, Gamaliel, the apostles

BOTTOM LINE:

Striving for excellence in small assignments prepares a person for greater responsibilities.

Real understanding of God always leads to practical and compassionate actions.

Stephen's story is told in Acts 6:1–8:2. He also is mentioned in Acts 11:19; 22:20.

STEPHEN

How serious are you about your faith in Jesus? Would you give your life for it?

Stephen did.

We first meet Stephen when he's chosen along with six others to manage the distribution of food among Christians in Jerusalem. Because many people lost jobs and belongings when they became Christians, other Christians had to share what they had with each other. Stephen and the other leaders were asked to make sure that the available food was handed out fairly. This probably was a job with more headaches than thank-yous.

Stephen also was a powerful speaker. When he was harassed in the Temple about his faith, he responded calmly and clearly. His logic devastated their arguments.

Consequently, Stephen was hauled before the official religious court, where he used a summary of the Jews' own history to show that Jesus was the Savior. Since the court was unable to answer him, they decided to silence him for good. They stoned him to death while he prayed for their forgiveness.

Stephen's final words show how much he had become like Jesus in a short time. His death had a lasting effect on a young man named Saul, who would later change from fiercely destroying the growing church to radically defending it.

How many risks do you take as a follower of Jesus? Would you die for him? Do you live for him?

also told him that his descendants would live in a foreign
land, where they would be oppressed as slaves for
400 years. 7 'But I will punish the nation that enslaves
them,' God said, 'and in the end they will come out and
worship me here in this place.'*

8 "God also gave Abraham the covenant of circumcision at that time. So when Abraham became the father of
Isaac, he circumcised him on the eighth day. And the
practice was continued when Isaac became the father of
Jacob, and when Jacob became the father of the twelve
patriarchs of the Israelite nation.

9 "These patriarchs were jealous of their brother Joseph, and they sold him to be a slave in Egypt. But God
was with him 10 and rescued him from all his troubles.
And God gave him favor before Pharaoh, king of Egypt.
God also gave Joseph unusual wisdom, so that Pharaoh
appointed him governor over all of Egypt and put him in
charge of the palace.

11 "But a famine came upon Egypt and Canaan. There was
great misery, and our ancestors ran out of food. 12 Jacob
heard that there was still grain in Egypt, so he sent his
sons—our ancestors—to buy some. 13 The second time they
went, Joseph revealed his identity to his brothers,* and they
were introduced to Pharaoh. 14 Then Joseph sent for his father, Jacob, and all his relatives to come to Egypt, seventy-
five persons in all. 15 So Jacob went to Egypt. He died there,
as did our ancestors. 16 Their bodies were taken to Shechem
and buried in the tomb Abraham had bought for a certain
price from Hamor's sons in Shechem.

17 "As the time drew near when God would fulfill his
promise to Abraham, the number of our people in
Egypt greatly increased. 18 But then a new king came to
the throne of Egypt who knew nothing about Joseph.
19 This king exploited our people and oppressed them,
forcing parents to abandon their newborn babies so
they would die.

7:5-7 Gen 12:7; 15:13-14; Exod 3:12. **7:13** Other manuscripts read *Joseph was recognized by his brothers.*

PAUL

UPS:
- Transformed by God from a persecutor of Christians to a preacher for Christ
- Preached for Christ throughout the Roman Empire on three missionary journeys
- Wrote letters, which became part of the New Testament, to various churches
- Was never afraid to face an issue head-on and deal with it
- Was sensitive to God's leading and, despite his strong personality, always did as God directed
- Often is called the apostle to the Gentiles

DOWNS:
- Witnessed and approved of Stephen's stoning
- Set out to destroy Christianity by persecuting Christians

STATS:
- Where: Born in Tarsus, but became a world traveler for Christ
- Occupations: Trained as a Pharisee; learned the tentmaking trade; served as a missionary
- Contemporaries: Gamaliel, Stephen, the apostles, Luke, Barnabas, Timothy

BOTTOM LINE:

The Good News is that forgiveness and eternal life are a gift of God's grace received by faith in Christ and available to all people.

Obedience results from a relationship with God, but obedience will never create or earn that relationship.

God will use our past and present so that we may serve him with our future.

Paul's story is told in Acts 7:58–28:31 and throughout his New Testament letters.

PAUL Have you ever thought you were totally right about something, but wound up being totally wrong? That was Paul in a nutshell.

Paul—or Saul as he was called early in his career—was a leader in the frenzied persecution of Christians following Stephen's death. Eventually, Paul met Christ personally and his life was changed. However, Paul never lost his intensity. Instead, it was redirected to spread the Gospel. No person, apart from Jesus himself, shaped the history of Christianity as much as the apostle Paul.

Paul was an expert on the Old Testament and was a member of the Jewish council. Since he was convinced that Christianity was dangerous to Judaism, Paul persecuted Christians without mercy. At one point, Paul received permission from the high priest to travel to Damascus to arrest Christians and bring them back to Jerusalem. His plans would have resulted in the deaths of many believers. But God had other plans. After an encounter with the risen Jesus on the road to Damascus, Paul's life changed forever.

He became God's ambassador to the Gentiles. Until Paul was converted, little had been done to carry Christ's message to non-Jewish people. Paul and his missionary teams eventually carried the gospel across the Roman Empire.

Although Paul worked hard to convince the Jews that Gentiles were acceptable to God, he spent even more time convincing Gentiles themselves that they were acceptable to God. Meeting Christ through Paul changed the lives of many people.

God used everything that made up Paul's life—his training, citizenship, mind, and even his weaknesses—to add people to the church, the body of Christ. Are you willing to let God do the same for you? You'll never know what he can do with you until you allow him to have all that you are!

[20]"At that time Moses was born—a beautiful child in
God's eyes. His parents cared for him at home for three
months. [21]When they had to abandon him, Pharaoh's
daughter adopted him and raised him as her own son.
[22]Moses was taught all the wisdom of the Egyptians, and
he was powerful in both speech and action.

[23]"One day when Moses was forty years old, he decided
to visit his relatives, the people of Israel. [24]He saw an
Egyptian mistreating an Israelite. So Moses came to the
man's defense and avenged him, killing the Egyptian.
[25]Moses assumed his fellow Israelites would realize that
God had sent him to rescue them, but they didn't.

[26]"The next day he visited them again and saw two men
of Israel fighting. He tried to be a peacemaker. 'Men,' he
said, 'you are brothers. Why are you fighting each other?'

[27]"But the man in the wrong pushed Moses aside.
'Who made you a ruler and judge over us?' he asked.
[28]'Are you going to kill me as you killed that Egyptian yesterday?' [29]When Moses heard that, he fled the country
and lived as a foreigner in the land of Midian. There his
two sons were born.

ACCUSED 6:8–7:60

When accused of a crime of speaking against the Temple and the Law of Moses, Stephen took the offensive, seizing the opportunity to summarize the history of the Jewish people. This history helped point the accusing finger back at the religious leaders. They failed to obey the laws they prided themselves in following so meticulously. Before his death, Jesus had leveled the same charge against the Pharisees (see Matt 23).

Like Stephen, we don't need to be on the defensive when we witness for Jesus. The truth of Christ is its own defense. ■

[30]"Forty years later, in the desert near Mount Sinai, an
angel appeared to Moses in the flame of a burning bush.
[31]When Moses saw it, he was amazed at the sight. As he
went to take a closer look, the voice of the LORD called out
to him, [32]'I am the God of your ancestors—the God of
Abraham, Isaac, and Jacob.' Moses shook with terror and
did not dare to look.

[33]"Then the LORD said to him, 'Take off your sandals,
for you are standing on holy ground. [34]I have certainly
seen the oppression of my people in Egypt. I have heard
their groans and have come down to rescue them. Now
go, for I am sending you back to Egypt.'*

[35]"So God sent back the same man his people had previously rejected when they demanded, 'Who made you
a ruler and judge over us?' Through the angel who appeared to him in the burning bush, God sent Moses to be
their ruler and savior. [36]And by means of many wonders
and miraculous signs, he led them out of Egypt, through
the Red Sea, and through the wilderness for forty years.

[37]"Moses himself told the people of Israel, 'God will
raise up for you a Prophet like me from among your own
people.'* [38]Moses was with our ancestors, the assembly
of God's people in the wilderness, when the angel spoke
to him at Mount Sinai. And there Moses received life-
giving words to pass on to us.*

[39]"But our ancestors refused to listen to Moses. They
rejected him and wanted to return to Egypt. [40]They told
Aaron, 'Make us some gods who can lead us, for we don't
know what has become of this Moses, who brought us
out of Egypt.' [41]So they made an idol shaped like a calf,
and they sacrificed to it and celebrated over this thing
they had made. [42]Then God turned away from them and
abandoned them to serve the stars of heaven as their
gods! In the book of the prophets it is written,

'Was it to me you were bringing sacrifices
    and offerings
  during those forty years in the wilderness, Israel?
[43] No, you carried your pagan gods—
  the shrine of Molech,
  the star of your god Rephan,
  and the images you made to worship them.
So I will send you into exile
  as far away as Babylon.'*

[44]"Our ancestors carried the Tabernacle* with them
through the wilderness. It was constructed according to
the plan God had shown to Moses. [45]Years later, when
Joshua led our ancestors in battle against the nations that
God drove out of this land, the Tabernacle was taken with
them into their new territory. And it stayed there until
the time of King David.

[46]"David found favor with God and asked for the privilege of building a permanent Temple for the God of
Jacob.* [47]But it was Solomon who actually built it.
[48]However, the Most High doesn't live in temples made
by human hands. As the prophet says,

[49] 'Heaven is my throne,
  and the earth is my footstool.
Could you build me a temple as good as that?'
  asks the LORD.
'Could you build me such a resting place?
[50] Didn't my hands make both heaven and earth?'*

[51]"You stubborn people! You are heathen* at heart and
deaf to the truth. Must you forever resist the Holy Spirit?
That's what your ancestors did, and so do you! [52]Name
one prophet your ancestors didn't persecute! They even
killed the ones who predicted the coming of the Righteous One—the Messiah whom you betrayed and murdered. [53]You deliberately disobeyed God's law, even
though you received it from the hands of angels."

[54]The Jewish leaders were infuriated by Stephen's accusation, and they shook their fists at him in rage.* [55]But
Stephen, full of the Holy Spirit, gazed steadily into

7:31-34 Exod 3:5-10. **7:37** Deut 18:15. **7:38** Some manuscripts read *to you.* **7:42-43** Amos 5:25-27 (Greek version). **7:44** Greek *the tent of witness.* **7:46** Some manuscripts read *the house of Jacob.* **7:49-50** Isa 66:1-2. **7:51** Greek *uncircumcised.* **7:54** Greek *they were grinding their teeth against him.*

heaven and saw the glory of God, and he saw Jesus standing in the place of honor at God's right hand. 56 And he
told them, "Look, I see the heavens opened and the Son of
Man standing in the place of honor at God's right hand!"
57 Then they put their hands over their ears and began
shouting. They rushed at him 58 and dragged him out of
the city and began to stone him. His accusers took off
their coats and laid them at the feet of a young man
named Saul.*
59 As they stoned him, Stephen prayed, "Lord Jesus, receive my spirit." 60 He fell to his knees, shouting, "Lord,
don't charge them with this sin!" And with that, he died.

8

Saul was one of the witnesses, and he agreed completely with the killing of Stephen.

PERSECUTION SCATTERS THE BELIEVERS

A great wave of persecution began that day, sweeping
over the church in Jerusalem; and all the believers except
the apostles were scattered through the regions of Judea
and Samaria. 2 (Some devout men came and buried Stephen with great mourning.) 3 But Saul was going everywhere to destroy the church. He went from house to
house, dragging out both men and women to throw them
into prison.

PHILIP PREACHES IN SAMARIA

4 But the believers who were scattered preached the Good
News about Jesus wherever they went. 5 Philip, for example, went to the city of Samaria and told the people there
about the Messiah. 6 Crowds listened intently to Philip because they were eager to hear his message and see the miraculous signs he did. 7 Many evil* spirits were cast out,
screaming as they left their victims. And many who had
been paralyzed or lame were healed. 8 So there was great
joy in that city.

PRODUCTIVE DISCOMFORT 8:4

Although persecuted believers were forced to move out of their homes in Jerusalem, the gospel was spread as a result. God can sometimes accomplish his purposes through the uncomfortable situations of our lives. Tempted to complain about uncomfortable or painful circumstances? Maybe God's preparing you for a special task. Why not check with him and see? ■

9 A man named Simon had been a sorcerer there for
many years, amazing the people of Samaria and claiming
to be someone great. 10 Everyone, from the least to the
greatest, often spoke of him as "the Great One—the
Power of God." 11 They listened closely to him because for
a long time he had astounded them with his magic.
12 But now the people believed Philip's message of
Good News concerning the Kingdom of God and the
name of Jesus Christ. As a result, many men and women
were baptized. 13 Then Simon himself believed and was
baptized. He began following Philip wherever he went,
and he was amazed by the signs and great miracles Philip
performed.
14 When the apostles in Jerusalem heard that the people of Samaria had accepted God's message, they sent Peter and John there. 15 As soon as they arrived, they prayed
for these new believers to receive the Holy Spirit. 16 The
Holy Spirit had not yet come upon any of them, for they
had only been baptized in the name of the Lord Jesus.
17 Then Peter and John laid their hands upon these believers, and they received the Holy Spirit.
18 When Simon saw that the Spirit was given when the
apostles laid their hands on people, he offered them
money to buy this power. 19 "Let me have this power, too,"
he exclaimed, "so that when I lay my hands on people,
they will receive the Holy Spirit!"
20 But Peter replied, "May your money be destroyed
with you for thinking God's gift can be bought! 21 You can
have no part in this, for your heart is not right with God.
22 Repent of your wickedness and pray to the Lord. Perhaps he will forgive your evil thoughts, 23 for I can see that
you are full of bitter jealousy and are held captive by sin."

THE WHOLE PACKAGE 8:18-24

Simon wanted the power of the Holy Spirit, but not the Holy Spirit himself. Having the Holy Spirit would have meant giving up the right to run his own life. Likewise, many people want the gifts of God (the peace, power, or other provisions), but not the giver of those gifts. In other words, they don't want the whole package. Or, they want just a part of God: his love and his grace, but not his judgment or discipline. How much do you want of God? Do you want the whole package or just a part? With God, it's all or nothing. ■

24 "Pray to the Lord for me," Simon exclaimed, "that
these terrible things you've said won't happen to me!"
25 After testifying and preaching the word of the Lord
in Samaria, Peter and John returned to Jerusalem. And
they stopped in many Samaritan villages along the way to
preach the Good News.

PHILIP AND THE ETHIOPIAN EUNUCH

26 As for Philip, an angel of the Lord said to him, "Go
south* down the desert road that runs from Jerusalem to
Gaza." 27 So he started out, and he met the treasurer of
Ethiopia, a eunuch of great authority under the Kandake,
the queen of Ethiopia. The eunuch had gone to Jerusalem
to worship, 28 and he was now returning. Seated in his carriage, he was reading aloud from the book of the prophet
Isaiah.
29 The Holy Spirit said to Philip, "Go over and walk
along beside the carriage."
30 Philip ran over and heard the man reading from the
prophet Isaiah. Philip asked, "Do you understand what
you are reading?"

7:58 *Saul* is later called Paul; see 13:9. **8:7** Greek *unclean.* **8:26** Or *Go at noon.*

31The man replied, "How can I, unless someone instructs me?" And he urged Philip to come up into the
carriage and sit with him.
32The passage of Scripture he had been reading was
this:

"He was led like a sheep to the slaughter.
And as a lamb is silent before the shearers,
he did not open his mouth.
33 He was humiliated and received no justice.
Who can speak of his descendants?
For his life was taken from the earth."*

34The eunuch asked Philip, "Tell me, was the prophet
talking about himself or someone else?" 35So beginning
with this same Scripture, Philip told him the Good News
about Jesus.
36As they rode along, they came to some water, and the
eunuch said, "Look! There's some water! Why can't I be
baptized?"* 38He ordered the carriage to stop, and they
went down into the water, and Philip baptized him.
39When they came up out of the water, the Spirit of the
Lord snatched Philip away. The eunuch never saw him
again but went on his way rejoicing. 40Meanwhile, Philip
found himself farther north at the town of Azotus. He
preached the Good News there and in every town along
the way until he came to Caesarea.

9

SAUL'S CONVERSION

Meanwhile, Saul was uttering threats with every breath
and was eager to kill the Lord's followers.* So he went to
the high priest. 2He requested letters addressed to the
synagogues in Damascus, asking for their cooperation in
the arrest of any followers of the Way he found there. He
wanted to bring them—both men and women—back to
Jerusalem in chains.
3As he was approaching Damascus on this mission, a
light from heaven suddenly shone down around him. 4He
fell to the ground and heard a voice saying to him, "Saul!
Saul! Why are you persecuting me?"
5"Who are you, lord?" Saul asked.
And the voice replied, "I am Jesus, the one you are persecuting! 6Now get up and go into the city, and you will be
told what you must do."
7The men with Saul stood speechless, for they heard
the sound of someone's voice but saw no one! 8Saul
picked himself up off the ground, but when he opened
his eyes he was blind. So his companions led him by the
hand to Damascus. 9He remained there blind for three
days and did not eat or drink.
10Now there was a believer* in Damascus named Ananias. The Lord spoke to him in a vision, calling, "Ananias!"
"Yes, Lord!" he replied.
11The Lord said, "Go over to Straight Street, to the
house of Judas. When you get there, ask for a man from
Tarsus named Saul. He is praying to me right now. 12I
have shown him a vision of a man named Ananias coming in and laying hands on him so he can see again."
13"But Lord," exclaimed Ananias, "I've heard many
people talk about the terrible things this man has done to
the believers* in Jerusalem! 14And he is authorized by the
leading priests to arrest everyone who calls upon your
name."
15But the Lord said, "Go, for Saul is my chosen instrument to take my message to the Gentiles and to kings, as
well as to the people of Israel. 16And I will show him how
much he must suffer for my name's sake."

REACHING THE UNREACHABLE 9:1-16

Ananias had trouble believing that Saul, the persecutor of Christians, was now a believer. Yet Saul had met the risen Christ in a dramatic way. Have you ever doubted that someone really believes in Jesus? Or, maybe you've thought that some people are impossible to reach for Christ. They're too hard, too stubborn, too whatever (fill in your own adjective) for God to change. With God, nothing is impossible (Gen 18:14; Luke 1:37). He can reach even the "unreachable." ■

17So Ananias went and found Saul. He laid his hands
on him and said, "Brother Saul, the Lord Jesus, who appeared to you on the road, has sent me so that you might
regain your sight and be filled with the Holy Spirit."
18Instantly something like scales fell from Saul's eyes,
and he regained his sight. Then he got up and was baptized. 19Afterward he ate some food and regained his
strength.

SAUL IN DAMASCUS AND JERUSALEM

Saul stayed with the believers* in Damascus for a few
days. 20And immediately he began preaching about Jesus
in the synagogues, saying, "He is indeed the Son of God!"
21All who heard him were amazed. "Isn't this the same
man who caused such devastation among Jesus' followers in Jerusalem?" they asked. "And didn't he come here
to arrest them and take them in chains to the leading
priests?"
22Saul's preaching became more and more powerful,
and the Jews in Damascus couldn't refute his proofs that
Jesus was indeed the Messiah. 23After a while some of the
Jews plotted together to kill him. 24They were watching
for him day and night at the city gate so they could murder him, but Saul was told about their plot. 25So during
the night, some of the other believers* lowered him in a
large basket through an opening in the city wall.
26When Saul arrived in Jerusalem, he tried to meet
with the believers, but they were all afraid of him. They
did not believe he had truly become a believer! 27Then
Barnabas brought him to the apostles and told them how
Saul had seen the Lord on the way to Damascus and how

8:32-33 Isa 53:7-8 (Greek version). **8:36** Some manuscripts add verse 37, *"You can," Philip answered, "if you believe with all your heart." And the eunuch replied, "I believe that Jesus Christ is the Son of God."* **9:1** Greek *disciples.* **9:10** Greek *disciple;* also in 9:26, 36. **9:13** Greek *God's holy people;* also in 9:32, 41. **9:19** Greek *disciples;* also in 9:26, 38. **9:25** Greek *his disciples.*

the Lord had spoken to Saul. He also told them that Saul had preached boldly in the name of Jesus in Damascus.

28So Saul stayed with the apostles and went all around Jerusalem with them, preaching boldly in the name of the Lord. 29He debated with some Greek-speaking Jews, but they tried to murder him. 30When the believers* heard about this, they took him down to Caesarea and sent him away to Tarsus, his hometown.

31The church then had peace throughout Judea, Galilee, and Samaria, and it became stronger as the believers lived in the fear of the Lord. And with the encouragement of the Holy Spirit, it also grew in numbers.

PETER HEALS AENEAS AND RAISES DORCAS

32Meanwhile, Peter traveled from place to place, and he came down to visit the believers in the town of Lydda. 33There he met a man named Aeneas, who had been paralyzed and bedridden for eight years. 34Peter said to him, "Aeneas, Jesus Christ heals you! Get up, and roll up your sleeping mat!" And he was healed instantly. 35Then the whole population of Lydda and Sharon saw Aeneas walking around, and they turned to the Lord.

KINDNESS 9:36-42

Dorcas never preached a sermon like Peter or Paul. Yet she had an enormous impact on her community by "doing kind things for others and helping the poor." When she died, the room was filled with mourners, people she had helped. Do you have this kind of impact on your community? Kindness is one "fruit" that all believers can have (see Gal 5:22). ■

36There was a believer in Joppa named Tabitha (which in Greek is Dorcas*). She was always doing kind things for others and helping the poor. 37About this time she became ill and died. Her body was washed for burial and laid in an upstairs room. 38But the believers had heard that Peter was nearby at Lydda, so they sent two men to beg him, "Please come as soon as possible!"

39So Peter returned with them; and as soon as he arrived, they took him to the upstairs room. The room was filled with widows who were weeping and showing him the coats and other clothes Dorcas had made for them. 40But Peter asked them all to leave the room; then he knelt and prayed. Turning to the body he said, "Get up, Tabitha." And she opened her eyes! When she saw Peter, she sat up! 41He gave her his hand and helped her up. Then he called in the widows and all the believers, and he presented her to them alive.

42The news spread through the whole town, and many believed in the Lord. 43And Peter stayed a long time in Joppa, living with Simon, a tanner of hides.

10 CORNELIUS CALLS FOR PETER

In Caesarea there lived a Roman army officer* named Cornelius, who was a captain of the Italian Regiment. 2He was a devout, God-fearing man, as was everyone in his household. He gave generously to the poor and prayed regularly to God. 3One afternoon about three o'clock, he had a vision in which he saw an angel of God coming toward him. "Cornelius!" the angel said.

4Cornelius stared at him in terror. "What is it, sir?" he asked the angel.

And the angel replied, "Your prayers and gifts to the poor have been received by God as an offering! 5Now send some men to Joppa, and summon a man named Simon Peter. 6He is staying with Simon, a tanner who lives near the seashore."

7As soon as the angel was gone, Cornelius called two of his household servants and a devout soldier, one of his personal attendants. 8He told them what had happened and sent them off to Joppa.

PETER VISITS CORNELIUS

9The next day as Cornelius's messengers were nearing the town, Peter went up on the flat roof to pray. It was about noon, 10and he was hungry. But while a meal was being prepared, he fell into a trance. 11He saw the sky open, and something like a large sheet was let down by its four corners. 12In the sheet were all sorts of animals, reptiles, and birds. 13Then a voice said to him, "Get up, Peter; kill and eat them."

14"No, Lord," Peter declared. "I have never eaten anything that our Jewish laws have declared impure and unclean.*"

15But the voice spoke again: "Do not call something unclean if God has made it clean." 16The same vision was repeated three times. Then the sheet was suddenly pulled up to heaven.

17Peter was very perplexed. What could the vision mean? Just then the men sent by Cornelius found Simon's house. Standing outside the gate, 18they asked if a man named Simon Peter was staying there.

19Meanwhile, as Peter was puzzling over the vision, the Holy Spirit said to him, "Three men have come looking for you. 20Get up, go downstairs, and go with them without hesitation. Don't worry, for I have sent them."

21So Peter went down and said, "I'm the man you are looking for. Why have you come?"

22They said, "We were sent by Cornelius, a Roman officer. He is a devout and God-fearing man, well respected by all the Jews. A holy angel instructed him to summon you to his house so that he can hear your message." 23So Peter invited the men to stay for the night. The next day he went with them, accompanied by some of the brothers from Joppa.

24They arrived in Caesarea the following day. Cornelius was waiting for them and had called together his relatives and close friends. 25As Peter entered his home, Cornelius fell at his feet and worshiped him. 26But Peter pulled him up and said, "Stand up! I'm a human being just like you!" 27So they talked together and went inside, where many others were assembled.

28Peter told them, "You know it is against our laws for a Jewish man to enter a Gentile home like this or to

9:30 Greek *brothers.* **9:36** The names *Tabitha* in Aramaic and *Dorcas* in Greek both mean "gazelle." **10:1** Greek *a centurion;* similarly in 10:22. **10:14** Greek *anything common and unclean.*

associate with you. But God has shown me that I should no longer think of anyone as impure or unclean. 29So I came without objection as soon as I was sent for. Now tell me why you sent for me."

30Cornelius replied, "Four days ago I was praying in my house about this same time, three o'clock in the afternoon. Suddenly, a man in dazzling clothes was standing in front of me. 31He told me, 'Cornelius, your prayer has been heard, and your gifts to the poor have been noticed by God! 32Now send messengers to Joppa, and summon a man named Simon Peter. He is staying in the home of Simon, a tanner who lives near the seashore.' 33So I sent for you at once, and it was good of you to come. Now we are all here, waiting before God to hear the message the Lord has given you."

THE GENTILES HEAR THE GOOD NEWS

34Then Peter replied, "I see very clearly that God shows no favoritism. 35In every nation he accepts those who fear him and do what is right. 36This is the message of Good News for the people of Israel—that there is peace with God through Jesus Christ, who is Lord of all. 37You know what happened throughout Judea, beginning in Galilee, after John began preaching his message of baptism. 38And you know that God anointed Jesus of Nazareth with the Holy Spirit and with power. Then Jesus went around doing good and healing all who were oppressed by the devil, for God was with him.

39"And we apostles are witnesses of all he did throughout Judea and in Jerusalem. They put him to death by hanging him on a cross,* 40but God raised him to life on the third day. Then God allowed him to appear, 41not to the general public,* but to us whom God had chosen in advance to be his witnesses. We were those who ate and drank with him after he rose from the dead. 42And he ordered us to preach everywhere and to testify that Jesus is the one appointed by God to be the judge of all—the living and the dead. 43He is the one all the prophets testified about, saying that everyone who believes in him will have their sins forgiven through his name."

THE GENTILES RECEIVE THE HOLY SPIRIT

44Even as Peter was saying these things, the Holy Spirit fell upon all who were listening to the message. 45The Jewish believers* who came with Peter were amazed that the gift of the Holy Spirit had been poured out on the Gentiles, too. 46For they heard them speaking in tongues and praising God.

Then Peter asked, 47"Can anyone object to their being baptized, now that they have received the Holy Spirit just as we did?" 48So he gave orders for them to be baptized in the name of Jesus Christ. Afterward Cornelius asked him to stay with them for several days.

11

PETER EXPLAINS HIS ACTIONS

Soon the news reached the apostles and other believers* in Judea that the Gentiles had received the word of God. 2But when Peter arrived back in Jerusalem, the Jewish believers* criticized him. 3"You entered the home of Gentiles* and even ate with them!" they said.

4Then Peter told them exactly what had happened. 5"I was in the town of Joppa," he said, "and while I was praying, I went into a trance and saw a vision. Something like a large sheet was let down by its four corners from the sky. And it came right down to me. 6When I looked inside the sheet, I saw all sorts of small animals, wild animals, reptiles, and birds. 7And I heard a voice say, 'Get up, Peter; kill and eat them.'

8"'No, Lord,' I replied. 'I have never eaten anything that our Jewish laws have declared impure or unclean.*'

9"But the voice from heaven spoke again: 'Do not call something unclean if God has made it clean.' 10This happened three times before the sheet and all it contained was pulled back up to heaven.

11"Just then three men who had been sent from Caesarea arrived at the house where we were staying. 12The Holy Spirit told me to go with them and not to worry that they were Gentiles. These six brothers here accompanied me, and we soon entered the home of the man who had sent for us. 13He told us how an angel had appeared to him in his home and had told him, 'Send messengers to Joppa, and summon a man named Simon Peter. 14He will tell you how you and everyone in your household can be saved!'

15"As I began to speak," Peter continued, "the Holy Spirit fell on them, just as he fell on us at the beginning. 16Then I thought of the Lord's words when he said, 'John baptized with* water, but you will be baptized with the Holy Spirit.' 17And since God gave these Gentiles the same gift he gave us when we believed in the Lord Jesus Christ, who was I to stand in God's way?"

18When the others heard this, they stopped objecting and began praising God. They said, "We can see that God has also given the Gentiles the privilege of repenting of their sins and receiving eternal life."

> **THE WHOLE STORY 11:1-18**
>
> **When Peter brought the news of Cornelius's conversion back to Jerusalem, the believers were shocked that he had eaten with Gentiles. Why were they shocked? Because of their laws (see Lev 11). After they heard the whole story, however, they began praising God (11:18). Their reactions teach us how to handle disagreements with other Christians. Before judging the behavior of fellow believers, we need to hear them out. The Holy Spirit may be using them to teach us something important. ■**

THE CHURCH IN ANTIOCH OF SYRIA

19Meanwhile, the believers who had been scattered during the persecution after Stephen's death traveled as far

10:39 Greek *on a tree.* 10:41 Greek *the people.* 10:45 Greek *The faithful ones of the circumcision.* 11:1 Greek *brothers.* 11:2 Greek *those of the circumcision.* 11:3 Greek *of uncircumcised men.* 11:8 Greek *anything common or unclean.* 11:16 Or *in;* also in 11:16b.

as Phoenicia, Cyprus, and Antioch of Syria. They preached
the word of God, but only to Jews. 20However, some of the
believers who went to Antioch from Cyprus and Cyrene
began preaching to the Gentiles* about the Lord Jesus.
21The power of the Lord was with them, and a large number of these Gentiles believed and turned to the Lord.

22When the church at Jerusalem heard what had happened, they sent Barnabas to Antioch. 23When he arrived
and saw this evidence of God's blessing, he was filled with
joy, and he encouraged the believers to stay true to the
Lord. 24Barnabas was a good man, full of the Holy Spirit and
strong in faith. And many people were brought to the Lord.

25Then Barnabas went on to Tarsus to look for Saul.
26When he found him, he brought him back to Antioch.
Both of them stayed there with the church for a full year,
teaching large crowds of people. (It was at Antioch that
the believers* were first called Christians.)

27During this time some prophets traveled from Jerusalem to Antioch. 28One of them named Agabus stood up
in one of the meetings and predicted by the Spirit that a
great famine was coming upon the entire Roman world.
(This was fulfilled during the reign of Claudius.) 29So the
believers in Antioch decided to send relief to the brothers and sisters* in Judea, everyone giving as much as they
could. 30This they did, entrusting their gifts to Barnabas
and Saul to take to the elders of the church in Jerusalem.

12

JAMES IS KILLED AND PETER IS IMPRISONED

About that time King Herod Agrippa* began to persecute
some believers in the church. 2He had the apostle James
(John's brother) killed with a sword. 3When Herod saw how
much this pleased the Jewish people, he also arrested Peter.
(This took place during the Passover celebration.*) 4Then
he imprisoned him, placing him under the guard of four
squads of four soldiers each. Herod intended to bring Peter
out for public trial after the Passover. 5But while Peter was
in prison, the church prayed very earnestly for him.

PETER'S MIRACULOUS ESCAPE FROM PRISON

6The night before Peter was to be placed on trial, he was
asleep, fastened with two chains between two soldiers.
Others stood guard at the prison gate. 7Suddenly, there
was a bright light in the cell, and an angel of the Lord
stood before Peter. The angel struck him on the side to
awaken him and said, "Quick! Get up!" And the chains fell
off his wrists. 8Then the angel told him, "Get dressed and
put on your sandals." And he did. "Now put on your coat
and follow me," the angel ordered.

9So Peter left the cell, following the angel. But all the
time he thought it was a vision. He didn't realize it was actually happening. 10They passed the first and second
guard posts and came to the iron gate leading to the city,
and this opened for them all by itself. So they passed
through and started walking down the street, and then
the angel suddenly left him.

11Peter finally came to his senses. "It's really true!" he
said. "The Lord has sent his angel and saved me from
Herod and from what the Jewish leaders* had planned to
do to me!"

12When he realized this, he went to the home of Mary,
the mother of John Mark, where many were gathered for
prayer. 13He knocked at the door in the gate, and a servant girl named Rhoda came to open it. 14When she recognized Peter's voice, she was so overjoyed that, instead
of opening the door, she ran back inside and told everyone, "Peter is standing at the door!"

15"You're out of your mind!" they said. When she insisted, they decided, "It must be his angel."

ANSWERS 12:5-15

The prayers of the little group of believers were answered, even as they prayed. But when the answer arrived at the door, they didn't believe it. Sometimes the answer to a prayer might be staring us in the face. When you pray, believe you'll get an answer. When the answer comes, don't be surprised! ■

16Meanwhile, Peter continued knocking. When they
finally opened the door and saw him, they were amazed.
17He motioned for them to quiet down and told them
how the Lord had led him out of prison. "Tell James and
the other brothers what happened," he said. And then he
went to another place.

18At dawn there was a great commotion among the soldiers about what had happened to Peter. 19Herod Agrippa ordered a thorough search for him. When he couldn't
be found, Herod interrogated the guards and sentenced
them to death. Afterward Herod left Judea to stay in
Caesarea for a while.

THE DEATH OF HEROD AGRIPPA

20Now Herod was very angry with the people of Tyre and
Sidon. So they sent a delegation to make peace with him
because their cities were dependent upon Herod's country for food. The delegates won the support of Blastus,
Herod's personal assistant, 21and an appointment with
Herod was granted. When the day arrived, Herod put on
his royal robes, sat on his throne, and made a speech to
them. 22The people gave him a great ovation, shouting,
"It's the voice of a god, not of a man!"

23Instantly, an angel of the Lord struck Herod with a
sickness, because he accepted the people's worship instead of giving the glory to God. So he was consumed
with worms and died.

24Meanwhile, the word of God continued to spread,
and there were many new believers.

25When Barnabas and Saul had finished their mission
to Jerusalem, they returned,* taking John Mark with
them.

11:20 Greek *the Hellenists* (i.e., those who speak Greek); other manuscripts read *the Greeks.* **11:26** Greek *disciples;* also in 11:29. **11:29** Greek *the brothers.* **12:1** Greek *Herod the king.* He was the nephew of Herod Antipas and a grandson of Herod the Great. **12:3** Greek *the days of unleavened bread.* **12:11** Or *the Jewish people.* **12:25** Or *mission, they returned to Jerusalem.* Other manuscripts read *mission, they returned from Jerusalem;* still others read *mission, they returned from Jerusalem to Antioch.*

PRIDE

Seventeen-year-old Leslie has always wanted to sing, but not just in the youth choir at church or the high school choir. She wants to be an "American Idol," performing in an auditorium packed with cheering fans.

Leslie is talented and practices a lot. Every now and then she gets to do solos at church. But last night, she finally got the big break she's been hoping for. She sang three songs at a huge youth rally (over 2,000 teens) in a city 250 miles away. There she was in the spotlight on a big stage, using professional sound equipment managed by top-notch technicians. For that she was paid $500! We're talking "big time"!

Well, it went great. The audience loved her. Afterward, a handful of youth pastors asked her, "Can I book you to sing for my group?" People complimented her like crazy, tossing around words and phrases like "wonderful," "beautiful," and "going places." Some even asked when her first CD would be out.

The day after, Leslie is still basking in her sudden success. She barely wants to talk to her friends, who suddenly don't seem as successful.

Why is success and/or admiration so difficult to handle sometimes? Where do our talents come from? What happens if we forget God and snatch all of the glory for ourselves? Check out Acts 12:19-23. What, if anything, would you say to Leslie based on this passage?

13 BARNABAS AND SAUL ARE COMMISSIONED

Among the prophets and teachers of the church at Antioch of Syria were Barnabas, Simeon (called "the black
man"*), Lucius (from Cyrene), Manaen (the childhood
companion of King Herod Antipas*), and Saul. 2One day
as these men were worshiping the Lord and fasting, the
Holy Spirit said, "Dedicate Barnabas and Saul for the special work to which I have called them." 3So after more
fasting and prayer, the men laid their hands on them and
sent them on their way.

PAUL'S FIRST MISSIONARY JOURNEY

4So Barnabas and Saul were sent out by the Holy Spirit.
They went down to the seaport of Seleucia and then sailed
for the island of Cyprus. 5There, in the town of Salamis,
they went to the Jewish synagogues and preached the
word of God. John Mark went with them as their assistant.
6Afterward they traveled from town to town across the
entire island until finally they reached Paphos, where
they met a Jewish sorcerer, a false prophet named Bar-
Jesus. 7He had attached himself to the governor, Sergius
Paulus, who was an intelligent man. The governor invited
Barnabas and Saul to visit him, for he wanted to hear the
word of God. 8But Elymas, the sorcerer (as his name
means in Greek), interfered and urged the governor to
pay no attention to what Barnabas and Saul said. He was
trying to keep the governor from believing.
9Saul, also known as Paul, was filled with the Holy
Spirit, and he looked the sorcerer in the eye. 10Then he
said, "You son of the devil, full of every sort of deceit and
fraud, and enemy of all that is good! Will you never stop
perverting the true ways of the Lord? 11Watch now, for
the Lord has laid his hand of punishment upon you, and
you will be struck blind. You will not see the sunlight for
some time." Instantly mist and darkness came over the
man's eyes, and he began groping around begging for
someone to take his hand and lead him.
12When the governor saw what had happened, he became a believer, for he was astonished at the teaching
about the Lord.

PAUL PREACHES IN ANTIOCH OF PISIDIA

13Paul and his companions then left Paphos by ship for
Pamphylia, landing at the port town of Perga. There John
Mark left them and returned to Jerusalem. 14But Paul and
Barnabas traveled inland to Antioch of Pisidia.*
On the Sabbath they went to the synagogue for the
services. 15After the usual readings from the books of
Moses* and the prophets, those in charge of the service
sent them this message: "Brothers, if you have any word
of encouragement for the people, come and give it."
16So Paul stood, lifted his hand to quiet them, and
started speaking. "Men of Israel," he said, "and you God-
fearing Gentiles, listen to me.
17"The God of this nation of Israel chose our ancestors
and made them multiply and grow strong during their
stay in Egypt. Then with a powerful arm he led them out
of their slavery. 18He put up with them* through forty
years of wandering in the wilderness. 19Then he destroyed seven nations in Canaan and gave their land to
Israel as an inheritance. 20All this took about 450 years.
"After that, God gave them judges to rule until the
time of Samuel the prophet. 21Then the people begged
for a king, and God gave them Saul son of Kish, a man of
the tribe of Benjamin, who reigned for forty years. 22But
God removed Saul and replaced him with David, a man
about whom God said, 'I have found David son of Jesse, a
man after my own heart. He will do everything I want
him to do.'*
23"And it is one of King David's descendants, Jesus,
who is God's promised Savior of Israel! 24Before he came,
John the Baptist preached that all the people of Israel
needed to repent of their sins and turn to God and be
baptized. 25As John was finishing his ministry he asked,
'Do you think I am the Messiah? No, I am not! But he is
coming soon—and I'm not even worthy to be his slave
and untie the sandals on his feet.'
26"Brothers—you sons of Abraham, and also you God-
fearing Gentiles—this message of salvation has been sent
to us! 27The people in Jerusalem and their leaders did not
recognize Jesus as the one the prophets had spoken
about. Instead, they condemned him, and in doing this

13:1a Greek *who was called Niger.* **13:1b** Greek *Herod the tetrarch.* **13:13-14** *Pamphylia* and *Pisidia* were districts in what is now Turkey. **13:15** Greek *from the law.* **13:18** Some manuscripts read *He cared for them;* compare Deut 1:31. **13:22** 1 Sam 13:14.

they fulfilled the prophets' words that are read every Sabbath. 28They found no legal reason to execute him, but
they asked Pilate to have him killed anyway.
29"When they had done all that the prophecies said
about him, they took him down from the cross* and
placed him in a tomb. 30But God raised him from the
dead! 31And over a period of many days he appeared to
those who had gone with him from Galilee to Jerusalem. They are now his witnesses to the people of Israel.
32"And now we are here to bring you this Good News.
The promise was made to our ancestors, 33and God has
now fulfilled it for us, their descendants, by raising Jesus.
This is what the second psalm says about Jesus:

'You are my Son.
Today I have become your Father.*'

34For God had promised to raise him from the dead, not
leaving him to rot in the grave. He said, 'I will give you the
sacred blessings I promised to David.'* 35Another psalm
explains it more fully: 'You will not allow your Holy One to
rot in the grave.'* 36This is not a reference to David, for after David had done the will of God in his own generation,
he died and was buried with his ancestors, and his body
decayed. 37No, it was a reference to someone else—someone whom God raised and whose body did not decay.
38*"Brothers, listen! We are here to proclaim that through
this man Jesus there is forgiveness for your sins. 39Everyone
who believes in him is declared right with God—something
the law of Moses could never do. 40Be careful! Don't let the
prophets' words apply to you. For they said,

41 'Look, you mockers,
be amazed and die!

13:29 Greek *from the tree.* 13:33 Or *Today I reveal you as my Son.* Ps 2:7. 13:34 Isa 55:3. 13:35 Ps 16:10. 13:38 English translations divide verses 38 and 39 in various ways.

JOHN MARK

UPS:
- Wrote the Gospel of Mark
- Allowed his home to be used as one of the main meeting places for Christians in Jerusalem
- Persisted beyond his youthful mistakes
- Was an assistant and traveling companion to three of the greatest early missionaries

DOWNS:
- Probably the nameless young man described in the Gospel of Mark who fled in panic when Jesus was arrested
- Left Paul and Barnabas during the first missionary journey

STATS:
- Where: Jerusalem
- Occupation: Missionary-in-training, Gospel writer, traveling companion
- Relatives: Mary (mother); Barnabas (cousin)
- Contemporaries: Paul, Peter, Timothy, Luke, Silas

BOTTOM LINE:
Maturity comes as a result of learning from mistakes, not the absence of them.
Effective living is not measured by what we accomplish so much as by what we overcome in order to accomplish our goals.
Encouragement can change a person's life.

John Mark's story is told in Acts 12:24–13:13 and 15:36-39. He also is mentioned in Col 4:10; 2 Tim 4:11; Philem 24; and 1 Pet 5:13.

JOHN MARK What did you learn from your last mistake? Mistakes can be effective teachers, because the consequences have a way of making lessons painfully clear. But those who learn from their mistakes gain wisdom.

John Mark, with the help of some time and encouragement, became a wise learner. Although he was eager to do the right thing, he had trouble staying on task. In his Gospel, Mark mentions a young man (probably himself) who fled in such fear during Jesus' arrest that he left his clothes behind (Mark 14:50-52). This tendency to run showed up again later in Mark's life when Paul and Barnabas took him as their assistant on their first missionary journey. Early in the trip, Mark left them and returned to Jerusalem. (See Acts 12:23–13:13.)

Paul didn't appreciate Mark's desertion. Two years later, Paul wouldn't even consider letting Mark try again. As a result, the team split up (Acts 15:36-39). Barnabas took his cousin Mark as his traveling companion, while Paul chose Silas.

Barnabas was patient with Mark, and the young man turned out to be a good investment. In fact, Paul and Mark were later reunited. The older apostle became a close friend of the young disciple (see 2 Tim 4:11).

Mark was able to watch closely the lives of three Christian leaders—Barnabas, Paul, and Peter. Peter probably provided much of the information in Mark's Gospel. As his helper, Mark had a chance to hear Peter's stories of the years with Jesus over and over. Mark became one of the first to put Jesus' life into writing.

Mark's experience can remind us to learn from our mistakes and to appreciate the patience of others. Who is the Barnabas or Peter in your life? How has he or she encouraged you?

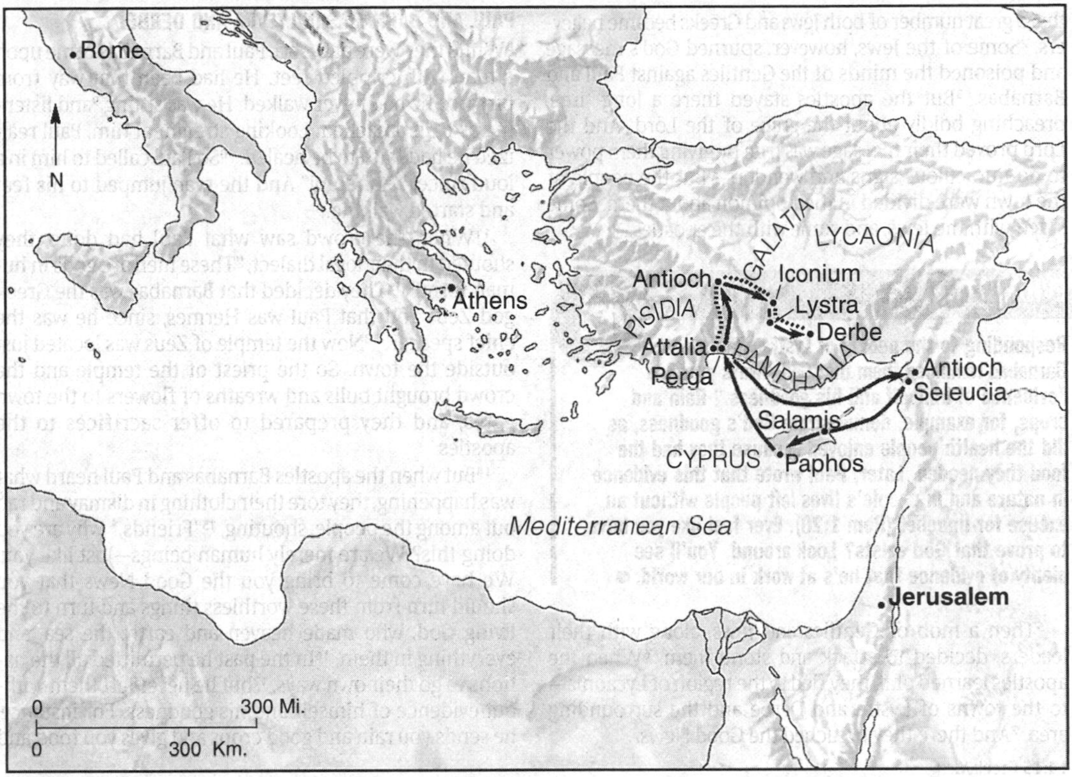

PAUL'S FIRST MISSIONARY JOURNEY (ACTS 13:1—14:28)

For I am doing something in your own day,
something you wouldn't believe
even if someone told you about it.'*"

FROM JEALOUSY TO JOY 13:42-45

Although the Jewish leaders brought theological arguments against Paul and Barnabas, jealousy was the real reason behind their denunciation. When we see others succeeding where we haven't or receiving the glory that we want, we sometimes feel envy instead of feeling happy for them. Is that your response? But with the help of the Holy Spirit, we can rise above envy or jealousy and rejoice. ■

42As Paul and Barnabas left the synagogue that day, the
people begged them to speak about these things again
the next week. 43Many Jews and devout converts to Judaism followed Paul and Barnabas, and the two men urged
them to continue to rely on the grace of God.

PAUL TURNS TO THE GENTILES

44The following week almost the entire city turned out to
hear them preach the word of the Lord. 45But when some
of the Jews saw the crowds, they were jealous; so they
slandered Paul and argued against whatever he said.
46Then Paul and Barnabas spoke out boldly and declared, "It was necessary that we first preach the word of
God to you Jews. But since you have rejected it and judged
yourselves unworthy of eternal life, we will offer it to the
Gentiles. 47For the Lord gave us this command when he
said,

'I have made you a light to the Gentiles,
to bring salvation to the farthest corners of the
earth.'*"

48When the Gentiles heard this, they were very glad
and thanked the Lord for his message; and all who were
chosen for eternal life became believers. 49So the Lord's
message spread throughout that region.
50Then the Jews stirred up the influential religious
women and the leaders of the city, and they incited a mob
against Paul and Barnabas and ran them out of town. 51So
they shook the dust from their feet as a sign of rejection
and went to the town of Iconium. 52And the believers*
were filled with joy and with the Holy Spirit.

14 PAUL AND BARNABAS IN ICONIUM

The same thing happened in Iconium.* Paul and Barnabas
went to the Jewish synagogue and preached with such power

13:41 Hab 1:5 (Greek version). 13:47 Isa 49:6. 13:52 Greek *the disciples.* 14:1 *Iconium,* as well as *Lystra* and *Derbe* (14:6), were towns in what is now Turkey.

that a great number of both Jews and Greeks became believers. 2Some of the Jews, however, spurned God's message
and poisoned the minds of the Gentiles against Paul and
Barnabas. 3But the apostles stayed there a long time,
preaching boldly about the grace of the Lord. And the
Lord proved their message was true by giving them power
to do miraculous signs and wonders. 4But the people of
the town were divided in their opinion about them. Some
sided with the Jews, and some with the apostles.

EVIDENCE 14:1-18

Responding to the people of Lystra, Paul and Barnabas reminded them that God always provided "evidence of himself and his goodness." Rain and crops, for example, demonstrate God's goodness, as did the health people enjoyed because they had the food they needed. Later, Paul wrote that this evidence in nature and in people's lives left people without an excuse for unbelief (Rom 1:20). Ever feel like you have to prove that God exists? Look around. You'll see plenty of evidence that he's at work in our world. ■

5Then a mob of Gentiles and Jews, along with their
leaders, decided to attack and stone them. 6When the
apostles learned of it, they fled to the region of Lycaonia—
to the towns of Lystra and Derbe and the surrounding
area. 7And there they preached the Good News.

PAUL AND BARNABAS IN LYSTRA AND DERBE

8While they were at Lystra, Paul and Barnabas came upon
a man with crippled feet. He had been that way from
birth, so he had never walked. He was sitting 9and listening as Paul preached. Looking straight at him, Paul realized he had faith to be healed. 10So Paul called to him in a
loud voice, "Stand up!" And the man jumped to his feet
and started walking.

11When the crowd saw what Paul had done, they
shouted in their local dialect, "These men are gods in human form!" 12They decided that Barnabas was the Greek
god Zeus and that Paul was Hermes, since he was the
chief speaker. 13Now the temple of Zeus was located just
outside the town. So the priest of the temple and the
crowd brought bulls and wreaths of flowers to the town
gates, and they prepared to offer sacrifices to the
apostles.

14But when the apostles Barnabas and Paul heard what
was happening, they tore their clothing in dismay and ran
out among the people, shouting, 15"Friends,* why are you
doing this? We are merely human beings—just like you!
We have come to bring you the Good News that you
should turn from these worthless things and turn to the
living God, who made heaven and earth, the sea, and
everything in them. 16In the past he permitted all the nations to go their own ways, 17but he never left them without evidence of himself and his goodness. For instance,
he sends you rain and good crops and gives you food and

14:15 Greek *Men.*

BARNABAS

UPS:
- One of the first to sell his possessions to help the Christians in Jerusalem
- Paul's first missionary partner
- Was an encourager, as his nickname shows, and thus one of the most quietly influential people in the early days of Christianity
- Called an apostle, although not one of the original Twelve

DOWN:
- Temporarily stayed aloof from Gentile believers until Paul corrected him

STATS:
- Where: Cyprus, Jerusalem, Antioch
- Occupation: Missionary, teacher
- Relatives: Mary (sister); John Mark (cousin)
- Contemporaries: Peter, Silas, Paul, Herod Agrippa I

BOTTOM LINE:

Encouragement is one of the most effective ways to help others.

Sooner or later, true obedience to God will involve risk.

Barnabas's story is told in Acts 4:36-37; 9:27; 11:25-30; 12:24–15:39. He also is mentioned in 1 Cor 9:6; Gal 2:1, 9-13; Col 4:10.

BARNABAS Think about the people who really matter in your life. Odds are that many of them are encouragers who have found ways to help you keep going. Good friends can tell when you're doing well and when you need to try harder. Mostly, they never give up on you! Everyone needs that kind of encouragement.

Among the first Christians, a man named Joseph was such an encourager that other believers nicknamed him "Son of Encouragement," or "Barnabas" (Acts 4:36-37). Barnabas had an unusual ability to find people he could help. Whenever Barnabas encouraged Christians, the result was that others became believers!

Barnabas's actions were crucial to the early church. In a way, we can thank him for most of the New Testament. God used Barnabas's relationship with Paul at one point and with Mark at another to help these two men when either might have failed. Barnabas did wonders with encouragement.

We're surrounded by people we can encourage. Think about this: Are you faster at encouraging others or criticizing them? Although showing people where they're wrong may be important at times, we'll be of greater help in the long run if we encourage people. How will you encourage others?

joyful hearts." 18But even with these words, Paul and Barnabas could scarcely restrain the people from sacrificing
to them.
19Then some Jews arrived from Antioch and Iconium
and won the crowds to their side. They stoned Paul and
dragged him out of town, thinking he was dead. 20But as
the believers* gathered around him, he got up and went
back into the town. The next day he left with Barnabas
for Derbe.

PAUL AND BARNABAS RETURN TO ANTIOCH OF SYRIA

21After preaching the Good News in Derbe and making
many disciples, Paul and Barnabas returned to Lystra,
Iconium, and Antioch of Pisidia, 22where they strengthened the believers. They encouraged them to continue in
the faith, reminding them that we must suffer many
hardships to enter the Kingdom of God. 23Paul and Barnabas also appointed elders in every church. With prayer
and fasting, they turned the elders over to the care of the
Lord, in whom they had put their trust. 24Then they traveled back through Pisidia to Pamphylia. 25They preached
the word in Perga, then went down to Attalia.
26Finally, they returned by ship to Antioch of Syria,
where their journey had begun. The believers there had
entrusted them to the grace of God to do the work they
had now completed. 27Upon arriving in Antioch, they
called the church together and reported everything God
had done through them and how he had opened the door
of faith to the Gentiles, too. 28And they stayed there with
the believers for a long time.

15 THE COUNCIL AT JERUSALEM

While Paul and Barnabas were at Antioch of Syria, some
men from Judea arrived and began to teach the believers*: "Unless you are circumcised as required by the law
of Moses, you cannot be saved." 2Paul and Barnabas
disagreed with them, arguing vehemently. Finally, the
church decided to send Paul and Barnabas to Jerusalem,
accompanied by some local believers, to talk to the apostles and elders about this question. 3The church sent the
delegates to Jerusalem, and they stopped along the way in
Phoenicia and Samaria to visit the believers. They told
them—much to everyone's joy—that the Gentiles, too,
were being converted.
4When they arrived in Jerusalem, Barnabas and Paul
were welcomed by the whole church, including the apostles and elders. They reported everything God had done
through them. 5But then some of the believers who belonged to the sect of the Pharisees stood up and insisted,
"The Gentile converts must be circumcised and required
to follow the law of Moses."
6So the apostles and elders met together to resolve this
issue. 7At the meeting, after a long discussion, Peter stood
and addressed them as follows: "Brothers, you all know
that God chose me from among you some time ago to

14:20 Greek *disciples;* also in 14:22, 28. **15:1** Greek *brothers;* also in 15:3, 23, 32, 33, 36, 40.

UPS:
- Represented the church in carrying the "acceptance letter" prepared by the Jerusalem council to the Gentile believers in Antioch
- Was closely associated with Paul from the second missionary journey on
- When imprisoned with Paul in Philippi, sang songs of praise to God
- Worked as a secretary for both Paul and Peter, using "Silvanus" as his pen name

STATS:
- Where: Roman citizen living in Jerusalem
- Occupation: One of the first career missionaries
- Contemporaries: Paul, Timothy, Peter, Mark, Barnabas

BOTTOM LINE:

Partnership is a significant part of effective ministry.

God never said that his servants will avoid suffering. In fact, he guarantees that they will suffer.

Obedience to God may mean giving up what makes us feel secure.

Silas's story is told in Acts 15:22–19:10. He also is mentioned in 2 Cor 1:19; 1 Thess 1:1; 2 Thess 1:1; 1 Pet 5:12.

SILAS One word that doesn't fit in the lives of the first Christians is *boring*. Too many exciting things happened. Christian missionaries took hazardous journeys over land and sea. Even preaching the gospel was sometimes dangerous, since resistance and hatred of the message often occurred.

Right in the middle of all the excitement was a young man named Silas. We first meet Silas when he acted as one of the representatives from Jerusalem to spread the official news that Gentiles did not have to be circumcised before they became Christians (see Acts 15). This was an important mission.

Later, Silas joined Paul and Timothy's ministry team. Life continued to be exciting. Paul and Silas spent a night singing in prison in Philippi after being severely beaten. Another time, they were almost beaten in Thessalonica but were able to pull off a daring escape in the night. Then after Paul left, Silas and Timothy continued to encourage the young believers in the Berean church.

We don't know what eventually happened to Silas. He spent some time with Peter and is acknowledged in 1 Peter. He continued to live the same faithful life that made him a good choice to represent the church in Jerusalem. Though he never sought the spotlight, his humility and consistency caused him to be remembered.

SILAS

preach to the Gentiles so that they could hear the Good
News and believe. 8God knows people's hearts, and he
confirmed that he accepts Gentiles by giving them the
Holy Spirit, just as he did to us. 9He made no distinction
between us and them, for he cleansed their hearts
through faith. 10So why are you now challenging God by
burdening the Gentile believers* with a yoke that neither
we nor our ancestors were able to bear? 11We believe that
we are all saved the same way, by the undeserved grace of
the Lord Jesus."
12Everyone listened quietly as Barnabas and Paul told
about the miraculous signs and wonders God had done
through them among the Gentiles.
13When they had finished, James stood and said,
"Brothers, listen to me. 14Peter* has told you about the
time God first visited the Gentiles to take from them a
people for himself. 15And this conversion of Gentiles is
exactly what the prophets predicted. As it is written:

16 'Afterward I will return
and restore the fallen house* of David.
I will rebuild its ruins
and restore it,
17 so that the rest of humanity might seek the LORD,
including the Gentiles—
all those I have called to be mine.
The LORD has spoken—
18 he who made these things known so long ago.'*

19"And so my judgment is that we should not make it
difficult for the Gentiles who are turning to God.
20Instead, we should write and tell them to abstain from
eating food offered to idols, from sexual immorality,
from eating the meat of strangled animals, and from
consuming blood. 21For these laws of Moses have been
preached in Jewish synagogues in every city on every
Sabbath for many generations."

THE LETTER FOR GENTILE BELIEVERS

22Then the apostles and elders together with the whole
church in Jerusalem chose delegates, and they sent them
to Antioch of Syria with Paul and Barnabas to report on
this decision. The men chosen were two of the church
leaders*—Judas (also called Barsabbas) and Silas. 23This
is the letter they took with them:

"This letter is from the apostles and elders, your
brothers in Jerusalem. It is written to the Gentile
believers in Antioch, Syria, and Cilicia. Greetings!
24"We understand that some men from here have
troubled you and upset you with their teaching, but
we did not send them! 25So we decided, having
come to complete agreement, to send you official
representatives, along with our beloved Barnabas and
Paul, 26who have risked their lives for the name of our
Lord Jesus Christ. 27We are sending Judas and Silas to
confirm what we have decided concerning your
question.
28"For it seemed good to the Holy Spirit and to us
to lay no greater burden on you than these few
requirements: 29You must abstain from eating food
offered to idols, from consuming blood or the meat
of strangled animals, and from sexual immorality. If
you do this, you will do well. Farewell."

30The messengers went at once to Antioch, where they
called a general meeting of the believers and delivered
the letter. 31And there was great joy throughout the
church that day as they read this encouraging message.
32Then Judas and Silas, both being prophets, spoke at
length to the believers, encouraging and strengthening
their faith. 33They stayed for a while, and then the believers sent them back to the church in Jerusalem with a
blessing of peace.* 35Paul and Barnabas stayed in Antioch. They and many others taught and preached the
word of the Lord there.

PAUL AND BARNABAS SEPARATE

36After some time Paul said to Barnabas, "Let's go back
and visit each city where we previously preached the
word of the Lord, to see how the new believers are doing."
37Barnabas agreed and wanted to take along John Mark.
38But Paul disagreed strongly, since John Mark had deserted them in Pamphylia and had not continued with
them in their work. 39Their disagreement was so sharp
that they separated. Barnabas took John Mark with him
and sailed for Cyprus. 40Paul chose Silas, and as he left,
the believers entrusted him to the Lord's gracious care.
41Then he traveled throughout Syria and Cilicia,
strengthening the churches there.

BARRIERS 16:1-3

Timothy was the son of a Jewish mother and a Greek father. Consequently, Paul asked Timothy to be circumcised, because he knew that some of the Jewish believers would have trouble accepting him if he wasn't circumcised. Although this act wasn't required (the Jerusalem council had voted against the necessity of it—see chapter 15), Timothy voluntarily did so to overcome barriers to his witness for Christ. Going beyond the minimum requirements is sometimes necessary to avoid giving anyone a reason to reject what we say about God. Is that your philosophy? ■

16

PAUL'S SECOND MISSIONARY JOURNEY

Paul went first to Derbe and then to Lystra, where there
was a young disciple named Timothy. His mother was a
Jewish believer, but his father was a Greek. 2Timothy was
well thought of by the believers* in Lystra and Iconium,
3so Paul wanted him to join them on their journey. In def-

15:10 Greek *disciples.* 15:14 Greek *Symeon.* 15:16 Or *kingdom;* Greek reads *tent.* 15:16-18 Amos 9:11-12 (Greek version); Isa 45:21.
15:22 Greek *were leaders among the brothers.* 15:33 Some manuscripts add verse 34, *But Silas decided to stay there.* 16:2 Greek *brothers;* also in 16:40.

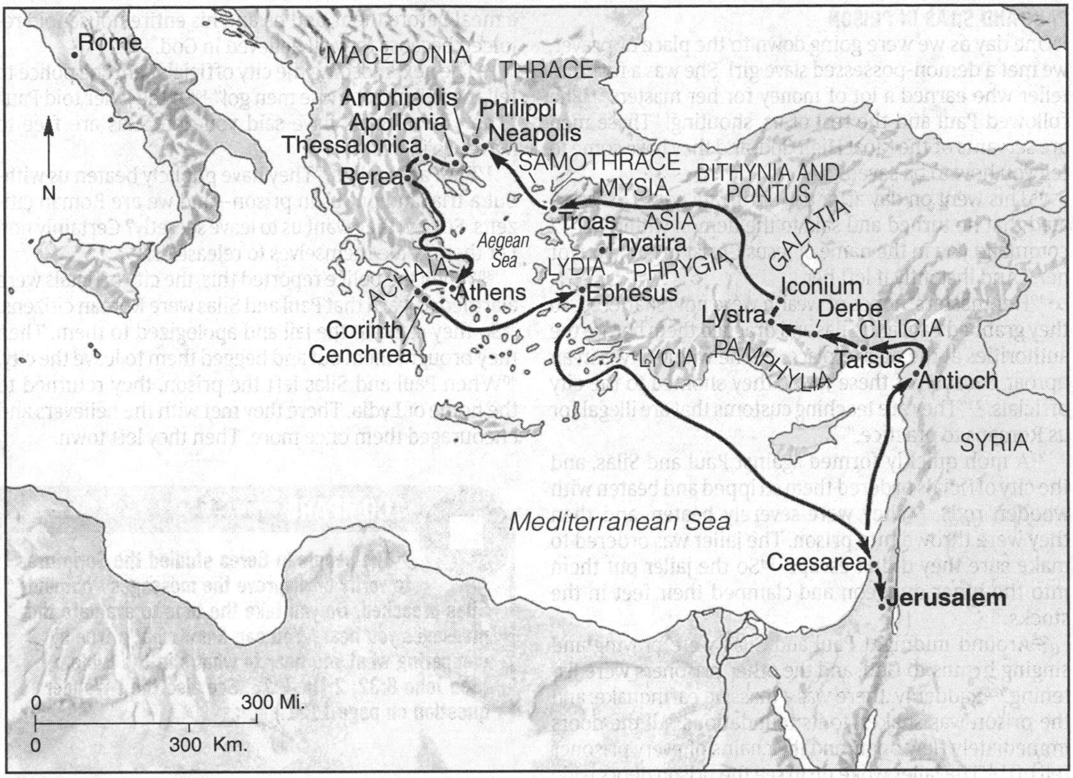

PAUL'S SECOND MISSIONARY JOURNEY (ACTS 15:36—18:22)

erence to the Jews of the area, he arranged for Timothy to
be circumcised before they left, for everyone knew that
his father was a Greek. 4Then they went from town to
town, instructing the believers to follow the decisions
made by the apostles and elders in Jerusalem. 5So the
churches were strengthened in their faith and grew
larger every day.

HOW GOD SPEAKS 16:6

We don't know how the Holy Spirit told Paul that he and his men were not to go into Asia. He may have spoken through a prophet, a vision, an inner conviction, or some other circumstance. Are you wondering what God is telling you to do? He often speaks through (1) well-chosen verses in the Bible; (2) the advice of mature Christians; (3) opportunities he provides; (4) prayer. Are you listening? ■

A CALL FROM MACEDONIA

6Next Paul and Silas traveled through the area of Phrygia
and Galatia, because the Holy Spirit had prevented them
from preaching the word in the province of Asia at that
time. 7Then coming to the borders of Mysia, they headed
north for the province of Bithynia,* but again the Spirit
of Jesus did not allow them to go there. 8So instead, they
went on through Mysia to the seaport of Troas.

9That night Paul had a vision: A man from Macedonia
in northern Greece was standing there, pleading with
him, "Come over to Macedonia and help us!" 10So we* decided to leave for Macedonia at once, having concluded
that God was calling us to preach the Good News there.

LYDIA OF PHILIPPI BELIEVES IN JESUS

11We boarded a boat at Troas and sailed straight across to
the island of Samothrace, and the next day we landed at
Neapolis. 12From there we reached Philippi, a major city
of that district of Macedonia and a Roman colony. And
we stayed there several days.

13On the Sabbath we went a little way outside the city
to a riverbank, where we thought people would be meeting for prayer, and we sat down to speak with some
women who had gathered there. 14One of them was Lydia from Thyatira, a merchant of expensive purple cloth,
who worshiped God. As she listened to us, the Lord
opened her heart, and she accepted what Paul was saying. 15She was baptized along with other members of
her household, and she asked us to be her guests. "If you
agree that I am a true believer in the Lord," she said,
"come and stay at my home." And she urged us until we
agreed.

16:6-7 *Phrygia, Galatia, Asia, Mysia,* and *Bithynia* were all districts in what is now Turkey. **16:10** Luke, the writer of this book, here joined Paul and accompanied him on his journey.

PAUL AND SILAS IN PRISON

16One day as we were going down to the place of prayer, we met a demon-possessed slave girl. She was a fortuneteller who earned a lot of money for her masters. 17She followed Paul and the rest of us, shouting, "These men are servants of the Most High God, and they have come to tell you how to be saved."

18This went on day after day until Paul got so exasperated that he turned and said to the demon within her, "I command you in the name of Jesus Christ to come out of her." And instantly it left her.

19Her masters' hopes of wealth were now shattered, so they grabbed Paul and Silas and dragged them before the authorities at the marketplace. 20"The whole city is in an uproar because of these Jews!" they shouted to the city officials. 21"They are teaching customs that are illegal for us Romans to practice."

22A mob quickly formed against Paul and Silas, and the city officials ordered them stripped and beaten with wooden rods. 23They were severely beaten, and then they were thrown into prison. The jailer was ordered to make sure they didn't escape. 24So the jailer put them into the inner dungeon and clamped their feet in the stocks.

25Around midnight Paul and Silas were praying and singing hymns to God, and the other prisoners were listening. 26Suddenly, there was a massive earthquake, and the prison was shaken to its foundations. All the doors immediately flew open, and the chains of every prisoner fell off! 27The jailer woke up to see the prison doors wide open. He assumed the prisoners had escaped, so he drew his sword to kill himself. 28But Paul shouted to him, "Stop! Don't kill yourself! We are all here!"

A GODLY RESPONSE 16:16-34

While in Philippi, Paul and Silas were beaten and placed in stocks in a dungeon. Instead of grumbling about how unfairly they had been treated, they sang praise songs to God while the other prisoners listened. Later, the jailer and his whole family became believers because of Paul and Silas's example.

How do you respond to unfair circumstances? Do you grumble or praise? Like Paul and Silas, you never know who might be listening. God may use your Christlike reaction to lead someone to him. ■

29The jailer called for lights and ran to the dungeon and fell down trembling before Paul and Silas. 30Then he brought them out and asked, "Sirs, what must I do to be saved?"

31They replied, "Believe in the Lord Jesus and you will be saved, along with everyone in your household." 32And they shared the word of the Lord with him and with all who lived in his household. 33Even at that hour of the night, the jailer cared for them and washed their wounds. Then he and everyone in his household were immediately baptized. 34He brought them into his house and set a meal before them, and he and his entire household rejoiced because they all believed in God.

35The next morning the city officials sent the police to tell the jailer, "Let those men go!" 36So the jailer told Paul, "The city officials have said you and Silas are free to leave. Go in peace."

37But Paul replied, "They have publicly beaten us without a trial and put us in prison—and we are Roman citizens. So now they want us to leave secretly? Certainly not! Let them come themselves to release us!"

38When the police reported this, the city officials were alarmed to learn that Paul and Silas were Roman citizens. 39So they came to the jail and apologized to them. Then they brought them out and begged them to leave the city. 40When Paul and Silas left the prison, they returned to the home of Lydia. There they met with the believers and encouraged them once more. Then they left town.

COMPARE 17:11

The people in Berea studied the Scriptures to verify or disprove the messages Paul and Silas preached. Do you take the time to evaluate the messages you hear? You can know what's true by comparing what you hear to what's in the Bible. (See John 8:32; 2 Tim 2:15. See also the I Wonder question on page 1121.) ■

17

PAUL PREACHES IN THESSALONICA

Paul and Silas then traveled through the towns of Amphipolis and Apollonia and came to Thessalonica, where there was a Jewish synagogue. 2As was Paul's custom, he went to the synagogue service, and for three Sabbaths in a row he used the Scriptures to reason with the people. 3He explained the prophecies and proved that the Messiah must suffer and rise from the dead. He said, "This Jesus I'm telling you about is the Messiah." 4Some of the Jews who listened were persuaded and joined Paul and Silas, along with many God-fearing Greek men and quite a few prominent women.*

5But some of the Jews were jealous, so they gathered some troublemakers from the marketplace to form a mob and start a riot. They attacked the home of Jason, searching for Paul and Silas so they could drag them out to the crowd.* 6Not finding them there, they dragged out Jason and some of the other believers* instead and took them before the city council. "Paul and Silas have caused trouble all over the world," they shouted, "and now they are here disturbing our city, too. 7And Jason has welcomed them into his home. They are all guilty of treason against Caesar, for they profess allegiance to another king, named Jesus."

8The people of the city, as well as the city council, were thrown into turmoil by these reports. 9So the officials forced Jason and the other believers to post bond, and then they released them.

17:4 Some manuscripts read *quite a few of the wives of the leading men.* 17:5 Or *the city council.* 17:6 Greek *brothers;* also in 17:10, 14.

PAUL AND SILAS IN BEREA

10 That very night the believers sent Paul and Silas to Berea. When they arrived there, they went to the Jewish synagogue. 11 And the people of Berea were more open-minded than those in Thessalonica, and they listened eagerly to Paul's message. They searched the Scriptures day after day to see if Paul and Silas were teaching the truth. 12 As a result, many Jews believed, as did many of the prominent Greek women and men.

13 But when some Jews in Thessalonica learned that Paul was preaching the word of God in Berea, they went there and stirred up trouble. 14 The believers acted at once, sending Paul on to the coast, while Silas and Timothy remained behind. 15 Those escorting Paul went with him all the way to Athens; then they returned to Berea with instructions for Silas and Timothy to hurry and join him.

PAUL PREACHES IN ATHENS

16 While Paul was waiting for them in Athens, he was deeply troubled by all the idols he saw everywhere in the city. 17 He went to the synagogue to reason with the Jews and the God-fearing Gentiles, and he spoke daily in the public square to all who happened to be there.

18 He also had a debate with some of the Epicurean and Stoic philosophers. When he told them about Jesus and his resurrection, they said, "What's this babbler trying to say with these strange ideas he's picked up?" Others said, "He seems to be preaching about some foreign gods."

19 Then they took him to the high council of the city.* "Come and tell us about this new teaching," they said. 20 "You are saying some rather strange things, and we want to know what it's all about." 21 (It should be explained that all the Athenians as well as the foreigners in Athens seemed to spend all their time discussing the latest ideas.)

WORTH IT 17:22-34

Paul's speech received a mixed reaction: Some people laughed, some kept searching for more information, and a few believed. As you tell others about Jesus, you might have this kind of mixed response. But the belief of only a few is still worth the effort. ■

22 So Paul, standing before the council,* addressed them as follows: "Men of Athens, I notice that you are very religious in every way, 23 for as I was walking along I saw your many shrines. And one of your altars had this inscription on it: 'To an Unknown God.' This God, whom you worship without knowing, is the one I'm telling you about.

24 "He is the God who made the world and everything in it. Since he is Lord of heaven and earth, he doesn't live in man-made temples, 25 and human hands can't serve his needs—for he has no needs. He himself gives life and breath to everything, and he satisfies every need. 26 From one man* he created all the nations throughout the whole earth. He decided beforehand when they should rise and fall, and he determined their boundaries.

27 "His purpose was for the nations to seek after God and perhaps feel their way toward him and find him—though he is not far from any one of us. 28 For in him we live and move and exist. As some of your* own poets have said, 'We are his offspring.' 29 And since this is true, we shouldn't think of God as an idol designed by craftsmen from gold or silver or stone.

30 "God overlooked people's ignorance about these things in earlier times, but now he commands everyone everywhere to repent of their sins and turn to him. 31 For he has set a day for judging the world with justice by the man he has appointed, and he proved to everyone who this is by raising him from the dead."

32 When they heard Paul speak about the resurrection of the dead, some laughed in contempt, but others said, "We want to hear more about this later." 33 That ended Paul's discussion with them, 34 but some joined him and became believers. Among them were Dionysius, a member of the council,* a woman named Damaris, and others with them.

17:19 Or *the most learned society of philosophers in the city.* Greek reads *the Areopagus.* **17:22** Traditionally rendered *standing in the middle of Mars Hill;* Greek reads *standing in the middle of the Areopagus.* **17:26** Greek *From one;* other manuscripts read *From one blood.* **17:28** Some manuscripts read *our.* **17:34** Greek *an Areopagite.*

I'm not the kind of person who can take everything at face value. Is it wrong to want to seek answers to questions I have about the Bible? Why or why not?

The Christians in Berea were complimented by Luke, the writer of Acts, because "they searched the Scriptures day after day to see if Paul and Silas were teaching the truth" (Acts 17:11).

Because being a Christian means accepting Christ's forgiveness by faith, some think we must believe everything just because another Christian said it. But getting your questions answered by studying the Bible is an important part of being a Christian. Although not every question can be answered, most of them can.

Some people are natural skeptics. They challenge everything in the Bible simply because they're looking for an argument, rather than answers. If, however, you really want answers, God will help you find them. "Keep on asking, and you will receive what you ask for. Keep on seeking, and you will find. Keep on knocking, and the door will be opened to you. For everyone who asks, receives. Everyone who seeks, finds. And to everyone who knocks, the door will be opened" (Matt 7:7-8).

Keep asking your questions and looking for answers.

18

PAUL MEETS PRISCILLA AND AQUILA IN CORINTH

Then Paul left Athens and went to Corinth.* 2There he became acquainted with a Jew named Aquila, born in Pontus, who had recently arrived from Italy with his wife, Priscilla. They had left Italy when Claudius Caesar deported all Jews from Rome. 3Paul lived and worked with them, for they were tentmakers* just as he was.

4Each Sabbath found Paul at the synagogue, trying to convince the Jews and Greeks alike. 5And after Silas and Timothy came down from Macedonia, Paul spent all his time preaching the word. He testified to the Jews that Jesus was the Messiah. 6But when they opposed and insulted him, Paul shook the dust from his clothes and said, "Your blood is upon your own heads—I am innocent. From now on I will go preach to the Gentiles."

7Then he left and went to the home of Titius Justus, a Gentile who worshiped God and lived next door to the synagogue. 8Crispus, the leader of the synagogue, and everyone in his household believed in the Lord. Many others in Corinth also heard Paul, became believers, and were baptized.

9One night the Lord spoke to Paul in a vision and told him, "Don't be afraid! Speak out! Don't be silent! 10For I am with you, and no one will attack and harm you, for many people in this city belong to me." 11So Paul stayed there for the next year and a half, teaching the word of God.

12But when Gallio became governor of Achaia, some Jews rose up together against Paul and brought him before the governor for judgment. 13They accused Paul of "persuading people to worship God in ways that are contrary to our law."

14But just as Paul started to make his defense, Gallio turned to Paul's accusers and said, "Listen, you Jews, if this were a case involving some wrongdoing or a serious crime, I would have a reason to accept your case. 15But since it is merely a question of words and names and your Jewish law, take care of it yourselves. I refuse to judge such matters." 16And he threw them out of the courtroom.

17The crowd* then grabbed Sosthenes, the leader of the synagogue, and beat him right there in the courtroom. But Gallio paid no attention.

PAUL RETURNS TO ANTIOCH OF SYRIA

18Paul stayed in Corinth for some time after that, then said good-bye to the brothers and sisters* and went to nearby Cenchrea. There he shaved his head according to Jewish custom, marking the end of a vow. Then he set sail for Syria, taking Priscilla and Aquila with him.

19They stopped first at the port of Ephesus, where Paul left the others behind. While he was there, he went to the synagogue to reason with the Jews. 20They asked him to stay longer, but he declined. 21As he left, however, he said, "I will come back later,* God willing." Then he set sail from Ephesus. 22The next stop was at the port of Caesarea. From there he went up and visited the church at Jerusalem* and then went back to Antioch.

23After spending some time in Antioch, Paul went back through Galatia and Phrygia, visiting and strengthening all the believers.*

A REASONABLE ARGUMENT 18:24-28

Apollos was from Alexandria in Egypt, the second largest city in the Roman Empire. He was a scholar as well as an eloquent speaker. After his knowledge about Christ was more complete, God greatly used his gifts to strengthen the church. Reason is a powerful tool in the right hands and in the right situation. Apollos used his reasoning ability to convince many in Greece of the truth of the gospel. You don't have to turn off your mind when you turn to Christ. You can use your reasoning skills to bring others to God. ■

APOLLOS INSTRUCTED AT EPHESUS

24Meanwhile, a Jew named Apollos, an eloquent speaker who knew the Scriptures well, had arrived in Ephesus from Alexandria in Egypt. 25He had been taught the way of the Lord, and he taught others about Jesus with an enthusiastic spirit* and with accuracy. However, he knew only about John's baptism. 26When Priscilla and Aquila heard him preaching boldly in the synagogue, they took him aside and explained the way of God even more accurately.

27Apollos had been thinking about going to Achaia, and the brothers and sisters in Ephesus encouraged him to go. They wrote to the believers in Achaia, asking them to welcome him. When he arrived there, he proved to be of great benefit to those who, by God's grace, had believed. 28He refuted the Jews with powerful arguments in public debate. Using the Scriptures, he explained to them that Jesus was the Messiah.

19

PAUL'S THIRD MISSIONARY JOURNEY

While Apollos was in Corinth, Paul traveled through the interior regions until he reached Ephesus, on the coast, where he found several believers.* 2"Did you receive the Holy Spirit when you believed?" he asked them.

"No," they replied, "we haven't even heard that there is a Holy Spirit."

3"Then what baptism did you experience?" he asked. And they replied, "The baptism of John."

4Paul said, "John's baptism called for repentance from sin. But John himself told the people to believe in the one who would come later, meaning Jesus."

5As soon as they heard this, they were baptized in the name of the Lord Jesus. 6Then when Paul laid his hands on them, the Holy Spirit came on them, and they spoke in

18:1 *Athens* and *Corinth* were major cities in Achaia, the region in the southern portion of the Greek peninsula. **18:3** Or *leatherworkers.* **18:17** Greek *Everyone;* other manuscripts read *All the Greeks.* **18:18** Greek *brothers;* also in 18:27. **18:21** Some manuscripts read *"I must by all means be at Jerusalem for the upcoming festival, but I will come back later."* **18:22** Greek *the church.* **18:23** Greek *disciples;* also in 18:27. **18:25** Or *with enthusiasm in the Spirit.* **19:1** Greek *disciples;* also in 19:9, 30.

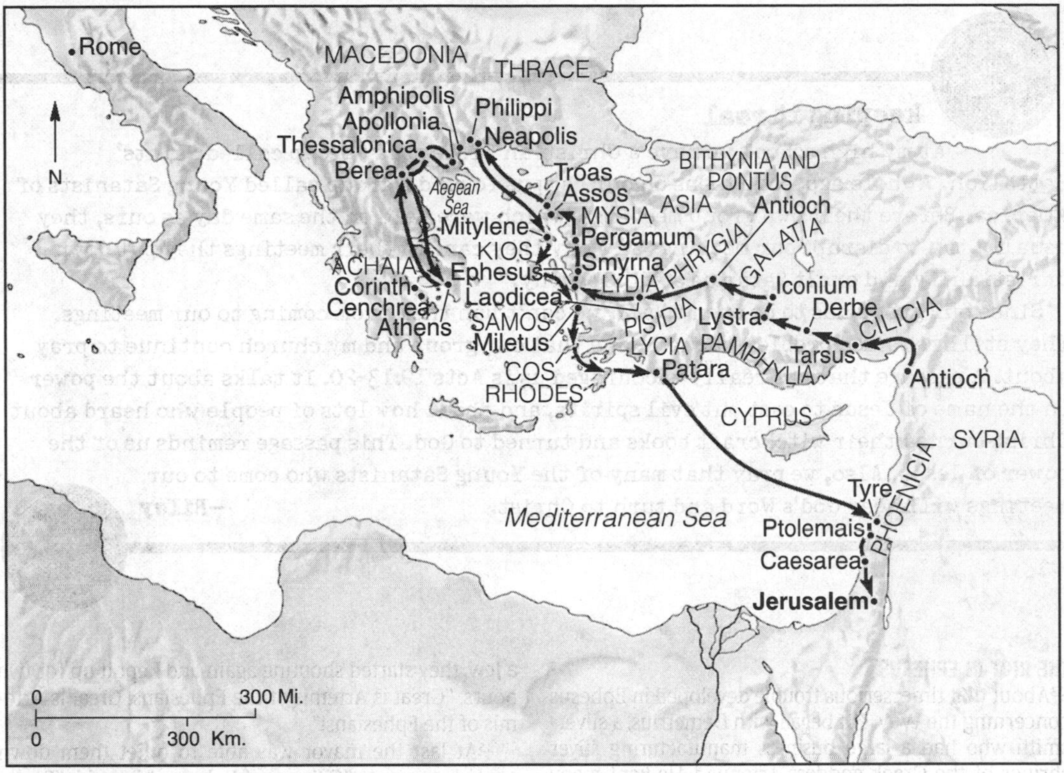

PAUL'S THIRD MISSIONARY JOURNEY (ACTS 18:23—21:16)

other tongues and prophesied. 7There were about twelve
men in all.

PAUL MINISTERS IN EPHESUS

8Then Paul went to the synagogue and preached boldly
for the next three months, arguing persuasively about the
Kingdom of God. 9But some became stubborn, rejecting
his message and publicly speaking against the Way. So
Paul left the synagogue and took the believers with him.
Then he held daily discussions at the lecture hall of Ty-
rannus. 10This went on for the next two years, so that people throughout the province of Asia—both Jews and
Greeks—heard the word of the Lord.
11God gave Paul the power to perform unusual miracles. 12When handkerchiefs or aprons that had merely
touched his skin were placed on sick people, they were
healed of their diseases, and evil spirits were expelled.
13A group of Jews was traveling from town to town
casting out evil spirits. They tried to use the name of the
Lord Jesus in their incantation, saying, "I command you
in the name of Jesus, whom Paul preaches, to come out!"
14Seven sons of Sceva, a leading priest, were doing this.
15But one time when they tried it, the evil spirit replied, "I
know Jesus, and I know Paul, but who are you?" 16Then
the man with the evil spirit leaped on them, overpowered
them, and attacked them with such violence that they
fled from the house, naked and battered.
17The story of what happened spread quickly all
through Ephesus, to Jews and Greeks alike. A solemn fear
descended on the city, and the name of the Lord Jesus
was greatly honored. 18Many who became believers confessed their sinful practices. 19A number of them who
had been practicing sorcery brought their incantation
books and burned them at a public bonfire. The value of
the books was several million dollars.* 20So the message
about the Lord spread widely and had a powerful effect.

THE POWER OF HIS NAME 19:13-19

The sons of Sceva were impressed by Paul, whose power to cast out demons came from the Holy Spirit. This power obviously was greater than theirs. They discovered the hard way that Jesus' name could not be used like a magic charm. No person can control or duplicate God's power. Only through a relationship with Jesus—one sealed by the presence of the Holy Spirit—can one experience the power of God. ■

21Afterward Paul felt compelled by the Spirit* to go
over to Macedonia and Achaia before going to Jerusalem.
"And after that," he said, "I must go on to Rome!" 22He sent
his two assistants, Timothy and Erastus, ahead to Macedonia while he stayed awhile longer in the province of Asia.

19:19 Greek *50,000 pieces of silver*, each of which was the equivalent of a day's wage. **19:21** Or *decided in his spirit*.

keeping it real

At my high school we have a Christian Bible study group called Saints' Battalion. Awhile ago, some teens on our campus formed a group called Young Satanists of America. Before their own group meetings, which were held on the same day as ours, they usually try to disrupt our meetings any way they can. In their meetings they put down Christianity and exalt Satan as a "philosophy."

Since our group has to be open to all, we can't ban them from coming to our meetings. They still remain a problem though—one that our group and my church continue to pray about. A passage that has really encouraged us is Acts 19:13-20. It talks about the power in the name of Jesus to cast out evil spirits, and about how lots of people who heard about Christ burned their witchcraft books and turned to God. This passage reminds us of the power of Jesus. Also, we pray that many of the Young Satanists who come to our meetings will hear God's Word and turn to Christ. —Riley

THE RIOT IN EPHESUS

23About that time, serious trouble developed in Ephesus concerning the Way. 24It began with Demetrius, a silversmith who had a large business manufacturing silver shrines of the Greek goddess Artemis.* He kept many craftsmen busy. 25He called them together, along with others employed in similar trades, and addressed them as follows:

"Gentlemen, you know that our wealth comes from this business. 26But as you have seen and heard, this man Paul has persuaded many people that handmade gods aren't really gods at all. And he's done this not only here in Ephesus but throughout the entire province! 27Of course, I'm not just talking about the loss of public respect for our business. I'm also concerned that the temple of the great goddess Artemis will lose its influence and that Artemis—this magnificent goddess worshiped throughout the province of Asia and all around the world—will be robbed of her great prestige!"

28At this their anger boiled, and they began shouting, "Great is Artemis of the Ephesians!" 29Soon the whole city was filled with confusion. Everyone rushed to the amphitheater, dragging along Gaius and Aristarchus, who were Paul's traveling companions from Macedonia. 30Paul wanted to go in, too, but the believers wouldn't let him. 31Some of the officials of the province, friends of Paul, also sent a message to him, begging him not to risk his life by entering the amphitheater.

32Inside, the people were all shouting, some one thing and some another. Everything was in confusion. In fact, most of them didn't even know why they were there. 33The Jews in the crowd pushed Alexander forward and told him to explain the situation. He motioned for silence and tried to speak. 34But when the crowd realized he was a Jew, they started shouting again and kept it up for two hours: "Great is Artemis of the Ephesians! Great is Artemis of the Ephesians!"

35At last the mayor was able to quiet them down enough to speak. "Citizens of Ephesus," he said. "Everyone knows that Ephesus is the official guardian of the temple of the great Artemis, whose image fell down to us from heaven. 36Since this is an undeniable fact, you should stay calm and not do anything rash. 37You have brought these men here, but they have stolen nothing from the temple and have not spoken against our goddess.

38"If Demetrius and the craftsmen have a case against them, the courts are in session and the officials can hear the case at once. Let them make formal charges. 39And if there are complaints about other matters, they can be settled in a legal assembly. 40I am afraid we are in danger of being charged with rioting by the Roman government, since there is no cause for all this commotion. And if Rome demands an explanation, we won't know what to say." 41*Then he dismissed them, and they dispersed.

20

PAUL GOES TO MACEDONIA AND GREECE

When the uproar was over, Paul sent for the believers* and encouraged them. Then he said good-bye and left for Macedonia. 2While there, he encouraged the believers in all the towns he passed through. Then he traveled down to Greece, 3where he stayed for three months. He was preparing to sail back to Syria when he discovered a plot by some Jews against his life, so he decided to return through Macedonia.

4Several men were traveling with him. They were Sopater

19:24 *Artemis* is otherwise known as Diana. **19:41** Some translations include verse 41 as part of verse 40. **20:1** Greek *disciples*.

son of Pyrrhus from Berea; Aristarchus and Secundus from Thessalonica; Gaius from Derbe; Timothy; and Tychicus and Trophimus from the province of Asia. 5They went on ahead and waited for us at Troas. 6After the Passover* ended, we boarded a ship at Philippi in Macedonia and five days later joined them in Troas, where we stayed a week.

PAUL'S FINAL VISIT TO TROAS

7On the first day of the week, we gathered with the local believers to share in the Lord's Supper.* Paul was preaching to them, and since he was leaving the next day, he kept talking until midnight. 8The upstairs room where we met was lighted with many flickering lamps. 9As Paul spoke on and on, a young man named Eutychus, sitting on the windowsill, became very drowsy. Finally, he fell sound asleep and dropped three stories to his death below. 10Paul went down, bent over him, and took him into his arms. "Don't worry," he said, "he's alive!" 11Then they all went back upstairs, shared in the Lord's Supper,* and ate together. Paul continued talking to them until dawn, and then he left. 12Meanwhile, the young man was taken home unhurt, and everyone was greatly relieved.

PAUL MEETS THE EPHESIAN ELDERS

13Paul went by land to Assos, where he had arranged for us to join him, while we traveled by ship. 14He joined us there, and we sailed together to Mitylene. 15The next day we sailed past the island of Kios. The following day we crossed to the island of Samos, and* a day later we arrived at Miletus.

16Paul had decided to sail on past Ephesus, for he didn't want to spend any more time in the province of Asia. He was hurrying to get to Jerusalem, if possible, in time for the Festival of Pentecost. 17But when we landed at Miletus, he sent a message to the elders of the church at Ephesus, asking them to come and meet him.

18When they arrived he declared, "You know that from the day I set foot in the province of Asia until now 19I have done the Lord's work humbly and with many tears. I have endured the trials that came to me from the plots of the Jews. 20I never shrank back from telling you what you needed to hear, either publicly or in your homes. 21I have had one message for Jews and Greeks alike—the necessity of repenting from sin and turning to God, and of having faith in our Lord Jesus.

22"And now I am bound by the Spirit* to go to Jerusalem. I don't know what awaits me, 23except that the Holy Spirit tells me in city after city that jail and suffering lie ahead. 24But my life is worth nothing to me unless I use it for finishing the work assigned me by the Lord Jesus—the work of telling others the Good News about the wonderful grace of God.

25"And now I know that none of you to whom I have preached the Kingdom will ever see me again. 26I declare today that I have been faithful. If anyone suffers eternal death, it's not my fault,* 27for I didn't shrink from declaring all that God wants you to know.

28"So guard yourselves and God's people. Feed and shepherd God's flock—his church, purchased with his own blood*—over which the Holy Spirit has appointed you as elders.* 29I know that false teachers, like vicious wolves, will come in among you after I leave, not sparing the flock. 30Even some men from your own group will rise up and distort the truth in order to draw a following. 31Watch out! Remember the three years I was with you—my constant watch and care over you night and day, and my many tears for you.

32"And now I entrust you to God and the message of his grace that is able to build you up and give you an inheritance with all those he has set apart for himself.

33"I have never coveted anyone's silver or gold or fine clothes. 34You know that these hands of mine have worked to supply my own needs and even the needs of those who were with me. 35And I have been a constant example of how you can help those in need by working hard. You should remember the words of the Lord Jesus: 'It is more blessed to give than to receive.'"

REAL SATISFACTION 20:24-34

Nowadays many people believe they won't be satisfied in life unless there's something in it for them: glory, fun, money, or popularity. Yet Paul was satisfied with whatever he had, wherever he was, as long as he could do God's work. Is that your definition of satisfaction? ■

36When he had finished speaking, he knelt and prayed with them. 37They all cried as they embraced and kissed him good-bye. 38They were sad most of all because he had said that they would never see him again. Then they escorted him down to the ship.

21

PAUL'S JOURNEY TO JERUSALEM

After saying farewell to the Ephesian elders, we sailed straight to the island of Cos. The next day we reached Rhodes and then went to Patara. 2There we boarded a ship sailing for Phoenicia. 3We sighted the island of Cyprus, passed it on our left, and landed at the harbor of Tyre, in Syria, where the ship was to unload its cargo.

4We went ashore, found the local believers,* and stayed with them a week. These believers prophesied through the Holy Spirit that Paul should not go on to Jerusalem. 5When we returned to the ship at the end of the week, the entire congregation, including women* and children, left the city and came down to the shore with us. There we knelt, prayed, 6and said our farewells. Then we went aboard, and they returned home.

7The next stop after leaving Tyre was Ptolemais, where we greeted the brothers and sisters* and stayed for one

20:6 Greek *the days of unleavened bread.* 20:7 Greek *to break bread.* 20:11 Greek *broke the bread.* 20:15 Some manuscripts read *and having stayed at Trogyllium.* 20:22 Or *by my spirit,* or *by an inner compulsion;* Greek reads *by the spirit.* 20:26 Greek *I am innocent of the blood of all.* 20:28a Or *with the blood of his own [Son].* 20:28b Greek *overseers.* 21:4 Greek *disciples;* also in 21:16. 21:5 Or *wives.* 21:7 Greek *brothers;* also in 21:17.

day. 8The next day we went on to Caesarea and stayed at
the home of Philip the Evangelist, one of the seven men
who had been chosen to distribute food. 9He had four
unmarried daughters who had the gift of prophecy.
10Several days later a man named Agabus, who also had
the gift of prophecy, arrived from Judea. 11He came over,
took Paul's belt, and bound his own feet and hands with
it. Then he said, "The Holy Spirit declares, 'So shall the
owner of this belt be bound by the Jewish leaders in Jerusalem and turned over to the Gentiles.'" 12When we heard
this, we and the local believers all begged Paul not to go
on to Jerusalem.
13But he said, "Why all this weeping? You are breaking
my heart! I am ready not only to be jailed at Jerusalem but
even to die for the sake of the Lord Jesus." 14When it was
clear that we couldn't persuade him, we gave up and said,
"The Lord's will be done."

THE WAY OF PAIN 21:10-14

Paul knew that he would be imprisoned in Jerusalem. Although his friends pleaded with him not to go, Paul knew that God wanted him to go. Although none of us wants to face hardship or suffering, obedience to God sometimes involves suffering. Jesus' life is proof of this. Like Paul's friends, are you willing to say, "The Lord's will be done," no matter what the circumstances? ■

PAUL ARRIVES AT JERUSALEM

15After this we packed our things and left for Jerusalem.
16Some believers from Caesarea accompanied us, and
they took us to the home of Mnason, a man originally
from Cyprus and one of the early believers. 17When we arrived, the brothers and sisters in Jerusalem welcomed us
warmly.
18The next day Paul went with us to meet with James,
and all the elders of the Jerusalem church were present.
19After greeting them, Paul gave a detailed account of the
things God had accomplished among the Gentiles
through his ministry.
20After hearing this, they praised God. And then they
said, "You know, dear brother, how many thousands of
Jews have also believed, and they all follow the law of
Moses very seriously. 21But the Jewish believers here in
Jerusalem have been told that you are teaching all the
Jews who live among the Gentiles to turn their backs on
the laws of Moses. They've heard that you teach them not
to circumcise their children or follow other Jewish customs. 22What should we do? They will certainly hear that
you have come.
23"Here's what we want you to do. We have four men
here who have completed their vow. 24Go with them to
the Temple and join them in the purification ceremony,
paying for them to have their heads ritually shaved. Then
everyone will know that the rumors are all false and that
you yourself observe the Jewish laws.
25"As for the Gentile believers, they should do what we
already told them in a letter: They should abstain from
eating food offered to idols, from consuming blood or the
meat of strangled animals, and from sexual immorality."

PAUL IS ARRESTED

26So Paul went to the Temple the next day with the other
men. They had already started the purification ritual, so
he publicly announced the date when their vows would
end and sacrifices would be offered for each of them.
27The seven days were almost ended when some Jews
from the province of Asia saw Paul in the Temple and
roused a mob against him. They grabbed him, 28yelling,
"Men of Israel, help us! This is the man who preaches
against our people everywhere and tells everybody to disobey the Jewish laws. He speaks against the Temple—and
even defiles this holy place by bringing in Gentiles.*"
29(For earlier that day they had seen him in the city with
Trophimus, a Gentile from Ephesus,* and they assumed
Paul had taken him into the Temple.)
30The whole city was rocked by these accusations, and
a great riot followed. Paul was grabbed and dragged out
of the Temple, and immediately the gates were closed behind him. 31As they were trying to kill him, word reached
the commander of the Roman regiment that all Jerusalem was in an uproar. 32He immediately called out his
soldiers and officers* and ran down among the crowd.
When the mob saw the commander and the troops coming, they stopped beating Paul.
33Then the commander arrested him and ordered him
bound with two chains. He asked the crowd who he was
and what he had done. 34Some shouted one thing and
some another. Since he couldn't find out the truth in all
the uproar and confusion, he ordered that Paul be taken to
the fortress. 35As Paul reached the stairs, the mob grew so
violent the soldiers had to lift him to their shoulders to
protect him. 36And the crowd followed behind, shouting,
"Kill him, kill him!"

PAUL SPEAKS TO THE CROWD

37As Paul was about to be taken inside, he said to the commander, "May I have a word with you?"
"Do you know Greek?" the commander asked, surprised. 38"Aren't you the Egyptian who led a rebellion
some time ago and took 4,000 members of the Assassins
out into the desert?"
39"No," Paul replied, "I am a Jew and a citizen of Tarsus
in Cilicia, which is an important city. Please, let me talk to
these people." 40The commander agreed, so Paul stood
on the stairs and motioned to the people to be quiet. Soon
a deep silence enveloped the crowd, and he addressed
them in their own language, Aramaic.*

22

"Brothers and esteemed fathers," Paul said,
"listen to me as I offer my defense." 2When they heard
him speaking in their own language,* the silence was
even greater.

21:28 Greek *Greeks*. 21:29 Greek *Trophimus, the Ephesian*. 21:32 Greek *centurions*. 21:40 Or *Hebrew*. 22:2 Greek *in Aramaic*, or *in Hebrew*.

3 Then Paul said, "I am a Jew, born in Tarsus, a city in Cilicia, and I was brought up and educated here in Jerusalem under Gamaliel. As his student, I was carefully trained in our Jewish laws and customs. I became very zealous to honor God in everything I did, just like all of you today. 4 And I persecuted the followers of the Way, hounding some to death, arresting both men and women and throwing them in prison. 5 The high priest and the whole council of elders can testify that this is so. For I received letters from them to our Jewish brothers in Damascus, authorizing me to bring the Christians from there to Jerusalem, in chains, to be punished.

SOMETHING IN COMMON 22:1-5

Before launching into a full-scale defense of Christianity, Paul usually tried to find something in common with his audience. By saying that at one time he was as zealous for God as any of his listeners, Paul acknowledged their sincere motives in trying to kill him. He also revealed that he had done the same to Christian leaders years earlier. Like Paul, are you ready to defend your faith? People are much more likely to listen to you if they feel they have something in common with you. ■

6 "As I was on the road, approaching Damascus about noon, a very bright light from heaven suddenly shone down around me. 7 I fell to the ground and heard a voice saying to me, 'Saul, Saul, why are you persecuting me?'

8 " 'Who are you, lord?' I asked.

"And the voice replied, 'I am Jesus the Nazarene,* the one you are persecuting.' 9 The people with me saw the light but didn't understand the voice speaking to me.

10 "I asked, 'What should I do, Lord?'

"And the Lord told me, 'Get up and go into Damascus, and there you will be told everything you are to do.'

11 "I was blinded by the intense light and had to be led by the hand to Damascus by my companions. 12 A man named Ananias lived there. He was a godly man, deeply devoted to the law, and well regarded by all the Jews of Damascus. 13 He came and stood beside me and said, 'Brother Saul, regain your sight.' And that very moment I could see him!

14 "Then he told me, 'The God of our ancestors has chosen you to know his will and to see the Righteous One and hear him speak. 15 For you are to be his witness, telling everyone what you have seen and heard. 16 What are you waiting for? Get up and be baptized. Have your sins washed away by calling on the name of the Lord.'

17 "After I returned to Jerusalem, I was praying in the Temple and fell into a trance. 18 I saw a vision of Jesus* saying to me, 'Hurry! Leave Jerusalem, for the people here won't accept your testimony about me.'

19 " 'But Lord,' I argued, 'they certainly know that in every synagogue I imprisoned and beat those who believed in you. 20 And I was in complete agreement when your witness Stephen was killed. I stood by and kept the coats they took off when they stoned him.'

21 "But the Lord said to me, 'Go, for I will send you far away to the Gentiles!' "

22 The crowd listened until Paul said that word. Then they all began to shout, "Away with such a fellow! He isn't fit to live!" 23 They yelled, threw off their coats, and tossed handfuls of dust into the air.

PAUL REVEALS HIS ROMAN CITIZENSHIP

24 The commander brought Paul inside and ordered him lashed with whips to make him confess his crime. He wanted to find out why the crowd had become so furious. 25 When they tied Paul down to lash him, Paul said to the officer* standing there, "Is it legal for you to whip a Roman citizen who hasn't even been tried?"

26 When the officer heard this, he went to the commander and asked, "What are you doing? This man is a Roman citizen!"

27 So the commander went over and asked Paul, "Tell me, are you a Roman citizen?"

"Yes, I certainly am," Paul replied.

28 "I am, too," the commander muttered, "and it cost me plenty!"

Paul answered, "But I am a citizen by birth!"

29 The soldiers who were about to interrogate Paul quickly withdrew when they heard he was a Roman citizen, and the commander was frightened because he had ordered him bound and whipped.

PAUL BEFORE THE HIGH COUNCIL

30 The next day the commander ordered the leading priests into session with the Jewish high council.* He wanted to find out what the trouble was all about, so he released Paul to have him stand before them.

23

Gazing intently at the high council,* Paul began: "Brothers, I have always lived before God with a clear conscience!"

2 Instantly Ananias the high priest commanded those close to Paul to slap him on the mouth. 3 But Paul said to him, "God will slap you, you corrupt hypocrite!* What kind of judge are you to break the law yourself by ordering me struck like that?"

4 Those standing near Paul said to him, "Do you dare to insult God's high priest?"

5 "I'm sorry, brothers. I didn't realize he was the high priest," Paul replied, "for the Scriptures say, 'You must not speak evil of any of your rulers.'*"

6 Paul realized that some members of the high council were Sadducees and some were Pharisees, so he shouted, "Brothers, I am a Pharisee, as were my ancestors! And I am on trial because my hope is in the resurrection of the dead!"

7 This divided the council—the Pharisees against the Sadducees—8 for the Sadducees say there is no resurrection

22:8 Or *Jesus of Nazareth.* 22:18 Greek *him.* 22:25 Greek *the centurion;* also in 22:26. 22:30 Greek *Sanhedrin.* 23:1 Greek *Sanhedrin;* also in 23:6, 15, 20, 28. 23:3 Greek *you whitewashed wall.* 23:5 Exod 22:28.

or angels or spirits, but the Pharisees believe in all of these. [9]So there was a great uproar. Some of the teachers of religious law who were Pharisees jumped up and began to argue forcefully. "We see nothing wrong with him," they shouted. "Perhaps a spirit or an angel spoke to him." [10]As the conflict grew more violent, the commander was afraid they would tear Paul apart. So he ordered his soldiers to go and rescue him by force and take him back to the fortress.

[11]That night the Lord appeared to Paul and said, "Be encouraged, Paul. Just as you have been a witness to me here in Jerusalem, you must preach the Good News in Rome as well."

A POWERFUL ALLY 23:12-24

Paul was no stranger to death threats or daring rescues. Not long after he became a believer, some Jewish leaders plotted to kill him (9:22-25). But God rescued him in the nick of time. Now, many years later, 40 Jews wanted him dead. But the same thing happened as before—God rescued him in a dramatic way. This pattern of death threats and daring rescues reminds us of two facts: (1) The Christian life isn't always easy; (2) God is powerful enough to overrule opposition. Feeling the heat of opposition? Don't worry. You've got a powerful ally. ■

THE PLAN TO KILL PAUL

[12]The next morning a group of Jews* got together and bound themselves with an oath not to eat or drink until they had killed Paul. [13]There were more than forty of them in the conspiracy. [14]They went to the leading priests and elders and told them, "We have bound ourselves with an oath to eat nothing until we have killed Paul. [15]So you and the high council should ask the commander to bring Paul back to the council again. Pretend you want to examine his case more fully. We will kill him on the way."

[16]But Paul's nephew—his sister's son—heard of their plan and went to the fortress and told Paul. [17]Paul called for one of the Roman officers* and said, "Take this young man to the commander. He has something important to tell him."

[18]So the officer did, explaining, "Paul, the prisoner, called me over and asked me to bring this young man to you because he has something to tell you."

[19]The commander took his hand, led him aside, and asked, "What is it you want to tell me?"

[20]Paul's nephew told him, "Some Jews are going to ask you to bring Paul before the high council tomorrow, pretending they want to get some more information. [21]But don't do it! There are more than forty men hiding along the way ready to ambush him. They have vowed not to eat or drink anything until they have killed him. They are ready now, just waiting for your consent."

[22]"Don't let anyone know you told me this," the commander warned the young man.

PAUL IS SENT TO CAESAREA

[23]Then the commander called two of his officers and ordered, "Get 200 soldiers ready to leave for Caesarea at nine o'clock tonight. Also take 200 spearmen and 70 mounted troops. [24]Provide horses for Paul to ride, and get him safely to Governor Felix." [25]Then he wrote this letter to the governor:

[26]"From Claudius Lysias, to his Excellency, Governor Felix: Greetings!

[27]"This man was seized by some Jews, and they were about to kill him when I arrived with the troops. When I learned that he was a Roman citizen, I removed him to safety. [28]Then I took him to their high council to try to learn the basis of the accusations against him. [29]I soon discovered the charge was something regarding their religious law—certainly nothing worthy of imprisonment or death. [30]But when I was informed of a plot to kill him, I immediately sent him on to you. I have told his accusers to bring their charges before you."

[31]So that night, as ordered, the soldiers took Paul as far as Antipatris. [32]They returned to the fortress the next morning, while the mounted troops took him on to Caesarea. [33]When they arrived in Caesarea, they presented Paul and the letter to Governor Felix. [34]He read it and then asked Paul what province he was from. "Cilicia," Paul answered.

[35]"I will hear your case myself when your accusers arrive," the governor told him. Then the governor ordered him kept in the prison at Herod's headquarters.*

24

PAUL APPEARS BEFORE FELIX

Five days later Ananias, the high priest, arrived with some of the Jewish elders and the lawyer* Tertullus, to present their case against Paul to the governor. [2]When Paul was called in, Tertullus presented the charges against Paul in the following address to the governor:

"Your Excellency, you have provided a long period of peace for us Jews and with foresight have enacted reforms for us. [3]For all of this we are very grateful to you. [4]But I don't want to bore you, so please give me your attention for only a moment. [5]We have found this man to be a troublemaker who is constantly stirring up riots among the Jews all over the world. He is a ringleader of the cult known as the Nazarenes. [6]Furthermore, he was trying to desecrate the Temple when we arrested him.* [8]You can find out the truth of our accusations by examining him yourself." [9]Then the other Jews chimed in, declaring that everything Tertullus said was true.

[10]The governor then motioned for Paul to speak. Paul said, "I know, sir, that you have been a judge of Jewish

23:12 Greek *the Jews.* **23:17** Greek *centurions;* also in 23:23. **23:35** Greek *Herod's Praetorium.* **24:1** Greek *some elders and an orator.* **24:6** Some manuscripts add an expanded conclusion to verse 6, all of verse 7, and an additional phrase in verse 8: *We would have judged him by our law, [7]but Lysias, the commander of the garrison, came and violently took him away from us, [8]commanding his accusers to come before you.*

affairs for many years, so I gladly present my defense before you. [11]You can quickly discover that I arrived in Jerusalem no more than twelve days ago to worship at the Temple. [12]My accusers never found me arguing with anyone in the Temple, nor stirring up a riot in any synagogue or on the streets of the city. [13]These men cannot prove the things they accuse me of doing.

[14]"But I admit that I follow the Way, which they call a cult. I worship the God of our ancestors, and I firmly believe the Jewish law and everything written in the prophets. [15]I have the same hope in God that these men have, that he will raise both the righteous and the unrighteous. [16]Because of this, I always try to maintain a clear conscience before God and all people.

> I always try to maintain a clear conscience before God and all people.
>
> *ACTS 24:16*

[17]"After several years away, I returned to Jerusalem with money to aid my people and to offer sacrifices to God. [18]My accusers saw me in the Temple as I was completing a purification ceremony. There was no crowd around me and no rioting. [19]But some Jews from the province of Asia were there—and they ought to be here to bring charges if they have anything against me! [20]Ask these men here what crime the Jewish high council* found me guilty of, [21]except for the one time I shouted out, 'I am on trial before you today because I believe in the resurrection of the dead!'"

[22]At that point Felix, who was quite familiar with the Way, adjourned the hearing and said, "Wait until Lysias, the garrison commander, arrives. Then I will decide the case." [23]He ordered an officer* to keep Paul in custody but to give him some freedom and allow his friends to visit him and take care of his needs.

A LIFE-CHANGING MESSAGE 24:24-25

Paul's talk with Felix became so personal that Felix felt convicted. Felix, like Herod Antipas (Mark 6:17-18), had taken another man's wife. Paul's words were interesting until they focused on "righteousness and self-control and the coming day of judgment." Like Felix, many people are glad to talk about the Bible or God as long as they don't have to change in any way. When truth hits home, they resist. But the gospel is all about God's power to change lives. Sometimes the truth hurts. How have you responded to the truth you've heard? ■

[24]A few days later Felix came back with his wife, Drusilla, who was Jewish. Sending for Paul, they listened as he told them about faith in Christ Jesus. [25]As he reasoned with them about righteousness and self-control and the coming day of judgment, Felix became frightened. "Go away for now," he replied. "When it is more convenient, I'll call for you again." [26]He also hoped that Paul would bribe him, so he sent for him quite often and talked with him.

[27]After two years went by in this way, Felix was succeeded by Porcius Festus. And because Felix wanted to gain favor with the Jewish people, he left Paul in prison.

25

PAUL APPEARS BEFORE FESTUS

Three days after Festus arrived in Caesarea to take over his new responsibilities, he left for Jerusalem, [2]where the leading priests and other Jewish leaders met with him and made their accusations against Paul. [3]They asked Festus as a favor to transfer Paul to Jerusalem (planning to ambush and kill him on the way). [4]But Festus replied that Paul was at Caesarea and he himself would be returning there soon. [5]So he said, "Those of you in authority can return with me. If Paul has done anything wrong, you can make your accusations."

[6]About eight or ten days later Festus returned to Caesarea, and on the following day he took his seat in court and ordered that Paul be brought in. [7]When Paul arrived, the Jewish leaders from Jerusalem gathered around and made many serious accusations they couldn't prove.

[8]Paul denied the charges. "I am not guilty of any crime against the Jewish laws or the Temple or the Roman government," he said.

[9]Then Festus, wanting to please the Jews, asked him, "Are you willing to go to Jerusalem and stand trial before me there?"

[10]But Paul replied, "No! This is the official Roman court, so I ought to be tried right here. You know very well I am not guilty of harming the Jews. [11]If I have done something worthy of death, I don't refuse to die. But if I am innocent, no one has a right to turn me over to these men to kill me. I appeal to Caesar!"

[12]Festus conferred with his advisers and then replied, "Very well! You have appealed to Caesar, and to Caesar you will go!"

[13]A few days later King Agrippa arrived with his sister, Bernice,* to pay their respects to Festus. [14]During their stay of several days, Festus discussed Paul's case with the king. "There is a prisoner here," he told him, "whose case was left for me by Felix. [15]When I was in Jerusalem, the leading priests and Jewish elders pressed charges against him and asked me to condemn him. [16]I pointed out to them that Roman law does not convict people without a trial. They must be given an opportunity to confront their accusers and defend themselves.

[17]"When his accusers came here for the trial, I didn't delay. I called the case the very next day and ordered Paul brought in. [18]But the accusations made against him weren't any of the crimes I expected. [19]Instead, it was

24:20 Greek *Sanhedrin.* 24:23 Greek *a centurion.* 25:13 Greek *Agrippa the king and Bernice arrived.*

something about their religion and a dead man named Jesus, who Paul insists is alive. 20I was at a loss to know how to investigate these things, so I asked him whether he would be willing to stand trial on these charges in Jerusalem. 21But Paul appealed to have his case decided by the emperor. So I ordered that he be held in custody until I could arrange to send him to Caesar."

22"I'd like to hear the man myself," Agrippa said.

And Festus replied, "You will—tomorrow!"

PAUL SPEAKS TO AGRIPPA

23So the next day Agrippa and Bernice arrived at the auditorium with great pomp, accompanied by military officers and prominent men of the city. Festus ordered that Paul be brought in. 24Then Festus said, "King Agrippa and all who are here, this is the man whose death is demanded by all the Jews, both here and in Jerusalem. 25But in my opinion he has done nothing deserving death. However, since he appealed his case to the emperor, I have decided to send him to Rome.

26"But what shall I write the emperor? For there is no clear charge against him. So I have brought him before all of you, and especially you, King Agrippa, so that after we examine him, I might have something to write. 27For it makes no sense to send a prisoner to the emperor without specifying the charges against him!"

26 Then Agrippa said to Paul, "You may speak in your defense."

So Paul, gesturing with his hand, started his defense: 2"I am fortunate, King Agrippa, that you are the one hearing my defense today against all these accusations made by the Jewish leaders, 3for I know you are an expert on all Jewish customs and controversies. Now please listen to me patiently!

4"As the Jewish leaders are well aware, I was given a thorough Jewish training from my earliest childhood among my own people and in Jerusalem. 5If they would admit it, they know that I have been a member of the Pharisees, the strictest sect of our religion. 6Now I am on trial because of my hope in the fulfillment of God's promise made to our ancestors. 7In fact, that is why the twelve tribes of Israel zealously worship God night and day, and they share the same hope I have. Yet, Your Majesty, they accuse me for having this hope! 8Why does it seem incredible to any of you that God can raise the dead?

9"I used to believe that I ought to do everything I could to oppose the very name of Jesus the Nazarene.* 10Indeed, I did just that in Jerusalem. Authorized by the leading priests, I caused many believers* there to be sent to prison. And I cast my vote against them when they were condemned to death. 11Many times I had them punished in the synagogues to get them to curse Jesus.* I was so violently opposed to them that I even chased them down in foreign cities.

12"One day I was on such a mission to Damascus, armed with the authority and commission of the leading priests. 13About noon, Your Majesty, as I was on the road, a light from heaven brighter than the sun shone down on me and my companions. 14We all fell down, and I heard a voice saying to me in Aramaic,* 'Saul, Saul, why are you persecuting me? It is useless for you to fight against my will.*'

15"'Who are you, lord?' I asked.

"And the Lord replied, 'I am Jesus, the one you are persecuting. 16Now get to your feet! For I have appeared to you to appoint you as my servant and witness. You are to tell the world what you have seen and what I will show you in the future. 17And I will rescue you from both your own people and the Gentiles. Yes, I am sending you to the Gentiles 18to open their eyes, so they may turn from darkness to light and from the power of Satan to God. Then they will receive forgiveness for their sins and be given a place among God's people, who are set apart by faith in me.'

19"And so, King Agrippa, I obeyed that vision from heaven. 20I preached first to those in Damascus, then in Jerusalem and throughout all Judea, and also to the Gentiles, that all must repent of their sins and turn to God—and prove they have changed by the good things they do. 21Some Jews arrested me in the Temple for preaching this, and they tried to kill me. 22But God has protected me right up to this present time so I can testify to everyone, from the least to the greatest. I teach nothing except what the prophets and Moses said would happen—23that the Messiah would suffer and be the first to rise from the dead, and in this way announce God's light to Jews and Gentiles alike."

24Suddenly, Festus shouted, "Paul, you are insane. Too much study has made you crazy!"

FACTS 26:26

When he defended the gospel message, Paul mentioned facts: People were still alive who had heard Jesus and seen his miracles; the empty tomb could still be seen; and the Christian message had "caused trouble all over the world" (17:6). Likewise, we can study the evidence that the Bible presents concerning Jesus' life as well as historical and archaeological records of the early church. Based on these facts, what are your conclusions? ■

25But Paul replied, "I am not insane, Most Excellent Festus. What I am saying is the sober truth. 26And King Agrippa knows about these things. I speak boldly, for I am sure these events are all familiar to him, for they were not done in a corner! 27King Agrippa, do you believe the prophets? I know you do—"

28Agrippa interrupted him. "Do you think you can persuade me to become a Christian so quickly?"*

29Paul replied, "Whether quickly or not, I pray to God that both you and everyone here in this audience might become the same as I am, except for these chains."

26:9 Or *Jesus of Nazareth.* **26:10** Greek *many of God's holy people.* **26:11** Greek *to blaspheme.* **26:14a** Or *Hebrew.* **26:14b** Greek *It is hard for you to kick against the oxgoads.* **26:28** Or *"A little more, and your arguments would make me a Christian."*

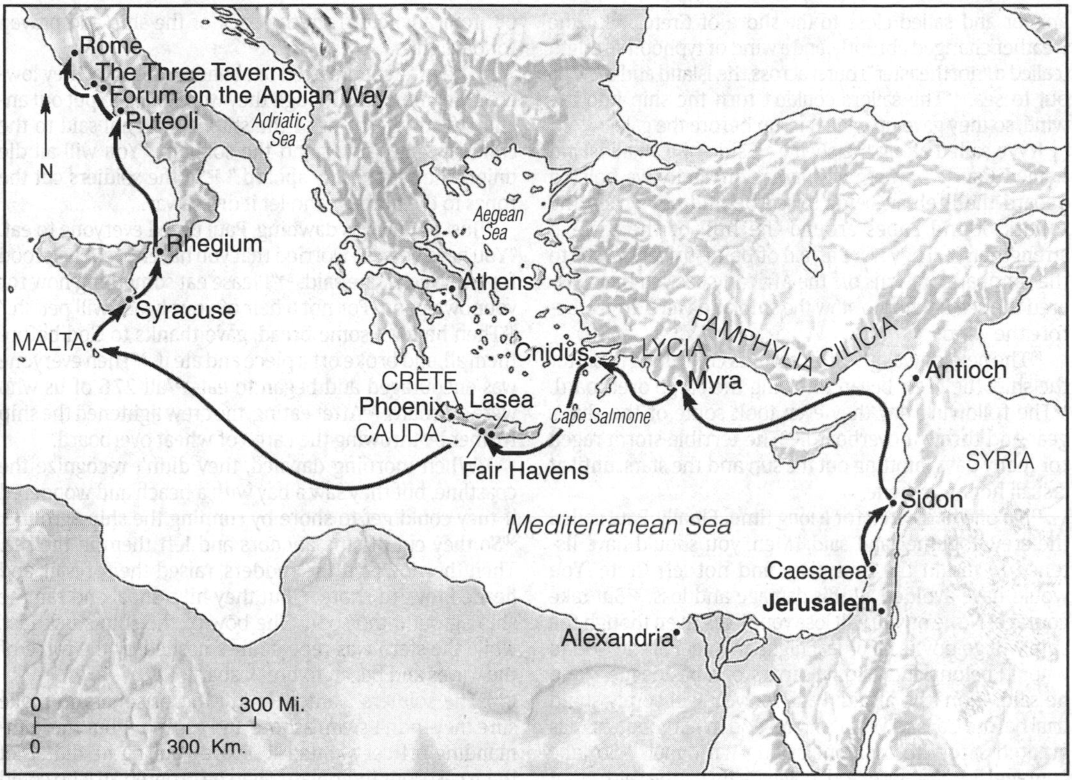

PAUL'S JOURNEY TO ROME (ACTS 21:17—28:31)

30Then the king, the governor, Bernice, and all the others stood and left. 31As they went out, they talked it over and agreed, "This man hasn't done anything to deserve death or imprisonment."

32And Agrippa said to Festus, "He could have been set free if he hadn't appealed to Caesar."

27

PAUL SAILS FOR ROME

When the time came, we set sail for Italy. Paul and several other prisoners were placed in the custody of a Roman officer* named Julius, a captain of the Imperial Regiment. 2Aristarchus, a Macedonian from Thessalonica, was also with us. We left on a ship whose home port was Adramyttium on the northwest coast of the province of Asia;* it was scheduled to make several stops at ports along the coast of the province.

3The next day when we docked at Sidon, Julius was very kind to Paul and let him go ashore to visit with friends so they could provide for his needs. 4Putting out to sea from there, we encountered strong headwinds that made it difficult to keep the ship on course, so we sailed north of Cyprus between the island and the mainland. 5Keeping to the open sea, we passed along the coast of Cilicia and Pamphylia, landing at Myra, in the province of Lycia. 6There the commanding officer found an Egyptian ship from Alexandria that was bound for Italy, and he put us on board.

7We had several days of slow sailing, and after great difficulty we finally neared Cnidus. But the wind was against us, so we sailed across to Crete and along the sheltered coast of the island, past the cape of Salmone. 8We struggled along the coast with great difficulty and finally arrived at Fair Havens, near the town of Lasea. 9We had lost a lot of time. The weather was becoming dangerous for sea travel because it was so late in the fall,* and Paul spoke to the ship's officers about it.

10"Men," he said, "I believe there is trouble ahead if we go on—shipwreck, loss of cargo, and danger to our lives as well." 11But the officer in charge of the prisoners listened more to the ship's captain and the owner than to Paul. 12And since Fair Havens was an exposed harbor—a poor place to spend the winter—most of the crew wanted to go on to Phoenix, farther up the coast of Crete, and spend the winter there. Phoenix was a good harbor with only a southwest and northwest exposure.

THE STORM AT SEA

13When a light wind began blowing from the south, the sailors thought they could make it. So they pulled up

27:1 Greek *centurion;* similarly in 27:6, 11, 31, 43. **27:2** *Asia* was a Roman province in what is now western Turkey. **27:9** Greek *because the fast was now already gone by.* This fast was associated with the Day of Atonement (*Yom Kippur*), which occurred in late September or early October.

anchor and sailed close to the shore of Crete. 14But the weather changed abruptly, and a wind of typhoon strength (called a "northeaster") burst across the island and blew us out to sea. 15The sailors couldn't turn the ship into the wind, so they gave up and let it run before the gale.

16We sailed along the sheltered side of a small island named Cauda,* where with great difficulty we hoisted aboard the lifeboat being towed behind us. 17Then the sailors bound ropes around the hull of the ship to strengthen it. They were afraid of being driven across to the sandbars of Syrtis off the African coast, so they lowered the sea anchor to slow the ship and were driven before the wind.

18The next day, as gale-force winds continued to batter the ship, the crew began throwing the cargo overboard. 19The following day they even took some of the ship's gear and threw it overboard. 20The terrible storm raged for many days, blotting out the sun and the stars, until at last all hope was gone.

21No one had eaten for a long time. Finally, Paul called the crew together and said, "Men, you should have listened to me in the first place and not left Crete. You would have avoided all this damage and loss. 22But take courage! None of you will lose your lives, even though the ship will go down. 23For last night an angel of the God to whom I belong and whom I serve stood beside me, 24and he said, 'Don't be afraid, Paul, for you will surely stand trial before Caesar! What's more, God in his goodness has granted safety to everyone sailing with you.' 25So take courage! For I believe God. It will be just as he said. 26But we will be shipwrecked on an island."

EVEN BETTER 27:1-28:24

One of Paul's most important journeys was to Rome. He didn't get there in quite the way he had expected, however. His journey turned out to be more of a legal one than a missionary journey, thanks to a series of trials and transactions. These events resulted in Paul being delivered to Rome, where he told the gospel message in places like the palace of the emperor.

Ever feel frustrated because your plans didn't work out the way you wanted them to? Just think: God is never out of control! He knows how to work things out so that the results are even better than we expected. Trusting God with your plans is a surefire plan for success! ■

THE SHIPWRECK

27About midnight on the fourteenth night of the storm, as we were being driven across the Sea of Adria,* the sailors sensed land was near. 28They dropped a weighted line and found that the water was 120 feet deep. But a little later they measured again and found it was only 90 feet deep.* 29At this rate they were afraid we would soon be driven against the rocks along the shore, so they threw out four anchors from the back of the ship and prayed for daylight.

30Then the sailors tried to abandon the ship; they lowered the lifeboat as though they were going to put out anchors from the front of the ship. 31But Paul said to the commanding officer and the soldiers, "You will all die unless the sailors stay aboard." 32So the soldiers cut the ropes to the lifeboat and let it drift away.

33Just as day was dawning, Paul urged everyone to eat. "You have been so worried that you haven't touched food for two weeks," he said. 34"Please eat something now for your own good. For not a hair of your heads will perish." 35Then he took some bread, gave thanks to God before them all, and broke off a piece and ate it. 36Then everyone was encouraged and began to eat—37all 276 of us who were on board. 38After eating, the crew lightened the ship further by throwing the cargo of wheat overboard.

39When morning dawned, they didn't recognize the coastline, but they saw a bay with a beach and wondered if they could get to shore by running the ship aground. 40So they cut off the anchors and left them in the sea. Then they lowered the rudders, raised the foresail, and headed toward shore. 41But they hit a shoal and ran the ship aground too soon. The bow of the ship stuck fast, while the stern was repeatedly smashed by the force of the waves and began to break apart.

42The soldiers wanted to kill the prisoners to make sure they didn't swim ashore and escape. 43But the commanding officer wanted to spare Paul, so he didn't let them carry out their plan. Then he ordered all who could swim to jump overboard first and make for land. 44The others held onto planks or debris from the broken ship.* So everyone escaped safely to shore.

28

PAUL ON THE ISLAND OF MALTA

Once we were safe on shore, we learned that we were on the island of Malta. 2The people of the island were very kind to us. It was cold and rainy, so they built a fire on the shore to welcome us.

3As Paul gathered an armful of sticks and was laying them on the fire, a poisonous snake, driven out by the heat, bit him on the hand. 4The people of the island saw it hanging from his hand and said to each other, "A murderer, no doubt! Though he escaped the sea, justice will not permit him to live." 5But Paul shook off the snake into the fire and was unharmed. 6The people waited for him to swell up or suddenly drop dead. But when they had waited a long time and saw that he wasn't harmed, they changed their minds and decided he was a god.

7Near the shore where we landed was an estate belonging to Publius, the chief official of the island. He welcomed us and treated us kindly for three days. 8As it happened, Publius's father was ill with fever and dysentery. Paul went in and prayed for him, and laying his hands on him, he healed him. 9Then all the other sick people on the island came and were healed. 10As a result

27:16 Some manuscripts read *Clauda*. **27:27** The *Sea of Adria* includes the central portion of the Mediterranean. **27:28** Greek *20 fathoms* . . . *15 fathoms* [37 meters . . . 27 meters]. **27:44** Or *or were helped by members of the ship's crew*.

HEARD THE GOOD NEWS?

ULTIMATE ISSUES

Ever wonder whether or not God would send someone to hell who has never heard of him?

For starters, God doesn't send anyone anywhere. God calls us, but each person has a choice. Concerning that question, however, the Bible doesn't deal with it directly. Instead, it talks about Jesus in rather exclusive terms. Take a look at Acts 4:12: "There is salvation in no one else! God has given no other name under heaven [other than Jesus Christ] by which we must be saved." Because the Bible doesn't talk directly about the problem, we must proceed with humility and caution. Still, we aren't left totally in the dark.

First, remember that God doesn't *owe* anyone a break. As the perfect, holy, righteous judge, he would be entirely justified in condemning everyone, for "everyone has sinned; we all fall short of God's glorious standard" (Rom 3:23). But Jesus offers forgiveness to all. That's grace—we get what we don't deserve, instead of what we do deserve.

Second, Romans 1 (especially verses 18-20) makes it clear that God has created us with the knowledge of our Creator. This truth is evident in other passages as well. Check out Psalm 19:1-2: "The heavens proclaim the glory of God. The skies display his craftsmanship. Day after day they continue to speak; night after night they make him known." Yet many people suppress that knowledge.

For all people, Christ is the only one who has opened the way for us to be restored to God. Missionaries have been sent all over the world to spread this news to people of *every* nation. They strive to reach all previously unreached people groups.

Is that your passion as well?

we were showered with honors, and when the time came to sail, people supplied us with everything we would need for the trip.

PAUL ARRIVES AT ROME

11It was three months after the shipwreck that we set sail
on another ship that had wintered at the island—an Alex-
andrian ship with the twin gods* as its figurehead. 12Our
first stop was Syracuse,* where we stayed three days.
13From there we sailed across to Rhegium.* A day later a
south wind began blowing, so the following day we sailed
up the coast to Puteoli. 14There we found some believers,* who invited us to spend a week with them. And so
we came to Rome.
15The brothers and sisters* in Rome had heard we were
coming, and they came to meet us at the Forum* on the
Appian Way. Others joined us at The Three Taverns.*
When Paul saw them, he was encouraged and thanked
God.
16When we arrived in Rome, Paul was permitted to
have his own private lodging, though he was guarded by a
soldier.

PAUL PREACHES AT ROME UNDER GUARD

17Three days after Paul's arrival, he called together the local Jewish leaders. He said to them, "Brothers, I was arrested in Jerusalem and handed over to the Roman
government, even though I had done nothing against our
people or the customs of our ancestors. 18The Romans
tried me and wanted to release me, because they found no
cause for the death sentence. 19But when the Jewish leaders protested the decision, I felt it necessary to appeal to
Caesar, even though I had no desire to press charges
against my own people. 20I asked you to come here today
so we could get acquainted and so I could explain to you
that I am bound with this chain because I believe that the
hope of Israel—the Messiah—has already come."
21They replied, "We have had no letters from Judea or
reports against you from anyone who has come here.
22But we want to hear what you believe, for the only thing
we know about this movement is that it is denounced
everywhere."
23So a time was set, and on that day a large number of people came to Paul's lodging. He explained and testified about
the Kingdom of God and tried to persuade them about Jesus

28:11 The *twin gods* were the Roman gods Castor and Pollux. **28:12** *Syracuse* was on the island of Sicily. **28:13** *Rhegium* was on the southern tip of Italy. **28:14** Greek *brothers.* **28:15a** Greek *brothers.* **28:15b** *The Forum* was about 43 miles (70 kilometers) from Rome. **28:15c** *The Three Taverns* was about 35 miles (57 kilometers) from Rome.

from the Scriptures. Using the law of Moses and the
books of the prophets, he spoke to them from morning
until evening. 24Some were persuaded by the things he
said, but others did not believe. 25And after they had argued back and forth among themselves, they left with this
final word from Paul: "The Holy Spirit was right when he
said to your ancestors through Isaiah the prophet,

26 'Go and say to this people:
When you hear what I say,
you will not understand.
When you see what I do,
you will not comprehend.
27 For the hearts of these people are hardened,
and their ears cannot hear,
and they have closed their eyes—
so their eyes cannot see,
and their ears cannot hear,
and their hearts cannot understand,
and they cannot turn to me
and let me heal them.'*

28So I want you to know that this salvation from God has
also been offered to the Gentiles, and they will accept it."*

CHURCH HISTORY 28:31

The book of Acts shows the history of the Christian church and its expansion in ever-widening circles to Jerusalem, Antioch, Ephesus, and Rome—the most influential cities in the western world. Acts also presents the stories of the members of the early church—people like Peter, Stephen, James, and Paul who acted through the power of the Holy Spirit.

Many unsung heroes of the faith continued the acts of the Holy Spirit, changing the world with a changeless message: Jesus Christ is Savior and Lord for all who call upon him. Today we can take part in the continuing story of the spread of the gospel, bringing that same message to our world so that others may hear and believe. ■

30For the next two years, Paul lived in Rome at his own
expense.* He welcomed all who visited him, 31boldly proclaiming the Kingdom of God and teaching about the
Lord Jesus Christ. And no one tried to stop him.

28:26-27 Isa 6:9-10 (Greek version). **28:28** Some manuscripts add verse 29, *And when he had said these words, the Jews departed, greatly disagreeing with each other.* **28:30** Or *in his own rented quarters.*

ROMANS

IMAGINE YOU'RE OUT on an evening run when you happen upon your dream car. As you admire its beauty, you notice a key in the ignition. The car seems to say, "Take me out for a quick spin." You glance around.

"But that would be stealing!" your conscience protests. "No way!" another voice cuts in. "You're not going to *keep* it." For an agonizingly long moment the inner voices battle—then adventure wins out. The engine hums to life.

"This is awesome!" you say, slipping the car into gear. You intend to make one slow trip around the block—but the speedometer goes up to 160 mph. . . . You head for the open road.

What happens next is a blur. You remember 143 mph, flashing lights, handcuffs, court, and the judge's gavel pounding out a guilty verdict: $20,000 and a six-month jail term. You deserve punishment, but that's severe!

Then the judge does something odd. He removes his robe, pays your fine, and serves your time. Then he looks you in the eyes and says, "I love you."

This analogy isn't perfect, but it *does* help explain how God deals with sinful humanity. The very penalty he demands (death), he provided (Christ's death). If you'd like an even better explanation of God's perfect justice and his intense love for you, read the book of Romans.

romans

stats

PURPOSE: To introduce Paul to the Romans and to give a sample of his message before he arrived in Rome

AUTHOR: Paul

TO WHOM WRITTEN: The Christians in Rome and believers everywhere

DATE WRITTEN: About A.D. 57, from Corinth, as Paul prepared for his visit to Jerusalem

SETTING: Paul had finished his work in the East, and planned to visit Rome on his way to Spain after first bringing a collection to Jerusalem for Christians in need (15:22-29). The Roman church was mostly Jewish, but also contained many Gentiles.

KEY PEOPLE: Paul, Phoebe

KEY PLACE: Rome

KEY points

SIN

Through Paul's writings to Rome, God revealed the destructiveness of sin. All of us were born with a desire to do wrong—a desire that comes with a consequence: death.

SALVATION

Paul explained God's plan of salvation: Christ's death paid the penalty for sin. Although we don't deserve it, God in his kindness reaches out to love and forgive us because of Jesus.

GROWTH

Paul revealed how the Holy Spirit provides freedom from the demands of the law and from the fear of God's judgment. Because we are free from sin's control and the fear of God's punishment, we can grow in our relationship with Christ.

SOVEREIGNTY

Throughout the ages, God shaped events to bring about his plan to save humans. Although God ultimately has control over all aspects of life, he still allows people to choose to accept or reject his forgiveness.

SERVICE

Paul discussed the spiritual gifts given to each member of the body of Christ. These gifts enable believers to serve God. Serving God unifies all believers and enables them to be loving and sensitive to others. By actively and vigorously building up other believers, Christians can be a symphony of service to God.

1

GREETINGS FROM PAUL

This letter is from Paul, a slave of Christ Jesus, chosen by God to be an apostle and sent out to preach his Good News. [2]God promised this Good News long ago through his prophets in the holy Scriptures. [3]The Good News is about his Son. In his earthly life he was born into King David's family line, [4]and he was shown to be* the Son of God when he was raised from the dead by the power of the Holy Spirit.* He is Jesus Christ our Lord. [5]Through Christ, God has given us the privilege* and authority as apostles to tell Gentiles everywhere what God has done for them, so that they will believe and obey him, bringing glory to his name.

[6]And you are included among those Gentiles who have been called to belong to Jesus Christ. [7]I am writing to all of you in Rome who are loved by God and are called to be his own holy people.

May God our Father and the Lord Jesus Christ give you grace and peace.

GOD'S GOOD NEWS

[8]Let me say first that I thank my God through Jesus Christ for all of you, because your faith in him is being talked about all over the world. [9]God knows how often I pray for you. Day and night I bring you and your needs in prayer to God, whom I serve with all my heart* by spreading the Good News about his Son.

[10]One of the things I always pray for is the opportunity, God willing, to come at last to see you. [11]For I long to visit you so I can bring you some spiritual gift that will help you grow strong in the Lord. [12]When we get together, I want to encourage you in your faith, but I also want to be encouraged by yours.

[13]I want you to know, dear brothers and sisters,* that I planned many times to visit you, but I was prevented until now. I want to work among you and see spiritual fruit, just as I have seen among other Gentiles. [14]For I have a great sense of obligation to people in both the civilized world and the rest of the world,* to the educated and uneducated alike. [15]So I am eager to come to you in Rome, too, to preach the Good News.

[16]For I am not ashamed of this Good News about Christ. It is the power of God at work, saving everyone who believes—the Jew first and also the Gentile.* [17]This Good News tells us how God makes us right in his sight. This is accomplished from start to finish by faith. As the Scriptures say, "It is through faith that a righteous person has life."*

GOD'S ANGER AT SIN

[18]But God shows his anger from heaven against all sinful, wicked people who suppress the truth by their wickedness.* [19]They know the truth about God because he has made it obvious to them. [20]For ever since the world was created, people have seen the earth and sky. Through everything God made, they can clearly see his invisible qualities—his eternal power and divine nature. So they have no excuse for not knowing God.

NO EXCUSE 1:18-20

Paul answers a common question: How could a loving God condemn someone who has never heard the Good News of Jesus? In fact, says Paul, God has revealed himself to *all* people. Although everyone knows what God requires, no one lives up to his standards. That's why Jesus died. But if people suppress God's truth in order to live their own way, they have no excuse. (See also "Heard the Good News?" in Acts.) ■

[21]Yes, they knew God, but they wouldn't worship him as God or even give him thanks. And they began to think up foolish ideas of what God was like. As a result, their minds became dark and confused. [22]Claiming to be wise, they instead became utter fools. [23]And instead of worshiping the glorious, ever-living God, they worshiped idols made to look like mere people and birds and animals and reptiles.

[24]So God abandoned them to do whatever shameful things their hearts desired. As a result, they did vile and degrading things with each other's bodies. [25]They traded the truth about God for a lie. So they worshiped and served the things God created instead of the Creator himself, who is worthy of eternal praise! Amen. [26]That is why God abandoned them to their shameful desires. Even the women turned against the natural way to have sex and instead indulged in sex with each other. [27]And the men, instead of having normal sexual relations with women, burned with lust for each other. Men did shameful things with other men, and as a result of this sin, they suffered within themselves the penalty they deserved.

[28]Since they thought it foolish to acknowledge God, he abandoned them to their foolish thinking and let them do things that should never be done. [29]Their lives became full of every kind of wickedness, sin, greed, hate, envy, murder, quarreling, deception, malicious behavior, and gossip. [30]They are backstabbers, haters of God, insolent, proud, and boastful. They invent new ways of sinning, and they disobey their parents. [31]They refuse to understand, break their promises, are heartless, and have no mercy. [32]They know God's justice requires that those who do these things deserve to die, yet they do them anyway. Worse yet, they encourage others to do them, too.

2

GOD'S JUDGMENT OF SIN

You may think you can condemn such people, but you are just as bad, and you have no excuse! When you say they are wicked and should be punished, you are condemning yourself, for you who judge others do these

1:4a Or *and was designated.* **1:4b** Or *by the Spirit of holiness;* or *in the new realm of the Spirit.* **1:5** Or *the grace.* **1:9** Or *in my spirit.* **1:13** Greek *brothers.* **1:14** Greek *to Greeks and barbarians.* **1:16** Greek *also the Greek.* **1:17** Or *"The righteous will live by faith."* Hab 2:4. **1:18** Or *who, by their wickedness, prevent the truth from being known.*

keeping it real

During my freshman and sophomore years in high school, I led a double life. Although I really wanted to live a committed Christian life, I only seemed to do that at home or at church. But at school I was too embarrassed to admit that I was a Christian. I was afraid of what people would think of me if they knew. So, whenever I was invited to parties where drinking and stuff would happen, I'd give in and go, then feel bad about myself for compromising.

The summer before my junior year, I knew things would have to change. That's when I read Romans 2:6-8. Verse 6 says God "will judge everyone according to what they have done." When I thought about what I've done, I realized how self-seeking I was. Yet I really did want to please God. So I decided right then to make my goal eternal life that God promises "to those who keep on doing good" (2:7).

So I memorized that passage and decided to let people at school know I'm a Christian. It's made a big difference. For one thing, I met other Christians who were there all the time, but whom I hadn't bothered to get to know before. The last two years have been much better than the first two. I found that taking a stand against certain things didn't really cost me friends. In fact, because I've found other friends who know what friendship is about, I actually have better friends than I had before. But most of all I have a clear conscience. I no longer live a double life. —Lisa

very same things. 2And we know that God, in his justice,
will punish anyone who does such things. 3Since you
judge others for doing these things, why do you think
you can avoid God's judgment when you do the same
things? 4Don't you see how wonderfully kind, tolerant,
and patient God is with you? Does this mean nothing to
you? Can't you see that his kindness is intended to turn
you from your sin?
5But because you are stubborn and refuse to turn from
your sin, you are storing up terrible punishment for yourself. For a day of anger is coming, when God's righteous
judgment will be revealed. 6He will judge everyone according to what they have done. 7He will give eternal life
to those who keep on doing good, seeking after the glory
and honor and immortality that God offers. 8But he will
pour out his anger and wrath on those who live for themselves, who refuse to obey the truth and instead live lives
of wickedness. 9There will be trouble and calamity for
everyone who keeps on doing what is evil—for the Jew
first and also for the Gentile.* 10But there will be glory
and honor and peace from God for all who do good—for
the Jew first and also for the Gentile. 11For God does not
show favoritism.
12When the Gentiles sin, they will be destroyed, even
though they never had God's written law. And the Jews,
who do have God's law, will be judged by that law when
they fail to obey it. 13For merely listening to the law
doesn't make us right with God. It is obeying the law that
makes us right in his sight. 14Even Gentiles, who do not
have God's written law, show that they know his law when
they instinctively obey it, even without having heard it.
15They demonstrate that God's law is written in their
hearts, for their own conscience and thoughts either accuse them or tell them they are doing right. 16And this is
the message I proclaim—that the day is coming when
God, through Christ Jesus, will judge everyone's secret
life.

THE JEWS AND THE LAW

17You who call yourselves Jews are relying on God's law,
and you boast about your special relationship with him.
18You know what he wants; you know what is right because you have been taught his law. 19You are convinced
that you are a guide for the blind and a light for people
who are lost in darkness. 20You think you can instruct the
ignorant and teach children the ways of God. For you are
certain that God's law gives you complete knowledge and
truth.
21Well then, if you teach others, why don't you teach
yourself? You tell others not to steal, but do you steal?
22You say it is wrong to commit adultery, but do you commit adultery? You condemn idolatry, but do you use
items stolen from pagan temples?* 23You are so proud of
knowing the law, but you dishonor God by breaking it.

2:9 Greek *also for the Greek;* also in 2:10. 2:22 Greek *do you steal from temples?*

Is the gay lifestyle really wrong? Shows like *Will & Grace, Boy Meets Boy,* and *Queer Eye for the Straight Guy* would say no. Instead, they would argue that homosexuality is "an alternative lifestyle"—one that you hear about more and more on TV and also in the courts.

For example, in 2003, the Massachusetts Supreme Judicial Court decided that denying same-sex couples the right to marriage was unconstitutional. They also decided that the definition of marriage needed to change from union of a man and a woman to the "voluntary union of two persons as spouses, to the exclusion of all others."

By now, you might wonder what the real scoop is. In the face of changing legislature, has God's view of homosexuality also changed?

Here's the short answer: No.

Now here's a longer one: in Romans 1:18-32, the apostle Paul has particularly harsh words for those who engage in idolatry and homosexuality. Men and women who practice homosexuality go against God's design for human sexuality and will experience consequences for their actions.

Two important messages need to be given on the subject of homosexuality. One is for our society, where biblical notions of right and wrong are sometimes viewed as outdated. That message is that some lifestyles are *not* acceptable "alternatives."

The second message is for Christians. While homosexuality is sin, it is not the *unforgivable* sin. (See Mark 3:29.) God loves homosexuals just as much as he loves other people who do wrong. Jesus' death on the cross paid for the sin of homosexuality, just as it paid for the sins of lying, greed, lust, hate, and pride.

Homosexuals, like all wrongdoers, stand guilty before God. If that were the whole story, there would be no hope. The great message of Romans—and of the entire Bible—is that Jesus can set us free, regardless of what we've done wrong.

24No wonder the Scriptures say, "The Gentiles blaspheme
the name of God because of you."*
25The Jewish ceremony of circumcision has value only
if you obey God's law. But if you don't obey God's law, you
are no better off than an uncircumcised Gentile. 26And if
the Gentiles obey God's law, won't God declare them to be
his own people? 27In fact, uncircumcised Gentiles who
keep God's law will condemn you Jews who are circumcised and possess God's law but don't obey it.
28For you are not a true Jew just because you were born
of Jewish parents or because you have gone through the
ceremony of circumcision. 29No, a true Jew is one whose
heart is right with God. And true circumcision is not merely obeying the letter of the law; rather, it is a change of heart produced by God's Spirit. And a person with a changed heart seeks praise* from God, not from people.

3 GOD REMAINS FAITHFUL

Then what's the advantage of being a Jew? Is there any
value in the ceremony of circumcision? 2Yes, there are
great benefits! First of all, the Jews were entrusted with
the whole revelation of God.*
3True, some of them were unfaithful; but just because
they were unfaithful, does that mean God will be unfaithful? 4Of course not! Even if everyone else is a liar, God is true. As the Scriptures say about him,

"You will be proved right in what you say,
and you will win your case in court."*

5"But," some might say, "our sinfulness serves a good
purpose, for it helps people see how righteous God is. Isn't it unfair, then, for him to punish us?" (This is merely a human point of view.) 6Of course not! If God were not entirely fair, how would he be qualified to judge the
world? 7"But," someone might still argue, "how can God condemn me as a sinner if my dishonesty highlights his truthfulness and brings him more glory?" 8And some
people even slander us by claiming that we say, "The more we sin, the better it is!" Those who say such things deserve to be condemned.

ALL PEOPLE ARE SINNERS

9Well then, should we conclude that we Jews are better
than others? No, not at all, for we have already shown that

2:24 Isa 52:5 (Greek version). 2:29 Or *receives praise.* 3:2 Greek *the oracles of God.* 3:4 Ps 51:4 (Greek version).

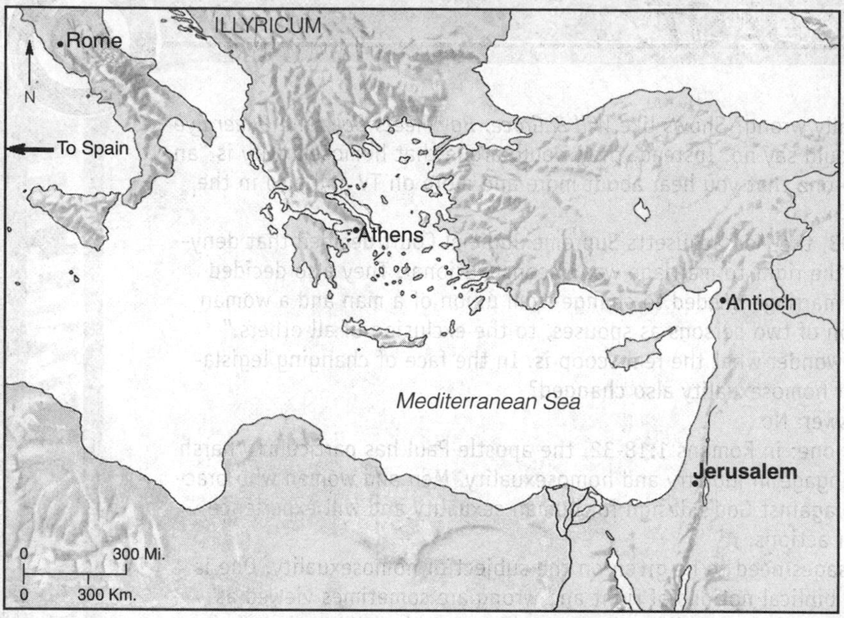

THE GOSPEL GOES TO ROME
When Paul wrote his letter to the church in Rome he had not yet been there, but he had taken the gospel "from Jerusalem all the way to Illyricum" (15:19). He planned to visit and preach in Rome one day, and hoped to continue to take the gospel farther west—even to Spain.

all people, whether Jews or Gentiles,* are under the
power of sin. 10As the Scriptures say,

"No one is righteous—
not even one.
11 No one is truly wise;
no one is seeking God.
12 All have turned away;
all have become useless.
No one does good,
not a single one."*
13 "Their talk is foul, like the stench from an
open grave.
Their tongues are filled with lies."
"Snake venom drips from their lips."*
14 "Their mouths are full of cursing and bitterness."*
15 "They rush to commit murder.
16 Destruction and misery always follow them.
17 They don't know where to find peace."*
18 "They have no fear of God at all."*

19Obviously, the law applies to those to whom it was
given, for its purpose is to keep people from having excuses, and to show that the entire world is guilty before
God. 20For no one can ever be made right with God by doing what the law commands. The law simply shows us
how sinful we are.

CHRIST TOOK OUR PUNISHMENT

21But now God has shown us a way to be made right with
him without keeping the requirements of the law, as was
promised in the writings of Moses* and the prophets
long ago. 22We are made right with God by placing our
faith in Jesus Christ. And this is true for everyone who believes, no matter who we are.

A HARD TRUTH 3:23

Paul revealed a hard truth: All people have blown it in some way. Some actions might seem "worse" than others because their obvious consequences are much more serious. Murder, for example, seems much worse than hatred; adultery seems worse than lust. Yet all wrong actions have the same consequence—death. (See Rom 6:23.) Thanks to Jesus, forgiveness is offered for all. See why they call it "good news"? ■

23For everyone has sinned; we all fall short of God's
glorious standard. 24Yet God, with undeserved kindness,
declares that we are righteous. He did this through Christ
Jesus when he freed us from the penalty for our sins.
25For God presented Jesus as the sacrifice for sin. People
are made right with God when they believe that Jesus sacrificed his life, shedding his blood. This sacrifice shows
that God was being fair when he held back and did not
punish those who sinned in times past, 26for he was looking ahead and including them in what he would do in this
present time. God did this to demonstrate his righteousness, for he himself is fair and just, and he declares sinners to be right in his sight when they believe in Jesus.
27Can we boast, then, that we have done anything to
be accepted by God? No, because our acquittal is not
based on obeying the law. It is based on faith. 28So we

3:9 Greek *or Greeks.* **3:10-12** Pss 14:1-3; 53:1-3 (Greek version). **3:13** Pss 5:9 (Greek version); 140:3. **3:14** Ps 10:7 (Greek version). **3:15-17** Isa 59:7-8. **3:18** Ps 36:1. **3:21** Greek *in the law.*

Salvation's Freeway

Everyone has sinned.
Romans 3:23

The penalty for our
sin is death.
Romans 6:23

Jesus Christ died for sin.
Romans 5:8

To be forgiven for our
sins, we must believe
and confess that Jesus is
Lord. Salvation comes
through Jesus Christ.
Romans 10:8-10

are made right with God through faith and not by obeying the law.
29After all, is God the God of the Jews only? Isn't he also
the God of the Gentiles? Of course he is. 30There is only
one God, and he makes people right with himself only by
faith, whether they are Jews or Gentiles.* 31Well then, if
we emphasize faith, does this mean that we can forget
about the law? Of course not! In fact, only when we have
faith do we truly fulfill the law.

4 THE FAITH OF ABRAHAM

Abraham was, humanly speaking, the founder of our Jewish nation. What did he discover about being made right
with God? 2If his good deeds had made him acceptable to
God, he would have had something to boast about. But
that was not God's way. 3For the Scriptures tell us, "Abraham believed God, and God counted him as righteous because of his faith."*

A GIFT 4:4-5

When some people learn that all can be saved through faith in Jesus, they start to worry: "Do I have enough faith?" "Is my faith strong enough to save me?" But they miss the point. Jesus, rather than our feelings or actions, saves us. He offers us forgiveness because he loves us, not because we earned it through our powerful faith. What, then, is the role of faith? Faith enables us to accept God's forgiveness. Have you accepted this gift? ■

4When people work, their wages are not a gift, but
something they have earned. 5But people are counted as
righteous, not because of their work, but because of their
faith in God who forgives sinners. 6David also spoke of
this when he described the happiness of those who are
declared righteous without working for it:

7 "Oh, what joy for those
whose disobedience is forgiven,
whose sins are put out of sight.
8 Yes, what joy for those
whose record the LORD has cleared of sin."*

9Now, is this blessing only for the Jews, or is it also for
uncircumcised Gentiles?* Well, we have been saying that
Abraham was counted as righteous by God because of his
faith. 10But how did this happen? Was he counted as
righteous only after he was circumcised, or was it before he was circumcised? Clearly, God accepted Abraham before he was circumcised!
11Circumcision was a sign that Abraham already had
faith and that God had already accepted him and declared him to be righteous—even before he was circumcised. So Abraham is the spiritual father of those who
have faith but have not been circumcised. They are
counted as righteous because of their faith. 12And Abraham is also the spiritual father of those who have been
circumcised, but only if they have the same kind of faith
Abraham had before he was circumcised.
13Clearly, God's promise to give the whole earth to
Abraham and his descendants was based not on his obedience to God's law, but on a right relationship with God
that comes by faith. 14If God's promise is only for those
who obey the law, then faith is not necessary and the
promise is pointless. 15For the law always brings punishment on those who try to obey it. (The only way to avoid
breaking the law is to have no law to break!)
16So the promise is received by faith. It is given as a
free gift. And we are all certain to receive it, whether or
not we live according to the law of Moses, if we have faith
like Abraham's. For Abraham is the father of all who believe. 17That is what the Scriptures mean when God told
him, "I have made you the father of many nations."* This
happened because Abraham believed in the God who
brings the dead back to life and who creates new things
out of nothing.
18Even when there was no reason for hope, Abraham
kept hoping—believing that he would become the father
of many nations. For God had said to him, "That's how
many descendants you will have!"* 19And Abraham's
faith did not weaken, even though, at about 100 years of
age, he figured his body was as good as dead—and so was
Sarah's womb.
20Abraham never wavered in believing God's promise.
In fact, his faith grew stronger, and in this he brought
glory to God. 21He was fully convinced that God is able to
do whatever he promises. 22And because of Abraham's
faith, God counted him as righteous. 23And when God

3:30 Greek *whether they are circumcised or uncircumcised.* 4:3 Gen 15:6. 4:7-8 Ps 32:1-2 (Greek version). 4:9 Greek *is this blessing only for the circumcised, or is it also for the uncircumcised?* 4:17 Gen 17:5. 4:18 Gen 15:5.

counted him as righteous, it wasn't just for Abraham's
benefit. It was recorded 24for our benefit, too, assuring us
that God will also count us as righteous if we believe in
him, the one who raised Jesus our Lord from the dead.
25He was handed over to die because of our sins, and he
was raised to life to make us right with God.

5 FAITH BRINGS JOY

Therefore, since we have been made right in God's sight
by faith, we have peace with God because of what Jesus
Christ our Lord has done for us. 2Because of our faith,
Christ has brought us into this place of undeserved privilege where we now stand, and we confidently and joyfully
look forward to sharing God's glory.
3We can rejoice, too, when we run into problems and
trials, for we know that they help us develop endurance.
4And endurance develops strength of character, and
character strengthens our confident hope of salvation.
5And this hope will not lead to disappointment. For we
know how dearly God loves us, because he has given us
the Holy Spirit to fill our hearts with his love.

OVERCOME 5:2-4

Paul tells us what we will *become* in the future. Until then we must *overcome*. This means we will experience difficulties that could help us grow. Problems we face will help develop our patience, which will strengthen our character, deepen our trust in God, and give us greater confidence about the future. As you find your patience tested in some way every day, how will you respond to these opportunities to grow? Check out James 1:2-4 and 1 Peter 1:6-7 for some advice. ■

6When we were utterly helpless, Christ came at just the
right time and died for us sinners. 7Now, most people
would not be willing to die for an upright person, though
someone might perhaps be willing to die for a person
who is especially good. 8But God showed his great love
for us by sending Christ to die for us while we were still
sinners. 9And since we have been made right in God's
sight by the blood of Christ, he will certainly save us from
God's condemnation. 10For since our friendship with
God was restored by the death of his Son while we were
still his enemies, we will certainly be saved through the
life of his Son. 11So now we can rejoice in our wonderful
new relationship with God because our Lord Jesus Christ
has made us friends of God.

ADAM AND CHRIST CONTRASTED

12When Adam sinned, sin entered the world. Adam's sin
brought death, so death spread to everyone, for everyone
sinned. 13Yes, people sinned even before the law was
given. But it was not counted as sin because there was
not yet any law to break. 14Still, everyone died—from the
time of Adam to the time of Moses—even those who did
not disobey an explicit commandment of God, as Adam
did. Now Adam is a symbol, a representation of Christ,
who was yet to come. 15But there is a great difference between Adam's sin and God's gracious gift. For the sin of
this one man, Adam, brought death to many. But even
greater is God's wonderful grace and his gift of forgiveness to many through this other man, Jesus Christ. 16And
the result of God's gracious gift is very different from
the result of that one man's sin. For Adam's sin led to
condemnation, but God's free gift leads to our being
made right with God, even though we are guilty of many
sins. 17For the sin of this one man, Adam, caused death to
rule over many. But even greater is God's wonderful
grace and his gift of righteousness, for all who receive it
will live in triumph over sin and death through this one
man, Jesus Christ.
18Yes, Adam's one sin brings condemnation for everyone, but Christ's one act of righteousness brings a right
relationship with God and new life for everyone.
19Because one person disobeyed God, many became sinners. But because one other person obeyed God, many
will be made righteous.
20God's law was given so that all people could see how
sinful they were. But as people sinned more and more,
God's wonderful grace became more abundant. 21So just
as sin ruled over all people and brought them to death,
now God's wonderful grace rules instead, giving us right
standing with God and resulting in eternal life through
Jesus Christ our Lord.

Ever since I became a Christian, I keep fighting against certain thoughts and habits that I used to never give a second thought about. Why is this happening?

Picture your life as a door. Before you became a Christian, wrong actions were like nails being pounded into the door and left there. When you asked Christ to forgive you, all of the nails you had collected were removed! Unfortunately, what was left was a door full of holes—not very pleasant to look at and not very useful.

Paul knew this all too well, as you can see if you read Romans 7:15–8:2. Like Paul, we're all tempted to give in to our desire to do wrong. Our new nature moves us to resist, however.

Likewise, you're experiencing a new sensitivity to sin. This new sensitivity means two things. First, this is a sign that the Spirit of God has truly entered your life (Rom 8:9). Otherwise you would still be numb to the nails (sin) if you had rejected Christ's forgiveness. Second, it means that God is reminding you of his love for you (Rom 8:38-39). He doesn't want you to be left scarred by the consequences of wrong actions, so he begins at the source of it—your thoughts.

6

SIN'S POWER IS BROKEN

Well then, should we keep on sinning so that God can show us more and more of his wonderful grace? 2Of course not! Since we have died to sin, how can we continue to live in it? 3Or have you forgotten that when we were joined with Christ Jesus in baptism, we joined him in his death? 4For we died and were buried with Christ by baptism. And just as Christ was raised from the dead by the glorious power of the Father, now we also may live new lives.

> For the wages of sin is death, but the free gift of God is eternal life through Christ Jesus our Lord.
>
> *ROMANS 6:23*

5Since we have been united with him in his death, we will also be raised to life as he was. 6We know that our old sinful selves were crucified with Christ so that sin might lose its power in our lives. We are no longer slaves to sin. 7For when we died with Christ we were set free from the power of sin. 8And since we died with Christ, we know we will also live with him. 9We are sure of this because Christ was raised from the dead, and he will never die again. Death no longer has any power over him. 10When he died, he died once to break the power of sin. But now that he lives, he lives for the glory of God. 11So you also should consider yourselves to be dead to the power of sin and alive to God through Christ Jesus.

12Do not let sin control the way you live;* do not give in to sinful desires. 13Do not let any part of your body become an instrument of evil to serve sin. Instead, give yourselves completely to God, for you were dead, but now you have new life. So use your whole body as an instrument to do what is right for the glory of God. 14Sin is no longer your master, for you no longer live under the requirements of the law. Instead, you live under the freedom of God's grace.

15Well then, since God's grace has set us free from the law, does that mean we can go on sinning? Of course not! 16Don't you realize that you become the slave of whatever you choose to obey? You can be a slave to sin, which leads to death, or you can choose to obey God, which leads to righteous living. 17Thank God! Once you were slaves of sin, but now you wholeheartedly obey this teaching we have given you. 18Now you are free from your slavery to sin, and you have become slaves to righteous living.

19Because of the weakness of your human nature, I am using the illustration of slavery to help you understand all this. Previously, you let yourselves be slaves to impurity and lawlessness, which led ever deeper into sin. Now you must give yourselves to be slaves to righteous living so that you will become holy.

20When you were slaves to sin, you were free from the obligation to do right. 21And what was the result? You are now ashamed of the things you used to do, things that end in eternal doom. 22But now you are free from the power of sin and have become slaves of God. Now you do those things that lead to holiness and result in eternal life. 23For the wages of sin is death, but the free gift of God is eternal life through Christ Jesus our Lord.

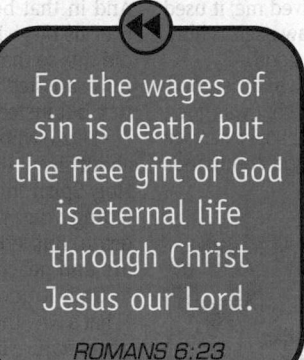

7

NO LONGER BOUND TO THE LAW

Now, dear brothers and sisters*—you who are familiar with the law—don't you know that the law applies only while a person is living? 2For example, when a woman marries, the law binds her to her husband as long as he is alive. But if he dies, the laws of marriage no longer apply to her. 3So while her husband is alive, she would be committing adultery if she married another man. But if her husband dies, she is free from that law and does not commit adultery when she remarries.

4So, my dear brothers and sisters, this is the point: You died to the power of the law when you died with Christ. And now you are united with the one who was raised from the dead. As a result, we can produce a harvest of good deeds for God. 5When we were controlled by our old nature,* sinful desires were at work within us, and the law aroused these evil desires that produced a harvest of sinful deeds, resulting in death. 6But now we have been released from the law, for we died to it and are no longer captive to its power. Now we can serve God, not in the old way of obeying the letter of the law, but in the new way of living in the Spirit.

> **WHY THE LAW? 7:9-11**
>
> **If people feel fine without the law, why did God give it? Because sin is real and dangerous. Imagine a sunny day at the beach. You have just plunged into the surf and you've never felt better. Suddenly you notice a sign on the pier: *No swimming: Sharks in water.* Your day is ruined. Is the sign responsible? Are you angry with the people who put it up? Of course not. The law is like the sign. It's essential, and we're grateful for it. But it isn't a solution for the sharks! ■**

GOD'S LAW REVEALS OUR SIN

7Well then, am I suggesting that the law of God is sinful? Of course not! In fact, it was the law that showed me my sin. I would never have known that coveting is wrong if the law had not said, "You must not covet."* 8But sin used this command to arouse all kinds of covetous desires within me! If there were no law, sin would not have that power. 9At one time I lived without understanding the law. But when I learned the command not to covet, for instance, the power of sin came to life, 10and I died. So I discovered that the law's commands, which were supposed to bring life, brought spiritual death instead. 11Sin took

6:12 Or *Do not let sin reign in your body, which is subject to death.* **7:1** Greek *brothers;* also in 7:4. **7:5** Greek *When we were in the flesh.* **7:7** Exod 20:17; Deut 5:21.

advantage of those commands and deceived me; it used the commands to kill me. 12But still, the law itself is holy, and its commands are holy and right and good.

13But how can that be? Did the law, which is good, cause my death? Of course not! Sin used what was good to bring about my condemnation to death. So we can see how terrible sin really is. It uses God's good commands for its own evil purposes.

A DESPERATE STRUGGLE 7:15

This is more than the cry of one desperate man—it describes the experience of any Christian struggling against a wrong desire. We must never underestimate the power of sin. While Satan is a crafty tempter, we also have a great ability to make excuses. Instead of trying to overcome sin with human willpower, we have access to the tremendous power of Christ through the Holy Spirit. And when we fall, God lovingly reaches out to us and helps us get up again. ■

STRUGGLING WITH SIN

14So the trouble is not with the law, for it is spiritual and good. The trouble is with me, for I am all too human, a slave to sin. 15I don't really understand myself, for I want to do what is right, but I don't do it. Instead, I do what I hate. 16But if I know that what I am doing is wrong, this shows that I agree that the law is good. 17So I am not the one doing wrong; it is sin living in me that does it.

18And I know that nothing good lives in me, that is, in my sinful nature.* I want to do what is right, but I can't. 19I want to do what is good, but I don't. I don't want to do what is wrong, but I do it anyway. 20But if I do what I don't want to do, I am not really the one doing wrong; it is sin living in me that does it.

21I have discovered this principle of life—that when I want to do what is right, I inevitably do what is wrong. 22I love God's law with all my heart. 23But there is another power* within me that is at war with my mind. This power makes me a slave to the sin that is still within me. 24Oh, what a miserable person I am! Who will free me from this life that is dominated by sin and death? 25Thank God! The answer is in Jesus Christ our Lord. So you see how it is: In my mind I really want to obey God's law, but because of my sinful nature I am a slave to sin.

8 LIFE IN THE SPIRIT

So now there is no condemnation for those who belong to Christ Jesus. 2And because you belong to him, the power* of the life-giving Spirit has freed you* from the power of sin that leads to death. 3The law of Moses was unable to save us because of the weakness of our sinful nature.* So God did what the law could not do. He sent his own Son in a body like the bodies we sinners have. And in that body God declared an end to sin's control over us by giving his Son as a sacrifice for our sins. 4He did this so that the just requirement of the law would be fully satisfied for us, who no longer follow our sinful nature but instead follow the Spirit.

5Those who are dominated by the sinful nature think about sinful things, but those who are controlled by the Holy Spirit think about things that please the Spirit. 6So letting your sinful nature control your mind leads to death. But letting the Spirit control your mind leads to life and peace. 7For the sinful nature is always hostile to God. It never did obey God's laws, and it never will. 8That's why those who are still under the control of their sinful nature can never please God.

9But you are not controlled by your sinful nature. You are controlled by the Spirit if you have the Spirit of God living in you. (And remember that those who do not have the Spirit of Christ living in them do not belong to him at all.) 10And Christ lives within you, so even though your body will die because of sin, the Spirit gives you life* because you have been made right with God. 11The Spirit of God, who raised Jesus from the dead, lives in you. And just as God raised Christ Jesus from the dead, he will give life to your mortal bodies by this same Spirit living within you.

12Therefore, dear brothers and sisters,* you have no obligation to do what your sinful nature urges you to do. 13For if you live by its dictates, you will die. But if through the power of the Spirit you put to death the deeds of your sinful nature,* you will live. 14For all who are led by the Spirit of God are children* of God.

15So you have not received a spirit that makes you fearful slaves. Instead, you received God's Spirit when he adopted you as his own children.* Now we call him, "Abba, Father."* 16For his Spirit joins with our spirit to affirm that we are God's children. 17And since we are his children, we are his heirs. In fact, together with Christ we are heirs of God's glory. But if we are to share his glory, we must also share his suffering.

THE FUTURE GLORY

18Yet what we suffer now is nothing compared to the glory he will reveal to us later. 19For all creation is waiting eagerly for that future day when God will reveal who his children really are. 20Against its will, all creation was subjected to God's curse. But with eager hope, 21the creation looks forward to the day when it will join God's children in glorious freedom from death and decay. 22For we know that all creation has been groaning as in the pains of childbirth right up to the present time. 23And we believers also groan, even though we have the Holy Spirit within us as a foretaste of future glory, for we long for our bodies to be released from sin and suffering. We, too, wait with eager hope for the day when God will give us our full rights as his adopted children,* including the new bodies he has promised us. 24We were given this hope when we were saved. (If we already

7:18 Greek *my flesh;* also in 7:25. **7:23** Greek *law;* also in 7:23b. **8:2a** Greek *the law;* also in 8:2b. **8:2b** Some manuscripts read *me.* **8:3** Greek *our flesh;* similarly in 8:4, 5, 6, 7, 8, 9, 12. **8:10** Or *your spirit is alive.* **8:12** Greek *brothers;* also in 8:29. **8:13** Greek *deeds of the body.* **8:14** Greek *sons;* also in 8:19. **8:15a** Greek *you received a spirit of sonship.* **8:15b** *Abba* is an Aramaic term for "father." **8:23** Greek *wait anxiously for sonship.*

have something, we don't need to
hope* for it. 25But if we look forward to
something we don't yet have, we must
wait patiently and confidently.)
26And the Holy Spirit helps us in our
weakness. For example, we don't know
what God wants us to pray for. But the
Holy Spirit prays for us with groanings
that cannot be expressed in words.
27And the Father who knows all hearts
knows what the Spirit is saying, for the
Spirit pleads for us believers* in harmony with God's own will. 28And we
know that God causes everything to
work together* for the good of those
who love God and are called according
to his purpose for them. 29For God knew
his people in advance, and he chose
them to become like his Son, so that his Son would be the
firstborn among many brothers and sisters. 30And having
chosen them, he called them to come to him. And having
called them, he gave them right standing with himself. And
having given them right standing, he gave them his glory.

> Nothing in all creation will ever be able to separate us from the love of God that is revealed in Christ Jesus our Lord.
>
> *ROMANS 8:39*

THE GREATER GOOD 8:28

God works all things—not just isolated incidents—for our good. This doesn't mean that all that happens to us is good. Although evil is prevalent in our world, God is able to turn it around for our long-range good. Note that God is not working to make us happy, but to fulfill his purpose. Note also that this promise is not for everybody—it is for those who trust Jesus. Such people have a new perspective, a new mind-set. They trust God, not their intellect or bank account. Does that describe you? ■

NOTHING CAN SEPARATE US FROM GOD'S LOVE

31What shall we say about such wonderful things as
these? If God is for us, who can ever be against us? 32Since
he did not spare even his own Son but gave him up for us
all, won't he also give us everything else? 33Who dares accuse us whom God has chosen for his own? No one—for
God himself has given us right standing with himself.
34Who then will condemn us? No one—for Christ Jesus
died for us and was raised to life for us, and he is sitting in
the place of honor at God's right hand, pleading for us.

35Can anything ever separate us from Christ's love? Does
it mean he no longer loves us if we have trouble or calamity,
or are persecuted, or hungry, or destitute, or in danger, or
threatened with death? 36(As the Scriptures say, "For your
sake we are killed every day; we are being slaughtered like
sheep."*) 37No, despite all these things, overwhelming victory is ours through Christ, who loved us.

38And I am convinced that nothing can ever separate us
from God's love. Neither death nor life,
neither angels nor demons,* neither
our fears for today nor our worries
about tomorrow—not even the powers
of hell can separate us from God's love.
39No power in the sky above or in the
earth below—indeed, nothing in all
creation will ever be able to separate us
from the love of God that is revealed in
Christ Jesus our Lord.

9

GOD'S SELECTION OF ISRAEL

With Christ as my witness, I speak
with utter truthfulness. My conscience and the Holy Spirit confirm
it. 2My heart is filled with bitter sorrow and unending grief 3for my people, my Jewish brothers and sisters.* I would be willing
to be forever cursed—cut off from Christ!—if that
would save them. 4They are the people of Israel, chosen
to be God's adopted children.* God revealed his glory to
them. He made covenants with them and gave them his
law. He gave them the privilege of worshiping him and
receiving his wonderful promises. 5Abraham, Isaac, and
Jacob are their ancestors, and Christ himself was an Israelite as far as his human nature is concerned. And he
is God, the one who rules over everything and is worthy
of eternal praise! Amen.*

6Well then, has God failed to fulfill his promise to Israel? No, for not all who are born into the nation of Israel are
truly members of God's people! 7Being descendants of
Abraham doesn't make them truly Abraham's children.
For the Scriptures say, "Isaac is the son through whom
your descendants will be counted,"* though Abraham
had other children, too. 8This means that Abraham's
physical descendants are not necessarily children of God.
Only the children of the promise are considered to be
Abraham's children. 9For God had promised, "I will return
about this time next year, and Sarah will have a son."*

10This son was our ancestor Isaac. When he married
Rebekah, she gave birth to twins.* 11But before they were
born, before they had done anything good or bad, she
received a message from God. (This message shows that
God chooses people according to his own purposes; 12he
calls people, but not according to their good or bad
works.) She was told, "Your older son will serve your
younger son."* 13In the words of the Scriptures, "I loved
Jacob, but I rejected Esau."*

14Are we saying, then, that God was unfair? Of course
not! 15For God said to Moses,

"I will show mercy to anyone I choose,
and I will show compassion to anyone I choose."*

16So it is God who decides to show mercy. We can neither
choose it nor work for it.

8:24 Some manuscripts read *wait.* **8:27** Greek *for God's holy people.* **8:28** Some manuscripts read *And we know that everything works together.* **8:36** Ps 44:22. **8:38** Greek *nor rulers.* **9:3** Greek *my brothers.* **9:4** Greek *chosen for sonship.* **9:5** Or *May God, the one who rules over everything, be praised forever. Amen.* **9:7** Gen 21:12. **9:9** Gen 18:10, 14. **9:10** Greek *she conceived children through this one man.* **9:12** Gen 25:23. **9:13** Mal 1:2-3. **9:15** Exod 33:19.

17For the Scriptures say that God told Pharaoh, "I have
appointed you for the very purpose of displaying my
power in you and to spread my fame throughout the
earth."* 18So you see, God chooses to show mercy to
some, and he chooses to harden the hearts of others so
they refuse to listen.

19Well then, you might say, "Why does God blame people for not responding? Haven't they simply done what
he makes them do?"

20No, don't say that. Who are you, a mere human being,
to argue with God? Should the thing that was created say to
the one who created it, "Why have you made me like this?"
21When a potter makes jars out of clay, doesn't he have a
right to use the same lump of clay to make one jar for deco-
ration and another to throw garbage into? 22In the same
way, even though God has the right to show his anger and
his power, he is very patient with those on whom his anger
falls, who are destined for destruction. 23He does this to
make the riches of his glory shine even brighter on those to
whom he shows mercy, who were prepared in advance for
glory. 24And we are among those whom he selected, both
from the Jews and from the Gentiles.

25Concerning the Gentiles, God says in the prophecy of
Hosea,

"Those who were not my people,
I will now call my people.
And I will love those
whom I did not love before."*

26And,

"Then, at the place where they were told,
'You are not my people,'
there they will be called
'children of the living God.'"*

27And concerning Israel, Isaiah the prophet cried out,

"Though the people of Israel are as numerous as the
sand of the seashore,
only a remnant will be saved.
28 For the LORD will carry out his sentence upon
the earth
quickly and with finality."*

29And Isaiah said the same thing in another place:

"If the LORD of Heaven's Armies
had not spared a few of our children,
we would have been wiped out like Sodom,
destroyed like Gomorrah."*

ISRAEL'S UNBELIEF

30What does all this mean? Even though the Gentiles
were not trying to follow God's standards, they were
made right with God. And it was by faith that this took
place. 31But the people of Israel, who tried so hard to get
right with God by keeping the law, never succeeded.
32Why not? Because they were trying to get right with
God by keeping the law* instead of by trusting in him.
They stumbled over the great rock in their path. 33God
warned them of this in the Scriptures when he said,

"I am placing a stone in Jerusalem* that makes
people stumble,
a rock that makes them fall.
But anyone who trusts in him
will never be disgraced."*

FOREVER TRYING 9:31-33

The people of Israel tried to get right with God by keeping his laws. In the same way, we may think activities like church work, giving offerings, and being nice will make us right with God. After all, we've played by the rules, haven't we? But as Paul explains, no one can earn God's favor. (See also Isa 64:6-7; Rom 11:6-7.) Only by putting our faith in what Jesus has done will we be saved. Because of Jesus, we "will never be disgraced." ■

10

Dear brothers and sisters,* the longing of my
heart and my prayer to God is for the people of Israel to
be saved. 2I know what enthusiasm they have for God, but
it is misdirected zeal. 3For they don't understand God's
way of making people right with himself. Refusing to accept God's way, they cling to their own way of getting
right with God by trying to keep the law. 4For Christ has
already accomplished the purpose for which the law was
given.* As a result, all who believe in him are made right
with God.

SALVATION IS FOR EVERYONE

5For Moses writes that the law's way of making a person
right with God requires obedience to all of its commands.* 6But faith's way of getting right with God says,
"Don't say in your heart, 'Who will go up to heaven' (to
bring Christ down to earth). 7And don't say, 'Who will go
down to the place of the dead' (to bring Christ back to life
again)." 8In fact, it says,

"The message is very close at hand;
it is on your lips and in your heart."*

And that message is the very message about faith that we
preach: 9If you confess with your mouth that Jesus is Lord
and believe in your heart that God raised him from the
dead, you will be saved. 10For it is by believing in your
heart that you are made right with God, and it is by confessing with your mouth that you are saved. 11As the
Scriptures tell us, "Anyone who trusts in him will never be

9:17 Exod 9:16 (Greek version). 9:25 Hos 2:23. 9:26 Greek *sons of the living God.* Hos 1:10. 9:27-28 Isa 10:22-23 (Greek version). 9:29 Isa 1:9. 9:32 Greek *by works.* 9:33a Greek *in Zion.* 9:33b Isa 8:14; 28:16 (Greek version). 10:1 Greek *Brothers.* 10:4 Or *For Christ is the end of the law.* 10:5 See Lev 18:5. 10:6-8 Deut 30:12-14.

disgraced."* 12Jew and Gentile* are the same in this respect. They have the same Lord, who gives generously to all who call on him. 13For "Everyone who calls on the name of the LORD will be saved."*

14But how can they call on him to save them unless they believe in him? And how can they believe in him if they have never heard about him? And how can they hear about him unless someone tells them? 15And how will anyone go and tell them without being sent? That is why the Scriptures say, "How beautiful are the feet of messengers who bring good news!"*

16But not everyone welcomes the Good News, for Isaiah the prophet said, "LORD, who has believed our message?"* 17So faith comes from hearing, that is, hearing the Good News about Christ. 18But I ask, have the people of Israel actually heard the message? Yes, they have:

"The message has gone throughout the earth,
and the words to all the world."*

19But I ask, did the people of Israel really understand? Yes, they did, for even in the time of Moses, God said,

"I will rouse your jealousy through people who are not even a nation.
I will provoke your anger through the foolish Gentiles."*

20And later Isaiah spoke boldly for God, saying,

"I was found by people who were not looking for me.
I showed myself to those who were not asking for me."*

21But regarding Israel, God said,

"All day long I opened my arms to them,
but they were disobedient and rebellious."*

11 GOD'S MERCY ON ISRAEL

I ask, then, has God rejected his own people, the nation of Israel? Of course not! I myself am an Israelite, a descendant of Abraham and a member of the tribe of Benjamin.

2No, God has not rejected his own people, whom he chose from the very beginning. Do you realize what the Scriptures say about this? Elijah the prophet complained to God about the people of Israel and said, 3"LORD, they have killed your prophets and torn down your altars. I am the only one left, and now they are trying to kill me, too."*

4And do you remember God's reply? He said, "No, I have 7,000 others who have never bowed down to Baal!"*

5It is the same today, for a few of the people of Israel* have remained faithful because of God's grace—his undeserved kindness in choosing them. 6And since it is through God's kindness, then it is not by their good works. For in that case, God's grace would not be what it really is—free and undeserved.

7So this is the situation: Most of the people of Israel have not found the favor of God they are looking for so earnestly. A few have—the ones God has chosen—but the hearts of the rest were hardened. 8As the Scriptures say,

"God has put them into a deep sleep.
To this day he has shut their eyes so they do not see,
and closed their ears so they do not hear."*

9Likewise, David said,

"Let their bountiful table become a snare,
a trap that makes them think all is well.
Let their blessings cause them to stumble,
and let them get what they deserve.
10 Let their eyes go blind so they cannot see,
and let their backs be bent forever."*

11Did God's people stumble and fall beyond recovery? Of course not! They were disobedient, so God made salvation available to the Gentiles. But he wanted his own people to become jealous and claim it for themselves. 12Now if the Gentiles were enriched because the people of Israel turned down God's offer of salvation, think how much greater a blessing the world will share when they finally accept it.

13I am saying all this especially for you Gentiles. God has appointed me as the apostle to the Gentiles. I stress this, 14for I want somehow to make the people of Israel jealous of what you Gentiles have, so I might save some of them. 15For since their rejection meant that God offered salvation to the rest of the world, their acceptance will be even more wonderful. It will be life for those who were dead! 16And since Abraham and the other patriarchs were holy, their descendants will also be holy—just as the entire batch of dough is holy because the portion given as an offering is holy. For if the roots of the tree are holy, the branches will be, too.

17But some of these branches from Abraham's tree—some of the people of Israel—have been broken off. And you Gentiles, who were branches from a wild olive tree, have been grafted in. So now you also receive the blessing God has promised Abraham and his children, sharing in the rich nourishment from the root of God's special olive tree. 18But you must not brag about being grafted in to replace the branches that were broken off. You are just a branch, not the root.

19"Well," you may say, "those branches were broken off to make room for me." 20Yes, but remember—those branches were broken off because they didn't believe in Christ, and you are there because you do believe. So don't think highly of yourself, but fear what could happen. 21For if God did not spare the original branches, he won't* spare you either.

22Notice how God is both kind and severe. He is severe

10:11 Isa 28:16 (Greek version). **10:12** Greek *and Greek*. **10:13** Joel 2:32. **10:15** Isa 52:7. **10:16** Isa 53:1. **10:18** Ps 19:4. **10:19** Deut 32:21. **10:20** Isa 65:1 (Greek version). **10:21** Isa 65:2 (Greek version). **11:3** 1 Kgs 19:10, 14. **11:4** 1 Kgs 19:18. **11:5** Greek *for a remnant*. **11:8** Isa 29:10; Deut 29:4. **11:9-10** Ps 69:22-23 (Greek version). **11:21** Some manuscripts read *perhaps he won't*.

toward those who disobeyed, but kind to you if you continue to trust in his kindness. But if you stop trusting, you
also will be cut off. [23]And if the people of Israel turn from
their unbelief, they will be grafted in again, for God has
the power to graft them back into the tree. [24]You, by nature, were a branch cut from a wild olive tree. So if God
was willing to do something contrary to nature by graft-
ing you into his cultivated tree, he will be far more eager
to graft the original branches back into the tree where
they belong.

GOD'S MERCY IS FOR EVERYONE

[25]I want you to understand this mystery, dear brothers
and sisters,* so that you will not feel proud about yourselves. Some of the people of Israel have hard hearts, but
this will last only until the full number of Gentiles comes
to Christ. [26]And so all Israel will be saved. As the Scriptures say,

"The one who rescues will come from Jerusalem,*
and he will turn Israel* away from ungodliness.
27 And this is my covenant with them,
that I will take away their sins."*

[28]Many of the people of Israel are now enemies of the
Good News, and this benefits you Gentiles. Yet they are
still the people he loves because he chose their ancestors
Abraham, Isaac, and Jacob. [29]For God's gifts and his call
can never be withdrawn. [30]Once, you Gentiles were rebels
against God, but when the people of Israel rebelled
against him, God was merciful to you instead. [31]Now they
are the rebels, and God's mercy has come to you so that
they, too, will share* in God's mercy. [32]For God has imprisoned everyone in disobedience so he could have
mercy on everyone.

[33]Oh, how great are God's riches and wisdom and
knowledge! How impossible it is for us to understand his
decisions and his ways!

34 For who can know the LORD's thoughts?
Who knows enough to give him advice?*
35 And who has given him so much
that he needs to pay it back?*

[36]For everything comes from him and exists by his
power and is intended for his glory. All glory to him forever! Amen.

12 A LIVING SACRIFICE TO GOD

And so, dear brothers and sisters,* I plead with you to give
your bodies to God because of all he has done for you. Let
them be a living and holy sacrifice—the kind he will find
acceptable. This is truly the way to worship him.* [2]Don't
copy the behavior and customs of this world, but let God
transform you into a new person by changing the way you
think. Then you will learn to know God's will for you,
which is good and pleasing and perfect.

A RENEWED MIND 12:2

"The behavior and customs of this world" are usually selfish and often corrupting. Therefore, many Christians wisely decide that such behavior is off-limits for them. Yet it is possible to avoid most worldly customs and still be proud, covetous, selfish, stubborn, and arrogant. That's why our refusal to conform to the world must go even deeper than the level of behavior and customs—it must become a mind-set. Only when our mind is renewed by the new attitude Christ gives us are we truly transformed. ■

[3]Because of the privilege and authority* God has
given me, I give each of you this warning: Don't think
you are better than you really are. Be honest in your evaluation of yourselves, measuring yourselves by the faith
God has given us.* [4]Just as our bodies have many parts
and each part has a special function, [5]so it is with
Christ's body. We are many parts of one body, and we all
belong to each other.

[6]In his grace, God has given us different gifts for doing
certain things well. So if God has given you the ability to
prophesy, speak out with as much faith as God has given
you. [7]If your gift is serving others, serve them well. If you
are a teacher, teach well. [8]If your gift is to encourage others, be encouraging. If it is giving, give generously. If God
has given you leadership ability, take the responsibility
seriously. And if you have a gift for showing kindness to
others, do it gladly.

GIFTS 12:4-8

God gives us abilities to use to build up his church. To use them effectively, we must (1) realize that the Holy Spirit works through us as we use these abilities; (2) understand that no ability is better than another; (3) be willing to serve at anytime, anywhere. (See also 1 Cor 12–14.) ■

[9]Don't just pretend to love others. Really love them.
Hate what is wrong. Hold tightly to what is good. [10]Love
each other with genuine affection,* and take delight in
honoring each other. [11]Never be lazy, but work hard and
serve the Lord enthusiastically.* [12]Rejoice in our confident hope. Be patient in trouble, and keep on praying.
[13]When God's people are in need, be ready to help them.
Always be eager to practice hospitality.

[14]Bless those who persecute you. Don't curse them;

11:25 Greek *brothers.* **11:26a** Greek *from Zion.* **11:26b** Greek *Jacob.* **11:26-27** Isa 59:20-21; 27:9 (Greek version). **11:31** Other manuscripts read *will now share;* still others read *will someday share.* **11:34** Isa 40:13 (Greek version). **11:35** See Job 41:11. **12:1a** Greek *brothers.* **12:1b** Or *This is your spiritual worship;* or *This is your reasonable service.* **12:3a** Or *Because of the grace;* compare 1:5. **12:3b** Or *by the faith God has given you;* or *by the standard of our God-given faith.* **12:10** Greek *with brotherly love.* **12:11** Or *but serve the Lord with a zealous spirit;* or *but let the Spirit excite you as you serve the Lord.*

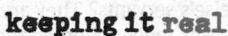

keeping it real

My boyfriend and I didn't have a very good relationship. We couldn't communicate much. So, I decided that we should break up. I tried to be as tactful as I could—I didn't want to hurt his feelings. His reaction was to call me a couple of names that were hurtful, demeaning, and completely untrue. Not only did he say these things to me, he said them to other people.

That enraged me! I immediately thought of different ways to get even. But then I thought about Romans 12:19, which tells us not to take revenge. The first part of the verse goes, "Dear friends, never take revenge. Leave that to the righteous anger of God." This helped me to remove any thoughts of revenge from my mind and to concentrate instead on forgiving him and praying for him. As I do this, concern for his spiritual life overshadows my feelings of anger and hurt. **—Yvonne**

pray that God will bless them. 15Be happy with those
who are happy, and weep with those who weep. 16Live in
harmony with each other. Don't be too proud to enjoy the company of ordinary people. And don't think you know it all!

17Never pay back evil with more evil. Do things in such a way that everyone can see you are honorable. 18Do all
that you can to live in peace with everyone.

19Dear friends, never take revenge. Leave that to the righteous anger of God. For the Scriptures say,

"I will take revenge;
I will pay them back,"*
says the LORD.

20Instead,

"If your enemies are hungry, feed them.
If they are thirsty, give them something to drink.
In doing this, you will heap
burning coals of shame on their heads."*

21Don't let evil conquer you, but conquer evil by doing good.

13 RESPECT FOR AUTHORITY

Everyone must submit to governing authorities. For all authority comes from God, and those in positions of authority have been placed there by God. 2So anyone who
rebels against authority is rebelling against what God has instituted, and they will be punished. 3For the authorities
do not strike fear in people who are doing right, but in those who are doing wrong. Would you like to live without fear of the authorities? Do what is right, and they will honor you. 4The authorities are God's servants, sent for
your good. But if you are doing wrong, of course you should be afraid, for they have the power to punish you. They are God's servants, sent for the very purpose of punishing those who do what is wrong. 5So you must submit
to them, not only to avoid punishment, but also to keep a clear conscience.

6Pay your taxes, too, for these same reasons. For government workers need to be paid. They are serving God in what they do. 7Give to everyone what you owe them:
Pay your taxes and government fees to those who collect them, and give respect and honor to those who are in authority.

IN DEBT 13:8

Why is love for others called a *debt*? We are permanently in debt to Christ for the love he lavished on us. The only way we can even begin to repay this debt is by loving others in turn. Because Christ's love will always be infinitely greater than ours, we will always have the obligation to love our neighbors. In what ways do you pay your debt? ■

LOVE FULFILLS GOD'S REQUIREMENTS

8Owe nothing to anyone—except for your obligation to love one another. If you love your neighbor, you will fulfill the requirements of God's law. 9For the command-
ments say, "You must not commit adultery. You must not murder. You must not steal. You must not covet."* These—and other such commandments—are summed up in this one commandment: "Love your neighbor as yourself."*
10Love does no wrong to others, so love fulfills the re-
quirements of God's law.

11This is all the more urgent, for you know how late it is; time is running out. Wake up, for our salvation is nearer

12:19 Deut 32:35. **12:20** Prov 25:21-22. **13:9a** Exod 20:13-15, 17. **13:9b** Lev 19:18.

AUTHORITY

"What a stupid law!" Logan complains. "How can they—"

"I know," Gabriel interrupts. "Can you believe it? An 11 o'clock curfew!"

"And," chimes in Abbie, "all because some losers from across town crashed a party and trashed a house. It's not fair!"

"Well," Logan concludes, "I don't know about you guys, but I'm not gonna let a bunch of 80-year-olds at city hall tell me what to do."

"What?" Abbie and Gabriel say together, as if they had rehearsed it.

"I mean, I'm gonna pretend the curfew doesn't exist. I'll be 18 in less than two months anyways."

"What are your parents gonna say?" Abbie asks. "Will they freak?"

"Aw, they're cool. They know I'm not gonna go out and make a big scene. See, we should keep doing what we're doing—just be quiet about it. The cops'll never even know."

Abbie nods. "The law is really just for people who do stupid things. But we're not like that."

"Right," Gabriel agrees. "What's wrong with a few Christian buds having a low-key party on the weekend—y'know, listening to some music or watching a few DVDs?"

"Nothin'!" Logan yells.

"Then, we're all agreed?" Abbie asks.

"Yep," Gabriel responds. "We're gonna ignore the curfew."

"What curfew?" Logan quips.

Everyone smiles.

Check out Romans 13:1-7. Is Logan, Abbie, and Gabriel's response to authority the same as what's suggested in this passage? Why or why not?

now than when we first believed. 12The night is almost
gone; the day of salvation will soon be here. So remove
your dark deeds like dirty clothes, and put on the shining
armor of right living. 13Because we belong to the day, we
must live decent lives for all to see. Don't participate in the
darkness of wild parties and drunkenness, or in sexual
promiscuity and immoral living, or in quarreling and jealousy. 14Instead, clothe yourself with the presence of the
Lord Jesus Christ. And don't let yourself think about ways
to indulge your evil desires.

14 THE DANGER OF CRITICISM

Accept other believers who are weak in faith, and don't
argue with them about what they think is right or wrong.
2For instance, one person believes it's all right to eat anything. But another believer with a sensitive conscience
will eat only vegetables. 3Those who feel free to eat anything must not look down on those who don't. And those
who don't eat certain foods must not condemn those
who do, for God has accepted them. 4Who are you to condemn someone else's servants? They are responsible to
the Lord, so let him judge whether they are right or
wrong. And with the Lord's help, they will do what is right
and will receive his approval.

5In the same way, some think one day is more holy
than another day, while others think every day is alike.
You should each be fully convinced that whichever day
you choose is acceptable. 6Those who worship the
Lord on a special day do it to honor him. Those who eat
any kind of food do so to honor the Lord, since they
give thanks to God before eating. And those who refuse to eat certain foods also want to please the Lord
and give thanks to God. 7For we don't live for ourselves
or die for ourselves. 8If we live, it's to honor the Lord.
And if we die, it's to honor the Lord. So whether we live
or die, we belong to the Lord. 9Christ died and rose
again for this very purpose—to be Lord both of the living and of the dead.

10So why do you condemn another believer*? Why do
you look down on another believer? Remember, we will
all stand before the judgment seat of God. 11For the
Scriptures say,

"'As surely as I live,' says the LORD,
'every knee will bend to me,
and every tongue will confess and give praise
to God.*'"

12Yes, each of us will give a personal account to God. 13So
let's stop condemning each other. Decide instead to live
in such a way that you will not cause another believer to
stumble and fall.

SELF-INVENTORY 14:1

Who is weak in faith and who is strong? We are all weak in some areas and strong in others. Our faith is strong in an area where we consistently avoid giving into temptation. It's weak if we must avoid certain activities or places in order to protect our spiritual life. We need to take a self-inventory to find our weaknesses and strengths. What are your weaknesses? Your strengths? No matter what your weaknesses may be, you can always count on God. Where you are weak, he is strong (2 Cor 12:10). ■

14I know and am convinced on the authority of the
Lord Jesus that no food, in and of itself, is wrong to eat.
But if someone believes it is wrong, then for that person it
is wrong. 15And if another believer is distressed by what
you eat, you are not acting in love if you eat it. Don't let
your eating ruin someone for whom Christ died. 16Then
you will not be criticized for doing something you believe
is good. 17For the Kingdom of God is not a matter of what
we eat or drink, but of living a life of goodness and peace

14:10 Greek *your brother;* also in 14:10b, 13, 15, 21. **14:11** Or *confess allegiance to God.* Isa 49:18; 45:23 (Greek version).

and joy in the Holy Spirit. 18If you serve Christ with this attitude, you will please God, and others will approve of you, too. 19So then, let us aim for harmony in the church and try to build each other up.

20Don't tear apart the work of God over what you eat. Remember, all foods are acceptable, but it is wrong to eat something if it makes another person stumble. 21It is better not to eat meat or drink wine or do anything else if it might cause another believer to stumble. 22You may believe there's nothing wrong with what you are doing, but keep it between yourself and God. Blessed are those who don't feel guilty for doing something they have decided is right. 23But if you have doubts about whether or not you should eat something, you are sinning if you go ahead and do it. For you are not following your convictions. If you do anything you believe is not right, you are sinning.

15

LIVING TO PLEASE OTHERS

We who are strong must be considerate of those who are sensitive about things like this. We must not just please ourselves. 2We should help others do what is right and build them up in the Lord. 3For even Christ didn't live to please himself. As the Scriptures say, "The insults of those who insult you, O God, have fallen on me."* 4Such things were written in the Scriptures long ago to teach us. And the Scriptures give us hope and encouragement as we wait patiently for God's promises to be fulfilled.

5May God, who gives this patience and encouragement, help you live in complete harmony with each other, as is fitting for followers of Christ Jesus. 6Then all of you can join together with one voice, giving praise and glory to God, the Father of our Lord Jesus Christ.

7Therefore, accept each other just as Christ has accepted you so that God will be given glory. 8Remember that Christ came as a servant to the Jews* to show that God is true to the promises he made to their ancestors. 9He also came so that the Gentiles might give glory to God for his mercies to them. That is what the psalmist meant when he wrote:

"For this, I will praise you among the Gentiles;
I will sing praises to your name."*

10And in another place it is written,

"Rejoice with his people,
you Gentiles."*

11And yet again,

"Praise the LORD, all you Gentiles.
Praise him, all you people of the earth."*

12And in another place Isaiah said,

"The heir to David's throne* will come,
and he will rule over the Gentiles.
They will place their hope on him."*

13I pray that God, the source of hope, will fill you completely with joy and peace because you trust in him. Then you will overflow with confident hope through the power of the Holy Spirit.

PAUL'S REASON FOR WRITING

14I am fully convinced, my dear brothers and sisters,* that you are full of goodness. You know these things so well you can teach each other all about them. 15Even so, I have been bold enough to write about some of these points, knowing that all you need is this reminder. For by God's grace, 16I am a special messenger from Christ Jesus to you Gentiles. I bring you the Good News so that I might present you as an acceptable offering to God, made holy by the Holy Spirit. 17So I have reason to be enthusiastic about all Christ Jesus has done through me in my service to God. 18Yet I dare not boast about anything except what Christ has done through me, bringing the Gentiles to God by my message and by the way I worked among them. 19They were convinced by the power of miraculous signs and wonders and by the power of God's Spirit.* In this way, I have fully presented the Good News of Christ from Jerusalem all the way to Illyricum.*

GOD'S WORK 15:17

Paul wasn't proud of what he had done, but of what God had done through him. Being proud of God's work isn't a sin—it's an act of worship. If you aren't sure whether your pride is selfish or holy, ask yourself this question: Are you just as proud of what God is doing through other people as you are of what he's doing through you?

20My ambition has always been to preach the Good News where the name of Christ has never been heard, rather than where a church has already been started by someone else. 21I have been following the plan spoken of in the Scriptures, where it says,

"Those who have never been told about him will see,
and those who have never heard of him will
understand."*

22In fact, my visit to you has been delayed so long because I have been preaching in these places.

PAUL'S TRAVEL PLANS

23But now I have finished my work in these regions, and after all these long years of waiting, I am eager to visit you.

15:3 Greek *who insult you have fallen on me.* Ps 69:9. 15:8 Greek *servant of circumcision.* 15:9 Ps 18:49. 15:10 Deut 32:43. 15:11 Ps 117:1. 15:12a Greek *The root of Jesse.* David was the son of Jesse. 15:12b Isa 11:10 (Greek version). 15:14 Greek *brothers;* also in 15:30. 15:19a Other manuscripts read *the Spirit;* still others read *the Holy Spirit.* 15:19b *Illyricum* was a region northeast of Italy. 15:21 Isa 52:15 (Greek version).

24I am planning to go to Spain, and when I do, I will stop off in Rome. And after I have enjoyed your fellowship for a little while, you can provide for my journey.

25But before I come, I must go to Jerusalem to take a gift to the believers* there. 26For you see, the believers in Macedonia and Achaia* have eagerly taken up an offering for the poor among the believers in Jerusalem. 27They were glad to do this because they feel they owe a real debt to them. Since the Gentiles received the spiritual blessings of the Good News from the believers in Jerusalem, they feel the least they can do in return is to help them financially. 28As soon as I have delivered this money and completed this good deed of theirs, I will come to see you on my way to Spain. 29And I am sure that when I come, Christ will richly bless our time together.

A BOND OF LOVE 15:25-27

Since the church in Rome was a mixture of Jews, Gentiles, slaves, free people, men, women, Roman citizens, and world travelers, it had potential for great influence and great conflict. But the Holy Spirit was the "glue" that held all of these believers together in a bond of love.

We also live in a world full of different kinds of people. Like the Roman Christians, we have the potential for widespread influence and terrible conflict. Yet the same God who unified the Roman Christians also unites us through his love. It is this love that causes us to influence others. ■

30Dear brothers and sisters, I urge you in the name of our Lord Jesus Christ to join in my struggle by praying to God for me. Do this because of your love for me, given to you by the Holy Spirit. 31Pray that I will be rescued from those in Judea who refuse to obey God. Pray also that the believers there will be willing to accept the donation* I am taking to Jerusalem. 32Then, by the will of God, I will be able to come to you with a joyful heart, and we will be an encouragement to each other.

33And now may God, who gives us his peace, be with you all. Amen.*

16 PAUL GREETS HIS FRIENDS

I commend to you our sister Phoebe, who is a deacon in the church in Cenchrea. 2Welcome her in the Lord as one who is worthy of honor among God's people. Help her in whatever she needs, for she has been helpful to many, and especially to me.

3Give my greetings to Priscilla and Aquila, my co-workers in the ministry of Christ Jesus. 4In fact, they once risked their lives for me. I am thankful to them, and so are all the Gentile churches. 5Also give my greetings to the church that meets in their home.

Greet my dear friend Epenetus. He was the first person from the province of Asia to become a follower of Christ. 6Give my greetings to Mary, who has worked so hard for your benefit. 7Greet Andronicus and Junia,* my fellow Jews,* who were in prison with me. They are highly respected among the apostles and became followers of Christ before I did. 8Greet Ampliatus, my dear friend in the Lord. 9Greet Urbanus, our co-worker in Christ, and my dear friend Stachys.

10Greet Apelles, a good man whom Christ approves. And give my greetings to the believers from the household of Aristobulus. 11Greet Herodion, my fellow Jew.* Greet the Lord's people from the household of Narcissus. 12Give my greetings to Tryphena and Tryphosa, the Lord's workers, and to dear Persis, who has worked so hard for the Lord. 13Greet Rufus, whom the Lord picked out to be his very own; and also his dear mother, who has been a mother to me.

14Give my greetings to Asyncritus, Phlegon, Hermes, Patrobas, Hermas, and the brothers and sisters* who meet with them. 15Give my greetings to Philologus, Julia, Nereus and his sister, and to Olympas and all the believers* who meet with them. 16Greet each other in Christian love.* All the churches of Christ send you their greetings.

PAUL'S FINAL INSTRUCTIONS

17And now I make one more appeal, my dear brothers and sisters. Watch out for people who cause divisions and upset people's faith by teaching things contrary to what you have been taught. Stay away from them. 18Such people are not serving Christ our Lord; they are serving their own personal interests. By smooth talk and glowing words they deceive innocent people. 19But everyone knows that you are obedient to the Lord. This makes me very happy. I want you to be wise in doing right and to stay innocent of any wrong. 20The God of peace will soon crush Satan under your feet. May the grace of our Lord Jesus* be with you.

21Timothy, my fellow worker, sends you his greetings, as do Lucius, Jason, and Sosipater, my fellow Jews.

22I, Tertius, the one writing this letter for Paul, send my greetings, too, as one of the Lord's followers.

23Gaius says hello to you. He is my host and also serves as host to the whole church. Erastus, the city treasurer, sends you his greetings, and so does our brother Quartus.*

25Now all glory to God, who is able to make you strong, just as my Good News says. This message about Jesus Christ has revealed his plan for you Gentiles, a plan kept secret from the beginning of time. 26But now as the prophets* foretold and as the eternal God has commanded, this message is made known to all Gentiles everywhere, so that they too might believe and obey him. 27All glory to the only wise God, through Jesus Christ, forever. Amen.

15:25 Greek *God's holy people;* also in 15:26, 31. **15:26** *Macedonia* and *Achaia* were the northern and southern regions of Greece. **15:31** Greek *the ministry;* other manuscripts read *the gift.* **15:33** Some manuscripts omit *Amen.* One very early manuscript places 16:25-27 here. **16:7a** *Junia* is a feminine name. Some late manuscripts accent the word so it reads *Junias,* a masculine name; still others read *Julia* (feminine). **16:7b** Or *compatriots;* also in 16:21. **16:11** Or *compatriot.* **16:14** Greek *brothers;* also in 16:17. **16:15** Greek *all of God's holy people.* **16:16** Greek *with a sacred kiss.* **16:20** Some manuscripts read *Lord Jesus Christ.* **16:23** Some manuscripts add verse 24, *May the grace of our Lord Jesus Christ be with you all. Amen.* Still others add this sentence after verse 27. **16:26** Greek *the prophetic writings.*

1 CORINTHIANS

ROB RECENTLY accepted Christ. Yesterday, the 15-year-old watched in disbelief as two "leaders" of his church got into a shouting (and shoving!) match after Sunday services. Rob quietly asks you why supposedly "mature" Christians act that way. What do you say?

Gemma has discovered that a man and woman who're active in the church aren't married, but live together. "Isn't that supposed to be wrong?" she asks. What would you tell her?

Abby knows that certain activities—drunkenness, premarital sex, lying, stealing—are wrong. But what about all those "gray areas" that aren't directly addressed? Is it okay to hang out in clubs ("I would just go to dance,") or buy expensive clothes? What about watching her favorite music videos on cable or listening to the radio? And how does God feel about movies she's watched? "I want to do what's right," she tells you, "but sometimes it's hard to know what's right. Aren't there some guidelines from the Bible that can help?" How do you answer?

Christians (and churches) have struggled with immaturity, division, and immorality since the first hymn was sung. But, the apostle Paul's first letter to the Corinthians has some real, practical answers. Got questions? Keep reading.

1 Corinthians

stats

PURPOSE: To identify problems in the Corinthian church, to offer solutions, and to teach the believers how to live for Christ in a corrupt society

AUTHOR: Paul

TO WHOM WRITTEN: The church in Corinth and Christians everywhere

DATE WRITTEN: About A.D. 55, near the end of Paul's three-year ministry in Ephesus during his third missionary journey

SETTING: The city of Corinth was a seaport and a major center of trade. It was the most important city in Achaia and also one of the most corrupt. The church in Corinth was largely made up of Gentiles. Paul had established this church during his second missionary journey.

KEY PEOPLE: Paul, Timothy, members of Chloe's household

KEY PLACES: Worship meetings in Corinth

KEY points

LOYALTIES

The Corinthians' loyalties to various church leaders and teachers—Peter, Paul, and Apollos—led to intellectual pride, which divided the church. We must guard against the division caused by misguided loyalty or pride in human wisdom.

IMMORALITY

Paul used tough love to deal with an incident of sexual sin in the church at Corinth. Paul's advice encourages us to avoid compromising, even if others seem to disagree with our moral stance.

FREEDOM

Paul taught freedom of choice on practices not expressly forbidden in Scripture. Although Jesus makes us free (see John 8:32, 36), we don't have the right to abuse that freedom by encouraging others to do wrong.

WORSHIP

Paul addressed disorder in worship. Worship must be carried out properly and orderly. Everything we do to worship God should be done in a manner worthy of his high honor.

LIFE AFTER DEATH

Some people denied that Jesus rose from the dead. Others believed that people would not be physically resurrected after death. Jesus' resurrection assures us that each of us will have a new, living body after we die.

1

GREETINGS FROM PAUL

This letter is from Paul, chosen by the will of God to be an
apostle of Christ Jesus, and from our brother Sosthenes.

USEFUL 1:1

Paul was chosen by God to be a missionary. Likewise, each Christian has a task to do. Although some tasks may seem more spectacular than others, all are necessary to carry out God's greater plans for the world. How will you use your abilities in his service? (Check out 1 Cor 12–14 for more on these abilities.) ■

2I am writing to God's church in Corinth,* to you who
have been called by God to be his own holy people. He
made you holy by means of Christ Jesus,* just as he did
for all people everywhere who call on the name of our
Lord Jesus Christ, their Lord and ours.
3May God our Father and the Lord Jesus Christ give you
grace and peace.

PAUL GIVES THANKS TO GOD

4I always thank my God for you and for the gracious gifts he
has given you, now that you belong to Christ Jesus.
5Through him, God has enriched your church in every
way—with all of your eloquent words and all of your knowledge. 6This confirms that what I told you about Christ is
true. 7Now you have every spiritual gift you need as you eagerly wait for the return of our Lord Jesus Christ. 8He will
keep you strong to the end so that you will be free from all
blame on the day when our Lord Jesus Christ returns. 9God
will do this, for he is faithful to do what he says, and he has
invited you into partnership with his Son, Jesus Christ our
Lord.

DIVISIONS IN THE CHURCH

10I appeal to you, dear brothers and sisters,* by the authority of our Lord Jesus Christ, to live in harmony with each
other. Let there be no divisions in the church. Rather, be of
one mind, united in thought and purpose. 11For some
members of Chloe's household have told me about your
quarrels, my dear brothers and sisters. 12Some of you are
saying, "I am a follower of Paul." Others are saying, "I follow Apollos," or "I follow Peter,*" or "I follow only Christ."
13Has Christ been divided into factions? Was I, Paul, crucified for you? Were any of you baptized in the name of
Paul? Of course not! 14I thank God that I did not baptize any
of you except Crispus and Gaius, 15for now no one can say
they were baptized in my name. 16(Oh yes, I also baptized
the household of Stephanas, but I don't remember baptizing anyone else.) 17For Christ didn't send me to baptize, but
to preach the Good News—and not with clever speech, for
fear that the cross of Christ would lose its power.

THE WISDOM OF GOD

18The message of the cross is foolish to those who are
headed for destruction! But we who are being saved
know it is the very power of God. 19As the Scriptures say,

1:2a *Corinth* was the capital city of Achaia, the southern region of the Greek peninsula. **1:2b** Or *because you belong to Christ Jesus.* **1:10** Greek *brothers,* also in 1:11, 26. **1:12** Greek *Cephas.*

Is temptation a sin? Why or why not?

For a quick answer to that, check out Matthew 4:1-11—the story of Jesus' temptation.

That story provides a basic truth: Temptation is not a sin. According to Matthew 18:7-9, it's the natural consequence of living in this world. Giving in to temptation, however, is where sin comes in.

Though temptation always will be present, we don't have to wave the white flag and admit defeat. The Holy Spirit provides any believer with the power to resist.

God's Word also teaches us how to overcome temptation. First Corinthians 10:13 has the scoop: "The temptations in your life are no different from what others experience. And God is faithful. He will not allow the temptation to be more than you can stand. When you are tempted, he will show you a way out so that you can endure."

God provides a way out of every temptation. We can choose to take his way out or to give in. If we stay close to God, we'll be more likely to resist and do what is right. We don't have to give in to temptation.

Why do we have to keep taking Communion? What's the point?

Have you ever saved something from a special event because you wanted to remember how great that moment was? Certain items help us remember special moments in our lives.

Before Jesus was arrested and placed on trial, he established a tradition by which his followers could remember him.

Communion (AKA the Lord's Supper or Eucharist) is that act. Paul reminds us of this in 1 Corinthians 11:23-26. (See also Matt 26:26-28.) By taking Communion, we remember how Jesus' body was broken and his blood shed for all people.

Because Communion is celebrated by believers throughout the world, it is a unifying act. And because we retell the message of Christ's death, we're reminded that he plans to return someday for his church.

There are many distractions that can cause us to lose our focus on what really matters in this life. Communion briefly reminds us that real life revolves not around us (surprise!), but around one incredible act of love at a certain time in history.

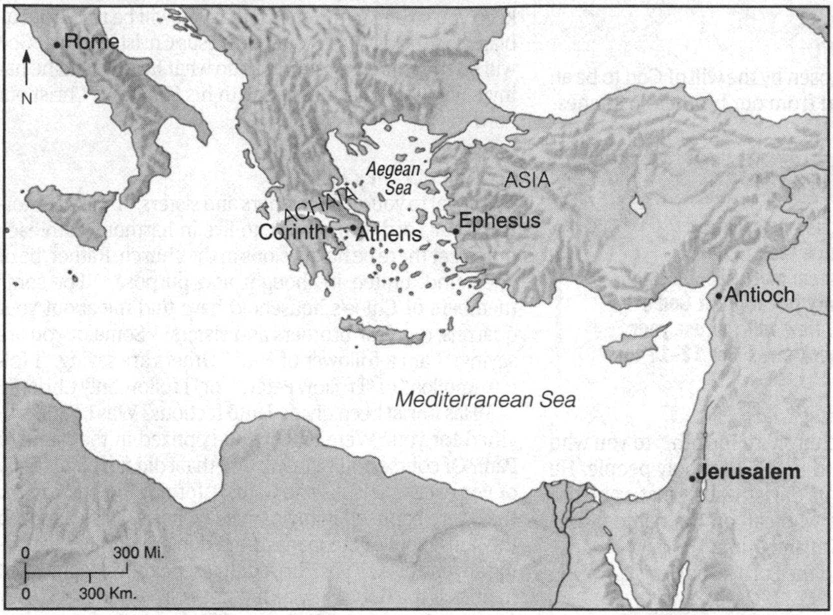

CORINTH AND EPHESUS
Paul wrote this letter to Corinth during his three-year visit in Ephesus during his third missionary journey. The two cities sat across from each other on the Aegean Sea—both were busy and important ports. Titus may have carried this letter from Ephesus to Corinth (2 Cor 12:18).

"I will destroy the wisdom of the wise
and discard the intelligence of the intelligent."*

20 So where does this leave the philosophers, the scholars, and the world's brilliant debaters? God has made the
wisdom of this world look foolish. 21 Since God in his
wisdom saw to it that the world would never know him through human wisdom, he has used our foolish preaching to save those who believe. 22 It is foolish to the Jews,
who ask for signs from heaven. And it is foolish to the Greeks, who seek human wisdom. 23 So when we preach
that Christ was crucified, the Jews are offended and the Gentiles say it's all nonsense.
24 But to those called by God to salvation, both Jews and Gentiles,* Christ is the power of God and the wisdom of
God. 25 This foolish plan of God is wiser than the wisest of human plans, and God's weakness is stronger than the greatest of human strength.
26 Remember, dear brothers and sisters, that few of you were wise in the world's eyes or powerful or wealthy* when God called you.
27 Instead, God chose things the world considers foolish in order to shame those who think they are wise. And he chose things that are powerless to shame those who are powerful.
28 God chose things despised by the world,* things counted as nothing at all, and used them to bring to nothing what the world considers important.
29 As a result, no one can ever boast in the presence of God.
30 God has united you with Christ Jesus. For our benefit God made him to be wisdom itself. Christ made us right with God; he made us pure and holy, and he freed us from sin.
31 Therefore, as the Scriptures say, "If you want to boast, boast only about the LORD."*

SIMPLE FAITH 1:18-31

Paul explained that faith in Jesus is the key to forgiveness and eternal life with God. God planned it this way so that no one could boast that his achievements helped him secure eternal life. (See also Eph 2:10.) Good intentions or actions do not make us acceptable to God. We need only accept what Jesus has already done for us. Have you? ■

2

PAUL'S MESSAGE OF WISDOM

When I first came to you, dear brothers and sisters,* I didn't use lofty words and impressive wisdom to tell you God's secret plan.*
2 For I decided that while I was with you I would forget everything except Jesus Christ, the one who was crucified.
3 I came to you in weakness—timid and trembling.
4 And my message and my preaching were very plain. Rather than using clever and persuasive speeches, I relied only on the power of the Holy Spirit.
5 I did this so you would trust not in human wisdom but in the power of God.
6 Yet when I am among mature believers, I do speak with words of wisdom, but not the kind of wisdom that belongs to this world or to the rulers of this world, who are soon forgotten.
7 No, the wisdom we speak of is the mystery of God*—his plan that was previously hidden, even though he made it for our ultimate glory before the world

1:19 Isa 29:14. **1:24** Greek *and Greeks.* **1:26** Or *high born.* **1:28** Or *God chose those who are low born.* **1:31** Jer 9:24. **2:1a** Greek *brothers.* **2:1b** Greek *God's mystery;* other manuscripts read *God's testimony.* **2:7** Greek *But we speak God's wisdom in a mystery.*

began. 8But the rulers of this world have not understood
it; if they had, they would not have crucified our glorious
Lord. 9That is what the Scriptures mean when they say,

"No eye has seen, no ear has heard,
and no mind has imagined
what God has prepared
for those who love him."*

WHAT'S IN STORE? 2:9

Paul quoted a promise in Isaiah concerning the amazing things God has in store for his people in this life and for eternity. He will create a new heaven and a new earth (Isa 65:17; Rev 21:1), and we will live with him forever. Until then, his Holy Spirit comforts and guides us. This promise of great things to come can give us hope and courage to press on in this life, even through hardship. Even when life seems at its most hopeless, we still have hope. ■

10But* it was to us that God revealed these things by his
Spirit. For his Spirit searches out everything and shows
us God's deep secrets. 11No one can know a person's
thoughts except that person's own spirit, and no one can
know God's thoughts except God's own Spirit. 12And we
have received God's Spirit (not the world's spirit), so we
can know the wonderful things God has freely given us.
13When we tell you these things, we do not use words
that come from human wisdom. Instead, we speak words
given to us by the Spirit, using the Spirit's words to explain spiritual truths.* 14But people who aren't spiritual*
can't receive these truths from God's Spirit. It all sounds
foolish to them and they can't understand it, for only
those who are spiritual can understand what the Spirit
means. 15Those who are spiritual can evaluate all things,
but they themselves cannot be evaluated by others. 16For,

"Who can know the LORD's thoughts?
Who knows enough to teach him?"*

But we understand these things, for we have the mind of
Christ.

3 PAUL AND APOLLOS, SERVANTS OF CHRIST

Dear brothers and sisters,* when I was with you I couldn't
talk to you as I would to spiritual people.* I had to talk as
though you belonged to this world or as though you were
infants in the Christian life.* 2I had to feed you with milk,
not with solid food, because you weren't ready for anything stronger. And you still aren't ready, 3for you are still
controlled by your sinful nature. You are jealous of one
another and quarrel with each other. Doesn't that prove
you are controlled by your sinful nature? Aren't you living
like people of the world? 4When one of you says, "I am a
follower of Paul," and another says, "I follow Apollos,"
aren't you acting just like people of the world?
5After all, who is Apollos? Who is Paul? We are only
God's servants through whom you believed the Good
News. Each of us did the work the Lord gave us. 6I planted
the seed in your hearts, and Apollos watered it, but it was
God who made it grow. 7It's not important who does the
planting, or who does the watering. What's important is
that God makes the seed grow. 8The one who plants and
the one who waters work together with the same purpose. And both will be rewarded for their own hard work.
9For we are both God's workers. And you are God's field.
You are God's building.

DESIRES 3:1-9

Paul called the Corinthians "infants" in the Christian life because they were not yet spiritually healthy and mature. The proof was that they quarreled like children. Baby Christians are controlled by their own desires, while mature believers are controlled by God's desires. Are your desires the same as God's? ■

10Because of God's grace to me, I have laid the foundation like an expert builder. Now others are building on it.
But whoever is building on this foundation must be very
careful. 11For no one can lay any foundation other than
the one we already have—Jesus Christ.
12Anyone who builds on that foundation may use a variety of materials—gold, silver, jewels, wood, hay, or straw.
13But on the judgment day, fire will reveal what kind of
work each builder has done. The fire will show if a person's
work has any value. 14If the work survives, that builder will
receive a reward. 15But if the work is burned up, the builder
will suffer great loss. The builder will be saved, but like
someone barely escaping through a wall of flames.
16Don't you realize that all of you together are the temple of God and that the Spirit of God lives in* you? 17God
will destroy anyone who destroys this temple. For God's
temple is holy, and you are that temple.
18Stop deceiving yourselves. If you think you are wise
by this world's standards, you need to become a fool to be
truly wise. 19For the wisdom of this world is foolishness
to God. As the Scriptures say,

"He traps the wise
in the snare of their own cleverness."*

20And again,

"The LORD knows the thoughts of the wise;
he knows they are worthless."*

21So don't boast about following a particular human
leader. For everything belongs to you—22whether Paul or

2:9 Isa 64:4. 2:10 Some manuscripts read *For*. 2:13 Or *explaining spiritual truths in spiritual language, or explaining spiritual truths to spiritual people*. 2:14 Or *who don't have the Spirit;* or *who have only physical life*. 2:16 Isa 40:13 (Greek version). 3:1a Greek *Brothers*. 3:1b Or *to people who have the Spirit*. 3:1c Greek *in Christ*. 3:16 Or *among*. 3:19 Job 5:13. 3:20 Ps 94:11.

Highlights of 1 Corinthians

The Meaning of the Cross, 1:18–2:16. Be considerate of one another because of what Christ has done for us. There is no place for pride or a know-it-all attitude. We are to have the mind of Christ.

The Story of the Lord's Supper, 11:23-29. The Lord's Supper is a time of reflection on Christ's final words to his disciples before he died on the cross; we must celebrate this in an orderly and correct manner.

The Poem of Love, 13:1-13. Love is to guide all we do. We have different gifts, abilities, likes, dislikes—but we are called, without exception, to love.

The Christian's Destiny, 15:42-58. We are promised by Christ, who died for us, that, just as he came back to life after death, our perishable bodies will be exchanged for heavenly bodies. Then we will live and reign with Christ.

Apollos or Peter,* or the world, or life and death, or the
present and the future. Everything belongs to you, 23and
you belong to Christ, and Christ belongs to God.

4

PAUL'S RELATIONSHIP WITH THE CORINTHIANS

So look at Apollos and me as mere servants of Christ who
have been put in charge of explaining God's mysteries.
2Now, a person who is put in charge as a manager must be
faithful. 3As for me, it matters very little how I might be
evaluated by you or by any human authority. I don't even
trust my own judgment on this point. 4My conscience is
clear, but that doesn't prove I'm right. It is the Lord himself who will examine me and decide.
5So don't make judgments about anyone ahead of
time—before the Lord returns. For he will bring our darkest secrets to light and will reveal our private motives.
Then God will give to each one whatever praise is due.

JUDGING 4:1-6

Paul warned the Corinthian believers to avoid judging one leader's performance by another's. Have you ever judged another person about the quality or sincerity of his or her relationship with God? Maybe you've even heard someone express skepticism as to whether or not someone really *is* a Christian. Only God has the perfect insight to correctly judge. ■

6Dear brothers and sisters,* I have used Apollos and
myself to illustrate what I've been saying. If you pay attention to what I have quoted from the Scriptures,* you
won't be proud of one of your leaders at the expense of
another. 7For what gives you the right to make such a
judgment? What do you have that God hasn't given you?
And if everything you have is from God, why boast as
though it were not a gift?
8You think you already have everything you need. You
think you are already rich. You have begun to reign in
God's kingdom without us! I wish you really were reigning already, for then we would be reigning with you.
9Instead, I sometimes think God has put us apostles on
display, like prisoners of war at the end of a victor's parade, condemned to die. We have become a spectacle to
the entire world—to people and angels alike.
10Our dedication to Christ makes us look like fools, but
you claim to be so wise in Christ! We are weak, but you
are so powerful! You are honored, but we are ridiculed.
11Even now we go hungry and thirsty, and we don't have
enough clothes to keep warm. We are often beaten and
have no home. 12We work wearily with our own hands to
earn our living. We bless those who curse us. We are patient with those who abuse us. 13We appeal gently when
evil things are said about us. Yet we are treated like the
world's garbage, like everybody's trash—right up to the
present moment.
14I am not writing these things to shame you, but to
warn you as my beloved children. 15For even if you had
ten thousand others to teach you about Christ, you have
only one spiritual father. For I became your father in
Christ Jesus when I preached the Good News to you. 16So I
urge you to imitate me.
17That's why I have sent Timothy, my beloved and
faithful child in the Lord. He will remind you of how I follow Christ Jesus, just as I teach in all the churches wherever I go.
18Some of you have become arrogant, thinking I will
not visit you again. 19But I will come—and soon—if the
Lord lets me, and then I'll find out whether these arrogant people just give pretentious speeches or whether
they really have God's power. 20For the Kingdom of God is
not just a lot of talk; it is living by God's power. 21Which
do you choose? Should I come with a rod to punish you,
or should I come with love and a gentle spirit?

5

PAUL CONDEMNS SPIRITUAL PRIDE

I can hardly believe the report about the sexual immorality going on among you—something that even pagans
don't do. I am told that a man in your church is living
in sin with his stepmother.* 2You are so proud of yourselves, but you should be mourning in sorrow and shame.
And you should remove this man from your fellowship.

3:22 Greek *Cephas.* **4:6a** Greek *Brothers.* **4:6b** Or *If you learn not to go beyond "what is written."* **5:1** Greek *his father's wife.*

3Even though I am not with you in person, I am with
you in the Spirit.* And as though I were there, I have already passed judgment on this man 4in the name of the
Lord Jesus. You must call a meeting of the church.* I will
be present with you in spirit, and so will the power of our
Lord Jesus. 5Then you must throw this man out and hand
him over to Satan so that his sinful nature will be destroyed* and he himself* will be saved on the day the
Lord* returns.
6Your boasting about this is terrible. Don't you realize
that this sin is like a little yeast that spreads through the
whole batch of dough? 7Get rid of the old "yeast" by removing this wicked person from among you. Then you
will be like a fresh batch of dough made without yeast,
which is what you really are. Christ, our Passover Lamb,
has been sacrificed for us.* 8So let us celebrate the festival, not with the old bread* of wickedness and evil, but
with the new bread* of sincerity and truth.
9When I wrote to you before, I told you not to associate
with people who indulge in sexual sin. 10But I wasn't talking about unbelievers who indulge in sexual sin, or are
greedy, or cheat people, or worship idols. You would have
to leave this world to avoid people like that. 11I meant that
you are not to associate with anyone who claims to be a
believer* yet indulges in sexual sin, or is greedy, or worships idols, or is abusive, or is a drunkard, or cheats people. Don't even eat with such people.
12It isn't my responsibility to judge outsiders, but it
certainly is your responsibility to judge those inside
the church who are sinning. 13God will judge those on the
outside; but as the Scriptures say, "You must remove the
evil person from among you."*

SEX

Melanie is confused about sex—not the how (she learned that a long time ago), but the when. Her mom tells her to wait. Her youth director gives her the same advice. But everywhere else the message is clearly, "Go for it!" Or, "If you're still a virgin, you're a total loser!"

- **Friends at school tell her how great sex is and how experienced they are.**
- **All of her favorite celebrities seem to hop from bed to bed on-screen and off-screen.**
- **During a health class lecture on birth control two weeks ago, the teacher stated, "Now, most normal young people are sexually active. I'm assuming you all are normal, so . . ."**
- **Melanie's boyfriend keeps telling her that having sex will strengthen their relationship.**
- **Almost every ad and billboard Melanie sees has a sexual twist or theme.**

"What am I supposed to think?" Melanie asks. "It seems like everybody's enjoying this really fantastic experience . . . and I'm like a nun or something. Is it really so wrong if I have sex now? Is saving myself for marriage really worth it?"

Check out 1 Corinthians 6:13-20 and 1 Thessalonians 4:1-4. How would you answer Melanie?

WARNING! 6:13-20

Next on Paul's list of warnings was one on sexual immorality. Such a warning may seem old-fashioned in light of what's regularly seen in movies and on television. But God's standards haven't changed. He doesn't put the kibosh on sex outside of marriage just to be difficult. He wants to prevent us from hurting ourselves and others. ■

6 **AVOIDING LAWSUITS WITH CHRISTIANS**
When one of you has a dispute with another believer,
how dare you file a lawsuit and ask a secular court to decide the matter instead of taking it to other believers*!
2Don't you realize that someday we believers will judge
the world? And since you are going to judge the world,
can't you decide even these little things among yourselves? 3Don't you realize that we will judge angels? So
you should surely be able to resolve ordinary disputes in
this life. 4If you have legal disputes about such matters,
why go to outside judges who are not respected by the
church? 5I am saying this to shame you. Isn't there anyone in all the church who is wise enough to decide these
issues? 6But instead, one believer* sues another—right in
front of unbelievers!
7Even to have such lawsuits with one another is a defeat for you. Why not just accept the injustice and leave it
at that? Why not let yourselves be cheated? 8Instead, you
yourselves are the ones who do wrong and cheat even
your fellow believers.*
9Don't you realize that those who do wrong will not
inherit the Kingdom of God? Don't fool yourselves.
Those who indulge in sexual sin, or who worship idols,
or commit adultery, or are male prostitutes, or practice
homosexuality, 10or are thieves, or greedy people, or
drunkards, or are abusive, or cheat people—none of
these will inherit the Kingdom of God. 11Some of you
were once like that. But you were cleansed; you were
made holy; you were made right with God by calling on
the name of the Lord Jesus Christ and by the Spirit of
our God.

AVOIDING SEXUAL SIN
12You say, "I am allowed to do anything"—but not everything is good for you. And even though "I am allowed to
do anything," I must not become a slave to anything.

5:3 Or *in spirit*. 5:4 Or *In the name of the Lord Jesus, you must call a meeting of the church.* 5:5a Or *so that his body will be destroyed;* Greek reads *for the destruction of the flesh*. 5:5b Greek *and the spirit*. 5:5c Other manuscripts read *the Lord Jesus;* still others read *our Lord Jesus Christ*. 5:7 Greek *has been sacrificed*. 5:8a Greek *not with old leaven*. 5:8b Greek *but with unleavened [bread]*. 5:11 Greek *a brother*. 5:13 Deut 17:7. 6:1 Greek *God's holy people;* also in 6:2. 6:6 Greek *one brother*. 6:8 Greek *even the brothers*.

ULTIMATE ISSUES

MARRIAGE

Think you know all there is to know about marriage? Relax. You aren't expected to. In fact, many married people wouldn't consider themselves experts on the subject!

Marriage was God's idea. He performed the first wedding in the Garden of Eden (Gen 2:18-25), thus establishing that marriage is for one man and one woman for life.

Our relationship with God is established through his commitment toward us. Therein lies another extremely important—but often overlooked—principle for a successful marriage: commitment.

Let's talk about emotions for a minute. The emotional rush two people experience when they "fall in love" and decide to marry is wonderful. It also is a terribly inadequate basis for marriage. That "rush," as powerful and enjoyable as it may be, will undoubtedly wear off at some point. If that's what the relationship is based on—physical attraction, romantic ideals, passion—the flame may burn brightly, but it won't burn for long.

Romance, sexual attraction, and passion are tremendous God-given elements of a love relationship. But don't mistake them for the foundation of a lifelong commitment. They're like icing on a cake. Icing makes the cake much sweeter, but a diet of 100 percent refined sugar doesn't make for good health.

To survive the pressure and temptations that attack a marriage, a husband and wife have to be totally committed to making their marriage work. Even when the romance is gone (as it sometimes will be in any marriage), when the money is tight, or the urge to run out is overwhelming, Christians must stand strong on the commitment they made.

Marriage, when seen from God's perspective, can be one of his greatest gifts to his children. Whether or not to marry—and what happens if you do marry—is up to you.

13You say, "Food was made for the stomach, and the
stomach for food." (This is true, though someday God will
do away with both of them.) But you can't say that our
bodies were made for sexual immorality. They were
made for the Lord, and the Lord cares about our bodies.
14And God will raise us from the dead by his power, just as
he raised our Lord from the dead.
15Don't you realize that your bodies are actually parts
of Christ? Should a man take his body, which is part of
Christ, and join it to a prostitute? Never! 16And don't you
realize that if a man joins himself to a prostitute, he becomes one body with her? For the Scriptures say, "The
two are united into one."* 17But the person who is joined
to the Lord is one spirit with him.
18Run from sexual sin! No other sin so clearly affects
the body as this one does. For sexual immorality is a sin
against your own body. 19Don't you realize that your body
is the temple of the Holy Spirit, who lives in you and was
given to you by God? You do not belong to yourself, 20for
God bought you with a high price. So you must honor God
with your body.

7

INSTRUCTION ON MARRIAGE

Now regarding the questions you asked in your letter.
Yes, it is good to live a celibate life.* 2But because there is
so much sexual immorality, each man should have his
own wife, and each woman should have her own husband.
3The husband should fulfill his wife's sexual needs,
and the wife should fulfill her husband's needs. 4The
wife gives authority over her body to her husband,
and the husband gives authority over his body to his
wife.
5Do not deprive each other of sexual relations, unless you both agree to refrain from sexual intimacy for
a limited time so you can give yourselves more completely to prayer. Afterward, you should come together
again so that Satan won't be able to tempt you because
of your lack of self-control. 6I say this as a concession,
not as a command. 7But I wish everyone were single,
just as I am. But God gives to some the gift of marriage,
and to others the gift of singleness.

6:16 Gen 2:24. **7:1** Greek *It is good for a man not to touch a woman.*

8So I say to those who aren't married and to widows—it's better to stay unmarried, just as I am. 9But if they can't control themselves, they should go ahead and marry. It's better to marry than to burn with lust.

TO MARRY OR NOT 7:1-9

Because many new believers in Corinth thought that everyone should remain celibate, some engaged couples decided not to get married. But Paul advised the couples who wanted to marry that they should not deny their normal sexual drives by avoiding marriage. This does not mean, however, that people who have trouble controlling their thoughts should marry the first person who comes along. It is better to deal with the pressure of sexual desire than to deal with an unhappy marriage. ■

10But for those who are married, I have a command that comes not from me, but from the Lord.* A wife must not leave her husband. 11But if she does leave him, let her remain single or else be reconciled to him. And the husband must not leave his wife.

12Now, I will speak to the rest of you, though I do not have a direct command from the Lord. If a Christian man* has a wife who is not a believer and she is willing to continue living with him, he must not leave her. 13And if a Christian woman has a husband who is not a believer and he is willing to continue living with her, she must not leave him. 14For the Christian wife brings holiness to her marriage, and the Christian husband* brings holiness to his marriage. Otherwise, your children would not be holy, but now they are holy. 15(But if the husband or wife who isn't a believer insists on leaving, let them go. In such cases the Christian husband or wife* is no longer bound to the other, for God has called you* to live in peace.) 16Don't you wives realize that your husbands might be saved because of you? And don't you husbands realize that your wives might be saved because of you?

17Each of you should continue to live in whatever situation the Lord has placed you, and remain as you were when God first called you. This is my rule for all the churches. 18For instance, a man who was circumcised before he became a believer should not try to reverse it. And the man who was uncircumcised when he became a believer should not be circumcised now. 19For it makes no difference whether or not a man has been circumcised. The important thing is to keep God's commandments.

20Yes, each of you should remain as you were when God called you. 21Are you a slave? Don't let that worry you—but if you get a chance to be free, take it. 22And remember, if you were a slave when the Lord called you, you are now free in the Lord. And if you were free when the Lord called you, you are now a slave of Christ. 23God paid a high price for you, so don't be enslaved by the world.* 24Each of you, dear brothers and sisters,* should remain as you were when God first called you.

25Now regarding your question about the young women who are not yet married. I do not have a command from the Lord for them. But the Lord in his mercy has given me wisdom that can be trusted, and I will share it with you. 26Because of the present crisis,* I think it is best to remain as you are. 27If you have a wife, do not seek to end the marriage. If you do not have a wife, do not seek to get married. 28But if you do get married, it is not a sin. And if a young woman gets married, it is not a sin. However, those who get married at this time will have troubles, and I am trying to spare you those problems.

29But let me say this, dear brothers and sisters: The time that remains is very short. So from now on, those with wives should not focus only on their marriage. 30Those who weep or who rejoice or who buy things should not be absorbed by their weeping or their joy or their possessions. 31Those who use the things of the world should not become attached to them. For this world as we know it will soon pass away.

32I want you to be free from the concerns of this life. An unmarried man can spend his time doing the Lord's work and thinking how to please him. 33But a married man has to think about his earthly responsibilities and how to please his wife. 34His interests are divided. In the same way, a woman who is no longer married or has never been married can be devoted to the Lord and holy in body and in spirit. But a married woman has to think about her earthly responsibilities and how to please her husband. 35I am saying this for your benefit, not to place restrictions on you. I want you to do whatever will help you serve the Lord best, with as few distractions as possible.

BE CONTENT 7:17-24

Have you ever had a bad case of the "If only" blues? These are the feelings you get when you think that life would be complete if only you had what you want. "Life would be perfect if only I had someone to go out with." "I would be successful if only I weren't stuck in the family I'm in." Paul advised the believers to "live in whatever situation the Lord has placed you" (7:17). In other words, be content. Does this mean you have to pretend that you're happy to be single when you don't really feel glad? Nope. It does mean accepting where you are instead of blaming God or demanding that he change your situation *right now*. ■

36But if a man thinks that he's treating his fiancée improperly and will inevitably give in to his passion, let him marry her as he wishes. It is not a sin. 37But if he has decided firmly not to marry and there is no urgency and he can control his passion, he does well not to marry. 38So the person who marries his fiancée does well, and the person who doesn't marry does even better.

39A wife is bound to her husband as long as he lives. If

7:10 See Matt 5:32; 19:9; Mark 10:11-12; Luke 16:18. **7:12** Greek *a brother*. **7:14** Greek *the brother*. **7:15a** Greek *the brother or sister*. **7:15b** Some manuscripts read *us*. **7:23** Greek *don't become slaves of people*. **7:24** Greek *brothers;* also in 7:29. **7:26** Or *the pressures of life*.

her husband dies, she is free to marry anyone she wishes, but only if he loves the Lord.* 40But in my opinion it would be better for her to stay single, and I think I am giving you counsel from God's Spirit when I say this.

NO PROBLEMS? 7:29-40

Many people think that finding the right boyfriend/girlfriend or getting married will solve all their problems. Having someone special in your life is cool. But no relationship—even a marriage—is a "cure for whatever ails you"! For example, here are a few of the problems marriage won't solve: (1) loneliness (some married people are really lonely), (2) sexual temptation, (3) satisfaction of one's deepest emotional needs. There is only one reliable solution for anyone: trust God to solve your problems. ■

8 FOOD SACRIFICED TO IDOLS

Now regarding your question about food that has been offered to idols. Yes, we know that "we all have knowledge" about this issue. But while knowledge makes us feel important, it is love that strengthens the church. 2Anyone who claims to know all the answers doesn't really know very much. 3But the person who loves God is the one whom God recognizes.*

4So, what about eating meat that has been offered to idols? Well, we all know that an idol is not really a god and that there is only one God. 5There may be so-called gods both in heaven and on earth, and some people actually worship many gods and many lords. 6But we know that there is only one God, the Father, who created everything, and we live for him. And there is only one Lord, Jesus Christ, through whom God made everything and through whom we have been given life.

7However, not all believers know this. Some are accustomed to thinking of idols as being real, so when they eat food that has been offered to idols, they think of it as the worship of real gods, and their weak consciences are violated. 8It's true that we can't win God's approval by what we eat. We don't lose anything if we don't eat it, and we don't gain anything if we do.

9But you must be careful so that your freedom does not cause others with a weaker conscience to stumble. 10For if others see you—with your "superior knowledge"—eating in the temple of an idol, won't they be encouraged to violate their conscience by eating food that has been offered to an idol? 11So because of your superior knowledge, a weak believer* for whom Christ died will be destroyed. 12And when you sin against other believers* by encouraging them to do something they believe is wrong, you are sinning against Christ. 13So if what I eat causes another believer to sin, I will never eat meat again as long as I live—for I don't want to cause another believer to stumble.

FREEDOM 8:1-13

You may have heard people talk about *legalism* and *freedom in Christ.* Although Paul doesn't mention the word *legalism,* it's implied in his message to the Corinthians. On one side is the freedom that Jesus offers through his forgiveness of sins. On the other side is legalism, which is all about keeping every rule in order to look "good" or to earn God's favor. Jesus often reprimanded the Pharisees for their love of rules, rather than people.

Still, with freedom comes responsibility. Some actions may be perfectly all right for us, but may harm someone new to the faith. As Paul warned, "You must be careful so that your freedom does not cause others with a weaker conscience to stumble." ■

9 PAUL GIVES UP HIS RIGHTS

Am I not as free as anyone else? Am I not an apostle? Haven't I seen Jesus our Lord with my own eyes? Isn't it because of my work that you belong to the Lord? 2Even if others think I am not an apostle, I certainly am to you. You yourselves are proof that I am the Lord's apostle.

3This is my answer to those who question my authority.* 4Don't we have the right to live in your homes and share your meals? 5Don't we have the right to bring a Christian wife with us as the other apostles and the Lord's brothers do, and as Peter* does? 6Or is it only Barnabas and I who have to work to support ourselves?

7What soldier has to pay his own expenses? What farmer plants a vineyard and doesn't have the right to eat some of its fruit? What shepherd cares for a flock of sheep and isn't allowed to drink some of the milk? 8Am I expressing merely a human opinion, or does the law say the same thing? 9For the law of Moses says, "You must not muzzle an ox to keep it from eating as it treads out the grain."* Was God thinking only about oxen when he said this? 10Wasn't he actually speaking to us? Yes, it was written for us, so that the one who plows and the one who threshes the grain might both expect a share of the harvest.

11Since we have planted spiritual seed among you, aren't we entitled to a harvest of physical food and drink? 12If you support others who preach to you, shouldn't we have an even greater right to be supported? But we have never used this right. We would rather put up with anything than be an obstacle to the Good News about Christ.

13Don't you realize that those who work in the temple get their meals from the offerings brought to the temple? And those who serve at the altar get a share of the sacrificial offerings. 14In the same way, the Lord ordered that those who preach the Good News should be supported by those who benefit from it. 15Yet I have never used any of these rights. And I am not writing this to suggest that I want to start now. In fact, I would rather die than lose my right to boast about preaching without charge. 16Yet

7:39 Greek *but only in the Lord.* 8:3 Some manuscripts read *the person who loves has full knowledge.* 8:11 Greek *brother;* also in 8:13. 8:12 Greek *brothers.* 9:3 Greek *those who examine me.* 9:5 Greek *Cephas.* 9:9 Deut 25:4.

Making Choices on Sensitive Issues

All of us make hundreds of choices every day. Most choices have no right or wrong attached to them—like what to wear or what to eat. But we always face decisions that carry a little more weight. We don't want to do wrong, and we don't want to cause others to do wrong. So how can we make right decisions?

IF I CHOOSE ONE COURSE OF ACTION . . .

. . .will it help my witness for Christ? (9:19-22)

. . .am I motivated by a desire to help others to know Christ? (9:23; 10:33)

. . .will it help me do my best? (9:25)

. . .is it against a specific command in Scripture and thus will cause me to sin? (10:12)

. . .will it be best and helpful? (10:23, 33)

. . .will I be thinking only of myself or do I truly care about the other person? (10:24)

. . .will I be acting lovingly or selfishly? (10:28-31)

. . .will it glorify God? (10:31)

. . .will it encourage someone else to sin? (10:32)

preaching the Good News is not something I can boast
about. I am compelled by God to do it. How terrible for
me if I didn't preach the Good News!
17If I were doing this on my own initiative, I would deserve payment. But I have no choice, for God has given me
this sacred trust. 18What then is my pay? It is the opportunity to preach the Good News without charging anyone.
That's why I never demand my rights when I preach the
Good News.
19Even though I am a free man with no master, I have
become a slave to all people to bring many to Christ.
20When I was with the Jews, I lived like
a Jew to bring the Jews to Christ. When
I was with those who follow the Jewish
law, I too lived under that law. Even
though I am not subject to the law, I did
this so I could bring to Christ those
who are under the law. 21When I am
with the Gentiles who do not follow
the Jewish law,* I too live apart from
that law so I can bring them to Christ.
But I do not ignore the law of God; I
obey the law of Christ.
22When I am with those who are
weak, I share their weakness, for I want
to bring the weak to Christ. Yes, I try to
find common ground with everyone,
doing everything I can to save some. 23I do everything to
spread the Good News and share in its blessings.
24Don't you realize that in a race everyone runs, but
only one person gets the prize? So run to win! 25All athletes are disciplined in their training. They do it to win a
prize that will fade away, but we do it for an eternal prize.
26So I run with purpose in every step. I am not just
shadowboxing. 27I discipline my body like an athlete,
training it to do what it should. Otherwise, I fear that after preaching to others I myself might be disqualified.

God is faithful. He will not allow the temptation to be more than you can stand.

1 CORINTHIANS 10:13

10 LESSONS FROM ISRAEL'S IDOLATRY

I don't want you to forget, dear brothers and sisters,*
about our ancestors in the wilderness long ago. All of
them were guided by a cloud that moved ahead of them,
and all of them walked through the sea on dry ground. 2In
the cloud and in the sea, all of them were baptized as followers of Moses. 3All of them ate the
same spiritual food, 4and all of them
drank the same spiritual water. For
they drank from the spiritual rock that
traveled with them, and that rock was
Christ. 5Yet God was not pleased with
most of them, and their bodies were
scattered in the wilderness.
6These things happened as a warning to us, so that we would not crave evil
things as they did, 7or worship idols as
some of them did. As the Scriptures
say, "The people celebrated with feasting and drinking, and they indulged in
pagan revelry."* 8And we must not engage in sexual immorality as some of
them did, causing 23,000 of them to die in one day.
9Nor should we put Christ* to the test, as some of them
did and then died from snakebites. 10And don't grumble
as some of them did, and then were destroyed by the angel of death. 11These things happened to them as examples for us. They were written down to warn us who live at
the end of the age.

9:21 Greek *those without the law.* **10:1** Greek *brothers.* **10:7** Exod 32:6. **10:9** Some manuscripts read *the Lord.*

keeping it real

For many years I had a problem with gossip. I knew it was wrong, but I kept giving in to temptation. I prayed about it a lot. Then the Lord gave me two Scriptures that have helped me begin to conquer this habit.

The first was 1 Corinthians 10:13. That verse says that God will always provide a way to escape temptation's power. So I reminded myself of this whenever the temptation to pass on any scoop that came my way. Although it helped somewhat, I still gave in more often than I wanted to.

Then God gave me another verse that's helped me even more. It's Psalm 141:3: "Take control of what I say, O LORD, and guard my lips." That's the prayer I pray whenever I'm tempted to gossip. Whenever I take the time to pray it, I find I can keep my mouth shut. But I have to take a moment to refocus my thoughts on the prayer rather than on the temptation to say something. Otherwise, I find myself giving in to temptation.

—Brooke

12If you think you are standing strong, be careful not to
fall. 13The temptations in your life are no different from
what others experience. And God is faithful. He will not
allow the temptation to be more than you can stand.
When you are tempted, he will show you a way out so that
you can endure.

TEMPTATION 10:13

Paul gave strong encouragement to the Corinthians about temptation. As with the Corinthian believers, God helps you resist temptation by first helping you to recognize it. He then gives you the courage to run from anything you know is wrong and to seek friends who love God and can offer help in times of temptation. Running from a tempting situation is the first step to victory (see 2 Tim 2:22).

14So, my dear friends, flee from the worship of idols.
15You are reasonable people. Decide for yourselves if
what I am saying is true. 16When we bless the cup at the
Lord's Table, aren't we sharing in the blood of Christ?
And when we break the bread, aren't we sharing in the
body of Christ? 17And though we are many, we all eat
from one loaf of bread, showing that we are one body.
18Think about the people of Israel. Weren't they united
by eating the sacrifices at the altar?

19What am I trying to say? Am I saying that food offered to idols has some significance, or that idols are real
gods? 20No, not at all. I am saying that these sacrifices are
offered to demons, not to God. And I don't want you to
participate with demons. 21You cannot drink from the
cup of the Lord and from the cup of demons, too. You
cannot eat at the Lord's Table and at the table of demons,
too. 22What? Do we dare to rouse the Lord's jealousy? Do
you think we are stronger than he is?

23You say, "I am allowed to do anything"*—but not
everything is good for you. You say, "I am allowed to do
anything"—but not everything is beneficial. 24Don't be
concerned for your own good but for the good of
others.

25So you may eat any meat that is sold in the marketplace without raising questions of conscience. 26For "the
earth is the LORD's, and everything in it."*

27If someone who isn't a believer asks you home for
dinner, accept the invitation if you want to. Eat whatever
is offered to you without raising questions of conscience.
28(But suppose someone tells you, "This meat was offered
to an idol." Don't eat it, out of consideration for the conscience of the one who told you. 29It might not be a matter of conscience for you, but it is for the other person.)
For why should my freedom be limited by what someone
else thinks? 30If I can thank God for the food and enjoy it,
why should I be condemned for eating it?

31So whether you eat or drink, or whatever you do, do it
all for the glory of God. 32Don't give offense to Jews or
Gentiles* or the church of God. 33I, too, try to please everyone in everything I do. I don't just do what is best for me; I
do what is best for others so that many may be saved.
11:1And you should imitate me, just as I imitate Christ.

11

INSTRUCTIONS FOR PUBLIC WORSHIP

2I am so glad that you always keep me in your thoughts,
and that you are following the teachings I passed on to
you. 3But there is one thing I want you to know: The head

10:23 Greek *All things are lawful;* also in 10:23b. 10:26 Ps 24:1. 10:32 Greek *or Greeks.*

of every man is Christ, the head of woman is man, and the
head of Christ is God.* 4A man dishonors his head* if he
covers his head while praying or prophesying. 5But a
woman dishonors her head* if she prays or prophesies
without a covering on her head, for this is the same as
shaving her head. 6Yes, if she refuses to wear a head covering, she should cut off all her hair! But since it is shameful for a woman to have her hair cut or her head shaved,
she should wear a covering.*

EQUALS 11:3

Submission is a key element in the smooth functioning of any business, government, or family. Yet submission is not surrender, withdrawal, apathy, or inferiority. Since God created all people in his image, all have equal value. Therefore, submission is mutual commitment and cooperation.

Thus God calls for submission among *equals.* Although Jesus was equal with God the Father, he submitted to the Father for the good of all. Likewise, although equal to man under God, a woman is called to submit to her husband for the sake of their marriage and family. Submission between equals is submission by choice, not force. In what ways do you submit to others? ■

7A man should not wear anything on his head when
worshiping, for man is made in God's image and reflects
God's glory. And woman reflects man's glory. 8For the
first man didn't come from woman, but the first woman
came from man. 9And man was not made for woman, but
woman was made for man. 10For this reason, and because
the angels are watching, a woman should wear a covering
on her head to show she is under authority.*

11But among the Lord's people, women are not independent of men, and men are not independent of
women. 12For although the first woman came from man,
every other man was born from a woman, and everything
comes from God.

13Judge for yourselves. Is it right for a woman to pray to
God in public without covering her head? 14Isn't it obvious that it's disgraceful for a man to have long hair?
15And isn't long hair a woman's pride and joy? For it has
been given to her as a covering. 16But if anyone wants to
argue about this, I simply say that we have no other custom than this, and neither do God's other churches.

ORDER AT THE LORD'S SUPPER

17But in the following instructions, I cannot praise you.
For it sounds as if more harm than good is done when you
meet together. 18First, I hear that there are divisions
among you when you meet as a church, and to some extent I believe it. 19But, of course, there must be divisions
among you so that you who have God's approval will be
recognized!

20When you meet together, you are not really interested in the Lord's Supper. 21For some of you hurry to eat
your own meal without sharing with others. As a result,
some go hungry while others get drunk. 22What? Don't
you have your own homes for eating and drinking? Or do
you really want to disgrace God's church and shame the
poor? What am I supposed to say? Do you want me to
praise you? Well, I certainly will not praise you for this!

23For I pass on to you what I received from the Lord
himself. On the night when he was betrayed, the Lord
Jesus took some bread 24and gave thanks to God for it.
Then he broke it in pieces and said, "This is my body,
which is given for you.* Do this to remember me." 25In
the same way, he took the cup of wine after supper, saying, "This cup is the new covenant between God and his
people—an agreement confirmed with my blood. Do this
to remember me as often as you drink it." 26For every
time you eat this bread and drink this cup, you are announcing the Lord's death until he comes again.

27So anyone who eats this bread or drinks this cup of
the Lord unworthily is guilty of sinning against* the body
and blood of the Lord. 28That is why you should examine
yourself before eating the bread and drinking the cup.
29For if you eat the bread or drink the cup without honoring the body of Christ,* you are eating and drinking God's
judgment upon yourself. 30That is why many of you are
weak and sick and some have even died.

31But if we would examine ourselves, we would not be
judged by God in this way. 32Yet when we are judged by
the Lord, we are being disciplined so that we will not be
condemned along with the world.

33So, my dear brothers and sisters,* when you gather
for the Lord's Supper, wait for each other. 34If you are
really hungry, eat at home so you won't bring judgment
upon yourselves when you meet together. I'll give you instructions about the other matters after I arrive.

12 SPIRITUAL GIFTS

Now, dear brothers and sisters,* regarding your question
about the special abilities the Spirit gives us. I don't want
you to misunderstand this. 2You know that when you
were still pagans, you were led astray and swept along in
worshiping speechless idols. 3So I want you to know that
no one speaking by the Spirit of God will curse Jesus, and
no one can say Jesus is Lord, except by the Holy Spirit.

4There are different kinds of spiritual gifts, but the
same Spirit is the source of them all. 5There are different
kinds of service, but we serve the same Lord. 6God works
in different ways, but it is the same God who does the
work in all of us.

7A spiritual gift is given to each of us so we can help
each other. 8To one person the Spirit gives the ability to

11:3 Or *to know: The source of every man is Christ, the source of woman is man, and the source of Christ is God.* Or *to know: Every man is responsible to Christ, a woman is responsible to her husband, and Christ is responsible to God.* 11:4 Or *dishonors Christ.* 11:5 Or *dishonors her husband.* 11:6 Or *should have long hair.* 11:10 Greek *should have an authority on her head.* 11:24 Greek *which is for you;* other manuscripts read *which is broken for you.* 11:27 Or *is responsible for.* 11:29 Greek *the body;* other manuscripts read *the Lord's body.* 11:33 Greek *brothers.* 12:1 Greek *brothers.*

THE CHURCH

ULTIMATE ISSUES

Please check the appropriate box:

The church is

☐ a building where religious people go on Sunday.

☐ a place where you're told all the things you shouldn't do.

☐ a place where a nice, respectable person tells a bunch of nice, respectable people to be nicer and more respectable (with apologies to Mark Twain).

☐ the people of God all over the world; those who follow Jesus and proclaim him as Lord.

Okay, you probably figured out that the last response is the best. But most of us probably feel there is some truth to the other statements as well.

Throughout 1 Corinthians, Paul refers to the church quite a bit. After all, this letter was written to educate the church—particularly the group in Corinth. He wanted to clear up any misconceptions they had about the Christian life. We want to clear up misconceptions you or someone else might have about the church. Are you ready?

Misconception #1: The church is a building. While most local churches in America *own* buildings, the church *isn't* a building. The church is wherever Christians gather.

Misconception #2: The church is where good people go to do religious things. Let's face it: There are no intrinsically "good" people. (If you're unclear on this concept, read Romans, particularly chapter 3.) Everyone is in need of forgiveness.

Misconception #3: The church is a human institution. Wrong. The church is God's own institution, called into being as his instrument on this planet. Through the power of the Holy Spirit, believers can influence society for the good of all people. We also have the responsibility of building up each member of the body of Christ.

The church isn't perfect, however. Since it's made up of imperfect humans, how could it be perfect? But the church *is* made up of God's people, called into existence by Jesus himself, and built on the rock-solid foundation of his promise that "all the powers of hell will not conquer it" (Matt 16:18).

give wise advice*; to another the same Spirit gives a message of special knowledge.* 9The same Spirit gives great
faith to another, and to someone else the one Spirit gives
the gift of healing. 10He gives one person the power to
perform miracles, and another the ability to prophesy.
He gives someone else the ability to discern whether a
message is from the Spirit of God or from another spirit.
Still another person is given the ability to speak in unknown languages,* while another is given the ability to
interpret what is being said. 11It is the one and only Spirit
who distributes all these gifts. He alone decides which
gift each person should have.

ONE BODY WITH MANY PARTS

12The human body has many parts, but the many parts
make up one whole body. So it is with the body of Christ.
13Some of us are Jews, some are Gentiles,* some are slaves,
and some are free. But we have all been baptized into one
body by one Spirit, and we all share the same Spirit.*

14Yes, the body has many different parts, not just one
part. 15If the foot says, "I am not a part of the body because I am not a hand," that does not make it any less a
part of the body. 16And if the ear says, "I am not part of
the body because I am not an eye," would that make it any
less a part of the body? 17If the whole body were an eye,
how would you hear? Or if your whole body were an ear,
how would you smell anything?

18But our bodies have many parts, and God has put
each part just where he wants it. 19How strange a body
would be if it had only one part! 20Yes, there are many
parts, but only one body. 21The eye can never say to the
hand, "I don't need you." The head can't say to the feet, "I
don't need you."

22In fact, some parts of the body that seem weakest and
least important are actually the most necessary. 23And the
parts we regard as less honorable are those we clothe with
the greatest care. So we carefully protect those parts that
should not be seen, 24while the more honorable parts do

12:8a Or *gives a word of wisdom.* **12:8b** Or *gives a word of knowledge.* **12:10** Or *in various tongues;* also in 12:28, 30. **12:13a** Greek *some are Greeks.* **12:13b** Greek *we were all given one Spirit to drink.*

keeping it real

After a bad dating experience, I decided to find out what God wanted a dating relationship to be. I talked to my youth pastor and studied Scripture. This time, when I felt ready to date again, I made sure I went out with a Christian.

Jenny and I talked about God's will right from the beginning and adopted 1 Corinthians 13 as the basis for our relationship. Even though Jenny and I didn't stay together forever, our relationship was a very positive experience. We both tried to let verses 4-7 guide all our thoughts and actions toward each other, even when we broke up. I learned a lot from that.

—Spencer

not require this special care. So God has put the body together such that extra honor and care are given to those parts that have less dignity. 25This makes for harmony among the members, so that all the members care for each other. 26If one part suffers, all the parts suffer with it, and if one part is honored, all the parts are glad.

THE BODY 12:4-31

Using the analogy of the human body, Paul emphasized the importance of each church member. The Holy Spirit gave each person an ability to use to serve others and to help build God's Kingdom. Now, there are some who believe that some abilities are more important than others. Yet no ability is insignificant. Check out the list of abilities in this passage. What is/are your spiritual gift(s)? How are you using it/them to build up the body? ■

27All of you together are Christ's body, and each of you is a part of it. 28Here are some of the parts God has appointed for the church:

first are apostles,
second are prophets,
third are teachers,
then those who do miracles,
those who have the gift of healing,
those who can help others,
those who have the gift of leadership,
those who speak in unknown languages.

29Are we all apostles? Are we all prophets? Are we all teachers? Do we all have the power to do miracles? 30Do we all have the gift of healing? Do we all have the ability to speak in unknown languages? Do we all have the ability to interpret unknown languages? Of course not! 31So you should earnestly desire the most helpful gifts.

But now let me show you a way of life that is best of all.

13 LOVE IS THE GREATEST

If I could speak all the languages of earth and of angels, but didn't love others, I would only be a noisy gong or a clanging cymbal. 2If I had the gift of prophecy, and if I understood all of God's secret plans and possessed all knowledge, and if I had such faith that I could move mountains, but didn't love others, I would be nothing. 3If I gave everything I have to the poor and even sacrificed my body, I could boast about it;* but if I didn't love others, I would have gained nothing.

4Love is patient and kind. Love is not jealous or boastful or proud 5or rude. It does not demand its own way. It is not irritable, and it keeps no record of being wronged. 6It does not rejoice about injustice but rejoices whenever the truth wins out. 7Love never gives up, never loses faith, is always hopeful, and endures through every circumstance.

REAL LOVE 13:4-7

Most people are pretty sure they know what real love is. Think about the last movie, song, or TV show where someone talked about love. How was love defined? More than likely, the described love was pretty conditional. "I love what you do for me." "I love the way you look." But when a change occurs, "love" disappears. Now check out this passage. What similarities or differences do you notice between what you've heard recently and what you read here? Is this the kind of love you have for others? ■

8Prophecy and speaking in unknown languages* and special knowledge will become useless. But love will last forever! 9Now our knowledge is partial and incomplete, and even the gift of prophecy reveals only part of the whole picture! 10But when full understanding comes, these partial things will become useless.

11When I was a child, I spoke and thought and reasoned

13:3 Some manuscripts read *sacrificed my body to be burned.* 13:8 Or *in tongues.*

as a child. But when I grew up, I put away childish things.
12 Now we see things imperfectly as in a cloudy mirror,
but then we will see everything with perfect clarity.* All
that I know now is partial and incomplete, but then I will
know everything completely, just as God now knows me
completely.
13 Three things will last forever—faith, hope, and love—
and the greatest of these is love.

14 TONGUES AND PROPHECY

Let love be your highest goal! But you should also desire
the special abilities the Spirit gives—especially the ability
to prophesy. 2 For if you have the ability to speak in
tongues,* you will be talking only to God, since people
won't be able to understand you. You will be speaking by
the power of the Spirit, but it will all be mysterious. 3 But
one who prophesies strengthens others, encourages
them, and comforts them. 4 A person who speaks in
tongues is strengthened personally, but one who speaks a
word of prophecy strengthens the entire church.
5 I wish you could all speak in tongues, but even more I
wish you could all prophesy. For prophecy is greater than
speaking in tongues, unless someone interprets what you
are saying so that the whole church will be strengthened.
6 Dear brothers and sisters,* if I should come to you
speaking in an unknown language,* how would that help
you? But if I bring you a revelation or some special knowledge or prophecy or teaching, that will be helpful. 7 Even
lifeless instruments like the flute or the harp must play
the notes clearly, or no one will recognize the melody.
8 And if the bugler doesn't sound a clear call, how will the
soldiers know they are being called to battle?
9 It's the same for you. If you speak to people in words
they don't understand, how will they know what you are
saying? You might as well be talking into empty space.
10 There are many different languages in the world, and
every language has meaning. 11 But if I don't understand a
language, I will be a foreigner to someone who speaks it,
and the one who speaks it will be a foreigner to me. 12 And
the same is true for you. Since you are so eager to have the
special abilities the Spirit gives, seek those that will
strengthen the whole church.
13 So anyone who speaks in tongues should pray also
for the ability to interpret what has been said. 14 For if I
pray in tongues, my spirit is praying, but I don't understand what I am saying.
15 Well then, what shall I do? I will pray in the spirit,*
and I will also pray in words I understand. I will sing in the
spirit, and I will also sing in words I understand. 16 For if
you praise God only in the spirit, how can those who don't
understand you praise God along with you? How can they
join you in giving thanks when they don't understand
what you are saying? 17 You will be giving thanks very well,
but it won't strengthen the people who hear you.
18 I thank God that I speak in tongues more than any of
you. 19 But in a church meeting I would rather speak five
understandable words to help others than ten thousand
words in an unknown language.
20 Dear brothers and sisters, don't be childish in your
understanding of these things. Be innocent as babies
when it comes to evil, but be mature in understanding
matters of this kind. 21 It is written in the Scriptures*:

"I will speak to my own people
through strange languages
and through the lips of foreigners.
But even then, they will not listen to me,"*
says the LORD.

22 So you see that speaking in tongues is a sign, not for
believers, but for unbelievers. Prophecy, however, is for
the benefit of believers, not unbelievers. 23 Even so, if unbelievers or people who don't understand these things
come into your church meeting and hear everyone
speaking in an unknown language, they will think you are
crazy. 24 But if all of you are prophesying, and unbelievers
or people who don't understand these things come into
your meeting, they will be convicted of sin and judged by
what you say. 25 As they listen, their secret thoughts will
be exposed, and they will fall to their knees and worship
God, declaring, "God is truly here among you."

A CALL TO ORDERLY WORSHIP

26 Well, my brothers and sisters, let's summarize. When you
meet together, one will sing, another will teach, another will
tell some special revelation God has given, one will speak in
tongues, and another will interpret what is said. But everything that is done must strengthen all of you.
27 No more than two or three should speak in tongues.
They must speak one at a time, and someone must interpret what they say. 28 But if no one is present who can interpret, they must be silent in your church meeting and
speak in tongues to God privately.
29 Let two or three people prophesy, and let the others
evaluate what is said. 30 But if someone is prophesying
and another person receives a revelation from the Lord,
the one who is speaking must stop. 31 In this way, all who
prophesy will have a turn to speak, one after the other, so
that everyone will learn and be encouraged. 32 Remember
that people who prophesy are in control of their spirit
and can take turns. 33 For God is not a God of disorder but
of peace, as in all the meetings of God's holy people.*
34 Women should be silent during the church meetings. It is not proper for them to speak. They should be
submissive, just as the law says. 35 If they have any questions, they should ask their husbands at home, for it is im-
proper for women to speak in church meetings.*
36 Or do you think God's word originated with you Corinthians? Are you the only ones to whom it was given?
37 If you claim to be a prophet or think you are spiritual,
you should recognize that what I am saying is a command

13:12 Greek *see face to face.* 14:2 Or *in unknown languages;* also in 14:4, 5, 13, 14, 18, 22, 26, 27, 28, 39. 14:6a Greek *brothers;* also in 14:20, 26, 39. 14:6b Or *in tongues;* also in 14:19, 23. 14:15 Or *in the Spirit;* also in 14:15b, 16. 14:21a Greek *in the law.* 14:21b Isa 28:11-12. 14:33 The phrase *as in all the meetings of God's holy people* could instead be joined to the beginning of 14:34. 14:35 Some manuscripts place verses 34-35 after 14:40.

from the Lord himself. 38But if you do not recognize this,
you yourself will not be recognized.*
39So, my dear brothers and sisters, be eager to prophesy, and don't forbid speaking in tongues. 40But be sure
that everything is done properly and in order.

15

THE RESURRECTION OF CHRIST

Let me now remind you, dear brothers and sisters,* of the
Good News I preached to you before. You welcomed it
then, and you still stand firm in it. 2It is this Good News
that saves you if you continue to believe the message I
told you—unless, of course, you believed something that
was never true in the first place.*
3I passed on to you what was most important and what
had also been passed on to me. Christ died for our sins,
just as the Scriptures said. 4He was buried, and he was
raised from the dead on the third day, just as the Scriptures said. 5He was seen by Peter* and then by the
Twelve. 6After that, he was seen by more than 500 of his
followers* at one time, most of whom are still alive,
though some have died. 7Then he was seen by James and
later by all the apostles. 8Last of all, as though I had been
born at the wrong time, I also saw him. 9For I am the least
of all the apostles. In fact, I'm not even worthy to be called
an apostle after the way I persecuted God's church.
10But whatever I am now, it is all because God poured
out his special favor on me—and not without results. For
I have worked harder than any of the other apostles; yet it
was not I but God who was working through me by his
grace. 11So it makes no difference whether I preach or
they preach, for we all preach the same message you have
already believed.

THE RESURRECTION OF THE DEAD

12But tell me this—since we preach that Christ rose from
the dead, why are some of you saying there will be no resurrection of the dead? 13For if there is no resurrection of
the dead, then Christ has not been raised either. 14And if
Christ has not been raised, then all our preaching is useless, and your faith is useless. 15And we apostles would all
be lying about God—for we have said that God raised
Christ from the grave. But that can't be true if there is no
resurrection of the dead. 16And if there is no resurrection
of the dead, then Christ has not been raised. 17And if
Christ has not been raised, then your faith is useless and
you are still guilty of your sins. 18In that case, all who have
died believing in Christ are lost! 19And if our hope in
Christ is only for this life, we are more to be pitied than
anyone in the world.
20But in fact, Christ has been raised from the dead. He
is the first of a great harvest of all who have died.
21So you see, just as death came into the world through a
man, now the resurrection from the dead has begun
through another man. 22Just as everyone dies because we
all belong to Adam, everyone who belongs to Christ will be
given new life. 23But there is an order to this resurrection:
Christ was raised as the first of the harvest; then all who
belong to Christ will be raised when he comes back.
24After that the end will come, when he will turn the
Kingdom over to God the Father, having destroyed every
ruler and authority and power. 25For Christ must reign
until he humbles all his enemies beneath his feet. 26And
the last enemy to be destroyed is death. 27For the Scriptures say, "God has put all things under his authority."*
(Of course, when it says "all things are under his authority," that does not include God himself, who gave Christ
his authority.) 28Then, when all things are under his authority, the Son will put himself under God's authority, so
that God, who gave his Son authority over all things, will
be utterly supreme over everything everywhere.
29If the dead will not be raised, what point is there in
people being baptized for those who are dead? Why do it
unless the dead will someday rise again?
30And why should we ourselves risk our lives hour by
hour? 31For I swear, dear brothers and sisters, that I face
death daily. This is as certain as my pride in what Christ
Jesus our Lord has done in you. 32And what value was
there in fighting wild beasts—those people of Ephesus*—
if there will be no resurrection from the dead? And if
there is no resurrection, "Let's feast and drink, for tomorrow we die!"* 33Don't be fooled by those who say
such things, for "bad company corrupts good character."
34Think carefully about what is right, and stop sinning. For
to your shame I say that some of you don't know God at all.

THE RESURRECTION BODY

35But someone may ask, "How will the dead be raised?
What kind of bodies will they have?" 36What a foolish
question! When you put a seed into the ground, it doesn't
grow into a plant unless it dies first. 37And what you put in
the ground is not the plant that will grow, but only a bare
seed of wheat or whatever you are planting. 38Then God
gives it the new body he wants it to have. A different plant
grows from each kind of seed. 39Similarly there are different kinds of flesh—one kind for humans, another for animals, another for birds, and another for fish.
40There are also bodies in the heavens and bodies on the
earth. The glory of the heavenly bodies is different from
the glory of the earthly bodies. 41The sun has one kind of
glory, while the moon and stars each have another kind.
And even the stars differ from each other in their glory.
42It is the same way with the resurrection of the dead.
Our earthly bodies are planted in the ground when we
die, but they will be raised to live forever. 43Our bodies
are buried in brokenness, but they will be raised in glory.
They are buried in weakness, but they will be raised in
strength. 44They are buried as natural human bodies, but
they will be raised as spiritual bodies. For just as there are
natural bodies, there are also spiritual bodies.
45The Scriptures tell us, "The first man, Adam, became
a living person."* But the last Adam—that is, Christ—is a
life-giving Spirit. 46What comes first is the natural body,
then the spiritual body comes later. 47Adam, the first

14:38 Some manuscripts read *If you are ignorant of this, stay in your ignorance.* 15:1 Greek *brothers;* also in 15:31, 50, 58. 15:2 Or *unless you never believed it in the first place.* 15:5 Greek *Cephas.* 15:6 Greek *the brothers.* 15:27 Ps 8:6. 15:32a Greek *fighting wild beasts in Ephesus.* 15:32b Isa 22:13. 15:45 Gen 2:7.

man, was made from the dust of the earth, while Christ, the second man, came from heaven. [48]Earthly people are like the earthly man, and heavenly people are like the heavenly man. [49]Just as we are now like the earthly man, we will someday be like* the heavenly man.

[50]What I am saying, dear brothers and sisters, is that our physical bodies cannot inherit the Kingdom of God. These dying bodies cannot inherit what will last forever.

[51]But let me reveal to you a wonderful secret. We will not all die, but we will all be transformed! [52]It will happen in a moment, in the blink of an eye, when the last trumpet is blown. For when the trumpet sounds, those who have died will be raised to live forever. And we who are living will also be transformed. [53]For our dying bodies must be transformed into bodies that will never die; our mortal bodies must be transformed into immortal bodies.

[54]Then, when our dying bodies have been transformed into bodies that will never die,* this Scripture will be fulfilled:

"Death is swallowed up in victory.*
55 O death, where is your victory?
O death, where is your sting?*"

[56]For sin is the sting that results in death, and the law gives sin its power. [57]But thank God! He gives us victory over sin and death through our Lord Jesus Christ.

[58]So, my dear brothers and sisters, be strong and immovable. Always work enthusiastically for the Lord, for you know that nothing you do for the Lord is ever useless.

RESULTS 15:58

Ever hesitate to tell someone about Jesus, because you haven't seen what good that does? Because of the Resurrection, nothing we do is useless. Yet in this lifetime, we might not see all of the good that results from our efforts. Don't let discouragement over an apparent lack of results keep you from working. Do the good that you have opportunity to do, knowing that your work will have eternal results. ■

16

THE COLLECTION FOR JERUSALEM

Now regarding your question about the money being collected for God's people in Jerusalem. You should follow the same procedure I gave to the churches in Galatia. [2]On the first day of each week, you should each put aside a portion of the money you have earned. Don't wait until I get there and then try to collect it all at once. [3]When I come, I will write letters of recommendation for the messengers you choose to deliver your gift to Jerusalem. [4]And if it seems appropriate for me to go along, they can travel with me.

PAUL'S FINAL INSTRUCTIONS

[5]I am coming to visit you after I have been to Macedonia,* for I am planning to travel through Macedonia. [6]Perhaps I will stay awhile with you, possibly all winter, and then you can send me on my way to my next destination. [7]This time I don't want to make just a short visit and then go right on. I want to come and stay awhile, if the Lord will let me. [8]In the meantime, I will be staying here at Ephesus until the Festival of Pentecost. [9]There is a wide-open door for a great work here, although many oppose me.

[10]When Timothy comes, don't intimidate him. He is doing the Lord's work, just as I am. [11]Don't let anyone treat him with contempt. Send him on his way with your blessing when he returns to me. I expect him to come with the other believers.*

[12]Now about our brother Apollos—I urged him to visit you with the other believers, but he was not willing to go right now. He will see you later when he has the opportunity.

[13]Be on guard. Stand firm in the faith. Be courageous.* Be strong. [14]And do everything with love.

[15]You know that Stephanas and his household were the first of the harvest of believers in Greece,* and they are spending their lives in service to God's people. I urge you, dear brothers and sisters,* [16]to submit to them and others like them who serve with such devotion. [17]I am very glad that Stephanas, Fortunatus, and Achaicus have come here. They have been providing the help you weren't here to give me. [18]They have been a wonderful encouragement to me, as they have been to you. You must show your appreciation to all who serve so well.

GRAND FINALE 16:22

Paul ended his letter with his hope for Jesus' swift return. To Paul, this was a glad hope, the best he could look forward to. He wasn't afraid of seeing Jesus—he could hardly wait! Do you share Paul's eager anticipation? Those who love Jesus look forward to "that wonderful day" (Titus 2:13). ■

PAUL'S FINAL GREETINGS

[19]The churches here in the province of Asia* send greetings in the Lord, as do Aquila and Priscilla* and all the others who gather in their home for church meetings. [20]All the brothers and sisters here send greetings to you. Greet each other with Christian love.*

[21]HERE IS MY GREETING IN MY OWN HANDWRITING—PAUL.

[22]If anyone does not love the Lord, that person is cursed. Our Lord, come!*

[23]May the grace of the Lord Jesus be with you.

[24]My love to all of you in Christ Jesus.*

15:49 Some manuscripts read *let us be like.* **15:54a** Some manuscripts add *and our mortal bodies have been transformed into immortal bodies.* **15:54b** Isa 25:8. **15:55** Hos 13:14 (Greek version). **16:5** *Macedonia* was in the northern region of Greece. **16:11** Greek *with the brothers;* also in 16:12. **16:13** Greek *Be men.* **16:15a** Greek *in Achaia,* the southern region of the Greek peninsula. **16:15b** Greek *brothers;* also in 16:20. **16:19a** *Asia* was a Roman province in what is now western Turkey. **16:19b** Greek *Prisca.* **16:20** Greek *with a sacred kiss.* **16:22** From Aramaic, *Marana tha.* Some manuscripts read *Maran atha, "Our Lord has come."* **16:24** Some manuscripts add *Amen.*

MINISTRY . . . OR MADNESS? A Quiz Just for You.

1. Your youth group gives 400 hard-earned dollars to a family whose house just burned down. The family never even acknowledges the gift! Do you: (a) Get on your soapbox about the importance of gratitude? (b) Think of all the ways *you* could have used the cash? (c) Ask for the money back? (d) Trust that God is in control?

2. During a church mission trip, some older teens surround you, call you names, shove you, and make fun of the Christian message on your T-shirt. Do you: (a) Introduce them to some kung fu moves like in the *Matrix* movies? (b) Change your shirt? (c) Vow never to stand up for Christ again? (d) Consider it an honor to suffer for Christ?

3. Second Corinthians discusses: (a) Living for the Lord when nothing seems to go right. (b) Why serving God and others *is* worth it (no matter what happens). (c) The amazing truth that we can't outgive God. (d) The importance of telling others about Jesus Christ. (e) All of the above.

Being Christ's ambassador may seem as crazy at times as the above quiz and twice as difficult. When you're faced with hard times, are you tempted to give up? Second Corinthians is just what you need.

stats

PURPOSE: To affirm Paul's own ministry, defend his authority as an apostle, and disprove the false teachers in Corinth

AUTHOR: Paul

TO WHOM WRITTEN: The church in Corinth, and Christians everywhere

DATE WRITTEN: About A.D. 55 through 57, from Macedonia

SETTING: Paul had already written three letters to the Corinthians. (Two are now lost.) In 1 Corinthians (the second of these letters), he used strong words to correct and teach. Most of the church had responded in the right spirit. There were, however, those who denied Paul's authority and questioned his motives.

KEY PEOPLE: Paul, Timothy, Titus, false teachers

KEY PLACES: Corinth, Jerusalem

KEY points

TRIALS
Paul depended on God to help him through some extremely difficult times. Likewise, we can look to God for comfort during trials. As he comforts us, we learn to comfort others.

CHURCH DISCIPLINE
As Paul explained, the church was to be neither too lax nor too severe in administering discipline. The goal of discipline in the church should be correction, not vengeance. An effective church confronts and solves problems, rather than ignoring them.

HOPE
Paul encouraged the Corinthians as they faced trials by reminding them that they would receive new bodies in heaven. This would be a great victory in contrast to their present suffering. Their hope also is ours.

GENEROSITY
Paul organized a collection of funds for the poor in the Jerusalem church. Our giving must be generous, sacrificial, according to a plan, and based on need. Generosity helps the needy, enabling them to thank God.

keeping it real

Last year, I went through a very difficult time. One thing after another happened. I wasn't sure I could take any more. Although God saw me through that time, I still had lots of unresolved questions about why those things had to happen to me.

Not long afterward, my friend's sister had a leukemia relapse. When I found out, I prayed and cried for a while. Then I decided to write her a note of encouragement. Later that night, I read 2 Corinthians 1:3-7. It was like God spoke tender words of comfort to me. I realized that there was a reason for the pain I had gone through not long before—so that I could relate to the pain of other people and offer true encouragement.

I was not only able to offer my friend's sister some sincere encouragement, but also my nagging questions over why God let me go through pain were answered. Since then, whenever something painful happens to me, it's much easier for me to believe that there's a good reason for it.

Lily

1

GREETINGS FROM PAUL

This letter is from Paul, chosen by the will of God to be an
apostle of Christ Jesus, and from our brother Timothy.
I am writing to God's church in Corinth and to all of his
holy people throughout Greece.*
2May God our Father and the Lord Jesus Christ give you
grace and peace.

COMFORT 1:3-7

Many people believe that when God comforts us, our hardships go away. If that were so, people would turn to God only to be relieved of pain and not out of love for him. Real comfort can also mean receiving the strength to deal with our hardships. The more we suffer, the more comfort God gives us (1:5). If you're feeling overwhelmed, allow God to comfort you. Remember, every trial you endure will later become an opportunity to help someone who suffers a similar hardship. ■

GOD OFFERS COMFORT TO ALL

3All praise to God, the Father of our Lord Jesus Christ.
God is our merciful Father and the source of all comfort.
4He comforts us in all our troubles so that we can comfort
others. When they are troubled, we will be able to give
them the same comfort God has given us. 5For the more
we suffer for Christ, the more God will shower us with his
comfort through Christ. 6Even when we are weighed
down with troubles, it is for your comfort and salvation!
For when we ourselves are comforted, we will certainly
comfort you. Then you can patiently endure the same
things we suffer. 7We are confident that as you share in
our sufferings, you will also share in the comfort God
gives us.
8We think you ought to know, dear brothers and sisters,* about the trouble we went through in the province of Asia. We were crushed and overwhelmed
beyond our ability to endure, and we thought we would
never live through it. 9In fact, we expected to die. But as
a result, we stopped relying on ourselves and learned to
rely only on God, who raises the dead. 10And he did rescue us from mortal danger, and he will rescue us again.
We have placed our confidence in him, and he will
continue to rescue us. 11And you are helping us by
praying for us. Then many people will give thanks because God has graciously answered so many prayers
for our safety.

PAUL'S CHANGE OF PLANS

12We can say with confidence and a clear conscience that
we have lived with a God-given holiness* and sincerity in
all our dealings. We have depended on God's grace, not
on our own human wisdom. That is how we have conducted ourselves before the world, and especially toward
you. 13Our letters have been straightforward, and there is
nothing written between the lines and nothing you can't
understand. I hope someday you will fully understand us,
14even if you don't understand us now. Then on the day
when the Lord Jesus* returns, you will be proud of us in
the same way we are proud of you.
15Since I was so sure of your understanding and trust, I
wanted to give you a double blessing by visiting you
twice—16first on my way to Macedonia and again when I
returned from Macedonia.* Then you could send me on
my way to Judea.

1:1 Greek *Achaia*, the southern region of the Greek peninsula. 1:8 Greek *brothers*. 1:12 Some manuscripts read *honesty*. 1:14 Some manuscripts read *our Lord Jesus*. 1:16 *Macedonia* was in the northern region of Greece.

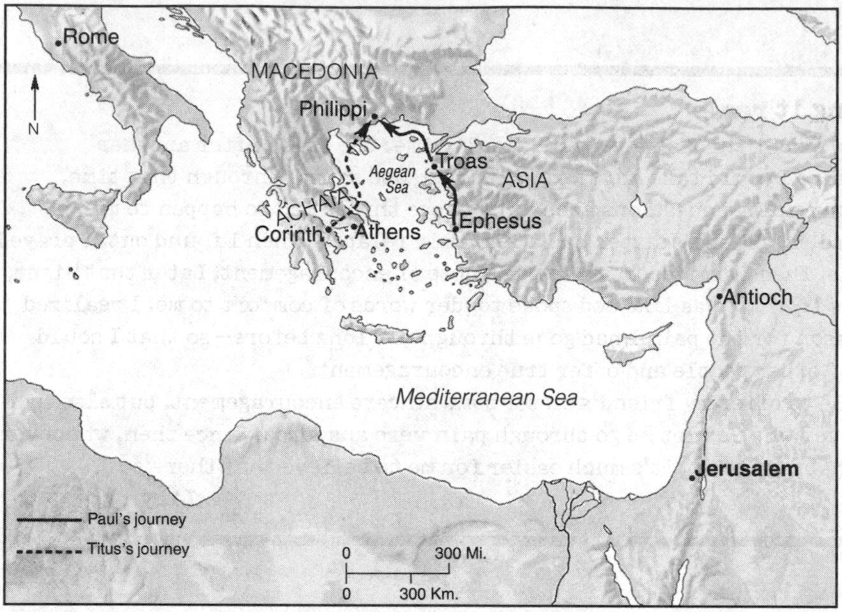

PAUL SEARCHES FOR TITUS
Paul had searched for Titus, hoping to meet him in Troas and receive news about the Corinthian church. When he did not find Titus in Troas, Paul went on to Macedonia (2:13), most likely to Philippi, where he found Titus.

17You may be asking why I changed my plan. Do you
think I make my plans carelessly? Do you think I am like
people of the world who say "Yes" when they really
mean "No"? 18As surely as God is faithful, my word to
you does not waver between "Yes" and "No." 19For Jesus
Christ, the Son of God, does not waver between "Yes"
and "No." He is the one whom Silas,* Timothy, and I
preached to you, and as God's ultimate "Yes," he always
does what he says. 20For all of God's promises have been
fulfilled in Christ with a resounding "Yes!" And through
Christ, our "Amen" (which means "Yes") ascends to God
for his glory.
21It is God who enables us, along with you, to stand
firm for Christ. He has commissioned us, 22and he has
identified us as his own by placing the Holy Spirit in our
hearts as the first installment that guarantees everything
he has promised us.

SEAL OF APPROVAL 1:21-22

When we become believers, God provides the Holy Spirit as a guarantee that we belong to him. (See also Eph 1:13-14.) With the privilege of belonging to God comes the responsibility of identifying ourselves as faithful representatives and servants of our master. How do you let others know you are his?

23Now I call upon God as my witness that I am telling
the truth. The reason I didn't return to Corinth was to
spare you from a severe rebuke. 24But that does not mean
we want to dominate you by telling you how to put your
faith into practice. We want to work together with you so
you will be full of joy, for it is by your own faith that you
stand firm.

2 So I decided that I would not bring you grief with
another painful visit. 2For if I cause you grief, who will
make me glad? Certainly not someone I have grieved.
3That is why I wrote to you as I did, so that when I do
come, I won't be grieved by the very ones who ought to
give me the greatest joy. Surely you all know that my joy
comes from your being joyful. 4I wrote that letter in great
anguish, with a troubled heart and many tears. I didn't
want to grieve you, but I wanted to let you know how
much love I have for you.

FORGIVENESS FOR THE SINNER

5I am not overstating it when I say that the man who
caused all the trouble hurt all of you more than he hurt
me. 6Most of you opposed him, and that was punishment
enough. 7Now, however, it is time to forgive and comfort
him. Otherwise he may be overcome by discouragement.
8So I urge you now to reaffirm your love for him.
9I wrote to you as I did to test you and see if you would
fully comply with my instructions. 10When you forgive
this man, I forgive him, too. And when I forgive whatever
needs to be forgiven, I do so with Christ's authority for
your benefit, 11so that Satan will not outsmart us. For we
are familiar with his evil schemes.
12When I came to the city of Troas to preach the Good
News of Christ, the Lord opened a door of opportunity
for me. 13But I had no peace of mind because my dear
brother Titus hadn't yet arrived with a report from you.
So I said good-bye and went on to Macedonia to find him.

1:19 Greek *Silvanus.*

MINISTERS OF THE NEW COVENANT

[14]But thank God! He has made us his captives and continues to lead us along in Christ's triumphal procession. Now he uses us to spread the knowledge of Christ everywhere, like a sweet perfume. [15]Our lives are a Christ-like fragrance rising up to God. But this fragrance is perceived differently by those who are being saved and by those who are perishing. [16]To those who are perishing, we are a dreadful smell of death and doom. But to those who are being saved, we are a life-giving perfume. And who is adequate for such a task as this?

[17]You see, we are not like the many hucksters* who preach for personal profit. We preach the word of God with sincerity and with Christ's authority, knowing that God is watching us.

3 Are we beginning to praise ourselves again? Are we like others, who need to bring you letters of recommendation, or who ask you to write such letters on their behalf? Surely not! [2]The only letter of recommendation we need is you yourselves. Your lives are a letter written in our* hearts; everyone can read it and recognize our good work among you. [3]Clearly, you are a letter from Christ showing the result of our ministry among you. This "letter" is written not with pen and ink, but with the Spirit of the living God. It is carved not on tablets of stone, but on human hearts.

[4]We are confident of all this because of our great trust in God through Christ. [5]It is not that we think we are qualified to do anything on our own. Our qualification comes from God. [6]He has enabled us to be ministers of his new covenant. This is a covenant not of written laws, but of the Spirit. The old written covenant ends in death; but under the new covenant, the Spirit gives life.

THE GLORY OF THE NEW COVENANT

[7]The old way,* with laws etched in stone, led to death, though it began with such glory that the people of Israel could not bear to look at Moses' face. For his face shone with the glory of God, even though the brightness was already fading away. [8]Shouldn't we expect far greater glory under the new way, now that the Holy Spirit is giving life? [9]If the old way, which brings condemnation, was glorious, how much more glorious is the new way, which makes us right with God! [10]In fact, that first glory was not glorious at all compared with the overwhelming glory of the new way. [11]So if the old way, which has been replaced, was glorious, how much more glorious is the new, which remains forever!

[12]Since this new way gives us such confidence, we can be very bold. [13]We are not like Moses, who put a veil over his face so the people of Israel would not see the glory, even though it was destined to fade away. [14]But the people's minds were hardened, and to this day whenever the old covenant is being read, the same veil covers their minds so they cannot understand the truth. And this veil can be removed only by believing in Christ. [15]Yes, even today when they read Moses' writings, their hearts are covered with that veil, and they do not understand.

[16]But whenever someone turns to the Lord, the veil is taken away. [17]For the Lord is the Spirit, and wherever the Spirit of the Lord is, there is freedom. [18]So all of us who have had that veil removed can see and reflect the glory of the Lord. And the Lord—who is the Spirit—makes us more and more like him as we are changed into his glorious image.

LIKE HIM 3:17-18

The glory that the Spirit imparts to the believer is greater both in quality and longevity than that which Moses experienced. (See Exod 34:33-35.) The glory gradually makes the believer more Christlike. Becoming Christlike is a progressive experience (see Gal 4:19; Phil 1:6; 1 John 3:2-3). The more closely we relate to Jesus, the more we will be like him. How closely do your actions resemble his? ■

4

TREASURE IN FRAGILE CLAY JARS

Therefore, since God in his mercy has given us this new way,* we never give up. [2]We reject all shameful deeds and underhanded methods. We don't try to trick anyone or distort the word of God. We tell the truth before God, and all who are honest know this.

[3]If the Good News we preach is hidden behind a veil, it is hidden only from people who are perishing. [4]Satan, who is the god of this world, has blinded the minds of those who don't believe. They are unable to see the glorious light of the Good News. They don't understand this message about the glory of Christ, who is the exact likeness of God.

[5]You see, we don't go around preaching about ourselves. We preach that Jesus Christ is Lord, and we ourselves are your servants for Jesus' sake. [6]For God, who said, "Let there be light in the darkness," has made this light shine in our hearts so we could know the glory of God that is seen in the face of Jesus Christ.

[7]We now have this light shining in our hearts, but we ourselves are like fragile clay jars containing this great treasure.* This makes it clear that our great power is from God, not from ourselves.

[8]We are pressed on every side by troubles, but we are not crushed. We are perplexed, but not driven to despair. [9]We are hunted down, but never abandoned by God. We get knocked down, but we are not destroyed. [10]Through suffering, our bodies continue to share in the death of Jesus so that the life of Jesus may also be seen in our bodies.

[11]Yes, we live under constant danger of death because we serve Jesus, so that the life of Jesus will be evident in

2:17 Some manuscripts read *the rest of the hucksters.* 3:2 Some manuscripts read *your.* 3:7 Or *ministry;* also in 3:8, 9, 10, 11, 12. 4:1 Or *ministry.* 4:7 Greek *We now have this treasure in clay jars.*

SERVING GOD

"Tom, maybe you've got the dates mixed up," Austin says.

"No way!" Tom replies. "The prison outreach is the same weekend."

"But what about Ethan's ski party?"

"I guess I'll have to miss it."

"Dude, you can't! Everybody will be at Ethan's–including the hottest girls in the whole sophomore class! It's the party of the year, man!"

"Look, I wish I could go. But I promised to sing with the group at this prison thing."

"Can't you get out of it?"

Tom shakes his head. "Austin, you just don't understand."

"Well, I say you're making a huge mistake. You'll regret it if you miss Ethan's party."

Two weeks later the big weekend has come and gone. Ethan's party was every bit as fun as advertised. Great weather, great skiing–it was a certified blast!

And the prison outreach? By comparison, it didn't seem as successful. The prisoners showered Tom's group with verbal abuse during the concert. Afterward, during a meal stop on the way home, someone broke into the church van and stole the sound equipment!

Does serving the Lord really pay? Is the hardship encountered worth all the effort? Take it from the apostle Paul, a guy who should know. Although he endured unbelievable difficulties (check out 2 Corinthians 4:8-10; 6:4-10; 11:23-33), he remained faithful to the end of his life. How do you respond to the difficulties you face? Want to live the way Paul lived? Why or why not?

our dying bodies. [12]So we live in the face of death, but this
has resulted in eternal life for you.
[13]But we continue to preach because we have the same
kind of faith the psalmist had when he said, "I believed in
God, so I spoke."* [14]We know that God, who raised the
Lord Jesus,* will also raise us with Jesus and present us to
himself together with you. [15]All of this is for your benefit.
And as God's grace reaches more and more people, there
will be great thanksgiving, and God will receive more and
more glory.
[16]That is why we never give up. Though our bodies
are dying, our spirits are* being renewed every day.
[17]For our present troubles are small and won't last very
long. Yet they produce for us a glory that vastly out-
weighs them and will last forever! [18]So we don't look at
the troubles we can see now; rather, we fix our gaze on
things that cannot be seen. For the things we see now
will soon be gone, but the things we cannot see will last
forever.

THE PURPOSE OF PROBLEMS 4:8-18

As Paul realized, there is a purpose in suffering. Problems and human limitations have several benefits: (1) They help us remember Christ's suffering for us; (2) they keep us humble; (3) they help us look beyond this brief life; (4) they prove our faith to others; and (5) they give God the opportunity to demonstrate his great power. Problems getting you down? Don't give up! ■

5

NEW BODIES

For we know that when this earthly tent we live in is taken
down (that is, when we die and leave this earthly body),
we will have a house in heaven, an eternal body made for
us by God himself and not by human hands. [2]We grow
weary in our present bodies, and we long to put on our
heavenly bodies like new clothing. [3]For we will put on
heavenly bodies; we will not be spirits without bodies.*
[4]While we live in these earthly bodies, we groan and sigh,
but it's not that we want to die and get rid of these bodies
that clothe us. Rather, we want to put on our new bodies
so that these dying bodies will be swallowed up by life.
[5]God himself has prepared us for this, and as a guarantee
he has given us his Holy Spirit.
[6]So we are always confident, even though we know
that as long as we live in these bodies we are not at home
with the Lord. [7]For we live by believing and not by seeing.
[8]Yes, we are fully confident, and we would rather be away
from these earthly bodies, for then we will be at home
with the Lord. [9]So whether we are here in this body or
away from this body, our goal is to please him. [10]For we
must all stand before Christ to be judged. We will each
receive whatever we deserve for the good or evil we have
done in this earthly body.

WE ARE GOD'S AMBASSADORS

[11]Because we understand our fearful responsibility to the
Lord, we work hard to persuade others. God knows we
are sincere, and I hope you know this, too. [12]Are we com-
mending ourselves to you again? No, we are giving you a
reason to be proud of us,* so you can answer those who
brag about having a spectacular ministry rather than having a sincere heart. [13]If it seems we are crazy, it is to bring
glory to God. And if we are in our right minds, it is for
your benefit. [14]Either way, Christ's love controls us.*
Since we believe that Christ died for all, we also believe
that we have all died to our old life.* [15]He died for everyone so that those who receive his new life will no longer
live for themselves. Instead, they will live for Christ, who
died and was raised for them.
[16]So we have stopped evaluating others from a human
point of view. At one time we thought of Christ merely
from a human point of view. How differently we know
him now! [17]This means that anyone who belongs to

4:13 Ps 116:10. **4:14** Some manuscripts read *who raised Jesus.* **4:16** Greek *our inner being is.* **5:3** Greek *we will not be naked.* **5:12** Some manuscripts read *proud of yourselves.* **5:14a** Or *urges us on.* **5:14b** Greek *Since one died for all, then all died.*

Christ has become a new person. The
old life is gone; a new life has begun!
[18]And all of this is a gift from God,
who brought us back to himself
through Christ. And God has given us
this task of reconciling people to
him. [19]For God was in Christ, reconciling the world to himself, no longer counting people's sins against
them. And he gave us this wonderful
message of reconciliation. [20]So we
are Christ's ambassadors; God is
making his appeal through us. We
speak for Christ when we plead,
"Come back to God!" [21]For God made
Christ, who never sinned, to be the
offering for our sin,* so that we
could be made right with God through Christ.

> Anyone who belongs to Christ has become a new person. The old life is gone; a new life has begun!
>
> 2 CORINTHIANS 5:17

MADE NEW 5:16-17

Christians are brand-new people on the *inside*. The Holy Spirit gives believers new life. Having new life isn't the same as being reformed or reeducated. Those who trust Christ learn to adjust to a new attitude and a new boss: God. Are you feeling like nothing's really new under the sun? There is: you. ■

6

As God's partners,* we beg you not to accept this
marvelous gift of God's kindness and then ignore it. [2]For
God says,

"At just the right time, I heard you.
On the day of salvation, I helped you."*

Indeed, the "right time" is now. Today is the day of
salvation.

PAUL'S HARDSHIPS

[3]We live in such a way that no one will stumble because of
us, and no one will find fault with our ministry. [4]In everything we do, we show that we are true ministers of God. We
patiently endure troubles and hardships and calamities of
every kind. [5]We have been beaten, been put in prison,
faced angry mobs, worked to exhaustion, endured sleepless nights, and gone without food. [6]We prove ourselves by
our purity, our understanding, our patience, our kindness,
by the Holy Spirit within us,* and by our sincere love. [7]We
faithfully preach the truth. God's power is working in us.
We use the weapons of righteousness in the right hand for
attack and the left hand for defense. [8]We serve God
whether people honor us or despise us, whether they slander us or praise us. We are honest, but they call us impostors. [9]We are ignored, even though we are well known. We
live close to death, but we are still alive. We have been
beaten, but we have not been killed. [10]Our hearts ache, but
we always have joy. We are poor, but we give spiritual
riches to others. We own nothing, and
yet we have everything.
[11]Oh, dear Corinthian friends! We
have spoken honestly with you, and
our hearts are open to you. [12]There is
no lack of love on our part, but you
have withheld your love from us. [13]I
am asking you to respond as if you
were my own children. Open your
hearts to us!

THE TEMPLE OF THE LIVING GOD

[14]Don't team up with those who are unbelievers. How can righteousness be a
partner with wickedness? How can
light live with darkness? [15]What harmony can there be between Christ and
the devil*? How can a believer be a partner with an unbe-
liever? [16]And what union can there be between God's
temple and idols? For we are the temple of the living God.
As God said:

5:21 Or *to become sin itself*. 6:1 Or *As we work together*. 6:2 Isa 49:8 (Greek version). 6:6 Or *by our holiness of spirit*. 6:15 Greek *Beliar*; various other manuscripts render this proper name of the devil as *Belian*, *Beliab*, or *Belial*.

I've been a Christian for about nine months. Although I've made a lot of friends who are Christians, I still have quite a few who aren't. Can I still hang out with friends who aren't Christians? Why or why not?

Find a quarter and two pennies. Place the quarter on a table. Put the two pennies about five inches below the quarter, one inch apart.

Now, pretend God is the quarter, you are the penny on the left, and your friend is the penny on the right. As you grow closer to God (move your penny up an inch or two), what happens to the distance between you and your friend? It gets wider! When only one person in a friendship moves closer to God, that's what happens to the relationship automatically!

Our closest friends have an effect on our behavior. That's why hanging around with old friends who aren't Christians will probably not help you become a stronger Christian. This is the message of 2 Corinthians 6:14. If you spend all of your time with unbelievers, you'll tend to become like them and not move closer to God.

In the early stages of your Christian life, you need friends who will help you grow spiritually. However, God doesn't want you to be totally isolated from those who aren't Christians. If you're going to be Christ's representative to those who don't know him (see 2 Cor 5:18-20), you have to be around them!

"I will live in them
and walk among them.
I will be their God,
and they will be my people.*
17 Therefore, come out from among unbelievers,
and separate yourselves from them, says the LORD.
Don't touch their filthy things,
and I will welcome you.*
18 And I will be your Father,
and you will be my sons and daughters,
says the LORD Almighty.*"

7

Because we have these promises, dear friends, let
us cleanse ourselves from everything that can defile our
body or spirit. And let us work toward complete holiness
because we fear God.
2Please open your hearts to us. We have not done
wrong to anyone, nor led anyone astray, nor taken advantage of anyone. 3I'm not saying this to condemn you. I
said before that you are in our hearts, and we live or die
together with you. 4I have the highest confidence in you,
and I take great pride in you. You have greatly encouraged me and made me happy despite all our troubles.

PAUL'S JOY AT THE CHURCH'S REPENTANCE

5When we arrived in Macedonia, there was no rest for us.
We faced conflict from every direction, with battles on
the outside and fear on the inside. 6But God, who encourages those who are discouraged, encouraged us by the arrival of Titus. 7His presence was a joy, but so was the news
he brought of the encouragement he received from you.
When he told us how much you long to see me, and how
sorry you are for what happened, and how loyal you are to
me, I was filled with joy!
8I am not sorry that I sent that severe letter to you,
though I was sorry at first, for I know it was painful to you
for a little while. 9Now I am glad I sent it, not because it
hurt you, but because the pain caused you to repent and
change your ways. It was the kind of sorrow God wants
his people to have, so you were not harmed by us in any
way. 10For the kind of sorrow God wants us to experience
leads us away from sin and results in salvation. There's no
regret for that kind of sorrow. But worldly sorrow, which
lacks repentance, results in spiritual death.
11Just see what this godly sorrow produced in you!
Such earnestness, such concern to clear yourselves, such
indignation, such alarm, such longing to see me, such
zeal, and such a readiness to punish wrong. You showed
that you have done everything necessary to make things
right. 12My purpose, then, was not to write about who did
the wrong or who was wronged. I wrote to you so that in
the sight of God you could see for yourselves how loyal
you are to us. 13We have been greatly encouraged by this.
In addition to our own encouragement, we were especially delighted to see how happy Titus was about the way
all of you welcomed him and set his mind* at ease. 14I had
told him how proud I was of you—and you didn't disappoint me. I have always told you the truth, and now my
boasting to Titus has also proved true! 15Now he cares for
you more than ever when he remembers the way all of
you obeyed him and welcomed him with such fear and
deep respect. 16I am very happy now because I have complete confidence in you.

ADMIT IT 7:11

Paul praised the Corinthians for clearing up an especially troublesome situation. How do you deal with correction for a fault? Do you tend to be defensive when confronted? Don't let pride keep you from admitting when you're wrong. Confrontation can be a tool for growth. ■

8

A CALL TO GENEROUS GIVING

Now I want you to know, dear brothers and sisters,* what
God in his kindness has done through the churches in
Macedonia. 2They are being tested by many troubles, and
they are very poor. But they are also filled with abundant
joy, which has overflowed in rich generosity.
3For I can testify that they gave not only what they
could afford, but far more. And they did it of their own
free will. 4They begged us again and again for the privilege of sharing in the gift for the believers* in Jerusalem.
5They even did more than we had hoped, for their first
action was to give themselves to the Lord and to us, just as
God wanted them to do.
6So we have urged Titus, who encouraged your giving
in the first place, to return to you and encourage you to
finish this ministry of giving. 7Since you excel in so many
ways—in your faith, your gifted speakers, your knowledge, your enthusiasm, and your love from us*—I want
you to excel also in this gracious act of giving.
8I am not commanding you to do this. But I am testing
how genuine your love is by comparing it with the eagerness of the other churches.
9You know the generous grace of our Lord Jesus Christ.
Though he was rich, yet for your sakes he became poor,
so that by his poverty he could make you rich.
10Here is my advice: It would be good for you to finish
what you started a year ago. Last year you were the first
who wanted to give, and you were the first to begin doing
it. 11Now you should finish what you started. Let the eagerness you showed in the beginning be matched now by
your giving. Give in proportion to what you have.
12Whatever you give is acceptable if you give it eagerly.
And give according to what you have, not what you don't
have. 13Of course, I don't mean your giving should make
life easy for others and hard for yourselves. I only mean
that there should be some equality. 14Right now you have
plenty and can help those who are in need. Later, they will

6:16 Lev 26:12; Ezek 37:27. **6:17** Isa 52:11; Ezek 20:34 (Greek version). **6:18** 2 Sam 7:14. **7:13** Greek *his spirit.* **8:1** Greek *brothers.* **8:4** Greek *for God's holy people.* **8:7** Some manuscripts read *your love for us.*

Principles of Confrontation in 2 Corinthians

Sometimes rebuke is necessary, but it must be used with caution. The purpose of any rebuke, confrontation, or discipline is to help people, not hurt them.

Be firm. (7:9; 10:2)

Affirm all you see that is good. (7:4)

Be accurate and honest. (7:14; 8:21)

Know the facts. (11:22-27)

Follow up after the confrontation. (7:13; 12:14)

Be gentle after being firm. (7:15; 13:11-13)

Speak words that reflect Christ's message, not your own ideas. (10:3, 12-13; 12:19)

Use discipline only when all else fails. (13:2)

have plenty and can share with you when you need it. In
this way, things will be equal. [15]As the Scriptures say,

"Those who gathered a lot had nothing left over,
and those who gathered only a little had enough."*

TITUS AND HIS COMPANIONS

[16]But thank God! He has given Titus the same enthusiasm
for you that I have. [17]Titus welcomed our request that he
visit you again. In fact, he himself was very eager to go and
see you. [18]We are also sending another brother with Titus.
All the churches praise him as a preacher of the Good
News. [19]He was appointed by the churches to accompany
us as we take the offering to Jerusalem*—a service that
glorifies the Lord and shows our eagerness to help.

[20]We are traveling together to guard against any criticism for the way we are handling this generous gift. [21]We
are careful to be honorable before the Lord, but we also
want everyone else to see that we are honorable.

[22]We are also sending with them another of our brothers who has proven himself many times and has shown
on many occasions how eager he is. He is now even more
enthusiastic because of his great confidence in you. [23]If
anyone asks about Titus, say that he is my partner who
works with me to help you. And the brothers with him
have been sent by the churches,* and they bring honor to
Christ. [24]So show them your love, and prove to all the
churches that our boasting about you is justified.

9 THE COLLECTION FOR CHRISTIANS IN JERUSALEM

I really don't need to write to you about this ministry of
giving for the believers in Jerusalem.* [2]For I know how
eager you are to help, and I have been boasting to the
churches in Macedonia that you in Greece* were ready to
send an offering a year ago. In fact, it was your enthusiasm that stirred up many of the Macedonian believers to
begin giving.

[3]But I am sending these brothers to be sure you really are
ready, as I have been telling them, and that your money is all
collected. I don't want to be wrong in my boasting about
you. [4]We would be embarrassed—not to mention your own
embarrassment—if some Macedonian believers came with
me and found that you weren't ready after all I had told
them! [5]So I thought I should send these brothers ahead of
me to make sure the gift you promised is ready. But I want
it to be a willing gift, not one given grudgingly.

THE POINT OF GIVING 9:6-15

Paul used the illustration of seeds to explain that the resources God gives us are not to be hidden, foolishly devoured, or thrown away. Instead, they should be used to help others. (See also 8:1-5.) When we invest what God has given us in his work, he will provide us with even more to give. What has God given you lately? How will you use what you've been given?

[6]Remember this—a farmer who plants only a few seeds
will get a small crop. But the one who plants generously will
get a generous crop. [7]You must each decide in your heart
how much to give. And don't give reluctantly or in response
to pressure. "For God loves a person who gives cheerfully."*
[8]And God will generously provide all you need. Then you will
always have everything you need and plenty left over to
share with others. [9]As the Scriptures say,

"They share freely and give generously to the poor.
Their good deeds will be remembered forever."*

[10]For God is the one who provides seed for the farmer
and then bread to eat. In the same way, he will provide

8:15 Exod 16:18. 8:19 See 1 Cor 16:3-4. 8:23 Greek *are apostles of the churches.* 9:1 Greek *about the offering for God's holy people.* 9:2 Greek *in Achaia,* the southern region of the Greek peninsula. *Macedonia* was in the northern region of Greece. 9:7 See footnote on Prov 22:8. 9:9 Ps 112:9.

and increase your resources and then produce a great harvest of generosity* in you.

[11]Yes, you will be enriched in every way so that you can always be generous. And when we take your gifts to those who need them, they will thank God. [12]So two good things will result from this ministry of giving—the needs of the believers in Jerusalem* will be met, and they will joyfully express their thanks to God.

[13]As a result of your ministry, they will give glory to God. For your generosity to them and to all believers will prove that you are obedient to the Good News of Christ. [14]And they will pray for you with deep affection because of the overflowing grace God has given to you. [15]Thank God for this gift* too wonderful for words!

10

PAUL DEFENDS HIS AUTHORITY

Now I, Paul, appeal to you with the gentleness and kindness of Christ—though I realize you think I am timid in person and bold only when I write from far away. [2]Well, I am begging you now so that when I come I won't have to be bold with those who think we act from human motives.

[3]We are human, but we don't wage war as humans do. [4]*We use God's mighty weapons, not worldly weapons, to knock down the strongholds of human reasoning and to destroy false arguments. [5]We destroy every proud obstacle that keeps people from knowing God. We capture their rebellious thoughts and teach them to obey Christ. [6]And after you have become fully obedient, we will punish everyone who remains disobedient.

WHICH WAY? 10:3-6

In some situations, Christians must choose between two strategies: God's or man's. Paul assures us that God's mighty weapons—prayer, faith, hope, love, God's Word, the Holy Spirit—are powerful and effective (see Eph 6:10-18)! When dealing with the pride that keeps people from a relationship with Christ, we may be tempted to use our own methods. But nothing can break down Satan's barriers like God's weapons. ■

[7]Look at the obvious facts.* Those who say they belong to Christ must recognize that we belong to Christ as much as they do. [8]I may seem to be boasting too much about the authority given to us by the Lord. But our authority builds you up; it doesn't tear you down. So I will not be ashamed of using my authority.

[9]I'm not trying to frighten you by my letters. [10]For some say, "Paul's letters are demanding and forceful, but in person he is weak, and his speeches are worthless!" [11]Those people should realize that our actions when we arrive in person will be as forceful as what we say in our letters from far away.

[12]Oh, don't worry; we wouldn't dare say that we are as wonderful as these other men who tell you how important they are! But they are only comparing themselves with each other, using themselves as the standard of measurement. How ignorant!

[13]We will not boast about things done outside our area of authority. We will boast only about what has happened within the boundaries of the work God has given us, which includes our working with you. [14]We are not reaching beyond these boundaries when we claim authority over you, as if we had never visited you. For we were the first to travel all the way to Corinth with the Good News of Christ.

[15]Nor do we boast and claim credit for the work someone else has done. Instead, we hope that your faith will grow so that the boundaries of our work among you will be extended. [16]Then we will be able to go and preach the Good News in other places far beyond you, where no one else is working. Then there will be no question of our boasting about work done in someone else's territory. [17]As the Scriptures say, "If you want to boast, boast only about the LORD."*

[18]When people commend themselves, it doesn't count for much. The important thing is for the Lord to commend them.

DON'T FALL FOR IT 11:3-4

The Corinthian believers fell for messages that sounded good and seemed to make sense. Yet these messages were false teachings. Today there are many false messages that seem to make sense. Don't believe anyone simply because he or she sounds like an authority or says things you like to hear. Search the Bible and check people's words against God's Word. (See Acts 17:11.) ■

11

PAUL AND THE FALSE APOSTLES

I hope you will put up with a little more of my foolishness. Please bear with me. [2]For I am jealous for you with the jealousy of God himself. I promised you as a pure bride* to one husband—Christ. [3]But I fear that somehow your pure and undivided devotion to Christ will be corrupted, just as Eve was deceived by the cunning ways of the serpent. [4]You happily put up with whatever anyone tells you, even if they preach a different Jesus than the one we preach, or a different kind of Spirit than the one you received, or a different kind of gospel than the one you believed.

[5]But I don't consider myself inferior in any way to these "super apostles" who teach such things. [6]I may be unskilled as a speaker, but I'm not lacking in knowledge. We have made this clear to you in every possible way.

[7]Was I wrong when I humbled myself and honored you by preaching God's Good News to you without expecting anything in return? [8]I "robbed" other churches by accepting their contributions so I could serve you at no cost. [9]And when I was with you and didn't have enough to live on, I did not become a financial burden to anyone. For the brothers who came from Macedonia brought me all that I needed. I have never been a burden

9:10 Greek *righteousness.* **9:12** Greek *of God's holy people.* **9:15** Greek *his gift.* **10:4** English translations divide verses 4 and 5 in various ways. **10:7** Or *You look at things only on the basis of appearance.* **10:17** Jer 9:24. **11:2** Greek *a virgin.*

to you, and I never will be. 10As surely as the truth of
Christ is in me, no one in all of Greece* will ever stop me
from boasting about this. 11Why? Because I don't love
you? God knows that I do.
12But I will continue doing what I have always done.
This will undercut those who are looking for an opportunity to boast that their work is just like ours. 13These people are false apostles. They are deceitful workers who
disguise themselves as apostles of Christ. 14But I am not
surprised! Even Satan disguises himself as an angel of
light. 15So it is no wonder that his servants also disguise
themselves as servants of righteousness. In the end they
will get the punishment their wicked deeds deserve.

PAUL'S MANY TRIALS

16Again I say, don't think that I am a fool to talk like this. But
even if you do, listen to me, as you would to a foolish person, while I also boast a little. 17Such boasting is not from
the Lord, but I am acting like a fool. 18And since others
boast about their human achievements, I will, too. 19After
all, you think you are so wise, but you enjoy putting up with
fools! 20You put up with it when someone enslaves you,
takes everything you have, takes advantage of you, takes
control of everything, and slaps you in the face. 21I'm
ashamed to say that we've been too "weak" to do that!
But whatever they dare to boast about—I'm talking like a
fool again—I dare to boast about it, too. 22Are they Hebrews?
So am I. Are they Israelites? So am I. Are they descendants
of Abraham? So am I. 23Are they servants of Christ? I know I
sound like a madman, but I have served him far more! I have
worked harder, been put in prison more often, been
whipped times without number, and faced death again and
again. 24Five different times the Jewish leaders gave me
thirty-nine lashes. 25Three times I was beaten with rods.
Once I was stoned. Three times I was shipwrecked. Once I
spent a whole night and a day adrift at sea. 26I have traveled
on many long journeys. I have faced
danger from rivers and from robbers. I
have faced danger from my own people,
the Jews, as well as from the Gentiles. I
have faced danger in the cities, in the
deserts, and on the seas. And I have
faced danger from men who claim to be
believers but are not.* 27I have worked
hard and long, enduring many sleepless
nights. I have been hungry and thirsty
and have often gone without food. I have
shivered in the cold, without enough
clothing to keep me warm.
28Then, besides all this, I have the
daily burden of my concern for all the
churches. 29Who is weak without my
feeling that weakness? Who is led
astray, and I do not burn with anger?
30If I must boast, I would rather boast about the things
that show how weak I am. 31God, the Father of our Lord
Jesus, who is worthy of eternal praise, knows I am not lying. 32When I was in Damascus, the governor under King
Aretas kept guards at the city gates to catch me. 33I had to
be lowered in a basket through a window in the city wall
to escape from him.

> I am glad to boast about my weaknesses, so that the power of Christ can work through me.
>
> *2 CORINTHIANS 12:9*

WHEN GOD SAYS NO 12:1-10

God said no to Paul's request for healing. What is your expectation when you pray? That God will always answer yes? Many of us that believe that Jesus' invitation to "Keep on asking" (Matt 7:7) is a guaranteed "yes." But sometimes, God says no.

Let's face it: a no can sometimes seem harsh. Think about how you would feel if someone turned you down for a date. But with God, a "no" could be the best answer you could receive. In Paul's case, "no" meant that he would experience more of God's strength. Has God said no to you recently? Like Paul, do you believe that he still has your best interests at heart? ■

12 PAUL'S VISION AND HIS THORN IN THE FLESH

This boasting will do no good, but I must go on. I will reluctantly tell about visions and revelations from the Lord.
2I* was caught up to the third heaven fourteen years
ago. Whether I was in my body or out of my body, I don't
know—only God knows. 3Yes, only God knows whether I
was in my body or outside my body. But I do know 4that I
was caught up* to paradise and heard things so astounding that they cannot be expressed in words, things no human is allowed to tell.
5That experience is worth boasting about, but I'm not going to do it. I will boast only about my weaknesses. 6If I
wanted to boast, I would be no fool in doing so, because I
would be telling the truth. But I won't do it, because I don't
want anyone to give me credit beyond what they can see in
my life or hear in my message, 7even
though I have received such wonderful
revelations from God. So to keep me from
becoming proud, I was given a thorn in my
flesh, a messenger from Satan to torment
me and keep me from becoming proud.
8Three different times I begged the
Lord to take it away. 9Each time he said,
"My grace is all you need. My power
works best in weakness." So now I am
glad to boast about my weaknesses, so
that the power of Christ can work
through me. 10That's why I take pleasure in my weaknesses, and in the insults, hardships, persecutions, and
troubles that I suffer for Christ. For
when I am weak, then I am strong.

PAUL'S CONCERN FOR THE CORINTHIANS

11You have made me act like a fool—boasting like this.*
You ought to be writing commendations for me, for I am
not at all inferior to these "super apostles," even though I

11:10 Greek *Achaia,* the southern region of the Greek peninsula. **11:26** Greek *from false brothers.* **12:2** Greek *I know a man in Christ who.* **12:3-4** Greek *But I know such a man, 4that he was caught up.* **12:11** Some manuscripts omit *boasting like this.*

am nothing at all. 12When I was with you, I certainly gave
you proof that I am an apostle. For I patiently did many
signs and wonders and miracles among you. 13The only
thing I failed to do, which I do in the other churches, was to
become a financial burden to you. Please forgive me for
this wrong!

14Now I am coming to you for the third time, and I will
not be a burden to you. I don't want what you have—I
want you. After all, children don't provide for their parents. Rather, parents provide for their children. 15I will
gladly spend myself and all I have for you, even though it
seems that the more I love you, the less you love me.

16Some of you admit I was not a burden to you. But others still think I was sneaky and took advantage of you by
trickery. 17But how? Did any of the men I sent to you take
advantage of you? 18When I urged Titus to visit you and
sent our other brother with him, did Titus take advantage
of you? No! For we have the same spirit and walk in each
other's steps, doing things the same way.

19Perhaps you think we're saying these things just to
defend ourselves. No, we tell you this as Christ's servants,
and with God as our witness. Everything we do, dear
friends, is to strengthen you. 20For I am afraid that when I
come I won't like what I find, and you won't like my response. I am afraid that I will find quarreling, jealousy,
anger, selfishness, slander, gossip, arrogance, and disorderly behavior. 21Yes, I am afraid that when I come
again, God will humble me in your presence. And I will be
grieved because many of you have not given up your old
sins. You have not repented of your impurity, sexual
immorality, and eagerness for lustful pleasure.

My grandma has been a Christian for 40 years. Her life has been hard, though. Why would God allow so much trouble to come into one person's life?

Do you or someone you know work out with weights? If so, you know that the goal of weight training is to develop the muscles and make them stronger. At first, the strain of lifting causes the person to feel weak. In the long run, however, it makes him or her strong. Like a muscle, faith grows stronger when it is exercised. (See James 1:2-4.) The book of Hebrews is all about faith—how to strengthen it, how it can help you endure.

One of God's goals for us is to learn to trust him more. When a Christian asks God for more faith, he or she is really asking for more trials. God knows that only through exercise can our faith be strengthened.

Another reason for hardships can be found in 2 Corinthians 1:3-5. Suffering helps us develop the compassion to help others. Our endurance through trials is very important to God. It allows him to use us to pass along comfort and encouragement to others.

Some Christians are glad that they have few problems. (Can you relate?) But our response to problems helps us to grow.

13 PAUL'S FINAL ADVICE

This is the third time I am coming to visit you (and as the
Scriptures say, "The facts of every case must be established by the testimony of two or three witnesses"*). 2I
have already warned those who had been sinning when I
was there on my second visit. Now I again warn them and
all others, just as I did before, that next time I will not spare
them.

3I will give you all the proof you want that Christ
speaks through me. Christ is not weak when he deals
with you; he is powerful among you. 4Although he was
crucified in weakness, he now lives by the power of God.
We, too, are weak, just as Christ was, but when we deal
with you we will be alive with him and will have God's
power.

5Examine yourselves to see if your faith is genuine.
Test yourselves. Surely you know that Jesus Christ is
among you*; if not, you have failed the test of genuine
faith. 6As you test yourselves, I hope you will recognize
that we have not failed the test of apostolic authority.

EXAMS 13:5

Just as we get physical examinations, Paul urges us to give ourselves spiritual examinations. We can do this by asking ourselves one question: *Am I becoming more Christlike?* If we're not taking active steps to grow closer to God, we're moving away from him. ■

7We pray to God that you will not do what is wrong by
refusing our correction. I hope we won't need to demonstrate our authority when we arrive. Do the right thing
before we come—even if that makes it look like we have
failed to demonstrate our authority. 8For we cannot oppose the truth, but must always stand for the truth. 9We
are glad to seem weak if it helps show that you are actually strong. We pray that you will become mature.

10I am writing this to you before I come, hoping that I
won't need to deal severely with you when I do come. For
I want to use the authority the Lord has given me to
strengthen you, not to tear you down.

PAUL'S FINAL GREETINGS

11Dear brothers and sisters,* I close my letter with these
last words: Be joyful. Grow to maturity. Encourage each
other. Live in harmony and peace. Then the God of love
and peace will be with you.

12Greet each other with Christian love.* 13All of God's
people here send you their greetings.

14*May the grace of the Lord Jesus Christ, the love of
God, and the fellowship of the Holy Spirit be with you all.

13:1 Deut 19:15. 13:5 Or *in you.* 13:11 Greek *Brothers.* 13:12 Greek *with a sacred kiss.* 13:14 Some English translations include verse 13 as part of verse 12, and then verse 14 becomes verse 13.

GALATIANS

EVER KNOWN A church like Luis's? Words like *different* and *strict* don't even begin to tell the story. Maybe Luis's best friend Esteban gave the best description. He attended Luis's church for several months—then quit. Luis wanted to know why.

"I just don't like it, okay?" Esteban finally said. "It's the 'don't church.' There's like about fifty million rules, man. Don't wear certain clothes. Don't go to parties. Don't be friends with non-Christians. And the list just keeps going. Who could keep up with them? Besides, some people there act like they're *better* than people who go to other churches."

"But you said you *liked* our youth pastor and some of the messages you heard."

"I guess I did—at first. But I came home feeling more and more guilty than ever. Sorry, *tipo* [dude], but if following all those rules is how I'm supposed to get close to God, I might as well forget it."

Almost 2,000 years ago another "don't church" tried to earn God's acceptance by following rules. That's what Paul's letter to the Galatians is all about. If you think that being a Christian is all about what you do or don't do, check out Galatians.

galatians

stats

PURPOSE: To contradict the Judaizers (who taught that Gentile believers must obey the Jewish law to be saved), and to remind Christians about faith and freedom in Christ

AUTHOR: Paul

TO WHOM WRITTEN: The churches in southern Galatia founded on Paul's first missionary journey (including Iconium, Lystra, Derbe), and Christians everywhere

DATE WRITTEN: About A.D. 49, from Antioch, prior to the Jerusalem council (A.D. 50)

SETTING: The most pressing controversy of the early church was the relationship of new believers, especially Gentiles, to the Jewish laws. When this issue arose, Paul wrote a letter to address it. Later, at the council in Jerusalem, the church leaders officially resolved the conflict.

KEY PEOPLE: Paul, Peter, Barnabas, Titus, Abraham, false teachers

KEY PLACES: Galatia, Jerusalem

KEY points

SAVED BY WORKS?

Paul opposed a group of Jewish teachers who insisted that Gentile believers obey Jewish laws in order to be saved. Rules and good works can't save anyone. Only Jesus can.

FREEDOM

Paul explained the freedom that believers have through Christ. Yet freedom is a privilege that comes with responsibilities.

THE WORK OF THE HOLY SPIRIT

Paul discussed the role of the Holy Spirit in the life of a believer. He instructs us, guides us, leads us, and empowers us. When the Holy Spirit controls us, he produces his fruit (love, joy, peace, and so on) in us.

1

GREETINGS FROM PAUL

This letter is from Paul, an apostle. I was not appointed by
any group of people or any human authority, but by Jesus
Christ himself and by God the Father, who raised Jesus
from the dead.
2All the brothers and sisters* here join me in sending
this letter to the churches of Galatia.
3May God our Father and the Lord Jesus Christ* give
you grace and peace. 4Jesus gave his life for our sins, just
as God our Father planned, in order to rescue us from this
evil world in which we live. 5All glory to God forever and
ever! Amen.

THERE IS ONLY ONE GOOD NEWS

6I am shocked that you are turning away so soon from
God, who called you to himself through the loving mercy
of Christ.* You are following a different way that pretends to be the Good News 7but is not the Good News at
all. You are being fooled by those who deliberately twist
the truth concerning Christ.

> **TWISTED TRUTH 1:6-7**
>
> **Twisted truth is sometimes more difficult to spot than outright lies. The Judaizers twisted the truth about Christ because they believed that all believers had to follow Jewish laws in order to be saved. Although they claimed to follow Jesus, they denied that his death was sufficient for salvation.**
>
> **There will always be people who twist the Good News. Either they don't understand what the Bible teaches, or they're uncomfortable with the truth as it stands. How can we tell when people are twisting the truth? Find out what they teach about Jesus Christ. If what they say doesn't match the truth in God's Word, then they're twisting the truth. ■**

8Let God's curse fall on anyone, including us or even an
angel from heaven, who preaches a different kind of
Good News than the one we preached to you. 9I say again
what we have said before: If anyone preaches any other
Good News than the one you welcomed, let that person
be cursed.
10Obviously, I'm not trying to win the approval of people, but of God. If pleasing people were my goal, I would
not be Christ's servant.

PAUL'S MESSAGE COMES FROM CHRIST

11Dear brothers and sisters, I want you to understand that
the gospel message I preach is not based on mere human
reasoning. 12I received my message from no human
source, and no one taught me. Instead, I received it by
direct revelation from Jesus Christ.*
13You know what I was like when I followed the Jewish
religion—how I violently persecuted God's church. I did
my best to destroy it. 14I was far ahead of my fellow Jews
in my zeal for the traditions of my ancestors.
15But even before I was born, God chose me and called
me by his marvelous grace. Then it pleased him 16to reveal his Son to me* so that I would proclaim the Good
News about Jesus to the Gentiles.
When this happened, I did not rush out to consult with
any human being.* 17Nor did I go up to Jerusalem to consult with those who were apostles before I was. Instead, I
went away into Arabia, and later I returned to the city of
Damascus.

> **A BIG CHANGE 1:13-24**
>
> **Paul's changed life inspired many comments from people who saw or heard of him. They praised God because only he could have turned this zealous persecutor of Christians into a believer. Although we may not have had as dramatic a change as Paul had, our new life should be noticeable. When people look at you, do they recognize that God has made changes in you? ■**

18Then three years later I went to Jerusalem to get to
know Peter,* and I stayed with him for fifteen days. 19The
only other apostle I met at that time was James, the Lord's
brother. 20I declare before God that what I am writing to
you is not a lie.
21After that visit I went north into the provinces of Syria and Cilicia. 22And still the Christians in the churches in
Judea didn't know me personally. 23All they knew was
that people were saying, "The one who used to persecute
us is now preaching the very faith he tried to destroy!"
24And they praised God because of me.

2

THE APOSTLES ACCEPT PAUL

Then fourteen years later I went back to Jerusalem again,
this time with Barnabas; and Titus came along, too. 2I
went there because God revealed to me that I should go.
While I was there I met privately with those considered
to be leaders of the church and shared with them the
message I had been preaching to the Gentiles. I wanted to
make sure that we were in agreement, for fear that all my
efforts had been wasted and I was running the race for
nothing. 3And they supported me and did not even demand that my companion Titus be circumcised, though
he was a Gentile.*
4Even that question came up only because of some so-
called Christians there—false ones, really*—who were
secretly brought in. They sneaked in to spy on us and take
away the freedom we have in Christ Jesus. They wanted to
enslave us and force us to follow their Jewish regulations.
5But we refused to give in to them for a single moment.
We wanted to preserve the truth of the gospel message
for you.

1:2 Greek *brothers;* also in 1:11. 1:3 Some manuscripts read *God the Father and our Lord Jesus Christ.* 1:6 Some manuscripts read *through loving mercy.* 1:12 Or *by the revelation of Jesus Christ.* 1:16a Or *in me.* 1:16b Greek *with flesh and blood.* 1:18 Greek *Cephas.* 2:3 Greek *a Greek.* 2:4 Greek *some false brothers.*

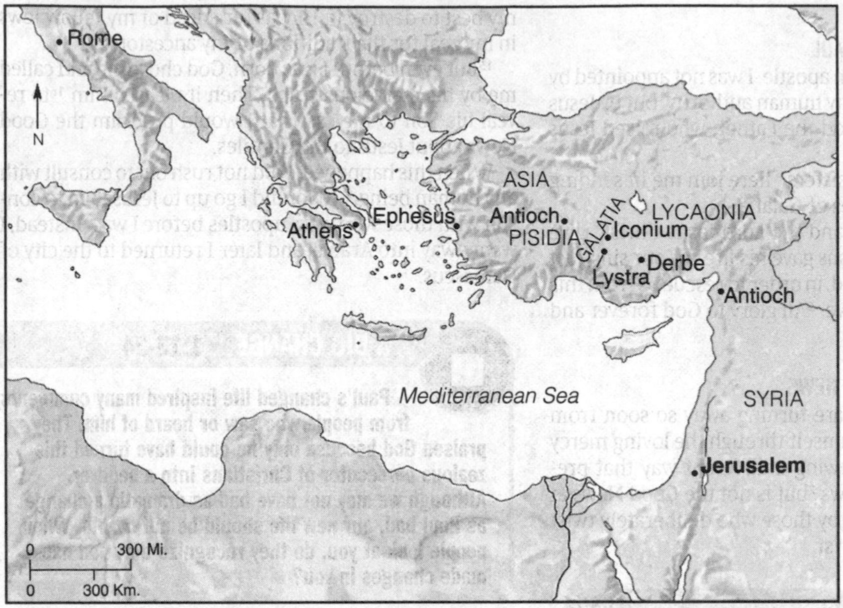

CITIES IN GALATIA
Paul visited several cities in Galatia on each of his three missionary journeys. On his first journey he went through Antioch in Pisidia, Iconium, Lystra, and Derbe, then retraced his steps. On his second journey he went by land from Antioch in Syria through the four cities in Galatia. On his third journey he also went through those cities on the main route to Ephesus.

[6]And the leaders of the church had nothing to add to
what I was preaching. (By the way, their reputation as
great leaders made no difference to me, for God has no
favorites.) [7]Instead, they saw that God had given me the
responsibility of preaching the gospel to the Gentiles,
just as he had given Peter the responsibility of preaching
to the Jews. [8]For the same God who worked through Peter
as the apostle to the Jews also worked through me as the
apostle to the Gentiles.
[9]In fact, James, Peter,* and John, who were known as
pillars of the church, recognized the gift God had given
me, and they accepted Barnabas and me as their co-
workers. They encouraged us to keep preaching to the
Gentiles, while they continued their work with the Jews.
[10]Their only suggestion was that we keep on helping the
poor, which I have always been eager to do.

CONCERN FOR THOSE IN NEED 2:10

Here the apostles referred to the poor people of Jerusalem. While many Gentile believers were financially comfortable, the Jerusalem church suffered from a famine in Palestine (see Acts 11:28-30). Much of Paul's time was spent gathering funds for the Jewish Christians (Acts 24:17; Rom 15:25-29; 1 Cor 16:1-4; 2 Cor 8). What can you do to show your concern for those in need? ■

PAUL CONFRONTS PETER

[11]But when Peter came to Antioch, I had to oppose him to
his face, for what he did was very wrong. [12]When he first
arrived, he ate with the Gentile Christians, who were not
circumcised. But afterward, when some friends of James
came, Peter wouldn't eat with the Gentiles anymore. He
was afraid of criticism from these people who insisted on
the necessity of circumcision. [13]As a result, other Jewish
Christians followed Peter's hypocrisy, and even Barnabas
was led astray by their hypocrisy.
[14]When I saw that they were not following the truth of
the gospel message, I said to Peter in front of all the others, "Since you, a Jew by birth, have discarded the Jewish
laws and are living like a Gentile, why are you now trying
to make these Gentiles follow the Jewish traditions?
[15]"You and I are Jews by birth, not 'sinners' like the
Gentiles. [16]Yet we know that a person is made right with
God by faith in Jesus Christ, not by obeying the law. And
we have believed in Christ Jesus, so that we might be
made right with God because of our faith in Christ, not
because we have obeyed the law. For no one will ever be
made right with God by obeying the law."*
[17]But suppose we seek to be made right with God
through faith in Christ and then we are found guilty
because we have abandoned the law. Would that mean
Christ has led us into sin? Absolutely not! [18]Rather, I am a
sinner if I rebuild the old system of law I already tore
down. [19]For when I tried to keep the law, it condemned
me. So I died to the law—I stopped trying to meet all its
requirements—so that I might live for God. [20]My old self
has been crucified with Christ.* It is no longer I who live,
but Christ lives in me. So I live in this earthly body by
trusting in the Son of God, who loved me and gave himself for me. [21]I do not treat the grace of God as meaningless. For if keeping the law could make us right with God,
then there was no need for Christ to die.

2:9 Greek *Cephas;* also in 2:11, 14. **2:16** Some translators hold that the quotation extends through verse 14; others through verse 16; and still others through verse 21. **2:20** Some English translations put this sentence in verse 19.

What Is the Law?

Part of the Jewish law included those laws found in the Old Testament. In the Old Testament there were three categories of law: ceremonial laws, civil laws, and moral laws. When Paul says that non-Jews (Gentiles) are no longer bound by these laws, he is not saying that the Old Testament laws do not apply to us today. He is saying certain types of laws may not apply to us.

CEREMONIAL LAW

This kind of law relates specifically to Israel's worship (for example, see Lev 1:1-13). Its primary purpose was to point forward to Jesus Christ. Therefore, these laws were no longer necessary after Jesus' death and resurrection. While we are no longer bound by ceremonial laws, the principles behind them—to worship and love a holy God—still apply. The Jewish Christians often accused the Gentile Christians of violating the ceremonial law.

CIVIL LAW

This type of law dictated Israel's daily living (for example, see Deut 24:10-11). Because modern society and culture are so radically different, some of these guidelines cannot be followed specifically. But the principles behind the commands should guide our conduct. At times, Paul asked Gentile Christians to follow some of these laws, not because they had to, but to promote unity.

MORAL LAW

This sort of law is the direct command of God—for example, the Ten Commandments (Exod 20:1-17). It requires strict obedience. It reveals the nature and will of God, and it still applies to us today. We are to obey this moral law, not to obtain salvation, but to live in ways pleasing to God.

3

THE LAW AND FAITH IN CHRIST

Oh, foolish Galatians! Who has cast an evil spell on you? For the meaning of Jesus Christ's death was made as clear to you as if you had seen a picture of his death on the cross. [2]Let me ask you this one question: Did you receive the Holy Spirit by obeying the law of Moses? Of course not! You received the Spirit because you believed the message you heard about Christ. [3]How foolish can you be? After starting your Christian lives in the Spirit, why are you now trying to become perfect by your own human effort? [4]Have you experienced* so much for nothing? Surely it was not in vain, was it?

[5]I ask you again, does God give you the Holy Spirit and work miracles among you because you obey the law? Of course not! It is because you believe the message you heard about Christ.

[6]In the same way, "Abraham believed God, and God counted him as righteous because of his faith."* [7]The real children of Abraham, then, are those who put their faith in God.

[8]What's more, the Scriptures looked forward to this time when God would declare the Gentiles to be righteous because of their faith. God proclaimed this good news to Abraham long ago when he said, "All nations will be blessed through you."* [9]So all who put their faith in Christ share the same blessing Abraham received because of his faith.

[10]But those who depend on the law to make them right with God are under his curse, for the Scriptures say, "Cursed is everyone who does not observe and obey all the commands that are written in God's Book of the Law."* [11]So it is clear that no one can be made right with God by trying to keep the law. For the Scriptures say, "It is through faith that a righteous person has life."* [12]This way of faith is very different from the way of law, which says, "It is through obeying the law that a person has life."*

[13]But Christ has rescued us from the curse pronounced by the law. When he was hung on the cross, he took upon himself the curse for our wrongdoing. For it is written in the Scriptures, "Cursed is everyone who is hung on a tree."* [14]Through Christ Jesus, God has blessed the Gentiles with the same blessing he promised to Abraham, so that we who are believers might receive the promised* Holy Spirit through faith.

THE LAW AND GOD'S PROMISE

[15]Dear brothers and sisters,* here's an example from everyday life. Just as no one can set aside or amend an irrevocable agreement, so it is in this case. [16]God gave the promises to Abraham and his child.* And notice that the Scripture doesn't say "to his children,*" as if it meant many descendants. Rather, it says "to his child"—and that, of course, means Christ. [17]This is what I am trying to say: The agreement God made with Abraham could not be canceled 430 years later when God gave the law to Moses. God would be breaking his promise. [18]For if the inheritance could be received by keeping the law, then it would not be the result of accepting God's promise. But God graciously gave it to Abraham as a promise.

[19]Why, then, was the law given? It was given alongside

3:4 Or *Have you suffered.* **3:6** Gen 15:6. **3:8** Gen 12:3; 18:18; 22:18. **3:10** Deut 27:26. **3:11** Hab 2:4. **3:12** Lev 18:5. **3:13** Deut 21:23 (Greek version). **3:14** Some manuscripts read *the blessing of the.* **3:15** Greek *Brothers.* **3:16a** Greek *seed;* also in 3:16c, 19. See notes on Gen 12:7 and 13:15. **3:16b** Greek *seeds.*

the promise to show people their sins. But the law was designed to last only until the coming of the child who was
promised. God gave his law through angels to Moses, who
was the mediator between God and the people. 20Now a
mediator is helpful if more than one party must reach an
agreement. But God, who is one, did not use a mediator
when he gave his promise to Abraham.

21Is there a conflict, then, between God's law and God's
promises?* Absolutely not! If the law could give us new
life, we could be made right with God by obeying it. 22But
the Scriptures declare that we are all prisoners of sin, so
we receive God's promise of freedom only by believing in
Jesus Christ.

GOD'S CHILDREN THROUGH FAITH

23Before the way of faith in Christ was available to us, we
were placed under guard by the law. We were kept in
protective custody, so to speak, until the way of faith was
revealed.

24Let me put it another way. The law was our guardian
until Christ came; it protected us until we could be made
right with God through faith. 25And now that the way of
faith has come, we no longer need the law as our
guardian.

26For you are all children* of God through faith in
Christ Jesus. 27And all who have been united with Christ
in baptism have put on Christ, like putting on new
clothes.* 28There is no longer Jew or Gentile,* slave or
free, male and female. For you are all one in Christ Jesus.
29And now that you belong to Christ, you are the true children* of Abraham. You are his heirs, and God's promise
to Abraham belongs to you.

DIFFERENCES 3:28

Race, social or economic status, gender, and age differences make no difference to God—all people are welcome. Yet these differences have often been the means of dividing us. In what ways do you show your belief in the unity of all believers in Christ? Is your faith not only color-blind, but also blind to status or age as well? ■

4

Think of it this way. If a father dies and leaves an inheritance for his young children, those children are not
much better off than slaves until they grow up, even
though they actually own everything their father had.
2They have to obey their guardians until they reach whatever age their father set. 3And that's the way it was with us
before Christ came. We were like children; we were
slaves to the basic spiritual principles* of this world.

4But when the right time came, God sent his Son, born
of a woman, subject to the law. 5God sent him to buy freedom for us who were slaves to the law, so that he could
adopt us as his very own children.* 6And because we* are
his children, God has sent the Spirit of his Son into our
hearts, prompting us to call out, "Abba, Father."* 7Now
you are no longer a slave but God's own child.* And since
you are his child, God has made you his heir.

PAUL'S CONCERN FOR THE GALATIANS

8Before you Gentiles knew God, you were slaves to so-
called gods that do not even exist. 9So now that you know
God (or should I say, now that God knows you), why do
you want to go back again and become slaves once more
to the weak and useless spiritual principles of this world?
10You are trying to earn favor with God by observing certain days or months or seasons or years. 11I fear for you.
Perhaps all my hard work with you was for nothing.
12Dear brothers and sisters,* I plead with you to live as I
do in freedom from these things, for I have become like
you Gentiles—free from those laws.

CORRECTED 4:1-16

Paul didn't become popular after he criticized the Galatians for turning away from their first faith in Christ. (See also 1:6-7.) Human nature hasn't changed much. We still get angry when we're scolded. How do you usually react when challenged? Are you willing to receive the correction with humility and to carefully think it over? ■

You did not mistreat me when I first preached to you.
13Surely you remember that I was sick when I first
brought you the Good News. 14But even though my condition tempted you to reject me, you did not despise me
or turn me away. No, you took me in and cared for me as
though I were an angel from God or even Christ Jesus
himself. 15Where is that joyful and grateful spirit you felt
then? I am sure you would have taken out your own eyes
and given them to me if it had been possible. 16Have I
now become your enemy because I am telling you the
truth?

17Those false teachers are so eager to win your favor,
but their intentions are not good. They are trying to shut
you off from me so that you will pay attention only to
them. 18If someone is eager to do good things for you,
that's all right; but let them do it all the time, not just
when I'm with you.

19Oh, my dear children! I feel as if I'm going through labor pains for you again, and they will continue until
Christ is fully developed in your lives. 20I wish I were with
you right now so I could change my tone. But at this distance I don't know how else to help you.

ABRAHAM'S TWO CHILDREN

21Tell me, you who want to live under the law, do you
know what the law actually says? 22The Scriptures say
that Abraham had two sons, one from his slave wife and
one from his freeborn wife.* 23The son of the slave wife

3:21 Some manuscripts read *and the promises?* 3:26 Greek *sons.* 3:27 Greek *have put on Christ.* 3:28 Greek *Jew or Greek.* 3:29 Greek *seed.* 4:3 Or *powers;* also in 4:9. 4:5 Greek *sons;* also in 4:6. 4:6a Greek *you.* 4:6b *Abba* is an Aramaic term for "father." 4:7 Greek *son;* also in 4:7b. 4:12 Greek *brothers;* also in 4:28, 31. 4:22 See Gen 16:15; 21:2-3.

FREEDOM

Hope storms upstairs, slams her bedroom door, and flings herself onto the bed. Burying her face in a pillow, she lets out a yell of disgust.

Rolling over, she stares at the ceiling and begins thinking:

Ooooh. I can't believe them! Why don't they just go ahead and put bars around my room? They don't let me do anything. They ask me six million questions about everything. They hate all my friends. They try to make me dress like a loser.

Hope glances at the calendar above her desk.

Nine more months—then I can go to college and do whatever I want. I'll be totally free. If I don't want to go to church, I won't go. If I want to trash my room and leave it that way the whole semester, I can. I'll be able to hang out whenever I want with whoever I want without Mom and Bill totally humiliating me. **She shakes her head at the thought of her mother and stepfather.**

I can't wait to leave! No more missing out on life. There'll be parties, tons of hot guys, and . . .

Hope's daydream is shattered by a voice yelling: "Hope! Come pick up your shoes from out of the middle of the living room floor—now!"

Hope groans and heads downstairs, mumbling, "Enjoy it now, Mother. Because in nine months, I'm so outta here!"

What's Hope's definition of freedom? Would she really be free? Why or why not? Check out Galatians 5:16-25. Can freedom have limits? Why or why not?

was born in a human attempt to bring about the fulfillment of God's promise. But the son of the freeborn wife
was born as God's own fulfillment of his promise.
[24]These two women serve as an illustration of God's
two covenants. The first woman, Hagar, represents
Mount Sinai where people received the law that enslaved
them. [25]And now Jerusalem is just like Mount Sinai in
Arabia,* because she and her children live in slavery to
the law. [26]But the other woman, Sarah, represents the
heavenly Jerusalem. She is the free woman, and she is our
mother. [27]As Isaiah said,

"Rejoice, O childless woman,
you who have never given birth!
Break into a joyful shout,
you who have never been in labor!
For the desolate woman now has more children
than the woman who lives with her husband!"*

[28]And you, dear brothers and sisters, are children of
the promise, just like Isaac. [29]But you are now being persecuted by those who want you to keep the law, just as
Ishmael, the child born by human effort, persecuted
Isaac, the child born by the power of the Spirit.
[30]But what do the Scriptures say about that? "Get rid
of the slave and her son, for the son of the slave woman
will not share the inheritance with the free woman's
son."* [31]So, dear brothers and sisters, we are not children of the slave woman; we are children of the free
woman.

5 FREEDOM IN CHRIST

So Christ has truly set us free. Now make sure that you
stay free, and don't get tied up again in slavery to the law.
[2]Listen! I, Paul, tell you this: If you are counting on circumcision to make you right with God, then Christ will be
of no benefit to you. [3]I'll say it again. If you are trying to
find favor with God by being circumcised, you must obey
every regulation in the whole law of Moses. [4]For if you are
trying to make yourselves right with God by keeping the
law, you have been cut off from Christ! You have fallen
away from God's grace.
[5]But we who live by the Spirit eagerly wait to receive by
faith the righteousness God has promised to us. [6]For
when we place our faith in Christ Jesus, there is no benefit in being circumcised or being uncircumcised. What is
important is faith expressing itself in love.

4:25 Greek *And Hagar, which is Mount Sinai in Arabia, is now like Jerusalem;* other manuscripts read *And Mount Sinai in Arabia is now like Jerusalem.* **4:27** Isa 54:1. **4:30** Gen 21:10.

Okay. Taking drugs is wrong. I get it. But what, if anything, does the Bible say about 'em?

There are some topics that the Bible doesn't mention directly. For example, you won't find a Scripture that discusses CDs with explicit lyrics. Maybe you would naturally avoid them or maybe you wouldn't, depending on what music you or your friends like. But you will find Scriptures on wisdom and the value of positive words.

You won't find a Scripture on drug usage (the illegal kind). But other Scriptures imply that this behavior is wrong.

In Galatians 5:21, Christians are warned against "envy, drunkenness, wild parties, and other sins like these." In other words, any situation that causes you to lose control—whether through drugs or alcohol—is dangerous.

In health class and on TV commercials, you've heard that drugs can cause permanent damage to the human body. For that reason alone, resisting the temporary thrill of a chemical high is wise. That's just common sense. But drug abuse doesn't always mean the illegal kind. Many people have become addicted to prescription drugs and have had a tough time kicking the habit.

The Bible *is* specific about the best kind of control to be under: the Holy Spirit's control. Check out Galatians 5:22-23. See also Romans 12:1-2; 1 Corinthians 6:19-20; and 3 John 1:2.

7You were running the race so well.
Who has held you back from following the truth? 8It certainly isn't God,
for he is the one who called you to
freedom. 9This false teaching is like a
little yeast that spreads through the
whole batch of dough! 10I am trusting
the Lord to keep you from believing
false teachings. God will judge that
person, whoever he is, who has been
confusing you.
11Dear brothers and sisters,* if I
were still preaching that you must be
circumcised—as some say I do—why
am I still being persecuted? If I were no
longer preaching salvation through the
cross of Christ, no one would be offended. 12I just wish that those troublemakers who want to mutilate you by circumcision would
mutilate themselves.*
13For you have been called to live in freedom, my
brothers and sisters. But don't use your freedom to satisfy your sinful nature. Instead, use your freedom to
serve one another in love. 14For the whole law can be
summed up in this one command: "Love your neighbor
as yourself."* 15But if you are always biting and devouring one another, watch out! Beware of destroying one
another.

> The Holy Spirit produces . . . fruit in our lives: love, joy, peace, patience, kindness, goodness, faithfulness, gentleness, and self-control.
>
> *GALATIANS 5:22-23*

LIVING BY THE SPIRIT'S POWER

16So I say, let the Holy Spirit guide your lives. Then you
won't be doing what your sinful nature craves. 17The sinful nature wants to do evil, which is just the opposite of
what the Spirit wants. And the Spirit gives us desires that
are the opposite of what the sinful nature desires. These
two forces are constantly fighting each other, so you are
not free to carry out your good intentions. 18But when
you are directed by the Spirit, you are not under obligation to the law of Moses.

FRUIT 5:22-23

The Holy Spirit produces character traits, not specific actions. If we want the fruit of the Holy Spirit to develop within us, we must recognize that all of these characteristics are found in Christ. The way to develop them is to first develop a relationship with him (see John 15:4-5). As a result, we'll fulfill the intended purpose of the law—loving God and people (5:14). Which of the qualities in this passage most needs further development in your life? ■

19When you follow the desires of your sinful nature,
the results are very clear: sexual immorality, impurity,
lustful pleasures, 20idolatry, sorcery, hostility, quarreling, jealousy, outbursts of anger, selfish ambition,
dissension, division, 21envy, drunk-
enness, wild parties, and other sins
like these. Let me tell you again, as I
have before, that anyone living that
sort of life will not inherit the Kingdom of God.
22But the Holy Spirit produces this
kind of fruit in our lives: love, joy,
peace, patience, kindness, goodness,
faithfulness, 23gentleness, and self-
control. There is no law against these
things!
24Those who belong to Christ Jesus
have nailed the passions and desires
of their sinful nature to his cross and
crucified them there. 25Since we are
living by the Spirit, let us follow the
Spirit's leading in every part of our
lives. 26Let us not become conceited, or provoke one another, or be jealous of one another.

EVERY PART 5:25

God is interested in all aspects of our lives, not just the spiritual part. As we live by the Holy Spirit's power, we need to submit every aspect of our lives—emotional, physical, social, intellectual, and vocational—to God. This is a process that requires perseverance. How much of your life does God control? ■

6 WE HARVEST WHAT WE PLANT

Dear brothers and sisters, if another believer* is overcome
by some sin, you who are godly* should gently and humbly
help that person back onto the right path. And be careful
not to fall into the same temptation yourself. 2Share each
other's burdens, and in this way obey the law of Christ. 3If
you think you are too important to help someone, you are
only fooling yourself. You are not that important.
4Pay careful attention to your own work, for then you
will get the satisfaction of a job well done, and you won't
need to compare yourself to anyone else. 5For we are
each responsible for our own conduct.
6Those who are taught the word of God should provide
for their teachers, sharing all good things with them.
7Don't be misled—you cannot mock the justice of God.
You will always harvest what you plant. 8Those who live
only to satisfy their own sinful nature will harvest decay
and death from that sinful nature. But those who live to
please the Spirit will harvest everlasting life from the
Spirit. 9So let's not get tired of doing what is good. At just
the right time we will reap a harvest of blessing if we
don't give up. 10Therefore, whenever we have the opportunity, we should do good to everyone—especially to
those in the family of faith.

5:11 Greek *Brothers;* similarly in 5:13. 5:12 Or *castrate themselves,* or *cut themselves off from you;* Greek reads *cut themselves off.*
5:14 Lev 19:18. 6:1a Greek *Brothers, if a man.* 6:1b Greek *spiritual.*

LOOK AT JESUS 6:4

When you do your very best, you feel good about the results. Consequently, there is no need to compare yourself with others. Yet people make comparisons for many reasons. Some point out others' flaws in order to feel better about themselves. Others simply want reassurance that they are doing well. When you're tempted to compare, look at Jesus Christ. His example will inspire you to do your very best. His loving acceptance will comfort you when you fall short of your goals. ■

PAUL'S FINAL ADVICE

11NOTICE WHAT LARGE LETTERS I USE AS I WRITE THESE
CLOSING WORDS IN MY OWN HANDWRITING.
12Those who are trying to force you to be circumcised
want to look good to others. They don't want to be
persecuted for teaching that the cross of Christ alone can
save. 13And even those who advocate circumcision don't
keep the whole law themselves. They only want you to be
circumcised so they can boast about it and claim you as
their disciples.
14As for me, may I never boast about anything except
the cross of our Lord Jesus Christ. Because of that
cross,* my interest in this world has been crucified,
and the world's interest in me has also died. 15It doesn't
matter whether we have been circumcised or not.
What counts is whether we have been transformed
into a new creation. 16May God's peace and mercy be
upon all who live by this principle; they are the new
people of God.*
17From now on, don't let anyone trouble me with these
things. For I bear on my body the scars that show I belong
to Jesus.
18Dear brothers and sisters,* may the grace of our Lord
Jesus Christ be with your spirit. Amen.

6:14 Or *Because of him.* **6:16** Greek *this principle, and upon the Israel of God.* **6:18** Greek *Brothers.*

EPHESIANS

AN ARGUMENT with a friend . . . A hug from Mom . . . A note in your locker . . . A prayer of thanks . . .

Every event of every day underlines this fundamental fact: *Life is made up of relationships.* We relate in a "horizontal" way to other people; we relate in a "vertical" manner to our Creator. Pretty basic stuff, right?

But here's where things get profound: Our problems, individual and national, are due to *broken relationships.* Because we fail to relate properly to God and to each other, we lie, cheat, drink and drive, abort our babies, fight wars, pollute, buy and sell drugs, ignore the needy, commit suicide, and do many other wrong things.

But *Jesus Christ can repair our broken relationships!*

First, Jesus pardons our sins, bringing us into a right relationship with God. (Get this—by faith in Christ we become his children . . . eternally!) Then Jesus gives us the wisdom and the power to build stronger horizontal ties—with parents, friends, bosses . . . even enemies!

Can your relationships stand a little improving? Check out Ephesians. The first three chapters explain how Jesus made knowing God in a personal way possible for us. The rest of the book provides practical tips for getting along with people.

Hey, it just might change your life!

ephesians

stats

PURPOSE: To strengthen the faith of the believers in Ephesus by explaining the nature and purpose of the church—the body of Christ

AUTHOR: Paul

TO WHOM WRITTEN: The church at Ephesus and believers everywhere

DATE WRITTEN: About A.D. 60, from Rome, during Paul's imprisonment there

SETTING: The letter was not written to confront any heresy or problem. It was sent with Tychicus (see Acts 20:4; Eph 6:21) to encourage area churches. Paul spent over three years with the believers at Ephesus; he was very close to them. His last meeting with the Ephesian elders was at Miletus (Acts 20:17-38)—a meeting filled with great sadness since Paul was leaving them forever.

KEY PEOPLE: Paul, Tychicus

KEY points

CHRIST, THE CENTER

Jesus is the focus of history as well as the head of his body, the church. Because Christ is central to everything, his priorities must be central to us.

NEW FAMILY

Because God through Christ paid our penalty for sin and forgave us, we have been reconciled to him. Being united with Christ means that we are one family in Christ. Because we all belong to him, we have the responsibility of living together in harmony.

CHRISTIAN CONDUCT

Paul encourages all Christians to make wise decisions. With that goal in mind, God provides his Holy Spirit to enable us to live his way.

1 GREETINGS FROM PAUL

This letter is from Paul, chosen by the will of God to be an
apostle of Christ Jesus.
I am writing to God's holy people in Ephesus,* who are
faithful followers of Christ Jesus.
2May God our Father and the Lord Jesus Christ give you
grace and peace.

UNSOLVED MYSTERY? 1:3-5

Paul's declaration that God "chose us in Christ" emphasizes that God made forgiveness possible. We didn't influence God's decision to save us; he did it according to his plan. (See also 2:10.) The mystery of salvation originated in the timeless mind of God long before we existed. Because of Christ, we are "holy and without fault in his eyes." This is one mystery you don't have to solve—just believe. ■

SPIRITUAL BLESSINGS

3All praise to God, the Father of our Lord Jesus Christ, who
has blessed us with every spiritual blessing in the heavenly realms because we are united with Christ. 4Even before he made the world, God loved us and chose us in
Christ to be holy and without fault in his eyes. 5God decided in advance to adopt us into his own family by bringing us to himself through Jesus Christ. This is what he
wanted to do, and it gave him great pleasure. 6So we praise
God for the glorious grace he has poured out on us who
belong to his dear Son.* 7He is so rich in kindness and
grace that he purchased our freedom with the blood of
his Son and forgave our sins. 8He has showered his kindness on us, along with all wisdom and understanding.
9God has now revealed to us his mysterious plan regarding Christ, a plan to fulfill his own good pleasure.
10And this is the plan: At the right time he will bring
everything together under the authority of Christ—
everything in heaven and on earth. 11Furthermore, because we are united with Christ, we have received an inheritance from God,* for he chose us in advance, and he
makes everything work out according to his plan.
12God's purpose was that we Jews who were the first to
trust in Christ would bring praise and glory to God. 13And
now you Gentiles have also heard the truth, the Good
News that God saves you. And when you believed in
Christ, he identified you as his own* by giving you the
Holy Spirit, whom he promised long ago. 14The Spirit is
God's guarantee that he will give us the inheritance he
promised and that he has purchased us to be his own
people. He did this so we would praise and glorify him.

PAUL'S PRAYER FOR SPIRITUAL WISDOM

15Ever since I first heard of your strong faith in the Lord
Jesus and your love for God's people everywhere,* 16I
have not stopped thanking God for you. I pray for you
constantly, 17asking God, the glorious Father of our Lord
Jesus Christ, to give you spiritual wisdom* and insight so
that you might grow in your knowledge of God. 18I pray
that your hearts will be flooded with light so that you can
understand the confident hope he has given to those he

1:1 The most ancient manuscripts do not include *in Ephesus*. **1:6** Greek *to us in the beloved*. **1:11** Or *we have become God's inheritance*. **1:13** Or *he put his seal on you*. **1:15** Some manuscripts read *your faithfulness to the Lord Jesus and to God's people everywhere*. **1:17** Or *to give you the Spirit of wisdom*.

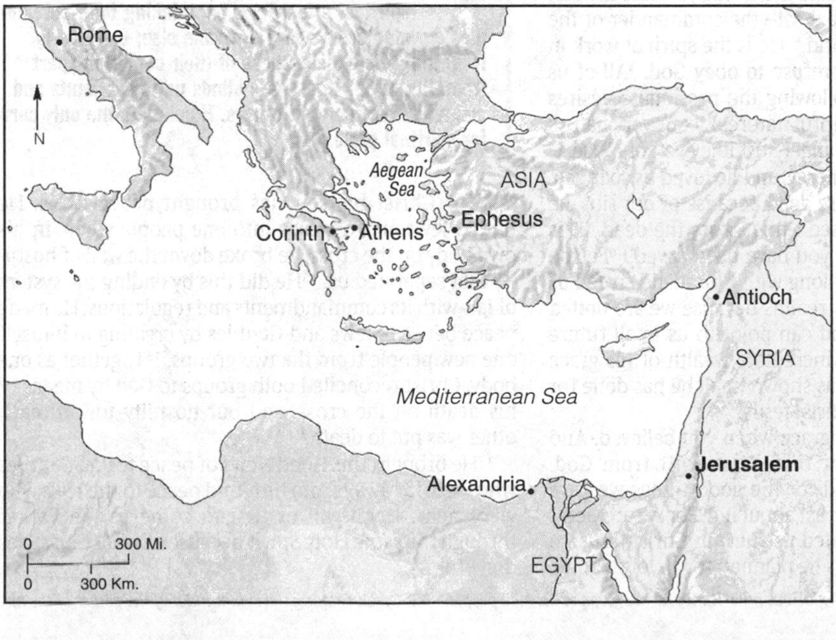

LOCATION OF EPHESUS
Ephesus was a strategic city, ranking in importance with Alexandria in Egypt and Antioch in Syria as a port. It lay on the western-most edge of Asia Minor (modern-day Turkey), the most important port on the Aegean Sea on the main route from Rome to the east.

Our Life Before and After Christ

BEFORE	AFTER
Under God's curse	Loved by God
Doomed because of our sins	Shown God's mercy and given salvation
Went along with the crowd	Stand for Christ and truth
God's enemies	God's children
Enslaved to Satan	Free to love and serve Christ
Followed our evil thoughts and passions	Seated with Christ in glory
Under God's anger	Given undeserved favor
Spiritually dead	Given new spiritual life in Christ

called—his holy people who are his rich and glorious inheritance.*
19I also pray that you will understand the incredible
greatness of God's power for us who believe him. This is
the same mighty power 20that raised Christ from the dead
and seated him in the place of honor at God's right hand
in the heavenly realms. 21Now he is far above any ruler or
authority or power or leader or anything else—not only in
this world but also in the world to come. 22God has put all
things under the authority of Christ and has made him
head over all things for the benefit of the church. 23And
the church is his body; it is made full and complete by
Christ, who fills all things everywhere with himself.

2 MADE ALIVE WITH CHRIST

Once you were dead because of your disobedience and
your many sins. 2You used to live in sin, just like the rest
of the world, obeying the devil—the commander of the
powers in the unseen world.* He is the spirit at work in
the hearts of those who refuse to obey God. 3All of us
used to live that way, following the passionate desires
and inclinations of our sinful nature. By our very nature
we were subject to God's anger, just like everyone else.
4But God is so rich in mercy, and he loved us so much,
5that even though we were dead because of our sins, he
gave us life when he raised Christ from the dead. (It is
only by God's grace that you have been saved!) 6For he
raised us from the dead along with Christ and seated us
with him in the heavenly realms because we are united
with Christ Jesus. 7So God can point to us in all future
ages as examples of the incredible wealth of his grace
and kindness toward us, as shown in all he has done for
us who are united with Christ Jesus.
8God saved you by his grace when you believed. And
you can't take credit for this; it is a gift from God.
9Salvation is not a reward for the good things we have
done, so none of us can boast about it. 10For we are God's
masterpiece. He has created us anew in Christ Jesus, so
we can do the good things he planned for us long ago.

ONENESS AND PEACE IN CHRIST

11Don't forget that you Gentiles used to be outsiders. You
were called "uncircumcised heathens" by the Jews, who
were proud of their circumcision, even though it affected only their bodies and not their hearts. 12In those
days you were living apart from Christ. You were excluded from citizenship among the people of Israel, and
you did not know the covenant promises God had made
to them. You lived in this world without God and without
hope. 13But now you have been united with Christ Jesus.
Once you were far away from God, but now you have
been brought near to him through the blood of Christ.

SPIRITUAL PRIDE 2:11-13

Jews and Gentiles alike could be guilty of spiritual pride: Jews for thinking their ceremonies elevated them above everyone else; Gentiles for forgetting the hopelessness of their condition apart from Christ. Spiritual pride blinds us to our faults and magnifies the faults of others. Humility is the only cure for spiritual pride. ■

14For Christ himself has brought peace to us. He
united Jews and Gentiles into one people when, in his
own body on the cross, he broke down the wall of hostility that separated us. 15He did this by ending the system
of law with its commandments and regulations. He made
peace between Jews and Gentiles by creating in himself
one new people from the two groups. 16Together as one
body, Christ reconciled both groups to God by means of
his death on the cross, and our hostility toward each
other was put to death.
17He brought this Good News of peace to you Gentiles
who were far away from him, and peace to the Jews who
were near. 18Now all of us can come to the Father
through the same Holy Spirit because of what Christ has
done for us.

1:18 Or *called, and the rich and glorious inheritance he has given to his holy people.* **2:2** Greek *obeying the commander of the power of the air.*

A TEMPLE FOR THE LORD

19So now you Gentiles are no longer strangers and foreigners. You are citizens along with all of God's holy people. You are members of God's family. 20Together, we are his house, built on the foundation of the apostles and the prophets. And the cornerstone is Christ Jesus himself. 21We are carefully joined together in him, becoming a holy temple for the Lord. 22Through him you Gentiles are also being made part of this dwelling where God lives by his Spirit.

3

GOD'S MYSTERIOUS PLAN REVEALED

When I think of all this, I, Paul, a prisoner of Christ Jesus for the benefit of you Gentiles* . . . 2assuming, by the way, that you know God gave me the special responsibility of extending his grace to you Gentiles. 3As I briefly wrote earlier, God himself revealed his mysterious plan to me. 4As you read what I have written, you will understand my insight into this plan regarding Christ. 5God did not reveal it to previous generations, but now by his Spirit he has revealed it to his holy apostles and prophets.

6And this is God's plan: Both Gentiles and Jews who believe the Good News share equally in the riches inherited by God's children. Both are part of the same body, and both enjoy the promise of blessings because they belong to Christ Jesus.* 7By God's grace and mighty power, I have been given the privilege of serving him by spreading this Good News.

8Though I am the least deserving of all God's people, he graciously gave me the privilege of telling the Gentiles about the endless treasures available to them in Christ. 9I was chosen to explain to everyone* this mysterious plan that God, the Creator of all things, had kept secret from the beginning.

10God's purpose in all this was to use the church to display his wisdom in its rich variety to all the unseen rulers and authorities in the heavenly places. 11This was his eternal plan, which he carried out through Christ Jesus our Lord.

12Because of Christ and our faith in him,* we can now come boldly and confidently into God's presence. 13So please don't lose heart because of my trials here. I am suffering for you, so you should feel honored.

PAUL'S PRAYER FOR SPIRITUAL GROWTH

14When I think of all this, I fall to my knees and pray to the Father,* 15the Creator of everything in heaven and on earth.* 16I pray that from his glorious, unlimited resources he will empower you with inner strength through his Spirit. 17Then Christ will make his home in your hearts as you trust in him. Your roots will grow down into God's love and keep you strong. 18And may you have the power to understand, as all God's people should, how wide, how long, how high, and how deep his love is. 19May you experience the love of Christ, though it is too great to understand fully. Then you will be made complete with all the fullness of life and power that comes from God.

20Now all glory to God, who is able, through his mighty power at work within us, to accomplish infinitely more than we might ask or think. 21Glory to him in the church and in Christ Jesus through all generations forever and ever! Amen.

4

UNITY IN THE BODY

Therefore I, a prisoner for serving the Lord, beg you to lead a life worthy of your calling, for you have been called by God. 2Always be humble and gentle. Be patient with each other, making allowance for each other's faults because of your love. 3Make every effort to keep yourselves united in the Spirit, binding yourselves together with peace. 4For there is one body and one Spirit, just as you have been called to one glorious hope for the future. 5There is one Lord, one faith, one baptism, 6and one God and Father, who is over all and in all and living through all.

7However, he has given each one of us a special gift* through the generosity of Christ. 8That is why the Scriptures say,

3:1 Paul resumes this thought in verse 14: "When I think of all this, I fall to my knees and pray to the Father." 3:6 Or *because they are united with Christ Jesus.* 3:9 Some manuscripts omit *to everyone.* 3:12 Or *Because of Christ's faithfulness.* 3:14 Some manuscripts read *the Father of our Lord Jesus Christ.* 3:15 Or *from whom every family in heaven and on earth takes its name.* 4:7 Greek *a grace.*

What does "spiritual growth" mean?

Spiritual growth is a lot like physical growth. To stay healthy and grow physically, we must eat the right foods, exercise, and get plenty of rest. You've heard that since you were a child. According to Scripture, especially passages like Ephesians 4:14-15, growing spiritually involves the same formula.

Christians must eat the right "spiritual food": God's Word. Yet many Christians try to survive on spiritual "fast food." That is, they watch Christian shows on TV, read Christian magazines, and listen to Christian music, while cutting the Bible out of their diet. But nothing builds the body—the body of Christ—like the Bible. Everything else is supplementary.

Exercise is another body builder. Christians exercise through resisting temptation, enduring trials, serving others, and telling others about their faith. Temptation and problems test our character; serving others stretches our faith; telling people about Christ strengthens our love for him.

Christians rest through worship. Our world has a tendency to pull us in different directions like a rubber band stretched to the limit. We need sleep, rest, and times of vacation to get our physical batteries recharged. In the same way, we need worship to keep us spiritually renewed.

Spiritual growth takes time—a lifetime! This means growing in a relationship, not just changing our behavior. Growing a strong Christian life means learning how to love Jesus more each day, staying close to him, and getting to know him better.

"When he ascended to the heights,
he led a crowd of captives
and gave gifts to his people."*

9Notice that it says "he ascended." This clearly means
that Christ also descended to our lowly world.* 10And the
same one who descended is the one who ascended
higher than all the heavens, so that he might fill the entire
universe with himself.
11Now these are the gifts Christ gave to the church: the
apostles, the prophets, the evangelists, and the pastors
and teachers. 12Their responsibility is to equip God's people to do his work and build up the church, the body of
Christ. 13This will continue until we all come to such
unity in our faith and knowledge of God's Son that we will
be mature in the Lord, measuring up to the full and complete standard of Christ.
14Then we will no longer be immature like children.
We won't be tossed and blown about by every wind of
new teaching. We will not be influenced when people try
to trick us with lies so clever they sound like the truth.
15Instead, we will speak the truth in love, growing in every
way more and more like Christ, who is the head of his
body, the church. 16He makes the whole body fit together
perfectly. As each part does its own special work, it helps
the other parts grow, so that the whole body is healthy
and growing and full of love.

LITTLE BY LITTLE 4:17-24

Paul encouraged the Ephesians to leave behind their old life of sin now that they were followers of Christ. The Christian life is a process. Despite our new nature in Christ, we don't automatically have all good thoughts and attitudes. Yet little by little, the Holy Spirit begins to change us.

As you look over the past year, do you see a process of change for the better in your thoughts, attitudes, and actions? Although change may be slow, it comes about if you trust God to change you. For more about our new nature as believers see 2 Corinthians 5:17; Romans 6:6; 8:9; Galatians 5:16-26; and Colossians 3:3-15. ■

LIVING AS CHILDREN OF LIGHT

17With the Lord's authority I say this: Live no longer as the
Gentiles do, for they are hopelessly confused. 18Their
minds are full of darkness; they wander far from the life
God gives because they have closed their minds and
hardened their hearts against him. 19They have no sense
of shame. They live for lustful pleasure and eagerly practice every kind of impurity.
20But that isn't what you learned about Christ. 21Since
you have heard about Jesus and have learned the truth
that comes from him, 22throw off your old sinful nature
and your former way of life, which is corrupted by lust
and deception. 23Instead, let the Spirit renew your
thoughts and attitudes. 24Put on your new nature, created
to be like God—truly righteous and holy.
25So stop telling lies. Let us tell our neighbors the truth,
for we are all parts of the same body. 26And "don't sin by
letting anger control you."* Don't let the sun go down while
you are still angry, 27for anger gives a foothold to the devil.
28If you are a thief, quit stealing. Instead, use your
hands for good hard work, and then give generously to
others in need. 29Don't use foul or abusive language. Let
everything you say be good and helpful, so that your
words will be an encouragement to those who hear them.
30And do not bring sorrow to God's Holy Spirit by the
way you live. Remember, he has identified you as his
own,* guaranteeing that you will be saved on the day of
redemption.
31Get rid of all bitterness, rage, anger, harsh words, and
slander, as well as all types of evil behavior. 32Instead, be
kind to each other, tenderhearted, forgiving one another,
just as God through Christ has forgiven you.

5 LIVING IN THE LIGHT

Imitate God, therefore, in everything you do, because you
are his dear children. 2Live a life filled with love, following
the example of Christ. He loved us* and offered himself
as a sacrifice for us, a pleasing aroma to God.
3Let there be no sexual immorality, impurity, or greed
among you. Such sins have no place among God's people.
4Obscene stories, foolish talk, and coarse jokes—these are
not for you. Instead, let there be thankfulness to God. 5You
can be sure that no immoral, impure, or greedy person will
inherit the Kingdom of Christ and of God. For a greedy person is an idolater, worshiping the things of this world.
6Don't be fooled by those who try to excuse these sins,
for the anger of God will fall on all who disobey him.
7Don't participate in the things these people do. 8For
once you were full of darkness, but now you have light
from the Lord. So live as people of light! 9For this light
within you produces only what is good and right and true.

SPEAK OUT 5:10-14

Paul advised the Ephesians to expose "worthless deeds of evil and darkness." That advice is for us as well. Often our silence is interpreted as approval. God needs people who will take a stand for what's right. Are you willing? ■

10Carefully determine what pleases the Lord. 11Take no
part in the worthless deeds of evil and darkness; instead,
expose them. 12It is shameful even to talk about the things
that ungodly people do in secret. 13But their evil intentions will be exposed when the light shines on them, 14for
the light makes everything visible. This is why it is said,

"Awake, O sleeper,
rise up from the dead,
and Christ will give you light."

4:8 Ps 68:18. 4:9 Or *to the lowest parts of the earth.* 4:26 Ps 4:4. 4:30 Or *has put his seal on you.* 5:2 Some manuscripts read *loved you.*

God's Armor for Us

We are engaged in a spiritual battle—all believers find themselves subject to Satan's attacks because they are no longer on Satan's side. Thus, Paul tells us in Ephesians 6:10-17 to use every piece of God's armor to resist Satan's attacks and to stand true to God in the midst of them.

Piece of Armor	*Use*	*Application*
BELT	Truth	Satan fights with lies, and sometimes his lies sound like truth; but believers have God's truth, which can defeat Satan's lies.
BODY ARMOR	God's righteousness	Satan often attacks our heart—the seat of our emotions, self-worth, and trust. God's righteousness is the breastplate that protects our heart and ensures his approval. He approves of us because we have trusted Christ to save us and cleanse our hearts from sin.
SHOES	The peace that comes from the Good News	Satan wants us to think that telling others the Good News is a worthless and hopeless task—the size of the task is too big, and the negative responses are too much to handle. But the "shoes" God gives us are the true peace that is available in God, which prepares us to share the news with others.
SHIELD	Faith	The shield of faith protects us from Satan's fiery darts in the form of insults, setbacks, and temptations. With God's perspective, we can see beyond our circumstances and know that ultimate victory is ours.
HELMET	Salvation	Satan wants to make us doubt God, Jesus, and our salvation. The helmet protects our mind from doubting God's saving work for us.
SWORD	The Word of God	The sword is the only weapon of offense in this list of armor. There are times when we need to take the offensive against Satan. When we are tempted, we need to trust in the truth of God's Word.

LIVING BY THE SPIRIT'S POWER
15So be careful how you live. Don't live like fools, but like
those who are wise. 16Make the most of every opportunity
in these evil days. 17Don't act thoughtlessly, but understand
what the Lord wants you to do. 18Don't be drunk with wine,
because that will ruin your life. Instead, be filled with the
Holy Spirit, 19singing psalms and hymns and spiritual songs
among yourselves, and making music to the Lord in your
hearts. 20And give thanks for everything to God the Father
in the name of our Lord Jesus Christ.

SPIRIT-GUIDED RELATIONSHIPS: WIVES AND HUSBANDS
21And further, submit to one another out of reverence for
Christ.
22For wives, this means submit to your husbands as to
the Lord. 23For a husband is the head of his wife as Christ
is the head of the church. He is the Savior of his body, the
church. 24As the church submits to Christ, so you wives
should submit to your husbands in everything.
25For husbands, this means love your wives, just as
Christ loved the church. He gave up his life for her 26to
make her holy and clean, washed by the cleansing of
God's word.* 27He did this to present her to himself as a
glorious church without a spot or wrinkle or any other
blemish. Instead, she will be holy and without fault. 28In
the same way, husbands ought to love their wives as they
love their own bodies. For a man who loves his wife actually shows love for himself. 29No one hates his own body
but feeds and cares for it, just as Christ cares for the
church. 30And we are members of his body.
31As the Scriptures say, "A man leaves his father and
mother and is joined to his wife, and the two are united
into one."* 32This is a great mystery, but it is an illustration of the way Christ and the church are one. 33So again I
say, each man must love his wife as he loves himself, and
the wife must respect her husband.

6
CHILDREN AND PARENTS
Children, obey your parents because you belong to the
Lord,* for this is the right thing to do. 2"Honor your father
and mother." This is the first commandment with a promise: 3If you honor your father and mother, "things will go well
for you, and you will have a long life on the earth."*
4Fathers, do not provoke your children to anger by the
way you treat them. Rather, bring them up with the discipline and instruction that comes from the Lord.

SLAVES AND MASTERS
5Slaves, obey your earthly masters with deep respect and
fear. Serve them sincerely as you would serve Christ.
6Try to please them all the time, not just when they are

5:26 Greek *washed by water with the word.* **5:31** Gen 2:24. **6:1** Or *Children, obey your parents who belong to the Lord;* some manuscripts read simply *Children, obey your parents.* **6:2-3** Exod 20:12; Deut 5:16.

keeping it real

"Connor, what've you decided about going to the college we talked about? The deadline is coming up, isn't it?"

Though my dad was trying to be casual, I could tell he wanted an answer.

"Yeah, I've decided I don't want to go to that school. But you won't take that for an answer," I said.

"Connor," Dad began, but I could tell by his tone what he was going to say. We'd been through this too many times before. I didn't want to go; he wanted me to. His pressuring me just made me angry.

I talked to my youth pastor about that the next day. He suggested that I read Ephesians. So I did. I began to understand that I can't always do what I want. Loving God means wanting to do his will, not mine.

When I read Ephesians 6:1-3, I realized that God often chooses to work through my earthly parents. So, I tried to think through all the reasons why Dad wanted me to go to that particular college and why I didn't want to go. Finally, I decided to trust God and believe that he was leading me there.

Now I'm glad I attend this college. I'm really growing in my faith here.

—Connor

watching you. As slaves of Christ, do the will of God with all your heart. [7]Work with enthusiasm, as though you were working for the Lord rather than for people. [8]Remember that the Lord will reward each one of us for the good we do, whether we are slaves or free.

[9]Masters, treat your slaves in the same way. Don't threaten them; remember, you both have the same Master in heaven, and he has no favorites.

THE WHOLE ARMOR OF GOD

[10]A final word: Be strong in the Lord and in his mighty power. [11]Put on all of God's armor so that you will be able to stand firm against all strategies of the devil. [12]For we* are not fighting against flesh-and-blood enemies, but against evil rulers and authorities of the unseen world, against mighty powers in this dark world, and against evil spirits in the heavenly places.

[13]Therefore, put on every piece of God's armor so you will be able to resist the enemy in the time of evil. Then after the battle you will still be standing firm. [14]Stand your ground, putting on the belt of truth and the body armor of God's righteousness. [15]For shoes, put on the peace that comes from the Good News so that you will be fully prepared.* [16]In addition to all of these, hold up the shield of faith to stop the fiery arrows of the devil.* [17]Put on salvation as your helmet, and take the sword of the Spirit, which is the word of God.

[18]Pray in the Spirit at all times and on every occasion. Stay alert and be persistent in your prayers for all believers everywhere.*

[19]And pray for me, too. Ask God to give me the right words so I can boldly explain God's mysterious plan that the Good News is for Jews and Gentiles alike.* [20]I am in chains now, still preaching this message as God's ambassador. So pray that I will keep on speaking boldly for him, as I should.

FINAL GREETINGS

[21]To bring you up to date, Tychicus will give you a full report about what I am doing and how I am getting along. He is a beloved brother and faithful helper in the Lord's work. [22]I have sent him to you for this very purpose—to let you know how we are doing and to encourage you.

[23]Peace be with you, dear brothers and sisters,* and may God the Father and the Lord Jesus Christ give you love with faithfulness. [24]May God's grace be eternally upon all who love our Lord Jesus Christ.

6:12 Some manuscripts read *you.* **6:15** Or *For shoes, put on the readiness to preach the Good News of peace with God.* **6:16** Greek *the evil one.* **6:18** Greek *all of God's holy people.* **6:19** Greek *explain the mystery of the Good News;* some manuscripts read simply *explain the mystery.* **6:23** Greek *brothers.*

PHILIPPIANS

TIME FOR A little daydreaming:

Scenario #1: You ace all of your exams.

Scenario #2: In the biggest game of the year, you score with one second left to give your school an upset victory.

Scenario #3: You learn that the most attractive member of the opposite sex (in your whole school!) likes you.

Exciting dreams, huh? Okay, let's daydream some more:

Scenario #4: While using the computer, your dad accidentally deletes your term paper—the one you worked on for over a month that's due today.

Scenario #5: You've trained for months for track team tryouts. On the way to school, you get in a car wreck and break your ankle.

Scenario #6: Your latest crush dumps you for your best friend!

Okay, so these are more like nightmares. Is it possible to be *joyful* in bad situations like these? Believe it or not, it *is* possible to be joyful in horrible circumstances.

Facing problems or trials? Get a fresh perspective. Read Philippians, Paul's letter to the Christians in Philippi. The message is clear: Joy and contentment really *can* be ours . . . as long as we keep trusting God even when bad times hit.

philippians

stats

PURPOSE: To thank the Philippians and to encourage them in the belief that true joy comes from Jesus Christ

AUTHOR: Paul

TO WHOM WRITTEN: Christians at Philippi and all believers

DATE WRITTEN: About A.D. 61, from Rome, during Paul's imprisonment there

SETTING: Paul and his companions founded the church at Philippi on the second missionary journey (Acts 16:11-40). This was the first church established on the European continent. This group of believers sent a gift with Epaphroditus (one of their members) to be delivered to Paul (4:18).

KEY PEOPLE: Paul, Timothy, Epaphroditus, Euodia, and Syntyche

KEY PLACE: Philippi

KEY points

HUMILITY

Christ showed true humility when he laid aside his rights and privileges as God to become human. Laying aside self-interest is essential to all our relationships. When we give up the need to receive credit and praise, we'll be able to serve with joy, love, and kindness.

UNITY

Paul encouraged the Philippians to agree with one another, stop complaining, and work together. In every church, in every generation, there are problems that divide people (issues, loyalties, and conflicts). Yet the love of Christ unites all believers.

CHRISTIAN LIVING

Paul provides tips for living a successful Christian life. Developing as a mature Christian requires discipline, obedience, and perseverance.

JOY

Believers can experience contentment and peace no matter what happens. This joy comes from knowing Christ personally and from depending on his strength rather than on our own.

1

GREETINGS FROM PAUL

This letter is from Paul and Timothy, slaves of Christ
Jesus.
I am writing to all of God's holy people in Philippi
who belong to Christ Jesus, including the elders* and
deacons.
2May God our Father and the Lord Jesus Christ give you
grace and peace.

PAUL'S THANKSGIVING AND PRAYER

3Every time I think of you, I give thanks to my God.
4Whenever I pray, I make my requests for all of you with
joy, 5for you have been my partners in spreading the
Good News about Christ from the time you first heard it
until now. 6And I am certain that God, who began the
good work within you, will continue his work until it is
finally finished on the day when Christ Jesus returns.

JOY SOURCE 1:4

This is the first of many times Paul uses the word *joy* in his letter. Here he says that the Philippians were a source of joy when he prayed. By helping Paul, they were helping to spread the Gospel. Paul knew that the Philippians were willing to be used by God for whatever task he had in store for them. Has anyone ever commented that you're a source of joy for him or her? (Anyone besides your grandma, that is!) In what ways do you show a willingness to do whatever God wants? ■

7So it is right that I should feel as I do about all of you,
for you have a special place in my heart. You share with
me the special favor of God, both in my imprisonment and
in defending and confirming the truth of the Good News.
8God knows how much I love you and long for you with the
tender compassion of Christ Jesus.
9I pray that your love will overflow more and more, and
that you will keep on growing in knowledge and understanding. 10For I want you to understand what really matters, so that you may live pure and blameless lives until
the day of Christ's return. 11May you always be filled with
the fruit of your salvation—the righteous character produced in your life by Jesus Christ*—for this will bring
much glory and praise to God.

PAUL'S JOY THAT CHRIST IS PREACHED

12And I want you to know, my dear brothers and sisters,*
that everything that has happened to me here has helped
to spread the Good News. 13For everyone here, including
the whole palace guard,* knows that I am in chains because of Christ. 14And because of my imprisonment,
most of the believers* here have gained confidence and
boldly speak God's message* without fear.
15It's true that some are preaching out of jealousy and
rivalry. But others preach about Christ with pure motives.
16They preach because they love me, for they know I have
been appointed to defend the Good News. 17Those others
do not have pure motives as they preach about Christ.
They preach with selfish ambition, not sincerely, intending to make my chains more painful to me. 18But that
doesn't matter. Whether their motives are false or
genuine, the message about Christ is being preached either way, so I rejoice. And I will continue to rejoice. 19For I
know that as you pray for me and the Spirit of Jesus
Christ helps me, this will lead to my deliverance.

PAUL'S LIFE FOR CHRIST

20For I fully expect and hope that I will never be
ashamed, but that I will continue to be bold for Christ, as
I have been in the past. And I trust that my life will bring
honor to Christ, whether I live or die. 21For to me, living
means living for Christ, and dying is even better. 22But if I
live, I can do more fruitful work for Christ. So I really
don't know which is better. 23I'm torn between two desires: I long to go and be with Christ, which would be far
better for me. 24But for your sakes, it is better that I continue to live.
25Knowing this, I am convinced that I will remain alive
so I can continue to help all of you grow and experience
the joy of your faith. 26And when I come to you again, you
will have even more reason to take pride in Christ Jesus
because of what he is doing through me.

SUFFERING 1:29-30

Suffering, in and of itself, is not a privilege. But when we suffer because we faithfully represent Jesus, we know that our message and example are having an effect and that God considers us worthy to represent him (see Acts 5:41). Suffering has these additional benefits: (1) It takes us out of our comfort zone; (2) it weeds out those who are only half-serious about God; (3) it strengthens the faith of those who endure; (4) it serves as an example to others who may follow us. Suffering for our faith doesn't mean we've done something wrong. In fact, the opposite is often true—it may verify that we have been faithful. ■

LIVE AS CITIZENS OF HEAVEN

27Above all, you must live as citizens of heaven, conducting yourselves in a manner worthy of the Good News
about Christ. Then, whether I come and see you again or
only hear about you, I will know that you are standing together with one spirit and one purpose, fighting together for the faith, which is the Good News. 28Don't be
intimidated in any way by your enemies. This will be a
sign to them that they are going to be destroyed, but that
you are going to be saved, even by God himself. 29For you
have been given not only the privilege of trusting in
Christ but also the privilege of suffering for him. 30We
are in this struggle together. You have seen my struggle
in the past, and you know that I am still in the midst of it.

1:1 Or *overseers;* or *bishops.* 1:11 Greek *with the fruit of righteousness through Jesus Christ.* 1:12 Greek *brothers.* 1:13 Greek *including all the Praetorium.* 1:14a Greek *brothers in the Lord.* 1:14b Some manuscripts read *speak the message.*

keeping it real

After years of friendship, Jessica was changing. We used to share so much—including faith. But after her parents' divorce, Jessica started hanging around with a different crowd. But her new friends didn't seem to do her much good.

I was concerned about Jessica, so I finally told her in a note that I felt bad that we were drifting apart. She told me that maybe I shouldn't expect our friendship to be the same as it was before.

That hurt! I turned to God with my confusion and pain. Several verses in the Bible seemed to reveal what he wanted me to do. For instance, Philippians 2:3-4 showed me that I should put her needs before my own. Yet I have to accept that she is unwilling or unable to be a better friend. But even though I can't expect much in return, the right thing to do is to continue trying to be her friend. Romans 12:9-10 also helped me see the need for balance. I can love her, but I must not compromise my own values. Finally, James 1:19 showed me that I should think before I speak.

It still hurts that Jess and I are no longer close. Yet I believe that as long as I continue trying to relate to others in God's way, he will provide the friends I need.

—Lila

2

HAVE THE ATTITUDE OF CHRIST

Is there any encouragement from belonging to Christ?
Any comfort from his love? Any fellowship together in
the Spirit? Are your hearts tender and compassionate?
2Then make me truly happy by agreeing wholeheartedly
with each other, loving one another, and working together with one mind and purpose.
3Don't be selfish; don't try to impress others. Be humble, thinking of others as better than yourselves. 4Don't
look out only for your own interests, but take an interest in others, too.
5You must have the same attitude that Christ Jesus had.

6 Though he was God,*
he did not think of equality with God
as something to cling to.
7 Instead, he gave up his divine privileges*;
he took the humble position of a slave*
and was born as a human being.
When he appeared in human form,*
8 he humbled himself in obedience to God
and died a criminal's death on a cross.

9 Therefore, God elevated him to the place of
highest honor
and gave him the name above all other names,
10 that at the name of Jesus every knee should bow,
in heaven and on earth and under the earth,
11 and every tongue confess that Jesus Christ is Lord,
to the glory of God the Father.

SHINE BRIGHTLY FOR CHRIST

12Dear friends, you always followed my instructions
when I was with you. And now that I am away, it is even
more important. Work hard to show the results of your
salvation, obeying God with deep reverence and fear.
13For God is working in you, giving you the desire and the
power to do what pleases him.
14Do everything without complaining and arguing, 15so
that no one can criticize you. Live clean, innocent lives as
children of God, shining like bright lights in a world full
of crooked and perverse people. 16Hold firmly to the
word of life; then, on the day of Christ's return, I will be
proud that I did not run the race in vain and that my work
was not useless. 17But I will rejoice even if I lose my life,
pouring it out like a liquid offering to God,* just like your
faithful service is an offering to God. And I want all of you
to share that joy. 18Yes, you should rejoice, and I will share
your joy.

PAUL COMMENDS TIMOTHY

19If the Lord Jesus is willing, I hope to send Timothy to
you soon for a visit. Then he can cheer me up by telling
me how you are getting along. 20I have no one else like
Timothy, who genuinely cares about your welfare. 21All
the others care only for themselves and not for what matters to Jesus Christ. 22But you know how Timothy has

2:6 Or *Being in the form of God*. 2:7a Greek *he emptied himself*. 2:7b Or *the form of a slave*. 2:7c Some English translations put this phrase in verse 8. 2:17 Greek *I will rejoice even if I am to be poured out as a liquid offering*.

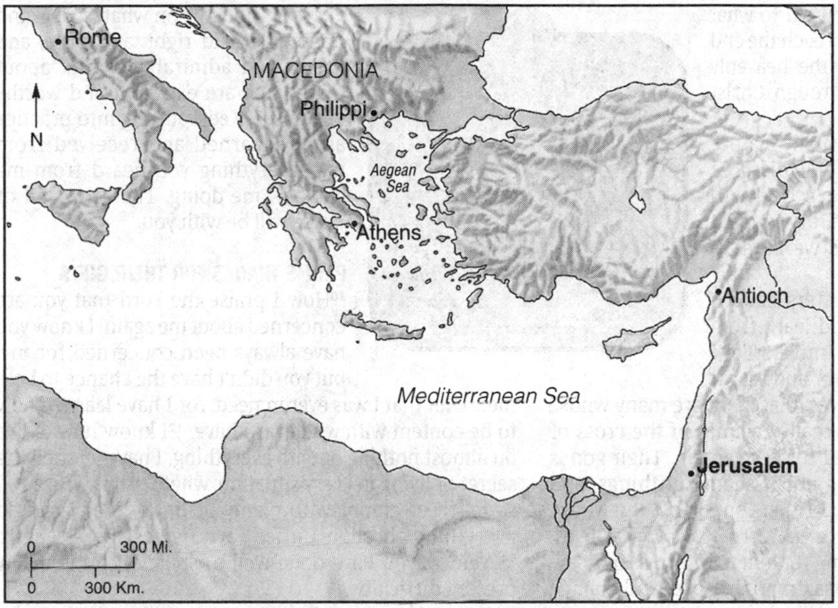

LOCATION OF PHILIPPI
Philippi sat on the Egnatian Way, the main transportation route in Macedonia, an extension of the Appian Way, which joined the eastern empire with Italy.

proved himself. Like a son with his father, he has served
with me in preaching the Good News. 23I hope to send
him to you just as soon as I find out what is going to happen to me here. 24And I have confidence from the Lord
that I myself will come to see you soon.

PAUL COMMENDS EPAPHRODITUS

25Meanwhile, I thought I should send Epaphroditus back
to you. He is a true brother, co-worker, and fellow soldier.
And he was your messenger to help me in my need. 26I am
sending him because he has been longing to see you, and
he was very distressed that you heard he was ill. 27And he
certainly was ill; in fact, he almost died. But God had
mercy on him—and also on me, so that I would not have
one sorrow after another.

28So I am all the more anxious to send him back to you,
for I know you will be glad to see him, and then I will not
be so worried about you. 29Welcome him with Christian
love* and with great joy, and give him the honor that people like him deserve. 30For he risked his life for the work
of Christ, and he was at the point of death while doing for
me what you couldn't do from far away.

3 THE PRICELESS VALUE OF KNOWING CHRIST

Whatever happens, my dear brothers and sisters,* rejoice in the Lord. I never get tired of telling you these
things, and I do it to safeguard your faith.

2Watch out for those dogs, those people who do evil,
those mutilators who say you must be circumcised to be
saved. 3For we who worship by the Spirit of God* are the
ones who are truly circumcised. We rely on what Christ
Jesus has done for us. We put no confidence in human
effort, 4though I could have confidence in my own effort
if anyone could. Indeed, if others have reason for confidence in their own efforts, I have even more!

5I was circumcised when I was eight days old. I am a
pure-blooded citizen of Israel and a member of the tribe
of Benjamin—a real Hebrew if there ever was one! I was a
member of the Pharisees, who demand the strictest obedience to the Jewish law. 6I was so zealous that I harshly
persecuted the church. And as for righteousness, I
obeyed the law without fault.

7I once thought these things were valuable, but now I
consider them worthless because of what Christ has
done. 8Yes, everything else is worthless when compared
with the infinite value of knowing Christ Jesus my Lord.
For his sake I have discarded everything else, counting it
all as garbage, so that I could gain Christ 9and become one
with him. I no longer count on my own righteousness
through obeying the law; rather, I become righteous
through faith in Christ.* For God's way of making us right
with himself depends on faith. 10I want to know Christ
and experience the mighty power that raised him from
the dead. I want to suffer with him, sharing in his death,
11so that one way or another I will experience the resurrection from the dead!

PRESSING TOWARD THE GOAL

12I don't mean to say that I have already achieved these
things or that I have already reached perfection. But I
press on to possess that perfection for which Christ Jesus
first possessed me. 13No, dear brothers and sisters, I have
not achieved it,* but I focus on this one thing: Forgetting

2:29 Greek *in the Lord.* 3:1 Greek *brothers;* also in 3:13, 17. 3:3 Some manuscripts read *worship God in spirit;* one early manuscript reads *worship in spirit.* 3:9 Or *through the faithfulness of Christ.* 3:13 Some manuscripts read *not yet achieved it.*

the past and looking forward to what lies ahead, [14]I press on to reach the end of the race and receive the heavenly prize for which God, through Christ Jesus, is calling us.

[15]Let all who are spiritually mature agree on these things. If you disagree on some point, I believe God will make it plain to you. [16]But we must hold on to the progress we have already made.

[17]Dear brothers and sisters, pattern your lives after mine, and learn from those who follow our example. [18]For I have told you often before, and I say it again with tears in my eyes, that there are many whose conduct shows they are really enemies of the cross of Christ. [19]They are headed for destruction. Their god is their appetite, they brag about shameful things, and they think only about this life here on earth. [20]But we are citizens of heaven, where the Lord Jesus Christ lives. And we are eagerly waiting for him to return as our Savior. [21]He will take our weak mortal bodies and change them into glorious bodies like his own, using the same power with which he will bring everything under his control.

> For I can do everything through Christ, who gives me strength.
>
> *PHILIPPIANS 4:13*

4

Therefore, my dear brothers and sisters,* stay true to the Lord. I love you and long to see you, dear friends, for you are my joy and the crown I receive for my work.

WORDS OF ENCOURAGEMENT

[2]Now I appeal to Euodia and Syntyche. Please, because you belong to the Lord, settle your disagreement. [3]And I ask you, my true partner,* to help these two women, for they worked hard with me in telling others the Good News. They worked along with Clement and the rest of my co-workers, whose names are written in the Book of Life.

[4]Always be full of joy in the Lord. I say it again—rejoice! [5]Let everyone see that you are considerate in all you do. Remember, the Lord is coming soon.

NO WORRIES 4:6-18

Imagine never being worried about anything! It seems like an impossibility. But Paul's advice is to turn our worries into prayers. Do you want to worry less? Then pray more! Whenever you start to worry, stop and pray. ■

[6]Don't worry about anything; instead, pray about everything. Tell God what you need, and thank him for all he has done. [7]Then you will experience God's peace, which exceeds anything we can understand. His peace will guard your hearts and minds as you live in Christ Jesus.

[8]And now, dear brothers and sisters, one final thing. Fix your thoughts on what is true, and honorable, and right, and pure, and lovely, and admirable. Think about things that are excellent and worthy of praise. [9]Keep putting into practice all you learned and received from me—everything you heard from me and saw me doing. Then the God of peace will be with you.

PAUL'S THANKS FOR THEIR GIFTS

[10]How I praise the Lord that you are concerned about me again. I know you have always been concerned for me, but you didn't have the chance to help me. [11]Not that I was ever in need, for I have learned how to be content with whatever I have. [12]I know how to live on almost nothing or with everything. I have learned the secret of living in every situation, whether it is with a full stomach or empty, with plenty or little. [13]For I can do everything through Christ,* who gives me strength. [14]Even so, you have done well to share with me in my present difficulty.

[15]As you know, you Philippians were the only ones who gave me financial help when I first brought you the Good News and then traveled on from Macedonia. No other church did this. [16]Even when I was in Thessalonica you sent help more than once. [17]I don't say this because I want a gift from you. Rather, I want you to receive a reward for your kindness.

[18]At the moment I have all I need—and more! I am generously supplied with the gifts you sent me with

4:1 Greek *brothers;* also in 4:8. 4:3 Or *loyal Syzygus.* 4:13 Greek *through the one.*

Before I became a Christian, I put some real garbage through my mind. How do I clean up my thought life?

Your mind works like a computer. If it's programmed to think about crud, that's what will happen. If it's programmed to think about things that are healthy, you'll think healthy thoughts. The hard part comes in trying to keep out the unhealthy thoughts.

So what's God's solution? Reprogram the mind! The reprogramming process begins when we realize that destructive thoughts and images are trying to get a foothold in our mind, and that we have the power to kick them out.

Philippians 4:8 provides the next step: "Fix your thoughts on what is true, and honorable, and right, and pure, and lovely, and admirable. Think about things that are excellent and worthy of praise." What will you think about?

keeping it real

Once when my grandmother was in the hospital, I heard my mom say over the phone to someone that the doctors weren't sure whether Grandma would make it.

I went to my room feeling agitated. As far as I knew, Grandma didn't know that Jesus died for her sins. I had always wanted to tell her, but how would I do it? I felt so unsure of myself. What would I say? Would she even listen to me?

I prayed about this for quite a while. Then I started reading my Bible. As I read Philippians, the thirteenth verse in chapter 4 leaped out at me: "I can do everything through Christ, who gives me strength." I believed that God was assuring me that I would know what to say to my grandmother.

I went to the hospital and told my grandmother about Jesus. She listened and later accepted Christ as her Lord and Savior!

One week later, she died. But I know she is now with the Lord. **—Jeff**

Epaphroditus. They are a sweet-smelling sacrifice that
is acceptable and pleasing to God. 19And this same God
who takes care of me will supply all your needs from his
glorious riches, which have been given to us in Christ
Jesus.
20Now all glory to God our Father forever and ever!
Amen.

PAUL'S FINAL GREETINGS

21Give my greetings to each of God's holy people—all who
belong to Christ Jesus. The brothers who are with me send
you their greetings. 22And all the rest of God's people send
you greetings, too, especially those in Caesar's household.
23May the grace of the Lord Jesus Christ be with your
spirit.

COLOSSIANS

WHO DO YOU say that Jesus is? Some believers call him God with skin on—the second person of the Trinity and the carpenter from Nazareth all rolled into one. But some nonbelievers insist that he was nothing more than just a good man. Still others regard him as a troublesome politician with a Messiah complex, who ended up being executed. Then there is the Hollywood Jesus—weak, wishy-washy, misguided, filled with contradictions, and surrounded by controversy.

So, was Jesus just a good man or a great moral teacher? Or was he, as Islam teaches, a prophet like Moses, Buddha, and Mohammed? Was he just one of many gods? Was he truly divine, or was he simply one manifestation of a divine, universal force?

There are hundreds of conflicting ideas floating around about who Jesus is. But only one of the views can be true.

Wondering what's true about Jesus? Check out the letter to the Colossians. See for yourself why the apostle Paul considered him to be "supreme over all creation" (1:15).

colossians

stats

PURPOSE: To combat errors in the church and to show that believers have everything they need in Christ

AUTHOR: Paul

TO WHOM WRITTEN: The church at Colosse, a city in Asia Minor, and believers everywhere

DATE WRITTEN: About A.D. 60, during Paul's imprisonment in Rome

SETTING: Paul had never visited Colosse. Evidently Epaphras and other converts from Paul's missionary travels had founded the church. But false teachers had infiltrated the church. Paul confronted their false doctrine with truths about Jesus.

KEY PEOPLE: Paul, Timothy, Tychicus, Onesimus, Aristarchus, Mark, Epaphras

KEY PLACES: Colosse, Laodicea (4:15-16)

KEY points

GOD WITH US

Jesus is the exact reflection of the invisible God. He is eternal, preexistent, all-powerful, and equal with the Father. To recognize Jesus as God means to allow him to call the shots in our lives.

HEAD OF THE CHURCH

Christ is the founder and leader of the church and the highest authority on earth. To acknowledge Christ as our leader, we must welcome his leadership in all we do or think.

UNITED WITH CHRIST

Jesus' death, burial, and resurrection makes forgiveness possible. Because our sin has been forgiven and we have been reconciled to God, we have a union with Christ that can never be broken.

MAN-MADE RELIGION

False teachers promoted the need to follow man-made rules. We must not let our hunger for a more fulfilling Christian experience cause us to trust in a teacher, group, or system of thought more than in Christ himself. Christ is our hope and our true source of wisdom.

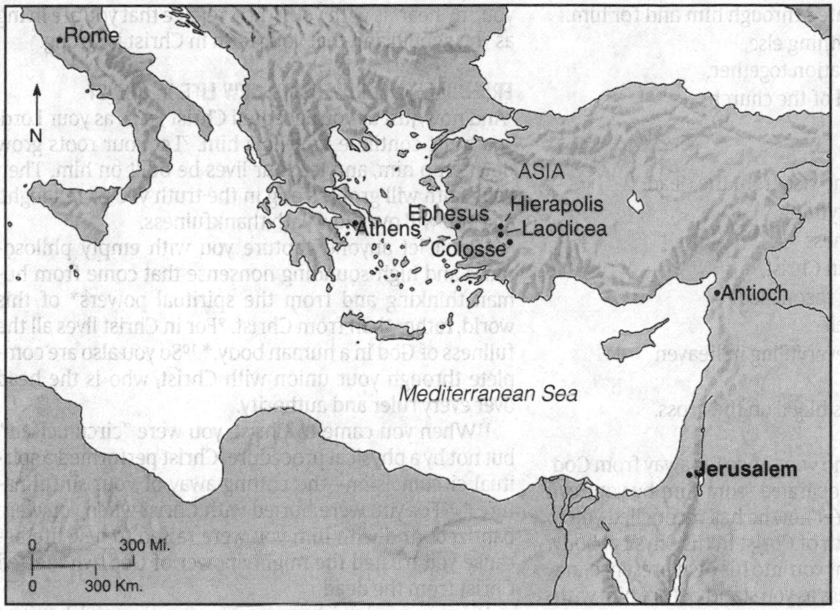

LOCATION OF COLOSSE
Paul had undoubtedly been through Laodicea on his third missionary journey because it lay on the main route to Ephesus, but he had never been to Colosse. Though a large city with a significant population, Colosse was smaller and less important than the nearby cities of Laodicea and Hieropolis.

1

GREETINGS FROM PAUL

This letter is from Paul, chosen by the will of God to be an apostle of Christ Jesus, and from our brother Timothy.

2We are writing to God's holy people in the city of Colosse, who are faithful brothers and sisters* in Christ.

May God our Father give you grace and peace.

PAUL'S THANKSGIVING AND PRAYER

3We always pray for you, and we give thanks to God, the
Father of our Lord Jesus Christ. 4For we have heard of
your faith in Christ Jesus and your love for all of God's
people, 5which come from your confident hope of what
God has reserved for you in heaven. You have had this expectation ever since you first heard the truth of the Good News.

6This same Good News that came to you is going out all over the world. It is bearing fruit everywhere by changing lives, just as it changed your lives from the day you first heard and understood the truth about God's wonderful grace.

7You learned about the Good News from Epaphras, our beloved co-worker. He is Christ's faithful servant, and he
is helping us on your behalf.* 8He has told us about the
love for others that the Holy Spirit has given you.

9So we have not stopped praying for you since we first heard about you. We ask God to give you complete knowledge of his will and to give you spiritual wisdom
and understanding. 10Then the way you live will always honor and please the Lord, and your lives will produce every kind of good fruit. All the while, you will grow as you learn to know God better and better.
11We also pray that you will be strengthened with all his glorious power so you will have all the endurance and
patience you need. May you be filled with joy,* 12always
thanking the Father. He has enabled you to share in the inheritance that belongs to his people, who live in the
light. 13For he has rescued us from the kingdom of darkness and transferred us into the Kingdom of his dear Son,
14who purchased our freedom* and forgave our sins.

HOW TO PRAY 1:9-14

Although Paul had never met the Colossians, he faithfully prayed for them. His prayers remind us to pray for others, whether we know them or not. All believers have a need to grow spiritually. You can pray for someone to (1) understand God's will, (2) gain wisdom and spiritual understanding, (3) honor God, (4) bear fruit (love, joy, peace, patience, etc.), (5) appreciate God in a deeper way, (6) be filled with God's strength, (7) stay full of Christ's joy, and (8) always be thankful. ■

CHRIST IS SUPREME

15 Christ is the visible image of the invisible God.
He existed before anything was created and is
supreme over all creation,*
16 for through him God created everything
in the heavenly realms and on earth.
He made the things we can see
and the things we can't see—
such as thrones, kingdoms, rulers, and authorities in
the unseen world.

1:2 Greek *faithful brothers.* 1:7 Or *he is ministering on your behalf;* some manuscripts read *he is ministering on our behalf.* 1:11 Or *all the patience and endurance you need with joy.* 1:14 Some manuscripts add *with his blood.* 1:15 Or *He is the firstborn of all creation.*

Everything was created through him and for him.
17 He existed before anything else,
and he holds all creation together.
18 Christ is also the head of the church,
which is his body.
He is the beginning,
supreme over all who rise from the dead.*
So he is first in everything.
19 For God in all his fullness
was pleased to live in Christ,
20 and through him God reconciled
everything to himself.
He made peace with everything in heaven
and on earth
by means of Christ's blood on the cross.

21This includes you who were once far away from God.
You were his enemies, separated from him by your evil
thoughts and actions. 22Yet now he has reconciled you to
himself through the death of Christ in his physical body.
As a result, he has brought you into his own presence, and
you are holy and blameless as you stand before him without a single fault.
23But you must continue to believe this truth and stand
firmly in it. Don't drift away from the assurance you received when you heard the Good News. The Good News
has been preached all over the world, and I, Paul, have
been appointed as God's servant to proclaim it.

PAUL'S WORK FOR THE CHURCH

24I am glad when I suffer for you in my body, for I am participating in the sufferings of Christ that continue for his
body, the church. 25God has given me the responsibility
of serving his church by proclaiming his entire message
to you. 26This message was kept secret for centuries and
generations past, but now it has been revealed to God's
people. 27For God wanted them to know that the riches
and glory of Christ are for you Gentiles, too. And this is
the secret: Christ lives in you. This gives you assurance of
sharing his glory.
28So we tell others about Christ, warning everyone and
teaching everyone with all the wisdom God has given
us. We want to present them to God, perfect* in their
relationship to Christ. 29That's why I work and struggle so
hard, depending on Christ's mighty power that works
within me.

2 I want you to know how much I have agonized for
you and for the church at Laodicea, and for many other
believers who have never met me personally. 2I want
them to be encouraged and knit together by strong ties of
love. I want them to have complete confidence that they
understand God's mysterious plan, which is Christ himself. 3In him lie hidden all the treasures of wisdom and
knowledge.
4I am telling you this so no one will deceive you with
well-crafted arguments. 5For though I am far away from
you, my heart is with you. And I rejoice that you are living
as you should and that your faith in Christ is strong.

FREEDOM FROM RULES AND NEW LIFE IN CHRIST

6And now, just as you accepted Christ Jesus as your Lord,
you must continue to follow him. 7Let your roots grow
down into him, and let your lives be built on him. Then
your faith will grow strong in the truth you were taught,
and you will overflow with thankfulness.
8Don't let anyone capture you with empty philosophies and high-sounding nonsense that come from human thinking and from the spiritual powers* of this
world, rather than from Christ. 9For in Christ lives all the
fullness of God in a human body.* 10So you also are complete through your union with Christ, who is the head
over every ruler and authority.
11When you came to Christ, you were "circumcised,"
but not by a physical procedure. Christ performed a spiritual circumcision—the cutting away of your sinful nature.* 12For you were buried with Christ when you were
baptized. And with him you were raised to new life because you trusted the mighty power of God, who raised
Christ from the dead.
13You were dead because of your sins and because
your sinful nature was not yet cut away. Then God made
you alive with Christ, for he forgave all our sins. 14He canceled the record of the charges against us and took it

1:18 Or *the firstborn from the dead.* **1:28** Or *mature.* **2:8** Or *the spiritual principles;* also in 2:20. **2:9** Or *in him dwells all the completeness of the Godhead bodily.* **2:11** Greek *the cutting away of the body of the flesh.*

I feel less mature spiritually than some of my friends who have been Christians longer. How do I catch up?

Have you ever planted a seed in a clear plastic cup? If the seed was planted close enough to the edge, you would see that the roots would grow downward first; then a few days later a plant would appear above the dirt. It was miraculous!

When you took the first step of faith to trust Christ with your life, that was like the seed being planted. From this point it's up to you and God to nourish the seed and let the roots grow deep (see Col 2:6-7).

The only difference between you and your friends is that they have had more time to get to know Jesus. This is accomplished by spending time with him. As with any relationship, time together helps you to appreciate God's character and will lead to a greater love for him (2 Pet 3:18).

As Christians, we never get to a point where we are totally mature. Our love and appreciation for God can always grow deeper as he shows us new areas in our life with which to trust him.

away by nailing it to the cross. 15In this way, he disarmed*
the spiritual rulers and authorities. He shamed them
publicly by his victory over them on the cross.
16So don't let anyone condemn you for what you eat or
drink, or for not celebrating certain holy days or new
moon ceremonies or Sabbaths. 17For these rules are only
shadows of the reality yet to come. And Christ himself is
that reality. 18Don't let anyone condemn you by insisting
on pious self-denial or the worship of angels,* saying
they have had visions about these things. Their sinful
minds have made them proud, 19and they are not connected to Christ, the head of the body. For he holds the
whole body together with its joints and ligaments, and it
grows as God nourishes it.
20You have died with Christ, and he has set you free
from the spiritual powers of this world. So why do you
keep on following the rules of the world, such as, 21"Don't
handle! Don't taste! Don't touch!"? 22Such rules are mere
human teachings about things that deteriorate as we use
them. 23These rules may seem wise because they require
strong devotion, pious self-denial, and severe bodily discipline. But they provide no help in conquering a person's evil desires.

SELF-CENTERED

Mackenzie's favorite topic for discussion, her major concern, the number one thing on her mind is . . . Mackenzie. Seriously, when we say she's stuck on herself, we're talking *really* stuck—Super-Glue style. Just look:

- **When Beth was extremely upset at not being asked to Homecoming, Mackenzie responded by going on and on about her date.**
- **When anyone asks, "How was your weekend?" Mackenzie goes on and on for twenty minutes. (Funny how she never asks anyone else that question.)**
- **When Mackenzie's neighbor called, desperately needing a baby-sitter at the last minute, Mackenzie wouldn't go, even though she had no other plans. She ended up going to work out at the health club.**
- **When Mackenzie receives money (allowance, pay, or cash from an unexpected source), she immediately goes to the mall and buys something for herself.**

Know anyone like Mackenzie? Are you like Mackenzie? Check out Colossians 1:9-12. How do Mackenzie's choices compare with the lifestyle mentioned in this passage?

CHANGES FOR THE BETTER 2:20-23

The Christian life is a process. Although we have a new nature, we don't automatically have all good thoughts and attitudes when we become new people in Christ. But if we keep listening to God, we will grow toward maturity. As you think about the events of the past year, what changes for the better have you noticed in your thoughts and attitudes? Change may be slow, but your life will change significantly if you trust God to work within you. ■

3 LIVING THE NEW LIFE

Since you have been raised to new life with Christ, set
your sights on the realities of heaven, where Christ sits in
the place of honor at God's right hand. 2Think about the
things of heaven, not the things of earth. 3For you died to
this life, and your real life is hidden with Christ in God.
4And when Christ, who is your* life, is revealed to the
whole world, you will share in all his glory.
5So put to death the sinful, earthly things lurking
within you. Have nothing to do with sexual immorality,
impurity, lust, and evil desires. Don't be greedy, for a
greedy person is an idolater, worshiping the things of
this world. 6Because of these sins, the anger of God is
coming.* 7You used to do these things when your life
was still part of this world. 8But now is the time to get rid
of anger, rage, malicious behavior, slander, and dirty
language. 9Don't lie to each other, for you have stripped
off your old sinful nature and all its wicked deeds. 10Put
on your new nature, and be renewed as you learn to
know your Creator and become like him. 11In this new
life, it doesn't matter if you are a Jew or a Gentile,* circumcised or uncircumcised, barbaric, uncivilized,*
slave, or free. Christ is all that matters, and he lives in all
of us.
12Since God chose you to be the holy people he loves,
you must clothe yourselves with tenderhearted mercy,
kindness, humility, gentleness, and patience. 13Make allowance for each other's faults, and forgive anyone who
offends you. Remember, the Lord forgave you, so you
must forgive others. 14Above all, clothe yourselves with
love, which binds us all together in perfect harmony.
15And let the peace that comes from Christ rule in your
hearts. For as members of one body you are called to live
in peace. And always be thankful.

PEACE RULES 3:15

The word *rule* comes from athletics: Paul tells us to let God's peace be the "umpire" in our heart. Our heart is the center of conflict because that's where our feelings and desires clash. How can we deal with these constant conflicts and live as God wants? Paul explains that we must decide between conflicting elements on the basis of peace. Ask yourself which choice will promote peace in your soul, your family, and your church. ■

16Let the message about Christ, in all its richness, fill
your lives. Teach and counsel each other with all the

2:15 Or *he stripped off*. **2:18** Or *or worshiping with angels*. **3:4** Some manuscripts read *our*. **3:6** Some manuscripts read *is coming on all who disobey him*. **3:11a** Greek *a Greek*. **3:11b** Greek *Barbarian, Scythian*.

keeping it real

For a couple of years, I didn't get along very well with my dad. It just seemed like everything he said irritated me. Dad seemed too restrictive. I began to rebel, not openly, but on the sly. For instance, I'd say yes when he had asked me to do something, but then I never would get around to doing what he asked. Then when he'd get angry, I'd tune him out. Or, I would tell Dad I was going somewhere that I knew he'd approve of. But I would really hang out with friends he didn't like very much.

I knew things weren't great between us, but I didn't think much about it until our youth group did a study on relationships. When we talked about parents, we studied Colossians 3:20 and Ephesians 6:1-3. We talked about why we should obey our parents, and what obedience means.

I felt cut to the heart, knowing how hurtful I'd been to my dad. Suddenly I understood that his rules were his way of showing that he loved me. If I was honest with myself, a lot of his rules made sense.

That evening I asked Dad to forgive me. Apologizing was hard, but it cleared the air. Dad took my apology well. He even admitted to some areas where he might have been too hard on me. That was the start of a much better father/son relationship, which has continued.

—Blake

wisdom he gives. Sing psalms and hymns and spiritual
songs to God with thankful hearts. 17And whatever you
do or say, do it as a representative of the Lord Jesus, giving
thanks through him to God the Father.

INSTRUCTIONS FOR CHRISTIAN HOUSEHOLDS

18Wives, submit to your husbands, as is fitting for those
who belong to the Lord.
19Husbands, love your wives and
never treat them harshly.
20Children, always obey your parents,
for this pleases the Lord. 21Fathers, do
not aggravate your children, or they will
become discouraged.
22Slaves, obey your earthly masters
in everything you do. Try to please
them all the time, not just when they
are watching you. Serve them sincerely because of your reverent fear of
the Lord. 23Work willingly at whatever
you do, as though you were working
for the Lord rather than for people.
24Remember that the Lord will give
you an inheritance as your reward, and
that the Master you are serving is
Christ.* 25But if you do what is wrong,
you will be paid back for the wrong you have done. For
God has no favorites.

> Work willingly at whatever you do, as though you were working for the Lord rather than for people.
>
> *COLOSSIANS 3:23*

4 Masters, be just and fair to your slaves. Remember
that you also have a Master—in heaven.

AN ENCOURAGEMENT FOR PRAYER

2Devote yourselves to prayer with an alert mind and a
thankful heart. 3Pray for us, too, that God will give us
many opportunities to speak about
his mysterious plan concerning Christ.
That is why I am here in chains. 4Pray
that I will proclaim this message as
clearly as I should.
5Live wisely among those who are
not believers, and make the most of
every opportunity. 6Let your conversation be gracious and attractive* so
that you will have the right response
for everyone.

PAUL'S FINAL INSTRUCTIONS AND GREETINGS

7Tychicus will give you a full report
about how I am getting along. He is a
beloved brother and faithful helper
who serves with me in the Lord's
work. 8I have sent him to you for this
very purpose—to let you know how we are doing and to
encourage you. 9I am also sending Onesimus, a faithful

3:24 Or *and serve Christ as your Master.* 4:6 Greek *and seasoned with salt.*

PERSIST 4:2

Have you ever grown tired of praying for something or someone? Paul says, "Devote yourselves to prayer with an alert mind and a thankful heart." Vigilance demonstrates our faith that God answers our prayers. Faith shouldn't die if the answers don't come immediately. The delay may be God's way of working his will in your life. When you feel weary in your prayers, know that God is present, always listening, always acting. ■

and beloved brother, one of your own people. He and
Tychicus will tell you everything that's happening here.
10Aristarchus, who is in prison with me, sends you his
greetings, and so does Mark, Barnabas's cousin. As you
were instructed before, make Mark welcome if he comes
your way. 11Jesus (the one we call Justus) also sends his
greetings. These are the only Jewish believers among my
co-workers; they are working with me here for the Kingdom of God. And what a comfort they have been!
12Epaphras, a member of your own fellowship and a
servant of Christ Jesus, sends you his greetings. He always
prays earnestly for you, asking God to make you strong
and perfect, fully confident that you are following the
whole will of God. 13I can assure you that he prays hard for
you and also for the believers in Laodicea and Hierapolis.
14Luke, the beloved doctor, sends his greetings, and so
does Demas. 15Please give my greetings to our brothers
and sisters* at Laodicea, and to Nympha and the church
that meets in her house.
16After you have read this letter, pass it on to the
church at Laodicea so they can read it, too. And you
should read the letter I wrote to them.
17And say to Archippus, "Be sure to carry out the ministry the Lord gave you."

THE SOURCE 4:18

The Colossian church was swayed by false teachers who promised a deeper spiritual life through secret knowledge. But Paul makes it clear in Colossians that Christ alone is the source of true spiritual maturity. He is the head of the body, the Lord of all. But is he the Lord of your life? ■

18HERE IS MY GREETING IN MY OWN HANDWRITING—PAUL.
Remember my chains.
May God's grace be with you.

4:15 Greek *brothers.*

1 THESSALONIANS

1 thessalonians

PHOBIAS ARE "phascinating" phenomena. Psychiatrists and psychologists have catalogued hundreds of them. Check out this list:

Anthophobia—fear of flowers

Belonophobia—fear of pins and needles

Decidophobia—fear of making decisions

Mysophobia—fear of dirt

Trichophobia/trichopathophobia—fear of hair

Arachibutyrophobia—fear of peanut butter sticking to the roof of the mouth

Okay, maybe you don't have these fears. Perhaps your worries are more about the concerns you hear about on the Internet or on the news. For example: Will researchers ever find a cure for AIDS and other deadly diseases? How are we going to deal with a generation of drug-addicted babies? How has war affected our lives? Will there ever be lasting peace in the Middle East?

These are scary issues. Yet Christians can have real hope and genuine peace even in uncertain times.

That's the message of this letter: Be comforted, for no matter what happens, God is with us. Rest in the reassuring truth that Jesus Christ is coming back soon, too. . . .

Read 1 Thessalonians. You won't believe your eyes.

stats

PURPOSE: To strengthen the faith of Christians in Thessalonica and to pass on the assurance of Christ's return

AUTHOR: Paul

TO WHOM WRITTEN: The church at Thessalonica and believers everywhere

DATE WRITTEN: About A.D. 51 from Corinth; this is one of Paul's earliest letters

SETTING: The church at Thessalonica had been established only two or three years before this letter was written. The Christians needed to mature in their faith. Also, there was a misunderstanding about Jesus' second coming. Some thought he would return immediately; others wondered if the dead would experience a bodily resurrection at his return.

KEY PEOPLE: Paul, Timothy, Silas

KEY PLACE: Thessalonica

KEY points

PERSECUTION
Paul and the new Christians at Thessalonica experienced persecution because of their faith in Christ. We can expect trials and troubles as well. The Holy Spirit helps our faith to remain strong even when we are persecuted.

PAUL'S MINISTRY
Paul expressed his concern for this church even when some of the members slandered him. Paul's commitment to share the gospel even through difficult times is an example for us to follow.

BE PREPARED
Paul encouraged believers to live as though they expected Jesus to return at any moment. No one knows when Jesus will return. While we wait, we are to remain faithful to God.

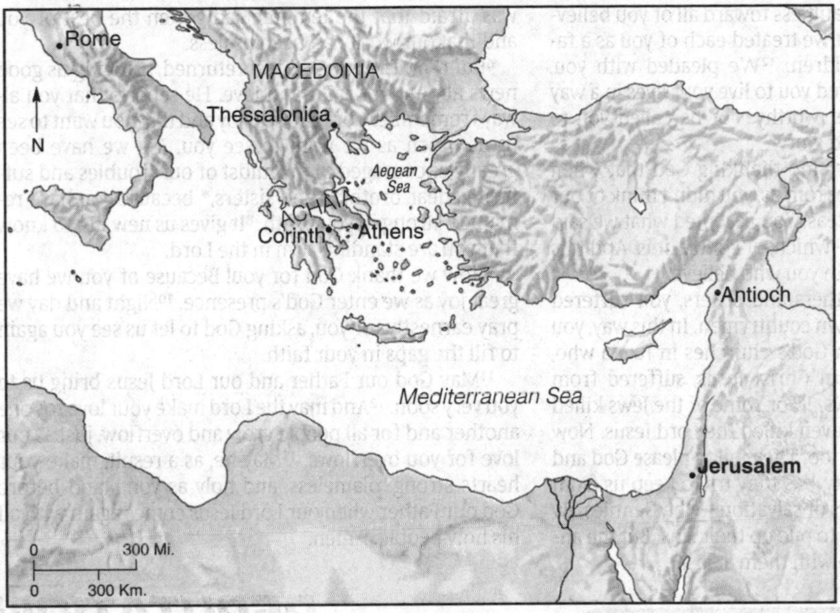

LOCATION OF THESSALONICA
Paul visited Thessalonica on his second and third missionary journeys. It was a seaport and trade center located on the Egnatian Way, a busy international highway. Paul probably wrote his two letters to the Thessalonians from Corinth.

1

GREETINGS FROM PAUL

This letter is from Paul, Silas,* and Timothy.
We are writing to the church in Thessalonica, to you
who belong to God the Father and the Lord Jesus Christ.
May God give you grace and peace.

THE FAITH OF THE THESSALONIAN BELIEVERS

2We always thank God for all of you and pray for you constantly. 3As we pray to our God and Father about you, we
think of your faithful work, your loving deeds, and the
enduring hope you have because of our Lord Jesus Christ.
4We know, dear brothers and sisters,* that God loves
you and has chosen you to be his own people. 5For when
we brought you the Good News, it was not only with
words but also with power, for the Holy Spirit gave you
full assurance* that what we said was true. And you know
of our concern for you from the way we lived when we
were with you. 6So you received the message with joy
from the Holy Spirit in spite of the severe suffering it
brought you. In this way, you imitated both us and the
Lord. 7As a result, you have become an example to all the
believers in Greece—throughout both Macedonia and
Achaia.*
8And now the word of the Lord is ringing out from you
to people everywhere, even beyond Macedonia and
Achaia, for wherever we go we find people telling us
about your faith in God. We don't need to tell them about
it, 9for they keep talking about the wonderful welcome
you gave us and how you turned away from idols to serve
the living and true God. 10And they speak of how you are
looking forward to the coming of God's Son from
heaven—Jesus, whom God raised from the dead. He is the
one who has rescued us from the terrors of the coming
judgment.

2

PAUL REMEMBERS HIS VISIT

You yourselves know, dear brothers and sisters,* that our
visit to you was not a failure. 2You know how badly we
had been treated at Philippi just before we came to you
and how much we suffered there. Yet our God gave us the
courage to declare his Good News to you boldly, in spite
of great opposition. 3So you can see we were not preaching with any deceit or impure motives or trickery.
4For we speak as messengers approved by God to be
entrusted with the Good News. Our purpose is to please
God, not people. He alone examines the motives of our
hearts. 5Never once did we try to win you with flattery, as
you well know. And God is our witness that we were not
pretending to be your friends just to get your money! 6As
for human praise, we have never sought it from you or
anyone else.
7As apostles of Christ we certainly had a right to make
some demands of you, but instead we were like children*
among you. Or we were like a mother feeding and caring
for her own children. 8We loved you so much that we
shared with you not only God's Good News but our own
lives, too.
9Don't you remember, dear brothers and sisters, how
hard we worked among you? Night and day we toiled to
earn a living so that we would not be a burden to any of
you as we preached God's Good News to you. 10You yourselves are our witnesses—and so is God—that we were

1:1 Greek *Silvanus*, the Greek form of the name. 1:4 Greek *brothers*. 1:5 Or *with the power of the Holy Spirit, so you can have full assurance*. 1:7 *Macedonia* and *Achaia* were the northern and southern regions of Greece. 2:1 Greek *brothers;* also in 2:9, 14, 17. 2:7 Some manuscripts read *we were gentle*.

devout and honest and faultless toward all of you believers. [11]And you know that we treated each of you as a father treats his own children. [12]We pleaded with you,
encouraged you, and urged you to live your lives in a way
that God would consider worthy. For he called you to
share in his Kingdom and glory.
[13]Therefore, we never stop thanking God that when
you received his message from us, you didn't think of our
words as mere human ideas. You accepted what we said
as the very word of God—which, of course, it is. And this
word continues to work in you who believe.
[14]And then, dear brothers and sisters, you suffered
persecution from your own countrymen. In this way, you
imitated the believers in God's churches in Judea who,
because of their belief in Christ Jesus, suffered from
their own people, the Jews. [15]For some of the Jews killed
the prophets, and some even killed the Lord Jesus. Now
they have persecuted us, too. They fail to please God and
work against all humanity [16]as they try to keep us from
preaching the Good News of salvation to the Gentiles. By
doing this, they continue to pile up their sins. But the anger of God has caught up with them at last.

OPPOSED 2:14

Just as the Jewish Christians in Jerusalem were persecuted by their own people, so the Gentile Christians in Thessalonica were persecuted by their fellow Gentiles. Persecution is discouraging, especially when it comes from family or friends. But taking a stand for Christ usually leads to persecution. Are you still willing to declare your faith even if doing so leads to persecution? ■

TIMOTHY'S GOOD REPORT ABOUT THE CHURCH

[17]Dear brothers and sisters, after we were separated from
you for a little while (though our hearts never left you), we
tried very hard to come back because of our intense longing to see you again. [18]We wanted very much to come to
you, and I, Paul, tried again and again, but Satan prevented us. [19]After all, what gives us hope and joy, and
what will be our proud reward and crown as we stand before our Lord Jesus when he returns? It is you! [20]Yes, you
are our pride and joy.

3

Finally, when we could stand it no longer, we decided to stay alone in Athens, [2]and we sent Timothy to
visit you. He is our brother and God's co-worker* in proclaiming the Good News of Christ. We sent him to
strengthen you, to encourage you in your faith, [3]and to
keep you from being shaken by the troubles you were going through. But you know that we are destined for such
troubles. [4]Even while we were with you, we warned you
that troubles would soon come—and they did, as you well
know. [5]That is why, when I could bear it no longer, I sent
Timothy to find out whether your faith was still strong. I
was afraid that the tempter had gotten the best of you
and that our work had been useless.
[6]But now Timothy has just returned, bringing us good
news about your faith and love. He reports that you always remember our visit with joy and that you want to see
us as much as we want to see you. [7]So we have been
greatly encouraged in the midst of our troubles and suffering, dear brothers and sisters,* because you have remained strong in your faith. [8]It gives us new life to know
that you are standing firm in the Lord.
[9]How we thank God for you! Because of you we have
great joy as we enter God's presence. [10]Night and day we
pray earnestly for you, asking God to let us see you again
to fill the gaps in your faith.
[11]May God our Father and our Lord Jesus bring us to
you very soon. [12]And may the Lord make your love for one
another and for all people grow and overflow, just as our
love for you overflows. [13]May he, as a result, make your
hearts strong, blameless, and holy as you stand before
God our Father when our Lord Jesus comes again with all
his holy people. Amen.

REPUTATION

The coach calls a time-out. The girls' varsity basketball team awaits a decision. Their decision, however, is not the most fascinating development in Butler Gymnasium.

Far more interesting are the thoughts that fill the minds of the students watching the game. If you could crawl through each set of watching eyes into each churning brain, what would you discover?

Well, you'd find that most of the students, when they glance at Ava (the player currently closest to the coach), are thinking words like *conceited, selfish, fake,* and *back-stabber*. Her reputation is, frankly, not the best.

Meanwhile, the player currently sitting on the bench—Roshonda—is regarded by almost everyone in the stands as *sweet, nice, friendly,* and *fun-to-be-with.*

Three quick questions:

- **What would you have to do consistently to earn either reputation?**
- **Who are the Avas and Roshondas in your life?**
- **How do other people regard you?**

Read 1 Thessalonians 4:1-12 for a fast lesson in reputation making. (See also Heb 13.) How would ignoring any of these commands affect your reputation?

4

LIVE TO PLEASE GOD

Finally, dear brothers and sisters,* we urge you in the
name of the Lord Jesus to live in a way that pleases God, as

3:2 Other manuscripts read *and God's servant;* still others read *and a co-worker,* or *and a servant and co-worker for God,* or *and God's servant and our co-worker.* 3:7 Greek *brothers.* 4:1 Greek *brothers;* also in 4:10, 13.

we have taught you. You live this way already, and we encourage you to do so even more. 2For you remember what
we taught you by the authority of the Lord Jesus.
3God's will is for you to be holy, so stay away from all
sexual sin. 4Then each of you will control his own body*
and live in holiness and honor—5not in lustful passion like
the pagans who do not know God and his ways. 6Never
harm or cheat a Christian brother in this matter by violating his wife,* for the Lord avenges all such sins, as we have
solemnly warned you before. 7God has called us to live
holy lives, not impure lives. 8Therefore, anyone who refuses to live by these rules is not disobeying human teaching but is rejecting God, who gives his Holy Spirit to you.
9But we don't need to write to you about the importance
of loving each other,* for God himself has taught you to
love one another. 10Indeed, you already show your love for
all the believers* throughout Macedonia. Even so, dear
brothers and sisters, we urge you to love them even more.
11Make it your goal to live a quiet life, minding your
own business and working with your hands, just as we instructed you before. 12Then people who are not Christians will respect the way you live, and you will not need
to depend on others.

THE HOPE OF THE RESURRECTION

13And now, dear brothers and sisters, we want you to
know what will happen to the believers who have died*
so you will not grieve like people who have no hope. 14For
since we believe that Jesus died and was raised to life
again, we also believe that when Jesus returns, God will
bring back with him the believers who have died.
15We tell you this directly from the Lord: We who are
still living when the Lord returns will not meet him
ahead of those who have died.* 16For the Lord himself
will come down from heaven with a commanding shout,
with the voice of the archangel, and with the trumpet
call of God. First, the Christians who have died* will rise
from their graves. 17Then, together with them, we who
are still alive and remain on the earth will be caught up
in the clouds to meet the Lord in the air. Then we will be
with the Lord forever. 18So encourage each other with
these words.

5 Now concerning how and when all this will happen,
dear brothers and sisters,* we don't really need to write
you. 2For you know quite well that the day of the Lord's
return will come unexpectedly, like a thief in the night.
3When people are saying, "Everything is peaceful and secure," then disaster will fall on them as suddenly as a
pregnant woman's labor pains begin. And there will be
no escape.
4But you aren't in the dark about these things, dear
brothers and sisters, and you won't be surprised when
the day of the Lord comes like a thief.* 5For you are all
children of the light and of the day; we don't belong to
darkness and night. 6So be on your guard, not asleep like
the others. Stay alert and be clearheaded. 7Night is the
time when people sleep and drinkers get drunk. 8But let
us who live in the light be clearheaded, protected by the
armor of faith and love, and wearing as our helmet the
confidence of our salvation.

Even though I know I'm going to heaven, I'm still afraid of dying. How can I quit being so afraid of death?

Many people have this fear. Death is an unknown for everyone—even for Christians. But fear is a learned response. Through the years we learned to fear certain things. Little kids aren't afraid of death because they don't understand it. Yet as they grow and see the response of adults and the media to death, they learn that it's something to be avoided at all costs.

After we become Christians, we need to go through a relearning process about death. Paul, the author of much of the New Testament, said this about death: "For to me, living means living for Christ, and dying is even better" (Phil 1:21).

Paul had learned that death would actually put an end to the struggles he faced on earth. He looked forward to the day when he could see Jesus face to face. In the meantime, though, he had work to do: winning people to Christ. Life wasn't a chore—it was a privilege!

Fear of dying doesn't disappear instantly. But as you spend time in the Bible and with other Christians who have the same hope you do, you will grow to realize that death is only a door to an eternity far better than your wildest dreams (see 1 Thess 4:13-14).

THE FINISH LINE 5:9-11

As you near the end of a foot race, your legs ache, your throat burns, and your whole body cries out for you to stop. This is when friends and fans are most valuable. Their encouragement helps you push through the pain and reach the finish line. In the same way, Christians are to encourage one another. A word of encouragement offered at the right moment can mean the difference between finishing well and collapsing along the way. Look around. Who needs your encouragement? ■

9For God chose to save us through our Lord Jesus
Christ, not to pour out his anger on us. 10Christ died for us
so that, whether we are dead or alive when he returns, we

4:4 Or *will know how to take a wife for himself;* or *will learn to live with his own wife;* Greek reads *will know how to possess his own vessel.* **4:6** Greek *Never harm or cheat a brother in this matter.* **4:9** Greek *about brotherly love.* **4:10** Greek *the brothers.* **4:13** Greek *those who have fallen asleep;* also in 4:14. **4:15** Greek *those who have fallen asleep.* **4:16** Greek *the dead in Christ.* **5:1** Greek *brothers;* also in 5:4, 12, 14, 25, 26, 27. **5:4** Some manuscripts read *comes upon you as if you were thieves.*

can live with him forever. [11]So encourage each other and build each other up, just as you are already doing.

PAUL'S FINAL ADVICE

[12]Dear brothers and sisters, honor those who are your leaders in the Lord's work. They work hard among you and give you spiritual guidance. [13]Show them great respect and wholehearted love because of their work. And live peacefully with each other.

[14]Brothers and sisters, we urge you to warn those who are lazy. Encourage those who are timid. Take tender care of those who are weak. Be patient with everyone.

> Never stop praying.
>
> 1 THESSALONIANS 5:17

[15]See that no one pays back evil for evil, but always try to do good to each other and to all people.

[16]Always be joyful. [17]Never stop praying. [18]Be thankful in all circumstances, for this is God's will for you who belong to Christ Jesus.

[19]Do not stifle the Holy Spirit. [20]Do not scoff at prophecies, [21]but test everything that is said. Hold on to what is good. [22]Stay away from every kind of evil.

PAUL'S FINAL GREETINGS

[23]Now may the God of peace make you holy in every way, and may your whole spirit and soul and body be kept blameless until our Lord Jesus Christ comes again. [24]God will make this happen, for he who calls you is faithful.

[25]Dear brothers and sisters, pray for us.

[26]Greet all the brothers and sisters with Christian love.*

[27]I command you in the name of the Lord to read this letter to all the brothers and sisters.

[28]May the grace of our Lord Jesus Christ be with you.

5:26 Greek *with a holy kiss.*

IN CONTROL 5:23

The spirit, soul, and body are integral parts of a person. This expression is Paul's way of saying that God must be involved in *every* aspect of our lives. We can't separate our spiritual life from everything else. Christ must control *all* of us, not just the part we give him on Sundays. How much of your life have you given to God? ■

2 THESSALONIANS

2 thessalonians

A PROMINENT author's best-selling new book has predicted that Jesus is coming back in a few days.

Shelby: "I guess I'm ready, but if it *does* happen, I'll never get my license—and I'll never get to . . . well, you know." (Everyone but Faith giggles.)

Jade: "I think it's *great*. I've got a *huge* algebra trig test on Monday that I can't possibly pass. *Now* I can just relax and forget about it."

Shelby: "Right, and no more abuse from Garrett Hampton and his atheist friends!"

Anne: "Oh yeah. *That* will be the best!"

Faith: "You guys *can't* be serious! You talk like you actually *believe* that stuff!"

Anne: "We do! It all fits together, and it's in the Bible. It's going to be this weekend. Better get ready."

Jesus *is* coming back. And his return *will* radically change things. But that doesn't mean we should start picking dates or sit around waiting. The prospect of Christ's return should motivate us to action, not laziness.

That's the message of 2 Thessalonians. Yes, the world can be gross. Yes, the Christian life is hard. But Jesus is coming back soon to make everything right. So keep watching, waiting—and working (or studying!).

stats

PURPOSE: To clear up the confusion about the second coming of Christ

AUTHOR: Paul

TO WHOM WRITTEN: The church at Thessalonica and believers everywhere

DATE WRITTEN: About A.D. 51 or 52, a few months after 1 Thessalonians, from Corinth

SETTING: Many in the church were confused about the timing of Christ's return. Because of increasing persecution, they assumed that the Second Coming would be at any moment. In light of this misunderstanding, some became lazy and disorderly.

KEY PEOPLE: Paul, Silas, Timothy

KEY PLACE: Thessalonica

SPECIAL FEATURES: This is a follow-up letter to 1 Thessalonians. In this epistle, Paul tells of various events that must precede the second coming of Christ.

KEY points

PERSECUTION

Paul encouraged the believers to have patience in spite of persecution. That encouragement is for us as well. Suffering for our faith can strengthen us to serve Christ.

CHRIST'S RETURN

Christ will return and bring total victory to all who trust in him. If we stand firm and keep working, we'll be ready. If we're ready, we don't have to be concerned about *when* he'll return.

THE GREAT REBELLION

Before Jesus' return, there will be a great rebellion against God led by the man of lawlessness (the Antichrist). We don't have to fear when we see evil increase. God is in control, no matter how much evil infects the world.

DON'T QUIT

Paul had harsh words for believers who stopped working and became disorderly. We must never get so tired of doing right that we quit. Instead, we are to persevere in the use of our time and talents.

1 GREETINGS FROM PAUL

This letter is from Paul, Silas,* and Timothy.

We are writing to the church in Thessalonica, to you who belong to God our Father and the Lord Jesus Christ.

2May God our Father* and the Lord Jesus Christ give you grace and peace.

ENCOURAGEMENT DURING PERSECUTION

3Dear brothers and sisters,* we can't help but thank God for you, because your faith is flourishing and your love for one another is growing. 4We proudly tell God's other churches about your endurance and faithfulness in all the persecutions and hardships you are suffering. 5And God will use this persecution to show his justice and to make you worthy of his Kingdom, for which you are suffering. 6In his justice he will pay back those who persecute you.

TROUBLES 1:5

As we live for Christ, we will experience trouble. Some say that hardships are a result of sin or lack of faith. Paul, however, teaches that they may be a part of God's plan for believers. Our problems help build strong character (Rom 5:3-4) and make us to be sensitive to others (2 Cor 1:3-5). ■

7And God will provide rest for you who are being persecuted and also for us when the Lord Jesus appears from heaven. He will come with his mighty angels, 8in flaming fire, bringing judgment on those who don't know God and on those who refuse to obey the Good News of our Lord Jesus. 9They will be punished with eternal destruction, forever separated from the Lord and from his glorious power. 10When he comes on that day, he will receive glory from his holy people—praise from all who believe. And this includes you, for you believed what we told you about him.

11So we keep on praying for you, asking our God to enable you to live a life worthy of his call. May he give you the power to accomplish all the good things your faith prompts you to do. 12Then the name of our Lord Jesus will be honored because of the way you live, and you will be honored along with him. This is all made possible because of the grace of our God and Lord, Jesus Christ.*

> The Lord is faithful; he will strengthen you and guard you from the evil one.
>
> 2 THESSALONIANS 3:3

2 EVENTS PRIOR TO THE LORD'S SECOND COMING

Now, dear brothers and sisters,* let us clarify some things about the coming of our Lord Jesus Christ and how we will be gathered to meet him. 2Don't be so easily shaken or alarmed by those who say that the day of the Lord has already begun. Don't believe them, even if they claim to have had a spiritual vision, a revelation, or a letter supposedly from us. 3Don't be fooled by what they say. For that day will not come until there is a great rebellion against God and the man of lawlessness* is revealed—the one who brings destruction.* 4He will exalt himself and defy everything that people call god and every object of worship. He will even sit in the temple of God, claiming that he himself is God.

5Don't you remember that I told you about all this when I was with you? 6And you know what is holding him back, for he can be revealed only when his time comes. 7For this lawlessness is already at work secretly, and it will remain secret until the one who is holding it back steps out of the way. 8Then the man of lawlessness will be revealed, but the Lord Jesus will kill him with the breath of his mouth and destroy him by the splendor of his coming.

9This man will come to do the work of Satan with counterfeit power and signs and miracles. 10He will use every kind of evil deception to fool those on their way to destruction, because they refuse to love and accept the truth that would save them. 11So God will cause them to be greatly deceived, and they will believe these lies. 12Then they will be condemned for enjoying evil rather than believing the truth.

BELIEVERS SHOULD STAND FIRM

13As for us, we can't help but thank God for you, dear brothers and sisters loved by the Lord. We are always thankful that God chose you to be among the first* to experience salvation—a salvation that came through the Spirit who makes you holy and through your belief in the truth. 14He called you to salvation when we told you the Good News; now you can share in the glory of our Lord Jesus Christ.

15With all these things in mind, dear brothers and sisters, stand firm and keep a strong grip on the teaching we passed on to you both in person and by letter.

16Now may our Lord Jesus Christ himself and God our Father, who loved us and by his grace gave us eternal comfort and a wonderful hope, 17comfort you and strengthen you in every good thing you do and say.

3 PAUL'S REQUEST FOR PRAYER

Finally, dear brothers and sisters,* we ask you to pray for us. Pray that the Lord's message will spread rapidly and be honored wherever it goes, just as when it came to you.

1:1 Greek *Silvanus,* the Greek form of the name. **1:2** Some manuscripts read *God the Father.* **1:3** Greek *Brothers.* **1:12** Or *of our God and our Lord Jesus Christ.* **2:1** Greek *brothers;* also in 2:13, 15. **2:3a** Some manuscripts read *the man of sin.* **2:3b** Greek *the son of destruction.* **2:13** Some manuscripts read *chose you from the very beginning.* **3:1** Greek *brothers;* also in 3:6, 13.

SPIRITUAL ATTACKS 3:1-3

Aside from the routine of daily life, a spiritual battle is taking place. Attacks from the forces of evil (discouragement, depression, etc.) can be devastating. But we're not without help! We have prayer and the Word of God. (See also Eph 6:10-19.)

The following guidelines can help you prepare for and survive satanic attacks: (1) Take the threat of spiritual attack seriously; (2) pray for strength and help from God; (3) study the Bible to recognize Satan's tactics; (4) memorize Scripture; (5) associate with those who speak the truth; and (6) practice what you're taught. ■

2Pray, too, that we will be rescued from wicked and evil
people, for not everyone is a believer. 3But the Lord is
faithful; he will strengthen you and guard you from the
evil one.* 4And we are confident in the Lord that you are
doing and will continue to do the things we commanded
you. 5May the Lord lead your hearts into a full understanding and expression of the love of God and the patient endurance that comes from Christ.

WORK AND PLAY? 3:6-15

Paul advised the Christians of Thessalonica to avoid lazy believers. There's a difference between leisure and laziness. Relaxation and recreation provide a necessary and much needed balance to the workday schedule. Yet Christians are still responsible to work. Is there a balance between your work schedule and your free time? Too much of one or the other can be hazardous. ■

AN EXHORTATION TO PROPER LIVING

6And now, dear brothers and sisters, we give you this command in the name of our Lord Jesus Christ: Stay away from all believers* who live idle lives and don't follow the tradition they received* from us. 7For you know
that you ought to imitate us. We were not idle when we
were with you. 8We never accepted food from anyone
without paying for it. We worked hard day and night so
we would not be a burden to any of you. 9We certainly
had the right to ask you to feed us, but we wanted to give
you an example to follow. 10Even while we were with you,
we gave you this command: "Those unwilling to work will not get to eat."
11Yet we hear that some of you are living idle lives, refusing to work and meddling in other people's business.

LAZINESS

Luke walks in the door, drops his backpack on the couch, and heads straight for the kitchen. Opening the pantry, he scans the shelves and scowls. "How come there's never anything to eat in this stupid house?" he mutters to no one in particular.

Grabbing a banana, he settles on the floor in front of the TV for a quick game of *Motorist Mayhem.* A "quick game" usually lasts five hours.

The phone rings. Luke doesn't budge.

"Luke, can you get the phone? I've got shaving cream all over my hands!" his dad suddenly yells from the bathroom.

***It'll stop soon,* Luke thinks. He continues playing the game.**

The phone continues to ring. The voice from the rear of the house gets louder. "Luke! Answer the phone!"

Just as the mystery caller gives up, Luke's mom staggers through the door, her arms loaded with grocery bags.

Luke watches her struggle from his easy chair and greets her by saying, "I hope you bought something decent to eat."

"Maybe if you help me carry the bags in, you'll find out," his mother quips.

Luke reluctantly gets up. "Why do I *always* have to do everything around here? You and Dad treat me like a slave!"

Check out 2 Thessalonians 3:6-13. What would you say to Luke?

12We command such people and urge them in the name
of the Lord Jesus Christ to settle down and work to earn
their own living. 13As for the rest of you, dear brothers
and sisters, never get tired of doing good.
14Take note of those who refuse to obey what we say in
this letter. Stay away from them so they will be ashamed.
15Don't think of them as enemies, but warn them as you
would a brother or sister.*

PAUL'S FINAL GREETINGS

16Now may the Lord of peace himself give you his peace at all times and in every situation. The Lord be with you all.
17HERE IS MY GREETING IN MY OWN HANDWRITING—PAUL. I DO THIS IN ALL MY LETTERS TO PROVE THEY ARE FROM ME.
18May the grace of our Lord Jesus Christ be with you all.

3:3 Or *from evil.* 3:6a Greek *from every brother.* 3:6b Some manuscripts read *you received.* 3:15 Greek *as a brother.*

1 TIMOTHY

WHAT DOES it take to be a leader? Super intelligence? Good looks? A magnetic personality? Persuasiveness? Obsession for power? That's what the world says.

But leadership is far more than being highly educated or multitalented. Jesus defined it as servanthood. It involves character, compassion, courage, and conviction.

So, here's the shocker: *Anyone who takes the time to develop those qualities can be a leader.* Even you.

"Me?! You're kidding! I don't have special talents. Besides, I'm young and kinda shy. I couldn't lead anyone."

Funny you should say that. A young man by the name of Timothy once felt the same way. He found himself facing big responsibilities and even bigger challenges. He wondered what to do and whether he could really be a leader.

Then he received the following letter from his friend and mentor, Paul. More than a mere letter, the Epistle of 1 Timothy is also an essay on leadership.

Hey, you may never be a major politician or CEO. But you'll always have friends, relatives, neighbors, and acquaintances whom you can influence for Christ.

So read about the character, compassion, courage, and conviction that leadership involves. Then give it a try. Be a leader.

stats

PURPOSE: To encourage and instruct Timothy

AUTHOR: Paul

TO WHOM WRITTEN: Timothy, young church leaders, and believers everywhere

DATE WRITTEN: About A.D. 64, from Rome or Macedonia (possibly Philippi), probably just prior to Paul's final imprisonment in Rome

SETTING: Timothy was one of Paul's closest companions. Paul had sent him to the church at Ephesus to counter the false teachings there (1 Tim 1:3-4). Timothy probably served for a time as a leader in the church at Ephesus. Paul hoped to visit Timothy (3:14-15; 4:13). In the meantime, he wrote this letter to give Timothy practical advice for the ministry.

KEY PEOPLE: Paul, Timothy

KEY PLACE: Ephesus

KEY points

TEACH AND MODEL

Paul instructed Timothy to preserve the Christian faith by correctly teaching the foundational truths of the Scriptures and modeling right living. Likewise, we must know the truth in order to defend it. We can know the truth by studying the Bible.

PUBLIC WORSHIP

Paul provided guidelines for conducting worship services. Christian character must be evident in every aspect of worship. We must rid ourselves of any attitudes that might disrupt worship or damage church unity.

CHURCH LEADERSHIP

Paul gave specific instructions concerning the qualifications for church leaders. These qualifications haven't changed. When church leaders live up to these standards, God is honored.

A LIFE OF DISCIPLINE

Timothy, like all church leaders, had to guard his motives, serve faithfully, and live a disciplined life. We can gain discipline by consistently studying God's Word and obeying it.

A CARING CHURCH

Paul wrote about the church's responsibility to care for the needs of all of its members. Caring for the family of believers demonstrates our Christlike attitude and genuine love.

1

GREETINGS FROM PAUL

This letter is from Paul, an apostle of Christ Jesus, appointed by the command of God our Savior and Christ
Jesus, who gives us hope.
[2]I am writing to Timothy, my true son in the faith.
May God the Father and Christ Jesus our Lord give you
grace, mercy, and peace.

WARNINGS AGAINST FALSE TEACHINGS

[3]When I left for Macedonia, I urged you to stay there in
Ephesus and stop those whose teaching is contrary to the
truth. [4]Don't let them waste their time in endless discussion of myths and spiritual pedigrees. These things only
lead to meaningless speculations,* which don't help people live a life of faith in God.*
[5]The purpose of my instruction is that all believers
would be filled with love that comes from a pure heart, a
clear conscience, and genuine faith. [6]But some people
have missed this whole point. They have turned away
from these things and spend their time in meaningless
discussions. [7]They want to be known as teachers of the
law of Moses, but they don't know what they are talking
about, even though they speak so confidently.
[8]We know that the law is good when used correctly. [9]For
the law was not intended for people who do what is right. It
is for people who are lawless and rebellious, who are ungodly and sinful, who consider nothing sacred and defile
what is holy, who kill their father or mother or commit
other murders. [10]The law is for people who are sexually immoral, or who practice homosexuality, or are slave traders,*
liars, promise breakers, or who do anything else that contradicts the wholesome teaching [11]that comes from the
glorious Good News entrusted to me by our blessed God.

FALSE TEACHING 1:3-11

Paul urged Timothy to put a stop to those who spread false information about God or the Scriptures. False teaching usually has these characteristics: (1) It stirs up questions and arguments instead of helping people come to Jesus (1:4). (2) It often is promoted by teachers whose motivation is to make a name for themselves (1:7). (3) It differs from what's taught in the Scriptures (1:6-7; 4:1-3). The best way to avoid being hurt by false teaching is have a firm grasp on what's really true. ■

PAUL'S GRATITUDE FOR GOD'S MERCY

[12]I thank Christ Jesus our Lord, who has given me
strength to do his work. He considered me trustworthy
and appointed me to serve him, [13]even though I used to
blaspheme the name of Christ. In my insolence, I persecuted his people. But God had mercy on me because I did
it in ignorance and unbelief. [14]Oh, how generous and gracious our Lord was! He filled me with the faith and love
that come from Christ Jesus.
[15]This is a trustworthy saying, and everyone should accept it: "Christ Jesus came into the world to save sinners"—and I am the worst of them all. [16]But God had
mercy on me so that Christ Jesus could use me as a prime
example of his great patience with even the worst sinners. Then others will realize that they, too, can believe in
him and receive eternal life. [17]All honor and glory to God
forever and ever! He is the eternal King, the unseen one
who never dies; he alone is God. Amen.

TIMOTHY'S RESPONSIBILITY

[18]Timothy, my son, here are my instructions for you,
based on the prophetic words spoken about you earlier.
May they help you fight well in the Lord's battles. [19]Cling
to your faith in Christ, and keep your conscience clear.
For some people have deliberately violated their consciences; as a result, their faith has been shipwrecked.
[20]Hymenaeus and Alexander are two examples. I threw
them out and handed them over to Satan so they might
learn not to blaspheme God.

CLEAR CONSCIENCE 1:19

How can you "keep your conscience clear"? Treasure your faith in Christ more than anything else and do what you know is right. Each time you deliberately ignore your conscience, you're hardening your heart. Your capacity to tell right from wrong slowly erodes. But when you stay close to God, he reminds you of what's right. Feeling the tug of your conscience? Don't ignore it! ■

2

INSTRUCTIONS ABOUT WORSHIP

I urge you, first of all, to pray for all people. Ask God to
help them; intercede on their behalf, and give thanks for
them. [2]Pray this way for kings and all who are in authority
so that we can live peaceful and quiet lives marked by
godliness and dignity. [3]This is good and pleases God our
Savior, [4]who wants everyone to be saved and to understand the truth. [5]For there is only one God and one Mediator who can reconcile God and humanity—the man
Christ Jesus. [6]He gave his life to purchase freedom for
everyone. This is the message God gave to the world at
just the right time. [7]And I have been chosen as a preacher
and apostle to teach the Gentiles this message about faith
and truth. I'm not exaggerating—just telling the truth.
[8]In every place of worship, I want men to pray with
holy hands lifted up to God, free from anger and
controversy.
[9]And I want women to be modest in their appearance.*
They should wear decent and appropriate clothing and
not draw attention to themselves by the way they fix their
hair or by wearing gold or pearls or expensive clothes.
[10]For women who claim to be devoted to God should
make themselves attractive by the good things they do.
[11]Women should learn quietly and submissively. [12]I do

1:4a Greek *in myths and endless genealogies, which cause speculation.* 1:4b Greek *a stewardship of God in faith.* 1:10 Or *kidnappers.*
2:9 Or *to pray in modest apparel.*

not let women teach men or have authority over them.* Let them listen quietly. 13For God made Adam first, and afterward he made Eve. 14And it was not Adam who was deceived by Satan. The woman was deceived, and sin was the result. 15But women will be saved through childbearing,* assuming they continue to live in faith, love, holiness, and modesty.

GREAT EXPECTATIONS 3:1-13

The word *elder* can refer to a pastor, church leader, or presiding elder over the church groups in an area. Paul stressed the high standards for spiritual leadership. Do you hold a position of spiritual leadership? Maybe you're a mentor for a younger teen or are a peer counselor in some way. Check yourself against Paul's standard of excellence. Those with great responsibility must meet high expectations. ■

3 LEADERS IN THE CHURCH

This is a trustworthy saying: "If someone aspires to be an elder,* he desires an honorable position." 2So an elder must be a man whose life is above reproach. He must be faithful to his wife.* He must exercise self-control, live wisely, and have a good reputation. He must enjoy having guests in his home, and he must be able to teach. 3He must not be a heavy drinker* or be violent. He must be gentle, not quarrelsome, and not love money. 4He must manage his own family well, having children who respect and obey him. 5For if a man cannot manage his own household, how can he take care of God's church?

6An elder must not be a new believer, because he might become proud, and the devil would cause him to fall.* 7Also, people outside the church must speak well of him so that he will not be disgraced and fall into the devil's trap.

8In the same way, deacons must be well respected and have integrity. They must not be heavy drinkers or dishonest with money. 9They must be committed to the mystery of the faith now revealed and must live with a clear conscience. 10Before they are appointed as deacons, let them be closely examined. If they pass the test, then let them serve as deacons.

11In the same way, their wives* must be respected and must not slander others. They must exercise self-control and be faithful in everything they do.

12A deacon must be faithful to his wife, and he must manage his children and household well. 13Those who do well as deacons will be rewarded with respect from others and will have increased confidence in their faith in Christ Jesus.

THE TRUTHS OF OUR FAITH

14I am writing these things to you now, even though I hope to be with you soon, 15so that if I am delayed, you will know how people must conduct themselves in the household of God. This is the church of the living God, which is the pillar and foundation of the truth.

16Without question, this is the great mystery of our faith*:

Christ* was revealed in a human body
  and vindicated by the Spirit.*
He was seen by angels
  and announced to the nations.
He was believed in throughout the world
  and taken to heaven in glory.

4 WARNINGS AGAINST FALSE TEACHERS

Now the Holy Spirit tells us clearly that in the last times some will turn away from the true faith; they will follow deceptive spirits and teachings that come from demons. 2These people are hypocrites and liars, and their consciences are dead.*

3They will say it is wrong to be married and wrong to eat certain foods. But God created those foods to be eaten with thanks by faithful people who know the truth. 4Since everything God created is good, we should not reject any of it but receive it with thanks. 5For we know it is made acceptable* by the word of God and prayer.

Don't let anyone think less of you because you are young. Be an example to all believers. . . .

1 TIMOTHY 4:12

A GOOD SERVANT OF CHRIST JESUS

6If you explain these things to the brothers and sisters,* Timothy, you will be a worthy servant of Christ Jesus, one who is nourished by the message of faith and the good teaching you have followed. 7Do not waste time arguing over godless ideas and old wives' tales. Instead, train yourself to be godly. 8"Physical training is good, but training for godliness is much better, promising benefits in this life and in the life to come." 9This is a trustworthy saying, and everyone should accept it. 10This is why we work hard and continue to struggle,* for our hope is in the living God, who is the Savior of all people and particularly of all believers.

11Teach these things and insist that everyone learn them. 12Don't let anyone think less of you because you are

2:12 Or *teach men or usurp their authority.* **2:15** Or *will be saved by accepting their role as mothers,* or *will be saved by the birth of the Child.* **3:1** Or *an overseer,* or *a bishop;* also in 3:2, 6. **3:2** Or *must have only one wife,* or *must be married only once;* Greek reads *must be the husband of one wife;* also in 3:12. **3:3** Greek *must not drink too much wine;* similarly in 3:8. **3:6** Or *he might fall into the same judgment as the devil.* **3:11** Or *the women deacons.* The Greek word can be translated *women* or *wives.* **3:16a** Or *of godliness.* **3:16b** Greek *He who;* other manuscripts read *God.* **3:16c** Or *in his spirit.* **4:2** Greek *are seared.* **4:5** Or *made holy.* **4:6** Greek *brothers.* **4:10** Some manuscripts read *continue to suffer.*

young. Be an example to all believers in what you say, in the way you live, in your love, your faith, and your purity. 13Until I get there, focus on reading the Scriptures to the church, encouraging the believers, and teaching them.

14Do not neglect the spiritual gift you received through the prophecy spoken over you when the elders of the church laid their hands on you. 15Give your complete attention to these matters. Throw yourself into your tasks so that everyone will see your progress. 16Keep a close watch on how you live and on your teaching. Stay true to what is right for the sake of your own salvation and the salvation of those who hear you.

YOUR FAMILY 5:8

Paul spoke out against those who refused to take care of their families. Almost everyone has relatives. According to Paul, a person who neglects his or her family responsibilities has denied the faith. Are you doing your part to meet the needs of those in your family circle—even your little brothers and sisters? ■

5 ADVICE ABOUT WIDOWS, ELDERS, AND SLAVES

Never speak harshly to an older man,* but appeal to him respectfully as you would to your own father. Talk to younger men as you would to your own brothers. 2Treat older women as you would your mother, and treat younger women with all purity as you would your own sisters.

3Take care of* any widow who has no one else to care for her. 4But if she has children or grandchildren, their first responsibility is to show godliness at home and repay their parents by taking care of them. This is something that pleases God.

5Now a true widow, a woman who is truly alone in this world, has placed her hope in God. She prays night and day, asking God for his help. 6But the widow who lives only for pleasure is spiritually dead even while she lives. 7Give these instructions to the church so that no one will be open to criticism.

8But those who won't care for their relatives, especially those in their own household, have denied the true faith. Such people are worse than unbelievers.

9A widow who is put on the list for support must be a woman who is at least sixty years old and was faithful to her husband.* 10She must be well respected by everyone because of the good she has done. Has she brought up her children well? Has she been kind to strangers and served other believers humbly?* Has she helped those who are in trouble? Has she always been ready to do good?

11The younger widows should not be on the list, because their physical desires will overpower their devotion to Christ and they will want to remarry. 12Then they would be guilty of breaking their previous pledge. 13And if they are on the list, they will learn to be lazy and will spend their time gossiping from house to house, meddling in other people's business and talking about things they shouldn't. 14So I advise these younger widows to marry again, have children, and take care of their own homes. Then the enemy will not be able to say anything against them. 15For I am afraid that some of them have already gone astray and now follow Satan.

16If a woman who is a believer has relatives who are widows, she must take care of them and not put the responsibility on the church. Then the church can care for the widows who are truly alone.

17Elders who do their work well should be respected and paid well,* especially those who work hard at both preaching and teaching. 18For the Scripture says, "You must not muzzle an ox to keep it from eating as it treads out the grain." And in another place, "Those who work deserve their pay!"*

19Do not listen to an accusation against an elder unless it is confirmed by two or three witnesses. 20Those who sin should be reprimanded in front of the whole church; this will serve as a strong warning to others.

21I solemnly command you in the presence of God and Christ Jesus and the holy angels to obey these instructions without taking sides or showing favoritism to anyone.

22Never be in a hurry about appointing a church leader.* Do not share in the sins of others. Keep yourself pure.

23Don't drink only water. You ought to drink a little wine for the sake of your stomach because you are sick so often.

24Remember, the sins of some people are obvious, leading them to certain judgment. But there are others whose sins will not be revealed until later. 25In the same way, the good deeds of some people are obvious. And the good deeds done in secret will someday come to light.

MONEY CYCLE 6:6-21

Despite almost overwhelming evidence to the contrary, some people still believe that money brings happiness. Rich people craving greater riches can be caught in an endless cycle that only ends in ruin and desperation. How can you avoid the love of money? Paul gives us some principles: (1) Realize that one day riches will all be gone (6:7, 17); (2) be content with what you have (6:8); (3) avoid compromising your principles just to gain money (6:9-10); (4) love people and God's work more than money (6:11); (5) freely share what you have with others (6:18). (See also Prov 30:7-9.) ■

6

All slaves should show full respect for their masters so they will not bring shame on the name of God and his teaching. 2If the masters are believers, that is no excuse for being disrespectful. Those slaves should work all the

5:1 Or *an elder.* 5:3 Or *Honor.* 5:9 Greek *was the wife of one husband.* 5:10 Greek *and washed the feet of God's holy people?* 5:17 Greek *should be worthy of double honor.* 5:18 Deut 25:4; Luke 10:7. 5:22 Greek *about the laying on of hands.*

harder because their efforts are helping other believers*
who are well loved.

MATERIALISM

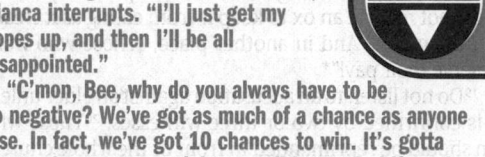

Jeremy and his girlfriend Bianca (whom he calls Bee) can hardly wait until next Saturday. That's the day when the winning numbers in the state lottery will be announced. Everybody is buzzing about the jackpot—now more than 170 million dollars!

"Just think what we could do if we won," Jeremy says. "We'd be able—"

"I'm not gonna even think about it," Bianca interrupts. "I'll just get my hopes up, and then I'll be all disappointed."

"C'mon, Bee, why do you always have to be so negative? We've got as much of a chance as anyone else. In fact, we've got 10 chances to win. It's gotta happen to someone—might as well be us. And if we *do* win, just think of all the stuff we could do, of all the things we could buy!"

"It *would* be great to be rich," Bianca admits. "Imagine going into the mall and picking up whatever you want and not even having to look at the price tag."

"Yeah, or going to any car dealership, walking over to the car you want, and saying, 'I'll take it.' Imagine that!"

"That'd be awesome!" Bianca exclaims.

The two dreamers sit thinking quietly for a few minutes. Finally Bianca breaks the silence. "Jeremy, I still can't help feeling like we just poured 10 dollars down the drain!"

"Bee!"

Ever felt like Bianca and Jeremy? Take a look at 1 Timothy 6:9-10. Why do you think Paul stressed this message?

FALSE TEACHING AND TRUE RICHES

Teach these things, Timothy, and encourage everyone to
obey them. 3Some people may contradict our teaching,
but these are the wholesome teachings of the Lord Jesus
Christ. These teachings promote a godly life. 4Anyone
who teaches something different is arrogant and lacks
understanding. Such a person has an unhealthy desire to
quibble over the meaning of words. This stirs up arguments ending in jealousy, division, slander, and evil suspicions. 5These people always cause trouble. Their minds
are corrupt, and they have turned their backs on the
truth. To them, a show of godliness is just a way to become wealthy.

6Yet true godliness with contentment is itself great
wealth. 7After all, we brought nothing with us when we
came into the world, and we can't take anything with us
when we leave it. 8So if we have enough food and clothing, let us be content.

9But people who long to be rich fall into temptation
and are trapped by many foolish and harmful desires
that plunge them into ruin and destruction. 10For the love
of money is the root of all kinds of evil. And some people,
craving money, have wandered from the true faith and
pierced themselves with many sorrows.

PAUL'S FINAL INSTRUCTIONS

11But you, Timothy, are a man of God; so run from all these
evil things. Pursue righteousness and a godly life, along
with faith, love, perseverance, and gentleness. 12Fight the
good fight for the true faith. Hold tightly to the eternal life
to which God has called you, which you have confessed so
well before many witnesses. 13And I charge you before
God, who gives life to all, and before Christ Jesus, who
gave a good testimony before Pontius Pilate, 14that you
obey this command without wavering. Then no one can
find fault with you from now until our Lord Jesus Christ
comes again. 15For at just the right time Christ will be revealed from heaven by the blessed and only almighty God,
the King of all kings and Lord of all lords. 16He alone can
never die, and he lives in light so brilliant that no human
can approach him. No human eye has ever seen him, nor
ever will. All honor and power to him forever! Amen.

17Teach those who are rich in this world not to be
proud and not to trust in their money, which is so unreliable. Their trust should be in God, who richly gives us all

6:2 Greek *brothers.*

Trying to be good and not sin seems like a full-time job. How can anyone stay pure? Why would anyone want to?

In 1 Timothy 6:11, Paul encouraged Timothy to "pursue righteousness and a godly life." In other words, keep doing what's right. But some try to seem holier than others in order to be admired or to earn their way to heaven.

Jesus talked a lot about the Pharisees. These men had created long lists of rules that they followed. They wanted to be admired for their discipline.

But in Matthew 5:20, Jesus made an incredible statement: "But I warn you—unless your righteousness is better than the righteousness of the teachers of religious law and the Pharisees, you will never enter the Kingdom of Heaven!" In other words, you have to have more than just correct behavior. You have to be pure on the inside. This inner purity begins by accepting Christ's death on the cross as taking the punishment for our sins. When we do this, we take on Christ's purity. In God's eyes, we are worthy of eternity in heaven! Now that's a pretty good deal!

It doesn't stop there, of course. God wants us to be like Jesus. This is a lifelong process of allowing God to change us (see John 15:1-17; 1 Tim 6:11-12).

A Christian who's really alive realizes that her eternity is settled. But she also genuinely wants to be more like the one who paid such a high price for her soul—Jesus. Her motivation—and yours—is not to parade her goodness in front of others, but rather to please God.

we need for our enjoyment. 18 Tell them to use their
money to do good. They should be rich in good works and
generous to those in need, always being ready to share
with others. 19 By doing this they will be storing up their
treasure as a good foundation for the future so that they
may experience true life.

20 Timothy, guard what God has entrusted to you.
Avoid godless, foolish discussions with those who oppose you with their so-called knowledge. 21 Some people
have wandered from the faith by following such
foolishness.

May God's grace be with you all.

TIMOTHY

Ever struggle with shyness or know someone who does? Real leadership abilities are sometimes buried under a person's shyness. Yet a friend with understanding and patience can uncover those strengths. That's what happened between the apostle Paul and a young man named Timothy.

Timothy probably became a Christian when Paul visited his hometown of Lystra during his first missionary journey (Acts 14:8-20). Timothy's Jewish mother and grandmother had prepared him by teaching him from the Old Testament. By the time Paul visited Lystra again, Timothy was a growing Christian who jumped at the chance to travel with Paul and Silas.

Away from home, Timothy struggled with shyness. But Paul chose to give Timothy important responsibilities in the ministry. Paul even made Timothy his personal representative on several occasions. Although Timothy sometimes failed, Paul never gave up on him.

Timothy was like a son to Paul, which is evident throughout 1 and 2 Timothy. The letters were intended to encourage and direct Timothy in Ephesus, where Paul had left him in charge of a young church (1 Tim 1:3-4). These letters also have encouraged countless other "Timothys" through the centuries. Are you a "Timothy"? Be encouraged!

When you face a challenge that seems beyond your abilities, you can find encouragement in 1 and 2 Timothy.

TIMOTHY

UPS:
- Became a believer after Paul's first missionary journey and joined him for two more journeys
- Was a respected Christian in his hometown
- Was Paul's special representative on several occasions
- Received two personal letters from Paul
- Probably knew Paul better than any other person, becoming like a son to him

DOWNS:
- Struggled with a timid and reserved nature
- Was disrespected because of his youthfulness
- Was apparently unable to correct some of the problems in the church at Corinth when Paul sent him there

STATS:
- Where: Lystra
- Occupations: Missionary, church leader
- Relatives: Eunice (mother); Lois (grandmother); Greek father
- Contemporaries: Paul, Silas, Luke, Mark, Peter, Barnabas

BOTTOM LINE:

Those who are young can have a great influence on others through the power of God.

Our inadequacies and inabilities should not keep us from being available to God.

Timothy's story is told in Acts, starting in chapter 16. He also is mentioned in Rom 16:21; 1 Cor 4:17; 16:10-11; 2 Cor 1:1, 19; Phil 1:1; 2:19-23; Col 1:1; 1 Thess 1:1-10; 2:3-4; 3:1-6; 1 and 2 Tim; Philem 1:1; Heb 13:23.

2 TIMOTHY

TRIVIA INCLUDES information that's often interesting but doesn't really matter much. For instance, did you know that:

- Grasshoppers are more nutritious than steak?
- The record for the most bowling balls stacked vertically without glue or tape is ten?
- Ben Franklin invented swim fins and the rocking chair?
- Mozart wrote the tune "Twinkle, Twinkle, Little Star" when he was five?
- Eating too many carrots can turn your skin yellow?

Though amusing—and helpful for filling the silence in an awkward conversation—the facts just cited are trivial. They won't change your life. Not so with 2 Timothy.

The apostle Paul's second letter to Timothy is serious stuff. History says that these were Paul's last words.

Perhaps the aged missionary recognized that his time was running out. If so, it's not surprising that he talked about important matters. Consider carefully Paul's final thoughts. He is, after all, one of the most influential individuals in history. And Paul's challenge to Timothy is just as appropriate 2,000 years later.

The bottom line? Second Timothy is no trivial pursuit!

stats

PURPOSE: To give final instructions and encouragement to Timothy, a leader of the church at Ephesus

AUTHOR: Paul

TO WHOM WRITTEN: Timothy

DATE WRITTEN: About A.D. 66 or 67 from prison in Rome. After a year or two of freedom, Paul was arrested again and executed under Emperor Nero.

SETTING: Paul was virtually alone in prison; only Luke was with him. He wrote this letter to pass the torch to the new generation of church leaders. He also asked for visits from his friends, for his books, and especially the parchments—possibly parts of the Old Testament, the Gospels, and other biblical manuscripts.

KEY PEOPLE: Paul, Timothy, Luke, Mark, and others

KEY PLACES: Rome, Ephesus

KEY points

BOLDNESS
In the face of opposition and persecution, Timothy was told to carry out his ministry unashamed and unafraid of the earthly consequences. To get over our fear of what people might say or do, we must take our eyes off people and look only to God.

FAITHFULNESS
Paul urged Timothy to maintain not only a firm knowledge of what's true, but also to be steadfast. As we trust Christ, he counts us worthy to suffer and will give us the strength we need to be steadfast.

PREACHING AND TEACHING
Paul encouraged Timothy not only to carry the torch of truth but also to train others, passing on to them his knowledge of the Scriptures and his enthusiasm for serving God's Kingdom. Likewise, each of us can look for ways to become better equipped to serve, as well as for ways to teach others what we have learned.

ERROR
In the final days before Christ returns, there will be false teachers, spiritual dropouts, and heresy. Therefore, we must be disciplined and ready to reject error. Knowing the Bible is a sure defense against error and confusion.

1

GREETINGS FROM PAUL

This letter is from Paul, chosen by the will of God to be an apostle of Christ Jesus. I have been sent out to tell others about the life he has promised through faith in Christ Jesus.

2I am writing to Timothy, my dear son.

May God the Father and Christ Jesus our Lord give you grace, mercy, and peace.

ENCOURAGEMENT TO BE FAITHFUL

3Timothy, I thank God for you—the God I serve with a clear conscience, just as my ancestors did. Night and day I constantly remember you in my prayers. 4I long to see you again, for I remember your tears as we parted. And I will be filled with joy when we are together again.

5I remember your genuine faith, for you share the faith that first filled your grandmother Lois and your mother, Eunice. And I know that same faith continues strong in you. 6This is why I remind you to fan into flames the spiritual gift God gave you when I laid my hands on you. 7For God has not given us a spirit of fear and timidity, but of power, love, and self-discipline.

8So never be ashamed to tell others about our Lord. And don't be ashamed of me, either, even though I'm in prison for him. With the strength God gives you, be ready to suffer with me for the sake of the Good News. 9For God saved us and called us to live a holy life. He did this, not because we deserved it, but because that was his plan from before the beginning of time—to show us his grace through Christ Jesus. 10And now he has made all of this plain to us by the appearing of Christ Jesus, our Savior. He broke the power of death and illuminated the way to life and immortality through the Good News. 11And God chose me to be a preacher, an apostle, and a teacher of this Good News.

BE BOLD 1:6-8

Timothy's youth, his association with Paul, and his leadership had come under fire. But Paul urged Timothy to be bold. When we allow people to intimidate us, we neutralize our effectiveness for God. The power of the Holy Spirit can help us overcome our fear of what some might say or do to us so we can continue to do God's work. ■

12That is why I am suffering here in prison. But I am not ashamed of it, for I know the one in whom I trust, and I am sure that he is able to guard what I have entrusted to him* until the day of his return.

13Hold on to the pattern of wholesome teaching you learned from me—a pattern shaped by the faith and love that you have in Christ Jesus. 14Through the power of the Holy Spirit who lives within us, carefully guard the precious truth that has been entrusted to you.

15As you know, everyone from the province of Asia has deserted me—even Phygelus and Hermogenes.

16May the Lord show special kindness to Onesiphorus and all his family because he often visited and encouraged me. He was never ashamed of me because I was in chains. 17When he came to Rome, he searched everywhere until he found me. 18May the Lord show him special kindness on the day of Christ's return. And you know very well how helpful he was in Ephesus.

2

A GOOD SOLDIER OF CHRIST JESUS

Timothy, my dear son, be strong through the grace that God gives you in Christ Jesus. 2You have heard me teach things that have been confirmed by many reliable witnesses. Now teach these truths to other trustworthy people who will be able to pass them on to others.

3Endure suffering along with me, as a good soldier of Christ Jesus. 4Soldiers don't get tied up in the affairs of civilian life, for then they cannot please the officer who enlisted them. 5And athletes cannot win the prize unless they follow the rules. 6And hardworking farmers should be the first to enjoy the fruit of their labor. 7Think about what I am saying. The Lord will help you understand all these things.

8Always remember that Jesus Christ, a descendant of King David, was raised from the dead. This is the Good News I preach. 9And because I preach this Good News, I am suffering and have been chained like a criminal. But the word of God cannot be chained. 10So I am willing to endure anything if it will bring salvation and eternal glory in Christ Jesus to those God has chosen.

11This is a trustworthy saying:

If we die with him,
  we will also live with him.
12 If we endure hardship,
  we will reign with him.
If we deny him,
  he will deny us.
13 If we are unfaithful,
  he remains faithful,
  for he cannot deny who he is.

14Remind everyone about these things, and command them in God's presence to stop fighting over words. Such arguments are useless, and they can ruin those who hear them.

AN APPROVED WORKER

15Work hard so you can present yourself to God and receive his approval. Be a good worker, one who does not need to be ashamed and who correctly explains the word of truth. 16Avoid worthless, foolish talk that only leads to more godless behavior. 17This kind of talk spreads like cancer, as in the case of Hymenaeus and Philetus. 18They have left the path of truth, claiming that the resurrection of the dead has already occurred; in this way, they have turned some people away from the faith.

19But God's truth stands firm like a foundation stone

1:12 Or *what has been entrusted to me.*

with this inscription: "The LORD knows those who are his,"* and "All who belong to the LORD must turn away from evil."*

20In a wealthy home some utensils are made of gold and silver, and some are made of wood and clay. The expensive utensils are used for special occasions, and the cheap ones are for everyday use. 21If you keep yourself pure, you will be a special utensil for honorable use. Your life will be clean, and you will be ready for the Master to use you for every good work.

22Run from anything that stimulates youthful lusts. Instead, pursue righteous living, faithfulness, love, and peace. Enjoy the companionship of those who call on the Lord with pure hearts.

23Again I say, don't get involved in foolish, ignorant arguments that only start fights. 24A servant of the Lord must not quarrel but must be kind to everyone, be able to teach, and be patient with difficult people. 25Gently instruct those who oppose the truth. Perhaps God will change those people's hearts, and they will learn the truth. 26Then they will come to their senses and escape from the devil's trap. For they have been held captive by him to do whatever he wants.

RUN! 2:22

Paul warned Timothy to run from anything that produced evil thoughts. Running away is sometimes considered cowardly. But wise people realize that removing themselves physically from temptation is often very wise. Perhaps you've experienced a temptation that seems difficult to resist. Knowing when to run is as important in a spiritual battle as knowing when and how to fight. (See also 1 Tim 6:11.) ■

3 THE DANGERS OF THE LAST DAYS

You should know this, Timothy, that in the last days there will be very difficult times. 2For people will love only themselves and their money. They will be boastful and proud, scoffing at God, disobedient to their parents, and ungrateful. They will consider nothing sacred. 3They will be unloving and unforgiving; they will slander others and have no self-control. They will be cruel and hate what is good. 4They will betray their friends, be reckless, be puffed up with pride, and love pleasure rather than God. 5They will act religious, but they will reject the power that could make them godly. Stay away from people like that!

6They are the kind who work their way into people's homes and win the confidence of* vulnerable women who are burdened with the guilt of sin and controlled by various desires. 7(Such women are forever following new teachings, but they are never able to understand the truth.) 8These teachers oppose the truth just as Jannes and Jambres opposed Moses. They have depraved minds and a counterfeit faith. 9But they won't get away with this for long. Someday everyone will recognize what fools they are, just as with Jannes and Jambres.

MUSIC

It's guaranteed to be the most spectacular concert tour ever. The members of Oozing Tumors are getting back together for one last show.

People begin lining up a week in advance for tickets! Among the O.T. faithful are three teens who happen to be Christians. Let's ask Emily (Em), Noah, and Angel a few questions.

"So you guys are pretty cranked, huh?"

Noah: "Oh, yeah! This is gonna be awesome! I saw O.T. on their last tour, and they were unbelievable. During the last song, the guitarist shattered nine guitars!"

"Isn't he the one who punched a photographer, trashed six hotel rooms, and spit on an old lady?"

Em: "Yeah, but he apologized later. I'd give anything for a front row seat. I want to see what he wears."

"You mean almost wears?" (Em and the guys laugh.)

"Does it bother you that these guys constantly brag about how many women they've slept with?"

Angel: "Naw, man. I just like their music."

"But should Christians support people who laugh at our beliefs and values?"

Em: "Chill, dude! It's just a concert!"

What's your view? Does the band's behavior outside of the auditorium really matter? Why or why not? Read 2 Timothy 3:1-5, noting especially the end of verse 5. Would this advice have any effect on your choice of music? Why or why not?

DIVINE INSPIRATION 3:16

The Bible is not a collection of stories, fables, myths, or merely human ideas about God. Through the Holy Spirit, God revealed his person and plan to godly men, who wrote down God's message for his people (see 2 Pet 1:20-21). This process is known as *inspiration*. The writers wrote from their own personal, historical, and cultural contexts. Yet, though they used their own minds, talents, languages, and styles, they wrote what God wanted them to write. Scripture is completely trustworthy because God was in control of its writing. How does this truth affect your view of the Bible? ■

PAUL'S CHARGE TO TIMOTHY

10But you, Timothy, certainly know what I teach, and how I live, and what my purpose in life is. You know my faith, my patience, my love, and my endurance. 11You know how much persecution and suffering I have endured.

2:19a Num 16:5. **2:19b** See Isa 52:11. **3:6** Greek *and take captive.*

You know all about how I was persecuted in Antioch, Iconium, and Lystra—but the Lord rescued me from all
of it. [12]Yes, and everyone who wants to
live a godly life in Christ Jesus will suffer persecution. [13]But evil people and
impostors will flourish. They will deceive others and will themselves be
deceived.
[14]But you must remain faithful to
the things you have been taught. You
know they are true, for you know
you can trust those who taught you.
[15]You have been taught the holy
Scriptures from childhood, and they
have given you the wisdom to receive
the salvation that comes by trusting
in Christ Jesus. [16]All Scripture is inspired by God and is useful to teach us what is true and
to make us realize what is wrong in our lives. It corrects
us when we are wrong and teaches us to do what is
right. [17]God uses it to prepare and equip his people to
do every good work.

> All Scripture is inspired by God and is useful to teach us what is true and to make us realize what is wrong in our lives.
>
> *2 TIMOTHY 3:16*

THIS LIFE 4:10

Demas had been one of Paul's co-workers (Col 4:14; Philem 1:24). Yet he deserted Paul because he loved "the things of this life." Do you love what the world has to offer—wealth, power, pleasure—even if gaining it means hurting people and neglecting the work God has given you to do? If so, the apostle John has this advice: "Do not love this world nor the things it offers you, for when you love the world, you do not have the love of the Father in you" (1 John 2:15). ■

4
I solemnly urge you in the presence of God and
Christ Jesus, who will someday judge the living and the
dead when he appears to set up his Kingdom: [2]Preach the
word of God. Be prepared, whether the time is favorable
or not. Patiently correct, rebuke, and encourage your
people with good teaching.
[3]For a time is coming when people will no longer listen
to sound and wholesome teaching. They will follow their
own desires and will look for teachers who will tell them
whatever their itching ears want to hear. [4]They will reject
the truth and chase after myths.
[5]But you should keep a clear mind in every situation.
Don't be afraid of suffering for the Lord. Work at telling
others the Good News, and fully carry out the ministry
God has given you.
[6]As for me, my life has already been poured out as an
offering to God. The time of my death is near. [7]I have
fought the good fight, I have finished the race, and I have
remained faithful. [8]And now the prize awaits me—the
crown of righteousness, which the Lord, the righteous
Judge, will give me on the day of his return. And the prize is not just for me
but for all who eagerly look forward to
his appearing.

PAUL'S FINAL WORDS

[9]Timothy, please come as soon as you
can. [10]Demas has deserted me because
he loves the things of this life and has
gone to Thessalonica. Crescens has
gone to Galatia, and Titus has gone to
Dalmatia. [11]Only Luke is with me. Bring
Mark with you when you come, for he
will be helpful to me in my ministry. [12]I
sent Tychicus to Ephesus. [13]When you
come, be sure to bring the coat I left
with Carpus at Troas. Also bring my
books, and especially my papers.*
[14]Alexander the coppersmith did me much harm, but
the Lord will judge him for what he has done. [15]Be careful
of him, for he fought against everything we said.
[16]The first time I was brought before the judge, no one
came with me. Everyone abandoned me. May it not be
counted against them. [17]But the Lord stood with me and
gave me strength so that I might preach the Good News in
its entirety for all the Gentiles to hear. And he rescued me
from certain death.* [18]Yes, and the Lord will deliver me

4:13 Greek *especially the parchments.* 4:17 Greek *from the mouth of a lion.*

A friend of mine stopped coming to church because he said that God had stopped answering his prayers. How do I answer him?

Like Demas, who deserted Paul (see 2 Tim 4:10), many Christians have a what-have-you-done-for-me-lately type of faith in God. Oh, they're willing to trust him in the good times. Yet when trouble hits, they figure God has "checked out on them"—so they "check out on God."

Because we live in a society where we often can get what we want when we want it, we may begin to think that God's only purpose is to meet our needs. When something doesn't work out or we think that God hasn't come through for us, we turn away from him.

God is in the business of molding our character. One way he does this is by allowing us to go through tough times. When Paul wrote 2 Timothy, the church was going through intense persecution. Demas got tired of it and left. He wanted his comforts more than he wanted God's will.

Encourage your friend to change the what-have-you-done-for-me-lately attitude. Help him realize that God wants to build his character. His goal is not to make us feel good, but to help us mature.

from every evil attack and will bring me safely into his
heavenly Kingdom. All glory to God forever and ever!
Amen.

PAUL'S FINAL GREETINGS

19Give my greetings to Priscilla and Aquila and those
living in the household of Onesiphorus. 20Erastus
stayed at Corinth, and I left Trophimus sick at Miletus.
21Do your best to get here before winter. Eubulus
sends you greetings, and so do Pudens, Linus, Claudia,
and all the brothers and sisters.*
22May the Lord be with your spirit. And may his grace
be with all of you.

4:21 Greek *brothers.*

IN MANY OF life's situations—whether from natural instinct, repeated instruction, or unpleasant experience—you know precisely what to do. For instance:

- If your clothing catches on fire, stop, drop, and roll.
- In case of emergency, call 9-1-1.
- Never stare at the sun during an eclipse.
- Always wash your hands after using the restroom and before eating.
- On a first date, never order pizza with extra garlic and onions.
- Never sign *anything* until you read the fine print.

No doubt you could handle each of these situations with ease. But what about the millions of other situations where you aren't sure what to do?

Now you see why Paul's epistle to Titus is so important. Through it we'll gain plenty of practical advice for living a pure life in an impure world. Wondering about commitment, discipline, self-control, purity, solid relationships, or civic duties? It's all here. By the way, here's a reminder of one more rule of life—one every mother seems to emphasize: Never cross your eyes while reading; they might get stuck that way.

stats

PURPOSE: To advise Titus in his responsibility of supervising the churches on the island of Crete

AUTHOR: Paul

TO WHOM WRITTEN: Titus, a Greek convert, who had become Paul's special representative to the island of Crete

DATE WRITTEN: About A.D. 64, around the same time 1 Timothy was written; probably from Macedonia while Paul traveled in between periods of imprisonment in Rome

SETTING: Paul had sent Titus to organize and oversee the churches on Crete. This letter tells him how to do this job.

KEY PEOPLE: Paul, Titus

KEY PLACES: Crete, Nicopolis

SPECIAL FEATURE: Titus is very similar to 1 Timothy with its instructions to church leaders.

KEY points

A GOOD LIFE
Paul gave Titus advice on living "the good life." This life consists of a belief in Jesus, along with the commitment and discipline to serve others.

CHARACTER
Titus's responsibility on Crete was to appoint church leaders (elders) to maintain proper organization and discipline. Their qualifications—self-control and integrity—are important qualities for all Christians.

CHURCH RELATIONSHIPS
Older Christians were to teach and to be examples to younger men and women. Every age and group has a lesson to learn and a role to play.

CITIZENSHIP
Christians must be good citizens in society, not just in church. Believers must obey the government and work honestly. How you fulfill your civic duties is a witness to the watching world.

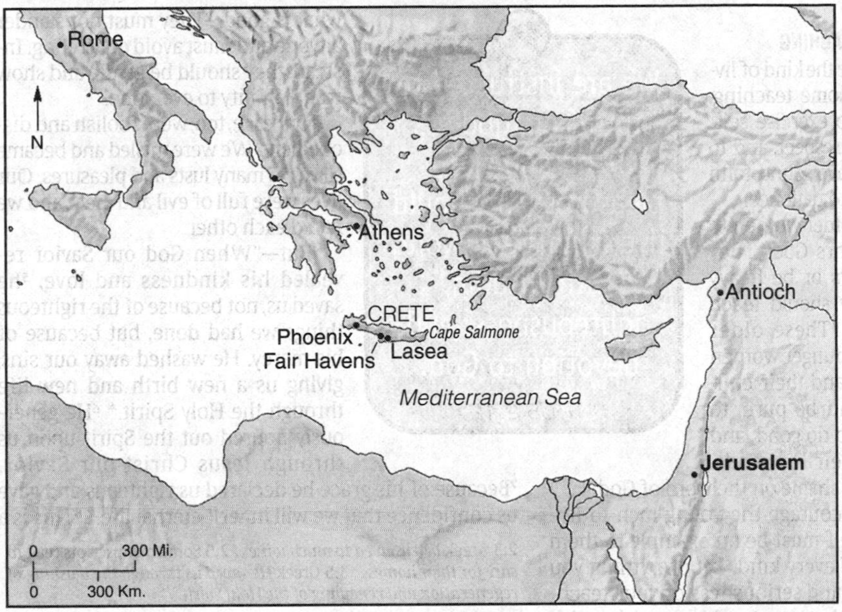

TITUS GOES TO CRETE
Tradition says that after Paul was released from prison in Rome, he and Titus traveled together for a while. They stopped in Crete. When it was time for Paul to go, he left Titus behind to help the churches there.

1

GREETINGS FROM PAUL

This letter is from Paul, a slave of God and an apostle of Jesus Christ. I have been sent to proclaim faith to* those God has chosen and to teach them to know the truth that shows them how to live godly lives. 2This truth gives them confidence that they have eternal life, which God—who does not lie—promised them before the world began. 3And now at just the right time he has revealed this message, which we announce to everyone. It is by the command of God our Savior that I have been entrusted with this work for him.

THE FOUNDATION OF FAITH 1:1-2

As Paul explained, the foundation of a believer's faith is trust in God's character. Because he is the source of all truth, he cannot lie. The eternal life he has promised will be ours because he keeps his promises. Is your faith built on that foundation? ■

4I am writing to Titus, my true son in the faith that we share.

May God the Father and Christ Jesus our Savior give you grace and peace.

TITUS'S WORK IN CRETE

5I left you on the island of Crete so you could complete our work there and appoint elders in each town as I instructed you. 6An elder must live a blameless life. He must be faithful to his wife,* and his children must be believers who don't have a reputation for being wild or rebellious. 7For an elder* must live a blameless life. He must not be arrogant or quick-tempered; he must not be a heavy drinker,* violent, or dishonest with money.

8Rather, he must enjoy having guests in his home, and he must love what is good. He must live wisely and be just. He must live a devout and disciplined life. 9He must have a strong belief in the trustworthy message he was taught; then he will be able to encourage others with wholesome teaching and show those who oppose it where they are wrong.

10For there are many rebellious people who engage in useless talk and deceive others. This is especially true of those who insist on circumcision for salvation. 11They must be silenced, because they are turning whole families away from the truth by their false teaching. And they do it only for money. 12Even one of their own men, a prophet from Crete, has said about them, "The people of Crete are all liars, cruel animals, and lazy gluttons."* 13This is true. So reprimand them sternly to make them strong in the faith. 14They must stop listening to Jewish myths and the commands of people who have turned away from the truth.

15Everything is pure to those whose hearts are pure. But nothing is pure to those who are corrupt and unbelieving, because their minds and consciences are corrupted. 16Such people claim they know God, but they deny him by the way they live. They are detestable and disobedient, worthless for doing anything good.

1:1 Or *to strengthen the faith of.* 1:6 Or *must have only one wife,* or *must be married only once;* Greek reads *must be the husband of one wife.* 1:7a Or *an overseer,* or *a bishop.* 1:7b Greek *must not drink too much wine.* 1:12 This quotation is from Epimenides of Knossos.

2 PROMOTE RIGHT TEACHING

As for you, Titus, promote the kind of living that reflects wholesome teaching. 2Teach the older men to exercise self-control, to be worthy of respect, and to live wisely. They must have sound faith and be filled with love and patience.

3Similarly, teach the older women to live in a way that honors God. They must not slander others or be heavy drinkers.* Instead, they should teach others what is good. 4These older women must train the younger women to love their husbands and their children, 5to live wisely and be pure, to work in their homes,* to do good, and to be submissive to their husbands. Then they will not bring shame on the word of God.

6In the same way, encourage the young men to live wisely. 7And you yourself must be an example to them by doing good works of every kind. Let everything you do reflect the integrity and seriousness of your teaching. 8Teach the truth so that your teaching can't be criticized. Then those who oppose us will be ashamed and have nothing bad to say about us.

> We are instructed to turn from godless living and sinful pleasures. We should live in this evil world with wisdom, righteousness, and devotion to God.
>
> *TITUS 2:12*

BE AN EXAMPLE 2:6-8

Paul urged Titus to be a good example to those around him so that others might see his good works and imitate him. Titus's life would give his words greater impact. If you want someone to act a certain way, be sure to live that way yourself. You then will earn the right to be heard. ■

9Slaves must always obey their masters and do their best to please them. They must not talk back 10or steal, but must show themselves to be entirely trustworthy and good. Then they will make the teaching about God our Savior attractive in every way.

11For the grace of God has been revealed, bringing salvation to all people. 12And we are instructed to turn from godless living and sinful pleasures. We should live in this evil world with wisdom, righteousness, and devotion to God, 13while we look forward with hope to that wonderful day when the glory of our great God and Savior, Jesus Christ, will be revealed. 14He gave his life to free us from every kind of sin, to cleanse us, and to make us his very own people, totally committed to doing good deeds.

15You must teach these things and encourage the believers to do them. You have the authority to correct them when necessary, so don't let anyone disregard what you say.

3 DO WHAT IS GOOD

Remind the believers to submit to the government and its officers. They should be obedient, always ready to do what is good. 2They must not slander anyone and must avoid quarreling. Instead, they should be gentle and show true humility to everyone.

3Once we, too, were foolish and disobedient. We were misled and became slaves to many lusts and pleasures. Our lives were full of evil and envy, and we hated each other.

4But—"When God our Savior revealed his kindness and love, 5he saved us, not because of the righteous things we had done, but because of his mercy. He washed away our sins, giving us a new birth and new life through the Holy Spirit.* 6He generously poured out the Spirit upon us through Jesus Christ our Savior. 7Because of his grace he declared us righteous and gave us confidence that we will inherit eternal life." 8This is a

2:3 Greek *be enslaved to much wine.* 2:5 Some manuscripts read *to care for their homes.* 3:5 Greek *He saved us through the washing of regeneration and renewing of the Holy Spirit.*

INTEGRITY

When Dawn sticks her head into her youth leader's office, it's plain to see that she's troubled. "Jane, can I talk to you?" she asks.

"Sure, Dawn," she tells her. "Come in."

"It's this whole youth group leadership team thing. I feel bad saying anything . . ."

"What do you mean?"

"Well, you know Kelly, the girl who's been coming with me to church the last few weeks?"

"Yeah."

"Well, she told me that she wants to be on the team. She wants to be in charge of publicity for the youth group."

"That's great. We've been looking for someone to fill that—"

"No, that's not great! You don't know Kelly. She's pretty wild . . . I mean, she's not exactly living like a Christian."

"I see."

"Don't get me wrong. I really love Kelly, and I'm trying to be a good influence on her and everything. I just don't think it's a very good idea to have her out there in charge of publicizing our group. At least not while she's living like she is. People might get the wrong idea, you know?"

"I agree. So, are you going to talk to her?"

"Oh, I guess so. Any advice?"

"Sure. If I were you, I'd . . ."

Christians in leadership positions are expected to be people of integrity. Read Titus 1:5-8; 2:11–3:8 for a quick glimpse at the qualities Christian leaders must possess.

SLAVE TO SIN 3:3

Following a life of pleasure and giving in to every desire leads to slavery. Many think freedom consists in doing anything they want. But this path leads to an addiction to gratification. A person is no longer free, but is a slave to what his or her body dictates (2 Pet 2:19). But Jesus frees us from the desires and control of sin. Have you been released? ■

AVOIDING ARGUMENTS 3:9-11

Paul warns Titus, as he warned Timothy, not to get involved in foolish and unprofitable disputes (2 Tim 2:14). This does not mean that we should refuse to study or discuss different interpretations of difficult Bible passages. Paul warned against petty quarrels, rather than honest discussion that leads to wisdom. You can stop an argument by turning the discussion back to a track that leads to a deeper understanding of the passage. ■

trustworthy saying, and I want you to insist on these teachings so that all who trust in God will devote themselves to doing good. These teachings are good and beneficial for everyone.
9Do not get involved in foolish discussions about
spiritual pedigrees* or in quarrels and fights about obedience to Jewish laws. These things are useless and a
waste of time. 10If people are causing divisions among
you, give a first and second warning. After that, have
nothing more to do with them. 11For people like that
have turned away from the truth, and their own sins condemn them.

3:9 Or *spiritual genealogies.*

PAUL'S FINAL REMARKS AND GREETINGS

12I am planning to send either Artemas or Tychicus to
you. As soon as one of them arrives, do your best to meet me at Nicopolis, for I have decided to stay there for the
winter. 13Do everything you can to help Zenas the lawyer and Apollos with their trip. See that they are given everything they need.
14Our people must learn to do good by meeting the urgent needs of others; then they will not be unproductive.
15Everybody here sends greetings. Please give my greetings to the believers—all who love us.

May God's grace be with you all.

PHILEMON

"I COULD *never* forgive her!"

"He'll *never* get serious about God!"

"I wish. My situation is *impossible!*"

Ever heard—or made—statements like those? If so, take this hint! Never say *never.* Many hard-to-believe things we declare "impossible!" eventually do come to pass . . . right before our embarrassed eyes.

Consider the Munich elementary school teacher who told ten-year-old Albert Einstein, "You will never amount to very much."

And you can be sure Simon Newcomb is red-faced in his grave. He's the guy who asserted in the 1800s that "flight by machines heavier than air is . . . utterly impossible."

Never say *never.* Don't end that friendship or relationship just because you've been wronged. Don't give up on that friend who claims to be an atheist. Don't write off your future based on your past experiences.

Never say *never.* The Gospel of Matthew states that same principle, while the book of Philemon illustrates it with the story of how a poor slave and his rich master ended up as Christian brothers.

So before you say, "That's *impossible!*" Or, "That could *never* happen!" read Paul's postcard to Philemon.

philemon

stats

PURPOSE: To convince Philemon to forgive—and accept as a brother in the faith—his runaway slave, Onesimus

AUTHOR: Paul

TO WHOM WRITTEN: Philemon, who probably was a wealthy member of the church in Colosse

DATE WRITTEN: About A.D. 60, during Paul's first imprisonment in Rome, at about the same time that the Epistles to the Ephesians and Colossians were written

SETTING: Slavery was very common in the Roman Empire. Evidently, some Christians had slaves. Paul makes a radical statement by declaring Onesimus, a slave, to be Philemon's brother in Christ.

KEY PEOPLE: Paul, Philemon, Onesimus

KEY PLACES: Colosse, Rome

KEY points

FORGIVENESS

Paul asked Philemon not to punish Onesimus for his infractions, but to forgive and restore him as a new Christian brother. In the same way, forgiving those who have wronged you is the appropriate response to Christ's forgiveness of you.

BARRIERS

While slavery was a barrier between people, Paul stressed that Christian love and fellowship could overcome such barriers. Although social and economic barriers still exist today, in Christ we are one family. Racial, economic, or political differences should not separate believers.

RESPECT

Paul had the authority as an apostle to tell Philemon what to do. Yet Paul chose to appeal to his friend in Christian love rather than order him to do what he wished. Like Paul, we can choose to use tactful persuasion when dealing with people. Tact often accomplishes a great deal more than commands.

GREETINGS FROM PAUL

1This letter is from Paul, a prisoner for preaching the Good News about Christ Jesus, and from our brother Timothy.

I am writing to Philemon, our beloved co-worker, 2and to our sister Apphia, and to our fellow soldier Archippus, and to the church that meets in your* house.

3May God our Father and the Lord Jesus Christ give you grace and peace.

PAUL'S THANKSGIVING AND PRAYER

4I always thank my God when I pray for you, Philemon, 5because I keep hearing about your faith in the Lord Jesus and your love for all of God's people. 6And I am praying that you will put into action the generosity that comes from your faith as you understand and experience all the good things we have in Christ. 7Your love has given me much joy and comfort, my brother, for your kindness has often refreshed the hearts of God's people.

> He is no longer like a slave to you. . . . He is a beloved brother. . . . Now he will mean much more to you. . . .
>
> *PHILEMON 1:16*

PAUL'S APPEAL FOR ONESIMUS

8That is why I am boldly asking a favor of you. I could demand it in the name of Christ because it is the right thing for you to do. 9But because of our love, I prefer simply to ask you. Consider this as a request from me—Paul, an old man and now also a prisoner for the sake of Christ Jesus.*

10I appeal to you to show kindness to my child, Onesimus. I became his father in the faith while here in prison. 11Onesimus* hasn't been of much use to you in the past, but now he is very useful to both of us. 12I am sending him back to you, and with him comes my own heart.

13I wanted to keep him here with me while I am in these chains for preaching the Good News, and he would have helped me on your behalf. 14But I didn't want to do anything without your consent. I wanted you to help because you were willing, not because you were forced. 15It seems you lost Onesimus for a little while so that you could have him back forever. 16He is no longer like a slave to you. He is more than a slave, for he is a beloved brother, especially to me. Now he will mean much more to you, both as a man and as a brother in the Lord.

RECONCILIATION

As roommates (and total opposites), college freshmen Arwen and Morgan had a very awkward relationship:

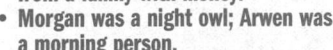

- **Morgan was totally into sports; Arwen preferred activities that didn't involve sweat.**
- **Morgan was loud; Arwen was quiet.**
- **Morgan had to get a scholarship since her family couldn't afford to send her to college; Arwen came from a family with money.**
- **Morgan was a night owl; Arwen was a morning person.**
- **Morgan was not a Christian; Arwen was.**

At the end of the fall semester, Arwen moved out of the dorm into an apartment. Right about that same time, she couldn't find her diamond earrings. Although she suspected Morgan, she never said a word.

The following summer, Arwen received a letter from Morgan. The first part of the letter told how Morgan had come to Christ during a beach outreach. The second half was a confession. Morgan had indeed taken the earrings and pawned them for some needed cash. She pleaded for forgiveness and promised to pay back the money.

Arwen immediately wrote back, welcoming Morgan to the family of God, granting the requested forgiveness, and suggesting that they get together first thing in the fall.

Could you have responded to Morgan as Arwen did? Their story isn't a fairy tale. Read Philemon to see for yourself the amazing reconciliation that Jesus makes possible.

DEALING WITH CONFLICT 1:8-9

Because Paul was an elder and an apostle, he could've used his authority with Philemon, commanding him to deal kindly with his runaway slave. But Paul based his request not on his own authority, but on Philemon's Christian commitment. Paul wanted Philemon's heartfelt obedience.

When you know something is right and you have the power to demand it, do you appeal to your authority or the other person's commitment? Here Paul provides a good example of how to deal with a possible conflict between Christian friends. When a conflict arises, what will you do? ■

17So if you consider me your partner, welcome him as you would welcome me. 18If he has wronged you in any way or owes you anything, charge it to me. 19I, PAUL, WRITE THIS WITH MY OWN HAND: I WILL REPAY IT. AND I WON'T MENTION THAT YOU OWE ME YOUR VERY SOUL!

20Yes, my brother, please do me this favor* for the Lord's sake. Give me this encouragement in Christ.

21I am confident as I write this letter that you will do what I ask and even more! 22One more thing—please prepare a guest room for me, for I am hoping

2 Throughout this letter, *you* and *your* are singular except in verses 3, 22, and 25. 9 Or *a prisoner of Christ Jesus.* 11 *Onesimus* means "useful." 20 Greek *onaimen,* a play on the name Onesimus.

that God will answer your prayers and let me return to you soon.

PAUL'S FINAL GREETINGS

23Epaphras, my fellow prisoner in Christ Jesus, sends you his greetings. 24So do Mark, Aristarchus, Demas, and Luke, my co-workers.

25May the grace of the Lord Jesus Christ be with your spirit.

FORGIVEN 1:10, 16

Paul asked Philemon not only to forgive his runaway slave who had become a Christian, but to accept him as a brother. As Christians, we have the responsibility of forgiving as we have been forgiven (Matt 6:12; Eph 4:31-32). True forgiveness means that we treat the person we've forgiven as we would want to be treated. Is there someone you say you have forgiven, but who still needs your kindness? ■

WOULD YOU:

- wear a diaper to school and suck on a pacifier during all of your classes?
- treat yourself to a lunch of jars of baby food: strained carrots, creamed spinach, and milk (out of a baby bottle, of course)?
- drool all over yourself in front of everyone?
- crawl from class to class?
- kick your legs, flail your arms, and cry uncontrollably anytime anything doesn't go your way?

You wouldn't do any of the above, would you? Such behavior is totally inappropriate and uncool for a teen. We expect this kind of immature behavior from babies. Sadly, we sometimes see these kinds of responses from fellow believers. Some remain "baby Christians" all of their lives.

In the same way that little kids grow physically, "baby" Christians need to grow in their relationship with Christ. The Epistle of Hebrews is all about spiritual maturity. You should know up front that Hebrews contains some tough challenges. It's a risky book to read—especially if you apply it. Are you up for the challenge?

stats

PURPOSE: To present Christ's superiority to angels and the great prophets of the Old Testament

AUTHOR: Unknown. Paul, Luke, Barnabas, Apollos, Silas, Philip, Priscilla, and others have been suggested as possible authors. This unknown author refers to Timothy as a "brother" (13:23).

TO WHOM WRITTEN: To believers everywhere, especially Hebrew Christians who may have considered a return to Judaism, perhaps because of their lack of understanding of biblical truths. They probably were "second-generation" Christians (2:3).

DATE WRITTEN: Probably before the destruction of the Temple in Jerusalem in A.D. 70 since sacrifices and ceremonies are referred to, while the Temple's destruction is not

SETTING: Jewish Christians probably experienced persecution, socially and physically, from fellow Jews and from Romans. The believers needed to be reassured that Christianity was true and that Jesus was the Messiah.

KEY PEOPLE: Old Testament men and women of faith (chapter 11)

KEY points

JESUS' SUPERIORITY

Hebrews affirms Jesus' identity as God. The testimonies in the Scriptures can help us conclude that he is greater than any religion or any angel, and superior to any Jewish leader (such as Abraham, Moses, or Joshua) or priest.

HIGH PRIEST

In the Old Testament, the high priest represented the Jews before God. As the ultimate high priest, Jesus guarantees our access to God the Father.

SACRIFICE

Jesus' sacrifice was the ultimate fulfillment of all that the Old Testament sacrifices represented—God's forgiveness for sin. But we must accept this sacrifice for us. By believing in him we are declared "not guilty" and reconciled to God.

MATURITY THROUGH ENDURANCE

Faith enables Christians to face trials. Genuine faith includes the commitment to stay true to God when we are under fire. Endurance builds character and leads to victory.

1 JESUS CHRIST IS GOD'S SON

Long ago God spoke many times and in many ways to our ancestors through the prophets. [2]And now in these final days, he has spoken to us through his Son. God promised everything to the Son as an inheritance, and through the Son he created the universe. [3]The Son radiates God's own glory and expresses the very character of God, and he sustains everything by the mighty power of his command. When he had cleansed us from our sins, he sat down in the place of honor at the right hand of the majestic God in heaven. [4]This shows that the Son is far greater than the angels, just as the name God gave him is greater than their names.

GOD REVEALED 1:2-3

Not only is Jesus God's exact representation, he is God himself. Christ is eternal; he worked with the Father in creating the world (John 1:3; Col 1:16). He is the full revelation of God. You can have no clearer view of God than by looking at Jesus. ■

THE SON IS GREATER THAN THE ANGELS

[5]For God never said to any angel what he said to Jesus:

"You are my Son.
Today I have become your Father.*"

God also said,

"I will be his Father,
and he will be my Son."*

[6]And when he brought his firstborn Son into the world, God said,*

"Let all of God's angels worship him."*

[7]Regarding the angels, he says,

"He sends his angels like the winds,
his servants like flames of fire."*

[8]But to the Son he says,

"Your throne, O God, endures forever and ever.
You rule with a scepter of justice.
[9] You love justice and hate evil.
Therefore, O God, your God has anointed you,
pouring out the oil of joy on you more than on
anyone else."*

[10]He also says to the Son,

"In the beginning, Lord, you laid the foundation
of the earth
and made the heavens with your hands.
[11] They will perish, but you remain forever.
They will wear out like old clothing.
[12] You will fold them up like a cloak
and discard them like old clothing.
But you are always the same;
you will live forever."*

[13]And God never said to any of the angels,

"Sit in the place of honor at my right hand
until I humble your enemies,
making them a footstool under your feet."*

[14]Therefore, angels are only servants—spirits sent to care for people who will inherit salvation.

2 A WARNING AGAINST DRIFTING AWAY

So we must listen very carefully to the truth we have heard, or we may drift away from it. [2]For the message God delivered through angels has always stood firm, and

1:5a Or *Today I reveal you as my Son.* Ps 2:7. 1:5b 2 Sam 7:14. 1:6a Or *when he again brings his firstborn son into the world, God will say.* 1:6b Deut 32:43. 1:7 Ps 104:4 (Greek version). 1:8-9 Ps 45:6-7. 1:10-12 Ps 102:25-27. 1:13 Ps 110:1.

I've heard so many different opinions on what God is really like that I'm beginning to wonder if anyone really knows. How can we really know God?

Have you ever assembled a complicated jigsaw puzzle? If so, you know how important the picture on the box is. As you put the puzzle together, you use the picture as a reference.

But what if you had the wrong box top, and the picture didn't match the puzzle? The puzzle would be nearly impossible to assemble (at least until you realized the mistake).

People throughout the world are trying to put the "God puzzle" together. But often they're trying to match the pieces to the wrong picture!

God isn't trying to hide. As Hebrews 1:1-3 tells us, God has clearly shown the world what he is like—through nature, through the Bible, and especially through Christ.

When Jesus was asked point-blank by Philip, he was straightforward in his reply. "Anyone who has seen me has seen the Father!" (John 14:9; see also John 10:30).

It doesn't get more obvious than that! To know what God is like, all you have to do is look at Jesus.

People get their God-pictures from friends who say they believe in God, but never act like it; coaches who pray before games and then swear the paint off of the walls at halftime; and so forth. But these aren't accurate pictures of God.

If you want to know what God is like, you don't have to settle for hearsay. Instead, look at the right picture—look at Christ.

every violation of the law and every act
of disobedience was punished. 3So
what makes us think we can escape if
we ignore this great salvation that was
first announced by the Lord Jesus himself and then delivered to us by those
who heard him speak? 4And God confirmed the message by giving signs and
wonders and various miracles and gifts
of the Holy Spirit whenever he chose.

> Since he himself has gone through suffering and testing, he is able to help us when we are being tested.
>
> *HEBREWS 2:18*

JESUS, THE MAN

5And furthermore, it is not angels who
will control the future world we are
talking about. 6For in one place the
Scriptures say,

"What are mere mortals that you should think about
them,
or a son of man* that you should care for him?
7 Yet you made them only a little lower than the angels
and crowned them with glory and honor.*
8 You gave them authority over all things."*

STILL IN CONTROL 2:8-9

Jesus has authority over everything. His authority is sometimes not apparent, especially when evil actions take place on a daily basis. These actions cause many to wonder whether or not God has totally abandoned the earth. Ever feel this way? But as this passage states, Jesus still is in control. Someday he *will* return to reign as King. Do you believe that? ■

Now when it says "all things," it means nothing is left out.
But we have not yet seen all things put under their authority. 9What we do see is Jesus, who was given a position "a
little lower than the angels"; and because he suffered
death for us, he is now "crowned with glory and honor."
Yes, by God's grace, Jesus tasted death for everyone. 10God,
for whom and through whom everything was made, chose
to bring many children into glory. And it was only right
that he should make Jesus, through his suffering, a perfect
leader, fit to bring them into their salvation.
11So now Jesus and the ones he makes holy have the
same Father. That is why Jesus is not ashamed to call
them his brothers and sisters.* 12For he said to God,

"I will proclaim your name to my brothers and sisters.
I will praise you among your assembled people."*

13He also said,

"I will put my trust in him,"
that is, "I and the children God has given me."*

14Because God's children are human beings—made of flesh and
blood—the Son also became flesh and
blood. For only as a human being
could he die, and only by dying could
he break the power of the devil, who
had* the power of death. 15Only in this
way could he set free all who have
lived their lives as slaves to the fear of
dying.
16We also know that the Son did not
come to help angels; he came to help
the descendants of Abraham. 17There-
fore, it was necessary for him to be
made in every respect like us, his
brothers and sisters,* so that he could
be our merciful and faithful High Priest before God.
Then he could offer a sacrifice that would take away the
sins of the people. 18Since he himself has gone through
suffering and testing, he is able to help us when we are
being tested.

3 JESUS IS GREATER THAN MOSES

And so, dear brothers and sisters who belong to God and*
are partners with those called to heaven, think carefully
about this Jesus whom we declare to be God's messenger* and High Priest. 2For he was faithful to God, who appointed him, just as Moses served faithfully when he was
entrusted with God's entire* house.
3But Jesus deserves far more glory than Moses, just as a
person who builds a house deserves more praise than the
house itself. 4For every house has a builder, but the one
who built everything is God.
5Moses was certainly faithful in God's house as a servant. His work was an illustration of the truths God would
reveal later. 6But Christ, as the Son, is in charge of God's
entire house. And we are God's house, if we keep our
courage and remain confident in our hope in Christ.*
7That is why the Holy Spirit says,

"Today when you hear his voice,
8 don't harden your hearts
as Israel did when they rebelled,
when they tested me in the wilderness.
9 There your ancestors tested and tried my patience,
even though they saw my miracles for forty years.
10 So I was angry with them, and I said,
'Their hearts always turn away from me.
They refuse to do what I tell them.'
11 So in my anger I took an oath:
'They will never enter my place of rest.'"*

12Be careful then, dear brothers and sisters.* Make sure
that your own hearts are not evil and unbelieving, turning
you away from the living God. 13You must warn each

2:6 Or *the Son of Man.* 2:7 Some manuscripts add *You gave them charge of everything you made.* 2:6-8 Ps 8:4-6 (Greek version). 2:11 Greek *brothers;* also in 2:12. 2:12 Ps 22:22. 2:13 Isa 8:17-18. 2:14 Or *has.* 2:17 Greek *like the brothers.* 3:1a Greek *And so, holy brothers who.* 3:1b Greek *God's apostle.* 3:2 Some manuscripts omit *entire.* 3:6 Some manuscripts add *faithful to the end.* 3:7-11 Ps 95:7-11. 3:12 Greek *brothers.*

other every day, while it is still "today," so that none of you will be deceived by sin and hardened against God. [14]For if we are faithful to the end, trusting God just as firmly as when we first believed, we will share in all that belongs to Christ. [15]Remember what it says:

"Today when you hear his voice,
don't harden your hearts
as Israel did when they
rebelled."*

[16]And who was it who rebelled against God, even though they heard his voice? Wasn't it the people Moses led out of Egypt? [17]And who made God angry for forty years? Wasn't it the people who sinned, whose corpses lay in the wilderness? [18]And to whom was God speaking when he took an oath that they would never enter his rest? Wasn't it the people who disobeyed him? [19]So we see that because of their unbelief they were not able to enter his rest.

> So let us come boldly to the throne of our gracious God. There we will receive his mercy, and we will find grace to help us when we need it most.
>
> *HEBREWS 4:16*

TRUE REST 4:1-3

In this passage *rest* refers to a belief in Jesus, whose death makes forgiveness possible. Some of the Jewish Christians who received this letter may have been on the verge of turning back from their promised rest in Christ, just as the people in Moses' day turned back from the Promised Land.

In both cases, the difficulties of the present moment overshadowed the reality of God's promise. Therefore, the people stopped believing that God was able to fulfill his promises. When we trust our own efforts instead of Christ, we too are in danger of turning back. Are you resting in the belief that God will keep his promises? ■

4

PROMISED REST FOR GOD'S PEOPLE

God's promise of entering his rest still stands, so we ought to tremble with fear that some of you might fail to experience it. [2]For this good news—that God has prepared this rest—has been announced to us just as it was to them. But it did them no good because they didn't share the faith of those who listened to God.* [3]For only we who believe can enter his rest. As for the others, God said,

"In my anger I took an oath:
'They will never enter my place of rest,'"*

even though this rest has been ready since he made the world. [4]We know it is ready because of the place in the Scriptures where it mentions the seventh day: "On the seventh day God rested from all his work."* [5]But in the other passage God said, "They will never enter my place of rest."*

[6]So God's rest is there for people to enter, but those who first heard this good news failed to enter because they disobeyed God. [7]So God set another time for entering his rest, and that time is today. God announced this through David much later in the words already quoted:

"Today when you hear his voice,
don't harden your hearts."*

[8]Now if Joshua had succeeded in giving them this rest, God would not have spoken about another day of rest still to come. [9]So there is a special rest* still waiting for the people of God. [10]For all who have entered into God's rest have rested from their labors, just as God did after creating the world. [11]So let us do our best to enter that rest. But if we disobey God, as the people of Israel did, we will fall.

[12]For the word of God is alive and powerful. It is sharper than the sharpest two-edged sword, cutting between soul and spirit, between joint and marrow. It exposes our innermost thoughts and desires. [13]Nothing in all creation is hidden from God. Everything is naked and exposed before his eyes, and he is the one to whom we are accountable.

CHRIST IS OUR HIGH PRIEST

[14]So then, since we have a great High Priest who has entered heaven, Jesus the Son of God, let us hold firmly to what we believe. [15]This High Priest of ours understands our weaknesses, for he faced all of the same testings we do, yet he did not sin. [16]So let us come boldly to the throne of our gracious God. There we will receive his mercy, and we will find grace to help us when we need it most.

5

Every high priest is a man chosen to represent other people in their dealings with God. He presents their gifts to God and offers sacrifices for their sins. [2]And he is able to deal gently with ignorant and wayward people because he himself is subject to the same weaknesses. [3]That is why he must offer sacrifices for his own sins as well as theirs.

[4]And no one can become a high priest simply because he wants such an honor. He must be called by God for this work, just as Aaron was. [5]That is why Christ did not honor himself by assuming he could become High Priest. No, he was chosen by God, who said to him,

"You are my Son.
Today I have become your Father.*"

3:15 Ps 95:7-8. **4:2** Some manuscripts read *they didn't combine what they heard with faith.* **4:3** Ps 95:11. **4:4** Gen 2:2. **4:5** Ps 95:11. **4:7** Ps 95:7-8. **4:9** Or *a Sabbath rest.* **5:5** Or *Today I reveal you as my Son.* Ps 2:7.

6And in another passage God said to him,

"You are a priest forever in the order of
Melchizedek."*

7While Jesus was here on earth, he offered prayers and pleadings, with a loud cry and tears, to the one who could rescue him from death. And God heard his prayers because of his deep reverence for God. 8Even though Jesus was God's Son, he learned obedience from the things he suffered. 9In this way, God qualified him as a perfect High Priest, and he became the source of eternal salvation for all those who obey him. 10And God designated him to be a High Priest in the order of Melchizedek.

PRUNING 6:7-8

Land that produces a good crop receives loving care, but land that produces thorns and briers has to be burned off so that the farmer can start over. In the same way, God prunes branches that haven't produced fruit, in order to encourage fruit to grow (see John 15:1-8). Although we aren't saved by works or conduct, what we do is the evidence of our faith. Being productive for Christ is serious business. How serious are you about your productivity? ■

A CALL TO SPIRITUAL GROWTH

11There is much more we would like to say about this, but it is difficult to explain, especially since you are spiritually dull and don't seem to listen. 12You have been believers so long now that you ought to be teaching others. Instead, you need someone to teach you again the basic things about God's word.* You are like babies who need milk and cannot eat solid food. 13For someone who lives on milk is still an infant and doesn't know how to do what is right. 14Solid food is for those who are mature, who through training have the skill to recognize the difference between right and wrong.

6

So let us stop going over the basic teachings about Christ again and again. Let us go on instead and become mature in our understanding. Surely we don't need to start again with the fundamental importance of repenting from evil deeds and placing our faith in God. 2You don't need further instruction about baptisms, the laying on of hands, the resurrection of the dead, and eternal judgment. 3And so, God willing, we will move forward to further understanding.

4For it is impossible to bring back to repentance those who were once enlightened—those who have experienced the good things of heaven and shared in the Holy Spirit, 5who have tasted the goodness of the word of God and the power of the age to come—6and who then turn away from God. It is impossible to bring such people back to repentance; by rejecting the Son of God, they themselves are nailing him to the cross once again and holding him up to public shame.

7When the ground soaks up the falling rain and bears a good crop for the farmer, it has God's blessing. 8But if a field bears thorns and thistles, it is useless. The farmer will soon condemn that field and burn it.

9Dear friends, even though we are talking this way, we really don't believe it applies to you. We are confident that you are meant for better things, things that come with salvation. 10For God is not unjust. He will not forget how hard you have worked for him and how you have shown your love to him by caring for other believers,* as you still do. 11Our great desire is that you will keep on loving others as long as life lasts, in order to make certain that what you hope for will come true. 12Then you will not become spiritually dull and indifferent. Instead, you will follow the example of those who are going to inherit God's promises because of their faith and endurance.

GOD'S PROMISES BRING HOPE

13For example, there was God's promise to Abraham. Since there was no one greater to swear by, God took an oath in his own name, saying:

14 "I will certainly bless you,
and I will multiply your descendants
beyond number."*

15Then Abraham waited patiently, and he received what God had promised.

16Now when people take an oath, they call on someone greater than themselves to hold them to it. And without any question that oath is binding. 17God also bound himself with an oath, so that those who received the promise could be perfectly sure that he would never change his mind. 18So God has given both his promise and his oath. These two things are unchangeable because it is impossible for God to lie. Therefore, we who have fled to him for refuge can have great confidence as we hold to the hope that lies before us. 19This hope is a strong and trustworthy anchor for our souls. It leads us through the curtain into God's inner sanctuary. 20Jesus has already gone in there for us. He has become our eternal High Priest in the order of Melchizedek.

7

MELCHIZEDEK IS GREATER THAN ABRAHAM

This Melchizedek was king of the city of Salem and also a priest of God Most High. When Abraham was returning home after winning a great battle against the kings, Melchizedek met him and blessed him. 2Then Abraham took a tenth of all he had captured in battle and gave it to Melchizedek. The name Melchizedek means "king of justice," and king of Salem means "king of peace." 3There is no record of his father or mother or any of his ancestors—no beginning or end to his life. He remains a priest forever, resembling the Son of God.

4Consider then how great this Melchizedek was. Even

5:6 Ps 110:4. 5:12 Or *about the oracles of God.* 6:10 Greek *for God's holy people.* 6:14 Gen 22:17.

Abraham, the great patriarch of Israel, recognized this by giving him a tenth of what he had taken in battle. 5Now the law of Moses required that the priests, who are descendants of Levi, must collect a tithe from the rest of the people of Israel,* who are also descendants of Abraham. 6But Melchizedek, who was not a descendant of Levi, collected a tenth from Abraham. And Melchizedek placed a blessing upon Abraham, the one who had already received the promises of God. 7And without question, the person who has the power to give a blessing is greater than the one who is blessed.

8The priests who collect tithes are men who die, so Melchizedek is greater than they are, because we are told that he lives on. 9In addition, we might even say that these Levites—the ones who collect the tithe—paid a tithe to Melchizedek when their ancestor Abraham paid a tithe to him. 10For although Levi wasn't born yet, the seed from which he came was in Abraham's body when Melchizedek collected the tithe from him.

11So if the priesthood of Levi, on which the law was based, could have achieved the perfection God intended, why did God need to establish a different priesthood, with a priest in the order of Melchizedek instead of the order of Levi and Aaron?*

12And if the priesthood is changed, the law must also be changed to permit it. 13For the priest we are talking about belongs to a different tribe, whose members have never served at the altar as priests. 14What I mean is, our Lord came from the tribe of Judah, and Moses never mentioned priests coming from that tribe.

JESUS IS LIKE MELCHIZEDEK

15This change has been made very clear since a different priest, who is like Melchizedek, has appeared. 16Jesus became a priest, not by meeting the physical requirement of belonging to the tribe of Levi, but by the power of a life that cannot be destroyed. 17And the psalmist pointed this out when he prophesied,

> "You are a priest forever in the order of
> Melchizedek."*

18Yes, the old requirement about the priesthood was set aside because it was weak and useless. 19For the law never made anything perfect. But now we have confidence in a better hope, through which we draw near to God.

20This new system was established with a solemn oath. Aaron's descendants became priests without such an oath, 21but there was an oath regarding Jesus. For God said to him,

> "The LORD has taken an oath and will not break
> his vow:
> 'You are a priest forever.'"*

22Because of this oath, Jesus is the one who guarantees this better covenant with God.

23There were many priests under the old system, for death prevented them from remaining in office. 24But because Jesus lives forever, his priesthood lasts forever. 25Therefore he is able, once and forever, to save* those who come to God through him. He lives forever to intercede with God on their behalf.

PAID IN FULL 7:25

The fact that Jesus "is able, once and forever, to save" everyone is staggering. No one else can add to what Jesus did to save us. Jesus is with the Father as a sign that every wrongdoing we could ever commit is already forgiven. (See also 9:24-28.) This, however, is not an encouragement for us to make bad choices simply because we can be forgiven. After all, our actions have consequences. Instead, we might do whatever we do when we receive a great gift: Say thank you. ■

26He is the kind of high priest we need because he is holy and blameless, unstained by sin. He has been set apart from sinners and has been given the highest place of honor in heaven.* 27Unlike those other high priests, he does not need to offer sacrifices every day. They did this for their own sins first and then for the sins of the people. But Jesus did this once for all when he offered himself as the sacrifice for the people's sins. 28The law appointed high priests who were limited by human weakness. But after the law was given, God appointed his Son with an oath, and his Son has been made the perfect High Priest forever.

8

CHRIST IS OUR HIGH PRIEST

Here is the main point: We have a High Priest who sat down in the place of honor beside the throne of the majestic God in heaven. 2There he ministers in the heavenly Tabernacle,* the true place of worship that was built by the Lord and not by human hands.

3And since every high priest is required to offer gifts and sacrifices, our High Priest must make an offering, too. 4If he were here on earth, he would not even be a priest, since there already are priests who offer the gifts required by the law. 5They serve in a system of worship that is only a copy, a shadow of the real one in heaven. For when Moses was getting ready to build the Tabernacle, God gave him this warning: "Be sure that you make everything according to the pattern I have shown you here on the mountain."*

6But now Jesus, our High Priest, has been given a ministry that is far superior to the old priesthood, for he is the one who mediates for us a far better covenant with God, based on better promises.

7If the first covenant had been faultless, there would have been no need for a second covenant to replace it. 8But when God found fault with the people, he said:

7:5 Greek *from their brothers.* 7:11 Greek *the order of Aaron?* 7:17 Ps 110:4. 7:21 Ps 110:4. 7:25 Or *is able to save completely.* 7:26 Or *has been exalted higher than the heavens.* 8:2 Or *tent;* also in 8:5. 8:5 Exod 25:40; 26:30.

"The day is coming, says the LORD,
when I will make a new covenant
with the people of Israel and Judah.
9 This covenant will not be like the one
I made with their ancestors
when I took them by the hand
and led them out of the land of Egypt.
They did not remain faithful to my covenant,
so I turned my back on them, says the LORD.
10 But this is the new covenant I will make
with the people of Israel on that day,* says
the LORD:
I will put my laws in their minds,
and I will write them on their hearts.
I will be their God,
and they will be my people.
11 And they will not need to teach their neighbors,
nor will they need to teach their relatives,*
saying, 'You should know the LORD.'
For everyone, from the least to the greatest,
will know me already.
12 And I will forgive their wickedness,
and I will never again remember their sins."*

[13]When God speaks of a "new" covenant, it means he has
made the first one obsolete. It is now out of date and will
soon disappear.

9 OLD RULES ABOUT WORSHIP

That first covenant between God and Israel had regulations for worship and a place of worship here on earth.
[2]There were two rooms in that Tabernacle.* In the first
room were a lampstand, a table, and sacred loaves of
bread on the table. This room was called the Holy Place.
[3]Then there was a curtain, and behind the curtain was the
second room* called the Most Holy Place. [4]In that room
were a gold incense altar and a wooden chest called the
Ark of the Covenant, which was covered with gold on all
sides. Inside the Ark were a gold jar containing manna,
Aaron's staff that sprouted leaves, and the stone tablets
of the covenant. [5]Above the Ark were the cherubim of divine glory, whose wings stretched out over the Ark's
cover, the place of atonement. But we cannot explain
these things in detail now.

[6]When these things were all in place, the priests regularly entered the first room* as they performed their religious duties. [7]But only the high priest ever entered the
Most Holy Place, and only once a year. And he always offered blood for his own sins and for the sins the people
had committed in ignorance. [8]By these regulations the
Holy Spirit revealed that the entrance to the Most Holy
Place was not freely open as long as the Tabernacle* and
the system it represented were still in use.

[9]This is an illustration pointing to the present time.
For the gifts and sacrifices that the priests offer are not
able to cleanse the consciences of the people who bring
them. [10]For that old system deals only with food and
drink and various cleansing ceremonies—physical regulations that were in effect only until a better system
could be established.

CHRIST IS THE PERFECT SACRIFICE

[11]So Christ has now become the High Priest over all the
good things that have come.* He has entered that greater,
more perfect Tabernacle in heaven, which was not made
by human hands and is not part of this created world.
[12]With his own blood—not the blood of goats and
calves—he entered the Most Holy Place once for all time
and secured our redemption forever.

[13]Under the old system, the blood of goats and bulls
and the ashes of a young cow could cleanse people's
bodies from ceremonial impurity. [14]Just think how
much more the blood of Christ will purify our consciences from sinful deeds* so that we can worship the
living God. For by the power of the eternal Spirit, Christ
offered himself to God as a perfect sacrifice for our
sins. [15]That is why he is the one who mediates a new covenant between God and people, so that all who are called
can receive the eternal inheritance God has promised
them. For Christ died to set them free from the penalty
of the sins they had committed under that first
covenant.

VALUE 9:15

Value, in our human way of thinking, is not measured by how *many* people can have something good, but by how *few*. "Limited edition" means "valuable" because only a few can have it. Eternal life, however, is dramatically different. Although it's the most valuable of all treasures, it's available to all. The more who have it, and the more they express their thankfulness for it, the greater its value! Got faith in God? How do your actions show its value to you? ■

[16]Now when someone leaves a will,* it is necessary to
prove that the person who made it is dead.* [17]The will
goes into effect only after the person's death. While the
person who made it is still alive, the will cannot be put
into effect.

[18]That is why even the first covenant was put into effect with the blood of an animal. [19]For after Moses had
read each of God's commandments to all the people, he
took the blood of calves and goats,* along with water, and
sprinkled both the book of God's law and all the people,
using hyssop branches and scarlet wool. [20]Then he said,
"This blood confirms the covenant God has made with
you."* [21]And in the same way, he sprinkled blood on the
Tabernacle and on everything used for worship. [22]In fact,
according to the law of Moses, nearly everything was

8:10 Greek *after those days.* **8:11** Greek *their brother.* **8:8-12** Jer 31:31-34. **9:2** Or *tent;* also in 9:11, 21. **9:3** Greek *second tent.* **9:6** Greek *first tent.* **9:8** Or *the first room;* Greek reads *the first tent.* **9:11** Some manuscripts read *that are about to come.* **9:14** Greek *from dead works.* **9:16a** Or *covenant;* also in 9:17. **9:16b** Or *Now when someone makes a covenant, it is necessary to ratify it with the death of a sacrifice.* **9:19** Some manuscripts omit *and goats.* **9:20** Exod 24:8.

Imagine you were about to meet someone famous—maybe the lead singer of your favorite band or an actor or politician you admire. Chances are you'd be nervous, wondering what to say and how to act. You wouldn't want to make a fool of yourself by doing or saying something inappropriate.

Now imagine you're just sitting around gabbing with your best friend. You don't worry about what to say or do. You can just be yourself; the talk flows freely.

These two situations illustrate something about the nature of prayer. On the one hand, prayer brings you into the presence of the King of the universe, the Lord and Creator of everything. (See Heb 4:16.) That's fairly intimidating! No wonder people feel tongue-tied when they pray. On the other hand, prayer is simply talking with your heavenly Father, the person who knows you better and loves you more than anyone else does.

When we talk with God, we can be ourselves. We don't need to change how we talk when we talk with him.

Prayer also trains us to hear what God has to say to us. Listening to God requires more patience and more practice than talking to him. Yet when we listen to God, he provides guidance as we seek his will. One caution: If you ever feel God is telling you to do something contrary to Scripture, you have misunderstood. God never contradicts himself or his inspired Word. Seek counsel from your parents, your pastor, your youth minister, or other Christians when this happens.

Time spent in the presence of God helps us to become more like him. Have you ever noticed that when two people spend a lot of time together, they begin to talk, act, and even think alike? The same principle applies to our relationship with God. The more we're with him, the more we become like him.

Prayer is more than simply asking God to give us what we want. It's living, active, and powerful communication with the Lord of all.

purified with blood. For without the shedding of blood, there is no forgiveness.

23That is why the Tabernacle and everything in it, which were copies of things in heaven, had to be purified by the blood of animals. But the real things in heaven had to be purified with far better sacrifices than the blood of animals.

24For Christ did not enter into a holy place made with human hands, which was only a copy of the true one in heaven. He entered into heaven itself to appear now before God on our behalf. 25And he did not enter heaven to offer himself again and again, like the high priest here on earth who enters the Most Holy Place year after year with the blood of an animal. 26If that had been necessary, Christ would have had to die again and again, ever since the world began. But now, once for all time, he has appeared at the end of the age* to remove sin by his own death as a sacrifice.

27And just as each person is destined to die once and after that comes judgment, 28so also Christ died once for all time as a sacrifice to take away the sins of many people. He will come again, not to deal with our sins, but to bring salvation to all who are eagerly waiting for him.

10 CHRIST'S SACRIFICE ONCE FOR ALL

The old system under the law of Moses was only a shadow, a dim preview of the good things to come, not the good things themselves. The sacrifices under that system were repeated again and again, year after year, but they were never able to provide perfect cleansing for those who came to worship. 2If they could have provided perfect cleansing, the sacrifices would have stopped, for the worshipers would have been purified once for all time, and their feelings of guilt would have disappeared.

3But instead, those sacrifices actually reminded them of their sins year after year. 4For it is not possible for the blood of bulls and goats to take away sins. 5That is why, when Christ* came into the world, he said to God,

"You did not want animal sacrifices or sin offerings.
But you have given me a body to offer.
6 You were not pleased with burnt offerings
or other offerings for sin.
7 Then I said, 'Look, I have come to do your will, O God—
as is written about me in the Scriptures.'"*

9:26 Greek *the ages.* **10:5** Greek *he;* also in 10:8. **10:5-7** Ps 40:6-8 (Greek version).

KEEP MEETING! 10:25

To neglect meeting with other Christians (for example, going to church) is to give up the encouragement and help of other Christians. We gather together to share our faith and strengthen each other in the Lord. As we get closer to the time of Christ's return, we may face many spiritual struggles. We'll need to pull together, just as any family would do in a crisis. (See also the "I Wonder" note below.) ■

8First, Christ said, "You did not want animal sacrifices or
sin offerings or burnt offerings or other offerings for sin,
nor were you pleased with them" (though they are required by the law of Moses). 9Then he said, "Look, I have
come to do your will." He cancels the first covenant in order to put the second into effect. 10For God's will was for
us to be made holy by the sacrifice of the body of Jesus
Christ, once for all time.

11Under the old covenant, the priest stands and ministers before the altar day after day, offering the same sacrifices again and again, which can never take away sins.
12But our High Priest offered himself to God as a single
sacrifice for sins, good for all time. Then he sat down in
the place of honor at God's right hand. 13There he waits
until his enemies are humbled and made a footstool
under his feet. 14For by that one offering he forever made
perfect those who are being made holy.

15And the Holy Spirit also testifies that this is so. For he
says,

16 "This is the new covenant I will make
with my people on that day,* says the LORD:
I will put my laws in their hearts,
and I will write them on their minds."*

17Then he says,

"I will never again remember
their sins and lawless deeds."*

18And when sins have been forgiven, there is no need to
offer any more sacrifices.

A CALL TO PERSEVERE

19And so, dear brothers and sisters,* we can boldly enter
heaven's Most Holy Place because of the blood of Jesus.
20By his death,* Jesus opened a new and life-giving way
through the curtain into the Most Holy Place. 21And since
we have a great High Priest who rules over God's house,
22let us go right into the presence of God with sincere
hearts fully trusting him. For our guilty consciences have
been sprinkled with Christ's blood to make us clean, and
our bodies have been washed with pure water.

23Let us hold tightly without wavering to the hope we
affirm, for God can be trusted to keep his promise. 24Let
us think of ways to motivate one another to acts of love
and good works. 25And let us not neglect our meeting together, as some people do, but encourage one another,
especially now that the day of his return is drawing near.

26Dear friends, if we deliberately continue sinning after we have received knowledge of the truth, there is no
longer any sacrifice that will cover these sins. 27There is
only the terrible expectation of God's judgment and the
raging fire that will consume his enemies. 28For anyone
who refused to obey the law of Moses was put to death
without mercy on the testimony of two or three witnesses. 29Just think how much worse the punishment will
be for those who have trampled on the Son of God, and
have treated the blood of the covenant, which made us
holy, as if it were common and unholy, and have insulted
and disdained the Holy Spirit who brings God's mercy to
us. 30For we know the one who said,

"I will take revenge.
I will pay them back."*

He also said,

"The LORD will judge his own people."*

31It is a terrible thing to fall into the hands of the living
God.

32Think back on those early days when you first
learned about Christ.* Remember how you remained
faithful even though it meant terrible suffering. 33Some-
times you were exposed to public ridicule and were
beaten, and sometimes you helped others who were
suffering the same things. 34You suffered along with

10:16a Greek *after those days.* **10:16b** Jer 31:33a. **10:17** Jer 31:34b. **10:19** Greek *brothers.* **10:20** Greek *Through his flesh.* **10:30a** Deut 32:35. **10:30b** Deut 32:36. **10:32** Greek *when you were first enlightened.*

Some of my friends who are Christians say they don't like going to church because it's boring. Why do we have to go?

Imagine growing up without a family. Families are designed to take care of your daily needs and to give you the continual love and guidance you need as you are growing up.

In Hebrews 10:24-25, we're warned against neglecting our church meetings. The body of Christ is our spiritual family. If we stay away from church gatherings, we are left to try to survive by ourselves.

The church, like the family, can often be undervalued for the role it plays in our spiritual growth. Some Christians don't recognize the positive influence of other Christians until years later. At that point, they realize that they would still be spiritual babies without the church's influence and love.

those who were thrown into jail, and when all you owned
was taken from you, you accepted it with joy. You knew
there were better things waiting for you that will last
forever.
35So do not throw away this confident trust in the Lord.
Remember the great reward it brings you! 36Patient endurance is what you need now, so that you will continue
to do God's will. Then you will receive all that he has
promised.

37 "For in just a little while,
the Coming One will come and not delay.
38 And my righteous ones will live by faith.*
But I will take no pleasure in anyone who
turns away."*

39But we are not like those who turn away from God to
their own destruction. We are the faithful ones, whose
souls will be saved.

11 GREAT EXAMPLES OF FAITH

Faith is the confidence that what we hope for will actually happen; it gives us assurance about things we cannot
see. 2Through their faith, the people in days of old earned
a good reputation.
3By faith we understand that the entire universe was
formed at God's command, that what we now see did not
come from anything that can be seen.
4It was by faith that Abel brought a more acceptable
offering to God than Cain did. Abel's offering gave evidence that he was a righteous man, and God showed his
approval of his gifts. Although Abel is long dead, he still
speaks to us by his example of faith.
5It was by faith that Enoch was taken up to heaven
without dying—"he disappeared, because God took him."*
For before he was taken up, he was known as a person
who pleased God. 6And it is impossible to please God
without faith. Anyone who wants to come to him must
believe that God exists and that he rewards those who
sincerely seek him.
7It was by faith that Noah built a large boat to save his
family from the flood. He obeyed God, who warned him
about things that had never happened before. By his faith
Noah condemned the rest of the world, and he received
the righteousness that comes by faith.
8It was by faith that Abraham obeyed when God called
him to leave home and go to another land that God would
give him as his inheritance. He went without knowing
where he was going. 9And even when he reached the land
God promised him, he lived there by faith—for he was
like a foreigner, living in tents. And so did Isaac and Jacob, who inherited the same promise. 10Abraham was
confidently looking forward to a city with eternal foundations, a city designed and built by God.
11It was by faith that even Sarah was able to have a
child, though she was barren and was too old. She
believed* that God would keep his promise. 12And so a
whole nation came from this one man who was as good as
dead—a nation with so many people that, like the stars in
the sky and the sand on the seashore, there is no way to
count them.
13All these people died still believing what God had
promised them. They did not receive what was promised,
but they saw it all from a distance and welcomed it. They
agreed that they were foreigners and nomads here on
earth. 14Obviously people who say such things are looking forward to a country they can call their own. 15If they
had longed for the country they came from, they could
have gone back. 16But they were looking for a better
place, a heavenly homeland. That is why God is not
ashamed to be called their God, for he has prepared a city
for them.

FAITHFUL 11:13-16

Although the people of faith listed here died without receiving all that God had promised, they still believed that God would keep his promises. Many Christians become frustrated and defeated because their needs, wants, expectations, and demands were not immediately met when they believed in Christ. They become impatient and want to quit. Are you discouraged because you're still waiting for a promise to be fulfilled? Take courage from these heroes of faith who lived and died without seeing the fruit of their faith on earth, yet continued to believe. ■

17It was by faith that Abraham offered Isaac as a sacrifice when God was testing him. Abraham, who had received God's promises, was ready to sacrifice his only
son, Isaac, 18even though God had told him, "Isaac is the
son through whom your descendants will be counted."*
19Abraham reasoned that if Isaac died, God was able to
bring him back to life again. And in a sense, Abraham did
receive his son back from the dead.
20It was by faith that Isaac promised blessings for the
future to his sons, Jacob and Esau.
21It was by faith that Jacob, when he was old and dying,
blessed each of Joseph's sons and bowed in worship as he
leaned on his staff.
22It was by faith that Joseph, when he was about to die,
said confidently that the people of Israel would leave
Egypt. He even commanded them to take his bones with
them when they left.
23It was by faith that Moses' parents hid him for three
months when he was born. They saw that God had given
them an unusual child, and they were not afraid to disobey the king's command.
24It was by faith that Moses, when he grew up, refused
to be called the son of Pharaoh's daughter. 25He chose to
share the oppression of God's people instead of enjoying
the fleeting pleasures of sin. 26He thought it was better to

10:38 Or *my righteous ones will live by their faithfulness;* Greek reads *my righteous one will live by faith.* **10:37-38** Hab 2:3-4. **11:5** Gen 5:24.
11:11 Or *It was by faith that he [Abraham] was able to have a child, even though Sarah was barren and he was too old. He believed.*
11:18 Gen 21:12.

suffer for the sake of Christ than to own the treasures of
Egypt, for he was looking ahead to his great reward. 27 It
was by faith that Moses left the land of Egypt, not fearing
the king's anger. He kept right on going because he kept
his eyes on the one who is invisible. 28 It was by faith that
Moses commanded the people of Israel to keep the Passover and to sprinkle blood on the doorposts so that the
angel of death would not kill their firstborn sons.
29 It was by faith that the people of Israel went right
through the Red Sea as though they were on dry ground.
But when the Egyptians tried to follow, they were all
drowned.
30 It was by faith that the people of Israel marched
around Jericho for seven days, and the walls came crashing down.
31 It was by faith that Rahab the prostitute was not destroyed with the people in her city who refused to obey
God. For she had given a friendly welcome to the spies.
32 How much more do I need to say? It would take too
long to recount the stories of the faith of Gideon, Barak,
Samson, Jephthah, David, Samuel, and all the prophets.
33 By faith these people overthrew kingdoms, ruled with
justice, and received what God had promised them. They
shut the mouths of lions, 34 quenched the flames of fire,
and escaped death by the edge of the sword. Their weakness was turned to strength. They became strong in battle and put whole armies to flight. 35 Women received
their loved ones back again from death.
But others were tortured, refusing to turn from God in
order to be set free. They placed their hope in a better life
after the resurrection. 36 Some were jeered at, and their
backs were cut open with whips. Others were chained in
prisons. 37 Some died by stoning, some were sawed in
half,* and others were killed with the sword. Some went
about wearing skins of sheep and goats, destitute and oppressed and mistreated. 38 They were too good for this
world, wandering over deserts and mountains, hiding in
caves and holes in the ground.
39 All these people earned a good reputation because of
their faith, yet none of them received all that God had
promised. 40 For God had something better in mind for
us, so that they would not reach perfection without us.

12 GOD'S DISCIPLINE PROVES HIS LOVE

Therefore, since we are surrounded by such a huge
crowd of witnesses to the life of faith, let us strip off
every weight that slows us down, especially the sin that so
easily trips us up. And let us run with endurance the race
God has set before us. 2 We do this by keeping our eyes on
Jesus, the champion who initiates and perfects our
faith.* Because of the joy* awaiting him, he endured the
cross, disregarding its shame. Now he is seated in the
place of honor beside God's throne. 3 Think of all the hostility he endured from sinful people;* then you won't become weary and give up. 4 After all, you have not yet given
your lives in your struggle against sin.

CONSISTENCY

Follow for six months the paths of Will and Jackson, two guys who made commitments to Christ in August at youth camp:

September: Both guys begin attending a midweek Bible study sponsored by a local church.

October: Both guys make a commitment to spend time with God and start digging into his Word.

November: Will shares his newfound faith in Christ with two friends on the football team. Jackson, claiming a busy schedule, begins skipping Bible study.

December: Will begins to be mentored by an "older brother" in the faith—his cousin Richard. Jackson no longer reads his Bible.

January: Will has signed up to go to a Christian discipleship conference over spring break. Jackson doesn't want to go to the conference. Also, he acts weird whenever Will tries to talk to him about spiritual matters.

February: Will leads his girlfriend to Christ. Jackson's girlfriend is pregnant and planning to get an abortion.

Why do you think Will was so consistent while Jackson fell away? For a possible answer, read Hebrews 12:1-4.

5 And have you forgotten the encouraging words God
spoke to you as his children?* He said,

"My child,* don't make light of the
LORD's discipline,
and don't give up when he corrects you.
6 For the LORD disciplines those he loves,
and he punishes each one he accepts as
his child."*

7 As you endure this divine discipline, remember that God
is treating you as his own children. Who ever heard of a
child who is never disciplined by its father? 8 If God
doesn't discipline you as he does all of his children, it
means that you are illegitimate and are not really his children at all. 9 Since we respected our earthly fathers who
disciplined us, shouldn't we submit even more to the discipline of the Father of our spirits, and live forever?*
10 For our earthly fathers disciplined us for a few years,
doing the best they knew how. But God's discipline is always good for us, so that we might share in his holiness.
11 No discipline is enjoyable while it is happening—it's
painful! But afterward there will be a peaceful harvest of
right living for those who are trained in this way.
12 So take a new grip with your tired hands and
strengthen your weak knees. 13 Mark out a straight path
for your feet so that those who are weak and lame will not
fall but become strong.

11:37 Some manuscripts add *some were tested.* **12:2a** Or *Jesus, the originator and perfecter of our faith.* **12:2b** Or *Instead of the joy.* **12:3** Some manuscripts read *Think of how people hurt themselves by opposing him.* **12:5a** Greek *sons;* also in 12:7, 8. **12:5b** Greek *son;* also in 12:6, 7. **12:5-6** Prov 3:11-12 (Greek version). **12:9** Or *and really live?*

keeping it real

Money and material things used to be very important to me. I cared a lot about the clothes I wore. I didn't think I had much in common with people who didn't have as much as I did.

Then I met Delaney. Even though she attended my school, I didn't know her, because we hung out with different groups. I got to know her at a Christian camp. She and I were worlds apart in lots of ways. Her parents didn't have much money and she didn't care about fashion at all. Yet Delaney was the most caring person I had ever met. That summer she turned out to be a good friend to me as I went through a rough time. Some other kids at the camp spread some untrue rumors about me, which hurt me a lot. But Delaney was always there to listen and encourage.

That fall when we returned to school, I began to see how shallow some of my other friendships were compared to what I'd experienced with Delaney. I began to do more things with her and her friends.

I asked Delaney why she didn't seem to care about money. She said, "Sometimes I do care that I don't have nice clothes like you. But I found a Bible verse that says we're not to love money. Instead, we should be satisfied with what we have. I try to do that." She showed me the verse: Hebrews 13:5. What struck me was that she seemed to be more satisfied with what she had than I was, even though she owned much less. I knew she had something that I was just beginning to appreciate: the sense that God really was with her.

My attitude toward money and toward people started to change as I prayed that God would help me to be satisfied with what I had and not care so much about externals. I saw that God—and true friends—look on the heart, not on whether you wear the latest fashions.

—**Katie**

A CALL TO LISTEN TO GOD

14Work at living in peace with everyone, and work at living a holy life, for those who are not holy will not see the
Lord. 15Look after each other so that none of you fails to
receive the grace of God. Watch out that no poisonous
root of bitterness grows up to trouble you, corrupting
many. 16Make sure that no one is immoral or godless
like Esau, who traded his birthright as the firstborn son
for a single meal. 17You know that afterward, when he
wanted his father's blessing, he was rejected. It was too
late for repentance, even though he begged with bitter
tears.

18You have not come to a physical mountain,* to a
place of flaming fire, darkness, gloom, and whirlwind, as
the Israelites did at Mount Sinai. 19For they heard an awesome trumpet blast and a voice so terrible that they
begged God to stop speaking. 20They staggered back
under God's command: "If even an animal touches the
mountain, it must be stoned to death."* 21Moses himself
was so frightened at the sight that he said, "I am terrified
and trembling."*

22No, you have come to Mount Zion, to the city of the
living God, the heavenly Jerusalem, and to countless
thousands of angels in a joyful gathering. 23You have
come to the assembly of God's firstborn children, whose
names are written in heaven. You have come to God himself, who is the judge over all things. You have come to the
spirits of the righteous ones in heaven who have now
been made perfect. 24You have come to Jesus, the one who
mediates the new covenant between God and people, and
to the sprinkled blood, which speaks of forgiveness instead of crying out for vengeance like the blood of Abel.

25Be careful that you do not refuse to listen to the One

12:18 Greek *to something that can be touched.* **12:20** Exod 19:13. **12:21** Deut 9:19.

OUR COACH 12:12-13

God is not only a disciplining parent, he also is a coach who sometimes pushes us beyond our comfort zone in order to help us to excel. Although we may not feel strong enough to push on to victory, we "can do everything through Christ, who gives [us] strength" (Phil 4:13). We can use this strength to help those around us who struggle. ■

who is speaking. For if the people of Israel did not escape when they refused to listen to Moses, the earthly messenger, we will certainly not escape if we reject the One who speaks to us from heaven! [26]When God spoke from Mount Sinai his voice shook the earth, but now he makes another promise: "Once again I will shake not only the earth but the heavens also."* [27]This means that all of creation will be shaken and removed, so that only unshakable things will remain.

[28]Since we are receiving a Kingdom that is unshakable, let us be thankful and please God by worshiping him with holy fear and awe. [29]For our God is a devouring fire.

13 CONCLUDING WORDS

Keep on loving each other as brothers and sisters.* [2]Don't forget to show hospitality to strangers, for some who have done this have entertained angels without realizing it! [3]Remember those in prison, as if you were there yourself. Remember also those being mistreated, as if you felt their pain in your own bodies.

[4]Give honor to marriage, and remain faithful to one another in marriage. God will surely judge people who are immoral and those who commit adultery.

[5]Don't love money; be satisfied with what you have. For God has said,

"I will never fail you.
I will never abandon you."*

[6]So we can say with confidence,

"The LORD is my helper,
so I will have no fear.
What can mere people do to me?"*

UNCHANGING 13:8

You change classes every day. Friendships begin and end. Someday you will leave your present school. Life seems to be in a constant state of change. Yet, there are some constants. Jesus "is the same yesterday, today, and forever." In a changing world we can trust our unchanging Lord. So, do you? ■

[7]Remember your leaders who taught you the word of God. Think of all the good that has come from their lives, and follow the example of their faith.

[8]Jesus Christ is the same yesterday, today, and forever. [9]So do not be attracted by strange, new ideas. Your strength comes from God's grace, not from rules about food, which don't help those who follow them.

[10]We have an altar from which the priests in the Tabernacle* have no right to eat. [11]Under the old system, the high priest brought the blood of animals into the Holy Place as a sacrifice for sin, and the bodies of the animals were burned outside the camp. [12]So also Jesus suffered and died outside the city gates to make his people holy by means of his own blood. [13]So let us go out to him, outside the camp, and bear the disgrace he bore. [14]For this world is not our permanent home; we are looking forward to a home yet to come.

MATURITY 13:15-25

Hebrews is a call to Christian maturity. Although this book was addressed to first-century Jewish Christians, it applies to Christians of any age or background. The road to Christian maturity begins when we make Christ the beginning and end of our faith. To mature, we have to be willing to submit our plans to him, rather than call our own shots. Is spiritual maturity your goal? ■

[15]Therefore, let us offer through Jesus a continual sacrifice of praise to God, proclaiming our allegiance to his name. [16]And don't forget to do good and to share with those in need. These are the sacrifices that please God.

[17]Obey your spiritual leaders, and do what they say. Their work is to watch over your souls, and they are accountable to God. Give them reason to do this with joy and not with sorrow. That would certainly not be for your benefit.

[18]Pray for us, for our conscience is clear and we want to live honorably in everything we do. [19]And especially pray that I will be able to come back to you soon.

20 Now may the God of peace—
who brought up from the dead our Lord Jesus,
the great Shepherd of the sheep,
and ratified an eternal covenant with his blood—
21 may he equip you with all you need
for doing his will.
May he produce in you,*
through the power of Jesus Christ,
every good thing that is pleasing to him.
All glory to him forever and ever! Amen.

[22]I urge you, dear brothers and sisters,* to pay attention to what I have written in this brief exhortation.

[23]I want you to know that our brother Timothy has been released from jail. If he comes here soon, I will bring him with me to see you.

[24]Greet all your leaders and all the believers there.* The believers from Italy send you their greetings.

[25]May God's grace be with you all.

12:26 Hag 2:6. 13:1 Greek *Continue in brotherly love.* 13:5 Deut 31:6, 8. 13:6 Ps 118:6. 13:10 Or *tent.* 13:21 Some manuscripts read *in us.* 13:22 Greek *brothers.* 13:24 Greek *all of God's holy people.*

AT FIRST you had trouble sleeping. Then came the headaches. Yesterday your teeth hurt and your fingernails turned blue for several hours. This morning your mom asked if you'd been sprayed by a skunk.

The doctor tries to hold her breath as she asks you questions. She nods knowingly as you tick off your symptoms. After looking in your eyes and noting your swollen eardrums, she orders some lab work.

A few hours later she returns to tell you, "Just what I suspected—you have an extremely high number of antibiomolecularsucrothyamin microbes in your liver."

"Huh?" you gulp.

"Oh, don't worry. You have a common ailment we call odoramonia. We'll put you on an antibiotic and get you eating a balanced diet, and you'll be fine."

Aren't doctors amazing?

God does the same thing for us spiritually.

By looking at our actions (or lack of action) God can tell us exactly what attitudes and desires need healing. His Word gives detailed prescriptions for curing behaviors.

Are you sick spiritually? Are you fighting worldly infections or the disease of disobedience? No matter what your ailment, the Epistle of James has the cure.

james

stats

PURPOSE: To expose unethical practices and to teach right Christian behavior

AUTHOR: James, Jesus' brother, a leader in the Jerusalem church

TO WHOM WRITTEN: First-century Jewish Christians residing in Gentile communities outside Palestine; Christians everywhere

DATE WRITTEN: Probably A.D. 49, prior to the Jerusalem council held in A.D. 50

SETTING: This letter expresses James's concern for persecuted Christians who were once part of the Jerusalem church.

KEY points

TRIALS
James, the brother of Jesus, warned believers about the inevitability of trials and temptations in life. Successfully overcoming these adversities produces maturity and strong character.

LIVING FAITH
James contrasted empty faith ("claims without conduct") with faith that works. Commitment to love and to serve is evidence of true faith.

LAW OF LOVE
James reminded believers of the "law of love"—the debt of love owed to others, as Jesus once commanded. (See also Matthew 19:19). Keeping the law of love shows that our faith is vital and real.

WISE SPEECH
James explained how God offers wisdom to control the tongue. This wisdom is shown by the way a person controls his or her speech.

WEALTH
James warned Christians not to compromise with worldly attitudes about wealth. Because the glory of wealth fades, Christians are encouraged to store up heavenly treasures through sincere, impartial service.

1

GREETINGS FROM JAMES

This letter is from James, a slave of God
and of the Lord Jesus Christ.
I am writing to the "twelve tribes"—
Jewish believers scattered abroad.
Greetings!

FAITH AND ENDURANCE

2Dear brothers and sisters,* when
troubles come your way, consider it an
opportunity for great joy. 3For you
know that when your faith is tested,
your endurance has a chance to grow.
4So let it grow, for when your endurance is fully developed, you will be perfect and complete, needing nothing.
5If you need wisdom, ask our gener-
ous God, and he will give it to you. He will not rebuke you
for asking. 6But when you ask him, be sure that your faith
is in God alone. Do not waver, for a person with divided
loyalty is as unsettled as a wave of the sea that is blown and
tossed by the wind. 7Such people should not expect to receive anything from the Lord. 8Their loyalty is divided between God and the world, and they are unstable in
everything they do.
9Believers who are* poor have something to boast
about, for God has honored them. 10And those who
are rich should boast that God has humbled them.
They will fade away like a little flower in the field.
11The hot sun rises and the grass withers; the little
flower droops and falls, and its beauty fades away. In
the same way, the rich will fade away with all of their
achievements.

> Understand this, my dear brothers and sisters: You must all be quick to listen, slow to speak, and slow to get angry.
>
> *JAMES 1:19*

ESCAPE! 1:12-15

Temptation begins with a thought. It becomes sin when we dwell on the thought and allow it to become an action. Like a snowball rolling downhill, sin's destruction grows the more we let that thought have its way. The best time to stop a snowball is at the top of the hill, before it's too big or moving too fast to control. In the same way, we can escape the destruction of bad choices by not giving in to temptation in the first place. (See Matt 4:1-11; 1 Cor 10:13; and 2 Tim 2:22 for more about escaping temptation.) ■

12God blesses those who patiently endure testing and
temptation. Afterward they will receive the crown of life
that God has promised to those who love him. 13And remember, when you are being tempted, do not say, "God is
tempting me." God is never tempted to do wrong,* and he
never tempts anyone else. 14Temptation comes from our
own desires, which entice us and drag us away. 15These
desires give birth to sinful actions.
And when sin is allowed to grow, it
gives birth to death.
16So don't be misled, my dear brothers and sisters. 17Whatever is good and
perfect comes down to us from God
our Father, who created all the lights in
the heavens.* He never changes or
casts a shifting shadow.* 18He chose to
give birth to us by giving us his true
word. And we, out of all creation, became his prized possession.*

LISTENING AND DOING

19Understand this, my dear brothers
and sisters: You must all be quick to
listen, slow to speak, and slow to get
angry. 20Human anger* does not pro-
duce the righteousness* God desires. 21So get rid of all
the filth and evil in your lives, and humbly accept the
word God has planted in your hearts, for it has the power
to save your souls.

OBEDIENCE

The First Church youth group has just heard a great talk about the importance of serving others. On the way home, three friends discuss the meeting:

"Ray is a great speaker! He's so funny! Don't you think so, dude?"

"*¡Por supuesto!* [Of course!] His talk was awesome."

"I'm sayin'! I feel so convicted. I never do anything for my mama or my pops."

"His suggestion about getting involved with the after school tutoring program is good."

"Yeah, I'm hyped about that. We should do that sometime."

Now, let's listen in on the conversation a few minutes later:

"So, what's up for this weekend?"

"Probably the same ol' stuff—go somewhere and hang out."

"Man, there's nothin' around here for us to do. I'm as bored as a board."

"I agree!"

What's wrong with that conversation? Anything? Check out James 1:21-27. Based on this passage, what would you suggest to the three friends?

22But don't just listen to God's word. You must do what
it says. Otherwise, you are only fooling yourselves. 23For if
you listen to the word and don't obey, it is like glancing at
your face in a mirror. 24You see yourself, walk away, and

1:2 Greek *brothers;* also in 1:16, 19. 1:9 Greek *The brother who is.* 1:13 Or *God should not be put to a test by evil people.* 1:17a Greek *from above, from the Father of lights.* 1:17b Some manuscripts read *He never changes, as a shifting shadow does.* 1:18 Greek *we became a kind of firstfruit of his creatures.* 1:20a Greek *A man's anger.* 1:20b Or *the justice.*

forget what you look like. 25But if you look carefully into the perfect law that sets you free, and if you do what it says and don't forget what you heard, then God will bless you for doing it.

26If you claim to be religious but don't control your tongue, you are fooling yourself, and your religion is worthless. 27Pure and genuine religion in the sight of God the Father means caring for orphans and widows in their distress and refusing to let the world corrupt you.

2

A WARNING AGAINST PREJUDICE

My dear brothers and sisters,* how can you claim to have faith in our glorious Lord Jesus Christ if you favor some people over others?

2For example, suppose someone comes into your meeting* dressed in fancy clothes and expensive jewelry, and another comes in who is poor and dressed in dirty clothes. 3If you give special attention and a good seat to the rich person, but you say to the poor one, "You can stand over there, or else sit on the floor"—well, 4doesn't this discrimination show that your judgments are guided by evil motives?

5Listen to me, dear brothers and sisters. Hasn't God chosen the poor in this world to be rich in faith? Aren't they the ones who will inherit the Kingdom he promised to those who love him? 6But you dishonor the poor! Isn't it the rich who oppress you and drag you into court? 7Aren't they the ones who slander Jesus Christ, whose noble name* you bear?

8Yes indeed, it is good when you obey the royal law as found in the Scriptures: "Love your neighbor as yourself."* 9But if you favor some people over others, you are committing a sin. You are guilty of breaking the law.

10For the person who keeps all of the laws except one is as guilty as a person who has broken all of God's laws. 11For the same God who said, "You must not commit adultery," also said, "You must not murder."* So if you murder someone but do not commit adultery, you have still broken the law.

12So whatever you say or whatever you do, remember that you will be judged by the law that sets you free. 13There will be no mercy for those who have not shown mercy to others. But if you have been merciful, God will be merciful when he judges you.

FAITH WITHOUT GOOD DEEDS IS DEAD

14What good is it, dear brothers and sisters, if you say you have faith but don't show it by your actions? Can that kind of faith save anyone? 15Suppose you see a brother or sister who has no food or clothing, 16and you say, "Good-bye and have a good day; stay warm and eat well"—but then you don't give that person any food or clothing. What good does that do?

17So you see, faith by itself isn't enough. Unless it produces good deeds, it is dead and useless.

18Now someone may argue, "Some people have faith; others have good deeds." But I say, "How can you show me your faith if you don't have good deeds? I will show you my faith by my good deeds."

19You say you have faith, for you believe that there is one God.* Good for you! Even the demons believe this, and they tremble in terror. 20How foolish! Can't you see that faith without good deeds is useless?

21Don't you remember that our ancestor Abraham was shown to be right with God by his actions when he offered his son Isaac on the altar? 22You see, his faith and his actions worked together. His actions made his faith complete. 23And so it happened just as the Scriptures say: "Abraham believed God, and God counted him as righteous because of his faith."* He was even called the friend of God.* 24So you see, we are shown to be right with God by what we do, not by faith alone.

25Rahab the prostitute is another example. She was shown to be right with God by her actions when she hid those messengers and sent them safely away by a different road. 26Just as the body is dead without breath,* so also faith is dead without good works.

2:1 Greek *brothers;* also in 2:5, 14. **2:2** Greek *your synagogue.* **2:7** Greek *slander the noble name.* **2:8** Lev 19:18. **2:11** Exod 20:13-14; Deut 5:17-18. **2:19** Some manuscripts read *that God is one;* see Deut 6:4. **2:23a** Gen 15:6. **2:23b** See Isa 41:8. **2:26** Or *without spirit.*

Okay, first we're told that we can't earn salvation. Next we're told that we have to do stuff to prove that we're saved. What's up with that?

James 1:22-27 and 2:14-26 have caused much debate. Here's a sample of both: "Don't just listen to God's word. You must do what it says. Otherwise, you are only fooling yourselves. . . . If you claim to be religious but don't control your tongue, you are fooling yourself, and your religion is worthless. Pure and genuine religion in the sight of God the Father means caring for orphans and widows in their distress and refusing to let the world corrupt you" (James 1:22-27). "Faith by itself isn't enough. Unless it produces good deeds, it is dead and useless" (2:17).

To put both passages simply, actions speak louder than words.

If someone declared his or her love for you, but within minutes began spreading vicious rumors about you, would you believe that he or she loved you? Not likely, right?

On the same token, many people claim to be Christians. Yet their lives don't reflect the fruit of the Spirit (see Gal 5:22-23) or a willingness to grow. In fact, they don't seem any different than they were B.C. (Before Christ).

We can't earn God's forgiveness. Jesus already paid the price for that by dying on the cross. We can, however, show our gratitude and acceptance of that act of love by showing his love toward others.

3

CONTROLLING THE TONGUE

Dear brothers and sisters,* not many of you should become teachers in the church, for we who teach will be
judged more strictly. 2Indeed, we all make many mistakes. For if we could control our tongues, we would be
perfect and could also control ourselves in every other
way.
3We can make a large horse go wherever we want by
means of a small bit in its mouth. 4And a small rudder
makes a huge ship turn wherever the pilot chooses to go,
even though the winds are strong. 5In the same way, the
tongue is a small thing that makes grand speeches.
But a tiny spark can set a great forest on fire. 6And the
tongue is a flame of fire. It is a whole world of wickedness, corrupting your entire body. It can set your whole
life on fire, for it is set on fire by hell itself.*
7People can tame all kinds of animals, birds, reptiles,
and fish, 8but no one can tame the tongue. It is restless
and evil, full of deadly poison. 9Sometimes it praises our
Lord and Father, and sometimes it curses those who have
been made in the image of God. 10And so blessing and
cursing come pouring out of the same mouth. Surely, my
brothers and sisters, this is not right! 11Does a spring of
water bubble out with both fresh water and bitter water?
12Does a fig tree produce olives, or a grapevine produce
figs? No, and you can't draw fresh water from a salty
spring.*

SAY WHAT? 3:1-12

According to James, "The tongue is a small thing that makes grand speeches. But a tiny spark can set a great forest on fire" (James 3:5). So, what you say and what you *don't* say are both important. Proper speech is not only saying the right words at the right time, but also controlling your desire to say what you shouldn't. Examples of wrongly using the tongue include gossiping, putting others down, bragging, manipulating, false teaching, exaggerating, complaining, flattering, and lying. Before you speak, you might ask, "Is it true, is it necessary, and is it kind?" ■

TRUE WISDOM COMES FROM GOD

13If you are wise and understand God's ways, prove it by
living an honorable life, doing good works with the humility that comes from wisdom. 14But if you are bitterly
jealous and there is selfish ambition in your heart, don't
cover up the truth with boasting and lying. 15For jealousy
and selfishness are not God's kind of wisdom. Such
things are earthly, unspiritual, and demonic. 16For wherever there is jealousy and selfish ambition, there you will
find disorder and evil of every kind.
17But the wisdom from above is first of all pure. It is
also peace loving, gentle at all times, and willing to yield
to others. It is full of mercy and good deeds. It shows no
favoritism and is always sincere. 18And those who are
peacemakers will plant seeds of peace and reap a harvest
of righteousness.*

4

DRAWING CLOSE TO GOD

What is causing the quarrels and fights among you?
Don't they come from the evil desires at war within you?
2You want what you don't have, so you scheme and kill to
get it. You are jealous of what others have, but you can't
get it, so you fight and wage war to take it away from
them. Yet you don't have what you want because you
don't ask God for it. 3And even when you ask, you don't
get it because your motives are all wrong—you want only
what will give you pleasure.
4You adulterers!* Don't you realize that friendship
with the world makes you an enemy of God? I say it again:
If you want to be a friend of the world, you make yourself
an enemy of God. 5What do you think the Scriptures
mean when they say that the spirit God has placed within
us is filled with envy?* 6But he gives us even more grace
to stand against such evil desires. As the Scriptures say,

"God opposes the proud
but favors the humble."*

7So humble yourselves before God. Resist the devil,
and he will flee from you. 8Come close to God, and God
will come close to you. Wash your hands, you sinners; purify your hearts, for your loyalty is divided between God
and the world. 9Let there be tears for what you have done.
Let there be sorrow and deep grief. Let there be sadness
instead of laughter, and gloom instead of joy. 10Humble
yourselves before the Lord, and he will lift you up in
honor.

WARNING AGAINST JUDGING OTHERS

11Don't speak evil against each other, dear brothers and
sisters.* If you criticize and judge each other, then you
are criticizing and judging God's law. But your job is to
obey the law, not to judge whether it applies to you. 12God
alone, who gave the law, is the Judge. He alone has the
power to save or to destroy. So what right do you have to
judge your neighbor?

WARNING ABOUT SELF-CONFIDENCE

13Look here, you who say, "Today or tomorrow we are going to a certain town and will stay there a year. We will do
business there and make a profit." 14How do you know
what your life will be like tomorrow? Your life is like the
morning fog—it's here a little while, then it's gone.
15What you ought to say is, "If the Lord wants us to, we
will live and do this or that." 16Otherwise you are boasting
about your own plans, and all such boasting is evil.
17Remember, it is sin to know what you ought to do and
then not do it.

3:1 Greek *brothers;* also in 3:10. **3:6** Or *for it will burn in hell* (Greek *Gehenna*). **3:12** Greek *from salt.* **3:18** Or *of good things,* or *of justice.* **4:4** Greek *You adulteresses!* **4:5** Or *that God longs jealously for the human spirit he has placed within us?* or *that the Holy Spirit, whom God has placed within us, opposes our envy?* **4:6** Prov 3:34 (Greek version). **4:11** Greek *brothers.*

GOALS 4:13-16

James cautioned against making plans without seeking God's opinion. Although goals are great to have, goals can disappoint us if we leave God out of them. God wants some say in the plans of his people. What would you like to be doing ten years from now? One year from now? Tomorrow? How will you react if God steps in and rearranges your plans? Plan ahead, but hang on to your plans lightly. If you put God's desires at the center of your planning, you will seldom be disappointed. ■

5

WARNING TO THE RICH

Look here, you rich people: Weep and groan with anguish
because of all the terrible troubles ahead of you. 2Your
wealth is rotting away, and your fine clothes are moth-
eaten rags. 3Your gold and silver have become worthless.
The very wealth you were counting on will eat away your
flesh like fire. This treasure you have accumulated will
stand as evidence against you on the day of judgment.
4For listen! Hear the cries of the field workers whom you
have cheated of their pay. The wages you held back cry
out against you. The cries of those who harvest your fields
have reached the ears of the LORD of Heaven's Armies.
5You have spent your years on earth in luxury, satisfying your every desire. You have fattened yourselves for
the day of slaughter. 6You have condemned and killed innocent people,* who do not resist you.*

PATIENCE AND ENDURANCE

7Dear brothers and sisters,* be patient as you wait for the
Lord's return. Consider the farmers who patiently wait
for the rains in the fall and in the spring. They eagerly
look for the valuable harvest to ripen. 8You, too, must be
patient. Take courage, for the coming of the Lord is near.
9Don't grumble about each other, brothers and sisters,
or you will be judged. For look—the Judge is standing at
the door!
10For examples of patience in suffering, dear brothers
and sisters, look at the prophets who spoke in the name of
the Lord. 11We give great honor to those who endure under
suffering. For instance, you know about Job, a man of great
endurance. You can see how the Lord was kind to him at
the end, for the Lord is full of tenderness and mercy.
12But most of all, my brothers and sisters, never take an
oath, by heaven or earth or anything else. Just say a simple
yes or no, so that you will not sin and be condemned.

THE POWER OF PRAYER

13Are any of you suffering hardships? You should pray.
Are any of you happy? You should sing praises. 14Are any
of you sick? You should call for the elders of the church
to come and pray over you, anointing you with oil in the
name of the Lord. 15Such a prayer offered in faith will
heal the sick, and the Lord will make you well. And if you
have committed any sins, you will be forgiven.
16Confess your sins to each other and pray for each
other so that you may be healed. The earnest prayer of a
righteous person has great power and produces wonderful results. 17Elijah was as human as we are, and yet when
he prayed earnestly that no rain would fall, none fell for
three and a half years! 18Then, when he prayed again, the
sky sent down rain and the earth began to yield its crops.

GREAT RESULTS 5:16-18

Prayer is a Christian's most powerful resource. The results often are greater than we thought were possible. Sadly, some people see prayer as a last resort—when all else fails. Because God's power is infinitely greater than our own, it only makes sense to rely on it, especially because God encourages us to do so. Do you? ■

RESTORE WANDERING BELIEVERS

19My dear brothers and sisters, if someone among you
wanders away from the truth and is brought back, 20you
can be sure that whoever brings the sinner back will save
that person from death and bring about the forgiveness
of many sins.

5:6a Or *killed the Righteous One*. **5:6b** Or *Don't they resist you?* or *Doesn't God oppose you?* or *Aren't they now accusing you before God?*
5:7 Greek *brothers;* also in 5:9, 10, 12, 19.

1 PETER

EACH YEAR a few individuals compete in what may be the most grueling athletic competition of all: a bicycle race across the U.S. Consider the obstacles: deserts, mountain ranges, inclement weather, 18- to 20-hour stretches of pedaling, flat tires, potholes, spills, inconsiderate motorists, and sheer fatigue. It's *amazing* anyone ever finishes. That some complete the 2,000-plus mile trip in *just over a week* is unbelievable!

How? Carefully trained support teams follow the cyclists in specially equipped vehicles and provide whatever they need—physically, mentally, and emotionally. These support teams make an impossible trip possible.

The Christian life is similar to that grueling bicycle marathon. The occasional joys of gliding downhill are obscured by the more frequent times of having to churn our way up steep mountain peaks. We get weary. We feel like quitting. The finish line seems far, far away.

Fortunately God has given us a first-rate support team to help us go the distance. With the Holy Spirit, the Word of God, and other believers to encourage us, we can not only finish the race, we can *win!*

Find out more about your spiritual support team in 1 Peter. (And the race has already started!)

1 peter

stats

PURPOSE: To offer encouragement to suffering Christians

AUTHOR: Peter

TO WHOM WRITTEN: Jewish Christians who had been driven out of Jerusalem and scattered throughout Asia Minor; believers everywhere

DATE WRITTEN: About A.D. 62 to 64; written from Rome

SETTING: Peter was probably in Rome when the great persecution under Emperor Nero began. (Peter eventually was executed during this time of persecution.) Throughout the Roman Empire, Christians were tortured and killed for their faith. Because of this persecution, the church in Jerusalem was scattered throughout the Mediterranean world.

KEY PEOPLE: Peter, Silas (Silvanus), Mark

KEY PLACES: Jerusalem, Rome, and the regions of Pontus, Galatia, Cappadocia, Asia Minor, and Bithynia

KEY points

GRATITUDE ATTITUDE
Because of Jesus, forgiveness and reconciliation with God are possible. Our hope in him motivates us to serve Christ even more.

PERSECUTION
Peter encouraged believers to persevere through persecution. Persecution makes us stronger because it refines our faith. We can face persecution victoriously as Christ did, if we rely on him.

GOD'S FAMILY
Believers are privileged to belong to God's family—a community with Christ as the Founder and Foundation. Through obedience, we show that we belong to this family.

FAMILY LIFE
Peter encouraged all family members to treat each other with sympathy, love, tenderness, and humility. Likewise, we must treat our family members lovingly. Relationships with parents, brothers and sisters, and spouses are important aspects of Christian discipleship.

JUDGMENT
God will judge everyone with perfect justice. He will punish evildoers; those who love God will be rewarded with life forever in his presence. Because all are accountable to God, we are free to avoid judging others.

1

GREETINGS FROM PETER

This letter is from Peter, an apostle of Jesus Christ.
I am writing to God's chosen people who are living as
foreigners in the provinces of Pontus, Galatia, Cappadocia, Asia, and Bithynia.* 2God the Father knew you and
chose you long ago, and his Spirit has made you holy. As a
result, you have obeyed him and have been cleansed by
the blood of Jesus Christ.
May God give you more and more grace and peace.

LIVE IN HOPE 1:3-6

Do you need encouragement? Peter's words offer joy and hope in times of trouble. He based his confidence on what God has done for us through Jesus. We're called into a *living* hope of eternal life (1:3). Our hope is not only for the future; eternal life begins when we believe in God and join his family. The eternal life we now have gives us hope and enables us to live with confidence in God. ■

THE HOPE OF ETERNAL LIFE

3All praise to God, the Father of our Lord Jesus Christ. It
is by his great mercy that we have been born again, because God raised Jesus Christ from the dead. Now we live
with great expectation, 4and we have a priceless inheritance—an inheritance that is kept in heaven for you,
pure and undefiled, beyond the reach of change and decay. 5And through your faith, God is protecting you by
his power until you receive this salvation, which is ready
to be revealed on the last day for all to see.
6So be truly glad.* There is wonderful joy ahead, even
though you have to endure many trials for a little while.
7These trials will show that your faith is genuine. It is being tested as fire tests and purifies gold—though your
faith is far more precious than mere gold. So when your
faith remains strong through many trials, it will bring
you much praise and glory and honor on the day when
Jesus Christ is revealed to the whole world.
8You love him even though you have never seen him.
Though you do not see him now, you trust him; and you
rejoice with a glorious, inexpressible joy. 9The reward for
trusting him will be the salvation of your souls.
10This salvation was something even the prophets
wanted to know more about when they prophesied
about this gracious salvation prepared for you. 11They
wondered what time or situation the Spirit of Christ
within them was talking about when he told them in advance about Christ's suffering and his great glory
afterward.
12They were told that their messages were not for
themselves, but for you. And now this Good News has
been announced to you by those who preached in the
power of the Holy Spirit sent from heaven. It is all so wonderful that even the angels are eagerly watching these
things happen.

It's hard to believe in anything you can't see. Why has God made it so difficult for people who would believe in him if they could only see him?

God could appear to anyone anyway he wants. But if he suddenly appeared, most people would feel forced or intimidated into following him, rather than loved into it. God wants us to respond out of love for him, not fear!

The truth is that people *can* see God . . . through the eyes of faith. This means taking God at his word—opening ourselves up to him. Some people say "seeing is believing." The truth is that "believing is seeing."

All of us believe in people or things we've never seen; for example, people in history, gravity, or the wind. Everyone has the capacity to believe things that aren't seen. The bottom line for most who say, "I can't believe in something I haven't seen," is "I won't believe in God, because I want to run my own life." God doesn't work that way. Each person must trust in Christ, acknowledging him as Savior.

Peter said that loving God, even though we have never seen him, will bring us "a glorious, inexpressible joy" (1 Pet 1:8). Jesus said, "Blessed are those who believe without seeing me" (John 20:29; see also Heb 11:1).

"We live by believing and not by seeing" (2 Cor 5:7).

BE HOLY 1:13-16

Peter tells us to be like our heavenly Father—holy in everything we do. Holiness means being totally dedicated to God and set apart for his special use. We're not to blend in with the crowd; yet we shouldn't be different just to be different. The fruit God develops in our lives—his characteristics in us—automatically make us different. Our focus and priorities must be his. All of this is in direct contrast to our old ways (1:14). Since we can't become holy on our own, God gives us his Holy Spirit to help us. He can turn an excuse like "I couldn't help it" into "I can do everything through Christ, who gives me strength" (Phil 4:13). ■

A CALL TO HOLY LIVING

13So think clearly and exercise self-control. Look forward to the gracious salvation that will come to you
when Jesus Christ is revealed to the world. 14So you must
live as God's obedient children. Don't slip back into your
old ways of living to satisfy your own desires. You didn't
know any better then. 15But now you must be holy in
everything you do, just as God who chose you is holy.

1:1 *Pontus, Galatia, Cappadocia, Asia,* and *Bithynia* were Roman provinces in what is now Turkey. 1:6 Or *So you are truly glad.*

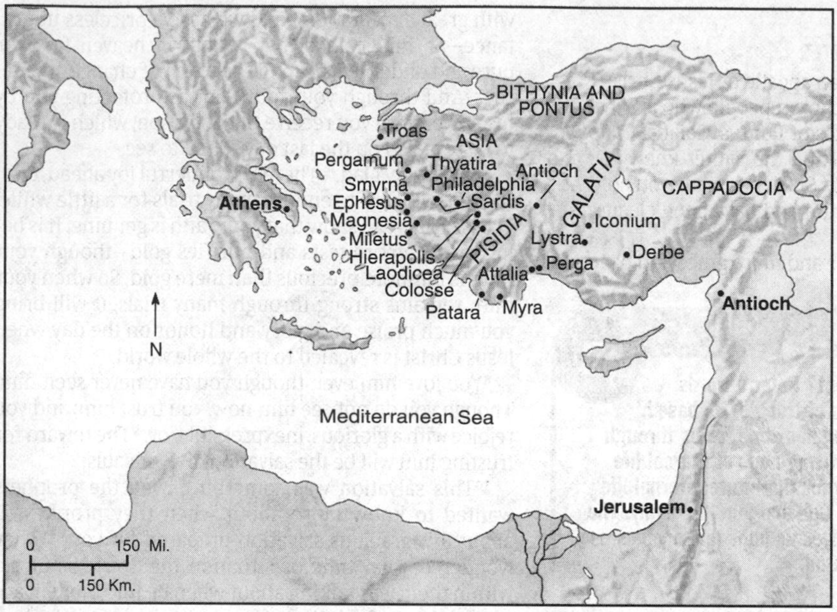

THE CHURCHES OF PETER'S LETTER
Peter addressed his letter to the churches located throughout Bithynia, Pontus, Asia, Galatia, and Cappadocia. Paul had evangelized many of these areas; others had churches that were begun by the Jews who were in Jerusalem on the day of Pentecost and had heard Peter's powerful sermon (see Acts 2:9-11).

16For the Scriptures say, "You must be holy because I am
holy."*
17And remember that the heavenly Father to whom
you pray has no favorites. He will judge or reward you
according to what you do. So you must live in reverent
fear of him during your time as "foreigners in the
land." 18For you know that God paid a ransom to save
you from the empty life you inherited from your ancestors. And the ransom he paid was not mere gold or silver. 19It was the precious blood of
Christ, the sinless, spotless Lamb of
God. 20God chose him as your ransom
long before the world began, but he
has now revealed him to you in these
last days.
21Through Christ you have come to
trust in God. And you have placed your
faith and hope in God because he
raised Christ from the dead and gave
him great glory.
22You were cleansed from your sins
when you obeyed the truth, so now you
must show sincere love to each other as
brothers and sisters.* Love each other
deeply with all your heart.*
23For you have been born again, but not to a life that
will quickly end. Your new life will last forever because it
comes from the eternal, living word of God. 24As the
Scriptures say,

"People are like grass;
their beauty is like a flower in the field.
The grass withers and the flower fades.
25 But the word of the Lord remains forever."*

And that word is the Good News that was preached to you.

The word of the Lord remains forever.

1 PETER 1:25

2

So get rid of all evil behavior. Be done with all deceit, hypocrisy, jealousy, and all unkind speech. 2Like
newborn babies, you must crave pure spiritual milk so
that you will grow into a full experi-
ence of salvation. Cry out for this
nourishment, 3now that you have had
a taste of the Lord's kindness.

LIVING STONES FOR GOD'S HOUSE

4You are coming to Christ, who is the
living cornerstone of God's temple. He
was rejected by people, but he was
chosen by God for great honor.
5And you are living stones that God
is building into his spiritual temple.
What's more, you are his holy priests.*
Through the mediation of Jesus Christ,
you offer spiritual sacrifices that
please God. 6As the Scriptures say,

"I am placing a cornerstone in Jerusalem,*
chosen for great honor,
and anyone who trusts in him
will never be disgraced."*

7Yes, you who trust him recognize the honor God has
given him. But for those who reject him,

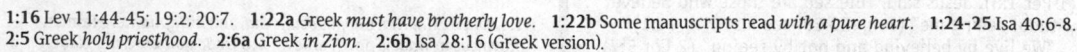

1:16 Lev 11:44-45; 19:2; 20:7. **1:22a** Greek *must have brotherly love.* **1:22b** Some manuscripts read *with a pure heart.* **1:24-25** Isa 40:6-8.
2:5 Greek *holy priesthood.* **2:6a** Greek *in Zion.* **2:6b** Isa 28:16 (Greek version).

"The stone that the builders rejected
has now become the cornerstone."*

8 And,

"He is the stone that makes people stumble,
the rock that makes them fall."*

They stumble because they do not obey God's word, and
so they meet the fate that was planned for them.
9 But you are not like that, for you are a chosen people.
You are royal priests,* a holy nation, God's very own possession. As a result, you can show others the goodness of God, for he called you out of the darkness into his wonderful light.

10 "Once you had no identity as a people;
now you are God's people.
Once you received no mercy;
now you have received God's mercy."*

11 Dear friends, I warn you as "temporary residents and
foreigners" to keep away from worldly desires that wage
war against your very souls. 12 Be careful to live properly
among your unbelieving neighbors. Then even if they accuse you of doing wrong, they will see your honorable behavior, and they will give honor to God when he judges the world.*

RESPECTING PEOPLE IN AUTHORITY

13 For the Lord's sake, respect all human authority—
whether the king as head of state, 14 or the officials he has
appointed. For the king has sent them to punish those who do wrong and to honor those who do right.
15 It is God's will that your honorable lives should silence those ignorant people who make foolish accusations against you. 16 For you are free, yet you are God's
slaves, so don't use your freedom as an excuse to do evil.
17 Respect everyone, and love your Christian brothers and
sisters.* Fear God, and respect the king.

SLAVES

18 You who are slaves must accept the authority of your
masters with all respect.* Do what they tell you—not only if they are kind and reasonable, but even if they are cruel.
19 For God is pleased with you when you do what you
know is right and patiently endure unfair treatment. 20 Of
course, you get no credit for being patient if you are beaten for doing wrong. But if you suffer for doing good and endure it patiently, God is pleased with you.
21 For God called you to do good, even if it means suf-
fering, just as Christ suffered* for you. He is your example, and you must follow in his steps.

22 He never sinned,
nor ever deceived anyone.*
23 He did not retaliate when he was insulted,
nor threaten revenge when he suffered.
He left his case in the hands of God,
who always judges fairly.
24 He personally carried our sins
in his body on the cross
so that we can be dead to sin
and live for what is right.
By his wounds
you are healed.
25 Once you were like sheep
who wandered away.
But now you have turned to your Shepherd,
the Guardian of your souls.

3 WIVES

In the same way, you wives must accept the authority of your husbands. Then, even if some refuse to obey the Good News, your godly lives will speak to them without
any words. They will be won over 2 by observing your pure
and reverent lives.
3 Don't be concerned about the outward beauty of
fancy hairstyles, expensive jewelry, or beautiful clothes.
4 You should clothe yourselves instead with the beauty
that comes from within, the unfading beauty of a gentle
and quiet spirit, which is so precious to God. 5 This is how
the holy women of old made themselves beautiful. They trusted God and accepted the authority of their hus-
bands. 6 For instance, Sarah obeyed her husband, Abraham, and called him her master. You are her daughters when you do what is right without fear of what your husbands might do.

HUSBANDS

7 In the same way, you husbands must give honor to your
wives. Treat your wife with understanding as you live together. She may be weaker than you are, but she is your equal partner in God's gift of new life. Treat her as you should so your prayers will not be hindered.

AN ALTERNATIVE TO REVENGE 3:8-12

Remembering Jesus' teaching to turn the other cheek (Matt 5:39-45), Peter encouraged his readers to pay back wrongs by praying for the offenders. In our society, tearing people down verbally or getting revenge is acceptable. In God's Kingdom, revenge and insults are both unacceptable. Want to rise above revenge or rudeness? Pray for those who hurt you. ■

ALL CHRISTIANS

8 Finally, all of you should be of one mind. Sympathize
with each other. Love each other as brothers and sisters.*
Be tenderhearted, and keep a humble attitude. 9 Don't re-
pay evil for evil. Don't retaliate with insults when people insult you. Instead, pay them back with a blessing. That is

2:7 Ps 118:22. 2:8 Isa 8:14. 2:9 Greek *a royal priesthood.* 2:10 Hos 1:6, 9; 2:23. 2:12 Or *on the day of visitation.* 2:17 Greek *love the brotherhood.* 2:18 Or *because you fear God.* 2:21 Some manuscripts read *died.* 2:22 Isa 53:9. 3:8 Greek *Show brotherly love.*

keeping it real

I attended a Christian school during junior high and the first year of high school. But after three years at Christian schools, I felt like God wanted me to go back to a public school. I talked it over in depth with my parents. They supported me, but reminded me of how difficult it could be because of all the pressures to live for yourself, not for God.

They were right—the pressures and temptations were greater. I didn't know quite how to be a Christian in that atmosphere. Although I was afraid that people would make fun of some of my beliefs, I was determined not to hide my faith.

I decided to take to heart the message of 1 Peter 3:15. This verse keeps me in line in difficult situations. For instance, if I'm at a party and drinking only Coke, often someone will ask me why I'm not drinking any alcohol. I usually tell them that I don't need alcohol to have a good time. Jesus helps me to enjoy life and people just as they are. Most people respect me when I say that. (Even when they don't, as it says in 1 Peter 3:16-17, it's better that they mock me for doing something right than for making a fool of myself by getting drunk.)

First Peter 3:15 reminds me of my purpose for being in a public school: to be ready to tell people of the hope I have in Jesus. —Jenny

what God has called you to do, and he will bless you for it.
10For the Scriptures say,

"If you want to enjoy life
and see many happy days,
keep your tongue from speaking evil
and your lips from telling lies.
11 Turn away from evil and do good.
Search for peace, and work to maintain it.
12 The eyes of the Lord watch over those who do right,
and his ears are open to their prayers.
But the Lord turns his face
against those who do evil."*

SPEAK UP 3:15

Some Christians believe that faith is a personal matter and should be kept to oneself. Although we don't have to be boisterous or obnoxious in sharing our faith, we *can* be ready at all times to answer—gently and respectfully—when asked about our beliefs, our lifestyle, or our Christian perspective. (See also 2 Tim 4:2.) Are you ready? ■

SUFFERING FOR DOING GOOD

13Now, who will want to harm you if you are eager to do
good? 14But even if you suffer for doing what is right, God
will reward you for it. So don't worry or be afraid of their
threats. 15Instead, you must worship Christ as Lord of
your life. And if someone asks about your Christian hope,
always be ready to explain it. 16But do this in a gentle and
respectful way.* Keep your conscience clear. Then if people speak against you, they will be ashamed when they see
what a good life you live because you belong to Christ.
17Remember, it is better to suffer for doing good, if that is
what God wants, than to suffer for doing wrong!

18Christ suffered* for our sins once for all time. He
never sinned, but he died for sinners to bring you safely
home to God. He suffered physical death, but he was
raised to life in the Spirit.*

19So he went and preached to the spirits in prison—
20those who disobeyed God long ago when God waited
patiently while Noah was building his boat. Only eight
people were saved from drowning in that terrible
flood.* 21And that water is a picture of baptism, which
now saves you, not by removing dirt from your body, but
as a response to God from* a clean conscience. It is effective because of the resurrection of Jesus Christ.

22Now Christ has gone to heaven. He is seated in the
place of honor next to God, and all the angels and authorities and powers accept his authority.

4 LIVING FOR GOD

So then, since Christ suffered physical pain, you must
arm yourselves with the same attitude he had, and be

3:10-12 Ps 34:12-16. 3:16 Some English translations put this sentence in verse 15. 3:18a Some manuscripts read *died*. 3:18b Or *in spirit*. 3:20 Greek *saved through water*. 3:21 Or *as an appeal to God for*.

ready to suffer, too. For if you have suffered physically
for Christ, you have finished with sin.* [2]You won't spend
the rest of your lives chasing your own desires, but you
will be anxious to do the will of God. [3]You have had
enough in the past of the evil things that godless people
enjoy—their immorality and lust, their feasting and
drunkenness and wild parties, and their terrible worship
of idols.

PARTIES

It's prom time, and Courtney and Samantha are getting nervous. Their problem? Getting their dates, Costa and Patrick, to forget the idea of an unchaperoned party in a hotel suite after the prom.

Maybe that situation seems simple to solve, but consider the facts:

- **The girls are sophomores. Their dates are seniors and are expected at the hotel.**
- **The party will feature an open bar and available beds.**
- **Costa and Patrick each have already kicked in $150 to pay for this private affair.**
- **A similar party last year featured some unbelievably wild activities.**

"What are we gonna do?" Courtney asks.

"Well, we could just tell our parents and let them get us out of this," Samantha says, not really believing that herself.

"Oh, right, Samantha! And get laughed out of school? We can't do that!"

"Okay, what if we fake like we're sick or something?"

"Samantha!! And miss the prom? It's our first one—and I don't want it to be our last. Look, this whole mess isn't our fault. Let's just pray about it. Maybe God wants us to go and be good examples or something."

"Okay," Samantha agrees.

The girls bow their heads.

Do Courtney and Samantha need to pray about such a decision? Why or why not? What would you do in this situation? Check out 1 Peter 4:3-6 and Galatians 5:19-21.

[4]Of course, your former friends are surprised when
you no longer plunge into the flood of wild and destructive things they do. So they slander you. [5]But remember
that they will have to face God, who will judge everyone,
both the living and the dead. [6]That is why the Good News
was preached to those who are now dead*—so although
they were destined to die like all people,* they now live
forever with God in the Spirit.*
[7]The end of the world is coming soon. Therefore, be
earnest and disciplined in your prayers. [8]Most important
of all, continue to show deep love for each other, for love
covers a multitude of sins. [9]Cheerfully share your home
with those who need a meal or a place to stay.
[10]God has given each of you a gift from his great variety
of spiritual gifts. Use them well to serve one another.
[11]Do you have the gift of speaking? Then speak as though
God himself were speaking through you. Do you have the
gift of helping others? Do it with all the strength and energy that God supplies. Then everything you do will bring
glory to God through Jesus Christ. All glory and power to
him forever and ever! Amen.

SUFFERING FOR BEING A CHRISTIAN

[12]Dear friends, don't be surprised at the fiery trials you
are going through, as if something strange were happening to you. [13]Instead, be very glad—for these trials make
you partners with Christ in his suffering, so that you will
have the wonderful joy of seeing his glory when it is revealed to all the world.

SUFFERING 4:16

Suffering for being a Christian isn't shameful. When Peter and the other apostles were persecuted for preaching the Good News, they rejoiced because such persecution was a mark of God's approval of their work (Acts 5:41). Are you willing to keep on doing what's right regardless of the suffering your actions might bring? ■

[14]So be happy when you are insulted for being a Christian,* for then the glorious Spirit of God* rests upon
you.* [15]If you suffer, however, it must not be for murder,
stealing, making trouble, or prying into other people's affairs. [16]But it is no shame to suffer for being a Christian.
Praise God for the privilege of being called by his name!
[17]For the time has come for judgment, and it must begin
with God's household. And if judgment begins with us,
what terrible fate awaits those who have never obeyed
God's Good News? [18]And also,

"If the righteous are barely saved,
what will happen to godless sinners?"*

[19]So if you are suffering in a manner that pleases God,
keep on doing what is right, and trust your lives to the
God who created you, for he will never fail you.

5 ADVICE FOR ELDERS AND YOUNG MEN

And now, a word to you who are elders in the churches. I,
too, am an elder and a witness to the sufferings of Christ.
And I, too, will share in his glory when he is revealed to
the whole world. As a fellow elder, I appeal to you: [2]Care
for the flock that God has entrusted to you. Watch over it
willingly, not grudgingly—not for what you will get out of

4:1 Or *For the one* [or *One*] *who has suffered physically has finished with sin.* **4:6a** Greek *preached even to the dead.* **4:6b** Or *so although people had judged them worthy of death.* **4:6c** Or *in spirit.* **4:14a** Greek *for the name of Christ.* **4:14b** Or *for the glory of God, which is his Spirit.* **4:14c** Some manuscripts add *On their part he is blasphemed, but on your part he is glorified.* **4:18** Prov 11:31 (Greek version).

it, but because you are eager to serve God. 3Don't lord it over the people assigned to your care, but lead them by your own good example. 4And when the Great Shepherd appears, you will receive a crown of never-ending glory and honor.

DIFFERENT SEASONS, SAME ADVICE 5:5

Pride sometimes keeps older people from trying to understand younger people and vice versa. Peter advised both young and old to be humble and serve each other. Young men could follow the leadership of older men, who could lead by example. What have you learned from someone older? What has someone older learned from you? ■

5In the same way, you younger men must accept the authority of the elders. And all of you, serve each other in humility, for

"God opposes the proud
but favors the humble."*

6So humble yourselves under the mighty power of God, and at the right time he will lift you up in honor. 7Give all your worries and cares to God, for he cares about you.

8Stay alert! Watch out for your great enemy, the devil. He prowls around like a roaring lion, looking for someone to devour. 9Stand firm against him, and be strong in your faith. Remember that your Christian brothers and sisters* all over the world are going through the same kind of suffering you are.

10In his kindness God called you to share in his eternal glory by means of Christ Jesus. So after you have suffered a little while, he will restore, support, and strengthen you, and he will place you on a firm foundation. 11All power to him forever! Amen.

PETER'S FINAL GREETINGS

12I have written and sent this short letter to you with the help of Silas,* whom I commend to you as a faithful brother. My purpose in writing is to encourage you and assure you that what you are experiencing is truly part of God's grace for you. Stand firm in this grace.

13Your sister church here in Babylon* sends you greetings, and so does my son Mark. 14Greet each other with Christian love.*

Peace be with all of you who are in Christ.

5:5 Prov 3:34 (Greek version). 5:9 Greek *your brothers*. 5:12 Greek *Silvanus*. 5:13 Greek *The elect one in Babylon*. Babylon was probably symbolic for Rome. 5:14 Greek *with a kiss of love*.

2 PETER

WE'VE ALL COME face to face with life's ironies. One man decided to make a list. The result? The famous "Murphy's Laws."

Some of the more interesting observations include:

- If anything *can* go wrong it *will*.
- "Broken" gadgets will operate perfectly in the presence of a repairman.
- Saying "Watch this!" guarantees that the behavior you want others to witness will not happen.
- The other line always moves faster.
- Failure to use a napkin ensures spillage.
- You'll only have to wait when you don't have time to.

We nod and smile at those "laws" because we've lived them. They're amazingly true to life. How about some other laws of life? Perhaps they're not as humorous, but they're just as true—and much more life-changing:

- Spiritual growth only happens when we get to know God and make an effort to serve him.
- The world will try to lead you astray.
- Jesus Christ is coming back.

Would you like to know more about these critical principles? They're all contained in the letter known as 2 Peter.

2 peter

stats

PURPOSE: To warn Christians about false teachers and to encourage them to grow in their faith and knowledge of Christ

AUTHOR: Peter

TO WHOM WRITTEN: The church at large

DATE WRITTEN: About A.D. 67, three years after 1 Peter was written, possibly from Rome

SETTING: Since Peter knew that his time on earth was limited (1:13-14), he wrote what was on his heart, warning believers of what would happen after he was gone. He especially wanted to warn them about false teachers and to remind them of the unchanging truth of the gospel.

KEY PEOPLE: Peter, Paul

SPECIAL FEATURES: The date and destination are uncertain, and the authorship has been disputed. Because of this, 2 Peter was the last epistle admitted to the canon of the New Testament. Also, there are similarities between 2 Peter and Jude.

KEY points

DILIGENCE

Peter encouraged believers to grow spiritually. Growth begins with faith and results in love for others. To keep growing, we need to be diligent in our relationship with God and remember what he taught us.

FALSE TEACHERS

Peter advised the church to beware of false teachers. God provides discernment through the Holy Spirit and his Word to recognize false teaching. The truth is our best defense.

JESUS' RETURN

One day Jesus will return to earth. But with his return comes his judgment on all who refuse to believe. The cure for unbelief, complacency, lawlessness, and heresy is found in the confident assurance that Jesus will return.

keeping it real

I didn't want to break up with my girlfriend. But the more I prayed about the relationship, the more I saw that it was interfering with my relationship with God. My girlfriend wasn't a Christian; her values were completely different from mine. I cared about her, but it came down to a choice: either her or God.

The clincher came when I read 2 Peter 1:5-8. The last part of it says: "The more you grow like this [in behavior that models Jesus'], the more productive and useful you will be in your knowledge of our Lord Jesus Christ."

I didn't need any more guidance. I knew I had to break up with Cate and concentrate on strengthening my relationship with the Lord. Though I felt bad after breaking up with her, I was confident that I had done the right thing and that the Lord still cared about me.

I also was encouraged. God showed me that I was slowly but surely becoming stronger spiritually. Every verse of that passage fit a part of my life. As I put God first and determined to obey him, I could see times when I put aside my own desires and how I was becoming more patient, etc.

Yes, breaking up was hard. But knowing that I did it to obey God made all the difference.

—Joel

1

GREETINGS FROM PETER

1This letter is from Simon* Peter, a slave and apostle of
Jesus Christ.
I am writing to you who share the same precious faith
we have. This faith was given to you because of the justice
and fairness* of Jesus Christ, our God and Savior.
2May God give you more and more grace and peace as
you grow in your knowledge of God and Jesus our Lord.

GROWING IN FAITH

3By his divine power, God has given us everything we
need for living a godly life. We have received all of this by
coming to know him, the one who called us to himself by
means of his marvelous glory and excellence. 4And because of his glory and excellence, he has given us great
and precious promises. These are the promises that enable you to share his divine nature and escape the world's
corruption caused by human desires.
5In view of all this, make every effort to respond to
God's promises. Supplement your faith with a generous
provision of moral excellence, and moral excellence with
knowledge, 6and knowledge with self-control, and self-
control with patient endurance, and patient endurance
with godliness, 7and godliness with brotherly affection,
and brotherly affection with love for everyone.
8The more you grow like this, the more productive and
useful you will be in your knowledge of our Lord Jesus
Christ. 9But those who fail to develop in this way are
shortsighted or blind, forgetting that they have been
cleansed from their old sins.
10So, dear brothers and sisters,* work hard to prove
that you really are among those God has called and chosen. Do these things, and you will never fall away. 11Then
God will give you a grand entrance into the eternal Kingdom of our Lord and Savior Jesus Christ.

BE ALL THAT YOU CAN BE 1:5-11

Faith must be more than belief in certain facts; it must result in action, growth in Christian character, and discipline, or it will die (James 2:14-17). Peter lists several actions of faith, including learning to know God better, developing endurance and godliness, and loving others. These actions don't come automatically; they require hard work. They're also not optional; all must be a continual part of the Christian life. But there's good news: God will help you "be all that you can be." ■

PAYING ATTENTION TO SCRIPTURE

12Therefore, I will always remind you about these things—
even though you already know them and are standing
firm in the truth you have been taught. 13And it is only
right that I should keep on reminding you as long as I

1:1a Greek *Symeon*. 1:1b Or *to you in the righteousness*. 1:10 Greek *brothers*.

live.* 14For our Lord Jesus Christ has shown me that I must
soon leave this earthly life,* 15so I will work hard to make
sure you always remember these things after I am gone.

16For we were not making up clever stories when we
told you about the powerful coming of our Lord Jesus
Christ. We saw his majestic splendor with our own eyes
17when he received honor and glory from God the Father.
The voice from the majestic glory of God said to him,
"This is my dearly loved Son, who brings me great joy."*
18We ourselves heard that voice from heaven when we
were with him on the holy mountain.

19Because of that experience, we have even greater
confidence in the message proclaimed by the prophets.
You must pay close attention to what they wrote, for
their words are like a lamp shining in a dark place—until
the Day dawns, and Christ the Morning Star shines* in
your hearts. 20Above all, you must realize that no prophecy in Scripture ever came from the prophet's own
understanding,* 21or from human initiative. No, those
prophets were moved by the Holy Spirit, and they spoke
from God.

2 THE DANGER OF FALSE TEACHERS

2 But there were also false prophets in Israel, just as there
will be false teachers among you. They will cleverly teach
destructive heresies and even deny the Master who
bought them. In this way, they will bring sudden destruction on themselves. 2Many will follow their evil teaching
and shameful immorality. And because of these teachers, the way of truth will be slandered. 3In their greed
they will make up clever lies to get hold of your money.
But God condemned them long ago, and their destruction will not be delayed.

4For God did not spare even the angels who sinned. He
threw them into hell,* in gloomy pits of darkness,* where
they are being held until the day of judgment. 5And God did
not spare the ancient world—except for Noah and the seven
others in his family. Noah warned the world of God's righteous judgment. So God protected Noah when he destroyed
the world of ungodly people with a vast flood. 6Later, God
condemned the cities of Sodom and Gomorrah and turned
them into heaps of ashes. He made them an example of
what will happen to ungodly people. 7But God also rescued
Lot out of Sodom because he was a righteous man who was
sick of the shameful immorality of the wicked people
around him. 8Yes, Lot was a righteous man who was tormented in his soul by the wickedness he saw and heard day
after day. 9So you see, the Lord knows how to rescue godly
people from their trials, even while keeping the wicked
under punishment until the day of final judgment. 10He is
especially hard on those who follow their own twisted sexual desire, and who despise authority.

These people are proud and arrogant, daring even to
scoff at supernatural beings* without so much as trembling. 11But the angels, who are far greater in power and
strength, do not dare to bring from the Lord* a charge of
blasphemy against those supernatural beings.

12These false teachers are like unthinking animals, creatures of instinct, born to be caught and destroyed. They
scoff at things they do not understand, and like animals,
they will be destroyed. 13Their destruction is their reward
for the harm they have done. They love to indulge in evil
pleasures in broad daylight. They are a disgrace and a stain
among you. They delight in deception* even as they eat
with you in your fellowship meals. 14They commit adultery
with their eyes, and their desire for sin is never satisfied.
They lure unstable people into sin, and they are well trained
in greed. They live under God's curse. 15They have wandered off the right road and followed the footsteps of Balaam son of Beor,* who loved to earn money by doing
wrong. 16But Balaam was stopped from his mad course
when his donkey rebuked him with a human voice.

CULTS

A month ago, while on a city bus, Hannah picked up a discarded leaflet advertising a free music festival and complimentary vegetarian meal. She called her friend Jasmine to go with her to check it out.

Throughout the afternoon Jasmine kept whispering, "Let's get out of here. This is weird!" But Hannah kept replying, "Chill, Jas! You're too intense."

On the way home, Jasmine made it clear what she thought. "Look, I don't care what you say. That group is some kind of cult."

"Why? Name one thing they did or said that was bad," Hannah challenged.

"Well, I dunno. . . . They just gave me the creeps, that's all!"

"Aw, I think you're paranoid. Who knows? I just might go to one of their classes."

Hannah returned on the following week. And now she's a full-fledged member of the "church"—The Society of Enlightened Minds. The members accept her and make her feel special.

Jasmine's parents did some checking. Hannah's "church" doesn't accept the Bible or the belief that Christ is God. It teaches that each of us is a god. We need each other to recreate the world—or so they believe.

With their popular, feel-good philosophies, many cults have captured millions of hungry hearts and uncritical minds. No wonder we're told in 2 Peter 2:12-22 to carefully consider the ideas that we hear every day. Do you? What would you say to Hannah?

17These people are as useless as dried-up springs or as
mist blown away by the wind. They are doomed to blackest darkness. 18They brag about themselves with empty,
foolish boasting. With an appeal to twisted sexual desires,

1:13 Greek *as long as I am in this tent* [or *tabernacle*]. **1:14** Greek *I must soon put off my tent* [or *tabernacle*]. **1:17** Matt 17:5; Mark 9:7; Luke 9:35. **1:19** Or *rises*. **1:20** Or *is a matter of one's own interpretation*. **2:4a** Greek *Tartarus*. **2:4b** Some manuscripts read *in chains of gloom*. **2:10** Greek *at glorious ones*, which are probably evil angels. **2:11** Other manuscripts read *to the Lord;* still others omit this phrase. **2:13** Some manuscripts read *in fellowship meals*. **2:15** Some manuscripts read *Bosor*.

they lure back into sin those who have
barely escaped from a lifestyle of deception. [19]They promise freedom, but
they themselves are slaves of sin and
corruption. For you are a slave to whatever controls you. [20]And when people
escape from the wickedness of the
world by knowing our Lord and Savior
Jesus Christ and then get tangled up
and enslaved by sin again, they are
worse off than before. [21]It would be
better if they had never known the way
to righteousness than to know it and
then reject the command they were
given to live a holy life. [22]They prove the
truth of this proverb: "A dog returns to its vomit."* And
another says, "A washed pig returns to the mud."

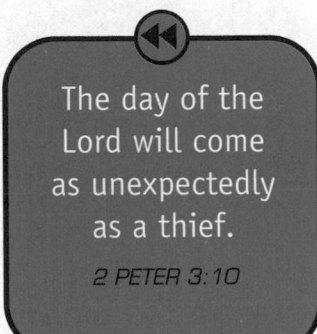

> The day of the Lord will come as unexpectedly as a thief.
>
> *2 PETER 3:10*

FREEDOM 2:19

As Peter warned, false teachers promised a freedom that in reality led to slavery. Ever wish that you didn't have to follow so many rules—that you could live whichever way you wanted to live? Many people would define freedom that way. But if we continually follow our own desires, we'll eventually become enslaved to those desires. But if we submit to Christ, he'll free us from slavery to wrong desires. (See also Titus 3:3.) Is that the kind of freedom you want? It's yours for the asking. ■

3 THE DAY OF THE LORD IS COMING

This is my second letter to you, dear friends, and in both
of them I have tried to stimulate your wholesome thinking and refresh your memory. [2]I want you to remember
what the holy prophets said long ago and what our Lord
and Savior commanded through your apostles.

[3]Most importantly, I want to remind you that in the last
days scoffers will come, mocking the truth and following
their own desires. [4]They will say, "What happened to
the promise that Jesus is coming again? From before the
times of our ancestors, everything has remained the
same since the world was first created."

[5]They deliberately forget that God made the heavens
by the word of his command, and he brought the earth
out from the water and surrounded it with water. [6]Then
he used the water to destroy the ancient world with a
mighty flood. [7]And by the same word, the present heavens and earth have been stored up for fire. They are being
kept for the day of judgment, when ungodly people will
be destroyed.

[8]But you must not forget this one
thing, dear friends: A day is like a thousand years to the Lord, and a thousand
years is like a day. [9]The Lord isn't really
being slow about his promise, as some
people think. No, he is being patient
for your sake. He does not want anyone to be destroyed, but wants everyone to repent. [10]But the day of the Lord
will come as unexpectedly as a thief.
Then the heavens will pass away with a
terrible noise, and the very elements
themselves will disappear in fire, and
the earth and everything on it will be
found to deserve judgment.*

[11]Since everything around us is going to be destroyed
like this, what holy and godly lives you should live,
[12]looking forward to the day of God and hurrying it along.
On that day, he will set the heavens on fire, and the elements will melt away in the flames. [13]But we are looking
forward to the new heavens and new earth he has promised, a world filled with God's righteousness.

[14]And so, dear friends, while you are waiting for these
things to happen, make every effort to be found living
peaceful lives that are pure and blameless in his sight.

ANY DAY NOW 3:14

Peter warned believers not to become complacent simply because Christ has not yet returned. Instead, believers are encouraged to live each day in the eager expectation of his coming. What would you like to be doing when Christ returns? Is that the way you're living now? ■

[15]And remember, the Lord's patience gives people
time to be saved. This is what our beloved brother Paul
also wrote to you with the wisdom God gave him—
[16]speaking of these things in all of his letters. Some of
his comments are hard to understand, and those who
are ignorant and unstable have twisted his letters to
mean something quite different, just as they do with
other parts of Scripture. And this will result in their
destruction.

PETER'S FINAL WORDS

[17]I am warning you ahead of time, dear friends. Be on
guard so that you will not be carried away by the errors of
these wicked people and lose your own secure footing.
[18]Rather, you must grow in the grace and knowledge of
our Lord and Savior Jesus Christ.

All glory to him, both now and forever! Amen.

2:22 Prov 26:11. **3:10** Other manuscripts read *will be burned up;* still others read *will be found destroyed.*

1 JOHN

LOVE.

We can't touch it, count it, bottle it, or even see it. But who among us would argue that love isn't real?

Love.

It makes sane people do and say crazy things. It prompts selfish people to do noble things. What else on earth has that kind of power?

Love.

It can hurt like nothing else in the world. And yet, paradoxically, *not* loving is much more painful.

Love.

The most talked-about, sung-about, and thought-about theme in the world—as well as the most misunderstood.

Love.

Would you like to know more about it and see it in a brand new light? Then read *1 John,* the most eloquent description of love ever penned.

Love.

It's not everything you think it is. It's more . . . much, much more.

1 john

stats

PURPOSE: To reassure Christians in their faith and to counter false teachings

AUTHOR: The apostle John

TO WHOM WRITTEN: The letter was sent to several Gentile congregations. It also was written to believers everywhere.

DATE WRITTEN: Probably between A.D. 85 and 90; written from Ephesus

SETTING: John was an older man—perhaps the only surviving apostle at this time. He had not yet been exiled to the island of Patmos. As an eyewitness of Christ, he wrote authoritatively to encourage a new generation of believers in their faith.

KEY PEOPLE: John, Jesus

SPECIAL FEATURES: The topic of love is mentioned throughout this letter. There are a number of similarities in vocabulary, style, and main ideas between this letter and John's Gospel. John uses brief statements and simple words, and he includes sharp contrasts—light and darkness, truth and error, God and Satan, life and death, love and hate.

KEY points

FORGIVENESS
John encouraged believers to confess their wrongdoings to God and receive his forgiveness. Although our wrong actions are our fault, we don't have to solve this problem on our own. Jesus offers forgiveness.

LOVE
Jesus commands us to love others as he did. Love means showing others we care, not just saying it.

THE FAMILY OF GOD
We become God's children by believing in Christ. How we treat others shows who our Father is.

TRUTH AND ERROR
False teachers encouraged believers to do whatever they wanted to do. As a result, many people became indifferent to sin. Believers need to know what's true to avoid being fooled by false teachers.

ASSURANCE
God is in control of heaven and earth. Because God's Word is true, we have an assurance of eternal life and victory over sin.

1

INTRODUCTION

We proclaim to you the one who existed from the beginning,* whom we have heard and seen. We saw him with our own eyes and touched him with our own hands. He is the Word of life. 2This one who is life itself was revealed to us, and we have seen him. And now we testify and proclaim to you that he is the one who is eternal life. He was with the Father, and then he was revealed to us. 3We proclaim to you what we ourselves have actually seen and heard so that you may have fellowship with us. And our fellowship is with the Father and with his Son, Jesus Christ. 4We are writing these things so that you may fully share our joy.*

LIVING IN THE LIGHT

5This is the message we heard from Jesus* and now declare to you: God is light, and there is no darkness in him at all. 6So we are lying if we say we have fellowship with God but go on living in spiritual darkness; we are not practicing the truth. 7But if we are living in the light, as God is in the light, then we have fellowship with each other, and the blood of Jesus, his Son, cleanses us from all sin.

8If we claim we have no sin, we are only fooling ourselves and not living in the truth. 9But if we confess our sins to him, he is faithful and just to forgive us our sins and to cleanse us from all wickedness. 10If we claim we have not sinned, we are calling God a liar and showing that his word has no place in our hearts.

OVER AND OVER 1:9

God offers forgiveness when we own up to what we've done wrong. Yet some Christians feel guilty because they've confessed the same actions over and over. Others believe that if they died with unconfessed sins, they would be lost forever. But *God wants to forgive us.* He allowed his beloved Son to die so that he could forgive us. We don't need to fear that God will reject us if we keep having to tell him about what we've done wrong. He won't. Instead, he offers forgiveness and the strength to defeat the temptation the next time it appears. ■

2

My dear children, I am writing this to you so that you will not sin. But if anyone does sin, we have an advocate who pleads our case before the Father. He is Jesus Christ, the one who is truly righteous. 2He himself is the sacrifice that atones for our sins—and not only our sins but the sins of all the world.

3And we can be sure that we know him if we obey his commandments. 4If someone claims, "I know God," but doesn't obey God's commandments, that person is a liar and is not living in the truth. 5But those who obey God's word truly show how completely they love him. That is how we know we are living in him. 6Those who say they live in God should live their lives as Jesus did.

A NEW COMMANDMENT

7Dear friends, I am not writing a new commandment for you; rather it is an old one you have had from the very beginning. This old commandment—to love one another—is the same message you heard before. 8Yet it is also new. Jesus lived the truth of this commandment, and you also are living it. For the darkness is disappearing, and the true light is already shining.

9If anyone claims, "I am living in the light," but hates a Christian brother or sister,* that person is still living in darkness. 10Anyone who loves another brother or sister* is living in the light and does not cause others to stumble. 11But anyone who hates another brother or sister is still living and walking in darkness. Such a person does not know the way to go, having been blinded by the darkness.

A CHOICE 2:9-11

Ever fear that if you can't like someone, you're not really a Christian? There will always be people we won't like as well as others. John's words focus on the attitude that causes us to ignore or despise others—to treat them as irritants, competitors, or enemies. But love isn't a feeling—it's a choice. We can choose to be concerned about the welfare of others and to treat them with respect, whether or not we feel affection toward them. If we choose to love others, God will give us the strength to express his love. ■

12 I am writing to you who are God's children
because your sins have been forgiven through Jesus.*
13 I am writing to you who are mature in the faith*
because you know Christ, who existed from the beginning.
I am writing to you who are young in the faith
because you have won your battle with the evil one.
14 I have written to you who are God's children
because you know the Father.
I have written to you who are mature in the faith
because you know Christ, who existed from the beginning.
I have written to you who are young in the faith
because you are strong.
God's word lives in your hearts,
and you have won your battle with the evil one.

DO NOT LOVE THIS WORLD

15Do not love this world nor the things it offers you, for when you love the world, you do not have the love of the Father in you. 16For the world offers only a craving for physical pleasure, a craving for everything we see, and pride in our achievements and possessions. These are

1:1 Greek *What was from the beginning.* 1:4 Or *so that our joy may be complete;* some manuscripts read *your joy.* 1:5 Greek *from him.* 2:9 Greek *hates his brother;* similarly in 2:11. 2:10 Greek *loves his brother.* 2:12 Greek *through his name.* 2:13 Or *to you fathers;* also in 2:14.

not from the Father, but are from this world. 17And this world is fading away, along with everything that people crave. But anyone who does what pleases God will live forever.

WARNING ABOUT ANTICHRISTS

18Dear children, the last hour is here. You have heard that the Antichrist is coming, and already many such antichrists have appeared. From this we know that the last hour has come. 19These people left our churches, but they never really belonged with us; otherwise they would have stayed with us. When they left, it proved that they did not belong with us.

> See how very much our Father loves us, for he calls us his children, and that is what we are!
>
> 1 JOHN 3:1

20But you are not like that, for the Holy One has given you his Spirit,* and all of you know the truth. 21So I am writing to you not because you don't know the truth but because you know the difference between truth and lies. 22And who is a liar? Anyone who says that Jesus is not the Christ.* Anyone who denies the Father and the Son is an antichrist.* 23Anyone who denies the Son doesn't have the Father, either. But anyone who acknowledges the Son has the Father also.

24So you must remain faithful to what you have been taught from the beginning. If you do, you will remain in fellowship with the Son and with the Father. 25And in this fellowship we enjoy the eternal life he promised us.

26I am writing these things to warn you about those who want to lead you astray. 27But you have received the Holy Spirit,* and he lives within you, so you don't need anyone to teach you what is true. For the Spirit* teaches you everything you need to know, and what he teaches is true—it is not a lie. So just as he has taught you, remain in fellowship with Christ.

LIVING AS CHILDREN OF GOD

28And now, dear children, remain in fellowship with Christ so that when he returns, you will be full of courage and not shrink back from him in shame.

29Since we know that Christ is righteous, we also know that all who do what is right are God's children.

3 See how very much our Father loves us, for he calls us his children, and that is what we are! But the people who belong to this world don't recognize that we are God's children because they don't know him. 2Dear friends, we are already God's children, but he has not yet shown us what we will be like when Christ appears. But we do know that we will be like him, for we will see him as he really is. 3And all who have this eager expectation will keep themselves pure, just as he is pure.

4Everyone who sins is breaking God's law, for all sin is contrary to the law of God. 5And you know that Jesus came to take away our sins, and there is no sin in him. 6Anyone who continues to live in him will not sin. But anyone who keeps on sinning does not know him or understand who he is.

7Dear children, don't let anyone deceive you about this: When people do what is right, it shows that they are righteous, even as Christ is righteous. 8But when people keep on sinning, it shows that they belong to the devil, who has been sinning since the beginning. But the Son of God came to destroy the works of the devil. 9Those who have been born into God's family do not make a practice of sinning, because God's life* is in them. So they can't keep on sinning, because they are children of God. 10So now we can tell who are children of God and who are children of the devil. Anyone who does not live righteously and does not love other believers* does not belong to God.

DON'T GIVE IN! 3:8-10

John warned believers against allowing Satan—the enemy of Christians—to tempt them to wrong actions. We all have areas where we feel especially tempted. However, this passage is not about people who are working to overcome a particular sin; it refers to people who constantly try to justify wrong actions. That attitude comes from the enemy. The Holy Spirit gives us the power to avoid giving in to temptation. But he won't force us to use his temptation escape route. We must choose to do so. Will you? ■

LOVE ONE ANOTHER

11This is the message you have heard from the beginning: We should love one another. 12We must not be like Cain, who belonged to the evil one and killed his brother. And why did he kill him? Because Cain had been doing what was evil, and his brother had been doing what was righteous. 13So don't be surprised, dear brothers and sisters,* if the world hates you.

14If we love our Christian brothers and sisters,* it proves that we have passed from death to life. But a person who has no love is still dead. 15Anyone who hates another brother or sister* is really a murderer at heart. And you know that murderers don't have eternal life within them.

16We know what real love is because Jesus gave up his life for us. So we also ought to give up our lives for our brothers and sisters. 17If someone has enough money to live well and sees a brother or sister* in need but shows no compassion—how can God's love be in that person?

18Dear children, let's not merely say that we love each

2:20 Greek *But you have an anointing from the Holy One.* 2:22a Or *not the Messiah.* 2:22b Or *the antichrist.* 2:27a Greek *the anointing from him.* 2:27b Greek *the anointing.* 3:9 Greek *because his seed.* 3:10 Greek *does not love his brother.* 3:13 Greek *brothers.* 3:14 Greek *the brothers;* similarly in 3:16. 3:15 Greek *hates his brother.* 3:17 Greek *sees his brother.*

other; let us show the truth by our actions. [19]Our actions will show that we belong to the truth, so we will be confident when we stand before God. [20]Even if we feel guilty, God is greater than our feelings, and he knows everything.

[21]Dear friends, if we don't feel guilty, we can come to God with bold confidence. [22]And we will receive from him whatever we ask because we obey him and do the things that please him.

[23]And this is his commandment: We must believe in the name of his Son, Jesus Christ, and love one another, just as he commanded us. [24]Those who obey God's commandments remain in fellowship with him, and he with them. And we know he lives in us because the Spirit he gave us lives in us.

4 DISCERNING FALSE PROPHETS

Dear friends, do not believe everyone who claims to speak by the Spirit. You must test them to see if the spirit they have comes from God. For there are many false prophets in the world. [2]This is how we know if they have the Spirit of God: If a person claiming to be a prophet* acknowledges that Jesus Christ came in a real body, that person has the Spirit of God. [3]But if someone claims to be a prophet and does not acknowledge the truth about Jesus, that person is not from God. Such a person has the spirit of the Antichrist, which you heard is coming into the world and indeed is already here.

[4]But you belong to God, my dear children. You have already won a victory over those people, because the Spirit who lives in you is greater than the spirit who lives in the world. [5]Those people belong to this world, so they speak from the world's viewpoint, and the world listens to them. [6]But we belong to God, and those who know God listen to us. If they do not belong to God, they do not listen to us. That is how we know if someone has the Spirit of truth or the spirit of deception.

A TEST 4:20-21

Saying we love God is easy when it doesn't cost us anything more than weekly attendance at a church service. But the real test of our love for God is how we treat the people right in front of us—our family members, fellow believers, and even enemies. We cannot truly love God while neglecting to love those who are created in his image. ■

LOVING ONE ANOTHER

[7]Dear friends, let us continue to love one another, for love comes from God. Anyone who loves is a child of God and knows God. [8]But anyone who does not love does not know God, for God is love.

[9]God showed how much he loved us by sending his one and only Son into the world so that we might have eternal life through him. [10]This is real love—not that we loved God, but that he loved us and sent his Son as a sacrifice to take away our sins.

[11]Dear friends, since God loved us that much, we surely ought to love each other. [12]No one has ever seen God. But if we love each other, God lives in us, and his love is brought to full expression in us.

4:2 Greek *If a spirit;* similarly in 4:3.

CAIN

Think about the last time you felt angry. What caused your anger? How did you deal with it?

Cain grew angry when God seemed to reject his offering while accepting that of his brother Abel. Although God warned Cain about his attitude, Cain didn't listen. Instead of making things right with God by changing his attitude, he chose to kill his brother. As a result, he became an outcast.

Anger is a powerful reaction. When something happens to us that we didn't expect, we get angry! Although anger is not a sin, uncontrolled anger can be. It's like a small flame on dry grass—unless it's snuffed out quickly, it can destroy a great deal of land.

Cain missed the opportunity to correct his attitude. We don't have to. Anger can remind us that we need God's help. Asking for his help to do the right thing may keep us from making mistakes we can't correct.

UP:
- Was the first human child and the first to follow in his father's profession (farming)

DOWNS:
- When disappointed, reacted out of anger and discouragement
- Took the negative choice even when a positive one was offered
- Was the first murderer

STATS:
- Where: Near Eden, which probably was located in either of the areas known today as Iraq or Iran
- Occupation: farmer
- Relatives: Adam and Eve (parents); Abel, Seth, and others not mentioned by name (siblings)

BOTTOM LINE:

Anger is not sin. What we do with our anger can be sinful.

What we offer to God must be from the heart—the best that we are and have.

The consequences of a wrongdoing are sometimes lifelong.

Cain's story is told in Gen 4:1-17. He also is mentioned in Heb 11:4 and Jude 1:11.

LOVE

Just as Alondra leaves the school cafeteria one day, she suddenly slips on a discarded French fry and a glob of gelatin and winds up sprawled on the floor. Not only does she hear laughter from every corner of the room, much of it comes from her two best friends. Neither asks whether or not she's okay. (She is, by the way.)

Guess how Alondra feels?

- **(a) Angry**
- **(b) Sad**
- **(c) Hurt**
- **(d) Totally humiliated**
- **(e) All of the above**

You guessed it: (e) describes *exactly* how she feels. Guess what Alondra wants to do?

- **(a) Go home immediately and beg her parents to enroll her in a different school**
- **(b) Sarcastically tell her friends, "Hope you enjoyed the show, traitors!"**
- **(c) Continue lying on the floor, pretending to be unconscious**
- **(d) Cry**
- **(e) All of the above**

That's right: (e) again. You are *so* smart! So what does Alondra *actually* do? Here's the shocker: She prays and asks the Lord to give her the strength to continue loving her friends instead of holding a grudge.

Check out 1 John 4:7-21. How is Alondra's attitude a reflection of this passage? Is this your attitude?

13 And God has given us his Spirit as proof that we live
in him and he in us. 14 Furthermore, we have seen with our
own eyes and now testify that the Father sent his Son to
be the Savior of the world. 15 All who confess that Jesus is
the Son of God have God living in them, and they live in
God. 16 We know how much God loves us, and we have put
our trust in his love.

God is love, and all who live in love live in God, and God
lives in them. 17 And as we live in God, our love grows
more perfect. So we will not be afraid on the day of judgment, but we can face him with confidence because we
live like Jesus here in this world.

18 Such love has no fear, because perfect love expels
all fear. If we are afraid, it is for fear of punishment, and
this shows that we have not fully experienced his perfect love. 19 We love each other* because he loved us
first.

20 If someone says, "I love God," but hates a Christian
brother or sister,* that person is a liar; for if we don't love
people we can see, how can we love God, whom we cannot see? 21 And he has given us this command: Those who
love God must also love their Christian brothers and
sisters.*

5

FAITH IN THE SON OF GOD

Everyone who believes that Jesus is the Christ* has become a child of God. And everyone who loves the Father
loves his children, too. 2 We know we love God's children
if we love God and obey his commandments. 3 Loving God
means keeping his commandments, and his commandments are not burdensome. 4 For every child of God defeats this evil world, and we achieve this victory through
our faith. 5 And who can win this battle against the world?
Only those who believe that Jesus is the Son of God.

6 And Jesus Christ was revealed as God's Son by his baptism in water and by shedding his blood on the cross*—
not by water only, but by water and blood. And the Spirit,
who is truth, confirms it with his testimony. 7 So we have
these three witnesses*—8 the Spirit, the water, and the
blood—and all three agree. 9 Since we believe human testimony, surely we can believe the greater testimony that
comes from God. And God has testified about his Son.
10 All who believe in the Son of God know in their hearts

4:19 Greek *We love.* Other manuscripts read *We love God;* still others read *We love him.* **4:20** Greek *hates his brother.* **4:21** Greek *The one who loves God must also love his brother.* **5:1** Or *the Messiah.* **5:6** Greek *This is he who came by water and blood.* **5:7** A few very late manuscripts add *in heaven—the Father, the Word, and the Holy Spirit, and these three are one. And we have three witnesses on earth.*

Although I felt hyped when I first became a Christian, my good feelings soon went away. Did I lose God? Why didn't the good feelings stay around?

Picture yourself meeting your favorite celebrity face to face. That would be an experience you would likely never forget. Yet over time you would forget the intensity of the emotion you once felt. But would that mean you didn't actually meet this person? Of course not! It shows that our feelings often come and go based on current experience.

Asking Jesus Christ into your life is far better than meeting another human, famous or not! You've begun a lifelong relationship with the God who created everything! Within this lifelong relationship will be some good feelings, but more often we won't have—or want—a continual, intense excitement.

The wonder of getting to know someone as loving and forgiving as Jesus Christ has similarities to other relationships you enjoy. There is the initial experience of meeting a person, followed by months and years of growing to appreciate his or her friendship and influence. (Anything worthwhile takes time.)

First John 5:12 assures us that "whoever has the Son has life." Once you've genuinely chosen to follow Jesus Christ, you can never lose him. As Jesus once said, "No one can snatch them away from me" (John 10:28). *Them* includes you. He'll always be there to guide and love you, even in hard times.

keeping it real

I was the master of rationalization—at least in some areas of my life. When I got into an argument with my parents, I always knew they were totally wrong. If I talked about someone behind her back, I told myself that I wasn't gossiping—I was providing information that person needed to know. When my boyfriend and I started having sex, I rationalized that it was okay, because we loved each other.

When my pastor preached on 1 John 1:8-10, I suddenly knew that I was just fooling myself. I never fooled God, though. He called these things—rebelliousness toward my parents, gossip, premarital sex—sins. That shook me up pretty bad.

I cried as I reread the passage after church. Before God that day, I owned up to the sins I had rationalized. It was hard to do because I knew I had to be willing to change, not just to say "I'm sorry." Change would be hard, particularly in my relationship with my boyfriend. But verse 9 encouraged me that God would not only forgive, he also would give me the strength to make a new start.

I ended up breaking up with my boyfriend. Our physical relationship made starting over impossible. The breakup hurt a lot. But underneath the pain, something felt very good, very right: I was no longer lying to myself or to God. **—Trish**

that this testimony is true. Those who don't believe this
are actually calling God a liar because they don't believe
what God has testified about his Son.
11And this is what God has testified: He has given us eternal life, and this life is in his Son. 12Whoever has the Son has
life; whoever does not have God's Son does not have life.

CONCLUSION

13I have written this to you who believe in the name of the
Son of God, so that you may know you have eternal life.
14And we are confident that he hears us whenever we ask
for anything that pleases him. 15And since we know he
hears us when we make our requests, we also know that
he will give us what we ask for.
16If you see a Christian brother or sister* sinning in a way
that does not lead to death, you should pray, and God will
give that person life. But there is a sin that leads to death, and
I am not saying you should pray for those who commit it.
17All wicked actions are sin, but not every sin leads to death.
18We know that God's children do not make a practice
of sinning, for God's Son holds them securely, and the
evil one cannot touch them. 19We know that we are children of God and that the world around us is under the
control of the evil one.
20And we know that the Son of God has come, and he
has given us understanding so that we can know the true
God.* And now we live in fellowship with the true God
because we live in fellowship with his Son, Jesus Christ.
He is the only true God, and he is eternal life.

YOU KNOW IT! 5:13

Some people *hope* they will spend eternity with God. John says that we can *know* we will. Our certainty is based on God's promise that he has given us eternal life through his Son. This is true whether you feel close to God or distant from him. Eternal life is not based on feelings, but on facts. You can know you have eternal life if you believe God's truth. If you lack assurance about your future destination, ask yourself whether or not you've honestly committed your life to Christ as your Savior and Lord. If so, by faith you know where you'll be—with your Father. ■

21Dear children, keep away from anything that might
take God's place in your hearts.*

5:16 Greek *a brother*. **5:20** Greek *the one who is true*. **5:21** Greek *keep yourselves from idols*.

2 JOHN

EVER PLAYED A practical joke on someone? Playing practical jokes on celebrities was the whole point of the MTV show *Punk'd.*

It's fun to fool people—or even to be fooled. Many people have tried the old favorites: a joy buzzer or a whoopee cushion. Others have short-sheeted beds or crank called neighbors. Perhaps you've attempted a more complicated stunt—turning a friend's dresser drawers upside down or freezing your brother's underwear.

Some enterprising university pals once lined a dorm mate's room with plastic and turned it into a giant aquarium—complete with a shark!

As long as no one gets hurt, no laws are broken, and there's no property damage, pranks are no big deal—except in the spiritual dimension. There we can't afford to be deceived because our enemy, the devil, packs his pranks with disaster!

One of Satan's favorite methods of suckering us is to get us to listen to *false teaching.* That's what the Epistle of 2 John is all about.

False teaching can come in many different forms, some of which might seem to make sense. But no matter how valid it may seem, false teaching is always deadly. And that's no joke.

2 john

stats

PURPOSE: To emphasize the basics of following Christ—truth and love—and to warn against the false teachers that had infiltrated the church

AUTHOR: The apostle John

TO WHOM WRITTEN: To "the chosen lady" and her children (which could refer to a local church) and to Christians everywhere

DATE WRITTEN: About the same time as 1 John, around A.D. 90, from Ephesus

SETTING: Evidently this woman and her family were involved in one of the churches under John's leadership. They had developed a strong friendship.

KEY PEOPLE: John, the chosen lady, and her children

KEY points

KNOW THE WORD

Following God's Word, the Bible, is essential to Christian living. A careful, consistent study of the Bible will help a believer to grow spiritually as well as provide the tools to recognize and counter false teaching.

LOVE

John repeated Jesus' command to his followers: love others. Helping, giving, and meeting needs puts love into practice. Love in deed is love indeed.

FOUNDATIONAL TRUTHS

ULTIMATE ISSUES

Mexico City is a fascinating place. Besides being one of the largest cities in the world, it's filled with interesting historical sights.

At the very center of the city, in the historical district known as the Zocalo, you'll find a huge square plaza surrounded by magnificent buildings. On the north side of the square is the beautiful Cathedral Metropolitana, which was begun in the late 1500s and dedicated in 1667 by the conquering Spaniards. Additions were put on in the 1800s.

For many years the cathedral had a slight problem: It sloped to the right. It wasn't built that way—the Spaniards built it straight. But they built it on a dry lakebed (formerly Lake Texcoco). The church had been sinking into the soft ground, little by little, year after year. But a restoration project has kept it from collapsing.

Do you wonder why John placed so much emphasis on knowing the Bible? Well, he's not alone—many biblical authors stress the importance of knowing God's Word.

In Psalm 119, the longest chapter in the Bible, all but three of the 176 verses mention God's Word. Throughout the chapter, the psalmist uses various synonyms for *Scriptures* interchangeably; synonyms like *law, instructions, rules*—not exactly favorites for any of us. Likewise, John refers to *the truth*—which comes only from God's Word—throughout this short letter. Why is knowing the Bible so important? And what in the world does this have to do with Mexico City's cathedral?

Just this: Like any structure, your life needs a foundation. The bigger the structure, the stronger the foundation has to be.

If you want to build a life that reflects God's glory, you need a firm base from which to start. You can gain that through time spent in the Word of God. When you study it—even when you don't feel like it—you're building a solid foundation—one that won't sink. (See Matt 7:24-27.)

GREETINGS

This letter is from John, the elder.*
I am writing to the chosen lady and to her children,*
whom I love in the truth—as does everyone else who
knows the truth—2because the truth lives in us and will
be with us forever.
3Grace, mercy, and peace, which come from God the
Father and from Jesus Christ—the Son of the Father—will
continue to be with us who live in truth and love.

LIVE IN THE TRUTH

4How happy I was to meet some of your children and find
them living according to the truth, just as the Father commanded.
5I am writing to remind you, dear friends,* that we
should love one another. This is not a new commandment, but one we have had from the beginning. 6Love
means doing what God has commanded us, and he has
commanded us to love one another, just as you heard
from the beginning.
7I say this because many deceivers have gone out into
the world. They deny that Jesus Christ came* in a real
body. Such a person is a deceiver and an antichrist.
8Watch out that you do not lose what we* have worked
so hard to achieve. Be diligent so that you receive your
full reward. 9Anyone who wanders away from this
teaching has no relationship with God. But anyone who
remains in the teaching of Christ has a relationship with
both the Father and the Son.
10If anyone comes to your meeting and does not teach
the truth about Christ, don't invite that person into your
home or give any kind of encouragement. 11Anyone who
encourages such people becomes a partner in their evil
work.

CONCLUSION

12I have much more to say to you, but I don't want to do it
with paper and ink. For I hope to visit you soon and talk
with you face to face. Then our joy will be complete.
13Greetings from the children of your sister,* chosen
by God.

1a Greek *From the elder.* **1b** Or *the church God has chosen and its members.* **5** Greek *I urge you, lady.* **7** Or *will come.* **8** Some manuscripts read *you.* **13** Or *from the members of your sister church.*

3 JOHN

"IT WAS OVER before it got started!" "Blink and you'll miss it." "Short, sweet, and to the point."

Those are just some of the expressions you might use to describe:

- The 1896 war between the United Kingdom and Zanzibar. (It lasted a mere 38 minutes!)
- The 20-minute reign of King Dom Luis III of Portugal in 1908.
- Montana's Roe River. (Its length? A measly 200 feet!)
- The 17-foot-long (or should we say "17-foot-*short*") McKinley Street in Bellefontaine, Ohio.

But just because things are brief or small or short doesn't mean they're unimportant.

Take 3 John for instance. With only 15 verses, it is one of the shortest books of the Bible—a quick contrast between godly living and worldly behavior.

In fact, this introduction is about as long as the book itself! So go ahead and read this warm, personal note from the apostle John to his friend Gaius.

When you do, another familiar expression may come to mind:

"Good things come in small packages."

stats

PURPOSE: To commend Gaius for his hospitality and to encourage him in his Christian life

AUTHOR: The apostle John

TO WHOM WRITTEN: Gaius, a prominent Christian in one of the churches known to John; Christians everywhere

DATE WRITTEN: About A.D. 90, from Ephesus

SETTING: Church leaders traveled from town to town helping to establish new congregations. They depended on the hospitality of fellow believers. Gaius welcomed them into his home.

KEY PEOPLE: John, Gaius, Diotrephes, Demetrius

KEY points

HOSPITALITY
John wrote to encourage the believers who showed hospitality to others. Genuine hospitality for traveling Christian workers was needed then and is still important.

PRIDE
John planned to reprimand Diotrephes for his pride and lack of hospitality. Pride is a disrupter of fellowship. Servanthood is the best defense against pride.

FAITHFULNESS
Gaius and Demetrius were commended for their faithful work in the church. Their examples of faithfulness are an encouragement for believers today.

GREETINGS

This letter is from John, the elder.*
I am writing to Gaius, my dear
friend, whom I love in the truth.
[2]Dear friend, I hope all is well with
you and that you are as healthy in
body as you are strong in spirit. [3]Some
of the traveling teachers* recently returned and made me very happy by
telling me about your faithfulness
and that you are living according to
the truth. [4]I could have no greater joy
than to hear that my children are following the truth.

> Don't let this bad example influence you. Follow only what is good.
>
> 3 JOHN 1:11

CARING FOR THE LORD'S WORKERS

[5]Dear friend, you are being faithful to God when you care
for the traveling teachers who pass through, even though
they are strangers to you. [6]They have told the church here
of your loving friendship. Please continue providing for
such teachers in a manner that pleases God. [7]For they are
traveling for the Lord,* and they accept nothing from
people who are not believers.* [8]So we ourselves should
support them so that we can be their partners as they
teach the truth.
[9]I wrote to the church about this, but Diotrephes, who
loves to be the leader, refuses to have anything to do with
us. [10]When I come, I will report some of the things he is
doing and the evil accusations he is making against us.
Not only does he refuse to welcome the traveling teachers, he also tells others not to help them. And when they
do help, he puts them out of the church.
[11]Dear friend, don't let this bad
example influence you. Follow only
what is good. Remember that those
who do good prove that they are
God's children, and those who do
evil prove that they do not know
God.*
[12]Everyone speaks highly of Demetrius, as does the truth itself. We ourselves can say the same for him, and
you know we speak the truth.

CONCLUSION

[13]I have much more to say to you, but I
don't want to write it with pen and
ink. [14]For I hope to see you soon, and then we will talk
face to face.

OPEN HOUSE 1:5

In the church's early days, traveling prophets, evangelists, and teachers depended on the hospitality of people like Gaius who housed and fed them. Hospitality is an active and much appreciated way to show your love. To whom will you show hospitality? ■

[15]*Peace be with you.
Your friends here send you their greetings. Please
give my personal greetings to each of our friends
there.

1 Greek *From the elder.* **3** Greek *the brothers;* also in verses 5 and 10. **7a** Greek *They went out on behalf of the Name.* **7b** Greek *from Gentiles.* **11** Greek *they have not seen God.* **15** Some English translations combine verses 14 and 15 into verse 14.

JUDE

COULD YOUR FAITH withstand a spiritual battle?

What would you say if the school agnostic called the resurrection of Christ a myth? What if a minister you respect admitted that he believes the Bible contains errors and contradictions?

What if your favorite teacher announced, "It's insensitive and downright *wrong* for one group of people to try to force its views on another group! Who really knows what's true?"

Imagine meeting someone full of joy and peace, a person *seemingly* very much in touch with God. As you converse, this person tells you that she is content and fulfilled because of an experience she recently had in which she journeyed back through her previous incarnations. She nods when you mention Jesus Christ and says, "If that works for you, great! But I found the truth another way."

If you haven't already had encounters like the ones just described, then just wait. Your time is definitely coming!

The fact of the matter is that our world is *full* of confused people who eagerly spread their confusing ideas.

Don't get caught off-guard! You can get in battle readiness by understanding what you believe and why. There's no better place to start your Bible Boot Camp Training than by reading the Epistle to Jude.

jude

stats

PURPOSE: To remind the church of the need for constant vigilance in order to keep strong in the faith and to defend it against false ideas about God and Scriptures

AUTHOR: Jude, James's brother and Jesus' half brother

TO WHOM WRITTEN: Jewish Christians and other believers everywhere

DATE WRITTEN: About A.D. 65

SETTING: From the first century on, heresy and false teaching have threatened the church.

KEY PEOPLE: Jude, James, Jesus

KEY points

FALSE TEACHERS

Jude warned believers about false teachers and leaders who rejected the lordship of Christ, undermined the faith of others, and led people astray. Genuine servants of God will faithfully portray Christ in their words and conduct.

APOSTASY

Jude also warned against apostasy—turning away from Christ. We must be careful not to drift away from a firm commitment to Christ.

GREETINGS FROM JUDE

This letter is from Jude, a slave of Jesus Christ and a brother of James.

I am writing to all who have been called by God the Father, who loves you and keeps you safe in the care of Jesus Christ.*

[2]May God give you more and more mercy, peace, and love.

THE DANGER OF FALSE TEACHERS

[3]Dear friends, I had been eagerly planning to write to
you about the salvation we all share. But now I find that
I must write about something else, urging you to defend the faith that God has entrusted once for all time
to his holy people. [4]I say this because some ungodly
people have wormed their way into your churches, saying that God's marvelous grace allows us to live immoral lives. The condemnation of such people was recorded long ago, for they have denied our only Master and Lord, Jesus Christ.

WHAT'S TRUE 1:4

Like the apostle John, Jude stressed the importance of knowing what's true about God and his Word. This is the only way to recognize false teaching. So, how do you know what's true? Study the Word. ■

[5]So I want to remind you, though you already know
these things, that Jesus* first rescued the nation of Israel from Egypt, but later he destroyed those who did
not remain faithful. [6]And I remind you of the angels
who did not stay within the limits of authority God gave them but left the place where they belonged. God has kept them securely chained in prisons of darkness,
waiting for the great day of judgment. [7]And don't forget Sodom and Gomorrah and their neighboring towns, which were filled with immorality and every kind of sexual perversion. Those cities were destroyed by fire and serve as a warning of the eternal fire of God's judgment.

WATCH OUT! 1:10

False teachers claimied to possess secret knowledge of God. In reality, we can never fully know everything there is to know about God. But God in his grace has chosen to reveal himself to us through his Word and through Jesus. Beware of those who claim to have all of the answers and who belittle what they don't understand. ■

PERSEVERANCE

Erin and Arianna met way back in eighth grade. Not only did they become fast friends, Erin had helped Arianna to become a Christian by the end of the school year. Throughout high school Erin always did her best to help Arianna grow in faith. She practically dragged Arianna to retreats and youth group events.

Had you known them in those years, you probably would've predicted that Erin would do great things for God. And you would have seriously doubted the long-term stability of Arianna's faith.

Boy, would you have been wrong!

During their first year of college, Erin got too physically involved with her boyfriend, a non-Christian. When she got pregnant, she married the guy and dropped out of sight. Meanwhile, Arianna has continued to mature in her walk with God. She's the one with the dynamic ministry on campus.

A sports figure once quipped, "The opera isn't over until the fat lady sings." The point? The Christian life is a long, long race. Are you willing to go the distance? Read about perseverance in the Epistle of Jude.

[8]In the same way, these people—who claim authority
from their dreams—live immoral lives, defy authority,
and scoff at supernatural beings.* [9]But even Michael,
one of the mightiest of the angels,* did not dare accuse the devil of blasphemy, but simply said, "The Lord rebuke you!" (This took place when Michael was arguing
with the devil about Moses' body.) [10]But these people
scoff at things they do not understand. Like unthinking animals, they do whatever their instincts tell them, and
so they bring about their own destruction. [11]What sorrow awaits them! For they follow in the footsteps of Cain, who killed his brother. Like Balaam, they deceive people for money. And like Korah, they perish in their rebellion.

DON'T SLIP 1:23

Jude warned his readers to avoid compromising when trying to help others. In trying to find something in common with the people we talk to about Jesus, we also must be careful not to fall into the quicksand of compromise. We are to influence others for Christ, rather than be influenced to make a bad choice! ■

[12]When these people eat with you in your fellowship
meals commemorating the Lord's love, they are like dangerous reefs that can shipwreck you.* They are like shameless shepherds who care only for themselves. They are like clouds blowing over the land without

1 Or *keeps you for Jesus Christ.* 5 As in the best manuscripts; various other manuscripts read *[the] Lord,* or *God,* or *Christ;* one reads *God Christ.* 8 Greek *at glorious ones,* which are probably evil angels. 9 Greek *Michael, the archangel.* 12 Or *they are contaminants among you;* or *they are stains.*

giving any rain. They are like trees in
autumn that are doubly dead, for they
bear no fruit and have been pulled up
by the roots. 13They are like wild waves
of the sea, churning up the foam of
their shameful deeds. They are like
wandering stars, doomed forever to
blackest darkness.

14Enoch, who lived in the seventh
generation after Adam, prophesied
about these people. He said, "Listen!
The Lord is coming with countless
thousands of his holy ones 15to execute judgment on the people of the
world. He will convict every person of
all the ungodly things they have done
and for all the insults that ungodly sinners have spoken against him."*

16These people are grumblers and complainers, living
only to satisfy their desires. They brag loudly about themselves, and they flatter others to get what they want.

A CALL TO REMAIN FAITHFUL

17But you, my dear friends, must remember what the
apostles of our Lord Jesus Christ said. 18They told you
that in the last times there would be scoffers whose purpose in life is to satisfy their ungodly desires. 19These
people are the ones who are creating
divisions among you. They follow
their natural instincts because they
do not have God's Spirit in them.

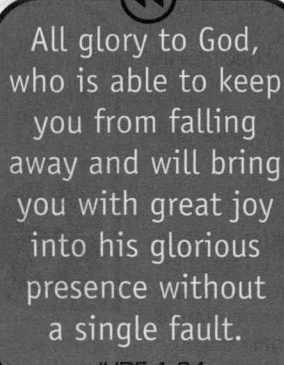

20But you, dear friends, must build
each other up in your most holy faith,
pray in the power of the Holy Spirit,*
21and await the mercy of our Lord
Jesus Christ, who will bring you eternal life. In this way, you will keep
yourselves safe in God's love.

22And you must show mercy to*
those whose faith is wavering. 23Rescue
others by snatching them from the
flames of judgment. Show mercy to
still others,* but do so with great caution, hating the sins that contaminate
their lives.*

> All glory to God, who is able to keep you from falling away and will bring you with great joy into his glorious presence without a single fault.
>
> *JUDE 1:24*

A PRAYER OF PRAISE

24Now all glory to God, who is able to keep you from falling away and will bring you with great joy into his glorious presence without a single fault. 25All glory to him
who alone is God, our Savior through Jesus Christ our
Lord. All glory, majesty, power, and authority are his before all time, and in the present, and beyond all time!
Amen.

14-15 The quotation comes from intertestamental literature: Enoch 1:9. **20** Greek *pray in the Holy Spirit*. **22** Some manuscripts read *must reprove*. **22-23a** Some manuscripts have only two categories of people: (1) those whose faith is wavering and therefore need to be snatched from the flames of judgment, and (2) those who need to be shown mercy. **23b** Greek *with fear, hating even the clothing stained sby the flesh.*

REVELATION

FAIRY TALES always end perfectly. The frog turns into a prince, the unloved stepsister becomes a beloved bride, and mean and greedy people get paid back for the rotten things they've done.

Unfortunately, fairy tales aren't true. "Happily ever after"? . . . The real world doesn't work that way, does it?

At the end of the Bible we find a book of prophecy: the book of Revelation. This strange vision of the apostle John's is one of the most discussed, mysterious, and controversial books ever written. And it's like a fairy tale.

Don't look so surprised! According to Revelation, those who have become God's children by faith in Christ will have the happiest of all endings: being in the very presence of God, untouched by sorrow or death.

And every evil being (including the devil) will "face the music." All injustices will be righted; all unforgiven sin will be judged. That, in a nutshell, is the message of Revelation: reward for God's people; punishment for all the guilty. A picture-perfect ending.

You have to admit that ending *does* sound like a fairy tale. There is, however, one important difference: This too-good-to-be-true story is truer than anything that ever existed. It *is* going to happen. You can count on it.

revelation

stats

PURPOSE: To reveal the full identity of Christ and to warn and provide hope for believers

AUTHOR: The apostle John

TO WHOM WRITTEN: Seven Asian churches and believers everywhere

DATE WRITTEN: About A.D. 95, from the island of Patmos

SETTING: Most scholars believe that the seven churches of Asia to whom John wrote had experienced persecution under the emperor Domitian (A.D. 90–95). Apparently the Roman authorities had exiled John to the island of Patmos (off the coast of Asia). John, an eyewitness of the incarnate Christ, had a vision of the glorified Christ. God also revealed to him what will take place in the future: judgment and the ultimate triumph of God over evil.

KEY PEOPLE: John, Jesus

KEY PLACES: The island of Patmos, the seven churches, New Jerusalem

KEY points

GOD'S SOVEREIGNTY

God is greater than any power in the universe. Knowing this can prevent us from despair when evil seems on the increase.

CHRIST'S RETURN

Jesus came to earth as a "Lamb," the symbol of his perfect sacrifice for our sin. He will return as the triumphant "Lion," the rightful ruler and conqueror. We can look forward to Christ's return as King and Judge. Because no one knows when he will appear, we must be ready at all times.

JUDGMENT

God's final judgment will put an end to evil and injustice. We must be certain of our commitment to Jesus if we want to escape this great final judgment. All who belong to him will receive their full reward.

HOPE FOR THE FUTURE

One day God will create a new heaven and a new earth. All believers will live with God forever in perfect peace and security. If we have confidence in our final destination, we will follow Christ with unwavering dedication no matter what trials we must face.

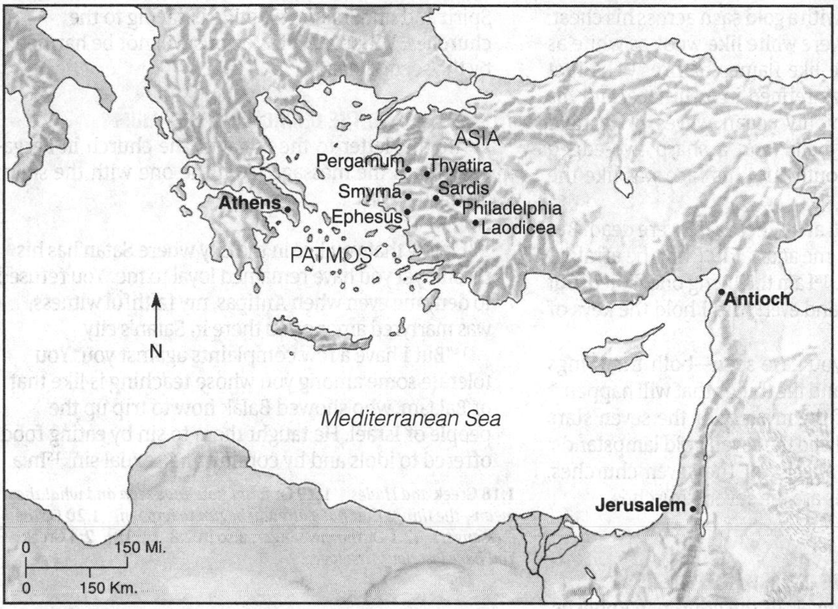

THE SEVEN CHURCHES
The seven churches were located on a major Roman road. A letter carrier would leave the island of Patmos (where John was exiled), arriving first at Ephesus. He would travel north to Smyrna and Pergamum (Pergamos), turn southeast to Thyatira, and continue on to Sardis, Philadelphia, and Laodicea—in the exact order in which the letters were dictated.

1 PROLOGUE

This is a revelation from* Jesus Christ, which God gave him
to show his servants the events that must soon* take place.
He sent an angel to present this revelation to his servant
John, 2who faithfully reported everything he saw. This is his
report of the word of God and the testimony of Jesus Christ.

INDESCRIBABLE? 1:1

Jesus gave his message to John in a vision, allowing John to see and record certain future events as an encouragement to all believers. What John saw, in most cases, was indescribable, so he used illustrations to show what an event or item was *like*. When reading this symbolic language, don't stress yourself by trying to understand every detail. After all, John didn't fully understand what he saw! But there's one thing you can understand: that Christ is the glorious, victorious Lord of all. ■

3God blesses the one who reads the words of this
prophecy to the church, and he blesses all who listen to
its message and obey what it says, for the time is near.

JOHN'S GREETING TO THE SEVEN CHURCHES

4This letter is from John to the seven churches in the
province of Asia.*

Grace and peace to you from the one who is, who always was, and who is still to come; from the sevenfold
Spirit* before his throne; 5and from Jesus Christ. He is
the faithful witness to these things, the first to rise from
the dead, and the ruler of all the kings of the world.

All glory to him who loves us and has freed us from our
sins by shedding his blood for us. 6He has made us a
Kingdom of priests for God his Father. All glory and
power to him forever and ever! Amen.

7 Look! He comes with the clouds of heaven.
And everyone will see him—
even those who pierced him.
And all the nations of the world
will mourn for him.
Yes! Amen!

8"I am the Alpha and the Omega—the beginning and
the end,"* says the Lord God. "I am the one who is, who always was, and who is still to come—the Almighty One."

VISION OF THE SON OF MAN

9I, John, am your brother and your partner in suffering
and in God's Kingdom and in the patient endurance to
which Jesus calls us. I was exiled to the island of Patmos
for preaching the word of God and for my testimony
about Jesus. 10It was the Lord's Day, and I was worshiping
in the Spirit.* Suddenly, I heard behind me a loud voice
like a trumpet blast. 11It said, "Write in a book* everything you see, and send it to the seven churches in the
cities of Ephesus, Smyrna, Pergamum, Thyatira, Sardis,
Philadelphia, and Laodicea."

12When I turned to see who was speaking to me, I saw
seven gold lampstands. 13And standing in the middle of
the lampstands was someone like the Son of Man.* He

1:1a Or *of.* **1:1b** Or *suddenly,* or *quickly.* **1:4a** *Asia* was a Roman province in what is now western Turkey. **1:4b** Greek *the seven spirits.* **1:8** Greek *I am the Alpha and the Omega,* referring to the first and last letters of the Greek alphabet. **1:10** Or *in spirit.* **1:11** Or *on a scroll.* **1:13** Or *like a son of man.* See Dan 7:13. "Son of Man" is a title Jesus used for himself.

was wearing a long robe with a gold sash across his chest.
14His head and his hair were white like wool, as white as
snow. And his eyes were like flames of fire. 15His feet
were like polished bronze refined in a furnace, and his
voice thundered like mighty ocean waves. 16He held
seven stars in his right hand, and a sharp two-edged
sword came from his mouth. And his face was like the
sun in all its brilliance.
17When I saw him, I fell at his feet as if I were dead. But
he laid his right hand on me and said, "Don't be afraid! I
am the First and the Last. 18I am the living one. I died, but
look—I am alive forever and ever! And I hold the keys of
death and the grave.*
19"Write down what you have seen—both the things
that are now happening and the things that will happen.*
20This is the meaning of the mystery of the seven stars
you saw in my right hand and the seven gold lampstands:
The seven stars are the angels* of the seven churches,
and the seven lampstands are the seven churches.

2

THE MESSAGE TO THE CHURCH IN EPHESUS

"Write this letter to the angel* of the church in Ephesus.
This is the message from the one who holds the seven
stars in his right hand, the one who walks among the
seven gold lampstands:

2"I know all the things you do. I have seen your hard
work and your patient endurance. I know you don't
tolerate evil people. You have examined the claims
of those who say they are apostles but are not. You
have discovered they are liars. 3You have patiently
suffered for me without quitting.
4"But I have this complaint against you. You don't
love me or each other as you did at first!* 5Look
how far you have fallen! Turn back to me and do the
works you did at first. If you don't repent, I will come
and remove your lampstand from its place among the
churches. 6But this is in your favor: You hate the evil
deeds of the Nicolaitans, just as I do.
7"Anyone with ears to hear must listen to the Spirit
and understand what he is saying to the churches.
To everyone who is victorious I will give fruit from
the tree of life in the paradise of God.

THE MESSAGE TO THE CHURCH IN SMYRNA

8"Write this letter to the angel of the church in Smyrna.
This is the message from the one who is the First and the
Last, who was dead but is now alive:

9"I know about your suffering and your poverty—but
you are rich! I know the blasphemy of those opposing
you. They say they are Jews, but they are not, because
their synagogue belongs to Satan. 10Don't be afraid
of what you are about to suffer. The devil will throw
some of you into prison to test you. You will suffer
for ten days. But if you remain faithful even when
facing death, I will give you the crown of life.
11"Anyone with ears to hear must listen to the
Spirit and understand what he is saying to the
churches. Whoever is victorious will not be harmed
by the second death.

THE MESSAGE TO THE CHURCH IN PERGAMUM

12"Write this letter to the angel of the church in Pergamum. This is the message from the one with the sharp
two-edged sword:

13"I know that you live in the city where Satan has his
throne, yet you have remained loyal to me. You refused
to deny me even when Antipas, my faithful witness,
was martyred among you there in Satan's city.
14"But I have a few complaints against you. You
tolerate some among you whose teaching is like that
of Balaam, who showed Balak how to trip up the
people of Israel. He taught them to sin by eating food
offered to idols and by committing sexual sin. 15In a

1:18 Greek *and Hades.* **1:19** Or *what you have seen and what they mean—the things that have already begun to happen.* **1:20** Or *the messengers.* **2:1** Or *the messenger;* also in 2:8, 12, 18. **2:4** Greek *You have lost your first love.*

Because of my shyness, I find it difficult to let people get close to me—even God. How involved in my life does God want to be?

As involved as you'll let him.

Although God knows everything about us, he still wants to be a Father to us. Isn't that amazing?

King David wrote about how much God thinks of us. "How precious are your thoughts about me, O God. They cannot be numbered! I can't even count them; they outnumber the grains of sand! And when I wake up, you are still with me!" (Ps 139:17-18).

Knowing how much God thinks about us (especially in light of how little we think of him) should give us an incredible feeling of worth. Our response to God's constant attentiveness, however, should never be out of obligation. God doesn't want us to hang out with him only because we feel we have to.

Revelation 2:4 warns us to avoid allowing our love for God to lessen or end. God wants us to grow beyond our initial commitment to him, just like in a marriage where love continues to grow. Unfortunately, this doesn't always happen. Many people who become Christians are really excited about their new relationship with God. But as problems come up, the excitement often wears off (just like what happens in some marriages).

To maintain a growing relationship with God, the key word is time: daily time with him, time with others who know him, and time (in years) to grow to appreciate his love for you.

Though God is anxious for an intimate relationship with us, he will wait for the day when we'll experience for ourselves what loving him really means. And what a wonderful day that will be!

The Names of Jesus

Scattered among the vivid images of the book of Revelation is a large collection of names for Jesus. Each one tells something of his character and highlights a particular aspect of his role within God's plan of redemption.

JESUS' NAME	REFERENCE
The Alpha and the Omega / The Beginning and the End	1:8
Lord	1:8
The Almighty One	1:8
Son of Man	1:13
The First and the Last	1:17
Son of God	2:18
Witness	3:14
Creator	4:11
Lion of the tribe of Judah	5:5
Heir to David's Throne	5:5
Lamb	5:6
Shepherd	7:17
Christ	12:10
Faithful and True	19:11
The Word of God	19:13
King of Kings	19:16
Lord of Lords	19:16
The Bright Morning Star	22:16

similar way, you have some Nicolaitans among you
who follow the same teaching. 16Repent of your sin,
or I will come to you suddenly and fight against them
with the sword of my mouth.
17"Anyone with ears to hear must listen to the
Spirit and understand what he is saying to the
churches. To everyone who is victorious I will give
some of the manna that has been hidden away in
heaven. And I will give to each one a white stone, and
on the stone will be engraved a new name that no one
understands except the one who receives it.

A SERIOUS PROBLEM 2:20

Why is sexual immorality serious? Because it always hurts someone. Sexual sin has tremendous power to destroy families, communities, and even nations, because it destroys the relationships upon which these institutions are built. But God wants to protect us from hurting ourselves and others—if we let him. ■

THE MESSAGE TO THE CHURCH IN THYATIRA

18"Write this letter to the angel of the church in Thyatira.
This is the message from the Son of God, whose eyes are
like flames of fire, whose feet are like polished bronze:

19"I know all the things you do. I have seen your love,
your faith, your service, and your patient endurance.
And I can see your constant improvement in all these
things.
20"But I have this complaint against you. You are
permitting that woman—that Jezebel who calls
herself a prophet—to lead my servants astray. She
teaches them to commit sexual sin and to eat food
offered to idols. 21I gave her time to repent, but she
does not want to turn away from her immorality.
22"Therefore, I will throw her on a bed of suffering,*
and those who commit adultery with her will suffer
greatly unless they repent and turn away from her
evil deeds. 23I will strike her children dead. Then all
the churches will know that I am the one who searches
out the thoughts and intentions of every person. And
I will give to each of you whatever you deserve.
24"But I also have a message for the rest of you in
Thyatira who have not followed this false teaching
('deeper truths,' as they call them—depths of Satan,
actually). I will ask nothing more of you 25except that
you hold tightly to what you have until I come. 26To
all who are victorious, who obey me to the very end,

To them I will give authority over all the nations.
27 They will rule the nations with an iron rod
and smash them like clay pots.*

28They will have the same authority I received from
my Father, and I will also give them the morning star!
29"Anyone with ears to hear must listen to the
Spirit and understand what he is saying to the
churches.

3 THE MESSAGE TO THE CHURCH IN SARDIS
"Write this letter to the angel* of the church in Sardis.
This is the message from the one who has the sevenfold
Spirit* of God and the seven stars:

2:22 Greek *a bed.* 2:26-27 Ps 2:8-9 (Greek Version). 3:1a Or *the messenger;* also in 3:7, 14. 3:1b Greek *the seven spirits.*

"I know all the things you do, and
that you have a reputation for
being alive—but you are dead.
2Wake up! Strengthen what little
remains, for even what is left
is almost dead. I find that
your actions do not meet the
requirements of my God. 3Go
back to what you heard and
believed at first; hold to it firmly.
Repent and turn to me again. If
you don't wake up, I will come to
you suddenly, as unexpected as
a thief.
4"Yet there are some in the
church in Sardis who have not
soiled their clothes with evil. They
will walk with me in white, for they
are worthy. 5All who are victorious will be clothed in
white. I will never erase their names from the Book
of Life, but I will announce before my Father and his
angels that they are mine.
6"Anyone with ears to hear must listen to the Spirit
and understand what he is saying to the churches.

> I stand at the door and knock. If you hear my voice and open the door, I will come in, and we will share a meal together as friends.
>
> *REVELATION 3:20*

THE MESSAGE TO THE CHURCH IN PHILADELPHIA

7"Write this letter to the angel of the church in Philadelphia.

This is the message from the one who is holy
and true,
the one who has the key of David.
What he opens, no one can close;
and what he closes, no one can open:*

8"I know all the things you do, and I have opened a
door for you that no one can close. You have little
strength, yet you obeyed my word and did not deny
me. 9Look, I will force those who belong to Satan's
synagogue—those liars who say they are Jews but are
not—to come and bow down at your feet. They will
acknowledge that you are the ones I love.
10"Because you have obeyed my command to
persevere, I will protect you from the great time
of testing that will come upon the whole world
to test those who belong to this world. 11I am
coming soon.* Hold on to what you have, so that
no one will take away your crown. 12All who are
victorious will become pillars in the Temple of
my God, and they will never have to leave it. And
I will write on them the name of my God, and
they will be citizens in the city of my God—the
new Jerusalem that comes down from heaven
from my God. And I will also write on them my
new name.
13"Anyone with ears to hear must listen to the
Spirit and understand what he is saying to the
churches.

THE MESSAGE TO THE CHURCH IN LAODICEA

14"Write this letter to the angel of the
church in Laodicea. This is the message from the one who is the Amen—
the faithful and true witness, the beginning* of God's new creation:

15"I know all the things you do, that
you are neither hot nor cold. I wish
that you were one or the other! 16But
since you are like lukewarm water,
neither hot nor cold, I will spit you
out of my mouth! 17You say, 'I am
rich. I have everything I want. I don't
need a thing!' And you don't realize
that you are wretched and miserable
and poor and blind and naked. 18So
I advise you to buy gold from me—gold that has been
purified by fire. Then you will be rich. Also buy white
garments from me so you will not be shamed by your
nakedness, and ointment for your eyes so you will be
able to see. 19I correct and discipline everyone I love.
So be diligent and turn from your indifference.

YOUR CHOICE 3:20

Think back to the days when you were a little kid in Sunday school. Remember seeing a picture of Jesus standing at a door knocking? (Just play along if you didn't.) Jesus knocks on the door of our hearts every time we sense that we should turn to him. This means he wants to hang out with us. He patiently and persistently knocks, rather than breaking and entering. He allows us to decide whether or not to open our lives to him. Have you? ■

20"Look! I stand at the door and knock. If you hear
my voice and open the door, I will come in, and we
will share a meal together as friends. 21Those who
are victorious will sit with me on my throne, just as
I was victorious and sat with my Father on his throne.
22"Anyone with ears to hear must listen to the
Spirit and understand what he is saying to the
churches."

4

WORSHIP IN HEAVEN

Then as I looked, I saw a door standing open in heaven,
and the same voice I had heard before spoke to me like a
trumpet blast. The voice said, "Come up here, and I will
show you what must happen after this." 2And instantly I
was in the Spirit,* and I saw a throne in heaven and someone sitting on it. 3The one sitting on the throne was as
brilliant as gemstones—like jasper and carnelian. And
the glow of an emerald circled his throne like a rainbow.
4Twenty-four thrones surrounded him, and twenty-four

3:7 Isa 22:22. 3:11 Or *suddenly*, or *quickly*. 3:14 Or *the ruler*, or *the source*. 4:2 Or *in spirit*.

The Beginning and the End

The Bible records for us the beginning of the world and the end of the world. The story of humanity, from beginning to end—from the fall into sin to the redemption of Christ and God's ultimate victory over evil—is found in the pages of the Bible.

GENESIS	REVELATION
The sun is created	The sun is not needed
Satan is victorious	Satan is defeated
Sin enters the human race	Sin is banished
People run and hide from God	People are invited to live with God forever
People are cursed	The curse is removed
Tears are shed, with sorrow for sin	No more sin, no more tears or sorrow
The garden and earth are cursed	God's city is glorified, the earth is made new
The fruit from the tree of life is not to be eaten	God's people may eat from the tree of life
Paradise is lost	Paradise is regained
People are doomed to death	Death is defeated, believers live forever with God

elders sat on them. They were all clothed in white and
had gold crowns on their heads. 5From the throne came
flashes of lightning and the rumble of thunder. And in
front of the throne were seven torches with burning
flames. This is the sevenfold Spirit* of God. 6In front of
the throne was a shiny sea of glass, sparkling like crystal.

NO FEAR 4–5

Chapters 4 and 5 are a glimpse of Christ's glory. Here we see into the throne room of heaven as God orchestrates the events that John records. Ever think that life seems out of control or that the forces of evil seem to be winning? God is never out of control. He will carry out his plans as Jesus initiates the final battle with the forces of evil—one that Jesus will win. John shows us heaven before showing us earth so we won't be frightened by future events. ■

In the center and around the throne were four living
beings, each covered with eyes, front and back. 7The first
of these living beings was like a lion; the second was like
an ox; the third had a human face; and the fourth was like
an eagle in flight. 8Each of these living beings had six
wings, and their wings were covered all over with eyes,
inside and out. Day after day and night after night they
keep on saying,

"Holy, holy, holy is the Lord God, the Almighty—
the one who always was, who is, and who is still
to come."

9Whenever the living beings give glory and honor and
thanks to the one sitting on the throne (the one who lives
forever and ever), 10the twenty-four elders fall down and
worship the one sitting on the throne (the one who lives
forever and ever). And they lay their crowns before the
throne and say,

11 "You are worthy, O Lord our God,
to receive glory and honor and power.
For you created all things,
and they exist because you created what
you pleased."

5

THE LAMB OPENS THE SCROLL

Then I saw a scroll* in the right hand of the one who was
sitting on the throne. There was writing on the inside and
the outside of the scroll, and it was sealed with seven
seals. 2And I saw a strong angel, who shouted with a loud
voice: "Who is worthy to break the seals on this scroll and
open it?" 3But no one in heaven or on earth or under the
earth was able to open the scroll and read it.
4Then I began to weep bitterly because no one was
found worthy to open the scroll and read it. 5But one of
the twenty-four elders said to me, "Stop weeping! Look,
the Lion of the tribe of Judah, the heir to David's throne,*
has won the victory. He is worthy to open the scroll and
its seven seals."
6Then I saw a Lamb that looked as if it had been
slaughtered, but it was now standing between the throne
and the four living beings and among the twenty-four
elders. He had seven horns and seven eyes, which represent

4:5 Greek *They are the seven spirits.* 5:1 Or *book;* also in 5:2, 3, 4, 5, 7, 8, 9. 5:5 Greek *the root of David.* See Isa 11:10.

the sevenfold Spirit* of God that is sent out into every part of the earth. 7He stepped forward and took the scroll from the right hand of the one sitting on the throne. 8And when he took the scroll, the four living beings and the twenty-four elders fell down before the Lamb. Each one had a harp, and they held gold bowls filled with incense, which are the prayers of God's people. 9And they sang a new song with these words:

"You are worthy to take the scroll
and break its seals and open it.
For you were slaughtered, and your blood has
ransomed people for God
from every tribe and language and people
and nation.
10 And you have caused them to become
a Kingdom of priests for our God.
And they will reign* on the earth."

11Then I looked again, and I heard the voices of thousands and millions of angels around the throne and of the living beings and the elders. 12And they sang in a mighty chorus:

"Worthy is the Lamb who was slaughtered—
to receive power and riches
and wisdom and strength
and honor and glory and blessing."

13And then I heard every creature in heaven and on earth and under the earth and in the sea. They sang:

"Blessing and honor and glory and power
belong to the one sitting on the throne
and to the Lamb forever and ever."

14And the four living beings said, "Amen!" And the twenty-four elders fell down and worshiped the Lamb.

6 THE LAMB BREAKS THE FIRST SIX SEALS

As I watched, the Lamb broke the first of the seven seals on the scroll.* Then I heard one of the four living beings say with a voice like thunder, "Come!" 2I looked up and saw a white horse standing there. Its rider carried a bow, and a crown was placed on his head. He rode out to win many battles and gain the victory.

3When the Lamb broke the second seal, I heard the second living being say, "Come!" 4Then another horse appeared, a red one. Its rider was given a mighty sword and the authority to take peace from the earth. And there was war and slaughter everywhere.

5When the Lamb broke the third seal, I heard the third living being say, "Come!" I looked up and saw a black horse, and its rider was holding a pair of scales in his hand. 6And I heard a voice from among the four living beings say, "A loaf of wheat bread or three loaves of barley will cost a day's pay.* And don't waste* the olive oil and wine."

7When the Lamb broke the fourth seal, I heard the fourth living being say, "Come!" 8I looked up and saw a horse whose color was pale green. Its rider was named Death, and his companion was the Grave.* These two were given authority over one-fourth of the earth, to kill with the sword and famine and disease* and wild animals.

9When the Lamb broke the fifth seal, I saw under the altar the souls of all who had been martyred for the word of God and for being faithful in their testimony. 10They shouted to the Lord and said, "O Sovereign Lord, holy and true, how long before you judge the people who belong to this world and avenge our blood for what they have done to us?" 11Then a white robe was given to each of them. And they were told to rest a little longer until the full number of their brothers and sisters*—their fellow servants of Jesus who were to be martyred—had joined them.

GOD'S TIME 6:9-11

Although the martyrs were eager for God to bring justice to the earth, they were told to wait. Those who suffer and die for their faith won't be forgotten, nor are their deaths in vain. Rather, God will single them out for special honor. Like these martyrs, we may wish for justice immediately. Yet we must be patient. Although God works on his own timetable, he promises justice. No suffering for the sake of God's Kingdom is wasted effort. ■

12I watched as the Lamb broke the sixth seal, and there was a great earthquake. The sun became as dark as black cloth, and the moon became as red as blood. 13Then the stars of the sky fell to the earth like green figs falling from a tree shaken by a strong wind. 14The sky was rolled up like a scroll, and all of the mountains and islands were moved from their places.

15Then everyone—the kings of the earth, the rulers, the generals, the wealthy, the powerful, and every slave and free person—all hid themselves in the caves and among the rocks of the mountains. 16And they cried to the mountains and the rocks, "Fall on us and hide us from the face of the one who sits on the throne and from the wrath of the Lamb. 17For the great day of their wrath has come, and who is able to survive?"

7 GOD'S PEOPLE WILL BE PRESERVED

Then I saw four angels standing at the four corners of the earth, holding back the four winds so they did not blow on the earth or the sea, or even on any tree. 2And I saw another angel coming up from the east, carrying the seal of the living God. And he shouted to those four an-

5:6 Greek *which are the seven spirits.* 5:10 Some manuscripts read *they are reigning.* 6:1 Or *book.* 6:6a Greek *A choinix* [1 quart or 1 liter] *of wheat for a denarius, and 3 choinix of barley for a denarius.* A denarius was equivalent to a laborer's full day's wage. 6:6b Or *harm.* 6:8a Greek *was Hades.* 6:8b Greek *death.* 6:11 Greek *their brothers.*

gels, who had been given power to harm land and sea,
3"Wait! Don't harm the land or the sea or the trees until
we have placed the seal of God on the foreheads of his
servants."
4And I heard how many were marked with the seal of
God—144,000 were sealed from all the tribes of Israel:

5 from Judah 12,000
from Reuben 12,000
from Gad 12,000
6 from Asher 12,000
from Naphtali 12,000
from Manasseh 12,000
7 from Simeon 12,000
from Levi 12,000
from Issachar 12,000
8 from Zebulun 12,000
from Joseph 12,000
from Benjamin. 12,000

PRAISE FROM THE GREAT CROWD

9After this I saw a vast crowd, too great to count, from
every nation and tribe and people and language, standing
in front of the throne and before the Lamb. They were
clothed in white robes and held palm branches in their
hands. 10And they were shouting with a mighty shout,

"Salvation comes from our God who sits on
the throne
and from the Lamb!"

ALL ARE WELCOME 7:9-10

John saw people from every nation praising God before his throne. The gospel is not limited to a specific culture, race, or country. God accepts anyone who comes in repentance and faith. Is that the kind of acceptance you have for others? ■

11And all the angels were standing around the throne
and around the elders and the four living beings. And
they fell before the throne with their faces to the ground
and worshiped God. 12They sang,

"Amen! Blessing and glory and wisdom
and thanksgiving and honor
and power and strength belong to our God
forever and ever! Amen."

13Then one of the twenty-four elders asked me, "Who
are these who are clothed in white? Where did they come
from?"
14And I said to him, "Sir, you are the one who knows."
Then he said to me, "These are the ones who died in*
the great tribulation.* They have washed their robes in
the blood of the Lamb and made them white.

15 "That is why they stand in front of God's throne
and serve him day and night in his Temple.
And he who sits on the throne
will give them shelter.
16 They will never again be hungry or thirsty;
they will never be scorched by the heat of the sun.
17 For the Lamb on the throne*
will be their Shepherd.
He will lead them to springs of life-giving water.
And God will wipe every tear from their eyes."

8 THE LAMB BREAKS THE SEVENTH SEAL

When the Lamb broke the seventh seal on the scroll,*
there was silence throughout heaven for about half an
hour. 2I saw the seven angels who stand before God, and
they were given seven trumpets.
3Then another angel with a gold incense burner came
and stood at the altar. And a great amount of incense was
given to him to mix with the prayers of God's people as an
offering on the gold altar before the throne. 4The smoke
of the incense, mixed with the prayers of God's holy people, ascended up to God from the altar where the angel
had poured them out. 5Then the angel filled the incense
burner with fire from the altar and threw it down upon
the earth; and thunder crashed, lightning flashed, and
there was a terrible earthquake.

MAKE SURE 8:6

A trumpet blast is usually a rallying call. These trumpet blasts had three purposes: (1) to warn that judgment is certain, (2) to call the forces of good and evil to battle, and (3) to announce the return of the King, the Messiah. These warnings urge us to make sure our faith is firmly fixed on Christ. Is that where your faith is? ■

THE FIRST FOUR TRUMPETS

6Then the seven angels with the seven trumpets prepared
to blow their mighty blasts.
7The first angel blew his trumpet, and hail and fire
mixed with blood were thrown down on the earth. One-
third of the earth was set on fire, one-third of the trees
were burned, and all the green grass was burned.
8Then the second angel blew his trumpet, and a great
mountain of fire was thrown into the sea. One-third of
the water in the sea became blood, 9one-third of all
things living in the sea died, and one-third of all the ships
on the sea were destroyed.
10Then the third angel blew his trumpet, and a great
star fell from the sky, burning like a torch. It fell on one-
third of the rivers and on the springs of water. 11The
name of the star was Bitterness.* It made one-third of
the water bitter, and many people died from drinking
the bitter water.
12Then the fourth angel blew his trumpet, and one-
third of the sun was struck, and one-third of the moon,
and one-third of the stars, and they became dark. And

7:14a Greek *who came out of.* **7:14b** Or *the great suffering.* **7:17** Greek *on the center of the throne.* **8:1** Or *book.* **8:11** Greek *Wormwood.*

one-third of the day was dark, and also one-third of the night.

13 Then I looked, and I heard a single eagle crying loudly as it flew through the air, "Terror, terror, terror to all who belong to this world because of what will happen when the last three angels blow their trumpets."

COMPLETELY ENTANGLED 9:20-21

These people were so hardhearted that even plagues couldn't drive them to God. People don't usually fall into immorality and evil suddenly—they slip into it a little at a time until they are completely entangled. Temptation entertained today can become a habit that eventually leads to separation from God forever (see James 1:15). To think you could never become this evil is the first step toward a hard heart. Do you feel yourself slipping? You know where to run: to God. ■

9

THE FIFTH TRUMPET BRINGS THE FIRST TERROR

Then the fifth angel blew his trumpet, and I saw a star that had fallen to earth from the sky, and he was given the key to the shaft of the bottomless pit.* 2 When he opened it, smoke poured out as though from a huge furnace, and the sunlight and air turned dark from the smoke.

3 Then locusts came from the smoke and descended on the earth, and they were given power to sting like scorpions. 4 They were told not to harm the grass or plants or trees, but only the people who did not have the seal of God on their foreheads. 5 They were told not to kill them but to torture them for five months with pain like the pain of a scorpion sting. 6 In those days people will seek death but will not find it. They will long to die, but death will flee from them!

7 The locusts looked like horses prepared for battle. They had what looked like gold crowns on their heads, and their faces looked like human faces. 8 They had hair like women's hair and teeth like the teeth of a lion. 9 They wore armor made of iron, and their wings roared like an army of chariots rushing into battle. 10 They had tails that stung like scorpions, and for five months they had the power to torment people. 11 Their king is the angel from the bottomless pit; his name in Hebrew is *Abaddon,* and in Greek, *Apollyon*—the Destroyer.

12 The first terror is past, but look, two more terrors are coming!

THE SIXTH TRUMPET BRINGS THE SECOND TERROR

13 Then the sixth angel blew his trumpet, and I heard a voice speaking from the four horns of the gold altar that stands in the presence of God. 14 And the voice said to the sixth angel who held the trumpet, "Release the four angels who are bound at the great Euphrates River." 15 Then the four angels who had been prepared for this hour and day and month and year were turned loose to kill one-third of all the people on earth. 16 I heard the size of their army, which was 200 million mounted troops.

17 And in my vision, I saw the horses and the riders sitting on them. The riders wore armor that was fiery red and dark blue and yellow. The horses had heads like lions, and fire and smoke and burning sulfur billowed from their mouths. 18 One-third of all the people on earth were killed by these three plagues—by the fire and smoke and burning sulfur that came from the mouths of the horses. 19 Their power was in their mouths and in their tails. For their tails had heads like snakes, with the power to injure people.

20 But the people who did not die in these plagues still refused to repent of their evil deeds and turn to God. They continued to worship demons and idols made of gold, silver, bronze, stone, and wood—idols that can neither see nor hear nor walk! 21 And they did not repent of their murders or their witchcraft or their sexual immorality or their thefts.

LIVE NOW 10:4

Throughout history people have wanted to know what would happen in the future. God revealed some future events in this book. But there are some events that he chose not to reveal. John was prevented from revealing certain parts of his vision. During Old Testament times, an angel also told the prophet Daniel that some things he saw were not to be revealed to everyone at that time (Dan 12:9). Hundreds of years later, Jesus told his disciples that only God knows what will happen during the end times (Mark 13:32-33).

God has revealed all we need to know in order to live for him now. In our desire to be ready for the end, we must not place more emphasis on what will happen during the last days than on living for God while we wait. ■

10

THE ANGEL AND THE SMALL SCROLL

Then I saw another mighty angel coming down from heaven, surrounded by a cloud, with a rainbow over his head. His face shone like the sun, and his feet were like pillars of fire. 2 And in his hand was a small scroll* that had been opened. He stood with his right foot on the sea and his left foot on the land. 3 And he gave a great shout like the roar of a lion. And when he shouted, the seven thunders answered.

4 When the seven thunders spoke, I was about to write. But I heard a voice from heaven saying, "Keep secret* what the seven thunders said, and do not write it down."

5 Then the angel I saw standing on the sea and on the land raised his right hand toward heaven. 6 He swore an oath in the name of the one who lives forever and ever, who created the heavens and everything in them, the earth and everything in it, and the sea and everything in

9:1 Or *the abyss,* or *the underworld;* also in 9:11. 10:2 Or *book;* also in 10:8, 9, 10. 10:4 Greek *Seal up.*

it. He said, "There will be no more delay. [7]When the seventh angel blows his trumpet, God's mysterious plan will be fulfilled. It will happen just as he announced it to his servants the prophets."

[8]Then the voice from heaven spoke to me again: "Go and take the open scroll from the hand of the angel who is standing on the sea and on the land."

[9]So I went to the angel and told him to give me the small scroll. "Yes, take it and eat it," he said. "It will be sweet as honey in your mouth, but it will turn sour in your stomach!" [10]So I took the small scroll from the hand of the angel, and I ate it! It was sweet in my mouth, but when I swallowed it, it turned sour in my stomach.

[11]Then I was told, "You must prophesy again about many peoples, nations, languages, and kings."

11 THE TWO WITNESSES

Then I was given a measuring stick, and I was told, "Go and measure the Temple of God and the altar, and count the number of worshipers. [2]But do not measure the outer courtyard, for it has been turned over to the nations. They will trample the holy city for 42 months. [3]And I will give power to my two witnesses, and they will be clothed in burlap and will prophesy during those 1,260 days."

[4]These two prophets are the two olive trees and the two lampstands that stand before the Lord of all the earth. [5]If anyone tries to harm them, fire flashes from their mouths and consumes their enemies. This is how anyone who tries to harm them must die. [6]They have power to shut the sky so that no rain will fall for as long as they prophesy. And they have the power to turn the rivers and oceans into blood, and to strike the earth with every kind of plague as often as they wish.

[7]When they complete their testimony, the beast that comes up out of the bottomless pit* will declare war against them, and he will conquer them and kill them. [8]And their bodies will lie in the main street of Jerusalem,* the city that is figuratively called "Sodom" and "Egypt," the city where their Lord was crucified. [9]And for three and a half days, all peoples, tribes, languages, and nations will stare at their bodies. No one will be allowed to bury them. [10]All the people who belong to this world will gloat over them and give presents to each other to celebrate the death of the two prophets who had tormented them.

[11]But after three and a half days, God breathed life into them, and they stood up! Terror struck all who were staring at them. [12]Then a loud voice from heaven called to the two prophets, "Come up here!" And they rose to heaven in a cloud as their enemies watched.

[13]At the same time there was a terrible earthquake that destroyed a tenth of the city. Seven thousand people died in that earthquake, and everyone else was terrified and gave glory to the God of heaven.

[14]The second terror is past, but look, the third terror is coming quickly.

THE SEVENTH TRUMPET BRINGS THE THIRD TERROR

[15]Then the seventh angel blew his trumpet, and there were loud voices shouting in heaven:

"The world has now become the Kingdom of our
  Lord and of his Christ,*
  and he will reign forever and ever."

[16]The twenty-four elders sitting on their thrones before God fell with their faces to the ground and worshiped him. [17]And they said,

"We give thanks to you, Lord God, the Almighty,
  the one who is and who always was,
for now you have assumed your great power
  and have begun to reign.
[18] The nations were filled with wrath,
  but now the time of your wrath has come.
It is time to judge the dead
  and reward your servants the prophets,
  as well as your holy people,
and all who fear your name,
  from the least to the greatest.
It is time to destroy
  all who have caused destruction on the earth."

[19]Then, in heaven, the Temple of God was opened and the Ark of his covenant could be seen inside the Temple. Lightning flashed, thunder crashed and roared, and there was an earthquake and a terrible hailstorm.

12 THE WOMAN AND THE DRAGON

Then I witnessed in heaven an event of great significance. I saw a woman clothed with the sun, with the moon beneath her feet, and a crown of twelve stars on her head. [2]She was pregnant, and she cried out because of her labor pains and the agony of giving birth.

[3]Then I witnessed in heaven another significant event. I saw a large red dragon with seven heads and ten horns, with seven crowns on his heads. [4]His tail swept away one-third of the stars in the sky, and he threw them to the earth. He stood in front of the woman as she was about to give birth, ready to devour her baby as soon as it was born.

[5]She gave birth to a son who was to rule all nations with an iron rod. And her child was snatched away from the dragon and was caught up to God and to his throne. [6]And the woman fled into the wilderness, where God had prepared a place to care for her for 1,260 days.

[7]Then there was war in heaven. Michael and his angels fought against the dragon and his angels. [8]And the dragon lost the battle, and he and his angels were forced out of heaven. [9]This great dragon—the ancient serpent called the devil, or Satan, the one deceiving the whole world—was thrown down to the earth with all his angels.

11:7 Or *the abyss*, or *the underworld*. 11:8 Greek *the great city*. 11:15 Or *his Messiah*.

ULTIMATE ISSUES

THE ENEMY

Forget about what you've heard about in horror flicks or in novels. Satan—the enemy of Christians—is real. The Bible has many names for him: the devil, Satan, the deceiver, the evil one, and the tempter. And today, interest in Satan and occult activities are on the rise. What does the Bible teach about this being and those under his command?

Old Testament passages such as 1 Chronicles 21:1, Job 1–2, and Zechariah 3 portray Satan as an accuser of God's people. It is historically believed that Satan was behind the serpent that deceived Eve in Genesis 3. Many interpret Isaiah 14:12 (the beginning of a prophecy about the "king of Babylon") as a reference to Satan: "How you are fallen from heaven, O shining star, son of the morning! You have been thrown down to the earth, you who destroyed the nations of the world."

Turning to the New Testament, Matthew 4:1-11 and Mark 1:12-13 describe Jesus' temptation by Satan. In Matthew 12, Jesus describes Satan as a powerful ruler over a demonic kingdom. John quotes Jesus as referring to Satan as "the ruler of this world" (John 12:31, 14:30, and 16:11). Passages such as Matthew 13:19, 2 Corinthians 4:4, and Ephesians 6:16 show that Satan's goal is to keep people from understanding and believing God's Word.

Okay. That's the bad news. Now here's the good news: God has already defeated this enemy. Just turn to the last book of the Bible, Revelation, to see how the battle turns out.

But even a defeated enemy still has claws. From time to time you'll find yourself in a skirmish or two with this enemy. But God doesn't leave you defenseless. That's the message of Ephesians 6:10-18. "Put on all of God's armor so that you will be able to stand firm against all strategies of the devil" (6:10). The rest of the passage talks about what you can do to defend yourself against an attack.

Although the enemy is not to be taken lightly, believers don't have to fear him. If you're a believer, you've got the power of God behind you.

10Then I heard a loud voice shouting across the
heavens,

"It has come at last—
salvation and power
and the Kingdom of our God,
and the authority of his Christ.*
For the accuser of our brothers and sisters*
has been thrown down to earth—
the one who accuses them
before our God day and night.
11 And they have defeated him by the blood of
the Lamb
and by their testimony.
And they did not love their lives so much
that they were afraid to die.
12 Therefore, rejoice, O heavens!
And you who live in the heavens, rejoice!
But terror will come on the earth and the sea,
for the devil has come down to you in great anger,
knowing that he has little time."

13When the dragon realized that he had been thrown
down to the earth, he pursued the woman who had given
birth to the male child. 14But she was given two wings like
those of a great eagle so she could fly to the place prepared for her in the wilderness. There she would be
cared for and protected from the dragon* for a time,
times, and half a time.

15Then the dragon tried to drown the woman with a
flood of water that flowed from his mouth. 16But the
earth helped her by opening its mouth and swallowing
the river that gushed out from the mouth of the dragon.
17And the dragon was angry at the woman and declared
war against the rest of her children—all who keep God's
commandments and maintain their testimony for Jesus.
18Then the dragon took his stand* on the shore beside
the sea.

12:10a Or *his Messiah.* **12:10b** Greek *brothers.* **12:14** Greek *the serpent;* also in 12:15. See 12:9. **12:18** Greek *Then he took his stand;* some manuscripts read *Then I took my stand.* Some translations put this entire sentence into 13:1.

13

THE BEAST OUT OF THE SEA

Then I saw a beast rising up out of the sea. It had seven heads and ten horns, with ten crowns on its horns. And written on each head were names that blasphemed God. [2]This beast looked like a leopard, but it had the feet of a bear and the mouth of a lion! And the dragon gave the beast his own power and throne and great authority.

[3]I saw that one of the heads of the beast seemed wounded beyond recovery—but the fatal wound was healed! The whole world marveled at this miracle and gave allegiance to the beast. [4]They worshiped the dragon for giving the beast such power, and they also worshiped the beast. "Who is as great as the beast?" they exclaimed. "Who is able to fight against him?"

[5]Then the beast was allowed to speak great blasphemies against God. And he was given authority to do whatever he wanted for forty-two months. [6]And he spoke terrible words of blasphemy against God, slandering his name and his dwelling—that is, those who dwell in heaven.* [7]And the beast was allowed to wage war against God's holy people and to conquer them. And he was given authority to rule over every tribe and people and language and nation. [8]And all the people who belong to this world worshiped the beast. They are the ones whose names were not written in the Book of Life before the world was made—the Book that belongs to the Lamb who was slaughtered.*

TERRIBLE TRIO 13:1-18

Satan (the dragon) has two evil accomplices: (1) the beast out of the sea (13:1-10) and (2) the beast out of the earth (13:11-18). Together, the three form an unholy trinity in direct opposition to the holy Trinity of God, Jesus, and the Holy Spirit. Their goal: to overthrow God. But there's good news. God will someday defeat them. Check out Revelation 19:19–20:10.

There may be some problems in your life that seem like an "unholy trinity." Maybe you're facing tons of homework, problems at home, and a constant state of "empty wallet." When problems come in bunches, we sometimes feel discouraged. But consider what God has in store for the unholy three above. A God with that kind of power can solve any problem you face. ■

[9] Anyone with ears to hear
should listen and understand.
[10] Anyone who is destined for prison
will be taken to prison.
Anyone destined to die by the sword
will die by the sword.

This means that God's holy people must endure persecution patiently and remain faithful.

THE BEAST OUT OF THE EARTH

[11]Then I saw another beast come up out of the earth. He had two horns like those of a lamb, but he spoke with the voice of a dragon. [12]He exercised all the authority of the first beast. And he required all the earth and its people to worship the first beast, whose fatal wound had been healed. [13]He did astounding miracles, even making fire flash down to earth from the sky while everyone was watching. [14]And with all the miracles he was allowed to perform on behalf of the first beast, he deceived all the people who belong to this world. He ordered the people to make a great statue of the first beast, who was fatally wounded and then came back to life. [15]He was then permitted to give life to this statue so that it could speak. Then the statue of the beast commanded that anyone refusing to worship it must die.

[16]He required everyone—small and great, rich and poor, free and slave—to be given a mark on the right hand or on the forehead. [17]And no one could buy or sell anything without that mark, which was either the name of the beast or the number representing his name. [18]Wisdom is needed here. Let the one with understanding solve the meaning of the number of the beast, for it is the number of a man.* His number is 666.*

14

THE LAMB AND THE 144,000

Then I saw the Lamb standing on Mount Zion, and with him were 144,000 who had his name and his Father's name written on their foreheads. [2]And I heard a sound from heaven like the roar of mighty ocean waves or the rolling of loud thunder. It was like the sound of many harpists playing together.

[3]This great choir sang a wonderful new song in front of the throne of God and before the four living beings and the twenty-four elders. No one could learn this song except the 144,000 who had been redeemed from the earth. [4]They have kept themselves as pure as virgins,* following the Lamb wherever he goes. They have been purchased from among the people on the earth as a special offering* to God and to the Lamb. [5]They have told no lies; they are without blame.

THE THREE ANGELS

[6]And I saw another angel flying through the sky, carrying the eternal Good News to proclaim to the people who belong to this world—to every nation, tribe, language, and people. [7]"Fear God," he shouted. "Give glory to him. For the time has come when he will sit as judge. Worship him who made the heavens, the earth, the sea, and all the springs of water."

[8]Then another angel followed him through the sky, shouting, "Babylon is fallen—that great city is fallen—because she made all the nations of the world drink the wine of her passionate immorality."

[9]Then a third angel followed them, shouting, "Anyone who worships the beast and his statue or who accepts his

13:6 Some manuscripts read *and his dwelling and all who dwell in heaven.* **13:8** Or *not written in the Book of Life that belongs to the Lamb who was slaughtered before the world was made.* **13:18a** Or *of humanity.* **13:18b** Some manuscripts read *616.* **14:4a** Greek *They are virgins who have not defiled themselves with women.* **14:4b** Greek *as firstfruits.*

keeping it real

I struggle with apathy. Maybe that's how one of the churches John talks about in Revelation 3 felt. I guess you can say I'm not very disciplined. This affects both my schoolwork and my Christian life. I have trouble applying myself to what I need to do if I don't feel like doing it at the moment.

In my youth group we studied 2 Timothy. One verse—2:15—has really challenged me directly. It says, "Work hard so you can present yourself to God and receive his approval. Be a good worker, one who does not need to be ashamed and who correctly explains the word of truth." These words remind me that my actions and attitudes are significant. Someday, I'll have to answer to God for them. The book of Revelation tells about when that will happen (14:7). Knowing this helps me make an extra effort to do the right thing, whether it's reading my Bible regularly or turning off the TV and opening a textbook.

—Spring

mark on the forehead or on the hand 10must drink the wine of God's anger. It has been poured full strength into God's cup of wrath. And they will be tormented with fire and burning sulfur in the presence of the holy angels and the Lamb. 11The smoke of their torment will rise forever and ever, and they will have no relief day or night, for they have worshiped the beast and his statue and have accepted the mark of his name."

12This means that God's holy people must endure persecution patiently, obeying his commands and maintaining their faith in Jesus.

13And I heard a voice from heaven saying, "Write this down: Blessed are those who die in the Lord from now on. Yes, says the Spirit, they are blessed indeed, for they will rest from their hard work; for their good deeds follow them!"

THE HARVEST OF THE EARTH

14Then I saw a white cloud, and seated on the cloud was someone like the Son of Man.* He had a gold crown on his head and a sharp sickle in his hand.

15Then another angel came from the Temple and shouted to the one sitting on the cloud, "Swing the sickle, for the time of harvest has come; the crop on earth is ripe." 16So the one sitting on the cloud swung his sickle over the earth, and the whole earth was harvested.

17After that, another angel came from the Temple in heaven, and he also had a sharp sickle. 18Then another angel, who had power to destroy with fire, came from the altar. He shouted to the angel with the sharp sickle, "Swing your sickle now to gather the clusters of grapes from the vines of the earth, for they are ripe for judgment." 19So the angel swung his sickle over the earth and loaded the grapes into the great winepress of God's wrath. 20The grapes were trampled in the winepress outside the city, and blood flowed from the winepress in a stream about 180 miles* long and as high as a horse's bridle.

JUDGMENT 14:14-20

The image of Jesus separating the faithful from the unfaithful—like a farmer harvesting his crops—is an image of judgment. This will be a time of joy for the Christians who have been persecuted and martyred. At last they will receive their long awaited reward. For this reason, Christians don't have to fear the last judgment. We have this assurance from Jesus: "Those who listen to my message and believe in God who sent me have eternal life. They will never be condemned for their sins, but they have already passed from death into life" (John 5:24). ■

15 THE SONG OF MOSES AND OF THE LAMB

Then I saw in heaven another marvelous event of great significance. Seven angels were holding the seven last plagues, which would bring God's wrath to completion. 2I saw before me what seemed to be a glass sea mixed with fire. And on it stood all the people who had been victorious over the beast and his statue and the number representing his name. They were all holding harps that God had given them. 3And they were singing the song of Moses, the servant of God, and the song of the Lamb:

"Great and marvelous are your works,
O Lord God, the Almighty.

14:14 Or *like a son of man*. See Dan 7:13. "Son of Man" is a title Jesus used for himself. 14:20 Greek *1,600 stadia* [296 kilometers].

Just and true are your ways,
O King of the nations.*
4 Who will not fear you, Lord,
and glorify your name?
For you alone are holy.
All nations will come and worship before you,
for your righteous deeds have been revealed."

THE SEVEN BOWLS OF THE SEVEN PLAGUES

5 Then I looked and saw that the Temple in heaven, God's Tabernacle, was thrown wide open. 6 The seven angels who were holding the seven plagues came out of the Temple. They were clothed in spotless white linen* with gold sashes across their chests. 7 Then one of the four living beings handed each of the seven angels a gold bowl filled with the wrath of God, who lives forever and ever. 8 The Temple was filled with smoke from God's glory and power. No one could enter the Temple until the seven angels had completed pouring out the seven plagues.

16

Then I heard a mighty voice from the Temple say to the seven angels, "Go your ways and pour out on the earth the seven bowls containing God's wrath."

2 So the first angel left the Temple and poured out his bowl on the earth, and horrible, malignant sores broke out on everyone who had the mark of the beast and who worshiped his statue.

3 Then the second angel poured out his bowl on the sea, and it became like the blood of a corpse. And everything in the sea died.

4 Then the third angel poured out his bowl on the rivers and springs, and they became blood. 5 And I heard the angel who had authority over all water saying,

"You are just, O Holy One, who is and who always was,
because you have sent these judgments.
6 Since they shed the blood
of your holy people and your prophets,
you have given them blood to drink.
It is their just reward."

7 And I heard a voice from the altar,* saying,

"Yes, O Lord God, the Almighty,
your judgments are true and just."

8 Then the fourth angel poured out his bowl on the sun, causing it to scorch everyone with its fire. 9 Everyone was burned by this blast of heat, and they cursed the name of God, who had control over all these plagues. They did not repent of their sins and turn to God and give him glory.

10 Then the fifth angel poured out his bowl on the throne of the beast, and his kingdom was plunged into darkness. His subjects ground their teeth in anguish, 11 and they cursed the God of heaven for their pains and sores. But they did not repent of their evil deeds and turn to God.

12 Then the sixth angel poured out his bowl on the great Euphrates River, and it dried up so that the kings from the east could march their armies toward the west without hindrance. 13 And I saw three evil* spirits that looked like frogs leap from the mouths of the dragon, the beast, and the false prophet. 14 They are demonic spirits who work miracles and go out to all the rulers of the world to gather them for battle against the Lord on that great judgment day of God the Almighty.

15 "Look, I will come as unexpectedly as a thief!
Blessed are all who are watching for me, who keep their clothing ready so they will not have to walk around naked and ashamed."

READY OR NOT? 16:15

Since Jesus will return unexpectedly (1 Thess 5:1-6), we must be ready when he returns. We can prepare ourselves by resisting temptation and by being committed to God's standards. In what ways does your life show your readiness for Jesus' return? ■

16 And the demonic spirits gathered all the rulers and their armies to a place with the Hebrew name *Armageddon.**

17 Then the seventh angel poured out his bowl into the air. And a mighty shout came from the throne in the Temple, saying, "It is finished!" 18 Then the thunder crashed and rolled, and lightning flashed. And a great earthquake struck—the worst since people were placed on the earth. 19 The great city of Babylon split into three sections, and the cities of many nations fell into heaps of rubble. So God remembered all of Babylon's sins, and he made her drink the cup that was filled with the wine of his fierce wrath. 20 And every island disappeared, and all the mountains were leveled. 21 There was a terrible hailstorm, and hailstones weighing seventy-five pounds* fell from the sky onto the people below. They cursed God because of the terrible plague of the hailstorm.

17 THE GREAT PROSTITUTE

One of the seven angels who had poured out the seven bowls came over and spoke to me. "Come with me," he said, "and I will show you the judgment that is going to come on the great prostitute, who rules over many waters. 2 The kings of the world have committed adultery with her, and the people who belong to this world have been made drunk by the wine of her immorality."

3 So the angel took me in the Spirit* into the wilderness.

15:3 Some manuscripts read *King of the ages.* 15:6 Other manuscripts read *white stone;* still others read *white [garments] made of linen.* 16:7 Greek *I heard the altar.* 16:13 Greek *unclean.* 16:16 Or *Harmagedon.* 16:21 Greek *1 talent* [34 kilograms]. 17:3 Or *inspirit.*

There I saw a woman sitting on a scarlet beast that had seven heads and ten horns, and blasphemies against God were written all over it. 4The woman wore purple and scarlet clothing and beautiful jewelry made of gold and precious gems and pearls. In her hand she held a gold goblet full of obscenities and the impurities of her immorality. 5A mysterious name was written on her forehead: "Babylon the Great, Mother of All Prostitutes and Obscenities in the World." 6I could see that she was drunk—drunk with the blood of God's holy people who were witnesses for Jesus. I stared at her in complete amazement.

7"Why are you so amazed?" the angel asked. "I will tell you the mystery of this woman and of the beast with seven heads and ten horns on which she sits. 8The beast you saw was once alive but isn't now. And yet he will soon come up out of the bottomless pit* and go to eternal destruction. And the people who belong to this world, whose names were not written in the Book of Life before the world was made, will be amazed at the reappearance of this beast who had died.

9"This calls for a mind with understanding: The seven heads of the beast represent the seven hills where the woman rules. They also represent seven kings. 10Five kings have already fallen, the sixth now reigns, and the seventh is yet to come, but his reign will be brief.

11"The scarlet beast that was, but is no longer, is the eighth king. He is like the other seven, and he, too, is headed for destruction. 12The ten horns of the beast are ten kings who have not yet risen to power. They will be appointed to their kingdoms for one brief moment to reign with the beast. 13They will all agree to give him their power and authority. 14Together they will go to war against the Lamb, but the Lamb will defeat them because he is Lord of all lords and King of all kings. And his called and chosen and faithful ones will be with him."

IN CHARGE 17:17

No matter what happens, we can still trust that God is in charge and that his plans will come to pass just as he promised. His control is shown in how he sometimes uses people opposed to him to execute his will. Although he allows evil to filter through this present world, evil will be completely abolished someday. ■

15Then the angel said to me, "The waters where the prostitute is ruling represent masses of people of every nation and language. 16The scarlet beast and his ten horns all hate the prostitute. They will strip her naked, eat her flesh, and burn her remains with fire. 17For God has put a plan into their minds, a plan that will carry out his purposes. They will agree to give their authority to the scarlet beast, and so the words of God will be fulfilled. 18And this woman you saw in your vision represents the great city that rules over the kings of the world."

18 THE FALL OF BABYLON

After all this I saw another angel come down from heaven with great authority, and the earth grew bright with his splendor. 2He gave a mighty shout:

"Babylon is fallen—that great city is fallen!
She has become a home for demons.
She is a hideout for every foul* spirit,
a hideout for every foul vulture
and every foul and dreadful animal.*
3 For all the nations have fallen*
because of the wine of her passionate immorality.
The kings of the world
have committed adultery with her.
Because of her desires for extravagant luxury,
the merchants of the world have grown rich."

4Then I heard another voice calling from heaven,

"Come away from her, my people.
Do not take part in her sins,
or you will be punished with her.
5 For her sins are piled as high as heaven,
and God remembers her evil deeds.
6 Do to her as she has done to others.
Double her penalty* for all her evil deeds.
She brewed a cup of terror for others,
so brew twice as much* for her.
7 She glorified herself and lived in luxury,
so match it now with torment and sorrow.
She boasted in her heart,
'I am queen on my throne.
I am no helpless widow,
and I have no reason to mourn.'
8 Therefore, these plagues will overtake her in
a single day—
death and mourning and famine.
She will be completely consumed by fire,
for the Lord God who judges her is mighty."

9And the kings of the world who committed adultery with her and enjoyed her great luxury will mourn for her as they see the smoke rising from her charred remains. 10They will stand at a distance, terrified by her great torment. They will cry out,

"How terrible, how terrible for you,
O Babylon, you great city!
In a single moment
God's judgment came on you."

11The merchants of the world will weep and mourn for her, for there is no one left to buy their goods. 12She bought great quantities of gold, silver, jewels, and pearls; fine linen, purple, silk, and scarlet cloth; things made of fragrant thyine wood, ivory goods, and objects made of

17:8 Or *the abyss,* or *the underworld.* 18:2a Greek *unclean;* also in each of the two following phrases. 18:2b Some manuscripts condense the last two lines to read *a hideout for every foul [unclean] and dreadful vulture.* 18:3 Some manuscripts read *have drunk.* 18:6a Or *Give her an equal penalty.* 18:6b Or *brew just as much.*

expensive wood; and bronze, iron, and marble. 13She also
bought cinnamon, spice, incense, myrrh, frankincense,
wine, olive oil, fine flour, wheat, cattle, sheep, horses,
chariots, and bodies—that is, human slaves.

14 "The fancy things you loved so much
are gone," they cry.
"All your luxuries and splendor
are gone forever,
never to be yours again."

15The merchants who became wealthy by selling her
these things will stand at a distance, terrified by her great
torment. They will weep and cry out,

16 "How terrible, how terrible for that great city!
She was clothed in finest purple and scarlet linens,
decked out with gold and precious stones
and pearls!
17 In a single moment
all the wealth of the city is gone!"

And all the captains of the merchant ships and their
passengers and sailors and crews will stand at a distance.
18They will cry out as they watch the smoke ascend, and
they will say, "Where is there another city as great as
this?" 19And they will weep and throw dust on their heads
to show their grief. And they will cry out,

"How terrible, how terrible for that great city!
The shipowners became wealthy
by transporting her great wealth on the seas.
In a single moment it is all gone."

GREED GUARD 18:11-19

John foresaw the eventual destruction of those caught up in greed. Recognize any similarities between this society and ours? Many people fall into the race to own more and more. Their motto is "Whoever dies with the most toys wins!" But no one has yet been able to take anything from this life into the next.

Many years before this vision, Jesus spoke a warning about greed: "Guard against every kind of greed. Life is not measured by how much you own" (Luke 12:15). Is that your motto? ■

20 Rejoice over her fate, O heaven
and people of God and apostles and prophets!
For at last God has judged her
for your sakes.

21Then a mighty angel picked up a boulder the size of a
huge millstone. He threw it into the ocean and shouted,

"Just like this, the great city Babylon
will be thrown down with violence
and will never be found again.
22 The sound of harps, singers, flutes, and trumpets
will never be heard in you again.
No craftsmen and no trades
will ever be found in you again.
The sound of the mill
will never be heard in you again.
23 The light of a lamp
will never shine in you again.
The happy voices of brides and grooms
will never be heard in you again.
For your merchants were the greatest in the world,
and you deceived the nations with your sorceries.
24 In your* streets flowed the blood of the prophets and
of God's holy people
and the blood of people slaughtered all over the world."

TRUE WORSHIP 19:1-10

Praise is the heartfelt response to God by those who love him. The more you get to know God and realize what he's done, the more you'll respond with praise. Praise is at the heart of true worship. Let your praise of God flow out of your realization of who he is and how much he loves you. ■

19 SONGS OF VICTORY IN HEAVEN

After this, I heard what sounded like a vast crowd in
heaven shouting,

"Praise the LORD!*
Salvation and glory and power belong to our God.
2 His judgments are true and just.
He has punished the great prostitute
who corrupted the earth with her immorality.
He has avenged the murder of his servants."

3And again their voices rang out:

"Praise the LORD!
The smoke from that city ascends forever
and ever!"

4Then the twenty-four elders and the four living beings fell down and worshiped God, who was sitting on the
throne. They cried out, "Amen! Praise the LORD!"
5And from the throne came a voice that said,

"Praise our God,
all his servants,
all who fear him,
from the least to the greatest."

6Then I heard again what sounded like the shout of a
vast crowd or the roar of mighty ocean waves or the crash
of loud thunder:

18:24 Greek *her*. 19:1 Greek *Hallelujah;* also in 19:3, 4, 6. *Hallelujah* is the transliteration of a Hebrew term that means "Praise the LORD."

"Praise the LORD!
For the Lord our God,* the Almighty, reigns.
7 Let us be glad and rejoice,
and let us give honor to him.
For the time has come for the wedding feast of
the Lamb,
and his bride has prepared herself.
8 She has been given the finest of pure white linen
to wear."
For the fine linen represents the good deeds of
God's holy people.

9 And the angel said to me, "Write this: Blessed are those
who are invited to the wedding feast of the Lamb." And he
added, "These are true words that come from God."
10 Then I fell down at his feet to worship him, but he
said, "No, don't worship me. I am a servant of God, just
like you and your brothers and sisters* who testify about
their faith in Jesus. Worship only God. For the essence of
prophecy is to give a clear witness for Jesus.*"

THE RIDER ON THE WHITE HORSE

11 Then I saw heaven opened, and a white horse was standing there. Its rider was named Faithful and True, for he
judges fairly and wages a righteous war.
12 His eyes were
like flames of fire, and on his head were many crowns. A
name was written on him that no one understood except
himself.
13 He wore a robe dipped in blood, and his title
was the Word of God.
14 The armies of heaven, dressed in
the finest of pure white linen, followed him on white
horses.
15 From his mouth came a sharp sword to strike
down the nations. He will rule them with an iron rod. He
will release the fierce wrath of God, the Almighty, like
juice flowing from a winepress.
16 On his robe at his thigh*
was written this title: King of all kings and Lord of all lords.
17 Then I saw an angel standing in the sun, shouting
to the vultures flying high in the sky: "Come! Gather together for the great banquet God has prepared.
18 Come
and eat the flesh of kings, generals, and strong warriors;
of horses and their riders; and of all humanity, both free
and slave, small and great."
19 Then I saw the beast and the kings of the world and
their armies gathered together to fight against the one sitting on the horse and his army.
20 And the beast was cap-
tured, and with him the false prophet who did mighty
miracles on behalf of the beast—miracles that deceived all
who had accepted the mark of the beast and who worshiped his statue. Both the beast and his false prophet were
thrown alive into the fiery lake of burning sulfur.
21 Their
entire army was killed by the sharp sword that came from
the mouth of the one riding the white horse. And the vultures all gorged themselves on the dead bodies.

20 THE THOUSAND YEARS

Then I saw an angel coming down from heaven with the
key to the bottomless pit* and a heavy chain in his hand.
2 He seized the dragon—that old serpent, who is the devil,
Satan—and bound him in chains for a thousand years.
3 The angel threw him into the bottomless pit, which he
then shut and locked so Satan could not deceive the nations anymore until the thousand years were finished.
Afterward he must be released for a little while.
4 Then I saw thrones, and the people sitting on them
had been given the authority to judge. And I saw the souls
of those who had been beheaded for their testimony
about Jesus and for proclaiming the word of God. They
had not worshiped the beast or his statue, nor accepted
his mark on their forehead or their hands. They all came
to life again, and they reigned with Christ for a thousand
years.
5 This is the first resurrection. (The rest of the dead did
not come back to life until the thousand years had
ended.)
6 Blessed and holy are those who share in the first
resurrection. For them the second death holds no power,
but they will be priests of God and of Christ and will reign
with him a thousand years.

NO CONTEST 20:7-10

This is not a typical battle where the outcome is in doubt during the heat of the conflict. We already know the outcome. Two mighty forces of evil—those of the beast (19:19) and of Satan (20:7-8)—unite to do battle against God. The Bible uses just two small passages to describe each battle. Here is the play-by-play: the evil beast and his forces are captured and thrown into the lake of fire or completely destroyed (19:20-21); fire from heaven consumes Satan's armies while Satan is thrown into the lake of fire (20:9-10). There will be no doubt, worry, or second thoughts for believers about whether they have chosen the right side. If you choose God, you'll experience a tremendous victory with Christ. ■

THE DEFEAT OF SATAN

7 When the thousand years come to an end, Satan will be
let out of his prison.
8 He will go out to deceive the na-
tions—called Gog and Magog—in every corner of the
earth. He will gather them together for battle—a mighty
army, as numberless as sand along the seashore.
9 And I
saw them as they went up on the broad plain of the earth
and surrounded God's people and the beloved city. But
fire from heaven came down on the attacking armies and
consumed them.
10 Then the devil, who had deceived them, was thrown
into the fiery lake of burning sulfur, joining the beast and
the false prophet. There they will be tormented day and
night forever and ever.

THE FINAL JUDGMENT

11 And I saw a great white throne and the one sitting on
it. The earth and sky fled from his presence, but they
found no place to hide.
12 I saw the dead, both great and

19:6 Some manuscripts read *the Lord God*. 19:10a Greek *brothers*. 19:10b Or *is the message confirmed by Jesus*. 19:16 Or *On his robe and thigh*. 20:1 Or *the abyss*, or *the underworld;* also in 20:3. 20:13 Greek *and Hades;* also in 20:14.

small, standing before God's throne. And the books were opened, including the Book of Life. And the dead were judged according to what they had done, as recorded in the books. 13The sea gave up its dead, and death and the grave* gave up their dead. And all were judged according to their deeds. 14Then death and the grave were thrown into the lake of fire. This lake of fire is the second death. 15And anyone whose name was not found recorded in the Book of Life was thrown into the lake of fire.

21 THE NEW JERUSALEM

Then I saw a new heaven and a new earth, for the old heaven and the old earth had disappeared. And the sea was also gone. 2And I saw the holy city, the new Jerusalem, coming down from God out of heaven like a bride beautifully dressed for her husband.

3I heard a loud shout from the throne, saying, "Look, God's home is now among his people! He will live with them, and they will be his people. God himself will be with them.* 4He will wipe every tear from their eyes, and there will be no more death or sorrow or crying or pain. All these things are gone forever."

5And the one sitting on the throne said, "Look, I am making everything new!" And then he said to me, "Write this down, for what I tell you is trustworthy and true." 6And he also said, "It is finished! I am the Alpha and the Omega—the Beginning and the End. To all who are thirsty I will give freely from the springs of the water of life. 7All who are victorious will inherit all these blessings, and I will be their God, and they will be my children.

8"But cowards, unbelievers, the corrupt, murderers, the immoral, those who practice witchcraft, idol worshipers, and all liars—their fate is in the fiery lake of burning sulfur. This is the second death."

9Then one of the seven angels who held the seven bowls containing the seven last plagues came and said to me, "Come with me! I will show you the bride, the wife of the Lamb."

10So he took me in the Spirit* to a great, high mountain, and he showed me the holy city, Jerusalem, descending out of heaven from God. 11It shone with the glory of God and sparkled like a precious stone—like jasper as clear as crystal. 12The city wall was broad and high, with twelve gates guarded by twelve angels. And the names of the twelve tribes of Israel were written on the gates. 13There were three gates on each side—east, north, south, and west. 14The wall of the city had twelve foundation stones, and on them were written the names of the twelve apostles of the Lamb.

15The angel who talked to me held in his hand a gold measuring stick to measure the city, its gates, and its wall. 16When he measured it, he found it was a square, as wide as it was long. In fact, its length and width and height were each 1,400 miles.* 17Then he measured the walls and found them to be 216 feet thick* (according to the human standard used by the angel).

18The wall was made of jasper, and the city was pure gold, as clear as glass. 19The wall of the city was built on foundation stones inlaid with twelve precious stones:* the first was jasper, the second sapphire, the third agate, the fourth emerald, 20the fifth onyx, the sixth carnelian, the seventh chrysolite, the eighth beryl, the ninth topaz, the tenth chrysoprase, the eleventh jacinth, the twelfth amethyst.

21The twelve gates were made of pearls—each gate from a single pearl! And the main street was pure gold, as clear as glass.

22I saw no temple in the city, for the Lord God Almighty and the Lamb are its temple. 23And the city has no need of sun or moon, for the glory of God illuminates the city, and the Lamb is its light. 24The nations will walk in its light, and the kings of the world will enter the city in all their glory. 25Its gates will never be closed at the end of day because there is no night there. 26And all the nations will

He will wipe every tear from their eyes, and there will be no more death or sorrow or crying or pain. All these things are gone forever.

REVELATION 21:4

DESPAIR

Blood, violence, murder, mayhem, images of doom and gloom. What have we got here? Some kind of horror movie?

No, just another edition of the nightly news. With smiling faces and playful banter, the channel 2 news anchors recite one horror story after another: Mad cow disease, killer flus, tragic accidents, a psychotic killer on the loose, a devastating flood in India, plus a host of other stories.

As Jeremiah turns off the TV, he sighs, then mutters to himself, "This world is *messed up!* What's the point? I mean, what do I have to live for? The way things are going, I won't even live to be 30."

Is it any wonder this dude's depressed? Is there any hope in a world that seems to be spinning out of control?

Yes! One of the greatest, most encouraging passages in the whole Bible is found right at the end. Read Revelation 21 and 22 for a fascinating and faith-building look at what the future holds for those who know Christ. (If you don't know Christ as your Savior, now is a perfect time to ask him to forgive your sins and to accept his offer of eternal life. So, what're you waiting for?)

21:3 Some manuscripts read *God himself will be with them, their God.* **21:10** Or *in spirit.* **21:16** Greek *12,000 stadia* [2,220 kilometers]. **21:17** Greek *144 cubits* [65 meters]. **21:19** The identification of some of these gemstones is uncertain.

bring their glory and honor into the city. [27]Nothing evil* will be allowed to enter, nor anyone who practices shameful idolatry and dishonesty—but only those whose names are written in the Lamb's Book of Life.

22 Then the angel showed me a river with the water of life, clear as crystal, flowing from the throne of God and of the Lamb. [2]It flowed down the center of the main street. On each side of the river grew a tree of life, bearing twelve crops of fruit,* with a fresh crop each month. The leaves were used for medicine to heal the nations.

[3]No longer will there be a curse upon anything. For the throne of God and of the Lamb will be there, and his servants will worship him. [4]And they will see his face, and his name will be written on their foreheads. [5]And there will be no night there—no need for lamps or sun—for the Lord God will shine on them. And they will reign forever and ever.

[6]Then the angel said to me, "Everything you have heard and seen is trustworthy and true. The Lord God, who inspires his prophets,* has sent his angel to tell his servants what will happen soon.*"

JESUS IS COMING

[7]"Look, I am coming soon! Blessed are those who
obey the words of prophecy written in this book.*"

EYEWITNESS 22:8-9

Hearing or reading an eyewitness account is the next best thing to seeing the event yourself. John witnessed the events reported in Revelation and wrote them down so we could "see" and believe as he did. If you have read this far, you have "seen." Have you also believed? ■

[8]I, John, am the one who heard and saw all these things. And when I heard and saw them, I fell down to worship at the feet of the angel who showed them to me. [9]But he said, "No, don't worship me. I am a servant of God, just like you and your brothers the prophets, as well as all who obey what is written in this book. Worship only God!"

[10]Then he instructed me, "Do not seal up the prophetic words in this book, for the time is near. [11]Let the one who is doing harm continue to do harm; let the one who is vile continue to be vile; let the one who is righteous continue to live righteously; let the one who is holy continue to be holy."

[12]"Look, I am coming soon, bringing my reward with
me to repay all people according to their deeds. [13]I
am the Alpha and the Omega, the First and the Last,
the Beginning and the End."

[14]Blessed are those who wash their robes. They will be permitted to enter through the gates of the city and eat the fruit from the tree of life. [15]Outside the city are the dogs—the sorcerers, the sexually immoral, the murderers, the idol worshipers, and all who love to live a lie.

[16]"I, Jesus, have sent my angel to give you this
message for the churches. I am both the source of
David and the heir to his throne.* I am the bright
morning star."

YOU'RE INVITED 22:17

When Jesus met the Samaritan woman at the well, he told her of the living water that he could supply (John 4:10-15). This image is used again as Jesus invites anyone to come and drink of the water of life. The gospel is unlimited in scope—all people, everywhere, may come. Salvation cannot be earned; God gives it freely. We live in a world desperately thirsty for living water; many are dying of thirst. Who will you invite to come and drink? ■

[17]The Spirit and the bride say, "Come." Let anyone who hears this say, "Come." Let anyone who is thirsty come. Let anyone who desires drink freely from the water of life. [18]And I solemnly declare to everyone who hears the words of prophecy written in this book: If anyone adds anything to what is written here, God will add to that person the plagues described in this book. [19]And if anyone removes any of the words from this book of prophecy, God will remove that person's share in the tree of life and in the holy city that are described in this book.

GOD WINS! 22:21

Revelation closes human history as Genesis opened it—in paradise. But there is one distinct difference: In Revelation, evil is gone forever. Genesis describes Adam and Eve walking and talking with God; Revelation describes people worshiping him face to face. Genesis describes a garden with an evil serpent; Revelation describes a perfect city with no evil.

The book of Revelation ends with an urgent request: "Come, Lord Jesus!" In a world of problems, persecution, evil, and immorality, Christ calls us to endure in our faith. Our efforts to better our world are important, but their results cannot compare with the transformation Jesus will bring about when he returns. He alone controls human history and forgives sin. Someday, he will recreate the earth and bring lasting peace.

"Come, Lord Jesus!" ■

[20]He who is the faithful witness to all these things says, "Yes, I am coming soon!"

Amen! Come, Lord Jesus!

[21]May the grace of the Lord Jesus be with God's holy people.*

21:27 Or *ceremonially unclean.* 22:2 Or *twelve kinds of fruit.* 22:6a Or *The Lord, the God of the spirits of the prophets.* 22:6b Or *suddenly,* or *quickly;* also in 22:7, 12, 20. 22:7 Or *scroll;* also in 22:9, 10, 18, 19. 22:16 Greek *I am the root and offspring of David.* 22:21 Other manuscripts read *be with all;* still others read *be with all of God's holy people.* Some manuscripts add *Amen.*

INTRODUCTION
We usually think of the Bible as one book. That's logical because it looks like one book and claims to come from one Author. We also speak of it as God's Word. But when we read and study the Bible, we discover that it is actually an entire library between two covers. Not one book, but 66 (39 in the Old Testament; 27 in the New Testament)! Each book has its own style and uniqueness—yet each book contributes to the message God wants to get across with the whole Bible. What's more, though we use the word *book,* some parts of the Bible are letters (like Paul's letter to the Romans) or collections (like the Psalms). Still, the overall message of the Bible is one message because it has one main Author—God. The reason the styles throughout the Bible vary is because God teamed up with dozens of people to write his Word.

HOW THIS PLAN IS DIFFERENT
There are many plans to help you read through the Bible library. You can even start at page one and read straight through. The approach taken here, however, is designed to help you get a flavor of the whole Bible by reading selections from it throughout a year. You'll read the best-known stories and many important lessons. Some parts of the Bible offer so much help that they can be read every day. Among these are the Gospels, Psalms, and Proverbs.

BEFORE YOU BEGIN
Each day's reading has a title and a question. These application questions can help you as you read. So, get ready. You're about to start the awesome adventure of reading God's Word and getting to know him.

OLD TESTAMENT

Genesis 1:1—2:3 How It All Began
Why do human beings have value and worth?

Genesis 2:15—3:24 Adam and Eve
In what ways are you like those first humans?

Genesis 4:1-16 Cain and Abel
How do you handle anger?

Genesis 6:9-22 Noah Builds a Boat
What is the most difficult act that God has asked you to do?

Genesis 7:1-24 All Aboard?
If you were alive at this time, would you have been invited to get on the boat? Why or why not? Would you have accepted? Why or why not?

Genesis 8:1-22 A Long Wait
How would you have spent your time on the boat?

Genesis 9:1-17 Rules and Rainbows
What could you do the next time you see a rainbow to show that you take God's covenant seriously?

Genesis 11:1-9 The Tower of Babel
Is there anyone you trust more than God? Why or why not?

Genesis 12:1-9; 17:1-8, 15-16 God's Promises to Abraham and Sarah
How do you usually make decisions? How is God involved in those decisions?

Genesis 18:1-15 Unusual Visitors
How do you make guests feel welcome in your home? at school?

Genesis 19:1-29 Destruction of Sodom and Gomorrah
How does God feel about sin?

Genesis 21:8-21 Hagar and Ishmael
In what ways have you seen God work through the messes in your life?

Genesis 22:1-19 Abraham's Painful Decision
Could you have made the same decision as Abraham? Why or why not?

Genesis 24:1-27 A Faithful Servant
How do you approach difficult tasks?

Genesis 24:28-67 Isaac and Rebekah
How has God surprised you recently?

Genesis 25:19-34 Jacob and Esau
How do you treat your brothers or sisters?

Genesis 27:1-40 Jacob Tricks His Father
On a scale of 1 to 5 (with 5 being really important) how important is honesty in your relationship with your parents? Why?

Genesis 28:10-22 Jacob Meets God
In what places in your life has God seemed the most real?

Genesis 29:14-30 Jacob's Marriages
How do you show your love for others?

Genesis 32:1—33:18 Jacob Returns Home
What happens inside you when you try to avoid a problem?

Genesis 37 Jacob's Children
How are disagreements settled in your family?

Genesis 39 Joseph in Trouble
How do you react when you're treat unfairly?

Genesis 40 Dreams in Prison
When have you helped someone even though you had your own problems?

Genesis 41:1-36 Dreams in the Palace
Whom has God used to give you guidance?

Genesis 41:37-57 Joseph in Charge
How well do you handle big responsibilities?

Genesis 42 Joseph Sees His Brothers Again
If you had the chance to get back at someone who wronged you, would you take it? Why or why not?

Genesis 43 Back to Joseph
How quick are you to forgive? Why?

Genesis 44 Crisis in the Palace
How do you react when someone points out a mistake you've made? Why?

Genesis 45; 46:26-30 Finding a Lost Son
What do you appreciate about your parents? How do you show your appreciation?

Genesis 49 Jacob's Final Words
What legacies have your parents or grandparents passed on to you?

Exodus 1:8—2:10 Moses Is Born
How has God protected you from birth till now?

Exodus 2:11-25 Moses on the Run
When was the last time you found yourself running from God? Explain.

Exodus 3 God's Burning Bush
In what ways has God made himself known to you?

Exodus 4:1-17 Moses Isn't Sure
How willing are you to do what you feel God wants you to do? Explain.

Exodus 5 Resistance
How do you handle others' resistance toward doing what's right?
Exodus 6:1-13 Rejection
What would it cost you to do what God wants?
Exodus 7:1-14 A Stubborn Ruler
What decisions, if any, have you tried to resist that you knew God wanted you to make?
Exodus 7:15—9:7 Five out of Ten Plagues
When do you try to bargain with God? Why?
Exodus 9:8—10:29 Four More Plagues
What are the worst consequences you've seen that were a result of wrong actions?
Exodus 11; 12:29-36 The Ultimate Plague
In what amazing way has God rescued you from a problem?
Exodus 13:17—14:31 A Narrow Escape
When have you experienced God's protection?
Exodus 15:22-27; 17:1-7 God Provides Water
When are you most tempted to complain? Why?
Exodus 16 God's Unusual Food Supply
For what specific gift did you last say thanks to God?
Exodus 18 Helpful Advice
Who are the dependable advisers in your life?
Exodus 19 An Appointment with God
How would you prepare to meet with God?
Exodus 20:1-21 The Ten Commandments
How important are these rules to you? Explain.
Exodus 32 The Gold Calf
What distracts you from obeying God?
Exodus 40 Instructions about God's Tent
When are you most aware of God's presence in your life?
Numbers 12 Trouble in the Family
What do you do when you find yourself feeling jealous of someone?
Numbers 13:1—14:4 Spying on the Promised Land
What do you usually do when you're faced with an impossible task?
Numbers 14:5-45 A Majority That Was Wrong
How often are your decisions based on peer pressure?
Numbers 21:4-9 Another Hard Lesson
What can you do to avoid repeating mistakes?
Numbers 22:5-35 Balaam and His Donkey
How do you avoid making a wrong choice when the right choice seems hard?
Deuteronomy 29 Moses Reviews God's Actions
How do you keep track of what God has done for you?
Deuteronomy 30 Moses Challenges the People
How do you show that you love God?
Deuteronomy 31:1-8 Moses Appoints New Leaders
In what ways have you been a leader?
Deuteronomy 34 The Death of Moses
How would you most like to be remembered?
Joshua 1 God Takes Over
Which of the qualities listed in this chapter would you most need to be like Joshua? Why?
Joshua 2 Spies Visit Jericho
What surprising individuals has God used in your life? Why do you think God chose them?
Joshua 3 The Invasion of Canaan
What instructions has God given you recently? How carefully did you follow them? Why?
Joshua 5:13—6:27 The Battle of Jericho
In what way has God worked through you to bring about something that would normally be impossible?
Joshua 7 Ultimate Consequences
What strongly negative or positive consequences have you experienced?
Joshua 10:1-15 The Longest Day
How do you know that God is powerful? Explain.
Joshua 23 Joshua Warns the Leaders
Which of Joshua's warnings do you most need to obey?
Joshua 24:1-31 Joshua's Last Words
How have the events of history provided hope for you?
Judges 4:4-24 Deborah Goes to War
What do you do to help suffering people?
Judges 6 Gideon Becomes a Judge
What examples of obedience can be found in your life?
Judges 7 Gideon and the Midianites
In what area of your life do you need to trust God more? Explain.

Judges 13 The Birth of Samson
In which part of your life do you need more discipline?

Judges 14 Samson's Riddle
How carefully do you consider the wisdom of your parents?

Judges 15 Samson and the Jawbone
What proof do you have that mistakes usually don't correct themselves?

Judges 16:1-21 Samson and Delilah
In what situations do you find yourself flirting with disaster?

Judges 16:22-31 Samson's Death
How well do you understand God's patience? Explain.

Ruth 1: Ruth and Naomi—A Friendship
How do difficulties affect your friendships?

Ruth 2 Ruth Meets Boaz
When have you found your reputation to be an advantage?

Ruth 3 Ruth Finds a Husband
What's the coolest thing that God has done for you lately?

Ruth 4 A Happy Ending
What future reasons could there be for obeying God today?

1 Samuel 1 A Serious Prayer
What promises have you made to God lately that you've kept?

1 Samuel 3 God Calls Samuel
When you read God's Word, what expectations do you have?

1 Samuel 8 The People Want a King
What has God taught you about being responsible for your own choices?

1 Samuel 8 Samuel's Disappointing Sons
What positive lessons have you learned from your parents' mistakes or the mistakes of other relatives?

1 Samuel 9:1-21 Saul and the Lost Donkeys
What is God's part in your daily decisions?

1 Samuel 10 Saul Becomes King
How do you evaluate people?

1 Samuel 14:1-23 Heroic Acts
What is the bravest thing you've ever done? Where did you find the courage to do it?

1 Samuel 16:1-13 Samuel Anoints David
Like God, do you choose to focus on a person's inner qualities? Why or why not?

1 Samuel 17:1-37 David Answers Goliath's Challenge
How does your confidence in God affect your decision to accept challenges?

1 Samuel 17:38-58 David Kills Goliath
What "giants" need to be defeated in your life?

1 Samuel 18 Trouble between Saul and David
How do you treat your friends who succeed?

1 Samuel 19:1-6; 20:1-42 David and Jonathan
How loyal are you to your friends? Would they agree? Why or why not?

1 Samuel 24:1-22 David Spares Saul's Life
Do you treat others the way you want to be treated? Why or why not?

1 Samuel 25:1-42 David and Abigail
How has God kept you from making big mistakes?

1 Samuel 28 Saul and the Occult
What kinds of things could be considered "occult practices"? How would God feel about your involvement in such things?

2 Samuel 5:1-12 David Becomes King over All Israel
How could you become a person who is more pleasing to God, as David was?

2 Samuel 9 The King's Kindness
How would you show kindness to an enemy?

2 Samuel 11 David and Bathsheba
How often are you tempted to correct one sin by committing another? Explain.

2 Samuel 12:1-25 David and Nathan
Which of your friends love you enough to correct you?

2 Samuel 13:1-19 Family Problems
What actions do you take to avoid temptation?

2 Samuel 13:20-39 Revenge
Why do you think taking revenge never fully solves the problem?

2 Samuel 15 Betrayal
Who helps you keep your motives clear?

2 Samuel 18:1-18 The Death of Absalom
In what situations are you most likely to lose control?

1 Kings 1:5-27 Conflict over the Throne
What happens when you don't make good decisions?

1 Kings 1:28-53 Solomon Becomes King
When things in your world get confusing, how do you know God is still in control?

1 Kings 3:1-15 Solomon's Choice
If you were told that you could have anything you wanted, what would you ask for? Why?

1 Kings 3:16-28 Solomon Solves a Problem
In what situation in your life do you presently need God's wisdom?

1 Kings 6 Solomon Builds the Temple
What can you learn from Solomon about making and carrying out plans?

1 Kings 10:1-13 Solomon and the Queen of Sheba
When are you tempted to try to impress people?

1 Kings 12:1-24 Solomon's Unwise Son
Who are the people you count on for advice? How helpful is this advice usually? Explain.

1 Kings 17 God Takes Care of Elijah
How do obeying and trusting God go together in your life?

1 Kings 18:16-46 Elijah versus the Priests of Baal
How willing are you to take a stand for God? Explain.

1 Kings 19 Spiritual Burnout
When was the last time you felt depressed? How did you handle that?

1 Kings 21 The Stolen Vineyard
How important is justice in your life?

1 Kings 22:29-40 The Death of King Ahab
When are you tempted to think that you can hide from God?

2 Kings 2:1-12 Elijah's Chariot
When you make a commitment, how far will you go to carry it out?

2 Kings 2:13-25 Elisha's Miracles
How would someone else know that you have a deep respect for God?

2 Kings 5 The Healing of Naaman
What "small" things, if there have been any, have you refused to do for God? What happened as a result?

2 Kings 11 A Seven-Year-Old King
Who were your best examples in childhood?

2 Kings 22:1—23:3 Discovery of the Lost Book
If your Bible turned up missing, what effect would that have on your life? Explain.

Ezra 3:7-13 Rebuilding the Temple
How do you feel when you're working on a large, important project? Explain.

Nehemiah 2 Nehemiah Returns to Jerusalem
What relationships in your past need to be rebuilt? Why?

Nehemiah 5: Nehemiah's Concern for the Poor
How do you express your concern for the poor?

Nehemiah 8 Reading God's Word
How much of a priority for you is the reading of God's Word? Explain.

Esther 1 A Queen Is Replaced
Have you ever taken the important people in your life for granted? Why or why not?

Esther 2:1-18 Esther Is Chosen
When have difficult or confusing events in your life actually been a preparation for something you would later experience?

Esther 3 The Jews in Danger
In what situations are you tempted to compromise your faith? Why?

Esther 4 The Queen Decides to Help
What hard decisions have you had to make because of your faith in God?

Esther 5 Esther Risks Her Life
When was the last time you did something scary in obedience to God? What happened as a result?

Esther 6:1—7:10 God Protects His People
When is it helpful to remember that God is still in control of the world?

Job 1 The Testing of Job
In what situations do you most quickly question God's concern for you?

Job 2 Job and His Friends
How do you normally respond to someone else's pain? Is this a helpful response? Why or why not?

Job 38 God Speaks to Job
What things around you remind you of God's greatness?

Job 42 The Rest of Job's Story
When has God turned a disaster around for your good?

Psalm 1 Two Kinds of Lives
What of the two kinds of people described in this passage do you really want to be? How do your actions reveal your choice?

Psalm 8 The Value of Humans
How do you know you have worth?

Psalm 23 A Sheep's Song
What is the most comforting phrase to you in this psalm?

Psalm 51 A Confession
How have your actions revealed your sorrow over a wrong choice?

Psalm 103 What God Is Like
Which picture in this psalm helps you understand God better?

Psalm 139 God Knows Us
What do you feel when you read this psalm?

Psalm 145 God for All People and Time
Which of God's qualities do you most need today?

Proverbs 4 Wise Words about Life
Is finding wisdom a priority for you? Why or why not?

Proverbs 5 Wise Words about Sex
How do these words compare with the messages you hear every day?

Ecclesiastes 12 A Summary of Life
In what way can you remember your Creator today?

Isaiah 6 God Chooses Isaiah
Can you relate to Isaiah's feelings in this chapter? If so, what did you do to express your need for forgiveness?

Isaiah 53 The Suffering Servant
How would you describe what Jesus did for you?

Jeremiah 1:1-9 God Calls a Prophet
If you were Jeremiah, how would you have responded to God's call? What do you think God wants to do through you?

Jeremiah 36 The Book Burning
How much risk is involved in your relationship with God?

Jeremiah 38:1-13 Jeremiah in the Well
What part of your life compares in any way with Jeremiah's time in the well?

Ezekiel 37:1-14 A Valley of Dry Bones
Have you ever experienced a time of spiritual "dryness"? Explain. How can you help people who are spiritually "dry"?

Daniel 1 Coping with Pressure to Conform
How do you usually respond when someone pressures you to go along with what everyone else is doing?

Daniel 2:1-24 A King's Dream
What qualities do seemingly hopeless situations bring out in you? Why?

Daniel 2:25-49 The Meaning of the Dream
Who gets the credit when things go right in your life? Why?

Daniel 3 Three Friends in a Furnace
What examples can you give of God's protection in your life?

Daniel 5 The Writing on the Wall
What message, if any, do you think God has for our society? Why?

Daniel 6 Daniel and the Lions
What do you do to spend time with God?

Jonah 1:1—2:10 Bending God's Directions
When did you last try to avoid doing what you knew God wanted you to do? What happened as a result?

Jonah 3:1—4:11 Wrong Motives
About what things do you complain to God? Why?

NEW TESTAMENT

You will read various parts of the four Gospels in order to have a fairly chronological biography of Jesus' life.

Luke 1:1-4; John 1:1-18 The Word Was God
What do you believe about Jesus?

Luke 1:5-25 The Angel and Zechariah
How would you react to an angel's visit?

Luke 1:26-56 Mary and Elizabeth
What makes you feel joyful?

Luke 1:57-80 John the Baptist Is Born
What hopes have your parents expressed to you about your life?

Matthew 1 A Family Tree
How has a family member's experience influenced your relationship with God?

Luke 2:1-20 Jesus Is Born!
What does Christmas mean to you?

Luke 2:21-3:8 Anna and Simeon See Jesus
What promise of God have you been waiting a long time to see fulfilled?

Matthew 2:1-12 Foreign Visitors
What gift would you offer to Jesus? Why?
Matthew 2:13-23 Escape and Return
How has knowing God brought excitement into your life?
Luke 2:41-52 Jesus in the Temple Again
What four words would summarize your teen years thus far? Why?
Mark 1:1-13 Baptism and Temptation
What are your most difficult temptations? How would they compare to Jesus' temptations? Explain.
John 1:19-34 John the Baptist and Jesus
To whom did you last talk about Christ? Why?
John 1:35-51 Jesus' First Disciples
How would someone know that you're a disciple of Jesus?
John 2 A Surprising Savior
How has Christ been unpredictable in your life?
John 3:1-21 Jesus and Nicodemus
How did you first meet Jesus?
John 3:22-36; Luke 3:19-20 John Gets into Trouble
When has knowing Christ ever gotten you into trouble?
John 4:1-42 Jesus Changes a Town
In what ways has Jesus affected your community?
John 4:43-54 Jesus' Ministry
In what practical ways has God met your needs recently?
Luke 4:16-30 Jesus Is Rejected
In what ways has Jesus been rejected by the people around you? Why?
Mark 1:16-39 Jesus Calls People to Follow
What specific things have you left behind to follow Christ?
Luke 5 Miracles and Questions
How do Jesus' miracles affect you today?
John 5 Honor for the Son
What do you find most attractive about Jesus? Why?
Mark 2:23—3:19 Jesus' Disciples
Based on what you know about Jesus' disciples, who do you most identify with? Why?
Matthew 5:1-16 The Beatitudes
Which of these attitudes do you struggle with most? Why?
Matthew 5:17-30 Rules for Living
How do Jesus' views on these subjects compare with yours?
Matthew 5:31-48 Jesus on Relationships
What part of your life could be most radically changed by these words? Why?
Matthew 6:1-18 The Pattern of Prayer
What do you find yourself praying for the most these days? Why?
Matthew 6:19-34 Money Matters
In what ways are money and worry related in your life?
Matthew 7:1-12 Judge or Pray?
Are you quicker to pray or to criticize? Why?
Matthew 7:13-29 Facts about Fruit and Foundations
What kind of fruit does your life show? What type of foundation is your life based upon? Explain.
Luke 7:1-10 A Roman Centurion's Request
What is your attitude toward people from other cultures? How can you show them God's love?
Matthew 11 Jesus Describes John
How would you want Jesus to summarize your life? Why?
Luke 7:36—8:3 Expressions of Faith
How do you express your faith in Jesus?
Matthew 12:22-50 Troubles for Jesus
When are you tempted to have Jesus prove himself to you?
Mark 4:1-29 Jesus Seeks, Seeds, and Weeds
What kind of soil is your life right now? Why?
Matthew 13:24-43 More of Jesus' Parables
How concerned are you about where your friends and family will spend eternity? Explain.
Matthew 13:44-52 Even More Parables
How and where did you find the hidden treasure?
Luke 8:22-56 Jesus in Control
Which of the events in this passage gives you greatest comfort? Why?
Matthew 9:27-38 The Compassion of Jesus
In what practical ways can you show Jesus' compassion to others?
Mark 6:1-13 The Mission
How clear an idea do you have of what God wants you to do? Explain.

Matthew 10:16-42 Jesus Prepares His Disciples
In what ways do Jesus' words speak to the fears you have?

Mark 6:14-29 Herod Kills John the Baptist
With what qualities of John the Baptist do you most identify? Why?

Matthew 14:13-36 Simply the Son of God
Would you have been more likely to step out with Peter or to stay in the boat? Why?

John 6:22-40 Bread from Heaven
How is Jesus "bread" to you?

John 6:41-71 Jesus Criticized and Deserted
How do you react when you hear critical comments about Jesus? Why?

Mark 7 Purity
If God were to describe what you're like inside, what do you think he would say? Why?

Matthew 15:32—16:12 Jesus Feeds and Warns
How do you evaluate what you hear about God? Explain.

Mark 8:22-38 Who Is Jesus?
In what specific ways have you come to understand Jesus better in the last few weeks?

Luke 9:28-36 Jesus Is Transfigured
Would you rather leave the world and be with Christ or be with Christ in the world? Why?

Matthew 17:24—18:5 Who's the Greatest?
When do you worry about status? Why?

Mark 9:38-50 Who's on Our Side?
How do you respond to the beliefs of others?

Matthew 18:10-20 Dealing with Wrong Choices
How do you react to the failures of others? Why?

John 7:1-31 Reactions to Jesus' Teachings
Which of Jesus' teachings is the most difficult for you to accept? Why?

John 7:32-53 A Warrant for Jesus' Arrest
What does it mean to have "rivers of living water" flowing from within you?

John 8:1-20 Jesus: Forgiveness and Light
Who is the last person you had to forgive? How easy/hard was it for you to forgive? Why?

John 8:21-59 Jesus: Giver of Freedom
How has Christ made you free?

Luke 10:1-24 Jesus Sends Seventy Messengers
What would have been most the exciting part of this trip for you? Why?

Luke 10:25-42 A Friend in Need
Who has been a good Samaritan to you? Explain.

Luke 11:1-13 Jesus Teaches about Prayer
What is your prayer routine like?

Luke 11:14-32 Accusations and Unbelief
What are your strongest reasons for being a faithful follower of Christ?

Luke 11:33-54 Real Faith
What comments have you heard about your faith lately?

Luke 12:1-21 Treasure Talk
Who or what do you treasure? Why?

Luke 12:22-48 Worry Warning
What worries you most these days? Why?

Luke 12:49-59 Troubles Ahead
What examples have you seen of the problems Jesus mentions in this passage?

Luke 13:1-21 Turn Around
What does repentance mean to you?

John 9 Jesus and a Blind Man
What does spiritual blindness mean?

John 10:1-18 The Good Shepherd
How have you experienced God's guidance in your life?

Luke:13:22-35 Jesus: The King Who Grieves
How do you feel about those around you who don't know Christ?

Luke 14:1-14 Pride or Humility?
What actions would taking "the lowest place" involve in your life?

Luke 14:15-35 Following Jesus
What are you willing to leave behind in order to be a follower of Jesus?

Luke 15:1-10 Two Parables of Losing and Finding
How do these stories help you understand God's love for you?

Luke 15:11-32 A Lost Son
In what ways is this story like your life?

Luke 16:1-18 A Good Servant
How can you be a good steward of God's resources?

Luke 16:19-31 The Rich Man and Lazarus
How can you help the poor in your community?

John 11:1-37 Lazarus Dies
In what situations have you been disappointed with God?

John 11:38-57 Jesus Raises Lazarus
How would you have felt watching Lazarus walk out of the tomb? Why?

Luke 17:1-19 Jesus and Ten Lepers
For what are you thankful to God?

Luke 17:20-37 Jesus and the Kingdom of God
What difference would it make in your life if Jesus returned today?

Luke 18:1-14 Jesus Teaches about Prayer
What is the attitude of your prayers?

Mark 10:1-16 Jesus on Family Matters
How far will you go to keep your word?

Mark 10:17-31 Jesus and the Rich Man
What is the most difficult thing Jesus could ask you to give up?

Matthew 20:1-19 A Parable about Equal Pay
Would you have felt the same way as the first workers in this story? Why or why not?

Mark 10:35-52 Jesus on Serving Others
In what ways are you learning to be a servant?

Luke 19:1-10 Jesus and Zacchaeus
What physical characteristic has most affected how you feel about yourself?

John 12:1-11 A Woman Anoints Jesus
What have you ever "wasted" as an expression of love for Christ?

Matthew 21:1-17 Jesus Rides into Jerusalem
If you had been part of the crowd that day, what would have been your most lasting memory?

John 12:20-36 Why Jesus Must Die
How would you explain to someone why Jesus had to die on the cross?

John 12:37-50 Jesus and His Message
What kinds of pressures make you hesitant to tell others about your belief in Christ?

Mark 11:20-33 Ask for Anything
How bold is your prayer life? Why?

Matthew 21:28-46 Two Parables
In the first parable, which son's actions most resemble yours? Why?

Matthew 22:1-14 Wedding Feast
At what point in your life did you realize that you were invited to this feast? How did you respond?

Luke 20:20-40 Jesus Answers Questions
How do you really feel about living forever?

Mark 12:28-37 Questions Given and Taken
Whom do you know who is close to believing in Jesus?

Matthew 23 Warnings
Which of these seven warnings most directly relate to your life? Why?

Luke 21:1-24 Signs of the Times
What concerns you most about the future? Why?

Luke 21:25-38 Jesus on Being Prepared
How do your actions reflect your belief that Jesus will return someday?

Matthew 25:1-30 Ready for His Return
With which of the people in these two stories do you identify most? Why?

Matthew 25:31-46 Just Like Jesus
How can you treat people in ways you would want to treat Christ?

Luke 22:1-13 Preparing the Last Supper
How do you prepare yourself for Communion?

John 13:1-20 Jesus Washes His Disciples' Feet
What is the greatest service someone has done for you? How do you serve others?

John 13:21-38 A Sad Prediction
How well do you feel Christ knows you? Explain.

John 14:1-14 Jesus Is the Way
How would you rate your present level of understanding of Christ and his teachings? Explain.

John 14:15-31 The Comforter
How are you aware of the Holy Spirit's presence in your life?

John 15:1-17 The Vine and the Branches
What kind of fruit has the Gardener produced in you?

John 15:18—16:4 The Test of Troubles
How do Jesus' words about persecution make you feel? Why?

John 16:5-33 The Power of the Holy Spirit
Have you ever been persecuted for your faith? If so, how did God help you through that experience?

John 17 Jesus Prays
How do you think this prayer of Jesus affects your life?

Mark 14:27-52 A Passionate Prayer
What problem have you most persisted in praying about? What answer, if any, have you received?

John 18:1-26 Jesus Betrayed and Abandoned
How close have you come to Peter's denial of Christ? Explain.

Matthew 26:57-75 Trial and Denial
In what ways has being a follower of Jesus complicated your life?

Matthew 27:1-10 Judas's Death
When you think of the consequences of wrong actions, what personal examples come to mind? Explain.

Luke 23:1-12 Two Political Trials
In what ways did your family situation or culture prepare you to respond to Jesus?

Mark 15:6-24 Sentenced to Die
Was there a time you chose to do the wrong thing on purpose? Why?

Luke 23:32-49 Jesus Crucified
What do you feel when you read the description of the Crucifixion? Explain.

Matthew 27:57-66 The Burial
What have you seen people do in their resistance to Christ?

John 20:1-18 Jesus Is Alive!
What makes Easter an important celebration in your life?

Matthew 28:8-15 Reactions to the Resurrection
What would be your first words to Jesus if he appeared to you? Why?

Luke 24:13-43 Appearances of Jesus
What convinced you that Jesus was who he said he was—the promised Savior?

John 20:24—21:14 More Appearances of Jesus
How has Jesus answered your doubts?

John 21:15-25 Jesus Talks with Peter
What difference would it make to you to read these verses with your name in the place of Peter's? Explain.

Matthew 28:16-20 The Great Commission
What are you doing to fulfill this mission?

Luke 24:44-53 Jesus Says Farewell
How have the Scriptures helped you recently in your relationship with God?

Acts 1:1-11 The Departure of Jesus
What one thing would you be sure to do if you knew Jesus was coming back today?

Acts 1:12-26 First Things First
What is your idea of the right amount of time for prayer? Explain.

Acts 2:1-13 An Amazing Gift
What is the main purpose of any gift God might have given you?

Acts 2:14-40 Peter's First Sermon
How would you put this sermon into your own words?

Acts 2:41—3:10 Daily Life in the Early Church
What part of these early days would you have enjoyed the most? Explain.

Acts 3:11—4:4 Peter's Second Sermon
If you were given three minutes to tell the story of your relationship with Jesus, what would you say?

Acts 4:5-22 Hostile Reactions
What excuses are you most likely to use to keep from sharing your faith? Explain.

Acts 4:23-37 Praying and Sharing
How is your church community like this one?

Acts 5:1-16 Strange Events
How often are you tempted to take God lightly?

Acts 5:17-42 Arrested!
How do you react when you are treated unfairly?

Acts 6 Stephen: Special Servant
What responsibilities do you have in your local church?

Acts 7:1-50 Family History
What events in your family history have helped you to reach the point where you are today?

Acts 7:51-60 Just Like Stephen
In what ways would you want to be more like Stephen? Explain.

Acts 8:1-25 Benefits of Persecution
Which difficulties in your life has God used to help you grow spiritually?

Acts 8:26-40 An Unexpected Appointment
What opportunities to share your faith have you taken recently? What happened?

Acts 9:1-19 Paul Meets Jesus
What unusual events has God used to catch your attention?

Acts 9:20-31 Paul's New Life
What are some of the ways that Jesus has changed your life?

Acts 9:32-42 God Uses Peter
This past week, what special ability did you use to meet someone's need?

Acts 10:1-23 God Speaks to Peter
Who is the last person you would expect to talk to about Jesus? Explain.

Acts 10:24-48 Peter Learns a Lesson
How has God helped you change your mind about some attitudes?

Acts 11:1-18 Gentiles Join the Family of God
Why should all people be treated the same? How do your actions show that you believe this?

Acts 11:19-29 Christians Helping One Another
What do you do when you hear stories of extreme poverty or hardship among Christians in other parts of the world?

Acts 12 A Great Escape
How do you react when God answers your prayers?

Acts 13:1-12 The Missionary Journey of Paul and Barnabas
What Christians do you know who might help you discover more clearly how God wants you to invest your time and abilities?

Acts 14 Response and Reaction
What responses have you had when you tried to share your faith?

Acts 15:1-21 A Church Conference
How important is it for you to talk problems over with other Christians? Explain.

Acts 15:22-41 The Gentiles Are Accepted
In what ways is God affecting your life and the goals you've set?

Acts 16:1-15 Paul, Silas, and Timothy
In what ways have you cooperated with others recently in order to spread the Gospel?

Acts 16:16-40 Adventures in Jail
How have your reactions to hard times help others to learn more about God?

Acts 17:1-15 Two Cities: Two Responses
What part does the Bible play in your evaluation of what you hear and read?

Acts 17:16-34 Paul in Athens
What aspects of God's presence do you notice in society?

Acts 19:1-20 Paul in Ephesus
In what situations are you most likely to become discouraged?

Acts 19:21-41 The Riot
When are you most likely to forget that God is in control? Explain.

Acts 20:1-12 Sleeping in Church
What does this story tell you about God's response to human weaknesses?

Acts 20:13-38 Saying Good-bye to Ephesus
When have painful good-byes worked for the best in your life?

Acts 21:1-14 Difficult Decision
What hard decisions do you have to make?

Acts 21:15-36 Paul in Jerusalem
What evidence do you see of God's leading in the lives of others (for example, friends or family members)?

Acts 21:37—22:29 Paul Speaks
How can you relate what Paul is saying to what God has done in your life?

Acts 22:30—23:22 A Plan to Kill Paul
How well do you know your rights and fulfill your responsibilities as a citizen of your country?

Acts 23:23—24:27 Paul in Prison
What would be harder for you—persecution or prison? Why?

Acts 25 Paul Speaks to Festus
If Christianity were outlawed, what evidence could be brought against you to prove you are a Christian?

Acts 26 Paul Speaks to Agrippa
How comfortable are you in explaining your faith? Why?

Acts 27:1-26 The Storm at Sea
Have you ever been part of a group that experienced difficulties? (For example, you experienced persecution for your faith or because you're from a different culture.) What was your attitude as you went through this experience?

Acts 27:27-44 The Shipwreck
How has God brought good out of a bad situation in your life?

Acts 28:1-14 The Winter on Malta
How do you notice about God in your daily routine?

Acts 28:15-31 Paul in Rome
What aspects of your daily routine show that you plan to persevere in your faith?

Romans 5:1-11 Faith Brings Joy
What caused you to thank God recently?

Romans 8:1-17 Truly Free from Sin
In what areas are you still struggling with temptation?

Romans 8:18-39 The Love of Christ
What people or things do you sometimes fear might separate you from the love of Christ? Explain.

Romans 12 Spiritual Gifts
What is your spiritual gift? How are you using it?

1 Corinthians 13 Real Love
Which quality of love mentioned in this passage do you most need to ask God to increase in your life? Why?

1 Corinthians 15:1-19 The Gospel
What parts of the gospel are especially helpful to you in times of doubt or stress?

1 Corinthians 15:42-58 Victory at Last
How has this passage affected your life after death?

2 Corinthians 4 Weak Containers; Strong Contents
With which difficult situation mentioned in this passage do you most clearly identify?

Galatians 5:13-26 Two Radically Different Lives
How can you "live by the Spirit"?

Ephesians 1 God's Actions
In what ways has God marked your life?

Ephesians 2 God's Plan
When have you recently reminded yourself and God that you want your life to be used for his purposes?

Ephesians 4:1-16 The Church
What is your role in Christ's body?

Ephesians 6:10-20 Armor of God
How quick are you to use the Christian's only offensive weapon—the Word of God?

Philippians 2:1-18 The Mind of Jesus
In what ways would having Christ's attitude make you face this day differently?

Philippians 3 Learning Joy
What areas of your life could God be using to teach you joy? Explain.

Colossians 2:1-15 What We Have in Christ
What information, if any, have you heard recently that could affect your relationship with Christ? What will you do about it?

Colossians 3:1-17 Christian Characteristics
What do you envision when you think about heaven? How does that affect the way you live now?

1 Thessalonians 1 Spiritual Reputation
How do you think others would evaluate your spiritual life? Explain.

1 Thessalonians 4 Living for God
What specific action could you take today simply out of obedience to God?

2 Thessalonians 1 Encouragement
What other Christians could you encourage today? Why?

2 Thessalonians 3 Final Requests
How aware and involved are you in the worldwide spread of the gospel?

1 Timothy 4 Always Going Forward
Which of these positive commands would you choose to make a higher priority in your life?

1 Timothy 6:3-21 A Friend's Final Words
How does your attitude toward money match Paul's advice?

2 Timothy 1 The Importance of Examples
Who has been a good spiritual example for you? How can you thank him or her?

2 Timothy 3 Last Days
How many of these characteristics are part of your world today?

Titus 3:1-11; Philemon 4-7 Good Counsel
Which of these commands seems best suited to your life right now? Why?

Hebrews 10:19-39 The New Life
What do your prayer habits and church involvement reveal about the real importance of faith in your life?

Hebrews 11 A Review of Faith
How deep is your commitment to Christ? Explain.

Hebrews 12:1-13 Our Turn
What do you need to do to follow the advice in this passage? Why?

James 1 Tough Times
What difficulty are you facing right now? How could the suggestions in this passage help?

James 2 Faith and Actions
How have you shown your faith recently by your actions?

James 3:1-12 Words as Weapons
How do you tame your tongue?

1 Peter 2 Living Stones
Which would you choose as the biggest personal challenge in these verses? Why?

1 Peter 3 Relationships and Pain
How willing are you to carry out your relationships God's way, even when there are difficulties?

2 Peter 1 Knowing God
How would you answer someone who asked you how a person can know God?

1 John 1 The Way of Forgiveness
What part does confession have in your life?

1 John 3 God Is Love
How do you put your love into action?

1 John 5 The Life God Gives
How do you know that you have eternal life? Explain.

2 John 4-6; 3 John 5-8; Jude 17-25 Family Matters
How often do you go out of your way to meet the needs of other Christians? Explain.

Revelation 1 Jesus the King
When you think of Jesus, what characteristics come to mind? Why?

Revelation 21 Everything Made New
Based on the description of the new world, what are you most looking forward to concerning it? Why?

Revelation 22 Life in the New City
How eagerly do you await the return of Jesus? Explain.

"So now we can rejoice in our wonderful new relationship with God because our Lord Jesus Christ has made us friends of God." (Romans 5:11).

You know someone who's just started a relationship with Jesus Christ . . . so what can you do to help?

First of all, you can be excited about this opportunity. Second, you need to be serious about this responsibility. Read Romans 5:11 again. You have the privilege of helping someone grow in his or her new relationship with your friend Jesus Christ. Here are some ways you can help a new Christian and Jesus grow closer. Remember, we all need FRIENDS.

Follow up with your new Christian friend by getting together regularly. Get together within 48 hours after your friend receives Christ, and at least once a week during the next six weeks (Matthew 28:20).

Reinforce what Christ has done in your friend's life. Do this by looking at Scriptures that affirm God's commitment to Christians (John 14:20; Hebrews 13:5; Colossians 2:13-14; 1 John 5:13; Galatians 5:25).

Involve your friend in your church activities. Take your friend with you and help answer any of his or her questions (Hebrews 10:24-25).

Exhibit Christ in your life through your actions and words. You don't have to be perfect, just someone who wants to obey and please God (Colossians 3:17).

Nurture your friend's spiritual growth. A new Christian is like a newborn baby who needs spiritual food and care. Try using the 14 encounters with God included in this section (1 Peter 2:2-3).

Do things together. Spending time together will give you opportunities to encourage your friend and put your faith into practice (Acts 14:21-22).

Stand by your friend in both the good and bad times. Your friend will fall down spiritually. Get ready to help him or her to get up and go again (Ephesians 4:11-16).

You have recently trusted Jesus Christ to be your Savior . . . so now what do you do?

First of all, you must know that through Christ you have become friends with God. Read Romans 5:11. Remember:

- You realized that your sin was keeping you from a relationship with God.
- You understood that Jesus Christ died on the cross to pay the penalty for your sin and that he rose again from the dead.
- You prayed, asking Jesus to forgive your sins and be your Savior.

Next, please understand that you have begun an exciting and lasting friendship. As in any relationship, getting to know someone takes time—it doesn't just happen by itself. (Make sure you have a friend who has been a Christian for a while who can help you grow in your new faith. If no one has contacted you, you should go back to the person who helped you become a Christian and ask for help.)

You can grow closer to God just like you grow closer to people. God created you to have a relationship with him, to be his very own son or daughter. Now that you're his child and friend, he will patiently help you get to know him better and better.

Here are some ideas you can use to help you and God become close friends. Remember, all it takes is TIME:

Talk to God through prayer. To help you learn how to talk to God, the 14 encounters with God include ideas for prayer. Give them a try. God will listen when you talk to him.

Investigate God's Word. Decide on a time and place to read the Bible each day. The schedule for 14 encounters with God will help you know what to read. This will help you grow.

Make it practical. One of the best ways to learn is by doing. The 14-encounter schedule includes action steps to help you make your friendship with God active and practical.

Express your thoughts. You know how important it is to show appreciation to a friend. As you finish your daily time with God, tell him thank you. During the next 14 encounters with God, try to keep a personal journal. Simply write down your thoughts, your questions, and, most important of all, why you're thankful to God!

Finally, to get to know God better, try using the following "14 Encounters with God" feature. These give you some great ways to spend time with God and find out more about who he is and who he wants you to be.

encounter 1 IT'S GUARANTEED

• ASSURANCE

You recently became a Christian. Have you had any doubts about whether or not Jesus really came into your life? Do you wonder if you'll really go to heaven someday?

Talk to God: "Father, thank you for giving me a relationship with you. Jesus, thank you for giving me life. Please teach me and help me learn more about you. Amen."

Investigate God's Word: Read 1 John 5:11-13. Memorize verse 13.

Make it Practical: Check out "I Wonder"—1 John 5:10-12, page 1290, or "Keeping It Real"—Matthew 7:24-27, page 969. How can you put the ideas presented here into action in your own life?

Express your thoughts: In your journal, write a description of when, where, and how you became a Christian. Say thanks to God!

encounter 2 PART OF THE FAMILY

• GOD, OUR FATHER

Everyone knows what it's like to not feel totally accepted by others. Did you know that when you became a Christian, God adopted you into his family and accepted you unconditionally?

Talk to God: "Dear God, thanks for making me part of your family. You accept me. That's awesome! Amen."

Investigate God's Word: Ephesians 1:3-8. Memorize verse 5.

Make it Practical: "I Wonder"—Hebrews 1:1-3, page 1253, or "Keeping It Real"—Mark 9–10, page 1011.

Express your thoughts: In your journal, make a list of what you like about being part of God's family. Don't forget to thank him.

encounter 3 NEW LIFE IN CHRIST

• GROWTH

OK, now that you're a new Christian, what's next? Well, the best relationships are those that grow and deepen. It's the same way in your relationship with Jesus Christ. It's time for growth.

Talk to God: "Lord, help me to let my roots sink down into you. Thanks for helping me grow. Amen."

Investigate God's Word: Colossians 2:6-7. Memorize the first part of verse 7.

Make it Practical: "I Wonder"—Colossians 2:6-7, page 1211, or "Keeping It Real"—2 Peter 1:5-8, page 1281.

Express your thoughts: Think of one way that you'd like to grow spiritually, share it with one friend, and write it in your journal. Then ask God to help you do what you've decided to do.

encounter 4 TIME TO TALK

• PRAYER

You know how good friends love to talk with each other. God, our heavenly Father, is ready for a heart-to-heart talk all the time. Conversation with God is a must!

Talk to God: "God, I'm so glad we can talk anytime. Thank you that you'll listen to my needs. Help me learn to listen to you. Amen."

Investigate God's Word: Philippians 4:6-7. Memorize verse 6.

Make it Practical: "I Wonder"—1 Kings 3:3-14, page 344 or "Keeping It Real"—Ecclesiastes 5:1-7, page 658.

Express your thoughts: Commit yourself to spending at least three minutes in prayer every day. In your journal, keep a record of your prayer requests and answers. Tell God thanks for those answers.

encounter 5 DIG IN

• BIBLE

When you get something new, you often receive an instruction manual. With your new life in Christ, you need God's instruction manual, the Bible. God communicates to us through his Word.

Talk to God: "Dear God, thank you for showing me what you're like through your Word. Help me to read it, study it, and obey it. Amen."

Investigate God's Word: 2 Timothy 3:14-17. Memorize verse 16.

Make it Practical: "I Wonder"—John 20:31, page 1093, or "Keeping It Real"—Isaiah 41:10, page 710.

Express your thoughts: Commit yourself to spending five minutes a day reading the Bible. As a result of something you read, write down in your journal something you will do. Ask God to help you.

encounter 6 JESUS DID IT ALL

• JESUS, OUR SAVIOR

Friendships get stronger when you really get to know the other person. You have trusted Christ to be your Savior and to give you new life. Really get to know who he is and what he has done! It's incredible!

Talk to God: "Jesus, you are so powerful! I'm thankful that you hold everything together, including me! Amen."

Investigate God's Word: Colossians 1:15-23. Memorize verse 17.

Make it Practical: "I Wonder"—Hebrews 1:1-3,5, page 1253.

Express your thoughts: Ask a friend to tell you what he or she really likes about Jesus. In your journal, write a note to Jesus about what you really appreciate about him.

encounter 7 SOLID ROCK

• OBEDIENCE

A good foundation is essential for a house to stand strong. Jesus wants you to realize that obeying God will give your life a solid foundation.

Talk to God: "Dear God, you know what's best for me. Help me to be strong and obey you in each area of my life. Amen."

Investigate God's Word: Luke 6:46-49. Memorize the first part of verse 47.

Make it Practical: "I Wonder"—Joshua 24:14-15, page 236 or "Keeping It Real"—Ephesians 6:1-3, page 1200.

Express your thoughts: In your journal, list one area of your life where you are obeying God and one where you are not. Say thanks to God for helping you to want to obey.

encounter 8 YOU HAVE INSIGHT

• HOLY SPIRIT

Nobody in this world knows you better than you know yourself. Nobody knows God like God's Spirit knows God. As a new Christian, you have been given God's Holy Spirit. He will give you insight into what God is like and what he wants you to do.

Talk to God: "Thank you, God, for giving me your Spirit. You know me so well, and I will trust your Spirit to help me know more about you. Amen."

Investigate God's Word: 1 Corinthians 2:9-16. Memorize verse 12.

Make it Practical: "I Wonder"—Romans 7:15–8:2, page 1142, or "Keeping It Real"—Isaiah 7:9, page 682.

Express your thoughts: In your journal, write down one question that you'd like the Holy Spirit to help you with. Now take a couple of minutes and just listen to God. Tell him thanks.

encounter 9 DON'T GIVE IN

• TEMPTATION

The Bible says in 1 Peter 5:8 that our enemy Satan is like a lion that wants to rip us apart. Satan will tempt us to disobey God, but God will show us a way out!

Talk to God: "Dear God, you know the temptations I struggle with. Thank you that you have promised me a way to escape. Amen."

Investigate God's Word: 1 Corinthians 10:13. Memorize verse 13.

Make it Practical: "Keeping It Real"—1 Peter 3:15, page 1276.

Express your thoughts: List the three temptations that Satan really uses on you. Now thank God ahead of time that he will show you how to not give in next time.

encounter 10 I'M SORRY

• FORGIVENESS

As a child in God's family, you'll still mess up. But God's love for you is so great that he will forgive you! He can do that because he loves you!

Talk to God: "Dear God, I confess to you my sin of _______. I admit that it was wrong. Thank you that Jesus died on the cross to forgive me for this sin. Amen."

Investigate God's Word: 1 John 1:8-10. Memorize verse 9.

Make it Practical: "I Wonder"—James 4:17, page 1268, or "Keeping It Real"—Lamentations 3:22-23, page 796.

Express your thoughts: Write down ways that you have disobeyed God recently. Look at each one and confess it through prayer. Cross out each sin. Let this remind you of God's loving forgiveness. Be sure to thank him!

encounter 11 WORSHIP HIM

• CHURCH

Christians are part of the body of Christ, which is called his church. Be sure you get together with other believers, members of the "body." It's an opportunity to love God and each other.

Talk to God: "Dear God, thank you for your body of believers, the church. Teach me how to get involved with other Christians and really worship you. Amen."

Investigate God's Word: Hebrews 10:22-25. Memorize verse 25.

Make it Practical: "I Wonder"—Hebrews 10:24-25, page 1260, or "Keeping It Real"—James 1, page 1268.

Express your thoughts: Go with some friends or family to church this week. List two ways you worshiped God.

encounter 12 I GOTTA TELL YOU SOMETHING

• WITNESSING

If you have a close friend, you can't keep from talking about that person. When you love someone, you can hardly contain yourself! Let your love for Christ motivate you to tell others about him.

Talk to God: "Lord, you have changed my life. Give me the courage and opportunities to tell others about you. Amen."

Investigate God's Word: Romans 1:16-17. Memorize verse 16.

Make it Practical: "I Wonder"—Luke 22:54-62, page 1054, or "Keeping It Real"—Acts 4:13, page 1102.

Express your thoughts: Write down the name of one person who needs to know Jesus Christ. Start praying for that person to become a Christian. Ask a Christian friend to pray with you for the person and to help you learn how to share your faith with him or her.

encounter 13 DO YOU REMEMBER?

• BIBLE MEMORY

To fight a battle you need powerful equipment. The Holy Spirit will use the power of God's Word like a sword to defeat Satan. So a great strategy is to memorize Scripture! What verses have you already learned?

Talk to God: "Lord, I need your power! Help me to memorize Scripture verses. I know this will help me live for you. Amen."

Investigate God's Word: Ephesians 6:10-17. Memorize verse 17.

Make it Practical: "I Wonder"—Philippians 4:8, page 1206, or "Keeping It Real"—Isaiah 46:4, page 716.

Express your thoughts: Review your memory verses from the past 12 days. In your journal, write down your favorite verse.

encounter 14 BE LIKE CHRIST

• SPIRITUAL GOAL

You've been a Christian for a short time now, and you're learning that you have a lifelong relationship with Christ. So what's your long-range plan? Becoming like Christ is the ultimate goal.

Talk to God: "Dear Jesus, more than anything else I want to become more like you. Thanks that you'll be patient and help me. Amen."

Investigate God's Word: Colossians 3:10-11. Memorize verse 10.

Make it Practical: "I Wonder"—Jeremiah 29:11-13, page 766 or "Keeping It Real"—Micah 4:6-13, page 912.

Express your thoughts: Make a list of at least five ways you want to become more like Jesus. Spend time asking God to help you. Remind yourself to read this part of your journal in one month to check on your spiritual growth.

life choices reference index

Need answers to nagging questions? Check out the Scriptures under each topic.

index to the "choices" notes

index to "I wonder"

index to the ultimate issues

index to the charts

index to the personality profiles

index to "keeping it real"

STORY

JESUS' MIRACLES